HARRY
WEBER

WINSTON S. CHURCHILL
1874—1965

OTHER BOOKS BY MARTIN GILBERT

The Appeasers (*with Richard Gott*)
The European Powers, 1900–1945
The Roots of Appeasement
Recent History Atlas, 1860–1960
British History Atlas
American History Atlas
Jewish History Atlas
First World War Atlas
Russian Imperial History Atlas
Soviet History Atlas
The Arab–Israeli Conflict: Its History in Maps
Sir Horace Rumbold: Portrait of a Diplomat
Churchill: A Photographic Portrait
The Jews of Russia: Their History in Maps and Photographs
Jerusalem Illustrated History Atlas
Exile and Return: The Struggle for Jewish Statehood
Children's Illustrated Bible Atlas
Auschwitz and the Allies
The Macmillan Atlas of the Holocaust
Churchill's Political Philosophy

Editions of documents

Britain and Germany Between the Wars
Plough My Own Furrow, the Life of Lord Allen of Hurtwood
Servant of India: Diaries of the Viceroy's Private Secretary, 1905–1910

WINSTON S. CHURCHILL

by

MARTIN GILBERT

VOLUME V
Companion Part 3
Documents

The Coming of War

1936–1939

HEINEMANN : LONDON

William Heinemann Ltd
10 Upper Grosvenor St, London W1X 9PA
LONDON   MELBOURNE   TORONTO
JOHANNESBURG   AUCKLAND

434 29188 9
First published 1982
© 1982 C & T Publications Limited

Printed in Great Britain by
Fletcher & Son Ltd, Norwich

Contents

PREFACE

ACKNOWLEDGEMENTS

Preface

THIS DOCUMENT VOLUME, *The Coming of War*, concludes the publication of the Churchill papers for the inter-war years. The largest of the volumes of this series, it covers more than three and a half years of Churchill's life, bringing together the documentary materials of one of the most intense periods of his work, outside the war years.

At the moment when this volume opens, in January 1936, Churchill had been out of office for six and a half years. For the previous five years he had been in constant conflict with the Conservative Party leadership, first, since 1930, over India, and then, since 1933, over defence, especially in relation to the Government's response to the rise of Nazi power in Germany.

Since 1933 Churchill had been urging a swifter rearmament, especially in the air, and the creation of a more effective administrative structure to make possible the gradual but definite transition from a peace-time to a war-time economy. He had written and spoken from the first months of Hitler's regime against what he saw as Britain's 'tired Ministers and flagging purpose' (see page 1411), caught, he believed, both by habit and by neglect, into 'a sort of catalepsy of action' (page 1482). 'Bold captains,' he argued, 'are required for perilous seas' (page 245, note 1).

By January 1936 Churchill's opposition on defence policy and method had ensured his isolation from the Conservative Party leadership, and thus his continued exclusion from the Cabinet lists of the National Government, in which the Conservatives predominated. Yet even at his apparently most isolated periods there were many people who expected him to be given office. This was particularly so at the time of speculation leading up to the appointment of a newly created Cabinet post, the Minister for the Co-ordination of Defence, established in March 1936. Those who advocated his return to the Cabinet at that time were surprised when the post went to Sir Thomas Inskip, a lawyer lacking either Churchill's experience or energy. Yet Churchill's own attitude to being passed over had been, and was to remain, one of philosophic disappointment. 'I do not mean to break my heart whatever happens,' he had written to his wife. And he added: 'If I am not wanted, we have many things to make us happy my darling beloved Clemmie' (page 62).

Throughout the three yesrs covered by this volume, there were occasions when Ministers sought Churchill's advice privately. There were many other occasions when he gave it. Nor did he hesitate to give it, and to draw on the well of experience to try to help them. But there were times when he found it frustrating to be outside the Cabinet circle, and this frustration was in many ways heightened by his presence on one secret Government discussion forum, the Air Defence Research committee of the Committee of Imperial Defence. Here he learnt of secret developments, such as Radar, but lacking the authority to follow them up Ministerially, could not ensure their exploitation at the speed or in the direction which he felt was needed.

Despite this sense of powerlessness, Churchill bore his isolation philosophically, and just as he retained his faith that in the end British people would respond to the threat of totalitarianism, so, in his personal life, he retained a calm and mature perspective on his apparently finished career. As he wrote to a friend, Sir Abe Bailey, in June 1936 (pages 182–3), shortly after he had been passed over for the Ministry for the Co-ordination of Defence:

Do not, my dear Abe, suppose that I mind. In the present posture of affairs I have no wish whatever for office. I would not join any Government which I do not feel was resolved to lift National Defence to an altogether different plane, nor would I join any Government in which I had not a real share of power for such a purpose. If all our fears are groundless and everything passes off smoothly in the next few years, as pray God indeed it may, obviously there is no need for me. If on the other hand the very dangerous times arise, I may be forced to take a part. Only in those conditions have I any desire to serve.

The documents in this volume also show the extent to which Government Ministers were concerned to answer or to forestall Churchill's criticisms, and at times to take him into their confidence. Each crisis, as it came, seemed to strengthen his warning powers, and to enhance public appreciation of his qualities. These three years, and the documents that reflect them, are dominated by a succession of crises in Europe, among them the German re-militarization of the Rhineland in March 1936, the repercussions of the Spanish Civil War, the German annexation of Austria in March 1938, 'Munich', the German occupation of Prague in March 1939, the Italian invasion of Albania in April 1939, and the Polish crisis leading to the outbreak of war in September 1939.

Observing these events closely, Churchill never despaired of the eventual response of the democratic States to the challenge of Nazism. 'There is no explosive so powerful,' he wrote in July 1938, 'as the soul of a free people' (page 1109, note 2). But his faith in this view was often tried, especially when, after 'Munich', troubles came in his own constituency, and an attempt was made to unseat him—an attempt in which even his Party's Central Office seemed to be involved (pages 1394–6).

As each crisis came, Churchill set out, in private correspondence, in public speeches, and in Parliament, his thoughts and suggestions. He was an outspoken advocate of collective action by the League of Nations to contain and if necessary to confront aggression. He was emphatic in his calls for the closest possible Anglo-French links, and for closer cooperation both with the United States and the Soviet Union. He sought, above all to stress the gulf between Dictatorship, whether Fascist or Communist, on the one side, and Democracy on the other, and to show that the threat to Democracy which had then to be faced came primarily, as he saw it, not from the Soviet Union, nor from Italy, but from Nazi Germany.

Churchill's reiterated assertion of the need to be willing to defend democratic values, and to make adequate and timely preparations to defend them, was also reflected in his many books and articles during these three and a half years. Quotation is made in this volume from forty-five of his political articles. Out of office, unlikely to be brought back into the Cabinet, approaching his mid-sixties, Churchill found in his writing, and in particular in his fortnightly political newspaper articles, an outlet for exhortation which he lacked in the Ministerial and Departmental sphere. He also set out his reflections and fears in articles for some of the mass circulation newspapers, including *The News of the World*, to whose owner he wrote of how pleased he was that 'the working people will hear my side of the tale' (page 1340).

Churchill's own sources of Intelligence, whether in the economic, military or political sphere, are shown here in full, together with the range of information with which his contacts provided him. Of considerable value to him was the information which he received about Germany, and about the scope and scale of British preparedness. In this connection, the part played by Desmond Morton and Wing-Commander Torr Anderson was paramount.

As the documents in this volume show, many other individuals, including Service personnel, also brought Churchill secret material, or confided to him their fears and experiences. His earlier links with the Foreign Office were maintained, as were his contacts in the Army, the Navy and the Air Force. Several of those who had worked under his Ministerial authority in the First World War came to him again with ideas and material. His friendship with Professor Lindemann enabled him to submit scientific facts for scrutiny. Other information he sent to individual experts for their appraisal, or direct to Cabinet Ministers, for their comments and use.

In the hope that this volume may be of service to those who study the

political and diplomatic debates of the late 1930s, I have included not only
those documents bearing on Churchill's own perspecive, but much material,
drawn from the papers of the Prime Minister of the day, the Cabinet, the
Foreign Office, the Admiralty, the Air Ministry, the India Office, and from
private archives, bearing on the evolution of Government policy, and the
Government's reaction to Churchill's reiterated arguments and protestations.

The views of Churchill's opponents are given a full showing, not only in
the letters which they themselves wrote to him direct, several hundred of
which are published here in full, but also in the letters which passed between
his critics and of which he knew nothing.

As Churchill worked, out of Office, to influence those in power, he received encouragement to continue in the political arena from an ever-
widening circle of former colleagues, friends and strangers. The love and
support of his family was likewise a factor of considerable importance. His
son Randolph, despite several outbursts of anger, emerges again and again in
these documents as a pugnacious ally. Churchill also enjoyed the determined
support of his three daughters, and cared deeply for them, as instanced in
this volume by his reiterated efforts to ensure that his daughter Sarah would
not make a dangerous marriage. Above all, he gained considerable strength
from the support of his wife, and was the first to acknowledge, as he wrote
to her at a time of intense isolation, 'The sense of gratitude in my heart to
you for all you give me is unfailing' (page 736). Her faith in his future was
constant, expressed succinctly in her 'telegraphic' prayer of 30 November
1937, on his 61st birthday: 'may your Star rise'.

*   *   *

Because this volume of documents contains nearly four times the number
of pages of the equivalent span of Main Volume Five, and because of new
material which has emerged in the six years since the publication of Main
Volume Five, it has been possible to include much previously unpublished
and unknown material. Each of Churchill's letters to his wife, with their
wide span of personal, political, domestic and philosophic reflections, as
well as their uninhibited reports on the events of the day, have been published here in full. Other documents published in full include Churchill's
submission to the Defence Deputation in July 1936 (see pages 267–94) and
his answers to the Palestine Royal Commission in March 1937 (pages 596–
617). On the lighter side, are, in November 1937 alone for example, Churchill's criticisms of a film script on Lawrence of Arabia, on both historic and
artistic grounds (pages 823–6) and his reflection on music, in a speech to
the Musicians Benevolent Fund (pages 833–5).

Churchill's personal perspective on the Abdication crisis is also published in full in this volume (pages 450–4), as are the letters which he received throughout the Abdication turmoil, both approving his attitude and critical of it. Also set out here in full are his own proposals to end the crisis without the need for Abdication, and the documents bearing on Churchill's momentary political eclipse, as a result of his intervention. Even while Abdication fever was at its height, Churchill asserted the primacy of Defence needs: this assertion is shown at its most forceful in his remarks to the 1922 Committee on 8 December 1936, as sent to the Cabinet by one of those present (pages 466–72).

One feature which emerges from the documents is the part played by Chartwell itself in Churchill's life. It was personal and also a political focus for him, a place in which to relax, and also in which to work, and the anguish involved in its impending sale for financial reasons, in April 1938, is particularly poignant. Among the documents relating to Chartwell is the Estate Agent's descriptive brochure at the time of the expected sale (pages 972–6), and the list of secretarial late night workings as the pressure of politics and authorship combined (page 1558, note 1).

For a view of Churchill's work methods as seen from the secretarial perspective, a remarkable document is the appeal by one of his most devoted secretaries, Violet Pearman, for a change of job (pages 443–5); she did not in fact leave, and through the index one can trace her continual service, and Churchill's response to the illness which forced her to cease her main task (page 1033). A further secretarial perspective is provided by the journal of the young lady who accompanied him to France in January 1939, and recorded his hourly progress (pages 1337–9 and 1352–4).

Each of the themes covered by this volume can be seen and followed in the subject-by-subject index entry under 'Churchill, (Sir) Winston Leonard Spencer'. Here the themes of the documents are listed according to topics, and there is also a complete listing of Churchill's political articles, speeches, statements to the Press and memoranda, as they appear in these pages. Each reader will, I hope, be able to trace through the 'Churchill' index entry those subjects of particular interest.

The range of Churchill's interests was so wide, his involvement in public affairs so intense, and his recourse to the written word so frequent, that hardly a week passed in the 'Coming of War' period without his being publicly involved, and making an impact by his involvement.

For those to whom Churchill's books are of interest, I have accorded space to those letters and documents which show how his books were commissioned, how research on them was conducted, how they were written, and how they were received. During the relatively short period covered by this volume, Churchill and his assistants compiled, and Churchill dictated more than 2,600 pages of history, beginning with the last two volumes of *Marlborough: His Life and Times*, a copiously documented biography of his ancestor 'Duke John', and continuing with *A History of the English Speaking Peoples* from the earliest times to the Victorian era, four volumes of which were virtually completed by the outbreak of war. This considerable literary productivity was in addition to a further three books also published during this period, *Great Contemporaries*, *Arms and the Covenant* and *Step By Step*, which were compilations of his articles and speeches.

The number of Churchill's helpers in his literary work was considerable, not only his research assistants, headed between 1936 and 1939 by F. W. Deakin, and his historical guides, among them Keith Feiling, Brigadier Pakenham-Walsh, G. M. Young, Sir James Edmonds and the young Alan Bullock, but also Adam Marshall Diston, who put together and even ghost-wrote articles for him (page 519, footnote 1); C. C. Wood, his devoted proof-reader; and Imre Revesz (Emery Reves), whose work in placing Churchill's political articles in Continental newspapers ensured that Churchill's opinions on current events were read regularly throughout Europe, until the Censors and nervous Editors decided to intervene (pages 1491-3). I have tried to give adequate representation to these devoted helpers, as to all those who enabled Churchill's writings to proceed at their staggering pace.

For a glimpse of the more private side of Churchill's daily life, I have printed in full several diary entries from visitors to Chartwell, as well as the recollections of his chauffeur, Sam Howes (pages 503-12) and of Dr Terence Brand, whom he called in at the time of his secretary's major illness (pages 1096-7). For Churchill as seen by the younger generation both in dinner-time conversation, and in an after-dinner speech on penguins, polar bears and the 'temperate zone', I have printed Judge Brown's recollections of Churchill's visit to the Ralegh Club, Oxford, in May 1937 (pages 676-81).

Readers who may be interested in Churchill's financial achievements, and problems, may follow these through the two index entries 'income and expenditure' and 'income from writing'. Churchill's literary earnings were so considerable that in many instances I have given the contemporary equivalent. Yet despite his substantial income, his financial affairs reached a crisis in the early months of 1938 with the collapse of his United States stocks. It was the willingness of a friend to come to his financial rescue (pages 950-1), that enabled him to remain in politics. This was the same friend, Sir Henry Strakosch, who had for several years provided Churchill with details of German arms expenditure, and was to continue to do so.

The reader of these documents will also obtain a view of Churchill's social life, of his wider friendships, of his travels, interests and amusements whether with his family and friends, or at weekends in English country houses, or on holiday in France, or at the theatre, or in his own garden, painting and entertaining. In the presentation of these documents I have tried to show Churchill in all his circumstances, as well as in all his moods.

Both Churchill's political and literary work are evidence of what the historian A. J. P. Taylor has called 'an extraordinary industry of mind'.[1] If these document volumes are able to show the extent of that industry, they will have served their purpose. With the publication of this 'Coming of War' volume, a total of 11,500 pages—more than five million words—of Churchill documents have now been published in this Companion form, together with the letters of others, and with annotations both biographical and historical. The first five document books were published in two sets, by Randolph Churchill, to whom is due both the concept itself and its initial fulfilment. The subsequent eight document books have been produced by the present author. In compiling this material, both Randolph Churchill and I were quickly made aware of the incredible energy of our subject, and came to realize that whatever view one might take of his often controversial actions and much-criticized opinions, both actions and opinions were on a remarkable scale, and expressed in language both magnificent and precise, based by 1936 upon more than three extremely active decades of public life, and on considerable past responsibilities, often at the centre of Government, in both peace and war.

Churchill's efforts in the late 1930s were carried out against the formidable and accumulated odds of political isolation, increasing age, ill-health, and, from time to time, a fear that he would fail to convince his fellow-countrymen of the dangers of the time, and of the needs to combat those dangers. Yet he always persevered and, as he wrote to his wife in the summer of 1937, at a time of intense political and literary work: 'I really don't know how I find all that I need, but the well flows freely: only time is needed to draw the water from it' (page 735).

'My life,' Churchill had written to his wife five months earlier, 'is probably in its closing decade' (page 575). He had, in fact, more than two and a half decades in prospect, including two periods as Prime Minister, one of more than five years in war, one of more than three years in peace. Yet whatever his achievements were to be during the years to come, it was in the years leading up to the Second World War that he established himself in the minds of the British public as a man of stature and integrity.

These massive volumes of documents are intended to make known the full

[1] Conversation with the author, 7 June 1982.

variety of Churchill's abilities, his efforts and achievements, and to show
something of the outstanding versatility of his mind: as shown here in his
praise for national unity 'across the gulfs of party' (page 1062); in his personal compassion, reflected in Lady Snowden's comment, writing as the
widow of a life-long political rival and critic that had she been in any trouble
which she could not control, 'there is none to whom I should have felt I
could come with more confidence that I should be gently treated' (page 675);
in his range of friendships, his sense of fun, his ability to draw facts and
strength from the events guarded in his memory; in his long experience of
power, politics and personalities; in his sense of history, and of the evolution
of British freedoms; in his ability to state in clear terms the fears and aspirations of ordinary people; in his vision; and in his tireless efforts to contribute to the quality and survival of British life and thought.

Acknowledgements

A S WITH EACH of the earlier volumes of this biography, I am grateful to Her Majesty the Queen, who graciously gave permission for me to have access to the Royal Archives; for help in answering my various queries relating to the Royal Family, I should like to thank Sir Robin Mackworth Young, Librarian, Windsor Castle.

My thanks are also due to those many people who have made possible the presentation of Churchill's story in its full historical scale and range. My particular thanks are due to Churchill's daughters, Sarah, Lady Audley, and Lady Soames DBE, both of whom have patiently watched the evolution of these volumes and have at each stage answered my various requests; and to the Churchill Trustees, Sir John Colville and Sir William Deakin, whose personal encouragement, and help on many specific points, have been much appreciated.

I am also extremely grateful to all those individuals who have provided me with the personal recollections which have been included in this volume:

The Rt. Hon. Julian Amery, Betty J. Anderson, the late Group-Captain Torr Anderson, the Rt. Hon. Anthony Wedgwood Benn, Dr Terence Brand, Judge Brown, TD, the Dowager Duchess of Buccleuch, Sybil, Lady Cholmondeley, Peregrine S. Churchill, the late Lord Coleraine, the late Sir Colin Coote, Sir Michael Creswell KCMG, William Deedes, the late Sir Reginald Dorman-Smith, the Rt. Hon. Lord Duncan-Sandys CH, Doris Edleston (in conversation with Grace Hamblin), Patrick Filmer-Sankey, Mrs L. J. Fox (Mary Penman), S. K. H. Goodenough, Norman Hamilton, Samuel M. Howes, the 2nd Baron Lloyd MBE, Professor Stefan Lorant, Maurice Nadin, Rowland Owen, Mrs Dorothy de Rothschild and Eric Wynn-Owen.

Although more than four-fifths of the documents in this volume are taken from the Churchill Papers in the care of the Chartwell Trust, and constitute the effective publication of those papers for the years 1936 to 1939, I have also incorporated documentary material from the following 79 collections of public and private papers: The Royal Archives; Admiralty papers; Air Ministry papers; Lord Allen of Hurtwood papers; Lord Altrincham papers; L. S. Amery papers; BBC Written Archives; Earl Baldwin papers; Bernard

Baruch papers; Lord Beaverbrook papers; G. D. Birla papers; Blenheim Palace archive; Lord Boothby papers; Cabinet papers; Viscount Camrose papers; Viscount Cecil of Chelwood papers; Sir Austen Chamberlain papers; Neville Chamberlain papers; Chartwell, Westerham, Kent (Library inscriptions and visitors book); Lord Chatfield papers; Viscount Cherwell papers; Christie's auction rooms; The Hon. Randolph Churchill papers; Cyril Clemens papers; Cranborne Visitors Book; Anthony Crossley papers; Geoffrey Dawson papers; Earl of Derby papers; Foreign Office papers; J. L. Garvin papers; Shiela Grant Duff papers; P. J. Grigg papers; Lord Hankey papers; George Harrap papers; Lord Harvey of Tasbrugh papers; Sir James Hawkey papers; William Heinemann Ltd, archive; Samuel M. Howes papers; India Office records and papers; Lord Ironside papers; Dr Thomas Jones papers; Harold Laski papers; Sir Shane Leslie papers; Sir Tresham Lever papers; Walter Lippman papers; Lord Lloyd papers; Stefan Lorant papers; Marquess of Lothian papers; Countess of Lytton papers; Sir Edward Marsh papers; Paul Maze papers; Harold Nicolson papers; Viscount Norwich papers; Major-General Pakenham-Walsh papers; Violet Pearman papers; Helen Pease papers; Mary Penman papers; Sir Eric Phipps papers; Premier papers; Martin Russell papers; Charles Sawyer Ltd (Supplement to catalogue 303); Earl of Selborne papers; Major-General Sir E. L. Spears papers: Lady Spears papers; Baroness Spencer-Churchill papers; Eugen Spier papers; G. R. Storry papers; Viscount Templewood papers; Viscount Thurso papers; V. V. Tilea papers; *The Times* archive; United Grand Lodge of England archive; Lord Vansittart papers; Viscountess Waverley papers; Lord Wedgwood papers; Viscount Weir papers; Dr Chaim Weizmann papers; H. E. Wimperis papers; and C. C. Wood papers.

For help in providing access to archives, or for answering specific queries, both in connection with the texts, and with the biographical and other notes, I should like to thank: Eldon Alexander, Public Research, Syndicated, California; Robert O. Anthony, Curator, Yale University Library; Major Robert and Mrs Cherrie Hill Archer; Maurice Ashley; Sarah, Lady Audley; James Barker; Beryl E. Beadle, The Royal Aeronautical Society; James Montgomery Beck; Dr B. S. Benedikz, The Library, University of Birmingham; Véronique Blum, Le Conservateur en Chef, Bibliothèque de Documentation International Contemporaine, Nanterre; Brian Bond; Marguerite Bowyer; Lord Bullock; John George Spencer Churchill; Michael Colefax; Sue Cowan, *Daily Express*; Clare Crossley; Richard Davenport-Hines; Le Général Delmas, Chef du Service Historique, Vincennes; Henry Douglas-Pennant; Derek Drescher; Harry E. Drew; the 11th Earl of Drogheda; H. J. Fawcus, Librarian, Blenheim Palace; Lord Fraser of Kilmorack; Ann Göranson, Information Department, Swedish Embassy; Richard Gott;

Mrs John Grimond; Richard Grunberger; Richard Gunston; Duff Hart
Davis; Lord Hartwell; Dr Cameron Hazlehurst; Kathleen Hill; David
Irving; Otis V. Jones Jr.; Claudia Josephs; Valerie Josephs; Wilfred Josephs;
Arthur Koestler; Martial de La Fournière, Ministère des Relations Ex-
terieures, Directeur des Archives et de la Documentation, Paris; Eustace
P. Lagacos, The Ambassador, Greek Embassy, London; the late Sir Tresham
Lever; Viscount Long of Wraxall; Elisabeth Lutyens; Lars-Olof Magnil,
Svenska Dagbladet, Stockholm; Nemanja Marčetić, Editor, *The South Slav
Journal*; Sir John Martin; Harford Montgomery Hyde; A. E. B. Owen,
Senior Under-Librarian, Cambridge University Library; Margaret Paken-
ham-Walsh; Colonel William Pakenham-Walsh; Hubert E. Powell; Alan
Palmer; K. St Pavlowitch; Dr Real, Bundesarchiv, Koblenz; Edmund de
Rothchild; Lord Rothschild; Martin Russell; the 6th Marquess of Salis-
bury; Julian Sandys; Elizabeth Sarachi; Dr Sareyko, Auswärtiges Amt,
Bonn; Willy Scally; Harry Shaberman; Diana Sheean; Naomi Shepherd;
Louise Sieminski; John J. Slonaker, Chief, Historical Reference Section,
Department of the Army, US Army Military History Institute, Pennsylvania;
Humphry Smith; Shiela Sokolov Grant; J. de Somogyi, Economic Infor-
mation Department, Marks & Spencer plc; Mrs Henny Spier; Marion
Stewart; the late G. R. Storry; the 4th Baron Tennyson; Rosemary Tufts;
Le Lieutenant-Colonel Turlotte, Service Historique, Vincennes; Dr Christ-
opher Watson; Minou Wellesley Wesley; John Wheldon; Miss Eirene M.
Wood; R. C. Yorke, Archivist and Assistant Librarian, The College of Arms.
I am also grateful for further material to Lord Home of the Hirsel; Dr
M. J. Jubb, Search Department, Public Record Office; G. F. Miles, Arch-
ivist, Barclays Bank plc; Miss E. Anne Monks, Library and Records
Department, Foreign and Commonwealth Office; and W. Roger Smith.
Quotation has been made from the following published works, to whose
authors, copyright holders and publishers my thanks are due: Earl of Avon,
The Eden Memoirs, volume 2, London 1965; Consuelo Vanderbilt Balsan,
The Glitter and the Gold, London 1953; Norman H. Baynes (editor), *The
Speeches of Adolf Hitler, April 1922–August 1939*, London 1942; Georges
Bonnet, *De Washington au Quai' d'Orsay*, Geneva 1946; Mary Borden, *Action
for Slander*, London 1937; Earl of Birkenhead, *Halifax*, London 1965; General
Sir Thomas Bridges, *Alarms and Excursions*, London 1938; *Burke's Peerage and
Baronetage*, 10th edition, London 1978; Lord Butler of Saffron Walden, *The
Art of the Possible*, London 1971; Alan Campbell Johnson, *Viscount Halifax,
A Biography*, London 1941; Barbara Cartland, *Ronald Cartland*, London 1945;
Arthur Christiansen, *Headlines All My Life*, London 1961; Sarah Churchill,
A Thread in the Trapestry, London 1967; Winston S. Churchill, *The Second
World War*, 6 volumes, 1948–54; Winston S. Churchill, *Great Contemporaries*,

London 1937; Winston S. Churchill, *A History of the English-speaking Peoples*, 4 volumes, London 1956-8; Winston S. Churchill, *Marlborough, His Life and Times*, 4 volumes, London 1933-8; Lord Citrine, *Men and Work, An Autobiography*, London 1964; Charles B. Cochran, *Cock-a-doodle-do*, London 1941; Lady Diana Cooper, *The Light of Common Day*, London 1959; Colin Coote, Editorial, *The Memoirs of Colin R. Coote*, London 1965; Geoffrey Dennis, *Coronation Commentary*, London 1937; David Dilks (editor), *The Diaries of Sir Alexander Cadogan OM, 1938-1945*, London 1971; Admiral Sir Barry Domvile, *By and Large*, London 1935; Frances Donaldson, *Edward VIII*, London 1974; Keith Feiling, *The Life of Neville Chamberlain*, London 1946; Martin Gilbert, *Britain and Germany Between the Wars*, London 1966; Martin Gilbert, *The Roots of Appeasement*, London 1968; Kay Halle, *Irrepressible Churchill*, Cleveland, Ohio 1966; General Sir Ian Hamilton, *Listening For the Drums*, London 1944; John Harvey (editor), *The Diplomatic Diaries of Lord Harvey of Tasburgh, 1937-1940*, London 1970; John F. Kennedy, *Why England Slept*, New York 1940; Valentine Lawford, *Bound For Diplomacy*, London 1963; Lord Londonderry, *Ourselves and Germany*, London 1938; Compton Mackenzie, *Octave Eight*, London 1969; Harold Macmillan, *Winds of Change 1914-39*, London 1966; Arthur J. Marder (editor), *Fear God and Dread Nought*, volume 2, London 1956; Paul Maze, *A Frenchman in Khaki*, London 1934; R. J. Minney, *The Private Papers of Hore-Belisha*, London 1960; *Planned ARP*, London 1939; Robert Rhodes James (editor), *Chips, The Diaries of Sir Henry Channon*, London 1967; Robert Rhodes James, *Victor Cazalet, A Portrait*, London 1976; Sidney Rogerson, *Twelve Days*, London 1933; N. A. Rose (editor), *Baffy*, London 1973; Stephen Roskill, *Churchill and the Admirals*, London 1977; Stephen Roskill, *Hankey, Man of Secrets 1931-1963*, volume 3, London 1974; Fabian von Schlabrendorff, *Offiziere gegen Hitler*, Zurich 1946; Vincent Sheean, *Between the Thunder and the Sun*, London 1943; R. C. Sheriff, *No Leading Lady*, London 1968; Mary Soames, *Clementine Churchill*, London 1976; Brigadier-General E. L. Spears, *Prelude to Victory*, London 1939; Eugen Spier, *Focus*, London 1963; R. H. Steel (editor), *Hitler's Interpreter*, London 1951; A. J. P. Taylor (editor), *The Abdication of King Edward VIII, by Lord Beaverbrook*, London 1966; A. J. P. Taylor, *Beaverbrook*, London 1972; Viscount Templewood, *Nine Troubled Years*, London 1954; W. H. Thompson, *Guard From The Yard*, London 1938; W. H. Thompson, *Sixty minutes with Winston Churchill*, London 1953; Loelia, Duchess of Westminster, *Grace and Favour*, London 1961; John W. Wheeler-Bennett, *King George VI, His Life and Reign*, London 1958; John W. Wheeler-Bennett, *The Nemesis of Power: The German Army in Politics, 1918-1945*, London 1954; Kenneth Young (editor), *The Diaries of Sir Robert Bruce Lockhart*, volume 1, London 1973; B. D. Zevin (editor), *Nothing to Fear: The Selected Addresses of Franklin Delano Roosevelt*,

1932–1945, London 1947; Special mention must be made of a published work which is an indispensable guide to anyone writing about Churchill, and the 398 pages of which reveal a mastery both of research and presentation: Frederick Woods, *A Bibliography of the Works of Sir Winston Churchill KG, OM, CH*, 2nd revised edition, London 1969.

I am also grateful to the as yet unpublished manuscript: Dr Cameron Hazlehurst, *The Founders of the Other Club: An Investigation*, Canberra, no date.

Quotation has been made from the following newspapers, journals and magazines, with grateful acknowledgement to their proprietors: *Angriff; The Annual Register* (for the years 1936, 1937, 1938 and 1939); *Birmingham Post; Collier's* magazine; *Daily Herald; Daily Mail; Daily Mirror; Daily Telegraph; Daily Worker; English Historical Review; Evening Standard; Hansard* (Parliamentary Debates); *The London Mercury; Manchester Guardian; Morning Post; The New Commonwealth; New Statesman and Nation; New York Times; News Chronicle; News of the World; Nineteenth Century and After; Observer; Oxford Times; Pall Mall* magazine; *Patriot; Stock Exchange Gazette; Strand* magazine; *Sunday Dispatch; Sunday Express; Sunday Pictorial; Sunday Times; The Times; The Times Literary Supplement; Truth; Winnipeg Free Press;* and *Yorkshire Post.*

One of the pleasures of preparing successive volumes of the Churchill Biography for publication has been my personal contact with the printers Richard Clay and Company Limited, Bungay, whose continuing and paternal interest in the text has led to printing of the highest order; I am particularly grateful to the Liaison Officer at Clay's, Bryan Jarvis, for his help, and considerable patience as each phase of printing and proof reading evolves; and would like also to thank the large number of individuals at Clay's—printers, binders, proof-readers and others—who have constituted for more than twenty years an indispensable 'back-up' team for the Biography.

When work on preparing this volume was begun in 1976, immediately following the publication of main volume 5, I was considerably helped both in collecting material, and in tracking down illusive references, by Larry P. Arnn, of Arkansas and California, whose efforts for each of the three document volumes to volume 5 have been both persistent and valuable. I am particularly grateful to the Winston S. Churchill Association of the United States, and its President, Professor Harry V. Jaffa, for having made Mr Arnn's services available and for help in other ways.

I was also helped in further footnote research by Taffy Sassoon, and in the early typing of documents by Mrs Wendy Rioch, Mrs Judy Holdsworth, Miss Sue Townshend, and Miss Penny Houghton (now Mrs Larry Arnn).

I am also particularly grateful to Dr Christopher Dowling, Keeper of the Department of Education and Publications, Imperial War Museum, for the time and energy which he has given to the Churchill Biography for more than a decade, on all matters relating to military personnel; to Miss Grace Hamblin, for guiding me so effectively on all questions concerning Churchill's life at Chartwell; and to Gordon Phillips, Archivist and Researcher of *The Times*, for answering so patiently my many queries.

For further help on answering queries and providing archival material, I should like to thank the Librarians and Staffs of the Bodleian Library; the British Library Newspaper Library, Colindale; Churchill College, Cambridge; the Daily Telegraph Information Bureau; the Imperial War Museum; the London Library; the National Maritime Museum, Greenwich; the National Trust; Nuffield College, Oxford; the Public Record Office, Kew; and the Welsh Guards Museum.

For help in scrutinizing this volume at its galley and page proof stages I am grateful to John Crusemann, Erica Hunningher, Sir John Hunt, Taffy Sassoon, Lloyd Thomas and Nigel Viney.

For help in the collation of readers' corrections, I am grateful to my daughter Natalie Gilbert, who gave up a portion of her half term to this task.

The footnotes were examined both in galley and page proof stage by Sir John Colville. In preparing the index I was helped by Andras Bereznay, Miriam Gilbert, Mary Miller and Sue Rampton, who also undertook both in Oxford and in London the arduous task of typing all of the footnotes, many of the texts, and the considerable correspondence involved in preparing this volume for publication.

For the past eleven years, the progress of the document volumes, as of the narrative volumes, has been watched over by my wife Susie. Without her archival research, historical guidance, and personal enthusiasm it would not have been possible to have maintained the pace of preparing for publication eleven large bound volumes in the course of eleven years—the equivalent of a volume a year. Undoubtedly, the pace would have been considerably slower had not my wife been at my side to help and to advise, and to provide encouragement. It is to her therefore, as much as to myself, that the thanks of the contented reader should be addressed.

Merton College,   Martin Gilbert
Oxford

10 June 1982

January 1936

P. J. Grigg[1] *to Winston S. Churchill*

(*Churchill papers: 2/261*)

1 January 1936   India
Private

My dear Winston,

The 'Marlborough' has come,[2] & I am most grateful to you for it. I am reading it aloud to my wife & we are delighted to find that none of your cunning has been lost.

But why James? That is only the miserable alternative to Percy & surely I am still PJ, to you.

I wish to God I could talk to you! There is so much that I could say but don't want to write. I am really very uncomfortable with the new regime out here[3] & often feel like chucking my hand in. (I shan't do it of course!)

However I arrive home on leave on May 28th & shall look forward to seeing you very soon thereafter.

Did you see that I had kicked out *my* Clarence Skinner[4] and, I may tell

---

[1] Percy James Grigg, 1890–1964. Educated at Bournemouth School and St John's College, Cambridge. Entered the Treasury, 1913. Served in the Royal Garrison Artillery, 1915–18. Principal Private Secretary to successive Chancellors of the Exchequer, 1921–30. Chairman, Board of Customs and Excise, 1930; Board of Inland Revenue, 1930–4. Knighted, 1932. Finance Member, Government of India, 1934–9. Elected to the Other Club, 1939. Permanent Under-Secretary of State for War, 1939–42. Secretary of State for War, 1942. Privy Councillor, 1942. National MP, East Cardiff, 1942–5. British Executive Director, International Bank for Reconstruction and Development, 1946–7. Subsequently Chairman of Bass, and a director of Imperial Tobacco, the Prudential Assurance Company and other companies.

[2] The second volume of Churchill's *Marlborough, His Life and Times*, which had been published in October 1934 (volume one had been published in October 1933, and Churchill was already well advanced on the work for the third volume, which was to be published in October 1936).

[3] India, following the passing of the Government of India Act, and the establishment of largely autonomous Provincial Councils, with Indian Ministers and administrations.

[4] Churchill did not understand this allusion when he read Grigg's letter. Later it was explained to him (see page 551). Clarence Skinner was the 'Treasury' nickname given to Montagu Norman, Governor of the Bank of England, and thus, by Grigg, to the Governor of the Bank of India. Ernest Skinner was Norman's Private Secretary, in whose name all Norman's travel reservations would be booked. Clarence Skinner was a real American Professor whose

you, in the face of the most bitter & treacherous opposition from *your* Clarence Skinner & Niemeyer.[1] I am afraid I must admit that you were right to hate the man—I do now.

Is there any chance of that whited sepulchre Baldwin[2] clearing out & allowing the country to be run by somebody with the normal number of faculties?

But I mustn't go on generating like this. Au revoir and with renewed thanks & affection.

Yours ever,
PJG

Sir Samuel Hoare[3] *to Winston Churchill*

(*Churchill papers: 2/251*)

2 January 1936

Hotel Castell,
Zuoz, Engadin,
Switzerland

Dear Winston,

I am greatly touched by your letter.[4] It was very friendly of you to think of writing it.

---

cabin on board ship was invaded by journalists who wrongly assumed him to be Norman, travelling incognito.

[1] Otto Ernst Niemeyer, 1883–1971. Educated at St Paul's and Balliol College, Oxford. Entered the Treasury, 1906; Controller of Finance, 1922–7. Member of the Financial Committee of the League of Nations, 1922–37. Knighted, 1924. A Director of the Bank for International Settlements, 1931–65, and of the Bank of England, 1938–52. Chairman of the Governors, London School of Economics, 1941–57.

[2] Stanley Baldwin, 1867–1947. Educated at Harrow and Trinity College, Cambridge. Conservative MP for Bewdley, 1908–37. Financial Secretary to the Treasury, 1917–21. President of the Board of Trade, 1921–2. Chancellor of the Exchequer, 1922–3. Prime Minister, 1923–4 and 1924–9. Lord President of the Council, 1931–5. Prime Minister (for the third time), 1935–7. Created Earl, and Knight of the Garter, 1937.

[3] Samuel John Gurney Hoare, 1880–1959. Educated at Harrow and New College, Oxford. Conservative MP for Chelsea, 1910–44. Succeeded his father as 2nd Baronet, 1915. Lieutenant-Colonel, British Military Mission to Russia, 1916–17 and to Italy, 1917–18. Deputy High Commissioner, League of Nations, for care of Russian refugees, 1921. Secretary of State for Air, October 1922–January 1924 and 1924–9. Secretary of State for India, 1931–5; for Foreign Affairs, 1935. First Lord of the Admiralty, 1936–7; Home Secretary, 1937–9; Lord Privy Seal, 1939–40; Secretary of State for Air, April–May 1940. Ambassador to Spain, 1940–4. Created Viscount Templewood, 1944.

[4] Nine days after Press publication on 9 December 1935 of the Hoare-Laval proposals, drafted in Paris, of a plan to allow certain Abyssinian territory to come under Italian economic control, Sir Samuel Hoare had resigned as Foreign Secretary. On 28 December 1935 Churchill had written to Hoare: 'My dear Sam, I must venture to write you a few lines to congratulate you on the dignity of yr speech of resignation, & to tell you how vy sorry I am at what has happened. It can only mean a brief interruption in yr career, and after so much work & worry I daresay the breathing space will be welcome. We are moving into a year of measureless perils' (*Templewood papers*).

Your last sentence sums up my attitude 'we are moving into a year of measureless perils'. I was not prepared in view of these perils to risk a European war with French opinion overwhelmingly opposed to it. As it is I must leave it to the future to judge between my critics and myself.

What, however, continues to worry me is the criminal indifference of the British world to the dangers that you and I foresee only too clearly. Every day the Abyssinian war continues, these dangers will be increased. We must talk over these grave issues when we are both returned.

In the meanwhile, many more thanks for your letter.

Yours ever,
Samuel Hoare

Clementine Churchill[1] to Winston S. Churchill

(*Spencer-Churchill papers*)

7 January 1936　　　　　　　　　　　　　　　　　　　Austria

My darling,

I was so very glad to get your interesting letter (of December 30). Here we are 5,500 feet up above the clouds in the eye of the sun completely enclosed in a little valley. On the steep slopes you can sometimes count over 400 human beings, struggling in the glistening powder-like snow. The ones near the top are the experts; (& there are many grades of them) they look like flies. It takes them $1\frac{1}{2}$ hours to climb up & perhaps 12 minutes to swirl down in lovely curves. Sometimes they come to grief on the way & get almost buried in the snow. Further down are the less good skiers—those who have only been out say 2 years and on the lower slopes are the 'ski babies' among them myself,

[1] Clementine Hozier, 1885–1977. Daughter of Lady Blanche Ogilvy (eldest daughter of the 10th Earl of Airlie) and Colonel Henry Hozier, soldier, war correspondent and (from 1874) Secretary to the Corporation of Lloyds of London, insurance under-writers. She married Churchill in 1908; they had five children, Diana (born 1909), Randolph (born 1911), Sarah (born 1914), Marigold (born 1919) and Mary (born 1922). In the First World War Clementine Churchill was active providing, through the YWCA, canteens for munitions workers; in the Second World War she presided over the Red Cross Aid to Russia Fund and the Fulmer Chase Maternity Home. From 1941 to 1947 she was also President of the YWCA War and National Fund, and from 1949 to 1951, Chairman of the YWCA National Hostels Committee. Created Baroness Spencer-Churchill, 1965; she took her seat on the cross benches, and not only attended the House of Lords thirteen times in seven months, but voted in favour of the abolition of the death penalty on 20 July 1965. A Trustee of Lord Attlee's Memorial Foundation, 1966. President of the National Benevolent Fund for the Aged, 1972. For a comprehensive account of her life, see Mary Soames, *Clementine Churchill*, London, 1976.

Maria,[1] Clarissa[2] and since yesterday Venetia,[3] her daughter Judy[4] and another little girl. It is extraordinarily difficult and laborious and it is a mystery to me why it is done at all, but there is a strange fascination about it & tremendous satisfaction at every minute stage of progress.

The idea of joining you in Morocco attracts me very much. For one thing I miss my Pig very much; but I want to stay out here till the 21st and I suppose by then you will be thinking of moving home? I hear that in February and March the weather is rainy in Morocco and that it improves again in April? Do get weather averages and statistics becos' as you like it so much I might accompany you another time? I hear Fez is deeply interesting but perhaps not so beautiful as Marrakech.

The political situation at home is depressing. I really would not like you to serve under Baldwin, unless he really gave you a great deal of power and you were able to inspire and vivify the Government. But as you say we are in it up to our necks and that cannot be altered now. All you could do would be to organise our armed forces. The very pussy foots who trust Baldwin are being misled by him (& not by policy but by muddle). Goodbye my darling.

Your loving,
Clemmie

---

[1] Mary Churchill, 1922–   . Churchill's fifth and youngest child. Served with the Auxiliary Territorial Service, 1940–5; accompanied her father on several of his wartime journeys. In 1947 she married Captain Christopher Soames (later Lord Soames). They have five children. In 1978 her husband was created a Life Peer, and in 1979 she published *Clementine Churchill*, a biography of her mother. Created DBE, 1980, after her husband's term as Governor of Rhodesia.

[2] Anne Clarissa Spencer Churchill, 1920–   . Daughter of Major John and Lady Gwendeline Churchill; Churchill's niece. In 1952 she married Sir Anthony Eden (later Earl of Avon), who died in 1977.

[3] Beatrice Venetia Stanley, 1887–1948. Clementine Churchill's cousin. The confidante of Asquith from 1912 to 1915, she married Edwin Montagu in July 1915. Her London house was at 62 Onslow Gardens, Kensington, and her country house, Breccles Hall, in Norfolk. Her husband died in 1924.

[4] Judy Montagu, 1923–1972. Only child of Edwin Montagu and Venetia Stanley (Clementine Churchill's cousin), and a close friend of Churchill's daughter Mary. Her father died before she was two years old. In 1962 she married Milton Gendel. After the Second World War, when she served in the ATS, she was active in the work of the Invalid Children's Aid Association.

Winston S. Churchill to Clementine Churchill

(Spencer-Churchill papers)

8 January 1936   Hotel Mamounia,
                                           Marrakech
                                           Morocco

My darling Clemmie,

Of course during last week the excitement here has been about the Ross and Cromarty by-election. The Unionist Association have unanimously and officially appealed to Randolph[1] to stand against Malcolm MacDonald.[2] The stubborn and spontaneous character of this invitation, and the refusal even to hear Malcolm MacDonald, are remarkable facts. You will see how unfortunate and inconvenient such a fight is to me. 'Churchill v MacDonald'. If they get in, it would seem very difficult for Baldwin to invite me to take the Admiralty or the co-ordinating job, and sit cheek by jowl with these wretched people. I therefore would greatly have preferred Randolph to damp it all down. Instead of this he has had his agent up there feeling around.

Quite apart from this, there is no doubt the thoughts of all Conservatives in the constituency turn naturally to him. It is a great insult to a Scottish constituency to be used as a mere utensil for Baldwin's purposes. Moreover this National Labour business is humbug. Here are these two MacDonalds, whom we are told must be elected, in order that the Labour element should be represented in a National Government, otherwise it cannot be called 'National'.

Yet when they stand they do not even call themselves Labour, so utterly

---

[1] Randolph Frederick Edward Spencer Churchill, 1911–1968. Churchill's only son. His godfathers were F. E. Smith and Sir Edward Grey. Educated at Eton and Christ Church, Oxford. On leaving Oxford in 1932, without taking his degree, he worked briefly for the Imperial Chemical Industries as assistant editor of their house magazine. Joined the staff of the *Sunday Graphic*, 1932; wrote subsequently for many newspapers, including the *Evening Standard* (1937–9). Reported during Hitler's election campaign of 1932, the Chaco War of 1935 and Spanish Civil War; accompanied the Duke of Windsor on his tour of Germany, 1937. Unsuccessful Parliamentary candidate 1935 (twice), 1936, 1945, 1950 and 1951. Conservative MP for Preston, 1940–5. On active service, North Africa and Italy, 1941–3. Major, British mission to the Yugoslav Army of National Liberation, 1943–4 (MBE, 1944). Historian; author of the first two volumes of this biography.

[2] Malcolm John MacDonald, 1901–1981. Son of Ramsay MacDonald. Educated at Bedales and Queen's College, Oxford. Labour MP for Bassetlaw, 1929–31 (National Labour 1931–5); for Ross and Cromarty, 1936–45. Parliamentary Under-Secretary, Dominions Office, 1931–5. Privy Councillor, 1935. Secretary of State for Dominion Affairs, 1935–8 and 1938–9; Colonial Secretary, 1935 and 1938–40. Minister of Health, 1940–1. High Commissioner, Canada, 1941–6. Governor-General of Malaya, Singapore and British Borneo, 1946–8. Commissioner General for South-East Asia, 1948–55. High Commissioner, India, 1955–60. Governor-General of Kenya, 1963–4; High Commissioner, 1964–5. British Special Representative in East and Central Africa, 1965–6; in Africa, 1966–9. Order of Merit, 1969.

are they repudiated by every section of Labour and Socialist opinion. The whole manoeuvre is an abuse of representative government, and I do not at all wonder that the Scottish electors are furious and insulted at being made a dump for these adventurers, whom no English constituency will receive. As I said, I should have been very glad if Randolph had put a stopper on the whole business, so far as he is concerned. But what with the insistent telegrams from the Ross and Cromarty Conservatives, and the press and broadcast references; and with Rothermere,[1] Beaverbrook[2] and Lloyd George[3] all goading him on, I really cannot blame him for accepting the official invitation of the local Conservative Association.

Neither do I think the fight hopeless. There will be four candidates. The Simonite Liberals will fight the Samuelite Liberals, splitting the Liberal vote at least half and half.[4] A good Socialist candidate will be out to down Malcolm MacDonald at all costs. Randolph, who will be the most live, powerful, presentable and also a consistent candidate in the field, might well get the five or six thousand votes which will win the seat. How will Baldwin take it? Will he regard it as a definite declaration of war by me? I have of course expressed no opinion whatever, and Randolph will make it clear he is acting entirely on his own.

[1] Harold Sidney Harmsworth, 1868–1940. Younger brother of Lord Northcliffe, with whom he had helped to establish the *Daily Mail* and *Evening News*. Created Baronet, 1910. Proprietor of the *Daily Mirror*, 1914. Created Baron Rothermere, 1914. Launched the *Sunday Pictorial*, 1915. Director-General of the Royal Army Clothing Factory, 1916. President of the Air Council, 1917–18. Created Viscount, 1919. Two of his three sons were killed in action in the First World War, one in November 1916, the other in February 1918.

[2] William Maxwell Aitken, 1879–1964. A Canadian financier. Conservative MP, 1910–16. Knighted, 1911. Elected to the Other Club, 1912. Canadian Expeditionary Force Eye-Witness in France, May-August 1915; Canadian Government Representative at the Front, September 1915–16. Newspaper proprietor: bought the *Daily Express*, his largest circulation newspaper, in December 1916. Created Baron Beaverbrook, 1917. Chancellor of the Duchy of Lancaster and Minister of Information, 1918. Minister for Aircraft Production, 1940–1. Minister of State, 1941. Minister of Supply, 1941–2. Lord Privy Seal, 1943–5. Known as 'Max'. On 28 May 1915, when Churchill's fortunes were at their lowest ebb following his removal as First Lord of the Admiralty at the height of the Gallipoli campaign, Beaverbrook (then Sir Max Aitken) had written, in an article commissioned by Lord Northcliffe but never published: 'Nor need Mr Churchill despair of his future. It will undoubtedly be high and even splendid, for he possesses many qualities which no other public man can claim. If his future were as dark as I believe it to be bright he would I think encounter it with the same composure' (*Churchill papers: 2/237*).

[3] David Lloyd George, 1863–1945. Educated at a Welsh Church school. Solicitor, 1884. Liberal MP for Caernarvon, 1890–1931. President of the Board of Trade, 1905-8. Privy Councillor, 1905. Chancellor of the Exchequer, 1908–15. An original member of the Other Club (founded by Churchill and F. E. Smith), 1911. Minister of Munitions, May 1915–July 1916. Secretary of State for War, July–December 1916. Prime Minister, December 1916–October 1922. Order of Merit, 1919. Independent Liberal MP, 1931–45. Created Earl, 1945.

[4] The Simonite Liberals supported the National Government, the Samuelite Liberals did not.

Rothermere is sending Oliver Baldwin[1] to write up Randolph, which he is apparently ready to do, and to write down Malcolm, which of course is what all other Socialists revel in. So we shall have Ramsay's[2] son, Baldwin's son and my son—all mauling each other in this remote constituency. However the people are very fine people and I should not be surprised if their strongest feeling was that they would not be made use of, and have their representation reduced to some London convenience. When the contest gets a little further developed, I propose to utter the following 'piece'. 'I wish Mr Baldwin would tell me the secret by which he keeps his son Oliver in such good order.' However for the present I am completely mum.

Randolph started last night, and tomorrow will be flying by aeroplane from Casablanca to Barcelona, this being the only means by which he can be in Dingwall on Friday. It will be a star contest, and will certainly have the sympathy of Conservatives, and all those who hate 'jobs' and humbug. In addition it will have the Rothermere–Beaverbrook support in a most vigorous manner. The Daily Express has an important circulation among the farmers of Ross and Cromarty.

I was reading what Marlborough wrote in 1708—'As I think most things are settled by destiny, when one has done one's best, the only thing is to await the result with patience.'

I think the Government greatly weakened by what has occurred over the Hoare–Laval agreement, and Baldwin greatly weakened too. Therefore I expect that either Baldwin will be looking for a chance to clear out, or he will want a strong reconstruction.

The Naval Conference is breaking down and Monsell[3] will soon be going. Thus everything comes to a head at once, and Destiny will decide. I thought you would like me to give you my views at length upon this unsought-for event.

[1] Oliver Ridsdale Baldwin, 1899–1958. Elder son of Stanley Baldwin. Educated at Eton. On active service in France, 1916–18. Vice-Consul, Boulogne, 1919. Fought in the Armeno-Turkish and Armeno-Russian wars, 1920 and 1921; imprisoned by both Bolsheviks and Turks, 1921. Parliamentary Labour candidate, 1924. Labour MP for Dudley, 1929–31; for Paisley, 1945–7. Succeeded his father as 2nd Earl, 1947. Governor of the Leeward Islands, 1948–50.
[2] James Ramsay MacDonald, 1866–1937. Labour MP for Leicester, 1906–18, for Aberavon, 1922–9 and for Seaham, 1929–31. Leader of the Labour Party, 1911–14. Prime Minister and Secretary of State for Foreign Affairs, January to November 1924. Prime Minister, 1929–35. National Labour MP for Seaham, 1931–5. Lord President of the Council, 1935–7. National Labour MP for the Combined Scottish Universities from 31 January 1936 until his death in November 1937.
[3] Bolton Meredith Monsell, 1881–1969. Known as 'Bobby'. Entered HMS Britannia, 1894; midshipman, 1896. Torpedo Lieutenant, 1903. Assumed the additional surname of Eyres, 1904. Conservative MP for South Worcestershire, 1910–35. A Conservative Whip, 1911. An original member of the Other Club, 1911. Returned to the Navy, 1914; on active service in Egypt, 1915; Commander, 1917. Treasurer of the Royal Household, 1919. Civil Lord of the Admiralty, 1921; Financial Secretary, Admiralty, 1922–3. Privy Councillor, 1923. Chief

This is a wonderful place. The hotel is incomparably superior to anything in Cairo. In my opinion it is better than any of the hotels I have stayed in on the Riviera. The food and service are excellent; the rooms beautifully constructed, and not much more expensive than Majorca. The country is wonderful with the fertile red and black soil, gushing streams of water, swarms of picturesque inhabitants, every one of whom is a picture, perfect cloudless days, brilliant sunshine, translucent air. We look through a tracery of palm trees at the wonderful snows of the Atlas mountains. It is pouring with rain in England and France. Spain is dismal. Tangier cloudy and showery. But here at Marrakech we have hardly had two hours of cloud or rain in three months. We are fifteen hundred feet high and the air is crisp, even sharp the moment one is out of the sun. But the sunlight is mellow and warm, and though the days are short, they are brilliant.

Esmond[1] is coming out here, and Rothermere has travelled north like a dutiful father to meet him at Tangier. He will probably bring him back here, or we shall go to Agadir and meet there. He has been good enough to arrange to have all the newspapers brought here each day by air for me and Lloyd George. This is a great convenience for we are only forty-eight hours behind the *Times*.

I have no plans and propose to stay here till I get bored. I spend the whole day painting and on Marlborough (apart from eating and drinking) but no neat spirits, according to the bet. Randolph is completely teetotal, though it does not seem to make him better tempered.

I have had one letter from you, but I look forward to some full account of your ski-ing, and how Mary is getting on. How I wish I had brought you out here straight away instead of that Barcelona–Formentor business. Lloyd George is staying here till the end of February. His daily routine is simple. He wakes at five and works on his *history* (save the mark) till breakfast. He plays golf on a very good course here till lunch. He sleeps from lunch till tea-time. His small wireless gives us what the BBC call the news bulletin, much twaddle, but here and there some facts. He dines early, then bed at 10.15. My roster is a little different, but equally satisfactory.

Conservative Whip, 1923–31. Parliamentary Secretary, Treasury, 1923–4, 1924–9 and 1931. Created Viscount Monsell, 1935. First Lord of the Admiralty, November 1931–June 1936.

[1] Esmond Cecil Harmsworth, 1898–1978. Only surviving son of the 1st Baron (later Viscount) Rothermere (whose other two sons were both killed in action on the western front). Served in the Royal Marine Artillery, 1917–18. ADC to Lloyd George at the Paris Peace Conference, 1919. Conservative MP for the Isle of Thanet, 1920–9. Supported Churchill at the Abbey by-election, 1924. Elected to the Other Club, 1928. Chairman of Associated Newspapers Ltd, 1932–71. Chairman of the Newspaper Proprietors' Association, 1934–61. Member of the Advisory Council, Ministry of Information, 1939. Succeeded his father as 2nd Viscount Rothermere, 1940. Chairman of the Daily Mail and General Trust Ltd.

Prof[1] has gone home on account of academic and scientific engagements. I think he enjoyed himself. So I am now alone with Duncan[2] and Diana.[3]

Please telegraph every day or so saying what you are doing. I have just sent you a long telegram to stir you up.

I sent three chapters of Marlborough in a very advanced condition home by the Prof.

I think this is the place to come out to for sunshine and comfort in the winter, in fact I have never seen the like. On Thursday the General[4] here

[1] Frederick Alexander Lindemann, 1886–1957. Born at Baden Baden (where his mother was taking the cure); son of Alsatian father who had emigrated to Britain in the early 1870s, and an American mother. Educated at Blair Lodge, Scotland; Darmstadt 1902–5, and Berlin University 1906–10. Doctor of Philosophy, Berlin, 1910. Studied physical chemistry in Paris, 1912–14. Worked at the Physical Laboratory, RAF, 1915–18, when he helped to organize the kite balloon barrage. Learned to fly, 1916. Personally investigated the aerodynamic effects of aircraft spin. Professor of Experimental Philosophy (physics), Oxford, 1919–56. Student of Christ Church (where he subsequently resided), 1921. Elected to the Other Club, 1927. Published his *Physical Significance of the Quantum Theory*, 1932. Member of the Expert Committee on Air Defence Research, Committee of Imperial Defence, 1935–9. Unsuccessful by-election candidate, Oxford University, 1937. Personal Assistant to the Prime Minister (Churchill) 1940–1; in 1953 Churchill's Private Secretary, John Martin, wrote to him, about the war years: 'Those without experience in the inner circle will never know the size of Winston's debt to you and how much stimulus and inspiration of ideas flowed from your office.' Created Baron Cherwell, 1941. Paymaster-General, 1942–5 and 1951–3. Privy Councillor, 1943. Viscount, 1956. His brother-in-law, Lieutenant Noel Musgrave Vickers (a barrister, born 1880, who had married Linda Lindemann in 1910) was killed in action on 24 March 1918, leaving a two-year-old son, James Oswald Noel Vickers (subsequently, from 1963–77, General Secretary of the Civil Service Union).

[2] Duncan Edwin Sandys, 1908–   . Educated at Eton and Magdalen College, Oxford. 3rd Secretary, British Embassy, Berlin, 1930. Conservative MP for Norwood, 1935–45; for Streatham, 1950–74. Political columnist, *Sunday Chronicle*, 1937–9. Member of the National Executive of the Conservative Party, 1938–9. Elected to the Other Club, 1939. On active service in Norway, 1940 (disabled; Lieutenant-Colonel, 1941). Financial Secretary, War Office, 1941–3. Chairman, War Cabinet Committee for defence against flying bombs and rockets, 1943–5. Privy Councillor, 1944. Minister of Works, 1944–5; of Supply, 1951–4; of Housing and Local Government, 1954–7; of Defence, 1957–9; of Aviation, 1959–60. Secretary of State for Commonwealth Relations, 1960–4 (and for Colonies, 1962–4). Created Baron Duncan-Sandys, 1974. In 1935 he married Churchill's daughter Diana (marriage dissolved, 1960). Companion of Honour, 1973.

[3] Diana Churchill. 1909–1963. Churchill's eldest child. In 1932 she married the eldest son of Sir Abe Bailey, John Milner Bailey (from whom she obtained a divorce in 1935). In 1935 she married Duncan Sandys MP.

[4] André Corap, 1878–1953. Entered the French Army as a cadet, 1896. On active service in Morocco, 1910–13. Served during the First World War on the Staffs of General Foch (1915) and General Pétain (1918). On active service in Morocco, 1925–6; it was to Colonel Corap that Abd el Krim surrendered on 26 May 1926. Général de brigade, 1929; de division, 1933. Chief of Staff to General Weygand (then Inspector-General of the Army), 1931–4. Commander-in-Chief of the French forces in Morocco, April 1935–December 1936. Commander of the Amiens Military Region, 1936–9. Commanded the IXth Army, September 1939–May 1940; forced by superior German arms and armour to withdraw from his position inside the Belgian frontier on 14 May 1940, he was relieved of his command, and severely criticized by the President of the Council, Paul Reynaud. He received no further military command.

has a great review, and is sending an aide-de-camp to conduct me to it.

The French have over fifty thousand men in Morocco, and we are to review three or four thousand which should be a fine spectacle. They govern the country with an iron hand, but great progress is being made and the whole apparatus of a pleasure resort is being established, where twenty years ago was chaos and war. There are fine expeditions to be made into the mountains. We are going to climb up to the big pass six thousand feet high, whence one can see, they say, as far as the Sahara Desert. No wonder the Germans were sulky over Agadir when they were jockeyed out of this grand country, where I don't see why white colonist-farmers should not live and breed. I am going to write an article for the Daily Mail about Morocco.[1]

We trafficked Morocco for our rights for a free hand in Egypt and are now throwing that away. The world seems to be divided between the confident nations who behave harshly, and the nations who have lost confidence in themselves and behave fatuously. Mussolini[2] is failing more and more in his Italian campaign. What I told you about the Italians being no good at

---

[1] Churchill's article 'I was Astonished By Morocco', published in the *Daily Mail* on his return to London, and illustrated by a photograph showing 'A Resident General and High Commissioner inspecting troops under the French flag'. The caption added: 'The remarkable efficiency of French colonisation is apparent in Morocco', and in his article he commented: 'The French are not at all infected with the apologetic diffidence which characterises British administration in African and Asiatic countries. They act, with something of the assurance which distinguished the builders of our Indian Empire in bygone times. They have a purpose and are not at all ashamed of it. Their purpose is not to hand over the country to its inhabitants, but on the contrary to develop it with the utmost energy for the enrichment of all classes in Morocco, and the important indirect advantage of France. They are by no means in the mood to be deprived of their rights, as they conceive them, by the agitation of a handful of students. They maintain an army of over fifty thousand men in Morocco; they offer its inhabitants logical, understanding, modern solutions of their problems. They govern to a large extent through the Arab chiefs, but in the ultimate issue their will is not to be questioned.'

In his article Churchill also wrote: 'If the world is designed to escape another hideous catastrophe, and the healing process can continue, one cannot doubt that Morocco has magnificent prospects.' But Churchill's own visit had angered the French Resident-General, of whom the British Consul-General in Rabat, Reader Bullard, wrote to Anthony Eden on 17 January 1936: 'I should hardly be surprised to find that M. Ponsot shared the view of the French newspaper which saw in the presence of Mr Lloyd George, Mr Winston Churchill and Lord Rothermere at Marrakech at the same time a dark conspiracy against the welfare and security of Morocco and France' (*Foreign Office papers: 371/20494*).

[2] Benito Mussolini, 1883–1945. Socialist journalist and agitator before 1914; editor of *Avanti*. Founded the patriotic *Il Popolo d'Italia*, 1914. Served on the Austrian front, 1917. Founded the Fascist Party at the end of the war. President of the Council of Ministers, 1922–6. Minister for Foreign Affairs, 1924–9 and 1932–6. Prime Minister 1926–43. Minister of War, 1926–9 and 1933–43. Left Rome as a prisoner, July 1943, first to Maddalena Island off Sardinia and then to Gran Sasso in the Abruzzi, where he was kept prisoner until rescued by glider on 12 September 1943. Head of the German-controlled Italian Social Republic, proclaimed on 23 September 1943 and set up at Saló on 19 October 1943. Murdered by Italian anti-Fascists, while attempting to cross into Switzerland, 28 April 1945.

fighting is being painfully proved. They are throwing away their wealth and their poor wedding rings on an absolutely shameful adventure. How it will end no one can tell. I am very sorry Austen[1] was not made Foreign Secretary. I think you will now see what a lightweight Eden[2] is. The League of Nations Union send me heaps of letters from the constituency clamouring for extreme measures, they having previously disarmed us, so that we are an easy prey!

It is vy nice having Diana & Duncan here. They are so happy. They say it is a second honeymoon. Anyhow sunshine, Love, & no expense or house-hold cares ought to be pretty good! The more I see of him, the better I like him. They read political books to each other under the palm trees while I paint. I think you will be surprised to see the pictures I have painted. I am. R[3] wishes to buy one to present to the Resident-General. I now have *seven*.

Randolph has just telegraphed his safe arrival at Toulouse. He left Casa Blanca this morning. Tomorrow he shd lunch in London!

I am longing to hear yr news. Is it true you have Venetia, Diana D.C.[4] & Duff[5] with you?

Tender love my darling pussy cat,
Your ever devoted husband,
W

PS. I wonder if the ginger cat misses me!

[1] Joseph Austen Chamberlain, 1863–1937. Educated at Rugby and Trinity College, Cambridge. Conservative MP, 1892–1937. Chancellor of the Exchequer, 1903–5. Unsuccessful candidate for the leadership of the Conservative Party, 1911. Secretary of State for India, 1915–17. Minister without Portfolio, 1918–19. Chancellor of the Exchequer, 1919–21. Lord Privy Seal, 1921–2. Foreign Secretary, 1924–9. Knight of the Garter, 1925. First Lord of the Admiralty, 1931. Half brother of Neville Chamberlain (see page 14, note 1).

[2] Robert Anthony Eden, 1897–1977. Educated at Eton and Christ Church, Oxford. Served on the western front, 1915–18, when he was awarded the Military Cross. Conservative MP, 1923–57. Parliamentary Under-Secretary, Foreign Office, 1931–3. Lord Privy Seal, 1934–5. Minister for League of Nations Affairs, 1935. Foreign Secretary, 1935–8, 1940–5 and 1951–5. Knight of the Garter, 1954. Prime Minister, 1955–7. Created Earl of Avon, 1961. One of his brothers was killed near Ypres in October 1914, another in 1916 at the battle of Jutland. His elder son was killed in action in Burma on 23 June 1945, aged 20.

[3] Lord Rothermere.

[4] Lady Diana Olivia Winifred Maud Manners, 1892–   . Daughter of the 8th Duke of Rutland. In 1919 she married Alfred Duff Cooper (later Viscount Norwich). After her husband's death in 1954 she was known as Lady Diana Cooper.

[5] Alfred Duff Cooper, 1890–1954. Known as 'Duff'. Educated at Eton and New College, Oxford. Entered the Foreign Office as a Clerk, 1913. On active service, Grenadier Guards, 1917–18 (DSO, despatches). Conservative MP for Oldham (Churchill's first constituency), 1924–9. Financial Secretary, War Office, 1928–9 and 1931–4. MP for St Georges Westminster, 1931–45. Financial Secretary, Treasury, 1934–5. Privy Councillor, 1935. Secretary of State for War, 1935–7. First Lord of the Admiralty, 1937–8. Minister of Information, 1940–1. British Representative, Singapore, 1941. Chancellor of the Duchy of Lancaster, 1941–3. British Representative, French Committee of National Liberation, 1943–4. Ambassador to France, 1944–7. Knighted, 1948. Created Viscount Norwich, 1952. In 1919 he married Lady Diana Manners. In 1928 he was elected to the Other Club (founded by Churchill and F. E. Smith in 1911).

Winston S. Churchill to Clementine Churchill

(*Spencer-Churchill papers*)

15 January 1936   Hotel Transatlantique
                                             Meknes, Morocco

My darling Clemmie,

We quitted Marrakech on the 14th with much regret, eighteen days having gone without count of time. Rothermere sent a motor which conveyed us 250 miles northwards to Meknes, where we still are. It is an excellent hotel, and is situated in most beautiful fertile foothills of the Atlas mountains, but does not compare with Marrakech. The weather is definitely colder, the sunlight less mellow and the vegetation Spanish rather than African. There is of course the great native city of Fez which we shall go to see tomorrow or the day after. Rothermere and Esmond are here, very friendly to us, and very pessimistic about everything.

Your letters of the 7th and 11th have arrived. The 11th pursued us from Marrakech, yet reached me on the 15th.

You will no doubt have read in the papers all about Randolph. Today he telegraphs that an unimportant Scottish paper alleges I am wholeheartedly supporting his candidature. I am reluctant to disavow him and have let things drift. Rothermere however is arranging for Oliver Baldwin to write an article examining the relations of fathers and sons in politics and pointing out that sons must take their own line and their fathers cannot be held responsible. I shall not make up my mind upon the matter further until I get home, but I should think that any question of my joining the Government was closed by the hostility which Randolph's campaign must excite. Kismet!

At Marrakech Ll G's party and ours dined with the Glaoui[1] or Pasha and ate a gargantuan endless Arab feast with our fingers. He is a very able man and keeps a great state in Marrakech. His son, aged 21, lives at Telouet, a hundred miles into the heart of the Atlas mountains. We visited him there by a splendid road with awful precipices on either side, and were entertained in his enormous castle which lies about the level of the snow line in a sombre valley. We were received with a great welcome and had another Arab banquet—I hope my last for a long time.

We were then entertained by a dance of about a hundred women, some quite goodlooking, all in their best silks and finery. The dance consisted of

---

[1] El Hadji T'hami El Glaoui, paramount Pasha of Marrakesh and Hereditary Sultan of the Atlas. Succeeded his brother as Pasha, 1911. Received an annual subvention from the French Government, in return for his loyalty to France. Noted for his particularly large harem, and for his infatuation with golf. Wounded seventeen times in suppressing local revolts against his authority. He died in 1956, aged 78. In 1957 his son Caid Brahim was exiled from Morocco for 15 years.

droning chants to kettle drums with rhythmic motions of the hands. Personally my taste is more attuned to the Russian ballet, but the natives seem to have been thrilled by this for hundreds of years. The mountain glens of the Atlas are full of men, villages every few miles, and great fertility at the bottom of the valleys. Here is where the warlike people are bred, and very dangerous they will be if ever they get weapons in their hands again. Ll G and I returned the Glaoui's hospitality by giving him a dinner at the hotel which went off very successfully.

I am very sorry that we did not carry out our original plan, staying longer at Marrakech and then going south to Agadir, and so back to Casablanca, instead of coming up to this quite pleasant, very healthy, but far less paintable and romantic north. I do like sunshine and palm trees and all the other delights of that charming part.

I must say I should like to take you there some day. The Pasha has an excellent private golf course, there is tennis and quite nice horses for riding. Everybody feels extremely well. This place too is very healthy.

I have been idle the last few days as we have been moving so much. Marlborough has advanced but little. I have four articles to do which I must manage somehow on the journey home.

17th January

I had been planning to return by ship from Casablanca which would have brought me to Paris by the 21st and London in time for the Birmingham banquet on the 25th. But thinking over the whole situation I decided yesterday to cancel my Birmingham fixture and go back to Marrakech for another week. The Paris Chamber of Commerce has invited me to address them at their annual dinner on the 30th. As the Ambassador[1] 'definitely advises' acceptance I have said 'Yes.' It does not matter chucking the Birmingham fixture. They have Austen[2] and Hailsham[3] and only wanted me to propose

---

[1] George Russell Clerk, 1874–1951. Educated at Eton and New College, Oxford. Entered the Foreign Office, 1899; served in Addis Ababa and Constantinople. Knighted, 1917. First Minister to Czechoslovakia, 1919–26. Ambassador to Turkey, 1926–33; to Belgium, 1933–4; to France, 1934–7. Retired, 1937.

[2] Sir Austen Chamberlain, a former Foreign Secretary (see page 11, note 1).

[3] Douglas McGarel Hogg, 1872–1950. Educated at Eton. A West India merchant. On active service in South Africa, 1900. Called to the Bar, 1902. King's Counsel, 1917. Attorney-General to the Prince of Wales, 1920–2. Knighted, 1922. Conservative MP, St Marylebone, 1922–8. Attorney-General, 1922–4 and 1924–8. Privy Councillor, 1922. Lord Chancellor, 1928–9. Acting Prime Minister, August–September 1928. Created Baron Hailsham, 1928; Viscount, 1929. Secretary of State for War, 1931–5. Lord Chancellor, 1935–8. His brother Ian (a friend of Churchill at Sandhurst) died of wounds received in action in France on 2 September 1914. Both his brothers-in-law also died on the western front, one in action in 1915, the other of illness in 1918.

the local toast about the industry of Birmingham. Moreover I think it is convenient for me to be out of England as long as possible and emphasises without any positive declaration that I am taking no part in Randolph's campaign. The moment I return I shall be asked to say whether I approve or not. Finally Duncan and Diana are enjoying themselves so much that I wish to prolong their stay and mine in these brilliant surroundings.

So here we are on our way in the train approaching Marrakech again amid sunshine once more warm and brilliant. They put a sleeping carriage on for us at Meknes at midnight and by noon we shall be back at the Mamounia hotel.

It is Ll G's birthday and we are all going to dine together to celebrate it.

Rothermere at last decided to go to Monte Carlo tomorrow and Esmond, who had been chafing at Meknes, is coming South to join us at Marrakech. We shall stay there till the 21st or 22nd, and then move over the mountains through the Arab town of Tarodant, of whose paintability I hear great tales, and so to Agadir, of byegone fame. Thence we shall motor northwards to Casablanca and embark on the 25th. I enclose you a little map so that you may follow our peregrinations.

I am delighted to know that you are enjoying yourself at Zürs. You certainly should do so with such agreeable company. Also to hear you and Mary are progressing in the art of ski-ing. I am afraid I must resign all attempts to emulate you. By the way they are making a winter sports centre here in the Atlas mountains and most years they have very good conditions at about 6,000 feet. This year however the weather has been so fine that all the snow is melting.

I telegraphed to you yesterday wondering whether you would now wish to join me in Paris at the Embassy on the 28th. Up to the present I have only proposed myself to the Ambassador, but if you would like to stay at the Embassy I have little doubt they have room for us both. When I get your answer I will telegraph to the Ambassador. On this showing I should not expect to return to England before the 2nd or 3rd February. Parliament meets on the 4th—to confront a situation which is steadily getting more difficult.

Evidently there is a deep division in the Cabinet between the Hoares and the anti-Hoares or Edens, the Edens pushed on by the febrile League of Nations Union and balloteers want oil sanctions and us to take a lead in them. They will be strengthened if things go worse with the Abyssinians than they have done so far. The other lot headed I suppose by Neville[1] and

---

[1] Arthur Neville Chamberlain, 1869–1940. Son of Joseph Chamberlain, his mother died in childbirth in 1875. Educated at Rugby and Mason College, Birmingham. In business in the Bahamas, 1890–7. Lord Mayor of Birmingham, 1915–16. Director-General of National

Runciman,[1] with Vansittart[2] in the background, are determined to play for safety. I fear they have some grave news about Germany and her aggressive intentions. Certainly our Ambassador at Berlin[3] found a very rough Hitler[4] when he went to talk about an air pact. They are getting stronger every moment. They have chosen to make their Press demonstrate vehemently against the Anglo-French military and naval conversations which were necessary upon the Italian danger.

The French papers all think that this outcry is a preliminary to a declaration that the Treaty of Locarno is not being observed in the spirit by England and only one-sidedly against Germany, and that consequently the German promise not to remilitarise the neutral zone can be repudiated.

Rothermere who has long letters and telegrams from Hitler and is in close touch with him, believes that on the 24th or it may be the 21st, Hitler is going to make a most important announcement. This may well be that Germany will violate Articles 46 and 47 of the Treaty and reoccupy the neutral zone with troops and forts. This would immediately raise a very grave European issue, and no one can tell what would come of it. Certainly the

---

Service, 1916–17 (when his cousin Norman, to whom he was devoted, was killed in action on the western front). Conservative MP for Ladywood, 1918–29; for Edgbaston, 1929–40. Postmaster-General, 1922–3. Paymaster-General, 1923. Minister of Health, 1923, 1924–9 and 1931. Chancellor of the Exchequer, 1923–4 and 1931–7. Leader of the Conservative Party, 1937. Prime Minister, 1937–40. Lord President of the Council, May–November 1940.

[1] Walter Runciman, 1870–1949. Educated at Trinity College, Cambridge. Liberal MP, 1899–1900; 1902–18. Shipowner. President of the Board of Education, 1908–11. President of the Board of Agriculture and Fisheries, 1911–14. President of the Board of Trade, 1914–16. Liberal MP, 1924–9; 1929–31. Liberal National MP, 1931–7. President of the Board of Trade, 1931–7. 2nd Baron, 1937. Created Viscount Runciman of Doxford, 1937. Head of Mission to Czechoslovakia, 1938. Lord President of the Council, October 1938–September 1939.

[2] Robert Gilbert Vansittart, 1881–1957. Educated at Eton. Entered the Diplomatic Service, 1902. Assistant Clerk, Foreign Office, 1914; 1st Secretary, 1918; Counsellor, 1920. Secretary to Lord Curzon, 1920–4. Principal Private Secretary to Ramsay MacDonald, 1928–30. Knighted, 1929. Permanent Under-Secretary of State for Foreign Affairs, 1930–8. Elected to the Other Club, 1933. Chief Diplomatic Adviser to the Foreign Secretary, 1938–41. Privy Councillor, 1940. Created Baron, 1941. His autobiography, *The Mist Procession*, was published posthumously, in 1958. His brother Arnold was killed in action in 1915.

[3] Eric Clare Edmund Phipps, 1875–1945. Diplomat; Attaché in Paris, 1899; Counsellor of Embassy in Brussels, 1920–2; Minister in Paris, 1922–8. Knighted, 1927. Minister in Vienna, 1928–33. Privy Councillor, 1933. Ambassador in Berlin, 1933–7; Ambassador in Paris, 1937–9.

[4] Adolf Hitler, 1889–1945. Born in Upper Austria. Served on the western front as a Corporal in the German Army, 1914–18; wounded and gassed; Iron Cross first and second class. Assumed the Leadership of the National Socialist Workers Party, July 1921. Staged an unsuccessful putsch in Munich, 8 November 1923. Imprisoned in the Landsberg Fortress, January–December 1924. Published *Mein Kampf*, 1925. Chancellor of the German Reich from 30 January 1933, until his death. Chief of State, 2 August 1934. He committed suicide in Berlin on 30 April 1945.

League of Nations would be obliged to declare the Germans guilty of 'aggression', and the French would be in a position to demand our specific aid in enforcing sanctions.

So the League of Nations Union folk who have done their best to get us disarmed may find themselves confronted by terrible consequences. Baldwin and Ramsay, guilty of neglecting our defences in spite of every warning, may well feel anxious not only for the public but for their own personal skins.

The Naval Conference has of course collapsed. Japan has ruptured it. The good thing is that we and the United States are working hand in glove and will encourage each other to strengthen the navies. Meanwhile Japan is seeking more provinces of China. Already more than half of their whole budget is spent upon armaments. Those figures I quoted about German expenditure on armaments are being admitted in the press to be only too true.

One must consider these two predatory military dictatorship nations, Germany and Japan, as working in accord. No wonder the Russian bear is quaking for his skin and seeking protectors among the capitalist powers he deserted in the war and sought to destroy at the close of it. What—to quote a famous phrase—'What a fearful concatenation of circumstances.'[1]

How melancholy that we have this helpless Baldwin and his valets in absolute possession of all power. I suppose now that the Naval Conference is over, Monsell will be going and it seems not at all unlikely to me that they may get Sam Hoare back as First Lord.[2] Evidently the reason why he made no complaint of his treatment was because of some promise of early reinstatement.

I doubt whether they will take any effective action however about coordinating the defence measures. Very likely some Minister without Portfolio may be assigned some of the duties in this respect. But all the three service Ministers will be very much against any higher control.

It is very nice to look forward to another week of sunshine and painting. I expect you will be surprised at my pictures when you see them. They are a cut above anything I have ever done so far. One more today! I am doing figures so much better than before. Indeed every person here however poor is a picture, & the crowds with their bright & varied colours are a pageant.

My darling pussycat—I must bring you to this place. I am sure we could spend some happy weeks here together in the sunshine, when perhaps at home all was gloomy & cold.

[1] A remark by the American orator, Daniel Webster (1772–1852).
[2] Sir Samuel Hoare returned to the Cabinet, as First Lord of the Admiralty, on 5 June 1936.

I will write again vy soon. Meanwhile give my fondest love to Maria, & tell her how glad I am she is getting on so well in ski-ing.

Your ever devoted & loving husband,

W

[sketch of pig]

Clementine Churchill to Winston S. Churchill
(*Spencer-Churchill papers*)

17 January 1936 Zürs

. . . I wonder how Randolph will do in this new Election. I feel rather dubious about it. It's lucky he enjoys elections so much. I do trust it will not prejudice your affairs.

Saturday the 18th. I see the Independent Liberal has stood down.[1] I do hope Randolph does not forfeit his deposit. I read a very well expressed letter from him in the Times of the 16th. The point he makes is a small one, but he makes it well & if his facts are correct it may make an impression.[2]

[1] The independent Liberal candidate was Provost Roderick Smith, of Stornoway. On 16 January 1936 *The Times* reported that he had been invited to stand as independent liberal candidate by the Scottish Liberal Federation. On January 15 Provost Smith attended a meeting at Dingwall 'to estimate the measure of support on which he might count', and decided, *The Times* reported, 'that it would be fatal to liberalism to go forward'. According to *The Times:* 'The meeting was of an extraordinary character. From the outset it was obvious that only a small proportion of those present were in favour of the adoption of an independent candidate. Members of the audience who did not want an independent liberal candidate were invited to leave the hall, so that others could form themselves into a committee. Three-quarters of those present made for the door, and, while they were still moving out, Provost Smith put an end to the proceedings by making it clear that in the circumstances it would be disastrous to go on with his candidature'.

[2] On 16 January 1936 *The Times* published a letter from Randolph Churchill which read: 'Sir, Under the heading "A Clear Issue in Ross" you expressed on Tuesday one point of view on the election in Ross and Cromarty. May I suggest that the issue would have been no less clear but your conclusion contrary if you had not burked most of the important issues involved in the present controversy? You make no mention of the long-established rule that constituencies are entitled to choose their own representatives rather than have them imposed by the executive. . . . The arrangements for foisting Mr Malcolm MacDonald on to the Liberal Association in Ross and Cromarty were the joint and prompt work of the Conservative Chief Whip and Sir Ian Macpherson, the retiring member. The timing of this intrigue is highly significant. . . . The arrangement which was thus concluded did violence to the Ross and Cromarty Unionists, who were not consulted, to the coordinating Committee, which never met, and to the National Liberals, whose vigilance was dormant and who found themselves on January 1 the unsuspecting donors of one of their best seats to the representative of another party whose name he was soon to deny. Finally, Sir, may I emphasize that I have been adopted as the official Unionist candidate in support of the National Government? My candidature is not hostile to the Government except in this one respect, that it is intended to be an effective protest against nomination by the executive in defiance of the principles of representative government. As I urged at my adoption meeting on Saturday, the real issue is whether Ross and Cromarty support of the Government is to be voluntary or coerced.'

Goodbye my darling. The post is going. A heavy fall of snow in the night and large woolly flakes still falling.

Your loving,
Clemmie

Brendan Bracken[1] *to Winston S. Churchill: telegram*

(*Churchill papers: 2/287*)

17 January 1936

Randolph's prospects very doubtful. Socialist win probable. More stags than Tories in Cromarty.

Brendan

Winston S. Churchill to Randolph S. Churchill: telegram

(*Churchill papers: 2/287*)

18 January 1936

Hope consider effect demise[2] on party feeling and your prospects. Wire nomination date Gerahty,[3] Minza Tangier.

Churchill

---

[1] Brendan Bracken, 1901–1958. Educated in Australia and at Sedbergh School. Journalist and financier. Conservative MP for North Paddington, 1929–45; for Bournemouth, 1950–1. Elected to the Other Club, 1932. Chairman of the *Financial News*. Managing Director of the *Economist*. Chairman of the *Financial Times*. Parliamentary Private Secretary to the Prime Minister (Churchill), 1940–1. Privy Councillor, 1940. Minister of Information, 1941–5. First Lord of the Admiralty, 1945. Created Viscount, 1952.

[2] The death of King George V was believed to be imminent (he died on 20 January 1936).

[3] Cecil Gerahty. Served in the Royal Navy, 1914–18. Employed in 1920 by a French firm to buy naval equipment in the Gibraltar Dockyard. *Daily Mail* correspondent in Morocco, 1934–7; he reported with the Moorish troops fighting in Spain (in the Cordoba mountains, and on the Madrid front). On 17 June 1937 Churchill wrote a letter of introduction on Gerahty's behalf for a job with the Empire Marketing Board. On 20 June 1937 Gerahty published his first book, *The Road to Madrid*, and in 1938 *The Spanish Avenue*.

Sir Reginald Barnes[1] to Winston S. Churchill

(*Churchill papers: 1/284*)

19 January 1936

Dear old Winston,

I wonder if you have seen the enclosed,[2] written & sent to me by my old French interpreter in the 111 Brigade, if not, it may amuse you to read & tear up. I wish you were in the Gov\u1d57 now as they look like wanting you. I had quite settled it for them that you would be First Lord of the Admiralty, and only hope that you will be so when the present stop-gap goes. The Italians seem to have their hands full, and it looks to me that Graziani[3] has gone too far forward in this last attack, & in the wrong direction. The Abyssinians ought to be able to make his rear very windy!

I hope Randolph will do well in Ross, but it will be a hard job with all the officials against him. Longing to see you again & have a quack, perhaps you will be in London when we come up for a bit later on.

Love to Mrs Winston.

Yours ever,
Reggie

[1] Reginald Walter Ralph Barnes, 1871–1946. Entered Army, 1890. Lieutenant, 4th Hussars, 1894, and one of Churchill's close Army friends. Went with Churchill to Cuba, 1895. Captain, 1901. Lieutenant-Colonel commanding the 10th Hussars, 1911–15. Colonel 1914. Brigadier-General, commanding the 116th Infantry Brigade, and the 14th Infantry Brigade, 1915–16. Commanded the 32nd Division, 1916–17 and the 57th Division, 1917–19. Major-General, 1918. Knighted, 1919.

[2] An article signed 'RCS', published in a French newspaper. The interpreter recalled Churchill saying, about a middle-aged, ambitious French politician: 'I know him. He is a good chap, but badly brought up. And then again, he has begun too late. Politics is like the piano, or prostitution. One must start young, or one will not succeed (l'on n'arrive à rien)'.

[3] Rudolfo Graziani, 1882–1955. A regular soldier, on active service in Libya, 1911, and on the Italian–Austrian front, 1915–18 (twice wounded, decorated for valour). Lieutenant-Colonel, Macedonian front, 1918. On active service (against rebel tribesmen) in Libya, 1921–31. Governor of Cyrenaica, 1931–5. Commanded the Italian forces which conquered Abyssinia from the South, 1935–6. Viceroy of Abyssinia 1936–7. Created Marquis of Neghelli, 1937. Commander of the Axis Forces in North Africa, 1940; defeated by the British in North Africa, 1941. Minister of War, 1943, in the Government of the Fascist Republic of Saló. Led the continuing Fascist armed resistance after the fall of Mussolini, 1943–4. Captured by Italian partisans near Lake Como, April 1945. Stripped of his rank, deprived of his decorations and sentenced to nineteen years imprisonment, for collaboration with the Germans, May 1950. Freed by Government amnesty, August 1950. Subsequently Honorary President of the neo-Fascist Italian Social Movement, from which he resigned in 1954, in protest against its opposition to the European Defence Community.

Sir Emsley Carr[1] *to Winston S. Churchill: telegram*

(*Churchill papers: 8/533*)

21 January 1936

Can you cable, collecting at this end, or send by airmail, appreciation of King George[2] for Great Men Series this week, 3,500 words, to arrive not later than Friday. Reply: Emsley Carr, Worldly Fleet, London.

Winston S. Churchill to Sir Emsley Carr: telegram

(*Churchill papers: 8/533*)

21 January 1936

Yes. Best cheapest method telegraph press rates Paris, forwarding thence by air mail. Who is your agent Paris. Churchill, Mamounia, Marrakech.

[1] Emsley Carr, 1867–1941. Newspaper proprietor; director of George Newnes Ltd; Chairman of the *News of the World*; Vice-Chairman of the *Western Mail*, Cardiff, the *South Wales Echo*, and the Cardiff *Evening Express*. Knighted, 1918. Delegate to the Imperial Press Conference, Canada, 1925; Australia, 1930. Chairman of the Press Gallery of the House of Commons, 1929–30. President of the Institute of Journalists, 1932 and 1933. Chairman of the Newspaper Press Fund, 1936, and the Printers' Pension Corporation, 1939. High Sheriff of Glamorgan, 1938.

[2] George Frederick Ernest Albert, of Saxe-Coburg and Gotha, 1865–1936. Second son of King Edward VII and Queen Alexandra. Navel Cadet, 1877; Midshipman, 1880. Created Prince of Wales, 1901, Ascended the throne on his father's death, 1910. Crowned, 1911. Announced the assumption of the surname of Windsor, 1917. He married Mary of Teck (later Queen Mary) in 1893. Churchill wrote, in his obituary of the King: 'Many were the changes which he saw in our habits, customs and moods. Women have acquired complete political enfranchisement and exercise enormous political power. The motor car has replaced the horse, with all that that implies. The wealth and well-being of every class has advanced, upon a giant scale. Crime, brutal violence, drunkenness, and the consumption of liquor, have diminished. We are gentler and a more decent people. The thriving free Press has become a faithful guardian of the Royal Family. The broadcast has enabled the Sovereign to speak to all his peoples. In a world of ruin and chaos King George V brought about a resplendent rebirth of the great office which fell to his lot.'

Winston S. Churchill to Sir Reginald Barnes

(*Churchill papers: 1/284*)

26 January 1936   Chartwell

Thank you so much for sending me the most agreeable appreciation written by your old interpreter. I must say I am very pleased with the mot with which it concludes. It is one of those things which I had forgotten I had said and which I will certainly take occasion to say again. I have just returned from six weeks in Marrakech's most lovely sunshine where I have been painting. I am consequently quite out of touch with the political situation here, but Randolph seems to be enjoying himself amid the snows of Cromarty. I have no idea what the future has in store for me, but you will find me vigorously advocating our rearmament while time remains by every channel that is open.

Let me know when you come to London.

Winston S. Churchill to Sir Michael O'Dwyer[1]

(*Churchill papers: 2/263*)

26 January 1936

Thank you so much for sending me your extremely disquieting letter to the Times.[2] This is the first fruit of that evil tree which has now begun to ripen. I will certainly see that it is raised in one form or another.

[1] Michael Francis O'Dwyer, 1864–1940. Born in County Tipperary. Entered the Indian Civil Service, 1885. Revenue Commissioner, North-West Frontier, 1901–8. Acting Resident Hyderabad, 1908–9. Viceroy's Agent in Central India, 1910–12. Knighted, 1913. Lieutenant-Governor of the Punjab, 1913–19. He published *India as I knew It* in 1925.

[2] On 10 January 1936 *The Times* published a letter from Sir Michael O'Dwyer, the theme of which was 'that the authorities here and in India are already seriously concerned at the difficulty of finding a sufficiency of suitable British candidates for the Indian Civil Service'. O'Dwyer's letter continued: 'The Joint Committee, whose report formed the basis of the Government of India Act, put it on record (paragraph 273) that "we are convinced that India for a long time to come will not be able to dispense with a strong British element in the Services". . . . If things go on in this way the "indispensable" British element will soon disappear, and it would be better to abolish the Service while it still has an honourable record.' The 'attractions' of the Indian Civil Service had, O'Dwyer wrote, 'been immensely reduced by the recent Act, which has deprived its members of nearly all the prize appointments they formerly held, or could aspire to' and he ended his letter: 'No one will regret the disappearance of those British officials more than the Indian masses, while their going will render the task of the remaining 1,000 British ICS and police officers—the sole survivors of the British administration—more arduous, their exile harder to bear, and the conditions of service generally less popular.'

Winston S. Churchill to Sir Robert Horne[1]

(Churchill papers: 1/284)

27 January 1936

On returning here from some weeks of delicious sunshine in Marrakech I received the extremely gratifying intimation that you had forwarded me a dozen bottles of sunshine in an even more compendious and mobile form. A thousand thanks for this most welcome Christmas present, which I greatly appreciate even more in practice.

Quite a lot seems to have happened while I have been away and I expect a few things more will go on happening in the near future. We must concentrate upon the defence danger.

Winston S. Churchill to Major Percy Davies[2]

(Churchill papers: 8/533)

27 January 1936

I am very glad you liked the article. It was rather a rush doing it at the very moment we were packing up and on the journey. Actually Mrs Pearman[3]

[1] Robert Stevenson Horne, 1871–1940. Lecturer in Philosophy, University College of North Wales, 1895. Examiner in Philosophy, Aberdeen University, 1896. Active at the Scottish Bar, 1900–14. Assistant Inspector-General of Transportation, with the rank of Lieutenant-Colonel, 1917. Director of Department of Materials and Priority, Admiralty, 1917. Director, Admiralty Labour Department, 1918. Third Civil Lord of Admiralty, 1918–19. Knighted, 1918. Conservative MP, 1918–37. Minister of Labour, 1919. President of the Board of Trade, 1920–1. Chancellor of the Exchequer, 1921–2. Declined office under Bonar Law and turned to the City for employment, where he became Chairman of the Great Western Railway Company, the Burma Corporation and several other companies. Created Viscount Horne of Slamannan, 1937. A member of the Other Club from 1920.

[2] David Percy Davies, 1892–1946. Educated at Llandovery College. Joined the editorial staff of the *News of the World*, 1914. Assistant editor of *Tit Bits*, 1914. Major commanding 12 Corps Cyclist Battalion in Italy and France, 1916–18. Captured by the Germans on the western front, April 1918. Called to the Bar 1919. Returned to the editorial staff of the *News of the World*, 1919; deputy editor, 1933; member of the Board, 1935; editor from 1941 until his death. High Sheriff of Glamorgan, 1943–4.

[3] Violet Constance Evelyn Williams, 1896–1941. Began secretarial work at the Treasury, 1915; worked subsequently in the Cabinet Office, Home Office and Irish Office (during the 'Troubles'). During the war she married George Edward Pearman (known as Alan), a Chartered Accountant. He enlisted, falsely declaring himself to be old enough to serve. Both his legs were blown off during fighting on the western front, and he suffered also from severe shell-shock. After the war he became a lift attendant. With one daughter aged nine, and another of only two months, Mrs Pearman began part-time work at Chartwell in July 1929, and became Churchill's principal, full-time secretary on 11 November 1929. In 1938 she was forced to retire, through illness, but continued to do part-time work for Churchill. Following her death on 17 March 1941, Churchill arranged for her monthly salary (of £12 a week)

had to type it in the train. I dare say if I had had more time I could have produced you something better.[1]

Mr Gerahty, the Daily Mail correspondent in Morocco, was very helpful in the transmission of this article. He advised me to send it by the French internal service to Paris. At press rates this is only about one tenth of the Eastern Telegraph Company's charge. I entrusted him with the despatch of the article after I had left Tangier,[2] specially with the checking of the punctuation etc. He used his Daily Mail press licence and sent it via the Daily Mail, Paris. I expect this saved a very considerable sum of money, possibly £70 or £80 for the cost of transmission. Anyhow I thought it right to pay Mr Gerahty a fee of £10 for his work and also £5 for his expenses for staying in Tangier an extra day for the purpose of transmitting the article. I gather from your conversation with Mrs Pearman that you would wish to reimburse me to this extent.

---

to be paid to her daughter Rosemary, then aged eleven; then for seven years from July 1943, Churchill paid £100 a year towards Rosemary Pearman's education. Violet Pearman's elder daughter, Marguerite, born in 1919, served first in a Munitions factory (1940), then in the Women's Auxiliary Air Force (1940–5), first with barrage balloons, then as a wireless operator with Coastal Command, Norfolk, and Ismailia. She married 1st, in 1945, Peter Savage; 2nd, in 1955, Leslie Bowyer.

[1] Churchill was paid £1,000 for this article, which was published in the *News of the World* on 26 January 1936. Of the world changes during the King's lifetime he wrote: 'A large part of the globe which in Victorian times lay in the mild sunshine of law and tranquillity is now scourged by storms of anarchy. Mighty nations which gained their liberties in the nineteenth century, and hopefully erected parliaments to preserve them, have fallen, or yielded themselves, to the iron sway of dictatorships. Over immense regions inhabited by the most gifted and educated races, as well as in barbarous countries, all enjoyment of individual freedom, all assertion of the rights of the individual against the State have utterly lapsed.' Defending British democracy, Churchill wrote: 'it is the people who own the Government, and not the Government the people'. As for the King's personal achievement, Churchill noted: 'He reconciled the new forces of Labour and Socialism to the Constitution and Monarchy. This prodigious event and enormous process of assimilation and rallying the spokesmen of left-out millions will be intently studied by historians of the future. To the astonishment of foreign countries and of our American kinsmen, the world beheld the spectacle of the King and Emperor working in the utmost ease and unaffected cordiality with politicians whose theories at any rate seemed to menace all existing institutions, and with leaders fresh from organizing the General Strike. The result has been to make a national unity upon Constitutional fundamentals, which is the wonder of the world. Such an evolution, which might well have occupied a tumultuous century, and perhaps in its process wrecked the continuity and tradition of our national life, was achieved by George V in the compass of his reign. In so doing he revived the idea of Constitutional Monarchy throughout the world.'

[2] Churchill had reached Tangier on the morning of 23 January 1936, after the night long journey from Marrakech, and had left that same morning for Spain, to return to London by train. Such was the popularity of holidaying in Tangier and Morocco that the visitors in January and February 1937 included Duff and Lady Diana Cooper, Lord Beaverbrook, Lord Camrose, Lord Rothermere, David Lloyd George, Admiral Sir Murray Sueter, Kenneth Lindsay, and the journalists George Ward Price and Hannen Swaffer.

Randolph S. Churchill to Winston S. Churchill

(*Churchill papers: 2/287*)

27 January 1936   Richmond House,
                                                   Strathpeffer

My dear Papa,

I will try to give you a fuller account of the conditions up here than was possible last night on the telephone.

The constituency stretches from the Atlantic to the North Sea and covers a million and a half acres. With an electorate of 27,000 odd this makes only one elector to every $55\frac{1}{2}$ acres. In effect, however, it is not as bad as it sounds as more than 70% of the electorate are on the East Coast in fairly populous districts. We can comfortably reach 20,000 of the electorate from our five Committee rooms at Tain, Invergordon, Dingwall, Strathpeffer and Fortrose. Between this strip on the East Coast and a much more sparsely populated strip on the West Coast there is no one at all, only vast deer forests and mountains.

I have not attempted to organise the West Coast, but am concentrating all my efforts on the 20,000 voters in the East. The electorate, as a whole, are by no means as dour as I had anticipated. The Highlander is a very different cup of tea from the Lowlander.

The distress in the farming community is quite appalling. The Government's agricultural policy, while it has been of benefit to England, has not helped Scotland at all and in many ways has been actually harmful. . . .

As to our support, we have 80% of the Unionist and probably 90% of the Unionist Association vote, and we only know of about a dozen farmers who are against us. Much will depend on the extent to which they can influence their own ploughmen and farmservants. We shall get a certain amount of the crofters' vote, but the bulk of it will be distributed between MacDonald and the Liberal, with a larger part, at any rate on the West Coast, going to the Liberal.

With the exception of a few county snobs who go to London and who come under the Baldwin influence, most people of substance are with us. Few people up here seem to care much for Baldwin, although there is a certain feeling for the National Government, but it is not as strong as in other parts of the country. . . .

We have two or three people in every district, even in those which I have not yet visited. In Cromarty, for instance, where I go this afternoon, the local doctor is working very hard for us. The same at Ullapool on the West Coast. We already have strong committees in Tain, Dingwall, Strathpeffer and Fortrose. There is no difficulty, as soon as one goes to these different towns and villages, in forming a strong local committee. Many people are holding back until they have heard the speeches before deciding. . . .

There is not the slightest doubt that we have made a large number of converts in the few places where I have already spoken. We have an overwhelming case, and it only needs to be stated to command support.

Whereas no one up here has heard Baldwin, you and Lloyd George are extremely popular, with you definitely in the lead. This is one of the most patriotic parts of the country I have ever struck. There are many retired people and the fisher folk all have a great opinion of your services to the Navy.

I was not invited to come here because of my reputation as a specialist in wrecking (as you suggested) but solely on account of you. They are all mystified and puzzled as to why you are not in the Government, and think it an abuse and a scandal. Of course I am besieged with requests that you should come and speak. I tell them all that if they make me their member you will doubtless come.

Many people are actuated by a fear of letting the Socialist in. If we can make the running in the next few days and appear to have our nose in the lead, we will probably get a big swing-over of waverers who will want to cast their votes on the winning side. Much will, of course, depend upon what happens in the Scottish Universities. If Dewar Gibb[1] wins or even polls well it will be very heartening to our people. . . .[2]

Early in the campaign I accepted £50 to £5 against myself from a local bookmaker, but these odds are no longer obtainable, particularly since the arrival of the Liberal candidate. No one here, friend, foe or pressman, thinks we can poll less than 3,000. The other side are bereft of argument and are forced to fall back upon the stale cry of 'personalities' and 'bad taste' when they are confronted with facts which they cannot deny and arguments which they cannot refute. No one can tell what MacDonald's following is at the moment, but subjected to an onslaught from three sides I am sure it is a vanishing asset.

The 'Scotsman' and the 'Glasgow Herald' which regarded our chances as derisory when we started, have started to become much more respectful

---

[1] Andrew Dewar Gibb, 1888–1974. Called to the Bar, 1914. Officer commanding D Company, 6th Royal Scots Fusiliers, 1915–16, Captain and Adjutant, 1916. He published *With Winston Churchill at the Front* in 1924. Regius Professor of Law, Glasgow, University 1934–58. Chairman of the Scottish National Party, 1936–40.

[2] Between 27 and 31 January 1936, ten days before the Ross and Cromarty poll (of 10 February 1936), Andrew Dewar Gibb, standing as a Scottish National Party (SNP) candidate, polled 9,034 votes, as against 16,393 votes cast for Ramsay MacDonald, and 3,597 votes cast for the Labour candidate, D. C. Thomson, at the Combined Scottish Universities seat. Ramsay MacDonald (standing as a National Labour candidate), had been defeated at Seaham in the General Election by the Labour Party candidate, Emanuel Shinwell.

since our meeting at Dingwall a week ago last Saturday. We had more than a thousand people in the Town Hall and I made the best speech I have ever made.

You will be shocked, or gratified, to hear that I have taken to using notes. This is not owing to any failing in fluency, but because there are only two telephone lines between Dingwall and Inverness. If, therefore, one is to get a good show in the press it is necessary to hand out the speech at about 4 o'clock. I do not find them nearly so much an impediment as I used to, and there is no doubt they improve the cohesion of the argument.

Your loving son,
Randolph

Sir Maurice Hankey[1] *to Winston S. Churchill*

(*Churchill papers: 25/7*)

29 January 1936   Committee of Imperial Defence
Confidential

Dear Winston,

I have been awaiting your return from abroad to write to you on the question of the correspondence which was exchanged between you and the Secretary of State for Air[2] on the Training and Organisation of the German Air Force. This correspondence resulted in the production of CID Papers Nos: 1198-B and 1205-B, which were considered by the Committee of Imperial Defence at their meeting held on December 20th, 1935.

As you are aware, the figures which you put forward challenged those in the possession of the Air Ministry, and in consequence it seems very desirable that the facts should be laid on the table and the figures checked. I therefore

---

[1] Maurice Pascal Alers Hankey, 1877–1963. Entered Royal Marine Artillery, 1895. Captain, 1899. Retired, 1912. Secretary to the Committee of Imperial Defence, 1912–38. Lieutenant-Colonel, Royal Marines, 1914. Knighted, February 1916. Secretary to the War Cabinet, 1916–18; to the Cabinet, 1919–38. Created Baron, 1939. Minister without Portfolio, September 1939–May 1940. Chancellor of the Duchy of Lancaster, 1940–1. Paymaster-General, 1941–2. His brother Hugh was killed in action in South Africa in March 1900. His brother Donald was killed in action on the western front in October 1916.

[2] Philip Lloyd-Greame, 1884–1972. Educated at Winchester and University College, Oxford. On active service, 1914–17 (Military Cross). Joint Secretary, Ministry of National Service, 1917–18. Conservative MP for Hendon, 1918–35. Parliamentary Secretary, Board of Trade, 1920–1. Knighted, 1920. Secretary of the Overseas Trade Department, 1921–2. President of the Board of Trade, 1922–3, 1924–9 and 1931. Assumed the name Cunliffe-Lister, 1924. Created Viscount Swinton, 1935. Secretary of State for the Colonies, 1931–5; for Air, 1935–8. Cabinet Minister Resident in West Africa, 1942–4. Minister of Civil Aviation, 1944–5. Minister of Materials, 1951–2. Secretary of State for Commonwealth Relations, 1952–5. Created Earl, 1955. His elder son died of wounds received in action in 1943.

write to ask whether you are prepared to communicate in confidence any special sources of intelligence on which your information is based.

You will, of course, appreciate that in answering your paper the Air Ministry produced information of a very secret character, and they are consequently anxious to avoid any possible leakage which might prejudice their sources of information at present available.

I feel sure you will agree that it is most desirable, in order to obtain a true picture of the German Air Force situation, that all information should be available to those responsible.

Yours very sincerely,
M. P. A. Hankey

Winston S. Churchill to Sir Maurice Hankey: not sent
(Churchill papers: 25/7)

30 January 1936   11 Morpeth Mansions

The figures in my last paper are of course only my own estimates based on such study as I have been able to make of the problem in the last three or four years. I have given them to you for your assistance as the fruits of my judgment. But I must emphasise that they are only minimum figures, and that I apprehend the real German strength may be far greater.

I hope however that though I cannot claim to possess 'any special sources of intelligence', you will not neglect my judgment, but weigh it carefully with the other opinions at your disposal. I would remind you that on August 13 1911 I wrote a paper for the CID which predicted accurately the exact course on land of the first two months of a possible war between France and Germany, and that I even specified the twentieth day of mobilisation as the date by which the French armies would be in full retreat by the frontiers upon Paris, and the period after the fortieth day of mobilisation as that in which an effective counterstroke might be expected. These dates were in fact borne out almost to the day by the event. In forming this conclusion I was running counter to the opinions of the General Staff and Henry Wilson,[1] with whom I was in very close touch, who taught us to expect a successful French offensive in the first instance. I do not mention this to claim daemonic powers for myself, but only to remind you of the very long and careful

[1] Henry Hughes Wilson, 1864–1922. Entered Army, 1884. Director of Military Operations, War Office, 1910–14. Lieutenant-General, 1914. Chief liaison officer with the French Army, January 1915. Knighted, 1915. Commanded the 4th Corps, 1916. Chief of the Imperial General Staff, 1918–22. Field-Marshal, July 1919. Created Baronet, August 1919, when he received the thanks of Parliament and a grant of £10,000 for his contribution to the war. Ulster Unionist MP, 1922. Shot dead by two Sinn Feiners on the steps of his London house.

thought I have given to these questions, and that it has sometimes been vindicated by the results.

Another instance occurred last year in November 1934 when I drew attention to the secret growth of the German military air force, and made certain statements about its strength relative to our own. These statements were disputed by Mr Baldwin, who I presume after full consideration of all the Intelligence information at the disposal of the Air Ministry, favoured other statements. But only a few months later in the Spring Mr Baldwin was forced to confess in the House of Commons that the Government with their official information were wrong, adding 'we were all in it'. Here then was a case in which an independent outside judgment was proved to be nearer the truth than the estimate from the Government based on all their secret sources. For these reasons I hope you will not brush aside my minimum estimates, although they have no other foundation than my own judgment.

In your penultimate paragraph you say that in answering my first paper which you printed, the Air Ministry provided information of a very secret character. This paper made a certain number of assertions and refrained from giving any authority for them except that they were based upon the consideration of a great number of Secret Service reports, and that these were the opinions formed on those reports by the officers responsible. It was to this attitude which no doubt was in every way appropriate, that I applied the word 'occultism'. I should therefore be much obliged to you if you would mark upon the Air Ministry's reply in DR 27 those passages that you consider constitute information of a very secret character in order that I may respect them and separate them from my general knowledge of this subject, and from the opinions I have formed by my independent study of it.

This appears to be the more necessary because we are now on the eve of a succession of important debates in Parliament upon the Air and upon Defence generally, in the course of which it will be my duty to unfold the full gravity of the Defence position, and I do not want to be hampered by any suggestions that I am using material placed at my disposal in my confidential capacity as a member of the CID Sub-Committee on Technical Research.

When Mr Baldwin asked me to join this Committee last Autumn I drew a very careful line between its purely technical aspects and the general questions of air strength and air policy, and received from him his written assurance that in any criticism on these larger aspects I should be 'as free as air'. I was therefore a little embarrassed when I received CID paper No 1189B because this volunteered information upon the Government view which went far beyond the purely technical aspects with which our Committee was concerned, and in regard to which I was ready to give my services. However as it seemed to me that the Government were allowing themselves to be misled even at this late hour, I felt myself bound to enter upon the correspondence with the Secretary of State to which your letter refers.

Would you kindly send me a printed copy of the last memorandum which I sent you before I left for Morocco.

Winston S. Churchill to Sir Maurice Hankey
(Cabinet papers: 21/419)

31 January 1936   Chartwell
Confidential

Dear Maurice,

I cannot claim any 'special sources of intelligence' for the figures given in my second memorandum. They are simply my personal estimate based on such study as I have been able to make of the problem in the last three or four years. I must however emphasise that they are only minimum figures, and that the real position is probably far more serious.

I shall be much obliged if you will send me a copy of the print made of the memorandum which I sent you in typescript before I went abroad.

Yours vy sincerely,
Winston S. Churchill

Winston S. Churchill to Sir Emsley Carr
(Churchill papers: 8/533)

31 January 1936   Chartwell

Thank you so much for your letter and for the cheque enclosed. I am so glad that your readers liked the article. Lord Rosebery,[1] who is a detached and instructed critic, told me he thought it the best of those that were written on this occasion.

I should like to hear from you how the new series is going and whether it is giving satisfaction to your readers. Presently when the Spring time comes and the country is more attractive, I hope you will come down to lunch here and we can have a talk about the new series. I am rather attracted by the idea of 'Great men of all time' as the sequel to 'Great men of our time'.

---

[1] Albert Edward Harry Mayer Archibald Primrose, 1882–1974. Son of the Liberal Prime Minister (the 5th Earl of Rosebery) and Hannah de Rothschild, who died in 1890. Educated at Eton and Sandhurst. Liberal MP for Edinburgh, 1906–10. On active service, 1914–18 (wounded, despatches, MC, DSO). Succeeded his father as 6th Earl 1929. Lord Lieutenant of Midlothian, 1929–64. President of the Thoroughbred Breeders Association. Regional Commissioner for Scotland, 1941–5. Secretary of State for Scotland (in Churchill's caretaker government), May–July 1945. Chairman of the Scottish Tourist Board, 1955–65. His younger brother, Neil Primrose, was killed in action on 18 November 1917. His elder son died in 1931, at the age of 21.

Lord Beaverbrook to Sir Samuel Hoare
(Beaverbrook papers)

31 January 1936

Winston is in some doubt. He evidently wants to speak for Randolph. Bracken advises him against it. Winston is not on good terms with me at present. He is very sulky about a caricature in the Evening Standard.[1] He spoke to me on the telephone last night for the first time since the affront. Maybe he will ask my advice tomorrow. If so, I shall urge him very strongly to go.

Desmond Morton:[2] note
(Churchill papers: 2/281)

31 January 1936   Industrial Intelligence Centre
Secret

INDUSTRIAL INTELLIGENCE

GERMANY: REPORTED MOVE TO CAPTURE WORLD TRADE
IN ARMAMENTS[3]

The following note is compiled from information received in the last fortnight from several independent sources. As yet the whole story is neither quite clear nor fully substantiated, but as it seems to rest on a sound foundation, it is thought desirable to circulate it at once, without waiting for further details, in view of its important implications.

D. Morton

---

[1] An *Evening Standard* cartoon on 15 January 1936, by Low, 'Rival Foundlings', showing Randolph Churchill and Malcolm MacDonald as babies on a doorstep, with their fathers dressed as women, lurking in the shadows, waiting for Ross and Cromarty to accept the foundlings.

[2] Desmond Morton, 1891–1971. 2nd Lieutenant, Royal Artillery, 1911. Converted to Roman Catholicism shortly before the First World War. Shot through the heart while commanding a Field Battery at the Battle of Arras, April 1917, but survived the wound. Later awarded the Military Cross. ADC to Sir Douglas Haig, 1917–18. Seconded to the Foreign Office, 1919. Head of the Committee of Imperial Defence's Industrial Intelligence Centre, January 1929–September 1939; its terms of reference were 'To discover and report the plans for manufacture of armaments and war stores in foreign countries.' A member of the Committee of Imperial Defence sub-committee on Economic Warfare, 1930–9. Principal Assistant Secretary, Ministry of Economic Warfare, 1939. Personal Assistant to Churchill throughout the Second World War. Knighted, 1945. Economic Survey Mission, Middle East, 1949. Seconded to the Ministry of Civil Aviation, 1950–3.

[3] Eleven copies of this note, and the accompanying document were circulated from the Industrial Intelligence Centre (reference ICF/185) to the Admiralty, the War Office, the Air Ministry, the Treasury, the Foreign Office, the Board of Trade, the Department of Overseas Trade, MI5 (Sir E. Holt Wilson), and others. Morton sent a twelfth copy to Churchill on 10 February 1936 (see page 40 of this volume).

Desmond Morton: memorandum

(*Churchill papers: 2/281*)

31 January 1936
Secret

1. On the instance of the German War Minister, General VON BLOM-BERG,[1] a 'Forschungs-apparat' (?Commission of Inquiry)[2] was set up, apparently in December 1935, to investigate ways and means of continuing rearmament in face of the difficulties being experienced from the shortage of foreign currency available for the purchase of essential raw materials.

2. The 'Forschungs-apparat' seems to have consisted firstly of a Committee composed of representatives of the following Government and public bodies:

  (a) The General, Naval and Air Staffs.
  (b) ?The 'Export Investigation Office' (? of the Reichswirtschafts-ministerium).
  (c) Statistisches Amt, Abt. IV. Betriebs- und Produktions-Statistik.
  (d) Auslands-Handelsstelle.
  (e) The Associations of German Engineering and Chemical Manufacturers.
  (f) Zentral-Beschaffungsstelle für Bekleidung und Ausrüstung (Berlin, W35, Tirpitzstr 72).

[1] Werner von Blomberg, 1878–1946. Born in Pomerania, the son of an officer. Minister of Defence, 1932–1938. The British Foreign Office confidential 'Record of Leading Personalities in Germany' of 4 January 1938 describes him as having 'served most of his time as a staff officer, specializing since the war on the training side, for which he has considerable gifts. He is much more a man of the world than his contemporaries in the army, having studied and travelled extensively in Russia, United States of America and Europe generally; he was also for a time head of the military delegation at Geneva. He was commanding the troops in East Prussia until brought to Berlin as Reichswehr Minister. He has been retained on the active list of the army. Decorated with the order Pour le mérite. Appointed Reichskriegsminister and Oberbefehlshaber der Wehrmacht in 1935. Promoted Field-Marshal the 20th April, 1936. He continues to carry out a large number of inspections in the services, particularly in the army. He has been subjected to a good deal of criticism in the army, as it is considered that he does not present the army's point of view sufficiently strongly to Herr Hitler. It is clear that Field-Marshal Blomberg is completely dominated by Herr Hitler, whose words he quotes on each and every occasion. He is markedly pro-British. Attended the coronation as the Chancellor's representative in May 1937' (*Vansittart papers: 1/22*). In March 1936 Blomberg urged Hitler to withdraw German troops from the Rhineland. Dismissed after the scandal which followed his second marriage (on 12 January 1938) to a typist-secretary in the War Ministry, with what was subsequently discovered to be an 'all too incontrovertibly established police record' as a prostitute. In exile for a year, he returned to Germany in January 1939, and lived in complete retreat in Wiessee, Bavaria, throughout the war.
   [2] 'Research Organization' would be a closer translation.

(g) Heeresverwaltungsamt, Abt I and II, and the Marine Verwal-
    tungsamt of the RKM.

3. The Commission, having reviewed the situation, appears to have reported somewhat along the following lines:

(a) That the reduction in the tempo of armament production below a
    certain point would inevitably result in a grave internal economic
    crisis, in view of the absence of alternative markets for civilian
    goods. Unemployment would rise, wages would fall, etc.
(b) That if, however, some measure of reduction in the output of
    armaments was essential, it was imperative to retain the armament
    industry in a position once more to produce all kinds of war material
    in large quantities at the shortest possible notice.
(c) That in order to do this, it was necessary to keep fully skilled arma-
    ment workers in employment to continue experimental work and to
    continue training additional skilled labour.
(d) As the means of effecting this and perhaps even of staving off an
    enforced reduction of armament output, every effort should be
    made to capture the world trade in armaments.

It was pointed out that British industry would be fully engaged for several
years in producing armaments to the order of the British Government,
and would thus leave the way clear for the Reich. Consequently, the Reich
should look for markets for war material in the Far East, Turkey, Iran,
Afghanistan, Siam, China, the *Union of South Africa* (sic), and in other
countries unable to manufacture their own arms and equipment.

4. It was thereafter decided that the offices represented on this Commission
should be utilised as an apparatus for furthering the scheme, as follows:

(a) The Government will give every assistance through its diplomatic
    missions and by other means, to representatives of German arma-
    ment firms in foreign countries.
(b) These representatives will be given power to offer to foreign Govern-
    ments war material for immediate delivery from the stocks now held
    by the German Army.
(c) Prices charged to foreign Governments for this 'second hand' material
    which in many cases will, in fact, be almost new, will be regulated
    by the Government and will be far below cost of foreign competitive
    prices.
(d) Any firm effecting a sale of this material will immediately receive
    a fresh order from the German Government.

5. It is said to have been pointed out by the Commission that by this means considerable sums in foreign value[1] would be received, and, in view of the fact that only a relatively small proportion of the cost of war material derives from the expenditure of foreign value on imported raw materials, the greater part of the cost being met by payment in Reichsmarks, whereas the whole of the price received as the result of these sales would be devoted to the purchase of selected raw materials, the result of the transaction would in the end be to increase the quantity of armaments which could be manufactured in Germany.

6. It is further reported that this scheme is now in actual operation and that sales have already been made to several countries in the last week or two.

It is confirmed by Messrs. Vickers that representatives of Vereinigte Stahlwerke, AG, are now in Greece, offering to provide second hand war material, as described, for the Greek Army, police, etc. Another source reports that the firms of MAN in Nuremberg and Bleichert in Leipzig have already received orders for export to Turkey and Afghanistan; while Professor Hermann Bohle,[2] leader of the Nazi Party in Cape Town, is on his way back to Germany to get his instructions for action in South Africa.

The General Staff (Intelligence) have received information from the India Office that the German Minister in Kabul[3] has opened negotiations with the Afghan Government for the sale of 4 or 5 batteries of mountain artillery, while there are reports from other quarters of German activity of the same kind in Uruguay, Siam and Turkey. In the latter connection attention is drawn to despatches from HM Ambassador in Turkey,[4] No 595 E dated November 23rd and No 606 E dated November 27th, 1935.

---

[1] 'Valuta', better translated as 'foreign exchange'.

[2] Hermann Bohle. A British subject, he went from Bradford to South Africa in 1914. Subsequently a Professor at Capetown University. Founder of the 'Landesgruppe Suedafrika' (County Group South Africa), 1932. He died in Berlin in 1943. The father of Ernst Wilhelm Bohle (see page 707, note 3).

[3] Kurt Ziemke, 1888–1965. Studied oriental languages at the universities of Berlin and Königsberg. Joined the German diplomatic service (in Constantinople), 1910. On active service on the western front, 1914–15 (wounded). Served successively in Constantinople, Rodosto and Jerusalem, 1915–18. German Vice-Consul in Poznan (Poland), 1920–2 and in Brno (Czechoslovakia). Consul in Beirut, 1931–2. Minister in Kabul, 1933–7. Served in Prague, 1939–40, and in south-eastern Europe, 1941–4. He published a volume on *The New Turkey*, in 1930, and his memoirs of Afghanistan in 1939.

[4] Percy Lyham Loraine, 1880–1961. Served as a 2nd Lieutenant in the South African War, 1900–1. Entered the Diplomatic Service as an Attaché at Constantinople, 1904. 12th Baronet, 1917. 1st Secretary, Warsaw, October 1919. Minister to Teheran, 1921–6; to Athens, 1926–9. High Commissioner for Egypt and the Sudan, 1929–33. Privy Councillor, 1933. Ambassador in Ankara, 1933–9; in Rome, 1939–40.

February 1936

Winston S. Churchill to King Edward VIII[1]

(*Churchill papers: 1/284*)

2 February 1936   Chartwell[2]

Sir,

I could not let these memorable days pass away without venturing to write how deeply I have felt for Your Majesty in the sorrow of a father's death, and in the ordeal of mounting a Throne.

I have many memories of the Prince of Wales since the Investiture at Carnarvon Castle twenty-five years ago,[3] which are joyous and gay in my mind, and also above all I have the sense of a friendship with which I was honoured.

Now I address myself to the King; and offer dutifully yet in no formal sense my faithful service and my heartfelt wishes that a reign which has been so nobly begun may be blessed with peace and true glory; and that in the long

---

[1] Edward Albert Christian George Andrew Patrick David, 1894–1972. Entered the Royal Navy as a Cadet, 1907. Prince of Wales, 1910–36. 2nd Lieutenant, Grenadier Guards, August 1914. Attached to Sir John French's Staff, November 1914. Served in France and Italy, 1914–18. Major, 1918. Succeeded his father as King, January 1936. Abdicated, December 1936. Duke of Windsor, 1936.

[2] Churchill's only weekend guest on his return to Chartwell from Morocco was Professor Lindemann (who again stayed at Chartwell during 1936 on March 7–9, March 21–22, April 25–27, May 10–11, May 27–28, July 6–7, July 19–20, August 8–12, September 18–21, October 7–8, November 21–23 and December 23–24). Other staying guests in 1936 included Robert Boothby (February 21–22 and April 13–14), Ava and Ralph Wigram (March 21–22), Sir Hugh Tudor (April 18–20), Sir Archibald Sinclair (April 25–27 and December 5–7), Edward Marsh (April 25–27 and November 21–23), F. W. Deakin (April 25–27), Patrick Buchan-Hepburn (June 20–21 and August 1–3), Sir Roger Keyes (August 8–10), William Astor (August 8–10), Bernard Baruch (August 14), Sir James Hawkey and his daughter (August 15), Patrick Donner (August 17–18), Lady Colefax (August 17–18), Sir William Nicholson (October 7–8 and November 22), Paul Maze (November 7–8), Sir Terence O'Connor (November 7–9), Margaret Countess of Birkenhead (November 7–9), Harcourt Johnstone (December 5–7) and Christopher Hassall (December 5–7). The guests for Christmas and New Year 1936–37 were Duncan, Diana and Julian Sandys (Duncan Sandys had also been at Chartwell during 1936 on March 7–8, March 14–15 and November 22).

[3] When Churchill, as Home Secretary, was the Cabinet Minister responsible for the ceremony.

swing of events Your Majesty's name will shine in history as the bravest and best beloved of all the sovereigns who have worn the island Crown.

Your Majesty's devoted servant and subject,

Winston S. Churchill to John Astor[1]

(Churchill papers: 2/287)

2 February 1936
Private

I was surprised to read in the leading article of Saturday's 'Times' on the Ross and Cromarty By Election, an insinuation that I had prompted my Son's candidature. As a matter of fact, I strongly advised him to have nothing to do with it. Naturally as a Father, I cannot watch his fight, now that it has begun, without sympathy; but I am taking no part in it, though much pressed to do so by the local people. In these circumstances the innuendo of your leading article is neither true nor fair.

Winston S. Churchill to Randolph S. Churchill: draft statement

(Churchill papers: 2/287)

[2] February 1936

You are pricking the bubble of an obvious sham. I hope that Mr Malcolm MacDonald will make a good career for himself in Parliament and I believe that he has many amiable qualities which will serve him. But to pretend that his return for Ross and Cromarty is required to give His Majesty's Government the right to call itself 'National' is humbug. Still more is it a departure from the verities that he should be portrayed as an indispensable representative of Labour. Anyone can see that that is not true. It is in fact the right-about reverse of the truth. This is proved when neither he nor his father dare call themselves Labour, let alone Socialist, in the contests in which they are now engaged. Thus we have one sham on top of another. No way through our present difficulties and dangers can be found by such pretences.

[1] John Jacob Astor, 1886–1971. Educated at Eton and New College, Oxford. 2nd Lieutenant, 1st Life Guards, 1908. ADC to the Viceroy of India, 1911–14. On active service, 1914–18 (severely wounded); Major, 1920. Conservative MP for Dover, 1922–45. Chief Proprietor of *The Times*. President of the Press Club, the Newspaper Press Fund, and the Commonwealth Press Union. Chairman of the Middlesex Hospital, 1938–62. Lieutenant-Colonel, 5th Battalion, City of London Home Guard, 1940–4. Created Baron Astor of Hever, 1956.

Winston S. Churchill to Queen Mary[1]

(*Churchill papers: 1/284*)

3 February 1936

Madam,

I venture to write to Your Majesty to express my most profound sympathy and sorrow in the measureless and indescribable loss which Your Majesty has sustained. The nation has found the means of giving vent to its grief, and the tributes it has paid have moved the world. But for the one on whom the blow falls directly with all the human pain of any humble home, there can be no relief from the awful severance and deprivation. Words are vain. Not all that the whole world can say or feel or do can be any help. Only in high and serene conceptions of existence and destiny can any solace be found. I feel that Your Majesty has been prepared by a lifetime's thought, faith and action to derive these consolations in their most perfect form. I trust and pray that Your Majesty may be so strengthened as to be able to go on helping us all in our anxious England, as has been done throughout the many years of King George's reign; and I read in Your Majesty's message to the Empire the hope that that would be so. As one who stood as Minister at the late King's side from the moment of his accession and served him in his great affairs for nearly fifteen years, I thought I might presume to write these few lines, and to mention how ineffaceable in the memories of myself and of my wife are the kindnesses and honours which we have received from King George and Your Majesty during all that glorious reign of perils and triumphs ending at last in peace and unfading fame.

Your Majesty's faithful and devoted servant,
Winston S. Churchill

Sir Emsley Carr to Winston S. Churchill

(*Churchill papers: 8/533*)

4 February 1936   News of the World

My dear Winston Churchill,

It is very gratifying to hear that Lord Rosebery, who is so great a critic, has so high an opinion of the article on the late King which you wrote for us.

But he is only voicing the views of all Fleet Street.

At a Directors' Meeting of George Newnes—of which firm I am a Director

---

[1] Victoria Mary, 1867–1953. Only daughter of Mary Adelaide, Duchess of Teck (a grand-daughter of King George III, and Queen Victoria's first cousin), and Francis, 1st Duke of Teck. In 1893 she married George, Duke of York, later King George V.

—we were congratulated on having obtained so instructive and valuable an article. They unanimously agreed it was the best article on King George that has appeared in the press.

Friends of mine on the 'Times', 'Morning Post' and 'Daily Telegraph' have also told me how delighted they were with the article, and again, in their opinion, it was the best that had been published, whilst the London Correspondents of the 'Western Mail' and the 'Scotsman' also expressed their admiration, not only for the article, but also the fact that it was written in so short a time and under such abnormal conditions.

The present series is also attracting attention, and we have had nothing but praise from our readers, with one exception, and that does not refer to the manner of the article but on a question of fact, about which there may be some doubt.

I need scarcely say it will give me the greatest pleasure when the spring arrives to motor down to Chartwell and discuss the new series which you have in mind. I like the idea 'Great Men of *All* Time'—it smacks of drama, and has the greatest possibilities.

With the best of wishes, I am,

Sincerely yours,
Emsley Carr

Winston S. Churchill to Edward Marsh[1]
(*Churchill papers: 4/2*)

6 February 1936

There was a very depressing review on St Helena in the Evening Standard.[2] I am glad to hear from you that you think I should be interested in it. I will see if I can have a night, but it would pain me to witness the death agony of a figure about which I have thought so much.

I have got $315\frac{1}{2}$ pages of Volume III in print, and I wonder whether you

---

[1] Edward Howard Marsh, 1872–1953. Known as 'Eddie'. Educated at Westminster and Trinity College, Cambridge. Entered the Colonial Office as a 2nd Class Clerk, 1896. Private Secretary to Churchill, December 1905–November 1915. Assistant Private Secretary to Asquith, November 1915–December 1916. Private Secretary to Churchill, 1917–22 and 1924–9. Private Secretary to successive Secretaries of State for the Colonies, 1929–36. Elected to the Other Club, 1932. Knighted, 1937.

[2] In a review signed 'D.B.' in the *Evening Standard* of 5 February 1936 the text of *St Helena* by R. C. Sherriff and Jeanne Casalis was described as 'a careful, scholarly piece of writing'. The reviewer went on, however, to say that the play 'performed last night at the Old Vic, was inexpressibly tedious'. 'D.B.' was Dudley Barker, who had been responsible for the theatrical reviews in the *Evening Standard* from 1933, and who in 1939 joined the editorial staff of the *Daily Herald*. From 1954 to 1959 he was associate editor of *John Bull*. Under the pseudonym Lionel Black, he wrote many crime novels and other books. He died in December 1980, aged 70.

would care to read them for me. There will be another 250 to come later on. I hope to publish in the autumn.

I have got another literary plan which is taking shape in which you might perhaps collaborate.[1]

Let me reciprocate your sentiments—you may imagine my divided feelings about Ross and Cromarty! I wish he had never gone, and I tried to persuade him not to. But now he is in it, of course I cannot help wishing him good fortune.

Winston S. Churchill to Sir Robert Vansittart
(*Churchill papers: 2/251*)

7 February 1936

When I was in Morocco recently I met a Mr Cecil Gerahty, whom I understand is applying for the post of Vice-Consul at Meknes. I was much impressed by him during my stay and saw a good deal of him. I think he is a very able man and a suitable applicant for the post. He was previously a naval officer who retired after the war and has for some years been the Moroccan correspondent inter alia of the Daily Mail. He has a very intimate knowledge of Morocco, speaks Arabic, and has been a resident in Meknes as well as other towns. I wonder whether his application has yet reached you, and if and when it does, I would be very much obliged if you would bear in mind my recommendation, without prejudice to the regulations governing such appointments.

Keith Feiling[2] to Winston S. Churchill
(*Churchill papers: 8/532*)

8 February 1936
Personal

My dear First Lord,

I enclose two receipted bills covering the work done[3] since October; £20.16.10 in total. Eleven chapters have reached you since Oct 1; three

---

[1] Churchill's plan to write a new book, *A History of the English-Speaking Peoples* (see also pages 114 and 310).

[2] Keith Grahame Feiling, 1884–1977. Lecturer and historian. Fellow of All Souls, Oxford, 1906–11; tutor at Christ Church, 1911–46. 2nd Lieutenant, Black Watch, 1915. Secretary to the Central Recruiting Board, India, 1917–19. OBE, 1918. University Lecturer in Modern History, Oxford, 1928–36; Chichele Professor of Modern History, 1946–50. Knighted, 1958. His first book, *The History of the Tory Party, 1640–1714*, was published in 1924. In 1946 he published a biography of Neville Chamberlain.

[3] On collecting the first materials for *A History of the English-Speaking Peoples*.

more are nearly done. That will leave only eight to complete the whole—except your Retrospect from 1914. As on the 31st May I shall have to stop any construction for you. I thought that I had better put down *something* for all those eight chapters, however jejune; although on some matters (the American Civil War, let us say) you know ten times more than I do, and in others (British Democracy) you have yourself helped to make the history.

If you still want a young man to do some work, either on Marlborough or on this, perhaps you will let me know; one good pupil of my own is still available, who might be useful to you in adding more detail or notes after I have stopped. . . .

Violet Pearman to T. W. Taylor[1]

(*Churchill papers: 8/539*)

9 February 1936

Dear Mr Taylor,

Thank you for both your letters. The reason the tickets were just over the expiry date is that until the last minute Mr Churchill could not make up his mind what to do, and then took the journey via Madrid to Paris and thence home. Consequently we arrived in Paris too late to do anything but give the tickets up to Cooks. It was an awful journey, so long and with so many changes.

The arrangements for our travelling on to Marrakech were made actually on Boxing Day. Mr Churchill wished to go on there on Christmas Day, but Cooks were of course shut, and he was persuaded to stay until the next day, which of course was only what could be done considering the late hour and the packing. All arrangements were made through the Daily Mail correspondent who made them for the whole party ie Lord Rothermere and party, and ours. Therefore I had nothing to do with it, and the excuse they have given you about your letter not arriving etc is I think quite wrong. But for the fact that Tangiers was cold and there did not seem to be a cessation of rain there either, I expect we should all have stayed on much longer. I hope that you do not have any difficulty over the matter now.

With many thanks for all your trouble and for your unfailing courtesy,

[1] T. W. Taylor. Known as 'Barcelona Taylor'. Joined Thomas Cook in the early 1920s; served in Spain until the outbreak of the Spanish Civil War, when he returned to London. Worked as a temporary staff member at Thomas Cook until the late 1940s, when he retired.

Desmond Morton to Winston S. Churchill

(*Churchill papers: 2/281*)

10 February 1936   21 Queen Anne's Gate

You might like to see the two attached papers in connection with any evidence you give before the Royal Commission on the Armament Industry.

ICF/62 of 7.2.36. is based on information publicly obtainable, but ICF/185 of 31.1.36 on the German attempt to capture the world armament trade is based on secret information.

Perhaps you could very kindly let me have these copies back in due course after you have made any notes that you require.

Yours sincerely,
Desmond Morton

Blanche Dugdale[1] to Robert Boothby[2]

(*Churchill papers: 2/251*)

11 February 1936

My dear Bob,

I have had an inspiration—I want Winston to be Minister of Defence—because I believe him to be the only person competent for that post on which the safety of us all may hang.

If *he* wants to be, let him try this—let him make a speech—stressing the need for *economy* of expenditure, or—not so much for economy—as for the need to get four farthings worth of efficiency out of every penny we spend on re-armament. That would take the wind out of the sails of all his critics—there are plenty of people who want Winston—but are frightened of him—and also frightened that the country would not trust him.

I *know* I'm right.

Yours,
Baffy

---

[1] Blanche Elizabeth Campbell Balfour, 1880–1948. A granddaughter of the 8th Duke of Argyll, and niece of A. J. Balfour. Known as 'Baffy'. Married to Edgar Dugdale. In 1936 she published a biography of her uncle, entitled *Arthur James Balfour*. An ardent supporter of the Zionist movement, she was a close friend of Chaim Weizmann, and a leading non-Jewish advocate of Jewish statehood in Palestine. She died on 15 May 1948, on the day after the establishment of the State of Israel.

[2] Robert John Graham Boothby, 1900–   . Educated at Eton and Magdalen College, Oxford. Conservative MP for East Aberdeenshire, 1924–58. Parliamentary Private Secretary to the Chancellor of the Exchequer (Churchill), 1926–9. Elected to the Other Club, 1928. Parliamentary Secretary, Ministry of Food, 1940–1. A British Delegate to the Consultative

Robert Boothby to Winston S. Churchill

(*Churchill papers: 2/251*)

12 February 1936

Dear Winston,

I am sorry about Randolph—although I feel that a little chastening at this particular juncture will not necessarily be to his ultimate disadvantage.[1] There is more sympathy & friendly feeling for him than he suspects.

But, my God, you don't challenge that machine with impunity. I enclose a letter from Baffy Dugdale. Its only significance is that she does see a certain amount of Baldwin. And is a clever old thing, with a good deal of influence amongst the younger ministers. She has written a thundering good life of AJB.

Yrs ever,
Bob

Victor Cazalet:[2] *diary*

(*Robert Rhodes James: 'Victor Cazalet, A Portrait'*)

13 February 1936

Made friends with Winston again. We went to Pratts and had supper. W friendly to me (after 2 years of silence) but he is obviously v irritated and unsettled. Furious at not being in government—contemptuous of present regime, and overwhelmed with German danger—v unbalanced I thought.

Assembly, Council of Europe, 1949–57. KBE, on Churchill's recommendation, 1953. Created Baron, 1958. President of the Anglo-Israel Association. Rector of St Andrews University, 1958–61. Chairman, Royal Philharmonic Orchestra, 1961–3. Published *The New Economy* (1943), *I Fight to Live* (1947), *My Yesterday, Your Tomorrow* (1962) and *Recollections of A Rebel* (1978).

[1] Randolph Churchill received 2,427 votes, as against 8,949 cast for Malcolm MacDonald (National Labour), 5,967 for H. McNeill (Labour), and 738 for W. S. R. Thomas (Liberal). Randolph had been the nominee of the local Conservative Association, which had refused to support the official National Government candidate. Randolph was returned to Parliament, for Preston, a two-member Constituency, on 25 September 1940, as a Conservative (unopposed). He was defeated (together with his fellow Conservative, Julian Amery) in the General Election of 1945.

[2] Victor Alexander Cazalet, 1896–1943. Educated at Eton and Christ Church, Oxford. Oxford half blue for tennis, racquets and squash, 1915. Served on the western front, 1915–18, when he won the Military Cross. A member of General Knox's Staff in Siberia, 1918–19. Conservative MP for Chippenham from 1924 until his death. Parliamentary Secretary, Board of Trade, 1924–6. Political Liaison Officer to General Sikorski, 1940–3. Killed in the air crash in which Sikorski died.

Winston S. Churchill to 'The Times'

(*Churchill papers: 1/284*)

14 February 1936   11 Morpeth Mansions

Sir,

I was discouraged from going to see St Helena at the 'Old Vic' by some unappreciative descriptions which I had read in various newspapers.

However, upon the advice of Mr Edward Marsh, a high connoisseur and keen supporter of the living stage, I went last night to see this remarkable play. In my humble judgement as a life-long but still voracious reader of Napoleonic literature, it is a work of art of a very high order. Moreover it is an entertainment which throughout rivets the attention of the audience. Nor need the sense of inexorable decline and doom sadden unduly those who have marvelled at Napoleon's prodigious career. There is a grandeur and human kindliness about the great Emperor in the toils which make a conquering appeal.[1] If it be the function of the playwright as of the historian 'to make the past the present, to bring the distant near, to place the reader in the society of a famous man, or on the eminence overlooking a great battle', this is certainly discharged. I was I think among the very first to acclaim the quality of *Journey's End*. Here is the end of the most astonishing journey ever made by mortal man.[2]

I am, etc.,
Winston S. Churchill[3]

[1] In the Old Vic production of *St Helena*, Napoleon was played by Kenneth Kent. Among the other actors were Leo Genn as General Count Montholon, Anthony Quayle as St Denis, and Glynis Johns (aged 12) as Hortense Bertrand. It was Glynis Johns' second stage appearance.

[2] In his memoirs, *No Leading Lady*, published in 1968, R. C. Sheriff wrote: 'The takings on the night before this letter was published added up to £17 12s 6d, which means about sixty people in a theatre that could seat a thousand. For the performance on the night following the letter more than five hundred people came, and on the next evening, the Saturday, the theatre was packed. Every seat sold, with people standing at the back of the pit and gallery. It must have been the most complete turnaround that had ever happened to a play before: all in a couple of nights. When I read the letter I got the car out and drove up to the theatre. I wanted to be around to see what happened, but I never expected things to happen as they did. When I got there at about ten o'clock there was already a trickle of people coming in to the Box office. This in itself was an event, because until that morning there hadn't been anybody at all. By lunchtime it had turned into a stream. There was a queue as people came across the bridge to book seats in their lunch hour. . . .'

[3] Eric Wynn-Owen, who played the Marine, writes: 'We were playing to all-but empty houses until the publication of Churchill's letter. The result was magical. The box-office was inundated as from that same day and houses so full from then on that the play had to be transferred to the West End, the last play at the old Daly's Theatre, now replaced by the Warner Cinema, in Leicester Square (*letter to the author, 16 January 1982*).

Desmond Morton to Violet Pearman

(*Churchill papers: 2/268*)

14 February 1936

1. These Völkerbund publications are very tendencious German propaganda. Some of the statements are true, but it is very difficult to pick out the truth. The papers, naturally, greatly exaggerate the naval, military and air power of Russia and France. I only wish they were true!

2. It is unfortunately quite incorrect to say that French aircraft are of the most modern type. Their own types are known and admitted by the French to be well behind those of most other countries, including Germany and England. The alleged strength of the Air Force on Page 8 is absolutely wrong. For Mr Churchill's confidential information, the true position is as follows:—

(a) In February 1935, the French stated they possessed 1,269 first line service aircraft, including all types, with a reserve of 100%, many of the reserves being out of date and possibly not even airworthy. Of the 1,269, only a proportion were of their own most modern type, and they were unsatisfactory compared with the most modern types of other countries.

(b) In May 1935, the French stated that they intended to raise the strength of their Air Force as soon as possible to 1,528, first line, with 100% reserve of modern aircraft.

(c) Early in June, the French stated that the figure in (b) above only referred to the Metropolitan Air Force, and that the total Air Force, when reconstituted, would be 1,707 first line modern aircraft, with 100% reserves.

(d) Late in June, the French stated that at the moment they only possessed a Metropolitan Air Force of 1,000 first line armed with machines which could in no way be described as modern. It was understood that their reserves were all old machines and that both first line and reserves, in the colonies were all old machines.

The statements about Russia's Naval Forces are also ridiculous. Soviet shipyards are quite unable to build a capital ship or even a cruiser of any tonnage at the moment. Except for a few small destroyers and some submarines, parts of which had to be imported, no serious naval construction has been done since the war. The pamphlet fails to point out that all the warships are obsolete and the capital ships probably not seaworthy.

A vivid example of exaggeration is the statement on page 19 that there are at present 17 factories in the U.S.S.R. exclusively producing poison gas. Possibly 17 chemical factories produce substances which, given the plant, knowledge and organisation, might be turned into war chemicals, but even the most war-minded and muddle-headed State would not keep special plant working in peace to turn out poison gas in the vast volumes suggested, if only for the reason that there would be no expenditure; while it is well nigh impossible to store some of the gases, and others cannot be stored for chemical reasons.

DM

Winston S. Churchill to Anthony Eden
(*Foreign Office papers: 371/20100*)

14 February 1936

My dear Anthony,

Winterton[1] and I are much concerned about the dangers of withdrawing our garrison from Cairo, & we find this anxiety widely shared among our friends. We are therefore going to ask the Prime Minister to receive a deputation next week before it is too late. But before doing this I write to let you know what is going forward, & in the hopes that perhaps you will be able to assure us that our fears that HMG would consent to such an evacuation are groundless.

Winston S. Churchill to Commander H. T. Bishop[2]
(*Churchill papers: 2/272*)

15 February 1936
Secret

I wish to compare the additions to the weight of the broadsides made by the United States, Germany, Italy, France and Japan with that of Britain in the last six published programmes. Since the Washington Treaty we have added no gun to the Fleet larger than 6″. I imagine we have built about fifteen 6″ gun cruisers mounting together about 100 6″ guns each firing 100

[1] Edward Turnour, 1883–1962. Educated at Eton and New College, Oxford. Conservative MP, 1904–18, 1918–40 and 1940–51. Succeeded his father as 6th Earl Winterton, 1907. As an Irish peer, he continued to sit in the House of Commons. An original member of the Other Club, 1911. Served at Gallipoli, in Palestine and in Arabia, 1915–18. Under-Secretary of State for India, 1922–4 and 1924–9. Chancellor of the Duchy of Lancaster, 1937–9. Paymaster-General, 1939. Chairman, Inter-Governmental Committee for Refugees, 1938–45.

[2] H. T. Bishop, 1899–1968. Assistant Clerk, HMS *Repulse*, 1917. Clerk, HMS *Furious*, 1918. Paymaster Midshipman, HMS *Monarch*, 1919. Paymaster Sub-Lieutenant, HMS *Cairo*, 1919. Paymaster Lieutenant, HMS *Courageous*, 1922. Retired from the Royal Navy, 1922. Subsequently General Secretary of the Navy League (of which Lord Lloyd was President).

lb shot, equalling 1,000 lb. broadside. It would seem that all foreign navies have added enormously more than this. For instance the Italians have built many 8″ gun cruisers firing 200 lb shot and mounting more guns than ours. In addition there are the two Italian super-Dreadnoughts now building carrying say ten 14″ guns apiece, either of them firing nearly double the broadside that the whole of our construction for the last six years has provided. France will tell a not less striking tale, and so will Germany when her two 26,000 ton Dreadnoughts are included. Thus it should be possible to show that during the last six years under the London Treaty we have added to the British Fleet perhaps one-fifth the broadside added to the Italian, say one-quarter added to the French, one-third added to the United States and one-fourth added to the German etc.[1] It is this that shd be checked. Calculation need not be complicated by bringing in the smaller natures of guns, although if some of these foreign navies have added a large range of 5″ guns, it might be noted.

The following point should be checked. Under the Anglo-German Naval Treaty Germany may if she desires build as much submarine tonnage as the British Navy. She has already nearly twenty or thirty submarines exercising, training crews etc. We do not know how many more she has on the stocks. There are tales of extensive preparation of parts for large submarines, and if these were true, this would permit very rapid assembly & commissioning once the crews were trained and ready for them. Thus we must expect that the same kind of rapid advance may be made in submarine construction by Germany as was made eighteen months ago when all their lay outs were completed for aircraft production. Thus it might be that by the summer of 1937 Germany would have certainly the tonnage of submarines we have in the British Navy. I do not know exactly what the tonnage or number is, but it may amount to about thirty serviceable craft.

But if the Germans contend, as they may easily do that circumstances have altered conditions under which the Treaty was made, they may easily produce more, and have perhaps fifty or sixty submarines by August 1937.

Now let us consider what our position will be if war broke out between us then. The first German submarine campaign of January 1915 was begun with no more than between thirty and forty German submarines. It was defeated in about two months. But how was it defeated? We had in those

[1] The Washington Naval Treaty was signed on 6 February 1922, the London Naval Treaty on 22 April 1930. Both were intended to promote Naval disarmament, the first in the Pacific, both Japan and the United States being among the signatories. Under the Anglo-German Naval Agreement, which was signed on 18th June 1935, the Versailles Treaty restrictions on German shipbuilding were abolished (without France having been consulted), and Germany was allowed to build at once, from scratch, a fleet of up to 35% the size of the British fleet.

days upward of two hundred and twenty-five destroyers. If we had not had this large force a different result would have followed. How many destroyers have we now under twenty years of age? I doubt if we have more than eighty, from which considerable deductions must be made for the Far East and the Mediterranean. It would seem therefore that at all costs and in priority of every other form of naval construction, we should lay down the largest possible number of destroyers which our yards and industry can accommodate.

It is to be hoped that these points may be kept quite secret as they are the fruits of my own personal reflection and I wish to use them in the general debate next month.

Sir Austen Chamberlain to Hilda Chamberlain
(*Austen Chamberlain papers*)

15 February 1936

. . . Well, I am wondering what Neville will say to you of my yesterday's speech.[1] It did rather flutter the journalistic dovecotes & I think rather surprised SB.

To tell the truth I thought that the time was overdue for trying to shake him out of his self-complacency. Of course it is true that no man can do all the work which in these days the Prime Minister is supposed to do, but what angers me is that the present Prime Minister does none of it; this, mustering all my self-restraint, I refrained from saying. But he had better show himself more alive to his duties or he will get into serious trouble, for discontent is spreading & becoming more serious. It is discontent bred of anxiety as to

---

[1] Sir Austen Chamberlain had spoken on 14 February 1936 during the Debate on whether to create a Ministry of Defence. He recalled several 'rude shocks' which the House and the country had recently experienced, including the repeated failure of the Government to estimate accurately the air strength of Germany. He cited these incidents because they 'could not have happened if the thinking machine of the Government was working properly, if their defence organization was really efficient'. During his speech he opposed setting up a specific Ministry of Defence 'not merely because I think it would place a quite intolerable burden— intolerable in the literal sense, for it is a burden that no man is strong enough to bear—on the shoulders of one man, but because it would lessen almost to vanishing point what I think it is vital to preserve, namely, the responsibility of the civilian heads of the three Services'. At the same time, he went on, he no longer thought that the Prime Minister could be an 'effective head' of the Committee of Imperial Defence, and he suggested the creation of 'a Minister there whose main business, whose almost exclusive business, except as a Member of the Cabinet, should be the work of that authority'. Such a Minister, he said, should not only be 'at the head of the Committee of Defence' but should also be 'the permanent chairman of the Chiefs of Staffs Committee'.

the results of his slackness & having done much to save him in December when an adverse vote would have been a direct vote of censure & necessitated his resignation, I decided to use this non-party debate when no vote would be taken to tell him what not only the older but many of the younger members are privately saying.

If there is any truth in the rumour—I don't believe there is—that he proposes to hand over Defence to Ramsay MacDonald there will be a howl of indignation & a vote of no confidence, nor is Eustace Percy[1] the man for that job. In my view there is only one man who by his studies & his special abilities & aptitudes is marked out for it, & that man is Winston Churchill! I don't suppose that SB will offer it to him & I don't think that Neville would wish to have him back, but they are both wrong. He is the right man for that post, & in such dangerous times that consideration ought to be decisive.

Winston S. Churchill to Captain Liddell Hart[2]

(*Churchill papers: 2/266*)

16 February 1936

On thinking over our talk the other night, I should be very much obliged if you would give me a note upon this idea of departing from the Cardwell

---

[1] Lord Eustace Sutherland Campbell Percy, 1887–1958. 7th son of the 7th Duke of Northumberland. Entered the Diplomatic Service, 1909; served in the Foreign Office, 1914–19. Conservative MP for Hastings, 1921–37. Parliamentary Secretary, Board of Education, 1923; Ministry of Health, 1923–4. President of the Board of Education, 1924–9. Minister without Portfolio, 1935–6. Rector of Newcastle University, and Vice-Chancellor of Durham University, 1939–41. Created Baron Percy of Newcastle, 1953. His brother-in-law, Lieutenant-Colonel A. E. Maxwell, was killed in action at Antwerp, 8 October 1914.

[2] Basil Henry Liddell Hart, 1895–1970. Educated at St Paul's School and Corpus Christi, Cambridge. 2nd Lieutenant, King's Own Yorkshire Light Infantry, 1914. On active service at Ypres, and on the Somme (company commander, wounded). Author of the revised Infantry Training Manual, 1919. Selected for the Royal Tank Corps, 1924, but found unfit for general service and placed on half pay. Began his journalistic career as Lawn Tennis Correspondent for the *Manchester Guardian*. Military Correspondent for the *Daily Telegraph*, 1924–34. A leading advocate of mechanization, in 1927 he was consulted officially about the creation of the Experimental Mechanical Force. Military Correspondent of *The Times*, 1934–9, and principal adviser on defence; he advocated a Minister of Defence with a combined staff drawn from all three services. Personal Adviser to Hore-Belisha (Secretary of State for War), 1937–8. In 1939 he opposed the British guarantee to Poland as impossible of fulfilment, and as likely to precipitate war while Britain's defences were still unprepared; this view was one of the reasons which led him to resign from *The Times*, which supported the guarantee. War Commentator for the *Daily Mail*, 1941–5. Knighted, 1966. In 1928 he told Churchill that it was his ambition to write a Churchill biography, but he never did so. In 1969, however, he published a forty-seven page essay, 'The Military Strategist', in *Churchill: Four*

link battalion system. I must have seen a dozen schemes influentially backed in the last forty years which have recoiled before its well proved economy, but I see the new point of the refusal of the Indian armies to imitate our mechanisation, and the derangement of the balance caused thereby. Clearly the right course is to make them do their share.

A point was made about the length of a mechanised division thirty-nine miles upon the road. But surely the true test is their speed in passing a given point.

I was very much surprised at your figures about March 21. I certainly thought they had fifty divisions on the front against about eleven.[1] Whether the whole of our divisions would be thrown in would of course be dependent upon the local fortunes of the battle. Still I think they had this preponderance on the front.

I thought the talk most interesting and stimulating, and I hope we may continue it before long.

Believe me,

Sir Austen Chamberlain to Duncan Sandys
(*Churchill papers: 2/251*)

17 February 1936

Dear Sandys,

Thank you for your kind letter. I thought that Baldwin had become too complacent and needed convincing that the situation was regarded by his

---

Faces and the Man. In *The British Way in Warfare*, published in July 1932, Liddell Hart had praised the conception of the Dardanelles attack, which should, he argued, have been given precedence over the offensives on the western front. In his essay in 1969 he wrote, of the Dardanelles: 'the vision apparent in his conception was marred partly by his own fault in overlooking practical difficulties and logistical needs. But nothing can detract from the value of his contribution towards getting the Navy ready and at its war stations in the nick of time. Nor from the part he played as foster-parent of the tank, the tactical key to victory that was at last fitted to the Western front lock at Cambrai in November 1917, and after that triumphal trial used with more consistent success from August 1918 onward.'

[1] In his *The War In Outline* (London, 1936), Liddell Hart considered the German predominance on the western front facing the British line not as 50 German divisions against 11 British, a ratio of nearly 5 to 1, but 58 German divisions including reserves against 30 British: a ratio of 2 to 1. On one sector of the front, however, the 5th Army front, Liddell Hart's estimated ratio was closer to 3 to 1, being 12 British divisions (one of which was a reserve division) against 35 German (of which 13 were in close reserve).

friends as serious, and I chose the occasion of Friday's debate because it was conducted entirely on non-party lines and could not be perverted in any way to the purpose of a Vote of Censure. I hope the speech will have done some good. I think that there will undoubtedly be changes but I am anxious lest Baldwin's selection for the post should not be adequate.

Yrs sincerely,
Austen Chamberlain

Sir Percy Loraine to Winston S. Churchill
(Churchill papers: 2/251)

17 February 1936

British Embassy,
Angora

Dear Mr Churchill,

A press telegram today states that you are going to be entrusted with a Special Mission to announce the King's accession in several capitals, including this one.[1]

I hope this report is true, for it would be a very pleasant duty for me to welcome you and to do what I was able to ensure the success of your mission and, I have no doubt, the Turkish authorities will give you a very cordial reception.

If the news is correct, it would be particularly useful to me to know about when you are likely to arrive in Turkey, and if there were any information you could give me on this point, it would be very welcome indeed. There are several local considerations involved, and in particular the circumstance that in recent years the President of the Republic[2] spends a good deal more time away from Angora than he used to do.

Yours sincerely,
Percy Loraine

[1] Churchill was given no such mission, nor any other task in connection with King Edward VIII's accession.

[2] Mustafa Kemal, 1881–1938. Served in the Libyan and Balkan campaigns, 1911–13. Military Attaché in Sofia, 1913–14. Served at Gallipoli, 1915, in the Caucasus, 1916, and in Syria, 1917. Assumed command of the Turkish national movement, 1919. First President of the Turkish Republic from 1922 until his death. Known as Atatürk.

Anthony Eden to Winston S. Churchill

(*Churchill papers: 2/251*)

17 February 1936   Foreign Office
Private

My dear Winston,

Many thanks for your letter regarding the question of the British troops in Cairo. I am afraid that it is not possible for me to give any specific assurance in the sense which you desire. The whole question of placing our relations with Egypt upon a more satisfactory and enduring basis is now under examination and will be the subject of negotiations in Cairo in the very near future. The final decision will necessarily lie with the Cabinet as a whole after taking into consideration all the many interests, political and military, and above all imperial, which are involved in this question.

In conclusion may I thank you very much for your kindness in letting me know your views in advance. I note that you may be bringing a deputation to see the Prime Minister next week.

Yours very sincerely,
Anthony Eden

Winston S. Churchill to John Gretton,[1] Sir Robert Horne and Frederick Guest[2]

(*Churchill papers: 2/251*)

17 February 1936

The Prime Minister has consented to receive a deputation of Members of Parliament, mostly Privy Councillors, upon the question of removing the British troops from Cairo which is now within the scope of the current Anglo-Egyptian negotiations. Lord Winterton, Mr George Lambert,[3] Colonel

---

[1] John Gretton, 1867–1947. Educated at Harrow. Conservative MP for South Derbyshire, 1895–1906, for Rutland, 1907–18, and for Burton, 1918–43. Chairman of Bass, Ratcliff and Gretton Ltd, brewers. Colonel, Territorial Army, 1912. Privy Councillor, 1926. A leader of the 'die hards' over India, 1929–35. Created Baron, 1944. One of his two brothers, a Captain in the Bedfordshire Regiment, was killed in action at Ypres on 18 December 1915.

[2] Frederick Edward Guest, 1875–1937. The third son of 1st Baron Wimborne. Churchill's cousin. Served in the South African War as a Captain, Life Guards, 1899–1902. Private Secretary to Churchill, 1906. An original member of the Other Club, 1911. Treasurer, HM Household, 1912–15. ADC to Sir John French, 1914–16. On active service in East Africa, 1916–17. Patronage Secretary, Treasury (Chief Whip), May 1917–April 1921. Privy Councillor, 1920. Secretary of State for Air, April 1921–October 1922. Liberal MP, 1910–22 and 1923–9. Joined the Conservative Party, 1930. Conservative MP, 1931–7.

[3] George Lambert, 1866–1958. Liberal MP for South Molton, 1891–1924; 1929–31. Civil Lord of Admiralty, 1905–15. Privy Councillor, 1912. Chairman of the Liberal Parliamentary Party, 1919–21; Liberal National MP, 1931–45. Created Viscount, 1945.

Spender-Clay,[1] Sir Edward Grigg,[2] Sir Roger Keyes[3] and myself propose to wait upon the Prime Minister in his room at the House at 4 pm on Thursday next.

If you are in principle opposed to the removal of these troops we should be very glad if you would join us on the deputation. In that case would you care to lunch with me at 11, Morpeth Mansions on Wednesday next at 1.30. Kindly reply by telephone on account of urgency.

Winston S. Churchill to Stanley Baldwin

(*Churchill papers: 2/251*)

18 February 1936

I am obliged to you for leaving the choice of the deputation to me. I think it might cause offence if it appeared that you drew a distinction between Privy Councillors and the other two gentlemen I mentioned in my letter in respect of observing confidence. Both have long been trusted with very secret business. I am asking three or four others who will all be Privy Councillors. Many thanks for your courtesy in receiving us.

[1] Herbert Henry Spender-Clay, 1875–1937. Educated at Eton and Sandhurst. Joined the 2nd Life Guards, 1896. On active service in South Africa, 1899–1900 and on the Western Front, 1914–18 (Military Cross, despatches three times). Lieutenant-Colonel, 1910. Conservative MP for Tonbridge from 1910 until his death. Charity Commissioner, 1923–4 and 1924–9. Privy Councillor, 1929.

[2] Edward William Macleay Grigg, 1879–1955. Educated at Winchester and New College, Oxford. Editorial staff of *The Times*, 1903–5; 1908–13. Served in the Grenadier Guards, 1914–18 (Churchill shared his frontline dugout in November 1915). Military Secretary to the Prince of Wales, 1919. Knighted, 1920. Private Secretary to Lloyd George, 1921–2. National Liberal MP for Oldham, 1922–5. Governor of Kenya, 1925–31. Elected to the Other Club, 1932. National Conservative MP for Altrincham, 1933–45. Parliamentary Secretary, Ministry of Information, 1939–40. Financial Secretary, War Office, 1940. Joint Parliamentary Under-Secretary of State for War, 1940–4. Minister Resident in the Middle East, 1944–5. Created Baron Altrincham, 1945. Editor of the *National Review*, 1948–55.

[3] Roger John Brownlow Keyes, 1872–1945. Entered Navy, 1885, Naval Attaché, Athens and Constantinople, 1905–7. Commodore in charge of submarines, North Sea and adjacent waters, August 1914–February 1915. Chief of Staff, Eastern Mediterranean Squadron (Dardanelles), 1915. Director of Plans, Admiralty, 1917. Vice-Admiral in command of the Dover Patrol (and Zeebrugge raid), 1918. Knighted, 1918. Created Baronet, 1919. Deputy Chief of the Naval Staff, 1921–5. Commander-in-Chief, Mediterranean, 1925–8; Portsmouth, 1929–31. Admiral of the Fleet, 1930. Elected to the Other Club, 1930. National Conservative MP, 1934–43. Director of Combined Operations, 1940–1. Created Baron, 1943. Churchill wrote the foreword to his memoirs, *Adventures Ashore & Afloat* (1939). His elder son was killed in action in Libya, leading a raid on Rommel's headquarters, 18 November 1941.

Winston S. Churchill to Commander H. T. Bishop

(*Churchill papers: 2/272*)

20 February 1936

Dear Sir,

I am very much obliged to you for the full details of the recent construction which you have given me so kindly. However what I meant to ask for was the weight of broadside comprised in the programme announced to Parliament in the Estimates of the last six years namely 1930 to 1935 inclusive. I do not wish to know the figures for ships actually joining the Fleet, but simply the accretions provided or proposed to be provided in these last six programmes, and to compare these with the similar last six programmes whether finished or not of other countries. This is after all what governs the future and the percentage results would I expect be very different from those obtained by adding up the actual vessels that have joined the Fleet in the programmes of previous years. The point I am anxious to make is that since the London Treaty we have not been entitled to propose to Parliament any ship above 6″ while others have proposed far larger programmes. Could you kindly make me an additional calculation for all countries concerned on these lines. There should be no difficulty in this as a statement only of countries showing what new construction they propose in any given year. I hope I have made things plain.

Yours faithfully,
Winston S. Churchill

Winston S. Churchill to Clementine Churchill

(*Spencer-Churchill papers*)

21 February 1936   House of Commons

My darling,

The interview took place on Saty at noon. He[1] professed himself quite ready to give the name & address of his mother & sister. His father was a well-known cloth manufacturer at Brünn named Victor Samek. He did not impress me with being a bad man; but common as dirt. An Austrian citizen,

[1] Victor Samek, 1898–1964. Born in Austria, the son of Baron Victor von Samek. Educated at the University of Vienna. Relinquished his father's title, 1922. A concert pianist, he worked in the United States from 1933 to 1935 under the stage name Vic Oliver; subsequently he worked on the stage and in revues in Britain and America. Married, as his third wife, Sarah Churchill, 1936 (from whom he obtained a divorce in 1945).

a resident in US, & here on license & an American passport: twice divorced: 36 so he says. A horrible mouth: a foul Austro-Yankee drawl. I did not offer to shake hands: but put him through a long examination. He described Sarah[1] as the 'brainiest & sweetest *gurl*' he had ever met. He said they would not think of getting married in a hurry, & 'that he would not force his way into my family agst my wishes': but he said they were always seen together at lunch supper etc: evil suggestions might be made, & the best thing was an engagement.

You may imagine that I confronted him with the hard side of things. I told him that if there was an engagement, it would force me to make an immediate public statement in terms wh wd be painful to them both. I then recapitulated the whole case agst their marriage or engagement. And I said that if they wd not see each other or communicate for one year, & were still in the same mood at the end, I would withdraw my resistance otherwise I wd do my best to persuade Sarah not to take a fatal step. On this he got up with gt emotion not without some dignity, & said 'You don't need to do it. I will do it myself.'

Sarah followed him downstairs & I have not seen her since. But I put Diana on to her & I learn that the idea of an engagement is off: & in my talks to her on the telephone she seems calm & in fairly good spirits. I don't think there is immediate cause to worry.

I am now going to try to get Sarah out of the revue, & started on the regular stage. Penelope Ward[2] is working in the Liverpool repertory theatre,

[1] Sarah Millicent Hermione Spencer Churchill, 1914– . Born while her father was returning from the siege of Antwerp, 7 October 1914. Edward Marsh was her godfather. She married Vic Oliver on 25 December 1936 (divorced, 1945). On stage in Birmingham, Southampton, Weston-Super-Mare and London, 1937–9; on tour with Vic Oliver in the play *Idiot's Delight*, 1938. Playing on the London stage in *Quiet Wedding*, 1939; in J. M. Barrie's *Mary Rose*, 1940. Appeared in the film *Spring Meeting*, 1940. Entered the Women's Auxiliary Air Force, October 1941; Assistant Section Officer (later Section Officer) at the Photographic Interpretation Unit, Medmenham, 1941–5. Accompanied her father (as ADC), to the Teheran Conference, November 1943, and to Yalta, February 1945. In 1949 she married Anthony Beauchamp, who died in 1957. In April 1962 she married the 23rd Baron Audley, MBE, who died in July 1963. An actress, in 1951 she had appeared on the stage in the United States in *Grammercy Ghost*. She published *The Empty Spaces* (poems) in 1966, and *A Thread in the Tapestry* (recollections) in 1967, *Collected Poems* in 1974 and *Keep on Dancing* (further recollections) in 1981.

[2] Penelope Dudley Ward, 1914–1982. Known as 'Pempy'. Born on the day Britain declared war on Germany, the daughter of William Dudley Ward and his wife Freda. Educated in London, Munich and Paris. An actress, she made her first appearance on the stage at the Playhouse, Liverpool, in November 1935. Remained with the Liverpool Repertory Company until April 1936. Played with the Theatre Royal, Brighton, repertory company, May 1936–March 1937. Made her first appearances on the New York stage on 28 September 1937. Appeared in several films between 1936 and 1939, including *Moscow Nights* and *Escape Me Never*. Brendan Bracken wanted to marry her. In 1948 she married (as his second wife) the film producer Carol Reed, who was knighted in 1953, and who died in 1976.

& I am finding out more about this from Brendan. Cochran[1] will I am sure do anything he can to help.

My darling, I am writing this to you while Bob Boothby is speaking just behind me.[2] But I wanted to give you a reasonable account.

The party was vy successful.[3] All enjoyed themselves. The house was warm, & the food good, the beds soft, & the cat made herself most agreeable to Austen.

There is no change in the uncertainty about my affairs. Evidently B desires above all things to avoid bringing me in. This I must now recognise. But his own position is much shaken, & the storm clouds gather.[4]

How are you getting on? I do hope you are happy healthy & making progress: & that the snow will not melt prematurely.

With innumerable kisses & tender love,

Your loving & devoted husband,

W

[sketch of pig]

---

[1] Charles Blake Cochran, 1872–1951. Theatrical manager, and producer of 128 plays and revues in London. First went on the stage in 1891 in New York; produced his first play in New York in 1895; in London, 1902. Introduced the wrestler Hackenschmidt to London; introduced roller-skating to France, Germany and Belgium. A promoter of boxing matches at Olympia; and of ballet and zoos. Brought the first rodeo to London, 1924. Manager of the Albert Hall, 1926–38. President of the Actors' Benevolent Fund, 1934–40. A Governor of the Shakespeare Memorial Theatre at Stratford-on-Avon. Knighted, 1948.

[2] During Oral Answers on 21 February 1936 Robert Boothby asked Baldwin 'whether the Committee of Civil Research is still in existence; and, if so, who is the chairman, how often it meets, and for what purpose'. He also asked 'whether the Economic Advisory Council is still in existence; if so, whether there have been any changes in its personnel; whether it is ever consulted by His Majesty's Government, how often it meets, and whether it issues any reports?' Baldwin replied that the Committee of Civil Research 'was absorbed in the Economic Advisory Council by Treasury Minute dated 27th January 1930'. As for the Economic Advisory Council, Baldwin said, its work was 'confidential', carried on by two main standing committees 'dealing respectively with economic information and scientific research, and through a number of specialist committees'. The two standing committees had held 26 meetings in 1935. Baldwin added: 'There have been no recent changes in the personnel of the Council.' Boothby went on to suggest the setting up of 'a permanent economic general staff' to help the Government 'in formulating a long-term policy'. But Baldwin replied: 'At the moment I have as much in the way of reconstruction as I can do.'

[3] See pages 56 and 57.

[4] On 27 January 1936 Clementine Churchill replied from Zürs: 'My darling—I think Baldwin must be mad not to ask you to help him. Perhaps it is a case of 'Those whom the Gods wish to destroy . . .'

Thomas Jones[1] *to a friend*

(*Jones papers*)

21 February 1936

In the meantime, Neville having refused, Sam will act as Deputy in the urgent matter of Defence. Those who desired Winston will be disappointed and those who dreaded Eustace Percy will be pleased.

Sir Samuel Hoare to Neville Chamberlain

(*Templewood papers*)

23 February 1936

He [Baldwin] hoped it would be Defence.[2] . . . On no account would he contemplate the possibility of Winston in the Cabinet for several obvious reasons, but chiefly for the risk that would be involved by having him in the Cabinet when the question of his (SB's) successor became imminent.

Austen is chiefly influenced by his wish to get in Winston.

Lord Rothermere to Winston S. Churchill

(*Churchill papers: 2/266*)

23 February 1936   Monte Carlo

My dear Winston,

Weir[3] is here but is returning. He gave me to understand that he is to co-ordinate the three Defence Departments.

[1] Thomas Jones, 1870–1955. Lecturer in Economics, Glasgow University, 1899–1909. Joined the Independent Labour Party, 1895. Special Investigator, Poor Law Commission, 1906–9. Professor in Economics, Belfast, 1909–10. Secretary, National Health Insurance Commissioners (Wales), 1912–16. Deputy–Secretary to the Cabinet, 1916–30. Companion of Honour, 1929. Member of the Unemployment Assistance Board, 1934–40.

[2] According to Sir Samuel Hoare, Baldwin had offered him the choice between First Lord of the Admiralty or Minister of Defence.

[3] William Douglas Weir, 1877–1959. Shipping contractor: his family won its first Royal Navy contract in 1896. A pioneer motor car manufacturer. Majority shareholder in G. & J. Weir Ltd, manufacturers of machinery for steamships. Scottish Director of Munitions, July 1915–January 1917. Controller of Aeronautical Supplies, and Member of the Air Board 1917. Knighted, 1917. Director-General of Aircraft Production, Ministry of Munitions, 1917–19. Created Baron, 1918. Secretary of State for Air, April–December 1918. Adviser, Air Ministry, 1935–9. Created Viscount, 1938. Director-General of Explosives, Ministry of Supply, 1939. Chairman of the Tank Board, 1942. A member of the Other Club from 1932.

As far as I can learn he has the final word. He has turned down a big scheme of artillery rearmament of the Army.

The Government are going to spend something under £300,000,000 in four years. I told him the sum was meagre and inadequate.

It looks as if Weir is going to be the big figure of the Government. The fact he holds no political office should give him great power.

I think he will stop any big battleship programme. This is all to the good because although it was possible for the battle fleet to hide in the Great War it is difficult to see where it would be able to hide in the next war when, in addition to submarine attacks, it will be attacked by great numbers of aeroplanes and speed boats. If it ever comes within striking distance of their weapons its fate will be immediately sealed.

I shall not be returning for some days.

Yours always,
Harold

Robert Boothby to Winston S. Churchill
(Churchill papers: 1/284)

24 February 1936   House of Commons

Dear Winston,

Thank you for an interesting and delightful week-end.[1]

It was good of you to ask me. And I couldn't have enjoyed it more.

Yours ever,
Bob

---

[1] The other Chartwell guests that weekend were Sir Edward Grigg, Sir Robert Horne, Sir Henry Page Croft, Sir Austen Chamberlain and Professor Lindemann.

Harold Nicolson:[1] *diary*

(*Nicolson papers*)

24 February 1936

Back to the House, where Winston makes a splendid speech on defence.[2]

Sir Edward Grigg to Winston S. Churchill

(*Churchill papers: 1/284*)

25 February 1936   House of Commons

My dear Winston,

Many thanks indeed for bidding me to Chartwell for the week-end. I enjoyed it immensely—talk, food, drink, setting—all equally delightful and stimulating.

Your people have just sent me this book, thinking I left it behind. I did not, but found it in the book-case in my room. It is, I observe, a wanderer from the WO Library, but I did not extract it thence!

Yrs ever,
Edward Grigg

Desmond Morton to Violet Pearman

(*Churchill papers: 2/278*)

26 February 1936   Department of Imperial Defence

The letter in German is from Mr Weiss,[3] who wrote to Mr Churchill several weeks ago telling him that he had two inventions in connection with fighting

[1] Harold George Nicolson, 1886–1968. Son of Sir Arthur Nicolson (1st Baron Carnock). Educated at Wellington and Balliol College, Oxford. Entered Foreign Office, 1909; Counsellor, 1925. Served at the Paris Peace Conference, 1919, Teheran, 1925–7 and Berlin, 1927–9. On editorial staff of *Evening Standard*, 1930. National Labour MP for West Leicester, 1935–45. Parliamentary Secretary, Ministry of Information, 1940–41. A Governor of the BBC, 1941–6. Joined the Labour Party, 1947. Author and biographer. Knighted, 1953.

[2] On 24 February 1936 Churchill spoke in the debate on the supplementary estimates for the Navy, supporting the Government's request for more destroyers, and attacking the Labour MP, A. V. Alexander, a former First Lord of the Admiralty, who had just opposed the increases. In his speech Churchill called attention to the number of submarines allotted to Germany in the Anglo-German Naval Treaty, which allowed for more total tonnage than Germany possessed in 1915, at the height of the submarine war. 'How was that attack defeated?' and he answered, with reference to A. V. Alexander: 'It was defeated by the fact that we had 220 destroyers. How many have we now? Not half; hardly a third; and now, when this tardy, this modest, this super-modest, this shrinking, timid tentative proposal, this beginning, this snowdrop—a few tender shoots that have come forward, he holds up his hands in holy horror.'

[3] I have been unable to trace either Mr Weiss or his letter.

aircraft and digging trenches which he would like to communicate to HM Government. Mr Weiss politely draws Mr Churchill's attention to the fact that he has not acknowledged his letter.

What happened was that you sent the letter to me, and I asked the Admiralty, with whom Mr Weiss appeared to be in touch, if they were dealing with the matter. They replied that they were in full contact with Mr Weiss and deprecated any other action.

I take the opportunity also of returning the two papers you passed to me over a week ago. I am sorry I did not send them back before.

Winston S. Churchill to Sir Maurice Hankey

(*Churchill papers: 25/10*)

26 February 1936   11 Morpeth Mansions
Secret

My dear Hankey,

I am much concerned at the slight and slow progress which we are making in Air Defence, in spite of the fact that we have such a very able and authoritative Committee. It is more than eighteen months since Professor Lindemann and I began to press for the experiments upon the proposals set out in various secret papers. It is just six months since we began working on these Committees. I cannot feel that enough progress has been made even in the experiments. The crisis which is approaching may be upon us long before any practical results are achieved. This causes me much anxiety as a member of the Committee.

There is of course no lack of bright and ingenious ideas and each time we meet we have most interesting discussions. But there seems no sufficient will and drive outside the Committee to get experiments done and one variant tried quickly after another. We must reach some conclusions and act upon them. I suggest that we now endeavour to concentrate upon two or three main lines of experiment with a view to speedy decision. I continue to ask for the experiments about making the shell-burst last longer, and laying mine curtains from aeroplanes, as previously discussed, and that these experiments should be undertaken without the loss of a single day, and day after day with the highest priorities.

Until these new shells are developed no confidence can be reposed in gunfire, except when many batteries are concentrated to protect some particular target. I have come gradually to the conclusion that the kite balloon affords greater prospects of giving protection both to focal points and to the fleet than gunfire, though there is no reason why they should not be combined. So far as defending London is concerned the kite balloon affords far better hopes at less expense than can be based on a long thin line of lights and guns. I suggest we ought to order immediately at least twenty of these balloons upon which experiments can be made, and if the experiments are successful, we should order forthwith on a large scale. The first lot can be assigned to the defence of the threatened focal points, and the bases of the fleet, and then as more come to hand they can be moved to form a general barrier line from south to north. So no time would be lost and every balloon play some part as soon as ready.

March 1936

Winston S. Churchill to Clementine Churchill
(Spencer-Churchill papers)

3 March 1936   11 Morpeth Mansions

My darling,

On Sunday when we went to feed Jupiter she would not eat from my hand. On Monday she was dead. She has been on the lake 10 years & was about 3 years old when she came. They only live about 12 years normally. So it was quite natural.

I send you a letter about the Liverpool Repertory Theatre. I am in corresp w this gentleman, & expect he will take her much sooner. Brendan seems to have irons in every fire. I told Sarah about it, & she said she would vy much like to go as soon as possible after this run of Follow the Sun is over. She has taken quite kindly to the plan. She knows all about the Repertory Theatre, & said it was much sought after & gt influence required to get in.

She came down to luncheon on Sunday & seemed quite cheerful. I said 'Does what you told me about "no need to worry" still hold good.' She replied 'Oh yes indeed it does.' I hope from her manner that this cloud will presently roll by. Once it has I will say a kind word to the man. However do not let us count our chickens before we have them all back in the hencoop.

The Defence business is at its height. Baldwin is still undecided. His own choice was Swinton (Cunliffe Lloyd Lister Greame).[1] But a really ugly snarl from the Commons has I believe scared him from appointing a Peer.

On Saturday Bendor[2] came out of the blue to luncheon at Chartwell, being

[1] On 29 November 1935 Sir Philip Cunliffe-Lister (formerly Philip Lloyd Greame) had been created Viscount Swinton.

[2] Hugh Richard Arthur Grosvenor, 1879–1953. Known as 'Bendor'. One of Churchill's closest friends. Educated at Eton. Succeeded his grandfather as 2nd Duke of Westminster, 1899. ADC to Lord Roberts, South Africa, 1900–2. DSO. Commanded an armoured car detachment, Royal Naval Division, 1914–15. Personal Assistant to the Controller, Mechanical Department, Ministry of Munitions, 1917. A member of the Other Club from 1917. A Vice-President (with Churchill) of the India Defence League, 1933–5. His uncle, Lord Hugh Grosvenor, a Captain in the Household Cavalry, was killed in action in November 1914.

much worked up on my behalf. He asked Gwynne[1] of the MP about it, who said 'there was reason to believe matters wd be settled as he wished.' Now this morning the DT comes out as the enclosed, wh is the most positive statement yet & the latest—& from a normally well-informed Governmental quarter.[2] Anyhow I seem to be still *en jeu*. I suppose that today or tomorrow it must be settled. Betty Cranborne[3] (whom I met at Jack[4] & Goonie's[5] dining last night) told me that Neville Ch said to her last week 'Of course if it is a question of military efficiency, Winston is no doubt the man.' Every other possible alternative is being considered & blown upon. Hoare because

[1] Howell Arthur Gwynne, 1865–1950. Reuter's chief war correspondent in South Africa, 1899–1902. Editor of the *Standard*, 1904–11. Editor of the *Morning Post*, 1911–37. One of Churchill's most outspoken public critics at the time of the siege of Antwerp in October 1914. Companion of Honour, 1938.

[2] On 3 March 1936 the *Daily Telegraph*, under the headline 'New Minister of Defence' added: 'Mr Churchill may be chosen'. The article itself, by the newspaper's Political Correspondent, reported that 'In Parliamentary circles yesterday the possibility that Mr Winston Churchill may become the new Defence Minister who will coordinate the fighting services was discussed with great interest. It is recognised in Government circles that the post must, almost of necessity, be filled by someone with a seat in the House of Commons. Mr Churchill's name is now prominently mentioned.'

[3] Elizabeth Vere Cavendish, 1897–1982. Granddaughter of the 8th Duke of Devonshire and of the 10th Duke of St Albans. She married Lord Cranborne (later 5th Marquess of Salisbury), in 1915. Their third son, Sergeant-Pilot Richard Hugh Vere Cecil, was killed during the Second World War, as a result of an accident, on 12 August 1944, aged 20.

[4] John Strange Spencer Churchill, 1880–1947. Churchill's younger brother, known as 'Jack'. Educated at Harrow. On active service in South Africa, 1900 (wounded). Major, Queen's Own Oxfordshire Hussars, 1914–18. Served at Dunkirk, 1914; on Sir John French's staff, Flanders, 1914–15; on Sir Ian Hamilton's staff at the Dardanelles, 1915; on General Birdwood's staff, France, 1916–18. A stockbroker he served as a partner with the City firm of Vickers da Costa, 1918–40. In 1931 he was elected to the Other Club, founded by his brother and F. E. Smith in 1911; asked once why he so enjoyed his brother's company, Churchill is said to have replied: 'Jack is unborable'.

[5] Lady Gwendeline Teresa Mary Bertie, 1885–1941. Known as 'Goonie'. Daughter of the 7th Earl of Abingdon. She married Churchill's brother Jack in 1908. Her first son, John George, was born in 1909 (he published his memoirs, *Crowded Canvas*, in 1961). Her second son, Henry Winston, known as Peregrine, was born in 1913. Her only daughter, Anne Clarissa, was born after the war, in 1920 (and married in 1952 Anthony Eden, later 1st Earl of Avon). On 11 July 1941 Lord David Cecil published in *The Times* an obituary of Lady Gwendeline Churchill which read: 'Lady Gwendeline Churchill's extraordinary charm was implicit in her appearance, her subtle twilight beauty, the fastidious grace of her dress. But it disclosed its power fully only in intimate conversation. Even then it was hard to analyse, so unexpectedly diverse were the elements of which it was compounded. Pensive, dreamy, with an intense refinement of feeling and a delicate sensibility to the beautiful, she exhaled romance. But unexpectedly mingled with romance was a touch of the eighteenth century, elegance, clear-eyed shrewdness, an amused scepticism, expressing itself in an enchanting mischievous irony which flickered over every phrase of her talk. Distinction was above all the keynote of her personality, an exquisite fineness of quality, beside which most people showed up as lamentably crude and commonplace. She was like the single flower of a high civilization, bred through generations to bloom once only, for the wonder and delight of mankind.'

of his FO position & Hoare-Laval pact: Swinton & Hankey[1] & Weir because Peers: Ramsay because all can see he is a walking ruin: Lord U Percy because of himself & his size: Neville because he sees the PM'ship not far off: K Wood[2] because he hopes to be Ch of Exch then, & anyhow does not know a Lieutenant General from a Whitehead torpedo: Horne because he will not give up his £25,000 a year directorships etc.

So at the end it may all come back to your poor [sketch of pig]. I do not mean to break my heart whatever happens. Destiny plays her part.

If I get it, I will work faithfully before God & man for *Peace*, & not allow pride or excitement to sway my spirit.

If I am not wanted, we have many things to make us happy my darling beloved Clemmie. I will wire if anything 'transpires'.

Your ever loving husband,
W

PS. It wd be the heaviest burden yet. They are *terribly* behindhand.

Professor Lindemann to Winston S. Churchill
(*Churchill papers: 25/10*)

5 March 1936   Christ Church

My dear Winston,

I enclose a few notes on the activities of the Committee.[3] So far as I can see

---

[1] Hankey did not become a Peer until 3 February 1939.

[2] Kingsley Wood, 1881–1943. Member of the London County Council, 1911–19. Chairman, London Insurance Committee, 1917–18. Conservative MP for Woolwich West, 1918–43. Knighted, 1918. Parliamentary Private Secretary to the Minister of Health, 1919–22. Parliamentary Secretary, Ministry of Health, 1924–9 (when Neville Chamberlain was Minister); Board of Education, 1931. Privy Councillor, 1928. Chairman, Executive Committee of the National Conservative and Unionist Association, 1930–2. Postmaster-General, 1931–5. Minister of Health, 1935–8. Secretary of State for Air, 1938–40. Lord Privy Seal, April–May 1940. Chancellor of the Exchequer from May 1940 until his death.

[3] The Scientific Committee of the Air Defence Research sub-committee set up under the auspices of the Committee of Imperial Defence, and chaired by Professor (later Sir) Henry Tizard. In his notes for Churchill, Lindemann wrote: 'it is submitted that if the Government is in earnest in desiring to develop a new mode of defence it should be given the power and responsibility to appropriate individuals and not try and act through a committee, the majority of whose members disbelieves in the method to be investigated. The RDF System has been successfully developed because it is entirely in the hands of Dr Watson-Watt, who suggested it and believes in it. When an invention is to be developed, each experiment is based upon the results of the last and all improvements must depend upon what happened on a previous occasion. It is clearly out of the question to proceed if each step must await a meeting of the committee which is not fully aware of all the details of the previous experiments and which is not in a position to determine and agree upon what experiments ought to be undertaken next.'

they have been to all intents and purposes nil, save for Watson-Watt's[1] very successful and commendable detection and location work. I do not know whether it would be worth your while to have a private talk with him and perhaps with A. P. Rowe,[2] the Secretary of the Committee. I have reason to know they are both most dissatisfied with the slowness and lack of drive which have been exhibited.[3]

I am very sorry I shall miss the Other Club to-night.[4] From some points of view I was delighted to read of Hartington's[5] appointment, but it may mean the thin edge of the wedge in more senses than one. I am looking forward to seeing you at the week-end and remain,

as ever,

yours,

FAL

[1] Robert Watson-Watt, 1892–1973. Engineer and inventor. Educated at St Andrews University. Joined the staff of the Meteorological Office, London, 1915, where he did successful research into the radio location of thunderstorms. Superintendent of the radio research stations at Aldershot and Slough, 1921; subsequently Superintendent of the radio department of the National Physical Laboratory. His radio wave experiments for detecting aircraft were sponsored by the Air Ministry in 1935. Superintendent at Bawdsey, 1936–8. Director of Communications Development, Air Ministry, 1938–40. After Pearl Harbor (December 1941) he advised the United States on radar defence. Knighted, 1942. After the war he received £50,000 for his contribution to radar development.

[2] Albert Percival Rowe, 1898–1976. Secretary of the Scientific Committee, and Joint Secretary of the Air Defence Research sub-committee, Committee of Imperial Defence, 1935–8. Chief Superintendent, Telecommunications Research Establishment, 1938–45. Deputy Controller of Research and Development, Admiralty, 1946–7. Defence Scientific Adviser to the Australian Government, 1947–8. Vice-Chancellor of the University of Adelaide, 1948–58.

[3] In his notes for Churchill, Lindemann wrote, of Watson-Watt's RDF (radar) experiments: 'Surely the RDF work has been given a very high priority; yet the recommendation to put Mr Watson-Watt in charge of these experiments under the Air Ministry has not been carried out though a quarter of a year has elapsed since it was made.'

[4] The Other Club had been founded by Churchill and F. E. Smith (later 1st Earl of Birkenhead) in 1911. According to the Rules, the object of the Club 'is to dine'. It was to consist of no more than 50 members, of whom not more than 24 should be Members of the House of Commons. It was to meet on alternate Thursdays 'at 8.15 punctually' when Parliament was in Session. The names of the Executive Committee 'shall be wrapped in impenetrable mystery' (rule 10). 'Nothing in the Rules or intercourse of the Club shall interfere with the rancour or asperity of party politics' (rule 12). I have indicated who were Other Club members in the biographical notes in this volume, on the basis that, as one member recently reflected, 'they were only elected to the Other Club if Winston thought well of them' (*conversation with the author, 1 February 1982*). For more about the Club's origins, see page 506, note 1.

[5] Edward William Spencer Cavendish, Marquess of Hartington, 1895–1950. Elder son of the 9th Duke of Devonshire. On active service, 1914–18. A member of the British Delegation at the Paris Peace Conference, 1919. Conservative MP for West Derbyshire, 1923–38. A Member of the Other Club from 1933. Parliamentary Under-Secretary for Dominion Affairs, 1936–40 (he was appointed on 4 March 1936). Succeeded his father, as 10th Duke of Devonshire, 1938. Chancellor of Leeds University, 1938. Parliamentary Under-Secretary of State for India and Burma, 1940–2; for the Colonies, 1942–5. Grand Master of the English

Sir Philip Sassoon[1] to Winston S. Churchill
(*Churchill papers: 25/7*)

6 March 1936   Air Ministry

My dear Winston,

You asked me for information concerning the number of additional Royal Air Force squadrons formed at home and overseas during the year ended 31st March, 1935, and the further number formed or to be formed at home during the year ended 31st March, 1936, one of which is destined for overseas. No additional squadrons were formed overseas during that year.

In the current year 17 squadrons (including 3 Auxiliary Air Force) have been or are in process of being formed, all for Home Defence. Some of these squadrons will not, of course, be up to establishment by the 31st March, 1936, but will be brought up to full strength in the ensuing months as personnel and aircraft become available.

So far as additions to the first line strength of the Fleet Air Arm are concerned, these are mostly brought about by a slight reorganisation of existing units but, during the two years ending 31st March, 1936, one new Squadron and one new Flight have actually come into being.

Yours sincerely,
Philip

Winston S. Churchill to Clementine Churchill: telegram
(*Churchill papers: 1/284*)

7 March 1936

Doubtful whether speaking Tuesday. Nothing yet settled. No need return till ready, but avoid travelling through Germany.[2] Tender love.

W

Lodge of Freemasons, 1947. His elder son William John Robert Cavendish, Major, Coldstream Guards, was killed in action in Belgium on 10 September 1944. His elder son's wife, Kathleen Kennedy (sister of President John F. Kennedy) was killed in a flying accident in France on 13 May 1948.

[1] Philip Albert Gustave Sassoon, 1888–1939. Educated at Eton and Christ Church, Oxford. Succeeded his father as 3rd Baronet, 1912. Conservative MP for Hythe, 1912–39. Private Secretary to Sir Douglas Haig, 1914–18. Parliamentary Private Secretary to Lloyd George, 1920–2. Trustee of the National Gallery, 1921–39. Under-Secretary of State for Air, 1924–9 and 1931–7. A special Regional Commissioner during the General Strike, 1926. Privy Councillor, 1929. First Commissioner of Works, 1937–9. His London house was 25 Park Lane, his country houses, Port Lympne and Trent Park.

[2] In a declaration to the Reichstag at noon on 7 March 1936, Hitler announced the remilitarization of the Rhineland and the abrogation of the Locarno Agreement (on account of the Franco-Soviet pact of 1935). At the same time, Hitler offered to negotiate another demilitarized zone on the German border, to sign a twenty-five year non-aggression pact with

Winston S. Churchill to Pierre-Etienne Flandin[1]

(Churchill papers: 2/274)

7 March 1936
Confidential

I should be much obliged if you felt able to give me information upon the following points:—

First. What is the latest French estimate of the present strength of the German Air Force. My own estimate, based on information drawn from a variety of sources, is that the Germans can put simultaneously in the air, and maintain in day-to-day action, 1,200 machines; that by June this number will be 1,500, and by the end of the year about 2,000. In their scientifically prepared industry they have of course an almost indefinite power of expansion so far as material is concerned. How do your estimates tally with this?

Secondly. What was the total French expenditure upon aviation services in 1935. My own estimate shows that it came to over sixty millions sterling. Such a sum was certainly voted, but whether it was all expended or not in the period I cannot tell.

I wish to check my information on both these points for the purpose of the debates about to take place in Parliament. If you are able to confirm or correct me, I should be indebted to you. I should not of course reveal the source of my information, although there is nothing that is not entirely natural and proper in my request. However, my dear M Flandin, if you feel any difficulty in complying with it, pray believe that I shall understand perfectly that you have good reason for it.

Believe me always,

France and Belgium and possibly the Netherlands (with Britain and Italy acting as guarantors), to enter non-aggression pacts with countries in the East including Lithuania, to join a Western Air Pact (an 'Air Locarno'), and to rejoin the League of Nations (in the 'expectation' of discussing Germany's claim to 'colonial equality of rights').

[1] Pierre Etienne Flandin, 1889–1958. Chef de Cabinet to the Prime Minister (Millerand), 1913–14. Entered the Chamber of Deputies, 1914. Director of the Allied Aeronautical Service, 1917. Under-Secretary for Air, 1920. President of the First International Conference on Aerial Navigation, 1921. Minister for Commerce, June 1924, November 1929 and March 1930. After 1930 he suffered constant pain from a broken arm which never properly healed. Minister for Finance, 1931 and 1932. Leader of the Right Centre group of Deputies, 1932. Prime Minister, November 1934–June 1935. Minister for Foreign Affairs, January–June 1936. After his visit to Germany in 1937, Blum's Government issued a communiqué declaring that he went as a private individual only. Arrested by the Allies in North Africa, 1943. Tried by the French Government, 1946, but acquitted of the charge of collaboration with the Germans (Randolph Churchill spoke in Flandin's defence at the trial, on his father's behalf). Following the trial Flandin was declared ineligible for Parliament.

PS. I am sending this letter by the shortest route, as I shall probably be speaking on Tuesday.[1] The information could be given in the very shortest general terms, for there is no need to go into detail. A cipher message through the French Embassy London would probably be the best way.[2]

Neville Chamberlain: diary

(*Neville Chamberlain papers*)

10 March 1936

. . . Winston made a constructive and helpful speech.[3]

[1] Churchill's only reference to France during his speech in the House of Commons on 10 March 1936 was to tell the House: 'we spent in the financial year which is now closing £29,000,000 on the air, under the original and supplementary estimates. In about the same period—the dates do not quite tally, the French voted nearly £70,000,000 and spent, I expect, at least £60,000,000. The Germans spent certainly far more, though I cannot hazard a figure; but both France and Germany spent on their air development at least twice what we were able to spend last year. . . .'

[2] Flandin replied to Churchill on the following day, from the Ministry of Foreign Affairs in Paris: 'My dear friend. I enclose the information for which you asked. I hope that it will be of use to you. I follow from afar your energetic and courageous efforts. I hope they will assure peace, which seems to me more and more threatened. I am very worried about the future, especially if the equivocal situation as regard to Italy is allowed to be prolonged. Italy must decide once and for all to rejoin the conservative powers in the Mediterranean as in central Europe, and this by our taking Mussolini at his word. I am always at your disposal, if I can be of help to you.' The information, on two typed sheets, gave Germany's air strength as 1,236 first line aircraft, with a reserve of 950 aircraft, together with a further 120 aircraft available on the mobilization of the Civil airline, Lufthansa. The document envisaged, for the end of 1938, a German first line strength of 2,280 with a further 1,500 in reserve, with a total of 216 Lufthansa aircraft, and an extra 540 from the special air reserve (Luftwaffen-reserve) which had been set up in 1935 (and which, by May 1936, had still not been equipped for military activity). This calculation envisaged a total German military strength of 4,536 aircraft by the end of 1938.

[3] Speaking in the defence debate on 10 March 1936, Churchill said, of the years 1932 and 1933: '*Then* was the moment when the change took place, and I think I may say that there were some of us in this House who gave full warnings on every occasion on which we had an opportunity to do so of the gravity of the change that was coming over the scene. The pages of the Official Report are dark with the warnings which we gave, and I cannot believe that the very admirable Intelligence Service of this country, which in the Great War was considered to be the best in the world, did not give its warnings through other channels. The gravamen of the criticism which is against the Government is that they did not realize effectively, or at any rate that they did not act in accordance with, the marked deterioration in world affairs which occurred in 1932 and 1933. They continued to adhere to a policy which was adapted to one set of circumstances after an entirely different set of circumstances had supervened.' Speaking only half an hour after Churchill, Lloyd George criticized Churchill's estimate of German strength, telling the House of Commons: 'We must not run away and work ourselves into a panic.' But he also urged that the jigs and gauges, 'of which you may need hundreds in one little machine and which must be meticulously accurate', 'ought to be manufactured by the State, and manufactured at once'. Lloyd George added: 'You will be making experiments, they must be State experiments . . . You may find that the machinery, or the jigs and gauges, must all be scrapped because of some new discovery which experiment has proved to be a complete success. You cannot pass that burden on to the private individuals, even if you can compensate them. It is a burden that the State must undertake.'

George Lloyd[1] to Winston S. Churchill: telegram

(*Churchill papers: 2/253*)

11 March 1936

Congratulations on your wonderful speech. All but you and LG seemed like Pygmies.

George Lloyd

Sir Henry Strakosch[2] to Winston S. Churchill

(*Churchill papers: 2/266*)

11 March 1936

My dear Winston,

. . . I should like to thank you again for the speech you made last night. In many ways I think it was the greatest speech I have ever heard you make, and I was very delighted in the way the House received it. It was rather a tragic debate in some ways. Your speech and Ll G's sounded like voices from the past in the days when there were really great men to serve the Government of our country.

However, we must hope for the best, and that the period of 'pussyfoot' will not last for ever.

Yours ever,
Henry

[1] George Ambrose Lloyd, 1879–1941. Educated at Eton and Cambridge. Travelled widely in the East as a young man. Honorary Attaché, Constantinople Embassy, 1905. Special Trade Commissioner to Turkey, including Mesopotamia, 1907. Conservative MP for West Staffordshire, 1910–18. A director of Lloyds Bank, 1911–18. Captain, 1914. On active service in Gallipoli, Mesopotamia and the Hedjaz; he accompanied T. E. Lawrence on one of his desert raids. Present at the capture of Gaza, 1917. Knighted, 1918. Governor of Bombay, 1918–23. Conservative MP for Eastbourne, 1924–5. Privy Councillor, 1924. Created Baron, 1925. High Commissioner for Egypt and the Sudan, 1925–9. One of the Vice-Presidents (with Churchill) of the India Defence League, 1933–5. Chairman, British Council, 1936. Elected to the Other Club, 1936. Secretary of State for the Colonies, 1940–1.

[2] Henry Strakosch, 1871–1943. Entered banking in the City of London, 1891; closely connected with South African industrial development and gold mining from 1895; Chairman of the Union Corporation Ltd, London. Author of the South African Currency and Banking Act, 1920. Knighted, 1921. Represented South Africa at the Genoa Conference, the League of Nations Assembly and the Imperial Conference, 1923. A Trustee of the League of Nations Loan for the Financial Reconstruction of Hungary, 1924. Member of the Royal Commission on Indian Currency and Finance, 1925–6. Member of the Council of India, 1930–7. Delegate of India, Imperial Economic Conference, Ottawa, 1932. Adviser to the Secretary of State for India, 1937–42. Chairman of the Economist Newspaper Ltd. Elected to the Other Club, 1939. In his will, published on 5 February 1944, he left Churchill £20,000.

Harold Laski[1] to Winston S. Churchill

(*Churchill papers: 2/252*)

11 March 1936   London School of Economics

My dear Mr Churchill,

I venture to send you a book, in the production of which I have had some part, that may, I hope, help in some degree to awaken our people to the menace of the new Germany.[2] Different as are our political views this at least is a subject on which I have followed your speeches with admiration and gratitude. Would you care to say some words about it that could be used for publication? That would indeed be generous for it would enable us to make the book known in circles that might otherwise remain strange to its documentation.

With warm regards to Mrs Churchill and yourself,

Yours sincerely,
Harold Laski

Winston S. Churchill to Pierre-Etienne Flandin

(*Churchill papers: 2/252*)

12 March 1936

I am delighted you can come and dine with me tomorrow Friday, at 1 Morpeth Mansions, at 8.15 pm. Sir Austen Chamberlain, Sir Samuel Hoare, and Sir Robert Horne will be the other guests.[3]

[1] Harold Joseph Laski, 1893–1950. Political philosopher and historian; the son of Nathan Laski (an influential member of the Jewish community in North-West Manchester, Churchill's former constituency). Lecturer in History, McGill University, Montreal, 1914–16; Harvard University, 1916–20. Vice-Chairman of the British Institute of Adult Education, 1921–30. Member of the Fabian Society Executive, 1922. Lecturer in Political Science, Magdalene College, Cambridge, 1922–5. Professor of Political Science, London, 1926–50. Member of Executive Committee of Labour Party, 1936–49.

[2] The book was *The Yellow Spot*, published by Victor Gollancz Ltd, and subtitled 'The Extermination of the Jews in Germany', with an introduction (dated 12 February 1936) by the Bishop of Durham, Herbert Hensley Henson. Its 287 pages documented and illustrated the anti-Jewish measures and propaganda in Germany from 1933 to 1935. The book also quoted the *Manchester Weekly Guardian* of 27 September 1935 to the effect that thirty-four Jews had been murdered in Dachau concentration camp, near Munich, between 1933 and 1935, and named fifteen of them, with the dates of their deaths, and their professions (students, businessmen, lawyers, a doctor, and a department store employee).

[3] Flandin, the French Foreign Minister, whom Churchill had met on a number of occasions, and who was a good friend of Ralph and Ava Wigram, had come to London on 11 March 1936 where the League of Nations Council was to discuss the Rhineland crisis. Ralph Wigram attended the League Council meeting, which was held at St James's Palace, and was seen at Eden's side 'inwardly increasingly disillusioned and depressed'. During the crisis, Wigram called the Press to his house in Lord North Street in an effort to alert public opinion.

Sir Christopher Bullock[1] to Winston S. Churchill
(*Churchill papers: 2/278*)

13 March 1936   Air Ministry
Private and Personal

My dear Mr Churchill,

This is in no sense an official, but a purely private and personal, letter which I am only justified in writing to you by virtue of the fact that I was once privileged to serve on your personal staff as Private Secretary, when you were Secretary of State for Air.

My reason for writing is my knowledge of your great Parliamentary influence, and of the keen interest you are taking in all questions bearing on the very difficult problems of war production, of which you have such unrivalled personal experience.

To save dictating a long letter at a time when I am very pressed, I am venturing to send you simply a copy of a semi-official letter which I wrote yesterday to Creedy,[2] and its attachments, which I think will be self-explanatory.

Whilst I hate the idea of any possible interference with amenities in the Highlands (and, incidentally, with salmon fishing, since fly fishing is my chief

---

There Flandin told the members of the Press: 'If you do not stop Germany now, all is over,' and he continued: 'France cannot guarantee Czechoslovakia anymore, because that will become geographically impossible.' (Valentine Lawford, *Bound For Diplomacy*, London 1963, pages 149–51.) On the evening of 11 March 1936 Wigram had driven specially to Chartwell to tell Churchill the full story of Flandin's mission. Early on the following morning Churchill drove up to London, to his flat in Morpeth Mansions, near Victoria Station, where he received Flandin, and wished him 'all success' in persuading the British Government to join the Allies of the last war in concerted opposition to Hitler. It was evident, Churchill later wrote, 'that superior strength still lay with the Allies of the former war. They had only to act, to win' (Winston S. Churchill, *The Second World War*, volume 1, pages 152–4). That evening Churchill set out this view to the Foreign Affairs Committee of the House of Commons, telling MPs of all parties that he believed that if the smaller nations of Europe were to support France and Britain against Germany, then Germany would back down. 'We must fulfil our obligations under the Covenant,' he told them; and it seemed, as one observer recorded, that a 'substantial proportion' of those present were prepared to go to war (*Premier papers: 1/194*).

[1] Christopher Llewellyn Bullock, 1891–1972. Educated at Rugby and Trinity College, Cambridge. Entered the Indian Civil Service, 1915. Captain, Rifle Brigade, France, 1915. Royal Flying Corps, Egypt, 1916 (wounded, despatches). On the Staff of the Air Ministry, 1917–18. Major, 1919. Principal Private Secretary to Churchill (when Secretary of State for Air), 1919, and to successive Secretaries of State, 1923–30. Permanent Secretary, Air Ministry, and Member of the Air Council, 1931–6. Knighted, 1932.

[2] Herbert Creedy, 1878–1973. Educated at Merchant Taylors School and St John's College, Oxford. Joined the War Office, 1901. On special duty in South Africa, 1903. Assistant Principal, War Office, 1908–20. Private Secretary to successive Secretaries of State for War, 1913–20 (including Kitchener from 1914 to 1916 and Churchill in 1919 and 1920). Knighted, 1919. Secretary of the War Office, 1920–4, and a member of the Army Council, 1920-39. Permanent Under-Secretary of State for War and Accounting Officer, 1924–39. A member (and later Chairman) of the Security Executive, 1940–5.

recreation when I have any leisure!), the scheme for producing Carbide put forward by the British Oxygen Company does seem to me, *prima facie*, of altogether outstanding national importance and that it would be the greatest pity in the world if it was blocked by factious opposition.

Incidentally, the promoters assure me that they are prepared to go to great lengths, and to incur any reasonable expense, with a view to safeguarding amenities and salmon fishing—which latter, however, they say is not really jeopardised.

You will, however, form your own judgment of the project. If you think well of it perhaps you will see fit to use your influence to see that it gets a fair hearing. If you do not, please consign these papers to the waste paper basket and think no more of it.

I hope you keep well.

Yours sincerely,
C. L. Bullock

PS. I understand the Bill is down for Second Reading early next week.[1]

Paul Maze[2] *to Winston S. Churchill*
(*Churchill papers: 2/252*)

13 March 1936

My dear Winston,

This is just to tell you that you are much in my thoughts during this crisis.

How right you have been, as events alas now prove. The public is slowly beginning to see it. I am hoping that a strong line will be taken. Hitler will come to heel if he knows that all the countries are against him as they surely will be. As you say in the Evening Standard 'it is a wonderful chance we are

---

[1] The Caledonian Power Bill, which would have relieved certain Scottish power companies of a portion of their rates, was debated in the House of Commons on 18 March 1936, when the House voted to postpone the Second Reading of the Bill for six months. Churchill took no part in the debate, nor was he present for the Division.

[2] Paul Lucien Maze, 1887–1979. Born in Le Havre. Painter. On active service, 1914–18 (DCM, MM and Bar, Légion d'Honneur, Croix de Guerre). He first met Churchill in 1916, on the western front, and subsequently encouraged him with his painting. Churchill wrote the preface to Maze's war memoirs, *A Frenchman in Khaki*, published in 1934. Left France after the German invasion, 1940; subsequently resident in England. Served with the Home Guard, and then with the RAF (intelligence), 1940–5. In his Introduction to Paul Maze's war memoirs, Churchill wrote of Maze: '. . . he is an artist of distinction whose quick comprehension, keen eye and nimble pencil could record impressions with revealing fidelity. As a British private, who watched him one day sketching in a heavily bombarded trench said, "Your pictures are done in shorthand." ' Churchill ended his Introduction: '. . . we have the battle-scenes of Armageddon recorded by one who not only loved the fighting troops and shared their perils, but perceived the beauties of light and shade, of form and colour, of which even the horrors of war cannot rob the progress of the sun. This volume should be acceptable alike to the artists and the soldiers of the two great nations whose cause of freedom its author so ardently and enduringly espoused.'

now offered & we must take it'. *Do* write to the papers all you can—the German propaganda spread about is most harmful especially in Mayfair society.[1]

Keep well—England needs you now more than ever, and I only hope that the Government will have the sense of putting you at the helm of defence.

Yours ever,
Paul

The Duke of Westminster to Winston S. Churchill: telegram

(*Churchill papers: 2/252*)

14 March 1936

My word, I never thought that would be their choice.[2]

Bendor

Charles Taylor[3] to Winston S. Churchill: telegram

(*Churchill papers: 2/252*)

14 March 1936

Unable to express my profound regret by telegram on hearing news.

Charles Taylor

[1] Writing in the *Evening Standard* on 13 March 1936, Churchill argued in favour of the League of Nations using the Rhineland crisis to resolve in future to assert its sovereign strength against an aggressor. If, he wrote, 'the forces at the disposal of the League of Nations are four or five times as strong as those which the Aggressor can as yet command, the chances of a peaceful and friendly solution are good'. It was, Churchill added, 'a wonderful chance we are now offered and we must take it'; there never was, he added, 'a moment or occasion when the League of Nations could command such overwhelming force. The Constabulary of the world is at hand. On every side of Geneva stand great nations, armed and ready, whose interests as well as whose obligations bind them to uphold, and, in the last resort, enforce, the public law. This may never come to pass again. The fateful moment has arrived for choice between the New Age and the Old.' The Germans could, however, make the League's action unneccessary, for as Churchill wrote: 'Herr Hitler and the great disconsolate Germany he leads have now the chance to place themselves in the very forefront of civilization. By a proud and voluntary submission, not to any single country or group of countries, but to the sanctity of Treaties and the authority of public law, by an immediate withdrawal from the Rhineland, they may open a new era for all mankind and create conditions in which German genius may gain its highest glory.'

[2] On 13 March 1936 Sir Thomas Inskip had been appointed Minister for Co-ordination of Defence.

[3] Charles Stuart Taylor, 1910–   . Educated at Epsom College and Trinity College, Cambridge (BA 1921). Conservative MP for Eastbourne, 1935–74 (returned unopposed at the by-election of March 1935 and at the General Election of November 1935; defeated both the Labour and Liberal challengers at the General Election of 1945). Captain, Royal Artillery, 1939; temporary Major, 1941. Managing Director of Unigate & Cow & Gate Ltd. President of the Residential Hotels Association of Great Britain. President of Grosvenor House (Park Lane) Ltd. Knighted, 1954.

Desmond Morton to Winston S. Churchill

(*Churchill papers: 2/252*)

14 March 1936   Earlylands,
                                                 Crockham Hill,
                                                 Edenbridge

Dear Winston,

I hardly need to write to let you know how sorry I am that, after all the tension of waiting, we are so disappointed in our hope that you would be now co-ordinating Defence. I feel, too, that you must have undergone no little strain. It is a horrible job awaiting the uncertain, as you and I learnt to recognise during the war.

Nevertheless, I really believe you are well out of it, as things stand. You have a great work to perform now. You have begun it without delay, I see and hear. Still, from my parochial point of view, I do regret what appears to me to be the intention of the Government once more to shelve really effective Defence measures. What else are we to read into the appointment of Inskip?[1] It is a little unfair to criticise without giving him a chance to prove what he is capable of doing, but there is a feeling abroad little short of dismay.

Apart from what is publicly known, I hear from legal friends of his, that he is bad at conducting Crown cases in the Court, that he revokes at Bridge more frequently than any other professed player of the game. The Navy as a whole, with whom, according to the Press, he might be supposed to have some support, is dumbfounded.

These are the merest superficialities. I think that very big movements are gaining momentum in the political world. At present the country will not show any real enthusiasm for resisting German frightfulness and consequently appears to approve the apparent attitude of HMG, but a slow current is setting in in the contrary direction. If this current gains momentum it is all up with the present PM whatever he does. If he resists it, it will sweep him away; if he swims with it, he will be looked upon as a time-server and, so soon as the World situation clears, public opinion will be too strong for him.

I feel I should have written this to-morrow—the 'Ides of March'—though Heaven knows SB does not appear to a simple minded person like me as a reincarnation of Julius Caesar!

                                    Yours very sincerely,
                                    Desmond Morton

[1] Thomas Walker Hobart Inskip, 1879–1947. Educated at Clifton and King's College, Cambridge. Barrister, 1899. Served in the Naval Intelligence Division, Admiralty, 1915–18. Conservative MP for Central Bristol, 1918–29 and for Fareham, 1931–9. Knighted, 1922. Solicitor-General, October 1922–January 1924, November 1924–March 1928 and September 1931–January 1932. Attorney-General, 1928–9 and 1932–6. Minister for the Co-ordination

Admiral Sir William Goodenough[1] to Winston S. Churchill

(*Churchill papers: 2/252*)

14 March 1936

My dear Winston,

I am sorry, but there it is.

That, after all the labour this great mountain shd give birth to such a small mouse as announced this morning, is deeply disappointing. It is enraging that we seem unable to get away from that safe, smug course of action or inaction that besets us. I had—we all had—hoped for someone who wld carry a torch to lead & light us on our way. The problem is essentially one to be solved by executive action.

DAMN.

Yrs,

W. E. Goodenough

Sir Leo Chiozza Money[2] to Winston S. Churchill

(*Churchill papers: 2/252*)

14 March 1936

Dear Churchill,

Thanks for your letter. Let me say how disgusted I am that the PM has not asked you to take the Defence Ministry. To me it is another and glaring instance of the stupidity of party politics, which always denies a nation the services of most of its best men.

I arrived at this conclusion long before the War. Now I observe that there

---

of Defence, 1936–9. Secretary of State for Dominion Affairs, January–September 1939 and May–October 1940. Lord Chancellor, September 1939–May 1940. Created Viscount Caldecote, 1939. Lord Chief Justice, 1940–6.

[1] William Edmund Goodenough, 1867–1945. A cousin by marriage of Clementine Churchill. Went to sea, 1882. Captain, 1905. Commanded the 2nd Light Cruiser Squadron, battles of Heligoland Bight, 1914; Dogger Bank, 1915; Jutland, 1916. Superintendent, Chatham Dockyard, 1918–20. Knighted, 1919. Vice-Admiral, 1920. Commanded the Africa Station, 1920–2; the Reserve Fleet, 1923–4; the Nore, 1924–7. Admiral, 1925. Retired list, 1930.

[2] Leo George Chiozza Money, 1870–1944. Born in Genoa. Economist, author and journalist. Managing editor, *Commercial Intelligence*, 1898–1903. Liberal MP, Paddington North, 1906–10; East Northants, 1910–18. Member, Restriction of Enemy's Supplies Committee, 1914–15; War Trade Advisory Committee, 1915–18. Knighted, 1915. Parliamentary Private Secretary to Lloyd George, 1915–16; to the Minister of Shipping, 1916–18. Unsuccessful Labour candidate, 1918. Member of the Royal Commission on the Coal Industry, 1919.

are three nations in adequate development of their resources—Italy, Germany and Russia. The development of Italy and her defeat of sanctions are an object-lesson; she is fortunately able to act as we did in 1917–1918.

Yours sincerely,
Leo Chiozza Money

Brigadier-General Sir Joseph Laycock[1] to Winston S. Churchill

(*Churchill papers: 2/252*)

14 March 1936

My dear Winston,

Just a line which please don't bother to answer, to say how disappointed I am that they didn't give you the position for which you were so obviously and eminently fitted.

It is very sad about poor David Beatty.[2]

Yours sincerely,
J. F. Laycock

Lord Lloyd to Winston S. Churchill

(*Churchill papers: 2/252*)

16 March 1936

My dear Winston,

Inskip's appointment is really a bit too steep even for Baldwin and I feel furious about it and that you were not asked to do it. It would have been a pretty tough job but you are the only person in the Country who could succeed at it. I am afraid moreover it is a sign that SB is only halfhearted about it all & wants someone who will give him no trouble or press any inconvenient questions or demands.

[1] Joseph Frederick Laycock, 1867–1952. Educated at Eton and Oxford. On active service in South Africa, 1899–1900 (despatches twice, DSO), and in the European war, 1914–18 (despatches). Extra ADC to Sir John French, 1914. Brigadier-General, 1918. Knighted, 1919.

[2] David Beatty, 1871–1936. Entered Navy, 1884. Commanded a gunboat near Omdurman, where he first met Churchill, 1898. Rear-Admiral, 1910. Churchill's Naval Secretary, 1912. Commander of the Battle Cruiser Squadron, 1913–16. Knighted, 1914. Vice-Admiral, 1915. Commander-in-Chief of the Grand Fleet, 1916–19. First Sea Lord, 1919–27. Created Earl, 1919. Admiral of the Fleet, 1919. Order of Merit, 1919. He died on 11 March 1936, aged 65.

One can only hope it is a nail in SB's coffin. How many have we suffered! I was *delighted* with Garvin's[1] leader yesterday.[2] Don't answer.

Yours ever,

George L

Lord Lloyd to his son[3]

(*Lloyd papers*)

17 March 1936

The Government here are feverishly engaged in restoring defences but they have left it so terribly late that whatever they do now the next three years are bound to be ones of great anxiety if not actual peril. Some of us, as you know, have long ago foreseen and constantly warned the Government, but were not heeded—were indeed abused and mocked for our warnings!

Baldwin has now appointed Inskip—a lawyer! to undertake the whole gigantic task of defence reorganisation and to preside over the Chief of Staffs Committee. He is much criticised for it and rightly.[4]

[1] James Louis Garvin, 1868–1947. Editor, *The Observer*, 1908–42. An original member of the Other Club (founded by Churchill and F. E. Smith), 1911. Editor, *Pall Mall Gazette*, 1912–15. Editor-in-Chief, *Encyclopaedia Britannica*, 1926–9. His only son was killed in action in 1916 on the western front.

[2] In his leading article in the *Observer* on Sunday 15 March 1936, Garvin wrote, of Inskip's appointment as Minister for Co-ordination of Defence: 'A more admirable man was never appointed to a more inappropriate office. Were the times more amusing it might be taken as the most diverting case on record of putting round pegs into square holes'. The public had been told, Garvin added, that Inskip's opinions on foreign affairs 'have been so inconspicuous that they cannot cause umbrage to any foreign country whatever. Had the same qualification been insisted on up to now, hardly one of the greatest statesmen in British annals would ever have been allowed to serve the Crown in any capacity. This queer apotheosis of negation, substituted for the positive requirements of momentous office, is part of Mr Baldwin's idiosyncrasy, like his long incomprehension and neglect of Defence itself. . . .'

[3] Alexander David Frederick Lloyd, 1912–   . Educated at Eton and Cambridge. Served in the British Council (of which his father was Chairman), 1935–9. On active service, 1939–45 (Palestine, Syria, north-west Europe). Succeeded his father as 2nd Baron, 1941. Joint Under-Secretary of State for the Home Department (with responsibility for Welsh affairs), 1952–4. Parliamentary Under-Secretary of State for the Colonies, 1954–7. Chairman of the National Bank of New Zealand, 1970–7; a Director of Lloyds Bank International, 1974–8.

[4] Eight days later Lord Lloyd wrote again to his son: '. . . when I asked the Prof. what he thought of Inskip's appointment as Defence coordinator by Baldwin he replied, "It is the most cynical thing that has been done since Caligula appointed his horse as consul" ' (*Lloyd papers*).

Winston S. Churchill to Harold Laski

(*Churchill papers: 2/252*)

17 March 1936

I have not yet had time to read the terrible book you have sent me, but as soon as I have done so I will write again. Pray think a little meanwhile of how to preserve the strength of England, the hope of freedom.

Harold Nicolson: diary

(*Nicolson papers*)

17 March 1936

I dined at the Belgian Embassy. A men's party to meet Van Zeeland,[1] the youthful Prime Minister of Belgium. . . .[2]

I sat next to Winston who was in superb form. Anthony Eden, who looked haggard with exhaustion, his lovely eyes rimmed with red and puffy with sleeplessness, expounded his policy. I shall not put that down on paper because that is not what one ought to do. But it seemed to me wise and honourable and clear. We all agreed. Winston said, 'Now here we are, elder statesmen plus heads of Opposition. We could sign a manifesto this very minute pledging ourselves to an agreed policy. Yet the world outside imagines that the House of Commons and the Government are torn by dissension.' 'And so they are,' said Anthony in a low, sad voice.

Neville Chamberlain to Winston S. Churchill

(*Churchill papers: 2/252*)

17 March 1936   11 Downing Street

My dear Winston,

I have now had an opportunity of reading your Birmingham speech, and must send you a word of thanks for your very kind references to myself.

---

[1] Paul van Zeeland, 1893–   . A Director of the Belgian National Bank, 1926; Deputy Governor, 1934. Prime Minister of Belgium, 1935–37 (when he devalued the franc by 28 per cent). President of the Co-ordinating Foundation for Refugees, 1939. In exile in England, 1940. Belgian Minister of Foreign Affairs, 1949–54.

[2] Those present were Van Zeeland, Anthony Eden, Sir Austen Chamberlain, Sir Herbert Samuel, Clement Attlee, Lord Snell, Sir Archibald Sinclair, Nicolson and Churchill.

Your packhorse quotation was most appropriate,[1] but I think you will find it comes not from Henry VI, but from a speech of Gloucester's in Richard III.[2]

Yours sincerely,
N. Chamberlain

Winston S. Churchill to Violet Pearman

(*Pearman papers*)

23 March 1936   Chartwell

Dear Mrs Pearman,

You must certainly stay in bed until you are fit to be ex-rayed, and then follow the Doctor's orders. Let me know when you are able to do any typing, and we will send you anything that is to be fair copied. But get well as soon

---

[1] During the course of his speech at the forty-first annual Banquet of the Birmingham Jewellers' and Silversmiths' Association on 14 March 1936 Churchill said: 'Mr Neville Chamberlain is the pack-horse in Shakespeare's phrase, "the pack-horse in our great affairs". Most of the weight of carrying on the burdens of the Government of this country has rested in the last four years on his shoulders. He will be for ever associated with the regeneration and restoration of our finances and our credit—(applause)—for which he became responsible in a dark hour—an unreasonably dark hour—when confidence was shattered and confusion reigned, and this wealthy, powerful country, with all its resources, was represented to the world as if it were a broken and bankrupt thing. He gathered up our finances, until today they bear bold comparison with the finances of any country in the world. And well it is that it should be so, because the credit he has carefully restored to our finances is now available to guard us in another sphere, the great sphere of defence, to which we must unhappily, but none the less with resolution turn our concentrated attention. And it is also remarkable that the Chancellor of the Exchequer who has saved the money and who stood fast for two or three bleak years against a great deal of pressure, has, according to all accounts, been the principal architect of the defence proposals now placed before the House of Commons' (report in the *Birmingham Post*, 16 March 1936).

[2] It was indeed Gloucester speaking, to Queen Margaret, widow of Henry VI, to whom Gloucester says: 'Ere you were Queen, ay, or your husband King, I was a pack-horse in his great affairs' (Richard III, 1:3, line 121). During his speech, to the Jewellers' Association, Churchill spoke of the Rhineland crisis. 'The issue which was at stake in Europe' he said, 'was not the difference between France and Germany, or between Germany and the Locarno Powers. It was a dispute between the Nazi Government and the League of Nations. It would make a profound difference to the history of the world if the League emerged from the ordeal with added credit and authority. If the authority of the League was destroyed, as it might well be, in the triumph of the Nazi regime, irrespective of law, events would continue to roll and slide remorselessly downhill towards the pit in which Western civilization might be fatally engulfed.' Austen Chamberlain also spoke at this meeting, commenting, on the appointment of Inskip as Minister for Co-ordination of Defence: 'Mr Churchill has great courage and infinite energy, and great and wide experience of the matters of defence, and there will be many of the House of Commons who regret that Mr Baldwin has not thought fit to call him to that new office, for which he has greater qualifications than any living politician.'

as you can, and do not worry about anything. If you are not insured I will pay for any necessary scientific treatment that is required, and your salary of course will continue during this illness. I am so sorry you have had this accident.[1]

Yours sincerely,
WSC

Winston S. Churchill to Oswald Frewen[2]

(*Shane Leslie papers*)

24 March 1936   11 Morpeth Mansions

My dear Oswald,

I am so deeply grieved to hear of your serious accident. I was delighted to learn from Shane that you are making steady progress, but I gather it will be a long job. Please let me know if there is anything I can do for you. In the meanwhile I venture to send a small cheque with which I hope you will buy any books or other things you may require to amuse you through your illness.

With every good wish,
Your affectionate cousin,
Winston S. Churchill

[1] Violet Pearman's deputy, Grace Hamblin, writes: 'I do remember very clearly Mrs Pearman's accident in 1936. In those days, the office floor was polished and partly covered with rugs. Mrs P came down from a session with Sir Winston in a great hurry (she was always in a hurry, but I imagine this time she was going to get a telephone call for him or something similar, for she really rushed into the room), caught her heel on the corner of a rug and fell heavily. X-rays revealed that she had cracked the bone at the base of her back, and she was obliged to rest for a long time' (*letter to the author, 17 January 1982*). Mrs Pearman had fallen backwards, hitting both the stone fireplace and the metal fender.

[2] Oswald Moreton Frewen, 1887–1958. Churchill's cousin. Son of Moreton Frewen and Clara Jerome. Lieutenant, Royal Navy, 1909. On active service in the Navy, 1914–18; Navigation Officer of HMS *Comus* during the Battle of Jutland, 1916. Travelled with his sister (Clare Sheridan) across the Soviet Union on a motor-bicycle, 1923–4. Drove his sister across the Sahara in his 'Baby Austin', 1930–1. On active service in the Second World War: served at the Normandy beachhead, 1944, on board HMS *Despatch*. In 1945 he married Lena Spilman.

Ralph Wigram[1] to Winston S. Churchill

(Churchill papers: 2/273)

26 March 1936   Foreign Office

Dear Mr Churchill,

I send you one or two papers which may help you. The note of Sept 1932 (it was published). A note on Hitler's 25 points (Oct 1930, before he came into power), a note of my own on the speech of May 1935, the White Papers about disarmament in case you haven't got them all—a despatch of Rumbold's[2] on Mein Kampf—the quotations you can evidently use—though the despatch is confidential.

The only thing I can find on the Hitler-Papen[3] talk in 1932 to which you & Lindemann referred—our records for the period are not very good.

A White Paper is coming out early next week containing all the important German correspondence between June 1934 and March of this year—it may be of a certain help to you.

Thank you so much for our delightful and interesting weekend.[4] It made us both feel much better in every way. It is such a privilege and encouragement to me to hear your views. I wish and wish they were the views of the Government.

Yours sincerely,
Ralph Wigram

[1] Ralph Follett Wigram, 1890–1936. Educated at Eton and University College, Oxford. Temporary Secretary, British Embassy, Washington, 1916–19. 3rd Secretary, Foreign Office, 1919; 2nd Secretary, 1920. 1st Secretary, British Embassy, Paris, 1924–33. CMG, 1933. A Counsellor in the Foreign Office, 1934, and head of the Central Department (among those who worked under him were Duncan Sandys, Michael Creswell and Anthony Rumbold).

[2] Horace Rumbold 1869–1941. Educated at Eton. Entered the Diplomatic Service, 1891. Succeeded his father as 9th Baronet, 1913. Chargé d'Affaires, Berlin, July 1914. Minister in Berne, 1916–19; in Warsaw, 1919–20. High Commissioner, Constantinople, 1920–4. Signed the Lausanne Treaty with Turkey on behalf of the British Empire, 24 July, 1923. Ambassador in Madrid, 1924–8; in Berlin, 1928–33. Vice-Chairman of the Royal Commission of Palestine, 1936–7.

[3] Franz von Papen, 1879–1969. Cavalry officer, and member of the Westphalian aristocracy. Military Attaché, Washington, 1914–16; expelled from the United States on a charge of sabotage. A leading shareholder in the Centre Party newspaper, *Germania*. Never elected to the Reichstag. Chancellor, June–November 1932. A member of Hitler's Cabinet, 1933–4. German Ambassador to Vienna, 1934–8; in Turkey, 1940–5. Tried at Nuremberg, and acquitted, 1946.

[4] At Chartwell.

Wing-Commander Warburton[1] to Winston S. Churchill

(*Churchill papers: 25/7*)

27 March 1936   Committee of Imperial Defence
Confidential

Dear Mr Churchill,

I am returning the draft of your paper in connection with CID Paper No: 1216-B,[2] and at your request I send you certain observations which I hope may be of value.

Paragraph 2.

Your whole paper is based mainly on the calculations contained in this paragraph. I suggest that the deduction which you make of a first-line strength of 1,210 German aircraft to 785 British is based upon a fallacy. If you are going to include the 40 squadrons, making a total of 360 aircraft (referred to in paragraph 10 of CID Paper No 1216-B), you must equally include the British equivalent. The British equivalent is, in fact, greater than 360, and is nearer 480. The comparison on this basis, therefore, becomes 1,210 Germans to 1,265 British. The Air Staff do not include these 40 squadrons in their first-line calculation, since they do not consider them of the same standard of efficiency as first-line formed units, because the pilots will not have done their courses or completed their training. Their military efficiency is therefore not comparable. But whether or not this is the case does not seem to matter, provided that a similar basis is taken for our own personnel in training establishments.

You may argue that the removal of these 40 squadrons will not hamper the training organisation and power to expand in the future, since behind that again the Germans have the DLV[3] (referred to in paragraphs 21–23 of CID Paper No 1216-B) and amounting to roughly 30 or 40 squadrons. But here again we are in the same position. We have a large reserve of trained pilots

---

[1] Peter Warburton, 1897–1950. Educated at Radley College. Lieutenant, Royal Garrison Artillery, 1915–17; transferred to the Royal Flying Corps, 1917 (MBE military, 1919). Flight Lieutenant RAF, 1922; Squadron Leader 1929. Air Adviser to the Iraq Government 1930. Air Adviser to the Committee of Imperial Defence, 1934–7. Wing-Commander, 1936. Air Commodore, 1937. Air Raid Precautions Department, Home Office, 1937–42; RAF, 1942–5; UNRRA, 1945–8. Both his sons were killed in action in the RAF in the Second World War.

[2] Committee of Imperial Defence Paper 1216B was the Air Staff's answer to Churchill's notes of 9 December 1935 (circulated to the CID on 17 December 1935 as Paper 1205B). These notes are printed in full in the previous document volume of this biography, pages 1345–8.

[3] The German Air Sports Association, ostensibly a civilian organization, but in fact an integral part of the German Air Force.

which should provide us not only with a numerical superiority to compare with the DLV, but with a distinctly higher standard of military efficiency.

If you accept the argument that our unformed squadrons must be taken into account if the Germans are so taken, certain of the remaining calculations in your paper require revision.

Paragraph 3.

I understand that the reason that the German industry worked only one shift instead of three and had to close down was due to a shortage of skilled personnel, and therefore to inability to spread adequately over the increased number of factories, and also due to a shortage of raw materials. You may think it desirable, perhaps, to modify the line of argument in your paragraph.

Paragraph 4.

I think there may be a misconception in the first sentence of this paragraph. It was only recently that a system was evolved to enable identification of German active squadrons to be made, and it was because of the adoption of this system that the number of identified squadrons rose by ten in the two months, December, 1935, and January, 1936. The rate of identification, therefore, does not provide a basis for calculating a rate of expansion.

Paragraph 7.

You quote the figure of 15 per cent peace-time wastage. This figure refers to pilot wastage, but I think if you are using it in connection with aircraft, wastage in the British service is between 30 and 40 per cent per annum of service type aircraft actually in service.[1] This is I understand, the figure which the Air Staff have used for their calculation of German wastage, but they have every reason to believe that it is, in fact, considerably higher. If you agree to this contention your figures quoted in paragraphs 8 and 9 will require some modification.

Paragraph 9.

It is of interest to note that in our own case we require approximately two-and-a-half times the number of pilots in our first-line strength to fill the requirements in training, staff and ground duties. In this respect it is believed that Germany is worse off than we are.

---

[1] Warburton wrote as a footnote at this point: 'Actual figures for last year were 25% Service aircraft in Squadrons, 55% All types training (incl. service type).'

Paragraph 10.

I have referred to the question of the DLV above. I do not think it is contended that we have the aircraft to form into squadrons to compare with the DLV, but it is contended that we have reserve pilots superior both numerically and in military efficiency.

Paragraph 11.

I recollect your (of course) correct contention that one should not under-rate one's enemy, but I understand that the Air Staff have every reason to believe that the Germans are suffering very seriously from the absence of a basic training system and an adequate supply of experienced instructors, and the many other disadvantages of trying to build up an air force quickly without a foundation such as we have been able to establish during the past sixteen years.

I trust that these observations will be of value, and I shall be very glad to give you any further assistance that I can.

Yours sincerely,
P. Warburton

Lord Davies[1] to Winston S. Churchill

(*Churchill papers: 2/284*)

29 March 1936

My dear Churchill,

I have just finished reading for the third time your speech in Thursday's debate.[2] May I congratulate you most heartily upon a historic pronouncement —which stands out by itself in a historic debate. I don't suppose you will remember but three or four years ago—I begged you to put yourself at the head of a movement in this country—for the establishment of an Int police

---

[1] David Davies, 1880–1944. Landed proprietor. Liberal MP for Montgomeryshire, 1906–29. Commanded the 14th Battalion, Royal Welsh Fusiliers, in France, 1915–16. Parliamentary Private Secretary to Lloyd George, 1916–22. Created Baron, 1932. Director of several colliery and railway companies. Founder and Chairman of the New Commonwealth Society.

[2] Speaking in the House of Commons on 26 March 1936, Churchill referred to the strength of German propaganda, and of the need to 'confront' the public with the realities of the European situation. The remilitarization of the Rhineland was, he said, 'Hitler's triumph'. It followed on several Nazi successes: the introduction of conscription, the Saar plebiscite and the Anglo-German Naval Treaty. Would Austria be next, he asked, and went on to urge an 'effective union' of all States alarmed by Germany, for mutual aid within the Covenant of the League of Nations. His aim, he said, was not the encirclement of Germany, but of any power that sought to impose its will by aggression.

force—I tried to point out that with your vast experience of politics—and your insight into military problems—you were cut out for this particular job—In all your books you have consistently advocated principles which lead inevitably to the creation of such a force as part of the machinery of the reign of law—Then why not lead a crusade to achieve this vital international reform? In this connection may I quote what Pres Theodore Roosevelt[1] said in 1910. 'As things are now such power to command peace throughout the world could best be assured by some combination between those great nations which sincerely desire peace & have no thought themselves of committing aggressions. . . . and the ruler or statesman who should bring about such a combination would have earned his place in history for all time & his title to the gratitude of all mankind—'

The problem at the moment is to bring about—as you say in your speech, a combination of *all* the European states members of the League—great & *small*—because the combined resources of the latter are almost equivalent to those of the four gt powers in Europe.

I would also suggest that such a combination can only be brought about by (a) education or propaganda and (b) investigation & research regarding the institutions which are necessary to make such a combination effective as part of the machinery of the League.

These are the two aims which the new Commonwealth Society has been trying to urge—to the best of its ability—but with meagre support & inadequate resources during the last three years—Will you consider putting yourself at the head of this movement by becoming the President of the British section of the Society? If you were willing to do so—we should be prepared to work loyally under your leadership in an enterprise which has no party affiliations, & which has contacts in about forty different countries.

Perhaps you will say—you don't want to be mixed up with a lot of fanatics! Well, the fanatic of today becomes the reformer of tomorrow—& we are not so fanatical as not to be prepared to advance by stages—Please will you let me come & talk to you about it—?

Yrs very sincerely,
Davies

PS. (a) The presidency of the British section only involves such time and activity as you would choose to give it—What we particularly desire is your blessing & moral support.

---

[1] Theodore Roosevelt, 1858–1919. Twenty-sixth President of the United States, 1901–10. As a result of his efforts to bring peace between Japan and Russia in 1905 he was awarded the Nobel Prize for peace. He was the first head of state to send an international dispute for settlement at the International Court of Arbitration at The Hague.

(b) I have already sent you particulars of the society—including a list of our VIPs, etc. If there is any further information you desire—I shall be delighted to give it.

(c) At the moment our Parliamentary group includes about 70 MPs of all parties. Major Entwhistle[1] is chairman & Vyvyan Adams[2] secty of the group.

Winston S. Churchill to Violet Pearman

(*Pearman papers*)

30 March 1936   Chartwell

Dear Mrs P,

I am very sorry that your accident is so serious, and you must take the greatest care. I have told the Doctor that I will pay for the extra treatment you may require, but I should like to know before any large expense is incurred. I have told Miss Hamblin[3] to make you out your salary cheques as you require them. Do not worry about typing for the present.

With good wishes, believe me,

Yours vy sincerely,
Winston S. Churchill

[1] Cyril Fullard Entwhistle, 1887–1974. Major, commanding the 235 Siege Battery, Royal Garrison Artillery, 1914–18 (despatches, Military Cross). Liberal MP for South-West Hull, 1918–24. Introduced (as a private members Bill,) the Matrimonial Causes Act, 1924. King's Counsel, 1931. Conservative MP for Bolton, 1931–45. Knighted, 1937. Chairman of the Decca Record Company.

[2] Samuel Vyvyan Trerice Adams, 1900–1951. Educated at Haileybury and King's College, Cambridge. Called to the Bar, 1927. Conservative MP for West Leeds, 1931–45. Member of the Executive of the League of Nation's Union, 1933–46. On active service, 1939–45 (Major, Duke of Cornwall's Light Infantry). In 1940, under the pen name 'Watchman', he published *Churchill: Architect of Victory*. Political researcher, 1946–51.

[3] Grace Hamblin, 1908– . Born in London. Educated at Crockham Hill Church of England school, near Chartwell, and at Secretarial Training College. Began secretarial work for Churchill in 1932. Worked as No 2 to Mrs Pearman from 1932 to 1938. Secretary to Mrs Churchill from 1939–66. In charge of the secretarial and accounts side at Chartwell, 1945–65. OBE, 1965. Administrator at Chartwell for the National Trust, 1965–73. Secretary to the Churchill Centenary Exhibition, 1974.

Lord Linlithgow[1] to Winston S. Churchill

(*Churchill papers: 1/284*)

30 March 1936

My dear Winston,

Wish me luck as I cope with the 320 million;[2] and I hope you find them —the 'stinkadoros'—consumable. I recall that you liked them some years ago when you made us happy by staying at Hopetoun.

My love to Clemmy and you

Yours ever,
Hopie

Winston S. Churchill to Lord Linlithgow: telegram

(*Churchill papers: 1/284*)

31 March 1936

Every wish for your good fortune.

Winston & Clementine Churchill

Winston S. Churchill to Desmond Morton

(*Churchill papers: 2/273*)

31 March 1936

I wish you would have a look at this. Warburton was authorised by Hankey to check my figures as they formed the basis of a paper I am writing for HMG. I have a feeling they still woefully underrate the German power. If they are right it is surely all the more important and all the more practicable to reach a conclusion, probably peaceful in the present year.

[1] Victor Alexander John Hope, 1887–1952. Earl of Hopetoun until 1908. Known as 'Hopey'. Educated at Eton. Succeeded his father as 2nd Marquess of Linlithgow, 1908. On active service, 1914–18 (despatches). Commanded the Border Armoured Car Company, 1920–6. Civil Lord of Admiralty, 1922–4. Deputy Chairman of the Conservative Party Organization, 1924–6. Chairman, Royal Commission on Indian Agriculture, 1926–8. Chairman, Joint Select Committee on Indian Constitutional Reform, 1933–4. Chairman, Medical Research Council, 1934–6. Privy Councillor, 1935. Viceroy of India, 1936–43. Knight of the Garter, 1943. Chairman of the Midland Bank. His country seat was Hopetoun House, South Queensferry, two miles west of the Forth Bridge.

[2] Lord Linlithgow was about to leave Britain to take up his appointment as Viceroy of India.

Winston S. Churchill to Wing-Commander Warburton

(Churchill papers: 25/7)

31 March 1936

Dear Wing-Commander Warburton,

I am greatly obliged to you for the trouble you have taken to give me this most valuable critique. I will study it at leisure with the closest attention. I trust indeed you may be right. I cannot help being impressed by your supreme confidence when danger may be so near, and I wish I could feel convinced. I will certainly reconsider my paper in the light of your letter.

Once more thanking you, believe me,

Ivan Maisky[1] to Winston S. Churchill

(Churchill papers: 2/252)

31 March 1936   Soviet Embassy,
London

My dear Churchill,

I am hoping that you will agree with me that the general outlook merits a chat between ourselves! If I am right, and you are free, I should be so delighted if you could lunch here on the 7th April—next Tuesday. If you can't do this, and would prefer that I should come to you some time in the near future please let me know. I shall try to keep any appointment you suggest.

Yours sincerely,
I. Maisky

[1] Ivan Mikhailovich Maisky, 1884–1975. Born in Omsk, the son of a Jewish doctor and a non-Jewish mother. A Menshevik, he was exiled by the Tsarist regime to Siberia, but escaped to Germany, and took a degree in economics at Munich University. Lived in London, 1912–17. Returned to Russia during the revolution. Became a Bolshevik, 1922. Counsellor at the Soviet Embassy in London, 1925–7. Soviet Ambassador to Britain, 1932–43. A Deputy Foreign Minister, 1943–5. Soviet member of the Reparations Committee, 1945–8. Arrested during one of Stalin's anti-Jewish purges, 1949. Imprisoned, 1949–53. Released from prison 1953. Worked at the Soviet Academy of Sciences from 1957 until his death, writing his memoirs, and preparing various historical studies.

April 1936

Desmond Morton to Winston S. Churchill

(*Churchill papers: 25/7*)

3 April 1936   21 Queen Anne's Gate
Private

Dear Winston,

Thank you very much for letting me see the papers which I return. My feelings are:—

Paragraph 2.

Warburton answers some of your points, but you may still calculate the British Metropolitan first line strength at 785, while the Air Ministry estimate of the German first line strength is 850, the French being 900. In respect of first line, therefore, the Germans are now stronger than we are. It is admitted elsewhere that Germany is also stronger than us in both actual production and capacity production of aircraft. It seems difficult, therefore, to contend that Great Britain is stronger in the air than Germany if the Metropolitan Air Forces are considered.

Paragraph 3.

I do not see that Warburton's argument has any effect on yours. Your point is that the Germans can now produce more aircraft than they need, therefore even if Warburton's information is correct—and I notice that he puts it forward somewhat diffidently—it is at the moment immaterial to the Germans whether or not they have enough skilled personnel to expand their existing industry to three shifts.

Paragraph 4.

Warburton says, in fact, that the apparent increase of ten squadrons in the German first line in the two months December 1935 and January 1936 was due to the unexpected discovery of their existence by the British Air Ministry, and there is no proof that they were only formed in those two months.

Does Warburton not lay himself open to an enquiry as to whether there may not be more German squadrons in existence which the Air Ministry have not yet discovered?

Paragraph 7.

In view of the wastage figures given by Warburton, your figures given in Paragraph 7 will require some modification, but I think the Prof would still show a discrepancy between the Air Ministry views and their own figures.

Paragraph 9.

Warburton's comment seems to me to leave your argument unimpaired, since the point of view seems to be different. I suggest you are trying to show what number of aircraft Germany might put in the air now if she went 'mad dog', and determined to try and make war according to Goering's theory, ie that the striking of a maximum blow from the air in the first two or three days of war might end the war. Warburton appears to be leaving this out of account and presuming that Germany's future action will develop along the lines laid down by the British Air Ministry. Of course he may be right.

Paragraph 10.

In both cases seems to be only a subsidiary argument to a main thesis.

Paragraph 11.

Warburton's answer seems in no way to affect your statement. Personally I feel that the S of S's covering note, to which you refer in this paragraph, is extremely significant, and appears to indicate a feeling on his part akin to yours, namely, that the Air Ministry are too complacent in their figures and calculations.

Yours very sincerely,
Desmond Morton

Winston S. Churchill to William Randolph Hearst:[1] *telegram*

(*Churchill papers: 8/813*)

3 April 1936

Ten days ago Mr Hillman[2] definitely accepted my article on the European situation but afterwards it was refused by New York. This week my first article in the new series although dealing with matters of American interest is also refused. I do not expect any other articles I write will be more suitable for American consumption than this. In these circumstances I hope you will agree that our projected agreement should lapse.

Regards
Winston Churchill

Anthony Eden to Winston S. Churchill

(*Churchill papers: 2/253*)

4 April 1936   Foreign Office

My dear Winston,

Thank you so much for sending me the enclosed papers regarding the staff conversations before the War. I was most interested to see them.

I want to take this opportunity to say 'thank you' to you for all your help & kindness to me in recent debates & during a critical period.

Yours ever,
Anthony Eden

[1] William Randolph Hearst, 1863–1951. Born in San Francisco, the son of a US Senator. Editor and Proprietor of the *New York American*, the *New York Evening Journal*, the *Boston American*, the *Boston Advertiser*, the *Chicago Herald and Examiner*, the *Chicago American*, the *San Francisco Examiner* and the *Los Angeles Examiner*. In 1903 he married Millicent Willson: they had five sons. Unsuccessful candidate for Mayor, New York, 1905. Congressman. Resident at his self-designed castle, the Hearst Ranch, San Simeon, a treasure house of medieval and renaissance European art and furniture which Churchill had visited in 1929.

[2] William Hillman, 1895–1962. A reporter for various news services, 1915–25. On active service with the American Expeditionary Force, France, 1917–18 (2nd Lieutenant, 310th Infantry). Correspondent for Hearst Newspapers in Paris, Berlin and London, 1926–31; Chief of Staff, Foreign Correspondents, Hearst Newspapers, 1934–9. British Isles Executive Director, King Features Syndicate, 1935–9. General European Manager of the International News Service, 1936–9. Foreign Editor of *Collier's* magazine, 1939–40. Washington commentator for the National Broadcasting Corporation, 1941–2. Commentator, Blue Network, 1942–5. Roving Correspondent, North American Newspaper Alliance.

Thomas Jones to a friend

(*Jones papers*)

4 April 1936

In two party meetings of back-benchers last week, the first, addressed by Austen and Winston, was on the whole pro-French; but two or three days later opinion had swung round to a majority of perhaps 5 to 4 for Germany. Part of the opposition to France is influenced by the fear of our being drawn in on the side of Russia.

Lieutenant-Colonel Denning[1] to Winston S. Churchill

(*Churchill papers: 2/278*)

6 April 1936

Dear Mr Winston Churchill,

I must ask forgiveness for taking the time of a busy public man but you have come to be regarded, in Service circles at least, as the best champion we have in matters connected with defence. A matter has come to my knowledge which I feel should be taken up & I feel equally that it is no use taking it up through Service channels. I am a serving officer & an instructor at this place, so I trust my name may be kept out of any discussion.

The matter is the problem of the air defence of London & the projected method of dealing with bombers, namely by the use of fighter aircraft. The Air Ministry I understand still advocate the use of fighters & are going into production in large numbers. I am advised by what I believe to be very highly qualified technical experts that the day of the fighter against the bomber is over. This conclusion is arrived at mainly because of the great increase in the speed of the bomber. I am advised (a) that bombers now approach fighters in speed, (b) that the speeds of both are approaching the probable maximum & (c) that without greatly superior speed, the fighter with its MG[2] rigid & firing through its propeller is no match for the bomber mounting several MGs on movable mountings. There are a number of other points making the fighter useless but this factor of relative speed is the outstanding one.

---

[1] Basil Cranmer Denning, 1894–1940. 2nd Lieutenant, Royal Engineers, 1914; Lieutenant, 1915; Captain, 1917. General Staff Officer, GHQ France, 1917–18; War Office, 1925–9. Major, 1929. Staff Officer, Royal Engineers, India, 1932–4. Lieutenant-Colonel, 1933. General Staff Officer, Staff College, 1935–9. Colonel, 1939. Killed in action at Dunkirk, 1 June 1940.

[2] Machine Gun.

If the contention of my informants is correct, not only is there tremendous waste of effort going on but, far worse, most of us are being deluded into the belief that we have in fighters some answer to enemy bombing. My informants are of [the] opinion that we have *nothing* that can prevent continuous & regular & relatively safe night bombing of London *now* with incendiary bombs & that our efforts are going to weapons that are no real defence, eg fighters, already discussed, retaliation in bombing (of no avail against Germany), guns & lights (of little avail in darkness, cloud, etc). They advocate balloon curtains as the only safe answer.

My informants both commanded fighter squadrons in the last war & are both technically very advanced. One has left the Air Force & the other is still in it. The latter is doing all he can to represent the case through the Air Ministry but finds his suggestions blocked there, he states through the inability of someone to admit that they are wrong. He is trying again to get through inside his Service. But the matter seems to me, though a mere outsider, so important, that I have ventured to trouble you, & you rather than anyone in office, for such are hampered.

The matter is one on which it is very difficult for any person outside the expert circle to act for he is at once faced with the departmental expert answer. At the same time the matter is so important that I feel it my duty to do something about it & I thought your private influence might at least see that some fatal error was not committed.

To return to some of the technical aspects, I understand that until recently, ie until the new bombers reached their great speeds, the theory of the use of the fighter in defence was perfectly sound & that it is this theory which still sways the Councils of the Air Ministry. As regards the balloon curtains, a small calculation will show that in point of cost, time, labour, industrial effort, etc the provision of a curtain of even 120 miles round London is very small compared to what we are otherwise undertaking. I understand from Army circles that the balloon curtain is not being seriously considered.

Please forgive me for troubling you but I see no other course open to me.

Yours sincerely,
B. C. Denning

Winston S. Churchill to Major Percy Davies
(*Churchill papers: 8/533*)

7 April 1936

I see that our series has come to an end, and I should like to know whether your readers were pleased with it. I have had a good many pleasant letters, and have heard much friendly comment. I hope it has been satisfactory from the point of view of circulation. I now send you a list of suggested figures for 'Great men of All time' which it was proposed I should complete before the end of this year. If you would pick a dozen of these names or put them in order and add any that occur to you, I would then make you a further suggestion and we could finally decide.

Believe me,

Yours very sincerely,

Winston S. Churchill to Lord Cranborne[1]

(Churchill papers: 2/253)

8 April 1936

At luncheon yesterday you said you thought my criticism about Abyssinia was 'unfair'. You probably do not know the past history of my opinions in the matter. When in August last I was consulted by Sam Hoare, I told him in Eden's presence that 'I thought he was justified in going as far with the League of Nations against Italy as he could carry France' but I added that he ought not to put any pressure upon France on account of her military connections with Italy and her German preoccupations, and that in these circumstances I did not expect France would go very far. Eden was in the room at the time, and will no doubt remember my remarks about the Italian divisions on the Brenner, the unguarded south front of France, etc.

The Government certainly did not follow this advice. On the contrary all through August and September, Eden was working up the strongest move for sanctions he possibly could at Geneva. Great pressure was put upon France in various ways. Finally Hoare went to Geneva and delivered his great speech which created a new situation. I naturally had to address myself to that, but I do not feel any responsibility for having brought it about, for I would myself either have gone much further at the very beginning, or nothing like so far.

Generally speaking, not to weary you with this account, you will find that

---

[1] Robert Arthur James Gascoyne-Cecil, Viscount Cranborne, 1893–1972. Eldest son of the 4th Marquess of Salisbury. Known as 'Bobbety'. Conservative MP for South Dorset, 1929–41. Parliamentary Secretary of State for Foreign Affairs, 1935–38; resigned with Anthony Eden, February 1938. Paymaster-General, 1940. Privy Councillor, 1940. Summoned to the House of Lords in his father's barony of Cecil of Essendon, 1941. Secretary of State for Dominion Affairs, 1940–2 and 1943–5; for the Colonies, 1942. Leader of the House of Lords, 1942–5. Knight of the Garter, 1946. Succeeded his father as 5th Marquess, 1947. Lord Privy Seal, 1951–2. Secretary of State for Commonwealth Relations, 1952. Lord President of the Council, 1952–7. Leader of the House of Lords, 1951–7. In 1937 he was elected to the Other Club (founded by Churchill and F. E. Smith in 1911). Nephew of Viscount Cecil of Chelwood.

throughout this business I have strongly advised the Government not to try to take a leading part or to put themselves forward so prominently. This I have done among other things because of the shocking plight to which our defences have been reduced by past neglect. I therefore feel fully entitled now that the policy, in the shaping of which I have had no hand, which has proceeded contrary to the lines which I myself advised, is coming to a most dismal and most disastrous end, to state facts and draw morals, and I shall certainly continue to do so. Any responsibility must rest with the Government and the Ministers concerned and not with private persons at all, even though they have from time to time tried to give the Government's policy as much support as possible. The case against the Government is that their policy has for a long time been designed to give satisfaction to powerful elements of opinion here rather than to seek the realities of the European situation and stand or fall by their convictions.

Winston S. Churchill to Lieutenant-Colonel Denning

(*Churchill papers: 2/278*)

9 April 1936
Confidential

I cannot write to you freely in reply to your letter, as I have been for eight months a member of the CID Committee which is dealing with this question. But I should like to let you know that I have read all that you say with an interest not born of novelty.

Winston S. Churchill to Viscount Cecil of Chelwood[1]

(*Cecil of Chelwood papers*)

9 April 1936   Chartwell

My dear Bob,
    After our talk I told Mr Richards[2] of the Anti Nazi Society that I thought

---

[1] Lord Edgar Algernon Robert Cecil, 1864–1958. Known as 'Bob'. Third son of the 3rd Marquess of Salisbury. Educated at Eton and University College, Oxford. Conservative MP for East Marylebone, 1906–10. Independent Conservative MP for Hitchin, 1911–23. Under-Secretary of State for Foreign Affairs, 1915–18. Minister of Blockade, 1916–18. Assistant Secretary of State for Foreign Affairs, 1918. Created Viscount Cecil of Chelwood, 1923. Lord Privy Seal, 1923–4. President of the League of Nations Union, 1923–45. Chancellor of the Duchy of Lancaster, 1924–7. Nobel Peace Prize, 1937.

[2] Arthur Harold Richards, 1889–1943. Publicity Manager of the *Daily News* (from 1930 the *News Chronicle*) and the *Star*, 1924 to 1935. In June 1930 he had organized a special feature on Churchill's life story to launch the new title, 'News Chronicle'. Employed by Chelsea

it would be absurd to have an Albert Hall meeting against the dangers of the German Dictatorship on April 29 within a few days of your AH meeting of May 8 against the *Italian* Dictatorship, and that it must be put off till later in the year. This has accordingly been done.

I think we are in pretty good agreement on several big things. There is a great danger that the Parliamentary nations and merciful, tolerant forces in the world will be knocked out quite soon by the heavily armed, unmoral dictatorships. But I believe there is still time to organise a European mass, and perhaps a world mass which would confront them, overawe them, and perhaps let their peoples loose upon them. Once you and your friends have formulated your principles you must face 'ways and means'. You need a secular arm. I might help in this.

It seems a mad business to confront these dictators without weapons or military force, and at the same time to try to tame and cow the spirit of our people with peace films, anti-recruiting propaganda and resistance to defence measures. Unless the free and law respecting nations are prepared to organise, arm and combine they are going to be smashed up. This is going to happen quite soon. But I believe we still have a year to combine and marshall superior forces in defence of the League and its Covenant.

Yours vy sincerely,
Winston S. Churchill

Winston S. Churchill to A. R. Wise[1]

(*Churchill papers: 2/254*)

9 April 1936

My dear Wise,

I am in agreement with much of your group's statement on the Foreign Policy, but pray consider the following:

The defensive pact between Great Britain, Belgium and France this year probably commands superior forces on the Western front. So far as I know the Germans have less than thirty divisions, but in 1937 they will have fifty,

---

Football Club as manager of their junior team, 1935–6. From 1936 to 1939, Organizing Secretary of the Anti-Nazi Council, to combat Nazi propaganda and to help its victims. Adviser to Lady Rhondda on *Time and Tide*, 1939. Worked at the Ministry of Information 1940–1. Active in charitable work for the British and Allied forces.

[1] Alfred Roy Wise, 1901–1974. Educated at Repton and Oriel College, Oxford. Assistant District Commissioner, Kenya Colony, 1923–6. Conservative MP for Smethwick, 1931–45; for Rugby, 1959–66. Served with British Intelligence Organization, Germany, 1946–54. Lieutenant-Colonel.

and in 1938 they will have, assuming they do not crack internally meanwhile, seventy, eighty, or even ninety. Our figures combined would be far less than this. Therefore it seems that in 1937 and certainly in 1938 we are bound to consider the aid of Russia and all the minor countries in the East and South of Europe. If meanwhile these, or any of these, were incorporated in the German system, the position you are willing to adopt in the West would be forlorn. On the other hand, this year, 1936, we have (I believe) a large plurality even in the West alone. Therefore if we can bring all the others in against German aggression before the end of the year, the forces with which we are ourselves associated would be overwhelming, and we might be able to come to terms with the Germans without a war. At the same time it would be folly to go in for such a policy unless we are prepared to face a war. The League of Nations is the only means by which all these overwhelming forces can be assembled. It is also the means by which the greatest unity can be obtained in this country. This also is the last year when this is possible.

Pray consider this in the spirit in which it is written. You may show it to the signatories of the document, but otherwise treat it as private.

Yours sincerely,
Winston S. Churchill

Lord Halsbury[1] to Winston S. Churchill

(*Churchill papers: 2/253*)

9 April 1936　　　　　　　　　　　　　　　　　　　　　　　　　Paris

My dear Churchill,

I am writing to you because I think I ought to do so. Perhaps everything that I am going to say you know far better than I, but I do know a considerable amount. I know France as well as I do England, and I happen to speak and write both languages equally well. Because of these things and because I had two years of my war with the French army, I have as many friends in France as in England. This is my apology for writing to you.

To-day the position between England and France is terrible. If a Frenchman does not like a person, he does not swear at him, nor does he curse him; he simply does not speak about him at all. They don't speak a word about England to-day, for them we are finished. My own very personal friends talk

---

[1] Hardinge Goulburn Giffard, 1880–1943. Educated at Eton and New College, Oxford. Barrister, 1906. Unsuccessful Conservative candidate, 1910. Major, RAF, 1918. Succeeded his father as 2nd Earl of Halsbury, 1921. Recorder of Carmarthen, 1923–5. King's Counsel 1923. Interned by the Germans in France, 1940. He died in an internment camp in France on 15 September 1943.

to me. According to them, the English navy is so rife with sabotage that it could not and would not fire a single shot. Nothing that I can say will persuade, as I have said, my best personal friends, friends of over twenty years to believe otherwise.

They are all convinced that England will talk and talk and back the League of Nations, but that she has made up her mind never to help France, no matter what happens.

They loathe sanctions and for that reason are going pro-Italian. Further, because they are sure that England will never help and has not got the armament to help, they are going pro-German against us.

It will not surprise either of us to know that they think that Eden at the FO is an insult to any nation to whom he has been sent.

My last reason for writing you is this, that everyone, everywhere asks me: 'Mais pourquoi on nous ne donnera pas Churchill? C'est le seul qui sait débruiller cette impasse.'

Sincerely yours,
Halsbury

Winston S. Churchill to the Fretwell Engineering Company
(*Churchill papers: 1/289*)

9 April 1936

I should be much obliged if you could send over here on Tuesday, one of your engineers at my expense who could check some calculations I am making about a catchment area which is needed in connection with the swimming pool. We have a spring water supply from both sides of the valley of fifteen gallons a minute, which equals about twenty-one thousand gallons in twenty four hours. Without filtering arrangements it is possible to keep the water in the pool clear, but the bottom tends to get greasy and dirty, and it is desirable to change the water completely during the Summer. But this must be done quickly or all bathing stopped. A catchment area can be provided half way up the hill into which all our supply can be directed from existing pipes. It is proposed to concrete a basin capable of holding at least one hundred and twenty thousand gallons. Our supply should fill this in a week. This water would be held as a reserve and when it was desired to change the water in the swimming pool it could be fed by gravity through the existing chemical filter and delivered in the pool at about five thousand gallons an hour, thus filling the bathing pool in about twenty-four hours. This would enable it to be cleaned once a fortnight if necessary in the Summer with the loss of only one day. As the whole process can be worked by gravity and from our own spring, it is a sound proposition. I have made my own calculations, but I should like it properly measured up for me, and also to have any other advice which occurs.[1]

Winston S. Churchill to Captain M. W. S. Boucher[2]
(Churchill papers: 2/272)

13 April 1936

I shall be away all this week, and next week is the Budget, which ties me to the House of Commons. I am, however, thinking a great deal about the Fleet Air Arm, and perhaps you will allow me to suggest to you some alternative dates for our meeting a little later on in the Spring. Meanwhile if you would like to write me a few short notes showing in detail the kind of difficulties and friction that arise at the present time, I shall be grateful.

Winston S. Churchill to Eleanor Rathbone[3]
(Churchill papers: 2/274)

13 April 1936
Private

Having seen the letter in the Manchester Guardian, in which you have been tackled for adopting my figures,[4] I send you in confidence a memoran-

---

[1] During April 1936 Churchill bought both brooms and a vacuum cleaner for his swimming pool. A heated and floodlit pool, one of the few heated outdoor pools in Britain, it cost him £600 for a year's supply of coal and coke. In March 1936 Philip Sassoon had sent him, for his other pool, four duck Rosybills and one drake Tufted, all 1935 hand-reared.

[2] Maitland Walter Sabine Boucher, 1888–1963. Entered the Navy as a cadet, 1904. On active service, 1914–18 (wounded). Served in the Operations Division, Admiralty, 1923–4. Qualified as a pilot, 1925. Directorate of Training, Air Ministry, 1929–31; Naval Air Division, Admiralty, 1933–4. Captain, 1930. Commanded HMS *Courageous*, 1935–7. Director of Air Matériel, Admiralty, 1938. Second Naval Member, Australian Naval Board, 1939–40. Rear-Admiral, 1941. Commodore, Royal Naval Reserve, in command of convoys, 1943–5. His only son, a Captain in the Royal Artillery, was killed in action in 1945.

[3] Eleanor Rathbone, 1872–1946. Educated Kensington High School and Somerville College, Oxford. The first woman member of the Liverpool City Council, 1909–34. Independent MP for the Combined English Universities, 1929–46. Chairman, Children's Nutrition Council and National Joint Committee for Spanish Relief. Secretary, Parliamentary Committee for Refugees. Vice-Chairman, National Committee for Rescue from Nazi Terror.

[4] On 13 April 1936 the *Manchester Guardian* published a letter from Professor Bone, of St Albans, in which he wrote: 'So it would seem that Miss Rathbone, so far from having any proof of her alleged fact about Germany having spent "£600,000,000 to £800,000,000 on rearmament in 1935 alone; perhaps £1,500,000,000 from 1933 to 1936, much of it secretly, while the Disarmament Conference was sitting", was merely endorsing an illusion of Mr Winston Churchill's fearful mind, which, as he told the House of Commons on March 26,

dum upon the subject prepared for me by Sir Henry Strakosch (who does not
desire his name to be mentioned). There are some points in this memorandum
which have not stood the test of the examination to which I have had it
subjected in various instructed quarters. Nevertheless its main conclusion is
true and the figures which I quote are well within the limits of the facts so
far as I can ascertain. Furthermore it was not upon this memorandum that I
first made the statement about Germany having spent eight hundred millions in a single year. This I obtained from other and even more confidential
sources. Sir Henry Strakosch sent me his memorandum as a detailed corro-
boration from quite a different angle. I hope you will believe that I do not
make any of my assertions without taking the very greatest pains to find out
the truth, and the trouble I had to find out about the air danger two years
ago was very considerable.

Will you kindly send me back the memorandum when you have digested it,
and I am sure that without going into details you are thoroughly justified in
standing to your guns. We are really in great danger.

Believe me,

Winston S. Churchill to Shane Leslie[1]
(*Churchill papers: 8/533*)

14 April 1936
Private

The 'News of the World' say that they think the project of twelve 'Great
Men of All Time' would not have 'sufficient popular appeal', and might be
'over the heads of our readers'. They suggest as an alternative a series en-

---

is "occupied with this idea of the great wheels revolving and the great hammers descending
day and night in Germany, making the whole industry of that country an arsenal, making
that gifted and valiant population into one great disciplined war machine", etc. Although
such is but a Churchillian nightmare, it seems to me deplorable that, in the midst of a grave
European crisis when above all calm reason and reflection are needed to ensure peace, one of
the members of the Combined English Universities should have endorsed it as a "fact". For
anyone with a proper sense of proportion and even a little knowledge of Germany's industrial organization and production might have apprised it as a canard.' Bone added: 'It is
impossible to say precisely what has been her expenditure on rearmament during the past
three years, although examination of her industrial statistics shows convincingly that it
cannot have been on anything like the Churchill-Rathbonian alarming scale. It is, however, a
factor now to be reckoned with and duly laid to heart.' See also page 129, notes 2 and 3.

[1] John Randolph Shane Leslie, 1885–1971. Son of Sir John Leslie and Leonie Jerome.
Churchill's first cousin. Educated at Eton and King's College, Cambridge. Author and
lecturer. Received into the Catholic Church, 1908. Contested Derry City as an Irish Nationalist, 1910, but defeated. Served in British Intelligence in the United States, 1915–16. Editor of
the *Dublin Review*, 1916–25. Succeeded his father as 3rd Baronet, 1944.

titled 'Great Events of our Time' covering the period of the last twenty-five years, and they are going to make out a list of suggested heads for my consideration. To these views I must of course defer. I have no doubt however that some of the incidents in the series would appeal to you. Meanwhile I should like to send you the enclosed for the trouble you took in thinking out the list of names for the other series.

Thornton Butterworth[1] *to Winston S. Churchill*

(*Churchill papers: 8/537*)

15 April 1936

Dear Mr Churchill,

It is very nice of you to have written me as you have done in your letter of the 9th instant. Dangerous, nevertheless, for it emboldens me to beg you to allow me to publish your book 'Great Contemporaries' this Autumn, which we contracted for, alas! as far back as September 1931. It would be very helpful to me, and I have little doubt that its publication would be good for both of us. I am quite sure that, being what it is, it would in no way conflict with the publication of the third volume of Marlborough.

Some time ago, you mentioned over the telephone that you proposed to continue your biography, which you thought would run into two further volumes. Can we not also do something in that direction? After our pleasant and profitable connection, I am unhappy to feel that there has been such a long interval since I published your last book.

Lord Cranborne to Winston S. Churchill

(*Churchill papers: 2/253*)

17 April 1936

My dear Winston,

Thank you so much for your letter. I am so sorry that you thought my comment on your speech unfair. I need not say that when I spoke I knew nothing of your private conversation with Sam Hoare & Anthony in August.

---

[1] Churchill's publisher; on 15 September 1942 *The Times* reported: 'Mr Thornton Butterworth, the publisher, died in London yesterday after a rather long illness. Mr Winston Churchill issued his series of works on "The World Crisis" and Lady Oxford her "Autobiography of Margot Asquith" under the imprint of the firm of Thornton Butterworth. In recent years the firm has published the Home University Library, which came originally from Williams and Norgate, and also memoirs, fiction, travel books. Before coming to London, Mr Thornton Butterworth spent some years in the Far East.' Thornton Butterworth also published Churchill's *My Early Life* (1930), *India* (1931), *Thoughts and Adventures* (1932), *Great Contemporaries* (1937) and *Step By Step* (1939). At his death, his firm was bankrupt, and owed Churchill some £600 in royalties.

I was judging merely by your public utterances. You will remember your speech in the House of Commons on October 24th last, in which you defined the Govt's right policy as 'the whole way with the whole lot'. Later in that speech you went on to say 'No one has suggested that we could do more than we have done, or that we shall take isolated action': and finally, in a most moving passage, you said that as a result of its action in this dispute 'The League of Nations has passed from shadow into substance', & you concluded that 'the case for perseverance holds the field'. I still feel that those quotations justified me in thinking that at that time, at any rate in public, you approved both the policy of the League with regard to the war in Abyssinia & the action of the British Government in supporting & giving an impulsion to that policy.

Moreover, the course which you now consider that we should have adopted, that of taking a less prominent part, was, I believe, at no time practicable. We are by far the greatest nation in the League, & we are bound to take a prominent part. The decision which the British Govt had to take was indeed not whether they should give a lead, but what lead they should give. To my mind the decisive factor governing this decision was inevitably our commitments under the covenant. As soon as the Emperor[1] had telegraphed to Geneva that Italian forces had violated the integrity of Abyssinia, & as soon as the League had decided that the Italian action constituted an unprovoked aggression, Art 16[2] came automatically into operation. Not to have indicated quite clearly that we were ready to honour our obligations under that Article

[1] Tafari Makonnen, 1892–1975. A cousin of the Emperor Menelik of Abyssinia. Appointed Governor of Salali at the age of 14, Governor of Sidamo at the age of 16, Governor of Harar (formerly ruled by his father) at the age of 18. Chosen as Regent and Heir to the Throne by a council of notables, 1916; one of his earliest acts was to abolish slavery. Visited Aden, 1922; toured Europe, 1924, winning Abyssinia's admittance to the League of Nations. Crowned King of Kings, 1928, and founded a new dynasty under his baptized name of Haile Selassie. Personally led his troops against the Italians, October 1935. In exile, 1936, first in Palestine, then in England. In 1940, from Khartoum, he helped organize partisan activity inside Abyssinia. Re-entered his country at the head of a partisan force, January 1941; after the Allied victory, he returned to his capital, May 1941. One of the founders of the Organization of African Unity (OAU), 1959. Received the baton of a Field-Marshal of the British Army, 1965. Deposed in favour of the Crown Prince, 1974 (the Crown itself was abolished in March 1975). Died in his former capital on 27 August 1975.

[2] Under Article 16 of the League of Nations Covenant, should any member of the League resort to war, 'it shall *ipso facto* be deemed to have committed an act of war against all other Members of the League, which hereby undertake immediately to subject it to the severance of all trade or financial relations, the prohibition of all intercourse between their nationals and the nationals of the covenant-breaking State, and the prevention of all financial, commercial, or personal intercourse between the nationals of the covenant-breaking State and the nationals of any other State, whether a Member of the League or not'. In such cases, according to Article 16, it would be the duty of the League Council 'to recommend to the several Governments concerned what effective military, naval, or air force the Members of the League shall severally contribute to the armed forces to be used to protect the covenants of the League'.

would have been so unjustifiable as for us not to indicate, in the Rhineland crisis, that we stood by the Treaty of Locarno. The fact that France may regard the Covenant not so much as a code of international law as an instrument of national policy, to be used when convenient, does not entitle us to take the same view.

For these reasons, I still believe that the Cab took the only possible course under difficult circumstances.

Yrs ever,
Bobbety

Winston S. Churchill: letter to 'The Times'

('*The Times*', 20 April 1936)

17 April 1936   Chartwell

Sir,—It is astonishing that Lord Hugh Cecil,[1] with his commanding mind and sincere desire to be just, should appear so utterly unconscious of the French side of the question.

The French are afraid of the Germans. In a hundred years they have been four times invaded. The memories of the last invasion fill their minds, and its wounds still smart. They see their tremendous neighbour arming night and day. His annual contingent of military youth conscribed for the army is already double that of France. He has spent the prodigious sum of £800,000,000 upon war preparations during the calendar year 1935 alone. Germany is ruled by a dictatorship which at an hour's notice, without the slightest reference to a Parliament or to public opinion, can launch the mighty forces, now ceaselessly and rapidly forming, into an aggressive war. If we were in the place of the French people I am sure we should take foreign affairs more seriously than we do.

For several years our Foreign Office continually sought to bring about a settlement of the differences between France and Italy. At the beginning of 1935 a Franco-Italian accord was effected. By it the French gained enormous advantages. They were able to dismantle their southern frontier against Italy and bring their troops back to help to man the ramparts they had built in the north against another 'avalanche of fire and steel'. They might also count upon the presence of a powerful Italian army on the Brenner Pass to prevent Austria from being incorporated in the German Nazi and military system.

---

[1] Lord Hugh Richard Heathcote Gascoyne Cecil, 1869–1956. Known as 'Linky'. Fifth son of the 3rd Marquess of Salisbury. Educated at Eton and University College, Oxford. Conservative MP for Greenwich, 1895–1906; for Oxford University, 1910–37. A prominent member of the Church Assembly. Provost of Eton, 1936–44. Created Baron Quickswood, 1941. In 1908 he was the 'best man' at Churchill's wedding.

The reliefs and aids secured by the French from their Italian agreement have been valued at at least 15 first-line French divisions available for their defence against what they regard as their supreme danger.

The ink was scarcely dry on these important transactions when an untoward quarrel broke out between Italy and Abyssinia. The League of Nations declared Italy the aggressor. Great Britain, which up to this moment had been regarded on the Continent as completely pacifist, wishing to be detached from the Continent, and, except for her Navy, disarmed, suddenly manifested a vehement desire to uphold the Covenant of the League of Nations and prevent Italy from conquering Abyssinia. It soon appeared that Great Britain was prepared to make exertions, spend money, and move ships and troops. She was even seen ready to face the risk of a war with Italy in which she would have borne practically the whole weight. In this spirited new mood she invited France to share the risks with her, and reminded her of the Covenant of the League.

The matter appeared in a different light to the French. The risks of the two countries did not seem equal. The British Navy and Air Force might well defeat the Italians, and Britain might easily reinsure herself with Germany against their subsequent hostility. To France a quarrel with Italy meant rearming her southern front and probably in a short time having to witness the inclusion of Austria in the German war-power. The equivalent of 15 French Regular divisions is not easy to procure. How many, for instance, would England be prepared to send, and at what dates? Many other questions like this the French may ask themselves, all dictated from a standpoint no higher and no lower than self-preservation. It is said that the French generals told the Cabinet of M. Laval[1] that a definite separation from Italy would mean the reestablishment of three years' military service for all Frenchman. Thus, to go the whole way with Britain in her splendid idealistic crusade meant that the French youth which already offers two years to the army would have to give a third. I wonder how many of the 11,000,000 balloteers would be prepared to enforce a similar sacrifice in time of peace upon the British people. I wonder what the British people would say to those who did. Yet this was the kind of thing we asked of the French.

[1] Pierre Laval, 1883–1945. A Socialist Deputy from 1914. Minister of Public Works, 1925; of Justice, 1926; of Labour, 1930 and 1932. Prime Minister and Foreign Minister, January 1931–February 1932. Minister of Colonies, 1934. Foreign Minister, October 1934–December 1935. Prime Minister, June 1935–January 1936. Deputy Prime Minister and Minister of Information, 1940. Foreign Minister, October–December 1940 and April 1941–November 1943. Minister of the Interior (and of Information and Propaganda), 1942. Deputy Head of State (to Pétain), April 1942–August 1944. Forced by the Germans to move his Government to Germany, August 1944. Escaped first to Switzerland, then to Spain, following Germany's defeat. Tried for treason in France, 1945, and executed.

However, torn between the fear of losing Italy and the hopes of gaining a reinvigorated, light-hearted, valiant Britain, apparently ready to take all risks upon the Continent in the name of the Covenant of the League of Nations, France decided on the whole to go with Britain. I was amazed at the lengths to which M. Laval went in rendering possible the imposition of sanctions by 52 nations upon the aggressor and bringing the League of Nations for the first time from theory into action, and by the assurance of the armed aid of France if we were attacked. He did not go far enough to please some of those who do not propose to run any risks themselves. But he went far enough to make a very definite estrangement between Italy and France. This estrangement gave Herr Hitler his opportunity. He struck his blow, and the safety of France suffered an injury so grievous that we are actually at this moment making our war plans, although we have virtually no Army, to defend France and Belgium if they should be attacked. In fact Mr Baldwin's Government, from the very highest motives, endorsed by the country at the General Election, has, without helping Abyssinia at all, got France into grievous trouble which has to be compensated by the precise engagement of our armed forces.

Surely in the light of these facts, undisputed as I deem them to be, we might at least judge the French, with whom our fortunes appear to be so decisively linked, with a reasonable understanding of their difficulties, which in the long run may also be our own.

I am, &c,
Winston S. Churchill

Winston S. Churchill to Thornton Butterworth
(*Churchill papers: 8/537*)

18 April 1936

I am keeping 'Great Contemporaries' for some year when my other literary activities are restricted through ill-health or some other cause. When that time comes I will not fail to let you have the first option. You will remember that in the meanwhile I have paid a considerable amount for the rent of the type. I hope indeed we shall before long embark again upon a common venture.

I cannot understand why 'My Early Life' does not have a better run. It had an enormous immediate success and now is produced in a cheaper edition; yet apparently nothing happens. Do drop me a line about it at your leisure.

With kindest regards, believe me,

Winston S. Churchill to Keith Feiling

(*Churchill papers: 8/532*)

18 April 1936

Many thanks for your letter of April 14. I fear you have been grievously distressed about your daughter's health. I should be very glad to hear from you that your anxieties are relieved. Events have taken some hold of me, and I have not been able to think about the 'English Speaking Peoples'. All that is for the future. I am labouring to finish 'Marlborough' in time for Autumn publication and I feel I have the measure of it in my mind. Wheldon[1] has left me, with my blessing, to join the cellulose trade, and I should now like to see your young man of whom you wrote to me if he is still available. There is no question of research, but only of attentive checking of the authorities, which I am actually consulting for every chapter, and also of course suggesting any omissions. Let me know when I can see the young gentleman.[2] It is best to telephone to my office.

PS. When is yr next cheque due.

[1] John Wheldon, 1911–   . Educated at Sedbergh and Balliol College, Oxford. Studied for nine months in Germany, 1930. Traffic Apprentice, London, Midland and Scottish Railway, 1933–4. Resident Research Assistant at Chartwell, 1934–5. Lecturer in Modern History at Balliol, 1935–6. Started the Tariffs and Quota Section, Courtaulds Limited, 1936. 2nd Lieutenant, Royal Artillery (Supplementary Reserve), 26 July 1939. Posted to France, October 1939. Wounded during the Dunkirk evacuation, 1940. Headquarters Staff, Medium Artillery, 8 Corps, 1940–1 (served in artillery liaison with beach defences). Captain, Special Operations Executive, 1941–4. Intelligence Officer attached to General Montgomery's staff during the Normandy landings, 1944. Major, 1944. Intelligence Officer on General Eisenhower's Staff, Versailles and Frankfurt, 1944–5. Second Secretary, Board of Trade, 1945. Member of the Allied Control Commission for Germany, 1945 (Press and Public Relations Officer). Rejoined Courtaulds, 1945; Director of their main export subsidiary, 1952–60.

[2] Frederick William Dampier Deakin, 1913–   . Educated at Westminster School, 1926–30. Studied for six months at the Sorbonne, 1931, then at Christ Church, Oxford, 1931–4, where he took a 1st class Honours degree in modern history. Teaching in Germany, 1934–5. Fellow and lecturer at Wadham College, Oxford, 1936–49. Research Assistant 1936–9. Churchill described him in a private letter on 15 February 1939 as 'a young man of great historical distinction', and wrote of him on 29 April 1939; 'I can say from my own intimate knowledge of him for several years that he is in every way fitted to make an excellent officer.' 2nd Lieutenant, Royal Artillery (Territorial Army), 8 July 1939. Served with the Queen's Own Oxfordshire Hussars, 1939–41. Special Operations, War Office, 1941; British Military Mission to Tito, 1943. DSO, 1943. Lieutenant-Colonel. First Secretary, British Embassy, Belgrade, 1945–6. Director of Researches for Churchill, 1946–9. Warden of St Antony's College Oxford, 1950–68. Historian. Author of *The Brutal Friendship* (a study of the relationship between Hitler and Mussolini), 1962. Knighted, 1975.

Winston S. Churchill to Lord Cecil of Chelwood

(Cecil of Chelwood papers)

18 April 1936   Chartwell

My dear Bob,

Thank you very much for your letter. I hope whatever happens the Government will not go on with futile half-hearted sanctions against Italy simply in order to save their own faces and put the pad of oblivion between the public and their past. What can you expect from a duel between Baldwin and Mussolini? The first has on this matter no convictions of any kind. The second is prepared to stake his life. We have been led into a horrible muddle, and we shall only make it worse by trying to throw the blame on France. It would have been easy last summer to have taken resolute action which would have prevented the whole affair.

Clemmie and I will be delighted to come over and see you[1] some time during the summer; may we propose ourselves a few days beforehand? And will you both promise to pay us a return visit? I should like to show you my swimming pool; it is limpid and tepid.

Yours vy sincerely,
Winston S. Churchill

Captain M. W. S. Boucher to Winston S. Churchill

(Churchill papers: 2/272)

19 April 1936   HMS Courageous
                                                 Portsmouth

Dear Mr Churchill,

Here are the notes you were kind enough to ask for. They are only part of what could be said on a large subject.

I first deck landed an aeroplane 12 years ago and have been in or near the Fleet Air Arm ever since, flying the aircraft, and knowing—for my sins—the conditions.

If I can assist any more I shall be delighted. As my ship is now in dock, I am free for a time whenever you should want me.

Yours sincerely,
M. W. S. Boucher

---

[1] Lord Cecil of Chelwood lived at Gale, Chelwood Gate, some sixteen miles by road from Chartwell.

Sir Maurice Hankey to Sir Thomas Inskip

(*Cabinet papers: 21/435*)

19 April 1936
Private and Confidential

NOTE OF A CONVERSATION WITH MR WINSTON CHURCHILL ON SUNDAY, 19th APRIL, 1936

During the Easter Recess Mr Winston Churchill, who is a neighbour of mine, sent me several pressing invitations to lunch or dine, and after my return from a short holiday, I dined with him on Sunday, 19th April. His son Randolph Churchill was present during part of our conversation. General Tudor,[1] a personal friend of the Churchills, who often visits Chartwell, was also present during part of the time.

The nominal object of our meeting was to arrange for the return of Mr Churchill's Cabinet Minutes, a subject on which I have been in correspondence with him for a long time. In this respect the result of our conversation was very satisfactory as he has now returned the whole of the Minutes which he had retained, and I am hoping also to recover a great part, if not all, of the Cabinet Papers in due course.

Apart from Cabinet Papers, our conversation ranged over a wide field. I do not usually make a note of private conversations, but some points arose which gave an indication of the line that Mr Churchill is likely to take in forthcoming Debates in Parliament.

I gathered that he and his associates propose to try and secure that when the various supplementary votes are under consideration in connection with the new programmes the discussion shall be general over Imperial Defence as a whole. Whether the Speaker[2] will allow that I do not pretend to know.

As regards the Minister for Defence Co-Ordination Mr Churchill's main criticism was on his assumption of the Chair at the Principal Supply Officers

---

[1] Henry Hugh Tudor, 1871–1965. 2nd Lieutenant, Royal Artillery, 1890. On active service in South Africa, 1899–1902. Brigadier-General commanding the Artillery of the 9th (Scottish) Division, 1916–18. Major-General commanding the 9th Division, 21 to 24 March 1918. Major-General commanding the Irregular Forces in Ireland (the 'Black and Tans') 1920-1. General Officer Commanding the special gendarmerie in Palestine (known as 'Tudor's lambs'), 1922, with the rank of Air Vice-Marshal. Knighted, 1923. Retired, 1923, and lived in Newfoundland. In 1959 he published his first-war diaries, entitled *The Fog of War*.

[2] Edward Algernon Fitzroy, 1869–1943. Son of the 3rd Baron Southampton. Educated at Eton and Sandhurst. A page of honour to Queen Victoria. Conservative MP for Daventry, 1900–6 and 1910–43. Captain, 1st Life Guards, 1914 (wounded at the first battle of Ypres). Commanded the mounted troops of the Guards Division, 1915–16. Deputy Chairman of Committees, House of Commons, 1922–8. Privy Councillor, 1924. Speaker of the House of Commons from 1928 until his death. His widow was created Viscountess Daventry in 1943. Their son Michael (born 1895) was killed in action on 15 April 1915.

Sub-Committee. When I asked him what rôle he would have contemplated for the Minister, he said he should be confined to questions of general policy, such as bombs versus battleships, the value of Russia as an ally, and so forth.

As regards the supply side, Mr Churchill takes a strong view that we ought to create a Ministry of Supply or Ministry of Munitions at once, and that a Minister of Munitions should be appointed. He went out of his way to explain that he did not want the job for himself. He had already held that post in war and would not touch it again. Sir Kingsley Wood was his nominee! I asked him if he remembered that the question of a Ministry of Supply had been gone into just after the War when he was Secretary of State for War as well as Secretary of State for Air, and that in both capacities he had put forward memoranda giving strong reasons against the maintenance of a Ministry of Munitions, with the result that the Cabinet decided to abolish it. He had forgotten and asked me to let him see the memoranda, but said that of course times had changed. I think he is sure to bring this up in the House of Commons.

He said that when the Minister for Defence Co-Ordination's salary was debated he intended to refer to my own position and to support the view that I ought to continue to hold the three offices. Clerk of the Council, as he rightly said, did not mean much work. The Secretaryships of the Cabinet and of the CID were, in his view, so closely interlocked that there were great advantages in my continuing to hold the two posts.

On the international side I found Mr Churchill's views disappointing— but he was talking rather at large, and probably without having thought the matters out.

As regards Italy, for example, he propounded a plan that we ought to make up our mind to deliver an ultimatum informing the Italians that unless they agreed to come to terms with the League we should close the Suez Canal. Shortly before the presentation of the ultimatum we should notify the French of our intention, demand their co-operation, and intimate that failing that co-operation we should ourselves come to terms with Germany. He talked in this connection of our delivering heavy bombing attacks on Italy which showed he had not thought out how it was to be done, from what bases or with what aircraft.

On the position *vis à vis* Germany he gave an admirable exposition of the dangers of the situation without his usual exaggerations as to German armaments. He is, however, still engaged in writing a commentary on the Air Staff's latest figures on German air strength which were communicated to him as a member of the Air Defence Research Sub-Committee—a task which I fancy he is finding not very easy. He favours continued support of the

League, and was very down on Conservative Members of Parliament who he said were widely criticising our League policy.

He himself of course has no illusions about the weakness of the League, but sees that the British people will not take re-armament seriously except as part of the League policy.

It was not this part of his remarks that disappointed me, but his positive suggestions. His general idea is to hammer away at the League for a complete encirclement of Germany (I do not think he used the word 'encirclement'). The various countries of the Baltic, Holland, Belgium, France, Italy, Switzerland, Austria, the Balkan States, Russia and Poland must all as Members of the League be induced to make such an effort as to deter and, if necessary, stop an aggression by Germany. As part of this plan he had a fantastic idea of sending to the Baltic a sufficient part of the British Fleet to ensure superiority over Germany in that sea. It would stay there, permanently based on a Russian port of which we should obtain the use as part of the plan. This Fleet would never come out of the Baltic in peace or war and would have to be replaced by building an equivalent number of ships for the North Sea. Its mere arrival in the Baltic, with its menace to German communications, would, he suggested, be a severe shock to German opinion and put a stop to further mischief.

All this seemed to be very fantastic and to ignore many realities some of which I mentioned to him, though they are so obvious that I need not mention them here. Mr Churchill developed some of this in greater detail next day to my Private Secretary, Mr Burgis,[1] who had gone to collect his Cabinet Minutes.

A point on which he was really concerned was how far Russia could be relied on as an ally. In view of the danger from Germany he has buried his violent anti-Russian complex of former days and is apparently a bosom friend of M Maisky. Until quite recently he has been inclined to believe in the strength of Russia. He has, however, been seriously shaken in this by reading a book with the curious title of 'Uncle give us Bread', which he urged me to read.[2] This book has awakened in his mind most serious misgivings of Russia, and he has evidently got the impression that Russia may perhaps present only a façade with nothing behind.

He suggested that Sir Thomas Inskip ought to collect all the evidence

---

[1] Lawrence Franklin Burgis, 1892–   . Private Secretary to Lord Esher, 1909–13. 2nd Lieutenant, Black Watch, 1913; Captain, 1917 (on active service, despatches). Military Assistant Secretary to the Committee of Imperial Defence, 1919–21. Assistant Secretary, Cabinet Office, 1922–39; War Cabinet, 1939–45.

[2] *Uncle Give Us Bread*. by Arne Strøm, a Danish poultry expert who had spent eighteen months in the Soviet Union, to help organize the State Poultry Farms. The book was published in Britain by Allen and Unwin.

official and otherwise that there is about Russia in order to determine whether she is an ally worth having or not, and that in particular we ought to ascertain from the French Government the detailed views of their General Staffs on Russia's naval, military and air strength, since it must have been on such views that the French Government based its decision to enter into the Treaty.

One other point of interest arose which is dealt with in a letter I am sending to Mr Duff Cooper of which I attach a copy.

M. P. A. Hankey

L. S. Amery[1] *to Winston S. Churchill*

(*Churchill papers: 2/253*)

20 April 1936

My dear Winston,

Just a line to express my admiration for your most effective letter in to-day's Times.[2] When I contrast it with the woolliness of SB's Bewdley speech, but then—!

Yours ever,

L. S. Amery

Sir Maurice Hankey to Alfred Duff Cooper

(*Hankey papers*)

21 April 1936   Committee of Imperial Defence
Private & Confidential

Dear Duff Cooper,

1. On Sunday evening I dined with Mr Winston Churchill who is a neighbour of mine. Apart from Mr Randolph Churchill, the only other person present was Major-General Sir Hugh Tudor who must be well known to the War Office as he commanded the 9th Division in France in 1918, and after the War was Chief of the Police in Ireland and GOC Palestine.

2. In the course of our conversation General Tudor who, since his retire-

---

[1] Leopold Charles Maurice Stennett Amery, 1873–1955. A contemporary of Churchill at Harrow. Fellow of All Souls College, Oxford, 1897. *Manchester Guardian* correspondent in the Balkans and Turkey, 1897–9. Served on the editorial staff of *The Times*, 1899–1909. Conservative MP, 1911–45. Intelligence Officer in the Balkans and eastern Mediterranean, 1915–16. Assistant Secretary, War Cabinet Secretariat, 1917–18. Parliamentary Under-Secretary, Colonial Office, 1919–21. First Lord of the Admiralty, 1922–4. Colonial Secretary, 1924–9. Secretary of State for India and Burma, 1940–5. Known as 'Leo'.

[2] Written by Churchill on 17 April 1936 (see pages 101–3).

ment, has lived a good deal in Newfoundland, propounded the view that we could obtain large numbers of recruits in that Dominion. He spoke of numbers as high as 2,000 to 3,000 men of a very fine type. He was not in favour of establishing separate battalions for Newfoundland men, but of scattering them through the Regular Army. His reason for this was that Newfoundland, being so close to the American Continent, is rather dominated by American ideas, and he thinks that associations of Newfoundlanders in British regiments would be of great value in combating this tendency when the men return to civil life in the Dominion. I asked how, if such a scheme were adopted, the passages would be defrayed. He admitted that the cost of the ordinary passage is at present £15. But he thought that if men were being taken in any considerable numbers, the shipping company that has the mail contract would make a big reduction. He thought that if a recruiting office were opened in Newfoundland, service in the British Army would be extremely popular, partly for the reason that there is a great deal of unemployment in the Island and the dole is only about 8/- a month. He himself would be glad to give any information on the subject and, if the scheme were adopted, to do his utmost to forward it in Newfoundland. He said that the late Governor, Admiral Sir Murray Anderson,[1] and the Governing Commission were in favour of the scheme, and that Admiral Anderson would be a good person to consult.

3. General Tudor also represented strongly that a naval recruiting office ought to be opened at St Johns, Newfoundland, as a very fine type of recruit for the Navy was obtained there before the War.

4. Mr Churchill asked me to pass on this information to the right quarter which I undertook to do, and that is the reason for this letter.

5. Mr Churchill was obviously very bitten with General Tudor's idea, and shortly before I left announced his intention of raising the matter in the House of Commons in two or three weeks' time, and I could not deter him from this. I dare say, however, that he could be induced to postpone inquiry until the Service Departments concerned have had an opportunity to consider the matter.

6. I am sending a copy of this letter to the First Lord of the Admiralty.

Yours sincerely,
M. P. A. Hankey

---

[1] David Murray Anderson, 1874–1936. Joined the Royal Navy, 1889; on active service in West Africa, 1895–6, in East Africa, 1915 (despatches), and with the Grand Fleet. Rear-Admiral, 1922. Senior Officer, Yangtse, 1923–5. Vice-Admiral, 1927. Commander-in-Chief, Africa Station, 1927–9. High Commissioner, South Africa, 1928. Admiralty Representative, League of Nations Permanent Advisory Commission, 1929–31. Knighted, 1930. Admiral, 1931. Retired from the Royal Navy, 1932. Governor and Commander-in-Chief, Newfoundland, 1933–6. Governor of New South Wales, 1936. He died on 30 October 1936.

Winston S. Churchill to Lord Cranborne

(*Churchill papers: 2/253*)

22 April 1936

I looked up the enclosed extract from a speech I made in the House last summer. From it you will see how strongly my personal judgment was expressed against our becoming a 'bell-wether or fugleman' of the League of Nations, and thus allowing Mussolini to speak of 'fifty nations led by one'. It is true that after Hoare and Eden had taken the bit between their teeth in the Autumn and had carried us so far afield, I did my best to support them in the new situation which they had created against my advice— such as it is—. But that in no way invalidates my right now that the adventure is coming to a dismal end to point out clearly where the original error lay.

Viscount Cecil of Chelwood to Winston S. Churchill

(*Churchill papers: 2/253*)

22 April 1936

My dear Winston,

I am delighted to hear that you and Mrs Winston may be able to visit us at Gale sometime, and I shall look forward very much to a return visit if that can be arranged.

I agree very much with what you say about the contrast between Baldwin and Mussolini; and indeed, it is not only Baldwin, for the initial mistakes— from which we have never recovered,—were committed by Simon[1] and Mac-Donald. The best time to stop the Abyssinian war was in January of last year, before Laval had committed himself to Mussolini and when it was known to everyone who had eyes in their head that the Italians were preparing to do something violent. On the other hand, I am unable to share your view that France is not to blame. Whatever may be said of the British Government, it is nothing to the perfidy of men like Laval and Flandin. I don't know Laval; but I do know Flandin and have always had a very bad opinion of

---

[1] John Allsebrook Simon, 1873–1954. Educated at Fettes and Wadham College, Oxford. Fellow of All Souls. Liberal MP for Walthamstow, 1906–18; for Spen Valley, 1922–31. Solicitor-General, 1910–13. Knighted, 1910. Attorney-General, with a seat in the Cabinet, 1913–15. Home Secretary, 1915–16, when he resigned in opposition to conscription. Major, Royal Air Force, serving in France, 1917–18. Liberal National MP for Spen Valley, 1931–40, Secretary of State for Foreign Affairs, 1931–5. Home Secretary, 1935–7. Chancellor of the Exchequer, 1937–40. Created Viscount, 1940. Lord Chancellor, 1940–5.

him. I am sure that he hates this country, and that all his pretended love for it is mere bunkum. Anyway, whether this is right or wrong, please do not underrate the very strong anti-French feeling that is raging in this country.

Yrs ever,
R C

Lawrence Burgis to Winston S. Churchill

(*Churchill papers: 1/284*)

22 April 1936   Offices of the Cabinet

Dear Mr Churchill,

Together with the official letter about your papers I feel I must add a personal word of thanks for your great kindness to me on Monday last. To have lunched with you at Chartwell was a very great honour and your book which you gave me I shall treasure quite as much, if not more, than you treasure your Mark Twain volumes![1]

Yours sincerely,
Lawrence Burgis

Eleanor Rathbone to Winston S. Churchill

(*Churchill papers: 2/274*)

22 April 1936

Dear Mr Churchill,

I now return the paper you kindly lent me, having taken notes of the figures.

I am not sufficiently acquainted with the technicalities to know whether the enclosed copy of a letter just received from a German correspondent gives information worth having, but as it sounds intelligent I send it.

The extent of pro-German feeling among my constituents, who send me more communications about international questions than about everything

---

[1] On his first American lecture tour in 1901, Churchill had been introduced to his New York audience (on 22 January 1901) by Mark Twain, who said: 'Mr Churchill by his father is an Englishman, by his mother he is an American, no doubt a blend that makes the perfect man. England and America; we are kin. And now that we are also kin in sin, there is nothing more to be desired. The harmony is perfect—like Mr Churchill himself . . .' The twin 'sins' were the Spanish-American and Anglo-Boer wars (of 1898 and 1899 respectively). Churchill asked Mark Twain to sign each of the twenty-five volumes of the collected *Writings of Mark Twain*. In the first volume Mark Twain wrote: 'To be good is noble; to teach others how to be good is nobler, & no trouble' (*Chartwell Library*).

else put together, is significant and deplorable, but there is no doubt that it is largely due to irritation with France on account of her selfish policy in blanketing sanctions against Italy. In your admirable speech of March 26th you indicated as the two practicable policies a strong Franco-British alliance and the establishment of real collective security throughout Europe; but some of us found it difficult to reconcile your preference for the latter with your opinion that we should not 'press France unduly' in the matter of Italy. If the League fails there because of France, is it not likely that both policies will become impossible, the former because public opinion will not stand it, and the latter because of the disheartenment that will follow upon failure in this test case?

A lead from you on the lines of an equally strong front towards both Germany and Italy would, I am sure, rally a very large and influential body of public opinion.

Of course this needs no answer.[1]

Yours sincerely,
Eleanor Rathbone

Harold Nicolson: diary

(*Nicolson papers*)

22 April 1936

Lunch with Sybil.[2] Party consists of Mrs Simpson,[3] Victor Cazalet, J. L. Garvin and Winston Churchill. Garvin, with unequalled eloquence, expounds the errors of the Government. He says that to have made an enemy

[1] Three months later Eleanor Rathbone told an Independent Labour Party summer school: 'I have described Winston Churchill as a new recruit to pro-League forces. Watch that man carefully. You may feel distrustful. So did I. I'm not certain yet. But I ask you to dispel prejudice and consider the facts. Churchill for three years has pointed out extensive German rearmaments. Later facts have justified his estimates. He was always in theory a pro-League man; but only recently has his imagination clearly been captivated by the potentialities of collective security through the League. I first noticed this when he spoke on the Abyssinian dispute on October 24th last year.'

[2] Sibyl Colefax, 1874–1950. The daughter of William Stirling Halsey, in 1901 she married Sir Arthur Colefax KBE, KC, an authority on Patent and Trade Mark Law, who died on 19 February 1936. One of London's most famous hostesses, she delighted in bringing together people from the worlds of literature and politics, first at Argyll House, in Chelsea, and then, after her husband's death, at 19 Lord North Street, Westminster.

[3] Wallis Warfield, 1896–   . Daughter of Teakle Wallis Warfield of Baltimore, Maryland. She married Edward, Duke of Windsor (as her third husband) on 3 June 1937. Duchess of Windsor, 1937. Resident in the Bahamas, where the Duke was Governor, 1940–5; in France from 1945.

of Italy is a mistake for which we shall pay heavily in after years. He contends that the Mediterranean is now untenable and that our only hope of maintaining our Empire is to have Italy as an ally. Winston, while agreeing naturally with his criticism of the Government, does not agree with the conclusions. Our communications cannot be left at the mercy of so unreliable a thing as Italian friendship. We must retain 'that command of the Mediterranean which Marlborough, my illustrious ancestor, first established'. Victor and I keep quite silent under this deluge of eloquence.

Drive back to the House with Winston. On the way he grumbles about the Budget and contends that Neville Chamberlain has been over-cautious. I say that the Government have been so weak in regard to public opinion that it is not a bad thing that NC should take a determinedly unpopular line. He rather agrees.

Winston S. Churchill to Newman Flower[1]

(Churchill papers: 8/532)

24 April 1936

I should be much obliged if you would kindly give instructions for a cheque for £500 to be sent to me this month, in accordance with our arrangement for the History of the English Speaking Peoples.

PS. As soon as I am free from Marlborough wh will be in the Autumn I shall go ahead on this 'monumental work'.

[1] Walter Newman Flower, 1879–1964. Educated at Whitgift School. Joined Cassells, publishers, 1906; purchased the firm in 1927; subsequently its Chairman and President. Knighted, 1938. A meeting between Flower and Churchill in August 1932 marked the beginning of the contractual stages of Churchill's new book, *A History of the English-Speaking Peoples*, which was planned for publication in 1940, but eventually published between 1956 and 1958, in four volumes. On 23 September 1932 Nancy Pearn of the Curtis Brown Literary Agency wrote to Churchill: 'Subject to the discussion of detail which no doubt that meeting will produce, we have now obtained the following definite proposal from Newman Flower on behalf of the firm of Cassell. On the basis of a manuscript of 400,000 words, to be delivered ready for press at a date to be mutually agreed, he will pay a sum of Twenty Thousand Pounds for all publication rights: all other rights—such as potential film—being left in your hands. Of this sum he will be prepared to pay Two Thousand Pounds on signature of the agreement by both parties; and contracts in principle to make further payments from time to time as may be agreed' *(Churchill papers: 8/313)*. In September 1981 the approximate equivalent of £20,000 was £350,000.

Winston S. Churchill to the Duke of Westminster

(*Churchill papers: 2/253*)

24 April 1936

It was kind of you to think of me for the Chester races. I should like so much to have a good talk with you. Alas I cannot come away in the Parliamentary week at this time, and on the 6th I have to go and give evidence about a case in my constituency. Do let me know when you come up to London so that we can dine.

Things are going from bad to worse and the Government are doing next to nothing about it. As Monty[1] would say 'That's what's so exasperating!'. Baldwin's stock continues to sag.

Please let me know when you come up.

Desmond Morton to Winston S. Churchill

(*Churchill papers: 2/266*)

24 April 1936   Earlylands,
                                                                Edenbridge

Dear Winston,

May I congratulate you most warmly and sincerely on your Budget speech.[2] You may be interested to hear that it seems to have had a profound

---

[1] Monty = James Milton Hayes, 1884–1940, who first appeared as a comedian, in Manchester, in 1899, and in London in 1910. Wrote and sang a series of 'Musical Monologues'; the one by which he became famous was *The Green Eye of The Little Yellow God*, 1911. On active service, 1914–18, 2nd Lieutenant, Manchester Regiment (Military Cross; prisoner-of-war). Returning to the theatre as 'The Laughsmith with a Philosophy', he drew on his war experiences in *The Road of Ten Thousand Crosses*, a savage outcry against the 'ten thousand Lancashires' killed at Passchendaele. His wireless career consisted of a two-part act, 'The Meanderings of Monty', of which there were twelve, followed by one of his Monologues, of which 'Monty Discusses the Empire Spirit' was one. A Christian Scientist, he retired on account of ill-health in 1927. Lived in Nice until his death in December 1940. His wife was to play a heroic part in the French resistance. 'If my memory serves me right,' Sir John Colville writes, 'Monty of the series of gramophone records enormously popular in the 1930s (I remember especially "Monty on the Empire") was always saying "that's what's so exasperating'" (*letter to the author, 20 April 1982*).

[2] During Churchill's speech of 23 April 1936 on Neville Chamberlain's Budget proposals, he told the House of Commons: 'When the Chancellor announced that the Supplementary Estimate would not in his opinion exceed £20,000,000, he proclaimed the failure and the inadequacy of our defence effort this year. One is told that you cannot spend more under peace conditions, however great the need may be, without disturbing the economic and social life of the country; and I noticed that my right hon. and learned Friend the Minister for the Co-ordination of Defence a few days after he had taken up his office, made a very important pronouncement. He explained that he was working under peace conditions. I was much concerned at that statement, and thought it premature for my right hon. and learned Friend to commit himself so early to such a limitation upon his powers. Surely, the question whether

effect in the City. Bodies like Lloyds' and the Stock Exchange could do little to-day save talk about it. Curiously enough, I wonder why. Although your speech was one of your masterpieces, the City did not hear you deliver it, and the facts you presented about German re-armament included little if anything that you have not already told them in other words. You will understand that in saying this, I intend no detraction whatever from my admiration for the speech itself. Somehow, this time, it appears to have 'got right across'. Unfortunately I cannot as yet add that the Government have been shewing signs of appreciating your points. They are delighted at your attitude towards the Budget, and perhaps a little disturbed at your unanswerable criticism of the new Minister of Defence Co-ordination; but I doubt if they are any more alive to the facts of the armament situation in Germany, France and this country.

I rather think they would be very apprehensive of an informed attack by you on the new Minister. After all, you *know*, and I am afraid he has, at best got to *learn*. Again, the appointment was clearly a fake; made in the hope that the international situation would so right itself that there would be no need for any hurry to rearm, or perhaps even to rearm at all. Recent events have destroyed this hope.

There is much speculation as to the source of your figures of German expenditure on armaments. I don't know and don't want to, but with the best will in the world and with the honest help of the Treasury cannot make the probable figure more than about half yours over the last three years. God knows that is alarming enough when compared with our own expenditure.

I see you told a Labour interrupter[1] that the cause of the relative cheapness of German armaments was probably lower wages. True enough, and of

we should continue working under peace conditions depends upon whether working under those conditions will give us the necessary deliveries of our munitions—upon whether the gun plants and the shell plants and, above all, the aeroplane factories, can fulfil the need in time. If they can do so, then peace conditions are no doubt very convenient; but if not, then we must substitute other conditions—not necessarily war conditions, but conditions which would impinge upon the ordinary daily life and business of this country. There are many other conditions apart from war conditions—preparatory conditions, precautionary conditions, emergency conditions—and these must be established in this country if any real progress is to be made, and if Parliament and the nation are not to find themselves deluded in the future by mere paper programmes and promises which in the result will be found to be utterly unfulfilled.'

[1] During his speech on the Budget on 23 April 1936, Churchill was interrupted when he spoke of 'the fact that armament production is much cheaper in Germany than here'. Asked 'Why?' he answered: 'Wages are much lower.' Allowing for this, and calculating a rate of exchange of 12 Marks to the pound, he pointed out that the German armaments expenditure had grown from 5 milliard marks (1933) to nearly 8 milliard (1934), to nearly 11 milliard (1935), a total of 24 milliards, or £2,000 million sterling, in three years.

course, a splendid riposte to the Labour party. Actually, however, as doubtless you recognise, there are many more causes than that. One is the old story of reduction of price on quantity. Overheads can be spread. Another is mass production methods. A third is a deliberate attempt to achieve simplicity of design and quantity rather than quality. Still, the quality achieved is quite adequate. We will persist in making our weapons, works of art. I do not agree with that policy. The old, old argument applics; on which side would you rather be? the side which can discharge a thousand projectiles of which 100% will be effective, or the side which can discharge a million, of which 50% will be effective?

With repeated congratulations,

Yours very sincerely,
Desmond Morton

Countess of Oxford and Asquith[1] *to Winston S. Churchill*

(*Churchill papers: 2/253*)

25 April 1936

Dearest Winston,

None of us minds praise, so I must congratulate you on yr *wonderful* speech of Thursday. Duffy & Diana also G. Dawson[2] (The Times) & others who lunched here yesterday were full of praise. It relieved the general depression wh ALL of us feel, & is terribly *true*. We are at the parting of the ways between war, & peace.[3]

Yrs ever always,
Margot

[1] Emma Alice Margaret Tennant, 1864–1945. Known as Margot, She married H. H. Asquith (as his second wife) in 1894, and published four separate volumes of memoirs, including *The Autobiography of Margot Asquith* in 1921. Her husband died in 1928.

[2] George Geoffrey Robinson, 1874–1944. Educated at Eton and Magdalen College, Oxford. Fellow of All Souls, 1898. Private Secretary to Milner in South Africa, 1901–5. Editor of the *Johannesburg Star*, 1905–10. Editor of *The Times*, 1912–19 and 1923–41. Took the surname of Dawson, 1917.

[3] During the debate on 23 April 1936 on the Budget Proposals, Churchill said: 'I trust we are going to have proper debates on Defence this year. We independent Conservatives who take an interest in these matters are in a very forlorn position as regards being able to bring to the attention of the House the matters in which we are particularly interested, but the Leaders of the two Oppositions have great facilities, and I trust the right hon. Gentleman opposite will not fail to rise to the level of his public responsibilities and make sure that his authority in the allocation of the different supply days is exercised in such a way as to cover, not merely the special views of his party, but the general wishes and requirements of the House of Commons.' At this point Clement Attlee rose and said: 'The right hon. Gentleman will realise that during the last four years, when we have been in Opposition, we have always done that, particularly in regard to matters of defence.' Churchill replied: 'I gladly welcome the right hon. Gentleman's accession to the appeal that I have made to him.'

Sir Henry Strakosch to Winston S. Churchill

(*Churchill papers: 2/277*)

27 April 1936
Confidential

My dear Churchill,

I enclose a copy of the promised note on German expenditure on war-like preparations, of which I gave you a short abstract over the telephone the other day.

The note I sent you on November 1st last, which includes an estimate of Germany's armaments expenditure based upon the figures of credit expansion in Germany through the issue of so-called commercial bills has, as you probably know, been challenged by Pinsent[1] (of the Treasury). He suggests that the figures of Governmental receipt on account of bill stamps, upon which this estimate is based, are misleading, because, latterly, stamp duty on such bills was paid not merely in respect of the normal period of renewal of three months, but for several renewals. I confess that I myself am sceptical about this line of reasoning. It was with a view to checking the result of my first investigation, that I tackled the problem on the several lines of approach mentioned in the enclosed Note. The result of these amply confirms my first impression that expenditure by Germany on war-like preparations since Hitler came into power has been on a gigantic scale, rising steeply from year to year, and corresponding pretty closely to the first estimate which I gave you in my note of 1st November last.

I hope that the unavoidable delay in sending you these figures will not cause you any inconvenience.

Yours sincerely,
H. Strakosch

PS. I am having the figures of Germany's imports of raw materials brought up to date & will let you have them as soon as they are ready.

[1] Gerald Hume Saverie Pinsent, 1888–1976. Educated at King's School, Canterbury, and Trinity College, Cambridge. Entered the Treasury, 1911; Assistant Secretary, 1931. Financial Adviser, British Embassy, Berlin, 1932–9; Washington 1939–41. British Food Mission, Ottawa, 1942–3. Principal Assistant Secretary, Board of Trade, 1943; Treasury, 1944. Comptroller-General, National Debt Office, 1946–51.

Sir Henry Strakosch: memorandum

(*Churchill papers: 2/277*)

27 April 1936

'ESTIMATE OF GERMAN CAPITAL EXPENDITURE ON WAR-LIKE PREPARATIONS'

FIRST LINE OF APPROACH

The following figures are compiled from official and semi-official statements:—

	In millions of Reichmarks (RM)
Increase of Public Debt from 31/3/33 to 30/6/35	7,227
Governmental Capital Expenditure covered by increased taxation from 31/3/33 to 31/3/36	5,000[1]
Probable minimum total	12,227

The foregoing total represents expenditure by the German Reich apart from current expenditure for the maintenance of her armed forces.

SECOND LINE OF APPROACH

Under the Hitler regime, German economy as a whole is subject to close supervision and regulation by the Government. Capital expenditure of private enterprise in particular is subject to the specific approval of the German Government. Owing to the limited supply of essential raw materials, the German Government permits capital expenditure of private enterprise only in so far as that expenditure is directly or indirectly devoted to armament purposes.

In its Bulletin issued at the end of 1935 (page 10), the Reichskredit Gesellschaft states that the extension of non-residential buildings, which began in 1933, is only to a very small extent due to building operations for purely private enterprise.

---

[1] Sir Henry Strakosch noted, at this point: 'The Bulletin of the Reichskredit Gesellschaft (a wholly Governmentally owned and controlled Bank), published at the end of 1935, page 53, states that most of the increased revenues amounting to RM *7,000 millions* from 30/3/33 to 31/3/35 has been spent by the Government for capital expenditure which must be presumed to be for armaments in the widest sense, i.e., including the construction of aerodromes, strategic roads, etc.'

The following figures are taken from the Bulletin of the Reichskredit Gesellschaft issued at the end of 1935:—

In millions of RM

Total capital expenditure for buildings, equipment and stores

1933	5,100	
1934	8,250	
1935	11,250 (provisional)	

24,600

Deduct estimated amounts spent on residential buildings (based on figures contained in the Reichskredit Gesellschaft Bulletin for the end of 1935, pp 9 & 10.

1933	360	
1934	550	
1935	550	
—	1,460	

Total capital expenditure, excluding residential buildings

23,140

THE THIRD LINE OF APPROACH

It may, in truth, be said that any increase in the national income of Germany during the last three years is due to expenditure by the German nation for capital purposes, and these, for the reasons set out above, are probably in the main for war-like preparations, for none of that increased income of the nation has gone into consumption owing to the fact that both wages and the cost-of-living have remained stationary during the period under review.

Moreover, the level of wholesale prices for all finished goods other than consumption goods has fallen during the period, while consumption goods have risen rather substantially.

The following figures are taken from the Statistical Year Book of the German Reich, 1935, page 485. The figure for 1935 is an estimate based on figures given in the Bulletin of the Reichskredit Gesellschaft issued at the end of 1935, page 33:—

In millions of Reichsmarks

Increase in National Income as com-pared with 1932		
	1933	1,200
	1934	7,200
	1935	11,500 (provisional)
		———
		19,900

It is to be noted that the 1935 figure of (about) 11 milliards of marks corresponds closely to Mr Winston Churchill's estimate of £800 millions sterling of expenditure on account of armaments in 1935.

Lord Weir to Winston S. Churchill

(Churchill papers: 2/253)

28 April 1936

Dear Winston,

Over the weekend I read the 'Hansard' with your Budget speech and I cannot help telling you how it affected me. Quite frankly, I say that without any doubt it is the most knowledgeable and educative speech I have ever read. It places every trend and policy of real importance in the last ten years in the truest sense of proportion and should serve as a perfect lesson to all who can understand the things which matter.

Late in the speech when you come to the key question of the moment, the degree of gravity and the consequent action covering definite interference with our existing industrial situation, I confess my inability to weigh up the pros and cons with your confidence.

Yours ever,
Weir

Winston S. Churchill to Sir Henry Strakosch

(Churchill papers: 2/277)

29 April 1936
Confidential

I am deeply indebted to you for the massive, cogent arguments with which you have supplied me. As you will see on Friday I have assumed responsibility for them, and put them forth in the series of articles I am now writing for the Evening Standard and other papers throughout the length and breadth of the land.[1] I thought this was the best way of making an impression. I may say that before I quoted your figures in the House, I told Neville what I meant to assert, the main fact of £800,000,000 in 1935, and that I would invite him to contradict me. He replied he would certainly not contradict me. So that I think we have done a public service in establishing a certain basis.

With regard to Lord Rennell,[2] he is an aged goose but virtuous and patriotic. I should like to write to him privately and ask him to put himself in touch with you. You could then explain to him these facts and figures. If you convince him—as I am pretty sure you would—I would then write him a public letter asking him to say that, having gone into the matter, he is satisfied that my statements were substantially true.

The Duchess of Atholl[3] *to Winston S. Churchill*

(*Churchill papers: 2/253*)

29 April 1936   House of Commons

Dear Mr Churchill,

I forgot, when I wrote the other day, to thank you for returning my copy of the English translation of *Mein Kampf*. I wonder if I now might have the

---

[1] The first of these articles, 'How Germany is Arming', in which Churchill gave prominence to the figure of £800 million as the minimum German arms expenditure for 1935, was published in the *Evening Standard* on 1 May 1936. It was followed by 'Our Navy *Must* Be Stronger' (15 May 1936), 'Organize Our Supplies' (29 May 1936) and 'How to Stop War', 12 June 1936. The first of these articles began: 'One looks at the people going about their daily round, crowding the streets on their business, earning their livelihood, filling the football grounds and cinemas. One reads their newspapers, always full of entertaining headlines whether the happenings are great or small. Do they realise the way events are trending? And how external forces may effect all their work and pleasure, all their happiness, all their freedom, all their property and all whom they love? I can only see one thing. I see it sharper and harsher day by day. Germany is arming more strenuously, more scientifically and upon a larger scale, than any nation has ever armed before.'

[2] James Rennell Rodd, 1858–1941. Educated at Haileybury and Balliol College, Oxford. Entered the Diplomatic Service, 1883. Knighted, 1899. Minister to Sweden, 1904–8. Ambassador to Italy, 1908–19. Conservative MP for St Marylebone, 1928–32. Created Baron, 1933. Chairman of the Executive Committee of the Parents' Association.

[3] Katharine Marjory Ramsay, 1874–1960. Educated at Wimbledon High School and the Royal College of Music. Married the 8th Duke of Atholl in 1899 (he died in 1942). Commandant, Blair Castle Auxiliary Hospital, 1917–19. DBE, 1918. A leading Scottish educationalist. Conservative MP for Kinross and West Perth, 1923–38. Parliamentary Secretary, Board of Education, 1924–9. Member of the Royal Commission on the Civil Service, 1929–31. Among her publications were *Searchlight on Spain* (1938) and *The Tragedy of Warsaw* (1945). An opponent, with Churchill, of the 1935 India Bill. Owing to her support for the Spanish Republicans in 1936, known as 'The Red Duchess'. Her husband fought with Churchill at Omdurman, 1898. Her elder brother, Lieutenant Nigel Ramsay, was killed in action in South Africa, 11 December 1899. Her nephew, Major David Ramsay, was killed in action in Normandy, 17 June 1944.

2 vols of the German original, & the black book 'Nazism: an assault on civilization' which I lent you along with the English translation? I have to write something this week end for which I shd like to refer to the German version, the other book if possible. I hope this won't be a bother.

Did I tell you when I wrote, of the very serious view of things taken by the Belgian Ambassador in Paris?[1] He thinks Germany will dominate Europe in about two years. He was Ambassador in Berlin for 4 years until 5 months ago, so has seen a good deal of the regime there. He thinks that every day adds to the strength of Germany in relation to the Western Powers, & is very frightened that she will make promises galore which she will break when it suits her.

Yrs sincerely,
Katharine Atholl

Winston S. Churchill to Louis Levy[2]
(*Churchill papers: 1/288*)

29 April 1936   Chartwell
Very private

Dear Mr Levy,

I should be grateful if you would assist me in the following personal matter. My second daughter, Sarah, wished to go on the stage and after a prolonged training, is playing in the chorus of Mr Cochran's revue 'Follow the Sun', and apparently enjoying it. One of the actors in this piece is a certain Vic Oliver, alias Victor Samek.

---

[1] André de Kerchove de Denterghem, 1885–1945. A Belgian diplomat, he served in London as Attaché, 1910–12, and as Secretary of Legation, 1912–16. Governor of East Flanders, 1921–31. Member of the Senate, 1929. Minister in Berlin, 1932–5. Ambassador in Paris, 1935–40. Ambassador in Charge of Food Supplies for Occupied Belgium (based in Lisbon), 1941–4.

[2] Louis Samter Levy, 1878–1952. Born in Alabama. Educated at Yale and Columbia Universities. Admitted to practice at the New York bar, 1902. A partner in several law firms, including Levy and Rosenthal (1905) and Stanchfield & Levy (1910–24 and 1936–52). Chairman of the Board of Art Associates Inc, which arranged a major exhibition of paintings at the New York World's Fair, 1939. Administrator and Trustee of several fine art donations and collections. In 1939 he was disbarred from practice before the Federal bar, and in 1940 he was disbarred as an attorney in state courts for obtaining a $250,000 loan for a business associate of a Federal Circuit Court of Appeals Judge, at a time when clients of Levy's firm were involved in a suit before the Federal Circuit Court of Appeals.

It has become necessary for me to know more about this man since he wishes to marry my daughter. All we know at present is that he was an Austrian subject, born, as he states, of good family; that his mother is living in Vienna at the present time; that his father (deceased) was an important wool merchant at Brünn in Moravia; that after the war he, the son, Victor, made his way to the United States where he played in Chicago in vaudeville or cabaret shows. He certainly lived for some years in Chicago and had some vogue which developed and he came to England. He is now a star turn, performing at hotels and cabarets, and also playing in Mr Cochran's revue.

Nothing that I have heard leads me to believe he is a bad, wicked or criminal man. He is probably making as much as £200 a week. He is in all probability twice the age of my daughter. He admits that he has been twice divorced. The first time was in Austria when, as he says, being quite a young man, he married 'beneath him'. He says the lady is still living in Vienna and is comfortably off. He states there were no children. The second marriage took place in Chicago. It was, he says, one of those relationships frequently entered into by artists on tour. Again it was unsuccessful, and he states that he is now paying her approximately £700 a year alimony, or compensation.

Having lost his Austrian nationality, he has not yet gained United States citizenship. He has what he calls a 'resident naturalization status'. He has, I understand, a United States passport. He is here on that passport subject to periodical renewals as a foreign performer.

The above facts will place the situation before you. We are making enquiries in Austria about his antecedents there, and he has certainly professed himself most anxious that we should do so.

What I ask you to do for me, if indeed it be in your power, is to make some enquiry into his American record, especially in Chicago. What was this marriage that he contracted? How was it terminated? What kind of divorce? What validity has that divorce under the laws of the United States (we can then check the validity under our laws)? Were there any children by this marriage? Where is the second wife? And in what condition? Are there any more of these marriages besides these two? Generally what sort of trail has this man left behind him in the United States, to which he proposes shortly to return, etc etc?

There is no need for any very elaborate investigation. Most of the facts ought to be ascertainable in theatrical circles in Chicago and records of any divorce proceedings which have taken place. I do not know whom else I could turn to better than you, who would probably be able, discreetly and without bringing my name into the matter at all, to put your hand upon a suitable agency. I feel it my duty as a father to ascertain these facts so far as possible, and my daughter is quite willing I should do so. It would give me pleasure to hear from you in the first instance what course you advise.[1]

I have hopes of coming to the States before the Presidential conventions, though all my plans are hampered by British politics. I look forward in that case to meeting you again. Meanwhile, believe me,

Yours sincerely,
Winston S. Churchill

Cabinet minutes

(Cabinet papers: 23/84)

29 April 1936

The Minister for Co-ordination of Defence[2] said that the course of the discussion impelled him to raise a matter that had lately been prominent in his mind. He had been feeling the urgency and the difficulty of the re-equipment programme and had been considering how far the assumption of 'peace conditions' on which our present preparations were based, was compatible with the growing anxieties of the international situation. . . .

He did not ask for a decision that day, but he warned the Cabinet that he might have to ask for authority to adopt more drastic measures such, for example, as would enable manufacturers to give priority to Government orders in connection with the Defence Requirements programme and to postpone commercial orders whether for home or foreign account.

The Chancellor of the Exchequer,[3] after recalling his own reply to some

[1] On 3 July 1936 Chadbourne, Stanchfield and Levy wrote to Churchill from New York: 'Upon receipt of your cables, dated June 30th and July 1st, respectively, we wired our Chicago correspondents and they have now found the record of the Cook County divorce. They have telegraphed us that from the record it appears that Victor Samek obtained a divorce from his wife, Elizabeth, on the ground of desertion. . . . The bill of complaint alleged that Victor Samek and his wife, Elizabeth, were married on or about September 30, 1916, at Vienna, Austria. It further alleged that the wife, Elizabeth, deserted Victor Samek on or about August 30, 1923. It stated that she was supposedly living at the time of the complaint at 106 West 74th Street, New York City. Mr Samek's address was given as 19 North Clark Street, Chicago, Illinois. . . . Two witnesses testified on behalf of Mr Samek to the effect that Mrs Samek deserted him. One of the witnesses was Margaret Crangle, who afterwards became his wife.' The Lawyers' letter added: 'We are writing you this, via Zeppelin "Hindenburg", to place it in your hands at the earliest opportunity. We will follow it up with such further information as we can obtain.'

[2] Sir Thomas Inskip.

[3] Neville Chamberlain. On 23 April 1936 Chamberlain told the House of Commons, in in reply to Churchill, that 'the Government had to bear the responsibility of taking special powers over industries in relation to Defence, but they would also be responsible if they took such powers prematurely and dislocated the country's industry and trade. The Government were watching the situation carefully, and they had reached the conclusion that it was not necessary for them at the present time to assume special powers'.

observations by Mr Winston Churchill in the House of Commons on this subject, asked that the Minister for Defence Co-ordination's question should be reserved until after decisions had been reached on the major policy of the Government.

Captain Ronald Oldham[1] *to Winston S. Churchill*

(*Churchill papers: 1/284*)

30 April 1936   HMS Ramillies
                                                       Sheerness

Dear Mr Churchill,

I hope you will forgive me for bothering you, but since taking command of this ship a short time ago, I have been trying to find out a little more than the official records tell, of the crest and motto with which she is honoured; and I felt sure that you would be able to help me.

It is stated that it is the crest and motto of the Churchill family, and that the motto—which was chosen by the great Duke of Marlborough—means 'Faithful but unfortunate' or alternatively 'Faithful throughout adversity'.

Would it be too much to ask you whether this is correct, and, if possible, the circumstances in which the motto was chosen? I have no doubt the crest goes even further back, but I felt that there must be some history attached to the motto that explains the apparently passive, or even pessimistic note which it conveys, and which seems contrary to the character of its originator.

I was hoping that perhaps our translation may be wrong, as a motto in which 'unfortunate' figures so prominently is a little difficult to 'carry off' effectively in a ship!

I hope you will forgive this intrusion into what is after all a family matter, but I am sure you will understand & sympathise with the reason for it.

Yours sincerely,
Ronald Oldham

[1] Ronald Wolseley Oldham. 1887–1980. Entered the Royal Navy as a cadet, 1903. Lieutenant, HMS *Irresistible* (Battleship), 1913–15; HMS *Inflexible* (Battle Cruiser), 1915–18. Lieutenant-Commander, 1916. A Gunnery specialist; OBE for war service. Training and Staff Duties Division, Admiralty, 1921–3. Captain, 1926. Naval Member of the Ordnance Committee of the Committee of Imperial Defence, 1927–9. Commanded the Cruiser *Shropshire* in the Mediterranean, 1929–31. Chief of Staff, Devonport, 1933. From 1937, Captain on *Ramillies* (Battleship). Rear-Admiral, retired, January 1938.

May 1936

Vice-Admiral Henderson[1] *to Winston S. Churchill*

(*Churchill papers: 2/272*)

1 May 1936

Dear Mr Churchill,

I am enclosing some notes on the Fleet Air Arm situation which I hope may be of some help.

As regards the destroyers, you will appreciate that within the last three months sixteen extra destroyers have been ordered and that there is a limitation to further new construction of such craft on account of the manning problem. You will also realise, I am sure, that from the anti-submarine point of view, we have relatively many more ships equipped with anti-submarine devices than in 1914–18. Further, we have only fifteen capital ships, and do not therefore have to lock up the same number of destroyers that we had to at Scapa Flow, with our 36 capital ships. Also, no foreign power to-day has more than 70 submarines, whereas Germany had 245. So I think that it is quite fair to say that the present destroyer position is not so bad as it would appear.

Yours sincerely,
R. G. H. Henderson

[1] Reginald Guy Hannam Henderson, 1881–1939. Entered the Royal Navy, 1896. Naval Mission to Greece, 1913. On active service, 1914–19 (despatches). Commanded the aircraft carrier HMS *Furious*, 1926–8. Rear-Admiral commanding Aircraft Carriers, 1931–3. Vice-Admiral, 1933. Third Sea Lord and Controller of the Navy, 1934–9. Knighted, 1936. Admiral, 1939. Churchill wrote in an unpublished draft of his second war memoirs: 'I also had a long and old friendship with Admiral Henderson, the Controller. He was one of our finest gunnery experts in 1912, and as I always used to go out and see the initial firings of battleships before their gun-mountings were accepted from the contractors, I was able to form a very high opinion of his work.'

Winston S. Churchill to Captain Oldham

(Churchill papers: 1/284)

2 May 1936

The motto 'Faithful but Unfortunate' also 'Faithful but Disinherited' was adopted by Sir Winston Churchill, the father of the Great Duke of Marlborough. He was a Cavalier who fought through the Civil War with great devotion on the Royalist side and was mercilessly plundered by the Roundheads when they won. At the Restoration he only recovered a portion of his estate, hence the motto which became that of Marlborough. I agree it is not very appropriate to a ship, and was not aware it had been adopted. You should not hesitate to change it if you think fit.

Captain Reginald Portal[1] to Winston S. Churchill

(Churchill papers: 2/272)

2 May 1936   Admiralty

Dear Mr Churchill,

Admiral Henderson asked me, last night, to prepare these notes on matters affecting the Navy's air services.

The notes have been somewhat hurriedly prepared but I shall be in London arriving the weekend and am available to give any further explanations, or information, that you may require.

My telephone no is Kens 6914.

Yours sincerely
Reginald Portal

[1] Reginald Henry Portal, 1894–1981. On active service, Royal Navy and Royal Naval Air Service, 1914–18 (DSC, 1916). Assistant Director, Naval Air Division, 1936. Commanded HMS *York*, 1939–41; HMS *Royal Sovereign*, 1941–2. Assistant Chief of the Naval Staff (Air), 1943–4. Flag Officer, Naval Air Stations, Australia, 1945. Naval Representative, Australian Joint Chiefs of Staff Committee, 1946–7. Flag Officer, Air (Home), 1947–51. Knighted, 1949. A brother of Marshal of the Royal Air Force, Viscount Portal of Hungerford.

Lord Londonderry[1] *to Winston S. Churchill*

(*Churchill papers: 2/266*)

4 May 1936

My dear Winston,

I read with amazement the figures which you gave in the House of Commons but I had no means of testing their correctness. I have however, just read in 'The Nineteenth Century' an article by Professor Bone[2] who deals very effectively with the whole matter.[3]

The whole European situation is so confused and the folly of our own Government has done so much harm that it is very difficult now to make any definite suggestion. I wish however, that I could get you to consider the German situation from a different angle. You may be quite right in your contention that war between Great Britain and Germany is inevitable. I do not take the same view, but I am not dwelling on that point now. The point is that

[1] Charles Stewart Henry Vane-Tempest-Stewart, 1878–1949. Educated at Eton and Sandhurst. As Viscount Castlereagh, Conservative MP for Maidstone, 1906–15. Succeeded his father as 7th Marquess of Londonderry, 1915. Served briefly on the western front as 2nd in Command, Royal Horse Guards, 1915. Under-Secretary of State for Air, 1920–1. Minister of Education and Leader of the Senate, Government of Northern Ireland, 1921–6. Returned to Westminster as First Commissioner of Works, 1928–9 and 1931; and as Secretary of State for Air and Lord Privy Seal, 1931–5. Churchill's second cousin.

[2] William Arthur Bone, 1871–1938. Lecturer in Chemistry, Owens College, Manchester, 1898–1905. Professor of Applied Chemistry, Leeds University, 1905–12. Chief Professor, and Head of the Department of Chemical Technology, Imperial College, London, 1912–36. Chairman of the British Association Committee on Fuel Economy, 1915–22. Consultant to the Government Fuel Research Board, 1917–18. Medalist of the Royal Society of Arts for his work on brown coals and lignites, 1922. Fellow of the Royal Society.

[3] In its May 1936 issue, the *Nineteenth Century and after* published an article by Professor William A. Bone, FRS, in which he wrote, of German rearmament: 'As an example of how palpably it is being exaggerated in certain quarters, it needs only to be recalled how in the House of Commons on March 10 last Mr Winston Churchill declared that "since the arrival of Herr Hitler in power three years ago the Germans have spent about £1,500,000,000 sterling upon warlike preparation directly or indirectly" and that in a single year (1935) from £600,000,000 to £800,000,000 was "spent on armaments in Germany". And on March 26 he said that he had been "occupied with the idea of the great wheels revolving and the great hammers descending day and night in Germany, making the whole industry of that country an arsenal, making the whole of that gifted and valiant population a great war machine." On April 20 *The Times* printed a letter from him to the same effect, claiming that the figures he had given were undisputed. Such being the Churchillian nightmare, it is perhaps not surprising that it scared Miss E. Rathbone, MP for the Combined English Universities, into inditing forthwith a letter to the *Manchester Guardian* in which she alleged as a "fact" that "Germany had spent £600,000,000 to £800,000,000 on rearmament in 1935 alone; perhaps £1,500,000,000 from 1933 to 1936, much of it secretly while the Disarmament Conference was still sitting", adding that the object thereof was "prestige" and "the annihilation of France". But when challenged by the writer to produce her evidence for such serious allegations, she had no more to say than that "I took my figures from Mr Churchill's speech on March 10 . . ." ' Churchill's figures, were, in Professor Bone's view (quoting Gilbert and Sullivan) 'a tale of Cock and Bull', which 'should be dismissed as gross exaggerations unworthy of credence'.

the Germans cannot risk a war for the best part of four years and it seems to me that our duty in those four years is to do everything in our power to create a situation in which war can be eliminated or at all events, postponed for a number of years. I never could convince you or Rothermere that there was no imminence of an invasion of Great Britain by Germany from the air. You have both been responsible by your speeches and writings for changing the attitude of the Government towards our defences and I certainly feel that we all owe you a debt of gratitude, but your success was due to your being able to frighten the people of this country by giving them wholly exaggerated figures. Rothermere obtained his figures from a source in Hungary which, when I was at the Ministry, we were fully aware of, and knew quite well, that their figures could always be divided by three.

I have been amazed about the lack of knowledge of Germany in this country, and at the same time that there is no desire on the part of leading men to find out any facts. I returned from Germany having seen all the leading people and having given our own Embassy in Berlin and our Air Attaché[1] information which came to them as a complete surprise and yet, when I returned to this country, there were only two people who were particularly anxious to see me and to discover what I had seen and the opinions which I had formed. These two were Maurice Hankey and Ellington[2] of the Air Ministry. Baldwin, who as he said was most anxious to see me, went on to say that as he had to make a Speech in ten days' time it was quite impossible for him to think of anything else. In the meantime, the Germans occupied the Demilitarised Zone, on which point I might perhaps have given some useful information but I was never asked for it, and I certainly had no intention of forcing myself on people who did not seem anxious to know anything about the German situation.

I would suggest that you should take an opportunity of going to Germany yourself and of seeing everything which the authorities are prepared to show you. I am quite convinced that with your professional knowledge of Service matters you will be able to form conclusions not at all wide of the mark, as I was myself. I returned fully aware of the developments which are going on in Germany, and which in three years time at the earliest and six years time at the latest, will make them the most powerful nation in the world,

[1] Group-Captain Don (see page 900, note 2).

[2] Edward Leonard Ellington, 1877–1967. 2nd Lieutenant, Royal Artillery, 1897; Major, 1914. Deputy Assistant Quartermaster-General, 1914–15. Lieutenant-Colonel, 1915. Major-General, Royal Air Force, 1918. Appointed by Churchill Director-General of Aircraft Production (later Supply) and Research, Air Ministry, 1919–21. Knighted, 1920. Air Vice-Marshal, Commanding the Royal Air Force, Middle East, 1922–3; India, 1923–6; Iraq, 1926–8. Air Officer Commanding-in-Chief, Air Defence of Britain, 1929–31. Chief of the Air Staff, 1933–7. Inspector-General, Royal Air Force, 1937–40.

assuming that no internal difficulties of an important nature hamper their progress.

I am bound to say however, that I regret what I may call the 'defeatist' attitude of this country in assuming that nothing can be done to avert hostilities between this country and Germany. When I saw Hitler in the course of a two hours' interview he spoke chiefly of the Communistic menace and I found myself in agreement with a great deal of what he said. His prophecies of the French Election[1] have been absolutely fulfilled, and I view with grave apprehension the Communistic influences, which have assumed such a large proportion in France. We in this country, owing to the fact that Communism is non-existent, take the view that Germany is exaggerating the Communistic danger, but I am quite sure that they are doing nothing of the kind and I deeply regret first of all, the Alliance which the French were forced to make with Russia owing to our foolish policy with regard to Sanctions, and the manner in which Russian influences are exercising their power over our Government.

I am viewing things at the moment from afar because our Government has done everything which I hoped it would not do and if I were to assume a critical attitude my methods might easily be impugned. I do look to you however, to play your part in the near future as your consistency in regard to re-armament, added to your many qualifications, has given you a very strong position in public opinion. I should like to get out of your mind what appears to be a strong anti-German obsession because all these great countries are required in the political settlement of the future and Great Britain can play a leading part if only we are not forced into ridiculous positions by people like Baldwin and Anthony Eden.

Yours ever,
Charlie

Air Ministry: memorandum
(Cabinet papers: 64/23)

4 May 1936

'NOTES ON SPEECH BY MR CHURCHILL
IN THE HOUSE OF COMMONS ON 4th MAY, 1936'

MR CHURCHILL
'All orders for stores and supplies for the FAA[2] serving in the ships very often

---

[1] Following the French General Election of 26 April 1936 (final Poll on May 3), Léon Blum became Prime Minister at head of a 'Popular Front' coalition of left wing Parties.
[2] The Fleet Air Arm.

get muddled and the articles themselves are almost invariably late. The movement of the Fleet does not correspond with the movement of the stores from one particular shore air base to another. For instance, longer time is required to make the air organisation conform ... There is now a Mediterranean cruiser which has its aeroplane administered from Singapore, while another in the same squadron has its aeroplane administered from Bermuda.'

AIR MINISTRY ANSWER

Instances of late arrival of stores may occasionally occur but the Air Ministry emphatically deny that the general standard of efficiency in this matter has been unsatisfactory. The fact that the Fleet may establish a new centre more quickly than stores could be moved from one shore base to another, might affect the supply of Naval equipment as much as that of air equipment. Actually, the circumstances of the recent Mediterranean crisis when the numbers of Fleet Air Arm aircraft in the Mediterranean had to be increased at very short notice, showed the advantage to the Fleet Air Arm of being within the same maintenance and supply organisation as the rest of the Air Force. On arrival of the aircraft carrying ships at Alexandria (where the Admiralty have no facilities) they were at once able to draw upon stores and facilities of the Depot maintained at Aboukir for the Royal Air Force in Egypt. An independent system of supply and maintenance for the Fleet Air Arm would make this pooling of resources in emergency much more difficult to operate, as differences in all forms of technical and other stores would inevitably follow.

It should be added that in the case of cruisers with catapult aircraft each ship is, as far as possible, supplied with three months' peace consumption of spares and stores. If the ship moves from one part of the world to another it can maintain its own aircraft for a period of three months which should be sufficient time for any further stores required to be sent out to its new base. The maintenance of the three months' stock on board depends, of course, upon the common sense of the personnel of the ship in demanding sufficiently far ahead. It may further be added that a reorganisation of the administration of the aircraft carried in capital ships and cruisers was agreed between the staffs of the Air Ministry and Admiralty in July 1935, the express object of which was to meet automatically any changes in the dispositions of the Fleet. This reorganisation was due to be brought into force on the 1st November 1935, but a few days before that date the Admiralty requested the Air Ministry to defer it because 'My Lords were of opinion that, during the present temporary distribution of catapult ships, the existing organisation should remain in force.' To this the Admiralty have adhered in spite of further suggestions from the Air Ministry that it should be brought into force.

2.

MR CHURCHILL

'A great aircraft carrier sent out in haste on emergency service to Alexandria had neither the proper numbers nor the proper type of wireless sets.'

AIR MINISTRY ANSWER

This charge clearly rests on statements made to Mr Churchill by some half informed individual. The aircraft carrier is obviously the 'Courageous' which was sent out by the Admiralty at short notice. All its aircraft were completely equipped with the standard type of wireless appropriate to their duties. The wireless sets referred to by Mr Churchill as the 'proper type' are a new general purpose type which were not due for completion and issue until some months after the time when the 'Courageous' went to the Mediterranean.

The Navy tend to expect that aircraft equipment of all kinds can be designed, ordered and purchased in a period much shorter than prudence and experience allow—(see remarks on Point 5 below).

3.

MR CHURCHILL

'Many of the aircraft (ie in a carrier sent to Alexandria) were supplied at the last minute without having even bomb racks fixed or the bombing release gear fitted.'

AIR MINISTRY ANSWER

This statement, again, is based on ignorance. The standard procedure in the Air Force from the earliest times is that whereby some items of equipment are not supplied fixed to the aircraft, but are installed by units to whom separate issue is made for that purpose. This is obviously convenient in the case of removable items such as bomb racks. In this case the numbers of the aircraft required had to be made up by drawing from reserve stocks. Such reserve stocks as were specific for the Fleet Air Arm were insufficient to make up the necessary numbers owing to the Admiralty (against the Air Ministry's advice) having refused to provide an adequate reserve. The remainder, therefore, were produced from the general reserves of the RAF at short notice, and most of them were not fitted with bomb racks or release gear. The Fleet Air Arm unit concerned, however, possessed the necessary items and if there was insufficient time to fit them before embarkation it was clearly the duty of the units to fit them as quickly as possible after embarkation, and this procedure was, presumably, carried out.

4.

MR CHURCHILL

'When an aircraft was sent to Alexandria—the necessary parts were not available to make certain engines serviceable for many months.'

AIR MINISTRY ANSWER

This presumably refers to the obsolescent Lion which was in course of normal replacement. As the type was going out of the Service in the very near future the supply of spare parts was deliberately cut down. A large number of complete engines were available and additional engines were therefore supplied in lieu of any deficiency of spare parts with the result that instead of a shortage, provision was made over and above the normal requirements of the unit in spare engines and spare parts.

5.

MR CHURCHILL

'When an aircraft carrier was sent to Alexandria—the aircraft of one of the squadrons which were of a new type were still so inefficient that they had to remain ashore and be replaced by others of an obsolescent type, and only half a squadron of these were ultimately available.'

AIR MINISTRY ANSWER

This obviously refers to the Shark Mark I aircraft supplied to 820 Squadron. These aircraft were the first of this type to be produced and were ordered for the Fleet Air Arm on the insistence of the Admiralty before they had completed their type trials at Martlesham and Felixstowe, or catapult trials, although the Admiralty were fully warned at a meeting of the Re-equipment Committee held at the Air Ministry on the 17th October 1934 of the risks which they ran. At that meeting it was pointed out to the Admiralty that the type had not been fully tested and that it was impossible for the Air Ministry to recommend its adoption at that time.

The withdrawal of the aircraft of this squadron through defects which had developed in the engine was due to the risks against which the Admiralty had thus been specifically warned. As a result the squadron had to revert temporarily to the type of aircraft with which it would have remained equipped but for the pressure from the Admiralty to equip it with a type that had not been fully tested. The statement that only half a squadron was available with which to replace this squadron is incorrect. In point of fact a squadron and a half of aircraft were supplied as replacement.

6.

MR CHURCHILL
'After that it seemed that there were no spare aircraft for the Fleet Air Arm in the country.'

AIR MINISTRY ANSWER
With reference to the statement that there were no spare aircraft for the Fleet Air Arm in the country, there existed the full numbers of reserve aircraft to the provision of which the Admiralty would agree. The Air Ministry had repeatedly pointed out to the Admiralty that their scale of reserve aircraft for the Fleet Air Arm was inadequate for even a minor emergency and had urged them to agree to it being increased. Despite constant pressure however it was not until after the 1935 crisis had arisen, when the Admiralty policy was exposed, that they agreed to make provision in the 1936-37 Estimates for the reserves considered by the Air Ministry to be the minimum requirements. Orders have already been placed for aircraft to meet this scale of reserves, but they will not of course be available for some time. On more than one occasion the reserve accepted by the Admiralty has proved to be inadequate in peace time, and the case referred to by Mr Winston Churchill emphasises their inadequacy at a time of emergency.

These considerations point to the desirability of some revision of the present arrangements whereby the Admiralty, and not the Air Ministry, is allowed to be the responsible authority for determining the scale of reserves, etc of the Fleet Air Arm. This is a matter on which the Admiralty should agree to accept the opinion of the Air Department.

Admiral of the Fleet Sir Ernle Chatfield[1] to Winston S. Churchill

(*Churchill papers: 2/272*)

5 May 1936
Private and Confidential

Dear Mr Churchill,
    I hope you will not mind my writing you a line of gratitude for your magnificent speech in the House about the Fleet Air Arm, a speech which

---

[1] Alfred Ernle Montacute Chatfield, 1873–1967. Entered Navy, 1886. Served at the battles of Heligoland (1914), Dogger Bank (1915) and Jutland (1916). Fourth Sea Lord, 1919–20. Knighted, 1919. Rear-Admiral, 1920. Assistant Chief of the Naval Staff, 1920–2. Third Sea Lord, 1925–8. Commander-in-Chief, Atlantic Fleet, 1929–31. Vice-Admiral, 1930. C-in-C

will not only be the greatest help to the Admiralty in this tiresome and difficult question, but one that will give the greatest happiness to the whole Navy. To have found a real champion of our cause, which we have been fighting for so many years in the House of Commons, and one whom, if I may say so with due respect, carries such tremendous weight in the country on such matters, is something for which we have long hoped, but for so long hoped in vain.

Sir Roger Keyes has done his best for us, but your advocacy is on an entirely different plane, and I think will compel the Government to hear the Admiralty case, which so far they have absolutely refused to do.

What is not understood, of course, is that not only is 'principle' involved, but the terrible consequences which we are now suffering under are a consequence of the old decisions; decisions which may have been the best that could have been made at the time, because we had no experience in the old days to show who was right in their forecast, the Admiralty or the Air Ministry; decisions which the experience of the last seven years has shown to be wholly unworkable and impracticable, loyally though the Admiralty and the whole Navy have tried to make the scheme work.

We are now in a position where we have not even got enough pilots in the Navy to man the miserable quota of aircraft which have been allotted to us. We have only been able to send out carriers to the Mediterranean properly equipped by stopping all the training of pilots in ordinary seamanlike duties in other ships which is laid down as essential in order to qualify for promotion. Still less have we been able to make any provision for pilots for the expansion of the Fleet Air Arm because the young officer will not come forward under the present conditions, which are so highly distasteful to him, and by absolute fiat of the Air Staff we have been refused our request to reinforce those officers by qualifying petty officers as pilots. However, I will not bother you with more on that matter. I will again repeat how grateful the Navy will be for your action.

May I, as I am writing to you, make two further points.

One about the destroyers. Nobody is more anxious to have a proper quota of destroyer tonnage than the Naval Staff, but I do not think it is realised that the destroyer problem which we shall be faced with in any future war will be a very different one from that which we had to face during the Great

---

Mediterranean, 1931–2. First Sea Lord, January 1933 to September 1938. Admiral of the Fleet, 1935. Created Baron, 1937. Privy Councillor, 1939. Minister for Co-ordination of Defence, 1939–40 (with a seat in the War Cabinet). Chairman, Civil Defence Honours Committee, 1940–6. Author of *The Navy and Defence* (1942), and *It might Happen Again* (1947). In 1937 he was elected to the Other Club (founded by Churchill and F. E. Smith in 1911).

War. As you know, of course, so well there are three principal roles for destroyers:—

(a) To be used in action to attack the enemy fleet; not as Stanley[1] said yesterday, unfortunately, to defend the Fleet against the enemy attack. The number of destroyers required for that purpose should properly be relative to the strength of destroyers that the enemy will have with its own fleet.

(b) Patrol work. Typically exemplified by the work of the Harwich Flotillas and the Dover Patrol.

(c) Escort and anti-submarine work.

Our problems have considerably changed. As regards (a) we can definitely measure what is a justifiable force in a well-balanced Fleet, considering finance, maintenance and personnel, for purely Fleet actions. As regards (b) here, again, there is some relativity to the numbers of the destroyer forces against which you may be patrolling. The more definite factor to determine is the factor (c) into which very important considerations enter. Our escort vessels, whether they be destroyers, sloops or small cruisers in narrow waters, have now a dual duty to protect our convoys against submarine attack and also against air attack.

Now, the submarine problem, as I have asked constantly to be explained in the House, is of an entirely different nature to what it was. Our anti-submarine methods are now so efficient, not, of course, 100 per cent efficiency, but I do not think that 80 per cent is too high an efficiency safely to place it at, that the number of destroyers and such like vessels that we shall require in a future war in the Channel, in the North Sea, and in the Mediterranean against submarine attack is greatly reduced. This is the combined experience of both the submarine and anti-submarine officers. Let me give you an example.

We are now facing Italy in the Mediterranean. Italy has a large number of submarines, far more, for instance, than Germany will have in the Anglo-German Naval Treaty and far bigger ships also, yet we consider that the five flotillas that we have been keeping in the Mediterranean will be able to crush the Italian submarine forces and drive them into port, and the experience those submarines will have will be so alarming to them that we believe it will demoralise them. The officers in charge of the Anti-Submarine School, Portland, and who are necessarily enthusiastic about our highly developed skill in this matter, hold the opinion that whereas we required something like 3,000 vessels in the late war to deal with submarine attack on trade, not more than 20 per cent of that number would be required to

[1] The Parliamentary Secretary, Admiralty (see page 1027, note 2).

carry out similar duties in future. Of course, I have to steer between these figures.

The Mediterranean problem you will, no doubt, immediately observe is not a true picture of what may happen, because in the Mediterranean in the case of war with Italy we have not necessarily to consider anti-submarine attack on merchant ships, at any rate in that sea, because we can deflect our trade elsewhere. Nevertheless, the intensive anti-submarine training and the tests that we have carried out in the last nine months in the Mediterranean have been very valuable and convincing, and the confidence of our destroyer Captains is very impressive.

But we have another problem, and that is anti-aircraft defence. Of course, it is almost incredible that aircraft attack on merchant ships can be carried out without not only offending all international law, but also offending all neutral Powers, because no aircraft can discern whether a ship disguised under a neutral flag is British or not, nor can aircraft operate at night in such work. If, however, such unrestricted attack is attempted, as it well may be by a desperate enemy, I do not think that they are going to find it a profitable operation; even one anti-aircraft gun in a merchant ship will keep the aircraft at a height, and the chance of destroying that merchant ship by a single bomb is going to be very small; even with highly trained pilots, whose life has been devoted to attacking ships over the sea, it is unlikely to be the case; but we must also be ready to meet a much heavier scale of air attack on convoys and ships, and therefore we must have vessels escorting our convoys so adequately equipped with anti-aircraft batteries that they also will be able to drive the aircraft up to such heights as to make the attack unfruitful and unprofitable. I am convinced that we can do this, indeed we *must* do it. Unless the Admiralty can ensure that our convoys can get to this country, not only over the oceans, but through the narrow waters, despite unrestricted air attack and submarine attack, then we are doomed, and if there is any doubt as to the Admiralty's ability to fulfil this responsibility then the whole nation and scientists ought to be working on the subject to see how this country and the Empire is to be saved.

I am sure you will not assume from what I have said above that I am happy about the existing situation. I am not. We have years of arrears to overtake. Anti-aircraft guns and anti-aircraft ships cannot be immediately produced by voting money, and for the next three or four years we are bound to be undergoing horrible risks, but we are fully alive to our responsibilities.

One other word about the battleship. Every country in the world, however air-minded, such as, shall we say, Italy and Germany, has come to the conclusion that battleships are essential. This country alone is hanging back mainly due to the fear that has been put into the mind of the public, in the

Press, that the day of the Navy is over, that we can defend this country and the Empire much cheaper and better by aircraft. I wonder if you know that in a time of peace for the cost of construction and maintenance of a battleship during her twenty-six years' life only forty aircraft can be maintained. This is a figure in which the Air Ministry are in agreement with us.

The Battleship Committee, as you know, is pursuing its labours. No one regretted the terms of reference more than myself. I should have liked them to have been complete and unlimited, and I should, above all things, have liked that you should have been one of the members of the committee, because I would far rather convince you of the absolute soundness of the Admiralty case than any one else. The committee we have is a very nice one, but of course it is not technical. It has a judicial chief,[1] and this is of great value because it enables our evidence to be judged on its merits, quite apart from the personalities who give that evidence. We have a complete case, indeed if we had not, and if we were presuming to build battleships without definite proof that we were wise in doing so, we should properly be driven out of office, and I should be hung in Trafalgar Square! But the fifteen years' exhaustive experiments that we have carried out since 1920, practically conceived and scientifically carried out with our scientific staff, our naval technical staff and our naval constructive staff, have given us ample facts on which to base the vulnerability of our battleships, not only to gunfire and torpedo attack, but also to bomb attack.

It will be a great mistake for Parliament to imagine that we believe that battleships can, or should, be made unsinkable or invulnerable. We are far from having any such crude idea. Ships, on the contrary, are meant to be sunk and unless battleships could be sunk no naval victory could ever be won. Our policy is not to build ships that cannot be sunk but to build ships so efficient and so strong, and with such highly trained personnel, that we shall sink the enemy battlefleet, whether by shell or torpedo or bomb, more rapidly than he will be able to destroy ours. That is the only fighting policy on which the Navy can rest. It is the basis of the policy that I have laid down here.

If the committee merely reports that they are satisfied by the Admiralty evidence on the terms of reference it will be highly unsatisfactory to me, and it would only lead, as I have said to them, to further questions and further discussions in the House and in the Press, discussions which are basically undesirable because they weaken our position internationally, and there is a feeling, as I am well aware, growing up in certain other countries that Britain has lost confidence in her Fleet, and that therefore they can do things which they would not have done before.

[1] General Sir Hugh Elles (see page 174, note 2), Master General of Ordnance, War Office, and the Chairman of the Vulnerability of Capital Ships Committee.

I very much hope that you will come before the Committee yourself, indeed, I should be so glad if the evidence given by the Admiralty could be placed at your disposal. It is essential, in my opinion, that the Committee should be able to completely assure Parliament, not only on the terms of reference, but that the Admiralty are a Department of State which can be trusted, that their conclusions are sound, that they are an alert Department, and that the reflections which have been made on them for over such a long period are unjustified and unwise.

Perhaps one day I may have an opportunity of discussing any of these matters with you personally, nothing would give me greater pleasure than to do so.

Yours sincerely
Ernle Chatfield

Herbert Williams[1] to Winston S. Churchill
(*Churchill papers: 2/280*)

5 May 1936

Dear Churchill,

Referring to our chat last night the man I met at dinner last night was Mr Allan G. Clark,[2] Plessey, Ilford. Telephone No Ilford 3040.

Mr Clark is a Contractor to the War Office, and I think the other two Defence Departments, for shells bombs etc. He recently had an opportunity of visiting some munition factories in Germany and from what he told me last night of the rate of output which the Germans are obtaining with the use of new methods I thought you would find it of very great interest to get Mr Clark to come and see you. He would be very willing to give you any information.

Yours sincerely,
Herbert Williams

His information was startling.

[1] Herbert Geraint Williams, 1884–1954. Educated at the University of Liverpool. Electrical and Marine Engineer. Secretary, Machine Tool Trades Association, 1911–28. Secretary, Machine Tool Department, Ministry of Munitions, 1917–18. Conservative MP for Reading, 1924–9; for South Croydon, 1932–45; for Croydon East, 1950–4. Parliamentary Secretary, Board of Trade, 1928–9. Knighted, 1939. Member of the House of Commons Select Committee on Expenditure, 1939–44. Chairman, London Conservative Union, 1939–48; National Union of Conservatives and Unionist Associations, 1948. Created Baronet, 1953.

[2] Allan George Clark, 1898–1962. Known as 'A.G.'. Educated at Felsted School Essex. Volunteered for service in France before his seventeenth birthday; wounded at Cambrai; 2nd Lieutenant, Royal Flying Corps, 1918. Established the Plessey Company, a small contract shop with a staff of six, in 1920, and built it up into a substantial manufacturer of radios, telephones and electronic equipment, with 40,000 employees; Joint Managing Director 1925; Chairman and Managing Director from 1946 until his death. Member of Council, Society of British Aircraft Constructors, 1960. Knighted, 1961.

Winston S. Churchill to Lord Weir

(*Weir papers*)

6 May 1936   11 Morpeth Mansions
Private

My dear Weir,

Thank you so much for your very kind letter, and I am glad you think my speech upon the budget was helpful. I always welcome any interchange of opinion with you because we both had opportunities to learn in a strenuous school. Will you forgive me if, upon the kindness of your letter, I venture to address you very frankly?

You are being laden with vast responsibilities. Everywhere use is being made of your name. Ministers quote it in public and in private. Are you quite sure you are right in lending all your reputation to keeping this country in a state of comfortable peace routine? All I hear makes me believe that the whole life and industry of Germany is organised for war preparation. Our efforts compared to theirs are puny. As to the Air, you know my views. As to the Army, we have none; and can get neither men nor, except very slowly, weapons. Even the Fleet, if there is more delay, may reach a relative position where the future will lie with the enormous gun-and-armour plants of Germany. What about German submarines? It is now two years since I explained to the House of Commons how I had ordered in the Great War from Schwab[1] the eighteen submarines which were made by components, and were actually, in consequence of neutrality objection, put on the rail in sections from Bethlehem for a Canadian yard, and yet delivered punctually.

I know how invaluable and disinterested you are in all your work for the Government. Would it not be a melancholy thing if in a year you felt that its main results had been to delay and paralyse till too late the supreme effort which is needed. At present you seem to me to have major responsibilities, no doubt with a great deal of influence, but without power. This is not fair to yourself and to your friends, or to your country. However, if you are contented to bear this load, I can only hope and pray that your judgment has not been deflected by detail and good nature from the true proportion of affairs.

With every good wish,
Believe me,
Yours vy sincerely,
Winston S. Churchill

[1] Charles Michael Schwab, 1862–1939. President, Carnegie Steel Corporation, 1897–1903. Chairman, Bethlehem Steel Corporation, 1903–39. Coming to England on board the *Olympic*, October 1914, he witnessed the sinking of the *Audacious:* on reaching London he pledged the

Winston S. Churchill to Keith Feiling

(*Churchill papers: 8/532*)

6 May 1936

I send you herewith your cheque.

I am so glad you are relieved in your anxiety about your daughter.

I like Mr Deakin very much and find him much more lively and sensible than Wheldon. I hope he will be able to help me. We shall see.

I find it a very great difficulty to finish Marlborough, with all this political distraction. Still I hope to accomplish my task.

Winston S. Churchill to Lord Londonderry

(*Churchill papers: 2/266*)

6 May 1936
Confidential

It is always very nice to hear from you. I certainly do not take the view that a war between England and Germany is inevitable. I fear very gravely however unless something happens to the Nazi regime in Germany there will be a devastating war in Europe, and it may come earlier than you expect. The only chance of stopping it is to have a union of nations, all well-armed and bound to defend each other, and thus confront the Nazi aggression with over-whelming force. In this way there is the best chance that an internal revolution rather than an external explosion may avert an ever-growing danger.

My figures about German rearmament have been collected by high authorities and they are not in principle contested by the Government. I have no doubt they will be contradicted as German propaganda in this country is very strong.

About the air. You ought not to confuse the moderate and precise figures given by me two years ago, and now proved to be understatements, with the extravagant figures which the Daily Mail published. You are, I am sure, wrong in supposing that anything I say, or said, made the slightest difference to the purblind complacency of the Government. What woke them up was a series of horrible shocks, and Intelligence from every quarter streaming in.

---

support of his factories to the allied cause. In charge of America's 'Shipbuilding Crusade', 1917–18; as Director-General of the Emergency Fleet Corporation, which built 495 ships in 16 months, including the 12,000 ton *Defiance* built in 38 days, and the 12,000 ton *Invincible* built in 24 days. Hon Vice-President of the Iron and Steel Institute of Great Britain, 1926–39.

You are also mistaken in supposing that I have an anti-German obsession. British policy for four hundred years has been to oppose the strongest power in Europe by weaving together a combination of other countries strong enough to face the bully. Sometimes it is Spain, sometimes the French monarchy, sometimes the French Empire, sometimes Germany. I have no doubt who it is now. But if France set up to claim the over-lordship of Europe, I should equally endeavour to oppose them. It is thus through the centuries we have kept our liberties and maintained our life and power.

I hope you will not become too prominently identified with the pro-German view. If I read the future aright Hitler's government will confront Europe with a series of outrageous events and ever-growing military might. It is events which will show our dangers, though for some the lesson will come too late.

I am amused at what you write about Baldwin. I think him fatally smitten in prestige and character by the Hoare-Laval episode. Considering his mediocre intellect he has had a very fair run. I do not suppose it will last much longer. As Arthur Balfour[1] used to say 'This is a singularly ill-contrived world, but not so ill-contrived as that.'

Let us see you when you come back to London.

PS. Professor Bone is a notorious Pro-German and his figures in no way weaken my faith in mine.

Winston S. Churchill to Lord Linlithgow

(*Churchill papers: 2/263*)

7 May 1936

. . . All the reports of your debut in India which have reached home are most gratifying to your friends and especially the note you have struck about being 'the peasants' Viceroy'. I have always been so sorry for these poor people. 'Famine is the horizon of the Indian villager, insufficient food the foreground.' What a task you have, and how many hopes are centred upon your success.

The collapse of Abyssinia and its effective conquest by Italy end a humiliating chapter in British foreign policy. It must also be made to end the sanction

---

[1] Arthur James Balfour, 1848–1930. Educated at Eton and Trinity College, Cambridge. Conservative MP, 1874–85; 1885–1906; 1906–22 (City of London). Prime Minister, 1902–5. First Lord of the Admiralty. 1915–16. Foreign Secretary, 1916–19. Lord President of the Council, 1919–22 and 1925–9. Created Earl, 1922.

quarrel between Britain and Italy. From this point of view the speedy cessation of the war is good for us. It will enable I expect, after a little while when
the bitter disappointment of many good people at home has faded, the
Stresa front to be reconstituted.[1] Certainly I expect developments have been
very unwelcome to Hitler.

Winston S. Churchill to Herbert G. Williams

(Churchill papers: 2/280)

9 May 1936

I shall be at the House on Thursday after questions. Why do you not bring
Mr Allan Clark to have a talk with me in the downstairs Smoking-room, or
in a private room, at 4 o'clock.

Desmond Morton to Winston S. Churchill

(Churchill papers: 2/266)

9 May 1936   Committee of Imperial Defence

Dear Winston,

Many thanks for letting me see Mr Pastfield's letter[2] which contains some
interesting points and suggestions. Surely we may take it, however, that even
if insufficient experiment is being carried out to compare the reaction of
artillery ammunition and air bombs on a modern battleship, the Admiralty
have carried out pretty exhaustive experiments on the penetrating effect of
modern Naval gun-fire. I am sure they have not published all their experiments.

In this connection, I am not sure that all is well with British armour-plate
in comparison with some continental products. There is a story of three
armour-plates being subjected to test under identical conditions by the
Dutch not so long ago. The plate from Vickers was smashed. The Dutch
plate from Siderius was badly damaged but the Bofors-Krupp plate was
undamaged.

[1] At the Stresa Conference, held in Italy between 11 and 14 April 1935, Britain, France
and Italy agreed to maintain the independence of Austria. No mention was made at Stresa
of the growing Italian pressures on Abyssinia. With the Italian invasion of Abyssinia in
October 1935, and the imposition of sanctions on Italy by the League of Nations, there had
been a rapid and severe worsening of Anglo-Italian relations, and considerable public hostility towards Italy.

[2] Not found.

The German who wrote the other letter, returned, is an amiable lunatic and it would take Drs Freud and Adler working together to understand what he means.

I take this opportunity also of returning the Review of 'Hitler's Motorisierte Stossarmee' from Lord Rothermere. This is the book I commented on to you the other day. Mrs Pearman will have the letter. The book may have its uses but is not nearly so good as the sister publication on the German Air Force, the information in which is far more accurate.

The copied published statistics in the present book are accurate enough but the interpretation is bad. The author is quite at sea about the German Army, actually giving them less armoured troops than they already possess, talking of Cavalry Divisions which the Germans have done away with and so on.[1] It would be dangerous, therefore, to rely on this book.

Yours very sincerely,
Desmond Morton

PS. The changed attitude of the Press which now reports you at considerable length is satisfactory & significant.

Lord Londonderry to Winston S. Churchill
(Churchill papers: 2/254)

9 May 1936

My dear Winston,

Thank you very much indeed for your letter. I was very glad to read what you say.

To-day I have read a speech of yours about Baldwin.[2] I suggest not hitting the poor little man too hard because it will evoke a wave of sympathy which he will be able to stimulate by platitudinous broadcasts.

With regard to the Nazi regime, I am not sure that I agree with you. Whatever the regime, if it creates efficient organisation, I feel a certain amount of admiration for it, and that is why I respect Hitler, Mussolini and

[1] But the last German Cavalry Division was not disbanded until December 1941, having served both in the Western campaign of 1940 and in the Soviet Union in 1941.

[2] Speaking in the House of Commons on 6 May 1936, immediately after Lord Cranborne (Under-Secretary of State for Foreign Affairs), during the Foreign Affairs debate on Abyssinia, Churchill declared: 'Lord Cranborne boasted of our leadership. Where had we led? Everyone knew how lamentable that leadership had been. The Prime Minister ought to have spoken in this debate. He was the man who had all the power, and one could not have the power without having the responsibility. He had changed his Foreign Secretaries as he chose, and sometimes he had two at once. . . . The idea of one man taking all the power to himself and not facing the realities of public discussion in debate in the House of Commons was one which had already produced great injury to our affairs and if continued must produce grave demoralization.'

Stalin. I should not like to live under these regimes myself because they are the negation of the freedom which we have learnt through the ages to claim and to enjoy, but still they do constitute an organisation and I feel that if the Nazi regime in Germany is destroyed, Germany will go Communist and we shall find a lining up of Communism between France, Germany and Russia and the menace of Communism, which people here are inclined to under-rate, the most powerful policy in the world. I am bound to say that I view the French Elections with grave apprehension, and this policy, which I am glad to see you condemned, of continuing sanctions is supported by Russia with the hope of bringing about a war in Europe.

As to sanctions themselves, I detest them altogether. The only sanction with which I have any sympathy is oil and it would have to be imposed by the united force of a really powerful League of Nations, which would mean that it would never have actually to come into being, but other sanctions are just as bad as a blockade or bombing from the air of women and children as they affect the life of the people and it is indirectly through these means that the sanctionists hope to compel an aggressor to capitulate.

I shall be in London at the end of May and will take the earliest opportunity of having a talk with you.

My last word is to go easy with Baldwin otherwise you will give him renewed strength as the British are very sentimental and sympathetic.

Yours ever,
Charley

Winston S. Churchill: memorandum[1]
(Churchill papers: 25/8)

10 May 1936

AERIAL MINES

At the first Meeting of the Committee which I attended, I pressed for work to be done for Aerial Mines. I understand that Professor Lindemann raised the same question at the Meetings of the Scientific Sub-Committee in July and that he wrote to Mr Tizard[2] on the 1st August pointing out how

[1] Printed as memorandum ADR 48 of the Committee of Imperial Defence, Sub-Committee on Air Defence Research, and circulated to all the members of the Sub-Committee, marked 'Secret', on 2 June 1936.

[2] Henry Thomas Tizard, 1885–1959. Educated at Westminster School, Magdalen College, Oxford and Imperial College. Lecturer in Natural Science, Oxford, 1911–21. Royal Garrison Artillery, 1914; Royal Flying Corps, 1915–18. Lieutenant-Colonel, and Assistant Controller of Experiments and Research, RAF, 1918–19. Permanent Secretary, Department of Scientific and Industrial Research, 1927–9. Rector of Imperial College, 1929–42. Chairman, Aeronautical Research Committee, 1933–43. Knighted, 1937. Member of Council, Ministry of Aircraft Production, 1941–3. President of Magdalen College, Oxford, 1942–6. Chairman, Advisory Council on Scientific Policy and Defence Research Policy, 1946–52.

urgent it was, and asking him to get experiments put in hand before the vacation.

Nothing was done, and Professor Lindemann raised the matter again at the first subsequent Meeting of the Scientific Sub-Committee on October 9th.

At the next Meeting on November 5th he again urged that work should be done on the amount of explosive required, and on the investigation of what happened if an aeroplane ran into a wire on which a weight was suspended.

All sorts of difficulties were raised concerning the danger of such experiments, but on December 4th it was stated that the Air Force would make the experiments, using fishing-lines instead of wire and small fragile vessels filled with paint in place of explosives.

At the next Meeting of the Scientific Sub-Committee on February 3rd it was stated that no experiments had been carried out, since the Authorities were afraid of damaging the machines, but that they were negotiating for the purchase of a secondhand machine on which the experiments might be tried.

At the same Meeting it was stated that some experiments had been tried at Shoeburyness on the effect of detonating high explosive charges against aeroplane wings, but that these experiments had not been very successful.

A few days afterwards Professor Lindemann wrote to Mr Wimperis[1] asking that the high explosive should be put into tubes 18 inches or so long, in order to spread the effect of the detonation when it hit the wing.

At the next Meeting of the Scientific Sub-Committee on February 25th it was stated that a few preliminary flying experiments had been made which seemed to shew that the mine would not be drawn up against the leading edge of the wing, but would swing round and hit the wing broadside on. It was also stated that fresh tests with the explosives would be made at Shoeburyness on March 13th.

Professor Lindemann attended the experiments at Shoeburyness which were actually carried out on March 12th. He found the authorities had not been told of the suggestion to put the explosive into tubes, but even without this it appeared clear that a wing would be so much damaged by the explosion of a four-ounce charge that the aeroplane would be effectively put out of action. He asked for further experiments to be carried out with the tubes, and on March 13th wrote a letter to the Superintendent of Experi-

[1] Harry Egerton Wimperis, 1876–1960. Engineer and inventor: inventor of the Wimperis Accelerometer (1909), the Gyro-Turn Indicator (1910), and the Course Setting Sight for Aircraft (1917). Experimental Officer, Royal Navy Air Service, 1915–18 and Royal Air Force, 1918–24. Director of Scientific Research at the Air Ministry, 1925–37. Member of the Executive Committee of the National Physical Laboratory, 1931–7. President of the Royal Aeronautical Society, 1934–8. Member of the Atomic Energy Study Group, Chatham House, 1946–50.

ments suggesting that the design of a suitable fuse should immediately be put in hand, and proposing what seemed to him a possible form of fuse.

Up till now (May 10th), it appears, no further experiments have been made on the explosives, though it is hoped that further work on the flying is being done.

As to the fuse, Professor Lindemann received a letter from the Superintendent of the Experiments saying that this question would be considered when the flying experiments had been completed.

Winston S. Churchill to Sir Austen Chamberlain

(Churchill papers: 2/272)

10 May 1936

I send you the enclosed letter from the First Sea Lord[1] which I am sure will interest you, also a copy of the letter of Air Vice-Marshal Swann[2] published in The Times.[3] Swann was the ablest Naval Officer I had promoted to Captain, far above his seniority in the days when we were making the Royal Naval Air Service. I have never seen him since. His conclusions are based upon previous knowledge. Thirdly I enclose a letter from another Officer who has twenty-five years experience, but whom I do not remember personally. I hope you will agree that we ought now to press, by whatever is thought to be the best method, for the speedy transference of the Fleet Air Arm to Admiralty control. . . .

Lindemann is with me here and he is preparing the case against the slow progress of all the experiments he wishes to have made for our defence against

[1] Admiral of the Fleet Sir Ernle Chatfield (see page 135, note 1).

[2] Oliver Swann, 1878–1948. Entered the Royal Navy, 1891; Post Captain, 1914. Commanded the Fleet aircraft carrier HMS *Campania*, 1915–17. Transferred to the RAF, 1919. Air Member for Personnel, Air Ministry, 1922. Air Officer Commanding Middle East, 1924. Knighted, 1924. Retired, 1926. Air Officer Commanding Halton, 1939. Air Liaison Officer, North Midland Region, 1940–3.

[3] On 7 May 1936 *The Times* published a letter from Air Vice-Marshal (retired) Oliver Swann, who wrote that he was encouraged by the report in *The Times* of Churchill's 'admirable criticism of the present dual control of the Fleet Air Arm' (House of Commons, 4 May 1936), 'to offer a few lines in support of his plea'. The existing 'chaotic state of dual control' over naval air which had been forseen by those at the Admiralty 'advising on air matters from 1912 to 1914', and the formation of the Royal Naval Air Service had been an attempt to avoid that chaos. Yet in 1936 'convoying of merchant ships and therefore safeguarding our food supplies, anti-submarine and anti-mining operations, guarding our coasts from attacks by ships are all under dual control, for the aircraft needed for these purposes, generally at short notice, are under Air Ministry control as they will generally emanate from shore bases, while the ships doing the same work are under naval control'. Such a situation, Swann warned, 'will not stand the test of war'.

Aircraft. I hope to let you have this early next week. I am proposing myself to present it to Hankey and Swinton as soon as possible, and to ask for a Meeting of our Committee to discuss it. If no satisfaction is given, it will be necessary to bring things to a head, both from within and from without.

I do not think that Grigg[1] and I will be able to present more than the heads of the case about re-armament to you when we meet on Tuesday night, but I have prepared a sheaf of questions which touch a number of crucial points which might be attacked from day to day.

Winston S. Churchill to the Editor of 'The Times' [2]

(*Churchill papers: 2/254*)

11 May 1936

Lord Hugh Cecil tells us that a long time must elapse before there can be any attitude of friendliness on our part towards Italy. He also tells us that we cannot have any friendly feelings towards France. As a devout Churchman and staunch Conservative he naturally cannot nourish any sympathy for the Soviet Republic. As a firm supporter of the League of Nations he must resist strongly the lawless aggression of Japan against China in defiance of the League. As a supporter of the Government he is committed to the Staff arrangements to protect France and Belgium against an unprovoked attack by Germany; nor as a champion of British individualism can he avoid disliking the Nazi regime and its persecutions. 'There is none that doeth good, no not one.'

It must be very painful to a man of Lord Hugh Cecil's natural benevolence and human charity to find so many of God's children wandering simultaneously so far astray. It is even more disconcerting to reflect that these five nations are also the five most warlike and heavily armed peoples in the world: that they are arming night and day; that except France they are all ruled by dictatorships, and, again except France, all are inspired by military aims. We on the other hand who are advised to cultivate such comprehensive antipathies are unhappily very feebly armed and unwarlike, and several years must pass before our weakness can be repaired. If meanwhile these ill-behaved but well-prepared and possibly quite tough nations should reciprocate our feelings of unfriendliness and disapproval, and come to some

---

[1] Sir Edward Grigg (see page 51, note 2).

[2] This was Churchill's second brush with Lord Hugh Cecil in the correspondence columns of *The Times*. On 16 April 1936 *The Times* had published a letter from Cecil criticizing the 'half-hearted actions of France about the Italian–Abyssinian war'. Churchill's reply had been printed in *The Times* of April 20 (see pages 101–3 of this volume).

common understanding among themselves, we might find it rather difficult to keep body and soul together.

In these circumstances I would venture to suggest to my noble friend, whose gifts and virtues I have all my life admired, that some further refinement is needed in the catholicity of his condemnation. It might be a good thing, for instance, for him to put his censures down in order of priority, and then try to think a little less severely of the two least bad, or least likely to endanger our own safety. The problem would then simplify itself; and the picture would acquire the charm of light and shade.

This is the more necessary because without at least three of these powerful nations actively associated with the League of Nations, that institution would afford no hope or refuge to all the small, weak or poorly armed states and peoples of Europe, and the reign of law and justice would be blasted at its birth.

Brigadier Pakenham-Walsh[1] to Winston S. Churchill

(*Churchill papers: 8/529*)

11 May 1936

Dear Mr Churchill,

I am sorry I was not able to answer your letter of 6th May before. It arrived while I was away on an army exercise, and then being the weekend I was unable to get any typing done and so I had to struggle with the diary of Malplaquet on my small machine. I only had a rough copy of the one I sent you about the time of our visit abroad. I must apologize for rather a messy job. . . .

I am pretty busy these days with my new Commander-in-Chief General Ironside,[2] and trying to organize training of troops short of men and equip-

[1] Ridley Pakenham Pakenham-Walsh, 1888–1966. Educated at Cheltenham College and the Royal Military Academy, Woolwich. 2nd Lieutenant, Royal Engineers, 1908; on active service at the Dardanelles, 1915–18 (Military Cross, despatches). British Representative, International Commission, Teschen, 1919–20. Instructor in Tactics, School of Military Engineering, 1923–6. Lieutenant-Colonel, 1928. Colonel, 1932. Assistant Adjutant-General, War Office, 1934–5. Brigadier, General Staff, Eastern Command, 1935–9. Major-General, June 1939. Commandant, School of Military Engineering, and Inspector, Royal Engineers, 1939. Engineer-in-Chief, British Expeditionary Force, 1939–40 (wounded, despatches). General Officer Commanding, Northern Ireland District, 1940–1; Salisbury Plain District, 1942. Lieutenant-General, 1941. Controller-General of Army Provision, 1943–6. Vice-Chairman, Harlow New Town Development Corporation, 1948–9.

[2] William Edmund Ironside, 1880–1959. 2nd Lieutenant, Royal Artillery, 1899. On active service in South Africa, 1899–1902. Major, 1914. Staff Officer, 4th Canadian Division, 1916–17. Took part in the battles for Vimy Ridge and Passchendaele. Commandant of the Machine

ment, and whose organization necessarily varies continuously owing to a sudden wave of the modernization which we have awaited so long. However I am managing to find time to press on steadily with my notes for 1710 and on the war in Spain.

You too judging by the Press have your hands pretty full.

Ralph Wigram to Winston S. Churchill
(Churchill papers: 2/273)

12 May 1936   Foreign Office

Dear Mr Churchill,

Thank you for letting me see those papers about Italy which are very interesting.

Here are the extracts from 'Mein Kampf'—they are worth reading.

I'm sorry now I missed out the following quotation from p 252 of the German edition.

'They started in this matter from the very wise principle that, if one tells big lies, people will always believe a part . . . something always remains of the most impudent lies.'

One ought to remember this when one reads Hitler's recent historical efforts.

Yours sincerely,
Ralph Wigram

Sir Henry Strakosch to Winston S. Churchill
(Churchill papers: 2/274)

12 May 1936

My dear Churchill,

Thank you for your note of the 9th. Needless to say, I am sorry you cannot manage to come to the Tuesday Club meeting to-morrow.

Gun Corps School, France, 1918. Brigadier-General commanding the 99th Infantry Brigade, 1918. Major-General commanding the Allied Troops, Archangel, October 1918–October 1919. Knighted, 1919. Head of the British Military Mission to Hungary, 1920. Commanded the Ismid Force, Turkey, 1920; the North Persian Force, 1920–1. Lieutenant-General, 1931. Quartermaster-General, India, 1933–6. General, 1935. General Officer Commanding-in-Chief, Eastern Command, 1936–8. Governor and Commander-in-Chief, Gibraltar, 1938–9. Head of the British Military Mission to Poland, August 1939. Chief of the Imperial General Staff, 1939–40. Commander in-Chief, Home Forces, May 1940. Field-Marshal, 1940. Created Baron, 1941. On 4 July 1938 Churchill wrote of Ironside, to Sir Abe Bailey: 'He is the finest military brain in the Army at the present time.'

On my return from Geneva, my attention was drawn to an article by Sir Arnold Wilson,[1] appearing in the 'Evening Standard' of the 5th instant, in which he tries to refute some of the points made by you in your article on 'How Germany is Arming.' It should not be too difficult to show up many of his arguments as fallacious, and I hope to let you have a short note on the subject in a day or so.

Yours very sincerely,
H. Strakosch

Sir Henry Strakosch: notes
(Churchill papers: 2/277)

13 May 1936

Sir Arnold Wilson's article is so deliberately misleading and confusing that one is drawn to the conclusion that it was probably inspired by the German Authorities. While at no point criticising the arguments put forward by Mr Churchill,[2] Sir Arnold endeavours to detract from the former's conclusions by carefully citing statistics which give but part of the story.

[1] Arnold Talbot Wilson, 1884–1940. Educated at Clifton and Sandhurst (Sword of Honour). 2nd Lieutenant, 1903; Indian Army, 1904. Entered the Indian Political Department, 1909; on duty in Persia, 1907–13, guarding the Ahwaz oilfields. British Commissioner, Turko-Persian Frontier Commission, 1914. Deputy Chief Political Officer with the Indian Expeditionary Force, Mesopotamia, 1915; Deputy Civil Commissioner, 1916. Acting Civil Commissioner and Political Resident, Persian Gulf, 1918–20. Knighted, 1920. Persian Gulf representative of the Anglo-Persian Oil Company, 1921–32. Author of *Loyalties* (1930) and *A Clash of Loyalties* (1931). Chairman of the Industrial Health Research Board, 1926–33; of the Home Office Committee on Structural Precautions Against Air Attack, 1936–8. Editor, *Nineteenth Century and After*, 1924–38. Conservative MP for Hitchin from 1933 until his death. A member of the Anglo-German Fellowship, and leading advocate of Anglo-German reconciliation after Hitler came to power in 1933. On the outbreak of war, he volunteered for active service in the RAF, and enlisted as a tail-gunner. He spoke eloquently in the defence of Chamberlain in the debate of 8/9 May 1940. He was killed in action over France on 31 May 1940, when his aeroplane crashed behind German lines.

[2] In his article, 'How Germany is Arming', published in the *Evening Standard* on 1 May 1936 (see page 122, note 1). In the course of this article Churchill wrote: 'Since 1932 German imports of iron ore have increased 309 per cent, kieselguhr by 145 per cent, bauxite by 153 per cent, asbestos by 197 per cent, nickel by 64 per cent, manganese by 273 per cent, wolfram ore by 345 per cent, chrome ore by 127 per cent, rubber by 64 per cent, and graphite by 220 per cent. All this has gone into making the most destructive war weapons and war arrangements that have ever been known: and there are four or five millions of active, intelligent, valiant Germans engaged in these processes, working, as General Goering has told us, night and day.' Churchill had ended his article: 'Surely these are facts which ought to bulk as large in ordinary peaceful peoples' minds as horse racing, a prize fight, a murder trial or nineteen-twentieths of the current newspaper bill of fare. What is it all for? Certainly it is not all for fun. Something quite extraordinary is afoot. All the signals are set for danger. The red lights flash through the gloom. Let peaceful folk beware. It is a time to pay attention and to be well prepared.'

Sir Arnold's argument hinges on his statement that 'to spend £1,500 millions in three years would involve an immense increase in employment and a vast dislocation of the German iron and steel industry'. He endeavours to disprove the enormous increase in employment and in iron and steel production since Hitler came into power by a careful selection of statistics.

He quotes a fall in unemployed from 4,000,000 in December 1933 to 2,500,000 in December 1935. But why choose December 1933 when Hitler came into power in March 1933? (The fact that the seasonal increase in unemployment in December 1935 was particularly severe may provide the answer). In March 1933 the number of unemployed was 5,599,000 and in March 1936 had fallen to 1,937,000, a drop in the first three years of the Hitler régime of over 3,600,000 persons (as compared with a fall of 1,500,000 between December 1933 and December 1935 so carefully selected by Sir Arnold!).

Moreover, why does Sir Arnold endeavour to get at the increase of employment by means of unemployment statistics when reliable figures of employment are available? Actually, as elsewhere, employment in Germany during the three years under review has risen substantially more than unemployment has decreased. In February 1936 (the last month for which figures are available) the total number of persons employed was 15,675,000, whereas in February 1933 the figure was 11,533,000. There has therefore been an increase in the number employed in Germany (excluding the Saar), since the advent of the Hitler régime, of some 4,000,000 persons and not 1,000,000 as Sir Arnold states.

Figures published by the German Institute for Business Research reveal further that whereas employment in industries producing goods for current consumption has increased during the three years under review by 25%, employment in producers' goods industries (which include armaments and auxiliary industries) has risen by over 90%.

Nor is this all. The average daily working time per worker in Germany has increased substantially in the last three years. Whereas the average working day was 7·00 hours in March 1933, it had risen by March 1936 to 7·55 hours. The increase was particularly striking in the producers' goods industries, whose working day rose from 6·99 hours in March 1933 to 7·71 hours in March 1936 (and to 7·87 hours in March 1936 in the industries engaged in construction). In consumers' goods industries the need for a longer working day was not so urgent, and here the working day during the same period was increased from 7·02 hours to 7·35 hours.

Finally, allowance must be made for a considerable increase in efficiency per workman-hour during the period, an increase which is more striking in heavy producers' goods industries, which, at the beginning of 1933, had a relatively larger proportion of plant idle than in consumers' goods industries. When production is increased by the utilisation of plant hitherto idle, a given increase of production usually requires less than the same percentage increase in workmen employed. Figures recently published by the German Institute for Business Research indicate, for example, that efficiency in the pig iron industry has increased by over 20% since 1932.

It is clear, therefore, that there has been a stupendous increase in activity in the producers' goods industries. This is borne out by the following production indices taken from the League of Nations Monthly Bulletin:—

Year	Production of All Industry	(1929 = 100) Production of Producers' Goods	Production of Goods for Current Consumption
1932	53·3	34·4	76·3
1933	60·7	43·6	82·6
1934	79·8	72·6	92·4
1935	94·0	99·4	88·3

It will be observed that whereas the German output of producers' goods industries was 190% higher in 1935 than in 1932, the corresponding increase in the output of consumers' goods industries was 16%, the production of the latter in 1935 being actually 4% lower than in 1934.

Sir Arnold endeavours to disprove the fact that an enormous increase in iron and steel production has taken place by reference to 'crucible and electric steels and steel castings'. It is not clear how he selects his figures, but he gives a 1934 output of 498,000 tons and compares this with 484,000 tons in 1929—the year in which the trade boom was at its height and with 536,000 tons in 1913. A 1935 figure is not given, nor is a figure for 1932 or 1933. But in any case, for Sir Arnold to indicate that the armament industry depends primarily on these steels is completely to mislead the reader. In the first place, armaments themselves are nowadays made largely from alloy steels (not necessarily derived from crucible and electric steel), which do not appear as such in the statistics. Secondly, enormous quantities of ordinary steel are required in industries which are auxiliary to armament production—such as defence works, bridges, bomb-proof underground shelters, machinery, etc etc. The total steel production figures reveal that whereas the output of crude steel ingots and castings in 1935, excluding the Saar, was 14,053,000 tons, the comparable figure in 1932 was 5,654,000—a rise in three years of 150%! The comparable production in 1913—a year of tremendous rearmament—

was 12,175,000 tons. It will be observed that the figures selected by Sir Arnold account for some 4% of the total steel production!

Sir Arnold contends that if Mr Churchill's arguments are true 'there should have been a great rise in the total of wages paid, and in prices'. Statistics of incomes of workers and salaried employees reveal that the total of such incomes had increased by 33% in 1935 as compared with 1932, and by 30% as compared with 1933, and this despite a decrease of wage rates. The fact that wage rates have decreased and not increased is, of course, perfectly understandable in a country where a demand for an increase in the rate of pay is followed by a journey to a concentration camp.

The fact that prices have not risen substantially is, of course, largely due to the fact that maximum prices are fixed by the Government, especially in the case of retail foods. Consequently such foods are frequently not available at all—as, for example, the shortage of butter, eggs, etc in Berlin a few months ago—while from time to time people are imprisoned for *paying* more than the maximum prices fixed.

Sir Arnold further contends that Mr Churchill's comparison of net imports of iron ore, nickel, tungsten, chrome, etc are misleading on the ground that 'these materials are not used solely, or even mainly, for armaments'. Sir Arnold states: 'Only a fraction (what fraction?) of these imports is going into armaments. Hitler is keeping German industry as busy in all its branches now as in earlier years.' The implications of these statements are quite contrary to the facts. It is quite untrue to say that only a *small* fraction of the imports mentioned by Mr Churchill is used for armament purposes. The imports of raw materials are carefully controlled, so that industries not connected directly or indirectly with armaments are unable to obtain supplies. Although, therefore, some of the materials quoted by Mr Churchill could have significant uses in peace time pursuits, they are, in fact, almost exclusively reserved for armament purposes. For Sir Arnold to point out that Germany is importing and producing greater amounts of copper, lead, zinc and aluminium than in 1933, in addition to the materials already cited, is merely to emphasise this point. The original list of materials given did not pretend to be complete. Copper, lead, zinc and aluminium, although capable of being used for peaceful purposes, have, in fact, been so used on an ever diminishing scale. Such manufacturing industries have, largely as a consequence of the impossibility of securing supplies of raw material, been compelled to curtail their operations and suffer a loss of their internal and external trade, in order to ensure an adequate supply of these metals for armament purposes.

Nor is Hitler keeping all branches of industry anything like equally busy. Private industry is severely handicapped by (1) the issue ban on the capital market which prevents the issue of new shares without special permission, and (2) the ban on new construction. In both of these cases, the bans are almost invariably only relaxed in the case of armament and armament accessory undertakings. An example of the effect of this strict Government control is seen, according to the 'Frankfurter Zeitung', and quoted in 'The Economist', in 'the different degrees of activity in the engineering trade— many branches have only half the amount of work, others have considerably more than the average'. A further example is to be seen in the poor state of residential building activity. In such circumstances, for Sir Arnold to query Mr Churchill's comparison of 1935 imports with 1932, on the ground that the latter year was the bottom of the slump, is ludicrous. If the effect of armaments is discounted what trade revival has there been?

Sir Arnold's endeavour to draw a red herring across the path of the discussion in the shape of the Russian bogey seems remarkably out of place in an analysis of German rearmament. Now-a-days the use of this bogey is, in Europe, usually confined to Germany.

Lord Weir to Winston S. Churchill

(Churchill papers: 2/254)

13 May 1936
Private

My dear Winston,

Many thanks indeed for your frank but kindly letter. Most of what you say has been closely in my mind for some time, especially since the Hitler declaration of 7th March.[1]

'The true proportion of affairs'—that is the real problem. Are we to take 'the whole life and industry of this nation and organise it for war preparation'? If I was completely confident that this was essential, I would not only advise it but push it hard in spite of its grave effects and dislocations. That is one extreme.

The other extreme is your reference to our comfortable peace routine. Frankly, that is not the case in regard to action in Air supply. As to the Army, I agree that existing action is inadequate and have said so. As to the Navy, I do not feel conscious of having any particular responsibility. Supply for the Navy is still a relatively simple task.

I admit that I have avoided official power and have confined myself to helping by advice in particular directions. My reason is simply this. Official responsibility covering political exposition would kill me. If we were at war

---

[1] See page 64, note 2.

that would not dismay me at all, but we are still at peace, although I grant it is a strained one.

Please believe me that I will bear closely in mind your cautions.

Yrs ever,
Weir

Sir Thomas Inskip to Winston S. Churchill

(*Churchill papers: 2/259*)

14 May 1936   2 Whitehall Gardens
Tuesday

Dear Churchill,

Thank you very much for your readiness to postpone your question till next Wedy.[1]

When I next see you perhaps you will let me have a word about the method I am following in trying to get to the bottom of the Fleet Air Arm question.

Yours sincerely,
T. W. H. Inskip

Winston S. Churchill to Sir Henry Strakosch

(*Churchill papers: 2/277*)

15 May 1936

Herewith the reply I have received from Rennell. Let me have it back when you have perused it. Would you now get in touch with him direct? I am sure you will soon convince him.

---

[1] Hansard recorded Churchill's question, and the response, as follows: 'Mr Churchill asked the Minister for Co-ordination of Defence whether he is yet in a position to make a statement upon the transference of the Fleet air-arm to the control of the Admiralty, or when he expects to be able to do so? Sir T. Inskip: No, Sir; but I am examining certain particular questions which have arisen as regards the working or organization of the Fleet air-arm. They are questions concerning the provision of personnel, the period of service and reserves. Mr Churchill: Is the right hon. Gentleman not considering the general question of the transference of the Fleet air-arm? Sir T. Inskip: I am taking the questions which arise first of all into consideration and, when I have satisfied myself as to the facts on those questions, I may be in a position to consider further questions. Captain Harold Balfour: In view of the contradictory statements of the right hon. Gentleman the member for Epping (Mr Churchill) in the Debate last week, that, first, some Admirals did not believe in the air-arm, and, secondly, that there is nobody more air minded than Admirals, should the Government be content to hand over the development of this new science to such doubtful minds?' (*Hansard*, 20 May 1936.)

Thank you very much for the memoranda you sent me disposing of Sir Arnold Wilson's figures. Have you seen the letter from F. W. Hirst[1] in the Times today?[2] Surely it is possible to contend that the rate of 12 RM to the £ is comparable as a guide to munition production, because of the lower wages received from the prominent industries of Germany compared to ours? Also the purchasing power of the mark internally is higher than what would be represented by 20 RM to the £.

About military roads, there is not the slightest doubt that they are war preparations of the most formidable kind. Perhaps you would ask your friends to look into this, and I will write a sweeping up answer presently to the Times.

Winston S. Churchill to Captain Boucher

(*Churchill papers: 2/278*)

18 May 1936
Private and Confidential

You will see that I was not idle in the matter upon which you wrote me. I am much obliged to you for your assistance, and I trust that there will be a good result for the public service. I have reason to know that the Admiralty were extremely pleased with the line I took, and are very hopeful that it will not be ineffective. Should we get into closer fighting in the matter, I hope you will allow me to write to you again.

[1] Francis W. Hirst, 1873–1953. Educated at Clifton, and Wadham College, Oxford. President of the Oxford Union Society. Barrister-at-Law, 1899. A member of the National Liberal Club. Editor of the *Economist*, 1907–16. Lectured on political economy, California, 1921; South Africa, 1923. A Governor of the London School of Economics. As a leading Liberal political economist, he published more than twenty-five books, including *Trusts and Cartels* (1905), *Political Economy of War* (1915), *Safeguarding and Protection* (1928), *Consequences of the War to Great Britain* (1934), *Liberty and Tyranny and Economic Freedom* (1935), *Armaments* (1937) and *Principles of Prosperity* (1945).

[2] F. W. Hirst's letter appeared in *The Times* under the headline 'The Budget and Defence'. In it Hirst declared that he detested 'every system of government that suppresses liberty', and that 'all nations which enjoy free institutions should protect themselves against aggression', but he went on to write that he did not think the proposed increase in defence spending to be justified. He took exception to Churchill's statement that Germany was spending £800,000,000 each year on arms, claiming that Churchill used an exaggerated exchange rate, and included road construction as armaments. The true figure would be, in Hirst's view, around £300,000,000 a year, and he ended by suggesting that 'the way of commercial appeasement' was preferable to military spending as a remedy for foreign danger.

Winston S. Churchill to Bernard Baruch:[1] *telegram*

(*Churchill papers: 1/284*)

18 May 1936

Have long cherished hope of seeing Democratic convention and you in its centre. Alas Parliament grips me. When will you come over. Kindest regards to all.

Winston

Winston S. Churchill to Marjorie Maxse[2]

(*Churchill papers: 2/254*)

19 May 1936

I think it very undesirable to add to the importance of the Oxford Union at the present time.[3] Only a very small proportion of the University belong to it, and these are almost entirely Socialists. Great harm has been done to our interests by the fact that it is still regarded abroad in the light of its old reputation.

In the first instance it would be much better to organise and stimulate the Conservative Clubs to endeavour to redeem the Union.

[1] Bernard Mannes Baruch, 1870–1965. Born in New York. Financier. Chairman of the Allied Purchasing Commission, 1917. Commissioner in Charge of Raw Materials, United States War Industries Board, 1917–18. Chairman of the War Industries Board, March 1918–January 1919. Economic Adviser to the American Peace Commission, 1919. Member of the President's Agricultural Conference, 1922. American Representative on the Atomic Energy Commission, 1946.

[2] Marjorie Maxse, 1891–1975. Chief Organization Officer, Conservative Central Office, 1921–39. Director of the Children's Overseas Reception Board, and Vice Chairman of the Women's Voluntary Services, 1940–4. Vice Chairman of the Conservative Party Organization, 1944–51. Created Dame Commander of the British Empire, 1952.

[3] On 18 May 1936 Miss Maxse had passed on a request to Churchill from the Oxford Union, to speak on the subject: 'That the torch of freedom is safe in the hands of the Conservative Party.'

Eugen Spier:[1] *recollections*

(*'Focus', pages 20-22*)

[19 May 1936]   [Hotel Victoria][2]

Churchill was at the head of the table with Lady Violet[3] beside him at his special request. I was seated between Mond[4] and Richards.[5] The atmosphere was pleasant and the conversation stimulating, although I felt that as an unknown quantity I was being carefully scrutinised. Churchill appeared to be enjoying a lively conversation with Lady Violet, but looked alternately grim and cheerful, cheerful about the gathering, grim about the political situation.

After lunch, armed with a cigar, he rose to address us. He began with some general references to the unsatisfactory state of our defences compared with the all-out effort being made by the Nazis. The government was just shutting its eyes to these disquieting facts. Virtually the whole population of Germany was being turned into a single gigantic war-machine, and the individual German was being denied every personal right and freedom, reduced to a mere cog in the wheel of destruction. For Great Britain rearmament was now a matter of life or death. At this Sir Archibald Sinclair[6] muttered his

---

[1] Eugen Spier, 1891–1971. Born in southern Germany, a German subject and a Jew, he came to Britain in 1922. Helped to organize and finance the 'Focus', 1936–9. Arrested, 1 September 1939, interned as an enemy alien, and deported to Canada. Released from internment in 1941. Became a British citizen after 1945. Resident in London until his death in 1971. In 1951 he published *The Protecting Power*, an account of his time as an internee. In 1953 he published *Reconciliation*, on the positive role of spiritual forces in politics. In 1963 he published *Focus*, an account of his work, and of his meetings, with Churchill.

[2] This was the first luncheon of a new group, later called the 'Focus' aimed at bringing together representatives of all Parties and groups opposed to Nazism.

[3] Helen Violet Asquith, 1887–1969. Elder daughter of H. H. Asquith. Educated in Dresden and Paris. Married, 1915, Sir Maurice Bonham Carter (who died in 1960). President of the Women's Liberal Federation, 1923–5 and 1939–45; President of the Liberal Party Organization, 1945–7. A Governor of the BBC, 1941–6. Member of the Royal Commission on the Press, 1947–9. Unsuccessful Liberal candidate, 1945 and 1951. DBE, 1953; created Baroness Asquith of Yarnbury, 1964. Published *Winston Churchill as I knew Him*, 1965.

[4] Robert Ludwig Mond, 1867–1938. An industrial chemist; President of the French Society of Chemical Industry. A Director of the South Staffordshire Mond Gas Company, the Mond Staffordshire Refining Company and the International Nickel Company of Canada. Knighted, 1932. Fellow of the Royal Society, 1938. A patron of music, the arts and archaeology; President of the Egypt Exploration Society, Treasurer of the Palestine Exploration Fund, Honorary Treasurer of the British School of Archaeology at Jerusalem and Vice-President of the Archaeological Institute. Founder of the Infant's Hospital, Westminster (in memory of his first wife, who died in 1905, seven years after their marriage).

[5] A. H. Richards (see Churchill's letter to Viscount Cecil of Chelwood, 9 April 1936).

[6] Archibald Henry Macdonald Sinclair, 1890–1970. Educated at Eton and Sandhurst. Entered Army, 1910. 4th Baronet, 1912. Captain, 1915. 2nd in Command of the 6th Royal Scots Fusiliers, while Churchill was in command, January–May 1916. Squadron-Commander,

disapproval, but Churchill would not give way and emphasised his point with even greater vigour. I admired the way in which he convincingly brushed aside Sinclair's opposition and how in the end Sinclair smiled approval.

Looking around to make certain that no waiter or other outsider was listening, he said to us: 'You will understand that this meeting is private; no notes are to be taken and no information whatsoever must be given to the press.' Thereupon he gave us some figures about the shortcomings of our rearmament effort, particularly about the Royal Air Force, figures that were gravely disquieting when compared to what the Nazis were doing. 'In this democratic country,' he went on, 'it is for the members of Parliament to bring their influence to bear on the Cabinet. And it is for us here to keep the public adequately and continuously informed so as to offset the damage done by German propaganda. At present the British public and press are very much the victims of the Nazi Ministry of Information and its lies; it has collared the press, the radio and every other instrument for spreading news. The task of this assembly is thus as difficult as it is indispensable and urgent. We must make an all-party effort, create a source from which unbiased and objective information will constantly flow to the government and to the whole country. We must spare no effort to enlist the support of men and women from every section of our community irrespective of party, creed and class. I fully realise that this is a task as difficult as it is worthy. I am also aware that this task is made more difficult on account of the most regrettable pro-Nazi attitude of a considerable section of the national press. I am there-fore greatly pleased and much encouraged to see already here, in this modest but truly representative meeting, a very promising omen for our future. For this I am most grateful. But it is only a beginning. We must march forward with faith and determination in order to overcome all the many obstacles which stand in our path.'

He then went on to say that, in order to get ourselves sufficiently organised, we should start by framing our policy in the form of a manifesto setting forth our aims, and on this basis enlist members and supporters from every section of the public. He proceeded to outline that policy in general terms and the sort of manifesto we should issue. We must ourselves be determined to resist, and to join others in resisting, any aggression, armed or unarmed, which

---

2nd Life Guards, 1916–18. Elected to the Other Club, 1917. Major, Guards Machine Gun Regiment, 1918. Private Secretary to Churchill, Ministry of Munitions, 1918–19. Churchill's personal Military Secretary, War Office, 1919–21. Churchill's Private Secretary, Colonial Office, 1921–2. Liberal MP for Caithness and Sutherland, 1922–45. Secretary of State for Scotland, 1931–3. Leader of the Parliamentary Liberal Party, 1935–45. Secretary of State for Air in Churchill's wartime Coalition, 1940–5. Knight of the Thistle, 1941. Created Viscount Thurso, 1952.

threatened our way of life in freedom, justice and peace, and to make it clear that Britain and the Commonwealth were prepared to stand for the defence of human rights and for the rule of law among nations. 'British leadership and action may yet save Europe and our grand civilisation whose very existence is being threatened by the Nazis.'

Churchill then suggested that the details of such a manifesto should be worked out by a special drafting committee, which was immediately established with Steed[1] as chairman. Waley-Cohen[2] and Lady Violet agreed to serve on the committee and promised their full assistance and co-operation. The secretary was instructed to take the necessary steps to meet the requirements of the committee, and to make arrangements for the next meeting at which the draft manifesto would be discussed.

The secretary agreed, but asked where the money to defray expenses was to come from. His bald request came like the explosion of a bomb. Expressions of embarrassment appeared on every side, and Churchill himself looked displeased, even angry.

For a moment it looked as if the whole effort was about to come to grief. To avert catastrophe I took Richards aside and asked him to announce that all our requirements had been taken care of. The tension was immediately eased. Churchill seemed greatly relieved. . . .[3]

Lady Violet Bonham Carter to Winston S. Churchill

(*Churchill papers: 2/282*)

19 May 1936

Dearest Winston,

'Arising out of' our luncheon to-day—the following considerations occur to me.

---

[1] Henry Wickham Steed, 1871–1956. Educated at Sudbury Grammar School; Jena, Berlin and Paris. Joined *The Times*, as acting correspondent, Berlin, 1896; correspondent, Rome, 1897–1902; Vienna, 1902–13. Foreign Editor of *The Times*, 1914–19. Editor of *The Times*, February 1919 to November 1922. Proprietor and Editor of the *Review of Reviews*, 1923–30. Broadcaster on World Affairs for the Overseas Service of the BBC, 1937–47. Author of twenty volumes of history and current affairs.

[2] Robert Waley-Cohen, 1877–1952. Educated at Clifton and Emmanuel College, Cambridge. Joined the Shell Company, 1901; subsequently Managing Director of the Shell Transport and Trading Co Ltd, and of United British Oilfields of Trinidad Ltd. Petroleum Adviser to the Army Council, 1914–18. Knighted, 1920. President of the United Synagogue. Vice-Chairman, University College, London.

[3] Between May 1936 and the summer of 1939 Spier contributed £9,600 towards the organization of the 'Focus' (letter to Churchill, 10 August 1953, *Spier papers*).

'Pointing the finger at Hitler' (advocated by Dr Dalton[1]—) is a futile policy. We have 'pointed the finger at Mussolini'—& it has done him no harm. Admonitory fingers do not deter dictators.

There are only two policies to be adopted towards Hitler: to hold out the hand or to clench the fist. The country at the moment is unwilling to pursue either.

If we advocate the second what does it amount to? Re-armament against & virtual encirclement of—Germany. This *may* be the only course consistent with our national self-preservation—but we cannot advocate it as a 'League' policy—

What is the alternative? Someone at lunch suggested a re-formed League —with commitments confined to Europe—& (I imagine) obligations of a more drastic & autocratic nature—Is this the suggestion that we are to amplify & work upon?

I feel strongly that we must have a plan of a more or less concrete & practical nature to put forward.

Our denunciations of tyranny do not move—or even *reach*—the people of the countries in which it exists—

I would love a word of guidance from you before the 'Committee' starts on its work.

Will the League be anything but a discredited corpse if Mussolini 'gets away with it' scot-free? & what can be done to revive or replace it? That is the question I *cannot* find an answer to.

Ever yours,
Violet

Winston S. Churchill to Sir Maurice Hankey
(*Churchill papers: 25/7*)

20 May 1936

I send you herewith two papers connected with the Air. Paper A is a continuation of the series of CID papers or Cabinet Papers, and I should be very glad if it were thought worth while to print them, and give them the same

---

[1] Edward Hugh John Neale Dalton, 1887–1962. Educated at Eton and King's College, Cambridge. Barrister, 1914. On active service in France and Italy 1914–18. Lecturer, London School of Economics, 1919. Reader in Commerce, University of London, 1920–5; Reader in Economics, 1925–6. Labour MP for Camberwell, 1924–9; for Bishop Auckland, 1929–31 and 1935–59. Parliamentary Under-Secretary, Foreign Office, 1929–31. Chairman, National Executive of the Labour Party, 1936–7. Minister of Economic Warfare, 1940–2. President of the Board of Trade, 1942–5. Chancellor of the Exchequer, 1945–7; resigned over a Budget leak, 1947. Minister of Town and Country Planning, 1950–1. Created Baron, 1960.

circulation as the others. Paper B entitled 'Aerial Mines' represents the sad treatment of Lindemann's idea. I should be glad if you would have this roneod, and ask the Secretary of State for Air to allow it to be circulated to the Sub-Committee for discussion when they meet again.

I was much concerned at the statement which he made in the House of Lords at the beginning of the session indicating that all was going well on this Committee. Certainly everything has been most agreeable, but the progress made is disquietingly small. I have no doubt in ten or twelve years something very fine will emerge, but where shall we all be then?

Violet Pearman to Winston S. Churchill

(*Churchill papers: 2/271*)

20 May 1936

Squadron-Leader C. T. Anderson[1] of the Air Ministry rang up to say that he would be very glad of a talk with you very soon. As a Service officer you would appreciate his position. He did not wish to write, but thought a talk was better. Would you speak to him tomorrow, if possible? He would come to the flat or the House. He mentioned that he was Director of the Training School, and he would confidently say you would be much interested in what he had to say. When can he come to see you? His number is at the Air Ministry, Holborn 3434 (Extension 673).

[1] Charles Torr Anderson, 1896–1979. Grandson of a former Chief Constable of Staffordshire. His father died when Anderson was seven. Educated at Christ's Hospital. A brewer's pupil, 1914. 2nd Lieutenant, 10th North Staffordshire Regiment, 1915. Badly wounded on the Somme, 29 September 1916, after which he spent a year in hospital. Transferred to the Royal Flying Corps, as an officer observer, 1917. Distinguished Flying Cross, August 1918. Permanent commission, 1919; served subsequently in India and Australia, where he was injured in an air crash which left him with frequent severe headaches. Commanded No 504 Bomber Squadron, 1931–4. Squadron-Leader, 1930. Directorate of Training, Air Ministry, 1934–6. Wing-Commander, 1 July 1936. Commanded RAF Hucknall, 1936–7. Commanded No 1 Armament Training School, Catfoss, Yorkshire, 1938–9. Senior Personnel Staff Officer, Headquarters No 5 Group, 1939–40. Group-Captain, 1940. Commanded two operational bomber squadrons at Waddington, Lincolnshire, 1940. Personal Assistant and Air Adviser to Lord Beaverbrook, 1940–1, when he helped to establish the Lancaster bomber on a proper production basis. A member of the Inspectorate of Flying Accidents, Training Command, 1941–2. Invalided out of the RAF, 1942. Joined the staff of Bass, Ratcliff and Gretton, 1944. Retired, 1959. His widow, Betty J. Anderson, writes: 'The wound he sustained at the Battle of the Somme was the beginning of many crashes and so on, but he never gave in, and the RAF was his life' (*letter to the author, 29 September 1981*).

Stanley Baldwin to Viscount Monsell
(*Premier papers: 1/282*)

20 May 1936

I am wholly opposed to the reopening of the general question of the control of the Fleet Air Arm at the present time. . . .[1]

Lord Weir to Stanley Baldwin
(*Premier papers: 1/282*)

20 May 1936

. . . If the Fleet Air Arm general question be reopened, I would have no hesitation but to disassociate myself from helping the Air Ministry and leave myself free to deal with this issue.

Winston S. Churchill to Sir Austen Chamberlain: telegram
(*Churchill papers: 2/266*)

20 May 1936

I propose speak anyhow tomorrow for about half an hour on Ministry Munitions.[2]

Sir Maurice Hankey to Sir Thomas Inskip
(*Cabinet papers: 21/573*)

22 May 1936

I feel constrained to submit to you my concern as to the rate at which our defence programmes are proceeding. I am not blaming anyone at all, and if there is blame I am, of course, prepared to take whatever share of the responsibility is my own. I feel, however, that somehow or other we ought to speed matters up and do better.

---

[1] This letter was drafted by Sir Maurice Hankey.

[2] On 21 May 1936, during a debate on the salary of the Minister for Co-ordination of Defence, Churchill said: 'it is incongruous and a serious fault in organization to make a Minister who has to concert the combined action of all four (Defence) Departments to be also the head of the Supply Branch—or the Ministry of Munitions into which it may broaden—which is also one of them'. Churchill went on to criticize the entire British defence effort, including the failure to establish a separate Ministry of Munitions, and the failure to make any progress towards overtaking Germany in air or land strength. His speech ended: 'I do not ask that war conditions be established in order to execute these programmes. All I ask is that these programmes to which the Government have attached their confidence shall be punctually executed, whatever may be the disturbance of our daily life.'

My own belief is that the starting-point of an acceleration is to speed up the existing administrative machine. Whether this should be followed by more heroic measures, such as constituting a ministry of supply or taking powers for control of industry, can come later.

An examination of the time-table since the process of re-conditioning our Defence Services was first started a year ago is not very flattering to efficiency.

This time-table tends to show that at all stages we have been rather slow.

Thomas Jones: diary

(*Jones papers*)

22 May 1936

CONVERSATION WITH STANLEY BALDWIN

BALDWIN: 'Neville told me that Austen had spoken to him about his (Austen's) present company, Winston, Horne and Winterton. They do not wish to embarrass the Government but they do mean to be inquisitive as they do not think we are active enough in defence matters.[1]

One of these days I'll make a few casual remarks about Winston. Not a speech—no oratory—just a few words in passing. I've got it all ready. I am going to say that when Winston was born lots of fairies swooped down on his cradle gifts—imagination, eloquence, industry, ability, and then came a fairy who said "No one person has a right to so many gifts", picked him up and gave him such a shake and twist that with all these gifts he was denied judgment and wisdom. And that is why while we delight to listen to him in this House we do not take his advice.'[2]

[1] On the day after hearing these remarks of Baldwin, Thomas Jones wrote to a friend: '. . . the hostile critics in the House are a formidable group: Austen, Winston, Horne and Winterton. On foreign policy L.G. is nearer to S.B. than he is to Winston.' On 25 May 1936 the *News Chronicle* published a banner headline across its whole front page: 'Anti-Baldwin "Shadow Cabinet" meets. Winston and Austen among Lord Winterton's Guests.' Churchill had spent the weekend at Shillinglee Park, Chiddingfold, Surrey, as a guest of Lord Winterton. Among the other guests were Sir Robert Horne, Sir Henry Page Croft and Sir Edward Grigg, as well as Sir Austen Chamberlain. There was considerable Press speculation that they were discussing the imminent Cabinet successors to J. H. Thomas and Lord Monsell: in the event, their successors were William Ormsby-Gore as Secretary of State for the Colonies (28 May 1936) and Sir Samuel Hoare as First Lord of the Admiralty (8 June 1936).

[2] And yet, on 26 May 1936, Percy Cater wrote in the *Daily Mail*, in his 'Spotlight on Politics' column: 'Despite the apparently profound differences between Mr Baldwin and Mr Churchill, Westminster gossip persists in the view that, before long, Mr Churchill will be associated, in some capacity, with defence. MPs cannot get over the anomaly that Mr Churchill's qualities should not be used by the nation at a time like this. The distinguished courtesies accorded by Sir Thomas Inskip and Mr Churchill to each other in the defence debate last week gave many observers the impression that they would work well together.'

Winston S. Churchill to Shane Leslie

(Shane Leslie papers)

22 May 1936   Chartwell
Private

My dear Shane,
    The Strand Magazine wants me to write an article about Parnell. I send you a copy of the correspondence which will show you what they want. You see the emphasis is to be laid upon the latter part of the tragedy of his life. This seems to lie very much in your country. If you would care to provide me with a preliminary étude on the basis we spoke of for other articles, I should be much obliged.[1]

Yours affectionately,
W

PS. I am relieved that Oswald is recovering.

Winston S. Churchill to Brigadier Pakenham-Walsh

(Churchill papers: 8/529

23 May 1936

    The inevitable has happened and Marlborough is to be four volumes. Volume III will end at the fall of Lille. We shall not therefore want any more about Malplaquet for the moment. Instead we want Spain 1705–6–7–8. We do not want to tell this in detail as twenty pages are about all we can spare. But Almanza is an important battle and so is the taking of Barcelona. Will you kindly go ahead on these four Spanish campaigns and note anything in the text you think might be brought in. Will you also prepare the maps to illustrate the Spanish affair. Will you also hurry on the rest of the maps for the Oudenarde–Lille campaign in so far as they are not already done. There was also some fighting on the upper Rhine in 1707 and 1708 and I think there

---

[1] Churchill's article 'The Tragic Story of Parnell' was published in the October 1936 issue of the *Strand* magazine, and subsequently reprinted in the revised edition of *Great Contemporaries* (published on 7 November 1938). Parnell, Churchill wrote, was a great moderate who 'held back the powers of revolution as an unflung weapon in his hand'. Churchill added: 'He met English hatred with obstruction, and coercion with a bitterness which destroyed the old amenities of Parliamentary debate. In Ireland, neither the Church nor the Revolutionaries liked him, but both had to submit to his policy. He was a Garibaldi who compelled at once the allegiance of the Pope and of the Carbonari in the national cause. When taunted with stimulating outrage and even murder, he thought it sufficient to reply, "I am answerable to Irish opinion, and Irish opinion alone."' Churchill's article contained a graphic account of Parnell's love for Kitty O'Shea, and of his downfall: 'as he had previously sacrificed all for Ireland, when the moment of choice came, he sacrificed all, even Ireland, for love'.

should be a couple of maps illustrating Villars'[1] operations there. It is a great relief to me not to have to hurry the finishing off of this work. Now I can concentrate on polishing what we have already done.[2]

Desmond Morton to Winston S. Churchill

(*Churchill papers: 2/266*)

25 May 1936   Committee of Imperial Defence

Dear Winston,

I return herewith, in registered envelope, the paper you kindly lent me on French Air expenditure. The figures coincide with those the Air Ministry already possess.

I was most interested to meet de la Grange,[3] and am going to try and get into touch with him later for a longer talk. I find he went back to France last night.

Though he struck me as being rather wordy and theoretic, some of his statements regarding the position in France strongly supported our view that the French are not nearly so ready for war as we should like them to be. We have been apprehensive about them for some time past.

Yours very sincerely,

Desmond Morton

[1] Marshal Claude-Louis-Hector de Villars, commander of the Grand French Army, and one of Marlborough's principal military opponents at the battles of Stollhofen, Tournai, Mons, Malplaquet, Douai, Arleux and Denain; described by Churchill as 'a being into every atom of whose texture vanity and valour entered in equal proportions' (*Marlborough: His Life and Times*, volume 4, page 37).

[2] The news of an extra Marlborough volume was not entirely welcome to Churchill's American publisher, Charles Scribner, who wrote to him from New York on 4 June 1936: '. . . I had not guessed that the *Marlborough* would run into another volume. It is difficult to say whether we shall be the gainers or losers in America through having the added volume. We certainly cannot hope to do very much with the third and fourth volumes on publication, as the work has grown to a so much greater size than originally planned that it has lost all semblance of general popularity and has become more of a library set. Let us hope however that when it is completed we may be able to find some ways of disposing of sets by subscription, emphasizing the fact that it is a history of England over a considerable period of years rather than the biography of a single character.' Scribner added: 'It is a miracle to me that you found time to do so much work on your book, as you are quoted at length in the papers here once or twice a week, and your Parliamentary and newspaper work must take up a great portion of your time.'

[3] Leo Lagrange, 1902–1940. Born in the Dordogne. Socialist Deputy for the Nord. Under-Secretary of State in the Blum Government for the Organization of Leisure and Sport (the first person to hold that post), June 1936. Encouraged popular sport and tourism linked to Blum's 'holidays with pay'. Under-Secretary of State for Physical Education, Sport and Leisure in the Chautemps Government of June 1937, and in the second Blum Government of March 1938. Killed in action at Evergnicourt on the Aisne, June 1940.

Winston S. Churchill: note on British Air Strength[1]

(*Churchill papers: 2/271*)

25 May 1936

Not a full programme of 2,000 machines until April 1939.

By the 1st July 1937 we shall have approximately 30 sqdrns only for Metropolitan war. Each sqdrn is about 14 aircraft. But no-one will commit themselves owing to contractor's difficulties.

Of these 30 sqdrns only 5 sqdrns will have new types of aircraft. All the rest will be obsolescent.

Winston S. Churchill to Sir Thomas Inskip

(*Churchill papers: 2/269*)

25 May 1936
Secret and Personal

I am very glad that you felt able to speak as you did about my various suggestions at the close of Thursday's debate. Of course you realise that it is my task and duty, as I conceive it, to arouse the Government and the country to the sense of the dangers by which we are being encompassed, but I shall always be ready to assist you in any way that you may at any time suggest.

There are two points on which you touched about which I venture to comment.

1. At the 1922 Committee you referred to me (without mentioning my name) about the progress made by the Committee on defence against air attack. You seem to have been led to believe that some very valuable discovery has been made which will improve our defence in the near future. It is true that some wonderful scientific progress has been made for locating hostile aircraft, but this is not likely to be perfected for a long time, and even when it is, the more difficult question arises of how to destroy the hostile plane when detected and located. On this no progress worth speaking of has

---

[1] This note is the first of many sets of information given to Churchill by Squadron Leader Anderson between May 1936 and the outbreak of war in September 1939. On the following day, 26 May 1936, Anderson sent Churchill an official Air Ministry minute giving the total Royal Air Force personnel strength at that date as 3,215 pilots already available, 1,131 pilots within five months of completing their training, 28,000 trained airman and 10,000 airmen under training. The minute commented: 'By 1.4.39 we aim at an Air Force comprising 5,600 pilots and 48,000 airmen.' The minute also gave Britain's projected air strength on 1 April 1937 as 1,500 aircraft 'at Home' (in 118 squadrons), 270 aircraft overseas and 217 Fleet Air Arm. On 1 April 1939 it was projected that there would be 1,750 aircraft at Home and 450 Overseas (*Churchill papers: 2/271*).

been made. In fact the main conclusion reached after eight months that I have been on the Committee is that anti-aircraft guns are practically useless with their present shells, except when concentrated for the defence of the Fleet or some special point. They are now all turning to the kite balloon, and I agree with this. But you will be shocked to see how slow, timid and insignificant is the progress made. I was astonished that Swinton in the Lords four months ago should have referred to the work of this Committee in such glowing terms. It is a very good Committee; it works most agreeably together; it has many bright ideas; but action and progress, except in the one respect I mentioned, are pitiful.

Accustomed as I was to see how things were done in the war, and how orders can be given for large scale experiment and supply, I have been deeply pained by the dilettante futility which has marked our action. The delays are dreadful. Lindemann whom you know and who is on the scientific committee, has been struggling vainly for eight months for certain not very costly experiments to be made. From time to time some little thing is done, and then another month before a variant is attempted, and so on. I have had, and am still having, a great deal of difficulty to prevent Lindemann from resigning. If you wish to confirm what I have said on this matter you might have a talk with Sir F. E. Smith.[1] I have never discussed it privately with him, nor indeed ever seen him except on the Committee, but I have very little doubt that he will tell you that what I have written is true. What Hopkinson[2] said about our having already some means which in the immediate future would spread a reign of terror among hostile aircraft, is utter rubbish. I do not doubt that ultimately the aeroplane will be conquered from the ground, but at the present rate of progress this will certainly not be in the next ten years. Much may happen in these ten years. In the meantime there is nothing—I do hope you realise that—absolutely nothing worth speaking of, except the power of the Fleet to protect itself by its immense concentration of gun power. For two or three years there will be nothing at home except retaliation as a deterrent.

[1] Frank Edward Smith, 1879–1970. Educated at the Royal College of Science. Superintendent, Electrical Department, National Physical Laboratory, 1901–20. Fellow of the Royal Society, 1918. Director of Scientific Research at the Admiralty, 1920–9. Secretary, Department of Scientific and Industrial Research, 1929–39. Knighted, 1931. Director of Instrument Production, and Controller of Bearings Production, Ministry of Supply 1939–42. Director of Research, Anglo-Iranian Oil Company, 1939–55. Controller of Telecommunications Equipment, Ministry of Aircraft Production, 1940–2. Chairman of the Technical Defence Committee, MI5, 1940–6; of the Scientific Advisory Council, Ministry of Supply, 1941–7. Chairman of the Road Research and Safety Research Board, 1945–54.

[2] Austin Hopkinson, 1879–1962. On active service in South Africa, 1900. 2nd Lieutenant, The Royal Dragoons, 1914–16; Private, 1918. Independent MP for Mossley, 1918–29 and 1931–45; a frequent speaker on air matters. Lieutenant, Fleet Air Arm, 1940.

2. You said you would refer to my query about the possibilities of landing considerable forces from the air to the Chiefs of Staff Committee. If you do I hope the issue, as I see it, will be put plainly to them. I should be willing if you desire it to put upon a sheet of paper the contingency, which I believe is now a practical one, in order that it may be considered. The pre-requisite of course is superior hostile air power. If you think it worth while I will draw you up a short paper defining the danger.

Your story about the machine tools and gauges is deeply alarming, and I shall have to refer to your statement in Parliament at the first opportunity. However I think you were absolutely right to make it, and that on any other basis your responsibility would be most unfair.

Winston S. Churchill to Lady Violet Bonham Carter

(*Churchill papers: 2/282*)

25 May 1936   Chartwell
Private & Personal

My dear Violet,

Human puzzles are not always capable of immediate solution; but often even a few weeks of time make them much easier. For this reason I prevented the Albert Hall meeting being held a month ago, and I would not advise one until we can, as Napoleon said 'See clear on our chessboard'. However I feel bound to respond to your request for an expression of opinion before your Sub-Committee meets. Pray be merciful in judgment.

We cannot whether on national or international grounds leave Mussolini and Abyssinia where they are now. That event has got to be regularised coûte que coûte. Therefore I would say to Mussolini 'Which do you mean to be, friend or foe? If a friend, you must regularise your position in Abyssinia. You must bring it into relation with the League of Nations. You must offer guarantees for the well-being of the Abyssinians. Your relationship with the outside world must be similar to that accepted by France in Morocco. You must not raise by compulsion large black armies etc. All this must constitute an act of submission to the League of Nations and the resumption of your place in that system of collective security. If you refuse and persist in your present wilful course you must leave the League of Nations, and we shall take persevering measures to build up a naval and air force in the Mediterranean which you will be forced to respect. We shall not recognise any of your actions. They will remain lawless and unrecognised actions. We shall endeavour to make a regional pact with other Mediterranean powers,

France, Greece and Turkey for mutual protection against your further aggression. (I believe the coming French Government under Blum[1] might well be got as far as this). From this pact you will be excluded unless or until you bring yourself in some effective sense within the law of nations. We are well aware, I would say, that you may throw in your lot with Hitler, and that is a prospect which we must face, and there is no other way round it. All the more therefore shall we be forced with our associates to take measures in the Mediterranean which will enable us to strangle you for certain if you are our enemy in a great war.'

Thus I would bring matters to a head quite soon with Mussolini. I do not think he would like at all the idea of regional encirclement, especially as it involves his being cut from his Abyssinian commitment. I would try to do all this under the auspices and with the assent at each stage of the League of Nations. But anyhow I would get on with it quite quickly.

The effect of the present half-hearted and sham sanctions is that although in a year or more they would be a serious injury to Italy, they would only mean a period of growing tension in Europe which at any moment might take an evil turn against us. Whereas by the policy I indicate we should come to a conclusion with Italy one way or another in the next two months.

If the conclusion is satisfactory, if Mussolini enters the regional pact having agreed to the terms prescribed, the League of Nations would then be strong enough to face the Hitler problem upon its present basis. I would then proceed by very similar methods under the authority of the League of Nations and by means of regional pacts linked together to make the strongest and closest encirclement of Nazidom which is possible. I would marshal all the countries including Soviet Russia from the Baltic southward right round to the Belgian coast, all agreeing to stand by any victim of unprovoked aggression. I would put combined pressure upon every country neighbouring to Germany to subscribe to this and to guarantee a quota of armed force for the purpose. I could of course offer Germany the right to enter this system, in which case she would receive from all these countries their guarantee pro tanto of support in the event of her becoming a victim of unprovoked aggression from any quarter. This I believe would ensure either the peace of the world or an overwhelming deterrent against aggression.

If on the other hand Mussolini refused to work with us and leaves the League of Nations, then I would say sorrowfully and openly that nothing

---

[1] Léon Blum, 1872–1950. Born in Paris, of Jewish parents. Chef de Cabinet, Minister of Public Works, 1914. Deputy for Paris, 1919. A leader of the 'Front Populaire', 1936. Prime Minister, June 1936–June 1937. Vice-President of the Cabinet, 1937–8. Prime Minister and Finance Minister, March–April 1938. Interned in Germany, 1941–5. Prime Minister and Foreign Minister, December 1946–January 1947. President of the French Socialist Party.

remains for us but to provide for our own interests and security. This would be done by a strictly limited regional pact among the Western States, Holland, Belgium, France and Britain for mutual aid in the event of unprovoked attack, and for keeping in being forces great enough to deter Germany from making such an attack. Secondly by the Mediterranean pact aforementioned.

In this second case we should have to expect that the Germans would soon begin a war of conquest east and south and that at the same time Japan would attack Russia in the Far East. But Britain and France would maintain a heavily-armed neutrality in the north and the Mediterranean powers would hold Mussolini completely gripped on all sides so that he would have to be neutral too. Very little would be left to the League of Nations in this second unhappy contingency, but still I hope those powers who held together for mutual protection and for the control of the Mediterranean would not divest themselves needlessly of any trappings of international society which they could rightly claim.

There my dear Violet, I have set forth my thoughts with every feeling of humility before such grievous and giant events. Now see how far with your friends you can formulate the more general principles which might form the basis, not necessarily of a manifesto, but of 'articles of association' to which eventually many men and women of courage and good-will might pledge their faith and hope.

Yours affectionately,
W

Winston S. Churchill to Captain Fitzroy[1]
(Churchill papers: 2/266)

26 May 1936

Some of us are anxious to raise upon the Adjournment Motion the question of a Ministry of Munitions in connection with the shortage of machine tools and the situation disclosed in the speech of the Minister for Co-ordination of Defence last week. I understand that the Labour Party will of course have precedence, but that the second topic is not yet selected. If you feel able to facilitate this debate, of which notice would of course be given to the Minister concerned, Sir Edward Grigg and Sir Robert Horne would in that order be willing to deal with the question. I myself would speak out now entirely as the course of the debate and the time available suggested, but in any case very briefly. Sir Edward Grigg would be about twenty minutes and Sir Robert Horne about half an hour. Perhaps you will allow me to have a word with you at the close of Questions.

[1] Speaker of the House of Commons (see page 106, note 2).

Harold Balfour[1] to Winston S. Churchill

(*Churchill papers: 2/272*)

26 May 1936

Dear Mr Churchill,

I am writing this line to let you know that when the Report State of the Navy Estimates comes up on Thursday, I want again to raise & debate the question of the Fleet Air Arm. Very respectfully and humbly, I propose to take the five points you made in your speech on Monday, the 4th and try to put the opposite view! I thought it only right to let you know this.

Although I may beg to differ on this particular aspect of defence, nevertheless I know that we all of us are united in the main desire to see *safety* achieved by efficiency in the *shortest possible* time.

Kind regards,
Yours sincerely,
Harold Balfour

Winston S. Churchill to Allan G. Clark

(*Churchill papers: 2/280*)

28 May 1936
Private and Confidential

I asked Sir Hugh Elles[2] to come to see me yesterday, and having obtained from him his assurance that you and your firm would be in no way prejudiced by the steps you have taken in coming to me, I told him the substance of what you had said and showed him your report. He seemed to be already well informed upon the subject and said at once 'No doubt it is the Plessey Com-

---

[1] Harold Harington Balfour, 1897–   . A great grandson of Field-Marshal Lord Napier of Magdala. Educated Royal Naval College, Osborne. Joined 60th Rifles, 1914; Royal Flying Corps, 1915–17 (Military Cross and bar). Served in the Royal Air Force, 1918–23. Conservative MP for the Isle of Thanet, 1929–45. Parliamentary Under-Secretary of State for Air, 1938–44. Privy Councillor, 1941. Minister Resident in West Africa, 1944–5. Created Baron Balfour of Inchrye, 1945. A member of the Board of British European Airways, 1955–66. Chairman, BEA Helicopters Ltd. He published *An Airman Marches* in 1935 and *Wings Over Westminster* in 1973. His elder brother, a Lieutenant-Commander, Royal Navy, was killed on active service in 1941.

[2] Hugh Jamieson Elles, 1880–1945. Entered Royal Engineers, 1899. Served in the South African War, 1901–2. Deputy Assistant Quartermaster-general, 4th Division, 1914. Brigade Major, 10th Division, 1915. Wounded in action, 1915. Lieutenant-Colonel commanding the Tank Corps in France, 1916–19. Promoted Brigadier-General, 1917; Major-General, 1918. Knighted, 1919. Commandant of the Tank Corps Training Centre, 1919–23. Director of Military Training, War Office, 1930–3. Master General of Ordnance, War Office, 1934–7. General, 1938. Regional Commissioner for South-West England, 1939–45.

pany'. He expressed himself greatly obliged by the action I had taken, and promised to give his personal attention to the matter, which as I have said, had already come to his notice. I am sure in these circumstances the right course will be taken. I should be glad to know whether I may retain your report and show it, also in confidence, to Lord Weir and Sir Thomas Inskip.

Ramsay MacDonald to Winston S. Churchill
(*Churchill papers: 2/266*)

28 May 1936 Privy Council Office

My dear Churchill,

I have been trying to arrange to be at the House today but find it quite impossible if I am to get away, as I really must, to Lossiemouth this evening. There is only one train in the day, and I think you will understand that as I am only to have 8 or 9 days' holiday I am anxious not to take a day off at this end. May I bring this point before you: The really effective matter is not the escalator clause but the obligations that Japan undertook to scrap seven cruisers of a considerably superior character to the five that we undertook to scrap. The position is that if Japan does not scrap—and privately I may say that I have good reason for believing that they will not—we have no obligations to scrap ourselves. I think that that is by far and away the best position for us to secure.

I do hope you will see that it is no lack of courtesy on my part if I do not put in an appearance at the House of Commons this afternoon.

Yours very sincerely,
J. Ramsay MacDonald

Winston S. Churchill to J. Ramsay MacDonald
(*Churchil papers: 2/266*)

29 May 1936

Many thanks for your letter of the 28th. I fully understand the reasons which made it impossible for you to be present at the debate.

It passed off quite peaceably.[1]

[1] During a debate on 28 May 1936, on the supplementary estimates for the Navy, Churchill supported the Government's request for a further £10,000,000 for naval construction, a request that was passed by 182 votes to 85. But he opposed the Admiralty's plan to scuttle five light cruisers in order to conform to the London Naval Treaty of 1930, urging the Government to invoke the escalator clause of the Treaty, which allowed any of the signatories to exceed the tonnage limits for any class of ship if it felt its security required it to do so.

Sir Thomas Inskip to Winston S. Churchill
(*Churchill papers: 2/269*)

29 May 1936
Secret and Personal

My dear Churchill,

Thank you for your letter. Believe me I shall always value your help and shall not resent your criticisms. I am naturally concerned at what you say of the scientific work and have it in mind to turn to it after Whitsun. You will no doubt yourself represent your opinion to the Committee. As to the second point, I should be grateful if you would let me have a short paper outlining your view of the problem.

Yours sincerely,
T. W. H. Inskip

Winston S. Churchill to Lord Swinton
(*Cabinet papers: 21/426*)

29 May 1936
Confidential

Dear Philip,

I have received from the French Government their latest estimate of the strength of the German Air Force, and think it my duty to send it to you. I must however ask that no comment or reference will be made to the French Government upon their having given me this information. You will see that their current estimate corresponds very closely, indeed almost exactly, to the figures which I gave in December, and which you somewhat unkindly characterised as 'a guess' in your introductory note to 1216B.[1]

Yours vy sincerely,
Winston S. Churchill

Sir Maurice Hankey to Winston S. Churchill
(*Churchill papers: 25/7*)

30 May 1936

Dear Winston,

Just a line to let you know that I spoke to Swinton about the French official information.

---

[1] Committee of Imperial Defence Paper 1216B was the Air Staff's answer to Churchill's notes of 9 December 1935 (circulated to the CID on 17 December 1935 as Paper 1205B). These notes are printed in full in the previous document volume of this biography, pages 1345–8. See also pages 178–9 of this volume.

He quite agreed that you should use it in your paper and that nothing should be done to interrupt your contact with the French. He added that if the information given by the French Staff to you differed from that given to the Air Staff they might have to make fresh inquiries, but he agreed that that could be taken up if necessary, by asking for their latest figures and estimates without referring to your information. My personal impression is that their latest information from the French does not differ materially from yours— though I am not quite certain.[1]

My personal advice to you would be to put in a paragraph asking that the Air Staff shall on no account mention your contact to the French.

I am just off to the sea-side for a few days.

Yours ever,
Maurice P. A. Hankey

Winston S. Churchill to Vice-Admiral Guépratte[2]
(*Churchill papers: 2/254*)

30 May 1936

I need scarcely say that I am very highly honoured by the invitation which you have tendered me to become a member of the Académie de Marine, and I am deeply grateful to you and your colleagues for this kind and complimentary thought. I feel however for reasons of politics, and in the existing situation, that it would be unwise for me to be formally identified with a branch of the French service, and that it might detract from my influence in dealing with the present dangerous situation in a manner which would serve the interests of our two countries, which as you know, is my earnest desire. Permit me therefore to leave this matter in suspense in the hopes that you may feel able to renew your invitation in calmer times.

[1] On 9 June 1936, in a 'most secret' letter, Sir Edward Ellington informed Sir Maurice Hankey, in connection with Churchill's French air strength figures: 'Actually our copy of the document written for the French Senatorial Commission was obtained from Morton's Industrial Intelligence Section' (*Cabinet papers: 21/426*).

[2] Emile Paul Aimable Guépratte, 1856–1939. Entered the French Navy, 1871. Rear-Admiral commanding the French naval forces at the Dardanelles, February–October 1915. Vice-Admiral, October 1915. Knighted, 1915. Subsequently Préfet Maritime at Brest and Commander-in-Chief and Préfet Maritime in Algeria–Tunisia.

June 1936

<hr>

Winston S. Churchill to A. H. Richards
(Churchill papers: 2/282)

1 June 1936

I have quite definitely reached the conclusion that a meeting on the 17th or 18th of June would be a mistake, and I could not myself take part in it. The present foreign situation is so obscure and difficult that almost any pronouncement by private persons would be futile. The Italian and German issues are so mixed up that it would be impossible to take a clear line, indeed any line, without being exposed not only to effective criticism but to early stultification. No pronouncement could be made at the moment which would not give great dis-satisfaction. However it is the duty of the Government to say what they are going to do about the mess into which they have led us.

On the other hand if we wait the situation must simplify itself, and meanwhile the growth of German armaments and our own inertia will increasingly impress itself upon the British mind. In the meantime however we should continue to interchange opinions and I will shortly write to you and suggest a small luncheon at my flat of six or seven of us to come a little closer to matters.

Believe me,

<hr>

Professor Lindemann: note prepared for Winston S. Churchill[1]
(Churchill papers: 25/10)

COMMENTS ON THE AIR STAFF
MEMORANDUM '1216 B'

1 June 1936

1216B estimates the German first line air strength on March 31st 1936

---

[1] Lindemann's introductory paragraph to this note read: 'Whilst I am not able to accept definitely the figures given in the Air Staff memoranda, I will in what follows, in order to save argument, utilize these figures only. But the conclusions which I draw from the Air Staff

at 850 to 900 machines. The British first line air strength is declared to consist on the same date of 785 Metropolitan machines, 260 overseas machines and 170 fleet air arm machines. As Germany possesses as yet no fleet air arm she can thus pit her whole force of admittedly at least 850 machines against our 785 machines. Hence, even on the Air Staff figures, without any further calculations or modification it is plain that the German Air Force on the 1st April 1936 was stronger than the Metropolitan British Air Force, contrary to all the undertakings and pledges given to Parliament.

This is the position as stated by the Air Staff.

The reality is certainly worse than this.

In comparing the relative strengths of the German Air Force and the RAF, we may proceed either upon the assumption of a war of duration (months or even years) or on the assumption, to which many influential Germans are said to adhere, that the war may be finished in ten days or so by annihilating air attack on the enemies' capital and principal cities. On either assumption our inferiority is disquieting.

We are told in 1216B that the German output, working only one shift instead of three, is 270 air-frames and 640 engines. As we are not entitled to assume that the German Government has erected three times as many factories as it is able to staff, one must count upon these factories in the event of war being utilised to their full capacity giving a monthly output of a thousand machines. I do not know what is the comparable British output, but I should be relieved to learn that it exceeds (or will exceed before the 1st April 1937) 300 to 350 machines a month.

If we assume a war wastage of 80% a month, which is I believe the French estimate, this output is not even sufficient to maintain our first line Metropolitan Air strength at its present number of 785 machines. Even if we have one machine in reserve for each first line aeroplane the number of machines which we can keep in commission will drop below 500 at the end of the fourth month. The German Air Force on the other hand, with its war-time output of a thousand per month, would be able to maintain a first line air strength of 1,250 machines for an indefinite period.

Thus, at the end of the fourth month the British Air Force would be nearer one third than one half of the German.

---

figures are far different and much more disagreeable.' Churchill's amended version of the introductory paragraph read: 'Without accepting definitely the figures of the Air Staff memoranda, I will in what follows, in order to save argument, utilize these figures mainly. But the conclusions which I draw on are different and more disagreeable.'

Allan G. Clark to Winston S. Churchill

(*Churchill papers: 2/280*)

2 June 1936   The Plessey Company Limited
Private and Confidential

Dear Mr Churchill,

Very many thanks for your letter of the 28th ultimo. I shall be glad if you will retain our report, and thank you for your assurance again that you will show this in confidence to Lord Weir and Sir Thomas Inskip.

I am glad to hear that the proper Authorities know about us, but you will appreciate that I am getting rather despondent on account of the delay in hearing from them as my friends are naturally anxious to hear from me as to whether we should be interested in obtaining this plant from them or not, and my feeling is that in view of the international situation the sooner a decision is arrived at the better it will be for this Country.

Yours faithfully,
A. G. Clark

Sir Thomas Inskip to Winston S. Churchill

(*Churchill papers: 2/269*)

3 June 1936

My dear Churchill,

I am taking advantage of your offer to give me any help in your power. Will you come & talk to me about your idea of a Minister of Supply. It is obviously in my own personal interest to pass over this part of my duties to someone else; my difficulty is in seeing what such a step involves and what advantage will be gained. It is here that you can help me if you will.

Monday or Tuesday would be convenient to me though I am fairly engaged on Tuesday. Of course I would come to you, if you prefer it.

I am very sorry to find that Grigg has taken umbrage at what I said last Friday. I have no idea what I could have said to hurt his feelings.

Yours sincerely,
T. W. H. Inskip

Winston S. Churchill to Sir Thomas Inskip

(*Churchill papers: 2/269*)

3 June 1936
Personal & Secret

I now send you in personal confidence two papers which have come into my hands. The first is from the Plessey Manufacturing Company. The Managing-Director, Mr Clark, came to see me a fortnight ago in great distress that no notice was apparently being taken of his report. He is a man who makes a very strong impression in conversation. I subsequently saw the Master-General of the Ordnance,[1] and after obtaining from him his promise that no grudge would be borne against the Plessey Company, I opened the matter to him. I was glad to find that he already knew something about it and I trust action is by now on the move. Nevertheless I thought the report of this German visit so interesting, and I may add so disturbing, that I asked permission to show it to you and to Weir. Not only is the scale of German war production at least ten times ours, but the pace and method of production are far superior.

The second paper was confided to me by the French government. It is their latest estimate of the German air strength at the beginning of May. This almost exactly confirms my estimate or 'guess' as Swinton somewhat unkindly described it, of the 9th of December of last year which is printed in 1216 B paragraph 3, page 2 of the Committee of Imperial Defence papers.

I hope the French are right in thinking the Germans no further advanced, for the accounts I receive of the French Air Force, though it is improving, are not at all satisfactory, and least of all in respect of their manufacturing capacity in wartime.

Lastly I enclose you the short note I mentioned about the dangers of invasion by troops from the air. Will you kindly let me have the first two documents back when you have made any use of them you may require.

Winston S. Churchill to Sir Thomas Inskip

(*Churchill papers: 2/269*)

3 June 1936   Chartwell

I shall not be in London till Tuesday, but it would be very nice if you could motor down here (one hour) and lunch or dine and sleep on Monday. If, however, your plans do not favour this, I can come to your room after

---

[1] Lieutenant-General Sir Hugh Elles (see page 174, note 2).

questions on Tuesday. I have an article to write that afternoon on 'How to stop War'[1] which, as you may well imagine, requires a little thought. Otherwise I am free.

Your job, like Gaul, seems divided into three parts. (i) Co-ordinating strategy and settling quarrels between the Services. (ii) Making sure the goods are delivered under the various programmes and (iii) Creating the structure of War industry and its organisation. These last two lie together. If you are going to be responsible for them, you will surely need a powerful machine which will grow from month to month and handle increasingly larger blocks of business as its strength and efficiency develop. The successive steps by which this machinery should be formed, the procuring of the necessary powers from Parliament, and the taking over by instalments all the Service Supply Departments, require to be scheduled. Wide powers should be taken in the act and applied in stages by Orders in Council as they are required, and as they can be used. Until you have got a fairly strong machine you cannot take over the work, and it would be most imprudent to accept the responsibility for the punctual execution of the programmes. This business is vast and complex, and no man can manage it without the necessary apparatus.

A Prime Minister may rightly hope for peace and resolve upon a policy of peace. But a Defence Minister must always contemplate the possibility of war at various dates in the future, and must plan accordingly. If, for instance, war comes in 1937, everyone will expect that a complete organisation of our industry for war purposes and a good system of control will be actually in being. It was my experience that while people oppose all precautions in time of peace, the very same people turn round within a fortnight of war and are furious about every shortcoming. I hope it may not be yours.

I will put down a few 'heads' of action in their sequence as I see it, so that you will have something to ask me questions about.

Grigg was, I think, upset at the idea that you would be so very good in Parliament and allay anxieties effectively, but that perhaps behind the scenes you would not single-handed be able to do very much. Personally I sympathise with you very much in your task. I would never have undertaken such a task knowing from experience how fierce opinions become upon these subjects once the nation is alarmed. It is an awful thing to take over masses of loosely defined responsibilities.

[1] Churchill's article 'How to Stop War' was published in the *Evening Standard* on 12 June 1936. In it he argued in favour of 'one world-wide organism' to resist aggression. 'Let all the nations and States be invited to band themselves together upon a simple, single principle: "Who touches one, touches all." Who attacks any, will be resisted by all, and resisted with such wrath and apparatus, with such comradeship and hearty zeal, that the very prospect may by its formidable majesty perhaps avert the crime.'

Perhaps you might think it worth while to send a note of four or five questions you wish to ask me about the Ministry of Supply, so that I can address my mind to them beforehand, apart from sending you my 'heads'.

Winston S. Churchill to Sir Abe Bailey[1]

(*Churchill papers: 2/255*)

3 June 1936

Indeed I have nothing to forgive. I was very much surprised when you showed me what you had written about me; and you will remember that I immediately said I was sure the Times would not print the letter with that in it.[2] Only a week before when Lord Bayford,[3] a respectable person, made friendly reference to me at a Conservative meeting, the Times which gave the longest report of his speech I have seen, omitted this reference which in every other paper was the only sentence printed from the speech.[4] I mention these facts because they show that the Times is not content in using its perfectly fair right to express its likes and dislikes in leading articles, but that it definitely distorts and suppresses news values where I am concerned.

Do not, my dear Abe, suppose that I mind. In the present posture of

---

[1] Abe Bailey, 1863–1940. One of the principal mine-owners of the Transvaal. Knighted, 1911, for his services in promoting South African union. Served as a Major on the staff of the South African forces which attacked German South-West Africa, 1915. Created Baronet, 1919. His son John married Churchill's eldest daughter, Diana, in 1932 (divorced 1935).

[2] In a letter published in *The Times* on 3 June 1936, Sir Abe Bailey had urged Britain to continue 'a resolute sanctions policy against Italy' for her 'aggressive designs' against Abyssinia, and had advised opposition to Italian expansion, in preference to building an alliance against Germany. 'In South Africa,' he wrote, 'and I believe in the other Dominions as well, we are not so convinced that Germany is our enemy as to feel any desire to create a "front" against her nor so conscious of our own weakness as to feel the need of an ally in Italy which has just broken most of the international agreements to which it was a party.' There was no reference to Churchill in the letter as published.

[3] Robert Arthur Sanders, 1867–1940. Educated at Harrow and Balliol College, Oxford. Barrister, Inner Temple, 1891. Conservative MP for Bridgewater, 1910–23; for Wells, 1924–9. Lieutenant-Colonel, on active service at Gallipoli, in Egypt and in Palestine, 1915–18. Treasurer of the Household, 1918–19. Junior Lord of the Treasury, 1919. Created Baronet, 1920. Under-Secretary for War, 1921–2. Privy Councillor, 1922. Minister of Agriculture and Fisheries, 1922–4. Created Baron Bayford, 1929.

[4] On Saturday 23 May 1936 Lord Bayford, Chairman of the Association of Conservative Clubs, speaking at a conference of Conservative Clubmen in Cardiff said (according to *The Times*, 25 May 1936) that 'if we wanted peace throughout the world there was no greater security than a strong and well-armed British Empire'. Under the headline 'Mr Churchill and Cabinet', the *Daily Telegraph* reported on 25 May 1936: 'Lord Bayford, addressing the Association of Conservative Clubs of South Wales and Monmouthshire at Cardiff on Saturday, discussed the possibility of Mr Churchill entering the Cabinet. His inclusion, said Lord Bayford, would "give great satisfaction in many Conservative circles".'

affairs I have no wish whatever for office. I would not join any Government which I do not feel was resolved to lift National Defence to an altogether different plane, nor would I join any Government in which I had not a real share of power for such a purpose. If all our fears are groundless and everything passes off smoothly in the next few years, as pray God indeed it may, obviously there is no need for me. If on the other hand the very dangerous times arise, I may be forced to take a part. Only in those conditions have I any desire to serve.

Desmond Morton to Winston S. Churchill
(*Churchill papers: 2/266*)

3 June 1936   Edenbridge

Dear Winston,

I have read Mr Peter Thomas'[1] memorandum several times, but I am not at all sure that I understand what practical action he recommends. If, however, the essence is that the Service Departments should remain responsible for supplying current needs for the existing forces, while a new Ministry of Supply should concern itself primarily with finding capacity to meet the requirements for (a) immediate expansion, and (b) further expansion in war, I am afraid I could not support the idea.

This is not altogether unlike the existing arrangements, which are so widely criticised.

In my opinion, nothing will be really satisfactory until there is one single authority responsible for all supply, and that authority is separate from the Armed Forces Departments, either singly or together.

You cannot separate current requirements to make good ordinary wastage, from immediate requirements for expansion or for reserve. You cannot separate either of these from planning for the great expansion which war will demand.

To set up a Minister with his Civil Servants, assisted by a council of private manufacturers, would be admirable. But this Ministry or body must be in charge of all manufacture, all contracting and all supply for the three armed forces. You can contract out for war-ships, leaving that to the

---

[1] Peter David Thomas, 1873–1952. Admitted a Solicitor, 1894. On active service, 1914–16 (despatches twice). MVO, 1918. Major, 1920. CBE, 1920. In his letter to Churchill he stated: 'I write the above as a result of experience of many years as a commercial lawyer and an active Director of numerous large firms engaged in most of the staple trades, and also of three years as Head of the Ministry of Munitions for the Yorkshire Area, including Sheffield. During the latter period all departments of the Ministry of Munitions were represented in the Area and were under my direct supervision. Consequently I had considerable experience of Supply, Co-ordination difficulties, and Labour.'

Admiralty in that case, the actual factories and Dockyards they can utilise. Moreover the Ministry of Supply must take the Naval guns, gun ammunition, explosives &c.

If I have misinterpreted Mr Thomas, I apologise to him, but must then confess that I do not know what he is suggesting. I have the feeling that Mr Thomas could write a far better and more intelligible memorandum, if he knew what the existing procedure was. I get the impression that he thinks it is the same as in 1913, or in war years. Both the system of supply and all questions of armament manufacture to-day have been revolutionised in certain essential particulars as a result of war time experience and the general adoption of the manufacture of armaments by components,—that is mass production—even in peace.

The chief trouble with us in this country is that we have failed to alter our system of supply in accordance with the automatic alteration of the system of manufacture. We have indeed altered it from prewar practice, but we have deluded ourselves into believing that war-time practice is only to be used in war.

The simplest form of the argument in favour of a single supply authority in peace as well as in war, is that in both periods, nowadays, the same factory may be required to manufacture at the same time bits of submarines, bits of aircraft engines, and bits of artillery ammunition. Chaos ensues if the unfortunate Manager has to deal with three totally unconnected ordering, contracting and inspecting authorities. Actually, under the present system, there may be four, since in the middle of it all, the fourth authority planning war-time expansion may descend upon him.

Given time, we shall make the stuff that is *now* so urgently required, and shall 'muddle through' somehow. After that—always provided we are given the time— we shall sit back with complacency and say, 'There you are. After all the fuss Winston made, we are all right after all'; quite forgetting that although we have somehow produced what we urgently require, these slip-shod methods will never do if war actually comes.

Yours very sincerely,
Desmond Morton

Lord Linlithgow to Winston S. Churchill
(*Churchill papers: 2/263*)

4 June 1936   Viceregal Lodge,
                                                     Simla

. . . It is good of you to write as you have of my beginnings out here. It is a great help to have got reasonably well off the mark, particularly in this country where first impressions are prone to persist. But my difficulties will come along soon enough, and you may be sure that I shall catch it hot before I am through with the thing!

I feel myself very fortunate to have had some previous drilling in agricultural matters, and you may count upon me to hold on to that side of the business, and to do all in my power to help the village folk.

I hope Clemmy is well; please give her my best messages.

Yours ever,
Hopie

Lieutenant-General Sir Hugh Elles to Winston S. Churchill

(*Churchill papers: 2/280*)

4 June 1936   War Office

Dear Mr Churchill,

I am sorry to have been so long in writing to you on the subject of *Plessey*. My expert on the subject was away when I got back after seeing you, and Whitsun has intervened. The Plessey proposition, I can assure you, has not been lost sight of, but it is one of a number of similar proposals, and we want to make the best of the job.

The whole question of the modern machine tools, especially those of German manufacture, is interesting us very much indeed. The matter is far from being an easy one, especially in the processes of peace administration. I can assure you that we are bending our energies in that direction.

I have just had from your Private Secretary a letter from Mr Frewen[1] on the subject of a streamline bullet and an Australian inventor. I will have the matter gone into at once, but you ought to know that we are producing a really first class anti-tank rifle as it is, which as far as penetration is concerned is superior to anything that we have seen up to date. We have explored the streamline question for the last two or three years, but there are immense difficulties as far as we have gone in the matter of mass production. This particular bullet may be free from these objections, and I will have the matter looked into.

Yours sincerely,
Hugh Elles

[1] Oswald Frewen, Churchill's cousin (see page 78, note 2).

Lord Davies and others[1] to Winston S. Churchill

(*Churchill papers: 2/284*)

4 June 1936

We, the undersigned members of the Parliamentary Group of The New Commonwealth Society, desire to give our unqualified support to the invitation which has been forwarded to you to become the President of the British Section of the Society.

Having observed with the greatest satisfaction your powerful advocacy of the fundamental principles upon which the programme of the Society is based, not only in your published works but also in your recent speeches and articles, we are confident that, by placing yourself at the head of this movement, you would be making an invaluable contribution to the cause of world peace and enabling the Society to intensify its efforts for the introduction of the reign of international law and order.

Winston S. Churchill to Lord Davies

(*Churchill papers: 2/284*)

5 June 1936   Chartwell

My dear Lord Davies,

I must regard it as my duty to accept the invitation with which you have honoured me. You and your friends certainly realise that I am doing my best to procure effective measures to put our country in a state of safety. The fact that you should consider these efforts of mine no barrier, but indeed rather an aid to the cause which you have so much at heart, makes me feel that there is a broad understanding across the gulfs of party both of the dangers in which we lie, and of the bold measures of thought and action which the crisis demands. I have long been, as you say, in fundamental agreement with your aims. Indeed the alternative to the reign of international law, supported by ample force to make it respected, can only be a horrible war and the probable ruin of civilisation.

The task which you have set yourselves, and in which I am willing to bear my part, is beset with every kind of difficulty and exposed to mockery and misunderstanding. But that we should persevere in it with faith, and practical measures, is surely a simple obligation. The fact that you and your friends

[1] The signatories of this letter included: Vyvyan Adams, Robert Bernays, Robert Boothby, F. Seymour Cocks, Clement Davies, Megan Lloyd George, Sir Patrick Hannon, G. le M. Mander, J. T. C. Moore-Brabazon, John P. Morris, Harold Nicolson, E. L. Spears, and Josiah Wedgwood.

wish for any small aid that I can give, is a proof that you recognise that a wider and higher order of human society can only be brought about through the championship of strong nations, willing and able through their strength to make exertions for weaker states and sacrifices for the larger hope, indeed the only hope.[1]

Yours sincerely,
Winston S. Churchill

Sir Thomas Inskip to Winston S. Churchill
(*Churchill papers: 2/269*)

6 June 1936

My dear Churchill,
    Many thanks for your letter of 3 June. I will make enquiries into the first two papers & let you have them back a little later on. As regards the third, I am very grateful to you for putting the idea into *writing* & I will certainly have it considered.[2]

Yours sincerely,
T. W. H. Inskip

We hope to reach you on Monday about 12 or perhaps a little earlier.

Lord Swinton to Sir Maurice Hankey
(*Cabinet papers: 64/5*)

9 June 1936
Secret

My dear Maurice,
    I am seeing you this afternoon about the Churchill-Lindemann affair, and I should like to deal with the Churchill French memorandum at the same time. As far as I can see, the mountain becomes rather a molehill. The

---

[1] On 8 June 1936, after his acceptance had been made public, Churchill wrote to Sir James Hawkey: 'I had a talk with Neville Chamberlain before accepting, and he told me he had subscribed and was a Member, and that he thought as the ultimate goal this was the right thing. I feel so strongly one ought to do all one can to get this country re-armed and to relieve people from feeling that re-armament means war. In my belief it is one of the few chances of peace' (*Churchill papers: 2/284*).

[2] On 6 June 1936 Churchill sent Inskip a memorandum on the need to establish a Supply Department under the Ministry of Co-ordination of Defence. Nearly two years later, Churchill received Inskip's permission to publish this memorandum in *The Times* (see pages 1034–5 of this volume, where it is reprinted in full).

document received with such empressement from the French Government is a document of no great secrecy, written by the French Air Ministry for the Senatorial Commission. I have no doubt that it will in due course receive the same publicity as the Report of the Senatorial Air Commission published last July, to which I drew the attention of the CID in an earlier paper.

As the Air Staff point out, the French Air Ministry would naturally tend to put the German position as high as they could. I think this is the more likely as the Senate Commission, in their previous report, had discounted and ridiculed a number of rumours and guesses, though, be it said in justice, none of them emanated from the French Air Ministry, but rather from the British press.

You will see from the Air Staff note that, even assuming the French figures to be correct, they have included immediate reserve in first-line strength, which we never do for ourselves or any other country; and the fair standard of comparison therefore is to write down the German figure by 30 per cent, or to write up ours by the same or more.

I think probably we are more likely to be right about numbers of squadrons formed. As you see from the note, we have more first-hand official information, but we also have another source of information, which I will explain to you.

As I told you, I very much dislike carrying on secret correspondence with Churchill on these matters by private letters, and I suggest, therefore, that we should issue as a CID paper the French memorandum, which is independently in our possession, and the notes of the Air Staff upon it.

Yours ever,
Swinton

Winston S. Churchill to Adam Marshall Diston[1]
(*Churchill papers: 8/536*)

9 June 1936

I am now thinking about the article 'The Shadow over the Pacific'. The bulk of it I have got in my mind, but as you made the suggestion about the title, would you let me have a two thousand word note upon it.

---

[1] Adam Marshall Diston, 1893–1956. Born in Scotland. Served in a Highland Regiment, 1914–18. Joined the Staff of Amalgamated Press after the war: subsequently Assistant Editor of *Answers*, and acting Editor (1934). An officer of the Trade and Periodical Branch of the National Union of Journalists. A Socialist, he joined Sir Oswald Mosley's New Party in 1931. Unsuccessful New Party Candidate for Wandsworth Central in the 1931 election (where he polled only 424 votes out of a total of 11,647, and lost his deposit); he never stood for Parliament again. In 1935 he tried in vain to be adopted as prospective Labour candidate for Aylesbury.

Stanley Baldwin to Sir Thomas Inskip

(*Cabinet papers: 64/31*)

10 June 1936   10 Downing Street

My dear Inskip,

I am very anxious about the programme of the Defence Services. I have followed the debates in the House and have seen some of the comments in the Press on the proposal to establish a Ministry of Supply which would take over the direction of everything necessary to get the programme completed in the time laid down if not earlier. The House and the Country are entitled to an assurance, which must rest on solid ground, that everything reasonably possible is being done to get the things which the Services need without any avoidable delay. Can this assurance be given? That is a question to which I should like to have your answer after the meeting of the DPR[1] to-morrow.

                                                        Yours sincerely,
                                                        Stanley Baldwin

Sir Thomas Inskip to Winston S. Churchill

(*Churchill papers: 2/269*)

11 June 1936
Personal

My dear Churchill,

I am now returning the two papers which you recently sent to me in confidence. A copy of the French Memorandum was in the possession of the

---

[1] The Defence Policy and Requirements Committee of the Cabinet. At its meeting on 11 June 1936 Inskip expressed his worries about the supply situation, believing that the period of 3 to 5 years laid down by the Cabinet as the years of preparation was too long and that 'the urgency of the situation might require us to alter the date, and to take new powers', such as making Austin turn their whole factory to war production. Vansittart, who was present at the meeting, agreed with Inskip that peace in Europe could not be guaranteed 'for the next five or even 3 years' and drew the Cabinet's attention to 'a marked change in the tone of Germany which was becoming distinctly sharper'. But Neville Chamberlain, as the minutes recorded, 'suggested that Germany's next forward step might not necessarily lead us into war'. Vansittart disagreed, warning that Germany's next forward move 'would probably be against Czechoslovakia'. Both Inskip and Swinton argued in favour of emergency powers, but Sir Samuel Hoare opposed them. 'Such powers', Hoare said, 'might come as a great shock to the country and result in an upheaval of industry.' This was also Neville Chamberlain's view, for, as he explained, 'The disturbance of industry produced by acceleration might result in grave consequences, financial, economic etc, and any alteration could only be justified by over-powering conditions.' At the end of the meeting Vansittart stated that there would not be 'any more marked symptoms of the foreign situation' than already existed. But

Air Ministry, and the Secretary of State has had it produced, with the Air Staff's notes upon it, in a CID Paper. A copy has, I understand, been sent to you.

I have made enquiries into the letter from the Plessey Company and understand that the writer had a personal interview with Mr Whitham[1] of the War Office at which the subject was discussed at length. From that it was assumed that a written acknowledgment was unnecessary. But the issues, which are undoubtedly very important, are before the Supply Board and I shall go into them personally.

Yours sincerely,
T. W. H. Inskip

Winston S. Churchill to Sir Maurice Hankey
(*Cabinet papers: 21/426*)

11 June 1936

My dear Maurice,

Thank you very much for your letters and for the new paper. I am sending you tonight a short comment upon it, which I hope may also be printed. I have left out all controversy about the past in order to arrive at a true estimate for the future.

I will at the Committee on Monday, if it is agreeable to the Secretary of State, make a short statement of a general character complaining of the slow rate of progress, and above all of achievement, which has characterised our work during the ten months I have served.

Yours vy sincerely,
Winston S. Churchill

Chamberlain insisted that only when 'the situation deteriorated' still further would there be sufficient 'accumulation of symptoms' to persuade public opinion to accept 'a more drastic move' (*Cabinet papers: 16/136*).

[1] Gilbert Shaw Whitham, 1889–1970. Born in Liverpool. Educated in Chile, 1910–14. A chemical engineer. On active service with the Yorks and Lancashire Regiment, 1914–16 (wounded). Ministry of Munitions, 1916–18 (Manager of the Sulphuric Acid Plant at Queenferry, 1916–17; technical officer for explosives supply, 1917–20; also Chemical Warfare Experimental Officer). War Office, 1919–43; serving as Assistant Director of the Dyestuffs Committee, and subsequently as Assistant Director of Ordnance Factories, and (from 1936) as Director of Industrial Planning. Director of Ammunition Production, 1939–41. Major-General, 1941. Head of British Supply Mission to Turkey, 1941. Deputy Director-General, Ministry of Supply, 1941. Head of Production Office, Palestine, 1942. Director-General, Production Services, Ministry of Supply, 1943–5. CMG, 1943. Chief of the Reparations Deliveries and Restitution Division, and Deputy Chief of the Economics Division, Control Commission for Germany, 1945–53.

Ralph Wigram to Winston S. Churchill

(*Churchill papers: 2/273*)

12 June 1936   Foreign Office

Dear Mr Churchill,

Here are the 3 despatches[1] containing the newspaper articles. Will you kindly destroy them when you have read them. I have marked the important passages.

I read your air paper with great interest, and I had an interesting talk today with one of the younger officers at the Air Ministry.

Have you noticed Ribbentrop's[2] 'blue book' to which he has just written a preface saying that it is 'a complete collection' of documents for those who want to know the truth in contradistinction to 'certain collections published lately in foreign countries which were of a tendentious & prejudiced character'. His 'complete collection' omits everything which could show that the British Govt had made any effort for peace. This is a stiffish act on the part of a man who comes here, pretending to work for Anglo-German understanding, and who is hospitably received. If the British Ambassador in Berlin did that kind of thing, he would be asked to go home.

Yours sincerely,
Ralph Wigram

Sir Hugh Tudor to Winston S. Churchill

(*Churchill papers: 2/266*)

12 June 1936   RMS Newfoundland,
                                                      Liverpool

My dear Winston,

I am sailing today. I went to the War Office about recruiting, and found they had already got the question about the Dominions & Newfoundland in particular under consideration, thanks to you.

---

[1] The despatches were: Sir Eric Phipps to Anthony Eden of 6 June 1936 (despatch No 575); Sir Eric Phipps to Anthony Eden of 4 June 1936 (despatch No 560); and Sir Eric Phipps to Anthony Eden of 3 June 1936 (despatch No 551). The third despatch contained a quotation from Dr Schacht that colonies 'are a vital necessity for an over-populated industrial country. For this reason it is impossible to withhold from Germany the possession of her old colonies which belong to her.'

[2] Joachim von Ribbentrop, 1893–1946. Champagne salesman in Canada, 1910–14. Lieutenant, Western Front, 1914–18, when he was wounded, and won the Iron Cross, first class. Aide-de-Camp to the German peace delegation in Paris, 1919. Head of a wine import-export business in Berlin, 1920–33. A National Socialist Deputy in the Reichstag, 1933. Ambassador to London, 1936–8. SS-Gruppenführer, 1936. Foreign Minister, 1938–45. Sentenced to death by the Allied Military Tribunal, Nuremberg, and hanged.

I gather from serving officers that the army is in a bad way for men. It seems to me that the nation must be got out of this false pacifism mood, and made to realize that if our forces are reasonably strong & capable of rapid expansion in case of need, we are hardly likely to be attacked. I loved your letter in the Times about Hugh Cecil about a fortnight ago.

I had a letter from Darling,[1] whom you will remember. He said that it was grotesque that the ablest mind in politics should be outside the government, & any little he could do would be done to increase the demand for your inclusion.

It is obvious to everybody I meet that the Defence job should have been given to you.

With all good wishes.

Yours ever,
Hugh Tudor

Henry Tizard to Lord Swinton

(*Cabinet 21/426*)

12 June 1936

My dear Swinton,

My immediate annoyance having subsided, I feel that I can write to you dispassionately about Lindemann's attack via Winston Churchill. I have come to the conclusion that I must ask you either to remove Lindemann from the Committee or to accept my resignation. Let me say at once that this is not a threat, and that if you prefer my resignation I should be left with no sense of grievance. I do not think that I am indispensable, nor that you would find it difficult to get someone just as good to act in my place.

My reasons are these. First, as I say in my note to the ADR Committee, I cannot have a member of my committee, who has failed to convince his colleagues, trying to force his views through outside influential people. As a result Mr Winston Churchill has circulated an attack on the Committee without taking the trouble to learn my views beforehand. This is an act of gross discourtesy.

But the more important thing I have to consider is whether the nation would lose or gain more by the severance of Lindemann's connection with the work. I am really sorry to say that I think that the gain would be greater than the loss. His querulousness when anybody differs from him, his inability to accept the views of the committee as a whole, and his consequent insistence

---

[1] Charles John Darling, 1849–1936. Barrister, 1874. Queen's Counsel, 1887. Conservative MP for Deptford, 1888–97. Knighted, 1897. Judge of the Queen's Bench Division of the High Court of Justice, 1897–1923. An original member of the Other Club, 1911. Chairman of the Committee on Courts Martial, 1919. Created Baron, 1924. He had died on 29 May 1936.

on talking about matters which we think are relatively unimportant, and hence preventing us getting on with more important matters, make him an impossible colleague. I have exercised the utmost patience with him throughout, and have done my best to get the best out of him, but when at the last meeting he accused a member of your Farnborough staff to his face with slackness and deliberate obstruction, without the smallest justification, I felt that the limit of my patience had been reached. I cannot be responsible to you for the success of our work under these conditions. Lindemann is a man of unusual scientific ability, and no one would be better pleased than I to work with him if he would use it in the right way. But the fact remains that he has contributed little of importance to our proceedings. The utmost I could say, in fairness to him, is that he has made some useful suggestions to Watson-Watt and that he has directed our attention to the least unpromising side of the short wire barrage schemes. But I believe, though I have no direct evidence, that outside the committee he decries the radio scheme. This, if true, is entirely unjustified. As for the short wire scheme, although it is still unpromising from a practical point of view, I think we must take the experiments to a decisive end, and that the progress will be faster and not slower if Lindemann goes. He has also been very insistent on the importance of infra-red detection. The rest of the committee decided to do nothing, before Lindemann joined, on infra-red detection, because we think that there is only a remote chance of practical success. But in deference to his views, we recommended that he should be given facilities to experiment in this direction, and if he goes off the committee, I should recommend that these facilities be continued.

Finally, I expect that it has already occurred to you that all this trouble may be part of a political move in which Lindemann is the willing tool of others. I cannot help suspecting that with the support of others he is waiting for a plausible pretext to resign, and 'make a row'. If so he has, with a typical lack of judgment, backed the wrong horse this time. He has no case. But he may be luckier next time, because other scientific men are also liable to make mistakes! If there is any possibility of this suspicion being correct, I suggest that the game had better be spoiled at the outset. But this is outside my beat: I merely throw it out as a suggestion.

I do dislike wasting your time and energies—and my own—in this way.[1]

Yours sincerely,

H. T. Tizard

[1] On 13 June 1936 Lord Swinton commented on Henry Tizard's letter, in a letter to Sir Thomas Inskip: 'This is all very tiresome, but I am bound to say my sympathies are entirely with Tizard. I have no doubt that if we lost Tizard we should lose the other two scientists as well. Tizard is dining with me tomorrow night, and I shall try to get him to hold his hand for the present' (*Cabinet papers: 64/5*).

Henry Tizard: Note on Mr Winston Churchill's Memorandum
(Cabinet papers: 21/426)[1]

12 June 1936

1. I propose in this note first to comment on Mr Winston Churchill's statements,[2] and then to add a general comment.

Paragraph 1 of Paper No: ADR 48.

The fact is that experiments on short-wire barrages (including 'Aerial Mines') were discussed by my Committee before Mr Winston Churchill raised the matter on the 25th July, 1935, and before Professor Lindemann joined the Committee. The idea is an old one. The problem to be attacked is that of deciding by experiment whether obvious difficulties and disadvantages can be overcome. In June, 1935, Mr Wimperis, on behalf of the Committee, was already discussing with the Royal Aircraft Establishment the nature of experiments to be carried out for the Committee.

2. Professor Lindemann joined my Committee at their meeting on the 25th July, 1935. A representative of the Royal Aircraft Establishment had been previously asked by me to attend the meeting in order to discuss the programme of experiments on short-wire barrages. There was a long discussion, during which Professor Lindemann had ample opportunity to put forward his views. Certain decisions for experimental work were unanimously reached.

3. On the 1st August Professor Lindemann wrote to me a private letter in which he urged that experiments on the type of explosive should be started at once. I replied on the 4th August that I had already asked the Secretary of the Committee to get such information as existed on the smallest explosive charge that would do serious damage to an aircraft, but that I did not feel inclined to go further without a decision of the Committee. I said: 'It is a pity you did not raise the point at our last meeting, when we were discussing wire barrages.'

Paragraph 2 of Paper No: ADR 48.
'Nothing was done.'

4. The fact is that during the summer months continuous experimental work was going on on the lines laid down by the Committee. At our next meeting on the 25th September (not the 9th October) a representative of the Royal Aircraft Establishment attended and described results of the experi-

---

[1] This note was circulated to the Sub-Committee on Air Defence Research as ADR 51.
[2] Churchill's memorandum of 2 June 1936, on Aerial Mines, printed on pages 146–8 of this volume.

ments. Two reports on results of experiment and calculation had previously been circulated. By the *next* meeting, on the 10th October, two further reports were ready. There was another long discussion, and further decisions were taken. It is true to say that investigations on 'what happened if an aeroplane ran into a wire on which a weight was suspended' have been continuously in progress since before Professor Lindemann joined the Committee, and have several times been discussed and modified in detail as a result of discussions at practically every meeting of the Committee since. It therefore seems faintly ludicrous to me to read that Professor Lindemann urged that this should be done, on the 5th November. Perhaps the day seemed appropriate—even more so, probably, to a discussion of the amount of explosive required. On this point I remark that experiments have been carried out, and in the opinion of the Committee as a whole (Professor Lindemann dissenting), further experiments on the nature and amount of explosive (though in progress) are not regarded as being of the highest priority. The reasons for this are technical; I can give them if necessary.

Paragraph 4 of Paper No: ADR 48.

5. I do not quite know what is meant by the phrase 'All sorts of difficulties were raised' etc. It is clearly the duty of my Committee to consider, as well as they can, the possible dangers of any full-scale experiments they may recommend. It is clearly also the responsibility of the Air Ministry to decide whether their recommendations shall be carried out.

On the last part of this paragraph, which reads like a criticism, I may remark that the recommendation to use small fragile vessels was made by Professor Lindemann.

6. In paragraph 7 it is stated that Professor Lindemann wrote to Mr Wimperis making a recommendation. In paragraph 9 it is stated that he wrote to the Superintendent of Experiments, Shoeburyness, making another recommendation. In my opinion Professor Lindemann should put his views before the Committee of which he is a member. The Superintendent of Experiments, Shoeburyness, can surely be forgiven for not attaching the importance to Professor Lindemann's request that he doubtless would have if it had come from the Committee.

7. My general comment on Paper No: ADR 48 is this: Professor Lindemann has not succeeded in convincing his colleagues on my Committee that certain of his views and recommendations are acceptable: nevertheless, as the above short sentence shews, the Committee hold that short-wire barrage ideas, old though they are in certain forms, require careful examination on lines laid down by them. Their object is finally to put before the Air Staff the technical data on which a decision will have to be made.

Unless a scientific committee is to be given unfettered discretion to decide what experiments are important and what are not, there is no point in having a scientific committee. I take the strongest exception to a member of my Committee, who has not succeeded in convincing his colleagues on scientific and technical questions, endeavouring to force his views through a member of this Committee, however distinguished.

When my Committee as a whole is seriously dissatisfied with the progress of experiment, or failure to carry out its recommendations, its dissatisfaction will be expressed by its Chairman to the proper authorities.

Winston S. Churchill: memorandum

(Foreign Office papers: 371/19933)

12 June 1936
Secret

To Be Kept Under Lock and Key[1]

GERMAN AIR STRENGTH

What is desired is to estimate the German air strength compared to ours now and at different dates in the future. For this purpose the standard of comparison adopted should be the one which gives the truest picture, rather than one which conforms to our own conventions, and on which past statements to Parliament have been based. The adoption of an arbitrary definition of 'first-line air strength' and its application to Germany, may have its bearing upon past controversies, but may not be a true guide to reality. After all, what we really want to know is the number at given dates of 'German war-planes simultaneously available for service and capable of indefinite maintenance'. It is suggested that comparison on this basis would be more helpful than the present method.

2. ADR 50, Annex 2, paragraph 2, disagrees with the French system of counting the three 'Immediate Reserve' aircraft in the strength of a German squadron. Is there any valid reason for this? We know from previous Air Staff papers that there is a very large surplus of German war-planes and pilots who have passed through the training schools available after the existing squadron formations have been filled. Why then should these three

---

[1] This was the instruction on Churchill's memorandum, as circulated to the Committee of Imperial Defence on 27 June 1936, by Sir Maurice Hankey. In his covering note Hankey wrote: 'I am instructed by the Secretary of State for Air to enclose herewith a Memorandum on German Air Strength by the Right Hon. Winston S. Churchill, CH, MP, together with Air Staff Notes thereon.'

Immediate Reserve trained pilots and war-planes in each squadron not be counted? In what respect do they differ from the other nine in each squadron? Unless there is some important difference it would surely be prudent to count them as the French do 'en ligne', and not rule them out as not according to our conventions. At any rate, 339 military aircraft incorporated with their squadrons, manned by pilots who have passed through the official training schools, is not a negligible factor in computing the danger we have to face. It would raise the German effective strength to 1,236 aeroplanes on the 1st May, 1936, to which one monthly increment of 60 has probably been added, making a total of 1,296, exclusive of the Lufthansa, which the French put at 120 and the Air Staff at 72.

3. The possibility envisaged by the French is that the German figure of machines in line will reach 2,000 by the end of the year. It may be, unfortunately, that we are still seriously under-estimating the number of German machines formed into squadrons. The Air Staff figures used in CID Paper No. 1216–B are derived from the number of squadrons which have been identified. An analysis of the papers 1186–B and 1189–B seems to show that a vastly greater number of machines has been constructed and pilots trained than corresponds to the number emerging from the process of identifying squadrons.

In Paper No FCI 78 we have an estimate of the monthly output of German aircraft from April 1933 to July 1935. Extrapolating up to the 1st April, 1936, and allowing for a wastage of 25 per cent per annum in service aircraft in squadrons and 55 per cent per annum in training aircraft, and reckoning 70 to 75 per cent of all machines produced as suitable for military purposes (in accordance with appendix 2 of FCI 78), some 3,200 machines should be available in Germany for military purposes. The question arises, what has happened to all these machines?

4. As to pilots, it is admitted in 1189–B that 2,530 pilots have been trained at the schools up to the 1st April, 1936. What has happened to all these pilots?

It is stated in CID Paper No 1216–B, in agreement with the French view, that many German squadrons of 9 machines have three pilots and machines in reserve. If we reckon, therefore, 12 pilots and 12 machines to the squadron, 88 squadrons will absorb 1,056 pilots and 1,056 machines. If we add 360 pilots and 360 war-machines in the training schools, this gives a total of 1,416. Thus, it seems that 1,200 machines and 1,114 pilots are unaccounted for. This would be amply sufficient to duplicate every one of the 88 squadrons now believed to have been identified. When we remember the fondness evinced by Germany in history for this particular form of surprise, and note the large number of machines and pilots which seem to have vanished into thin air and the hundred odd aerodromes which have been constructed, this possibility cannot be excluded.

5. Another set of calculations must also be borne in mind. We are told in CID Paper No 1216–B that the German output, working only one shift of three, is 270 air-frames and 640 engines. We can hardly assume that the German Government has erected three times as many factories as it is able to staff, and we must therefore count upon these factories in the event of war being utilised to their full capacity, giving a monthly output of perhaps a thousand machines. I do not know what is the comparable British output, but I should be relieved to learn that it exceeds 300 to 350 machines a month.

If we assume a war wastage of 80 per cent a month, which is, I believe, the French estimate, this output (350) is not even sufficient to maintain our first line Metropolitan Air strength at its present number of 785 machines. Even if we have one machine in reserve for each first line aeroplane, the number of machines which we can keep in commission will drop below 500 at the end of the fourth month. The German Air Force, on the other hand, with its war-time output of a thousand per month, would be able to maintain a first line air strength of 1,200–1,500 machines for an indefinite period.

Thus at the end of the fourth month the British Air Force would be nearer one-third than one-half of the German.[1]

Robert Watson-Watt to Sir Frank Smith

(Churchill papers: 25/10)

12 June 1936   Roehampton
Secret

Dear Sir Frank,

Lindemann, as a member of the Tizard Committee, asked me to see him today to discuss the matters, within the scope of that committee, with which I was concerned. He added that Mr Churchill, as member of a higher committee, would like to meet me and to have similar information. After a preliminary talk, Lindemann and I went to see Mr Churchill. The essence of what I said to them, separately or together, was as under:—

In the RDF[2] field, including RDF2, very generous facilities had been put at my disposal, with a general indication that there was no financial or material limit to facilities for which I might establish a case. This wide scope was limited only by the scale on which the normal machinery of the Air Ministry could operate at abnormal speed, as opposed to the higher speed

---

[1] For the Air Staff notes on Churchill's memorandum, see page 217–20 of this volume.

[2] RDF, an early designation for Radar, see page 209, note 1.

at which emergency machinery might have been made to work. It was clear to me that the Ministry wished to avoid setting up emergency machinery in place of the accelerated normal machinery. Even after acceleration, this normal machinery has held down my rate of advance.

On the wider field of Defence Communications (as I have defined them elsewhere) I said that I found myself in a very embarrassing position. This was the thirteenth Friday since Friday the 13th March, the day on which a Tizard recommendation concerning myself had been considered by the higher committee. Three weeks had passed since I stated to you my willingness to recede by one more step (the third) from the position which I still regarded as most desirable in the public interest. Despite these generous time intervals the Committee could not, at its meeting on Monday next, be informed of any concluded action in the sense of the Tizard recommendation.

This apparently personal issue was of public importance in two ways. It indicated again the Air Ministry's unwillingness to take emergency measures, although nothing but the pressure of national emergency led me to give so much as a moment's thought to rejoining the Air Ministry. It also inhibited me from full immediate usefulness, since I could not, in face of the Air Ministry's immutable attitude, bring myself to make large-scale recommendations of great urgency so long as they might be interpreted in Air Ministry as manoeuvres to magnify the importance of my prospective post.

I cited as examples of the matters calling for urgent action (1) the direction-finding organisation, which had never, so far as I knew, been tested in conditions at all comparable to war conditions, (2) the acoustic detection system, similarly restricted in tests to artificially simple conditions, and (3) the elaboration by Air Ministry and Post Office of ground communication systems for the Observer Corps before the probable wartime utility of the Corps had been adequately examined.

On the argument that there must be only one Director of Research in any one Department I pointed out that Research on radio communications was specifically excluded from the instructions of the Director of Scientific Research, Air Ministry, whence it must be concluded (a) that no research on radio communications was conducted by the Ministry or (b) that there already existed in effect two or more directors of research in the Ministry.

In sum, I felt that it was urgently necessary to make emergency provision of a full-scale and full-time organisation for the investigation of Defence Communications, but that the measure of urgency and emergency urged on me by and for the Ministry differed from that adopted by the Ministry in its own internal operations.

Answering Mr Churchill I said that I would have no objection to stating my views to any appropriate committee before which I might be summoned.

In the interests of clarity I am handing copies of this note to Mr Churchill and to Lindemann.

Yours sincerely
R.A.W-W.

Robert Watson-Watt to Winston S. Churchill
(*Churchill papers: 25/10*)

13 June 1936   London

Dear Mr Churchill,

I have thought it desirable to shorten to its essentials the rather rambling story I gave you yesterday, in the hope that it may be of use to you to have the two salient points, pruned of detail.

I have also thought it proper to inform my present Chief, Sir Frank Smith, of our conversation, and I have combined the two purposes by putting the story in a letter to him, of which I enclose a copy for your information.

I very much appreciated the privilege of meeting you yesterday, and am much encouraged by your generous interest in our work.[1] I look forward to the visit which we hope to persuade you to pay to Bawdsey Research Station.

I am, as you suggested, taking no action to hasten Air Ministry until I hear from you again.

Yours sincerely,
R. A. Watson-Watt

---

[1] A year earlier, at the Air Defence Research sub-committee of the Committee of Imperial 'Defence, held on 25 July 1935, and to which Churchill had been invited for the first time, Robert Watson-Watt had outlined the nature and potential of Radar (then known as Radio Location). Watson-Watt's paper 'Detection and Location of Aircraft by Radio Methods' had been received by the Air Ministry on 12 February 1935. At the Air Defence Research sub-committee meeting on 25 July 1935 there had been what H. E. Wimperis called in his diary 'a fine discussion' about the new invention. During this discussion, Churchill had given his views in a four-line pencilled note passed across the table to Wimperis and Swinton:

'Seeking, Finding, Following, Keeping,
Is he sure to bless?
Angels, Martyrs, Prophets, Virgins,
Answer: "M, Yes".' (*Wimperis papers*)

David Lloyd George: remarks to Dr Thomas Jones

(Jones papers)

14 June 1936

Winston has no following in the country. He has no 'region' on which he is based for support like the Chamberlains in the Midlands, the Stanleys in Lancashire, the Aclands in the West. He's a stunter. He can put things neatly: 'SB has to choose between the devil and Neville', and last year 'between the devil and the deep LG'.

Sir Thomas Inskip to Winston S. Churchill

(Churchill papers: 2/269)

17 June 1936
Secret

My dear Churchill,

As was recently announced in the House of Commons a Sub-Committee of the Committee of Imperial Defence has been set up with the following terms of reference:

'to consider the experiments that have taken place or are proposed in connection with the defence against aircraft, and the vulnerability from the air, of capital ships'.

The Sub-Committee have now obtained the views of a number of non-official persons who have made public statements on the subject, whether in the Press or in Parliament.

There are, however, others who, whilst they have not given open expression to their opinions, have had special opportunity, from valuable experience in the past, to arrive at well weighed conclusions on the subject.

In this connection, I am authorised by my colleagues of the Committee to enquire whether you would give us the benefit of your views.

I might say that the Committee do not confine their enquiry to the purely technical and material aspects of their Terms of Reference, but are prepared to consider other points arising therefrom, provided, of course, they are relevant to the general object of the enquiry.

I attach a copy of a memorandum which may help you in formulating any statement which you may be good enough to make to us. Although we do not wish to restrict you to these points we should be glad to have your views on these matters in particular.

If you are willing to give the Committee the benefit of your experience, we gladly leave to you the alternatives of attending a meeting of the Committee or submitting a Memorandum. Perhaps you would be good enough to inform me which of these alternatives you prefer. Meetings are held either at the House of Commons or at 2, Whitehall Gardens, as often as the engagements of Ministers concerned permit, roughly once or twice a week and if you prefer to come to a meeting, a convenient day will be arranged. If, on the other hand, you prefer to let us have your views in writing and would forward me a copy of a Memorandum, I would have it circulated.

Yours sincerely,
T. W. H. Inskip

MEMORANDUM

The Committee would be glad to be informed on the following points:

(i) Any technical knowledge and experience of your own bearing on the Terms of Reference of the Committee:

(ii) General experience (not necessarily purely technical) on the same questions:

(iii) Your opinion (based on either your own knowledge and experience or that of other persons) as to the degree of risk of loss or damage incurred by capital ships:

(iv) Arising from the matters above, views as to the future usefulness of capital ships in the role they may have to play in Imperial Defence, having regard to your opinion as to their liability to loss or damage resulting from air attack.

Henry Tizard to Professor Lindemann
(Churchill papers: 25/10)

18 June 1936

Dear Lindemann,

No doubt you already know that as a result of your personal criticisms to Winston Churchill he made a written attack on the Research Committee without taking the trouble to ascertain my views first. I was obliged to answer this categorically, whereupon he followed up in Committee with other wild criticisms presumably based on information from you. Needless to say I have no objection to your discussing with him the work of our Committee—on the contrary everyone concerned would welcome this if the object were to produce fresh ideas and constructive suggestions. But if the only result is to produce ill-founded criticisms then I am bound to say that however good your ultimate motives are, the only effect of your actions is to retard progress. I should really enjoy working with you if you were ready to work as a member of a team, but if you are playing another game I don't think it is possible for us to go on collaborating without continual friction. I have told Swinton this —so you ought to know.

I wish we could have settled such differences of opinion that exist in a friendly manner in our own Committee, but you have made this very difficult, if not impossible.

I am writing a general statement about the policy underlying the priority attached to different items of our work. I will let you have this next week. If agreed by members it will be circulated to the CID Committee.

Yours sincerely,
H. Tizard

Lord Wolmer[1] to Winston S. Churchill

(*Churchill papers: 2/255*)

18 June 1936

My dear Winston,

I am afraid I failed you this afternoon. I am so sorry. Having delivered my 'preface' the rest of my speech 'disappeared' & I had to sit down.[2]

---

[1] Roundell Cecil Palmer, Viscount Wolmer, 1887–1971. Known as 'Top'. Eldest son of the 2nd Earl of Selborne and a grandson of the 3rd Marquess of Salisbury. Educated at Winchester and University College, Oxford. In 1910 he married Churchill's cousin, Grace Ridley, daughter of the 1st Viscount Ridley. Conservative MP for Newton, Lancashire, 1910–18; and for Aldershot, 1918–40. Assistant-Director, War Trade Department, 1917–18. Parliamentary Secretary, Board of Trade, 1922–4. Assistant Postmaster-General, 1924–9. A member of the Executive Committee of the India Defence League, 1933–5. A member of the Other Club from 1938. Succeeded his father as 3rd Earl, 1942. Minister of Economic Warfare, 1942–5. President of the Church Army, 1949–61. His brother Robert was killed in action in Mesopotamia in 1916. His eldest son was killed accidentally by a shell while on active service in 1942.

[2] On 18 June 1936 Lord Wolmer spoke for ten minutes in the House of Commons on Foreign Affairs. His theme was very much Churchill's own, that in order to assert its authority, the League of Nations needed the force and arms 'of those nations who are loyal supporters of peace', and he added: 'That is where I think we are entitled to criticize the Government. They have led this country into this position because they have too long delayed the rearming of Britain. They have committed that mistake in spite of the gravest warnings, which they have belittled and denied during the past three years until about a year ago. When the history of this episode comes to be written it will be seen that the parting of the ways in regard to disarmament occurred about 1933 or 1934. In that time it became clear to more candid and well-informed observers that the ideal of disarmament had definitely failed, at any rate for the time being, but the Government unfortunately refused to look facts in the face. Too long

This (I suppose) due to

1. Insufficient preparation—I had not conceived it possible I should get in until it was obvious that SB could not last out.
2. The feeling that SB had made such a shit of himself that it was impossible to 'gild the lily' (excuse change in metaphors) and I was afraid of spoiling things by rubbing in the obvious.

Anyhow I am conscious that I failed to make use of an opportunity and am so sorry. I had quite a good speech in the back of my head about

falling between 2 stools
3 foreign secretaries & 6 foreign policies in the last 12 months.

What are you doing re armaments *now*?

Yours,
Top

Frederick Guest to Winston S. Churchill
(*Churchill papers: 2/255*)

19 June 1936
Private & Confidential

Dear Win,

It is very seldom that I butt in nowadays in your private affairs, but I cannot resist sending this note for your consideration.

Let me say at the outset that it is dictated to a confidential private secretary, who has been with me for a great many years, and it is therefore completely secret.

It seems to me and to many other friends that you have in the House of Commons, particularly the new Members since 1935, that you have a God-given chance of coming straight to the top of the great Conservative Party; if you were to come to the rescue of the Government by smashing the hypocritical humbug of the Pacifist Socialist Party, and, incidentally, destroy the Lloyd George speech of yesterday, you would gain hundreds of adherents in the H of C.

---

they clung to the hope that there was still some method of getting general disarmament, and all the while the armaments of Italy and Germany were daily contributing towards the situation that has now developed.' Wolmer ended his short speech: 'The terrible tragedy is that this country is found in a position so ill-prepared, that the League of Nations is dishonoured, the League of Nations is weakened, and the prestige of this country is lowered, all because we did not grasp time by the forelock and prepare to carry out the old doctrine, in which so many of us were brought up, that if you want peace you must prepare for war.'

The rank and file know quite well that Baldwin is tired and that you could do it much better than anyone else and with the greatest ease. On the other hand they will not see the old man bullied as they are intensely and pathetically loyal to him.

I need not say any more, but this is the advice from someone who has been trying to help you one way and another for nearly thirty years.

I am convinced that this is the psychological moment in your career.

On the other hand if you drive out or break down SB the party will simply & immediately crown NC.

You can lead the Conservative party but you cannot break the Party machine.

Bless you. Good luck.

Yrs,
Freddie

Winston S. Churchill to Lord Wolmer

(*Churchill papers: 2/255*)

22 June 1936

I thought you were quite good, but the House was rather jaded. I am very glad you said what you did. You ought to speak again this session especially if there is a Defence Debate.

Winston S. Churchill to Sir Thomas Inskip

(*Churchill papers: 2/269*)

22 June 1936   Chartwell
Confidential

As the Government have decided to build these capital ships in any case, I do not see what more there is to be said. The reference for your Committee has been strictly limited by you, or by the Government, to the consideration of certain experiments which the Admiralty have made into the resistance of steel structures to explosions of various kinds. As I do not know the nature of these experiments it is impossible for me to express even a layman's opinion upon their results. I do not feel therefore that I have anything to add to the general observations which I made in the debate on the Navy Estimates on the 28th May. These were very carefully considered by me and if they are pondered over, they will I believe supply the general answer to your questionnaire.

The fundamental question is whether capital ships can be constructed to withstand the mines, larger torpedoes and aerial bombs of modern warfare without their importance and their vulnerability imposing in practice an undue deterrent upon their use in war. If you are sure of that, there is no doubt that on strategic grounds they are pre-eminently desirable. It is also true that the larger the hull, the greater the possibility of obtaining the necessary protection.

As I told you when you kindly visited me here,[1] I am entirely at your service if you wish to cross-examine me.

Winston S. Churchill to Lord Swinton

(Cabinet papers: 21/426)

22 June 1936
Confidential

My dear Philip,

I am sorry you do not feel able to allow an impartial examination to be made of the points in dispute. I certainly did not agree to the procedure which you say was 'decided' at the end of our meeting. In fact I well remember saying that I was not at all satisfied. I will however await Tizard's promised report. His first step has been to write a very offensive letter to Lindemann which I should have thought would make, and was perhaps intended to make, their future relations impossible.

What surprises and grieves me is your attitude and that you should be apparently contented with the way the work is going. We are at present entirely defenceless from the ground (except for a few vulnerable points where batteries are massed) against any attack from the air: and it must be at least more than a year before anything practical can be done. During the ten months I have sat upon the Committee I have been shocked at the slowness with which every investigation proceeds. I well know that this branch is a very small part of your labours. All the more therefore I should have thought you would welcome the assistance of others in trying to get things done.

The differences upon the Scientific Committee are not as you suggest of a technical or abstruse character. They are differences about the method and procedure to be used in testing certain ideas, which if found sound would open a new domain to anti-aircraft artillery, as well as helping in other ways known to you. The experiments are neither large nor expensive, but they must be numerous, and can only advance by repeated trial and error.

---

[1] Inskip had lunched at Chartwell on Monday, 15 June 1936.

Last August we decided to try to find out what happened when an aeroplane was brought in contact with a thin wire at the end of which was an explosive charge, and how big that explosive charge should be. If this enquiry had been entrusted to a private firm, it could have been completed in two or three months at the outside at a cost I should suppose of less than £1,000. Instead of this we have the long series of delays set forth by Lindemann in the paper which you have circulated at my desire. Apart from knowing that a very modest explosive charge will suffice to do serious damage, we have not made any progress. I certainly thought that an idea like this if adopted provisionally would be tested day in, day out, until it would either be proved sound or futile. But if these small experiments are to be agreed to one by one, and then fitted in with the mass of important experimental work being discharged at Shoeburyness and elsewhere, with reports in each case back to the Committee which meets about once a month, and with no one person given the means to pursue the quest, then it is certain that nothing will result before the period of maximum danger has come.

It is always difficult to have a public controversy about unmentionable topics. I am however quite sure that if instead of serving on your Committee Lindemann and I had pressed our points by all the various methods and channels open to us, these ideas would have had better treatment than they have received.

I have dwelt upon this particular set of experiments because I have followed them more closely. But I fear that a similar slowness and inter-mittence characterises other lines of research in this field.

I hope you will weigh what I write without resentment or prejudice.

Yours sincerely,
Winston

Professor Lindemann to Henry Tizard

(*Cherwell papers*)

23 June 1936

Dear Tizard

I thank you for your letter of the 18th June.

It is not worth while for me to attempt to discuss the relative wildness of the various statements which may or may not have been made in my absence at the meeting of the CID Committee, but I am sure that anything deriving from me was strictly accurate. If you would send me a copy of the statement of which you complain and of your 'categorical' reply I would be glad to deal with the matter.

The point on which we seem to be in complete disagreement is the different urgency which we attach to our endeavours to find some method to deal with air attack. Your procedure would no doubt be excellent if we had 10 or 15 years' time. I believe that the period available is to be measured in months.

Apart from Watson-Watt's work you will scarcely claim that any appreciable advance towards a solution of the problem has been made since the Committee has been in being. You appear to be perfectly satisfied with the rate of progress. I am not.

In view of the immense importance of the question and holding the views I do as to its urgency, you will not be surprised that I have used every means at my disposal to accelerate progress and that I am determined to continue to do so. I am very sorry if this offends you, but the matter is too vital to justify one in refraining from action in order to salve anybody's *amour propre*.

Professor Lindemann to Winston S. Churchill

(*Churchill papers: 25/10*)

24 June 1936   Claridge's

My dear Winston

You asked me to let you know whether there was reason to complain of slowness in pursuing Air Defence Research in directions other than in the development of Aerial Mines. I regret to say that this particular item is only too typical of all the rest. I will give you a few instances.

The method of location known as RDF[1] due to Mr Watson-Watt is as you know most promising and important. But it only represents a solution to half the problem. To be effective it is not sufficient for the Air Staff to know where the enemy is, it is essential that the fighter should be able to close with him. In order to do this the fighter must discover where he himself is relative to the enemy and be able to detect him at some relatively short distance, (eg 1 to 3 miles) and close with him. There is little doubt this could be achieved on lines similar to those proposed and developed by Watson-Watt, but it obviously requires a lot of staff and facilities if the work is to progress quickly.

Another method to locate the enemy is to use an instrument capable of detecting the heat rays emitted by the hot exhaust etc. It is true the enemy might ultimately shield these but he has not done so. In any event the method

---

[1] RDF = Radio Direction-Finding. Its existence was not publicly acknowledged until 1941, when it was referred to as Radiolocation. Radar, an American term (= Radio Direction and Ranging), was adopted in 1943 as part of the effort to establish a joint Anglo-American nomenclature.

should be explored as it would enable an aeroplane on a dark night to detect, say, a factory chimney or other target. Though not very promising great weight is at present attached to sound locating. If this is to be of any use it is essential that observers be capable of using their apparatus when several machines simultaneously are overhead and of transmitting their information to headquarters, and furthermore that GHQ be able to inform the appropriate defence units where & when to find the enemy.

All this is of course a very complicated business and the Sub-committee therefore recommended 13 weeks ago that Watson-Watt be put in charge of research connected with all these questions.

Though 3 months have elapsed this has not been done; to the great detriment of progress.

Though the Sub-Committee agreed early in December to experiment with Infra-Red methods it was not till the end of January that authority to engage one man for four months at £100 was given. This man has now been given a four months extension, but it is clear that only his patriotism will enable him to give of his best in such conditions. It is work of the most difficult character and only an absolutely first-class man can do it at all. (I gather he has been offered over £600 a year outside).

I submit that if the work is worth doing at all the scale of endeavour should be of a different order of magnitude. The man in question should be given adequate assistance and reasonable prospects and pay.

Another case in point is the request that has been made again & again for experiments on sound-location with several machines simultaneously within ear-shot. These experiments may damn sound-location but it is better to know where one stands. So far no results have reached the Committee.

A proposal has been put forward to try lighting clouds from below with a view to silhouetting bombers against the surface when observed from higher up. Months have elapsed but nothing happens.

All of these instances individually may appear insignificant (except perhaps the very gross case of the Aerial Mines), but their cumulative effect is to suggest that more push and drive is required.

Anyone used to this sort of work will further agree that each experiment suggests new lines of development so that one nipped in the bud really sterilises a whole field. And it is impossible to predict in which field & where salvation may lie. Unless they are explored we may miss the essential discovery.

Personally, I am afraid that the present organisation is not calculated to achieve success.

If a committee can research at all, which is doubtful, it must meet at least twice a week & keep track of all experiments. For dozens or hundreds of experiments invariably precede any successful results; intervals of months spell such delays as to be equivalent to failure.

In my view there should be a Director of Air Defence Research who has priority for his work accorded to him in all service research departments & a nucleus of laboratories & staff of his own. He should be under the CID not the Air Ministry. One does not ask butchers to make researches to prove that vegetarianism is the best dietary.

He should report periodically to the CID committee to which more scientists could be added, or if preferred through a sub-committee.

What is essential is that he should be able to get things done without going back to the Committee & be keen & enthusiastic himself.

Despite the handicaps and delays Watson-Watt acting in this way has achieved a great deal. If his results are taken away precious little is left. Let us profit from the experience.

Please forgive this hasty note & believe me as ever

Yours,

FAL

Sir Thomas Inskip to Winston S. Churchill

(*Churchill papers: 2/289*)

24 June 1936

My dear Churchill,

I am much obliged for your letter of 22nd June recording your views on the future of the Capital Ship, and, if I may say so, I agree with your definition of the fundamental question which underlies the whole matter.

We are, of course, aware of the views which you expressed in the debate on the Navy Estimates, and in the circumstances I don't think the Committee would wish to press you to discuss them in person.

Yours sincerely,

T. W. H. Inskip

Sir Thomas Inskip to Winston S. Churchill

(*Churchill papers: 2/269*)

24 June 1936

My dear Churchill,

You will remember sending me a letter from the Plessey Company giving an account of a visit to some German munition works. I have been making enquiry into the letter and I find that a demonstration of the Haase & Wrede machine was witnessed by British representatives in September of last year and a full report made. Plessey's statement that they were the first foreigners ever to have seen the plant was therefore made under a misapprehension.

The Borsig factory mentioned by Plessey's was not visited on this occasion, but enough information was obtained for an estimate of the value of the process to be made. I have in fact seen a copy of the report that was produced. I thought you would be interested to know this.

Yours sincerely,
T. W. H. Inskip

PS. I can't help being sorry that I should be supposed to be unwilling to 'disturb the peacetime atmosphere of normal production'. That is exactly what I *am* doing.

TWHI

Winston S. Churchill to Sir Thomas Inskip

(*Churchill papers: 2/269*)

24 June 1936

The fact that official knowledge was obtained last September of the matters contained in the letter from the Plessey Company which I sent you only makes things worse if no action has been taken upon it or unless there has been a decision after full consideration that it does not require any action. I doubt very much whether any effective action has been taken unless quite recently, or whether indeed a definite decision has been taken by superior authority. Perhaps you could reassure me upon this point.

With regard to your postscript, I can of course only base myself upon your public statements. You declared a few days after taking office that you must observe the limitations not to disturb the normal course of trade, and you have argued in Parliament against emergency measures. No one would be more pleased than I to learn by some public statement of yours that you have freed yourself from these restrictions. Nothing that you have said to me even in private has led me to believe that you have reached any such decision.

J. H. Thomas[1] *to Winston S. Churchill*

(*Churchill papers: 1/285*)

24 June 1936

My dear Winston,

I can only say thank you, for your note. I do indeed appreciate it, & my wife who is keeping up very well asks me to thank your wife for her kindly thoughts. I feel like a Rat in a Trap, & the future is all a Blank to me, but whatever my fate, I shall always keep in mind the Interests of my Country.[2]

Yours sincerely,
J. H. Thomas

Lord Swinton to Winston S. Churchill

(*Churchill papers: 25/7*)

25 June 1936   Air Ministry
Secret

My dear Winston,

Thank you for your letter of the 22nd of June. I am sure I can say with truth that neither resentment nor prejudice have affected me or will affect me

---

[1] James Henry Thomas, 1874-1949. Began work as an errand boy at the age of nine; subsequently an engine-cleaner, fireman and engine-driver. Labour MP for Derby, 1910–31; National Labour MP, 1931–6. General Secretary, National Union of Railwaymen, 1918–24, and 1924–31. President of the International Federation of Trade Unions, 1920–4. Vice-Chairman of the Parliamentary Labour Party, 1921. Secretary of State for the Colonies in the first Labour Government, 1924. Elected to the Other Club, 1925, but resigned in 1930. Minister of Employment and Lord Privy Seal, 1929–30. Secretary of State for the Dominions, 1930–5; for the Colonies, 1935–6.

[2] At the beginning of May 1936 Lloyd's of London informed the Chancellor of the Exchequer that 'an undue amount of insurance against budget risks had been taken at a late date' by a certain Alfred Bates. Bates was an old friend of J. H. Thomas, and an investigation revealed (1) that Bates had given Thomas £15,000 advance for the rights to Thomas's memoirs on April 8; (2) that Thomas was informed of a rise in income tax of three pence on April 9, during a Cabinet meeting; (3) that Thomas had been frequently in Bates' company between April 10 and 12; and (4) that on April 14 Bates had begun to take out insurance against income tax increases. The investigation received much publicity, some of it unfavourable to Thomas, and on 20 May 1936 he resigned from the Cabinet, in which he had been Secretary of State for the Colonies, because, as he expressed it, his 'private affairs have been bandied about rendering his continuation as a member of the Government impossible'. On 2 June 1936 an official Tribunal of Inquiry reported: 'that there was an unauthorized disclosure of information relating to the Budget by Mr J. H. Thomas to Mr Bates, and that use was made of this information by Mr Bates for his private gain'. Thomas gave his farewell speech to Parliament on 11 June 1936, claiming to have made 'no conscious leakage of Budget secrets', but at the same time accepting the findings of the Tribunal. He then resigned as a Member of Parliament, and retired from politics. In 1945 he called on Churchill unexpectedly and unannounced, to tell him how to win the forthcoming General Election.

in my work; and I am sure all members of the Committee welcome all the constructive help which they can get.

I am definitely of opinion, and I know Inskip fully shares this view, and I think other members of the Committee do too, that responsibility for deciding what broad lines of experiments should be undertaken must rest with the Scientists Committee, and the CID Committee. As soon as a line of experiment has been approved, it is my desire, and I am sure everyone else's, that it should be pursued resolutely and effectively. I am quite sure that the CID Committee welcome criticism on these lines.

Leaving aside for the moment the particular matter referred to in your letter, and which is now under the consideration of the CID Committee, I do not think there is any ground for your suggestion that 'a similar slowness and intermittence characterises other lines of research'. On the two subjects for which I am particularly responsible departmentally—interception and location, and balloons—certainly no such charge could possibly be made. I should welcome the fullest discussion in the Committee, and any suggestion by which work in either of these directions could be speeded up. I am trying to give of my best, and I know all my people are; and I am sure it is up to all of us to do the same.

Yours sincerely,
Swinton

Sir Thomas Inskip to Winston S. Churchill

(*Churchill papers: 2/269*)

26 June 1936
Confidential

My dear Churchill,

I have discussed with the Chiefs of Staff your note on the possibility of invasion by air, and should like you to have a brief resumé of their views.

As you said in your first letter, the idea presupposes that the enemy have achieved air superiority. It would have to be very great air superiority, coupled with the availability of a large number of machines designed for troop and store carrying—a superiority which would have to continue if the Force is to be maintained in military stores and personnel so that it might remain for any length of time.

I think the first comment is that, if through some disaster or combination of unforeseen circumstances we were so reduced, the enemy could probably exploit the superiority more effectively by increasing the scale of bombing attacks against vulnerable points. The Staff feel that this would be the more likely development. Should, however, the enemy prefer the alternative of invasion and achieve a successful landing, superior military forces could be concentrated at short notice. Taking the situation in the early stages of hostilities and considering the territorial force alone, there would be twelve territorial divisions in this country of which four at least would be ready to move quickly to any threatened point.

A small scale raid with the object of destroying some vulnerable point and not involving the strain of maintenance might be a more practicable proposition. It would have to penetrate the Air Defence Organisation, as of course would the major proposition; and again military forces would be available at short notice.

I am grateful to you for calling attention to the idea.

Yours sincerely,
T. W. H. Inskip

Sir Thomas Inskip to Winston S. Churchill

(*Churchill papers: 2/269*)

26 June 1936

My dear Churchill,

Thank you for your letter of the 24th June. As you and I had a very full discussion of the matters mentioned in your letter, which I gather you had already dictated when we had the conversation, I need say no more except that I am sure you did not wish to give a wrong impression as to my statements, although I know the impression you gave to your audience was very different from that which I think any statements I have made justified. However, you and I don't want to waste each other's time with a wrangle, and believe me I have found some of your suggestions helpful and I welcome any stimulus that you can apply to me.

Yours very sincerely,
T. W. H. Inskip

Lord Swinton to Sir Maurice Hankey
(*Cabinet papers: 21/426*)

26 June 1936   Air Ministry
Secret

My dear Hankey,

I return Churchill's further paper about air strength, together with the comments of the Air Staff. I have no objection at all to both these being circulated to the CID; indeed, I think it would be a good thing to do so. But a question of principle arises here on which I think we should have Inskip's ruling. The Air Research Committee of the CID is concerned with research, and only indirectly with general policy. It is the object of the Air Research Committee to explore and undertake any useful research and experimental work in connection with air defence. It is not the business of that Committee to discuss German air strength, except insofar as an appreciation of probable German air strength affords us a test of the magnitude and character of the problem of air defence. Still less is it the business of that Committee to consider or advise upon the strength of the British Air Force. That is the function of the CID and the Cabinet.

In accordance with this obvious principle, all papers relating to German air strength and manufacturing capacity go direct to the CID, and are considered by them. The Prime Minister decided a good while ago that it would be reasonable to let the members of the Air Defence Research Committee have these papers. The reason for this was that Churchill was constantly propounding fallacious statements about German strength, and that as he was a member of the CID Sub-Committee on Air Defence Research, it would be a good thing to let him see the appreciations (which of course represent the combined work of the Air Staff, the Board of Trade Intelligence, and the Secret Service) on which the CID works. But that is a very different matter from discussing these questions on the ADR Sub-Committee. If an attempt is made to do so, I suggest that Inskip, as Deputy Chairman of the CID, must take the line that that would be quite out of order. Moreover, in view of recent events, it is for consideration how far these secret papers should any longer be given to Mr Churchill. I do not think we can avoid circulating the present paper and comments to the CID, but I expect Inskip will want to consider whether the time has not come when this practice should cease.

I should add that, as you will recollect, one of the reasons that weighed with us was the great undesirability of my supplying secret information to Churchill in any other way except by a CID paper, which he would receive by the Prime Minister's instructions, and with all the obligation of secrecy attaching thereto. I must make it plain that I should flatly refuse to afford secret information in any other way except by a CID paper.

Yours ever,
Swinton

Air Staff: notes on Churchill's memorandum of 12 June 1936 [1]

(*Foreign Office papers: 371/19933*)

26 June 1936

Paragraphs 1 and 2.

The reason the Air Staff omits immediate reserve aircraft in assessing Germany's first line strength is given by Mr Churchill himself in his opening paragraph. Namely, that the standard comparison should be the one which gives the truest picture. An Air Force comprises operational aircraft in the squadrons, together with sufficient reserves judged adequate to cover war wastage during the period when industry is turning over from a peace to war output. Germany considers that her requirements in this respect are met by 100 per cent reserves, ie, 9 aircraft per squadron, of which 3 are in immediate reserve with the unit and 6 in stored reserve at the aircraft park.

2. British policy follows the same lines except that we consider that our reserve should be on a higher scale than that adopted by the Germans. No two countries have the same ideas on the number of reserve aircraft to maintain in peace, because the time to turn their respective aircraft industries from a peace to a war footing will differ. The same principle, however, applies to every country, namely, to hold sufficient reserves to maintain the first line strength in face of war wastage during the change over of her industry from peace to war output. Therefore the inclusion of reserve aircraft in a comparison of operational aircraft in formed units (ie, first line strength) would be totally misleading. The *principle* underlying the policy of reserve aircraft is the important point to be borne in mind. For example, of two countries A has a first line strength of 1,500 aircraft with a big industry behind her which she considers can be placed on to a war footing in two months. She assumes that her war wastage will be 50 per cent per month, therefore she maintains 100 per cent reserve, that is to say, a total of 3,000 military aircraft. Country B has the same first line strength as A, namely 1,500, but it takes longer to turn her aircraft industry from peace to war

---

[1] Churchill's memorandum of 12 June 1936 is published in full on pages 197–9 of this volume.

production. She considers that 200 per cent reserves are necessary to bridge the gap before output will meet war wastage. She therefore maintains 4,500 aircraft in peace. Were Mr Churchill's method of comparison to be adopted, we should have a misleading estimate of the strength of A and B, each of which is actually organised to maintain the same number of first line aircraft in war.

Paragraph 3.

3. Mr Churchill is incorrect in stating that Air Staff figures used in CID Paper No 1216–B are derived from the number of squadrons which have been identified. The passage to which Mr Churchill refers reads as follows:—

'By the 31st January, 1936, this had risen to 59 Service units identified or located, which, with those thought to have been formed, but not identified, gave a first line figure of 710 aircraft.'

The Air Staff realise that information concerning formed units is always slightly out of date and therefore allowance is made for a reasonable proportion of units formed, but not identified. For instance, at the 31st May, 1936, the Air Staff estimates show that 90 Squadrons have been identified, making a total of 861 aircraft, but allowing for units not identified, a grand total of 920 first line aircraft is given.

4. As regards the number of military aircraft available in Germany, Mr Churchill's total of 3,200 is only slightly in excess of the Air Staff estimate, which, at the 31st May, 1936, was 3,115. Assuming, for the sake of argument, that the Air Staff figure of 920 first line aircraft is correct, then 1,840 aircraft are taken up in first line and reserve, leaving 1,275 to be accounted for. The Air Attaché has now visited a large number of the schools given in CID Paper No 1189–B, and from conversations which he has had with various German officers, is in a position to assess the number of aircraft used in their training schools. The average number of military type actually in use at schools varies between 70 and 80 at each. This alone accounts for over 800 aircraft. Besides these aircraft in use there is a number (which varies greatly in the different schools) of reserve training aircraft, amounting to something in the nature of 30 to 50 per cent. We find therefore that at the schools there are nearly 1,200 aircraft for training purposes. A large number of these are of obsolescent type and are fitted up for instructional purposes rendering them almost useless for military purposes until considerable reconditioning has been carried out. It is clear, therefore, that the balance of 1,275 aircraft, over and above those for first line and reserve, is easily accounted for without considering the appreciable number of military type aircraft used for communication, experimental and other such purposes.

Paragraph 4.

5. In CID Paper No 1198–B, enclosure 2, paragraph 1, dated November 1935, the Air Staff explain the so-called discrepancy between the total number of pilots and estimated first line strength in the German Air Force. Our own experience shows that in a well-established Air Force the ratio of pilots to first line strength is rather greater than 2·5 : 1. In a newly formed Air Force in which training, organisation and administrative needs absorb a far greater percentage of pilots than in an old-established one, a greater ratio may well be expected. The Air Staff estimated that at the 31st May, 1936, Germany had available 2,565 trained pilots. Of this number, 1,140 are absorbed in actual operational units, leaving a balance of 1,415 to fill all headquarters, staff, administrative, training and other appointments. These estimates show a ratio rather smaller than 2·5 : 1.

Flying instructional staff in training units, according to estimates based on Air Attachés' reports, absorbs nearly 750 pilots, leaving approximately 700 to fill other appointments. We know of the formation of 82 station or other headquarters and, allowing only 3 pilots for each of these headquarters, a total of 246 are required. Only 450 are thus left to man the experimental stations, recruit depots, aircraft parks, staff college, Air Ministry and the instructional posts in the RLK.[1] In fact, the number of pilots is known to be insufficient for the German Air Force needs and has resulted in non-flying Air Force officers and other officers transferred from the Army and Navy being employed in posts which normally would, and which eventually will, be filled by flying personnel. The fact that there are insufficient pilots to go round has often been mentioned by the German Air Attaché in conversations with officers in the Air Ministry.

6. The Air Staff fully share Mr Churchill's apprehensions as regards German ability to spring a surprise on their enemy on the outbreak of war by some unexpected manoeuvre. They do not, however, feel that the method envisaged by Mr Churchill would be employed since the execution of such a plan would not be in keeping with Germany's well-known love of method and organisation and would be contrary to the first and main principle of sound Air Force organisation.

The Air Staff, however, would again draw attention to the creation of the Air Force reserve (Luftwaffe) through the medium of the DLV (Air Sports Association), mentioned in paragraphs 21–23 of CID Paper No 1216–B, dated the 4th March, 1936.

It is felt that any unexpected addition to first line strength on the outbreak of war will be found by this organisation which is now constituted on a

---

[1] RLK = *Reichs Luftkreis*, a regional division of the German Air Force before the Second World War.

military basis. Admittedly the growth within the framework is to-day a negligible quantity because it would be an impossible feat to form a regular air force and an air force reserve 'ab initio' simultaneously.

In 18 months or two years' time, however, when the framework has been filled out and many of the personnel are trained officers and airmen who have completed their short-term engagements in the regular air force it may be a force seriously to be reckoned with and trained to a standard not far short of the regular air force.

The Air Staff suggest, therefore, that it is in this direction that attention should be focused.

Paragraph 5.

7. As regards output of airframes and engines it may be said that Germany at present is ahead of us in her organisation for war production, but the Air Ministry is working to the principle quoted in paragraph 1 above, namely, that sufficient reserves should be maintained in peace to make good war wastage during the period when factories turn from peace to war production.

8. We have based the German peace wastage rate of machines upon our own experience. We know as a fact that their death rate under training is very much higher than ours; from which it is reasonable to suppose that their wastage of aircraft is also higher than our own. We have, however, made no reduction for this, as we felt it right to leave a margin to countervail the possibility of German production being in excess of our estimates.

Sir Maurice Hankey to Sir Thomas Inskip
(Cabinet papers: 21/426)

29 June 1936
Secret

I attach a written letter I have received from Lord Swinton on the subject of a controversy that has been going on some time between Mr Churchill and himself on the question of the German air strength.

On the 11th July, 1935, Mr Churchill was added to the Air Defence Research Sub-Committee.

On the 19th September, 1935, the Secretary of State for Air circulated to the CID some notes by the Air Staff on the training organisation of the German Air Force as at 1st August, 1935.

Copies of these were circulated, with the approval of the Prime Minister and on the initiative of the Secretary of State for Air, to the ADR Committee of which Mr Churchill was a member. This paper had no direct bearing on ADR work, but it was sent to that Committee as being a convenient way of giving Mr Churchill a look at a CID paper and some inside knowledge on the subject on which he was making difficulties in Parliament. Mr Churchill replied with some criticisms. These were replied to by the Air Staff—the two papers being circulated in CID paper 1189–B.

This process has continued and there have been further criticisms by Mr Churchill and replies by the Air Staff which have been circulated as in the case of the original paper as CID documents communicated for information to the ADR Committee.

The latest development consisting once more of a criticism by Mr Churchill and a reply by the Air Staff has been submitted to the Secretary of State for Air, who has no objection to their being circulated to the CID. He points out, however, quite correctly that this is not really a subject for the Air Defence Research Committee and that they ought not to be discussed by that Committee.

Up to the present time, there has been no discussion at the ADR Committee on any of these figures, and the memoranda have never appeared on the agenda of the Sub-Committee. I have no reason to believe that Mr Churchill wishes to raise them at the Sub-Committee and they certainly will not appear on the agenda without the instructions of the Chairman.

In the circumstances, I think you could quite safely acquiesce in Lord Swinton's suggestion that if Mr Churchill tries to bring the matter up with the ADR Committee you should take the line that this would be out of order. You could support this by pointing out that the documents were CID documents only, communicated (like the ADGB[1] reports for example) to the ADR Committee solely as a matter of information and background: up to now they never had been discussed at the ADR Committee and their discussion would be outside its terms of reference. Do you agree?

Lord Swinton raises a second point, namely, as to how far these secret papers should any longer be given to Mr Churchill. As already mentioned, he agrees that the two latest papers should go to Mr Churchill, but he suggests that you 'will want to consider whether the time has not come when this practice should cease'.

If Mr Churchill accepts the latest reply of the Air Staff, the matter will automatically come to an end. Wing Commander Warburton assures me that it is very convincing—but of course Mr Churchill does not want to be convinced!

If Mr Churchill sends in another reply, I am inclined to think that the best plan would be for us to try and close the correspondence.

M. P. A. Hankey

---

[1] Air Defence of Great Britain sub-committee of the Committee of Imperial Defence.

Winston S. Churchill to Sir Thomas Inskip

(*Churchill papers: 2/269*)

29 June 1936   11 Morpeth Mansions

I agree, so far as it goes, with the argument about more tempting objectives. At the same time I still think the danger real, and one that will increase every year. Surely four Territorial Divisions in their present state of training and equipment could not make head against a quarter their number of trained Regular storm troops. If they were raised to full strength and given at least three months training in each year, and mechanised to a high degree, they would be an effective deterrent. Under present conditions it would be most unwise to count upon them until they had been three or four months mobilised. The fact however that they are counted upon would be a stimulant to recruiting if it were known.

If you had time I would discuss with you the Question and Answer following upon my original suggestion in debate.

Alfred Duff Cooper to Winston S. Churchill

(*Churchill papers: 2/266*)

29 June 1936   War Office

My dear Winston,

You will remember that I spoke to you at Blenheim[1] about the desire of the Imperial Defence College for you to go and address them on July 29th, either in the morning or the afternoon. That is the date that would suit them best, but they could manage on the afternoon of either the 13th or the 15th of July.

As you know, the numbers there are small, but it is an audience that is well worth addressing, and as you had so much to do with the inception of the College I think you ought to see how it is working. You will probably choose as your subject 'The Higher Direction of War', but you might also perhaps discuss with the students there the subject of 'Invasion from the Air', with the possibilities of which I know you are much concerned.

You said something about my taking the chair on the occasion, but it is

[1] On 27 June 1936 Churchill and his wife had been among the guests at a Blenheim weekend. The other guests, as signed in the visitors' book, were King Edward VIII, Wallis Simpson, Ernest Simpson, Diana Cooper, Duff Cooper, the Duke and Duchess of Buccleuch, and Lady Cunard (*Blenheim Palace archive*).

not their custom to have any Chairman there. The Head of the College, Major-General R. H. Haining,[1] would introduce you and would initiate any discussion that followed your remarks.[2]

Yours ever,
Duff Cooper

Sir Maurice Hankey to Stanley Baldwin

(*Cabinet papers: 21/573*)

29 June 1936

I have received a certain amount of evidence that the push and drive required in connection with the Defence Requirements programme—or perhaps I should say the realisation of the need for push and drive—has not penetrated very far below those who hold immediate responsibility. In particular, it has been suggested that it does not extend to establishments maintained by the Services.

I have been told that some of those establishments are still being run very much on peace-time lines: that for relatively small and approved expenditure, authority has to be obtained from the Headquarter Department and tenders calling for contracts passed by Directors of Contracts.

The result, if my information is correct, is interminable delays involved by the bandying about of minutes and correspondence between the Service Departments and Technical Experts on specifications. This was given to me as one of the causes of noticeable delays in experimental work.

Sir Thomas Inskip to Sir Maurice Hankey

(*Cabinet papers: 21/426*)

30 June 1936

The ADR Committee must not be turned into something else, and if questions of air-strength are debated that is what will happen. I agree there-

---

[1] Robert Hadden Haining, 1882–1959. 2nd Lieutenant, 1901; Major, 1915. On active service, 1914–18 (despatches six times, DSO); Major-General, 1934. Commandant, Imperial Defence College, 1935–6. Deputy Director of Military Operations and Intelligence, War Office, 1936–8. General Officer Commanding the British Forces in Palestine and Transjordan, 1938–9. Knighted, 1940. Vice-Chief of the Imperial General Staff, 1940–1. Intendant-General, Middle East, 1941–2.

[2] On 1 July 1936 Churchill replied to Duff Cooper: 'Alas, I cannot spare the time and thought for this important lecture. I have to finish my proofs by the end of this month, and every minute I can snatch from politics is already bespoke. I am so sorry' (*Churchill papers: 2/266*).

fore with the suggestion of the S/S for Air that objection should be taken if Churchill raises issues as to the accuracy of information contained in CID documents.

As to the best way of ending the paper Controversy, I should be inclined to let the matter drop whether or not Mr Churchill accepts the last reply of the Air Staff. If he sends a controversial reply, the best answer is that the S/S for Air will take care to put Mr Churchill's comments & information before the CID.

Allan G. Clark to Winston S. Churchill

(*Churchill papers: 2/280*)

30 June 1936   The Plessey Company Limited

Dear Mr Churchill,

I am taking the liberty of writing to you once again owing to the fact that since I saw you last, I have had absolutely no communication from the War Office regarding my proposal for the installation of a Bomb Shell Plant. I am very concerned with the whole situation, especially as I have had advice from the Continent, that my friends are exceedingly busy on foreign orders, and naturally any orders we place would have to take their turn.

From various enquiries I have made I can find absolutely no trace of movement regarding my report, and I was wondering whether you would be good enough to mention the matter again to Sir Hugh Elles.

Yours faithfully,
A. G. Clark

S. D. Waley:[1] *memorandum*

(*Foreign Office papers: 371/19946*)

30 June 1936

GERMANY'S EXPENDITURE ON ARMAMENTS

I understand that Mr Churchill proposes to raise this question on the third reading of the Finance Bill on Friday. The German Government no longer

---

[1] Sigismund David Schloss, 1887–1962. Educated at Rugby and Balliol College, Oxford. Entered the Treasury, 1910. Assumed the name of Waley (his mother's surname) in 1914. On active service, 1916–18 (Military Cross, 1917). Assistant Secretary, Treasury, 1924; Principal Assistant Secretary, 1931; Third Secretary, 1946–7. Knighted, 1943. Chairman of the Furniture Development Council, 1949–57. Chairman of Sadler's Wells Trust, 1957–62.

publish figures of their expenditure so that any estimate of their expenditure on armaments must be conjectural.

(1) Mr Churchill's estimate
Mr Churchill's estimate is £1,500 million for the three years of Hitler's regime and £800 million for the year 1935 only. Sir Henry Strakosch told me that he had supplied Mr Churchill with these estimates. They are based on such factors as the increase in German revenue from taxation, the expenditure in Germany on capital account, and the increase in Germany's national income. Dr Schacht[1] told Mr Pinsent recently that the figures used by Mr Churchill were remarkably accurate and only slightly exaggerated.

(2) The 'Morning Post's' estimate
1935
     Current expenditure—£240 million
     Capital expenditure —£400 million to £500 million
1936
     Current expenditure—£400 million to £500 million
     Capital expenditure —£400 million to £500 million
Total for 1935—£640 million to £740 million
Total for 1936—£800 million to £1,000 million
Total expenditure on armaments since Hitler came into power—£1,600 million.

(3) Mr Pinsent's estimate
1935
     Current expenditure—£250 million
     Capital expenditure —£400 million to £500 million
1936
     Current expenditure—£400 million to £500 million
     Capital expenditure —£400 million to £500 million

It will be seen that there is a very close resemblance between the three estimates. But Mr Pinsent, who is in a better position to ascertain the facts than most people, bases his estimate largely on conjecture. For example he says that the figure of £250 million for current expenditure in 1935 'is a sheer guess; but acquaintances of mine both German and foreign have made guesses of about the same order of magnitude'. As regards the current

---

[1] Hjalmar Horace Greely Schacht, 1877–1970. Economist and banker. Assistant Manager, Dresdener Bank, 1908–15. Managing Partner, National Bank of Germany, 1915–22. Senior Partner, Schacht & Co, Bankers, of Düsseldorff. Reich Currency Commissioner, 1923. President of the Reichsbank, 1924–30; reappointed by Hitler, March 1933. Minister of Economics, 1934–7. Tried by the Nuremberg War Crimes Tribunal, 1946, but acquitted.

expenditure for 1936 Mr Pinsent says 'I have been told by a German friend who is usually well informed that the strictly ordinary expenses of the Budget will rise from £640 million in 1935 to £1,080 million in 1936. These figures I find almost beyond belief; but it might well be the case that the ordinary expenditure of the Armed Forces might rise from £250 million in 1935 to £400 million or even £500 million in 1936.' As regards capital expenditure in 1935, Mr Pinsent says 'It seems probable that an additional £400 million to £500 million must have been borrowed for the purpose of capital expenditure on armaments' and also says 'There is every reason to expect that in 1936 the capital expenditure of the Forces as a whole will be at least as high as in 1935.'

It is of course difficult to draw any sharp line between expenditure on armaments and expenditure on unemployment which takes the form of building roads required for strategic purposes and similar work. The current expenditure on armaments is met out of revenue, which is estimated to have increased from £470 million in 1933 to £700 million in 1935 (taking $12\frac{1}{2}$ RM = £1 in both cases). The capital expenditure is financed largely by means of Treasury bills which are held by special financial institutions created for the purpose.

The methods in which armament expenditure has been financed in Germany are extremely skilful, but it is clear that the process is not one which can be continued indefinitely. Germany has in fact been living on her capital, since a considerable part of the national production which ought to have gone to the capital expenditure required to keep machinery in good working order and similar purposes has been expended on armaments. Moreover as soon as armament expenditure is slowed down, Germany will be faced with a formidable unemployment problem.

S. D. Waley

Foreign Office memorandum

(*Foreign Office papers: 371/19946*)

30 June 1936

1. In a statement in the House of Commons on April 23rd last, Mr Churchill estimated that *in 1933, 1934 and 1935* the Germans had spent on capital expenditure on armaments a sum of from 20 to 24 milliards of Reichsmarks. This converted at RM$12\frac{1}{2}$ to the £ gives a sum in sterling of some £1,600 millions to £1,900 millions. *For 1935 alone* he estimated a *total* capital and *current* expenditure of some £600 to £800 millions.

2. Last week the 'Morning Post' estimated that *in 1933, 1934 and 1935* the Germans had spent some £1,240 millions on capital expenditure on armaments and a further £300 to £400 millions on current (maintenance) expenditure. The 'Morning Post' further estimated that *in 1935 alone* £240 millions had been spent on current (maintenance) expenditure on armaments and a further £400 to £500 millions on capital expenditure; and that *in 1936* Germany would spend £400 to £500 millions on current expenditure and a similar sum on capital expenditure.

3. Estimates we have received from the Berlin Embassy (Berlin despatches Nos 162 and 553 of February 5th and June 4th) suggest *for 1933, 1934 and 1935* a total capital expenditure of £1,200 millions. *For 1935* capital expenditure is estimated at £400 to £480 millions plus £240 millions on current expenditure; and *for 1936* £400 to £480 millions on capital expenditure plus a similar sum on current expenditure.

4. Thus, for each of the years 1935 and 1936, according to the Berlin Embassy's estimates, a total sum is being spent which is comparable for each year to the whole of the expenditure on the British Budget. A still more significant fact is that, even if expansion comes to an end now, the maintenance of the German armed forces seems likely to require an annual expenditure of some £400 to £480 millions as against our present annual expenditure on similar services of £140 millions.

Ralph Wigram: minute
(Foreign Office papers: 371/19946)

30 June 1936

I see that it was not possible in the answer to yesterday's question to make the reference which the Department had suggested to Mr Churchill's figures and the estimate given by the 'Morning Post' on June 25th, which the Department meant by the reference to 'others'.

It seems to me that it is very important to let the country know the gigantic sums which the Germans are spending on armaments. The information in our possession, which generally coincides with that given by Mr Churchill and the 'Morning Post', shows that in 1935 the Germans spent on armaments a sum about equivalent to the whole of the British Budget, ie about £800 million: and are likely to spend as much, if not more, this year.

Surely some means ought to be found of making people here realise this.

I submit within a memorandum which states the position and which I would suggest might be given to whichever Minister is going to take the debate in the House which, I understand from Mr Mason,[1] will take place on this subject next Friday.

Would it not be possible for the Government spokesman in this debate, if the opportunity arises, at least to indicate that from such information as is available, the estimates of Mr Churchill and the 'Morning Post' do not seem to be very wide of the mark? This is the only way I see of making clear the position. We can scarcely make a statement on our own seeing that our figures are estimates.

It will be remembered that Dr Schacht himself (see paragraph 18 of Berlin despatch No 553) has informed Mr Pinsent that Mr Churchill's estimate is only slightly exaggerated.

Since writing above, the Treasury have sent over the memo submitted herewith (C4960). It appears that the Chancellor will be answering in Friday's debate, and Mr Waley tells me that he thinks that, if pressed by Mr Churchill, the Chancellor will say with all proper safeguards, that all these calculations are estimates, but if he himself may estimate, he would say that the figures published are not very wide of the mark. I think, for the reasons stated above, that it is desirable that something should be said.

R. F. Wigram

---

[1] Paul Mason, 1904–   . Educated at Eton and King's College, Cambridge. Entered the Foreign Office, 1928. Private Secretary to the Parliamentary Under-Secretary of State, 1936–7. Minister at Sofia, 1949–51. Assistant Under-Secretary of State, 1951–4. Knighted, 1954. Ambassador to the Netherlands, 1954–60. United Kingdom Permanent Representative on the North Atlantic Council, 1960–2.

[2] Chamberlain made no reference to German arms expenditure when he spoke in the debate on Friday 3 July 1936.   But during Oral Answers on July 20, when Churchill asked him 'whether he is aware that the expenditure by Germany upon purposes directly and indirectly concerned with military preparations, including strategic roads, may well have amounted to the equivalent of £800,000,000 during the calendar year 1935; and whether this rate of expenditure seems to be continuing in the current calendar year?' Chamberlain replied: 'The Government have no official figures, but from such information as they have I see no reason to think that the figure mentioned in my right hon Friend's question is necessarily excessive as applied to either year although, as he himself would agree, there are elements of conjecture'.

July 1936

Winston S. Churchill to Allan G. Clark

(*Churchill papers: 2/280*)

1 July 1936

Not only did I bring the matter before Sir Hugh Elles, but also, after stipulating that you should not be victimised in any way, I showed your letter to the Minister for Co-Ordination of Defence. After some time I received from him a letter saying that you were in error in supposing that you were the first who had seen these plants, that they had in fact been examined in September. Apparently this was thought to dispose of the whole matter and prove that the Government were doing all that could be expected. Upon enquiry I learned also what you told me, namely that two machines had been purchased. I explained the futility of this to Sir Thomas Inskip. I can do no more in that quarter. I will however make a further enquiry of Sir Hugh Elles.

King Edward VIII to Winston S. Churchill

(*Churchill papers: 2/264*)

2 July 1936   St James's Palace

Dear Winston

Thank you very much for providing me with such an admirable speech for the occasion of presenting Colours to the Battalions of the three senior Regiments of the Brigade of Guards.

I may change a word here and there in a sentence, but certainly not the sense of the address, which I would like to have emphasised as well as you have.[1]

---

[1] On 16 July 1936 King Edward VIII addressed his 'Grenadiers, Coldstreamers, and Scots Guardsmen'. His address ended: 'Only a few of us on parade this morning have known the awful weight of war, with all its horrors, and yet its comradeships, during the world struggle of 20 years ago. With all my heart I hope, and indeed I pray, that never again will our age

I told Alec Hardinge[1] to communicate with you in connection with a speech to 6,000 Canadians at Vimy, which would be broadcast to Canada. If you would like some notes he can supply them, but I feel you would prefer to write it on your own.[2]

It was nice to see you and have an opportunity of talking again, and at Blenheim. What a magnificent and stately home! and how well Mary[3] and Blandford[4] have adapted it to modern comfort and enjoyment!

Yours sincerely,
Edward R. I.

Winston S. Churchill to Sir Austen Chamberlain
(Austen Chamberlain papers)

3 July 1936   11 Morpeth Mansions
Secret

My dear Austen,

Surely it would be well to proceed upon the basis of your original Motion 'for a Secret Committee of the whole House to consider the state of the

---

and generation be called upon to face such stern and terrible days. Humanity cries out for peace and the assurance of peace, and you will find in peace opportunities of duty and service as noble as any that bygone battlefields can show. Keep, then, the message of these Colours ever before you, and the honour of your Regiment and of your Country will rest safe and sure in your hands.' (*Royal Archives*)

[1] Alexander Henry Louis Hardinge, 1894–1960. Educated at Harrow and Trinity College, Cambridge. On active service, 1915–18 (wounded, Military Cross). Adjutant, Grenadier Guards, 1919–20. Assistant Private Secretary to King George V, 1920–36. Private Secretary to King Edward VIII, 1936; and to King George VI, 1936–43. Privy Councillor, 1936. Knighted, 1937. Succeeded his father, as 2nd Baron Hardinge of Penshurst, 1944 (his elder brother having died of wounds received in action on 18 December 1914).

[2] For Churchill's help with another of King Edward VIII's speeches, see page 247.

[3] Alexandra Mary Cadogan, 1900–1961. A granddaughter of the 5th Earl Cadogan, and one of the five daughters of Henry Arthur, Viscount Chelsea. Worked in a London hospital, 1917–18. She married the Earl of Sunderland (later 10th Duke of Marlborough) in 1920: Sarah Churchill was one of the child bridesmaids, and both Churchill and Balfour signed the register. From 1938 to 1940 she was Chief Commandant of the Auxiliary Territorial Service (ATS) and from 1940 to 1945 she helped to administer eight Red Cross auxiliary hospitals and convalescent homes. A member of the Executive Committee of the Red Cross, 1944. Chairman of the Nuffield Orthopaedic Centre, Oxford, for 23 years. Mayor of Woodstock, 1946–51. Her uncle, Alexander Cadogan was (from 1938 to 1946) Permanent Under-Secretary of State for Foreign Affairs. Another of her uncles, William George Sydney Cadogan, Major, 10th Hussars, had been killed in action in France on 14 November 1914.

[4] John Albert Edward William Spencer-Churchill, 1897–1972. Elder son of the 9th Duke of Marlborough and Consuelo Vanderbilt (Balsan). Marquess of Blandford. Captain, 1st Life Guards, 1916; retired, 1927. Succeeded his father as 10th Duke of Marlborough, 1934. Mayor of Woodstock, 1937–42. Military Liaison Officer to the Regional Commander, Southern Region, 1942. Lieutenant-Colonel, Liaison Officer, US Forces in Britain, 1942–5. In 1972, shortly before his death, he married, as his second wife, Mrs Laura Canfield, formerly Countess of Dudley and Viscountess Long.

nation'. It would then be for the Government to argue that the secret procedure would be ineffective and make their counter proposal, which would certainly afford us ample excuse for not dividing.

Baldwin seems to have recovered and entered the lists again, and there can be no reason that the necessary public action should not proceed.

On the merits of the various proposals:

1. The secret committee of the whole House. This could be achieved by a simple motion to espy strangers and declaration that the House would regard any report of their secret proceedings as a breach of privilege. I believe this would be quite effective for the limited purpose desired. We do not wish to know all the secrets of defence. Indeed all that I want is to be able to debate the defence position with the same freedom as was possible in less dangerous years, and to receive answers from the Government which they would certainly give in ordinary times. I think I could make a considerable case that a secret non-reported session would enable a far more searching debate to take place upon defence, particularly air defence, than is possible in public, and that little more would be known than what is current talk in the Smoking Room and the Lobbies.

2. A meeting of the CID[1] to which a considerable number, say a dozen, Private Members of standing in all parties were invited might not be accepted by the Socialists on the grounds that it would hamper their freedom of criticism. This applies also to any of us. Certainly six or eight hours would be required merely to cover the main ground. Of course if the Government were prepared to give the same measure of attention and time to such a conference as they gave to Lloyd George's unemployment proposals, we could undoubtedly get to the root of the matter. But it is hardly to be expected that at the end of July and August they would face all this labour.

Surveying the whole question, I can see nothing so good as the original proposal, namely that a day should be granted for the public discussion of a Motion to go into a secret Committee.

Yours always,
Winston S. C.

---

[1] The Committee of Imperial Defence; the members of which, as opposed to those of the Cabinet, had always been drawn from all political parties.

Sir Austen Chamberlain to Winston S. Churchill
(Churchill papers: 2/266)

4 July 1936
Personal

My dear Winston,

About my motion I shall do nothing until I have seen Margesson[1] again, which I hope to do on Monday. If the Government were to make such a proposal to us as he foreshadowed, I feel it would be a great mistake not to accept it and that it would put us right out of court. This does not exclude the possibility of a motion to which such an offer might be the answer.

I return Mr Purbrick's[2] letter. I am afraid I differ from him *in toto*. I regard it as impossible to maintain the Demilitarized zone on the Straits since we have allowed Germany to occupy and fortify the demilitarised zone on her Western frontier. These things stood together and were part of the same order of ideas and common settlement at the close of the War. I do not think it possible to maintain a servitude in one case which we have allowed to perish in the other.[3]

Secondly, I do not regard Russia as a military menace to us or to Europe. Nor do I regard Germany as a defence of Europe against Communism. That is part of Hitler's propaganda, but if my safety depended upon him, I should think myself very insecure. Communism is an internal menace in many countries and no doubt wherever it appears to have a chance to flourish, it is encouraged and aided by the Third International which is indistinguishable from the Soviet Government, but against this kind of attack Germany can offer no guarantees to other countries, and I think the German menace to our own safety so real and so imminent that it would be folly to dissipate our strength and energies over a number of minor points when we need to concentrate them all to save us from the greater peril.

I dictate in haste and therefore, I fear, rather dogmatically, but 'them's my sentiments' shortly put.

Yours sincerely,
Austen Chamberlain

[1] Henry David Reginald Margesson, 1890–1965. Educated at Harrow and Magdalene College, Cambridge. On active service, 1914–18 (Military Cross). Captain, 1918. Conservative MP for Upton, 1922–3; for Rugby, 1924–42. Assistant Government Whip, 1924. Junior Lord of the Treasury, 1926, 1926–9 and 1931. Chief Government Whip, 1931–40. Privy Councillor, 1933. Secretary of State for War, 1940–2. Created Viscount, 1942.

[2] Reginald Purbrick, 1877–1950. Educated in Melbourne. Amateur boxing and walking champion, Australia. In commerce, 1900–21. Conservative MP for the Walton Division of Liverpool, 1929–45.

[3] But on 26 June 1936 Churchill had written to Purbrick, about the ending of the Demilitarized Zone of the Dardanelles: 'This is only one of the many losses we are suffering in these bad days of Baldwinism. I will talk it over with Austen, and see if there is anything we can try to do' (*Churchill papers: 2/255*).

Winston S. Churchill to A. H. Richards

(*Churchill papers: 2/282*)

4 July 1936

Would Wednesday 22nd be suitable for the small lunch at my flat which you mentioned? Who should be asked besides Citrine[1] and Lady Violet Bonham Carter? Would it not be possible for Sir Robert Mond to come at the same time? I am afraid I cannot spare a separate day as I am busy completing the proofs of my book this month for press.

Cabinet minutes

(*Cabinet papers: 23/85*)

6 July 1936

The Chancellor of the Exchequer[2] said that during the previous week his brother, Sir Austen Chamberlain, had visited him and told him how concerned he was with the situation of this country, of Europe and of the Government. For the first time since the late Marquess of Salisbury's Government he noticed that the House of Commons was divided on foreign policy. Sir Austen was anxious to help, and had consulted friends, who agreed on his general line. Sir Austen had also made a similar communication to the Parliamentary Secretary to the Treasury.[3] His idea had been to present a Motion that the House should go into Committee in order to discuss the state of the nation. His idea was that there should be a Secret Session, at which the Government could give information which could not be given in ordinary debate, with a view to bringing the various Parties together and securing a united front. . . .

The Chancellor said he would probably see his brother some time that afternoon. He had discussed the matter with the Parliamentary Secretary to the Treasury, and on the previous evening had had an opportunity to talk it over with the Prime Minister. Assuming, as he felt justified in doing, that the idea of a Secret Session had probably been dropped, he himself felt that

---

[1] Walter McLennan Citrine, 1887–1981. Secretary of the Electrical Trades Union, 1914–20; Assistant General Secretary, 1920–3. Assistant Secretary, Trade Union Congress, 1924–5; General Secretary, 1926–46. Director of the *Daily Herald*, 1929–46. Knighted, 1935. Visited Russia, 1936 and 1938. Privy Councillor, 1940. Member of the National Production Advisory Council, 1942–6, and 1949–57. Created Baron, 1946. Member of the National Coal Board, 1946–47. Chairman of the Central Electricity Authority, 1947–57. GBE, 1958.

[2] Neville Chamberlain.

[3] David Margesson, the Conservative Chief Whip (see page 232, note 1).

the Leader of the Labour Opposition[1] would probably refuse the alternative. If other influential Members of Parliament attended a meeting of this kind it would lead to a series of conferences at each of which Mr Winston Churchill would probably adopt an increasingly aggressive line. Very likely he and Mr Lloyd George would work together and would accuse the Government of not taking Defence sufficiently seriously, and eventually they might insist on telling the country, or at any rate Parliament, what they thought about it. On the other hand it was rather difficult to give a categorical refusal. The answer might be that the Government could not consider the proposal unless there was a reasonable prospect of reaching a united front, including the Opposition Labour Party. If this line were adopted Sir Austen Chamberlain might be asked to sound the Leader of the Opposition Labour Party and ask if he would be willing to collaborate. If the Leader of the Labour Opposition accepted, then the meetings might take place; but if he refused it would at least show that the Government was not to blame for the failure of the proposal. This view was shared by the Prime Minister and the Parliamentary Secretary to the Treasury.

The Prime Minister said he had spoken to the Lord President of the Council[2] on the subject. Mr Winston Churchill, he understood, was contemplating the delivery of a speech four hours in length. As he could not get a platform for a sufficiently comprehensive speech on any of the Estimates, he proposed to make it on the Consolidated Fund Bill.

The Lord President of the Council was reluctant to reject the proposal both for a Secret Session and a private meeting. He asked, however, whether the Cabinet would welcome the prospect of having to face Mr Churchill's criticisms in Parliament. If not, one method that had occurred to him for meeting the difficulty was by inviting influential Members of Parliament to a Meeting of the Committee of Imperial Defence, for which there were numerous precedents. That course should not be adopted, however, if the Leader of the Labour Opposition Party refused. The more he thought of it

[1] Clement Richard Attlee, 1883–1967. Educated at Haileybury and University College Oxford. Called to the Bar, 1906. Tutor and lecturer, London School of Economics, 1913–23. On active service at Gallipoli, Mesopotamia (wounded) and France, 1914–19; Major, 1917. First Labour Mayor of Stepney, 1919, 1920; Alderman, 1920–7. Labour MP for Limehouse 1922–50; for West Walthamstow, 1950–5. Parliamentary Private Secretary to Ramsay MacDonald, 1922–4. Under-Secretary of State for War, 1924. Chancellor of the Duchy of Lancaster, 1930–1. Postmaster-General, 1931. Deputy Leader of the Labour Party in the House of Commons, 1931–5. Leader of the Opposition, 1935–40. Lord Privy Seal, 1940–2. Deputy Prime Minister, 1942–5. Lord President of the Council, 1943–5. Prime Minister, 1945–51 (Minister of Defence, 1945–6). Leader of the Opposition, 1951–5. Created Earl, 1955.
[2] Ramsay MacDonald (from his resignation as Prime Minister in June 1935, until the end of Baldwin's Premiership in May 1937).

the less he liked the idea of a meeting attended by Mr Winston Churchill, whether Major Attlee accepted or not. At the same time he did not like to reject both proposals. If asked for a meeting by the Leader of the Labour Opposition and other influential MPs he would not refuse.

The Prime Minister agreed that a Secret Session was out of the question. It might easily throw the country into a panic, and there was no precedent for it except during war. The position would be a very awkward one if the Government invited Sir Austen Chamberlain and his friends to a meeting without any representatives of other Parties. It was sure to leak out in the House of Commons and would create a bad impression.

The Secretary of State for Air[1] said there was a history behind this question. He recalled that the Lord President of the Council, when Prime Minister, had asked him to be Chairman of the Air Defence Research Sub-Committee. The Prime Minister and the Lord President had thought it wise to invite Sir Austen Chamberlain to be a member of that Committee, but Sir Austen had refused, owing to his preoccupation with the India Committee. When the India Committee came to an end another approach had been made to Sir Austen Chamberlain, but he had again refused and had proposed that Mr Winston Churchill should become a member. Mr Churchill had accepted, but his attitude had throughout been unhelpful. Instead of confining himself to the Research questions he had raised wider issues. As Chairman he himself had refused to allow the work of the Committee to be extended, and he had also declined to receive any Papers privately from Mr Churchill on such subjects. Such Papers as he had received from Mr Churchill had been made available to the Air Defence Research Sub-Committee but had been reproduced as documents for the whole Committee of Imperial Defence in the ordinary course. Mr Churchill had never really considered the Air Ministry's comments on his Papers on their merits, although they were probably fairly accurate, and actually had turned out to be within one per cent of the French estimates of German air strength.

Mr Churchill had also been working in close alliance with Professor Lindemann, who was a member of the Expert Committee on Air Defence Research. The latter had put forward two proposals, one of which was so fantastic that it had been rejected by all his scientific colleagues, including Sir Frank Smith; and the other had also not commended itself at all strongly. At the last meeting of the Air Defence Research Sub-Committee Mr Churchill's attitude had been very intransigent; he had adopted an attitude of pique and seemed to be about to resign from the Committee. He thought that the present proposal was not unconnected with Mr Churchill's attitude. . . .

[1] Viscount Swinton.

The Minister for Co-ordination of Defence[1] described how, during the previous week, Mr Churchill, at a late hour in the Library of the House of Commons, had unfolded his plan, after explaining that he now rejected the idea of a Secret Session. In reply to his own question as to what would happen if Mr Churchill and his friends found the Government's attitude unsatisfactory, he had said that they would then have to tell the country or the House of Commons. Mr Churchill's ultimate idea appeared to be to create a great Office supervised by business men with a total staff of a thousand, and at a given moment, so to speak, to pull the lever and switch the whole of the munitions supply over to this new Department.

Ralph Wigram: minute

(*Foreign Office papers: 371/19933*)

8 July 1936

I have already commented on this paper in a note for the Foreign Office Representative on the Committee of Imperial Defence.

The interesting points seem to be:

(1) The Air Ministry explanation that the peace reserve is intended to be adequate to cover the war wastage during the period after the outbreak of war prior to the completion of the change over of industry from a peace to a war basis. As the Germans are ahead of us in the organisation of industry, the change over will take a shorter period for them; and therefore, as I understand it, our peace-time reserve has to be larger than theirs. This is, I understand, the case.

(2) The fact that Mr Churchill's estimate of the total number of machines available in Germany for military purposes is 3,200, while that of the Air Ministry is 3,115.

(3) The attention directed to the potential reserve which will be constituted for Germany in 12 to 18 months time by the development of the Air Sports Association.

R. F. Wigram

[1] Sir Thomas Inskip.

Desmond Morton to Winston S. Churchill

(*Churchill papers: 25/7*)

10 July 1936   Industrial Intelligence
Secret

Dear Winston,

I return herewith the paper you kindly sent me, and agree with you that it is no use carrying the controversy further along these lines. May I suggest that you reserve yourself for an enquiry into the progress of our own air rearmament, and as to whether it has proceeded satisfactorily along the line promised in Parliament?

As regards the Air Staff comments on your Memorandum: there is apparently a misprint in the first paragraph, the last two lines, which should read 'ie 12 aircraft per squadron, of which 3 are in immediate reserve, &c'. This is evidently only a misprint, as if read as printed it does not make sense.

Apart from this negligible point, I was interested in their comments on your Paragraph 4. The Air Staff seems to demand that a great number of posts in the German Air Force, which would not seem to call for the appointment of an officer with a pilot's certificate, should nevertheless be filled by such an officer. It may be in accordance with our own procedure, but as a layman I am surprised that 'all HQ, Staff, administrative, training and other appointments, experimental stations, recruit depots, aircraft parks, Staff College, Air Ministry, and the instructional posts in the RLK' should all apparently require a proportion of pilots.

Paragraph 6 of the Air Staff's comments reads to me as an acceptance of your views, though perhaps not a whole hearted one.

There is still no desire on the part of the Air Staff to estimate the total number of German aircraft that might take the air on the first day of war.

My comments above do not alter my agreement expressed at the beginning of this letter with your view that further discussion on these lines will hardly be profitable.

Yours very sincerely,
Desmond Morton

Winston S. Churchill to Walter Monckton[1]

(Churchill papers: 2/264)

10 July 1936
Confidential

Dear Mr Monckton,

I sat next to our friend[2] last night, and he surprised me by saying that you had told him what I had said about not allowing gossip to be repeated in my presence. He said he thought it very nice of me. However, he then asked where I had seen you. Was it at dinner? To which, concluding that you had told him of our interview, I replied, that you had come to see me. He then asked 'about what'? and I replied 'about gossip'. He seemed somewhat startled at this, but proceeded, after a pause, to speak in very warm terms about you.

I do not think the incident is of much importance, but as he may mention the matter to you, I let you know exactly what he said; if he should raise the matter, I hope you will say that, knowing I was a friend, you asked me generally what my view was about gossip, and whether it was serious and growing, or not: and that I said, provided the conventions were observed, I thought it would die down. There appears to be no need to go into any further details.

Walter Monckton to Winston S. Churchill

(Churchill papers: 2/264)

11 July 1936
Confidential

Dear Mr Churchill,

I am very grateful to you for your letter.

I will certainly take the course you propose should our friend discuss his talk with you, as well he may.

I will also be careful to limit any conversation on the subject, as you suggest.

Yours very sincerely,
Walter Monckton

[1] Walter Turner Monckton, 1891–1965. Educated at Harrow and Balliol College, Oxford. President of the Oxford Union Society, 1913. On active service, 1915–19 (Military Cross). Called to the Bar, 1919. King's Counsel, 1930. Attorney-General to the Prince of Wales, 1932–6. Knighted, 1937. Director-General of the Press Censorship Bureau, 1939–40. Director-General, Ministry of Information, 1940–1; of British Propaganda and Information Services, Cairo, 1941–2. Solicitor-General, 1945. Conservative MP for Bristol West, 1951–7. Minister of Labour and National Service, 1951–5. Minister of Defence, 1955–6. Paymaster-General, 1956–7. Created Viscount, 1957.

[2] King Edward VIII.

Lieutenant-General Sir Hugh Elles to Winston S. Churchill

(Churchill papers: 2/280)

11 July 1936   War Office

Dear Mr Churchill,

I have delayed answering your letter of the 1st July on the subject of Plessey because I wished to make certain of the position.

I do not propose to go on with the proposition for the following main reasons:

Firstly, the firm has no forging experience.

Secondly, if we are to install a special plant at considerable expense for mortar bombs it should be nearer the sources of supply and certainly not in a vulnerable place like Ilford.

My people have discussed the matter very fully with Mr Clark to whom we are much obliged for putting up the scheme and giving us the benefit of his information.

Yours sincerely,
Hugh Elles

Harold Balfour to Winston S. Churchill

(Churchill papers: 2/256)

11 July 1936

Dear Mr Churchill,

May I please be allowed to thank you most genuinely & sincerely for your speech yesterday.[1] Not only was it a great help to me, personally, in my

---

[1] Speaking at Birchington, in Kent, on 10 July 1936, Churchill declared: 'The Government are at last making strenuous efforts to remedy the deficiencies in our defence. It is a great pity that they did not begin to do this earlier.' Churchill added: 'People must not allow themselves to be lulled into a sense of false security by the large sums of money now being spent.' His speech continued: 'Socialists talk of these sums we are spending as huge sums of money, and so they are, but everything is relative. Certainly they (the Germans) are spending more than four times as much as we are spending now. It seems to me that a far greater effort is necessary, and that we should set up a Ministry of Supply to organize industry and to make the necessary expansion in our weapons without delay'. Churchill wanted the Government to 'declare without delay a period of emergency preparation—something more than peace conditions, something less than war conditions'. He also mentioned the recent flight of the German zeppelin over England, criticizing British protests as weak and ineffective.

Division but I am glad to see by its treatment in the Press today, that it is regarded as a pronouncement of national importance.[1]

I hope you got back safely and you took back with you the warmest regards from Thanet[2] and including those of,

Yours sincerely,
Harold Balfour

Winston S. Churchill to Sir Hugh Tudor

(*Churchill papers: 2/266*)

11 July 1936

Thank you so much for your letter. I was sorry not to see you when you came through England on your way back. Everything is getting steadily worse upon the continent. A good deal of work is of course going on here, but all about two years behind. What will these two years bring forth?

Let me know what happens about the recruiting in Newfoundland. I will press again for a small training cruiser. The new First Lord is a great improvement on the old.[3]

Let me know when you are coming over again.

All good wishes,

[1] But not all Press comment was favourable. On 11 July 1936 the *Manchester Guardian* leading article, headed 'Mr Churchill as Bogey-man', commented: 'Mr Churchill was asking yesterday what would have happened if a British airship or aeroplane had flown over a German fortified district. Something very different, he thought from the "bleating expostulations" which are "all we have been able to make" when the Hindenburg "passes and repasses, now across this dockyard and port of entry of our foodstuffs and now another". Mr Churchill's oratory seems strangely impervious to facts. Sir Philip Sassoon distinctly stated in the Commons that the Hindenburg passed over no British prohibited area and that in fact, none of our national regulations was known to have been infringed. In addition, it seems worth pointing out that even now a British private aeroplane can still, so long as it keeps the regulations, fly almost as freely over Germany as the Hindenburg over England. The prohibited areas are certainly more numerous, though a glowing article in the current "Shell Aviation News", pointing out the delights of Germany to air tourists, asserts that they only exist over "artillery ranges, kite-flying stations, and training areas for blind flying, and over industrial districts where considerable damage might be done in the event of a landing". The same article, based on information supplied by the German Aero Club, tells us that pilots from countries with no air traffic agreement with Germany may enter without permits between July 1 and August 16 and be given a "certificate to the effect that the pilot is a visitor to the Olympic Games; this will ensure that no difficulties are encountered". We may take this special and sports-period amiability for what it may be worth. But is there really any reason yet for Mr Churchill to start stimulating spy-mania on the best pre-1914 model?'

[2] Harold Balfour had been Conservative MP for Kent, Isle of Thanet, since the General Election of 1929.

[3] On 5 June 1936 Sir Samuel Hoare had become First Lord, in place of Viscount Monsell. This appointment marked Hoare's return to the Cabinet, five and a half months after his resignation as a result of the Hoare-Laval 'Pact'.

Vice-Admiral Sir Reginald Henderson to Winston S. Churchill

(*Churchill papers: 2/266*)

13 July 1936

Dear Mr Churchill,

From the information we have in the Admiralty, Colonel Garforth's[1] figures certainly seem to be exaggerations.

He does not state from what height his 500 lb SAP[2] bomb is dropped, but I understand that in recent trials this bomb, when dropped from 10,000 feet, only penetrated a maximum of 17 feet into a variety of soils.

The burst of the bomb, acting as a mine in the ground, at this depth would do damage several feet further down. From Military Engineering, Vol IV, (a book which is on sale to the public) it can be calculated that the bomb would blow in a tunnel in the ground from 25 to 30 feet below its point of burst depending on the nature of the soil. It would not, of course, damage the roof of a concrete underground shelter at this distance.

The German pillboxes to which you refer, and which stood up to 8-inch and 9-inch guns, were probably attacked by HE shell fitted with direct action fuzes, which burst the shell immediately on impact. They would probably have been defeated by armour-piercing shell fuzed with a slight delay, and a 500 lb SAP bomb dropped from 12,000 feet would have about the same striking energy as the shell in this case.

The 12 ft craters which you saw in France were also probably caused by HE shell which go off on graze or impact in the same way as does the General Purpose bomb, half the explosive effect going up into the air. The effect of fitting a fuze with slight delay to an Armour Piercing bomb or shell is, as I am sure you know, that one gets a tamping effect due to the delay in the fuze, resulting in a much more violent explosive effect.

I have no precise figures for the penetration of heavy AP shell into the earth, but we know that 15-inch shell do sometimes go 60 feet into the wet sands at Shoeburyness. The striking energy of a 15-inch shell at 20,000 yards, however, is, as you estimate, almost exactly ten times that of a 500 lb bomb dropped from 12,000 feet.

There is one more point. I do not see why we should expect that the use of Armour Piercing bombs would find a place in the general bombing pro-

[1] William Garforth, 1882–1965. Educated at Rugby. 2nd Lieutenant, Royal Engineers, 1901. Captain, 1912. Major, 1916. General Staff Officer, New Zealand Reserve Group, 1916–18. Lieutenant-Colonel, 1926; Colonel, 1930. Deputy Chief Engineer, Eastern Command, 1932. Retired from the Army, 1935.

[2] SAP = Semi-armour-piercing. A type of bomb or shell designed for use against lightly armoured targets. It had a thinner casing than the armour-piercing type and contained more high explosive.

gramme of an enemy except against ships. As far as I know, we are not making such bombs for use against land objects.

I hope this is a satisfactory answer.

Yours sincerely,
R. G. Henderson

Alfred Duff Cooper to Winston S. Churchill
(*Churchill papers: 2/278*)

14 July 1936   War Office

Dear Winston,

On the 7th July you handed me a letter which you had received from Mr Martin Lindsay,[1] and which I now return.[2]

I can assure you that there is no foundation whatever for Mr Lindsay's suspicion that Messrs Hitchins Jarvis may be buying surplus machine guns from the War Department for re-conditioning and sale to Germany.

There are about 30,000 surplus Hotchkiss machine guns, not 21,000 as Mr Lindsay states, and they are at Weedon, not Didcot. Nobody except the War Office possesses the selling rights of these guns (the Soley Armament

---

[1] Martin Alexander Lindsay, 1905–1980. 2nd Lieutenant, Royal Scots Fusiliers, 1925; served in the Army, 1925–36. 4th Battalion, Nigeria Regiment, 1927. Travelled through the Ituri Forest, Belgian Congo, 1929. Surveyor to the British Arctic Air-Route Expedition to Greenland, 1930–1. Published *Those Greenland Days*, 1932, and *The Epic of Captain Scott*, 1933. Leader of the British Trans-Greenland Expedition, 1934. Prospective National Government candidate, Brigg Division, 1936–9. On active service, Norway, 1940. Commanded the 1st Battalion, Gordon Highlanders, in sixteen operations, July 1944–May 1945 (despatches, wounded, DSO); Lieutenant-Colonel. Conservative MP for Solihull, 1945–64. In 1946 he published *So Few Got Through: the Diary of an Infantry Officer*, and in 1947 *Three Got Through: Memoirs of an Arctic Explorer*. Chairman, West Midlands Area of Conservative and Unionist Associations, 1949–52. Created Baronet, 1962. In 1969 he married, as his second wife, Loelia, Duchess of Westminster, divorced wife of Churchill's friend 'Bendor' and daughter of the 1st Baron Sysonby.

[2] On 6 July 1936 Martin Lindsay, Prospective Conservative candidate for the Brigg Division, wrote to Churchill from the Marlborough Club, Pall Mall: 'last night one of the directors of Hitchins Jarvis (armament manufacturers) told me that this firm is about to supply Germany with 28,000 re-conditioned machine guns. He said that 7,000 of this number were to be provided by Germany for re-conditioning, from stocks captured during the war, and that the work would be done at the Soley Armament Coy Depôt at Liège. The remaining 21,000 his firm were buying from Government surplus stocks at Didcot, and exporting them (after reconditioning) nominally to the Soley Coy in Belgium, whence they will go to Germany. I put this information at the disposal of the War Office this morning, and there I was told that the Government has precisely the figure quoted by my friend—21,000 surplus Hotchkiss M.G.s for sale at Didcot. As I mistrust Government Departments (specially the War Office) I am also putting this information at your disposal for such action as you may think necessary.'

Company's agreement expired on the 30th June last). There has been no offer to purchase them, and if such an offer were made it would not be considered unless it had the approval of the Foreign Office and of the General Staff.

The weapon proved to be so unreliable and unsuited to the needs of the Cavalry that it was withdrawn from use, hence the surplus. Apart from the facts it is difficult to imagine that Germany would contemplate using or purchasing inferior weapons such as these.

Yours ever,
Duff Cooper

Winston S. Churchill to Sir Henry Page Croft [1]

(Churchill papers: 2/256)

14 July 1936

I return you Charley's [2] letter herewith. I do not agree with his version of events, nor with his figures. I wish I could believe him right. I warned him as a friend of his childhood and as a cousin three years ago that if he did not exert himself he would be victimised. This is exactly what happened!

Harold Nicolson: diary

(Nicolson papers)

16 July 1936

Foreign Affairs Committee. Winston argues from the premise, which everyone accepts, that our main duty is to defend the British Empire and the Rhine frontier. This in itself, in modern conditions, is 'a gigantic task'. What we have got to ask ourselves is whether that task would in the end be facilitated by our telling Germany that she could take what she liked in the East. Were we to say this, Germany, within the course of a single year, would become dominant from Hamburg to the Black Sea, and we should be faced by a confederacy such as had never been seen since Napoleon.

[1] Henry Page Croft, 1881–1947. Educated at Eton, Shrewsbury and Trinity Hall, Cambridge. Conservative MP for Christchurch, 1910–18; for Bournemouth, 1918–40. Served in the Great War, 1914–16 (despatches); Brigadier-General, 1916. One of the Vice-Presidents, with Churchill, of the India Defence League, 1933–5. Member of the Speaker's Conference on the Franchise, 1918; Civil List Committee, 1936; Committee of Privileges, 1939. Created Baronet, 1924; Baron, 1940. Parliamentary Under-Secretary of State for War, 1940–5. Privy Councillor, 1945.

[2] Lord Londonderry, see page 129, note 1.

The general impression left was that the majority of the National Party are at heart anti-League and anti-Russian, and that what they would really like would be a firm agreement with Germany and possibly Italy by which we could purchase peace at the expense of the smaller states. This purely selfish policy would to my mind make an Anglo-German war quite certain within twenty years. I do not believe that this mood will last, and I think that eventually Winston will be able to get a solid block for his League of restricted commitments and unlimited liabilities.

Winston S. Churchill to Alfred Duff Cooper

(*Churchill papers: 2/278*)

16 July 1936

Many thanks for your letter of the 14th, which disposes of the allegations of my correspondent. May I express the hope that these 30,000 machine guns, even if they are unsatisfactory and obsolete, should be carefully locked up and on no account disposed of until at least an equal number of better weapons are available.

At one time early in the Great War I had to ransack the gunsmiths for sporting rifles wherewith to arm some of the ancillary services of the Navy. Beggars must not be choosers!

Major-General Sir Henry Thuillier[1] to Winston S. Churchill

(*Churchill papers: 2/266*)

16 July 1936

Dear Mr Churchill,

I venture to send you a copy of a lecture I gave some months ago on the subject of restrictions of certain methods of warfare, as I think the subject is

---

[1] Henry Fleetwood Thuillier, 1868–1953. 2nd Lieutenant, Royal Engineers, 1887. On active service, Chitral, 1895, and on the western front, 1914–18. Director of Gas Services GHQ, France, 1916. Controller, Chemical Warfare, Ministry of Munitions, 1917–18. Commanded the 23rd Division, 1918 (despatches five times, Major-General). Commandant of the School of Military Engineering, 1919–23. Director of Fortifications and Works, War Office, 1924–7. General Officer Commanding the 52nd Division of the Territorial Army, 1927–30. Knighted, 1930. Colonel Commandant, Royal Engineers, 1935–40. Served with the rank of Major in the Ministry of Supply, 1940–5. His younger son, Captain George Fleetwood Thuillier, Devon Regiment, fought on the Somme, 1916–17, received the Military Cross, 1 January 1918, and was killed in action at St Christ on the Somme while commanding his company, 26 March 1918.

one that would interest you. I was much attacked in the Press for saying that gas is the most humane weapon used in war!

I am exceedingly glad to see that you have consented to become president of the British Section of the 'New Commonwealth', since your powerful advocacy will do much to educate the public up to the realization of the fact that the only way of avoiding war is to equip the League of Nations with the means of enforcing its decrees by military action & that the first step to that end is to put our own country into a condition of strength.

Yours sincerely,
H. F. Thuillier

Lord Rothermere to Winston S. Churchill
(Churchill papers: 2/266)

16 July 1936   At Sea
Confidential

My dear Winston,

I read your gloomy article in the 'Evening Standard'.[1] But you are a blazing optimist compared with myself.

With the Austrian agreement[2] Germany has started her grand diplomatic offensive to be followed in a short time by war.

[1] In an article in the *Evening Standard* on 13 July 1936, headed 'Dusk Approaches', Churchill criticized what he called the 'Baldwin–MacDonald regime', and the Government's failure to rearm soon enough against 'the Teutonic giant' who, from 1933, 'was stealthily regathering the weapons with which he had almost conquered the world'. He went on to tell his readers: 'The country is slowly but undoubtedly awakening to the fact that world peace is menaced, and that our island safety is no longer unquestioned. Gradually it is being understood that whereas four years ago all was sure and easy, all has now become dark, doubtful and hazardous in the extreme. It is this growing comprehension that the times have changed, that woeful miscalculations have been made, that a violent period is drawing near, and that we ourselves are neither ready for it nor even making the exertions which are now possible, that has affected so profoundly the position of the Prime Minister.' The article ended: 'National leaders flourish or fade, and ought to do so, only in proportion as they express and meet the public need. Bold captains are required for perilous seas. However unpalatable it may be to docile adherents of the powers that be, the Baldwin–MacDonald regime is passing out of life into history. Let us hope there is still time to turn the affairs of the British Empire to a different fortune.'

[2] Of 11 July 1936, signed by Schuschnigg and Hitler, at Hitler's insistence, whereby Germany and Austria agreed to 'recognise the mutual interests of the two Germanic States, Germany and Austria, and to put on record Germany's recognition of the sovereignty of Austria and her pledge that she would not interfere in Austrian internal affairs'. As a corollary to this agreement, Schuschnigg was forced to appoint two Cabinet Ministers with strong Nazi sympathies: Dr Guido Schmidt (as Foreign Secretary) and General Glaise von Horstenau. Among the secret clauses to the agreement of 11 July 1936 was one which ended the prohibition on the sale of *Mein Kampf* in Austria, while books critical of the Nazi regime in Germany were to be withdrawn.

At the best I hope that war will not break out before 1938 but it may come at any moment.

Single-handed Germany can win a two or three weeks' war against Britain and France. Against ourselves I think the war would be over in 72 hours. France may put up a scattered resistance which it may take Germany two or three weeks to overcome.

Any more talk about the Rhine being Britain's frontier or the frontiers of France being our own may lead instantly to the catastrophe. We are in increasing disfavour in Berlin. Three or four months ago there was quite a friendly feeling towards us but this is changing all the time. The oligarchs there have a complete contempt for our Government. They shew it by failing for four months to appoint a new ambassador in London and by failing for ten weeks to reply to the questionnaire which after all is one of the most important diplomatic documents ever sent out by the British Foreign Office.

With Berlin and Rome now friendly there may be short shrift for London and Paris.

Africa, except possibly South Africa, will change ownership well within the present decade.

We live in times when frontier changes of the most far-reaching character may take place. Who knows that you and I may not be citizens within three years' time of a vassal state with Scapa Flow a great naval and air arsenal of Germany.

Yours always,
Harold

PS. I have come away for a short holiday. I find fretting and fuming over our failure to arm is bad for my health.

King Edward VIII to Winston S. Churchill

(Churchill papers: 2/264)

17 July 1936   St James's Palace

Dear Winston,

I want to thank you again for your help over yesterday's speech on the occasion of the presentation of new Colours to the three senior Regiments of the Brigade of Guards. I hear from all sides how well it has been received and appreciated, not only as a suitable address for that occasion, but as introducing a peaceful note at this somewhat disturbed time.

I enclose one of the copies which were handed to every Guardsman after the Parade, and have signed it under the facsimile autograph in case you care to keep it as a souvenir.

I am also very grateful that you are dealing with the speech for Vimy, which I understand I shall have over the weekend. I am sure that Tommy Lascelles[1] feels highly commended at your remarking on the excellence of his draft.

Yours sincerely,
Edward R.I.

Winston S. Churchill to Sir Maurice Hankey
(Churchill papers: 25/7)

17 July 1936

Many thanks for sending me the print of my last air strength paper together with the Air Staff comments thereupon. These do not at all alter my opinion. It is no use carrying the controversy further, but I should like to put it on record that the French official figures which I quoted and which confirm my December forecast, are the very least that should be accepted. Indeed I fear the position may be considerably worse. If you think fit, show this letter to the Secretary of State.

If all the military machines mentioned in my last paper have been unaccounted for, in fact they make every appearance of formed squadrons.

King Edward VIII to Winston S. Churchill
(Churchill papers: 2/264)

20 July 1936   St James's Palace

Dear Winston

Thank you again for another admirable speech. I received your suggestions

---

[1] Alan Frederick Lascelles, 1887–1981. On active service in France, 1914–18. Captain, 1916; Military Cross. ADC to Lord Lloyd (then Governor of Bombay), 1919–20. Assistant Private Secretary to the Prince of Wales, 1920–9. Secretary to the Governor-General of Canada, 1931–5. Assistant Private Secretary to King George V, 1935; to King Edward VIII, 1936 and to King George VI, 1936–43. Knighted, 1939. Privy Councillor, 1943. Private Secretary to King George VI, 1943–52; to Queen Elizabeth II, 1952–3.

for Vimy yesterday. I have not changed a word, but only added a personal allusion to my having dedicated the altar at Ottawa nine years ago.[1]

Thank you also for your kind remarks about Thursday's unpleasant incident.[2] Mercifully no one was injured, but it was a very unsuitable ending to such a grand and impressive ceremony.

Yours sincerely,
Edward R. I.

Desmond Morton: notes on a speech by Sir Thomas Inskip
(Churchill papers: 2/268)

20 July 1936

Numbered paragraphs refer to numbers in blue on the margin of Mr Churchill's copy of Hansard.

1. The Minister said that the Supplementary Estimates were evidence of a swelling tide of production.

They are in fact nothing of the kind, though they are evidence that steps are now being taken to get industry into a condition eventually to produce what is required. The whole speech avoids giving evidence of what is actually required to be produced. Of course it would be impossible to give such facts in the House of Commons, since to do so would be to betray the state of our defences to foreign countries.

2. The Minister stated that regular sources of supply are being used to their utmost capacity.

This means very little, since it is well known that the regular sources of supply have nowadays an insignificant capacity relative to what is required, either to make up the deficiencies in reserves, or to arm the nation's forces in war.

---

[1] On 26 July 1936, King Edward VIII unveiled the memorial to the Canadian war dead on Vimy Ridge. During his speech of dedication, the King said: 'Already the scars of war have well-nigh vanished from the fair landscape spread before us. Around us here to-day there is peace and the re-building of hope. And so also in dedicating this memorial to our fallen comrades our thoughts turn rather to the splendour of their sacrifice, and to the consecration of our love for them, than to the cannonade which beat upon this ridge a score of years ago.'

[2] On 17 July 1936, while the King was riding at the head of six battalions of the Guards between Hyde Park and Buckingham Palace, a man broke through the crowd of spectators and hurled a revolver loaded in four of its six chambers between the King and his troops. The King paused briefly to look at the revolver, and then proceeded calmly on his way. George Andrew McMahon, a journalist, was arrested at the scene of the incident, and charged with unlawfully possessing a loaded revolver, with intent to endanger life and property, with presenting a firearm near the King with intent to break the public peace, and with producing a firearm with intent to alarm the King.

3. The Minister confessed that new firms, by which it is clear that he means all firms other than those referred to above as the regular sources of supply, have to be inspected, or classified etc and then have to learn a new technique of armament production.

This is ample evidence of the long delay that must ensue before output is reached.

4. The Minister said that the preliminary stages have been passed.

This however only applies to 52 firms of which only 14 have accepted definite contracts. The suggestion in the statement that the preliminary stage has been passed is therefore unacceptable. It has only been passed in the case of these 52 firms. How foreign countries must laugh when they learn that 52 firms—or in point of fact only 14—are the total now accepted upon which we can draw for armament manufacture! While the United States has inspected and planned several thousand firms, Germany is known to be employing at the moment several hundred firms in the manufacture of projectiles alone, and all other first class powers have at least planned on the same scale.

5. The Minister said that when all 52 firms are in production seven-eighths of the total requirements of the Government in shells and fuses and cartridge cases will have been provided.

Presumably this refers to the provision of ammunition to make up past deficiencies. Certainly the qualifying phrase that they have entered into production is therefore necessary, since apparently none of the 52, not even the 14 who have accepted firm contracts, have yet entered into production. Later in his speech the Minister admits that new firms have to be supplied with additional plant and machinery. Moreover, then when that has been supplied and set up in the new factories, output cannot be reached for some further considerable time.

Even if these facts mean that in a year or so deficiencies in reserves of ammunition will have been made good, what steps have yet been taken to ensure an adequate supply in war?

6. The Minister admits that firms do not yet possess the necessary jigs to perform their contract.

How then can they enter into production?

7. It is admitted that 18 months or two years must elapse before the new filling factories proposed will be able to start work.

8. As regards the provision of labour, by which presumably the Minister refers to skilled labour, all he can say is that he hopes and trusts that there will be no difficulty in finding it.

Seeing that the chief factor limiting industrial production today in all first class countries, is the provision of skilled labour, even in Germany special steps have been taken to train large numbers of apprentices, it is extraordinary that the Minister should merely hope and trust, and not propose some clear course of action.

9. The Minister states that the speed of service aircraft in production today, would five years ago have made them serious competitors for the Schneider Cup.

But this is a fact which applies to modern service types of aircraft in every country in the world. Moreover at 10, he admits only that 'some have been delivered'. It would be of the highest importance to know what proportion of the estimated requirements of different types of service aircraft, day bombers, night bombers, reconnaissance and fighters, will have been delivered by the 1st April 1937. Even though the necessary 4,000 for a 1,500 Metropolitan first line can be counted at that date, it will not be truly 1,500 first line, unless the proportion of the different types of aircraft are correct.

11. It is satisfactory to find that new types of aircraft have been accepted after a much briefer trial than was hitherto deemed necessary; but it would seem essential for the Government to take powers to enforce the manufacture of types they have accepted by factories other than the one responsible for its design.

12. Forty new aerodromes have been or are being acquired.

It is a pity that the Minister found it impossible to say that the whole 40 had not only been acquired, but were in process of transformation into aerodromes. Like factories and industrial production it is quite inadequate to buy a piece of ground and then call it an aerodrome. In this present case it appears that an unknown proportion of the forty pieces of ground have not yet even been acquired.

This piece of information is valueless, unless it be known how many new aerodromes in all it is considered necessary for our defence to set up, and what proportion of these are emergency landing grounds, and what proportion aerodromes at which units will be stationed.

13. The Minister stated that in April, May and June of this year about three and a half times as many air frames, and twice as many engines had been delivered, as in the same months of the previous year.

Surely this confession betrays absolutely an unbalanced production. What is the good of an air frame without an engine? Seeing that a large proportion of air frames require, or should require if they are to be bombers, more than one engine, it is really necessary for at least one spare engine to be manufactured for every engine used in a machine. The engine proportion in this country appears to be hopelessly inadequate, relatively, to airframe production—which we know to be only too small.

In this connection, is it not a fact that three quarters of the special purpose machine tools necessary to the manufacture of aircraft, are not made in this country, but have to be imported from the United States? What steps have been taken either to set up manufacture of these essential tools in this country, or to lay in a large reserve stock of such tools? It has surely not been forgotten that the United States have placed an embargo in respect of armaments to belligerents, and that in some quarters it is confidently expected to apply also to special purpose machine tools for the manufacture of these armaments.

14. The Minister implies that the British optical industry is able to manufacture all service requirements both in quantity and quality, with one exception.

The industry may be able to do so in time, but in war it is time that counts; and is the British optical industry in a position to produce the necessary instruments at the rate at which they will be required in war?

15. The Minister says that the imports of machine tools in May this year are double the value of similar imports a year ago.

This alone betrays the weakness of our position, in that when machine tools are required, we have to import them. Alternatively, if it be argued in answer to this that the £1,000,000 of machine tools is a mere fleabite to what is being produced in this country, then the £1,000,000 which is being voted in the Supplementary Estimates for provision of machine tools is likewise a fleabite to what is required.

16. The Minister states that we are still having a very careful examination of war material requirements in the event of war.

What a confession of slackness in the past, that this essential enquiry should not have been completed years ago, and in addition definite arrangements made for the supply of these raw materials should war come, and a reserve already collected of those raw materials the supply of which in war may be unduly difficult or delayed.

Winston S. Churchill: memorandum

(*Churchill papers: 2/268*)

20 July 1936

For more than two years it has been common knowledge that Germany was creating a military Air Force in breach of the Treaty, and that her civil and sports aviation were a vast training-ground for war purposes.

I warned the House of Commons about this in March 1933. A whole year was wasted in vain attempt by the first Eden Mission to induce France, Italy and other European powers to reduce their air force to the British level. There was never the slightest chance of these proposals, which did not affect Germany, being accepted. Further warnings were addressed to the Government in the Air debate of March 1934, and it was on this occasion that the Lord President[1] gave his assurance to Parliament that our Air Force should not be allowed to fall below the strength of any power within striking distance of our shores.

In August 1934 the new Air Force expansion programme was ʼnnounced. The Government still maintained the fiction that Germany had no military Air Force, but it was clearly of Germany that the Lord President was speaking when he used the expression 'our frontiers are the Rhine'. Nevertheless the five years' expansion programme then proposed was inadequate in scale and too slow in pace of execution.

In November 1934 by an amendment to the Address a formal complaint was made that our defences, and particularly our Air defences, were insufficient to provide for national safety. During this debate I made the definite statement that the Germans had already created an illegal military Air Force. This was acknowledged by the Government. I also asserted that the German military Air Force was rapidly approaching equality with our own. The Lord President strenuously denied this. He declared—I presume on figures supplied by the Air Ministry—that the German Air Force on that date (ie November 1934) was not 'rapidly approaching equality with our own', but was in fact not 50% (ie not half) our own. He stated further 'that by this time next year' (ie November 1935) 'we should still have a 50% superiority' (ie three to two) over Germany. These statements were wrong, but they were everywhere accepted as most reassuring by the British public.

The next opportunity for raising the issue was upon the Air Estimates of the current year in March 1935. On this occasion the Under-Secretary of State[2] was instructed to say that we still had a substantial superiority over Germany, and that even in November 1935 we should have a superiority. These statements, although widely different from those made by the Lord President in November, were still far from the truth. A fortnight later Herr Hitler announced that he already had a German Air Force of first line strength equal to ours, or words to that effect. This statement was confirmed by the Foreign Secretary without its facts being contradicted in any way.

Let us now come to some of the actual figures which have emerged in the debates. In November 1934 the Lord President stated the British first-line strength for home defence at 880, including the auxiliary squadrons (127) and the Fleet Air Arm (about 100). He also suggested that remarkably large reserves of aircraft existed behind our first line strength which it was not in the public interest to disclose.

[1] Stanley Baldwin, Lord President of the Council from August 1931 until becoming Prime Minister in June 1935.
[2] Sir Philip Sassoon.

In March 1935, the last debate upon the subject, the Under-Secretary of State corrected the Lord President's figure of the strength of the British home defence Air Force from 880 to 690, including the auxiliary squadrons and Fleet Air Arm. The 127 auxiliary squadron machines ought not to be counted in the first line Air strength, as they are no more comparable to the regular units of the Royal Air Force than are the Territorial battalions to those of the whole-time professional Army. Neither ought the 100 or more machines of the Fleet Air Arm to be included as first line strength for home defence; for the machines are only scouting machines and the Fleet itself may be absent.

The total British first line strength available for home defence is thus shown to be not 880, as stated by the Lord President, but under 460, or little more than half his figure.

Parliament has not been given any information about the basis upon which Herr Hitler made his statement that he had already reached parity with Great Britain. Whether he was basing himself upon the 880 of the Lord President in November 1934, or upon the 690 of the Under-Secretary of State in March 1935; or whether he deducted the Fleet Air Arm and the auxiliary squadrons from the British strength before making his calculations, is a point upon which information must be sought. If it should prove that Herr Hitler was basing himself upon the Lord President's assertion of November (viz a first-line strength of 880 machines), and that he claims to have equality with that at the present time, then it is certain that he has not merely equality, but a very large superiority at the present time over our first line with its Home Defence strength of under 460. This fact would show how far astray were the statements of the Lord President in November 1934 and of the Under Secretary of State in March 1935.[1]

Hitherto the Government have argued the question of relative air strengths on the basis of numbers either of 'first line strength' or of military machines. But it is now necessary to note the quality.

No doubt the conditions of secrecy in which the German military Air Force has been created have impeded training in formation flying. The great mass of Material and Personnel which they have prepared was only from April 1 openly assembled in large units. There is however no reason from all we have ever learned of the Germans as warriors, to impugn the quality of their flying personnel. We know on the contrary that this service has been

[1] Churchill inserted a footnote at this point: 'Since the above was written the Daily Telegraph has published the fact evidently supplied from official sources, that actually the figure mentioned by Herr Hitler was the 1,020 cited by the Under Secretary of State on March 19 as the first line strength of the British Air Force "*all the world over*"; and that in consequence the German Air Power is already "established on a basis of 2–1 superiority over the Air Forces of the United Kingdom".'

nourished by the full force of devoted patriotism, inflamed by the bitterness of defeat, and has been regarded throughout the Reich as the instrument by which Germany will regain dominance in Europe. We know that large numbers,—at least three or four times as numerous as ours,—of young Germans have qualified as aeroplane or glider pilots. It is presumably the best of these who have been selected for the expanding military units. A survey of the known facts of German civil and military aviation reveals accommodation now ready or nearly ready for at least 150 squadrons. In a few months of this summer all German flying squadrons that may be formed from the trained personnel and machines now assembled at the various centres, will easily acquire proficiency in formation flying. In fact no less than 36 military aeroplanes were flying over Berlin in perfect formation on April 1 of this year. Photographs of this array, equal to four squadrons of the Royal Air Force, were published in the Evening Standard. It is therefore concluded that any superiority we may now possess in formation flying will be effaced during the summer, and that it would be most imprudent to rate the personnel of the German Air Force, whether as individuals or in organised units, as in any way inferior to our own.

Consideration of the relative quality of material causes further disquiet. The only sure guide for measuring this lies in the age not merely of the machines but of their designs. Practically all the military machines possessed by Germany have been produced within the last two years after prolonged previous research in designs.

It is impossible to make a detailed analysis of the British material within the limits of a non-technical memorandum; but the bulk of the data is accessible to the public. Colonel Moore-Brabazon[1] made statements in the debate of March 1935 of a very alarming character. One of our bombing squadrons is equipped with the Virginia, a machine of the 1922 pattern. Other squadrons are being equipped with the 'Heyford' and 'Hendon' type of design, which itself is seven years old. It has been stated in Parliament that in the present organisation of the Air Ministry and the air industry it has hitherto taken from five to seven years from the first decision to adopt a new type before that type is actually in the possession of squadrons. A simple calculation of the average age of the designs of the first-line military machines

---

[1] John Theodore Cuthbert Moore-Brabazon, 1884–1964. Educated at Harrow and Trinity College, Cambridge. Pioneer motorist and aviator; holder of pilot's Certificate No. 1. Won the *Daily Mail* £1,000 for flying a circular mile, 1909. Lieutenant-Colonel in charge of the Royal Flying Corps Photographic Section, 1914–18 (Military Cross, despatches thrice). Conservative MP for Chatham, 1918–29; for Wallasey, 1931–42. Chairman, Air Mails Committee, 1923. Elected to the Other Club, 1936, Minister of Transport, 1940–1. Minister of Aircraft Production, 1941–2. Created Baron, 1942. He published *The Brabazon Story* in 1956.

now belonging to the Royal Air Force would reveal an average age at least double that of the comparable German machines.

It is when we consider dynamics that the full gravity of the position appears. Under our existing programme as provided by the estimates of March 1935, we are to add eleven squadrons of 12 machines to the Royal Air Force during the current financial year, and the actual constructive addition to our first line air strength was stated by the Under Secretary of State to be 151. He also stated that 1,000 new machines had been ordered. As however Vote 3 is only increased from £6 to 7 millions, it is obvious that the great bulk of these machines are not expected to mature for payment during the current financial year, and are therefore only orders for delivery in 1936/7. On every account given to the House therefore our output addition to first line air strength, including the Fleet Air Arm, will not under present arrangements exceed from 200 to 250 modern first line machines during the current year.

What of Germany? It is believed that the Germans have already, including their convertible civil-aviation fast-bombers, from 1,500 to 2,000 modern military machines, the majority of which have been actually manufactured in the last 12 months. Their aircraft industry has therefore already acquired the momentum which produced last year at least 1,000 military machines. On this basis and judging by the experience of the Ministry of Munitions in 1917–18, it should be easy for them to produce two to three thousand new machines by March 21, 1938. Statements have been made that their present rate of production is between 200 and 250 per month. This probably includes training, sport or purely commercial machines, of which three to four thousand already exist in Germany, together with a pool of pilots, mechanics and aviation grounds etc many times exceeding our own.

Behind this stands the industry of Germany organized for immediate transition to war and capable of producing under war conditions a steady mass production of aeroplanes and engines which in the very first year of war would produce at least 10,000 military aircraft.

It is possible that all these figures are woeful understatements of the real facts. The possession however of 10,000 aeroplanes by Germany at the present time, or during the present year, would not identify the maximum gravity of the situation disclosed by the figures here cited; for it is clear that the limiting factor of German air power will not be first class modern aeroplanes. The limiting factor has now become for Germany the rate at which the squadrons can be marshalled and exercised. There is however no reason to doubt the capacity of Germany to achieve an organised military air force of two hundred squadrons during the currency of the present year, comparable in every way to the British home defence force under the arrangements of the recent estimates, of 54 squadrons, from which should be deducted the 13 auxiliary squadrons and the Fleet Air Arm.

The conclusions which cannot be avoided are that the Government have allowed themselves to be mistaken in their estimates of British and German strength at particular dates; and that the statements made by Ministers in Parliament are wrong, are admitted to be wrong, and will be proved still more grievously wrong, with every month that passes. The German superiority, already large, will now grow upon all counts with progressive speed, to an extent determinable only by the decisions of the German Government.

The declaration and promise made by the Lord President to Parliament in March 1934 that His Majesty's Government would maintain an Air Force equal to that of any power within striking distance of our shores, is not being made good. We are in a position of perilous weakness compared to Germany at a time when we are involved by our existing commitments in the European situation, and when that situation is degenerating. The realisation of these facts explains the confident attitude which Herr Hitler, no doubt with the assent of the German General Staff, permits himself to adopt not only to all the neighbours of Germany, but to the League of Nations.

WSC

Winston S. Churchill to Lord Rothermere
(*Churchill papers: 2/266*)

21 July 1936

Very many thanks for your letter. As you will see I keep on trying my best. If as you say we are going to be vassals of Germany, I can only hope I shall not live to see it!

You have been wonderfully right in your talks with me:

1. At Christmas predicting the violation of the Rhineland;
2. The collapse of the Abyssinian resistance; and
3. That Mussolini had squared Hitler about Austria.

My information tallies with yours that Czecho-Slovakia will soon be in the news.

Oliver Locker Lampson[1] *to Winston S. Churchill: telegram*

(*Churchill papers: 2/256*)

21 July 1936

Your speech last night and the reactions in today's press mark a peak point in your national importance.[2]

Oliver Locker Lampson

Winston S. Churchill to Sir Austen Chamberlain

(*Churchill papers: 2/270*)

21 July 1936

Here is the letter which I propose to send to Baldwin. It only remains to add the list of Members whom we would bring. I have spoken to Sinclair[3] and Lloyd George and also to Attlee, and I shall know tomorrow afternoon their answers. I think it would be well if we met tomorrow in Committee Room 9 in the House of Commons in order to settle the Members and dispatch the letter. The matter ought not to hang fire. I have therefore invited our Group to meet there at 5.30, time being so short.

When we have settled our own deputation it will be necessary to have one meeting in order to concert the general line we take, and to divide up the work.

PS. I must ask for Freddie Guest's inclusion—ex S of S for Air, PC, 20 yrs H/C,[4] one of the supporters of our Amendment to the Address 1934. Please consider this favourably.

[1] Oliver Stillingfleet Locker Lampson, 1881–1954. Educated at Eton and Trinity College, Cambridge. Editor of *Granta*, 1900. Called to the Bar, 1907. Conservative MP, 1910–45. Lieutenant-Commander, Royal Naval Air Service, December 1914; Commander, July 1915. Commanded the British Armoured Car detachment in Russia, 1916–17. Parliamentary Private Secretary to Austen Chamberlain, 1919–21. Churchill's Private Secretary, 1926. A member of the Other Club (founded by Churchill and F. E. Smith) from 1925.

[2] Churchill had spoken during a Debate on defence policy in the House of Commons on the evening of 20 July 1936, claiming that the efforts of the Government although improving, were still insufficient. Germany, he said, was spending £800,000,000 each year on armaments (a figure which Neville Chamberlain admitted during the Debate to be 'not necessarily excessive') and Britain was slipping further behind with each month that passed. In a leading article on 21 July 1936, *The Times* disagreed with what it called Churchill's demands for declaration of a state of emergency, and it went on to argue: 'it has yet to be shown that the Government's decision to interfere as little as possible with normal industry has so far delayed the delivery of a shell, an aeroplane, a gun, or a ship'. But *The Times* added that Churchill's figure 'tentatively endorsed by Mr Chamberlain yesterday', of £800,000,000 a year military expenditure by Germany 'makes our own expenditure appear modest indeed'.

[3] Sir Archibald Sinclair, Leader of the Parliamentary Liberal Party (see page 160, note 6).

[4] Churchill's cousin, Frederick Guest, had been Secretary of State for Air from April 1921 (when he succeeded Churchill) until the fall of the Lloyd George Coalition in October 1922 (when he was succeeded at the Air Ministry by Sir Samuel Hoare). He had first entered the House of Commons in 1911, and had been created Privy Councillor in 1920.

Winston S. Churchill to Stanley Baldwin: draft
(*Churchill papers: 2/270*)

21 July 1936   Chartwell

My dear Prime Minister,

Following upon the Chancellor of the Exchequer's kind acceptance on your behalf of my suggestion that you should receive a deputation of Members of the House of Commons upon the general subjects of National Defence, I write to say that Sir Austen Chamberlain will lead this deputation, and the gentlemen whose names are on the attached slip would be glad if you would receive them. We understand that Lord Salisbury[1] wishes to bring a deputation from the House of Lords upon the same general subject, and it might perhaps be convenient to you to receive both deputations simultaneously. This would be entirely satisfactory to us.

The object of the House of Commons deputation of your supporters is to present to you, and any of your colleagues you may invite, statements of fact which, according to our belief and present information, are true and cause us serious anxiety. In ordinary circumstances the bulk of what we have to say could be said openly in the House of Commons in any of the Defence Debates. We do not aver that it is of a specially secret or unknown character; but we feel that this is not the time when any detailed technical disparagement of our position, particularly as to the Air, the Army or to the Munitions accumulation or supply, could be made without public disadvantage. Nor do we feel that even if as we hope, you are in a position to remove many of our anxieties, the Government would care, at this juncture, to make the kind of precise rebuttal which could so safely be made in calmer times. On the other hand we do not wish to see Parliament disperse without enabling you to be in possession of our thoughts and apprehensions. We are therefore grateful to you and to the Chancellor of the Exchequer for having consented to receive us.

Naturally we desire to save you all possible inconvenience and burden. Nevertheless it would not be possible for us to submit our statements to you at a single meeting. The progress of the expansion of our Air Force; the condition of the Army and Territorial Army and their recruiting; the organisation of our Munition and Equipment supply under present conditions or in case of war, are topics which require to be unfolded with some particularity.

[1] James Edward Hubert Gascoyne-Cecil, Viscount Cranborne, 1861–1947. Educated at Eton and University College, Oxford. Conservative MP, 1885–92 and 1893–1903. Succeeded his father (the former Prime Minister) as 4th Marquess of Salisbury, 1903. President of the Board of Trade, 1905. Lord President of the Council, October 1922–January 1924. Lord Privy Seal, 1924–9. Leader of the House of Lords, 1925–9.

We understand from the Chancellor of the Exchequer's speech on Monday last that you would not feel at liberty to give more information to a deputation not formally representative of the House than you would give to the House itself. At present Parliament has only received the vaguest indications of the progress made in executing the Air expansion programme or the Munitions programme, nor are we in presence of any effective plan for bringing the land Forces up to strength.

It may be that you will feel that after hearing what we have to say, that there are certain further statements which, without detriment to the public, you might make to Parliament before the Session closes; and these perhaps might be shaped as a result of our visit in a manner to give greater reassurance to the public.

Once more thanking you for your courtesy in consenting to receive us,

Believe me,

Clement Attlee to Winston S. Churchill

(*Churchill papers: 2/270*)

21 July 1936

Thank you for your invitation to join in your deputation to the Prime Minister on the Government's Arms Programme. I have considered the matter with my friends and I do not think that it would be desirable for His Majesty's Opposition to follow this procedure at this juncture.[1]

Yours sincerely,
C. R. Attlee

Eric Long[2] to Winston S. Churchill

(*Churchill papers: 2/266*)

22 July 1936 [Road Haulage Association]

My dear Winston,

In your magnificent speech on the debate upon the work done by Sir Thomas Inskip you did just mention that the question of transport within

[1] Having received Attlee's letter, Churchill sent the above draft to Stanley Baldwin, with no changes. But the copy as received by Baldwin is dated 22 July 1936, from 11 Morpeth Mansions (*Cabinet papers: 21/437*).

[2] Richard Eric Onslow Long, 1892–1967. Son of the 1st Viscount Long (Walter Long). Educated at Harrow. In business in the City, 1911–14. On active service in France and at the Dardanelles (despatches). Major, 1923. A Member of the London Stock Exchange. Conservative MP for Westbury, 1927–31. President, West Wiltshire Constitutional Association,

the country would necessarily have to be looked into by the Minister either now or at a future date.

The reason I am writing to you is the paragraph in the Times of Wednesday, 22nd July, which states quite definitely that Sir Thomas Inskip is relying on the work of a sub-Committee which 'has included a thorough examination of the internal transport system as it would affect the movement of foodstuffs in wartime'.

Repeated efforts have been made by my Association to impress upon Inskip and Belisha[1] the grave anxiety that all road operators in the country feel that nothing *whatever*, so far as they are aware, has been done to warrant such a statement being made by Sir Thomas Inskip. On the contrary we have been entirely ignored by the Minister of Transport and almost as badly treated by Inskip.

A memorandum has been in their possession for weeks, and this Association, the largest of its kind in the country, having 16,000 operators, over 400,000 employees and 150,000 vehicles, is completely ignored. Surely, if the Minister was really considering these grave problems, this Association would have had an opportunity of placing its services at his disposal, prepared as we are to organise and carry out any scheme which the Government desires for our internal security both for moving troops and ammunition and foodstuffs.

Archie Sinclair raised all these points, but the Minister's reply, so far as I can ascertain from Hansard, practically ignored the whole problem. Knowing, as I do, how much we are relying upon you personally to safeguard the Empire by your magnificent fighting speeches and work, I venture to hope that this grave problem of transport will not be overlooked in your deputation to the Prime Minister next week.

Yours ever,

Eric Long

1927–33, and 1948. Officer Commanding the 75th Searchlight Regiment, Royal Artillery, 1939–43. His only brother was killed in action on 27 January 1917. His elder son, Lieutenant Walter Reginald Basil Long, was drowned while on active service in Greece, 28 April 1941, aged 22. His nephew (whom he succeeded as third Viscount) was killed in action in north-west Europe on 23 September 1944.

[1] Leslie Hore-Belisha, 1893–1957. His father, an Army officer, died when Hore-Belisha was nine months old. Known, on account of his Jewish origins, as 'Horeb Elisha'. Educated at Clifton and St John's College, Oxford. On active service in France, 1915–16 and at Salonica, 1916–18. President of the Oxford Union, 1919. Liberal MP for Plymouth Devonport, 1923–42 (National Liberal from 1931; Independent from 1942–5). Parliamentary Secretary, Board of Trade, 1931–2. Financial Secretary, Treasury, 1932–4. Minister of Transport, 1934–7 (with a seat in the Cabinet from October 1936). Privy Councillor, 1935. Secretary of State for War, 1937–40 (Member of the War Cabinet, 1939–40). Minister of National Insurance, 1945. Created Baron, 1954.

Sir Maurice Hankey: notes for Stanley Baldwin

(*Premier papers: 1/193*)

24 July 1936

I. THE 'TEN YEAR RULE'

As I[1] myself pointed out in the House of Commons on the 9th March,[2] the greater part of the present deficiencies in the Defence Services grew up under the *régime* of the assumption that for ten years there would be no major war in Europe. It would be impossible to over-state the influence exercised by such a rule on defensive preparation, especially after 1928, when it was intensified by a decision that the ten years was to apply *from any given date*. That meant that every morning when the sun rose we were to assume that there would be ten years in which no major war would occur. When proposals were made by the Committee of Imperial Defence or its Sub-Committees, or by the Defence Departments, they all had to be submitted to the rigours of that rule. Was the proposal required for a major war within ten years? If the answer was 'Yes', then it was ruled out. If the answer was 'No', it might be approved. Naturally the effect was tremendous. No accumulation of reserves could be justified; little or no expenditure could take place on such essential items as the completion of the Singapore Base and its defence, which was actually stopped for a time; the renovation of obsolescent coast defences; the creation of modern anti-aircraft defences; air raid precaution services; the development of new armaments for all three Services; and many other defensive needs which had to be relegated to a distant future. This was the more important as the extension of the rule came at a time when the war equipment of the Services was becoming obsolescent and when some forms of material reserves were getting low. When a new Government came into office it was extremely difficult for it to reverse the decision of its predecessor, or for those in opposition to challenge their attitude.

[1] Written in the first person, by Sir Maurice Hankey, for use by Stanley Baldwin.

[2] The reference which Sir Maurice Hankey inserted at this point was to *Hansard*, volume 309, number 45, column 1832, where Baldwin had said that 'the present inadequacy of the defensive services' was not due to inter-Service quarrels but because of the need of successive Governments 'to conserve our finances'. To this end, he explained, there had been a rule applied 'by successive Governments for many years that, in working out their Estimates, the Services were to presume that for 10 years there would be no major war in Europe'. It was during these years of that assumption, Baldwin had said, 'that most of the present deficiencies accumulated'. The Services, he added, 'were held by finance as in a vice. . . . They could not make preparations involving expenditure. They could only live from hand to mouth.' These financial restraints were not however, Baldwin had explained, 'the only factors. There was the Disarmament Conference which opened four years ago.' While the Disarmament Conference was sitting, Baldwin explained, 'we refrained from any increase, and, indeed, we concluded the paring down of the Services, so far as preparation for the future goes, to the very bone' (*Hansard, 9 March 1936*). See also Main Volume 5 of this biography, pages 289–92.

The rule was re-examined every year, and sometimes even more often, in accordance with the original decision of 1928, but it was not until 1932 that the Government of the day decided to cancel it. Even then it was extremely difficult to embark on any considerable expenditure on armaments, in the first place because the national crisis had brought the National Government into existence, with the rehabilitation of our finances as its first and paramount task; and, second, because the Disarmament Conference had begun work and a temporary truce in armaments had been agreed to.

The long continuance of this rule had created a state of mind in Government Departments from which recovery was slow. Even when the situation had become menacing it took some time before Departments as a whole realised that serious expenditure on armaments was to be undertaken. Meanwhile, contractors, kept short of orders for years and years, had perforce been compelled to close shops, leave their machinery to become obsolete, and dismiss skilled labour. The knowledge possessed by Governments is always greater than that of their Departmental Officers, and still more of the contractors. Hence it has been a heavy task to obtain full realisation of the urgency of the problem.

The responsibility for the 'Ten Year Rule' was shared by a good many people. If we, on this side of the table, have our share, so have many members of the Deputation. *If some of my Right Hon friends search their memories, and still more if they refresh their memories from the records—as I myself have done—they will find that their responsibility for the 'Ten Year Rule', perhaps the root cause of our accumulation of deficiencies, is very great indeed.*

NOTE: It is presumed that Mr Churchill will bring up his old point about our information as to German aircraft. Presumably no attempt will be made to answer it there and then in detail, but the following observations might be useful.

II. MR CHURCHILL AND THE GERMAN AIR FIGURES

The Service Departments have, of course, their Intelligence Departments. Information reaches the Departments from a considerable number of sources. Some of these are public: Parliamentary returns; statements in Parliament in countries where there is Parliamentary Government; public speeches; information communicated officially to the Service *Attachés* or given occasionally in the course of a Diplomatic interview, and so forth. Sometimes information may be obtained from the Press or from individuals who have had exceptional opportunities for observation, or conversation with those concerned. There are, of course, in addition, other sources of information known to some of those present, but these are not developed rapidly, nor without considerable expenditure of money. They do not grow up like mushrooms in a night, however carefully they may be tilled.

In the days of the 'Ten Year Rule' it was not easy to obtain additional money for such developments. Again I would appeal to some of my Right Hon Friends who are present to search their memories as to whether it occurred to them that that was the time for building up sources of information which might prove useful in the future.

From time to time within the last year or two we have been severely taxed in Parliament as to the value of our information on certain matters which I need not refer to more specifically. I will frankly admit that such attacks are an embarrassment to the Government. They have their own sources of information, some of which I have mentioned. There is not the slightest doubt that those sources of information are far more widespread and likely to be more accurate than those of any private individual. Some of them, however, are sources which the Government are not in a position to quote without possibly drying them up. If alarmist statements are made by Private Members and authority is claimed for them, Parliament is naturally interested, and the Government is placed on the defensive in peculiarly awkward circumstances.

As a matter of fact the information which has been given to us by the Air Staff has been proved by the passage of time to have been substantially correct. Not only have forecasts given in one year worked out with considerable accuracy in the next, but it has been possible to apply counter-checks from independent sources.[1] Perhaps the differences between the critics and our official advisers have been not so much in the material facts as in the deductions drawn from them. It is surely obvious that in order to make a true diagnosis it is essential to scrutinise carefully information from all the various sources. The deductions of a single individual, however brilliant he may be, are less likely to provide a correct basis of calculation than those of the Government Departments with their infinitely larger sources of information.[2]

[1] Hankey noted at this point: 'e.g., French Government information'.

[2] On the same day that Sir Maurice Hankey prepared these notes for Stanley Baldwin, he also wrote to Lord Swinton that Baldwin had not decided whether the three Service Ministers (Lord Swinton himself, Alfred Duff Cooper and Sir Samuel Hoare—who had become First Lord of the Admiralty on 5 June 1936) should meet the Deputation. Hankey added: 'I think what is in his mind is that to do so would lend too much importance to the proceedings and might also render it more difficult to avoid answering questions put by the Deputation' (*Cabinet papers: 21/437*).

Winston S. Churchill to Lord Trenchard [1]

(*Churchill papers: 2/266*)

25 July 1936

Salisbury told me you were a little disturbed by my criticism of the new Short Service Entry of Air Pilots. I hope you realise exactly the category to which I am referring. It is nothing to do with Cranwell and its successive generations. All that maintains the highest quality. I am thinking about two classes. First the Short Service Commission pilots at 17/- a day and £300 at the end of four years. This is educationally far below all previous standards. Three-quarters have not received any education beyond the public elementary schools. Hardly any have been to the University. The Public School entry has of course completely dried up. Although this system worked on a small scale, and on rather better terms, very well in by-gone years, the attempt to engage twelve or fourteen hundred pilots in a single year on this plan gives results which are disquieting. Secondly there are the Direct Entry Airmen pilots of which there are about six hundred trained and in training. These men are taken direct from the streets and made sergeants immediately, thus cutting out almost entirely the Halton [2] entry which was such an object of ambition there.

No one knows as well as you how vital quality is in men who have to face the ordeal of air war. Without going back at all on what has been done in the past, I think the time has come to stiffen up the new pilot class. This could only be done by widening the permanent entry both through Cranwell and through the Universities. Here there are large waiting lists of admirable candidates, but they would not be attracted without the promise of a permanent career, or an entirely different type of Short Service Commission.

---

[1] Hugh Montague Trenchard, 1873–1956. Entered Army, 1893. Active service, South Africa, 1899–1902 (dangerously wounded). Major, 1902. Assistant Commandant, Central Flying School, 1913–14. Lieutenant-Colonel, 1915. General Officer Commanding the Royal Flying Corps in the Field, 1915–17. Major-General, 1916. Knighted, 1918. Chief of the Air Staff, 1918–29. Air Marshal, 1919. Created Baronet, 1919. Air Chief Marshal, 1922. Marshal of the Royal Air Force, 1927. Created Baron, 1930. Commissioner, Metropolitan Police, 1931–5. Created Viscount, 1936. Trustee of the Imperial War Museum, 1937–45. A member of the Other Club from 1926. His elder son, and both his stepsons, were killed in action in the Second World War.

[2] In 1918 Lord Trenchard had selected Halton Park, near Tring, as the site of a training establishment. The house and park were bought by the Royal Air Force that same year, on the death of their owner, Alfred Rothschild. The Halton entry was for boy trainees. On passing a final examination, the boys were graded as Leading Aircraftsmen. A certain number were then specially selected for a further course of training, at the end of which they were promoted to Corporal, or granted a Commission. Those Commissioned would then join the Royal Air Force Officer Cadet College at Cranwell.

Alfred Duff Cooper to Winston S. Churchill

(*Churchill papers: 2/278*)

28 July 1936   War Office

Dear Winston,

In reply to your letter of the 16th July I write to assure you that the War Office has no intention of parting with any of the 30,000 surplus Hotchkiss machine guns at Weedon until there is something better to put in their place.

Yours ever,
Duff Cooper

Winston S. Churchill to Sir Arnold Wilson

(*Churchill papers: 2/266*)

28 July 1936   11 Morpeth Mansions

I am still incredulous, but will send this memorandum to my friend for his opinion.

The decisive point to my mind is that no-one is going to use AP[1] bombs against ordinary houses, shelters and civil population. It would be a shocking waste of air power to carry so much steel and so little explosive. AP bombs would never be used except against the fleet or against some vital power station or magazine etc. So far as the protection of the civil population is concerned, I am sure you ought to exclude anything but ordinary bombs, explosive, incendiary and gas together.

I was sorry to see that Colonel Garforth committed himself in public to several statements which I am sure will not bear reasonable examination. I am glad you are continuing your cross-examination. What are the respective weights in a 500 SAP bomb of steel and explosive?

Record of a Discussion between Stanley Baldwin and a Deputation from both Houses of Parliament [2]

(*Premier papers: 1/193*)

28 July 1936

1. SIR AUSTEN CHAMBERLAIN: First of all we desire to thank you and Sir Thomas Inskip for receiving us. We come to you, not as critics of the

---

[1] Armour-piercing.

[2] The Government was represented by Stanley Baldwin, Lord Halifax and Sir Thomas Inskip. The Deputation consisted of five members of the House of Lords (Lords Salisbury,

past, and in no unfriendly mood in the present, but we are profoundly anxious about the European conditions, which seem to us extremely menacing, and about our own position faced with these conditions. We have members of the deputation from the two Houses who have, of course, given long study to these questions. Others of us who know much less have done our best to inform ourselves, and the information that reaches us is disquieting us. I do not think there is much dispute about the enormous preparations which Germany has made and is making, for what purpose we may guess, but the information that reaches us as to the progress of our own programme and the adequacy of our programme does leave us with grave anxieties and doubts. We wish to put that information before you. If you can remove our doubts and fears, no one will be more pleased than we. It may be we are too widely representative, and it may be in all points we do not agree among ourselves, but we come to you to put to you our anxieties in the hope that you will be able to relieve some of them, and feeling it a duty to put whatever information we have at your disposal. . . .

2. LORD SALISBURY: I, of course, share with Sir Austen Chamberlain, indeed, I suppose, with every single individual in this room a feeling of great anxiety. We are profoundly disquieted, as you no doubt are, and as everybody else is, at the contrast between the high degree of preparation which appears to have taken place abroad among those who might be our adversaries and the want of promptness with which we originally responded to that challenge. We are therefore profoundly disquieted, but we do not come in any way to hamper His Majesty's Government. On the contrary, the whole object is to help them in every possible way we can. Years and years ago when some of us were in office who are no longer in office, in those days the Committee of Imperial Defence was proud of the fact that they were prepared for all emergencies, they had everything ready so far as preparation was concerned upon paper, and they knew exactly what they were going to do and they knew exactly how it was to be done so far as circumstances would permit. Now we do not know whether that is still the case. We are anxious about the material; whether we have the necessary materials if we were called upon to make head against those who might be our opponents. We are not sure whether the Government have thought out the military policy which they would pursue in the various events which might take place, and we are not yet certain whether there is that co-ordination between

Trenchard, Milne, Lloyd and Fitzalan) and thirteen Members of Parliament (Sir Austen Chamberlain, Churchill, Sir Robert Horne, L. S. Amery, Sir John Gilmour, Captain Guest, Lord Winterton, Brigadier-General Sir Henry Page Croft, Sir Edward Grigg, Lord Wolmer, Lieutenant-Colonel Moore-Barbazon, Admiral Sir Roger Keyes and Sir Hugh O'Neill). The minutes were kept by Sir Maurice Hankey and Colonel Pownall.

the Services without which it is impossible to produce the best results. In all those three respects we feel anxious, and we want to be re-assured. . . .

3. MR CHURCHILL: I was given confidentially by the French Government their estimate of the German air strength to the beginning of May 1936, as follows: Regular Air Force, 103 squadrons, 1,236 first-line aeroplanes (with a reserve of 950 aeroplanes). To this should be added 3 months' increment at 60 per month, which equals 180. To this should be added 10 Auxiliary Squadrons, which equals 120 aeroplanes. Total, 1,556. Possible position at the end of 1936: 2,000 first line aeroplanes, with corresponding reserves of material and perhaps personnel. This tallies closely with the figures I forecasted to the Committee of Imperial Defence in December. The Air Staff thought the French estimate too high. Personally, I think it is too low. The number of service machines constructed in Germany and the number of pilots trained leads me to the conclusion that they could already put into action simultaneously nearer 2,000 than 1,500 aeroplanes. Moreover, there is no reason to assume that they mean to stop at 2,000.

4. The whole plant and lay-out of the German Air Force is on an enormous scale, and they may be already at work upon a development perhaps double anything yet mentioned. Even if we accept the French figures of about 1,500, the German strength at this moment is double that of our metropolitan or Home Defence air force, judged by trained service pilots and military machines that could go into action by squadrons and be maintained in action.

5. But the relative strength of two countries cannot be judged without reference to their power of replenishing their fighting force. The German industry is so organised that it can certainly produce at full blast a thousand a month and increase the number as the months pass.

6. Can the British industry at the present time produce more than 300 to 350 a month? Can it even produce so many? How long will it be before we can reach a war-potential output equal to the Germans? Certainly not within two years. When we allow for the extremely high rate of war wastage, a duel between the two countries would mean that, before six months were out, our force would not be a third of theirs. The preparation for war-time expansion at least three times the present size of the industry seems urgent in the highest degree.

7. Speaking generally upon the scale and quantity, it shows the vigorous efforts made by the Secretary of State, that we are able to spend as much as £50 millions this year.

8. It is probable, however, that Germany is spending out of her £800 millions on warlike preparation, not less than £120 millions on her air force this year. It is clear, therefore, that so far as *this* year is concerned we are not

catching up. On the contrary, we are falling further behind. How long will this continue into next year? No one can tell. But in the present conditions there seems to be no hope of preventing the Germans, unless they change their minds, increasing their numerical preponderance at any rate till after the end of 1937.

9. It may be worth while to review the course the Germans have pursued. First, after several years of profound study, a great plan of production was made on the basis of widespread manufacture of components to be fitted together in large assembling plants. When the Hitler régime decided to put this in motion at full speed, a tremendous production resulted, and they were able after a very short time to declare that they had an air force equal numerically to our own. That was fifteen months ago, and ever since they have been putting the polish on it. The German Government expected to be challenged by England and France for breaking the treaty. Therefore they wished to make their first bound forward in complete secrecy, and reach a position where they could give a good account of themselves if attacked.

10. When they saw that no one was going to interfere with them, they slowed down this rapid development, reduced their factories to single shifts and began a more steady progress. That is what is going on now. So far as air frames and engines are concerned, they are running very easy and have an enormous power of expansion at any moment.

11. It would be most imprudent to assume that in the two years which have passed since they put their secretly-prepared, surprise air force manufacture into full activity and made a great quantity of machines, they have not made preparations for introducing new and superior types. By all accounts, in every branch of war manufacture they are not hesitating to scrap old patterns for the sake of better, and at any time we may hear that they have put upon their plants another outfit of machines superior to those they launched two years ago. The condition of their industry and the moderate pressure at which it is working would render this easy.

12. It may be said that mass production machines assembled by components will not yield the highest results. That may be so. Modern war is based upon wholesale mass production rather than upon the superfine.

13. If, as seems likely, the German Government has concentrated on night-bombing as its objective, quality is less important than quantity. If the bomber will always get through, the *load* and *numbers* count chiefly. The whole organisation of German air industry, and, indeed, of German war industry, has this in view.

14. They aim at numbers, averages, mass effects, above all at simplification of production, the use to as large an extent as possible of unskilled labour, and concentration upon a few leading types.

15. One of the complaints against our organisation is that we have far too many types, even in our new machines, and have not the power to deal with patent rights so as to secure the widespread or universal manufacture by all aircraft firms of the proved best patterns. It is said of the new machines we are making, that we are aiming at producing more than double as many patterns as those to which the Germans confine themselves. This will be a fertile cause of friction and difficulty, shortage of spare parts, &c, should we be put to full strain. We are up against a vast simplex symmetrical production machine in Germany which can move forward in a succession of great waves without any appreciable diminution in volume.

16. I now come to the question of *quality*. The German air force, of course, suffers from newness. The pinch is in personnel. Nevertheless, when we consider the tremendous development of 'Air Sport' and the fact that the cream of the German youth was burning to avenge their country's defeat, and that the air seemed the swiftest and most dominating means, we must not underrate the quality or the spirit of German pilots. We are told they are suffering an enormous rate of casualties in the training schools, which, so far as it goes, is all to the good. As many as seven hundred in a single year are quoted. But it cuts both ways. It may mean that enormous numbers are being trained. It may also mean, as is said, that they are doing a large amount of night-flying under war conditions. It certainly shows the ruthless intensity of the effort they are making to make their air force personnel catch up their immense aircraft potentiality. However, I am not going to say they are superhuman.

17. Now I come to the quality of our own air force personnel. The old unexpanded air force was, of course, far superior in quality to anything the Germans have yet attained. It was a plant of slow and long growth and we still have it as the core of our great recent expansion. But Cranwell has not been expanded. Generally speaking, the permanent Air Force has not been enlarged. Apart from the recall of a small number of old officers, it has merely had a large temporary addition attached to it.

18. What is the quality of our own new air pilots? Two distinct classes have been recruited. First, the Short Service Entry. The terms offered were not very attractive, 16s 6d a day and £300 with no vocational training at the end of four years. It is not much for men who will have to handle machines costing £15,000. We could hardly expect that in a time of rising trade this would be sufficient to induce the best class of our educated youth to give up the four most critical years of their life, apart from the dangerous risks of their calling; and then be turned out on the world with only £300. I believe the physical standard up to three months ago was very good. The educational standard is by no means high. A school certificate is not necessary. Many of

them have received no education after leaving the Secondary Board Schools. What is called the Public School Entry has entirely dried up. Very few indeed have University qualifications. Yet far more is needed than the art of flying. A background is needed either of inspiration or prolonged training or habit of command and obedience—preferably both. For there is no service in the world which calls for the highest attributes, moral and mental, so much as the modern Air Pilot.

19. The second class are called Airmen Pilots. These are simply recruited by direct entry in answer to advertisement, given eight months' training, and then are qualified as pilots with the rank of Sergeant. It may be noted that the demand for skilled mechanics has led to the Halton entry to Sergeant-pilots class, which was so much coveted, having to be restricted to the very narrowest limits. Yet Halton Airmen have behind them a considerable period of discipline, training and association with flying. There are, I understand, about 1,200 Short-Service entry pilots trained or in training, and about 500 of the Direct Entry Airmen pilots. No doubt both will improve with time. Shall we have time?

20. I think it a pity that the Air Ministry did not, as I ventured to recommend a year ago, call for two or three hundred volunteers from the young officers seconded to the Army and Navy, and make it worth their while to come for four years. These would be men with permanent careers, whose future would be assured, and behind whom lay a full educational and vocational training and experience. Their places in the Army and Navy could have been filled by opening Sandhurst, Woolwich and Dartmouth wider. Everything turns on the intelligence, daring, the spirit and firmness of character of the Air pilots. The need of the Air Service is far greater than that of either of the other two Services. Even now I should hope that might be done.

21. But there is another practical step above all which should be taken now. The permanent commission pilots of the Royal Air Force should be increased at least 50 per cent as fast as possible. At the Universities, I am told, there are long waiting lists of admirable candidates of very high mental and personal quality. Only fifty are allowed to be commissioned each year. These are men of 22 and 23, many of whom have taken their degrees or are about to take them. Their parents do not object to their learning flying, as is shown by the strength of University Air Force squadrons and their long waiting lists. We want this quality among the pilots of the regular permanent Air Force, and none of these men are attracted by the conditions of the short-service entry. The moment you open the permanent Air Force widely to University entrants, you will get a stream of the very best brains and quality of our youth. The offer of a permanent career will give you the quality needed. Nothing

else will give it to you. Can there be any doubt that Germany is going to maintain for many years an Air Force upon a scale much larger than our present permanent Air Force? Were we not promised 'parity'? What will it matter if in a few years the war clouds pass and general disarmament comes, and you have to pay a million or two in compensation to pilots who will no longer be required?

22. I am told that in some quarters in the Civil Service there is a prejudice against having too many of what is called 'the officer class' trained to handle these very potent war machines. Why, for instance, should the new Royal Volunteer Air Force which the Secretary of State has announced be only open to the Sergeant pilot class? This is no time for class prejudice. I think we should choose the best, irrespective of whether they belong to the officer class or not. At the same time, Cranwell should be expanded with all speed to take a larger flow through that channel.

23. But pilots are little use without observers who navigate the aeroplanes and aim the bombs. To use pilots as observers is almost to halve your pilot strength. Is it true that the supply of observers is wholly insufficient in numbers and inadequate in quality? There is urgent need to institute a corps of observers drawn from persons of a high level of intelligence and education and given a permanent career. The training of such observers need not conflict with the training of Pilots and mechanics. It can be conducted in separate additional establishments. Some flying training, in case the pilot is shot, can be added as convenient.

24. Under the revised expansion scheme announced to Parliament in May 1935 the programme of 123 squadrons, comprising 1,512 first-line aeroplanes, for Home Defence, or what is called 'the Metropolitan air force', was to be completed by the 31st March, 1937. Great stress was laid upon the definition 'first-line aircraft' to include our reserves of aeroplanes with all the reserve pilots, ground organisations, mechanics, training schools, &c, and we were told how much more thorough we are in all that than Germany, for instance. You may say that 1,500 first-line aeroplanes would imply something like 3,500 machines altogether. Parliament has not been given any information how this programme is being carried out in aeroplanes, in personnel, in organisation or in the ancillary supplies. We have been told nothing about it at all, except Sir Thomas very kindly mentioned in the House that the engines were being produced at double and the air frames at $3\frac{1}{2}$ times the rate of last year. If that is so, it looks as though it is a very unbalanced production, because more engines are needed than air frames, but anyhow we know nothing. We have no means of judging from any statement that has been made to us what is the progress in completing this Air Force. I do not blame the Government for not giving particulars. I have not commented

upon it in public. Naturally, however, in the absence of any information at all, there must be great anxiety and much private discussion.

25. For instance, how many squadrons set out in the Air Force List are up to their full strength in airmen? I heard of one that had only 30 airmen instead of 140. How many of them have their full outfit of machines together with their reserves? When such strict interpretations are put forward of first-line air strength for the purpose of comparison with Germany, it is disconcerting to hear that many of our regular squadrons, not new ones in process of formation, but regular long-formed squadrons, are far below their strength, and have a large proportion, if not the whole, of their reserve aircraft either taken away for service in the Flying training schools or unprovided with the necessary equipment or even, in some cases, without engines. Great allowance must be made for the disturbance of the Mediterranean scare, but the fact remains that a very large proportion of our regular formed Air Force squadrons at home are and must long remain far below their establishment in personnel, aeroplanes, reserves, and indispensable miscellaneous equipment.

26. The same kind of difference between establishment and strength in personnel manifests itself between the programme and the deliveries of machines. The Minister for Co-ordination of Defence spoke in a late debate as if a broad flow of new machines of the latest design were 'in production'. 'In production' is a very elastic term. The only test is *deliveries with perfect equipment to the squadrons*. Great play is made with a fine quality of our new types—Schneider Cup speeds, &c. How many squadrons will be equipped with the new types by this time next year, July 1937?

27. Is it true that the bulk of the aeroplanes reaching the squadrons this year are what is called the Hind type, which is simply the former Hart type of 6-year old design with an extra tank added to increase its range at the expense of its performance? If it is true, I think the Secretary of State, coming into Office only a year ago in an emergency, was quite right to set the factories at work on a machine they could make by mass production in the largest possible numbers; for it was better to have any kind of aeroplane than no aeroplane at all. I am not criticizing his decision. On the contrary, it was the best thing to do. But then I do not think it should be suggested in Parliament that there is any appreciable supply of new types of Schneider Cup speed now reaching the squadrons, or likely to reach them for many months to come. I doubt very much whether by this time next year—by July not March—we shall have 30 squadrons equipped with the new types. I understand that the deliveries of the new machines will not really begin to flow in large numbers for a year or fifteen months. Meanwhile, we have very old-fashioned and obsolete tackle, and even in numbers there is no question

of the programme being completed or nearly completed at the appointed date.

28. Is it true that we are still selling aeroplanes to foreign countries, although our own production and programmes are so lamentably in arrears? One can hardly believe it.

29. There is a second question about these new machines. When they begin to flow out of the factories in large numbers fifteen months hence, will they be equipped with all necessary appliances? Take, for instance, the machine guns. If we are aiming at having, say, 2,500 of the latest machines, ie, 1,500 first line plus, say, 1,000 in reserve in 18 months from now, what arrangements have been made for their machine guns? Some of these modern fighting machines are to have no fewer than eight machine guns in their wings. If that is so and we are aiming at making an Air Force on that scale and you have proper reserves of these machine guns, you will have to be thinking of a production of something like 10,000 machine guns very quickly. Is it not a fact that the large scale manufacture of the Browning and Bren machine guns was only decided upon a few months ago? Any one acquainted with munition production will ask 'When will these deliveries come in'? Is it not a fact that even if you get the new machines 15 or 18 months ahead, there may be another 6 or 9 months' delay before the machine guns, without which they are of no use, will come from the factories? In this case, are they being ordered from abroad? I hope so.

30. The same query holds good about the miscellaneous equipment; bomb sights, bomb gears, ammunition shoots, flying instruments, &c. Does not the same apply to a great proportion of the indispensable spare parts? I may emphasise the fact that in this superfine sphere of the air, an aeroplane without everything is for all practical purposes an aeroplane with nothing. It may figure on your lists. It will not be a factor in actual fighting. Surveying the whole of this aspect, is it not true that it must be more than two years from now before the 123 squadrons which Parliament is led to believe will be ready by the 1st April, 1937, will be furnished with new machines thoroughly equipped in all particulars?

31. Let us now try the aeroplane fleet we have built and are building by the test of bombing power as measured by load and range. Here I must again make comparison with Germany. Germany has the power at any time henceforward to send a fleet of aeroplanes capable of discharging in a single voyage at least 500 tons of bombs upon London. We know from our war statistics what the destruction of lives and property was per ton dropped. One ton of explosive bombs killed 10 people and wounded 30, and did £50,000 worth of damage. Of course, it would be absurd to assume that the whole bombing fleet of Germany would make an endless succession of voyages to and from

this country. All kinds of other considerations intervene. Still, as a practical measure of the relative power of the bombing fleets of the two countries, the weight of discharge per voyage is a very reasonable measure. Now, if we take the German potential discharge upon London at a minimum of 500 tons per voyage of their entire bombing fleet—and that is an extremely modest basis—what is our potential reply?

32. *They* can do this from now on. What can we do? First of all, how could we retaliate upon Berlin? We have not at the present time a single squadron of machines which could carry an appreciable load of bombs to Berlin. What shall we have at this time next year? I submit for your examination that this time next year, when it may well be that the potential discharge of the German fleet is in the neighbourhood of 1,000 tons, we shall not be able to discharge in retaliation more than 60 tons upon Berlin.

33. But leave Berlin out of the question. Nothing is more striking about our new fleet of bombers than their short range. The great bulk of our new heavy and medium bombers—even when they are produced—cannot do much more than reach the coasts of Germany from this island. Only the nearest German cities would be within their reach. In fact, the retaliation of which we should be capable this time next year from this Island would be puerile judged by the weight of explosive dropped, and would be limited only to the fringes of Germany.

34. Of course a better tale can be told if it is assumed that we can operate from French and Belgian jumping-off grounds. Then much larger and more important districts of Germany would be within reach of our machines. This very important point will, I believe, be elaborated by Lord Trenchard. It certainly affects both strategy and foreign policy. Our Air Force will be incomparably more effective if used in conjunction with those of France and Belgium, than it would be in a duel with Germany alone. But even so, the fact remains that the maximum load of bombs which our air fleet would carry across the lines *this time next year* would only be in the neighbourhood of 400 tons per voyage, or less than what Germany can send to London now, and less than half what she will be able to send to London then.

35. I now pass to the next stage. Our defence, passive and active, ground and air, at home. Evidently, we might have to endure an ordeal in our great cities and vital feeding ports such as no community has ever been subjected to before. What arrangements have been made in this field?

36. Take London and its seven or eight million inhabitants. Nearly two years ago I explained in the House of Commons the danger of an attack by thermite bombs. These small bombs, little bigger than an orange, had even then been manufactured by millions in Germany. A single medium aeroplane can scatter 500. One must expect in a small raid literally tens of thousands

of these bombs which burn through from storey to storey. Supposing only 100 fires were started and there were only 90 fire brigades, what happens? Obviously the attack would be on a far more formidable scale than that. One must expect that a proportion of heavy bombs would be dropped at the same time, and that water, light, gas, telephone systems, &c, would be seriously deranged. What happens then? Nothing like it has ever been seen in world history. I ventured to warn the House of Commons two years ago that there would be a vast exodus of the population of London into the surrounding country. This would present to the Government problems of public order, of sanitation and food supply which would dominate their attention, and probably involve the use of all their disciplined forces.

37. What happens if the attack is directed upon the feeding ports, particularly the Thames, Southampton, Bristol and the Mersey, none of which are out of range? What arrangements have been made to bring in the food through a far greater number of subsidiary channels?

38. What arrangements have been made to protect our defence centres? By defence centres I mean the centres upon which our power to continue resistance depends. The problem of the civil population and their miseries is one thing; the means by which we could carry on the war is another. Have we in our turn got an adequate supply of thermite bombs or of sodium potassium bombs which are a later improvement? Have we the fuses and bomb containers for our thermite, observing that the fuse is of special construction. Certainly nothing had been done for eighteen months after I gave my warning.

39. Have we organised and created an alternative centre of Government if London is thrown into confusion? No doubt there has been discussion of this on paper, but has anything been done to provide one or two alternative centres of command with adequate deep-laid telephone connections, and wireless from which the necessary orders can be given by some coherent thinking mechanism to the vast panic-striken or infuriated population with whom we may have to deal.

40. First among all the vital elements is the protection of our oil supply. Great provision has been made in foreign countries against this danger. I hear of large underground storage of fuel oil in France. What have we done? Is not all our oil contained in these open, thin-skinned defenceless tanks, concentrated at well-known points, no doubt now duly photographed from the air? Does this not touch the life of the fleet upon which our own life depends absolutely? Have we made any arrangements to protect our oil fuel stores from attack by incendiary bombs scattered wholesale in showers, some of which must certainly hit the target? Ought the Admiralty not immediately to undertake the storage of enough oil in large underground

receptacles to keep the Fleet alive? What can they do to strengthen the existing receptacles meanwhile? Destruction of property and a great loss of civilian life in our large cities might be borne and we could still come through, but the paralysis of the Fleet would be fatal. The oil reserve must be made safe. Has this been done? I say it has not been done. It may have been talked of, but it has not been begun. I hope you will forgive me for mentioning these matters even though they may have occurred to you beforehand.

41. What methods are there of destroying the raiding aeroplanes from the ground, or by the Home Defence forces? Having served on the Sub-Committee of the Committee of Imperial Defence upon Air Defence for one year, I do not propose to go into technical details of any kind. But I will say this. The practical results so far, of our investigation, have been almost entirely negative. There are many promising ideas, and at least one potent discovery, but there is nothing that will give us any effective protection in the next year, and I fear in the next two or three years. I have been disappointed in the rate of progress, and in the reluctance to make large-scale experiments in rapid succession.

42. Everyone is agreed that AA guns are only useful when massed in batteries around small specific targets, and operated by highly-trained personnel. If a large target is being attacked, the bomber can zig-zag and anti-aircraft fire is useless. In the case of the Fleet, anti-aircraft gun defence will probably defeat or deter any aerial attack. In the two square miles covered by the Fleet, you have enormous numbers of guns served by the most skilful gunners in the world. The destruction of attacking aeroplanes in the air above the Fleet must reach a very high percentage. But no one can feel any confidence in zones of scattered guns, or batteries in the hands of Territorials for the defence of London. Nevertheless, we are still converting two divisions of Territorials to this Anti-Aircraft Service, which will probably be perfectly useless. Another method for protecting London is now being developed. It is at any rate more promising, but we are probably two years away from any general security by this method, even if it is found effective. In the meantime we are highly vulnerable and completely defenceless against night bombing.

43. What are the conclusions which may be drawn from this section of our problem of National Defence? First, we are facing the greatest danger and emergency of our history. Second, we have no hope of solving our problem except in conjunction with the French Republic. The Union of the British Fleet and the French Army, together with their combined Air Forces operating from close behind the French and Belgian frontiers, together with all that Britain and France stand for, constitutes a deterrent in which salvation may reside. Anyhow, it is the best hope; coming down to detail;

ought we not to lay aside every impediment in raising our own strength? We cannot possibly provide against all possible dangers. We must concentrate upon what is vital and take our punishment elsewhere.

44. In first priority stands the protection of the Home bases of the Fleet, and the protection of the centres of aeroplane production. Secondly, the control and preservation of the panic-stricken multitudes driven out of the bombed cities and the rearrangement of our feeding ports to meet evil conditions. Coming to still more definite propositions, ought we not to increase the development of our Air power in priority over every other consideration? At all costs we must draw the flower of our youth into piloting aeroplanes and observing from them. We must draw from every source by every means. We must accelerate and simplify our aeroplane production and push it to the largest scale, and not hesitate to make contracts with the United States and elsewhere for the largest possible quantities of aviation material and equipment of all kinds. I say there is a state of emergency. We are in danger as we have never been in danger before—no, not in the height of the submarine campaign. I will return to this to-morrow in connection with the supply of munitions and equipment.

Meanwhile, permit me to end upon this thought which preys upon me. The months slip by rapidly. If we delay too long in repairing our defences, we may be forbidden by superior power to complete the process.

Record of a Discussion between Stanley Baldwin and a Deputation from both Houses of Parliament

(Premier papers: 1/193)

29 July 1936

90. MR BALDWIN: There is no engagement of any kind with the French to send an Expeditionary Force.

SIR EDWARD GRIGG: I am very glad to hear that. The important point is I think and believe there is in the country—we are discussing this from the aspect of recruiting. . . .

MR BALDWIN: I know nothing about that, but I am able to relieve your mind on that. There is no undertaking at all, and I think now they do know what our position is, we are not in a position to give an undertaking for very much at present. It would be a ghastly thing if our undertaking was called upon. There is no question at this moment; the only undertaking is—it is reciprocal—that each goes to the aid of the other in the event of attack by a wanton aggressor.

SIR EDWARD GRIGG: I am deeply concerned about the impression in this country, because that is what I think is affecting recruiting.

MR BALDWIN: I do not want to make a pledge and say we have no engagement.

MR CHURCHILL: No. Having lived through the time before the War, when although there was no engagement there was a sort of tacit understanding that if we came in we should put six Divisions on the left of the line of the French armies, I feel very strongly that it would be very much better if France and Belgium were taught to make their own arrangements for manpower to defend their frontiers, and we made it quite clear that they have to do that by themselves. What we do we then do in addition, extra, if we can, but there would not be any gap in the line about which, if it was not filled, we should be told we had failed. That is a very serious point, and I think you are in a much better position than we were then because none of them has at the moment the right to say a British Army must take its stand here or take its stand there.

MR BALDWIN: That is perfectly true, but this is only a standstill pending Locarno. If Locarno comes off, no question. If it does not, we shall have to get into touch with them, and I imagine they will want fresh discussions, and I am hoping that this obligation, which is the only one we have, may possibly come to an end in two or three months. I hope so.

MR CHURCHILL: It does not mean we should not consent afterwards—that is another matter.

MR BALDWIN: Not at all.

MR CHURCHILL: Or that we should not get forces capable of going.

MR BALDWIN: I quite agree, but at the moment it is understood perfectly that we have not the responsibility of sending an Expeditionary Force in the event of trouble arising in the future.

99. SIR AUSTEN CHAMBERLAIN: To turn to munitions, I will ask Mr Churchill to speak, and then Sir Robert Horne.

MR CHURCHILL: In time of peace the needs of our small Army and to some extent of the Air Force and Admiralty for particular weapons and any ammunition are supplied by the War Office through certain Government Factories which they have, and through their habitual private contractors. This organisation is capable of meeting the ordinary peace-time requirements and providing an accumulation of reserves, modest reserves sufficient for a few weeks' war by very limited forces. Outside this there was nothing until a few months ago. The War Office had no money and no mandate. Whether this position ought to have arisen is not a matter to be discussed here, but the fact remains.

100. About three or four months ago authority was given to extend the

scope of War Office orders in certain directions to ordinary civil industry. Of course, for some years before a good deal of paper work had been done in surveying the possibilities of civil industry, and that is helpful to us now, but no practical steps were taken to enlist and prepare civil industry by any concrete act until April or May of the present year. Up to that date there had been nothing but examination, a certain amount of enquiry, and inspection of a cursory and superficial character. I do not use those terms in any invidious sense, but marking down firms and seeing whether they would be really useful or not. This was conducted at first by a handful of officials, which was gradually broadened out to a considerable number in the last year or year and a half.

101. On the other hand, all the leading Continental countries have had their whole industry for some time scientifically organised to turn over from peace to war. It is extraordinary, the refinement with which that has been carried out in all the countries on the Continent, not only great countries but some of the small States too, a complete dual purpose has been woven through the whole texture of their manufacturing firms. In Germany, of course, above all others, it was this process of transferring industry to war which was the supreme study of the Government even before the Hitler régime—in fact some years before the Hitler régime. Indeed, under the impulse of revenge—whatever you call it, revanche—Germany, forbidden by Treaty to have a Fleet, Army or Air Force, concentrated with an intense compression upon effecting the transformation of her whole industry to war purposes. We alone began seriously to examine the problem when everyone else had solved it. Still, there was time in 1932 and 1933 to make a great advance in our organisation of industry for the alternative function. Three years ago, when Hitler came into power, we had perhaps a dozen officials studying the war organisation of industry as compared with 500 or 600 who had been working for some time continuously in Germany. The Hitler régime set this vast machinery in motion. They did not venture to break the Treaty until they had such a head of steam on in every war industry that they felt pretty sure would make them speedily an armed nation. Once they let it go, in a few months the transference from being apparently defenceless to being suddenly possessed of a great volume of arms would have been made. They did not venture to break their Treaties until they had that, and their only doubt was whether they would be immediately attacked by the Allies. When they found there was not that, then they were able to fall back, as I said yesterday, into a more comfortable compass.

102. What is being done now in this country? Nothing has been given to Parliament except fragmentary items which by themselves are liable to mislead ignorant people. I am not blaming the Government for not putting all

the cards on the table, that is why we are talking here, but it is the fact. For instance, we were told last week that 52 firms had been inspected and offered contracts, that the old former gun factory was to be re-opened at Nottingham, that the Woolwich filling station was to be removed to the West Coast, and certain other facts of that kind were mentioned by Sir Thomas Inskip, but no orders were given until three months ago, and there was no prospect of our reaching the stage of mass deliveries for at least eighteen months from the date of order. If by ammunition, which is the term the Minister used, is meant projectiles, bombs and shells, cartridge cases containing propellant, air bombs, trench mortar bombs, grenades and so forth, it will be necessary to equip factories with a certain amount of additional special purpose machine tools, and to modify their existing lay-out. The jigs and gauges for actual manufacture must be made. Eight to twelve months—probably twelve in the case of most firms—will be required for this. Until the process is completed not a single shell or bomb can be made except by hand or individual process outside the old-established habitual War Office firms which I mentioned at the beginning of my remarks, and which of course have been turned on to full power. The manufacture of the special machine tools, jigs and gauges, has to be done in most cases by firms quite different from those to whom the output of projectiles is entrusted. After the delivery of the machine tools, jigs and gauges, a further delay intervenes while they are being set up in the producing factories, while the process of production is being started. It may well be a further three or four months would be found to be required for this. Then, and only then, first in a trickle, then in a stream, finally in a flood, then and not until then when the deliveries begin to come can we begin to accumulate the war reserves. Inevitably, Sir, this lengthy process is being applied on what, compared to other countries, is a minute scale. We were told that 52 firms had been offered contracts and that 14 up to last week had accepted. This announcement, and the pathetic satisfaction with which it was received by the public, must have caused no little amusement in Europe.

103. At the present moment it is no exaggeration to state that the German ammunition plants—I am using the word ammunition to cover all categories of projectiles—may well amount to 400 or 500; already they are very nearly two years in full swing. They have accumulated an enormous amount. I am told—I cannot vouch for it at all, but I am told—that they have got something like the supplies that were needed to fight the campaign of 1918— enormous masses, mountains of projectiles have been accumulated of all kinds, with the explosives and so forth; and they do not hesitate to re-cast their preparations; if they design a bomb better than the one they already have, they run the explosive out and re-forge the metal into the new shape, and so on.

104. They have a forging process in Germany to which I ventured to draw the attention of the Minister some weeks ago, and also somewhat earlier the Master-General of the Ordnance, which of course he knew about beforehand. It seems to me to be very important; they have a process of forging projectiles which is different from the methods hitherto adopted, which is probably more efficient; enormous presses come down on the hard metal and squeeze it actually into shape with wonderful refinement and accuracy, and this process enables the same number of men to turn out six or seven times as much as could be turned out from any plant existing in England. Oddly enough, unhappily, we in our industry in England have not mastered this forging process to any extent. We have been bringing to the Minister's attention some proposals. Apparently it would be possible now to purchase whole installations of this from Germany, and I have no scruples about it. If you can buy what you need from anywhere, get it into this country as quickly as possible. I would not hesitate for a moment. I think we should not hesitate a moment to buy from Germany or anywhere else, if we can get the deliveries and make sure we get the delivery before we actually pay the money. But they have a very much improved method of forging, and apparently the second-best process they are willing to part with now. It seems to me that this forging process is of the utmost importance. One of the advantages of it is that you do not require skilled labour once the thing is laid out—or little skilled labour; in fact, once it is running they say the men can go away and their places in war can be taken by women. Anyhow, it multiplies the power of making projectiles four or five or six times anything we possess.

105. Turning now to cannon—by cannon I mean guns firing explosive shells. I am not talking of the smaller cannon which fire solid projectiles—the process of their manufacture is necessarily more lengthy, the special plant and machine tools and the lay out are more elaborate. The normal peace-time output of cannon in the last ten years, apart from the Fleet, has been negligible, almost nil. Certainly we are separated by at least two years from any large supplies of field guns or anti-aircraft guns. Two years I put it at.

106. Last year it is probable that at least 5,000 guns were made in Germany, and this process could be largely amplified in war. In fact, they are not worrying at all about material, they are in such a strong position that they would only seek to sell surplus plant, surplus stores, to other countries and in order to keep their wheels turning. At any moment they may pull a big lever and out will come a supply capable of maintaining our Army's greatest force in 1918. Of course, Sir, you probably remember that all countries were very short of munitions shortly after the war began in 1914. They all had got their paper plans and their reserves which the War Offices of the different countries

had made, and they rushed to conflict and terrible collisions occurred in the first few weeks, but then everybody ran short, the Germans, the French and everybody ran short, and so trench warfare began. There was practically nothing, there was a sort of long pause which to us was invaluable, it enabled us to begin to catch up and use our industry and world industry to catch up. Nothing like that can be expected this time. The plants which are created in Europe will enable this hellish process once started to proceed at full supply to a conclusion.

107. I am not going to compare the German needs with the British needs. The cases are not similar. We do not need a great Continental Army like the Germans do, and of course naturally they would have far larger plant for that purpose; but surely we ought to call into being now the plant which would enable us, if need be, to create a national Army of considerable size. Leave out the question of its employment, but if a great war arises and we are either in it or in great danger of being drawn into it, we ought to have here plant from which, with the pull of a lever, a tremendous process of delivery takes place. That means an enormous amount of preparation, and I am afraid an enormous amount of expense. Whether your Army is to be one million or two million or only 500,000 or 600,000, an enormous plant will be needed because you will have, as we had in those days, millions of people volunteering, clamouring to be given weapons, and there were then no weapons except for our Regular Forces and the ones which had been fore-seen, which were pretty good.

108. I have taken projectiles and cannon because that is the core of defence. The same arguments and conditions with certain modifications apply to the whole field of equipment. The flexibility of British industry should make it possible to produce many forms of equipment, motor lorries, kindred weapons like tanks and armoured cars and many slighter forms of material, in a much shorter time than shells and cannon if that industry is once set going. Has it been set going? Why should we be told that the Territorial Army cannot be equipped until after the Regular Army is equipped? Surely the industry of this country—I am not now talking of rifles and cannon, but of nearly all other equipment which they require—surely our industry, which is so comprehensive and variegated, could carry out that process concurrently if it is set in motion?

109. I must say a word upon the hard case of the Territorial Volunteer. His is a very hard case. I wonder they come forward at all, these young men and young officers; they alone in this country have to sign an engagement to go and fight almost anywhere in almost any quarrel; they do not know, they cannot tell, they may have to go anywhere at a moment's notice, they alone, those 150,000 of them out of this population, devoting themselves to a fate

and fortune of which no human being can tell them the limit, and even then there is no equipment, there are no weapons, to put into their hands. I wonder they come forward. That they do is a most remarkable and wonderful thing.

110. I do not know the position about rifles and rifle ammunition, but I hope at least you have a million. At any rate, it is the last reserve of a free community, that there shall be a large number of rifles with which they can sell their lives at the end. But the delivery of rifles from new sources is a very lengthy process. I was surprised to find at the beginning of the war that it took much longer to start a rifle factory and get a flow of rifles than it did even to make cannon. But if we get the jigs and gauges and the lay out all planned, so that on the day if trouble comes—and I join in the general prayer that it may never come—you will be able to set to work and begin immediately a flow of small arms and ammunition. There ought to be that standing ready. The more people you have, the more necessary is it that you can set up that, because you will want millions of rifles.

111. Even more pertinent almost is the production of machine guns. I touched on this yesterday, but it comes in here too. I do not know what is the programme for the production of the Browning and Bren guns, but even if orders for setting up the necessary plant were only given a few months ago one cannot expect appreciable deliveries except by direct purchase from abroad before the beginning of 1938, if then. This great factory in Czecho-Slovakia is running now. If you could get 10,000 or 20,000 of these in from there and got them into this country with the spare parts and with the ammunition, setting up your own ammunition plant, at any rate that is an enormous blessing, an enormous act of safety. The comparable German plants, of course, which are already in operation, are capable of producing supplies of machine guns, rifles and so forth, which are limited only by the national manhood available to use them. There is absolutely no limit to what they can produce and produce with great celerity.

112. This same argument can be followed through the processes of producing explosives, propellants, fuses, poison-gas, gas-masks, searchlights, trench mortars, grenades, air bombs, all the special adaptations which affect the Navy for depth charges, mines, &c; and it must not be forgotten that the Navy is dependent upon the War Office and upon an expansion of national industry for a hundred and one minor articles, shortage in any one of which would cause grave injury to the Navy.

113. Behind all this is the supply of raw materials, with its infinite complications, but I am quite ready to admit that they are not the same as they are with other countries. As long as we can retain command of the sea we can certainly feel the whole world is part of our reserves, but what Lord Lloyd

has said about the stringency of shipping, of mercantile marine, is a qualification on that.

What is the conclusion? It is that we are separated by at least two years
from any appreciable improvement in the material processes of national
defence so far as concerns the volume of supplies for which the War Office has
hitherto been responsible, with all the reactions which that entails on the
Navy and War Office, but on the scale on which we are now acting even at
the end of two years the supply will be petty compared to the needs of a
national war, and melancholy compared to what others have already secured
in time of peace.

114. Sir Thomas said the other day that if these 52 firms all got into
working order, together with the old-established War Office contractors who
are working at full speed, this would eventually supply seven-eighths of our
requirements. What does that mean? Seven-eighths of what? Certainly it
cannot mean seven-eighths of our requirements in a major war. It can only
mean our requirements in what is called the deficiency programme—I am
quoting there the published document in which the expression 'deficiency
programme' is used—it can only mean seven-eighths of that—but the
deficiency programme merely means making up the proper supplies, reserves
with the existing forces on their first entry into war if they were at full
strength, the Army and Territorials. Besides that, if you have to fight for your
lives, you must have the power to call into being a great draft from the manhood of the nation, and there must be preparation to put arms in their hands
and give them missiles to fire from their weapons.

115. If these facts are even approximately true—and I believe they are
mostly under-statements—how can it be contended that there is no emergency, that we must not do anything to interfere with the ordinary trade of
the country, that there is no need to approach the Trade Unions about
dilution and trainees, that we can safely trust to what Sir Thomas has
described as training additional labour as required on the job, that nothing
must be done which would cause alarm to the public or lead them to feel that
their ordinary habit of life is deranged or going to be deranged? Complaint is
made that the nation is unresponsive to the national needs, that Trade
Unions are unhelpful, that recruiting for the Army and Territorial Forces is
very slow, and even obstructed by certain elements of public opinion. We
see the Socialists even voting against the Estimates, and so forth. As long as
they are assured by the Government that there is no emergency those
obstacles will continue, but I believe they will all disappear if the true
position about foreign armaments is set before the public and if the true
position about our own condition is placed before them, placed before them
not by words, not by confessions, but placed before them by actions which

speak louder than words, measures of State ordering this, that and the other, by events, by facts which would make themselves felt when people see this was happening here and that happening there. It is that which will make the serious impression which they ought to gather of our position; and that could be done without telling foreign Powers more about our weakness than they know already.

116. I plead that whatever is said, action should be taken in the sense of an emergency. I do not at all ask that we should proceed to turn ourselves into a country under war conditions, but I believe that to carry forward our progress of munitions we ought not to hestitate to impinge to a certain percentage—25 per cent, 30 per cent—upon the ordinary industries of the country, and force them and ourselves to that sacrifice at this time.

117. Moreover, I think you ought to have Legislation. You ought to have a Bill in two Parts, a Bill which gives you power of claiming priorities in organising as far as you propose to use it in time of peace, and then you ought to have Part Two, which comes into operation on the outbreak of war, if war ever should come, and it would be a very good thing to bring people up against that and let them see. The first part of the Bill would give you the powers you require to use now—you need not use them on all occasions unless you required to—the other part would show what the country would pass into if war broke out; and if this matter were handled not in an atmosphere of political warfare, I believe you would turn the flank to a very large extent on all this profiteering argument, because you cannot stop profiteering in time of peace.

118. When you are preparing and trying to repair your defences and make up your deficiencies, there must be a lot of profit made by firms who make an outlay and run the risk, and who have been waiting many years without much to do. There must undoubtedly be profits made, and we ought to appreciate that. If you prevent anyone making profit you will stop people making munitions in time of peace, but when it comes to war, Parliament should make it quite clear that no one is going to make any profits out of the war, and that on the day war is declared you would impose the most stringent discouragements against people getting richer out of making munitions, while those who had to serve might be shot down at the Front.

If those propositions were placed before the country, they would not only give you much more facility and ease in your present production, but place our affairs upon a very solid basis upon which appeal could be made to the nation to support the whole process of national rearmament.

119. SIR ROBERT HORNE: I should only like to point the moral of the concluding part of Mr Churchill's speech. He alluded to our condition at the beginning of the last War, and I am sure that no one in this country would

ever again wish to see our people who were fighting on the war front so
inadequately provided with the necessary munitions. That is a thing which all
of us will wish to guard against. . . .

130. PRIME MINISTER: I hope you realise my difficulty in this. I have
listened to a great deal. I did not know what was going to be said. I have
not had a minute since yesterday, you will realise that, you know the circumstances of our work at the present time. I am afraid anything I may have to
say must be of a rather general nature because I cannot attempt to deal in
detail with the many detailed points that have been raised. We shall have to
study them very carefully when we have the shorthand note. That we shall
do. Sir Thomas Inskip will be able to deal with several of the general
questions in so far as he can without saying anything he ought not to and
such as he has had time to look at, but as you have been good enough to give
us plenty of time I should like to begin by pointing out some of the earlier
difficulties of the situation, with no desire to dwell on old history, but just to
see how we have got into the present position. You may feel, many of you,
that we might have got on faster than we have. I will say something about
that by-and-by. There was one remark Lord Salisbury made yesterday when
he began, I do not think I need say anything about that, when he hoped we
felt as deeply as you do about these things. There is not an anxiety mentioned
that is not weighing on me. I can assure you of that, and all of us, and has
done night and day for the last three or four years. This country, of course,
when the war stopped suffered from the usual relapse she usually has had
after wars. We know the temper of our people. The moment war is over they
think there will never be another one and undoubtedly we have suffered from
what all of us who have held office is concerned with, that is the ten years' rule.

131. I do not want to say anything about what took place in Cabinets,
but the ten years' rule existed until we abolished it in 1932 and you will
remember at one time—I do not think I am saying anything I should not
here—at one time the ten years' rule was more narrowly defined as ten years
from any given date, and of course, at that time in the state of the world
it did look safe, but of course, it did have this effect. It had the effect, an
effect aided by the economies we have had to practise since the war and very
much by the economies we had to practise in 1931, 1932 and 1933, at the
time of the financial crisis, the result was every Service was skinned. It was
done before we went out in 1929 and I do not think there is any secret about
this. I think we should all agree. Partly owing to the admirable management
of the then Secretary of State, I think probably the War Office was skinned
more than any of them. I think we should all agree the Army paid a larger
price at that time than the Navy or the Air Force. They all paid a price and
a big price it was.

132. Then another bad effect it had was when orders were curtailed to the minimum, gradually, and here I come to part of Lord Lloyd's point and it was a very serious thing, with the depression in trade in certain lines that came owing to the interruptions in international trade and so forth, the skilled men in so many of the most important trades of the country got broken up, particularly in ship-building and in munition making. A good many emigrated at one time, but they did get broken up. One of the great difficulties today is in the re-assembling of such skilled men as you have got and the teaching of the younger generation to do that work. That was a very great loss.

133. Then it was I think in 1933 when the Nazi Government came into power and very soon after that although it was extremely difficult to get absolutely accurate and reliable information, we, and the world, knew re-armament on some scale was beginning in Germany. This was the great difficulty we were up against, and I do beg you to realise what an awful responsibility this was. I was not Prime Minister at the time, but as somebody who had some influence in the country I have said in many speeches and it is a tragic fact, but it is a true statement and I want to drive it into the heads of other people, a democracy is about two years behind an autocracy and it has proved so in this case.

134. It would have been an extremely difficult thing in a free country to have started arming freely in 1934. This was a thing which was in my mind tremendously, and during the winter of 1933 we began to study this question and what the requirements of the country would be to bring it up to a perfectly equipped force, to the extent of such forces as we thought this country would require for her defence, and we began to consider the speeding up of the existing air programmes. When that was done, of course, starting from scratch took a long time to do. It was done extremely thoroughly. Then we had a ministerial examination upon which the Chancellor and I, among others, were on, and we went through everything ourselves. It took a long time; it was a very careful examination and, if I remember rightly, we got it finished in about July 1934. The only outcome of that practically was—I am speaking from memory here; I have honestly not had time to look up all these things, and I expect Mr Winston Churchill can correct me if I am wrong; he has a good memory for these things—we proposed an increase in the air, not as much as you wanted, but an increase, but not in anything else. This was the problem in my mind.

135. Most of you sit for safe seats. You do not represent industrial con-stituencies; at least, not many of you. There was a very strong, I do not know about pacifist, but pacific feeling in the country after the war. They all wanted to have nothing more to do with it, and the League of Nations

Union have done a great deal of their propaganda in making people believe they could rely upon collective security, and it was a question in 1934 whether if you tried to do much you might not have imperilled and more than imperilled, you might have lost the General Election when it came. I personally felt that very strongly, and the one thing in my mind was the necessity of winning an election as soon as you could and getting a perfectly free hand with arms. That was the first thing to do in a democracy, the first thing to do, and I think we took it at the first moment possible. For some time a great many powerful influences were against me on that. They wanted to postpone the election until 1936, and I think the Central Office was against me, as we are all Tories here together, but it was wrong. We took it at the first moment we could and we had two elements with us, and I think we used them to the full. The first was people had begun to realise what Hitler meant, and, secondly, that time coincided with a great wave of feeling for what they called collective security. The position was complicated by Lloyd George and his Council of Action, which was meant to rally in the pacifists and appeal to the Non-Conformists in the country, but, fortunately for us, there was some delay in bringing it into action. There was a good deal of examination needed of the programme which he submitted to us, and we fought the election immediately after the holidays before he had a chance of getting to work, so it did not function at the election though it looked at one time as though it might be a dangerous element. We fought the election, and we won it and won it more handsomely than anyone in this room, I think, would have expected before the election. That was a great thing done. It was done and you had the support of the democracy for your armaments. I think we were perfectly honest about it because we did try out, both before the election and into this year, we did try out at the first opportunity we had of trying out, collective security. We tried it out short of war. We tried it out and showed the people—people will only learn, unfortunately, in a democracy by putting their heads against a brick wall; they would never believe or realise what sanctions meant unless they tried them. They tried them and they saw what they meant. I was able to take the line at the election broadcast that I would never be responsible for sanctions again until the country had re-armed. That made them think a bit, and you all know what the history of that has been.

136. We started, of course, as I said, from scratch. I do not know, looking back, I do not know whether starting in peace conditions we could have done much better or got on much faster. The spade work to be done in beginning, and Sir Thomas Inskip will say something about this, the spade work to be done is very heavy and very difficult, and it is being gone on with every day. He will be able to tell you something about that, and we have had

in our minds, very present to our minds, the point, I think, has been perhaps latent in a good many observations that have been made, could we do better if we were to turn over, Mr Churchill did not say definitely to war conditions, but to some kind of half-way house. That is a question which I have thought about a good deal and mainly discussed with the Chancellor of the Exchequer; it touches him so closely, and we have always felt up to now, we have felt to do that might throw back the ordinary trade of the country perhaps for many years. It has never been done in peace time, throw it back for many years and damage very seriously at a time when we might want all our credit, the credit of the country. If the emergency were such as obviously demanded it, of course, it would have to be done, and I am not afraid of emergency powers. I am not afraid of anything if it has to be done.

137. Then you come to the peril itself. Some observations were made yesterday by one of the speakers that seemed to me to envisage—I may have misunderstood them—a possibility of a war between ourselves and Germany alone. I do not know if anybody does envisage that, but unless Germany goes mad and attacks us and France refuses to come in, which she is bound to do, I do not think that can happen. I mean, if there is going to be a war it will be with France and Belgium and possibly Holland and ourselves on the one side, and Germany on the other. But a good deal has been said, and I have great sympathy with it, and I would like to ask one or two questions about it and in no captious spirit because we want to help each other, that is as to how you would propose to warn people; what would you tell them? Germany is arming to fight us? It is not easy when you get on a platform to tell people what the dangers are. I have not dotted the i's and crossed the t's, but I have often spoken of the danger to democracy from dictators which I think is the one line whereby you can get people to sit up in this country, if they think dictators are likely to attack them. I think that is so, but I have always found it, but I have never quite seen the clear line by which you can approach people to scare them but not scare them into fits. I am not sure that Duff Cooper's programme in that famous speech of his in Paris about which I was asked a question, I do not know that that would quite meet the case and I have faced a very real difficulty. I think it could be done if we had a meeting such as Sir Austen Chamberlain suggested; I should like it very much.

138. Again speaking in confidence in this room, there is one very important man in the Labour Party with whom I am on very good terms, that is Sir Walter Citrine of the TUC. He has just come back from Russia. I have had some interesting talks with him. I had a talk with him before bringing out the programme. I told Sir Walter Citrine about the situation in Europe and about organised labour and how we should all have to play up—this was a

few months ago—and I said 'I am in a little difficulty; I am pushing forward'—as a matter of fact, I think it must have been before the Election I saw him, it was last September I think I saw him. When he heard all I had to say he thanked me for what I had said, and he said 'take your courage in both hands and go to the country with it', and intimated he for one would not complain. Of course, that is in the minds of a good many of them, though they do not come out and say so. I wish you could go to a body like that and tell them the same thing. You could talk to the Privy Councillors. I believe most of those fellows of the George Hicks[1] type would come in and you would have Labour with you, and it would arm them against the Communistic influence which at the moment is causing a great deal of anxiety both to them and to us.

139. It is quite natural when we are all talking together like this that I should ask a question or two, when you have a case to put before us—I do not use that in any unpleasant sense at all, but the case of course is your anxiety and what you want to see done; is it in the mind of most of you that a war with Germany is inevitable?

SIR AUSTEN CHAMBERLAIN: I never call a war inevitable.

PRIME MINISTER: I am not trying to lessen my responsibilities, but I hope you do not feel that.

SIR AUSTEN CHAMBERLAIN: I do not feel that.

PRIME MINISTER: Because I do not frankly. I am not sanguine, and I think the times are most anxious.

SIR AUSTEN CHAMBERLAIN: May I just say, you put the question, I never call a war inevitable in advance because there have been so many that looked almost certain and which have not been realised, but I put it this way, that all the omens are, in my opinion, worse to-day than they were in the years which preceded the Great War.

140. PRIME MINISTER: The worst of it is we none of us know what goes on in that strange man's mind; I am referring to Hitler. We all know the German desire, and he has come out with it in his book, to move East, and if he should move East I should not break my heart, but that is another thing. I do not believe she wants to move West because West would be a difficult

---

[1] Ernest George Hicks, 1879–1954. Began work as a general builder at the age of 11; later became a bricklayer. National Organizer for the Bricklayers' Society, 1912. President of the National Federation of Building Trade Operatives, 1919 (and 1936–7); first General Secretary of the Amalgamated Union of Building Trade Workers, 1921–41. President of the Trades Union Congress, 1926–7. Labour MP for East Woolwich, 1931–50. Member of the Central Housing Advisory Committee (which led to the Housing Act, 1935), and the Holidays with Pay Committee. Member of the Anglo-Russian Parliamentary Committee, and of the Empire Parliamentary Association. Parliamentary Secretary, Ministry of Works, throughout Churchill's war-time premiership, 1940–5. CBE, 1946.

programme for her, and if she does it before we are ready I quite agree the picture is perfectly awful and will be perfectly awful. I do quite agree with you, and every effort of our work and diplomacy must keep us out of it if it can be done. If the man goes stark mad and is determined to fight, as in a small way Mussolini did with the Abyssinians, we must try and get everybody against them and have the whole of Europe in the war again, which is too ghastly for anything. We may know more about it if we get talking, but, as you said the other day, you would not believe a word they say. That is one of the tragedies. No engagements, no treaties, no promises, no anything, seem to be worth while with anybody. That is one of the terrible features of it. If they come to talk we may find out what the value of all the speeches he has made about peace, and peace in the West, is, and what his undertaking not to effect changes except by peaceful means may be. I do not know.

141. I am not going to get this country into a war with anybody for the League of Nations or anybody else or for anything else. There is one danger, of course, which has probably been in all your minds—supposing the Russians and Germans got fighting and the French went in as the allies of Russia owing to that appalling pact they made, you would not feel you were obliged to go and help France, would you? If there is any fighting in Europe to be done, I should like to see the Bolshies and the Nazis doing it. You are dealing more with specific points and I have made general observations, but I do not want you to believe that everything you have said is not most powerfully present to our minds and most of it has been for some time.

142. SIR THOMAS INSKIP: Prime Minister, I hardly know what to say lest either I should give a false impression as to what is being done within my knowledge or arouse any feeling that might lead anyone to suppose as the result of what I said that we are on opposite sides of the table in spirit as well as in fact. I am sure you will forgive me for saying there are some statements that have been made as facts which, if I were minded to be controversial, I think I should have to correct a little.

143. I may take one rather colourless statement that has been made to-day —I mean colourless because it is not the kernel, the heart of the question, about the opinion that the Canadian Ministers expressed as to the possibility of storing food. I have discussed it in detail twice with them both, the Minister of Finance and the Treasurer. They both assured me, Dunning[1] in

---

[1] Charles Avery Dunning, 1885–1953. Born in England. Went to Canada in 1903, becoming Director of the Saskatchewan Grain Growers' Association in 1910, and serving as General Manager of the Saskatchewan Elevator Company from 1911 to 1916. Member of the Canadian Council of Agriculture, 1911–16. Provincial Treasurer, Saskatchewan, 1916–17. Director of Food Production for Canada, 1918. Premier of Saskatchewan, 1922–6. Minister of Railways, Canada, 1926–29; Minister of Finance, 1929–30 and 1935–9.

particular, that if we were to attempt to store No 1 Manitoba wheat in this country we should be mad.

LORD LLOYD: I can only rely upon what they say in public themselves. I have speeches in which they say the contrary.

144. SIR THOMAS INSKIP: I can only repeat what the Prime Minister said, everything will be studied and checked and considered. May I say one word about the sources of information. I think it was Lord Salisbury who said you had sources of information not open to the Government. I should rather doubt that statement. At any rate, if the sources of information are to be regarded as equally valuable, Sir Austen knows better than any of us the Government has means of checking and cross-checking even statements made by responsible persons from sources which I need not indicate to see whether they are correct, and, indeed, a whole structure of information can be built up with pieces of information obtained in a variety of ways which I think does really put the Government in the possession of the truest picture which can probably be painted on the facts. So far as Mr Churchill's statement is concerned, my information does not justify me in criticising, even if I wanted to, the statement as to the facts so far as German capacity and output in munitions are concerned. I should not like to say there is not a case that can be made on some of them.

145. For instance, take the air statement that was made at the beginning. There the information was in the Government's possession, as Mr Churchill I think knows, some time ago and certain analysis has been prepared and certain criticisms made of the accuracy of the French information, or, rather, of its balance.

MR CHURCHILL: Of the interpretation which the French Government put on certain facts.

SIR THOMAS INSKIP: Of the interpretation the French Government put, but I can assure you that it is not because we doubt the seriousness of the position of the immense undertaking which Germany has set on foot to arm herself and make herself the strongest Power in Europe. It does not seem to me to matter very much whether it is 2,000 or 3,000 or 5,000 aeroplanes; the fact is she has made herself supremely strong and has organised herself and that is sufficient to say on that point.

146. Lord Salisbury asked for an assurance that we are whole-hearted and single-hearted in our determination to do our very utmost. I think I can say that of myself. I live with this problem. I literally go to bed with it. I wake up with it. If it were not that it is good for no man to think of nothing else and if I did not firmly put it out of my mind I should think of nothing else because I am so impressed—I do not use the word appalled—I am so impressed with the position at the present time, but then I find myself when dealing with

these questions face to face with the fact, which I am sure Mr Churchill realises because he has indeed expressed it in his own inimitable fashion, that you cannot work impossibilities. If I could wave a conjuror's wand I should do a great deal.

147. For good or for ill we were all parties to that process of disarmament. Sir Austen Chamberlain will remember the All-Party Conference which I used to attend in 1931 to see if we could agree upon some programme for the Disarmament Conference. I think I may say that a great many people have said we have disarmed to the point of danger, but I think everyone recognises that it was a deliberate policy on the part of successive Governments. Nobody can dispute that, at any rate, because that was the real meaning of the perpetual pushing forward of the ten-year rule until it was abandoned in 1932 and, as long as that was pushed forward, disarmament took place whether it was a political necessity or not and the fact is that the sources both in men, and I mean by that skilled labour, and material and machines did dry up and diminish to such an extent that it takes a long time, of necessity, to recover them. So far as machines are concerned, I agree with Mr Churchill that a great deal, or something at any rate, can be done by going abroad, by purchasing.

148. So far as material is concerned, raw material, apart from what Sir Robert Horne suggested, and I am not very sure how far it goes, I am not aware of any shortage or possible shortage of raw material.

149. But the shortage of men, that is to say skilled men, cannot be made up by going abroad; you have to get the men in this country. There is a way, of course, in which we might increase the reservoir of skilled labour in order to produce things that are urgent, and that is by going to all the engineering firms in the country and taking the eyes out of their organisation by taking the skilled men, the key men. That would supplement our resources, but I hesitate to advise the Government, if it is my duty to advise them, I hesitate to advise them to take that very drastic step. In wartime, of course, it would be done, but I am not sure whether it is possible, I do not know what would happen to all the rest of the labour.

150. You cannot turn over a motor-car firm, however easy it seems at the first moment, to produce aero engines. They are two different pieces of engineering. The fineness of the work in the aero engine for war aircraft is a very different proposition from the mass production of motor-car engines. There is a great deal that has got to be done and organised. I only point that out, not to palliate, not to defend any delay there has been, but to point out that really there is not any power in me or anybody else to perform impossibilities and, in Mr Churchill's words to-day, it is bound to be first a trickle, then a stream, and then a flood. I think we are all agreed that it is about a

three years' business, or, to take his own expression in the House of Commons it is ploughing the first year, it is sowing the next year, and it is reaping the third year, and, humanly speaking, if we can be kept out of a conflict, of war, until 1938, that is a twelve months' period, I should like to say the end of 1938 or the middle of 1938 I should expect by that time, and before that, a stream to be flowing which will put us in a very much happier position than we are in to-day.

164. MR CHURCHILL: I only wanted to say one word. I ventured to suggest to Sir Thomas, when we had a talk the other day, that one of the means by which you could get, for instance, a greater supply of machine guns and a greater capacity would be, for instance, if you went to all the cycle makers and, instead of taking one firm and saying: 'We will compensate you for making things,' you got the trade together and said: 'In a fortnight come back with a scheme which affords twenty-five per cent of your existing capacity,' and then they would settle between themselves all the difficult trading points that arose about goodwill and loss of subsequent reputation and so on, they would settle that between them and come back to you with a cut-and-dried plan and, if you had the power, of course, eventually you would say: 'If you cannot make a plan I will have to make one for you.' That is the sort of power you ought to have. A great deal could be done in that way, and I strongly urge that a definite proportion in the necessary trades should be taken from the trades engaged on the work at present, and that they should settle it up between themselves. However, I do not want to go into that any more.

I want to say that, of course, what you have told us we will treat as absolutely confidential because any statement you feel able to make on that you must make in your own time to the public.

165. The only other thing I wanted to say was on the Prime Minister's question to you: 'Do you consider war with Germany inevitable?' I certainly do not consider war with Germany inevitable, but I am sure the way to make it much less likely is to afford concrete evidence of our determination in setting about re-armament.

PRIME MINISTER: I am with you on that.

MR CHURCHILL: I am sure that is a Bull point.

PRIME MINISTER: I am with you there whole-heartedly.

A. H. Richards to Winston S. Churchill

(*Churchill papers: 2/283*)

29 July 1936
Private & Confidential

Dear Mr Churchill,

I have much pleasure to enclose summary of the proceedings recording the decisions at the private luncheon in your flat Friday last.

I am happy to inform you Sir Robert Mond has sent Mr Wickham Steed cheque for £500 to organise research work.

From time to time the results of the research organisation will be circulated through me.

Yours sincerely,
A. H. Richards

A. H. Richards: memorandum

(*Churchill papers: 2/283*)

29 July 1936

As a sequel to the luncheon recently held at the Hotel Victoria, Mr Winston Churchill kindly invited to a private luncheon, in his flat on Friday, July 24th, a small number of those present at the Hotel Victoria.

There were present the Rt Hon Winston Churchill, PC, MP, Sir Walter Citrine, KBE, Sir Robert Mond, Sir Norman Angell,[1] Lady Violet Bonham Carter, Commander Locker Lampson, DSO, MP, Mr Duncan Sandys, MP, Mr Wickham Steed, Mr Philip Guedalla,[2] Mr A. H. Richards.

The purpose was to consider the international situation and plans for action in the autumn. Both Mr Winston Churchill and Sir Walter Citrine expressed their views upon the situation, agreed upon its dangerous character, not least in relation to this country, and dwelt on the need for the enlightenment of public opinion.

[1] Ralph Norman Angell Lane, 1874–1967. Educated in France and Switzerland. Worked as a rancher, prospector and journalist in California, 1894–8. Using the name Norman Angell, he published in 1910 *The Great Illusion*, which warned of the economic catastrophe even of a victorious war. Henceforth known as Norman Angell. General Manager of the *Paris Daily Mail*, 1905–14. Editor, *Foreign Affairs*, 1928–31. Labour MP for North Bradford, 1929–31. Knighted, 1931. Nobel Peace Prize, 1933.

[2] Philip Guedalla, 1889–1944. Educated at Rugby and Balliol College Oxford. President of the Oxford Union, 1911. Barrister, 1913. Legal Adviser, Contracts Department, War Office and Ministry of Munitions, 1915–17. Organizer and Secretary, Flax Control Board, 1917–20. A friend of Lloyd George. Unsuccessful Liberal candidate, 1922, 1923, 1924, 1929 and 1931. Historian; author of *Mr Churchill: A Portrait*, 1941. Squadron-Leader, RAF, 1943.

Sir Walter Citrine thought it important that this matter should be kept clear of party politics, and that the people should be told the truth, especially in regard to the battle of ideas behind the situation. Germany and Italy, he thought, were the only nations aiming at the imposition of their ideas by force. Of the two Germany was the greatest present menace.

It was also urged that efforts should be made to gather all available information which could be communicated to the Government as well as to the public. To this end it was decided that a research organisation should be set up with the immediate purpose of keeping members of the Group informed of the latest developments and of the issues that might lie behind them.

To illustrate the kind of information that could be gathered in this way, and the need for an outline of firm peace policy which the Group could advocate, Mr Wickham Steed submitted a draft memorandum of which a copy was given to all present.

It was agreed that this work of research should be under the general supervision of Mr Wickham Steed.

In the course of the discussion the position of this country in regard to Soviet Russia was repeatedly mentioned. The prevailing view was that, however undesirable Russian economic methods and political propaganda might be, the main difference between Soviet Russia, Nazi Germany and Fascist Italy is that Russia has every reason not to promote war and is under no constraint, from the exigencies of her internal position, to make war. Therefore Russia can for the present be looked upon as an asset to the cause of peace.

It was decided that, early in September, a dinner should be given to selected representatives of the press so as to inform them of the objects of the Group and to enlist their sympathy in the public campaign of education to be begun by a large public meeting at the Queen's Hall in October.

Sir Samuel Hoare to Winston S. Churchill

(Churchill papers: 2/272)

30 July 1936   Admiralty

Dear Winston,

I find that it is very difficult for me to manage the talk about the 16″ guns on Wednesday afternoon. I am coming up from the country for the Trinity House installation and the only possible train back is at 3.30 in the afternoon. This being so, would you care to stick to coming to the Admiralty after luncheon and having a talk with Chatfield? I have told him your views and he has asked me to say that he will be at your disposal if it suits you. Will you send him a line direct as to whether you will be coming and if so, at what time.

Yrs ever,
Samuel Hoare

Winston S. Churchill to the French Ambassador[1]

(*Churchill papers: 2/256*)

31 July 1936

I think I ought to let you know that in my judgment the great bulk of the Conservative Party are very much inclined to cheer the so-called Spanish rebels. One of the greatest difficulties I meet with in trying to hold on to the old position is the German talk that the anti-Communist countries should stand together. I am sure if France sent aeroplanes etc to the present Madrid Government, and the Germans and Italians pushed in from the other angle, the dominant forces here would be pleased with Germany and Italy, and estranged from France. I hope you will not mind my writing this, which I do of course entirely on my own account. I do not like to hear people talking of England, Germany and Italy forming up against European Communism. It is too easy to be good.

I am sure that an absolutely rigid neutrality with the strongest protection against any breach of it is the only correct and safe course at the present time. A day may come if there is a stalemate, when the League of Nations may intervene to wind up the horrors. But even that is very doubtful.

---

[1] André Charles Corbin, 1881–1970. Attaché, 1906; Chief of the Press Service, French Foreign Office, 1920. French Ambassador to Madrid, 1929–31; to Brussels, 1931–3; to London, 1933–40. Honorary knighthood, 1938.

Sir Maurice Hankey to Lord Swinton

(*Cabinet papers: 21/437*)

30 July 1936   Committee of Imperial Defence
Secret

Dear Secretary of State,

You will have received copies of the stenographic note of the meetings between the Prime Minister and the Deputation on the 28th and 29th July. No attempt was made of course to answer the very numerous points of detail raised by the Deputation and particularly by Mr Churchill.

I have been told by the Prime Minister that he wishes that the records of the meeting should be thoroughly examined and that in due course he would like to receive the observations of the Service Departments on the various criticisms or enquiries that were made, in order that he may himself be informed of the facts.

We will undertake a similar examination in this office in matters in which we may be chiefly concerned but I expect the majority of questions can best be treated within one or other of the Departments.

I understand that there is no great urgency for this examination and suggest that if the Departments forward their comments to this office on the 15th September I should submit a collated paper to the Prime Minister.

I am writing similarly to the other Service Ministers with copies to Sir Arthur Robinson[1] and the Air Raids Precautions Department of the Home Office.

It is the facts and not an answer for public consumption that the Prime Minister has asked for.

Yours sincerely,
M. P. A. Hankey

[1] William Arthur Robinson, 1874–1950. Educated at Appleby School and Queen's College, Oxford. Entered Colonial Office, 1897 (first place in Civil Service Examination). Permanent Secretary, Air Ministry, 1917–20. Knighted, 1919. Secretary to the Ministry of Health. 1920–35. Chairman of the Supply Board, Committee of Imperial Defence, 1935–9. Secretary to the Ministry of Supply, 1939–40.

August 1936

Winston S. Churchill to Leslie Hore-Belisha: telegram

(*Churchill papers: 1/285*)

1 August 1936   Chartwell

When will you come here.

Winston

Winston S. Churchill to Dr Colijn:[1] *telegram*

(*Churchill papers: 1/285*)

1 August 1936   Chartwell

It would give me so much pleasure if you could motor over to visit me here and lunch or dine any day within the next three weeks. We are only half an hour away.

Winston

Winston S. Churchill to Lord Rothermere: telegram

(*Churchill papers: 1/285*)

1 August 1936   Chartwell

Do choose a sunny day next week and come down here to lunch. I want to show you my swimming pool.

Winston

[1] Hendrikus Colijn, 1869–1944. The son of a farmer. Entered the Dutch Army, and served with distinction in the Dutch East Indies. Retired with the rank of Major. An administrator in the Dutch East Indies until 1909, when he returned to Holland, and was elected to the Dutch Parliament. Minister of War, 1911–13. Minister of Finance, August 1923 to March 1926. Prime Minister of Holland, July 1925 to March 1926 and May 1933 to August 1939; Minister of War, July 1935 to May 1937; Foreign Minister, June to September 1937. As Chief Editor of the Calvinist newspaper, *De Standaard*, 1939–41, he was an uncompromising opponent of the Nazi ideology. Forced to resign the editorship, he was arrested by the Germans in July 1941, and interned in Germany, 1942. He died in internment.

Winston S. Churchill to G. M. Trevelyan[1]

(*Churchill papers: 8/530*)

1 August 1936   Chartwell

I wonder whether you would allow me to send you the page proofs of Marlborough Volume III to read as before? You will probably read it some day, so why not read it when perhaps something may catch your erudite eye before it is too late?

You always predicted that I should have to run to a fourth volume, and this is now correct.

How are you getting on with Grey? We live in gloomy times.

Winston S. Churchill to C. C. Wood[2]

(*Wood papers*)

1 August 1936   Chartwell

You sent me a new copy of the enclosed map. It is already in the text, and I commented on it on the proofs 'Where is Villeroy?' Also Ghent and Bruges should (I think) be black as they were in Marlborough's hands. I am sending a duplicate of this letter to the Brigadier.[3]

It is of the utmost importance now to know where the remaining maps are.

I will get on with the preface as soon as I have completed the chapters.

I agree with what you say about the spelling of Wynendael. By all means continue the spelling as 'dale'.

[1] George Macaulay Trevelyan, 1876–1962. A great nephew of the historian Lord Macaulay. Educated at Harrow and Trinity College, Cambridge. Historian; author of seven books before 1914, including a trilogy about Garibaldi. Commandant, 1st British Ambulance Unit for Italy, 1915–18. Regius Professor of Modern History at Cambridge, 1927–40. Order of Merit, 1930. Master of Trinity College, Cambridge, 1940. Chancellor of Durham University, 1949–57. Among his books was *Blenheim* (1930), and a biography of Sir Edward Grey (1937). In 1944 he published his *English Social History, A Survey of Six Centuries*.

[2] Charles Carlyle Wood, 1875–1959. An expert on typography and literary form, he worked first with Spottiswoode & Co, where he was apprenticed in 1891, and then, from 1912, with Harraps, where he became Head of the Editorial Department. He retired from Harraps in 1940. Proof-reader for Churchill's biography of *Marlborough*, for the *Second World War* and for the *History of the English Speaking Peoples*. At Chartwell, the process of proof-reading was known as 'wooding'.

[3] Brigadier Pakenham-Walsh (see page 150, note 1).

Winston S. Churchill to C. C. Wood

(*Wood papers*)

1 August 1936   Chartwell

I have altered the Ramillies text so as not to be dependent upon the old map, which I cannot find. I must ask the Brigadier to make a folder map of Ramillies as well as the one of Oudenarde now under construction. There will have to be a general map of the Low Countries, but that can be repeated from Volume II, also a general map of Europe and the theatres which can likewise be repeated.

The Ramillies playing card was photographed by the King's librarian.[1] It is very old, small and well-worn, and I doubt if any new photograph would be any better. There is no reason why you should not make a print of it slightly larger, and let us see how it looks. I return it to you herewith meanwhile.

You have everything now, so far as illustrations and facsimiles are concerned. I shall keep you well supplied day by day with chapters.

WSC

Winston S. Churchill to Brigadier Pakenham-Walsh

(*Churchill papers: 8/530*)

1 August 1936

I think this map should be altered as indicated to illustrate the text. Will you very kindly explain it to the draughtsman.

The word Villeroy should be spread out widely to show how he is dispersed. The Prussians, Hanoverians and Palatines are certainly a feature. Helchin, Marlborough's head-quarters, much mentioned in the correspondence is required, and surely Ghent and Bruges had already fallen into Marlborough's hands.

I cannot find the old map of Ramillies on which I was relying. It has disappeared. So a folder map of Ramillies will be required in colour as well as the similar one of Oudenarde. Could you let me know the ones you have that are not finished yet or are with the draughtsman. There are I think only three or four.

---

[1] Owen Frederick Morshead, 1893–1977. On active service in France, and Italy, 1914–19 (MC, DSO, despatches five times). Fellow of Magdalene College, Cambridge, 1920. Librarian, Windsor Castle, 1926–58. Commanded the 9th Berkshire Battalion, Home Guard, 1940–5. Knighted, 1953.

I enclose also the two general maps of the Netherlands and of Europe which figured in volume II. I think we have shown every place mentioned in Northern Italy on the Eugene's march map and I do not think a general map of Northern Italy is necessary. What do you say? About Spain: there must surely be a general map of Spain showing all the places mentioned in the text and the important places as well. This would be a folder too. I do not think any alterations are required in the map of Europe, but a certain number of new places mentioned in this text should go in the Western side of the Netherlands.

I hope to get these sent to the printers very quickly now. The page proofs are coming in well.

Winston S. Churchill to Sir Samuel Hoare: not sent

(Churchill papers: 2/272)

1 August 1936   Chartwell
Private

My dear Sam,

I shall be very glad, if you think it worth while, to have a talk with Chatfield (and the Comptroller)[1] after lunch on Wednesday. I suppose I could get there at 3.15 pm. It is very civil of you to attach any importance to my opinion, and prima facie there is a case. I cannot answer the argument about the long delay involved. Once again we alone are injured by Treaties. I cannot doubt that a far stronger ship could be built with three triple 16″ gun turrets in a 35,000 ton hull, than any combination of 14″. Not only would it be a better ship, but it would be rated a better ship, and a more powerful token of naval power by everyone, including those who serve in her. Remember the Germans get far better results out of their guns per calibre than we do. They throw a heavier shell farther and more accurately. The answer is a Big Punch. Not only is there an enormous increase in the weight of broadside, but in addition the explosive charge of a 16″ shell must be far larger than that of a 14″. If you can get through the armour, it is worth while doing something inside with the explosion.

Another aspect is the number of turrets. What a waste to have four turrets which I suppose weigh 2,000 tons each, when three will give a bigger punch! With three turrets the centralisation of armour against gunfire and torpedoes can be much more intense; and the decks all the more clear for the anti-

---

[1] Vice-Admiral Sir Reginald Henderson (see page 127, note 1).

aircraft batteries. If you ask your people to give you a legend for a 16″ gun ship, I am persuaded they would show you decidedly better proportions than could be achieved at 14″. Of course there may be an argument about gunnery control, the spread of shot etc, with which I am not familiar. Still I should have thought that the optimum gunnery effect could be reached with salvos of four and five alternatively.

Nothing would induce me to succumb to 14″ if I were in your shoes. The Admiralty will look rather silly if they are committed to two 14″ gun ships, and both Japan and the United States go in for 16″ a few months later. I should have thought it was quite possible to lie back and save six months in construction. Terrible to deliberately build British battleships costing £7,000,000 apiece that are not the strongest in the world! As old Fisher[1] used to say 'The British Navy always travels first class.'

However these are only vaticinations![2] I went through all this in byegone years, or I would not venture to obtrude it on you. I will get in touch with Chatfield as you suggest.

Lord Davies to Winston S. Churchill

(*Churchill papers: 2/285*)

1 August 1936

My dear Churchill,

When we had a talk after dinner a few weeks ago you said something like this: 'It is a forlorn hope, but when they come to the edge of the abyss they may recoil at the last moment.' This has stuck in my mind ever since, and the problem is how to make them recoil and to execute an about-turn. Obviously, such a manoeuvre cannot be planned and consummated without a leader. Europe is leaderless today, just as she was in the days of Sully when he penned his grand design. Rousseau was right when he said that when Henry IV was assassinated the grand design also perished at that moment because he was the only man in Europe who could have put it across.

Now let me assure you, my friend, I am not trying to flatter you, but I honestly believe that you are almost the only person in Europe today who

[1] John Arbuthnot Fisher, 1841–1920. Known both as 'Jackie' and, because of his somewhat oriental appearance, 'the old Malay'. Entered Navy, 1854. First Sea Lord, 1904–10. Admiral of the Fleet, 1905. Created Baron, 1909. Retired, 1911. Head of the Royal Commission on Fuel and Engines, 1912–14. Reappointed First Sea Lord, October 1914; resigned, May 1915. Chairman of the Admiralty Inventions Board, 1915–16.

[2] Vaticination: a prediction of an oracular or inspired nature; a prognostication or prophecy, a prophetic utterance or forecast.

possesses the qualifications to see the thing through. I will give you my reasons. First, you are an Englishman. It is true that our stock is much below par at the moment, but everyone realises that only Great Britain, and only an Englishman, can pull Europe out of the mess she is in today. No Frenchman can do it, no German can do it; no-one but an Englishman can build the bridge between these two great nations. Secondly, you are what is known as an elder Statesman. You have had a wide Ministerial experience both in domestic and international affairs. Thirdly, you are an author whose works have been widely read and whose name is familiar in every country. Fourthly, you are a strategist—amateur, if you like, but with a profound knowledge of military subjects and with first hand experience of the military, economic and financial problems which had to be solved by the Allies during the World War. Lastly—and this is the most important consideration—you have a vision of the future. You are not blinded, like most of your colleagues, with pre-conceived notions and obsolete ideas which belong to a bygone age, and you have the courage of your convictions. Therefore, I repeat, you are the man for the job, a great and noble enterprise, nothing less than the federation and reorganisation of Europe. I doubt whether you will be successful, but as you told me yourself, it is better to go down fighting on the side of the angels than of the devil.

Consequently I would plead with you to concentrate upon the role of the saviour of Europe—nothing less—the leader of a last, it may be a futile attempt, to save her from plunging over the abyss. As Theodore Roosevelt once remarked in a similar connection: 'The ruler or statesman who should bring about such a combination would have earned his place in history for all time and his title to the gratitude of all mankind.'

To achieve this position it will obviously be necessary to rally all good Europeans to your banner, on which will be inscribed your motto 'The Rule of Law'. This will involve the formation of groups and parties in all those European countries where they may be tolerated, and the mobilisation of all those forces—the press, wireless, authors and the best brains—in order to exert a powerful influence upon public opinion. Péréfixe[1] tells us that your predecessor, Henry IV, had 'enlisted all the good writers in Christendom on his side: for indeed he would have chosen rather to persuade than force people, and instruct them so well in his intentions that they should regard his arms as forces held in reserve, to be used only as a last resort'. In short, it means taking the offensive against reactionary and ultra-nationalistic elements in all these countries. Given a leader, I believe there will be a far

[1] Hardouin de Beaumont de Péréfixe (Bishop of Rodez, and Archbishop of Paris), author of *Histoire du roi Henri le Grand*, 1749 (reissued, with an additional essay on Henry IV, by M. Andrieux, 1822).

bigger response than anyone could reasonably have anticipated. If the necessary resources are forthcoming you will soon have all the progressive forces behind you. They are waiting for a lead, and the reaction to the ultra-nationalistic tendencies of the last ten years is now about due. . . .

Winston S. Churchill to C. C. Wood

(Wood papers)

3 August 1936   Chartwell

Dear Mr Wood,

I send you now everything except the last five chapters. Mr Deakin will be with you tomorrow. There are a number of points for him marked by me from 'The Jacobite Raid' chapter onwards, nor are Mr Marsh's corrections in from that point. Some of these chapters are a good deal pulled about, and if you think fit you had better put them into slip again, keeping enough of the earlier chapters to go on continuously with the page proofing. Chapter 19 about Ghent and Bruges is now split in two, altering the numbers thereafter. I do not feel like a lengthy preface, nor is it worth your while to await it. I will, however, do it next before I finish the last chapter if you wish. What maps are still outstanding? Please discuss all these points with Mr Deakin.

Would you mind asking your proof readers to put down quite clearly their rule about hyphened words. I do not like Mr Marsh's very full use of hyphens, but what rule do you follow? Macaulay frequently runs the words together without a hyphen, eg 'panicstricken'. The great thing is to have a principle and stick to it.[1]

With regard to modernization of letters, here is the rule. All letters which have been printed before, unless specially marked by me, should be modernized as you have proposed. All original letters or letters inserted because of their archaic character should only be corrected here and there as I have done, for punctuation and to make sense.

Contrary to what is said in the preliminary note, all starred documents will have in addition a footnote, Blenheim Mss or other source. All spellings of places must agree with the maps unless the maps are definitely wrong. With regard to numbers, I think the following will work: viz when there is a confrontation of armies in battalions, squadrons, etc numerals should be

---

[1] Churchill's anguish concerning the proper use of hyphens was not without precedent. H. W. Fowler (author of *A Dictionary of Modern English Usage*) wrote, in a special pamphlet on hyphens: 'The chaos prevailing among writers or printers or both regarding the use of hyphens is discreditable to English education.'

used. When there are broken numbers, eg 7,500 ditto. When numerals are used in some old quoted letter ditto. Otherwise it is better to *spell*. In sending these proofs to the printers, please enforce this system. I find we are in practice spelling almost everything and I must say it runs better except as mentioned.

I do not like the high punctuation, however, indeed etc.

Yours vy truly,
Winston S. Churchill

Winston S. Churchill to Sir Abe Bailey: telegram
(*Churchill papers: 1/285*)

4 August 1936   Chartwell

Do lunch here one day. Much want to see you. The cranes are magnificent.

Winston

Sir Hugh Tudor to Winston S. Churchill
(*Churchill papers: 2/257*)

4 August 1936   Newfoundland

My dear Winston,

Thank you so much for your letter.

The situation in Europe certainly seems to be getting worse. Spain is a new complication. If the rebels win the Fascist group will be strengthened in Europe, & Spain may line up with Italy & Germany.

If the red Government wins Bolshevism will come very near us. With Spain Bolshie, France half Bolshie, & Russia subsidising our communists are we going to line up with them & Russia?

I know how important even vital our friendship with France is, but I feel many in England would rather make a strong western pact with Germany & France & let Germany settle Russia & Bolshevism in her own way. No doubt Germany would *eventually* be stronger after defeating Russia but in the meantime we & France would have time to get our defences right; & it would take years before Germany would be in a position to make war again, nor do I suppose she would want to having got a satisfactory expansion. Even Germany cannot like war.

Russia deserves what is coming to her, as she will never stop undermining capitalistic governments in every way she can. If she is left alone, in 10 years or so she will be the strongest power on earth & *she* may want to take in India and may be a more dangerous enemy than Germany.

I am so glad you are having success in bradawling[1] the Government about the rearmament. It must take several years before we are safely rearmed even with the utmost energy.

I have had another letter from the Aldershot command to ask me what sort of date I can go there & give my experiences of smoke tactics & ideas about the use of smoke to suit the latest tactical developments. But I am afraid I cannot come over till after Xmas at earliest. I didn't go to Norway after all, as I was doubtful about my left hip, & had intense X-ray treatment in London for arthritis, which seems to have got me right.

Yours ever,
Hugh Tudor

Winston S. Churchill to Anthony Eden

(*Churchill papers: 2/257*)

7 August 1936

Many thanks for sending me 'Twelve Days' which I read with pleasure. It is a very straight-forward account and obviously based on facts and experience in every line.[2]

This Spanish business cuts across my thoughts. It seems to me most important to make Blum stay with us strictly neutral, even if Germany and Italy continue to back the rebels and Russia sends money to the government. If the French government take sides against the rebels it will be a god-send to the Germans and pro-Germans. In case you have a spare moment, look at my article in the Evening Standard on Monday.[3]

---

[1] To bradawl: to bore holes in, to bore away at (from the act of using an awl to make holes to insert brads—thin, flattish nails—into wood). Used mainly by carpenters and cobblers.

[2] Sidney Rogerson, *Twelve Days*, with a foreword by Basil Liddell Hart, had been published in November 1933. The book was a narrative history of twelve days of the Great War, as seen by Captain Sidney Rogerson, who had served during the winter of 1916 in the trenches on the Somme. Rogerson called his book 'a plain, unvarnished version of one short tour in the Somme trenches, written in the hope of recalling to the soldier the scenes with which he was familiar, and of presenting the younger generation with an accurate picture of life as we lived it in those days'.

[3] On 10 August 1936 the *Evening Standard* published Churchill's article, 'The Spanish Tragedy', in which he wrote: 'The worst quarrels only arise when both sides are in the right and in the wrong' and he added: 'The cruelties and ruthless executions extorted by the desperation of both sides, the appalling hatreds unloosed, the clash of creed and interest, make it only too probable that victory will be followed by the merciless extermination of the active elements of the vanquished and by a prolonged period of iron rule.' In Spain, Churchill

I have ordered my bookseller to send you 'Uncle, give us Bread'. I hope your rest has done you good.

Winston S. Churchill to N. B. Foot [1]

(Churchill papers: 2/285)

7 August 1936

I do not wish to go beyond the Resolutions which we passed in the House of Commons. I think it would be a mistake at this juncture to dwell too much on the past. It may be true, and also agreeable, to apply the word 'dastardly' to the conduct of Italy. The question is whether it will be helpful for the future. There is no doubt that the League of Nations could not have gone into action on a worse ground than Abyssinia which was a backward slave-owning state not fit for inclusion in the League of Nations, and in regard to which the whole military brunt must fall on Great Britain alone. One would hope that in an European cause, a great many countries would be involved which would form the nucleus of a real resolve around which all the others could rally. There is a lot in this declaration which I think might be stated in a manner more likely to influence events. To say that there must be no regional pacts in any area smaller than Europe, is to run I think counter to an irresistible tide. It is much better to stick to the formula that regional pacts must be subordinated to the principle of the Covenant, and that their obligation in any given instance may be governed by zones of varying responsibility. However as I understand this is only to be a declaration signed by individuals and not a formal pronouncement of the New Commonwealth I naturally only suggest these points for your friends' consideration.

---

wrote, 'Fascism confronts Communism. The spirit and prowess of Mussolini and Hitler strive with those of Trotsky and of Bela Kun,' and he advised Britain and France both to pursue a strictly neutral policy, and to urge neutrality on others. His article ended: 'French partisanship for the Spanish Communists, or British partisanship for the Spanish rebels, might injure profoundly the bonds which unite the British Empire and the French Republic. This Spanish welter is not the business of either of us. Neither of these Spanish factions expresses our conception of civilization. We cannot afford in our perilous position to indulge a sentimental or a sporting view. All that is happening increases the power of those evil forces which from both extremes menace the existence of Parliamentary democracy and individual liberty in Great Britain and France. Let us stand aloof with redoubled vigilance and ever-increasing defences!'

[1] N. B. Foot. General Secretary of the New Commonwealth, a Society 'for the promotion of International Law and Order through the creation of a Tribunal in Equity and an International Police Force'. The President of the International Section of the Society was George Barnes (a former Labour member of Lloyd George's War Cabinet); the Chairman was Lord Davies. Churchill was President of the British Section of the Society. The Society published a monthly newspaper, *The New Commonwealth*.

Winston S. Churchill to Vyvyan Adams
(*Churchill papers: 2/286*)

7 August 1936

I have not heard from Lord Cecil and I shall shortly be going abroad. I would consider his invitation should it arrive. I am thinking over the invitation of the League of Nations Union Executive.

This Spanish business is distracting. I think we must be very strictly neutral, and I hope we can persuade France to be neutral too. Everything seems to play into German hands.

Violet Pearman to Winston S. Churchill
(*Churchill papers: 2/285*)

7 August 1936

Lord Davies is enquiring about the dedication of the book, about which he spoke to you. The book is nearly finished and therefore he would like to know your wishes.

Winston S. Churchill to Lord Davies
(*Churchill papers: 2/285*)

7 August 1936

Of course I shall be much honoured if you would dedicate your book to me. The only thing is that I hope you will not be disappointed in any contribution I can make towards the furtherance of your ideas.

I am up to my neck in passing the proofs for Marlborough Volume III, but I hope later to reply to your long and most interesting letter.

I hope that your health continues to improve.

Winston S. Churchill to John Wheldon
(*Churchill papers: 8/530*)

7 August 1936

. . . It would be very nice of you to read through the page proofs in case anything catches your eye. They are in a very advanced condition so that no more work can be done upon them but there might still be time to leave out a mistake. Do not let me trouble you with these, if you are otherwise engaged. I am looking forward to sending you a copy in October.

I am very glad to hear that my letter was of service to you, and that you are making good progress in your new work.

Winston S. Churchill to Newman Flower
(*Churchill papers: 8/532*)

7 August 1936   Chartwell

A HISTORY OF THE ENGLISH-SPEAKING PEOPLES

The contract only says 'by April 30th 1937 or by such later date prior to April 30th 1939 as may be mutually agreed. . . .' I am afraid it will not be possible for me to complete this work before April 1939. I have been very much ridden in upon by politics owing to the need of urging this country to rearm. This has delayed me with 'Marlborough' which will not now be finished till the Spring or Autumn next year—I hope by the Spring. However a great deal of work has been done upon the English Speaking Peoples. Not only has the ground been surveyed, and the whole plan made out, but I have a very large mass of material which has been carefully collected under my supervision covering every chapter. I have spent over £2,500 of the advance upon this work of preparation and I am greatly impressed with the possibilities. As soon as I can complete the proofs of Marlborough, Volume III, which are now in page form, I will make you out a copy of the provisional plan so that you will be able to see the character and scope of the work for yourself. I hope you will agree to the later date, as I am sure this will be needed in order to produce good results.

I shall be here till the 24th. Could I not persuade you to come over and lunch one day? If you can give me a day or two's notice, I could prepare the plan in a shape which would interest you.

WSC

Winston S. Churchill to Lord Cecil of Chelwood: telegram

(*Cecil of Chelwood papers*)

10 August 1936   Westerham

Much complimented by your invitation.[1] Must consult before accepting. Will wire in few days. Writing.

Winston

Winston S. Churchill to Lord Cecil of Chelwood

(*Churchill papers: 2/286*)

10 August 1936

Naturally I would consider most carefully the important invitation you have sent me. So far as the meeting is concerned I have every disposition to comply. But I fear I cannot undertake to write an article. I have so much literary work to do, and am now in the throes of another volume of Marlborough.

I may add that I am not at all in agreement with the suppression of private manufacture of armaments. This seems to me quite absurd, when the entire industry of every country is being converted to war, and when the manufacture of components is carried to such enormous lengths. However I do not suppose that everyone attending the Conference has to agree on everything beforehand.

Ought you not, by the way, to have a Liberal speaker or do they exist no more as an international force?

Winston S. Churchill to Bernard Baruch: telegram

(*Churchill papers: 1/285*)

11 August 1936

Delighted you are coming. Suggest you dine with me Embassy Club London. Wire arrival and which hotel. Will come and see you early.

Winston

---

[1] Lord Cecil of Chelwood had asked Churchill to be the main speaker, in Brussels, at the first big demonstration of the International Peace Campaign.

Winston S. Churchill to Collin Brooks[1]

(Churchill papers: 1/257)

12 August 1936

Thank you so very much for your very friendly article last Sunday, which I read with great pleasure.[2] It is terrible to watch the slow motion picture of our rearmament.

Anthony Eden to Winston S. Churchill

(Churchill papers: 2/257)

12 August 1936
Personal

Dear Winston,

Thank you so much for sending me 'Uncle give us Bread', which I found here today, on my way through London. I shall take it with me to read in the country, where I hope to spend another week before I return definitely under the yoke.

I was most interested to read your article in the Evening Standard which should be timely & helpful. While I do not pretend to agree with every sentence, I do agree emphatically with its concluding paragraphs.

Blum has behaved very well in this business, which is more difficult for him than for us. So far I think that the 'collective neutrality' policy—dreadful phrase—has achieved as much support as we could reasonably expect. We must clearly continue to work for it.

Yours ever,
Anthony Eden

[1] William Collin Brooks, 1893–1959. Member of the Manchester Produce Exchange, 1905–15. Founder of the Manchester Press Agency, 1913–15. On active service, 1915–18; when he was awarded the Military Cross. Literary Editor and chief leader writer, *Liverpool Courier*, 1920–3; Assistant Editor, leader writer and chief reviewer, *Yorkshire Post*, 1923–8; Assistant Editor, *Financial News*, 1928–33; London Correspondent of the *New York Journal of Commerce*, and *The Business Week*, 1928–38. Editor, City Editor, and feature writer of the *Sunday Dispatch*, 1936–8. Chairman and Editor of Truth, 1940–53. Chief leader writer of the *Statist* from 1942 until his death.

[2] Collin Brooks' article, entitled 'Mysteries of British Politics', was published in the *Sunday Dispatch* on 9 August 1936. In it Brooks wrote that Churchill was 'by common consent, the most forceful and dynamic statesman of his age, a man who has held high office and whose almost super-human energy was harnessed to the vital supply and fighting departments during the last war'. Brooks described many differences he had had with Churchill. 'But today,' he wrote, 'these points of difference do not blind any sensible mind to the urgent need which the nation has of his services in executive office. It is a tragedy of waste that his magnificent brain, his unresting energy and his driving, eager personality should be unharnessed.'

Winston S. Churchill to F. W. Deakin
(*Churchill papers: 8/530*)

14 August 1936

Dear Deakin,

I have sent all the chapters to the printer except this last which has been less carefully studied than earlier ones. You will see the points I have marked. I think the chapter requires to be enriched at various points and clamped together. Pray study the points marked and bring this back with you on Monday. I also enclose the former proofs. The last chapter is specially important.

Yours sincerely,
Winston S. Churchill

Winston S. Churchill to Sir Hugh Tudor
(*Churchill papers: 2/257*)

16 August 1936

Very many thanks for your letter. I have, as you divine, been much perturbed in my thoughts by the Spanish explosion. I feel acutely the weight of what you say in the earlier part of your letter. I am sure it represents the strong and growing section of Conservative opinion, and events seem to be driving us in that direction.

Every good wish. Let me know when you return.

Winston S. Churchill to Sir Maurice Hankey
(*Cabinet papers: 21/437*)

16 August 1936   Chartwell

My dear Maurice,

I should be much obliged if you would send me a copy of the following extracts from the transcript of our deputation on Defence—

1. My statement upon the Air,
2. Lord Trenchard's statement on the Air,
3. Grigg's statement upon the Army,
4. Lord Lloyd's statement on Shipping,
5. My statement on munitions production,
6. Sir Robert Horne's supporting speech.

You will realise that these statements contain only the views put forward by the deputation and do not involve the Government in any way. It would be possible to collect and reconstruct them without troubling you, but this I think would involve unnecessary labour, as you have a full record. I hope you may feel able to do what I ask as a matter of courtesy and convenience.

Yours vy sincerely,

PS. When are you coming over to swim? The pool is at its best and if we have sunny weather this week it would be very nice to see you and any of your family. You need only telephone.

Do please,
WSC

Sir Thomas Inskip to Winston S. Churchill
(*Churchill papers: 2/269*)

17 August 1936

My dear Churchill,

Thank you for sending me the information you had received from Colonel A. S. Keates[1] relating to the Suomi machine pistol. I had as a matter of fact already received these particulars from Colonel Keates himself, and understand that the matter is receiving attention in the War Office and that Colonel Keates has had an invitation to demonstrate his pistol. The authorities here are aware of the activity on the Continent with regard to weapons of this type and they have obtained several kinds for examination and trial.

You added that you hoped that I would not mind your sending me various letters you get in respect of defence matters in case they should contain material of value. I shall be, of course, more than glad to see anything which may be of use and it is, I realise, unnecessary for me to make the reservation to you that some of the questions raised may very possibly be more properly for examination by Hoare, Duff Cooper, or Swinton and their experts than by myself. But I like to know of anything that is being considered.

Yours sincerely,
T. W. H. Inskip

---

[1] Arthur Sidney Keates, 1881–1961. Joined the Army as a private, 1900. 2nd Lieutenant, East Kent Regiment, 1915; Lieutenant, 1917; temporary Lieutenant-Colonel, 1917–19. Captain, Scottish Rifles, 1920; Lieutenant-Colonel, 1921. Retired, 1921.

Edward Marsh to Winston S. Churchill

(*Churchill papers: 8/530*)

18 August 1936   Bath

My dear Winston,

I found yr telegram when I got here this afternoon, & I've been trying to formulate principles of hyphenation; but I don't know if I shall satisfy you. I think there are three main branches of the question:—

(1) words compounded of two nouns—for these, my principle has been, when in doubt as to the accepted usage, to consult the Oxford Dictionary. I have never been able to discover any system in the matter. For instance, dinner-table has a hyphen, & apple tree none—why I don't know.

(2) adjectives or participles preceded by an adverb. Here it wd be difficult to lay down a rule, the cases must be decided on their merits. The idea is that if the two are felt to coalesce into a single epithet, there shd be a hyphen. For instance, I shd write 'a well-established fact', but 'a needlessly complicated argument'. In such cases I haven't inserted hyphens in yr proofs except where I thought they were clearly necessary.

(3) participles followed by prepositions, eg a made-up tie. I don't think these present any difficulty.

Yours ever,
Eddie

Violet Pearman to C. C. Wood

(*Wood papers*)

18 August 1936   Chartwell

Dear Mr Wood,

I am asked by Mr Churchill to send you the Preface to the Third Volume, which he dictated during the week end, so that you could have it as soon as possible.[1] Would you mind letting me know whether you receive it safely, as the posts get rather delayed here lately, which is such a nuisance.

---

[1] Dictated to Mrs Pearman on 13 August 1936, Churchill's eight-page preface to his third Marlborough volume began: 'I had purposed to finish the story of Marlborough and his Times in this volume; but as the massive range of the material came fully into view it was clear that this could not be done without altering the balance and proportion of the work and failing to give a level, comprehensive account. I have therefore ended this volume after the campaign of 1708.' Later in the Preface, Churchill wrote: 'In one other main aspect the story of this volume has a peculiar interest for us to-day. We see a world war of a League of Nations against a mighty, central military monarchy, hungering for domination not only over the lands but over the politics and religion of its neighbours. We see in their extremes the

Collin Brooks to Winston S. Churchill
(*Churchill papers: 2/257*)

18 August 1936   The Sunday Dispatch

Dear Mr Churchill,

Many thanks for your very kind letter, which only reached me this morning. You will be interested to hear that a great many people wrote to me
approving the article, including my colleague who represents us at Geneva,
who says: 'I am constantly being told by foreign Statesmen that if Winston
had been PM we should have had no reoccupation of demilitarised zones, no
Abyssinia . . . and consequently no new problems of Empire defence which,
as many people think, can only be solved by war. Foreigners have a whole-
some respect for WC but they have none for the dear old "English gentlemen"
whose main occupation appears to be "turning the other cheek".'

I hope we may meet and talk together some time again soon.

Yours sincerely,
Collin Brooks

Winston S. Churchill to the Duke of Norfolk[1]
(*Churchill papers: 1/285*)

18 August 1936

Dear Duke of Norfolk,

Pray see the enclosed cutting from the Daily Telegraph. I should be very
glad if you would consider my brother-in-law Colonel Bertram Romilly,[2]
late of the Scots Guards, as one of the ushers at the Coronation.

---

feebleness and selfish shortcomings of a numerous coalition, and how its weaker members cast
their burdens upon the strong, and sought to exploit the unstinted efforts of England and
Holland for their own advantage. We see all these evils redeemed by the statecraft and
personality of Marlborough, and by his military genius and that of his twin captain, Eugene.
Thus the causes in which were wrapped the liberties of Europe were carried to safety for
several generations.'

[1] Bernard Marmaduke Fitzalan-Howard, Earl of Surrey, 1908–1975. Succeeded his grandfather, as 16th Duke of Norfolk, 1917. Earl Marshal, and Heriditary Marshal and Chief
Butler of England; Premier Duke and Earl. Knight of the Garter, 1937. One of his three
brothers-in-law (Lieutenant-Colonel Davidson) was killed in action in Tunisia on 2 March
1943. Joint Parliamentary Secretary, Ministry of Agriculture, 1941–45. In 1965 he supervised
the organization of Churchill's State Funeral.

[2] Bertram Henry Samuel Romilly, 1878–1940. 2nd Lieutenant, Scots Guards, 1898. On
active service in South Africa, 1900–2 (DSO). Attached to the Egyptian Camel Corps, 1903.
On active service 1914–17; Lieutenant-Colonel, 1915. Military Governor of the Galilee,
1919–20. Chief Instructor, Cairo Military School, Egyptian Army, 1925–8. He had married
Clementine Churchill's sister, Nellie Hozier, in 1915: they had two sons, Giles and Esmond.
Colonel Romilly died four days before Churchill became Prime Minister.   Esmond Romilly
was killed in action in November 1941.

This officer had a most distinguished career in the Sudan Camel Corps and commanded the Scots Guards in the Great War. In 1915 he received a terrible wound from a large shrapnel bullet in the head, and it was deemed extraordinary that he survived. He however recovered sufficiently after a year or more to be able to resume command of his battalion during the Passchendaele offensive, when he was again wounded and seriously shell shocked by an explosion which destroyed the headquarters dug-out of the battalion, and killed many of its occupants. After that he again returned to France, but was only able to serve on the staff. At the close of the war he received further employment in Egypt, but the effects of his first wound marred his prospects of high promotion.

He is however perfectly fit to discharge the duties now in question and his social standing makes him acquainted with many well-known people. I am sure he would appreciate as a very high compliment an invitation to serve as an usher, and I feel it would be in every way an appropriate choice, and one that would be in full harmony with His Majesty's deep interest in his wartime comrades.[1]

Yours very truly,
Winston S. Churchill

Desmond Morton to Winston S. Churchill

(*Churchill papers: 2/266*)

21 August 1936 Committee of Imperial Defence

Dear Winston,

Might I suggest your getting a copy of:—

'When Japan goes to War' by O. Tanin and E. Yohan, Vanguard Press, New York, Published 1936.

Though Japan is not our first potential enemy, all the figures and statistics in this book are correct and if you ever want to quote figures about Japanese war potential, here you are. In addition, it shows you what a modern war of national effort entails.

---

[1] Edward VIII was never crowned; but Colonel Romilly did serve as one of the Gold Staff Officers at the Coronation of George VI and Queen Elizabeth in Westminster Abbey on 12 May 1937.

Doubtless you will anyhow get a copy of Ludendorff's[1] book to be published next week—'The Nation at War'.

In the words of the Morning Post: 'This book shows how a vast and all powerful military machine can be created and how a whole nation can be mobilised for War'.

Yours very sincerely,
Desmond Morton

G. M. Trevelyan to Winston S. Churchill

(*Churchill papers: 8/530*)

21 August 1936 Hallington Hall,
Newcastle-on-Tyne

Dear Churchill,

I am getting on fast with your proofs, though grouse shooting and guests curtail the time. I think it is the best volume so far, which is saying a lot. I think the technique and proportion are now perfect both in the political parts and the fighting. The great cavalry fight at Ramillies is about as good a description of a battle as can be given. And the politics of the reign were never told more truly or more clearly.

You have not said *when* you want the proofs back, I mean if you are in a hurry. I seem to have (so far) no suggestions or corrections. If I find any I will put them on a pc at once. No doubt you are sending me the rest.

Yrs very truly,
G. M. Trevelyan

Winston S. Churchill to G. M. Trevelyan

(*Churchill papers: 8/530*)

22 August 1936

Your letter just arrived. I am most relieved to learn that you do not think the new volume below the level. It has taken me two years and has perhaps

---

[1] Erich von Ludendorff, 1865–1937. Entered the Prussian Army, 1883. Served on the German General Staff, 1894–1913. Quartermaster-General of the 2nd Army, August 1914, when he took over command of the 14th Brigade of Infantry, whose General had been killed, and captured Liège. Chief of Staff to Hindenburg in East Prussia, 1914–15; First Quarter-master-General of the German armies, 1916–18. With Hindenburg, he controlled the making of German war policy. Fled to Sweden, November 1918. Returned to Germany, April 1919. Published *My War Memoirs* in 1919. Joined Hitler's unsuccessful attempt to seize power in Munich, November 1923. Entered the Reichstag as a National Socialist, 1924.

gained by being done at leisure. Although it now seems to me very dull in parts, I count on the structural effect. I shall be most interested to know what you think of Oudenarde, a peculiarly difficult battle to describe.

There is no hurry about returning the proofs. But if you see anything wrong I should be grateful if you would send me a postcard with just the number of the page, and the correction required. We shall be going to press in about a fortnight. Of course the proofs you are reading have been heavily corrected by me since.

Once more, many thanks.

Winston S. Churchill to Sir Thomas Inskip

(Churchill papers: 2/269)

22 August 1936

Many thanks for your letter. I did not mean you to be personally troubled in the matter. I thought it was my duty to forward the suggestions and had no doubt your secretary would hand it to the appropriate department. A good many people write to me, and when there seems any substance in what they write, I pass it on to the Government without taking any responsibility for it. Unless I write to you personally myself, I hope you will not be burdened with these communications.

Winston S. Churchill to Lord Cecil of Chelwood: telegram

(Cecil of Chelwood papers)

22 August 1936

Much regret that after full consideration I cannot come to your meeting at Brussels. On many grounds it would have given me great pleasure to support you, but I am convinced that in the present situation in Europe I should have to make too many reservations to be helpful. Thank you so much for inviting me.[1]

Winston

---

[1] At a conference of the International Peace Campaign, held in Brussels from 2 to 6 September 1936, there were a thousand delegates from forty countries. The main speeches at the opening session were by Lord Cecil of Chelwood, Pierre Cot (the French Air Minister), Edouard Herriot, the President of the French Chamber of Deputies, and Emile Vandervelde, Vice President of the Belgian Council of Ministers. Cecil and Cot were Joint Presidents of the Campaign.

Thomas Hunt[1] to Winston S. Churchill

(*Churchill papers: 1/285*)

22 August 1936

Dear Mr Churchill,

I am delighted that the X Rays show no sign of any Ulcer, and the Gall bladder is perfectly healthy.

The stomach is a very active one—too active in fact—and I have no doubt the indigestion is due to nothing more than this, as the wind will get held up at times and the stomach will contract too energetically and secrete too much acid. I feel very confident that I can help this—and have little doubt that your smoking plays some part in keeping the stomach too much stimulated. The most important thing is to keep meals fairly small and *frequent*—not going longer than about 3 hours without taking something to eat.

Will you try the enclosed prescription with a little water before lunch and dinner, and a teaspoonful of the powder if you have the indigestion, up to 3 or 4 times in the 24 hours.

I hope you will let me know if my advice is not clear, and again am very glad you let us have the X Rays done which give me a proper knowledge to work on.

Yours sincerely,
Thomas Hunt

Dr Thomas Hunt to Winston S. Churchill: diet sheet

(*Churchill papers: 1/351*)

DIET

Avoid Highly seasoned food—cooked cheese, high game; strong coffee; marmalade peel; pickles; coarse vegetables etc celery, watercress stalks, radish, cucumbers; raw apples; pineapple; Rich pastries: new bread.

---

[1] Thomas Cecil Hunt, 1901–1980. Educated at St Paul's School and Magdalen College, Oxford. Demonstrator and Tutor in Physiology, Oxford, 1924–5. Medical Registrar, St. Mary's Hospital, Paddington, 1928–30. A founder member, 1937, and later President of the British Society of Gastro-enterology. Lieutenant-Colonel, Royal Army Medical Corps, 1940–4 (on active service in North Africa; mentioned in despatches). Consultant, Persia Iraq Command; Brigadier, 1944–5. President of the World Organization of Gastro-enterology, 1962–66. Examiner in Medicine, Royal College of Physicians and London University. Author of several articles in medical journals on digestive diseases. Consulting Physician, St Mary's Hospital, Paddington, the Royal Masonic Hospital, and the King Edward VII Hospital for Officers. CBE, 1964. Vice-President of the Royal College of Physicians, 1967. Founder and Chairman of the British Digestive Foundation, 1970.

Do not go more than 3 hours without some food, eg half glass milk, or biscuits.

The *Medicine* twice a day, before lunch and dinner. The *powder* occasionally *when* the indigestion occurs (up to 4 times in 24 hours).

The *Exercises* not MORE than twice a day—and not longer than 15 minutes.

Cigars—to use a holder and reduce the number.

Port One glass after dinner. Brandy will suit better than port.

Vegetable soups are better than meat soups or broth.

Winston S. Churchill to Sir George Hennessy[1]

(Churchill papers: 2/257)

22 August 1936

Miss Joan Vickers[2] tells me she had a talk with you about coming forward as a candidate at the next County Council election. She did not think you were very encouraging but then of course I do not know the class of candidates who are now presenting themselves as you do.

She is a very clever young lady, who has done a good many years political work in Islington. She is a brilliant horsewoman and an independent and attractive spinster. She wishes to devote herself seriously to municipal politics. She could pay her own expenses at a County Council election.

[1] George Richard James Hennessy, 1877–1953. Educated at Eton. Joined the Militia, 1896. On active service in South Africa, 1899–1901. Retired with the rank of Major, 1907. Member of the Hampshire County Council, 1910–19. On active service on the western front, 1914–18 (despatches twice). Conservative MP for Winchester, 1918–31. Parliamentary Private Secretary, Ministry of Labour, 1921–2. Junior Lord of the Treasury, 1922–4 and 1924–5. Vice-Chamberlain of the Household, 1925–7; Treasurer, 1928–9 and 1931. Civil Commissioner for the North West of England, and for Liverpool, during the General Strike, 1926. Created Baronet, 1927. Vice-Chairman of the Conservative Party Organisation, 1931–41. Created Baron Windlesham, 1937.

[2] Joan Helen Vickers, 1907–   . Daughter of Churchill's stockbroker, H. C. Vickers. Her mother having died when she was 13 years old, Clementine Churchill had presented her at Court. Rode horses for the Irish Free State Army, in ladies' classes; show-jumped horses at the Dublin Show, and other shows in Eire. Hunted in both Eire and England. Member of the London County Council (for Norwood), 1937–45. Served with the British Red Cross in South-East Asia, 1944–5 (MBE). Unsuccessful Conservative candidate for Poplar, 1945. Colonial Service, Malaya, 1946–50. Conservative MP for Plymouth, Devonport, 1955–74. United Kingdom Delegate (Conservative) to the Council of Europe, 1967–74. Created Baroness (Life Peer), 1974. President of the Status of Women Committee, the International Friendship League, the Institute of Qualified Private Secretaries, and the International Bureau for the Suppression of Traffic in Persons.

I should be much obliged if you would let me know what her chances are, as she has asked me to advise her. I have known her and her father[1] for many years.

Adam Marshall Diston to Violet Pearman

(*Churchill papers: 8/533*)

22 August 1936

Dear Mrs Pearman,

I am enclosing notes on the General Strike and the Crisis of 1931, which I hope Mr Churchill may find useful. I'm afraid I have been a little unkind to Mr Ramsay MacDonald in certain passages—I don't seem to like him very much.

Only one set of notes is still to do—on the Statute of Westminster. I haven't yet got all the material I want for that, but I'll do it as soon as possible and send it on. If I address it to Chartwell will it be forwarded, or can you give me an address to which to send it? Once the Notes are out of the way, I shall get on with the articles, so as to have one or two drafts ready for Mr Churchill when he comes back. . . .

Winston S. Churchill to Anthony Eden

(*Churchill papers: 2/257*)

22 August 1936

You asked me dates for France. I am going to stay with Madame Balsan,[2] St Georges Motel, Dreux from Monday 24th to Saturday 29th, and I thought of staying Sunday 30th in Paris. I shall only be $1\frac{1}{2}$ hours from Paris by motor and could meet M Blum whenever convenient on Thursday, Friday, Saturday or Sunday. I do not expect I should do any harm. Will you perhaps ask the Embassy to get in touch with me.

---

[1] Horace Cecil Vickers, 1882–1944. Churchill's stockbroker. Apprenticed to a firm of stockbrokers as a clerk at the age of 12. Member of the London Stock Exchange, 1904. Founded the firm of Vickers, da Costa, of which he became the Senior Partner, 1917 (his son Ralph Cecil Vickers, MC, became its Chairman in 1972).

[2] Consuelo Vanderbilt, 1877–1964. Born in New York. She married Churchill's cousin the 9th Duke of Marlborough in 1895, at the age of 18, and obtained a divorce in 1921 (after which she married Lieutenant-Colonel Jacques Balsan, CMG). Mother of the 10th Duke of Marlborough and Lord Ivor Charles Spencer-Churchill. In the 1920s and 1930s Churchill was a frequent visitor at her château, St Georges Motel, near Dreux (some 50 miles to the west of Paris), and at her villa, Lou Seuil, at Eze in the South of France. In 1952 she published her memoirs, *The Glitter and the Gold*.

I have decided not to speak at Brussels, as I should have had to make too many explanations about appearing at this juncture on the same platform with Communists.

Thank you for inviting me to your Egyptian dinner, but I am afraid I should be the skeleton at the feast and anyhow I am going away. I am sending you a separate letter about Egypt.

All good wishes to you in your many difficulties.

Winston S. Churchill to Anthony Eden

(*Foreign Office papers: 371/20118*)

22 August 1936

My dear Anthony,

I asked Lloyd to give me a note of his conversation with Halifax, in order that I could circulate it to my friends.[1] As you know we were dissuaded by Lloyd from taking any action during the closing weeks of Parliament, and it is distressing to find that he feels himself misled, of course unintentionally, by the scope of the Treaty. This note was not of course written for your eye, but it seems to me that it might be useful for you to see it and realise some of the objections which are entertained by people who on general grounds would much like to support the Government, and particularly you.

I am personally deeply disturbed about what is being done without Parliament having any inkling. No doubt with the aid of the Socialists the

---

[1] Lord Lloyd had gone to see Lord Halifax at the Foreign Office on 11 August 1936, as Halifax was then deputizing for Eden, to say how 'perturbed' he was about the new and 'far more hurried' procedure now adopted towards the Egyptian Treaty. 'It seemed clear,' Lloyd told Halifax, that both Eden and Miles Lampson (the British High Commissioner in Egypt) 'were in full cry of the negotiation for a wholesale settlement in the civil as well as the military spheres and that this course was being pursued without any consultation with or authority from Parliament, and that the settlement was being rushed through at a time when Parliament would have no kind of opportunity to get information or to exert any influence over the final settlement of so delicate and vital a question. It was clear that Parliament was to be presented with a fait accompli; and be asked to choose whether it would support the terms of the Treaty—be they good or bad. . . .' After setting out his criticisms in detail, Lloyd ended his conversation with Halifax: 'I reminded Halifax that the Government had really shown a remarkable lack of candour about the whole affair. When Eden had addressed the House of Commons Egyptian Committee in July, he had given no inkling that anything so swift or so comprehensive was to be undertaken. Indeed he spoke so vaguely and gave so little information that after asking him whether he had no information at all to give the Committee who had come especially to hear about his proposal, and after he had expressed his regret that he could not do so, I left the room.' ('Note by Lord Lloyd on his conversation at Foreign Office with Lord Halifax on Egyptian Affairs, August 11th, 1936, sent to Mr Churchill on August 16th,' *Foreign Office papers, 371/20118, folios 36–9*).

Government will be able to carry anything of this kind, but it seems to me there is a tremendous case against it so far as I am at present informed.

Surely at least you should ask Russell Pasha[1] for his personal opinion about the police arrangements in Cairo. Will you kindly return the Lloyd memorandum when you have done with it.

Yours very sincerely,
Winston S. Churchill

Winston S. Churchill to George Harrap[2]

(*Churchill papers: 8/530*)

22 August 1936

Volume III is now so far completed that I feel I may ask you to send me a cheque, at your convenience. I am going away on Monday for a few weeks, but hope to have everything finished up then, except perhaps a few odd points which Mr Deakin will settle for me.

I think this is a pretty good volume. It certainly represents a most careful and far-reaching study. It has a good structure and I daresay anyone reading it for the first time will be caught up in the argument of the story, and not easily be able to escape. Mr Wood tells me that all is now in a thoroughly satisfactory condition for publication as early as you like in October.

---

[1] Thomas Wentworth Russell, 1879–1954. A great-grandson of the 6th Duke of Bedford, and of the 8th Baron Middleton. Educated at Haileybury and Trinity College, Cambridge. Entered the Egyptian Civil Service in 1902, as an Inspector, Ministry of the Interior. Assistant Commandant of Police, Alexandria, 1911. Commandant, Cairo City Police, 1917–46 (with the civil rank of Pasha, and the military rank of Major-General). Director of the Egyptian Central Narcotics Intelligence Bureau, 1929–46. Knighted, 1938. Vice-President of the League of Nations Advisory Committee on the Opium Traffic, 1939. In 1949 he published his memoirs, *Egyptian Service*.

[2] George Godfrey Harrap, 1867–1938. Educated at West Ham Model School; left school at the age of 14. In publishing all his life; began publishing modern language and other textbooks, 1901. Managing Director, George G. Harrap and Company Limited. Planned and launched Harrap's Standard French Dictionary, 1919–34. Published Churchill's biography of *Marlborough* (in four volumes 1933–8) and *Arms and the Covenant*, 1938; but declined to publish Churchill's *History of the English-Speaking Peoples* (which was published by Cassell).

Winston S. Churchill to F. W. Deakin

(*Churchill papers: 8/530*)

23 August 1936

I shall be sending the page proofs each day to Harraps. On them I shall mark the various queries for you. Settle these for the final re-print with Harraps without consulting me. I hope I can have the re-print of the Preface and preliminary matter by Mrs Pearman when she leaves on Thursday, also as much of the final revise as possible. Arrange with Harraps about any foot-notes or minor alterations that are required without reference to me. All I want to see in the final revise is outstanding queries. I have seen the General[1] and arranged with him about the maps. Please act in liaison between him and Harraps. You have no doubt got your notes of the various small points I mentioned to you. Any others will be found marked by me on the text I am now returning.

Winston S. Churchill to F. W. Deakin

(*Churchill papers: 8/530*)

23 August 1936   Chartwell

I send you a few miscellaneous papers here in case they may be of any use to you for the final revises. Return them all to me when you are finished. These papers were carefully sorted out. I do not suppose you will need them much. Pray come down here and make use of any books etc you may require.

Winston S. Churchill to C. C. Wood

(*Churchill papers: 8/530*)

23 August 1936

1. P. 292. *Valley* of Enz should read *Line* of the Enz.

2. The folder map of Oudenarde should portray the situation shown on page 423, with of course the French left and the princes round the Mill of Royegem. Hachures will illustrate this better than contours.

---

[1] Pakenham-Walsh; in fact a Brigadier, and referred to as such in Churchill's letter to C. C. Wood of the same date. He was appointed Major-General in June 1939.

3. Upon further consideration, I remain of the opinion that the folder map of Ramillies is not necessary. The old map will do, and I find the draftsman would have to re-draw the folder. The old map will be put at the end of the Chapter.

4. P. 145. Map 12A was originally designed for this, but it is not required here and it is better where it is now, on page 395.

5. I agree with you that the map of Spain on page 179 should go to 175. It will not be quite a full page, but there is enough matter to adjust the paging to the end of the chapter.

6. You have not sent me your list of folder maps. I presume it will be as follows:—

a. The old map of Ramillies.
b. Coloured folder map of Oudenarde.
c. Folder map of Spain (which need not be coloured) showing the provinces, all names mentioned in the text, and the principal places.
d. Coloured folder map of Europe showing the two sides in the war. This is the big red and blue map taken from Volume II.
e. Folder map of the Western Netherlands. This is already drawn by the Brigadier. Note: The folder map of the whole of the Netherlands which figured in Vol. II is not now required.

All these are now in train, and I have settled the above points in concert with the Brigadier.

I leave tomorrow (Monday). I will send you the rest of the page proofs in the next three days. Mrs Pearman who leaves on Thursday will bring out as much of the second revise as you have done. I wish myself to interleave the illustrations, and will do so in the final revise. Practically everything has been cleared up and I do not expect there will be any alterations worth speaking of in the next revise. All questions of footnotes etc should be settled between you and Mr Deakin without reference to me. The Brigadier has all the maps now and I do not wish to see any of them again except the Oudenarde sketch which can be sent to me in Paris next Sunday. I am counting on you to let Mrs Pearman have the revise of the preliminary matter including the preface when she leaves on Thursday. I do not propose to read the final revises, but only to look at the points you mark. Therefore let everything be marked clearly about which there is any doubt.

Winston S. Churchill to Thomas Hunt

(*Churchill papers: 1/285*)

23 August 1936

Many thanks for your letter, directions and medicines.

You do not say how long before meals the medicine should be taken, nor how many bottles of it. Should I leave off as soon as I feel better, or take it for a certain period?

About the powder. You do not say whether it may be taken before or after meals, and how long before or after. Do I understand it can be taken any time when there is indigestion?

Diet. I note what you wish me to avoid. I presume if I get stronger I can get bolder. I do not like vegetable soups and always have chicken broth, or some variant of it, made for me. I hope you do not attach importance to this.

Cigars. The holder is being employed and numbers will, I trust, be reduced.

Port—noted. I must not drink brandy before the end of the year, as I have a wager.[1]

I will endeavour to cat a few sandwiches for tea, and have a little soup and sandwiches before I go to bed about midnight. As I do not breakfast till 8.30 and lunch at 1.15 there is no need to eat anything between whiles.

I may say I have been quite all right these last few days and slept extremely well last night, after eating sandwiches before retiring. I will let you know how I get on.

If you will address your letter to my secretary, Mrs Pearman, who is coming out to France on Wednesday next, she can if necessary bring extra bottles of the medicine, assuming they are needed.

Desmond Morton to Military Intelligence [2]

(*Cabinet papers: 21/437*)

25 August 1936   Industrial Intelligence Centre [3]

With reference to DPM 3—Discussion between the Prime Minister and a Delegation from Parliament on 29th July, 1936:—

[1] The wager was with Lord Rothermere (see page 6, note 1). If Churchill drank no brandy between his 61st and 62nd birthdays, that is between 30 November 1935 and 30 November 1936, he would receive £600. This was the equivalent of more than £10,000 in September 1981.

[2] Addressed to MI1, a copy of this memorandum was sent by Morton to Colonel Ismay at the Committee of Imperial Defence.

[3] This document was number ICF 505 of the Industrial Intelligence Centre's numbered memoranda.

MI3B have asked for our assistance in commenting on certain points raised regarding German armaments. Our views on these points are as follows:—

1. *Page 9, line 6 and on.*

The statement that Germany was planning the mobilisation of industry with a view to rearmament for some years before the National Socialist Government came to power, is correct. This process was well under way soon after the IAMCC[1] left the country—say in 1928/29.

2. *Page 11, line 13. 'Ammunition plants'.*

If this wording can be read to mean that between February 1933 and the present time, some 400 to 500 different factories have, at one time or another, received an order for the manufacture of some component of 'ammunition' as that word is defined in the text, it may be correct. In the absence of detailed supporting information, we would, however, find it impossible to believe that anything like 400 factories have been delivering complete filled or unfilled 'ammunition' to the German Government.

3. *Page 11, line 17.*

It is not clear to us what is meant by the suggestion that Germany now possesses stocks of ammunition approaching in size the quantities 'that were needed to fight the campaign of 1918'. If it is suggested that German stocks of ammunition approach the total quantity manufactured in that country in the whole of 1918, it is, in our opinion, quite incorrect. Nor could the suggestion be justified that at the moment the same number of factories or factory-hands are employed on ammunition manufacture in Germany as in 1918.

On the other hand, if a slip has been made in the date, it can readily be accepted that more factories and workmen are actually employed on ammunition manufacture today than were so employed at the outbreak of the last war in 1914.

4. *Page 11, line 23.*

The idea conveyed that the Germans do not hesitate to scrap accumulated armament stores in the event of the discovery and acceptance of definitely improved types, is correct. Incidentally, this is one of the more striking features of the present German rearmament policy.

[1] The Inter-Allied Military Control Commission, set up in 1920 as a result of the Treaty of Versailles.

5. *Page 11, line 25.*

The 'forging process' referred to is doubtless the EUMOCO shell forging plant, of which full particulars are in the possession of the War Office. The German Government actually holds the patents of several improved patterns, which are not for sale. The best of these is reported to be the invention of the BORSIG WERKE, and to have been manufactured and installed in several works.

6. *Page 13, line 7.*

According to our information about 11,000 guns of calibres between 3·7 cm and 30·5 cm will have been delivered by German industry between 1933 and the end of 1936. The rate of delivery was greater last year than in 1933 or 1934. It is not impossible that 4,000 or more guns of the calibres mentioned were delivered in 1935, but 5,000 appears rather too large an estimate.

7. *Page 13, line 12.*

It is an exaggeration to suggest that German industry can at once maintain in the field a force as large as was maintained by the UK in 1918, if the wastage and expenditure is to be anything like on the scale of that year. According to our information Germany might forthwith be able to maintain about 36 divisions with a high rate of wastage and expenditure or perhaps up to 50 divisions with a rate of expenditure comparable to that of 1914.

I am sending a copy of this note to the Deputy Secretary[1] of the Committee of Imperial Defence.

D. Morton

[1] Hastings Lionel Ismay, 1887–1965. Educated at Charterhouse and Sandhurst. 2nd Lieutenant, 1905; Captain, 1914. On active service in India, 1908 and the Somaliland, 1914–20 (DSO). Staff College, Quetta, 1922. Assistant Secretary, Committee of Imperial Defence, 1925–30. Military Secretary to the Viceroy of India (Lord Willingdon), 1931–3. Colonel, 1932. Deputy Secretary, Committee of Imperial Defence, 1936–8; Secretary (in succession to Sir Maurice Hankey), 1938. Major General, 1939. Chief of Staff to the Minister of Defence (Churchill), 1940–5. Knighted, 1940. Deputy Secretary (military) to the War Cabinet, 1940–5. Lieutenant-General, 1942. General, 1944. Chief of Staff to the Viceroy of India (Lord Mountbatten), 1947. Created Baron, 1947. Secretary of State for Commonwealth Relations, 1951–2. Secretary-General of NATO, 1952–7. Knight of the Garter, 1957. He published his memoirs in 1960.

Neville Chamberlain to Winston S. Churchill

(*Churchill papers: 2/257*)

25 August 1936   11 Downing Street

My dear Winston,

Many thanks for your note. I was very sorry myself (for more reasons than one) that I could not be at the meeting about defence but I have told my people to keep the transcript till I get back next month when I shall certainly read it carefully. I daresay you will have an interesting time in Paris. I have just been reading Bodley's[1] France written nearly 40 years ago & have been astonished to find how applicable it is to modern conditions in that country.

Yours sincerely,
N. Chamberlain

Winston S. Churchill to C. C. Wood

(*Churchill papers: 8/530*)

28 August 1936   Saint-Georges-Motel

I telegraphed to Mr Deakin asking him to meet me at the Ritz Hotel, Paris, at noon on Monday, and I hope to give him then everything that is outstanding. I will send back the final proofs by him in one block.

There are one or two general points:—

1. Numbers of battalions, squadrons and cannons.

We have followed no general principle. You will find in the revises of the page proofs which I have just completed, numerous instances both of spelling and figures in the same circumstances. In the final revises pray make the treatment uniform on the following lines:—

When numbers of battalions etc are used in the course of the narrative they should be spelt eg 'Cadogan brought up six battalions.' Where there is the enumeration of the strength of armies, figures may be used eg 'Marlborough mustered 120 battalions and 230 squadrons.' All other numbers seem to be satisfactorily adjusted.

I think it would be a very good thing if you got one of your proof-readers

[1] John Edward Courtenay Bodley, 1853–1925. Educated at Balliol College, Oxford. Barrister, Inner Temple, 1874. Private Secretary to Sir Charles Dilke, 1882–5. Published his first book, *France*, in 1898. His subsequent books included *The Church in France* (1906), and *Romance of the Battle Line in France* (1920). One of his daughters, Ava, married Ralph Wigram, who in 1936 was head of the Central Department of the Foreign Office.

who has not read it before, and whose eye is clear, to read through and enforce this principle.

Your letter of the 25th, about the folder map of Spain. This had best be at the end of the book facing the reader, just behind the Netherlands map and just before the blue and red one of Europe. All these three follow each other in that order.

I have noted three frightful mistakes altering the whole sense in the corrections of my last revise, in the first 80 pages. I am of course checking every correction. All the more therefore does this make it necessary that a fresh eye should read it through. In two cases utter nonsense followed from the correction.

Commas. The book about stops which I have read says that when a single word, or two words are interpolated it is optional whether you use a comma or not. I do not like the high punctuation. But it doesn't matter so long as the same thing is done all through.

Yours sincerely,
Winston S. Churchill

Winston S. Churchill to Thomas Hunt

(*Churchill papers: 1/285*)

28 August 1936 Saint-Georges-Motel

Many thanks for your letter of the 24th. I have had a good deal of indigestion since arriving here. Of course painting always tries me highly, but I cannot give it up on my holidays. It is the mental concentration which seems to affect the stomach. I always paint standing up, as otherwise the indigestion would be very severe. I mention this as it may give you some clue.

I have taken the brown medicine regularly, and have eaten a few mouthfuls of soup or sandwiches at five o'clock and at midnight. The indigestion comes on during the night but disappears after the exercises in the morning.

Kindly say whether if the powder is taken the other medicine should be discontinued, or can they both be taken within half an hour of one another? I gather you do not mind whether the powder is taken before or after meals nor how close to them. I have only taken it three times so far. It does not make much difference.

Winston S. Churchill to Brigadier Pakenham-Walsh

(*Churchill papers: 8/530*)

31 August 1936

Oudenarde. This is I suppose about 7.30 pm. The map looks all right subject to your corrections, but there is no need to use colours, either blue or red, for the names of the generals. These should be printed according to our ordinary rule, in black, the French being slanting cap letters and the Allies ordinary upright. This will simplify the appearance. Lottum and Cadogan cannot be printed where they are now and must be brought to the other side of the road. Now that they are in black it will be all right. Have you got enough French troops inside the net? Vendôme's personal position should be shown opposite Herlegem. It would be better to put Marlborough behind the line of the Hanoverians and the word 'Hanoverians' in front. Similarly Eugene should be behind the line of troops, while Argyle, Lottum and Cadogan could be printed not quite as large from left to right, in front of him. The troops can advance almost to the Diepenbeck and almost up to the French to make room for these names. The troops were in close contact. All the map details should be black except blue for the Scheldt and the streams. Overkirk's name must be inserted. Would it not be well to have a few more of Overkirk's troops further up the arrow in advance of those you now have, mentioning the Prince of Orange? I should show troops crossing the bridges in Oudenarde in column route by simply prolonging the red discontinuous dots, also coming over the pontoon bridges. Remember Eugene said they were crossing late in the night. If possible have a dotted line showing Lottum as arriving from Marlborough's front. I have made a few scribbles.

No border is required for the map which may if convenient run the whole length of the page.

Winston S. Churchill to C. C. Wood

(*Churchill papers: 8/530*)

31 August 1936   As from The Ritz Hotel,
                                                                          Paris

Dear Mr Wood,

Your first batch of final revises sent off on Thursday reached me at Dreux this morning (Monday). The French reject a letter over a certain weight, class it as a parcel, and it arrives four or five days late. Consequently I had to leave Dreux without receiving sections from 370 to 435. I have given Mr Deakin these missing sections provisionally corrected and will send the others as soon as I receive your missing package. It would always be better to employ several envelopes when sending proofs to France. I am now remaining over till tomorrow in Paris, so I hope to retrieve the package before leaving.

2. Map 271 of the Lines of Stollhofen. Clearly this will require alteration as I had not noticed that it no longer was up to date. A new block must be made. Mr Deakin brings the corrections. I hope there will be time for these.

3. The words 'French advance barred' should be omitted. Likewise the arrow indicating their march. The fortifications should be prolonged as shown by me in red from the word Stollhofen to the town of Philippsburg. The line is not continuous and in black. Durlach and Rastadt mentioned on page 272 should both be inserted if they come into the picture.

The Order of Battle for Oudenarde comes out so poor and dull when not reproduced in colour, that it is not worth including. Moreover we have not been able to get in touch with the gentleman whose permission appears to be required.

September 1936

Violet Pearman to Percy Cudlipp [1]
(Churchill papers: 8/534)

1 September 1936   Paris [2]

Dear Mr Cudlipp,

Herewith Mr Churchill's article for this week.[3] As he goes to Cannes to-night at 8 pm from Paris, he will not be able to see a proof, but will telegraph to you any amendments that may be necessary, after he has carefully perused the carbon copy on his journey down.

Winston S. Churchill to C. C. Wood
(Churchill papers: 8/530)

2 September 1936   As from
                                                    Château de l'Horizon,
                                                             Cannes

I must renew my request about numbers of battalions and squadrons. I notice, reading through for the last time, that we are following no principle. I hope this will be looked into.

---

[1] Percy Cudlipp, 1905–1962. Educated in Cardiff. Dramatic critic and humorous column-ist, *Sunday News* (London), 1925–9. Joined the *Evening Standard*, as its film critic, 1929; Assistant Editor, 1931; Editor, 1933–8. Editorial Manager, *Daily Herald*, 1938–40; Editor, 1940–53. Columnist, *News Chronicle*, 1954–6. Editor, *New Scientist*, 1956–62.

[2] At 8 pm on 1 September 1936 Churchill left Paris, where he had been staying at the Ritz hotel, for the Château de l'Horizon, Maxine Elliot's villa at Golfe Juan, in the South of France.

[3] 'Enemies to the Left', published in the *Evening Standard* on 4 September 1936, and subse-quently reprinted in Churchill's volume of collected articles *Step by Step*. 'Everywhere,' Churchill wrote, 'the manufacture of munitions proceeds apace, and science burrows its insulted head in the filth of slaughterous inventions. Only unarmed, unthinking Britain nurses the illusion of security.' The rest of the article was about the Soviet Purge trials. In Moscow, Churchill pointed out, many of the Bolshevik leaders of 1917 were being executed. 'The odd thing is,' he wrote, 'that such an exhibition should be expected to make a good impression outside Russia. We see the gulf between the Communist mentality and the wider world.' Churchill continued: 'The second point to notice is that these victims were nearly all

The second packet has not yet reached me. I hope it will come tomorrow. I shall be glad to receive the final proofs as they are struck, but do not delay printing. Settle all outstanding points with Mr Deakin. In sending out the final proofs, send them in three or four signatures at a time in separate envelopes and by air mail.

Violet Pearman to Percy Cudlipp

(*Churchill papers: 8/534*)

3 September 1936

Dear Mr Cudlipp,

I enclose herewith a copy of the telegram I sent to you regarding the corrections in the typescript of Mr Churchill's article, and cannot imagine why they were unintelligible. I suppose in the usual French fashion words had been misspelled making complete nonsense of the whole lot. This often happens, but apparently this time they had done their very worst. But fortunately I had just time before the aeroplane departed to make Mr Churchill's most important amendments on the top copy, and the others for Curtis Brown[1] were actually made by someone else on the journey here.

Winston S. Churchill to the Duchess of Marlborough: telegram

(*Churchill papers: 1/285*)

3 September 1936   Château de l'Horizon

Was unable get painting outfit going through Paris. Now ordering England. Give my love to Consuelo.

Winston

Jews. Evidently the Nationalist elements represented by Stalin and the Soviet armies are developing the same prejudices against the Chosen People as are so painfully evident in Germany. Here again extremes meet, and meet on a common platform of hate and cruelty. Perhaps, Churchill concluded, the Purge trials were 'less a manifestation of world propaganda than an act of self-preservation by a community which fears, and has reason to fear, the sharp German sword'.

[1] Adam Curtis Brown, 1866–1945. Educated in the United States. Editorial Staff, *Buffalo Express*, 1884–94. *New York Press* Sunday Editor, 1894–8; London correspondent, 1898–1910. Established the International Publishing Bureau, London, 1900; Managing Director, 1900–16. Managing Director, Curtis Brown Ltd, Literary Agents, 1916–45.

Winston S. Churchill to Clementine Churchill

(*Spencer-Churchill papers*)

5 September 1936   Château de l'Horizon

My darling.

I have been painting all day & every day. I have found a beautiful clear river—the Loup—& a quiet wild spot, & I study the clear water. I have done two variants which I hope you will admire as much as I do! Wow! Tomorrow I go to lunch with Muriel[1] (who came over here) at Maryland. She is asking the Lloyds who are near by. After lunch I shall have another go at the little port of St Jean Cap Ferrat—wh you know I have several times attempted.

The weather has been bright & warm, but tonight there is more wind & also cloud & mist. Loelia[2] left yesterday & we have here only Doris,[3] a young French film actress (vy pretty but not vy successful), Lord Queensberry's younger brother[4] (who lost a leg in the war). But many come as usual to bathe & lunch—among others the Polignacs[5] (I can't remember them all— or indeed any) bathe. We were all taken to lunch with Mrs Corrigan![6] I could not avoid it without being abrupt. . . .

---

[1] Muriel Thetis Wilson, 1871–1964. Daughter of Arthur Wilson of Tranby Croft. A friend of Churchill since his twenties, she declined his proposal of marriage. In 1917 she married Major Richard Edward Warde (1884–1932).

[2] Loelia Mary Ponsonby, only daughter of the 1st Baron Sysonby. In 1930 she married the 2nd Duke of Westminster (as his third wife). The marriage was dissolved in 1947. In 1969 she married Sir Martin Alexander Lindsay of Dowhill, CBE, DSO.

[3] Jessica Doris de le Vigne, 1901–1942. Born in Streatham, the daughter of a Belgian who had come to London as a boy, and became a general merchant, as well as Secretary of the London Chess Club. His daughter changed her surname to 'Delavigne' and declared to a friend: 'I'm going to marry a Lord.' In 1928 she married Viscount Castlerosse (later 6th Earl of Kenmare). They were divorced in 1938. In the United States, 1940; returned to Britain, 1941; died of an overdose of drugs, 1942.

[4] Lord Cecil Charles Douglas, 1898–1953. Brother of the 11th Marquess of Queensberry. Educated at Lancing and Sandhurst. On active service, 1916–18. Lieutenant, King's Own Scottish Borderers, and Royal Flying Corps, (when he was wounded, losing a leg).

[5] On 11 June 1936 Harold Nicolson wrote in his diary, of Sibyl Colefax's dinner party for King Edward VIII: 'Rubinstein started to play Chopin. More people drifted in—the Winston Churchills, Madame de Polignac, Daisy Fellowes, Noel Coward, the Kenneth Clarks. Madame de Polignac sat herself down near the piano to listen to Rubinstein. I have seldom seen a woman sit so firmly: there was determination in every line of her bum'.

[6] Laura Corrigan. Described by Loelia, Duchess of Westminster as one of those hostesses 'who make a sort of hobby of it, and collect a salon as deliberately as one might collect stamps . . . the speciality of Lady Colefax was entertaining the intelligentsia; Mrs Corrigan, on the other hand went in for titles. Immensely rich and with a docile husband, she engaged a brilliant social secretary who knew everybody and how things should be run, rented a large house and set out to have the most sensational parties in London. However, money by itself is never enough, it is ultimately the personality of the hostess which matters and if Mrs

The hostess[1] was so attentive to her guests that she seemed to have no time to eat or even sit down. No one could cavil at this: & she affirmed to enjoy it. I have just completed the first of my new articles for the News of the W. I mean to do at least three before I leave. They are vy lucrative. It wd be folly not to work them off in view of many uncertainties.[2]

I have arranged to go to the manoeuvres at Aix in Provence on Wed 9th & 10th.

I am to have a formal invitation. I return here, & leave Sunday night 13th for Paris. The 14th & 15th I go to visit the Maginot line. It entails sleeping at Metz one night. I may stay 17th in Paris if there are any interesting people to see. I will be with you for the week end—if not sooner.

Corrigan has not been such a "character" she could never have stormed Society and won. She had a painted face and was small and sprightly and I have seen her stand on her head at a party (having first tied a scarf round her skirt for modesty's sake), from which position she assured everyone that it was delightfully comfortable and good for the health. She was badly educated and every sort of malapropism was attributed to her, most of them probably apocryphal. She is supposed to have said of some cathedral that the flying buttocks were magnificent; when, after a cruise, she was asked if she had seen the Dardanelles she replied that she did have a letter of introduction to them but she hadn't sent it. She was rumoured to be bald as the result of some accident in her obscure early life and her guests took a morbid interest in her wig, or rather wigs, for there appeared to be a number of them . . . .' (*Grace and Favour*, 1961).

[1] Jessie Dermot, 1871–1940. Born in Rockland, Maine, USA, the daughter of Captain Tom Dermot, a New England Republican. Educated at Notre Dame Academy, Roxbury, Massachusetts. Took the name 'Maxine Elliot' for her stage career. Made her first stage appearance in New York in 1890, at the age of 19, in the melodrama, *The Middleman*. First appeared on the London stage in 1895, as Silvia in *The Two Gentlemen of Verona* and as Hermia in *A Midsummer Night's Dream*. In 1896 she married (as her second husband) the American comic actor, Nat Goodwin, whom she accompanied that year on a tour of Australia; this marriage was later dissolved. She was first seen as a 'star' in *Her Own Way* in Buffalo and New York, 1903, and in London, 1905. In 1908 she opened her own theatre, the Maxine Elliot Theatre in New York. In 1914 she organized a Belgian Relief Barge, from which in fifteen months she fed and clothed some 350,000 refugees. Appeared in films, 1916–17, including *The Eternal Magdalen* and *Fighting Odds*. From 1920 until her death she lived at the Château de l'Horizon, Golfe Juan, just east of Cannes.

[2] Churchill's *News of the World* articles were eventually published as a series of thirteen, entitled 'Great Events of Our Time', the first on 30 May 1937 ('The Awful Crime that Shook Civilization—Sarajevo'), followed by 'Tragedy of the Torpedoed Lusitania' (6 June 1937), 'The Decisive Factor in the Allied Victory' (13 June 1937), 'When the Crash came to the United States' (20 June 1937), 'The Dominions are Partners of Empire' (27 June 1937), 'Chief Factors in our Social Revolution' (4 July 1937), 'This Age of Government by Great Dictators' (10 October 1937), 'Japan's Swift Rise to her Place in the Sun' (17 October 1937), 'Will Japan Decide to Accept the Olive Branch?' (24 October 1937), 'Vision of the Future through Eyes of Science' (31 October 1937), 'Life in a World Controlled by the Scientists' (7 November 1937), 'Mankind is Confronted with one Supreme Task (14 November 1937), 'A Federation for Peace is the Hope of the World' (21 November 1937). For the way in which these articles were prepared, see Adam Marshall Diston's letter of 18 September 1936, quoted on page 345.

I think the Doctor's medicine is doing me good. I have been better today (although painting) than for a long time.

I am thankful the Spanish Nationalists are making progress. They are the only ones who have the power of attack. The others can only die sitting. Horrible! But better for the safety of all if the Communists are crushed. I see B did not turn up at the Council, in spite of Palestine becoming so grievous & all the rest of it.[1]

My darling I do hope yr swimming has been arranged for. It was indeed unfortunate that Arnold's[2] holiday shd come at this moment, for I expect it will be difficult for anyone else to make the filter work well. I wish I could be with you to adjust it.

Tender love my sweet Clemmie,
Always your devoted loving husband,
W

[sketch of pig]

Lord Lloyd to his son

(*Lloyd papers*)

6 September 1936

Yesterday we went to lunch with Muriel Wilson at the villa near by. Winston had come over from Maxine Elliot's at the Château de l'Horizon at Cannes (the villa which the king *had* been going to take) to meet us at lunch. He arrived in an enormous Texan hat, the car full of easels & painting appliances plus the faithful Inches[3] and was in very good form, but anxious & distressed as we all are at the increasing gravity of the Palestine situation as well as Government's ineptitude in dealing with it. I warned Billy Gore[4]

---

[1] Baldwin had not attended the recent meeting of the Council of the League of Nations, a body made up of 14 member States (including 5 permanent members, of whom Great Britain was one). The Council which met three times a year, and was authorized by the League of Nations Assembly to deal at its meetings 'with any matter within the sphere of action of the League or affecting the peace of the world', in particular Disarmament, the Private Manufacture of Arms, Disputes, Expulsions and Mandates.

[2] The estate carpenter and odd-job man at Chartwell.

[3] Churchill's valet. Grace Hamblin recalls: 'he was a tremendous character—always overworked, always perspiring, sometimes drunk! He was the Valet, and we also had a rather grand Butler and Footman, in those days' (*letter to the author, 12 June 1978*).

[4] William George Arthur Ormsby Gore, 1885–1965. Educated at Eton and New College, Oxford. Conservative MP, 1910–38. Intelligence Officer, Arab Bureau, Cairo, 1916. Assistant Secretary, War Cabinet, 1917–18. Member of the British Delegation (Middle East Section) to the Paris Peace Conference, 1919. British Official Representative on the Permanent Mandates Commission of the League of Nations, 1920. Under-Secretary of State for the Colonies, 1922–4, and 1924–9. Privy Councillor, 1927. First Commissioner of Works,

before I left London that he would be compelled to concede the perfectly reasonable Arab demand in respect of Jewish immigration & at the same time would need far more action & intensive military preparation. He disbelieved me as regards the latter.

Winston S. Churchill to Pierre-Etienne Flandin: telegram

(*Churchill papers: 1/285*)

8 September 1936   Cannes

Should like very much to arrive by train from Cannes 7.30 Sunday morning and leave for Paris Monday 10.9 if agreeable to you. Looking forward much to seeing you.

Winston Churchill

Winston S. Churchill to Lloyd Thomas: [1] *telegram*

(*Churchill papers: 2/267*)

8 September 1936

Should be glad bring Lord Lloyd instead of Lord Winterton. Will you tell Ambassador delighted accept his invitation dine and sleep Monday night. Arrive Paris Monday morning eight o'clock. Trust will be convenient.

Churchill

1932–6. Secretary of State for the Colonies, 1936–8. Succeeded his father as 4th Baron Harlech, 1938. High Commisioner, South Africa, 1941–4. Chairman of both the Midland Bank, and the Bank of West Africa. A Trustee of both the Tate and National Galleries.

[1] Hugh Lloyd Thomas, 1888–1938. Educated at Eton and New College, Oxford. Entered the Foreign Office, 1912. Assigned to Constantinople, 1913. Granted an allowance for knowledge of Turkish, 1914. Promoted 3rd Secretary, 1914. Transferred to Cairo on the outbreak of hostilities between Great Britain and Turkey, November 1914. Passed an examination in International Law, and granted an allowance for knowledge of Arabic, 1915. Transferred to Rome and promoted to 2nd Secretary, 1919; 1st Secretary 1920. Transferred to Madrid, 1922; transferred to the Foreign Office, and promoted to Assistant Private Secretary to the Secretary of State, 1924. Attached to the Garter Mission to Japan, promoted to Counsellor in the Diplomatic Service, 1929. Assistant Private Secretary to the Prince of Wales, 1929–35. CVO, 1929. Minister Plenipotentiary, Paris, from 1935 until his death (he was killed by a fall while steeple-chasing).

Clementine Churchill to Winston S. Churchill

(*Spencer-Churchill papers*)

8 September 1936 Chartwell

My Darling Winston,

How wise you are to be in the South for here it is autumnal. I have had the furnace let out under the pool as no one bathes, but the filter is kept working so that in the pale fitful sunlight the pool looks like a great aquamarine. I have been home (this evening) a week, but altho' nothing of consequence has really been happening I have hardly had a moment to sit down!

Winston S. Churchill to Léon Blum

(*Churchill papers: 2/267*)

9 September 1936

I promised to write to you about my visit to the fortress line which you so kindly approved. However that is being all satisfactorily arranged through the Embassy, no doubt with your consent.

I have had a most interesting day with General Gamelin[1] at the manoeuvres. I was very pleased with all I saw.

I thought you might be interested to see the enclosed cutting from The Morning Post, which has hitherto been very much opposed to you.[2]

---

[1] Maurice Gustave Gamelin, 1872–1958. Born in Paris. 2nd Lieutenant, 1893. Lieutenant-Colonel, 1914. Served on General Joffre's Staff, 1911–17; drafted the principal directives at the battle of the Marne, 1914. Commanded a brigade during the battle of the Somme, 1916. Commanded the 9th Infantry Division, 1917–18. Military Assistant to the Syrian High Commissioner, 1925–8, when he defeated the Druse rebellion. Commanded the 20th Army Corps (Nancy), 1929. Army Chief of Staff, 1931. Inspector-General of the Army and Vice-President of the War Council, 1935–7. Chief of the General Staff of National Defence, January 1938–September 1939. Honorary knighthood, 1938. Generalissimo, commanding the French Land Forces, September 1939–May 1940, when he was superseded and later interned by the Vichy regime. Tried for having 'weakened the spirit of the French armies', 1941. Deported to Buchenwald Concentration Camp, 1943–5. Liberated by American troops, May 1945.

[2] In its leading article on 8 September 1936 the *Morning Post* described Léon Blum as 'a courageous man' who had not 'flinched' during the international crisis, and had gained and guided the support of a 'motley assortment of politicians, from palest pink to brightest red'. Although Blum was a Socialist who sympathized with the Spanish Government, he had 'Proposed the pact of non-intervention which is the one hope of localising the Spanish Civil War', and although he was a Jew he welcomed Dr Schacht to Paris because of what he described as 'the will to maintain peace'. But Blum was not a pacifist, and he had renewed the Franco-Polish alliance and introduced measures to strengthen the French Army. The *Morning Post* approved of these decisions, telling its readers: 'This Jew has shown some European statesmen what a good European should be'.

Winston S. Churchill to Clementine Churchill
(*Spencer-Churchill papers*)

13 September 1936   Domecy-sur-Cure, Yonne

My darling,

I arrived here this morning It is 120 kilometres from Dijon by car. We are in the heart of France: Flandin's home, by the banks of the clear swift-flowing Cure. We have exhausted the possibilities of conversation on politics, & I have retired to bed to write to you.

The eleven days I passed with Maxine were pleasant—The weather beautiful, every comfort, & I have painted six beautiful pictures, besides the three at Dreux. I am sending them home tomorrow or next day by Mrs P: but do not unpack them till I come: for I want to do the honours with them for yr benefit myself.

I dined near Toulon with Frau Friedlander Fuld now Mrs Goldsmith Rothschild.[1] She was pathetic about the treatment of the Jews in Germany. They have a terrible time. She is a remarkable woman.

I caught the night train to Dijon. I have been reconverted to Mah Jong: & I propose to introduce it into Chartwell. It all comes back in a few games, & really it is most amusing. I was vy lucky & beat them all.

They came over to luncheon at the pool, a Miss Cecile de Rothschild,[2] daughter of Robert,[3] who has one of the most beautiful oval faces I have ever seen. The perfect Madonna. She was a Jewess we often forget—or Rachel at the Well. A sweet girl with whom I made some progress. I shd like you to see her—she lives at St Raphael or Paris.

The manoeuvres were vy interesting. I drove about all day with General Gamelin the Generalissimo, who was communicative on serious topics. There was nothing to see, as all the troops were hidden in holes or under bushes.

---

[1] Marie-Anne Friedländer-Fuld, 1892–1973. The only daughter of a German coal magnate, Herr von Friedländer-Fuld, of Berlin, who died in 1916; leaving her coal mines worth £5 million. In January 1914 she married Clementine Churchill's cousin, Jack Mitford, son of the first Baron Redesdale; the marriage was annulled later in the same year, and she subsequently married Baron Rudolph de Goldschmidt-Rothschild, a cousin of James de Rothschild, MP. In May 1940 she fled to the United States. On learning of the liberation of Paris in August 1944 she donated Van Gogh's *L'Arlesienne* to the Louvre. Later a convert to Catholicism.

[2] Cecile de Rothschild, 1913–   . Only daughter of Baron Robert de Rothschild. A first-class golfer, later famous for her superb collection of objets d'art. Resident in England and America, 1939–45. Active in the Free French Committee for Prisoners of War, 1940–5. Resident in Paris since 1945. Unmarried.

[3] Robert Phillip Gustav de Rothschild, 1880–1946. An Ingénieur des Mines. The present Lord Rothschild writes: 'he is to be distinguished from most other Rothschild collectors in that he bought contemporary pictures' (*letter to the author, 14 November 1978*). His nephew Edmund de Rothschild writes: 'He supported polo matches at Laversine, entertained widely and was greatly admired (*letter to the author, 5 November 1981*). His two sons, Alain and Elie, who saw active service in the French Army in 1940, were both prisoners-of-war in Germany, 1940–5.

But to anyone with military knowledge it was most instructive. The officers of the French army are impressive by their gravity & competence. One feels the strength of the nation resides in its army. Tomorrow I go to Paris, dine & sleep at the Embassy, & then the Tuesday go to the fortress line. The military attaché[1] & Lloyd are coming with me. It will be a pilgrimage well worth making. I shall perhaps stay 17th in Paris, and perhaps make a little 'discours' to the journalists, before returning.

Everything gets worse, except that the Nationalists (as they insist on being called) are winning. *Secret.* F thinks that the French communists were paid at the election, not by Russia, but by *Germany*—in order to weaken France! Pretty cynical if true. This would explain why Stalin executed the Bolshevik old guard: ie in order to break the Orthodox Communists who were disobeying his orders about not disturbing France. On this showing it looks as if the Russians are trying to move to the right—& with sincerity. Of course this is only surmise.

My darling I got yr letter, & was much pleased by all yr Chartwell news.

I wonder how Diana is getting on. It must be vy near now.[2] F has the same family as we have. One married & 2 unmarried daughters, & a son. You would like to see this charming little place in a lovely valley. He has a special office & waiting room at the gate to receive his constituents; & once a month about eighty come to a levée. I explained the advantages of not having a home in one's constituency.

People are vy anxious here: but I do not feel that there will be a disaster internally. Read what I have written in the Evening Standard next Friday.[2]

---

[1] Colonel Beaumont-Nesbitt, see page 355–6, note 1.

[2] Diana Sandys was expecting her first child, and Churchill's first grandchild.

[3] On Friday, 18 September 1936, the *Evening Standard* published Churchill's article, 'A Testing Time For France'. Some people, he wrote, believed that the French Communists were about to plunge France 'into the same ferocious welter as they have plunged Spain' or that, alternatively Nazi propaganda would triumph in France. Churchill disagreed, writing in his article: 'I am very decidedly of the opinion that France is going to come through her troubles this autumn and winter, not only without any fatal catastrophe, but with an actual accretion of moral and material strength. No doubt parliamentary countries cannot present the same show of unity as can be commanded by Nazi or Communist regimes. Not to criticize the government of the day is, in a parliamentary country, to be out of the fashion. To criticize it in a Nazi or Communist State is to be sent to the concentration camp, the gaol or the grave. It must not, however, be supposed that because no expression is allowed to Russian and German feelings, everyone in those countries are entirely satisfied with their lot. In France as in England every form of discontent can manifest itself. Troubles rise to the surface, and at the same time also there often rise forces to control or remedy them.' Churchill added: 'English people who speak slightingly of the strength of the French Republic should remember that it is common ground between all parties in France at the present moment that at least two years' compulsory military service should be required of every Frenchman in time of peace. The sense of national comradeship and unity which calls forth this immense and ungrudged sacrifice gives us the measure of patriotism with which French people in the mass confront

My darling I hope you got my wire & flowers on September 12. How time flies![1] My sweet Clemmie how much I owe you.

With a thousand kisses, I remain

Your loving devoted husband,

[sketch of a pig]

Indigestion definitely better.

PS. One of the daughters keeps & breeds yellow Persian cats. She has nine. I have been introduced to all of them. Good news about Baldwin![2] I must get these N of W articles done the moment I come home. I have been so idle as to have only done one out here.

W

Minutes of the 50th Progress Meeting, Committee of Imperial Defence

(Air Ministry papers: 2/1873)

15 September 1936

Secretary of State[3] again emphasised that the memorandum[4] was intended for the Prime Minister's information only and in no circumstances for communication to Mr Winston Churchill, or other members of the Deputation. The inevitable result of such a step would be a counterblast from the Deputation with all the waste of time which this would involve.

LORD WEIR agreed, and said that a good deal of the information contained in the memorandum was of such a nature that it would be highly dangerous to let members of the Deputation have it. He considered that the memorandum was a very fair statement of the position.

---

their dangers. . . . It will take a lot to convince me that the qualities and devotion which have made and preserved the greatness of France have suddenly departed from the French people.'

[1] Churchill and his wife had been married on 12 September 1908.

[2] On 25 July 1936 Baldwin had been ordered by his doctor to take three months complete rest because 'worry and loss of sleep had made his nervous reserves bankrupt' (Keith Middlemas and John Barnes, *Baldwin: A Biography*, London 1969, page 962). In September it was rumoured that he was about to resign. But see Baldwin's own letter to Churchill of 9 October 1936, quoted on page 359, and Desmond Morton's letter to Churchill of 16 October 1936, quoted on page 364.

[3] Lord Swinton, Secretary of State for Air from June 1935 to May 1938.

[4] The Air Ministry memorandum, for use by Inskip on 23 November 1936 (see pages 427–31). On 16 September 1936 Lord Swinton wrote of these Air Ministry notes, to Sir Maurice Hankey: 'I must stress that they have been prepared for the Prime Minister's information only, and not for transmission in whole or in part to members of the deputation.'

Winston S. Churchill to Maurice Ashley [1]

(*Churchill papers: 8/530*)

17 September 1936

I did not trouble you with the revised proofs as you had already read the slips. Of course the work has been read thoroughly since the Sunday Times version. I am very much obliged to you for the corrections which you have been so kind as to send me. The most serious is that of Abigail's relations with Sarah and Harley. I have only just returned from abroad and do not know how far the printer has got with the final printing. I will have all your points carefully examined and if not too late will make the alterations in the text, but if too late, by erratas.

The reason why there is no Malplaquet is that this volume stops at the end of 1708 and there is to be a fourth volume to wind up. I should be very glad if you would read the proofs of this for me and will make you a new proposal upon this subject.

Winston S. Churchill to Sarah Churchill: telegram [2]

(*Churchill papers: 1/288*)

18 September 1936

Have asked Levy's legal firm send responsible representative meet you. He will advise you and place various facts before you without in any way dictating your action. Pray use him to guard your interests whatever course you adopt.

Father

---

[1] Maurice Percy Ashley, 1907–   . Educated at St Paul's School, London and New College, Oxford (History Scholar). Historical Research Assistant to Churchill, 1929–33. On the editorial staff of the *Manchester Guardian*, 1933–7; *The Times*, 1937–9. Editor of *Britain Today*, 1939–40. Served in the Army, 1940–5. (Major, Military Intelligence, becoming a specialist in the order of battle of the Japanese army.) Deputy Editor of the *Listener*, 1946–58; Editor, 1958–67. Research Fellow, Loughborough University of Technology, 1968–70. Author of more than twenty-five historical works, many on Cromwellian and Stuart England, including biographies of Cromwell (1937), Marlborough (1939) and Charles II (1971). In 1968 he published *Churchill as Historian*, and in 1978 he was awarded the CBE for his historical writings, and in 1979 a Doctorate of Letters at Oxford University.

[2] Sarah Churchill was on board the steamship *Bremen*, on her way to New York.

Winston S. Churchill to Louis Levy: telegram

(Churchill papers: 1/288)

18 September 1936

Please send competent representative meet Sarah Bremen. He should say he represents parents and comes to guard her interests without dictating to her in any way. He should ask her to wait in New York for Randolph before taking any final decision or going away with Samek. He should inform her of grave doubts about validity Samek's second divorce on account of domicile. Think probable if issue put on legal rather than personal grounds both will agree delay investigate point. Onus should be put on Samek to prove validity divorce. Paramount object is to prevent hasty marriage.

Churchill

Adam Marshall Diston to Winston S. Churchill

(Churchill papers: 8/536)

18 September 1936

Dear Mr Churchill,

I am enclosing drafts of 'The Crime that Shook Civilisation' and 'The Lusitania Tragedy'. They are both about 4,300 words.

In the case of the first, I have worked on the first five chapters of 'The Eastern Front'. After the introduction, the story is told very largely in the words of the book, but the arrangement is different. Naturally, there has been a good deal of condensation. That, combined with the alterations in arrangement, the connecting links here and there, and occasional minor alterations in phrasing, will, I think, probably be sufficient for the 'News of the World' purposes. It is essentially an article, moving at speed, although its actual words are largely drawn from the longer and more detailed narrative.

For the 'Lusitania', I have worked on the 'World Crisis, 1915' and the chapter, 'The Intervention of the United States in 1916–18'. For the actual sinking I have supplemented the 'Evening Standard' information with another account. And I have taken quotations from House, Roosevelt and Spring-Rice from the Lloyd George 'War Memoirs'.

I am also enclosing the suggestions for 'Collier's' which you said you would like to see on your return. I have done eight, as there are two, 'A King is Crowned' and 'The New British Prime Minister', which, however popular they might be in the States, you may have reasons for not doing. I hope, however, that there may be at least something which you will find useful in the list.

Yours very sincerely,
A. Marshall Diston

Winston S. Churchill to Geoffrey Dawson

(*Dawson papers*)

22 September 1936   11 Morpeth Mansions
Private & Confidential

Dear Sir,

I send you herewith a draft copy of my Paris speech. It is not in its final form and another version will be sent you tomorrow. Meanwhile I should be very glad to know privately how it strikes you.

Yours vy faithfully,
Winston S. Churchill

R. M. Barrington Ward[1] to Winston S. Churchill

(*Churchill papers: 2/258*)

23 September 1936
Private and Confidential

Dear Mr Churchill,

In Geoffrey Dawson's absence I write to thank you for having allowed us to see an advance copy of the speech which you will be delivering in Paris. Naturally any suggestion which it has occurred to me to make with regard to the general course of your argument will be in line with opinions that have been frequently expressed in leading articles in *The Times*. Like yourself, *The Times* attaches great importance both to effective readiness in the defence of democratic civilization and to the maintenance of close relations among like-minded Powers. At the same time we have always taken the view that it is the negative, if indispensable, side of national duty. On the positive side, *The Times* has always held that this country should most firmly decline

[1] Robert McGowan Barrington Ward, 1891–1948. Educated at Westminster and Balliol College, Oxford. President, Oxford Union Society, 1911. On active service, 1914–18 (Military Cross, DSO, despatches twice). Assistant Editor, the *Observer*, 1919–27; *The Times*, 1927–41. Editor of *The Times*, 1941–8.

to take part in the formation of 'fronts' until or unless the choice of a 'front' is positively forced upon us. However alien to your way of thinking may be the governing philosophies of other countries, we feel that the only safe and impartial test to apply to them is whether or not they are ready for practical collaboration, political and economic. We should, for example, certainly be against premature abandonment of the hope, supported by many authoritative pronouncements on the German side, that Germany is prepared to reach a general understanding and settlement with the British Empire. *The Times* has consistently endeavoured to argue—and I well remember your stating the same case in several speeches some years ago—that there is no other ultimate basis for stability in Europe but an understanding between France, Germany and Britain on lines designed eventually to embrace Europe generally.

All these contentions are, I know, more than familiar. But—since you have been good enough to invite an opinion—they may suggest a more immediate and specific definition of the purpose ('no narrowly national purpose') which you will set before your audience and they might help to guard an appeal for Franco-British collaboration against the risks of misunderstanding and controversy.

Yours sincerely,
R. M. Barrington Ward

H. A. L. Fisher [1] *to Winston S. Churchill*

(*Churchill papers: 2/258*)

24 September 1936

My dear Winston,

I have read with enthusiastic assent your splendid and timely defence of democratic civilization delivered to the Parisians. You have never done any-

---

[1] Herbert Albert Laurens Fisher, 1865–1940. Historian. He published his first book, *The Medieval Empire* in 1898, and a further seven works by 1914. Member of the Royal Commission on the Public Services of India, 1912–15 and of the Government Committee on alleged German outrages, 1915. Liberal MP, 1916–18 and 1918–26. President of the Board of Education, 1916–22. A British delegate to the League of Nations Assembly, 1920–2. Warden of New College, Oxford from 1925 until his death. He published his *History of Europe* in 3 volumes in 1935. Governor of the BBC, 1935–9. He died after being knocked down by a truck in the black-out, on his way to sit on a Conscientious Objectors' Tribunal. Two of his four brothers died in the First World War: Lieutenant Charles Dennis Fisher, RN, editor of Tacitus' *Annals* and *Histories* for the Clarendon Press, who was killed in action at the Battle of Jutland, 31 May 1916, at the age of 39; and 2nd Lieutenant Edmund Montagu Prinsep Fisher, who died on Easter Sunday 1918, through an illness contracted on the western front, at the age of 46. In 1937 Fisher was awarded the Order of Merit.

thing better, and I hope that your speech will be widely circulated through France.[1]

George Trevelyan tells me that your third volume is the finest of the three. I look forward to it with eagerness now that, after a pretty long spell of illness, my old zest for reading has returned.

Yours very sincerely,
Herbert Fisher

A. J. Cummings[2] to Winston S. Churchill
(*Churchill papers: 2/258*)

24 September 1936   News Chronicle

Dear Mr Churchill,

May I offer you my respectful and sincere congratulations on your magnificent defence of democracy in Paris today. Could you not send a copy of your address to LG with the request that he should pass it on clearly annotated, to Hitler?[3]

Yours very sincerely,
Arthur J. Cummings

[1] Speaking in English at the Théâtre des Ambassadeurs on 24 September 1936, Churchill urged the need to uphold parliamentary democracy and liberal civilization. Of the Nazi and Communist alternative he asked: 'How could we bear, nursed as we have been in a free atmosphere, to be gagged and muzzled; to have spies, eavesdroppers and delators at every corner; to have even private conversation caught up and used against us by the Secret Police and all their agents and creatures; to be arrested and interned without trial; or to be tried by political or Party courts for crimes hitherto unknown to civil law.' Churchill also told his audience: 'Between the doctrines of Comrade Trotsky and those of Dr Goebbels there ought to be room for you and me, and a few others, to cultivate opinions of our own,' and he added: 'We are in the midst of dangers so great and increasing, we are the guardians of causes so precious to the world that we must, as the Bible says, "Lay aside every impediment" and prepare ourselves night and day to be worthy of the Faith that is in us.'

[2] Arthur John Cummings, 1882–1957. On active service on the western front, 1915–18. Assistant Editor, *Yorkshire Post*, 1919; *Daily News*, 1920 (later Deputy Editor). Political Editor and chief commentator, *News Chronicle* 1932–55. Selfridge Award for Journalism and foreign reporting, 1933. President of the Institute of Journalists, 1952–3.

[3] Lloyd George met Hitler at Berchtesgaden on 4 and 5 September 1936. Notes of both meetings were taken by his friend T. P. Conwell-Evans. According to these notes, at their first meeting Lloyd George agreed with Hitler 'that Russia was a military danger', and he told Hitler: 'Lately, two Englishmen, who had been in Russia, had informed him of the terrific armaments that were proceeding there.' Hitler told Lloyd George: 'Czechoslovakia was a positive danger on account of her alliance with Soviet Russia.' At one moment in their conversation Lloyd George told Hitler: 'After fourteen years of political campaigning and popular education he had created in the German people a new spirit. He had given them confidence and faith in the future of the country and a new outlook affecting every sphere of their life. . . .' At their second meeting Lloyd George told Hitler that he was 'the greatest German of the age . . . . in the latest Volume of his Memoirs, which he was now preparing, he had stated that if in September, October, and November 1918, Hitler had been Germany's Führer a better Peace would have been negotiated'. For the full text of these two talks, see Martin Gilbert, *The Roots of Appeasement*, Appendix 2, pages 197–211.

Kenneth Lindsay[1] to Winston S. Churchill

(*Churchill papers: 2/258*)

25 September 1936   Admiralty

Dear Mr Churchill,

May I in great humility say with what joy I read your Paris lecture? At last it would seem one heard the authentic note struck, with authority & dignity.

Please forgive this invasion of the Parliamentary recess, but I have just returned from Central Europe.

Yours sincerely,
Kenneth Lindsay

Winston S. Churchill to Sir Charles Mendl[2]

(*Churchill papers: 2/258*)

26 September 1936

My dear Charles,

I really must thank you again for all the pains you took to make my adventure a success. That it was a success is undoubted. The whole English Press has taken it extremely well, and if your friends are pleased, it is indeed an achievement.[3]

I have a bill here for £6 which I have paid to the lady who made the translation of the speech which we discarded. This I think would be a fair charge against the moneys they gave you for me. Will you also pay out of them any telephone calls or incidental expenses to which you or the Embassy were put,

---

[1] Kenneth Lindsay, 1897–   . Educated at St Olave's school. On active service, 1916–18. At Worcester College, Oxford, 1921–2; President of the Oxford Union, 1922. Secretary, Political and Economic Planning (PEP), 1931–5. Independent National MP for Kilmarnock Burghs, 1933–45; Independent MP for the Combined English Universities, 1945–50. Civil Lord of the Admiralty, 1935–7. Parliamentary Secretary, Board of Education, 1937–40. Director of the Anglo-Israel Association, 1962–73. A Vice-President of the Educational Interchange Council (sometime Chairman), 1968–73.

[2] Charles Mendl, 1871–1958. Educated at Harrow. On active service with the 25th Infantry Brigade, 1914–15 (invalided out). Worked for the Admiralty, 1918; for the Foreign Office News Department, 1920–5. Knighted, 1924. Press Attaché, British Embassy, Paris, 1926–40. Subsequently resident in California. Married to the American interior decorator and hostess, Elsie de Wolff, resident in Paris in the 1930s.

[3] On 24 September 1936 Robert Bruce Lockhart recorded in his diary, after a talk with Rex Leeper, head of the News Department at the Foreign Office: 'Rex says Winston is making great recovery in the Conservative Party. Many regard him as only PM in a crisis.' (Kenneth Young, editor, *The Diaries of Sir Robert Bruce Lockhart*, page 356).

and then hand the rest over, as you propose, to the British hospitals in Paris. I really am delighted that all went off so well, and without you it would never have succeeded. Every good wish,

Lady Sinclair [1] *to Winston S. Churchill*
(*Churchill papers: 2/258*)

26 September 1936

My dear Winston,
I feel I must send you our line of thanks for your magnificent speech in Paris.
Everyone who loves democracy & dreads war must be grateful to you. Congratulations on your grandson! [2]

Love from,
Marigold

Adam Marshall Diston to Winston S. Churchill
(*Churchill papers: 8/536*)

26 September 1936

Dear Mr Churchill,
I am enclosing 'All the Wealth of America Turns to Dust', and hope that you will find the draft useful. It is between 4,200 and 4,300 words in length. I have drawn on two articles, written, I think, during the earlier period of the depression 'The American Mind and Ours' and 'Gold versus Wealth', and have added about 2,500 words of new matter.
I am proposing to tackle 'Japan' next.

Yours very sincerely,
A. Marshall Diston

---

[1] Marigold Forbes. Daughter of Colonel J. S. Forbes, DSO, and Lady Angela St Clair Erskine. She married Sir Archibald Sinclair (later 1st Viscount Thurso) in 1918. She died in 1975.
[2] Julian Sandys, 1936–   . Educated at Eton, Salem and Trinity College, Melbourne. 2nd Lieutenant, 4th Hussars; subsequently Captain, Queen's Royal Irish Hussars. Contested Ashfield (as a Conservative), October 1959. Called to the Bar, November 1959. Married, October 1970, Elizabeth, daughter of Alderman John Martin CBE. They have one daughter and three sons.

Lord Craigavon[1] to Winston S. Churchill

(*Churchill papers: 2/258*)

27 September 1936   Stormont Castle,
                                                    Belfast

My dear Winston,

You really are a wonder! I feel impelled to repeat the platitude on reading your remarkable Paris speech; quite the most brilliant of my time.

Hearty congratulations & all good wishes to you both.

We are now happy & content in these parts, though naturally anxious as to the outcome of the European situation.

Again, cordial felicitations.

Yrs ever,
James

Jacob Landau[2] to Winston S. Churchill

(*Churchill papers: 2/283*)

27 September 1936

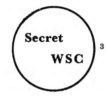

Secret
WSC [3]

Dear Mr Churchill,

I would like to summarise the conversation I had the pleasure of having with you regarding your visiting the United States. The visit would take

---

[1] James Craig, 1871–1940. A Protestant. Born in Dublin, the son of a wealthy distiller. A stockbroker by profession. Served in the South African War, 1899–1902. Unionist MP, 1906–21. A leading opponent of Irish Home Rule before 1914. On active service against the Germans in South-west Africa, 1914–15. Created Baronet, 1918. Parliamentary Secretary, Ministry of Pensions, 1919–20. Financial Secretary, Admiralty, 1920–1. First Prime Minister of Northern Ireland (under the Government of Ireland Act), from June 1921 until his death. Created Viscount Craigavon, 1927. In 1930 he was made an honorary member of the Other Club (founded by Churchill and F. E. Smith in 1911).

[2] Jacob Landau, 1892–1952. Born in Vienna. A journalist, he established the first international Jewish news service, the Jewish Correspondence Bureau, at the Hague, in 1914. Paris Peace Conference correspondent for the Amsterdam newspaper, *De Telegraaf*, 1919. Founder and Managing Director of the Jewish Telegraphic Agency Ltd (of London, New York, Paris, Berlin, Warsaw, Jerusalem and Prague), with its headquarters first in London, then in New York. Founded the Overseas News Agency, 1940, which specialized in covering news of minority peoples of all races, religions and nationalities.

[3] Note added by Churchill in his own handwriting.

place preferably in January, but perhaps in November, and would not extend over a period of more than a fortnight, during which you would address three meetings in New York, Philadelphia and Chicago, and some additional luncheons and dinners, for the sum of £5,000 as compensation.[1]

The purpose of your visit would be to extend your assistance to a movement similar to the 'Peace with Freedom' movement, to be launched in America soon after it is started in England.

I spoke to Mr Swope[2] over the telephone. He was delighted to hear of your willingness to come to the States.

I intend to return to the States immediately upon receipt of your letter in which you would confirm your readiness to pay this visit. Upon my arrival in New York, a meeting of our committee will be convened in order to adopt a formal resolution making the arrangements final, and to write you accordingly.

Yours sincerely,
Jacob Landau

Winston S. Churchill to Commander Owen[3]
(Churchill papers: 8/530)

28 September 1936   Morpeth Mansions

Dear Commander Owen,

I am indebted to you for a most valuable and important series of corrections as the result of your reading the semi-final proofs. Some of these were

---

[1] In September 1981, the approximate equivalent of £5,000 was £90,000.

[2] Herbert Bayard Swope, 1882–1958. Born in St Louis, Missouri. A journalist, he worked successively as a reporter for the *St Louis Post-Dispatch*, the New York *Herald*, and the New York *World*. Served as a War Correspondent for the *World* with the German armies, 1914–16. In 1914 he sent several exclusive despatches of German U-boat sinkings, including those of the battleships *Crecy*, *Aboukir* and *Hogue*. Awarded the Pulitzer prize for best reporting, 1917. Commissioned Lieutenant-Commander, US Navy, 1918. Appointed to the War Industries Board as Assistant to Bernard Baruch, 1919. Chief correspondent for the *World* at the Paris Peace Conference, 1919. Member of the International Press Commission, 1919, and a leading advocate of greater publicity for the Conference. He was the first journalist to publish both the terms of the League of Nations covenant, and full text of the reparations agreement. Executive Editor of the *World*, 1920–9, during which period he received further Pulitzer Prizes. In retirement, 1929–42. Consultant to the Secretary of War, 1942–6. Author of several books, including *Inside the German Empire*, *War Censorship* and *Free Speech*.

[3] John Hely Owen, 1890–1970. Born in Yorkshire, the son of a solicitor. Entered the Royal Navy at the age of fifteen. Midshipman, 1907. Lieutenant, 1912. Second in command of the submarine, C.10, May 1913–October 1915. Commanded the submarine C.5, operating in the North Sea, 1916. Commanded the submarine H.1, operating with the Italians in the Adriatic, against the Austrians, September 1916–May 1918. Among his subsequent commands was the submarine L.4 on the China Station, 1921–2. Second-in-Command of the

put right in the final revise, but I am sorry to say that several very stupid mistakes have now definitely been printed. I am inserting an erratum slip. How we wrote May 12 for December 13 about Barcelona I cannot conceive. I blame myself for not sending you the page proofs in time. I did not wish to burden you unduly and it was very kind of you to write and ask for them. I am looking forward to sending you a copy of the book when it comes out, and your corrections will be incorporated in any reprint that may be needed.

Sir Charles Mendl to Winston S. Churchill

(*Churchill papers: 2/258*)

28 September 1936   British Embassy,
                                                        Paris

Dear Mr Churchill,

Enclosed are all the press cuttings on your conference. As you will see they are uniformly favourable & enthusiastic & there is no question that no foreigner has ever given a Conference since I have been here that has been so enthusiastically received. . . .

Winston S. Churchill to Thomas Hunt

(*Churchill papers: 1/285*)

30 September 1936

Dear Mr Hunt,

As I gather you have returned from your holidays I write to let you know how I have got on. The indigestion is definitely very much better, in fact it hardly troubles me at all except in the early morning. But then my exercises take it away. I have taken three bottles of the medicine sometimes missing a day and sometimes taking it only once, and have used the powder about fifteen times. I have not been very good about eating at the extra occasions.

---

cruiser *Calliope*, 1925–6. Served with the Naval Intelligence Division, 1931–3. Commander, retired list, 1932. Author of historical articles in the *Naval Review* from 1925 and of a confidential history of mutiny in the Royal Navy (written in 1933, 'classified' until 1973). Author of *War at Sea Under Queen Anne*, 1938. Served in the Naval Historical Section of the Admiralty, 1939–45, writing battle summaries to provide guidance for Admirals and their staffs. His only brother, a Lieutenant in the West Riding Regiment, was killed in the second battle of Ypres in April 1915.

When I take soup or a sandwich just before going to bed I do not find the result very good. I have used the holder for the cigars ever since, but have eaten whatever came along.

I should be glad if you would let me know whether I should go on taking the medicine before luncheon or dinner if ever I feel the need. What exactly does the medicine do, and what is the prescription? Is it the kind of medicine one could take for a long time without it doing one any harm? What does the powder do and what are its ingredients? When I come to London I will come to see you again. Meanwhile I shall be glad if you will write.

October 1936

Winston S. Churchill to Colonel Beaumont-Nesbitt [1]
(*Churchill papers: 2/267*)

1 October 1936

Dear Colonel Beaumont-Nesbitt,
   Thank you so much for your letter and for forwarding me the one from General Gamelin, which was most complimentary. It was a great pleasure to me to make your acquaintance, and I do not think our journeys together have done any harm.

Winston S. Churchill to F. W. Deakin
(*Churchill papers: 8/530*)

1 October 1936

My dear Deakin,
   I hope all is well in your family.
   Commander Owen sent in a very heavy batch of corrections, some of which are serious and all of which were too late. The Brigadier satisfied me that Owen is not right about the 16,000 and that stands. All the other corrections appear valid. You will see that we have inserted an erratum covering some of them. Most of these mistakes noticed by Owen occur in the Spanish naval part which we did at the end. He certainly is very searching in his studies. Perhaps you will check the points he makes as we must insert them in a later edition, even when they are only improvements.

---

[1] Frederick George Beaumont-Nesbitt, 1893–1971. Educated at Eton and Sandhurst. 2nd Lieutenant, Grenadier Guards, 1912. On active service, 1914–18 (Military Cross). Commanded the 2nd Battalion, Grenadier Guards, 1932–5. Military Attaché, Paris, 1936–8. Deputy Director of Military Intelligence, 1938–9; Director, 1939–40. Military Attaché, Washington, 1941. Major-General, General Staff, 1941–5.

Winston S. Churchill to Brendan Bracken

(Churchill papers: 1/286)

1 October 1936

My dear Brendan,

Will you have the two breakfast dishes engraved with the following inscription 'To Brendan Bracken from Winston Spencer Churchill, September 1936' and tell them to send the account to me.

Brendan Bracken to Winston S. Churchill

(Churchill papers: 1/286)

2 October 1936

My dear Winston

A word of thanks for your beautiful present.

If I had any heirs I wd mark it as an heirloom. Having none I can only tell you that I shall always look upon it as the best of my possessions.

Bless you.

Brendan

Winston S. Churchill to Adam Marshall Diston

(Churchill papers: 8/536)

5 October 1936

The Japanese outline is very good. Of course the quid pro quo over the Japanese Treaty of 1902 was that Japan should send a quarter of a million soldiers to defend India against a Russian invasion. Otherwise I think the picture extremely well drawn.

Pray now go forward upon the subject 'Our own Social Revolution with National Health Insurance etc'. I am getting some technical advice about the 'Marvels of Land, Sea and Air' and shall probably do that myself. I am now working upon the deciding factor in the Great War. There only remains to provide for the Vision of the Future. I do not know what they really want for this, but let me have the Insurance Old Age Pension one as soon as convenient. I want these all out of the way before Parliament begins.

Thomas Hunt to Winston S. Churchill

(*Churchill papers: 1/286*)

5 October 1936

Dear Mr Churchill,

Thank you so much for your letter which reached me on Saturday. I am delighted to hear the indigestion is so much better.

As regards your questions, the medicine is quite a simple prescription which aims at relaxing the contractions of the stomach which, in your case, are really too strong. Also to make it relax satisfactorily when wind collects. It is a kind of medicine that can be taken almost indefinitely without doing any possible harm. The Powder is a similar thing but has an absorbent effect which aims at counteracting excessively gastric secretion which I have little doubt your active stomach is liable to form.

I am particularly pleased that you have been so much better in spite of eating whatever came along, but imagine that the cigar holder has been some help in your improvement. I shall look forward to seeing you again whenever you are in London and wish to see me.

Yours sincerely,
Thomas Hunt

Winston S. Churchill to Thomas Hunt

(*Churchill papers: 1/286*)

6 October 1936   11 Morpeth Mansions

Dear Mr Hunt,

Many thanks for your letter. Of course ever since I wrote to you in such sanguine terms, I have had a set back, and have had to take both medicine and powder frequently.

When Parliament meets and I am more regularly in London, I will come to see you. Meanwhile I have asked you for another supply of the powder.

Winston S. Churchill to Wilfred Fish[1]

(Churchill papers: 1/286)

7 October 1936

Dear Dr Fish,

The back tooth cannot be cleaned properly by a toothbrush. Will you send me a dental syringe with a right angle bend in it, so that I can wash the cavity out when I am brushing my teeth.[2]

Winston S. Churchill to Sir Abe Bailey

(Churchill papers: 2/259)

8 October 1936

. . . The Times on Monday had a full report of the Lawrence speech.[3] Geoffrey Dawson came down and dined at All Souls to meet me and we had a friendly talk. The Times have done me all the harm they can. Whether they will come round or not I do not know.

Things are going from bad to worse abroad, and Baldwin is perfectly incompetent at home.

[1] Eric Wilfred Fish, 1894–1974. Studied dentistry at University College, London and Manchester University, 1911–14. Registered as a dentist, 1915. Resident at Sevenoaks, near Chartwell, and at 9 Cavendish Square, London. Captain, Royal Army Medical Corps, 1915–18; Temporary Surgical Specialist, Bombay Brigade. Postgraduate Lecturer, Victoria and South Australia Dental Board, 1935. Chairman of the Dental Board of United Kingdom, 1944–5. CBE, 1947. Knighted, 1954. President of the General Dental Council, 1956–64. Honorary Consulting Dental Surgeon to the Royal Dental Hospital, and to St Mary's Hospital, Paddington. Vice-President of the International Dental Federation.

[2] On 10 October 1936 Churchill wrote again to Fish: 'I did not know that there was only a dressing in one of those upper teeth. Certainly the teeth there are still sensitive to heat and cold. I will propose myself to see you as soon as I come again to London.'

[3] On 3 October 1936 Churchill spoke at the unveiling of a memorial to Lawrence of Arabia at the City of Oxford High School for Boys. His speech began: 'Although more than a year has passed since Lawrence was taken from us, the impression of his personality remains living and vivid upon the minds of his friends, and the sense of his loss is in no way dimmed among his countrymen. All feel the poorer that he has gone from us. In these days dangers and difficulties gather upon Britain and her Empire, and we are also conscious of a lack of outstanding figures with which to overcome them. Here was a man in whom there existed not only an immense capacity for service, but that touch of genius which every one recognizes and no one can define. Whether in his great period of adventure and command or in these later years of self-suppression and self-imposed eclipse, he always reigned over those with whom he came in contact. They felt themselves in the presence of an extraordinary being. They felt that his latent reserves of force and willpower were beyond measurement. If he roused himself to action, who should say what crisis he could not surmount or quell? If things were going very badly how glad one would be to see him come round the corner.' The full text of Churchill's speech was published in *Proceedings at the Unveiling of the Memorial to Lawrence of Arabia*, Oxford 1937.

I look forward to dining with you on the 21st.

Mary's saddle. It would be better to wait a year before giving her your charming present. She is growing fast and so is the size of the horses which she rides.

I am very glad to see from your excellent hand that you are in full vigour.

Winston S. Churchill to Major Percy Davies
(Churchill papers: 8/533)

9 October 1936   Chartwell

My dear Major Davies,

You will be surprised and I hope glad to hear that I have almost completed the whole series of articles for the News of the World. I have made only one alteration in the series of titles which you gave me, which I hope you will approve. The article entitled 'Freedom of Sea, Land and Air, marvels of transport and wireless' would run better as I have written it under the heading 'The Vision of the Future'; whereas the article 'The Vision of the Future' might be better called 'Our Supreme Task'. These articles have taken me a good deal longer than those of last year as they consist so largely of entirely new matter. I think they make a very varied and readable series and I hope you will be thoroughly pleased with them. If not I will gladly make any alterations which you may desire.

I must thank you for the skill and thought with which you selected the topics, showing how well you knew the kind of subjects it would be easy and congenial for me to write upon. In fact I have taken every single one of them, only suggesting one change of title. I shall have the whole series faircopied and completed by the end of this week and it would be very nice if you could come down here and lunch either on Monday or Tuesday next as I should like to hand them to you personally.

Stanley Baldwin to Winston S. Churchill
(Churchill papers: 8/531)

9 October 1936

My dear Winston,

The arrival of your book[1] and its accompanying letter gave me great pleasure. I thank you for both most warmly.

---

[1] The third volume of *Marlborough, His Life and Times*, which was formally published on 23 October 1936. Ten thousand copies were published, and a further 155 copies in a specially bound and inscribed edition, which Churchill gave to his closest friends.

I am all right again. I only needed rest. I was just tired out in the summer. Not to be wondered at for I haven't had a carefree holiday for many years and it was only when I was definitely ordered to rest that I did so with easier conscience.

I nearly wrote you a line last month and then I hesitated. But I do want you to know that I felt with you from my heart when I read in the papers of certain domestic anxieties that must have caused you pain. I know you well enough to realise how closely these things touch you.[1]

I go to London on Monday, and shall then be up and down, from and to Chequers.

Yours very sincerely,
Stanley Baldwin

Sir Reginald Barnes to Winston S. Churchill
(*Churchill papers: 8/531*)

9 October 1936

My dear Winston,

Thank you ever so much for sending me your Marlborough book. I do so appreciate your giving it to me, and I am looking forward enormously to reading it, with the deliberation it is worthy of. The reviews of it are very flattering, so I hope you will benefit substantially as well as morally.

Winston S. Churchill to Jacques Doriot [2]
(*Churchill papers: 2/259*)

10 October 1936

I am much indebted to you for the kindness of your letter, and for your book with its inscription. I do not understand much about French politics.

---

[1] On 15 September 1936, without telling her parents, but only her sister Mary, Sarah Churchill had gone to the United States to be with Vic Oliver (see page 52, note 1, and page 422 n.1).

[2] Jacques Doriot, 1898–1945. Son of a French factory worker of Italian origin. Worked in a motor car factory, 1915–17. Mobilized, 1917. On active service, 1917–18 (when almost the whole of the regiment in which he was serving was killed at the Chemin des Dames). Awarded the Croix de Guerre for having carried a wounded soldier out of the firing line on his back. Served with the French forces in Hungary, 1919 (where he witnessed the Bela Kun revolution, and the Horthy counter-revolution). While serving in Fiume in 1919, he was briefly taken prisoner by D'Annunzio's forces. Served later in Albania. Demobilized, 1920. Returned to the motor car factory, 1920. Active in trade union politics. Spent fourteen months in Moscow, 1921–2 (when he was received by Lenin). Secretary of the French Young Communists, 1923. Arrested December 1923. Elected to the Chamber of Deputies as a Communist, May 1924 (the youngest Deputy in the Chamber). Denounced the Moroccan campaign, 1925, claiming that French financiers were arming both the French and native

It is hard enough to understand what happens in one's own country. I have the feeling that you work for the strength of France which is so vital to the world in these grave critical years.

I shall look forward when I come over to Paris again to meeting you and I will not fail to communicate with you and suggest a rendezvous.

Winston S. Churchill to Sir Ian Hamilton [1]

(*Churchill papers: 1/286*)

10 October 1936

You will be grieved to hear that my beautiful cow is not in calf. Would you allow me therefore to send her back to you one day, so that your bull may endeavour to repair his past shortcomings.

I see Lullenden [2] has been sold again. Do you happen to know the price.

---

forces. Proclaimed the formula: 'Morocco for the Moroccans'. Sent by Stalin on a mission to China, 1926 (at the time of Chiang Kai-shek's breach with the Chinese communists). Following an appeal for violence in the Chamber, he was imprisoned for sedition in 1927. Expelled from the Communist Party, June 1934. Publicly denounced the 'machiavellianism of the Soviets', February 1936. Standing as a 'Workers Unity' candidate, he defeated the Communist candidate in the election of April 1936. Founded the Parti Populaire Français, June 1936, based on the leadership principle. Defeated by a Communist candidate in June 1937. Mobilized, August 1939. A leading advocate of collaboration with the Nazis, May 1940; he urged even greater collaboration than that offered by the Vichy Government. Raised a force to fight alongside the German Army, July 1941. Himself fought with the German forces attacking Moscow during 1942, and again in 1943. After a meeting with Hitler in December 1944, he agreed to get up a Government of Franco-German collaboration. Killed in Baden (Germany) on 23 February 1945 (aged 47) by gunfire from a British aeroplane.

[1] Ian Standish Monteith Hamilton, 1853–1947. Entered Army, 1872. Major-General, 1900. Knighted, 1900. Chief of Staff to Lord Kitchener, 1901–2. General, 1914. Commander of the Central Force, responsible for the defence of England in the event of invasion, August 1914–March 1915. Commanded the Mediterranean Expeditionary Force at Gallipoli, March–October 1915, after which he received no further military command.

[2] A manor house at Dormansland near East Grinstead, less than eight miles from Chartwell. Churchill had bought it in October 1917 and sold it (to Sir Ian Hamilton) in October 1919. 'It was a low building,' writes his daughter Mary, 'built in grey stone, with a large barn nearby, and a small farmery. Downstairs, running the full length of the house, was a big high room with a large open fireplace, which made a delightful "studio-like" nursery, from where a staircase led to a gallery, off which were the children's bedrooms. There was a good deal to be done to the place, including the laying on of piped water, and as the house was not over large, Clementine set about converting the barn for the children's use as well' (Mary Soames, *Clementine Churchill*, London 1979, page 185). The house itself dated from the early seventeenth century, the barn from the sixteenth century, with about 20 acres of garden, 7 of woods and 60 of fields. Below a natural stone cliff at the side of the house, Churchill had dammed the water to make a pool (*conversation with Minou Wellesley Wesley, 1 June 1982*).

Winston S. Churchill to N. B. Foot

(Churchill papers: 2/285)

12 October 1936

I think luncheons are better reported than dinners, and I could give you Wednesday 25th November if that would be agreeable to Sir Montague Burton.[1] I should like to be informed as to the character and numbers of the company. I would speak for half an hour more or less on the lines of my address to the Parliamentary Group brought up to date.

I cannot make any other engagements at present, nor do I feel able to arrange an interview. You must understand that my work is extremely heavy as I not only have many political engagements in my constituency, and elsewhere, but I have to earn my living by writing.

Winston S. Churchill: remarks at a private luncheon[2]

(Churchill papers: 2/283)

15 October 1936   Pinafore Room
noon   Savoy Hotel

Since we met six months ago, everything has vindicated our outlook then, except that events have moved more quickly abroad, and opinion has moved more and faster in our direction at home. A double reaction has taken place.

I see a great reaction of opinion at home. I think it is a sign that things are very dangerous. Nothing could have been more admirable than the action of the Trades Union Congress and the representatives of the Trades Unions at the Labour Party meeting. Whether our volume of thought has been at all contributory to that decision or not I do not know, but at any rate it is in entire harmony with it, and I think the two decisions which they took—first, to draw a line against Communism, such as we drew it against Nazism, and secondly to support the principle of necessary re-armament in order that free countries should not be trampled down, are of the utmost help. It does not matter so much about a vote in the House of Commons because they are in a minority, though a very influential minority. Opposition is always looking for excuses to oppose, while it would be very much

---

[1] Montague Maurice Burton, 1885–1952. Chairman of Montague Burton Ltd., tailors. Knighted, 1931.

[2] The luncheon was given and organized by A. H. Richards. Among those present were Sir Norman Angell, Sir Walter Citrine, Henry Wickham Steed, Philip Guedalla and Philip Noel-Baker. During the meeting, it was agreed to set up a new movement, 'Defence of Freedom and Peace', under the auspices of the League of Nations' Union.

better if they could come to agreement on the main principles. It shows that Labour is more alive than many of the Conservatives.

That seems to clear the way for our work to go forward more vigorously and more openly. I see no reason why we should not now have our opening meeting in November at the Albert Hall or Queen's Hall and marshal the widest platform we can possibly get.

We must have some Tories to show up the others. We can certainly now get—after the decision taken by the Labour Party—large numbers of their leading men. Of course Sir Walter Citrine must be in the Chair. We cannot have the meeting until he can take the Chair. I certainly would not speak with any lesser authority than Sir Walter in the Chair.

Then about ten days before the meeting let us bring out this Manifesto booming the meeting and bringing the position forward. I think the Manifesto might well be signed by a certain number of people. You must get some of the Right too, or else it will look as if it were sectional, whereas the whole point of this is that we represent men of all opinions, however divided, coming together upon the essential points.

As to the question of policy, we have a most important statement issued by our friend here, (Mr Wickham Steed), who has been working for the last three or four months upon it, and we have also a Draft Manifesto; and I have had a letter from Sir Norman Angell with whom I am in the most hearty accord. All these point quite clearly to what our policy is. Our policy is that we adhere to the Covenant of the League of Nations; that is our rock. We do not in the slightest degree allow that to be departed from or whittled down in any respect. 'We will make every effort in our power to rally around that Covenant all the effective aid that we can get from any quarter without respect to party or nation.'

Then we hope that, armed with this, we shall get a great measure of support to arming this country, to the importance of putting this country in a position to be a strength and not a weakness to any system of collective security.

I feel myself that these ideas really ought not to offend the Conservative position at all. I think we require an opportunity to proclaim the liberties and rights of British Parliamentarianism which everybody values and cherishes very much in this country. I feel with the aid and effort of these institutions you will have an indefinite faculty of progressive self-improvement.

But how are these principles to be defended? How is this great body of principle to be defended? It certainly won't be defended by milksops and mugwumps and pussyfoots. It will only be defended if the cause of Freedom and reasonable ordered Progress and Liberty can find champions as vigorous, and hands as strong, and if need be, as ruthless as either of the violent parties at either end of politics.

Why is it that a man can be proud to strut about in some ridiculous Black Shirt, and another man will go along and say he is proud because he is in full line with Moscow, if we are not to have people who can go and preach of that vast body of doctrine which has made our country almost the only home of freedom, civilisation, and good fellowship.

No, we have got to find a policy of moderation defended by vigour, peace defended by force. Why not? I cannot see why. We have a people of just as good heart as these extremist fanatics at both ends, and with great skill the line has been drawn by Sir Walter Citrine to leave Communists on one side and these ridiculous Nazis on the other.

We have the means of being the spear-point of all this vast mass of opinion which guards our rights.

Desmond Morton to Winston S. Churchill

(Churchill papers: 2/259)

16 October 1936

Earlylands
Crockham Hill
Edenbridge

. . . When you spoke to me on the telephone last Sunday I had to be careful in my answers as I had several people with me, and in this tiny cottage everything can be overheard. Still, I had little to add then, but in the last week a good deal has happened.

The opinion of the Carlton Club seems to be almost unanimous that SB is not going until Death or the Coronation. There is trouble brewing about Eden, however. The FO is singularly united in a desire to curtail his activities as a peripatetic ambassador à la Ribbentrop and seem to be hammering out a line of policy for the approval of the Cabinet; briefly that until rearmament is real we must avoid commitments at all costs.

According to my information, rearmament is now progressing at last, though it cannot be anything like adequate for at least another three years unless steps are taken really to prefer the claims of the country's defences before those of ordinary trade and commerce.

In the Air, greater success has been realised than was anticipated in the sphere of material; personnel is a different matter. The Navy is reasonably content with proposals and progress. In other spheres—Army, Coast Defences and Anti-Aircraft Defences the situation is bad.

I have just learnt that the Germans have something new in AA Defence. They have concentrated on cannon; but have devised some new method of controlling the fire of AA artillery from their own aircraft, which, in their opinion, wholly alters the potentialities of anti-aircraft artillery. So pleased are they with the results that they have abandoned research into balloon aprons &c.

I should very much like to talk to you about this.

The Belgian news is not unexpected.[1] Again I had rather talk than write.

There is troublesome news about France—the undermining of efficiency by the intrigues of that rather sinister body the Comité des Forges, and, though I hate seeming to be sensational, the Grand Orient Masonry.[2]

The brightest light is given out by the reactions of Germany and Italy to the speeches of Sam Hoare and the resolutions of the Conservative Party Congress. How clear it is that we have only to speak with a clear, proud voice and these upstart peoples run to confess their sins. Still, we must not bluff too high; better could we not bluff at all.

I feel so deeply that if only the people were given a lead and did respond to that lead as they have done in the past and have it in them to do again, there is no nation of the world or combination of nations which would not scurry, however grudgingly, to do our bidding. Not that we may rule the world for the gratification of a common will to power, but that we may compel the world to peace and law and order.

Your article in the Evening Standard to-night scouts the idea that Germany is providing funds for the Old Guard of Communism. I feel sure you may bank on that. Germany has not the foreign exchange at her disposal to do such a thing. I have information, however, that strongly suggests the hand of Moscow in support of the very movement, whose alleged leaders Moscow has just exterminated.

At first glance this seems ridiculous; but further consideration of the ways of Communism leads to other conclusions.

---

[1] On 14 October 1936, speaking to a Council of Ministers for the first time since his accession, King Leopold of the Belgians gave his support to widespread Belgian fears that were Belgium to sign a regional pact with France, she would be drawn into a European war. 'Even a purely defensive alliance,' the King averred, 'would not lead to the desired end, for however prompt the assistance of an ally might be, he could not intervene until after the invader's attack, which would be a lightning attack, had been launched' ('The Times', 15 October 1936). This remark was interpreted by many listeners as confirming 'a tendency in favour of a more independent policy, and even of a return to neutrality'. The King's speech was particularly praised by the Flemish nationalists, who had campaigned for many months against the proposed Franco-Belgian military agreement. All the Cabinet ministers—Catholic, Liberal and Socialist—had approved publication of the King's speech, which was also given prominence in the German press: 'whether or not the Brussels pronouncement will turn out in the long run to be an advantage to Germany, it is certainly regarded at the moment as a matter of moderate self-congratulation' ('The Times', 16 October 1936).

[2] Unknown perhaps, even to Desmond Morton, Churchill had himself become a Freemason in May 1901, remaining a member of the United Studholme Lodge, London, until July 1912 (Archives of the United Grand Lodge of England).

I personally cannot agree that the Government of Moscow has changed its original intentions and objective one iota. Time after time in the past the Jekyll and Hyde theory has been put into practice in a manner impossible to a nation with the least moral consistency. The old game was the denial of responsibility for the activities of the IIIrd International. Now my information states that in destroying the well known leaders of the latter, the Soviet Government has retained in its own hands, secretly, the machinery. Through that machinery the Soviet Government is distributing funds to the Spanish Communists and other disruptive forces.

Stalin's excuse that he had no control over the International is more than threadbare; but it is far harder to prove openly the continuation of similar activities through a secret agency; one, moreover which he appears to have destroyed by killing its apparent leaders.

I am very much intrigued by your last paragraph about the Jews. I am no anti-semitist, no more are you. It is a matter I do not remember your having touched upon in public before. The paragraph seemed to me to hint at more than it expressed.[1]

I hope I may be allowed to see you soon.

Yours very sincerely,
Desmond Morton

David Lloyd George to Winston S. Churchill
(*Churchill papers: 1/286*)

16 October 1936
Bron-y-de,
Churt,
Surrey

My dear Winston,

Your picture is a real joy. I have never professed to be an art critic but I know when a picture gives me a thrill which increases every time I see it. That is certainly my experience so far with yours. I was so delighted with it that, although I had already taken my tickets for the West Indies, I was half persuaded to cancel them and return to that dream of colour which you so effectively depict.

I am very grateful to you. I have fixed the picture already in my new room

---

[1] Churchill's *Evening Standard* article, 'The Communist Schism', published on 16 October 1936, ended: 'It is especially important that British Jewry should keep itself absolutely clear from this brawling. In Great Britain the law-abiding Jew need not look to the Communist for protection. He will get that as his right from the Constable.'

where I now do all my work, and I am sure you will feel glad to know that it will cheer an old fellow who is a friend and an admirer of your genius.

I am so glad you are coming to the private Dinner organised by Ivor Nicholson[1] to celebrate the completion of my labours.[2]

When are you coming to see us here as you promised?

D Ll G

Winston S. Churchill to Sir Austen Chamberlain

(*Churchill papers: 2/283*)

17 October 1936

I think you will be interested to see the letter which Norman Angell has written me and which shows clearly the robust spirit of this small group who are gathered together under the title of 'Freedom and Peace Union'. I have been surprised to find the resolution and clarity of thought which have prevailed among them, and the profound sense of approaching danger from the growing German power. Citrine was not able to be with us on Thursday as he was away, but he sent a remarkable deputy, a Mr Wall,[3] who is the head of the London Trades Council, a very authoritative Trade Unionist and model of common sense.

We shall have another luncheon at the Savoy on the 29th and I hope you will be able to come. I will see there is no mistake about the invitation this time. You would be committed to nothing except a friendly talk with highly intelligent and sensible people.

[1] Ivor Percy Nicholson, 1881–1937. Son of a Welsh preacher. Became a free-lance writer after leaving Mill Hill School in 1910. On the advertising staff of *The Times*, 1912–14. In charge of the Pictorial Propaganda Branch of the Ministry of Information, 1916–18. Private Secretary in the Department of Overseas Trade. On the staff of Cassell's, Publishers. Director of the National Magazine Company. Founder and Chairman of Ivor Nicholson and Watson Ltd, Publishers, of 44 Essex Street, Strand, from 1931 until his death.

[2] The fifth and final volume of Lloyd George's *War Memoirs* was published in November 1936.

[3] Alfred Mervyn Wall, 1890–1957. The son of a Shropshire farmer. A printer by trade. Secretary of the London Trades Council, and Secretary of British Actors Equity Association. Obtained recognition of collective bargaining in the cinema trade following the formation of the London and Home Counties Conciliation Board for the cinema industry. A supporter of Roosevelt's 'new Deal', on 18 October 1937 the *Manchester Guardian* reported that: 'He expressed the hope that Britain would see fit to take the sound advice of "Doctor" Roosevelt instead of replying on the advice of quacks and charlatans.' In 1938 he became General Secretary of the London Society of Compositors. In 1944 he took charge of the industrial relations and union-management co-operation of C and E Layton Ltd, Blockmakers and Typesetters. In December 1944 he appealed to the Labour Party not to break up the National Government, but to seek to join with Churchill in achieving a four-year programme of peace-time social reforms.

Ivan Maisky to Winston S. Churchill

(*Churchill papers: 2/259*)

19 October 1936   13 Kensington Palace Gardens
                                                              London

My dear Churchill,

I tried to get you by telephone today to see whether you could lunch or dine with me in the near future, as I should so much like to have the opportunity of a talk with you. As you are out of town I am sending this note to say how gladly I should welcome you here for lunch or dinner on Thursday of this week (the 22nd) or Tuesday of next (the 27th). Would you be so good as to telephone me about this? Of course if these dates are not convenient I shall be glad to fix another—and if you would prefer a different rendezvous please suggest it.

I hope you are well. I am just back from a very stimulating holiday in the USSR, mostly in the Caucasus.

Yours sincerely,
I. Maisky

Winston S. Churchill to the Duchess of Marlborough

(*Churchill papers: 1/286*)

20 October 1936

I send you herewith a painting table and a small outfit of paints and brushes. These paints are the set of colours selected by Sir William Nicholson,[1] and are supposed to contain everything you require. But no doubt as you continue to paint you will add other ones to them.

I also send you a copy of M III. Blandford[2] will not receive his till next week, as it is being specially bound for the library. Please explain to him. It will be very nice to see you on the 30th.

---

[1] William Newzam Prior Nicholson, 1872–1949. Painter. Co-author (with Rudyard Kipling) of *An Almanac of Twelve Sports*, 1898. As well as portrait, landscape and still-life painting, he worked in stained glass windows and woodcuts. A Trustee of the Tate Gallery, 1934–9. A member of the Other Club from 1934. Knighted, 1936. Called by Churchill 'Le cher maître'.

[2] The 10th Duke of Marlborough (see page 230, note 4), formerly Marquess of Blandford, and known to his family as 'Blandford'.

Vyvyan Adams to Winston S. Churchill
(Churchill papers: 2/259)

20 October 1936

Dear Mr Churchill,

I was very much impressed by your speech which is to-day reported,[1] and wonder if, when Parliament reassembles, what you said could be effectively impressed upon the Government. I have been apprehensive for some time— and so have many of my friends—that the Government may be contemplating some kind of an accommodation with Germany which leaves her free to attack Eastwards or Southwards. Your speech precisely exposes the dangers which would accompany any such policy. Would it be possible, in the debate on the Address, to put down an amendment expressing the need for a collective security which embraces the East and South-East of Europe? If you would sponsor such an amendment I am sure it would have two results: first, it would reassure the French; and secondly it would have a tremendous effect upon public opinion in this country.

If I can assist in this matter you have only to let me know.

Yours sincerely,
Vyvyan Adams

Winston S. Churchill to A. H. Richards
(Churchill papers: 2/283)

21 October 1936

... What I have in mind is a demonstration at the Albert Hall with Citrine in the Chair and the League of Nations Union and the New Commonwealth Society, together with some important Trade Union organisations, all officially represented. Such a meeting addressed by Sir Austen and myself, with one or two other speeches, might give the 'Freedom and Peace' movement a great impetus. I do not contemplate the building up of a new and rival society to the existing organisations, but only a welding together of those organisations and galvanising them into effective use. Pray comment freely upon what I have written.

[1] Speaking at Chingford on the evening of 19 October 1936, Churchill argued in favour of the principle of collective security. 'Unhappily,' he said, 'in the present state of the world collective security is no substitute for national self-defence. But collective security might be a great reinforcement of it. If many nations great and small, each of which had strong defences, were to bind themselves together to uphold the reign of law in Europe, and to protect each other mutually against unprovoked aggression, it might well be possible to prevent another great war.' Churchill ended his speech: 'We ought to try to make a further effort to prevent this immense and measureless catastrophe, and to weld all the nations of Europe without exception into a strong structure of law and good will which would enable them to benefit by the wonders of science instead of being destroyed by them.'

Winston S. Churchill to Lord Cecil of Chelwood
(*Cecil of Chelwood papers*)

21 October 1936   Chartwell
Confidential

My dear Bob,

Many thanks for your letter. I wonder if Noel-Baker[1] gave you any account of the private luncheon at which some of us, who are deeply alarmed, considered what steps could be taken to mobilise the moral as well as the material forces available at the present time in Europe, to resist the potential Aggressor.

I am also President of the New Commonwealth Society (British Section). Though I do not naturally consider myself bound by all their views, I am very clear they have the root of the matter in them. What I have in my mind is joint action by all of those who (save the paradox!) are prepared to keep the peace by force (as is done inside every country), and exalt the reign of Law and Freedom. This naturally involves further effort to be made this year (while time remains) to constitute and gather at Geneva the strongest possible force that will resist unprovoked aggression and tyranny whencesoever threatened. When you have talked with Noel-Baker and received his report, perhaps you will write to me again.

There is no question of the eclipse of the New Commonwealth Society nor the League of Nations Union, but only for a fusion of practical working effort and for united advance. This is almost certainly the last twelve months in which it will be possible to hope for a good solution.

Even if our efforts are already too late, working in this direction will be helpful to preserving what is left.

Yours vy sincerely,
Winston S. Churchill

[1] Philip John Noel-Baker, 1889–   . Educated at Bootham School and King's College, Cambridge. President of the Cambridge Union Society, 1912. Vice-Principal, Ruskin College, Oxford, 1914. First Commandant, Friend's Ambulance Unit, August 1914–July 1915. An officer in the Friend's Ambulance Unit, Italy, 1915–18; Italian Silver Medal for Valour, 1917 and Croce di Guerra, 1918. Served in the League of Nations Section, Paris Peace Conference, 1919; League of Nations Secretariat, Geneva, 1920–2. Labour MP for Coventry, 1929–31; for Derby, 1935–50; for Derby South, 1950–70. Parliamentary Private Secretary to the Secretary of State for Foreign Affairs, 1929–31. Parliamentary Secretary, Ministry of War Transport, 1942–5. Privy Councillor, 1945. Secretary of State for Air, 1946–7; for Commonwealth Relations, 1947–50. Minister of Fuel and Power, 1950–1. Chairman, Foreign Affairs Group, Parliamentary Labour Party, 1964–70. Nobel Peace Prize, 1959. Created a Life Peer, 1977.

Wing-Commander Anderson to Violet Pearman
(*Churchill papers: 2/271*)

21 October 1936

Dear Mrs Pearman,

I thought you would be interested to see the attached Air Ministry Press Summary, particularly C [1] and I would be pleased if you would bring this to the notice of —.

Yours very sincerely,
C. T. Anderson

A. P. Herbert [2] to Winston S. Churchill
(*Churchill papers: 2/267*)

21 October 1936
Private

Dear Winston

I am sending you a little collection of literary oddments. But my main purpose in writing to you is to say that I wish you could find time to meet my friend Brigadier P. C. S. Hobart,[3] DSO, who is top dog, I think, (or very nearly so) of Tanks, and has a lot of interesting things he wants to say to someone who like you knows about defence. His address is Burdenshott

---

[1] The enclosure was the Air Ministry Daily Press Summary No. 244/1936, dated Monday 19 October 1936. Section C read: 'RAF expansion—(a) American fighting and bombing planes are to be bought for the RAF. Orders are shortly to be placed for high speed dive-bombers and 1,000 horse-power fighting planes, the latest and most powerful machines with which the US Air Force is equipped. This step has been made necessary because British aircraft manufacturers cannot meet the new requirements of the Royal Air Force.' This item was summarized from the *Sunday Chronicle* and *Sunday Dispatch* of 17 October 1936.

[2] Alan Patrick Herbert, 1890–1971. Educated at Winchester and New College, Oxford. Humorist; began writing for *Punch*, 1910. On active service with the Royal Naval Division, Antwerp, Gallipoli and France (wounded), 1914–18. Called to the Bar, 1918. Joined the staff of *Punch* 1924. Independent MP for Oxford University 1935–50 (when the University seats were abolished). Petty Officer, River Thames Naval Auxiliary Patrol, June 1940. Knighted, 1945. A Trustee of the National Maritime Museum, 1947–53. Author of more than sixty works of prose and verse, including a novel about Gallipoli, *The Secret Battle*.

[3] Percy Cleghorn Stanley Hobart, 1885–1957. Joined the Royal Engineers 1904. Served on the North-West Frontier of India, 1908. On active service on the western front, 1915, and in Mesopotamia, 1916–18, when he was wounded, and taken prisoner. MC, DSO (1916) and OBE (1918). Served in Palestine, 1918; in Waziristan, 1921. Joined the Royal Tank Corps, 1923; Inspector, Royal Tank Corps, 1933–6. Commander, Tank Brigade, 1934–7. Deputy Director of Staff Duties, War Office, 1937. Major-General, 1937. Director of Military Training, War Office, 1937–8. Raised the 7th Armoured Division, Egypt, 1938–9; the 11th Armoured Division, 1941–2; the 79th Armoured Division, 1942 (commanding it in north-west Europe, 1944–5). Knighted, 1943. His sister married (in 1927) Bernard Montgomery, (later Viscount Montgomery of Alamein). She died in 1937.

Farm, Worplesdon, Surrey, and I happen to know that he will be in London for a few days from the 26th. Probably the simplest thing would be if he could come and see you somewhere. He is one of the most intelligent and interesting soldiers I have met. Hoping you are all well.

Yours sincerely,
Alan Herbert

His phone number is Worplesdon 46.

Desmond Morton to Winston S. Churchill
(Churchill papers: 2/267)

22 October 1936   3 Beaufort Gardens

Dear Winston,

Last Saturday I mentioned to you the Marquis del Moral[1] now in this country acting as a link between Franco[2] and affairs in England. You suggested my bringing him to lunch with you.

He has today sent you a copy of the official record (Vol I) of the atrocities committed by the Communists & Anarchists in Spain, but has enclosed not his own card but that of the Duke of Alba.[3]

I have suggested he should write to you mentioning my name. He can give you first hand information on the Spanish situation including the military position & plans. He speaks better English than I do & was on the British Staff in the S African War. Aged 65; a little apt to go on talking but a most sincere and honourable Spanish gentleman.

PS. The Atrocities book is one of the most horrible things I have ever read. The tale of German atrocities in 1914 pales to insignificance beside it.

[1] Frederick Ramón de Bertodano, 1871–1955. Succeeded his uncle as 8th Marquis del Moral, 1924. (The Marquisate had been created in 1765, in Spain, but the family had been resident in Britain since the 1830s.) On active service with the British Army in Matabeleland 1896; in South Africa, 1899–1902; and in the First World War, 1914–18 (General Staff Officer). In 1907 he had married Lady Ida Dalzell, eldest daughter of the 14th Earl of Carnwath, and in 1934 he married Gytha Stourton, a granddaughter of the 4th Viscount Southwell. His eldest son married Lady Mary Savile, 3rd daughter of the 6th Earl of Mexborough. Born in Australia, the Marquis died in Rhodesia.

[2] Francisco Franco Bahamonde, 1892–1975. Entered the Spanish Army, 1907. Second-in-Command of the Spanish Foreign Legion, 1920. During the Republican regime he served abroad, in the Balearic Islands, Morocco and the Canary Islands. One of the leaders of the Nationalist revolt, July 1936. Head of the State, 1939. Sent Spanish volunteers to fight with Germany against Russia, June 1941.

[3] Jacobo Maria del Pilar Carlos Manuel Fitz-James Stuart, 1878–1953. 17th Duque de Alba and (but for the Act of Attainder of 1695) 10th Duke of Berwick. Minister of Education, Spain, 1930. Spanish Foreign Minister, 1930–1. Spanish Ambassador to London, 1939–45. Author and historian. Corresponding Member of the British Academy.

Sir Eric Phipps to the Foreign Office: telegram

(*Foreign Office papers: 371/19914*)

22 October 1936

The 'Deutsche diplomatisch-politische Korrespondenz' of 21st October attacks Mr Winston Churchill's Chingford speech, which it regards as an example of an attempt to camouflage personal dislike of Germany under the appearance of practical reasoning.[1]

Mr Churchill had declared that an understanding with Germany must practically mean a war and that German policy consisted in furthering security in the west in order to have a freer hand in Eastern and South-Eastern Europe. His proposal—'Co-operation of Great and Small Powers on a basis of reciprocity to protect themselves against unprovoked attack'—was a policy which, far from hiding its object of encirclement, regarded encirclement as a necessity and a virtue. The commentary is not surprised at the tone of the speech but merely at the publicity given to it in England, in view of its manifest absurdity. Germany's policy was to restore normal relations among her neighbours by the regular removal one by one of the factors of disturbance, while each such step is misrepresented by Mr Churchill as preparation for warlike intentions in another quarter.[2]

If this method of interpretation were to be generally applied, all confidence would disappear from international relations. But it was applied to Germany alone and thus represented a discrimination which could not be without its effect. One could only conclude that those who thought in this way were merely trying to camouflage their interest in the maintenance of the harmful spirit of the encirclement and suppression of Germany. Those who refused to see the value of the removal of sources of disturbance merely gave cause for suspicion of their own intentions: and it was surprising that the very same circles regarded the peaceful desire of Belgium to keep herself

---

[1] Speaking at Chingford, in his constituency, on 19 October 1936, Churchill commented: 'Many people said to him, why not make a good arrangement with Germany? It would no doubt be easy for Great Britain and perhaps France to make an arrangement with Germany. All Germany asked, apart from the return of her colonies, was a free hand in the East and South of Europe. That sounded very smooth spoken. But what did it mean in fact? It meant, it seemed to him—he hoped he was wrong—one of the most fearful wars of history. No one knew what would happen in the course of such a war, nor what the position of Great Britain would be if as a result of it Nazi Germany became the overwhelming master of Europe. Therefore, in his view, we ought to try to make a further effort to prevent this immense and measureless catastrophe, and to weld all the nations of Europe without exception into a strong structure of law and good will which would enable them to benefit by the wonders of science instead of being destroyed by them.' (Report in *The Times*, 20 October 1936.)

[2] On 24 October 1936 Churchill issued a public rebuttal of these charges (see page 375 of this volume).

out of foreign conflict not as a reduction in the risks of European war but as a limitation of certain possibilities of intervention against Germany, and that they regretted that one more territory was no longer accessible to them as a base of operations against the Reich. . . .

Charles Peake [1] *to Winston S. Churchill*

(*Churchill papers: 8/531*)

23 October 1936 Foreign Office

Dear Mr Churchill,

The book you sent me has only arrived today from Paris, where parcels seem to have accumulated since I transferred myself to the News Department here.

I am most grateful for it, and looking forward to reading it at an early date.

Your last speech at Chingford was much admired here and has fluttered the dove cotes at Berlin considerably which is an excellent thing in the circumstances.

It is good that the Germans shd realize that there is one English statesman, who instead of apologizing for democracy stands up for it.

Again with many thanks,

Yours sincerely,
Charles Peake

Sir Edward Marsh to Winston S. Churchill

(*Churchill papers: 4/2*)

23 October 1936

My dear Winston,

Very many thanks indeed for Vol III. It is a delight to see it so finely presented & illustrated—I shall begin reading it at once, with the new freedom of not having to peer for misprints (I was disconcerted at seeing the list of

---

[1] Charles Brinsley Pemberton Peake, 1897–1958. On active service 1914–18 (Military Cross, despatches). Entered the Diplomatic Service, 1922; 1st Secretary, 1934; Counsellor of Embassy, 1939. Chief Press Adviser, Ministry of Information, 1939. Personal Assistant to Lord Halifax (in Washington), 1941. British Representative to the French National Committee, 1942–4. Political Adviser to General Eisenhower, 1944–5. Consul-General, Tangier, 1945–6. Ambassador to Yugoslavia, 1946–51. Knighted, 1948. Ambassador to Greece, 1951–7.

errata, but relieved to find most of them were hardly in my province—at any rate I hope you think so!). I don't feel that I've quite pulled my weight in this volume, as I only had one reading, & that not of quite the whole. The two *Times* reviews & the *DT* are most satisfactory.[1]

As you always take a kindly interest in my affairs, you will be glad to hear that my pension, which had been tentatively estimated by the Dept at £700, has now been definitely fixed by the Treasury at £933, which makes a great difference—& I think now I shall be able to 'manage'—my retiring date is Feb 15th.

I've vy much admired all your recent speeches, & so has everybody.

Yr,
Eddie

Winston S. Churchill: Press Statement[2]

(*Foreign Office papers: 371/19914*)

24 October 1936

It is an entire mistake to suppose that I am in favour of 'the encirclement and oppression of Germany'. I should, however, like to see the largest possible forces combined against the aggressor, whoever he might be. There is nothing which England and France seek for their own safety that they would not gladly extend to Germany.

When the Eastern Pact was first announced nearly two years ago it offered to Germany exactly the same protection as was offered to Russia. Even now, if Germany desired it, I have no doubt that guarantees to assist her in one

---

[1] Among the reviews of volume III of *Marlborough, His Life and Times* on 23 October 1936 was one in *The Times*, unsigned, which stated that 'there is much to be learnt from Mr Churchill's writings besides the splendid story of the Duke's career', and called the volume 'a more magnificent reconstruction of history than even its much-praised predecessor'. The review in *The Daily Telegraph*, also unsigned, said: 'This is a remarkable picture of a man who was remarkable in an age when many men stood out by reason of their ambitions and energies. The opportunities which this period in Marlborough's life offer to his historian are many and tempting, but also exacting. It cannot be said that Mr Churchill has failed with any of them.' Also on 23 October 1936, Sir Charles Petrie wrote in the *Morning Post*: 'Mr Churchill has frequently shown his skill in making history live, but never so successfully as in these pages,' while 'H' wrote in the *Manchester Guardian*: 'This brilliant and fascinating book sustains expectancy to the end and leaves us eager for the final volume, which will tell the story of Marlborough's fate and gather up the public lessons of his life. No book has ever made military operations clearer or political intrigue more fascinating. One is compelled to add that Mr Churchill's opinions on current politics have coloured many of his judgments. Only the Mr Churchill who is a politician as well as a writer could have written this book.'

[2] This statement was published in full in *The Times* on 25 October 1936.

way or another, if she were the victim of unprovoked aggression, would readily be forthcoming. The whole meaning of collective security is that none should be left out. If Soviet Russia, for instance, were to make an unprovoked attack on Germany, British sympathy would be wholeheartedly upon the German side, and Germany would be entitled to the assistance which could be given under the Covenant of the League of Nations. Unless, therefore, the German Government contemplates an act of aggression, it is idle to talk about encirclement or oppression.

There is no nation in Europe which is more safe than Germany at the present time or less afraid of its neighbours. Even as long ago as the discussions about the Eastern Pact the German Government felt themselves so strong that they abruptly dismissed all idea of their requiring aid if they were the victims of Russian invasion.

But now, in the meantime, they have been spending at the rate of over £800,000,000 sterling a year on warlike preparations. Their armed forces are far more than double what they were only a year ago, and next year they will be far stronger still. The German people are being subjected during this winter to many privations and are making many sacrifices in order to perfect their terrible war machine. This cannot be required only for defence, in view of the great strength of Germany and the additional guarantees which would so readily be given to her by almost all Europe.

Those who agree with me in Great Britain in supporting the idea of collective security as a reinforcement of individual security are certainly not anti-German. On the contrary, there is nothing they would welcome more than the sincere association of Germany in a renewed effort to establish the reign of law in Europe, supported by adequate forces, and thereafter an earnest attempt in a friendly atmosphere to remove just causes of grievance. It would be easy for Germany to test the truth of those statements at any time, and if she does not do so it is because her ideas are moving along other channels.

Sir Maurice Hankey to Winston S. Churchill
(*Churchill papers: 8/531*)

25 October 1936

Dear Winston,

I find it difficult to express my delight at receiving the third volume of 'Marlborough', and—though I have too little time for reading these days— I plunged straight into the preface last night. You put all the other historians into the shade because you tell us the things we really want to know and—having made history yourself—you are able to reconstruct that curious interplay of politics, strategy, personalities from which real history is built up and thus to give us a picture that we recognise as true.

I am distressed at never having plunged into your swimming pool this summer. Cold weather, over-work (that infernal Arms Commission[1] on top of everything else), week-end visitors of the non-bathing type, August leave, and in September banishment from my home to make room for a terribly ill relative from Central Africa with his nurses,—these were the causes.

I read all your speeches and follow your doings with interest. We shall meet soon.

Yours ever,
M. P. A. Hankey

PS. We both sympathise so much with you two over the way these cursed newspapers gassed about Sarah.

MH

Neville Chamberlain to Winston S. Churchill

(*Churchill papers: 8/531*)

25 October 1936   11 Downing Street

My dear Winston,

Thank you once again very much for your continued kindness in sending me the new volume of your Marlborough. From the reviews which I have seen it appears that you have surpassed even yourself in the account of your great ancestor's career and I shall look forward to reading it with keen anticipation, of interest & pleasure. I remember your speaking to me of the parallel you had found with current affairs and this will give the volume special piquancy.

Yours sincerely,
N. Chamberlain

---

[1] Like Churchill, Hankey had given evidence to the Royal Commission on the Private Manufacture of Arms. In two memoranda, and in a total of nine hours of cross-examination on 8 and 21 May 1936, Hankey had argued against the nationalization of major firms like Vickers, and the steel manufacturers, on the grounds that nationalization was bound to disrupt the rearmament programme. 'One of his objects,' added his biographer, 'was, he admitted "to keep the Royal Commission away from (recommending) a Ministry of Supply", for which Churchill had recently been pressing. . . .', Stephen Roskill, *Hankey, Man of Secrets*, volume III, page 247. For several months after giving evidence, Hankey was much abused and publicly, particularly by Labour MPs, for having supported the private manufacturers of arms, but he was defended in Parliament both by Alfred Duff Cooper and Sir Thomas Inskip.

Desmond Morton to Winston S. Churchill

(*Churchill papers: 2/267*)

25 October 1936   Earlylands,
                                                                  Edenbridge

My dear Winston,

I suggest that it is important not to form a final judgment on the Air dispute until the points at issue are made much clearer. Nuffield's[1] charges are as yet not very specific, save as regards discourteous and cavalier treatment. Evidence of this has been produced and I do not know how Swinton proposes to answer this unless he can shew that certain actions on Nuffield's part, at present unrevealed, merited so severe a rebuke.[2]

Two other matters appear to be involved, but in my opinion, they must not be confused. They are

(a) The provision of engines for the expansion of the Air Force now in progress, including the accumulation of reserves of engines.
(b) Preparations being made to expand the aircraft industry in war, far above anything that could possibly be needed in peace.

Nuffield's complaint on the first issue seems to be that the Air Ministry refused to give him orders for engines for present needs. A part answer to this would be to shew that such engines as his factory was capable of manufacturing were not required. But, if this is the official answer, I would ask why advice and assistance was not given to Nuffield to enable his factory to

---

[1] William Richard Morris, 1877–1963. Motor car manufacturer. Chairman of Morris Motors Ltd, and its associated companies, 1919–52. Created Baronet, 1929; Baron Nuffield, 1934; Viscount, 1938. A philanthropist of note, he caused both his ancestry and his philanthropic gifts to be listed in appendices of volume XIII to *The Complete Peerage* (1940), towards whose publication costs he provided £50,000. His largest listed benefaction was £2,368,000 to Oxford University, for a Medical Research and Scholarship Fund. Among his other large benefactions were £2,031,000 in trust for Distressed Areas, £1,650,000 for Recreational Facilities for Forces of the Crown, and £1,036,000 for Nuffield College, Oxford. In 1952 Churchill offered him an earldom, which he declined.

[2] In October 1936 Lord Nuffield announced his withdrawal from the 'shadow' scheme devised by the Air Ministry. In a statement (published in full in the *Oxford Times* on 23 October 1936) he said: 'One reason for my not cooperating in the shadow scheme is that, when I had a fully equipped aero factory ready, the Air Ministry wished me to put up another factory in which to make components for new engines. If that is not a waste of public money I do not know what is'. It was difficult to manufacture an aero engine under one roof, but what would happen if parts were made in seven different factories 'he did not know'. Nuffield had earlier said publicly that the Air Ministry were paying prices for aero engines that in his judgement were too high. 'That statement got back to certain political interests in the Air Ministry,' he said, 'where apparently it was not received with favour. Throughout the whole development of our aero engines my venture was characterised by a complete lack of support by political interests in the Ministry.'

make types of engines that *are* required *now*. Surely it cannot be contended that we have ample capacity to manufacture all our immediate requirements of engines of *all* types.

On the second point Nuffield seems rather vaguely but forcibly to disagree with the whole scheme devised for wartime expansion. It does not seem possible to take sides unless he will make it clear why he considers the scheme unpractical. This can only be treated as a highly technical argument in which manufacturing experts must take part and which is not immediately susceptible to public understanding and discussion.

Thank you so very much for the copy of Marlborough Vol III. It is most kind of you to send it to me and to autograph it. I look forward immensely to studying it and will let you know if I have anything worth considering to say after I have done so.

Yours very sincerely,
Desmond Morton

Winston S. Churchill to Ivan Maisky
(*Churchill papers: 2/259*)

26 October 1936   Morpeth Mansions

I am in London all this week, but I am grieved to find every single luncheon and dinner is already engaged. I should be very glad however if you would be so kind as to come to 11, Morpeth Mansions on Wednesday afternoon at 6 o'clock, if that will be convenient. If not let me fix some other time.

Squadron-Leader Rowley[1] to Wing-Commander Anderson
(*Churchill papers: 2/271*)

26 October 1936

Dear Anderson,

I have just returned from a visit to Germany in company with Dick Atcherley.[2] During our stay in Berlin we were fortunate enough to make

---

[1] Herbert Victor Rowley, 1898–1966. Commissioned into the Royal Naval Air Service, April 1916; into the Royal Air Force, April 1918. Squadron-Leader, 1930. Wing-Commander 1937, at the Air Ministry, Directorate of Operations and Intelligence where, under Group Captain R. D. Oxland, he was responsible for policy regarding new aircraft. Air Commodore, 1941. Served in Fighter Command, 1939–41; South-East Asia Command, 1942–5.

[2] Richard Llewellyn Roger Atcherley, 1904–1970. Entered the Royal Air Force, 1924. Central Flying School Instructor, 1925–8. Served in Jordan (14 Squadron), 1930–4. Royal Aircraft Establishment, Farnborough, 1934–7; RAF Staff College, 1937–8. Officer Commanding 219 Night Fighter Squadron, 1939–40; Garrison Commander, Badu-Foss (Narvik), 1940.

friends with many people in the German Air Ministry and consequently saw a great deal of interesting things and people.

They flew us out to Heinkel works and Junkers works and took us all over the DLV[1] and out to a fighter squadron.

The development of air power in Germany has left me in a somewhat dazed condition but with one fact firmly in my mind and that fact is that they are *now* stronger in the air than England and France combined. I have been busy writing out a report—being on leave I had no shorthand typist—but I hope my girl at Martlesham will have it ready by Friday.

I am coming up to the Air Ministry to have luncheon and a talk to AMRD[2] on Friday next and should like to see you on Friday or Saturday morning.[3]

J. L. Garvin to Winston S. Churchill

(*Churchill papers: 8/531*)

29 October 1936

My dear Winston,

Many and warmhearted thanks to you for this inscribed copy of your third noble volume. It will always be treasured by your friend. My chance to read it right through is not just yet, for one is overwhelmed and civilised leisure quite extinct, but even a flight over it shows me that it is grandly done; and above all with that terse masculine clarity which belongs to action. The work never can be displaced from its rank as a foremost classic of our language in the great field of historical biography. I long for the time when I shall be able to read the whole four volumes just for my joy and instruction.

(Air Force Cross). Officer Commanding RAF Station Drem, 1940; No 54 Night Fighter Officers' Training Unit, 1941. Sector Commander, Fairwood Common, 1942; Kenley, 1942. Air Officer Commanding 211 Group, Desert Air Force, 1943; Air Support Training HQ, Allied Expeditionary Air Force, 1944. Commandant, Central Fighter Establishment, 1945; RAF College, Cranwell, 1946–8. Commander-in-Chief of the Royal Pakistan Air Force, 1949–51. Commander, Royal Air Force Staff, British Joint Services Mission, Washington, 1953–5. Air Officer Commander-in-Chief, Flying Training Command, 1955–8. Knighted, 1956.

[1] The German Air Sports Association (see page 80, note 3). Established in 1920, by 1929 it had 50,000 members. The main source of encouragement was the Defence Ministry, as it was realised that the Association's gliding training and development was a means of circumventing the Treaty of Versailles. The first courses in gliding instruction were organised in 1920 by Captain Student (who, as General, commanded the paratroops in the invasion of Holland in 1939 and the landings on Crete in 1941).

[2] The Air Member (of the Air Council) for Research Development and Production, since April 1936, Air Vice-Marshal W. R. Freeman, CB, DSO, MC (see page 641, note 2).

[3] Anderson sent a copy of this letter to Churchill.

My own job on Joe IV (and last)[1] very slow and dogged just now; like threading needles in the dark. Nor have I any happiness, the least about politics. Never in my life was I so uneasy about politics. So far as they mean 'the future of the country'. No leadership. On June 1st 1935 I asked Baldwin in writing, giving grave reasons, to make you Minister of Air & Göring's[2] opposite number. He refused and the whole of his third Premiership has been a calamity.

Ever yours,
J. L. Garvin

Donald Fergusson[3] to Winston S. Churchill
(*Churchill papers: 8/531*)

[29] October 1936   Ministry of Agriculture
                                 and Fisheries

Dear Winston,

It was most kind of you to remember me again & send me a signed copy of your new volume of Marlborough's life. My warmest thanks.

My treasured collection of your books—nearly all inscribed—now extends the length of one of my library shelves. I am almost ashamed to think how little, owing to your generosity & kindness I have contributed to the emoluments you have received from them.

This Ministry is in these days an interesting & busy place, & I am enjoying my new job. You'll be glad to know that we are actively engaged on the agricultural preparation for war emergencies.

Yours ever & most gratefully,
Donald Fergusson

[1] Garvin's biography of Joseph Chamberlain: volume I (1836–1885) was published in 1932, volume II (1885–1895) in 1933 and volume III (1895–1900) in 1934. Garvin, who died in 1947, never completed the fourth volume, which was written by Julian Amery (the son of L. S. Amery) and published as three separate volumes in 1951 (the volume for the years 1901–3) and 1969 (the volumes for 1901–14).

[2] Hermann Goering, 1893–1946. Served as a Lieutenant in the German Infantry, 1914. Commander of the Richthofen fighter squadron, 1918. A follower of Hitler from 1923. Wounded during the unsuccessful Munich putsch of November 1923, after which he lived in Austria, Italy and Sweden. Air Adviser in Denmark and Sweden, 1924–8. Returned to Germany, and elected to the Reichstag, 1928. President of the Reichstag, 1932–3. Prime Minister of Prussia, 1933. Commander-in-Chief of the German Air Force, 1933–45. Air Chief Marshal, 1935. Commissioner for the Four-Year Plan, 1936. Field-Marshal, 1938. President of the General Council for the War Economy, 1940. Sentenced to death at Nuremberg, October 1946, but committed suicide the night before his intended execution.

[3] John Donald Balfour Fergusson, 1891–1963. Educated at Berkhamsted School and Magdalen College, Oxford. On active service, 1914–18. Entered Treasury, 1919; Private Secretary to successive Chancellors of the Exchequer, 1920–36. Permanent Secretary, Ministry of Agriculture and Fisheries, 1936–45; Ministry of Fuel and Power, 1945–52. Knighted, 1937. One of his three sons was killed on active service in the Second World War.

Violet Pearman to Winston S. Churchill

(*Churchill papers: 2/271*)

29 October 1936

This is the Air Force List 'at a glance', but Wng Cmdr A says it is merely a paper one. He thinks Professor Lindemann would be most interested to see it.

Major Percy Davies to Winston S. Churchill

(*Churchill papers: 1/292*)

30 October 1936

Dear Mr Churchill,

I have much pleasure in enclosing herewith cheque for £5,000 in payment of the series of twelve articles entitled 'Great Events of Our Time'. As you will see, I have adopted your suggestion that we should take the round figure of 50,000 words, and have, as requested, dated the cheque January 1st next.

Both Sir Emsley and I are very pleased with the series, which we believe will prove even more brilliant and successful than the previous one.

I hope in the course of a few weeks' time to send you the proofs, and shall be glad if you will kindly go through them, and make any corrections you wish.

I hope to start publication about the second week of January next.

Violet Pearman to Clifford Norton[1]

(*Churchill papers: 2/267*)

31 October 1936

Dear Private Secretary,

Mr Churchill had an interview with the Marquis del Moral, the informal representative of the insurgents, and stressed to him the extreme importance of the victors showing mercy to the rank and file. Mr Churchill thinks that the views in this enclosed letter might be of interest to Mr Eden, though he has no doubts that he has already had them put before him from other quarters.

---

[1] Clifford John Norton, 1891– . Educated at Rugby and Queen's College, Oxford. On active service at Gallipoli, 1915 and in Palestine, 1916–18. Political Officer, Damascus, Deraa and Haifa, 1919–20. Entered the Diplomatic Service, 1921. Private Secretary to Sir Robert Vansittart, 1930-7. Counsellor, British Embassy, Warsaw, 1937–9. Minister to Switzerland, Berne, 1942–6. Knighted, 1946. Ambassador in Athens, 1946–51.

November 1936

Sarah Churchill to Winston S. Churchill
(*Churchill papers: 1/288*)

[1] November 1936

The Lombardy Hotel
New York City

Everyone speaks so highly of you here and all your speeches are well reported. You must be very worried over the turn of events in England. It is impossible to know what is happening. The press here is pure hysteria.[1]

I hope you are in the best of health. I think of you all and Chartwell often.

All my love to you,
Sarah

Sir Bindon Blood[2] to Winston S. Churchill
(*Churchill papers: 8/531*)

1 November 1936

My dear Winston,

I write to send you my very best thanks for so kindly sending me your third volume of 'Marlborough and his Times', which I am reading with very great interest and pleasure. I congratulate you on the success of your great work, which contains a worthy record of the glorious life of your famous ancestor. I see great danger that England may be ruined by its 'proletariat', and I am in great hope that it may fall to you to steer our country clear of

---

[1] A reference to the growing gossip about Edward VIII and Mrs Simpson, gossip which had for some months been a dominant feature of newspaper reports throughout the United States (see pages 238, 399 and 438–9).

[2] Bindon Blood, 1842–1940. Entered the Royal Engineers in 1860. On active service in the Jowaki Expedition, 1877–8; the Zulu War, 1879; the Afghan War, 1880; the Egyptian Campaign, 1882. Brigadier-General, and Chief Staff Officer, Chitral Relief Force, 1895. Knighted, 1896. Major-General Commanding the Malakand Field Force, and Buner Field Force, 1897–8 (when he was Churchill's Commanding Officer). Lieutenant-General commanding the troops in the Eastern Transvaal, 1901. Retired from the Army, 1907. GCB, 1909; GCVO, 1932. Chief Royal Engineer of the Corps of Royal Engineers, 1936–40.

the dangers that threaten us. Our worst enemies seem to be of our own household, and our 'authorities' seem to be neglecting to face obvious facts.

I hope you and all your family are well and flourishing.

With all good wishes.

Yours ever,
B. Blood

Desmond Morton to Violet Pearman

(*Churchill papers: 2/267*)

2 November 1936

Dear Mrs Pearman,

Enclosed thanks Mr Churchill for his article in the 'Diplomatische Korrespondenz' and recognises that Mr Churchill as a patriotic Englishman is no enemy of Germany but Germany's best friend.

Between these two statements is a mass of academic argument apparently trying to prove

(a) Germany only rearmed because she had to.

(b) Germany has armed against the USSR.

(c) Germany hasn't rearmed at all,

with which varied conclusions the writer is happy to see Mr Churchill agrees!

Curious!

Yours sincerely,
D. Morton

Professor Lindemann to Winston S. Churchill

(*Cherwell papers*)[1]

2 November 1936

Your address evidently made a great impression; in fact, one tutor told me three of his pupils had given up Socialism on the strength of it. As each tutor has about twelve pupils, this is not a bad yield.[2]

---

[1] On 24 October 1936 the Oxford University Conservative Association Committee had decided (by 14 votes to 11) not to support Lindemann's candidature at the forthcoming by-election for the University seat. He had therefore decided to stand as an Independent.

[2] Churchill was in Oxford on the evening of Friday 30 October 1936, to talk to the Oxford University Conservative Association in support of Lindemann's candidature at the forthcoming by-election. He spoke in the Oxford Union, attracting, according to the *Oxford Times*

Winston S. Churchill to Lord Cromer[1]

(Churchill papers: 1/286)

4 November 1936

I hear that one of the readers of plays has died, and I venture to make a very strong appeal to you on behalf of Eddie Marsh. There is surely no one who has his qualifications. His immense knowledge of literature, his fine taste, his long official experience, his love of the theatre as well as the drama are no doubt well-known to you. May I then add my appeal as one of his oldest friends and his Chief for nearly a quarter of a century of public office in so many departments.[2]

Winston S. Churchill to Stanley Baldwin

(Churchill papers: 2/267)

4 November 1936

Some of my friends suggested that I should write to you to ask for a two days' debate on Defence, and I hope you will allow me to question you upon this point tomorrow when business is discussed. I have put down an Amendment to the Address about Defence on the Paper. The Liberals also want to raise it. Thus I suppose there will certainly be a one day's debate on the Address. But have you not also promised a debate on 'Nuffield'? Will not

---

of 6 November 1936, 'the largest crowd of undergraduates since Mr Lloyd George came to the same hall in 1912'. Speaking of the official Conservatives, who had opposed Lindemann's candidature, and were likewise opposed to close involvement in Europe, Churchill said: 'The idea that every kind of principle can be smirched away and that all can be united in a kind of vague, smudgy amalgam is a very grave danger!' Isolation, he argued, was impossible. 'If we could only get a few large steamers to tow this island of ours a couple of thousand miles across the Atlantic and anchor us off the coast of New Brunswick, I think our future would be covered with sunshine. Unhappily, we are only a few minutes by air flight from Europe. We are involved in the affairs of Europe. We cannot turn our backs on Europe without the greatest danger of finding a hostile Europe.' Churchill argued in favour of British support for the League of Nations, in order to give Europe 'the hope of collective security against unprovoked aggression and reasonable opportunity by which grievances might be redressed'. When a woman member of the audience asked how these powers latent in the Covenant of the League could be made more effective, Churchill replied: 'By every young woman making every young man join the Territorials.'

[1] Rowland Thomas Baring, 1877–1953. Served in the Diplomatic Service, 1900–7; in the Foreign Office, 1907–11. Entered merchant banking as Managing Director of Baring Bros & Co Ltd, 1913. ADC to the Viceroy of India, 1915–16. Succeeded his father as 2nd Earl of Cromer, 1916. Assistant Private Secretary to King George V, 1916–20; Lord Chamberlain of His Majesty's Household, 1922–38. Privy Councillor, 1922. British Government Director of the Suez Canal Co, 1926–50.

[2] As Sir Edward Marsh's name does not appear in the Lord Chamberlain's Warrant Book, it would seem that Churchill's effort on his behalf was unsuccessful.

the official Opposition expect this? Would it not therefore be better to have a two days' debate in one? This enables a statement to be made by the Government at the beginning, and thoroughly considered by the House. There are so many who wish to speak that one day's treatment would be very inconvenient. Whether these debates take place on the Amendment to the Address or separately, makes no difference to Government time. Will you kindly take this letter as notice that we shall be raising the matter tomorrow.

Lord Winterton to Winston S. Churchill: telephone message

(Churchill papers: 2/267)

4 November 1936

I have seen the Chief Whip.[1] I put our case very strongly and even fiercely. In principle he was friendly, but as happens in such cases he was very sticky when it came to detail. The most I could get was a provisional promise to have the defence debate on the Liberal amendment which would last all Tuesday and extend until 7.30 on Thursday. Wednesday is Private Members day and he is unwilling to take away the Private Members, and in any case it being Armistice Day, it is not an appropriate occasion for an Armament debate. I have subsequently seen Archie Sinclair. He says that he thinks that he can induce his people to allow him to word his amendment in such a fashion as to make it possible to discuss all aspects of defence, though primarily on the report of the Royal Commission on Armaments, and will add about the need of the creation of a Ministry of Supply. But the first words in the Amendment, referring as they do to the extension of the services, should make it possible to discuss everything. I strongly advise that you ring up Margesson tonight before dinner, and discuss with him personally this question of the time. I feel pretty sure he won't offer more than a day and a half, and I was rather inclined to accept the offer, though I gave him no indication of my views, especially as I think we could get him to promise two or three days debate early in the New Year in addition.

[1] David Margesson, see page 232, note 1.

A. H. Richards to Winston S. Churchill

(*Churchill papers: 2/283*)

4 November 1936
Private and confidential

Dear Mr Winston Churchill,

DEFENCE OF PEACE AND FREEDOM

It is practically certain that Sir Archibald Sinclair will be present at to-morrow's luncheon.

I also hope Dr J. J. Mallon,[1] Warden of Toynbee Hall, will be present.

His Grace the Archbishop of Canterbury[2] is Chairman of Toynbee Hall.

May I respectfully suggest that you do not press for Lord Lloyd to be a speaker at the Albert Hall meeting.

Yesterday during my interview with Sir Walter Citrine I very tactfully broached the question of speakers, and if Lord Lloyd were invited to speak it really would create difficulties for Sir Walter Citrine.

By all means let His Lordship be invited to the platform—and to a prominent position.

Yours sincerely,
A. H. Richards

Eugen Spier:[3] recollections

(*Spier papers: November 1953*)

[5 November 1936]

After one of our Focus Luncheons,[4] Winston Churchill, Commander Locker-Lampson and myself withdrew to a quiet chat over a cup of coffee,

---

[1] James Joseph Mallon, 1875–1961. Secretary of the National League to establish a Minimum Wage, 1906. Member of the first thirteen Trade Boards (established by Churchill under the Trade Boards Act), 1909. Warden of Toynbee Hall, 1919–54. Member of the Board of Governors of the BBC, 1937–9 and 1941–6. Companion of Honour, 1939. Adviser to the Ministry of Food on Feeding in Air Raid Shelters, 1940–5. Member of the National Assistance Board, 1948.

[2] Cosmo Gordon Lang, 1864–1945. Educated at Glasgow University and Balliol College, Oxford; Fellow of All Souls, 1889–93. Dean of Divinity, Magdalen College, Oxford, 1893–6. Honorary Chaplain to Queen Victoria. Bishop of Stepney, 1901–8. Archbishop of York, 1908–28. Privy Councillor, 1909. Archbishop of Canterbury, 1928–42. GCVO, 1937. Created Baron, 1942.

[3] See page 160, note 1.

[4] Possibly the luncheon of 5 November 1936, at the Dorchester.

cigar and brandy. Commander Locker-Lampson addressed Churchill and asked him: 'Winston what do you say to your daughter marrying that Austrian Comedian.' To this Churchill replied: 'Ah yes Oliver, I believe she inherited the adventurous spirit of her father.'

Churchill always insisted that at our luncheons etc he should be seated next to Lady Violet Bonham Carter. He also requested that he should get always his special vintage port. When he was asked whether there was any connection between the two requests he said: 'Both of them generate a unique degree of warmth.'

Lady Houston[1] to Winston S. Churchill

(*Churchill papers: 2/260*)

6 November 1936

Dear Mr Churchill,

I do not think you can realise what an immensity of harm you are doing yourself by trying to resuscitate the League of Nations. It is as dead as a doornail and everyone knows it is and surely it has done harm enough already for most people to be glad to be done with it. You are backing the wrong horse.

Yours sincerely,
Lucy Houston

PS. Please realize that these words are *friendly* & remember that everything I have foreseen for the last 5 years & more *has happened* alas!

Sir Austen Chamberlain to Hilda Chamberlain

(*Austen Chamberlain papers*)

7 November 1936

I have just finished the third volume of Winston's Marlborough. It is brilliantly written on the political as well as on the military side & leaves one with a profound admiration for the hero; but it will not do for reading aloud, as it needs constant reference to the maps which are freely scattered through its pages. Now for Volume II of Balfour's Life.[2]

---

[1] Fanny Lucy Radnall, 1857–1936. Married, 1901, the 9th Baron Byron (who died in 1917); 1924, Sir Robert Houston (who died in 1926). A keen suffragist. Founded and administered the first Rest Home for Tired Nurses, 1914–18; DBE, 1917. Gave £100,000 for the Schneider Air Trophy Contest, 1931. Helped to finance aircraft and air experiments.

[2] *Arthur James Balfour, First Earl Balfour*, Blanche Dugdale's two volume biography of her uncle, published in 1936.

Sir Robert Vansittart to Winston S. Churchill

(*Churchill papers: 2/302*)

7 November 1936 Foreign Office

My dear Winston,

Very many thanks for your letter of October 19th enclosing your article on the Pacific, which I have read with the greatest interest.[1]

There are only two points that I should like to put to you. In the first place, in the paragraph which begins at the bottom of page 10 you argue that it is completely immaterial to us what America builds, and that therefore the idea of naval parity is rather ridiculous. There are, however, certain considerations to be borne in mind. If America were to increase her building programme beyond the point of parity with us and if Japan were to follow suit (as she certainly would) this could not be immaterial to us because we

---

[1] Published in *Collier's* on 20 February 1937, entitled 'The Mission of Japan'. One paragraph read: 'It would be a great mistake if a gallant nation like the Japanese thought too little of the United States because of the clatter of Presidential elections; or of France because of the political ferment that always goes on there; or even of Old England, because she cannot get recruits for her Army—until there is a war. It will be far better if we all treat each other with justice and mutual respect, and with an earnest desire to find out, not how we can gratify our own ambitions, but how we can meet the reasonable grievances of others.' The article continued: 'I have been in Parliament since the year 1900, and I am one of the dwindling band of Members who voted for the ratification of the original Anglo-Japanese Alliance. I watched with enthusiasm the loyal co-operation of Japan in the Great War. The impression left on my mind by many years of working with the Governments of the Mikado has been that the Japanese are a sober, steady, grave and mature people; that they can be trusted to measure forces and factors with great care, and that they do not lose their heads, or plunge into mad, uncalculated adventures. But of late years we have been confronted with a somewhat different Japan. The elder statesmen and their sagacious power seem to have dispersed. For the last four or five years the political movement of Japan has seemed to effect itself through the murder of statesmen who were deemed too prudent or circumspect, or in other ways were objectionable to secret societies of Army officers. Great and honourable Japanese leaders have fallen in a swift succession to the sword or bullet of honourable assassins. The Mikado's Government and his august and sacred authority have been exerted to punish the criminals. We have been conscious in Britain and the United States that it was only with a grievous effort that this indispensable process was accomplished. A state or empire possessing brave, powerful fleets and armies, whose supreme direction may be affected by systematized murder, is one about which ordinary civilized neighbours must feel serious anxieties. It is so easy to launch a modern war. Somebody signs a paper or utters an ejaculation: someone presses a button, and terrible things begin. Where they end no one can say, least of all those who begin them. The lesson of the Great War was that those who fix the moment for the beginning of wars are not those who fix the hour of their cessation. All these admonitions would be quite valueless unless the ocean Powers, the English-speaking peoples, and the Western democracies took all the necessary measures for their self-defence, and as I hope, mutual protection. But since these processes are now in progress on both sides of the Channel and on both sides of the Atlantic, we may hope that the Shadow which now falls upon the Pacific will only be a shadow ever shortening as the sun of world-confidence and goodwill rises again to the zenith.'

should have to follow in our turn. Whether we like it or not, the building of the three countries is really interconnected. Even if *we* do not mind what America builds, the same is not true of the United States, who watch our building with the greatest care and regard parity not as an abstract theory but as a real necessity. If the purpose of your article is to appeal to Japanese opinion, I suggest it might be a mistake to say that so much do we trust America that we do not mind what she builds, but that we shall be most careful to watch and match every ship which Japan builds. Finally, the chances of our bringing Japan into the new Naval Treaty will be diminished in proportion as she regards this as a frame-up between the Americans and ourselves.

In view of these considerations I must confess that I should have preferred to see the suppression of that paragraph beginning with the words 'To-day all these disputes' and ending 'Mistress of the Yellow Seas'.

To turn to the second and less important point. At the top of page 6 you seem to classify Chiang Kai-shek[1] and Wang Ching-wei[2] as pro-Japanese. This is hardly true of the former without a lot of qualification, and I suggest it might be a pity for such a statement to appear over your signature. It is probably more true of the latter, but I should have preferred to see both names left out.

[1] Chiang Kai-Shek, 1887–1975. Joined Sun Yat-sen's revolutionary party in 1907. A member of the revolutionary army, Shanghai, on the outbreak of the Chinese revolution, 1911. Served at Chinese General Headquarters, 1918–20. Visited the Soviet Union to study its military and social systems, 1923. Founder and Principal, Whanpoa Military Academy, Canton, 1924. Member of the Central Executive Committee of the Kuomintang, 1926. Commander-in-Chief, Northern Expeditionary Forces, 1926–8. Chairman of State, and Generalissimo of all fighting services, 1928–31. Resigned, 1931. Director-General of the Kuomintang Party, 1938. Chairman of the Supreme National Defence Council, 1939–47. President of the Republic of China, 1948. Retired, 1948. Formed a Government on behalf of the Chinese Nationalists in Formosa (Taiwan), 1949.

[2] Wang Ching-wei, 1883–1944. Born in Canton. Passed a Government examination in 1903, to win a scholarship to study law in Tokyo. While in Tokyo, in 1906, he joined Sun Yat-sen's patriotic society, which was opposed to the Manchu dynasty then ruling Peking. In 1910 he attempted to assassinate the Prince Regent in Peking. He was caught, and though he confessed was given only a prison sentence by the tottering Manchu regime. He was released, a national hero, in 1911. In France, as a teacher, 1912–17. An aide to Sun Yat-sen, Canton, 1917–24. Elected to the Central Executive Committee of the Kuomintang, 1924. After Sun Yat-sen's death in 1925, Wang Ching-wei became leader of the left wing of the Kuomintang, in opposition to Chiang Kai-Shek, who did not want to co-operate with Chinese communists. Co-operated with Chiang Kai-Shek, 1927–38. Administrative head of the National Government, 1932–6. In 1938 he broke with Chiang and advocated peace with the Japanese. Wounded in an assassination attempt, 1939. In 1939 he visited Tokyo and signed an agreement with the Japanese. In 1940 the Japanese helped him establish a government in Nanking over all occupied areas. In 1943 his government declared war on the Allies. In November 1944 he went to Japan for treatment of wounds he had sustained in the 1939 assassination attempt, and died within a week.

I do not know whether it may be of assistance to you to draw attention to some very small verbal points:—

Page 1, line 10. The words 'and primitive peoples' might possibly give offence, and the sentence would not suffer much if they were dropped.

Page 8, 2nd line of 2nd paragraph. The words 'if a rise it be' are not very clear. I suppose they are intended to cast a cynical (rather Chinese) doubt on the value of modern Western civilisation. I have no objection to them.

Page 9, line 2. The word 'tripartite' is not strictly accurate, as I suppose you are referring to the Four-Power Treaty, of which France was also a signatory.

Page 13, 6 lines from the end, 'a hundred years' would be more accurate than 'a hundred and fifty years'.

Finally, on page 17, last line of the first paragraph, the word 'honourable' might be queried. You may have intended that the assassins of whom you are writing were actuated by honourable patriotic motives, but the context does not altogether support this, and it occurred to me that it might be a slip for 'dishonourable'. In any event, I question whether we should be serving any purpose by letting the Japanese Government think that we view these assassins as honourable gentlemen. We ourselves have rather tried to express our horror at their acts.

Yours ever,
Van

Winston S. Churchill to Sir Charles Mendl
(*Churchill papers: 2/274*)

8 November 1936

My dear Charles,

I should be much obliged if you would deliver the enclosed letter to Monsieur Blum. It is asking him to bring some figures about the German air strength which Flandin gave me in May, up to date, and I am anxious to have the information not for public use, but as a guide to the forming of my own opinion, before I speak in the forthcoming debate. If you think proper, pray deliver the letter yourself, and tell him what I have told you in this letter. He will I am sure immediately give orders that the information should be given me. He has already offered me the fullest information. You then perhaps could obtain the answer which the Air department no doubt can give almost immediately, and could send it to me at 11, Morpeth Mansions, Westminster. I do not trouble the Embassy with the matter as it might seem to make the request look official. If you have the slightest doubts about whether you yourself should intervene, will you have the letter sent by a trusty messenger in the ordinary way. I do not think it should go through the post, as it contains a copy of a secret French document given to me by Flandin. All I am anxious is that it should reach its destination safely and promptly.

Winston S. Churchill to Léon Blum
(*Churchill papers: 2/274*)

8 November 1936

Monsieur Flandin some months ago kindly gave me the enclosed French official estimate of the strength, actual and prospective, of the German air force. I should be very much obliged to you if you would let me know whether this estimate still holds good, or in what respect it has been changed by later information. You may rely upon my using such information with all necessary discretion.

I hope you will allow me to offer my earnest congratulations upon all the great improvements that have taken place in French affairs since I first had the pleasure of meeting you at the Quay D'Orsai. It is very much appreciated in England how much this is due to your personal influence, and I am sure if you were able to come to this country you would receive the warmest welcome from all parties. It is very pleasant to remember, as Mr Eden said, that France and England are now more closely in accord than at any time since the Great War ended. It is less agreeable to remember our common perils.[1]

---

[1] On 13 November 1936 André Blumel, Blum's Director of Cabinet, sent Churchill, at Blum's request, a two-page typed summary of French estimates of German air strength. At the beginning of January 1937, the French believed, Germany would have 1,764 first line aircraft, 200 Lufthansa aircraft, 1,500 general reserve aircraft and 540 special reserve; an increase in first-line strength of 608 since the beginning of May 1936. By the end of 1938, the summary stated, the number of second-line aircraft would be substantially increased, but first-line increases were hampered by personnel difficulties. The summary concluded:'The numerical strength of the German Air Force is in the process of rapid increase. The development of the quality of the personnel is evolving more slowly. At the present time the German air squadrons have only 50% of the military value of the corresponding English or French units' (*Churchill papers: 2/274*).

Thornton Butterworth to Winston S. Churchill

(*Churchill papers: 8/537*)

9 November 1936

Dear Mr Churchill,
We propose putting the 'The Eastern Front' into the Keystone Library after the turn of the year; and I am now writing to enquire whether you would object to our entitling it, as follows:—

'THE UNKNOWN WAR'
(The Eastern Front)[1]

Anthony Eden to Winston S. Churchill

(*Churchill papers: 2/260*)

9 November 1936   Foreign Office

My dear Winston,
This is to say 'Thank you' for your speech last Thursday.[2] You will probably have seen that the reaction of the whole debate in Europe has been good, & the effect steadying. A very large measure of this we owe to you. I am most grateful.

Yours ever,
Anthony Eden

[1] When it was first published in November 1931, the fifth and final volume of Churchill's first world war memoirs, *The World Crisis*, had been entitled 'The Eastern Front' in Britain, and 'The Unknown War' in the United States. Churchill had preferred this latter title. In 1937 Thornton Butterworth reissued the volume in his Keystone Library edition, using the United States title as indicated here. Four years later, the book was again reissued, this time by Macmillan, who again used 'The Unknown War' as the book's main title, but adding the dates 1914–1917. Also in 1941, Hodder and Stoughton published a cheap edition (for sixpence).

[2] On 8 November 1936 Churchill spoke in the House of Commons about the need for a precise plan in foreign policy. 'The repeated chops and changes', he said, 'hot fits and cold fits, with which even the last melancholy twelve months have acquainted us, have sensibly diminished our influence and augmented the dangers which menace us and others.' Anglo-French cooperation was essential: 'Together they will be very hard to destroy.' No nation sought to encircle Germany. All legitimate grievances were capable of peaceful resolution. And he continued: 'It is said that there must not be a front against any nation, against Germany. All I can say is that unless there is a front against potential aggression there will be no settlement. All the nations of Europe will just be driven helter-skelter across the diplomatic chessboard until the limits of retreat are exhausted, and then out of desperation, perhaps in some most unlikely quarter, the explosion of war will take place, probably under conditions not very favourable to whose who have been engaged in this long retreat.'

Winston S. Churchill to Joseph Beck[1]

(Churchill papers: 2/260)

9 November 1936

I am most deeply grateful to you for your kindness in sending me the handsome volume by the late Marshal Pilsudski,[2] the Father of his country, statesman, warrior and patriot, who played so grand a part in the liberation and reunion of Poland. I have always been warmly attached to the Polish cause, and it gives me the greatest pleasure to receive marks of consideration from those who are guiding Poland in these anxious days.

Sir Guy Fleetwood Wilson[3] *to Winston S. Churchill*

(Churchill papers: 2/260)

9 November 1936

My dear Churchill,

I am very glad indeed to think that you have not forgotten me because I think it must have been at your instigation that I was sent an invitation to the Luncheon on the 25 November at which you propose to speak on the International situation. One of my greatest pleasures is to dwell on the happy Sundays I used to spend when I had my cottage near Dormansland and you

---

[1] Joseph Beck, 1894–1944. An undergraduate at Vienna on the outbreak of war in 1914, when he joined Pilsudski's Legion and took part in the war against Russia. Served first in the Artillery, then on the General Staff. Colonel, 1918. Polish Military Attaché in Paris, 1922–5. Chef de Cabinet to Pilsudski, 1926–9. Minister without Portfolio, 1929–32. Appointed Foreign Minister (at the age of 38) in 1932; remained in office until the German invasion of Poland in 1939. Escaped to Rumania, 1939. Arrested near Bucharest, 1940; died four years later, while still in captivity.

[2] Joseph Clemens Pilsudski, 1867–1935. Born in the Vilna Province, under Russian rule. Involved in an anti-Tsarist plot and deported to Siberia, 1887–92. Edited, printed and distributed a secret Radical paper, *Robotnik*, 1894–1900, when he was arrested in Lodz and imprisoned. Escaped from prison in St Petersburg, 1901. In exile in London, 1901–2. Established a Polish army in Austrian Poland, 1908–14; in 1914 his 10,000 men fought in the Austro-Hungarian Army. Minister of War in the Council of State, Warsaw (under Central Power auspices), 1916–17. His army refused to support the Germans in July 1917; he was imprisoned by the Germans, July 1917–November 1918. Chief of the Polish State, November 1918–December 1922. Chief of the General Staff, 1923. Retired from public life, July 1923. Occupied Warsaw, May 1926. Minister of War, 1926–35. Prime Minister, 1927–8 and 1930.

[3] Guy Douglas Arthur Fleetwood Wilson, 1850–1940. A Clerk in the Paymaster-General's Office, 1870. Private Secretary to Gladstone, 1886; to Campbell-Bannerman, 1892–93. Financial Adviser to Kitchener in South Africa, 1901. Knighted, 1902. Privy Councillor, 1904. Director-General of Army Finance, 1904–8. Finance Member of the Supreme Council of India, 1908–13. Vice-President of the Legislative Council of India, 1911–13. Commissioner, Special Government Enquiry, Dublin, 1916. Chairman of the Financial Committee, Flying Corps, 1917. Member of the High Court Tribunal for Naval Prize, 1918–28.

had a house within a couple of miles towards Sussex.[1] I shall never forget my Sunday visits to you and to Mrs Churchill who was always so nice to me and your delightful children to whom I became very greatly attached.

I find that most people have quite forgotten my existence and the latter day folk 'know not Joseph'. Only the other day a man met me and said 'You must have had a very interesting experience when you were Governor of the Isle of Man!'

I should like of all things to hear your speech on the 25th, but I do not feel justified in going, as I am mad. I must be mad, because it is absurd to suppose that all the very distinguished people who are shown as being members of the New Commonwealth Society can be mad!

I personally think it is madness to meddle with any International anything and my views were given expression to recently in answer to Cecil who sent me a pressing invitation to join the International Peace Campaign and to go to the meeting which you attended at Brussels. I send you a copy of my letter to Cecil. I think that the only sound, sensible and safe attitude and action of the English people is to state concisely what they will fight for, that is, in defence of themselves and their Colonies and their possessions generally, and in my opinion also the defence of Belgium not only from the standpoint of sentiment, but because it is essential for us to control their coast line in the interests of our Navy and further I consider that we ought to keep entirely out of any wars of disagreements which may occur in respect of the other countries of Europe, including of course Russia.

You will realise that holding the views I do it would not be right of me to attend a meeting of very distinguished people who hold the exactly opposite view.

I presume your speech will be published in the newspapers and I shall read it with the greatest interest.

I have been immensely interested and greatly delighted with the very able articles by you which have appeared in the EVENING STANDARD [2] and I

[1] Lullenden: see page 361, note 2.

[2] Between 13 March 1936 and 5 April 1938 Churchill wrote a regular fortnightly article for the *Evening Standard*. These articles were subsequently reprinted in Churchill's book *Step By Step* (published in June 1939). The first of the articles was entitled 'Britain, Germany and Locarno', and in it Churchill wrote that if the League of Nations were to act decisively over the German re-militarization of the Rhineland, 'there is no reason why the horrible, dull, remorseless drift to war in 1937 or 1938. and the preparatory piling up of enormous armaments in every country, should not be decisively arrested. . . . There is a simple method: the assembly of overwhelming force, moral and physical, in support of international law. . . . if the forces at the disposal of the League of Nations are four or five times as strong as those which the Aggressor can yet command, the chances of a peaceful and friendly solution are very good. Therefore every nation, great or small, should play its part according to the Covenant of the League.'

confess that I find it quite difficult to reconcile some of your articles with your membership of this New Commonwealth Society which is essentially meddling with what does not concern us and will probably end by having what my excellent friend Lord Davies has always advocated—an International Police Air Force.

Forgive me for writing so frankly and so freely.

I am sure you will appreciate that it is only because I wish you to understand my feelings and my reasons for not attending the Dorchester Hotel Luncheon.

Yours sincerely,
Guy Fleetwood Wilson

Winston S. Churchill to Lady Houston

(*Churchill papers: 2/260*)

9 November 1936   11 Morpeth Mansions

Many thanks for your letter. You may be sure I have very carefully considered the course I am taking, from the point of view of the safety of England from the German Nazi menace. If you will read my speech in the House on Thursday last you will see the arguments on which I rely. I am well aware you do not take the same view. I share to the full your regrets for the misguided policy of the MacDonald–Baldwin regime during the last five years in defence and external affairs.

Ivan Maisky to Winston S. Churchill

(*Churchill papers: 2/260*)

10 November 1936

My dear Churchill,

I was sorry not to be able to get to the House of Commons for the debate last Thursday (as a matter of fact I went down to Dover to meet my wife on her return from the USSR). Knowing that you had spoken in the debate I was especially keen to read the next day's Hansard, because I always find your speeches interesting and stimulating.

But, on this occasion I must confess that though I found most of your contribution excellent, I was very disappointed by that part which had reference to my country.

I do not understand why you seem to think that 'Moscow' is primarily responsible for the outbreak of civil war in Spain; certainly this is not the case, although certain elements would no doubt like such a view fostered.

I am sure that you are aware of the position in the constellation of political parties in the Spanish Republic; it is not at all favourably disposed to 'Moscow'. Apart from the 'left' Republicans which certainly can't be suspected of any dealings with 'Moscow' there are two main political forces in Spain: First, the Socialists (left and right wing) who have always belonged to the Second (Labour & Socialist) International and, on the Trade Union side, to the Amsterdam International Federation of Trade Unions; and secondly, the Anarchists and Anarcho-Syndicalists (especially strong in Catalonia) who always bitterly opposed 'Moscow' as 'reactionary' and 'statebound'. The Communists, who may reasonably be expected to look to Moscow are a very small and uninfluential party.

And when you talk of the 'importation of the most skilled agitators, Bela Kun[1] and others'—you are quite misled, for none of these men have been visiting Spain.

In the circumstances I do not see how you can say: 'But for Russia and but for the Russian Communist Propaganda and intrigues which for more than six months racked Spain before the outbreak, the Spanish horror need never have occurred.'

There is, on the other hand, one point which you must not lose sight of: Immediately after the last Spanish elections which, in the recognised democratic way, returned a 'left-wing' Government, the Germans and Italians, and more particularly the Germans, set to work to foster anti-republican propaganda and to prepare carefully military rebellion against that Government.

I expect you saw the documents which were published in the 'Manchester Guardian' on August 19, 20, 24 etc, and which fully confirmed the existence of a widespread net of German 'cells' and agents all over Spain, working at high pressure to upset the legitimate government of the country. (I had confirmation of this from other sources.)

It is also common knowledge that before embarking on their military venture the Spanish rebels had dealings in Berlin with certain very important

---

[1] Bela Kun, 1886–1939. A Hungarian Jew, he worked before 1914 as a journalist on a Socialist newspaper in Budapest. Served as a Lieutenant-Commander of an ammunition Supply column, 1914. Captured by the Russians on the Eastern Front and imprisoned in Russia, 1915–17. He supported the Bolsheviks in 1917; in October 1918 he returned to Hungary as leader of a revolutionary party. Prime Minister of Hungary, March–August 1919, when he instituted a communist regime. In July 1919 the Allies halted his invasion of Slovakia. He fled to Vienna in August 1919, and was interned in a lunatic asylum. Allowed by the Allies to go to Russia, 1920, he became a leading figure of the Comintern. Eventually he was imprisoned, then murdered on Stalin's orders.

personalities there, securing German aid for their venture in advance. That these dealings were not wholly unsuccessful is amply proved by the abundance of German aeroplanes, guns, tanks, etc in the service of the rebels. It is with these supplies that they have been able to beat their way to Madrid, fighting all the time against the ill-equipped, ill-trained militia-men of the Spanish Government.

Would it not be far truer to say that German propaganda and German intrigues are largely responsible for the outbreak of civil war in Spain?

And to wind up let me just reaffirm that the reason which occasions such great interest on the part of the Soviet Government and the peoples of the Soviet Union in the affairs of Spain is the deep conviction (and you will remember that I talked to you about this when we last met) that there is going on at the present time in Spain, an advance battle between the forces of peace and the forces of war in Europe. The outcome of this battle will have an enormous effect on the whole situation in our part of the world, and on the question of whether a general conflagration comes soon—within the next twelve months—or whether it may be postponed. We have not the slightest doubt that a victory for General Franco would mean such an encouragement to the forces of aggression, of hatred, of destruction in Europe that such conflagration could not be long averted.

It is because of this—apart from any sympathy which our peoples feel for the democratic elements in Spain—that we consider in this momentous struggle between the forces of peace and the forces of war that our sympathies must be on the side of the forces of peace.

It is a matter of very real regret to us that people in other countries who also sincerely desire to avoid war do not see their way to supporting the cause of the Spanish Government.

Yours sincerely,
I. Maisky

Lady Desborough[1] *to Winston S. Churchill*
(*Churchill papers: 8/531*)

10 November 1936

Winston my dearest,

I meant to write & thank you not until I had finished reading that en-

---

[1] Ethel Anne Priscilla Fane, 1867–1952. Known as 'Ettie'. Married, 1887, William Henry Grenfell, 1st Baron Desborough. Their homes at Taplow Court in Buckinghamshire, and at Panshanger in Hertfordshire, were two of the great social houses of the pre-1914 and post-war decades. Lady Desborough was a Lady of the Bedchamber to Queen Mary, 1911–36. Two of her sons were killed in action on the western front (in May and July 1915). Her third son died in 1926 as a result of a motor car accident.

thralling volume, but cannot wait so long. I am most entranced in the very middle, rolling every syllable separately in my ears.

What a treat, what a feast, you are giving us. I wish there were to be forty volumes. Never could there be another hero like Marlborough, what a perfect character. Each actor in the drama is as present in one's eye as Mrs S![1] Thank you & bless you, & a whole Pacific Ocean of love to you & darling Clemmie.

Your devoted,
E

Guy Eden[2] *to Winston S. Churchill*

(*Churchill papers: 2/279*)

11 November 1936   Press Gallery
Private and Confidential   House of Commons

Dear Mr Churchill,

An important industrialist closely connected with the 'shadow airplane industry' suggested that I might ask you to put and press this question in the debate:

'How soon does the Govt expect to get its first airplane engine, completed and assembled and tested, as a result of the work of the shadow scheme.'

I am told that the answer, if a truthful one, should be that there can be no delivery for two years or so.

I pass on the suggestion, as requested, but I know you will not quote me or bring me into the discussion in any way.

Yours faithfully,
Guy Eden

[1] Mrs Simpson. An allusion to the crisis then growing, and in which Churchill himself was soon to become embroiled.

[2] Guy Ernest Morton Eden, 1864–1954. Educated at Westminster. Called to the Bar, Inner Temple, 1901. Board of Education, Legal Branch, 1903–5 and 1906–14. Attached to the Directorate of Military Intelligence, War Office, 1914–18. Novelist, poet and lyricist. Editor of *The Navy*, 1918–39. Author of *Bush Ballads*, 1930; *Portrait of Churchill*, 1945; *What You Pay, What You Get*, 1947 and *The Parliament Book*, 1949. Political Correspondent, *Daily Express*, 1933–52; subsequently on the *Sunday Despatch*.

Lord Salisbury to Stanley Baldwin

(*Baldwin papers*)

12 November 1936
Confidential

My dear SB,

I am told that the feeling in the House of Commons upon the subject[1] of which you told us at Hatfield (and at the House on Thursday) is intense. Selborne[2] suggests a deputation to *you* of the elder statesmen. Useless of course except perhaps to strengthen your hands. Would you like it? It is of course a thing for you to decide. The idea would be Austen, Winston, Crewe,[3] Derby[4] etc—and perhaps Attlee though he is not quite an elder statesman.

Tell your secretary to telephone to me here tomorrow morning if you have any wishes.

Yours ever,
Salisbury

Of course Selborne and myself too and perhaps others.

[1] Rumours of a possible marriage between the King and Mrs Simpson.

[2] William Waldegrave Palmer, 1859–1942. Educated at Winchester and University College, Oxford. Liberal MP, 1885–6; Unionist MP, 1886–95. 2nd Earl of Selborne, 1895. First Lord of the Admiralty, 1900–5. High Commissioner for South Africa, 1905–10. President of the Board of Agriculture and Fisheries in Asquith's Coalition Government, from May 1915 to June 1916, after which he received no further Cabinet appointment. Served in the Ministry of Economic Warfare, 1940. His second son, Robert, was killed in action in Mesopotamia in 1916.

[3] Robert Offley Ashburton Crewe-Milnes, 1858–1945. Educated at Harrow and Trinity College, Cambridge. Succeeded his father as 2nd Baron Houghton, 1885. Lord Lieutenant of Ireland, 1892–5. Created Earl of Crewe, 1895. Secretary of State for the Colonies (when Churchill was his Under-Secretary of State), 1908–10. Secretary of State for India, 1910–15. Created Marquess, 1911. President of the Board of Education, 1916. Ambassador to Paris, 1922–8. Secretary of State for War, 1931. In 1899 he married (as his second wife) Lady Margaret Primrose, daughter of the 5th Earl of Rosebery. His two sons predeceased him, one aged 7, the other aged 11. One of his sons-in-law (by his first marriage) was killed in action on the western front on 5 November 1914; a grandson, (Sir) John Colville, was one of Churchill's Private Secretaries, 1940–1, 1943–5, and 1951–5.

[4] Edward George Villiers Stanley, 1865–1948. Educated at Wellington College. Lieutenant, Grenadier Guards, 1885–95. Conservative MP for West Houghton, 1892–1906. Postmaster-General, 1903–5. 17th Earl of Derby, 1908. Director-General of Recruiting, October 1915. Under-Secretary of State at the War Office, July–December 1916. Secretary of State for War, December 1916–18. Ambassador to France, 1918–20. Secretary of State for War, 1922–4. Member of the Joint Select Committee on the Indian Constitution, 1933–4.

Winston S. Churchill to Randolph S. Churchill

(*Churchill papers: 2/283*)

13 November 1936   Chartwell

My dear Randolph,

You will remember a luncheon you attended at the Hotel Victoria to meet Citrine and others connected with the Anti Nazi League. This is living under another form and arrangements are now in train for an Albert Hall meeting at which I speak, with Citrine in the Chair. All the Left Wing intelligencia are coming to look to me for protection of their ideas, and I will give it wholeheartedly in return for their aid in the rearmament of Britain. The basis of the Anti Nazi League is of course Jewish resentment at their abominable persecution. But we are now taking broader ground rather on the lines of my Paris speech which perhaps you read. A Peace with Freedom committee has been formed. I enclose a copy of the formula at length adopted. This committee aims at focusing and concentrating the efforts of all the Peace societies like the New Commonwealth and the League of Nations Union in so far as they are prepared to support genuine military action to resist tyranny or aggression.

So much for what is happening here.

It appears however, that there is a similar movement similarly actuated in the United States, and I received the enclosed letter from Herbert Bayard Swope introducing a Mr Landau. These people want me to come to the United States and deliver a few speeches or lectures of the kind which I gave in Paris, and on the lines on which I am speaking here. I said that my plans were to go to Marrakech for the Winter and that nothing would induce me to cross the Atlantic. On further pressure I said that if I went it could only be on a business footing. Thereupon I received the enclosed letter from Mr Landau, with which it would clearly be my duty to comply. A list of American gentlemen behind this American branch was also furnished to me. It appears however that these are only people whom Herbert Bayard Swope thought of approaching and I do not gather that they or any large number of them have signified their adhesion to the Committee. This is indeed not essential for I am perfectly prepared to lecture for the fee mentioned as proposed. However it is naturally necessary for me to know whether everything is all right on that side. I shall therefore probably ask Mr Landau to get in touch with you, and if you receive any communication from him you will know from this what it is about.

After Mr Landau has seen you and you have mastered the case you should talk it over with Baruch whose advice would be invaluable, as to the standing, bona fides of the parties, and whether he would think it advisable on general grounds. Subject to everything being satisfactory I am prepared to sail after Christmas for New York and would make a programme for the lectures and speeches as indicated. I should stay in America during January and would spend at least a fortnight with Consuelo Balsan at Palm Beach. It would probably be more agreeable to me to fix the engagements so as to have a clear fortnight in the south. It would be desirable if the contract or exchange of letters to be made in the United States as I did in the case of my lecture contract and I will if necessary send you power of attorney to act for me. I do not suppose it will be necessary to trouble Levy with this, as he has done so much for me already.

Diana and Duncan are coming here for Christmas and I hope you will be with us too.

H. W. Woollett [1] *to Winston S. Churchill*

(*Churchill papers: 2/279*)

13 November 1936

Sir,

May I commence by saying I know about what I wish to say. I was for 18 years an officer in the RAF & I now hold 9 decorations.

On Wednesday in the House, Sir Thomas Inskip said, 'The number of squadrons *at home* in present circumstances today is *80*, and that figure includes 16 auxiliary squadrons, but excludes The Fleet Air Arm.'

From the November Air Force List it will be seen that there are over *43 fully formed* regular squadrons, and 12 *fully formed* auxiliary squadrons!

A total of 55—but on paper 80!!

I am Sir,

Yours truly,
H. W. Woollett

[1] Henry Winslow Woollett, 1895–   . Educated at Wellingborough School. Medical Student, London Hospital, 1912–14. Enlisted as a 2nd Lieutenant, Lincolnshire Regiment, 1914. Transferred to the Royal Flying Corps, 1916. Military Cross, 1917 (and bar, 1918). DSO, 1918. Légion d'Honneur, 1918. French Croix de Guerre with palm, 1919. Captain, Royal Air Force, 1918. Served with 208 (Army Co-operation) Squadron, 1924. Resigned from the RAF with the rank of Squadron Leader, 1932. Granted a Commission, as Acting Pilot Officer, Royal Air Force Volunteer Reserve, 1941. Resigned his commission, 1942.

Winston S. Churchill to Sir Guy Fleetwood Wilson

(*Churchill papers: 2/260*)

13 November 1936

It is very nice to hear from you again, and I quite understand the point of view which you hold. I am trying to marshal all the forces I can to prevent this coming war, and to strengthen Britain. If you will read the speech I shall make on November 25 you will I think see that there is not so much between us.[1]

Lord Cavan[2] to Winston S. Churchill

(*Churchill papers: 25/7*)

13 November 1936

My dear Winston,

I can't tell you with what delight I have read of Ramillies & Oudenarde in your Vol III. I wish my memory was retentive, but the 3 Vols are all in my Library next to the World Crisis—& however old, one can refresh.

I cannot help regretting one stroke only of bad luck in my career—that from 1924 to 1926 your orders as Chancellor were—reduce two million a year on Army estimates.

---

[1] Churchill's luncheon speech on 25 November 1936, as President of the New Commonwealth Society, was heard by more than 450 people, including Ivan Maisky, the Soviet Ambassador. In his speech, Churchill argued that British foreign policy 'should strive to build up under the League of Nations a great structure of combined defensive strength, so that not only should we be taking the measures for defending ourselves, and be a help and not a burden to others, but also that we should be ourselves a worthy and acceptable partner in a general scheme of mutual defence and insurance against unprovoked aggression'. Churchill added: 'Where we differ from most other peace societies is that we contemplate and advocate the use of force against the aggressor, in support of law. We think it utterly futile to have a League of Nations or an International Court, unless behind that there is an armed, organized force, capable of procuring respect for their decisions.' Churchill's speech was printed in full in the December 1936 issue of *The New Commonwealth*. Lord Davies, in expressing his thanks, declared: 'Gentlemen, no cause has ever succeeded without a leader. Here is a great and noble cause: here is a courageous leader whose sterling gifts and high attainments are respected, not only in his own country and in the British Commonwealth, but throughout the length and breadth of Europe. I would therefore appeal to you to enrol under the banner which he has unfurled here to-day, the banner of Equity and Justice, supported by might.'

[2] Frederick Rudolph Lambart, 1865–1946. Entered Army, 1885. 10th Earl of Cavan, 1900. Major-General commanding the 4th (Guards) Brigade, September 1914–June 1915. Commanded the Guards Division, August 1915–January 1916. Commanded the XIV Corps in France and Italy, January 1916–18. Commander-in-Chief, Aldershot, 1920–2. Chief of he Imperial General Staff, 1922–6. Field-Marshal, 1932. Private, Home Guard, 1940.

No doubt right—but so dull from my point of view as CIGS. I rejoice to see your efforts to get more than 8 millions back!!

Do press for a simple frame of steel girders with *two* nets of steel over the 5 or 6 big Power Stations of London. So simple: and underground Parking Places—for Peace—gas proof refuges for War.

Yrs ever,
Cavan

Winston S. Churchill to Major Percy Davies

(Churchill papers: 8/533)

13 November 1936

I have been so busy that this is the first moment I find to thank you and the News of the World for the extremely handsome manner in which you have treated me about the articles. I shall be glad if you will tell Sir Emsley Carr how much I appreciate his consideration.

With regard to the Biblical series I should be glad if this could be provisionally settled in writing. My political affairs are still in the uncertainty which lapped them last year and it would be convenient to me to have an agreement made as before. There will be plenty of time to settle which Biblical characters are to be dealt with.

Sir Archibald Boyd-Carpenter [1] to Winston S. Churchill

(Churchill papers: 2/260)

13 November 1936   Carlton Club

My dear Winston,

I must send you a few words of congratulation on your wonderful & inspiring speech yesterday.[2] I said to myself 'Thank God someone has courage'

---

[1] Archibald Boyd-Carpenter, 1873–1937. One of Churchill's contemporaries at Harrow. Son of the Rt Rev Dr W. Boyd-Carpenter, Bishop of Ripon and Canon of Westminster. Educated at Balliol College, Oxford. President of the Oxford Union. British Vice-consul, Menton. Joined the Highland Light Infantry, 1900. Served as a Staff Captain in South Africa, 1901–2, and as a Major in the European War, 1914–19. Conservative MP for North Bradford, 1918–23, for Coventry, 1924–9 and for Chertsey, 1931–7. Parliamentary Secretary, Ministry of Labour, November 1922–March 1923. Financial Secretary to the Treasury, 1923; to the Admiralty, 1923–4. Paymaster–General, 1923 and 1924. Knighted, 1926.

[2] Speaking in the Defence Debate on 12 November 1936, Churchill told his fellow MPs: 'I have heard it said that the Government had no mandate for rearmament until the General Election. Such a doctrine is wholly inadmissible. The responsibility of Ministers for the public

& I feel it all the more after the pathetic effort of SB which makes one feel almost ill.

Good luck & good health to you.

Yours ever,
Archie Boyd-Carpenter

Winston S. Churchill to Sir Archibald Boyd-Carpenter

(*Churchill papers: 2/260*)

13 November 1936

Thank you so much for your most kind letter. I have never heard such a squalid confession from a public man as Baldwin offered us yesterday.[1]

---

safety is absolute and requires no mandate. It is in fact the prime object for which Governments come into existence. The Prime Minister had the command of enormous majorities in both Houses of Parliament ready to vote for any necessary measures of defence. The country has never yet failed to do its duty when the true facts have been put before it, and I cannot see where there is a defence for this delay.' Churchill ended his speech with the words: 'I say that unless the House resolves to find out the truth for itself it will have committed an act of abdication of duty without parallel in its long history.'

[1] Seeking to explain why he had not rearmed more forcefully between the autumn of 1933 and the General Election in the summer of 1935, Baldwin told the House of Commons on 12 November 1936—in answer to a critical speech by Churchill: 'I would remind the House that not once but on many occasions in speeches and in various places, when I have been speaking and advocating as far as I am able the democratic principles, I have stated that a democracy is always two years behind the dictator. I believe that to be true. It has been true in this case. I put before the whole House my own views with an appalling frankness. You will remember at that time the Disarmament Conference was sitting in Geneva. You will remember at that time there was probably a stronger pacifist feeling running through this country than at any time since the War. You will remember the election at Fulham in the autumn of 1933, when a seat which the National Government held was lost by about 7,000 votes on no issue but the pacifist . . . My position as the leader of a great party was not altogether a comfortable one. I asked myself what chance was there—when the feeling that was given expression to in Fulham was common throughout the country—what chance was there within the next year or two of that feeling being so changed that the country would give a mandate for rearmament? Supposing I had gone to the country and said that Germany was rearming and that we must rearm, does anybody think that this pacific democracy would have rallied to that cry at that moment? I cannot think of anything that would have made the loss of the election from my point of view more certain.'

Winston S. Churchill to Geoffrey Dawson

(*Churchill papers: 2/260*)

13 November 1936

Sir,

In my speech in the House yesterday I complained of the difficulty of forcing new ideas upon the Government. The context makes this appear as if this complaint was directed at the War Office. Such was not my intention. I meant the criticism to apply generally, and in so far as any particular department was concerned, it was not the War Office.[1]

Lord Londonderry to Winston S. Churchill

(*Churchill papers: 2/267*)

13 November 1936

My dear Winston,

Many congratulations on a speech which I am glad to see was characterized in the leading article of the 'Times' as brilliant. You will forgive me for noting that your estimated number of German aeroplanes has been considerably reduced and I am very glad indeed. As a matter of fact, your figure is still too high as the Germans have about eighty squadrons in being now; if however they were to break up their Training Schools, the number of squadrons could be considerably increased but only at the expense of expansion, as with the break up of the Training Schools the training of new pilots would practically come to an end.

SB's admission was a very remarkable one, and it is interesting to me to know that no indication of his opinion that the country was running deadly risks was ever divulged by him as his opinion. In fact his lips were sealed. We

---

[1] On 12 November 1936, during his speech in the House of Commons, Churchill had referred to deficiencies in the strength and weaponry of the Territorial Army and the Tank Corps, and urged the establishment of a Ministry of Supply to make good all deficiencies. 'A very long period must intervene,' he said 'before any effectual flow of munitions can be expected, even for the small forces of which we dispose. Still we are told there is no necessity for a Ministry of Supply, no emergency which should induce us to impinge on the normal course of trade.' His speech continued: 'The First Lord of the Admiralty in his speech the other night went even further. He said, "We are always reviewing the position." Everything, he assured us, is entirely fluid. I am sure that that is true. Anyone can see what the position is. The Government simply cannot make up their mind, or they cannot get the Prime Minister to make up his mind. So they go on in strange paradox, decided only to be undecided, resolved to be irresolute, adamant for drift, solid for fluidity, all powerful to be impotent. So we go on preparing more months and years—precious, perhaps vital, to the greatness of Britain—for the locusts to eat.'

told him and Neville of the risks, but they were much too frightened of losing bye elections.

Yours ever,
Charley

Neville was really the villain of the piece because he as Chancellor blocked everything on the grounds of Finance.

Winston S. Churchill to Lord Davies
(*Churchill papers: 2/285*)

14 November 1936

I was so sorry not to be able to have a talk this week. The Defence Debate weighed me down. Speaking on these extremely precise technical subjects is a very laborious and exacting task.

I am looking forward to our luncheon on the 25th, and it will take two or three of my days to prepare an adequate speech for such an important occasion. Mr Foot tells me that 350 people have already accepted. With regard to Abe Bailey's proposed dinner I do not know that such a gathering would do very much good. The propagation of ideas rather than the enlistment of individuals seems to be the best way of advancing. I do not advise therefore embarking upon this plan. With regard to the appeal which is to be sent out after the luncheon, surely it should go in your name. I have never yet signed any of these appeals for funds, and I would rather not do so on this occasion. I think my best contribution will be to make you as good a speech as I can at your luncheon. I hope they will report it well.

With all good wishes, believe me,

Desmond Morton to Winston S. Churchill
(*Churchill papers: 2/267*)

14 November 1936   Crockham Hill

Dear Winston,

I have burnt Moral's letter and enclosure as you asked. Thank you for letting me see it. The enclosure translated from 'Gringoire' may be genuine, but that newspaper is not a very sure source of information.

The post-card you also enclosed was from an Italian, who says you are wrong in blaming the Communists for everything evil in this world, and that the Socialists are nearly as bad. 'The Socialist of today is the Communist of to-morrow', says he.

Thank you for the book in German, but as a matter of fact I have it in English. It is rather an interesting economic analysis of Japan in war-time.

I return a cutting you sent me, as I think it is necessary to point a moral from it. The cutting claims that a 'shadow' scheme for aero-engine construction broke down during the Great War, and draws the conclusion therefrom that the present scheme is unsound. That argument is bad. The wartime shadow factories had never been taught in peace how to make aero-engines. One of the chief points of the present scheme is to train the shadow factories in peace by giving them 'educational orders'.

I have to admit that I have not quite comprehended the full meaning of the French figures of German Air strength, which you read to me on the telephone. The qualification that the German Air Force is 50% in value in comparison with the British and French force is a new departure. That the German force is not yet man for man and machine for machine the equal of the British or French may be upheld; but it would be a bold man who dared to define the exact arithmetical equivalent. For our purposes it seems to me sound that we should regard a German squadron as the equal of a French or a British squadron, and leave it at that.

Yours very sincerely,
Desmond Morton

Winston S. Churchill to Sir Austen Chamberlain
(Churchill papers: 2/260)

14 November 1936

How very kind of you to send me your book about our pre-war battles.[1] I am starting at once upon reading it. It will be intensely interesting to me, and I shall look forward to talking it over with you when I have finished it. It will always fill an honoured place in my library. What days those were!

---

[1] *Politics from Inside: An Epistolary Chronicle 1906–1914.* By Sir Austen Chamberlain, published by Cassell and Company Limited. Churchill was frequently mentioned in the letters, particularly on naval and Irish matters.

Winston S. Churchill to Ivan Maisky
(*Churchill papers: 2/260*)

14 November 1936

I am very much obliged to you for your long and interesting letter, and for the information and assurances which it contains. I hope that you read my speech in Hansard where it was fully reported, and that you will give as much weight to the latter part of my references to your Government as to the former.[1] This, I am sure, was the effect produced upon the greater part of my hearers.

Once more thanking you,

Believe me,

Sir Leo Chiozza Money to Winston S. Churchill
(*Churchill papers: 2/260*)

14 November 1936

My dear Churchill,

I joined in the applause of your Commons speech and again deplore the fact that the Party Game (falsely termed Democracy) robs us of your services as a minister of state. I wanted a Ministry of Supply in the War and nearly got it, but they funked (more 'democracy') Liberal opposition to yet another department. That Ministry, if established in the War and continued in peace, would have saved us from economic collapse and military danger.

I wonder what they are doing about *stocks*. I send you copy of a letter I wrote to Hoare about it.

May I add something about the general situation? Surely we cannot enter war as an ally of the Soviet! It would, of course, be the end of the British Commonwealth and many other things, whatever the military determination. If that is accepted, why not face the necessity of making friends with

---

[1] Speaking in the House of Commons on 5 November 1936, Churchill declared: 'Russia is in very great peril. She has to consider dangers from the East as well as from the West. Mighty military nations glare at Soviet Russia, and it is most surprising that a State thus threatened should act with such insensitive folly'—the Russian intervention in Spain. But, Churchill went on, 'there is another Russia, which seems to be growing stronger as the years pass, which only wishes to be left alone in peace, which only wishes to be allowed to live whatever kind of life it can work out for itself. Such a Russia has its rights in the comity of nations, if, by foolish conduct, these rights are not destroyed.' One day, Russia could be 'an indispensable element in the equipoise of peace both in the West and in the East, but we have not such a Russia at the moment'. In the Russia of 1936 'everything is so obscure, so double-faced, so transitional'. As a result, 'we must await with patience, however strained, developments which are taking place in Russia in the hope that she may play a part in preserving the general peace'.

Germany and Italy and of giving a true lead to France? The French need to be saved from themselves.

It is population that will count, and France has doomed herself by sterility. Why link ourselves with a degenerate, *reddening* France leaning vainly on Russia?

The ancient trouble between France and Germany is the main obstacle to peace. Because of it, France seeks alliances, knowing her man power to be sadly lacking. Britain can be the friend of both parties and set an example which would call all the world to reason.

Germany feels herself deprived and frustrated. She makes plans to improve her economy while pointing to needs her own efforts, however skilled, cannot supply. Her 66 million people have the right to live and prosper. Why should we not allow her, out of our own abundance (including as it does a fourth of all the world) once more to rule the lands she lost in the war of 1914–1918, so far as we now rule them. France has not the resources to develop her share of the German spoils; our action could hardly fail to induce her to follow our example.

As for Italy, I am convinced that she has no hostile intentions, and that she is only seeking to protect herself. Her friendship with Germany, the formation of the Roman Group, the surprising Yugo-Slavian development,[1] all aid the cause of peace if we care to express ourselves in deeds. If we do not, the issue is plain. Can a number of Whites, fewer than the Germans in Germany, however they tax themselves for arms, hold a fourth of the world (a third in point of value) against all nations? To ask the question is to answer it.

About population, may I ask you to read an article on the subject which is to appear in the 'Nineteenth Century' for December?[2]

With good wishes always,
Leo Chiozza Money

[1] See page 448, note 1.
[2] In an article entitled 'Renew or Die!' in the December 1936 issue of *The Nineteenth Century*, Sir Leo Chiozza Money argued that 'nothing short of drastic action' could halt the decline in the population of Britain. In 1913 a total of 881,890 children had been born in England and Wales, in 1930 it had fallen to 648,811 and in 1935 to 599,167. For the population of Britain to 'hold its own', it was necessary for those who did marry to produce three children each. In Britain and the Empire combined, Chiozza Money pointed out, there were 64,000,000 Englishmen, Welshmen, Scotsmen and Irishmen (of whom 46,700,000 lived in the United Kingdom); but this was smaller than the population of the German Reich 'which in 1935, with the restored Saar, was about 66,000,000'. Chiozza Money went on to suggest the setting up of a Department of Maternity and Child Welfare, under a Cabinet Minister, to 'promote respect for motherhood' and to erect 'splendid maternity homes in every district, as is done in Italy'. He also proposed income tax and wage reforms, and State dowries, to encourage family life 'in a section of the community that is leading the nation in race suicide'.

Patrick Donner[1] to Winston S. Churchill
(*Churchill papers: 2/260*)

15 November 1936

Dear Mr Churchill,

You will not I feel sure misunderstand me if I send you these few lines to express my wholehearted admiration of your superb exposition during the debate on defence. I do not know the nature of the probable consequences of your speech but I cannot recall seeing the House *as a whole* so uneasy. For my own part I have, with the exception of your speech on the second reading of the India bill, never heard you more effective, and feel justified for that very reason, in troubling you with a letter.

Yours sincerely,
Patrick

Paul Maze to Winston S. Churchill
(*Churchill papers: 1/268*)

My dear Winston,

I was thrilled by every word you said in the House yesterday—as I went down, the usher downstairs said to me 'you chose a good day to come, he is always fine—none left like him—he always does one good'. I nearly embraced him—I feel so much what he said!

I have sent you some brushes—you should destroy most of your old brushes which can't help you in your work. Paint like you write or speak. You can do it—every stroke of the brush must be a statement felt & seen— Remember that 'En peinture il faut que a tout moment le tableau soit beau— il ne faut jamais mettre quelques touches qui ne le sert pas—il est toujours plus facile de pousser une toile loin *quand on est parti de la verité*.'

Do come & have lunch here the first moment you are free—just telephone.

Thank you again for getting me into the House yesterday.[2]

Affectionately,
Paul

---

[1] Patrick William Donner, 1904– . Son of Ossian Donner, Finnish diplomat and first Finnish Minister to London, 1919–26. Educated at Exeter College, Oxford. Conservative MP for West Islington, 1931–5; for Basingstoke, 1935–55. Honorary Secretary, India Defence League, 1933–5. Member of the Advisory Committee on Education in the Colonies, 1939– 41. Parliamentary Private Secretary to Sir Samuel Hoare at the Home Office, 1939; to Oliver Stanley at the Colonial Office, 1944. Royal Air Force Volunteer Reserve, 1939. Acting Squadron Leader, 1941. Knighted, 1953. High Sheriff of Hampshire 1967–8.

[2] Paul Maze's letter, although undated, must have been written on 12 November 1936; both he and Patrick Donner were referring to Churchill's 'adamant for drift' speech of 12 November 1936 (see pages 404 note 2 and 406, note 1).

Alfred Duff Cooper to Winston S. Churchill

(*Churchill papers: 2/267*)

16 November 1936   War Office

My dear Winston,
    Many thanks for the kind word you gave us in the Times on Saturday.[1]
We are doing our best and are very grateful for a little encouragement.

Yours,
Duff

Sir Herbert Creedy to Winston S. Churchill

(*Churchill papers: 2/260*)

16 November 1936   War Office

My dear Mr Churchill,
    Your letter to 'The Times' comes as a comfort and an encouragement in
these difficult days.
    We should indeed have fallen away if we had forgotten that, among the
lessons you taught me when you were S of S, was that of readiness to welcome
new ideas.
    Have we not warmly embraced an Engineer Admiral[2] as a Member of
Council?

Yours very sincerely,
Herbert Creedy

Lord Cecil of Chelwood to Winston S. Churchill

(*Cecil of Chelwood papers*)

16 November 1936

My dear Winston,
    A thousand thanks for your note.
    The present people that I am asking in this country are:—the Archbishop

---

[1] Churchill's letter of 13 November 1936, published in *The Times* on November 14 (see
page 406).
[2] Harold Arthur Brown, 1878–1968. Educated at the Royal Naval Engineers College.
Entered Navy, 1894. In 1912, when Churchill was First Lord of the Admiralty, Brown was
the Engineer-Lieutenant on board the destroyer *Cameleon*. Vice-Admiral, 1932. Engineer-in-
Chief of the Fleet, Admiralty, 1932–6. Knighted, 1934. Retired, 1936. Director-General of
Munitions Production, Army Council, 1936–9. Director-General of Munitions Production,
Ministry of Supply, 1939–40. Controller-General of Munitions Production, 1941–2. Chair-
man of the Armament Development Board, Ministry of Supply, 1942–6. Chairman of the
Fuel Research Board, 1947–50.

of Canterbury, Sinclair, Lytton,[1] Dalton, and Gilbert Murray[2] & Walter Citrine. I am doubtful about adding Austen, because he has got such a passion for saying 'no'; however, I think I shall ask him in the end. Do not say anything to him about it at present.

Lloyd George has already accepted.

Yours very sincerely,

Winston S. Churchill to Léon Blum

(*Churchill papers: 2/274*)

16 November 1936 11 Morpeth Mansions

I am extremely obliged to you for the information which has reached me about the Air. I do not know whether you have yourself seen the paper. I think the conclusion on page 2 is a dangerous one to adopt as a working rule. It may be that the French and English squadrons are more matured than the German and that the permanent headquarters staff and cadres rest on a more solid foundation. But all we have known of the Germans in every sphere has taught me, at any rate, to rate their efficiency very high. I am afraid from my own sources of information that they are very nearly as strong, perhaps quite as strong, as both the English and French put together. You will see that we are discussing armaments here with increasing seriousness.

Once more thanking you,

Believe me,

[1] Victor Alexander George Robert Lytton, 1876–1947. Educated at Eton and Trinity College, Cambridge. Succeeded his father as 2nd Earl of Lytton, 1891. Civil Lord of the Admiralty, 1916; Additional Parliamentary Secretary, Admiralty, 1917; British Commissioner for Propaganda in France, 1918; Civil Lord of the Admiralty, 1919–20. Under-Secretary of State for India, 1920–2. Governor of Bengal, 1922–7; Acting Viceroy of India, April-August 1925. Head of the League of Nations' Mission to Manchuria, 1932. Chairman of Palestine Potash Ltd, Central London Electricity Ltd, the London Power Company, and the Hampstead Garden Suburb Trust Ltd.

[2] George Gilbert Aimé Murray, 1866–1957. Professor of Greek at Glasgow University, 1888–9. Regius Professor of Greek at Oxford University, 1908–36. Chairman of the League of Nations Union, 1923–38.

Winston S. Churchill to Paul Maze

(Churchill papers: 1/286)

17 November 1936

It would be very nice of you if you would care to go to Neville Lytton's[1] studio which I have rented and see the kind of lamp which you would advise me to have at Chartwell, and I will have it put in the London studio and later on move it to Chartwell.

Many thanks for the brushes. I am glad you were interested at H of C. Your letter most encouraging.

Winston S. Churchill to Lord Cavan

(Churchill papers: 25/7)

17 November 1936   11 Morpeth Mansions

Thank you so much for your letter. I am delighted you liked Ramillies and Oudenarde.

I think the idea of underground parking places for peace which would be gas proof refuges for war is extraordinarily good, and I will certainly try to push it. If you will put your point on the frame of steel girders over the power houses in a separate letter, I will put it before the Air Defence Committee, of which I am still a member.

I did not become Chancellor till the last months of 1924, therefore my guilt, if guilt there be, at any rate is halved.

[1] Neville Stephen Lytton, 1879–1951. Son of the 1st Earl of Lytton. Painter. Amateur Tennis Champion, 1911 and 1913. Major, 11th Battalion, Royal Sussex Regiment, 1914–18. In 1915 he gave Churchill a series of notes on the technique of oil painting. Wounded, 1916; mentioned in despatches four times. Secretary, Société Nationale des Beaux Arts, Paris, 1936. Succeeded his elder brother as 3rd Earl of Lytton, 1947. In 1921 he published *The Press and the General Staff*, and in 1942 *The English Country Gentleman: Life in Unoccupied France*.

Sir Norman Angell to Lord Allen of Hurtwood [1]

(*Allen papers*)

17 November 1936

My dear Allen,

The group to which you refer started life as the 'Anti-Nazi Council',[2] which in its turn was, I think in some way connected with 'The World Committee Against War and Fascism' whose headquarters are in Paris. At the request of Romain Rolland[3] I had succeeded Henri Bataille[4] as a member of the 'Presidium' and was supposed to represent the British end of it. Thus my connection with the Anti-Nazi Council when it was formed.

Some semi-private luncheons were held in connection with the 'Anti-Nazi Council', and at one of these Churchill was present and an ad hoc committee was formed to further an Albert Hall meeting to awaken the public to the danger of the general growth of Fascism. It has now been decided, I understand, to hold the meeting under the auspices of the LNU, though Churchill's committee will defray the cost.

The 'slant' of his committee is a bit more anti-Fascist and anti-German than I think you would approve, and has nothing whatever to do with domestic policy—social reform of any kind. I don't think it will strike across the efforts of the Next Five Years Group, both because it doesn't concern itself with social legislation in any way, and because it does not, I imagine, contemplate anything in the way of a definite or permanent organisation. It is by way of being an ad hoc demonstration to check the pro-German ten-

---

[1] Reginald Clifford Allen, 1889–1939. Educated at Berkhamsted, University College, Bristol, and Peterhouse, Cambridge. Secretary and General Manager of the *Daily Citizen*, 1911–15. Chairman of the No-Conscription Fellowship, 1915–19. Imprisoned three times for refusing military service, 1917–19. A Labour Party delegate to Russia, 1920. Treasurer and Chairman of the Independent Labour Party, 1922–6. Chairman, the *New Leader*, 1922–6. Director of the *Daily Herald*, 1925–30. Created Baron Allen of Hurtwood, 1932. A leading advocate of conciliation with Germany, 1933–7, when he twice visited Hitler.

[2] The Anti-Nazi Council's full name was: 'British Non-Sectarian Anti-Nazi Council to Champion Human Rights.' Its President was the Trade Union leader, Sir Walter Citrine. Its Vice-Presidents included Sir Norman Angell, Sylvia Pankhurst and Eleanor Rathbone. On its notepaper were the slogans: 'Nazi Germany is the Enemy of Civilization' and 'Refuse to Trade with the Enemy.'

[3] Romain Rolland, 1866–1944. Born in France. Author and dramatist. Author of a ten-volume novel, *Jean-Christophe* (1904 to 1912). Professor of Music at the Sorbonne, 1910. Biographer of Michelangelo (1906), Beethoven (1910), Handel (1910), Tolstoy (1911) and Gandhi (1924). Nobel Prize for Literature, 1915. During the First World War his pacifist writings, written in Switzerland, aroused much hostility in France; resident in Switzerland, 1915–38. A leading opponent of Fascism and Nazism from 1933 until his death.

[4] Henri Bataille, 1872–1922. Born in Nimes; French poet and dramatist, his first play was performed in France when he was 22. He wrote principally on modern subjects. In 1916 he published *La Divine Tragédie*, a book of war poems.

dencies of the Lothian[1] type, and the tendency to turn away from association with France. Churchill is a good man to make this protest and at a time when Ribbentrop and his henchmen are so exceedingly active it seemed a useful thing to do. If and when Churchill goes into the cabinet it will, I think, simply dissolve, and whatever measure of success it has could be capitalised I think later by the Next Five Years Group. All this is for your ear alone.

I hope to be at the Executive of the Group on Friday. . . .

Winston S. Churchill to Lady Houston

(*Churchill papers: 2/260*)

18 November 1936   11 Morpeth Mansions

Dear Lady Houston,

Many thanks for your letter. We are agreed on so many things and have so many powerful antagonists, that we ought to be tolerant with one another about differences.[2]

If the League of Nations' collective security (or combined defensive strength, as I call it) were to be based as formerly upon weak and disarmed nations, I should share all your prejudices against them.

What is now proposed is an association of strong and well-armed States to resist an aggressor, and especially that Britain should be made strong again as fast as possible. This means a greater measure of national unity behind our rearmament effort which will be a great advantage. At the present time

---

[1] Philip Henry Kerr, 1882–1940. Educated at the Oratory School, Birmingham and New College, Oxford. Worked as a civil servant in South Africa, 1905–8. Editor, *The Round Table*, 1910–16. Secretary to Lloyd George, 1916–21. Secretary of the Rhodes Trust, 1925–39. Succeeded his cousin as 11th Marquess of Lothian, 1930. Chancellor of the Duchy of Lancaster, 1931. Chairman of the Indian Franchise Committee, 1932. Ambassador in Washington from 1939 until his death.

[2] Lady Houston had written to Churchill: '*Why*—when you can *be* so great—so devastating do you demean yrself by truckling to that *unreal* thing of the League of Nations & that awful little ass Mr Eden?—who isn't fit to black your shoes! You can be magnificent & could if you only would carry the country with you—but I am now *dreading* to hear you say you didn't mean anything personal etc. etc., thereby undo all the wonderful effect of your splendid words. I have always *wanted you so much* to go to those heights you rose to the other day, & I would most gladly have financed you to run out Baldwin but what good would that be if you tied yrself up, with the League. You have made a tremendous effect, why don't you *keep it up* until you demolish them entirely. I believe in a few weeks you would have them out, & yrself in as a *true* Conservative' (*Churchill papers: 2/260*). On the same day as Churchill's reply, Neville Chamberlain told the Cabinet, in relation to the proposed Five Power Pact, that 'the League of Nations was in a tottering position', and would not therefore be a suitable base for such a Pact (*Cabinet papers: 23/86*).

I am most anxious to marshal all worthy forces behind this process of rearmament.

I offer you this explanation because of your kindness in writing to me, but I do not expect you to agree.

Blanche Dugdale: diary

(*N. A. Rose, editor, 'Baffy'*)

18 November 1936

I predict that Winston will take on LNU[1] and use it! Also that he will shortly form a Government, drawing the Right by his Armament programme, the Left by his support of the League.

Shane[2] says Winston's admiration of Blum, knows no bounds. All these are strange portents of coming changes.

Wing-Commander Anderson: note dictated to Violet Pearman

(*Churchill papers: 2/271*)

18 November 1936

June 1937

Bombers only	Machines	Mobilisation Strength	Position in March 1939
Hart	6	3	nil
Hind	24	14	nil
Overstrand	1	nil	nil
Wellesley	5	2	nil
Battle	6	2	26
Blenheim	9	2	14
HP 69/32	nil	nil	8
Heyford	6	4	nil
Hendon	8	1	nil
Whitley	5	2	9
Harrow	5	1	3
Wellington	nil	nil	8
Sqdrn total	75	31	68
Aeroplane total	744	372	990

[1] The League of Nations Union, of which Viscount Cecil of Chelwood was President.
[2] Churchill's cousin, Sir Shane Leslie (see page 98, note 1).

Explanation:

Column 1 is 'shop window dressing' for Parliament. Column 2 is actual mobilisation strength. In other words to maintain 31 squadrons with 372 aircraft we should require the full 744 aircraft.

In 1939 mobilisation strength will be 990 and the type of aircraft will be better in performance, speed, and bomb carrying capacity.

Arrangements are being made with the French Government now for the Hind, Hart and Hendon squadrons to operate from French landing grounds, and French airmen have been detailed on paper to assist in maintenance, bomb loading etc. A further conference regarding this is being held in December.

The number of squadrons promised to Parliament by 1st April 1937 will be deficient by 23. Parliament is going to be openly informed of this. The reason is lack of equipment and the failure on the part of manufacturers to supply. Should Parliament bring pressure to bear, then further shop window dressing will take place, and squadrons which have at present two flights, will be split up into an additional squadron of one flight, to operate from the same aerodrome.

Up to 1938 it is the intention to operate 25 squadrons in North East France.

A new type of aeroplane is on the drawing board called P12/36. It is designed to carry 14,000 lbs of bombs with a range of 2,000 miles.

America has at present a 4 engine Boeing aircraft. This aeroplane has this carrying capacity and could be built in this country immediately.

The Wellington and the Wellesley have a cruising speed of 220 miles per hour and can carry 4,000 lbs of bombs with a range of 1,500 miles.

We require on the outbreak of war 3,000 additional aeroplanes for wastage. It will be necessary to hold 7,000 aeroplanes in storage.

The CID have recommended that we should hold 34,000 tons of petrol. The Air Staff consider the minimum should be 60,000 tons. There is no underground storage, and it has been agreed that a portion of this petrol should be stored in open tanks in the Western counties.

At present we have 10,000 air bombs in the country.

Scheme F has cost the country £200,000,000. This is for aircraft and buildings alone, and does not include personnel, upkeep or overhead charges.

The Battle and Blenheim have only 800 miles of safe range owing to the consumption of petrol and sensitivity of the throttle.

The mobilisation orders for the Air Force are in preparation, and it is agreed that it would take between 3 to 6 days to mobilise, whereas the Metropolitan Air Force should always be mobilised and ready to strike immediately.

Winston S. Churchill to Air Commodore J. A. Chamier: [1] *extract*

(*Churchill papers: 2/272*)

19 November 1936   11 Morpeth Mansions

I wish at this stage to have the Fleet Air Arm under the control of the Navy because I am anxious to see the aggregate air power of Britain increased as fast as possible, and I believe that the Naval personnel, commissioned and other ranks, will be an important additional rivulet of supply.

In addition I feel that the Air Ministry is overweighted at the present time and the gigantic expansion which is being attempted is failing alarmingly at many points. The needs of the Navy are forcing the Air Ministry to use for the Naval wing a very large proportion of the Cranwell entry, thus leaving the Metropolitan squadrons deprived of a very essential element in their pilot strength. There are also many other reasons which make me feel that the present system is detrimental both to the Fleet and the Air service.

Winston S. Churchill to Lord Swinton

(*Churchill papers: 25/7*)

19 November 1936   11 Morpeth Mansions
Private and Confidential

I am very sorry that you have finally decided to extrude Lindemann. I noticed a certain tension between him and Tizard a year ago when we all three attended the fleet firings together. This arose from the pressure which Lindemann put upon the late Prime Minister through various influential friends to have the Air Defence Committee constituted separately from the Air Ministry and under the CID. At that time there was, and still is, very strong support from all parties in the House of Commons to urge a most earnest effort to discover some means of Air Defence. Tizard, who had been in charge of this for some time on the scientific side, resented the implied reflection on his work. I cannot feel that Lindemann's ideas have received fair play.

In losing Lindemann you are in my judgment losing one of the best scientists and finest brains in the country, and a man whose chief thought for many years has been fixed upon these problems. I am sure a good many

[1] John Adrian Chamier, 1883–1974. Indian Army: on active service in Somaliland, 1904, and in the war of 1914–18 (despatches, DSO). Director of Technical Development, Air Ministry, 1927–8. Retired from the RAF, 1928. Technical Director of Vickers and Supermarine Aviation, 1929–32. Recalled to the RAF, 1939. Commandant of the Air Training Corps, 1941. Knighted, 1944. Author of *The Birth of the Royal Air Force*, 1944.

people will be distressed when they hear that he has gone, and I have no doubt this will lead to a controversy. Upon the broad merits I cannot help feeling that Lindemann is right. Although Tizard's committee have done a great deal of excellent work, it has given me a feeling during this year of watching a slow motion picture.

It is certain that we have no defence at present, and only too probable that nothing will be ready should danger come in the next two years. I feel also a certain responsibility for bringing this complaint of Lindemann's before you and thus leading his colleagues to form up against him. Moreover he and I have been so long together upon this question of air defence that I cannot feel it would be much use my remaining a member of your Committee any longer. I hope you will therefore not mind my asking the Prime Minister to allow me to withdraw. I am writing him a formal letter on the subject.

Violet Pearman to Winston S. Churchill

(*Churchill papers: 2/271*)

19 November 1936

Cmdr Anderson came again today and dictated the following!—

It is impossible to give the exact strength of bombers and fighter aircraft as numbers vary daily owing to crashes and unserviceability etc. But the approximate number including all types of bombers fighters and army co-operation is 600, of which 66% are bombers and 34% are fighters. The types are of course obsolescent and we should have to operate from France. If we required to mobilise and to use our squadrons as efficient instruments of war in tactical formation, and maintain a force for say four days, the number 600 would have to be halved.

Plans state that the expected output of new aircraft when deliveries commence will be approximately 5 complete aeroplanes and engines per week per factory. . . . This would apply to certain factories Vickers, Avro-Armstrongs, Blackburns, Bristols, Hawkers, and Super-Marines.

The present output of obsolescent aircraft is approximately 2 aeroplanes per day. Bristol output is approximately 22 engines per week, likewise Rolls Royce.

The variable pitch propeller is now regarded by the USA as obsolete and they have completely gone over to the constant pitch propeller. This propeller varies its pitch automatically according to the climb or dive of the aeroplane.

The Air Ministry are still purchasing Wrights and experimenting and giving orders for large quantities of the obsolete variable pitch propeller.

Violet Pearman to Winston S. Churchill

(*Churchill papers: 2/271*)

19 November 1936

Cmdr Anderson called this afternoon again and gave me the following dictation—

'This information is obtained from Wing Cmdr Goddard[1] who is head of the German Intelligence Section. I asked for it in connection with some lectures I am giving tomorrow.

The Chief of the Air Staff[2] will only accept the German bomber strength as 550. Their fighter strength is 250. Both bombers and fighters have 100% reserve in aircraft. Their squadrons are established on a 9 aircraft basis. Their accepted pilot strength is *8,500*. It is agreed that few of these have been fully trained in the full arts of applied flying, ie bombing, gunnery etc. But are capable nevertheless of piloting an aeroplane and dropping bombs over a target, such as London. These reports are obtained direct from the Secret Service through agents.

It is agreed that these Agents have little technical knowledge.

The German squadrons are faced with a shortage of trained personnel ie fitters and riggers, and many civilians are seen working in the squadrons.

In May 1937 the German estimated bomber strength will be 800 and fighter strength 250, again with 100% reserve.

The Chief of Air Staff will not accept the principle of the Germans using training aircraft for offensive operations, although he realises that such aircraft have the necessary radius of action capable of reaching this country. He considers that if such is the case, when war is likely to take place, our own training aircraft could do likewise.'

[1] Robert Victor Goddard, 1897–   . On active service with the Royal Navy, Royal Naval Air Service, Royal Flying Corps and Royal Air Force, 1914–19. Air Ministry, 1919; head of the German Intelligence Section, Air Ministry, 1936–8; Deputy-Director of Intelligence, 1938–9; Director of Military Co-operation, 1940–1. Chief of the Air Staff, New Zealand, 1941–3. Air Officer in charge of administration, Air Command, South East Asia, 1943–6. RAF Representative, Washington, 1946–8. Knighted, 1947. Member of the Air Council for Technical Services, 1948–51.

[2] Air Vice-Marshal Sir Edward Ellington (see page 130, note 2).

Violet Pearman to Winston S. Churchill

(*Churchill papers: 2/271*)

19 November 1936
Secret
Personal

Cmdr Anderson told me very seriously that he had never been frightened in his life before, but he is of this, ie that the fact of the vast number of German pilots may come out. IT MUST NOT BE DIVULGED OPENLY as it would implicate not only him, but Wing Commander Goddard, whom he must not harm. The number must be camouflaged. Nothing that can recoil on Cmdr Goddard must come out.

After the lectures they seemed curious to know why Cmdr Anderson should wish to know about the pilots. He does not know whether they are suspicious of him, and may try to trace him. The figures are accurate, and so accurate and staggering, that he thinks this is the reason those who know are frightened of facts coming out.

He has gone back to Hucknall, and hopes that his help has been of real use to you.

Winston S. Churchill to C. B. Cochran

(*Churchill papers: 1/286*)

19 November 1936

I have now found a moment in the press of events to tell you how much we both appreciate the kindly thought that made you cable your offer to Sarah while she was on her voyage. We shall always remember your courtesy and kindness.[1]

---

[1] Sarah Churchill has recorded: 'Everyone from the call-boy to CB himself was to give me advice and tell me not to take this affection seriously. Even Mrs Cochran was induced to invite me to tea to discourage me from the folly of any serious commitment. She poured out the tea in an abstracted way and wandered vaguely about the room. Suddenly she plucked up courage: "Cocky is most distressed at the news that you might marry Vic. You are so young. At the beginning of your career. Life is so long". I felt she had memorized these lines. "My dear", she said, "he is eighteen years older than you, and has been married twice before. You are so young, so inexperienced . . ." Her voice trailed away. Silence filled the room. I could not think of anything helpful to say. I was so sorry for her in her embarrassment that I almost wanted to join in and help her with her arguments. Suddenly she smiled and said: "Of course I ran away from home to marry Cocky and have never regretted it". I bade her a smiling farewell' (*A Thread in the Tapestry*, page 51).

Major G. P. Myers[1] *to Winston S. Churchill*

(*Churchill papers: 2/267*)

20 November 1936

Dear Sir,

In view of the 're-armament' position and the questions asked in the House and answered by responsible ministers, the following may be of interest to you, though only a small item in the re-armament programme, if it is not already known to you.

General Aircraft Ltd, (Hanworth Aerodrome, Feltham) in October 1935, had a contract placed with them by the Air Ministry for 89 Hawker 'FURY' aeroplanes. Up to the 13th: of the present month only 23 machines of this contract had been delivered, 23 machines in more than twelve months.

The 'FURY' is of course a modified type of the original 'FURY' which dates I think from about 1930 and it can hardly be described as the latest type of 'fighter'.

May I ask you to note that I am an employee of General Aircraft Ltd: and as such would lose my position were the source of this information disclosed by some mischance.

Yours faithfully,
G. P. Myers

Winston S. Churchill to Oswald Frewen

(*Shane Leslie papers*)

20 November 1936   Chartwell

I have known Commander Oswald Frewen, who is my cousin, since childhood, and am very pleased to give him my strong personal recommendation for the post of Air Raids Precautions Organizer.

His naval service at Heligoland, Dogger Bank and Jutland has of course given him experience of warfare, and I have every confidence that his impeccable sense of duty, his imagination, tact and organizing ability suit him most admirably for the appointment under consideration.

I feel that if the choice falls on him, it is one which will meet with complete approval hereafter.

I should be very glad to give any further information if it is required.

Winston S. Churchill

[1] Gilbert Percival Louis Myers, 1881–   . 2nd Lieutenant, 1900; Lieutenant, 1904–7 (when he resigned). Captain, Machine Gun Corps, 1915; Major, 1916. Instructor in Gunnery, Royal Flying Corps, 1917–18. Mentioned in despatches, 1917. Retired, 1919. Subsequently an employee of General Aircraft Limited.

Winston S. Churchill to Sir Richard Hopkins[1]

(*Churchill papers: 2/260*)

20 November 1936

My dear Hopkins,

I should be very much obliged if you would advise me with regard to this request, with which I am in sympathy though of course I have no personal interest of any kind.

The Baroness Goldschmidt-Rothschild is a very able and agreeable woman who is still possessed of an enormous fortune. Being a Jewess she is under the Nazi ban. As she is so wealthy she is not interfered with at all herself, but her children have no future whatever in Germany. Both she and her husband are anxious to acquire British nationality. They could then live here on the proceeds of their great estates in Poland, which would in fact become the property of British subjects. They would of course pay very substantial taxes in this country, and also maintain a large and beneficial expenditure. I am of opinion that the public interest and the revenue would be served if they could be naturalized. But there appear to be complications. It would be kind of you to let me know how the financial aspect could be arranged, and I would then myself approach the Home Secretary.

Lord Cecil of Chelwood to Winston S. Churchill

(*Cecil of Chelwood papers*)

23 November 1936

My dear Winston,

I have asked Attlee whether he would sign the Declaration, and he has agreed subject to one alteration. He wants some reference to the peaceful settlement of international disputes. I have therefore put in two amendments, one at the end of paragraph 2, and one at the end of paragraph 4. You will see in the new declaration I send you how it now reads. I hope you will not think that this makes any serious change. It undoubtedly will conciliate a considerable body of opinion who are afraid of treating the League as merely a warlike machine.

[1] Richard Valentine Nind Hopkins, 1880–1955. Educated at King Edward's School, Birmingham, and Emmanuel College, Cambridge. Member of the Board of Inland Revenue, 1916; Chairman, 1922–7. Knighted, 1920. Controller of Finance and Supply Services, Treasury, 1927–32; Second Secretary, Treasury, 1932–42; Permanent Secretary, 1942–5. Privy Councillor, 1945. Member of the Imperial War Graves Commission. Chairman of the Central Board of Finance of the Church Assembly.

There is another change in the plan, which I think will appeal to you. It is now proposed that each country shall have a separate set of signatures, though the documents signed will be issued more or less simultaneously. That is to say, there will be one set of signatures here, and one in France, and so on; so that you will only be associated with those who sign here. I think I have already given you the list of those whom I propose to ask, and they are all highly respectable. I shall be very glad to hear whether Austen has also assented: his name will be very valuable. It follows from this new arrangement that it will not be necessary to have any meeting of the signatories, which I personally rejoice at, because meetings almost always do something silly.

Frederick Guest to Winston S. Churchill

(*Churchill papers: 2/260*)

23 November 1936

Dear Win,

Attlee will support you on any rearmament programme. He admires & likes you. The door is open if you want to talk to him.

Record of a Discussion[1]

(*Premier papers: 1/193*)

23 November 1936

SIR AUSTEN CHAMBERLAIN: We are very much obliged to you and your colleagues for offering to see us again and giving us at any rate some of the results of your consideration of what we laid before you.

PRIME MINISTER: Thank you very much. It will be within the memory of everyone here the discussions which we had at the end of July. At that time I think it was recognised that there was some difficulty in seeing Members of the House of Commons as it was apt to arouse jealousies, and you will have seen the statement I have made, the willingness I have

---

[1] Between Baldwin and a Deputation from both Houses of Parliament. Those present were (for the Government), Baldwin, Sir Thomas Inskip, Neville Chamberlain and Lord Halifax; (for the House of Lords), Lords Salisbury, Fitzalan, Trenchard, Lloyd and Milne; (for the House of Commons), Sir Austen Chamberlain, Churchill, Sir Robert Horne, L. S. Amery, Sir John Gilmour, F. E. Guest, Earl Winterton, Brigadier-General Sir Henry Page Croft, Sir Edward Grigg, Viscount Wolmer, Lieutenant-Colonel J. T. C. Moore-Brabazon, Sir Roger Keyes and Sir Hugh O'Neill. The minutes were kept by Colonel H. L. Ismay.

expressed to meet responsible Delegations from the Opposition Parties if they so desire; and when we parted I remember Mr. Churchill saying to me he hoped very much I would have the whole of his speech very carefully examined because he had raised an enormous number of points.

MR CHURCHILL: I meant the other speeches, too.

PRIME MINISTER: I know, but you were speaking about some particular points you raised, because what you said to me, and what I remember so well, was that you did not expect a reply but did want me to satisfy myself—that was the phrase you used.

MR CHURCHILL: That is it.

PRIME MINISTER: I thought a little more than that was due to so representative a body as this. While, of course, there is the greatest difficulty on our part in going beyond what we might say on certain questions in the House, yet we have had all the speeches gone very carefully into. It has taken an immense amount of time, and you will not misunderstand me what I say, time on the part of very busy men; but they have given time and they have done it, and the Minister for Co-ordination of Defence will give you so far as he can the results, and will be prepared to elucidate, again as far as he can, points on which you may desire to question him.

There is one little difficulty which will appeal to all those of you with experience in Governments. There is always a certain tendency in meetings of this kind for both of us perhaps to be a little like advocates, the one side naturally going for the weak spots, and there is a natural tendency on the part of the Government to defend itself; but I hope we will eliminate that in what we are going to say as far as possible. We can point to some things which I think are better than you feared; we have spots about which we are anxious; we are all aware of them and are anxious and willing to remedy them; but the less we talk of our difficulties, in public at any rate, the better, I think. Now, Sir Thomas.

LORD SALISBURY: May we take a note or two, or would you rather that we did not?

PRIME MINISTER: I had not thought of it. I hope I can trust everyone, but the fewer the notes left about, the better; there is always the danger, if you take a note, of leaving it somewhere.

MR CHURCHILL: I do not want to be told anything which, if I am not satisfied, would prevent me from criticising. Anything I know myself or put in myself from bona fide sources I feel free to raise, subject only to my discretion whether it will do harm to the country or not. Therefore, of course, anything which you say or is said here that we do not know is obviously completely bound in secrecy. But I hope you will feel it will not be a complaint against us if we continue to criticise.

PRIME MINISTER: I have never put an impossible strain on any of my friends.

MR CHURCHILL: Thank you very much. I like to get it nicely 'taped out' beforehand.

SIR THOMAS INSKIP: As it apparently rests with me to be the vehicle of communicating this information to the Deputation, I will do my best. I have written out what I propose to say. So far as I am concerned, if anyone wants to interrupt me, I personally shall take no objection at all, if there is any sentence obscure—which is quite likely—or any statement which requires elaboration.

May I begin with a general observation? The Government have at no time underrated the importance of the air. They are fully alive to the menace which a powerful German Air Force presents to this country. We are basing our arrangements on the hypothesis that Germany will attempt to defeat the forces of Great Britain by a sustained and intensive air bombardment of London and other selected targets where vital industries or dense populations are concentrated. That is the hypothesis which underlies the whole of our arrangements both for the defence of this country and for the conduct of any war in which we may be engaged.

Mr Churchill, in his speech, speaking as he was in July, took the position with regard to air strength in May, 1936. In his recent speech in the Debate on the Address, he took 1st November for the purpose of a comparison of German and British air strengths. On both occasions he gave figures which do not agree with the information of the Air Staff. The Prime Minister stated in the Debate on the Address that Mr Churchill's estimate of German strength on 1st November was too high. I repeat that statement; and it is equally true of the May estimate. The discrepancy is due to the difference between our way and the French way of estimating air strength. It is obvious that if you are making comparisons the same method of calculation must be used. That is what our Air Staff has done. I am not in a position to give the figures; but it is, I hope, useful that I should say what the Government's view is of Mr Churchill's statements of the relative strengths of Great Britain and Germany at the present time.

SIR AUSTEN CHAMBERLAIN: Might I ask if you find it possible, and if so, convenient, to explain in what way the basis of calculation differs? I venture to ask this because primarily I should, for defensive purposes, be disposed to base an estimate on the calculation most unfavourable to us; if there are two ways of counting, one which is more favourable and another which is less favourable, the only safe way would, I think, be to take the less favourable as our basis.

SIR THOMAS INSKIP: The basis which the French Government have always adopted does not correspond to our basis so far as the inclusion of the reserves is concerned: this has been fully explained, I think, in some correspondence between Mr Churchill and, I think, the Secretary of State for Air. The French Government put into their first-line strength machines and men which for our purposes are included in the reserves and, therefore, are not included in the calculation of the first-line air strength. That is in substance the difference between the two methods of calculation; and that is what makes the French figures higher than the British figures.

MR CHURCHILL: I have of course had for the last year prolonged correspondence, through the Committee of Imperial Defence, upon this question of the German air strength, and I think there are five or six printed papers on the interchanges that have taken place. But I agree with what Sir Thomas Inskip says, that one of the principal points is that the Air Staff will not accept the same method of calculation as the French: they count the German squadrons as 9 only, whereas the French count them as 12. When you get to 120 or 130 squadrons, it is obvious that a matter of 400 machines is in question. I personally should be prepared to argue and to submit that from all points of reality and effective strength, these 3 additional machines which the Air Ministry will not recognise and which the French do, are every whit as good—pilots, crews to keep them in order, superiority of machines—every whit as good as the 9 which you count; and it seems to me very odd, purely for purposes of estimate and figures, to rule out as many as 400 machines manned by the best pilots in Germany, interchangeable with all the others, with the very best kind of machines and with the rigging parties all ready standing by them. Of course, you can rule them out and say 'We do not count them'; but they are there all the same from every point of view. I do not know whether it would be of interest to hear the actual French figures? I only got them after the debate, but from their latest figures. . . .

SIR THOMAS INSKIP: At what date?

MR CHURCHILL: 1st January, 1937. Germany can put in line at the beginning of January, 1937 (a) under a form of active aerial squadrons 147 *escadrilles*—that is to say 1,764 *avions de combat* [1] of the first line; (b) 200 machines (Luft-Hansa)—those are the big Luft-Hansa bombers which are ready for immediate action. Those two, added together, make a total of 1,964 '*avions de première ligne*' compared with 1,356 at the beginning of May, an increase of about 600. Then they say that behind these are about

---

[1] Churchill noted at this point: 'This expression no doubt includes bombers.'

1,500 *appareils 'en deuxième ligne'*. Those would, I suppose, correspond to our stored reserve. They are, I suppose, machines without pilots. This material reserve would work out at about 75 per cent of the 2,000 roughly that the French credit the Germans with having. Behind that again are the 45 *escadrilles* in the training squadrons which they count as 540 machines. These *escadrilles* in the training squadrons cannot be moved at present from the training squadrons without interrupting the whole method of training future pilots in Germany, but these 45 squadrons have the best pilots in Germany, they are the teachers, they are mostly instructors instructing the pupils, and if the Germans at any time—which they may do quite easily—get from their sports aviation the squadrons which can take the place of those 45 and keep the work of the training schools going in mobilisation, the whole 45 are available to fight in addition to the other figures. If you take 1,964 at 12 in a squadron, you knock off 450 which brings the figure probably near, we should not be very much out, but you are knocking off 450 live things, things which can absolutely work and are of the highest quality. You can knock them off, but you must put them down somewhere.

SIR THOMAS INSKIP: I am not in a position to follow the details of those figures, but Mr Churchill will not object to my saying that he suggested that he and I, perhaps by exchange of documents, should try to arrive at a common understanding as to what the differences are.

MR CHURCHILL: Yes.

SIR THOMAS INSKIP: I am perfectly prepared to do that. Let me say this. Take Sir Austen Chamberlain's point. If we adopt the same method of calculation that the French adopt, our figures would be higher.

SIR AUSTEN CHAMBERLAIN: Yes.

SIR THOMAS INSKIP: It is a question of making a balance, but what happened, if Mr Churchill will allow me to say so with great respect, was that in his statement he has taken the French basis as the proper calculation of German figures, and the British basis as the calculation of our figures.

MR CHURCHILL: No, I counted the 80 and multiplied by 12, which makes 960, which you estimated was practically right.

SIR THOMAS INSKIP: That is the figure you gave in the Debate. But I do not think it is useful to pursue this now. . . .

MR CHURCHILL: No.

SIR THOMAS INSKIP: . . . because I could not follow these details here. But I will gladly take part in any discussion with Mr Churchill to enable him and me at any rate to agree where it is that we differ in the basis of calculation.

MR CHURCHILL: Yes, I would like that. I beg your pardon for interrupting.

SIR THOMAS INSKIP: Not at all. Mr Churchill's next point in order was what we call the war potential. The potential war output of the British aircraft industry is not equal to that of Germany. Our efforts hitherto have been directed to the immediate exigencies of the existing programme, but we are now planning for a larger expansion of our war potential. The creation of the shadow industry will have the effect of giving valuable educative experience, and will greatly broaden the basis of engine and airframe war-production. Estimates have been made of the expansion necessary to meet war requirements; and it is substantial. I do not want to blink that fact. That will show that this serious question has not been overlooked. The relation of our production to German production varies from month to month. At present it is roughly the same, but undoubtedly in Mr Churchill's phrase Germany is, so far as air-frames and engines are concerned, 'running easy'. I am sure the Deputation will follow the anxiety it gives the Government, because, when they have dealt with what in our jargon we call the deficiency programme there is still that gap between the war potential that it is necessary to fill in order to meet the wastage and the demands which war would make upon use. . . .

Mr Churchill passed on to deal with the quality of the personnel. With his general warning against underrating the quality or spirit of German pilots, we entirely agree. Moreover the number of their fatalities, which incidentally is five times as many as ours, shows the intensity of the German effort. . . .

Arrangements have been made for the production of machine guns.

MR CHURCHILL: What kind of machine guns? Bren?

SIR THOMAS INSKIP: Not the Bren, the Browning: the Bren gun is not used for aircraft. Mr Churchill suggested something like 10,000 machine guns would be required, and suggested we ought to lose no time in thinking about it. That was his phrase. But before the Deputation, orders had in fact been placed for approximately not 10,000 but 20,000 new type of guns, and a conversion of 1,300 Vickers guns. The manufacture of the Browning gun was decided upon more than a year ago and deliveries commence in December 1936, and the new type Vickers gun at the same time.

MR CHURCHILL: Deliveries in bulk? Large numbers, or what?

SIR THOMAS INSKIP: Yes. I am not speaking of the first month or two, but as soon as production really begins these machine guns are turned out quickly in substantial bulk numbers.

MR CHURCHILL: Will you get 10,000 in 1937—that sort of scale?

SIR THOMAS INSKIP: No, not in 1937. I do not like to give the figure.

MR CHURCHILL: No, I do not want the actual figure.

MR CHURCHILL: Have any of the new type of aircraft gun been ordered?

SIR THOMAS INSKIP: I cannot answer that.

SIR THOMAS INSKIP: . . . There was a suggestion that one Ministry—the Air Ministry—should control the whole organisation of anti-aircraft defence at home. That would be taking a step further than the existing decision that the Royal Air Force are responsible for the operational control of the active defences. The Army provide the equipment; the Air Force are responsible wholly for operational control. On general grounds the suggestion is attractive, but it is really impossible to carry it out. In addition to the units for Air Defence of Great Britain, the Army has to provide the anti-aircraft defences for the field force and ports abroad, which defences the Royal Air Force could not take over.

MR CHURCHILL: Before you leave that, I take it that at present there are none of these new guns, and that up to the present the manufacture of none has been commenced? All that is happening is that you are preparing a factory at Nottingham for the output of these guns as fast as you can?

SIR THOMAS INSKIP: And others.

MR CHURCHILL: I do not know what sort of numbers; but supposing you required a thousand guns have you any prospect of getting that amount from this scheme in two years from now?

SIR THOMAS INSKIP: I forget whether it is two years. I do not think it is. I do not want anybody here to suppose that anyone could be easy about the non-existence of the gun of the most up-to-date character which has been designed, but no rule about interference with civil industry—I do not want to get on to King Charles's head—and no Ministry of Supply could increase the production of these guns of a heavier type than the three-inch guns, which is all we have at the present time.

LORD SALISBURY: Are we fully equipped with the three-inch guns?

SIR THOMAS INSKIP: No, not in sufficient numbers for the equipment of the zone and the targets which we think require defending.

LORD LLOYD: Have we enough for practice?

SIR THOMAS INSKIP: Just enough for the training purposes of the three-inch guns. But something has to be done even to the three-inch guns. If it were a question of having enough for War purposes—I do not want to dwell upon the bright spots—this undoubtedly is one of the major anxieties of the Government, and if there were any means by which they could be produced more quickly than they will begin to be in the New Year then the Government would take that course.

MR CHURCHILL: Nothing would stand in the way?

SIR THOMAS INSKIP: Nothing would stand in the way. We can multiply the sources, we can increase the people who will make them, and we have done. We have started on Woolwich, and added Nottingham, and put Vickers into the programme, and by allotting certain other supplies—and we contemplate a source of supply in the Clyde District—and therefore we are supplementing the sources of supply; but apart from that there is no power on earth to get them more quickly than we hope to get them. I think, therefore, for practical reasons the present arrangements must stand as to the Air Force having the operational control and the Army responsibility for equipment. About three quarters of the units required have already been formed, or are in process of formation; the remainder will probably be formed next year. Change at the present juncture would in any case be undesirable.

SIR THOMAS INSKIP: The Bren gun is to be used for the Army.

MR CHURCHILL: You are making that at home?

SIR THOMAS INSKIP: We are going to. There must be some misapprehension as to the facts. So far as the purchase of Bren guns in Czechoslovakia is concerned inquiry has been made and although there was quite recently no plant available for the production of the British type of weapon, we have been informed more lately that such a plant has been or is being erected. The information is being verified and Mr Churchill's suggestion that it may be deemed advisable to purchase some of our earlier requirements from this source, will be, if possible, carried out. With regard to machine guns, supplies are adequate both for the equipment of the army and for war reserves.

We have stocks of rifles to cover at least eighteen months of War.

MR CHURCHILL: On a front of five divisions?

SIR THOMAS INSKIP: More than the five division basis. We have in fact. ...

MR CHURCHILL: More than a million, anyhow?

SIR THOMAS INSKIP: Well over a million rifles: In the case of anti-tank rifles, this is a newly designed equipment, but supplies will start coming forward in quantity early in 1937. (It is a very remarkable type of anti-tank weapon which is one of the factors that has made the old tank obsolete.) There has been some delay in the production of trench mortars on a full scale but all battalions will shortly have sufficient for training purposes, and two divisions will have their war scale also, it is hoped, by the end of the year. With regard to the manufacture of Bren guns in this country, a second source of supply is being arranged as soon as the necessary erection of plant can be completed. The output from Enfield will not begin until next year. As soon as it begins a type of weapon will be turned out very rapidly in large quantities.

Mr Churchill begged the Government not to hesitate to make contracts with the United States and elsewhere for the largest possible quantities of aviation material and equipment of all kinds. Contracts have been placed abroad for items of equipment when such action would prove of clear assistance to the expansion programme. In illustration it may be mentioned that a large number of machine guns are being obtained from the United States of America to tide over the period before the British manufacturers are in full production. I can give other illustrations of contracts which have been placed abroad for instruments and a large number of smaller items. So far as aircraft and engines are concerned, Mr Churchill would be the first to appreciate the maintenance difficulties that would arise in the case of foreign-bought aircraft and engines, with entirely different parts and equipment from our own. Nevertheless we are not unmindful of foreign resources. I am bearing in mind information which if given here we might have to give to another Deputation.

MR CHURCHILL: Are you adopting at all the method of making a contract with an American aeroplane firm to start a branch establishment over here? because I have been advised by people high up in American affairs that that is our most safe method of getting round neutrality laws; nothing would prevent the American engineers and skilled workmen, and so forth, coming over to keep the thing running over here. Nobody could stop them and a branch of that kind over here would give you an additional element of production in connection with your War expansion scheme.

SIR THOMAS INSKIP: I will bear that in mind. I do not know quite how the Government would approach that. We should have to approach the American firms, and their willingness would be conditioned by the possibility of getting the skilled labour over here at this present juncture. It is true that labour is being trained in an amazing way. I have seen some of these places and been shewn tools and people: skilled men are now produced and put on these powerful machines in nine to twelve months instead of four years. Nevertheless I do not know how the American firms would get over the skilled labour difficulty, at the moment.

Mr Churchill made one observation as to the range of our new heavy and medium bombers, which, if I understood it aright requires correction. He said, 'the great bulk of our new heavy and medium bombers, even when they are produced, could not do much more than reach the coasts of Germany from this Island. Only the nearest German cities would be within their reach.' The fact is of our new type bombers operating from this country some types will be able to reach Berlin, while other types will be able to penetrate some 150 miles beyond the German frontier. If operating from French or Belgian aerodromes, these distances would, of course, be very materially increased.

MR CHURCHILL: I doubt very much whether by this time next year we shall have thirty squadrons equipped with the new type.

SIR THOMAS INSKIP: I am not in a position to say about thirty squadrons. The production of these new heavy squadrons is beginning in driblets, and I hope by the summer of next year it will be not in floods, but greater than driblets. 'The great bulk of our new heavy and medium bombers, even when they are produced, could not do much more than reach the coasts of Germany from this Island.' It is that statement that I wanted to correct.

A number of points important in themselves but subsidiary to the bigger questions were raised during the discussion. There was the question of the type and supply of aircraft bombs. Arrangements are being made for war reserves in sufficient quantities of the bombs of the type which the Air Ministry consider most effective.

MR CHURCHILL: Before you leave the air, could you give us some information about the eighty squadrons of the Metropolitan Air Force, which you mentioned in the House? It is a matter less secret than many things.

SIR THOMAS INSKIP: It is all in the Air List.

MR CHURCHILL: How many squadrons have got their proper supply of aeroplanes and how many have their proper reserves and are up to strength? November Air List only thinks it worth while to mention fifty squadrons, the others being in a rudimentary condition. If that can be stated, what is the strength we shall have at the end of this year?

SIR THOMAS INSKIP: The Metropolitan First Line strength?

MR CHURCHILL: How many squadrons have we in the Metropolitan Air Force with their full complement?

SIR THOMAS INSKIP: The number of squadrons is the figure I gave, eighty. I see I have been charged during the week with having been inaccurate—a stronger word was used—because I over-stated it by two. Two of the latest were formed on the 1st November, and no doubt their information is not up-to-date. Eighty is right. They have not all their full complement because it has not been thought right to keep back the formation of squadrons because they cannot have their full personnel. But I am not able to answer the question as to the extent to which they are equipped.

MR CHURCHILL: I am sure a very large number of them have not got half their establishment strength; and I am taking it at twelve, because there is a theoretical establishment strength of eighteen, which is not approached anywhere.

SIR THOMAS INSKIP: I can give the figure computed on the basis that I gave at the beginning, this afternoon. I should think I had better not give the figure.

MR CHURCHILL: I took your average of twelve. I took it 960, which perhaps is not very far different from what the Paper calculation would be; but I do not think anything like that figure will be capable of going into, and being kept in, action.

SIR THOMAS INSKIP: I am not in a position to say that. But I should be surprised to hear it is 600. It is 984 and you have mentioned 960.

MR CHURCHILL: I could certainly name the number of a dozen squadrons which have nothing like their proper outfit of aeroplanes. Others, where there are a great number of pilots but so few aeroplanes for them that the pilots cannot go on with their training. I have also heard 150 at a time are to go to Uxbridge for physical training, so that they do not get toned down and slipshod, and so forth. I am not asking for this information particularly, but I do suggest that if the Minister could for his own satisfaction have a most strict 'field state' made of the strength of the different squadrons on a given day, because your case is you have not only aeroplanes that go into action, behind them you have six per squadron in immediate reserve; behind them again are to be the one hundred per cent stored reserve that is what you call a First Line aeroplane, and that is what you judge the German scale so strictly about. But if you looked you would find hardly half of your own status was achieved. At any rate I do suggest if you called for a strict field state for every squadron as it is now and looked at it, it would reveal a very grave deficiency.

SIR THOMAS INSKIP: Well, Mr Churchill will not expect me to be armed with figures, nor will he think any disrespect is intended to him if I say I think he must be cautious about some statements which are made to him by other people, but I will certainly, when I have the transcript, examine this and see. But what I think the Deputation realise is that while we are going through a rapid expansion of the Air Force it would be the wrong policy to postpone the formation of your Squadrons until they could be fully equipped with pilots and with machines. You have to train with skilled men. To that extent you are using the personnel and machines which would otherwise be available for forming complete squadrons.

MR CHURCHILL: Yes. Well, the fact remains that we have not got eighty effective Metropolitan Squadrons, or anything like that, to guard us in the coming year.

SIR THOMAS INSKIP: If the emphasis is on 'effective', I agree: but I am not prepared, because I have not got the figures and I am not fully armed on that.

MR CHURCHILL: I think you have given a very full and interesting answer to the points which have been raised, but I do not feel you have made us a party to the grave situation which you have before you except in regard to one or two particular points where you have not contradicted the assertions which were made. I certainly do not feel that you would wish it to be thought that you had imparted to us, as I see some of the papers indicate, all the most deadly secrets of the State. You have not. What we have had is a talk.

PRIME MINISTER: It would make for a lot more questions in the House to-morrow, if anybody thought that, which would be difficult to answer.

SIR AUSTEN CHAMBERLAIN: We have had some kind of a conversation with you, which you had offered to hold with some responsible representatives of the House.

PRIME MINISTER: That is so.

SIR THOMAS INSKIP: I find no statement was issued last time. Is it desirable to say more than that the deputation saw the Prime Minister and his colleagues, and certain statements were made—or simply not to issue a communique, as no communique was issued last time.

MR CHURCHILL: I saw something.

SIR THOMAS INSKIP: By the Press—they invented it.

MR CHURCHILL: That is quite true, but if you do not say anything you will find something will be invented again. It was in the papers that we were coming.

SIR THOMAS INSKIP: May I draft something and show it to Sir Austen Chamberlain?

CAPTAIN GUEST: I think it would be the easiest thing to say that answers and explanations were given to the questions raised by the deputation at the previous meeting. That is precisely what you said in the House.

SIR AUSTEN CHAMBERLAIN: The danger of that is that frankly I am not quite satisfied with the answers, and that kind of communique would give the impression that we were quite satisfied with the answers. Would it not be better to leave it as last time?

MR CHURCHILL: Would it not be better to say that the Prime Minister and other Ministers conferred with the deputation on certain matters arising out of the interview which took place at the end of July?

SIR THOMAS INSKIP: Yes.[1]

(The proceedings terminated).

[1] On 24 November 1936 *The Times* reported: 'There was a further meeting yesterday afternoon between Ministers and the deputation led by Sir Austen Chamberlain and Mr Churchill on the question of defence. There were two meetings in July, and during the recent Commons debate Mr Baldwin expressed the hope that a further meeting might be arranged

Winston S. Churchill to Lord Cecil of Chelwood

(*Cecil of Chelwood papers*)

26 November 1936   11 Morpeth Mansions

My dear Bob,

I have sent your document to Austen with a letter asking him to sign. I do not think there is much value in the additions in pencilled brackets, but apparently they please the Labour members. They do not improve the swing. I should myself like the second paragraph to read 'We the under-signed declare that the best hope by which war can be averted and a stable peace permanently maintained, is that the nations which are members of the League should now make plain. . . .' I doubt very much whether anything we can do will prevent what is coming.[1]

Yours vy sincerely,
Winston S. Churchill

---

in order that the Government might communicate the information it had collected in reply to the case presented in the summer. The Prime Minister, as in July, was accompanied by Lord Halifax and Sir Thomas Inskip, and also, for the first time, by Mr Chamberlain, Chancellor of the Exchequer. The House of Lords was represented on the deputation by Lord Salisbury, Lord Lloyd, Lord Trenchard, Lord Fitzalan and Lord Milne, and the House of Commons by Sir Austen Chamberlain, Mr Churchill, Lord Winterton, Lord Wolmer, Sir Henry Page Croft, Sir John Gilmour, Mr Amery, Sir Robert Horne, Sir Edward Grigg, Sir Roger Keyes, Lieutenant-Colonel Moore-Brabazon, Captain Guest, and Sir Hugh O'Neill. The meeting lasted for an hour and 50 minutes, and it was afterwards announced that the Ministers had conferred with the deputation "on certain matters arising out of the interview which took place at the end of July". No further meeting was arranged, and it is understood that the meetings are now at an end. Ministers and members of the deputation alike realize that there is a growing feeling in the House of Commons that information on defence subjects ought to be communicated to all sections, and not to a deputation from a limited section—which is not wholly confined to Privy Councillors, as Sir John Simon suggested in reply to a question in the House of Commons last week.'

[1] On the following day, in an article entitled 'Germany and Japan', published in the *Evening Standard* on 27 November 1936, Churchill wrote: 'Let us gaze for a moment at Japan. Here again is a martial race of more than sixty millions straining every nerve to arm in spite of serious financial difficulties. Here again is a nation imbued with dreams of war and conquest. Here again is a State where the military mind is supreme; where the export trade is used not so much for profit as to acquire the means of bringing in necessary war materials; where every voice of moderation is silenced by death; where the murder of political oppo-nents has been for some years accepted practice: where even trusted commanders may be slaughtered by their supporters for suspected luke-warmness. Communism in Japan as in Germany is held fast in the grip of a highly efficient, all-pervading police force, eagerly wait-ing to smite the smallest manifestation. Yet these two great powers in opposite quarters of the globe use the pretext of their fears of communism to proclaim an association the purpose of which, and the consequences of which, can only be the furtherance of their national designs.' Should Germany make war in Europe, Churchill added, 'We may be sure that Japan will immediately light a second conflagration in the Far East.'

Winston S. Churchill to Clementine Churchill

(*Spencer-Churchill papers*)

27 November 1936   Eaton[1]
                                                   Chester

My darling,

We had a jolly day. I shot 112 birds. Indeed a year without Brandy seems to have improved my eye.[2]

You would not have been particularly amused by the party, or by the sport.

Ursula's[3] son is at a Catholic school about ten miles from us. Would it not be nice to ask her for a weekend. She looks so unhappy, & she said she wd love to come. She could have her boy over to luncheon. She lives quite alone now—except for Benny.

There is no less than £6,000 to pay in Income & super tax during 1937. This being so I feel it necessary to take this US offer, & I am satisfied that it is quite proper for me to do so. I plan therefore to sail on the Normandie on December 18, going to Consuelo (if she has room) till Jan 10. Then do the speeches, & return by the Berengaria about 20th reaching England in time for Parlt wh reopens 26th Jan.

I am disappointed not to be with you all at Christmas: & I don't know how I shall spend my poor Christmas day. But everything is so uncertain (except taxation) that it would be wise to have this large sum safely banked in US. I have always hitherto managed to provide the necessaries, & I feel that this particular toil is a measure of prudence.

I am to see yr house carpenter on Monday I hope. We must get Chartwell down to a smaller scale if we are to keep it.

Max rang me up to say he had seen the gent,[4] & told him the Cornwall

---

[1] The Duke of Westminster's principal country house.

[2] Churchill had drunk no spirits since his 61st birthday, on 30 November 1935, in response to a wager by Lord Rothermere, who had offered him £600 as a challenge. On 17 December 1936 Rothermere wrote to Churchill: 'My dear Winston, Here is the cheque for £600, which you have so bravely earned. I have never with more pleasure paid money to anyone, but all through the year I felt that you were a certain winner. With affectionate regards, Yours always, Harold R.'

[3] Lady Ursula Mary Olivia Grosvenor, 1902–   . Eldest daughter of the 2nd Duke of Westminster (Churchill's friend 'Bendor' or 'Benny'). In 1924 she married William Patrick Filmer-Sankey, 1st Life Guards (marriage dissolved by divorce in 1940). In 1940 she married Major Stephen Vernon. Her son Patrick Filmer-Sankey, who was then at Worth Priory, a preparatory school near Crawley, Surrey, near Chartwell. Later he became an industrial film producer. In a conversation with the author he recalled: 'The visit to Chartwell was nothing special; just another day out from school.'

[4] King Edward VIII.

plan was my idea.[1] The gent was definitely for it. It now turns on what the Cabinet will say. I don't see any other way though.

Good night my darling one. I will telegraph whether I return tomorrow late or Sunday early.

Fondest love,

Your ever loving husband,

W

Lord Zetland[2] *to Lord Linlithgow*

(*India Office records*)

27 November 1936
Secret

My dear Hopie,

This is the most secret letter that I have ever written. We were summoned at short notice to a Cabinet meeting this morning and the PM proceeded to give us an account of certain talks which he had had with the King, on October 18th, November 16th and November 25th. I have seldom listened to a more dramatic narrative. The first talk took place after the visit of Mrs Simpson to Balmoral and the announcement in the Press of the divorce of Mr Simpson. SB it seems spoke with great frankness and said that the situation was a serious one; that the press of America was commenting freely on

---

[1] Churchill had hoped that Mrs Simpson could be persuaded to renounce all idea of marriage, morganatic or otherwise to King Edward VIII (see pages 464 and 472). But in the last two weeks of November 1936 the idea being canvassed was for a morganatic marriage, whereby the King would remain King, but any children of the marriage would have no claim to the throne. Lord Beaverbrook later recalled his conversation with the King on November 27: 'He then said that on 21st November Mr Esmond Harmsworth had taken Mrs Simpson to lunch and had propounded to her the project of a morganatic marriage. Mrs Simpson, the King said, preferred the morganatic marriage to any other solution of the problem. He told me also that Mr Harmsworth had laid the morganatic proposal before Mr Baldwin and he understood that it originally came from Mr Churchill' (A. J. P. Taylor, editor, *The Abdication of King Edward VIII, by Lord Beaverbrook*, London 1966, page 50). The 'Cornwall plan' was for Mrs Simpson to become, not Queen, but Duchess of Cornwall, as had once been proposed for Queen Caroline (see pages 475–6).

[2] Lawrence John Lumley Dundas, 1876–1961. Educated at Harrow and Trinity College, Cambridge. Earl of Ronaldshay, 1892 (when his father became 1st Marquess of Zetland). Conservative MP for Hornsey, 1907–16. Governor of Bengal, 1917–22. Privy Councillor, 1922. President of the Royal India Society, 1923–50; of the Royal Asiatic Society, 1928–31. Succeeded his father as 2nd Marquess of Zetland, 1929. President of the Society for the Study of Religions, 1930–51. A member of the Indian Round Table Conference, 1930–1, and of the Parliamentary Joint Select Committee on India, 1933–5. Secretary of State for India, 1935–40, and for Burma, 1937–40. Governor of the National Bank of Scotland, 1940–52. Biographer of both Curzon and Cromer. His younger son was killed on active service in 1943.

the prospect of Mrs Simpson becoming Queen of England and that serious concern was being displayed in the Dominions at these widespread rumours. He asked the King what his intentions were? It seems that the Monarch replied that he was determined to marry the lady. SB asked him if he realised that this would probably mean abdication? He agreed that this would be a probable consequence and that he was prepared for it. He was willing to abdicate voluntarily and to make things as easy as possible for his successor.

This held good until the talk on the 25th, when his attitude changed. He now said that he believed that he would have the sympathy and support of a very large part of the people, and that while he realised that they might be unwilling to accept her as Queen, they would accept a morganatic marriage if the Government were willing to introduce legislation authorising it. SB told him bluntly that if he thought that he was going to get away with it in that way he was making a huge mistake. It is significant that a proposal to this effect was printed in an American newspaper before the King made it to SB. We were told that we were not asked for a decision at the moment. He hoped to see the King again; but his present intention seemed to be to refuse to withdraw from his position.

It was pointed out at the Cabinet that this might involve the resignation of the Government and that in this case it would give rise to a Constitutional issue of the first magnitude, viz the King v. the Government. It seems that the King has been encouraged to believe that Winston Churchill would in these circumstances be prepared to form an alternative Government. If this were true there would be a grave risk of the country being divided into two camps—for and against the King. This clearly would be fraught with danger of the most formidable kind.

So now, my dear Hopie, we are faced with a problem compared with which even the international issues, grave as they assuredly are, pale into comparative insignificance. I sometimes ask myself if these things are really happening, or if they are made of the stuff that dreams are made of, the insubstantial phantasmagoria of some incredible form of mass hallucination? Yet here they are, thrusting themselves upon the attention of perfectly sane and ordinary persons of whom the Cabinet is composed.

I am making no copy of this letter; but I thought it only fair to warn you of a storm of incalculable possibility which is brewing and which, so far as I can see, may at any moment break upon us. Keep it in your most secret repository. What the effect of it may be in India I scarcely dare try to imagine.

Winston S. Churchill to Anthony Eden
(*Churchill papers: 2/260*)

27 November 1936

Suggestions have been made to me that at my Albert Hall meeting on Thursday I should propose intervention by the League of Nations in Spain, with a view to (a) parting the combatants; (b) procuring declarations from both sides against vengeance on the vanquished, whoever they may be; and (c) the setting on foot of conferences to establish a broad constitutional regime. Under Article XI of the Covenant[1] it might now be alleged that a case exists of the danger of war spreading outside the bounds of Spain, and perhaps some locus for the League might arise therefrom. The initiative would obviously come from Great Britain and France. It would I think be difficult for Germany and Italy not to comply. I cannot think in present circumstances Russia would not come along. There may be during the winter months a deadlock in the fighting. The two sides seem both still to have a chance of victory, and broadly speaking they divide Spain fifty-fifty.

Naturally nothing that I say will commit you. All the same as you know I try to keep as much in step with the Foreign Office and you as I can. I shall be in London on Monday, and perhaps you would tell me how you feel about it.

Anthony Eden to Winston S. Churchill
(*Churchill papers: 8/531*)

27 November 1936

My dear Winston,

It was very kind of you to think of sending me the Third volume of the 'Life'. I have embarked upon it already and promise myself many an enjoyable hour in its company. Moreover it is excellent news that there is to be a fourth. You write of the appositeness of the book to our present day problems, and that is certainly true. But what I have found most helpful so far is that it induces a sense of proportion in one's analysis of our present difficulties.

---

[1] Article XI of the Covenant of the League of Nations, which read: 'Any war or threat of war, whether immediately affecting any of the Members of the League or not, is hereby declared a matter of concern to the whole League, and the League shall take any action that may be deemed wise and effectual to safeguard the peace of nations. In case any such emergency should arise the Secretary-General shall on the request of any Member of the League forthwith summon a meeting of the Council. It is also declared to be the friendly right of each Member of the League to bring to the attention of the Assembly or of the Council any circumstances whatever affecting international relations which threatens to disturb international peace or the good understanding between nations upon which peace depends.'

The speed of present day events, the rapidity of the reaction to every incident in the international sphere is apt to make us think that our task is more difficult than that of, say, Salisbury's days. To read of Marlborough is to realise what nonsense that all is. Perhaps just as well that the pigmies (self) are not called upon for the feats of the prodigies.

Anyway, thank you very much indeed. It is splendidly stimulating reading, & written as only you can today.

Yours ever,
Anthony Eden

Eleanor Rathbone to Violet Pearman

(*Churchill papers: 2/260*)

27 November 1936

Thank you for your letter, saying that Mr Churchill can see me on Tuesday after questions. I am not sure whether he has a room in the House; but if so, I will go there, and if not, I will sit in one of the cross benches just at the bar of the House so that he can find me quickly as soon as he is free.[1]

Winston S. Churchill to Paul Reynaud[2]

(*Churchill papers: 2/260*)

27 November 1936

It would give me great pleasure if you could lunch with me at 11, Morpeth Mansions on Tuesday, December 8. I would ask a few political friends to meet you, and we could talk a little more then than at the Luncheon Club the day before.

---

[1] On 18 November 1936 Eleanor Rathbone had written to Churchill: 'My only claim on your attention is that my success in holding a University seat as a complete Independent during three Parliaments, and before that a seat in the extremely Conservative Liverpool City Council for twenty years, also as a complete Independent, does perhaps show that I have some *flair* for what people not strongly attached to any party are thinking and feeling, and it is these people who often decide elections. I am quite sure that what these people, and also many who do belong to parties, are longing for just now is a Leader who can reconcile their conflicting desires for Peace and for the defence of Democracy, for others as well as themselves. If only you would lead a really big campaign in favour of collective security through the League, I believe you would secure an immense response. But it would need a much bigger and more coordinated campaign than anyone seems yet to have attempted.'

[2] Paul Reynaud, 1878–1966. On active service, 1914–18 (twice decorated). Entered the Chamber of Deputies, 1919. Minister of Colonies, 1931–2. Minister of Justice, April–November 1938. Minister of Finance, 1930, and November 1938–March 1940. Prime Minister, 21 March to 17 June 1940 (Foreign Minister, 21 March–18 May and 6 June–17 June 1940). Arrested by the Vichy Government, September 1940. Deported to Germany, 1943–5. Released, 1945. Minister of Finance, 1948. Deputy Prime Minister, 1953. President of the Finance Committee of the National Assembly, 1958.

Violet Pearman to A. H. Richards

(*Churchill papers: 2/283*)

27 November 1936

Dear Mr Richards,

Following your conversation yesterday Mr Churchill is thinking of sailing on December 18, arriving New York on the 23rd or 24th. After a preliminary luncheon or dinner with the Committee to concert the detailed arrangements for the meetings, he would leave for Florida where he would stay with Madame Balsan till after the New Year. About the 10th January would probably be a good time for the public meetings. Mr Churchill has to be home in England for the opening of Parliament on January 26. The Berengaria seems to be sailing about the 20th. But all the above must be considered to be purely provisional unless confirmed by Mr Churchill during the course of the next week.

Violet Pearman to Sir James Hawkey[1]

(*Pearman papers*)

27 November 1936
Confidential

Sleepy Hollow,
Spitals Cross,
Edenbridge,
Kent

Dear Sir James,

I have never approached you personally on any matter, because I have never needed to, and therefore write to you now in some trepidation, yet knowing you will understand.

For some weeks I have been seriously thinking of giving up my post, and getting another, much though I hate doing it. As you know for nearly eight years now I have been a loyal, devoted secretary to Mr Churchill. I can

---

[1] Alfred James Hawkey, 1877–1952. Educated at Woodford Collegiate School. A baker; Chairman of Clark's Bread Company; Vice-Chairman, Aerated Bread Company. Elected to the Woodford Urban District Council, 1909; Chairman, 1916–34; Chairman of the Wanstead and Woodford UDC, 1934–7. Organized Food Control in Woodford, 1914–18. Deputy Chairman of the Epping Conservative Association, 1922–6; Chairman, 1927–52. Knighted, 1926. A member of the Executive Committee of the India Defence League, 1933–5. Mayor of Wanstead and Woodford, 1937–8 and 1943–5; responsible for emergency feeding and information services in the Borough during the blitz, 1940–1. Member of the Essex County Council. Created Baronet, 1945. In his war memoirs Churchill described Hawkey as 'my ever faithful and tireless champion'.

confidently say that I fill the post as no other woman secretary for him has done in the past, though I hold no degree, and am not brilliant. This is due I think mainly to the fact that I understand him so well, can anticipate his moods, whims and fancies, and deal accordingly with crises. Also I am not afraid of him in the least, and can stand up for whoever or whatever is the cause of his wrath—if justice is to be done. And I have loved doing it.

It has however meant giving up my whole life to him, sacrificing my friends, seeing hardly anything of my children, and having no rest, recreation or anything else. As you know a twelve hour office day is the average, with week end duty if required. Many a time does it extend to a fifteen hour day, dividing one's time between country and town, week in, week out. This often happens to secretaries. But one gets so stale, never having the chance to improve one's mind, even get out of the atmosphere of the place. This state of things is deplorable, and getting groovy is detrimental to one's work, also the health.

Since 1915, except for a short interval when I married during the war, I have had a home to keep, first one and then two children. Circumstances have made it that I do so entirely unaided, though not a widow. Fortunately I was able to go back to my Governmental Department job, and held the highest reference from them for the various posts I filled at their discretion. I have been in the Treasury, Cabinet offices, Home Office, Irish Office (during rebellion) and on many conferences etc etc. This has given me valuable insight into the workings of such places, and has brought me in touch with many people known to Mr Churchill which again has been useful. In 1922 I left the Treasury (on whose staff I had been all this while, lent by them to these other posts). This was on account of their regulations to make such people as myself 'permanent', which they wished to do although I was not a widow—a special ruling having to be made for this—but it meant reverting to half my salary, and a lower position, to make it in accord with other 'permanents'. This I could not do in view of my responsibilities, and one is not allowed to do other work while in their employ. I changed to the City after this, for seven years, being lucky in meeting an old friend of mine one day who was junior partner in a big firm. It was interesting, but not progressive enough for a woman who wanted to get on. Then I came to Mr Churchill, again by pure chance, and have remained with him ever since.

Although I have more than once tried to make Mr Churchill understand the inexorable grip he has on my life, and that if he expects the best from me, I must be allowed to live a more human life, he thoughtlessly drifts back into the old ways before the week is out. You know the struggle I have to get things done in time etc the fights I have over some things; and what you don't actually know, I am sure you can guess. I have always loved work and plenty of it. (This has been fully borne out by all for whom I have worked.) But I must have a change or something will snap.

But, posts are difficult to get, especially when one is 42. Nothing has been saved, for expenses have more than filled the bill. Neither is my remuneration what people have thought, and of course no overtime charge. Posts like mine very rarely come 'on the market' as no agency touches them. Chiefly they seem to go by chance or recommendation. Hence the snag.

No one is ever indispensable or else the world would not go on, and I am sure you will find someone who loves working for the good of constituents as much as I have done.

If as a City gentleman with many irons in the fire, and a large circle of friends and acquaintances, you ever hear of a good post, I should be very grateful to you.[1]

Randolph Churchill to Winston S. Churchill: telegram

(*Churchill papers: 2/283*)

28 November 1936   New York

Somewhat mystified by plans indicated your cable, since my information is that conditions specified your letter as necessary your visit are absent. No committee yet formed nor cash raised. Bernie advises against coming under Landau's sole auspices since it merely representative Jewish telegraph agency. Have not seen Landau but from talks with Bernie and Swope judge plans this end very unformed. Would appreciate further details. Love,

Randolph

---

[1] Violet Pearman did not change her job. Two and a half years earlier, in its series 'Secretaries of Famous Men', the *Sunday Express* had written: 'Mrs Pearman has heard nearly all Winston Churchill's speeches—in private, but never one in public. That is her great regret. Follows him to the House, but is always too busy to go into a gallery. Keeps pace with him between London and Westerham, absorbing cigar smoke, wit and wisdom. Stenographs his books and articles. Has no interest in politics. Got the post by enterprise. Lives near him at Westerham, heard he was wanting a secretary, and applied for the job. Got it, five and a half years ago. Would like to see him Prime Minister. Works in a room with a view. View thirty miles of Kent uplands, room stacked with books, mostly reference. No hours, no time for hobbies. Believes a secretary's chief value lies in taking burdens from her employer's shoulders' (*Sunday Express, 25 March 1934*).

Sir Henry Strakosch to Winston S. Churchill

(*Churchill papers: 2/277*)

30 November 1936

Thank you for your letter of the 27th, and for Mr B.R.'s letter and note on German Armaments. I return these documents herewith.

Mr R.'s figures of the estimated deficit—and therefore the figure of 13 milliards of marks for armament expenditure—lack support; yet I believe they are probably not far wide of the mark.

Quite recently, information reached me, from an apparently reliable source, which suggests that Germany has increased her indebtedness during the last $3\frac{1}{2}$ years by some $37\frac{1}{2}$ milliards of marks. I gather, further, that her annual expenditure on armaments—excluding upkeep of the Army, Navy and Air Force, and also excluding expenditure on industrial equipment for armament purposes—is at the rate of 600 million marks per month, that is 7·2 milliards of marks a year. It is not an unreasonable guess that, if the items excluded from these figures were added, the total annual expenditure would reach 13 milliards of marks (the figure assumed by Mr R.).

Yours sincerely,
H. Strakosch

Lord Cecil of Chelwood to Winston S. Churchill

(*Cecil of Chelwood papers*)

30 November 1936

My dear Winston,

Thank you very much for your letter and for writing to Austen. He wrote me a very stiff refusal but perhaps you will have better luck. He certainly has a gift for saying No,—'er ist der Geist der stets verneint'![1] As for your re-draft, I expect it is a great improvement, but I am a little nervous about changing. We have acceptances from the Duchess of Atholl (I thought the female sex should be represented), Archie Sinclair, Attlee, Dalton, Lytton, G. Murray, Noel-Baker, Lloyd George and self—and it may be difficult to get them all to approve,—anyhow it means delay and one never knows what may happen. I will, however, do my best.

Yours ever,
RC

[1] In Act One of Goethe's *Faust*, Mephisto says of himself: '*Ich bin der Geist der stets verneint, denn Alles, Alles das entsteht ist wert dass es zugrunde geht*' ('I am the spirit that ever denies, for everything that is created deserves to perish').

December 1936

Lord Cecil of Chelwood to Winston S. Churchill

(Cecil of Chelwood papers)

1 December 1936

My dear Winston,

On further consideration of your amendment I cannot help expressing the earnest hope that you will not insist. To say to the peoples of Europe war *can* be averted if the League Powers do their duty will be a great encouragement. It may make all the difference and may well ward off the immediate imminence of war. I am convinced that time is on our side. Nazism and Fascism cannot last. Even in oriental Russia, Stalin[1] feels the necessity of making some concession to Democracy. And there must remain considerable deposits of sanity in Germany and Italy which have not been destroyed by these few years of tyranny. On the other hand to say that the League is our 'best hope' seems rather cold comfort. It is the kind of thing doctors say

---

[1] Joseph Vissarionovich Dzhugashvili, 1879–1953. Born at Gori, in Georgia, the son of a cobbler of peasant origin, who died when Joseph was eleven. Studied in Tiflis, Georgia, at a church school and Seminary. Joined a clandestine socialist organization, 1898. Expelled from the Seminary, 1899. Elected to the Tiflis Social Democratic Committee, 1901. Active in illegal work in Baku. Exiled to Siberia, 1902, but escaped. Known first as 'Koba', then as 'Stalin': his revolutionary cover name. Sided with the Bolsheviks in the Menshevik–Bolshevik split, 1903. Rearrested, 1908, but escaped again. Rearrested, 1910. Released 1911. In prison in Siberia, February 1913 to February 1917. Temporary editor of *Pravda*, Petrograd, 1917. People's Commissar of Nationalities, October 1917. Secretary-General of the party, March 1922. Criticized by Lenin (4 January 1923) for having 'concentrated in his hands an immense power' and for being 'too rough'. Succeeded Lenin as party leader, 1924. Expelled his principal rival, Trotsky, from the party, 1927. Undertook the collectivization of agriculture, 1928. Brought to trial all his prominent Bolshevik rivals and fellow party leaders in three main 'show trials', 1935, 1936 and 1937: after so-called confessions for 'treason', almost all (including Zinoviev, Kamenev and Bukharin) were shot. Executed the head of the NKVD, 1938. Signed a non-aggression pact with Nazi Germany, August 1939. Partitioned Poland with Germany, October 1939. Invaded Finland, November 1939. Commanded the Soviet forces following the German invasion of the Soviet Union, June 1941. Met Churchill at a series of wartime conferences (August 1942, December 1943, October 1944, February 1945 and July 1945). Annexed eastern Poland, northern East Prussia, and Ruthenia to the Soviet Union, 1945.

when they believe that the death of their patient is practically certain. The Declaration as it stands is true *if* the League Powers can be trusted. And it says no more than that.

Yours ever,
R C

Winston S. Churchill to Lord Cecil of Chelwood

(*Cecil of Chelwood papers*)

2 December 1936   Chartwell
Private

My dear Bob,

Austen gave me various reasons against his signing, the chief being that suggestions about Treaty revision will estrange the Little Entente. At the present time the improved attitude of Poland and the Little Entente gives me hopes that these four countries in more or less good relations with Russia, will form an eastern insurance group similar to that which now exists in the west between England, France and Belgium.[1]

In my speech tomorrow I shall be indicating that the mutual association of these groups through the League of Nations and under the Covenant give the League for the first time a very great nucleus of solid strength against at least one potential aggressor. Nothing could give better hope of preventing a war. Any undue stressing of Russia would simply drive an overwhelming amount of Tories into violent opposition to the League of Nations cause. But I think on the whole matters are moving in the direction you wish, and the League may well become more powerful.

I must confess that I do not see the advantage of your manifesto at this stage. The list of names you have sent me is not at all impressive, in fact it is nothing but the League of Nations Union notabilities, plus your humble servant. I sympathise deeply with you in your intense desire to take some action to uphold the League; but I feel as far as I am concerned, the inclusion of my name would weaken me seriously in the work I am trying to do. In these circumstances I hope you will reconsider the whole plan.

---

[1] The 'Little Entente' was already under strain as a result of Yugoslavia's decision to seek closer relations with Italy and Bulgaria, at the expense both of France, and of the other 'Little Entente' members, Czechoslovakia and Rumania. On 6 November 1936 *The Times* had commented that the recent action by Mussolini in 'pointedly offering Yugoslavia friendship while ignoring the two other Little Entente States, which have most to fear from Hungarian claims, may have cast a shadow over promising schemes'.

Unless you have hope of strong Conservative support, it will only concentrate the Tory antagonism upon the League of Nations Union, whereas the actual movements of events is favourable in many ways.

You said after the luncheon at the Dorchester Hotel[1] that you wish I had made a speech two years ago. I send you an extract from the speech which I made in the House of Commons on July 13, 1934, which is $2\frac{1}{2}$ years ago.[2] I had forgotten about it, or it would have saved me the trouble of preparing a new one for the Dorchester luncheon.

Lord Citrine: recollections

('Men and Work')

3 December 1936

We had several speakers, in addition to Winston Churchill, drawn from people in public life. Lady Violet Bonham Carter was amongst them. We all assembled in a private room behind the platform, except for Winston who was late.

The minutes were ticking by and we were all becoming anxious. I hate to keep an audience waiting and I am a firm believer in starting meetings at the advertised time. So I said to my colleagues, 'If Winston isn't here in three minutes we are going on the platform without him.' I didn't ask whether anyone agreed with me, but I was relieved when a few moments later Churchill rushed up.

'I must speak to you,' he said rather excitedly, calling me aside.

'What about?' I asked rather gruffly.

'About the King,' he replied, referring to the rumours of his abdicating.

'What's that got to do with this meeting?' I demanded.

'People will expect a statement from me,' Churchill answered.

'I don't see that at all,' I said. 'We have come here to demonstrate our unity in standing up to the Nazis. We haven't come to talk about the King, or anything else. If you make a statement others may want to do so. You will certainly be challenged, and if no one else does it I will.'

---

[1] Of 25 November 1936, see page 403, note 1.

[2] Speaking in the House of Commons on 13 July 1934 Churchill said: 'The League of Nations should be the great instrument upon which all forces resolved to maintain peace should centre, and we should all make our contribution to the League.' Churchill continued, as *The Times* reported on the following day: 'He could not see how better they could prevent war than to confront an aggressor with the prospect of such a vast concentration of force, moral and material, that even the most reckless and infuriated leader would not dare to challenge those great forces.' Possibly, he added, 'this process of agreements under the sanction of the League of Nations might eventually lead on to a step we should never exclude, the ultimate creation of some international force'.

Churchill was a little taken aback at this, and simply replied, 'I must consider my position.'

Some may wonder at my abruptness and may think me churlish. They must remember that in those days Winston was an active Tory politician whom few people in the Labour Party either trusted or admired. He had not then shown his great qualities as the leader of the nation who installed himself in the affections of us all.

With that we went upon the platform. The meeting passed off successfully without the least vestige of discord. Winston read his speech throughout in the most masterly fashion.[1]

Winston S. Churchill: notes[2]

(Churchill papers: 2/264)

December 1936
Secret

THE ABDICATION OF KING EDWARD VIII

1. Upon the King's coming to the Throne, it was known through wide circles of politics and society that he had formed a deep attachment for Mrs Simpson. He delighted in her company, and found in her qualities as necessary to his happiness as the air he breathed. Those who knew him well and watched him closely noticed that many little tricks and fidgetings of nervousness fell away from him. He was a completed being instead of a sick

---

[1] Speaking at the Albert Hall on 3 December 1936, under the auspices of the League of Nations Union, and the Movement for the Defence of Freedom and Peace, Churchill said, as reported in *The Times* on the following day, that 'they were gathered together on that platform with one object. They wanted to stop this war of which they had heard so much talk.' During the course of his speech Churchill declared: 'If we wish to stop this coming war—if coming it is—we must in the year that lies before us—nay, in the next six months—gather together the great nations, all as well armed as possible and united under the Covenant of the League in accordance with the principles of the League, and in this way we may reach a position where we can invite the German people to join this organization of world security; where we can invite them to take their place in the circle of nations to preserve peace, and where we shall be able to assure them that we seek no security for ourselves, which we do not extend most freely to them.' 'We should rally and invite under the League of Nations the greatest number of strongly armed nations that we could marshal. Let us invite Germany to take her part among us. Then we should, he believed, sincerely have done not only our best but have succeeded in warding off from the world calamities and horrors the end of which no man could foresee.'

[2] Written shortly after the Abdication, these notes were never published but were kept by Churchill among his private papers.

and harassed soul. This experience which happens to a great many people in the flower of their youth, came late in life for him, and was all the more precious and compulsive from that fact. The association was psychical rather than sexual, and certainly not sensual except incidentally. Although branded with the stigma of a guilty love, no companionship could have appeared more natural, more free from impropriety or grossness. Both were forty-two years old. While profoundly interested in all his duties as King, and discharging with dignity and punctilio the laborious regal routine, Edward VIII found in his mature paramour a joy and a comfort without which his life and burden seemed insupportable.

2. There is no need to be an apologist for a lax morality in order to state that in no other period in the history of monarchy and upon no other Throne than that of the British Empire would such an attachment have brought about the abdication from his Throne of such a Prince. Upon him had been bestowed many of the rarest and most splendid gifts of personal charm, of insight, of sympathy, and above all of courage and honour. For twenty-five years as Prince of Wales he had faithfully and diligently discharged public duties of a ceremonial character most serviceable to all sorts and conditions of people in all parts of British dominions, but most wearing and exhausting to himself. 'How would you like' he exclaimed once to the present writer, 'to have to make a thousand speeches, and never once to be allowed to say what you think yourself?' The sense of unreality, of discharging a function which though blatant to the world, must always be kept clear of controversy of any kind, cast its shadows upon the servant of constitutional requirements. To have to seek harmony and reality in his private life such as is granted to the vast masses of men and women the world over, was an intense desire, and might at any moment become an abnormal obsession. A life of glittering public pomp without a home and some human comfort in the background would not be endurable to the vast majority of men. One must have something real somewhere. Otherwise far better die.

3. The character and record of the lady upon whom the affection of Edward VIII became so fatally fixed is relevant only upon a lower plane to the constitutional and moral issues which have been raised. No one has been more victimised by gossip and scandal, but gossip and scandal would not in themselves have been decisive. The only fact of which the Church could take notice was that she had divorced one husband and was in the process of divorcing another. Now the law of England under the liberal reforms of the nineteenth century affirms the validity of civil marriage, the right of divorced persons to re-marry, and the right of the legally innocent party of a divorce to be remarried within the sanction of the Church.

4. At the end of July Mr Walter Monckton, attorney for the Duchy of

Cornwall and in the King's intimate confidence, asked to see me, and I received him at 11, Morpeth Mansions. He told me that Mrs Simpson was contemplating divorcing her husband who was more than ready to comply as he was already living with someone else. Mr Monckton assured me that the King had no thought of marrying Mrs Simpson, but would be glad to see her free, as his 'possessive sense' was strong. What did I think about this? He also enquired what I thought about Mrs Simpson being invited to Balmoral. In reply I said that such a divorce would be most dangerous; that people were free to believe or ignore gossip as they chose; but that court proceedings were in another sphere. If any judgment was given in court against Mr Simpson it would be open to any Minister of Religion to say from the pulpit that an innocent man had allowed himself to be divorced on account of the King's intimacies with his wife. I urged most strongly that every effort should be made to prevent such a suit.

About Balmoral: I deprecated strongly Mrs Simpson going to such a highly official place upon which the eyes of Scotland were concentrated and which was already sacred to the memories of Queen Victoria and John Brown.[1] What I said as reported was not at all pleasing to Mrs Simpson and I heard that she had expressed herself with surprise that I should have shown myself to be 'against her'. I dined at York House with the King two days later. He had not yet received any account of our conversation from Mr Monckton, and he asked me whether I had seen him. He asked me what we had talked about. I replied in one word 'Gossip'. His Majesty looked at me hard, but did not pursue the subject.

I had no access to or communication with the King, nor did I seek any, until Friday December 4. At about 5 o'clock on that afternoon, Mr Monckton telephoned from Fort Belvedere asking me whether I was free to come down and see the King that night, that he would confirm the invitation later, and that it would be for dinner. Two hours later he telephoned that the King wished me to dine with him, and that he had asked Mr Baldwin's leave which had been granted. On arrival at the Fort I saw the King at once. HM was most gay and debonair for the first quarter of an hour, and no one would have thought him in a serious crisis. But after this effort it was obvious that the personal strain he had been so long under, and which was now at its climax had exhausted him to a most painful degree. On the way down I had made up my mind that never having been consulted at all for so many months, I would not advise on any point except one, viz: time. He must

---

[1] Queen Victoria's favourite Highland servant. On his accession to the throne in 1901, Edward VII had ordered the immediate destruction or removal of all the statues, busts and other memorials which Queen Victoria had erected after John Brown's death nearly twenty years earlier, in 1883.

have full time for his decision. During the course of a long evening I confined myself strictly to this point. The King told me that he had said to Mr Baldwin, '*You* can see anyone you like. You can send for anyone you like. You can consult with any number of people. You can arrange with the newspapers and with the Church; you can bring the Dominions High Commissioners together; you can set the Whips to work upon the MPs. But I cannot see anyone except those you send me, like the Archbishop of Canterbury or Mr Geoffrey Dawson of the "Times". I want to see someone who is independent of all that. I want to see Mr Churchill.' Mr Baldwin had replied 'Certainly'. The King also said 'I have not abdicated. I never used the word abdication in my conversation with the Prime Minister. I had Mr Monckton in the room with his permission all the time and he will bear me out.' HM told me that he had desired to issue a broadcast message to his peoples and that his Ministers had forbidden him, but had told him that there would be no objection if he had abdicated. Then he would speak as a private person and not 'on advice'. Meanwhile if he desired the Government would make a statement on his behalf, and Mr Baldwin would bring him this tomorrow (Saturday) evening. The King went on 'I am sure that in this statement they will insert a declaration that I have renounced the Throne.' He was evidently most strongly adverse from this. He said he wanted a fortnight to weigh the whole matter. He felt himself a prisoner in the Fort. If he could go to Switzerland with a couple of equerries he would be able to think out his decision without undue pressure. He asked me what would happen if he made this request to Mr Baldwin when he saw him the next day. Did I think that the Ministers would resign unless he immediately consented to abdication.

In reply as the conversation proceeded, I said 'Your Majesty need not have the slightest fear about time. If you require time there is no force in this country which would or could deny it you. Mr Baldwin would certainly not resist you. If he did you could remind him that he himself took nearly three months rest in order to recover from the strain of the session. Your strain was far more intense and prolonged. Mr Baldwin is a fatherly man and nothing would induce him to treat you harshly in such a matter. Ministers could not possibly resign on such an issue as your request for time.' In order that there should be no mistake I dictated to a shorthand writer in the King's presence the substance of the position he should adopt towards the Prime Minister. To this I added two other counsels. First that he should not on any account leave the country. That would produce the worst possible impression. Everyone would say that he had gone to meet Mrs Simpson (then at Cannes). His Majesty demurred to this; said he had no intention of seeing her, but that a complete change in the Alps was what he required.

Secondly I urged him strongly to send for Lord Dawson[1] and Sir Thomas Horder.[2] I was sure that he was in no condition to take so grave a decision as that which lay upon him. He twice in my presence completely lost the thread of what he was saying, and appeared to me driven to the last extremity of endurance. Most of this conversation took place in the presence of Mr Monckton and some other member of his household was there from time to time.

The next morning I wrote the following letter to the Prime Minister.[3]

And I also published on the Sunday an appeal for time and patience.[4]

I must add that throughout I was aware that very strenuous efforts were being made by Lord Beaverbrook through Lord Brownlow[5] to induce Mrs Simpson who was at Cannes to renounce all idea of marriage, morganatic or otherwise, with the King. This could have been rendered decisive at any moment by withdrawing her petition for divorce upon which she had obtained the decree nisi. It is my belief that if this had been obtained, the intense pressure then at work both upon His Majesty and Mrs Simpson would have resulted in her taking this step and thus ending the crisis.

---

[1] Bertrand Dawson, 1864–1945. BSc, London, 1888. Member of the Royal College of Surgeons, 1890. Assistant Physician, London Hospital, 1896; Physician, 1906. Physician-in-ordinary to King Edward VII, 1906–10; to King George V, 1910–36. Knighted, 1911. Consulting Physician to the Army in France, 1915–18; temporary Major-General, Army Medical Service, 1917–18. Created Baron 1920. Physician-in-ordinary to the Prince of Wales, 1923–36; to King Edward VIII, 1936. Member of the Medical Research Council, 1931–35. Created Viscount Dawson of Penn, 1936. It was he who, as King George V was dying, wrote the words 'The King's life is moving peacefully towards its close' which were repeated at 15 minute intervals over the BBC on the night of 20 January 1936.

[2] Thomas Jeeves Horder, 1871–1955. Physician to the Prince of Wales (both as Prince of Wales, 1923–36, and as King Edward VIII, 1936). Subsequently Physician to King George VI. Consulting Physician to the Ministry of Pensions, to the Cancer Hospital, Fulham, and to many other hospitals and institutions. Knighted, 1918. Created Baronet, 1923. Created Baron, 1933. Chairman of the Empire Rheumatism Council, 1936–53; of Wireless for the Bedridden; and of the Nursing Reconstruction Committee, and of the Anti-Noise League. President of the Food Education Society, of the Industrial Education Society, and of the Eugenics Society.

[3] Churchill's letter to Baldwin of 5 December 1936 is printed as the following letter of this volume.

[4] Churchill's Press Statement of 5 December 1936 is printed in full on pages 457–9 of this volume.

[5] Peregrine Francis Adelbert Cust, 1899–1978. Educated at Eton and Sandhurst. 2nd Lieutenant, Grenadier Guards 1918; Adjutant, 3rd Battalion, 1923–6. Succeeded his father as 6th Baron Brownlow, 1927. Lord in Waiting to King Edward VIII, 1936. Flight Lieutenant, RAF Volunteer Reserve, 1939. Parliamentary Private Secretary to Lord Beaverbrook (Minister of Aircraft Production), 1940. Attached to Bomber Command, 1941. Staff Officer Air Staff, 1942; attached to US Air Force Staff, 1943. Squadron Leader, 1944.

Winston S. Churchill to Stanley Baldwin

(*Churchill papers: 2/264*)

5 December 1936   11 Morpeth Mansions

My dear Prime Minister,

The King having told me that he had your permission to see me, I dined with His Majesty last night, and had a long talk with him.

I strongly urged his staff to call in a doctor. HM appeared to me to be under the vy greatest strain and vy near breaking point. He had two marked and prolonged 'black-outs' in which he completely lost the thread of his conversation. Although he was very gallant and debonaire at the outset, this soon wore off, even to hardwon politeness. His mental exhaustion was vy painful. The combination of public and private stresses is the hardest of all to endure.

I told the King that if he appealed to you to allow him time to recover himself and to consider now that things have reached this chaos the grave issues constitutional and personal with which you have found it your duty to confront him, you would I was sure not fail in kindness and consideration. It would be most cruel and wrong to extort a decision from him in his present state.

WSC

Winston S. Churchill to King Edward VIII

(*Churchill papers: 2/264*)

5 December 1936   11 Morpeth Mansions
Evening

Sir,

News from all fronts! No pistol to be held at the King's head. No doubt that this request for time will be granted. Therefore no final decision or Bill till after Christmas—probably February or March.

2. *On no account must the King leave the country.* Windsor Castle is his battle station (poste de commandment). When so much is at stake, no minor inclinations can be indulged. It would be far better for Mrs Simpson to return to England for a day or two, than for the King to go abroad now. Please let me talk to you about this if there is any doubt. (This would at any rate show she had not been driven out of the country.) But of course better still if she preferred to remain where she is for this critical time.

3. Lord Craigavon, Prime Minister of Northern Ireland, is deeply moved

by loyalty to the King, and all for time. Could not he be invited to luncheon tomorrow? He has a constitutional right of access (I think) & anyhow there could be no objection. His visit should be made public. He shares my hopes such as they are of an ultimate happy ending. It's a long way to Tipperary.

4. Max. The King brought him back across the world. He is a tiger to fight. I gave him the King's message &—please telephone or write—better telephone. I cannot see it would do harm to see him if it could be arranged. Important however to make contact with him. A *devoted* tiger! Very scarce breed.

5. For real wit Bernard Shaw's article in tonight's Evening Standard should be read. He is joyous.[1]

Summary.

Good advances on all parts giving prospects of gaining good positions and assembling large forces behind them.

Your Majesty's faithful devoted servant & subject,
WSC

Lord Salisbury to Winston S. Churchill
(Churchill papers: 2/264)

5 December 1936 Hatfield House

My dear Winston

When I met you in the House of Lords two or three weeks ago and you explained to me why you could not come with the elder statesmen to signify

---

[1] Writing in the *Evening Standard* on 5 December 1936, under the heading 'The King, The Constitution and The Lady, Another Fictitious Dialogue', George Bernard Shaw wrote: 'In the Kingdom of the Half Mad, that same prince whose difficulties over his father's illness I formerly chronicled, succeeded to the throne on the death of that same father, and almost at once found himself in difficulties with his Cabinet and with the Church.' Shaw went on to describe how the Prime Minister and the Archbishop called on the Prince. The Archbishop admitted that a civil marriage ceremony would solve his problems, but the Prime Minister was adamant. The King demanded alternative suggestions if he were to be barred from marrying the woman he loved, and told his visitors: 'You are dreaming of a seventeenth century dynastic marriage. I the King of England and Emperor of Britain, am to go a-begging through Europe for some cousin, five or six times removed, of a dethroned down-and-out Bourbon, or Habsburg, or Hohenzollern, or Romanoff. . . . I shall do nothing so unpopular and so silly . . . . I am living in a world of republics, of mighty Powers governed by ex-housepainters, stonemasons, promoted ranker soldiers, sons of operators in boot factories. . . . That is the royal stock of to-day. I wonder would any of these great rulers elbow a relative of his to marry an old-fashioned King! I doubt it. I tell you there is not a royal house left in Europe to-day into which I could marry without weakening England's position.' After the King had refused to abdicate, he invited his two guests to stay for lunch. Shaw ended: 'The Prime Minister ate hardly anything; but the Archbishop left nothing on his plate.'

their support to Baldwin in this crisis you intimated that while you shared our views you would by joining this deputation lose all influence over the King, that he was sure to consult you and that you wanted to say to him that just as you and others had made every sacrifice in the War (so I understood), so he must now be willing to make every sacrifice for his Country.

I did not press you then, but I am watching your attitude now with great anxiety. If your purpose now is the same as it was in our conversation and you are still intent upon persuading him to make every sacrifice of his personal interests and desires for his Country it would enable us to be less anxious. It does not shock me that a man should want to marry his mistress nor worry me that a man should be willing to marry a woman who has two other living husbands, but it is very different that a man born to sublime responsibilities should be ready to jeopardise them, as it seems, in order to gratify his passion for a woman of any sort.

Yours ever,
Salisbury

Winston S. Churchill: Press statement

(Churchill papers: 2/264)

5 December 1936

I plead for time and patience. The nation must realise the character of the constitutional issue. There is no question of any conflict between the King and Parliament. Parliament has not been consulted in any way, nor allowed to express any opinion.

The question is whether the King is to abdicate upon the advice of the Ministry of the day. No such advice has ever before been tendered to a Sovereign in Parliamentary times. This is not a case where differences have arisen between the Sovereign and his Ministers on any particular measure. These could certainly be resolved by normal processes of Parliament or dissolution. In this case we are in presence of a wish expressed by the Sovereign to perform an act which in no circumstances can be accomplished for nearly five months, and may conceivably for various reasons never be accomplished at all. That on such a hypothetical and supposititious basis the supreme sacrifice of abdication and potential exile of the Sovereign should be demanded, finds no support whatever in the British constitution. No Ministry has the authority to advise the abdication of the Sovereign. Only the most serious Parliamentary processes could ever raise the issue in a decisive form.

The Cabinet has no right to prejudge such a question without having previously ascertained at the very least the will of Parliament. This could perhaps be obtained by Messages from the Sovereign to Parliament, and by Addresses of both Houses after due consideration of these Messages. For the Sovereign to abdicate incontinently in the present circumstances would inflict an injury upon the constitutional position of the monarchy which is measureless and cannot fail to be grievous to the Institution itself, irrespective of the existing occupant of the Throne.

Parliament would also fail entirely in its duty if it allowed such an event to occur as the signing of an Abdication in response to the advice of Ministers without taking all precautions to make sure that these same processes may not be repeated with equal uncanny facility at no distant date in unforeseen circumstances. Clearly time is needed for searching constitutional debate.

The next question is—what has the King done? If it be true, as is alleged, that the King has proposed to his Ministers legislation which they are not prepared to introduce, the answer of Ministers should be not to call for Abdication, but to refuse to act upon the King's request, which thereupon becomes inoperative. If the King refuses to take the advice of his Ministers they are of course free to resign. They have no right whatever to put pressure upon him to accept their advice by soliciting beforehand assurances from the Leader of the Opposition that he will not form an alternative administration in the event of their resignation, and thus confronting the King with an ultimatum. Again there is cause for time and patience.

Why cannot time be granted? The fact that it is beyond the King's power to accomplish the purpose which Ministers oppose until the end of April, surely strips the matter of constitutional urgency. There may be some inconvenience, but that inconvenience stands on a different plane altogether from the grave constitutional issues I have set forth. National and Imperial considerations alike require that before such a dread step as a demand for abdication is taken, not only should the constitutional position be newly defined by Parliament, but that every method should be exhausted which gives the hope of a happier solution.

Lastly, but surely not least, there is the human and personal aspect. The King has been for many weeks under the greatest strain, moral and mental, that can fall upon a man. Not only has he been inevitably subjected to the extreme stress of his public duty, but also to the agony of his own personal feelings. Surely if he asks for time to consider the advice of his Ministers, now that at length matters have been brought to this dire culmination, he should not be denied.

Howsoever this matter may turn it is pregnant with calamity and inseparable from inconvenience. But all the evil aspects will be aggravated beyond measure if the utmost chivalry and compassion is not shown by both Ministers and by the British nation, towards a gifted and beloved King torn between private and public obligations of love and duty.

The Churches state their claims at the highest. They believe in the efficacy of prayer. Surely their influence must not oppose a period of reflection. I plead, I pray that time and tolerance will not be denied.

The King has no means of personal access to his Parliament or his people. Between him and them stand in their office the Ministers of the Crown. If they thought it their duty to engage all their power and influence against him, still he must remain silent. All the more must they be careful not to be the judge in their own case, and to show a loyal and Christian patience even at some political embarrassment to themselves.

If an abdication were to be hastily extorted, the outrage so committed would cast its shadow forward across many chapters of the history of the British Empire.

Desmond Morton to Winston S. Churchill

(Churchill papers: 2/264)

6 December 1936   Crockham Hill

My dear Winston

I think your statement to the Press is magnificent. I am sure you are doing all you can to make both parties see reason. Pray God, you may be successful. As you know better than I, there is an overwhelming desire in the country that he should remain our King. Persons of all classes to whom I have spoken, are unanimous in that. True, I find that they cannot acclimatise themselves to Mrs S as Queen, and I think that the great majority would be very much distressed were she his wife, without the Royal dignity.

If, however, he can by any means give her up, his popularity would be so great that he could make himself Dictator of England, if so he chose. The whole of this business would be regarded as forging an unbreakable bond between himself in person and his subjects. There is nothing, in my opinion, that he could not do with them afterwards.

The belief is, I find, widely held that this is a Baldwin and Parlimentary plot; that Parliament led by SB is determined to reduce the Monarchy to an utterly impotent symbol, lacking even those powers still enjoyed by it and so wisely used on rare occasions by King George. An immense number of people rightly or wrongly believe that although the Monarchy is highly circumscribed, it does, at times, act as a court of disinterested equity, to prevent the rasher acts of no matter what Party being carried through without sufficient consideration, in the heat of political strife and controversy. They believe that SB has with set purpose taken advantage of an unfortunate situation to destroy the last vestige of Kingly power and dignity, in favour of himself and Parliament.

However well or ill-founded these ideas may be, they are held, and I believe that if the King should abdicate it will give an enormous impetus to those misguided persons who believe in Fascism or Communism, and that, before long, a Dictatorship of the 'Right' or the 'Left' will become a real possibility.

Naturally, do not answer this but I wanted to congratulate you on your stand.

Yours very sincerely,
Desmond Morton

Walton Newbold [1] *to Winston S. Churchill*

(*Churchill papers: 2/264*)

6 December 1936

Dear Churchill

Count me all in once more with yourself in the line you are taking in respect of the King. If it comes to an issue my voice and pen are at the service of those who take the stand you are doing. It is time that something shook up this country and Empire to the dimensions of the world crisis in all its ramifications of thought and action. The sooner the old gang are de-bunked the better.

Yours very truly,
Walton Newbold

[1] John Turner Walton Newbold, 1888–1943. Born in Lancashire. Educated at the University of Manchester. Joined the Fabian Society, 1908; the Independent Labour Party, 1910; the Communist Party of Great Britain, 1921. Communist MP for Motherwell, 1922–3. Member of the Executive of the Communist Party, 1924. Unsuccessful Labour Candidate at Epping, 1929. Member of the Macmillan Committee on Finance and Industry, 1929–31. Resigned from the Labour Party, 1931. Author of several books on capitalism and democracy.

Professor J. H. Morgan[1] *to Winston S. Churchill*

(*Churchill papers: 2/264*)

6 December 1936
Private and Confidential

My dear Churchill

It has occurred to me, since our conversation yesterday afternoon, that His Majesty the King has still a powerful weapon available to him in the most painful dilemma in which the action of his present Ministers has placed him. Failing the consent of the Labour Opposition to accept office in the event of the resignation of Mr Baldwin and his colleagues, the King can with perfect propriety send for you and invite you to form a new Administration. In such a case you, with equal constitutional propriety, can accept such an invitation and 'carry on', even if you have a following of only forty or fifty members of the House of Commons. You would then have the right to ask His Majesty for a Dissolution and it would be perfectly in accord with constitutional propriety, and indeed with actual precedent, for His Majesty to grant you an immediate Dissolution. It is quite possible that in such a case and on so grave an issue you might 'sweep the country'.

If, in such an event, you experienced any difficulty in finding men of sufficient eminence in the Commons to take office under you, you would also be acting quite constitutionally, and following precedents, in advising his Majesty to appoint competent men of eminence to such offices even though they had not at the time of such appointment yet got a seat in either House. This statement of mine is equally true of the legal appointments, ie the Woolsack and the Law Offices of the Crown, and of the purely political offices.

If I can be of any further service to you, pray let me know. I am returning to London on Monday afternoon and leaving for India on Thursday, having been retained and instructed to advise the Chamber of Princes in the pending negotiations with the Viceroy on the subject of Federation.

As I intimated to you yesterday, I shall be obliged if, for the present, you do not quote my name in connection with the statements on the constitu-

---

[1] John Hartman Morgan, 1876–1955. Educated at Oxford, Berlin and London. Joined the *Daily Chronicle*, 1901; leader writer, *Manchester Guardian*, 1904–5. Unsuccessful Liberal candidate, 1910 (twice). Home Office Commissioner with the BEF, 1914–15. Staff Captain, Adjutant-General's Staff, 1915. Adjutant-General's Office, Paris Peace Conference, 1919; Inter-Allied Military Mission of Control, Germany, 1919–23. Brigadier-General, 1923. King's Counsel, 1926. Reader in Constitutional Law, Inns of Court, 1926–36. Counsel to the India Defence League, 1933–4; to the Indian Chamber of Princes, 1934–7; to the State of Gwalior and the Central Indian States, 1939–45; to the Parliamentary Post-War Policy Group, 1942–5. Adviser to the United States War Crimes Commission at Nuremberg, 1947–9.

tional position which you are about to make. But I have no objection to your quoting me as your authority at any time after Friday Dec 11th.

Yours sincerely,
J. H. Morgan

J. A. Spender [1] *to Winston S. Churchill*

(*Churchill papers: 2/264*)

6 December 1936

Dear Churchill

Forgive me for the sake of old times, but I have read your statement in the Sunday papers to-day with consternation. How can you suggest that the present state of things should be prolonged for five months—five months of raging & tearing controversy, quite possibly a King's party being formed against the Government, the Crown a centre of schism tearing Country and Commonwealth to pieces & all this at this moment in world affairs! It is a grotesque situation for the British Constitution & Monarchy & will set all the Agitators jeering, if it is allowed to go on. The danger of its going on is that the K may suppose that he will have the backing of influential people like yourself in fighting the Government & damning the consequences & I am sure you can't mean that. The one use of the Crown to us in these days is as a unifier; if it becomes a centre of discord it will be a deadly menace to the whole British System.

The thing ought to be settled *at once*. Every day it goes on is irreparable mischief. You will be snowed under with letters of thoughtless approval—which makes me risk sending you this.

Yours ever,
J. A. Spender

---

[1] John Alfred Spender, 1862–1942. Educated at Balliol College, Oxford. Entered journalism, 1886. Editor of the *Westminster Gazette*, 1896–1922. A friend of Asquith, and a staunch Asquithian Liberal. Co-author of *The Life of Lord Oxford and Asquith* (1932), and of seventeen other volumes, including a memoir, *Life, Journalism and Politics* (1927).

Henry Wickham Steed to Winston S. Churchill

(*Churchill papers: 2/264*)

7 December 1936
Personal

Dear Mr Winston Churchill,

As one who has recently been associated with you in advocating certain principles of foreign policy, including the defence of democratic freedom, you will perhaps pardon me if I say that I feel unable to agree with the position you have taken up in regard to the present constitutional crisis. While I feel that both the Government and the leading organs of the press have been very remiss in not bringing this painful matter to the knowledge of Parliament and of the public much earlier, so that the King might have been guided by expressions of feeling here and in the Dominions before making up his mind, I think that once the issue had been raised the Government took the only proper constitutional course in regard to it. Any other course would, it seems to me, have endangered both the principle of Parliamentary supremacy over the wishes of the Crown in matters of national and imperial interest, and would have opened the door to an agitation which must have 'brought the King into politics'.

I do not for a moment expect or desire that my views should in any way influence your own judgment in this grave matter. I wish only to lay it before you personally so that, should events make it expedient or desirable for those of us who have worked with you in the Freedom and Peace movement to dissociate ourselves publicly from your standpoint, you will not feel that we have done this lightly or out of any lack of deference to you.

I trust that the King may be moved to make a decision which we shall all be able to welcome and to respect. In this event the storm will blow over, and it may be possible to resume work on the lines of 'Freedom and Peace'. Otherwise I cannot well see how we can stand up for democracy and parliamentary institutions, if, when the issue is raised, we do not dissociate ourselves from a course calculated to endanger the principle of parliamentary supremacy over the Crown.

Believe me, dear Mr Churchill,
Yours very sincerely,
Wickham Steed

PS. I am writing this before knowing what may have been said in the House this afternoon.

Winston S. Churchill to King Edward VIII

(*Churchill papers: 2/264*)

7 December 1936   House of Commons

Sir,

You kindly said I might write to Your Majesty about the opinion I encounter.

The only possibility of Your Majesty remaining on the Throne is if you could subscribe to some such Declaration as the following:—

'The King will not enter into any contract of marriage contrary to the advice of His Ministers.'

I forbear to use any argument because all that will be apparent to Your Majesty.

Sir, I cannot claim any authority behind this suggestion except my own belief. But I earnestly hope it may be considered.

With my humble duty,

Your Majesty's most faithful servant & subject,
Winston S. Churchill

L. S. Amery: diary

(*Amery papers*)

7 December 1936

So to the House where at the end of questions Baldwin explained that he had no further statement to make for the moment. Winston got up again and tried to get an assurance that 'no irrevocable step would be taken before the House had received a full statement' and tried to develop the question into a little speech. He was completely staggered by the unanimous hostility of the House, as well as by being called to order by the Speaker.

Lambert[1] followed by asking whether the Prime Minister was aware of the deep personal sympathy with him felt by the House, which raised a tremendous cheer. There is no doubt that over the week-end opinion in the country had settled down steadily behind the Government, and that outside the London area, less puritan, perhaps, and influenced by the Harmsworth and Beaverbrook press, the country as a whole was getting progressively more shocked at the idea that the King could hesitate between his duty to the Throne and his affection for a woman, and Members had been in touch with them.

[1] George Lambert (see page 50, note 3).

Robert Boothby to Winston S. Churchill

(*Churchill papers: 2/264*)

7 December 1936

Dear Winston,

I understood last night that we had *agreed* upon a formula, and a course, designed to save the King from abdication, if that is possible. I thought you were going to use all your powers—decisive, as I believe, in the present circumstances—to secure a happy issue, on the lines that were suggested.

But this afternoon you have delivered a blow to the King, both in the House and in the country, far harder than any that Baldwin ever conceived of.

You have reduced the number of potential supporters to the minimum possible—I shd think now about seven in all.

And you have done it without any consultation with your best friends and supporters.

I have never in my life said anything to you that I did not sincerely believe. And I never will.

What happened this afternoon makes me feel that it is almost impossible for those who are most devoted to you personally to follow you blindly (as they wd like to do) in politics. Because they cannot be sure where the hell they are going to be landed next.

I'm afraid this letter will make you very angry. But not, I hope, irretrievably angry.

I could not leave what I feel unsaid.

Yours ever,
Bob

Harold Nicolson: diary

(*Nicolson papers*)

8 December 1936

Winston collapsed utterly in the House yesterday. Bob Boothby was so funny about it. 'I knew,' he said, 'that Winston was going to do something dreadful. I had been staying the weekend with him. He was silent and restless and glancing into corners. Now when a dog does that, you know that he is about to be sick on the carpet. It is the same with Winston. He managed to hold it for three days, and then comes up to the House and is sick right across the floor.' Which is literally true. He has undone in five minutes the patient reconstruction work of two years.

Two things emerge, I think. First the supremacy of Baldwin. A leading

Labour man said to me yesterday, 'Thank God we have SB at the top. No other man in England could have coped with this.' And, secondly, how unanimous the House really is in times of crisis. There has been no hysteria and no party politics. One really feels that at such moments the House is a Council of State. What a *solid* people we are under all our sentimentality!

Blanche Dugdale: diary

(N. A. Rose, editor, 'Baffy')

8 December 1936

Rob Bernays[1] drove me home. He says Winston was absolutely howled down yesterday, and is in a very chastened mood today, and told him (Rob) that when he put his question he really had not read Baldwin's Statement! I think he is done for. In three minutes his hopes of return to power and influence are shattered. But God is once more behind his servant Stanley Baldwin.

Meeting of the 1922 Committee: report to the Cabinet

(Cabinet papers: 64/5)

8 December 1936

1. Mr Winston Churchill addressed the 1922 Committee of the House of Commons last night on 'Defence'. There was a large attendance.

2. In his opening remarks, he drew attention to the years which this country had lost, and developed his familiar argument that a sum of 2 or 3 million pounds expended at the proper time would have enabled the productive capacity of British industry to deal with the demands that are now required. His remarks were not framed in an obviously hostile manner.

NAVY

3. Referring to the Navy, Mr Churchill emphasised that, relative to Euro-

---

[1] Robert Hamilton Bernays, 1902–1945. Educated at Rossall and Worcester College, Oxford. President, Oxford Union, 1925. *News Chronicle* leader-writer, 1925; correspondent in India, 1931; in Germany and Austria, 1934. Liberal MP for Bristol North, 1931–45 (Liberal National after 1936). Parliamentary Secretary, Ministry of Health, 1937–9; Ministry of Transport, 1939–40. Deputy Regional Commissioner, Southern Civil Defence Region, 1940–2. Sapper, Royal Engineers, 1942; 2nd Lieutenant, 1943; Captain, 1944. Author of *Naked Fakir: A Study of Gandhi* and *Special Correspondent*. Killed in an aeroplane accident while flying from Italy to Greece, March 1945.

pean powers, our position was better than in 1914. It should not be forgotten, however, that we had lost our world supremacy.

4. He felt that the British Navy was unprepared at the time of the Italo-Abyssinian crisis. Today, however, deficiencies of great consequence had been repaired and he felt we could pride ourselves on having a fleet which was prepared and well equipped.

5. Referring to Japan, he strongly urged that the work on the defence of Singapore should be expedited. Our naval base should be made impregnable. It was impossible, he said, for Japan to conceive an attack on Australia provided we had battleships with their proper complements of cruisers and destroyers working from a strong base. He emphasised, however, that Japan would always have complete supremacy in the yellow seas. To challenge this supremacy would be impossible and futile.

6. Mr Churchill proceeded to make a passing reference to the Fleet Air Arm. The position should be clarified forthwith. He felt the Navy should have supreme control from start to finish of aeroplanes working from ships, and of all aircraft, whether working from ships or land bases, when engaged in defending our commerce or lines of communication.

7. Commenting on the Report of the Committee charged with investigating the problems of bombs v battleships, Mr Churchill said that the findings and recommendations of that Committee should be accepted. Battleships would undoubtedly play a great part in any future war, and no aeroplanes would invalidate their use.

ARMY

8. Referring to recruiting of the Army, he deplored that the difficulties had not yet been overcome. He hoped that measures would shortly be introduced which would enable this problem to be tackled.

9. He dwelt on the possibility of a foreign invasion of our shores by air. A few hundred men descending unexpectedly by parachute could incapacitate certain vital centres such as factories, arsenals, storage tanks, bridges, and such like. He did not develop his theme or deal with the many problems which an enemy power would presumably find inseparable from such an exploit. He urged, however, that it was essential for us to create and maintain strong mobile units which could be despatched with all possible speed to places of danger.

10. Mr Churchill concluded his remarks on the Army by insisting that we had lost our supremacy in the manufacture of tanks. The quality did not come up to that obtained by foreign powers. Making special reference to medium tanks, he said we were deplorably short in numbers, and a long time

would have to elapse before this could be rectified. No substantial mechanisation could take place in the Army for two years.

THE AIR FORCE

11. Mr Churchill then turned to the British Air Force. His observations
under this heading appeared to form the principal substance of his speech.
The picture which he drew was indeed melancholy. Our position was not
only bad, but was daily growing worse. We were not only incapable of
defending ourselves from aerial attack from without, but did not possess a
striking force of such power or dimensions as would inspire fear into others
and act as a possible deterrent. It might be useful if I [1] attempt to develop in
greater detail the various points which he made.

12. We were the victims of our geographical position. Our ports, arsenals
and factories were fatally vulnerable. We were at this moment in a position
of extreme danger. Our weakness was such as had probably never been
known before.

13. What was the relative strength of the British and German metropolitan
air forces? He frankly admitted the difficulty of forming a true estimate or
of appraising the situation correctly. First, he took first-line air strength.
What did he understand by this? He meant an aeroplane with its pilot, and
also probably with its observer and wireless operator, together with the
requisite number of ground staff and personnel, also reserve stocks of spare
parts for that particular machine. Behind that would be a reserve which he
thought would probably be in the neighbourhood of *75%–100%* of the first-
line strength, all composed of first-class machines. Behind that stood the war
potential of the industry.

14. By the strength of Germany's metropolitan air force he meant the
force which Germany could put into effective action forthwith on the outbreak of war, and which she could maintain at any rate for a substantial
time without serious diminution.

15. What was the size of this force? He understood ('a little bird had told
him') that on the 1st January 1937 Germany would have 150 squadrons.
Taking 12 aeroplanes to one squadron (9 in front and 3 in reserve) this
would mean at least *1,750 first-line machines*, all thoroughly equipped. They
also possessed 250 Luft Hansa civil machines which could be transformed

---

[1] Stuart Hugh Minto Russell, 1909–1943. Educated at Rugby and Trinity College, Cambridge. Conservative MP for Darwen, 1935–43. Parliamentary Private Secretary to Sir
Philip Sassoon (Under-Secretary of State for Air), 1936–7. Parliamentary Private Secretary
to Sir John Simon (Chancellor of the Exchequer), 1937–8. Captain, Coldstream Guards.
He died in Egypt on 30 October 1943, while on active service.

almost immediately into bombing machines. This brought their number up to 2,000 machines. Behind this lay a stored reserve of 1,500 machines, all well equipped. Furthermore, they had 45 squadrons which form the centre of their training schools, and it had to be remembered that instructors were with these squadrons, ie, the pick of Germany's pilots. This meant a further 400–500 machines, bringing the total up to nearly 4,000 machines. It might be argued, he continued, that Germany could not contemplate bringing in these squadrons which, in the event of war, would be more than ever necessary for training purposes. It would be most unwise to make any such assumption. He understood that they could bring in 45 squadrons from the sport platz (?)—(it was impossible to catch this word correctly—I am not quite certain what it was)—to replace the 45 squadrons released for war.

16. What was our position? Now, in December 1936, the metropolitan air force of this country consisted of 80 squadrons (only 50 odd, he added, were mentioned in the Air Force List). Many of these were skeleton squadrons. Many of them were only up to half to one-third strength, with great deficiencies of observers and mechanics. This, he admitted, was inevitable. The Air Ministry was, in his opinion, quite right to reduce the immediate efficiency of our fighting force to facilitate and expedite the expansion which was so urgently required. This meant, however, that our first-line strength at the present time consisted of only 960 machines. In round figures, therefore, the first-line strength of Germany consisted of 2,000 machines, while we had 1,000 only, or exactly half. (Mr Churchill would appear to be including in these calculations of first-line machines, the 45 squadrons employed at training schools).

17. This, moreover, was only half of the picture. In Germany there was no military machine more than three years old. In this country, per contra, we were still ordering a large amount of obsolete machines. 'We hear a good deal,' he said, 'of new machines and new designs.' 'They may be good; there may be none better, but how many of these machines have we at the present time? When will they reach the squadrons?' For the next twelve months our air force would be armed with old and short-ranged machines. In comparing the potential bombing power of the German and British Air Forces, the balance was weighed heavily against us. At the moment we had no machines which could bomb Berlin. We should have only a very few next year. Germany, on the other hand, could bomb London from her bases with the greatest of ease.

18. This led Mr Churchill to say that the effectiveness of our Air Force would be trebled if it operated from French and Belgian bases. It was this thought which so deeply disturbed him when he heard the Belgian statement about neutrality. Without these bases the odds against us would be im-

measurable. It was of the utmost importance, therefore, that we should work in the closest possible harmony with France and Belgium. The combined air forces of France and Britain, working from French or Belgian bases, would possess sufficient power to make Germany exceedingly shy of attack. More than this, however, he could not say, as he sincerely felt that *the combined air forces of the two countries (France and Britain) were not as strong as that of Germany.* Moreover, when one took into account the war potential, the position became even worse. He believed Germany could work up to a *monthly* output of *1,000–1,500 machines almost immediately*, on the outbreak of hostilities. The combined industrial resources of Great Britain and France did not admit of anything approaching this output being attained.

19. Mr Churchill then made a reference to the defence of London from aerial attack. It could not be defended. It was true that the fleet or certain vulnerable points might be defended by means of intensive anti-aircraft barrage. It was foolhardy, however, to imagine that London as such could rely on any protection from 'Saturday evening gunners'. The only hope lay in our own fighter aeroplanes.

20. Mr Churchill concluded his speech by saying that 1937 would be the most critical and mournful year we had ever approached. We had no choice in the matter. If we did not keep in with the French republic we should be doomed. Such a policy was vital and essential, and he was proud to think that, together with Sir Austen Chamberlain, he had put pressure on a certain French statesman a very short time ago which might at any rate have been partly responsible for the clear policy recently enunciated by Mr Delbos[1] with reference to the explicit assurances given to this country by France in the event of unprovoked attack.

21. Little applause was forthcoming while Mr Churchill spoke. The general impression, however, was that it was a good speech and it was well received. The remarks about the British Air Force have been the subject of some considerable discussion, and while some frankly feel that he has exaggerated his case, yet at the same time there are, in my opinion, many people who are genuinely disturbed on this account, and Mr Churchill's speech of last night has certainly done nothing to allay their anxieties.

[1] Yvon Delbos, 1885–1956. Born in the Dordogne. Editor-in-Chief of *Radical*, 1914. On active service in the infantry, 1914–15; wounded. In the French air service, 1916–18; wounded a second time. Political Editor of the *Dépêche de Toulouse*, 1920–4. Deputy for the Dordogne, 1924–40. Minister of Public Instruction and Fine Arts, 1925. Vice-President of the Council, 1936. Minister of Foreign Affairs, June 1936–March 1938. Minister of Education, September 1939–March 1940 and 5–16 June 1940. Arrested by the Germans April 1943 and held at Oranienburg concentration camp until May 1945. A delegate at the National Provisional Consultative Assembly, 1945. Deputy for the Dordogne, 1946–55. Minister of State, 1947; Minister of Education, 1948–50. Unsuccessful candidate for the Presidency of the Republic, 1953.

At the conclusion of the speech certain questions were addressed to Mr Churchill.

MR ——:[1] Asked was it not true that there was a great wastage of pilots in the German Air Force?

MR CHURCHILL: That was certainly true. Their wastage was probably larger than ours. He did not believe, however, that this was due to faulty machines or of 'clumsy' training. Probably it was due to the 'ruthlessness' of their training and that the proficiency of the German people in the air was not so high as it was in certain other directions.

SIR GIFFORD FOX:[2] Is it not true that we are the only nation which has not practised a 'black-out'?

MR CHURCHILL: Thought that that was so. It would be wrong, however, to suppose that there was any real passive defence against aerial attack. He felt sure that the Air Ministry must be making detailed plans for all contingencies. If they were not doing that, they would be failing in their duties.

SIR ARNOLD WILSON: Would he be prepared to appoint a Director-General of Recruiting to work under Sir Thomas Inskip?

MR CHURCHILL: Said that he was not in favour of this at the present stage. He was primarily concerned about the state of our factories. To get them harmoniously working was the immediate and imperative need.

SIR MERVYN MANNINGHAM-BULLER:[3] Asked whether it was possible to hope for the development of our Air Force by drawing on the productive capacity of the British Empire?

MR CHURCHILL: Said he hoped that this would be encouraged. It would certainly not, however, be a sure shield in 1937.

MR MOREING:[4] Said that much information of a disquieting nature had been received. This showed that the Air Ministry was not only not getting

[1] This name was left blank in the original report, as sent to the Cabinet.

[2] Gifford Wheaton Grey Fox, 1903–1959. Educated at Eton and Magdalen College, Oxford. Succeeded his father as 2nd Baronet, 1925. Barrister-at-law, Middle Temple, 1926. Conservative MP for Henley, 1932–50. Assistant Provost Marshal, 1940–6.

[3] Mervyn Edward Manningham-Buller, 1876–1956. On active service in South Africa, 1900 (despatches). Unsuccessful Conservative Candidate, 1906 and 1910. Succeeded his uncle as 3rd Baronet, 1910. Lieutenant-Colonel, Commanding the 12th Battalion Rifle Brigade, 1914–16. Conservative MP for Kettering, 1924–9; for Northampton, 1931–40.

[4] Adrian Charles Moreing, 1892–1940. Educated at Winchester and Trinity College, Cambridge. Partner in his family firm of mining engineers. Conservative MP for Preston from 1931 until his death. Following Moreing's death, Churchill's son Randolph was elected, unopposed, for the Preston seat (and defeated by the Labour candidate in the 1945 election). Moreing had joined the Territorial Army in February 1914, and served in the Royal Fusiliers (Captain, 1916). In 1940 he was a member of the Territorial reserve.

value for money expended but also that there was complete and utter confusion with reference to the placing of orders and contracts. This applied, he said, to all the Defence Departments. Enquiry from the Department always elicited the reply that all was going well. The facts, however, belied the assurances which were given. No answer was given to this question.

Frederick Guest to Winston S. Churchill

(*Churchill papers: 2/261*)

8 December 1936

Dear Win,

Your speech at the 1922 Committee on defence was admirable, and very well received.

Yrs,
Freddie

Winston S. Churchill to Captain Diggle[1]

(*Churchill papers: 2/264*)

8 December 1936

I am sorry to receive such a letter from you after all these years when we have been in accord.[2] Before you dismiss me from your mind, kindly remember that I am still bound by the Oath of Allegiance which I so recently took to His present Majesty. According to my belief an Act of Abdication will produce a profound lesion in the unity of this country, with parallel degeneration in the Dominions. I am still of opinion that given time and patience this disaster will be averted, and the news recently received from Cannes seems to indicate increasingly hopeful possibilities. An abdication was very nearly made effective last week, and might well have been announced on Monday. If in a few days we find that a happy solution has been achieved in which this disastrous marriage has been renounced and abdication avoided, I shall expect you to make your amends to me, for I have never diverged by a hair's breadth from the path of loyalty and honour.

[1] Nestor William Diggle, 1880–1963. Entered the Royal Navy, 1901. Commander, 1913. Served on the China Station, with the Dover Patrol, and at the Dardanelles, 1914–18; Assistant Beach Master during the V Beach Landing, Gallipoli, April 1915. Naval Attaché, Rome, 1919–22. CMG 1919. Employed at the Admiralty, 1922–6. Retired with the rank of Captain, 1926. Member of the Executive Committee of the India Defence League, 1933.

[2] Captain Diggle's letter to Churchill has not been found among the Churchill papers.

P. C. Loftus[1] *to Winston S. Churchill*

(*Churchill papers: 2/264*)

8 December 1936   House of Commons
5 pm

Dear Churchill

If you would forgive me the impertinence I would like to say first this.

That I admire and respect loyalty however impulsive and even if expressed in an unfavourable atmosphere and at an inopportune moment.

It is more admirable to those with any trace of generous feeling than is the cold mentality so admirable in politicians & I imagine that the future, perhaps even the near future, may be of my opinion.

For myself I am torn by conflicting emotions. I feel the tide turning against the King hour by hour—and I cannot contemplate except with disgust & horror a political controversy (or worse a General Election) in which the past of the lady—the American reputation included—would be broadcast on every platform & chewed & wrangled over & the Crown bespattered with filth. The prospect would be so distasteful that I would retire from politics.

Yours very sincerely,
P. C. Loftus

Winston S. Churchill to J. A. Spender

(*Churchill papers: 2/264*)

9 December 1936   11 Morpeth Mansions

I have never thought of such a thing as five months' raging propaganda, but I have asked for ten days or a fortnight. Also that before the irrevocable act of abdication is accomplished, Parliament should examine the matter and also the consequences.

---

[1] Pierse Creagh Loftus, 1877–1956. Served in South Africa (Maritzburg Defence Force), 1899. Worked in the brewery and hotel business from 1902. On active service in France, 1916–18 (despatches). Captain, Suffolk Regiment, 1919. Member of the East Suffolk County Council, 1922. Vice-President of the Lowestoft Conservative Association, 1923. Alderman, East Suffolk County Council, 1930. Conservative MP for Lowestoft, 1934–45. Chairman of the Rural Construction Association, 1948.

Winston S. Churchill to Henry Wickham Steed: unsent
(Churchill papers: 2/264)

9 December 1936   11 Morpeth Mansions
Private

Dear Wickham Steed,

I expect that the issue will be settled in the sense you probably desire before the week is out, so that I do not expect it will be necessary for you to dis-associate yourself publicly from my standpoint. All the more is that unlikely as our association in no way fetters our individual action in any other direction. If of course there is any danger of the principle of Parliamentary supremacy over the Crown being challenged, you may count upon my effective assistance in any measures which you may desire to take.

As I see the story, the King asked his Ministers whether they would adopt a particular course, and they said No, and he has bowed to their decision. I should be prepared if necessary in all the circumstances to see the Ministers advise the Sovereign to send a Message to Parliament that he will not contract any marriage contrary to the advice of his Ministers. I think this is a very necessary improvement of the constitution.

I cannot believe that the King would resist this advice. What is all this talk of abdication? It has nothing to do with the issue. It might well be that the monarch, weary of the burden, may ask Parliament to relieve him, and that Parliament—after due protest and examination of all the issues involved—might agree. But I cannot see what that has got to do with the immediate problem.

As you have been good enough to write, you will forgive me for replying at some length.

Winston S. Churchill to Geoffrey Dawson
(Churchill papers: 2/264)

9 December 1936
Personal and Private

A great deal that you have written lately has caused me pain but I am in entire agreement with the last paragraph of your leader this morning. I have never pleaded for anything except the King's unhurried judgment. Where I differ has been the alternatives with which he is now unhappily presented. As you point out 'He has proposed a certain course of action, and has been advised in constitutional form that it is impracticable. There is no reason to doubt that he has accepted the advice.'

If this is so there is no conflict between the Crown and Parliament, or between the King and His Ministers. Why then should he have been all last week and now, so far as I know, upon the verge of abdication? In my view if the Ministers feel that something more is required in the circumstances from the King, they should advise him to send a Message to Parliament stating that he will not enter into any contract of marriage contrary to the advice of His Ministers. Is it certain that any conflict would arise upon this? If no conflict arose, would not the crisis be terminated? If this procedure were followed it would not require from the Sovereign any particular act of renunciation in any particular quarter. It would simply narrow for the future the liberty hitherto enjoyed by Sovereigns in respect of marriage. This clearly is a necessary constitutional reform.

Nothing can however deprive the Sovereign of the right of laying down his burden if at any time he finds it unbearable or for any other reason. In this case the Sovereign would himself of his own free will, should the occasion arise, send a Message to Parliament explaining that he desired to abdicate the Crown, and asking them to make all the necessary provisions. Parliament then, after a period of suitable expostulation, during which the grave constitutional reactions were thoroughly explained (as they have never been yet) might decide to liberate their Sovereign in accordance with his wishes. But this situation might never arise for a year or two ahead, or never arise at all, because many things happen to human beings in a year or two.

It may well be that all will have been settled one way or another before you get this, and I send it to you of course in your private capacity and for your own information.

Roger Fulford[1] *to Winston S. Churchill*

(*Churchill papers: 2/264*)

9 December 1936   Reform Club

Dear Mr Churchill

I am sending you the facts about Queen Caroline, although I am afraid they wd have been more use to you last week.

On his accession George IV asked the Cabinet to introduce special legis-

---

[1] Roger Thomas Baldwin Fulford, 1902–   . Educated at Lancing and Worcester College, Oxford. President of the Oxford Union, 1931. Unsuccessful Liberal candidate for Parliament, 1929, 1945 and 1950. Joined the editorial staff of *The Times*, 1933. Historian and biographer, he published his first book, *Royal Dukes*, in 1933. Civil Assistant, War Office, 1940–2. Assistant Private Secretary to the Secretary of State for Air (Sir Archibald Sinclair), 1942–4.

lation to enable him to divorce the Queen. They replied in a long minute
refusing to do this, but suggesting the following alternative:

1. That they shd introduce into Parlt a bill for settling a provision on the
   Princess of Wales (throughout all these negotiations she was never
   referred to as Queen).
2. That it shd be arranged *by agreement* between the King and the Princess
   (there was no suggestion of an Act of Parlt being necessary)

that

a. She shd use some other title than Queen (Dchss of Cornwall was suggested).
b. She shd forgo the legal rights and privileges of Queen.

There is also the point that her name was omitted from the Liturgy without any sanction from Parliament.

The negotiations which lasted for 3 weeks amply justify yr protest against
this Govt's endeavours to rush the King into an immediate decision. They
certainly do not justify Mr Baldwin's blunt statement about the status of the
King's wife. Ld Liverpool—not generally regarded as one of our most
eminent statesmen—certainly showed far greater consideration for the King
than has been the case now.

How dreadful the genteel Press is!

Don't, please, trouble to answer this treatise.

Yours sincerely,
Roger Fulford

Winston S. Churchill to Lord Salisbury
(*Churchill papers: 2/264*)

9 December 1936   11 Morpeth Mansions
Secret

I am glad to give you some account of my action. In July I was approached
upon the question of the Simpson divorce, and advised against it in such
terms that I did not see the King till this crisis developed. It is obvious that
the difficulty which arose after the divorce, was that point of honour that a
man should marry the woman who divorces herself or is divorced on his
account. This difficulty seemed to be insuperable, unless the lady in question
herself spontaneously gave the release. Owing to the well-meant, but unwise
stifling of the British Press, the blasts of public opinion did not begin to make

themselves felt until last Tuesday. I have always been hopeful that given time and patience a satisfactory result would be achieved. However the pressure which the Government put upon the King, and the press campaign directed against him with so much brutality by the Times, together with the personal strain to which he was inevitably subjected, might well have led to his abdication any day last week. In fact the Deeds were all drawn and in my view the Government expected to announce the abdication on Monday.

On Friday the King, who had been quite alone apart from his household staff, asked Baldwin if he might see me. I dined and spent the evening with him. He was very apprehensive that he would be faced with a demand by Baldwin on Saturday for abdication, and that the Government would resign unless he immediately complied. I assured him that he had only to ask for a reasonable period of time, and no Minister could deny him.

I wrote to the Prime Minister on Saturday morning urging that time should be granted, especially on account of the King's condition of overstrain. Subsequently or perhaps in consequence, a very much easier line was taken by the Prime Minister at the interview on Saturday evening than the King had feared. I published my statement on Sunday, which you may perhaps have read, to which I adhere. It is strictly true in all respects. The statement made by Baldwin on Monday in the House was not unsatisfactory to me, provided that the King was not hurried even if he required a week or ten days.

Meanwhile I was always aware of efforts which were being made in another direction, and which I rejoice to see have now proved to some extent effectual.

My main difference with the Government has consisted in the fact that I regarded abdication as a far greater disaster than they did, and I would have put up with the disadvantages and dangers of a prolongation of the controversy within moderate limits, in the hope, which may yet be justified, that the weakest link would snap.

What has impressed me most during this crisis has been the King's virtues of courage, manliness and honour; and of his loyalty to his Ministers and respect for the Constitution.

PS. I shall be glad if you will preserve the secrecy of this letter, as it is one I could only write to so senior a Privy Counsellor as yourself.[1]

---

[1] Lord Salisbury had been sworn of the Privy Council in 1903, Churchill in 1907.

Sir James Albery[1] *to Winston S. Churchill*

(*Churchill papers: 2/275*)

9 December 1936
Confidential

Dear Churchill,

With reference to our conversation yesterday—

1. My German letter of the 15th November, read as follows—

'It just occurs to me to give you a friendly hint that, on the Continent, war is considered probable before the Coronation. You will be well advised to arrange your business so as to face a very sudden, over-night so to speak, outbreak of war.'

The writer is an old friend, with military connections in Germany: not a man whose judgment I value very highly, but he is probably quoting others: had not communicated with me for a long time, and only did so in the belief that he was giving me a warning.

2. A Swiss business friend, on about the 24th November, informed me that Germany was expected to go to war some time next year: that France was expected to be the objective: that two English Peers had done a lot of damage by encouraging the Germans to believe that the pro-German feeling in this country was so extensive that this country would not go to the assistance of France. Also, there had been a nasty incident in Switzerland, involving a Swiss Staff-Officer and Germany.

3. A Swedish business friend sent me, about a week ago, the information that as a result of the Laval negotiations with Italy, transferring North Somaliland, the Italians had recently placed big guns in position commanding the bottom of the Red Sea, opposite Perim, and that if our access to the Mediterranean from the West were blocked, access to Egypt round the Cape and Red Sea, would also be blocked.

I do not want to attach undue importance to these indications, which have reached me in a time which is full of rumours, but it is, nevertheless, significant that they should all come to me from foreign friends, and from entirely different directions.

As regards food-stuffs in Germany, I understand that there is at present

---

[1] Irving James Albery, 1879–1967. On active service in South Africa, 1900. A member of the Stock Exchange, 1902–64. On active service, 1914–18 (Military Cross, despatches). Conservative MP for Gravesend, 1924–45. Knighted, 1936.

the largest hog population on record, but that feeding stuffs are down: also that drastic grain regulations have been put into operation.

Yours sincerely,
James Albery

PS. I visited Germany about 7 months ago & what I saw did not make me discount the indications over page. Personally, in view of the German–Italian–Jap entente I cannot regard an attack on this country as outside possibility, but I am not sufficiently well informed from a military point of view to measure the chances![1]

Winston S. Churchill to Sir Terence O'Connor[2]
(Churchill papers: 1/286)

9 December 1936

I am now smoking your delicious cigars. It was indeed kind of you to mark my birthday[3] in this way, and I am always deeply grateful to you for your renewed marks of friendship.

Philip Guedalla to Winston S. Churchill
(Churchill papers: 2/261)

10 December 1936

Dear Mr Churchill,

I have never felt so much respect for anyone as for you and for the stand which you have made in the past week.

Yours sincerely,
Philip Guedalla

---

[1] Churchill sent this letter for comment to Desmond Morton (see page 492).

[2] Terence James O'Connor, 1891–1940. On active service, 1914–18, with the Highland Light Infantry and the West African Frontier Force. Barrister, 1919. Conservative MP for Luton, 1924–9; for Central Nottingham, 1930–9. King's Counsel, 1929. Elected to the Other Club, 1933. Knighted, 1936. Solicitor-General, 1936–40. He died on 8 May 1940, two days before Churchill became Prime Minister.

[3] On 30 November 1936 Churchill had celebrated his 62nd birthday.

Harold Nicolson: diary

(*Nicolson papers*)

10 December 1936

I went off to the library to sign some letters. On leaving it, I bumped straight into Baldwin in the corridor. It was impossible not to say something. I murmured a few kind words. He took me by the arm.

'You are very kind,' he said, 'but what did you really think of it?' I detected in him that intoxication that comes to a man, even a tired man, after a triumphant success.

'It was superb,' I answered. 'I regretted only that Hitler, Mussolini and Lord Beaverbrook had not been in the Peers Gallery.'

'Yes', he said, 'it was a success. I know it. It was almost wholly unprepared. I had a success, my dear Nicolson, at the moment I most needed it. *Now is the time to go.*'

I made no answer.

Then he got on to Winston. He said, 'Do you know, my dear Nicolson, I think Winston is the most suspicious man I know. Just now I said that the King had said to me, "Let this be settled between you and me alone. I don't want outside interference." I meant to indicate by that the reasons why I had not made it a Cabinet question from the start. But Winston thought it was a thrust aimed at him, and has been at my Private Secretary within the last five minutes. What can one do with a man like that?'

I suggested that Winston had put himself in a false position. The PM flung up his hand. 'We are all in false positions!'

No man has ever dominated the House as he dominated it tonight, and he knows it.

L. S. Amery: diary

(*Amery papers*)

10 December 1936

After an adjournment of an hour and a half Attlee followed and received an ovation both at the outset and when he finished. His speech was in perfect good taste and sympathetic. Snell[1] in the other House was even better. The Socialists responded to the situation with an instinctive good sense and good feeling that lie deeper than party. Archie Sinclair could not help a little long-winded pomposity, but it wasn't bad. Winston rose in face of a hostile House

---

[1] Henry Snell, 1865–1944. Labour MP, 1922–31. Parliamentary Under-Secretary, India Office, 1931. Created Baron, 1931. Vice-Chairman of the British Council. Chairman of the London County Council, 1933–8. Deputy Leader of the House of Lords, 1940–44.

and in an admirably phrased little speech executed a strategical retreat, and did his best to convey the impression that he had never asked for more than the delay and the full statement which had, in fact, been given.[1]

Lord Hamilton of Dalzell[2] to Winston S. Churchill

(*Churchill papers: 2/264*)

11 December 1936   House of Lords Library

My dear Winston,

I have followed your intervention in the recent happenings with an appreciation and an understanding that few can have had.

It recalled to me something which you have probably forgotten, but which remains vividly in my mind. At Holyhead, on King George's yacht, you walked long up and down the deck, urging me to hesitate long before I took certain action which I contemplated. The circumstances bore some resemblance to those in which King Edward has been placed. I remember vividly one phrase you used. You said that you had a deep distrust of the decisions that were taken by people who thought that they had come to 'the parting of the ways'. That more unwise decisions had been taken in that frame of mind than in any other.

---

[1] Speaking in the House of Commons on 10 December 1936, after Baldwin, Attlee and Sinclair had each spoken, Churchill stressed the dangers of any further 'recrimination or controversy', telling the House: 'What is done is done. What has been done or left undone belongs to history, and to history, so far as I am concerned, it shall be left.' Churchill went on to say that he accepted 'wholeheartedly' what Baldwin had proved, 'namely, that the decision taken this week has been taken by His Majesty freely, voluntarily, spontaneously, in his own time and in his own way'. As a friend of Edward for more than twenty-five years, Churchill said, 'I should have been ashamed if, in my independent and unofficial position, I had not cast about for every lawful means, even the most forlorn, to keep him on the Throne of his fathers, to which he had only just succeeded amid the hopes and prayers of all.' Churchill ended with a plea to look to the future, and above all to Europe, telling the House of Commons: 'Danger gathers upon our path. We cannot afford—we have no right—to look back. We must look forward; we must obey the exhortation of the Prime Minister to look forward. The stronger the advocate of monarchical principle a man may be, the more zealously must he now endeavour to fortify the Throne and to give to his Majesty's successor that strength which can only come from the love of a united nation and Empire.'

[2] Gavin George Hamilton of Dalzell, 1872–1952. Educated at Eton and Sandhurst. Succeeded his father as 2nd Baron, 1900. Lord in Waiting to King Edward VII and King George V, 1906–11. On active service in South Africa, 1900, and on the western front, 1915–18. Military Cross, 1917. Chairman of the Royal Fine Art Commission for Scotland, 1932–52. Owner of some 2,500 acres in Scotland. One of his three brothers was killed in action on the western front on 29 October 1914. One of his brothers-in-law was killed in action on the western front on 25 January 1916. In July 1912 Lord Hamilton of Dalzell married Sybil Mary, Mrs Lawson (who died in 1933), daughter of Lieutenant-General Sir Frederick Marshall KCMG.

I knew that your advice was kind, and I knew that it was wise. I was very grateful, but I could not follow it.

You spoke yesterday of your part in the ceremony at Caernarvon at that time. I was also thinking of the shy loveable lad who came repeatedly into my cabin (& representing King George), in rehearsal of the part he had to play that day.

Sad, sad.

I have been horror-struck—as I am sure you have been—by the readiness with which the word 'Abdication' has come to men's lips in the recent crisis. It is a word that can only be spoken, without treason, by one man.

He has spoken it, and we can only bow to his decision, and serve his successor in all loyalty.

Yours,
Hamilton of Dalzell

Robert Boothby to Winston S. Churchill
(*Churchill papers: 2/264*)

11 December 1936   House of Commons
Private

Dear Winston,

I am sorry I wrote that letter.

We were all, I think, strung up at the time. And you can imagine how bitterly disappointed I was that our talk the night before seemed to have borne no fruit.

Even now, I don't quite understand what happened. When I said good-night to you at Chartwell you were resolved to try and persuade the King to accept the formula which we had all helped to devise.

Next morning, quite by chance, I received a letter from Godfrey Thomas:[1] and in my reply which—again by chance—I sent by hand, I told him of our hopes; and added that it was essential that the King should be shown the words of the formula and, if possible, see you, at the earliest moment.

When I reached the House of Commons you would not speak to me; and Archie told me that when you came down at Chartwell that morning your 'mood had changed'.

---

[1] Godfrey John Vignoles Thomas, 1889–1968. Educated at Harrow. Entered the Diplomatic Service, 1912; Third Secretary, Berlin, 1913–14. Succeeded his father as 10th Baronet, 1919. Private Secretary to the Prince of Wales, 1919–36. Assistant Private Secretary to King Edward VIII, 1936. Private Secretary to the Duke of Gloucester, 1937–57. Employed in the Foreign Office, 1939–44. Privy Councillor, 1958.

I was dismayed, and feared the worst; and, at question-time, the worst seemed to have happened.

Afterwards in the smoking-room I found several members of the particular group you always imagine are your most loyal supporters, roundly abusing you, & accusing you of 'playing for your own hand'. And I wrote to you, in a ferment of indignation and disappointment, the letter which I now wish I had not sent. At that particular moment the tension was very great; and I am sure you will make due allowances.

The aftermath was extraordinary.

I got a message from Walter Monckton asking me to dine with him. He came straight from Fort Belvedere, and told me he was afraid the game was up.

The King remained obdurate, and the Duke of York[1] was dining with him.

I showed him the formula, *which he had not seen before*. He became quite excited, and telephoned the King in the middle of dinner, asking him to hold his hand, as he had a new suggestion to make.

The King agreed; and Walter left for Fort Belvedere immediately after dinner, saying there was a hope once more. What happened afterwards I know not. At least further delay. But can you blame me for thinking, at the time, that if you had done what you said you intended to do the night before, and pressed the King to accept the formula that morning, the result might have been different?

I am now convinced that no human effort could have altered the course of events.

The one thing I regret is that your intervention at question-time last Monday may have temporarily diminished your power and authority in the House, which prior to that had seldom been greater, and certainly had never been so necessary to the country.

But this raises an old issue between us.

I have made many mistakes in my life, and paid for them; but I still don't think my political judgement is altogether bad, although you have never attached any value to it.

For ten years, as one of your most devoted followers, I have fought a losing battle against the influence of the Die-hards, the Press Lords, and Brendan.

Because I believe that the Die-hards are not fundamentally loyal to you, that the Press Lords (and especially one of them) are your most dangerous

---

[1] Albert Arthur Frederick George, 1895–1952. Second son of King George V. Midshipman, Royal Navy, 1913; on active service 1914–18 (including the Battle of Jutland, 1916); Lieutenant RN, 1920. Created Duke of York, 1920. Privy Councillor, 1925. Succeeded his brother (Edward VIII) as King, 11 December 1936. Crowned at Westminster Abbey, 12 May 1937.

enemies, and that Brendan is the best friend and the worst counsellor in the world. For instance, only this morning Clive Baillieu[1] told me he thanked God he had refused to send a series of cables to friends of his in the Australian Government—at Brendan's instigation, but under the aegis of your authority —which were not only wild and mischievous, but bore no relation to any of the facts which had since been made public. All these people give you advice which is immediately the most alluring, and ultimately the most fatal. And I cannot help feeling that one of them got at you last Monday morning.

It is only when you rely on the power of clear disinterested argument, based on your unrivalled intellect and experience, with *the solid central mass of the House of Commons*, that you rise to the position of commanding authority which you should always occupy.

You have done it during recent weeks & months.

You can, and must, do it again.

I believe, passionately, that you are the only man who can save this country, and the world, during the next two critical years.

And that must be my excuse for writing this letter.

Yours ever,
Bob

Geoffrey Dawson to Winston S. Churchill

(*Churchill papers: 2/264*)

11 December 1936   The Times
Private

My dear Churchill,

I should be very sorry to think that anything I had written in *The Times* should have caused you pain. I have, as a matter of fact, written nothing about you myself; but that is a small matter, for of course I am responsible for the whole paper, and I expect that you are referring to the various accounts of the proceedings in Parliament.

However, this wretched business is now over, and I am bound to say that

---

[1] Clive Latham Baillieu, 1889–1967. Educated at Melbourne University and Magdalen College, Oxford. On active service 1915–18. An Australian Representative on the Imperial Economic Committee, 1930–47. Knighted, 1938. Director-General, British Purchasing Commission, Washington, 1941–2. Member of the British Supply Council in North America, 1941–3. Chairman, Fairey Aviation Company, 1943–5; of Central Mining, 1945–59; and of Dunlop, 1949–57. Chairman of the English Speaking Union, 1951–65. Created Baron 1953. Company Director. First President of the British Institute of Management, 1959.

your speech of yesterday, which I have just been reading, seems to me to present a thoroughly sound, constitutional point of view.

Yours sincerely,
Geoffrey Dawson

Winston S. Churchill to Geoffrey Dawson
(*Churchill papers: 2/264*)

12 December 1936
Private

Nothing that was written about me caused me pain, because I have had forty years of such buffettings. I was referring only to the sledge-hammer blows The Times dealt the late King.

Now of course the only thing is to look forward and repair the damage that has been done to the Throne. I am hoping that the Duke of Windsor will be able soon to come back and live here quietly as a private gentleman. For this purpose the dust of controversy must be laid, and the new reign established on unshakable foundations. I am sure he has no other wish but to live quietly in England, and it seems very hard if he should not be allowed to do this. May I enlist your chivalry in trying to bring this about, after a suitable lapse of time. Perhaps the Newspaper Proprietors' Association might be induced to give him the same kind of immunity as was such a comfort to Colonel Lindbergh.[1] Perhaps you will let me have a talk with you about this later on.

PS. No doubt you saw the AG's[2] statement that he could live here if he liked.

---

[1] Charles Augustus Lindbergh, 1902–1974. Born in Detroit. Educated at the University of Wisconsin. Enrolled in flying school, 1922, becoming an air mail line pilot at St Louis. Flew alone from New York to Paris, 1927 (the first solo transatlantic non-stop flight). Flew from the United States to Denmark via Greenland, Ireland, and the Shetland Islands, with a view to establishing a Transatlantic air route, 1933. In 1932, following the kidnapping and murder of his son, the Press agreed not to pursue him for stories. A leading isolationist; subsequently, from April 1939, recalled to service as Special Adviser on technical matters to the Office of the Chief of the Air Corps, charged with making a survey of United States' aviation facilities. Brigadier-General, 1940. Awarded the Pulitzer Prize for his book *The Spirit of Saint Louis* (1953).

[2] Donald Bradley Somervell, 1889–1960. Educated at Harrow and Magdalen College, Oxford. Fellow of All Souls College, Oxford. On active service, 1914–18. King's Counsel, 1929. Conservative MP for Crewe, 1931–45. Knighted, 1933. Solicitor-General, 1933–6. Attorney-General, 1936–45. Privy Councillor, 1938. Home Secretary, 1945. A Lord Justice of Appeal, 1946–54. Created Baron Somervell of Harrow, 1954. A Lord of Appeal in Ordinary, 1954–60. A member of the Other Club from 1939. His father was Churchill's English teacher at Harrow.

Winston S. Churchill to Robert Boothby

(*Boothby papers*)

12 December 1936
Personal

My dear Bob

Thank you so much for your letter. Even if you had not written it, our old relations would have been unchanged.

I reached the House on Monday rather prepared in my mind to be attacked for what I had written over the weekend, and addressing myself too attentively to that possibility, I did not sufficiently realise how far the Prime Minister had gone to meet the views I had expressed. I ought of course to have welcomed what he said. I cannot however think that it was wrong to repeat the request that no irrevocable decision should be taken.

I made careful enquiries yesterday at Belvedere and am absolutely satisfied that the point was put to the King most fully, Archie's name and mine being used; and that he turned it aside on the grounds that it would not be honourable to play for time when his fundamental resolve was unchanged, and as he declared unchangeable. It was certainly this very strict point of honour which cost him his Crown. Whether I could have prevailed upon him personally, I do not know. It is however certain that I should not have been allowed access to him, as the Ministers were already angry with Baldwin for having given him permission to see me on Friday, and he had been made aware of this fact. Therefore I feel you are right in saying that no human effort could have altered the course of events.

The only thing now to do is to make it easy for him to live in this country quietly as a private gentleman as soon as possible and to that we must bend our efforts by discouraging noisy controversy and (apart from quasi historical investigation) refusing to take part in it. The more firmly the new King is established, the more easy it will be for the old one to come back to his house.

Yours ever,
W

Winston S. Churchill to Josiah Wedgwood[1]

(Churchill papers: 2/264)

12 December 1936
Personal

I told the late King yesterday what you said about his having cast aside royalty to remain a man, and I thought you would like to know how visibly moved he was by this remark. His mettle was marvellous.

H. V. Evatt[2] *to Winston S. Churchill*

(Churchill papers: 2/264)

12 December 1936   Judges Chambers,
                                          High Court of Australia

Dear Mr Winston Churchill,
    The writer is a Justice of this, the Federal Supreme Court of Australia and the author of a recent work called 'The King and His Dominion Governors', which studies the Reserve Powers of the Monarch. He is also a close student of English and Imperial Affairs, and is well acquainted with your own masterly contribution to historical and social research.
    I write to express my personal gratitude that there was at least one man in the Parliament at Westminster who in a time of unexampled crisis, served his late Monarch so loyally and so well.
    Unfortunately no means existed for ascertaining the guidance and extent of the 'public opinion' (in the Dominions or England) to which the newspapers so glibly referred.

---

[1] Josiah Clement Wedgwood, 1872–1943. Naval architect, 1896–1900. On active service in South Africa, 1900. Liberal MP for Newcastle-under-Lyme, 1906–19. Commanded armoured cars in France, Antwerp, Gallipoli and East Africa, 1914–17 (DSO, wounded, despatches twice). Assistant Director, Trench Warfare Department, Ministry of Munitions, 1917. War Office Mission to Siberia, 1918. Elected to the Other Club, 1918 (resigned, 1930). Granted the Labour Whip, May 1919. Labour MP, 1919–42. Vice-Chairman of the Labour Party, 1921–4. Chancellor of the Duchy of Lancaster, 1924. Created Baron, 1942. Known as 'Josh'.

[2] Herbert Vere Evatt, 1894–1965. Born in Australia. Member of the New South Wales Legislative Assembly (Labour), 1925–9. King's Counsel, 1929. Justice of the High Court of Australia, 1930–40. Attorney-General and Minister for External Affairs, 1941–9; Deputy Prime Minister, 1946–9. Member of the Advisory War Council, 1941–5; of the Australian War Cabinet, 1941–6. Australian Representative in the UK War Cabinet, 1942 and 1943. Australian Member of the Pacific War Council, 1942–3. Leader of the Australian Delegation to the UN General Assembly, 1946 and 1947. Chairman of the United Nations Palestine Commission, 1947. In 1945 he received the Freedom of the City of Athens for defending the interests of small nations. Leader of the Parliamentary Labour Party, Australia, 1951–60.

What a Whip triumph! That a Parliament with no Shadow of relevant popular mandate should effectuate such a charge! And what a triumph for Dictatorship! That a Government should carry through such an affair before any reference to Parliament was made!

Here in Australia, for many years the people, and especially the children, have been taught to love and venerate not the chattel which is placed upon the Monarch's head nor the Seat upon which he sat but the man in person. A sentiment so built up cannot be suddenly replaced upon the theory that the 'Crown' or the 'Throne' is a sufficient symbol. In the hurry and bustle of a week-end, all this was forgotten or seemed to be.

All this has passed into History. Will not history contrast the two men, the politician who by innuendo, by the over emphasis on personal friendship, and by downright misrepresentation, gave the Iago touch to the crisis and the man, the monarch, who was too great for the Parliament and too noble for the individuals who purported to speak for the Dominions.

If ever I get the opportunity, I shall examine the crisis from the point of view I have stated which is both realistic and true. In doing so, I shall have a further opportunity of stating publicly what I now can state only privately, that all loyal subjects as well as loving hearts admired your courage and devotion.

Believe me, Sir,

Yours most sincerely,
H. V. Evatt

The Duke of Windsor [1] to Winston S. Churchill: telegram

(Churchill papers: 2/264)

12 December 1936

Thank you again for all your great help and understanding. Au revoir.

Edward

---

[1] When Sir John Reith introduced the former King over the wireless, on 11 December 1936, he had intended to call him 'Mr Windsor'. But Edward pointed out that he was still a Royal Prince, and he was introduced as 'His Royal Highness Prince Edward'. On the following day, December 12, at the Accession Council at St James's Palace—at which Churchill was present—the new King, George VI, announced that his first act was to confer a Dukedom on the late King, who would henceforth be known as 'His Royal Highness the Duke of Windsor'.

Lord Tweedsmuir [1] to Stanley Baldwin

(*Baldwin papers*)

12 December 1936   Ottawa

. . . A third gain is, I hope, that the power for mischief in Winston and his like has now been killed.

Robert Boothby to Winston S. Churchill

(*Churchill papers: 2/264*)

14 December 1936   House of Commons

Dear Winston,

Thank you so much for your letter.

I am delighted to learn that he contemplates coming back to live in this country.

If such a project were publicly mentioned at this juncture there would, no doubt, be angry protests from certain quarters. But I do not think this will be the case six months hence.

Yrs ever,
Bob

Winston S. Churchill to Mackenzie King [2]

(*Churchill papers: 1/286*)

14 December 1936

I have been deeply distressed by all that has happened here, and I cannot help feeling that earlier and more skilful treatment would have prevented this catastrophe. However we must look forward. I feel, as I told you, that most perilous years lie ahead. It is a comfort to me that you are at your post in Canada, because I am sure the best will be done for all our difficult affairs.

[1] John Buchan, 1875–1940. Author, historian and novelist. Private Secretary to Lord Milner in South Africa, 1901–3. Lieutenant-Colonel, GHQ France, 1916–17. Director, Department of Information, 1917–18. Conservative MP, 1927–35. Created Baron Tweedsmuir, 1935. Governor-General of Canada 1937–40. His brother Alastair served in Churchill's battalion on the western front in 1916, and died of wounds received in action in 1917.

[2] William Lyon Mackenzie King, 1874–1950. Born in Ontario, Canada. Fellow in Political Science, Harvard University, 1897–1900. Deputy Minister of Labour, Canada, 1900–8. Liberal MP in the Canadian Parliament, 1908–11 and 1919–49. Minister of Labour, 1909–11. Leader of the Liberal Party of Canada, 1919–48. Leader of the Opposition, 1919–21 and 1930–5. Prime Minister of Canada, 1921–6, 1926–30 and 1935–48. Secretary of State for External Affairs, 1921–6, 1926–30 and 1935–46. Order of Merit, 1947.

Wing Commander Warburton to Violet Pearman

(*Churchill papers: 25/7*)

14 December 1936   Committee of Imperial Defence

Dear Private Secretary,

With reference to your letter to me of the 29th November enclosing two papers from a correspondent of Mr Winston Churchill's, I have had the two points investigated and the following is an extract from the report I have received from the Air Raid Precautions Department—

PROTECTION OF POWER HOUSES WITH STEEL NETS

In the first place these steel nets would be penetrated by all but the very smallest bombs. It is conceivable that the 2-lb incendiary bomb might be caught but as this bomb is only two inches in diameter, the mesh would have to be very small. It is also conceivable that a high explosive bomb might be detonated if fitted with a percussion fuse but with a delay action fuse it would enter the building before detonating as the steel nets would offer little resistance to its fall.

Secondly, the practical difficulties of erecting such a net are much greater than they might appear at first sight. The weight of the net would be tremendous and to support this weight the steel staunchions would have to be very strong steel structures. Some idea can be obtained as to the size that would be necessary for these structures by considering the pylons erected for carrying aerial electric cables. These only support three or four wires at a comparatively low height. In this case a multitude of wires at a much higher altitude would be required, and the 'pylons' necessary would have to be enormous structures. The suggestion, therefore, does not seem to be of any practical value.

UNDERGROUND PARKING PLACES

The question of providing underground parking places to be used as air raid shelters in times of emergency is being considered. Our present view is that to protect a large area such as would be necessary for a car park against a 500-lb high explosive bomb, such a tremendous thickness of concrete is required that it becomes impracticable. If a lesser protection is given, the result of such a bomb exploding in the shelter among hundreds and possibly thousands of people is too horrible to contemplate. The possibility of dividing up such shelters to localise the effect of any bomb which might enter is being considered. Such division into small compartments is very difficult from the point of view of the use of the shelter as a car park and it is doubtful whether a satisfactory solution will be found.

Yours sincerely,
P. Warburton

Josiah Wedgwood to Winston S. Churchill
(*Churchill papers: 2/264*)

15 December 1936 House of Commons

My dear Winston,

I think your little letter was one of the kindest and most thoughtful things you have done. It will go among my heirlooms, and I shall not forget.

Yours ever,
Josiah C. Wedgwood

Winston S. Churchill to the Duke of Westminster
(*Churchill papers: 1/286*)

16 December 1936

I am going to Palm Beach for a little sunshine, sailing on Tuesday. I have so many things to settle up at Chartwell before I go, that I must forego, what I have been looking forward to so much, your famous shoot.

Our friend was very much pleased by your kind offers. He said he was going to write to you as soon as he could get his head above water. I managed to stop his going to a hotel, and he is now in very good hands in Austria.[1]

---

[1] On leaving Britain, the Duke of Windsor had travelled direct to Schloss Enzesfeld, in Austria, the home of Baron Eugene de Rothschild, and his wife, Baroness Kitty de Rothschild. The Baron was away, but the Baroness remained at the Schloss until the following February. Mrs Simpson remained at Cannes. On 21 January 1937 a friend of the Duke, Major Metcalfe, wrote to his wife from the Schloss: 'I think Kitty has got on his nerves—she won't leave—he gets quite short with her at times. Says he wants men only & doesn't want any women about. Three times Kitty said she was leaving but never does. (He takes over the place, servants & all when she does)'. On 3 February 1937 Metcalfe wrote again: 'Kitty left yesterday!! *Terrible show*! as HRH was late getting dressed owing to his infernal telephone call!! *& missed her*! *Never saw her to say good-bye or thank her*! She was *frightfully hurt* & I don't blame her. He *is* awfully difficult at times & this is the worst thing he's done yet. I went down to the station with a letter which I got him to write & that made things a bit better.' The Duke and Mrs Simpson were married at the Chateau de Candé, near Tours, in France, on 3 June 1937. Only seven English people were present, among them Randolph Churchill. After his marriage the Duke leased Wasserleonburg-bei-Notsch castle in Carinthia from Count Paul Munster, for the rest of the summer. In October 1937 the Duke and Duchess visited Germany, where they met Hitler.

It is extraordinary how Baldwin gets stronger every time he knocks out someone or something important to our country. I greatly fear the dangers of 1937.

All my good wishes dear Bennie for Christmas and the New Year. It gives me comfort to think how long our friendship has lasted in this world of shock and change.

Desmond Morton to Winston S. Churchill

(*Churchill papers: 2/275*)

17 December 1936   Department of Overseas Trade
Personal & Secret

Dear Winston,

Thank you for letting me see Sir James Albery's letter.

I do not think that the Germans will be ready for war in 1937 unless a considerable and unexpected change takes place in the relative war potential of those countries likely to be their enemies.

There is every sign in Germany of the intention further to extend the army at the end of 1937 or beginning of 1938. Steps to this end are now being taken to allow each regular division to throw off a new reserve division in between 12 and 24 months' time. These steps necessarily disorganise the regular army, and temporarily lower its cohesion and fighting value. The naval building programme is not completed. The air expansion is continuing.

Furthermore, the economic condition of Germany is bad for war. She is very short of raw materials. If she did go to war her only hope would be in forcing a conclusion through military superiority in a few weeks. Failure would be disastrous. Taking all the measures of arms and defence into account Germany cannot be said yet to be so much stronger than France, let alone France, Belgium and England, that she could have any hopes of a rapid decision. In 12 or 24 months this position may possibly be very different.

There remains the question of a German–Italian combined attack. In my opinion the Germans are most unlikely to make war so long as they have to rely utterly on Italian assistance. They do not trust the Italians. If, however, a German–Italian attack did come, which I do not believe will happen in 1937, the same conditions would apply, namely, that if their joint attack can be withstood successfully for three months, at no matter what cost, it will have proved a cataclysmic disaster for the Italo-German side. This fact must be apparent to the Italians as well as to the Germans.

I am making further enquiries regarding paragraph 3 of Sir James' letter, but I do not think the big guns described have been put into position, nor would I be prepared to agree that, if they had, the contention is supported that our access to the Red Sea would be blocked by them. The Italian Air Force in Abyssinia and Eritrea would be far more dangerous.

The last paragraph of Sir James' letter is correct.

Yours very sincerely,
Desmond Morton

Winston S. Churchill to the Duke of Windsor

(*Churchill papers: 2/264*)

17 December 1936

I was so glad to learn that Your Royal Highness had found a convenient agreeable shelter for the moment. I know your charming hostess well, having been a guest with her at Maxine's villa.

From all accounts the broadcast was successful, and all over the world people were deeply moved; millions wept. The Government were grateful. They certainly ought to be. Very different was the reception accorded to the Archbishop of Canterbury's performance on Sunday night.[1] There has been a perfect storm of anger raised against him for his unchivalrous reference to the late reign. Even those who were very hostile to your standpoint turned round and salved their feelings by censuring the Archbishop. All the newspapers were inundated with letters of protest. Some are worth reading in today's Daily Telegraph.[2] I am sure that what you would wish however is that all controversy should die, and I shall act in that sense myself.

I went to see Sam Hoare yesterday and had an hour with him. I am sure Your RH can count on him as a friend and a friend in a very important position. He promised to keep in touch with me in order to watch over your interests so far as Parliament and the Cabinet are concerned. From some

[1] In a broadcast on Sunday 13 December 1936, the Archbishop of Canterbury, Cosmo Gordon Lang, criticized Edward VIII for having 'sought his happiness in a manner inconsistent with the Christian principles of marriage, and within a social circle whose standard and way of life are alien to all the best instincts and traditions of his people. Let those who belong to this circle know that today they stand rebuked by the judgement of the nation which had loved King Edward.'

[2] On 17 December 1936 the *Daily Telegraph* published five letters in a special letters section on the Archbishop of Canterbury's broadcast, which one of the writers described as 'unnecessary and needlessly unkind' (J. B. Calvert of Doncaster). One of the letters published supported the Archbishop describing his words as 'necessary and timely' (Mary E. Haythonthwaite, from Lancashire).

words I had with Neville when we went to present the Commons' Address I gathered that what he attached great importance to was your living absolutely separate until everything is settled and the new Civil List is voted. He was rather grim and bleak, but I am sure he is right on this point. There is an enormous amount of sympathy and goodwill towards you here, and many people are quite stunned. Feeling rather battered myself I am off to Palm Beach on Tuesday where I shall get some peace and sunshine with Consuelo Balsan. I shall of course be back at the beginning of February in time to take my place upon the Civil List Committee. Max also sails again for Arizona.

The new reign has started very smoothly. The King looked to me very anxious and strained but is being helped by everyone as you would yourself desire.

I suppose, Sir, you saw that the Attorney General in the Debate on the Abdication Bill declared formally that there was no obligation upon Your RH to reside outside the British Dominions. So I earnestly hope that it will not be very many months before I have the honour to pay my respects to you at the Fort.

Bendor would be delighted if you cared to use Saint Saens. [1] His horses and hounds are there and every facility for the chase. I do not know whether Your RH has ever hunted the boar. It is pretty good sport and I like it because although there is a great deal of rough and tricky riding through woodland and up and down hill, there are no fences to jump. This I fear you would regard as a disadvantage.

Sir, pray command me in any way I can be of any use for I am sure Your RH will believe that there could be no greater honour or pleasure to me at any time than to be of service.

PS. Do not, Sir, I beg you trouble to answer this, for I know what a mass of letters you must have upon you.

Winston S. Churchill to Roger Fulford
(*Churchill papers: 2/264*)

17 December 1936   11 Morpeth Mansions

Thank you so much for your most interesting letter which I am going to keep by me in case I find it possible to write some monograph on this subject when we are clear of current controversy.

---

[1] Twenty miles south-east of Dieppe, where the Duke of Westminster had a hunting lodge.

Winston S. Churchill to Sir John Simon

(*Churchill papers: 2/261*)

17 December 1936

I should be glad if you could give your personal attention to the enclosed upon which I have already addressed the Treasury.[1]

The Baroness is possessed of several millions derived from Poland. If she and her husband were naturalised British subjects their difficulties of remittance would be removed. They wish to qualify by the full residential period, but how are they to draw their moneys until they are naturalized? It would be kind of you to see whether anything can be done. Certainly I should have thought it a distinct advantage to this country to have these victims of Nazi Jewish persecution resident here. Their contribution to the income tax and super tax would be very substantial, and on other grounds they would be worthy citizens. Is there no way in which this period of residence can be speeded up?

Winston S. Churchill to Pierre Etienne Flandin

(*Churchill papers: 2/261*)

17 December 1936   11 Morpeth Mansions

I am so grateful to you for your letter of the 28th November. It was a great pleasure to me and my wife to receive you during your all too short visit here.

The declarations which you made yourself and procured from M Delbos mark I am sure the most important milestone in the conscious association of our two anxious peoples. Everything has been overshadowed by the distressing constitutional events.

I am going away to America for a few weeks' sunshine at Palm Beach, but I shall be back early in February and will not fail to get in touch with you.

Every good wish, in which my wife joins,

---

[1] Churchill was continuing in his efforts to help the Baroness Goldschmidt-Rothschild (see also pages 424 and 539).

Winston S. Churchill to Ian Colvin[1]
(Churchill papers: 8/531)

17 December 1936

I am so glad you like the third volume. It gives me great pleasure to think it has whiled away some hours of your convalescence. I am so grieved that you are out of action and trust indeed you will soon be fully recovered. The leaders in the Morning Post are very different in style and spirit from what we have got to relish from your pen.

Thank you also for what you say about the melancholy happenings of the last fortnight. Avoidable havoc is what I call it. I am much battered myself and am going abroad for some sunshine.

Every good wish.

Winston S. Churchill to Maxwell Garnett[2]
(Churchill papers: 2/283)

17 December 1936

Many thanks for your letter and for the kindly message you conveyed to me from your Executive Committee. I have been greatly distressed by what has happened in the last fortnight, and find it absolutely necessary to go abroad for some rest and sunshine. I am sailing for America on the 22nd. I do not wish to commit myself to any further engagements until I return at the end of January. But thereafter I would gladly hear from you again.

---

[1] Ian Duncan Colvin, 1877–1938. Educated at Inverness College and Edinburgh University. A journalist, he began work on the *Inverness Courier*. Subsequently he was on the staff of the *Allahabad Pioneer*, 1900–3 and served as Assistant Editor of the *Cape Times*, 1903–7. Leader writer of the *Morning Post* from 1909 until his death. Biographer of General Dyer (1929) and Lord Carson (1934 and 1936). For his son's contacts with Churchill, see pages 879, 1117–8 and 1285–8 of this volume.

[2] James Clerk Maxwell Garnett, 1880–1958. Educated at St Paul's School and Trinity College, Cambridge. Lecturer in Applied Mathematics, University College, London, 1903; examiner, Board of Education, 1904–12. Dean of the Faculty of Technology, Manchester University, 1912–20. CBE, 1919. Secretary of the League of Nations Union, 1920–38. Chairman of the British Association's Committee on Post-War University Education, 1941–4. Among his books were *Education and World Citizenship* (1921), *Organising Peace* (1936) and *The World We Mean To Make* (1943).

Lord Davies to Winston S. Churchill

(*Churchill papers: 2/285*)

18 December 1936

My dear Churchill,

I saw Sir Abe this week, and he told me that you were leaving for America. This is to wish you bon voyage and a safe and speedy return.

Events during the past few weeks have unfortunately distracted people's minds from the vital issue of Peace or War. But I am sure you will forgive me for returning to the theme which I ventured to propound to you some months ago.

I remember suggesting to you six or seven years ago that you should concentrate your efforts in bringing to fruition the plan you had described so admirably and convincingly in 'The Aftermath'. Obviously, if you intend becoming the champion of a supreme cause, you must cast all else aside and concentrate all your vigour and energy upon its achievement.

May I suggest that the first step is to win the confidence of your own people, and to make them believe in your sincerity and wholehearted devotion to the cause which you espouse and advocate. To do this, could you not embark early next year upon not merely a political stunt, but upon a long, intense and vigorous campaign—preaching a new gospel and introducing a new idea. This means that you will assume the mantle of the prophet, not the cloak of the politician, and in your speeches you will expound great moral principles—the right use of force in the governance of the world, the function of equity in international relationships, etc—rather than deal with immediate day to day controversies, which are useful only insofar as they serve to illustrate and to prove your main thesis.

Further, may I also venture to suggest that it is wise to refrain from attacks either upon nations or individuals, because should you indulge in these onslaughts, you may only create the impression that you are looking for a job. I am sure it is sound strategy that the job should come to you; not that you should go after the job!

Therefore, let the country resound with your speeches, in which you expound the doctrine of international toleration and non-intervention, the restraint of violence, a peaceful procedure for the settlement of all disputes and the organisation of force to uphold the rule of law in Europe.

Surely, my friend, here is material for innumerable speeches and addresses upon a subject of which you possess first-hand knowledge and experience.

With your wonderful powers of exposition, you could convert the vast majority of your fellow-countrymen in about six months, and then you could appeal to the nations of the Continent. You could demonstrate to them the only means of averting a catastrophic struggle which, day by day, is steadily approaching and must eventually engulf Europe, unless a leader appears who is capable of galvanising and mobilising all those forces which make for justice, and organising the potential resources of those nations who are determined to maintain the peace, against the aggressor.

No doubt, it is a colossal job, but it is surely worth every ounce you can put into it, and if you succeed in preventing a war you will have eclipsed your distinguished ancestor who, after all, only won a war! Therefore, as a sincere friend and admirer, I would beg of you to throw everything else to the winds and to set out upon this crusade. A few weeks ago a request came from Manchester inviting you to address a meeting in the Free Trade Hall, and in the last few days, another has come from Austria. I imagine there will be no lack of invitations if you are prepared to undertake a strenuous and prolonged campaign, for which it will be necessary to husband your strength and to keep yourself fit.

Such a glorious opportunity to serve your country, to serve Europe, to serve humanity, very seldom comes to any man. I implore you to seize it before it is too late. I know you agree that the time factor is all important, and therefore isn't it possible to arrange something—some plan of campaign for next year—before you cross the Atlantic?

I am sure you will forgive me for being so frank. I feel I have no right to address you in this fashion, but you remember the old proverb—'Faithful are the wounds of a friend, but the kisses of an enemy are deceitful.' This is my only excuse.

With best wishes for Christmas and the coming New Year.

Believe me to be,
Yours very sincerely,
Davies

George Harrap to Winston S. Churchill

(*Churchill papers: 8/530*)

18 December 1936

Dear Mr Churchill,

I have just read the last word of your third volume and I feel impelled to express my admiration of your success in maintaining the proud standard of this monumental survey. Indeed, so far from falling below the previous two volumes this third section of your great narrative in some respects surpasses its predecessors. It is unfolded with a lucid eloquence that makes it easy and delightful to follow every thread; the dramatic intensity is often so great that at times you compelled an extra beat or two from my pulse.

I read your chapter on the Fall of Harley in the midst of the recent crisis and that historical moment was no more absorbing than the dramatic scene in which Anne was stricken and defeated. One feels that Marlborough in Volume Three is moving like a majestic figure in Greek tragedy to eventual catastrophe. His triumphs contribute to the mesh within which the Fates are encircling him, and you inspire in the reader, after 200 years, emotions which he would feel were he contemplating world-shaking events of which the issue is still in doubt.

Your work so far has been untiring; you have not spared yourself, and you deserve every word of the high praise from every quarter that has greeted each volume. For my part I thank you sincerely for this sustained effort, so full of promise for the happy fulfilment of your task next year.

Yours very sincerely,
George G. Harrap

Winston S. Churchill to George Harrap

(*Churchill papers: 8/530*)

19 December 1936

I am touched by the extreme kindness of your letter. It is a great satisfaction to me to feel that although this book on Marlborough has taken so very much more extended a form than what we had contemplated, nevertheless you are still its champion. Your praise of my work and all the business relations I have had with your firm make one of the most pleasant experiences of my life. I am greatly encouraged to throw myself into the new volume which I trust may be ready by the Autumn.

After these four volumes have had what in your judgment is their full run, I hope if I survive, to make a reduced or concentrated story in a single volume.[1]

With all kindest regards to you and yours for Christmas and the New Year,

Believe me,

---

[1] No single volume edition of *Marlborough: His Life and Times* has yet been published (as of 1982), but in December 1947 George Harrap published a two-volume edition, reset but not revised, price 50 shillings. A total of 17,000 sets was printed. In February 1941 the battle of Blenheim section of volume 2 had been published in book form, as *Blenheim*, by Guild Books. Of this shorter book, a total of 64,750 copies were sold (Frederick Woods, *A Bibliography of the Works of Sir Winston Churchill KG, OM, CH*, London 1969, pages 74–6).

Winston S. Churchill: memorandum[1]

(Foreign Office papers: 371/20733)

20 December 1936
Most secret
To be Kept Under Lock and Key

It is requested that special care may be taken to ensure the secrecy of this document.

GERMAN AIR STRENGTH

1. As in my previous memoranda, I will base my calculations entirely on figures given by the Air Ministry.

2. In Paper No ADR 52,[2] enclosure 2, paragraph 3, it is admitted that on the 31st May, 1936, 3,115 military aircraft were available in Germany. This figure is in close agreement with my figure of 3,200 calculated from the date for German output given in CID Paper No 1186–B. Since the 1st June six months have elapsed. Calculating on the same basis, and allowing for wastage at the same rates (assuming, as the Air Staff does in CID Paper No 1264–B a basis of 810 front-line machines and 800 training machines), there would be an accretion in these six months to the number of military aircraft available of 924 machines, making a total of approximately 4,040 military aircraft in being in Germany to-day.

3. In Paper No ADR 52, enclosure 2, paragraph 4, the Air Staff estimates that the number of trained pilots available in Germany on the 31st May, 1936, was 2,565. Taking their figure for the monthly accretion given in CID Paper No 1189–B, namely, 110 pilots per month, we may therefore conclude that there are now 3,225 fully-trained pilots available.

4. We therefore have on the Air Staff's own figures over 4,000 modern military machines constructed within the last 3 years, and over 3,200 fully-trained pilots at the disposal of the German Government today. Yet we are asked in CID Paper No 1216–B to believe that their front-line strength should be reckoned at no more than 810 machines (ie, 90 squadrons of 9 each). In other words, only 20 per cent of the machines and 25 per cent of the fully-trained pilots known to be available are to be reckoned in the German front line.

---

[1] This memorandum was circulated to the Committee of Imperial Defence by Sir Maurice Hankey on 11 January 1937, as Committee of Imperial Defence Paper No 1295–B. This copy printed here was the one sent to Sir Robert Vansittart at the Foreign Office. Churchill also kept a copy in his own archive (*Churchill papers 25/10*).
[2] Churchill noted at this point: 'Also CID Paper No. 1241–B'.

5. In CID Paper No 1264–B the Air Staff notes with satisfaction that the information leading us to suppose that only 90 German squadrons were in being on the 1st September, 1936, has been completely confirmed by German official information. It is well to compare this with the Air Staff estimate for the 31st May, 1936. In Paper No ADR 52, paragraph 3, we are told that on that date 90 squadrons had been identified, so that we must conclude, if the Air Staff information is correct, that between the 1st June and the 1st September, ie, in 3 months, not one single squadron has been added to the German Air Force. In fact, if we take the German official figure of 88 squadrons, 2 squadrons have been removed—an unexpected gesture of disarmament.

6. The Air Staff figures in CID Paper No 1216–B are in complete disagreement with the information of the French Government. According to a résumé received from Paris, the Germans will be able to put into the front line on the 1st January, 1937, 147 squadrons. The French Government reckons 12 machines to a squadron, and thus counts 1,764 military machines in the first line. According to the French view, 200 commercial machines (Lufthansa) should be added to this and 45 training squadrons which they count as 540 machines. Thus, according to their reckoning, there are 1,964 machines in the first line, 540 machines in the training squadrons, and they add 1,500 machines 'in the second line', which probably means in stored reserve. This would be a 75 per cent reserve for 2,000 front-line machines.

7. Even if we take the conventional view of the Air Ministry that we must only reckon 9 machines to the squadron, the 147 first-line squadrons which the French Government believe to exist would contain 1,323 machines, which, together with the 200 civil aeroplanes, would make 1,523 immediately available in the front line. If we add to this the 45 training squadrons, counting 9 aeroplanes each, a further 405 machines would be available with the 1,500 machines of the second line in stored reserve. If we also add the 3 reserve machines in each of the 147 active squadrons, ie, 441, which the Air Ministry prefer to ignore, the total becomes 1,523, plus 405, plus 441, equals 2,369.

8. It should be noted that the total of military aeroplanes which the French Government believe Germany to possess, ie, 1,964, plus 540, plus 1,500, adds up to nearly exactly 4,000 in close accord with the figure worked out above from Air Staff papers.

9. A point of some interest is that the French Government believes the German first-line strength to have risen from 1,356 machines at the beginning of May to 1,964 at the end of December, ie, 608 machines, or, in their mode of counting, over 50 squadrons. This is, of course, in flagrant contradiction with the Air Staff view that the present strength is only 90 squadrons which

had already been identified on the 31st May, ie, that no increase has occurred in the last six months.

WSC

Winston S. Churchill to Bernard Baruch: telegram

(*Churchill papers: 1/286*)

20 December 1936

Sailing Berengaria 22nd arrive 28th. Propose going straight Palm Beach for two or three weeks. Please unalter your plans but let me know them so as arrange meeting. Propose visit Washington, New York, on return, third fourth week January. No speeches this time. Possibly second visit for lecture purposes in April.

Winston S. Churchill: To Whom it May Concern

(*Howes papers*)

20 December 1936   Chartwell

Samuel Howes[1] has been in my employ as chauffeur since July 1928, and I have much pleasure in recommending him. He is trustworthy, sober, a skilful mechanic, splendid driver, and a reliable man with whom I am sorry to part.

I shall be quite ready to give further particulars if applied to.

Winston S. Churchill

[1] Samuel Musgrove Howes, 1907–   . Born in West Ham, London. The youngest of ten children. Educated (by Trade Scholarship) at the London County Council School of Engineering and Navigation, Poplar, 1921–3. Apprenticed as a motor mechanic at a Ford Service Depot, Nottingham, 1923–6. Began work as a chauffeur, 1926. First Class Chauffeur's Certificate, Royal Automobile Club, 1928. Churchill's chauffeur, 1928–36. Married Clementine Churchill's parlour maid, Olive, in 1932. Worked in the Ministry of Supply, Aeronautical Inspection Directorate, 1940–2; on the development of the Jet Engine, 1942–5. Engineer Sub-Lieutenant Royal Navy, 1943, but not released by the Ministry of Supply, despite an appeal. Worked in the Gas Turbine Department of the Bristol Aeroplane Company, Filton, 1945–55. Followed his chief from Filton to Canada. Assistant Chief Mechanical Engineer, Engineering Division of A.V. Roe, Malton, Ontario, Canada, 1955–7; an engineer with the Solar Aircraft Company in San Diego, California, 1957–70 (retired, 1970, as Group Engineer). Resident in California since 1957.

Samuel M. Howes: recollections

(letter to the author, 19 November 1981)

[20 December 1936]

In July 1928 Mrs Churchill interviewed me at No 11 and engaged me, albeit with some misgivings because I was so young (I was 21 years of age and single). There was a house on the country estate in Kent for the chauffeur.

After 3 weeks, without warning I was called in by Mrs Churchill and relieved of my post because she had decided that the unoccupied chauffeur's house was deteriorating, and she had an elderly married man in view for the post.

A few days after I left, I called at No 11 to pick up some personal items I had left behind. When I saw the butler he said, 'Sam, Mr Churchill has been asking for you.' A formal dinner party was in progress in the dining room. Nevertheless I asked the butler to let Mr Churchill know I was there because I hadn't much time to catch my last bus home. He did, and to my surprise Mr Churchill left the table immediately and saw me in the adjoining room, where a pleasant fire was burning in the fireplace.

I still remember the scene vividly. Mr Churchill stood, back to the fire holding the tails of his evening coat apart to get the warmth. 'Howes,' he said. 'I wanted to see you because I did not know you were going to leave us and I didn't say goodbye.' Then he proceeded to praise my driving expertise, to assure me that my leaving was in no way due to any shortcomings on my part, and to wish me good luck in my future.

Then we shook hands and he said a gracious goodbye to me and returned to his dinner guests.

This action of his marked him as a good man in my mind, and I left the house happy but regretting that I had had to leave his employ.

At that time I was driving, temporarily for 3 months, a General Thompson Rtd, who was the head of the Dunlop Rubber plantation in Malaya, home on 3 months furlough.

About 3 weeks later, when we were in Somerset I received a telegram from Mrs Churchill, via the RAC, asking me if I was willing to return to Mr Churchill's employ. I answered 'perhaps' and an interview was set up a few days later at No 11 Downing Street, when General Thompson would be in London. At this interview I was re-engaged with assurances that my being single would be accepted, and the position was secured and permanent.

This, then, for me was the beginning of a long and happy though arduous association with the family.

Although the following years were the 'Wilderness Years' for Mr Churchill they were politically busy years for him, particularly the 'thirties' when Hitler was a growing menace in a sleeping world and seemingly only Winston Churchill had the true measure of the danger.

In the period 1928–1936 inclusive, driving this man around I had many experiences that showed me clearly that here was a man of great personal courage, wisdom and decency. Intensely patriotic and a staunch royalist. These experiences built up in me a personal feeling that a great destiny awaited him and was saving the man for the hour when he would be called upon.

We had close calls on the road. The kind of driving he demanded made this inevitable. Also, off the road, he had serious illnesses and made remarkable recoveries. Several times I have been asked during this period, if I thought he would ever be Prime Minister. I used to say 'no, I thought not—unless there is a war'.

In the following I will attempt to describe accurately and briefly some of the experiences I have in mind which, to me, were very illuminating as to the kind of man I was serving.

Item 1.

Very early in my association with Mr Churchill I dared to cross swords with him and the event bears telling as an example of his honesty and fairness.

He was a very impatient man, very volatile but non-grudge-bearing. I was a young brash cockney boy brought up in an East End neighbourhood where one stood up for oneself or else! The car was ordered for an early start for London (from Chartwell). Mr Churchill had just come down to the car with Mrs Pearman the senior secretary and both were seated in the car waiting for the bags to come out. The harassed valet[1] was hastily packing them. He waited several minutes, all the time muttering and mumbling about 'where's that luggage?' Down came the bags. I had had a case of bags being lost by coming loose on the outside luggage grid that cars of that day sported, and was being careful and thorough in strapping the bags on. All the time Mr Churchill was roaring at me to 'come on, let's go' 'Hurry up' etc. etc. in very rough peremptory terms. When the bags were securely strapped on, without premeditation I opened the rear door of the car and stuck my head in as close to him as I could reach, he sat on the other side of the car, and I said quietly but clearly, 'Excuse me Sir, I'm not a pig and I don't like to be spoken to like one.' Then I realized what I had done but I maintained a straight face and waited for his reply, expecting to be fired at once, or worse. Poor Mrs Pearman just stared at her shoes, embarrassed. Mr Churchill's

---

[1] Inches (see page 338, note 3).

face coloured up and he said nothing for what seemed an eternity to me, then he said that I should not take any notice of his way of speaking. 'It's my military manner and it doesn't mean anything.' I closed the door and we drove to London. That incident was never mentioned again by him or anyone else after that—but noticeably he never again abused me like that. I like to think that it was the beginning of a mutual respect between he and me. I was not proud of my action but I was for ever proud of the way he handled it.

Item 2.

Soon after the above (we still had the old Wolseley car) the following incident took place on the road. The car had places on the flywheel where the teeth were worn off and if the engine happened to stop in such a position the electric starter would not turn the engine and the starting handle had to be used. However, to put the starting handle in position the front number plate had to be swung down to disclose the hole behind it into which the handle had to be pushed. I'm waiting at his entrance to the House of Commons in the Speaker's yard and I know he is late and we are going to Chartwell. To save time I swing down the number plate and insert the starting handle in case the electric starter is ineffective. Out he comes and I put him into the car. Get into my seat and press the starter button. Presto! the engine starts and off I go, forgetting about the number plate. Out of the House yard, around the Parliament Square. No traffic lights then, a police constable regulating traffic at the end of Whitehall holding up our line of traffic. When it is our turn to go the constable notices our number plate, lets the other traffic go and stops me. I immediately remember the plate and I got down, said 'sorry' to the constable, fixed the plate and got back in my seat. By that time my line of traffic was held up again. Again the constable let the rest of the traffic go and stopped me and came over and officiously gave me another telling off. Not satisfied with this he made to do it to me again. Winston, who had been perfectly quiet so far, saw the constable coming over to me again. He flung the rear door open on the constable's side and treated him to a glorious dressing down. 'Take a good look at this car, and never, never stop me again. I heard my chauffeur apologise to you. Now let us go.' This the young constable did right away. I never saw that officer on that or any other corner again. I often wonder, and think that perhaps he requested a transfer.

Item 3—Whimsy.

'The Other Club.' This was a group of prominent right-wing statesmen and politicians who met, usually with guests, on the third Thursday evening of every month at the Savoy Hotel, using the entrance on the Embankment. Winston never missed this if it was possible to attend, and he always, but always enjoyed himself there, always coming out at around 2 am give or take an hour, in a very happy frame of mind. I have many reminiscences of these occasions.

On one occasion that springs to mind he came out alone in the 'wee small hours' and instead of getting into the car he backed out into the drive looking up at the upper windows of the hotel and burst into song as though serenading someone up there. He did a whole verse and chorus of Gilbert and Sullivan's 'When there's constabulary duties to be done' which I think was the regimental song of the 4th Queens Own Hussars, his old regiment.

He was really letting forth with gusto and the uniformed doorman watched him for a while, then he came over to me, sitting in the car by the hotel door, and asked, 'Say, can you get your old man out of here, he's making a nuisance of himself.' I was highly amused and I got down and walked over to Mr Churchill and put my hand on his arm and said, 'Come on Sir, let's go home, I'm tired.' He came right away saying 'goodnight' to the doorman and off we went to Chartwell.

As he always did on these late drives he put the black blindfold around his eyes and straight off to sleep he went.[1]

---

[1] A further footnote on the Other Club may be in order here. Together with all other historians to date, I have repeated (both in this and earlier volumes of the biography) the widely-held belief that the Other Club was founded in 1911 by Churchill and his friend F. E. Smith. To this day, members of the Club itself (which continues to flourish) believe this to be true. But the Anglo-Australian historian Cameron Hazlehurst, of the Institute of Advanced Studies, Australian National University, has found, in the private papers of one of the Club's original 'distinguished outsiders', a letter of invitation to join the Club, which credits, not F. E. Smith, but the then Chancellor of the Exchequer, David Lloyd George, with being the co-founder. As the letter was written by Churchill himself, this claim cannot lightly be dismissed. Writing from the Home Office on 9 May 1911, Churchill informs Sir Francis Hopwood (later 1st Baron Southborough): 'The Chancellor of the Exchequer and I are getting up a small Club for the purpose of pleasant fortnightly dinners. It is to be non-political, 12 Members on each side in the House of Commons have joined, and we are asking a few distinguished outsiders to come in. It would be a great pleasure to us all if I could persuade you to be one of these. The first dinner will be held at the Savoy on Thursday, May 18th, and if you say yes to this letter a notice will be sent to you. Lord Knollys will be our Chairman on the first occasion.' There was no mention of F. E. Smith in this letter. Having attended the first dinner, Hopwood noted in his diary the names of some of his fellow diners. His list read: 'Churchill, Lloyd George, Tree, Bigge, C. Beresford, F. E. Smith etc' (diary entry, 18 May 1911). Dr Hazlehurst comments: 'Knowing what we do of Churchill and Smith's relationship, the sorts of men they were, it is not difficult to picture them deciding that a select club, consisting largely of men they knew in politics and public affairs, would be agreeable. When they contemplated how the club could be set up, they may well have recognised that Smith's status—he was still a backbencher, having been in Parliament only five years—might make him not quite the most appropriate person to be proffering invitations to eminent courtiers and civil servants, distinguished soldiers, or even to politicians whose positions were more

Item 4—Memories.

On another occasion at the 'Other Club' Winston came out alone to go down to Chartwell. About 1.30 am. Beautiful clear, starry night. Much to my surprise, instead of getting into the back of the car he said 'I'll ride with you, Howes' and sat beside me in the Daimler car. Almost as soon as we got under way he looked up at the stars and pointed out 'Orion' the constellation to me. 'You see that, Howes,' he said. 'That group of stars saved my life,' and he proceeded to tell me at length about his escape from the Boers on the veldt and how he decided to follow where Orion led and reached the house at the mine workings, and moreover to the only room in that house occupied by two Scottish engineers, who hid him and later got him away. The rest of the house was occupied by Boers. It was extremely interesting to me and I had never heard the story before. His telling occupied almost the whole journey home.

Item 5—Fish.

Winston had the big lake stocked with trout in the early thirties. A few years later and the fish were getting quite a good size and I had never known the lake to be fished. One Sunday Winston had a visitor, I think it was Sir Ian Hamilton the well known army general retired. He evidently loved to fish and had a good catch. About mid afternoon I was in my living room and Winston came and tapped on my window carrying a large dish of fresh-caught trout. I opened the window and he said, 'Howes, would Olive like these trout for your dinner?' I said, 'Yes I'm sure she would but I doubt if she knows how to cook them' (Olive is my wife and I knew that we had never had fresh trout before). By that time Olive appeared on the scene and Winston proceeded at great length to explain each step in the cooking of fresh trout. We thanked him and off he went leaving us with the plate of several nice fish which we did indeed have and enjoy for our dinner. However I was informed by Olive that I should not have said she could not cook fresh trout. Informed in no uncertain terms.

---

solidly established than his own. Their friend, Lloyd George, however, was in a different category. Whatever his social antecedents, and no matter how controversial his political style, he was undeniably by 1911 a political figure of the very highest rank. The Chancellor's reputation would be an attraction for other potential members. His seniority, and his obvious commitment and participation might also have been conceived of as a protection should the party leaders, Asquith or Balfour, decide that bipartisan dinners were an impermissible interruption to the vehement posturing of party conflict' (Cameron Hazlehurst, *The Founders of the Other Club: An Investigation*, Canberra, no date, pages 12–13).

Item 6—Bricks and Mortar.

As is well known now, among Winston's hobbies and diversions were picture painting and bricklaying. He became quite professional at the latter and was a card carrying member of the bricklayers' union. In the mid-thirties he was having a house built just south of the manor house on the road, and he personally was laying bricks on the project whenever he could get the time.

One Sunday afternoon I was in my living room relaxing with the Sunday paper. My living room looked out into the garage yard. After a while Winston appeared in his blue overalls, Wellington boots and Stetson hat and started mixing mortar by hand on the concrete paving of the yard, loading the mortar into a wheelbarrow and pushing it up the quite steep hill to the building site at the top. After a little while, having used that load laying bricks in the wall he was building, he would be down mixing another load. I was young, in my twenties and he in his fifties and I just could not relax and see him doing that heavy work alone. I went out to him and asked to help him somehow. He would not hear of it. 'It's your day of rest,' he said. 'I can do this.' I replied that was fine but I couldn't rest seeing him struggling with that heavy barrow. He demurred and I persisted and finally he grudgingly agreed to let me help on one condition, that he pushed the barrow half way up the hill and I pushed it the rest. In this way he and I worked until he had to go and dress for dinner.

Item 7—Courage.

In the 1929 election campaign I drove him to Bermondsey Town Hall to make a speech for the Conservative aspirant. Arriving at the front entrance to the building I let him out of the car and he entered accompanied by the local police inspector. Winston's own bodyguard was not with us on this occasion. Whilst I was waiting there a knot of rough belligerent individuals gathered between the car and the entrance. These people began to talk loudly of what they were going to do to him when he emerged. After a while the police inspector came out and told me that there had been ugly incidents among cars parked in the vicinity—tyres slashed and threatening behaviour and he instructed me to pick up Mr Churchill around at the rear entrance to the building. I drove off and this group of people literally ran after me screaming out 'He's in the car', 'He's hiding under the rug in the back,' and other stupid but malicious cries. Almost as soon as I arrived at the rear entrance the whole group of vicious men were there continuing with their threatening behaviour.

I had not long to wait, wondering what was about to happen, (I had provided myself with a tyre iron by my side on the seat), when out bustled

Winston. The group parted like the Red Sea and he walked through them waving his 'John Bull' hat and smiling broadly as though among friends. Nothing untoward happened and we drove off. He was a man without fear—I was proud of him.

Item 8—Humility.

During his term as Chancellor of the Exchequer I was to drive Winston, Mrs Churchill and Miss Diana to a weekend with Lord[1] and Lady Desborough, at Panshangar Park near St Albans. At this time the M1 motorway, or St Albans by-pass as it then was had not been completed but some sections of it were open, with detours in between. I knew this but couldn't convince Mrs Churchill. She had had a letter from Lady Desborough saying that the best way to come was on the by-pass, that it was open all the way. On this Saturday afternoon in 1928—weather misty but visibility quite good—we left No 11 Downing Street. Mr Churchill, Mrs Churchill and Miss Diana in the back. Sergeant Thompson[2] had the weekend off and was not with us.

Through the parks and up the Edgware Road and on to the new Barnet by-pass. All looked fine for a few miles, then barriers across the road and detour signs. Local roads became country lanes and we were suddenly fog bound—a real London pea souper. We were slowed down and time was going on. I knew not where I was going, only a vague sense of direction. No one around to ask. We came to a sort of village green with a solitary wooden signpost. I thought I recognised Elstree crossroads but was unsure. I pulled up and went to the signpost but in the darkness and fog and the height of the board, even flicking my cigarette lighter, could not read the words on the board. It was 8.30 pm and I could hear sobs of frustration coming from Mrs C and Miss Diana in the back of the car. Winston flung the door of the car open violently, breaking the door-strap, and almost ran over to me. 'Where are we?' he said to me. I said, 'I think at Elstree crossroads but I can't read the board.' He said angrily, 'No you're not, you're lost.' Then he bent right

---

[1] William Henry Grenfell, 1855–1945. Liberal MP for Salisbury, 1880–2 and 1885–6; for Hereford, 1892–3; Conservative MP for Wycombe, 1900–5. A famous athlete. Created Baron Desborough, 1905. President of the London Chamber of Commerce, and Chairman of the Thames Conservancy Board. Two of his sons were killed in action (in May and July 1915). His third son died in 1926, as a result of a motor car accident, aged 28.

[2] Walter H. Thompson. Detective Constable, Special Branch, Scotland Yard, 1913. Bodyguard to Lloyd George, 1917–20. Bodyguard to Churchill, 1920–32 and accompanied Churchill to the United States, 1929 and 1931–2. Retired from the police force with the rank of Detective Inspector, 1936. Worked as a grocer, 1936–9. Recalled to the police force, 1939, and served as Churchill's personal bodyguard from September 1939 until May 1945. Married, as his second wife, Churchill's secretary, Mary Shearburn. His son, Flight-Lieutenant F. D. J. Thompson, DFC and Bar, was killed in action over enemy territory in March 1943, after 43 missions.

over making a back. 'Get on my back,' he said. I promptly knelt and then stood on his back and could, with my lighter, read the board. We were indeed at Elstree crossroads, and in another 30 minutes or so we were at Panshangar—then after 9 pm. The ladies were red-eyed and furious and said nothing to me, but Winston was now calm and dismissed me with instructions to find lodgings in the village and take them home on the Sunday afternoon. Which I did.

Had I been allowed to come by the old route I knew we would have been there hours before. I felt vindicated. What Winston and the ladies thought I never knew. Still I'm sure that few if any gentlemen on his level would have bent down for me to stand on their back. Would probably have demanded the reverse situation—them on my back.

Item 9—Deep feelings.

When Winston was recuperating from his relapse of the para-typhoid attack that hit him on a visit to the continent, he came down the garden at Chartwell to get into his studio. Found it locked and the odd-job man was off for the afternoon. No one else knew where the key was kept so Winston was locked out. In desperation he came to me at my house and asked me if I could get him into the studio. I said if he didn't mind my breaking one of the small diamond panes in the narrow window beside the door of the studio, I would get into the place and let him in the door. He agreed and we walked round to the studio next to my house and I did break the glass, opened the window intending to climb through. This window was no more than 12″ wide. Before I could climb in he did so and looked at me from inside. I was shocked and without thinking I said, 'Sir, you would not have got through that window before your illness.' His jaw dropped and sadly he said, 'Have I lost so much weight.' I could have cut my tongue out, I was so sorry to have said such a thing to him. I asked if there was anything else he wanted. He said 'no thank you Howes' and I returned to my house leaving him to get reacquainted with his store of paintings. That scene has stayed in my mind ever since.

Item 10—Loyalty.

The abdication of King Edward VIII took place in the last days of my service with Mr Churchill, and gave rise to what I think was a noteworthy instance of Winston's great loyalty to an old friend.

The abdication took place on the 11th December 1936 and for the 3 final days I had been driving Winston from Chartwell over to Fort Belvedere before lunch and returning to Chartwell in the late evening. Over the years he had been a regular visitor to Edward at York House and elsewhere, and I had got to know George Ladbrook,[1] Edward's chauffeur from these meetings. He and I spent our time on these visits to the Fort playing billiards down in the servants' hall.

On the final night the King's car and Mr Churchill's car were ordered to the front door after dinner. The King and Winston came out and after talking together for a few minutes they both made their final farewells, the King got into his Buick car and George drove him off to Windsor to make his abdication address to his people and then to Dover to board the destroyer for France. Winston got into my car with tears flowing and silently we drove home to Chartwell.

The late nights with Mr C began to tell on me, young as I was, and at the end of 1936 after a severe 'telling off' I received from Mrs C I impulsively gave notice to leave. I tendered my notice to leave personally to Winston. He was shocked and tried repeatedly to get me to change my mind.

Sequel.

This event happened in 1941, 5 years after I had left Winston's employ but I think is worth relating as it reflects on his kindness to me and his good nature.

I was posted to Armstrong Siddeley works in Coventry (I was there during the terrible blitz). The Prime Minister was to visit us. He arrived during our lunch hour. Crowds lining the road in front of the works. I was standing near the kerb when the cortège of cars appeared. Inspector Walter Thompson was on the front of Mr Churchill's car as he used to be with me when Winston was Chancellor of the Exchequer and I was his chauffeur. Thompson saw me and called out, 'Sam, what are you doing here?' I replied, 'Working here.' He stopped the car and spoke a few words to Winston who was in the back with, I think, the Mayor of Coventry. Thompson beckoned me to come over and I had a few words with Winston. He was genuinely glad to see me and interested in what I was doing there. Then he said, 'Mrs Churchill is in the car behind and she will want a word with you.' I said goodbye and good luck to him and went to the next car and had a pleasant few words with Mrs C. The whole line of cars at a standstill meanwhile.

My Chief came to see me in the afternoon a bit miffed because Mr C had given the welcoming committee waiting in the foyer the slip and gone straight to the shops. Then he learned that one of his staff had been seen

---

[1] George Ladbrook, Edward VIII's trusted chauffeur. According to Press reports, he weighed 17 stone. It was he who drove Mrs Simpson across France when she left England shortly before the Abdication. Remained with the Windsors in France, 1936–40, and drove them across France to Spain after the German invasion of France, May 1940.

having a conversation with the Prime Minister in the street. I had to tell him why.

21 December 1936

After all impossible escape. Parliament now meeting January 19. Must abandon plan. Thousand thanks for your kindness.

Winston

21 December 1936

Many thanks for your letter and for the visit of your secretary.

I have agreed to do an all-Party meeting in Glasgow for the Defence of Freedom and Peace Council on March 15, otherwise I have not felt able to make any engagements in the New Year.

I am afraid it would not be possible for me to devote my entire life to the New Commonwealth as you suggest I should do. I have to earn my living by writing books and articles which consumes a very great part of my time and strength. Besides this I have my work in Parliament, especially on Defence, which is very heavy; and a constituency which requires at least twenty-five meetings every year.

I warmly appreciate the kind things you say. With every good wish for Christmas and the New Year,

Believe me,

21 December 1936

My dear Churchill,

I have now made enquiries into the two cases in regard to our supply arrangements, which you mentioned in the House on the 12th November

(Col 1109) and of which you sent me some particulars on the 19th November.

With regard to the first case, may I summarise the statement you made. A British firm had received an order from a French firm for bearings used in gun lathes. The British firm had an order for similar bearings from Germany, and as the French price was not tempting the British firm accepted the German order. By chance some weeks later the Director of the British firm heard that the French firm wanted the bearings for gun lathes which had been ordered by Woolwich Arsenal: it was too late to do the work in England. The British firm, however, had a branch in America which quickly arranged for the order to be executed in America and delivered the bearings to the French firm who would in turn deliver them to Woolwich Arsenal (Hansard, 12th November, Col 1109).

The facts are that the British Timken Company and the French Timken Company are both off-shoots of an international organisation, the Timken Bearing Company of USA. Woolwich Arsenal, in order to equip the new Nottingham gun factory without any avoidable delay with the best machines, did what you have more than once urged me to encourage: they placed an order for gun lathes abroad where they could get not only earlier delivery but a better machine than in this country. Berthiez, the suppliers of the gun lathes, wanted some bearings—a comparatively small part of the lathes. These bearings are invariably 'bought out' components and are only made by a few specialist firms. One such firm is the Timken Bearing Company and its off-shoots. Berthiez first placed their enquiry for these bearings with the French Timken Company who in turn passed it to the British Timken Company. In the end the order was executed by the American Timken Company in the USA.

You cited the case as an example of confusion of organisation and of misuse of our resources. I must, with all respect to you, entirely traverse any such suggestion. In the urgent circumstances that existed a Ministry of Supply would have been wise to do precisely what Woolwich Arsenal did, namely, order the best lathes obtainable. If the Ministry had used their powers of control and had had the whole order executed in this country in such time as was possible, it would have resulted in the sacrifice to no purpose of production power for private and export trade.

I derive very little satisfaction from writing this letter. No one can now be expected to take the trouble to understand the incident and unravel the facts. I do not even want you to trouble yourself, when you are going to get a holiday, to acknowledge this letter, but you will not object to my placing on record the facts, if only in fairness to those concerned.

The second case you mentioned is that of the Cincinnati Milling Machines, Limited. They are an American Company with a British branch at Birmingham, which has been providing the War Office with machine tools, orders to the value of approximately £30,000 having been placed in the last six months. It is true that the Government have not asked for powers to enable them to insist upon priority of Government orders, but I am satisfied that by the methods we have used we are now getting substantial priority for all orders for the Government programme, and I am in close touch with the leading representatives of the industry on this question. You are aware of the Government's decision not to interfere with normal industry. I know you do not approve this decision but I feel no doubt at all about its wisdom, at any rate in connection with the machine tool industry. We should be running a very grave risk if we were to ask the industry to abandon all their ordinary trade. When the urgent Government programme is concluded the industry would have to face a bleak prospect, and we should more than ever be dependent on foreign suppliers.

Yours sincerely,
T. W. H. Inskip

Winston S. Churchill to Desmond Morton

(Churchill papers: 2/272)

21 December 1936

I wonder if you would let your organising eye run over these papers. My idea was that the Air League and Navy League should try to reach an agreement about the Fleet Air Arm, which agreement would probably impose itself upon the indecision of His Majesty's Government. The First Lord[1] was much interested in such a project. You will see there is not much between the parties.

If you will let me have your views as to how it could be settled, I will then write a paper which could serve as the basis for a conference, which might take place early in the New Year.

---

[1] Sir Samuel Hoare.

Winston S. Churchill to Stanley Baldwin

(*Churchill papers: 2/264*)

22 December 1936

I venture on the strength of old associations and your invariable courtesy to me to write these few lines for your consideration.

If for any reason the Simpson divorce does not go through it will be felt by many millions of people throughout the Empire that the abdication could have been avoided and that the choice between renunciation and abdication should never have been presented to the ex-King. 'Why' it will be asked, 'were the legal aspects now apparently so plain, not thoroughly explored? Was there any occasion when the Prime Minister said to King Edward, "What is the use of talking about marrying Mrs Simpson? The law officers advise me that the divorce will not go through, or is very unlikely to go through".' I should have thought that nothing was more likely to start a faction in this country than that King Edward had been left or even forced to take his decision without this indispensable fact or probability being made known to him, and also the lady. Surely you will be held responsible for not having brought all the legal aspects to the notice of the Cabinet; for not having drawn their attention to the change of venue and any other circumstances which might have been made known at a time when matters could be remedied? Surely the Prime Minister will lie under the charge of having left his Sovereign in ignorance of the legal facts, and thus confronting him with an unreal dilemma? It is only my desire that this disaster, for such I at least regard it, may now pass from us with the least injury and unhappiness to all concerned and with the least distress in the public mind, that forces me thus to intrude upon you.

Believe me,

Yours very sincerely,

The Duke of Windsor to Winston S. Churchill: telegram

(*Churchill papers: 2/264*)

22 December 1936

Many thanks your kind letter. Hope you have a nice trip. Happy Christmas and New Year.

Edward

Winston S. Churchill to Sir Maurice Hankey

(*Churchill papers: 25/7*)

23 December 1936

You will see that Lord Cavan returns to the charge about underground shelters.[1] I think the statements made about this are not well founded. I had some correspondence upon the subject some time ago with Sir Arnold Wilson who is on the Home Office Committee, and I question altogether the statements of the Home Office executive about the penetration of air bombs. It is true that the armour piercing bombs may penetrate deeply, but these would scarcely ever be used except against ships or perhaps a few to destroy water mains, gas and electrical centres. You may be interested to see the correspondence. I think the whole question of underground shelters is made too difficult through the acceptance of exaggerated data. You really ought to look into this yourself because an immense amount of thought and argument is proceeding on wrong lines.

Winston S. Churchill to Bernard Baruch

(*Churchill papers: 2/264*)

25 December 1936

Thank you so much for sending me these most interesting cuttings. It has been a terrible time here, and I am profoundly grieved at what has happened. I believe the abdication to have been altogether premature and probably quite unnecessary. However, the vast majority is on the other side. You have done well to be out of it.

---

[1] Lord Cavan was an advocate of the construction of bombproof shelters. 'I cannot accept the arguments used against underground parking places', he had written to Violet Pearman on 21 December 1936, and he added: 'A 500 lb bomb cannot penetrate deeper than the 17 inch Howitzer the projectile of which weighed 2,400 lb. The depth of the crater made by these into *earth* with no concrete was only 15 feet. Why is it "impossible & impracticable" to excavate underground chambers 30 to 50 feet below the surface? The Maginot lines in France are bomb proof for many consecutive miles, & in these, shelters are of various strength. May I suggest a visit to these as illustration of the point I still insist upon—that it *is* practicable to use Mother Earth as protection'. (*Churchill papers: 25/7*).

Winston S. Churchill to Stanley Williams[1]

(*Churchill papers: 1/292*)

28 December 1936

I expect to pay in during the next few days about £400, and the cheque for £5,000 will also be collected by you. Thus I suppose we shall start the New Year with the overdraft at about £2,600. Will you kindly let me know the value of the securities you hold against this, and the present surrender value of the £10,000 insurance policy.

I have made literary contracts for the coming year comprising:

Six months' Evening Standard articles	£1,440
Coronation series	1,250
Volume IV Marlborough	3,500
Another News of the World series	4,200
Six articles for Collier's	1,800
totalling	£12,190
to which add approximately	3,000
for income, salary fees etc Total	£15,190

say *£15,000*.[2]

This does not include any contracts that may be made to write fortnightly articles in the last six months of the year.

I have however to pay in the first half of the year £3,400 super tax and at least £1,000 income tax, as against only £1,000 income tax inuring in the second half year. Besides this the payments for Marlborough IV and the News of the World series (ie £3,400 plus £4,200) will not accrue till the third or fourth quarter.[3] I should therefore be glad if the Bank would allow the overdraft to stand at £7,000 for the year, on the understanding that it is reduced to £5,000 by December 31, 1937. I should hope it would not be necessary for me to use this overdraft to the full, but I cannot tell how the literary payments will be made in relation to the taxes. Perhaps you would

---

[1] Stanley Williams, 1887–1954. Entered Cox's bank in 1907. Transferred to the employ of Lloyd's on the absorption of Cox's by Lloyds in 1923. 2nd Clerk, in charge of the Guards Section, Pall Mall Branch, 1923–33; 1st Clerk, 1934–41. Sub-Manager, Administration, Pall Mall Branch, 1941–7. Retired, 1947.

[2] In the money values of September 1981, Churchill's projected income for the year 1937 was in excess of £260,000.

[3] During which period Churchill was paying his principal research assistant, F. W. Deakin, £33.6.8 a month.

let me know at your convenience whether my wishes can be met. Also what is the rate of interest you charge on overdraft accounts.

I also wish to renew the other two loans of £4,000 as in previous years.

Winston S. Churchill to Sir Maurice Hankey
(*Churchill papers: 2/267*)

28 December 1936
Confidential

My dear Maurice,

Included among the file I sent you a few days ago, was a letter from Admiral Henderson.[1] Please treat this as absolutely private and do not mention or quote him to anyone. The point upon which I consulted him was one on which it was quite proper that he should express a purely scientific opinion; but I do not think he would expect his opinions to be cited. May I have your assurance therefore that all will be well?

Sir Maurice Hankey to Winston S. Churchill
(*Churchill papers: 2/267*)

28 December 1936
Confidential

My dear Winston,

I have taken steps to withdraw Henderson's letter from the file, and, in reproducing, to eliminate all reference to the letter. I will treat it as absolutely private.

I am going away for three days.

Yours ever,
M. P. A. Hankey

---

[1] Admiral Henderson's letter to Churchill of 13 July 1936 (see page 241).

Winston S. Churchill to Viscount Cecil of Chelwood

(*Churchill papers: 8/531*)

29 December 1936

I am so glad that Marlborough Volumes I and II have beguiled your influenza. May I encourage you to persevere in the story by sending you Volume III.

With all good wishes,

Winston S. Churchill to Marshall Diston

(*Churchill papers: 8/536*)

29 December 1936

I have found your draft for the article on King George the Sixth so very helpful that instead of the usual fee, I hope you will let me increase it to £20.[1]

---

[1] An article by Churchill entitled 'His Majesty King George VI' was published in the May 1937 issue of the *Strand* magazine. Churchill accepted Diston's draft for the article, but he did add several sentences. Of the Royal Navy in 1914 Churchill added: 'neither the Empire nor the Allies would have been saved without the British Navy. It carried the troops & stores. It conquered the U-boats' (Diston had written: 'It strewed the waves with the wreakage of the U-boats'). Of King George VI, when he served, as Prince Albert, at the battle of Jutland, Churchill added to Diston's draft: 'Thus he shares with William IV & James II the distinction of having fought in a first class naval engagement'. Of air power Churchill added: 'The menace of hostile Air Power darkens our island life. To be safe we must be strong in this new Arm'. Of the 'new Radicalism' of 1906 to 1914 Churchill added that it was 'forever associated in its practical application with Mr Lloyd George'. Of George VI having said he was 'deprived of a close friendship' as a result of the Abdication, Churchill added: 'But we may hope that this close friendship will not always be obstructed by distance, & that it will last all his life. Certainly he will find in the Duke of Windsor the most faithful of his subjects, no rival for popular applause, but a loving brother who will aid him to the utmost of his opportunity'. Of the marriage of King George VI and Queen Elizabeth, Churchill added: 'Two daughters have been born to this marriage, & in the Heir Presumptive to the Crown, the Princess Elizabeth, the Houses of Stuart & Hanover both find a representative of their blood, cheering even to the White Rose League, and reconciling in the fullness of time one of the most prolonged & poignant quarrels of British history'. Of Royalty. Churchill added: 'It is the barrier against Dictatorship'.

January 1937

Winston S. Churchill to Bernard Baruch
(*Churchill papers: 1/298*)

1 January 1937

Sarah and her husband came to luncheon with us yesterday. You have indeed been a good friend through all this tiresome business, and Clemmie and I are most deeply grateful for all you have done.

I gathered from Randolph that you formed the opinion that Mr Oliver's attachment was serious, and did not think ill of him. Certainly I feel that after what has been virtually an engagement of almost a year, it would be wrong of us to withhold our consent. We are bound to wish for nothing but their future happiness. Moreover one has neither the right nor the power to do more than advise and make sure that everything is in order.

I feel also under a great obligation to Levy. Randolph tells me how perfectly magnificent he was in all his personal handling of the couple. I am writing to him in this sense today and will ask him to let me know what the charges of his firm will be. Quite apart from the personal service which he gave, there must have been a definite out of pocket expense for cables, looking up registers etc.

I was much disappointed at having to give up at the last moment my trip to the United States. I had booked a passage and the Cunard people had given me their best cabins. But I felt that the situation here was difficult for me to leave. Parliament is meeting as early as the 19th, and almost immediately will begin upon the Civil List for the new King—and the old. I am certain to be on the Committee, and I must be there to watch over the interests about which I have an enduring sentiment.

The Abdication has been most painful and has left far deeper marks among the people than Parliament or the newspapers show. I cannot convince myself that with time and patience it could not have been avoided. The voluntary muzzling of the British Press for so many months gave the worst forms of rumour and gossip their chance, and then suddenly when the explosion of publicity took place, no time was allowed for its pressures to operate on either of the parties. We English must now make the best of things as no doubt we shall do. But Lloyd George's telegram stirred the pulse of scores of millions.[1]

I do not feel that my own political position is much affected by the line I took; but even if it were, I should not wish to have acted otherwise. As you know in politics I always prefer to accept the guidance of my heart to calculations of public feeling. Baldwin has got a new lease of life. Indeed he throve on the job. He is practically sure now to hang on till after the Coronation.

This makes it easier for me to plan ahead. I have every hope that I shall be able to come over to the States in April and hope to inaugurate the Defence of Peace and Freedom movement about which Randolph consulted you. It would have been a great pity to hurry it unduly. I am therefore keeping April more or less provisionally free. Neville is introducing his Budget then, but I do not think it will raise any controversy. Everyone is prepared to provide all that is necessary for rearmament, or rather all that it is possible to spend upon rearmament.

In Europe the situation becomes increasingly tense and next year the German army will become definitely stronger than the French. However there has recently come to me the feeling that the balance is tilting rather decidedly against Hitler. England and France have now declared what is virtually a defensive alliance. Italy is by no means 'vendue à la Prusse'. The Eastern group of States with Russia behind them are drawing together much better than I expected. The internal discontent in Germany is most serious beneath the surface. This of course cuts both ways, but if we can gather enough strongly armed nations at Geneva upon the Basis of the Covenant of the League, there is a good chance of overawing the Aggressor, however desperate he may become; and then perhaps the explosion will take place inside Germany rather than upon her neighbours. How you must regret, how we all regret, that Wilson's dream[2] was not carried through, for I have no

---

[1] On Christmas Eve, 1936 Lloyd George had sent the Duke of Windsor a telegram which read: 'Best Christmas greetings from an old Minister of the Crown who holds you in as high esteem as ever and regards you with deep and loyal affection, deplores the mean and unchivalrous attacks upon you, and regrets the loss sustained by the British Empire of a monarch who sympathized with the lowliest of his subjects.' The Duke of Windsor replied on the following day: 'Very touched by your kind telegram and good wishes, which I heartily reciprocate. Edward. *Cymru Am Byth.*' (Wales for Ever).

[2] The hope of President Woodrow Wilson, after America had entered the war on 6 April 1917, that a peace settlement could be both fair and lasting. Wilson's plan had been set out in his '14 Points', in a public speech on 8 January 1918, including the right of all peoples to self-determination, and open agreements 'openly arrived at'. In November 1918 the German, Turkish and Austro-Hungarian Governments accepted the 14 points as the basis of peace-making, but during the course of the Paris Peace Conference of 1919, and in the Treaties of Versailles, Trianon and St Germain which resulted from it, many of the principles insisted upon by Wilson had been compromised or whittled away.

doubt it would have made the difference between a safe, happy and prosperous world and the present hideous panorama.

With every good wish for peace and happiness in the coming year,

Winston S. Churchill to Louis Levy
(*Churchill papers: 1/298*)

1 January 1937

Sarah and her husband arrived home and lunched with us here yesterday. There is nothing for us now but to make the best of things and hope they will be happy. I am extremely glad the naturalization was effected before the marriage and above all that they were persuaded to wait until the Austrian divorce was in all respects valid.

My wife and I are deeply indebted to you for the kindness and personal interest with which you handled the affair. Randolph tells me how magnificent you were in personal contact with the couple. Apart from all your own trouble you took yourself there must be expenses for cables, looking up registers etc. I should be very glad if you would let me know what I owe you in money.

I put off my journey at the last moment because of the situation here, but I hope to be over in the States in April, when we must meet.

With kindest regards,

Winston S. Churchill to Dr Colijn
(*Churchill papers: 8/547*)

1 January 1937   Chartwell

My dear Dr Colijn,

I send you by the hand of my literary secretary, Mr F. W. Deakin, a copy of the new volume of Marlborough. Mr Deakin, who is a Fellow of Wadham College Oxford, is hoping to be allowed to consult the archives at the Hague for the Marlborough-Heinsius correspondence of the year 1709. Our Foreign Office have been kind enough to ask our Embassy to put him upon the right track, so that there is no need to trouble you in any way. But I thought I would take advantage of his journey to send you this small token of my respect for you, my good wishes to you, and to your country in this anxious year.

It may be that in this Volume III you will find some of those criticisms which are customary between Allies. However if I am able in another year to send you Volume IV, you will find I shall not spare my own country for the shameful desertion of the Grand Alliance which led to the Treaty of Utrecht.

With all good wishes, believe me,

Yours vy sincerely,
Winston S. Churchill

Winston S. Churchill to Clementine Churchill

(*Spencer-Churchill papers*)

2 January 1937

Trent[1]
New Barnet

My darling,

I fear you had an uncomfortable crossing. Howes[2] said the sea & wind were vy high, the boat small, crowded, French, & that you had no private cabin. I bewailed yr misfortunes, but anyhow they are now over.[3]

I was deeply shocked & grieved to learn from Vansittart by chance on the telephone that poor Ralph Wigram died suddenly on New Year's Eve in his wife's arms. I thought him a grand fellow. A bright steady flame burning in a broken lamp, wh guided us towards safety & honour.

Brendan & I are going on Monday to the Funeral wh is at Cuckfield, near Hayward's Heath. Afterwards I shall bring him & Van back to luncheon at Chartwell. I am taking a wreath from us both. Poor little Ava[4] is all adrift now. She cherished him & kept him alive. He was her contact with gt affairs. Now she has only the idiot child.[5]

[1] Trent Park, the Hertfordshire home of Sir Philip Sassoon.

[2] Churchill's chauffeur since 1928 (see page 502, note 1).

[3] Clementine Churchill had gone to the Austrian Alps with their 14-year-old daughter Mary. They stayed at the Flexenhotel, Zürs am Arlberg. Among the other guests there were Venetia and Judy Montagu, and Churchill's niece Clarissa Churchill. On 3 January 1937 Clementine Churchill wrote to her husband from Zürs, about the Abdication crisis: 'My darling I hope you are having a happy visit at Trent. Do not be sad my Dear One. There is nothing which you have done which in perspective will not seem generous & courageous— which is indeed the truth.'

[4] Ava Bodley, 1897–1975. Daughter of the historian J. E. C. Bodley (see page 330, note 1). In 1925 she married Ralph Wigram, and in 1941 John Anderson, later 1st Viscount Waverley (who died in 1958). She and Ralph Wigram had one child, a mongol son, who died in 1951 at the age of 21. In her will she left £5,000 to the London Federation of Boys Clubs, for the benefit of physically and mentally handicapped boys.

[5] Charles Edward Thomas Bodley Wigram. Only son of Ralph and Ava Wigram. He was born on 27 November 1929 and died on 14 August 1951, aged 21.

We have an odd party here, but one you wd like. Mrs Belloc Lowndes,[1] the Kenneth Clarks,[2] Brendan, little Ivor,[3] Lord Stanmore,[4] Hannah[5] & one or two old tabbies I have not identified.

Quite different from the usual outfit; but peaceful.

The King's business forms a constant theme. I have worked at Marl, & am also painting a little daub indoors.

I hope by now you are safe & teed up at Zurs.

With all my fondest love,

Your devoted loving husband,

W

[sketch of pig]

[1] Marie Adelaide Belloc Lowndes, –1947. The sister of Hilaire Belloc. Author of more than forty books, many about crime. Published her first book, *The Heart of Penelope*, in 1904. In 1937, she published two books, *The House by the Sea* and *The Marriage-Broker*. Her last book, *She Dwelt with Beauty*, was published posthumously in 1949. A contemporary writes: 'She was a great gossip and seemed to know most of the writers. There was usually a sting in the tail of her remarks, but she was very entertaining' (*letter to the author, 22 July 1981*).

[2] Kenneth Mackenzie Clark, 1903– . Art historian. Director of the National Gallery, 1934–45. Knighted, 1938. Controller, Home Publicity, Ministry of Information, 1939–41. Slade Professor of Fine Art, Oxford, 1946–50 and 1961–2. Companion of Honour, 1959. Created Baron, 1969. Order of Merit, 1976. In 1927 he married Elizabeth Martin, who died in 1976. In 1977 he married Madame Nolwen de Janzé-Rice.

[3] Ivor Grosvenor Guest, 1903–1967. Eldest son of Churchill's cousin, the 1st Viscount Wimborne. Educated at Eton and Trinity College, Cambridge. Liberal MP for Brecon and Radnor, November 1935–June 1939. Succeeded his father as second Viscount, June 1939. On active service in the Second World War; Major, Royal Armoured Corps, 1943. Parliamentary Private Secretary to the Under-Secretary of State for Air (Lord Sherwood), 1943–5. Liberal Whip in the House of Lords, 1944–8. Chairman of the Governors of Stowe School, 1952–60. OBE, 1953.

[4] George Arthur Maurice Hamilton-Gordon, 1871–1957. Succeeded his father as 2nd Baron Stanmore, 1912. A Lord in Waiting to King George V, 1914–22. Chief Liberal Whip in the House of Lords, 1923–44. Privy Councillor, 1932. Chairman of Committees and Deputy Speaker, House of Lords, 1944–6.

[5] Hannah Gubbay, a cousin of Sir Philip Sassoon. Beginning in 1928, she had organized a series of exhibitions of British painting and decorative art, in aid of the Royal Northern Hospital. These exhibitions included paintings by Gainsborough (1936) and Reynolds (1937), and the Old London Exhibition (1938). In 1967 she left the National Trust a cash endowment of £1 million, but because she died within a year of making the gift, £900,000 of it was taken in taxation. She also left her art collection to the National Trust; it is housed at Clandon Park, near Guildford, Surrey. She died in 1968. In an obituary notice in *The Times*, John Pope-Hennessy wrote (2 March 1968): 'When the term "sense of quality" is used to describe the talent of a collector, it can mean many different things. In Hannah Gubbay's case it connoted a liking for excellence—her incomparable food was an expression of this interest as much as the magnificent red lacquer cabinet from Hornby Castle which stood in her dining-room—and a sometimes aggressive honest-mindedness which ensured that she was never taken in.'

Winston S. Churchill to Ava Wigram

(*Viscountess Waverley papers*)

2 January 1937

. . . I admired always so much his courage, integrity of purpose, high comprehending vision. He was one of those—how few—who guard the life of Britain. Now he is gone—and on the eve of this fateful year. Indeed it is a blow to England and to all the best that England means. It is only a week or so that he rang me up to speak about the late King. I can hear his voice in my memory. And you? What must be your loss? But you still will have a right to dwell on all that you did for him. You shielded that bright steady flame that burned in the broken lamp. But for you it would long ago have been extinguished, and its light would not have guided us thus far upon our journey.

Ava Wigram to Winston S. Churchill

(*Churchill papers: 1/300*)

2 January 1937

Van says you rang up to ask about Ralph's funeral. If you'd like to come I'd be very glad—as it's only for people Ralph specially cared for—& the memorial service is for those less close—

I don't know what to do at all—I'm feeling so stunned. I can't believe that in five minutes our whole wonderful life together was shattered for always—It can't be true, can it.

Private. I wanted to ask you to write a little thing in the papers, but I thought perhaps it was a bother. He adored you so—& always said you were the greatest Englishman alive. Please come on Monday.

Ava Wigram to Winston S. Churchill

(*Churchill papers: 1/300*)

2 January 1937

I'm grateful you are coming to the funeral—It is 11 o'clock Cuckfield Parish Church—Hayward's Heath. Would you be there in good time so I can have you by me—to be helped by you—none of his relations are coming—NOT his father or mother[1]—or anybody so I need you very much.

---

[1] Eustace Rochester Wigram, 1860–1940, sometime Lieutenant, Coldstream Guards, and Mary Grace Wigram (died 1951), daughter of Colonel Ralph Bradford-Atkinson of Morpeth.

Leslie Hore-Belisha to Winston S. Churchill

(*Churchill papers: 1/298*)

5 January 1937   War Office

My dear Winston,

It was a most generous act of yours to give me the chain, so that I shall
never be able to forget my keys or your thoughtfulness. Such gifts really do
give pleasure to the recipient & in this case a most unexpected one.

My very good New Year wishes.

Yours sincerely,
Leslie Hore-Belisha

Clementine Churchill to Winston S. Churchill

(*Spencer-Churchill papers*)

5 January 1937   Zürs am Arlberg

My Darling,

I am horrified & astonished to read in last Saturday's Times an 'appreciation' of your friend Ralph Wigram by Vansittart. Did you know he was ill?
I did not see any announcement of his death in Friday's Times, the day I
left; & I think you must have missed it or you would have mentioned it to
me—I am so very sorry—He was a true friend of yours & in his eye you could
see the spark which showed an inner light was burning—

His poor little wife will be overwhelmed with grief—

In these troubled times one is astonished to be standing up—with head
'bloody but unbowed'—

I wonder if you have seen our Sarah. I'm glad I waited. She is unchanged
—as virginal & aloof as ever.

Yesterday at Noon the Sun was dazzling, the sky blue & it was so hot that
a cotton shirt with short sleeves & an open neck seemed the only thing to
wear on the slopes—

I wonder if you will go to Blenheim[1]—

---

[1] Churchill went to Blenheim on the 9 and 10 January 1937. The only other guest was his
cousin Lord Ivor Churchill, brother of the 10th Duke of Marlborough. He returned to Blenheim four days later, for the weekend of 14 to 16 January 1937 (see page 528), and was again
at Blenheim, with Clementine Churchill, from 22 to 24 May 1937, when the other guests
included Lord Curzon's widow, Grace, Marchioness Curzon of Kedleston, Euan and Barbara
Wallace, the Earl and Countess of Birkenhead, Evelyn Fitzgerald (a stockbroker) and his
wife Helen (Lord Beaverbrook's sister-in-law), and Terence Philip (one of Clementine
Churchill's fellow voyagers on her cruise to the Dutch East Indies at the end of 1934).

Mary has been promoted & is now more than half way up the Ski school.
I am more pedestrian but still creditable.

Your loving,
Clemmie

Winston S. Churchill to Clementine Churchill
(Spencer-Churchill papers)

7 January 1937   Chartwell

My darling,

Yr second letter arrived this morning. I am so glad you have health, snow
& sunshine.

I went to Cuckfield (Sussex) for the funeral of poor Wigram. The widow
was ravaged with grief, & it was a harrowing experience. Vansittart & his
wife have taken her in for ten days at Denham[1]—a good act. There appears
to be no pension or anything for Foreign Office widows: but she says she can
manage on her own resources. Her future seems blank & restricted. A sombre
world!

After the funeral I brought the Vansittarts & other FO people back here
to luncheon. Ivor C,[2] Brendan & P. Maze came also. The remnants of the
influenza stricken staff rose to the occasion.

Sarah came to luncheon yesterday (Wed) & we had a nice talk. She was
vy sweet & loving, & seems to want vy much to keep in touch with us. I told
her what we proposed financially. She seemed vy pleased, & liked the idea of
all except yr £100 pin money rolling up for a rainy day. 'Vic'—I suppose we
must call him that—is making about £200 a week[3] for 8 to 10 weeks over
here. They get special terms at the hotel. But what a life—hand to mouth,
no home, no baby!

I thought Sarah serious & gentle. Like the ill starred D of W, she has done
what she liked, & has now to like what she has done. We shall have to take
special care & make excuses for her. She spoke with gt affection of you.

---

[1] Churchill himself was the guest of the Vansittarts at Denham Place on 17 August 1937.
During 1937 he also saw Vansittart (at either the Foreign Office, Morpeth Mansions, or
Vansittart's house in Park Street) on March 3, April 4, May 25, May 26, October 11, October
21 and December 8.

[2] Lord Ivor Charles Spencer-Churchill, 1898–1956. Second son of Churchill's cousin
'Sunny', 9th Duke of Marlborough. Educated at Eton and Magdalen College, Oxford. On
active service, 1917-18 (Lieutenant, Royal Army Service Corps). In 1947, after his marriage
to Elizabeth Cunningham, he lived at Rogate, Hampshire, in the next village to Churchill's
friend Paul Maze, the painter.

[3] Half the *annual* salary of a Member of Parliament. In June 1937 an MP's salary was raised
from £400 (which it had been since 1911), to £600, on the grounds that the cost of living had
risen 50% in those twenty-six years. The September 1981 equivalent of £200 in 1937 was
just over £7,000.

I have been painting indoors a good deal & have been using one end of the drawing room—with a dust sheet.

Deakin has been here 4 days & has helped me a lot. He shows more quality & serviceableness than any of the others. We have reached definite conclusions about the abortive Peace negotiations of 1709. They are a terrible tangle, & have never been satisfactorily or even intelligibly explained, before. It is quite an effort to keep all the points of this complicated argument in one's mind when so much else is afoot.

Arnold caught about 15 of the large golden orfes with his landing net when the middle lake was empty. They are wonderful fish—15 inches long & thick in proportion. I have now 25 in the garden pool. I told them to eat all that they wish. But I expect they will miss their mud & weeds.

I go to Consuelo at Blenheim for the week end—to paint & look at archives.[1] I shall not go to Italy, & indeed hardly leave this garden till you return. The days pass quickly for I have so much to do. Marlborough alone is a crusher— then there are always articles to boil the pot!

My darling I do hope you & Mary are going to have good fun. I do feel so happy when I think of you enjoying yourselves. Venetia shd be with you now. Write me all about it.

Your ever loving husband,
W

PS. HMG are preparing a dossier about the D of W's finances, debts, & spendings on acct of Mrs S wh I fear they mean to use to his detriment when the Civil List is considered. 'Odi quem laeseris' (Hate whom you have injured) as the Romans used to say.[2]

W

[sketch of pig]

Winston S. Churchill to Sir William Nicholson
(Churchill papers: 1/298)

7 January 1937

You shall have the autograph your schoolboy seeks.

When will you come to see me? I am all alone now, and am painting a bit.

---

[1] As well as visiting Blenheim, and painting there, Churchill also visited during 1937 (and was normally seen with his easel) Trent Park (1–3 January and 18–20 June), Paul Maze's studio in London (9 January), Knebworth (29 January), Ashby St. Legers (13–14 March), Waddesdon (3–4 July), Stoke D'Abernon (24–25 July), Hever Castle (9 August and 5 November), Peper Harow (23–24 October), Eaton Hall (25–29 November), Houghton Hall (4–6 December) and Panshanger (18–20 December). *Churchill papers: 2/327*.

[2] An abbreviation of a sentence of Tacitus (*Agricola*, 42): 'proprium humani ingenii est odisse quem laeseris': it is the peculiar quality of man to hate someone he has wronged.

Lord Davies to Winston S. Churchill

(*Churchill papers: 2/312*)

7 January 1937

My dear Churchill,

Many thanks for your kind letter of the 21st December. I am afraid I must have expressed myself very badly in my previous letter, because I never intended to convey the suggestion that you should devote your entire life to the New Commonwealth. On the contrary, what I tried to convey was, that the objectives of the New Commonwealth—not the New Commonwealth itself—might become the vehicle in which you could ride to power as the first Minister in this country: I believe it is the only vehicle. Honestly, I prefer to see you in the wilderness than play the part of second, third, or any other kind of Minister.

I don't care two hoots about the New Commonwealth quâ New Commonwealth, but I do worry a great deal about the safety and security of my country, and the vital importance of preventing another war. Believing that you are probably the one man who can prevent it, by becoming Prime Minister, I naturally plead with you to employ and conserve your time and energies in such a way as to bring all your forces to bear at the *decisive point* which is the first essential in all strategy.

What is your constituency compared with Europe? What is our defence programme compared with the combined strength of all the countries included in the League, provided it can be pooled, consolidated and organised in defence of the rule of law? There are lots of people who can hammer away at the government on the subject of defence and keep them up to the scratch; but unfortunately there are few, if any, possessing the necessary qualifications and gifts which will enable them to tackle the larger issues successfully. And I am sure you will agree that it is the big issues which alone will count in the long run.

Honestly, I am not trying to lure you into boosting the New Commonwealth, although as a Society, we are naturally grateful whenever you give us a leg up, as you so kindly did at the Luncheon a few weeks ago. The New Commonwealth after all is only one vehicle, and there are many vehicles. All we are concerned about are our objectives, which cannot be achieved without a leader, whose constituency is not confined to this country, but embraces all Europe, or at least the nations in Europe who are willing to support the rule of law.

Recognition of your leadership will come when public opinion demands that you assume the office of Prime Minister. But what I venture to suggest is that you will not win that recognition unless you go all out to get it, and lay your plans accordingly. Why not make an experiment during the next six or twelve months, using the Defence of Freedom and Peace Council, the League of Nations Union, or the New Commonwealth as a vehicle? Concentrate on a procedure of peaceful change—revision of treaties—sanctions and an International Police Force, and you will be astonished at the amount of support you will get. I cannot help feeling that, in the long run, speeches in the country are just, if not more important, than speeches in Parliament. In the end, the electorate calls the tune. But why not both?

If you will forgive me for saying so, I think you treat your constituents far too generously, and give them much more consideration than they probably expect or, at any rate, deserve. I used to think I was doing my constituency proud if I tried to deliver three or four speeches to them in the course of the year. Perhaps it was a case of least said—soonest mended!!

To wind up, here is a true story which will amuse you. Two Radnorshire farmers met at Rhayader Fair during the recent crisis.

Farmer A. 'Now man, can you tell me what all this old bother is in London. They do say there is some dreadful bother there.'

Farmer B. 'Man, man, don't you know—there is an awful bother there indeed, and no mistake. They do say as how the king has got some 'ooman into trouble there, and he be trying to put the fault on old Baldwin.'

May I heartily reciprocate your good wishes for the New Year. I trust it will bestow upon you the precious boon of a good conscience, which brings in its train joy and happiness, and that it will become a landmark, not only in your brilliant and already distinguished career, but also in the development of your plan for the enthronement of Justice and the defence of Peace.

Believe me to be,

Yours very sincerely,
Davies

Winston S. Churchill to Sir Archdale Parkhill[1]
(*Churchill papers: 2/267*)

7 January 1937

I am extremely grateful to you for your kindness in sending me these very valuable and interesting papers upon the subject of Imperial defence. I shall not fail to study them with care.

[1] Robert Archdale Parkhill, 1879–1947. Born in Australia. A member of the Australian Liberal Party. Australian Minister for Home Affairs and Minister for Transport, 1932; Minister for the Interior, 1932; Postmaster-General, 1932–4; Minister for Defence, 1934–7. Knighted, 1936. Australian Delegate to the International Postal Congress, Cairo, 1934; to the Imperial Conference, London, 1937.

There are good hopes that our tardy rearmament may not be too late to ward off the growing continental danger from the air. The close association of France and England for defence against unprovoked aggression is a very considerable insurance. Nevertheless the years 1937 and 1938 will be most anxious for us at home. Assuming that the home position is not compromised, Singapore is the next most important feature. It is not a menace to Japan, but it gives us power to come to the aid of Australia with all our strength if the Commonwealth were attacked. Its existence when completed will in itself be a very considerable safeguard. No one in England whatever party is in power will ever forget the debt we owe to the Anzacs. Singapore gives us the means of paying it should the worst happen.

With every good wish,

Air Staff: note[1]

(*Churchill papers: 25/13*)

7 January 1937
Most Secret
To Be Kept under Lock and Key

GERMAN AIR STRENGTH

1. The calculations made in paragraphs 2 and 3 of the memorandum, resulting in totals of 4,040 military aircraft and 3,225 fully trained pilots on the 1st December, 1936, approximate to the Air Staff estimates for the same date, but are slightly higher than the Air Staff figures which have taken into account factors for which Mr Churchill has apparently made no allowance, eg, monthly wastage is not a fixed figure but is more likely to be a fixed proportion, and the actual wastage numbers should therefore increase as the totals increase.

2. The Air Staff believe that the first-line strength corresponding to these totals on that date was 1,230 aircraft representing a potential of 137 squadrons. This first-line strength would absorb 32 per cent of the total aircraft and 39 per cent of the total trained pilots, proportions which the Air Staff do not regard as at all unreasonable. This matter was explained in CID Paper No 1241–B (also ADR 52), enclosure No 2, paragraph 4.

3. The comment contained in paragraph 4 of the memorandum is based on two misconceptions. Firstly, Mr Churchill assumes that the 90 squadrons

---

[1] This note, a reply to Churchill's memorandum of 20 December 1936 (quoted on pages 500–2 of this volume), was circulated to the Committee of Imperial Defence by Sir Maurice Hankey on 11 January 1937, as Committee of Imperial Defence paper 1296-B.

mentioned in CID Paper No 1264–B constitute the whole of the German military first-line strength, whereas it specifically excluded Luftkreis VI, consisting of 11 squadrons. Secondly, he omits to notice that the paper in question deals with the German position on the 1st September, 1936, whereas he has calculated the total number of aircraft and pilots in his paragraphs 2 and 3 as at the 1st December, 1936, ie, three months later.

4. The first of these misconceptions has also led Mr Churchill to the quite fallacious conclusion which he reaches in paragraph 5 of his memorandum, that the Germans removed two squadrons between the 1st June and the 1st September, 1936. In point of fact, the number identified on the former date was, as Mr Churchill says, 90 squadrons. But on the latter date the number identified was 101 squadrons. It is agreed that these figures show but a small increase in three months, but they must not be regarded by themselves as an indication of the mean rate of increase in the strength of the German Air Force. In the first place, it is known that immediately before the occupation of the Rhineland there was a sudden increase in the number of squadrons, which was achieved partly by a curtailment of the normal training system and temporarily closing certain tactical training schools. This sudden increase alone would cause an apparent falling-off in the rate of increase in squadrons from May to September. In the second place the German process of forming a squadron is not gradual from a nucleus: complete units, when ready, are thrown-off from expanded units. Thus the first-line strength expressed in terms of aircraft is always in excess of the number which would be arrived at by multiplying the number of formed and identified squadrons by 9. The Air Staff estimate of a first-line strength of 1,070 aircraft at the 1st September allowed for this building-up of additional aircraft and personnel in squadrons, and it represented a *potential* squadron strength of 119 squadrons, which has since been justified by identifications of newly formed squadrons. There is therefore no question of a reduction in the average rate of increase: it has apparently been maintained in accordance with Air Staff expectations.

5. The statement in paragraph 6 of Mr Churchill's memorandum that the Air Staff figures in CID Paper No 1216–B are in complete disagreement with the information of the French Government is difficult to accept, since the figures given in parts II and III of that paper (which was produced in February 1936) led to the conclusion that 'the French estimate, at any rate until the 1st May, 1936, follows closely the Air Staff estimate'. If it was CID Paper No 1264–B to which Mr Churchill intended to refer, his statement is equally obscure, since the information in that paper is dated the 1st September, 1936, whereas the French information which he quotes refers to the 1st January, 1937.

6. The Air Staff estimates for this latter date have not hitherto been given in CID Papers, but for purposes of comparison it may be stated that we estimate 144 *potential* squadrons at that date, against the French figure of 147.

7. The reasons for not including immediate reserve aircraft in the calculation of first-line strength were fully explained in CID Paper No 1241–B (also ADR 52), enclosure No 2, paragraphs 1 and 2. It is not possible to give a complete picture of the Reserve situation of the German or any other Air Force, because we have not sufficient information; and it is also not possible to compare reserves between two Air Forces because conditions are not the same. For instance, an Air Force with a strong industry can afford to do with less reserves than one with a weak industry or none at all. Consequently the Air Staff believe that the best estimate of the relative strengths of Air Forces is a comparison between the first-line strength; that is, as regards aircraft, initial equipment, to the exclusion of the immediate and all other reserves. The British and German Air Forces have immediate reserves on the same scale, so if the German immediate reserve is included, the British should be included, too, and relatively the comparison would be unaltered. An assumption that immediate reserve aircraft should be included in the *British* first line would have entailed very material increases in the figures given to Parliament.

8. The French view that 200 commercial aircraft should be included in the first-line strength certainly cannot be accepted. It is true that the Germans originally arranged for their Junkers 52 aircraft to be convertible for use as bombers, but this policy dates back to the days before the formation of an air force was publicly announced. These aircraft are now in course of replacement by later types which have no such dual function, and, even if those of the older type that remain were to be used for military purposes, they could not be regarded as part of the first-line owing to the time taken to mobilise the aircraft and personnel into squadrons and convert these commercial aircraft into Service bombers. On the other hand, the availability in Luft Hansa of a fine body of pilots and ground staff, all of whom undergo training in Service units each year, has, of course, been allowed for in calculations of personnel available on the outbreak of war.

9. To include, as Mr Churchill suggests, the 45 training 'squadrons' in first-line calculations is, in the view of the Air Staff, equally unsound. The pilots which would go to make up these 'squadrons' would be, for the most part, only partially trained, and we know from bitter experience in the war of 1914–18 the result of any such policy. Whatever opinions may be held on this matter, it should be remembered that we ourselves would have comparable resources in our own training establishments on the outbreak of war.

10. Mr Churchill's final paragraph has, for the most part, been dealt with in the foregoing paragraphs of this note. But it should perhaps be emphasised that the difference between British and French estimates of German first-line strength is, for all material purposes, limited to the following points:—

(i) We estimate 9 aircraft per squadron while the French estimate 12 per squadron.

(The difference is explained by the fact that in our estimate of 9 we exclude the immediate reserve, which the French include. We exclude immediate Reserve in the German figure, because we exclude it in our own British figure. If we adopted the French calculation, we should have to make a similar addition in the case of British squadrons.)

(ii) The French include Luft Hansa aircraft and we do not.

Even the French do not claim that the 45 training squadrons should be counted as first-line.

11. Finally, perhaps, it is relevant to quote, for what it is worth, an extract from the French intelligence résumé, which Mr Churchill has omitted to mention:—

'At the present moment, the German air squadrons probably possess only about 50 per cent of the military value of the corresponding British or French units.'

Desmond Morton to Winston S. Churchill: report

(*Churchill papers: 2/306*)

8 January 1937

So far as can be seen there is no dispute on questions of fact between Sir Thomas Inskip and Mr Churchill. On the other hand, the Minister clearly disagrees with the interpretation placed upon these facts by Mr Churchill.

Mr Churchill quotes these facts as evidence of confusion in defence planning. The Minister contends that the course taken by events was inevitable; that it is not the duty of the Government to know exactly where their orders for material will be manufactured but only to ensure that the goods ordered will be delivered to specification in the quickest possible time.

It is respectfully suggested that no advantage can accrue from pursuing this matter at the present juncture. On the other hand, the main issue is still open, viz,

(a) whether the Government promises in regard to the relative strength of the British Air Force compared with the Air Forces of foreign powers within striking distance of these shores are being fulfilled in practice;

(b) whether the agreed minimum rearmament of this country is in fact being carried out with the maximum speed possible or desirable in view of the international situation.[1]

Winston S. Churchill to Clementine Churchill: telegram

(*Churchill papers: 1/298*)

9 January 1937

Weather here bright. Hope good sport. Much love to both.

W

Sir Philip Gibbs[2] to Winston S. Churchill

(*Churchill papers: 2/302*)

9 January 1937

Dear Mr Churchill

I have information which I believe to be reliable about the alarming inefficiency and most dangerous conditions of the Royal Air Force under the present expansion scheme. I feel that you ought to have these facts but hesitate to put them on paper.

---

[1] On 14 January 1937 the Secretary of State for Air, Lord Swinton, circulated a memorandum to his Cabinet colleagues, urging them to agree to 'an equal number of first line bomber aircraft, with adequate reserves' as that which Germany would possess by 1939. The Air Staff estimated that by April 1939 the German front line strength would be 2,500 aircraft, of which 1,700 would be bombers. The British programme envisaged a total front-line strength of 1,750, of which 1,022 would be bombers. Swinton added: 'It would be impossible without a complete dislocation of industry to increase this programme by 1939, and in any case it is likely that the full execution of the present programme of production will be some months late. In my view, however, it is vital to create a larger deterrent force by the earliest possible date.' Swinton added, of the plan to create a front line strength of 1,750: 'As this cannot be carried out by 1939 as an addition to our present programme, an interim plan has been devised. The essence of this temporary plan is that we should temporarily draw on our reserves to create a much larger first line strength.' The new plan, scheme H, would create a front line strength of 2,422 aircraft by April 1939, as against the 1,736 of the existing programme: but with reduced reserves (*Cabinet papers: 24/267: Cabinet paper 18 of 1937*).

[2] Philip Gibbs, 1877–1962. An editor at Cassell and Company, publishers, 1898. Entered journalism, 1902; Literary editor, the *Daily Mail*. War correspondent for the *Daily Chronicle* in the Balkans, 1912, and on the western front, 1914–18. Author of over fifty novels and a further twenty-five historical works, including *Realities of War* (1920). Knighted, 1920.

Could you by any chance spare the time to see me for half an hour one day in the coming week?

Very faithfully yours,
Philip Gibbs

Clementine Churchill to Winston S. Churchill
(*Spencer-Churchill papers*)

11 January 1937   Zürs am Arlberg
                                                              Austria

Moppett[1] tells me you are painting a lovely picture of the two little silver sugar urns (& also of a little gold box?). I am so glad that you went to Blenheim for a visit—Mary is devoted to you & she & Blandford have transformed it into a pleasant home.

My Darling I hope that what with Marlborough weighing you down & the Pot Boilers nagging at you, that you are not worn out—I wish you liked snow—If you saw it glistening under a royal sun & a limpid blue sky I think you might—It is sweet of you to let Mary & me have this holiday. She returns to you next Tuesday & I go on to Davos where I shall be from the 21st to the 24th. . . .

I notice in the latest Times I have seen, January the 9th, an attack on the War Office on account of the new scales laid down for Territorial Units. These are said to be quite insufficient & to be a deterrent to recruiting. I fear this will do Duff harm. It shows a lack of grasp of the problem & an utter inability to get the job even in hand, let alone done.

Yesterday while Mary & I were slowly & laboriously climbing a mountain we were overtaken by a good looking young man accompanied by two guides—It was Prince Starhemberg.[2] We greeted each other, but I'm not sure

---

[1] Maryott Whyte, 1895–1973. Known as 'Cousin Moppett' and 'Nana'. Clementine Churchill's first cousin. A 'Norland' nanny. She lived at Chartwell between the wars, and was Mary Churchill's nanny, as well as looking after Chartwell when Mrs Churchill was in London. During the Second World War, when Chartwell was closed, she lived in a cottage near the house to supervise the estate.

[2] Prince Ernst Rüdiger von Starhemberg, 1899–1956. Born near Linz. A member of the Freikorps forces in Upper Silesia, 1921–2. Participated in Hitler's Munich putsch, 1923. Leader of the *Heimwehr* military forces in Upper Austria in the 1920s; subsequently leader of the *Heimwehr* forces throughout Austria. Minister of the Interior, 1930. Vice-Chancellor May 1934–May 1936. Represented Austria at the funeral of George V, January 1936. Dropped from the Austrian Cabinet, on Mussolini's advice, and on the eve of the Austro-German Agreement, July 1936. Leader of the Fatherland Front, 1936–8. When the Germans occupied Vienna in March 1938, the Nazis forced his mother 'to wash out the men's urinals at the railway station' (*Harold Nicolson diary*, 16 June 1938). In exile, 1938–55; on active service with the Fighting French Air Force, 1940–5. Returned to Austria, 1955; died at Schruns, 1956.

if he recognised me—Later I asked my Guide about him & if he now had any political status—He said 'No'. And that first Dollfuss[1] & now Schuschnigg[2] found him difficult to work with. His 'Heim wehr' has been taken away from him & made into Militia—He is quite personally popular the guide said, but it was thought he wanted to try some Fascist trick with the Heimwehr—I asked about Otto's[3] prospects & was told that in the present European turmoil 'no change' from present arrangements was the feeling. There are lots of German Fascists here & the feeling is quite friendly to them. They are thought to be having a 'breather' from over strenuous conditions at home.

Your loving,
Clemmie

Sir Eustace Tennyson d'Eyncourt[4] to Winston S. Churchill

(*Churchill papers: 2/302*)

12 January 1937

Dear Mr Churchill,

I wonder whether you would be able to give me a few minutes some time soon.

I am rather disturbed about the position of the Tank design and production, and would very much like to consult you about the matter, if you

[1] Engelbert Dollfuss, 1892–1934. Leader of the Austrian Christian Socialist Party. Chancellor of Austria, 1932–4. Suspended Parliamentary Government, 1933, and crushed the Socialist opposition. Murdered by the Nazis, 25 July 1934.

[2] Kurt von Schuschnigg, 1897–1975. On active service in the First World War (several times decorated). Elected to the Austrian Parliament, 1927. Minister of Justice, 1932; of Justice and Education, 1933–34. Chancellor of Austria, 1934–38. Imprisoned by the German Government after the Anschluss, 1938, and held in prison until 1945. Professor of Government at St Louis (USA), 1948.

[3] Otto von Habsburg, 1912–   . Eldest son of the Emperor Karl (Emperor, 1916–18; died, 1922), and great-nephew of the Emperor Francis Joseph (Emperor, 1848–1916). In exile in Switzerland, Madeira and Spain, 1919–29; in Belgium 1929–40. Doctor of Science, Louvain University, 1935 (his dissertation being on peasant property rights and customs in Austria). In exile in the United States, 1940–4. Returned to Europe in 1944. In 1951 he married Princess Regina von Sachsen-Meiningen, Duchess of Saxe; they had seven children. At present (1981) resident in Austria. Author of several books on political and international affairs. President of the Pan European Union. Honorary citizen of over 1,500 Austrian towns and villages. A Member of the European Parliament.

[4] Eustace Henry William Tennyson d'Eyncourt, 1868–1951. A naval architect, 1898–1912. Director of Naval Construction and Chief Technical Adviser at the Admiralty, 1912–23. President of the Landships Committee of the Admiralty, 1915–16. Knighted, 1917. Vice-President of the Tank Board, 1918. Managing Director of Armstrong Whitworth's shipyards at Newcastle, 1924–8. Director of the Parsons Marine Steam Turbine Company, 1928–48. Created Baronet, 1930. One of the principal inventors of the Tank.

will mention a time and place that would suit you; or I should be very glad
if you would lunch with me at the Marlborough Club.[1]

With very kind regards,
Yours sincerely,
Eustace H. T. d'Eyncourt

Michael Dewar[2] *to Winston S. Churchill*

(*Churchill papers: 2/306*)

12 January 1937

My dear Mr Churchill,

I am so sorry I did not get your letter of the 9th until this morning, as I
was out of town.

Many thanks for sending me Sir Thomas Inskip's letter.

He is, of course, not aware of all the circumstances. To begin with, the
British and French Timken Companies are controlled by me, not by the
American Timken Company which he rather leads one to surmise. Secondly,
although the Roller Bearings for these lathes are a small part, the lathe is
entirely useless without the Bearings, and there are very few people who can
make them.

If I had been responsible for the purchase of the Gun Lathes in question,
I should certainly have asked my sub-contractors to advise anyone with
whom they placed the order that they were for urgent munition purposes.
Any British firm receiving such an enquiry naturally would put other things
aside.

With regard to the Cincinnati Milling Machine Company, it may be true
that only £30,000 of orders have been placed by the War Office in the last
six months, but the fact remains that General Goering is prepared to pay
higher prices for essential machinery than Sir Thomas Inskip. It is also true
that we shall probably have a large number of machines ready for Govern-

---

[1] Tennyson d'Eyncourt saw Churchill on 1 February 1937, at Morpeth Mansions.

[2] Michael Bruce Urquhart Dewar, 1886–1950. Educated at Rugby and Trinity College,
Cambridge. An engineer, he served his apprenticeship at Vickers, 1908. On active service with
the Royal Engineers, 1914–15. War Office (munitions production), 1915–16; Ministry of
Munitions, 1916. Director of the National Projectile Factories, and Assistant Controller of
Shell Manufacture, 1916–17; Director-General of Shell and Gun Manufacture, 1918; OBE,
1918. Joined the Leeds Forge Company, 1919; later Managing Director. Managing Director,
Metropolitan Carriage and Finance Company, 1922–7. Member of the Committee of Enquiry
into Employment Exchanges, 1920. Head of a special Tank Mission to the United States,
1940; played a leading part in the design and production of the Sherman Tank. Deputy
Director-General, British Purchasing Commission, and British Supply Mission, Washington
1942–4. One of his three sons was killed in action in 1941.

ment Factories when the Government Factories will be able to take them. Perhaps that is why it is better not to have any control!!

Sir Thomas says we should be running a very grave risk if we were to ask the industry to abandon all their ordinary trade. Does he regard the supply of machines to equip the German Air Force as one's ordinary trade?

Yours very sincerely,
M. S. C. Dewar

Winston S. Churchill to Clementine Churchill: telegram
(*Churchill papers: 1/298*)

12 January 1937

Everything alright. Going Blenheim again week end. Much love. Writing.
W

Winston S. Churchill to the Duchess of Marlborough: telegram
(*Churchill papers: 1/298*)

13 January 1937

Shall be delighted to come Saturday for week end. Will motor down arriving after tea.

Winston

Winston S. Churchill to Baroness Goldschmidt-Rothschild
(*Churchill papers: 2/294*)

13 January 1937

I made enquiries from the highest quarter at the Home Office, and they say they have no power to alter the law which requires a five year period. So there is nothing doing. I forbear being more explicit but will explain the position to you when we next meet.[1]

With every good wish for the New Year,

[1] On her father's death in 1916 the Baroness had inherited the coal mines at Rybnik (then in German Silesia, since 1919 in Polish Silesia), worth then £5 million. By 1936 a million tons of coal and coke were being produced there annually. The Baroness wished to become a British subject, and to transfer funds to Britain. But under British law, it was practically impossible to transfer money from Germany or Poland on such a scale, unless she were a British citizen. Churchill had made enquiries about the possibility of accelerating the citizenship process.

Winston S. Churchill to H. V. Evatt

(Churchill papers: 2/264)

13 January 1937

Your letter of December 12 gave me lively pleasure. I hope you will persevere in your intention to examine this most grave and untoward constitutional episode from the high standpoint which you occupy in Australia. I have never felt myself so much apart from what is called public opinion. I am sure that with some time and patience this evil could have been averted and that the lady would have withdrawn from the scene. In the new circumstances we have to do our duty and uphold our institutions. But that is no reason at all that the true facts and arguments should not be set forth. Some great new impulse will have to manifest itself among the British peoples similar to the strong virility of their ancestors if the British Empire is to cope with the problems the future is casting upon us. In this I trust the spirit of the Anzacs will play a galvanising part.

In case it may be a convenience to you I send you a little book[1] published only last week, which gives a dispassionate and tolerably accurate account of what is known publicly about the crisis.

Winston S. Churchill to Lord Davies

(Churchill papers: 2/312)

13 January 1937

Many thanks for your kind letter. I certainly will continue to do what I can, and feel every day more sure that we are upon the right lines. You must not however overrate the value of public meetings. At the present time non-official personages count for very little. One poor wretch may easily exhaust himself without his even making a ripple upon the current of opinion. If we could get access to the broadcast some progress could be made. All that is very carefully sewn up over here.

On the other hand I do not think you should be at all despondent. There is no doubt that the balance of European opinion is tilting heavily against Germany, and that the idea of strong confederations of armed nations to resist an Aggressor is moving steadily in a concrete and practical way towards reality.

Every good wish,

---

[1] J. Lincoln White (editor), *The Abdication of Edward VIII: A Record of All the Published Documents*. According to the review in *The Times Literary Supplement* of 9 January 1937, 'until the inner story can be told by the chief actors and critically studied by historians, it is a convenient summary of events'.

Winston S. Churchill to Sir Thomas Inskip

(*Churchill papers: 2/306*)

14 January 1937

Many thanks for your letter of December 21.

We appear to be agreed on all essential facts and the only questions open are those of interpretation. In my view it is proof of a serious lack of organization that when the British Government put out an order for say, gun lathes, they do not know what the consequential reactions of that order are upon industry, nor where nor how it will in fact be executed. With a proper system of control the whole capacity of British industry could be brought in review, and the Government then, when placing the order abroad, would have warned the British firm producing one vital part, that their services would be required, and they would not then be bespoken by the German Government.

I cited this instance not, as you appear to suppose, to deprecate the policy of placing orders abroad, or to suggest that it would have been better to have executed this particular order in Great Britain, but to show the very loose manner in which war production demands by the Government are in fact being placed. I think it is a pity that there should be British firms who have spare capacity to execute urgent orders for our national defence, which should in fact be employed by Germany, because they have not been told that their services would be involved. I feel quite justified in quoting these facts as evidence of confusion in defence planning.

In the second case again we appear to be in agreement upon the facts. They show that a British firm is at this juncture engaged in making machine tools to supply machines for the military equipment of Germany, while our own shortage of machine tools is most grievously in arrears. You say that it is the Government policy not to interfere with normal trade. It may be Government policy and yet not be right. You are under a misapprehension when you suggest that I wish you to ask the machine tool industry 'to abandon *all* their ordinary trade'. I should be quite content if instead of 'all' were written 'all the Government requires' of their ordinary trade.

Of course if the Government promises about the relative strength of the British Air Force compared to the Air Forces of foreign powers within striking distance of these shores, are being fulfilled in practice; and also if the re-armament of this country is being carried out punctually, no case arises. If not, however, if the programmes are falling ever more into arrears, as I am assured, and if the relative weakness of Britain in the air compared to Germany is at the present time marked and deplorable, and not likely to be alleviated probably during 1937, then I submit that not only were my facts correct but the moral which I drew from them was timely and apposite.

I postponed writing this letter to you until I was delighted to hear you were rapidly recovering from your influenza. I am telling your secretary not to show it to you till you are quite restored. Grave as are the times, I hope you will make sure you have the necessary period of convalescence. All my household has been down with this minor scourge, and a certain number of days of complete relief from work of any kind is absolutely necessary for perfect recovery. So far I have survived and if I escape altogether I shall attribute it to a good conscience as well as a good constitution.

Winston S. Churchill to Anne, Lady Islington[1]

(Grigg papers)

17 January 1937   Chartwell

My dear Anne,

I have thought so much about you and your gt sorrow during these last weeks. Clemmie showed me yr brave letter. I do beg you to accept my heartfelt sympathy. How lucky Jack was to have you to look after him in all these long years of pain & illness! My mind is full of memories of all those old days at Hartham. What jolly times we had when our world was young! And then politics—so fierce and active. Do you remember the meeting outside the station when trains made such a noise—and that other meeting interrupted by the Tory trumpeter? Jack enjoyed it all, from the day of Mr Brodrick's[2] Army Corps—& the Free Trade Split. He had a vy full & fine life. I was so glad to find we were together in opinion on India & some other things in these last years.

As one gets old—the scene contracts, and the colours fade. Dear Anne I hope & pray that there will still be some mellow sunshine left for you, & that you will think kindly of your sincere friend

                                                                   Winston

---

[1] Anne Beauclerk Dundas, 1868–1958. A granddaughter of Field-Marshal Lord Napier of Magdala. In 1896 she married John Poynder Dickson-Poynder, who had been created Baron Islington in 1910, and had died on 6 December 1936. (A Conservative MP from 1892 to 1910, he had been Governor of New Zealand, 1910–12; Parliamentary Under Secretary of State for India, 1915–18; and Chairman of the National Savings Committee, 1920–6.) Before 1914 they lived at Hartham Park, Corsham. Her grandson John Grigg became a journalist and writer, and biographer of Lloyd George.

[2] St John Brodrick, 1856–1942. Educated at Eton and Balliol College, Oxford. Conservative MP, 1880–5 and 1885–1906. Privy Councillor, 1897. Secretary of State for War, 1900–3; for India, 1903–5. Succeeded his father as 9th Viscount Midleton, 1907; created Earl, 1920. He published his memoirs, *Records and Reactions 1856–1939* in 1939. In 1903 Churchill had attacked his military policy, and in particular his proposed increases in military expenditure, in a series of speeches published in pamphlet form with the title *Mr Brodrick's Army*.

Desmond Morton to Winston S. Churchill

(*Churchill papers: 2/307*)

17 January 1937   Earlylands

Dear Winston,

The letter returned herewith from the Secretary of the 'Black Front' is of no importance. The book he enclosed has been sent to you before by the author, Otto Strasser,[1] whose brother Gregory[2] was shot by Hitler on the night of the famous purge.

The 'Black Front' is a violent anti-Hitler organisation with HQ at Prague and has as its objective the destruction of Hitler and the Nazi Regime at any price. They have a good information bureau, in the sense that they are well informed as to the situation in Germany, but, unfortunately, they distort all the information they receive before distributing it, in order to make it more in accordance with their own views of what *ought* to be happening in Germany.

I think the Czechs are very unwise not to close them down on a suitable pretext. If, as may well be the case, the Czechs have access to their information before it is distorted for political ends, they ought, nevertheless, to restrain them. They are not helpful and are as much as anything else, a cause of legitimate and unnecessary irritation to Berlin.

Much as I distrust the Nazis, and much as I sympathise with the Czechs I think that the latter are criminally stupid in their internal policy vis à vis National Socialism and secondly, that no sound issue can be based on mere calumny of your enemy and a distortion of the truth.

I feel certain that you agree with the latter sentiment at least.

Yours sincerely,
Desmond Morton

---

[1] Otto Strasser, 1897–1974. Born in Bavaria. On active service in the First World War. Lieutenant, 1917. After the war he studied Political Economy at the universities of Munich, Würzburg and Berlin. Worked as a shorthand writer in the Reichstag. Established a small Literary Agency, 1922. A Clerk in the Ministry of Supply, 1922–3. Worked for an industrial concern, 1923–5. Under the influence of his elder brother, Gregor, he joined the Nazi Party in 1925. In 1930 he broke away from Hitler, founding his own Black Front Party. His brother, who remained loyal to Hitler, was murdered by the Nazis during the 'night of the long knives', 30 June 1934. Otto Strasser's own death having been ordered by Goering, he fled in 1934 to Vienna. In exile subsequently in Prague, Zurich and Paris. Founded the Free German Movement in France, 1939. In exile in Canada and the United States, 1940–5. In Germany after 1945 he organized a League for German Revival. Deprived of his citizenship (the Allies feared his alleged Nazi sympathies) he lived in Canada until 1955, when he returned to Germany again, and founded the German Social Union. He died in Munich.

[2] In 1914, Gregory (Gregor) Strasser had volunteered for active service with his brother Otto. In 1925 he became Leader of the Gauleiters of the Nazi Party in Northern and Western Germany, and between 1925 and 1934 sought to influence Hitler in favour of a more Socialist orientation of Nazism.

Winston S. Churchill to F. W. Deakin

(*Churchill papers: 8/547*)

18 January 1937

It would be a good thing if you could come here on Friday night[1] which would give more time as I shall be making up my speech on Sunday. I send you some of the translations of Klopp[2] which bear on these chapters now being re-printed. I should be glad if you would read them through before coming, and notice where I have made underlinings. You will see that Klopp differs from us on several points. He certainly makes a very interesting tale of the negotiations.

C. J. W. Torr:[3] *Foreign Office minute*

(*Foreign Office papers: 371/20733*)

20 January 1937

The Air Staff seem to have disposed of Mr Churchill pretty thoroughly but there is one point on which their explanation does not seem to be quite satisfactory. It is in paragraph 7. They there state that 'the British and German Air Forces have "immediate reserves on the same scale" '. Yet when in July (C 4922/G) the Air Ministry sought to dispose of Mr Churchill's previous memorandum they stated that 'we consider that our reserves should be on a "higher scale than that adopted by the Germans" '; and they went on to explain that the size of the reserve must depend on the country's industrial production-capacity and on the rapidity with which industry could turn over from peace time to war time production. Unless, therefore, our industry is now equal to the German in these respects it would seem that we are falling behind in the matter of reserves.

---

[1] Deakin had been at Chartwell for several days from 4 January 1937, and during the year was to stay again on January 22, February 20, February 27, April 17, April 24, May 15, June 11, June 26, October 30 and November 20 (*Churchill papers: 2/327*).

[2] Onno Klopp's *Der Fall des Hauses Stuart*, volumes ten and eleven of which were published in 1881 and 1885 respectively. In his own second Marlborough volume, Churchill described Klopp as 'usually censorious' (page 244), and noted, of one incident (page 489), how 'Klopp devotes twice as much space to this example of Marlborough's pettiness as to the battle of Blenheim.' At Chartwell, the word 'Klopp' was also used to describe the metal hole-puncher which Churchill often used to keep pages tied together with 'treasury' tags: hence the request 'Bring me the "klopp"' could cause some confusion to a new secretary unaware of the two meanings.

[3] Cyril James Wenceslas Torr, 1896–1940. Entered the Foreign Office, 1920; Second Secretary, 1923; First Secretary, 1932. Transferred to Riga, 1934. Returned to the Foreign Office, 1936. Chargé d'Affaires, Vatican, 1937–8; Berne, 1939–40.

Winston S. Churchill to the Duke of Marlborough: telegram

(Churchill papers: 1/298)

20 January 1937

Fear cannot come Blenheim Sunday. Thank you so much for these very pleasant visits.

Winston

Winston S. Churchill to Clementine Churchill

(Churchill papers: 1/298)

20 January 1937　　　　　　　　　11 Morpeth Mansions

Sarah and her husband lunched here yesterday. They are contemplating taking a flat. There is one vacant under Randolph's at about half the rent they are paying in the hotel. I have no doubt they could let it furnished when they are in America to take off the greater part of the rent. It is possible that Oliver will stay in England even till the autumn as he has got a good list of engagements.

We have not yet given her any present on her wedding and I think if they do decide to have some small fixed abode we might well see them into it. There must be a certain amount of gear at Chartwell, and I would myself find £200 or £300. I send you meanwhile a copy of the letter I have written to Sarah after seeing Nicholl Manisty.[1] Actually she is entitled to about £230 a year under what is called the Elder Children's settlement which I made in 1920. With your £100 she will be getting considerably more than Diana, but I gave Diana £1,000 for a wedding present and you gave a motor car, so that it works out fairly equally between them.

I went to Blenheim again last week-end to finish the picture. It is getting on slowly and is not yet spoilt. The new chauffeur[2] took five hours, so I arrived late for dinner which was to be held at Ditchley, Ronald Tree's[3] house.

---

[1] Nicholl Manisty & Co, Solicitors, who had acted for Churchill since the turn of the century (see also page 574, note 1).

[2] Cale, Howes' successor.

[3] Ronald Tree, 1897–1976. Son of Arthur Tree and Countess Beatty. Educated at Winchester. On active service in France and Italy, 1917–18. Managing Editor of *Forum* magazine, New York, 1922–6. Joint Master of the Pytchley Hounds, 1927–33. Conservative MP for Harborough, 1933–45. Parliamentary Private Secretary to Robert Hudson, 1936–8; to Sir John Reith, 1940; to Alfred Duff Cooper, 1940–1 and to Brendan Bracken, 1941–3. Parliamentary Secretary, Ministry of Town and Country Planning, 1945. In 1920 he married, as his first wife, Nancy Parkins, of Richmond Virginia, a niece of Nancy Astor, and widow of Henry Field of Chicago. In 1947 he married Mrs Mary Endicott Fitzgerald, daughter of the

However I was most warmly welcomed and in chouette bezique took nearly £40 off Rex Benson[1] and my hostess. We came back to Chartwell in much better time. The young chauffeur is a very nice fellow and I am taking great pains with him.

Yesterday I moved up to the flat to do the fortnightly article. These are getting on quite well, and I think will yield from all sources, British, Imperial and Foreign, £120 each. There must be nearly forty papers publishing it in all the different countries. Some only pay two or three guineas, but they all mount up. Randolph is here so I have moved downstairs and have encamped in the drawing room and dining room. I slept in Sarah's old room which is much nicer than the one I have upstairs. I like the bed better than the one I have upstairs, and perhaps with your approval when Randolph departs would make an exchange. It is a particular kind of hard-soft-springy bed which I sleep on very well.

Would you not like me to give you a nice washing basin in your bathroom? It seems to me a nice green marble basin with well finished taps and two thin silvery legs would be much better than the one you have. I have done myself the honour of installing a superior basin upstairs and would be glad to do this for you, if you would like it.

Walter Monckton came to see me today. He is going out to the D of W on Friday week, and I am to see him again beforehand. He said that the D would very much like me to come out and stay with him, but I said that we would wait and see how the Civil List Pensions went first, and then I would certainly like to go if all was well. But I must not run any risk of compromising on the Civil List Committee.

Herr von Ribbentrop promised the Leeds Chamber of Commerce to dine with them on Monday at their annual dinner, but then he threw them over on account of his preoccupation in Germany. So the Yorkshire Post which is apparently running their affairs made vehement appeals to me to take his place. No one else apparently would serve. (They could not have the German Eagle, so they must have the Blenheim pup. At least that is how I put it to myself!) I therefore consented to meet their wishes. They say it is to be a record attendance.

Rt Rev Malcolm Peabody of New York. Nancy Tree married, in 1948, as her third husband, Colonel Claude Granville Lancaster, a Conservative MP, 1938–70, and Chairman of the Tory Reform Committee, 1946. During the second world war, at times of a full moon, Churchill would spend his weekends at Ditchley, instead of at Chequers, because of the danger of air attack.

[1] Rex Lindsay Benson, 1889–1968. Educated at Eton and Oxford. On active service, 1914–18 (despatches, DSO, MC). Lieutenant-Colonel, 1918. Merchant banker. Deputy President of the English-Speaking Union of the Commonwealth. Served in the French Army, 1939–40. British Military Attaché, Washington, 1941–4. Knighted, 1958.

Parliament has met in a dead-alive condition. I do not feel much desire to take part in their affairs. People are very unhappy about the sudden death from influenza and pneumonia of Phyllis Brand (Bob Brand's[1] wife) which occurred this morning. Also I am very unhappy about poor Clare[2] who has lost her son.[3] I showed you the queer letter she wrote to me asking me to come to his twenty-first birthday party, and referring to the curse which lay on the Sheridan family. She will be frightfully broken now by this blow. Poor Clare, I am indeed sorry for her. I hope however that as he did attain the age of 21 in spite of the curse, his inheritance will pass to her. I seem to spend my time writing sad letters. Yesterday I wrote both to Kitty Lambton[4] and Anne Islington.

The most remarkable thing happened on Saturday last. I was sitting at lunch, drinking my port, smoking my cigar. I found myself thinking quite subconsciously about the sheep, Friendly, and how I would like to give him some bread. But I knew he was too far away, right on the opposite side of the

[1] Robert Henry Brand, 1878–1963. Fourth son of the 2nd Viscount Hampden. Banker. Member of the Imperial Munitions Board of Canada, 1915–18. Deputy-Chairman, British Mission in Washington, 1917–18. Financial Representative of South Africa at the Genoa Conference, 1922. Member of the Macmillan Committee on Finance and Industry, 1930–1. Head of the British Food Mission, Washington, 1941–4. Treasury Representative in Washington, 1944–6. Created Baron, 1946. President of the Royal Economic Society, 1952–3. A Director of Lazard Bros and Co Ltd. In 1917 he married Phyllis Langhorne (Nancy Astor's sister) who died in 1937. On 23 January 1937 Clementine Churchill wrote to her husband: 'Poor Phyllis Brand, she was a contrast to Nancy, dark & gentle' (*Spencer-Churchill papers*). Lord Brand's only son, Robert James Brand, Lieutenant, Coldstream Guards, was killed in action in western Europe in March 1945, aged 21.

[2] Clare Consuelo Frewen, 1885–1970. Churchill's cousin. Daughter of Moreton Frewen and Clara Jerome. Educated in Paris and Germany. Sculptress and writer. European correspondent of the *New York World*, 1922. Her husband, Wilfred Sheridan, whom she married in 1910, was killed in action in France in September 1915 (his elder brother had been killed in action in the Boer War). Of her two daughters, Margaret married Comte Guy de Renéville, and became an authoress under the name 'Mary Motley'; Elizabeth Anne Linley, died in 1913 of tuberculosis, aged thirteen months. For the fate of her son, see below.

[3] Richard Brinsley Sheridan, 1915–1937. He was five days old when his father, Captain Wilfred Sheridan, was killed in action on the western front. At the age of 21 he would inherit 6,000 acres at Frampton; land which his father had himself inherited on the death of his own elder brother in the Boer War. Since the reign of Henry VIII, no first-born son had ever lived to inherit the Frampton lands, of which he was the heir. In 1934 he sailed to Australia before the mast on a windjammer, and described his experiences graphically in a book entitled *Heavenly Hell* (1935). Came of age, 20 September 1936. Within four months, on 17 January 1937, following an operation for appendicitis in North Africa, he died of peritonitis in a hospital in Constantine. In 1939 his mother published a memoir of her son, entitled *Without End*.

[4] Lady Katharine de Vere Beauclerk, 1877–1958. Fourth daughter of the 10th Duke of St Albans. In 1896 she married Henry Somerset, a grandson of the 8th Duke of Beaufort (divorced 1920). In 1921 she married the sixth son of the 2nd Earl of Durham, Major-General Sir William Lambton (who died on 11 October 1936). Her third son by her first marriage, Edward Victor Somerset, died in 1929, at the age of 26, as a result of an aeroplane accident. Her grandson by her first marriage, Lieutenant John Alexander Somerset, Coldstream Guards, was killed in action in Germany on 15 April 1945, at the age of 20.

valley beyond the Gainsborough road where the thorn bushes have recently been cut down. I looked up and down the opposite hill Friendly was marching. At first he walked and then he trotted and finally he cantered, until he came to the little gate on the middle dam where there was once a may tree which perished. It was an amazing case of thought transference and this most intelligent animal realised my intention to give him bread. Needless to say I gathered up whatever bread there was on the table and hastened down to the lake where I rewarded him for his occult intelligence. If you had seen what happened you would have thought it remarkable. It appears to me these things do not depend on the will power at all or on any conscious exercise of the intellect. It is only when there is a thought which forms subconsciously that sometimes it is transferred. In this case the key was simple, namely bread, which Friendly could understand as well as I.[1]

Winston S. Churchill to Sir Akbar Hydari[2]

(Churchill papers: 2/294)

21 January 1937

How very kind of you to send me your card of good wishes for the New Year.

It is nearly half a century since I used to come to Hyderabad to play against the famous Golconda team, and also against the Vicar al Umra team at polo. But I preserve a vivid memory of riding through the streets of Hyderabad upon an elephant with the daughter of the then Resident, Sir Chichele-Plowden, now Lady Lytton.[3] Consequently it gives me great pleasure to hear from you, and also to learn that I may have the opportunity of meeting you when you come over to the Coronation. I pray you to let me know when I may expect to see you.

---

[1] Clementine Churchill replied from Davos on 23 January 1937: 'What you tell me about Friendly is extraordinary. You might show him at the Circus at Olympia next year as your occult sheep' (*Spencer-Churchill papers*).

[2] Akbar Hydari, 1869–1942. A leading Hyderabad politician and administrator. Knighted, 1928. Head of the Hyderabad Delegation to the Round Table Conferences, and to the Joint Select Committee, 1933. President of the Hyderabad State Executive Council, 1937–41. Member of the Viceroy's Executive Council, 1941–2.

[3] Pamela Frances Audrey Plowden, 1874–1971. Daughter of Sir Trevor Chichele-Plowden. On 4 November 1896 Churchill wrote to his mother: 'I must say that she is the most beautiful girl I have ever seen.' Later Churchill proposed to her (at Warwick Castle) but was refused. In 1902 she married Victor Lytton, later 2nd Earl of Lytton. Their elder son, Edward, Viscount Knebworth, died in 1933 as a result of an aeroplane accident; their younger son, Alexander, Viscount Knebworth, was killed in action at El Alamein in 1942.

Lady Lambton to Winston S. Churchill

(*Churchill papers: 1/298*)

21 January 1937

Dear Winston,

You really are an adorable creature! And I am more deeply touched by your kind letter than I can say. Thank you so very much. I feel very sad and lonely without my Billy.[1] I can't get Poor Clare Sheridan out of my mind, what a cruel tragedy that is. All her plans to save that boy from war—What a heart break for her.

Yours ever,
Kitty Lambton

Neville Chamberlain to Winston S. Churchill

(*Churchill papers: 2/294*)

22 January 1937   11 Downing Street

My dear Winston,

Alas, you have all my sympathy.[2]
Fortunately, you are by now inured to the hardest knocks of fate.

Yours sincerely,
N. Chamberlain

Winston S. Churchill to Clementine Churchill

(*Spencer-Churchill papers*)

25 January 1937

My darling,

We have had tremendous rains and the valley is soaking. Nevertheless I have finished your new wire fencing near the crane house, and I hope you

---

[1] William Lambton, 1863–1936. Known as Billy. Sixth son of the 2nd Earl of Durham. Educated at Eton and Sandhurst. 2nd Lieutenant, Coldstream Guards, 1884. Captain, 1892. On active service at the battle of Omdurman, 1898, (despatches). Major 1898. On active service in South Africa, 1899 (despatches twice, wounded twice). DSO 1899. Military Secretary to Lord Milner, High Commissioner for South Africa, 1900–4. Colonel, 1910. On active service on the western front, 1914–17. Military Secretary to Sir John French, 1914. Major-General. Commanded the 4th Division, 1915, leading his troops at the Battle of the Somme, 1916, Le Transloy, 1917, and Arras, 1917. Fell from his horse in 1917, incapacitating himself entirely. Knighted, 1918. Retired, 1920. He died on 11 October 1936.

[2] On the death of his cousin, Richard Sheridan.

will like it. A big beech tree has fallen down in the gale on the other side of the valley on the top of the little pool which I cemented in last year.

The Arnolds have found a house and are going next Saturday. Moppett says they have been very dignified about going; but I think they are most anxious about the future.

Two wild white swans have arrived this morning. Perhaps they will stay on the lake. A pair of black swans are nesting on the island and have laid a number of eggs. It is very early days for them and I hope they will not get caught by some heavy February frost.

I dined with Venetia[1] on Saturday. Diana and Duff were there. Duff got into such a rage and was apoplectic on two occasions. Finally Diana and Venetia fell upon him in the most merciless manner and rebuked him so severely, that I, who was the victim of his violence, had to appeal for mercy for him. All three are coming to spend the next week end at Chartwell. I hope you will not mind Venetia or Diana sleeping in your bedroom. If you do, will you let me know, and I will sleep there myself, and give up my room.

Monckton is coming to lunch on Wednesday. I think there is no doubt that our friend gave Mrs S an enormous sum of money, so that it will be very difficult to have anything in the Civil List, as this would entail bringing out all the facts and would be most injurious to many interests.

Rothermere returned to London for the funeral of his brother.[2] I went to see him and got Randolph to join me there. He told Randolph that he intended to keep up his payments of £500 a year to him for being teetotal as long as he (Rothermere) lived. So that Randolph must give up all intentions of ever being allowed to drink again. I should not be surprised if he made some provision in his Will, as he seems most keen and delighted with the improvement in Randolph's appearance.

Randolph will be moving into his flat in about a fortnight or so. Sarah and her husband have taken the flat below. I am glad Sarah has done this because it is good for her to have some fixed resting place where she can put her belongings. I have told her that I would give £200 towards it. Perhaps you may be able to find some furniture. Anyhow there are a number of pictures.

Duncan and Diana and Sarah and her husband all came to lunch on Sunday. Everything has been very quiet there,[3] and I think we have spent very little this month. I am seeing the wine lists regularly and they are very

---

[1] Venetia Montagu (see page 4, note 3).

[2] Robert Leicester Harmsworth, 1870–1937. Liberal MP for Caithness, 1900–18; for Caithness-Sutherland, 1918–22. Created Baronet, 1918. Chairman of the Companies owning the *Western Morning News*, the *Western Times*, and the *Field*. He died on 19 January 1937. His eldest son was severely wounded in the Battle of the Somme, 1916.

[3] At Chartwell.

small. Also I get the telephone account every fortnight and check it with the past.

I am now on my way to Leeds to make a speech. I do not know how on earth I let myself in for this jaunt. However they say that many more applied to come to see me than for the German Ambassador! Randolph is joining me there. We will sleep at the house of a local worthy.

It went off all right.[1]

Winston S. Churchill to P. J. Grigg

(*Churchill papers: 2/294*)

25 January 1937   11 Morpeth Mansions

I did not realise all you meant in your references to Skinner[2] until the other day when Strakosch and Brendan explained it to me. I did not of course show them yr letter. They stated the topic independently.

You must have had a devil of a fight, in which by all accounts you showed not only your well-known pugnacity but great firmness of mind. Now that the elections are over I expect you will have a lot to amuse you in the behaviour of the various Provincial Councils. Some of us will watch with deep

---

[1] On 25 January 1937 Churchill spoke at the Annual Dinner of the Leeds Chamber of Commerce, on the subject: Fascism and Communism. 'There are those non-God religions,' he said, 'Nazism and Communism. We are urged from the continent that we must choose which side we are on. I repudiate both, and will have nothing to do with either. As a matter of fact, they are as like as two peas. Tweedledum and Tweedledee were violently contrasted compared with them. You leave out God and you substitute the devil. You leave out love and you substitute hate.' Churchill added: 'But do not let us blind our eyes to the power that these new thoughts are gaining. They have powerful arms on either side. Let us first arm and be strong. Let us be conscious of our meaning and proclaim it with conviction. Let us join ourselves to other great countries similarly minded and similarly seeking peace. Let us associate ourselves in that great structure of the League of Nations, which weaves together all forces of peace in the world, which, if it has been found weak in the past, need not necessarily be found weak in the future.' Churchill then spoke of his reiterated warnings of 'the enormous growth of the German army', warnings which 'could not be disputed now'. Churchill added: 'I have on all occasions endeavoured to rouse this country in good time to the need of putting its defences in order. That is now admitted. It is common ground between all parties. But owing to the delays which have taken place I have to tell you that the next two years are going to be years of great anxiety and danger, which might have been easily avoided by common fore-sight.' Britain's ideological stance, he said, was opposition to 'all forms of totalitarian tyran-nies' and he ended: 'We stood for tolerance, resistance to religious or racial persecution of any kind. We desired to see a system of Government which enabled individual families to make the best of themselves. It was better to go down with our ideals unsmirched than to be afraid to stand up for the truth that was in us.'

[2] 'Professor Skinner' was the name given to Montagu Norman (see page 1, note 4).

interest the unfolding of this wonderful scheme of self-government. The Princes who we were told demanded it do not seem very eager. The Indian Civil Service has now to depend on nomination, no candidates of high ability caring to compete in the examinations. The British import trade with India is less than that of South Africa and of course Lancashire trade is practically at an end. However Mr Baldwin and all those responsible for the new policy gained great honour and political advantage from it. Therefore I suppose we must be quite content.

I look forward to seeing you when you come home on leave in May. It will be very nice to have some good long talks. Baldwin flourishes like the green baytree. He has risen somewhat like the Phoenix (though not quite on all fours like that animal) from the pyre upon which the late monarch committed suttee. I suppose you are a regular koi hai[1] now.

All good wishes,

Winston S. Churchill to Clementine Churchill: telegram[2]

(Churchill papers: 1/298)

25 January 1937

Hope all well. Love

Winston

Wing-Commander Anderson: notes dictated for Winston S. Churchill

(Churchill papers: 2/303)

27 January 1937

Page 11.

The Hind has a superior climb to the Hart, but has only a radius of action of 180 miles due to the greater consumption of petrol of the engine, whereas the Hart has a radius of 280 miles.

Accumulation of German pilots due to intensity of effort. They even have flying class rooms and give instruction to 16 pupils at a time in navigation etc.

---

[1] A Hindustani phrase, meaning a person who had seen long service in British India; derived from the way in which servants were summoned in a club, 'Koi hai?', 'Is there anyone there?'

[2] Clementine Churchill was at the Palace Hotel, St Moritz, Switzerland.

Page 12.

Cranwell was increased in January 1937 by 30 cadets ie from an intake of 120 to 150, the course being two years.

Only 5 apprentices from Halton are allotted cadetships and there are at present 3,000 boys in training, the majority of whom entered Halton with the idea and object of getting into Cranwell, or at any rate flying. I should like to stress one point. The Air Force is increasing daily in its personnel. Inefficiency cannot be kept back from the public, as there very shortly will be hardly an aunt, an uncle or a cousin that has not some relation in the Air Force.

Page 13.

The educational standard of the short service officer and direct entry airman pilot is still very low. We only ask for a certificate that the boy is up to the school certificate standard. I have at Hucknall in my two regular squadrons 16 pilot officers. They underwent examination last Tuesday in simple mathematics with a view to increasing their knowledge in navigation. Only 2 of the 16 obtained the necessary standard and the general ignorance was appalling.

Page 15.

There is still a distinct prejudice by the Civil Service against the officer and public school class. The secretary of the Personnel department, Mr Lindsay Scott,[1] is entirely responsible for this policy. He overrules the Air Member for personnel[2] and is the only man that Ellington[3] will listen to.

In 98 and 104 squadrons I only have two air observers in each although I should have 12.

---

[1] Warwick Lindsay Scott, 1892–1952. Lieutenant, RNVR. Employed on mine-sweeping duties, 1914–19; DSC, 1918. Entered Colonial Office, 1919; transferred to Air Ministry, 1919. Secretary, Personnel Department, Air Ministry, 1936–7; Deputy Under-Secretary of State, 1940. Second Secretary, Ministry of Aircraft Production, 1940–46; Ministry of Supply, 1945–6. Knighted, 1942. A Director of Power Jets (Research and Development) Ltd, the the company that pioneered the jet engine.

[2] Frederick William Bowhill, 1880–1960. An officer in the Merchant Navy, 1896–1912. Lieutenant, Royal Navy, 1913. Served in the Royal Flying Corps, Royal Naval Air Service and Royal Air Force, 1914–18 (DSO and bar, despatches six times). Member of the Air Council for Personnel, 1933–7. Knighted, 1936. Air Officer Commanding-in-Chief, Coastal Command, 1937–41; Ferry Command, 1941–3; Transport Command, 1943–5, Chief Aeronautical Adviser, Ministry of Civil Aviation, 1946–57.

[3] Air Vice-Marshal Sir Edward Ellington, Chief of the Air Staff (see page 130, note 2).

Page 19

No squadrons in the Air Force at home or abroad are equipped with either Browning front gun or Vickers gas rear gun. We are still using the obsolete Vickers front and Lewis rear gun. We have not even skeleton guns for instructional purposes of the Browning and Vickers gas gun. Not even at the School of Armament training Eastchurch have they this skeleton gun to train 150 boy entry armourers.

Page 46.

No squadrons are up to their full strength of 18 aircraft and those squadrons which should have 12 are deficient of spare engines etc and in many cases only have 7 or 8 effective aircraft.

Not one squadron of the Air Force at home **or abro**ad are flying an aeroplane which was not designed prior to 1927.

Miscellaneous equipment ie wireless, oxygen apparatus, bomb gears etc are all sadly lacking even in our obsolescent aircraft. When we ask for these spares we are told 'Not available. Contractor cannot supply.' I have at the moment 3 Rolls Kestrel engines which are unserviceable because I am unable to get the necessary spare parts.

Miscellaneous equipment will be sadly lacking with our new types when they are delivered.

There is not a single aircraft at present under construction which is capable of flying to Berlin and back with a full warload. For example the Blenheims, Whitleys, Harrows, Battles etc when we can get them, in all cases we shall have to land in France on our return journey for petrol. It is true that we have on the drawing board aircraft which will be capable of going to Berlin and back, but such aircraft will not be available at the earliest till 1939 and then owing to design will all have to be launched by catapult, as there are no aerodromes in this country sufficiently large for them to take off with a full warload.

Wing-Commander Anderson to Winston S. Churchill: notes

(*Churchill papers: 2/303*)

27 January 1937

In the regular Air Force we shall require between now and the end of 1938, a further 1,500 pilots. The standard of man which is now going through our Civil Training Schools is definitely below the average, and the Instructors are amazed at the type of man they are being asked to train and are horrified when they think of our future Air Force. The reason is not far to seek; industry has improved; the Air Force is getting large; conditions under which the present pilot is called upon to serve are deplorable and it should not be forgotten that the recruiter of the future officer and pilot is the man who is serving today.

Many of our new aerodromes are equipped with temporary hutments of a type far worse than that which existed in 1915/16. Has the Secretary of State visited one of these Camps and seen the airmen's quarters, officers' quarters, mess, sergeants' mess, canteen, etc? Take, for example, UPWOOD which will be occupied by two Squadrons in March; or WYTTON, Hunts which is at present occupied by two Squadrons. The difficulties regarding bricklayers and so forth are appreciable, but as many of these wooden camps will be in existence for two years, a superior type of wood construction, giving better facilities and greater comfort, at a very small additional cost, could have been provided. The economy principle, when it reaches the welfare of the officers and men, will only hit back on the esprit de corps and efficiency of the future Air Force.

The Air Ministry Technical Departments are hampering and hindering Bristols, and other Contractors, by continually altering the new types with a view to the fitting of miscellaneous equipment. At the present rate, no Squadrons will be equipped with new aircraft before March of this year.

Although the BROWNING and the VICKERS gas guns have been accepted as a firing weapon for all aircraft, no Squadron has a sectioned or instructional BROWNING or VICKERS gun on which to train our pilots, armourers, and fitter-armourers, etc.

Although we carry a Reserve of 10,000 airmen, Class E, who come up to Squadrons for 12 days annual training, it has now been ascertained that some 7,000 of these men are being employed in the aircraft industry and are thus 'key' industry men who could not be released for the Air Force in War. Our Effective Reserve, without 'window dressing' is slightly under 2,000.

As an example of the position, out of 32 Class E Reservists who were attached to Hucknall during December last year 3 men are employed as civilian fitters at No 2 Flying Training School at Digby and assist in the overhauling and maintenance of the Kestrel engine. They were completely at a loss to understand why they should have to attend for 12 days at a service unit carrying out the same work.

Considerable obstacles are still being met, followed by delays in connection with the Royal Air Force Volunteer Reserve. We were originally to take in 800 during 1937; this number has now been increased to 2,000. The main difficulties which arise are due to the Navy, Army, and other Government Departments stating that we should not overlap their requirements and take in civilians to be trained as pilots who, during their normal work, are engaged in a capacity which would become a 'key' industry in war, ie,

> 'Jones works at Ericssons in Nottingham, making telephones, and can give up his week-ends and wants to learn to fly; is suitable in all respects. The Army say that Jones will be required to make field telephones in War.'

And so the muddle goes on.

The only solution would appear to be to have a complete census of the population which is recorded in the various Labour Exchanges and, before he is accepted, his ultimate future as a possible 'key' industry man should be known.

No Squadron is, at present, equipped with the BLENHEIM type aircraft, and Squadrons in the Metropolitan Air Force are equipped with aircraft in use prior to the Expansion, and of a design not later than 1927.

Our existing Squadrons equipped with the HIND and the Kestrel engine are desperately short of spare engines, and it is impossible to get replacement of spare parts for these engines. These Squadrons, with an establishment of 12 aircraft and 16 pilots, are often left with only 8 or 9 serviceable aeroplanes.

The additional Expansion, called Scheme 'H', has been generally approved by the Cabinet; this will involve an additional 39 Squadrons on the top of the 71. To meet this Expansion many thousands of airmen will be required. This will throw a heavy strain on the Instructional Establishments for Technical Training, and it is said that no Firms can supply the Royal Air Force with lathes, tools etc for instructional purposes under 52 weeks. This will mean that airmen will not be trained properly and they will eventually arrive at Squadrons having little technical knowledge, working on aircraft which, in most cases, will be of a new type suffering from teething troubles, retractable and hydraulic under-carriages, variable pitch propellors, flaps, etc, thus endangering the lives of our unsuitable and rapidly-trained pilots.[1]

---

[1] Churchill used Anderson's notes of 27 January 1937 as background material during the debate on the following day in the House of Commons, when his main point was that, according to Sir Thomas Inskip, of the 124 squadrons promised for 31 March 1937, only 100 were now to be ready by that day, of which 22 would consist only of one flight each, instead of three flight, and he commented: 'I suppose others will consist of only two flights each. These squadrons are formed very much in the way in which the human race was formed. A rib is taken from one body and starts out on an independent existence of its own. But 22 squadrons, consisting of only one flight each, really cannot bear their part as complete squadrons. They are not in a condition to take part in fighting. They are only nuclei around which are built up new drafts and semi-trained personnel. If we take 22 from 100 it leaves 78 and that is the number which we shall have on 31st March in place of 124. That is to say we shall be 46 short of the promised total. Now, 46 out of 124 is a considerable proportion, and it must be remembered that when the first programme was mentioned in March, 1935, we

Wing-Commander Torr Anderson: recollections

(Conversation with the author, 15 April 1975)

[27 January 1937]

Churchill would say: 'You must always turn every disadvantage into an advantage. Whatever comes your way, if it is a disadvantage, turn it into an advantage.' He would bate Baldwin with facts in order to get Baldwin to answer it.

Churchill said to me, 'Never make a point of over-emphasising. Cut it down. If the need is action you can always do it again.'

Churchill loved Lindemann. If you could get a point to Lindemann, you would get it to him.

You would give Churchill a new idea, he would say nothing. Two hours later, while feeding the goldfish he would come out with the flaw in what you said. He had the power to use the unconscious mind.

He said to me once speaking of Britain, and, as it were to Britain: 'You came into big things as an accident of naval power when you are an island. The world had confidence in you. You became the workshop of the world. You populated the island beyond its capacity. Through an accident of air power you will probably cease to exist.'

One day when he was in bed he said to me: 'I know what is troubling you it is loyalty to the Service and loyalty to the State. You must realise that loyalty to the State *must* come before loyalty to the Service.'

I was so determined that if there was a war we should at least be strong enough *either* to remain neutral *or* to declare war.

Churchill threatened Baldwin that he would bring me to the Bar of the House in uniform and he recited to me the speech that he would make.

Churchill brought me into the family life at Chartwell. He did it to protect me. He could then say—he is a member of the family.[1]

---

already had 52 or 53 squadrons. So we have actually had 25 or 26 squadrons in 20 months and we shall be 46 short of what we hoped to have on 31st March. In order to be punctual in the fulfilment of the programme outlined we would require to do in nine weeks nearly double what we have done in 20 months. It is clearly a serious deficiency. There is no good in pretending that it is a comparatively small thing, that it is just a little falling-short. It is an enormous percentage of deficiency.' Churchill also pointed out that 'even if the full programme of 124 had been completed by 31st March it would still not have given us parity with the German strength at that date, or anything like it'.

[1] During 1937 Wing-Commander Anderson visited Churchill at Chartwell or Morpeth Mansions on March 21, April 7, June 6, June 27, August 1, (together with Group-Captain Lachlan MacLean), October 2 and October 15 (*Churchill papers: 2/327*).

Winston S. Churchill to Clementine Churchill: telegram

(*Churchill papers: 1/298*)

27 January 1937

Wire date return. Am possibly going Rothermere, Riviera, for ten days painting. Much love.

Winston

Clementine Churchill to Winston S. Churchill: telegram

(*Churchill papers: 1/322*)

29 January 1937   St Moritz

Heavenly if you could come here. Lovely colours in the snow for painting. Love.

Clemmie

Clementine Churchill to Winston S. Churchill

(*Spencer-Churchill papers*)

29 January 1937   Palace Hotel
                                                          St Moritz

My darling,

I was overjoyed when I read your telegram saying that perhaps on your way to the Riviera you might join me here for a few days. Oh please do—I should love it so much & really I believe you would like this place. The air is like champagne & you could sit in the sun & paint without a great coat. You could paint the most fairy like pale dazzling pictures—The fir trees weighted down with sparkling snow are too beautiful—The snow itself is mauve pink & every shade of warm white—Then you could do a portrait of *me* like on this post card—Don't I look big in front of the Alps? I wish I could really master them!

Then this hotel is extremely comfortable & cosmopolitan—The food is hot & good—There is such a nice man staying here, Sir John Maffey[1]—He

---

[1] John Loader Maffey, 1877–1969. Entered the Indian Civil Service, 1899. Private Secretary to the Viceroy, 1916. Chief Political Officer with the forces in Afghanistan, 1919. Knighted, 1921. Chief Commissioner, North West Frontier Province, 1921–3. Governor-General of the Sudan, 1926–33. Permanent Under-Secretary of State at the Colonial Office, 1933–7. United Kingdom Representative in Eire, 1939–49. Created Baron Rugby, 1947.

is permanent Head of the Colonial Office & in 3 years has had 3 chiefs, J. H. Uhomas, Malcolm MacDonald & now Mr Ormsby Gore. . . .[1]

I'm waiting impatiently for yesterday's Times, to read your speech in the Air Debate.[2] So far only the Continental Daily Mail has come to hand, & of course it does not give a full report—It is astonishing that Cunliffe Lister[3] can survive the reversal of his decision about the aircraft factory—The Daily Mail (Continental) says Baldwin has now decided to stay on for another 2 or 3 years! I must say that as the country does not seem to mind the way it is governed by a system of 'trial & error' he might just as well maunder on.

Tender love my Darling from your alert & expectant
[sketch of pig]

But I'm not as fat as this.

Violet Pearman to Paul Maze

(*Churchill papers: 1/298*)

29 January 1937

Dear Mr Maze,

Mr Churchill wants me to ask you if you would be good enough to tell him where he gets the tubes of fine madder crimson paint, so that he can order some.

---

[1] In fact, Malcolm MacDonald from 7 June 1935 to 22 November 1935; J. H. Thomas from 22 November 1935 to 28 May 1936, and William Ormsby-Gore from 28 May 1936 to 16 May 1938 (when Malcolm MacDonald became Secretary of State for the Colonies for the second time).

[2] In his speech during the Air debate on 28 January 1937, Churchill had declared: 'We have been most solemnly promised parity. We have not got parity' and he added: 'We have not nearly got it, we have not nearly approached it. Nor shall we get it during the whole of 1937, and I doubt whether we shall have it, or anything approaching it, during 1938. I feel bound to make these statements.' On the previous day, in anticipation of Churchill's criticisms, the Cabinet had discussed the situation in detail. According to the official minutes, Neville Chamberlain told his colleagues: 'He understood that at present we were a long way behind Germany numerically,' while Baldwin thought that, in defending the Government's position, Sir Thomas Inskip 'might, with advantage, remind members of the danger of referring directly to Germany at a time when we were trying to get on terms with that country' (*Cabinet papers: 23/87*).

[3] Lord Swinton, see page 26, note 2.

Sir Charles Mendl to Winston S. Churchill

(*Churchill papers: 8/561*)

29 January 1937   British Embassy
                                                          Paris

My dear Winston,

Would you receive Dr Revesz[1] who owns & runs an organization called 'Co-operation'.

His organ publishes & pays well for articles of Statesmen in nearly all the big newspapers of Europe & America. He covers 25 countries in Europe. He lately published some articles of Sir A. Chamberlain in about 75 papers & I believe that he might be a very useful channel for your excellent views. You will find him a most interesting person, a Hungarian by birth who has lived the last 10 years in Paris. He publishes articles of about 80 statesmen & his organ wishes to create better international understanding by informing the public of other countries the views held by the statesmen of the different nations.

If you will receive him & listen to what he has to say I shall be grateful.

Yours ever,
Charles Mendl

PS. Dr Revesz says that for reference if you required then you could refer to Sir A. Chamberlain, Lord Cecil & Sir Herbert Samuel.[2]

---

[1] Imre Revesz (later Emery Reves), 1904–1981. Born in southern Hungary. Studied at the universities of Berlin and Paris. Doctorate in political economics, Zurich, 1926. Founded the Co-Operation Press Service for International Understanding, 1930, and syndicated articles by public figures in some 400 newspapers in 60 countries. By 1937, when he first met Churchill his authors included Austen Chamberlain, Clement Attlee, Anthony Eden, Leon Blum, Paul Reynaud, Eduard Beneš and Einstein. In February 1940 Revesz became a British subject. Concerned with propaganda to the USA and neutral countries, June–December 1940. Severely wounded by a bomb during the London blitz, December 1940. In January 1941 he went to New York, where he published several important anti-Nazi works, including two books of his own, *A Democratic Manifesto* (1942) and *The Anatomy of Peace* (1945). Most of his relatives were murdered in German-occupied Yugoslavia. Helped to negotiate the American rights of Churchill's war memoirs, 1946. He himself purchased all the foreign language rights to the war memoirs, as well as to the *History of the English-Speaking Peoples*. Between 1956 and 1960 Churchill was a frequent guest at his villa, La Pausa, in the South of France.

[2] Herbert Louis Samuel, 1870–1963. Educated at University College School and Balliol College, Oxford. Liberal MP, 1902–18; 1929–35. Chancellor of the Duchy of Lancaster, 1909–10. Postmaster-General, 1910–14. President of the Local Government Board, 1914–15. Home Secretary, 1916. Chairman of the Select Committee on National Expenditure, 1917–18. Knighted, 1920. High Commissioner for Palestine, 1920–5. Chairman of the Royal Commission of the Coal Industry, 1925–6. Home Secretary, 1931–2. Leader of the Parliamentary Liberal Party, 1931–5. Created Viscount, 1937. Order of Merit, 1968.

Group-Captain Lachlan MacLean:[1] *notes for Winston S. Churchill*

(*Churchill papers: 2/303*)

29 January 1937
Secret

On November 10th the Minister for Defence, after reassuring the House on the progress of the Royal Air Force expansion scheme and the general state of technical efficiency in the Air Force, enunciated the Government's policy with regard to air power by saying—'It is our aim and purpose to develop, as a deterrent, as powerful a striking force as we can.'

In view of the many conflicting and some astonishing statements that are being made from time to time, both in Parliament and in the Press, with regard to the air, it is of vital importance at the present juncture to analyse the real circumstances of the Air Force as they are, in relation to the projects for its future development, to see how nearly this 'aim and purpose' of the Government is being, or can be, attained.

What is meant by 'a striking force' and what will actually be required of it, in order that it may be a deterrent? Such a force, to be of any value at all must be able to reach those 'centres' in the enemy's country which are vital to his existence and the attack of which will react immediately on his will or ability to continue the war; furthermore it must be able to attack the correct targets with accuracy and intensity. This requires that:—

I. The aircraft with which the force is equipped should have a sufficient radius of action to reach the various vital centres.

II. The aircraft must be equipped with adequate apparatus and crews to permit of accurate navigation, self defence and bombing, and furthermore it must carry a reasonable load of bombs.

III. The crews must be sufficiently skilled in the science of navigation to reach their objectives, and in the art and science of bombing, to attack them.

IV. The personnel forming the maintenance organization on the ground to keep the 'striking force' in the air must be competent and experienced, and above all enjoy the confidence of the flying personnel.

---

[1] Lachlan Loudoun MacLean, 1890–1979. 2nd Lieutenant, Indian Army, 1911; Captain, Gurkha Rifles, 1915; wounded, western front. Royal Flying Corps, 1916. Served in the Middle East, 1916–18 (despatches); Flight Commander, 1917. Captain, RAF, 1918; Squadron-Leader, 1921; Wing-Commander, 1929; Group-Captain, 1935. Served as British Air Representative at the League of Nations, 1935–6 and from 1937 to 1939 as Senior Air Staff Officer, Headquarters No 3 (Bomber) Group; acting officer commanding at the time of the Munich agreement, 1938. Resigned from the RAF, January 1939; recalled, August 1939. Air Commodore, 1939–44 (despatches twice). Commanded Heavy Bomber Group, Middle East, 1940–2; formed the Operational Training Group, Canada, 1943.

If Germany be accepted as the potential enemy, the preceding four requirements can be expressed in specific terms as follows:—

I. The ranges of our aircraft must be governed by the following factors.

Assuming that Belgian neutrality is observed, the flight to the Ruhr round Belgium is 500 miles out and 500 miles back, ie 1,000 miles all told—superimpose on this at least 25% extra to allow for climb, bad weather, inaccuracies in navigation, deliberate deviations from course to avoid AA defences, etc and it is apparent that a minimum range of 1,250 miles is necessary. On the other hand the distance to Berlin and other towns in the centre of Germany is 650 miles out and 650 miles back, ie, the whole flight 1,300 miles. Add the margin of 25% already explained and it is apparent that the minimum operational range for objectives deep seated in Germany is something over 1,600 miles.

Against these distances compare the maximum range of our biggest aircraft. Our standard heavy bomber, the HEYFORD, has an effective range of something less than 700 miles, whereas the HIND, the standard light bomber, has an effective range of about 400 miles. It is obvious, therefore, that the Air Force at present can not strike a blow of any sort at Germany from England. Furthermore, our new heavy bomber squadrons under the expansion scheme are being equipped with the HEYFORD, just as most of the other new squadrons are being equipped with HINDS. Therefore none of the existing squadrons, or those in the process of forming, can be counted in a striking force at all, until types of aircraft with a 1,250 and 1,600 miles range are not only in production, but actually in the service. As not even a prototype of the 1,600 mile range machine is in existence, it would be impossible to hazard a guess as to how many years must elapse before re-equipment on these lines can take place. . . .

At the present time the proportion of inexperienced to experienced personnel in twin engine squadrons is about 5 to 1 and hardly any of the squadrons can maintain their full establishment of aircraft serviceable. In addition there is a serious shortage of wireless operators, so that crew training as such has literally ceased and it cannot start on a proper basis until the present congestion in these squadrons has been relieved—a condition of which there is no indication at present, since the dilution of experienced personnel still continues and the influx of semi-trained personnel grows.

In comparing training in the past with the training of the immediate future it must be realised that the demands on crews in the next war will be immeasurably more severe than ever in the past and training will have to be correspondingly more thorough.

Even the most interested and best informed people, if one may judge from the questions in Parliament and articles in the Press, have no real appreciation of what the RAF expansion really involves. The fundamental fallacies that appear to be general are that the expansion is being carried out on the new fast type of aircraft, whereas the new squadrons are all equipped with the types that were already in the Service, and secondly, that the expansion has been built on the base of 57 squadrons of all kinds which composed the RAF in 1935, whereas the real base on which the expansion has taken place was the 36 squadrons which existed in England when the expansion commenced.

It is these 36 squadrons which, while finding the full reinforcements for the squadrons abroad, the Fleet Air Arm and the Flying Boat Squadrons, and suffering in addition the normal losses through time expiry of short service commissions, periods of enlistment, etc, have expanded to 64 squadrons and will, if the present project continues, become 106 squadrons. It must be realised that, in addition, these squadrons have been subjected to ruthless robbery of old hands to form and maintain the large number of Flying Training Schools created within the expansion scheme.

It is only when viewed in this light that the appalling dilution of skilled personnel under a spate of hastily trained learners begins to be apparent, and the realization comes that each one of the 106 squadrons will be, to all intents and purposes, a squadron of raw material and that until these squadrons have, in the process of time, become experienced, we shall have in England no seasoned units ready for any sort of serious operation. . . .

We appear to have become obsessed by the necessity for numbers: numbers of aircraft, numbers of pilots, numbers of mechanics, regardless of whether the aircraft will serve the purpose for which they are required, or the personnel be capable of doing what will be demanded of them.

While numbers may possibly serve the needs of the Germans, the problem before us is peculiar to ourselves and demands, in the first place, quality— fast, high ceiling, long endurance aeroplanes, and pilots and navigators capable of taking them to many and dispersed objectives long distances away. Given quality, we can then seek quantity, but never at the expense of quality.

The foregoing review of the present situation reveals that, technically, we haven't the aircraft, the instruments, the equipment, the weapons, or the organization in keeping with modern requirements, and that, having been starved of the technical equipment, the scope and degree of our training has correspondingly suffered, and that we haven't, in fact, the men trained for the work in front of them.

As a Service, we in the past thought almost entirely in terms of the small single engined aeroplane operating with small loads over short distances. This has had its repercussions in every direction—We have done no training in the various forms of advanced navigation that will be essential if we are to operate against Germany. We haven't even got the equipment and instruments that will enable such long distance navigation to be carried out.

Such big aeroplanes as we have, the Virginia and the Heyford, are so slow that they couldn't hope to survive a long flight across hostile country, and, slow as they are, even they do not possess the air endurance to permit of them operating from home bases into Germany at all.

Furthermore, our aeroplanes haven't got the gun armament that would give them a reasonable chance of fighting their way out, if intercepted. Our guns and mountings are the guns and mountings of 1916 and worn out at that.

Lacking modern aeroplanes and adequate equipment, not only are we not ready for war but our whole training for war must wait on the provision of such aircraft and equipment. In the meantime, training on the old lines and on obsolete aeroplanes is just so much waste and furthermore a delusion. For example, our bombing training has hitherto been done at speeds of 75–120 mph, circumstances that permit of the bomb being released while the target is in full view and only some hundreds of yards away. At 300 miles per hour the bomb dropped from 15,000 feet will have to be released some four miles away; the target will therefore actually have to be sighted some seven or eight miles away. What technique can be evolved to meet these conditions, and particularly at night? Obviously night bombing requires the use of some sort of illumination, but we haven't got a suitable flare and certainly haven't any experience on which to evolve a technique of bombing by flares.

On completion of the expansion programme we shall have a complete 'raw' air force and it will take not less than two to three years from that date to train it up to a pitch of instant readiness for war that must be the essential characteristic of any 'striking' force.

This is assuming that expansion, re-equipment, and the wholesale improvisation that is already taking place, can in fact be carried out concurrently. An assumption which I think is unwarrantable.

In brief, if we have a war forced on us in the next three, possibly five years, we shall be powerless to retaliate, at any rate in the air. A fact which ought to provide food for thought.[1]

[1] These notes were passed on to Churchill by Wing-Commander Anderson. Amounting in all to ten typed pages, the first six are printed here in full. The remaining four pages stressed the need for advances in bombing techniques, pilot training, and maintenance standards to meet the coming advances in aircraft design. In this final section MacLean noted: 'These new aircraft are, in short, going to be something inherently utterly different to anything we have previously experienced and it is obvious to the thinking pilot that they will require a new and different flying technique. If this technique is not given time to evolve itself, the inevitable result will be wholesale crashing, useless loss of life, and more important still, the destruction of a carefully built up "morale". Lack of skill on the part of the pilots, however,

Winston S. Churchill to Clementine Churchill: telegram

(Churchill papers: 1/298)

29 January 1937

Quite alright. Am making plans. Perhaps bring you back myself. Anyhow meet Paris. Write about snow effects for painting, especially sunshine. Fondest love.

W

Winston S. Churchill to Sir Thomas Inskip

(Churchill papers: 2/269)

30 January 1937

My dear Inskip,

You are reported as saying at Cosham on Friday night[1] 'I am sometimes astonished at the complacency with which critics of the Government use their own sources of information as if they were 100 per cent reliable, and pour scorn on what is believed by the Government to be the case. The Government is naturally in a better position to obtain and assess a great deal of information in relation to the strengths of foreign Powers.' You should remember that in 1934 I made a whole series of detailed statements to the House upon the strength and future development of the German Air Force. These statements were denied and others made in their place by the Prime Minister upon this very same official information, which you now suggest should not be disputed. However, in March 1935 the Prime Minister found himself compelled to make an open public confession of error, and all the facts which have come to light since have proved how well grounded that

---

is not the only cause of accidents, the second and equally contributory cause is lack of skill on the part of the so-called technical trades maintaining the aircraft. It is just this maintenance skill which has already suffered so seriously and must continue to deteriorate under the present expansion scheme.'

[1] Friday, 26 January 1937. Inskip's speech was reported in *The Times* four days later, on January 30. In the section quoted verbatim, Inskip was reported as saying: 'I am sometimes astonished at the complacency with which critics of the Government use their own sources of information as if they were 100 per cent reliable, and pour scorn on what is believed by the Government to be the case.' He had gone on to say: 'The Government is naturally in a better position to obtain and assess a great deal of information in relation to the strengths of foreign Powers. It is the duty of the Government to satisfy itself that its information is as complete as possible, and to determine its policy in the light of such information. That is regularly and thoroughly done.'

confession was. This then is one of the explanations why some people, of whom I am one, cannot always accept with blind confidence, statements made on behalf of the Air Ministry about the strength of Foreign Powers.

In November last, 1936, I made a further statement upon German Air strength to the effect that their front line strength was certainly not less than 1,500 front line aeroplanes, by which I meant their capacity to put in the air and maintain in action 1,500 machines. I was careful however to add that this was a minimum estimate, and that the true figure might conceivably be very much higher. Upon this the Prime Minister was moved to a direct contradiction in your presence and I believe with your assent, stated that the true figure was substantially below 1,500. I do not believe that there is any Government in Europe that would endorse that statement. I am sure from long and patient study of this subject that it is not a true estimate of the real military facts. I wish to place on record my repudiation of such a statement and my profound regret that it should have been made.

I notice however that in your speech you use the word 'assess'. Such an expression avoids all controversy about facts. It amounts to nothing less than a claim of the Air Ministry to pronounce judgment without disclosing facts, which judgment must be unquestioningly accepted. But then we have the trouble of March 1935 when this assessment and judgment was confessed by the Prime Minister to be erroneous, and we also have the widely known facts of the mighty German Air strength.

At some risks for a private person of controversial reprisals, I will venture to publish the facts on which I based my assertion of November that the German front line Air strength was at least 1,500. They had at that time at least 140 fully formed squadrons. These squadrons are organized in three flights of 3 machines each with 3 reserve machines in every respect similar to the others and inter-changeable with them. $140 \times 12 = 1,680$. In addition the German Air Force contains 200 Lufthansa machines which are immediately convertible into long range bombers. There were in addition 45 training squadrons of 12 machines a piece $= 540$. It must be remembered that these training squadrons contain the highest class personnel instructors. If these 45 squadrons were removed from the training schools for what is called 'a ten days war' they would all come into the front line, though at the cost of interrupting the training establishments. If, however, arrangements can be made to substitute for the training squadrons other training squadrons from the Sports Verein or Auxiliary Air Force, then these 45 squadrons would be free to enter the front line not merely for a ten days war, but for a war of indefinite duration. Thus in stating 1,500 as the minimum front line Air strength of Germany on November 12 last I was, with the knowledge of all these facts, making a marked and deliberate understatement in the hopes of reaching with you and the Government common ground upon facts potentially vital to our safety. The Government contradiction constitutes a second great public error which should certainly not have been committed.

I now come to your statement about the British Air Force. You stated on Wednesday last that by March 31 1937 we should have, including 16 auxiliary squadrons, 100 squadrons of which 22 would be 'on a one-flight basis'. This term 'squadron on a one-flight basis' is a new one. No-one has hitherto called a flight of aeroplanes which is one-third or one-fourth of a squadron, a squadron. On such a process of debasing the currency one could easily meet any argumentative difficulty. We might even get squadrons on 'a one-aeroplane' basis. There would be no difficulty in making good every promise on their paper, nominal and pretentially basis. Unhappily all military matters ultimately subject themselves to the test of reality. Neither the arbitrary 'assessment' or whittling down of the German Air Force, nor the inclusion in the British strength of 100 squadrons of which 22 are in fact only flights, can alter the actualities. If a Parliamentary Select Committee were to examine the situation with full power to call for persons and papers, as would have been done in almost any other period than the present in the history of the House of Commons, they would soon find themselves in a position either to reassure or to arouse the public. I should very readily submit my statements to such an examination. Would you, for your part, submit yours?

It must be remembered that we were solemnly promised by the Prime Minister in 1934 that air parity with Germany would be maintained. I assert that this promise has not been kept and cannot be kept in any period which we can now foresee. Secondly, until your speech on Wednesday last, we have been assured that the programmes of expansion, whether adequate or not for the purposes of parity, were being fully and punctually executed. It is now admitted that this is not true. It is not yet realized how far short the facts fall from the truth.

Lastly in your speech on Wednesday you said that our Air Defence, ie ground defence, was the best that could be devised. I grieve deeply that you should be so misinformed. Any honest intelligent person serving in any of the Anti-Aircraft Defence Units would, I think, very easily be able to convince you that your statement, made no doubt in all good faith, bears not even the most remote relation to the truth.

It may be said 'nothing can be done in a hurry. Time is needed to develop and mature all these complicated arrangements.' That is the very reason why some of us four years ago began unceasing efforts to have the necessary steps taken while all could still have been well arranged.

Sir William Beveridge[1] *to Winston S. Churchill*

(*Churchill papers: 2/302*)

31 January 1937

My dear Churchill

   If you have time to look at the enclosed before I come tomorrow at 4:30, you'll know the sort of thing I want to talk about.

Yours sincerely,
W. H. Beveridge

Sir William Beveridge: notes[2]

(*Churchill papers: 2/302*)

31 January 1937

   . . . Defence of urban populations under aerial attack is not a question of gas masks or fire brigades; it involves every side of life in great cities. Food plans for war, to take another instance, must affect and must be affected by agricultural policy in peace. But the former is now the concern of the Board of Trade; the latter is the responsibility of the Ministry of Agriculture. Peace Policy to-day ought to yield to war plans, without departmental disputes. It may well be doubted whether, without calling on the cumbrous and over-worked machinery of the Cabinet, this predominance of war planning in food will be secured. Logic suggests that the Food (Defence Plans) Department should have been part, not of the Board of Trade, but of the Committee of Imperial Defence. This need for weaving together food plans for war and peace policy in agriculture has been illustrated repeatedly in the discussion of food control. It is itself an illustration of the last point named above the third objective of a General Staff for Home Defence.

   This third objective is in some ways the most difficult and most important of the three. War preparedness means both having plans in pigeon-holes for

---

   [1] William Henry Beveridge, 1879–1963. Educated at Charterhouse and Balliol College, Oxford. Civil servant at the Board of Trade, 1908–16, when first Lloyd George and then Churchill gave him considerable responsibilities in connection with the creation of a scheme of compulsory state-aided national insurance; Ministry of Munitions, 1915–16; Ministry of Food, 1917–18 (Permanent Secretary, 1919). Knighted, 1919. Director of the London School of Economics and Political Science, 1919–37. Member of the Royal Commission on the Coal Industry, 1925. Master of University College, Oxford, 1937–45. Chairman, at Churchill's suggestion, of the Interdepartmental Committee of Social Insurance, 1941–2. Liberal MP, 1944–5. Baron, 1946. Author of more than twenty books on politics and political science; and of the Beveridge Report.

   [2] These notes covered ten typed pages. The last three pages are printed here. Beveridge went to 11 Morpeth Mansions to discuss his ideas with Churchill on 1 February 1937.

action when war comes and taking certain action now, to be less vulnerable later.

Some may object that war is likely to come so soon that we have no time for substantial changes beforehand. It is true that the third objective grows in importance, the more time we are likely to have before war comes: changes to lesser vulnerability which would be impossible in one or two years might be accomplished in ten years. But some things could and should be done, however short the time. And the other things that will take longer should be begun at once, however small the hope of completion before the storm may burst. We have to become less vulnerable for all time, so as to be for all time less inviting to attack.

From now on, till the fear of war is banished finally from earth, all the economic activities of the country—governmental and private—should be reviewed from the standpoint of better preparedness for war. Location of stores and of factories of every kind, development of ports, regulation of transport, planning of towns and designing of houses, agricultural policy, organisation of police and fire brigades, of hospitals and water supply—none of these things can be left any longer to be guided by the old criterion of greater wealth or more comfort in peace. Defence is more than opulence; in a new war, defence means largely defence on the home front.

Is this a dismal conclusion—that in all our daily lives of peace we must be thinking of the possibility of war? In the main course, it is dismal, as the world is rather dismal to-day. But the reason for this conclusion should not be misunderstood. The reason is not that war must now be regarded as instant or as probable. The reason is that war, like other misfortunes of mankind, is now totalitarian. If we prepare for war at all, we must prepare for it completely; otherwise, all our expenditure on military defence is likely to prove futile.

And, however dreary the main conclusion, it has two brighter features:

First, many of the things that we ought to do now for preparedness in war, will make a better country in peace. Restoration of the depressed areas of the West and North, stopping the growth of London, scattering population in place of letting it crowd yearly closer into the cities, increase of dairy herds and milk consumption, better housing and better roads, are all measures to be desired for their own sake and not for war preparedness alone.

Second, whatever hesitation we may have about armaments as a way to peace, our scruples do not apply to preparedness on the home front. To become more dangerous to others is a doubtful road to peace; to become less vulnerable threatens no man and raises no doubts. To-day we cannot escape making swords to rattle at the foe: let us put ourselves into position as swiftly as we can to rattle a shield as well. In this perhaps lies the best hope of never having to use either shield or sword. If we can escape, as I for one believe that we can escape, any war in the near future, we might in ten years have made a country at once better to live in in peace, and less inviting to attack; the postponed war might never come at all.

WHB

February 1937

Winston S. Churchill to Lady Lytton

(*Lytton papers*)

2 February 1937   Chartwell

Dearest Pamela,

    I enjoyed our day so much.[1] Do let me come again & finish the masterpiece. Always yr loving friend,

                                           W

Winston S. Churchill to Clementine Churchill

(*Spencer-Churchill papers*)

2 February 1937   Chartwell

My darling,

    I am off tomorrow, & look forward much to joining you 10th or 11th either at St M or Davos—as you decide.

    A lovely picture you sent me of the jocund cat perching amid the snows! I am so glad you have found all this fun.

    I will get in touch with you from Monte Carlo. The world gets no better.

                           Always yr loving husband,

                                      W

[sketch of pig]

---

[1] At Knebworth House, Knebworth, 25 miles north of London.

Winston S. Churchill to Clementine Churchill

(*Spencer-Churchill papers*)

2 February 1937

CHARTWELL BULLETIN

The Arnolds left on Saturday, and Hill[1] has taken over all the extra services I wrote to you about. I am very pleased with Cale who drives well and seems an excellent chauffeur, and a nice boy. I have therefore confirmed him in his appointment. Both the cottages are empty now, and the Arnolds' has been scrubbed out and thoroughly cleaned. Jackson arrives on Monday 8th with his wife. I thought this following week when we shall neither of us be here would be the time for them both to get into their cottages. Cale has asked if he may distemper his cottage. I said 'yes' and that Jackson would very likely help him. Jackson will also fit up the old harness room as a carpenter's shop. He will make his own bench out of wood which Moppett will sign for. Therefore I hope when we come back all will be in working order.

I think we have had a very cheap month here. The wine has been very strictly controlled and little drunk. We get our fuel in for the central heating in five ton batches at £9.11.0 each. This used to last a fortnight. I have been talking to Ernest about saving as much as possible. The last lot lasted three weeks instead of a fortnight, although the weather has been raw and generally damnable. The telephones also show a marked reduction. We are having fortnightly accounts from the Post Office which enables us to check it. I am not taking Inches with me abroad as we thought it well to give him a holiday now. He had none last year, and was very pleased.

The making of the new croquet court is going forward at intervals, but there have been such floods of rain that the men have been much interrupted.

Randolph and I start tomorrow on the 10.25 am aeroplane from Gatwick (weather permitting). It seems to be blowing up for a storm tonight. We

---

[1] Albert Edwin Hill, the gardener at Chartwell from 1926 to 1944; he died, of leukaemia, on D-Day, aged 49. His daughter, Doris Edleston recalled, (in a conversation with Grace Hamblin in April 1979) 'the "belted Galloways" which her father looked after when everyone else had gone to the War, and the Flamingoes which were once presented to Sir Winston and were in his care until they were sent to the Zoo; and the pony named Judy. And the Canadian soldiers who were camped round about. And how her Father had to care for the "Fox light" (a rather super amateur electric light fixed to a bicycle wheel, which threw intermittent lighting across the lake at night to guard the swans from Mr Fox). . . . She said how she and her family had hidden in the silver safe in the "big house" when the raids were on: that Hill was an ARP Warden: and how he packed hampers of fruit and veg. each Monday morning, which were taken by Taxi to the station and thence by train and to No. 10.' (*letter from Grace Hamblin to the author, 25 April 1979*).

cannot get tickets for Wed night on either the Rapide or the Blue train so great is the crowd. We shall stay in Paris on Wednesday night and go south on Thursday. This will enable me to see a few French ministers and politicians and keep in touch there. We are lunching with Lloyd Thomas tomorrow who will arrange it. So I shall not need to stay in Paris on the return journey with you unless you particularly wish. I must be back for the 18th. You remember Colonel Theodore Roosevelt[1] whom we met in New York at the Fosters before he went out to become the Governor of the Philippines and on the eve of my accident. I have asked him to lunch on Thursday, 18th at the flat. He does not want company, only to talk. In the evening I have the Steel banquet,[2] so we need not therefore be back in London till the evening of the 17th, which means we need not leave your Alps till the 16th. I propose to stay with Rothermere till the night of Tuesday 9 or perhaps Wednesday 10, reaching you the next day. You should write to La Dragonnière, Cap Martin.

I am much looking forward to painting your lovely coloured snows on which Lavery,[3] years ago, dilated and enthused me. (You remember you did not go because you were afraid of your heart at the altitude). There is no difficulty in getting from Milan to St Moritz or Davos, though the latter is 25 miles further off. The road over the Moloja and Julian Passes is kept clear

[1] Theodore Roosevelt, 1886–1944. Son of Theodore Roosevelt ('Teddy'), 26th President of the United States. Educated at Harvard University. On active service with the American Expeditionary Force in France, 1917–18, being wounded in the St Mihiel offensive, attaining the rank of Lieutenant-Colonel, and receiving the Distinguished Service Cross and the Distinguished Service Medal. Elected to the Assembly of New York, 1919. Assistant Secretary of the Navy, 1921–4. Unsuccessful candidate for Governor of New York, 1924. Leader of two scientific expeditions to Asia, 1927–32. Governor of the Philippines, 1932–3. Chairman of the Board of the American Express Company, 1934–5. Editor, Doubleday, Doran & Co, 1935–44. Author of several books recounting his travels and adventures, including *Average Americans* 1919; *All in the Family*, 1928, and *Trailing the Giant Panda*, 1929. In 1937 he published *Colonial Policies of the United States*. On active service, Sardinia and Corsica, 1943; Brigadier-General.

[2] On 18 February 1937 Churchill addressed the British Iron and Steel Federation at their annual dinner in Grosvenor House, London. During his speech he praised the Government's policy of introducing tariffs; a policy which, he believed, had restored confidence and stimulated trade and prosperity. He also applauded the Government's action in borrowing £400,000,000 for national defence. This, he said, had 'sensibly impressed the world and the Empire', and would 'have the effect of enormously diminishing unemployment'. Churchill was likewise pleased by the plan to build five new battleships, as he had never held the view, he said, that 'the Air would displace the Navy, especially in our case'. He concluded: 'Science in five or six years time, perhaps, will be able to claw down from the air raiding aeroplanes, but at the present time this is not possible, and before then some catastrophe may break out in the world because mankind has diverted the use which science intended for this wonderful discovery and made it a menace to nations.'

[3] John Lavery, 1856–1941. Painter. Knighted, 1918. President, Royal Society of Portrait Painters, 1932–41. In 1910 he married, as his second wife, Hazel Martyn, who died in 1935. Churchill described her influence on his own paintings in his book *Painting As A Pastime* (1948). In 1932 Lavery was elected to the Other Club.

by snow ploughs, but if through exceptional weather it should be closed, there is a train via Zurich which will bring me to you that same night.

Mrs P comes with me, at any rate, as far as Mentone. I am not sure whether Randolph will come on. He may have to go back to England.

Both Sarah and Randolph are getting into their respective flats in Westminster Gardens, one under the other. I have told Sarah I will give her £200 towards expenses. When you come back we may find some furniture, bedding or plate for them. Randolph took the fat maid of all work who helped us out at Christmas as his duenna. No one is likely to cast any aspersions upon him at any rate in this respect! Sarah has equipped herself with Jefferies as you know.

I will tell you all about the business affairs connected with Sarah and the Children's Trust when we meet. She has the right under the Children's Trust which I made in 1919 for reasons I have explained to you, to have about £4,500 worth of capital, without any restrictions. I am making the necessary arrangements to raise this as I do not wish to have a mortgage on the Garron Towers property which may be foreclosed at any time. I feel however it is of real importance to persuade her to tie this small sum up in a friendly trust, so that it cannot be disturbed without good cause shown. It will be her stand-by against those bleaker years to which so many must look forward, and against which they should prepare. I am going to suggest to you that your £100 a year pin-money and some extra money which I will pay to make up for the reduction of interest on the paying-off of the Garron Tower mortgage, should be contingent upon this capital payment remaining untouched in the hands of the trustees. Mr Osborne[1] told me that while Sarah had wished to leave the mortgage where it now lies in the hands of the trustees, Mr Oliver seemed insistent that it should be handed over to her, which of course would mean to him, should he at any time persuade her. However I will discuss this all with you when we meet.

Mr Capon[2] told Osborne, and now tells me, that there is a lady nibbling

---

[1] Henry C. Osborne, 1869–1950. Joined the staff of Nicholl Manisty & Co, Solicitors, in 1883, and remained with that firm for the rest of his life. As Managing Clerk, he handled Churchill's legal and financial affairs during the inter-war years. In 1941–2, when his health failed, this aspect of his work was taken over by G. W. Pardy, who acted for Churchill until 1951–2, when Nicholl Manisty & Co was taken over by Messrs Fladgate & Co.

[2] Frank Capon. Joined Knight, Frank and Rutley, estate agents, before 1918. Retired as a result of ill-health, during the Second World War. S. K. H. Goodenough, senior partner, writes: 'During his long period in the firm he became chief surveyor and was widely respected for his knowledge of agricultural land values and the meticulous records he kept. His work covered a very wide field and it is alleged that while carrying out a timber valuation in Poland in winter time his sleigh was chased by wolves but luckily the horses galloped faster than the wolves!' (letter to the author, 18 July 1978).

around for a house like Chartwell, and even mentioning Chartwell. Capon said he would on no account mention any figure less than £30,000. If I could see £25,000 I should close with it.[1] If we do not get a good price we can quite well carry on for a year or two more. But no good offer should be refused, having regard to the fact that our children are almost all flown, and my life is probably in its closing decade.

Venetia and the Prof spent the week end here and Brendan, Diana and Duff came to luncheon on Sunday. We played a great deal of bezique and rummy to amuse Brendan. In the upshot Venetia went off with about £40, to which I only contributed £12 as the result of a hard stern bezique duel. Brendan supplied the rest.

I am very taken with this new form of bezique which Venetia taught me. It brings about a tremendous situation before the declaration of trumps. If clubs are trumps, the queen of clubs and the knave of hearts are bezique and vice versa. You would be surprised what a shock it is the first time you play it. I will teach it to you.

I have what seems to be almost absolutely certain information from the most sure sources inside the Cabinet and from B's intimate entourage that he is resolved to go after the Coronation.[2] He has practically announced it to his colleagues. Neville who is already in fact doing the work, will without any doubt or question succeed him. It will be a great relief and simplification of our affairs to have all uncertainty cleared up at that date one way or the other. I really do not care very much which.

Wolmer's dinner was very pleasant and there I met Leathers,[3] of whom I have told you, who is the leading man at Cory's and connected with my small

---

[1] This is the first documentary evidence that Churchill contemplated the sale of Chartwell in 1937 or 1938. A year later, a financial setback forced him to put it, momentarily, on the open market (see pages 971–6).

[2] The Coronation of King George VI and Queen Elizabeth took place on 12 May 1937. Baldwin was succeeded as Prime Minister by Neville Chamberlain on 28 May 1937.

[3] Frederick James Leathers, 1883–1965. Shipowner and company director. Served at the Ministry of Shipping, 1915–18. Chairman of William Cory and Son Ltd; Mann, George and Co Ltd; R. and J. H. Rea Ltd; and the Steamship Owners' Coal Association Ltd. A director of several steamship companies. Adviser to the Ministry of Shipping on all matters relating to Coal, 1940–41. Created Baron, 1941. Minister of War Transport, 1941–5. Companion of Honour, 1943. Secretary of State for the Co-ordination of Transport, Fuel and Power, 1951–3. Created Viscount, 1954.

Boards.[1] If I am not required for public work he gives me great expectations of important business administrative employment. Then I should be able to do my books more slowly and not have to face the truly stupendous task like Marlborough Vol IV being finished in 4 or 5 months, simply for current expenses. For 1938–9 we have the History of the English-speaking Peoples, worth £16,000, but entailing an immense amount of reading and solitary reflection if justice is to be done to so tremendous a topic.

Always yrs,
W

Winston S. Churchill to Newman Flower

(Churchill papers: 8/550)

2 February 1937

Dear Mr Newman Flower,

I should be very much obliged if you would kindly send me the fifth and final Thousand pounds of the advance which is now due to me. I am making good progress with the last volume of Marlborough, and hope to begin the Magnum Opus in earnest in the late Autumn. Meanwhile all the preliminary work is going steadily forward at considerable expense. As I am going abroad for a fortnight, would you very kindly pay the money into my account with Lloyd's Bank at 6, Pall Mall.

---

[1] In volume 3 of his war memoirs Churchill wrote (pages 131–2): 'In 1930, when I was out of office, I accepted for the first and only time in my life a directorship. It was in one of the subsidiary companies of Lord Inchcape's far-spreading organisation of the Peninsular and Oriental shipping lines. For eight years I regularly attended the monthly board meetings, and discharged my duties with care. At these meetings I gradually became aware of a very remarkable man. He presided over thirty or forty companies, of which the one with which I was connected was a small unit. I soon perceived that Frederick Leathers was the central brain and controlling power of this combination. He knew everything and commanded absolute confidence. Year after year I watched him from my small position at close quarters. I said to myself, "If ever there is another war, here is a man who will play the same kind of part as the great business leaders who served under me at the Ministry of Munitions in 1917 and 1918." ' In July 1929, at the invitation of Lord Inchcape, Churchill had become a Director of two companies, R. & J. H. Rea Limited, and Mann, George and Co. Limited, both of which were concerned with the transport and storage of coal. Churchill's total annual salary was £1,000 a year (the equivalent in 1981 of £15,000).

Sir Austen Chamberlain to Winston S. Churchill

(*Churchill papers: 8/561*)

4 February 1937

My dear Winston,

Dr Revesz, founder and director of 'Co-operation' would like very much to make, if possible, arrangements with you for the publication of your articles on the continent of Europe, as he has done for those of mine published in the Daily Telegraph. He has certainly given them a wide distribution and my relations with him have been very satisfactory. I venture, therefore, to give him this letter of introduction and to express the hope that you will receive him.

Yours sincerely,
Austen Chamberlain

Robert Boothby to Winston S. Churchill

(*Churchill papers: 2/294*)

5 February 1937

Dear Winston,

Many congratulations on your magnificent article in the 'Evening Standard' to-night.[1]

---

[1] Entitled 'Europe's Peace', Churchill's *Evening Standard* article on 5 February 1937 reflected on Hitler's 'blast of propaganda' against Czechoslovakia, and pointed out that 'This community of fifteen million more or less educated Christian people dwells from day to day under the fear of violent invasion with iron conquest in its wake. At any moment a quarrel may be picked with them by a mighty neighbour. Already they see the directions given to the unregimented German Press to write them down, to accuse them of being Communists, and, in particular, of preparing their airports for a Russian assault upon Germany. Vain to protest their innocence, vain to offer every facility for German or neutral inspection of their arrangements. The hate-culture continues, fostered by printing-press and broadcast—the very instruments, in fact, which philosophers might have hoped would liberate mankind from such perils. Thus we see the Czechs in the nineteen-hundred-and-thirty-seventh year of our Lord frantically fortifying their frontiers, and for the rest sombrely resigned as in the Stone Age to the possible deprivation of life, home and freedom. To this point, then, has the public law of Europe sunk. To this lamentable pit of degradation has Christendom and the circle of the European family drifted or strayed.' Hitler's propaganda, Churchill added, could be turned just as easily against Belguim, Holland, Sweden, Switzerland, Britain, and he ended: 'If ever there was a moment when a League of mutual defence against unprovoked aggression should be formed it is now during this present year, 1937. Then any possible German explosion might well take place internally, instead of devastating the surrounding lands.'

I venture to enclose one of mine written last week for a Scottish periodical, which you may find time to glance at.[1]

I do hope you will have a good rest in lovely weather.

Yours ever,
Bob

Winston S. Churchill to the Marquess of Dufferin and Ava[2]

(Churchill papers: 2/294)

7 February 1937

I much appreciate your kind invitation to me to speak to the University of London students this term to help the Conservative Association in its struggle against Socialism and Communism. I should much have liked to do so, had my engagements permitted me to add to their number. The amount of work I have to fulfil this year in a literary capacity is so great, that I have been compelled to limit myself to as little pressure outside that sphere as is possible. I am therefore sure you will excuse me in these circumstances.[3]

---

[1] In his article, 'Peace or War?' Boothby had written 'So long as the German Government continues to pursue a policy of economic isolation and re-armament on an unlimited scale, we must arm and arm and arm again, and seek all the support we can get in resisting aggression, from any quarter.' Boothby ended his article: 'Is humanity going to achieve a greater prosperity than it has ever known, or are we going to destroy such civilization as has been built up through the centuries? That, and no less than that, is the question now posed. The answer to it will probably be given within the next three years.'

[2] Basil Sheridan Hamilton-Temple-Blackwood, 1909–1945. Son of the 3rd Marquess of Dufferin and Ava. Educated at Eton and Balliol College, Oxford. Succeeded his father (who was killed in an aeroplane accident) as 4th Marquess of Dufferin and Ava, 1930. A member of the Indian Franchise Committee, 1932. Parliamentary Private Secretary to the President of the Board of Education, 1932–5; to the Secretary of State for War, 1935; to the Lord Privy Seal, 1935–6. Parliamentary Under-Secretary of State for the Colonies, 1937–40. Director of the Empire Division of the Ministry of Information, 1941. On active service, HQ Staff, Mandalay Sector, Burma. Killed in action in Burma, 25 March 1945. His uncle Archibald had died of wounds received in the Boer War, at Ladysmith on 11 January 1900, and his uncle Basil had been killed in action in the First World War, on 3 July 1917. He was outlived by two of his aunts, Hermione (who died in 1960, aged 91) and Victoria (who died in 1968, aged 94).

[3] Churchill wrote sixty-four articles for the Press during 1937: thirty-three for the *Evening Standard*, thirteen for the *News of the World*, eleven for the *Sunday Chronicle*, four for *Colliers*, one for the *Strand*, one for the *Jewish Chronicle* and one for *John O'London's*. In addition, he published two letters in *The Times* and the text of a broadcast, 'Freedom and Progress for All', in the *Listener*.

Winston S. Churchill to Brigadier-General Spears[1]

(*Churchill papers: 1/298*)

19 February 1937   Switzerland[2]

I read 'Action for Slander' with the very greatest interest.[3] It held me from beginning to end. I lent it to several good judges who all had the same pleasurable experience. I offer your wife[4] my sincere congratulations on her brilliant book.

Winston S. Churchill to Lord Rothermere

(*Churchill papers: 2/294*)

21 February 1937   Chartwell

I am sending you (1) a better frame which I have had made for the picture. (2) The second little picture in case you like it. If you have not room for it send it back. I shall not be at all ruffled. (3) One of my bed-tables which I

---

[1] Edward Louis Spears, 1886–1974. Joined the Kildare Militia, 1903. Captain, 11th Hussars, 1914. Four times wounded, 1914–15 (Military Cross). Liaison officer with French 10th Army, 1915–16. Head of the British Military Mission to Paris, 1917–20. Brigadier-General, 1918. National Liberal MP for Loughborough, 1922–4; Conservative MP for Carlisle, 1931–45. Churchill's Personal Representative with the French Prime Minister, May–June 1940. Head of British Mission to de Gaulle, 1940. Head of Mission to Syria and the Lebanon, 1941. First Minister to Syria and the Lebanon, 1942–4. Knighted, 1942; created Baronet, 1953. Elected to the Other Club, 1954. Chairman of Ashanti Goldfields. Chairman (later President) of the Institute of Directors.

[2] Churchill had joined his wife in Switzerland on 11 February 1937. Returning to England ten days later, on 22 February 1937 he spoke at Paddington in support of the Conservative Party in the London County Council elections. Encouraging a large turnout of voters, he said: 'Democracy can only operate if the enormous mass of the electorate give their votes as a result of individual consideration of what it is their duty to do.' He also attacked the Labour Party, calling Socialism 'the curse of the world' and the enemy of ordered, liberal progress in every country. Of the international situation, Churchill warned: 'The next three years, it seems to me, may well be climacteric in the long history of Britain. The great cities of the world are exposed to danger from the air. In every city strong, effective measures are being taken, and undoubtedly a great deal has still to be done here. It may unfortunately be necessary for the municipal rulers of London at some future time to take measures vital to the lives of the city's inhabitants. How can we confide the rule of the City to a party which opposes the Government's plans for rearmament?'

[3] Published by William Heinemann Ltd. in 1936, Mary Borden's novel *Action For Slander* was based upon the events which followed an accusation of cheating at poker, and centred upon a series of courtroom dramas, set in November 1930, in which the principal figures included a Peer, and two leading politicians of whom Mary Borden wrote: 'your children's children will read of them in their history books'.

[4] Mary Borden, 1886–1968. Daughter of William Borden of Chicago, and wife of George Douglas Turner. She married General Spears (as her second husband) on 30 March 1918. She published over twenty books, including her first novel in 1924, *Action for Slander* in 1936, and *Passport for a Girl* (set at the time of the Munich Conference) in 1939. Head of the Hadleigh-Spears Mobile Field Hospital Unit, France, 1939–40.

am certain will be a convenience to you. I noticed how often you had your dinner in bed leaning forward on a side table, whereas with these little bed-tables which I have carried about with me all my life for breakfasting, one has no inconvenience whatever.

Randolph started in much ardour two days ago.[1] I can't pretend to be without anxiety because there is always the outside chance. Still, it is not for me to stand in his way, and I hope he will gather a valuable experience.

There is an overwhelming wave of optimism and confidence about our position in Parliament. There was no need to publish this grangerized[2] fore-cast of what our expenditure will be for the next five years.[3] I doubt very much whether over and above the estimates the contractors can earn this year more than forty or fifty millions. Therefore the fall in the gilt-edged stocks shows only how silly the City is, for only very small borrowings will be needed for a long time to come—worse luck.

The effect, however, of the announcement has been largely to paralyse criticism at home. People say 'What is the use of crabbing them when they are doing all you wish.' I know too much to feel easier about it all. But there is no doubt that the effect upon the Empire is beneficial and that the Dominions in their own way will gradually get on the move. Moreover the effect, in my point of view, in Europe will be salutary as a declaration of the general military revival of Britain.

The danger is that something will happen in the meanwhile.

Once more thanking you for your charming hospitality which I enjoyed enormously,

Believe me,

---

[1] Randolph Churchill had left England for Spain, on a journalistic assignment to the Nationalist Forces. On 15 February 1937 Lord Rothermere had written to him: 'My dear Randolph, I am consenting to your going to Spain on the very strict understanding that you will under no circumstances expose yourself to any risk. You will be under the tutelage of Cardozo who has similar instructions from me. I suggest you stay in Spain for six weeks. You ought to collect quite a lot of material for a good book. Regarding my bet with you, you have my full permission to drink the wine of the country and beer but no spirits or foreign wines. When you return you will of course go out to win your bet in regard to a strict teetotal regime. Affectionately yours, PS Never forget you are an only son.' Rothermere sent Churchill a copy of this letter (*Churchill papers: 1/301*). Randolph Churchill reported on, but wrote no book about, his Spanish experiences.

[2] Overlavish. In 1769 James Granger published a *Biographical History of England*, with blank leaves for the reception of engraved portraits, or other pictorial illustrations of the text. The filling up of a 'Granger' became a favourite hobby, and soon other books were produced with similar blanks.

[3] On 16 February 1937 the Government had published a Defence White Paper, envisaging a total defence expenditure of £1,500 million over the five years between 1937 and 1942.

Anthony Eden to Winston S. Churchill

(*Churchill papers: 2/203*)

24 February 1937   Foreign Office

My dear Winston,

Very many thanks for the loan of the document about the Air Force which you gave me in the South of France. I was very interested to read it and am now sending it back to you herewith.[1]

Yours ever,
Anthony Eden

PS. Glad to hear that you had a good wind up in the rooms!

Winston and Clementine Churchill to Professor Lindemann: telegram[2]

(*Churchill papers: 2/321*)

27 February 1937

Congratulate you on your gallant fight, which although not now successful will I am sure bear fruit in future. It constitutes definite entry into politics and leaves you with many friends throughout country among whom please always count

Winston and Clementine Churchill

[1] The document which Churchill had sent Eden contained a note that 'A fairly large number of Senior Officers, prior to the Expansion were informed by an Air Council letter that they would not be eligible for promotion and that they would be retired on reaching the compulsory retiring age for their Rank. Since the Expansion several of the Officers have been given an option of remaining in the Service in their present Rank, such increase of service giving a slight increase of pension; a number of such Officers are now filling "key" positions in the Air Ministry, Fighter, and Training Groups and Commands. . . . These Officers are unhappy regarding their inability to be considered for promotion and their discontent is being felt through the service generally, even by the most junior Officers. If such Officers are fit to hold these important "key" positions which are, in nearly all cases established for a rank higher than that to which they are appointed then, without doubt, they should be promoted to fulfil that establishment, or other senior Officers be given these appointments with Brevet Rank. There are at present 16 vacancies for Air Vice-Marshals' (*Churchill papers: 2/303*).

[2] On 23 February 1937, following the resignation of Lord Hugh Cecil on his appointment as Provost of Eton College, a by-election was held for one of the two Oxford University seats (the second seat being held by A. P. Herbert). The result was declared on the last day of the Poll four days later, the seat being won by Sir Arthur Salter (Independent) with 7,580 votes. Sir E. F. Buzzard (Conservative) was second with 3,917 votes, and Lindemann (Independent Conservative) was third with 3,608 votes.

Blanche Dugdale: diary

(*N. A. Rose, editor, 'Baffy'*)

27 February 1937

Neville Chamberlain and Victor[1] came in when we were half through lunch; they had been inspecting orchids at Tonbridge. At lunch, talk about Winston and Stanley Baldwin—it seems clear that Winston will *not* be invited to join Chamberlain's Cabinet. He quoted with approval a description of him made (I think) by Haldane[2] when they were in Asquith's Cabinet; 'It is like arguing with a Brass band.' He also said to me later how deficient in judgement Churchill is. He told, very amusingly, how Baldwin had scored an enormous success when speaking at the Oxford Union by saying: 'I have always been a great admirer of Randolph Churchill'—then a pause—'I mean *Lord* Randolph Churchill.'

Winston S. Churchill to Percy Cudlipp

(*Churchill papers: 8/552*)

28 February 1937

I have managed after all to complete the 'Great Reigns' Coronation series by the date you mentioned, March 1. Some of them are a little longer than others and in the aggregate are nearer twelve thousand than ten thousand words. If this is a disadvantage pray let one of your people make suggested cuts for me to consider. It is always easier for another hand to use the knife.

There may be a few mistakes and misprints in the text. Will you kindly have the articles set up as soon as possible on decent paper, and send me four proofs of them? I will then revise them finally and settle the proposed cuts if any. I hope you will feel they make a good series. They have been quite interesting to do. You say you want them to be 'factual', so I have indulged in very few generalisations.[3]

---

[1] Victor Cazalet, see page 41, note 2.

[2] Richard Burdon Haldane, 1856–1928. Liberal MP, 1885–1911. Secretary of State for War, 1905–12. Created Viscount, 1911. Lord Chancellor, first under Asquith, 1912–15; then under Ramsay MacDonald, 1924.

[3] Beginning on 26 April 1937, the *Evening Standard* published the following articles by Churchill in a series entitled 'The Great Reigns': 'The Heroic Story of Alfred the Great' (April 26), 'William the Conqueror' (April 27), 'Conqueror of Wales, Hammer of the Scots (Edward I)' (April 28), 'Here was a Man for the People' (Henry VIII) (April 29), 'A Queen Indeed' (Elizabeth I) (April 30), 'A Reign of Splendour' (Anne) (May 1), '"Mother of Many Nations"' (Victoria) (May 3).

March 1937

Winston S. Churchill to Lord Rothermere

(*Churchill papers: 2/295*)

1 March 1937   11 Morpeth Mansions

I am still not satisfied with the little picture, but if you kept it handy in the villa some day when I am in the neighbourhood, or visit you again, I can in a morning's sunshine put on the true effect.

The bed table I am sending in spite of what you said. Its value does not exceed ten shillings, so that if it is no use just leave it behind. But I think you will find it exactly the thing for dinner in bed.

I am very pleased with the interview Randolph has had with Franco which is featured in today's Daily Mail.[1] I think it most important that Franco should keep on this note of mercy to the rank and file. That is much the wisest course he could pursue both to win opinion here and get the other side to desert to him. Quarter was instituted in war not out of mercy but because it is so costly to make men desperate.

There is no news here. Parliament is dead as mutton and the Tory party feel that everything is being done for the best and the country is perfectly safe.

We are having horrid weather. I strongly recommend you not to return to it.

---

[1] On 1 March 1937 the *Daily Mail* published a report from Randolph Churchill in Salamanca, following his interview with General Franco. 'A humane and equitable clemency is a policy which can ensure a reconciled and united Spain'; this, Randolph Churchill wrote, was the 'keynote' of Franco's remarks. Franco also told him: 'Our Red opponents have committed innumerable crimes and atrocities which cry out to Heaven for a just retribution. This they will assuredly receive. For the ringleaders and those who are guilty of murder, death must be the penalty. But to the ordinary rank and file of our opponents we shall continue to show leniency and mercy. Many now serving in the Red ranks are there against their will. Many have been helplessly caught up in the enemy's web through the accident of chance and war. Many are ignorant and credulous people who have been led away by the specious words of crafty agitators. The mere fact that a man has borne arms against our forces is not regarded by us as a crime. We prefer to think it a folly or misfortune.' Franco added: 'We are strong enough to be humane.'

Poor Freddie Guest is very ill and I fear he will not be with us very long. He is very calm and courageous, but does not know how bad he is. We play a little backgammon together each day. Not a very brilliant world is it?

Imre Revesz to Winston S. Churchill
(*Churchill papers: 8/561*)

1 March 1937   Paris

Dear Mr Churchill,

I have pleasure in confirming our conversation of this afternoon as follows:

1. COOPERATION will have the exclusive rights of publication of all your articles of international interest, outside the British Empire and North America.

2. You will let us have in Paris, at your earliest possible convenience, three copies of all your articles, so that we should be able to arrange for translations and, if possible, simultaneous publication in all countries.

3. The arrangements existing between you and continental newspapers will be taken over and carried out by COOPERATION. These newspapers are the following which now pay for each article:

Paris Soir	£9.	9.	0.
Telegraaf, Amsterdam	£5.	5.	0.
Dagens Nyheter, Stockholm	£4.	4.	0.
Berlingske Tidende, Copenhagen	£4.	9.	0.

Needless to say we shall do our utmost to retain friendly relations with these newspapers. We shall try, however, after some time to improve the terms for the publication of your articles in France, Holland, Denmark and Sweden, but we shall give you information in advance of all possible changes, and nothing will be undertaken with-out your consent.

4. We shall collect the payments of these four newspapers which shall be remitted to you entirely without any deduction.

5. Concerning publication in other countries, 50% of the gross proceeds will be remitted to you as remuneration. All our expenses, such as travelling, telegrams, telephones, stereotyping, circulating, etc, will be covered out of the remaining 50%.

6. This arrangement will come into force in the middle of March. . . .[1]

---

[1] Churchill had met Revesz at Morpeth Mansions on 25 February 1937 and again on 1 March 1937. As a result of these two meetings, Churchill agreed that 'Cooperation' would handle all Churchill's non-British, non-Empire and non-USA rights, and would pay Churchill

Sir Maurice Hankey to Sir Thomas Inskip and Stanley Baldwin

(*Hankey papers*)

1 March 1937   Committee of Imperial Defence
Confidential

Yesterday (Sunday) Mr Churchill telephoned me from his home, which is near to my own, to enquire, first, whether his latest Memorandum on the strength of the German Air Force had been circulated to the Committee of Imperial Defence, and, second, whether he was to receive a copy of the Air Staff's comments.

I replied that I could not carry these matters completely in my head, but that, according to my own recollection, both Mr Churchill's Memorandum and the Air Staff Comments had been printed and circulated to the Committee of Imperial Defence, but that I had not had authority for any further distribution. This I have since found to be correct. He asked me to look into the question, and made the observation that if he was not to receive the Comments he would consider himself free to circulate his own Memorandum to any of his friends whom he might think fit. His manner was irritable.

I have spoken on the telephone to Lord Swinton on this subject, and he has suggested that as the matter has a political bearing I should submit to the Minister for Co-ordination of Defence and the Prime Minister the question of whether Mr Churchill should receive a copy of the Air Staff's criticisms. I am sending a copy also to the Chancellor of the Exchequer.

In order to appreciate the circumstances in which Mr Churchill's latest Memorandum came to be written it is necessary to go back to the early days of the Air Defence Research Committee.

The exchange of information with Mr Churchill began in September, 1935, when an Air Staff Paper on the Training and Organisation of the

---

60% of the proceeds, with a guaranteed minimum of £25 for each article sold. Other users of 'Cooperation', which called itself a 'Press Service for International Understanding', were Sir Austen Chamberlain, Lord Cecil of Chelwood, Sir Herbert Samuel, Leon Blum and Pierre-Etienne Flandin. On 31 May 1937 Churchill wrote to Revesz: 'I am considering the whole of the question of the handling of my foreign material with a strong desire that you should undertake it,' and Revesz was formally appointed on 17 June 1937. In October, when some of Churchill's articles were reprinted without permission, Revesz tracked down the culprits and obtained payments. Churchill wrote to him on 29 October 1937; 'I do not think we shall be pirated again. However you must be the judge of this. I really can do no more at this end.' By the end of 1937 Revesz had placed Churchill's articles in twenty-two European newspapers, in Paris, Copenhagen, Stockholm, Brussels, Luxembourg, Rotterdam, Oslo, Trondheim, Helsinki, Riga, Kovno, Tallinn, Prague, Zurich, St Gallen, Lucerne, Geneva, Vienna, Warsaw, Belgrade, Bucharest and Budapest. Thus Churchill's views became known, not only in the capital cities of Europe, but in many provincial towns. Revesz had also placed Churchill's articles in Sao Paolo, Buenos Aires and Cairo.

German Air Force (CID 1189–B) was placed before the Air Defence Research Committee, of which Mr Churchill is a member. The Paper at present under consideration is the third critique of Air Staff information which Mr Churchill has put forward.

It will be noticed that until the present occasion, Mr Churchill's Memoranda and the Air Staff replies were circulated not only to the Committee of Imperial Defence but also to the Air Defence Research Committee. The reason for not circulating it to the Air Defence Research Committee on the present occasion was partly that the Secretary of State for Air was not encouraged by Mr Churchill's attitude to give him further inside information, and partly that some specially secret information, happening to confirm our information from other sources, has been received, which, for reasons I need not enter into, has been communicated only to members of the Cabinet and not to any of the Sub-Committees of the Committee of Imperial Defence, and which, therefore, would not be communicated to Mr Churchill.

So far as I can see, there is no advantage in continuing this controversy with Mr Churchill. The real disagreement is not so much on the figures as on the deductions to be drawn from the figures. So far as I can judge from the Papers, Mr Churchill's deductions have always been made on the same basis, and the Air Staff have always made substantially the same reply. But, as political considerations are involved, I hesitate to recommend the cessation of the exchange of views.

If Ministers should decide to discontinue the controversy I suggest that the best way of ending it would be for them to instruct me to inform Mr Churchill quite frankly that within the last few weeks we have opened up new sources of information which we believe to be of great realiability and which it has been possible to test for accuracy in many details by other reliable information, but which is of so secret a character that it has been decided to communicate it only to members of the Cabinet. To continue the exchange of views with Mr Churchill without this information involves so much unreality that it is really not worth while, as probably he himself will agree.

I should add that, so far as I am able to judge, the Air Staff criticisms of Mr Churchill's latest Paper do not use the latest source of information, and, consequently, if it were desired to end the discussion on a friendly note, there would appear to be no objection to sending the criticism to him at the same time as a confidential letter to the above effect.

M. P. A. Hankey

Sir Maurice Hankey to Winston S. Churchill

(*Churchill papers: 25/12*)

1 March 1937   Committee of Imperial Defence
Confidential

Dear Winston,

I have looked into the facts as regards the circulation of your last Paper on the German figures.

You will remember that shortly after its receipt we sent you a roneo-ed or typewritten copy.

Your Paper was, as before, sent to the Air Ministry, and in due course we received the Air Staff's comments. Your Paper and the Comments were printed separately and sent to the Committee of Imperial Defence. On this occasion, however, it was decided not to send them to the Air Defence Research Committee. Consequently I had no authority to give them any distribution beyond the normal Committee of Imperial Defence distribution.

I am re-opening the question and hope to send you a further letter in a day or two.

Yours sincerely,
M. P. A. Hankey

Winston S. Churchill to Sir Maurice Hankey

(*Churchill papers: 25/12*)

2 March 1937

I am glad the paper in question has been circulated to the members of the CID. It is a matter of indifference to me whether I am shown the Departmental reply. The first of this series of papers was sent me more than a year ago. I was surprised at receiving it, as it clearly stood altogether outside the work of the Research Committee. Since then there has been this long interchange of argument. I consider my responsibility is discharged when I have commented on any paper which is sent me. A civil acknowledgment promising consideration of the views expressed is all that could be asked, and that is not necessary now.

Sir Maurice Hankey to Winston S. Churchill

(*Churchill papers: 25/12*)

4 March 1937   Committee of Imperial Defence
Confidential

Dear Winston,

Many thanks for your letter of the 2nd March. Before receiving it, as I mentioned in my last letter, I had raised the question as to sending you the Air Staff's comments on your latest Memorandum on the German Air figures.

Although the observations of the Air Staff have not been communicated to the Air Defence Research Committee, the Secretary of State for Air has decided that he would like you to see them. I accordingly enclose a copy (CID 1296–B).[1]

As you say in your letter, Memoranda of this kind are altogether outside the work of the Research Committee, and it is not proposed in future to send them to that body.

Yours sincerely,
M. P. A. Hankey

Lord Rothermere to Winston S. Churchill

(*Churchill papers: 2/295*)

4 March 1937   La Dragonnière
                               Cap Martin

My dear Winston

Many thanks for the picture and frame which have arrived. I prefer the picture you have sent to the one you left here. They are both good but the second one has more atmosphere about it.

I am returning to London for a few days when I shall hope to use the bed-table you so kindly sent.

This is a very cold dreary day. However I do not doubt that it is better than London.

Randolph's interview with Franco was extraordinarily good. It seems to me that Franco is acting very wisely and will make a good dictator.

Yours always,
Harold R

---

[1] For Professor Lindemann's comment on Committee of Imperial Defence paper 1296–B, see pages 617–19.

Winston S. Churchill to Allan Clark

(*Churchill papers: 2/309*)

4 March 1937
Confidential

I should be interested to know what has happened about your forging plant. I gathered that your interview with Sir Thomas Inskip was fruitless, that the Government did nothing, but that you at your own risk and expense brought the plans over here. At any rate the Air Minister, speaking confidentially the other day, dilated upon the enormous advantages of this plant, and explained how he had acquired and set one up, I believe in South Wales. In view of the interest you have taken in this matter, I should be glad to know whether this was your plant, and generally how the matter stands. Perhaps you will kindly let me know confidentially.

Winston S. Churchill to Sir Robert Vansittart

(*Churchill papers: 2/295*)

5 March 1937
Secret

This letter[1] touches on what you mentioned to me the other evening last week. I have been reflecting upon it and am very much inclined to make a move. Can you give me in a nutshell the outlines of the danger you had in mind. Naturally I should not bring you in in any way.

PS. I made a preliminary reference to it yesterday in the House.[2] It was taken up by all sides.

[1] A letter from A. W. F. Garnier, of Singapore.

[2] During the course of his speech on the Defence Loans Bill on 4 March 1937, Churchill said: 'There is a serious issue, which I am bringing forward on another occasion, raised by the fact of the large number of foreigners in this country who now since the war are all held together by bonds of Nazi and Fascist organisation. That is a new feature, and it is a matter which certainly will have to be considered. In my view there are any number of facts about which we have no good information in this House, on which probably foreign general staffs are perfectly well informed. When the Fleet went to the Mediterranean a year and a half ago the movements of every ship were printed in every paper on the Continent. The only country which was unable to form any opinion about it was the one which was vitally interested.'

Andrew McLaren[1] to Winston S. Churchill

(Churchill papers: 2/295)

5 March 1937

My dear Winston,

Sorry I was called out of the House before you concluded your speech. I was very much interested in and in hearty agreement with what you said.

Your point about foreigners floating about England needs driving home. Thanks for the speech.

Yours sincerely,
Andrew McLaren

Violet Pearman to Winston S. Churchill

(Churchill papers: 2/317)

5 March 1937

Mr Boothby rang up to say that he has just spoken to Dr Weizmann[2] and passed his message on to you at once.

Dr Weizmann is most anxious to see you before you give your evidence before the Palestine Cttee[3] and would not take up much of your time. He has some very important facts to lay before you of some new development, and thinks you should hear this.

His number is Museum 3817 and will you please get into direct touch with him.

---

[1] Andrew MacLaren, 1883–1975. Educated at Technical College and Glasgow School of Art. An engineer, later engaged in journalism and art. Labour MP for Burslem, 1922–3, 1924–31 and 1935–45. His principal political interest was in the taxation of land values.

[2] Chaim Weizmann, 1874–1952. Born in Russia, educated in Germany. Reader in Biochemistry, University of Manchester, 1906. Naturalized as a British subject, 1910. Director Admiralty Laboratories, 1916–19. President of the World Zionist Organization, and of the Jewish Agency for Palestine, 1921–31 and 1935–46. Chairman, Board of Governors, Hebrew University of Jerusalem, 1932–50. Adviser to the Ministry of Supply, London, 1939–45. First President of the State of Israel from 1949 until his death. His eldest son, Flight-Lieutenant Michael Weizmann, RAF, was killed in action in 1942.

[3] The Royal Commission on Palestine, headed by Lord Peel. For a verbatim transcript of Churchill's secret evidence, given on 12 March 1937, printed in this volume in full, see pages 596–617.

Wing-Commander Anderson to Violet Pearman

(*Churchill papers: 2/303*)

5 March 1937

Station Headquarters,
Royal Air Force,
Hucknall, Notts.

Dear Mrs Pearman,

I am trying to obtain what you require; as far as I can remember I also sent the Professor a copy. In the meantime I am sending three letters of interest. One is from Air Commodore Tedder,[1] Air Officer Commanding, Singapore and the reference refers to the Navy; the combined Air Forces in these exercises have completely shaken the Admiralty. The letter marked 'B' is from an aircraft apprentice at Halton.

We at present have 4,000 boys under training at Halton and this number is to be increased to 7,000, but the letter does show that all is not well, and the information is from the man on the spot. I gave this letter to the Officer in Charge of Technical Training at the Air Ministry who, incidentally, is an Officer who was informed prior to the expansion that he would not be promoted, and is merely permitted to extend his service year by year. His answer was, 'who cares' and 'in any case he was not going to worry'.

The other letter marked 'C' gives indication that all is not well with our new Pilots. I appreciate all three letters are rather a waste of time, but it will give you a true atmosphere. I would awfully like Rothermere to have the Halton letter ('B').

Wing Commander Rowley has now been posted to the Air Ministry and is working in the Directorate of Operations and Intelligence under Group Captain R. D. Oxland,[2] and is responsible for the policy regarding new aircraft.

Your very sincerely,
C. T. Anderson

[1] Arthur William Tedder, 1890–1967. Educated at Whitgift and Magdalene College, Cambridge. Colonial Service (Fiji), 1914. On active service, Royal Flying Corps, France, 1915–17 and Egypt, 1918–19 (despatches thrice). Commanded 207 Squadron, Constantinople, 1922–3; Royal Naval Staff College, 1923–4; No 2 Flying Training School, 1924–6. Director, RAF Staff College, 1921–9. Director of Training, Air Ministry, 1934–6. Air Officer Commanding RAF Singapore, 1936–8. Director-General, Research and Development, Air Ministry, 1938–40. Deputy Air Officer C-in-C, RAF Middle East, 1940–1; Air Officer C-in-C, RAF, Middle East, 1941–3. Knighted, 1942. Air Commander-in-Chief, Mediterranean Air Command, 1943. Deputy Supreme Commander (under General Eisenhower), 1943–5. Created Baron, 1946. Chief of the Air Staff, and First and Senior Air Member, Air Council, 1946–50. Chairman, British Joint Services Mission, Washington, 1950–1. Chancellor of the University of Cambridge from 1950 until his death.

[2] Robert Dickenson Oxland, 1889–1959. Joined the Royal Flying Corps, 1915; Royal Air Force, 1918. Director of Operations and Intelligence, Air Ministry, 1937. Retired, 1946, with the rank of Air Vice-Marshal.

Winston S. Churchill to Bernard Baruch: telegram

(*Churchill papers: 1/298*)

5 March 1937

Deepest gratitude for your wonderful neutrality Bill. Would it do harm if we showed ourselves pleased about it over here.[1] Warmest regards.

W

Winston S. Churchill to Bernard Baruch: telegram

(*Churchill papers: 1/298*)

8 March 1937

Was only congratulating you on cash and carry bill passing Senate.[2] Will it do harm with your public opinion if I praise this Commons Thursday as most friendly act.[3] Regards

Winston

[1] During his speech on the Defence Loans Bill on 4 March 1937, Churchill had said: 'We must not undervalue the enormous power and security which we would derive from the British Navy in any quarrel in which the right feeling of the United States was not withdrawn from the British Empire.'

[2] In the early months of 1937, as a result of the Spanish Civil War, President Roosevelt took the opportunity to amend the 1935 and 1936 Neutrality Acts, in order to allow United States arms to be delivered to other States, with the 'cash-and-carry' proviso that consignments should be paid for in cash and collected by their purchasers. This provision finally came into effect by a joint resolution of Congress on 1 May 1937.

[3] Churchill did not speak about the new American bill when he next spoke in the House of Commons, on 11 March 1937, during the Navy Estimate debate. But he did say, about the Washington Naval Agreement: 'I earnestly hope that the United States will not fall below the level of that parity and will not fail to produce their equal quota. Indeed, I think there is not much danger that they will fail to do so. Thus we must contemplate the immediate and simultaneous construction of the capital ships (the combined British and American construction for the coming year) of the highest class, not obsolete in type or invalid, but with all the new developments . . . we must contemplate, I say, the construction simultaneously of ten of these great ships by the English-speaking Powers.' Churchill made his first public comment on the amended Neutrality Act in his *Evening Standard* article of 31 May 1937, 'America Looks At Europe', when he wrote: 'The doctrine of "cash and carry" means that no American ships will carry supplies to the warring countries, but if these countries choose to present themselves in ships at the American doorstep with ready money in their hands they will be allowed to buy non-military supplies. This arrangement certainly has the merit of rendering to superior sea power its full deserts. It avoids for Great Britain, if engaged in war, the danger of any dispute with the United States such as caused so much anxiety in 1914 and 1915. It may be rather chilling comfort, but it is comfort none the less.'

Allan Clark to Winston S. Churchill

(*Churchill papers: 2/309*)

8 March 1937 The Plessey Company Limited

Dear Mr Churchill,

Many thanks for your letter of the 4th instant to which I regret I have not replied before, but I have only just returned from Germany.

The position is this. As I wrote you on the 26th October, up to that time we had been definitely turned down by the War Office, and we ourselves had ordered a complete unit of plant for delivery in April of this year. I however, did not let this matter rest after writing to you, and in the beginning of November I approached the Air Ministry and told them the same story as I told the War Office in April of last year. They believed what I said, and accepted my invitation to take over one of their principal technical Officers to see the German plant working. As a result of that trip, they authorised us to act as Agents on their behalf to order another unit of plant which is to be set up in South Wales.

This we have done, but unfortunately so much time has been lost that delivery of this particular plant will not be until round about next August.

One of the reasons of our recent visit to Berlin was to see whether we could not urge forward delivery, but I am afraid that in view of the tremendous commitments with the German Manufacturers for plant suitable for armament production, together with armaments of all descriptions, it is practically an impossibility to get a better delivery promise than next August.

Therefore the position is this, that we have our own plant which we are erecting at our own expense near to us here on the North Circular Road. We are also installing on behalf of the Air Ministry a plant in South Wales.

We have once again approached the War Office and told them exactly what we are doing, and have offered them the first refusal of the facilities of our own plant. Up to the moment they inform us that they will invite us to tender sometime in the near future.

Such is the present position, and if you so desire it, I shall be glad to call on you if you are interested in hearing a few facts about production of armaments on the Continent.

I take the liberty of enclosing a couple of tickets for our annual exhibition at Grosvenor House, and to inform you that I shall be in attendance every afternoon and evening. I should feel greatly honoured if you could pay us a visit.

Yours faithfully,
A. G. Clark

Violet Pearman to Neville Chamberlain's Private Secretary

(*Churchill papers: 2/303*)

8 March 1937

Dear Private Secretary,

Mr Churchill finds that the Conclusions of the long Report from the officer who visited Germany were not attached to the report which he gave to the Chancellor recently; and as these conclusions seem to Mr Churchill particularly interesting, he thought the Chancellor would like to see them, and has asked me to send them herewith.[1]

The value of this report is that it is not upholding any particular point of view. Mr Churchill would like you to tell the Chancellor that he does not necessarily accept the views of these various reports, but forms his own opinions afterwards from these and other sources.

When the Chancellor has finished with these documents, would you very kindly return them to Mr Churchill, as they are the only copies which he has.

Sir Stafford Cripps[2] *to Winston S. Churchill*

(*Churchill papers: 2/295*)

9 March 1937

Dear Winston Churchill,

I am writing to ask your assistance in a personal matter which I believe to be of some importance. I know you have often expressed yourself in favour

---

[1] The document was a thirty-one page Report on a visit to Germany by Squadron Leader H. V. Rowley and Flight Lieutenant R. L. Atcherley between 6 October and 15 October 1936. Churchill had received the document from Wing-Commander Anderson. The Report stressed the advanced state of Germany's air preparations. Of their visit to the main Junkers factory they wrote: 'The size and efficiency of this great mass production plant was far too large to assimilate in such a brief time.'

[2] Richard Stafford Cripps, 1889–1952. Fifth son of Charles Cripps, later first Baron Parmoor. Educated at Winchester and New College, Oxford, where he excelled in chemistry. A barrister. Medically unfit for military service, he became a lorry driver for the Red Cross, France, 1914. Recalled, to become Assistant Superintendent, Queen's Ferry Munitions Factory, 1915–18. Called to the Bar, 1919. KC, 1927. Treasurer of the World Alliance 'to promote international friendship through the Churches', 1923–9. Solicitor-General, 1930-1. Knighted, 1930. Advocated a Popular Front to link Labour, Liberal radicals, the Independent Labour Party and the Communists, 1936; the journal *Tribune* was launched to further this cause, 1937. Expelled from the Labour Party for advocating a Popular Front against Neville Chamberlain, including Conservatives and Communists, January 1939; not readmitted until 1945. Ambassador to Moscow, 1940–2. Minister of Aircraft Production, 1942–5. President of the Board of Trade, 1945. Minister for Economic Affairs, 1947. Chancellor of the Exchequer, 1947–50.

of freedom of speech in the past and I therefore ask you, in the concrete case mentioned below, to put those beliefs into practice by using your influence as a well known figure in the political life of the country.

I applied for the use of the Albert Hall on a date upon which I had ascertained that it was free, but the Trustees have refused it to me without assigning any reason. The only conceivable reason can be that they disapprove of my political views. I have, like others, often spoken there in the past. The Trustees permit Conservatives, Fascists, Liberals and the Labour Party to use the Hall and I am certain that you will agree with me that it is absolutely wrong that they should refuse its use to any individual on the ground of his political opinions.

I would ask you therefore to write a letter to the Trustees—in your personal capacity—protesting against the action that they have taken and thus help in making a reality of the professions of freedom of speech of which this is a most flagrant denial. I have no doubt that if you and others to whom I have addressed a similar letter will do this the Trustees will alter their views.

May I ask you for an early answer as the matter is very pressing.

Yours sincerely,
Stafford Cripps

Josiah Wedgwood to Winston S. Churchill
(*Churchill papers: 2/315*)

10 March 1937   House of Commons

Dear Winston,

I see you are reported as 'going to give' evidence before the Palestine Comm. I hear from several quarters that they are going to divide Palestine & set up a Jewish state & annex the rest to Trans-Jordan.

This is an admission of failure, scuttle, & the end of British expansion in those parts. Both new countries will curse us for all & hate us in future. We shall never again have the Jews on our side in war. The Christian Arabs & fellaheen are deserted & handed over to the Mufti.[1] The prestige of GB goes

[1] Haj Amin el-Husseini, 1891–1974. Left Palestine after the Arab riots of 1920; sentenced to fifteen years' imprisonment *in absentia* for his part in arousing the Arabs against the Jews. Appointed Mufti of Jerusalem (by Herbert Samuel), March 1921, in succession to his half-brother. A senior member of the Executive Committee of the Supreme Moslem Council, and leader of the anti-Jewish movement among the Arabs of Palestine. Fled Palestine in disguise after the murder of Lewis Andrews in 1937. In exile in Baghdad in 1941, he helped to direct a pro-German uprising. Broadcast from Berlin, 1942; while in Berlin he protested to Hitler when some small exceptions were made to Jewish children being sent to Concentration Camps. Imprisoned in France, 1945–6. Went to Cairo, 1946; there the Arab League Council transferred to him all funds for Palestinian purposes. In 1948 he urged the total expulsion of all Jews from Palestine. Living in Beirut (1972).

into the mud: & all for want of a little resolute rule such as our forbears would have seen thro' with courage & success. Damn these rotten Scotsmen![1]

Winston S. Churchill to Consuelo Balsan: telegram
(Churchill papers: 1/298)

11 March 1937

We were so disappointed we could not come to you in Florida. Hear you will be at Eze Eastertime. Could you have us both for a week, Wednesday 31st March. Love

Winston

Winston S. Churchill to Sir Stafford Cripps
(Churchill papers: 2/295)

12 March 1937

I cannot feel that the right of free speech is directly involved in the inability of a particular person to procure a particular hall. I do not therefore feel myself impelled to come to your assistance. You are, unless I am misinformed, working in political association with the Communists at the present time, and it has always been their rule whenever they have the power, forcibly to suppress all opinions but their own. This also would make the case you mention by no means a good occasion on which to make a protest to the public. Most people will think that the Communists have a pretty good run over here, certainly much better than they are given by the German Nazis, by whom, if I remember rightly, you declared it would be a good thing if we were conquered. Excuse my frankness in dealing with the points you raise.

Palestine Royal Commission: notes of evidence
(Churchill papers: 2/317)

12 March 1937

WITNESS: THE RT HON WINSTON CHURCHILL, CH, MP

8626. CHAIRMAN:[2] We do not want to limit you to the questions, but we have suggested certain questions to you upon which we should very much

[1] A reference to the High Commissioner for Palestine since 1931, Sir Arthur Wauchope.
[2] William Robert Wellesley Peel, 1867–1937. Educated at Harrow and Balliol College,

like to have your views. The first one has given rise to a lot of discussion, the principle of the economic absorptive capacity in the control of immigration. Your words are:—

'This immigration cannot be so great in volume as to exceed whatever may be the economic capacity of the country at the time to absorb new arrivals.'

Of course, Jews have interpreted that in this way, that whatever is in a year the absorptive economic capacity of the country that number of Jews should be admitted. Obviously there is, I will not say an ambiguity, but there is another interpretation to be put on your words—that Jews should come in, but those who come in in any year should never exceed the economic capacity of the country; that is to say, the economic capacity should be an upper limit?—Yes, a limiting factor, but not the sole limiting factor.

8627. One is inclined to take the view that there must be other considerations than mere economic capacity for the amount of immigrants you wanted to admit in any year into the country?—Certainly, I think that follows from the whole text of the paper.

8628. You will see in the letter on page 29, the letter of the 18th June, signed by Dr Weizmann, he slightly alters the meaning of that there by saying 'that the volume of such immigration is to be determined by the economic capacity of the country from time to time to absorb new arrivals', and that has gradually grown to mean that that is the number that should come in. It gives a slight variant?—I am sure it was not intended to make that an absolute gauge of the rate of immigration. It was to be, as it were, a maximum. You should not go beyond that, but it was not intended to make it the sole test, still less the foundation; certainly not. Of course, it is always governed on the other side—I must point out—by the fact that we are trying to bring in as many as we possibly can in accordance with the original Balfour Declaration.

Oxford. Conservative MP, 1900–6 and 1909–12. Succeeded his father as Viscount Peel, 1912. Chairman of the London County Council, 1914. Chairman of the Committee on the Detention of Neutral Vessels, 1916. Under-Secretary of State for War, 1919–21. Chancellor of the Duchy of Lancaster and Minister of Transport, 1921–2. Secretary of State for India, 1922–4, 1928–9. Created Earl, 1929. Lord Privy Seal, 1931. Member of the Indian Round-Table Conference, 1930–1; and of the Joint Select Committee on the Indian Constitution, 1933–4. Chairman of the Burma Round-Table Conference, 1931–2; and of the Palestine Royal Commission, 1936–7. He died on 28 September 1937.

SIR LAURIE HAMMOND:[1] Then there is the Prime Minister's letter of the 13th February, 1931, which carries it still further.

8629. CHAIRMAN: 'It is for that reason that His Majesty's Government have insisted and are compelled to insist that Government control of immigration must be maintained and that immigration regulations must be properly applied. The considerations relevant to the limits of absorptive capacity are purely economic considerations?'—I should have used the word 'primarily'.

8630. There is an ambiguity there?—I should have used the word 'primarily economic considerations'.

8631. You see, particular importance, if I may say so, is attached to your paper of 1922, because I think it was issued a month or two before the Mandate and therefore the Jews claim that yours is the authoritative interpretation issued before the Mandate, which really governs the whole thing, and that it would be a breach of faith if anything was suggested contrary to that. That is why I lay much stress upon that point?—The paper must be taken as a whole, but we undertook to try to bring them in as quickly as we could without upsetting the economic life of the country or throwing it into political confusion. I certainly never considered they were entitled, no matter what other consequences arose, to bring in up to the limit of the economic absorptive capacity. That was not intended. On the other hand, it must be made clear our loyalty is on the side of bringing in as many as we can.

8632. Subject to these considerations which you have stated?—Yes.

8633. I only interpolate this: I am not exactly asking a question upon it. That economic absorptive capacity has given rise to all sorts of arrangements. For instance, businesses are started; protection is asked for them by the Jewish Agency prospectively. They say, 'We shall be able to employ twenty, thirty or fifty men: therefore, our figures for the distribution of licences to come in this year ought to be increased by so much.' It is twisted into all sorts of different shapes, that economic absorptive capacity?—I have always thought the British Government is the final judge, acting with sincerity in accordance with its pledges and obligations. It is the final judge. It holds its hands upon the regulating wheel. It knows which way it would like to turn that wheel, but it is under no obligation to turn it further or faster than they feel right. It is not as if it were a matter of £ s d or a percentage inserted in a business contract.

8634. But as you know, the Jews insist very much upon the letter of the

[1] Egbert Laurie Lucas Hammond, 1873–1939. Educated at Keble College, Oxford. Member of the Executive Council, Bihar and Orissa, 1924–7. Knighted, 1927. Governor of Assam, 1927–9. Chairman of the Indian Delineation Committee, 1935–6. Member of the Royal Commission on Palestine, 1936–7. Author of a three-volume work on Indian Election Petitions, and a further volume, *The Indian Candidate and Returning Officer*.

bond and it is purely for that reason we put that question to you?—I insist upon loyalty and upon the good faith of England to the Jews, to which I attach the most enormous importance, because we gained great advantages in the War. We did not adopt Zionism entirely out of altruistic love of starting a Zionist colony: it was a matter of great importance to this country. It was a potent factor on public opinion in America and we are bound by honour, and I think upon the merits, to push this thing as far as we can, but we are not bound to any particular detail, nor has anybody a right to say, 'You have said at a certain date there must be so many.'

8635. SIR LAURIE HAMMOND: The Jews have taken this as their Magna Charta. No other consideration at all comes into it?—I do not think they put it as high as that.

8636. Yes, they do?—They put it because they are making their case.

8637. PROFESSOR COUPLAND:[1] Dr Weizmann said—and this is a good debating point—that if you have any other criterion than economic absorptive capacity, the person who decides the rate of immigration is the Mufti—a good point?—I hope to see the British Government so strong it will not be swayed by them. If I may go a little outside, I think the root of the evil was the abolition of the Gendarmerie. I formed that Gendarmerie. They were very good class, the officer class and the sergeant class. They did very well in Palestine. They had a good reputation and gained the confidence of the people. To compare Gendarmerie with troops is absurd. Five hundred Gendarmerie living in the place, established there with their cars and weapons and at the same time with their knowledge of the people, are worth five thousand soldiers.

8638. SIR LAURIE HAMMOND: Exactly why were they disbanded?— When you come to soldiers, you put brigades and a division in the field and all they can do is to advance and fire. They can do nothing else, but these people living the lives of the ordinary people in the village, knowing their men, talking to this man, helping that man—they win the confidence of the people and are an invaluable influence, and can bend the bough when it is still a twig and can nip danger when it is only in the bud, and so forth. It was, to my mind, a most disastrous thing when they were disbanded. They were disbanded either in the Bonar Law–Baldwin Government, which lasted only a few months, or in the first MacDonald Government. I cannot tell you at the moment.

[1] Reginald Coupland, 1884–1952. Lecturer in Ancient History, Oxford, 1907–14; Lecturer in Colonial History, 1913–18. Editor of the *Round Table* 1917–19 and 1939–41. Fellow of All Souls College, 1920–48. Beit Professor of the History of the British Empire, Oxford, 1920–48. Adviser, Burma Round Table Conference, 1931. Member of the Palestine Royal Commission, 1936–7. Member of the Cripps' Mission to India, 1942. Author of many books on Indian and colonial history. Knighted, 1944.

8639. SIR HAROLD MORRIS:[1] They were not disbanded in 1923. They were not disbanded until after Sir Herbert Samuel left?—At any rate, when I came back to office at the end of 1924, the Gendarmerie was practically non-existent. It was petering out under a decision which had previously been taken. No proposals were made to revive it. The decision to destroy the Gendarmerie, to abolish it, was taken in those two short Parliaments. The actual death may have come later. I remember being surprised about it when I was at the Exchequer.

8640. SIR LAURIE HAMMOND: I had an idea the reason given was economic?—This is an extract from the Shaw Commission Report:—

'In 1921 a unit of mounted Palestine Gendarmerie had been raised consisting of 500 rank and file, locally recruited, with British officers. In 1922 a battalion of British Gendarmerie was enlisted, mostly from ex-members of the Royal Irish Constabulary. In consequence of these measures and of the improved state of public order, the garrison was reduced by progressive stages until at the beginning of 1925 it consisted of a regiment of cavalry, a squadron of aeroplanes, a company of armoured cars, and the British Gendarmerie, which by that time had been reduced from their original complement of 762 to a strength of about 500.

'At a conference held in Jerusalem in April, 1925, an agreement was reached between the Secretaries of State for Air and the Colonies and the High Commissioner to the effect that the Palestine Gendarmerie should have an establishment of 500 (with a possible increase later), that the British Gendarmerie should be reduced to 200 and absorbed in the civil police.'

—That was a mistaken decision. I was in office at the time, but it was not in my departmental purview.

8641. Lord Plumer[2] was the High Commissioner?—I think it was a great mistake. It may have come before me in relation to the proposed

---

[1] Harold Morris, 1876–1967. Educated at Clifton and Magdalen College, Oxford. Called to the Bar, Inner Temple, 1899. On active service, 1914–18 (despatches). National Liberal MP for East Bristol, 1922–3. Chairman of the National Wages Board for Railways, 1925. President of the Industrial Court, 1926–45. Knighted, 1927.

[2] Herbert Charles Onslow Plumer, 1857–1932. Entered the Army, 1876. On active service in the Sudan, 1884 and in South Africa, 1899–1902. Brigadier-General, 1902. Major-General, 1903. Knighted, 1906. Lieutenant-General, 1908. Commanded the II Corps in France, 1914–15; the Second Army, 1915–17. Commanded the Franco-British Forces in Italy, 1917–18. Resumed Command of the Second Army, March 1918. Commanded the British Army of Occupation in Germany, 1918–19. Created Baron, appointed Field-Marshal, and granted £30,000 by Parliament, 1919. Governor of Malta, 1919–24. High Commissioner to Palestine, 1925–8. Created Viscount, 1929.

expenditure, but when we look back upon it I must regard it as a great misfortune, because it destroyed the means of the white people getting into really friendly touch with the competing, quarrelling races, and that you must have.

8642. CHAIRMAN: I think we might deal now with the second point?—May I just say I think, whatever you do, you should recreate a Gendarmerie.

8643. Now we come to the meaning of the Jewish National Home. There are several aspects of that. First of all, did you intend that there should be a sort of corps of Jews organized in, as it were, a Home of their own, with self-governing institutions inside the Palestine State, or did you mean that the Jews should come into the country, really amalgamate as far as they could with the Arabs and then form a body of Palestinians who were not so much Jews and Arabs as Palestinians? That leads I think to a further point. There is nothing laid down as far as one can see in the Mandate itself as to the numbers of Jews who should come in or their relation to the Arabs. Now they have increased, as you know, very much, and there are 400,000 Jews and a million Arabs and the fear is very intense on the part of the Arabs that the Jews coming in, if they come in at the same rate—and 60,000 came in in the year 1935—will, within a limited number of years, overtop the Arabs, and in that case, instead of being a Jewish Home, in Palestine, become a Jewish State. The Jews, on the other hand, when they are challenged on this point, say, 'We cannot submit to be considered in a position of permanent inferiority': they do not say they want to have a majority, but they do not want to be in a permanent minority, and moreover, they say, 'If we have this majority, we do not want to dominate the Arabs,' but the point is that nobody really knows and it is not defined in the Mandate as to whether you did contemplate that, in the course of immigration and so on, the Jews should be in a majority. That terrifies the Arabs, of course. They know they are—I call them—an inferior race in many ways to the Jews. The Jews will have what they consider is their country and the Jews will rule them financially, culturally and educationally. They will be their rulers. The point I am putting to you is—what is the conception you have formed yourself of the Jewish National Home?—The conception undoubtedly was that, if the absorptive capacity over a number of years and the breeding over a number of years, all guided by the British Government, gave an increasing Jewish population, that population should not in any way be restricted from reaching a majority position. Certainly not. On the contrary, I think in the main that would be the spirit of the Balfour Declaration. As to what arrangement would be made to safeguard the rights of the new minority, that obviously remains open, but certainly we committed ourselves to the idea that some day, somehow, far off in the future, subject to justice and economic convenience, there might well be a great Jewish State there, numbered by millions, far exceeding the present inhabitants of the country and to cut them off from that would be a wrong. But, on this question, we never committed ourselves to making Palestine a Jewish Home. We said there should be a Jewish Home in Palestine, but if more and more Jews gather to that Home and all is worked from age to age, from generation to generation, with justice and fair consideration to those displaced and so forth, certainly it was contemplated and intended that they might in the course of time become an overwhelmingly Jewish State.

8644. Over the centuries?—Over the generations or the centuries. No one has ever said what is to be the rate at which it is to be done. The British Government is the judge and should keep the power to be the judge.

8645. SIR HORACE RUMBOLD:[1] You used the expression on page 19 of the White Paper:—

'When it is asked what is meant by the development of a Jewish National Home in Palestine,' it is so and so 'in order that it may become a centre in which the Jewish people may take a pride.'

—May become a centre.

8646. It seems to me it would attract Jews from outside, but not be actually more than a nucleus for the great Jewry of the world?—Naturally all the Jews in the world would not go and live there, but if it is a centre which will attract Jews from outside and if the attraction can be kept within the limits of the economic absorptive capacity, and also what I may call the management of the British Government, which is the responsible Government, there are no limits assigned at all. If more Jews rally to this Home, the Home will become all Palestine eventually, provided that at each stage there is no harsh injustice done to the other residents. Why is there harsh injustice done if people come in and make a livelihood for more and make the desert into palm groves and orange groves? Why is it injustice because there is more work and wealth for everybody? There is no injustice. The injustice is when those who live in the country leave it to be a desert for thousands of years.

8647. All that has been strengthened by things like the policy of the Nazi Government in Germany and the economic pressure on the Jews in Poland? —That makes it more poignant, but it does not oblige us to do any active injustice to Arabs because of the injustice done to Jews in Europe. We have to see that they do not come in in such numbers that they upset the country and create unfair conditions and we are the judges of that, and the sole judges in my opinion.

---

[1] Former British Ambassador to Berlin, and Deputy Chairman of the Peel Commission (see page 79, note 2).

8648. If this policy results in periodical disturbances, costing us the lives of our men and so on?—I would have a good Gendarmerie out there to get a good hold of the place. In my opinon, all questions of self-government in Palestine are subordinate to the discharge of the Balfour Declaration—the idea of creating a National Home for the Jews and facing all the consequences which may ultimately in the slow passage of time result from that. That is the prime and dominating pledge upon which Britain must act. In certain circumstances, if we became very weak, we might have to abandon the whole thing, somebody else might have to take it on; but, while there, that is what we are undoubtedly pledged to.

8649. CHAIRMAN: As you know, in the Mandate, no declaration was laid down upon this point. It was left, I will not say vague, but it was left unsettled and controversy is going on about it. The Arabs have fears upon the subject. Would you be in favour, then, that being your view, of having a declaration made which would anyhow satisfy doubts among the Arabs that the Government did intend, if there was sufficient Jewish immigration, that they should be a Jewish State and that the Jews would, in fact, under the Mandate, if you like, be the rulers of the country?—I do not say it should be a Jewish State necessarily. It might be a State in which there would be a great majority of Jews. That is the only question you have put to me so far. It would, no doubt, be a Palestinian State.

8650. But you did contemplate the possibility of a Jewish majority? At present, I do not think that has ever been stated in so many words. It might anyhow lay down a definite line of policy?—I am sure it would be contrary to the whole spirit of the Balfour Declaration if we were to declare that in no circumstances, however naturally it might arise, would we contemplate a Jewish majority.

8651. Put it the other way. If the Jews are approaching the limit—they are increasing very fast now—would you, to allay fears and doubts among the Arabs, simply lay it down that it was the view of the Government that if in the course of time sufficient Jews come in there should be a Jewish majority and that is a thing you did contemplate?—As Burke says, if I cannot have reform without injustice, I will not have reform. I am dealing with the facts. If we displace so-and-so from this place and so-and-so from that place and he and his family are subject to harsh usage, we cannot have that; but to say this great idea of a Jewish National Home in Palestine was to have a limit put on it and say it is not to be a Jewish National Home if more people get to it than the Arab population, that would not be right.

8652. It is so difficult to know what injustice is. Land is being acquired from the Arabs by the Jews and when that land is acquired by the Jews or a great deal of it is acquired from the Arabs by the Jews it is declared it shall never be alienable to the Arabs again and Arabs are not, in fact, employed upon it. That frightens them?—I think the Mandatory Power should talk to the Jewish people about it and say how foolish they are to do it and how wrong. 'If you cannot ease the situation in the way of employing more Arabs, if you cannot get on better terms with these Arabs, that is a reason for our reducing immigration in any given year.' I see this thing only from the point of view of British mastery. If British mastery disappears you had better be quit of the whole show.

8653. SIR LAURIE HAMMOND: That argument of yours hits the bottom out of the Prime Minister's letter of 1931, in which he said the immigration is limited purely by economic considerations, because you are taking in political considerations?—Certainly, I always have done. I said it was only one limiting factor, the economic capacity. I look upon it like this. We have to manage this thing above board and fairly and decently, a gentleman's agreement and everything else. If we feel we cannot do it, better clear out. If we do it, we must have the power and we must have our plan and we must absolutely turn the wheel this way or that according as we think is best; but we are always aiming at the fact that, if enough Jews come, eventually it may be a great Palestinian State, in which the large majority of the inhabitants would be Jews. It is not a thing which will happen for a century or more.

8654. If this policy provokes, as Sir Horace Rumbold put it, periodical disturbances, is it right for the Mandatory Power to sacrifice the lives of its own subjects in order to fulfil its obligation?—Either do that or give it up.

8655. Or clear out?—Or clear out.

8656. PROFESSOR COUPLAND: I cannot help thinking there was a moral assumption from the outset, not expressed, and that was that sooner or later or somehow or other, the Arabs, recognizing the economic advantage which people expected to come from the Jewish immigration, recognizing that they have got that, would come to acquiesce even in the gradual development of the Jewish majority. That has not come about. Surely, the assumption was that, if for any reason, such as pure pigheadedness, if you like, or still more, through the rise of Arab nationalism, they did not acquiesce, and even your policy could not persuade them to acquiesce—surely the moral assumption was that you could not go on forcing it, that you should not make it a creeping invasion and conquest of Palestine spread over half a century, which is a thing unheard of in history?—It is not a creeping conquest.

8657. If you are always hitting them on the head?—These Arabs were a poor people, conquered, living under the Turks fairly well, but they hated the Turks, though they lived fairly easily in a flat squalor typical of pre-war Turkish Empire provinces, and then when the war came they became our enemies and they filled the armies against us and fired their rifles and shot our men.

8658. Certainly?—But our armies advanced and they were conquered. It is not a question of a slow creeping conquest. They were beaten then and at our disposition. Mercy may impose many restraints. The question is how you give back to them in accordance with the new facts which have emerged in the great struggle some of the positions which they held. They were defeated in the open field. It is not a question of creeping conquest. They were beaten out of the place. Not a dog could bark. And then we decided in the process of the conquest of these people to make certain pledges to the Jews. Now the question is how to administer in a humane and enlightened fashion and certain facts have emerged.

8659. Every few years—I am not suggesting this is my view; but I think it wants meeting—every few years you go on shooting Arabs down because they dislike the Jews coming in?—Have there not been many more Jews murdered than Arabs?

8660. More Arabs get killed in the end?—You cannot say we go on shooting down the Arabs.

8661. SIR LAURIE HAMMOND: More Arabs are killed than Jews?—That follows because we are the stronger power.

8662. SIR HAROLD MORRIS: But what makes you say we conquered the Arabs? I thought they were our allies?—The actual inhabitants, the Palestinian Arabs, were making their quota to the Turkish Army. The Arabs from the Hedjaz were our allies.

8663. That may be, because they were compelled to by the Turk; but they came in and fought with us?—Not the Palestinian Arab.

8664. As many of them as could join?—No, they were all in the Turkish army. You have to take people from the area in which they live. There may have been individuals. I give you that.

8665. SIR HORACE RUMBOLD: It would logically follow that as we conquered Palestine we can dispose of it as we like?—In accordance with the pledges we gave in the process of conquest.

8666. You conquer a nation: you have given certain pledges the result of which has been that the indigenous population is subject to the invasion of a foreign race?—A foreign race? Not at all. The people who had it before that indigenous population came in and inhabited it. In the time of Christ the population of Palestine was much greater, when it was a Roman province. When the Mohammedan upset occurred in world history and the great hordes of Islam swept over these places they broke it all up, smashed it all up. You have seen the terraces on the hills which used to be cultivated, which under Arab rule have remained a desert.

8667. Would it not be more just to say under Turkish rule?—I do not know about that. I have a great regard for Arabs, but at the same time you find where the Arab goes it is often desert.

8668. They created a good deal of civilization in Spain?—I am glad they were thrown out.

8669. They were there six or seven hundred years and they did a great deal there. It has gone back since they left Cordova?—It is a lower manifestation, the Arab. Now I have heard about some plan of dividing the place into two. When I talk of a Jewish Home in Palestine instead of making Palestine a Jewish Home, I do not want it to be understood I am thinking of any particular plan, because I have not addressed my mind to such a plan; I have not thought about it. It is a tremendous proposition and I should like to think about it, but anything I say is in ignorance of that. I might or might not agree to it, but it seems to me it may be a thing you have been thinking of for some time.

8670. CHAIRMAN: I should like, if I may, to put one question to you on that point we have been discussing. There is a good deal of evidence—indeed, I think it may be accepted as a fact—that in the last few years that feeling of Arab nationalism has very largely developed. It is far stronger than it used to be and it is not only a matter of a few *effendis* who thought they were losing caste or position because of our rule: but younger people have rather taken charge; the men and women and everyone else in the villages and the Arab world in Palestine has really become solid against this increase of Jewish immigration and the fears of Jewish domination. Would you not pay much attention to that exhibition of national sentiment?—You might have to soft pedal a bit, but you will not alter your purpose. Your purpose is declared. You may go a little bit slower. I regard it as being a thing for England. If she cannot do it she had better give it up. She can perfectly well mark time for a lustrum or a decade. The Jews have no right to say, 'You have promised us we can have a further million immigrants.' England is the judge.

8671. SIR LAURIE HAMMOND: It is open to England to say 'We will have a standstill, no immigration for four or five years?'—You would not say no immigration.

8672. The bare minimum?—Are we going too fast? We want these races to live together and to minister to their well-being. Their well-being would be greatly enhanced if they did not quarrel. Where there is now a desert would become a really lovely place and the Arabs would reap the benefit. We want them to; but if you go too fast and you have these furious outbreaks, then you must go a bit slower. But you must not give in to the furious outbreaks; you must quell them. You may go a bit slower, but do not be diverted from your purpose, which is, that you will preserve a nucleus in Palestine round which as many Jews as can get a living will be gathered, without regard to the racial balance of population in the country. That is my view.

8673. CHAIRMAN: Of course, the relations between the two races unfortunately in the last few years have been getting worse and worse. That is a factor you can take into consideration, because you do not really look forward to a mixed population or a Jewish Home, or a Jewish State—any-how, a country containing a majority of Jews—where there are the worst possible relations between Jews and Arabs?—No, the relationship between the two races must be considered just as much as the economic absorptive capacity; because we have to foot the bill, we have to do the work.

8674. Putting aside outbreaks, you can say people should not make out-breaks when they do, but when there are great grievances and great feelings in the country you get the outbreaks, and I do not want to lay emphasis on the outbreaks but on the position between the two races?—That clashes with our giving them self-governing institutions in accordance with the Mandate, and in my opinion the Mandate over-rides the self-governing institutions.

8675. I should like your view on that. That is the next point I was going to ask you about. Article 2 of the Mandate?—'The Mandatory shall be respon-sible for placing the country under such administrative, political and economic conditions as will secure the establishment of a Jewish national home.' There is a great positive thing. And 'the development of self-governing institutions' and also 'safeguarding the civil and religious rights of all the inhabitants of Palestine irrespective of race and religion'. That is perfectly all right.

8676. I am not bothering so much about the last few words as about the development of self-governing institutions. Do you consider these as two parallel duties? They would place it under such conditions and also be responsible for the development of self-governing institutions, because the argument of the Arabs is that they are prevented from having these because the Mandatory Power says, 'No, if you have them, you will use them in order to diminish the obligation, as it were, and perhaps put the Jews out of the country.' A curious thing happens. I presume if the Jews get a majority, as soon as they have a majority you might establish self-governing institu-tions, because it would not then conflict with the establishment of a Jewish National Home. The Arabs say, 'That is very odd self-government: it is only when the Jews are in a majority that we can have it?'—I think that is inherent in the conditions under which the country fell under our charge, so quite definitely, in my opinion, the self-governing aspect, although important, is not superior but inferior to the prime obligation in the declaration under which we went into this country. But in all these things it is not a question of laying down the law on one side or the other. It is a question of administrative capacity, one side to concede and the other side to forbear, but to do that you have to have your force, your power, your control. If you are not prepared to take the measures to have the control and the force and to do things fairly in an equitable manner for both, you had better clear out, give it up and—I put this as a *reductio ad absurdum*—say, the Italians come in if they want to. They would love to. They would have no trouble at all. They would use ruthless force: they would kill the whole lot of their opponents; kill them all off. I have been told that they made an offer to the Jews that if they could get their support and help they would clear the Arabs out. Then the Arabs have to think of that, too. The Arabs would never get on with the Italians. The Jews could perfectly well manage to do it. Both races have to think of all these things. We are a very gentle and kindly power. We have done nothing to hurt these people. We have every right to strike hard in support of our authority.

8677. The Arabs are so far right in saying that it is the entry of the Jews and the Jewish Home and so on which prevent them from having these self-governing institutions, to which they think, as the people of the country, they have a claim?—It limits the rate at which those can be developed as long as they do not accept the spirit of the Balfour Declaration. The moment they accept that spirit, with all the pledges of their civil liberties, the question falls to the ground. They resist and they do not want it. If I were an Arab I should not like it, but it is for the good of the world that the place should be cultivated and it never will be cultivated by the Arabs.

8678. The Arabs are doing a lot in their plantations. I daresay it is following the Jews; but they have a lot of fine orange plantations of their own?—I am very glad to hear it.

SIR HORACE RUMBOLD: They are limited in their resources. The Jews can pour money into Palestine. I think they have already poured in £80,000,000. The Arabs have no money.

8679. PROFESSOR COUPLAND: It is very like Ireland in the nineteenth century. The majority of people were refused Home Rule because the minority were in the way, Ulster. It is the Irish analogy of the nineteenth century. What was in the path of Home Rule for Ireland was the resistance of the minority in Ulster. Presumably Arab nationalism sees it cannot get the self-government which Iraq, Syria, Trans-Jordan and Egypt have all got, for one reason only, because the Jewish National Home is there?—Because England entered into obligations.

8680. Certainly?—England can resign the Mandate. That is the only way in which you can possibly avoid your obligation. Mind you, the threat to do it would probably make a lot of people very reasonable who are now very truculent; but you can always resign. A king may always abdicate, there is nothing to prevent it. He can say the burden is too heavy. Everyone can do that.

8681. If you were able, as to some extent you were in Ireland, however difficult we believe it will be to find a compromise, it would be a great relief I should have thought to the average Englishman to find he had not got to go on denying self-government to these Arabs, had not got to go on shooting the Arabs down because of keeping his promise to the Jews. It is a most disagreeable position to be in?—I should like to know more about this suggested compromise, dividing up the country and so on, keeping them in groups as the Turks and Greeks have been sorted out in Asia Minor, before expressing any opinion on it.

8682. It is within reach of our power. It is not like the Assyrian tragedy in Iraq?—My view is that you should go on and persevere with the task, holding the balance in accordance with the declaration, allowing the influx of new immigrants to take place as fast as can be, but having the right to slow it down when you like and having power and force of the right kind to support you, but if you cannot do that, give it up and let Mussolini take it on, which he would be very anxious to do. Someone else might come in. You would have to face that. A power like Italy would have no trouble. There are powers in the world which are the rising powers which are unmoral powers; they admit no morals at all.

8683. The friction in Palestine is alienating the Arab world. We have had much evidence to show the relations with the Arab States are being irritated by this fact that British troops are fighting Arabs and shooting them down?— I think it is much exaggerated. I have heard it so often.

8684. SIR HORACE RUMBOLD: In present circumstances I do not see how you can apply Article 6 of the Mandate, because it says, 'Jewish immigration shall be facilitated under suitable conditions.' What does 'suitable conditions' mean? At present the atmosphere is one of unconcealed hostility. That is not a proper atmosphere for doing anything in. If you take a plant or any organism it will not flourish in certain conditions?—That means you must not push too hard. Perhaps they have, with the Germans treating the Jews so badly, pushed in too many. There has been an extra drive and that drive started up the Arabs. I should have thought the Jews would have been clever enough to have conciliated the Arabs. Money helps things. When land is bought, perhaps the Arab might be given land more suitable to him. That is how they should go on.

8685. PROFESSOR COUPLAND: They have been for eighteen years?— There were 80,000 when I wrote that paper. Now there are 400,000.

8686. SIR LAURIE HAMMOND: At the time you wrote that paper do you think for a moment anyone envisaged the idea of there being by 1936, 400,000 Jews there?—Yes, certainly, I hoped for it.

8687. SIR HORACE RUMBOLD: The immigration was very moderate indeed, except for two periods. It never went over 9,000 at the outset?—It certainly did; but, mind you, I have no illusions about some of these Jews who are coming in there. We ought to stiffen the standard up.

8688. CHAIRMAN: Somehow the economic capacity of the country seems to have been very flexible at that time; anyhow, more were allowed in? —They made a mistake in saying they would only employ their own people on their own work. It was never intended that that should happen. It was intended that the two races should intermingle.

8689. There is one minor point I should like to ask. That is about the position of the Jewish Agency, which, as you know, is recognized in the Mandate, 'for the purpose of advising and co-operating with the Administration of Palestine in such economic, social and other matters as may affect the establishment of the Jewish national home' and so on. That was composed originally of Zionists in the different countries. In about 1929 or 1930 the non-Zionists also took their part, a fifty/fifty part, in the Jewish Agency?— Non-Zionist Jews.

8690. Yes, non-Zionist Jews. That added enormously to the influence and prestige of this Jewish Agency. They have pretty well the control of those who come into the country from Poland and Germany. They agree with the Government of Palestine beforehand as to the number of certificates that shall be allowed, but they have grown into a very very important body in Palestine. Their buildings in Jerusalem seem to dominate the place. They have all sorts of departments. There is nothing of that kind on the Arab side at all. Do you think this might have been very useful to start with, in order to push Jewish immigration, but that, now that the Jews are so many, such an Agency of this kind, representing the whole weight of Jewry, in Palestine, influencing the Government of Palestine, is not too much of another Government being set up side by side with the existing Government and that their powers should be diminished?—As to their scale I cannot say, but as to their limit, it is clear their function is in respect of facilitating the immigration of Jews into Palestine, but they have no status of any sort or kind as to the Government of the Palestinian State, none whatever. They ought never to be allowed to be in that position at all.

8691. They have, as a matter of fact, I will call it encroached—it is a tendencious word—in this way. Every action of the Government affects that economic capacity. For instance, the whole of the fiscal system and the taxation are urged upon the Government, they say put duties on this, that and the other. You can see how in that way they have penetrated into all the sections of the Government and their influence is very great. There is no corresponding Arab influence to meet it?—I think it should be kept within bounds. The Jewish Agency has nothing whatever to do with the title-deeds of the Government of the country.

8692. It ought not. It has its representatives in London and they can speak to the Colonial Office and the Arabs feel on their side they are rather left in the cold. They have not the great engine the Jews have?—It is a question of which civilization you prefer.

8693. I was going to say, to sum up your argument, that you would say we ought to go on more or less as we are, limiting, if necessary, immigration of the Jews, sternly putting down any uprisings or disturbances on the part of the Arabs, and really allowing the movement to develop so that the Jews gradually, as they will if they go on being admitted in large numbers, get into charge of the country?—No—becoming a majority in the country, but nothing will supersede the Mandate. At that moment, the Mandatory will rest its weight on the other foot and say . . . .

8694. SIR LAURIE HAMMOND: Now you can start your self-governing institutions; but you do contemplate, do you not, a sort of permanent Mandate on your principles?—Certainly.

8695. Our remaining there, I will not say for ever, but for a long, long time?—Certainly. We are engaged in an operation which is establishing a Jewish National Home in Palestine. That is the operation, the positive operation. When we cannot carry that any further, we ought to give up the Mandate.

8696. SIR HORACE RUMBOLD: I was going to ask you when do you consider the Jewish Home to be established? You have no ideas of numbers? When would you say we have implemented our undertaking and the Jewish National Home is established? At what point?—When it was quite clear the Jewish preponderance in Palestine was very marked, decisive, and when we were satisfied that we had no further duties to discharge to the Arab population, the Arab minority.

8697. SIR LAURIE HAMMOND: It was put before us that there have been these recurrent troubles, which began before the Mandate, in 1920, and again in 1923 and 1929, and so on, and if you wanted to do anything that would really stop it and, as you say, enforce on the Arabs the idea that we are determined there shall be a National Home, it is not only a matter of Gendarmerie, but it is a matter of disarming the Arabs. Every village is full of arms, and it is a question of disarming them. That is a very big undertaking? —Yes.

8698. And it would mean using rather brutal methods to accomplish it. I do not say the methods of the Italians at Addis Ababa, but it would mean the blowing up of villages and that sort of thing?—What do you mean by blowing them up?

8699. Dynamiting them?—They blew up part of Jaffa. Why did they blow it up? Because it was a slum full of disagreeable people?

CHAIRMAN: They blew up a lot of houses all over the place in order to awe the population. I have seen photographs of these things going up in the air.

SIR MORRIS CARTER:[1] In the Jaffa case, it was in order to make a military road.

8700. SIR LAURIE HAMMOND: They have had to blow up houses in the search for arms. They have gone to a village and said, 'You were sniping our people the last three or four days. You must have arms and you must produce them. If you do not produce them we shall blow up *that* house to-morrow at two o'clock?'—I have not heard about that. Tell me about it. Then what happens?

8701. On a further search of the house perhaps they will reluctantly bring out four or five old rifles which were left in some dump at Kantara after the War and have found their way up there; but, meanwhile, the four good rifles with which they have been shooting at our people are still buried in the dump?—If you cannot put down banditry or guerilla or a murder campaign directed at the humble agents of the British Government, if you cannot do that, then you have to give in as we did in Ireland. If that is the position, that is a reason for abandoning the Mandate.

8702. PROFESSOR COUPLAND: If the good thing is done, I do not mind what the reason for it is, and I am one of those who think that the partition of Ireland was a good thing under the circumstances and for all time?—I beg you not to think either that I have given any evidence which is in support of the idea I have heard talked about of the partition of Palestine, or that I am opposed to it. I have not thought sufficiently about it.

8703. SIR LAURIE HAMMOND: The point I was putting to you was rather this. Assuming we have, as you say, to go on and fulfil the obligations and implement the promises we have made to the world, if we are to do it properly and to safeguard the Jews, it must mean taking very stern action. It means martial law and martial law in Palestine, under the conditions there, which you have seen, means a great deal of trouble?—Yes.

8704. It means what you might almost call Turkish measures?—Martial law done by generals, with two brigadiers and eight colonels and so forth—that will be a great failure. You must build up your Gendarmerie, and build

---

[1] William Morris Carter, 1873–1960. Magistrate, Mombasa, 1902. Knighted, 1919. Chief Justice, Tanganyika Territory, 1920–24. Chairman, Kenya Land Commission, 1932–3. Member, Palestine Royal Commission, 1936–7.

it up with people who care about the Arabs as much as they care about the Jews, who are friends of both sides.

8705. We have had the case put before us that some of the Gendarmerie had recourse to Turkish methods. I think that was one of the complaints?—I do not know what Gendarmerie you mean? A white Gendarmerie?

8706. Yes?—Have they got any white police left?

SIR LAURIE HAMMOND: Yes. They have a regular police force formed on the lines of the Ceylon Police Force, with an Inspector-General. The Police Budget for this next year is £750,000. It is double and treble what it was when you were Colonial Secretary and, as far as I can see, comparatively ineffective. They can get no information from any Arabs and they cannot rely on their own Arab Police Force.

8707. SIR HORACE RUMBOLD: They cannot put Arabs into Jewish Districts, and *vice versa*?—Did you see Peake?[1]

8708. CHAIRMAN: Not this time. He was away; but we saw Glubb,[2] the second in command. You have put very forcibly, as you always put it, your view as to what should be done, but I was going to ask you this. Do you not think public opinion in this country, which is rather sentimental, as you know, might get rather tired and rather inquisitive, if every two or three years there was a sort of campaign against the Arabs and we sent out troops and shot them down? They would begin to enquire, 'Why is it done?' 'What is the fault of these people?' 'Is it not simply because they want to live in what they say is their own country?' Might not people say, 'Why are you doing it? In order to get a Home for the Jews?'—I do not think that would happen. We have passed through that exhausted shell-shock period and England is becoming a strong country again. I think that epoch of ten years or so which we had to live through to gather force is passing away. So far as politics are concerned, I can only judge of what they are in this Parliament and this Parliament is overwhelmingly in support of the Jews. Try it out in debate and see.

8709. I know that was so in the debate of last March?—Try it in a debate and see. If the Government went violently against it, I suppose they could

[1] Frederick Gerard Peake, 1886–1970. 2nd Lieutenant, 1906. Served in India, 1906–13; Sudan Camel Corps, 1913–16; Royal Flying Corps, Salonica, 1916; Hedjaz sector of the Egyptian Expeditionary Force, 1917–18. Inspector-General of Gendarmerie, Transjordan, 1921–3; raised the Arab Legion, 1922; Director of Public Security, 1923. Author of the *History and Tribes of Jordan*.

[2] John Bagot Glubb, 1897–   . 2nd Lieutenant, Royal Engineers, 1915. On active service in France, 1915–18 (wounded thrice, Military Cross). Lieutenant, Royal Engineers, Iraq, 1920–6. Administrative Inspector, Iraq Government, 1926–30. Officer Commanding the Desert Area (Colonial Service), Transjordan, 1932. Lieutenant-General Commanding the Arab Legion, Transjordan, 1939. Chief of the General Staff, Arab Legion, 1939–56. Knighted, 1956. Relieved of his command by King Hussein, March 1956.

swing Parliament, with the Whips, and that kind of thing; but, as a matter of fact, the Government will not depart from the main principles of the Balfour Declaration.

8710. SIR HAROLD MORRIS: Do you think there is any possibility of fusion between Arabs and Jews? Is that not one of the reasons why Jews may accept partition?—It may be difficult to make them fuse.

8711. Did you contemplate that the National Home would be a thing that would really never be established, but would always go on growing and never be complete?—The view I took was as to our fostering certain processes and as to our having a duty not to arrest certain other processes. My vision was not able to project itself upon that distant future and to say what would be the result of following that line.

8712. The difficulty of that is this. Knowing that the Arabs were opposed to it, how could you possibly get administrative government or self-govern-ment in Palestine, unless you had got a majority?—That is what I said. Self-government must yield to the obligations of the Mandate. You must not abandon the prime obligation of the Mandate for the sake of self-government —self-government, subject to not interfering with the prior right. When you buy an estate it has certain charges upon it and you have to pay those charges.

8713. I think the Mandates Commission contemplated a rather different state of affairs. They did contemplate the completion of the National Home within a certain length of time. What they meant by it I do not know, but this is what they say in June, 1930:—

'It would be unfair to make it a complaint against the Mandatory that eight years after the entry into force of the Mandate Palestine has not yet been granted a *régime* of self-government, and it would be equally unfair to reproach the Mandatory because the Jewish national home has not yet reached its full development.'

They evidently contemplate completion?—Who are the people who do that?

8714. This is the Mandates Commission. I cannot tell you who they were, but I take it they were in Geneva?—They wanted to have it both ways. Either we are to carry out our mandatory obligation to facilitate the estab-lishment of the Jewish National Home, or we are to hand over the govern-ment of the country to the people who happen to live there at the moment. You cannot do both.

8715. You cannot do both, and has it not been assumed throughout, both by yourself in 1922, and by the Mandates Commission, that the only way in which this can be carried out is if the two races agree?—Oh, no.

8716. Come to some form of agreement, do not fight?—No. Obviously, some process of friction was inevitable.

8717. I think, perhaps, that is contemplated here. This is the way they go on:—

'Those are the objects of the Mandate . . . that is, the national home and self-government . . . and it is not one of the Mandatory's obligations to bring them to an immediate completion. The Mandatory's immediate obligation is slowly to create and maintain in Palestine conditions favourable to the gradual accomplishment of the two objects of the Mandate.'

—That is all right.

8718. After seventeen years, or fifteen years, is it not about time we tried something else?—Not at all. What is seventeen years?

8719. Is it your view that it should go on until there is a Jewish majority?— I think it should go on as we are. The time to think about changing our policy is in another fifty or hundred years, not to be turned off after you have done it for fifteen years and say now you must do something else. The whole point is to keep on a steady line.

8720. Then you are bound to delay self-government?—Certainly. I have said so. If it is the fact that the proper application of the British Mandate obliges us to impinge upon and restrict to some extent the desire which we have to associate the people of the country in the governing authority—yes, I have said so.

8721. SIR LAURIE HAMMOND: And in the interval we have to go on as the Mandatory Power, governing the country against the wishes of the majority of the people in the country?—Certainly, against the wishes of both of them, because the Jews will not be satisfied with your soft-pedalling of immigration, and the others will hate the fact that you are saying, 'We are going to work up to this goal.'

8722. With disturbances recurring at intervals of about three years?—If you had had a proper Gendarmerie they would not have gone on in this way. Now it has got into a very bad condition. I think mistakes were made in the early stages. I have heard a great deal about that. Terrible mistakes were made and small things were allowed to grow into great things, but the races were not so frightfully apart eighteen months or two years ago. The officers were in touch with both, and we had a large proportion of the Arab community working with us; but the Arab leaders and all of them are now bitterly hostile. They have been alienated and it may take a long time to get back to the position we were in only two or three years ago.

8723. Here is this little country, the size of one ordinary District in India, and they have had to take two Divisions out there?—As I say, if you had a proper Gendarmerie, I believe you could have kept it quite quiet. However, if you feel you have to give up, then say so. A great many people would say, 'All right, give it up.' A lot of people would say, 'Return the Mandate'; but not a single one would say, 'Hold the Mandate and abandon the pledge to the Jews.'

8724. If you hold the Mandate you have to carry it out, *ça va sans dire*?— You must take what I say as just a contribution *de bene esse*.

8725. CHAIRMAN: We are very much obliged to you, because you have made very clear to us all the points we did not feel quite clear about, the 1922 White Paper, the Mandate, and so on?—It is only my recollection, but I remember how we felt about it after the War. It was understood that it was not all going to be done by kindness.

8726. The warlike mood was still there?—No, it was over then.

8727. SIR LAURIE HAMMOND: The 1922 Cabinet had before them the findings of the Military Commission that sat in 1920 to consider the troubles in Jerusalem and they pointed out then everything, very much as we have placed it before you now—the difficulty about immigration, the transfer of land, and the Arab fear of Jewish domination. It was all placed before them, so that it was all before you when you drew up the Mandate?—Yes. The argument is that England may not be strong enough and she cannot do it; let us lay the burden down then, but if she is strong enough. . . .

8728. CHAIRMAN: Might I say there that it is not only a question of being strong enough, but she might have some compunction if she felt she was downing the Arabs year after year when they wanted to remain in their own country?—I do not admit that the dog in the manger has the final right to the manger, even though he may have lain there for a very long time. I do not admit that right. I do not admit, for instance, that a great wrong has been done to the Red Indians of America, or the black people of Australia. I do not admit that a wrong has been done to those people by the fact that a stronger race, a higher grade race, or, at any rate, a more worldly-wise race, to put it that way, has come in and taken their place. I do not admit it. I do not think the Red Indians had any right to say, 'The American Continent belongs to us and we are not going to have any of these European settlers coming in here.' They had not the right, nor had they the power.

8729. May I say we are very much obliged to you indeed?—Is there anything I have said which at any one point appears to be contradictory to anything else I have said? If there is, I would like to clear it up.

SIR LAURIE HAMMOND: Only one thing. You did refer to the fact that the idea of the Cabinet was the intermingling of the races?

8730. CHAIRMAN: You thought it was based upon the fact that they should be brought together?—I thought it was part of the responsibility of the Jews to make it worth the while of the Arabs, and they have failed in that respect.

8731. SIR LAURIE HAMMOND: If I may say so, the Mandate itself contains articles which are the most ingenious devices for keeping the two races apart, such as the three languages. From the word 'go' the whole thing was laid down so as to force these two nations apart?—We do not want to do that.

8732. There were inherent conditions in the Mandate which will remain so long as the Mandate remains, and the effect of which it seems to me must increase year by year. You did say, I think, that the Mandate was based on the assumption of the intermingling of the races, but that you qualify now by saying it would be the duty of the Jews to see that that took place?—I did not mean the intermingling of the races by blood.

8733. No, but by satisfactory relations between them?—The Arabs were very poor and I thought a lot of them would be working for good wages and others would be starting their own plantations and would find a market for their goods because close by there was a Jewish settlement.

8734. That was the case before the War and for a certain time afterwards, but now there is not a sign of it in any way whatever?—It is a terrible situation now.

8735. CHAIRMAN: Even the old Jews who used to get on so well with the Arabs have now been roped into the hatred of the Arabs and they are now treated just as badly as the newer Jews?—It is a serious situation.

Professor Lindemann: comments dictated to Violet Pearman

(*Churchill papers: 25/12*)

12 March 1937

1. Allowance has been made for monthly wastage on the basis of the figures accepted by the Air Staff. But the difference between the numbers they accept and those given ie 3,850 military aircraft as against 4,040 and 3,150 pilots to 3,325 is scarcely worth arguing about.

2. The Air Staff maintain that it is not unreasonable to believe that the Germans have two modern military machines in reserve for every one in the first line, and three pilots fully trained on such modern machines for every two in the first line in reserve. Hitherto no endeavour has been made to compare the British and German Air Forces in these respects, but it would be a great relief to learn that we have even half this reserve of modern machines and pilots fully trained on such modern machines.

3. If it is known that Luftkreis VI contains eleven squadrons, why were they not added to the ninety, making 101 ? If we take this figure and the 137 squadrons admitted for the 1st December in paragraph 2, the Air Staff appear to believe that 36 squadrons were added between the 1st September and the 1st December ie 12 a month.

4. By adding in the 11 squadrons in Luftkreis VI the Air Staff have now constructed an accretion of 11 squadrons in the 3 months 1st June to 1st September. Making an allowance for the push to get extra squadrons ready for the 7th March, it seems odd that 12 squadrons a month should have been added between 1st September and 1st December, but only 4 per month between 1st June and 1st September.

A new red herring is introduced in this paragraph ie the concept of a potential squadron strength. This, we are told, is always in excess of the number of formed and identified squadrons, and is arrived at by dividing the first line strength by 9. Hitherto it had seemed that the Air Staff arrived at the first line strength by multiplying the number of identified squadrons by 9, but evidently this is wrong. If this were the method there would be no difference between the potential strength and the actual squadron strength ie the number of machines actually in use. It would seem, according to this paper that the Air Staff calculates the 1st line strength in machines in some manner not disclosed, subtracts one quarter for immediate reserve, which it refuses to count, and divides the remainder by 9, thus obtaining a potential squadron strength in excess of the squadron strength actually formed and identified.

5. Impossible to comment on this without the relevant papers.

6. As to the introduction of the new potential squadrons it is difficult to make a clear comparison between the previous papers of the Air Staff and the present one. It does appear however that in their view between 1st June and 1st September squadrons were added at the rate of rather less than 4 a month; between 1st September and 1st December at the rate of 12 a month and between 1st December and 1st January at the rate of 7 per month. These fluctuations appear strange.

7. Comparison between the German and British Air Forces has not been undertaken. But paragraph 7 gives rise to two reflections ie

(a) It is stated that an Air Force with a strong industry can afford to do with less reserves than one with a weak industry. Our industry is incomparably weaker than the German, consequently we ought to have a much greater reserve. The contrary seems to be true.

(b) Quite apart from any question of immediate reserves, the Air Force memorandum gives rise to the following disquieting conclusions. Whereas according to paragraph 4 the number of machines in the first line in Germany is in excess of the number arrived at by multiplying the number of formed squadrons by 9, the number of machines in the first line in Great Britain is less than the number of squadrons multiplied by 9.

8. It seems strange that Germany, which previously insisted that all commercial aircraft should be convertible, should have abandoned this attitude.

9. It is true that the pupils in training squadrons would only be partially trained, but instructors would be the flower of the German Air Force.

10. Impossible to comment on this without the relevant papers.

11. When people are frightened some of them say the enemy is big but inefficient, and others say he is not as big as he looks. The Air Staff would like to have the best of both worlds.

Sir Edward Marsh to Winston S. Churchill
(Churchill papers: 4/2)

12 March 1937

My dear Winston,

I finished my *War & Peace* this morning & have sent it to be typed, so I hope to let you have it at Morpeth M early next week. I *couldn't* get it done before, it's been the most gruelling job I ever did, & I've worked like a galley-slave at *every* spare moment.

I'm not very well pleased with it, but I doubt if the greatest artist in pemmican cd have made it really readable—& I only hope you may think it will serve yr purpose.

How you will hate Tolstoi's contempt for Napoleon, & his absurd theory that 'Great Men' are flies on the wheel of History! I wonder what he wd have said if he'd read yr Marlborough.

At the thought of my dinner on Wed 'at once with joy & fear my heart rebounds'. It is splendid of you to be taking the chair.

Yours,
Eddie

I will get to work immediately on the proofs you sent me.[1]

---

[1] The proofs of Churchill's fourth volume of *Marlborough: His Life and Times*. Marsh had been knighted at the end of more than thirty years service at the Colonial Office, having been seconded to work as Churchill's Private Secretary for a total of 19 years.

Lionel Curtis[1] to Winston S. Churchill

(*Churchill papers: 1/298*)

12 March 1937

My dear Winston,

A few days ago I met a young man who had just come out of the exam for Mods and learned that the examiners had set an extract from your speech on Lawrence[2] for translation into Latin prose; so I got a copy of the paper from one of the examiners to send you. It is not often that Oxford recognises a writer during his life time as a classic. *Sic itur ad astra*, which is, I think, the motto of the Air Force.[3]

Yours ever,
L. Curtis

PS. Observe that we prefer your prose to your candidates!!![4]

Sir Norman Angell to Winston S. Churchill

(*Churchill papers: 2/311*)

15 March 1937

Dear Mr Churchill,

As you are, of course, aware there is growing up among sections of the Conservative Party, support of a policy which is, in fact, a reversal of the

---

[1] Lionel George Curtis, 1872–1955. Served in the South African War as a Private, 1899. Secretary to Sir Alfred Milner in South Africa, 1900. Town Clerk, Johannesburg, 1902–3. Assistant Colonial Secretary, Transvaal, 1903–9. Editor of the *Round Table*, 1909. Professor of Colonial History, Oxford, 1912. Member of the British League of Nations Section at the Paris Peace Conference, 1919. Secretary to the British Delegation at the Irish Conference, London, 1921. Colonial Office Adviser on Irish Affairs, 1921–4. Companion of Honour, 1949.

[2] Thomas Edward Lawrence, 1888–1935. Born in North Wales. Educated at Oxford. Travelled in Syria and Palestine while still an undergraduate. Obtained a first-class degree in history, 1910. On archaeological work at Carchemish, 1911–14. Explored, with Leonard Woolley, the Negev desert south of Beersheba, 1914. Served in the Geographical Section, General Staff, War Office, 1914–15; military intelligence, Egypt, 1915–16. Accompanied Ronald Storrs to Jedda, 1916, at the inauguration of the Arab revolt against the Turks. Liaison officer and adviser to the Emir Feisal, 1917–18. Took part in the capture of Akaba from the Turks, July 1917, and the capture of Damascus, October 1918. Accompanied Feisal to the Paris Peace Conference, 1919. Elected a Fellow of All Souls, Oxford, 1919. At Churchill's request he joined the Middle East Department of the Colonial Office, January 1921; resigned, 1922. Enlisted in the Tank Corps (as J. H. Ross), 1922 and in the Royal Air Force (as T. E. Shaw), 1925. Served in India, 1927–8. Retired from the RAF, 1935. Killed in a motor-cycle accident. His memoirs of the Arab revolt, *The Seven Pillars of Wisdom*, was first published in 1926.

[3] It is, in fact: *Per ardua ad astra*.

[4] A reference to Professor Lindemann coming bottom of the poll at the Oxford by-election, held between 23 and 27 February 1937 (see page 581, note 2).

purpose of the Great War—a surrender to the German hegemony which would place the British Empire at the mercy of an all-powerful Mittel-Europa. Garvin's article yesterday, which urges that Poland, Austria, Czecho-Slovakia, Jugo-Slavia, Roumania, Hungary and Bulgaria be brought under German domination, constituting a German Federation, is merely a more than usually naked expression of the policy. This German hegemony is to be encouraged while at the same time we maintain our enmity to Russia.

If, when we had the support of Japan, Italy, Russia and the United States we could only barely cope with the Austro-German combination, what is likely to be the situation of the British Empire when, without the support of Italy, Japan, Russia or the United States, it has to face demands coming from a Mittel-Europa of the character just described?

Thus, while the nation is making immense sacrifices for defence on its military and material side, that defence is in fact being neutralised (betrayed?) on its political side. The motive is, I take it, largely a fear of Russian Communism—a fear which at this date, does not take account of the virtually complete turn over of Moscow policy. Capitalism is to-day certainly as much menaced by Nazi Germany as by Communist Russia. Russia has become Nationalist in the sense of withdrawing more and more from the old conception of world revolution, and Conservative in the sense of a readiness to co-operate for political purposes with Capitalist states; Conservative also in the sense of erecting a bourgeois state in which the bureaucracy have become the bourgeoisie.

The only alternative to this surrender to the German hegemony of Europe is the policy which you yourself have advocated: an alliance of the Western Democracies and of Russia standing for a system which offers to 'the other side' the same means of security and peaceful change which we claim— briefly the League system, built up, bit by bit, from the nucleus of a firm Anglo-French alliance.

The case for this alternative to surrender is not understood by the rank and file of the Conservative Party, whose not very realist anti-Russian, anti-League prejudices, prompt instinctively its rejection. Unless the 'education' of these rather slow-moving elements can be brought about, they may become numerically so strong as to paralyse any action of the Government designed to check the German domination of Europe.

The purpose of my writing to you is, briefly, to urge you to use your influence with a few of your Conservative colleagues to start some 'process of education'. The simplest way to do that would be for a few Conservatives to join the League of Nations Union and prevent it becoming a purely Left organisation. If such an organisation is captured by the Left, more and more will that collective resistance to German domination which you have urged become unpalatable to Conservatives, and the greater will be the tendency to accept the surrender solution.

I have been impertinent enough to write you this longish letter as I understand I am having the pleasure of meeting you at luncheon on Wednesday and may perhaps take the opportunity of raising some of its points.

Yours very sincerely,
Norman Angell

Sir Stafford Cripps to Winston S. Churchill
(*Churchill papers: 2/295*)

15 March 1937

Dear Winston Churchill,

Thank you for your letter of the 12th of March. You are quite right that I am working in political association with the Communists at the present time in order, not to obtain power for the Communists but in order to obtain power for the Labour Party, who like myself have always expressed the view that freedom of speech is essential to Democracy, even to the extent of supporting your belief that you should be allowed to use the Broadcasting.

I do not appreciate your reference to the Communists being allowed a pretty good run over here. They are as entitled in a democratic country to a good run and the use of a recognised public Hall as are the Fascists, yourself or Mr Baldwin.

If you will take the trouble to refer to the Press and the correction which I issued as regards my Stockport speech to which you refer, you will see that you are misquoting me.[1]

I am delighted at your frankness because it shows as I suspected that you are keener on downing the Communists than on supporting freedom of speech.

[1] On 3 December 1936, during the Albert Hall meeting arranged by the League of Nations Union in defence of freedom and peace, Churchill had said, listing those who did not support them: 'Then there was Sir Stafford Cripps, who was in a class by himself. He wished the British people to be conquered by the Nazis in order to urge them into becoming Bolsheviks. It seemed a long way round. And not much enlightenment when they got to the end of their journey.' On 24 January 1937 Cripps had launched his United Front Campaign for Labour. According to *The Times* on the following day, he had said: 'Russia alone among the countries of Europe had shown herself a champion of working class power, and had done what she could in a world over-ridden with capitalism to stem the tide of Fascist aggression.' Three days later, on 27 January 1937 the Executive Committee of the Labour Party disaffiliated Cripp's Socialist League for 'disloyalty' (another MP who was a member of the League was Aneurin Bevan).

I shall probably be sending to the Press the whole of the correspondence with respect to the Albert Hall.

Yours sincerely,
R. Stafford Cripps

Wing-Commander Anderson to Violet Pearman

(*Churchill papers: 2/303*)

16 March 1937   Station Headquarters,
Royal Air Force,
Hucknall, Notts.

Dear Mrs Pearman,

I attach two small Papers, marked 'A'[1] and 'B'.

In the Paper marked 'B' I strongly criticise Contracts; but I think you know that I am unbuyable, and have no financial interests.[2]

Ever yours,
C. T. Anderson

[1] The paper marked 'A' was the original of a letter, dated 16 February 1937, from Air Commodore Tedder, in Singapore in which Tedder wrote: 'A good deal of muck of all sorts to be cleared away, training & organisation for the exercises to be done which should have been done years ago, preparation for the reinforcement & finally the combined training & the exercises themselves. *And* an appalling aftermath of functions & entertainments. The social side here is hell!! However thanks to a certain amount of good fortune & some damned good work by a lot of people things went with a bang which has shaken the old gentlemen to the core'.

[2] The paper marked 'B' was a three page unsigned note about the establishment of the Royal Air Force Volunteer Reserve (RAFVR). It contained the following statements: 'The essence of the scheme was to take training to the "back doors" of young men who were willing to give up their weekends. From the initiation of this policy which, incidentally, I was personally responsible for at the Air Ministry, the Service side was continually up against Mr Meadowcroft, who is now the Director of Contracts. He wished that the only Schools to be given these Contracts and Centres should be those already in existence and allied with the Ring of Aircraft Constructors and Manufactories. It will be seen by the Appendix, which I attach to Pamphlet 62, that all these Schools are owned by the Industry: Filton, by Bristols; Ansty, by Air Service Training and the Avro Group; Prestwick, by Scottish Colleges and de Havillands have 70% interest; Brough, Blackburnes; Desford, Reid and Sigrist, the Avro; Hanworth, Blackburnes; Hatfield and White Waltham, de Havillands; Sywell, the Sigrist Air Group; Perth, Alan Munks Airworks; Hamble, Air Service Training, Avro Group; Yatesbury, Bristols. Now, it is quite apparent that the majority of these Centres are entirely unsuited for recruiting the right type of volunteer. Hanworth, Hatfield and White Waltham for London are too far away, and are badly served by transport, and the other Centres have not the necessary population from which to select out best material . . .' and 'I know that Swinton is particularly unhappy regarding all the difficulties that have been put in his way regarding this Scheme; difficulties which have been manufactured entirely by Contracts in

Winston S. Churchill to Lord Peel

(Churchill papers: 2/317)

16 March 1937

I return you the transcript of my evidence in the form in which I wish it to stand. You assured me that our conversation was confidential and private. It certainly became somewhat informal at the end, and there are a few references to nationalities which would not be suited to appear in a permanent record. I shall be very glad to hear from you that you will make my corrections effective. Perhaps you will let me have a fair copy.

Victor Rothschild[1] to Winston S. Churchill

(Churchill papers: 1/298)

16 March 1937

Dear Mr Churchill,

Some time ago I saw Randolph, and he told me that you were very fond of Pol Roger 1921, but that you were having great difficulty in finding any.

---

order to keep these Schools in the hands of the vested interests. When I was at the Air Ministry Mr Meadowcroft tried to persuade me in every possible way, and brought pressure to bear on me to agree to contracts being given only to Firms who were running these present schools. A strong Reserve is just as essential as a strong First Line Air Force, and what will happen is just this; the personnel will not be obtainable from these Centres, but, as the average contract rate per hour for flying is £6, the firms will encourage their own employees, who are key industry men to undergo these courses, and, in the event of War, our Reserve is just a blind bluff, [?thus] we are to rob Peter to pay Paul. In carrying out the old Class "A" and "F" Reserve this is exactly what happened, and I personally am quite prepared to address an open Court of Enquiry and call for the necessary files showing the pressure unnecessarily placed on Service Officers by the Director of Contracts, Mr Meadowcroft.' The letter ended: 'I can prove that, in quoting for previous prices, luncheons and dinners were held in London by Blackburnes and Air Service Training Avros, and including Clydesdale, in order that prices could be fixed. The only honest man who would not agree to these Ring prices was Reid, from Desford' *(Churchill papers: 2/303)*.

[1] Nathaniel Mayer Victor Rothschild, 1910–   . Educated at Harrow and Trinity College, Cambridge. Fellow of Trinity College, 1935–9. Succeeded his uncle as 3rd Baron Rothschild, 1937. On active service (Military Intelligence), 1939–45 (George Medal, American Legion of Merit, American Bronze Star). Director, British Overseas Airways Corporation, (BOAC), 1946–58. Chairman of the Agricultural Research Council, 1948–58. Assistant Director of Research, Department of Zoology, Cambridge University, 1950–70. Member of the BBC General Advisory Council, 1952–6. Vice-Chairman, Shell Research Limited, 1961–3; Chairman, 1963–70. Research Co-ordinator, Royal Dutch Shell Group, 1965–70. Director-General, and First Permanent Under-Secretary, Central Policy Review Staff (the 'Think Tank'), Cabinet Office, 1971–4. Chairman, N. M. Rothschild & Sons, 1975–6. In 1977 he published a volume of memoirs, *Meditations of a Broomstick*.

I have a few dozen left, and I wonder whether you would care to accept a dozen bottles. It sounds rather mingy, a dozen, but, as you have found out, it is difficult to acquire these days, and I've got very little of it. Anyway, I hope you will accept it with my best wishes.

Yours sincerely,
Victor Rothschild

Winston S. Churchill to Bernard Baruch: telegram

(*Churchill papers: 1/298*)

17 March 1937

Your bet made with Ladbroke thirteen to one. Have obtained two places for coronation procession in Foreign Office stand for junior and his wife.[1] Hope this will suit them. Am greatly pleased at trend American opinion.

Winston

Patrick Donner to Winston S. Churchill

(*Churchill papers: 1/298*)

17 March 1937

Dear Mr Churchill,

I fear the death of Sir Austen Chamberlain will come as a great personal grief to you and one quite apart from the realisation of his loss to the nation at the present time.[2] It is for this reason that I venture to send you these few lines of sincere sympathy. The only times when I had the opportunity of speaking to Sir Austen Chamberlain at any length was under your roof and I shall ever remember this with gratitude to you.

When the news came through on the tape I was on the point of writing to you in order to make a request. I should so much value—more than I can say—a photograph of yourself as a souvenir of India days when I had the privilege of working in such small but splendid company under your leadership, and if therefore you could spare me one I should be most grateful.

Yours sincerely,
Patrick

---

[1] The Foreign Office register of correspondence shows that in 1937 Churchill had written to suggest the provision of Coronation Seats 'for distinguished US citizens' (*reference Treaty section, 6845/308/379*). The file itself, however, does not appear to have survived; in failing to locate it at the Public Record Office, Kew, I was told (15 January 1982) that 'it doesn't exist any longer'.

[2] Sir Austen Chamberlain had died on 16 March 1937.

Winston S. Churchill to Ivy, Lady Chamberlain

(*Austen Chamberlain papers*)

18 March 1937   11 Morpeth Mansions

My dear Ivy,

Accept my deepest sympathy in your overwhelming loss. I was shocked and shaken to the depths when on arriving at the Foreign Office Anthony told me. What must your sorrow be at this sudden severance of your long & glorious companionship! I pray indeed that you may find the resources in your spirit to enable you to bear this supreme stroke. Nothing can soften the loneliness or fill the void. Great happiness long enjoyed, casts its own shadow. All his friends of whom I am proud to be one will miss him painfully. In this last year I have seen more of him & worked more closely with him than at any time in a political & personal association of vy nearly forty years. I feel that almost the one remaining link with the old days indeed the great days has snapped.

Yet when one surveys the scene of our brief lives from an impersonal standpoint, I must confess that my strongest impression is of his wonderful good fortune. To preserve up to the vy last a complete mental & physical efficiency, & to die at 73 in a peaceful flash is surely the reward which should attend a lifetime of fidelity & honour. The tributes the like of which I have never heard surpassed in the House of Commons are only one measure of the esteem & love which Austen commanded on all sides. His life added lustre to the famous name he bore. We shall never see his like again—a great gentleman, a true friend of England, an example & an inspiration to all.

Do not try to answer this but let me know when I may come to see you, & always I beg you believe me

Your sincere friend,
Winston

Winston S. Churchill to Neville Chamberlain

(*Austen Chamberlain papers*)

18 March 1937   11 Morpeth Mansions

My dear Neville,

So many will be writing to you that I do so with some hesitation, & in the hope that you will not think it necessary to send me a personal answer.

But I saw so much of Austen all through his life, & especially in these later years, that I began to understand how strong & vital were the ties that bound you to one another; & so I can also realize the poignancy of the loss & severance wh has befallen you at this time above all of boundless care.

Pray accept my deepest sympathy.

Yours vy sincerely,
Winston S. Churchill

Neville Chamberlain to Winston S. Churchill

(*Churchill papers: 1/298*)

18 March 1937

My dear Winston,

I was very glad to have your letter for as I expect you know Austen had a great admiration and affection for you.

It was a shattering blow to me for I had no premonition of such a thing. But for him it was the end we should all have wished. And he has done what seemed almost impossible. He has added to the reputation which my father left behind him, something all his own, arising out of the shining nobility of his character.

I am deeply grateful for your sympathy.

Yours sincerely,
N. Chamberlain

Dr Colijn to Winston S. Churchill

(*Churchill papers: 2/295*)

18 March 1937

My dear Churchill,

Your literary secretary, Mr Deakin, handed me a copy of the third volume of Marlborough for which I most cordially thank you. I did not see Mr Deakin because I was in a conference when he presented himself, but I sent him a message that I would be only too glad to be of assistance if there was any reason for him.

As I intend to take a holiday of a week before Easter I hope to read the book very shortly, but I am already sure in my mind that I will find it very interesting. You have a most wonderful gift of expression and you have the advantage of treating a part of European history which belongs to the decisive periods of that history.

Allow me to tell you how impressed I am by the splendid effort Great-Britain is making to regain its proper influence on world politics. My

decided opinion is that the re-armament program is the best possible guarantee for maintaining world peace. In proportion to our means I am doing the
same since the beginning of last year.

With my good wishes for yourself, your family and country, believe me,

Yours very sincerely,
H. Colijn

Bernard M. Baruch to Winston S. Churchill
(Churchill papers: 2/295)

19 March 1937   New York

I do not want you to get over-enthusiastic about the trend of American
opinion. I believe the trend would take a very decided turn if we could find
some way of getting the debt question settled. I dislike to talk about this, but
you and I can be very frank with each other. I do not think we are going to
get very far until we get that out of the way. It is just too bad that England
did not continue to pay something, because when England last paid, the
others had defaulted and all over the country one heard 'Let's go English and
pay.'

We ought to be thinking hard about this matter, although neither one of
us has anything to do with the governments. But, I want you to keep that in
the back of your mind always when we talk about establishing the kind of
relations that should exist between the great commonwealths of England and
the United States.

With kindest regards, I am

Sincerely yours,
Bernie

Winston S. Churchill to Sir Thomas Inskip
(Churchill papers: 2/309)

19 March 1937

You will remember that in May last I approached you about the desire of
the Plessey Company to bring over and install one of the new German
forging plants. You were kind enough to see the Managing Director, Mr

Clark, and I also addressed myself to Sir Hugh Elles, the Master-General of the Ordnance, in this matter which I regarded as of high importance and urgency. You did not however feel able to take any action except to inform me that you had long had that under consideration. I therefore think you may be interested to see what has actually happened since the proposal was rejected.

My attention was directed afresh to this subject by a report which reached me of a confidential statement by Lord Swinton to the 1922 Committee in the House of Commons in which he had dilated upon the great advantages of this plant, and plumed himself upon its acquisition. Actually however it appears it cannot now begin to be in operation until August next!

Ivy, Lady Chamberlain to Winston S. Churchill

(*Churchill papers: 1/298*)

20 March 1937   24 Egerton Terrace,
                                                                    London

My dear Winston,

I am deeply touched by your letter. I know that you loved Austen & will feel his loss greatly. He always had a great affection & admiration for you even when you did not agree! I am thankful to say that his end was swift & peaceful & for him I would not have it otherwise. The wonderful world-wide tributes to his character & memory are a great solace to me & my children. After 31 years of perfect happiness & companionship I must not complain.

I want to thank you again for the help that you gave us, & which made it possible for us to have a home again. Austen was *so happy* in this home, & had planned & ordered plants for the rock garden at the last horticultural show. The plants arrived yesterday & I have today planted them as he wished.

Will you come & see me one day next week either morning or afternoon. I would like to show you the house & garden before I leave it. Just telephone when convenient to you. My loving thanks to Clemmie for her letter—I will write later.

Yours v sincerely,
Ivy Chamberlain

Ivy, Lady Chamberlain to Winston S. Churchill

(*Churchill papers: 1/299*)

Undated

My dear Winston

I am sending you a cigar case that Austen always carried, as a souvenir of the many years of friendship & affection that he had for you.

Yours v sincerely,
Ivy Chamberlain

Sir Thomas Inskip to Winston S. Churchill

(*Churchill papers: 2/306*)

23 March 1937
Confidential

My dear Churchill,

It was kind of you to send me a message last night telling me why you had to leave early. As I did not have an opportunity of seeing you after the debate I am sending you this note to explain, for your private information, my statement with regard to our present first-line strength. I am anxious that you should not misunderstand what I said, and I feel justified in giving you, as a Privy Councillor, this further confidential information, especially as you have already had so much secret information in this connection.

As I stated last night there will be 103 squadrons (and not 100 as stated in the Memorandum on Air Estimates) at home on the 1st April. All the regular squadrons will be at full strength in pilots and mechanics, but 10 will still be under strength in aircraft pending the delivery of further machines. At present the total deficiency in these squadrons is in the neighbourhood of 50 aircraft. The position changes from week to week. Moreover some of the Auxiliary Air Force squadrons which were recently formed will not be up to establishment.

In a comparison with what would have been the position if Scheme C had been continued, there are two factors to be borne in mind. I explained that the 1936 scheme required the continuance of the training organisation at its peak longer than would have been necessary under Scheme C. In consequence 11 flying training schools instead of 8 are still being maintained. This is the equivalent of 12 squadrons in personnel and aircraft.

The second factor is this. For tactical reasons the number of aircraft in fighter squadrons has been increased and the number of squadrons accordingly reduced. There are the same number of fighter aircraft, but 30 squadrons which have been formed under the 1936 scheme become the equivalent of 35 under the previous scheme. If I were to give in public particulars of partially formed squadrons I should be disclosing the tactical reorganisation of fighter squadrons: that is undesirable.

Wing-Commander Anderson to Winston S. Churchill

(*Churchill papers: 2/303*)

23 March 1937   Station Headquarters,
                                                 Royal Air Force,
                                                 Hucknall, Notts

The attached letter is of interest.[1]

I raised the question as I considered it was useless to train key-industry men in Auxiliary Squadrons, but have received the attached reply, dated 16th March, signed by a Civil Servant of the low grade of Junior Staff Officer.

2. No 116 Squadron, Andover, are the first Squadron to receive Blenheim aircraft, and have been equipped with 3. In the past week, one Blenheim has been completely smashed and written off beyond repair by one of our Acting Pilot Officers which Lord Trenchard considers are the cream of Britain.[2]

---

[1] The enclosed document was a copy of a letter from J. E. Lambert of the Air Ministry to the Air Officer Commanding No 6 (Auxiliary) Group, Royal Air Force. The letter read: 'I am directed to inform you that Messrs Rolls-Royce Ltd, Derby, have brought to the notice of this department that their employees are being refused enlistment into No 504 (County of Nottingham) (Bomber) Squadron. On the grounds that they would not be available on embodiment of the Auxiliary Air Force. It has been decided, after careful consideration of the question, that such employees should not be refused enlistment, and I am to request that you will instruct No 504 Squadron accordingly. Messrs Rolls-Royce Ltd have been informed that whilst the department recognises that this may involve the enlistment of key-men, it is anticipated that their release for industry in time of war would present no great difficulty' (*Churchill papers: 2/303*).

[2] Three weeks later, on 12 April 1937, Anderson sent Churchill an internal Royal Air Force letter, written by the Air Vice-Marshal commanding No 3 (Bomber Group), on the question of pilot training in heavy bomber squadrons. The letter dated 25 March 1937, read in part: 'A further indication of the degree to which dilution of experience has occurred within the squadrons of this Group is indicated by the shortage of Officers of the rank of Flight Lieutenant and above. The Group is deficient of 2 Group Captains, 11 Wing-Commanders, 18 Squadron Leaders and 37 Flight Lieutenants, and the position must deteriorate with the formation of new squadrons. Lacking the leaven of experience, it is inevitable that a condition will soon be reached when even elementary night flying training will diminish and the progress of those partially qualified will cease.'

Josiah Wedgwood to Winston S. Churchill

(*Churchill papers: 2/315*)

23 March 1937   House of Commons

My dear Winston,

You know the situation of the Jews in Poland.[1] Public opinion here and in America still counts. They have had a conference in America to which Senators & Governors sent messages (& La Guardia[2] spoke!). They are trying the same thing here on Apr 6.

I offered to get messages from you & LG. So I have drafted the enclosed for you to cut about or rewrite. I think you might, because so much still depends on the words of an Englishman. . . .

Yours ever,
Josiah C. Wedgwood

Josiah Wedgwood: draft message for Winston S. Churchill

(*Churchill papers: 2/315*)

23 March 1937

No Englishman can read without distress and indignation of the barbarous assaults directed against the Jewish population in Poland. The Polish Republic can never hope to make good its claim to be a bulwark of Western Civilization so long as it fails to afford adequate protection to a tenth of its population against the organised hooliganism whose successes in Germany have spread horror and apprehension throughout Europe. Nor can an economic policy which counts multitudes of law-abiding Polish citizens among its

---

[1] Beginning in 1935, and continuing until 1938, several hundred of Poland's three million Jews had been attacked in the streets by anti-semitic groups in towns and villages throughout Poland. Thousands of homes and shops had been broken into and looted. From 9 March 1936, when three Jews were murdered in the remote hamlet of Przytyk (fifty miles south of Warsaw), many thousands of Polish Jews had sought to emigrate to Europe, the United States and Palestine; others had formed local self-defence groups to try to beat off their attackers.

[2] Fiorello Henry La Guardia, 1882–1947. Born in New York City, of Italian parents. Educated in Arizona, and at the New York University. Served in the American consular service in Hungary and Italy, 1895–1906. Received his Law Degree at New York University, 1910. Deputy State Attorney-General, New York, 1914. Member of the Federal House of Representatives, 1916. On active service with the Air Corps, commanding a squadron on the Italian front, 1917–18. Defeated Tammany Hall, to become Mayor of New York, 1933. Re-elected in 1937 and 1941. An outspoken critic of the policies and methods of Hitler and Mussolini. Director-General of the United Nations Relief and Rehabilitation Agency (UNRRA), 1946–7, when he succeeded in bringing home to his fellow countrymen the extent of the hunger and suffering in post-war Europe.

victims promote the internal peace and stability without which Poland cannot fulfil the high destiny which history has assigned to her.

I hope that the Polish Government may yet be persuaded to afford to its Jewish citizens the full measure of aid and protection guaranteed to them by the Polish Constitution and the Peace Treaties.

Winston S. Churchill to Sir Edward Marsh

(*Churchill papers: 4/2*)

24 March 1937   Chartwell

Cheque herewith. I thought the digest admirable, and can quite understand that it must have been gruelling. You certainly covered the whole field and at the same time produced a version which was most readable and easy to follow.

Thank you also very much for the correction of the opening chapters of Volume IV.[1] I feel that as they stand they are a bit too stodgy and not equal in interest to the rest of the narrative. They will very likely be severely cut when the whole book is finished.

I thought the tributes paid to you were very fine because they were so true and sincere.[2] Do let me know how things go. You must come and stay here when the weather improves. I am at the present time on the brink of a trip to the Riviera and indulging all my customary vacillation where alternative forms of pleasure are concerned.

Winston S. Churchill to Josiah Wedgwood

(*Churchill papers: 2/315*)

24 March 1937
Private

I am reluctant to take up a position antagonistic to Poland at this time when our dangers are so great, and we have to pick our steps so carefully. We do not want these people, as well as Italy, to go into the Nazi camp. If only we had not neglected our defences we might indeed play a more spacious role. Pray therefore excuse me.

---

[1] Churchill had begun work on the fourth and final volume of his Marlborough biography.

[2] Following Marsh's retirement, Churchill had attended two dinners in his honour, one at the May Fair Hotel on 17 March 1937, (see page 656, note 3), the other on 22 April 1937, at Brooks's Club.

Winston S. Churchill to Neville Chamberlain

(*Churchill papers: 2/300*)

24 March 1937
Secret

CIVIL LIST COMMITTEE

Lloyd George and I would be much obliged if you could see us before the Committee meets. I shall certainly be back in England by the 7th, and should be glad if that date were convenient to you.

We should be glad to know whether you would tell us, privately, what will be the financial position of the Duke of Windsor. Baldwin mentioned to me that he possessed a large capital sum, which I gather is from £800–£950,000 —a large part of which was at one time settled on the lady, though I believe she has renounced all except £10,000 a year. Besides this I am aware that there is an agreement signed by the present King to pay the Duke £25,000 a year—I presume free of tax. However there has lately been some discussion about this, and meanwhile the Duke has not yet made over to the King his life interest in Balmoral and Sandringham. Let me say at once that if the signed agreement holds good, that the £25,000 is free of tax, and if the capital sum is what I have been led to believe, these assets would in my opinion together constitute a satisfactory and proper provision.

If you were able to assure us of this privately it would not be necessary for us to raise the question at all in the Civil List Committee, still less elsewhere. It would be a great advantage if the whole business of the Civil List could be conducted without the slightest reference to the ex-King. This is I am sure what you would yourself advise and wish. But we both feel that we ought to know definitely how the matter lies, because a proper establishment for the Duke with the formalities due to royalty seems to us to be an essential part of 'the maintenance of the honour and dignity of the Crown'.

If you will tell your secretary to let me know whether you can receive us on the 7th, we should be much obliged.

Winston S. Churchill to the Duke of Windsor

(*Churchill papers: 2/300*)

24 March 1937

I have not inflicted any letter upon Your Royal Highness knowing well how you must be burdened by the 'fan mail'. But my thoughts have strayed very often to Enzesfeld and I have been unhappy to think that these many weeks must have lain very heavy on your hands. Bendor told me your project of going to Saint Saens, and how it was all arranged, also all the reasons which prevented it. How very wise and prudent, Sir, you have been in all that you have done since leaving England. Now I am very glad to think this trying period is drawing to a close and better days are in store.

The specific reason which now makes me write is that Lloyd George and I are on the Civil List Committee, and naturally we wish to make sure, as far as our influence goes, that proper provision will be made in one form or another for that part of 'the honour and dignity of the Crown' represented by Your Royal Highness. Before the Committee meets we seek an interview with Neville and hope to hear from him that all is settled in an acceptable and agreeable manner.

Accordingly I saw Monckton who gave me some information about how things stand. But if there is any point about which Your Royal Highness feels concern, I hope you will let me know either through him or otherwise, so that we may consider whether we can do anything to further your wishes. I hope we shall receive assurances from the Chancellor of the Exchequer which will make it unnecessary for the matter even to be mentioned in the Civil List Committee, still less in the House of Commons.

I am sure Your Royal Highness will be grieved to hear that poor Freddie Guest has cancer and that no operation is possible. He insisted upon knowing the whole truth, and has now gone to Brussels where there is a Belgian doctor who holds out some hopes of a cure. They are, I fear, very slender hopes. Nothing could be more admirable than the gallant manner in which he faces this melancholy ordeal. I know he would value immensely a message from you now that polo days are over for him once and for all.

The European situation has not improved at all, except that a great many small countries are comforted by British rearmament. This is now of course in full swing, but as the Government started so late in spite of all the warnings some of us gave, we have at least two very dangerous years to go through. I pray indeed that we may have the time necessary to put our house in order, for then peace will stand on far surer foundations.

I should like above all things to come and see you as Your Royal Highness so kindly suggested after the Civil List business is satisfactorily disposed of.

Winston S. Churchill to David Lloyd George

(*Churchill papers: 2/300*)

25 March 1937   Chartwell
Secret

I sent the enclosed letter to Monckton who is to see the King this week, because I thought it was just as well that he should let it be known that we were taking an interest in the matter. I have also written the enclosed letter to Neville. If you approve please seal it up and send it on as quickly as possible for time is short. If you do not like it telephone me any amendments that may occur to you. I am going abroad on Saturday. Anyhow I shall be back on the 7th.

The weather has been delightful here today, most pleasant sunshine after so much sleet and drizzle.

Lord Louis Mountbatten[1] to Winston S. Churchill

(*Churchill papers: 2/305*)

25 March 1937

Dear Mr Churchill,

As promised over the telephone I am sending you some arguments in favour of placing all craft concerned in the defence of trade, be they warships, flying boats or specialised shore-based aircraft, under the control of a single service. The enclosed memorandum has been prepared by officers who have had more experience of air operations over the sea than any other officers on the active list.

It is almost inevitable that you should wish to obtain further information on some points, and, as time will not permit of your doing so by correspondence, I would like to suggest an alternative method. It happens that Captain Graham,[2] of the Naval Air Division, lives near you. He is spending the Easter holiday at home and would be very pleased to answer any further questions you wish to put, either over the telephone or in person. If you care to send a telephone message to Wadhurst 167, he could drive over at any time to see you.

[1] Prince Louis Francis Albert Victor Nicholas of Battenberg, 1900–1979. Second son of Prince Louis of Battenberg. A Naval Cadet, 1913–15. Midshipman, 1916. His father was created Marquess of Milford Haven, and assumed the surname of Mountbatten in 1917. Commander, 1932. Naval Air Division, Admiralty, 1936. Captain, 1937. Commanded HMS *Kelly* 1939 (despatches twice). Chief of Combined Operations, 1942–3. Supreme Allied Commander, South-East Asia, 1943–6. Created Viscount Mountbatten of Burma, 1946. Viceroy of India, 1947. Created Earl, 1947. Governor-General of India, 1947–8. First Sea Lord, 1955–9. Admiral of the Fleet, 1956. Chief of the Defence Staff, 1959–65. Murdered by Irish terrorists of the Irish Republican Army (IRA), 27 August 1979, at Mullaghmore in the Irish Republic. Also murdered in the same explosion were his daughter's mother-in-law (aged 82), his grandson Nicholas (aged 14), and a 17-year-old boatman. On the same day, 18 British soldiers were killed in a landmine explosion in County Down, Northern Ireland.

[2] Cosmo Moray Graham, 1887–1946. Lieutenant, Royal Navy, 1909. Served on the destroyer *Nubian* in 1911, while Churchill was First Lord. On active service, 1914–18; as Commander of an aircraft carrier, he was the first commander to learn to fly under the dual control scheme. Captain, 1930. Deputy Director of the Naval Air Division, 1936–9. Commanded HMS *Shoreham*, 1939–41. Rear-Admiral, 1941, and Flag Officer Commanding the Humber Area. He lived at Wadhurst, twenty-two miles from Chartwell, and went to see Churchill, as Mountbatten had suggested.

He has been closely associated with the Fleet Air Arm since its inception, has served twice in the Naval Division of the Admiralty, been Commander of an Aircraft Carrier and was the first Commander to learn to fly under the dual control scheme. There is no officer serving in the RAF or RN with a greater knowledge of the whole question, or who has made a deeper study, but I can't guarantee that his views will necessarily coincide with any of the 'high-up' views, which you may have had put before you. I hope you don't mind my having rung you up and that you won't mention it!

Yours very sincerely,
Dickie Mountbatten

Winston S. Churchill to Sir Thomas Inskip
(*Churchill papers: 2/306*)

26 March 1937

Many thanks for your letter about the RAF strength. It is of course inevitable that there should be a great deal of disorganisation and weakness during a period of rapid expansion. I send you, in personal confidence, a paper which was written a few weeks ago by a Staff Officer of the Air Force which throws a revealing light upon the present situation. I must ask you not to show it to anybody else as, though it is not an official document, it was written in confidence.

I wonder you do not get a list made out of everything that a regular Air Squadron should have—pilots, machines, spare engines, spare parts, machine guns, bombing sights etc together with the reserves of all kinds which should be kept at the station. And then, armed with this, go down accompanied by three or four competent persons to visit, quite by chance, some Air Squadron by surprise. If then during the course of a whole day your people went through the list while you cross-examined the officers, you would have some information on which you could rest with some security.

It must never be forgotten that the structure of the Air Force both civil and military, is very much weaker, slighter and newer than that of the Army or the Navy. On the other hand a strain has been thrown upon them incomparably more severe than either of the two older services are bearing. The reason why I am not dwelling upon these matters in public is because of the fear I have of exposing our weakness even more than is already known abroad.

I am sending you in a separate envelope a note on the Fleet Air Arm controversy. I shall be back from the Riviera on the 7th and of course you are free to send for me at any time.

April 1937

Winston S. Churchill to David Lloyd George

(*Churchill papers: 2/300*)

1 April 1937   Cap Martin

I have had the enclosed answer from Neville[1] which seems satisfactory so far as it goes. I hope to be back on Tuesday, and will meet you in the House after questions. I am asking Monckton, who will know the Duke's latest wishes, to luncheon on Wednesday and hope you will come too. 1.30 at 11 Morpeth Mansions. We shall then know where we are.

The weather here is cold but brilliant. Max has returned from his long holiday cured of his asthma, but looking somewhat aged. We look as if we are going to have another Baldwin triumph in India.[2]

Sir Thomas Inskip to Winston S. Churchill

(*Churchill papers: 2/306*)

1 April 1937

My dear Churchill

Many thanks for your letter of 26 March. I have read rather hastily the memorandum you enclose, and I will of course read it again more carefully.

---

[1] On the question of the Duke of Windsor's finances (see pages 634, 643 and 644).

[2] Under the Government of India Act, 1 April 1937 was the day set for the start of Provincial Autonomy in India. But the Congress Party, under the Presidency of Jawaharlal Nehru, had agreed, on 18 March 1937, that the leader in each province would only accept office as Prime Minister provided that the Governor of the province agreed that so long as the Prime Minister and his Cabinet acted within the constitution 'the Governor will not use his special powers of interference or set aside the advice of his Ministers'. The Governors at once replied that no such pledge could be given consistent with the India Act. The convening of the new Legislatures was therefore postponed. On June 21 Lord Linlithgow proposed a compromise: Prime Ministers would not be dismissed, but would resign, in the event of serious disagreement with their Provincial Governor. On July 7, after Gandhi had intervened to prevent a stalemate, this proposal was accepted, on the understanding that individual Congress members would accept office for the specific purpose of furthering the Congress policy of combating the India Act on the one hand, and presenting a 'constructive programme' of Provincial Government on the other.

There are some statements which I find at variance with facts within my own knowledge, but I have no doubt there is a great deal that deserves attention in the memorandum. Perhaps the date at which it was written would explain the discrepancy between the facts as I know them & some of the statements. The document is undated. I will take care that it is not seen by anyone except myself.

Thank you for your suggestion. I will consider this—it might be very useful.

Vice-Admiral Sir Reginald Henderson to Winston S. Churchill

(*Churchill papers: 2/302*)

5 April 1937   Admiralty

Dear Mr Churchill,

I have read the attached letter from Mr Harrison[1] which you sent me, and have the following comments to make.

No one pretends that, other things being equal, a 'six inch' cruiser is the match for an 'eight inch' cruiser. It is, therefore, perfectly true that the three large eight inch cruisers at present being built by Germany are superior to any of the cruisers at present being built by Britain. We must also concede that, by virtue of their newness, the German cruisers may be somewhat superior to our own 'eight inch' cruisers. But it is wholly untrue to suggest that the German construction is the result of the Anglo-German 35% agreement. It is the result of the German Government's repudiation of the disarmament clauses of the Treaty of Versailles. Faced with that repudiation, the former allied powers had three courses of action open to them:—

---

[1] On 22 March 1937 B. Howard Harrison wrote to Churchill from Devon: 'I am sending you an article by the Naval Correspondent of the Morning Post, in case you have not seen it (very unlikely!). When the present Government was elected with Rearmament as one of the chief planks in its programme many Conservatives must have heaved a sigh of relief. Their relief and satisfaction must be shattered by this article. To expect 6 in gun cruisers to success-fully fight 8 in gun cruisers seems to my lay mind like setting a fox-terrier onto a bull-terrier. I apparently in my lay ignorance, thought that Coronel had proved the futility of 6 in guns as against 8 in. And further why have we adopted the 14 in gun for battleships as against the 15 in gun of certain foreign navies? I hope you will not resent my writing to you on this subject.' The article in the *Morning Post* read, in part: 'The London Naval Treaty of 1930 instituted a "holiday" in the building of cruisers with 8 in guns. This "holiday" is designed to last six years and applies only to the Powers signatory to the Treaty. Moreover, that Treaty fixed the maximum displacement for cruisers mounting 6 in guns at 8,000 tons. The Treaty has so far been ratified only by America, but Great Britain is considering herself bound by it in the framing of her building programmes.'

(i) To protest, but otherwise do nothing.
(ii) To acquiesce, and attempt to control the extent of German re-armament by agreement.
(iii) To wage a preventive war against Germany.

Perhaps Mr Harrison and the naval correspondent of the 'Morning Post'[1] would have favoured war, and history may decide that they were right. However, that was plainly out of the question & there remained a choice between protest and agreement. For land and air force the Powers concerned failed to reach agreement, with the result that Germany is already credited with the greatest army and the most formidable air force in Europe. For naval forces, we chose the path of agreement, with result that for two years, at least, we have been spared the anxiety of naval rivalry with Germany.

On the wider question of the future of 8 inch cruisers, as a whole, this country has consistently worked for their abolition as a type. This would plainly be in our interest because we have an absolute requirement for a large number of cruisers for trade protection, and, for obvious reasons, we should like them to be as small as possible. The eight inch cruiser is unnecessarily large, and if we were forced to adopt it as the standard size, the additional cost would be extremely heavy. That, briefly, was our reason for pressing for a building holiday in eight inch cruisers, and we attach so much importance to getting the holiday that we are prepared to run some risk at present by building to designs which anticipate the 1936 Treaty's ratification.

If, however, our hopes of ratification are disappointed a new situation will arise in which no one should assume that we shall necessarily continue building 8,000 ton 6 inch cruisers. Neither should it be assumed that the reply to renewed building of 8 inch cruisers abroad will necessarily be a corresponding building programme by ourselves.

As regards battleships, the Admiralty contention is that one cannot build a really well balanced ship of 35,000 tons with a gun larger than 14″. What will happen, in view of Japan's refusal to be limited to 14″, yet remains to be seen.

It also remains to be seen whether she is going to limit herself to 35,000 tons. If she does so, I do not think she can build a well-balanced ship with 16″ guns—the maximum she can go to would be 15″.

My own personal view is that, now Japan's 'armour propre' has been satisfied, in that she is no longer stigmatised as relatively a smaller power, she

---

[1] Kenneth Philip Mackenzie Edwards. A submariner. Described by his colleague the Air Correspondent (Major Oliver Stewart) as 'Good looking, rather German type. Average height. Square face. Fair wavy hair, with a sardonic manner.' (*Daily Telegraph* archives)

may fall into line of her own accord, put her thumb in her mouth and say 'What a good girl am I'.

Yours sincerely,
R. G. H. Henderson

William Elliott[1] *to Violet Pearman*

(*Churchill papers: 25/12*)

6 April 1937   Committee of Imperial Defence
Secret

Dear Private Secretary,

I am directed to thank you for your letter of the 27th March, 1937, forwarding a copy of Mr Winston Churchill's comments on the draft conclusions of the 12th Meeting of the Sub-Committee on Air Defence Research.

The point which Mr Churchill wishes to emphasise regarding the development of a system of deceptive, as opposed to restricted, lighting on the lines of the silhouette scheme was, in fact, included in the Minutes of the Meeting, but it is agreed that it was not, perhaps, sufficiently emphasised in the conclusions. Mr Churchill's remarks were therefore passed on to Air Marshal Freeman,[2] Air Member for Research and Development, who is dealing with the question at the Air Ministry in order that Mr Churchill's proposals may receive the emphasis which he desires.

Meanwhile, if Mr Churchill will agree, it is suggested that instead of including his remarks in the conclusion these should be recorded in full in the Minutes and the conclusion redrafted with a summary of his proposals. I attach a copy of the original conclusion with the suggested redraft and I

---

[1] William Elliott, 1896–1971. On active service, 1914–18, (despatches, DFC and bar). Assistant Secretary, Committee of Imperial Defence, 1937–9; to the War Cabinet, 1939–41. Director of Plans, Air Ministry, 1942–4. Air Officer Commanding Gibraltar, 1944; Balkan Air Force, 1944–5. Assistant Chief Executive, Ministry of Aircraft Production, 1945–6. Knighted, 1946. Assistant Chief of the Air Staff (Policy), 1946–7. C-in-C Fighter Command, 1947–9. Deputy Secretary (Military) to the Cabinet, 1949–51. Chairman of the British Joint Services Mission to Washington, 1951–4. ADC to the Queen, 1952–4.

[2] Wilfrid Rhodes Freeman, 1888–1953. Major, Manchester Regiment, on active service in France, 1914–18 (despatches, DSO, MC). Deputy Director of Operations and Intelligence, Air Ministry, 1927–30. Chief Staff Officer, Inland Area, 1930. Air Officer Commanding Palestine and Transjordan, 1930–1. Commandant, Royal Air Force Staff College, 1933–6. Member of the Air Council for Research Development and Production, 1936–40. Knighted, 1937. Air Chief Marshal, 1940. Vice-Chief of the Air Staff, 1940. Chief Executive, Ministry of Aircraft Production, 1942–5. Created Baronet, 1945.

would be grateful if you could let me know if this meets with Mr Churchill's approval.[1]

Yours sincerely,
William Elliott

Sir Thomas Inskip to Winston S. Churchill

(*Churchill papers: 2/303*)

8 April 1937
Personal & Confidential

My dear Churchill,

I am writing a further letter with reference to the paper which you sent me privately on the 26th March about the RAF. I have now read it carefully and am returning it, as it is undesirable that it should be among my papers in view of your wish that I should treat it as very confidential. You will not wish me to discuss or reply to it in detail; before doing that I should naturally want to consult the Air Ministry. But some passages strike me at once as being written with incomplete knowledge—direction-flying is an example and on tactical training you yourself are in touch with the location and interception developments; some broach on what are disputable questions such as the size and load of bombers—on that we must obviously be guided by expert opinion; and some make scanty allowance for such inevitable difficulties as the shortage of building labour.

The essence of the paper, however, does not seem so much a criticism of the Air Ministry's methods, or a plea for more activity or for alternatives, as a picture of the magnitude of the task of rapidly expanding the Air Service, especially in the light of our particular strategic requirements and at a time when great strides are being made in aeronautics. I rather infer that the writer thinks we have been trying to go too fast. He feels that the magnitude of the task is not generally appreciated and also, I think, that I have been drawn into giving too reassuring a picture of the efficiency of the Force as it stands to-day. We have often discussed the dual requirements of immediate expansion, and the introduction of new types. I feel convinced that there is nothing more that we can do to expedite the production of new machines. Incidentally it is useless for the production of material to outrun the training of personnel. I have been informed that we are not behind other countries in

---

[1] On 9 April 1937 Violet Pearman wrote to William Elliott: 'I am desired by Mr Churchill to thank you for your letter to me of the 6th instant, Reference ID/D/132, and to say that he is entirely satisfied with the suggested redraft.'

the development of new instruments—guns, bomb sights, for instance. There will, anyway, be no relaxation of our efforts, and I take note of the very great importance of these items. As regards numbers, I have myself been at pains to explain that in judging our progress figures are not everything. I have been troubled from time to time by the tendency in our debates to adopt figures of first-line strength as a full criterion. As regards training, obviously time is required. I do not think we have ever minimized the importance of quality in every sense, and we have generally, at any rate, the advantage of building upon an efficient, if small, organisation.

I will certainly keep in mind the writer's apprehensions, and that is, I think, what you want me to do.

Yours very sincerely,
T. W. H. Inskip

Winston S. Churchill to David Lloyd George

(*Churchill papers: 2/300*)

8 April 1937
Secret

Everything went off quietly today. Only two points of significance were raised.

First, Attlee asked for information about the private fortunes and savings of members of the Royal Family. You will see the drift of this. I suggested that we should be guided by precedent, and Neville promised to look up the precedent. Evidently they would not favour disclosure.

Secondly, on the other hand, Amery quite unexpectedly raised the question of the Duke of Windsor. He ought, he said, to be treated like one of the King's sons. His marriage might unfit him for the position of Sovereign, but we could not adopt an air of unctuous rectitude and pretend that thereby he was cast out altogether from the Royal Family and from our society. The Chancellor and SB were disconcerted and said nothing, so I said that in this very preliminary and provisional survey we had been making of our problem, I thought it would be premature to enter upon such a very extensive subject, but that it might be necessary to do so later on. Neville endorsed this and the matter dropped.

We agreed to meet again on Tuesday at 11 am and Thursday at 5 pm.

Winston S. Churchill to Neville Chamberlain

(*Churchill papers: 2/300*)

8 April 1937

Attlee's question about the private fortunes of the Royal Family and Amery's unexpected reference to the Duke of Windsor's position, show how easily we might find ourselves immersed in awkward topics. The best solution would surely be that the King should honour his signature about the £25,000 a year, and that the Duke of Windsor should intimate to you that he does not desire to make any request for provision in the Civil List. Whether he would do this I do not of course know. This could then if necessary be stated in public. It would certainly put everything on the best footing.

If on the other hand a dispute arises about an annuity of £25,000 a year, and if the question about the provision for the Duke of Windsor is raised in the Committee it seems to me that you will have no choice but to disclose the capital figure mentioned yesterday; and the moment this is disclosed the Labour Party could hardly help drawing the moral of the very large savings which it is possible for Royal persons to make, and to argue that the existing Civil List should be reduced. Thus it seems to me that the King's interest, no less than that of the Duke of Windsor, is directly involved in an amicable settlement of the kind outlined.

I should have thought it would not be a hardship for the King to pay the £25,000 on the assumption that the Civil List is voted at the figure now proposed by you. It is true that it is £36,000 less than the previous Civil List but on the other hand there is the £50,000 a year saving on account of the Duke of York. Thus there is a balance of £14,000, practically the £25,000 he promised to provide for his brother.

The idea of a dispute between the two brothers upon the question of good faith, and still more of legal process, would of course be a disaster of the first order to the monarchy.

I write these few lines for your consideration before you have your audience.

Desmond Morton to Winston S. Churchill

(*Churchill papers: 2/305*)

14 April 1937 Earlylands

Dear Winston,

I enclose a further draft of the paper on the Fleet Air Arm. The liberties I have taken have, for their object, primarily the elimination of repetition and a suggested rearrangement. Apart from this, I have suggested a new Paragraph 2. Even if you do not like my wording, I do recommend the insertion of some answer to the objection that the Air Force is always raising, namely, that since the Army makes no demand for a separate Air Force to undertake Army co-operation, the Navy has no case.

You will see that I have omitted a few sentences of your original draft. This is intentional, as I doubt if they are necessary to your case.

Any other suggested alterations will be clear to you in the reading.

As often before, I am astonished at your knowledge of detail in Defence matters. How many Cabinet Ministers or Privy Councillors have ever heard of a Fortress Commander? Or, as you do, appreciate the delicacy of his position.

In this connection, I have just been looking at the new Handbook of Coastal Defence, which was published in 1936 after ten years of wrangling. I am afraid it is nothing like the last word on the subject, though an improvement on previous thought. Too many paragraphs have, at present, to end with the suggestion that, owing to disagreement, the exact responsibilities of the various interested authorities cannot be determined. So far as I can see, however, there is nothing in it necessarily impeding your present proposals.

I gather that there would be considerable opposition on the part of the Army to the suggestion to place the AA guns and lights under the Air Ministry. I, personally, am undeterred. I am sure that an Anti-Air Department of the Air Ministry is the correct solution.

In this connection you will see that, in the present draft, I have restricted its functions to 'active' AA Defence. I find that this covers all that you intend. 'Passive' AA Defence is the term now used to describe 'Air Raid Precautions' under the Home Office. Whereas it is not impossible that eventually the Air Ministry may have to take this over too, the question is perhaps outside the scope of the present paper.[1]

---

[1] As well as their correspondence, and frequent meetings at Chartwell, during 1937 Desmond Morton dined with Churchill on January 24, February 21, May 16, July 17, August 15, September 6, September 12 and November 21; lunched with him on September 26 and October 10, and visited him at Morpeth Mansions on February 24.

Winston S. Churchill: draft memorandum[1]

(Churchill papers: 2/305)

15 April 1937

FLEET AIR ARM

1. It is impossible to resist an Admiral's claim that he must have complete control of and confidence in the aircraft of the battle fleet, whether used for reconnaissance, gun-fire or air attack on a hostile fleet. These are his very eyes. Therefore the Admiralty view must prevail in all that is required to secure this result.

2. The argument that similar conditions obtain in respect of Army co-operation aircraft cannot be countenanced. In one case the aircraft take flight from aerodromes and operate under precisely similar conditions to those of normal independent Air Force action. Flight from warships and action in connection with naval operations is a totally different matter. One is truly an affair of co-operation only; the other an integral part of modern naval operations.

3. A division must therefore be made between the Air Force controlled by the Admiralty and that controlled by the Air Ministry. This division does not depend upon the type of the undercarriage of the aircraft, nor necessarily the base from which it is flown. It depends upon the function. Is it predominantly a naval function or not?

4. Most of these defence functions can clearly be assigned. For instance, all functions which require aircraft of any description (whether with wheels, floats, or boats; whether reconnaissance, spotters or fighters, bombers or torpedo seaplanes) to be carried regularly in warships or in aircraft carriers naturally fall to the naval sphere.

5. The question thus reduces itself to the assignment of no matter what type operating over the sea from shore bases. This again can only be decided in relation to the functions and responsibilities placed upon the Navy. Aircraft borne afloat could discharge a considerable function of trade protection. This would be especially true in the broad waters, where a squadron of cruisers with their own scouting planes or a pair of small aircraft carriers could search upon a front of a thousand miles. But the Navy could never be required to maintain an air strength sufficient to cope with a concentrated attack upon merchant shipping in the narrow waters by a large hostile Air Force of great power. In fact, the maxim must be applied of Air Force versus

---

[1] On 15 April 1937 Churchill sent copies of this memorandum to Lord Trenchard and Lieutenant-Colonel Moore-Brabazon; and on April 16 to Sir Thomas Inskip.

Air Force and Navy versus Navy. When the main hostile Air Force is to be encountered, it must be by the British Royal Air Force.

6. In this connection it should not be forgotten that a ship or ships may have to be selected and adapted for purely Air Force operations, like a raid on some deep-seated enemy base, canal or vital centre. This is an Air Force operation and necessitates the use of types of aircraft not normally associated with the Fleet. In this case the roles of the Admiralty and the Air Ministry will be reversed, and the Navy would swim the ship in accordance with the tactical or strategic wishes of the Air Ministry. Far from becoming a baffle, this special case exemplifies the logic of the 'division of Command according to function'.

7. What is conceded to the Navy should, within the limits assigned, be fully given. The Admiralty should have plenary control and provide the entire personnel of the Fleet Air Arm. Officers, cadets, petty officers, artificers, etc for this force would be selected from the Royal Navy by the Admiralty. They would then acquire the art of flying and the management of aircraft in the RAF training schools, but after acquiring the necessary degree of proficiency as air chauffeurs and mechanics they would pass to shore establishments under the Admiralty, for their training in Fleet Air Arm duties. Thus, the personnel employed upon fleet air functions will be an integral part of the Navy, dependent for discipline and advancement as well as for their careers and pensions solely upon the Admiralty. This would apply to every rank and every trade involved, whether afloat or ashore.

8. Coincident with this arrangement whereby the Fleet Air Arm becomes wholly a naval service, a further rearrangement of functions should be made, whereby the Air Ministry becomes responsible for active anti-aircraft defence. This implies, in so far as the Navy is concerned, that, at every naval port, shore anti-aircraft batteries, lights, aircraft, balloons and other devices will be combined under one operational control, though the officer commanding would, of course, with his command, be subordinate to the Fortress Commander.

9. In the same way, the control of the air defences of London and of such other vulnerable areas as it may be necessary to equip with anti-air defences on a considerable scale should also be unified under one command and placed under the Air Ministry. The consequent control should cover not only the operations, but as far as may conveniently be arranged, the training, the raising and administration of the entire personnel for active air defence.

10. The Air Ministry have as clear a title to control active anti-air defence as have the Navy to their own 'eyes'. For this purpose a new Department should be brought into being in the Air Ministry, to be called 'Anti-Air' to control all guns, searchlights, balloons and personnel of every kind connected

with this function, as well as such portion of the Royal Air Force as may from time to time be assigned to it for this duty. Under this Department there will be Air Force officers, assisted by appropriate staffs, in command of all active air defences in specified localities and areas.

11. It is not suggested that the Air Ministry or Air Staff are at present capable of assuming unaided this heavy new responsibility. In the formation of the Anti-Air Command recourse must be had to both the older Services. Well-trained staff officers, both from the Army and the Navy, must be mingled with officers of the existing Air Staff.

NB. The question of the recruitment and of the interior administration of the units handed over to the Anti-Air Command for operations and training need not be a stumbling block. They could be provided from the present sources unless and until a more convenient solution was apparent.

12. This memorandum has not hitherto dealt with material, but that is extremely simple. The Admiralty will decide upon the types of aircraft which their approved functions demand. The extent of the inroad which they require to make upon the finances and resources of the country must be decided by the Cabinet, operating through a Priorities Committee under the Minister for the Co-ordination of Defence. At the present stage this Minister would, no doubt, give his directions to the existing personnel, but in the event of war or the intensification of the preparations for war, he would give them to a Ministry of Supply. There could, of course, be no question of Admiralty priorities being allowed to override other claims in the general sphere of air production. All must be decided from the supreme standpoint.

13. It is not intended that the Admiralty should develop technical departments for aircraft design, separate from those existing in the Air Ministry or under a Ministry of Supply. They would, however, be free to form a nucleus technical staff to advise them on the possibilities of scientific development and to prescribe their special naval requirements in suitable technical language to the supply department.

14. To sum up, therefore, we have:

First—The Admiralty should have plenary control of the Fleet Air Arm for all purposes which are defined as naval.

Secondly—A new Department must be formed under the Air Ministry from the three Services for active anti-aircraft defence operations.

Thirdly—The question of material supply must be decided by a Priorities Committee under the Minister for the Co-ordination of Defence, and executed at present through existing channels, but eventually by a Ministry of Supply.[1]

---

[1] Churchill had first argued publicly for a Ministry of Supply on 23 April 1936. It was announced three years later, on 14 April 1939.

Winston S. Churchill to Sir Thomas Inskip

(*Churchill papers: 2/306*)

16 April 1937

I send you herewith some notes upon the Fleet Air Arm in case it may be of any assistance. I told you before the Easter holidays I propose publishing my views on this question in the near future, possibly in the Times, and you said that nevertheless you would like to have them.

I take this occasion to thank you for your letter about the present efficiency of the RAF and for returning me the paper which I sent you. Later on when you are less pressed I should like to send you some more information on this subject.

Anthony Eden to Winston S. Churchill

(*Churchill papers: 2/296*)

16 April 1937   Foreign Office

My dear Winston,

Thank you so much for the kind things you said, during Wednesday's debate, about our work here.[1] I can assure you that they were much appreciated by the occupant of this anxious office.

May I also say how very good I thought your speech as a whole; indeed I heard many opinions that the speech must be ranked among your very best. It was difficult to make with the House in that tempestuous and unreasoning mood, and you contrived to sober them and cause them to reflect.[2] Many

---

[1] Speaking in the House of Commons on 14 April 1937, during a debate on the situation at Bilbao, where Nationalist forces were blockading the Republican controlled port, Churchill defended the Government's decision not to use British naval forces to break the blockade. 'It is easy,' Churchill said, 'to point the finger of scorn and to accuse the Government of fear, but there is no need to fear. Overwhelming naval power is in our hands. But our policy is not to be drawn, certainly not single-handed, into this dismal welter. I thought we had decided to be neutral, and I earnestly hope the Government will bear the harsh reproaches that are addressed to them and move steadily upon the path they have taken.'

[2] During his speech on the situation at Bilbao, Churchill reflected on the Spanish Civil War as a whole, telling the House of Commons: 'I have not been able to work up the same state of passionate indignation or enthusiasm about either side in Spain that I see is so sincerely present in the breasts of many Members, not all by any means on one side in the Spanish matter, or on one side of the House. I have tried very sincerely to be neutral, and to adopt a neutral attitude of mind; I refuse to become the partisan of either side. I will not pretend that, if I had to choose between Communism and Nazi-ism, I would choose Communism. I hope not to be called upon to survive in the world under a Government of either of those dispensations. It is not a question of opposing Nazi-ism or Communism; it is a question of opposing tyranny in whatever form it presents itself; and, having a strong feeling

congratulations, and again thanks for what you said about our Foreign policy.

No answer please.

Yours ever,
Anthony Eden

Sir Thomas Inskip to Winston S. Churchill
(*Churchill papers: 2/306*)

19 April 1937

My dear Churchill,

Many thanks for your letter of the 16th April. I am anxious to have your views on the Fleet Air Arm question, and should like to keep your notes. But I think that in this copy a page is missing. It runs from paragraph 7 on the Fleet Air Arm to what seems a broken ending of paragraph 8, the earlier part of which may develop the argument on shore-based aircraft. If this is right, could your Secretary add the page and return the notes to me?

Yours sincerely,
T. W. H. Inskip

Winston S. Churchill to N. B. Foot
(*Churchill papers: 2/312*)

19 April 1937

I am obliged to you for the draft statement of policy which you have sent me.[1] I am very doubtful about the expediency of publishing it at the present

---

in regard to the preservation of individual rights as against Governments, and as I do not find in either of these two Spanish factions which are at war any satisfactory guarantee that the ideas which I personally care about, and to which I have been brought up in this House to attach some importance, would be preserved.' A few moments later Churchill said: 'There is nothing in this world, it appears to me, more horrible than the taking out of great masses of men, quite simple men, in batches, sometimes for no fault greater than to have been the secretary of a trade union or to have voted Conservative at the previous election, and shooting them by firing parties against a wall, yet that is proceeding on both sides to a terrible extent every day'.

[1] The draft statement urged the setting up of an 'Equity Tribunal' to settle international disputes 'which cannot be settled by negotiation and conciliation'. The Tribunal's decisions would be supported by an 'International Police Force', which would take the place of 'national competitive armaments'. Once this system was established, the New Commonwealth would support 'a review of the whole problem of conflicting colonial claims on the principles of safe-guarding the welfare of native populations, of securing to all nations equitable access to sources of raw materials and of submitting to an Equity Tribunal for investigation and settlement, any claims not susceptible of amicable adjustment through the existing machinery of the League'.

time. It would certainly arouse a lot of opposition to our movement among Conservatives. The circumstances which it contemplates are hypothetical and certainly not likely to be realised immediately. It is so fenced about that it would give no satisfaction to the Germans; and on the other hand you know how averse the English people are from giving pledges about hypothetical situations. Is it not much better to stick to our general position which provides for not only an International Police Force, but for an Equity Tribunal. Shall we not make these ideas more unpopular by holding out to the British public the prospect that when our work is done, they will at a very early stage have to submit the Colonies question to International arbitration. From their point of view therefore I see little gain and much antagonism. In any case before it is published I think we should have a discussion in the Parliamentary Committee.

Wing-Commander Anderson to Winston S. Churchill

(*Churchill papers: 2/303*)

22 April 1937

Air Chief Marshal Sir John Steel[1] attains the age of 60 in September of this year, and he has been informed by the Air Council that he will be placed on the Retired List.

I consider it criminal, during the Expansion time, that a man such as this should be compulsorily retired.

Winston S. Churchill: note of remarks to Lord Wigram[2]

(*Churchill papers: 2/300*)

25 April 1937

I understood that the allowance, apart from certain business elements, was a matter of family affection arising out of the King's promise to the Duke

---

[1] John Miles Steel, 1877–1965. A naval cadet, 1892. On active service in South Africa (relief of Ladysmith; wounded). 2nd in Command, HMS *Conqueror*, at the battle of Jutland, 1916 (despatches). Captain, 1916. Royal Air Service, 1917. Brigadier-General, RAF, 1918. Director of the Air Division, Admiralty, 1918–19. Air Commodore, RAF, 1919. Deputy Chief of the Air Staff, 1926. Knighted, 1926. Air Officer Commanding the Wessex Bombing Area, 1926–31; the RAF in India, 1931–5. Air Chief Marshal, 1936. Air Officer Commanding-in-Chief, Air Defence of Great Britain, 1935–6; Bomber Command, 1936–7. Retired list, 1937. Air Officer Commanding Reserve Command, 1939–40. Controller-General of Economy, Air Ministry, 1941–5.

[2] Clive Wigram, 1873–1960. Served in the Indian Army, 1897–9. Aide-de-Camp to Lord Curzon (then Viceroy of India), 1899–1904. Assistant Private Secretary to King George V, 1910–31; Private Secretary, 1931–5. Knighted, 1928. Created Baron, 1935. His second son was killed in action in 1943.

before the latter's abdication. It is altogether a personal and brotherly affair. It would not be right for Ministers to advise the King to make the payment of this allowance contingent upon the Duke not returning to England without the King's permission. Such advice would tend to involve the King in what might become very distressing publicity. Above all Ministers should not advise that such a condition should be presented to the Duke through the lawyers. The Duke would have no option but to refuse to receive such a communication; for otherwise he would put himself in the position of bartering his right to return to his native land for pecuniary advantage. It is to be hoped therefore that Ministers will not persist in such advice to the King.

It was stated to Parliament by the Attorney-General during the passage of the Abdication Bill that no condition of exile followed a voluntary abdication. As this declaration preceded the abdication, it must stand as a formal and solemn pledge both to Parliament and to the late King. It would therefore be all the more undesirable that Ministers, especially those personally involved in the said pledge, should advise the King to take the burden of preventing the return of the Duke upon himself and to use the allowance given in family affection for that purpose. If for any grave public reason Ministers considered that the return of the Duke of Windsor to England could not be allowed, their only course is to pass an Act of Parliament forbidding or regulating his return. This they could no doubt do. But it would not be right to take such a step, which would cause much pain and scandal throughout the British Dominions and the world, merely upon grounds of social convenience and etiquette. It would however be preferable to Ministers tendering advice which would bring the King himself personally into the centre of any controversy that might arise. The duty of Ministers is to take the burden on themselves, to use the powers at their disposal, in the public interest, and above all, to shield the Sovereign whom they serve from being involved in painful personal and family disputes.

I have given you my opinion as invited upon this point. But I wish to make it clear that far from advising the Duke to return at the present time, I would urge him most strongly to allow several years to pass before taking up his residence in England. Time is a healer of many things. The great and growing popularity of the present King and Queen among all classes of their subjects, reveals the unique and supreme position of the Sovereign far above all other members of the Royal Family; and when this fact is realised upon all sides the conditions for the Duke's return would be more favourable. What is important in these intervening years is to make the relations between the Duke and the King, or other members of the Royal Family, those of warm and easy friendship and affection, all doing their utmost for mutual benefit and in the public interest, and trying to help each other in every way they possibly can. The better this feeling is, the easier would it be for the Duke to exercise his undoubted right to return without detriment to interests which are precious to him. For this purpose one would have hoped that the Duke would make himself a home not too far away from England where he could be visited by members of his family, and by persons of distinction in England and Europe.

You have asked me my opinion upon the possibility of the Duchess of Windsor being recognised as a Royal Highness. I do not think that any Government will be found in England which would advise the Crown to take such a step. On the contrary I am sure that they would advise insistently against it. The fact that such an issue was still being proposed would certainly be an obstacle to the Duke's wishes in other respects. I have heard that HRH at one time contemplated renouncing his own royal status and ranking only as a Duke. Such a course would undoubtedly give much greater freedom in many ways, but it should only be adopted after consultation with the King, or otherwise it might make matters worse and not better.

Winston S. Churchill to H. Osborne

(*Churchill papers: 1/303*)

26 April 1937

In a book 'Coronation Commentary' by Geoffrey Dennis,[1] Heinemann, London, the following passage occurs—

'Those who came out as King's champions were an unprepossessing company. An unstable ambitious politician, flitting from party to party, extreme reactionary, himself the first-fruit of the first famous snob-dollar marriage; "half an alien and wholly undesirable" as long ago was said.'

This passage in the context plainly refers to me, and no answer could be given to the question 'If you did not mean me, who did you mean?' I should like to know whether this is not ground for libel. I do not wish to be advised on the policy of taking action, but only on the legal aspect.

It is to be observed that this book has been challenged by the Duke of Windsor's solicitors and there is a demand it should be withdrawn from circulation. The publishers who have some reputation are probably perturbed at this issue being unexpectedly raised upon them. It would seem therefore that they might be little inclined to endure the chastisement of a legal process for these extremely offensive statements about me. Surely these

---

[1] See page 660, note 1.

words are defamatory and calculated to hold their object up to hatred and contempt.

Violet Pearman to Adam Marshall Diston
(*Churchill papers: 8/546*)

26 April 1937

Dear Mr Diston,

Mr Churchill wishes me to thank you for your letter, and to say that he would be glad if you would make the amendments etc of The Middle Way (which I send herewith) take priority over the Jewish article.

Here are some suggestions which he would make regarding the latter article:—

'Obviously there are four things. The first is to be a good citizen of the country to which he belongs. The second is to avoid too exclusive an association in ordinary matters of business and daily life, and to mingle as much as possible with non-Jews everywhere, apart from race and religion. The third is to keep the Jewish movement free from Communism. The fourth is a perfectly legitimate use of their influence throughout the world to bring pressure, economic and financial, to bear upon the Governments which persecute them.'

Winston S. Churchill to Nathan Laski[1]
(*Churchill papers: 2/296*)

26 April 1937

I am planning to spend the winter on the other side of the Atlantic, and therefore fear that I cannot be with you on November 30th.[2] I can however

---

[1] Nathan Laski, 1863–1941. A Manchester merchant, trading with India for more than fifty years. Chairman of the Manchester Jewish Hospital and of the Jewish Board of Guardians. From 1904–1908 he was one of Churchill's principal supporters at Manchester North-West. Member of the War Pensions Committee. Retired, 1930, to devote himself to social work. Author of *A Week in Palestine* (1924) and *India As I Know it* (1928). On 31 October 1941 Churchill wrote to Laski's son Harold: 'I know how much you and your brother will feel his loss. It is for you the severance of a link with childhood which can never be replaced. He was a very good man whose heart overflowed with human feeling and whose energies were tirelessly used for other people and large causes. I feel I have lost a friend, and all my memories of Manchester and Cheetham are veiled in mourning.' (*Harold Laski papers*)

[2] Nathan Laski had asked Churchill to speak at the 70th anniversary meeting of the Manchester Jewish Board of Guardians, of which Laski himself (then aged 73), was President. Laski noted, in his letter to Churchill on 22 April 1937: 'The Jewish Community will give you the heartiest welcome a man could possibly have.'

send you a message of goodwill, and if it would be of any use to you, I would send a few of my books which perhaps could be sold or raffled.

What a mess they have made of things in India!

Joachim von Ribbentrop to Winston S. Churchill

(*Churchill papers: 2/296*)

27 April 1937

German Embassy,
Carlton House Terrace,
London

My dear Mr Churchill!

I am giving a smaller luncheon for Generalfeldmarschall v Blomberg, the representative of the Führer at the Coronation, on Saturday, May 15th, at 1.30. A number of men of the political life will be present to meet Herr v Blomberg in a less formal atmosphere.

Will you, my dear Mr Churchill, and Mrs Churchill give us the pleasure of joining us at this occasion? My wife and myself would be very pleased, if the many engagements in those days will allow you to come.

I do not know whether you have met Generalfeldmarschall v Blomberg before, but I am sure you will like him, and a talk between you and him might be useful from every point of view.

Believe me, my dear Mr Churchill

Yours faithfully,
J. Ribbentrop

Winston S. Churchill to Joachim von Ribbentrop

(*Churchill papers: 2/296*)

28 April 1937

It would give my wife and me great pleasure to accept your kind invitation to meet Field Marshal Blomberg at luncheon on May 15th. I have never yet made his acquaintance, but some time ago our Military Attaché in Berlin, Colonel Hotblack,[1] told me that the Field Marshal had spoken to him

---

[1] Frederick Elliot Hotblack, 1887–1979. On active service, 1914–18 (Military Cross and bar, DSO and bar, Legion of Honour, despatches four times, wounded five times). Royal Tank Corps, 1916. Brigade Major, 1st Rhine Brigade, 1921. General Staff Officer, War Office, 1927. Colonel, 1932. Instructor, Staff College, Camberley, 1932–5. Military Attaché, British Embassy, Berlin, 1935–7. Deputy Director of Staff Duties, War Office, 1937–9. Major-General, British Expeditionary Force, 1939–40. Retired, 1941.

appreciatively about some of my writings on the war. In consequence I ventured to send him a copy of one of my volumes, receiving in response a most agreeable acknowledgement.

Sir Edward Marsh to Winston S. Churchill
(Churchill papers: 4/2)

29 April 1937

My dear Winston,

You must have been very much surprised when you read Coronation Commentary at my having recommended it to you without mentioning that it contained an outrageous attack on you. The truth is that (tho' you may find it difficult to believe) I had for the moment forgotten the attack, tho' it had filled me with indignation. I remembered on my way home, and realized what an ass I had made of myself.

When I wrote to Dennis[1] about the book (before the row started) I told him that while I admired it very much I must strongly protest against the paragraph about you; that he had got your attitude entirely wrong and that the remark about the 'snob-dollar marriage' was completely unjustified.

I heard nothing from him till this morning, when he has twice rung me up, first asking me to make his apologies to you, and later, from the publisher's office to tell me of the letter which had just come in from your solicitors, and to ask if I could give him any advice. I told him that he knew from my letter what I thought, and that in my opinion there was nothing for him or Heinemann's to do but to accept your terms without demur.

This letter is written in a faint hope of putting myself right with you for the extraordinary and unaccountable étourderie[2] with which I spoke to you at Malcolm's dinner.[3] The only excuse is that I was so much excited by the honour you were all doing me, I had no brains left for conversation.

---

[1] Geoffrey Dennis, author of *Coronation Commentary* (see page 660, note 1).

[2] 'Etourderie': thoughtlessness, absent-mindedness, a careless act or blunder.

[3] On 17 March 1937 a dinner was given at the May Fair Hotel in honour of Sir Edward Marsh, who had retired from the Dominions Office the previous month. Among those present were the Earl and Countess of Lytton, Professor G. M. Trevelyan, Lady Colefax, H. G. Wells, John Masefield, Walter de la Mare, Sir James Barrie, Victor Cazalet, Brigadier-General E. L. Spears, Horatia Seymour, Sir John Squire, C. B. Cochran, Siegfried Sassoon, Kenneth Clark and Duncan Grant. Churchill, who presided, presented Marsh with two etchings by Augustus John, and an illuminated address. Marsh had rendered, said Churchill, 'a solid contribution to the strength and maintenance of our life as a nation', and he added: 'I don't know what I shall do now. I have never been in office without Eddie Marsh and now I shall never be in office with Eddie Marsh.'

You must be feeling Freddie's death deeply, tho' no one could wish it delayed.[1] He will be a happy memory to very many.

Yours,
Eddie

G. D. Birla:[2] *report to M. K. Gandhi*[3]

(Birla papers)

[30 April 1937]

... I had the temerity to write to Mr Churchill early in 1937 and say that I was disappointed with his utterances in the Press about the political situation in India, reminding him that I had told him that the personal touch between the representatives of the Congress and the former Government had been lacking and the spirit of mutual distrust prevailed. I told him that during the elections in some Provinces the highest officials openly sided against the Congress, and it was in this atmosphere that the Congress was now approaching the new Constitution. I went on to say:

'Let me assure you that Mr Gandhi and others of his way of thinking honestly wish to work the Constitution for the good of the people. I conveyed your words to Mr Gandhi. "I will be entirely satisfied if you can give more bread and butter to your people. Not more loyalty to Great Britain. I am always for more bread and butter." The Election Manifesto of the Congress was prepared with a view to giving more bread and butter. And the Congress, in asking for certain assurances, rightly or wrongly felt that there would be interference from the Governors in carrying out their programme. You may

---

[1] Frederick Guest, Churchill's cousin and life-long friend, had died on 28 April 1937.

[2] Ghanshyam Das Birla, 1894– . Industrialist. President of the Indian Chamber of Commerce, 1924. Member of the Bengal Legislative Council Fiscal Committee. Member of the Indian Legislative Assembly (he resigned in protest against legislation favouring imperial preference, 1930). Unofficial adviser to the Government of India on Indo-British trade negotiations, 1936–7. Member of a family of wealthy financiers and a personal friend of Gandhi; throughout the 1930s he paid monthly allowances to many leading members of the Indian National Congress. Subsequently one of the principal financiers of the Congress Party, and a donor of large sums for charitable and educational purposes.

[3] Mohandas Karamchand Gandhi, 1869–1948. Born in India. Called to the Bar, London, 1889; practised as a barrister in South Africa, 1889–1908; gave up his practice in order to devote himself to championing the rights of Indian settlers in South Africa, 1908; leader of the Passive Resistance Campaign in South Africa, 1908–14; started the Non-Cooperation Movement in India, 1918; given sole authority to lead the national movement by the Indian National Congress, 1921; inaugurated the Civil Disobedience Campaign, 1930; frequently imprisoned; opposed the partition of India into Hindu and Muslim states; severely critical of the Hindu caste-system; assassinated by an orthodox Hindu in 1948, within a year of the creation of India and Pakistan as independent states.

criticise this suspicion or, as Lord Lothian[1] says, it may be due to lack of experience of democracy, but all the same it is there. And I also feel that with statesmanship and the personal touch this misunderstanding could be removed.

'Don't you think that an eminent statesman like you could be of great help in solving the problem?'

I quoted from memory and it may also be that at the time I misunderstood Mr Churchill, and that he did not say 'not more loyalty' but 'and more loyalty' or 'with more loyalty'. Anyhow Mr Churchill was not prepared to admit that he had said that he did not look for more loyalty to the British from India.[2] Here is his reply. . . .

Winston S. Churchill to G. D. Birla

(Birla papers)

30 April 1937   11 Morpeth Mansions
Private

Dear Mr Birla,

Many thanks for your letter. I shall always be interested to hear from you. But you have not quoted me correctly in the sentence you mention. I certainly did not say the words you use.

You should seriously consider the present state of the world. If Great Britain were persuaded or forced for any cause, Indian or European, to withdraw her protection from India, it would continuously become the prey of Fascist dictator nations, Italy, Germany or Japan, and then indeed with the modern facilities there would be a severity of Government even worse than any experienced in bygone ages. The duty of the Indian electorate and of Congress is to take up the great task which has been offered them, and show that they can make India a happier country; and at the same time do everything they can to win the confidence of Great Britain, and offer to her

[1] Lord Lothian had gone to India in 1932 as Chairman of the Indian Franchise Committee (see page 416, note 1).

[2] According to Birla's report to Gandhi of 25 August 1935, Churchill had said to him: "You have got immense powers. Theoretically the Governors have all the powers, but in practice they have none. The king has all the powers in theory but none in practice. Socialists here had all the powers when they came into office, but they did not do anything radical. The Governors will never use the safeguards. So make it a success." I said, "What is your test of success?" He said, "My test is improvement in the lot of the masses, morally as well as materially. I do not care whether you are more or less loyal to Great Britain" (Companion volume 5, part II, of this biography, pages 1244–5: The Wilderness Years).

gratitude and loyalty for being the guardian of Parliamentary government and Indian peace.

Yours sincerely,
Winston S. Churchill

Winston S. Churchill to the Duke of Windsor

(*Churchill papers: 2/300*)

30 April 1937

I have waited to answer Your Royal Highness's most kind letter until I had some news. I look forward very much to paying you a visit, and am honoured by the invitation. I do not think it would be wise for me to leave the country till after Whitsuntide. The Government will all be in process of reconstruction, and although I am not very keen upon office, I should like to help in defence. I think therefore I had better stay on the spot till this is settled. I could be more help in many ways if I were inside. May I therefore suggest a date later in May.

Monckton showed me Your Royal Highness's correspondence with the King, and I was very sorry that the Ministerial advice had caused both you and the King so much distress. It is very painful to me to see how much hard feeling there is in some quarters and all the malice of the small fry. This rascal Bolitho[1] has exposed himself as a miserable creature. I have written a review of his book for Collier's weekly magazine which I think will amuse you when it is printed.[2] Then there is the scurrilous publication of Geoffrey

---

[1] Henry Hector Bolitho, 1898– . Born in New Zealand. Came to England in 1922. Traveller, lecturer and author, he published his first book, *With the Prince in New Zealand* in 1922; his biography, *Edward VIII, his life and reign* in 1937.

[2] On 5 June 1937 *Collier's* published Churchill's review of Hector Bolitho's book *Edward VIII*. Churchill described the book as a Coronation Ode 'transmogrified into abdication odium'. During the course of his review, Churchill wrote: 'Mr Bolitho who marks every peccadillo, and apologises for them in a heavy-footed style, speaks of "his love of popularity" as if it was a vice and introduces the word "conceit" which would certainly not have appeared in a coronation volume. He reminds us of several small things in the Prince's management of his fortune and household to which it would be thought impertinent to refer in the case of a statesman, a general, an admiral, an artist or a bishop. Now was the time to make the full catalogue of shortcomings, errors of judgment, minor controversies which arose here or there, and pepper these hundreds of pages of sterling endeavour and achievement with an adverse comment appropriate to the unfriendly account required for the final phase. In the main, and with much consistency, this story of the life of this brilliant, gifted, charming and warm-hearted prince represents him as being below the average of mankind. We are given a picture, alleged to be intimate, claiming to be drawn by a friend and admirer, of a character vitiated by grave defects of temperament and conduct, at which the wise, the good, the healthy, and above all, the average British man and woman would frown or blush. A whole

Dennis[1] of which Heinemann have been guilty, and about which I see you have very properly issued a Writ. I came across a poisonous sentence about myself and received Counsel's Opinion that it is a gross libel.[2] I have instructed my own solicitors to demand an apology and damages. These people require a lesson and the only thing they appreciate is being made to pay.

Last Monday I had a visit from Wigram who brought me privately the King's assurance about the financial affair, that 'I could be sure he would not let you down'. I told Wigram that he ought to talk to Lloyd George also, which he did. In consequence of this assurance, which I felt bound to accept, coming as it did directly from His Majesty, neither of us raised the matter on the Civil List Committee, and as Your Royal Highness may have seen, the Committee has agreed upon its report on terms which seem to me very favourable to the new Sovereigns and their Family, and which certainly leave resources out of which the promised provision can be met. I therefore hope and trust that all will be well.

---

series of excuses and explanations are offered for him by his disillusioned defender. All is done in the guise of sorrowing friendship. This heightens the effect of the general depreciation. An atmosphere of insulting pity is made to pervade the story and thus prepare the reader for the final chapters which the author found it so horrible to write, but which he nevertheless wrote unflinchingly. By the time King Edward ascended the throne our author without excising the long account of his many public services and successes has contrived to draw a picture of a delinquent on whom long-delayed but inevitable retribution is about to fall.'

[1] Geoffrey Pomeroy Dennis, 1892–1963. Articled to an estate agent and auctioneer, 1907–10. At Exeter College, Oxford, 1910–14; Librarian of the Oxford Union. On active service, 1915–18; GHQ, Cologne, 1919–20, with the rank of Captain. Chief Editor, and Chief of Documents Services, League of Nations, Geneva, 1920–37. Adviser to the Institute of Agriculture, Rome, 1938–9. Major, Intelligence Corps, 1940–5. Head of the Italian section of the BBC, 1945–9. The English Editor, UNESCO, 1949–57. He published his first book, *Mary Lee*, in 1922; *Coronation Commentary* in 1937.

[2] The phrases which caused Churchill offence were the descriptions of him as 'an unstable politician', 'an ambitious politician', 'flitting from Party to Party', 'Extreme Reactionary', 'the first-fruit of the first famous snob-dollar marriage' and 'half-alien and wholly undesirable'. For the last of these phrases, Geoffrey Dennis's defence was that it had been published in the *National Review* by Leo Maxse shortly before the First World War. 'I of course did not see it in the National Review myself,' Dennis wrote to Heinemann, 'but heard it freely quoted at the time of the abdication' (letter of 8 January 1938, *Heinemann papers*). As a result of a separate action by the Duke of Windsor, the book was withdrawn having already sold 9,732 copies out of a print order of 18,078. In the United States, more than 35,000 copies were sold. Churchill's action was suspended in March 1939 when he was paid £500 plus £250 costs by Heinemann. The only condition laid down by Heinemann was 'that we shall not be called upon to make a public apology in Court: and we feel this very strongly' (Managing Director's letter of 3 March 1939, *Heinemann papers*). See also Heinemann's letter to Churchill of 18 March 1939. The copy of Dennis's book in the Bodleian Library, Oxford is, as the catalogue states, 'not available for consultation', apparently during the lifetime of the Duchess of Windsor.

Winston S. Churchill to King George VI

(*Churchill papers: 2/300*)

30 April 1937   11 Morpeth Mansions

Sir,

I feel I should be wanting in respect if I did not express to Your Majesty my thanks for the message of assurance that I received through Lord Wigram about certain matters. In consequence of this I did not raise the question in the Civil List Committee, and as Your Majesty has perhaps learned the Committee has agreed upon what I think is a satisfactory report without any question being raised which would lead to public discussion about the Duke of Windsor. Of course the Report has still to be debated in the House of Commons, I believe on May 24. If any member should ask a question, nothing could be better than that Ministers should be able to reply that the matter has been settled within the Royal Family on a basis of natural affection and good will—or words to that effect. This I am sure would be good from every point of view.

Sir, let me take this occasion of offering Your Majesty my heartfelt congratulations upon ascending the Throne. I have served your Majesty's grandfather, father and brother for very many years and I earnestly hope that Your Majesty's reign will be blessed by Providence and will add new strength and lustre to our ancient Monarchy.

I am, Sir, with humble duty,

Your Majesty's faithful servant and subject,
Winston S. Churchill

Winston S. Churchill to Sir Edward Marsh

(*Marsh papers*)

30 April 1937   Chartwell

Dismiss altogether from your mind my feeling of reproach against you. I looked into the book to find the passage about which the Duke of Windsor is taking action, and I came across this very offensive, wounding and insulting libel on myself. As you know I have some experience of libel cases and I saw at once that this was grave. On taking two separate high legal opinions I find my view absolutely confirmed.

In these circumstances you will see that I have no choice but to proceed as I am doing, for I think that not only individuals but the public ought to be protected from profit making by writing cruel things about well-known people.

The reference to my mother and father's marriage is not only painful to me, but as you know is utterly devoid of foundation. This was a love match if ever there was one, with very little money on either side. In fact they could only live in the very smallest way possible to people in London society. If the marriage became famous afterwards it was because my father, an unknown sprig of the aristocracy, became famous, and also because my mother, as all her photographs attest, was by general consent, one of the beauties of her time. To construct insults out of such materials must indeed be a malicious task.

Other parts of the passage are even more offensive and the cumulative effect is the worst of all. Although this book has now been withdrawn in England it has already, I am told, sold 7,000 copies which will eagerly be passed from hand to hand.

I see from the papers that it is circulating very widely in America, and that a new edition is being hurried out. As you know I have considerable literary and other connections in the United States, and of course I am also considering what action can be taken there.

Freddie's death was a great blow to me. We were very fond of each other. But the pain of his loss is lessened when I knew about two months ago that he had cancer in a hopeless form, and it is a relief that he should have had so painless an end. I have never seen anyone show such a complete contempt of death and make so little fuss about it.

Yours ever,
W

Winston S. Churchill to Neville Chamberlain
(Churchill papers: 2/302)

30 April 1937

I have been wondering whether your purpose, with which I sympathise, could be achieved on the following lines viz:—

Any firm receiving a contract from the Admiralty, War Office or Air Ministry must, as a condition of that contract, allow itself to be scheduled as an Armament firm. Or where the contract was only a small part of their business accept the contract being scheduled as an armament contract. Firms and contracts so described would pay the appropriate National Defence Contribution and the scale would be made sufficient to raise the amount you require in 1938. The test is not the character of the goods required but the fact that the contract is given by the military departments, or if preferable by Government departments. This would seem to me justified in view of the enormous Government expenditure flowing into specialised channels.

I should not attempt to follow the process into the firms which supply the materials to the scheduled armament firms. These are less recognisable as military materials. It can also be argued that as they had an alternative rising market from the trade revival in which to sell their goods, they are not on the same footing as the Armament firms. I do not think those who tender for Government contracts—certainly not the great bulk—would hesitate to accept the burden in order to gain the Government custom on which they live and thrive.

On the other hand if they combined to put up their prices against the Government this would be corrected, at one end by the costings system which is already in force, and at the other by the fact that as they increase their profits they would increase their tax liability. The armament firms would themselves recover by private bargaining with their sub-contractors, a portion of the tax, and thus spread the incidence more widely. Lastly, in the event of intensified preparations involving ever more widely civil industry in the defence sphere, the radius of the tax would extend automatically, and in time of major war would be probably coincident with all industry.

Of course this is purely my own idea, and I have not discussed it with any experts. Very likely it can be riddled, though I do not myself see how. At any rate almost anything would be better than a prolongation of the present uncertainty, and also having to rummage the accounts of every firm in the country in order to ascertain their contribution, and whether they deserve any of the concessions you have promised, or those which may have to be given in Committee.

John Martin[1] *to Winston S. Churchill*

(*Churchill papers: 2/317*)

30 April 1937

Palestine Royal Commission
Whitehall

Dear Sir,

The Palestine Royal Commission have instructed me to inform you that they propose in their Report to quote the enclosed extract from your 1922 Statement of Policy, and then to continue:—

[1] John Miller Martin, 1904–   . Entered the Dominions Office, 1927. Seconded to the Malayan Civil Service, 1931–4. Secretary, Palestine Royal Commission, 1936–7. Private Secretary to the Prime Minister (Winston Churchill), 1940–1; Principal Private Secretary, 1941–5. Assistant Under-Secretary of State, Colonial Office, 1945–56. Deputy Under-Secretary of State, 1956–65. Knighted, 1952. High Commissioner, Malta, 1965–7.

'This definition of the National Home has sometimes been taken to preclude the establishment of a Jewish State. But, though the phraseology was clearly intended to conciliate, as far as might be, Arab antagonism to the National Home, there is nothing in it to prohibit the ultimate establishment of a Jewish State, and Mr Churchill himself has told us in evidence that no such prohibition was intended.'

The Members trust that you will see no objection to their referring to your evidence in this way.[1]

Yours faithfully,

J. M. Martin

[1] Churchill had no objection to the paragraph as proposed; but none of the evidence to the Palestine Royal Commission was made public, and the full text of Churchill's evidence is published in this volume in full for the first time (on pages 596–617). The 'enclosed extract' from Churchill's statement of British policy in Palestine (the 'Churchill' White Paper of 1922) as printed in the Royal Commission Report, pointed out that already (by 1922) the Jews had 'recreated in Palestine a community, now numbering 80,000, of whom about one-fourth are farmers or workers upon the land'. The extract also declared: 'When it is asked what is meant by the development of the Jewish National Home in Palestine, it may be answered that it is not the imposition of a Jewish nationality upon the inhabitants of Palestine as a whole, but the further development of the existing Jewish community, with the assistance of Jews in other parts of the world, in order that it may become a centre in which the Jewish people as a whole may take, on grounds of religion and race, an interest and a pride. But in order that this community should have the best prospect of free development and provide a full opportunity for the Jewish people to display its capacities, it is essential that it should know that it is in Palestine as of right and not on sufferance. That is the reason why it is necessary that the existence of a Jewish National Home in Palestine should be internationally guaranteed, and that it should be formally recognized to rest upon ancient historic connection'.

May 1937

Winston S. Churchill to Sir Samuel Hoare

(Churchill papers: 2/302)

3 May 1937
Secret

About our brief conversation in the Lobby. I cannot help feeling anxious upon the following points:—

First: there was a case that you could not afford the delays entailed in redesigning the first two battleships, and that the action of other countries was uncertain. But if quite soon we know that the United States, Japan, Germany and Italy, or most of them, are laying down vessels with 16″ guns, I am sure that ours will be considered undergunned and will be consequently written down as factors of Naval strength by all other countries. I fear it will be a reproach against the Admiralty in future years. The difference in weight and broadside and also in the striking power and explosive charge of the projectiles are so enormous, considering the very small increase in cost, that the comparison with heavier guns and foreign ships will be detrimental. Of course I understand some of the more detailed arguments and with your permission, as you will remember, I had a long talk with the First Sea Lord in October last.

The comparison of nine 16″ guns in three turrets against ten 14″ in four turrets is on paper very heavily adverse to the second alternative. The extra turret required makes a serious inroad in space and weight of armour. This weight used in a three turret ship would afford not only the extra weight of the heavier guns and mountings, but also provide, at least this is my belief, a large surplus which could be used for deck armour and other requirements.

The issue seems to me to turn entirely upon the triple turret. I know the Admiralty have now turned against the triple turret on the ground of the interference of the projectiles with one another in flight. I have not of course heard the details of this argument, though I remember it played a large part in our discussions before the war. Is it however admitted that the Hood,

Nelson and Rodney cannot compete with other ships in gunnery? Are other nations convinced that triple turrets are a failure? I remember shortly before the war broke out I persuaded the Board to put a triple turret in the stern of one of the new battleships, in order that we might make real experiments. But these matters are now no longer novelties, and there must be an immense amount of data upon the subject. Even if there was a slight interference it by no means follows that it would outweigh the grave disadvantage of losing nearly 40% striking power.

I write all this only because the five ships now projected will probably play an important part in our whole Naval strength for twenty or twenty-five years to come, and if opinion should judge them adversely, the injury will be grave and irremediable.

Secondly: am I right in supposing that the Germans are building, or going to build, seven 10,000 ton 8″ gun cruisers of the most modern kind? By the time these are ready what shall we have to master them? All our earlier 8″ gun cruisers are poor ships with very weak protection and now ageing. They are certainly inferior in strength and stiffness to the great batch of later American 8″ vessels. The Americans have built far stiffer ships, and no doubt the Germans with all the modern improvements will be better still. What then are we building that will be ready when these seven German cruisers are built?

It would seem to me that these seven German ships might be the successors to the Emden & Co[1] as commerce destroyers. What shall we have to catch *and kill them*? All the more does this seem important when aircraft give a squadron searching the broad waters, such an enormously increased radius of vision. It should be easy to find the raider. But if the raider, who will also know the position of our ships, is not afraid to encounter any one of them, you may easily have a disastrous single-ship action instead of a victory. Remember that though it took more than thirty ships to find the Emden an hour sufficed to destroy her once she was found and a more powerful vessel had reached her.

It is no use finding without having a killer to send. The moral effect of the enemy having heavier metal and stiffer ships is also serious, and you will certainly find it affects strategic decisions in the broad waters. To build a

---

[1] The *Emden*, a German light cruiser, was one of a number of German warships that successfully sank allied merchant ships on the high seas in the first eighteen months of the First World War. The *Emden*, which steamed from the China coast on the outbreak of war, sank fifteen unarmed merchant ships, and captured eight, in the Indian Ocean. She also sank a Russian cruiser and a French destroyer which were inside Penang harbour, and bombarded the oil depot at Madras. As a disguise, the ship's funnel was altered, to look like that on an English cruiser. She was herself sunk by the Australian light cruiser, the *Sydney*, on 9 November 1915.

10,000 ton ship at the cost of over £2 millions, and put only 6″ guns into her, seems to me open to most serious criticism.

With regard to the smaller type of cruisers, or later developments of the Arethusa type, presumably for attendance on the battle fleet, it will be a long time before any power, except the United States and Japan, can draw out a line of battle, and before conditions of a major fleet action will return in European waters. Therefore I cannot think the multiplication of small weak cruisers, costing I believe nearly £1½ millions, can be good. The development of aircraft working with the Fleet make numbers for trade protection less important. What is all-important is to be able to kill when found. At any rate the seven German big cruisers will be a terrible war weapon on the broad waters when completed, which it seems to me could on present procedure only be countered by the dispersing of battle cruisers on trade protection duty. I doubt very much whether a Commander in Chief of some future Grand Fleet would like very much to have them taken away and assigned to distant oceans.

Thirdly, all this brings me to the Treaty obligation. I have for many years expressed the view that all Naval agreements, other than the Washington Agreement, have proved injurious to the Royal Navy, and it is my personal belief, though of course it cannot be proved—and anyhow is purely academic— that the navies of the world would indeed be not much stronger, or have cost more money if there had been no regulations. The Treaties hampered us especially in our freedom of design. Of course we are bound by Treaties and Agreements. If that is the reason for our having to do something greatly to our disadvantage, it ought to be made clear, and measures should be taken to obtain relief in the best possible manner and as soon as possible.

Your coming to the Admiralty has been followed by a magnificent programme, and has synchronised with the time when financial obstacles have not operated. All the more therefore do I hope that you will not take amiss these thoughts, from one who shares your views on the general issues.

Sir Samuel Hoare to Winston S. Churchill
(*Churchill papers: 2/302*)

4 May 1937   Admiralty

Dear Winston,

Many thanks for your letter of May 3rd. You raise several questions of vital importance in it. These I will discuss with the Staff and either write you a letter or have a talk with you about them in the course of the next week or so.[1]

Yours ever,
Samuel Hoare

Neville Chamberlain to Winston S. Churchill
(*Churchill papers: 2/302*)

6 May 1937   Treasury Chambers

My dear Winston,

Your letter of 30th April, unlike most of those which I have been receiving about the National Defence Contribution, contains a constructive suggestion, and if I have delayed my answer it has been in order that I might consider it more carefully.

I may say at once that this consideration has led me to the conclusion that I could not adopt it, but you may like to see the general and particular grounds which have influenced me.

Your proposal is strictly confined to the profits on armament manufacture. To my mind this would be an admission that those profits were excessive and

---

[1] An Admiralty note, written for Sir Samuel Hoare, and headed: 'Unexpurgated edition *Not* sent to Mr Churchill,' included the paragraph: 'With the advent of the London Navy Treaty in 1930, we achieved our object of limiting the laying down of more 8 inch cruisers, and during the next three years we laid down eight 6 inch cruisers (LEANDER class) of about 7,000 tons (the size which after exhaustive investigation had been selected as the minimum for a satisfactory 6 inch gun cruiser for general work). Under the terms of the Treaty we were allowed to build up to 10,000 tons displacement, but we preferred the smaller tonnage, partly because our *total* tonnage was limited and we needed numbers of ships, and partly in the hope that our example would be followed. We thus equipped ourselves with a class of cruiser of the smallest size which could efficiently be used on the trade routes, but which was admittedly inferior to certain of the six inch cruisers building or projected by foreign powers. In the end this foreign building forced us to adopt a larger design, and the ten SOUTHAMPTON cruisers followed with displacements ranging from 9,000 to 10,000 tons. (Only the first 2 of these ships are at present complete.) From a technical point of view the LEANDERS and SOUTHAMPTONS are very fine ships, and could no doubt give a good account of themselves against any foreign cruisers of corresponding size. From a strategical point of view, however, they are less satisfactory because they could not be expected to stand against an 8 inch raider. Moreover the 7,000 ton LEANDERS are naturally weaker than certain of the larger Japanese and Italian cruisers, but it would be highly uneconomical to operate them on the trade routes in company in pairs. The great weakness in the policy of building large 6 inch cruisers lies in the risk that for the same cost and on the same tonnage a foreign power may build a more powerful 8 inch cruiser. Yet there is no choice but to accept this risk so long as we are trying to secure the abolition by treaty of the 8 inch type. We need feel no regrets therefore at the LEANDER or SOUTHAMPTON classes, but we shall have to exercise caution when operating them singly in time of war.' (*Templewood papers*)

that there was something inherently vicious in making any profits from such a source. That of course is the view taken by many people. I do not share it myself because I consider that the vice consists in the use of armaments for aggressive purposes, not in the mere manufacture of them, the purpose of which may, as in our case, be essentially defensive.

On this broad ground of principle then your suggestion would be inconsistent with the fundamental idea of my proposal; namely, that *increases* of profits in industry which, whether derived from armaments or from commercial business, are mainly due to the favourable conditions created by Government policy, are the fairest source from which to look for our requirements.

In the second place, I think your proposal would be extremely unfair to the main armament contractors whose profits are being strictly limited by our contract procedure. I doubt if you have realised that in all probability the *whole* of their profits, such as they are, would have to be taken to provide the necessary revenue and even then would very likely be insufficient. What an unjustifiable contrast with the sub-contractors who *are* making good profits free from Government control and who would be exempt! I can't believe that we should get the big contractors to take contracts at all in such circumstances.

Apart from these main considerations I fail to see how in practice it would be possible to dissect out the taxable profits on scheduled contracts in the case of firms whose activities embraced a wide range of goods both for service use and for the general public.

I feel sure that the growth of profits is the thing to tax. Then no one can be worse off than they were.

Yours sincerely,
N. Chamberlain

Winston S. Churchill to Brigadier Pakenham-Walsh
(*Churchill papers: 8/547*)

7 May 1937

I am toiling now at Marlborough and am quite ready for the campaign of 1710 and 1711. Meanwhile I send you the new chapter which, although not quite complete, deals with Tournai and the opening of the Malplaquet campaign. I thought your maps of this were very good.

Adam Marshall Diston to Winston S. Churchill

(*Churchill papers: 8/546*)

10 May 1937

Dear Mr Churchill,

I am enclosing the draft article, 'How the Jews Can Combat Persecution', and hope that it may be on the right lines. It is, I think, nearer 3,000 words than the 2,500 required, but there are certain things which you may want to cut.

Mrs Pearman did not tell me for what paper it was wanted. If it is for a Jewish journal, it may in places be rather outspoken.[1] Even then, however, I do not know that that is altogether a bad thing. There are quite a number of Jews who might, with advantage, reflect on the epigram:

'How odd
Of God
To choose
The Jews.'

Yours very sincerely,
A. Marshall Diston

Sir Patrick Hastings:[2] *Legal opinion*

(*Churchill papers: 1/303*)

10 May 1937

I find it difficult to say that this most offensive paragraph amounts to an actionable libel. To say of a politician that he is 'unstable, ambitious or reactionary' would not of itself in my opinion be defamatory. On the other hand to say that he is 'a flitter from party to party and wholly undesirable' might but not necessarily would be held to be prima facie actionable. I must however point out that a plea of justification would of course be open to a

---

[1] In having Diston's article retyped for possible publication, Churchill made no changes in it, nor is there any record in the Churchill papers, or in Frederick Woods, *A Bibliography of the Works of Sir Winston Churchill* (revised edition, 1969), that this article was ever published. Churchill was paid $1,000 (£200) for it, and paid Diston £25 for his help. On 10 October 1937 Churchill wrote to Diston: 'I hope you found my notes a help. Do not let them cramp your style or feel any obligation to use them' (*Churchill papers: 8/546*).

[2] Patrick Hastings, 1880–1952. A mining engineer, 1898–9. On active service in South Africa, 1900–1. A journalist, 1902–3. Called to the Bar, Middle Temple, 1904. Labour MP for Wallsend, 1922–6. Attorney-General, 1924. Knighted, 1924. A leading barrister; author of three plays, and *The Autobiography of Sir Patrick Hastings* (published in 1948).

Defendant as well as the much more dangerous plea of fair comment. Under the latter plea the defence has a very great latitude and in the present case an action would in my view only have a reasonable prospect of success if it could be proved that the Author was expressing his views dishonestly as opposed to unreasonably and offensively. For the purpose of this opinion I am of course assuming that Mr Churchill is in a position to prove by evidence that he is the person and is understood to be the person indicated by the offending paragraph.

I notice from Mr Churchill's letter that he does not wish to be advised upon the question of policy in bringing an action and consequently I offer no advice although I hold a strong opinion on the matter.

Finally in this as in every other case of libel I must point out the great danger of starting an action unless it is intended to bring it to trial in the event of the defendant setting up a defence. Such an action once started and thereafter abandoned is a most unfortunate occurrence.

Patrick Hastings

Winston S. Churchill to Lady Violet Bonham Carter
(Churchill papers: 2/312)

15 May 1937

I do not expect to have a completely prepared speech on the occasion of the New Commonwealth luncheon on the 25th. I shall recite the general justification for our Society. It is the sublime of logic and the quintessence of militant pacifism. But if I do have anything ready the day before I will not fail to let you have it.[1]

Winston S. Churchill to the Duke of Windsor
(Churchill papers: 2/300)

17 May 1937

I and your other friends with whom I consort have had many thoughts about Your Royal Highness in these moving days. The Coronation[2] has been a brilliant success and the King and Queen went through it extremely well, and were the objects of magnificent demonstrations of loyalty.

---

[1] Churchill spoke at the New Commonwealth luncheon on 25 May 1937. His Press Statement before the meeting is printed on page 682 of this volume.

[2] The Coronation of King George VI and Queen Elizabeth took place on 12 May 1937.

Outside the circle of friends there is a great deal of bitterness from those who are hostile to you, and from those who are hostile because of their disappointment. The line I take is 'I wish to see the King reign gloriously, and the Duke of Windsor live happily.'

I have had a letter from an MP Mr Michael Beaumont,[1] who proposes to raise the question of a Civil List provision for you when Parliament meets on the 24th. I send you a copy of his letter, and also the answer I have sent. I do trust at least the financial business will be settled by then. I have sent a copy of Beaumont's letter and my answer to Wigram, because I thought it might speed up matters. If Beaumont raises the question, and the answer were unsatisfactory Lloyd George would certainly speak, and then there might be a most vexatious debate out of which no good could come to anyone.

Sir, I have been wondering whether it would not be wise for Your Royal Highness to try and bring about a general arrangement, covering a period of, say, three years, not only on finance, but on other matters, and have it all settled in the best possible way. Sometimes it is easier to settle a lot of things together than dispute over each one separately. I must say I think time is needed before we can attain the ideal, namely that Your Royal Highness and future wife could live pleasantly in England in the same sort of position as the Duke of Connaught or the old Duke of Cambridge. This it seems is what we have got to work for and I believe patience and perseverance will secure it. It seems to me that everything, apart from a proper financial settlement, should be subordinate to this ultimate objective.

I hope I may be forgiven if I presume in making this suggestion, which I only do because Your Royal Highness has not many around you who are in touch with all that is going on here.

I took Patrick Hastings' Opinion upon the very offensive passage in 'Coronation Commentary' which affected me. He says it is more vulgar abuse than a libel and is doubtful whether a case would arise. It is always best to take the highest Opinion on this occasion and association. The Counsel my solicitors consulted pronounced it a libel at once, but a man like Hastings with his immense experience knows what happens when you come into Court. At present I am undecided what to do, but I believe it will be possible to obtain a public apology from the publishers and the little rascal.

---

[1] Michael Wentworth Beaumont, 1903–1958. Educated at Eton, Oundle and Sandhurst. 2nd Lieutenant, Coldstream Guards, 1923–4; Captain, 1931; Major, 1939. Conservative MP for Aylesbury, 1929–38.

Winston S. Churchill to Sir Abe Bailey

(Churchill papers: 1/299)

17 May 1937

I was enchanted to hear from you. I learned only a few days ago that you had been in England a month. I hope you are all the better for your African sojourn.

Do not make the mistake of supposing that we have got over our dangers. On the contrary 1937 and 1938 are years of our maximum weakness, and it is not until after that that we begin to improve our position relatively to Germany.

I nearly telegraphed to you in Africa to tell you that the female crane fell into a small pool and most stupidly drowned herself. The male bird is magnificent, but seems restless and fretful now that Spring is here and he has no mate. Do you think it would be possible for you to get me another female from Africa? They walk about most agreeably around the bathing pool and in the gardens, and I think it is rather hard on him having to remain a widower.

Let me see you some time when Parliament meets. We might have one of our luncheons together.

I am very glad Baldwin is going.[1] I think we shall come to some real and straightforward politics now he is out of the way.

King George VI to Winston S. Churchill

(Churchill papers: 2/296)

18 May 1937   The Royal Lodge
                                                Windsor

My dear Mr Churchill,

I am writing to thank you for your very nice letter to me. I know how devoted you have been, & still are, to my dear brother, & I feel touched beyond words by your sympathy and understanding in the very difficult problems that have arisen since he left us in December. I fully realise the great responsibilities & cares that I have taken on as King, & I feel most encouraged to receive your good wishes, as one of our great statesmen, & from one who has served his country so faithfully. I can only hope & trust

---

[1] On 28 May 1937 Neville Chamberlain succeeded Stanley Baldwin as Prime Minister.

that the good feeling & hope that exists in the Country & Empire now, will prove a good example to other Nations in the World.[1]

Believe me,
Yours very sincerely,
George R.I.

Rear-Admiral Bertram Ramsay[2] to Winston S. Churchill

(Churchill papers: 2/310)

18 May 1937

Dear Mr Winston Churchill,

As the son of your old Colonel in the 4th Hussars,[3] I venture to approach you on a subject which I know you have at heart, the welfare & efficiency of the Defence Forces.

In this connection I have first hand information regarding certain proceedings in the Fleet which would interest you, information which I think you should possess, whether you make use of it or not!

I should like therefore to make use of the opportunity of being in London next week, to meet & discuss the matter with you if you would care to do so.

Tuesday or Wednesday are free, as far as I am concerned, up to six o'clock, & I shall be leaving London again on Thursday. It will be unnecessary to remind you that it is undesirable that any action in approaching you should be known, as I am still on the Active List, & I trust that you will treat this communication as in every respect confidential.

I have only to add that the purport of this letter is one in which I am personally disinterested.

---

[1] On 25 May 1937 Churchill wrote to the King from Chartwell: 'Sir, The letter which Your Majesty has written me amid the stresses of the Coronation will ever be treasured in my family and home. I am, Sir, Your Majesty's faithful and devoted servant and subject Winston S. Churchill.'

[2] Bertram Home Ramsay, 1883–1945. Entered the Royal Navy, 1898; commanded Monitor 25, Dover Patrol, 1915; HMS *Broke*, 1916–18. Chief of Staff, China Station, 1929–31. On the Staff of the Imperial Defence College, 1931–3. Commanded HMS *Royal Sovereign*, 1933–5. Rear-Admiral and Chief of Staff, Home Fleet, 1935. Retired, 1938. Recalled, 1939. Flag Officer, Dover, 1939–42. Knighted, 1940. Naval Commander, Eastern Task Force, Mediterranean, 1943. Allied Naval Commander-in-Chief, Expeditionary Force, 1944–5. Killed in an aeroplane accident in France, January 1945. His 'finest hour' was as the naval officer in command of 'Operation Dynamo', the evacuation of the Dunkirk beachhead, in June 1940.

[3] William Alexander Ramsay, 1848–1933. Son of Captain Francis Ramsay, Royal Artillery. 2nd Lieutenant, 1869. Colonel, 4th Hussars, 1895. Retired, 1905, with the rank of Colonel. Honorary Brigadier-General, 1912. Lived in retirement at Cheltenham.

Lady Snowden[1] to Winston S. Churchill

(*Churchill papers: 1/299*)

20 May 1937

Dear Mr Churchill,

I am writing to thank you for your beautiful article on my husband.[2] It is the finest thing which has appeared and bears the brand of sincerity. I am deeply grateful to you, and touched by your kindness beyond the power of adequate expression.[3]

Your generosity to a political opponent marks you for ever in my eyes the 'great gentleman' I have always thought you. Had I been in trouble which I could not control myself, there is none to whom I should have felt I could come with more confidence that I should be gently treated. Accept my warmest and most grateful thanks.

[1] Ethel Annakin, 1881–1951. Married Snowden in 1905. An active advocate of women's suffrage, and temperance. Member of the Labour Commission of Enquiry to Russia, 1920, and author of *Through Bolshevik Russia*, critical of Bolshevism. Member of the Royal Commission on Food Prices, 1925. Member of the first Board of Governors of the BBC, 1927–33. Her husband had died on 15 May 1937.

[2] Philip Snowden, 1864–1937. Educated at Board School. Entered the Civil Service, 1886; retired, 1893. Chairman of the Independent Labour Party, 1903–6 and 1917–20. Labour MP for Blackburn, 1906–18; for Colne Valley, 1922–31. Privy Councillor, 1924. Chancellor of the Exchequer, 1924 and 1929–31. Created Viscount, 1931. Lord Privy Seal, 1931–2. One of Churchill's principal critics while Churchill himself was Chancellor of the Exchequer (1924–9).

[3] In a tribute to Snowden, published in the *Sunday Express* on 16 May 1937, Churchill wrote: 'I first met him many years ago when I was a young Liberal Minister and he was one of the small band of Independent Labour men who nevertheless found themselves forced to conform to the main policy of the Asquith Government. We travelled for four hours together to Lancashire. Then for the first time I saw beneath this apparently bitter and even spiteful spirit and regard something of the charm and kindliness of his nature. His face, though in a way twisted by pain, ill-health and the mood of revolt, was lighted by a smile truly disarming, comprehending and delightful. Afterwards it fell to my lot for seven years to wrangle with him about finance as Chancellor of the Exchequer, or in opposition to his Chancellorship, and we hit each other as hard as we could within the wide rules of Order. But never have I had any feeling towards him which destroyed the impression that he was a generous, chivalrous, honourable, true-hearted man.' Churchill added: 'The British democracy should be proud of Philip Snowden. He was a man capable of maintaining the structure of Society while at the same time championing the interests of the masses. His long life of struggle against poverty and physical affliction was crowned by honourable success. His fearlessness, his rectitude, his austerity, his sobriety of judgment, his deep love of Britain and his studiously-concealed, but intense, pride in British greatness, distinguish him as one of the true worthies of our age. His life of privation, of affliction, of self-denial, of war-time odium, had a grand culmination. The history of Parliament will not ignore the scene when the House of Commons rose to their feet in enthusiasm as he recited the famous lines: "All our past proclaims the future: Shakespeare's voice and Nelson's hand, Milton's faith and Wordsworth's trust in this our chosen and chainless land, Bear us witness . . . Come the world against her, England yet shall stand!" ' Churchill ended: 'One supreme comfort was also his. In the brilliant and gifted woman whom he married he found a dear companionship of thought and aim and nature.'

If others had been more like you and had glimpsed something of the inner as well as the outer man, they would have known that Philip's strength was matched by his gentleness, and that the sweetness of his smile and not the bitterness of his tongue was the truer indication of his character. I never knew a human being who so combined strength with tenderness, and I had 32 years of happy comradeship.

I wish you two had met more often. I wish you had talked with him by his own fireside. I wish you had seen something of his love of birds and dogs and flowers. I never met an individual who had the power to the same extent, and used it, to 'rejoice with them that do rejoice and weep with them that weep'— almost the whole of the law and the prophets when one comes to think of it.

He had always an affection for yourself. We often spoke of you. And when I told him of our meeting at the Czech luncheon and that you had sent him messages, his face lit up with pleasure.

I am desperately lonely in spirit, but the pain is mitigated by the knowledge and thought of the kindness of friends like yourself, who understood him and have had thought for me.

Please remember me to Mrs Churchill, and believe me to be, dear Mr Churchill,

Yours very sincerely,
Ethel Snowdon

Judge Brown: [1] *recollectons*

(*letter to the author, 31 October 1981*)

[22 May 1937]   [Oxford]

He arrived late from Blenheim in a black mood. (I never discovered the reason for the anger). He refused a pre-drink & went in to sit on my left. On my right was the Gaekwar of Baroda [2] who was very old by then but still making pronouncements on Indian politics. He had caused a stir at the

---

[1] James Alexander Brown, 1914–   . Educated at Campbell College, Belfast and Balliol College, Oxford. President of the Oxford Union, 1936. On active service with the Royal Ulster Rifles, 1939–45 (wounded; Captain). Called to the Bar of Northern Ireland, 1946; to the English Bar, 1950. Queen's Counsel, 1956. County Court Judge, County Down, 1967–78. Recorder of Belfast, 1978–   .

[2] Sayaji Rao III, 1863–1939. Maharaja Gaekwar of Baroda from the age of twelve until his death sixty-four years later. His state had a population of two and a half million people. Invested with full powers, and knighted, 1881. During the First World War he gave the British Government substantial sums of money for aeroplanes, Ford vans etc as well as a personal gift of 154 horses and 13 tents. Doctor of Laws, Benares Hindu University, 1924. Representative of India at the Imperial Conference, 1937.

Delhi Durbar of 1911 by turning his back on George V. Much more recently he had been the only substantial Indian prince to support the India Bill. He had rather a vague reputation of being an Indian nationalist.

As we began dinner, Churchill still would not speak. I tried many subjects but received only grunts 'Yes', 'No' & 'Oh'. He refused sherry with the soup (& white wine with the fish, red wine with the meat & port). He asked for a decanter of whiskey & a syphon of soda water. Cad that I was, I counted the number of drinks he had. It was eleven. Much later when the Gaekwar was reading his short speech & came to a passage mildly criticising Churchill for his illiberal attitude to Indian affairs, Churchill held his glass under the empty (or almost empty) syphon & pressed the handle hard for four or five seconds. The resulting splutter was quite loud & caused general, though politely subdued amusement.

To return to the early part of the dinner, I finally despaired of getting him to talk (either to me or to the South African Rhodes Scholar on his left), so I said rather abruptly 'What was it like thinking you were going to be lynched in Belfast in 1912?'[1] He was surprised & asked 'What do you know

---

[1] According to *The Times*, a hostile crowd of 10,000 had greeted the Churchills outside the Grand Central Hotel in Belfast, where they were staying. On 9 February 1912 *The Times*, describing the drive from the hotel to the Celtic Road, reported, 'As each car made its way through, men thrust their heads in and uttered fearful menaces and imprecations. It seemed to me,' wrote *The Times* reporter, 'that Mr Churchill was taking a greater risk than ever he expected ... Yet he never flinched and took hostility visualised as well as vocalised calmly and no harm befell him.' The *Manchester Guardian* said that the back wheels of Churchill's car were lifted eighteen inches off the ground by the angry crowd before the police beat them off. Four battalions of infantry guarded the route. When Churchill reached the Roman Catholic district of Belfast, there was 'a transition from scowls to smiles'. *The Times* reported Churchill as having commented: 'It was splendid. The wicked dug the pit and they tumbled into it themselves.' Churchill then told a crowd of 5,000 Irish Nationalists, and a handful of Unionist hecklers, that the main safeguard for the Protestants of Ulster and Ireland would be the Irish Parliament, 'which will be so constituted, both in its House of Commons and in its Senate, as to be fully and fairly representative of the Irish nation; of Protestants as well as Catholics of urban interests as well as of agricultural interests, of minorities even more than majorities'. He went on to set out six further safeguards which would provide the 'additional rampart' for the protection of the Protestants: 'First, the Crown will be able to refuse assent to an unjust Bill. Secondly, the Imperial Parliament will be able to repeal such a Bill or enact another law. Thirdly, the Home Rule Bill will contain provisions safeguarding religious freedom and fair play for both Protestants and Roman Catholics. Fourthly, if any law passed in Ireland transgressed the limit laid down by the Home Rule Act, then the Privy Council would be able to declare it void. Fifthly, the Home Rule System will be worked in the face of Great Britain as well as Ireland. The Imperial Parliament is overwhelmingly Protestant, and would certainly resent any attempt to act in a spirit of religious intolerance or unfairness. Sixthly, the power of the Imperial Parliament to interfere is unquestioned in law, and equally unquestioned in fact, for all military forces will be under the Imperial control.' Churchill continued: 'We look forward to a time which has long been retarded and which we believe is now, when this island—instead of being a disruptive force in the British Empire—shall be transformed into a new centre of Union, when the harsh and

about that? You weren't born then.' I told him that I had in fact been born a few weeks before the outbreak of war, but that my interest stemmed from the fact that I was an Ulsterman. At once he became animated & gave me a detailed account of the whole affair. 'I had no idea, nor had any of us in the Cabinet, of the intensity of Protestant opposition to Home Rule. That old fool Augustine Birrell[1] had not kept us fully informed. My wife & I were staying in the best hotel in Belfast & we went up to our room. As we came downstairs for our meal, the foyer was packed with respectably-dressed people, all of them standing there in total silence. When our feet touched some step (perhaps the sixth from the bottom) they all hissed, & continued to hiss until we went into the dining-room & went to our table. Then they all poured into the dining-room & occupied all the other tables, where they all had their meal in total silence. When we were on our way to the meeting at the football ground, the crowds jostled our car & at one time we thought it was going to be overturned.'

I asked him if it was true that the crowd was prevented from doing so, by urgent waves from Carson[2] & all the other prominent Unionist leaders who were standing on the steps of the Reform Club, which the car had to pass immediately before turning right into the Falls Road (where a very different welcome awaited him). He did not remember that. He was very amused when I asked him if it was true that when he landed at Larne earlier that day & pointed to his suit-case, the porter snarled at him 'Ah, carry yer ain bag.' He did not remember that, but I assured him that whether it was true or false the porter had been dining out on the story ever since.

He added 'We all thought that Carson & the Unionists were bluffing. I began to realise that day that we were wrong.'

He then said 'When I was Chancellor of the Exchequer ten years ago I

---

lamentable cry of reproach which so long jarred upon the concert of Empire will die away, when the accursed machinery, by which the hatred manufactured and preserved will be broken for ever.'

[1] Augustine Birrell, 1850–1933. Quain Professor of Law, University College, London, 1896–9. Liberal MP, 1899–1900 and 1906–18. President of the Board of Education, 1905–7; Chief Secretary to the Lord Lieutenant of Ireland, 1907–16. Author and editor of several works of literature, including an edition of Boswell's Life of Johnson, first published in 1897. His memoirs, *Things Past Redress*, were published posthumously in 1937.

[2] Edward Henry Carson, 1854–1935. Educated at Trinity College, Dublin. Barrister. Conservative MP, 1892–1921. Knighted, 1900. Solicitor-General, 1900–6. Leader of the Ulster Unionists in the House of Commons, 1910–21. Attorney-General, May–October 1915. First Lord of the Admiralty, December 1916–July 1917. Minister without Portfolio in the War Cabinet, July 1917–January 1918. Created Baron, 1921. A Lord of Appeal in Ordinary, 1921–9.

put Ulster's financial position on a firm footing & that saved you from being financially cut off by Great Britain. If I had not done so, Snowden would probably have starved you out.'[1]

He learned that I would be going to USA in October for a 2-month debating tour & was delighted. 'It's a great country, but they're touchy. When you've made an anti-American remark, say something anti-British immediately afterwards—& tell them that I told you to do so. Americans' worst fault is that they can't carry their drink which is generally of poor quality. Anyway one doesn't need much drink there owing to the climate.

'I never go to the Oxford Union now, & won't go until its members acquire a sense of responsibility.' This was said four years after the debate ('That this house will in no circumstances fight for King & Country') & after which Randolph Churchill & Lord Stanley of Alderley[2] made fools of themselves in an effort to have the record of the debate expunged from the Minutes.

He went on to talk about Joad[3] (who had just published his controversial autobiography 'Testament of Joad'). 'He is not only a pacifist but also doesn't wash.'

He was very bitter about Baldwin. 'The legacy of Baldwinism is incompetence because of the sentimental all-men-are-brothers-so-don't-let's-wrangle attitude'.

I was a devout Liberal at the time & he said: 'I believe in Liberalism. I am still a Liberal. I have a great admiration for Sir Archibald Sinclair. I will not rejoin the party because it didn't back me over India nor over

---

[1] In December 1925, at Stanley Baldwin's request, Churchill had presided over the British delegation at the Irish Boundary Commission. The other British members were Lord Salisbury (Lord Privy Seal), Lord Birkenhead (Secretary of State for India), Sir John Anderson (Permanent Under-Secretary of State, Home Office), G. G. Whiskard (Assistant Secretary, Dominions Office) and P. J. Grigg (Treasury). The Irish Free State members were William Cosgrave (President of the Executive Council), Kevin O'Higgins (Vice-President) and J. O'Byrne (Attorney-General). The full text of the Commission's deliberations is published in *The Exchequer Years* volume of the Churchill Biography (Companion volume 5, part 1), pages 603 to 616. When the negotiations were over, L. S. Amery noted in his diary: '. . . if the Free State settlement is to succeed at all, or succeed for a generation, this new agreement has given it its chance' (*Amery papers*).

[2] Edward John Stanley, 1907–1971. Son of the 5th Baron Stanley of Alderley (Clementine Churchill's cousin). Educated at Eton and Balliol College, Oxford. Succeeded his father as 6th Baron, 1931. Lieutenant-Commander, Royal Naval Volunteer Reserve, 1939–45. He married four times.

[3] Cyril Edwin Mitchinson Joad, 1891–1953. Educated at Blundell's and Balliol College, Oxford; John Locke Scholar in Moral Philosophy, 1914. A civil servant in the Board of Trade (later Ministry of Labour), 1914–30. Head of the Department of Philosophy, Birkbeck College, University of London, from 1930 until his death. Doctor of Letters, London, 1936. Author of more than 45 books on philoshical themes, including *The Book of Joad*, *The Testament of Joad*, *Why War?* and *The Recovery of Belief*. A member of the Brains Trust, BBC.

rearmament. It was John Morley[1] who taught me Liberalism & he would have been with me on both issues. Our last chance lay with LG's pre-war social services, etc & when that was played out our day was over.'

Incidentally there was no reason to doubt that Morley would have shared his views on Indian self-government (at least in part), but rearmament![2]

He said that he had been busy painting at Blenheim all day & so had not had a chance to prepare anything. Nevertheless he spoke for 50 minutes & not one of us wanted him to stop. As he spoke, he shuffled his feet about & on one occasion gave a mighty kick which only just missed me. L. S. Amery was a guest (who did not make a speech) & Churchill referred to him & said 'so far he & I have kept in step, but now I come to the League of Nations & there we part company'. The kick came with the word 'step'.

[1] John Morley, 1838–1923. Editor of the *Fortnightly Review*, 1867–82, strongly supporting Liberalism and Liberal policies. Editor of the *Pall Mall Gazette*, 1880–3, changing the paper's outlook from conservatism to radicalism. Biographer of Burke (1867), Voltaire (1872), Rousseau (1873), Cobden (1881), Cromwell (1899) and Gladstone (in three volumes, 1903). Liberal MP for Newcastle, 1883–95 and 1896–1908. Irish Secretary, 1892–5. Secretary of State for India, 1905–10. Created Viscount, 1908. Lord Privy Seal 1910–14. Resigned from the Cabinet on the outbreak of war. A fifteen volume edition of his historical and political writings was published in 1921. On 12 May 1912 Churchill wrote to Morley (after entertaining him on board the Admiralty yacht *Enchantress*): 'It was a great treat & honour to me to entertain you, & I am delighted to think that in spite of the weather upsetting all my best plans, you were so much pleased. Men like you & Arthur Balfour are independent of external conditions. You can always turn to one of your great treasure houses & take out some rare, instructive or curious topic & play with it & polish it & throw it from one to the other for you to enjoy & for others to admire. And yet your interest in new things, & different things from those of your usual life is keen and strong. T''is a balance & gift of mind & nature that carries pleasure with it ready made for all. But for none more than me. Towards you besides I feel as you rightly desire a sincere affection, & always cherish your friendship as one of my most precious possessions' (*Christie's auction rooms, 24 October 1979*).

[2] On India: in 1909 Morley published his *Indian Speeches 1907–1909*. In one of the speeches quoted, delivered at Arbroath on 21 October 1907, Morley had declared: 'I would only say this to my idealist friends, whether Indian or European, that for every passage that they can find in Mill, or Burke, or Macaulay, or any other of our lofty sages with their noble hearts and potent brains, I will find them a dozen passages in which history is shown to admonish us, in the language of Burke—"How weary a step do those take who endeavour to make out of a great mass a true political personality." They are words much to be commended to those zealots in India—how many a weary step has to be taken before they can form themselves into a mass that has a true political personality.' On rearmament: in 1914 Morley had resigned from Asquith's Cabinet in protest against Britain's declaration of war on Germany; his *Memorandum on Resignation* was published posthumously in 1928. But Morley had not been among those Liberal Ministers who challenged Churchill's proposed increase in naval expenditure in January 1914 (the opponents being Lloyd George, John Simon, Herbert Samuel, Walter Runciman, Reginald McKenna, Charles Hobhouse and Lord Beauchamp). On 13 January 1914 Churchill had sent Morley details of his proposals, and of the increase in German shipbuilding which they were designed to meet, with a covering note: 'Here is my case; & I wonder vy much what you will think of it. The situation has been rendered serious by LG's astonishing behaviour, the various aspects of wh have no doubt not been lost on you. I am absolutely fixed, & can do nothing more. The 4 ships are vital & no compromise of any sort is possible' (*Christie's auction rooms, 24 October 1979*).

He stressed the need for rearmanent & a defensive alliance with France. 'We must co-operate with America as far as she is willing. Above all, we must support the League. Wherever war threatens or breaks out, we are on the side of the victim of aggression & in each case we shall do what we can, through the League, to aid the victim.'[1]

He ended with an attack on both Communism & Fascism. 'Sometimes it is said that they are poles apart. Perhaps they are. But what difference is there for the inhabitants of the North Pole from those at the South? Perhaps when one crawls out of one's igloo in the morning there may be a few more penguins at one or polar bears at the other. But otherwise they are alike & alike as miserable. For my part I propose to remain in the temperate zone.'[2]

It was great & we were all spell-bound.

After dinner he returned to Blenheim & Amery to All Souls.

Next evening Amery gave quite a long informal address to the under-graduate members of the Club. He devoted much of it to attacking Churchill's speech, particularly the part about the League, which he said, was not so much useless as dangerous. It would get us into wars from which we could be saved by ordinary conventional diplomacy, e.g. Abyssinia. He also attacked the notion that the victim of aggression was always in the right. With great erudition (& without a note) he gave a long list of 19th century wars in which, he alleged, history backed the cause of the aggressor. Most of us had never heard of any of these wars. Not one of us was convinced. Churchill was an easy victor over Amery.

[1] Churchill's re-iterated criticisms of Nazism were in contrast to the views of Geoffrey Dawson, editor of *The Times*, who wrote privately to Lord Lothian on 23 May 1937: 'I should like to get going with the Germans. I simply cannot understand why they should apparently be so much annoyed with *The Times* at this moment. I spend my nights in taking out anything which I think will hurt their susceptibilities and in dropping in little things which are in-tended to soothe them' (*Lothian papers*).

[2] In an article entitled 'The Infernal Twins', published in *Colliers* on 3 July 1937, Churchill wrote, of Nazism and Communism: 'I am reminded of the North Pole and South Pole. They are at opposite ends of the earth, but if you woke up at either Pole tomorrow morning you could not tell which one it was. Perhaps there might be more penguins at one, or more Polar bears at the other; but all around would be ice and snow and the blast of a biting wind. I have made up my mind, however far I may travel, whatever countries I may see, I will not go to the Arctic or to the Antarctic regions. Give me London, give me Paris, give me New York, give me some of the beautiful capitals of the British Dominions. Let us go some-where where our breath is not frozen on our lips because of the Secret Police. Let us go somewhere where there are green pastures and the shade of venerable trees. Let us not wander away from the broad fertile fields of freedom into these gaunt, grim, dim, gloomy abstrac-tions of morbid and sterile thought.'

A. L. Rowse[1] to Winston S. Churchill

(*Churchill papers: 2/296*)

24 May 1937   All Souls College
                                                            Oxford

Sir,

   I am writing to ask if you will pardon the liberty I have taken in asking
my publisher, Jonathan Cape, to send you an advance-copy of my Life of
Sir Richard Grenville of the *Revenge*. I have often been tempted to write to
you to say that, though on the other side in politics, I am strongly in agreement with your views on the organisation of peace in Europe, the menace
of German armaments and the necessity of our own rearmament; and it was
a matter of the greatest regret to me that I was away from college at the
time of your recent visit to us here. . . .[2]

Winston S. Churchill: Press statement

(*Churchill papers: 2/312*)

25 May 1937

   In the confusion and darkness of these times, it is clear that in order to
prevent the horror and ruin of another World War we must work towards the
permanent organisation, first of Europe, but as soon as possible of the whole
world, to redress legitimate grievances, to overawe aggression, and thus prevent the brutal explosion of war.

   The programme of The New Commonwealth Society offers a constructive
plan for the organisation of such a system. It is the paramount duty of the
peoples of the British Empire to play their part in bringing about its inauguration. I therefore urge all men and women of goodwill, both in the Mother
Country and in the Dominions and Colonies, to acquaint themselves of
these proposals, and to lend this movement their aid in the task which it
has undertaken.

                                                   Winston S. Churchill

---

   [1] Alfred Leslie Rowse, 1903–   . Historian and poet. Fellow of All Souls College, Oxford,
1925–74. Unsuccessful Labour Party candidate at Penryn and Falmouth, 1931 and 1935.
Author of *The Early Churchills* (1956) and *The Later Churchills* (1958).
   [2] On June 24 A. L. Rowse wrote to Churchill again: 'May I say, though I am myself a
member of the Labour Party, how much I wish you were a member of the Government at
such a juncture as this! It seems to me that we are now paying the penalty for all these years
of forebearing and divided aims.'

Lieutenant-Colonel Sir John Sandeman Allen[1] to Winston S. Churchill

(*Churchill papers: 2/302*)

26 May 1937   House of Commons

Dear Mr Churchill,

I should very much like to have a talk with you in the near future and to introduce to you Colonel H. W. Hill,[2] CMG, DSO, who is an expert on the question of Anti-Air Artillery and, in fact, the Anti-Air Craft problem in general. He has a mass of very interesting data and is not at all satisfied with the way things are going at the present moment.

I feel that with the possession of the facts something must be done and I am afraid I do not quite know how to handle it myself. Your advice and assistance would be invaluable.

Yours sincerely,
J. Sandeman Allen

Field-Marshal Sir Cyril Deverell[3] to Winston S. Churchill

(*Churchill papers: 2/302*)

27 May 1937   War Office

Dear Mr Churchill,

With reference to our conversation on the subject of the mechanization of the cavalry, I send you a paper which I hope will explain the situation.

---

[1] John Sandeman Allen, 1865–1949. Entered marine insurance, 1882. Chairman of the Liverpool Chamber of Commerce, 1922–6. Chairman of Technical and Commercial Education, Liverpool, 1924–8. Conversative MP for Birkenhead West, 1931–45. Knighted, 1928. Chairman of the Commercial Committee of the House of Commons; of the Coastal Trade Development Council; and of the Federation of Chambers of Commerce of the British Empire.

[2] Henry Warburton Hill, 1877–1951. A grandson of Sir Rowland Hill, inventor of the penny post. Educated at Bradfield and Woolwich. On active service in South Africa, 1900 (despatches). Artillery experimental work, 1906–9. On active service in Flanders, 1914–18 (wounded at Ypres, despatches thrice, CMG, DSO, Croix de Guerre). Commandant, Anti-Aircraft Defence School, 1925–9. Commander of the 26th (London) Air Defence Brigade (a Territorial Brigade), 1929–33. Retired, 1934.

[3] Cyril John Deverell, 1874–1947. 2nd Lieutenant, 1892; Major, General Staff, India, 1913–14. On active service in France, 1914–18; promoted Major-General for distinguished service in the field (despatches seven times). In India, 1921–31; knighted, 1926; Quarter-master-General, 1927–30; General, 1933; Field-Marshal, 1936. Chief of the Imperial General Staff, 1936–7. Retired (aged 63) in December 1937.

I hope that in the circumstances as explained, you will find that the best is being done.[1]

Yours sincerely,
C. J. Deverell

Robert Bernays to Winston S. Churchill

(*Churchill papers: 2/296*)

28 May 1937

Dear Mr Churchill,

It was very kind of you to send me a telegram of congratulation on my promotion.[2]

I have only one regret—and that is that I am now removed too far to hear your whispered and pungent comments on the passing Parliamentary scene—which were always so exhilarating.

I shall always be grateful—as must be every young man in the House to-day—for the way in which you continuously demonstrate to what heights the arts of Parliamentary debate can be made to attain.

Yours very sincerely,
Robert Bernays

---

[1] The War Office paper, on which Churchill wrote 'Major Morton to see', was dated 25 May 1937, and entitled 'Mechanization of Cavalry'. The paper described the five steps being taken to turn cavalry regiments into tank regiments. The first step was 'the removal of all horses', as the retention of horses prevented the 'efficient' carrying out of mechanized training. The second step was a year's training on 'mechanized wheeled vehicles', the third was 'the provision of tracked vehicles to enable training to take place in tracked driving', the fourth was the provision 'of sufficient of the older types of light tanks' to enable tactical training to be carried out, and the fifth was 'the issue of the complete peace establishment of light tanks and other vehicles of the latest types, as soon as the regiments are sufficiently trained to be able to handle and maintain them, and as soon as production permits'. The paper then outlined the stage of mechanization reached in the various regiments concerned, and noted that 'During the winter 1937/38 all the above regiments will receive sufficient light tanks and unarmoured carriers for carrying out their individual training. It is hoped that by the summer of 1938 they will all receive sufficient light tanks and carriers for training that year, and that the completion of their war establishment of those vehicles will be in progress'.

[2] Robert Bernays (see page 466, note 1) had just been appointed Parliamentary Secretary to the Ministry of Health. Maurice Nadin writes: 'I knew Bernays well, because he was the only MP to join the Services during the war without telling the authorities he was an MP. He & I joined the Army on the same day. He told me that when he was offered this post in the Government, he did not want to accept it, and asked Churchill if he could join him (WSC) in his campaign for re-armament, to which the reply was that he strongly recommended Bernays to accept the Government post he had been offered. He made it clear that the experience of office was all-important and that he (Bernays) ought to consider his own political future. For his own sake he ought to accept the position he had been offered' (*letter to the author, 15 January 1982*).

Lord Derby to Winston S. Churchill

(*Derby papers*)

28 May 1937
Private

I see in the papers today a report, which I sincerely hope is true, namely that whilst I am to propose that Neville Chamberlain be appointed our Leader you are to second it. The report is true as far as I am concerned and I trust it is with regard to yourself, as it would give me the greatest possible pleasure to be once again acting in close co-operation with you.

I am afraid mine will be somewhat of a dull oration. I do not mind that because I know that you will make up for any of my deficiencies.

I shall be at the Caxton Hall a little before 12 should you be there then. We might compare notes in case there is anything likely to clash, not that I think there will be.[1]

Winston S. Churchill: magazine article, extract

('*Colliers*', *16 October 1937*)

[28 May 1937]

There never was any doubt that Neville Chamberlain would succeed Baldwin. No rival candidature was even discussed by serious people. Thus we see him securely installed in the great office, which while it by no means possesses the high direct authority of a President of the United States,

---

[1] On 31 May 1937 Churchill spoke at the Caxton Hall, in support of a motion nominating Neville Chamberlain to the Leadership of the Conservative Party. In his diary, Henry Channon described Churchill's speech as 'an able, fiery speech not untouched by bitterness'. It was his duty, Churchill told the assembled MPs, Peers and prospective candidates, as the senior Conservative Privy Councillor in the House of Commons, to second the resolution nominating Chamberlain to the party leadership. After recalling Chamberlain's 'memorable achievement' as Chancellor of the Exchequer in restoring Britain's financial credit and stimulating foreign trade, Churchill told the meeting that the leadership of the party had never been interpreted 'in a dictatorial or despotic sense', and he appealed for the continued recognition of the rights of those who disagreed with party policy: 'The House of Commons,' he said, 'still survives as the arena of free debate. We feel sure that the leader we are about to choose will, as a distinguished Parliamentarian and a House of Commons man, not resent honest differences of opinion arising between those who mean the same thing, and that party opinion will not be denied its subordinate but still rightful place in his mind.'

nevertheless combines in one single man the guidance of the executive, leadership of the House of Commons and the control of the strongest party machine.

Curiously enough, at the moment of succeeding to all these commanding powers Neville Chamberlain made the most obvious mistake of his political career. He added to his budget, quite needlessly so far as the current year was concerned, a tax which was at once injurious, unworkable and infertile. The city, at first puzzled, was soon thoroughly estranged. The manufacturers and traders who, for so many years, had reposed their confidence in a Chancellor of the Exchequer who, like themselves, was a trained and experienced businessman, were infuriated. The markets collapsed in an exaggerated but none the less alarming slump. He was the last man from whom such an excursion was expected. Reaction was all the more severe. After a month of bargaining, bickerings and hagglings it gradually became clear that the House of Commons would not have the tax, or would have it forced upon them only at the price of the prestige of the new cabinet and the popularity of the new Prime Minister.

No one impugned his motives. They arose from a very sincere desire to absolve the government from all suspicion of tolerating readily profiteering in the firms inevitably enriched by the great flood of government rearmament. They arose from a desire to make the munition workers realise that the imperative, long-delayed rearmament of Britain would not be converted into a rich man's ramp. They arose from the habit of looking ahead and from a grave view of the European and world situation.

But still, for ten or twenty millions out of a budget of over eight hundred and fifty millions no one should compromise the larger issues involved. Least of all should this be done when the money could so easily be found from the same quarters by different and simpler means.

It was with enormous relief that the House of Commons learned that the new Prime Minister was not incapable of making a timely, judicious and coolly executed withdrawal. So far from his prestige being affected by his retreat, it was, strangely, enhanced.

There has grown up a conception of Neville Chamberlain as a cold, aloof, rather inhuman figure, set apart, not only by the loneliness of leadership, but also by a certain arctic quality in himself. His strength is unadorned with graces. There is a bleakness in it. It is true that he has few friends and that he shuns society. He dislikes and mistrusts facile enthusiasms. He has taken no pains to invite or encourage those affectionate loyalties that so often centre upon the personality of a party chief. He has the typical Englishman's distaste for emotionalism. This certainly does not imply that he is cold and unfeeling. He had inherited a great deal of his father's passion for social justice. Like Joseph Chamberlain, he believes that the well-being of the people is the touchstone of political success. And he interprets well-being in no narrow sense. The extensive scheme for the physical education of British youth, of which he is the principal architect, bears the impress alike of boldness of conception and generosity of spirit.

But there is one sphere especially in which the real man has revealed himself. There are many homes in England that would be motherless today but for the impetus which, as Minister of Health, Neville Chamberlain gave to the campaign against maternal mortality. Behind his interest in this subject lay a deep intensity of feeling which had its origin in personal tragedy. 'My own mother,' he said in a speech some years ago at Leeds, 'died in childbirth. And I know how great is the injury to the family when the mother is taken away.' It is possible that this early bereavement, so deeply felt, drove the boy in upon himself and led to the creation of that cloak of icy reserve in which, at times, the man appears to be wrapped.

His chosen recreations—fishing and bird-watching—are of a kind best pursued alone. They have perhaps confirmed him, not in misanthropy, but in self-sufficiency. But it is difficult to fit the friend of birds, who feeds a flock of sparrows, blackbirds and thrushes every morning at No 10 Downing Street before sitting down to his own breakfast, into the picture that is sometimes painted of him. It is not any lack of normal human feeling that makes him hold aloof from society. The happy comradeship of his home life shows that. But Neville Chamberlain, throughout his career, has been too busy doing things to bother about meeting people.

In his wife he found the ideal help-mate. She has, he said on one occasion, 'rejoiced in my successes, encouraged me in my disappointments, guided me with her counsel, warned me of dangers, and never allowed me to forget the humanity underlying all politics'. And he added: 'She has been privy to all my secrets, and she has never divulged one.'

He has never spared himself. When he was doing war work as Lord Mayor of Birmingham he allowed himself only twenty minutes for lunch and had no break for tea. He still rises early and goes to bed late. The days are too short for the work that he wants to crowd into them. A man who has thus to fight every inch of the upward way, and in whom habits of un-remitting industry and self-discipline have become ingrained—one, more-over, whose chosen recreations take him to scenes where nature is still un-spoiled and man is dwarfed by the immemorial hills—may well regard the standards of society and the easy eminence which birth or wealth can give, with a measure of suspicion.

Chamberlain undertook his heavy burden at a time when most men are thinking of retirement. Still, as he has said: he has led a sober, temperate life, and he is sound in wind and limb and capable of hard, long and tiring effort.[1]

He is a man of the highest character, equipped with many years' experience, and supported on all sides by the hopes and wishes of his fellow countrymen. He has a most agreeable voice on the broadcast; he has a disarming smile, a charming wife, and carries the flag of righteous endeavour.

Winston S. Churchill to Alfred Duff Cooper: telegram

(*Churchill papers: 1/299*)

29 May 1937

Heartiest congratulations on your great promotion.[2]

Winston and Clemmie

---

[1] On 31 May 1937 Chamberlain had told the Caxton Hall meeting, at which he was elected Leader of the Conservative Party: 'I am informed that I am sound in wind and limb, and I am not afraid of the physical labour which may be entailed upon me. I am entering on the duties and responsibilities of Prime Minister at an age when most people would think of retiring from active work, but I have hitherto led a sober and temperate life.'

[2] On 28 May 1937 Duff Cooper had succeeded Sir Samuel Hoare as First Lord of the Admiralty. Hoare became Home Secretary, and Sir John Simon (the former Home Secretary) became Chancellor of the Exchequer. Duff Cooper was succeeded at the War Office by Leslie Hore-Belisha On 13 July 1937, after they had dined together, Duff Cooper wrote to Churchill: 'Dear Winston, Herewith a reward for good play at bézique and for being the most charming of guests in the worst of weather. Yours ever, Duff' (*Churchill papers: 1/299*).

June 1937

Winston S. Churchill: speech on the Finance Bill, extract
(Hansard)

1 June 1937   House of Commons

Let me now say that I hope that the free and full discussion to which Parliament is entitled will not be complicated by any question of personal prestige. In China, face-saving is usual, but it is less important in this country. Indeed, the successful avowal of mistakes was one of the most important arts in the armoury of the late Prime Minister, and one that was frequently practised to the discomfiture of those who had pointed out, with much precision and much toil, the error which he had committed.

The doctrine that the Chancellor of the Exchequer is infallible and that the Budget statement is one of the laws of the Medes and Persians has no foundation in our Parliamentary life. I seem to remember having heard that Mr Gladstone, or perhaps it was Mr Disraeli or some very eminent and respectable statesman in the past, said, when he was reproached for giving way on some point, something to this effect: 'In a democratically governed country, possessing powerful, representative, Parliamentary institutions, it is sometimes necessary to defer to the opinion of other people.'

In House of Commons finance and on questions of ways and means, it is right that the Executive should, from time to time, yield to the sense of the House. In nine times out of 10, and 19 times out of 20, the Government will prevail; but their status will be increased and not decreased, if, on the tenth or the twentieth occasion, they bow to the opinion of the Assembly.

There were many such occasions in our history. There was Walpole, who, after the Division on the Excise Bill, came into the Chamber and said to his colleagues: 'This dance can no further go.' Then there was Mr Lowe with his tax on matches '*Ex luce lucellum*.'[1] I myself remember Sir Michael Hicks-Beach, in 1901, when he increased the tax on cheques. We have got used to it nowadays, but in those days it seemed infinitely horrible; the shock was almost intolerable when the tax was raised from 1d to 2d. He introduced this tax, which had a most chilling effect upon the Conservative party and the

---

[1] 'A little profit from light'.

Liberal leaders. Two days later, I saw him come down to the House. I pushed my way through the crowd at the Gangway, which was enormous. It was a moment of great excitement and they said to me: 'Black Michael is giving up the tax.' But what happened? Was he regarded as having done anything wrong? On the contrary; he was praised. He was cheered.

In those days, the Conservative party used to live, or at any rate, used to lunch, at the Carlton Club, and for weeks afterwards they were talking about the magnificent way in which Black Michael had extricated himself from this difficult situation, and of the courage and good feeling he had shown.

Perhaps the House may remember that only seven or eight years ago I got into some trouble myself about the Kerosene Tax. It was a very good tax. I was quite right about it. My right hon Friend slipped it through a year or two later without the slightest trouble and it never ruined the homes of the people at all. Anyhow, the Chief Whip[1] of those days telephoned me. I was resting in the country after the Budget speech. He said: 'You had better come up. All our fellows are against the tax, and all the others too.'

I do not know whether any similar communication has been made by the present occupant of that most important office. Anyhow, I acted with great promptitude. I came up to London immediately. It was said to be very difficult to withdraw the Kerosene Tax; it was said to me by the experts, who so often turn out to be wrong, to be impossible to withdraw it without wrecking the whole of the oil tax, which was a very good tax. May I remind hon Members that more than £50,000,000 from the oil tax is being derived this year? It was so much abused but, so far as I can make out, it has not stopped motoring.

I came down to the House in the nick of time. Lord Snowden—Mr. Snowden, he was then—was rising, full of pent-up, overwhelming fury, to fall upon me. I got up. I withdrew the tax. Was I humiliated? Was I called weak? Was I accused of running away? Not at all. There were loud and prolonged cheers. Not only did people say: 'How clever; how quick; how very well he has outwitted them'; but others came along and said: 'How very right it is to meet with respect the opinion of the House of Commons.'

I hope you will pardon me, Mr Speaker, for referring to those matters, but that was one of my best days.[2]

[1] Sir Bolton Eyres-Monsell (see page 7, note 3), the Chief Conservative Whip from 1923 to 1931, and Chief Whip during the second Baldwin Government of 1924 to 1929.

[2] Commenting on Neville Chamberlain's decision to withdraw his proposed National Defence Contribution scheme, *The Times* wrote, on 1 June 1937: 'The real turn of the tide was produced by Mr Churchill, who brilliantly and wittily, as the sole surviving ex-Chancellor present, offered "avuncular advice" . . . Amid loud laughter Mr Churchill recalled Mr Baldwin's method of discomfiting critics by a "Successful avowel of his mistakes" and his own happy experience ("one of my best days") when he withdrew the Kerosene tax. It was one of Mr Churchill's most entertaining Parliamentary successes.'

Lord Melchett[1] to Winston S. Churchill

(*Churchill papers: 2/302*)

2 June 1937

My dear Winston,

One of your best ever,[2] and I believe it was due to the facts you presented, to the tactful manner in which you handled the Prime Minister—grave and gay—that you gave him the courage to abandon NDC. You are indeed a very great man, and God knows why you are not in the Cabinet to help to guide this old country of ours in the difficult times we are going through.

Yrs ever,
Harry

Nathan Laski to Winston S. Churchill

(*Churchill papers: 2/296*)

2 June 1937   Cheetham,
                                                  Manchester

My dear Mr Churchill,

I seize the first opportunity to congratulate you most sincerely upon the wonderful speech you made regarding the Chamberlain National Scheme.

---

[1] Henry Ludwig Mond, 1898–1949. Educated at Winchester. On active service in France, 1915–18 (wounded, 1916). Liberal MP, Isle of Ely, 1923–4; East Toxteth, 1929–30. Succeeded his father as 2nd Baron Melchett, 1930. Deputy Chairman, Imperial Chemical Industries, 1940–7. Director of the International Nickel Company of Canada. His elder son was killed in a flying accident at sea in April 1945.

[2] On 1 June 1937 Churchill spoke in the House of Commons during the second reading of the Finance Bill. A small part of the speech is quoted above. Churchill had begun his speech by saying, of his decision to speak in the debate at all: 'I certainly do not do so in any hostile spirit to the new Government and to the new Prime Minister. On the contrary, I take a friendly interest in this new Government. I do not quite know why I do. I cannot go so far as to call it a paternal interest, because, speaking candidly, it is not quite the sort of Government I should have bred myself. If it is not paternal, at any rate I think I may call it an avuncular interest.' Churchill went on to oppose the Government's proposed National Defence Contribution, a tax devised to raise revenue from arms manufacturers, on the grounds that this 'most healthy tax', as he expressed it, 'is one whose sole purpose is revenue. Taxation to give effect to some political purpose, or even to inculcate some moral principle, is usually found to fall short of the highest standard of financial economy. All the best authorities prescribe as the true test of any tax that it should yield the largest sum of money with the least possible disturbance of the life and business of the nation.' Of 'individual enterprise', Churchill said: 'I know that it is the Socialist idea that making profits is a vice, and that making large profits is something of which a man ought to be ashamed. I hold the other view. I consider that the real vice is making losses.' Of war profiteering Churchill said: 'Personally, I do not mind saying that I would have gone as far as after the War as a capital levy—(An Hon Member: "Why did you not?")—I have always suffered from a lack of power to give full effect to my wishes. I know that Mr Bonar Law was very much inclined that way. It seemed to me, and I think to others, that it would have been quite fair to say that no one should come out of the War richer than he went in.'

Even 'The Times' who in recent years has been no friend of yours tells us today that it is one of the best speeches you have ever made in your whole career.

For the last three general elections I have been a whole-hearted supporter of the National Government and I think I may say that I have done as much as any single man in Lancashire to support the Government although I must admit that Lancashire made a great mistake in supporting the India Bill. It seems that you were right when you said that goodwill would not make the Indians recognise the claims of Lancashire and our trade, I am sorry to say, is dwindling every year as the figures recently made public show.

The object of my letter is that there are hundreds of thousands of people in this country who like myself thought you would be a member of the new Government. It is our opinion, without any flattery whatsoever, that there is no great enterprising power existing in Parliament today equal to yourself and it is a great loss to the country that you are not at its disposal. Many of us wish to know why this is so and what steps we could take to make the people understand that if we have to have a Government representing brain power, you should be one of its members.

Could you possibly tell me in absolute confidence what you consider should be done to bring this matter to the notice of the Prime Minister? Certainly I shall not use any efforts towards this Government if it is made up of such nonentities as many of them are.

Yours very sincerely,
Nathan Laski

Winston S. Churchill to the Marquess of Cholmondeley[1]

(Churchill papers: 8/547)

2 June 1937

From 1708 onwards Walpole[2] was Secretary of War and thus worked in close contact with Marlborough. The association became very intimate in

---

[1] George Horatio Charles Cholmondeley, Earl of Rocksavage, 1883–1968. On active service in South Africa, 1901–2. Married, 1913, Sybil, sister of Sir Philip Sassoon. On active service in France and Flanders, 1914–18. Major, RAF, 1920. Succeeded his father, 1923, as 5th Marquess of Cholmondeley. Joint Hereditary Lord Great Chamberlain, he bore the Royal Standard at the coronation of King George VI.

[2] Robert Walpole, 1679–1745. Secretary of State for War, 1708–12. Prime Minister from 1721 to 1742. Created Earl of Orford, 1742. His only daughter married the 3rd Earl of Cholmondeley, whose country seat was Houghton Hall, the home of the Cholmondeleys, and residence of the 5th Marquess. For Churchill's own visit to Houghton Hall on 5 December 1937, see pages 853–5.

1709, 1710 and 1711. Both were driven out of office and accused of peculation, and at the beginning of 1712 Walpole was sent to the Tower, while Marlborough a little later went into voluntary exile. However they seem to have preserved contact during the early part of the reign of George I. Later after the death of Marlborough Sarah had a bitter quarrel with Walpole.

My interest is in the years 1709–12 inclusive, and I wonder whether you have at Houghton Hall any papers on this period, or any letters from Marlborough to Walpole which have not yet seen the light of day. I would be greatly obliged if you would allow my literary secretary, Mr Deakin, who is a Fellow of Wadham College, Oxford and a young gentleman of high distinction and agreeable manners, to come and see your Librarian. Thereafter if it is thought that any material exists bearing on my life of Marlborough, would you allow him access to it?

Winston S. Churchill to Lord Stanhope[1]

(Churchill papers: 8/547)

2 June 1937

I find increasing evidence that from 1709 onwards Stanhope and Marlborough were working in the very closest contact. Marlborough seemed to have relied on Stanhope for everything connected with the Spanish War; but afterwards in 1711 and 1712 when they were both under the frown of the Tory Government, Stanhope was working with the Whigs at home and again in Marlborough's most intimate confidence.

Do you think you have any letters bearing upon the historical association of these two warrior-statesmen? In this case I should be grateful if you would allow my literary secretary, Mr Deakin, who is a Fellow of Wadham College, Oxford, and a young gentleman of high attainments and agreeable manners, to come over to Chevening and see any material that might be of use to me in my life of Marlborough.

Pray accept my congratulations on your new appointment.[2]

[1] James Richard Stanhope, 1880–1967. Educated at Eton and Magdalen College, Oxford. Grenadier Guards, 1901–8. Succeeded his father as 7th Earl Stanhope, 1905. Served with the Grenadier Guards in France, 1914–18 (despatches twice, Military Cross 1916, DSO 1917). Parliamentary Secretary, War Office, 1918–19. Civil Lord of Admiralty, 1924–9. Privy Councillor, 1929. Under-Secretary of State for War, 1931–4. Knight of the Garter, 1934. Parliamentary Under-Secretary of State for Foreign Affairs, 1934–6. First Commissioner of Works, 1936–7. President of the Board of Education, 1937–8. First Lord of the Admiralty, 1938–9. Leader of the House of Lords, 1938–40. Lord President of the Council, 1939–40. In 1952 he succeeded a distant cousin as the last Earl of Chesterfield. He was also the last Earl Stanhope, and bequeathed his country house, Chevening, to the nation. His only brother, a Captain in the Grenadier Guards, was killed in action in France on 16 September 1916.

[2] As President of the Board of Education.

Desmond Morton to Winston S. Churchill

(*Churchill papers: 2/307*)

2 June 1937

Dear Winston,

Thank you very much for letting me see M Pierre Cot's[1] Memorandum, which I return, having attached some brief comments.

May I congratulate you on your great triumph in the House last night, as, undoubtedly, whatever may have been the intention of the Government with regard to NDC, your speech settled the matter.

Yours very sincerely,
Desmond Morton

PS. I have not shown the French Memorandum to anyone else, but I rather think that a copy of it was sent to the AM[2] via the Air Attaché in Paris.[3] The big point now is not so much any dispute between the AM and the French figures, but a comparison between our own position and that of the Germans.

Desmond Morton: notes

(*Churchill papers: 2/307*)

2 June 1937

1. The statements and estimates in Parts II and III regarding the German Army and Navy are the same as those made by the War Office and Admiralty.

2. There is still some divergence of opinion between the French figure estimates of the German air strength and those of the Air Ministry, but the difference is more apparent than real.

The AM steadily refuse to consider for purposes of calculating first line strength more than 9 aircraft per squadron, though admit the existence of an

---

[1] Pierre Cot, 1895–   . Elected to the Chamber of Deputies, 1919. Under-Secretary for Foreign Affairs, 1932. Air Minister in successive Governments, 1933–7. A pilot himself, he headed several flights to Russia. Reorganized French civil aviation under a single company, Air France. Urged Daladier to take emergency powers to deal with the rioters in Paris, 1934. In political eclipse after January 1938. Cot had visited Chartwell on 3 May 1937, and on his return to Paris had sent Churchill a nineteen-page memorandum on German air strength.

[2] AM = the Air Ministry.

[3] The British Air Attaché in Paris in 1936 was Douglas Colyer, subsequently Assistant Chief of the Air Staff, Policy (1943–4) and Head of the Royal Air Force Delegation in the United States (1945–6). In 1947 he returned to Paris as Civil Air Attaché at the British Embassy.

additional 3, complete with pilots. They agree, however to the total number of aircraft with each squadron and in immediate reserve, ie 9 + 3 + 3, though the last 3 have no pilot.

Referring to Page 2, the AM would count 7 less squadrons of fighters than do the French in the Aviation Terrestre. See French Note 2.

3. By *October 1937* the German air strength will be:

	No of squadrons
Aviation terrestre	170–190
Aviation maritime	15
Lufthansa squadrons	6
School squadrons	23

According as to whether you count 9 or 12 with the squadron and whether you count in the school squadrons, a different 'first line' can be arrived at.

Page 8, 4th Para: It is a great pity that the French do not also compare the output strength, both actual and potential of the French and German aircraft industries. The French are worse than ourselves in appreciating the meaning of the 'Fourth Arm of Defence' in modern war, but in this particular instance they may well be unwilling to disclose their own desperate position in this respect, which we can only hope is temporary. It is due to the socialist legislation recently passed nationalising the aircraft industry, imposing the 40-hour week, etc. At the moment the result is chaos.

4. Attention is drawn to the first paragraph on the top of Page 9, claiming that the unification of command of the anti-aircraft artillery and Air Force in Germany has been inspired by French proposals to that end, which the French themselves have not yet been able to put into effect. Evidently, however, the French also intend to move in that direction.

Winston S. Churchill to Field-Marshal Sir Cyril Deverell
(*Churchill papers: 2/302*)

2 June 1937

I am very much obliged to you for sending me the paper on the process of Cavalry Mechanization. As you know I have for a very long time urged this course and in 1927 pressed Sir Laming Worthington-Evans[1] very strongly

---

[1] Laming Evans, 1868–1931. Admitted solicitor, 1890; retired, 1910. Conservative MP for Colchester, 1910–18. 1918–29, and for Westminster St Georges, 1929–31. Inspector of Administrative Services, War Office, 1914–15. Controller, Foreign Trade Department, Foreign Office, 1916. Assumed the prefix surname of Worthington, 1916, and known as 'Worthy'. Created Baronet, 1916. Parliamentary Secretary, Ministry of Munitions, 1916–18. Minister of Blockade, 1918. Minister of Pensions, 1919–20. Minister without Portfolio, 1920–1. Secretary of State for War, 1921–2 and 1924–9. Elected to the Other Club in 1920.

to abolish the horses altogether, and I offered to supply all the money from the Exchequer for a complete mechanization. I have no doubt the general process of training which you are carrying out is the best that can be devised. It is very disheartening for regiments like my old regiment, the 4th Hussars, to be for a whole year without horses or mechanized vehicles except those for training.

I am not of course apprised of all the later developments in tanks. I have no doubt that the Cavalry light tank regiments will be incomparably stronger than the ordinary horse regiment for every purpose, offensive and defensive, except in very exceptional country. On the other hand I wonder whether all small tanks will not be powerless against a properly dug ditch. It seems very alarming that no medium tank is now in production. I have heard that the design has not even yet been approved. The original tank was devised for the purpose of crossing trenches, and these are certain to be encountered at an early stage in a European war.

I hope you will allow me to keep the paper for the present, and perhaps you will allow me to write to you again later.

Winston S. Churchill to Lieutenant-Colonel John Sandeman Allen
(Churchill papers: 2/302)

2 June 1937

I wonder if in the first instance Colonel Hill would be willing to talk to my friend Professor Lindemann. He has a vast knowledge and experience. I am rather hard pressed myself at the present time, but should be glad later on to meet Colonel Hill.

Winston S. Churchill to Nathan Laski
(Churchill papers: 2/296)

3 June 1937

Thank you so much for your very kind letter.[1]

I am not anxious to join the Government unless there is some real task they want me to do. They are very pleased with themselves at present.

[1] Of 2 June 1937 (see page 691).

Winston S. Churchill to Marjorie Maxse

(*Churchill papers: 2/319*)

3 June 1937

I am very much obliged to you for the several invitations you have sent me to speak in the country at Bye-Elections.[1] I regret I am not able to accept any of these up to the present. I think it would be a serious matter for me to start going to Bye-Elections, except perhaps in some cases where Mr Lloyd George goes. If I began I should find myself pressed to go every time. I have a great deal of work to do in Parliament and elsewhere.

Winston S. Churchill to Sir Samuel Hoare

(*Churchill papers: 4/143*)

4 June 1937   Chartwell

If the view about battleship armament set forth in this paper is accepted for the first five as is perhaps now inevitable, it would seem most necessary without prejudice to any future decision to have the designs for the larger guns and turrets completed without delay. It would also seem a wise precaution to have the tools and appliances necessary to adapt the gun plants etc to the larger calibre actually made, even at a considerable expense. There would perhaps be no objection to foreign countries knowing later on that we were in full readiness to take an upward step. Indeed this might make them more ready to adhere to the existing limits.

I am glad to find that the views I expressed about the triple turrets are not unsound, and especially that those already mounted in HM ships are satisfactory.

I do not know whether a sixteen inch gun can be fired as quickly as a

---

[1] Between June and December 1937, Churchill declined more than twenty invitations to speak in public. Among those which he refused were the Cambridge Conservative Association, the Anglo-Hungarian Society, the National Safety First Association, the Royal Photographic Society and the Empire Parliamentary Association. As Violet Pearman wrote to Randolph Churchill on 22 September 1937, about his father: 'He is very averse from making any engagements' (*Churchill papers: 2/298*). To Fenner Brockway, who had asked him to speak to the Independent Labour Party Summer School he replied, on 2 June 1937, that he was 'much complimented' by the invitation, but that he would be abroad.

fourteen-inch. If so, the advantage of the larger gun is not expressed only in the weight of the shell, but in its superior damaging capacity; for surely the explosive content increases rapidly in relation to the steel envelope. Moreover does not the smashing power increase very rapidly with the weight of the projectile at any given velocity.

The Dido class seems now to be entirely justified on the two main grounds, first of releasing larger cruisers for the trade routes, and second its anti-air value.

I notice that the case for the larger six-inch gun cruisers is not considered so complete as that for the Didos. Do I understand that we are still bound by some obligation to the United States not to build any more eight-inch gun cruisers. If so, this would appear a most crippling restriction and every effort should be made to persuade the American Admiralty to release us in a friendly way.

The fact stares us in the face that when the five (not seven) modern eight-inch gun cruisers are complete, any one of these five spread on the trade routes would be more than a match for any British cruisers in a single ship action. It would be necessary to detach the battle-cruisers from the main fleets in order to have killers in every theatre. Even so there would not be enough, and we know from past experience what a Commander-in-Chief would say if asked to give up his battle cruisers. I am quite sure strategy will be hampered unless we can match every modern cruiser possessed by Germany with at least its equal. They only had five cruisers out at the beginning of the war. These did enormous damage to trade. Everyone of them sunk a warship besides before being destroyed herself; and it took five months to clear the outer seas.

I should like to express my thanks for the attention which has been given to the entirely friendly comments I have ventured to make.

Violet Pearman to Rosalind Culhane[1]

(Churchill papers: 2/303)

8 June 1937
Very confidential

Dear Private Secretary,

You will remember a little while ago I spoke to you about a report which Mr Chamberlain had received from Mr Churchill personally, I think after a

---

[1] Neville Chamberlain's Personal Private Secretary.

talk he had had with him either at the Treasury or at the House, and which was highly confidential. This has not been returned to Mr Churchill, and as it is probably among Mr Chamberlain's personal belongings which are now no doubt in course of removal to No 10, Mr Churchill would be glad if it could be found and returned to him here. It was a report of a visit to Germany by two of our English Air Force officers, and was written in an amusing un-official form, but contained quite a number of important points of interest. Mr Churchill has not got another copy, and as he would like to see it again, he wonders whether you can let him have it as soon as possible.

The Duke of Windsor to Winston S. Churchill
(*Churchill papers: 2/300*)

9 June 1937   Schloss Wasserleonburg,
Austria

Dear Winston,

Thank you and Mrs Churchill very much indeed, for the lovely piece of plate you have been kind enough to send for a wedding present. The Duchess joins me in an assurance of deep appreciation of your thought of us.

This is a charming place, and we find it very peaceful after all we have been through during the past few months. If you happen to be in this vicinity later on in the Summer, we should be delighted if you were to propose yourself to stop here. I am afraid there are no gambling facilities in the neighbour-hood, but we can guarantee you really lovely subjects for your brush and canvas.

Besides, I am anxious for the opportunity of discussing many things with you. Randolph was most helpful to us at Candé, and we both thought that his article, intended for the Daily Mail but eventually published in the Express, was charming.[1]

With our renewed thanks to you both for your kind thought of us,

Yours sincerely,
Edward

---

[1] Randolph Churchill had been one of seven English guests at the Duke of Windsor's marriage to Mrs Simpson at the Château de Candé, near Tours, on 3 June 1937. The other guests were Lady Selby, Lady Alexandra Metcalfe, Major Edward Dudley Metcalfe, Sir Walter Monckton, George E. Allen (the Duke's solicitor), and Hugh Lloyd Thomas (the Duke's Assistant Private Secretary). On the evening after the wedding the Duke and his wife left France for Count Munster's castle, Schloss Wasserleonburg, in Austria.

Winston S. Churchill to Pierre Cot

(*Churchill papers: 2/307*)

9 June 1937

I am extremely obliged to you for your courtesy in sending me the deeply interesting confidential information for which I asked when you so kindly visited me at Chartwell. I do not feel at all happy about the relative Anglo-French air strength compared to Germany in 1938. Not only do these misgivings apply to the actual formations, but even more to what we call 'the war potential of production'. I am told the German peace time monthly output is in the neighbourhood of 400.

Once more thanking you, believe me.

Winston S. Churchill to George Harrap

(*Churchill papers: 8/547*)

11 June 1937

I grieve to reach the conclusion that it is impossible for me to produce the fourth and final volume of Marlborough ready for press by the end of August. Such an effort, even if physically possible, would not be worthy of the work as a whole. On the other hand, apart from events over which I have no control, I have every hope and expectation of letting you have the final copy by the end of the year. This will enable you to publish in the Spring or Autumn as you think best.

I should mention that it will be necessary for me to publish in the Autumn, through Thornton Butterworth, a collection of articles about Great Contemporaries, which have been written by me for various magazines during the last few years. These will in no way interfere with Marlborough, as the work is already done except for proof reading and a few adjustments.

W. H. Bernau[1] to Winston S. Churchill

(*Churchill papers: 2/297*)

12 June 1937

I have made a point of not discussing politics with you, but I must say I was very much disappointed when you were not made Minister for Co-

---

[1] William Henry Bernau, 1870–1937. Started work at Cox & Co, bankers, 1889; in charge of the Insurance Department, 1910–35; retired 1935. Churchill's insurance broker.

ordination of Defence, when that post was created, as it is one for which I consider you are better adapted & prepared than any other man. I do hope if there is any further shopping of offices that you will be given that job.[1]

Winston S. Churchill to Lord Salisbury

(*Churchill papers: 2/303*)

14 June 1937

I send a paper, not official, written for me by a Staff Officer of the highest attainments employed in one of the largest and most important Commands. It was written, as you see, last year. I sent it to Inskip, and also Neville Chamberlain early this year. Inskip made the observation that things had improved since. No doubt this is true to a small extent. I therefore two months ago asked the officer to write another impression bringing his view up to date. I will send you this from Chartwell tomorrow as I have not got it in London. Kindly let me have the papers back when you have done with them and please do not show them to anyone else whose knowledge of the Air Force would enable him to locate the individual.

Chaim Weizmann to Winston S. Churchill

(*Churchill papers: 2/315*)

14 June 1937

My dear Mr Churchill,

I have not yet had time to write to you since I had the pleasure of seeing you at Sir Archibald's house last Tuesday evening,[2] but I am anxious to let you know that I have followed your advice, and have made it clear, both to

---

[1] It was at about this time that Churchill invited Cecil Roberts, who, as a journalist, had supported him at Leicester during the 1923 General Election, to visit him at Chartwell. Roberts later recalled: 'He was full of foreboding. Chamberlain, like Baldwin, had by-passed him and the House was hostile. He gave me a cold douche when I told him about my overture to Hore-Belisha. "There's no plan of any kind for anything. It is no good. They walk in a fog. Everything is very black, very black," he said, looking at his black swans on the lake. I wondered if they had given him the adjective. Here was the best man in Britain excluded from office.' On 11 June 1937 at a dinner given by the Australia Club, Churchill had appealed for a more vigorous defence and foreign policy, telling his listeners: 'Lots of people fight for hearth and home. Even sheep bleat at the approach of the wolf.'

[2] Tuesday, 8 June 1937. Sir Archibald Sinclair's London house was at 1 Thorney Court, Kensington.

members of the Commission and to Mr Ormsby-Gore (whom I saw yesterday), that they should not assume that I am in any way committed to the
acceptance of any project of partition which the Government may propose.
I think that both the Commission and Mr Ormsby-Gore now understand
this quite clearly.

The Secretary of State told me something, when I saw him, of your own
conversation with him, and from what he told me I gathered that you have
pressed very strongly the idea that the Southern part of Palestine should not
be incorporated into the Arab State—if and when such a State comes to be
set up. This is a point which worries us a great deal, for obvious reasons, and
I would like to express to you my heartiest thanks, both for the advice you
gave me last Tuesday, and for all you have done with Mr Ormsby-Gore to
endeavour to make the project (if such a project comes off) as acceptable as
possible in the circumstances.[1]

I had a long conversation with Mr Ormsby-Gore, the main points of which
I intend to embody in a letter to him, of which I should like, if I may, to
send you a copy in due course.

With kind regards, and renewed and most grateful thanks for all your
help, I am

Very sincerely yours,
Ch. Weizmann

Eugen Spier: recollections [2]
(*'Focus'*, pages *104–5*)

[14 June 1937]

Titulescu[3] gave a brief survey of the situation in south-eastern Europe.
Nazi Germany, he said, was definitely bent on extending its influence over

---

[1] Weizmann saw Churchill again at Morpeth Mansions on the evening of 16 July 1937.

[2] Titulescu had been invited to London at the suggestion of Ivy, Lady Chamberlain who
feared 'that Roumania would go Nazi and be lost to the democracies'. He was the guest of
honour at a luncheon party given by Churchill and a group of likeminded friends, known
as the 'Focus', on 14 June 1937. 'Churchill presided as usual,' wrote Eugen Spier, 'and introduced our guest to the small but very representative gathering, paying tribute to the courage
and energy with which Titulescu had faced difficult and trying years and maintained his
policy of co-operation with the Western democracies (Eugen Spier, *Focus*, London 1963, pages
51 and 104). Titulescu had lunched at Chartwell on 8 June 1937.

[3] Nicolae Titulescu, 1883–1941. Professor of Law at Bucharest University before the First
World War. Entered the Rumanian Parliament, 1913. Minister of Finance, 1916. Fled to
London, 1917. Minister of Finance for the second time, 1919; one of the founders of the
'Little Entente' between Rumania, Yugoslavia and Czechoslovakia. Ambassador to London,
1921. Foreign Minister of Rumania, July 1927 to August 1928; October 1932 to October
1934; and October 1934 to May 1936. Finance Minister for the third time, 1932. A leading
anti-Nazi, he was dismissed from the Rumanian Cabinet in 1936.

the whole Danube basin, and was doing so by the usual Nazi methods. Their present tactics consisted of organising an artificial demand by the indigenous population for political co-ordination with Germany. The end would be military occupation and Nazi government. The plans had been prepared to the last detail. There was no organised opposition, no counter-action by the West, and their success seemed assured. The dream of an eastern Locarno had been finally shattered when the western Locarno was broken a year before. The alliance of France with the Little Entente was now no longer of any practical value. Rumania could not count on any assistance from France alone.

But, although the West had failed, and the Nazis were representing both the Western democracies and democracy itself as spent forces, Titulescu said that he did not believe it. It was still in the power of the Western allies to upset all the Nazi calculations. Besides there were at that very moment millions of Germans who would collaborate in breaking Hitler's power. The German army was not yet ready to fight the wars which Hitler has planned, and in south-eastern Europe there were still other millions of people who would gladly follow if only the West were to give a lead. But without aid they could not alone oppose the Nazis and their agents who at once flattered, bribed and terrified. Emissaries from Hitler had approached him with the most tempting offers to secure his co-operation, and simultaneously he was threatened by the murder gangs operating outside the frontiers of the Reich. He further stated that he had very reliable information that Hitler had already given instructions to the German General Staff to draft plans for the invasion of Austria and Czechoslovakia in 1938. He wished our organisation every success, for through it and others like it the sad face of the earth could be changed.

Nicolae Titulescu to Winston S. Churchill

(*Churchill papers: 1/299*)

15 June 1937
Ritz Hotel,
London, W.1.

Dear Mr Churchill,

I feel I must just thank you once again for all your kindness during my visit to London. I carry away with me the happiest recollection of the delightful hospitality shown to me by your wife and yourself at your country home. I very much appreciate your thoughtfulness in arranging for me to meet so many of your friends at luncheon on Monday and it was a most enjoyable affair for me.

I leave London early to-morrow en route for Prague, so this is just a hurried note of thanks.—With kindest regards and every good wish,

Believe me,
Yours very sincerely,
N. Titulescu

Winston S. Churchill: notes[1]

(Eugen Spier, 'Focus', pages 122–3)

[15 June 1937]

The Nazi and Communist creeds seek to divide the world between them by hurling the democratic nations at one another in ferocious conflict. At home a secret police continually spies on and threatens the safety and life of every citizen, under its power to arrest anybody where, for merely venturing to criticise the government, he will be worked and tortured to death. Rather than submit to such oppression there is no length to which the people of Britain will not go. Communism and Nazism both worship 'One Man Power,' the power which the parliamentary system in Britain and the constitution of the United States equally reject as a thing odious, pernicious and degrading to man. It is the first duty of the English-speaking democracies to guard against it. . . .

In neither the Nazi nor the Communist state is there any sense of abstract justice. Justice is entirely in the service of the one-party state. Men can be tried by courts composed of their political opponents for crimes never yet placed upon the pages of the statute book. Such arbitrary power can be kept in being only if backed by a great war-machine, the existence of which forces the rest of the world to produce arms on as large a scale in order to resist the threat of destruction. There is nothing new in this 'One Man Power' worship; it can be seen in the history of every despot. The great theories of government which the British race devised and which the English-speaking peoples have adopted and made their systems are the foundation upon which civilisation rests and without which it will fall. We believe it is the duty of the state to guard the rights of the individual. We are opponents of totalitarian tyranny in all its forms. We believe in tolerance.

---

[1] Eugen Spier wrote, of September 1937: 'Some time previously Churchill had promised the Focus to write an essay on the meaning and danger of Nazism and Communism to the civilised world. It was to be made available to the Focus's writers and speakers; actually they made good use of it.' The notes are published here as they were reprinted by Spier in his book, *Focus*, in extract only.

We should value these treasures—glories I call them—as we do our lives; and there should be no sacrifice we would not make, and no length to which we would not go conformably with honour and justice so as to hand them over unmutilated and unbesmirched to our children. In Britain the good cause will never lack hearts as resolute, swords as sharp, as have those who champion evil. But we must arm ourselves so that the good cause may not find itself at a hopeless disadvantage against the aggressor.

Winston S. Churchill to Newman Flower

(Churchill papers: 8/550)

16 June 1937

. . . I believe it will be possible for us to complete our business by December 31, 1939. I write this in view of what you said that once you were able to go ahead upon the serials I could have the best part of a year for the improvements and corrections, desirable for volume form. Many thanks for having arranged this easement. I have every hope of finishing Marlborough in the Autumn of this year; but it will not be published till the Spring, and thereafter I shall press on with the English Speaking Peoples.

Winston S. Churchill to F. W. Deakin

(Churchill papers: 8/547)

17 June 1937

I have sent between 20,000 and 25,000 words to Harraps covering Sacheverell, Shrewsbury, Hill etc. I hope this will be in proof next week. They will require a lot of checking and correction. Will you do your best to get the interleaving, with any material of the first half dozen printed chapters, completed as soon as possible, as it would be a pity to let this part fade from one's mind, and have to work it all up again. Remember you have my own personal proof of this part of the text.

PS. What a beautiful handwriting your wife[1] has. Please express to her my thanks for the trouble she took.

[1] Margaret Ogilvy Bell (daughter of Sir Nicholas Dodd Beatson Bell, KCSI, KCIE, former Governor of Assam). They were married in 1935, and had two sons, Michael and Nicholas. Their marriage was dissolved in 1940. In 1943 Deakin married Livia Stela, daughter of Liviu Nasta, of Bucharest.

Winston S. Churchill to Brigadier Pakenham-Walsh

(*Churchill papers: 8/547*)

18 June 1937

In your various campaign notes there are about a dozen sketches illustrating operations. Have you duplicates of these? If not I will send them to you and put you in touch with our former draughtsman. I am not publishing till the Spring, so that we shall have plenty of time to finish in style. Have you any plans and maps for Malplaquet, both strategic and tactical. I should be very much obliged if you could rough me out some. I am leaving Malplaquet behind for the present and pushing forward with the politics which are the staple of this volume.

Shiela Grant Duff[1] to Winston S. Churchill

(*Churchill papers: 2/307*)

19 June 1937   Prague
Confidential

Dear Mr Winston Churchill,

I believe I am a cousin of Mrs Winston Churchill so I hope you will forgive the liberty which it is to write to you when I do not know you, but the matter is itself so important that I think it should justify itself.

It is about the relations between Germany and Czechoslovakia. The tension has never been so great as it is at the present moment and this is saying much when it is remembered that in March and in November, War councils were held in Berlin as to whether Germany should or should not attack Czechoslovakia. The reason for the present tension is that the internal crises in France and Russia have practically isolated this country. The only protec-

---

[1] Shiela Grant Duff, 1913–   . A granddaughter of Lady Avebury and cousin of Clementine Churchill. Her father, Lieutenant-Colonel Adrian Grant Duff, was killed in action on the western front on 14 September 1914. An undergraduate at Oxford, 1931–4, when she visited Germany (1932) and Sub-Carpathian Ruthenia (Eastern Czechoslovakia, 1933). Graduated, 1934. Worked in Paris for the *Chicago Daily News*, 1934. Covered the Saar Plebiscite for the *Observer*, 1935. Secretary to Hugh Dalton, 1935, and to Jawaharlal Nehru. Lived in Prague, 1936–7, as correspondent of the *Observer*. Resigned, June 1937; worked subsequently for the *Manchester Guardian* and *Spectator*, 1937–8. In Prague at the time of the Anschluss (March 1938). Published *Europe and the Czechs* (a Penguin special), 1938. Travelled in Germany and the Balkans, 1938. Helped Vernon Bartlett and the Duchess of Atholl in their by-elections, 1938. Czechoslovak editor at the BBC Overseas Service, 1940–2; worked on 'London Calling Europe', 1943–4. Published the *Czech Protectorate*, 1941; *The Parting of Ways: A Personal Account of the Thirties*, 1982.

tion left is the moral support of England. The two incidents, of Weigl[1] and Stauber,[2] which have come up during the last three days are calculated to alienate the sympathy of England from Czechoslovakia and make her hesitate to interfere if Germany should begin the 'gegenmassnahmen'[3] which the German press have threatened.

Information has reached this country that our foreign office is hesitating. I am writing to you to ask you to do everything in your power to make our attitude firm and unfaltering. The crisis has never been so great and I am convinced that only a stand on our part can overcome it. Czechoslovakia is, for the moment, almost entirely dependent on us. . . .

Winston S. Churchill to Sir Samuel Hoare

(*Churchill papers: 2/296*)

21 June 1937
Private and Personal

My dear Sam,

Perhaps you may remember that about six weeks ago I referred in a speech to the new dangers arising from the external organisation of foreign communities in England. Of course there are always the Communists and they are pretty well looked after by the police. But now we have over 18,000 German and 20,000 Italian males residing here, and all woven together in the Nazi and Fascist organisations. The Germans have appointed an official called Bohle[4] as Minister for Germans resident abroad. He certainly gives many

---

[1] Bruno Weigl was a German who had been arrested in Prague in November 1936, on a charge of pro-Nazi activities. He had been released in May 1937, whereupon he claimed that he had been ill-treated in prison. On the insistence of the German Government, the Czech Government was forced to agree to the case being re-investigated, although it was convinced that Weigel's charge was totally without foundation. The German Government also accused the Czech Government of providing sites inside Czechoslovakia for Soviet aerodromes.

[2] A Henleinist who alleged ill-treatment by the Czechs. Such incidents were to become even more frequent during the municipal elections, begun on 22 May 1938. On 6 June 1938 two 'British observers' arrived in Prague to report to the British Government on all such incidents which might occur between Czechs and Germans. On 12 June 1938 the Henleinist won 90.9 per cent of the votes cast in German-speaking districts, but in the industrial areas up to 30% of the German-speaking votes was cast against them.

[3] Counter measures.

[4] Ernst Wilhelm Bohle, 1902– . Born in Bradford, of naturalized British parents. Went to South Africa with his parents at the age of twelve. Educated in Capetown. In 1920 he went to Germany, where he studied political economy and commerce at Cologne and Berlin universities. In 1931 he joined the Nazi Party, and began at once to organize Germans living

instructions in respect of all Germans dwelling in England. They are told to keep in touch with particular centres at frequent intervals. Here they learn what they are to observe and report, and also know about what language they are to hold. Nothing like this has ever occurred before. Foreigners living in England have lived here as individuals, and not as part of an organised national and political unit. You will see in a moment the dangers that might arise if we had a period of strained relations, and sabotage became important. There are many other aspects which will, I am sure, appeal to you.

I propose to ask you some Questions about this position on lines which will be apparent from this letter. Before doing so I should like to give you the fullest possible notice, and to learn how you feel about it. In my opinion the organisation of foreigners into bodies of this kind ought not to be permitted, and unless redress were given by the Governments in question, special measures should be taken against members of the organisation in the sense of inviting them either to report at much more frequent intervals, or to return to their native land. Generally speaking a state of much more active vigilance would seem to be required than in pre-war days.

Perhaps you will let me hear from you at your convenience.[1]

Yours very sincerely,
Winston S. Churchill

Winston S. Churchill to Adam Marshall Diston
(*Churchill papers: 8/548*)

21 June 1937

Could you find me—perhaps through your office—the speech delivered by Lord Curzon at the end of his career at a dinner in London, in which

---

outside Germany into a 'German Society'. From May 1933, Gauleiter, and from October 1933 Head of the Organization of Germans Resident Abroad, German Foreign Ministry, under the 'personal command' of Hitler. Repudiated his British nationality, and adopted German nationality, by the legal means of a public declaration, August 1937. Believed by British intelligence to be 'very near the throne', and possibly to 'entertain ideas of succeeding Hitler', he was also described as having 'a pleasant personality'. Living in Berlin during the Second World War.

[1] On 25 June 1937 Sir Samuel Hoare wrote to Anthony Eden from the Home Office, enclosing a copy of Churchill's letter. In his covering letter, Hoare asked Eden whether, 'in the event of it being decided to embark on an active policy, the Foreign Office would be able to give adequate support in the diplomatic sphere so as to ensure that it would not be necessary for us to withdraw from our position'. Hoare added: 'I feel somewhat doubtful as to the wisdom of pressing the issue at the present moment' (*Foreign Office papers: 371/20739*).

he spoke of having been haunted all his life by the rhyme about being 'a most superior person', suggesting that this had blighted his career.[1]

Secondly could you find me the speech delivered by Lord Birkenhead at the end of the 1929 election at Portsmouth, (very late in the polling) when he fell upon the Communists. 'You run a Government! You couldn't run a whelk stall! We will slit your soft throats' etc. There is extant, I know, some official version given of this fine specimen of his rhetoric.

Violet Pearman to Adam Marshall Diston

(*Churchill papers: 8/555*)

23 June 1937

Herewith the article on Mr Neville Chamberlain for you to see, and to confirm that I asked you on behalf of Mr Churchill to supply him with a further 400 or 500 words mentioned in the cable below: 'Article received, thanks. Publication late August. Can you send insert three or four hundred words description aloof personality and anecdotes of man. If ship mail impracticable by July tenth, please cable press rate, Chenery.'

Mr Churchill has replied that he will mail by the 10th, and so would like your addition as soon as you can possibly manage it.[2]

Colonel Hill to Professor Lindemann

(*Cherwell papers*)

24 June 1937

ANTI-AIRCRAFT DEFENCE[3]

Now that I have retired from the service, I am endeavouring to widen

---

[1] While Curzon was an undergraduate at Oxford, from 1878 to 1882, the following rhyme was in circulation:

> 'My name is George Nathaniel Curzon,
> I am a most superior person,
> My cheek is pink, my hair is sleek,
> I dine at Blenheim once a week.'

[2] Entitled 'England's "No" Man', Churchill's article on Neville Chamberlain was published in Collier's on 16 October 1937 (part of which is printed on pages 685–8 of this volume).

[3] On 21 June 1937 Colonel Hill wrote to Professor Lindemann: 'I was very glad to have the opportunity of discussing the anti-aircraft artillery part of Air Defence with you. I enclose a further paper which I should be glad to have back fairly soon (to Chislehurst address). At

these efforts and am through Sandeman Allen bringing to the notice of Mr Winston Churchill the present state of affairs showing where they fail and how they can be improved.

There has been no perceptible improvement in AA shooting as judged from the effect on the target in the past 7 years with the present service equipment. The rate of fire is slow, the accuracy is poor. . . .

Mr Churchill is desirous that before taking any action, I should put before you my various proposals. I can claim to have some practical knowledge of certain branches of the Air Defence problem as for 2 years I was an Air Defence Commander in France, 4 years Commandant of the School of Air Defence, 4 years in command of a London Territorial Air Defence Brigade; prior to that I have held a number of technical appointments.

Winston S. Churchill to Captain McEwen[1]

(*Churchill papers: 2/296*)

25 June 1937

Very many thanks for your letter. Things are so very slack just now at Westminster, and I personally am so much occupied with my literary toils that I should much prefer to put this off till the autumn session.[2]

Don't you think this would be better?

PS. Besides things are moving along lines of agreement; tho we are getting a little too anti-Franco!

---

present I have with me a complete fire control instrument and a course and speed finding instrument which I am certain will produce double the present service effect in the same time. . . . if Mr Winston Churchill decides to interest himself in this question a meeting might be arranged in, say, October, when the results of the AA shooting might be available' (*Cherwell papers*).

[1] John Helias Finnie McEwen, 1894–1962. Educated at Eton and Trinity College, Cambridge. On active service, 1914–18 (Captain, 1915; prisoner of war). Diplomatic Service, 1920–8. Conservative MP for Berwick and Haddington, 1931–45. Assistant Government Whip, 1938–9. Member of the Council of Aliens (Foreign Office), 1939–40. Parliamentary Under-Secretary of State for Scotland, 1939–40. A Lord Commissioner of the Treasury, 1942–4. Created Baronet, 1953.

[2] Captain McEwen had asked Churchill if he would address the Foreign Affairs Committee of the House of Commons on July 8.

Kathleen Hill[1] to Violet Pearman

(*Churchill papers: 1/299*)

27 June 1937   Morden,
                                                      Surrey

Dear Mrs Pearman,

Thank you very much for your letter of the 24th.

I am very pleased indeed that Mr and Mrs Churchill have chosen me for the post of resident Secretary, and I should like to assure them that I will do my utmost to render them loyal and efficient service.

I propose to arrive at Oxted Station on Tuesday 6th July, by the train that reaches there at 9.58 am from East Croydon. If you would be kind enough to arrange for a car to be sent to the station, I should be very grateful.[2]

Yours sincerely,
R. E. K. Hill

Wing-Commander Anderson to Winston S. Churchill

(*Churchill papers: 2/303*)

29 June 1937

The attached statement is correct,[3] and a point is made that it will not be for some months that all the new Squadrons will be fully equipped with

---

[1] Rose Ethel Kathleen Hill, 1900–   . Chief Clerk, Automobile Association and Motor Union Insurance Company, Portsmouth, 1917–24, and a member of the Portsmouth Philharmonic Society (first violins), 1918–24. District Commissioner of Girl Guides, Bengal-Nagpur Railway, 1928–30. Secretary to the Chief Commissioner of Girl Guides for All-India, 1930–2. Broadcast as a solo violinist, Calcutta, Bombay and Delhi, 1935–6. Returned to England, 1937. Churchill's first Residential Secretary, July 1937; lived at Chartwell from July 1937 to September 1939. Churchill's Personal Private Secretary from 1939 to 1946. MBE, 1941. Curator of Chequers, 1946–69.

[2] On 29 June 1937 Violet Pearman sent this letter to Clementine Churchill with the covering note: 'Mrs Hill's letter herewith for you to see. Mr Churchill thought it very nice. She comes in on the 6th, as the 7th would be rather a muddling rushing day for a beginner, and the 6th will allow her a day to find her way round and get used a little to things.'

[3] A report in *The Times* of 29 June 1937, in which it was stated that 'With the formation yesterday if Nos 53 and 59 (Army Cooperation) Squadrons at Farnborough and Old Sarum, the total number of new squadrons formed since the expansion scheme was started two years ago is brought up to 71. This is for home defence, and excluded one squadron formed in December last for service in Kenya.' The article continued: 'Before the expansion scheme there were 53 squadrons at home, so that the present total is 124. One of them, No 33 (Bomber) Squadron, is temporarily detached from the Bomber Squadron for service at Ismailia. It will not be for some months that all the new squadrons will be fully equipped with aircraft and pilots; certain of them are as yet on a one-flight basis. But all the squadrons required to complete the home defence programme are now in being. . . '.

aircraft and pilots. This statement may, of course, be interpreted in its widest sense.

At least 100 squadrons of 124 are equipped with obsolete aircraft, and some of the new squadrons being formed even on a one-flight basis are being equipped with training type aircraft only, ie TUTOR.

Lord Salisbury to Winston S. Churchill

(*Churchill papers: 2/303*)

29 June 1937

My dear Winston,

You sent me a week or so ago some papers on Re-armament, according to your kind promise. I read them, I need not say, with all the respect which they deserve, and I would have sent them back to you long ago but that I thought you indicated in your covering letter that you proposed to supplement them by some further papers which would bring what you contended for up to date. This in the midst of your multifarious obligations, even if I rightly understood you, you would naturally have forgotten. But that is the reason why I did not sooner send the papers back to you.

Of course things may be as bad as you make out (I don't doubt you have access to first-rate information), but it is curiously different from what I hear from Ministers when I talk to them privately. I don't mean to say that they are satisfied, but their attitude is quite different from the sort of acute apprehension which they had a year ago; and you will notice that in Inskip's speech reported this morning his line is optimistic. No doubt his optimism is exaggerated: I wish it were not. I think it a great mistake this Ministerial pose of self satisfaction; but apparently it cannot be avoided. All Ministers do it in all Governments. Nevertheless by making a certain discount one ought to arrive at something like the truth, and it does not seem to agree with the papers you sent me and which I return herewith. Thank you very much all the same for letting me see them. I need not say they deeply interest me.

Yours ever,
Salisbury

Winston S. Churchill to George Harrap

(*Churchill papers: 8/547*)

30 June 1937

I am very reluctant not to fall in with any wish of yours, but I really do not like the idea of making a harangue on the broadcast in order to sell my book. On the other hand I should be very glad, so far as I am concerned, to allow a record which was made of my speech on the Coronation, broadcast by Radio Luxembourg, to be repeated on this occasion, or if desired a shorter variant of it.

I am working very hard at Marlborough now, night and day in fact.

July 1937

Anthony Eden to Winston S. Churchill

(Churchill papers: 2/314)

2 July 1937   Foreign Office
Personal

Dear Winston,

Since I saw you yesterday I have received from the French Government a very definite intimation that they would be opposed to the granting of belligerent rights to the two parties in Spain at the present time. Whilst I have no objection to the line which you propose to take in your speech on Saturday, I feel sure you will wish to bear in mind what we know to be the French view on the subject.

Thank you so much for coming to see me before making your speech.[1]

Yours,
Anthony Eden

---

[1] Speaking at Wanstead on the evening of Saturday 3 July 1937, Churchill deferred to Eden's wishes, telling his constituency (as reported in *The Times* two days later): 'In spite of the mockery which has marked the work of the London Non-Intervention Committee, I am sure that the policy has been right and that the Foreign Secretary deserves full approval for it. For a whole year the Spanish conflict has raged and every kind of evil has taken place in Europe without our being drawn any nearer the vortex than when it began. During this last year we have grown in strength and reputation; we have more friends in the world; we are more closely united to our old friends; we have not abandoned the principle of the covenant of the League of Nations; we never have been on terms of greater good will and understanding with the United States. The vital thing now is not to change our policy, for if we march steadfastly along the road of peace and freedom we shall find ourselves attended by a very large and ever better armed company of nations, great and small.' The Spanish Civil War had been on Churchill's mind for some time. In May, when dining with Lady Colefax he had heard a first hand account from an American journalist, H. R. Knickerbocker. Henry Channon, who was present, wrote in his diary for 4 May 1937: 'Winston Churchill, gay and plump, gave us a dramatic 10-minutes account of the horrors that are taking place, and how all the original motives of the war have long been obscured in the general ghastliness and barbarity' (Robert Rhodes James, editor *Chips, The Diaries of Sir Henry Channon*, page 122).

Malcolm MacDonald to Winston S. Churchill

(*Churchill papers: 8/547*)

5 July 1937

Dear Winston Churchill,

Here is the 'Account of the Conduct of the Dowager Duchess of Marl-borough'. She was a great character—alike in youth, middle life and old age. There are few more glorious stories in our national history than that of the faithful and brilliant partnership between Sarah and John Churchill. This present of a first edition of the old lady's book is a small token of gratitude for the many hours of delight which I have passed reading your own superb rendering of the story.

Yours sincerely,
Malcolm MacDonald

Air Vice-Marshal Richard Peirse[1] to Winston S. Churchill

(*Churchill papers: 2/310*)

6 July 1937   Air Ministry

Dear Mr Churchill,

After yesterday's ADR meeting[2] you will remember that Lord Swinton asked me to arrange a visit for you to Biggin Hill. I have this morning been in

---

[1] Richard Edmund Charles Peirse, 1892–1970. A pilot in the Royal Naval Air Service, 1913–14, and one of Churchill's flying instructors at that time. On active service, 1914–18 (DSO, AFC). Deputy Director of Operations and Intelligence, Air Ministry, 1930–3. Air Officer Commanding British Forces, Palestine and Transjordan, 1933–6. Deputy Chief of the Air Staff, 1937–40. Knighted, 1940. Vice-Chief of the Air Staff, 1940. Air Officer Commanding-in-Chief, Bomber Command, 1940–2; India, 1942–3; Allied Air Commander-in-Chief, South-East Asia, 1943–4.

[2] On 5 July 1937 Churchill had been present at the 13th meeting of the Committee of Imperial Defence's Sub-Committee on Air Defence Research, held at 2 Whitehall Gardens, London SW1. The two Cabinet Ministers present were Lord Swinton (Chairman) and Sir Thomas Inskip. Among the others attending were Sir Warren Fisher, Vice-Admiral Sir Reginald Henderson, Sir Maurice Hankey, Sir Hugh Elles and Sir Henry Tizard. With reference to 'Radar', the Sub-Committee agreed: 'To take note that satisfactory progress was being made in the matter of inland location by RDF, and that it was hoped that the experimental inland location set would be in operation by October 1937.' It was also agreed: 'That the experiments now being conducted at Oxford on Infra-red radiation should continue in the hope that they will have an application to air defence other than the detection of aircraft from the air' (*Churchill papers: 25/13*). Churchill attended a further Air Defence Research meeting on 3 October 1937.

touch with Air Chief Marshal Sir Hugh Dowding's[1] headquarters (Head-quarters, Fighter Command, Stanmore, Middlesex) and I learn that certain interception exercises will take place this week on Thursday morning, Friday morning and Friday afternoon.

I would suggest that the simplest thing would be for you to communicate direct with Wing Commander Lock,[2] who commands Biggin Hill—telephone Ravensbourne 0194—and let him know what time and day is convenient. If neither of these days is suitable it will be quite a simple matter for Lock to arrange a demonstration for you on some other occasion, if you will suggest a date and time.

Yours sincerely,
R. E. C. Peirse

Clifford Norton to Violet Pearman

(*Churchill papers: 8/548*)

7 July 1937   Foreign Office
Private

Dear Mrs Pearman,

Thank you for your letter of July 2nd enclosing the proofs of an article, which I return herewith.

I am afraid that Sir Robert Vansittart is taking a fortnight's leave and for the time-being cannot be got at. If, however, the views of myself and an Under Secretary whom I consulted in confidence are of any interest they are, with all deference, that it is hardly to be thought that this article would be at all palatable to the powers that be in Germany. In the present rather delicate state of our relations with that country, when one does not know which way

---

[1] Hugh Caswall Tremenheere Dowding, 1882–1970. Educated at Winchester. Joined the Royal Artillery, 1900; Royal Flying Corps, 1914. On active service, 1914–19 (despatches). Director of Training , Air Ministry, 1926–9. Commanding the Fighting Area, Air Defence of Great Britain, 1929–30. Air Member for Research and Development, 1930–6. Knighted, 1933. Air Officer Commanding-in-Chief, Fighter Command, 1936–40. Mission to the USA for the Ministry of Aircraft Production, 1940–4. Created Baron, 1943.

[2] Henry George Watts Lock, 1893– . Educated at Clapham College. Wireless Operator, 1913–14. Enlisted as an Airman, 2nd Class, Royal Flying Corps, 1915; 2nd Lieutenant, 1917. Awarded the Italian Bronze Medal for Valour while on active service in Italy, 1917. Served with 13 (Training) Squadron, 1917–18. Awarded the Distinguished Flying Cross while on active service in Mesopotamia, 1921. Served with 84 (Bomber) Squadron, 1928, and with 12 (Bomber) Squadron, 1930. Officer Commanding RAF Biggin Hill, 1937. On active service, 1939–45 (including Burma). Retired with the rank of Group Captain, 1945.

the cat will jump, it might therefore be questioned whether republication just now was advisable.[1]

Violet Pearman to Clifford Norton

(*Churchill papers: 8/548*)

8 July 1937
Confidential

Dear Mr Norton,

Mr Churchill thanks you very much indeed for your letter returning the proof on 'Hitler' and for your remarks upon it. He would now like to know whether the excisions proposed, as marked by him on the enclosed article in red ink, take the sting out of the article. The rest is no more than he is accustomed to say on public platforms.

Mr Churchill wishes me to add that of course the fact that he has consulted Sir Robert Vansittart privately could never be mentioned, or that he has been in communication with anyone at the Foreign Office. The responsibility is solely Mr Churchill's own.

Winston S. Churchill to J. L. Garvin

(*Churchill papers: 8/548*)

8 July 1937

I am publishing in September a book on Great Contemporaries. There are more than twenty of these essays, but one of the chief is on Joe. I should be very much obliged if you could find time to read this over for me and let me know what you think of it. Of course I was, and in my heart still am, an opponent, but I have tried to do full justice to this remarkable electric figure whom we both knew and liked so well.[2]

---

[1] When Churchill's original article was published in the *Strand* magazine in November 1935, there had been considerable German protests (see *The Wilderness Years* companion volume of documents of this biography, pages 1304 and 1308). Even the slightly abridged article led to renewed German protests (see pages 748 and 772 of this volume).

[2] During the course of his essay on Joseph Chamberlain, Churchill wrote: 'The career of this eminent man and strong actuator of world movements is divided between the period when he was making his way towards the world scene and the period when he acted upon it. In the first he was a ruthless Radical and, if you challenged him, a Republican; in the second he was a Jingo Tory and Empire Builder. All followed naturally and sincerely from the particular pressures and environment affecting an exceptional being at one stage or the other of his life.' In Lloyd George's copy of *Great Contemporaries*, this passage was sidelined.

Winston S. Churchill to J. L. Garvin

(Churchill papers: 8/548)

13 July 1937

What a splendid and informative letter you have written me! The reason why I sent you the proof was that I felt the need of pulling out a somewhat bigger stop in doing credit to 'Old Joe'. You have given me just the turn I wanted, and I will bend this in to my text.

I read your third volume, but as I was not called upon to review it for the Daily Mail, I did not remember there were three. I have made the necessary correction.

I daresay you are getting in the same position as I am over Marlborough. I want increasingly to get rid of it, and to do justice to it, but so many things intervene!

For the life of me I cannot see on what grounds we should refuse belligerent rights to the Spanish nationalists. They seem to me to have established every condition presented by the Confederate States. However I am not worrying much about the House now.

Winston S. Churchill to Brigadier-General Sir James Edmonds[1]

(Churchill papers: 8/548)

13 July 1937

I venture to send you the enclosed very short epitome of French's[2] command. I should be so much obliged if you would very kindly vet it for me. It is required to form part of a biographical essay upon him which will come into my new book, Great Contemporaries, which I am publishing at the end of September.

I think it is all right. It follows on the lines we worked out together some years ago, and I think is in accord with your monumental and decisive work.

---

[1] James Edward Edmonds, 1861–1956. Educated at King's College School, London. 2nd Lieutenant, Royal Engineers, 1881; Major, 1899. On active service in South Africa, 1901–2, and on the Western Front, 1914–18. British Delegate to the Red Cross Conference, 1907. Colonel, 1909. Deputy Engineer-in-Chief, BEF, 1918 (despatches six times). Officer in charge of the Military Branch of the Historical Section of the Committee of Imperial Defence, 1919–49. Brigadier-General. Knighted, 1928.

[2] John Denton Pinkstone French, 1852–1925. Entered Navy, 1866. Transferred to Army, 1874. Lieutenant-General, commanding the Cavalry in South Africa, 1899–1902. Knighted, 1900. Chief of the Imperial General Staff, 1912–14. Field-Marshal, 1913. Commander-in-Chief of the British Expeditionary Force in France, August 1914–December 1915. Commander-in-Chief, Home Forces, 1915–18. Created Viscount French of Ypres, 1916. Lord Lieutenant of Ireland, 1918–21. Created Earl of Ypres, 1922. In 1911 he was one of the nine 'distinguished outsiders' elected to the Other Club.

Still there may be some statements not quite justified and a place or a river here and there which is not correct.

I do not think French has had justice done to him. He is allowed to go down to this generation at least as a dud who was happily replaced by Haig.[1] I consider French was a finer soldier than Haig and that if he had remained at the head of the Armies we should not have had the horrible slaughter of Passchendaele. However this is a personal contention.[2]

Winston S. Churchill to A. H. Richards

(Churchill papers: 2/311)

15 July 1937

Many thanks for your letter telling of the breakdown of the American plan. As you know I was never very much set upon it and extremely sceptical as to its substance. Pray let the matter drop now therefore altogether so far as I am concerned. I hope if Mr Wickham Steed goes over to the United States he will not bring me into his negotiations. If there is a demand from that side let it come, but I do not want it worked up in my interests.

I am not prepared at the present time to make any plan about Central and Southern Europe. If I should make a tour there I should go to various countries and I should certainly hope to visit Yugo-Slavia. I am not at all sure about making speeches in such a dangerous area.

I could give you Wednesday 21st for another luncheon of the Focus at which the statement of policy can be discussed.

[1] Douglas Haig, 1861–1928. Entered the Army, 1885. Knighted, 1909. Chief of Staff, India, 1909–11. Lieutenant-General, 1910. Commander of the 1st Army Corps, 1914–15. His successful defence of Ypres, 19 October–22 November 1914, made him a national figure. Commanded the 1st Army at Loos, November 1915. Succeeded Sir John French as Commander-in-Chief, British Expeditionary Force, 19 December 1915. Field-Marshal, 1917. Created Earl, 1919.

[2] In his essay on Sir John French in *Great Contemporaries* Churchill wrote: 'French was a natural soldier. Although he had not the intellectual capacity of Haig, nor perhaps his underlying endurance, he had a deeper military insight. He was not equal to Haig in precision of detail; but he had more imagination, and he would never have run the British Army into the same long drawn-out slaughters.' Churchill also recalled how French, in July 1914, faced 'long, empty years of retirement and idleness. I remember that we scrambled ashore from a picket-boat before daybreak one morning to watch the first trials of a circular aeroplane upon which a young friend of mine, Sir Archibald Sinclair, had spent a great deal of money. I remember, too, long walks with the general up and down the esplanade at Deal. My impression of French, for all his composure, was that he was a heart-broken man. Now, observe how swiftly Fortune can change the scene and switch on the lights! Within a fortnight of this melancholy voyage Sir John French realized his fondest dream. He was Commander-in-Chief of the best and largest army Britain had ever sent abroad, at the beginning of the greatest war men have ever fought!' (see also pages 786 and 854).

Anthony Eden to Winston S. Churchill

(*Churchill papers: 2/314*)

15 July 1937   Foreign Office
Strictly Confidential

My dear Winston,

You will remember speaking to me on the telephone this morning with regard to the mounting of guns by General Franco in a position, on Spanish soil, which dominates Gibraltar. You drew attention to the obligation which lies on the Spanish authorities not to take such action, in view of the provision of the Treaty of Utrecht, and said, if I understood right, that you proposed to raise this matter in the Debate on Monday. I said at the time that I feared that our position under the Treaty was not so strong as might at first sight appear. I have now looked into the question further and find that legally it is, if anything, even weaker than I had recollected. Under the circumstances, I hope very much that you will not think it desirable to raise the Treaty aspect, or at least not ask me what I think of it! I am, as you will appreciate, not anxious to have to expose the weakness of the Treaty position, and even if I could avoid this, it would only be possible to give you so unsatisfactory an answer as must do more harm than good.

At the same time I can tell you confidentially that the position from the military point of view is not such as to cause any immediate alarm. The larger calibre guns at present in position are beyond range of Gibraltar or the harbour, and appear to be intended rather to dominate the Straits. The smaller calibre guns, I understand, do not cause anxiety.

Yours ever,
Anthony Eden

PS. This position may well have to be taken up again with the Spaniards, but I am by no means convinced for reasons I had rather not put into a letter, that the moment is now.

AE

Winston S. Churchill to Brigadier-General Sir James Edmonds

(*Churchill papers: 8/548*)

16 July 1937

Thank you so much for your invaluable notes. They seem to knock out practically everything I had written, but I will recast it.

Perhaps I might also send you what I have touched upon about Haig, which is the counter-part of the French chapter.[1]

I shd so like to see you again and will make a suggestion as soon as I get the book off my hands.

Violet Bonham Carter to Winston S. Churchill

(*Churchill papers: 2/316*)

16 July 1937

Dearest Winston,

Here is a memorandum by Mr Jabotinsky[2] in case you feel disposed to speak on Wed. It does set forth some very relevant objections to the present scheme—even if the principle of partition is acceptable. Above all one feels that it should not be rushed through in a fortnight. People are so ignorant of the geographical proportions & strategic position of the *tiny* corner now allotted to the Jews—Forgive my bothering you.

Ever yrs,
Violet

[1] Of Sir Douglas Haig, Churchill wrote in *Great Contemporaries*: 'He does not appear to have had any original ideas; no one can discern a spark of that mysterious, visionary, often sinister genius which has enabled the great captains of history to dominate the material factors, save slaughter, and confront their foes with the triumph of novel apparitions. He was, we are told, quite friendly to the tanks, but the manoeuvre of making them would never have occurred to him. He appeared at all times quite unconscious of any theatre but the Western Front. There were the Germans in their trenches. Here he stood at the head of an army corps, then of an army, and finally of a group of mighty armies. Hurl them on and keep slogging at it in the best possible way—that was war. It was undoubtedly one way of making war, and in the end there was certainly overwhelming victory. But these truisms will not be accepted by history as exhaustive.'

[2] Vladimir Jabotinsky, 1880–1940. Born in Odessa, into a middle-class Jewish family. Studied law in Berne and Rome, 1898. On the editorial staff of, and columnist for, *Odesskiya Novosti*. Organized a Jewish self-defence group in Odessa, against anti-Jewish attacks, 1903. A Zionist lecturer in Russia before 1914. Active in Zionist work in Constantinople, 1909. In London in 1914, he urged the formation of a Jewish Legion. Lieutenant, 38th Battalion, Royal Fusiliers, 1917; decorated for heading the first company to cross the Jordan river against the Turks. Organized the Jewish defence force, or Haganah, in Jerusalem, 1920; sentenced to 15 years imprisonment by a British military court for seeking to check an Arab mob in Jerusalem during the Passover riots of 1920. Amnestied, 1921. Formed a break-away Zionist movement, the World Union of Zionist Revisionists, 1925. Lived in Jerusalem, as director of the Judaea Insurance Company, 1928–9. Banned from Palestine, 1930. Urged the Zionists to demand 'the establishment of a Jewish State', 1931. Founded the New Zionist Organization, 1935, to further this aim; wanted a ten-year plan to bring 1,500,000 East European Jews to Palestine. After the Arab riots of 1936 he accepted, as against the majority Zionist view, the principle of violent reprisals against the Arabs. Supreme Commander of the Irgun Zvai Leumi, 1937–40. On the outbreak of war in 1939 he came to London to urge the formation of a Jewish army to fight the Nazis alongside the allies.

Vladimir Jabotinsky to Winston S. Churchill
(*Churchill papers: 2/316*)

16 July 1937

Sir,

I apologise for my informal approach, and for disturbing whatever there may be of repose in your week-end seclusion.

Lady Violet Bonham Carter told me that you are not sure whether you intend to speak on the partition of Palestine. This letter is an attempt to urge you to intervene. To me as a Jew—and even opponents never deny that I do represent the *feelings* of the Jewish masses—you are one of the very limited inner circle of British statesmen responsible for the birth of the Jewish Commonwealth idea between 1917 and 1922; and we expect you to defend it now that it is so dangerously threatened, and would be grievously disappointed if your voice were not heard.

The Note I enclose expresses, I am sure, feelings most widely shared by my fellow-Jews throughout the world. It is possible that not all of them as yet, have fully realised every point raised in my Note—they know very little about densities of population, dry farming, or especially about the military aspects of the situation. But they surely want, above all, room for colonisation and a Holyland that is Holyland, and as they gradually realise that partition kills all their hopes their opposition crystallises. It is the worst feature of the whole business that we shall have no time even to state our case. I hope it will be stated by friends, in the first place by you.[1]

If I can be of any use, please let me see you before next Wednesday. I would come to Chartwell if necessary. My home telephone (the office is closed on Saturdays) is Primrose 2118.

Yours faithfully,
V. Jabotinsky

Vladimir Jabotinsky to Winston S. Churchill
(*Churchill papers: 2/316*)

16 July 1937

NOTE ON THE PALESTINE PARTITION SCHEME

The Partition scheme is to be rejected even if the area of the 'Jewish State' proposed in the Report[2] could be increased, as suggested by some

---

[1] For Churchill's speech in the House of Commons on 21 July 1937, see page 728, note 1.
[2] The *Palestine Royal Commission Report*, known as the 'Peel Commission Report', which had been presented to Parliament on 7 July 1937.

friends of the scheme, by adding to it a big slice of the South ('Negeb') and a part, or even the whole, of Jerusalem.

The reasons for such rejection are:

I. The area in question, even if increased as above, offers no room for any considerable Jewish immigration;

II. It is a fallacy to assume that this 'Jewish State' would only be a 'first step', a sort of Jewish Piedmont destined to expand. Once prematurely formed, it could never expand either by peaceful penetration or by conquest;

III. On the contrary, such a Jewish State would be destined to be eventually captured by the neighbouring Arab States, the conquest being probably accompanied by destruction and massacre.

In the following, brief explanations of the above three points are offered.

I. No Room For Immigration

1. The area as outlined in the Report on p. 383–4 comprises about 4,600 square kilometres and contains (excluding Jaffa and the British corridor) about 645,000 inhabitants. In other words; the density of population in the area proposed to form the 'Jewish State' is already now about 140 inhabitants per square kilometre.

2. This is a very high density, equal to that of Germany and almost double that of France (76). There is no reason to believe that it can be considerably increased by methods of sound economy.

3. More than one half of the 645,000 inhabitants occupying that area are not Jews but Arabs; but the hope that they could be induced to 'trek' away is a fallacy. The 'Jewish State' would be a rich and busy place, and people do not, as a rule, *voluntarily* emigrate from rich into poor districts. Nor would there be any room for them to go to in the Arab State deprived of Jewish energy and capital.

4. No such increase of the area as can be reasonably expected even by optimists can substantially change this situation. The addition of Jerusalem (whether the modern city only or the whole of it) would be of no account as 'area'. As to the Negeb, even optimist Jews do not expect to get more than one half of the Beersheba area, or about 5,000 sq kilometres. This is an area where no water has so far been found, an area destined at best for dry or semi-dry farming. All precedents show that the limit of density of population an area of that kind may reach—and that only in the future—would be about 25 inhabitants per sq kilometre; or a total of 125,000 settlers—in the future.

5. The homeless Jewish masses in Eastern and Central Europe constitute a reservoir of distress numbering 8 to 9 millions.

6. In some of these Eastern countries, the only argument against Anti-semitism is the hope that Palestine will some day be able to absorb large masses of Jewish emigrants. The moment this prospect becomes obviously impossible, an unprecedented outburst of anti-Jewish feeling is to be expected, and governments will be powerfully urged to follow the Nazi example in placing Antisemitism on the Statute book.

7. For comparison, it may be useful to mention that Palestine on both sides of the Jordan contains 116,000 sq kilometres (26,000 West of the Jordan, 90,000 East). Densities of population: West of the Jordan—52, the whole country (both East and West)—14. Should the country *as a whole* be made some day to reach, as all Zionists wish, the rather moderate average density of 100 or even 75 inhabitants per sq kilometre, it would mean a refuge for several million Jews, without any need to displace the 1,000,000 Arabs who live there now, or their progeny.

II. No Jewish 'Piedmont'

1. All those who favour the partition idea trust and repeat that the little 'Jewish State' would only be a beginning, eventually to expand into a larger area. This is an irredentism as unreal as it is dangerous, for no territorial expansion will be possible either by peaceful penetration or by conquest.

2. The moment the Balfour Declaration is abolished outside the limits of the 'Jewish State', immigration of Jews into the Arab State will only be possible within limits which the Arab government will tolerate. Even if such immigration will be allowed at all (it may even be encouraged, in small numbers bringing in big capitals), it will never be suffered to reach such a size as to change the predominantly Arab character of any district. The Jews may be allowed to form new ghettos in Arab territory, but not to form new Jewish majorities with the consent of an Arab government.

3. Any hope to use the 'Jewish State' for organising a Jewish army which would eventually conquer the rest of Palestine by force, is utterly absurd. The Jewish army will be unable even to defend the 'Jewish State' if, or rather when, it will be attacked by the Arab countries: the 'Jewish State' consists essentially of plains dominated by hills which will belong to the Arabs, Tel Aviv being within 15 miles from the nearest Arab mountain gun and Haifa within 18 miles.

4. At the same time, the *spirit* of 'irredenta' among the Jews will of course be ineradicable, both because of nationalist stimuli and under the pressure of their homeless masses abroad. Sterile and hopeless, it will only foster eternal

tension—until the inevitable capture of the 'Jewish State' by its Arab neighbours.

III.

1. The capture of the 'Jewish State' by its Arab neighbours will be inevitable. A dwarfish area, whose defenders can never grow to more than a handful, but full of riches and culture, will be surrounded not by the Arab Palestine only, but by an Arab Federation from Aleppo to Basra and Sanaa (for the Report openly invites the proposed 'Arab State' to join such a Federation). It will inevitably be coveted, and inevitably attacked at the first opportunity; and the meaning of 'opportunity' is—any moment when the British Empire will be in trouble elsewhere.

2. The Royal Commission probably intended, while benefiting Jews and Arabs, also to ease the Empire's burden of responsibility; but its proposal means a responsibility tenfold increased. In the present mandated territory, the danger of riots would gradually decrease with the growth of the Jewish population; and in any case it would be a danger of 'rioters', badly drilled, ill equipped, and never numerous. Under the partition scheme, the danger will be represented by regular troops.

In conclusion, I wish to protest against the haste and hurry with which this scheme is being rushed through Parliament, the Mandates Commission, and the Council of the League. Unprecedented pressure is being used to get final and fateful decisions before even that evidence, on which the Report is supposed to be based, has been read by all concerned, and especially before the Jews to whom it is a matter of life and death have had time properly to confer.

Winston S. Churchill to Lord Beaverbrook

(*Beaverbrook papers*)

16 July 1937   Chartwell

My dear Max,

I send you herewith the passage in Curzon about which you have so kindly helped me.[1] I will send you the whole article as soon as I get another proof

---

[1] In his essay on Lord Curzon in *Great Contemporaries*, Churchill told the story of how Curzon failed to become Prime Minister in 1923. One new fact which he was able to reveal concerned Balfour's attitude. Churchill had received this information from Lord Beaverbrook,

back. What you tell me makes everything quite clear and orderly. There is only one point about which I am in doubt, Stamfordham's[1] telegram to Curzon to come to London. Was this sent at a moment when the King actually thought of asking him to form a Government, or was it only sent so that Stamfordham could explain to him why he could not have the commission? Perhaps you can throw some light on this.[2]

Would it be agreeable to you for me to say that I have these details about Mr Bonar Law[3] from you, his closest friend and confidant at every stage, or words to that effect?

I left out the bit about Salisbury saying that he would recommend Curzon but much against the grain, and also about his waiting all day in London, because he is still alive and would probably argue about it all.

Once more many thanks,

Yours always,

W

---

who had obtained it from Venetia Montagu, who had been present at the episode described. Churchill's account read: '. . . as the inquiries of the King had proceeded, what may at first have seemed the obvious choice appeared in a new and doubtful light. Lord Balfour's great influence was thrown into the scales against the former Viceroy. He was summoned specially from Sheringham in Norfolk where he lay ill of phlebitis. The doctors protested that travelling would be dangerous. Balfour was undeterred. He felt he had a duty to perform. Arrived at the Palace, he expressed with conviction the view that in these days a Prime Minister must be in the House of Commons. He confined himself strictly to this point. He was careful to use no other argument. It was enough. When late that night Balfour returned to his sick-bed at Sheringham after his fatiguing journey, he was asked by some of his most cherished friends who were staying with him, "And will dear George be chosen?" "No," he replied placidly, "dear George will not."'

[1] Arthur John Bigge, 1849–1931. Entered Army, 1869. Entered the Royal Household, 1880. Private Secretary to Queen Victoria, 1895–1901. Private Secretary to George V, 1910–31. One of the nine 'distinguished' outsiders elected to the Other Club in 1911 (when it was founded by Churchill and F. E. Smith). Created Baron Stamfordham, 1911. His only son, Captain the Hon. John Neville Bigge, was killed in action on 15 May 1915. His son-in-law, Captain H. R. A. Adeane, having already been killed in action on 2 November 1914, leaving a son aged 4, who, as Sir Michael Adeane, was to be Private Secretary to Queen Elizabeth II from 1953 to 1972.

[2] Churchill wrote in *Great Contemporaries*: 'While Curzon was journeying to London, debating what he should do with No 10, Downing Street, the King sent for Mr Baldwin. When, that afternoon, Lord Stamfordham was announced at Carlton House Terrace, it was only to tell him that Mr Baldwin was already at Buckingham Palace. The blow was bitter, and for the moment overwhelming.'

[3] Andrew Bonar Law, 1858–1923. Born in Canada. Brought to Scotland at the age of twelve. Conservative MP, 1900–10 and 1911–23. Parliamentary Secretary, Board of Trade, 1902–5. Leader of the Conservatives in the House of Commons, 1911. Secretary of State for the Colonies, May 1915–December 1916. Chancellor of the Exchequer, 1916–19. Lord Privy Seal, 1919–21. Prime Minister, 1922–3. Two of his four sons were killed in action in the First World War.

Sir Ian Hamilton to Winston S. Churchill

(*Churchill papers: 2/297*)

19 July 1937

My dear Winston,

I am rather glad I missed Miss Grant Duff because I should have differed from her too violently. Except the Masaryks[1] there are no distinguished persons amongst the Czechs. They are, in fact, a most harsh and disagreeable lot and to put those 3,000,000 *Sudeten* Germans under them has been very bad business indeed. . . .

Sir Robert Waley Cohen to Winston S. Churchill

(*Churchill papers: 2/315*)

20 July 1937

My dear Churchill,

I write as you kindly asked to record the suggestion which I made to you tonight about the Palestine report. It arose out of a discussion among a number of English Jews who command general respect and who have been considering, from a British point of view, the effect of the Royal Commission's proposals.

It is I think recognised on all sides that the scheme proposed by the Royal Commission is a policy of despair. If it has to be carried into effect it will be disastrous to all the three parties concerned, namely the British Empire, the Jews and the Arabs. Nobody would wish to see it carried into effect if any better solution can be found. The Royal Commission expressed the view that agreement between the Zionists and the Arabs of Palestine could not be achieved, but since the publication of their Report there have been many indications—and notably from Arab quarters—that, rather than see the country mutilated by partition, there would be a willingness to concede and forbear to an extent that had not previously been contemplated. Thus, as a result of this threat of partition, agreement might be achieved on terms which would not have been possible before the Report was published.

My suggestion is, therefore, to ask you to plead for delay in carrying out the policy of despair to which the Commissioners felt themselves reduced,

---

[1] Jan Masaryk, the Czechoslovak Minister to London from 1925 to 1938 (see page 1020, note 1) and his father Thomas Garrigue Masaryk, the first President of the Czechoslovak Republic, from the foundation of the State in 1918 until his death in 1935.

and that the Government should be asked to make it clear that if the Jews and the Arabs could now agree upon a basis on which peace could be established and the country remain intact, the Government of the United Kingdom would be prepared to call the parties together in London and to use their good offices to press this infinitely preferable solution. No-one doubts that the economic possibilities of a united Palestine, whether forming part of the British Empire or continuing as a territory over which Great Britain exercises a mandate, are infinitely greater than could ever be attained by the separate sections of the country after partition.

If, therefore, by giving time for the devastating realities of partition to be appreciated by all those whose future is bound up with Palestine and by those who care for its welfare, the Jews and Arabs were to come to agreement with one another, an infinitely better solution of the problem would have been achieved than that which the Royal Commission put forward when no agreement seemed possible.

The Royal Commission, in the face of what they regarded as implacable opposition between the two sections, were reduced to partition, but it must be remembered that the conditions of their Enquiry favoured the putting forward of the maximum conceivable claims by both sides, whereas the threat of partition as the only alternative to agreement creates an entirely new atmosphere in which both sides, anxious to meet the other, might find a means of avoiding the dismemberment of their country. Partition will not relieve the British Government of its liabilities: we should surely be bound to intervene before long, if a country so important to our imperial position were to be given over to the unrestrained hostility of two races facing one another along unnatural frontiers and increasingly animated by a sense of the injury caused by the dismemberment of their country. All this will be avoided if agreement can be achieved.

Surely it is worth while to allow a period of delay during which the threat of partition may exert its sobering and moderating influence?[1]

Yours sincerely,
Robert Waley Cohen

---

[1] During the debate on Palestine in the House of Commons on 21 July 1937, Churchill opposed any final commitment to the Partition of Palestine into two States, one Jewish and the other Arab, telling the House: 'Take the military aspect alone. The gravest anxieties arise about that. There are two sovereign States, one a rich and small State more crowded than Germany, with double the population to the kilometre of France, and then in the mountains in the surrounding regions, stretching up to Bagdad with the Assyrians and the desert tribes to the south, the whole of this great Arab area confronting this new Jewish State, and in between the two the British holding a number of extremely important positions with responsibilities at present altogether undefined.' Arguing in favour of delay, Churchill spoke of 'the question of the value of time' and of 'some time' passing before approval of

Winston S. Churchill to Imre Revesz: telegram

(*Churchill papers: 8/561*)

21 July 1937

Article this week deals with Palestine Zionist question. Should be of special interest. Please press it upon your clients. Do they object to 1,500 words or shall I cut to 1,100.[1]

Churchill

Harold Nicolson to Winston S. Churchill

(*Churchill papers: 8/548*)

21 July 1937

Dear Winston Churchill,

I have read through the enclosed article on Lord Curzon with a special eye upon whether there was anything in it either ungenerous or unfair. I cannot find a single word which goes beyond reasonable criticism. On the contrary, not merely have you been gentle to his faults but you have also made the best of all favourable fact. I particularly relish your phrase about his being able to domineer but not to dominate; and you are absolutely correct in saying that once Curzon had stated his case in clear and orderly fashion he seemed to believe that there was nothing more to be done.

There is one point where, (although justifiably), I think you have been too kind. You say that he had 'plenty of pluck'. I often feel that the central cause of his failure was that although he was all too combative in little things he was not heroic in great. He would defend his front line trenches with great tenacity and at moments would launch powerful counter-attacks; but once his outer defences had been pierced or encircled he would surrender the inner fortress without a blow.

Your final words regarding the three metals, each finely polished after its

---

Partition, and he went on to explain: 'There are, I believe, signs on both sides that people are thinking that perhaps rather than this they might make some mutual concessions. They have heard of the judgment of Solomon, and how wise that was, in which a baby was held up in order to see which was the true mother. But if sufficient time had not been given for the true mother to proclaim herself by her feelings, I very much doubt whether that parable would have commended itself so much to subsequent generations.'

[1] For Churchill's article, see page 735, note 3.

fashion, are a brilliant summary of that metallic but brittle temperament.[1] Whatever harshness of judgment may be felt in some passages is utterly redeemed by your story of the 'magnificent compulsive gesture' with which he greeted you after his Carlton Club betrayal.[2]

Incidentally, the name of the governess mentioned in the fifth line of your second paragraph was Miss Paraman, not Miss Paranor.

Yours sincerely,
Harold Nicolson

G. D. Birla to M. K. Gandhi

(Birla papers)

22 July 1937

I was lunching today with Churchill at his house and again enjoyed his company for two hours. As usual he was very cordial and charming, but very ill-informed about India.

Immediately on seeing me, he said, 'Well, a big experiment has begun' and when I said 'Yes, it has begun but it will require all your sympathy and good wishes' he assured me of these, but all the same said 'It depends entirely on you. You know I have not spoken a word against the Act after the King's signature was put on it, and if you can make this experiment a success, you will reach your goal automatically. You know how democracy is attacked all over the world. It is only Great Britain that has preserved democracy, and if you can show by your actions that you can make democracy a success, you will have no difficulty in advancing further. Play fair and we will play fair.'

'What do you mean by "Play Fair"' I asked. He replied 'Make the Provinces contented, peaceful and prosperous. Don't allow violence and don't murder Englishmen.' I said, 'I am simply shocked at what you say.

---

[1] Churchill's last paragraph on Lord Curzon read: 'These heavy reverses were supported after the initial shocks with goodwill and dignity. But undoubtedly they invested the long and strenuous career with ultimate disappointment. The morning had been golden; the noontide was bronze; and the evening lead. But all were solid, and each was polished till it shone after its fashion.'

[2] The Carlton Club meeting took place on 19 October 1922. In his essay on Curzon, Churchill wrote: 'It was not for nine months that I saw him again. We met at a large private dinner in London. He was a leading minister and we were knocked out, so I did not press myself upon him. But as the ladies left the dining-room he came round to me and threw out his hand in a most magnificent, compulsive gesture which swept everything away. Here was the real man.'

Do you seriously believe that we are going to murder Englishmen?' He was rather surprised at my own complacence but accepted the assurance that India did not believe in violence. I added, 'Even the most extremist Congressman is not anti-British. He is certainly for independence, but this does not mean that one should become anti-British.' He asked whether I could say this about Jawaharlal[1] also. I replied 'I can. I am a capitalist and he is a socialist and we have got different views on economic and social matters, but all the same, in fairness to him, I must say that he is a great man, very sincere and not at all anti-British. You must go to India to see things for yourself, because then you will be of great help to us.' He said, 'Yes, I will go. Linlithgow has already invited me to go, but if Mr Gandhi also desires it, I will go. Give your leader my greetings and tell him that I wish him all success. Don't feel shy of fighting socialism. Accumulation of wealth is a good thing because it creates initiative, but of course capitalists have to be servants and not masters.'

He was very sceptical about the future of the European political situation. For one more year he did not expect any war, but he would not say about the far future. He said, 'The dictators are getting mad and they may do anything in order to preserve their power. Russia is getting less communistic and Germany is getting more socialistic. So they are finding common ground to some extent. England is the only country which has preserved democracy. I started agitating for rearming England because I believe nations are ruled either by right or by force. Right is the better method of ruling, but you cannot establish right unless you have force. And now we have got force with the help of which we can establish right. Italy is dreaming of establishing an Empire.'

He went on in this mood for a pretty long time. This time he himself suggested that I should keep him well informed about the situation in India and I have promised to do so.[2]

---

[1] Jawaharlal Nehru, 1889–1964. Educated at Harrow and Trinity College, Cambridge. Barrister-at-Law, Inner Temple, 1912. Secretary, Home Rule League, Allahabad, 1918. Member of the All-India Congress Committee, 1918; General Secretary, 1929. Imprisoned several times. President of the Indian National Congress, 1924, 1936, 1937 and 1946. Chairman of the National Planning Committee, 1939. Vice-President, Interim Government of India, 1946. Prime Minister and Minister for External Affairs from 1947 until his death.

[2] On 28 July 1937 Birla wrote to Churchill: 'This is just to remind you of your kind promise to send me a copy of your photograph with your autograph on it. I extremely enjoyed the lunch at your house and I am very thankful to you for your kindness (*Churchill papers: 1/299*).

Réné Léon[1] to Winston S. Churchill

(*Churchill papers: 2/297*)

23 July 1937   New York

Dear Mr Churchill,

I have just returned from Washington whither I had been called to appear as a witness before certain Congressional Committees now holding hearings on pending bills.

Despite the great demands upon his time the President[2] was good enough to afford me an opportunity to communicate to him the impressions which I gathered during my recent visit to England. First of all let me say that Mr Roosevelt was delighted to have good news of you and to learn that you plan coming to America next September.[3] He was particularly pleased to hear that that section of enlightened British opinion with which I came in contact was so definitely in favor of closer Anglo-American co-operation in the monetary field. I hardly needed this further confirmation of that of which I had always been convinced, namely, that the President is an ardent cooperator by nature, so that his quick response will always greet any genuine gesture of rapprochement.

The practical test of the genuineness of any proposal is its ultimate success or failure and, as I see it, the trouble hitherto has been not so much in the method of approach as in the underlying policies which have been formulated by a school of thought self convicted by its very own record. Thus if success is to crown future effort we necessarily must seek our inspiration from wiser counsel.

---

[1] Réné Leon, 1882–1965. Born in Egypt, of French parents. Emigrated to the United States at the age of 14. Naturalized a United States citizen, 1903. Entered the brokerage business in New York; served in Mexico City, 1909–12. With the Equitable Trust Company of New York City, 1914–19; the Guaranty Trust Company, 1919–24 (in charge of bullion and Far Eastern exchanges). A partner in W. C. Langley and Company, bankers and brokers, 1924–30. Retired, 1930. An adviser to President Roosevelt, 1933, and instrumental in Roosevelt's decision to place an embargo on gold exports. In 1937 he published *Money and Trade*. Léon had lunched with Churchill on 25 June 1937.

[2] Franklin Delano Roosevelt, 1882–1945. United States Assistant Secretary of the Navy, 1913–20. Governor of New York State, 1929–33. President of the United States, 1933–45. Churchill's support for Roosevelt was frequently repeated in his articles in both Britain and America. 'I am,' he wrote in *Colliers* magazine in the first year of Roosevelt's presidency, 'though a foreigner, an ardent admirer of the main drift and impulse which President Roosevelt has given to the economic and financial policy of the United States.' And when, at Oxford, an undergraduate echoed the prevailing anti-American feeling by asking Churchill if he approved Roosevelt's policy 'of neglecting the affairs of the rest of the world for the especial benefit of the United States', Churchill replied with feeling: 'The President is a bold fellow, I like his spirit' (*G. R. Storry papers*, note of 23 February 1934).

[3] A visit that did not take place (see page 762).

I make bold to say to you in strict confidence, and on no one's authority but my own, that if your Exchequer will formulate a simple plan of action and submit it to America as the basis for a cooperative effort, it will meet the whole-hearted and sincere welcome and support of the Government and the Nation. I accompany herewith a memorandum, of which you may make such use as you see fit, detailing my own idea of a workable proposal.

If those who examine it will consider its broader implications; if they will trouble to give the features peculiar to America's problem as much weight as they do to Britain's, then I believe that we can make considerable progress.

In conclusion I should like to make just one request: At Chartwell last month you pencilled a drawing of the Pound Sterling and the Dollar together marching to glory. I want another such drawing which please be good enough to initial as I propose to use it as the frontispiece of a booklet on which I now am working. I had meant to use the drawing you gave me but am unable to do so. As I walked out of the President's office, Mr Roosevelt had it on his desk and was gazing at it with considerable interest.[1]

Cordially yours,
René Léon

Winston S. Churchill to Professor G. M. Trevelyan
(*Churchill papers: 8/547*)

23 July 1937

We have found in the Sunderland papers a whole series of reports from a spy in Paris, covering 1709 and 1710. I am inclined to think that this was a part of Marlborough's secret service. The reports often deal with military matters, and they would have been quite useless if they had to reach the Army only through Whitehall. Dates of the letters and of their receipt in London, often show that the journey took a month, though we have some

[1] This was not the first time that Churchill had sent Roosevelt his intertwined Pound-Dollar design. Nearly four years earlier, on 8 October 1933, Roosevelt's elder son James had been among the dinner guests at Chartwell. 'After dinner on this particular weekend Mr Churchill initiated a guessing game, drawing from each of us a confession of our fondest wish. His guests fumbled and qualified their answers. But when the question was put to him, he shot back without a flicker of hesitation, "I wish to be Prime Minister and in close and daily communication by telephone with the President of the United States. There is nothing we could not do if we were together." Then, turning to a secretary, he called for a piece of paper on which he inscribed the insignias of a pound and a dollar sign intertwined. "Pray, bear this to your father from me," he said to James Roosevelt. "Tell him this must be the currency of the future".' (Kay Halle, *Irrepressible Churchill*, Cleveland Ohio, 1966, pages 7–8, including a facsimile of the ₤ design dated 8 October 1933.)

cases where it only took eleven days. In most cases, three reports are sent forward together. Therefore, I think they went to Marlborough's headquarters, and were thence transmitted for custody to his son-in-law, Sunderland. We have found no copies of them in the Record Office, nor, so far, anywhere else.

These reports are remarkable in many ways. Evidently the chief spy was a person who had access to everyone, and who employed some Agents to lunch with the Foreign Office and military officials, and also servants in close contact with the King. These reports contain very intimate side-lights on the French Court, and information about many matters only treated upon by Saint Simon, and published much later.

I thought you would like to see them, and therefore I send you what we have so far transcribed. There must be more than three hundred, and I am drawing upon them in my last volume. It may be, however, that with your knowledge, you have heard of them, or copies of them, elsewhere, and that they are not a new discovery. If so, I should be grateful if you would let me know. I cannot publish now until the spring.

With kind regards,

Believe me,

Winston S. Churchill to Bernard Baruch: telegram

(*Churchill papers: 1/299*)

23 July 1937

Clemmie Badgastein. Hope you will stay with me both at flat and Chartwell during whole visit. Comfort and freedom guaranteed. Will meet you Waterloo Tuesday. Every welcome.

Winston

Winston S. Churchill to Clementine Churchill

(*Spencer-Churchill papers*)

25 July 1937

The Manor House
Stoke D'Abernon
Surrey

My darling Clemmie,

I am overwhelmed with work. Three days H of C last week: the new book in its final birth throes: articles, & always Marlborough: & now ahead on

Tuesday next another debate on Inskip's salary. I really don't know how I find all that I need, but the well flows freely: only the time is needed to draw the water from it.

Let this be some apology for my not having written, do not think you have not been always in my thoughts. I do hope the cure is benefiting you: & that now Kommer[1] is with you, you will not be bored or lonely.[2]

I hope you have seen the papers wh show how important was the change of procedure I induced the Government to make over Palestine. I expect now to beat the partition scheme. I will send you what I wrote in ES about it.[3]

[1] Rudolf Kommer. Born in Czernowitz (then in the Austro-Hungarian Empire; from 1919 to 1939 in Rumania; since 1945 in the Soviet Union). A close friend of Lady Diana Cooper. He died in New York in 1943. Kommer, who always wrote after his signature: 'fr. Cz.' (from Czernowitz), sent Churchill on 28 December 1938 an invitation on behalf of the American Committee for Jewish Palestine for Churchill to speak at the New York World's Fair, for a fee of five thousand dollars (£20,000 sterling in the values of September 1981), and added: 'Should you not be in a position to come, I should be very much obliged, if you would kindly mention the matter to Duff Cooper. Alas, they don't want to spend quite so much on him. But they say that they "could come to terms with him". This might be undue oriental optimism, but there it is. To accelerate matters I would like to suggest that if you should decline and if Duff Cooper should feel like accepting, you might ask him to cable me his terms. It would, therefore, perhaps be advisable not to mention to him the figure that was offered you, for he might consider himself much more valuable than you are in the eyes of the committee. . . .' (*Churchill papers: 2/357*).

[2] Clementine Churchill was staying at Haus Hirt, in Badgastein, Austria. A small hotel, run by Heinrich Hirt. Among the other guests taking the cure (thermal baths) was the German Crown Prince, of whom Clementine Churchill had written to her husband on 18 July 1937: 'He has very good royal manners; but he does not look at all intelligent' (*Churchill papers: 1/322*). The Crown Prince had last met Churchill at the coronation of King George V in 1911.

[3] Writing in the *Evening Standard* on 23 July 1937, Churchill opposed the recommendation of the Peel Commission for the partition of Palestine into two States, one Jewish and one Arab, (with Jerusalem and Bethlehem excluded, and remaining under British control). The 'plan of cutting Palestine into three parts', he wrote, 'is a counsel of despair. One wonders whether, in reality, the difficulties of carrying out the Zionist scheme are so great as they are portrayed, and whether in fact there has not been a very considerable measure of success. In the sixteen years that have passed since the mandate, many troubles have been overcome, and great developments have taken place in Palestine. When I paid my last visit, only three years ago, I was delighted at the aspect of the countryside. The fine roads, the new buildings and plantations, the evidences of prosperity, both among Jews and Arabs, presented on every side, all gave a sense of real encouragement . . .' The change since then was due, he explained 'to outside events' which were not Britain's fault: 'The persecutions of the Jews in Germany, the exploitation of anti-Semitism as a means by which violent and reactionary forces seize, or attempt to seize, despotic power, afflicted the civilised world with a refugee problem similar to that of the Huguenots in the seventeenth century. The brunt of this has fallen upon this very small country and administration of Palestine. Jewish immigration, suddenly raised to 30,000 or 40,000 a year, may not have exceeded the "economic absorptive capacity" of the settled districts, but it naturally confronted the Arabs with the prospect, not of an evolutionary growth of the Jewish population, but of actual flooding and swamping which seemed to bring near to them the prospect of domination. Too much current was put on the cables. And the cables have fused. That may be a reason for mending the cables and

Here we have a tiny party. Ettie,[1] a young man from FO & his wife, and Ld Stanmore whom you know. Edgar[2] is much the same as when we saw him 2 years ago—perhaps a little frailer. His mind is intact. Ettie says he is much weaker. Helen looks after him with tender & noble solicitude. I return tonight home, as I must work all tomorrow. I will send you a Chartwell bulletin of news.

My darling I send you by this only my fondest love. The sense of gratitude in my heart to you for all you give me is unfailing. God bless you sweet pussie.

Always your ever loving husband,

W

[sketch of pig with 10 tons weight on back]

Evan[3] and Dorothy[4] have arrived.

---

reducing the current. It is surely no reason for declaring that electricity is a fluid too dangerous for civilisation to handle. While I hold myself free to study the whole situation anew, I do so under the strong impression that the case for perserverence holds the field. I am quite sure that the genius of a man like Lawrence of Arabia, if Fate untimely had not swept him from the human scene, would in a few months restore the situation, persuade one side to concede and the other to forbear, and lead both races to bathe their hands together in the ever-growing prosperity and culture of their native land.'

[1] Lady Desborough (see page 398, note 1).

[2] Edgar Vincent, 1857–1941. Served in the Coldstream Guards, 1877–82. Financial Adviser to the Egyptian Government, 1883–9. Knighted, 1887 (at the age of thirty). Governor of the Imperial Ottoman Bank, 1889–97. Conservative MP, 1899–1906. Created Baron D'Abernon, 1914. Chairman, Central Control Board (Liquor Traffic), 1915–20. Mission to Poland, 1920. Ambassador to Berlin, 1920–6. Created Viscount, 1926. Chairman, Medical Research Council, 1929–33. In 1931 he published an account of the battle of Warsaw, *The Eighteenth Decisive Battle of the World*. In 1890 he married Lady Helen Venetia Duncombe, daughter of the 1st Earl of Feversham.

[3] Evan Edward Charteris, 1864–1940, 6th son of the 10th Earl of Wemyss. Educated at Eton. Staff Captain, Royal Flying Corps, 1916; General Staff Officer, Grade 3, Tank Corps, 1916–18. King's Counsel, 1919. Knighted, 1932. A Trustee of the National Gallery, 1932–9. Chairman of the Tate Gallery, 1934–40. His nephew Ivo Alan, 2nd Lieutenant, Grenadier Guards, was killed in action in France on 17 October 1915; his nephew Hugo was killed in action in Egypt on 23 April 1916.

[4] Lady Dorothy Margaret Browne, 1888–1961. Elder daughter of the 5th Earl of Kenmare. In 1914 she married Lord Edward Arthur Grosvenor, youngest son of the 1st Duke of Westminster. Lord Edward died in 1929. In 1930 she married the Hon. Sir Evan Charteris K.C. Her brother, Lieutenant Maurice Henry Dermot Browne, Coldstream Guards, was killed in action on 29 September 1915, aged 21.

Violet Pearman to Commander Owen

(*Churchill papers: 8/547*)

26 July 1937

Dear Cmdr Owen,

Herewith Mr Churchill asks me to send a copy of The Battle of the Nile which he has written for Harraps as the caption for a jig-saw puzzle which they are doing for school children on educational lines. The matter has had to be condensed into a small space. Mr Churchill wonders if you would let him have your comments upon the wording, and if it is quite correct. As the matter is urgent, would you be very kind and reply at once.[1]

Winston S. Churchill to Captain Fitzroy[2]

(*Churchill papers: 2/302*)

26 July 1937

I will, with your permission, ask you tomorrow to give some general guidance about the scope of discussion on the salary of the Minister for Co-Ordination of Defence. I conceive that this Minister's functions are such that any general question affecting Defence is in order, especially if it should concern more than one arm of the service. The Minister has been formally constituted the Prime Minister's deputy in presiding over the Committee of Imperial Defence. He also presides over the meetings of the three Chiefs of Staff.

The general index of the Session 1935–6, Vol 316, pages 370–373 inclusive for instance, sets out a numerous range and multiplicity of questions upon which the Minister has spoken or answered Questions. As a key example of his dealing with large strategic issues may I draw your attention to his answer to Mr Mander[3] on April 8, 1936 (Vol 310, cols 2785–6) upon 'whether or not a military expeditionary force should form part of the British contribution to collective security' etc.

---

[1] A further jig-saw puzzle caption for Rorke's Drift, was sent by Brigadier-General Sir James Edmonds. Both the Battle of the Nile and Rorke's Drift notes were prepared for Churchill by F. W. Deakin, and then re-drafted by Churchill himself. Churchill also prepared captions for the battles of Blenheim and Jutland. The jig-saw puzzles were published by John Waddington Ltd.

[2] The Speaker of the House of Commons (see page 106, note 2).

[3] Geoffrey Le Mesurier Mander, 1882–1962. Educated at Harrow and Trinity College, Cambridge. Liberal MP for East Wolverhampton, 1929–45. Parliamentary Private Secretary to Sir Archibald Sinclair (Secretary of State for Air), 1942–5. Knighted, 1945.

Also his speech on May 21, 1936 (Vol 312, cols 1509 et seq). In his speech it was both assumed by the House and accepted by the Minister that the discussion should cover the whole field of Defence policy. See particularly Cols 1511 and 1512. Also his remarks about the strategic functions of the Army, Cols 1512 and 1513.

A case which seems particularly in point is covered by the Question about the military conditions around the fortress of Singapore, found in Vol 310, col 2956–7 where Commander Fletcher[1] asked the Minister if any decision had been formed about cutting a canal through the isthmus of Kra at Singapore, and its effect upon the strategic questions involved in the Singapore base. In this case the Minister accepted fully the responsibility of replying and did so at length.

I only venture to cite these instances out of a number which could be found with more diligence if it were necessary. I will therefore venture to ask your ruling to submit these instances to you after Questions tomorrow. I shall of course put my Questions on the general basis of the topics confided to the Minister's responsibility as I am well aware that this particular debate is in Committee and therefore within the scope of the Chairman of Committees. I therefore feel I may ask for a ruling on the general principle.

If, sir, you would prefer that the issue shd be put to the Chairman of Committees, I shd of course do so. But the issue seems to be of wider character than one governed by a particular occasion. I remain,

Winston S. Churchill to Leslie Hore-Belisha

(*Churchill papers: 2/314*)

26 July 1937

I hope you will be able to give us more information on Tuesday about the guns around Gibraltar and the Straits. There was no time to discuss the matter on the last occasion, but there should be plenty on Tuesday. Hundreds of people, possibly thousands, have seen these guns and howitzers in transit to their various batteries. Some were a fortnight on the road, and in the early days, anybody could enquire about them. Latterly, while they were being

---

[1] Reginald Thomas Herbert Fletcher, 1885–1961. Joined the Royal Navy, 1899; on active service, 1914–19. Retired with the rank of Lieutenant-Commander. Liberal MP for Basingstoke, 1923–4. Unsuccessful Liberal candidate for Tavistock at a by-election in 1928. Labour MP for Nuneaton, 1935–42. Parliamentary Private Secretary to the First Lord of the Admiralty, 1940–1. Created Baron Winster, 1942. Minister of Aviation, 1945–6. Privy Councillor, 1945.

placed on their concrete platforms, very strict cordons have been maintained around the area.

If nothing is said by the Government beyond Lord Cranborne's speech last Monday, the only result will be the kind of exaggeration which appears in the News Chronicle Chart, which I enclose. (Kindly return.) I hope, therefore, further and better particulars will be given, and I propose to ask for them on Tuesday.

I should have thought you might at least say, for instance if true:—'No primary guns have been mounted which can bombard the dockyard or anchorage of Gibraltar. The medium guns which the Spanish Nationalists have mounted around the Bay of Algeciras, are, of course, inferior to the fortress cannon, and their position is fully explained by the conditions of the Spanish Civil War. There are, however, several batteries which have been mounted further to the west of Gibraltar, or on the opposite African shore. These batteries consist of primary guns. I hope I shall not be pressed to give the exact position of these batteries, or to specify their range and calibre. Sometimes we are told things in a friendly way; sometimes we find them out for ourselves. The House may rest assured that we are thoroughly informed about these guns. They constitute a menace to the free navigation of the Straits, that is to say, the maximum discharges from the two sides would overlap each other, and vessels passing through the Straits might have to run the gauntlet of their fire. We cannot regard this in any way as a light or negligible matter. It cannot be considered by itself. It must be considered in relation to other manifestations of a similar character which have recently appeared, not only in various parts of the Mediterranean, but also in the Red Sea.'

Violet Pearman to Winston S. Churchill

(*Churchill papers: 1/299*)

28 July 1937   Chartwell

General Spears says that Dr Bruning[1] will be delighted to come to luncheon here on the 4th. . . .

---

[1] Heinrich Brüning, 1885–1970. Fought in the First World War, winning the Iron Cross second and first class. Served in the Prussian Ministry of Health, 1919–21. Adviser to the German Christian Trade Union Movement, 1922–9. Centre Party Member of the Reichstag, 1924–33. Chancellor of the Reich, March 1930 to June 1932 (when he was succeeded by von Papen). Emigrated to the United States, 1934. Research Fellow, Queen's College, Oxford, 1937–9. Professor of Government, Harvard University, 1939–52. Returned to Germany as Professor of Political Science, University of Cologne, 1951–5. Died in the United States.

Winston S. Churchill to Brigadier Pakenham-Walsh

(Churchill papers: 8/547)

30 July 1937

My dear Pakenham-Walsh,

Mrs Pearman is sending you by post some of the chapters which, in very provisional form, have been put into proof. You will see that I have left Malplaquet and Douay behind for the present while clearing up the political situation. I think it would be a help to me now if I could have as soon as possible your campaign of 1711. I do not think you have sent me this yet. The passing of the lines and the siege of Bouchain require very careful study. The capture of this great fortress in the presence of a relieving army larger than Marlborough's, is often spoken of as the finest example of his art. It is all the more remarkable when one remembers how the army was honeycombed with political intrigue, how his power had sunk to the lowest ebb, and he was serving as a General only, the government of bitter political opponents.

Winston S. Churchill: Statement to the Press Association

(Churchill papers: 9/126)

30 July 1937
5.30 pm

When asked his opinion about the Government decision on the Fleet Air Arm, Mr Churchill said 'I think a wise decision has been reached. It was always useless to try to divide the Services on the basis of whether aircraft used wheels or floats or boats. It is not a question to be settled according to the under-carriages. The Admiralty have a right to the full integral control of all the aircraft and personnel which start from ships of war or aircraft carriers. This is essential to the operation of British ships of war whether in squadrons or fleets. It implies not only operational control but the right to administer and develop the service in their own way and with their own Naval personnel. It carries with it the control by the Admiralty of such bases and training schools on shore as are found in practice to be necessary for the highest development of the Fleet Air Arm. This the Government have fully conceded.

However there is no reason why the preliminary training in the art of flying by Naval officers destined for the Fleet Air Arm should not be conducted at the Central Flying School, or in some other Air Ministry establishment. As soon as they have received this general training they should go to the specialised Naval schools to learn the particular work of the Fleet. Above all it is important that the Naval pilots should go back to the Navy after their service as airmen, thus securing their permanent career. The Navy will now be able to bring a strong new stream of high-class personnel to reinforce the British air strength. So much for the Admiralty.

On the other hand the Air Ministry is entitled to the full control of all major air operations. This can only be achieved through their administration of all squadrons of aircraft starting from the shore, irrespective of whether they are flying boats or on wheels. This also is fully provided for by the Government decision. I believe the Air Ministry will gain just as much as the Admiralty by the new arrangements.

It is a great pity that this decision was not taken eighteen months ago. I have been pressing for it all this time. There really is no excuse for it not having been settled earlier. Now that at last a sound decision has been made, we must have an absolute stoppage to this controversy, for a good many years to come. Both the Admiralty and the Air Ministry have agreed and they must loyally work together to execute the scheme in the smoothest and most efficient manner. I am sure they will do this. The times are much too dangerous for any further jealousies or bickerings. Sir Thomas Inskip is to be cordially congratulated on the outcome.[1]

[1] On 19 January 1940 Churchill (then First Lord of the Admiralty) wrote to Admiral Pound, the First Sea Lord: 'I have always been a strong advocate of the FAA, in fact I drafted for Sir T. Inskip the compromise decision to which he eventually came in 1938' (*Admiralty papers: 205/31*).

August 1937

Winston S. Churchill to Clementine Churchill
(*Spencer-Churchill papers*)

3 August 1937   Chartwell

My darling one,

Tomorrow we have a luncheon party: E. L. Spears wife & son,[1] 'Prof',
Brüning the banished German Prime Minister, Treviranus[2] the banished
Trade Minister, Hawkey, Dinah[3] and another constituent! What a pot
pourri! But I expect it will go all right.

I was worried by what you said about yr eyes, & if you are near Vienna
you shd certainly go & see their best man. If not there are good men in
England. Perhaps it is the waters that have affected you. Anyhow we must
clear it up, so that you can jump over the moon with yr eyes open—Darling!

Here all goes peacefully. I am working night & day and the progress on
M is enormous—I have done nearly 20,000 words this week alone. Deakin
arrives this evening so the pace will not slacken.

Julian[4] is vy sweet, but you will have to come back by the 14th if you want
to see him.

The fish pool has now become quite clear in a mysterious way & I do not
doubt that it will eventually be crystal. Four Herons, the old 2 & 2 children,

---

[1] Michael Spears, 1919–1969. Educated at Eton. A victim of osteomyelitis at school. A
pupil of A. J. P. Taylor at Magdalen College, Oxford, 1939–40. Progressively incapacitated
by his disease, he was disabled by a stroke, 1956.

[2] Gottfried Reinhold Treviranus, 1891–1971. Served in the Imperial German Navy,
1909–18; commanded a destroyer during the First World War. Retired with the rank of
Lieutenant-Commander, 1918. Farmer, 1919–21; Director of the Lippe Agricultural Board,
1921–8. Nationalist Member of the Reichstag, 1924–33; Leader of the People's Conservative
Party, 1929–34. Minister of Communications, and Minister without Portfolio, in the Brüning
Cabinet, 1930–2. He evaded his Nazi would-be executioners, June 1934, and escaped to
England. Deprived of his German citizenship, 1938. Emigrated to Canada, 1939. Returned
to Germany, 1948. Living in Switzerland, 1964.

[3] Dinah Pratt, Sir James Hawkey's daughter, and herself an active constituency worker
on Churchill's behalf.

[4] Julian Sandys, Churchill's first grandchild (see page 350, note 2).

were watching our fish in the middle lake morosely yesterday. We told them to move on: & they did. Everything here goes quietly & peacefully, I am certainly not wasting the days.

We need not settle plans for going abroad till you come back.

With fondest love my sweet Clemmie

Always yr loving husband,
W

[sketch of pig with 10 ton weight on his head]
doing it on his head

Winston S. Churchill to Heinrich Brüning

(*Churchill papers: 8/548*)

4 August 1937

In my new book there are these three articles upon Hitler, Hindenburg,[1] and the ex-Kaiser.[2] I should be grateful to you if you have the time to glance through them, and entirely of course for my private information, make any comments which occur.[3] The Hitler article has been softened a good deal since it first appeared in The Strand Magazine.

It was very agreeable to see you today.

[1] Paul von Beneckendorff und Hindenburg, 1847–1934. 2nd Lieutenant, 1866. Fought in the Austro-Prussian and Franco-Prussian wars of 1866 and 1870–1. Retired from the Army with the rank of General, 1911. Recalled, 1914. Commander-in-Chief, 7th Army, 1914. In August 1914 he moved German troops rapidly by rail from Gumbinnen, where they had been defeated by the Russians, to Tannenberg, where they were victorious. Marshal and Commander-in-Chief of all German Forces in the East, 1915. Chief of the General Staff, 1916–18. President of the Reich, 1925–34.

[2] Wilhelm II, 1859–1941. A grandson of Queen Victoria, and first cousin of King George V. Succeeded his father as German Emperor in 1888. Known to the British as 'Kaiser Bill'. Abdicated, November 1918. In exile in Holland from 1918 until his death. While in exile he published his *Memoirs 1878–1918* (translated into English in 1922).

[3] For Brüning's comments, see pages 752–5.

Mahadeo Desai[1] to G. D. Birla

(*Birla papers*)

4 August 1937

What you say about Churchill is most interesting. When he uttered that sentence about violence, and Indians murdering Englishmen why did you not remind him of his article in which he threatened us with dread consequences if we refused to accept office? The cruel word that he used about Bapu's statement still smarts in my memory. Do you know the word? He described those statements as 'Gandhi's barbed-wire blandishments'. But that is Churchill all over. At the time of the Irish settlement it was he who invited Michael Collins[2] to his place and laughed and joked with him and told him that whereas the British Government had set a price of 1,000 pounds on his (Collins') head, the Boers had set a price of only 10 pounds[3] on his (ie Churchill's) head. I am quite sure his greetings to Bapu[4] are perfectly genuine. And you must convey Bapu's thanks to him. In 1931 he declined to

---

[1] Mahadeo Haribhai Desai, 1892–1942. Born in the Surat District, son of a school teacher, of the Anavil Brahmin caste, one of the leading communities in the district. Educated at the Elphinstone College, Bombay, 1907–10; at Law College, Bombay, 1910–13. Translated Lord Morley's *On Compromise* into Gujarati, 1914. Worked in a Cooperative Bank, 1914–17 (but left on account of his distaste for the irregularities practised there, and the amount of travelling involved). First met Gandhi on 31 August 1917; and served thereafter as Gandhi's secretary. Sent by Gandhi to Allahabad to edit the periodical, the *Independent*; whereupon he was arrested and imprisoned. Released from prison, 1923. Supervised the editorial work of *Navjivan*, 1923–4. Author of *With Gandhi in Ceylon*, 1928; *Eclipse of Faith*, 1929, and several other works. Accompanied Gandhi to London for the Round Table Conference, 1931. Author of many newspaper articles attacking untouchability, and urging Hindu–Muslim unity. On 10 August 1942 *The Times* reported the arrest on the previous day of Gandhi, Mahadeo Desai and Miraben, and their imprisonment in Poona, following a Government of India declaration that the Congress Party bodies which they represented were illegal. A week later, on 17 August 1942, *The Times* reported: 'Mahadeo Desai, the principal secretary to Mr Gandhi, which whom he was under detention near Poona, died suddenly yesterday of heart failure.' Mahadeo Desai was described by *The Times* as 'one of the few men who thoroughly understood and interpreted Mr Gandhi's philosophy'. His diary was published after his death, in eight volumes. Gandhi said of him: 'I wonder if half a dozen secretaries would do the work which Mahadeo did alone'.

[2] Michael Collins, 1890–1922. Born in County Cork, the son of a Catholic farmer. Worked at first as a Post Office employee, then as a bank clerk in London, 1906–16. Took part in the Easter rebellion in Dublin, 1916. Imprisoned for eight months, 1916. A leader of the Sinn Fein movement, and Adjutant-General of the Irish Republican Army, 1917–18. Imprisoned for a second time, 1918. Minister of Home Affairs, and Finance Minister, in the Sinn Fein Government, 1918–21. One of the Delegates who negotiated the Irish Treaty with Britain, 1921–2. Chairman of the Provisional Free State Government, and Minister of Finance, 1922. Commanded the Irish Free State army against the opponents of the Treaty, June 1922. Ambushed and killed by Irish Irregulars, 22 August 1922.

[3] In fact, £25.

[4] Bapu = Gandhi.

see Bapu but now if he comes to India at Bapu's insistance, I suppose he will ask for the interview himself.

Wing-Commander Anderson to Winston S. Churchill
(Churchill papers: 2/304)

5 August 1937 RAF Hucknall

Dear Mr Churchill,

I spoke last Sunday regarding the retirement of Air Commodore Brock[1] at the early age of 48, and I attach his history taken from 'THE TIMES', dated 5th August, 1937.

In all sincerity I was very impressed by that incident in the life of the Duke of Marlborough which you read, and by your conclusion as to the power of personal example and inspiration. It is just that influence which is so disastrously absent from the Air Force at this moment. We are, as a Service, peculiarly dependent on, and susceptible to, the genuine inspiration of leadership, far more so than either the Navy or the Army, since in War work is mainly done as individuals and not in groups or companies.

I do hope that a real effort will be made to draw from Parliament that the RAF Expansion is permanent; this will give a feeling of security and stability which is so desperately needed to the Service and the Aircraft Industry.

For the next few weeks I may be on sick leave, or in Hospital, as I am most anxious to get really fit, and I attach a copy of a letter giving the cause of the temporary trouble.

I had a long talk with Rowley[2] the other day, and I will bring him along one Sunday.

Violet Pearman to C. C. Wood
(Churchill papers: 8/547)

5 August 1937

Dear Mr Wood,

Herewith a good batch. Pray let me have them back as soon as you can,

[1] Henry Le Marchant Brock, 1889–1964. 2nd Lieutenant, Royal Warwickshire Regiment, 1909; Lieutenant, 1912. Learned to fly, 1913 (Royal Aero Club Certificate No 551). Royal Flying Corps, 1913. On active service in France, Salonica and the Middle East, 1914–17, (DSO, despatches six times); and on the north-west frontier of India, 1930. Air Commodore, 1931. Air Officer Commanding No 22 (Army Co-operation) Group, 1931–6. Air Officer in charge of administration, Bomber Command, 1936–7. Retired List, at his own request, 1 August 1937. Deputy Commandant, Royal Observer Corps, 1938–42.

[2] Wing-Commander Rowley, of the Directorate of Operations and Intelligence, Air Ministry (see page 379, note 1).

as we are working here continuously now on Marlborough and nothing else.
I hope to send you another chapter in two or three days.
It will be sufficient if four sets only of these proofs are sent to me.

Winston S. Churchill to Imre Revesz

(*Churchill papers: 8/561*)

6 August 1937

Dear Dr Revesz,

. . . I may be going on a tour of the Continent in the Autumn in which
case I will get in touch with the papers or the proprietors of the papers who
are taking my articles, and show them a civility.

Winston S. Churchill to Joachim von Ribbentrop

(*Churchill papers: 8/547*)

14 August 1937

I am thinking of sending my literary secretary Mr F. W. Deakin, a Fellow
of Wadham College, Oxford, to Hanover to study the archives there. We
have reason to believe that there must be most interesting reports from Von
Bothmar and other Hanoverian representatives in England covering the
'Marlborough' period, and particularly the years 1709, 1710 and 1711. One
imagines that access is readily given to responsible students and historians to
these documents. It would probably not be necessary for me to trouble you
at all, but for the fact that as Mr Deakin is connected with me, I should
like you to know about the purpose of his visit to Germany and his activities
there. Of course if you could speak a word to help him in his work and contacts, I should be much obliged. He would come over in the last week in
August, and would stay for two or three days.

Sarah Churchill to Winston S. Churchill

(*Churchill papers: 1/299*)

14 August 1937   Chicago

My darling Papa,

We motored out here two days after we landed. We had the most lovely
crossing. Next time you come to America, do try to take the Normandie, it is

really amazing—very comfortable no vibration—marvellous food—and because of the veneration the French have for you, I was sent flowers and chocolates all day long by the Purser, and given an all silver (solid!) plaque with the Normandie on it—in fact they spoilt me so that I think that if you travelled on the boat, they might almost give you the 'Normandie' herself. . . .

Winston S. Churchill to C. C. Wood

(*Churchill papers: 8/547*)

15 August 1937

Dear Mr Wood,

We have had a great week's work, and I send you nearly 20,000 words and over 60 pages in a very mature condition. I should greatly like to have them back, if possible, by the end of the week.

I also send you a rough outline of the present state of the book. You will see that 340 pages are done, and there are still 12 chapters to do. At 5,000 words a chapter this would be 60,000 words; or at 330 to the page, about 180 pages. Say a total of about 520 pages. This with appendages, preliminary matter, etc, should make a volume comparable to the others.

If more material develops, this will be met by cutting or summarising severely some of the correspondence, of which there is too much in the present proofs.

I should like to hear from you that 520 pages of actual text would be all that you would require.

G. D. Birla to Mahadeo Desai

(*Birla papers*)

16 August 1937

About Churchill, he is a politician, pure and simple and I think perhaps his philosophy is to have one policy in public and the other in private. But I tell you that as a man he is full of warmth. There is no vanity about him and he has got a childlike simplicity. He had the honesty to admit to me that when he stood up in favour of the ex-King, he did not know that public opinion was so much against him. I also discussed with him the general position of the monarchy in England and why he was not in the Cabinet. I felt that he is one of the half-dozen persons who rule England and I was impressed with his frankness in private talks. He was very straight in telling me that I should not expect him to write articles in favour of India. He reminded me what politics were.

C. W. Baxter:[1] *Foreign Office minute*

(Foreign Office papers: 371/20740)

21 August 1937

Herr von Selzam[2] of the German Embassy called yesterday evening to draw attention to Mr Winston Churchill's article in the 'Evening Standard' entitled 'A Plain Word to the Nazis'. He referred to a recent conversation between Herr Woermann[3] and Mr Strang[4] in which it had been agreed that it would be unfortunate if the alleged activities of Nazi organizations in this country should become a major cause of controversy in the British and German press. Mr Churchill's article seemed to him most unfortunate, and indeed quite unjustified by the facts. For example, it was quite untrue that Nazi Germans living in England were obliged 'to report at frequent intervals to regular centres, where they receive instructions as to . . . what they should do in case of an emergency'. Again, it was monstrous that Mr Churchill should compare the Nazi organizations in this country with Communist organizations, since the members of the Nazi organizations, unlike the

---

[1] Charles William Baxter, 1895–1969. Educated at Charterhouse and Trinity College, Cambridge. On active service, 1914–18 (Military Cross). Third Secretary, Diplomatic Service, 1919. Served in Teheran, 1919–22. Second Secretary, 1920. Transferred to the Foreign Office, 1922. First Secretary, 1928. Transferred to Berlin, 1932. Returned to the Foreign Office, 1933; Acting Counsellor, 1938. British Minister to Iceland, 1947–50.

[2] Eduard von Selzam, 1897–1980. Born in Darmstadt. A law student, and Doctor of Laws (1921). Entered the German Foreign Ministry in the Department of Foreign Trade, Bremen, 1921. Served in Washington, 1925; in the Press Department, Berlin, 1928 and in the Consulate-General, Calcutta, 1931–4. Counsellor of Embassy, London, January 1937 to September 1939; in the Hague, September 1939 to July 1940; in Bern, 1940–2. Served in the Trade Department, Berlin, 1942–4. Retired, 1944. Resident in the United States since 1945, he died in Charlottesville, Virginia, in November 1980.

[3] Ernst Woermann, German diplomat. Minister First Class in Great Britain, 1937–8; Head of the Political Department of the Foreign Ministry, 1938–43; Ambassador to China, 1943–5.

[4] William Strang, 1893–1978. Educated, University College, London, and the Sorbonne. On active service, 1914–18. Entered Foreign Office, 1919; Counsellor of Embassy, Moscow, 1930; Mission to Moscow, 1939; Assistant Under-Secretary of State, Foreign Office, 1939–43. Knighted, 1943. UK Representative, European Advisory Commission, 1943–5. Political Adviser, British Forces of Occupation, Germany, 1945–7. Permanent Under-Secretary, German Section, Foreign Office, 1947–9; Permanent Under-Secretary of State, Foreign Office, 1949–53. Created Baron, 1954.

Communists, had definite instructions not to intervene in any way in the internal affairs of the country whose guests they were; Herr von Selzam drew attention to the ten rules on page 11 of the Party Handbook recently communicated to Mr Strang. The article would certainly be ill received in Berlin, and the last paragraph, in which the German Government were adjured in the interests of good relations to 'meet our reasonable desires' as regards these organizations, would be regarded as merely sarcastic. Herr von Selzam feared that the article would have further repercussions, if only because other British papers would take the matter up, whereupon the German press would also be bound to take the matter up, and we should have a serious Anglo-German press controversy with its inevitable effects upon Anglo-German relations. He wondered whether the Foreign Office could take some action to prevent this undesirable press campaign from developing.

I replied that I agreed that the matter would very likely be taken up by other papers in this country, but that I did not think that the Foreign Office could do anything to prevent a subject of this kind being discussed in the press. Herr von Selzam would be aware that Mr Churchill, who was not a member of the Government, had held strong views on this subject for some time, and had made them clear in Parliament. He obviously could not be prevented from also stating them in the press. As for what Herr von Selzam had said about the likelihood of a counter campaign in the German press, I very much hoped the German Embassy in London would use its influence to prevent such a development.[1]

Winston S. Churchill to Anthony Eden
(Churchill papers: 2/313)

23 August 1937

I told you I had some idea of paying a visit to Yugo-Slavia at the end of September. Some of my friends in this 'focus' of Peace and Freedom—of which you may have heard mention—are anxious that I should do so, and invitations are being sent from that country through the medium of Dr Mazuranic,[2] I believe with the concurrence of the Government. However I

---

[1] On 26 August 1937 Anthony Eden minuted: 'Certainly we can do nothing to stop Mr Churchill, with whose point of view I have personally a considerable measure of sympathy.'

[2] Želimir Mažuranić, 1882–1941. Grandson of the poet and politician Ivan Mažuranić (1814–1890), son of the legal historian Vladimir Mažuranić (1845–1928). One of the best known barristers-at-law in inter-war Yugoslavia. Minister of Trade, January 1929 to Sep-

should certainly not go, except with your approval, and under the auspices of the British Embassy. Vansittart, who has been consulted, seems to think it would be a very good thing; that I should do no harm, and might do good.[1] Clemmie would come with me, and I should take my paintbox and spend perhaps ten days in the country, primarily for pleasure and sightseeing. But of course I should no doubt receive visits from the leaders of the different parties there, and would very likely make some statement when I leave, either in public, or to the Press. You know my general line, so I need not trouble you with it.

Our Minister at Belgrade[2] is coming to lunch with me on Tuesday, as Vansittart suggested, and I am going to discuss with him the situation in Yugo-Slavia—which seems hectic—before making up my mind finally. But I need not say that I shall be guided by you.

---

tember 1931. Acting Foreign Minister for a short time in 1931. Subsequently President of the Yugoslav Senate. Head of the State Department for Elections, 1938. Committed suicide, 6 July 1941. A correspondent writes: 'He left a letter, which the authorities of the Independent State of Croatia immediately destroyed. It was only seen by a relative of his who was the first to enter his home. In this letter he said that he did not wish to live to see the end of the war, which would be won either by the Germans or by the Soviets. In the first case, there would be no more Yugoslavia and his country Croatia would continue to be ruled by the Ustashis. Neither as a Yugoslav nor as a Croat did he want to live to see that. In the second case, if the war were won by the Soviets, Yugoslavia would be restored, but it would be ruled by other totalitarians, the communists. Neither as a democrat nor as a human being did he want to live to see that. He had forseen the future and cut his throat with a razor' (*letter to the author, 8 January 1982*). His brother Božidar Mažuranić, a Commander in the Royal Yugolav Navy, had lost a leg while saving the lives of the Allied Military Mission in Budapest in 1920, was later ADC to King Alexander, was in London during the Second World War, and died in exile in Argentina in 1952.

[1] In formally inviting Churchill to visit Yugoslavia, Mažuranić wrote (from Zagreb, on 25 August 1937): 'We know from your writings and speeches how convinced a supporter you are of democratic principles and of the cause of freedom and peace. A visit from you might therefore be of the greatest service to our people and a contribution of inestimable value to the cause of peace in South Eastern Europe. At the same time I feel sure that you would gain from your visit fuller knowledge of Yugoslavia and a feeling of certainly that our people are animated by ideals not very different from those of Great Britain and the British Commonwealth of Nations. I trust you may give this invitation your favourable consideration and to let our people have the honour and the pleasure as receiving you as the bringer of message of goodwill from Britain to Yugoslavia.'

[2] Ronald Hugh Campbell, 1883–1953. Entered the Foreign Office in 1907. Private Secretary to Lord Carnock, 1913–16; to Lord Hardinge of Penshurst, 1916–19 and to Lord Curzon, 1919–20. British Minister in Paris, 1929–35; at Belgrade, 1935–9. Knighted, 1936. Ambassador to France, 1939–40; to Portugal, 1940–5.

Anthony Eden to Winston S. Churchill
(*Churchill papers: 2/313*)

25 August 1937   Foreign Office

My dear Winston,

Very many thanks for your letter of the 23rd August. I much appreciated your consulting me about your proposed visit to Yugoslavia at the end of September. I need hardly say that I see no objection at all to your proposed visit, quite the contrary. I am sure it would be a very good thing, and frankly envy you the trip and the holiday, for I hope it will be the latter for you as well as an interesting experience.

I have returned to a world more than ever troubled, and wonder more & more how long the British Empire can continue like a Noah's ark on the waves of strife. . . .

All good wishes again for the journey.[1]

Yours ever,
Anthony Eden

Winston S. Churchill to J. J. Astor
(*Churchill papers: 1/299*)

28 August 1937

I am sending round to Hever[2] today the painting table I ordered for you which I hope you will accept as the gateway to a new amusement.

These tables are made by a little man in Norfolk whom Lavery put me in touch with. They have the convenience that they can be easily carried in the one hand with everything inside, including if necessary two wet paintings. It can be used for water colours equally and the attachment with the elastic is intended for this purpose. I have added a small selection of paints and brushes so that you can start on the first Sunday that the grouse allow.

'La peinture a l'huile est bien difficile,
     Mais c'est beaucoup plus beau que la peinture a l'eau.'
For my own part I think the technique is less difficult and far more satisfactory.

Many thanks for your invitation for December 18th. If we are in England at that time we should like very much to come and stay with you for your shoot.

---

[1] In the event, Churchill did not travel to Yugoslavia, see pages 761–2.
[2] Hever Castle, Kent, the home of J. J. Astor (created Baron Astor of Hever in 1956), five miles south east of Chartwell.

Leslie Hore-Belisha to Clementine Churchill

(*Churchill papers: 1/299*)

28 August 1937   War Office

My dear Mrs Churchill,

Although the recollection of my pleasant visit to Chartwell has not been absent from my thoughts, I suddenly remembered that I had not written to thank you. Do forgive me for this. The omission is all the greater on my part because I was, as a bachelor, so wistfully impressed by the happiness of your home. You have all my good wishes for the perpetual lasting of your happiness. Please apologize to your daughter for my failure on this occasion either to play tennis or swim. Another delinquency of mine was to find that I had misappropriated that wonderful eye-lotion which Winston lent me!

Leslie Hore-Belisha

Heinrich Brüning to Winston S. Churchill

(*Churchill papers: 2/307*)

28 August 1937

I do not know if I can say very much about your article: 'Hitler and his Choice'. I admire very much your description of the feelings of the German people in these fourteen years after the War and the characteristics of the British policy at that time.

I would like to add that in all the years after the War beginning from 1919 a few former General Staff Officers have worked very hard and persistently for rearmament of the German nation. The best of them are scarcely known to the outside world. They were no longer on active service as in spite of their political loyalty they could not take the Oath on the new Constitution. Like my old friend Willisen[1] they were in business but spent ten hours of the day or night for the Army. They had plans ready for every possibility but they were never carried away by the *rage du nombre*. They never wanted to re-introduce the two years' service. They were working somewhat on the model of the Swiss military system. For that reason they wanted always to be in close touch with the Trade Unions, slowly persuading them that democracy

---

[1] Freiherr von Willisen. A pupil of General Gröner. In charge of the German Government's four Schools of Aviation (outlawed in 1919 by the Treaty of Versailles), 1926–33. Described by Sir John Wheeler-Bennett (*The Nemesis of Power*, 1953) as 'the "mystery man" of the Reichswehr, and regarded by many, in contradistinction to von Schleicher, as its "*good* secret genius".' Refused to be a 'competitor' to Schleicher for the Chancellorship, 1932.

could only be saved in Germany if the workmen like in Switzerland were prepared to fight for it.

Although, for instance, Willisen was running from his business office the four Schools of Aviation which we had in Germany since 1926 he supported me to ask at the Disarmament Conference for the abolition of bombing aeroplanes. It was only necessary to talk with him ¼-hour to convince him that a big re-armament of Germany in the air would automatically lead to a new military alliance between England and France.

I may say that no actual preparations were made for re-armament during the time I was in office; plans were only made for every eventuality, and a skeleton organisation was built up for a militia system on the Swiss model, but that was confined upon my wish to the provinces east of the Elbe. We had only samples of weapons with which we experimented. The War Ministry resisted a long time against the enormous increase of the Army and the Air Fleet which were proposed by Hitler for prestige sake. Only when the War Ministry saw that in the summer and autumn of 1933 nickel and other metals necessary for re-armament were delivered to Germany by foreign nations in enormous quantities on a credit basis did they give in as they came to the conclusion that the commercial point of view in other nations was quite dominant over purely military reasons. There is no doubt about it that the heavy steel industries on the Continent were very much afraid of disarmament. After I had made the German propositions for disarmament in April 1932 in the Villa of Mr Stimson,[1] two German industrialists coming back from the Meeting of European Steel Industrialists came to see me and told me how silly we were to make such modest demands.

The real rise of Hitler only started in 1929 when the German big industries and other people refused to pay money any longer for a lot of patriotic organisations which, so far, had done all the work for German *risorgimento*. These people were persuaded that all the other organisations had too advanced social ideas. They were satisfied that only Hitler would do away radically with all rights of the workmen; therefore, in stopping their subsidies to all others they forced them to join Hitler's organisation. This is, of course, the normal beginning of Fascism everywhere.

Hitler kept his own organisation away from any collaboration with the army. He refused to join any defence preparations for the Eastern Provinces

---

[1] Henry Lewis Stimson, 1867–1950. A lawyer, and a Republican. Secretary of War, 1911–13. On active service in France, 1918, as a Colonel in the Field Artillery, United States Expeditionary Force. Personal Representative of President Coolidge in the Nicaragua fighting of 1927 (when he arranged a settlement). Governor of the Philippines, 1928–9. Secretary of State, 1929–33. Secretary of War, June 1940 to September 1945. In 1948 he published his memoirs, *On Active Service*.

against an attack by Poland. He was the only leader of a patriotic organisation who also refused to join the passive resistance in the Ruhr. He refused to
have any responsibility whatsoever or any collaboration with any other Party
for the most urgent task of the nation as he was only interested in keeping his
force prepared for the internal struggle. This was all very well known to President Hindenburg. The reason why he detested Hitler and in his heart never
ceased to detest him was that he was quite aware of the fact that Hitler's
policy was concentrated only upon destroying all those national organisations
and trade unions which had fought so bravely and suffered so heavily in
Upper Silesia and in the fight against the French in the Ruhr district and the
Separatists in the Rhineland.

But of course the years of the ascendency of Hitler are full of complexities.
In German books published about these years the policy of Hitler is either
extolled or ridiculed. Most of the people as far as they were known to the
public which were killed on 30th June 1934 or disappeared elsewhere, or
living in exile, were a cause of great fear to Hitler. He wanted to get rid of
them as witnesses of a very dark period in his life. Many of the former Separatists and the Communist leaders, on the other hand, are in a high position
at present in the Nazi Party. Only slowly the German nation is realizing this
fact, but it does not make a very great impression upon the rank and file of
the Army. For these people to whom, of course, types like General von
Fritsch[1] do not belong, the essential thing is that Germany has again an
Army of 800,000 men. Hitler succeeded in getting hold of Blomberg and other
Army Officers already in 1932 after I had made my statements at the Conference in Mr Stimson's House in April 1932 because he promised them to
re-introduce a big front line Army instead of the militia proposed by Hammerstein[2] and Willisen. I suppose it will be always amazing for later his-

[1] Werner, Baron von Fritsch, 1880–1939. Born in the Rhineland. Served as a staff Captain,
4th German Army, 1914–17; Major, 1917. An expert in the use of aeroplanes in warfare.
After the Versailles Treaty he became a member of a secret German general staff, which
immediately began the training of a new army. Commander-in-Chief of the German Army
February 1934–February 1938; 'framed' by the Gestapo in February 1938, and deprived
of his post. For several years he had been an opponent of Hitler's policies, not believing that
the German Army was strong enough to fight Britain and France in 1938, opposing the
annexation of Austria, and opposing Nazi propaganda inside the German Army. Acquitted by
the 'Court of Honour' on all charges, August 1939. His death was reported by the official
German news agency as having taken place while serving with the German Army on 22
September 1939, near Warsaw, and gave rise to much speculation in the western Press; so
much so that *The Times* headlined his obituary: 'Mysterious death in German Army'.

[2] Kurt von Hammerstein-Equord, 1878–1943. Entered the German Army, 1898; Captain,
General Staff, 1913; Major, 1914; General, 1930. Chief of Staff of the German Army,
1930–4. Commanded Army Group A, based on Cologne, 1939. An outspoken opponent
of the Nazis, from 1938 until his death he was a leading member of the anti-Hitler circle;
in September 1939 he had hoped to entice Hitler to Cologne in order to arrest him. After his
death his widow and daughter were confined in Buchenwald Concentration Camp.

torians that the European Powers did not see this fact and not realise its importance.

It has been a very great pleasure for me to dictate these few remarks to which your admirable articles give rise. . . .[1]

Winston S. Churchill to 'Colliers' magazine: telegram

(*Churchill papers: 8/576*)

30 August 1937

The lamentable events now taking place in the Far East[2] bring this question into the arena of practical and current politics. The United States like Great Britain has enormous interests commercial, moral and cultural in China. These interests have been built up over several generations. The construction by Japan of a modern Navy has during the last twenty years completely transformed the position in the Yellow Sea and upon the Asiatic side of the Pacific Ocean. Unless at some future date the position in Europe is so secure and the feeling in the United States is so strong that joint Anglo-American action with a very serious purpose behind it becomes possible, we must expect in common with the other European nations to suffer a ceaseless encroachment upon our interests.

Japan is in the hands of leaders who are themselves controlled under pain of imminent death by a military secret society, whose ideas are far removed from modern conceptions. The remorseless conquest and subjugation of parts of China by Japan, will be driven forward by these primordial forces. The spectacle will not be pleasant to witness nor the experience agreeable to endure. Nevertheless it is not likely that the present renewed

---

[1] Churchill replied to Brüning on 4 September 1937: 'I have to thank Your Excellency most sincerely for the great pains you have taken in reading my essays, and for the most interesting and informing letter which you have written me upon them. I wish indeed it had been possible to delay the publication sufficiently long enough to enable me to incorporate these ideas, or some of them, in the text. However I found myself compelled to go to press. None the less I greatly value the document you have sent me and your courtesy in writing it. Perhaps you will give me an opportunity of seeing you again (*Churchill papers: 8/548*).

[2] At the beginning of August 1937 full-scale fighting had broken out between China and Japan, with concerted Japanese military and air attacks on Peking, Tientsin and Shanghai. On August 9 the Japanese seized Peking. On August 17, as the fighting intensified, Chinese aeroplanes had mistakenly killed 1,700 civilians in Shanghai, including 3 Americans. As a result of this incident, Roosevelt had ordered an additional 1,200 United States marines to China, to reinforce the 2,300 American troops already there, charged with the task of protecting US nationals. In the last week of August, the Japanese Government announced a naval blockade of the China coast (Shanghai fell to the Japanese on November 9, Nanking on December 13).

Japanese inroad upon China will lead to a world conflagration. On the contrary the fact that Japan finds the moment opportune to expand her energies and entangle her troops in China, looks as if her military men do not expect a major war this year. The great danger to the world at the present time still lies, not in the Far East, not in the quarrels of the yellow peoples, but in the heart of Christendom and Europe.

September 1937

Group-Captain Lachlan MacLean to Professor Lindemann

(*Churchill papers: 2/304*)

1 September 1937   RAF Station
                                                              Mildenhall

Dear Professor Lindemann

I am afraid when we met at Chartwell I did not realize who you were, & it was only when we were in the car, going away, that Anderson told me your name.

I understand that you are not happy about the 'times of flight & trajectory tables' which I attached to that air fighting paper of mine. Actually those figures were worked out for me by Vickers & the explanation is on the attached paper.

The object of the figures, in fact the object of the whole paper, was to stimulate the Air Ministry to sufficient interest to investigate that aspect of a vitally important problem, & to produce some ballistic tables of their own, applicable to velocities of 3,000 fs & over—information which was not in possession of the Air Ministry, & which was of vital importance.

I have had an almost childish reply about my parachute cum cable bomb & should very much like an opportunity of discussing that, amongst other things, with you.

I would particularly like advice on a proposal, whose basis is astronomical navigation by starting & maintaining flight along a known line of latitude & fixing position over towns by means of a heat or some other energy detector.

Yours sincerely,
Lachlan MacLean

Winston S. Churchill to Anthony Eden

(*Churchill papers: 2/302*)

3 September 1937
Secret

Two thoughts occur to me on reading the very anxious news.[1] First, we ought not to make ourselves responsible for ships which are only nominally British, being chartered and manned by Greeks, Spaniards, etc, and run simply to make a profit out of the war. The stakes are now becoming too high for us to take on any burden beyond our own absolute duty.

Secondly, I thought of writing to Chatfield about decoy ships. We started these very early in the War. Why not arrange with Mustapha Kemal to slip a few parties of RN personnel and a modern 4″ gun on to tankers or other merchantmen coming from the Black Sea, with a trapdoor, etc., and let these vessels offer themselves to the pirate submarines, and get a few? This is a dodge which comes off best when it is first tried, but is very good then. I should think Mustapha would like the idea very much, would be a good confederate, and all the better friend thereby. Probably you and the Admiralty have already got the matter in train.

It seems to me very important to find out now whether the Admiralty can really find and kill submarines as they declare so confidently. If the submarine that fired at the 'Havock' was in fact sunk, it ought to be easy with the detector apparatus to spot the mass of metal lying on the Mediterranean floor in this area. If I am not wrong on this technical point, you should surely make certain of this. A great deal of our safety, and of your policy, depends upon whether the Admiralty are right in their belief that they have the submarines beaten.

LG told me to ask you whether you would care to dine with him and me, and one or two men he would get, in the near future. He mentioned Liddell Hart and Wilfred Greene,[2] the Judge; and I suggested George Lloyd (if he is

---

[1] On Friday, 3 September 1937, *The Times* reported a Cabinet decision to send more destroyers to the Western Mediterranean in response to a series of attacks on shipping by unidentified submarines and airplanes. These attacks included a submarine attack on HMS *Havock*, a destroyer, on 31 August 1937, and the sinking of the tanker *Woodford* on September 1. On September 6 the French and British Governments invited twelve Mediterranean and Black Sea Powers and Germany to a conference to consider measures to stop the piracy. Germany and Italy refused to attend the conference, which began at Nyon on September 11, and decided that Britain and France would patrol the Mediterranean with authority to seek out and destroy any vessel attacking a non-Spanish merchant ship 'if such attack is contrary to the rules of international law'.

[2] Wilfred Arthur Greene, 1883–1952. Fellow of All Souls College, Oxford, 1907. Called to the Bar, Inner Temple, 1908. On active service in France, Flanders and Italy, 1914–18 (Major, Military Cross, OBE). King's Counsel, 1922. Standing Counsel to Oxford University, 1926–35. Knighted, 1935. Lord Justice of Appeal, 1935–7. Master of the Rolls, 1937–49. Created Baron, 1941. A Lord of Appeal in Ordinary, 1949–50.

in England). Perhaps even Max might come too. The object would be to discuss the danger in which we stand, and the enormous deterioration in our position all over the world. I have gathered from you that you would be very willing to come, and unless I hear to the contrary, I shall tell Lloyd George, who will write to you. It would be before the middle of this month.

Bernie Baruch was greatly impressed with you, and it is by no means improbable that you may receive an American reaction after he has talked to the President.

Anthony Eden[1] to Winston S. Churchill

(*Churchill papers: 2/302*)

3 September 1937   Foreign Office
Personal & Confidential

My dear Winston,

Thank you very much for your letter of September 3rd. I quite agree with you about the difficulties of the present position.

You will have seen from the papers that we have agreed to the meeting of the Mediterranean Powers at Geneva and we hope to put forward some very definite proposals for discussion at this meeting. The present situation clearly cannot be allowed to continue. In the meantime I am passing on your suggestions to the Admiralty and will take an early opportunity of ascertaining their views on the subject.

I am anxious that the Mediterranean meeting at Geneva should take place early—Friday is the latest date. This means I am afraid that I shall have to start off for Geneva on Thursday and that it will therefore be really impossible for me to dine with you and LG before I leave, much as I should have liked to do. If, however, either you or LG would care to come and discuss matters with me one day early next week, I shall be delighted to see you here.

Yours ever,
Anthony Eden

---

[1] On 31 August 1937 Churchill had given a private luncheon in the Patience Room at the Savoy. Four days later there was a dispute over the bill, for, as Violet Pearman wrote to the Hotel's manager on September 4, 'Mr Churchill himself drank no liqueurs'. The manager replied two days later that 'The "7/6d Liqueurs" is for the Brandy which Mr A. Eden had', while in addition, two of the cigars for which Churchill had been charged 'were taken away by Mr Churchill's son' (*Churchill papers: 1/315*).

Desmond Morton to Violet Pearman

(*Churchill papers: 2/307*)

3 September 1937

Dear Mrs Pearman,

The letter in German is from a man who was for a short time President of the short-lived Rhineland Republic.[1] He is of no political importance, however, and is now, of course, a refugee in France. He dislikes the Nazis, Bolsheviks, English and French apparently more or less equally, and it is a little hard to discover whom he does like.

The letter is quite polite. The first part is critical of certain remarks of Mr Churchill's regarding Nazidom in essence, which Herr Matthes considers were uncalled for. Herr Matthes claims that National Socialist policy is an internal affair of Germany's and nothing to do with Mr Churchill. After all, he suggests, the British cannot throw stones, since they have in their history the story of the concentration camps for Boer prisoners in South Africa, etc. On the other hand, the letter goes on to applaud Mr Churchill's objection to Nazis trying to organise their Party in foreign countries, and says they are doing the same thing everywhere.

I, personally, do not think there is much in the other letter in English. The possibility of German petrol-filling stations for submarines or aircraft being set up in Ireland in the event of war has received attention, but there is no evidence whatever of any such measures being taken now. I would seriously doubt any attempt being made to take such action in Scotland.

Yours sincerely,
D. Morton

Winston S. Churchill to Maxine Elliot: telegram

(*Churchill papers: 1/300*)

4 September 1937

Thinking much of you all and the pool. Alas am tied here by work on Marlborough. If a chance comes later, will propose myself. Love,

Winston

---

[1] J. F. Matthes. President of the Rhineland republic, 1919. A refugee in France from 1933. In 1937 Director of the International Press Bureau, Paris.

Violet Pearman to Randolph Churchill

(Churchill papers: 1/301)

5 September 1937

Dear Mr Randolph,

Mr Churchill sends herewith two cuttings from a German newspaper with the following message:—

'Here are a couple of points which have been shown to me. (A) is remarkable because people in Germany have now to mark themselves on the forms as either (i) members of some of the Christian Churches, or (ii) believers in God, or (iii) atheists. By implication therefore to declare oneself a Protestant or Catholic etc one has to leave unfilled the question "Are you a believer in God?" This will no doubt lead to many people choosing the second and enabling the German statisticians to declare how small are the Protestants, Catholics etc and how large those who believe in God and his prophet the Führer.

(B) Here is a certain speech by Göbbels[1] showing all the people who are against them in Germany and how necessary it is for the SA to be ready to face these hostile forces. This contrasts curiously with the statements of two years ago when almost everybody was supposed to have voted for Hitler.'

Winston S. Churchill to Dr Mažuranić

(Churchill papers: 2/313)

7 September 1937
Private & Confidential

My dear Excellency,

I am deeply indebted to you for the most kind and hospitable invitation which you have extended to me to visit Yugoslavia. I read with deep interest the illuminating memorandum which you enclosed. It has given me an insight of the situation in Yugoslavia which I had hitherto lacked.

I very much regret that I do not feel able at the present time to make a plan for a foreign journey which would involve so many important personages. The situation in the Mediterranean is so uncertain, that I might not

---

[1] Joseph Goebbels, 1897–1945. Rejected for military service because of a deformed foot. Doctor of Philosophy at Heidelberg, 1921. Unsuccessful playwright. Joined the Hitler movement in 1922. Appointed by Hitler to be Gauleiter of Berlin, 1926. Founder of *Der Angriff* ('The Attack'), a Berlin Nazi newspaper, 1927. Elected to the Reichstag, 1929. Propaganda Leader of the Nazi Party, 1929. Minister of Enlightenment and Propaganda, 1933–45. Committed suicide in Berlin, after poisoning his six children, 1 May 1945.

care to leave the country when the time came; or again, Parliament might be called together. In these circumstances, I hope you will allow me to seek another opportunity of visiting your country, towards which I nourish feelings of the warmest regard.

Believe me,

Winston S. Churchill to Sir Ronald Campbell
(Churchill papers: 2/313)

8 September 1937

I have decided not to visit Yugo-Slavia at the present time. Things are so uncertain, and I do not like to make plans ahead involving important people. I trust that you have yourself suffered no inconvenience in consequence of my having examined the project. It was so very kind of you to entertain it in so friendly a spirit.

Winston S. Churchill to Nicholas Murray Butler[1]
(Churchill papers: 2/298)

8 September 1937

Thank you very much indeed for your most kind letter,[2] and I will certainly apprise you should I come to the United States. I fear I shall not be able to leave England this Autumn. Everything is so uncertain, and the powers of evil are so strong.

---

[1] Nicholas Murray Butler, 1862–1947. Born in New Jersey. Educated at Columbia University, New York, receiving his Doctorate of Philosophy in 1884. Assistant in Philosophy at Columbia, 1885–6; Tutor, 1886–9; Professor, 1889–90; Dean, Faculty of Philosophy, 1890–1902. President of Columbia University, 1902–45. President of Barnard College and Teacher's College, 1904–45; of Bard College, 1928–45; of the New York Post-Graduate Medical College, 1931–45. Butler was also president of many charitable foundations and professional associations; Editor of six journals in three languages; and the author of seventeen books on philosophy, politics and informational relations. He received honorary degrees from thirty-eight universities in the United States, Canada and Britain.

[2] Inviting Churchill to lecture at Columbia University, New York, during his forthcoming visit to the United States.

Winston S. Churchill to Lord Swinton

(Churchill papers: 2/298)

9 September 1937

This gentleman[1] lives close by me at Westerham. His father and family are much respected in the district, and he is a neighbour and friend of ours.

He already holds a pilot's certificate. He has a very good knowledge of engineering, radio and television. I should have thought, in these circumstances, he was well suited to receive a commission in an auxiliary squadron, as he has good intelligence, character and qualities, as well as the special aptitudes I have mentioned. He is, however, already 29 years old, and apparently this is beyond the limit.

I wondered whether you had any dispensing power. Certainly many good men have learnt to fly over 30, and distinguished themselves in the War. I thought you would not mind my bringing the case to your notice, for I know how anxious you are to build up the strength of these auxiliary units, and to get men of the right stamp for them.

I visited the Biggin Hill Aerodrome as you authorised, and was much interested by the demonstration which they gave of interception methods. I had not realised the vital important change which has been made in effecting contact with the enemy from the ground, instead of leaving the squadron leader in the air to find them for himself. The officers assured me that provided 'Cuckoo' was accurate, the percentage of interception was extraordinarily high. This has greatly affected my thought upon the subject, and I think of writing a short paper for our Committee upon the tactical aspects, so far as they affect design. When I have finished it, I will send it to you in the first instance.

Winston S. Churchill to Sir Hubert Young[2]

(Churchill papers: 2/298)

10 September 1937

. . . I hope all is going well with you. I always look back with great

---

[1] Cecil Patrick Fox, 1908– . Lived at Mearing, Kent Hatch, near Edenbridge. Although he was not accepted at the Royal Air Force Volunteer Reserve in 1937, he did eventually receive his commission as an Acting Pilot Officer, Technical Branch (Electrical Engineers) in December 1941 (subsequently Pilot Officer, April 1942 and Flying Officer, October 1942).

[2] Hubert Winthrop Young, 1885–1950. 2nd Lieutenant, Royal Artillery, 1904. Transferred to the Indian Army, 1908. Adjutant, 116th Mahrattas, 1913. Assistant Political

pleasure to the days when we worked together—and I think accomplished some things that have lasted.[1] I do not believe this partition scheme for Palestine will work. It would be much better to persevere along the old lines. However we are oppressed by so many larger burdens and dangers that I could wish we had only Palestine and its troubles on our hands.

Winston S. Churchill to Bernard Baruch: telegram

(*Churchill papers: 1/300*)

10 September 1937
11 pm

Grateful your opinion American prices now on basis no major war this year. Regards.

W. Chartwell

Anthony Eden to Winston S. Churchill

(*Churchill papers: 2/302*)

14 September 1937   United Kingdom Delegation
Confidential   to the League of Nations,
                                                      Geneva

My dear Winston,

Thank you so much for your letter which I should have answered long since, but I have had not one moment to myself. Apart from the immediate cares of the Nyon Conference, other Spanish troubles and the situation in the Far East have been persistently knocking at my door.

Officer, Mesopotamia, 1915. Deputy Director, Local Resources Department, Mesopotamia, 1917. Transferred to the Hedjaz operations at the request of T. E. Lawrence, March 1918, where he organized transport and supplies for the Arab forces. President of the Local Resources Board, Damascus, 1918. Major, 1919. Member of the Eastern Department of the Foreign Office, 1919–21. Assistant Secretary, Middle East Department, Colonial Office, 1921–6. Colonial Secretary, Gibraltar, 1926–9. Counsellor for the High Commissioner, Iraq, 1929–32. Knighted, 1932. Minister to Baghdad, 1932. Governor and Commander-in-Chief, Nyasaland, 1932–4; Northern Rhodesia, 1934–8; Trinidad and Tobago, 1938–42. Unsuccessful Liberal candidate at the 1945 election. In 1933 he published *The Independent Arab*.

[1] From March 1921 until October 1922, Major Young was an Assistant Secretary in the newly created Middle Eastern Department at the Colonial Office (T. E. Lawrence having been appointed as Churchill's Adviser on Arabian Affairs in the same department).

You will now have seen the line which we have taken at Nyon which, in part at least, coincides with that suggested in your letter. I hope you will agree that the results of the Conference are satisfactory. They seem so as viewed from here. The really important political fact is that we have emphasised that co-operation between Britain and France can be effective, and that the two Western democracies can still play a decisive part in European affairs. It is all the more satisfactory that we have been able to do this without having to call for the active co-operation of the Soviet Government. The programme upon which we eventually agreed was worked out jointly by the French and ourselves. I must say that they could not have co-operated more sincerely and we have been surprised at the extent of the naval co-operation which they have been ready to offer. It is fair to say that if we include their help in the air we shall be working on a fifty-fifty basis.

I agree that what we have done here only deals with one aspect of the Spanish problem. But it has much increased our authority among the nations at a time when we needed such an increase badly. The attitude of the smaller Powers of the Mediterranean was no less satisfactory. They played up well under the almost effusively friendly lead of Turkey. Chatfield had been a great success with everyone and I feel that the Nyon Conference, by its brevity and success, has done something to put us on the map again. I hope that this may be your feeling too.

At least it has heartened the French and ourselves to tackle our immensely formidable task together.

Yours ever,
Anthony Eden

Professor Lindemann to Group-Captain Lachlan MacLean
(*Churchill papers: 2/304*)

17 September 1937

Very many thanks for your letter which I found on my return to Oxford from a holiday abroad.

I am sure your figures are right. The point I had overlooked was that you were considering such long ranges as 600 yards. Personally I should not have thought it worth while to start firing until one was very much closer, and in that case the difference in velocity is of course not very important. It is of course a real point, but to my mind not a vital one.

The fact that attack from astern can be so easily countered by small mines on the other hand, seems to me of the utmost importance: but whether one can induce the authorities to take it into account is a very different matter.

I hope there may soon be a chance of seeing you again, and remain,

Yours sincerely,

PS. I do not know whether you want to have the papers back, but I have left them with Mrs Pearman in case you do.

Winston S. Churchill to the Duke of Westminster: telegram

(Churchill papers: 1/300)

19 September 1937   Chartwell

So glad hear from you again. Am dwelling here in peace and health writing books and painting. Let me know when you come to London. Should like so much to have a talk. Every good wish my dear Bendor,

Winston

Winston S. Churchill to Anthony Eden

(Churchill papers: 2/302)

20 September 1937
Confidential

It was very good of you, when so busy, to write to me. Indeed I congratulate you on a very considerable achievement. It is only rarely that an opportunity comes when stern and effective measures can be brought to bear upon an evil doer, without incurring the risk of war. I have no doubt that the House of Commons will be very much pleased with the result.

I was very glad to see that Neville has been backing you up, and not, as represented by the Popular Press, held you back by the coat-tails. My hope is that the advantages you have gained will be firmly held on to. Mussolini only understands superior force, such as he is now confronted with in the Mediterranean. The whole naval position there is transformed from the moment that the French bases are at our disposal. Italy cannot resist an effective Anglo-French combination. I hope, therefore, that Mussolini will be left to find his own way out.

Winston S. Churchill to Lord Linlithgow

(*Churchill papers: 2/301*)

23 September 1937 Chartwell

I have not troubled you with letters all this time, though you and India have been often in my thoughts. You have proceeded with great steadfastness on the formidable course upon which our fortunes in India are now embarked. I wonder very much what you feel about it all now that you are at close quarters with events. I need not say I hope and trust your hopes will be wiser than my fears. I and my friends have done nothing to make more difficult the task of bringing the India Constitution into being. We were, as you remember, always ready to submit to the Provincial scheme minus the police. I gather now that the Federal scheme cannot come into operation for some time until that stage is reached we certainly have no grounds for criticism. I sympathise much with you in your anxieties, and your toils will always have my fervent wishes for success.

Here everyone is united in dealing with our deficiencies as fast as possible without interfering with the ordinary life of the country. This is a serious limitation. The Navy is overwhelmingly strong, so far as Europe is concerned, and the gigantic programme now being executed can only increase our lead. The Air Force, alas, is but a fraction of the German, and I do not think we shall catch up. On the contrary it would seem that 1938 will see Germany relatively stronger to the British Air Force and the French Army than now. I do not believe in a major war this year because the French army at present is as large as that of Germany and far more mature. But next year and the year after may carry these Dictator-ridden countries to the climax of their armament and of their domestic embarrassments. We shall certainly need to be ready by then.

I expect you will have on top of you before very long proposals for a separate army for India. I gather that is the line upon which the new War Minister's[1] thoughts are proceeding. He knows little about the problem at the present time, and I have begged him not to commit himself until he has thoroughly mastered all the implications of the Cardwell[2] system.

Neville has begun very well and is certainly being given a very fair chance

---

[1] Leslie Hore-Belisha, Secretary of State for War from 28 May 1937 to 5 January 1940.

[2] Edward, Viscount Cardwell, 1813–86. As Secretary of State for the Colonies in 1864 he reformed the system of Colonial defence by refusing to keep British troops in the Colonies in time of peace unless their expense was paid for by the Colony. In 1868, as Secretary of State for War, he abolished army commissions acquired by purchase, and introduced both the short service, and reserve systems of army organization: known together as the 'Cardwell system'.

by all parties. The Socialists have gone to pieces completely and I have no doubt we could go to the country now and secure a good working majority.

I have been living a perfectly placid life here painting and working at Marlborough, in fact I have hardly moved outside the garden since Parliament rose.

I send you a copy of my new book. It may amuse you to read about some of these men you knew so well.

I venture to give a letter of introduction to a German[1] who is visiting India shortly. He is associated with the International Nitrogen Association, but it is not in that capacity that I recommend him to you. He is the eldest son of Grand Admiral von Tirpitz[2] and I knew him when I was at the Admiralty before the war. He has been to see me several times since. We took him prisoner in the Heligoland Bight where he fought most bravely, and went down with his ship, refusing Roger Keyes' appeal to come on board the destroyer which was rescuing the German wounded. However he came up again and our fellows hauled him on board.

He came down here to see me the other day and we had a long talk. He is no Nazi but belongs to what he calls 'the old Germany' which indeed I wish we could see back again. He is a man of exceptional ability and high character and I am sure a conversation with him about Germany would be interesting to you. I should be grateful for any courtesy you may extend to him.[3]

With all good wishes and kind regards to you and your wife,[4] believe me,

[1] Wolfgang von Tirpitz, son of Grand Admiral Tirpitz. He lunched at Chartwell on 15 September 1937. After his capture in 1914, Churchill had sent a message to his father through neutral channels: 'Your son is safe'.

[2] Alfred von Tirpitz, 1849–1930. As Chief of Staff of Supreme Naval Command 1892 he laid down plans for a powerful German Navy; as Secretary of State for Naval Affairs 1897 he supervised the construction of that Navy. He saw the Navy as an important instrument of diplomacy; not as a weapon of war. Favoured a fixed ratio for the Anglo-German Navies; wished to give up supplementary estimates in return for an Anglo-German Naval Agreement, 1912; in 1914 he advocated an early naval engagement to decide the war as quickly as possible. He resigned all offices on 15 March 1916. Entered politics as a Nationalist Member of the Reichstag 1924–8; urged German co-operation with Britain and the United States 1925–30. His daughter Ilse (who died in 1982) married the German diplomat, and later Ambassador in Rome, Ulrich von Hassell, who was hanged by Hitler after the July Plot of 1944.

[3] On 13 April 1965 Wolfgang von Tirpitz wrote to Lady Churchill (from Irschenhausen near Munich): 'I only want to tell you, how grateful I am and shall be to the end of my life for the many signs of Sir Winston's kind-hearted and noble feeling to the son of a man who certainly was for a long time a political/not personal adversary of your country. I hope you are as healthy and good-looking as I remember you at my last visit in Chartwell. I am sure you will bravely endure the void which is left to you by the death of Sir Winston and which cannot be filled . . .' (*Spencer-Churchill papers*).

[4] Doreen Maud Milner, younger daughter of Lord Randolph Churchill's friend, Sir Frederick Milner 7th Baronet, PC, GCVO. She married the Marquess of Linlithgow (then Earl of Hopetoun) in 1900.

Violet Pearman to Winston S. Churchill

(*Churchill papers: 2/304*)

23 September 1937

Mr Churchill

Cmdr Anderson is now out of hospital and is resting at home. A nearby neighbour of his Lord Addison[1] (who used to be Dr Christopher Addison) came to see his cottage which was up for sale. He stayed and had tea with him and chatted. He told Cmdr that he viewed with much anxiety what was coming in the future, and appeared to hold much the same views as him. Cmdr A says that he was very discreet in what he said, and thought you would like to know he called, as he seemed quite a good ally in the large common cause. Is this so?

Anthony Eden to Winston S. Churchill

(*Churchill papers: 2/302*)

25 September 1937   Foreign Office
Confidential

My dear Winston,

Thank you so much for your letter of the 20th September and for the generous things you have written about Nyon, which I much appreciate. I thought your summing up of the postition at Nyon: 'It is only rarely that an opportunity comes when stern and effective measures can be brought to bear upon an evil doer, without incurring the risk of war' effectively described the position. Mussolini has been unwise enough to overstep the limits and he has had to pay the penalty. There is no doubt that the spectacle of eighty Anglo-French destroyers patrolling the Mediterranean assisted by a considerable force of aircraft has made a profound impression on opinion in Europe. From reports which I have received Germany herself has not been slow to take note of this fact. It was a great relief both to Delbos and me to be able

---

[1] Christopher Addison, 1869–1951. Hunterian Professor of Anatomy, Cambridge, 1901. Liberal MP for Hoxton, 1910–22. Parliamentary Secretary to the Board of Education, 1914–15. Parliamentary Secretary, Ministry of Munitions, 1915–16. Minister of Munitions, 1916–17. Minister in Charge of Reconstruction, 1917. President of the Local Government Board, 1919. Minister of Health, 1919–21. Minister without Portfolio, 1921. He published a volume of *Memoirs* in 1924; and his war-time diary, *Four-and-a-half-Years* in 1934. Joined the Labour Party before the General Election of 1929. Labour MP for Swindon, 1929–31; 1934–5. Minister of Agriculture and Fisheries, 1930–1. Created Baron, 1937; Viscount, 1945. Secretary of State for Commonwealth Relations in Clement Attlee's Labour Government, 1945–7; Paymaster-General, 1948–9; Lord Privy Seal, 1949–51. Knight of the Garter, 1946.

to assert the position of our respective countries in this way in the autumn of a year in which we have inevitably had to be so much on the defensive. There is plenty of trouble ahead and we are not yet, of course, anything like as strong in the military sense as I would wish, but Nyon has enabled us to improve our position and to gain more time.

I also cordially agree with you on the importance of the Anglo-French co-operation which we have now created in the Mediterranean. The whole French attitude was, of course, fundamentally different from that which prevailed when Laval was in command. The French Naval Staff could not have been more helpful and they really made a great effort to make an important contribution to the joint force. Our Admiralty were, I am sure, impressed. Moreover the mutual advantages to which you refer in respect of the use of each other's bases are very valuable. Nor will Italian participation, whatever its ultimate form, be able to affect the realities of the situation.

I hope to get away from London after the Cabinet on Wednesday for ten days' break before the strenuous labours of the autumn session begin. If I may I will get in touch with you as soon as I get back and I shall be most glad if you can dine with me, when we could, I hope, have a discussion on the world and its woes!

Yours ever,
Anthony Eden

Ernst Woermann to Winston S. Churchill: telegram

(Churchill papers: 2/307)

28 September 1937

Herr Bohle asked me to get into touch with you in view of your answer to him published in Evening Standard September 17.[1] Bohle arrives Thursday afternoon and leaves London Sunday. Best day for interview seems to be Saturday. Owing to other appointments it is difficult for Bohle to leave London during his stay. Would interview be convenient to you Saturday morning in German Embassy. If not please make other suggestions.

Woermann

---

[1] See page 772, note 1.

Kathleen Hill to Winston S. Churchill

(*Churchill papers: 2/307*)

28 September 1937

Herr Bohle will call on you at the flat at *12.15 pm* on Friday next, 1st October.

Desmond Morton to Winston S. Churchill

(*Churchill papers: 2/307*)

29 September 1937

Dear Winston,

With regard to Bohle, I have been on to the Foreign Office and to K,[1] and understand that Van rang up K this morning and told him to send you before Friday a note giving all they know about Bohle.

I have no idea what he will send, and in case it does not come to hand, or is insufficient to your purpose, I am sending you a short note which I have tried to compound myself from various documents I have got. I have not many of these, as Bohle is well outside my normal activities; therefore, if any of the facts I give are contradicted by K's, please take his as being correct.

I hope that by one of these two means you will be fully primed.

Yours very sincerely,
Desmond Morton

G. W. Liddell[2] to Winston S. Churchill

(*Churchill papers: 2/307*)

30 September 1937

Dear Mr Winston Churchill,

I have been asked by Major Morton to send you the attached note which will give you the dry bones of the Auslands Organisation and its leader.[3]

---

[1] 'K', of Military Intelligence. During the Second World War MI14 (K) was the section concerned with German military maintenance and supply throughout Europe, as well as German operations against the Soviet Union.

[2] Geoffrey William Liddell, 1884–1955. Educated at Eton and Sandhurst. 2nd Lieutenant, Rifle Brigade, 1904; Captain, 1913. On active service in France and Belgium, 1914–15 (wounded). Commander of a Company of Gentlemen Cadets, Sandhurst, 1915–18. On active service, 1918 (DSO). Major, 1919. Lieutenant-Colonel (retired), 1921. Served at the War Office (Military Intelligence), between the wars.

[3] For the details sent to Churchill about Bohle, see page 707, note 3.

I am also enclosing an official publication by the Union of South Africa which will give you some idea how things work out or are likely to work out in practice. I should be glad if you could let me have this document back in due course through Major Morton.[1]

Yours sincerely,
G. W. Liddell

---

[1] In an article in the *Evening Standard* on 17 September 1937, entitled 'Friendship with Germany', Churchill wrote: 'I find myself pilloried by Dr Goebbels' Press as an enemy of Germany. That description is quite untrue.' In the past he had made many efforts on Germany's behalf. But it was his duty to warn against German rearmament. 'I can quite understand that this action of mine would not be popular in Germany. Indeed, it was not popular anywhere. I was told I was making ill-will between the two countries. Similarly, for the last few months, in Parliament and in these articles which are so widely published throughout Europe I drew attention to a serious danger to Anglo-German relations which arises out of the organisation of German residents in Britain into a closely-knit, strictly disciplined body. We could never allow foreign visitors to pursue their national feuds in the bosom of our country, still less to be organised in such a way as to effect our military security. The Germans would not tolerate it for a moment in their country, nor should they take it amiss because we do not like it in ours.' Churchill went on to write that he would be glad to meet Herr Bohle, and would tell the Germans: 'We cannot say that we admire your treatment of the Jews or of the Protestants and Catholics of Germany. . . . But, after all, these matters, as long as they are confined inside Germany, are not our business.' Churchill added: 'We cannot be expected to help Germany financially while she is spending nearly a thousand millions sterling a year upon her tremendous rearmament. . . . We cannot hand over colonies irrespective of the wishes of their inhabitants. To feel deep concern about the armed power of Germany is in no way derogatory to Germany. On the contrary. . . . ' Churchill's article continued: 'One may dislike Hitler's system and yet admire his patriotic achievement', and he ended with an appeal that 'the Fuehrer of Germany should now become the Hitler of peace'. The essay on Hitler, as published in *Great Contemporaries* in October 1937, contained a similar appeal that 'we may yet live to see Hitler a gentler figure in a happier age'. For the stronger ending of this finally published version, see page 903, note 2.

October 1937

<hr/>

Sir Maurice Hankey to Winston S. Churchill

(*Churchill papers: 8/549*)

3 October 1937

My dear Winston,

Many thanks indeed for 'Great Contemporaries'—a most valuable contribution to history, as I have already discovered.[1] Someone ought to add to the list by writing a sketch of the author, and he would have to cover a lot of ground!

I spent my leave 'nosing' about in a small car in Italy—but I did not get anywhere near the official crowd in Rome.

Since my return I have had a run round some of the new aircraft factories in the Midlands. It was heartening to find half a dozen huge factories, covering acres of ground (27 acres in Austin's case), full of the most modern machine tools, and carrying a large-scale production in places where, twelve months ago there was nothing but rolling, unlevelled grassland.

We shall meet soon at our Committee. There is good progress, but heaps to be done yet. Robin[2] writes from Warsaw that he is reading and absorbed in the Third Volume of the World Crisis. Henry,[3] by the way, to whom I

<hr/>

[1] *Great Contemporaries* was formally published on 4 October 1937. 5,000 copies were printed, but demand was so large that a further 4,000 had been printed before the end of the month. Within three months of publication, a total of 15,000 copies had been printed. On 7 November 1938 a further 5,000 copies were printed of a new edition with four extra sketches (Admiral Fisher, Charles Parnell, Baden-Powell and President Roosevelt), and in August 1939 a second impression of 28,000 copies was printed.

[2] Robert Maurice Alers Hankey, 1905–   . Educated at Rugby and New College, Oxford. Entered the Diplomatic Service, 1927. Served in Berlin, Paris, London, Warsaw, Bucharest, Cairo, Teheran, Madrid and Budapest. British Ambassador at Stockholm, 1954–60. Knighted, 1955. Permanent UK Delegate to the OEEC and the OECD, 1954–60; Chairman of the Economic Policy Committee, 1960–5. President of the Anglo-Swedish Society, 1969–75. A Director of the Alliance Building Society, 1970. Succeeded his father as 2nd Baron, 1963.

[3] Henry Arthur Alers Hankey, 1914–   . Educated at Rugby and New College, Oxford. Entered the Diplomatic Service, 1937. Third Secretary, Paris, 1939. Second Secretary, Madrid, 1942. First Secretary, Rome, 1946. Consul, San Francisco, 1950. Head of the

think you once gave a 'character' has just passed into the Foreign Office & diplomatic service.

I hope all goes well with you all. Randolph seems to be establishing a position for himself.

Yours ever,
M. P. A. Hankey

PS. On the whole my spirits are rising.

General Sir Bindon Blood to Winston S. Churchill
(*Churchill papers: 8/549*)

3 October 1937

Dear Winston,

Very many thanks for your charming & interesting new book, which I do think it most kind of you to send me. I shall get my wife to read it to me as I have 'out lived' my eyes, and cannot see to read or write, which is not astonishing as I shall be 95 next month. We hope you are all flourishing.

Yours ever,
B. Blood

Winston S. Churchill to Anthony Eden
(*Churchill papers: 2/311*)

3 October 1937
Confidential

As I think we told you some time ago, we have a small 'focus' of people who advocate the cause of 'freedom and peace'. We lunch occasionally at the Savoy, and we should all very much like you to come one day. The proceedings are strictly confidential, and nothing in the nature of a formal speech would be required. I should preside, and would introduce you.

Originally, I was concerned in bringing this 'focus' together in order to gather 'left-wing' support for re-armament. In this we have been most successful. We held a meeting at the Albert Hall, where Citrine presided, and all parties and denominations were represented. We hold meetings all over the

American Department of the Foreign Office, 1956. Counsellor of Embassy, Beirut, 1962–6. Ambassador to Panama, 1966–9. Assistant Under-Secretary of State, Foreign and Commonwealth Office, 1969–74. A Director of Lloyd's Bank International, 1975.

country, at which the municipal authorities usually preside, and Socialists, Liberals and Tories advocate organised resistance to Nazi and Communist propaganda. Our greatest common principle is resistance to the Lansbury[1] Pacifist movement. Many of these people are very influential in Socialist and Liberal circles, but of course we always have a proportion of live Conservatives as well.

The League of Nations Union and the New Commonwealth, of which I am President, are both closely associated, and many of our meetings are held under their aegis. So far as I know, our views are yours, and your views are ours. They would be very pleased to see you after Nyon, and I can guarantee it would not cost you any trouble or embarrassment.

I hope you will be able to give me a date in the first week of November. We lunch at one sharp, so as not to make the MPs late for Questions.

I may add that our contacts enable us to go right into the heart of the Trade Union world, and to act with them in the utmost harmony. Without the support of Trade Unions, our munition programme cannot be properly executed. This aspect is of real public importance. It may well be in the future that the Trade Unionists will detach themselves from particular political parties. This would be a gain enormous to our political life.

Pray treat all this as for your private information only. I send you a list of those who came to the luncheon we gave to Titulescu.

We should make a special effort to bring the Trade Unionists in.

Neville Chamberlain to Winston S. Churchill

(Churchill papers: 8/549)

4 October 1937   10 Downing Street

My dear Winston,

I was very delighted to find on my table yesterday a copy of your new book, inscribed in your own hand.

[1] George Lansbury, 1859–1940. Left school at the age of 14. Was employed unloading coal trucks for the Great Eastern Railway. First attempted to enter Parliament, 1895. Labour MP for Bow and Bromley, 1910–12. Resigned to fight the seat as a supporter of women's suffrage. Not re-elected until 1922. Mayor of Poplar, 1919–20 and 1936–7. Editor of the *Daily Herald*, 1919–25. First Commissioner of Works in the second Labour Government, 1929–31. Leader of the Labour Party, 1931–5. On 11 May 1937, after a private meeting with Hitler, Lansbury wrote to a friend: 'He is a very lonely man and has no spiritual background to fall back upon, except that he believes he has saved Germany and is determined she shall not slip back again. He is ruthless and quite cynical with everything that seems to stand in his way. He will *not* go to war unless pushed into it by others. He knows how a European war will end. He is a good conversationalist and did *not* monopolise more time than I did' (quoted in Martin Gilbert, *Britain and Germany Between the Wars*, London 1966, pages 102–3).

How you can go on throwing off these sparkling sketches with such apparent ease & such sustained brilliance, in the midst of all your other occupations is a constant source of wonder to me. But the result is to give great pleasure and entertainment to your numerous admirers, of whom not the least sincere is

Yours very gratefully,
Neville Chamberlain

Cyril Clemens[1] to Winston S. Churchill

(*Churchill papers: 8/546*)

4 October 1937   Missouri

Dear Mr Churchill,

If the rumor is true that you are about to write a biography of Campbell-Bannerman, we shall be most happy to send you letters and documents which may prove useful.[2] I myself am writing the biography of G. K. Chesterton who held you in the highest esteem. Do you recall your first meeting with him either in the flesh or through his books.

Your *Marlborough* is so magnificent that we feel it deserves the Nobel prize in literature![3]

---

[1] Cyril Clemens, a descendent of Mark Twain, and founder and President of the International Mark Twain Society, which Churchill had joined on 12 September 1929. Editor of the *Mark Twain Journal* (established 1936). On 25 October 1943 Churchill wrote to Clemens from 10 Downing Street. 'I am writing to express my thanks to the International Mark Twain Society for their Gold Medal, which has been handed to me by Mr Philip Guedalla. It will serve to keep fresh my memory of a great American, who showed me much kindness when I visited New York as a young man by taking the Chair at my first public lecture and by autographing copies of his works, which still form a valued part of my library' (*Cyril Clemens papers*).

[2] The rumour was untrue, nor did Churchill publish an essay on Campbell-Bannerman (the Liberal Prime Minister under whom he received his first Government post in December 1905, as Under Secretary of State for the Colonies), in his collection of essays, *Great Contemporaries*, which was published in London on 4 October 1937, the day of Clemens' letter.

[3] Churchill received the Nobel Prize for Literature in 1953, following the publication of five of the six volumes of his war memoirs *The Second World War*.

Thornton Butterworth to Winston S. Churchill

(*Churchill papers: 8/559*)

5 October 1937

Dear Mr Churchill,

. . . The review in The Evening Standard was excellent;[1] and so they have all been with the exception of that by Squire[2] in the Daily Telegraph. He appears to be prejudiced for some reason or other, or possibly he had looked upon the wine when it was red. It will be, I am sorry to say, far from helpful.[3]

---

[1] In the *Evening Standard* on 4 October 1937, George Malcolm Thomson wrote, of the twenty-one portraits in *Great Contemporaries*: 'each becomes a mirror in which another contemporary is reflected—Mr Churchill gleams back at us from 21 looking-glasses, formidable, affectionate and lovable'. As for Churchill's prejudices, the reviewer noted, 'they sprinkle these pages like grains of pepper: the Irish Free State is dismissed as "a group of ill-mannered agricultural counties"; "the dull, squalid figures of the Russian Bolshevists are not redeemed in interest even by the magnitude of their crimes".' George Malcolm Thomson added: 'How well the book is written! Here is the old love of fine words and heartening military metaphors; the gift for the majestic sentence unfolding great events in stately drapery. But let no one think that a brave rotundity is the sole strength of the writing. Mr Churchill can be pithy, he can even be simple.'

[2] John Collings Squire, 1884–1958. Poet and literary critic. Educated at Blundell's and St John's College, Cambridge. Literary Editor of the *New Statesman*, 1913; acting Editor, 1917–18. Unsuccessful Parliamentary Candidate (Labour), 1918 and 1924. Editor of the *London Mercury*, 1919–34. Knighted, 1933. Author of more than forty volumes of poetry and essays.

[3] Writing in the *Daily Telegraph* on 5 October 1937, Sir John Squire described *Great Contemporaries* as not one of Churchill's 'major performances'. It was, he wrote, 'a collection of articles of magazine length by the accomplished journalist rather than the eloquent historian'. The essays, like all essays of their kind about persons alive or recently dead, were, in his view 'necessarily limited by good taste, imperfect information and paucity of space', while Churchill's new lights on recent history were 'few and trifling'. Churchill had, however, 'an eye for character and has never been such a prig as to disapprove of a man because he disagreed with him'. Among the favourable reviews of *Great Contemporaries* were those of George Malcolm Thomson in the *Evening Standard* ('How well the book is written!'), Lloyd George in the *Listener* ('stimulating, brilliant, vivid'), Leonard Woolf in the *New Statesmen and Nation* ('some of the essays are brilliant'), Herbert Sidebotham in the *Sunday Times* ('he has the art in a greater degree than any other writer of creating the atmosphere of emotion and excitement') and A. J. Cummings in the *News Chronicle* ('Mr Churchill certainly has the seeing eye. Sometimes he sees further and more clearly than almost anybody else'). Cummings' review ended with a political reflection: 'On the whole I would rather see him in charge of British affairs in these critical times than any member of the Government from which he is so jealously excluded.'

Roy Fedden:[1] *extract from a letter*[2]

(Churchill papers: 2/328)

5 October 1937

I have been twice to Germany this summer, once in June and once again in September and have had the most wonderful time under the official aegis of my friend, General Milch,[3] and inspected the latest German aero engine and aircraft plants. I also had an invitation, and a most interesting time, at the Nurnberg Congress. I am absolutely shattered at the tremendous progress of aircraft and engine production in Germany, not from the technical aspect so much as in quantity and organisation. What they are doing is quite astounding.

Winston S. Churchill to F. W. Deakin

(Churchill papers: 8/547)

6 October 1937

The first twenty-one chapters now only lack VIII the actual battle of Malplaquet, X Three Women, XVII a two-page appreciation of Godolphin and XXI two pages on Sarah's final dismissal by Anne.

On the next page of the Contents Table 'Exile' is begun by me. Here is a point on which you should now concentrate. We want all the facts and documents to be assembled which bear on Marlborough's life abroad. If you will let me have this part explored as soon as possible, I shall be much obliged. Marlborough's rare correspondence at this time should be collected. His relations with Robethon; his advising Hanover to have a spy with the Pretender in Lorraine. His visits to Frankfort and Mindleheim. Sarah's letters

---

[1] Alfred Hubert Roy Fedden, 1885–1973. Educated at Clifton and Bristol Technical College. Works Manager and Chief Engineer, Brazil Straker & Co, Bristol (manufacturing aero engines and shells), 1909–20. Founded the Engine Department Bristol Aeroplane Co. 1920; Chief Engineer, 1920–42. President of the Royal Aeronautical Society, 1938, 1939 and 1945. Knighted, 1942. Special Technical Adviser, Ministry of Aircraft Production, 1942–4. Research Work, Ministry of Supply, 1945–7. Aeronautical Adviser to NATO, 1952–3.

[2] A copy of this extract was sent to Churchill by Wing-Commander Anderson.

[3] Erhard Milch, 1892–1972. Born at Wilhelmshaven. Served as a pilot, 1909–20. Head of the air traffic department of Junkers, 1920–3. Board member of Lufthansa, 1923–6; head of the Lufthansa Finance Department, 1928–33; President of Lufthansa, 1942. Secretary of State for Aviation, 1933–44. General, 1936. Inspector-General of the Air Force, 1938–44. Appointed deputy to Albert Speer, Minister of Armament and War Production, and Plenipotentiary for Armament in the four-year plan, June 1944. Captured by the Allies, May 1945. Sentenced to life imprisonment at the Nuremberg trials, 1947; released, 1954.

from exile. His announcement in 1714 to Robethon, I think, of his intention to return to England. His stay at Antwerp. His relations with the Elector. The attempts of Harley to undermine him with the Elector by sending him copies of his Jacobite letters. His relations with St Germains in this period. The question of a pardon in return for a gift of money. The £20,000 promised by him to the Elector. The upshot of all this. His refusal to sign the association paper sent by the Whigs. His reception by the Royal Irish regiment described in Parker. His contacts with the Whigs in England, and with his officers and friends like Cadogan, Stair, Craggs, Stanhope etc. The more you can get together about all this the better. Bring it to me when you come on Friday week.

After Chapter XXXI 'Exile' there is very little more. I have done about 5,000 words on the death of the Queen. There will only be one more chapter to the book after the accession of George I. We need not think of this at present. Meanwhile I will concentrate upon Malplaquet and Three Women. I should like some references to guide me in the tribute to Godolphin. You need only send the references—I have the books.

Desmond Morton to Winston S. Churchill

(*Churchill papers: 2/311*)

6 October 1937

Dear Winston,

I return with many thanks Wickham Steed's letter to you and its enclosures.

I have to confess that at the moment I have no knowledge whatever bearing on an alleged attempt by the Germans to establish a naval base in Ecuador, and it seems to me a little far-fetched. However, there is evidently something going on there which gives rise to this rumour, and I am making enquiries.

As regards Wickham Steed's note, I think he over-emphasises any antagonism which may exist between the Nazi Party and the Reichswehr. I certainly doubt if there is any intrigue against Hitler, since, if the Reichswehr decided to take full charge of German affairs, they would, in my opinion, probably retain Hitler in person as Chancellor and merely suppress the Party.

I believe it to be true that the Reichswehr does not like the idea of an Italian alliance, having a considerable contempt for the Italian as a fighting man. On the other hand, I cannot confirm that the Reichswehr are really actively pursuing a policy aiming at friendship with the USSR in lieu of

Italy, but would suppose that their policy is to wait until in their own minds they are strong enough to conquer the world alone.

The Reichswehr talks fairly openly of a military parade against Czecho-slovakia, but not yet, unless circumstances are favourable, ie there is certainty that neither France nor England will intervene on the Czechs' behalf.

I am told that the question of Austria was not discussed during the Hitler–Mussolini meeting, neither party wishing to open so thorny a subject, but I feel that if Germany did go to war, with or without Italian help, Austria would almost at once be included within the German frontiers.

I do not understand Wickham Steed's reference to the object of the Reichswehr being to get raw materials from Russia to make good the present shortage holding up German rearmament. Russia cannot at present provide these, while the trade returns show conclusively that she is not doing so.

My information from Hungary strongly emphasises the anti-German feeling in that country. The Hungarians are being more and more drawn into the orbit of Italy, it is true, and therefore may through that channel prolong the Berlin–Rome axis. This axis will, however, then be a rum shape in more ways than one.

I will let you know later if I get anything of interest in regard to Ecuador.

Yours very sincerely,
Desmond Morton

Lord Samuel to Winston S. Churchill
(*Churchill papers: 2/315*)

6 October 1937
Confidential

Dear Winston,

I read Tudor's letter with much interest, and am glad to know that his experience of Palestine has led him to agree in the proposal which I made. He has not understood it altogether correctly, however, for on a few points— though somewhat minor ones—the report which he has read has misled him.

1. I suggested a 40 per cent limitation for Jewish immigration, and not a limitation to one-third. The latter represents almost the existing position, and would nearly preclude any further immigration. The 40% would give a very considerable margin.

2. This was to be only a temporary arrangement for a period of years. I had in mind that if the country quieted down and the two races had become reconciled, the immigration position might be reviewed.

3. I did not make any arithmetical proposal with regard to immigration into Trans-Jordan, but only suggested that it should be such as would be agreed to by the TJ Government.

I do not know, also, whether Tudor fully realises that I hold no representative position in the Jewish community, and had made it clear that I spoke in the House of Lords only for myself. As a matter of fact, as I had anticipated, my proposals have proved very unwelcome to the whole body of Zionists on account, particularly, of the suggestion for a limitation of immigration on a principle other than economic absorptive capacity.

The Zionist position, in fact, is to say, 'We are most anxious to arrive at an arrangement with the Arabs, but it must of course be clearly understood that we surrender no point in our demands. Since the Arabs—or the dominant section of them—say similarly that they are quite ready to come to an accommodation with the Jews, but only on the basis that the Balfour Declaration is dropped and further immigration stopped, the prospect of agreement is not bright!

I was sorry that the Royal Commission, in the first place, and the Mandates Commission of the L of N afterwards, did not propose a second scheme on a compromise basis as a possible alternative to partition, with partition in the background as the only recourse if the parties did not accept the other. It is just possible that had they done so, a compromise might have been reached; and conceivably that might still be done. The Government, in my view, made a great mistake in hurrying to announce their acceptance of partition, without waiting for an expression of the views of either of the parties directly concerned. If only the Nashashibi section of the Arabs and the non-Zionist section of the Jewish Agency could agree together on some alternative, it is still just possible that they might draw to their side a sufficient body of opinion among both races to enable some alternative to partition to be brought into effect. I fully agree with you that the partition scheme is a folly.

Yours sincerely,
Samuel

Lord Londonderry to Winston S. Churchill

(*Churchill papers: 8/549*)

7 October 1937

My dear Winston,

Your last book shows you at your very best. The beautiful style and your very accurate and generous descriptions give one a real pleasure to read, and the underlying note is one of freshness and encouragement. I have spent some delightful moments with it and shall spend many more. I will get you to inscribe my copy so that the book can live with my other valued volumes of which you are the distinguished author. I admire your strenuous efforts but I do not always agree with them in toto, though there can never be much difference of opinion between us on anything. Perhaps I do not care as much as you do and believe that so many things which evoke such passionate expressions really do not matter at all. I want to avoid another war but I think our Government whose actions you praised at Scarborough[1] are heading straight for one and the way they muddle this Spanish drama, is frought with desperate danger.

I wish NC had made you Minister of Defence. I feel you would have liked it and you could have co-ordinated contending forces and developed that strength which is vitally necessary. Our friends here have never known how to control Hitler and Mussolini and they never will. Mussolini is the more difficult of the two and we have let it all run on so long, that difficulties have increased and accumulated. So long as the FO as at present constituted is influenced and dominated by France, so long will we be completely misunderstood. However as I have said I am not bothering about it very much; I have so many other interests and it really bars me criticizing the mistakes of other people: finding the mote in other people's eyes when I am fully conscious of the beam in my own.

Yours ever,
Charley

Sir Reginald Barnes to Winston S. Churchill

(*Churchill papers: 8/549*)

7 October 1937

My dear old Winston,

I do so appreciate your sending me your last book with your name in it. I have got most of them now, & I love having them. So far I have only read the soldier contemporaries—strange to say!! but I am going to read them all.

---

[1] In addressing the Conservative Annual Conference at Scarborough on 7 October 1937, Churchill began: ' I used to come here year after year when we had some differences between ourselves about rearmament and also about a place called India. So I thought it would only be right that I should come here when we are all agreed.' He went on to praise the Government's 'great effort for rearmament', and concluded: 'let us indeed support the foreign policy of our Government, which commands the trust, comprehension, and the comradeship of peaceloving and law-respecting nations in all parts of the world.'

You were kind to dear old Pinkstones,[1] I so agree with you that he had a 'flair'—which DH had not—& he was a man easy to work for. I think it is remarkable how you manage to get that sort of 'aerated' quality in your English—it makes reading you so interesting, even if it is about say—Snowden!

I am so sorry I shan't see you at the OC dinner on the 23rd, it would have been a joy if you could have had a talk to the men.

Poor old Joss Underwood[2] has moved on, no doubt you will remember the old boy.

Don't forget the pay of the soldier—vis-à-vis the agricultural labourer. I am reading what I think is an interesting book about the war called 'Vain Glory' by Guy Chapman.[3]

Best love,
Reggie

Anthony Eden to Winston S. Churchill

(*Churchill papers: 2/311*)

8 October 1937   Foreign Office

My dear Winston,

I have just read the reports of your speech at the Scarborough Conference and hasten to send these few lines of warmest thanks. Your tribute was most generous and a real tonic for these troublous times. We have, I fear, some rough weather ahead in the Mediterranean during the next few weeks, but the unity of the Conference and more especially the speech in which you

---

[1] Sir John (Pinkstone) French, see page 718, note 2.

[2] Joseph William Underwood, 1865–1937. 2nd Lieutenant, 4th Queen's Own Hussars 1888. Major, 1905. Retired from the army, 1913. He died on 28 September 1937.

[3] Guy Patterson Chapman, 1889–1972. Educated at Westminster School and Christ Church, Oxford. Called to the Bar, 1913. Rejected the legal profession and went to work for a publishing firm as an unpaid trainee, 1914. 2nd Lieutenant, Royal Fusiliers, 1914; on active service on the western front, 1915–18 (Military Cross; twice mentioned in despatches). Served with the Army of Occupation on the Rhine, 1919. A publisher between the wars, in 1930 he co-authored his own first book, a bibliography of Beckford, the 'abbot' of Fonthill. That same year he published his first novel, *A Painted Cloth*. His book *A Passionate Prodigality* (1933) was described by *The Times* as 'an uncommonly vivid, truthful and memorable description' of trench warfare. Director of the Army Bureau of Current Affairs, 1940–5. Professor of Modern History at Leeds University, 1945–53. Author of important books on *The Dreyfus Case* (1955) and *Why France Collapsed* (1969). His memoirs, *A Kind of Survivor*, were published in 1975 by his wife from notes he had left for such a work. The book *Vain Glory*, edited by Chapman, was a collection of personal recollections of the war, first published in 1937, and reissued in 1968.

underlined that unity should do much to steady opinion abroad just where it is in most need of that process.

You have written to me about the 'focus' of people who advocate the cause of 'Freedom and peace'. I shall be very glad to lunch with them in the first week in November. As to the actual date, perhaps your secretary could let mine know what day of the week suits you best and I will do my utmost to fit it in.

Finally, I am proud to have on my bookshelves an inscribed copy of 'Great Contemporaries' from a great contemporary. It will ever be a greatly valued possession and I look forward to a week-end when I hope to forget present troubles in reading of what I see Feiling has called 'a book of the mighty men of yesterday'.[1]

Again sincere thanks for your many acts of kindness and help.

Yours ever,
Anthony Eden

Professor G. M. Trevelyan to Winston S. Churchill

(*Churchill papers: 8/549*)

10 October 1937   Cambridge

Dear Churchill,

. . . Professional historians most of them haven't the art of getting themselves read, and the unprofessional ones, like Wells and Belloc, usually have bees in their bonnet. So you fill a gap. When you have finally buried the great Duke, if you are not back in office at some call of England's, write Napoleon.[2] The English speaking world will read it 'as long as the English language is spoken in any quarter of the globe', or if that is rather a tall order, at least as long as Lawrence's Seven Pillars.

Yrs sincerely,
G. M. Trevelyan

---

[1] Reviewing *Great Contemporaries* in the *Observer* on 3 October 1937, Keith Feiling wrote: 'A book of the mighty men of yesterday; but a book for the present and the future to read; for all who take interest in the present art of politics, and for History when it comes to assess the leaders and achievement of an epoch charged with significance in the annals of mankind. In those, its substantial pages, it is a delight to read, a work not unworthy of the historian of Marlborough and the critic of the World War. If one begins to reckon them up, this sort of essay is rare in our history, and even more rarely of value. . . . after the indiscriminate diatribe which some public men have purveyed, this tonic is good; this sanguine, warmhearted and generous dealing.'

[2] For further suggestions that Churchill write a biography of Napoleon, see page 790 and 1153.

Sir John Simon to Winston S. Churchill

(*Churchill papers: 8/549*)

10 October 1937 Treasury Chambers

My dear Winston,

I send you my warmest thanks for the copy of your *Great Contemporaries*. I have enjoyed it all very much: most of all, I think, your picture of FE, which does justice to his really great qualities—courage, loyalty, vigour of speech, above all judgement.[1] You are right, I think, in implying that he was not at his best in the H of C (and, really he was not quite first-rate in the Courts) but he was tremendous in other ways—and public men, like poets, should be judged by their best work. (In your case. I don't know whether that would be the written or the spoken word!)

I send you a little memoir I wrote about my Mother.[2] She was a darling.

Yours ever,
John Simon

By the way, it may well be that the German Emperor (page 37) wrote down 'Sic volo, sic jubeo, stet pro ratione voluntas' but if he did, he made two mistakes in one line. Juvenal wrote '*Hoc* volo, sic jubeo, *sit* pro ratione voluntas'.[3]

---

[1] Reflecting on the career of Lord Birkenhead (F. E. Smith) in *Great Contemporaries*, Churchill wrote: 'F.E. was the only one of my contemporaries from conversation with whom I have derived the same pleasure and profit as I got from Balfour, Morley, Asquith, Rosebery and Lloyd George. One did feel after a talk with these men that things were simpler and easier, and that Britain would be strong enough to come through all her troubles.' Of Birkenhead's loyalty, Churchill wrote: 'In every affair, public or personal, if he was with you on the Monday, you would find him the same on the Wednesday, and on the Friday when things looked blue, he would still be marching forward with strong reinforcements. The opposite type of comrade or ally is so very common that I single this out as a magnificent characteristic.' And of Birkenhead's power of work, Churchill wrote: 'He had a singular power of concentration, and five or six hours sustained thought upon a particular matter was always within his compass. He possessed what Napoleon praised, the mental power "*de fixer les objets longtemps sans être fatigué*".'

[2] Fanny Allsebrook, wife of the Rev Edwin Simon, a Congregational Minister. After her death, at the age of 90, in 1936, her son, Sir John Simon, wrote a tribute to her in *The Times*; it was subsequently published as a small book, *Portrait of My Mother*.

[3] 'I will it, I insist on it, let my will stand instead of reason': Juvenal, *Satires*, vi, 223.

Sir Archibald Sinclair to Winston S. Churchill

(*Churchill papers: 8/549*)

10 October 1937

My dear Winston,

Of all the people to whom you send your books I am probably the least distinguished but, by the same token, the most appreciative. Thank you so much, dear Winston,—and this is a grand book!

Of course the thing that pleases me most is to find (to my astonishment!) that you haven't forgotten that morning (7 am!) at Shoreham when I introduced you to my round machine—and I can still feel my bitter disappointment that there was just too much wind to fly it!

Of course, I was delighted, too, that you included Savinkov.[1] Do you remember the story of him following the man in Brussels? He grew more & more certain that it was Azeff[2]—his height, his build, the peculiarity of his walk—and then, just as he was drawing his revolver, the man turned round —a stranger!

You scored a big triumph at Scarborough—but I was glad to observe that one little epithet of criticism 'so-called'! An Italian Spain would weigh heavily in the balance of power against all the ships, guns & aeroplanes which we shall be turning out during the next few months.

Our maternal cousins[3] are waking up. Pittman's[4] support is most reassur-

[1] Boris Viktorovitch Savinkoff, 1877–1925. Russian nihilist. Exiled to Siberia as a student, for revolutionary activity. Escaped to Switzerland. Returned to Russia, 1905; and took part in the assassination of the Grand Duke Serge. Condemned to death. Escaped to Switzerland for a second time. He described his revolutionary work in a novel, *The Pale Horse*, published in 1909. Political commissar for the Provisional Government, charged with restoring discipline on the eastern front, July–August 1917. Deputy Minister of War in the Provisional Government, August 1917. An opponent of Bolshevism, he joined General Alexeiev's forces on the Don, November 1917. Accredited Agent in Paris, first of Alexeiev, then of Kolchak and finally of Denikin, 1918–20. Organized an anti-Bolshevik army in Poland, 1920. Returned to the Soviet Union voluntarily, 1924. Tried, condemned to death, and given a commuted sentence of ten years in prison, 1924. Died in prison, possibly by suicide, 1925.

[2] Yevno Fishlevich Azeff, 1869–1918. A founder of the Russian Socialist Revolutionary Party. Head of the Party's 'fighting organization', 1903–8, organizing several assassinations, including the assassination of the Russian Minister of the Interior, Pleve. In 1908 he was revealed to have been, throughout his 'revolutionary' career, a police spy. After 1908 he lived in Berlin, under an assumed name, and was a dealer on the Berlin stock exchange. Known as 'The Russian Judas'.

[3] Both Churchill and Sinclair had American mothers.

[4] Key Pittman, 1872–1940. Born in Vicksburg, Mississippi. Practised law in Seattle, 1892–7. Mined for gold in the Klondyke, 1897–9, when he entered politics in the Klondyke. For two years he fought for 'clean government' for Alaska. Moved to Nevada and set up a private law practive, 1901. Democratic Senator for Nevada, 1912–35. Received honorary law degrees from Southwestern Presbyterian University, 1921. Four times Democratic candidate for President *pro tempore* of the Senate, and elected once, 1933–5. United States delegate to the World Economic Conference, London, 1933.

ing. Wilson had the Republicans against him & the Senate Foreign Affairs Committee, but Roosevelt is supported by both Pittman & Stimson. Simon rebuffed Stimson (not indefinitely) over Manchuria; SB & Sam Hoare failed to impose the oil sanction in the Abyssinian dispute when Roosevelt was moving in Congress to obtain powers to co-operate; Hull[1] pleads in vain for a commercial treaty; don't let Neville fail to respond to the latest & most important advance from Roosevelt, Pittman & Stimson. Please give my love to Clemmie & Mary.

Archie

Winston S. Churchill to Sir Edward Marsh

(*Churchill papers: 8/547*)

11 October 1937

I send you a copy of the Marlborough proofs as far as they have got, together with a list of chapters, which will show the omissions. I have marked on this list the chapters you have already read, and I shall be glad if you will look through the others at your convenience. You will see we are within sight of port, and therefore it is time to take the pilot on board.

You will be glad to hear that 'Great Contemporaries' has gone like hot cakes. The first edition of five thousand is exhausted; the second of two thousand nearly finished, and they are printing a third edition, making ten thousand in all up to date. This is a remarkable result for a guinea book, and fully justifies your expectations. The only really disparaging review was Jack Squire's in the 'Daily Telegraph'. This might well have done a good deal of harm. However the book has overridden it. The best of all the reviews was in the Literary Supplement of 'The Times',[2] and the worst in 'The Daily Telegraph'.

The Tories were very pleased with me at Scarborough.

Yours always,

[1] Cordell Hull, 1871–1955. Admitted to the Bar of Tennessee, 1891. Member of the Tennessee House of Representatives, 1893–7. On active service in Cuba, 1898. Member of the United States House of Representatives, 1907–21 and 1923–31. Author of the Federal Inheritance Act, 1916. Chairman of the Democratic National Committee, 1921–31. United States Senator for Tennessee, 1931–7; resigned upon appointment as Secretary of State of the United States, 1933–44. Nobel Peace Prize, 1945. He published his war memoirs, in two volumes, in 1948.

[2] The anonymous reviewer in *The Times Literary Supplement*, called *Great Contemporaries* 'this rich and penetrating book' and noted that 'The author's personality is exceptional in the range and diversity of its sympathies'. In all his writings, the reviewer added, 'Mr Churchill has a peculiar gift for conveying atmosphere and a peculiar appreciation of great military strokes.'

Lady D'Abernon to Winston S. Churchill

(*Churchill papers: 8/549*)

11 October 1937

Dearest Winston,

I was at Stoke today and found there the copy of 'Great Contemporaries' you have so kindly sent us. They had been already eagerly and most appreciatively devoured by Edgar (as well as by myself) and to possess a copy inscribed by your hand is a real joy and will be an enduring memento of an author who—'en passant'—is himself far the Greatest Contemporary of them all.

Yrs affectionately,
Helen D'A

Edgar asks me to tell you that he thinks the portraits are 'perfect'.

Lord Linlithgow to Winston S. Churchill

(*Churchill papers: 2/301*)

11 October 1937   Viceregal Lodge,
Private   Simla

My dear Winston,

I am delighted for your letter of 23rd Sept. and by the kind things you say. Anxieties there are, but the position today is better than—12 months ago— I thought it likely to be at this time. I wish you could (both) come out and have a look at things for yourself. Ministers in all provinces are doing pretty well, and responding to responsibility and experience. The enclosed, which is an extract from a speech in the Bihar legislature by the Premier,[1]

[1] Shrikrishna Sinha, 1887–1961. A student at Patna College, 1907, when he was much impressed by the French Revolution. Joined Gandhi's Non-Cooperation Movement, 1921, and was active as a fund-raiser. Took a leading part in the boycott of the Simon Commission, 1929, and in the refusal to pay the salt-tax, 1930. A popular orator, he was imprisoned in 1931. Elected to the Imperial Legislative Assembly, 1934; and to the Bihar Legislative Assembly, 1937. Elected Leader of the Congress Party in Bihar, and Premier 1937; he at once ordered the release of all political prisoners, but was opposed by the (British) Governor of Bihar. Only after his right to issue the order was conceded, did he in fact withdraw it. Unable to satisfy the expectations of the peasants, he found himself ordering the imprisonment of several peasant leaders. In September 1939 he resigned the Premiership, in protest against Britain's decision to involve India in the war against Germany. Imprisoned for nine months in 1940, and for three years, 1942–5. Chief Minister for Bihar from 1946 until his death. An avid reader, his library of 20,000 books is now one of the most important collections in Bihar: he used always to say that his ambition in life was to become a Professor, but that he had strayed into politics.

is typical of speeches made by most of the Congress Ministers. I think you will agree that it is a very impressive performance. My strong impression is that these men are sincere in what they say. They are being very hard hunted by their own left wings; and, worse than that, are being constantly messed about by Gandhi & Nehru, a process that they are beginning strongly to resent. My impression is that this interference, made as a rule on strictly doctrinaire lines and without the least regard for the peculiarities of each individual province, is not likely to cease so long as the Mahatma can wield his pen. The Ministers admit freely to Governor that the proposals forced upon them by the old gentleman are for the most part quite impracticable; but a Mahatma is on the verge of being divine, and not one of them shows the least sign of having pluck enough to stand up to him.

Three months ago, I thought it about 50:50 that Nehru would pull the Congress Ministers out of office some time in '38. Now I think of it as about 5 to 1 against him being able to do so. I think, however, that when Congress find themselves under criticism in their constituencies on the eve of the next series of general elections, they will be greatly tempted to mobilize, in their own electoral favour, the prejudice that exists (and it is widely distributed) against the British. No one, and certainly not a foreigner, can hold the reins of government for 150 years and avoid picking up a little unpopularity!

I think you will have to do some more thinking about the federal issue. The Central legislature is now completely in the air—a narrower franchise than the legislatures in the provinces, and no element of responsibility by the government to the legislature. My view is that we cannot sustain this position at the centre for very long if parliamentary govt. in the provinces catches hold and grows. I am, too, very seriously alarmed by the signs already available to me that the provinces, unless held together by some central system in which Indians can play a substantial part and which will be reasonably attractive to the provinces, will tend to group themselves according to their natural affinities rather than to look to a common all-India centre. The other day, one of the most trusted and distinguished Muslims in the Punjab, a man very prominent in public life and a Minister, came and asked me if I had any objection to his advocating in public, a political union between the Punjab, Sind, the NWFP and the Punjab States. One has known for long of this idea, which takes account of the 500,000 rifles on the frontier and of Afghanistan behind them. I need say no more of this, for you will appreciate its significance without further word from me. I myself hope very strongly that we may not contemplate, and that you & your friends will not contemplate, a federation of *British* India. Take it from me, the old order in the Indian States is dying fast. If you build on its survival, you will build upon that which cannot long endure. Communications are extending everywhere

& the road vehicle is rapidly destroying the calm and isolation of the greater number of States. I cannot—putting the best judgment I can upon it—contemplate a time-horizon of more than 15 to 20 years for the States as we know them, and I think 10 years nearer the mark. In many of the larger States, a political ferment in the direction of calling for a liberalising of their systems of government is evident and is increasing. I myself should regard it as unwise in the extreme to attempt to perpetuate the political separation of the 2 Indias, and I venture to feel that if you spent a year in this country you would come to be of the same way of thinking.

As I think you know, I should not be in the least afraid to admit a change of view if such had come to me as a result of experience & of unceasing contact with the realities of the position over the past 18 months. But the simple truth is that the effect of that experience and of much thought leaves me the more convinced that the federal scheme drawn in the Act of '35 is about the best that could be devised, that it is the only one holding promise of federation within a reasonable time, and that—when the matter is put to the final issue—it will be accepted and worked by both the Princes and provinces of British India. I have still a good deal of adjustment and negotiation to get through, nor is it possible, in a case of that kind, to prophesy with confidence as to the precise date by which all the multifarious preliminaries will have been completed. It does however seem to me as I read your letter that you overestimate the time likely to elapse before the Federation is started.

Thank you very much for sending me your book, it has not yet arrived, but is no doubt travelling by the safe and sensible method of a good ship. I look forward much to reading it.

What are you going to do after Marlborough? Is there any hope of a Napoleon?

Well, Winston, I have given you a little of the thing I most lack—time, but I must stop now and tackle the mounting files. The pressure since March has been uncomfortably heavy but never unmanageable, given the will to do a couple to $2\frac{1}{2}$ hours after dinner every night, and no week ends off. Now we —my lady and I—are off on a few days tour, and I only hope the papers may not find me too easily.

Von Tirpitz shall receive such help & kindness as I am able to afford him. I only hope he may turn up at a time when I am settled in New Delhi.

I hope you have been able to read my handwriting.

My love to Clemmy & the best of good wishes to you both,
                                                        Yours ever,
                                                        Hopie

Lord Trenchard to Winston S. Churchill

(*Churchill papers: 2/299*)

11 October 1937

My dear Churchill,

You may know that the German Official Air Mission is coming over to this country next Sunday, 17th, and is going to stop a week.

I have asked them privately to dinner at Brooks's Club on 20th October at 8.15 pm to meet only unofficials, and the German Secretary of State for Air has accepted with two or three of his colleagues. His name, as you probably know from the papers, is General Milch—he has just been to Paris.

I saw them all when I was in Berlin not long ago and had rather an amusing talk with them, and I thought it would be rather a good thing to get them to come and dine with unofficial people.

I wonder if you would come to dinner? *I hope you will,* because I think it might amuse you and interest them enormously. You may like to know who I have got coming as well—I have got Camrose,[1] Sir Robert Kindersley,[2] Weir, Amery, D'Arcy Cooper[3] and one or two others. Do come if you can. . . .

---

[1] William Ewart Berry, 1879–1954. Newspaper proprietor. Founder of *Advertising World*, 1901. Editor-in-Chief of the *Sunday Times*, 1915–36. Chairman, Financial Times Limited, 1919–45; Allied Newspapers Limited, 1924–36. Created Baron Camrose, 1929. Chief Proprietor and Editor-in-Chief of the *Daily Telegraph and Morning Post*, 1936–54. Principal Adviser, Ministry of Information, 1939. Advanced to a Viscounty, 1941. One of Churchill's close friends (he was elected to the Other Club in 1926), and from 1945 a principal financial adviser; in 1946 he negotiated both the sale of Churchill's war memoirs, and also the purchase of Chartwell by a group of Churchill's friends and its conveyance to the National Trust (Camrose himself contributing £15,000 and sixteen other friends £5,000 each).

[2] Robert Molesworth Kindersley, 1871–1954. A Director of the Bank of England, 1914–46. Knighted, 1917. President of the National Savings Committee, 1920–46. Created Baron, 1941. The oldest of his four sons was killed in action on the western front on 24 November 1917. Two of his other sons fought in the Second World War, one being wounded, and the other being taken prisoner-of-war. Member of the Bankers' Committee on German Finance, 1922. Senior British Representative on the Dawes Committee, 1924. Merchant banker: Chairman of Lazard Bros and Co Ltd.

[3] Francis D'Arcy Cooper, 1882–1941. A Chartered Accountant. On active service, 1914–19; Lieutenant, Royal Field Artillery (wounded on the Somme, August 1916). Vice-Chairman of Lever Brothers, 1923; Chairman, 1925. Subsequently Chairman of Unilever Limited, of MacFisheries Limited, and of the Niger Company Limited. Chairman of the Executive Committee of the Board of Trade Industrial Export Council. Undertook a mission to the USA for closer Anglo-American trade co-operation, 1940–1. Created Baronet, 12 June 1941. Died, 18 December 1941. In his will he left The Drovers estate in Sussex (of over 1,000 acres) to the National Trust.

Winston S. Churchill to F. W. Deakin

(Churchill papers: 8/547)

11 October 1937

I send you Chapters XV and XVa which I have now revised. You will see a good many references to queries to you and also the notes of the publishers' reader. Will you kindly supply these as soon as possible and then send the two Chapters for second revise to Harraps.

You will see I have broken the Sunderland chapter into two of more manageable size. I am not particularly pleased with either of these chapters and they certainly offer room for compression when the final revise of the book is begun.

Winston S. Churchill to Maurice Ashley

(Churchill papers: 8/547)

11 October 1937

My dear Ashley,

I was very glad to learn from your letter that you have come to live in London, and I hope your work on 'The Times' will prove congenial and prosperous.

I have now got nearly 200,000 words of Marlborough IV in print, some of it in an advanced condition, and I wonder whether you could spare the time to read it for me? You will understand that these later volumes are not so profitable to me in the way in which the earlier ones were. I could pay you an honorarium of fifty guineas for reading the proofs for me. This would not entail any research beyond your present wide knowledge, nor should I consider you responsible for accuracy. It would be enough if you would give me your careful eye and full opinion, correcting any mistake which you notice, and giving me your views as to omissions, proportion, etc.

Perhaps you will let me know whether this task would be agreeable to you.

PS. Do come and see us here one Sunday—both please.

Winston S. Churchill to Brigadier Pakenham-Walsh

(*Churchill papers: 8/547*)

12 October 1937

My dear Brigadier,

It would be very nice if you could, when you come on Sunday next, give me and Deakin a lecture on the battle of Malplaquet, as you see it. I have plenty of maps here and no doubt you have your own notes. We went over it on the ground together,[1] but it would greatly refresh my memory, and I should like to hear the emphasis which you put on the different incidents.

Stanley Baldwin to Winston S. Churchill

(*Churchill papers: 8/549*)

12 October 1937   69 Eaton Square,
London

My dear Winston,

I arrived here last night and found your book awaiting me.

Your generous thought of me gave me real pleasure and I shall enjoy reading it as I always enjoy reading your books.

Thank you.

Yours very sincerely,
SB

Group-Captain MacLean to Wing-Commander Anderson

(*Churchill papers: 2/304*)

12 October 1937

You have probably seen that a German Mission consisting of Milch, Stumff[2] and Udet,[3] are visiting this country next week to see the Air Force.

---

[1] At the end of August 1932 Pakenham-Walsh had acted as Churchill's guide on a visit to Marlborough's principal battlefields. For Churchill's own account of that visit, see Companion Volume 5 of this biography, Part Two, 'The Wilderness Years', pages 475 and 477–8.

[2] Hans-Jürgen Stumpff, 1889–1968. Head of the Personnel Section of the Luftwaffe, 1933–6. Chief of the General Staff of the Luftwaffe, July 1937–January 1939. Chief of Luftflotte 1, on the western front, January to May 1940; of Luftflotte 5, Norway and Finland, May 1940–October 1943; of the Luftflotte 'Reich', 1944–5. One of the signatories (with Keitel and Friedeburg) of the German surrender in Berlin-Karlshorst, 9 May 1945. In October 1947 he was acquitted of war crimes by a British military tribunal. He died in Bonn.

[3] Ernst Udet, 1896–1941. Born in Frankfurt-am-Main. As a fighter pilot from 1915 to 1918 he shot down 62 enemy aeroplanes. After 1918, a stunt pilot and electrical engineer. Director

Unlike our mission to Germany, the German mission is a practical flying body, with a particularly astute and highly trained technical observer in Udet, who is the German AMRD.[1]

How we have been let in for this visitation at the present moment is beyond imagination.

The attached notes[2] are a pretty incisive commentary on our state of preparedness to receive such a mission. Everyone concerned must realize that the impression created on these people now, must inevitably influence German policy with regard to us and foreign policy generally.

At present we are bluffing with the sky as the limit, without holding a single card and we have then invited our opponents to come round and see what cards we hold, trusting to sleight of hand to put across a second bluff.

We know that Milch heads the group which suspects the real state of affairs and that the mission is out to find confirmation of their suspicions.

I suppose this is simply the culminating instance of being caught in the net which we ourselves have woven. Having gone on reiterating that expansion is beyond our most sanguine hopes, and re-equipment well up to expectation—no one dare now call a halt, and disclose the real situation. So the wholesale deceptions and deceits that have been practised, are to continue, in order to prevent a disclosure of the past—even at the risk of wrecking civilization in order to ensure that our various nabobs at any cost hold their jobs & continue with the havoc that they have wrought.

Not a day passes, that the situation does not deteriorate.

Conference at Headquarters, Bomber Command: notes
(Churchill papers: 2/304)

[12 October 1937]

The Chairman[3] opened the proceedings by saying that we should have to comb the country in order to produce sufficient aircraft to put up any sort of show.

Groups were asked to state the number of aircraft that would be available

---

of the Technical Department of the German Air Ministry, 1936. Member for Research and Development, German Air Staff, 1937. Major-General, 1937. Master of the Ordnance (Generalluftzeugleiter), 1938–40. Director-General of Air Force Equipment, 1940–1. Committed suicide in Berlin, 17 November 1941.

[1] Air Member for Research and Development.
[2] Printed as the following document.
[3] Sir Edgar Ludlow-Hewitt (see page 798, note 2), Churchill's Private Secretary at the Air Ministry, 1919–21.

to commence practice on Monday, the 11th October. By types, the following figures were given. . . .[1]

It was hoped to be able to put up a Fly-Past by types of two squadrons each, but it soon became apparent that it would not be possible to put up two squadrons either of Battles or Whitleys, and in consequence the proposal was made that the Fly-Past should be made by squadron formations flying in subformations of flights of three, line astern, stepped up or down.

In this way, the equivalent of perhaps two squadrons of Harrows, two of Wellesleys, two of Blenheims and one each of Battles and Whitleys could be scraped together by amalgamating all the resources available for the purpose, ie, borrowing from one squadron, machines or trained pilots, to make up deficiencies in other squadrons of the same types.

Violet Pearman to Winston S. Churchill

(*Churchill papers: 9/129*)

[12 October] 1937

The Commander wants you particularly to read through this and study it, as it may be very useful to you.

Wing-Commander Anderson: note for Winston S. Churchill

(*Churchill papers: 9/129*)

[12 October] 1937[2]

RAF EXPANSION

A programme of further expansion has been drawn up and it is known as Scheme 'J'.

The proposal is to bring the first line strength of the Royal Air Force up to 2,500 first line aircraft, with a nine to one Reserve; this will mean 20,000

---

[1] Listed were *Battles* (12, 'possibly' 16 aeroplanes), *Blenheims* (22, 'possibly' 25 aeroplanes), *Wellesleys* (31 aeroplanes), *Whitleys* (13 aeroplanes) and *Harrows* (31 aeroplanes). Of the Blenheim it was noted that 144 Squadron 'had only just received theirs from the Makers'.

[2] On 12 October 1937 Lord Swinton had circulated to the Cabinet a memorandum by the Air Staff, recommending a new expansion scheme, J, 'for our minimum requirements for security' to create a total of 2,331 front-line aircraft, including 1,442 bombers, which should be provided 'by the summer of 1941'. This was still 900 less than the German strength estimated by the Air Staff for December 1939 (*Cabinet papers: 27/648*).

aircraft and in round figures we shall have an Air Force as strong in numbers as we had at the end of the Great War.

In taking the figures nine to one, this includes all forms of Reserves ie War Training Reserve to meet the needs on Mobilization of a further additional 35 Flying Training Schools.

Expansion Scheme 'L' has been referred several times to INSKIP and the Cabinet Sub-Committee but is waiting final approval by the Government.

As regards pilots our present output is 3,000 trained pilots every five weeks. As soon as Scheme 'L' is approved a further 8 Flying Training Schools will be opened making our total 17, excluding the Fleet Air Arm, with an output of 600 pilots every five weeks.

We have ordered 1,700 Battle aeroplanes and it has now been agreed that a Navigation Officer is necessary. No provision was made for this in the design of the Battle and delays are now occurring in production to provide the necessary alteration in the seating.

We have received 8,000,000 Links (required for making cartridges into belts). These 8,000,000 Links are out of true and will have to be scrapped.

Winston S. Churchill to F. W. Deakin
(Churchill papers: 8/547)

12 October 1937

Dear Deakin,

Have you found the references in Klopp under the paragraph headed 'Deaths in France'. Let me know the volume and page so that I can see whether I have got the missing bundle of Klopp translations.

We must certainly know what Klopp says about Marlborough's behaviour in exile and about the death of the Queen period. Perhaps you could read some of this to me at the week end. Salomon is also important and I have no translation. Please bring the Klopps with you. Also please get Sergeant Millner[1] from the London Library.

The Brigadier is coming on Sunday and I hope he will be able to give us a lecture on Malplaquet.

---

[1] F. Salomon, *Geschichte des letzten Ministeriums Königin Annas von England, 1710–14*, published in 1894, and used by Churchill as a better authority for the date of Queen Anne's secret letter to Harley than Dean Swift; and Sergeant John Millner, *Journal, 1701–12*, published in 1733, an eye-witness of the events leading up to the battle of Blenheim, as well as the source for the fullest list of the killed, the wounded and prisoners at the battle itself.

Violet Pearman to Thornton Butterworth
(Churchill papers: 8/559)

16 October 1937

Dear Mr Butterworth,

I am asked by Mr Churchill to say that his attention has been called to some more corrections in his new book which he would be glad if you would have made in the future editions.

In the sketch on Alfonso,[1] General Gough[2] has pointed out that the regiment at the wedding was not the Royal Dragoons but the 16th Lancers of which Alfonso was Colonel in Chief.

Mr Bernard Shaw[3] has also written to say that the Red Flag march was described by him as the funeral march of a fried eel, and not as Mr Churchill calls it the burial march of a monkey.[4]

[1] Leon Fernando Maria Jaime Isidoro Pascual Antonio, 1886–1941. Posthumous son of King Alfonso XII of Spain, he was proclaimed King at birth (as Alfonso XIII). He married Victoria Eugénie, a granddaughter of Queen Victoria, in 1906. He fled the country following the Republican majority in the 1931 local elections. He died in exile in Rome.

[2] Hubert de la Poer Gough, 1870–1963. Entered Army, 1889. On active service in the Tirah, 1897–8 and South Africa 1899–1902 (severely wounded). Professor, Staff College 1904–6. Major-General, 1914; Lieutenant-General, 1917. Knighted, 1916. Commanded the 3rd Cavalry Brigade, 1914; the 2nd Cavalry Division, 1914–15; the 1st Army Corps, 1915–16; the Fifth Army, 1916–18. Chief, Allied Mission to the Baltic, 1919. He published *The Fifth Army* (1931) and *Soldiering On* (1954).

[3] George Bernard Shaw, 1856–1950. Novelist, essayist, playwright and dramatist. Awarded the Nobel Prize for Literature, 1925. Among his specifically political works were *Fabianism and the Empire* (1900), *Common Sense About the War* (1914), *How to Settle the Irish Question* (1917), *Peace Conference Hints* (1919), and *Everybody's Political What's What* (1944). In 1938 he published a play about the League of Nations, entitled *Geneva*. In August 1929 Churchill published an essay on Shaw in the *Pall Mall* magazine; it was subsequently reprinted in book form in *Great Contemporaries* (1937). In it Churchill wrote: 'Mr Bernard Shaw was one of my earliest antipathies. Indeed, almost my first literary effusion, written when I was serving as a subaltern in India in 1897 (it never saw the light of day), was a ferocious onslaught upon him, and upon an article which he had written disparaging and deriding the British Army in some minor war. Four or five years passed before I made his acquaintance. My mother, always in agreeable contact with artistic and dramatic circles, took me to luncheon with him. I was instantly attracted by the sparkle and gaiety of his conversation, and impressed by his eating only fruit and vegetables, and drinking only water. I railled him on the latter habit, asking: "Do you really never drink any wine at all?" "I am hard enough to keep in order as it is," he replied. Perhaps he had heard of my youthful prejudice against him. . . . At any rate, I possess a lively image of this bright, nimble, fierce, and comprehending being, Jack Frost dancing bespangled in the sunshine, which I should be very sorry to lose.'

[4] In his essay on Shaw, Churchill had written: '"The Red Flag", the international hymn of the Labour Party, is dubbed by this most brilliant of Socialist intellectuals "the burial march of a monkey",' and he added: 'Everyone has been excoriated, every idea has been rattled, and everything goes on the same as before. We are in the presence of a thinker, original, suggestive, profound; but a thinker who depends on contradiction, and deals out thought as it flashes upon his mind without troubling about its relation to what he has said before, or its results upon the convictions of others. Yet, and it is the essence of the paradox, no one can say that Bernard Shaw is not at heart sincere, or that his life's message has not been consistent.'

Winston S. Churchill to Sir Maurice Hankey

(*Hankey papers*)

16 October 1937   Chartwell
Secret and Personal

My dear Maurice,

As one small instalment of the alarming accounts I have received of the RAF, I send you the enclosed.[1] It is for your own personal information, and I trust to our friendship and your honour that its origin is not probed. But look at the facts!

We have invited the German Mission over—why I cannot tell. Highly competent men are coming. A desperate effort is now being made to present a sham. A power-drive turret is to be shown, as if it was the kind of thing we are doing in the regular way. Ought it to be shown at all? You will see that a special telegram has to be sent to fetch one of the only men acquainted with this turret to give a demonstration. You will also see the feelings of some of the high officers concerned. You will also see from the statement, made by the Air Officer Commanding-in-Chief Bomber Command (paper C. marked in red), Ludlow-Hewitt,[2] how he is forced to address himself to the task of making a show; and what exertions are necessary to put little more than a hundred bombers in the air—the great majority of which (as the Germans will readily see) can barely reach the coast of Germany with a bomb load.

I shall be very glad to know your reaction upon this. I remember how you played an essential part in saving the country over the convoy system, and how when young officers came to you and told you the truth, against Service rules, you saw that the seed did not fall on stony ground. If I had opportunity I could unfold a most shocking state of affairs in the Air Force, and no one would be more pleased than I if I could be refuted categorically. But you have a great responsibility—perhaps on the whole second to none—and therefore I leave the matter for the moment in your hands.

---

[1] Lachlan Maclean's letter of 12 October 1937 (page 793), and its enclosed notes.

[2] Edgar Rainey Ludlow-Hewitt, 1886–1973. 2nd Lieutenant, Royal Irish Rifles, 1905. Transferred to the Royal Flying Corps, 1914. Major, 1915. Commanded the 10th Brigade, Royal Air Force, 1918. Awarded the DSO and the MC. Chief Staff Officer, Royal Air Force Headquarters, France, 1918–19. Group Captain, 1919. Private Secretary to the Secretary of State for Air, 1919–21. Commandant, Royal Air Force Staff College, 1926–30. Air Officer Commanding, Iraq, 1930–2. Knighted, 1933. Elected to the Other Club, 1933. Director of Operations and Intelligence, Air Ministry, 1933–5. Commanded RAF India, 1935–7. Commander-in-Chief, Bomber Command, 1937–40. Inspector-General of the RAF, 1940–5. A member of the Other Club from 1933, he resigned in 1935 (on leaving for India) but rejoined in 1938.

Is it credible that we are sending fifty or sixty Gladiators to China while our own squadrons have to carry on with an even less up-to-date machine? Is it true that a great many of the 3 inch AA guns have been sold to foreign countries or given away, although the new pattern has not yet begun to come into production. Is it true that there are under twenty AA guns at Malta and these only of an old pattern? But I forbear.

Please send me the stuff back when you have done with it, for I am much inclined to make a Memorial to the Prime Minister upon the whole position. Obviously it cannot be dealt with in public.

Yours vy sincerely,
Winston S. Churchill

Brigadier Pakenham-Walsh: diary

(*Pakenham-Walsh papers*)

17 October 1937

Motored over to Chartwell. Winston did not appear till lunch. Mrs C fighting a cold. Diana & Sarah there with their husbands. Sandys I know and like, but I found Sarah's Vic Oliver too much of the American comedian. Mary has grown up a lot in the last year. Deakin of Oxford staying there with his wife and baby. . . .

After lunch I lectured Winston & Deakin for about $2\frac{1}{2}$ hours on Malplaquet. Winston was rather disappointed with my theory about Withers,[1] but Deakin on examining the evidence thought I was right. Winston very interested in my idea of a partial parallel with Blenheim more especially of the combined use of all arms in the centre.

Winston has drafted all but about 4 chapters of Vol IV. So it is an advanced condition. He has I am glad to say decided to continue to use Wood[2] as draughtsman. He was inclined to try his nephew John Churchill.[3]

Winston plied me with a number of questions about Germany, as indeed did they all. He is very concerned about Palestine & Italian movements in

---

[1] General Henry Withers, who commanded nineteen battalions on the right flank of the Allied forces at the battle of Malplaquet, 11 September 1709.

[2] Robert Cavers Wood, 1877–1966. A talented commercial and freelance artist; the younger brother of Churchill's proof-reader, C. C. Wood.

[3] John George Spencer Churchill, 1909–   . Churchill's nephew; son of Jack and Lady Gwendeline Churchill. Educated at Harrow and Pembroke College, Oxford. Artist and designer of murals; he painted the Marlborough pavilion at Chartwell, 1938. Served in the Royal Engineers, 1939–45; Major, 1945. He published his memoirs, *Crowded Canvas*, in 1961.

the Mediterranean. I told him the story of Jack Evetts[1] and the Mayor of Nablus, which excited him greatly.[2]

Sandys wants to form a group of Conservative MPs to make a special study of Palestine.

Winston says at heart he is for Franco, but is very frightened if F is successful of a Spanish alliance with Italy, and the consequent impossible position for Britain & France in the Mediterranean. He suggested Britain & France should occupy Minorca as Trustees for Spain. We asked him what he would do if Franco won & was acknowledged, and he replied laughingly 'Oh then I suppose we would say, what we have we hold.'

He gave me a signed copy of his latest book 'Great Contemporaries' which has had very good reviews. As may be imagined from all this I did not get home till 7.30.

Commander Bishop to Winston S. Churchill

(*Churchill papers: 9/126*)

18 October 1937   The Navy League

Dear Mr Churchill,

I enclose some notes on the Merchant Shipping position, brief because I gather you will not want a great deal, as the Merchant Shipping question will be only one part of your speech; also a rather longer pamphlet, being a recent speech by Lord Lloyd, dealing with the whole question, in case you want to reinforce any of your remarks.

The facts and figures contained therein are all vouched for either by promi-

---

[1] John Fullerton Evetts, 1891–   . Educated at Sandhurst. Entered the Army in 1911. On active service, 1914–18 (Military Cross, despatches; Major, Machine Gun Corps, 1916). Employed with the Iraq Army, 1925–8. Lieutenant-Colonel, Royal Ulster Rifles, 1934. Colonel, 1935. Commander of the British Troops in Palestine, 1935; Brigade Commander, 16th Infantry Brigade, Palestine and Transjordan, 1936–9 (despatches). Commander of the Western District, India, 1940–1. Major-General, 1941. Assistant Chief of the Imperial General Staff, 1942. Senior Military Adviser, Ministry of Supply, 1944–6. Head of the British Ministry of Supply Staff in Australia, 1946–51. Knighted, 1951.

[2] Pakenham-Walsh recorded in his diary for 15 February 1937: 'There was sniping at Nablus & Jack Evetts in command of the Bde there sent for the Mayor, & then gave him a blanket & said "Now you sleep on my roof".The Mayor was furious & returned his MBE. HE [Wauchope, the High Commissioner for Palestine] sent for Dill & said the Army must apologize. Dill said they would be damned first. So HE made the District Commissioner apologize & did so himself as well!! NC [Napier-Clavering, a fellow officer stationed in Palestine] says the whole civil administration are completely disloyal to Wauchope & some definitely traitors' (*Pakenham-Walsh papers*).

nent shipowners, whose names are quoted, or are taken from official Chamber of Shipping documents.

I have sent to-day tickets for the Dinner to Mr and Mrs Duncan Sandys.

Commander Bishop: Notes on the Merchant Shipping Position
(Churchill papers: 9/126)

18 October 1937

Fact that Merchant Shipping is doing better and freights rising at present has little to do with the question of dependence on Merchant Shipping in time of war. Requirements are an adequate number of Cargo Carriers of all types and a sufficiency of men not only to man them but to provide a reserve for the Navy.

Present Position Grave

Compared with 1914, we have 1000 less Cargo Carriers, yet requirements have increased. Increase of population means more mouths to feed. Increasingly dependent upon foreign fuel. 1914 petroleum imports 646 million gallons. In 1935 2,808 million gallons.

An estimate of present shortage of ships to requirements on outbreak of war by a well-known shipowner is 700. Others would put it much higher—1,000 to 1,500.

Reliance on Neutrals

Shortage of British ships means reliance on neutrals. Dangerous position, since at best it means the possibility of blackmail, at worst disaster, since many neutral countries are now within reach of air raid threats, which might force them to preserve absolute neutrality.

Manning

Result of years of depression means thousands of seamen have abandoned the sea and there is now a serious shortage of efficient deckhands, bos'ns and junior engineers being almost unobtainable. Considered by Shipping Federation there would be no men available for the Navy from Merchant Service, whereas in 1914, 16,000 were taken on the outbreak of war.

Causes of decline, British Shipping
　　Government-aided foreign competition.
　　Building and running subsidies.

Coastal restrictions.

Various forms of privilege.

British Merchant Shipping has had to fight foreign Governments almost entirely by its own resources. It is only recently, after damage has been done, Government granted small subsidy, which is to end this year, to Tramp section.

Essential if British Shipping Industry is to be built up to a size adequate to our needs that Government should use whole weight of authority; of British buying power in Trade Agreements: and if necessary grant further protection and assistance to preserve British ships from being driven off the seas.

Public Education

Contributory cause to this state of affairs is public ignorance. Navy League doing what it can to dispel ignorance and rouse public opinion in a matter of National importance.

Winston S. Churchill to Bernard Baruch: telegram
(Churchill papers: 1/300)

18 October 1937

Should be grateful your private opinion market. Have small holdings and indisposed quit. We cannot here conceive reason your collapse. No war Europe this year and immense production including armaments.

Kindest regards,
Chartwell[1]

Sir Maurice Hankey to Winston S. Churchill
(Churchill papers: 2/304)

19 October 1937
Secret and Personal

My dear Winston

In replying to your Secret and Personal letter of the 16th October, let me begin by saying that you may rely on me, on the present occasion, not to

[1] Churchill's code in sending telegrams to Bernard Baruch when dealing with financial matters. For the fate of Churchill's 'small holdings', see pages 950–1.

probe the origin of the information you send about the RAF and other matters. Nevertheless I cannot conceal that I am a good deal troubled by the fact of your receiving so many confidences of this kind.

You and I are very old friends who have hunted together in circumstances of supreme danger and difficulty. I have always valued your friendship. The frequent commendation of one for whom I have an immense admiration has been, and remains, a tremendous encouragement, especially in the parlous times through which we are passing. I feel, therefore, that I can open my mind quite frankly to you on the subject.

It shocks me not a little that high Officers in disciplined Forces should be in direct communication with a leading Statesman who, though notoriously patriotic beyond criticism, is nevertheless in popular estimation regarded as a critic of the Departments under whom these Officers serve.

I do not question the motives of these Officers. They can only be of the highest, for the reason that they have personally nothing to gain from their supposed revelations. On the contrary, they jeopardise their official careers by their action, for a slip might prove disastrous to them, and even though they escape this possibility, it may all come out years after and damage their reputations before posterity. Nothing injured Henry Wilson's[1] reputation so seriously as the revelations from his own diary of his trafficking with the Opposition Leaders before the War.

I am prepared to admit also that it is a very difficult position for an Officer who honestly believes (though he is usually in ignorance of the wider factors that control national policy) that his superiors are not doing their job properly. He has, of course, official channels, eg, his official superiors, Inspecting Officers, even an approach to his Government Department, or, in the last resort, to its political Head. But he may be inexperienced or may shrink from representations that might result in his being marked down as a litigious person or a bore by some red-tapey official superior. So he turns to some unofficial channel.

Nevertheless I feel in my bones that these unofficial communications are all wrong, that the thing is infectious, and subversive to discipline and that the damage done to the Services far outweighs any advantage that may accrue—especially as, when the matters in question are investigated, there is almost invariably a perfectly sound explanation forthcoming.

The position of the recipient of such illicit information is also embarrassing.

[1] Sir Henry Wilson (see page 27, note 1). His diary, in two volumes, was published in 1927, edited and annotated by Major-General Sir Charles Callwell. In an 'author's note', Callwell wrote: 'Outspoken in conversation and outspoken by nature, Sir Henry was no less outspoken on paper—so much so that it has been found expedient to omit some passages, even though of undoubted interest. . . .' Many of these diary extracts were first published in their unexpurgated form in Companion Volume IV of the Churchill biography.

As you may imagine, I am not without experience in the matter. I have sometimes been the recipient of embarrassing confidences of the kind which you enclose. The course which I seek to follow is to try and contrive a way in which the giver of the information can himself get it into the official channel in a perfectly above-board manner and without risk to himself. If, from the circumstances of the case, this is impossible and *prima facie* the matter seems to need probing, I go direct to the Minister or to some friendly official in the Department concerned and put the case before him. That, however, is a delicate matter, as he may demand the source. I am certain that if I had come to you, when you were First Lord of the Admiralty before the War, with material comparable to that with which you have furnished me, you would have turned on me pretty hard. You might well have demanded a searching Inquiry, in which both my informant and I should have found ourselves up against Official Regulations. I have a vague recollection that you once gave me a sharp but friendly rap over the knuckles (perhaps well-deserved) for making a nuisance of myself over submarine mines.

Broadly, then, I do my best to discourage the habit of 'backstairs' information because it breeds distrust and has a disintegrating effect on the discipline of the Services. At the same time I am not so bound up with red tape that I do not try in some cases to get to the bottom of the matter, usually by steering it somehow or other into the official machine. For example, in the case you mention of the convoy system, my Memorandum to the Prime Minister, which is published in the Official History, was in the hands of Carson, Jellicoe and Duff,[1] and was discussed with them collectively, within 48 hours of the completion of the first draft.

I do not know and, as I have said, I do not seek to know, the names of your correspondents in the present instance, but in your case I should, if the circumstances permit, give them friendly counsel, first and above all in the interests of their Service and also, no doubt, of their own careers and reputations, to go to their Commanding Officers, or, if in a position to do so, to some friend in the Department, and frankly to open their minds as to their troubles. I believe that in more than nine cases out of ten they would get a satisfactory explanation and peace of mind. Moreover, if there is truth and substance in their criticism, it is much more likely to find its proper target by a direct course.

We have to remember that everyone is now working under the greatest difficulties, and this applies especially to the RAF in the expansion period. New squadrons are being formed. As the butter of experience gets spread

---

[1] Sir Edward Carson (First Lord of the Admiralty in 1917), Sir John Jellicoe (First Sea Lord) and Rear-Admiral Alexander Duff (Director of the Anti-Submarine Division, Admiralty, 1917, and subsequently Assistant Chief of the Naval Staff).

more thinly over a greatly enlarged Air Force, senior personnel are no doubt constantly being pulled out of their present posts either to join a new squadron or to undergo some course to fit them for specialist activity. All this is happening at a time when new machines, perhaps harder to fly than the old ones, and a new personnel are coming in. The new machines require, no doubt, new tactics, longer flights, and new apparatus, all of which means more intensive training. Probably also all sorts of annoying things happen. Arrivals of machines and their equipment may not synchronise. All this sort of thing must be very harassing, and the tendency must be rather to set people on edge. Although this will rectify itself in the later stages of the expansion, one has to make allowances.

One has also to make allowances for those responsible in the Air Ministry. They are all very hard driven. They, again, must meet with many exasperations, such as delays due to contractors' failures; or, maybe, unavoidable alterations in designs, machines or apparatus that on trial do not come up to expectations.

If they were not doing their best, or were not doing it competently, there would be a case for appropriate action by the Government or, if they do not realise the position, from outside. That is not true at the present time of the Air Ministry. I believe there is tremendous enthusiasm and competence in the face of a very difficult problem. I believe we are aware of our deficiencies (which do not necessarily arise from incompetence) and that every effort is being made to rectify them.

I have seen something myself of the immense effort which is involved in answering long strings of questions. They put an extra load on an overburdened machine, and especially on to those at the top, through whom the replies must necessarily pass, with the consequence that again and again I have seen more harm than good result from that procedure.

I should like to see you using your great influence to get all concerned to appreciate each other's point of view and difficulties, and thus to strengthen mutual trust and confidence. As a nation we need 'jollying' along rather than frightening, and I think in recent writings you have recognised this.

In coming now to the actual details of your communication, I again feel embarrassed unless I know what you are going to do. The material was sent along for my personal information. Some of it I could answer straightaway, but I should not like to do so without Ministerial authority, especially if there is a question of your making representations to the Prime Minister. There are other matters into which I should need inquiry. At least two of the allegations are, I believe, a complete mare's-nest, though here again I should have to check my statement.

You speak here, as you have spoken before, of my responsibility. I do not shirk whatever responsibility is mine. I felt it even more keenly than I do now in the days of the disarmament era, and I did my utmost again and again to bring out the dangers of our course. Since the advent of the re-armament period I am happier in the ceaseless activity that it entails. I have passed the normal age of retirement, and my Chiefs have long known and have repeatedly been told that they will meet with no obstacle or resentment from me if and when they think that a change is necessary in my post. Until the public interest renders my retirement desirable, or inexorable age limits apply, I shall continue to devote my utmost energies to the discharge of my responsibilities, and I hope that I shall continue to have your good will.

I return the enclosures.

Yours ever,
M. P. A. Hankey

Winston S. Churchill to Professor Lindemann

(*Churchill papers: 8/551*)

19 October 1937

I have contracted to write an article on the Future of Invention. You helped me in one on this point four or five years ago which is now published in an altered form in Thoughts and Adventures. I wonder if you would be so kind as to help me in bringing this up to date? If you would take this article as a foundation and give me some new ideas which have come into being since then, and any other improvement which you can suggest, I shall be greatly obliged.[1]

---

[1] Almost a year later, on 16 October 1938, the *News of the World* published Churchill's article, 'The Future of Invention'. In it he wrote, of inventions in the area of biological science: 'It seems not altogether fantastic to imagine that new forms of animals, or even men, breeding true to type, might be produced in some such manner. Supermen, or perhaps submen: angels, or perhaps devils: according to the decision of mere human intelligence. There is an almost universal innate revulsion against interventions in the biological scheme of things. We none of us quite like them, and custom and religion will probably resist them. And custom and religion are probably right, for we do not seem to be making such a wonderful success of our present system that we can afford to have thrust upon us political problems, such as will arise if the very make-up of mankind becomes the plaything of the bureaucrat. But whatever the resistance, such inventions seem likely to be made, and in certain countries to be exploited. Whether they will lead to a Utopia or to the extinction of the human race, one cannot say; but to offer almost limitless possibilities to the very limited intelligence which will be able to use them may well spell, not only the ruin of the civilization we know, but the end of human dominance on this planet. Still, although we are jogging along, happily we are not there yet'.

Bernard Baruch to Winston S. Churchill: telegram

(Churchill papers: 1/300)

20 October 1937

Think America on bargain counter.[1]

Winston S. Churchill to Lord Beaverbrook

(Beaverbrook papers)

20 October 1937   Chartwell
Personal

My dear Max,

I return you Frank Owen's[2] note of our very private and informal after-dinner conversation, which certainly gives a loose and sloppy impression of what I said, or did not say. I think it is a pity that he took the trouble to put it down, and it would certainly be a gross offence if it were ever published. I only asked him from a disinterested friendly impulse and with no object of any kind. *It gives a vy much better picture of FO than it does of me.*

I read your paragraphs in the Evening Standard about FE's and Bonar's Privy Councillorships. I wrote this originally four years ago in the preface of young Freddie's[3] Life of FE and of course I only recorded the impression left on my memory at that time, viz that there was a deadlock for a fortnight or so, at the end of which I was told 'It is all right, Bonar Law has been added too'. Of course I only heard it from our side, and you may well be right that

[1] As far as Churchill's United States stocks were concerned, Baruch was wrong (see pages 950–1).

[2] H. Frank Owen, 1905–1979. Liberal MP for Hereford, 1929–31. Defeated by the Conservative candidate in the General Election of 1931. Became a 'ghost' for all Lord Beaverbrook's articles on economic policy. One of Beaverbrook's 'young eagles'. Editor of the *Evening Standard*, 1938–42, and a pre-war supporter of the grand alliance against the fascist powers. In June 1938 Beaverbrook wrote to him: 'Frank, be careful of your attacks on Ribbentrop. If you get making attacks on Ribbentrop, you are going to disturb the immense efforts that are now being made for an accommodation with Germany.' Co-editor, with Michael Foot, of *Guilty Men*, 1941 (a fierce attack on Neville Chamberlain and the 'appeasers'). Edited a Forces newspaper in India, 1943–5. Biographer of Lloyd George, 1954.

[3] Frederick Winston Furneaux Smith, 1907–1975. Churchill's godson. Only son of the 1st Earl of Birkenhead, to whose earldom he succeeded in 1930. Educated at Eton and Christ Church, Oxford. Parliamentary Private Secretary to Lord Halifax (when Foreign Secretary), 1938–9. Joined the 53rd Anti-Tank Regiment, 1938. Captain, 1940; Major, 1942; Political Intelligence Department, Foreign Office, 1942; British Military Mission to the Yugoslav Partisans, 1944–5. Biographer of his father (1933), of Strafford (1938), of Lord Cherwell (1961), of Lord Halifax (1965), of Walter Monckton (1969), of Kipling (published posthumously in 1978) and of Churchill (being completed by his son, the 3rd Earl).

Bonar Law was always included. I will see if I can make the corrections for the third edition, though I fear it has already gone to press. If any slight was conveyed by what I wrote on Bonar Law, it was certainly not intended, for although he did me damage on many occasions, I do not think I have ever said an unkind word about him in public, and as you know I am not re-vengeful.[1] You will be glad to hear the book has been a great success and we hope to sell 10,000.

You must be having good weather at Cannes or I suppose you would not stay there so long. The Americans have gone quite cracky and I have locked up my few shares till they come to their senses, which I expect they will do in the course of the next year. I am told that Esmond[2] has bought a lot of firstclass stuff very cheap.

The Tories received me very well at Scarborough, and I do not feel my pilgrimage there was in vain.

When are you coming home?

Yours ever,
W

Winston S. Churchill to Sir Maurice Hankey
(Hankey papers)

21 October 1937   11 Morpeth Mansions
Strictly personal

My dear Maurice,

I certainly did not expect to receive from you a lengthy lecture when I went out of my way to give you, in strict confidence, information in the public interest. I thank you for sending me the papers back, and you may be sure I shall not trouble you again in such matters.

Yours vy sincerely,
Winston S. Churchill

---

[1] In his essay on F.E. (first published in 1933 as a preface to the 2nd Earl of Birkenhead's biography of his father, and reprinted in 1937 in *Great Contemporaries*) Churchill wrote: 'His son tells us of his becoming a Privy Councillor at the Coronation in 1910. I think I had something to do with that. I knew Mr Asquith thought highly of him and, liked his mind with refined professional appreciation. I urged his inclusion as a Privy Councillor in the non-party honours list. The author tells us of the curious reaction which this proposal when made by the Prime Minister produced upon Mr Balfour, then leader of the Opposition. I do not think it was jealousy or fear of subsequent complications. Mr Balfour had his long-built ideas about how patronage and promotion should be distributed among members of the party over which he and his uncle had reigned for a generation. At any rate he opposed it, and in order to carry the proposal it was found necessary to confer another Privy Councillor-ship upon Mr Bonar Law. This probably turned the scale in favour of Mr Bonar Law's leadership, and may traceably have altered the course of history. However, it is always being altered by something or other.'

[2] Esmond Harmsworth (see page 8, note 1).

Lord Wigram to Winston S. Churchill

(*Churchill papers: 8/549*)

21 October 1937   Windsor Castle

My dear Churchill,

I have just read your appreciation of King George V in 'Great Contemporaries'. It is quite charming and you have been very clever in describing the man as he was and thought.[1] HM always had a high regard for you. . . .

Winston S. Churchill to Lord Wigram

(*Churchill papers: 8/549*)

22 October 1937

I am so glad you liked what I wrote about King George. Several times in my life he went out of his way to pay me a compliment, and there were times (Mylius[2] etc) when I had intimate business to do for him.

[1] In his essay on King George V, Churchill wrote, of the aftermath of the First World War: 'The shadow of victory is disillusion. The reaction from extreme effort is prostration. The aftermath even of successful war is long and bitter. The years that followed the Great War, and such peace as the infuriated democracies would allow their statesmen to make, were years of turbulence and depression. Shrill voices, unheard amidst the cannonade and the hum of national exertion, were now the loudest notes. Subversive processes, arrested by the danger, resumed their course. Weak peoples, protected by the shield of Britain from conquest or invasion, used their nursed-up and hoarded strength against their successful guardians. But the King preserved his sense of proportion. When Mr Lloyd George returned from Paris with the Treaty of Victory, he took the unprecedented course of himself meeting his deserving subject at Victoria Station and driving him in his own carriage to Buckingham Palace. History will not overlook the significance of this act.' Of the King, and the first Labour Government of 1924, Churchill wrote: 'He reconciled the new forces of Labour and Socialism to the Constitution and the Monarchy. This enormous process of assimilating and rallying the spokesmen of left-out millions, will be intently studied by historians of the future. To the astonishment of foreign countries and of our American kinsmen, the spectacle was seen of the King and Emperor working in the utmost ease and unaffected cordiality with politicians whose theories at any rate seemed to menace all existing institutions, and with leaders fresh from organizing a General Strike. The result has been to make a national unity upon Constitutional fundamentals which is the wonder of the world.'

[2] In November 1910, shortly after George V had come to the throne, and before the Coronation, Edward F. Mylius, a Republican and an anarchist, alleged, in the Paris published magazine the *Liberator*, that the King's marriage to Princess (later Queen) Mary in 1893 had been a 'sham, shameful and bigamous and an offence against the Church', in that he had already been married, in Malta, to a daughter of Admiral Sir Michael Culme-Seymour. As Home Secretary, Churchill initiated steps to prosecute Mylius for a criminal libel against the King, and himself urged the King 'to strike at the libel and sweep the falsehood out of existence once and for all'. The case took place before the Lord Chief Justice, and a jury in 1 February 1911. Mylius was convicted, and sentenced to a year's imprisonment. Later that day the King wrote to Churchill from Windsor: 'I hasten to send you these lines

I wonder whether the present King would allow me to send him a copy of Great Contemporaries? If so, I will have one suitably bound. Most of my other books were received by the late Sovereigns and are in the Royal Library. Perhaps you will drop me a line.

Winston S. Churchill to David B. Cunynghame[1]

(*Churchill papers: 8/557*)

22 October 1937
Private and Confidential

It happens that in these months I am very heavily engaged in literary work, extremely important to me for next year. I have undertaken to finish by December 31 the last volume of Marlborough, for which I am to receive £3,500. This is far advanced. I am also writing another series of twelve articles for the News of the World for which I am to receive £4,500. Although these contracts would not be voided by a month's delay, I was counting upon the money for certain heavy payments which fall due at the end of the year.

If I am to make a strong personal contribution to this Lawrence film,[2] I

---

to say how deeply I appreciate the very thorough manner in which you have carried through the most disagreeable case, which has caused both the Queen & myself much pain & anxiety, to a successful conclusion. I am afraid it must have given you a great deal of trouble & work. I desire to express my most grateful thanks to you for your valuable assistance in your position as Home Secretary, in carrying out my wishes to prove to the world at large the baseness of this cruel & abominable libel' (*Spencer-Churchill papers*).

[1] Henry David St Leger Brooke Selwyn Cunynghame, 1905–78. Educated at Eton. A motion picture producer. Squadron Leader, RAFVR, 1940–4. Succeeded his father as 11th Baronet, 1941. Dallas Bower writes: 'Very much Alexander Korda's *eminence grise*, his organizing ability made him the primary motive power behind the extension of the Isleworth studios—one of the oldest in the country—the creation of the huge production centre at Denham and subsequently the enlargement of facilities at Shepperton. Not only a champion of ideas but determined supporter of the necessity for technical excellence in the production of films, he was at the very centre of the Korda 'golden' period ranging from *The Private Life of Henry VIII* to the immensely ambitious *Things to Come* of H. G. Wells. . . . Cunynghame learnt film making the hard way having at some time or another served in a junior capacity in nearly every department of production thereby equipping himself to a high degree of technical skill and knowledge and thus enriching his managerial expertise. An intensely shy man, his manner was often mistaken for brusqueness by those who knew him only superficially but those closer to him knew him to be quintessentially a warm-hearted generous and kind man' (*The Times, 25 August 1978*).

[2] Churchill had been asked to act as historical adviser, on a full length feature film about Lawrence of Arabia, to be made by Alexander Korda, the script of which had already been written (see pages 817–9 and 823–6).

must derange all my existing plans, and let the subject play a large part in my thoughts during the month of November. I have some ideas upon the subject, but it will be necessary for me to re-read the Seven Pillars as well as the scenario. I have no doubt I shall get much interested in it and my other work will fall into the shade.

In all these circumstances, of which I inform you confidentially, I think I should be paid £2,000 for giving my best services in opinion, criticism and assistance on the film during the month of November—£1,000 on the signing of the contract, and £1,000 on November 30 when the bulk of the work so far as it affects me would be over.[1] I should furnish both written and oral commentaries on different points and would attend or arrange conferences with you as might be necessary and convenient. If the above is satisfactory to you I suggest that the first meeting should take place at my flat on Tuesday morning at 11 o'clock, by which time I shall have read the scenario and first impressions can be interchanged.

If however my contribution should be found of sufficient importance to warrant my name being used with the editing or preparation of the scenario, which might perhaps be of advantage to the film, I should then ask for a percentage additional to the foregoing fee which we could discuss at a later stage in case this further aspect was found to be advantageous by your directors.

Winston S. Churchill to Lord Derby

(*Churchill papers: 2/311*)

23 October 1937

We have a small 'focus' which aims at gathering support from all Parties, especially those of the 'left', for British re-armament, for the association of the two Western democracies (France and Britain), and for the maintenance of peace through British strength.

We are entertaining Anthony Eden on November 2nd at the Savoy Hotel. Your friend Mr Toole,[2] the Socialist Mayor of Manchester is coming, and all Parties will be there,—about thirty-five people altogether. It would be

---

[1] In the money values of September 1981, Churchill wished to receive £35,000 for his work on the Lawrence film script, and would receive more than £60,000 for his last Marlborough volume, and nearly £80,000 for his twelve *News of the World* articles.

[2] Joseph Toole, 1887–1945. Educated at Mount Carmel Roman Catholic School, Salford. Worked first as a newsboy, then as a labourer in an iron foundry and in electrical shops. Labour MP for Salford, 1923–4 and 1929–31. Lord Mayor of Manchester, 1936–7.

splendid if you would join us at the luncheon. It would involve no political commitments, and is of course strictly private.

We usually have interesting luncheons.[1]

Winston S. Churchill to Lord Londonderry

(*Churchill papers: 2/299*)

23 October 1937

It is very good of you to write to me so fully about your anxieties concerning our foreign policy.

I am afraid we take very different and almost opposite views. I am in general agreement with the present Foreign Office policy, and only wish they had a freer scope.

You cannot expect English people to be attracted by the brutal intolerances of Nazidom, though these may fade with time. On the other hand, we all wish to live on friendly terms with Germany. We know that the best Germans are ashamed of the Nazi excesses, and recoil from the paganism on which they are based. We certainly do not wish to pursue a policy inimical to the legitimate interests of Germany, but you must surely be aware that when the German Government speaks of friendship with England, what they mean is that we shall give them back their former Colonies, and also agree to their having a free hand so far as we are concerned in Central and Southern Europe. This means that they would devour Austria and Czecho-Slovakia as a preliminary to making a gigantic middle-Europa-block. It would certainly not be in our interests to connive at such policies of aggression.

It would be wrong and cynical in the last degree to buy immunity for ourselves at the expense of the smaller countries of Central Europe. It would be contrary to the whole tide of British and United States opinion for us to facilitate the spread of Nazi tyranny over countries which now have a considerable measure of democratic freedom.

In my view, we should build up so strong a Federation by regional agreements under the League of Nations, that Germany will be content to live within her own bounds in a law-abiding manner, instead of seeking to invade her smaller neighbours, slay them and take their farms and houses for themselves. The idea that the 'have-nots' should forcibly pillage the 'haves' is not

---

[1] Lord Derby replied, on 26 October 1937: 'Nothing will give me greater pleasure than to accept your invitation and attend the luncheon on November 2nd. Unless anything unforeseen occurs I will be there. You don't mention the time. Would you telephone that?' (*Derby papers*).

one I have been brought up to admire, either in international or domestic affairs. If Germany likes to live like any other non-aggressive country, she will receive no obstruction from us, and we should be very glad to see her prosperous internally. As her population is now on the decline, there is no need for her to expand. All Germany has to do to win British goodwill is not to commit crimes.

One must hope that in the passage of years, these Dictators will disappear like other ugly creatures of the aftermath.

Winston S. Churchill to Imre Revesz
(*Churchill papers: 8/561*)

23 October 1937

Dear Doctor Revesz,

I send you the article 'Yugo-Slavia and Europe' in very good time. It will not be published here until Friday, 29th October. You can have it translated as soon as possible, but there may be a few corrections, which I will telephone at latest on Monday. Thus you could despatch it for certain by the night mails of Monday, for release Saturday morning.[1]

I think my next article will probably study the problems of Czecho-Slovakia.

---

[1] On 29 October 1937 the *Evening Standard* published Churchill's article 'A Key State in Europe', in which he wrote that 'the need of national survival and prosperity should foster a broad-based settlement. These are not times when young nations can afford to have needless friction.' Churchill urged the Yugoslavs to 'proclaim high ideals for the rights of the individuals, the conscious share of all citizens in the Government of their country, the respect for law, the freedom of speech and writing, and free Parliamentary debate'. His article declared: 'It would be a disaster, far reaching in its consequences, if Yugoslavia were quite needlessly ranged among the dictatorial or totalitarian states. Great internal stresses would immediately arise. The Little Entente would be completely ruptured. The fate of Czechoslovakia might be sealed. Bohemia and Moravia would soon be incorporated in Nazidom, and these convulsions might well produce a world war with its incalculable possibilities. The position of Yugoslavia as a poor relation to Rome and Berlin would be pitiful in the last degree. In fact, from the moment when the armed Western democracies, Britain and France, lost their interest in the fortunes of South-Eastern Europe, Yugoslavia would be left to bargain for her existence with the two dictators, one of whom, the Italian, views the Dalmatian coast and its harbours with avid eyes. Far safer and wiser would it be for this new kingdom of the Southern Slavs to throw in her lot boldly upon the side of Peace, Freedom and Parliamentary democracy. In this way alone would she realise that internal strength and unity which is vital to her in these critical decades of her life.'

Winston S. Churchill to Sir Edward Marsh

(*Churchill papers: 8/547*)

23 October 1937

My dear Eddie,

Thank you so much for the corrections, which I am incorporating. All your criticisms are so just and enlightening. I hope you think the work gains by its structure. The use of many documents can only be defended if an irresistible impression is produced upon the faithful reader.

Do you think it is up to the standard of the previous volumes? Of course it will be clapped together and pruned a good deal before it finally sees the light.

All this period is marked by a double calendar difficulty. Old Style and New Style run at their interval of eleven days, and in addition in England the year only ended in April. Consequently when an English person wrote 'January 3, 1710', what he really meant was January 14, 1711. Funny!

I hope to see you soon.

P. J. Grigg to Winston S. Churchill

(*Churchill papers: 8/549*)

24 October 1937   Financial Member of Council,
                                                         India

My dear Winston,

It is kind of you to go on sending me your books & I am most grateful. If you could know what an encouragement it is out here to get reminders of another & friendlier country and of other & kinder & greater people I think that you would be pleased.

When I first got back it looked as if there was going to be a change for the better in official relationships but it didn't last long & as the deterioration coincided in time with a refusal on my part to give an increase of £900 a year in pay to the Viceroy's private secretary[1] I am assuming that the trouble is

[1] John Gilbert Laithwaite, 1894–   . Educated at Trinity College, Oxford. On active service in France, 1917–18 (wounded). Appointed to the India Office, 1919; Principal, 1924; specially attached to the Prime Minister (Ramsay MacDonald) for the second Indian Round Table Conference, 1931. Secretary of the Indian Franchise (Lothian) Committee, 1932; of the Indian Delimitation Committee, 1935–6. Private Secretary to the Viceroy (Linlithgow), 1936–43. Knighted, 1941. Under-Secretary (Civil), War Cabinet, 1944–5. Deputy Under-Secretary of State for India, 1944–5; for Burma, 1945–7; for India, 1947; for Commonwealth Relations, 1948–9. British Ambassador to Dublin, 1950–1; High Commissioner to Pakistan, 1951–4. Permanent Under-Secretary of State for Commonwealth Relations, 1955–9.

entirely caused by His Jesuitical Sub-Excellency. I think we are in for big trouble out here though what form it will take is not certain. It looks at the moment as if it will start by fierce communal clashes but big strikes may pre-cede. Or the Mahatma may pull his puppets out of office when he is ready for a row, or anything. The extremists are counting on a European war which they won't get & so the odds are a communal trouble which Indian Ministers will handle very feebly. However I will lay you fair odds that Federation is dead though, as in this country the prophet is always wrong, not in a very large sum.

My love & thanks to you,
Yours ever,
PJ

Lord Wigram to Winston S. Churchill
(*Churchill papers: 8/549*)

25 October 1937 Windsor

My dear Churchill,

I know that the King would much appreciate your sending him a copy of 'Great Contemporaries' and it certainly should have an honoured place in the Royal library. His Majesty prefers books in their ordinary binding and not specially bound. He also likes a little inscription in the fly leaf from the author. So will you kindly send a copy direct to the King?

Yours sincerely,
Wigram

Lord Londonderry to Winston S. Churchill
(*Churchill papers: 2/299*)

26 October 1937

My dear Winston,

I have returned to London and we must have a conversation. Much as you desire to make out that there is a difference of opinion between us, I am quite sure there is none. I do feel however, that Hitler is looked upon in this country and by so many of our leading men, as a complete bogey and I am quite sure that careful handling would, in the past, have made him do a great deal that we wanted and in the present may stop him taking steps which a Dictator and what you call 'these ugly creatures of the aftermath', are compelled to take so as to maintain public opinion.

I am sending you 'Great Contemporaries' and shall be most grateful if you will inscribe it for me.

Yours affectionately,
Charley

Winston S. Churchill to Louis Levy: telegram

(*Churchill papers: 1/407*)

26 October 1937

Most grateful for your cable and invitation. Have so much work over here that I could not undertake visit US unless assured minimum twenty-five thousand dollars.[1] Several other proposals have been made also suggestions other broadcasts also possibly few lectures. Can you let me know what are prospects. Imagine now things much restricted. Do not anticipate difficulty about topics.

Kindest regards,
Churchill

Winston S. Churchill to Louis Levy: telegram

(*Churchill papers: 1/407*)

27 October 1937

My friend Brendan Bracken sailing today on Queen Mary will communicate with you on arrival New York. Herbert Swope had a plan and Sarnoff [2] talked to Randolph about some broadcast. If all could be arranged would

---

[1] The equivalent in pounds sterling in September 1981 of more than £85,000.

[2] David Sarnoff, 1891–1971. Born in Minsk, Russia, of Jewish parentage. Brought to the United States by his parents, 1900. A messenger boy with the Commercial Cable Company, New York, 1906. A Junior Telegraph operator with the Marconi Wireless Telegraph Company of America, 1907. Wireless Operator, Nantucket Island, 1908. Chief Radio Inspector, and Assistant Chief Engineer, Marconi Company, 1913–15; Assistant Traffic Manager, 1915–16; Commercial Manager, 1917–19. Commercial Manager of the Radio Corporation of America (RCA) when it absorbed the Marconi Company, 1919; General Manager, 1921; Vice-President, 1922; Executive Vice President, 1929; President, 1930; Chairman and Chief Executive Officer, 1947–66; Chairman, 1966–70. Brigadier-General, Signal Corps, US Army, 1944; Legion of Merit, 1944.

come States December and do some work both before and after Christmas which should spend in Jamaica. Will keep my plans open till November 15 otherwise shall winter Riviera where I can do my literary work. You will like Brendan who is a friend of Bernie.

Churchill

Lord Winterton to Winston S. Churchill

(Churchill papers: 8/567)

27 October 1937

My dear Winston,

I have read the script of the proposed Lawrence film, and my views are as follows:

Speaking with some slight knowledge (possibly here the old proverb 'A little knowledge is a dangerous thing' applies) of the film industry as a former director of two cinema theatres, I should say that the film had distinct possibilities of a moderate Box Office success, because Lawrence's personality should have a good drawing power if he is portrayed at all adequately, and also because there should be a number of good scenes if well 'shot' in the play—eg:

(a) The interview between Feisal and Auda.
(b) The attack on the Turkish post.
(c) Lawrence's execution of the criminal.
(d) As a 'comic' (here I thought the dialogue was very good), the episode of the two sergeants riding camels.
(e) Auda and his wife and child in the former's tent.

What I have said above as to the drawing power of the film would only apply if it were produced on a really good and grand scale, which the dramatic greatness of the theme and the principal character in it demand; if, as I understand, Korda[1] intends to produce it, Cadit Quaestio,[2] because a genius like him would not dream of producing it on any other scale.

The film of course falsifies history, but so must one sadly confess does every

---

[1] Alexander Korda, 1893–1956. Born in Hungary. Educated at Budapest University. Film producer in Budapest, Vienna, Berlin, Hollywood and Paris. Founder and Chairman of London Film Productions Ltd, 1932. Became a British subject, 1936. Founded Alexander Korda Productions, 1939. Made 112 films, including The Scarlet Pimpernel (1934), The Third Man (1949) and Richard III (1956). Knighted, 1942.

[2] Literally: 'the question falls to the ground'. In use as: 'so be it'.

film purporting to be historical; for example, so far as I know Allenby,[1] when he entered Jerusalem in December 1917, never talked about an immediate advance to Damascus. In fact the EEF, very properly, rested, waited and re-organised before the great offensive in September 1918. As having some bearing on this matter I might mention a conversation which I had with Allenby when I was going home on leave in June 1918. He very kindly gave me a lift to Suez, where I was to catch my boat, from Cairo in his special train, and when he said good-bye to me his last words were: 'You might tell some of your Politician friends in England if you see any of the 'powers that be' that they have taken away the meat and left me only the bone.'

By this, of course, he meant the fact that several of his best divisions had been removed after the March 1918 offensive. You might argue that if it had not been for the removal of these divisions he would have advanced in the early Summer of 1918, but I do not think he had any intention of doing so. What he meant was that the troops which he was training for the big offensive which he contemplated in the Autumn would no longer be avail-able, and he would have to begin all over again with fresh troops from India.

There is one falsification of history to which I do take real exception, not because I was personally concerned (because I did not join the Arab Bureau until later), but because of the reflection upon friends of mine.

In the early part of the script the people under whom Lawrence was work-ing are made to look absolute fools, and he (Lawrence) to be the sole originator of the idea of the Arab Campaign. Of course this is the most com-plete nonsense as every document of authority, official and unofficial, shows (eg See Ronald Storr's[2] book 'Orientations' with its history of how the Arab Revolt started); the author has completely missed the real point. It

---

[1] Edmund Henry Hynman Allenby, 1861–1936. Entered Army, 1882. Major-General, 1909. Commanded 1st Cavalry Division, British Expeditionary Force, 1914. Commanded the Cavalry Corps, 1914–15. Commanded 5th Army Corps, 1915. Knighted, 1915. Com-manded 3rd Army, 1915–17. Lieutenant-General, 1916. General, 1917. Commander-in-Chief, Egyptian Expeditionary Force, 1917–19. Received the surrender of Jerusalem, 9 December 1917. Drove the Turks from Palestine at the Battle of Megiddo, 19 September 1918. Created Viscount Allenby of Megiddo, 1919. Field-Marshal, 1919. High Commissioner for Egypt and the Sudan, 1919–25. His only son was killed in action in France in 1917.

[2] Ronald Storrs, 1881–1955. Educated at Charterhouse and Pembroke College, Cambridge. Entered the Ministry of Finance of the Egyptian Government, 1904; Oriental Secretary, British Agency, Egypt, 1909–14. Assistant Political Officer, Egyptian Expeditionary Force, 1916 (despatches). Liaison Officer, Mission to Baghdad and Mesopotamia, 1917 (despatches). A member of the War Cabinet Secretariat, London, autumn 1917. Military Governor of Jerusalem, 1917–20 (despatches). Civil Governor of Jerusalem and Judaea, 1920–6. Knighted, 1924. Governor and Commander-in-Chief, Cyprus, 1926–32; Northern Rhodesia, 1932–4. Invalided from tropical service, 1934. Member of the London County Council (East Isling-ton), 1937–45. Broadcaster and writer for the Ministry of Information, 1940–5. Special Correspondent of the *Sunday Times* from Portugal to Persia, 1942–3. He published his diary and memoirs of Palestine, entitled *Orientations*, in 1937 (reprinted in 1949).

was in the execution of the plan that Lawrence showed his genius, and where he was undoubtedly thwarted until Allenby arrived on the scene was by the ordinary stupid type of 'brass hat', but *never* by either his superiors or colleagues in the Arab Bureau; they recognised his genius from the first.

I think you ought to use your immense influence in the matter to get this portion of the script altered; the writer can have a 'go' at the 'stupid soldiers', if he wishes, by showing the way in which Lawrence was undoubtedly thwarted at first when he had actually set to work.

I have to go this afternoon to speak for Ivor Guest[1] in Brecon, but shall be in the House to-morrow afternoon if you want to see me.

Yours sincerely,
Winterton

Winston S. Churchill to the Duke of Windsor
(*Churchill papers: 2/300*)

28 October 1937

Sir,

I am indeed grieved not to be able to see your Royal Highness before you start for the United States.

I have followed with great interest your German tour. I am told that when scenes of it were produced in the news reels in the cinemas here, your Royal Highness' pictures were always very loudly cheered. I was rather afraid beforehand that your tour in Germany would offend the great numbers of Anti-Nazis in this country, many of whom are your friends and admirers; but I must admit that it does not seem to have had that effect, and I am glad it all passed off with so much distinction and success.[2]

---

[1] Churchill's cousin, the Liberal MP for Brecon and Radnor (see page 524, note 3).

[2] Reaching Berlin on 11 October 1937, the Duke and Duchess of Windsor, were met by Dr Robert Ley, and visited among others Himmler, Hess, Goebbels and Göring. The Duke was shocked in Göring's home to find a map on which Austria was shown as a part of Germany. On the last day of their visit they were Hitler's guests at Berchtesgaden. Hitler's interpreter Paul Schmidt later recalled: 'Hitler was evidently making an effort to be as amiable as possible towards the Duke, whom he regarded as Germany's friend, having especially in mind a speech the Duke had made several years before, extending the hand of friendship to German ex-serviceman's associations. In these conversations there was, so far as I could see, nothing whatever to indicate whether the Duke of Windsor really sympathized with the ideology and practices of the Third Reich, as Hitler seemed to assume he did. Apart from some appreciative words for the measures taken in Germany in the field of social welfare the Duke did not discuss political questions. He was frank and friendly with Hitler, and displayed the social charm for which he is known throughout the world. The Duchess joined only occasionally in the conversation, and then with great reserve, when any question of special interest to women arose. She was simply and appropriately dressed and made a lasting impression on Hitler. "She would have made a good Queen," he said when they had gone' (R. H. Steel, editor, *Hitler's Interpreter*, London 1951, page 75).

The American journey I feel sure will be prosperous and you will get a reception from that vast public which no Englishman has ever had before. There is only one point on which I would presume to make a suggestion. Would it not be wiser to cross the Atlantic in the 'Normandie' rather than in the 'Bremen' or 'Europa'? Nothing can beat the 'Normandie' for comfort; but what makes me write is the importance of not running counter needlessly to the overwhelming Anti-Nazi feeling in the United States. As you know, the mob in New York a few months ago actually raided the 'Bremen' and tore down the Swastika flag. There are millions of Jews in the United States, and they have a great deal of influence there. I do not think that your tour in Germany will be a serious impediment, but if you arrive in a French ship, you will have effectively made a gap between the German and the American tour. Moreover, travelling by the 'Normandie' would enable you to pay a compliment to France, which after all is the country with whom our fortunes at the present time are bound up.

I hope, Sir, you will forgive me for venturing to put this point before you, for I, like your many friends in England, have only one desire, namely for your continued happiness, good fortune and influence for good.[1]

Politics here are horribly dull. We used to have such fun before the War, but now it is all drab. There are no quarrels, no vehement debates, no stormy scenes,—nothing in fact to make the House of Commons worth attending; and I do so as little as possible.

The Duke of Windsor to Winston S. Churchill
(*Churchill papers: 2/300*)

29 October 1937   Hotel Meurice,
                                                       Paris

Dear Winston,

Thank you for your letter just received; the Duchess of Windsor and I are also sorry that we shall not see you before we leave for America.

---

[1] In the event, the Duke of Windsor cancelled his United States visit, and stayed instead in France. Among the reasons for the cancellation was the hostile reaction in the United States to his German visit. On 23 October 1937, five days before Churchill's warning, the *New York Times* carried the following report: 'The Duke's decision to see for himself the Third Reich's industries and social institutions and his gestures and remarks during the last two weeks have demonstrated adequately that the Abdication did rob Germany of a firm friend, if not indeed a devoted admirer, on the British throne. He has lent himself, perhaps unconsciously but easily, to National Socialist propaganda. There can be no doubt that his tour has strengthened the regime's hold on the working classes. . . . The Duke is reported to have become critical of English politics as he sees them and is reported as declaring that the British ministers of today and their possible successors are no match for the German or Italian dictators.'

I quite understand, and appreciate, what you say regarding possible criticism of our crossing the Atlantic in a German ship, from anti-Nazi quarters, and am glad of the opportunity of explaining why the 'Bremen' was the only ship available to suit our plans.

I have to remain in Paris until November 4th in order to deal with certain papers now being prepared in London, and must start my Industrial Tour of the United States on November 14th in order to avoid clashing with the Christmas Season. I may also add that we have to go to Washington first, to see the President, then for me to make a short broadcast, and finally to dine with the Lindsays[1] at the British Embassy. This last information, how-ever, will not be released until later, so I am asking you to regard it as confi-dential.

Our visit to Germany was intensely interesting, and I am glad to hear it has not given offence, though as I went there without any political considera-tions and merely as an independent observer studying housing and industrial conditions, I cannot see that it could have. After all, one cannot ignore a country with a population of sixty-five millions, or the system dealing with the problem, even though it may not have one's entire approval. I am gratified to hear that the news-reels of the visit have been well received in England.

We are looking forward to America with the greatest interest and hope to be able to tell you about it on our return to Europe next year.

The Duchess and I have seen as much of Randolph as we have dared without creating too much jealousy among his colleagues of the press. I think you will find that he also regards his tour with us in Germany as a great experience.

Thank you for your good wishes for our journey.

Yours sincerely,
Edward

---

[1] Ronald Charles Lindsay, 1877–1945. 5th son of the 26th Earl of Crawford. Entered the diplomatic service in 1898. Under-Secretary of State for Finance to the Egyptian Govern-ment, 1913–19. Minister Plenipotentiary at Paris, 1920. British Government representative at Constantinople, 1924–5; Ambassador to Turkey, 1925–6. Knighted, 1925. Ambassador at Berlin, 1926–8. Permanent Under-Secretary of State at the Foreign Office, 1928–30. Ambassador at Washington, 1930–9. His first wife was Martha (who died in 1918), daughter of former Senator James Donald Cameron, of Pennsylvania. He married again, in 1924, Elizabeth Sherman, daughter of Colgate Hoyt of New York. He died on 21 August, and his second wife on 3 September 1945. They had no children.

Sir Emsley Carr to Winston S. Churchill

(*Churchill papers: 8/551*)

30 October 1937   News of the World

My dear Winston,

Hearty congratulations on this week's article.[1] It is, I think, one of the most interesting so far as our general readers are concerned.

To-day our circulation exceeds four millions net, and it requires no imagination on your part to realise what an enormous public—probably the largest in the world—you are addressing. Four readers to every paper issued—some say five—is the usual computation, and the power behind this number is what you will comprehend.

I cannot say how delighted we are to have you as our chief contributor, and we are looking forward to your promise to dine with us one Saturday night and see our production in active operation.[2]

And, with kindest remembrances to Mrs Winston,

I am,
Very sincerely yours,
Emsley Carr

[1] On 31 October 1937 the *News of the World* published Churchill's article, 'Vision of the Future through the Eyes of Science'. After commenting on the revolution brought about by the use of coal fuel as a substitute for food, Churchill wrote: 'Today we know that there is another source of energy a million times greater. We have not yet learned how to harness it or apply it, but it is there. Occasionally in complicated processes in the laboratory a scientist observed transmutations, re-arrangements in the core of the atom, which is known as the nucleus, which generated power at a rate hundreds of thousands of times greater than is produced when coal is burned and when, as the scientists put it, a carbon atom satisfied its affinity for an oxygen molecule. It can scarcely be doubted that a way to induce and control these effects will be found. The new fire is laid, but the particular kind of match is missing. If, and when, these sources of power become available our whole outlook will be changed. Geography and climate, which have conditioned all human history, will become our servants rather than our masters.'

[2] Also on 31 October 1937, the *Sunday Chronicle* had published the last of a series of six articles by Churchill. This series had begun with 'Big Navy' (21 February 1937), and had continued with 'A King is Crowned' (9 May 1937), 'The Creeds of the Devil', on fascism and communism (27 June 1937), 'menace over Europe' (17 October 1937), and 'Jellicoe' (24 October 1937) ending with 'Kitchener' (31 October 1937).

November 1937

[1 November] 1937

Have not answered your September 20 because I had nothing to say. Weight of European situation presses so heavily on all minds here. Brendan should arrive today. Please let me know after seeing him whether there is any advantageous step I can take. Hope our poor little man[1] will have kindly welcome. Warmest regards.

W

3 November 1937

Dear Mr Cunynghame,

I do not know whether you have heard from Mr Korda, or what was the result. However, I have now consulted Lord Winterton about the scenario, which he has read. I send you his comments. You must remember that he was with Lawrence during some of the most important phases in this story. You will of course treat his comments as confidential, and as made only to me. It seems to me that Paragraph 4 of his letter will be tiresome, and might entail considerable recasting of this part of the story. Yet I do not see why a good tale could not be told more in accordance with the truth. The picture of the Arab Bureau, all burning and toiling around Lawrence, should fill all this scene and would be good, especially when one saw them hampered and shut down by the 'brass-hats' outside. There is no doubt they were all as keen as mustard, and I can see this part of the tale well told—Lawrence mak-

---

[1] The Duke of Windsor; but he never made his intended visit (see page 820, note 1).

ing his way with them and converting them. Anyhow I think you will have
to try to re-draw this part more in accordance with the truth.

Generally, I think Lord Winterton's comments are very valuable. My own
were largely imparted to you in our talk. I think the 'Lawrence touch' in the
early dialogue is good and characteristic.

Page 18. You can hardly talk of arousing the Arabs to a *Crusade*, which were
things instituted to do them in. *Jehad* is the real word. Anyhow, they have no
use for the Cross.

It would be a good thing to check this whole story up with the map. *Page
24.* What is the distance from Damascus to Wejd? It is 500 miles. Any ordinary film 'fan' reading this would suppose that it was a stepping-stone and
quite close to Damascus. As a matter of fact it is hundreds of miles in the
opposite direction. I do not think this tale can be told properly unless the
geography is driven into the minds of the audience early in the day; otherwise they get a wrong impression, and keep on wondering why the hell
people turn up here and there, and what it is all about. It is above all important to avoid confusion of mind in the audience. Unless you can carry
them with you in thought at each stage, with pictures moving so quickly,
they just get blurred, if not bored. Therefore I counsel forcing the audience
to know where they are at each stage.

Another notable instance occurs on *Page 16*, where Feisal and his fellow-
conspirators gallop out of the gates of Damascus, and in less than half of one
second are in an Arab encampment outside the walls of Medina. Any ordinary ignorant person would suppose that Medina was a few hours' gallop
from the gates of Damascus. Actually, it is about 650 miles.

These points bring me to what I think should be a feature in the film,
viz:—the great distances, and the enormous weight of the sun. This was the
strongest impression left on my mind after reading 'The Seven Pillars'. One
felt the unending toil of these immense marches by camel; with the most
severe privations; barely enough food and water to keep body and soul
together;—on and on each day under brazen skies through hot, crisp sand,
and over black jagged rocks. The script fails to give the impression of the
rigours of the desert in which these strange Arabs live, and to which they are
habituated. The words at the top of *Page 52* show that the author has this
idea, but I suggest it should be emphasized more elaborately. It is a case of
Ramsay MacDonald's 'On, and on, and on, and up, and up, and up!'

I think you should make more of Lawrence's execution of the murderer.
It is a terrible story, and a high-spot in the story. It is very well done as it is.

You will see that Lord Winterton likes your comic relief of the two sergeants riding in the desert. I can well see the necessity for this feature, but
sergeants of the British Army do not talk in this common way. A sergeant is

a fairly intelligent person who has risen to that position through a great deal of competition. The idea of a conventional British Tommy (odious expression!) being a person whose language is that of a half-boozed coster, is not in accordance with the facts. I am well aware that on the screen the idea is that a private soldier or sergeant begins every sentence with 'Gor blimey' etc, but I wonder whether in this film you could not afford to shake off this rubbish?

Page 100. If Allenby was going to start his final drive on Damascus from Jerusalem ('tomorrow'), Lawrence would have to go a long way into the desert to get to his people in time. Perhaps however he flew. I have not re-read this story.

The latter part of the film. When eventually Allenby's army—it was of course about fifty times as strong as Lawrence's force—drove the Turks back from their lines north of Jerusalem, Lawrence was far out in the desert, and in a position to ride across the communications of the retreating Turks. The remarkable episode which should be chronicled was that in defiance of all military advice, he took his little Arab force of perhaps twelve hundred men, and planted them in the path of this vast retreating Turkish mass, perhaps two hundred thousand strong. There are some grand pages in his book about what happened, but they do not tell the tense scene which occurred when the regular officers with him begged him not to sacrifice needlessly his small valuable force. He paid no attention whatever to them, and stood straight in the path of the avalanche. It was a miracle that he or any of them survived. No doubt they killed a lot of Turks and some Germans, but it was like throwing pebbles at a wave. I suggest that this episode requires further study and recasting. It certainly reveals Lawrence in his most heroic and Napoleonic aspect. Again, however, the point cannot be made without the audience having the geographical lay-out in their minds.

I am quite sure Auda's home did not lie in this place. Was not Auda a desert Arab who had nothing whatever to do with the wretched Palestinian Arabs?

Finally, this film falls away, as they nearly all do, towards the end. We have vague galloperaverings of horsemen doing impossible charges, in the style of some of the absurdities of 'Bengal Lancer'.[1] Nearly always the audience fails to keep up with the reel under these conditions. With horses galloping five times faster than animals' feet ever touched the ground, a sense of flurry is about all that results in the spectators' minds. 'On ne règne sur les

---

[1] *Lives Of A Bengal Lancer*, based on the book by Frances Yeats-Brown, and issued by Paramount Pictures in 1935, presented by Adolph Zukor, producer Louis B. Lighton, director Henry Hathaway, and starring Gary Cooper. It lasted 109 minutes, and was said by Hitler to be his favourite film.

âmes que par le calme.' Indeed I feel films ought to be begun from the end, because that is what strikes home, and what the audience take home. I cannot suggest alternatives at the present time, but this ending is the weak part of what is in many ways an excellent piece of work.

I forgot to say that the blowing-up of the trains should be more emphasized. It lends itself very well to your technique. Surely you should blow up half-a-dozen in different ways!—The approach in the distance; the scene in the railway carriage; the tense excitement of the ambush; the terrible explosion; the wreck of the locomotive, etc, and the fact of the sole communications of an army being cut off . . .—all very pretty! And also the means by which the Turks were hunted away from Medina, and made to fight hundreds of miles to the north. It was because of these expeditions that the fame of Lawrence spread about Arabia, and it was not till after this process that anyone thought of asking for 'Lurens'.

I have sent you these few impressions hoping they may be of use, but of course I have not been able to give very much time or thought to the problem. Let me know if you want me to have talks with your story-group.

I return you the script.

Yours very truly,

Winston S. Churchill to Sir Emsley Carr

(*Churchill papers: 8/551*)

3 November 1937

I am delighted to receive your letter and to learn that you are satisfied with the work I have been doing for the News of the World. It is indeed a wonderful platform from which to address the stable, sagacious, good-humoured, kind-hearted central mass of the British nation, and I value the opportunity of doing so, quite apart from the handsome payment which you make.

I have been for some time at work upon the new series. Eight are now finished and I hope to complete the series—the fifth in succession—by the end of this month.

Many thanks for your compliments to my wife. We should both much like to come one Saturday evening and see the News of the World hurled out upon its sixteen million readers.

Winston S. Churchill to Lord Linlithgow

(*Churchill papers: 2/301*)

3 November 1937
Private

It is very good of you to be so generous with what you lack more—Time, and to write me such a deeply interesting letter upon the vast Indian scene over which you preside. I have read it several times very carefully and am grateful for the insight which it gives me into your difficulties and hopes. You may be sure I shall keep it entirely to myself.

I think the main difference between us is that you consider a united All-India an end desirable in itself; whereas I regard it as an abstraction, which in so far as it becomes real will be fundamentally injurious to British interests. I look upon India as on the same scale as Europe with all its divisions and counter-poises, and upon the British function being to preserve the balance between these great masses, and thus maintain our own control for our advantage and their salvation. Following this line of thought I should rather like to see the Moslems of the North joining together as a counter-check upon the anti-British tendencies of Congress. I hope that 'Princes' India' will preserve a separate entity and outlook from the rather dismal and bleak manifestations of British India. I should have thought that it was in the preservation of these forms of culture and organisation, that one of the essentials of British strength rested. I am not at all attracted by the prospect of one united India, which will show us the door. We might not be able to prevent it, but that we should devote our best efforts to producing it, is to my mind distressing and repugnant in the last degree.

Our British mission in India which is to raise the level of Indian life far above what it can be under Indian management, requires a greater and not a diminishing measure of influence and control. I have always predicted 1st, that Congress would gain the main power; 2ndly, that they would electioneer against the British connection, and, incapable of satisfying the material needs of their own people, would find it easy to lay the burden upon us. How simple it must be for an Indian minister, leading the life of an ascetic, to direct popular hatred upon the British official with his expensive standard of life—his meat, his liquor, his club, his chuprassis, his children being educated in England, his pension accumulating year by year—costing in fact ten times what the Indian would do, who could beat him at examinations, and probably argue his head off in any Parliament. I fear the whole process will be to freeze them out and cut them down, and that this degeneration (which you told me seven years ago you had noticed in the agricultural field) will extend rapidly to all spheres.

LG in private the other day threw out this remark to me 'Now, in war time we must regard India as a liability not as an asset.' The trade of Britain with India has now fallen to less than our trade with South Africa; and after all we are only at the beginning of the path.

I did not mean, when I began, to be drawn into these sombre reflections, and yet now they have come out, I will let them stand, feeling always that you are a man capable of confronting the new emergencies of the day with the resources which are at hand. I have come to think myself in the last lap of life that one should always look back upon the history of the past, study it and meditate upon it. Thus one learns the main line of advance. On the other hand it is wrong to be bound by the events and commitments of the last few years, unless these are sound and compatible with the main historic line. I am sure the right course is to know as much as possible about all that has happened in the world, and then to act entirely upon the merits from day to day. Of course my ideal is narrow and limited. I want to see the British Empire preserved for a few more generations in its strength and splendour. Only the most prodigious exertions of British genius will achieve this result.

Here the concourse of events is increasingly grim. Germany is about to make a demand upon us for her former colonies. Mussolini is fortifying the Mediterranean and the Red Sea against us in extraordinary detail from end to end. Japan has linked herself with these Dictator powers. Apart from the Navy, which is preponderant in Europe, our defences are rudimentary. The Air Force will for another two years be far inferior to that of Italy. The peace of Europe dwells under the shield of the French Army. But in a few years the German army will be much larger than the French and increasingly its equal in maturity. The deadly years of our policy were 1932 and 1935. 'The years that the locusts have eaten.' I expect we shall experience the consequences of these years in the near future.

Meanwhile our people are united and healthy. The spirit of Britain is reviving. The working people are ready to defend the cause of Liberty with their lives. The United States signals encouragement to us, for what that is worth. We must all fight our corners as well as we can, each in his station great or small, and I am very glad when I think of you holding this tremendous station, and from the bottom of my heart wish you all good fortune and success.

Winston S. Churchill to Sir Ronald Campbell

(*Churchill papers: 2/313*)

3 November 1937

You may be interested to see the enclosed article which I wrote on the position of Yugo-Slavia, on which I consulted some friends here. I was rather surprised to find that the Military Censor cut it out of the paper in which my articles usually appear. Perhaps you might think it worth while to show it to Prince Paul,[1] or M Stoyadinovitch[2] or his Chef du Cabinet,[3] whom I met over here.

Winston S. Churchill to Maurice Ashley

(*Churchill papers: 8/547*)

5 November 1937

My dear Ashley,

Very many thanks for your letter, and for the proofs with your instructive comments.

I am not at this stage cutting down the letters. They have already been printed, and until the book is finished I do not know how much I have to cut. I expect to prune about 100 pages, or 40,000 words in the final revise. Meanwhile it is convenient to keep the text of these letters as they are. I agree with you there are far too many, but when I began I did not know how much I should want.

I now send you a substantial batch. 'The Battle of Malplaquet' is not begun, though all the material is prepared, and I know what to say. I hope to do it within the next fortnight. The chapter 'After Malplaquet' requires expansion to include the political movement at home, and the beginning of

---

[1] Prince Regent of Yugoslavia, see page 831, note 2.

[2] Prime Minister and Foreign Minister of Yugoslavia, see page 832, note 1.

[3] Dragoslav-Dragan Protić, 1902–1972. Entered Yugoslav civil service, Ministry of Finance, 1923. Transferred to the diplomatic service, 1926; held posts in Brussels, Vienna, Hamburg and London, before becoming *chef de cabinet* to the Foreign Minister, Vojislav Marinković, in 1932. He held a similar post under the Prime Minister, Milan Stojadinović, 1935–9, where his financial experience was of particular value. From 1938 to 1941 Protić served at the Yugoslav legation in Athens, subsequently coming to London (by way of Cairo) and accepting the post of Yugoslav Ambassador to the allied governments in exile. In July 1944 he assisted the royal Yugoslav Prime Minister, Ivan Subašić, in talks in London with Tito's envoy, Vladimir Velebit. Protić later emigrated to the United States and spent his last years as a member of the United Nations Secretariat in New York.

the Conference at Geertruidenberg.[1] Chapter X ('Three Women') is not yet done, and may eventually be distributed among other chapters. Chapters XI to XX inclusive are all fairly far advanced, and may be read continuously. From Chapter XIV onwards I send you Eddie Marsh's copy with his corrections. My own of course contains a good many others that have come to hand. The references for the Spanish War are being prepared, and will be incorporated at each stage. Apart from this, the articulation of this centre part of the book is now fairly complete. The later chapters are being rapidly revised, and I will send you the latest editions when they come in.

You will be surprised at the detail in which the political drama is told. I do not think anything on this scale has been done before; yet I think if the reader will lend himself to the process, he will not find it too tiresome.

I also send you a supplement on the spy letters we found in the Sunderland papers. The introduction to these will now be inserted in the earlier chapters, and the letters themselves, of which there are a good many more, will form an appendix. We do not think they have ever been published before, nor does Trevelyan.

By the time you have read all this, I shall have another lot ready for you in an advanced condition.

Winston S. Churchill to Major Percy Davies

(Churchill papers: 8/551)

6 November 1937
Confidential

I now send you eight of the twelve articles for the 1938 series and I hope to let you have the other four before the end of the month. The scientific facts quoted in the Inventions article have the authority of Professor Lindemann, and therefore are not likely to be overset. If you think the end a little recondite let me know and I will have it modified.

I had a charming letter from Sir Emsley Carr praising very much the Scientific article which appeared last Sunday, and generally expressing great satisfaction with my work. Perhaps therefore your readers will like the future forecast of Invention, in spite of its being a little stiff and startling at the end.

---

[1] Spelt by contemporaries, Gerturenberg, and by Churchill in the volume itself, Gertruyd-enberg, where, as he wrote (*Marlborough*, volume 4, page 235) 'the diplomatists and plenipotentiaries, surrounded by a host of agents and busybodies, official and unofficial, manoeuvred sedately around the clauses of the peace treaty, incapable as were the armies of reaching a decision'.

The article on Parliamentary institutions reproduces parts of an article I wrote four years ago for Pearson's monthly magazine. These passages can be recast if you desire it, but personally I think it reads extraordinarily well as it is.

I hope you will feel that the series is lively and varied, but if you can suggest any improvements I will immediately attend to them.

I may possibly leave for the United States on December 1, and hope to leave this all behind me satisfactorily settled before then. It would be a great convenience to me if I could hear from you, as I did last year, that you will want another series for 1939. I have to try to parcel out my work as well as possible in the year, and as you know it might in certain circumstances be a help to me to say 'the contract is already made'.

The success of Great Contemporaries makes me wonder whether you might not care to have another batch. I have never done Admiral Beatty, General Botha, Mark Twain, Rudyard Kipling, Sir Edward Grey, King Edward VII, Sir Austen Chamberlain, or Baden-Powell. These men I knew, and no doubt I could think of others.[1]

Sir Ronald Campbell to Winston S. Churchill

(*Churchill papers: 2/313*)

8 November 1937   British Legation,
Private & Confidential   Belgrade

Dear Mr Churchill,

Thank you for your letter enclosing a copy of your article in the 'Evening Standard'. Owing to the action of the censor I should not in the ordinary way have seen it. In point of fact, however, I had just procured a copy for the reason that your article was mentioned to me by Prince Paul[2] when I saw

---

[1] The second, enlarged edition of *Great Contemporaries*, published a year later, on 8 November 1938, included extra articles on Baden Powell, Parnell, Lord Fisher and Franklin Roosevelt. But none of the other individuals mentioned here were included in the book, nor were Churchill's further newspaper biographical sketches collected together in book form during his lifetime, or in the two decades after his death. Churchill's 'Homage to Kipling', originally a speech at the Rudyard Kipling Memorial Fund banquet on 17 November 1937, was published that same year as a twelve-page pamphlet (see page 845, note 1).

[2] Paul Karageorgevich, 1893–1976. Born in St Petersburg, nephew of King Peter I of Serbia. Studied modern history at Christ Church, Oxford, 1913–14 and 1920–1; BA, 1921. In 1923 he married Princess Olga of Greece, whose sister, Princess Marina, was later Duchess of Kent. A patron of the arts in the newly created kingdom of Yugoslavia, of which his first cousin, Alexander, was King. Following the assassination of Alexander at Marseilles, in 1934, Prince Paul became head of a regency, and Prince Regent, for the young King Peter II.

him a few days after its appearance. I have since ascertained that no opposition paper in Belgrade attempted to publish it as they knew that it would get them into trouble. An attempt was made to publish it in Zagreb but was frustrated by the censor. A translation of all the more important articles in the foreign press is made every day for the benefit of Prince Paul (and members of the Government) and it was through that agency no doubt that he saw it. As I had not however seen it myself at the time when he mentioned it to me, I was unable to discuss it with him. He did not say very much, but it was clear that it was not very welcome to him. . . .

From *my* point of view there is much in your article which I should be glad to see digested by Prince Paul and Stoyadinovitch.[1] (I like especially the bit about the fate of Yugoslavia if she became 'a poor relation to Rome and Berlin'). I propose, at the risk of annoying them, to take an opportunity of inviting them to read it carefully, on the plea that what they did read was probably only a summarised translation.[2]

Yours sincerely,
Ronald Campbell

Negotiated the *Sporazum* (agreement) of 26 August 1936, which brought the Croats into participation in the government, and gave them a wide measure of autonomy. Sought for more than six years to combat Nazi influence in Yugoslavia, and to resist German pressures for an alliance, but because of British inability to give military aid in 1940 and 1941, he bowed to the will of the majority in the government, and signed the Yugoslav pact with Nazi Germany, 25 March 1941. Two days later, in a coup d'état encouraged by Britain, the regency was overthrown. Left Yugoslavia for Greece, but was refused permission to stay there. Taken by the British to Kenya, and interned there. Brought to South Africa by General Smuts. Resident in Paris, and near Florence, from 1945 until his death. One of his two sons was killed in a road accident in 1954.

[1] Milan Stoyadinovitch, 1888–1961. Educated at the University of Belgrade, and subsequently in England, France and Germany. Entered the Accountancy Section of the Serbian Ministry of Finance, 1914; head of the section, 1917–19. Lecturer in Economics at Belgrade University, 1920–2. Yugoslav Minister of Finance, 1922–6. President of the Finance Committee of the Yugoslav National Assembly, 1927. Prime Minister of Yugoslavia, June 1935 to February 1939. As his own Foreign Minister from 1935 to 1939, he aligned Yugoslavia more closely with Germany and Italy. Narrowly escaped assassination at the hands of a fellow member of Parliament, who shot at him while he was speaking, 1936. Interned by the Yugoslav Government in April 1940. Handed over to the British, and held on the island of Mauritius, 1941–8. Emigrated to South America, 1948. Settled in Argentina, 1950, becoming editor of the economic weekly, *La Economista*. He died in Buenos Aires.

[2] For the gist of Churchill's article on Yugoslavia, see page 813, note 1.

Winston S. Churchill: statement for the National Book Fair[1]

(Churchill papers: 8/624)

8 November 1937

The glory of literature in any free country is its variety, and the most fertile means from which happiness may be obtained is variety.

The issues in the world to-day are such that readers should be on their guard against any attempt to warp their intellects or to narrow or enfeeble their judgements. They should read widely, choosing only those books which will inform them accurately, avoiding any which contain tendentious propaganda whatever its source.

Books, in all their variety, offer the human intellect the means whereby civilisation may be carried triumphantly forward.

Books guard the highest manifestation of man's spirit, conserving that freedom of thought without which our Western culture cannot survive.

Winston S. Churchill: notes for a speech[2]

(Churchill papers: 9/126)

9 November 1937

British music and Brit. musicians.

No intention delivering lecture.

---

[1] The National Book Fair, which was organized by the *Sunday Times* in conjunction with the National Book Council, was opened in London on 8 November 1937. Opening the fair, Churchill told the assembled publishers, authors and readers: 'The mission of the book trade is to disseminate impartial knowledge. Nothing can be worse than to introduce totalitarianism into literature and to try to breed in a single country races of men and women fundamentally incapable of understanding one another. The glory of literature in any free country is its variety. I urge readers to guard against tendential literature dealing with "coloured" facts and carefully selected statistics. We see great nations slaves of propaganda, great States in which only one opinion is tolerated, all of which is contrary, not only to the genius of man, but to the most vehement urge of human nature. The author is the source of a spring from which there comes the ever-broadening flow of intellectual and commercial activity. He is therefore a highly desirable citizen and ought to be cherished and honoured and substantially rewarded by an enlightened community. A wise Chancellor of the Exchequer would allow authors to write off every year against income tax a substantial sum for the depreciation of their mental machinery through wear and tear and through age and use. When I was Chancellor of the Exchequer I refrained from motives of delicacy, but all of my successors may not be equally hampered. The English-speaking people comprise more than 150,000,000 potential readers. England and the United States ought therefore to have the greatest outputs of the very best books, and thus lead the world in thought as well as in trade.'

[2] Churchill spoke at the Musicians Benevolent Fund on 9 November 1937. These were the notes from which he read his speech.

Yesterday Book Fair.
　　I know something about that.

Many other topics upon wh cd make speech,
　　politics, parties I have worked for,
　　　　national defence.

But Music—pleasure wh I enjoy with awe.

Never succeeded in learning any instrument.

Had feeling for big drum,
　　but they only gave me triangle.

What I really shd like wd be conducting.

Political training wd come in there.

Co-ordination—Inskip
　　generally slow time,
　　　　occasionally b flat.

Party leader wd be useful training.
　　'I am their leader
　　I must follow them.'

Trust orchestra help him out in Div lobby
　　if not in performance.

However decided at my age
　　I shall leave field of conducting
　　　　to Sir T. Beecham.[1]

I am most respectful
　　even thrilled auditor of Music.

But I have definite predilection
　　for a tune.

You cannot run a Church,
　　cinema, theatre,
　　　　political meeting, football final,
　　　　　　seaside resort, pleasure cruise,
　　　　　　　　successful restaurant,
　　　　　　　　　　strike, revolution,
　　　　　　　　　　　　certainly not a war,
　　　　　　　　　　　　　　without Music.

[1] Thomas Beecham, 1879–1961. Conductor, composer and operatic impressario. Succeeded his father as 2nd Baronet, 1916. Knighted, 1916. Companion of Honour, 1957.

Only place where not been tried—Parlt.
Perhaps why not successful on Continent.

Many tunes have made history—
Lillibulero,
Marseillaise,
Racokowski's march Hungary,
John Brown's body,
Tipperary.

By the way, find I have done injustice
to Bernard Shaw.
Red Flag not Burial march of Monkey
but Funeral march of Fried Eel.

Old tunes and memory.
Nothing recalls past so well.

Music universal language.
Wd it be some use to L/N?[1]
Might introduce *Harmony*,
but perhaps some nations wd prefer
thorough bass.

So much for Music.

But serious purpose tonight is MBF.[1]

Financial position of Fund lamentable.

Call in some German,—Schacht—Italian or Japanese
adviser to put it in good order.

Tragedy of fallen artist.
Living stage, and living orchestra,
pressed out of existence
by vast new mechanism
wh has given joy to millions,
at cruel expense to few.

Thank HRH[3] for coming.

Worthy cause.

[1] L/N = League of Nations.
[2] MBF = Musicians' Benevolent Fund.
[3] Prince George Edward Alexander Edmund, 1902–1942. Fourth son of King George V. Served in the Royal Navy, 1921–7; on the staff of the Commander-in-Chief, Atlantic Fleet, 1927. Attached to the Foreign Office, 1929. Married Princess Marina of Greece, 1934. Created Duke of Kent, 1934; Privy Councillor, 1937. Group Captain, RAF, 1937. Rear-Admiral, Major-General and Air Vice-Marshal, 1939. Governor-General Designate of Australia. Killed in an air crash while on active service.

Winston S. Churchill to the Editor of 'The Times'[1]

(*Randolph Churchill papers*)

10 November 1937   11 Morpeth Mansions

Sir,

May I through your columns draw attention to the growth at public banquets of discourteous practice on the part of certain photographic agencies? While the guests are seated eating their dinner photographers walk about the room taking unexpected close-up snapshots of well-known people of both sexes which are afterwards published by the newspapers. In the United States, this practice is carried to a very unpleasant degree, and I recently saw a photograph of President Roosevelt with his mouth half-open in the act of eating or drinking. Similar tendencies are already manifesting themselves here, and I could give numerous illustrations, but the effrontery is at present confined to a small circle of publications. May I point out that the society or public body holding the dinner is through its president or chairman in the position of host to its guests, many of whom attend at personal inconvenience to further public objects. It is the responsibility of the host to protect his guests from annoyance of this kind, and guests should not hesitate to ask for this protection when necessary. It might also be a good thing for public men, when invited to attend dinners as speakers, to stipulate beforehand that such practices shall not be allowed. No one could possibly object to the regular photographs which are taken of banquets and preserved by many attending them as souvenirs. But the abuse to which I refer should surely be brought to an end.

Yours faithfully,
Winston S. Churchill

Winston S. Churchill to Sir Ronald Campbell

(*Churchill papers: 2/313*)

12 November 1937

Many thanks for your most interesting letter. It is very kind of you to give me such a full explanation. I told Mr Eden that the article had been vetoed by the Censor, but that I had sent it to you hoping that you would show it

---

[1] Churchill's letter was published in *The Times* on 12 November 1937, with the headings:
SNAPSHOT AT BANQUETS
A GROWING ABUSE
RESPONSIBILITY OF THE HOST

to Prince Paul. He said he was very glad I had done so. The censoring of this article shows very clearly that Stoyadinovitch is moving steadily towards the Rome–Berlin axis, and is another sign of the bias to Nazi-ism of his Government. One can only hope that the liberal and democratic forces in Yugo-Slavia who would like to work with France and Great Britain, will be able to assert themselves before the tyranny settles finally down upon them. I have felt for some time that there was a great deal of tension in Yugo-Slavia, and it was purely for this reason that I thought it best not to get mixed up in it personally. It may interest you to know that the article was also excluded from the following countries—Austria, Hungary, Czecho-Slovakia and Poland—where the papers usually print it. It was however printed in about thirty European newspapers. I am afraid the powers of evil are getting too strong for us in Central and Southern Europe.

Group-Captain Lachlan MacLean: memorandum
(Churchill papers: 2/304)

15 November 1937

It is difficult to understand the reasons which prompted the authorities to permit the visit of the German Mission to England at this particular juncture —Whatever the reasons, however, and whatever the effect on our visitors, the visit had, on our side at any rate, this one result; it threw into clear relief the exact state of the Royal Air Force as regards re-equipment, and the degree of its preparedness for war on October 19th, 1937.

On the other hand, the reasons which actuated the German Government in desiring to send an air mission to this country are not so incomprehensible—General Milch, as the result of previous visits to England, had reported strongly on the thoroughly backward state of our air development. While Field Marshal Blomberg, during his visit to England early this year, was impressed by what he had seen and had been told at Andover, and on his return to Germany he joined issue with Milch over the latter's report.

It was only natural, therefore, that Milch, anxious to verify his earlier impressions, should come over here, somewhat biased and certainly in a highly critical frame of mind—Furthermore, he brought with him a particularly astute, technical and practical mission.

It is therefore not unreasonable to assume that the Royal Air Force, knowing this, used all the resources at its disposal, and made every endeavour to stage a display which would create in the minds of the Germans an impression of our readiness and immediate efficiency. In fact, every such effort was made and it may be confidently assumed that the Mission was shown the best of all that we had.

It is obvious that in the present state of international affairs, it was of far greater importance to create a strong impression of our actual fighting efficiency than, to leave as the chief impression, a promise of a big potential strength, likely to materialise at some distant date: since, as things are, a weak actual, backed only by a future potential, might merely prove an inducement to a possible opponent to forestall the practical development of that potential.

That this psychological factor was taken into consideration in planning the tour for the Mission is doubtful, since the greater part of what the Germans saw, indicated potential rather than actual strength. Their programme provided for a visit to a 'typical Heavy Bomber Station', a 'typical Fighter Station', the Cadet College at Cranwell, the Technical Training Establishment at Halton, the Bristol Aircraft Works and a shadow factory—of these, the Bomber and Fighter Stations alone, provided the possibility of staging a demonstration of our actual air strength. Therefore their visits to these stations were of primary importance and it is worth while examining in detail what these visits provided, particularly at the Bomber Station (Mildenhall), at which they commenced their tour.

Mildenhall Station consists of two Heavy Bomber Squadrons armed with the HEYFORD biplane. These two Squadrons therefore, with their crews, formed the basis of the display on the ground—Behind the HEYFORDS, obviously as a special exhibit, was a display of one specimen of each new type bomber, a Blenheim, a Battle, a Whitley, a Harrow and a Wellesley, which the Mission was free to examine. Behind these aircraft was a background exhibition of various ground equipment such as flood-lighting, bomb-loading gear, bombsights, camera guns etc—

While the visitors were inspecting these aircraft on the ground, a 'fly past' of new types took place, by Blenheims, followed considerably later by formations of 9 Wellesleys, 18 Battles, 18 Harrows, 9 Blenheims, followed considerably later by 6 more Blenheims which passed over unseen, because the Mission was by then in one of the hangars looking at ground exhibits.

The Germans were told that another squadron of Wellesleys and a squadron of Whitleys ought also to have 'flown past', but that they were fogbound on their aerodromes. This was an unfortunate admission, because at Mildenhall the day was clear and the Mission itself was flown to Cranwell after lunch.

Summarized—the Mission saw that the standard equipment of two service squadrons was the Heyford biplane—whose range, performance and capacity was doubtless fully known to them. The Heyfords did actually evoke the question 'are these training aircraft?'

They were shown, rather obviously as a special exhibit, single aircraft of five new types—Four of these types they saw in the air in significantly varying and somewhat unimpressive numbers, ie, 9–18–18–9, and finally they were told that two more squadrons, due to have taken part in this parade, could not leave their home aerodrome because of bad weather.

This then is the data on which the Mission would base its estimate of our striking strength.

The question which must inevitably form itself in any mind is—'Why was a station armed with an obsolete type of aircraft selected as the show station in preference to one with modern equipment.' There can only be one explanation, which is, that there is no station so equipped, for although there are Stations whose equipment is a monoplane type aircraft, there is no single Squadron in the Air Force which is armed with one of the new types complete with all the essential equipment for war purposes—for instance, no aircraft have wireless loops for Direction Finding, none of the Harrows or Blenheims is fitted with guns and working turrets or efficient blind flying panels.—There are no automatic pilots, high speed bombsights or gun sights. Had the Mission visited a newly equipped station these vital deficiencies would have been glaringly obvious and the essence of our unreadiness would have been apparent beyond all concealment.—As it is, the only new types, which the Mission saw at close quarters, were almost complete and they did see similar types in the air.—Conclusions as to deficiencies and shortages will therefore be inferential and conjectural and not the result of direct evidence.

Nevertheless, much evidence of an unfortunate nature was available. Wherever the Mission went the standard equipment was of the biplane type —Heyfords at Mildenhall, Gladiators at Hornchurch, various Tutor types at the instructional establishments and finally the 'DH.86' in which they themselves were transported, must have shown clearly that we were still in the biplane era, with all that it implies.

The foregoing has been deliberately elaborated in some detail to emphasise that in answer to an urgent call of some importance, the authorities were able, by mustering the whole resources of all the re-armed squadrons to create a composite group, equivalent to one squadron (18 aircraft) of each of the following types, Wellesley, Battle and Blenheim, one squadron (12 aircraft) of Whitleys, and one squadron and a half (18 aircraft) of Harrows. Of these not one aircraft was fitted with war equipment, and it was only by a great deal of hard work and complicated borrowing of special instruments and apparatus from here, there and everywhere, that one specimen aircraft of each type was completed for demonstration purposes.

It is therefore hardly an exaggeration to say that the effective war strength of the Royal Air Force today differs but little from its strength prior to the reorientation of our defence system from South to East in September, 1934. This in turn is equivalent to saying that after three years of intensive effort we have not succeeded in re-equipping a single squadron for war and it is obvious that it must be at least two years before the air force as a whole can be re-equipped. That is to say, that five years, probably more, will have elapsed in the process of rearmament and the aircraft then coming into the Service may be as many years out of date, with their useful life in service still to run, ie another three to four years.

This time lag between the conception of the right aircraft for the needs of the Service and its ultimate production in sufficient numbers to equip the Service deserves a searching analysis, since it may well prove the decisive factor in air warfare, giving, as in certain circumstances it undoubtedly will, to the nation, which starts one step ahead of its opponent in technical efficiency, an initial advantage which it need never lose.

The lessons of the last war showed clearly enough the decisive advantages that resulted from even a slight margin of superiority in aircraft performance, an advantage that changed from one side to the other, as either we or the enemy produced the superior aeroplane.

In those days it did not take five years to produce a fighting machine nor was it necessary to lay down plant to produce hundreds of a type in order to make the venture an economical possibility. The machines being chiefly made of wood, and not requiring the jigs, tools and machinery layout of the modern all-metal types, permitted an elasticity of production which is essential in war, and may prove to be essential in the period of instability and tension which possibly precedes war.

It is just this elasticity of production which we have so light-heartedly sacrificed at a time when we most need it.

Lack of this flexibility has forced us to trust our immediate future to types such as the Blenheim, Battle, Wellesley, Harrow and Whitley whose suitability for the work required of them is at least doubtful, and doubtful as it is, these types have to go into production in mass.

Group-Captain Lachlan MacLean to Violet Pearman

(*Churchill papers: 2/304*)

16 November 1937
RAF Station
Mildenhall

Dear Mrs Pearman,

I met Wing Commander Anderson at a conference yesterday. I showed him the enclosed paper & he thought that Mr Churchill might be interested in the views expressed in it.

Though actually self contained, this paper was intended only as the first part of a considerably more comprehensive examination of some of the problems of aircraft types & production. The last half is not yet complete.

Yours sincerely,
Lachlan MacLean

Violet Pearman to Winston S. Churchill

(*Churchill papers: 2/304*)

16 November 1937

Mr Churchill

Cmdr A rang up yesterday and I had a long talk to him. He said he was not 'huffy' at all, only a little worried. He is too devoted to you to think of being offended over trifles. He says that the conference, about which he had been speaking to you, has gone all in his favour, and that everything will be all right. But please do *not* use what he gave you on Sunday.[1] Bear the fact in mind, and say if you like that it had come to your ear, but do not show the copies to anyone.

He said HIMSELF that you were *not* to think he was not 'balanced', because he was so pessimistic. I explained that I had said this was because he brooded too much owing to his lonely life, therefore being thrown back into his thoughts and worries, and he agreed that this was so.

---

[1] Wing-Commander Anderson had given Churchill a copy of a secret Air Council circular of 12 October 1937, warning of 'the extent to which officers are continuing to resort to money-lenders for financial assistance'. The circular continued: 'The dangers arising from this practice, involving in some cases the careers of the officers themselves, have already been pointed out, and cannot be too strongly emphasised; in addition the Council are seriously concerned lest the good name of the Royal Air Force be jeopardised should the alleged extent of the practice be given undesirable publicity.' The normal charge made by private money-lenders was 60% per annum, which the circular described as 'grossly excessive'. For Churchill's use of this information, see pages 844 and 850.

He is 'lying low' after this conference for some time, and asks that you do not do anything with anything he has given you, for the present at any rate.[1]

Charles Schwab to Winston S. Churchill

(*Churchill papers: 8/549*)

16 November 1937   New York

My dear friend:

I have read your book, 'Contemporaries', which you sent me a short time ago.

Nothing that I have read in a long time gave me so much pleasure, as I knew most of the characters which you so well describe. The one idea left with me after reading the book, was the kindly and praiseworthy attitude you took towards all these great men; no harsh criticisms but frank appreciation, just like your own good self.

> With best regards, and all good wishes, I am,
> Sincerely yours,
> C. M. Schwab

---

[1] It was thought that Churchill would speak in the House of Commons on 15 November 1937. But, as the *Daily Telegraph* reported two days later: 'Mr Churchill surprised some MPs by being a silent listener to Monday's debate on the Air Raids Bill. His silence was tactical. By rising at 10.59 that evening he secured the right to speak first yesterday and thus ensure wider attention both in and out of Parliament. That Mr Churchill is still the best orator in the House he made plain when he turned his guns on Mr Herbert Morrison. The House revelled in the way he unfolded his final sentence: "He has entered a region which baffles even the most extensive vocabulary: the facetious monstrosities of his assertions defy rejoinder, but happily do not need it because of their inherent folly." ' The *Daily Telegraph* report of the debate of 16 November 1937 continued: 'Salvoes from Mr Churchill's guns were fired in various directions. At the beginning it was the Socialists who cheered him most, for he was attacking the past delays at the Home Office in the matter of air-raid precautions. Mr Churchill silenced his Socialist supporters with the remark that his speech would be applauded by every part of the House in turn, but never by all together. His prophecy was amply justified.' In this, as in all his air speeches, Churchill was conscious of the need not to use Anderson's information in too obvious a way. Eventually, however, the fact of Anderson's help became known to the Air Ministry (see page 1551, note 1).

Robert McCormick[1] to Winston S. Churchill

(*Churchill papers: 8/549*)

18 November 1937   The Chicago Tribune

Dear Churchill,

There was I in an armchair by the fire, with a glass of gingerale and orange juice on the table, and the Life of the Duke of Marlborough in my hands, looking forward to a voyage into the romantic and glorious past . . . and somebody brings in a package, that, opened up, turns out to be GREAT CONTEMPORARIES.

History was forgotten while I met your friends and some of my acquaintances.

The evening was just as well spent and I still have Marlborough to look forward to.

The inscribed Churchilliana are of great sentimental value to me, and in years to come, when you and I are using clouds as balls, and harps as mallets, they will probably make some book dealer independently rich.[2]

I hope the Christmas season will bring you what cheer and comfort it can in this lunatic world.

Yours sincerely,
Robert McCormick

Winston S. Churchill to Lord Camrose

(*Churchill papers: 2/302*)

18 November 1937

If you will glance through the report of my speech in yesterday's *Daily Telegraph* (and morning post) you will see that though it is shorter than the one in the Times, it is incomparably more readable and gives a much truer

---

[1] Robert Rutherford McCormick, 1880–1955. Born in Chicago. Educated partly in England. Member of the Chicago City Council, 1904–6. President of the *Chicago Tribune*, 1911. War Correspondent with the British, French and Russian forces, 1915. Major, First Illinois Cavalry, US–Mexico border, 1916. On active service in France, 1918. Colonel, General Staff, 1918. Editor and publisher of the bitterly anti-British *Chicago Tribune*, from 1919 until his death. Chairman of the Board of the *New York Daily News*. President of the *Washington Times Herald*, 1949–54.

[2] An inscribed *Marlborough: His Life and Times* could be expected to realize (in 1982) between £250 and £300, and an inscribed *Great Contemporaries* between £175 and £200. An even larger price might be realized if the inscription itself were particularly interesting or personal.

effect of what was actually said. I am sure with the limited space for reporting speeches now-a-days it is much better to select, as your reporters do, the salient points and give them intelligently instead of making a long jumble, which is what appears in the Times.[1]

Many thanks also for the leading article upon the lag. Arrangements are at present in a chaotic condition and the delay has been more regrettable.[2]

I am very glad to see the enormous figures of the Daily Telegraph circulation.[3]

Winston S. Churchill to Lord Swinton

(Churchill papers: 2/299)

18 November 1937
Personal

The circular letter about the money lending, which I mentioned to you, was sent out from the appropriate department of the Air Ministry on October 12 last. If you ask to see it it will explain itself. There are also letters which have been written in the commands throwing further light upon the subject. The effect of these letters is to show the proper attitude adopted by officials and officers in endeavouring to cope with this serious abuse. It seems to me however that the matter would greatly gain by your personal intervention. Money may be needed which your authority alone could procure, to pull these young fellows out of their scrapes. I was told that the money lending firm most active is called Increased Power Co Ltd, Sentinel House, Southampton Row, WC 1.

[1] Churchill had spoken on 17 November 1937 at a dinner to inaugurate the Rudyard Kipling Memorial Fund. *The Times* quoted his remarks in full, in 218 lines. The *Daily Telegraph* gave 70 lines to the same speech. On 26 November 1937 the speech was reprinted in full in *John O'London's* and it was subsequently published as a pamphlet by the Rudyard Kipling Memorial Fund.

[2] On 17 November 1937 the leading article in the *Daily Telegraph*, headed 'The Lag in Air Raid Precautions' warned that the 'financial wrangle' over ARP had occupied 'a wholly disproportionate amount of time and attention', and that it had 'seriously delayed the progress of work that is of the utmost national importance'. The House of Commons had divided on the issue on November 16, 'despite Mr Churchill's statesmanlike plea for a demonstration of unity on this vital issue'. Although 200,000 volunteers had been recruited, by comparison with the 'less vulnerable' countries, the leading article declared, 'our preparations are still almost rudimentary'. The article ended: 'Mr Churchill enunciated a profound truth when he remarked that the more efficient our defensive preparations against this hideous new mode of attack the less likely will be the emergency.'

[3] In November 1935 the circulation of the *Daily Telegraph* was 472,121. By November 1937 it had risen to 646,645 (in November 1981 it stood at 1,325,494).

If you find the facts are substantiated, it certainly is a great argument for increasing the proportion of senior officers from other Services, so as to give a stronger framework to all this flood of new young pilots necessitated by the rapid expansion. You can certainly rely on my support in the House of Commons for any steps you may take in this direction, unpopular as they will be.

Pray make your own enquiries now from this, and let our correspondence remain entirely secret and personal.

Winston S. Churchill to J. J. Astor

(*Churchill papers: 1/300*)

20 November 1937

I am very sorry indeed to have got into a muddle about your most kind invitation to shoot with you at Hever the week-end of the 18th December. Your letter arrived when Clemmie was abroad and by some error it was not marked on my card or hers. In the meantime she had made other plans for us both. As she is going abroad on the Monday for a month's ski-ing, I think I ought to go with her. I do hope that this will not cause you any inconvenience.

It was very nice of the Times to print a full report of my speech on Kipling.[1] I took a lot of trouble about it, and was glad to see it in an unmutilated form.

I am going to propose myself one day to come over to have another go at the gallery alcove. I expect you will have made good progress with it by now.

---

[1] Churchill said at the Kipling dinner: 'The light of genius expressed in Literature does not fail with the death of the author. His galleries are still displayed for our instruction and enjoyment. But the magic key which could have opened new ones to our eager desire has gone for ever. Let us, then, guard the treasures which he has bequeathed.' Of Kipling and India Churchill said: 'To read with faithful eye Kipling's Indian stories, short or long, is to gain a truer knowledge of that great episode, the British contact with India, than will be found in many ponderous Blue-books, or in much of the glib, smooth patter which is now in fashion.' Churchill added: 'Although in my political actions I was often fiercely opposed to him, yet there never was a moment when I did not feel the surge of his appeal upon the great verities of our race and State. But what has always thrilled me most in Kipling was the occult power which he had to roll back the Time Curtain and bring the past to life again. We read a few pages in "Puck of Pook's Hill" of unpretentious prose, and then suddenly with a gasp we realize that we are on the Roman Wall.' Of the death of Kipling's son on the western front, Churchill said: 'He endured that inch by inch devouring, wasting of hope which makes the word "missing" much more tragical than "killed in action". Yet we hope that his own lines which gave comfort to so many were some solace to him. He bore his grief with stoic fortitude. He was never the same again. Victory came, the victory in which he had believed, and to which he had conspicuously contributed. It came in all its fullness and all its disillusion. The Old World had passed away.'

Violet Pearman to N. B. Foot [1]

(*Churchill papers: 2/312*)

21 November 1937

Dear Mr Foot,

In reply to your letter of the 12th instant, I am asked by Mr Churchill to say that he does not think that this is a good moment for such a circular as you propose in your letter of the 25th October. The feeling, he says, at the Committee last week was that the form of the Nyon Resolution was the most practical step we could take. People are thoroughly frightened of going into a war with Japan, Italy and Germany at the same time, no matter what the cause might be, especially when our own defences have been so lamentably neglected. Nyon was a flash of success, but the general situation is increasingly depressing and formidable. There could be no objection to recirculating the original aims of the Society to MPs coupled to the statement that the three party leaders are all in sympathy with it. But, Mr Churchill thinks, this should not be tagged on to a condemnation of any particular country, though he shares to the full your indignation about it.

Brendan Bracken to Winston S. Churchill

(*Churchill papers: 1/407*)

26 November 1937   Waldorf Astoria,
                                                 New York

Winston,

Levy's odd offer was not improved by the manner in which it was made. [2] He appeared to be overcome by his own generosity when he said 'he was prepared to advise his friends to make a contribution of one thousand dollars towards Mr Churchill's expenses'. When I politely suggested that this sum wd hardly pay the fare, he replied that it was a great honour to be invited to

---

[1] On 12 November 1937 N. B. Foot had written to Mrs Pearman: 'You will remember that you suggested on the telephone some time ago that I might get an opportunity of having a word with Mr Churchill at our meeting last Monday evening in connection with the question of the circular letter which we propose to send out to all MPs. Unfortunately he seemed to be in rather a hurry to get away, and before I could disentangle myself from the table at which I was sitting he had walked out through the door with the Duchess of Atholl.' The draft resolution on Nyon condemned Japan's aggression against China and urged 'immediate and determined collective action' by the League States, and the United States 'with the object of compelling Japan to terminate her aggressive campaign'.

[2] On 10 November 1937 Brendan Bracken had telegraphed to Churchill from New York: 'Manufacturers offer only one thousand dollars. Advise refusal. Brendan.'

address the American manufacturers & that they were adopting an unusual and most generous course in offering any expense contribution. By giving you this opportunity they were creating a favourable atmosphere for any lecture tour you decided to make.

Levy is a greasy, not to say nasty, creature. He certainly tempted me to qualify my dislike of Hitlerism.

I had a lot of difficulty in finding him as there are no less than three Louis Levys in Corporation Lawyers offices here. Two are in William Street!

America is full of encircling gloom without a sign of a kindly light. The industrial recession is serious & there is no small risk of a crisis of confidence. The Government's economic experts announce that they fully expect a recovery next summer. This statement is likely to increase the possibility of grave trouble during the bitter winter months.

Yrs
Brendan

Ivone Kirkpatrick:[1] *report on the German Air Mission's visit*

(Cabinet papers: 64/18)

30 November 1937

. . . They were pleased to meet Mr Churchill at Lord Trenchard's dinner. He made the impression of a great personality, but it was clear that he was an implacable enemy of German aspirations. On this account I gather the mission had not really taken to him.

---

[1] Ivone Augustine Kirkpatrick, 1897–1964. On active service, 1914–18 (wounded, despatches twice). Diplomatic Service, 1919. First Secretary, Rome, 1930–2; Counsellor, Berlin, 1933–8. Director of the Foreign Division, Ministry of Information, 1940. Controller, European Services, BBC, 1941. Assistant Under-Secretary of State, Foreign Office, 1945; Deputy Under-Secretary, 1948; Permanent Under-Secretary (German Section), 1949; Permanent Under-Secretary of State, 1953–7. Knighted, 1948. Chairman of the Independent Television Authority, 1957–62.

Ivan Maisky to Winston S. Churchill

(*Churchill papers: 2/299*)

30 November 1937

My dear Mr Churchill,

On occasion of your birthday anniversary[1] I would like to send you this brief message of congratulation and my sincere wishes for your future happiness and good health.

Yours sincerely,
I. Maisky

Clementine Churchill to Winston S. Churchill: telegram

(*Churchill papers: 1/322*)

30 November 1937

Many Happy Returns, my darling one, and may your Star rise.

Clemmie

[1] Churchill's 61st birthday.

December 1937

Malcolm MacDonald to Winston S. Churchill

(*Churchill papers: 1/300*)

1 December 1937

My dear Winston Churchill,

These are just a few lines to thank you for your kind note of sympathy on my father's death.[1] It is of course a terrible grief to me; there is a gap in my life which can never be filled. But you know as well as anyone what a source of everlasting pride to a son is the memory of a great father; and, as you say, I had the additional rare privilege of working with and for mine for many years.

Though his and your political paths crossed more often than they met, he always had a high regard for you. After that last occasion on which you both met he spoke to me with pleasure of the afternoon and with particular pleasure of your and his association together in friendly speeches.

Yours very sincerely,
Malcolm MacDonald

Winston S. Churchill to Lord Swinton

(*Churchill papers: 2/299*)

1 December 1937
Personal & Secret

I am very glad you have given your personal attention to the matter on which I wrote you. It seemed to me your Department was doing exactly the right thing, but that probably some money was needed which your influence alone could procure.[2]

---

[1] Ramsay MacDonald had died, at sea, on 9 November 1937.

[2] On 29 November 1937 Lord Swinton had written to Churchill, in a letter marked 'Personal and Secret': '. . . There is very little evidence of circulars from moneylenders at the present time. Various methods were adopted to guard against the activities of the particular

The importance of the personal functions discharged by an air pilot, not only in war but in peace, makes it most necessary in the public interest that he should be well looked after and strongly supported by the State. I am sure Parliament would be with you in all measures to stabilize and dignify the status and life of the pilot officer. The bringing in of these great numbers which the expansion required, makes it necessary to give them quite exceptional assistance, both in the way of maintenance and discipline. The greater the sense of permanence that can be given, the better it seems to me would be the result to the Force. We ought not to assume that air expansion is temporary, and every really worthy pilot should be given a career or a substantial gratuity.

I am told you could get a great many more pilots into the Air Force through the Oxford and Cambridge squadrons if more permanent commissions were given. Officers who have been recalled to service are in many cases working at three months' notice. Many of the young pilots you have trained by the thousand can feel very little assurance of their immediate future. If they are really good, surely they should be taken on to permanent strength and compensated if there is some reduction later on. When it comes to fighting, it will be found that quality counts first in the air.

Forgive these truisms. I shall be very ready to support you in the House of Commons if you are criticized for giving appropriate rank to Army or Navy officers who join the Air Force temporarily or permanently. The military background is indispensable, and there ought to be a good sprinkling of older men.

Many thanks for your letter.

Winston S. Churchill to Anthony Eden
(Churchill papers: 2/302)

3 December 1937
Private & Personal

My dear Anthony,

I thought perhaps you might be interested to see the enclosed correspondence which epitomises some of the most important current issues in naval architecture. I think they will probably come round now to my view.

---

company you mention, and I think they have been successful. On the information carefully, confidentially and understandingly collected, I should say that the regular moneylender is very little in the picture, but there is a good deal of indebtedness to certain tailors, who, where an officer runs up bills he cannot pay, tend to become what I may call a "tied house"'
(Churchill papers: 2/299).

Will you please not show it to anybody, or mention it to anyone, that I have sent it to you, as it is entirely between me and the Admiralty Board, including of course the First Lord concerned.

If your secretary will let me know when you have done with it, I will say where I will be to receive it personally.

Yours vy sincerely,
Winston S. Churchill

PS. I did not send any answer to the Admiralty paper, but I am not wholly in agreement with it. It is a vy able paper. I thought time would answer it.

Anthony Eden to Winston S. Churchill

(*Churchill papers: 2/302*)

3 December 1937
Private & Personal

My dear Winston,

Thank you very much for sending me the enclosed to read. I was much interested. Much must, I presume, depend upon the efficiency of our 8″ cruisers once the 'extensive reconstruction' is complete. I know something of the battleship problem and the Admiralty made a strong case considering the dilemma in which they were placed.[1]

I so much enjoyed our dinner the other evening. This Far Eastern situation is very anxious, but we must keep calm & above all avoid ineffective action.

Yours ever,
Anthony Eden

Winston S. Churchill to Brigadier Pakenham-Walsh

(*Churchill papers: 8/547*)

4 December 1937

My dear Pakenham-Walsh,

I have had the devil of a time with Malplaquet, but after about four complete days and nights, I have covered the ground. I have sent my copy to the printer, but let you have this typescript, as it will be about a week before we get the proofs.

---

[1] For Churchill's correspondence on naval gunnery, see pages 639–40, 689 and 697–8.

You will see there are a good many things which have cropped up, some of which may be new to you. The Dutch attack on the left is not yet finished, and will have to be more sharply pointed.

I shall be greatly interested to know what you think of the general picture. This time next week I will send it to you in print.

Major A. H. Burne,[1] RA, who wrote the article on Malplaquet in the Journal of the Royal Society, would be worth talking to. Is he still alive, and in the Service? Do you know him? Could you give me an introduction to him? He confesses not to have read Schulenberg.[2] I should rather like to reproduce one of his photographs of the terrain.

I am sorry on personal grounds about your old Chief,[3] but I am sure the changes will lead to the Army being put more than ever as you said 'on the map'.

Yours sincerely,
Winston S. Churchill

[1] Alfred Higgins Burne, 1896–1956. Educated at Winchester and the Royal Military Academy, Woolwich. Second Lieutenant, Royal Artillery, 1906. Lieutenant, 1909. Captain, 1914. Major, 1917. Brigade-Major, Royal Artillery, France, 1918–19. Lieutenant-Colonel, 1934. Retired, 1935. Editor of *The Gunner Magazine*, 1938–57. Commandant, 121st Officer Cadet Training Unit, Royal Artillery, 1939–42. Military historian. Author of *Mesopotamia: The Last Phase* (1937), *The Art of War on Land* (1944), *Battlefields of England* (1949) and many other works. The article mentioned by Churchill had in fact been published in the *Journal* of the Royal United Services Institute.

[2] *Leben und Denkwürdigkeiten Johann Mathias Reichsgrafen von der Schulenburg*, published in 2 volumes in 1834. Churchill wrote, in *Marlborough His Life and Times*, volume three, pages 309–10: 'General Schulenburg gives us a convincing instance of Marlborough's judgment and of his comprehension, which held all Europe in its gaze. He recounts a conversation which he had with him in 1708 in the presence of Eugene upon Charles XII's affairs. "Milord duke believes that one cannot do better than let him act exactly as he wishes in the direction of Moscow, where he could never reach his end (*venir au bout*) but will ruin himself to such an extent that he will not be able to do any more mischief and that we shall find ourselves altogether rid of him." ' Churchill commented: 'It is curious that Prince Eugene, with all his knowledge of Europe, took the opposite view. He thought that "the attack upon the Czar might go too far and might well produce regrettable consequences; and that the King of Sweden at the head of forty thousand men would be able to overturn the Empire as often as he chose". But Marlborough was right. His measurements of men and affairs were so sure that he seems almost gifted with prophetic power. By the end of 1709 Charles XII was irretrievably ruined by the battle of Pultawa. Every word of Marlborough's had come true.'

[3] Field-Marshal Sir Cyril Deverell, who had been succeeded as Chief of the Imperial General Staff by Viscount Gort. A public announcement to this effect had been made on 3 December 1937.

Group-Captain Lachlan MacLean to Violet Pearman
(*Churchill papers: 2/304*)

5 December 1937 United Service Club

Dear Mrs Pearman,

I am enclosing some notes which might possibly be of some use, if Mr Churchill is doing a tour of RAF Stations.[1]

General Sir Edmund Ironside: [2] *diary*
(*Ironside papers*)

6 December 1937

We drove to Houghton near Fakenham [yesterday] where we found the Winston Churchills.[3] He had said he wished to see me, and I thought that I ought not to miss the chance, even from the point of view of interest. Winston was most cordial and kept reiterating that he must see that I was not done down. He was horrified that Hore-Belisha had not seen me before he made his decision to change to Gort.[4] He talked about the *Conseil Supérieur* and

---

[1] MacLean's notes concerned aircraft speeds, aircraft ranges, direction finding, training. and instrument finding. He also enclosed a letter from Wing-Commander Vincent, Commanding Officer of RAF Wyton, dated 10 June 1937, on the problems of formation flying practice and traffic control. Of traffic control the Commanding Officer wrote: 'I get very little support, but it will come, and we must have a control staff specially trained in that work to do nothing else, like the staff at Croydon for instance. We have also suggested a signalling device to eliminate as far as possible the possibility of collision when manoeuvering a formation of Blenheims. The leader cannot turn his formation successfully if he cannot see all the members, or give some indication of his intentions.' A further letter, dated 2 September 1937, from Wing-Commander Drew, Officer Commanding RAF Feltwell, concerned instrument flying. The Wing-Commander wrote: 'A case has occurred at this Station of an aircraft running into a patch of low cloud at night directly after the initial take-off. Due to the venturi system of working the flying instruments, these were inoperative and the pilot was immediately in difficulties with no safety margin of height.'

[2] General Officer Commanding-in-Chief, Eastern Command, resident at Hingham, Norfolk (see page 860, note 1).

[3] Churchill and his wife were the guests of Lord and Lady Cholmondeley at Houghton Hall, Norfolk.

[4] John Standish Surtees Prendergast Vereker, 1886–1946. Succeeded his father as 6th Viscount Gort, 1902. Educated at Harrow and Sandhurst. 2nd Lieutenant, 1905; Captain, 1914. On active service, 1914–18 (despatches 9 times, Victoria Cross, Military Cross, DSO and 2 bars). General, 1937. Chief of the Imperial General Staff, 1937–9. Commander-in-Chief of the British Field Force, 1939–40. Inspector-General to the Forces for Training, 1940. Governor and Commander-in-Chief, Gibraltar, 1941–2; Malta, 1942–4. High Commissioner and Commander-in-Chief, Palestine, 1944–5. In 1938 he became a member of the Other Club.

more than once said that he would see Belisha this next week and impress upon him that I was not to be thrown over. He told me that I should not go abroad and that I should resist being sent because I was the man that would be called upon to lead the Army were we unfortunate enough to have to go to war. I told him that the whole future of the Army was in the melting pot. That neither the Cabinet nor Belisha had any idea what the Army was wanted for. That they were groping about for a solution and hadn't even begun to formulate a policy. . . .

He then told me the story of Lord French. How he had had in view the chance of commanding the British Army in the field all his life. How he had been thrown out at the critical moment over politics. Chiefly Ulster. How he had come on the Admiralty yacht with Winston a broken man. And within a fortnight he was the Commander-in-Chief of the greatest Army we had ever put in the field. A dramatic turn of fortune. He then agreed with me that things were 'written'. They may or may not be 'written' for you, he said, but you must do nothing to prevent the fulfilment. I told him that I had never influenced my career in one single way by asking or intriguing for things. He told me that he had not either, and added 'I have had my ups and downs.'

Winston loves to hold forth. We touched upon every kind of subject. He told me that he was now more than profoundly upset with things. He set forth the European situation from his view with blistering clearness. Very pro-British and very pro-French for our goodselves' interest. He thought the French Army an incomparable machine at the moment. It would be so during 1938 and 1939. Unassailable. But from then on he thought the Germans would have caught up the French and distanced them. He catechized me over the Germans as to their lack of training, lack of staff and lack of leading experience. An Army in the making. But by 1940 the annual contingent in Germany would be double that of France. He said that the power of France to defend herself was terrific. . . . He was in agreement with me that 1940 was a very bad time for us.

I could get nothing out of him as to our need of sending an Army to France. He launched out into the action of the Air and the Navy. He said that the Navy was all right. Absolutely efficient. That a modern fleet was unassailable from the air. A floating movable dock that was guarded by anti-aircraft gun-fire from hulks. A curtain of fire could be put up which would make it impossible for aeroplanes to come. He even thought Malta was unassailable. I simply couldn't agree. The Navy cannot mend ships in Malta and they would go away. I wasn't sure how the AA defences of Malta had progressed, so I didn't join issue; but I believed that we had done nothing.

The Far East he dealt with in a way that left me gasping, though I believe that he is right. He thought that we shouldn't have Hong-Kong very long.

Declare war against Japan and retire to Singapore. . . . Don't send troops out there. No mention was once made of the USA, and I had no time to bring in about Australia and New Zealand. After all, Japan is a long way from Australia, and our big Fleet should be able to compete with Japan. What about oil for the Japanese?

Then Mussolini. Winston thought that there was a good deal of bluff. That we had a good many cards in our hands. He pictured a very different picture to myself in the Mediterranean. He was definitely of opinion that we ought to have done with Mussolini before 1940; that it was very imperative to do so. The Germans wouldn't come in before 1940. He foresaw our Fleet paramount in the Mediterranean having dealt with the Italian Air and Submarine Forces. He saw the Italians in Libya and Abyssinia hopelessly cut off. He saw our Fleet bombarding the Italian coast ports. . . . He could not picture to me any Army landing, though he said it might be necessary. . . . He thought the time was not very far off when Mussolini must crash. . . .

I am afraid that I still think the situation in the Mediterranean most precarious. I am inclined to think that the British Navy is optimistic. Supposing Japan is at war with us, that Italy starts operations, and Germany asks questions. Have our political leaders the power to stop such a set of circumstances?

Winston then said that he was afraid of the RAF expansion. That it was not going as well as it should. That it was behind-hand in many ways. . . .

He ought to be the Minister of Supply if we are in for a crisis. His energy and fiery brain seem unimpaired with age. He is certainly not dismayed by our difficulties. He says that our rulers are now beginning to get frightened. . . . He said that sometimes he couldn't sleep at night thinking of our dangers, how all this wonderful Empire which had been built up so slowly and so steadily might all be dissipated in a minute.

He was just the stuff required in an emergency. The thing is to say when the emergency has arrived.

Lord Rothermere to Winston S. Churchill

(Churchill papers: 1/300)

9 December 1937

My dear Winston,
    You have won your bet for this year and I am enclosing a cheque.[1]

---

[1] For the second year in succession, Churchill had drunk no spirits, in response to a wager from Lord Rothermere. In two years, this self-imposed abstinence had won him £1,100 (the equivalent in September 1981 of nearly £20,000).

If agreeable to you, I am willing to make the same bet for next year.

Personally I would rather you did not have a break from Christmas to New Year, but I leave that to you.

I am off to the South in a few days, and looking forward to seeing you.

Yours always affectionately,
Harold R

Wing-Commander Anderson to Violet Pearman

(*Churchill papers: 2/304*)

10 December 1937   Royal Air Force Station,
Hucknall,
Nottingham

Dear Mrs Pearman,

The attached Xmas card is being sent to my Pilot Officers from this money lending firm.

I thought it would be of interest.

All goes well at Hucknall and I am finding plenty to do.

Best wishes,
C. T. Anderson

Winston S. Churchill to Merry del Val [1]

(*Churchill papers: 2/314*)

10 December 1937

My dear Ambassador,

I have read your letter with very great interest. You know the sympathy I feel for you and your country, and how deep is my desire to see Spain rise once again, happy and glorious. But mercy will have to play its part in that resurrection, and every country ought to be a home for all its people. [2]

---

[1] Merry del Val, 1864–1943. Born in London (where his father was Secretary of the Spanish Legation). Educated at Louvain University, Belgium. Entered the Spanish diplomatic service in 1882. On special missions to Moscow (1896) and London (1897). Sometime Assistant Private Secretary and later Chamberlain to the King of Spain. Ambassador to London from 1913 to 1931. Created Marquis by Royal decree, 1925.

[2] Churchill had personally intervened during 1937 to try to procure the release from a Franco prison at Malaga of Arthur Koestler, then reporting on the Spanish Civil War for the *News Chronicle*. The fact of his intervention on Koestler's behalf is indexed in the Foreign Office records (reference Western Department, 7352/2/41). The file itself, however, does not appear to have survived, and in failing to locate it at the Public Record Office, Kew, I was told (15 January 1982) that it had been 'probably weeded'.

With many thanks for your most kind messages,

Believe me,
Yours sincerely,

PS. I remember well how you prophesied Civil War to me the day the King was driven out.[1]

Imre Revesz to Winston S. Churchill
(Churchill papers: 8/561)

12 December 1937   Paris

Dear Mr Churchill,

As you were kind enough to ask me, I venture to make a suggestion regarding the subject of your next article.

The changements in the high command of the army undertaken by Mr Hore-Belisha have been widely commented abroad but General Gort and his colleagues are hardly known. I think if you could write an article on the reorganization of the army it would be of great interest. I am all the more convinced of that as every information regarding British rearmament is always published by the great newspapers abroad.[2]

Yours very sincerely,
Revesz

[1] King Alfonso XIII, (see page 797, note 1) had left Spain in 1931, after Republican gains in the municipal elections in the principal cities had shown a significant movement against him, and after the Army had withdrawn its support for the Monarchy.

[2] In his article 'Britain rearms', published in the *Evening Standard* on 7 January 1938, Churchill wrote: 'Great Britain has never had a large army in time of peace. She has a small professional force which is little more than an Imperial police reserve. Indeed, it is a prodigy to see the vast tracts of the world, and multitudes of people who dwell in composure, and for the most part in goodwill under the British Flag, protected by smaller military forces than even a third-class European State could mobilise. Nevertheless, it is necessary that the modest military establishment we maintain should be kept at its full strength, and should be equipped with the latest appliances and fullest supplies. Recruiting has greatly improved, and the rejuvenation of the High Command, for which the new Secretary for War Mr Hore-Belisha, has been praised, should initiate a period of overhaul and replenishment throughout our small army.' For further extracts from this article, see page 885, note 1). As for Revesz's suggestion, see Churchill's reply of 19 December 1937, printed on page 863.

Merry del Val to Winston S. Churchill

(*Churchill papers: 2/314*)

14 December 1937   Biarritz

Dear Mr Winston Churchill,

All my thanks for your kind letter of 10th inst just received.

You may be sure that mercy is and will be shown by General Franco and his Administration. No one suffers any penalty in his territory unless convicted of a crime. Even the prisoners of war who for reasons of military prudence are kept in labour camps are paid at the same rate as the Regular troops or the same wage as the ordinary workman if employed on any task of public utility such as road mending or repairing the damage they have done. Those who volunteer for the front and inspire confidence are allowed to join the ranks of the Army. Several thousands have been drafted into Franco's Regiments while more than a million Reds are living quietly in the cities and villages behind his lines. That they have never risen is a tribute to his beneficent rule and explains why thousands of Spanish refugees when obliged to leave this country by the French Government chose to enter his zone.

The authors and instigators of the terrible agony through which Spain is passing will meet the fate they deserve if captured. Public opinion in Nationalist Spain demands this and Franco will not be given the chance to follow any other course. Much less will they be allowed to govern in the future.

I sent you an interesting cutting yesterday.

With every good wish for Christmas I remain

Sincerely yours,
Merry del Val

Winston S. Churchill to Anthony Eden

(*Churchill papers: 2/311*)

14 December 1937

We are all looking forward very much to your coming to luncheon with our 'Focus' on Thursday next. I have no doubt Mr Richards has sent you a list of those who will be present, and as you will see, though not very numerous, they cover the whole political field. Although many are life-long pacifists they are all in favour of rearmament to meet the aggression of the Dictators. They are all for standing by the League of Nations and using it as part of our apparatus against aggression and tyranny. All are pro-French

and most of them anti-Franco. All are prepared to make exertions in common with other nations to preserve the rule of law in Europe.

I shall make a short speech on these lines. The more you can say to us the
better we shall be pleased. Afterwards you will be asked a few queries, or
preached some brief homilies. Everything will be entirely secret.

Anthony Eden to Winston S. Churchill

(*Churchill papers: 2/311*)

15 December 1937   Foreign Office

My dear Winston,

Very many thanks for your letter of December 14th. I am much looking
forward to the luncheon tomorrow and am grateful to you for the details
which you have sent me.[1]

It all sounds rather alarming, but I shall feel sustained by the chair![2]

Yours ever,
Anthony Eden

[1] A 'Strictly Private and Confidential' note in the Churchill papers gives the names of all
those present at the 'Pinafore' Room private luncheon at the Savoy Hotel on 16 December
1937. They were Anthony Eden MP (Guest of Honour), Churchill (Chairman), Clementine
Churchill, the Earl of Stamford, the Earl of Lytton, and the Earl of Derby, J. R. Clynes, MP,
Sir Walter Layton, Sir Arthur Salter, MP, Sir Malcolm Robertson, Sir Robert Waley Cohen,
Sir Norman Angell, Sir Archibald Sinclair, MP, Lady Violet Bonham Carter, the Duchess
of Atholl, MP, Eleanor Rathbone, MP, Henry Wickham Steed, A. M. Wall, Alderman
Toole, James de Rothschild, MP, Paul Emrys Evans, MP, Lieutenant Commander Reginald
Fletcher, MP, Arthur Henderson, MP, Duncan Sandys, MP, Ronald Cartland, MP, J.
McEwen, MP, the Rev Alan Don, John Eppstein (Political Secretary of the League of
Nations Union), the Rev Dr S. M. Berry (Congregational), the Rev Dr Archibald Alexander
(Presbyterian), and the Rev Dr Benjamin Gregory (Wesleyan Methodist). Including
Churchill, a total of fourteen MPs were present. (*Churchill papers: 2/343*).

[2] According to one of those who was present: 'Eden's speech was short but very revealing.
He made clear his growing anxieties about the international situation created by the practices
of the two dictators, Hitler and Mussolini. He thought it important not to yield in negotiation
on any important issue. Firmness and patience would be needed and the support of the
nation. He gave us some detailed information about his own personal views and it became
evident to all of us that there was a deep-rooted divergence of views between the Foreign
Secretary and Mr Chamberlain. This position was not evident from Chamberlain's speech
in the House on October 3rd when he had nothing but praise for Eden's co-operation and
thereby created the impression that a state of complete harmony existed between the two of
them. The Foreign Secretary had much to say in praise of the Focus. He was, he said, greatly
impressed and encouraged at seeing so many prominent people supporting it. To Churchill
he paid special tribute . . .' (Eugene Spier, *Focus*, London 1963, page 129.

Brigadier Pakenham-Walsh: diary

(Pakenham-Walsh papers)

15 December 1937

Lunch, taking A. H. Burne, with Winston at Morpeth Mansions. Deakin also there. WSC in great form. He asked me what I thought of Tiny[1] & I begged to be excused as he was my Chief, but made it clear how much I thought of him as a Commander. Winston says he ought to have been CIGS and that he was runner up the two last times. I do not agree that he would make a good CIGS. He is too much the Commander to suffer the necessary limitations of the job.

The chief business was to discuss Malplaquet, and we really only discussed what Withers did. I think I convinced Deakin & Burne that he did not start on an entirely different line from the rest. Winston is not keen as it spoils his story!

A very good lunch, Lobster, chicken, & sparkling moselle.

Major Percy Davies to Winston S. Churchill

(Churchill papers: 8/551)

16 December 1937   News of the World

Dear Mr Churchill,

As I informed you on the telephone this morning, I have now had an op-portunity of discussing with Sir Emsley Carr the matter you raised with me at dinner here last Saturday night and also on the telephone last Monday.

I am glad to be able to inform you that we shall be very pleased to adopt your suggestion. This, briefly, is that the present arrangement by which you will write for us a series of articles for publication in the early part of 1939 on the terms and conditions set out in my letter to you of Novr 13th last shall be extended for a further period of two years. That is to say, you will write a similar series on the same terms for publication in 1940 and a third series for publication in 1941.

In consideration of us extending the contract for this further period of two years, you agree, on your part, not to write until the end of 1941 for any other Sunday newspaper published in this country, subject to the existing contracts that you have already entered into. These, I understand, concern

---

[1] General Sir Edmund Ironside (see page 150, note 2), known as 'Tiny' on account of his considerable height. He was to become Chief of the Imperial General Staff on the out-break of war in September 1939. In 1937 Ironside was the General Officer Commanding-in-Chief, Eastern Command, on whose staff Pakenham-Walsh was serving.

only the series which is at present running in the 'Sunday Chronicle', and which will conclude next February,[1] and the publication in the 'Sunday Times' of your fourth book on the Life of Marlborough.

I trust this sets out fairly the effect of our verbal agreement, and I shall be very glad of a line in confirmation.

Winston S. Churchill to Major Percy Davies

(Churchill papers: 8/551)

17 December 1937

I am very glad indeed to accept the arrangements set forth in your letter of the 16th instant. It is a great satisfaction to me to be able to make some plans ahead, and to keep the course clear for my work for the News of the World.

With regard to the existing contracts, these are as follows. The present series now running in the Sunday Chronicle will not be finished until the end of February. They also made a contract to have the option of purchasing the English rights of the six articles I have written for Colliers during the present year at £100 apiece. This added to the £350 which Colliers pays make these articles very attractive to me. Four of the six articles have already been published in England by the Sunday Chronicle. Two, namely one on Divorce and one on Mr Neville Chamberlain, have not yet been published. I have the right to withhold any article from them if I do not think it suitable for the British public or for any other reason. This right I can exercise if I desire it. Besides this the Sunday Chronicle have renewed their contract for the six articles which Colliers has commissioned for 1938 which will probably not be written till later in the year. I talked to Mr Drawbell[2] on the telephone and found him most obliging and considerate. He is willing to waive altogether the contract for 1938 for the Colliers articles, but he asked particularly that the two remaining articles of the 1937 contract might be given to him for

---

[1] Beginning on 5 December 1937 and ending on 13 February 1938, the *Sunday Chronicle* published a weekly series of ten articles by Churchill, entitled 'My Childhood' (December 5), 'Under Fire' (December 12), 'Charge!' (December 19), 'I Was a Prisoner of War' (December 26), 'How I Escaped' (January 2), 'The True Story of the Tank' (January 16), 'When Britain nearly Starved' (January 23), 'Drama of the Dardanelles' (January 30), 'My Spy Chase' (February 6), 'Would I Live my Life Again?' (February 13).

[2] James Wedgwood Drawbell, 1899–   . On active service with the Royal Scots Fusiliers 1917–18. Worked on the New York *World*, the Montreal *Star*, and the Edinburgh *Evening Despatch*. Assistant Editor of *The People*, 1921–4. Editor of the *Sunday Chronicle*, 1925–46. Managing Editor with Newnes-Pearson publications.

publication at some time when the News of the World is not running any series. I told him that I would ask you about it. I am quite willing to exercise my right to veto if you desire it. I could on the other hand very likely persuade Mr Drawbell to use these other six articles, as he suggested, in some other paper or magazine of his group other than a Sunday paper. So do not hesitate to say exactly what you feel about these two articles. I have cancelled the six for 1938 anyhow. If Mr Drawbell does not want them for one of the non-Sunday papers or magazines of his group I daresay I can place them with the Strand magazine. Naturally I wish to be as agreeable as possible to Mr Drawbell as he could, in virtue of our agreement, have prevented any of these six from appearing anywhere in England except in his own columns. But this he waived in the most obliging manner and with cordial expressions about the News of the World and yourself in particular.

I have had a contract with Lord Camrose running over a good many years now for the serial rights of Marlborough. Volume IV will be appearing, I suppose, in March or April in the Sunday Times. I am much obliged to you for the intimation in your letter that you will not object to this serialisation, as it lies in an altogether different field.

With the arrangement covering the years 1939, 1940 and 1941, added to the five now completed, I shall (DV) have been working for you for eight consecutive years. In these circumstances I shall certainly expect an invitation to the annual outing of the staff.

With all seasonable wishes to you and Sir Emsley,

Lady Cholmondeley[1] *to Winston S. Churchill*

(*Churchill papers: 1/300*)

18 December 1937

My dear Winston,

I was quite confused to receive such a large cheque from you & I hope you will win it all back when we meet in February on the Riviera. Rock & I have *never* enjoyed any visit as much as yours to Houghton, it was really wonderfully enjoyable, & exhilarating for us!

Yrs affectionately,
Sybil

[1] Sybil Rachel Betty Cecile Sassoon, 1894–   . Sister of Sir Philip Sassoon. In 1913 she married Lord Rocksavage (known as 'Rock'), later 5th Marquess of Cholmondeley, who died in 1968. Resident at Houghton Hall, Norfolk, at 'Le Roc', Golfe Juan, in the South of France, and in the last private residence in Kensington Palace Gardens.

Desmond Morton to Winston S. Churchill

(*Churchill papers: 2/299*)

18 December 1937   Industrial Intelligence Centre

Dear Winston,

. . . The German Government now strictly controls all raw materials, which the country is obliged to purchase abroad, and takes wartime measures to prevent waste.[1] Jute is one of these raw materials since, as you know, India has a practical monopoly of production. By insisting that all used jute bags should be returned to the Government purchasing centres, the German authorities can reduce waste by re-issuing usable sacks to manufacturers requiring them, a procedure which in point of fact is taking place.

Yours very sincerely,
Desmond Morton

Winston S. Churchill to Imre Revesz

(*Churchill papers: 8/561*)

19 December 1937

Dear Dr Revesz,

Herewith the article for this week, which is a resumé of the year 1937, and not upon the changes in the army here. You should get it first thing on Sunday morning this time, as I am putting it on the boat-train tonight, ie the late-fee box in Victoria Station.[2]

---

[1] On 6 December 1937 Churchill had been sent, by R. E. Clark, of Rickmansworth, a cutting from the *Daily Telegraph*, citing an order just published in Berlin 'for the surrender of all sacks made of jute'. The order added that it was 'forbidden to cut, tear, or mend such sacks or to use them in the interval before surrender for holding coal, firewood or coke'.

[2] Entitled 'Panorama of 1937', the article was published in the *Evening Standard* on 23 December 1937, as well as throughout Dr Revesz's European syndication. It surveyed the civil war in Spain ('fought feebly but cruelly and incessantly throughout the year'), the Japanese invasion of China ('marked by a succession of outrages against neutral powers, particularly Great Britain and the United States, followed in all cases by apologies. So far these apologies have had to be accepted, but it may be that further injuries are in store and that little else than the destruction of British, United States and European interests in the Far East may be in contemplation') and the Italian occupation of Abyssinia ('seething with sporadic rebellion'). But Churchill saw hope in Anglo-French unity and 'the goodwill extended towards the free Governments of Europe by the United States', which had become 'more apparent as the months have passed'. His article ended: 'On Christmas Day, 1914, the German soldiers on the Western Front ceased firing. They placed small Christmas trees on their trenches and declared that on this day there should be peace and goodwill among suffering men. Both sides came out of their trenches and met in the blasted No-Man's Land. They clasped each other's hands, they exchanged gifts and kind words. Together they buried the dead hitherto inaccessible and deprived of the rites which raise man above the brute. Let no man worthy of human stature banish this inspiration from his mind.'

Desmond Morton to Winston S. Churchill

(*Churchill papers: 2/299*)

22 December 1937   Earlylands

Warmest congratulations on your brilliant speech last night which I have just read with the greatest pleasure and profit. I only wish I could have heard it. The view I have heard expressed is that your speech alone gave a clear indication of a line of policy. At the same time your ridicule of Mussolini, which admittedly neither the PM or Foreign Secretary could have expressed with propriety, whatever they may feel about it, was beautifully calculated.[1]

I hope there may be a chance of seeing you next week after you get back from Blenheim. Meanwhile I wish you and Mrs Churchill a very happy Christmas,

Yours very sincerely,
Desmond Morton

Winston S. Churchill to Desmond Morton

(*Churchill papers: 2/299*)

23 December 1937

I am told that at 28, Victoria Street there is a group of Japanese, about a dozen. They employ an English secretary who has heard them frequently talking about the coming war. If her name was mentioned she would of course be dismissed. Indeed after giving this information she was greatly alarmed lest it should be brought home to her. I pass this information on to you as it came from a source which I am sure is trustworthy.[2]

---

[1] During his speech on 21 December 1937 Churchill told the House of Commons: 'I do not see why the League should be weakened by the departure of a Country which has, to put it as politely as I possibly can, broken every engagement into which it has entered, and whose spokesmen have rejoiced in mocking and insulting every principle on which the League is founded. The one small service Signor Mussolini had left to render to the League was to leave it.' As for the success of the Nyon Conference in ending the sinking of ships in the Mediterranean, Churchill praised the British Government for its firm policy, adding, with sarcasm: 'but I must pay my tribute to Signor Mussolini, who joined the common exertions of the Mediterranean Powers, and whose prestige and authority—by the mere terror of his name—quelled the wicked depredations of these pirates. Since the days of Caesar himself there has been no more salutory clearance of pirates from the Mediterranean.'

[2] In one of his regular fortnightly articles in the *Evening Standard*, on 21 January 1938, Churchill wrote: '. . . it is said that Japan has already embarked upon the construction of several battleships which exceed in tonnage and size of cannon those that are being built in Britain and America. The United States Navy Board will of course be compelled to review its

Wing-Commander Anderson to Violet Pearman

(*Churchill papers: 2/304*)

23 December 1937

Smedley's Hydro
Matlock
Derbyshire

Dear Mrs Pearman

I am staying at this place for a week. But go to Hucknall for Xmas day & help with the dinner for the Airmen. I will reply in full to S[1] letter & return same.

The Air Ministry are now very worried over the large number of accidents. 150 killed during the last 12 months & 97 died as result of accidents. The cost of each new Aeroplane is between £15,000 ; £25,000 each, prior to 2 years ago the average price was £3,000. So on the grounds of finance alone we deserve officers holding Permanent Commissions.

All the best & long to have a real talk to you.

Yours ever,
C. T. Anderson

Lord Rothermere to Winston S. Churchill

(*Churchill papers: 2/302*)

23 December 1937

La Dragonnière
Cap Martin

My dear Winston,

I see from your speech in the House of Commons the night before last that you are still harping on what I suppose is your belief in the invincibility of the French Army.[2] *You are utterly mistaken.*

---

programmes and types very searchingly. President Roosevelt's declarations seem to show that the Government of the United States would not be willing to see their naval power seriously rivalled in the Pacific Ocean at the present time. They have an ample superiority, but this might pass in a few years unless timely measures are taken. It seems probable that a large programme of naval expansion will be undertaken in the United States, and that the American Navy will keep good pace with the British Navy in accordance with the principles of parity which govern our relations. Neither Government need be afraid of what is called starting a naval race with Japan. It is quite certain that Japan cannot possibly compete with the productive energies of either branch of the English-speaking peoples.'

[1] Lord Swinton's letter of 29 November 1937 (see page 849, note 2).

[2] Speaking in the House of Commons on 21 December 1937 Churchill said: 'I comfort and fortify myself with the conviction that France and Britain together, with all their worldwide connections, in spite of their tardiness in making air preparations, constitute so vast and formidable a body that they will very likely be left alone undisturbed, at any rate for some

The French Army is slowly but surely sinking into a condition of chaos and confusion such as is beginning to distinguish the life of France. I hear that in some districts officers' pay is in arrears. There is a loosening of discipline. The artillery ammunition is deficient in quality and quantity.

Prominent Frenchmen do not hesitate to say in private that in many parts of France a high proportion of the Reservists would not respond to the orders of mobilisation. Anything like a suicidal attempt to come to the aid of Czecho-Slovakia or Austria, in case of German intervention, would expose the fact that the French Government was trying out a policy to which nearly all the fighting men of France are utterly opposed.

The Air Force is beneath contempt. France still has a number of fine pilots but the number of fine aeroplanes is so small as to be almost negligible. Whereas in other countries like Germany new types of aeroplanes are manufactured within three or four months, it takes three or four years in France. Today nearly all the aeroplanes being delivered to the French Air Force are completely out of date. Moreover, the material used in their manufacture is of poor quality and not properly tested out before being utilised. Corruption in this vital branch of national defence reigns supreme.

Major-General Fuller[1] states that the Maginot Line can be easily pierced. He says the German General Staff are fully aware of this and count in the next war on the defeat of France in the first few weeks at most.

In my opinion nothing should be said which might induce our ignorant mob electorate to believe that Britain and France have any fighting chance against the enemies they would have to encounter once war started.

The Western damocracies—the correct way to spell democracies— would be completely smashed and there would be an end of our wonderful and glorious country.

----

time to come.' During his speech Churchill also told the House of Commons: 'I attach the greatest significance to the relations which we have with France. Those relations are founded on the power of the French Army and the power of the British Fleet. They are also founded on the known and proved desire of these two countries to keep out of war, and to the best of their ability to help others to keep out of war.' For Churchill's worries about the future preponderance of the German Army, see General Ironside's diary extract for 6 December 1937 (quoted on pages 853–5), Churchill's own reply to Lord Rothermere on 29 December 1937 (page 869), and his letter to William Chenery of 21 April 1938 (pages 1001–2).

[1] John Frederick Charles Fuller, 1878–1966. 2nd Lieutenant, Oxford Light Infantry, 1898. On active service in South Africa, 1899–1902 and on the western front, 1914–18 (despatches, DSO, Lieutenant-Colonel). Major-General, 1930. Retired from the Army, 1933. A guest (with Lord Brocket) at Hitler's 50th birthday celebrations in Berlin, April 1939. One of the leading advocates of mechanical warfare, he published some thirty books on military history, the first, *Tanks in the Great War*, 1914–18, in 1920; the last, a biography of Julius Caesar, in 1965.

I wish you would keep this letter.

Yours always,
Harold R

PS. Above all things I desire you should not be one of those who will be arraigned for misleading our ignorant people if war breaks out with its inevitable result.

Lord Lloyd to Winston S. Churchill

(*Churchill papers: 1/323*)

23 December 1937

My dear Winston,

Something impels me to send you this line of Christmas greeting & to wish you more power to your elbow in the coming year. I think it is because I never cease to be grateful to you for all you did for us over the India fight which some forget & I do not. Neither you nor I will ever fight in a greater cause however badly we may seem to have been beaten & we could have done nothing without you.

Yours ever,
George L

Duncan Sandys to Winston S. Churchill

(*Churchill papers: 1/300*)

Christmas Day 1937

Hotel Lenzerhorn,
Lenzerheide,
Austria

My dear Winston,

Thank you so very much for the very lovely silver inkstand you gave us for Christmas. Diana & I are so delighted to possess it. The inscription on it makes it all the more interesting.

I want to congratulate you on your grand speech in the House on Tuesday. I wish I could have heard it. Your remarks about 'not giving a scrap of territory to keep the Nazi kettle boiling' were just what was needed at this moment.[1]

---

[1] In his speech on 21 December 1937 Churchill commented, on the current discussion about the possible return of German colonies to Germany: 'I do not know in any definite way what the real intentions of His Majesty's Government are, and I am certainly not asking for any immediate declaration, but I should like to say that, though there are a very large

Apart from daily tobogganing Diana & I are not taking winter sports very seriously. But we are thoroughly enjoying ourselves and feeling the better for it already. It's nice being here with Clemmie & Mary.

We return on Jan 2nd & hope to see you before you go to the Riviera. Again with many thanks for the beautiful inkstand.

Yours affectionately,
Duncan

Clementine Churchill to Winston S. Churchill
(*Churchill papers: 1/322*)

27 December 1937   Hotel Lenzerhorn

My Darling Winston

Everything is going very well here. Mary is very happy & enjoying the crisp powder snow & Duncan & Diana are having a renewed honeymoon. . . .

I do hope you enjoyed Blenheim & also Randolph.[1]

On Christmas night we all went to a dance at one of the big hotels & I provided Champagne for dinner! I expect you are returning to Blenheim for the New Year or perhaps staying right on. But I'm sending this by Air Mail to Chartwell.

Your loving,
Clemmie

---

number of people in this country who would be willing to make sacrifices to meet German wishes about the colonies if they could be assured that it meant genuine lasting peace to Europe, none of them would yield one scrap of territory just to keep the Nazi kettle boiling. I therefore welcome very much the declarations we have heard at different times, and renewed this afternoon by the Prime Minister, to the effect that there is no question whatever of any isolated retrocession of colonial war conquests; that we could only discuss such matters in company with our former Allies; that we should only approach the many difficulties involved if it were part of a general return by Europe to the old standards of tolerance and the final healing of outstanding quarrels; and, above all, leading in the end to an all-round reduction of armaments.'

[1] Churchill and his son were at Blenheim from 24 to 27 December 1937. Among the other guests were Paul Maze (the painter), Lord Ivor Churchill, Gerard and Elizabeth Koch de Gooreynd, Victoria Gilmour and her children Diana, aged 14 (later, as Lady Beith, the wife of the British Ambassador to Belgium) and Ian, then aged eleven (later Secretary of State for Defence; and Lord Privy Seal in Margaret Thatcher's Conservative Government of 1979).

Winston S. Churchill to Lord Rothermere

(*Churchill papers: 2/302*)

29 December 1937

Thank you very much for both your letters. As I gather you are at Cap Martin, and I shall very likely be in the neighbourhood, I will come over and see you, and help you bear the many damnable oppressions under which we are compelled to pass the evening of our lives. I will then unfold you arguments for believing that at the present time the French army can defend France against Germany, and is in fact a stronger military organisation. This condition will of course pass as Germany's numbers increase, and as the officer and NCO cadres mature.

What a horrible responsibility these men bear in England who refused either to arm themselves in the air, or to stop Germany from doing so while we had the power.

I have sent your message to Randolph and he will write to you himself. He is very grateful to you for all your kindness and so am I.

Winston S. Churchill to Sir Eric Phipps

(*Churchill papers: 2/299*)

29 December 1937

I hope to arrive by the Ferry at 9 o'clock on Monday morning. It is very kind of you to put me up. I shall be much interested to meet Léger[1] and Daladier[2] if they are available at this holiday moment. I should particularly like to meet Blum, with whom I established pleasant relations when he was Premier. I am anxious to persuade him to pay us a visit over here and I

---

[1] Marie–René August Alexis Saint-Léger Léger, 1887–1975. Poet, writing under the pseudonym St-John Perse. Joined the French Foreign Service, 1914. Secretary, Peking, 1916–21. Chef de Cabinet, Ministry of Foreign Affairs, 1925–32; Secretary-General, 1933–40. Honorary knighthood, 1938. Left France for the United States, 1940. Deprived by the Vichy Government of his nationality, property and civil honours, October 1940. Consultant on French Literature to the Library of Congress, 1941–5. Returned to France in 1957, to live in a house presented to him by American friends and admirers. Awarded the Nobel Prize for Literature, 1960 (*Anabase* had first been published in 1921, and was translated by T. S. Elliot in 1931).

[2] Edouard Daladier, 1884–1970. Mayor of Carpentras, 1912–58. Member of the Chamber of Deputies, 1919. Minister of Colonies, 1924. Minister of War, 1933. Minister of Foreign Affairs, 1934. Minister of War and Defence, 1936–8. Prime Minister, April 1938–March 1940; also Minister of War and Defence.

would give him a luncheon at our 'focus' of which I will tell you more when I come. Also I would give a dinner in the House for him to meet MPs. I talked to Anthony about this and he seemed to think well of the project of Blum coming over, so very likely the FO would do something too. Anyhow if I meet him this would be the topic I should ventilate. I warned Blum two years ago that French aviation was falling far behind but alas I could not alarm him sufficiently.

With regard to the British Chamber of Commerce, I shall very likely be passing through Paris on my way home about that date, and I will tell my wife about your kind invitation. Let us talk this over when we meet.

Winston S. Churchill to Vice-Admiral Guépratte
(*Churchill papers: 2/299*)

30 December 1937

I am most grateful to you for your kind letter and good wishes. It always gives me great pleasure to hear from you, and to collaborate with you in maintaining that unbreakable friendship between our two countries, which appears to be our only means of safety at the present time.

I venture to send you a copy of a book of mine[1] which has been translated into French and deals with very early days.

Winston S. Churchill to H. G. Wells[2]
(*Churchill papers: 1/407*)

30 December 1937

An American lecture agent, Mr Harold Peat,[3] called on me yesterday and made me serious proposals for a tour next Autumn. I do not think we should have any difficulty in reaching an agreement on terms. But of course I know

---

[1] *My Early Life*, first published in English in 1930, and subsequently translated into French, German, Italian, Swedish, Norwegian, Danish, Spanish, Portuguese, Hebrew, Dutch, Islandic, Japanese and Finnish.

[2] Herbert George Wells, 1866–1946. Author and novelist. Among his earliest works were *The Time Machine* (1895), *The War of the Worlds* (1898) and *The First Men in the Moon* (1901). On his return from a visit to Russia in 1920 he published *Russia in the Shadows*. He parodied Churchill in his novel *Men Like Gods* (1923), where he wrote, of 'Rupert Catskill', that 'his wild imaginings have led to the deaths of thousands of people'. A member of the Other Club (founded by 'Rupert Catskill' and F. E. Smith) from 1934.

[3] Harold R. Peat Incorporated, Management of Distinguished Personalities: one of the leading lecture agencies in the United States. Its offices were at 2 West 45th Street, New York City.

very little about him. He tells me that he has just managed your lecture tour, and that I should apply to you for an expression of opinion. He makes good impression upon me at first sight, but of course none of these people are in a very strong position. I should be very glad if you would let me know whether you were satisfied with the way you were managed, and looked after, and with the results of the tour; and whether in your opinion I can trust Mr Peat.[1]

All good wishes for the New Year. When are we going to meet again. I am off to Cannes on Sunday night.[2]

Winston S. Churchill to Maxine Elliot

(*Churchill papers: 1/300*)

30 December 1937   Chartwell

I was delighted to get your letter. I shall arrive by the morning train on the 5th and look forward very much to seeing you again. There is just one uncertainty that faces me on the 5th. The Duke of Windsor is leaving on the 6th and I am to go to see him some time or other on the 5th. Very likely it will be for luncheon. Whatever he suggests I shall have to do, as I have not seen him since that dark day when he left our country, and as you know I am a devoted servant.

The weather here is cold, grey and cheerless. I have a horrible cold which has kept me indoors for the best part of a fortnight. I have turned on all the electric heaters, and sealed up all the windows; so it will be very nice to come into your brilliant sunshine. Please do your very best not to let it escape before I can enjoy it.

I am coming quite alone with no servant but Mrs Pearman whom you know will overtake me with mails etc and the usual consignment of book proofs, a few days later.

---

[1] A note on the carbon copy of this letter, in Mrs Pearman's handwriting, states: 'Spoke to H. G. Wells on 31st Dec & he recommended.' Wells had stayed at Chartwell on 11 August 1937.

[2] Before leaving for the South of France, Churchill spent New Year's Day 1938 at Blenheim. The other guests included Euan and Barbara Wallace and three of their sons, Peter, William and John (see page 1591, note 1).

Desmond Morton to Winston S. Churchill

(*Churchill papers: 2/302*)

31 December 1937   Earlylands

Dear Winston,

You asked me to put a few words on paper about the change in the MGO's branch at the War Office.

Yours ever,
Desmond Morton

Desmond Morton: notes for Winston S. Churchill

(*Churchill papers: 2/302*)

31 December 1937

The appointment of Admiral Brown as Army Council Member for Supply, at the recommendation of the Master General of the Ordnance, had elements of soundness, but was vitiated by the extent to which Supply and Design were separated—the MGO remaining virtually entirely responsible for Design.

The present counter-march, whereby the Admiral becomes virtually MGO as well as Member for Supply, being assisted in MGO duties by a Deputy MGO, the post of MGO itself being temporarily unfilled, is a necessary retrograde movement. It is, however, little more than 'as you were', and entirely fails to tackle the real problem.

It is first of all essential to establish a clear division of responsibility between the Soldier and the Civilian Manufacturer, due regard being paid to the rights and difficulties of either party. The mass production of armament stores of all kinds, including warships and aircraft, is at least as technical a problem as training Armed Forces and fighting a campaign. The military man, particularly the soldier, knows far less about industrial production than the Industrialist knows about warfare. Many Industrialists have been military men, no military man has been a practical Industrialist.

I can see no really sound solution outside of a Ministry of Supply, though it would not be impossible to camouflage such a Ministry in peace-time under other titles. The point remains in the necessity to separate the Authority responsible to Parliament for the Supply of Armament Stores in peace and war from the Authority responsible for the Fighting Forces.

The Military man must first decide what types of weapons he requires, in what quantity and in what order and at what rate of delivery. To do this he must, indeed, have his own advisory designing staff, who will, within reasonable limits design the ideal weapon. This design and the necessary additional information anent quantity and rate of delivery will be passed to the Supply Authority, who, in consultation with the actual manufacturers, will comment on the demands from the Industrialist's standpoint, ie making it clear to the military man that if he insists on certain details of the ideal design he will get no delivery for the first year of war; suggesting modifications which will speed up delivery without seriously impairing the efficiency of the weapon &c.

Responsibility for final decision upon types must rest with the Military in the light of the additional information the Industrialist is thus able to provide. Responsibility for delivery in accordance with the agreement thus reached must rest with the Supply Authority.

The chief cause of failure in this country to turn out armament stores and aircraft (I exclude warships, since the Navy have long adopted a procedure which conforms to the essential principle) must lie at the door of the military man. He has failed because he has interfered in the Industrialist's job. He has not made up his mind what types of armaments he requires. Having apparently done so, he has constantly changed detail of design, quite oblivious of the effect of such action on eventual production. He has constantly demanded the impossible, namely the marriage of highly complicated design with rapid output.

In modern warfare there are four arms of Defence; Industry taking its place alongside the three Fighting Forces. Until the Military man recognises this fact in deed as well as in words, we shall continue to fail to make adequate preparations to defend the Empire against aggression.

Winston S. Churchill to J. W. Drawbell
(*Churchill papers: 8/553*)

31 December 1937

Dear Mr Drawbell,

I am very much obliged to you for having arranged that the six Colliers' articles will be published in your other papers.

There is only one point which I must stipulate, and that is that the articles must always be published in the most prominent position in the various morning papers. I am advised that it is injurious to me if the articles are not so treated.

You are still free to publish the two outstanding articles of the 1937 contract in the 'Sunday Chronicle' at some time not inconvenient to the 'News of the World'. If you will let me know when you would like to do this, I will find out for you.

January 1938

Wing-Commander Anderson to Violet Pearman

(Churchill papers: 2/338)

1 January 1938   Royal Air Force
                                                   Hucknall
                                                   Nottingham

Dear Mrs Pearman,

Will you give the attached papers to Papa. He asked for them to be sent on as he wishes to reply further to S.[1]

Yours ever,
C. T. Anderson

---

[1] Anderson had prepared for Churchill a two-page note about pilot training, stressing what he considered to be the weaknesses of the Short Service and Medium Service commissions, and writing: 'The financial responsibility of our new aircraft costing some £25,000 apiece makes it imperative that a responsible and contented officer should be in charge. Is it fair that some 106 aircraft in Bomber Command—in England alone—should be written off each Quarter? This loss of life; injuries resulting frequently in permanent incapacity; and loss of equipment can be attributed, in a large measure, to the personnel. The financial responsibility alone warrants that pilots be given a permanent career in their service. Instability of type and lack of continuity, are fundamental causes of the present state of inefficiency and discontent; the attached analysis speaks for itself.' The analysis, of five Bomber squadrons, showed, for example, No 37 Squadron with 15 Pilot Officers 'of whom only 1 is permanent', No 12 Squadron with 11 Pilot Officers 'of whom only 1 is permanent' and No 211 Squadron with '1 permanent Squadron Leader, no Flying Officers', and 13 Pilot Officers 'all short service'. Anderson also sent Churchill a copy of a confidential letter to all Bomber Group Headquarters, dated 13 December 1937, and circulated by the Senior Air Staff Officer of Bomber Command, analysing the causes of the flying accidents in the quarter ending 30 September 1937. Of these accidents, 70 were listed as 'avoidable', 38 of them being officially ascribed to 'Inexperience of pilot or crew in piloting or navigating and communications due to insufficient instruction, or failure in emergency which more experienced personnel might have overcome successfully.'

Clementine Churchill to Winston S. Churchill

(Churchill papers: 1/332)

2 January 1938   Hotel Lenzerhorn

My Darling Winston,

I like to think of you to-day speeding towards the South &, I hope sunshine.

Do not work too hard there. Has 'Marlborough' reached a point where you can leave it until you return? I do hope so. . . .

Lord Rothermere to Winston S. Churchill

(Churchill papers: 2/328)

2 January 1938   La Dragonnière,
                                                  Cap Martin

My dear Winston,

Read the accompanying page from the Stock Exchange Gazette dealing with French finance.[1] How you or anyone else can think present day France can fight another war successfully is entirely beyond my comprehension. Germany and Italy could strangle France in a few weeks. If we tie our fortunes to France we shall be strangled at the same time.

Hoping to see you quite soon.

Yours,
Harold

[1] In an article in the *Stock Exchange Gazette*, published on 4 December 1937, and dated 'Paris December 1, from our own Correspondent', it was reported that Bonnet's 'well-laid plans for financial restoration received their first real check at the hands of the Chamber at the week-end, when he was compelled to give way to demands for increased expenditure which will far more than swallow up his estimated surplus of Frs 1,600,000,000, at the end of 1938'. According to the article, the cause of the increased expenditure was a demand by Civil Servants for increased pay and measures, supported by Communists and Socialists, for increased expenditure in respect of aged workers, agricultural calamities, and unemployment insurance. There was, the correspondent of the *Stock Exchange Gazette* warned, 'a steadily growing belief . . . that a policy of overturning the present social and economic order by financial bankruptcy is now being applied, in substitution for that of revolutionary violence and disorder'.

Winston S. Churchill to the Dowager Lady Leconfield [1]

(*Churchill papers: 8/594*)

2 January 1938

It gave me exceptional pleasure to receive your letter of December 11 and to learn that you liked the chapter I wrote about your dear and venerated brother, the friend and patron of my youth, and my father's friend before me. Many people think that this sketch, necessarily only slight and brief, is the best in the book. Bob and Peggy [2] helped me with it a great deal, and it gave me a deep satisfaction to feel that those who knew and loved Rosebery best are contented with what I have written about him. [3]

Winston S. Churchill to Eugene Spier

(*Churchill papers: 2/328*)

3 January 1938

Dear Mr Spier,

Thank you very much for sending me the translation (through Mr Richards) of the far too complimentary article which has appeared in several Yugo-Slavian papers. Indeed I hope I shall be able to visit that country one day.

[1] Constance Evelyn Primrose, 1846–1939. A granddaughter of the 4th Earl of Rosebery, and sister of the 5th Earl. In 1867 she married Henry Wyndham, 2nd Baron Leconfield, who had died in 1901. One of their six sons was killed in action in November 1914. One of their grandsons was killed in action at El Alamein in October 1942, and another grandson was killed in action in Normandy in November 1944. She died on 27 June 1939.

[2] The Marquess and Marchioness of Crewe (see page 400, note 3).

[3] Churchill's chapter in *Great Contemporaries*, 'The Earl of Rosebery' had first been published in the *Pall Mall* magazine in October 1929. In it Churchill wrote: 'He was keenly curious about every aspect of life. Sportsman, epicure, bookworm, literary critic, magpie collector of historical relics, appreciative owner of veritable museums of art treasures, he never needed to tear a theme to tatters. In lighter vein he flitted jauntily from flower to flower like a glittering insect, by no means unprovided with a sting. And then in contrast, out would come his wise, matured judgements upon the great men and events of the past. But these treats were not always given. He was at his best with two or three and on his day; and sometimes in larger company he seemed shy and ill at ease. When he was out of humour, he could cast a chill over all, and did not hesitate to freeze and snub. On these occasions his face became expressionless, almost a slab, and his eyes lost their light and fire. One saw an altogether different person. But after a bit one knew the real man was there all the time, hiding perversely behind a curtain. And all the more agreeable was it when he came out.' Churchill added: 'Hardest of all is it to revive the impression which he produced upon his hearers when dealing with the greatest affairs. His life was set in an atmosphere of tradition. The Past stood ever at his elbow and was the counsellor upon whom he most relied. He seemed to be attended by Learning and History, and to carry into current events an air of ancient majesty. His voice was melodious and deep, and often, when listening, one felt in living contact with the centuries which are gone, and perceived the long continuity of our island tale.'

But I must tell you that I have been greatly concerned at the recent policy of the present Prime Minister of Yugo-Slavia which seems to me contrary to the interests of Peace and Freedom in Europe.[1] A very mild article which I wrote for the Evening Standard, which in the ordinary course would have been printed in the Belgrade paper, was cut by the military censor, much to the regret of that paper. I have informed the Foreign Office of this incident.

With best wishes to you and your wife for the New Year.

Yours sincerely
Winston S. Churchill

Winston S. Churchill to Clementine Churchill

(*Spencer-Churchill papers*)

3 January 1938   British Embassy,
Secret   Paris

My darling Clemmie,

Blum lunched here today and we had a long talk, with the Ambassador.[2] Blum began by admitting the bad state of French Aviation & that I had warned him about it 18 months ago. It is difficult to persuade people of facts till too late.

When Chautemps[3] & Daladier were in London Neville told them that we

---

[1] The Yugoslav Prime Minister, Stoyadinovich, had made it his object to keep on good terms with the totalitarian States, and in the first week of December 1937, he had visited Rome. 'Although he protested that he had entered into no commitments, the public showed its dislike of his foreign policy by enthusiastic Francophil demonstrations, in the course of which conflicts took place between students and the police, resulting in one death and several injuries.' (*The Annual Register*, for the year 1937, London 1938, p. 212.) In the middle of January Stoyadinovich visited Germany, where he was given a very flattering reception.

[2] Sir Eric Phipps, see page 15, note 3.

[3] Camille Chautemps, 1885–1963. A lawyer, son of a former Minister of the Colonies. Mayor of Tours, and a leading French freemason. Elected as a Socialist Radical Deputy, 1919. Minister of the Interior, 1924; of Justice, 1925; of the Interior, 1925, and 1926. Prime Minister for three days in 1930. Minister of the Interior, 1932 and 1933. Prime Minister, November 1933–January 1934. Minister of Public Works, January 1936; Minister of State, June 1936; Prime Minister, June 1937–March 1938. Honorary knighthood, 1938. A member of the Reynaud Cabinet, 1940; as Vice-President of the Council, he continued to hold this office for a brief period in Marshal Petain's Vichy Government. While on a mission, for Vichy, to the United States, in the late autumn of 1940, be broke with the Vichy Government, and on 10 March 1944 he offered his services to General de Gaulle's Free French Provisional Government in Algiers. No position of trust was offered to him. In 1946 he was sentenced to five years imprisonment, and national degradation for life, for 'collaboration with the enemy', but he was already living in the United States. The sentence was later annulled. He died in the United States.

were making 350 machines a month. They were deeply impressed. But now it turns out N C was wrongly informed, the true figure being only $\frac{1}{2}$! Consequently there is a certain reproaching going on between N C & the Air M. What happened was that poor Neville believed the lie that the Air M circulated for public purposes & did not know the true figures. This gives you some idea of the looseness w wh we are governed in these vital matters. I had heard all about this from a quarter you can guess, Ⓜ,[1] so I led the talk into this channel & got full confirmation. It ought to make Neville think. He does not know the truth: & perhaps he does not want to.

Anthony E is passing through here tonight on his way S so perhaps I shall see him.

The French were much excited by the rumour I was going to join the Govt. They have been sprouting eulogistic articles—of one of which I send you a copy.

To-night we are going to a review: viz Amb, Ch Mendl, Lloyd Thomas & self. Tomorrow Leger lunches. Otherwise I stay in my room & work.

Randolph is going to embark upon a course of physical fitness & beauty culture in the New Year. He was vy agreeable to me last night. We only just caught the train.

My darling how are you going on? I see there has been another bad avalanche in Austria. But I hope you will not run needless risks, or go too far from home. I had a lovely letter from Mary. Do thank her for it & give her many kisses from yr own ever loving husband.

W

[Sketch of pig] Tender love my sweet darling.

PS. The Amb asked much after you. She[2] is most agreeable. I don't think I shall do the Ch glorious speech. I will write you later.

It wd be vy nice if you would write a line to the D of W and thank him for his Christmas Card. You can refer to her as The Duchess thus avoiding the awkward point.[3]

More love

---

[1] Desmond Morton: Churchill himself drew a circle around the letter 'M'.

[2] Frances Ward, daughter of Herbert Ward. She married Eric Phipps, as his second wife, in 1911. Her sister Sarita married, first, in 1912, Sir Colville Barclay, and, second, in 1931, Sir Robert Vansittart.

[3] The Duke of Windsor had been insisting that the Duchess should be addressed as 'Her Royal Highness', which she specifically was not. For Churchill's view of this controversy, see page 653.

Darling, I have just returned from R[1] at Cap Martin. I had meant to add a separate letter to this, but now I am too late, as I am off to dine with LG. I will write again tomorrow.

Always my darling your ever loving husband

W

[Sketch]

Love to Mary from whom I have a delightful letter. The Times today (11th) say the south wind makes avalanches likely, be careful, & don't make long wild expeditions.

PS. Poem about the cat—lovely
Tell him about it when you return.

W

Ian Colvin[2] to Winston S. Churchill

(*Churchill papers: 2/341*)

4 January 1938   Berlin

Dear Mr Winston Churchill,

Since you heard my story of mobilisation of 3 Army Corps, I should like to let you know that the plan of occupation was cancelled when the News Chronicle report reached Germany. The third Army Corps was therefore not mobilised at all. But the occupation will take place at a later date (probably March) and there will be German garrisons in important Czech and Slovak cities and towns.

I will write more fully later.

Yours sincerely,
Ian Colvin

---

[1] Lord Rothermere. This postscript was dated 10 January 1938.

[2] Ian Goodhope Colvin, 1913–1975. Son of Ian D. Colvin, the journalist and editor. Joined the *Morning Post* as a reporter, 1932. Transferred to Reuters, 1933. *News Chronicle* correspondent in Berlin, 1938–39. Served in the News Department of the Foreign Office, 1939–40; in the Royal Marines and at Combined Operation's Headquarters, 1940–4. Landing craft Flotilla Commander, 1944–5. On the staff of Kemsley newspapers, 1946–52; Foreign Editor of the *Sunday Express*, 1953–5. Leader writer and foreign correspondent on the *Daily Telegraph* from 1955 to his death, specializing in African affairs. Author of two historical works, *Vansittart in Office* (1965) and *The Chamberlain Cabinet*, as well as *The Rise and Fall of Moishe Tshombe*. Of Colvin's work in Berlin, Churchill wrote in his war memoirs: 'He plunged very deeply into German politics and established contacts of a most secret character with some of the important German generals and also with independent men of character and quality in Germany who saw in the Hitler movement the approaching ruin of their native land.'

Winston S. Churchill to Ludwig Noé [1]

(Churchill papers: 2/328)

8 January 1938

Dear Dr Noé,

Many thanks for your letter with the sentiments of which I am in full accord. I was not aware however there was ever any question between Germany and England which required settlement, except that of the return of war conquests, upon which our position has already been defined. England is seeking nothing from Germany except that the Germans should live in a happy contented manner in their own country without attacking any of their neighbours. As long as Germany does not embark upon a policy of aggression there can be no possible quarrel between our two countries, though of course it is painful to every country to see the cruel persecution of the Jews, Protestants and Catholics, and the general suppression of Parliamentary life.

Reciprocating your good wishes for the New Year,

Winston S. Churchill to Brigadier-General Sir Henry Page Croft

(Churchill papers: 2/328)

8 January 1938

I am very glad you and your friends are pleased with the article I wrote in the Evening Standard about the Spanish Civil War.[2] It would not be in accordance with the position I have taken of even-handed neutrality for me

---

[1] Ludwig Noé. Born in the Rhineland, 1871. Doctor of Mechanical Engineering. Professor at the Technical College, Danzig, 1919–39. Consul-General in Danzig for the Finnish Government, and a Director of the Danziger Werf. President of the International Shipbuilding and Engineering Company, Danzig.

[2] In an article in the Evening Standard, 'Spain's Road to Peace', on 26 November 1937, Churchill argued in favour of 'formal friendly diplomatic relations' with both sides in the Spanish conflict, in order to encourage moderation and humanity on both sides. 'It is just as wrong,' he wrote, 'to call the Valencian and Catalonian Governments a mob of savage Bolshevists as to dub the Nationalist movement a mere body of rebels, traitors and reactionaries.' Churchill went on to propose the restoration in Spain of a constitutional monarchy, as a guarantee 'that all Spaniards who have not committed crimes of moral turpitude will find their places in the New Spain.' Churchill's article ended: 'This week in Austria, when the Monarchists were celebrating the natal day of the Habsburg heir to the throne, they were assaulted by a combination of Nazis and Communists. Does not such an episode strike a note which should be audible to all that great majority of Europeans who wish to see totalitarian tyrannies pass from the life of Europe, and to that end would rejoice to see Spain resume a united and independent place among its leading nations?'

to attend or speak at your meeting on the 23rd March, but I am extremely grateful to you for inviting me.[1]

With every good wish, believe me,

Violet Pearman to A. H. Richards

(*Churchill papers: 2/343*)

8 January 1938
As from Château de l'Horizon,
Golfe Juan, AM

Dear Mr Richards,

I find that unfortunately your letter of the 29th December had got caught up behind another one and therefore the answer was delayed. Mr Churchill was away at Blenheim Palace for Christmas, then home for two days and returned again there, from whence he came on here, so things have been a little bit moving around in boxes and cases. You have, I see, explained to The Ban[2] that Mr Churchill was going away, for which very many thanks. He came away on the 2nd, not before he needed it, as he looked very tired.

---

[1] The invitation, to speak at the Queen's Hall on 23 March 1938, came from the 'Friends of Spain', of which Lord Phillimore was Chairman. Page Croft, a member of the Executive, explained to Churchill (in his letter of 5 January 1938): 'The Friends of Spain are wholeheartedly opposed to the Socialist–Anarchist–Syndicalist combination of Valentia and are endeavouring to see that the true facts with regard to Nationalist Spain are made known in the country as a counter to Red propaganda. We also feel that in view of the fact that two-thirds of Spain is now under General Franco's Nationalist Government and the inhabitants are living in peace and good order such as they have not known for many years, that the time has come when his Government should receive the same recognition as is granted to the Government of remnants at Valentia, which is now merely a military dictatorship responsible to no one.'

[2] Viktor Ružić, Ban of Croatia from April 1936 to August 1939; the head, or Prefect, of the Sava province of Yugoslavia, with its administrative centre and Ban's Palace at Zagreb. The Sava province was one of the nine administrative divisions of Yugoslavia established by King Alexander. On 29 December 1937 A. H. Richards had written to Churchill: 'You will recollect that when you were considering the proposed visit to Yugoslavia, The Ban of Croatia graciously and spontaneously placed his Palace at your disposal for as long as you might desire to stay. The Ban has come to England—primarily to place his daughter, aged 19, at an English school—and whilst staying in England, will be Mr Spier's guest'. Richards added: 'The Ban is returning to Yugoslavia on the 8th January. If, between now and that date, you will be coming to London, I do hope a meeting can be arranged, as I am sure it will be mutually profitable. I shall be only too pleased to reserve a special private room in the Savoy for luncheon or dinner, as you wish, and it would be particularly pleasing to The Ban if Mrs Churchill is able to accompany you, and to meet his daughter. For your information, The Ban exerts considerable influence throughout Yugoslavia, being one of Prince Paul's principal and most trusted advisers' (*Churchill papers: 2/311*).

I have not been well myself, and have followed him here for a short rest too. Mrs Churchill is away in Switzerland and has been since the 20th December, so the family has been scattered.

With regard to your other letter about M Blum, I know Mr Churchill was going to invite him to the focus and looked forward to doing so. I have not yet heard his account of what he did when he was alone in Paris this week, and will let you know as soon as I do.

Violet Pearman to Professor Lindemann

(Cherwell papers)

8 January 1938

Mr Churchill looks better even for his short change, but the sunshine he expected has, alas, sadly disappointed him. . . .

He is working very, very hard on his book and has not had time to paint. I am so glad he has come away at last, because I think he would have tired himself out at Chartwell. Contrary to our expectations he has not lost a single thing on his journeyings alone, and is very pleased.

Winston S. Churchill to F. W. Deakin

(Churchill papers: 8/595)

9 January 1938

My dear Deakin,

The enclosed will show you what I have been doing. I should be much obliged if you would get in touch with Harraps and authorities and get the footnotes and references corrected in green ink on my copy. Pray also incorporate in the same colour any corrections or improvements which you think desirable. Then when I return it will not take long to finish.

You will see that only $2\frac{1}{2}$ pages (1,000 words) can be allowed for the Treaty of Utrecht, Catalans etc and only 25 pages for Marlborough in the New Regime, and the Old Corporal, of which 6 are already done. Everything has now to wind up. Pray let me have any notes you have written, as I shall have to summarise it myself.

The text will not be reprinted until I have gone through your corrections with you.

Sir Eric Phipps to Sir Maurice Hankey

(*Phipps papers*)

9 January 1938 British Embassy
Paris

My dear Maurice,

. . . I am honestly perturbed at the fuss made over Van's appointment.[1]

Winston Churchill invited himself to stay with us for two nights on his way South, and could hardly talk of anything else. He told us that he thought Van's displacement was a very dangerous thing, that it would be represented as a victory for the pro-Germans in England, that it would arouse the suspicions of the French, etc etc. The result of his appointment has been an exaggerated Press campaign over here to magnify its importance, and to make out that it is on the contrary a big victory for the pro-French party in England. Winston's last words to Frances[2] on saying goodbye were 'I hope it is all right about Van?'

I have no idea myself what the meaning is of Van's new post, but the danger is that, divested of all routine work, he will spread himself unduly and end by causing trouble, unless put on the right lines from the start.

I feel sure that you will realise that if Van were in effect charged with a mission by the PM I would do all in my power to help. You will remember that in August 1936, I insisted upon Van and his wife[3] coming to stay with me at Berlin for over a fortnight, in order to convince the Germans that the head of our FO was not possessed of any personal feelings of animosity towards them!

[1] In the second week of December Neville Chamberlain had decided to remove Sir Robert Vansittart from his position as Permanent Under-Secretary of State at the Foreign Office, and to offer him the position of Chief Diplomatic Adviser to the Government. On 12 December 1937 Chamberlain wrote to one of his sisters: 'Van has accepted my proposal. Indeed I did not give him any alternative. I think the change will make a great difference in the FO, and when Anthony can work out his ideas with a sane, slow man, like Alick Cadogan, he will be much steadier. Van has had the effect of multiplying the extent of Anthony's natural vibrations and I am afraid his instincts were all against my policy.' News of Vansittart's new appointment was made public in a Press communiqué on 1 January 1938.

[2] Lady Phipps (see page 878, note 2).

[3] Sarita Eriqueta, widow of Rt. Hon. Sir Colville Adrian de Rune Barclay, and daughter of Herbert Ward of Paris. After Vansittart's death she lived first at Denham Place, and subsequently in London. Elder sister of Lady Phipps.

Winston S. Churchill to Clementine Churchill

(*Spencer-Churchill papers*)

10 January 1938   Château de l'Horizon

My darling Clemmie,

I have been here nearly a week practically without quitting the house. I do not get up till luncheon time, but work in bed and have a masseur. After lunch we play Mah Jong till 5 o'clock, when I again retire to rest and work. I have not played bezique nor have I been to the Rooms. MJ has been amusing and very inexpensive. I have lost about £2 after all these hours of harmless amusement. I have not unpacked my painting things, nor indeed done anything of any sort or kind, except to dine once at the Windsors and once with Flandin.

The dinner to which the Windsors came was a great success. LG was the only guest outside the house and Maxine never ceases to declare that she has not enjoyed any dinner in her own house since the days at Hartsbourne when she used to entertain the politicians and celebrities.[1] The W's are very pathetic, but also very happy. She made an excellent impression on me, and it looks as if it would be a most happy marriage.

On Wednesday Anthony Eden and LG are coming to dine. Tomorrow I am lunching with Rothermere at Cap Martin, and dining with LG in the evening. I was going to lunch with Van, but he has just telegraphed that his father[2] has died and that he must return at once to London.

The dinner with Flandin was very depressing, the food lamentable. But the account he gave of France was most pessimistic. Making every allowance for what people feel when they are out of office, and what we should feel if an extreme Left-Wing Government were ruling the roost in London, I still came away very seriously concerned about their position, and consequently our own. It looks as if these French Right-Wing politicians thought that Germany would become undisputed ruler of Europe in the near future. All was the fault of the years 1932–35 when Ramsay, Baldwin and Simon would neither make friends with Germany, nor prevent her rearming. A thousand years hence it will be incredible to historians that the victorious Allies delivered themselves over to the vengeance of the foe they had overcome.

There is much talk about the bad state of the Air Force, upon which a great deal of information has been sent me through sources of which you are aware. I do not propose at the present time to say a word upon the subject.

---

[1] Maxine Elliot's pre-war house, Hartsbourne Manor, at Bushey Heath, twelve miles north-west of Marble Arch, to the north of Harrow.

[2] Captain Robert Arnold Vansittart, a retired Army officer.

The Ministers are at last realising all these facts which I explained and predicted in detail two or three years ago.

I send you my latest article in the Evening Standard in which I tried to put the most hopeful view upon things for my large European audience.[1]

I have had to cut nearly 100 pages out of Marlborough which I had in print, and this has been a very long, tiresome business, like cutting off your own fingers and toes; but I think the result will be much more readable. I am longing to get this book finished, but I am still far from satisfied with it as a whole. The more I read it the more I want to put in new matter and leave out the old. It is a massive work of good structural quality, but I fear lacking in originality and distinction. I am determined to have it off my hands by the end of February, come what may.

I shall not stay more than a week at the outside with Daisy,[2] and unless something very attractive opens up, I shall return home. Therefore keep me well informed of all your plans. It is no good painting here after lunch, as you said, because of the dark coming on so soon. On the other hand the mornings pass very agreeably with my papers and books. It is the afternoon and evening lights which are so good and that one only gets in the summer. The weather here is bright and not too cold.

I sent on your letter to the Duke of W, and I am sure he will be very pleased.

[1] This article, 'Britain rearms', was published in the *Evening Standard* on 7 January 1938, and syndicated in eight British regional newspapers, as well as in New Zealand, South Africa and Malta. During the course of it Churchill stressed the 'immense programme' of. British naval construction, and noted: 'At the present time no other Power in Europe, except the British, can attempt to form a line of battle, nor, indeed all the Powers of Europe together. By treaty the United States is entitled to build to full parity with Great Britain. As far as we can see, President Roosevelt has every intention of acting up to the spirit of that agreement. Therefore we may be easy on that score. A feeble, ill-armed United States Navy would at the present time be an additional danger to the world. A strong and efficient United States fleet inspires no one with fear but evil-doers.' The article ended: 'Money for defence is certainly pouring out in all directions in Britain. The Co-ordination Minister assures us that the expenditure will far exceed the estimate of fifteen hundred millions sterling forecasted less than a year ago. Happily, British credit is so good that no difficulty in financing these enormous charges need be expected. The friends of political and democratic freedom in Europe need not therefore look upon the sombre year now opening with undue despondency and alarm.'

[2] Marguerite Severine Philipinne, daughter of the 4th Duc Decazes and de Glücksbjerg. Known as 'Daisy'. In 1910 she married Prince Jean de Broglie (who died in 1918), hence her nickname 'the Imbroglio'. In 1919 she married the Hon Reginald Ailwyn Fellowes (who died in 1953). In 1929 Daisy Fellowes published *Cats in the Isle of Man*. Her villa in the south of France was Les Zoraïdes; she also lived in Paris and Newbury. She died in 1962.

L. S. Amery to Winston S. Churchill

(Churchill papers: 2/348)

11 January 1938

My dear Winston,

Weizmann has asked me, as you will see at the end of his letter, to let you see both his letter to myself and the copy of his letter to Shuckburgh.[1] It was written of course before the recent White Paper announcing the leisurely progress which the Government mean to make with this question of partition, and I should think the White Paper has probably added to Weizmann's anxieties.[2]

I feel more than ever that with the kind of Government that we have got, both here and on the spot, the only solution now is to go ahead with partition and give the Jews a chance of seeing what they can do for themselves on a reduced area, providing it is not so reduced as to be ridiculous and practically to exclude further immigration on any large scale. It is of course a second best policy, and a consistent, vigorous carrying out of the policy of equal rights, as laid down by you in 1922, and no nonsense about it, would have been much better. But that policy has never been wholeheartedly carried out, in recent years, and I don't see the slightest chance of the present Government screwing itself up again to such a pitch.

I see a poor devil of an archaeologist has now been murdered simply because he is British. If Billy Gore[3] had any real courage he would let it be known that every additional murder would mean an enlargement of the Jewish State. As it is it looks unpleasantly like the old Irish business, a gradual acceptance of murder as the natural expression of political opposition, in fact as an argument whose reasonableness we end by acknowledging.

---

[1] John Evelyn Shuckburgh, 1877–1953. Entered the India Office, 1900. Secretary, Political Department, India Office, 1917–21. Appointed by Churchill to be Assistant Under-Secretary of State, Colonial Office, 1921. Knighted, 1922. Remained Assistant Under-Secretary of State until 1931; Deputy Under-Secretary of State, 1931–42. Appointed Governor of Nigeria, 1939, but did not assume office owing to the outbreak of war. Worked in the historical section of the Cabinet Office, 1942–8. His son Evelyn was Principal Private Secretary to Anthony Eden from 1951–1954 (knighted, 1959).

[2] Following the publication of the Peel Commission Report on 7 July 1937, advocating the Partition of Palestine into a Jewish and an Arab State (with Jerusalem, Bethlehem and a corridor to the sea to remain under British control), a new Commission had been set up to recommend the precise border of the proposed new States. Headed by Sir John Woodhead, it published its various plans on 19 October 1938. The Government decided, however, to abandon all idea of Partition, and to try instead to limit Jewish immigration in order to prevent for all time a Jewish majority (see also pages 1289–91 and 1505–6).

[3] William Ormsby-Gore, Secretary of State for Colonial Affairs (see page 338, note 4). The archaeologist, J. L. Starkey, had been murdered near Hebron on 10 January 1938. Twelve days later, two Arabs were hanged for his murder.

Clementine Churchill to Winston S. Churchill
(Churchill papers: 1/322)

14 January 1938

Hotel Lenzerhorn,
Lenzerheide,
Austria

Your letter of January the 10th has just arrived. I am so glad you are combining a much needed rest with so much agreeable & varied company.

Talking of the Air Force, there is here a very competent & stocky looking little man, Air Vice Marshal Gossage[1] in whose charge, I am told, is the whole Air Defence of London. He looks as tho' he would make the best use of everything he has at his disposal.

I have not pumped him about the shortages & deficiencies as he looks as if he would never give away a superior.

I do hope the last Volume of Marlboro' will equal its predecessors. I feel sure it will. All the concentrated energy, research & revision are sure to bear fruit.

Wing-Commander Anderson to Violet Pearman
(Churchill papers: 2/338)

16 January 1938

Station Headquarters
Royal Air Force
Hucknall, Notts

Dear Mrs Pearman,

I attach information which, I think, will be of use; the figures are accurate in all respects.

Something at once should be done to prevent the loss of our best Short Service Officers as the new type which are coming in are definitely unfitted by character and general bearing to fulfil the responsibilities of piloting these expensive aircraft.

Our own production of aircraft, viz 200 per month is poor showing against Germany's 600.

Ever so sincerely,
C. T. Anderson

[1] Leslie Gossage, 1891–1949. 2nd Lieutenant, Royal Field Artillery, 1912. Seconded to the Royal Flying Corps, 1915. Squadron-Commander, 1916; Wing-Commander, 1917. Served on the western front, 1915–18 where he won the Military Cross. Served at the Air Ministry 1919–21, on the Staff of Sir Hugh Trenchard. Group Captain, 1928. Deputy Director of Staff Duties, 1928–30. Air Attaché, Berlin, 1930–1. Air Commodore, 1932. Senior Air Staff Officer, Air Defence of Britain, 1931–4; of Iraq, 1934–5. Air Officer Commanding the British Forces in Aden, 1935–6. Air Vice-Marshal, 1936. Knighted, 1941. Air Officer Commanding No. 11 Group, 1936–40; Balloon Command, 1941–4. One of his two sons was killed on active service in the Second World War.

Wing-Commander Anderson: notes for Winston S. Churchill

(Churchill papers: 2/238)

16 January 1938

Output of Airframes, December, 1937.

GERMANY	600 per month.
ITALY	175 per month.

Italy has slowed down her production of aircraft from 300 to 175 per month for economic reasons. Her output of engines, however, remains at approximately 400 per month. (These figures appear in the Committee of Imperial Defence Papers.)

In December, 1937, the output of the British aircraft industry was 200 aircraft per month—all types. No aircraft have yet been produced by the Shadow Industry.

The Air Ministry and the Staff College are now discussing the advisability of determining strengths of aircraft by tonnage, instead of numbers. For example, 1 4-engined aircraft might be able to drop $1\frac{1}{2}$ tons of bombs; thus, three aircraft of this type would be termed as equal to $4\frac{1}{2}$ tons of destructive capacity per day.

Considerable discussion is now taking place at the Air Ministry regarding the size of the future Bomber, ie whether it should be a 2-engined aircraft, or 4-engined aircraft, the former carrying a medium load and the latter carrying a large load. It will be seen that the larger the aircraft the greater the economy in pilots, crews and maintenance. The balance of opinion is in favour of a compromise allowing for large production of both types. The 4-engined bomber would cost (in mass production) in the neighbourhood of £50,000 and it would be fitted with 4 engines capable of 1,600 hp, ie, the Rolls-Royce 'Vulture' or Bristol 'Hercules' developing a total hp of 6,400 per aircraft using a combined total of petrol at the rate of 240 gallons per hour.

It is apparent that the best possible type of pilot should be in charge of these expensive war machines.

Attached on a separate minute sheet it will be seen that large numbers of Short Service Officers are being refused Permanent Commissions; also Officers who have attended Courses at Cambridge University are being allowed to retire at their own request at the age of 40.

The aircraft production figures quoted above were given by the Director of Aeronautical Production, Colonel Disney,[1] at a lecture to the Royal Air

[1] Henry Anthony Patrick Disney, 1893-1974. Educated at Marlborough and Caius College, Cambridge. On active service, 1914-18 (pilot, Royal Flying Corps; War Office Staff; Deputy Assistant Quarter-Master General, Italy; Wing-Commander, Royal Air

Force Staff College in December, 1937. It will, of course, be a considerable time before the Shadow Industry can reach a figure of 500 aircraft per week; but the design, buildings and plant, etc, would be capable of reaching this figure by 1942.

Colonel Beaumont-Nesbitt to Winston S. Churchill

(*Churchill papers: 2/328*)

17 January 1938   British Embassy
Personal   Paris

Dear Mr Winston Churchill:—

I must first apologise for the very long delay between the time you handed me your book for presentation to General Gamelin, and this letter to let you know that it has been done. My excuse is that I was suddenly called home, at the beginning of last week, owing to the serious illness of my boy.

Unfortunately, I was not able to hand the book to General Gamelin personally, as he was away; so I did the next best thing, and left it with his Staff Officer, Colonel Petibon.[1] I have no doubt that, ere this, you will have received some direct acknowledgement from the General.

As regards the Memorandum on the French Army which you asked me to write for you: I had begun a draft of it before leaving for England, and while there, mentioned the fact that I was doing this in the War Office. It was as well that I did so, as I found that they do not like Military Attachés giving information in this manner on the countries to which they are accredited. I very much regret, therefore, that I am unable to comply with your request. I suggest that if, on your return to London, you were to ask the War Office direct, they could give you what you want—and are even better qualified to do so than I am, since they view the problem from every angle, whereas I only see one side of it.

Force, 1918). In commerce, 1918–35, with the International Telephone and Telegraph Company (to 1932), Standard Telephone and Cables (Director) and Standard Radio Relay Services Limited. Director of Aeronautical Production, Air Ministry, 1936–8. Director of Armament and Equipment Production, Air Ministry, 1938–40; Ministry of Aircraft Production 1940. Rejoined the Royal Air Force active list, 1940; subsequently Group Captain, South East Asia Command.

[1] Jean Louis Marie Petibon, 1892–1973. Born in Le Havre. Entered the French Army in 1912. On active service, 1914-18 (six times mentioned in despatches; Croix de Guerre 1914–18 with 2 palms and 3 stars). Lieutenant-Colonel, 1936. Colonel, 1939. On active service, 1939–40. Temporary commander of the Infantry of the 20th Division, 7 June 1940; taken prisoner-of-war, 29 June 1940. Released, October 1940. Demobilized, November 1942. Général de Brigade, January 1945 (Croix de Guerre 1939–45 with 1 palm and 1 star).

I met Colonel Fuller[1] (American MA) soon after you left Paris: he asked to be remembered to you, and hopes very much to see you on your return.

Yours sincerely,
F. Beaumont-Nesbitt

Winston S. Churchill to L. S. Amery

(*Churchill papers: 2/348*)

18 January 1938

My dear Leo,

Many thanks for what you have sent me from Weizmann. I have not at all altered my views about Palestine, and am quite certain that the only thing to do is to persevere upon the old lines, having a strong British Gendarmerie, with native contingents, and keeping immigration within moderate bounds. The plan of Partition will only make everything much worse. I agree with you in not liking the general situation at all. Let us meet when the House reassembles.

Winston S. Churchill to Clementine Churchill

(*Spencer-Churchill papers*)

18 January 1938   Les Zoraïdes,[2]
Cap Martin

My darling Clemmie,

I was very glad to hear that you had had a good passage, because by all accounts forty-eight hours before there had been a tempest.

I motored on here yesterday with all my belongings and am very comfortably installed. No one but the family is here. Poor Daisy is still recovering

---

[1] Horace Hayes Fuller, 1886–1966. Born in South Dakota, the son of an army officer. Graduated from West Point, 1909. A cavalry officer, 1909–16. Transferred to the artillery, 1916. Served on the western front, 1918, temporary Lieutenant-Colonel, 1918. Served in the Motor Transports Corps, 1919, and the Graves Registration Service, 1920. Graduate of the Army War College, Washington, 1928. American Military Attaché in Paris, 1936–40. On active service, commanding the 41st Infantry Division, South West Pacific, 1942–4. Distinguished Service Medal, 1944: 'in all attacks', the citation read, 'he inflicted decisive defeat on an experienced enemy. His personal courage and inspiring leadership made possible the able execution of assigned missions, and contributed materially to our success in dislodging the enemy and forcing him to relinquish his conquests.' On the staff of Lord Louis Mountbatten in India, 1945. Retired, 1946.

[2] The villa of Daisy Fellowes (see page 885, note 2).

from the frightful blow on her face which she received in these disgraceful trains. The wounds have healed without leaving any scar, but her face still seems to me to be swollen in parts. I have no doubt that in two or three months it will all contract again. Reggie[1] has quite recovered from his recent attack and is able to play golf regularly.

To show how small the world is—his step-daughter, Jacqueline, had been for six months engaged to marry a young American, Johnson. This young man was killed in Spain by the same shell that killed Dick Sheepshanks,[2] Sarah's friend. She is very stoical about it, but letters from him arrived for ten days after he was no more.

Everyone here is of course excited about the French Government crisis. I am very glad that the Communists are not to be included in the Government, although with my knowledge of politics and of France, I should not have been alarmed by this, the impression produced in Europe would have been very weakening.[3]

My twelve days with Maxine were most peaceful and agreeable. Although I have spent all my mornings in bed correcting and recasting the proofs, this is not at all fatiguing. The book is gaining a great deal by the severe compression, and if it is sometimes hard to leave out the tit-bits, no one but me will ever know about them, and I shall not tell.

Maxine was genuinely upset at my departure, and made me promise to come back again, and if possible bring you. She declared that she had not had such pleasant dinners since her great days at Hartsbourne, when she gathered political stars into her orbit. The Windsor–LG dinner was a great success, and the poor duke gay and charming, although he had to fight for his place in the conversation like other people. The other dinner to which the

---

[1] Reginald Ailwyn Fellowes, 1884–1953. Son of Churchill's aunt Rosamond (2nd daughter of the 7th Duke of Marlborough) and the 2nd Baron de Ramsey. Captain, 4th Volunteer Battalion, Bedfordshire Regiment. A Justice of the Peace for Huntingdonshire. He married Daisy de Broglie in 1919.

[2] Ernest Richard Sheepshanks, 1909–1937. Educated at Eton and Trinity College, Cambridge. Joined Reuter's head office, 1933, becoming assistant editor of the mail and features department. One of Reuter's war correspondents in Abyssinia, October 1935; invalided home suffering from dysentry, December 1935. Reuter's special correspondent with General Franco, June 1937. Killed by flying shrapnel with three other war correspondents while driving in an open jeep, on the Aragon front, at the battle of Teruel, December 1937.

[3] Léon Blum's Popular Front Government had lasted from June 1936 until June 1937, when he was succeeded as Prime Minister by Camille Chautemps. Following a political crisis in the second week of January, Chautemps had temporarily survived. On 23 January 1938 Neville Chamberlain wrote to his sister: 'Chautemps is back in the saddle and though regarded in Paris as merely a stopgap, his Govt may prove an example of the proverb that threatened men live long' (*Neville Chamberlain papers*). Léon Blum was Prime Minister of France for a second time from 13 March to 10 April 1938, when he was succeeded as Prime Minister by Edouard Daladier.

Edens and LGs, including Megan,[1] came, was equally pleasant. We had no one staying in the house except two local residents (Dutch), friends of Maxines, whose house is being rebuilt. I took them all out to dinner at the Casino one night where there is the most lovely parrot I ever saw. He is a millionaire and keeps a sailor to look after him. The sailor is evidently well paid and is extremely fat on his rations. The parrot first of all made speeches to the company using all kinds of French endearments such as 'Bon soir, coco' 'Au revoir, coco' 'Merde' etc. In addition he had a very cunning trick of whispering into the sailor's ear and then roaring with laughter. He imitated a cat with beautiful miaows, and also the drums of a military band marching off. Finally he sang like a prima donna, accompanied by the band, and really you would have thought it was a human voice. He was marvellous and not at all strident, and when he did the high notes, he brought the house down.

Now the thing to be decided is, whether you will come and join me at Maxine's. In this case I will return there to meet you on Sunday 23, and we could stay till the beginning of February. Will you telephone me on receipt of this, as I must let Maxine know my plans. It would be lovely if you would come. There is golf both at Moujins, and the old course, which everybody says is very good. And even if I did not play myself, there would be no difficulty in finding you excellent partners. At Moujins, which is high up, the lunch is excellent and I could certainly keep you company in this. They, though I have not seen it, say it is lovely to paint up there. So you could play golf, while I painted. However I do not exclude the possibility of playing myself. So if you come do not forget to bring my clubs with you—if they are still in existence. I have no doubt I could arrange some tennis for you too. Maxine says the weather will get much warmer, but it is quite warm and bright now in the day time, though a little misty. I doubt whether Maxine has any other visitors till February. If you will not come I think I shall come home, as there is a meeting of my Committee[2] on the 24th. In that case I should come home on Sunday 23. But I strongly advise you to come out here. The days pass very pleasantly, and I believe you would find it restful. If you come I advise the ferry from Victoria at 10 pm. Go to bed and take a cachet and you will wake up in Paris at 9 am. There is a day train very highly spoken of which would get you to Cannes the same evening. I am not sure whether

[1] Megan Lloyd George, 1902–1966. Younger daughter of David Lloyd George. Liberal MP for Anglesey, 1929–51 and for Carmarthenshire, 1957–66. President of the Women's Liberal Federation, 1936 and 1945. Chairman of the Welsh Parliamentary Party, 1944–5. Deputy Leader of the Liberal Party, 1949–51. Joined the Labour Party, 1957. Companion of Honour, 1966.

[2] The Air Defence Research Committee. Churchill did not return in time for it (see pages 904–5).

you can catch that connection. If not there are always things to see in Paris for the day, and then you could come on by the night train. If you are here by the 24th I will give a luncheon at the Carlton in honour of the LGs golden wedding anniversary.

Thinking it over, I see that you could not get this letter till rather late to make your plans, so I am telegraphing you and will tell you the trains.

I enclose you a little poem which I have never seen before which I found in a book which Randolph gave me on grammar etc. It was included as an example of the metre and rhyming of the old French ballade and seems to me a very beautiful specimen of English poetry. I have never read anything of Austin Dobson's[1] before. If you have time bring out a book of his poems.

Bernie has telegraphed that his wife is dead.[2]

My darling I am just hoping to talk to you on the telephone, so I will end this with my fondest love. Always your loving husband.

W

[Sketch of pig]

Winston S. Churchill to Randolph Churchill
(Randolph Churchill papers)

19 January 1938   Les Zoraïdes,
                                                   Cap Martin

My dear Randolph,

I have been much pleased with the book you gave me, and find it most interesting, though I do not see why one should treat a word like 'valiant' as unsuitable. There is a very jolly little poem on page 600. I wish you would find out whether the author of the book is alive or dead. I can think of no one else whose comments on my present proofs would be more valuable.

It has been very peaceful out here, but I have not painted at all. I have spent all the mornings in bed correcting proofs, and doing nothing of a strenuous character.

Many thanks for sending me the cutting about the Air Force. As it happened I was anxious to get hold of that copy of the News Chronicle and missed it.

I am going back to Maxine's to stay for another week, and your mother is

---

[1] Henry Austin Dobson, 1840–1921. Educated at Coventry and Strasbourg (then a French city). Served in the Board of Trade from the age of 16; Principal Clerk, Marine Department, Board of Trade, 1884–1901. He published his first verses in 1864, and his first volume of poetry in 1873. His first prose volume was published in 1874. Father of ten children.

[2] Bernard Baruch had married Anne Griffen in 1893. They had one son and two daughters. After her death in 1938 he did not remarry.

joining me out there. I expect to be back at the end of the month. I am giving
LG a luncheon on his golden wedding day.

I hope all is well with you,

your loving Father,
Winston S. Churchill

Winston S. Churchill to Léon Blum
(*Churchill papers: 2/328*)

20 January 1938

I was touched by your kindness in writing to me so appreciative a letter at
a time when you had such grave preoccupations. I have followed the political
changes in France with great attention. Although from one point of view I
am sorry that you are no longer a Minister, yet I feel that your power to help
forward the causes in which we are jointly interested, will in no way be
diminished—and may indeed be increased—by your being for a while in a
private station. I also flatter myself that the hope that some opportunities of
your paying a visit to London may occur in the future.

I earnestly trust that Madame Blum's health is improving.[1]

F. W. Deakin to Winston S. Churchill
(*Churchill papers: 8/458*)

21 January 1938   Wadham College
                                                   Oxford

My dear Mr Churchill,

I have been giving some attention to the points raised in your letter of
January 12. . . . I found & copied the enclosed notes of Sarah's investments
in South Sea stocks. . . . I shall be going to Blenheim again at the beginning
of next week. . . .

The work on the proofs is advancing, and should be completed by your
return. Hoping that you are enjoying your holiday.

Yours very sincerely,
F. W. Deakin

---

[1] Blum's wife died three months later (see page 960).

Winston S. Churchill to F. W. Deakin

(*Churchill papers: 8/595*)

22 January 1938

I have sent you various 'pieces' from out here which I hope you have duly received. I have not so far done any new work, but I have been very busy remodelling chapters and cutting down the text. I think we shall have about fifty pages in hand for the final chapters. The book has gained by the compression from the point of view of the reader. We must have a clean slip proof as soon as possible after I get back. Could you therefore manage to come to Chartwell on the night of Friday 4th, and stay till Monday; but if that is impossible, come anyway on Saturday.[1]

Winston S. Churchill to Brendan Bracken

(*Churchill papers: 8/594*)

22 January 1938 Les Zoraïdes
Cap Martin

I will certainly look up Strakosch when I go back to Cannes next week. I am very glad he has so far recovered.

I sent you on the message about Mrs Baruch as he asked me by cable.

I am returning in the early days of February, having had a very peaceful time both at Maxine's and here. Clemmie is coming out to join me tomorrow, and we shall be a week more at Cannes.

I remember that a couple of years ago you were very clever in suggesting some subjects for American articles. I have my usual six to prepare for Colliers who are very difficult to suit in the way of topics, as it must be of American interest, or something very out of the way. I have more difficulty in thinking of the subjects than in writing upon them once they are chosen. It would be very kind of you if you would give me any ideas that may occur to you after you have turned your fertile mind upon the matter.

I am glad to see you are writing against any Italian loan at the present time. To give them money or trade facilities to fortify the Mediterranean against us, and prepare to invade Egypt through Libya, would indeed be the acme of folly.

---

[1] Other than Deakin, the only overnight guests at Chartwell during 1938 were Diana and Duncan Sandys (in July, October and November); Jack Churchill and his daughter Clarissa (August); Professor Lindemann (March, May, July, September—twice, October—twice, and December—twice); Lloyd George (June); William Nicholson (July); Bernard Baruch (July); Edward Marsh (August); Sir Archibald Sinclair (September and October—twice) and Horatia Seymour (December).

Winston S. Churchill to Sir Russell Scott [1]

(*Churchill papers: 1/407*)

22 January 1938

In the autumn of 1931 when I proposed to make a lecture tour in the United States Sir Ernley Blackwell[2] sent me warning that my life might be in danger in California. There is, it appeared, a Sikh colony there which has a secret society and it had been responsible for several political murders. I was thought to be obnoxious on account of my opposition to the Indian Constitution, and information had been obtained by the Home Office that a plan had been made to assassinate me. In these circumstances the Home Office sent with me at my expense a Scotland Yard detective,[3] and the Federal Police of the United States took various special precautions. As my tour was curtailed by the motor car accident which I sustained, I did not in fact visit the Pacific Coast, though precautions were taken in many other cities.

I desire now to know whether the conditions of 1931/2 have entirely disappeared. I should myself suppose they had, because the Indian question is in a different atmosphere, and I myself am not prominent in it at the present time. But what has happened to the secret society, and have you any other information or advice upon the subject?

I am now contemplating another tour this autumn in the course of which I shall certainly visit the Pacific Coast, and I should be much obliged for your advice.

---

[1] Robert Russell Scott, 1877–1960. Educated at Manchester Grammar School and Wadham College, Oxford. Clerk, Class I, Admiralty, 1901; Private Secretary to the Civil Lord, 1904–7. Joint Secretary to the Royal Commission on Indian Public Services, 1912–15, Member of the Central Control Board (Liquor Traffic), 1915. Acting Assistant Secretary, Admiralty, 1917. Controller of Establishments, Treasury, 1921–32. Knighted, 1922. Permanent Under-Secretary of State at the Home Office, 1932–8.

[2] Ernley Robertson Hays Blackwell, 1868–1941. Called to the Bar, Inner Temple, 1892. Legal Assistant and Under-Secretary of State, Home Office, 1913–38. Knighted, 1916. Chairman of the Statutory Committee of the Pharmaceutical Society, 1934–9.

[3] Walter H. Thompson (see page 509, note 2). His first volume of memoirs—the first of three about his guarding Churchill—*Guard From the Yard*, by Ex-Detective-Inspector W. H. Thompson, was published at the end of 1938. In his Foreword, Churchill wrote: 'It is astonishing to me, looking back on those times, how many different kinds of people—Suffragettes, Sinn Feiners, Communists, Egyptians, Indians and the usual percentage of ordinary lunatics—have from time to time shown a very great want of appreciation of my public work. It is sad to reflect that though most of them have carried their causes to success, they do not seem any happier nor the world any better for all the trouble they took!' Churchill also noted: 'To be guarded and shadowed day and night for years on end is not a pleasant experience. It is only rendered tolerable by grim necessity, and still more by the extraordinary tact, courtesy and skill of those entrusted with the duty of watching over public persons, who, at particular times, are thought to be worthy of powder and shot.'

Daisy Fellowes to Winston S. Churchill

(*Churchill papers: 1/300*)

[22 January] 1938   Les Zoraïdes,
                                                    Cap Martin

Dear Winston,

Here is a book that may make you smile. It amused me very much to write it, during a cure of mud-baths, at Dax. I don't think I'll come in to the sporting before dinner but hope to see you there after dinner.

Love,
Daisy

PS. Rather stuck with an anagram HE MAY GRIP NO CAT (14),[1] if you find it you might telephone.

Josiah Wedgwood to Winston S. Churchill

(*Churchill papers: 2/348*)

23 January 1938   House of Commons

My dear Winston,

I have to write to you for other reasons, but first come your 'Great Contemporaries'. I don't think I know anything in English prose to compare with the account of Clemenceau.[2] It makes me regret that there will be no one left to paint you comparably. But all is so good. You make me like them once more—Morley, Asquith, all figures now from the remote past. Grand merci! It makes one sentimental; I can only remember that I have known you in fair and foul weather for 34 years and that is better than knowing all the rest. I wish they would call you in as they did the Tiger. Our situation is nearly as desperate as in 1917, but we shall not realize it in time.

The Jews, not too late I think, have resolved and decided at last that they would gladly see Palestine in the British Empire, ultimately as a Dominion. They used to think that such a declaration would cut their American sub-

---

[1] 'Cinematography'. Also, in phrases of three words: 'Charming Toy Ape', 'A Grimy Cenotaph', 'No Magic Therapy' and 'Oi, Try Champagne' (I am grateful to Humphry Smith for these solutions, *letter of 24 October 1981*).

[2] Georges Clemenceau, 1841–1929. Mayor of Montmartre, 1870. Member of the Chamber of Deputies, 1876–93 and 1902–29. Radical journalist; editor of *Justice*. Minister of the Interior, 1906. Prime Minister, 1906–8. Prime Minister and Minister of War, November 1917–January 1920. Known during the war as 'the Tiger'. In *Great Contemporaries* (1937) Churchill wrote of him: 'Happy the nation which when its fate quivers in the balance can find such a tyrant and such a champion.'

scriptions, now they know otherwise, perceive that the hostility of our officials will ruin them and close Palestine to Jewish refugees, and hope by declaring for Britain as against Italy that we shall neither go nor leave them in the lurch. Weizmann always feels it a bit of a wrench to come round to my point of view, but he has done so.

Now they want within the next month a meeting in Central Hall, Westminster, no Jews on the platform, you and LG speaking. I shall be in the chair, but I need not conceal from you that the adequate reason is that I might get you to speak. Can I? 8.30 any day after next week. We shall get— Archie,[1] Morrison,[2] Citrine if possible. Before I write to them you must fix the day. If, as I hope, you will accept, name two or three days. If you feel like saying No! don't say it till I have a chance to explain to you why we must have you. We shall have a press crush first, so that the send-off for the new Dominion shall be made a great occasion. You probably know the line I want from yourself; but if not I will do as I have done before![3]

Yours ever,
Josiah C. Wedgwood

Diana Churchill to Winston S. Churchill

(*Churchill papers: 1/328*)

28 January 1938   19 Vincent Square
                                                   Westminster

Darling Papa,

I am so sorry to read in the newspapers of your sea-sickness.[4] We have a fellow-feeling for you.

We have just returned from Belfast and had the worst crossing of the year. However, when we got there, we had a wonderful time. Duncan made two speeches and everyone was very enthusiastic. No apathy there.

---

[1] Sir Archibald Sinclair (see page 160, note 6).

[2] Herbert Morrison, 1888–1965. Errand boy, shop assistant and telephone operator before he joined the *Daily Citizen*; Labour MP, 1923–4, 1929–31, 1935–59; Minister of Transport in Ramsay MacDonald's second Labour Government, 1929–31; Home Secretary and Minister of Home Security in Churchill's wartime Coalition, 1940–5; Deputy Prime Minister, in Clement Attlee's Labour Government 1945–51, and Foreign Secretary, 1950–1; created Baron, as Lord Morrison of Lambeth, 1959. He was active in London as well as national politics, being a Member of the L.C.C. from 1922 to 1945 and Leader of the Council, 1934–40. He published *How Greater London is Governed* in 1925 and *Herbert Morrison: An Autobiography* in 1960.

[3] Churchill replied, on 4 February 1938: 'Many thanks for your letter. Alas I find myself far too heavily engaged to undertake the task to which you so kindly invite me. Thank you for all the kind things you say.'

[4] Churchill had crossed the Channel to France on 2 January 1938. His return journey a month later was less disturbed (see page 905).

We stayed with Lord Craigavon, who was so charming to us. He sent many messages to you & Mummie. I am afraid he is not very well—tho' one is not supposed to say so. He looks alright and has plenty of fight—but he is on a very strict diet & has to have injections before each meal. I think he is one of the most charming people I have ever met.

Randolph is in Holland—I don't know whether he is waiting for the BABY or the Kaiser![1]

I do hope you are having a lovely holiday.

We are all well & longing to see you & Mummie soon.

With love to you both,

Your,
Diana

Winston S. Churchill to Louis Levy

(Churchill papers: 1/407)

28 January 1938   Château de l'Horizon,
Private and Confidential   Golfe Juan

I have decided to make another lecture tour next October in the United States. A provisional agreement has been drafted over here, but I wish the contract to be made in New York. I should be very much obliged to you if you would sign the contract on my behalf, and I am sending you by the next mail the necessary Power of Attorney. I have been into the details carefully with Mr Harold Peat and have formed a good opinion of him. He conducted Mr H. G. Wells's short lecture tour last year, and Mr Wells, who is an old friend of mine, spoke very strongly in his favour. The draft agreement follows lines which are familiar to me, and unless you see some extraordinary reason to the contrary I think it is all right. I am telling Mr Peat to put himself in touch with you.

I have spent the best part of this month here and now my wife has joined me. Maxine is looking very handsome, and though her health is frail, she is very active.

I have had a good rest, which I needed, doing very little and hardly even painting. The sunshine has been pleasant nearly every day, and as you know this house is beautifully warm for all weathers.

[1] Kaiser Wilhelm II had been in exile in Holland since 1918, and was ill (he lived until 1942). Princess Juliana of the Netherlands, daughter of Queen Wilhelmina, was expecting her first baby, whom many hoped would be a boy. On 31 January 1938 a daughter was born (Beatrix Wilhelmina Arongard). Princess Juliana had three more daughters, Irene (born on 5 August 1939), Margriet (born in Canada, 19 January 1943) and Maria (born in Holland on 18 February 1947). Juliana succeeded as Queen in 1948. In 1980 she abdicated in favour of Beatrix, who became Queen.

Lord Munster¹ to Winston S. Churchill

(*Churchill papers: 2/336*)

31 January 1938   Sandhills
                                                   Bletchingley

I have a cousin of mine—Frank Don²—by name, who will be staying here
for the week-end of Feb 19th and I should so like to bring him to see you on
Sunday 20th.

He has just returned from 3½ years as British Air Attaché in Berlin and although he is still in the RAF I know he would much like to see you. He has,
of course, to be careful what he repeats but I know if you would care to meet
him he would like to come and see you.³ I hope you and Mrs Churchill enjoyed your trip to Cannes.

                                                   Yours ever,
                                                   Munster

Wing-Commander Anderson to Violet Pearman

(*Churchill papers: 2/338*)

                                   No 1 Armament Training Camp,
                                        Royal Air Force,
31 January 1938   Catfoss,
                                        nr Hull, E Yorks

My dear Mrs Pearman,

I have now taken over the Command of No 1 Armament Training Camp,
and my address and telephone number are as above.

¹ Geoffrey William Richard Hugh FitzClarence, 1906–1975. Succeeded his uncle as 5th
Earl of Munster, 1928. Member of the LCC for North Paddington, 1931–7. A Lord-in
Waiting to the King, 1932–9. Paymaster-General, June 1938—January 1939. Parliamentary
Under-Secretary of State for War, February-September 1939. ADC and Military Secretary
to Lord Gort, 1939–41. Parliamentary Under-Secretary of State for India and Burma, 1943–
4; at the Home Office, 1944–5; at the Colonial Office, 1951–4. Minister without Portfolio
1954–7. Privy Councillor 1954. Among his cousins, Charles FitzClarence (related by marriage to Churchill), was killed in action in France in November 1914; Edward FitzClarence
was killed in action in the Sudan in 1897.

² Francis Percival Don, 1886–1964. Educated at Rugby and Trinity College, Cambridge.
Qualified as an engineer; in business 1906–14. On active service at Gallipoli, 1915. Royal
Flying Corps, 1916. Served in Egypt, 1916 and France, 1916–17 (wounded, prisoner of war).
After the war he commanded the Cambridge University Air Squadron. Air Attaché Berlin,
1934–7. Head of Mission to the French Air Forces in the Field, 1939. Air Officer in charge of
Administration, British Forces in France, 1940. Senior Air Staff Officer, Ferry Command,
Canada, 1941–2. Retired as Air Vice-Marshal, 1942. Regional Air Liaison Officer, Northern
Region Civil Defence, 1943–5.

³ Lord Munster brought Group Captain Don to Chartwell on the afternoon of 20 February 1938.

I do hope you have had a good holiday and benefited by the rest.
I will write to you at length in a few days. . . .

Yours ever so sincerely,
C. Torr Anderson

Wing-Commander Anderson: note for Winston S. Churchill

(Churchill papers: 2/338)

31 January 1938

ANALYSIS OF CRASHES IN FIGHTER COMMAND

For the quarter ending September, 1937, there were 47 Fighter Aircraft crashed beyond repair. 69% of these crashes were due to culpable negligence.

For the quarter ending June, 1937, the number was 43 aircraft crashed beyond repair, 63% being due to culpable negligence.[1]

Sir Alexander Maxwell [2] to Winston S. Churchill

(Churchill papers: 1/407)

31 January 1938   Home Office

Dear Mr Churchill,

Before Sir Russell Scott retired last week he handed me your letter of the 22nd about your proposed lecture tour in the United States.

The India Office tell me that the secret society to which you refer, known as the Ghadr Party, still exists and carries on a certain amount of virulently anti-British propaganda; but there is no reason to suppose that it would attempt to interfere with you in any way, unless any of your remarks on Indian affairs were so reported or misreported in the American Press as to excite signal hostility. Even in that event it is thought doubtful whether the Ghadr Party would resort to personal violence.

---

[1] Wing-Commander Anderson enclosed the official notice of the setting up of a Court of Inquiry, held on 26 January 1938, at No 8 Armament Training Camp, RAF Evanton, Ross-Shire, Scotland, 'to enquire into circumstances involving damage to aircraft of Nos 7 and 99 (Bomber) Squadrons, on the night of 22/23 January 1938, and to apportion blame if any'. On the bottom of the notice Anderson had written, in his own handwriting, '12 Aircraft destroyed, 22/1/38' *(Churchill papers: 2/338)*.

[2] Alexander Maxwell, 1880–1963. Entered the Home Office in 1904 (and served under Churchill, 1910–11); Chairman of the Prison Commissioners, 1928–32. Deputy Under-Secretary of State, Home Office, 1932–8; Permanent Under-Secretary of State, 1938–48. Knighted, 1936.

If the Indian question should take on a different atmosphere before the autumn, we should like to think about the matter again, but at present the information given us by the India Office does not suggest that the precautions taken in 1931 are necessary.

Yours sincerely,

A. Maxwell

Sir Horace Wilson[1] *to P. J. Grigg*

(*Grigg papers*)

31 January 1938   10 Downing Street

If—as I hope is to be the case—we get ahead with our talks with Germany & Italy and are seen to be making progress, the effect here would be a considerable revival of confidence. There had been & still is a great deal of personal depression, the result of the war talk, and it would make a good deal of difference if the idea got about that the outlook was less dangerous. . . .

Before you get this, Roosevelt may have obscured the horizon by another cloud of words, but it should clear off after a bit.[2]

We begin tomorrow a long stretch of Parliamentary hard labour, with very few apples in our basket, but there is no sign of a major crisis. WSC has been very quiet for months, which is rather a long time for him.

[1] Horace John Wilson, 1882–1972. Entered the Civil Service, 1900; Permanent Secretary, Ministry of Labour, 1921–30. Knighted, 1924. Chief Industrial Adviser to the Government, 1930–9. Seconded to the Treasury for special service with Stanley Baldwin, 1935–7, and with Neville Chamberlain, 1937–40 (when he had a room at 10 Downing Street). Permanent Secretary to the Treasury and Head of the Civil Service, 1939–42.

[2] In his message to Congress on 4 January 1938 Roosevelt had spoken vigorously in defence of Democracy and had offered to join negotiations with the Dictators to ensure that aggression did not take place. Eden wished to follow up this initiative, but Chamberlain, as Eden recalled, 'said it was vague and would fail'. On 20 January 1938 Eden's Private Secretary, J. P. L. Thomas saw Sir Horace Wilson, as Eden wrote in *Facing the Dictators* (page 562). But Wilson 'dismissed the Roosevelt initiative as "woolly rubbish" and made it perfectly plain that he was using all his powers to persuade the Prime Minister to pour cold water on the American effort, while going ahead with his own plans to appease the dictators'.

February 1938

Sir Maurice Hankey to Air Chief Marshal Sir Cyril Newall[1]

(*Cabinet papers: 21/517*)

1 February 1938

This is the critical year.

It now looks as if we were going to get into conversations both with Italy and Germany. Provided we are strong, we shall have some chance of doing a deal.

If we show the smallest signs of letting up: in other words if we give the Parliamentary critics any case which they can develop to the detriment of the Government and which can be interpreted abroad as weakening, we shall do no good at all with our conversations.

The Marquess of Cholmondeley to Winston S. Churchill

(*Churchill papers: 8/595*)

6 February 1938

Le Roc
Golfe Juan

My dear Winston,

As you saw, on my writing table was your pamphlet, The Truth about Hitler.[2] This was meant to remind me to give you the photos of Sir

---

[1] Cyril Louis Norton Newall, 1886–1963. 2nd Lieutenant, Royal Warwickshire Regiment, 1905; Indian Army, 1909; Royal Flying Corps, 1914. On active service in India, 1908, and on the western front, 1914–18 (despatches thrice; Major). Royal Air Force, 1919. Deputy Director of Personnel, Air Ministry, 1919–22. Director of Operations and Intelligence, and Deputy Chief of the Air Staff, 1926–31. Air Officer Commanding the RAF, Middle East 1931–4. Knighted, 1935. Member of the Air Council for Supply and Organization, 1935–7. Air Chief Marshal, 1937. Chief of the Air Staff, 1937–40. Marshal of the Royal Air Force, 1940. Order of Merit, 1940. Governor-General and Commander-in-Chief, New Zealand, 1941–6. Created Baron, 1946.

[2] Churchill's article on Hitler, first published in the *Strand* magazine in November 1935, reprinted in October 1937 as one of the essays in *Great Contemporaries*, and issued by the Anti-Nazi Society as its Leaflet No 1, entitled, 'The Truth About Hitler'. The essay ended: '. . . the world lives on hopes that the worst is over, and that we may yet live to see Hitler

Robert,[1] it miscarried. So I am sending them to you, so choose which you want & get your sec to return them to our London house. I like the one marked X.

I think you were so right to choose the bust in preference to one of his portraits. None do him justice but in the bust it brings out his strength of character. If only my gym had been in existence & the method of PT that I have persuaded Clemmie to adopt, those double chins would not be there & he would be a handsome Roman type.

You don't know how Sybil & I enjoyed our lunch with you. It is the finest free education a few hours in your company & I appreciate it very much.

I will send you the negative of George I. Had another interesting character to lunch—Sasha Guitry,[2] wish you had been there, he was most delightful. . . .

Sir Maurice Hankey to Winston S. Churchill
(Churchill papers: 25/14)

7 February 1938   Committee of Imperial Defence
Secret

My dear Winston,

I send you the Papers of the Air Defence Research Committee which were issued during your absence.

The meeting, which was held on the 24th January, was called as a matter

---

a gentler figure in a happier age. Meanwhile, he makes speeches to the nations, which are sometimes characterized by candour and moderation. Recently he has offered many words of reassurance, eagerly lapped up by those who have been so tragically wrong about Germany in the past. Only time can show, but, meanwhile, the great wheels revolve; the rifles, the cannon, the tanks, the shot and shell, the air-bombs, the poison-gas cylinders, the aeroplanes, the submarines, and now the beginnings of a fleet flow in ever-broadening streams from the already largely war-mobilized arsenals and factories of Germany.'

[1] Sir Robert Walpole. George, 3rd Earl of Cholmondeley (1703–1770) had married, in 1723, Mary Walpole only daughter of Sir Robert Walpole, Prime Minister from 1721–42, (who was created Earl of Orford on his resignation). Their grandson—Walpole's great grandson—was created Marquess of Cholmondeley in 1815, and it was his great-great grandson, the Earl of Rocksavage (later 6th Marquess of Cholmondeley), who gave Churchill access to the Walpole papers at Houghton Hall.

[2] Sasha Guitry, 1885–1957. Born in St Petersburg, the son of the Russian actor-manager, Lucien Guitry. Educated in France. First appeared on the stage with his father's company in Russia, then, in 1902, with his father's company in Paris. Author of nearly a hundred plays, mostly light comedies, the first of which, *Le Page*, was written in 1902, when he was sixteen. In 1920 he came to London with the play *Nono* (in which the leading lady was Yvonne Printemps, the second of his five wives). Scriptwriter and director of several films, including *The Cheat, Pasteur, Talleyrand* and *Napoleon*.

of urgency at the request of Hugh Elles, who was anxious that his two Memoranda should be considered without delay. These two Memoranda—considered under Item Nos 1 and 2 respectively—were, in fact, the most important matters with which we dealt.

The first (Paper No ABE 41) was concerned with setting up an establishment at Teddington for the special purpose of investigating the design and production of fire control instruments, and, as you will see from the Conclusions, we recommended that this should be done as soon as possible.

Elles's second Paper (Paper No ABE 42) was a plea for the development of a low balloon barrage as a protection against low-flying attacks, on the score that existing methods of gun defence against this form of attack seem unlikely to give the necessary protection at heights below 2,000 feet. As you will see from the Conclusions of the meeting we were all in favour of getting on with this without delay. You will note, however, that emphasis was laid on the fact that the low balloon barrage should supplement and not replace the gun.

I hope you have had a good holiday in the south of France, and that the change has done you good.

Yours ever,
M. P. A. Hankey

Winston S. Churchill to Maxine Elliot

(*Churchill papers: 1/323*)

8 February 1938

We had a very smooth crossing and were back home less than twenty-four hours after leaving you. The weather for a wonder is quite mild and decent, still I do wish I could have stayed longer with you.

I found a great deal of work awaiting me here, but am addressing myself to it with a vigour renewed by the first really good rest I have had for a long time. I do not know when I have had such a peaceful pleasant month, and I am so glad to think that looking after me did not tire you out.

I do not find things any better. On the contrary the latest convulsion in Germany has undoubtedly increased the danger of war.[1] One has always

---

[1] On 4 February 1938 Field-Marshal von Blomberg, Commander-in-Chief of the German Army since 1935, resigned, together with a number of other high ranking officers, including General von Fritsch. Hitler thereupon declared himself to be Commander-in-Chief, and appointed General Keitel as Chief of Staff. That same day, the Foreign Minister, von Neurath, was replaced by Joachim von Ribbentrop. Eight days later the Austrian Chancellor, Kurt von Schuschnigg, was forced to meet Hitler at Berchtesgaden, to agree to an amnesty for all Nazis arrested in Austria, and to appoint Hitler's nominee, Artur von Seyss-Inquart, as Minister of the Interior in the Austrian Government.

hitherto had the feeling that the generals oddly enough, had the power to restrain the Nazi party violence. Now the whole place is in the hands of the violent party men, and I fear very much lest something should happen in Central Europe.

How are you getting on with your Italian Duchess? I think perhaps it was just as well that I did not get into arguments with her. I feel I can confidently leave our cause in your hands and Clare's.[1]

Rothermere it appears has gone to South America after staying only two days at La Dragonnière.

Randolph flew over to Berlin to 'cover' the crisis there and has been sending some excellent despatches back.[2]

I am toiling away at Marlborough IV and am determined to get it finished by the end of this month. I am therefore not paying much attention to the House of Commons, at which I expect the Ministers will not be at all vexed!

[1] Clarissa Madeline Georgiana Felicite Tennant, 1896–1960. Known as Clare. Daughter of the 1st Baron Glenconner. Margot Asquith's niece. In 1915 she married Captain W. A. V. Bethell, 2nd Life Guards (marriage dissolved, 1918). In 1918 she married Major Hon. Lionel Tennyson, later 3rd Baron Tennyson (marriage dissolved, 1928). In 1928 she married James M. Beck, the American financier. Her brother Edward Wyndham Tennant, Lieutenant, Grenadier Guards, was killed in action on the Somme on 22 September 1916, aged 19, six days after her cousin Mark Tennant, Lieutenant Scots Guards and Machine Gun Corps, had likewise been killed in action on the Somme, aged 24.

[2] On 2 February 1938 the 'special correspondent' of the *Evening Standard* reported on Field-Marshal von Blomberg's resignation, quoting 'a military source in Berlin'. The resignation arose, he said, despite opposition from Hitler and Goering, because 'a strong movement of discontent arose in the Reichswehr at the news that the Minister had chosen a wife from a class from which officers are forbidden to obtain their brides'. In a second front page report on February 3, the special correspondent noted: 'The Jewish question is also an issue. Herr Himmler, chief of the dreaded Gestapo, proposed a new and intense anti-semitic campaign directed not against Jewish small shopkeepers, but against important Jewish industrialists. General Goering opposed this. He said the "big Jews" were essential to the Four-Year-Plan for which he is responsible. There was an angry scene between Goering and Himmler in which Dr Goebbels, the Propaganda Minister, took Himmler's side. . . .' On 5 February the *Evening Standard* announced that Randolph Churchill would be writing a regular Saturday column for the paper, and published the first of the columns that same day. The first item was about von Blomberg's romance. 'Women have succeeded,' Randolph wrote, 'in building up conventional bans which may exclude husband as well as wife from the society in which they have been accustomed to move in those cases where snobbishness, a zealous moral code, or their own self-interest suggest to them the wisdom of excluding the wife.' Randolph's second article, on February 12, was on German womanhood.

Violet Pearman to N. B. Foot

(*Churchill papers: 2/344*)

10 February 1938

Dear Mr Foot,

I thank you for your letter of the 2nd.[1] Unhappily the same conditions still prevail, and I am afraid they will do so for a long time! The literary work is very heavy, and as it is scheduled for certain dates it has to be done to time. Mr Churchill has had to decline many invitations because of this, especially those some distance away from home. He is very sorry to be unable to serve you as he would wish, but in the circumstances he is sure you will forgive him if he does not commit himself to a mass meeting in Birmingham before the end of the winter.

Violet Pearman to Winston S. Churchill

(*Churchill papers: 2/348*)

13 February 1938

Mr Churchill

I spoke to Capt Cazalet, who said he quite understood about tonight. He wd propose himself for another night, say Friday next. In the meantime he will see you in the House about the message which he gave me as follows:—

'The Palestine Commission are very anxious that Mr Churchill should lead the deputation to the PM and Colonial Secretary on the Palestine question. They think they have a far better chance of the PM receiving them if Mr Churchill comes with them. Will Mr C consider this and let him have a reply this coming week.'[2]

[1] On 2 February 1938 Foot had written Violet Pearman to ask if Churchill could speak 'before the end of the winter' at a mass meeting of the Birmingham Regional Committee of the New Commonwealth.

[2] On 16 February 1938 Violet Pearman wrote to Victor Cazalet: 'I gave Mr Churchill your message of Sunday last which he has carefully considered. He is very sorry indeed but he does not feel he can lead the Deputation to the Prime Minister on the 17th, which you so kindly asked him to do.'

Winston S. Churchill to Sir Edward Marsh

(*Churchill papers: 8/595*)

14 February 1938

My dear Eddie,

I send herewith the first 19 chapters in what is virtually their final slip form.

I wonder if you could bear to read them through again, not to make many corrections, but merely in case there are some blemishes in the new matter and the few chapters you have not yet seen.

I think you will find that it reads more easily this time.

Randolph S. Churchill to Winston S. Churchill

(*Churchill papers: 1/325*)

14 February 1938   70 Westminster Gardens

My dear Papa—

I am sorry that you took my jocular remark so seriously. You yourself are apt in conversation to permit yourself many extravagant images and phrases, but I notice that if ever I say anything that is intended ironically you insist on taking it literally.

I quite agree that this particular remark was clumsily worded, but its very crudity would have been enough, I should have thought, to have obviated any chance of your thinking that I meant it seriously.

Yet you proceeded to 'cut' me for the rest of dinner. If there had not been a stranger present I should certainly have left rather than submit to such extraordinary treatment from my host and my father.

I only obtained the information I did from the Daily Mail because I thought it would interest you, but you refused in a very marked manner to discuss it at all and when I was injudicious enough to press the point you merely started abusing Hore Belisha who is a friend of mine.

Your abuse was obviously not intended seriously and I tried to expose its lack of substance by reminding you of your gift to him and ironically explaining it in view of your vigorous onslaught.

I only set this down lest by any chance you should still think that I was in earnest.

If you realised that from the outset, that I was not and had merely been guilty of a somewhat clumsy phrase induced by your own invective, I am at a loss to know why you should seek to punish your own son by refusing to talk to him for the remainder of dinner and thereby humiliating him in front of someone he scarcely knows.

An expression of surprise at my clumsiness would have been quite enough to have brought from me an apology for my stupidity.

When two people know each other as well as we do, it ought to be possible to solve misunderstandings other than by relapsing into moody silence.

Your loving son,
Randolph

Winston S. Churchill to Randolph Churchill
(Churchill papers: 1/325)

14 February 1938   Chartwell

My dear Randolph,

I thought yr remark singularly unkind, offensive & untrue; and I am sure no son shd have made it to his father. Your letter in no way removes the pain it caused me, not only on my own account but on yours, & also on account of our relationship. I was about to write to you to ask you to excuse me from coming to luncheon with you on Thursday, as I really cannot run the risk of such insults being offered to me, & do not feel I want to see you at the present time.

Your loving Father,

Winston S. Churchill to Keith Feiling
(Churchill papers: 8/595)

15 February 1938

My dear Feiling,

Marlborough IV and final has now reached a stage when I should be very grateful if you could read it. I have no doubt you will read it some day, perhaps indeed review it, and it will be a great help to me to have your comments before the axe falls. As I know how busy you are I venture to suggest an honorarium of twenty-five guineas, so that you may not feel you are entirely wasting your time.

With kind regards,

Yours sincerely,
Winston S. Churchill

PS. I will send you the whole of the proofs (39 chapters) during the course of the present week.

Winston S. Churchill to G. M. Trevelyan

(Churchill papers: 8/595)

15 February 1938

My dear Trevelyan,

Marlborough IV at last has now reached the final slip proof stage. I expect you will have to read it one day, and why not read it as you did the other volumes before my errors are crystallized beyond repair? If you will so kindly oblige me, I will have the chapters sent you during the course of the present week. I may say that in my final reading I may slightly soften or mitigate the picture of Bolingbroke.[1] What a virile and magnificent age it was!

Yours sincerely,
Winston S. Churchill

Winston S. Churchill to Jack Imber[2]

(Churchill papers: 2/342)

15 February 1938
Confidential

Commander Oliver Locker-Lampson having sent me your scheme, I have forwarded it to the Secretary of the Air Defence Research Committee. I may say that the principle is by no means new. I myself two and a half years ago

---

[1] Of Bolingbroke's treatment of Marlborough, Churchill wrote (*Marlborough*, volume 4, page 630): 'He had turned Swift loose upon him to traduce his character and libel his wife. In his hour of authority he had lectured and patronized him. He had written scores of letters about him in terms of hostility and contempt. He had largely destroyed his European work. He had removed him from the command of the allied armies, broken his faithful officers, and involved the British troops in the foulest dishonour. He had led and persuaded the House of Commons, in spite of truth or justice, to brand him for all time as guilty of peculation and corruption. His had been the hand that would have denied him even an asylum abroad. He had even written to Torcy that he would cut off his head, and only a few months before had threatened to send him to the Tower if he set foot in his native land. Now, in all the disreputable inconsequence of his nature, he came to beg his help and advice. . . .'

[2] Jack Imber, 1892–1970. Born in Somerset. Emigrated to Canada in his late teens. Joined the Canadian Cavalry on the outbreak of war in 1914. On active service in the First World War (where he became an expert on shells and fuses, which he collected in no-man's land). Badly wounded at the 3rd Battle of Ypres, 1917. Transferred to the British Army, 1918, when he worked on armaments inventions. Founder, in 1919, of Aladdin Industries Ltd (manufacturers of incandescent paraffin lamps), of which he became Chairman and Managing Director. Founder, in 1940, of Imber Research Ltd, for the development of armaments. In 1946 he was awarded £90,000 in relation to his inventions in the field of Air Burst Fuses, which had greatly improved the accuracy of the Pathfinder Forces during the operations of Bomber Command. In 1978 the Institute of Patentees and Inventors founded an annual lecture in his memory.

pressed these ideas upon the Committee and a certain number of experiments have been made during the period. I very much regret that they have advanced no further.

Obviously if the danger effects of shell action can be made to last for a longer period, the danger zone before and around an aeroplane is enormously increased. From numerous quarters the parachute idea has been brought before the authorities. As you know everything goes at a snail's pace here. Perhaps your project will give it a further impulse. Pray treat this matter as confidential.

Randolph Churchill to Winston S. Churchill

(Churchill papers: 1/325)

15 February 1938   70 Westminster Gardens

My dear Papa—

Thank you for your letter. I am most upset by your attitude. You described my remark as untrue. I agree. It was so absurdly untrue that I cannot conceive how you ever supposed that it was other than ironic.

But since you chose, I know not why, to take it seriously I took the earliest opportunity of writing to you to explain that it was only an inept jest and to apologise for it.

I don't see what more I can do.

If you still wish to bear me a grudge for it I cannot prevent you, though it seems to me somewhat strange to make so big a quarrel out of so trivial an occasion.

I did not mean to be unkind or offensive or I should have thought that you knew me well enough and had enough proof of love for you to know that I would never be so deliberately.

If, infected by the violence of your own language, and in the heat of an argument I used words unbecoming for a Son, I should have thought you might have excused such conduct, particularly when assured that it was accidental.

Your unforgiving and ungenerous attitude can only be explained by supposing that you reject my assurance that I had no intention of insulting you.

If that is so it is clearly useless for me to say more. If on the other hand you do accept my explanation your present attitude is inexplicable.

I am sorry you will not lunch with me on Thursday.

Your loving Son,

Winston S. Churchill to Randolph Churchill

(Churchill papers: 1/325)

16 February 1938   11 Morpeth Mansions

My dear Randolph,

I do not understand how what you said could be looked upon as 'jocular' or ironic. It was grossly rude & as such wounded me deeply. It is not enough when you have insulted someone to say it was a joke & to reproach them with attaching importance to small things. If, as you protest, you did not mean to be offensive, surely when you saw that I was hurt, you cd have said 'I am sorry. I ought not to have said such a thing.' Instead you complain in yr first letter that I did not continue to converse with you as if nothing had happened. I really did not & do not want such a thing to happen again. I do not see why at my age I shd be subjected to such taunts from a son I have tried to do my best for.

It was a vy base thing for you to suggest that the small gift I gave was given to curry favour, presumably in the hopes of gaining political or personal advantage. It was given out of kindness of heart, & of some pity wh I felt, for a man I do not much like, but who had appealed to me for advice & spoken much of his loneliness etc. I wonder you are not even now ashamed that such a thought shd have sprung so readily to yr mind & yr lips. I have not deserved it of you.

There is no question of my 'bearing you a grudge'. I shall always do my best to help you, and I have no doubt the extremely unpleasant impression wh I sustained will wear out & pass away in a little while. Meantime you are welcome to yr own self-justifications wh appear to be in your eyes complete.

Your loving Father,

Winston S. Churchill to Sir Robert Vansittart

(Churchill papers: 8/600)

16 February 1938

My dear Van,

I send the article herewith. Would you be kind enough to read it and then make any amendments which you think are necessary. As it is urgent, may I have it back tonight? My chauffeur will call after dinner for it.

Sir Robert Vansittart to Winston S. Churchill

(*Churchill papers: 8/600*)

16 February 1938

My dear Winston,

Excuse a hurried note in pencil. You are too hard, I think, on the army in your 2nd paragraph column 2. After all they have been the party of caution & anti-adventure. You do not allude to this, but treat them as 'Prussians' only.

And column 2 leaves one with the impression that you are avoiding saying what you think or know about the course of recent events in Germany. I don't suggest anything provocative of course.[1]

Otherwise no comment, and the rest of what you say is clear-cut & to the point. But you seem to me very veiled, and overcautious perhaps, in that passage. That is only an impression perhaps—enhanced because the rest *is* so outspoken.

Yours ever,

R V

You might perhaps say a little more about Austria—even at this stage.[2]

---

[1] Of the German internal situation, Churchill wrote in his article as published in the *Evening Standard* on 17 February 1938: 'Why should men's opinions be condemned as crimes, and buzzing functionaries conduct an inquisition into the political or party views of law-abiding folk? Why should religion be the subject of oppression? Why should racial persecution endure? Was it not Frederick the Great who said, "In Prussia every man must get to Heaven in his own way"? Can anyone help being born with red hair or a hook nose?' And of the German army, Churchill commented: 'The German army may continue to preserve under its iron discipline the breath of tolerance and freedom: in which case there will be a considerable gain in international security. On the other hand, the Nazi party, aided by the Secret Police, may succeed in creating a party-army dominated by Nazi principles in this world, and by the Nazi religion as their guide to the next. In this case also we should all breathe easier, because no army can be formed on party lines without very serious diminution of its military efficiency. Once the process of heresy-hunting pervades an army, true comradeship dies. Officers are promoted not for professional knowledge but for being glib in the party patter. Pretence infects every rank and every unit. A bad officer gets on by mouthing orthodox political doctrines. Resolute men needed to stand the strain of battle are no good at this game.'

[2] In his *Evening Standard* article of 17 February 1938, Churchill wrote of the Nazi threats to Austria: 'It is not at all certain yet what the reactions in Austria will be, and whether the violent scenes at Berchtesgaden will produce all the recruits for the Nazi cause in Austria which were expected from them. If there is any general rally by the Austrian people, deeply religious as they are, to the cause of national independence, it may be that some breathing space will be secured. Peoples do not like being bullied into an ideology. In Rumania, the Jew-baiter, Goga, has been pitched out of his brief authority, and the munition contracts of the Rumanian army are once again restored to France.'

Winston S. Churchill to Anthony Eden

(*Churchill papers: 2/328*)

21 February 1938

My dear Anthony,

Forgive me for intruding upon yr immediate preoccuptns.[1]

It seems to me vital that you shd not allow your personal feelings of friendship to yr late colleagues to hamper you in doing full justice to yr case and above all you shd not say anything that fetters yr action in the future. You owe this not only to yrself which you no doubt feel the least part of the event —but to yr cause wh is also the cause of England.

Yours ever,
WSC

'Alle zoll recht Kommen.'[2]

Lord Askwith[3] to Winston S. Churchill: telegram[4]

(*Churchill papers: 2/346*)

21 February 1938

Strongly urge no compromise with Fascist Powers.

Askwith

[1] During a Cabinet meeting on 16 February 1938 it had become clear that Eden, in his insistence on a firmer attitude towards Italy, did not have Chamberlain's support. But Chamberlain was determined to open direct negotiations with Mussolini, and Eden resigned from the Cabinet on February 18. During his resignation speech in the House of Commons, Eden explained that in his view the time had not yet come for Britain to open negotiations with Italy. Italian propaganda against Britain was rife throughout the world. Italians troops were still fighting alongside the nationalists in Spain. The moment had come, he said, 'for this country to stand firm'. There could be no constructive appeasement in Europe 'if we allow the impression to gain currency abroad that we yield to constant pressure'.

[2] 'All will come right': a phrase which Churchill remembered from his time in South Africa during the Boer War, and which he often quoted. The favourite motto of President Steyn, the phrase is more usually spelt 'Alle sal reg kom'.

[3] George Ranken Askwith, 1861–1942. Barrister, 1886. Industrial arbitrator. Assistant Secretary, Board of Trade, 1907. Chairman of the Fair Wages Advisory Committee, 1909–19. Knighted, 1911. Chief Industrial Commissioner, Board of Trade, 1911–19. Created Baron, 1919. President of the British Science Guild, 1922–5. Vice-President, Royal Society of Arts, 1927–41. President of the Institute of Arbitrators, 1933–41.

[4] Churchill received seventeen telegrams on the day of Eden's resignation debate. One, signed 'Group of Leeds Patriots', read: 'Give it Neville Hot'. Another, signed 'Six Leeds Tories', read: 'Lash Italophile Cowards'. Churchill also received 39 letters and postcards from members of the public (*Churchill papers: 2/346*).

Bernard Pares[1] to Winston S. Churchill

(*Churchill papers: 2/346*)

23 February 1938 University of London

Dear Mr Churchill,

Will you allow me to congratulate you on your perfectly splendid speech of yesterday,—its perspective, its fairness, its form, and its sure touch on this most disturbing episode. I particularly liked your last sentence, and I hope people will go on thinking about it.[2]

Yours sincerely,
Bernard Pares

Georg Franckenstein[3] to Winston S. Churchill

(*Churchill papers: 2/328*)

24 February 1938 Austrian Legation
London

Dear Churchill,

I listened with great interest and much admiration to your brilliant speech in the House the other day and want to thank you very warmly for what you said about Austria.[4]

Sincerely yrs,
Georg Franckenstein

[1] Bernard Pares, 1867–1949. Educated at Harrow and Trinity College, Cambridge. Historian, he published his first book on Russian history, in 1907. Professor of Russian History, Language and Literature, Liverpool, 1908–17. Attached to the Russian Army, 1914–17. Attached to the British Embassy in Petrograd, 1917. Knighted, 1919. Director, School of Slavonic and East European Studies, London, 1922–39.

[2] Churchill's last sentence in his speech of 22 January 1938, on Eden's resignation, was: 'I predict that the day will come when at some point or other or on some issue or other you will have to make a stand, and I pray God that when that day comes we may not find that through an unwise policy we are left to make that stand alone.'

[3] Georg Franckenstein, 1878–1953. Before 1914, served in the Austro-Hungarian embassies in Washington, St Petersburg, Rome, Tokyo and London. Member of the Austrian Peace Delegation, Paris, 1919. Austrian Minister to London, 1920–38. Knight Grand Cross of the Royal Victorian Order, 1937. Became a British subject, 1938. He published *Facts and Features of My Life* in 1939. Killed in an air crash at Frankfurt.

[4] On 22 February 1938, during the debate on Anthony Eden's resignation as Foreign Secretary, Churchill criticized Lord Halifax's recent visit to Germany, during which he had seen Hitler. The visit has been ill-timed, Churchill said, and the Germans had used the occasion to increase pressure on Austria, making it seem that—as a friend from Vienna had reported to Churchill—'England would not object to Germany's authority over Austria.' This, Churchill continued, 'shows the danger of these unofficial visits, and how use may be made of conversations, which are entered into in quite good faith, in order to procure support for other policies'.

Harcourt Johnstone[1] to Winston S. Churchill

(*Churchill papers: 2/229*)

24 February 1938

My dear Winston,

. . . I am writing a line to say—with great respect—how much I have admired your speeches during the Eden-Austria period. They seem to me to have been a marvellous contribution to the steadiness, good judgement and courage of the nation.

Yrs ever,
Crinks Johnstone

Victor Cazalet to Stanley Baldwin

(*'Victor Cazalet: a portrait'*)

24 February 1938

Last Thursday evening,[2] that is the day before the crisis, Winston came up to the Foreign Affairs Committee and for a quarter of an hour gave us an enthusiastic eulogy of Anthony and ended by saying that we must support him. This struck me as somewhat unnecessary as we were all devoted to Anthony and no one had even faintly criticised him. I smelt, if not a rat, at any rate, a mouse. I remembered that three prominent gentlemen had all been on the Riviera together.

The only thing that relieved my anxiety was the conviction that a combination of Lloyd George and Winston was fatal to any attack on the Government and as good as a combination of Beaverbrook and Rothermere against you.

I hope I have been as objective and dispassionate as I intended in the recital of the above story. . . .

---

[1] Harcourt Johnstone, 1895–1945. Known as 'Crinks'. Educated at Eton and Balliol College, Oxford. On active service, 1914–18. Liberal MP for Willesden East, 1923–4. Unsuccessful Liberal Candidate for Eastbourne, 1925. MP, South Shields, 1931–5, and for West Middlesborough, 1940–5. Secretary, Department of Overseas Trade, 1940–5. A member of the Other Club from 1932, and its Joint Honorary Secretary (with Brendan Bracken) from 1937.

[2] Thursday, 17 February 1938.

Sir Edward Marsh to Winston S. Churchill

(*Churchill papers: 4/2*)

25 February 1938

My dear Winston,

My warmest congratulations on the accomplishment of this great task. The end is fully worthy of the whole—I can't say handsomer than that. It is certainly one of the great biographies.

Yours ever,
Eddie

Winston S. Churchill to Sir Edward Marsh

(*Marsh papers*)

26 February 1938

I am deeply grateful to you for the enormous pains you have taken in your second revision of Marlborough IV. There is hardly one of your comments that I have not accepted, and I could easily explain the two or three exceptions to you. I am now beginning my own final reading, and should be very glad if you would let me know whether there is any part which seems to drag unduly.

This book is not to be commended by its purple patches, but by its structure, which I hope will bring home to modern readers the life and drama of that great age. How like their forerunners the modern Tories are!

I still want you to give an afternoon to Deakin in checking the French translations. I have translated them for the most part myself and rather freely, so perhaps I have not brought out the full strength of the passages.

Winston S. Churchill to G. M. Trevelyan

(*Churchill papers: 8/595*)

26 February 1938

Thank you so much for sending me back the rest of the proofs and for your most agreeable letter. I am dealing with the various points you mention and am relieved to find they are so few. Most of the Tories of the present day seem uncommonly like their predecessors. The Daily Express is a lively descendant of the Examiner, without of course the malicious genius of Swift behind it.

Winston S. Churchill to Keith Feiling

(Churchill papers: 8/595)

26 February 1938
Private

I am much obliged to you for your kindness in reading through my proofs and relieved that, with your great knowledge, you do not find much to criticise. I should indeed have been unhappy if you had felt it your duty to launch out upon another of those exercises of literary ferocity to which you treated the unfortunate Chidsey![1] I am attending to all the points you have noted.

How like the Tory party of those days our present lot is! I wish I had studied history at the beginning of my life, instead of at the end.

Winston S. Churchill to Sir James Hawkey

(Churchill papers: 7/46)

26 February 1938   Chartwell

In case some of our friends in the constituency are asking about my attitude towards our foreign policy, will you very kindly tell them that it is, and will be, in strict accordance with the following two paragraphs from my election address in 1935:—

'We have pledged our faith to the Covenant of the League of Nations and to the Kellogg Pact.[2] We have thus renounced for ever all idea of war for national aggrandisement or for any selfish purpose. We look forward to the building up of a system of collective security, to the prevention of violence and bloodshed through the united action of many Nations, States and Races,

---

[1] Donald Barr Chidsey, 1902–   . Born and educated in New Jersey. After high school he spent several years doing odd jobs, many of them with newspaper firms. Began to travel as a reporter for various newspapers, visiting all the continents and living continually abroad. Besides reporting, he also worked as manager of a copra plantation in Tahiti, and of a tea room in Bermuda. From 1942 to 1945 he was on active service as an ambulance driver in North Africa. He published his first book, *Bonnie Prince Charlie*, in 1929. His biography of the first Duke of Marlborough was published in 1929. He also wrote biographies of Sir Walter Raleigh (1931), Roscoe Conkling (1935) and John L. Sullivan (1942), and more than ten adventure novels.

[2] The Kellogg Pact for the 'outlawry of war', signed on 27 August 1928 by representatives of fifteen nations, including Britain, France, Germany and the United States. The pact was named after its principal negotiator, Frank B. Kellogg, 1856–1937, formerly United States Secretary of State (to Calvin Coolidge), 1925–9.

and to the reign of world law. We submit ourselves to that law, and we must be ready to take our share in making it respected.'

'We cannot do more than our share, but the British Empire moving with the broad opinion of the world is a mighty power for peace and for good. We must be worthy of the greatness of our task and not unequal to it. The alternative to the growing strength of the League of Nations is the return to the ferocious appetites of the jungle, and the blotting out of the new light which has begun to shine, though as yet faintly and fitfully, upon mankind.'

Nothing that has happened in the interval has led me in any way to modify these views which, as you may remember, were endorsed by an even larger majority than we had at the election in 1931.[1] I may add that I have no reason to believe that His Majesty's Government do not adhere to these general principles. Of course you will remember that I always urged that the idea of 'collective security' can be no substitute for strong and effective national defences in this and other peace-seeking countries until such time as it has been made real and effective. You will see therefore that an even greater effort is needed in Great Britain to give us the necessary security from external menace, and especially from blackmail by air-murder.

[1] In 1931 Churchill's majority at Epping was 20,286. In 1935 it rose to 20,419. In both elections the Liberal candidate had come second (and in 1931 the Labour candidate had lost his deposit).

March 1938

Randolph Churchill to Winston S. Churchill

(*Churchill papers: 1/325*)

1 March 1938   70 Westminster Gardens

My dear Papa—

I'm afraid I was rather de trop at your party tonight. I put off a dinner engagement in order to dine with you. Subsequently you told me that you were going to make a speech and suggested that we should have supper afterwards. I was delighted at the opportunity of hearing you speak and was in the House from 8.30 onwards.[1]

When I asked for you after the debate I found that you had gone without leaving any message for me.

After a good deal of telephoning I discovered where you were and came along.

Your reception of me was not very cordial and I felt that I was butting in. In the course of the evening you twice went out of your way to warn me against repeating what you said without making any such admonition to the rest of the company.

As I wrote to you before, I do not think I have ever betrayed anything you have told me, and I find it intolerable that you should publicly treat me with less confidence than you show towards others whose love and devotion for you is scarcely likely to equal mine.

---

[1] At 10.08 pm on 28 February 1938 Churchill spoke in the debate on the new Secretary of State for Foreign Affairs, Lord Halifax, and whether it was derogatory to the House of Commons to have the Foreign Secretary in the House of Lords. When you have a Prime Minister, he said, 'what is the good of worrying about the Foreign Secretary? What is the point of crying out for the moon, when you have the sun, and you have that bright orb of day from whose effulgent beams the lesser luminaries derive their radiance. It is no use working up a grievance on that.' As to the desire of some that Samuel Hoare should return to the Foreign Office, Churchill remarked that, quite apart from the importance of his new work as Home Secretary, especially the preparation of air raid precautions, 'I understand that there is another obstacle to the right hon. Gentleman being appointed Foreign Secretary, namely, that nothing in the world would induce him to accept the office again. Once bitten, twice shy. It is a case of the burnt child dreading the fire.'

I should have thought a sensitive man like yourself could easily envisage the deep humiliation I feel when my discretion is repeatedly called in question by you in front of hacks like David Margesson and Victor Warrender[1] and that amiable flibbertigibbert, Brendan.

Apart from the humiliation I feel at the time, how can you suppose these men will treat me when you are not there? They will naturally (except in so far as I strenuously combat such tendencies), presume to patronise me to the full and treat me, as you do, as a somewhat inferior creature.

You will doubtless think me very silly to make so much of this, but I feel it very acutely.

All evening I had waited around and sought you out to congratulate you on your truly magnificent speech; yet even at the end of the evening you preferred to go off with David Margesson.

You may think it presumptuous of me to complain of the manner in which you treat me. I would not do so if I had not been deeply wounded by your attitude on so many occasions.

I do not see why you should not show the same marks of friendship & respect to me that you show to Brendan—to put it at its lowest.

I do not think that you will find me a less reliable friend than him, to say nothing of such stray acquaintances as Margesson and Warrender. Yet whoever is present, even if it is only Victor Cazalet, you always treat me as a combination of sneak guest and odd man out!

When I was thirteen and fourteen years old you did me the compliment of treating me almost as if I were a grown up. Now that I am about 27 you treat me as a wayward and untrustworthy child.

Despite your example no-one else treats me the way you do, nor do you behave towards anyone else as you do to me.

Please forgive this lengthy outburst. I hope you will not think it bitter. I know that you are fond of me, and I think you know the love & respect and admiration I have for you. But I cannot comprehend why you should crucify all these feelings by treating me with such obvious contempt before such men of straw.

Your loving Son,
Randolph

---

[1] Victor Alexander George Anthony Warrender, 1899–   . Queen Victoria's last god-child. Educated at Eton. On active service with the Grenadier Guards, 1917–18 (Military Cross, 1918). Conservative MP for Grantham, 1923–42. An Assistant Whip, 1928–31. A Junior Lord of the Treasury, 1931–2. Vice-Chamberlain of HM Household, 1932–5. Financial Secretary, War Office, 1935–40. Parliamentary and Financial Secretary, Admiralty, 1940–2; Parliamentary Secretary, Admiralty, 1942–5. Created Baron Bruntisfield, 1942.

Harold Nicolson to his wife

(*Nicolson papers*)

2 March 1938

I went to such an odd luncheon yesterday. It is called 'The Focus Group', and is one of Winston's things. It consists of Winston, Norman Angell, Wickham Steed, Walter Layton,[1] Robert Cecil, Violet Bonham Carter, Clynes[2] and some other of the Labour people. I was made to make a speech without any notice and was a trifle embarrassed. But one gets a thick skin and an easy habit about these things and my speech was rather a hit. Winston was enormously witty. He spoke of 'this great country nosing from door to door like a cow that has lost its calf, mooing dolefully now in Berlin and now in Rome —when all the time the tiger and the alligator wait for its undoing'.

Don't be worried, my darling. I am not going to become one of the Winston brigade. My leaders are Anthony and Malcolm.[3]

Violet Pearman to Anthony Eden

(*Churchill papers: 8/595*)

2 March 1938

Dear Sir,

I am asked by Mr Churchill to send you herewith the chapters, in proof, of his last volume of Marlborough. There are thirty-nine chapters in all, so the set is complete, although tagged in two separate bundles. Mr Churchill apologises for their bulkiness, but the book has not yet gone into page-proof, as he is still revising parts of it.

[1] Walter Thomas Layton, 1884–1966. Lecturer in economics, University College, London, 1909–12. Represented the Ministry of Munitions on the Milner Mission to Russia, 1917. Statistical Adviser, Ministry of Munitions, 1917–18. Unsuccessful Liberal candidate at the Elections of 1922 and 1923. Editor of *The Economist*, 1922–38. Knighted, 1930. Chairman, *News Chronicle* Ltd, 1930–50; Vice-Chairman, *Daily News* Ltd, 1930–63. Head of the Joint War Production Staff, 1942–3. Director, Reuters Ltd, 1945–53. Created Baron, 1947. Vice-President, Consultative Assembly of the Council of Europe, 1949–57. Deputy Leader of the Liberal Party in the House of Lords, 1952–5. Director, Tyne-Tees Television Ltd, 1958–61.

[2] John Robert Clynes, 1869–1949. Labour MP, Manchester Platting, 1906–31; 1935–45. President, National Union of General and Municipal Workers. Parliamentary Secretary, Ministry of Food, 1917–18. Privy Councillor, 1918. Food Controller, 1918–19. Chairman, Parliamentary Labour Party, 1921–2. Lord Privy Seal, 1924. Home Secretary, 1929–31.

[3] Anthony Eden and Malcolm MacDonald.

Winston S. Churchill to Anthony Eden
(Churchill papers: 8/595)

3 March 1938
Personal

I am quite ashamed for dumping these proofs upon you to comfort you in your exile. On no account bore yourself with them. My father wrote that there was nothing so relaxing as reading history, and I have certainly found it so in my later life.

It occurred to me that you would be amused to see what rascals the Tories were at the beginning of the eighteenth century. Of course it is all quite different now.[1] I had some fun with them nevertheless the other day.

With all good wishes,

Squadron-Leader John A. McDonald [2] to Violet Pearman
(Churchill papers: 2/339)

4 March 1938   Royal Air Force Club

Dear Mrs Pearman,

I find I am on duty this weekend and cannot therefore get out of London on Sunday. I shall be unable to come to lunch.

---

[1] Writing in the *Strand* magazine for August 1939, Churchill commented on Eden's political fate after his resignation: 'With its permeating and far-reaching social and political influence the power of the Conservative Party to break a resigning Minister has often been proved. It extinguished Lord Randolph Churchill at the height of his popularity. It crushed the brilliant George Wyndham. All this force was now applied to Eden. The papers addicted to the policy of appeasing the Dictators simply ceased to report his speeches, or reported them in a manner which was an insult. Even in the courageous constituency of Warwick and Leamington it was possible to raise opposition among the elders. Many of his adherents throughout this island and in the United States have blamed him for not striking back with sufficient vigour. One can only say that he had been restrained by his inherent loyalty to the Conservative Party. For indeed there is no one else of his age and experience who has a greater hold upon the sympathy and imagination of what may, in its widest sense, be called "the liberal forces of England".' Churchill added: 'Let us hope the Conservative Party will one of these days recognize that they will have need of him and that, with them, he will be able to render high service to the causes which in their hearts they value most.'

[2] John Alexander McDonald, 1897–   . Educated at Dumfries Academy, 1909–13. Worked as a Post Office Telegraphist, 1913–15. Enlisted in the Royal Flying Corps as an Airman 2nd Class, 1915. Belgian Croix de Guerre, 1918. 2nd Lieutenant (administration), 1918. Served with 208 Squadron, Constantinople, 1922; with 55 (Bomber) Squadron, Iraq, 1935. Squadron-Leader, 1935. Services Staff (Signals), No 11 (Fighter) Group, Fighter Command, June 1937–January 1938. Directorate of Signals, Department of the Chief of the Air Staff, January 1938–September 1939. On active service, 1939–45, including Burma (mentioned in despatches, June 1945). Group Captain, 1944. CBE (Military), 1946. AFC, 1947. Retired, 1947.

Commander Anderson: notes dictated for Winston S. Churchill

(Churchill papers: 2/338)

..., ... Force. 19 AAF squadrons equipped with Harts and Hinds.

Note. These 19 squadrons are included in the 123 squadrons of the Metropolitan Air Force.

Regular Air Force.

Lympne	2 squadrons Hinds		
Hucknall	2	,,	,,
Andover	2	,,	,,
Waddington	2	,,	,,
Turnhouse	1	,,	,,
	28		

30 Fighter Squadrons

Only 1 squadron is equipped with Hurricanes. The remaining 29 are equipped with Furies, Gauntlets and Gladiators, all designed before 1932.

Conclusions—Bombers 336 old types
Fighters 522 ,, ,,

858

Unity Mitford [1] to Winston S. Churchill

(Churchill papers: 2/328)

5 March 1938   Old Mill Cottage
High Wycombe

Dear Cousin Winston,

I read your article last night in the 'Evening Standard', and I was particularly interested in the part about Austria.[2] I really do think that you, in

---

[1] Unity Valkyrie Mitford, 1914–1948. Daughter of the 2nd Baron Redesdale; sister of Diana, Nancy and Jessica Mitford; and Clementine Churchill's cousin. From 1933, as an admirer of Hitler and the Nazi regime, she was frequently in Hitler's company, and on the outbreak of war in 1939, while still in Germany, she tried to commit suicide. The Germans arranged for her to be sent back to Britain. Her brother Tom died of wounds received in action in Burma in March 1945. Her brother-in-law Esmond Romilly (Clementine Churchill's nephew) was killed in action in November 1941.

[2] Churchill's article 'Carry On!' published in the *Evening Standard* on 4 March 1938, in which he wrote: '. . . this crowded fortnight has revealed in several quarters the innate strength of the cause of freedom in Europe. The brutal bullying of Herr Schuschnigg at

common with most English people, are very misinformed about Austrian affairs, which are consistently misrepresented by the British press. I know Austria fairly well, and have been there a lot in recent years; and I was lucky enough to be there when the Hitler–Schuschnigg meeting took place, and for a week or so after. The jubilation which broke out among all classes of the population must have been one of the most tremendous demonstrations of belief the world has ever seen. One could notice it immediately in the streets of Vienna; on one day, the entire population looked pathetically oppressed and hopeless, as they had done for years; on the next, everyone looked happy & full of hope for the future. I often heard people say that it was like waking up from a frightful nightmare. In Graz, Linz and Vienna I witnessed demonstrations in which the population went mad with joy and one could not move in the streets for people shouting 'Heil Hitler! Anschluss!' & waving Swastika flags. By night, the hills around Vienna were ablaze with bonfires in the shape of Swastikas.

For anyone who knew and loved Austria, it used to be an unhappy experience to go there, though it was wonderful to see how bravely the people carried on, risking the loss of their jobs and imprisonment for the sake of their ideals. Now, it is a joy to be there & see the Austrians at last being justly treated.

Of course, you undoubtedly know that Anschluss with the Reich was the great wish of the entire German population of the Austro-Hungarian Empire, long before the war & long before Hitler was even born, though the English press would make one believe that it was the Führer who invented the idea. Altogether, the idea of Germany trying to 'eat up poor little Austria, who is struggling for her independence', seems unbelievably ridiculous to all Austrians except the aristocracy, who cling to the idea of a restoration for selfish motives, and the Reds, who are obviously against Anschluss with Nazi Germany.

Most Austrians have no doubt at all that a free plebiscite would result in *at least* 80% for the Nazis. I do not know where you got your information that the Austrian government 'have now probably two-thirds of the people of Austria behind them', but I think that, with the person who made this estimate, it is a case of the wish being father to the thought.

You probably won't bother to read this letter, for I know you are very busy

---

Berchtesgaden, where the most horrible threats were uttered, is in its secondary stage producing a very strong national rally throughout Austria. The union of the Socialists with the Catholics gives a broad foundation to the Vienna Government which they have never had before. They have now probably two-thirds of the people of Austria behind them in defence of their independence. They could now probably face a plebiscite conducted under fair conditions without fear. But no one can tell what the reactions in Nazi Germany will be, or what new shattering blows impend upon a small unhappy State.'

but I hope you will because I am sure you are not a person who would consciously misrepresent the facts in order to prove your case, and I wish you
would visit Austria yourself, and see how happy the recent events have made
a whole people.[1]

Yours,
Unity Mitford

Winston S. Churchill to Georg Franckenstein

(*Churchill papers: 2/328*)

7 March 1938

This letter is from one of the young ladies who have been so attracted to
Herr Hitler. Perhaps you will give me a little material from which to answer
her. Naturally it will never appear to have come from you.

Brendan Bracken to Winston S. Churchill

(*Churchill papers: 8/604*)

8 March 1938

My dear Winston,
Here are a few suggestions for your Collier's articles.

1. 'Is the Capitalist System Hopeless?' This subject should appeal to the
mass of Americans. It has given them their relative prosperity. And if it were
only allowed to work America's financial and unemployment woes would
diminish.

2. 'The Case for a Non-Political Civil Service.' The recent immense
increase in the bureaucracy makes this a live issue in America. You can
show how much the British Empire owes to the Civil Service. Politicians can
do little without the aid of well trained permanent officials.

3. 'Japan and the Prussian Spirit.' The astonishing development of Japan
seems to fascinate and irritate the Yanks. When the Duke of Connaught went
to Japan in 1875 there were but two carriages in the country. It is now one of
the leading industrial nations. Japan's worst import was the Prussian spirit.
Her belief in brute force is as great a menace to the world as Nazism. (I can
give you some good stuff about Japan).

---

[1] On 15 March 1938 Churchill telegraphed to Unity Mitford: 'Thank you dear Unity
for your clearly written letter which I am answering in a few days. Winston.'

4. 'Eden and Chamberlain—Two Incompatible Temperaments.' Americans are interested by all they hear about Eden, and they know little about Chamberlain. You could write an interesting article on these two conflicting personalities.

5. 'Is Speculation Wholly Harmful?' The Yanks are ingrained speculators. They would like to read the argument that a large part of the trade of the world cannot be carried on if all 'gambling' is eliminated. And you might have some fun in showing that less reputable types of gambling, like betting and football pools, relieve the drabness of millions of lives. It may be censurable, but it is part of the nature of many human beings.

6. 'A Foreigner's View of a Third Term.' Americans are agog about the question whether Roosevelt will run again. The prejudice against giving a President a Third Term is very deep rooted. The President exercises so much power and patronage that people feel that Washington was right when he thought that the nation benefited by a change in the executive after eight years. The growth of dictatorships in many parts of the world probably increases American prejudice against a Third Term Presidency. In Europe the executive Head of a State can continue in office for twenty years.

7. 'Ataturk.' A great deal is written in American papers about Hitler and Mussolini, but few people realise the quality of Kemal.

Yours,
BB

Georg Franckenstein to Winston S. Churchill

(*Churchill papers: 2/328*)

9 March 1938

Austrian Legation
London

Dear Churchill

I am returning enclosed the letter you gave me. It is well known that by means of great activity and noisy demonstrations the National Socialists are trying to create the impression that they are the most powerful factor in Austria and that their followers form the majority in the country. Their tactics have apparently been most successful in the case of your correspondent.

As regards what she says about the rejoicing in Austria, I agree that there was much jubilation among the National Socialists after Hitler's speech. But the tremendous enthusiasm aroused in other sections of the population by Dr

Schuschnigg's speech on February 24th must not be overlooked. As Dr Schuschnigg wishes at all costs to avoid conflict and bloodshed which might lead to German intervention in Austria, his followers are remaining quiet and orderly, while the Nazis are displaying the greatest possible activity. In these circumstances the impression might easily be gained that the majority of Austrians are Nazis, but this is undoubtedly not the case. I have consulted quite a number of people recently whom I know to be objectively minded and well informed about Austrian conditions as to the present strength of the National Socialists in Austria. It is apparently difficult to estimate what percentage they constitute of the population; some suggested 25%, others 35%, but all were agreed that the majority in the country is in favour of an independent Austria. Well-informed political observers have expressed the opinion that if a plebiscite were held now, there would be a large majority against Anschluss. So far there have been a number of reasons why it is not possible to hold a plebiscite at the present time—chief among them being the fact that Germany would undoubtedly throw all her political and financial strength into the scales in order to influence the result and that Nazis would thus be in a position to intimidate the rest of the population into voting as they wished them to.

The remark in your correspondent's letter that 'Anschluss with the Reich was the great wish of the entire German population of the Austro-Hungarian Empire long before the war' is of course absurd. It is true that there was a pan-German party before the war, but their programme was one that lay quite outside the realm of practical politics and their membership was comparatively speaking small.

The National Socialists often make capital out of the fact that after the breakdown of the Monarchy the Austrian Social Democrats advocated union with Germany. But it is important to remember that this policy was prompted by the wish of the Socialists to strengthen their own regime by joining forces with the powerful Socialist movement in Germany and of course also by the hope that union with their big neighbour would alleviate the desperate shortage of food and raw materials with which Austria was faced in 1918 and 1919. All this has now changed, however, and since the advent of the Hitler regime in Germany there has been a complete volte face on the part of the Socialists and the workers as a whole in Austria. I am sending you enclosed a copy of an interesting proclamation issued in February by spokesmen of the trade union movement, in which they declare themselves determined to defend to the utmost the independence of Austria.

It is of course by no means only the working classes and Monarchists who are opposed to National Socialism. There are great numbers of patriotically minded people in Austria belonging to neither of those groups who are vigorously opposed to having a regime alien in aims and methods to Austrian traditions forced upon them.

Soon after listening to Dr Schuschnigg's stirring speech I wrote down the thoughts which had occurred to me. I am sending you a copy here as I think you may care to glance at them.

Sincerely yours,
George Franckenstein

PS. We have just been informed by Reuters that a plebiscite will be held in Austria next Sunday. If this news is true it will decide the 'American duel' between Miss Unity Mitford and myself.

Wing-Commander Anderson to Violet Pearman

(*Churchill papers: 2/338*)

9 March 1938

Royal Air Force Station
Catfoss
Nr Hull

Dear Mrs Pearman,

I forward a complete copy of the attached Report.[1] Taken from the Orderly Room. Copy also letter the Link Trainer.[2]

Will you please file these.

Yours,
C. T. Anderson

[1] The 'attached Report' was the 1937 Annual Training Report of Bomber Command, issued from the Headquarters of Bomber Command on 4 February 1938, and marked 'Secret'. The 16-page report was signed by Air Chief Marshal E. R. Ludlow-Hewitt, Commander-in-Chief of Bomber Command, who noted that the Report itself 'would seem to be pre-occupied mainly with the difficulties and impediments to efficient training' and added: 'I fear this is, under present conditions unavoidable, as the essence and gravamen of the whole situation is the fact that in many respects our organisation and ancillary equipment has not kept pace with the requirements of operational flying with modern fast aircraft.' The Report ended: 'In conclusion I must repeat that particularly in view of the unsettled international situation I cannot but regard the present low level of operational efficiency generally prevailing throughout the Command with concern and anxiety. Nevertheless in the circumstances described in this report, to press on with operational training in advance of our equipment and services would be to risk an increase in wastage and a serious decrease in confidence which would not be counter-balanced by any real improvement in efficiency. As soon as they are equipped to do so, I have complete confidence that the officers and airmen of this Command will see to it that their units attain full operational efficiency in the shortest possible time.'

[2] A letter dated 2 March 1938, from the Senior Air Staff Officer, Training Command, Royal Air Force, sent to No 1, Armament Training Camp. The letter read: 'With reference to your letter 1ATC/1402/E, dated 24th February, 1938, subject – Link Trainer, it is regretted that your request cannot be granted at the present time. As soon as it has been established whether or not Air Ministry are prepared to furnish Armament Training Camps with the Link Trainer your request will be given every consideration.'

Violet Pearman to Winston S. Churchill

(*Churchill papers: 2/336*)

10 March 1938

Cmdr A rang up to say that perhaps it would be as well to omit the *actual figures* of the crashes, as this would most probably give the source from which they were obtained. Anyhow it may arouse curiosity.

He says also another point to mention would be, and it is important, that the ability to cope with new aircraft is dependent upon trained airmen mechanics in the squadrons, and in this respect we are 600 wireless operator mechanics deficient now.

The servicing of the new aircraft, which is very different from the old aircraft, requires skilled instrument mechanics for the variable pitch propellers, the undercarriages etc. These men take some time to train to be of any use, and they will not have these trained men for another 18 months or so.

Sir Horace Wilson: note of a conversation with Neville Chamberlain

(*Premier papers: 1/238*)

10 March 1938

It is to be anticipated that Mr Churchill will repeat the suggestion for an enquiry which he threw out tentatively during the Defence Debate last Monday.[1]

The Prime Minister decided that an enquiry should be refused and should be refused flatly and firmly, the decision to be adhered to notwithstanding any criticisms that may be raised during the debate.

This decision is to hold good in spite of anything which Mr Churchill may say.

[1] Speaking in the House of Commons on 7 March 1938, Churchill said: '. . . I hold strongly that the House of Commons should satisfy itself more thoroughly than it can do in these Debates about the exact conditions of our Air Force and expansion programme. We have had an inquiry, much resisted, but soon to be published, into civil aviation. The least we can do at the present time is to have a similar inquiry into the state of our military aviation. It might well be that the results of that inquiry would not be a fit subject for publication to foreign Powers; in that case, the Prime Minister could do as his predecessors have done in such matters, he could summon to the Committee of Imperial Defence the representatives of other parties, and there should be an agreement, such as one would expect under a National system of Government, both upon what should be said and upon what should be done. When the Air Force Estimates are considered, I shall certainly press this request—whether by Select Committee, or by a committee like the Cadman Committee, or by the Cadman Committee itself, I care not. There should be some tribunal, independent of the Executive, before which statements of detail could be made. They certainly cannot be made in this House, where we cannot converse about our vital affairs without having it all read abroad.'

(The Chief Whip[1] did not think that Mr Churchill is getting, or is likely to get, much support for his request for an enquiry.)

Desmond Morton to Winston S. Churchill
(*Churchill papers: 2/336*)

11 March 1938

I have only three comments.

Paragraph 1. It does not follow that, because a formed squadron is shown in the Air Force list, the said squadron possesses the established number of first-line aircraft, let alone reserves. Have you not counted the 123 squadrons as possessing each about 12 machines, ie 4 flights of 3, but surely it is admitted that some of these squadrons are still only on a one-flight basis?

The fact that 50% of the first-line aircraft whatever be the figure, are of old types is not disputed by me!

Paragraph 2. I think it is a little under the mark in para 2 to suggest that the number of metropolitan first-line aircraft of a relatively modern type which would go into action to-day is 'certainly less than 500'. I would put that at 30% higher.

Paragraph 5. I expect you would be prepared to recognise that the *very latest* types of British aircraft are superior to the *very latest* types of German aircraft, but whereas there may be several hundred of the latter in use, the number of the former in service can be counted on the fingers of both hands.

On the other hand, even if it be said that, technically speaking, the very latest types of British aircraft are superior to the very latest types of German aircraft, it could not be said that the former are superior to the very latest types developed everywhere in the world. Certain recent types of US aircraft appear undoubtedly to be of superior design, performance and construction to British types.

I apologise for the messiness of these notes: speed is the excuse.

DM

[1] David Margesson (see page 232, note 1).

Winston S. Churchill to Neville Chamberlain

(Premier papers: 1/237)

12 March 1938
Personal

My dear Neville

I send you a few of the points which, if we lived in less dangerous times, I should feel bound to bring up in debate in support of what I think is a reasonable request for an Enquiry.

Yours vy sincerely,
Winston S. Churchill

Winston S. Churchill: memorandum on aircraft types

(Churchill papers: 2/336)

12 March 1938

1. Of the 123 squadrons Metropolitan Air Force now formed more than half are still armed with obsolete types. In fact out of 1,500–1,700 machines at least 850 consist of Hinds, Harts, Heyfords, Gauntlets etc the designs of which are in most cases more than ten years old.

2. Such new machines as have reached the squadrons mostly lack essential armament and equipment, namely, Browning guns, turrets, sights and modern blind-flying equipment. Without these elements the machines have no war value and even training is obstructed. The number of Metropolitan first-line aircraft of a relatively modern type which could go into action to-day properly equipped in all respects and be so maintained is certainly less than 700.

3. The slow rate of delivery of aircraft and appurtenances in the third year of rearmament is astonishing. The monthly output of about 200 machines is perhaps only one-third of the German, although the latter are not pressing their factories. Since less than one-half of the Regular squadrons have received their outfit of new machines, it would seem to follow that there are no reserves of such new machines available. Thus the picture of 'British first line aircraft' with 100% reserves behind it is an illusion. Every new machine as it emerges is devoured by the squadrons, few are left for training, either in the schools or for the reserve pilots, and none for the reserves of the squadrons. These conditions can only be gradually and partially modified during the present year.

4. In the paper which I sent you in January 1937 an important paragraph

forecasted the inevitability of a high and excessive rate of crashes when the new aircraft reached the squadrons. The results justified the prediction. In the last quarter of 1937 nearly 350 machines—old and new—were written off in the various Home Commands. These crash figures, although operative mainly over old machines, are a grievous subtraction from the new deliveries, already so meagre.

5. What of the new types with which we are assured the 123 squadrons will be fully equipped by March 31, 1939? Owing to the slow production some of these types are already becoming outclassed. For instance the Hurricane fighter of which a dozen or two have been delivered, was ordered by the Air Ministry in 1935, and a specimen was actually available at the end of 1936. It is only now being delivered at a present rate of perhaps 200 a year.

Meanwhile it can hardly be doubted that the Germans have laid new types of fighters and bombers dating from 1936 and 1937 upon their mass production plants. As they order wholesale from a unified industry, full supplies of these should be available on March 31, 1939. It is not therefore true that we are overtaking them in the quality of the machines which will be in general use in the regular squadrons by that date.

6. All questions of design relate to air strategy and tactics and are consequently disputable. We have concentrated upon the forward-firing fixed-gun Fighter (Hurricane and Spitfire). The latest developments increasingly suggest that hostile aircraft can only be engaged with certainty on parallel or nearly parallel courses, hence that the current type of equipment will become obsolete.

7. The idea that the expanded Air Force is upon a temporary basis should be discarded. A far larger proportion of wholetime careers should be offered to proved men. If the foreign danger passes, the cost of compensating them on being axed will be petty compared to the general savings. Aircraft costing £25,000 should be in the hands of matured, experienced pilots and crews who are entitled to regard the Service as their future and their life. Only with this class of permanent personnel will the new machines yield their operational efficiency.

8. As you know I have been a member of the Air Defence Research Committee since July 1935. Many wonderful ideas are being developed and it may well be that we are ahead of our rivals in some important respects. Nevertheless it would be untrue to suggest that any decisive protection will be available on a nation-wide scale for a long time to come.

Cabinet minutes

(Cabinet papers: 23/92)

12 March 1938

The Cabinet were reminded that the House of Commons, after recent events, would be in a different frame of mind for discussing the defence estimates next week than had been the case in the present week.

The Cabinet were informed that the Right Hon Winston Churchill was intending to attack the Government on the ground of the inadequacy of their Air Force Programme and to support the motion of the opposition for an enquiry into the Air Ministry. It was suggested that a speech belittling our efforts might have a very adverse effect on the international position just now when the only hope of saving Czechoslovakia from the German menace was by creating an impression of force.

The Secretary of State for Air recalled that in connection with the recent enquiry by the Minister for Coordination of Defence into our future defence programmes, he had submitted a scheme 'K', which was below the minimum scheme considered necessary by the Air Staff for security. The Cabinet had decided that it was more than we could afford to undertake.

Winston S. Churchill to Unity Mitford

(Churchill papers: 2/328)

12 March 1938

There can be no doubt that a fair plebiscite would have shown that a large majority of the people of Austria loathe the idea of coming under Nazi rule. It was because Herr Hitler feared the free expression of opinion that we are compelled to witness the present dastardly outrage.[1]

[1] On 9 March 1938, speaking at Innsbruck, Schuschnigg had announced that he would hold a plebiscite on March 13, on the question of whether or not the Austrians wanted an independent Austria. As this gave the Germans no time to organize their influence against continuing independence, the Austrian Nazis had been instructed to begin anti-plebiscite demonstrations, and general disorder throughout Austria, and on the morning of March 11 the Austrian Minister of the Interior, General Glaise von Horstenau, brought to Schuschnigg, from Berlin, an ultimatum demanding the cancellation of the plebiscite. That same afternoon von Horstenau and the Minister of Security, Artur Seyss-Inquart insisted on either immediate postponement, or a German invasion, by some 200,000 German troops, already massed on the frontier. That evening Schuschnigg accepted the ultimatum (half an hour before it was due to expire), and broadcast to his nation the facts of the day's events. That same night, German troops crossed into Austria.

Wing-Commander Anderson: telephone message for Winston S. Churchill

(Churchill papers: 9/129)

13 March 1938

He has been looking through both the White Paper and the Air Estimates and has found some rather misleading language.

Page 7, paragraphs 23 and 24 of the White Paper.

The word 'pilots' is used in connection with them being trained for RAF volunteer reserve. The true use of the word means 'fit to carry out work of applied flying ie bombing, gunnery, wireless etc etc.' These men have not done all this, and therefore are not fully trained. On the face of it one would think there were a fine lot of pilots ready.

Page 7, paragraph 22.

This says that there are now 11 flying training schools instead of 4, and gives the impression that all this has been done during the last year. But it actually was done 3 years ago and is not a new thing.

Confirming his note to you the other day by telephone:—

He has in his own office a letter, replying to his demand for wireless operators of which he is short, saying that he cannot have them, as the service is already deficient of 600 wireless operators. This he thinks is important, as it shows a lack of foresight. What is the good of training pilots, making aircraft etc and being deficient of an important part? The training should embrace *all* branches at the same time, to make a coherent whole.

He is at home all day should you wish to speak to him.

Page 11 of Air Estimates.

This deals with Cranwell and says it is being extended to its full capacity. This is not true. It is only taking in 25 University entrants, for instance, and any of these could supply very large numbers.

His comment on both White Paper and Air Estimates is that they both read well until one digs beneath the fine language.

VP

Neville Chamberlain to Winston S. Churchill

(*Churchill papers: 2/336*)

13 March 1938

My dear Winston,

I write to thank you for your letter enclosing your Secret notes on Air questions, which was handed to me last night.

Yours sincerely,
N. Chamberlain

H. Beckett-Overy[1] to Winston S. Churchill

(*Churchill papers: 2/328*)

14 March 1938

My dear Mr Churchill,

I trust you will not think I am presumptuous in writing to you and will forget our professional relations! I have only two real interests in my life—the first my job, the second politics. One of the nights of my life was that first night of the 1906 elections when largely owing to your work the Liberals swept Lancashire. I was in the old Automobile Club before it was the RAC and the only Liberal there!! I was brought up a Liberal in one of the last feudal strongholds of Sussex where we were ostracised though my father was by far the most cultured man in the village! You will understand that I can never be other than a Liberal. The Labour Party with its insularity and narrowness cannot appeal to me nor does it to thousands and hundreds of thousands like me.

I have been impressed these last few weeks by the number of people of conservative leanings—and thought who are profoundly disgusted with the present government and who feel you voice their dissatisfaction. I believe that throughout the land there is a large body probably a majority who favour at least collective security with our rearmament. To all of us the attitude of the Prime Minister is contrary to our best instincts. To tell us he has urged other nations not to look to the League and to turn instead to Great Britain for help seems the apotheosis of self interest.

I lunched with a member of one of the smaller Embassies today and he said. 'It is 1914—again—what is Great Britain going to do!!' We wonder

---

[1] Harry Beckett-Overy, 1875–1950. Graduated from Edinburgh University, 1902. Fellow of the Royal College of Surgeons, 1904; MD, 1906. Pathologist at the Metropolitan Hospital, London, 1903; later assistant surgeon at the Kensington General Hospital. Practised as a gynaecological surgeon in Kensington. Medical Officer in charge of the Londonderry House hospital for officers in Park Lane, 1914–18. Honorary Secretary of the British Gynaecologist Society, and of its successor, the obstetrics and gynaecology section of Royal Society of Medicine. In 1927 he published an article on varicose veins in the Franco-British Medical Review.

whether the country would not follow a real lead for the League, a national service suited to us, and armaments necessary (with the prevention of larger profits!!).

Believe me,

Yours sincerely and admiringly,

H. Beckett-Overy

Cabinet minutes

(Cabinet papers: 23/92)

14 March 1938

The Chancellor of the Duchy of Lancaster[1] urged that it was as important for the Cabinet to consider the views of the 'Right' as well as of the 'Left' in Parliament. He himself had had exceptional opportunities for knowing Mr Winston Churchill's views. Since joining the Cabinet and having access to Cabinet documents, he was deeply concerned at our inability to fulfil the pledges of the late Prime Minister. He could see the reason for the difficulties, but the Government were going to be faced with a strong demand. Even the News Chronicle urged that we should press on with rearmament.[2]

Harold Nicolson: diary

(Nicolson papers)

14 March 1938

Chamberlain makes a dry statement threatening a double rearmament effort but giving little indication of real policy. The Opposition behave beautifully and do not hoot or scream. There is a sense of real national crisis. Winston makes the speech of his life in favour of the League.[3]

[1] Lord Winterton, who had entered the Government as Chancellor of the Duchy of Lancaster in May 1937 (he had been granted Cabinet rank on 11 March 1938).

[2] The Chairman of the *News Chronicle*, Sir Walter Layton, was a member of Churchill's 'Focus' Group. See also the *News Chronicle* leading article of 16 March 1938, quoted on page 940, note 1.

[3] Speaking in the House of Commons on 14 March 1938, Churchill advocated 'a solemn treaty for mutual defence against aggression', organized by Britain and France, 'in what you may call a Grand Alliance', and he added: '. . . if they had their Staff arrangements concerted; if all this rested, as it can honourably rest, upon the Covenant of the League of Nations, in pursuance of all the purposes and ideals of the League of Nations; if that were sustained, as it would be, by the moral sense of the world; and if it were done in the year 1938—and, believe me, it may be the last chance there will be for doing it—then I say that you might even now arrest this approaching war'. Churchill ended with a solemn warning, telling the House of Commons: 'Before we cast away this hope, this cause and this plan, which I do not at all disguise has an element of risk, let those who wish to reject it ponder well and earnestly upon what will happen to us if, when all else has been thrown to the wolves, we are left to face our fate alone.'

M. J. Creswell[1] to Winston S. Churchill

(Churchill papers: 2/307)

15 March 1938   St James' Club

Dear Mr Churchill,

I have recently been at the Embassy in Berlin—for two and a half years—and am now, since the beginning of this month, in the Southern Dept of the FO (Austria and Czechoslovakia).

Before going to Berlin, though I never had the honour to meet you personally, I became familiar with your views when I was working under Wigram on the question of the German Air Force, and if I may say so I much admired your speeches on that subject.

When listening to your speech yesterday from the gallery I noticed a remark you made about the strength of the German Army[2] which is at variance with most of the information I have on the subject, and the purpose of this letter is to ask you if you would be good enough to receive me (some evening after 7 pm) to enable me to discuss this point with you.

I would be grateful if your Secretary would send me a reply to this address and not to the Foreign Office.[3]

Yours sincerely,
M. J. Creswell

[1] Michael Justin Creswell, 1909–   . Educated at Rugby and New College, Oxford. Served in the Foreign Office, 1933–5; 3rd Secretary, Berlin, 1935–8; 2nd Secretary, Madrid, 1939–44; Athens, 1944. Counsellor, Teheran, 1947–9; Singapore, 1949–51. Minister to Cairo, 1951–4. Ambassador to Finland, 1954–8. Senior Civilian Instructor, Imperial Defence College, 1958–60. Knighted, 1960. Ambassador to Yugoslavia, 1960–4. Ambassador to the Argentine, 1964–9. On 8 June 1935 Sir Robert Vansittart wrote of how Creswell 'has greatly distinguished himself during his time in the FO by his papers on aviation, and is himself a very competent aviator'.

[2] On 14 March 1938, during a Foreign Affairs (Austria) debate, Churchill asked: 'Where are we going to be two years hence, for instance, when the German Army will certainly be much larger than the French Army, and when all the small nations will have fled from Geneva to pay homage to the ever waxing power of the Nazi system, and to make the best terms they can for themselves?'

[3] Churchill saw Michael Creswell at Morpeth Mansions, where they discussed the relative strengths of the French and German armies, and their potential. Creswell had returned from Berlin three weeks before, on the day after Eden's resignation. From the knowledge he had acquired in Germany, Creswell was convinced that the German army would be superior to the French army in much less than the two years mentioned by Churchill in the debate. Sir Michael Creswell recalls: 'I was rather taken aback by what he had said in the House. I thought it was a very dangerous assumption. My feeling was that he was being too optimistic, because the Germans already had a very powerful military instrument. They had made such progress, that they were *already* a superior instrument of war to the French: a brand new army, the mechanized equipment. It was really a question of feel. I didn't have any figures to quote. He didn't like this at all. I think he thought I was tarred with the brush of Nevile Henderson; that I was therefore a suspect person. I was speaking very much out of turn. I was simply on the Austrian desk at the Foreign Office, dealing with refugees' (*conversation with the author, 14 January 1982*).

Irene Noel-Baker[1] to Winston S. Churchill

(*Churchill papers: 2/328*)

16 March 1938   In the Simplon Express to
                                           Athens.

My dear Winston Churchill,

Your speech on Monday in the House was quite magnificent and is the one hopeful thing that has happened in these last disastrous days.[2] I feel that I must write to thank you for it & to beg you—as *thousands* of men and women now want to beg you—to take up the fight for the League & collective security with *all* the great intelligence and marvellous compelling force that you can give to it. Why must we leave all initiative and courage to the two madmen of Europe?

You, Ld Bd,[3] Eden, Archie Sinclair, Attlee, Alexander,[4] my Philip & Lloyd George are a band of warriors in the House & in the country who surely ought to beat that miserable middle class business man with no scrap of imagination, who to our immense misfortune is now Prime Minister of Great Britain.

Wherever I go it is the same story—despair & amazement among the people of every country at the complete feebleness of British policy. And as you say this is our last chance, & the people everywhere know it & are passionately longing for us to act. Ask Philip to tell you of my long talk with the conductor on my part of this train—most indicative at this moment & all the conductors—waiters on the train think as he does he tells me.

For God's sake lead now and put an end to this most ghastly nightmare in which we are all living.

Most sincerely yours,
Irene Noel Baker

I *do* hope you agreed to speak in Paris, or if you haven't, you *will*.

[1] Irene Noel, only daughter of Frank Noel, a British landowner of Achmetaga, Greece. She married Philip Baker in 1915, when they both took the surname of Noel-Baker. Her husband was a Labour MP 1929–31 and 1936–70; their son Francis Noel-Baker was a Labour MP from 1945–69. She died in 1956.

[2] Speaking in the debate of 15 March 1938, and supporting Robert Boothby's appeal for an Anglo-French 'common cause', Churchill declared: 'Not so lightly will the two great Liberal democracies of the West be challenged, and not so easily, if challenged, will they be subjugated.'

[3] Lord Baldwin.

[4] Albert Victor Alexander, 1885–1965. Educated at an elementary school, and technical classes, in Bristol. Labour (Co-operative) MP for Hillsborough, 1922–31 and 1935–50. Parliamentary Secretary, Board of Trade, 1924. First Lord of the Admiralty in Ramsay MacDonald's second Labour Government, 1929–31; in Churchill's war-time Coalition Government, 1940–5; and in Attlee's Labour Government, 1945–6. Member of the Cabinet Delegation to India, 1946. Minister of Defence, 1947–50. Created Viscount, 1950. Chancellor of the Duchy of Lancaster, 1950–1. Leader of the Labour Peers in the House of Lords, 1955–65. Created Earl, 1963. Knight of the Garter, 1964.

Lord Beaverbrook to Winston S. Churchill

(*Churchill papers: 2/328*)

16 March 1938

My dear Winston,

I send you a letter from A. J. Cummings to me. It is the origin of the leader in the News Chronicle this morning.[1]

Cummings dined with me last night. He is very strong and very firm in his views, and appears to have become one of your followers.

He will follow you anywhere, if only you will say now that you will fight for Czecho-Slovakia.

Yours ever,
Max

Harold Nicolson: diary

(*Nicolson papers*)

16 March 1938

. . . go to Pratt's with Winston Churchill, Randolph and R. Boothby. Winston doesn't fully agree with us about Spain but mainly because of his personal friendship with Spanish Grandees. He admits however that the strategic argument is almost unanswerable and he understands that Hore-Belisha has become converted to it and has rather shaken the Cabinet.

He says that never has any man inherited a more ghastly situation than has Neville Chamberlain and he places the blame wholly upon Mr Baldwin. He also says that in his long experience he has never known a Conservative Party composed of so many blind and obstinate men. He says that he will wait for a day or two in the hope that the negotiations which are now going on between Chamberlain, Attlee and Sinclair for a formula of policy which will command the assent of the whole House have either failed or come to fruition. But if no clear statement is issued between now and Wednesday next he will himself refuse the Whip and take some fifty people with him. This

---

[1] On 16 March 1938 a *News Chronicle* leader, entitled 'Act Now', stated: 'Mr Churchill demanded that effect should be given to his policy now, in the year 1938, which might be the last chance. He pertinently asked why we should assume that time is on our side. No empty peroration, but a "practical and realistic conception", closed Mr Churchill's speech. He wants to see a number of States assembled around Great Britain and France in a solemn treaty for mutual defence against aggression. He wants their forces marshalled and their staff arrangements co-ordinated. We hope the Government will give heed to Mr Churchill's advice. It contains risks. The alternative, as Mr Churchill warned the Government, is that we may be left to face our fate alone.'

threat should in itself suffice to determine the Government. He says that the situation is worse than in 1914. 'We stand to lose everything by failing to take strong action. Yet if we take strong action, London will be a shambles after half-an-hour.'

Winston S. Churchill to Clement Attlee

(*Churchill papers: 2/328*)

17 March 1938

My dear Attlee,

Bob Cecil told me that he had been asking you to join a Party Committee sponsoring a campaign for the Covenant of the League, and rearmament, which I and some other members of our Focus contemplate in the near future unless the decision of the Government is satisfactory. He said you had some doubts about whether this was advantageous. For myself I think that if we do decide to have a Committee it would be better to confine it to un-official members of your party, as otherwise it would look as if there was a significance quite beyond anything which our educative campaign implies. Probably moreover we shall run it under the L of N Union and New Commonwealth.

Helen Wedgwood[1] to her father

(*Pease papers*)

17 March 1938

For God's sake can't you shift Chamberlain. Couldn't Sinclair & Attlee tell Churchill their parties would support him if he will take the premiership? We haven't a hope of a Labour Govt, even if we could force an election, which we can't. But Churchill with the decent Tories & our support could force one, & could get the country's support. *Anything* is better than drifting into war with that miserable wobbler Chamberlain. Churchill may be a reactionary in most ways, but he is sound about foreign affairs, & his speeches are a joy to read.[2]

[1] Helen Bowen Wedgwood, 1895–   . Eldest daughter of Josiah Wedgwood. Educated at Newnham College, Cambridge. In 1920 she married Michael Pease, OBE (who died in 1966), and in 1925 she became a Justice of the Peace.

[2] On 17 March 1938 Oliver Harvey, Halifax's Principal Private Secretary (and formerly Anthony Eden's) wrote in his diary: 'I would like to see Winston as Air Minister or Minister of Co-ordination—but definitely not PM; I would rather see AE as Foreign Secretary than PM at this stage provided always he had his hands free and the loyal support of a PM—but who is to be PM?' (*Harvey of Tasbrugh papers*).

Harold Nicolson: diary

(*Nicolson papers*)

17 March 1938

I confer with Winston Churchill and Boothby as to the Resolution to be put to our Bankers Meeting later. We agree on the text assuring the Government full support 'in any measure they may think fit to resist aggression on the part of the Nazi Powers'. We then go down to the City and have a meeting of some 300 bankers. Edgar Mowrer[1] and Jacques Kayser[2] (Vice Chairman of the Radical Socialist party) fly across from Paris and assist us in our efforts. We three speak on Spain and Boothby ends up with the more general appeal. We then put it to the vote and to our astonishment the motion is carried with only two against it . . .

Dine with Violet Bonham Carter there and some of the Liberals. A long talk afterwards with Winston Churchill who is in tremendous form. I have never heard him so witty or so brilliant, and yet when I tried afterwards to remember what he had said I found that his remarks, if written down, would look quite trivial. It is more his tremendous radiating personality and his immense courage. There we were in the Smoking Room terrified and depressed by the alternatives between a disastrous war and the surrender of our independence. And this old battlehorse remains determined and im-

---

[1] Edgar Ansel Mowrer, 1892–1977. Born in Illinois. Educated at the University of Chicago and the Sorbonne. A war reporter for the *Chicago Daily News*, France and Italy, 1914–18; Rome correspondent in the 1920s; Berlin correspondent in the 1930s; Paris correspondent until June 1940. Awarded the Pullitzer Prize, 1932. Deputy Director of the Office of Facts and Figures (later called the Office of War Information), Washington, 1942–3. American Editor, *Western World Magazine*, 1957–60. His publications included *Immortal Italy* (1923), *Germany Puts the Clock Back* (1932), *Mowrer in China* (1938), *Global War* (1942), *The Nightmare of American Foreign Policy* (1948), *A Good Time to be Alive* (1959) and *Triumph and Turmoil: A Personal History of Our Time* (1968).

[2] Jacques Kayser, 1900–   . A journalist, writing in the Left and Left Centre press. He published his first book, a life of Lafayette, in 1928, and a book on the Dreyfus Affair in 1931. Vice-President of the Socialist Radical Party. Sir Eric Phipps wrote (in his 'Report on Leading Personalities in France', July 1939, enclosure to Lord Halifax of 13 July 1939): 'Possesses very sound judgment and great political sense. Reliable and well-disposed towards Great Britain. Most pleasant to meet. Visited the United States in 1937. Specialises in foreign affairs. Has an American wife. Is liked and trusted, and expected to have a future if he enters the Chamber. Attached to the Cabinet of M. Daladier since April 1938' (*Vansittart papers*). After the war he published more books, including *One Week's News* (a comparative study of 17 major daily newspapers for a 7 day period), 1953; a book on the Provincial Press in the Third Republic, 1958; *From Kronstadt to Kruschev* 1962; a book on the great struggles of French Radicalism, 1820–1901, 1962; and a study of French daily newspapers, 1963. On 26 April 1933 Spears had written to Kayser, after a talk with Churchill, that in Churchill's view 'France would be well advised to take advantage of the present position to demand that Germany should respect all her treaty obligations and should take whatever steps are best calculated to impose treaty obligations upon her. He thinks that Germany would recognize a strong lead and submit. . . . In Mr Churchill's view England would today stand aside and not be hostile' (*Spears papers*).

perturbable. Someone comes up to us and says to Winston: 'isn't this situation absolutely ghastly?' Winston takes a long puff at his cigar, smiles and
answers: 'myself I always find that occasions which demand the display of
great moral and physical courage are very invigorating occasions'. Somebody else said that Franco would be strong enough to turn out the Germans
and Italians. 'You are talking,' said Winston, 'of something which has no
existence—as of a chicken that barks.'

Winston S. Churchill to Arthur J. Cummings

(*Churchill papers: 2/328*)

18 March 1938

Lord Beaverbrook allowed me to see your letter to him about me. I value
very much the spontaneous agreement of so many Liberals on the views I
have been expressing on foreign policy, and especially yours. I believe it
should still be possible by pursuing the kind of policy I have outlined in the
Evening Standard of today,[1] to arrest the onward march of the Dictators
and prevent a war.

Once more thanking you,

Believe me,

Sir Henry Strakosch: memorandum on British rearmament

(*Churchill papers: 2/336*)

18 March 1938

There can be no doubt that the international situation is one of great
gravity and danger for this country and the Empire, and that, to meet that

---

[1] In his article 'The Austrian Eye-Opener' in the *Evening Standard* of 18 March 1938,
Churchill argued: '. . . if concerted diplomatic action is now taken upon the basis of active
rearmament, it ought to be possible to accumulate a mass of deterrents against further acts
of aggression. These deterrents must then be assembled upon the basis of the Covenant of the
League of Nations and must be in strict harmony with the principles and ideals of the League.
It must be made plain that any combination of Powers, who may find themselves prepared to
act as special mandatories of the League, will carry their action as far as may be necessary to
deter or, failing that, to resist, further instances of unprovoked aggression. In such a policy
Mr Chamberlain and his Government would have behind them the united support of all
parties in Great Britain, and by proceeding on the basis of the Covenant they might confidently expect the broad concurrence of the Dominions, over whose individual decisions the
Mother Country has, of course, no control. The urgency of the undertaking arises from the
fact that the hope of producing peace by concerted action is greater in 1938 than it would be
in 1939, and far greater than in 1940. To continue delaying from month to month while the
degeneration of European morale proceeds apace, would seem to make war certain at a
later date.'

danger, a substantial speed-up, as well as an extension of our armaments programme, has become an urgent necessity.

The absorption of Austria—with a population of about 6½ million people—into the German Reich means a corresponding increase of man-power for the Reich, thus not only increasing its fighting forces, but its capacity to increase its armaments production. There are, in the old Austria, extensive and efficient armaments plants, and iron ore deposits which may be ranked as some of the finest in Europe. In addition, Austria is rich in timber, and is therefore able to produce all the many products, including explosives, in which cellulose is required.

In order to speed up and increase our own armaments production, ordinary economic production will undoubtedly have to be subordinated to the vitally important task of increasing our means of defence. Such a re-arrangement of our productive forces, however, is a slow process, and, as time is of the very essence in the present situation, a reorientation in the matter of armaments production seems to me indispensable.

The most effective means by which a speeding-up and extension of our armaments can be attained is to acquire abroad not only a large part of those armaments, but also the equipment for the production of armaments within this country. No country is better able to furnish such additional requirements than the United States of America, and this is particularly true of aeroplanes, machine guns, as well as jigs and machine tools. It is able to do so owing to the recent very substantial recession of its own economic activity. America has at present standing idle a very substantial proportion of its industrial equipment. At this stage, therefore, America would no doubt welcome any orders that we might place with them, and would be able to make deliveries at far shorter notice than we could hope to produce the same equipment in this country. It is perhaps unnecessary to add that America is producing aeroplanes of a quality which compares favourably with that of aeroplanes produced in any other country.

America has no doubt already produced, or has in course of production, a substantial number of planes for military purposes on behalf of the United States Government, and it is perhaps not unreasonable to anticipate that, having regard to the dangerous European situation, that Government would be ready to cede to us planes and equipment which are at present in the last stages of production. This is a process which need not cause any political difficulties, as it is probably a departmental matter under the control of the Administration, and would thus not necessitate an Act, or even the knowledge, of Congress.

The objection may be raised that a policy of this kind would weigh heavily on our Balance of Payments. That objection is not well-founded.

If we divert plant, equipment and man-power from the production of ordinary economic goods to armaments production, we shall undoubtedly have to reduce our export of ordinary commercial goods. If the value of this reduction in our ordinary exports is as great as our expenditure on the purchase of armaments abroad, the position of our balance of payments clearly remains unaltered. But, even if our expenditure on armaments abroad should be greater, and if thus our Balance of Payments should be worsened to that extent, we need feel no anxiety, for our foreign investments are huge, and a good part of those foreign investments is in the form of readily realisable securities.

When considering the question of the Balance of Payments, it should be remembered that we must not look narrowly at the Balance of Payments of the United Kingdom. What we have to look at is the Balance of Payments of the British Empire as a whole, for the currency systems of the Dominions and Colonies are closely linked to our own, and will no doubt remain so, particularly in times of stress such as we are facing at the present time.

It is commonly overlooked that, during the last two years, the adverse Balance of Payments of this country has been largely offset by the credit balance of the Overseas parts of the Empire. Whereas, in 1936 and 1937, this country had, on the average, a debit balance of approximately £35 millions per annum, the Overseas parts of the Empire had, on the average, a credit balance of £18 millions per annum. In the period 1930 to 1932, when the pressure on our Exchange was heavy, a debit balance of £43 millions per annum for the United Kingdom was not only counter-balanced by a credit balance in the rest of the Empire, but, on the contrary, was topped by an additional debit balance of as much as £100 millions per annum, so that, in the present period, an average debit balance of some £17 millions per annum for the total British Empire compares favourably with the £143 millions per annum in 1930/32. In the current year, a debit balance in the United Kingdom may once more be offset, to a considerable extent, by a credit balance in the rest of the Empire.

There is an aspect of a psychological character which the acquisition of war material in the United States of America would create which seems to me to be of great importance in the present situation of tension and danger. It is a usual occurrence in business life that the regular flow of orders creates a sympathetic understanding of the interests of the customer. This sympathy is not restricted to the entrepreneur class, but probably extends to all classes dependent for their livelihood on the industries concerned. Sentiments of this kind were engendered in the United States of America in respect of the United Kingdom in 1914/16, and I believe it to be true that similar sentiments have been engendered in favour of Germany in countries of the

Danubian Basin in spite of the intense political suspicions of Germany in this part of Central Europe. The value of an increased sympathetic understanding by America of the British Empire's present needs might prove ample compensation for the possible worsening of the Empire's Balance of Payments due to purchases of arms and equipment in that country.

Winston S. Churchill to Sir Eric Phipps

(*Churchill papers: 2/328*)

18 March 1938
Personal

I send you this letter to apologise for my change of plan and to beg of you to tell Charles[1] how sorry I am to have inconvenienced him.

I have some hopes that we shall have declarations of greater solidarity with France from the Government next week, and I think it would be better for me to talk with my French friends after the Government policy has been defined. I am greatly obliged to you for the trouble you have taken, and I beg of you to convey to Reynaud and Daladier my excuses.

I have had a message from a round-about source from Paul-Boncour[2] saying he hoped to see me when I came to Paris. Perhaps you will be so kind as to tell him privately of my change of plan. I should like to come over on Friday next the 25th, arriving in time for dinner and returning on Monday morning. Would this be convenient? I beg you not to hesitate to say.

There is a M. Kayser[3] who flew over here to address a meeting in the City, and is I believe influential. He has expressed a great desire to see me, and I might perhaps meet him some time on one of the afternoons.

Once more thanking you,

[1] Sir Charles Mendl, Press Attaché at the British Embassy in Paris (see page 349, note 2).
[2] Joseph Paul-Boncour, 1873–1972. A barrister. Private Secretary to the Prime Minister (Waldeck-Rousseau), 1900–2 and to the Minister of Labour (Viviani), 1906–9. Republican (independent) Socialist deputy for Blois. Minister of Labour, 1911. On active service, 1914–18 (Battalion commander, twice decorated). A member of the French delegation to the League of Nations in the 1920s, devoted to the cause of the League. A member of the League Council, 1924–7. President of the Foreign Affairs Committee of the Chamber of Deputies, 1927. Senator, 1931. Minister of War, 3 June to 17 December 1932. Prime Minister from 18 December 1932 to 30 January 1933. Foreign Minister 18 December 1932 to 30 January 1933 and 13 March to 9 April 1938 (when he was succeeded by Georges Bonnet). French delegate to the first United Nations Assembly in London after the Second World War.
[3] Jacques Kayser (see page 942, note 2).

Lord Halifax:[1] *Cabinet memorandum*

(*Cabinet papers: 27/623*)

18 March 1938

. . . There are, in the main, three courses open to us:

The grand alliance.

This proposal has been described in the following terms by Mr Winston Churchill in the House of Commons on March 14th:—

'If a number of States were assembled round Great Britain and France in a solemn treaty for mutual defence against aggression; if they had their forces marshalled in what you may call a grand alliance; if they had their staff arrangements concerted; if all this rested, as it can honourably rest, on the Covenant of the League of Nations; if that were sustained, as it would be, by the moral sense of the world; and if it were done in the year 1938—and, believe me, it may be the last chance there will be for doing it—then I say that you might even now arrest this approaching war.'[2]

This is an attractive proposal, and there is a good deal that might be said both for and against it: but there is one decisive objection against it for our present purposes.

In order to achieve it, it would be necessary to draw up a formal instrument in Treaty form, and this would be a long and complicated matter. If any undertaking is to be given by us which will help to save the situation in Central Europe, this must be done without undue delay. The long and difficult negotiations which would be necessary to conclude the Grand Alliance would afford both a provocation and an opportunity to Germany to dispose of Czechoslovakia before the grand alliance had been organised.[3]

[1] Edward Frederick Lindley Wood, 1881–1959. Educated at Eton and Christ Church, Oxford. Conservative MP for Ripon, 1910–25. Parliamentary Under-Secretary of State for the Colonies, 1921–2. President of the Board of Education, 1922–4. Minister of Agriculture, 1924–5. Created Baron Irwin, 1925. Viceroy of India, 1926–31. President of the Board of Education, 1931–4. Succeeded his father as 3rd Viscount Halifax, 1934. Secretary of State for War, 1935. Lord Privy Seal, 1935–7. Lord President of the Council, 1937–8. Foreign Secretary, 1938–40. Ambassador in Washington, 1941–6. Order of Merit, 1946. One of his three sons was killed in action in Egypt in October 1942.

[2] In his article in the *Evening Standard* of 18 March 1938, Churchill wrote that if the smaller State of Europe were unwilling to join Britain and France 'for special action, not excluding armed resistance, under the Covenant of the League . . . then Nazi domination over the greater part of Europe is inevitable at no distant date. Alone, Great Britain and France cannot save Europe and avert war. If the larger hope fails through the weakness of the States of Second rank, a mutually defensive role will alone be open to France and Britain. With their backs to the ocean and the command of the seas, they will be the heavily armed spectators of the horrible events and indefinite tyranny which will involve all countries from the Baltic to the Black Sea, and after that Holland and Belgium and the Scandinavian countries.'

[3] The two other courses which Halifax outlined were first 'a new commitment to France', as a first step to 'some more comprehensive arrangement', to which it would be possible for

Cabinet Committee on Foreign Policy: minutes

(Cabinet papers: 27/623)

18 March 1938
4 pm
Secret

THE SECRETARY OF STATE FOR FOREIGN AFFAIRS[1] wondered what the French General Staff thought of the prospects of successful offensive operations to relieve Czechoslovakia. The proposition must be a most formidable and dangerous one. France was admittedly helpless in the Air. Germany was in a strong position to hold up any advance by land. No doubt the French authorities would face up to the facts but when he had put the difficulties to M Corbin[2] the latter had replied to the effect that these were matters which could profitably be discussed with us. Mr Winston Churchill had a plan under which the French Army was to act on the defensive behind the Maginot Line and there detain large German forces while Czechoslovakia engaged Germany's remaining forces. This seemed to have no relation to the realities of the situation.[3]

'Powers other than the original parties to accede to', if they wished. Halifax's memorandum ended: 'His Majesty's Minister in Prague has suggested in a recent telegram that "having regard to her geographical situation her history and the racial divisions of her population, Czechoslovakia's present political position is not permanently tenable", and for that reason he submits that "His Majesty's Government are entitled to decline the risk of involving Great Britain in a fresh war in order to shore up the present position if it is one which seems to us fundamentally unsound". If, however, we are prepared to go to great lengths in bringing the Czechoslovak Government to agree to measures which will settle the Sudeten question in conformity with the realities of the situation, unpleasant as those realities may be, then I would not say that we should not be justified in taking whatever risk there might be in trying to deter Germany from making war on Czechoslovakia to enforce a solution of the question, since in that event Germany would have less reason to risk the hazards of war in order to obtain what she could have some hope of obtaining by peaceful negotiation' (*Cabinet papers: 27/623*).

[1] Lord Halifax.

[2] The French Ambassador (see page 297, note 1).

[3] At this same meeting of the Cabinet's Foreign Policy Committee on 18 March 1938, Inskip told his colleagues that in his view Czechoslovakia was 'an unstable unit in Central Europe', and that 'he could see no reason why we should take any steps to maintain such a unit in being'. According to Sir John Simon, 'Czechoslovakia was a modern and very artificial creation with no real roots in the past'. Neville Chamberlain asked his colleagues 'whether it would not be possible to make some arrangement which would prove more acceptable to Germany', while Lord Halifax warned his colleagues that 'the more closely we associated ourselves with France and Russia the more we produced on German minds the impression that we were plotting to encircle Germany'. Halifax added that 'He (Lord Halifax) distinguished in his own mind between Germany's racial efforts, which no one could question, and a lust for conquest on a Napoleonic scale which he himself did not credit.' Halifax then set out for his colleagues his view of what British policy should be: 'We should try to persuade France and Czechoslovakia that the best course would be for the latter to make the best terms she could with Germany while there was yet time and that we would use any influence we might

David Hindley-Smith[1] to Winston S. Churchill

(*Churchill papers: 2/328*)

18 March 1938   Vienna

Dear Mr Churchill,

'The Times' still reaches me. It gives the impression that here in Vienna, as in the rest of what was recently Austria, an overwhelming majority enthusiastically support the new regime. To anyone of English upbringing and outlook who knows the Viennese at all well this idea must seem like heaping insult on injury.

The Viennese are a sentimental intensely patriotic people who love liberty quite as much as we do and whose cultured outlook is very like our own. All my many friends in this city are in the depths of despair. The cultural life of the city must die for it is these people—together with the Embassies and the Jews—who upheld it.

Many hundred lorry-loads of NS[2] supporters from Graz and Linz were brought into Vienna to make it a hell hot enough to hold the Führer—and everyone knows what a noise University students can make.

It avails nothing to speak of the many sickening incidents. A family of six Jews have just shot themselves, a few houses down the street. They are well out of it. Yesterday morning I saw two well-dressed women forced to their knees to scrub out a 'Heil Schuschnigg!' on the pavement. But these things seem to be all part of the Totalitarian's stock in trade.[3]

Yours sincerely,
David Hindley-Smith

PS. Letters to me are opened.

---

have with Germany to induce her to take up a reasonable attitude. If in the result a satisfactory solution of the Sudeten problem was reached we might offer in that event to join with Germany in guaranteeing Czechoslovakia's independence.' The other Cabinet Ministers present at this meeting were Sir Samuel Hoare, Malcolm MacDonald, Lord Hailsham, William Ormsby-Gore and Oliver Stanley. R. A. Butler was also present (*Cabinet papers: 27/623*).

[1] David Dury Hindley-Smith, 1916–   . Educated at Uppingham and King's College, Cambridge. Studied in Paris and Vienna, 1937–8. Passed the Diplomatic Service examination, 1939. On active service, 1939–45; Liason Officer to General Leclerc, 1942 and to General de Gaulle's first administration, 1944. Acting Colonel, 1944. Registrar, Dental Board of the UK (later the General Dental Council), since 1947. Executive Chairman, National Association of Youth Clubs, 1970–4. CBE, 1972.

[2] NS = National Socialist (or Nazi) Party.

[3] Churchill sent this letter to Geoffrey Dawson on 22 March 1938, with the covering note: 'This letter reached me from a man I know, and I thought you would like to see it. Please let me have it back again.' For Dawson's reply, see page 956.

Winston S. Churchill: notes on his financial difficulties

(Churchill papers: 1/328)

19 March 1938

Against the foregoing,[1] the following assets can, if desired, be immediately produced:—

Irish ground rents, not readily marketable, but valued at . .	£7,500
Cash	2,500
Life policy for	6,000

In addition the present holder, apart from the regular literary contracts on which he lives, has a contract for a book[2] on which some progress has been made, deliverable on December 31, 1939 for £15,000. He could accomplish this task within the specified time by laying everything aside; but how is he to do this while events run at this pitch, still less if he should be required to devote his whole energies to public work.

It is suggested that the account should be taken over from Vickers da Costa and be held for, say three years, with full discretion to sell or vary holdings at any time, but on the basis that no risk of greater liability to the present holder arises, thus removing altogether the speculative element.

Interest amounting to about £800 a year on the whole account will of course be paid.

Winston S. Churchill to Brendan Bracken

(Churchill papers: 1/328)

19 March 1938

My dear Brendan,

I was profoundly touched and relieved by what you told me last night of the kindness of our friend.[3]

If it were not for public affairs and my evident duty I shd be able to manage all right. But it is unsuitable as well as harassing to have to watch an account

---

[1] The United States' stocks which had fallen had cost Churchill £18,162.1.10. When this note was written, their value had dropped to £5,692, a loss to Churchill of over £12,000. By 10 October 1938 they had recovered more than £3,300 *(Churchill papers: 1/328)*. In September 1981 the equivalent value of Churchill's loss of £12,000 was in excess of £200,000.

[2] The History of the English-Speaking Peoples.

[3] Sir Henry Strakosch, who had agreed to cover all Churchill's share losses, and to purchase his United States stocks at the price he had paid for them (see page 959).

from day to day when one's mind ought to be concentrated upon the great world issues now at stake. I shd indeed be grateful if I cd be liberated during these next few critical years from this particular worry, wh descended upon me so unexpectedly; to the chance of which I shall certainly never expose myself again. I cannot tell you what a relief it would be if I could put it out of my mind; and take the large decisions wh perhaps may be required of me without this distraction and anxiety.

I send you a short note which explains the position; and perhaps you will show this to our friend.

Yours always,
WSC

Covering note:—

My dear B,
    Enclosed is a letter wh you can show to our friend. This is only to tell *you* that as Hitler said to Mussolini, on a recent and less worthy occasion 'I shall never forget' this inestimable service.[1]

Sir Eric Phipps to Winston S. Churchill

(*Churchill papers: 2/328*)

19 March 1938
British Embassy,
Paris

My dear Churchill,
    Many thanks for your letter.
    All is well and the change of plan is no inconvenience whatever.
    On Friday night I have Herriot[2] to dinner: on Saturday Mendl has

---

[1] In a telegram to Mussolini on 13 March 1938, Hitler thanked him for not having moved across the Brenner Pass when German troops entered Austria. The telegram read 'I shall never forget this.' Two days earlier Hitler had written to Mussolini, in explanation of the annexation of Austria: 'Whatever may be the consequences of recent events, I have marked a clear German frontier towards France and now I trace another, equally clear, towards Italy. It is the Brenner. This decision will never be either questioned or violated. This decision I have not taken in the year 1938 but immediately after the close of the Great War, and I have never made any secret of that decision.' German troops crossed the French frontier in May 1940, and marched across the Brenner into Italy in July 1943 (immediately after the collapse of Mussolini's power).

[2] Edouard Herriot, 1872–1957. Mayor of Lyons, 1905–40. Senator, 1912–19. Minister of Public Works, 1916–17. President of the Radical Party, 1919–40; of the Socialist-Radical Party, 1945–57. Deputy, 1919–40. Prime Minister, June 1924–April 1925 and July 1926. Held numerous Ministerial posts, 1926–36. President of the Chamber, 1936–40. Arrested by the Vichy Government, 1940. Interned near Berlin, 1944–5; liberated by Soviet troops. President of the National Assembly, 1947–54.

Reynaud to lunch: on Saturday I have Blum and probably Paul-Boncour to dinner: on Sunday I have Daladier to dinner. I will arrange meetings for you with Léger and Flandin besides.

Please let me know later on what time you arrive and where, and I will send the car to meet you.

Yours sincerely,

Eric Phipps

Neville Chamberlain to Ida Chamberlain

(*Neville Chamberlain papers*)

20 March 1938   Chequers

My idea at present is that we should again approach Hitler following up our Halifax–Henderson[1] conversations & say something like this. 'We gave you fair warning that if you used violence to Austria you would shock public opinion to such an extent as to give rise to the most disagreeable repercussions. Yet you obstinately went your way & now you can see for yourselves how right we were. Incidentally it has made it quite impossible for us in present circumstances to continue talking over colonies.

'But it is of no use crying over spilt milk & what we have to do now is to consider how we can restore the confidence you have shattered. Everyone is thinking that you are going to repeat the Austria coup in Czechoslovakia. I know you say you aren't, but nobody believes you. The best thing you can do is to tell us exactly what you want for your Sudeten Deutsch. If it is reasonable we will urge the Czechs to accept it and if they do you must give assurances that you will let them alone in future'. I am not sure that in such circumstances I might not be willing to join in some joint guarantee *with Germany* of Czech independence. I should have to consider that further according as conversations developed but what I have written will show how I would start. I believe the Germans might listen. I have a letter from a man who met Ribbentrop after his last conversation with me and said he was quite changed (he knows him well). From another source I heard that after Henderson's conversation with Hitler the latter for the first time declared his belief that we meant business. Moreover we are getting on so well with the Italians that H must be a bit anxious on that side. And in any case the plan seems likely to postpone a crisis & perhaps to prevent it.

[1] Nevile Meyrick Henderson, 1882–1942. Educated at Eton. Entered the Diplomatic Service, 1905. 3rd Secretary, Tokyo, 1909–11. Counsellor, Constantinople, 1921–4. Minister at Belgrade, 1929–35. Knighted, 1932. Ambassador at Buenos Aires, 1935–7; at Berlin, 1937–9. He published an account of his Berlin Embassy, *Failure of a Mission*, in 1940.

The FO are, I think, rapidly coming round to this idea though at present they don't want us to approach Hitler but to tell Beneš[1] to go to him direct. There I think the FO is wrong but I shall have further talks on the subject with Halifax today or tomorrow. What a comfort he is to me & how thankful I am that I have not to deal with Anthony in these troubled times.

. . . the plan of the 'Grand Alliance', as Winston calls it, had occurred to me long before he mentioned it. I was thinking about it all last week end. I talked about it to Halifax, and we submitted it to the Chiefs of the Staff and the FO experts. It is a very attractive idea; indeed, there is almost everything to be said for it until you come to examine its practicability. From that moment its attraction vanishes. You have only to look at the map to see that nothing that France or we could do could possibly save Czecho-Slovakia from being overrun by the Germans if they wanted to do it. The Austrian frontier is practically open; the great Skoda munition works are within easy bombing distance of the German aerodromes, the railways all pass through German territory, Russia is 100 miles away. Therefore we could not help Czecho-Slovakia—she would simply be a pretext for going to war with Germany. That we could not think of unless we had a reasonable prospect of being able to beat her to her knees in a reasonable time, and of that I see no sign. I have therefore abandoned any idea of giving guarantees to Czecho-Slovakia, or to France in connection with her obligations to that country.[2]

[1] Eduard Beneš, 1884–1948. Born in Bohemia, the son of a farmer. Educated in Prague, Berlin and London. A leading member of the Czechoslovak National Council, Paris, 1917–18. Czech Minister for Foreign Affairs, 1918–35; Prime Minister, 1921–2. President of the Czechoslovak Republic, 1935–8. In exile, 1939–45; President of the Czechoslovak National Committee in London, 1939–45. Re-elected as President of the Republic, Prague, 1945. Resigned, 1948. Author of many books and pamphlets on the Czech question.

[2] Speaking at his constituency on 18 March 1938, Alan Lennox-Boyd, Parliamentary Secretary to the Ministry of Labour, had said, according to a report in *The Times* on the following day, 'that he could countenance nothing more ridiculous than a guarantee that the frontiers of Czechoslovakia should not be violated when half the people in that country could not be relied upon to be loyal to the Government of the day; and from what he knew of Mr Chamberlain, he did not think he would make a move to give a guarantee of that kind. Germany, he said, could absorb Czechoslovakia and Great Britain would remain secure.' Lennox-Boyd had gone on to say: 'but Germany could not invade France without threatening us. We should therefore reaffirm our undertaking to France to defend her if she should be invaded. He could think of Governments he liked better than M Blum's. Nevertheless we should give him support at this moment. He did not think we should tie ourselves in advance by giving undertakings to go to the aid of European countries if they were invaded unless their security was a vital concern to us.'

Thomas Jones to an American friend

(*Jones papers*)

20 March 1938

The last few days have seen a revival of the wish to see Winston in the Government and I should welcome him at the Air Ministry for his driving power would soon be felt throughout the department down to the typists and messengers. But on policy he would have to be kept in chains. He has commended himself to the Labour Party by his support of the League in his recent speeches and articles. Many would like a reconstruction of the Government on more national lines for this emergency.

Arthur J. Cummings to Winston S. Churchill

(*Churchill papers: 2/328*)

21 March 1938   News Chronicle

Dear Mr Churchill,

I am glad Lord Beaverbrook showed you my letter. I am in agreement with almost the whole of your views on the present situation; and I know that large numbers of people share my sincere hope that it will be possible before long for you to be in a position to put your views into effect. There are however many formidable obstacles to be overcome before that can happen. What a pity that Lord Beaverbrook has gone into the jungle of isolation. His help would have been of the utmost value.

Yours very sincerely,
Arthur J. Cummings

Professor J. H. Morgan to Winston S. Churchill

(*Churchill papers: 2/328*)

21 March 1938

I have read with lively appreciation your speech in the House on Germany's latest coup-d'état. That speech has made a profound impression. I was discussing it at a dinner party the other night at which some Conservative MP's were present and one of them said that there was a strong and growing feeling in the House that our 'Defence Programme' would never be complete until you were a member of the Cabinet. You may be interested to know his exact words. They were 'Winston Churchill's presence in the Cabinet would be worth two battleships to us and would put the fear of God into the Germans as nothing else could do.' And so say all of us.[1]

Yours sincerely,
J. H. Morgan

Sir Henry Strakosch to Winston S. Churchill

(*Churchill papers: 2/336*)

21 March 1938

My dear Winston,

As promised the other night, I now send a note on 'Our Armaments Programme' which may be of some little service to you.

Ever yours,
H. Strakosch

Ava Wigram to Winston S. Churchill

(*Churchill papers: 1/323*)

21 March 1938

My dear Winston,

Your speeches have been so magnificent that I feel I must send you a little word to tell you how with all my heart I thank God that you are there.

What would Ralph say today? I miss him more & more as the events accelerate—Don't you?

I will not trouble you with a long letter—I only wanted to tell you how much my thoughts are with you in your great work.

Love from,
Ava

---

[1] Two days later, on 23 March 1938, J. M. Keynes wrote to Churchill: 'I have shared the general admiration of your magnificent speeches in the House of Commons.'

Winston S. Churchill to Ava Wigram

(Churchill papers: 1/323)

22 March 1938

Thank you so much for your letter. I am sorry I cannot come to luncheon on Friday next, but I shall be on my way to Paris. Flandin has been behaving very badly, and doing all manner of harm. Indeed we miss Ralph now!

All good wishes,

Geoffrey Dawson to Winston S. Churchill

(Churchill papers: 2/328)

23 March 1938   The Times

My dear Churchill,

Very many thanks for letting me see this letter—a most distressing document. I have seen others like it. No doubt it is true that *The Times*, like every other paper, gave the impression of an enthusiastic street welcome for the new régime. Our Correspondent in Vienna,[1] who is an extreme anti-Nazi and lost no time in leaving the country, talked, for instance, about 'the extraordinarily complete emotional surrender of the Austrians' and of 'an apparent change in the Austrian character as the outer world has understood it. Nobody,' he concluded his message, 'can believe Austria could be like that.' There is no doubt, I think, that the impression of jubilation was overwhelming. But we all knew, and said, that this was not the whole of the story. I remember writing myself that same day that the exuberant crowds were composed for the most part of youths and that others had hidden their faces.

Many thanks again for letting me see the letter, which I return.

Yours sincerely,
Geoffrey Dawson

---

[1] Douglas Launcelot Reed, 1895–1976. Joined a publishing firm as an office boy at the age of 13. Became a bank clerk at the age of 19. On active service, first in the infantry and then in the Royal Flying Corps, 1914–18 (twice wounded, and mentioned in despatches). Joined the staff of *The Times*, 1921; worked as a clerk in the paper's office, 1921–2; appointed a sub-editor, 1925; Assistant Berlin Correspondent, 1928–35; Central European Correspondent (based on Vienna), 1935–8; resigned, October 1938. In 1938 he published *Insanity Fair*, describing his experiences of Nazism and stressing Nazi world-ambitions, but the book was marred for many readers by its virulent anti-semitism. In 1935 he published *Disgrace Abounding*. A War Correspondent in Normandy, 1944. Later Foreign Editor of Kemsley Newspapers. Resident after the war in South Africa; in 1967 he published an assessment of the Rhodesian situation entitled *Insanity Fair 1967*.

Robert Boothby to Winston S. Churchill

(*Churchill papers: 2/328*)

24 March 1938   House of Commons

Dear Winston,

I can't help writing a line of very sincere congratulation and appreciation. Your speech was *magnificent*—from the first word to the last.[1] It makes one very proud to have been associated with you in public life.

Yours ever,
Bob

Harold Nicolson: diary

(*Nicolson papers*)

24 March 1938

Winston makes a fine oration and ends with a magnificent epilogue. I hope to get in but as Winston has said everything I meant to say, I creep out.

R. J. Thompson[2] *to Winston S. Churchill: extract*

(*Churchill papers: 8/600*)

24 March 1938   Evening Standard

Dear Mr Churchill,

I write this letter with considerable regret.

The purpose is to end an association which has been most agreeable to us, and from a literary point of view has given our columns a rare lustre.

---

[1] Churchill ended his speech of 24 March 1938: '. . . if mortal catastrophe should overtake the British Nation and the British Empire, historians a thousand years hence will still be baffled by the mystery of our affairs. They will never understand how it was that a victorious nation, with everything in hand, suffered themselves to be brought low, and to cast away all that they had gained by measureless sacrifice and absolute victory—gone with the wind! Now the victors are the vanquished, and those who threw down their arms in the field and sued for an armistice are striding on to world mastery. That is the position—that is the terrible transformation that has taken place bit by bit. I rejoice to hear from the Prime Minister that a further supreme effort is to be made to place us in a position of security. Now is the time at last to rouse the nation. Perhaps it is the last time it can be roused with a chance of preventing war, or with a chance of coming through to victory should our efforts to prevent war fail. We should lay aside every hindrance and endeavour by uniting the whole force and spirit of our people to raise again a great British nation standing up before all the world; for such a nation, rising in its ancient vigour, can even at this hour save civilization'.

[2] Reginald John Tanner Thompson, 1896–1956. On active service, Royal Fusiliers and 18th Division, western front, 1914–18. Journalist; worked on the *Daily Express* and the *Evening News*. Editor of the *Evening Standard*, 1938–9. Editor and Managing Director of the Essex Chronicle Series Limited, publishers of the *Essex Chronicle*. His father, mother, brother and two nephews were killed during a raid by a solitary bomber on Chelmsford, 1940.

We feel the time has come for a new policy with regard to our Page Seven articles on foreign affairs. We find it necessary to have articles based, as far as possible, on the news of the day. As your articles have to be written some days in advance of publication, it occasionally happens that there is little difference—so far as argument goes—between the speech which you make in the House of Commons on an important issue and the article based on the same subject which you write for us.

Further, as it is my duty to be completely frank, it has been evident that your views on foreign affairs and the part which this country should play are entirely opposed to those held by us.[1]

Wing-Commander Anderson for Winston S. Churchill
(Churchill papers: 2/338)

24 March 1938   Royal Air Force Station,
                                                    Catfoss, Nr. Hull

Dear Mrs Pearman,

I spoke some time ago regarding the unserviceability of the service aero-dromes in this country and that with our new low winged monoplanes carrying their full load it would be impossible for these machines to take the air.

I enclose a letter regarding CATFOSS and you will see that £10,000 has now been allotted for a drainage scheme.

Drainage schemes have, however, been of little value in the past and there is only one real solution ie the construction of concrete run-ways.

Regarding Link Trainers I am attaching a letter from Air Commodore R. LECKIE,[2] D of T, and you will see that when the White Paper was issued there were 48 of these Trainers and it is only in the last few weeks that this has been increased to 150.

Yours very sincerely,
C. T. Anderson

---

[1] For Churchill's response to this letter, and for the new outlet for his fortnightly articles, see pages 980–2, 986 and 987–8.

[2] Robert Leckie, 1895–1975. Joined the Royal Naval Air Service, 1915. On Active service in the North Sea, 1915–18 (despatches, DSC, DFC, DSO). Director of Flying Operations Canadian Air Board, 1920. Commanded the aircraft carrier HMS *Hermes*, 1925–7, and HMS *Courageous*, 1927–9. Commanded 210 Flying Boat Squadron, 1931. Director of Training, Air Ministry, 1935–8. Commanded RAF Mediterranean (Malta), 1938–9. Director of Training, Royal Canadian Air Force, 1940. Chief of the Air Staff, Royal Canadian Air Force, 1944–7, when he retired.

Sir Henry Strakosch to Winston S. Churchill
(*Churchill papers: 1/328*)

24 March 1938

My dear Winston,

I have to-day paid to Vickers da Costa & Co £18,162.1.10 being the amount due to them by you, & arrangements are being made for them to deliver to me the securities they are holding for you viz.

400 Otis Elevator shares
500 Worthington Pumps & Co
1000 Consolidated Paper
400 Abitibi Paper Pref shs.
200 d° Common
200 New York Central

As agreed between us I shall carry this position for three years, you giving me full discretion to sell or vary the holdings at any time, but on the understanding that you incur no further liability.

Sir Eric Phipps to Sir Alexander Cadogan [1]
(*Phipps papers*)

24 March 1938   Paris

I fervently hope that all these meetings will not unduly excite the French.[2] In any case I shall do my best to calm them down and to convince them that Winston is not the arbiter of our destinies.

Sir Eric Phipps to Lord Halifax
(*Foreign Office papers: 800/311*)

27 March 1938   British Embassy,
Private   Paris

My dear Secretary of State,

Winston Churchill was of course present at the dinner the night before last with Herriot and last night with Blum and Paul-Boncour, reported by my Saving Telegrams of yesterday and today.

---

[1] Sir Alexander Cadogan (see page 1199, note 1), Sir Robert Vansittart's successor as Permanent Under-Secretary of State for Foreign Affairs.

[2] The arrangements made for Churchill were: Friday 25 March am Léger (Quai d'Orsay), lunch Reynaud, dinner Herriot; Saturday 26 March dine Léon Blum and Paul Boncour (British Embassy); Sunday 27 March, lunch Flandin (British Embassy), dinner Daladier (British Embassy) (*Phipps papers*).

Churchill's share in the conversation was chiefly devoted to the urgent necessity of forming a solid Anglo-French block against Germany in the first instance, with a kind of Central European and Balkan Grand Alliance joined thereto as the next step. He advocated close and immediate Anglo-French staff talks, not merely air, but military and naval, and the placing at our disposal of all French ports in the Mediterranean. These suggestions fell in the main on willing ears, though when he proposed to Herriot speedy publication of these steps, Herriot showed commendable caution, and said that that would have to be very carefully considered.

Churchill's French interlocutors naturally realise that he only speaks for himself and a very small section of British public opinion, and I lay great stress on this, and urge liberal sprinklings of salt on what he says.

Today Flandin will lunch and Daladier will dine with us. Tomorrow I have thought it well for Churchill to meet two distinguished writers of the Right in Andre Chaumeix,[1] of the Académie Française and 'Journal des Débats', and Wladimir d'Ormesson,[2] of the 'Figaro'.

Poor Blum is terribly broken over his wife's death. Last night when Winston took leave of him their eyes filled with tears.

Very sincerely yours,
Eric Phipps

Sir Eric Phipps to Lord Halifax: telegram

(*Phipps papers*)

27 March 1938   Paris

M Flandin lunched at the Embassy to-day with Lady Phipps, Mr Winston Churchill and myself.

He thinks M Blum has two alternatives before him, viz (1) to propose such Socialistic financial measures that even the Socialist-Radicals in his own Government would decline to accept them, in which case he would resign and would withdraw into opposition, thus breaking up the Front Populaire,

---

[1] Andre Chaumeix, 1874–1955. Editor of the *Journal des Débats*, 1900–40. Counsellor of the French Legation, Berne, 1917–18. Directeur, *La Revue de Paris*, 1920–6. Political Editor of *Figaro*, 1926–30. Appointed Directeur of the *Revue des Deux Mondes*, 1937. President of the Franco-American Committee, 1942.

[2] Wladimir Oliver Marie François de Paule Le Fèvre D'Ormesson, 1888–1981. Born in St Petersburg, the son of Count D'Ormesson. Educated in France. Leader-writer of the *Figaro*. Foreign Political editor of the *Temps*. French Ambassador to the Vatican, 1940; to the Argentine Republic, 1945–8; to the Vatican, 1948–58. Author of several books on European current affairs.

or (2) to produce a series of financial measures amongst which some might be acceptable to the Senate, and thus prolong his ministerial existence for some time to come.

M Flandin does not believe in the likelihood of a Government of National Union or in its efficacity if it were formed. For instance, if M Blum agreed inside such a Government to the passing of certain conservative but indispensable financial measures his followers in Parliament and outside would decline to support him. Even now his authority and influence with his Party were greatly weakened.

M Flandin painted the situation in black. He feels that things will have to get much worse before they get better and that the general public do not yet realise how bad they are. The remedy he advocates is, briefly, for a Government of Socialist-Radicals and Centre, after the break up of the Front Populaire, to obtain parliamentary assent (he admits by a majority of only about 20 votes) for government by decree for a certain specified time, perhaps until the next elections in May, 1940. He admitted that a General Strike might well be declared as a result, but affected to be hopeful of being able easily to crush it.

Mr Churchill warned M Flandin that if such procedure were followed it would alienate all Left sympathies in Great Britain for France, and render most difficult that close and loyal collaboration between our two countries now more than ever essential to check further German aggression and to prevent German hegemony.

We asked M Flandin whether a dissolution would not be preferable to his suggested remedy, but he made the usual French objection to the effect that a dissolution except at the normal electoral period was regarded as a kind of 'coup d'état' and had not been indulged in since the days of Marshal MacMahon.[1] Moreover, it would in any case mean at least two months of electioneering and recrimination, which would be dangerous in the present international situation. He added that a general strike would be quite likely to break out during the electoral campaign.

We both accused M Flandin of black pessimism, but he smilingly denied the soft impeachment, and reiterated that his remedy would, after a short period of disturbance, provide a satisfactory solution to the present difficulties. He feels strongly that a series of weak Front Populaire Governments has

---

[1] Marie Edmé Patrice Maurice de MacMahon 1808–1893. Descended from an Irish Jacobite family, MacMahon was a regular officer in the French Army and distinguished himself in the Algerian, Italian and Crimean campaigns, becoming a Marshal of France and Duke of Magenta. In the Franco-Prussian war he commanded the First Army Corps, but was defeated at Wörth, and captured at Sedan. In 1871, in command of the Army of Versailles, he suppressed the Paris Commune. In 1873 he was elected President of the Republic for seven years, but resigned in 1879.

given such encouragement to the extremists that firm action and even repression will be necessary to cure the malady from which France is suffering.

Foreign affairs were only mentioned in passing and the following is the substance of what M Flandin said:—

·SPAIN

The very great majority of the French people were strongly opposed to intervention, and this was apparent in view of the fact that, despite the present Front Populaire Government, non-intervention was still officially adhered to. General Gamelin had vetoed French intervention at a recent meeting of the National Defence Committee; but nevertheless large quantities of arms and ammunition (not from French arsenals), including guns, were pouring across the frontier.

Negrin,[1] when he was in Paris about ten days ago actually offered to place Catalonia under the protectorate of France, and M Paul-Boncour had wished to accept this compromising offer.

It was highly desirable that the conflict in Spain should end as soon as possible, but this seemed unlikely till May or June, owing to the increased unofficial help the Government forces were receiving from France.

CZECHOSLOVAKIA

That country was impossible to defend, and it would therefore be folly to attempt to defend it. M Flandin agreed, moreover, that its surrender to Hitler would most likely be effected by economic strangulation, which we were all powerless to prevent.

ITALY

It was very wise to have entered upon our talks with Italy, and it was to be hoped that they would reach a successful termination. For the gallery we should pretend to talk to Germany at the same time, but success there seemed most doubtful. We should never admit that we wished to break the Berlin–Rome axis, but that might well be the eventual result when German pressure on the Brenner increased and Italy realised what German hegemony meant for her. As for the German menace, we must console ourselves with the thought that no Power in the past had ever succeeded in gaining or maintaining complete hegemony in Europe.

[1] Juan Negrin, 1887–1956. Born in Teneriffe, Canary Islands. Practised as a Doctor of Medicine in Madrid. A Militant socialist. Became a Republican Deputy, 1931. Minister of Finance, 1936. Prime Minister of Spain (when the Republic Government's capital was at Valencia) from 17 May 1937 to 1 February 1938. Minister of War (at Barcelona) 6 April 1938 to 6 March 1939. In exile in France, 1939. Head of the Spanish Republican Government in Exile (at Paris) 1939–45. He died in exile in Paris.

Sir Eric Phipps to Lord Halifax

(Foreign Office papers: 800/311)

28 March 1938   British Embassy
Private   Paris

My dear Secretary of State

My private letter of yesterday.

Winston Churchill's stay here has continued in an increasingly kaleido-
scopic manner. Almost every facet of French political life has been presented
to him at and between meals.

In addition to the interviews, all too inadequately reported in my Saving
Telegrams, he has seen (mostly 'en tête à tête') Louis Marin,[1] General
Gamelin, Mandel,[2] Chautemps, Chastenet[3] of the 'Temps', Sauerwein[4] of

---

[1] Louis Marin, 1871–1960. Born in Lorraine (on the French side of the Franco-German
frontier). Deputy for Meurthe-et-Moselle, 1905–42. Served as a volunteer, 1914–18. National
President of the Republican Federation, 1924. A noted liberal and social reformer. Founder
and editorial writer of *La Nation*. Minister of the Liberated Regions, 1924; of Pensions,
1926–8; of Public Health and Physical Education, 1934. Minister of State, November
1934–January 1936 and 19 May–16 June 1940. One of the strongest opponents of the armistice in Reynaud's Cabinet, faithful to his beliefs, he refused to take part in the vote of 10
July 1940, which conferred full powers on Marshal Pétain. Joined the Resistance, 1942.
Member of the Provisional Consultative Assembly, 1944. Elected to the National Assembly,
1946–51. An advocate of equal pay for women.

[2] Georges Mandel, former Chef de Cabinet to Clemenceau (see page 967, note 1).

[3] Jacques Chastenet de Castaing, 1893–1978. The son of a French Senator. On active
service, 1914–18 (Croix de Guerre); Liaison Officer with the American Expeditionary Force,
1918. Secretary, Rhineland Inter-Allied Commission, 1920. Diplomatic correspondent,
L'Opinion, 1926–31. Editor of *Le Temps*, 1931–40. CBE, 1938. Major, French Military
Mission, Egypt, 1945. Author of many historical works, especially on British history, including
William Pitt (1941), *Wellington* (1945), *Elizabeth the 1st* (1953) and *Winston Churchill et l'Angle-
terre du XX Siécle* (1958). Member of the French Academy, 1956.

[4] Jules August Sauerwein, 1880–   . Born in Marseilles. French journalist; Foreign
Editor of *Paris Soir*, 1933. A frequent correspondent of the *New York Times*, for which he
worked for eight years. Author of *Que Va Faire l'Amérique* (1932) and *Les Événements de Septembre
1938* (1939). Commander of the Légion d'Honneur. In an article published in *Le Matin* on
15 January 1925 he wrote, of the Anglo-French debt dispute: 'If it were up to Churchill alone
to decide, I am certain that his reply would be generous and practical. I had the good fortune
of speaking to him several times during his visit to Paris. This is a man of courage. He does not
allow himself to be stopped by the arguments of demagogues. If the opposition tell him that
he is giving up the English share of reparations in unholding the principles of the Balfour
note, he replies that it is better to get rid of all cause of friction with France than to bind
oneself to the illusory hopes of total repayment.' According to Sir Eric Phipp's 'Report on
Leading Personalities' in France, July 1939 (despatch 903, 13 July 1939), in 1937 and 1938
Sauerwein 'increased his contacts with Italy, and is believed to have accepted money to
accompany Mussolini on his African tour in 1937. In 1937–39 he favoured an agreement
with Germany and Italy on every possible occasion, and supported M. Bonnet's policy.
Although he sent his son to Oxford and professes friendship for Great Britain, his enemies
say that his pen cannot be relied upon unless subsidised' (*Vansittart papers: 1/25*).

the 'Paris-Soir', and others. He wanted to see a Communist, but I strongly advised against this and he abstained.

At nearly all the conversations at which I was present Churchill strongly advocated a close Anglo-French alliance, with staff talks, military, naval and air; and also the joint attempt by France and Great Britain to galvanise the Central European and Balkan Powers to join together in resisting German pressure.[1]

On taking leave of Daladier last night Churchill said that he would consult you and the Prime Minister on this matter and let him know the result.

If and when a strong French Government is formed I feel it will be very useful for you and the Prime Minister to come over here and put things into somewhat better proportion than they have been left by Winston.

His French is most strange and at times quite incomprehensible. For instance, to Blum and Boncour the other night he shouted out a literal translation of 'We must make good', by 'Nous devons faire bonne (not even "bon")'. This clearly stumped Boncour, who may even have attributed some improper meaning to it.

You will get a most eloquent first-hand account of this hectic and electric week-end from its brilliant animator.

Sir Henry Strakosch to Winston S. Churchill

(*Churchill papers: 2/328*)

29 March 1938
Personal

My dear Winston,

How nice of you to have taken the trouble to write to me from Paris when your time must have been so fully occupied with your conversations.

It was reassuring to read in your letter that you think it will not be long before a broad Government is formed in France.

I will try to let you have a note on the economic and financial effect on the Danubian countries of the incorporation of Austria into the German Reich to explain more fully what I said to you the other night. I will also endeavour,

---

[1] Speaking in the House of Commons on 24 March 1938, Churchill argued that peace in Europe could only be preserved by an 'accumulation of deterrents against the aggressor'. Commenting on Chamberlain's statement earlier in the debate that France and Britain would work together for their mutual defence, he asked whether it was an actual alliance. If so, 'Why not say so?' His speech continued: 'Why not make it effective by a military convention of the most detailed character? Are we, once again, to have all the disadvantages of an alliance without its advantages, and to have commitments without full security?'

in that note, to deal with the altered situation in regard to railway communications which has been created, for I believe that that question is perhaps not as grave as you thought, except, of course, so far as Czechoslovakia is concerned. A closer investigation will probably show that the other countries of the Danubian Basin will not be as hard pressed as might appear at first blush, for they have the Danube as a means of getting their products out by the Black Sea and the Mediterranean.

Violet Pearman to James Watts[1]

(*Churchill papers: 2/343*)

29 March 1938

Dear Mr Watts,

On Mr Churchill's arrival home today he was given your message, and also received your letter, for both of which he thanks you. He quite agrees with you about the seriousness of the situation, and as a matter of fact had made tentative arrangements for some big meetings in various parts of the country during April. One of these was to take place in Manchester. He has heard that he would be sure of a great meeting there. As you know he is a member both of the New Commonwealth Society and also the Defence of Freedom and Peace. The meetings are all being arranged with Mr A. H. Richards, who is the Secretary of the Defence of Freedom and Peace movement. Mr Churchill thinks the best that can be done for all is for yourself and Mr Richards to communicate with each other, and he is sure that a splendid meeting at Manchester will result. . . .

Mr Churchill much appreciates the kindness of your offer to come all the way down south to see him for this reason, but thinks that he could not possibly put you to all this trouble. Once you have got in touch with Mr Richards —who is managing all for Mr Churchill—I am sure everything will go well.

Cabinet minutes

(*Cabinet papers: 23/93*)

30 March 1938

The Secretary of State for Foreign Affairs read a personal letter from His Majesty's Ambassador in Paris giving some account of Mr Winston Chur-

---

[1] James Watts, 1903–1961. Educated at Shrewsbury and New College, Oxford. Worked in his family's textile firm, S. and J. Watts, Manchester. A nephew of Agatha Christie. Treasurer of the Manchester Conservative Association, 1933–51; Chairman 1951–3. Elected to the Manchester City Council, 1933. Resigned, 1939, to join the Cheshire Regiment. On active service in France, Iraq and Persia, 1939–45. Conservative MP for Moss Side, 1959–61.

chill's recent visit to Paris, where he had advocated an Anglo-French alliance, staff talks and an effort by the two countries to bring various democratic European countries into combination with a view to resisting the Dictator countries. . . .

The Foreign Secretary added that he himself had seen Mr Winston Churchill since his return. The conversation did not add very much to what might have been expected from his visit. He said that Mr Churchill had pressed for staff conversations and he had added two useful items of information, namely, first that the French had dropped any idea of intervention in Spain because General Gamelin had told the Government that, in the event of intervention, they would have to mobilise the Army, and second, certain information (which Lord Halifax gave the Cabinet) of a highly secret character as to French plans in the event of a German aggression against Czecho-Slovakia.[1]

Lord Halifax to Sir Eric Phipps

(*Foreign Office papers: 800/311*)

30 March 1938   Foreign Office
                                                 London

My dear Phipps,

One line to thank you for your letter of the 28th reporting about Winston's visit to Paris. I read it to the Cabinet this morning, who were greatly amused with the last paragraph of it.

Some of them were disposed to be a little critical of my having encouraged you, as I think I did, to show hospitality to him and generally to keep an eye on his movements. I still think that it was better so, and the Prime Minister was on the whole of the same opinion. Winston came to see me yesterday and we had some talk. He repeated his desire to see France and Great Britain together forming the nucleus for the rally of smaller Central European and Balkan Powers. I pointed out some of the obvious difficulties in the way of this to him and he did not seem violently interested in that side of the subject.[2]

It would, I think, be useful if, as you get an opportunity of seeing any of those with whom he came in contact, especially perhaps Daladier and Herriot, you were to warn them, as you have no doubt done already, that the right source from which to ascertain British Government policy is the decla-

---

[1] For this secret matter, see Oliver Harvey's diary for 4 April 1938 (page 980)

[2] For Churchill's version of his conversation with Lord Halifax, see his letter to Sir Eric Phipps of 1 April 1938 (page 969).

rations of the British Government, rather than Winston's exuberant inter-pretations of it. I am always a little bit anxious lest his enthusiasm should lead him, quite unwittingly, to misrepresent HMG's attitude.

Halifax

Sir Eric Phipps to Lord Halifax

(*Foreign Office papers: 800/311*)

30 March 1938   British Embassy
Private   Paris

My dear Secretary of State,
  My letter of March 28th.
  An important point made by Winston Churchill to several Frenchmen was the following:—

'Why do you French bother to vote large sums of money to increase your navy, when we English have relatively a much bigger superiority over the German and Italian navies than we had before the war? *You* should concentrate on your air force, *we* will answer for your maritime communications in the Mediterranean.'

Mandel,[1] whom I met at luncheon today, said to me that the above argument was perfectly sound, but only on one condition, viz, that Great Britain should give France a definite guarantee to the above effect.
  I took advantage of this remark to rub in, as I have done to all concerned, that Churchill was speaking for himself only during his recent visit to Paris, and that much salt must be taken with what he said.

[1] Louis Rothschild, 1885–1944. Of Jewish parentage, born near Paris. A journalist, he took the name of Georges Mandel. Joined Clemenceau's Staff on *L'Aurore*, 1903. Chef de Cabinet to Clemenceau, 1906–9 and 1917–19 (during Clemenceau's two premierships). In charge of the trials dealing with treason and defeatism, 1917–18. Elected to the Chamber of Deputies, 1920. Minister of Posts and Telegraphs, 1934–6 (when he introduced the first French television broadcast, in November 1935). Minister of Colonies, April 1938–May 1940. Minister of the Interior, May–June 1940, (when he arrested many Nazi sympathizers). Churchill's choice to lead a Free French movement in Britain, but refused to leave France, June 1940. Imprisoned in France, 1940–2; in Germany, 1943–4. Sent back to France, 4 July 1944. Assassinated by Vichy militia, 7 July 1944.

Winston S. Churchill to Duncan Sandys

(Churchill papers: 1/323)

31 March 1938

My dear Duncan,

You will do a very wrong act and one which the world would judge harshly if you take Diana with you to Barcelona.[1] There is no excuse whatever for bringing her into this scene of misery, privation and danger. You may easily have great difficulty in getting out if the front breaks while you are there. I am bound to let you know how very strong my opinion is.[2]

Yours ever,

---

[1] Duncan Sandys did not take his wife to Barcelona, but travelled there with a fellow Conservative MP, Oliver Simmonds, the former Chairman of the Parliamentary Air Committee (1933–5), their aim being to examine the effect of air raid precautions in Barcelona, a city under frequent air bombardment, with a view to learning something for British needs in the event of war. During a three-day period earlier that month, more than 500 civilians had been killed during air raids on Barcelona. 'It seemed to me,' Sandys later recalled, 'that we were neglecting Air Raid Precautions. I formed a Committee with Simmonds, the Parliamentary Air Raid Precautions Committee. We wanted to attract attention as to the seriousness of air raids. We thought it best to go to Spain and to be photographed in front of bombed buildings and inside shelters. We went out for a few days, and we were all photographed as we had hoped. As a result of our efforts, they sent out Home Office officials to Spain, and then they set up a Civil Defence section at the Home Office, with one of our Committee members as Under Secretary' (*conversation with the author, 16 December 1981*).

[2] On 24 April 1938 the *News of the World* published an article by Churchill entitled 'How Wars of the Future will be Waged'. In it he wrote, of air power: 'The air has altered the picture. It spreads the war over the whole country instead of it being fought only on the fronts. Not only will aeroplanes throw their bombs upon the enemy, but they will also carry quite large bodies of troops through the air, and descend suddenly, without five minutes warning, now here, now there, in a zone hundreds of miles beyond the front lines. Every factory, every railway junction, every important bridge will have to be guarded, not, as heretofore, by a few reservists or militia, but by effective, well-organised forces.' Of the nature of air warfare in the future Churchill wrote: 'It seems very likely that if both air forces are fairly equal, the one that concentrates on attacking military objectives, and breaking up the communications of the enemy armies, and beating the other air force both in the air and in its nests, will soon have a great advantage over the side which just goes bombing and murdering the mass of the civil population in the hope of terrorising them into making peace.' Churchill's article ended: 'I do not myself believe that the deliberate massacre of the inhabitants of the great cities will decide the future struggle; though, of course, we in England are particularly vulnerable. But I am sure that the best defence yet available is to fight the enemy's armed forces in the air and in their nests, and to leave the women and children alone. This may be found to be not only chivalrous, but profitable. Better still: have no war!'

April 1938

1 April 1938
Confidential

My dear Ambassador,

I had talks both with the PM and your Chief, and I pressed very strongly for Staff conversations and detailed arrangements with the French. I was pleased to find both were responsive.

Halifax told me that he had come round to the view that this would be wise, and even that publicity would be helpful.

Neville also spoke in the same sense, so I hope this at least may be done.

I do hope the French will get their Government settled soon. How can they expect us to open these serious matters to Ministers who expect to quit at any moment?

I enjoyed very much my stay with you and the deeply interesting conversations which filled the days and nights. I gather that your accounts of it were much appreciated and anyhow I am sure no harm was done, perhaps even a little good.

Once more thanking you for your hospitality and kindness.

Believe me,
Yours vy sincerely,
Winston S. Churchill

Winston S. Churchill to Eduard Beneš
(*Churchill papers: 8/595*)

1 April 1938

I venture to commend to you my literary secretary Mr F. W. Deakin, a Fellow of Wadham College, Oxford, who is paying a short visit to Czechoslovakia and will be in Prague on the 11th or 12th. Mr Deakin is a young man of the highest character and intelligence and shares my outlook on European affairs. For this reason I send the letter direct to you through the Embassy bag rather than leave him to carry it himself on his journey through Germany. Any consideration you may be able to show him will be much appreciated by me. I wish I could come myself, but Spears gave me a full account of his talks with you.

Winston S. Churchill to Robert Boothby
(Churchill papers: 2/329)

1 April 1938

Alas, I cannot undertake to come and speak at your fête. I have a very exacting constituency of my own, and it is all I can do to get through my work. Do please forgive me.

Randolph Churchill to Winston S. Churchill
(Churchill papers: 1/325)

1 April 1938

My dearest Papa—

I do hope you will not think it impertinent if I make you a suggestion in regard to your handling of the Press, which is probably the only subject in the whole world which I may claim to know more about than you.

When you are engaged or about to be engaged in some activity which, in the nature of things, is bound to become public, it is far better to have a controlled release of this information rather than allow it to leak out into the hands of those who may maliciously or accidentally distort it, or, because they have it exclusively to themselves, play it up beyond its real importance.

Naturally a different technique is desirable according to whether you wish the piece of information to obtain the minimum or the maximum of attention. But in either case if you are to get the desired result it is essential to place the release of the information in reliable and friendly hands.

In the case of your visit to Paris you issued a communiqué to the Press. In nine cases out of ten this might have been all right, but it so happened that your communiqué coincided with Ll G's departure for Paris, with the resulting unfortunate headline in the 'Evening Standard'.[1] If I had had the handling of that story there would have been a discreet yet pregnant paragraph in the 'Londoner's Diary' which would have put your visit in its right setting but which would not have quoted you as the authority for the story. Thus, when you later postponed your visit to the following week, it would have looked as if we had made an error about the date and not, as it did, as if you had altered your plans because of the unfavourable reaction which the disclosure had aroused.

In the case of the sale of Chartwell[2] and your forthcoming campaign, the stories were allowed to leak out. In the case of the sale of Chartwell the story got into the worst possible hands—the 'Daily Express'—with the consequent distasteful story in this morning's paper.[3]

You were more lucky about the campaign story since it was got hold of by the 'News Chronicle' who are naturally friendly on this topic. But I would submit that in both cases I could have dealt with the matter much better and have written paragraphs which would have filled the bill satisfactorily.

When an atmosphere of mystery is created about any topic, it inevitably leads to far greater publicity. I have found with innumerable stories which we have handled in the Diary that our publication of the story has been the end of the matter. It all depends, of course, upon the way in which it is handled. If you tell the story in an intriguing and dramatic way you can create great public interest and encourage all the morning papers to take it up, but if you want no more done about it, it is usually quite easy by deliberately making the story seem dull and of small importance to discourage any further publicity.

[1] On 17 March 1938 the front page of the *Evening Standard* had the headline 'Churchill following L. G. to Paris'. Under a photograph of Lloyd George and his daughter Megan it commented: 'Mr Lloyd George went to Paris today. Mr Winston Churchill announced that he too was spending the week-end in Paris.' Churchill subsequently had to postpone his departure, and on 25 March 1938 the main item in the 'Londoner's Diary' in the *Evening Standard* was on Churchill's rescheduled Paris visit, which had begun (by air) that morning. 'In some quarters' the article read, 'there has been a disposition to question the desirability of British politicians visiting Paris at this juncture. I am told that Mr Churchill observed to a friend in this connection: "If it's right for Lord Londonderry and Lord Lothian to go to Berlin I don't see what's wrong in my going to Paris." '

[2] Churchill had decided to sell Chartwell for financial reasons, and to buy instead a house in London. But after a few weeks, Chartwell was withdrawn from the market. For the estate agent's description of Chartwell see the following document.

[3] On 1 April 1938 the front page of the *Daily Express* included the headline: 'Winston Puts His Mansion Up For Sale', and on page 2 the continuation of the story was headed 'Winston Selling Home'. The article, by a 'Daily Express Staff Reporter', ended: 'He loved his country home. I remember his eloquence as he pointed out the views from his windows of the Kentish Weald. "A home in one of England's loveliest spots," he called it. I remember accompanying Mr and Mrs Churchill from Westerham on a car tour of his Epping constituency. He said: "We'll drop you after the meetings in London. We always like to get back to Chartwell." It was foggy, and it was midnight. But they got back to Chartwell.'

I do hope you will not think I write all this merely because I would like to do myself good with the 'Evening Standard' by getting an occasional scoop about yourself. That is a very small consideration. But I do feel that these matters are not being properly handled at the moment and it is naturally a matter of regret to me that you should always be so suspicious and procrastinating whenever I suggest to you the desirability of my handling some particular piece of news.

You must know that I would always handle it as your agent rather than as a journalist who wanted to exploit a good story for the maximum headline. The worst possible method for any information to become public is by its leaking out accidentally. A general communique is better than this, but I am sure that in nine cases out of ten far the best method would be through myself. A paragraph in the 'Londoner's Diary', written on our own authority, commits you far less and enables us to put an interpretation upon the facts which you yourself could hardly do by the formal means of a communique.

These considerations apply with even greater force when, as in the case of the Chartwell story, there is some disagreeable twist which can be given to the report. More than ever in such a case is it expedient to have the matter handled by friends. It follows from the above that if there is any information which is bound to become public, the sooner you let me have it the better.

Your loving son,
Randolph

Chartwell: Estate Agent's descriptive brochure[1]

(*Pearman papers*)

[2 April 1938]

Privately for Sale by Direction of the Rt Hon WINSTON CHURCHILL, PC, MP

'CHARTWELL'

Westerham.

2¼ miles from Westerham Station.	10 miles from Tonbridge.
6 miles from Sevenoaks and Oxted Stations.	23 miles from London.

About 80 Acres.

---

[1] On 2 April 1938 *The Times* published an item on its main news page entitled 'Mr Churchill's Home in Kent for Sale'. The item read: 'In view of inquiries which have been made, Mr Churchill has authorized Messrs Knight, Frank and Rutley to state that he is prepared to consider the private sale of Chartwell, Westerham, Kent, provided that a sufficient offer is obtained. He has placed the sale in their hands, and also in the hands of Messrs Ralph Pay and Taylor. Chartwell is situated on the southern slope of the Kentish Hills; it adjoins Crockham Hill Common and the common land which will remain open spaces in perpetuity.'

Hall, Five Reception Rooms; Nineteen Bed and Dressing Rooms, Eight Bath Rooms; Usual Domestic Offices; Company's Electric Light and Water, Central Heating throughout, Modern Drainage; Stabling and Three Garages; Large Studio; Three Cottages.

HEATED AND FILTERED OPEN AIR SWIMMING POOL. TWO LAKES.
HARD TENNIS COURT. BEAUTIFUL GROUNDS AND GARDENS.
PARK AND WOODLAND.

KENT AND SURREY BORDERS.

Occupying a magnificent position in a valley **on the Southern slope of the Kentish Hills**; one of the most beautiful districts in the Home Counties, entirely unspoilt by building development, and **adjoining Crockham Hill Common and other Common Land** which will remain open spaces in perpetuity.

THE HOUSE

which stands

About 550 Feet Above Sea Level

has a pleasing elevation and is built of brick with tiled roof, being partly covered with Wisteria and Lemon-scented Magnolia. It commands wide views over the Kentish Weald, along the Valley to the South and also over a considerable stretch of undulating and wooded country to the Downs in the distance. The House is completely sheltered from the North and West by a high bank of woodland which actually adjoins and has access to the Crockham Hill Common.

The property has been the subject of very considerable expenditure, care and attention by the present owner who has modernised and fitted it throughout with every convenience and comfort.

It is now in first-rate order throughout, and the approach is from a quiet road by a Carriage Drive, the Main Entrance to the House being through double oak doors to the

HALL with beamed ceiling; from this is the

BLUE SITTING ROOM (East and West), 22-ft by 18-ft, with doors to tiled Terrace, having lovely views over the grounds and parkland and lakes to the South.

On the West is the LIBRARY OR SMOKING Room, 22-ft by 18-ft,

The Drawing Room

(South and East), about 40-ft by 21-ft, is delightful and well lighted. On this floor there is a **Bachelor's Bed Room** with hot and cold water, large Bath Room with hand-basin and WC. **Business Room or Bed Room** (West).

ON THE LOWER LEVEL (owing to the House being built on a slope) is

The Very Fine Dining Room

measuring 40-ft by 21-ft with five arched windows. This room has lovely views over the grounds, gardens, lakes and parkland.

On this level are also the well-arranged

Domestic Offices

comprising: Kitchen, Scullery, Larder, Butler's Pantry with tiled floor and sink, hot plate; Servants' Hall with built-in safe, ample cupboard accommodation; Butler's Room.

There is a Separate Staircase to **Three Servants' Bed Rooms**, also an outside **Men's Bath Room** and WC.

Useful **Range of Out-Offices**; Stoke Hole with two boilers, one for domestic hot water and Central Heating; Outside WC; Coal House; Knife and Boot Room.

There is a large **Wine Cellar**, Housekeeper's Room; Store cupboard, etc; large South room used as **Day Nursery** with Separate Staircase to **Bed Room** above, facing South and with large bow window.

The fine Oak Staircase from the Hall gives access to the Corridor from which is entered

The Upstairs Library

MR WINSTON CHURCHILL'S SUITE, comprising a very fine well-proportioned room with open raftered ceiling, which has access to another **Bed Room**, facing full South, and a Separate Staircase to a **Third Room**. There is a particularly well-fitted **Bath Room** with hand-basin and WC en suite.

The second principal Suite, comprising **MRS WINSTON CHURCHILL'S BED ROOM** (facing South and East), 26-ft by 22-ft, with arched ceiling; **Bath Room** en suite, hand-basin, etc.; **Visitor's Bed Room**, 22-ft by 18-ft, known as Henry VIIIth room, well-fitted **Bath Room** en suite; **Three other**

Bed Rooms, one now used as Work Room, two of them with fitted hand-basins; another **Bath Room** and WC.

The **South Tower Bed Room**, 18-ft square, with **Bath Room** and WC en suite.

The **North Tower Bed Room** with fitted hand-basin (h and c); House-maid's cupboard and sink.

ON THE SECOND FLOOR

there is **Staff Bath Room**, WC, **Four Servants' Rooms** one with hand-basin (h and c), another smaller ditto; Linen Room; Tank Room.

THE GROUNDS, GARDEN AND PARKLAND

which for their size are inexpensive to maintain, are studded with specimen trees among which are Cedars and Wellingtonia, Cryptomeria, Japonica, Araucaria Imbricata, as well as fine forest trees.

One of the ideal features of the Estate are the belts of beech and other woodland which afford absolute protection to the House.

Other features worthy of note are the Terraced Gardens and Terraced Lawn, grass path and Lavender Bank, Upper Lawn surrounded by low yew hedge, Summer House, en-tout-cas Tennis Court, surrounded by yew hedge, rose garden enclosed by stone wall, steps to Croquet Lawn from the upper level, stone-built **Italian Pergola** with flagged walk leading to the Summer House.

A FEATURE OF THE GARDEN IS THE 'CHARTWELL',

a Clear Pool fed from a Spring rising in the greensand 600 ft up, giving approximately 24,000 gallons of water a day. This Pool supplies the fish pond. From the Pond there are a series of Cascades and small Pools forming the Water Garden.

THE FLOODLIT SWIMMING POOL

of about 35,000 gallons is a special feature. It is arranged so as to be supplied by a system of filtered hot water, and is one of the few heated outdoor Swimming Pools in this country. There is a Furnace Room[1] with three large 'Britannia' furnaces, and also a special filtration system.

---

[1] Churchill had designed this Furnace (or boiler) Room himself, ensuring that it was made with sufficient thickness of concrete to be able to serve as an air-raid shelter in the event of war.

The Park slopes gently away to the Two Large Lakes in the Valley, one Lake having a small Island.

Conveniently placed to the House is the **HEATED GARAGE** for three cars, with Work Shop, also **ANOTHER GARAGE** for three cars. Near by is a further **GARAGE** with Two Rooms over; Harness Room, etc.

STABLING of Three Stalls and Loose Box.

COTTAGE, containing Two Rooms downstairs and Four Rooms upstairs, Outside Bath Room and WC.

CHAUFFEUR'S COTTAGE, containing Sitting Room, Bath Room, WC; Kitchen and Living Room, with three rooms over.

LARGE STUDIO with North Light—this is connected with Electric Light and Telephone, and also has hand-basin.

There is a large completely **WALLED KITCHEN GARDEN**, Apple Orchard, and an abundance of walled Fruit, Morello Cherries, Peaches, Nectarines, etc. In this Garden is the Herbaceous Walk with sundial, and **CHILDREN'S SUMMER HOUSE**. There is a range of Eighteen Frames, Potting Shed and Men's Room.

GARDENER'S COTTAGE, containing Three Bed Rooms, Kitchen, Bath Room and Living Room.

THE OTHER OUTBUILDINGS

comprise: a range of three brick-built Pigstyes, range of old Cow Sheds, Open Cart Shed, large open brick-built Wood Shed, weather-board Loose Box, now used as Goat House, another ditto for storage.

The balance of the property comprises Parkland and attractive Woodland, and extends in all to approximately

80 Acres.

GOLF—Excellent Golf Links at Tandridge, 7 miles, and Limpsfield Common, 2½ miles' distant.

HUNTING with the West Kent Foxhounds, Surrey Staghounds, and Old Surrey and Burstow Hounds.

Price, Freehold—£20,000.[1]

---

[1] In property values, £20,000 in April 1938 was the equivalent of more than £1 million in January 1982.

Winston S. Churchill to George Harrap

(*Churchill papers: 8/547*)

2 April 1938

Two years ago we had some correspondence about publishing a critical examination of the Baldwin/MacDonald foreign policy. Please see your letter of the 19th March 1936. This project has revived again in my mind but in a somewhat different form. I am now pressed from many quarters to publish an edited and annotated selection of speeches which I have made on these crises during the last five years, and indeed when I look at them they make a coherent whole. The publication is one which would require to be made very quickly and I should like to know your views about it. Meanwhile I should like at my expense to have the copy set up by your printers. Then one can see what it looks like, and if you should decide to take them over, you could of course credit me with the cost of printing. Will you kindly let me know what will be the charge for printing on my present sheets per thousand words, assuming there will be 40,000 or 50,000. Will you also consider how this can be fitted in with Marlborough publication in June.

Winston S. Churchill to Randolph Churchill

(*Churchill papers: 8/598*)

3 April 1938

I shall be very glad if you will prepare these speeches for publication, and submit the copy to me when completed. I will assist you to the best of my ability, but must have the final word in a matter which so closely concerns myself, upon what goes in or out.

I will arrange the business part and I am more or less committed to Harrap by an agreement made two years ago. I do not expect there will be much profit, but you shall have half of whatever there is. The publication will of course be in your name.

I enclose a letter I wrote to Harrap yesterday. I have no doubt his reply will be satisfactory. In that case as soon as your copy is ready and I have skimmed it over, we will have it set up in an agreeable form for further consideration.

We do not want any speeches or parts of speeches except those bearing on Foreign Policy and Rearmament. They run from 1931 down to last week. I have looked through the Hansards and send you the enclosed list of the principal dates, so far as I have gone. But there are certainly about a dozen more that I have not yet found but have in my mind. There was one in 1932 about putting the factories in order.

I recommend you to use the daily Hansards of the dates in question, which will save expenses of buying and mutilating the bound full volumes. You can get these from the Stationery Office. (I send you sixteen I have by me here.) Meanwhile I will continue to look up the others which occur to me.

It may possibly be worth while including some in 1919 at the time of the Peace Conference when I seem to remember having made several appeals for lenient treatment of the Germans. These I will have looked up in my boxes of that date.

There is no need to wait till the whole work is complete before printing. As soon as you can, send me a good big batch and I will skim through them. Irrelevancies have to be cut out and there is a certain alteration between the spoken and written word. A pleasant effect must be produced to the reader if any good is to be done.

If you like this idea let me have a line.[1]

Adam Marshall Diston to Violet Pearman
(*Churchill papers: 8/594*)

3 April 1938   Gerrards Cross

Dear Mrs Pearman,

I am enclosing draft of the German colonies article, 'Germany Wants a Place in the Sun'. Unfortunately, I haven't been able to finish this so quickly as I had hoped. My wife has been ill and that slowed me up. However, she is better now and I should be able to get ahead with the other two subjects, if Mr Churchill wants me to tackle them. I propose to do next the article on the shipbuilding race and Japan.

'Germany Wants a Place in the Sun' is again on the long side. But there are some references to Germany's colonial record which Mr Churchill may think go a bit too far, though they are based on official sources. If these stay in, the account of Bismarck's colonial drive, and its origin, could, I think, be condensed. I hope that Mr Churchill will like the article.[2]

---

[1] Randolph agreed to his father's proposal, as did George Harrap. The result was the volume *Arms and the Covenant*, 41 speeches made by Churchill between 25 October 1928 and 24 March 1938, 'compiled by Randolph S. Churchill', and published on 24 June 1938. The American edition, entitled *While England Slept*, was published by Putnam on 30 September 1938 (and was to give John F. Kennedy the idea for the title of his own book, *Why England Slept*, published in 1939).

[2] Marshall Diston had based much of the historical section of his article on a new book, *Germany's First Bid for Colonies, 1884–85*, by the young Manchester historian, A. J. P. Taylor. It was Taylor's second book (of more than 25).

Winston S. Churchill: notes for Adam Marshall Diston

(*Churchill papers: 8/594*)

[3] April 1938

This requires completely recasting and the introduction of perhaps a thousand words of new matter. It should feature the more prominent psychological contrast between Hitler and Mussolini. It should also be brought up to date by references to the latest performances of both. Mussolini is the greater man who is on a small moke,[1] while the other is on an elephant or a tiger. This is only as a guide. It should be easy to do this. The News of the World article has never been published in the United States.[2]

Winston S. Churchill to L. S. Amery

(*Churchill papers: 2/329*)

4 April 1938

I have been asked to write an article for an American paper on the ex-German colonies. I wonder if you have any material which you could give me. Of course I am going to argue against giving them back to the present Nazi regime.

Winston S. Churchill to F. W. Deakin

(*Churchill papers: 2/341*)

4 April 1938

I have written a letter to President Beneš, and have asked the Foreign Office to mention your name to the Embassy at Prague. You should call at the Embassy, and ask the best way of getting in touch with the President. Remember he is the head of a State. You should encourage him, or anyone he puts you in touch with, to talk to you confidentially for my information about their position, and what they think we can do to help. Is it true that the fortifications are already complete opposite the new Austrian front? What sort of communications have they from Roumania into Russia? What are their relations with Roumania and Yugoslavia? Is it worth while working

---

[1] Moke = a donkey. In Australian slang, a very inferior horse.

[2] Of three articles which Marshall Diston drafted for Churchill in 1938, 'Japan Guesses Wrong', and 'Dictators on Dynamite' were published in *Collier's Magazine* on 30 July and 3 September 1938 respectively, and the third article. 'The Colony Racket', was published in *Collier's Magazine* on 19 November 1938.

out the plan I outlined in the House of Commons for a block of Danubian States planned for economic and ultimately military purposes?

Oliver Harvey:[1] *Foreign Office minute*

(Foreign Office papers: 371/21616)

4 April 1938

. . . what Mr Churchill said was that he had discussed the matter with General Gamelin and that the latter had said that in the event of war breaking out France would not attack Germany by advancing beyond the Maginot line, but would attack in Libya on the assumption I suppose that Italy had joined hand with Germany at the outset.[2]

I think Sir O. Sargent[3] would like to see this as he also wondered what Mr Churchill had said to the S of S.

Winston S. Churchill to Lord Camrose

(Camrose papers)

4 April 1938

My dear Camrose,

I am very glad you have returned to these troubled scenes.

There is a matter of business which I want to discuss with you. For the last two years I have written fortnightly mainly on foreign politics for the Evening Standard. They have paid £70 per article of 1,000 to 1,100 words.

[1] Oliver Charles Harvey, 1893–1968. Educated Malvern and Trinity College, Cambridge. On active service in France, Egypt and Palestine (despatches), 1914–18. Entered Foreign Office, 1919. First Secretary, Paris, 1931–6. Counsellor, and Principal Private Secretary to successive Secretaries of State for Foreign Affairs, 1936–9, and 1941–3. Minister to Paris 1940. Assistant Under-Secretary of State, 1943–6. Knighted, 1946. Deputy Under-Secretary of State (Political), 1946–7. Ambassador to France, 1948–54. Created Baron Harvey of Tasburgh, 1954.

[2] On reading Churchill's report of his interview with General Gamelin, J. M. Roberts of the Foreign Office noted on 6 April 1938: 'This is what Col Petibon has been saying lately, but it will not help the Czechs much. Nor does there seem any special reason why Italy should be engaged at all, if the French refrain from attacking Germany.' Two days later Ivo Mallet noted: 'It is a poor look-out if the French General staff are really reduced to thinking on these lines' (*Foreign Office papers: 371/21616*).

[3] Orme Garton Sargent, 1884–1962. Educated at Radley. Entered Foreign Office, 1906. Second Secretary, Berne, 1917; 1st Secretary, 1919. At the Paris Peace Conference, 1919. Counsellor, Foreign Office, 1926. Head of the Central Department of the Foreign Office, 1928–33. Assistant Under-Secretary of State for Foreign Affairs, 1933. Knighted, 1937. Deputy Under-Secretary of State, 1939; Permanent Under-Secretary, 1946–9. Known in the Foreign Office as 'Moley'.

In addition they have syndicated it in England for my benefit to the papers on the attached list A,[1] yielding from £25 to £30 per article. Besides this outside the United Kingdom they have syndicated it for my benefit to the papers on list B,[2] yielding about £15 per article. This they have done through their own office without any trouble or expense to me.

Finally however a remarkable development has grown up on the Continent for translations of these articles. These I now manage myself through the agency of Co-operation, and the yield on a 60/40 basis is between £40 and £50 per article. The list of Continental papers taking these articles includes those on list C.[3] As you will see it is a very fine platform, though as Nazi power advances, as in Vienna, planks are pulled out of it. The acceptances vary slightly from fortnight to fortnight, but I should think on the whole the articles have reached £140–£150 apiece. I have not made any satisfactory arrangement about the American rights, though occasionally an article is sold. I am looking into this and hope to develop syndication there during the course of the present year.

The Evening Standard have now terminated the series so far as they are concerned, on the grounds that my views are not in accordance with the policy of the paper, and I should like to know whether the Daily Telegraph would care to carry on the series, and if so on what terms. Of course as the Daily Telegraph is a National paper publication therein would prevent syndication in the United Kingdom to the papers in Class A, whereas with a London evening paper like the Star, this syndication should continue.

I should be much obliged if you would let me know as soon as possible whether you are interested or not. Of course I am going on with the series in one form or another.

Randolph talked to Seymour[4] about this so perhaps you are already familiar with the subject.

Yours vy sincerely,
Winston S. Churchill

[1] List 'A' included the *Glasgow Evening News*, the *Aberdeen Evening Express* and the *Belfast Telegraph*, all of which regularly printed Churchill's fortnightly articles.

[2] List 'B' included the *Adelaide Advertiser*, the *East African Standard*, the *Times of Malta* and the *Madras Mail*.

[3] List 'C' for the scope of which Imre Revesz had been responsible, included newspapers in Holland (Rotterdam), Belgium (Brussels) Denmark (Copenhagen), Sweden (Stockholm), Norway (Oslo and Trondheim), Estonia (Tallin), Latvia (Kovno), Switzerland (Lausaune, Lucerne and Zurich), Czechoslovakia (Prague), Hungary (Budapest), Poland (Warsaw and Cracow), Rumania (Bucharest) and Argentina (Buenos Aires).

[4] John Seymour Berry, 1909– . Elder son of the 1st Baron (later Viscount) Camrose. Educated at Eton and Christ Church, Oxford. Conservative MP for Hitchen, 1941–5. On active service in North Africa and Italy, 1942–5 (despatches). Vice-Chairman of the Amalgamated Press Ltd., 1942–59. Succeeded his father, as 2nd Viscount, 1954. Subsequently Chairman of Daily Telegraph Ltd.

Lord Camrose to Winston S. Churchill

(*Churchill papers: 8/601*)

6 April 1938

My dear Winston,

Thank you for your letter.

I only got back on Friday and have been very heavily engaged; but Seymour had told me during the week-end of his talks with Randolph so that I knew something about the matter before receiving your note.

It is a little difficult for us to enter into a definite agreement for any lengthy period to publish a series of articles on political subjects, having regard to the fact that our policies might well be at serious variance.

I would be willing to try the experiment for six months at a fee of £70 per article, undertaking to pay you for the whole 13 articles, but reserving the right of non-publication in such cases as we so decided.

I am afraid, as you say, that if the articles appeared in a London morning paper, serialisation in the provincial evening papers, other than those of Scotland and Ireland, would not be practicable. As things are in this country the two methods are irreconcilable.

I would like to have a chat with you before the holidays. Are you by any chance free for lunch to-morrow (Thursday)? I will get my Secretary to telephone yours in the morning.

Yours,
Camrose

Winston S. Churchill to Pierre Cot

(*Churchill papers: 2/329*)

6 April 1938

My dear Monsieur Pierre Cot,

I am appalled to find that your most kind letter of February 15 has been overlooked by me. It was put aside together with the more important letters I received on that occasion, for my personal attention, and by this very precaution it got mislaid. I trust you will pardon my very bad manners, though quite involuntary, in not acknowledging sooner your extremely courteous letter to me.[1]

---

[1] C. B. Cochran recalled a similarly courteous apology by Churchill at about this same time, when he had arranged to see Churchill at Morpeth Mansions at 11.30 one evening, arrived, found Churchill was not there, waited until 2 in the morning and, as Churchill had still not arrived, returned home. 'Next morning, however,' Cochran later recalled, 'as I was

Harold Nicolson: diary

(*Nicolson papers*)

6 April 1938

On to the Focus. This is a mysterious organization. I do not understand who pays. We lunch excellently in the Pinafore Room of the Savoy. Who pays?[1] Anyhow there are present Winston (in the Chair), Wickham Steed, Gilbert Murray, Archie Sinclair, Arthur Salter.[2]

The point is that Winston pledges himself to a League programme. He makes a good speech.

---

dressing, a taxicab arrived, with a letter in Mr Churchill's own hand, offering me profuse apologies. He had dined with friends, he said, and, instead of coming home, "forgot entirely", and was carried off to a club. "It is only now," he continued, "returning at this hour, that I remembered my engagement with you, and your great kindness in coming to see me. I do trust that you will forgive this hiatus in my behaviour. Pray prove it to me by letting me know when I may call upon you to-morrow. Any time you specify, from 10 to 1, or 5.30 to 7.30, I will faithfully observe. I am so ashamed of my lapse." (Charles B. Cochran, *Cock-a-doodle-do*, London 1941, page 242.)

[1] The 'Focus' activities were paid for by Eugen Spier (see page 160, note 1). He has recorded how, after the first of its luncheon meetings in June 1936, a special drafting committee was set up, at Churchill's suggestion, to prepare a manifesto. 'The secretary was instructed,' Spier recalled, 'to take the necessary steps to meet the requirements of the committee, and to make arrangements for the next meeting at which the draft manifesto would be discussed. The secretary agreed, but asked where the money to defray expenses was to come from. His bald request came like the explosion of a bomb. Expressions of embarrassment appeared on every side, and Churchill himself looked displeased, even angry. For a moment it looked as if the whole effort was about to come to grief. To avert catastrophe I took Richards aside and asked him to announce that all our requirements had been taken care of. The tension was immediately eased. Churchill seemed greatly relieved and the other guests were clearly delighted' (Eugen Spier, *Focus*, London 1963, page 22).

[2] James Arthur Salter, 1881–1975. Educated at Oxford High School and Brasenose College, Oxford. Admiralty Transport Department, 1904; Director of Ship Requisitioning, 1917. General Secretary of the Reparations Commission, 1920–2. Knighted, 1922. Gladstone Professor of Political Theory and Institutions, Oxford, 1933–44. Independent MP for Oxford University, 1937–50. Parliamentary Secretary, Ministry of Shipping, 1939–41. Joint Parliamentary Secretary, Ministry of War Transport, 1941. Privy Councillor, 1941. Head of the British Merchant Shipping Mission to Washington, 1941–3. Chancellor of the Duchy of Lancaster, 1945. Conservative MP for Ormskirk, 1951–3. Minister of State of Economic Affairs, 1951–2. Minister of Materials, 1952–3. Created Baron, 1953.

Sir Henry Strakosch to Winston S. Churchill

(Churchill papers: 2/340)

6 April 1938
Personal

My dear Winston,

I have attempted to summarise, in the enclosed Note, the economic and financial aspects of the new situation which has been created for the Danubian and Balkan countries through the absorption of Austria into Greater Germany. I hope the Note may be of some service to you.[1]

Looking forward to our evening together on Thursday.

Ever yours,
H S

Group-Captain Lachlan MacLean to Violet Pearman

(Churchill papers: 2/339)

7 April 1938   United Service Club

Dear Mrs Pearman

I don't know if Mr Churchill will find the enclosed paper on 'first line air strength' of interest, but I am sending it in case it may be of some use.

It attempts to deal, in a perhaps somewhat academic manner, with the principles which should govern our 1st line strength in aircraft.[2]

---

[1] Entitled 'Greater Germany's Economic Threat to the Danubian Countries', this five-page Note was the second Note that Sir Henry Strakosch had sent Churchill, on the same theme, in three weeks. For the text of his earlier, and fuller Note, dated 18 March 1938, see pages 943–6 of this volume. This second Note, which was undated, ended: 'the dominant position of Greater Germany is not so much based on a natural economic dependence of the Danubian countries on Greater Germany, but on the superior position she occupies as a single and closely controlled market and her power to use her political strength in her economic interests. There is, on the other hand, at present no co-ordinated effort by the Danubian countries *inter se* and the Western world to secure the maintenance or broadening of their trade relations so as to prevent the complete dominance of Greater Germany. To remedy this situation a concerted effort by the Western world is urgently called for' (*Churchill papers: 2/350*).

[2] During the course of his five-page paper, headed 'Parity of Air Forces', Lachlan MacLean wrote: 'A dogma, which by age-long repetition has reached acceptance as an axiom, is that "the armed strength of a State is not necessarily the real indication of the potential strength of that State for war". That this was true, as long as the armed forces of the State could interpose themselves as a barrier against hostile advance and so give time for the momentum of potential strength to develop, is probably incontrovertible; but that it is true now, when the opening gambit in warfare has moved from the ground into the air, is questionable. Air attack can be carried out so swiftly, and, as technical development proceeds, may be so widespread in its scope, that the peace industries of a country, surprised by such attack, may never be afforded the opportunity of mobilizing their latent war potential, even if deliberately organized to that end in peace. The opening move in air warfare may therefore be the decisive move, and a failure in the initial stages may be irremediable.'

I am continuing with a second part in which I hope to reach, as the result of a more detailed analysis of facts and figures, concrete conclusions.

The second part may be rather delayed, because I am finding it difficult these days, to spare from the demands of ordinary routine work, the time that is really necessary to devote to the proper study for these papers. I will however send it as soon as it is ready, if it will be of interest.

Winston S. Churchill to Lord Camrose

(*Camrose papers*)

8 April 1938   Chartwell

My dear Camrose,

Following your letter of April 6 and our talk last night, I write to say that the arrangements you propose are most agreeable to me. I have asked the Syndication Department of the Evening Standard to notify all the English provincial papers that the series is no longer available to them. There are two papers, one in Glasgow and one in Belfast, which I am proposing still to supply in view of your letter. However if later on you find this clashes with the interests of the Daily Telegraph, perhaps you will let me know. The English provincial papers affected have expressed great regret at the prospect of losing the articles.

If you wish the next article to be ready by Wednesday perhaps you will ask your Editor to ring me up on Saturday or Sunday so that we can discuss the topic. In this case it would seem to be 'The new French Government' which would have special interest in view of my recent visit to Paris, of which I have hitherto said nothing.

I will also mention to the Editor[1] the special line at the bottom of the articles safeguarding their copyright in the interests of the foreign syndication.

Yours vy sincerely,
Winston S. Churchill

---

[1] Arthur E. Watson, 1880–1969. Educated at Armstrong College, Newcastle. Began his journalistic career on the *Newcastle Daily Leader*. Joined the *Daily Telegraph*, 1902. On active service in France, Royal Field Artillery, 1914–18; acting Major, 1918. Assistant Editor, *Daily Telegraph*, 1923. Honorary Treasurer of the Institute of Journalists, 1923–8. Editor of the *Daily Telegraph*, 1924–50. President of the Merton and Morden Conservation Association, 1962–8. The present editor of the *Daily Telegraph* writes: 'A shy, self-effacing man, non-writing editor, he was a lifelong teetotaller and non-smoker (rare for a journalist) and his only indulgence was driving fast cars' (letter to the author, 30 October 1981). Arthur Watson's brother was Sir Alfred Watson, former editor of the Calcutta *Statesman*.

Winston S. Churchill to Imre Revesz

(Churchill papers: 8/607)

8 April 1938

Dear Dr Revesz,

The Evening Standard notified me of their wish to terminate the series of articles at a month's notice on account of divergence from the policy of the paper. I replied that in these circumstances I did not wish to write any more for them.

I have now transferred the publication of the parent article on the same terms to the Daily Telegraph. I gather they would prefer Wednesday for publication instead of Friday, and also that they will insert any line safeguarding copyright which I may require. I will therefore insert it in the form you wish, thus there will not be the same difficulty about concerting the publications abroad.

Obviously the first article will be about the French Government which should command special interest in view of my visit.

I am sending under separate cover, a letter enquiring about the various newspapers which have not taken the last four articles at particular times.

It may amuse you to know that there was a rush of papers to secure the articles the moment it was rumoured in Fleet Street that the Standard had stopped them. Both the News Chronicle and the Sunday Pictorial were eager with offers, but the Daily Telegraph is a far more powerful and suitable platform for me.

Victor Cazalet: diary

(Robert Rhodes James: 'Victor Cazalet, A Portrait')

11 April 1938

Dined with Winston last night. Just he and Clemmie. Delightful! We talked over, round, through, the present problems. He is v anti-Govt for not having got on with rearmament. We are, apparently, lamentably behind, but of course it's all a matter of degree. He views German aggression as inevitable. Equality perhaps today. Submission tomorrow. French army still very good. We play bezique, but we talk most of the time. I suppose he ought to be in Government. He has had experience, he has the drive. Buck de la Warr,[1]

---

[1] Herbrand Edward Dundonald Brassey Sackville, Lord Buckhurst, 1900–1976. Known as 'Buck'. Educated at Eton and Magdalen College, Oxford. Succeeded his father as 9th Earl De La Warr, 1915. Parliamentary Under-Secretary at the War Office in Ramsay MacDonald's second Labour Government, 1929–30. Parliamentary Secretary, Ministry of Agriculture and

whom I saw on Friday, is all for him being in, but I know there must be a great deal of opposition.

Winston S. Churchill to R. J. Thompson
(*Churchill papers: 8/600*)

11 April 1938

Dear Mr Thompson,

I have made arrangements with the Daily Telegraph to carry on the series of articles which I have been writing for the Evening Standard, without any intermission, and am now able to reply to your letter of the 24th March.

I was not aware that you had any reason to be dissatisfied with my articles, or the time and conditions in which they were presented. It was always understood that if circumstances changed and an emergency arose, you could have a new topic chosen up till almost the last moment. As to any speech I made entrenching upon the sphere of the current article, it was always open to you to draw my attention to this, and I should have been very ready to meet your wishes.

With regard to the divergence from Lord Beaverbrook's policy, that of course has been obvious from the beginning, but it clearly appears to me to be less marked than in the case of the Low[1] cartoons. I rather thought that Lord Beaverbrook prided himself upon forming a platform in the Evening Standard for various opinions including of course his own.

With regard to the method of terminating the contract by a month's notice, this was clearly within the formal agreement but the understanding which I had with Mr Cudlipp certainly never led me to expect such abrupt treatment, and I admit I was surprised to receive your communication.

It may interest you to know that I could have placed the articles in three, if not four, different quarters at the same fee, and I understand that the provincial papers, who must now be struck off, expressed regret. The very wide circulation which these articles were commanding throughout Europe also encourages me to feel that you had no reasonable case for dissatisfaction.

Fisheries, 1930–5; Board of Education, 1935–6. Chairman of the National Labour Party, 1931–43. Elected to the Other Club, of which he was Joint Secretary, 1935. Parliamentary Under-Secretary of State for the Colonies, 1936–7. Lord Privy Seal, 1937–8. President of the Board of Education, 1938–40. First Commissioner of Works, April-May 1940. Chairman of the Agricultural Research Council, and Director of Home Flax Production, 1943–9. Postmaster-General in Churchill's post-war Government, 1951–5. Chairman of the Joint East and Central African Board, 1956–9. His younger son was posted missing, presumed killed, on air operations in the Second World War, aged twenty.

[1] David Low (see page 1548, note 1).

I am writing separately to Mr Monkhouse[1] and Mr Robertson[2] to thank them for their assistance, and for the trouble they took in making this series a success.

Leslie Hore-Belisha to Winston S. Churchill

(*Churchill papers: 2/336*)

11 April 1938   War Office
Secret and Confidential

My dear Winston,

Your Private Secretary wrote to mine on the 2nd April enclosing a document entitled 'Summary of the Fortifications, Artillery, etc, on the Coasts and in the Naval Bases of the Peninsula and of Morocco'.

I am always pleased to receive information of this kind, particularly when it comes from a reliable source, as your Private Secretary said in her letter. The information contained in the document which she forwarded does not entirely agree with the information at the disposal of the War Office, particularly with regard to the guns sited on the African side of the Straits, although the actual number of the guns is approximately the same.

You will have noted, however, that certain rather vague expressions such as 'a very large cannon' etc are used in the document indicating that the observations made were either rather vague or made under conditions of difficulty.

You may be interested to know that my military advisers also received a

[1] Patrick Monkhouse, 1905–1981. Known as 'Paddy'. Educated at Trinity College, Oxford; editor of *Oxford Poetry*; member of the Oxford Union debating tour of the United States. Joined the *Manchester Guardian* (on which his father was Literary Editor) in 1927; worked as a reporter, leader writer and critic, and 1934–6, as Night News Editor. Worked on the *Evening Standard*, 1936–40; Member of the National Executive of the National Union of Journalists. Enlisted in the Royal Ulster Rifles, 1940; Lieutenant, 1941 (worked in the Personnel Selection Branch of the War Office). Returned to the *Manchester Guardian* as News Editor, 1946; subsequently Deputy Editor. Author of three books for walkers in the hills; and a member of the Peak Park Planning Board. OBE, 1972. His obituary in *The Times* records: 'He survived with dignity the keen disappointment of not being chosen to succeed A. P. Wadsworth as editor, and in the crisis of 1966 played an important part as a member of the Scott Trust in resisting a proposal for a merger between *The Times* and *The Guardian*' (*The Times*, 15 April 1981).

[2] William Harris Robertson, 1894–1972. Born in Aberdeen. Left school at the age of 14. Served with the Cameron Highlanders on the western front, 1914–18 (twice wounded). Went to London University after the war. Subsequently editor of the Singapore *Free Press*, then Syndication Manager of the *Daily Express*. Worked with the BBC monitoring service, 1939–45. After the war he edited *Coal*, the magazine of the newly founded National Coal Board. Purchased the *Montrose Review*, 1959; the *Mearns Leader*, 1959 and the *Kincardineshire Observer*, 1965.

copy of the document which you forwarded and have been informed of its source. Although I cannot, of course, comment on the reliability of the information, I think you will agree with me that the source could not fairly be described as either disinterested or unbiased.

Yours very sincerely,
Leslie Hore-Belisha

Winston S. Churchill to Leslie Hore-Belisha

(*Churchill papers: 2/336*)

12 April 1938

Surely the point is not whether the source is disinterested or unbiassed, but whether the information obtained is, broadly speaking, true? If it is true, it is very serious; and the Government cannot slur over, for political reasons, matters of this consequence without incurring invidious responsibilities. I consider my part discharged when I placed the information before you.

Winston S. Churchill to Lord Derby

(*Churchill papers: 2/343*)

12 April 1938

I am very glad you feel able to take the Chair for me at Manchester on the 9th. I have felt it my duty to make exertions—so far as I can—to rouse the country in the face of our ever-growing dangers. Nothing less than a national effort will suffice. We must have the men who make the weapons as well as those who may have to use them. We must be in the main a united nation. A far greater effort is needed in rearmament. The volunteer and Territorial army must be stimulated in the highest degree. The ARP activities and organisation are rudimentary at the present time. England must speak with a confident voice. Our party must carry the Trade Unions with them. Non-Conformists, Churchmen and Catholics must work for a common end. The unattached flowing mass (which can nevertheless decide elections) must have a real awakening and a clear goal. The time is very short in which war may be averted. It can only be averted by a great England standing boldly for Peace and Freedom—Freedom first. Even if every effort is made I cannot feel sure that we shall succeed; but I am certain that if we do not make an effort we shall live to see all that we have guarded, lost.

We are all pretty well agreed upon a French alliance if only we can find a solid and coherent France. But our own attitude is of vital aid to France. They although armed lean on us, although we as yet are largely unarmed. There must be an attempt to rally the secondary Powers, all of whose interests are the same as ours, to resistance against aggression. This means a system of regional pacts—Danubian, Balkan, Scandinavian—perhaps even Anglo-Italian.[1] These can only be made acceptable to a united country by reference to the Covenant of the League of Nations. To mock at the League of Nations commends itself to many in our party, but we cannot defend upon a party basis. We must be national. Moreover the machinery already in existence at Geneva carries with it a moral sanction with which it would be the highest improvidence to dispense.

Finally these aspirations to establish the reign of law against brutal or calculated violence command today the approval of the world. In all the struggles of four centuries England has always marched with the mass opinion of the world and has stood for the general interest of all nations, to dwell in peace and toleration with one another. It is upon this theme that I shall dwell at Manchester and elsewhere.

Forgive this lengthy statement which I feel I ought to render you.

Winston S. Churchill to Anthony Eden
(Churchill papers: 2/329)

13 April 1938   Chartwell

We are looking forward so much to having you here, and will make you quiet and comfortable. Do try to give me two nights and let me know which.

I notice signs in the Daily Herald and the Star that they are coming round to an Anglo-Italian pact involving the recognition of the Abyssinian conquest. It is a good thing that the agreement will not be published till the House is up, as it will give time to think it over before anything need be said. From what I can learn the Government are very confident of producing a good impression.

My all-party campaign begins on May 9 in the Free Trade Hall, Manchester and Derby is going to preside. . . .

---

[1] Under the Anglo-Italian agreement signed in Rome on 16 April 1938, Mussolini agreed to evacuate all Italian soldiers from Spain and Libya, while Britain agreed not to fortify Cyprus without prior consultation with Italy. Britain also agreed to support at the League of Nations the *de jure* recognition of the Italian conquest of Abyssinia (see also pages 993, 995, 1010–1 and 1011 note 2). The agreement was not presented to the House of Commons until 2 November 1938, when it was approved.

Winston S. Churchill to Lord Camrose

(*Camrose papers*)

13 April 1938   Chartwell

My dear Camrose,

I presume you would not object to Answers publishing occasional re-prints. They are of course only second serials and appear about a fortnight after.

We put off the first article until Thursday so as to see what happened in France. It looks as though there has been a very considerable forward step.[1]

Winston S. Churchill to Léon Blum

(*Churchill papers: 20/24*)

14 April 1938   Chartwell

My dear Monsieur Blum:

I have thought much about you in these anxious and trying days, and I feel bound to express to you the gratitude which so many English people cherish towards you for the so great and real advance in the understanding between our two countries which marked your memorable Premierships. It is not for a foreigner, however friendly, to meddle in French politics. But I have never seen the good feeling between Britain and France so strong as during your tenure of power.

I am sure that in a private station for a while you will have immense opportunities of carrying forward this good work, so necessary for the rights

---

[1] Following a political crisis in France, Blum had been replaced by Daladier as Prime Minister, and Bonnet had replaced Paul-Boncour as Foreign Minister. On 14 April 1938 the *Daily Telegraph* published Churchill's article 'France's New Government', which began: 'If France broke, everything would break, and the Nazi domination of Europe, and potentially of a large part of the world, would seem to be inevitable. It is therefore with a keen and somewhat strained attention that all countries—especially friendly countries, great and small—have watched the prolonged deadlock in French Parliamentary affairs.' Commenting on the prolonged political crisis in France, Churchill wrote: 'I wonder whether the French people realise how bitter and persistent is the pro-German propaganda in this island? The strongest point, repeatedly made, is that France is on the verge of collapse. She is portrayed as about to go down the same bloody sewer as Spain has done. All the "Heil Hitler" brigade in London society exploit and gloat over what they are pleased to call "the Parliamentary impotence of the French democracy". Thus the amusing game in which French politicians rejoice is turned in deadly fashion to their detriment—and to our common danger. There surely ought to be an effort to put this right.' It was therefore welcome, he wrote, that Daladier, 'a very capable and sincere man', had emerged as Prime Minister: 'He has for nearly two years been identified with the French army and the defence of France.'

of the common people in every land, and for the Peace and Freedom of the world.

As a very old minister now in retirement (!) I thought I might without presumption send these few lines to you, and believe me,

Yours vy sincerely,
Winston S. Churchill

PS. Let us keep in touch.[1]

Anthony Eden to Winston S. Churchill

(*Churchill papers: 2/329*)

16 April 1938   Kirkdale Manor
Personal & Confidential   Yorkshire

My dear Winston,

Thank you for your letter. I should so much like to be able to come to Chartwell soon. Unhappily my plans have been a little disarranged by the fact that my Mother[2] has not been well lately, and I must devote a day or two to going to see her at Windlestone some forty miles away before I go to London.

The week-end of the 23rd to the 25th I promised while I was out at Cannes to spend with SB[3] in Worcestershire. Consequently, I cannot now reach London before Monday the 25th. This is tiresome, but I am afraid it cannot be helped. You may not, I suppose, be at Chartwell during Budget week? If not, I hope you would, in any event, be free to dine with me any night you

---

[1] At the end of May 1941 the Foreign Office was asked if this letter could be published on Blum's birthday (8 April 1941). They advised against publication, and Churchill deferred to their judgement. As W. H. B. Mack minuted to Sir Alexander Cadogan on 3 April 1941: 'The implication sedulously conveyed by German propaganda and believed by many Frenchmen that it is one of our war aims to restore the Front Populaire has done our cause a lot of harm in France. We have during the last three months been countering this propaganda by declaring that it will be for the French themselves to choose their own regime after the war and that we are prepared to work with any Frenchmen who are prepared to work with us. We have had indications that this propaganda of ours has had considerable success. I fear that the publication now of the letter proposed, even though Mr Churchill was not at the time a member of HM Government, would certainly be used by the Germans and Vichy to our detriment. I hope therefore that the Prime Minister will refuse permission to "show the letter".' (*Churchill papers: 20/24*)

[2] Sybil Frances Grey, daughter of Sir William Grey, Lieutenant Governor of Bengal and subsequently Governor of Jamaica. In 1886 she married Sir William Eden (who died in 1915). She died on 17 June 1945, six days before her grandson (Eden's elder son) was killed in action in Burma.

[3] Stanley Baldwin, who had been created a Knight of the Garter on 28 May 1937, and raised to the peerage as Earl Baldwin of Bewdley on 8 June 1937.

liked during that week. There is in point of fact perhaps some advantage in having our talk a little later, for I imagine that the Italian Agreement will not be debated in Parliament before the beginning of May.

As to that Agreement itself, it is in many respects a strange document, for it does not apparently enter into force at once. It may not do so for many months and in the interval much may happen. There is not apparently to be a marriage as yet, but only the announcement of the banns, coupled with the admission that there is a 'just impediment'. The Italian part of the bargain seems to consist principally of the re-affirmation of pledges, which up to now they have consistently broken, and which they are breaking to-day. While it appears that we are to bless the annexation of Abyssinia, Italy will not apparently bless our policy in Palestine. But I am, of course, writing before I have seen the terms of the agreement.

Fundamentally, however, I suppose that one's attitude towards negotiations with either Germany or Italy depends upon what one's conceptions are of the ambitions of these two Powers. As to Germany, you know my views. As to Italy, I do not believe that Mussolini has abandoned his dream of creating a Mare Nostrum. If so, every step we take in negotiations with Italy must be judged from the standpoint of whether or not it has facilitated Mussolini's main plan. I only hope we shall not fulfil the statement which I saw attributed to Mussolini in the 'New Statesman' the other day. 'Chamberlain will let me conquer Spain and then pay me to get out,' or words to that effect.

Quite naturally the Government will make all they can of the Agreement, even though it is as yet only of a hypothetical character, but I find it hard to believe that it will arouse great enthusiasm in the Country, while amongst those who care ardently about the Spanish issue, it is likely to be interpreted as giving Mussolini and Hitler a free hand to finish their campaign. . . .

I was most interested to hear about your Manchester meeting. I cannot imagine a better place for the opening of your campaign, or better auspices. It seems to me that the chief danger of the present time is complacency. A section of the British people is always so ready to take an optimistic view of the European situation. Perhaps the trouble is that we continue to be mentally an island long after we have ceased to be one geographically.

Many apologies for so long a letter!

Yours ever,
Anthony

Winston S. Churchill to Edouard Daladier

(*Churchill papers: 2/329*)

17 April 1938
Private

My dear Monsieur Daladier,

Accept my cordial congratulations upon the brilliant manner in which your Administration has assumed power, and my earnest wishes for its success.

The time now seems ripe to carry forward those plans for the common safety of our two countries which we talked over together when I had the pleasure to meet you in Paris. You will find the ground well-prepared for you over here; and I do not doubt of success. But strike while the iron is hot.

With every good wish,
Yours sincerely,

Lord Derby to Winston S. Churchill

(*Churchill papers: 2/343*)

17 April 1938

Dear Winston,

Many thanks. I quite understand the position and am very glad to be able to take the chair for you. I am sure the meeting will do good.

I am rather anti-the League of Nations but will not say that, only emphasise the fact that it is neither a party nor a League of Nations meeting, only a really National non-political gathering.

Yours ever,
E

Winston S. Churchill to Sir James Hawkey

(*Churchill papers: 2/343*)

18 April 1938

I dare say you will be interested to see the letter I wrote to Derby after he had consented, upon local representations, to preside at Manchester on the 9th, and also his reply thereto. You will see that his feeling about the League of Nations is much the same as yours. But he certainly does not think it should be made the means of barring national unity. Let me have the letters back when you have read them.

What a triumph for Mussolini this Italian pact is. If we had only rearmed in time we should never have had to submit to such humiliations.

I hope you had some holiday.

Winston S. Churchill to Anthony Eden

(*Churchill papers: 2/329*)

18 April 1938   Chartwell

I am sorry indeed you cannot come here this week, but as you say, we have plenty of time before the debate. It will, I imagine, take place on the 2nd or 3rd of May. The only night I have free in the preceding week is Friday the 29th. It would be very nice if you would come down here then. We should be alone and could have a good talk, and I should like to show you this place the next morning. If you cannot get away from London, I will come up myself, as I think it most necessary we should discuss together what should be done about the Italian pact.

It is of course a complete triumph for Mussolini who gains our cordial acceptance for his fortification of the Mediterranean against us; for his conquest of Abyssinia; and for his violence in Spain. The fact that we are not to fortify Cyprus without 'previous consultation' is highly detrimental. The rest of it is to my mind only padding.

Nevertheless I feel that considerable caution is necessary in opposing the agreement bluntly. It is a done thing. It is called a move towards peace. It undoubtedly makes it less likely that sparks from the Mediterranean should light a European conflagration. France will have to follow suit for her own protection, in order not to be divided from Britain. Finally, there is the possibility that Mussolini may be drawn by his interests to discourage German interference in the Danube basin.

Before making up my mind, I should like to know your views and intentions. I think the Anglo-Italian pact is only the first step, and that the second will be an attempt to patch up something even more specious with Germany which will lull the British public, while letting the German armed strength grow, and German designs in the East of Europe develop.

Chamberlain last week told the Executive of the National Union in secret that he 'had not abandoned hopes of similar arrangements with Germany'. They took this rather coldly.

Meanwhile our progress in the Air is increasingly disappointing, and what I told you about internal discontents continues to be true.

I am sorry that your speech could not be changed to another date, but I think, having regard to the broadcast facilities, it will hold its own with the Budget statement. It seems to me a very important speech for you, and so also is the line you take next month about the pact.[1]

Winston S. Churchill to Sir Maurice Hankey
(*Churchill papers: 25/14*)

18 April 1938

I think the time has come when the Air Defence Research Committee should take stock of the progress made to date. Many bright ideas of a highly technical character have been examined, and many experiments made. It is surely time to focus results, such as they are, severely eliminating items that give no practical defence service for, say, three years to come. Perhaps you will very kindly mention this to the Secretary of State.

Winston S. Churchill to Neville Chamberlain
(*Premier papers: 1/237*)

18 April 1938
Private

My dear Neville

Before the Air debate on the 15th March, I sent you a note containing a number of points about the failure of our Air extension programme, and I received an acknowledgment, for which I thank you. I had however hoped that you would be able to reassure me that you had looked yourself personally into these points, which I had selected from many with much care. I still hope that you will find time to do so.

I am sorry to add to your business on your well-deserved holiday, from which I hope you are benefiting.

Yours vy sincerely,
Winston S. Churchill

[1] For Churchill's published comments on the Anglo-Italian agreement, see page 1011, note 2.

Winston S. Churchill: message given on the telephone to the Press Association

(Churchill papers: 2/343)

18 April 1938

A series of meetings is being planned throughout the country with the object of helping the public to realise the increasing danger of the situation, and the need for a united national effort to cope with it. It is hoped to rally the great mass of latent opinion irrespective of party to those measures most conducive to the safety of Britain and the peace of the world.

The principle of these meetings is the support of national rearmament for the defence of Great Britain and for the maintenance of Freedom and Peace in accordance with the Covenant of the League.

The meetings will be held in association with the League of Nations Union and the New Commonwealth. Mr Winston Churchill has undertaken to address several of these meetings and various fixtures have already been made for him, the first at Manchester on the 9th May. Others are being fixed at Sheffield, Birmingham and Bristol, and particulars of these will be announced later. Mr Churchill will also speak in the Epping Division during the month of May.

Harold R. Peat to Winston S. Churchill

(Churchill papers: 1/407)

18 April 1938   New York

Dear Mr Churchill:

This is to acknowledge your cable to which I replied today.

No doubt you have received word from your attorneys to the effect that the contracts were signed and everything is satisfactory.

So far, we have actual signed contracts for your appearance in the twelve following cities:

Chicago, Ill (Northwestern University)	Oct	25
Kansas City, Mo (Kansas City Forum)	,,	27
Cincinnati, Ohio (Univ of Cincinnati)	Nov	1
New York, NY (Town Hall)	,,	10
Philadelphia, Pa (Phil Forum)	,,	15[1]
Dallas, Texas (Town Hall)	,,	21

---

[1] Churchill had drawn a line at this point, thinking that he might begin the projected lecture tour only after the planned Philadelphia lecture on 15 November 1938 (see Churchill's letter to J. Arthur Leve of 17 August 1938, quoted on pages 1118–9).

Fort Worth, Texas (Town Hall) . . . . ,, 22
Los Angeles, Calif (Los Angeles Forum) . . . . ,, 28
Pasadena, Calif (Pasadena Forum) . . . . ,, 29
San Francisco, Calif (Town Hall) . . . . Dec 6
Washington, DC (Town Hall) . . . . ,, 13
New York[1] Economic Club . . . . ,, 14

Please do not let this schedule frighten you because the other engagements will be fitted in as consecutively as possible with a view toward making your traveling as easy as possible. I expect to accompany you on the tour and all in all we are looking forward to a most successful visit for you.

The fees, so far, have averaged $2,000.00 a lecture.[2] Not really as much as I had anticipated but no doubt you are well aware of economic conditions in the United States. The indications are, however, for an upturn from now on. There is no question in our minds but that we will have the tour completely sold out. I would like to inquire regarding other engagements in addition to the twenty-five. I refer to those that we spoke about for the Luncheon Clubs and smaller Colleges where these can be fitted in, in conjunction with your main engagements. How many of these are you inclined to take, and on what basis? My suggestion is that for all engagements other than those guaranteed you, you permit me to book them on a straight fifty-fifty basis, with a guarantee that your share, in any case, shall not be less than Three Hundred ($300.00) Dollars.

Major T. M. Barlow[3] to Winston S. Churchill
(Churchill papers: 2/343)

20 April 1938   Fairey Aviation Company

Dear Sir,

I hear from a friend of mine, Alderman J. Toole (formerly Lord Mayor of Manchester) that you are speaking in Manchester at a public meeting on

[1] On 30 June 1938 the Secretary of the Pilgrims of the United States, Elihu Church, wrote to Churchill from New York: 'Dr Nicholas Murray Butler has written me saying he understands you are coming to this country in the autumn for a lecture tour covering several weeks. I am, in consequence, directed to write and tell you that The Pilgrims would appreciate the opportunity of giving a dinner in your honor while you are in New York. We are most hopeful that you may be pleased to accept our invitation and that a satisfactory date can be arranged' *(Churchill papers: 1/407)*.

[2] Two thousand dollars in April 1938 was the approximate equivalent of seven thousand pounds sterling in September 1981.

[3] Thomas Morgan Barlow, 1886–1950. MSc, Engineering, Birmingham. Lieutenant, RNVR, attached to the Air Department, Admiralty, June 1915. Transferred to the Air Board, April 1917. Designed a single seater flying boat, 1917. Major, 1918, and Chief Technical Officer, Martlesham Heath. Fellow of the Royal Aeronautical Society, 1921. Chief Engineer, and a director of the Fairey Aviation Company, Stockport, from 1931.

May 9th. Knowing your keen interest in the Rearmament Programme I should be very pleased if you will visit this Factory on May 10th as I feel sure you will be impressed with what has been done to date as regards aircraft production.

Winston S. Churchill to George Harrap

(Churchill papers: 8/595)

20 April 1938

Dear Mr Harrap,

. . . My son tells me he has sent you the 'copy' of the speeches. There are forty. They are all directed to foreign policy and rearmament, and they tell a perfectly consistent story, forming a running commentary upon the events of these disastrous years. They will be annotated to explain the points, and where necessary a timetable will be given of intervening events, and a few extracts from Lord Baldwin's and other speeches will be inserted.

I do not see why they should not be read. Certainly I have taken as much trouble in preparing them as about any book I ever wrote.

Will you kindly have them set up, and let me have slip proofs in the usual form as fast as they can be delivered from the printer.

By the end of this week, you shall have my last version of 'Marlborough' IV. You will be relieved to see that it falls within your limit of 652 pages.

Eugen Spier to Winston S. Churchill

(Spier papers)

20 April 1938

Dear Mr Churchill,

Mr Richards has communicated to me your wish to hear from me how my friends[1] judge the present position. I can briefly summarize their impressions as follows:

There appears to be undoubtedly a growing desire to oppose the Hitler influences in Eastern Europe. Such desire must however remain latent fo the following reasons. A moral opposition is discouraged as long as the very representatives of aggression and brutal force receive moral support from England. Neither can there be any encouragement for material opposition as long as the mighty British Empire officially proclaims its own weakness.

---

[1] In Yugoslavia, especially Mažuranić (see page 749, note 2).

Under such circumstances there seems no likelihood to stop the further advance of the victorious and unchecked practise and glorification of brutal force and lawlessness. Every possible device is organised by Hitler to intimate and discriminate in all countries especially in Eastern Europe including Turkey against any citizen who is not supporting unconditionally Nazi demands.

These thoroughfares, communications, waterways, transport of imports, exports and tourists are at the mercy of Nazism.

Industrialists, traders, caterers are given preference, directly and indirectly subsidized if they submit to the Nazi demands whilst those loyal to their country and law are faced with ruin. The passive attitude or rather the encouraging attitude of Great Britain is still less understandable as there seems no doubt that Great Britain will have to pay in the end the bill for this policy of wholesale destruction and impoverishment.

In this connection it is well to remember that Hitler has originally cemented his power in Germany by rallying all the discontented, displeased and bankrupt elements in Germany (Harzburger Front), as he believes in the maxim that such elements provide a more powerful fighting force than all content and saturated supporters. According to these principles of the 'hungry wolves' he expects from the control of the comparatively poor Balkan States a formidable fighting spirit which may easily be directed against those nations who are in a more satisfactory position. In comparison he declares the wealth of the British Empire as immoral and untenable. Leading National Sozialists are saying that to consider England's possessions as permanent or morally justifiable means only to recognize the strength of the British Empire and to admit ones own weakness. These statements are supported by Hitler's own saying that the frontiers of nations have not been drawn up by God or nature but by men's brutal force.

It has also been lately recognized that it appears more tempting from a military point of view and more profitable from an economic point of view to isolate and attack the vulnerable British Isles than the vast Russian Empire. Hitler however is anxious to avoid a repetition of 1914 by having to fight at one and the same time against 'God and the whole world', and his aim is therefore concentrated at the isolation of Great Britain. His propaganda for isolation is especially successful in England. In carrying through this propaganda he now repeatedly asserts that the frontiers of France are sacred and unviolable whilst at the same time the Nazis in France blame England for all Franco-German wars and quarrels. On the other hand the Nazi propaganda in England does not cease to assert how akin the German and English races are and what a crime to civilization it would be if the English would ever support the French. Furthermore it is believed that

Hitler must have very good reasons to assume that Italy will remain neutral in Eastern Europe as long as France remains neutral and further that Italy will also remain neutral in any dispute between Great Britain and the Greater Germany provided that France also remains neutral in such a dispute.

These statements are the summary of my friend's observations.

In my own humble opinion I still think as I always did that it is now more than ever a vital and urgent need in this country to fight the appalling ignorance about Nazi totalitarian aims and I again suggest to proceed in the way which I previously indicated to members of our Focus and in particular to Mr Wickham Steed, who I think principally agrees with my suggestions.

I definitely believe that such a procedure of enlightenment will enable this country to take such measures which will result to preserve in Europe the principle of Freedom and Peace within the reign of law. Only on such a basis is it possible to establish a lasting peace and friendship with Germany and this country. Such measures alone provide a last chance to avoid a catastrophe. I further respectfully submit that the piling up of armaments alone however urgent and necessary this is will certainly not prevent by itself a war.

I should be very pleased indeed to avail myself of the privilege to continue our last conversation any time you should desire to do so.

Yours very sincerely
Eugen Spier

Winston S. Churchill to W. L. Chenery[1]
(Churchill papers: 8/604)

21 April 1938

Dear Mr Chenery,

I send you herewith four articles:—

Great Britain and the German Colonies,
The De Valera,[2]

[1] William Ludlow Chenery, 1884–1949. Born in Virginia. Educated at the University of Chicago. Reporter for the *Chicago Evening Post*, 1910–14. Edited the leader page of the *Rocky Mountain News*, 1914. Editorial writer on the *Chicago Herald*, 1914–18. Associate-editor of *The Survey*, 1919; the *New York Globe*, 1921–3. Editorial writer, New York Herald, 1923. Managing Editor, *New York Sun*, 1923. Editor, *New York Telegram-Mail*, 1924. Editor of *Collier's Weekly*, 1925–43. President, Pelham (New York) Board of Education, 1937. Publisher of *Collier's Weekly* from 1943 until his death.

[2] Eamon De Valera, 1882–1975. Born in New York. A leading figure in the Easter Rebellion, 1916. Sentenced to death; sentence commuted to life penal servitude on account of his American birth. Released under the general amnesty, June 1917. President of the Sinn Fein, 1917–26. Elected to Parliament as a Sinn Fein MP, 1918. Imprisoned with other Sinn Fein

The Problem of the Labour Unions,
Challenge in the Pacific,

upon the lines you suggested to me. They are all a little over the 4,000 words limit, and you should cut them as you desire. I should recommend 'Challenge in the Pacific' being published as soon as convenient. The article on the relative demerits of Dictators will follow in a mail or two.

Surely you would like to have an article on the broad drift of events in Europe, and whether the war-clouds are coming nearer or tending to dissipate. So much has happened that could be woven into an important story. Never forget that the Germans are adding an army corps of three divisions to their already vast army every six weeks; and that by 1940 they will soon be double the strength of the French. I am delighted to see the Japanese apparently for the moment in the toils.[1]

Unless the unexpected happens, I shall be in New York in the third week of October, as my lecture tour has taken definite shape. I shall look forward to seeing you then. [2]

Winston S. Churchill to Vice-Admiral Sir Reginald Henderson
(*Churchill papers: 8/604*)

21 April 1938

I venture to send you a draft of an article I have written for Collier's Magazine in the United States on the situation in the Pacific, and should be much obliged if you could find time to read it through in order to let me

---

leaders, 1918; escaped from Lincoln Jail, February 1919. 'President' of the Irish Republic, 1919–22. Rejected the Irish Treaty and fought with the Irregulars against the Free State Army, 1922–3. President of Fianna Fail, 1926–59. Leader of the Opposition in the Free State Parliament, 1927–32. Prime Minister and Minister for External Affairs, 1932–48. Prime Minister for a second and third time, 1951–4 and 1957–9. President of the Republic of Ireland, 1959–73.

[1] On 19 April 1938 some 80,000 Japanese troops took part in an offensive in the southern Shantung region of China. A Chinese report published in *The Times* on 20 April 1938 told of 'a dozen places where their guerillas have killed hundreds of Japanese, disrupted communications and seized supplies' within thirty miles of Shanghai. The Chinese also claimed to have re-occupied Hanchwang. A further report published in *The Times* on 21 April 1938 told of the Japanese advancing against Linyi, but with Chinese forces apparently attacking their right flank. There was said to be 'severe street fighting' in Suchow, while 'The Chinese also report that reinforcements are on the way, and they appear to be hopeful of being able to stem the Japanese advance.' These hopes proved illusory.

[2] This visit never took place (see pages 1117, 1118–9 and 1124–5).

know whether anything I say in it would, if published, be detrimental to our interests. I do not think it contains anything which has not already appeared in public.[1]

Believe me,

Winston S. Churchill to Major T. M. Barlow

(Churchill papers: 2/343)

22 April 1938

I should like very much to come and see the Fairey Aviation factory the day after my meeting at Manchester. The only obstacle might be some debate in Parliament which would oblige me to return by the night train. I hope however that this will not arise, and in any case I could let you know if I could not come four or five days beforehand, so that no inconvenience would arise.

---

[1] In an article published in *Collier's* for 30 July 1938, and entitled 'Japan Guesses Wrong, Churchill wrote: 'The Japanese government has refused to contradict the allegation that it is building battleships of over 35,000 tons. In consequence, the British and the United States admiralties have invoked the Escalator Clause, and are free to build capital ships of whatever tonnage and of whatever cannon they may desire. This decision has been taken with pious regrets but with a strong underlying alacrity by the two English-speaking naval powers. They have absolutely nothing to do with each other, but their minds were moving on parallel lines and they both came simultaneously to the conclusion that they should agree to free themselves from their mutually imposed treaty restrictions about the size of battleships. Some people say, loud and often, that we are launched upon another naval race. Certainly it is not a naval race between our two countries. We have for many years abandoned all rivalry. But there was a foolish epoch in which Americans were trying to cut down British warship building and the British were arguing with the United States delegation about the exact interpretation of "parity". That crazy time is over. Nothing resulted from it except that the two peace-keeping powers nagged each other as far as possible, and the pirate powers took the fullest advantage of their stupidity. Now these follies have been discarded. The only question asked in England about the American Navy is whether it is strong enough. . . .' The article ended: 'The superior resources of the English-speaking nations can easily carry naval rivalry in this, as in other spheres, to a level at which it is quite impossible for Japan to compete. She would be well advised therefore, not to provoke such rivalry but, on the contrary, to have conversations in a frank and friendly spirit with the two English-speaking powers. The excited elements and militaristic secret societies that have now laid their grip upon Japanese policy should ponder long and anxiously before they commit their country to tasks beyond its strength. Japan has plunged into a war of almost measureless dimensions, which, at any moment, may take for her a much graver turn. Her finances are in the gravest disorder. The masses of her people are bowed beneath their burdens. There is rising discontent at home and increasing inability to purchase war materials across the exchange. In these circumstances, it would not be prudent to challenge Britain and the United States in their now buoyant and robust temper to a trial of naval shipbuilding capacity. It would be madness; but sometimes nations are mad. Anyhow, our course is clear.'

Winston S. Churchill to Herbert B. Swope

(*Churchill papers: 2/329*)

22 April 1938

It is very nice to hear from you again, and I thank you for your news of Bernie.

We are very anxious here about the trend of events, and I am thankful not to have any responsibility for past neglects.

I plan to come to the States on a lecture tour in the latter part of October and hope to see you then.

Winston S. Churchill to Philip Guedalla

(*Churchill papers: 2/329*)

22 April 1938

Very many thanks for your letter. I feel sure that what has happened has done no end of harm in the United States.[1]

We must have another of our Focus lunches soon.

---

[1] Churchill's concern for the support of the United States was expressed in an article for the *News of the World*, published on 15 May 1938, entitled 'The Union of the English-Speaking Peoples', which began: 'It is a relief to turn from the quarrels and jealousies of distracted Europe to contemplate the majestic edifice of Anglo-American friendship. But let us not deceive ourselves. Look more closely: in places the facing stone has been eaten away by acids in the atmosphere. There are cracks in the pillars that support the mighty dome. Pierce to the foundations: beneath a crust that sometimes seems all too thin are bitter waters of suspicion, a marsh of misunderstanding. No one is really afraid that the building will collapse. Something stronger than any masonry holds it together—a cement of the spirit. But it would be well to strengthen the foundations: to grout and bind the great structure till the great structure is indeed secure.' The article ended with a discussion of the risk to Britain of war, in which Churchill wrote: 'If Britain and the United States were agreed to act together the risk would be slight. These two great kindred powers, in collaboration could prevent—or at least localize and limit—almost any quarrel that might break out among men. They could do this, almost certainly, without any resort to force themselves by moral, economic and financial power, provided that in reserve there were armaments of sufficient strength to ensure that moral, economic and financial powers were not violently ruptured and suspended. Collaboration of this kind does not imply any formal union of the English-speaking peoples. It is a union of spirit, not of forms, that we seek. There need not even be an alliance. All that is necessary is a willingness to consult together, an understanding that Britain and America shall pursue, side by side, their mutual good and the good of the whole world. There would be nothing in such an understanding that need arouse fears elsewhere. Collaboration of the English-speaking peoples threatens no one. It might safeguard all.'

R. W. B. Clarke[1] to Brendan Bracken

(Churchill papers: 8/604)

24 April 1938

Dear Mr Bracken,

Here, at long last, are the notes for your friend's two articles. They are both rather academic and objective, because I imagine that he will be able to put in any epithets and abuse of the President that may be required. Also, presumably they are meant to be serious articles, and not just blah.

I hope they will provide the backbone of what he wants to say: if what he wants is something different, I'll see what I can do about it.

Winston S. Churchill to E. L. Spears

(Churchill papers: 2/329)

25 April 1938

I opened 'Liaison 1914' on Sunday to look up something, and never stopped until I read it all through again. What an excellent book it is. When is the second volume coming out? I understood you were at work upon it some years ago.[2]

I have not yet made up my mind about going to Czecho-Slovakia. It might be embarrassing from several points of view. Let us have a talk about it when we meet. Meanwhile I must not obstruct your plans of taking someone else.

---

[1] Richard William Barnes Clarke, 1910–1975. Known as 'Otto'. Educated at Christ's Hospital and Clare College, Cambridge. Wrangler, 1931. A chess enthusiast, he played for Cambridge against Oxford in 1931 (when Cambridge lost) and 1932 (when Cambridge won). Prizeman of the Royal Statistical Society, 1932. A writer on *Financial News*, 1933–9. In 1935 he devised an 'index' of ordinary share prices, which was to become famous as the 'Financial Times Index'. Visiting Lecturer, Cambridge University, 1935–6. Worked for the Ministries of Information, Economic Warfare and Supply and Production, 1939–45; member of the Combined Production and References Board, Washington, 1942–3. OBE, 1944. Assistant Secretary, Treasury, 1945; Under-Secretary, 1947; Third Secretary, 1955; Second Secretary, 1962. Permanent Secretary, Ministry of Aviation, 1966; Ministry of Technology, 1966–70. Knighted, 1964.

[2] *Prelude to Victory*, by Brigadier-General E. L. Spears, was published by Jonathan Cape, London, in 1939. In his Introduction, Churchill wrote: 'It is one of the best books which have been written about the Great War. It has a particular bearing upon present events. It should be read with attention by every officer of field rank and upwards in the French and British Armies. It will reveal to them a hundred mistakes and honest shortcomings which could be avoided in the light of experience already so dearly bought. It should also be read by the widest public as a record of wonderful exertions and glorious sacrifices, ending after tribulation in victory.'

Vice-Admiral Sir Reginald Henderson to Winston S. Churchill

(Churchill papers: 8/604)

26 April 1938   Admiralty

Dear Mr Churchill,

Thank you for sending me your article 'Challenge in the Pacific' which I have read with very great interest and which I return herewith. If I may say so, I have never seen Japan's folly so clearly expressed and in so few words, and in my opinion there is nothing in the article that is in any way detrimental to our interests. I only wish it had been published for Japanese consumption some months before the London Treaty discussions.

There are possibly one or two technical details with which I am not in entire agreement. I think that speed in battleships is important. Perhaps this is especially the case for operations against the German pocket battleships on the trade routes when speed (in conjunction with air) will be required to hunt them down; I assume that the whole of the German plan is for a concentration of effort—surface, under the surface and in the air—against British shipping and ports. What Japan may build in the heavier type of cruiser we do not know; but if she does so, she would get at the very least a year's start which really means more and, at the moment, we have only our four battle cruisers to deal with such a type. In my opinion, therefore, for the achievement of our object and for the best security of this country, it is best (without knowing Japan's intentions) to build, and go on building, fast battleships which may have to perform the role of a battleship cruiser on the trade routes. I think it would be a mistake to break off to some special design to meet something which is still indefinite.

Yours sincerely,
R. G. H. Henderson

Winston S. Churchill to the 2nd Earl of Birkenhead

(Churchill papers: 1/323)

26 April 1938

I most heartily congratulate you upon 'Stafford'.[1] It is a very fine piece of work, and once I began it, it held me tight to the end. The chapter called 'London and the Men in Power' is brilliantly written and leaves a most vivid, agreeable impression on the mind. What are you going to write now?

---

[1] Lord Birkenhead's *Stafford* was published in 1938. His next published biographies were a memoir of Lady Eleanor Smith in 1953 and a biography of Lord Cherwell, published in 1961.

One feels almost bereaved when one has finished writing a book, but I expect you have already embarked upon several flirtations, if not indeed an actual engagement!

Neville Chamberlain to Winston S. Churchill

(*Churchill papers: 2/336*)

26 April 1938   10 Downing Street

My dear Winston,

Thank you for your letter of the 18th April about the Air programme. Let me say at once that I have not overlooked the points that were raised in the note which you sent me with your letter of the 12th March. I have in fact been giving the whole of this subject my very close personal attention, together with Inskip and Swinton. A number of decisions have now been taken, most, if not all, of which you would, I feel sure, approve. You may be quite sure that I shall not cease to give the matter very close personal attention.[1]

Yours sincerely,
N. Chamberlain

[1] On 26 April 1938 Sir Horace Wilson wrote to Neville Chamberlain, about Churchill's letter: 'It might, I think, be a good thing if he were to be seen in the course of the next 48 hours and told of the changes that are being made at the Air Ministry and of the way in which arrangements are being made to cover the next two years' (*Premier papers: 1/237*). On the following day, 27 April 1938, the Cabinet were asked to endorse the opinion of a special Cabinet Committee consisting of Chamberlain, Simon, Inskip and Sir Kingsley Wood that Britain 'should aim at the dual purpose both of securing acceleration of suitable types and of bringing into production as early as possible the latest improved types'. The Committee believed that the production of 2,373 first-line aircraft by 31 March 1940 (Scheme L), 'ought to be substantially achieved'. The Cabinet minutes also recorded Chamberlain's remarks: 'Criticism must still be expected, especially from Mr Winston Churchill, but he hoped that the Chancellor of the Duchy of Lancaster now felt that he had a good answer, and everything possible was being done to meet the situation and keep the firms extended to their uttermost capacity. It would of course be said that other firms might have been called in to do the work, but that proposal probably emanated from interested quarters who did not really know the business' (*Cabinet papers: 23/93*). The Chancellor of the Duchy of Lancaster (an Office held by Churchill from May to November 1915), was Earl Winterton, who had entered the Government, but not the Cabinet, on 11 March 1938.

Winston S. Churchill to George Harrap

(Churchill papers: 8/598)

27 April 1938

Dear Mr Harrap,

We have provisionally decided on the title as 'War in Masquerade' from Dryden's Absalom and Achitophel—'and peace itself is war in masquerade'.

It is possible that we may later think of a better title, and I suppose it would always be possible to change it, even if the initial blurb has gone out. But for my part I am fully satisfied with it as it stands. The cover should then read:

WAR IN MASQUERADE[1]

by

Winston S. Churchill

(compiled by

Randolph S. Churchill)

Winston S. Churchill to Sir Maurice Hankey

(Churchill papers: 8/598)

[27] April 1938   Chartwell

My dear Hankey,

I propose to publish in a volume of speeches on Defence which is being prepared, the two statements which I made when I accompanied the deputation to Baldwin and Inskip at the end of July, 1936. The facts then set forth by me are now 21 months old, and in consequence have no relevance to the existing situation. You will remember I stipulated that the fact that I made these statements in the course of a confidential deputation should in no way debar me from making use of what I said myself, (apart from anything said by others) if at any time I considered in my discretion the public interest so required. You will see in the record of the proceedings, (Nov 23) page 2,

---

[1] The title eventually chosen was *Arms and the Covenant*, but not before another possibility 'The Locust Years', had been discussed. The American publishers chose *While England Slept* as their title. Churchill proposed to share the royalties with his son, and a year later, on 4 April 1939 Randolph Churchill's secretary, L. H. Buck, wrote to Kathleen Hill that in June 1938 Randolph had received his share of the American and Swedish royalties (£333.6.8) and in August 1938 his share of the American and Swedish royalties (£100). In addition, Churchill had made Randolph two private payments of £200 (5 September 1938) and £100 (16 January 1939): a total of more than £700, or approximately £12,000 in 1981 values.

that Mr Baldwin explicitly recognised my right to do so.[1] I shall of course practise a certain amount of editing abridgement, as for instance the reference to information obtained from the French General Staff, etc, and I shall be quite willing to consider any suggestions from you on particular points, phrases or figures.[2]

Meanwhile I return to you the record of the proceedings which you sent me after the deputation. It has remained in one of my locked boxes ever since, and except for my own two statements no one has seen it. I am retaining only my own two statements. I have of course the original draft from which I read them on the deputation, but there are slight differences between the written and the spoken words. I have also kept a copy of my colloquy with Baldwin in which I made clear what I have mentioned above.

Looking back now, I regret very much that I did not make these two main statements, or the bulk of them, in the House of Commons. They might perhaps then have led to more effective action being taken.

Sir Henry Page Croft to Winston S. Churchill

(*Churchill papers: 2/239*)

28 April 1938

My dear Winston,

I have talked to some of our friends who are interested in the Irish side of affairs, and whilst I find a feeling of discomfort, there seems to be a general consensus of opinion that any attempt to divide the House would result in a very small minority.

Under these circumstances, I think that it is better to make such protest as can be made in the debate. If there was the slightest chance of stopping the Treaty going through I would be prepared to make a long and sustained fight but I do not think that any useful purpose would be served at this anxious moment in taking any steps which might seriously impair the unity of the forces supporting the Government.[3]

[1] See page 426 of this volume, where Churchill said to Baldwin 'I do not want to be told anything which, if I am not satisfied, would prevent me from criticising,' to which Baldwin replied: 'I have never put an impossible strain on any of my friends.'

[2] Churchill did not publish any of the Defence Deputation proceedings in *Arms and the Covenant*; his own contribution to these proceedings is published here in full for the first time, in this volume, pages 265–94.

[3] The British Government had agreed with the Government of Eire to give up all British naval rights at Queenstown, Berehaven and Lough Swilly. These rights had been secured as part of the Irish Treaty of 1922, at which time Churchill, as one of the principal negotiators, had placed the highest importance on Britain retaining control of these three naval bases. On

The real danger now as for the last 6 years is Germany, and my own view is that we should concentrate on doing everything in our power to get air production speeded up without parading the nakedness of the land to the world in such a way as to encourage Germany to undertake further adventures.

To this end I am prepared to co-operate and to the same end I am anxious to see everything possible done to bring Italy nearer to ourselves. If we can get close to Italy we may be able to stiffen up South-Eastern Europe, and in this way help the whole European situation.

Yrs ever,
H. Page Croft

Anthony Eden to Winston S. Churchill
(Churchill papers: 2/329)

28 April 1938

. . . With regard to the Italian Pact, I agree with what you write. Mussolini gives us nothing more than the repetition of promises previously made and broken by him except for the withdrawal of troops from Libya, troops which were probably originally sent there for their nuisance value. It has now become clear that, as I expected, Mussolini continued his intervention in Spain after the conversations in Rome had opened. He must be an optimist indeed who believes that Mussolini will cease increasing that intervention now should it be required to secure Franco's victory.

As a diplomatic instrument the Pact embodies a machinery which is likely to be found very troublesome to work. It is not to come into force until after the Italians leave Spain. It is almost certain, however, that many months will elapse before that occurs, and since what is important is not the presence of Italian infantry, but the authority of their experts and the Germans, it will be difficult to establish with certainty that the withdrawal has taken place. But maybe some do not mind much about that.

Then there is the Italian position in Abyssinia which, from what I hear, so far from improving grows steadily worse. I am afraid that the moment we

---

5 May 1938, during a debate in the House of Commons, he attacked the decision as 'an improvident example of appeasement', comparable to the abandonment of Gibraltar or Malta. The House of Commons listened to him with what he later described as 'a patient air of scepticism'. There were frequent, angry interruptions, and his criticisms of Chamberlain were widely resented by his fellow Conservative MPs. Bitterly he told them: 'You are casting away real and important means of security and survival for vain shadows and for ease'.

are choosing for its recognition will not benefit our authority among the many millions of the King's coloured subjects.

None the less I equally agree as to the need for caution in any attitude taken up towards the Agreement. After all it is not an Agreement yet, and it would be wrong certainly for me to say anything which could be considered as making its fruition more difficult. After all this is precisely what I promised I would not do in my Resignation speech and at Leamington.

The most anxious feature of the international situation, as I see it, is that temporary relaxation of tension may be taken as a pretext for the relaxation of national effort, which is already inadequate to the gravity of the times.

Did you notice a paragraph in the *City* column of 'The Times' of the 20th April, headed 'The Italian Agreement'? It is, I think, worth reading.[1]

I am much looking forward to our talk & to hear your views.[2]

Yours ever,
Anthony Eden

[1] On 20 April 1938 an article on the City page of *The Times* stated that the Anglo-Italian agreement had not had any appreciable effect on financial relations between the two countries. Italian credits were still being withheld by British banks. Italian bills were still expensive to discount on the British market. *The Times* speculated, however, that British banks might soon take a more liberal policy in lending money for Italian trade. This would help to improve commercial relations, and would lead to a 'finer rate' for Italian bills. 'Both parties', *The Times* argued, would then 'be advantaged by the agreement.' However, a caution was added to the effect that the Anglo-Italian agreement had not altered Italy's 'financial status', and the granting of credits to Italy should be 'conditioned primarily by the standing of the borrower'.

[2] On 12 May 1938, in an article in the *Daily Telegraph* entitled 'Britain and Italy', Churchill wrote critically of the recently signed Anglo-Italian Agreement, but added: 'Mr Chamberlain's policy towards Italy and France must be judged as a whole. France and Britain, more closely associated than ever, are both entering into arrangements with Italy, designed if possible, and if they are kept, to make the Mediterranean an area excluded from a possible war. This leads directly to the question of the Danube basin, to the States of the "Little Entente" and the Balkan League. Undoubtedly all these countries have heard with relief that all the Mediterranean Powers are trying to keep war out of the Mediterranean, and all of them feel a strong sense of easement and an added freedom of action as the result of the hope—and growing belief—that common interests will increasingly unite Italy with France and Britain. No one can pretend that what is called the "Berlin–Rome axis" has been broken, but at least we may feel that no sparks from Vesuvius or Etna will light up the forests of the North. It would be foolish to undervalue this hope at the present time. If Europe is to be stabilised and the destruction of civilisation averted, it is imperative that as many Powers as possible, all heavily armed, should be linked together in a non-war area and system. From such an association, a more practical form of collective security may develop.'

Anthony Eden to Winston S. Churchill

(*Churchill papers: 2/329*)

28 April 1938   Kirkdale Manor
                                                 Yorkshire

My dear Winston,

Many thanks for your telegram. I shall be delighted to go to Bristol to receive my Degree on July 2nd.

As to the Debate on Monday, I have thought matters over and come to the conclusion that it is preferable that I should not speak then. It is virtually impossible for me to say anything without going into the merits of the case, more especially in respect of Spain. While if I were to do this, I could, with some show of reason, be accused of departing from my undertaking not to do anything to hamper the course of the negotiations. This is all the more true since the Agreement has not come into force and may not do so for many months to come. I agree with you, however, that there may be some who will complain of my absence (though I think there would have been more who would have complained of my presence!); but this situation can be dealt with in a couple of sentences at my Annual Meeting on Friday, the 6th.

I feel pretty sure that this is the right line to take, but if for any reason I have to modify my decision between now and Monday, I will, of course, telegraph to you.[1]

Thank you so much for my luncheon & our talk, both of which I much enjoyed.

                                                 Yours ever,
                                                 Anthony Eden

Lord Derby to Alderman Joseph Toole

(*Derby papers*)

30 April 1938
Private

I was very sorry not to fulfil my engagement with you and Mr Winston Churchill, but that night at Manchester I found things were so bitter and everybody was telling me that it was so purely a political meeting that if I wanted to keep to my resolution of not attending a political meeting while I was Lord Lieutenant I certainly could not go to that meeting.

---

[1] Eden did not in fact speak in the debate on Monday 2 May 1938, nor did Churchill.

Randolph Churchill was very nice about it. He telephoned to me and I told him the circumstances of the case. It was agreed there should be a paragraph in the papers to say that I had not realised how political the meeting might be and therefore as Lord Lieutenant I felt I could not preside at it.

Winston S. Churchill to Lord Derby

(*Derby papers*)

30 April 1938   Chartwell
Private

My dear Eddie,

Randolph showed me your letter to him. I was very pleased when I heard that you were willing to take the Chair, though I was not aware you were to be approached by Toole. I was also rather surprised, because although my meetings are no campaign against the Government, they are a campaign for a policy which differs not in facts or in principle but in emphasis from the official policy, and I thought this might be a worry to you. I thought it very nice of you to be willing on personal grounds to preside, and I quite understand the reasons which have led you to decline. Indeed I should have been so careful not to put you in a false position that I might well have been put off my stroke.

With kindest regards,

Believe me,
Yours vy sincerely,
Winston S. Churchill

May 1938

Lord Derby to Winston S. Churchill
(Derby papers)

2 May 1938

I regret that I feel myself unable to take the Chair at your meeting in Manchester as I had originally intended to do. I have always made it a rule, since I became Lord Lieutenant, not to preside over any political meeting and though your meeting is not really a Party political meeting but a National meeting, I cannot help feeling that most people will regard it as being a political one, and for that reason I have asked to be allowed to withdraw from presiding.

I am glad to think, from what you have told me and from what you have written to me, that you quite agree with my decision.

May I say that my chief regret in not presiding is that I shall not be able to show to Manchester people, how completely you and I have refused to allow the differences of a few years ago to alter our personal feelings towards one another, and our feelings of loyalty to our Party.

Lord Derby to Winston S. Churchill
(Derby papers)

2 May 1938
Private

Very many thanks for your letter which confirms what you told me personally on Saturday night. I am so glad that you do not think that I let you down by my decision. I really only promised to take the Chair because I thought it was an excellent way of showing to Manchester that you and I had buried the hatchet.

I am writing a short message to you which you can read or not read, as you like, at the meeting. Anyhow, I hope you will have a successful one.[1]

Wing-Commander Anderson to Violet Pearman

(*Churchill papers: 9/129*)

2 May 1938   Royal Air Force Station,
                                             Catfoss,
                                             Nr Hull

Dear Mrs Pearman,

I have made out eleven points regarding the delay in re-arming the Royal Air Force together with a possible remedy. Would you add this to the other papers, also a letter from a pupil pilot which shows how short we are of aircraft to meet the needs of the old expansion. The letter gives an insight into the poor living conditions of our pupil pilots.

Yours very sincerely,
C. T. Anderson

Winston S. Churchill to Edouard Daladier

(*Churchill papers: 2/341*)

3 May 1938

Your predecessors, Mm Blum and Flandin, were both kind enough to give me the French estimates of the German Air strength at particular

---

[1] On 9 May 1938 Churchill spoke at the Free Trade Hall, Manchester, at a meeting organized by the Defence of Freedom and Peace Movement, on the theme 'Arm—and Stand by the Covenant'. His speech opened the Movement's campaign to draw in, as Churchill phrased it, 'church and chapel, Protestant and Catholic, Jew and Gentile . . . Trade Union leaders, co-operators, merchants, traders, industrialists, those who are reviving the strength of our Territorial forces, those who are working on ARP—none', he added, 'have felt themselves debarred'. Among those who listened to his speech were his son Randolph and daughter Diana, and the editor of the *Manchester Guardian*, W. P. Crozier. During the course of his speech Churchill told the audience: '. . . . we are told that we must not involve ourselves in a quarrel about ideologies. If this means that we are not to back Communism against Nazism, or vice versa, we all agree. Both doctrines are equally obnoxious to the principles of freedom. But surely we must have an opinion between right and wrong. This is no question of resisting dictators because they are dictators, but only if they attack other people. Surely we must have an opinion between aggressor and victim. Have we not an ideology, if we must use this ugly word, of our own—freedom in a liberal Constitution, in democratic and Parliamentary government, Magna Charta, and Petition of Right? Ought we not to be ready to make as many sacrifices and exertions for our own broad central theme and cause as the fanatics of either of these new creeds? Ought we not to produce in defence of right champions as bold, missionaries as eager, and if need be swords as sharp as are at the disposal of totalitarian States?'

periods in recent years. I should be much obliged if you could let me know what your view is now. I have several sources of information which have proved accurate in the past, but am anxious to have a cross-check from an independent source.

I am so glad that your visit here was so successful, and I hope now that all those staff arrangements will be made, the need for which I have pressed upon our Ministers.

Lord Londonderry to Winston S. Churchill

(Churchill papers: 2/347)

6 May 1938

My dear Winston,

Many congratulations on a very courageous speech.[1] I think your experiences have told you very clearly the value of the present arrangement, and as soon as De Valera loses his authority, we shall have another Party in Ireland repudiating all the present arrangements. I am inclined to think that our friend James Craig has played rather a poor part; he has been satisfied by the promise of a battleship and by the verbal undertaking of the British Government to maintain the social services in Northern Ireland on the same scale as in this country. At least, that is what I understand to be the position, and James knows quite well that his tenure will not be for very long, but he does not seem to appreciate the fact that very soon Northern Ireland will be a

---

[1] Churchill's speech of 5 May 1938, see page 1009, note 2 of this volume. During his speech Churchill also said, of the ports that were now to be given up: 'Queenstown and Berehaven shelter the flotillas which keep clear the approaches to the Bristol and English Channels, and Lough Swilly is the base from which the access to the Mersey and the Clyde is covered. In a war against an enemy possessing a numerous and powerful fleet of submarines these are the essential bases from which the whole operation of hunting submarines and protecting incoming convoys is conducted. I am very sorry to have to strike a jarring note this afternoon, but all opinions should be heard and put on record. If we are denied the use of Lough Swilly and have to work from Lamlash, we would strike 200 miles from the effective radius of our flotillas, out and home; and if we are denied Berehaven and Queenstown, and have to work from Pembroke Dock, we should strike 400 miles from their effective radius out and home. These ports are, in fact, the sentinel towers of the western approaches, by which the 45,000,000 people in this Island so enormously depend on foreign food for their daily bread, and by which they can carry on their trade, which is equally important to their existence. In 1922 the Irish delegates made no difficulty about this. They saw that it was vital to our safety that we should be able to use these ports and, therefore, the matter passed into the structure of the Treaty without any serious controversy. Now we are to give them up, unconditionally, to an Irish Government led by men—I do not want to use hard words—whose rise to power has been proportionate to the animosity with which they have acted against this country, no doubt in pursuance of their own patriotic impulses, and whose present position in power is based upon the violation of solemn Treaty engagements.'

derelict area with the great mass of an elderly population entirely unemployed.

I am quite sure that this is De Valera's plan, and he feels that what he
believes to be the artificial existence of Northern Ireland is maintained
solely by the British Government coming to the rescue with money, when
otherwise the Ulstermen would be compelled to make terms with him.
However, I think the British public are thoroughly tired of Ireland and do
not really care what happens so long as they are quit of her. I am quite sure
that Castlereagh[1] was right when he brought about the Act of Union, and I
think that connection could have been maintained but for the dependence
of the Liberal Administration after 1910 on the Irish vote.

I was so glad to see that Chartwell had been withdrawn from the market.
I was terribly disturbed to think of you giving up your lovely home.

Yours ever,
Charley

Winston S. Churchill to George Harrap

(Churchill papers: 8/595)

7 May 1938

It is most important to bring out the speeches as soon as possible. I am
reading rapidly through the revises a second time, and they can be put into
page proof as soon as Mr Randolph clears them. I think the right-hand
headline is most important. I am sure 'The Locust Years' is the best title.
Let us settle on that. . . .[2]

Winston S. Churchill to Sir Edward Marsh

(Churchill papers: 8/595)

7 May 1938

My dear Eddie,

I wonder if you would look through these proofs for me. It is of course the
spoken style. I have felt myself free to make some compressions.

---

[1] The 7th Marquess of Londonderry was the great-grandson of the 3rd Marquess, who was
half brother to the statesman Viscount Castlereagh (Foreign Secretary 1812–22).

[2] Churchill's speech volume was published by Harrap on 24 June 1938, entitled *Arms and
The Covenant*. It was dedicated by Randolph Churchill 'To my Father, without whose help this
book could never have been written.' 5,000 copies were published, price 18s. A total of 3,381
copies had sold by June 1940 when the book was reissued as a cheap 7/6d. edition, of which
1,382 were sold. A new edition was published by Odhams in 1947.

I shall be very glad if you will read it for defective grammar and particularly gross inelegancies. Taken altogether, it is a pretty remarkable indictment.

Do mark what you think is wrong, contradictory, repetitious or boring. It would be very good to cut 10,000 words, but one must have a fresh eye to do it.

Yours sincerely,
Winston S. Churchill

Winston S. Churchill to H. C. Vickers
(Churchill papers: 2/340)

7 May 1938

Many thanks for your letter about Czechoslovakia, the enclosure to which I will keep. It is of course a violently one-sided tale. There is no doubt that the Sudeten–Deutsche are the best treated minority in Europe.[1]

Winston S. Churchill to Sir Archibald Sinclair
(Churchill papers: 2/329)

10 May 1938
Secret

My dear Archie,

Henlein[2] of Czechoslovakia is lunching with me at 1.30 pm here on Friday, May 13th. Van has asked me to receive him. His visit is being kept

---

[1] On 16 May 1938 Churchill spoke at Bristol. As reported in *The Times* on the following day: 'He saw no reason why the Sudeten Deutsche should not become trusted and honoured partners in what was, after all, the most progressive and democratic of the new States in Europe. If this happy result should be achieved it would be due to the fact that the pressure by Germany in one direction had been balanced by the firm and courageous declarations of France, supported to a very considerable extent by Mr Chamberlain and his Majesty's Government, upon the other.' The inhabitants of Czechoslovakia, he added, 'were for the time being in a position to settle their own difficulties among themselves. How long these healthy conditions would last no one could foretell.'

[2] Conrad Henlein. A schoolteacher by profession. Founded the Sudetendeutsche Heimatfront, 30 September 1933, to replace the banned Nazi Party in Czechoslovakia; renamed the Sudeten German Party (SdP), 1935; Chairman of the Party, 1933-8. Advocated (in a letter to Hitler on 19 November 1937) that not only the Sudetenland, but also the whole of Bohemia should become a part of Germany. Appointed by Hitler to be Reich's Commissioner for the Sudeten German territories, 1 October 1938. Gauleiter of the Sudetengau, May 1939–May 1945. Captured by the US 7th Army, 9 May 1945; committed suicide on the following day.

a secret. It may be that he is not in transit. At any rate his wish to come to London to see Van and a few others is a hopeful sign. He will bring an interpreter. If you will come too we shall be four. Please tell no one.

I am sorry you could not come tomorrow as we might, together with Attlee, have discussed the Air debate. I hope Hugh Seely's[1] case will be well marshalled. I shall vote for the enquiry, but I think it would be better to do this on the second day, Wednesday 18, and not to force a division on the first day when the House will still be soaked with Winterton's pail of white-wash.[2]

Yours ever,

W

[1] Hugh Michael Seely, 1898–1970. Succeeded his father as 3rd Baronet, 1926. Liberal MP for East Norfolk, 1932–4 and for Berwick upon Tweed, 1935–41. Elected to the Other Club, 1932. Assistant Liberal Whip, 1935. Parliamentary Private Secretary to the Secretary of State for Air (Sir Archibald Sinclair), 1940. Joint Under-Secretary of State for Air, 1941–5. Treasurer of the Liberal Central Association, 1941–80. Created Baron Sherwood, 1941. His eldest brother, Captain Charles Grant Seely, was killed in action on 19 April 1917, aged 22. one of his younger brothers Victor Seely, was a prisoner-of-war, 1941–3. but escaped.

[2] On 12 May 1938, during a debate on the Air Estimates, Sir Hugh Seely moved the reduction of the salary of the Secretary of State for Air by £100, a traditional method of protest against Government policy. His aim, he said, was 'that there must be a committee of enquiry into what is happening in order to decide whether there should or should not be what we believe to be necessary, that is, a Ministry of Supply', and he went on to ask: 'Have the Government taken the necessary steps for raw material? Can they produce the necessary plant for fabricating aluminium? They cannot deny that the present state is highly unsatisfactory among the aeroplanes today, and that it is worse in many regards as to armaments.' The Government was opposed to any enquiry, and Seely's motion was rejected by 299 votes to 131. Among those Conservatives who voted against the Government in support of Seely, and of a Ministry of Supply, were Richard Acland and Harold Macmillan. Other supporters included the Liberal MP, James de Rothschild, and, among the Labour Party leaders, Clement Attlee, Aneurin Bevan, Sir Stafford Cripps, Hugh Dalton, Emanuel Shinwell and Josiah Wedgwood. Seely reiterated his call for a Ministry of Supply in the Air Defence Debate on 25 May 1938, urging that the Air Ministry would need the help of such a co-ordinating Ministry. It would not obtain, for example, the necessary anti-aircraft guns and searchlights (the sphere of the War Office) or air raid precautions (the sphere of the Home Office) without the 'strong and built up unity' which a Ministry of Supply would create.

Harold Nicolson: diary

(*Nicolson papers*)

10 May 1938

December Club dinner. Jan Masaryk[1] is our guest. I sit next to Spears and Bob Boothby. Jan makes what is rather a too slangy and simple speech—facetious. And yet behind it all one has a feeling of a man on the edge of a nervous breakdown. He says the Czechs are prepared to make any sacrifice to avoid war, but will we please tell them exactly where they stand? What he means is that they will make concessions provided that in return we guarantee their independence and no British Government can do that. On afterwards to Randolph Churchill's flat. He is editing a book of his father's speeches which show how right he has always been. His adoration for his father is really touching.

Winston S. Churchill: note

(*Churchill papers: 9/129*)

[11] May 1938

Fairey's wh I visited on Tuesday told me that in September last 189 Battle bombers were cancelled. They had to undo all their sub contracts.
In April these same 189 were restored owing presumably to the outcry.

Wing-Commander Anderson to Violet Pearman

(*Churchill papers: 9/129*)

12 May 1938

Dear Mrs Pearman,
    The attached Paper on delays of Armament equipment is worth reading I have marked out in red the points to read.

Yours,
C. T. Anderson

---

[1] Jan Garrigue Masaryk, 1886–1948. Son of Thomas Masaryk. Leader of the Czechoslovak Delegation, Paris Peace Conference, 1919. Czechoslovak Minister to London, 1925–38; resigned after the Munich Conference. Minister of Foreign Affairs, Czechoslovak Government in Exile, 1940–5; in Prague, 1945–8 (Deputy Prime Minister, 1941–5). Died after falling from a high window in Prague; whether his death was suicide, or murder by the Communist authorities, is a much-disputed question.

Wing-Commander Anderson to Violet Pearman

(Churchill papers: 9/129)

12 May 1938

Dear Mrs Pearman,

I would like the enclosed placed with the other papers as not a single pilot trained has fired a gun or dropped a bomb. Yet the RAFVR was formed 2 years ago. So we have not a trained pilot in the RAFVR.

I have decided to take the appointment as Commandant of the Oxford RAFVR in August.

Yours ever,
CTA

Winston S. Churchill: press statement

(Churchill papers: 2/329)

13 May 1938

As Herr Henlein was coming to England, it was thought by mutual friends that it would be a good thing if we had a talk together about the situation in Central Europe. So a luncheon was arranged, at which the other two guests were Sir Archibald Sinclair and Professor Lindemann. The conversations were strictly private.

Note of a conversation between Winston S. Churchill, Sir Archibald Sinclair and Konrad Henlein

(Churchill papers: 2/329)

13 May 1938

Herr Henlein was challenged as to the meaning of his Carlsbad speech.[1] Said that he claimed the right to profess the Nazi ideology, but he did not

---

[1] On 24 April 1938 Henlein had announced the 'Carlsbad Programme' of his Sudeten German Party. In it he demanded not only full autonomy for the Germans of the Sudetenland, but also full liberty for the Sudeten Germans to proclaim their adhesion to the 'ideology of Germans', whose true policy was, as he expressed it, 'inspired by the principles and ideals of National Socialism'. Henlein also demanded that the Czechoslovak Government should carry out 'a complete revision of the Czech foreign policy which up to today had led the State into the ranks of the enemies of the German people'. In rejecting these demands on 25 April 1938, the Czech Prime Minister, Milan Hodza, announced that he was pressing forward with the Nationality Statute, designed to meet the requirements of all minorities within the State and on which the coalition parties had agreed. It was his hope that this legislation would be hastened through Parliament and placed on the Statute Book by July.

claim to impose it on others. On being told English anxiety was caused by
the fear that he might be used as a pawn in Germany's 'Drang nach Osten',
he insisted, and offered to give his word of honour that he had never received
orders or even recommendations ('Weisungen') from Berlin.

He said the position in his country was intolerable, and gave instances,
and was told he would have complete British sympathy in an endeavour to
improve the position of his followers within the Czecho-Slovakian State. He
said that the Czechs must no longer maintain that it was their State in which
others were allowed to live, but accept the position that it was the common
country of all the various races; and he insisted that the other minorities
were just as dissatisfied as the Sudeten Deutsche.

He was asked whether he claimed a veto, eg about the Czecho-Russian
alliance regarding foreign policy. He said 'Certainly not'. He disapproved
of this Pact, and claimed the right to advocate its rescission, but he did not
consider this a 'sine qua non' for agreement. He said that it would be un-
thinkable, however, that Germans should be asked to fight Germans in
support of Russia. He appeared to be attracted by the possibility of a
guarantee by Britain and France to come to the assistance of Germany if she
were attacked by Russia, as also by the suggestion that the Czecho-Russian
Pact against German aggression might be extended on Locarno lines to a
bi-lateral Pact made between Cz and Germany against the possibility of
Russian aggression.

On being pressed not only about his Carlsbad speech but about his speech
a week later, when he said his demands at Carlsbad had been minimum
demands not maximum demands, he said that this had been necessary
because the Cz newspapers had insisted that his Carlsbad demands had been
merely put forward for electioneering purposes, and were bargaining points
from which he was prepared to recede.

He realised that an incident between the Sudeten Deutsche and the Czechs
might easily set Europe alight, as if Germany marched, France would come
in and England would follow. He was assured this was correct,[1] and adjured
to avoid incidents even though he might be in the right. He stated that an
emissary of his who had a discussion with the Cz Minister in Paris, who had

---

[1] During his speech in Manchester on 9 May 1938, Churchill had said: 'Although we have
not gone as far as France in giving a pledge to Czecho-Slovakia, Mr Chamberlain has gone a
long way. We are the ally of France, who would certainly be involved. We may be drawn in,
says the Prime Minister, by the force of circumstances even in cases where there is no legal
engagement. Finally, we are at this moment offering advice to Czecho-Slovakia, and if she
takes that advice and makes the concessions we think right and finds herself attacked none
the less, is it not clear that we are morally entangled? We have thus in this case, the most
urgent, undertaken in the name of detachment engagements beyond what the Covenant
prescribes.'

said there were certain circles amongst the Czechs who thought it would be a good thing to provoke an incident. They reckoned that Germany, knowing France and England were behind Prague, would not act, and this 'Ohnmachts probe' could be exploited to destroy the Sudeten Deutsche party: he insisted on the danger of such a proceeding.

He said that in his view there were three possibilities: The first was some form of Autonomy within the Czecho State. The second was a plebiscite probably leading to the Anschluss. The third was war. His policy was to make a last attempt to arrive at agreement on some form of Autonomy, but it must be reached soon, and by agreement, as his followers were impatient, and undoubtedly at the moment would prefer the Anschluss. (He seemed to feel some sense of grievance that a minority statute was now being settled in Prague without any discussion or negotiation with his party.)

If no settlement could be reached, he proposed to appeal to the Great Powers for a plebiscite to be held under International supervision, in which the two questions would be:

(1) The maintenance of the status quo.
(2) Autonomy.

Herr Henlein was asked whether he thought any agreement on Autonomy was possible which would not destroy the integrity of the Cz State, and which would enable him and his followers to act as loyal members of the State prepared to defend it against aggression from whatsoever side it might come. He thought this should be quite feasible on the following lines:—

There should be a central Parliament in Prague, which should have control of foreign policy, defence, finance and communications. All parties should be entitled to express their views there, and the Government would act on majority decisions. The frontier fortresses could be manned by Czech troops, who would of course have unhindered access thereto. The Sudeten Deutsche regions, and possibly the other minority districts, should enjoy local autonomy; that is to say, they should have their own Town and County Councils, and a Diet in which matters of common regional concern could be debated within definitely delimited frontiers. He would be prepared to submit questions of fact, eg the tracing of the boundary to an impartial tribunal, perhaps even appointed by the League of Nations. All parties would be free to organise and offer themselves for election, and impartial Courts of Justice would function in autonomous districts. The officials, ie postal, railway and police officers, in the German-speaking regions, would of course be German-speaking, and a reasonable proportion of the total taxes collected should be returned to these regions for their administration.

M Masaryk, who was afterwards informed of this conversation professed himself contented with a settlement on these lines.

Winston S. Churchill to Neville Chamberlain

(*Churchill papers: 2/329*)

15 May 1938
Private

I send you a short precis prepared by Professor Lindemann of the conversation which we had with Henlein on Friday.

I was very much pleased with the result of the talk, and still more so when I found the proposals on the last page were quite agreeable to Masaryk, whom we visited afterwards.[1]

I must add that we made it clear to Masaryk that nothing we had said to Henlein constituted any pledge to aid Czecho-Slovakia which went beyond your statement in the House of Commons.[2]

Sir Robert Vansittart: minute

(*Foreign Office papers: 371/1719*)

16 May 1938

Since, however, it was impossible for members of the Government to receive Herr Henlein lest some sort of negotiations be suspected, it was necessary to arrange that Herr Henlein should see not only myself but some persons of consequence in the House of Commons where he has already made some acquaintances during his previous visits. I therefore suggested that he might be seen by Mr Churchill and Sir Archibald Sinclair. . . .

I questioned Herr Henlein upon his other contacts and conversations, and he appeared to have been pleased with them. There had been certain differences of opinion, but on the whole he felt the conversations had been

---

[1] On 16 May 1938 Neville Chamberlain replied to Churchill: 'Thank you very much for your letter of the 15th May. I am grateful to you for sending me such full notes of the conversation which Sinclair and you had with Herr Henlein last Friday. I agree with you that what you gathered from him was encouraging rather than the reverse.' Churchill had also sent a copy of the notes of the discussion to Halifax, who replied on the same day as Chamberlain: 'I am very glad you saw him, and I think it will have done much good. Provided that no mischievous influences are intruded into his talks with the Czechoslovak Government, it looks as though there might be a chance of making real progress' (*Cherwell papers*).

[2] For Chamberlain's pledge concerning Czechoslovakia, see page 1122 of this volume.

both frank and helpful. He had taken all that had been said to him in very good part and felt that he had seen a good deal of various sections of British opinion.

Lord Halifax to Basil Newton[1]

(Foreign Office papers: 371/1719)

16 May 1938

I am encouraged by what would appear to be Herr Henlein's attitude, but I feel that if advantage is to be taken of his present disposition by which Vansittart was impressed, it is essential that the Czechoslovak Government should make a sincere and thorough going offer at the earliest possible moment, since if the present opportunity is boldly seized a large offer of basis of negotiations made quickly may lay the foundation of an agreement.

Professor Lindemann to Winston S. Churchill

(Churchill papers: 25/16)

16 May 1938   Christ Church,
                                                           Oxford

My dear Winston,

As promised I enclose a few notes which I have endeavoured to put together of what we discussed the other night.[2] I have cast it into the form of

---

[1] Basil Cochrane Newton, 1889–1965. Educated at Wellington and King's College, Cambridge. Entered the Foreign Office, 1912. Acting Counsellor, Peking, 1927–9. Counsellor, Berlin, 1930–5; Minister, Berlin, 1935–7. Minister to Prague, 1937–9. Knighted, 1939. Ambassador to Baghdad, 1939–41.

[2] Lindemann's notes concerned 'certain difficulties' that might be encountered in the use of RDF (radar), and the need to experiment with aerial mines as a means of bringing down enemy bombers. Of the latter, Lindemann wrote: 'Supported by a parachute or possibly a small balloon and hanging at the end of a wire of appropriate length, comparatively few mines of this nature will be enough to form a curtain impassable to aeroplanes without grave risk. (About one hundred such mines, weighing, say, 50 pounds altogether, spread in a curtain of a mile width and a thousand feet deep, would bring down one aeroplane in five).' Of radar, Lindemann wrote: 'Though undoubtedly excellent for detecting single aircraft or squadrons thereof, flying together, it seems likely that great difficulties may be encountered when large numbers of aeroplanes attacking and defending are simultaneously in the air, each sending back its signals. This difficulty may be very materially increased if the enemy chooses to blind the RDF operator by strewing numbers of oscillators in the appropriate region. Such oscillators need consist merely of thin wires fifty to a hundred feet long which could easily be suspended in suitable positions from toy balloons or even, if only required for half-an-hour or so, from small parachutes. As far as the RDF detector is concerned each one would return an echo just like an aeroplane. It is quite true of course that a single oscillator of this type could after a few minutes be distinguished from an aeroplane, since it would only move with the

a speech, though obviously it is no good as quâ speech, but merely as an aide memoire in composing your own. Anyhow it may be out of date as I gather Kingsley Wood has been appointed.[1]

Until I heard this I was much tempted to write a letter to the Times or Telegraph, calling attention to the fact that all our difficulties would have been reduced if the technical problem of stopping aeroplanes getting over had been solved, and pointing out how curious it is so little interest in this matter has been evinced.

It seemed to me if the question were raised now, that a new Air Minister might consider it one of the scandals which ought to be removed, whereas once he gets into the saddle, Tizard and Co will explain to him that all is for the best in this particular world and it will be impossible to get him to stir things up.

I will ring you up to-morrow morning and hope you may advise whether you think it well or not to send such a letter. If it is to do any good, presumably it should appear not later than Thursday morning.

Once more with many thanks for my delightful evening at Chartwell, believe me,

as ever,
yours,
FAL

Harold Nicolson to his wife
(Nicolson papers)

17 May 1938

We had an excitement yesterday, Swinton sacked. At once I telephoned (or rather got Duncan to telephone) to Winston saying that his motion[2] must

---

velocity of the wind instead of approaching or receding at several miles a minute. But if some hundreds or even thousands were scattered about in the relevant region by one or more aeroplanes flying ahead of the main attack, it is difficult to believe that it would be possible to sort out all the hundreds of incoming signals and distinguish the genuine aeroplanes from the dummy oscillators floating about over the sea. Indeed, if sufficient were used the individual echoes would vanish in a confused blur' (*Churchill papers: 25/16*).

[1] Sir Kingsley Wood succeeded Lord Swinton as Secretary of State for Air on 16 May 1938.

[2] Instead of Churchill's motion, the Labour Party foreign affairs spokesman, Hugh Dalton, moved, on 25 May 1938, 'That, in the opinion of this House, the growing public concern regarding the state of our air defences and the administration of the departments concerned, calls for a complete and searching independent enquiry conducted with despatch under conditions consistent with the national interest.' In his speech, Dalton asked: 'have we to go on drifting, with these weaknesses in our air defences unexposed and unrepaired until, it may be, the tragedy comes and the first bombs fall upon this ill-defended native land of ours?' Dalton was not supported in the debate by Churchill, who explained that 'since the broad

be withdrawn. He assented grumpily. But how silly the whole thing is! Here we are at the gravest crisis in our history, with a genius like Winston doing nothing and Kingsley Wood as our Minister for Air with Harold Balfour as his Number Two. It is all due to David Margesson. I admire David, since he is strong and efficient and kind. But I do not believe that he is a good Cabinet-maker. Much sickness left behind. Nobody understands why Euan Wallace[1] is sent to the Treasury. Nobody understands why on earth Stanley[2] (who is amiable but stone-deaf) is given the Dominions. Nobody understands anything. There is a real impression that the whole show is going to crack up. This view is held, not only by protagonists like Winston, but by the silent useful members of whom nobody ever hears. They think that a new Government will emerge on a far wider basis, possibly a Coalition Government.

---

fact of a very serious breakdown is now admitted, and there is now to be a fresh start and a new surge of impulse, it seems to me that some, at least, of the arguments for an enquiry are now removed'. Churchill then urged upon Ministers the immediate creation of a Ministry of Supply to 'rise to the level of events and give more effective defence protection and service to the nation which has trusted them so long'. Dalton's motion was defeated by 329 to 144. But Churchill did not vote with the Government; instead, he abstained.

[1] David Euan Wallace, 1892–1941. Educated at Harrow and Sandhurst. Joined the 2nd Life Guards, 1911. On active service in France, 1914–18 (wounded, despatches four times, Military Cross). Captain, Reserve of Officers, 1919. Assistant Military Attaché, Washington, 1919–20. Conservative MP for Rugby, 1922–3; for Hornsey, 1924–41. Parliamentary Private Secretary to the First Lord of the Admiralty, 1922–3; to the Colonial Secretary, 1924–8. An Assistant Government Whip, 1928–9. Civil Lord of Admiralty, 1931–5. Secretary, Department of Overseas Trade, 1935–7. Privy Councillor, 1936. Parliamentary Secretary, Board of Trade, 1937–8. Financial Secretary to the Treasury, 1938–9. Minister of Transport, 1939–40. For the fate of his five sons, see page 1591, note 1.

[2] Edward Montagu Cavendish, Lord Stanley, 1894–1938. Elder son of the 17th Earl of Derby. On active service 1914–18 (wounded, Military Cross). Conservative MP, 1917–18 and 1922–38. A Junior Lord of the Treasury, 1924–7. Deputy Chairman of the Conservative Organization, 1927–9. Parliamentary Under-Secretary at the Admiralty, 1931–5; Parliamentary Secretary, 1935–7. Elected to the Other Club 1936. Parliamentary Under-Secretary of State for India and Burma, 1937–8. Secretary of State for Dominion Affairs, 16 May 1938. He died on 16 October 1938.

Sir Thomas Inskip's notes: 'WSC's plan' [1]

(Cabinet papers: 64/31)

17 May 1938

Wrongly grouped functions.

Strategic coordin is different from work of Minister securing existing programme & planning British Industry.

Form Separate Department

    Min Supply with MCD [Minister for Co-ordination of Defence] at summit. With final voice on priorities.

Com^{ee}. not able to do work.

Command needed.

Chain of resp^{ble}. authority must descend through whole of British Industry.

Unify supply command into one organism also commanding war expansion.

Design must go with supply.

Progr^{mmes}. cannot be achieved in present atmosphere of 'ordinary peace time preparation'.

Don't take *war* powers.

    Declare Emergency Period.

Legislation Part I. Emerg Prep^{n}.

        — II. War.

    Part I into force now, 'Gliding into war with whole design foreseen'.

∴. First create M/S^{y} [Ministry of Supply] with S^{y} [Supply] Council.

    Each member study production in his sphere.

    Transfer S^{y}. Des^{n}. Contr^{acts}. [Supply, Design, Contracts] by instalments to M/S. Finance dealt with between M/S & Treas^{y}.

'Note on Mr Churchill's proposal to appoint a Minister of Supply'

(Cabinet papers: 64/31)

17 May 1938

    Mr Churchill's proposal is to appoint a Minister of Supply in addition to the Minister for Co-ordination of Defence.

    1. His intention is that the present Minister should deal with strategic coordination, and the new Minister with:

    (1) securing the execution of existing programmes;

---

[1] These are Inskip's own notes of Churchill's suggestions. For Churchill's formal memorandum, published in *The Times* on 20 May 1938, and discussed in a letter from Colonel Ismay to Inskip, see pages 1040–2 of this volume.

(2) planning British industry to spring quickly into war time conditions and creating a high effective control for this and the previous purpose.

His ultimate aim is that the new Minister should create a Ministry of Supply.

2. Up to the present the policy of His Majesty's Government has been that a Minister or Ministry of Supply in addition to the Minister for Co-ordination is not required.

In CP 297(36) Sir Thomas Inskip said he saw no need for a second Minister, not executively managing supply but co-ordinating the work of the Departments.

Mr Churchill seems to suggest that the new Minister should have executive responsibility for supply. He suggests that there should be four departments, Navy, Army, Air Force and Supply, with the new Minister at the top having the final voice on priorities.

If the proposal is accepted it will mean a Ministry of Munitions in peace in the full sense of the term, responsible for design as well as supply.

He also advocates legislation—

(a) to be brought into force in peace in a precautionary stage, and
(b) to be brought in on the outbreak of the war.

It would be generally admitted that a Ministry of Supply could not function effectively if they were not responsible for design. This, however, is a question which has raised much Departmental controversy and it will be remembered that it was on this question that the Admiralty would not come within the orbit of the Ministry of Munitions in the Great War.

It is quite possible that a similar issue would be raised by the Air Ministry if the Admiralty were permitted to stand out from the new Ministry.

It would take a long time to reach Departmental agreement in peace as to the various branches of the Service Departments to be transferred to the new Ministry and, from the point of view of our present preparation, there would be very little expedition of the Service programmes.

In addition, owing to the increased complexity of modern armaments, such as ships, aircraft, anti-aircraft equipments etc, tending to specialization within the Departments, the problem of centralization of design within a new Department would be one of great difficulty which would take a long time to solve.

Each Department has its own problems and organization to deal with them. Design is interlocked with problems of strategy and the transfer of this responsibility would involve the transfer not only of the design staffs but other sections of the Service staffs.

3. Mr Churchill's proposals to introduce legislation in peace are also fraught with many difficulties.

It will be remembered that, in introducing the Ministry of Munitions Bill in 1915, Mr Lloyd George referred to compulsory powers on a very wide scale. These included—

(1) Power to obtain information as to stocks of raw and semi-raw materials and machinery in the country.

(2) Power to release Trade Union practices and regulations.

(3) Application of the principle of compulsory arbitration to prevent stoppages of work by strikes and lock-outs.

(4) Compulsion to secure adequate supplies of labour.

(5) Limitation of profits.[1]

If it was to be effective Mr Churchill's proposal would presumably cover similar points.[2]

The question of the introduction of emergency legislation in peace has already been considered by the Committee of Imperial Defence.

Most of the legislation required in war has already been drafted. The Committee of Imperial Defence (CID/295th Meeting, Minute 1) approved the Draft Emergency Powers (Defence) Bill and Draft Defence Regulations,

---

[1] The limitation of war profits was something on which Churchill had felt strongly in the aftermath of the First World War. On 4 August 1919 (when Secretary of State for War) he wrote to Lloyd George: 'I do not see how we can look the working classes in the face while these enormous war fortunes remain untouched. No one had any right to make money out of the war or during the war: & if they have, no matter how, they are a good subject for taxation. I am assured it wd be perfectly practicable to devise a system. Payment cd be made in War Loan at par & if necessary spread over 3 years. I wd forgo £10,000 to leave out the small people & take 80% of the remaining excess over pre-war capital (inheritance of course being excluded). I don't wonder there is an ugly spirit abroad when everyone can see a whole new class of millionaires who made their fortunes while 5/6th of the industries of the country were in suspension or abeyance & every little shop-keeper who cd march was serving in the trenches. This sense of injustice rankles in every heart and is in my opinion at the root of our troubles & governmental weakness' (Churchill papers: 2/106).

[2] As Minister of Munitions from July 1917 until November 1918, Churchill had supported Lloyd George's concept of compulsory powers, as listed above, and on 10 July 1918, after a strike at the Alliance Aeroplane Works had spread to other munitions factories throughout the London area, he had announced that the Government were to take over the Works. In his announcement, Churchill censured the owners of the factory, Waring and Gillow, as follows: 'It is believed by the workmen that the firm in question has opposed the legitimate development of the shop steward and shop committee movement. The Minister, without pronouncing a final opinion, has formed the view that this belief is not wholly unfounded.' At the same time, the announcement warned the strikers that 'as soon as the firm against whom they have struck has been taken over by the Government, they are no longer strikers but merely unemployed or idle workmen. It is accordingly the duty of these men and all others on strike in sympathy to resume work immediately. Failing such resumption, the Minister will use his powers against them under the Defence of the Realm Act and the Munitions of War Acts.' The strikers returned to work, and Churchill then met their principal grievances, reinstating the shop committee movement which the owners had opposed.

but they also agreed that such regulations should not be introduced in peace (CID/315th Meeting, Minute 3), and that legislation—

(1) designed to compel civilian workers to remain at their posts in time of war, and
(2) to prohibit strikes,

should not be prepared in advance.[1]

It is very doubtful whether the legislation suggested by Mr Churchill would pass through Parliament in peace without being so whittled down as to make it completely ineffective.

Mr Churchill's suggestion for partial legislation, in what he calls the period of emergency preparation, does not seem to be practicable. There appears to be no immediate stage possible between—

(a) full war control with full compulsory powers, and
(b) the normal peace-time method of voluntary co-operation with industry which His Majesty's Government has adopted.

4. Mr Churchill considers that supply cannot be achieved without command, and that a definite chain of responsible authority must descend through the whole of British industry affected.

In this regard he criticizes the present planning authority, ie the Principal Supply Officers Committee, in that it is purely consultative, and that it is only based on the war need divorced from present supply.

This criticism is quite unwarranted. It is true that the primary function of the Committee of Imperial Defence Supply Organization is to plan for the first twelve months but the officers who represent the Departments on that organization are the officers concerned with executive supply functions in the Departments and thus a very effective link between planning and execution is secured.[2]

[1] The documents to which this note referred were Cabinet Paper 297 of 1936, of 30 October 1936; conclusions of the 295th meeting of the Committee of Imperial Defence on 1 July 1937; and the 315th meeting of the Committee of Imperial Defence of 25 March 1938.
[2] On 18 May 1938 Sir Thomas Inskip told the Cabinet 'that Mr Winston Churchill predicted an Act in two parts dealing respectively with (1) emergency preparation service, and (2) war. He had asked him to specify what powers he thought should be provided under the first heading, and Mr Churchill had refused to say.' A few moments later Lord Winterton said that the 'real issue' was whether Britain 'could compete in peace and war with Germany as at present organised', to which Lord Halifax commented that 'frank discussions with our own leaders of industry' would alone give the answer to that question (*Cabinet papers: 23/93*).

Winston S. Churchill to Violet Pearman: telegram

(Pearman papers)

17 May 1938   London

So grieved your illness.[1] Don't worry about anything but just get well. Will come and see you soon. Affectionate regards.

Winston

Colonel Christie[2] to Winston S. Churchill

(Churchill papers: 2/329)

18 May 1938

Dear Mr Churchill,

Thank you so much for including me amongst your guests at the excellent lunch you gave to Herr Henlein last Friday. I would have written sooner, had I not been indisposed. Henlein took away with him the firm impression that you incorporated & represented the *real* strength of the British, the intent to tolerate no aggression against the ČSR, but at the same time to see fairplay given to the SD minority. It seemed to me of utmost importance that Henlein should meet he-men & fighters at this juncture & *not* those wretched defeatists whose gutless attitude encourages both ends of the Axis to rev up their demands relentlessly in spite of their own faulty bearings.

Thank you again for your big contribution.

Sincerely yours,
M. G. Christie

[1] Violet Pearman's illness was complete mental and physical exhaustion caused by her husband's refusal to give her a divorce, despite the fact that they had not lived together for nearly ten years.

[2] Malcolm Grahame Christie, 1881–1971. An engineer; and graduate of Aachen University. General Manager of the Otto Cokeoven Company of Leeds and President of the Otto Coking Corporation of New York. Served in the Royal Flying Corps, 1914–18, and in the Royal Air Force, 1919–30 (retiring with the rank of Group Captain). Air Attaché, Washington, 1922–6; Berlin, 1927–30. A friend of Göring, he worked closely with Sir Robert Vansittart in obtaining information about the German air force, and about German military plans, while on business journeys inside Germany between 1930 and 1938.

Winston S. Churchill to Violet Pearman

(*Pearman papers*)

18 May 1938   Chartwell

Dearest Mrs P,

I am so grieved at yr illness—due I fear largely to yr devotion to my interests & fortunes. I am sure that all you need is a good long rest without worries of any kind. Now do help in this. Lie absolutely fallow & you will recover. There is no need to fret about anything—tho I don't pretend I do not miss you badly.

Do not let yr case be a burden. Why don't you tell yr solicitor to come to me. I will have it all properly looked after. Remember you can count on me for the £50 I promised.

All I want you to do is to get well, & this you can do by a good holiday. I will look after you.

Yours affectionately,
Winston S. Churchill

Violet Pearman to Winston S. Churchill: telegram

(*Pearman papers*)

19 May 1938

Will always treasure your lovely letter thank you with all my heart.

VP

Winston S. Churchill to Colonel Christie

(*Churchill papers: 2/329*)

20 May 1938

Thank you very much for your letter.

I am so glad you think the meeting was useful. I shall be glad to know what Henlein's action was on his return home. Perhaps you will keep me informed.

Winston S. Churchill to Major-General Sir Reginald Barnes

(*Churchill papers: 1/323*)

20 May 1938

How nice to hear from you again!

Alas, I have to make a speech at Sheffield on the 31st, and cannot come to the dinner. Let me know sometime when you come to London, so that we can meet.

I am sorry indeed that you have had to give up farming, as I know what an occupation it was to you.

I am filled with anxiety about the increasing danger into which we are moving. I look forward to sending you a book upon the subject which I am publishing in a few weeks.

With every good wish,

Winston S. Churchill: memorandum

(*Cabinet papers: 64/31*)

20 May 1938

SUPPLY ORGANIZATION[1]

(1) The existing office of the Minister for the Coordination of Defence comprises unrelated and wrongly grouped functions. The work of the Minister charged with strategic coordination is different, though not in the higher ranges disconnected, from the work of the Minister charged with: (*a*) securing the execution of the existing programmes; and (*b*) planning British industry to spring quickly into wartime conditions and creating a high control effective for both this and the present purpose.

(2) The first step therefore is to separate the functions of strategic thought from those of material supply in peace and war and form the organization to direct this latter process. An harmonious arrangement would be four separate departments—Navy, Army, Air Force, and Supply—with the Coordinating Minister at the summit of the four having the final voice upon priorities.

(3) No multiplication of committees, however expert or elaborate, can achieve this purpose. Supply cannot be achieved without command. A

---

[1] This memorandum was published in *The Times* on 20 May 1938, with the covering note: 'Mr Winston Churchill announced last night that Sir Thomas Inskip, Minister for the Coordination of Defence, had consented to the publication of a memorandum which Mr Churchill wrote for him two years ago. He added that it had a bearing on the present defence discussions.' Churchill had written the memorandum on 6 June 1936.

definite chain of responsible authority must descend through the whole of British industry affected. (This must not be thought to imply State interference in the actual functions of industry.) At the present time the three Service authorities exercise separate command over their particular supply, and the fourth, or planning, authority is purely consultative, and that only upon the war need divorced from present supply. What is needed is to unify the supply command of the three Service Departments into an organism which also exercises command over the war expansion. (The Admiralty would retain control over the construction of warships and certain special Naval stores.)

(4) This unification should comprise not only the function of supply but that of design. The Service Departments prescribe in general technical terms their need in type, quality, and quantity, and the supply organization executes these in a manner best calculated to serve its customers. In other words, the Supply Department engages itself to deliver the approved types of war stores of all kinds to the Services when and where the latter require them.[1]

Winston S. Churchill to Lord Londonderry

(*Churchill papers: 2/347*)

21 May 1938

Many thanks for your letter of May 6th. I am very glad to find there is one subject upon which we are in agreement.

I have also to thank you for sending me through your publishers a copy of your book, which seems to have excited much interest.[2]

[1] For an official comment on this memorandum, and on how it differed from Churchill's original memorandum of 6 June 1936, see pages 1040–2. For Churchill's explanation of these differences, see his letter to *The Times* of 24 May 1938, quoted on pages 1042–3.

[2] Lord Londonderry's book *Ourselves and Germany*. In it, he reflected on Hitler's coming to power five years before: 'Herr Hitler restored the sense of national pride and self-respect. He carried out his programme in the face of the tremendous difficulties which had assailed his country—of being defeated, of suffering acute privation, of passing through various stages of political revolution, of having an army of occupation within the German frontiers for a decade, finally of being disappointed and refused a fair hearing in the councils of Europe. On becoming Chancellor in 1933, Herr Hitler challenged these disabilities; and by his example and inspiration he inculcated in the people he was leading the spirit of self-respect and the desire for equality with other nations in their rights and responsibilities.' In a new edition published immediately after the Munich Agreement in October 1938, which Hitler and Chamberlain declared was a 'symbolic desire of our two peoples never to go to war with one another again', Londonderry wrote: 'Let us hope that the signing of the declaration not only opens up a prospect of more friendly and secure Anglo-German relations than have existed at any time since the War, but let us hope, too, that it also may rank merely as a prelude to the greater settlement of all the outstanding international differences in Europe.'

It is difficult to talk much when one feels so strongly about things: but as you know I always wish you well in every way of friendship, and kinship.

Clementine Churchill to Violet Pearman [1]
(Pearman papers)

21 May 1938 [2]   Manor House,
                                                  Cranborne,
                                                  Dorset.

My Dear Mrs Pearman,

I must write to you to say how very very sorry I am about your illness & how much I feel for you. You have been working so very hard, & I know you have private anxieties. And combined, it has been too much.

Nervous exhaustion cannot be hurried—I do hope after you have partly recovered from the shock that you won't hate being in bed for a time. I feel sure you will get quite well sooner than you or your doctor expects.

Later on when you feel like it I should much like to come & see you. You have done so much for Mr Churchill & he is so sad that you are ill.

Miss Whyte keeps me informed every day.

Please try not to worry. Peace of mind is the great cure.

Yours affectionately,
Clementine S. Churchill

---

[1] This letter was written on a Saturday. The Churchills were staying with Lord and Lady Cranborne (see also page 1045, note 2). But Churchill was among the guests who broke off the weekend on the Sunday and returned early to London. During Friday 20 May 1938 news had reached the Czech Government from the British Secret Service that several German divisions were concentrating in Saxony, just behind the Czechoslovak Frontier. That night the Czech Cabinet mobilized all specialist troops of the reserves, and a whole year's class of reservists. The news published in the Sunday papers on May 22, made a German invasion seem imminent, perhaps only a matter of hours. That same day, in municipal elections, the Henleinists won a large majority in the German-speaking areas. Nine days later, it was learnt that the German troop concentrations had dispersed. Dorothy de Rothschild writes: 'I remember that party at Cranborne so vividly with both the Churchills & the Duff Coopers who were recalled to London on the Sunday afternoon' (letter to the author, 7 August 1977).

[2] 'The events of May 21' were to be much discussed in Britain, some arguing that the stern Anglo-French response had caused Hitler to give up a planned invasion of Czechoslovakia, others to say that the mobilization had been a test during which substantial German military weakness had been revealed (see for example pages 1119 and 1140, note 1). Churchill himself wrote, on 22 June 1938 in the Daily Telegraph: '. . . no one who remembers the past can doubt that circumstances and national feeling may upon occasion pass beyond the control even of the most sincerely peace-loving British Administration. It may be that some of these reflections played their part in the very definite easement of the Czechoslovakian problem which occurred a month ago'.

James Watts to Winston S. Churchill
(*Churchill papers: 2/329*)

22 May 1938   Manchester
Private and Confidential

My dear Mr Churchill,

I have been thinking over what conclusions should be drawn from your wonderful meeting, and think that if we could have a real National Government pledged to defend the at-present unattacked countries from any new menaces, and also pledged to rearm 'all-out' for this object *and none other*, and if this plan was accompanied by a social policy for the removal of malnutrition and were to include inter alia a plan for the bettering of nurses' conditions and hours in hospitals, we should have a united England behind us and could on a popular vote even get National Service in some form made compulsory and have class privilege in such a cause eliminated.

I do not see how mere meetings in the country however successful can do any active good when the Government have such an enormous majority in the House, but a revolt in Parliament run by all those who care for decency and equality and who are alive to the menace to the world from German frightfulness, would surely rally the country to fight for its liberties as one family.

But members of a family share what goods there are and if there is malnutrition in one section and too much food in another there cannot be the unity we need for National Service, nor will our Country be healthy enough to fight to its best advantage while such a large portion of its people remain underfed. Only social justice will at once enlist all classes to prepare for the fight against brute force which it seems must come. I am sure that in the day of battle there would be unity but our object is to get the unity before the battle is started.

Yours sincerely,
James Watts

Winston S. Churchill to James Watts
(*Churchill papers: 2/329*)

23 May 1938

Thank you very much for your letter. I am so glad you think the Meeting was a success.

There is no chance whatever of any action in Parliament being effective. The present majority will remain dumb to the end.

Richard Acland[1] *to Winston S. Churchill*

(*Churchill papers: 2/329*)

23 May 1938

Dear Mr Churchill,

Without having any shadow of right to do so, I venture to put before you some reflections which arise on my reading the best reports I can get of your meetings at Manchester and Bristol.[2]

You will build up a very large personal following from these meetings out of the people who distrust equally the present policy and the leaders of the Labour Party, and at any forthcoming election you will be able to turn this following in one direction or the other.

This will enable you at a not very distant date, to present Mr Chamberlain with an ultimatum in the form 'I can break you unless. . . .'

In private this might cause him pain, but it seems to me he might yield to your pressure without any public loss of face at all. . . .

To my mind the only government which would stand a chance of commanding the unity of our own people, the only government in which you would find a spontaneous willingness to take the courageous decisions necessary for success would be a government led by yourself, Eden, Sinclair and Attlee. I don't put in Sinclair because he or his followers are essential in themselves, but because we happen to be there and to fit in.

---

[1] Richard Thomas Dyke Acland, 1906–   . Educated at Rugby and Balliol College Oxford. Unsuccessful Liberal candidate, 1929 and 1931. Liberal MP for Barnstaple, 1935–45. Succeeded his father as 13th Baronet, 1939. Founded the Commonwealth Party during the war. Labour MP for Gravesend, 1947–55. Second Church Estates Commissioner, 1950–1. Lecturer, St Luke's Training College, Exeter, from 1959.

[2] For Churchill's speech at Bristol on 16 May 1938, see page 1018, note 1. At Manchester, on 9 May 1938, he had told his audience that Yugoslavia, Rumania, Hungary and Czechoslovakia ought to be asked to join Britain and France in a 'special duty' to the League. And he went on: 'But even that would only be a beginning. To the east of Europe lies the enormous power of Russia, a country whose form of government I detest, but which at any rate seeks no military aggression upon its neighbours, a country whose interests are peace, a country profoundly menaced by Nazi hostility, a country which lies as a great background and counterpoise at this moment to all those states of Middle Europe I have mentioned. We should certainly not go cap in hand to Soviet Russia, or count in any definite manner upon Russian action. But how improvidently foolish we should be, when dangers are so great, to put needless barriers in the way of the general association of the great Russian mass with resistance to an act of Nazi aggression. There is, however, a third stage in the process. There is Poland; and the countries of the north, the Baltic states, the Scandinavian powers. If we had once gathered together the forces I have mentioned, we should then be in a position to offer these countries a very great measures of armed security for peace. At the present time they do not know which way to turn. But if they saw a strong, armed association, such as I have described, whose interest in peace was the same as theirs, they might easily be induced to throw in their lot with us and "make assurance double sure". But what is this but a recreated League of Nations, devoted to its original purpose, namely the prevention of war?'

I am aware that as things now stand you could not alone get enough support to get such a government without an election, and the prospect of an election campaign is not attractive at the present moment. But if you were joined by Eden, I believe you could get such a government without an election not at one step, but at two.

You could, at the first step, secure enough government supporters who would agree that if there were an election they would come and fight with you for such a government. Armed with those, you would make it so certain that well over half the remaining government supporters would lose their seats in any forthcoming election that sufficient of them would come over at the second step to give you your government without your election.

Yours sincerely,
Richard Acland

I need hardly say that I would be delighted to meet you to discuss any points arising out of this *if* you would like me to.

Ronald Bell[1] to Winston S. Churchill

(*Churchill papers: 2/329*)

23 May 1938   Cardiff

Dear Mr Churchill,

I am standing as the Government candidate at the approaching bye-election in the Caerphilly Division of Glamorganshire, and I would appreciate it very much indeed if you would spare about five minutes of your very valuable time to see me at some place convenient to you before the election.

I do not think I am known to you now, as it is some three or four years since I last met you, when I was an undergraduate at Oxford, but I should be very grateful if you could manage to see me some time in the near future.

Yours sincerely,
Ronald Bell

---

[1] Ronald McMillan Bell, 1914–1982. Educated at Cardiff High School and Magdalen College, Oxford. Treasurer of the Oxford Union, 1935. President of the Oxford University Conservative Society, 1935. Called to the Bar, Gray's Inn, 1938. Unsuccessful Conservative candidate at the Caerphilly by-election, 4 July 1939. Served in the RNVR, 1939–46. Conservative MP for Newport, May–July 1945. Unsuccessful Conservative candidate for Newport, July 1945. Member of the Paddington Borough Council, 1947–9. Conservative MP for South Buckinghamshire, 1950–1982. Queen's Counsel, 1966.

Colonel Ismay to Sir Thomas Inskip

(Cabinet papers: 64/31)

23 May 1938   Committee of Imperial Defence

Minister,

On Friday night we drew attention to the fact that the Memorandum published by Mr Churchill in 'The Times' did not exactly correspond with the note which he gave you some two years ago.

You instructed us to let you have a note on the subject. It is attached herewith.

1. The printed version of Mr Churchill's statement as published in the Times on 20th May, differs from the statement handed to Sir Thomas Inskip in 1936, in some important respects, in that to certain paragraphs he has added what he terms explanatory notes, which largely alter the complexion of parts of his proposals. These are indicated by red underlining in the copy of the statement attached hereto.

2. *Paragraph 3.*

There are two additions:

(i) In the first he qualifies his statement that 'a definite chain of responsible authority must descend through the whole of British Industry' by adding the following—

'*This must not be thought to imply State interference in the actual functions of industry.*'

It is difficult to imagine a definite chain of responsibility throughout industry without some form of control, and one can hardly imagine an effective control which does not, in some measure, interfere with industry, if, as it is presumed, Mr Churchill intends a more effective use of industry than is being made at present could result from his proposals.

The question of control has been fully dealt with in Note B attached to the Notes on Lord Mottistone's[1] Motion for a Minister of Supply.[2]

---

[1] John Edward Bernard Seely, 1868–1947. Educated at Harrow and Trinity College, Cambridge. Liberal MP, 1900–22; 1923–4. Under-Secretary of State for the Colonies, 1908–11. An original member of the Other Club, 1911. Secretary of State for War, 1912–14. Resigned in March 1914, following the Curragh incident. Commanded the Canadian Cavalry Brigade, 1915–18. Gassed, 1918, and retired from Army with rank of Major-General. Under-Secretary of State to Churchill, Ministry of Munitions and Deputy Minister of Munitions, 1918. Under-Secretary of State for Air, 1919. Created Baron Mottistone, 1933. Chairman of the National Savings Committee, 1926–43. His son Frank was killed leading his company at the battle of Arras, 1917.

[2] On 23 May 1938 Mottistone moved in the House of Lords 'that it was essential in the interests of national security that a Ministry of Supply for the three Defence Services be

Mr Churchill, although he advocates a chain of command through industry, and also legislation in peace to better our preparations, is presumably well aware of the difficulties of instituting either legislation or any effective control in peace.

The Statement therefore that there should be no interference with industry, takes all the force out of his proposal for a chain of command through industry.

He knows as well as we do that there is no intermediate stage possible between—

(a) full war control with full compulsory powers, and
(b) the normal peace-time method of voluntary co-operation with industry which His Majesty's Government has adopted.

See Note B to Brief which deals with this subject at length.

(ii) Towards the end of paragraph 3 Mr Churchill says 'what is needed is to unify the supply command of the three Service Departments into an organism which also exercises command over war expansion'.

But he now adds—

'The Admiralty would retain control over the construction of warships and certain special naval stores.'

It must also be remembered that in paragraph 4 of his Statement the unification of supply he suggests must comprise not only supply but design. This question is fully dealt with in Note B to the Brief.

Mr Churchill's new sentence excluding certain Admiralty functions from the new Ministry has been presumably inserted because he is well aware of the difficulties, and the enormous time it would take to bring about the unification of supply and design of the Admiralty, War Office and Air Ministry; but if he advocates the exclusion of the Admiralty for warships and special naval stores (it will be noted that he does not define the latter), does not this argument apply equally to the Air Ministry for aircraft and special Air Ministry stores of which there are a good many?

It is difficult to see where Mr Churchill's proposal in this respect leads us to. If his intention is to have a Ministry of Supply not controlling the whole supply situation, would we be better off than we are at present? He would only create an additional Government machine, and unless this was responsible for the whole supply and had full powers of control over industry in

_____

established forthwith', a motion, he added, 'not conceived in my feeling of hostility to the Prime Minister'. The motion was supported by Lord Trenchard and Lord Addison. It was opposed, for the Government, by Lord Zetland, and negatived by 54 votes to 12.

peace, it would seem that his arrangement would give no better results than does our present system.

3. The only other addition is to paragraph 7 which explains what he means when he says the new supply authority will alone deal with the Treasury upon Finance. This is rather vague and also somewhat illogical when we have regard to the fact that he has now excluded certain Admiralty functions from the new Ministry.

Lord Cecil of Chelwood to Winston S. Churchill
(*Churchill papers: 2/343*)

24 May 1938

My dear Winston,

I should just like to write you a line of thanks for your two speeches, at Manchester and Bristol.[1] I thought they were admirable and most useful, particularly the Bristol one. I hope you had good audiences and that all went well.

It was very provoking of the Labour people not to attend the Bristol meeting, but they seem to be determined to keep this Government in for as long as they can!

We had quite an interesting debate in the Lords the other day, and I thought there were some symptoms that Halifax was inclined to repent of the earlier speeches of himself and Neville.

Yours ever,
R C

Winston S. Churchill to the Editor of 'The Times'
(*Churchill papers: 2/337*)

24 May 1938

Sir,

The Memorandum on the formation of a Ministry of Supply, which you were good enough to publish on Friday last, was sent to you with a covering note stating that I had added a few explanatory footnotes. Those footnotes were as follows:—

(1) This must not be thought to imply State interference in the actual functions of industry.

---

[1] For these two speeches, see pages 1015, note 1 and 1018, note 1.

(2) The Admiralty would retain control over the construction of warships and certain special naval stores.

(3) By 'finance' is meant payments within the scope of the authorized programmes.

When you printed the Memorandum, these footnotes, no doubt for typographical convenience, were included in brackets in the text. Thus it would appear that they had been an integral part of the original Memorandum. This of course was not so, and I should be very much obliged if you would allow me to make it clear. These footnotes however were not in any sense afterthoughts, but simply explanatory comments upon the general scheme. For instance, I had never contemplated that the Admiralty should be deprived of their full control of the design and construction of ships and special stores, but only of those commodities used by the Navy which are common to all three Services. I may cite in illustration what I said in the House of Commons on this point on May 21, 1936:

'Let the Government transfer to this Ministry, by instalments, as soon as it is willing to undertake the task, the whole business of supply and design for the Air Force and for the Army, and such portions of Naval supply as are not concerned in the construction of warships and certain special Naval stores. These, and certain ancillaries, I would leave to the Admiralty because, to a very large extent, they have already their own great plants in existence and in operation, because they have the Royal Corps of Naval Constructors, and because expansion for defence purposes does not strain the Navy in the same degree as it does the other two Services. The Navy is already upon a European or a world scale. . . .'

I am, Sir,
Yours faithfully,

Winston S. Churchill to Richard Acland
(*Churchill papers: 2/329*)

26 May 1938
Private

My dear Acland,

Many thanks for your letter, which I have read and thought about.

I don't think any of the considerations you mention will arise in the present Parliament. The Government have a solid majority, and Chamberlain will certainly not wish to work with me. If of course the foreign situation darkens, something in the nature of a National Government may be forced upon us; but events, and great events alone will rule.

Winston S. Churchill to General Sir Hugh Tudor

(*Churchill papers: 2/329*)

26 May 1938

I have been so hunted lately that I have hardly had time to turn round, so please forgive me for not having answered your letter earlier.

It would be very nice if you could come to lunch with me at 11, Morpeth Mansions on Thursday, June 2nd. I have to make a speech in Birmingham that night, but I should so much like to have a talk.

We are in an awful mess and it is the Tory Party, above all others, who have failed in their duty to the country.

Winston S. Churchill to Robert Graves[1]

(*Churchill papers: 1/323*)

26 May 1938

I have delayed thanking you for the copy of 'Belisarius', which your publishers sent me, at your kind request, until I was able to read it. This, I have now done with the very greatest pleasure and profit.

I most heartily congratulate you upon this brilliant piece of work. You have rolled back the time curtain in a magical way and made all this strange epoch young again. I daresay some of your readers will have felt there was too much war, but the vivid accounts you give of these long forgotten campaigns, in my mind, only enhance the value of the work.

I delight also in the theological discussions which blend so amusingly with the easy morals.

Once I began the book, I could not put it down.

Again thanking you,

Believe me,

[1] Robert Ranke Graves, 1895—   . Writer and poet: author of more than 137 books. On active service in France with the Royal Welch Fusiliers, 1915–18. Professor of English Literature, Cairo, 1926. Published his war memoirs, *Goodbye to All That*, in 1929. Author of *I, Claudius* and *Claudius the God* (both in 1934) and *Count Belisarius* (1938), for which he received the Stock Prize. Professor of Poetry at Oxford University, 1961–6. Queen's Gold Medal for Poetry, 1968. One of his two sons was killed in action in Burma in the Second World War.

James de Rothschild [1] *to Winston S. Churchill*

(*Churchill papers: 2/329*)

27 May 1938

Dear Winston,

When you spoke with such sympathy last week at Cranborne [2] about the Jewish situation in Germany, you mentioned that the number of Jews in the various professions and occupations had been, in the days before Hitler, very high in comparison with the proportion which Jews bore to the total population. The idea that this was so was fostered by Nazi propaganda, and has been widely accepted.

I am enclosing an article which appeared in the 'Manchester Guardian' of 3rd January 1936, which disproves this by official German statistics. [3] I

---

[1] James Armand de Rothschild, 1878–1957. Known as 'Jimmy'. Born in Paris, the son of Baron Edmond de Rothschild, (patron of Jewish agricultural enterprise in Palestine). Educated in Paris and at Trinity College, Cambridge. On active service, 1914–18, on the western front and in Palestine; Major, Royal Fusiliers, 1918. Liaison Officer with the Zionist Commission in Palestine, 1918. President of the Palestine Jewish Colonization Association, 1924. A Director of the Palestine Electric Corporation, and a patron of the Hebrew University of Jerusalem. A member of the Other Club from 1925. Liberal MP for the Isle of Ely, 1929–45. Trustee of the Wallace Collection, 1941–55. Joint Parliamentary Secretary, Ministry of Supply, 1945. An advocate of making Palestine a British colony, in order to preserve the rights of both Jews and Arabs. In 1946 he contributed £5,000 towards the purchase of Chartwell for the National Trust. He left his own country house at Waddesdon and its contents to the National Trust.

[2] Churchill had stayed at Cranborne, as the guest of the Lord and Lady Cranborne, on 21–22 May 1938. The other guests were Duff and Diana Cooper, Sir John Carew Pole and Lady Carew Pole, James de Rothschild and his wife (Dorothy de Rothschild), Peter Loxley (Foreign Office), the Countess de Mun, Clarissa Churchill, Carlos de Beistigui, the Duke of St Albans and Colonel C. G. Lancaster MP (*Cranborne Visitors Book*). For a note of why Churchill had left early, see page 1036, note 1.

[3] On 3 January 1936 the *Manchester Guardian* published an article, based on official German statistics published at that time. It read, in part: '. . . Nazi propaganda speaks of a Jewish monopoly and complains that non-Jewish Germans were unable to find a place in these professions. A glance at the official statistics proves the contrary. The highest Jewish percentage was among the lawyers (there is no distinction between barristers and solicitors in Germany), amounting to 16.25. The percentage of Jewish doctors was 10.88. Of the State-appointed lawyers (judges, magistrates, and State attorneys) no more than 2.76 per cent were Jews. What about the stranglehold of the Jews on the universities? The percentage here was 2.64. The percentage of Jews among the teachers in the elementary and secondary schools was no higher than 0.53. And in cultural life? The figures show that 5.61 per cent of the producers in the theatres were Jews, 3 per cent of the actors and dancers, 2.04 per cent of the musicians and singers, 2.5 per cent of the booksellers, 2.44 per cent of the painters and sculptors, and 5.05 per cent of editors and authors. This is neither a stranglehold nor a monopoly.' The *Manchester Guardian* article did not give the percentage of Jews among the total population, which was, at the Jewish population's peak in 1910, 0.95% (615,000 out of a total population of 61,470,000) By 1925 the Jewish population of Germany (then excluding Danzig and the western provinces of Poland) had fallen to 564,379; 0.9% of the German population then.

thought it might interest you; but perhaps you will be good enough to let me have the cutting back, as it is the only copy I have.

Yours ever,
James Rothschild

Desmond Morton to Winston S. Churchill
(*Churchill papers: 2/341*)

27 May 1938
Personal & Secret

Dear Winston,

I have read and examined personally with great interest the document you lent me and there is no doubt that it is a deeply thought out preparation by the French Air Staff. So far as I can make out, it agrees in every essential with the independent opinions formed by the British Air Staff on the basis of their own information.[1]

The French estimate of the size of the German Air Force is slightly higher than the British estimate, the latter being calculated on the principle enunciated on page 4 of the French memorandum, not on that given on page 5 of the French memorandum.

The only point where I personally think the French have gone off the lines is in respect of the production of airframes and aero-engines given at the bottom of page 12. In this matter we are known to be well ahead of the French, since they have failed to grasp the necessity of having all defence/economic questions studied by a staff composed not of military staff officers but of civilians who know about these matters.

Admittedly the French phraseology is strictly correct, since they call it 'production connue'. The figures they give are roughly correct for the deliveries by German industry to the German Air Force, but omit deliveries of military aircraft for export and deliveries to Franco in Spain. In fact, I suspect that the French have estimated the output of the German industry on the basis of the growth of the German Air Force, without having very much information about the activity of industry itself to use as a cross check.

They are certainly also wrong in saying, at the top of page 13, that the aircraft factories have only been working on an average a 48-hour week, ie one-third of capacity. They have not been working on night shifts, but several factories have been working 16 hours a day, while, anyway, capacity is not three times that of a 48-hour week but only something less than $2\frac{1}{2}$ times.

However, these are relatively minor points.

[1] For the origin of this document, and Churchill's own comment, see page 1055.

Perhaps a more important point, with reference to the top of page 14, is that we anticipate the German Air Force, stated by the French on page 4 to consist on January 1st, 1938, of 207 squadrons, to reach 300 squadrons on or before 1st April 1939 at the present rate of formation and, if they continue expansion at the same rate, to consist of 400 squadrons by the 1st April, 1940. This is a more rapid expansion than the French allow.

Yours very sincerely,
Desmond Morton

Winston S. Churchill to Lord Cecil of Chelwood

(*Cecil of Chelwood papers*)

27 May 1938   Chartwell

My dear Bob,

I am very glad you were pleased with these speeches. I think the Government are going a great deal in our direction, and Chamberlain seems to have said things to the Labour Deputation which would be most satisfactory if repeated in public.

I have got two big Meetings next week,[1] and am much pressed with work.

Yours ever,
W

[1] On 31 May 1938 Churchill spoke at Sheffield, and on 2 June 1938 at Birmingham. At Birmingham, under the auspices of the League of Nations Union, he criticized the Anglo-Italian agreement, and opposed 'any attempt to give financial aid to Italy, directly or indirectly', while Italian troops were still fighting in Spain as part of Franco's forces. Churchill also told his audience: 'Volcanic forces are moving in Europe. Sombre figures are at the head of the most powerful races of man. The dictator countries are preparing night and day to advance their ambitions, if possible by peace, if necessary by force. I must say I come here tonight under the impression that we and other countries stand in great danger. For four years Germany has been arming with might and main. More than £800,000,000 a year has been spent in the effective currency of that country upon rearmaments. Families are made to bring their children up on the strongest ideas of race aspiration and of spreading wider the boundaries of their State. Nearly an army corps—that is to say, three divisions, 50,000 or 60,000 men—is added to the strength of the German Army every six or seven weeks, and it is going on. There has never been seen such an outpouring of the means of war. At present we are sheltered to some extent by the strength of the French Army, but the German numbers are overtaking this, and in the course of the next two years they will be much more numerous. We still have our Navy, never happily so supreme in European waters as it is tonight. But our Air Force, on which much depends, so far from overtaking Germany's, is falling farther and farther behind.'

Winston S. Churchill to Captain Fitzroy

(*Churchill papers: 2/336*)

28 May 1938

Dear Mr Speaker,

I propose with your approval to raise the question of a Ministry of Supply upon the Whitsuntide Adjournment.

I gather that both the Opposition Parties would be agreeable to this, though probably the Labour Party will have a short topic of their own at the beginning.

Perhaps I may speak to you on Monday about this.

Colonel Moore-Brabazon to Winston S. Churchill

(*Churchill papers: 2/336*)

30 May 1938

Dear Winston,

I read your article in the News of the World and I must say I was enthralled by it. I really do congratulate you on it.[1] It was absolutely superb, and I am sure many people hundreds of years hence will look back at it and say:— 'Here was a man thinking far in advance of his time'—as you so often do.

I told you in person how much I enjoyed your speech. I thought that you took exactly the right line.

---

[1] On 29 May 1938 the *News of the World* published an article by Churchill entitled 'Why Not "The United States of Europe"?' In it he urged a unified European community, based on the unity of those states 'with a tradition of liberty'. His article ended: 'But we have our own dream and our own task. We are with Europe, but not of it. We are linked, but not comprised. We are interested and associated, but not absorbed. And should European statesmen address us in the words which were used of old— "Shall I speak for thee to the King or the Captain of the host?"—we should reply with the Shunamite woman: "Nay, Sir, for we dwell among our own people." The conception of a "United States of Europe" is right. Every step taken to that end which appeases the obsolete hatreds and vanished oppressions, which makes easier the traffic and reciprocal services of Europe, which encourages its nations to lay aside their threatening arms or precautionary panoply, is good in itself, is good for them and good for all. It is, however, imperative that as Europe advances towards higher internal unity there shall be a proportionate growth of solidarity throughout the British Empire, and also a deepening self-knowledge and mutual recognition among the English-speaking peoples. Then without misgiving and without detachment we can watch and aid the assuagement of the European tragedy, and without envy survey their sure and sound approach to mass-wealth; being very conscious that every stride towards European cohesion which is beneficial to the general welfare will make us a partner in their good fortune.'

I spent the week-end fishing with Dick Fairey,[1] he had had a report from Barber[2] on your visit to Stockport. Very frank opinions on people pass between fellow-Directors of a firm and Barber's report to Fairey was that he was staggered at your general knowledge of the subject.

Yours ever,
'Brab'

[1] Charles Richard Fairey, 1887–1956. Manager of the Blair-Atholl Aeroplane Syndicate, 1912–13. Chief Engineer to Short Bros, 1913–15. Founded the Fairey Aviation Co Ltd, 1915; subsequently Chairman and Managing Director. Chairman of the Society of British Aircraft Constructors, 1922–4. Member of the Aeronautical Research Committee, 1923–6. President of the Royal Aeronautical Society, 1930–1 and 1932–3. Knighted, 1942. Director-General of the British Air Commission, Washington, 1942–5. Member of the Joint Aircraft Committee, Washington, 1942–5.

[2] A director of the Fairey Aviation Company Limited.

June 1938

Harold Nicolson: diary

(*Nicolson papers*)

1 June 1938

Winston in great form. He attacks the Tory party for being worms about the bombing of British ships by Franco.

Winston S. Churchill: note

(*Churchill papers: 2/341*)

1 June 1938

The German army at this date, June 1, consists of 66 regular divisions, and 4 armoured divisions, the whole at full war-strength. The non-armoured divisions are rapidly acquiring the power to triple themselves, and could at the present time (at least duplicate themselves). The artillery beyond 70 divisions is markedly incomplete. The Officer-Corps is thin over the whole force. Nevertheless by October 1, 1938, we cannot expect less than 108 well equipped and 66 + 4 armoured = 70 *fully* equipped and armed divisional formations. Behind these will stand a reservoir of trained men equal in man power to about another 36 divisions for which skeleton formations have been devised, and for which armaments and small arms & a *very* low complement of artillery munitions would be available if a lower standard were accepted for part of the active army. This takes no account of the manpower of Austria which at the extreme computation could provide 12 divisions, whose formations are well-matured, but without arms, but ready to draw on the general pool of German munition industry. In addition there are a number of men and formations of an 'unbrigaded' nature—frontier defence forces— Landwehr divisions & so on who are relatively unarmed.[1]

[1] Churchill sent a copy of this note to the French Prime Minister on 6 June 1938 (see page 1055).

General Sir Thomas Bridges[1] *to Winston S. Churchill*

(*Churchill papers: 2/330*)

1 June 1938

My dear Winston,

Bravo! for your speech at Sheffield.[2] I do hope you will keep up the pressure, you have done such a lot of real good lately.

I do hope the PM will stick to his guns & promise conscription of the whole country in war.

It would have a calming effect on the continent & *he would have the country behind him*. I did not write & thank you for that *excellent* preface to my book, it made the sale.[3]

Yours ever,
Tom Bridges

[1] George Tom Molesworth Bridges, 1871–1939. Entered Royal Artillery, 1892. Lieutenant-Colonel 4th Hussars, 1914. Head of British Military Mission, Belgian Field Army, 1914–16. Major-General commanding the 19th Division, 1916–17. Wounded five times; lost a leg at Passchendaele. Head of British War Mission, USA, 1918. Head of British Mission, Allied Armies of the Orient, 1918–20. Knighted, 1919. Governor of South Australia, 1922–7. He published his memoirs, *Alarms & Excursions*, in 1938 (with a Foreword by Churchill).

[2] Speaking at Sheffield on 31 May 1938, Churchill declared: 'If Britain today had what Mr Baldwin, Mr MacDonald, and others pledged themselves to give us—an Air Force equal to that of Germany, not only we but all Europe would sleep safer in our beds. We can hardly imagine the miseries and horrors which may flow out over us and over the whole world as the result of that most wrongful act of negligence. The plainest warnings were given in Parliament, and I cannot believe that the British Intelligence Service, which in the Great War was considered by friend and foe the finest in the world, did not place the obvious facts before the Government. We hear a great deal,' he continued, 'of the wonderful collection of deliberative and advisory committees which have been brought into being under the Committee of Imperial Defence. How was it, we may ask—in Sheffield of all places: in the armourers' shop of England—that none of these committees had the wit and foresight even to order the jigs and gauges, and make the preparations in the factories which, at the cost of a few millions, would, in 1933 and 1934, have enabled the whole business of making aeroplanes and other weapons to get into its stride two years earlier? They deliberated, and they advised no doubt, but no one seems to have thought of that elementary and vital precaution. If the Ministers responsible had used one-half the vigour in providing for the defence of the country, which was their bounden duty, as they did in contradicting and discrediting private members who gave the warnings, how much brighter would be our prospects today.'

[3] In his Foreword to *Alarms and Excursions*, dated 31 January 1938, Churchill wrote: 'My first impression of the author of this attractive story was gained a few days before Spion Kop. In the first light of dawn I saw three or four horsemen swimming back to us across the Tugela River amid a rattle of Mauser fire. A few minutes later Tom Bridges, still dripping, joined us in the dip of ground from which we had watched his adventure. We soldiered together in Dundonald's Brigade during the relief of Ladysmith, and ever since I have preserved a lively friendship and admiration for him . . .' Surveying Bridges' career, Churchill wrote, at one point: 'We see our author, who was wounded five times in the War, struck down by a high-explosive shell during one of the battles at Passchendaele. This incident, which cost him his leg, is certainly of peculiar interest for me. I was indignant when General Plumer, the Army Commander, refused to allow me as Minister of Munitions to be with Bridges on that day; but

Winston S. Churchill to General Sir Thomas Bridges

(*Churchill papers: 2/330*)

4 June 1938

Thank you so much for your letter.

I try to do all I can, and it is a comfort to feel you are thinking along the same lines.

Winston S. Churchill to Colonel Moore-Brabazon

(*Churchill papers: 2/336*)

4 June 1938

Thank you so much for your very kind letter of May 30th, which gave me great pleasure to read.

After Whitsuntide we must have a serious talk. I went over Austin's Shadow Factory yesterday, which seems to be a very fine affair, but what a target, and utterly unprotected. The very first thing they would do would be to send daylight bombers to these places, probably before any declaration of war.

Winston S. Churchill to Leslie Hore-Belisha

(*Churchill papers: 2/336*)

4 June 1938

Thank you very much for the excellent map which has arrived here. It certainly gives a very graphic picture of Europe. My eye rests often on it, hoping that it will not soon be out of date.

I heard that you were pained by my references to War Office affairs in my last speech.[1] There is nothing in the anti-aircraft position for which you can

---

when I learned what had happened to him, I was by no means sure that I had ground for complaint.' As Secretary of State for the Colonies in 1922, Churchill had supported Bridges nomination to the Governorship of South Australia.

[1] On 25 May 1938, during a debate in the House of Commons on Air Defence, Churchill had criticized the 'extraordinarily cumbrous and complex organisation' of supply for the armed services. He specifically criticized the War Office, which one year before, had defended its Department of Master General of Ordnance as 'working splendidly', only to discover it in a disorganized condition a few months later. 'I assert,' Churchill said, 'that the Air Ministry and the War Office are absolutely incompetent to produce the great flow of weapons now required from British industry.' Only the creation of a Ministry of Supply and the declaration of a national emergency, would, he concluded, meet the urgency of the situation.

be blamed, unless of course you commit yourself to the impossible task of white-washing this horrid scandal. Undoubtedly the whole position will have to be probed by the House of Commons. We ought to have at least two thousand modern AA guns. Although the three-inch re-lined may be better than nothing, it is no substitute for the three-point-seven of which I suppose we have a dozen, and a trickle of eights and tens coming in through the present year. The position of the four-point-five is even worse, as it is said that the design of the carriages is not yet even approved. Of course you realise that people serving in the existing units are indignant at the failure to supply them with effective arms. They make no secret of the state they are in. The Germans are certainly not making less than three thousand cannon a year, although they have already an enormous accumulation. Yesterday I went over the Austin Shadow Factory near Birmingham,—a magnificent plant, totally undefended. It could be wrecked for many months in a few minutes by a single aeroplane. There is no attempt even at camouflage or artificial fog.

I am hoping that we shall have your vote down before the end of the Session, and I propose myself to make a very considerable examination of our present military system. I do not know whether you have at any time given in public an explanation (a) of the size of the Expeditionary Force, and (b) of the means by which draft-producing units are to be created. I am assured that the scale of the Expeditionary Force has been steadily reduced in the past few years. Remember, we had fifteen divisions in action before Christmas 1914, and your Army Estimates are far above those of pre-War days.

What I hope above all things to hear from you is that you are preparing the weapons, munitions and equipment for at least twenty divisions. If we should unhappily be drawn into a great war, you will have a million volunteers crowding your recruiting stations in the first few weeks. It will be very bad for all if there are no weapons for them. The new factor of air bombing will infuriate people. There will be no need for compulsion to bring them forward. I do hope you will not consent to reduce the provision for the army, and even if you cannot make new formations, make sure that the weapons are ready when the numbers come forward. The idea that Britain will in time of war become a great military power is one of the most important deterrents against war.

As I understand you questioned some of the facts I mentioned the other day, I hope you will yourself look into the deficiencies which I alleged existed in the equipment, even of the Guards. Of one battalion it is said there are only five Bren guns out of forty, and one anti-tank rifle out of twenty-four. The rest are represented, or were a month ago by coloured rags on sticks. It is incomprehensible to me that such deficiencies can exist now that we are at the end of the third year of re-armament. The fact that none of this is yr fault shld give you the greater power to rectify it.

Winston S. Churchill to Major Percy Davies

(*Churchill papers: 8/602*)

5 June 1938
Private & Secret

My dear Major Davies,

As I know how earnestly you desire not to mislead the readers of the 'News of the World', I venture to write you a line upon the enclosed article, which I read with much astonishment.[1]

There is at present time an almost total absence of defence, apart from the RAF, for our cities and vulnerable points. We have not got a dozen modern anti-aircraft guns in the country. The 3·7 guns which are modern, are now trickling out in small numbers every month, but the total order is itself on a scale hopelessly below our requirements. The Germans have actually between 3,000 and 4,000 modern anti-aircraft guns, all made since 1933. While I would not say the War-time reclined 3″ gun is of no value, it is not comparable with modern weapons. The balloon barrage is at present on a very small scale, and I doubt if it will affect the problem. As for the wonderful inventions of the scientists, I have served on the CID Committee, which deals with this subject, for nearly three years, and while there are many hopeful lines which are being explored and some developed, it is a delusion to think that for the next two or three years there will be any substantial contribution to our defence from this source. As to the RAF, it is at present less than one-third of the German Air Force, and the rate of production is at present less than one-third. Only about half the Squadrons are equipped with modern machines, and the German fast bombers are so fast that we have not a

[1] The *News of the World*, in its leading article of 5 June 1938 headed 'What Britain's enemies may expect!' Commenting on a recent broadcast by Sir Thomas Inskip, the leading article declared: 'Air power is no less vital to our security. On that subject Sir Thomas Inskip was specially reassuring. Joint plans have been prepared by the Navy and the Air Force to fit every emergency. Should the day come when an enemy sends his aeroplanes to destroy our docks and wharves, our warehouses and aerodromes, our roads and railways, he will be welcomed by the finest airmen and the finest machines in the world. Those of his machines which pass will encounter myriads of guns and balloon barrages. They will encounter something more, for we are told that "some of our greatest scientists are helping in the task of air defence", and that "some of their very latest discoveries are now coming into use". Never in the whole course of her history has Britain prepared with such thoroughness as today to wield the sword.'

sufficient margin of speed to catch them, except under very lucky circumstances. In any case, we should be heavily outnumbered.

The Germans know our position very accurately, and it is our own people who are living in a 'Fool's Paradise'.

Excuse my writing this to you for your own private eye, and that of Sir Emsley Carr; but I take a great interest in all that the 'News of the World' says.

Winston S. Churchill to Edouard Daladier

(*Churchill papers: 2/341*)

6 June 1938

I am very much obliged to you for the invaluable information which I have received through the French Military Attaché.[1] You may be sure I shall use it only with the greatest discretion, and in our common interests.

The general estimate of the German Air Force at the present time agrees with the private views I have been able to form. I am inclined to think, however, that the German Aircraft industry is turning out aircraft at a somewhat higher rate than is allowed, and that the figure given is that for the actual deliveries of aircraft of military types to the German Air Force, excluding deliveries for export, and to General Franco. One also considers that the German Air Force will consist of 300 Squadrons by April 1, 1939, and 400 Squadrons by April 1, 1940.

I venture to enclose a very short note of the information I have been able to gather from various sources about the present and prospective strength of the German army. It would be a convenience to me to know whether this agrees broadly with your estimates. It would be quite sufficient if the figures, as you understand them, could be pencilled in in any case where you think I am in error.[2]

[1] Pierre Paul Lelong, 1891–1947. 2nd Lieutenant, 1914; wounded on the western front, September 1914. Severely wounded, February 1915, and taken prisoner-of-war. Escaped from a prisoner-of-war camp in Poland, 1918, and joined General Janin's French-led forces in Siberia. On active service in Syria, 1920–2, in Morocco, 1928–30 and in Dahomey, 1931–3. Lieutenant-Colonel, 1933. French Military Attaché in London, 1937–9. On active service in France, 1940. Subsequently joined the Free French Forces at Gibraltar, to command the 1st Brigade; on active service with the resistance in Morocco, February to August 1942. On missions to London, 1942 and to Madagascar, 1943. Commandant of the French Troops in Madagascar, 1943–5. Military Governor of Corsica, 1946–7, when he was killed.

[2] On 18 June 1938 Edouard Daladier wrote to Churchill from Paris that, of the 36 German Divisions, four were entirely motorized, and two were in the process of becoming motorized. On 30 June 1938 Desmond Morton commented both on Churchill's memorandum, and on Daladier's letter: 'Thank you so much for letting me see the paper which I return. I would agree with Daladier's amendment. It is satisfactory to know that the French opinions & estimates coincide with ours' (*Churchill papers: 2/341*).

Jan Masaryk to Winston S. Churchill

(*Churchill papers: 2/330*)

8 June 1938   Czechoslovak Minister
                                                    London

My dear Mr Churchill,

The Xth Sokol Congress takes place in Prague from 2nd–5th July this year. It is a specifically Czechoslovak institution which has played a big role in our national life: I venture to say that the mass exercises are quite unique.

Dr Beneš, my Government and the Municipality of Prague would be very happy if you and Mrs Churchill could visit Prague as their guests on this occasion. There is an excellent connection with Prague by air.

Do let me know if it is possible for you to get away. Needless to say, I would be very happy if you could. I know it is daring of us to ask you.

With best wishes,

Ever sincerely yours,
Jan Masaryk

Brigadier-General Sir James Edmonds to Winston S. Churchill

(*Churchill papers: 2/330*)

8 June 1938   Committee of Imperial Defence

My dear Mr Churchill,

I am delighted to hear that the 2nd draft meets with your approval.

Yes! I still think that war is NOT imminent. First Germany is far more frightened of our joining a confederation against her than we are of her. She is not ready for war yet. Italy is now inclined to keep friends with us; she is afraid of Germany, having had a taste of Hitler's way. Japan would like to clear us [out] of the Far East, but dare not try as long as the USA are prepared to unite with us in the Far East in a common cause; besides she is hopelessly involved in China & reduced to methods of frightfulness.

Providence looks after us and confounds our enemies, but expects 'works' as well as faith. To ensure peace we must be strong. It would impress our enemies if Gilbert Murray[1] and the LNU were sent to a concentration camp!

Yours sincerely,
J. E. Edmonds

---

[1] Chairman of the League of Nations Union (see page 413, note 2).

Winston S. Churchill to Sir Kingsley Wood

(*Churchill papers: 25/17*)

9 June 1938

I send you a copy of my new book (which does not appear until the 24th). Will you kindly keep it in your possession.

May I draw your attention to my speech on 'Air Defence Research', June 7, 1935, page 239. I should be glad if you could find time to read this. You will see at the beginning of page 242 how far we had advanced in thought on that date and from the rest of the speech the past history of this effort will be plain.

I have been summoned to a Meeting of the ADR Committee on the afternoon of June 21, and I shall come. But I must tell you that the two and three-quarter years I have been a member of this Committee have been very disappointing. I regret that Professor Lindemann and I accepted Baldwin's invitation to take part in these studies. I am sure that with the support we had from Austen Chamberlain and the Liberal and Labour Parties in the House, we could have enforced more attention to this subject, than by being members of these committees.

The secret information to which we became parties, although going very little further than what we knew ourselves imposed silence.

In all my experience of public offices, I have never seen anything like the slow-motion picture which the work of this Committee has presented; and I fear it is typical of a whole group of committees which have been in existence during these vital years. One could not have devised a better method of soothing this whole matter down and laying it politely in repose than the elaborate process which has been followed. It proved impossible to get any experiments upon new types of shells carried out except at such lengthy intervals and on so petty a scale as to be futile.

Professor Lindemann, who has a far greater insight in this sphere than anyone I know, was very soon turned out of the Technical Committee for pressing more vigorous action. The kite balloons mentioned in my speech were for a long time condemned by the Technical Committee. Now that they have at last been adopted, it is upon so small a scale as to give us no appreciable protection during the coming critical two years. Even the rocket plan of the Technical Committee (minus Lindemann), which seemed so hopeful, has not yet reached the mass production stage; and I see from the latest War Office circulation that there is to be a further delay negativing the decision taken at our last Meeting.

So far as the ADR Committee is concerned, there seems to be a complete lack of driving power. The final result is that we have nothing that will be of

any effective use in the next two years, when much either in war or humiliation may be in store for us all.

Now that you have succeeded Swinton, can we not hope for a renewed
effort, for more readiness to carry experiments forward from day to day, and
more resolve to take action leading to more tangible result. I earnestly hope
so. When you look into this subject yourself, you will no doubt be given
excellent answers to these complaints and quite enough to baffle protests in
Parliament, but this will not remove the glaring reproach that we have
nothing to shield ourselves with at the present moment. Dark hints have been
thrown out from time to time of wonderful secrets which will be our shield,
but if you come to ask what actually we shall have to destroy raiding aircraft
in 1938 and 1939, I venture to believe you will be seriously concerned.[1]

Brendan Bracken to Violet Pearman

(*Pearman papers*)

10 June 1938   London

Dear Mrs Pearman,

I was most grieved by the news of your illness.

I & all who know you pray that you will get well quickly. Your devoted

---

[1] This letter had considerable repercussions. On 16 June 1938 Professor Tizard was warned
by Kingsley Wood's Secretary: 'I think you should be aware that Mr Churchill is on the war-
path again and has written to the Secretary of State with all sorts of allegations about delays
in the work of the ADR Committee' (*Air Ministry papers, 19/25*). That same day Tizard wrote
to Sir Maurice Hankey: 'I have received Churchill's outrageous memorandum. He is hindering the work of the Committee in every possible way and doing nothing to help it' (*Cabinet
papers: 21/634*). But Sir Thomas Inskip wrote that same day to Kingsley Wood: 'I think it
will be necessary to go very carefully into the whole of Winston's allegations' (*Cabinet papers:
21/631*). William Elliot, the Assistant Secretary to the Committee of Imperial Defence, wrote to
Kingsley Wood on 17 June 1938: 'Sir Henry Tizard feels that in view of Mr Churchill's letter
to you of the 9th June you may think it better not to have his Note discussed at the meeting
on the 27th' (*Cabinet papers: 21/631*). On 17 June 1938 Kingsley Wood proposed including in
his reply to Churchill the phrase 'and I should naturally also be willing to consider any
suggestions that you may have for possible new lines of research'. But Kingsley Wood's
Secretary advised leaving out this phrase as 'Churchill might suggest something quite fantastic and the Secretary of State for Air does not want to be obliged to consider anything
Churchill throws up' (*Air Ministry papers, 19/25*). On 21 June 1938 Elliot suggested that,
despite Kingsley Wood's inclination to do so, Churchill's criticisms should not be discussed at
the next Air Defence Research meeting. As Elliot noted: 'Personally, I feel that it would be
a mere waste of time to wash this dirty linen in Committee' (*Cabinet papers: 21/634*). Kingsley
Wood agreed to this, but still wanted to send Churchill material. On 19 July 1938 William
Elliot was to write to Kingsley Wood's Secretary: 'As Sir Kingsley Wood undertook to supply
this information personally to Mr Churchill I suppose it must go, but I cannot help feeling
that this special treatment, if continued, will eventually land us in trouble' (*Cabinet papers:
21/634*). See also pages 1066–7 and 1071–2 and 1075–6 of this volume.

service to Mr Churchill is beyond valuation. No one has helped him more than you during these last five years when he has been fighting an uphill battle for things very precious to England.

Yours sincerely,
Brendan Bracken

Winston S. Churchill to J. L. Garvin

(*Garvin papers*)

15 June 1938   Boughton House,
Private   Kettering[1]

My dear Jim,

It wd give me pleasure if you could find time to read this book:[2] because it wd I think show you that the differences wh have emerged between us on the supreme issues to which our lives have been devoted are vy much less than the gt body of doctrine & knowledge which unite us still in a common cause.

I fear that at no gt distance there lies before us a trial more grievous than any we have known—aye & surmounted. We have been cruelly mismanaged,

[1] The dowager Duchess of Buccleuch writes (from Boughton House): 'I do indeed remember every moment of the Churchill visit. I can't think how we could have subjected him to such a dull week end! except that he had said he would like to see this house, which is magical.' The other guests that week end were the Princess Royal and her husband Lord Harewood, Lord and Lady Elphinstone (she the sister of Queen Elizabeth, later Queen Mother), and Lord and Lady Pembroke. Of Lady Pembroke, the dowager Duchess of Buccleuch writes: 'She at least could play Bezique with Winston (*but* as it turned out it was *I* who played with him, an interesting experience—as he was notoriously known to be an erratic scorer, flicking up the ivory markers 100 & even *1,000* at a time!).' Her account continues: 'We had had a Charity Fête here Saturday afternoon. News spread that "Royalty" was coming to stay, & by the evening a considerable crowd had gathered by the front door to see the guests arrive from the station (in those days everybody travelled by train). Winston was delighted and drew the cheers by waving his hat & cigar at the crowd.' During the week end 'someone had mentioned *ghosts* to Winston, and he complained that "*someone*" had been in his room "taking exschepschion to my being there".' Later that summer Neville Chamberlain was to be at Boughton House 'at a huge Midlands Conservative Fête. I consulted Winston where to place the platform for the PM's speech, at 5 pm. The obvious place was on the terrace looking *due West*, so I was suggesting we put up the dais under the trees, on the *South* of the lawn looking *North*. Winston, with that delicious impish grin, and chortle, said, "Put Neville Chamberlain with the shun in his eyes, and the wind in his Teesch" ' (*letter to the author, 12 February 1982*).

[2] Churchill's collection of speeches made between 1936 and 1938, and entitled *Arms and the Covenant*, was published on 24 June 1938. That same day *The Times* noted, in its review: 'Mr Churchill himself has done his utmost both to profit by experience and to instruct his fellow-citizens. The lessons of 1914 are never far from his mind, and one of his besetting fears is that the next war, particularly if it comes suddenly, may catch us, as the last war caught us, inadequately prepared.'

& chances wh are inestimable have been thrown away. Still let us proclaim the only hope that makes later life endurable—Never give in!

The Italian references in this volume as you will see bear the imprint of yr advice.[1]

Yours ever,
Winston S.C.

Sir Henry Strakosch to Winston S. Churchill

(*Churchill papers: 2/336*)

15 June 1938
Personal

My dear Winston,

I made the acquaintance last night of Sir Robert McLean,[2] who is Chairman of Vickers (Aviation) Limited—an offshoot of the great Vickers Company—engaged in large-scale aeroplane production. Their works are near the Brooklands Motor Racing Track, which, as you know, is not far from Weybridge. Sir Robert struck me as a very level-headed fellow who knows his business well, and has a very sound conception of what our policy in regard to the production of aircraft for military purposes should be. On parting, he invited me to inspect their Works, and hear from their Engineering Staff what they have to say about the type of aircraft which is being produced there (on the geodetic system) and as to the method of manufacture.

---

[1] Thus on 5 November 1936 Churchill had told the House of Commons: 'What ought to be our policy towards Italy? At any rate, we can see what it ought not to be. It ought not to be a policy of nagging. Very serious antagonism existed between Great Britain, doing her part as a member of the League of Nations, and Italy over the conquest of Abyssinia. In that antagonism we have not prevailed. We have been humiliated, but we have not been dishonoured. However we may have been guided, we are not regarded either as knaves or cowards. Friends of mine tell me that the Italian Dictator has repeatedly said that he both understands and respects the British point of view. He has also made public a statement of certain submissions which Italy will make to the League of Nations about the character of Italian rule in Abyssinia. I do not know whether those have been departed from or not, or whether they still apply. It seems to me that any statements of that kind are of value and importance. The relations between Great Britain and Italy in the Mediterranean have always been those of special amity' (*quoted in 'Arms and the Covenant', page 367*).

[2] Robert McLean, 1884–1964. Worked on the Indian State Railways before the First World War; Assistant Secretary, Indian Railway Board, 1916; Secretary, 1919. On active service in Mesopotamia and France, 1915–18. General Manager, Great Indian Peninsular Railway, 1922–9. Trustee, Port of Bombay, 1922–7. Knighted, 1926. Chairman, Vickers (Aviation) Limited, and Super-marine Aviation Works Limited, 1927–38. Chairman of the Society of British Aircraft Constructors, 1935–7.

I told him that you were keenly interested in all matters of military aviation, and that you, too, would no doubt like to have a look at the Works. He very much welcomed the idea of your seeing them. We are asked to lunch at the Works. Would you care to come out with me on Wednesday next, the 22nd? I would motor you out, and I suggest that we might leave London about 12 o'clock noon, which should enable us to be back in town between four and five o'clock in the afternoon. This would give us ample time to have a good look at the Works. I may say that work is now proceeding there on mass production lines.

As soon as I hear from you, I will make a definite appointment with Sir Robert.

Ever yours,
H. Strakosch

Winston S. Churchill to Sir Maurice Hankey
(Churchill papers: 2/330)

15 June 1938
Private

My dear Maurice,

Although we have been in late years divided by differences of view about national safety and the measures to procure it, I cannot allow the momentous announcement of your impending retirement to pass without writing you these few lines of earnest tribute to the magnitude of the services you have rendered in the great days which are gone. At several crises of mortal danger your personal initiative brought about the measures needful to success. The imprint of your long work upon the structure of National Defence, and also upon the workings of the Cabinet system, will form a definite chapter in our history—unless that history is about to be cut short—a fate which even in my most anxious moods I still believe can be averted. I look back with pleasure upon our own association from the day when Ottley[1] came to me at the Admiralty to tell me about the qualities of a young Captain of Marines who above all men was qualified to guide the CID, and when old Fisher[2] sang your praises in his vibrant tones. I must thank you for many acts of courtesy

---

[1] Charles Langdale Ottley, 1858–1932. Entered Navy, 1871. Present at the bombardment of Alexandria, 1882. Senior Naval Officer at Constantinople, 1898. Captain, 1899. Director of Naval Intelligence, 1905–7. Knighted, 1907. Secretary to the Committee of Imperial Defence, 1907–12. Retired from Navy with rank of Rear-Admiral, 1912. Director of Armstrong Whitworth, 1912–19.

[2] Admiral of the Fleet Lord Fisher (see page 773, note 1). On 20 August 1911 Fisher wrote to the First Lord, Reginald McKenna: 'I hope you continue to put your whole trust in Hankey, for it is true what Esher says of him that he is a Napoleon!' To Lord Esher, Fisher wrote on

to me throughout this period—generation-long—when you have so tirelessly discharged your immense function, and formed the chain of continuity which united phases and ministers across the gulfs of party. I wish you all content-ment and good fortune in your easier life of rest after unexampled toils.

Yours very sincerely,

Sir Maurice Hankey to Winston S. Churchill

(*Churchill papers: 2/330*)

16 June 1938

My dear Winston,

Your letter has touched me more than I can express. What inimitable power you have to touch the hearts of men!

I am a little upset at your suggestion that we have been divided by differences over national defence. That we have been divided, or rather parted, I agree, but that has been due more to my position as a Public Servant than to fundamental differences of opinion, which a frank talk would probably have reconciled.[1]

A few nights ago I dined alone with Lloyd George. He told me he had avoided me lately, because he was a frequent critic of the Government and had felt it might be embarrassing to me to meet. In the same way, my dear Winston, I have avoided you! For me, in the complete confidence of the Cabinet, their trusted servant, with all their inside knowledge, to discuss the

---

9 November 1911 (shortly after Churchill had become First Lord): '. . . why I am writing to you now is to entreat you to *make sure* with the Prime Minister that Hankey succeeds Ottley if there is any change. This is VERY, VERY secret. But you know Hankey's great value! I feel you are the only one who could see this through, so I write. *I consider it absolutely vital for the future of the CID!* Winston promised me he would do his utmost for Hankey if any change, but you know what politicians are!' (quoted in Arthur J. Marder (editor), *Fear God and Dread Nought*, volume II, London 1956).

[1] In speaking at Sheffield on 31 May 1938, of the need for a Ministry of Supply, Churchill had told his audience: 'Even now the right methods are not being used, nor are the measures taken proportionate to the scale of events or to the dangers of our position. Sir Maurice Han-key, that great public servant, who in his day rendered invaluable service, is resigning, but the extraordinary labyrinth of Advisory Committees to which it was said he alone knew the key amid which the unfortunate Minister for the Co-ordination of Defence wanders, forlorn and overburdened, is still to be maintained. A Ministry of Supply to grapple with the whole problem of armament production is still refused, and refused upon the extraordinary ground that there is no emergency. The anxieties of the public are quieted by the appointment of a new Air Minister, and by the association of a well-known figure, Lord Nuffield, in the work of air production, and hardly a day passes without some grandiose paper scheme being splashed in the headlines of the popular Press. But I am here to tell you tonight that far more vehement effort, more powerful executive organization, and, I will add, a sterner temper, will be needed before we can even say that, late as it is, we are doing our best.'

sort of question which you and I can't help discussing, with an intimate friend of many years standing, who is a critic of the Government, was I felt too difficult. I know that you know a lot. But I never know how much you know! I think Bacon expresses my position:—

> 'For if a man have that penetration of judgement as he can discern what things are to be laid open, and what to be secreted, and what to be shewed at half lights, and to whom, and when (which indeed are arts of state and arts of life, as Tacitus well calleth them), to him a habit of dissimulation is a hindrance and a poorness.' (Essay—Of simulation and dissimulation).

Yes, after copying it I think that hits it off. I cannot dissemble or hide with you, and I cannot quite reconcile it with my official position to talk freely.

I once hid something terrific from you. I think it must have been the first news of Kitchener's death.[1] I did so because I received the information (in your presence) by telephone with a strict injunction not to tell anyone but the Prime Minister. I hated myself for it, but I comforted myself with the thought that when you came back to Office you would trust me the more.

My code you know. I let my chiefs know what I think, but when they have taken their decision, as a public servant, as part of the official machine, I give all the help I can in carrying out their policy.

But all this has never abated my admiration for you nor my affection. And that is why I am so deeply moved by your all too kind references to my past services and to our long and profitable association.

In a few weeks I shall be quit of my official shackles, and then we can meet on the old terms and I hope we shall.[2]

Yours ever,

M. P. A. Hankey

---

[1] Lord Kitchener was drowned at sea on 5 June 1916, on his way to Russia. When the news became known publicly, Churchill was with Sir Ian Hamilton, preparing his evidence for the Dardanelles Commission. In his book *Listening for the Drums* Hamilton recalled how as the two men worked, they heard somebody calling Kitchener's name: 'We jumped up and Winston threw the window open. As he did so an apparition passed beneath us, I can use no other word to describe the strange looks of this newsvendor of wild and uncouth aspect. He had his bundle of newspapers under his arm and as we opened the window was crying out, "Kitchener drowned! No survivors!" The fact that he should have vanished,' Hamilton wrote in his book, 'at the very moment Winston and I were making out an unanswerable case against him was one of those *coups* with which his career was crowded—he was not going to answer!' At lunch that day, Hamilton recalled, 'Winston signed to everyone to be seated and then, before taking his own seat very solemnly quoted: "Fortunate was he in the moment of his death!" It was,' Hamilton recorded, 'a nightmare lunch—no small talk—Winston said K might yet turn up but I told the company that he always had a horror of cold water, and that the shock of the icy sea would at once extinguish his life.'

[2] Hankey formally retired on 31 July 1938. His duties as Secretary of the Committee of Imperial Defence were taken over by Colonel Hastings Ismay.

Sir Edward Grigg to Winston S. Churchill
(*Churchill papers: 2/330*)

16 June 1938

My dear Winston,

I am sending you herewith a copy of my new book, 'Britain looks at Germany', which is to be published on Thursday next, the 23rd. . . .

I was delighted to read your article on National Service in the DT on Thursday last.[1] I hope you will keep hammering at it.

Yours ever,
Scribe

Winston S. Churchill to Lord Chatfield
(*Chatfield papers*)

18 June 1938   Chartwell

My Dear Chatfield

I keenly enjoyed our expedition and think it a great compliment that you should have conducted me personally upon it. A visit to the Fleet is a tonic in every sense.

I have reflected constantly on all that you showed me, and I am sure the Nation owes the Admiralty, and those who have guided it, an inestimable debt for the faithful effort sustained over so many years which has, as I feel convinced, relieved us of one of our great dangers.

What surprised me was the clarity and force of the indications.[2] I had

---

[1] Writing in the *Daily Telegraph* on 9 June 1938, in an article entitled 'National Service', Churchill urged the establishment of a National Register, 'enabling a survey to be made of all our resources in man power'. Churchill added: 'Having gone so far, the Government cannot stop short of a complete scheme for national service, which would come into operation on the outbreak of war if Parliament approved. Such measures would naturally have to be accompanied by legislation "to take the profit out of war", upon the study of which great progress has been made in the United States of America. The idea of large numbers of men being made liable to be sent abroad on military service is not compatible with others remaining at home to pile up inflated wartime profits, under conditions when free competition is largely suspended. The principle that no man, whatever his calling, shall become richer out of war should be proclaimed, and a special financial bill should be drafted for this purpose. . .'

[2] A reference to Asdic, a method of submarine location. Captain Roskill writes: '. . . Churchill cannot be blamed for accepting the Naval Staff's view that the Asdic had conquered the submarine, and that ships could defend themselves successfully against air attacks. The responsibility for the propagation of such fallacies rests firmly with the Admiralty, and their exposure probably aggravated Churchill's mistrust of service "experts", and contributed to his determination to equip himself with independent scientific advice in the shape of Professor Lindemann and his associates' (Stephen Roskill, *Churchill and the Admirals*, London 1977, page 89).

imagined something almost imperceptible, certainly vague and doubtful. I never imagined I should hear one of these creatures asking to be destroyed, both orally and literally. It is a marvellous system and achievement.

There is one more point which occurs to me, which no doubt has already been considered; but I write of it on the chance. I refer to that target apparatus. Does it echo the same note as the real thing? Can it be easily distinguished from the real thing? If not, there is this danger. One of those creatures, if they understood the whole story, might take half a dozen targets on its back and release them in different directions when pursued or in danger; thus, half a dozen false scents would be laid and much disappointment encountered. If this were so, it might be better not to proceed with the target idea, however convenient. I hope, however, that there is no difficulty in telling turtle from mock-turtle.

I venture to send you a copy of my new book, which really constitutes my public work for the last five years. You will find a lot that you do not agree with; but I hope you will also find some things of which some notice might well have been taken betimes.

Brigadier Pakenham-Walsh to Winston S. Churchill

(*Churchill papers: 8/595*)

18 June 1938

My dear Mr Churchill,

. . . I was intensely interested in what you said about your hope of a peaceable debate on the Army. As a serving soldier one cannot say much, but many like myself, who are perhaps not fully 'in the know', are very disturbed at the situation, and we can only pray that war will not come till we are much more ready. Even when we get equipment we have to learn to use it, and develop suitable tactics. One cannot do everything by imagination.

Winston S. Churchill to Sir Alexander Maxwell

(*Churchill papers: 1/326*)

18 June 1938

Dear Sir Alexander,

I venture to bring to your notice the desire of my son-in-law, Mr Victor Oliver, to become naturalised as a British subject.

He is at present an American citizen of Austrian origin.

He is an actor and public entertainer, who has had for many years a considerable vogue in the United States. Since marrying my daughter Sarah, he has become closely attached to this country and has developed important connections here. He has always been treated with much consideration by Mr Humbert Wolfe[1] of the Ministry of Labour. He makes a very large income here and holds himself available for public and charitable work whenever required.

Although, in the first instance, as you may have heard, I opposed his marriage with my daughter, I have come to like and esteem him greatly and I am sure that any assistance you can give to his wish would be well bestowed.

I shall be in London Tuesday, Wednesday and Thursday, and could call upon you if that were necessary. Perhaps you will drop me a line.

Sir Maurice Hankey to Sir Thomas Inskip

(Cabinet papers: 64/5)

20 June 1938

Minister

I wrote a letter to Sir Henry Tizard, Air Ministry and War Office (with copy to the Admiralty for information) asking for their comments and material to assist in the reply to Mr Churchill's letter on the ADR Committee.

Sir Henry Tizard called on me on Friday morning. He was boiling with indignation at Mr Churchill's letter. In fact he had already written to me to hint that if they were to be criticised in this way, his whole Committee of scientists would resign. However, he quietened down in the course of our conversation and promised on no account to inform his Committee of the criticisms and to let me have a reply containing comments within a few days.

As I am going down to the Fleet at Portland Monday and Tuesday (leaving by a train at 12.30 pm) I thought it best to get my own ideas blocked in during the weekend, without waiting for the replies from Sir Henry Tizard and the Departments. I therefore prepared rather a full memorandum with a view to informing Sir Kingsley Wood as to the facts. The memo-

---

[1] Humbert Wolfe, 1886–1940. Born in Milan, of German-Italian Jewish parentage. Educated at Bradford Grammar School and Wadham College, Oxford. Entered the civil service, 1908. At the Board of Trade he played a leading part in the organization of Labour Exchanges and Unemployment Insurance. Controller, Labour Regulation Department, Ministry of Munitions, 1915–18. Director of Services and Establishments, Ministry of Labour, 1919–21; Head of the Department of Employment and Training, 1934–7; Deputy Secretary, 1938. A poet and literary critic, his first volumes of poetry were published in 1920 and 1924. He wrote or edited over forty books, and did translations of Greek, German and French poems and plays.

randum could be sent to Mr Churchill, but could not be published, even if later this should be thought necessary, as it contains a good deal of confidential matter. In fact nothing could be published until the RDF and rockets become more or less public property—and I imagine they cannot be kept secret very much longer. From a tactical point of view, I think the Government ought to avoid an open clash with Mr Churchill on this subject until the RDF can be mentioned publicly, because that is the great success that has been achieved, and as you know is being followed up with promising results in many fields.

On the whole, therefore, I suggest that it is desirable to keep Churchill in the Committee. I do not think, however, that his intolerable accusations ought to remain unanswered. What we really want is a reply which shows him that we do not accept his criticism, and that we have ample material to rebut it, but does not, so to speak, reveal our whole case.

In addition to the memorandum, therefore, I have prepared the draft of a letter from Sir Kingsley Wood to Churchill. I am afraid it reveals rather more than I intended of our case, but I think it will be sufficient to stop his mouth.

The position is very unsatisfactory, because after reading Mr Churchill's letter, I cannot but believe that it is prompted by Professor Lindemann, and the latter is in Churchill's entire confidence and very likely sees our secret papers. I cannot prove it. Nevertheless I do not think the moment has come for calling Mr Churchill's bluff openly. On the whole the course I suggest seems to be the best in the circumstances.

I am leaving copies of my draft memorandum and draft letter with Wing Commander Elliot. Immediately the replies from Sir Henry Tizard and the Departments are received, he will re-cast my drafts as necessary and submit them to you. I have left him an entirely free hand in this matter, though it is possible that in spite of rather a heavy week, I may be able to take a further hand in the matter.

M. P. A. Hankey

Princess Bibesco[1] to Winston S. Churchill
(Churchill papers: 2/330)

20 June 1938

My dear Winston,

Tatarescu[2] the late—and near future—Roumanian Prime Minister is over here till Thursday. Feeling as you and I do about the Nazis and indeed the world in general I think it would be *most* useful if you could see him for a few minutes. It is curious how blind everyone is in this country to the vital importance of the Balkan States not falling under German tutelage—owing to their belief in our weakness.

Would you come here (I would introduce you and then leave you alone) or would you rather see him somewhere else?

Yours affectionately,
Elizabeth

Could you send a telephone message?

Lord Cranborne to Winston S. Churchill
(Churchill papers: 2/330)

20 June 1938

My dear Winston,

After a good deal of discussion, Anthony & I decided that we would neither of us speak tomorrow. There is obviously something up with regard to the Anglo-Italian Pact, & it looks as if, up to now, the Govt have stood firm. If Anthony were to press them in debate tomorrow, it might merely make it more difficult for them to take a firm line, as it would seem to be the result of pressure from him, & would be so interpreted by Musso. For this reason, it is clearly not the moment for him to speak.

I am admittedly not quite in the same position. But we all felt that, if I were to speak and he were to remain silent, it would give rise to misconception. Either I should be regarded as his mouthpiece, in which case the position

---

[1] Elizabeth Charlotte Lucy Asquith, 1897–1945. Daughter of H. H. Asquith (Prime Minister, 1908–15) by his second wife, Margot Tennant. In 1919 she married Prince Antoine Bibesco, sometime Rumanian Minister to Madrid (who died in 1951).

[2] Gheorge Tatarescu, 1892–1957. Prime Minister of Rumania, January 1934–December 1937 and November 1939 to July 1940. (Also Foreign Minister, October 1934, and February to March 1938). Arrested, September 1940. Rescued from the Iron Guard, December 1940. Ambassador to France, 1941–44. Deputy Prime Minister, and Foreign Minister, from March 1945 to November 1947 when he resigned in protest against arrests by the Soviet controlled Communists and the overthrow of the monarchy while the King of Rumania was in London for Princess Elizabeth's wedding. Resigned the Chairmanship of the Liberal Party, 1947. Under house arrest, 1949.

would be the same as if he had spoken himself, or I should be regarded as differing from him, which would be embarrassing for us both. Once he has had a go, this argument will of course no longer apply. But until then, at any rate if he is in the House, it has to my mind considerable force. The last thing I want to do is to make things more difficult for him than they already are.

Yours ever,
Bobbety

J. L. Garvin to Winston S. Churchill

(*Churchill papers: 2/330*)

20 June 1938

My dear Winston,

I have just got the book, love having it and will make time somehow to read every word—perhaps tomorrow for I am called off today. Your letter enhances the sending and I shall write again after having finished the pages. Between you and me it is 'no disagreement except in opinion' and on defence —that is over the formation of things—not even a difference of view but an identity of minds and convictions. I feel more hopeful of our getting this summer through without general war: and if we don't use this further and perhaps final respite to strengthen our hands even God won't help us for we shan't deserve. But another word to you soon.

Ever yours affectionately,
Jim

Lord Chatfield to Winston S. Churchill

(*Churchill papers: 2/336*)

20 June 1938   Admiralty

My dear Churchill,

Thank you so much for your letter of the 18th June, the terms of which I greatly appreciate. It was a pleasure to me to take you to Portland and show you the results of our concentrated effort of the last 18 years.

As I am just off to The Fleet with The King, I am sending to-day this brief acknowledgment of your letter and I shall hope later on to be able to give you some information on the point you raise about the Target Apparatus.

Thank you also very much for sending me a copy of your book. I shall look forward to reading it. I enjoyed our day as much as yourself.

Yours very sincerely,
Chatfield

Winston S. Churchill to Jan Masaryk

(Churchill papers: 2/330)

21 June 1938

Indeed I should like to visit Prague, and especially on such an occasion as you describe in your letter of June 8. I am quite clear, however, that I ought not to go at the present time. All kinds of suggestions would be made, and harm would be done to grave interests, which, as you know, I am earnestly seeking to safeguard.

Forgive my delay in answering.

Kathleen Hill to Winston S. Churchill: telephone message

(Churchill papers: 2/330)

21 June 1938

The Private Secretary to Mons. Masaryk has telephoned to say that a Mr Ripka[1] is in London for two or three days, and he would appreciate it if you could possibly give him a short interview.

This Mr Ripka is an intimate friend of President Beneš, and is the owner of one of the most important Czechoslovakian newspapers, so the ambassador considers it would be worth your while seeing him, although naturally he does not want to worry you.

Winston S. Churchill to Lord Birkenhead

(Churchill papers: 2/330)

22 June 1938

You may be interested to see the record of the conversation which we had with Henlein. This note was prepared by Lindemann, whom you know.

As far as I can see, Henlein is adhering to what he said to us, and we understood from Masaryk that the Czech Government would agree to terms

---

[1] Hubert Ripka, 1895–1958. Lecturer in International Politics at Prague University, 1930. Combining university work with journalism, he edited a Prague daily newspaper, *Lidove Noviny* from 1934–9, warning that Hitler always meant to attack Bohemia. Escaped to Paris, March 1939, where he began to organize pro-Czech propaganda. Escaped from France, June 1940. Deputy Secretary of State for Foreign Affairs of the Czechoslovak Government in Exile (in London), 1940–5. Czechoslovak Minister of Foreign Trade, Prague, 1945–8; resigned in February 1948 in protest against the growing power of the Communists. Escaped from Czechoslovakia, 1948. In exile in England from 1948 until his death.

like these. I have every reason to believe that is also true. Therefore, if the negotiations break down, it will almost certainly be because of malignant outside interference.

Will you let me have the note back when you have read it, as it is my only copy.

Lady Violet Bonham Carter to Winston S. Churchill

(*Churchill papers: 2/330*)

22 June 1938

Dearest Winston,

I was so *miserable* to have to leave in the middle of your marvellous speech to-day.[1] (I am on the Foreign Office Board examining young men—& only get an hour's interval for lunch). I could have *killed* Wickham Steed for getting up before you while my precious minutes were oozing away—I wish I had heard the end.

The Govt's *abject* & supine behaviour over our ships is a humiliation to us all. What my Father wld have said about it you know. You are the only trustee left of our national honour whom the world will listen to—so speak on.

Ever yours,
Violet

Sir Henry Tizard: memorandum

(*Cabinet papers: 64/5*)

22 June 1938

. . . I do most strongly resent Mr Churchill's continual pin pricking, especially as he is in a position which enables him to use large and poisonous pins quite irresponsibly. The effect of these pin pricks is that very many busy people, both inside and outside the Government Service, who are devoting themselves to the solution of the problems instead of devoting themselves to criticism of people who are trying to solve them, are forced to do a great deal of unnecessary work.

If it were not for this irritating feature of Mr Churchill's attacks his remarks would be highly entertaining. He says that in all his experience he has never

---

[1] At a meeting of the 'Focus'; see also A. H. Richards' letter to Churchill of 24 June 1938, quoted on page 1075 of this volume.

seen anything like the slow-motion picture which the work of the ADR Committee has presented. Contrast the development of the last few years with the state of affairs when Mr Churchill was First Lord of the Admiralty before the War. As a result of his total lack of real scientific imagination and foresight we entered the War without any defence whatsoever against submarines, and without any method of locating them.

It is well known that the Country only narrowly escaped defeat and 'humiliation' because of this, and that the defeat was only avoided by (a) the convoy system which was opposed by the Admiralty, and (b) the efforts of scientists in developing means for locating submarines.

I rather fancy there is evidence to show that Mr Churchill did very little to promote these efforts.[1]

[1] On 7 June 1935 Churchill told the House of Commons of the First World War years: 'We were told that it was impossible to grapple with submarines, but methods were found which enabled us to strangle the submarine below water. . . .' As to the convoy system, Churchill was no longer First Lord of the Admiralty when the sinking of merchant ships reached a crisis. As he wrote in *The World Crisis, 1916–1918*: 'I had instituted the convoy system for troopships crossing the oceans at the beginning of the war. Then the attack by faster German light cruisers was the danger. The guns of an obsolete battleship or heavy cruiser could certainly drive away any hostile raiders then loose upon the surface of the seas. We had also from the beginning used destroyer escorts to convoy troopships in and out through the submarine zone. In no case did any mishap occur. It did not however seem reasonable to expect similar results from the convoy system in the case of attack by submarines upon merchant ships' (page 363). The sinking of merchant ships became a factor only in 1916. As Churchill wrote: 'When under the pressure of ever-increasing losses the remedy of convoys was again advocated by the younger officers of the Admiralty War Staff, it encountered opposition from practically every quarter. Every squadron and every naval base was clamant for destroyers, and convoy meant taking from them even those that they had. There would be delays due to assembling. There must be reduction in speed of the faster vessels and congestion of ships in port. The scale and difficulties of the task were exaggerated, and it was argued that the larger the number of ships in company, the greater the risk from submarines' (page 364). Churchill concluded: 'It fell to Sir Edward Carson's lot during his tenure as First Lord to face the most anxious and trying period of the naval war. During those eight months the U-boat sinkings of merchantmen reached their terrible climax. It was under his administration that the peak was surmounted and most of the important decisions of principle were taken by which the peril was ultimately overcome. The trial of the convoy system was urged upon the naval authorities by the Cabinet, and in this the Prime Minister [David Lloyd George] took a decisive part. At the end of April, 1917, the Director of the Anti-Submarine Division definitely advocated the introduction of convoys, and the first one left Gibraltar on May 10. It was entirely successful, and regular convoys commenced from the United States on June 4' (page 367).

Leslie Hore-Belisha to Winston S. Churchill

(*Churchill papers: 2/336*)

23 June 1938   War Office
Private

My dear Winston,

I have now given my personal investigation to the matters which concerned my Department in your letter of the 4th June.

I can assure you that the information which you have obtained does not accurately summarise the present facts. I naturally have put and am putting all my energy into accelerating production, but you know well, and have stated publicly, the inevitable time that elapses between conception and fulfilment. Having regard to this, I think you would not be dissatisfied with the present rate of production. I may tell you that this, at any rate, was the view of representative industrialists with whom I conferred at the War Office last week.

I decided to make to them a particular appeal for acceleration and made certain proposals to them, which, with the goodwill they showed, may give us a certain advance of date.

You would not wish me within the scope of a letter to go into details, but I can understand your desire to be assured that everything that can be done will be done.

Yours sincerely,
Leslie Hore-Belisha

Sir Maurice Hankey to Sir Kingsley Wood

(*Cabinet papers: 64/5*)

23 June 1938

Dear Kingsley Wood,

With reference to my letter of the 13th June, enclosing a copy of a letter from Mr Churchill on the subject of the lessons to be learned from the War in Spain, I have now received the Reports from the three Deputy Chiefs of Staff.

All three confirm the impression which I had that technical information of the kind which would be useful to the Air Defence Research Committee has been meagre.

While the fact that this is so may be partly due to the difficulties which we have had in accrediting Service representatives to the Nationalist Headquarters—the War Office observer is actually now leaving for Burgos—the reasons for the comparative failure to obtain technical information appear to be as follows:—

In order to obtain an adequate record of the essential factors—eg speed and height of aircraft and details of equipment and methods of air defence—from observation, it would be necessary to have expert observers wherever air-action might be expected. The presence of one observer, who would normally be located at Headquarters, would not suffice. Expert observers have not been, and for practical reasons cannot be forthcoming, nor is it probable that they could be received in sufficient numbers by Governments which are not bound to us by any particularly friendly ties.

Even were the number of accredited representatives to be satisfactory it would not necessarily follow that satisfactory results would result. It is most improbable that in present conditions in Spain and China our observers would be given facilities for prosecuting enquiries unhindered by any form of restriction; it is, for instance, highly unlikely that the German technical advisers of General Franco would accept close enquiry and analysis of their methods by foreign observers.

Facts—not surmises—about the technical methods of attack and defence are required. Presumably statistics and reports on these points are compiled at the headquarters of the Nationalist and Government Armies in Spain and probably the 'volunteer allies' on both sides have drawn up a set of conclusions from them. Until we can obtain information from such sources—and the difficulties of doing so are very great—our technical information will, I fear, continue to remain inexact and unsatisfactory.

In the circumstances I feel that there is no alternative but to inform Mr Churchill that whereas we have received a number of Reports on War in Spain which have proved of considerable value from the tactical point of view these Reports do not contain information which merits their being circulated to the Air Defence Research Committee.

With this in mind I have drafted the attached letter which I suggest that you might send as a reply to Mr Churchill.

M. P. A. Hankey

A. H. Richards to Winston S. Churchill

(*Churchill papers: 8/599*)

24 June 1938
Confidential

Dear Mr Churchill,

. . . Your hint at Wednesday's luncheon of a National Opposition has been surprisingly well received, revealing strength of unity within our Focus. We must steadfastly pursue our way without haste and without rest. We of the Focus at any rate must not be found feeble in action and leadership for through the Focus the day is at hand when British leadership and action may yet save Peace and civilisation.

Headway[1] agreement is now sealed, signed and delivered, this should be a powerful instrument for the advocacy and the advancement of our Aims and Objects. . . .

Sir Maurice Hankey to Neville Chamberlain

(*Premier papers: 1/253*)

24 June 1938

What might interest you in particular is the material available, not only for rebutting Mr Churchill's allegations, but for counter-attacking him. . . .

Obviously the moment has not yet come to join issue with him because it would not yet be in the public interest to divulge the epoch-making inventions that have been adopted. But the time is not very distant, now that they are coming into use, when they will leak out. Then the Government will be in a position to deliver a withering counter-blast if need be.

In the meantime the obvious tactic is to play for time.

[1] *Headway* had been the League of Nations Union magazine since 1918. In October 1938 it was re-issued, aimed at a wider public, beyond the actual members of the LNU. The front cover of the first number consisted of seven photographs captioned: 'These men wish success to the new Headway.' The seven were Viscount Cecil of Chelwood, J. R. Clynes, Cardinal Hinsley, the Archbishop of York, Churchill, Professor Gilbert Murray, Lord Horder, S. M. Berry and Chief Rabbi J. H. Hertz. The second page of the magazine was an advertisement for the *News Chronicle*. The first issue contained articles by Harold Nicolson ('Before Godesberg'), Sir Norman Angell ('The Great Confusion'), Lady Violet Bonham Carter ('Not an Inch Further'), Captain Liddell Hart ('Britain's Foreign Policy'), Lord Cranborne, Wickham Steed, Harper Poulson, Sir John Orr, Roger Fortune, Vandaleur Robinson, and an unnamed refugee ('It Happened in Vienna').

Sir Kingsley Wood to Winston S. Churchill

(*Churchill papers: 25/14*)

24 June 1938   Air Ministry
Secret

My dear Winston,

As soon as I received your letter, I called for a report on the work of the Air Defence Research Committee, and I think that I can assure you that I have been into this report critically and with an open mind. I have been a good deal impressed by the particulars of the comprehensive programme of research with which I have been furnished, and with the manner in which very different lines of research are being followed up, so far as I can judge, with considerable energy. But I should, of course, wish to take up any particular points on which you may think that there are delays or difficulties which are not warranted.

I notice that you do not mention in your letter the line of research which my advisers consider as the most important of all. In this particular case research carried out along the lines approved by the Committee has resulted in the development of a new technique which already forms part of the training of the Royal Air Force.

I am a little tempted to take up your statement that you have never in the past known anything so slow as the work of this Committee, but I hope very much that it will not be necessary for us to go into past history, and that we shall be able to work together to secure the maximum drive behind the experiments on which we are now engaged, and any further experiments which may be necessary to initiate new lines of development.

Yours ever,
Kingsley Wood

Sir Kingsley Wood to Winston S. Churchill

(*Churchill papers: 25/14*)

25 June 1938   Air Ministry
Secret

My dear Winston,

I have been going into the suggestion contained in your letter of the 10th June to Wing Commander Elliot that a report should be circulated to the Air Defence Research Committee on the conclusions drawn up by the

Service Departments from information at their disposal about the War in Spain.

I understand that when you raised at a meeting of the ADR Committee last October the question of the lessons to be learned from air warfare in Spain, Swinton mentioned that there was in fact a Committee studying this, but that it had been obliged to concentrate almost entirely on the tactical aspect. Inskip added that it had been very difficult to obtain any precise technical information and that certainly there had been insufficient technical information to be of any value in the kind of work with which the ADR Committee was concerned. I regret to find from the enquiries that I have made that the position, in so far as technical information is concerned, remains much the same. We have received a number of most valuable reports from the tactical point of view but the technical information which they contain is meagre.

In the circumstances you will, I think, agree that there would be no advantage in circulating to the ADR Committee reports which contain information of tactical but not technical value.

Yours ever,
Kingsley Wood

Desmond Morton to Winston S. Churchill
(*Churchill papers: 8/599*)

25 June 1938 Earlylands

Dear Winston,

Thank you so very much for the copy of 'Arms and the Covenant', which reached me yesterday and not less for having written my name and yours therein. It is a memory to me of years of struggle and not a little bitterness, as it must in some ways be to you. But you, and in an infinitely less degree I, are not the first to have told the truth to the people and become heartily unpopular for having done so. Modern Governments, whether it be that of an Autocrat or a Party caucus, which Randolph rightly spurns in his able Preface,[1] hate to be told uncomfortable truths. To that extent both are

[1] In his preface (dated 28 May 1938) to *Arms and the Covenant*, Randolph Churchill wrote, of his father: 'As a politician, Mr Churchill suffers from the disadvantage of being strangely free from the prejudices and ideologies which constitute such a large part of the mental equipment of our more successful public men. He always finds it difficult to subordinate his views on public affairs to the current exigencies of party position. Such independence of thought and speech is a handicap in the days when party machines are steadily increasing their power.' Randolph Churchill added, as a comment on the 41 speeches which he had chosen for the book: 'If British interests are set in the foremost place, it is only upon the

intensely human. But whether they recognise the truth and mend their ways or reject it, both have the habit of crucifying the prophet of truth or, if this less virile epoch shrinks at such drastic action, they exterminate him with a gas cloud—of propaganda.

However they have not silenced you yet, thank God, so there is some hope for the Empire still.

I have just had a long and most interesting talk with our Military Attaché in Berlin—Colonel Mason-Macfarlane[1]—a very able officer. Taking it all round his information is comforting, compared with what might be. I have also spoken with people back from Rome, where our apparent rearmament has created an impression out of all proportion with the facts. Solely on account of our increasing strength, several smaller countries have been along to see us hat in hand and they have not been sent away empty.

Never was there such proof of your thesis that England rearmed and strong would attract all the world into her orbit—save Germany. If only our rearmament were more real and our political leaders more truly enthusiastic in regard to it.

Lord Chatfield to Winston S. Churchill
(Churchill papers: 2/336)

25 June 1938   Admiralty

My dear Churchill

I am grateful for the book which I shall particularly value in remembrance of our visit to Portland. I found the Anti s/m school last Tuesday, *much* interested in your suggestion about the s/m Target being used as a means of defence, the opinion seemed to be that a good operator would distinguish it from a s/m, but that there was much interest in the idea. I will write you again about it.

---

condition that they shall serve the cause of a free and progressive world. Mr Churchill's attitude towards foreign countries seems to be mainly influenced by whether their character and policy is likely to prove helpful or harmful to these larger conceptions. His natural liberalism is as much affronted by tyranny and cruelty in Nazi Germany as by similar acts in Communist Russia, but he does not allow the interior politics of foreign countries to cloud his judgement upon the practical question whether these countries are likely to prove themselves serviceable or dangerous to the high interests he sets himself to guard.'

[1] Frank Noel Mason-Macfarlane, 1889–1953. Educated at Rugby and Woolwich. On active service in South Africa, 1900; France, Belgium and Mesopotamia, 1914–18 (Military Cross and two bars); Afghan war, 1919. Military Attaché in Budapest, Vienna and Berne, 1931–4; in Berlin and Copenhagen, 1937–9. Director of Military Intelligence, BEF, 1939–40. Head of British Military Mission to Moscow, 1941–2. Governor and Commander-in-Chief, Gibraltar, 1942–4. Knighted, 1943. Chief Commissioner, Allied Control Commission for Italy, 1944. Lieutenant-General, 1944. Labour MP for North Paddington, 1945–6.

Many thanks also for your information about the Air in Germany which I am studying.

I wish you had been in Nelson on Tuesday last to see the Queen Bee[1] shot down. We shall master that too *soon*.

Yours very sincerely,
Chatfield

Lord Rothermere to Winston S. Churchill
(*Churchill papers: 8/599*)

26 June 1938

My dear Winston,

Many thanks for your book. I am sure it was a good thing that Randolph suggested you should put on permanent record your plea for the rearmament of Britain.

My firm, implacable belief is that no parliamentary democracy can hope to wage war on any terms promising victory with a dictator state like Germany. The contest would be so unequal that in such a war the very existence of the country might be at hazard.

Yours always,
Harold R

Sir Henry Strakosch to Winston S. Churchill
(*Churchill papers: 8/599*)

26 June 1938

My dear Winston,

It was nice of you to send me a copy of Randolph's compilation of your speeches on 'Arms & the Covenant'. I am so glad to have the book. Many

---

[1] Captain Stephen Roskill writes: 'Queen Bees were the unmanned, pilotless wireless controlled aircraft at which ships carried out rather more realistic A-A firing practices than against the towed sleeve targets which had been in general use before about 1930. They were controlled by a specially equipped destroyer and could be made to manoeuvre—to a small extent'. Roskill adds: 'Ships were not allowed to use High Explosive shells against them because of their cost; so we always used what were called "Practice Innocuous Shells" when firing at them. I recall that in 1939 when I did the first trials with the Swiss 20 mm Oerlikon gun we shot down so many Queen Bees that the trials had to be stopped'. In Roskill's opinion, the Admiralty 'was as wrong about A-A defence as it was about the defeat of the Submarine by Asdic' (*letter to the author, 2 June 1981*).

thanks. Even a cursory perusal of the earlier pages of the book brings out most strikingly how right you have been in your numerous warnings on the armament question. No man could have done as much as you have. It is almost incredible that so many years should have been allowed to elapse before your advice was taken. If it had been taken, I feel sure that the situation in Europe would be far less grim than it is to-day & we should have been spared the ignominy & discomfort of the fits of indignation from which we have been suffering owing to our all too copious indulgence in the eating of humble pie.

Lady Cholmondeley to Winston S. Churchill

(Churchill papers: 8/599)

26 June 1938

My dear Winston,

I am proud to receive a copy of your book & have found it deeply interesting. I should imagine that *even you* must have been amazed at the clairvoyance of your earlier speeches when you read them again. As the Bible says 'Sa bouche J'ouvre avec sagesse' & this sturdy, unwavering & wise note of warning is a fine demonstration of your foresight & rightful anxiety. I have always thought of Germany as the cat in the fable to whom the rabbit & the stoat brought their several grievances for arbitration & who 'mis les plaîdeurs d'accord en croquant *l'un* et *l'autre*'.

I hope Clemmie is better now, do give her my love.

Thank you again so much for the book.

Yrs ever,
Sybil

J. L. Garvin to Winston S. Churchill

(Churchill papers: 8/599)

26 June 1938

My dear Winston,

. . . Astonishing how the defence speeches keep their life and colour; and to my mind are more forcible and gripping than even they seemed at the time. Which almost never happens with speeches. From the Abyssinian crisis my great desire, perhaps not practicable for *you*, was that you should concentrate on defence as the indispensable foundation for any successful policy whatever;

and so get behind you the whole country irrespective of party. It's the only subject that unites the nation.

On foreign policy we are wide apart for the time. But it's a difference with a difference! It's like this. As I have known, in my clambering days, two men on a mountain may go in the same direction with a formidable valley between them, and yet find themselves together at the top. Personally I would gain time for re-arming with the grimmest stone-walling in defence of a policy of avoidance. And though I want the very strongest coalition possible if we have to fight, I think the League the worst conceivable agency through which to organise a solid combination. But I won't go on. I beg and beg you—keep defence predominant in *your* part of it.

Ever yours,
J. L. Garvin

Lord Wolmer to Winston S. Churchill

(Churchill papers: 8/599)

27 June 1938

My dear Winston,

How extraordinarily nice of you to send to me a copy of your book with your usual charming inscription. I shall enjoy immensely reading the speeches over again, some of which I was privileged to listen to and will ever rank among the great Parliamentary utterances of our generation. I do appreciate the gift immensely.

Clement Attlee to Winston S. Churchill

(Churchill papers: 8/599)

27 June 1938   House of Commons

My dear Churchill,

It is extremely kind of you to send me a copy of your collected speeches on Defence. I shall value it very much. They make a formidable array. The earlier ones might be entitled 'in the steps of Cassandra'.

I do not know if you have been informed that K. Wood is making a statement on the control of responsibility for Air Craft Construction this afternoon in answer to a private notice question from me. If not I hope this reaches you in time to inform you.

Yours sincerely,
C. R. Attlee

Committee of Imperial Defence, Sub-Committee on Air Defence Research:
minutes[1]

(*Churchill papers: 25/15*)

27 June 1938
11 am
Secret
To Be Kept Under Lock and Key

3. POINTS RAISED BY MR CHURCHILL
CONCLUSION (3)
  THE SUB-COMMITTEE agreed:—
To take note that the Chairman would take up personally with Mr Churchill
the following points which were raised by Mr Churchill at this meeting:—

(a) Special measures for the protection of the Austin shadow factory at
Birmingham, including the possible provision of a contiguous 'war house'.
(b) That the prior claim to protection of such vital centres of war production
as the Austin shadow factory should be recognised over that of the
protection of the general public.
(c) The present position regarding the balloon barrage.

---

[1] Those members present at the seventeenth meeting of the Committee of Imperial Defence's
Sub-Committee on Air Defence Research, held on 27 June 1938, were Sir Kingsley Wood (in
the Chair), Sir Thomas Inskip, Churchill, Sir Warren Fisher, Vice-Admiral Sir Reginald
Henderson (Third Sea Lord and Controller of the Navy), Lieutenant-General Sir Hugh
Elles, Lieutenant-General Sir Maurice Taylor (Deputy Master-General of the Ordnance,
War Office), Sir Frank Smith (Secretary, Department of Scientific and Imperial Defence),
Air Marshal Sir Wilfrid Freeman (Air Member for Research and Development, Air Ministry),
Sir Henry Tizard (Rector of the Imperial College of Science and Technology), Air Vice-
Marshal Richard Peirse (Deputy Chief of the Air Staff) and Wing-Commander E. J. Hodsoll
(Inspector-General, Air Raid Precautions Department, Home Office). Also present were Sir
Maurice Hankey, Engineer Vice-Admiral Sir Harold Brown (Director-General of Munitions
Production, War Office), General Sir Ronald Adam (Deputy Chief of the Imperial General
Staff), D. R. Pye (Director of Scientific Research, Air Ministry), Dr H. J. Gough (Director
of Scientific Research, War Office), Colonel F. G. Wrisberg (War Office) and Dr A. D.
Crow (Research Department, Royal Arsenal, Woolwich). The Joint Secretaries to the Sub-
Committee were Wing-Commander W. Elliot (Committee of Imperial Defence) and A. E.
Woodward Nutt (Air Ministry), both of whom were also present.

Winston S. Churchill to Sir Kingsley Wood

(*Churchill papers: 25/14*)

27 June 1938
Secret

My dear Kingsley Wood,

Information as to the tactical aspect is indispensable as a foundation for research into the technical. Without a true view of what is happening in the Air, the basis for invention does not exist.

I may add that I am proposing to write you a paper on the tactical and technical aspects of Air Defence and counter-attack and their influence on design, which I trust you will be willing to receive. It will be similar to the original paper which I wrote when the Committee was first started, and which was printed as a CID paper. I hope, therefore, that you will let us have the information, such as it is.

Violet Pearman to Winston S. Churchill

(*Churchill papers: 1/323*)

28 June 1938   Sleepy Hollow
                                                    Edenbridge

Dear Mr Churchill,

I am delighted to read in today's paper of the stand Mr Sandys is making (with of course you behind him as I can guess) over the Official Secrets Act. Every shock the Government has of this kind brings to light the appalling lethargy over defence preparation of which they are guilty. I wish you *every success* in your fight, and only wish I were there to help you. I shall watch eagerly for news and if there is a spare Hansard, I should love to read the full debate.[1]

---

[1] On 17 June 1938 Duncan Sandys had sent Leslie Hore-Belisha the draft of a question which he wished to ask on London's air defences. As the question was clearly based on secret information, Hore-Belisha, with Churchill's approval, told Sandys to call on the Attorney-General, Sir Donald Somervell. This Sandys did on the 23 June and again on 24 June. Somervell told Sandys, as Sandys later declared, that unless he disclosed the name of his informant, he would be liable to prosecution under the Official Secrets Act of 1920. On June 28 Sandys unfolded this story in the House of Commons, and asked for a Select Committee of the House to look into the applicability of the Official Secrets Act to members of the House in the discharge of their Parliamentary duties. On June 29 Sandys informed the House that, in his capacity as a junior officer in the Territorial Army, he had received orders to appear in uniform before the Military Court of Inquiry. This he submitted, was a 'gross breach' of the privileges of the House. His submission was at once upheld, and a Committee of Privileges set up. It reported on the following day that a breach of privileges had indeed been committed, and

With regard to my health, I am still progressing at the same steady level and gaining vitality in the sunshine in my garden. I am to go out for a car ride this week (quite a 'gentle' one) and am beginning to walk out in the fields. So I feel real progress has been made. Don't you think my writing shows more strength in my hand. It is still very uncertain of itself however, and soon gets tired and weak. But my speech is much better.

Again wishing 'more power to your elbow' in the debate.

Sir Roger Keyes to Winston S. Churchill
(Churchill papers: 8/599)

29 June 1938

My dear Winston,

Thank you very much for sending me 'Arms and the Covenant' which I am very glad to have—I listened to nearly all the speeches and it is very interesting reading them again in the light of what has happened since. The next generation will not easily forgive Baldwin and Chamberlain for not getting you to help in the restoration of our defences.

Frederick Leathers to Winston S. Churchill
(Churchill papers: 8/599)

29 June 1938

My dear Mr Churchill,

I send you my warmest thanks for the copy of your new book and I count myself fortunate in having yet another of your works inscribed with your signature.

Although many are aware of the consistency and strength of your advocacy

---

on June 30 the House debated a motion to set up a Select Committee to enquire into Sandys' original complaint. The motion was supported by Attlee and Sinclair, as well as by Churchill, who commented caustically that an Act devised to protect the national defence should not be used to shield Ministers who had neglected national defence. The motion was accepted without dissent. 'I hear Winston is in the brightest spirits over it,' Oliver Harvey noted in his diary on July 2. Within a few days, however, it emerged that Sandys had not in fact been summoned by the Military Court of Inquiry, but had been ordered to attend the court by Eastern Command. This detail, small in itself, invalidated the decision of the Committee of Privileges. There was at once a demand for a new enquiry. The matter was finally left in the hands of a Select Committee.

for peace by adequate defence preparation the publication of your speeches
at this time is well chosen and I shall read the book with intense interest.

Believe me,
Yours sincerely,
F. Leathers

Sir Philip Sassoon to Winston S. Churchill

(*Churchill papers: 8/596*)

Thursday   45 Park Lane

My dear Winston,

I did not want to write & thank you for your book, until I had had the
time to read it properly. Now I can at the same time tell you how very grateful I am to you for thinking of sending me a copy & also how much I enjoyed
& admired it. I think it the best of all the volumes & I am proud to have it on
my shelves along side of the others that you have been kind enough to send
me. Thank you a million times, Winston, & hoping to see you & Clemmie
soon.

Yours ever,
Philip

July 1938

H. C. Vickers to Winston S. Churchill

(Churchill papers: 8/599)

1 July 1938

. . . It was a fine idea to publish these speeches and events have justified you in all you said. There can be no doubt that the public know you are to a great extent responsible for the Government's present energetic programme and I have heard hundreds of expressions of regret that you are not in the Cabinet.

Sir Abe Bailey to Winston S. Churchill

(Churchill papers: 2/330)

1 July 1938

My dear friend Winston,

I am so sorry I have not seen you lately, however I have watched your movements & read your speeches. The two cranes from the farm I understand will appear in England, & Chartwell soon I hope. I believe Mae West[1] said, 'who is that Hore-Belisha, I don't know her'.

From what I hear he has misled the public on the air defence question—England's security is before political or party privileges. I don't know enough about all that has happened to form an opinion. I was sorry to see

---

[1] Mae West, 1892–1980. Born in Brooklyn. First appeared on the stage at the age of five. In 'vaudeville' for several years in New York and San Francisco (1913). She wrote much of her own material, and was imprisoned for eight days in New York for her book and play *Sex*. Appeared in films continuously from 1932. Her first starring role, *She Done Him Wrong* (1933) broke box office records by taking two million dollars in three months. To combat her influence, the National Legion of Decency was formed in Chicago in October 1933; among the lines it objected to was: 'Is that a gun in your pocket, or are you just glad to see me'. The Hearst newspapers denounced her in 1936 as a 'menace to the Sacred Institution of the American Family'. Returned to the New York stage, 1944. Appeared in the films *Myra Breckinridge* (1970) and *Sextette* (1978). Her oft-quoted quips included: 'I always say, keep a diary and one day it will keep you' and 'I used to be Snow White but I drifted'.

Ironside had been appointed to Gibraltar. I knew him in the Boer War, & have always thought him very able.

Well here I am still as you saw me helpless & all pain. The Doctors say it will all go in time & I told them so will I.

With love to you all.

I am your old & affectionate friend,

Abe

Sir Alexander Cadogan: diary

('*The Diaries of Sir Alexander Cadogan*')

1 July 1938   Foreign Office

Winston came to get material for an article on Austria. I got Sargent to help, but we couldn't tell him much. . . .[1]

Desmond Morton to Winston S. Churchill

(*Churchill papers: 2/336*)

3 July 1938   Earlylands

Dear Winston,

Longmore,[2] Commandant of the Imperial Defence College, has asked me to sound you as to whether you would honour the IDC by addressing them

---

[1] Churchill's article 'The Rape of Austria' was published in the *Daily Telegraph* on 6 July 1938. In it he wrote of the most recent news reaching London from Vienna: 'It is easy to ruin and persecute the Jews; to steal their private property; to drive them out of every profession and employment; to fling a Rothschild into a prison or a sponging-house; to compel Jewish ladies to scrub the pavements; and to maroon clusters of helpless refugees on islands in the Danube; and these sports continue to give satisfaction. But 300,000 Jews in Vienna present a problem of large dimensions and intractable quality to a policy of extirpation. Already it is admitted the process will take some years. Meanwhile, a very serious loss to the already straitened economic life of Vienna is incurred when a busy, ingenious, industrious community, making themselves useful in a thousand ways is reduced to a mass of helpless, miserable folk, who nevertheless cannot quite be allowed to starve wholesale. The tale of their tribulations preads widely through the world, and it is astonishing that the German rulers are not more concerned at the tides of abhorrence and anger which are rising ceaselessly against them throughout the heavily-arming United States.'

[2] Arthur Murray Longmore, 1885–1970. Entered Navy, 1904. Squadron-Commander, Royal Flying Corps (Naval Wing) 1912; transferred to the Royal Naval Air Service, 1914. Commanded No 1 Royal Naval Air Service Squadron, Dunkirk, December 1914. Served in Flanders, at the Battle of Jutland, and in Italy, 1914–18. Director of Equipment, Air Ministry, 1925–9. Commandant, RAF College Cranwell, 1929–33. Air Officer Commanding Inland Area, 1933–4; Coastal Command, 1934–6. Knighted, 1935. Commandant, Imperial Defence College, 1936–8. Air Officer Commanding in Chief, Training Command, 1939; Middle East, 1940–1. Inspector-General of the RAF, 1941. Retired with the rank of Air Chief Marshal, 1942. Vice-Chairman, Imperial War Graves Commission, 1954–7.

some time this Autumn. Both Inskip and Attlee do so, as well as other public men of the first rank. It is solemnly pledged that anything said at such times is secret and confidential.

Inskip has given his views on the organisation of Defence—the King attended his address—Attlee has told them plainly what he would do if he became Prime Minister.

If you would consider giving them the benefit of your views the subject would be entirely left to your choice.

My own view, for what it is worth, is that you would be rendering a considerable service to the country, if you delivered a lecture. As you know, the students are all men selected from the fighting services and the Civil services with a few Dominions officers, who, on leaving the College are assured of high posts.

Longmore's idea in approaching me was that he did not wish to cause you any possible embarrassment by a direct application, were you not willing to undertake the matter.

Yours very sincerely,
Desmond Morton

Winston S. Churchill to Sir Abe Bailey

(*Churchill papers: 2/330*)

4 July 1938

. . . Do let me know when you are in London again so that I can come to see you.

I agree with Mae West and think the personage[1] deserves to be exposed. It is a disaster that Ironside should have been smashed up by this advertising creature. He is the finest military brain in the Army at the present time.

I look forward to the crane.[2] The old bird will be very glad to see her. He

---

[1] The Secretary of State for War, Leslie Hore-Belisha (see page 260, note 1). On 27 July 1938 Lord Camrose recorded a conversation he had had that day with Neville Chamberlain, who told him: 'Belisha was in a highly nervous state and seemed incapable of tackling any serious problem at the present time.' Camrose added: 'The PM asked me my opinion of him and agreed with my suggestion that he suffered from an inferiority complex (partly born of his race) and that he was too fond of the limelight to settle down to tackling awkward problems. The PM had found him react in a similar way when he was at the Treasury. He would not hesitate to have Belisha on the carpet in the autumn if he felt in the least degree it was necessary to do so' (*Camrose papers*).

[2] Abe Bailey's gift came at an opportune moment, for on 4 July 1938 the 'Londoner's Diary' of the *Evening Standard* reported: 'Mr Winston Churchill has lost three of his black swans. Preoccupied with Politics, he forgot to give orders for their wings to be clipped, and they took flight in the middle of last week. Mr Churchill is offering a reward of £1 per head for their safe return, or five shillings per head for a report leading to their capture. Mr

now walks about quite tamely everywhere, and looks magnificent.[1] I have told Mary who sends you her love.

Winston S. Churchill to Mortimer Wheeler [2]

(Churchill papers: 8/597)

4 July 1938

Dear Mr Wheeler,

The happy chance which brought us together emboldens me to make a suggestion to you, which I hope you will entertain kindly.

You will realise that in my new work I can only spare about 15,000 words for the whole story of Early Britain, down to the obliteration of the Roman power; and perhaps another 10,000 or 15,000 must carry me to the Norman Conquest. Therefore my task is one essentially selective and generalising. I am most anxious, however, to be rightly guided and up-to-date in these early chapters where the spade is mightier than the pen.

I wonder whether you would come here for the week-end of Saturday 16 to Monday 18, and also for the week-end Saturday 23 to Monday 25? Would you then be willing to give me three informal lectures or talks on (1) pre-Roman Britain, (2) Roman Britain and its downfall, and (3) the Saxon kingdoms to Alfred. Your audience would be attentive and select,—Mr Deakin and me!

As I know how busy you are, I hope you will not mind my suggesting an honorarium of fifty guineas, so that you will not be entirely wasting your time.

We might go over and look at the villa near Arundel, or the one at Richborough, and I would try to make your stay amusing.

Dr Feiling of Oxford helped me in this way in regard to the general historical basis of the first volume of Marlborough.

Believe me,

Yours sincerely,

Churchill has had black swans on his lake at Chartwell for many years. He imported the first pair from Australia. Unused to the change in seasons, they successfully hatched six cygnets on Christmas Day, despite the fact that there was snow on the ground.'

[1] On 23 June 1938 Churchill telegraphed to Lindemann: 'Most grateful for polaroid glasses.' They were meant for Churchill to look at the fish in his pond.

[2] Robert Eric Mortimer Wheeler, 1890–1976. Franks Student in archaeology, 1913. Major, Royal Field Artillery, 1917, France and Italy (Military Cross, despatches). Lecturer in Archaeology, University of Wales, 1920–4. Keeper and Secretary of the London Museum, 1926–44. Lecturer in Archaeology, University College London, 1934–44. Raised and commanded a Royal Artillery Regiment, North Africa, 1943 (from El Alamein to Tunis). Served with the 10th Corps in Italy (Salerno landing). Director-General of Archaeology in India, 1944–8. Professor of Roman Archaeology, University of London, 1948–55. Knighted, 1952.

Winston S. Churchill to Anthony Crossley[1]

(Churchill papers: 2/330)

4 July 1938

Thank you so much for sending me your witty lines, which I shall have great pleasure in keeping, together with your kind letter.[2]

It is curious how one's mood changes. In the Spring of 1936, or better still the Autumn of 1935, I should have esteemed it a great privilege to help in the work of rearmament, but now the whole scene has changed. Much has been done, much can never be done. A great deal more is being tried, and I cannot feel that the particular knowledge I possessed in those days is required at the present time. I am, therefore, quite content with my corner seat.

Winston S. Churchill to Sir Reginald Barnes

(Churchill papers: 1/323)

6 July 1938

I wonder if, as Colonel of the regiment, you could give me any information on a personal matter? My son Randolph who is twenty-seven years of age and who, as you know, has pushed about a bit in politics, is extremely anxious to join the supplementary reserve of a regular regiment. Although his

---

[1] Anthony Crommelin Crossley, 1903–1939. Educated at Eton and Magdalen College Oxford. Published three volumes of poetry, 1929, 1931 and 1935. Conservative MP for Oldham, 1931–5 and for Stretford, 1935–9. Parliamentary Secretary, Ministry of Transport, 1932–8. Killed in a civilian aeroplane crash on 15 August 1939.

[2] Enclosing a poem written in 1936, in which Crossley parodied the arguments of the Cabinet in discussing the possibility of Churchill as Minister of Defence. Three of the stanzas read:

> But Winston were worst, with his logic accursed
>   For he'll scorn our impartial endeavour.
> He'll make up his mind, right or wrong, with the first,
>   And how should we temporise ever?
> Let's have soldier or sailor or peer or civilian,
>   Whatever his faults, so they be not Churchillian.

> Did you dare, Father Churchill, did you dare to expect
>   A summons to council again,
> In face of the feeling that haunts the elect
>   That they scoffed at your warnings in vain?

> You're polite to the small and you're rude to the great,
>   Your opinions are bolder and surer
> Than is seemly today in an office of state—
>   You've even insulted the Führer.

work as one of the chief contributors to 'The Londoner's Diary' in the Evening Standard makes considerable demands upon him he would be able to go through the necessary courses and to attend such other drills and training as is required. He thinks it his duty to acquire military training and to have a space marked out for himself should trouble come.

I do not know whether cavalry regiments have a supplementary reserve, but if so I thought perhaps you might be able to help me in getting him such a commission in the 4th Hussars. Although we have such a small army it seems frightfully difficult for anyone to get into it.

Brigadier Pakenham-Walsh to Winston S. Churchill

(Churchill papers: 8/595)

6 July 1938

My dear Mr Churchill,

. . . I hope that with the completion of 'Marlborough' our very happy association will not come entirely to an end. Apart from everything else it is a great delight to a soldier who takes the welfare of the Army & Country much to heart, to hear the views first hand of one who has always been one of the Army's best & most loyal friends.

I would very much like to hear you on the 'Sandys' affair, but perhaps it is best for one on the Staff of the Eastern Command, though thank goodness our 'General' Staff are only indirectly concerned, not to give tongue too much at the moment.

I heard a murmur from political circles that, if a way out could be found, it might be possible that my Chief, Ironside, would not be banished to Gib after all.[1] I only hope it may be so. We cannot waste men like that. I wish they would make him Commander-in-Chief Home Defence to co-ordinate the unorganized arrangements in conjunction with Naval, Air & Civil authorities.

Yours v sincerely,
R. P. Pakenham-Walsh

---

[1] General Ironside (see page 150, note 2) was indeed 'banished' to Gibraltar, as Governor and Commander-in-Chief, Gibraltar. He returned in 1939 as Chief of the Imperial General Staff, and in May 1940 was appointed Commander-in-Chief, Home Forces, when Churchill himself had become Prime Minister.

Winston S. Churchill to Anthony Crossley
(Churchill papers: 2/330)

7 July 1938

Thank you so much for sending me this book, but I do not know when I shall have time to read it. I think, however, I understand the main point.[1]

It is incredible that we have not ever used, and are not now using our economic power to check the growth of German armaments.

You will by now already have received my letter thanking you for your verses.

Winston S. Churchill to Clementine Churchill
(Spencer-Churchill papers)

8 July 1938   Chartwell

My darling one,

We have had a strenuous day in the old building. You will not know its interior when you return. I have put a good floor down in the loft, good ceilings in both rooms, larger metal windows, and everything is painted bright cream colour. I hope in a few more days to be able to begin installing the tin boxes. The new workshop is going to be occupied tomorrow. The cost has been very small, as nearly all the bricks etc were found on the place.

The difficulty about the dirt in the pool was due to the fact that the alumina was not working in the filter. As soon as Jackson discovered this, he was able to put it right, and that filthy, dirty water you saw is now crystal clear. But we had to run the filter night and day for three days.

Three reports have come to hand about the swans. One on the way to Sundridge, which we have tried in vain to recapture so far. Another reported in Hampshire and a third on a lake near Dartford. I doubt very much whether we shall be able to get them. It is very tiresome.

The rose-garden is a veritable explosion of colour. I have never seen so many roses in my life. As it has been pouring all day, I have not been out

---

[1] The book was *The Strategy of Raw Material*, by Brooks Emery, born in Ohio in 1901. Educated at Princeton, the Sorbonne, the London School of Economics, the Konsular Akademic, Vienna, the University of Madrid, and Yale. Married, 1928, a granddaughter of John D. Rockefeller. Instructor in International Politics at Yale, 1927–31. Between 1931–5 he wrote three books on foreign affairs: *The Great Powers in World Politics* (1931), *The Price of Peace* (1935), and *The Strategy of Raw Materials* (1935), the first two in collaboration with Frank H. Simonds. From 1935 to 1947 he was Associate Professor of International Relations at Cleveland College, 1935–51, and from 1936–1950 a member of the Board of Directors of Oberlin College, 1936–50. Consultant with the Department of State, 1941–59. Professor at Princeton, 1957–74.

to see your lilies, but I will do so tomorrow. Moppet says they are in very good order, though not very tall.

The cow has been shut up pending an event which is expected daily.

The cat slept two nights in the work-room under the table on which the dove-cage stood though without the dove being frightened at all, which is very much to the credit of the cat. It reminds me of Brab's[1] famous saying: 'My Sergeant-Major's wife is sacwed to me.'

Duncan's case, I hear from inside, is going quite well. To-day his Colonel[2] went to give evidence and, as you know, he very strongly supports Duncan, and the Adjutant.[3] As he is an independent banker, this will add to the Government's difficulties. The debate on the privilege section of the affair comes on on Monday. I shall speak, though not at length.

Chamberlain, having said that we could not be self-contained in the matter of food (perfectly true), Max is insulting him daily in his papers and the Tory County Members are all up in arms. Some of these people only think of defence in terms of getting money for their own interests. I think Max's quarrel with Chamberlain looks likely to last, which is a very good thing. Generally, he seems like finishing the Session in a much more draggle-tailed condition than could have been expected a few weeks ago.

All our arrangements are complete for Paris, and I will meet you there the night of the 18th. I think Betty,[4] and possibly Bobity,[5] are coming too, and I have written to her to make up her mind. We shall know by Monday. It looks as if we shall be well looked after, and anyhow, we will amuse our-selves. I am looking forward to it very much.

My lunch on Monday is as follows:-

2 Phipps, 2 WS Morrisons,[6] Masaryk, myself, and perhaps Venetia—7. All is being looked after.

---

[1] Colonel (later Brigadier-General) Sir John Brabazon, 1843–1922, Churchill's first commanding officer (in 1895).

[2] Clifford White Gourlay, 1888–1975. Joined Barclays Bank, 1904. On active service, Royal Field Artillery, 1916–18 (severely wounded, 1917; Military Cross). Lieutenant, Special Reserve, 1918. Lieutenant-Colonel, 1936. Commanded 51st (London) Heavy Anti-Aircraft Brigade, 1936–1939; his guns were stationed in Hyde Park. Duncan Sandy's Bank Manager at Barclays, 106 Piccadilly, a Branch which he had opened in 1927. Known as 'Colonel Overdraft', he loaned the first £100,000 from which Qantas airlines was started. Retired from Barclays, 1948.

[3] Henry Tanner Hogan, 1900–1980. 2nd Lieutenant, Royal Artillery, 1919. Major, 1938. Retired, 1947.

[4] Lady Cranborne, see page 61, note 3.

[5] Lord Cranborne, see page 92, note 1. He spelt his own nickname 'Bobbety'.

[6] William Shepherd Morrison, 1893–1961. Known as 'Shakes' Morrison. Served in the Royal Field Artillery, France, 1914–18 (wounded, Military Cross, despatches three times). Captain, 1919. President of the Edinburgh University Union, 1920. Called to the Bar, 1923. Conservative MP for Cirencester and Tewkesbury, 1929–59. King's Counsel, 1934. Financial Secretary to the Treasury, 1935–6. Privy Councillor, 1936. Minister of Agriculture and

I invited the Duff Coopers when the Cranbornes failed, but Diana replied laconically on the telephone: 'The Phipps's are a menace.'

'Arms and the Covenant' has not gone as well as we expected. They have sold 4,000, but the price is high, and it is by no means certain that a second edition will be required. The reviews have been very good and I am glad we collected and published the speeches.

Dr Brand[1] rang me up about Mrs Pearman, saying that he found her definitely improved on his return from his holiday, but her blood pressure is still nearly 200, and she will not be well enough to do any serious work for some months. All this causes me much perplexity.

I have been here quite alone for the last three days, except that Morton dined with me last night, and I have no one coming until I go up for the Monday debate. Bernie Baruch came down for lunch before going off by the plane, and I also gave him a dinner in London (5 people). We had a good talk. It looks, from what he says, as if he would quite soon become a sort of Minister for co-ordinating war munitions production in America. The President has talked about it to him seriously. This would be a very good thing. The President is breast-high on our side and will do everything in his power to help. Baruch admitted opinion in the States had never yet been so friendly to us. It is a great pity matters cannot be carried further now. Apparently, you always have to have a disaster before anything sensible can be done which would prevent it.

I have practically settled not to go to the United States. I have to pay £400 damages up to August 1, and £600 after that. On the other hand, if HMG were reconstructed to affect me by Oct 15—there wd be nothing to pay! I will let you know by next how I settle this.

Fisheries, 1936–9. Chancellor of the Duchy of Lancaster, 1939–40. Postmaster-General, 1940–3. Minister of Town and Country Planning, 1943–5. Speaker of the House of Commons, 1951–9. Created Viscount Dunrossil, 1959. Governor-General of Australia, 1960–1. A member of the Other Club from 1936. His wife, Catherine, was the daughter of Rev. William Swan, D.D. Minister of South Leith parish; they were married in 1924, and had four sons, the youngest of whom had been born in April 1937. One of 'Shakes' Morrison's eight brothers, Alexander, had been killed in action at Loos in 1915.

[1] Terence Astley Brand, 1904–   . Born in Canterbury. Bachelor of Medicine (MB) and Bachelor of Surgery (ChB), 1927 (Bristol, and London Hospital). Paul Bush Gold Medal, 1929. Doctor of Medicine (MD), Bristol, 1930. Honorary Medical Officer, Edenbridge Memorial Hospital, and Four Elms Infant Welfare Centre. Surgeon Lieutenant Commander, Royal Naval Volunteer Reserve, 1937; served at sea, Red Sea, 1940; Indian Ocean, 1941. Deputy Principal Medical Officer, Fleet Air Arm (United Kingdom, 1943–4; Principal Medical Officer, HMS *Colossus* Far East, 1945). Surgeon Commander, 1945. Diploma in Child Health, England, 1948; Paediatric Registrar, St George's Hospital, London, 1948–50. Consultant Paediatrician, Royal Gwent Hospital (Newport and Monmouth Hospital Group), 1950. Author or joint author of several articles on tuberculosis (1949, 1951) and on 'Cat Scratch Fever', 1956. Member of the British Paediatric Association, 1958.

I should like to have some lovely warm sunshiny weather. To-day has been all gales and rain. However, the last helps to fill the lake.

Randolph flies off tomorrow in the Imperial Airways machine. They start at 5 am and stop at Marseilles and Rome, reaching Athens at 7 the same evening. Marvellous! Randolph and Co stay in Southampton tonight where they will see Sarah performing.

I am dining Monday night with Betty, who has the Edens. She is full of revolt and, apparently, Lord Salisbury is all for vigorous action. Anthony made a rather truculent speech yesterday, but it is well boycotted by the Tory Press.

I have not yet lost the impression of that lovely play of Noel Coward's,[1] and I am ashamed to say I have not written him as I meant to do.

My sweet one—it grieves me to hear you are tired & lonely at yr retreat. Now that yr garden is so beautiful & all sorts of things in wh you take an interest are alive & growing it is vexing that you shd not be here. But I am sure a change wh cuts you out of the household routine and leaves you free to recharge yr batteries is a wise step. In another fortnight we shall meet in Paris; & then you can decide whether to return to Cauterets or home. I am longing to hear from you that the altitude, change, & treatment are doing you good.[2]

After I had dictated the Chartwell bulletin last night I opened the Polly's cage to encourage him to sit on my hand. He gave me a frightful peck & got out. It took Edna (& her young man) an hour to get him back. He is vy naughty. But still a companion.

I keep my weight steady at 5–6 lbs less. But it seems difficult to push it further. I am persevering strictly.

I am puzzling about the secretarial problem for August. We cannot be bunged up with 'residents'. But I must have 3 for that busy month on 'Early Britain'. It will be all right.

With my tender love to you my darling Clemmie.

Your ever loving husband
W

[Sketch of pig] Privilege!

---

[1] *Operette*, a musical play written and composed by Noel Coward, which had opened at His Majesty's on 16 March 1938. In it the part of the Countess of Messiter was played by Irene Vanbrugh. Three years earlier, in March 1935, Churchill had so enjoyed the play *Viceroy Sarah*, in which Irene Vanburgh took the title role, that he had sent her a strong letter of praise with the note: 'If it would be any use to publish the substance of my comments on the play I should be delighted' (*Churchill papers: 8/503*).

[2] Clementine Churchill was at Cauterets, a spa and health resort in the French Pyrenees (see page 1099, note 1).

Dr Terence Brand: recollections

(Letter to the author, 19 November 1981)

[8 July 1938]

I remember Mrs Pearman well. I saw her often because of her high blood pressure and her massive cerebral stroke at a very early age. . . .

She lived in a very neatly kept bungalow at Spitals Cross, Edenbridge. She was of medium height, always very tidy and with a pleasant appearance and manner. She impressed as a most competent and well organised person. I believe she was a widow and certainly have no recollection of a husband. She seemed completely involved in her secretarial duties for Mr Churchill whom she clearly greatly admired, but she only rarely spoke of her work and then only in general terms, she was always most discreet.

Mrs Pearman was the senior of three secretaries employed by Mr Churchill at that time when, as well as his political activities, he was very much engaged on his 'Marlborough: His Life and Times'. I understand that a great deal of the research for this was carried out by historians at Oxford for him. On receiving the reports, Mrs Pearman told me, he would study them all day and, after dinner and with his three secretaries working in shifts, he would walk up and down his long study dictating steadily as he walked. This often went on till the early hours of the morning. His secretaries, as in the case of Mrs Pearman who lived out, were then sent home by taxi. The next day, as soon as he was given the typescripts, he subjected them to a rigorous review making many alterations and additions until he was satisfied with the final texts.

In contrast, Mrs Pearman told me, when he was expecting to make a speech in the House, he would travel up to London in the morning with her by local taxi and dictate his speech to her as they went up. She would then type this out and hand it to him before he went into the Chamber. She often listened to these speeches from the gallery and although he only rarely referred to his notes, he seldom departed by a word from the typescript she had given to him.

Shortly after Mrs Pearman's stroke, I had a telephone call from Chartwell to ask if I would go out there to discuss her case with Mr Churchill, as he was anxious to know if he could help her in any way. I drove out after lunch and was taken up to his study where he greeted me, I believe he was wearing some sort of boiler suit and open necked shirt, I don't think this is a figment of my imagination! He said he was very concerned about her and was very complimentary about her loyal service. He listened to my account of her case and to the poor prognosis which had been confirmed by one of the Consultant Physicians to Edenbridge Hospital. . . .

Mrs Pearman was being looked after at her home by the very able District Nurse and friendly neighbours. After asking me various relevant questions, Mr Churchill then asked what I thought of the very recent paper on the subject of high blood pressure by a Paris physician. I had to say that I had not seen this reported in the British journals. He then gave me a very lucid account of this and I was tremendously impressed by his command of quite rarified medical terminology which he used very accurately. Unfortunately the treatment was not suitable or applicable to Mrs Pearman's case.[1]

Winston S. Churchill to Lord Camrose

(*Camrose papers*)

10 July 1938   Chartwell

My dear Camrose,

Time passes quickly, but I was surprised to find I had already completed four out of the six months covered by our correspondence for articles in the Daily Telegraph. I hope you have been pleased with these articles, and I am glad that no divergence of any kind has arisen about them.

I should like to know whether you would like to go on with them for a further period, because if I have to seek for a new home for the 'parent' article I should like to have a little notice. But I hope very much that you will feel inclined to continue the arrangement.

Yours vy sincerely,
Winston S. Churchill

[1] Of Desmond Morton, Dr Terence Brand wrote, 'He was a patient with whom my wife and I were on friendly terms and with whom we occasionally had lunch and then were taken round his very interesting woodland garden. Though he never discussed the nature of his work for Mr Churchill, it was obvious he had tremendous respect and admiration for him and spoke affectionately of the latter's little eccentricities with not a little wit. Sir Desmond lived at the foot of Crockham Hill not more than two miles from Chartwell.' In this same letter Dr Terence Brand also recalled, 'a bricklayer who lived in Edenbridge and worked at Chartwell at the time "the wall" was being built. He was one of the gang Mr Churchill used to join in the mornings. He liked him because he insisted on taking his turn with the unpopular chores as well as the bricklaying and this included going up to the house to collect the drinks for the tea break.' (*Letter to the author: 19 November 1981*).

10 July 1938

Dear Doctor Revesz,

Many thanks for your letter of July 1. The sales of the articles are growing well under your care, and I am very satisfied with all you do for me. I now address myself to the other points mentioned therein.

I think all you have done about the Dominion rights is very good. I only wish you could develop something of the same kind in the United States. It is incredible that this market has not been tapped. There must be at least half a dozen papers who would pay from five to ten guineas apiece. I am not so sure that I am going there this Autumn after all.

At present I have put the marketing of the articles in the hands of the representative of Curtis Brown.[1] He does not appear to have achieved anything so far.

I am very glad that the last few articles have had a wider circulation on the Continent.

With regard to Sweden I think you should try to keep the two going on the present basis. Anyhow, I leave it entirely to you.

I am coming over on July 18 and shall be in Paris until 21 or 22. I shall probably do one of the Daily Telegraph articles on the Royal Visit. In these circumstances it would be difficult for me to write a preliminary puff for the PARIS SOIR.

I hope you liked the last article about Austria. I see that the Daily Telegraph was confiscated in Germany for publishing it.

I shall look forward to seeing you in Paris.

12 July 1938   Cauterets

My Darling,

It was a great joy to get your letter—I am longing to see you. The weather is now glorious, brilliant sun with freshness in the air.

The 'cure' is most thorough & searching & takes $2\frac{1}{2}$ hours in the morning & $\frac{3}{4}$ of an hour in the afternoon. You have to be up betimes, as at 11.30 am the cure establishments close down till 3.30 pm. It's a long mid-day pause!

---

[1] Alan M. Collins, whom Churchill replaced by Revesz as his American literary agent five months later.

& as the weather is far from tropical rather unnecessary. I am reversing the process & doing the long bout in the afternoons so as not to be rushed in the morning. . . .[1]

I'm sorry Darling you are disappointed at the sale of the Book. I'm sure it's the price—The sort of people who want to hear that the Government is all wrong are not the rich ones—The Tories don't want to be made to think. It's too painful!

I hope you have got a lovely grey suit for Versailles etc—I *am* looking forward to it all; but my French local rag tells me the King has a tummy ache?

Your loving,
Clemmie

Winston S. Churchill to Lord Ivor Spencer-Churchill

(Churchill papers: 2/330)

13 July 1938

It was a great pleasure to see you, dear Ivor. Thank you so much for all you have done about our Paris trip. We are replying direct to the French authorities with all ceremony. . . .

Lord Horne to Winston S. Churchill

(Churchill papers: 8/599)

13 July 1938

My dear Winston,

I apologise for not acknowledging your handsome Book of Defence Speeches sooner. I now do so with great fervour after having dipped into them at such leisure moments as I have been able to snatch. It is the finest eloquence we have had in Parliament in my time & deserved to be made immortal apart from the importance of the theme at this critical time. . . .

---

[1] Clementine Churchill's daughter Mary writes: '. . . the apparent causes of her periods of fatigue and tension were nearly always in themselves relatively trivial. Winston had to force himself to accept—even when he could not understand—that Clementine's bouts of mental and physical exhaustion were as much "illnesses" as influenza or measles. Nor was he oblivious to the fact that he himself (however unwittingly) somehow contributed to her troubles. And although he hated her leaving him, he ruefully recognised that a "let-up" away from home—and away from him—was from time to time necessary for her poise and health' (Mary Soames, *Clementine Churchill*, London 1979, page 254).

'Memorandum of Mr Churchill's Interview with Herr Foerster'[1]

(*Churchill papers: 2/340*)

14 July 1938

After the usual preliminaries, I remarked that I was glad they had not introduced the Anti-Jewish laws in Dantzig.[2] Herr Foerster said the Jewish problem was not acute in Dantzig, but he was anxious to know whether this type of legislation in Germany would prevent an understanding with England. I replied that it was a hindrance and an irritation, but probably not a complete obstacle to a working agreement, though it might be to comprehension. He appeared to attach great importance to this point, and returned to it at a later stage.

Herr F asked whether I had ever been in his country, and suggested I should pay a visit. I replied that if I went to Poland, I would make a point of passing through Dantzig. He then pressed me, if going to Poland, to pass through Germany and to meet Hitler. I replied that it would be difficult to carry on a useful conversation between an all-powerful Dictator and a private individual, and asked whether August and September would not be unhealthy months to visit Germany. He replied that nobody in Germany was thinking of war; that they had immense social and cultural plans which it would take them years to work out: that the Party Meeting took place in September, and that there was no question of incidents or serious complications. Returning to this point later, his interpreter, Herr Noé said the situation was similar to 1914, when no one in Germany thought of war, but everyone in England feared it. To this I replied that we had unfortunately been right.

Herr Foerster asked what possible reason there could be, in reply to which I mentioned the Czecho-Slovak position. He said this ought to be capable of settlement, and I told him that after our discussion with Henlein and

---

[1] Albert Foerster. Born in Fürth, Bavaria, in 1902, the son of the Superintendent of Prisons in Fürth. A Catholic. Apprenticed as a bank clerk, but dismissed because of his Nazi affiliations, having joined the Nazi Party in 1923. Ortsgruppenführer (Local Group Leader) of the Nazi Party in Fürth, 1925–30. Elected to the Reichstag, September 1930. Gauleiter of Danzig, 1930–45. Won more than half the seats in the Danzig Assembly for the Nazi Party, 1933. Editor of *Der Vorposten*. Imprisoned for life by the Polish Government, 1948. Reported killed in Gdansk (Danzig) Military Prison, 1953.

[2] In 1924 there were 4,678 Jews in Danzig (protected by the League of Nations minority protection Statute). But in 1937 Foerster had dismissed almost all the professional Jews from their practices (doctors, lawyers etc). More than 2,000 Jews had emigrated from Danzig by early 1938. On 12 and 14 November 1938 two synagogues were burnt down and others desecrated; many shops and homes were looted. More Jews fled, and by September 1939 only 1,200 remained, mostly elderly people. Of these, only 22 Jews (all partners of mixed marriages) survived the war; the rest were sent by the Nazis to concentration camps, and murdered.

Masaryk, I felt this should be possible within the frame-work of the Czecho-Slovak State. I assured him that England and France were making every effort to persuade the Prague Government to agree, but he said that the Moscow influence had caused them to stiffen their attitude recently, and to make them impudent. He asked what would happen if they refused to accept the advice of England and France, to which I replied that I was sure they would do so. He commented, somewhat truculently, that he hoped this would happen soon.

I remarked that I did not believe Germany was really afraid of Russia, to which he replied that they had definite evidence of the existence of Russian aerodromes in Czecho-Slovakia, from which Berlin could be assailed in half-an-hour. I replied that in my view, it would be quite possible as part of the general European settlement for England and France to engage to come to the help of Germany with all their power, if she were the victim of an unprovoked attack by Russia, through Czecho-Slovakia or otherwise. He asked, who is to define the aggressor? To this I replied it was the nation which first crossed the other's frontiers in force.

I said that Herr Hitler had it in his power to achieve lasting fame for himself and immense benefits for Germany and the whole world, by relieving us of this oppression of the fear of war. He said that Hitler had again and again offered to disarm pari-passu with the other nations: that they had tried unilateral disarmament without success: and could not remain a country of second order in danger of attack from heavily-armed neighbours. I said at any rate we might try and agree on rules of air-warfare, to which he replied that Hitler had offered to abolish bombers, but had met with no response: if the matter was to be taken up again, it was for England to make the first approach.

I said that I was not an opponent of the greatness of Germany, and that most people in England wanted to see her take her place as one of the two or three leading powers in the world: that we would not resent gradual peaceful increase of German commercial influence in the Danube basin, but that any violent move would almost inevitably lead to a world war. The situation was going from bad to worse. All countries were wasting their substance on armaments. We had even started factories in Canada, so that in the third and fourth year of a war, we could enjoy an unlimited supply of aeroplanes. It was in Hitler's power to lift the shadow. We would help.

Herr F said he could see no real points of dispute between England and Germany: that if England and Germany would only agree together they could divide the world between them. (This latter remark the interpreter thought it wiser not to translate.)

The visit concluded with a repetition of the invitation to visit Herr Hitler, and a question as to whether I would come if officially requested; to which I gave a non-committal answer.

Winston S. Churchill to Lord Halifax

(*Churchill papers: 2/330*)

16 July 1938

I send you a note which Professor Lindemann took of the talk I had with Herr Foerster, who asked to see me on Thursday last. He did not make a bad impression on me, though I am told he is 'a tough'. There is nothing in the conversation to make it necessary for you to read it, but I always send a record of any talk I have with these sort of people.

I should like to have a talk with you before we separate, and when we met at No 10 on that Day of Wrath[1] you said you would come and dine. I am going to Paris for the French show on Monday (barring Privilege), but will you be free to dine with me on Friday night, July 22, at No 11 Morpeth Mansions? (In this House there are many Mansions). Perhaps you will be going away for a long week-end, in which case I will suggest another date.

---

[1] In the first volume of his war memoirs, *The Gathering Storm*, Churchill recalled, of a luncheon given by Chamberlain on 11 March 1938 for Ribbentrop, who was about to leave the London Embassy to become Foreign Minister: 'My wife and I accepted the Prime Minister's invitation to attend. There were perhaps sixteen people present. My wife sat next to Sir Alexander Cadogan near one end of the table. About half-way through the meal a Foreign Office messenger brought him an envelope. He opened it and was absorbed in the contents. . . . The meal proceeded without the slightest interruption, but quite soon Mrs Chamberlain, who had received some signal from her husband, got up saying, "Let us *all* have coffee in the drawing-room." We trooped in there, and it was evident to me and perhaps to some others that Mr and Mrs Chamberlain wished to bring the proceedings to an end. A kind of general restlessness pervaded the company, and everyone stood about ready to say good-bye to the guests of honour. However Herr von Ribbentrop and his wife did not seem at all conscious of this atmosphere. On the contrary, they tarried for nearly half-an-hour engaging their host and hostess in voluble conversation. At one moment I came in contact with Frau von Ribbentrop, and in a valedictory vein I said, "I hope England and Germany will preserve their friendship." "Be careful you don't spoil it," was her graceful rejoinder. I am sure they both knew perfectly well what had happened, but thought it was a good manoeuvre to keep the Prime Minister away from his work and the telephone. At length, Mr Chamberlain said to the Ambassador, "I am sorry I have to go now to attend to urgent business," and without more ado he left the room. The Ribbentrops lingered on, so that most of us made our excuses and our way home. . . .' The message which had been brought in had contained news of German troop movements on the Austrian border, on the day of the German annexation of Austria.

Winston S. Churchill to Sir Alexander Cadogan

(*Churchill papers: 2/330*)

16 July 1938

I wonder if I might have a talk with someone in your United States Department on Monday morning, July 18? I am going to write about Anglo-American relations this time, and ten minutes conversation is quite enough for me to see if there are any points one ought specially to avoid. In principle, I am urging that the Commercial Treaty should be carried through, even at some inconvenience to the Dominions.

If this request is a bore, please do not hesitate to say so. Otherwise I shall await a call to the telephone (*Victoria 1826*) at noon on Monday.[1]

Winston S. Churchill to Lord Camrose

(*Camrose papers*)

16 July 1938   Chartwell

My dear Camrose,

With you, I was surprised to find that we have now completed four out of the six months' arrangement, or rather, that we shall have done at the end of this month.

I should like to go on, at any rate, for a full year, which would end in March next, and then review the situation.

A feature of this sort is not one which we would continue indefinitely, and

---

[1] In his regular fortnightly article in the *Daily Telegraph*, on 4 August 1938, entitled 'The United States and Europe', Churchill argued that the economic stability of the United States was as important as her growing armaments. 'As a contribution to trade revival,' he wrote, 'and as an expression of the goodwill prevailing in the English-speaking world, the British–American Trade Agreement is of real importance. There is every prospect of a good arrangement being reached in the near future. The debt question, on the other hand, has encountered a new complication. The isolation forces in the United States are not favourable to a settlement which would free Great Britain from the ban imposed upon foreign loans to defaulting countries by the Johnson Act. These forces would naturally press for the most rigorous terms, and make it difficult for a reasonable compromise to be reached. The stirring of this question at this juncture, and when Congressional Elections are already looming, would not be helpful. Nevertheless there is an earnest desire in Great Britain for a fair and friendly agreement.' Churchill ended his article: 'It would be foolish of the European democracies, in their military arrangements, to count on any direct aid from the United States. It would be still more foolish for war-making forces in the Dictator Governments of Europe to ignore or treat with contempt this slow but ceaseless marshalling of United States opinion around the standards of freedom and tolerance. The more weightily the personality of the United States is accounted in Europe in these years, perhaps even in these months, the better are our chances of escaping another lurch into the pit.'

it is possible that you might like to make other arrangements yourself at the end of the time. Any way, we would certainly like to have the articles for twelve months, and I suggest that we leave the matter until a month or two before the year is up.

I had hoped to be at the Other Club last night or I would have written you earlier.

Yours vy sincerely,
Winston S. Churchill

Lady Diana Cooper: diary

(*'The Light of Common Day'*)

18 July 1938

We had a merry dinner with the Rothschildren and Winston and Venetia, Winston packed for the Ferry with bezique-cards in hand for plucking me. But a message came from the Chief Whip that trouble would be debated next day.[1] Too disappointed to believe it, Winston tore round to the House, only to meet us again at Victoria with the news endorsed. He'll start tomorrow night instead.[2]

---

[1] The continuing discussion of the Sandys Case. During the debate of July 19 Churchill told the House of Commons: 'We hear a great deal about the time that is being wasted upon this affair, but that is certainly not our fault. I do not know whether it is being wasted, provided that it inculcates valuable lessons for the future. We are told that the House and still more the country are sick and tired of this matter. As to the country, we have to take that from the Press, some of whose organs have a necessity for providing new topics at least every few days, but the House of Commons must not be wearied in pursuing its themes. It must persevere and persist, and it must enforce accountability, as was done in days of old. Anyone looking around the House can see how utterly bored and sick and deficient in interest the Members are in the whole of this matter, how they are all longing to get away from it to more important topics—great issues of agriculture or of unemployment—on which during long hours this Chamber will be lamentably empty. I do not agree with those who say, "Cut the cackle and get on with the job". Why, Sir, it was about trying to make people get on with the job of rearming that all this cackle started, and it is about that that the cackle will proceed.'

[2] Churchill and his wife were among the official British guests in Paris at the time of the royal visit of King George VI and Queen Elizabeth. Commenting on the visit in the *Daily Telegraph* on 26 July 1938, Churchill wrote: '. . . the entertainment offered to the British Sovereigns had a charm and elegance, a quality of gentle peace and culture, of art and poetry, of music and dance, which only French genius can command. The scenes at Bagatelle, at the Opera, in the chapel of Versailles, at the Bosquet d'Apollon, might well have been devised to show how much there is in human life above and beyond the blare of trumpets or the webs of diplomacy. It was as if a clear voice were calling upon the peoples of Europe to turn their thoughts from harsh ambition, iron regimentation, bitter creeds and hatreds, to all the joy and fun and splendour to be gained without pain or crime. Poor indeed must be the heart which could not delight in this day-dream amid the mellow sunshine of freedom and of France. How fair the world could be, how bountiful the gifts of Nature, how bright the inheritance of man, if only the great States and Governments of Europe would take unitedly a few resolute and simple steps together!'

Harold Nicolson: diary

(*Nicolson papers*)

19 July 1938

There is another debate on the Sandys thing. The Tories take it as an attack on the PM, and the herd hoots. Winston makes an unnecessary speech and so does A. P. Herbert.

Sir Robert Waley Cohen to Winston S. Churchill

(*Churchill papers: 2/330*)

20 July 1938

My dear Mr Churchill,

We have all been exceedingly anxious about the situation of the persecuted Jewish community in Danzig and I noticed a statement in the Press that you have been seeing the Gauleiter of that unhappy city.

I know how much you will have wished to try to say something to him about the cruelties and persecutions which the Nazis are introducing there and I wonder whether you would be willing to tell me something of your talk with the Gauleiter? If by any chance you are free at some time on Friday, may I come and have a word with you about it?

Yours sincerely,
Robert Waley Cohen

Dr Ludwig Noé to Winston S. Churchill

(*Churchill papers: 2/340*)

21 July 1938   Danzig

Dear Sir,

Gauleiter Foerster and myself have returned from our trip to England and I hasten to express to you my heartiest thanks for the opportunity you kindly offered us for such a thorough conversation with your goodself.

I am absolutely aware that in your country we can scarcely find a person who with greater clearness could have answered our questions as to what could be done to bring about the urgently necessary improvement of relations between your country and ours, than you who by decades of political experience to such an extraordinary extent have accumulated knowledge and experience in the field of international politics.

With absolute frankness, which I really welcomed, you have expressed your views during the call I could pay you in November last, and this time also. I am sure that nothing could serve better to promote an understanding between our two nations than frank conversations which might clear the situation.

Everything you told me in November last regarding foreign policy has absolutely become true. My urgent desire is now that your pessimistic prophecy for the next future, however, may not be realized and that collaboration, based on mutual understanding, of the responsible men of our two countries may succeed in finding a way, together with France, to maintain peace in Europe, so that there remains no annoyance with one party or another.

As intelligent beings, we should have learned from history. One must be careful to avoid repeating the faults once made. The nationalities dispute on the Balkans which for years has disquietened Europe and finally led to the most terrible of wars, should for us be a warning that never-more similar occurrences must arise within the heart of Europe.—With good will it must be made possible that the justified demands of minorities within the Czechoslovakian Republic are met. If this is not done, one may be quite certain that Czechoslovakia will remain the source of unrest and danger for Europe.

With the expression of my great esteem, I remain,

Dear Sir,
Yours very sincerely,
Dr Noé

Sir Kingsley Wood to Winston S. Churchill

(*Churchill papers: 25/14*)

23 July 1938   Air Ministry[1]
Secret

My dear Winston,

You will remember that at the last meeting of the Air Defence Research Committee, it was agreed that a meeting of the Sub-Committee would be

---

[1] Kingsley Wood's letter to Churchill had been the subject of some discussion. On 22 July 1938 Wing-Commander Elliot (Assistant Secretary, Committee of Imperial Defence), informed Folliott Sandford at the Air Ministry that while both Sir Thomas Inskip and Sir Maurice Hankey approved of the letter, 'At the same time they instruct me to say that they think it would be undesirable to make this a precedent for according Mr Churchill special treatment on any future occasion. They point out that the questions which have been raised by Mr Churchill, and to which Sir Kingsley Wood's notes reply, are not really proper to the research problems with which the Air Defence Research Sub-Committee is concerned, and therefore suggest that any future requests of a similar nature should be discouraged on the grounds that these matters are outside the province of the committee' (*Cabinet papers: 21/634*).

held about the end of July to consider the reports of the trials of the 3" rocket. I have now heard from General Taylor[1] that though the trials are progressing satisfactorily, it will take some little time yet to enable the War Office to draw a true average picture of the results from which to deduce final data. In consequence the War Office feel that they would not be able to give us a full report by the end of July.

In the circumstances, I think that we should wait until there is some substantial progress to report before we have our next meeting. I shall myself be available throughout the Recess, and I should propose to call a meeting of such members of the Committee as are available towards the end of August or early in September to consider the results of the War Office trials. Perhaps you could let me know what your plans for the Recess will be so that we can, if possible, arrange a meeting when you would be available.

Meanwhile, I am instructing Wing Commander Elliot to circulate a notice that there will be no further meeting before the Recess.

You will also remember that it was agreed that I would take up with you certain points which you raised at the meeting, and I am enclosing some notes which have been prepared on these points. I also took the opportunity of a visit to the Austin factory yesterday to talk the air raid precautions aspect over with Lord Austin.[2]

Yours ever,
Kingsley Wood

Winston S. Churchill to Sir Kingsley Wood
(*Churchill papers: 25/14*)

26 July 1938   Chartwell
Secret

Very many thanks for your letter, and for the reassurances you give me on the various points I raised.

I am still despondent about the Committee, which has been little more than

[1] Maurice Grove Taylor, 1881–1960. Joined the Royal Engineers, 1900. On active service, 1914–18 (DSO, CMG). Major-General in charge of Administration, Aldershot Command, 1934–7. Deputy Master-General of the Ordnance, War Office, 1938–9. Knighted, 1938. Senior Military Adviser to the Ministry of Supply, 1939–41.

[2] Herbert Austin, 1866–1941. An engineering apprentice in Australia. Came to England 1890, to control the manufacture of the Wolseley Sheep Shearing Machine. Manager of the Wolseley Tool and Motor Car Co Ltd, Birmingham, 1900–5. Began manufacture of his own motor cars in 1900; Chairman of the Austin Motor Co Ltd. Knighted, 1917. Conservative MP for King's Norton, 1919–24. President of the Society of Motor Manufacturers and Traders, 1934. Created Baron, 1936.

a damping-down apparatus. Do you realise that 3 whole years have passed since it was sought to make it a real pioneer of discovery? When I think of what might have been done in this period to make us all safe, I find it difficult to express my grief.

I am most appreciative of all you are doing (so far as I understand it) in the Air Ministry. You carry my most profound good wishes, and if there is anything in which I can help you, pray command me; for I am sure you will not turn and ask me, under penalty, where I got my information from!

I am preparing a note, which I will send you in a few days, on:—

    (a) The inevitability of fighting on a parallel course, and the consequences upon the design of fighter-aircraft.

    (b) The paramount need of making projectiles the evil effects of which last in the air for perhaps as much as 2 or 3 minutes, and thus infect a very large cubic area, and

    (c) An operation for which a special study should be made, and the necessary apparatus provided.[1]

I shall be here all August, within easy reach of London, so perhaps if you are in the neighbourhood you will come one day to lunch or dine, when we can have a talk.[2]

Winston S. Churchill to Harold R. Peat: telegram

(*Churchill papers: 1/407*)

26 July 1938

Regret that political outlook in autumn makes it impossible for me to lecture this year in United States. Still hope however to do so later on under your auspices. Mr Levy who is shortly returning to States will act for me in winding up present arrangements.

                                    Winston Churchill

[1] For this mysterious 'operation', see page 1246.
[2] Churchill added at the bottom of this letter: 'But now that I see you will be at Tunbridge Wells, I need do no more than draw yr attention to this address where I shall be always at yr service. Pray propose yourself & your wife to come to lunch one day . . .' (*Air Ministry papers: 2/3354*).

Winston S. Churchill to Bernard Baruch

(Churchill papers: 1/323)

26 July 1938

My dear Bernie,

I am very glad to hear the cure is doing you good.[1] I shall be at Chartwell all August, so pray let me know when you are coming to London. If you give me a little notice, I have no doubt I can arrange for you to meet Eden at dinner, that is unless he stays in Yorkshire all the time.

The situation has not, in my opinion, much improved, though the Royal Visit to Paris has had a stabilising effect.[2]

Randolph is still on his holiday in Greece, but I hope to see him back at the beginning of August.

Every good wish,

Winston S. Churchill to Dr Noé

(Churchill papers: 2/340)

26 July 1938

Dear Dr Noé,

Thank you very much for your letter. I am glad you thought our talk was useful.

I was particularly pleased to receive from you and Gauleiter Forster such explicit promises that Germany would not attack Czechoslovakia. As you know, we are working to try and secure a reasonable and friendly settlement, but I am quite sure that any crossing of the Czechoslovakian frontier by German troops would lead to a general war. The French would certainly march and, in my opinion, England would be drawn in. Such a war would

---

[1] Baruch was taking the cure at Vichy, staying at the Hotels du Parc & Majestic.

[2] During the course of his article on the royal visit to France (see page 1104, note 2), Churchill wrote: 'The visit of King George VI and Queen Elizabeth, with the overwhelming assent of the Parliaments and peoples of the British Empire, must be regarded as a new and additional security against the sudden onset of catastrophe. It has strengthened and emphasised the deep accord which unites the Governments and masses of France and Britain. It has enabled France to see herself once again in her true greatness.' Of the atmosphere in Paris, Churchill wrote: 'It is wonderful to observe the calm of a people where the nation is the army, where the people own the Government, who have been pledged openly by their leaders to enter upon the most terrible of ordeals if certain events, over which they can have no control, should take place in countries far removed from their own frontiers, and with whose people they have no contact but that of a common cause. There is no high explosive so powerful as the soul of a free people.'

be a most terrible catastrophe, as it would last until all the great nations were utterly ruined and exhausted.

The feeling in the United States against Germany is now far stronger than it was even in 1914. In fact, there never has been in time of peace so fierce a feeling against any European country. It seems to me very likely that the United States would not wait so long this time before coming in themselves. Thus what we should see would be a world struggle in which numbers would be once more heavily against Germany.

Therefore, I am especially glad to learn from you and your friend that there is no thought of military violence being used against Czechoslovakia.

Once more thanking you for your letter.

Clarice Fisher[1] *to Winston S. Churchill*

(*Churchill papers: 1/324*)

27 July 1938   Geneva

Dear Mr Churchill,

Your last words to me when you were in Geneva a few years ago were, 'Be sure to let me know if ever I can do anything for you.' It is because of those words and similar ones when I left you in 1929, that I am writing to you now.

I am still very happy in Geneva and enjoy my work in the International Labour Office, but soon after I came out here I lost my father and now I have just lost my mother. Consequently I am feeling lonely and depressed, and am wondering whether I should not do well to return to England where I could be with my sister. Were I to make this move, I know that in applying for another post a testimonial from you would count for more than any of the others I possess. May I therefore take advantage of your offer and ask you to let me have something in writing that would help me in this way?

What I should like is a statement to the effect that I was your personal secretary from 1923 to 1929, that I left of my own accord, and that you were 'sorry to lose me' (words you used when we parted in Eze). Of course anything you felt disposed to add in my favour would be very welcome and would carry weight. For instance, when I was with you, you often remarked on my initiative which you seemed to consider somewhat exceptional. I am

---

[1] Clarice M. Fisher, Churchill's secretary from 1923 to 1929, including his four and a half years as Chancellor of the Exchequer. Churchill wrote in reply, on 3 August 1938: 'Dear Miss Fisher, Certainly I will give you a testimonial, but perhaps you will write out for me the sort of thing you think would be helpful, and let me improve upon it. It seems to me, at this distance, that it would be a very serious step for you to give up the position you have built up for yourself in Geneva, and I hope you will not do it until you have made definite arrangements.'

explaining this, because it is now so long since I left that I am sure you can have only a vague recollection of the time I spent as your secretary, whereas of course to me that period stands out vividly among the years I have been engaged in secretarial work.

I continue to read all your articles and speeches which I see in the press, and am always keenly interested in what you have to say; and I should like to take this opportunity to tell you that I feel our Government is greatly weakened by your absence from the Cabinet, and that I trust you will soon be back and in a position to see that we keep the peace as long as possible but that we are ready when war is again forced upon us. There is no one in all England who would have the foresight and courage to do this as well as you would, of that I am sure.

Yours sincerely
Clarice M. Fisher

PS. Perhaps you have not yet seen some new Swiss stamps which were brought out a couple of months ago. This one shows the ILO building. Possibly Mary is now a stamp collector.

Winston S. Churchill to Sir Kingsley Wood
(Churchill papers: 25/14)

28 July 1938

Aeroplanes flying over 250 mph can only plan to fight on parallel courses or thereabouts. Obviously meeting and flying past happens too quickly for human action. Pursuing from behind is open to deadly retort. How easy to throw out aerial mines! Following in the wake is therefore to incur needless and possibly fatal risk. Perhaps occasionally an oblique intersection of fire at a lucky angle may strike home: but nothing except resolute engagement on the beam will be decisive.

The only sure method is to swim along side by side and let him have it. Assuming the 'Cuckoo'[1] story is correct and will work out (!), it should be possible to get the height and turn the intercepting machines into parallel courses before the attack has been delivered. It should be possible at least to see the visitor home.

All tactical arguments depend upon physical superiority at the moment of action. But why should the home force lack this superiority? A raider comes for the sole purpose of carrying a ton of bombs. He probably requires more

---

[1] An experimental height 'radar' device, it never went into production. A wartime device, however, IFF (identification friend or foe) was later able to distinguish friendly aircraft from 'hostiles'.

than a ton of petrol to get him there and back. Two tons is a lot for the defending aeroplane to have in hand. Two tons put into speed, armour or cannon, should yield decisive results. Once machines of this character are known to have been created in large numbers it is improbable, providing the enemy believe in 'Cuckoo', that long-range bombing will be attempted. Here then, (provided 'Cuckoo' works), we may see finality and certainty. Even a 25% penalty will stop the business.

Therefore, we should now build, as quickly and in as large numbers as we can, fast heavily-armed aeroplanes designed with turrets for fighting on the beam on parallel courses. The urgency for action arises from the fact that the Germans must know we have banked upon the forward-shooting plunging 'Spit-fire', whose attack must most likely resolve itself into a pursuit which, if not instantly effective, exposes the pursuer to destruction.

Shiela Grant Duff to Winston S. Churchill
(Churchill papers: 2/330)

28 July 1938

Dear Mr Churchill,

I am very disturbed by the use which the Germans and Sudeten Germans are making of your words and actions.[1] They claim to have your support against the Czechs and this is used by the more extreme to force the more moderate to raise their claims. You will remember telling me that Herr Henlein had shown himself to be most moderate in his conversation with you, and that he had told you that the fulfilment of *all* his Carlsbad demands was not the necessary condition of agreement with the Czechs. Since his return to Prague, he has in fact raised his original demands. The explanation is partly that Herr Henlein is not a free agent, (and therefore it is of no account that he himself is not an ardent nazi), partly that he is apt to tell a different story in different places, partly that the Henlein party, like any other political party, is out to get the most it can.

When I told Henlein leaders that this was the impression Henlein had made

[1] At the end of July 1938, Churchill warned publicly against Czech obduracy, writing, in his regular fortnightly article in the *Daily Telegraph* on 26 July 1938: 'The Czech Government owe it to the Western Powers that every concession compatible with the sovereignty and integrity of their State shall be made, and made promptly. Just as we demand that Germany shall not stir up strife beyond her borders, so we must make sure that the clear definitions of our attitude which have become visible shall be no encouragement to obduracy on the part of a small State whose existence depends upon the conscience and the exertions of others. Having myself heard at first hand the case for both sides in Czechoslovakia, I am sure that all the essential elements of a good and lasting settlement are present, unless it is wrecked by obstinacy on the one hand, or mischievous fomentations upon the other.'

in London, they very indignantly denied that it was intentional. He is too weak to doublecross his own party even if he wished to do so.

You are the one British statesman of whom the Germans are afraid. If you are conciliated, they consider that they can expect much greater support from the British Government whom they think are afraid. They have therefore raised their demands concurrently with British pressure on the Czechoslovak Government. Henlein is more radical since he saw you.

The Czechs recognise you to be the bravest and most outspoken of British statesmen and very strongly opposed to the German advance. The fact that in the Czech–German conflict you stress the acceptability of the *German* claims and the necessity for the *Czechs* to give way still further is interpreted in many Czech and German circles to mean that our armed forces are catastrophically weak and that therefore we will surrender Prague to the Germans rather than fight. The Czechs, for whom it is a matter of life and death in any case, whether they fight or not, will fight even without us, therefore any intimation which we give to the Germans that we will not fight, only increases the likelihood of a German attack. If we will not fight ourselves, they only ask that we do not make it more necessary for them to do so.

You were in Paris during the Royal visit and therefore will know that Lord Halifax spoke very strongly to M Bonnet[1] and that the French were even given the impression that, in our opinion, they should have threatened Prague with a denunciation of the French alliance. The only issue now in which the Germans are interested is in the independence of Czechoslovakia and the danger with which it threatens them of having again to fight on two frontiers. It is this which the Czechs are determined to preserve and they can do so only if they maintain their foreign alliances and if the Sudeten Germans do not have a controlling influence over their policy and above all their military defences. This is the only issue on which they have refused to give way. Lord Halifax's conversation with M Bonnet and our own renewed pressure in Prague is taken to mean that we are willing to see them surrender their independence to Berlin. The Sudeten Germans are encouraged to believe that they need content themselves with no less.

If it is Lord Runciman's[2] object to find another solution and not merely to

[1] Georges Bonnet, 1889–1973. Born in the Dordogne, for which he was elected a Socialist-Radical Deputy in 1924. Minister for the Budget, 1925; for Pensions, 1926; for Commerce, 1930. President of the Stresa Conference, 1932. Minister of Finance, 1933; of Commerce, 1935. Ambassador to Washington, 1937. Minister of Finance, June-December 1937; of Foreign Affairs, April 1938–September 1939. Honorary knighthood, 1938. Minister of Justice, 1939–40. Member of the National Council, 1941. Member of the Council of State, 1946.

[2] Lord Runciman of Doxford (see page 15, note 1), the Liberal National Peer who had been sent to Czechoslovakia by Neville Chamberlain at the head of a Mission to promote a solution of the Czech–Sudeten dispute.

advise the Czechs as to the best method of surrendering their independence with the most dignified and courageous appearance, his visit is of the greatest importance. It is unfortunate, however, that the Czechs must know even if this country does not, that the British Prime Minister was lying to Parliament when he said that the Czechs had asked for a mediator and that the British Government had never hustled them. In fact, as you know, we suggested an 'arbitrator' and it was Paris who said he should only 'observe'. I am told that our Foreign Office is in possession of secret information from Germany more alarming than that which they possessed on May 19th. I am told the only thing to do if one meets a grizzly bear and has no gun, is to wave at him with an umbrella. Yours is the biggest umbrella in the country and, after all, Swift might have said of the Germans 'A servile race in folly nursed, Who truckle most when treated worst.' Is there a necessity I do not know of to hand over Czechoslovakia to the German nazis? What did Wiedermann[1] have to say?

Yours sincerely,
Shiela Grant Duff

Victor Oliver to Winston S. Churchill

(*Churchill papers: 1/326*)

29 July 1938

My dear Mr Churchill,

I am deeply grateful to you for having taken so much trouble regarding my status in this country. I am re-enclosing Sir Alexander Maxwell's letter, and I have also written to Sir Alexander Maxwell, thanking him for his decision.

I feel greatly relieved at having received permission to remain in this country indefinitely as now I shall only have to wait two more years before I

---

[1] Captain Fritz Wiedermann. Hitler's company commander in the First World War, and a member of Hitler's personal staff, as Personal Adjutant, from 1936–8. German Consul-General in San Francisco, 1938–41. Sent on a Special Mission to the Far East, 1942. Arrested as a war criminal by the United States' authorities in China, 1945. On 16 July 1938 he had arrived in London on a special mission, bringing with him Hitler's personal assurance of goodwill towards England and his renewed desire for a peaceful solution of the Sudeten problem: The Führer's patience was being sorely tried by the dilatory processes of the Czechs in redressing the wrongs of their German minority. He would restrain himself for six months, perhaps even for a year, provided no further burden of grievance was added to the sad lot of his fellow Germans, but let but one *Sudetendeutsch* be murdered and he would take immediate action. Once, however, the Sudeten problem had been satisfactorily dispensed with, the way would be clear not only for an Anglo-German understanding but for a Four-Power Pact.

can apply for naturalization, which, of course was the ultimate goal in my mind.

I feel that I can now settle down here permanently, and make my plans for the future financially and otherwise; buy a residence which will give me a sense of security and real citizenship.[1]

Once again thanking you, I am,
Yours sincerely,
Victor Oliver

Sir Abe Bailey to Winston S. Churchill

(*Churchill papers: 1/323*)

29 July 1938

My dear friend Winston,

I was so pleased to meet you again on Monday. You cannot realise Winston my affection for you & my admiration too—you must not over work, you looked as if you wanted a good rest. Why not take a cruise to S. Africa? I will be your host—pay your expenses & stay 14 days . . . & return in the same ship—you, Mrs W, & Mary. You would love it all. Peace for once for you. . . .

Abe

---

[1] On 28 July 1938 Churchill wrote to Sir Alexander Maxwell: 'I am very much obliged for the consideration you have given to my request on behalf of my son-in-law. He will, I am sure, be most grateful for the courtesy extended to him' (*Churchill papers: 1/326*).

August 1938

Winston S. Churchill to Sir Newman Flower

(*Churchill papers: 8/595*)

12 August 1938   Chartwell

At last I send you herewith the first tentative and provisional instalment of the new book.[1]

It comprises the first and part of the second chapters.

Winston S. Churchill to C. C. Wood

(*Churchill papers: 8/595*)

13 August 1938

Dear Mr Wood,

Thank you very much indeed for the three copies you have sent me of the last volume of 'Marlborough'.[2] This is on a level in excellence of production with all the others, and I congratulate you on a beautiful book. I hope the inside will be on the same plane as the outside!

---

[1] *The History of the English-Speaking Peoples*, on which Churchill had worked at Chartwell throughout the first two weeks of August. Under his contract, he was due to deliver the completed volume by the end of 1939, and by 6 June 1939 some 450,000 words were already in print (see page 1513). Among Churchill's visitors at Chartwell during the first two weeks of August were Bernard Baruch and Alfred Wall, Secretary of the London Trades Council. Churchill was also asked, on 10 August 1938, to open a series of broadcast talks on the BBC, on the subject of the Mediterranean, to begin on 6 October 1938, the subsequent speakers to include Professor E. H. Carr, F. A. Voigt, Sir Ronald Storrs, Professor R. W. Seton-Watson, Geoffrey Crowther and Arnold Toynbee.

[2] The first bound copies of Churchill's fourth Marlborough volume, which was to be published on 2 September 1938.

Winston S. Churchill to David Lloyd George

(*Churchill papers: 2/331*)

13 August 1938

Everything is overshadowed by the impending trial of will-power which is developing in Europe. I think we shall have to choose in the next few weeks between war and shame, and I have very little doubt what the decision will be.

Winston S. Churchill to J. Arthur Leve:[1] telegram

(*Churchill papers: 1/407*)

15 August 1938

Felt bound give Peat formal notice cancellation because cannot measure situation when Parliament meets November. My paramount duty almost certainly will lie here apart from provisions clause ten. Kinder to him cancel in ample time as provided in contract. Please explain this to him Mr Levy concurs many thanks.

Ian Colvin to Randolph Churchill

(*Randolph Churchill papers*)

15 August 1938   Hotel Adlon
                                                                              Berlin

Dear Randolph,

Miss Stewart will give you this letter and a message from me. A friend of mine[2] will be staying at the Park Lane Hotel from the 18th to the 23rd. I think it essential that he should meet your father. Please put nothing about him in your column or mention his presence to your colleagues. Miss Stewart will tell you why.[3]

---

[1] J. Arthur Leve, 1889–1975. A graduate of Columbia University Law School. A partner in the law firms of Coudert Brothers, and of Chadbourne, Stanchfield and Levy. Among his clients were the Pierre Hotel and Oscar Hammerstein.

[2] Ewald von Kleist-Schmenzin. A gentleman farmer from East Elbia, descendant of the poet Kleist. A member of the German Conservative Party before 1914, and a convinced anti-Nazi since 1933. Author of a pamphlet attacking Hitler's regime. Hanged by the Nazis on 16 April 1945, nine months after the failure of the plot to kill Hitler, and three weeks before the end of the war in Europe.

[3] Beginning on 15 August 1938, German military manoeuvres took place both along the Rhine frontier with France and on the approaches to Czechoslovakia (see also page 1122, note 1 and page 1140, notes 1 and 3).

I honestly think it worth while for your father to return from the country for a day, if he is anywhere near London, as the occasion won't offer itself again. I rely on your absolute discretion in this matter. The visitor will have some information of great interest to your father, and maybe your father could talk to him on the same lines as he did to the Sudeten chief Conrad Henlein.

I am not giving my friend a letter of introduction, for obvious reasons; but you may rely on his integrity and desire for understanding.

Yours ever,
Ian G. Colvin

Winston S. Churchill to J. Arthur Leve
(*Churchill papers: 1/407*)

17 August 1938

Dear Sir,

Many thanks for your cablegram. My difficulty is that I cannot forsee what conditions will prevail when Parliament meets in November. Even if clause 10 does not apply, it may be, probably it will be, my duty to be in attendance upon the House and give my counsel. Peat must realise how extremely critical and dangerous the whole European situation is, and the reaction this must have upon British politics.

I greatly regret with him the loss of this opportunity, but I thought it right to give him the fullest notice that I cannot be bound in the circumstances which have developed.

With regard to his own position towards the various societies with whom he has made contracts, I should, of course, be willing to write him a letter he could show to these bodies and so convince them of his authority and bona fides in having offered me as lecturer. I should further be prepared to make an arrangement with him if he so desires to give him the first refusal on any lecture contract I may make in the United States in the next three years. But the forfeit would have to be taken into consideration in this.

There remains one further point which is both difficult and delicate. It may be that everything will blow over and that after Parliament has met and the situation is clear I could come for a portion of the tour. The series of lectures beginning at Fort Worth and Dallas, Texas, on November 21 and comprising the Pacific Coast finishing in New York December 14 is a fairly compact block. This would entail my leaving England about November 11, and would mean that everything in front of November 21 would have to be definitely cancelled or indefinitely postponed. If Peat likes to take a chance upon this he might at his own risk let these engagements stand for a few weeks, but I can give no guarantee beyond my natural desire to undertake the tour.

'Note of Conversation at Chartwell between Monsieur de K [1] and
Mr Winston Churchill'

(*Churchill papers: 2/340*)

19 August 1938

K started by saying that he thought that an attack upon Czechoslovakia was imminent and would most likely occur between the Nuremburg Conference and the end of September. C asked if an ultimatum would be sent and was told 'No'. The troops and air forces would be asked to attack straightaway. K continued there was nobody in Germany who wanted war except H who regarded the events of May 21 as a personal rebuff the recurrence of which he must avoid and the memory of which he must obliterate. Even Goering, though he would not say a word against war, is not keen on it. The generals, including Reichenau,[2] are for peace and K believed that if only they could receive a little encouragement they might refuse to march. At least half of them were convinced that an attack upon Czechoslovakia would involve Germany in war with France and Britain & that Germany could not last three months.[3] But there was extreme dread of facing H personally on account of his fury and his power.

C observed that these generals were correct in their view and that though many people in England were not prepared to say in cold blood that they would march for Czechoslovakia, there would be few who would wish to stand idly by once the fighting started. He pointed out that the successive Nazi coups had hardened public opinion in Britain. Our patience in Spain was not so much a sign of weakness as of the conserving of resources for the real struggle which must come if fighting started in Central Europe; he added

[1] Ewald von Kleist.

[2] Walther von Reichenau, 1884–1942. Born in Karslruhe. An artillery officer, he spent most of his time on the staff. Showed strong Nazi leanings from 1931. Chief of Staff, Königsberg Command, East Prussia, 1932–3. A member of the Reich Defence Council, and Chief of Staff of the German Army, 1933–5. Commander of the Bavarian Corps, 1935. Promoted General of Artillery, November 1936. Commanding Officer of the Sixth Army, 1939–41. One of the twelve Generals to be created Field-Marshals on 19 July 1940. Replaced von Rundstedt as Commander-in-Chief, Army Group South, during the German invasion of the Soviet Union, 22 June 1941; on 10 October 1941 he issued an order calling for the 'complete annihilation of the false bolshevist doctrine of the Soviet State and its armed forces and the pitiless extermination of foreign treachery and cruelty' (International Military Tribunal, Nuremberg, document D-411). He died at Poltava in January 1942.

[3] Churchill noted at this point: 'That is his view not mine.'

that public opinion in the United States was immeasurably more advanced than in 1914. He stressed the fact that those who thought as he did were anti-Nazi and anti-war, and not anti-German.

K said that he knew what C said was true and that he would continue to emphasise these facts to his friends. He thought, however, that some gesture was needed to crystallize the wide-spread and indeed, universal anti-war sentiment in Germany. Particularly was it necessary to do all that was possible to encourage the generals who alone had the power to stop the war. He realised the difficulties of action by a democratic government, but inquired whether it was not possible for private members of parliament by letters in the press or by private communications to friends in Germany to stress the dangers of the situation, and to appeal to the peaceful elements in Germany to assert themselves without delay. He was convinced that in the event of the generals deciding to insist on peace, there would be a new system of government within forty-eight hours. Such a government, probably of a monarchist character, could guarantee stability and end the fear of war for ever.

C stated that once the world was assured of a peaceful tolerant and law-abiding government in Germany such questions as the colonies and commercial treaties would be much easier of adjustment. Neither Britain nor France would prove ungenerous. On the contrary, there would be a cordial desire to mark the end of the crisis in a manner that would strengthen a peaceful regime, once the shadow of aggression and war had passed from Europe. At this point K mentioned that his friends were not greatly concerned about the colonies, but that the Polish Corridor was the matter that affected them most. C said that before H had started, he (C) had always wished to see this difficulty cleared up; but that now it had been officially dropped by Germany, and this was certainly not the moment to discuss it. It would only throw Poland on to the side of H.

K recognised this, but said it was the real grievance in the military mind.

C told K that his conversations with V[1] had been reported to the Foreign Secretary and the Prime Minister and that the former had authorised C to state that the Prime Minister's declaration in the House of Commons on March 24 still stood. C undertook to embody this assurance together with his own view in the form of a letter.[2]

---

[1] Sir Robert Vansittart, to whom Ian Colvin had also sent von Kleist.

[2] Churchill himself sent copies of this memorandum, and of his letter to von Kleist, to Neville Chamberlain, Lord Halifax and Anthony Eden. To Eden he wrote, on 31 August 1938: 'You may be interested to see the enclosed. Both Edward and Neville wrote subsequently approving my letter; though, of course, it was only sent on my responsibility. Hope you are having a pleasant holiday' (*Churchill papers: 2/331*).

Winston S. Churchill to Ewald von Kleist

(*Churchill papers: 2/340*)

19 August 1938   Chartwell

My dear Sir,

I have welcomed you here as one who is ready to run risks to preserve the peace of Europe and to achieve a lasting friendship between the British, French and German peoples for their mutual advantage.

I am sure that the crossing of the frontier of Czecho-Slovakia by German armies or aviation in force will bring about a renewal of the world war. I am as certain as I was at the end of July 1914 that England will march with France and certainly the United States is now strongly anti-Nazi. It is difficult for democracies in advance and in cold blood to make precise declarations; but the spectacle of an armed attack by Germany upon a small neighbour and the bloody fighting that will follow will rouse the whole British Empire and compel the gravest decisions.

Do not, I pray you, be misled upon this point. Such a war, once started, would be fought out like the last to the bitter end, and one must consider not what might happen in the first few months, but where we should all be at the end of the third or fourth year.

It would be a great mistake to imagine that the slaughter of the civil population following upon air-raids would prevent the British Empire from developing its full war power. Though, of course, we should suffer more at the beginning than we did last time. But the submarine is practically mastered by scientific methods, and we shall have the freedom of the seas and the support of the greater part of the world. The worse the air-slaughter at the beginning, the more inexpiable would be the war. Evidently, all the great Nations engaged in the struggle, once started, would fight on for victory or death.

As I feel you should have some definite message to take back to your friends in Germany who wish to see peace preserved and who look forward to a great Europe in which England, France and Germany will be working together for the prosperity of the wage-earning masses, I communicated with Lord Halifax.[1] His Lordship asks me to say, on his behalf, that the position of His Majesty's Government, in relation to Czechoslovakia, is defined by the Prime Minister's speech in the House of Commons of March 24, 1938. The speech must be read as a whole, and I have no authority to select any particular passage out of its context; but I must draw your attention to the final passage

---

[1] At the point in Churchill's letter where Churchill had written: 'I communicated with Lord Halifax', Sir Horace Wilson noted, on 25 August 1938: 'This is mischievous; it might be taken to mean that H had concurred in what is said on p.1' (*Premier papers: 1/249*).

on this subject—columns 1405–6, Official Report of the Parliamentary Debates 1937–8:—

'Where peace and war are concerned, legal obligations are not alone involved, and, if war broke out, it would be unlikely to be confined to those who have assumed such obligations. It would be quite impossible to say where it would end and what Governments might become involved. The inexorable pressure of facts might well prove more powerful than formal pronouncements, and in that event it would be well within the bounds of probability that other countries, besides those which were parties to the original dispute, would almost immediately become involved. This is especially true in the case of two countries like Great Britain and France, with long associations of friendship, with interests closely interwoven, devoted to the same ideals of democratic liberty, and determined to uphold them.'

May I say that, speaking for myself, I believe that a peaceful and friendly solution of the Czecho-Slovak problem would pave the way for the true reunion of our countries on the basis of the greatness and the freedom of both.[1]

Winston S. Churchill to Lord Halifax

(*Foreign Office papers: 800/309*)

20 August 1938

My dear Edward,

I send you herewith a note made by Randolph of my talk with Herr von Kleist and also the letter I have given him.

K was also very emphatic that all the Generals were convinced that they

---

[1] On 18 August 1938, in an article in the *Daily Telegraph* entitled 'German Manoeuvres', Churchill wrote: 'The British Government have sent Lord Runciman to Prague with a sincere desire to find the way to a fair and friendly settlement of the Sudeten-German problem. Those who know him are sure that he would feel in honour bound to state the truth and not to deny justice to either party. Assuming that his mission runs its normal course we shall presently have a practical working compromise which will give the Sudeten-German a free and equal chance with other races inside a more broadly based Czechoslovak Republic. Such a plan might be the rallying ground of all the good forces which sustain the cause of world peace . . .' The immediate fortunes of the world lay, however, with Hitler, of whom Churchill wrote: 'He entertains Sir Ian Hamilton in his mountain retreat. Apparently there, according to the General's account, it is all birds' nests and goodwill. The idea, says the General, of war being planned in such surroundings is absurd. He may be right, and, if so, this period of increasing strain drawing to its climax will be succeeded by a far more solidly founded peace than we have at this moment.' Nevertheless, Churchill warned, 'An episode like the trampling-down of Czechoslovakia by an overwhelming force would change the whole current of human ideas and would eventually draw upon the aggressor a wrath which would in the end involve all the greatest nations of the world.'

could not possibly fight for more than three months and that defeat was certain, but I did not like what he said about there being no ultimatum, merely an order to troops to advance from all sides at some unexpected moment.

My hope is, however, that the evident distress of the German people at being dragged into a war will create an atmosphere affecting the Generals and the Fuehrer in opposite senses.

I am very glad you enjoyed Mademoiselle Curie's[1] book about her mother. She is a friend of mine, and is as beautiful as she is clever. . . . I am ashamed to say I have not yet found time to read it being at the moment horribly entangled with the ancient Britons, the Romans, the Angles, Saxons and Jutes, all of whom I thought I had escaped from for ever when I left school!

Winston S. Churchill to Violet Pearman

(*Pearman papers*)

20 August 1938   Chartwell

Dear Mrs P,

Thank you so very much for the black bands; they fit me perfectly.

Please do not worry about coming to Chartwell at all this month, and do not overdo the homework, but give yourself plenty of rest and fresh air.

I will try to come and see you again either next week or the week after.

Yours vy sincerely,
Winston S. Churchill

Sir Edward Marsh: diary

(*Marsh papers*)

22 August 1938   Chartwell

Winston very apprehensive, thinks Hitler means to attack Czecho-S without ultimatum in Sept, but he *may* be stopped.

Bézique with Clemmie. Long talk with Winston on way to bed.

---

[1] Eve Curie, 1904–   . Born in Paris, the daughter of Marie Curie. A pianist, she gave her first concert in Paris in 1925. Musical critic of *Candide*. After her mother's death in 1934, she collected and classified all her papers, and wrote her biography (published in 1937; translated into 32 languages). Co-ordinator of Women's War Activities, Paris, 1939–40. Returned to Paris from a lecture tour in the United States, 2 May 1940. Went to London June 1940. Deprived of her French citizenship by the Vichy Government, April 1941. War Correspondent, Libya, Russia, Burma and China, 1941–3. Enlisted as a Private in the Fighting French Corps; Lieutenant, 1944. Co-publisher of *Paris-Presse*, an evening paper, 1944–9. Special Adviser to the Secretary-General of NATO (in Paris), 1952–4.

Winston S. Churchill to Major Percy Davies

(*Churchill papers: 8/602*)

23 August 1938   Chartwell

My dear Major Davies,

The months slip by so quickly that it is with a sense of surprise and even of Autumn chill that I remind myself that the time is drawing near when we should settle the articles for next year.

It helps me very much in my work if I know some time ahead because I can then begin thinking about the subjects.

Would you, therefore, very kindly, if possible in the course of the next month, let me have your ideas so that I can make contributory or counter suggestions? I should hope to begin work upon these articles during the month of October, and let you have them as usual before Christmas.

I suppose the second series is going to start quite soon. If there are any points in it which have been upset by the time which has passed, please let me know.

I shall be here up to September 15, and it would be very agreeable if you could come down one day and have a talk.

Harold R. Peat to Winston S. Churchill

(*Churchill papers: 1/407*)

23 August 1938   New York

Dear Mr Churchill:

I have waited two weeks since your cable stating you were writing and to date I have not received the promised letter. Really, Mr Churchill, my position is a most desperate one. I am not concerned about the legality of the situation. The following facts, we, both you and I, must face.

As I informed you at your home, and again in France, and in which you concurred, the only basis of cancellation as far as my contracts with your local sponsors would permit, is war, and the Cabinet. You told me yourself that you recognized that, and even though I gave you a legal 'out' in the agreement between us, you would not let me down. You definitely told me that regardless of our personal written contract, you would be here for the tour and only an election or war, or illness, would prevent your presence in the USA. Your word, your assurance, Mr Churchill, mean more to me than any legal agreement.

You are now scheduled for 25 lectures for such outstanding institutions as

Columbia University, University of Cincinnati, Northwestern University, University of Minnesota, University of Washington, University of California, University of Oklahoma and the Institute of Arts and Sciences in New York, Brooklyn, Washington, Los Angeles and San Francisco, etc. etc. I am informed that never before was a tour so arranged giving the speaker the largest and at the same time the most influential groups in the USA. At this moment, so opportune indeed, (after the President's speech in Canada)[1] for the ripening of Anglo-American cooperation—the opportunity, sir, for a genuine service to mankind is obvious. On the other hand, should you fail the American people now, do you frankly believe that another such tour could ever again be arranged? War, or an Election can be the only honorable excuse for postponement or cancellation. You are, I presume, safe legally, but I am not, and as I informed you in my letter of July 30, I cannot brusquely tell your local sponsors, 'Mr Churchill has decided to break his agreement with you.' No doubt the majority of them will sue me—my business, which I have given a life in building, will be wrecked because I have no legal 'out'. I took your word—an Englishman's word is always good. I am not being emotional, Mr Churchill, I am frankly being honest with you—advising you by all means to come. If, after you arrive here, there is an Election in England or a War, or some extraordinary situation that dictates your departure, you can then immediately quit and be back *in four days*.

We have shipped cards, circulars and general advance publicity material to the 25 cities in which you are to appear—we have long since manufactured this material. Samples have been mailed to you. Your local sponsors have all heralded your appearance as the event of the year, season tickets have been sold, brochures and programs printed. Your importance as an international personality has commanded such anticipation of your arrival to the extent that no explanation will cure the disastrous effects of your non-appearance. The prestige that will be destroyed can never be remedied.

I plead with you that you cable me today that you will be here as agreed, but if the circumstances presently are such that you cannot depart as agreed, then when you can appear.

Sincerely yours,

Harold R. Peat

[1] Roosevelt's speech of 18 August 1938, opening the new International Bridge between New York State and Canada. The editor of Franklin Roosevelt's Presidential speeches noted: 'It was the first time that a Chief Executive of this country had ever extended the Monroe Doctrine to Canada. Germany, engaged in plans for the dismemberment of Czechoslovakia, dismissed the speech curtly as "moral preachment".' B. D. Zevin (editor), *Nothing to Fear: The Selected Addresses of Franklin Delano Roosevelt, 1932–1945*, London 1947, page 158.

Winston S. Churchill to Imre Revesz
(*Churchill papers: 8/607*)

25 August 1938

Many thanks for your letter and cheque.

Do you happen to know anything about a Monsieur Ferdinand Lot.[1] He is an archaeologist and a great authority on Roman and Anglo-Saxon Britain. He delivered a lecture here in 1931 which was greatly esteemed. I gather he is now very old. Could you find out for me what his circumstances are? Because if I could get in touch with him it might help in the work upon which I am now engaged.

What has happened to the Japanese Naval article? Did the Swedes take it? I was very pleased to see how well you had disposed of the article 'Women in War'. The sales of the articles are growing well under your care, and I am very satisfied with all you do for me.

I do not like the look of things at all.[2]

Neville Chamberlain to Winston S. Churchill
(*Churchill papers: 2/331*)

26 August 1938   The Manor House,
                                                 Great Durnford[3]

My dear Winston,

Many thanks for your letter of 24th with enclosures. I had seen these already as Halifax had shown them to me & I hope your letter may help. Our latest information from Prague is rather more encouraging.

I have had rather a poor sort of holiday so far, but I am glad to say that I

---

[1] Ferdinand Lot, 1866–1952. A professor at the Sorbonne, historian and philologist, he published his first book, on the later Carolingians, in 1891. His widely acclaimed history of the end of the ancient world and the beginning of the middle ages was published in 1927, after which he wrote a history of the invasions of the German tribes (1935) and a study of the barbarian invasions and the settlement of Europe (1937). His last book, on Gaul, was published in 1947.

[2] On 26 August 1938 Revesz wrote to Churchill: 'The situation in Paris is not good, the days of Daladier seem to be counted. His speech was a great mistake, the Trade-Unions were prepared to make every concession, but instead of negotiating he has made this public attitude which awoke the fighting spirit on both sides again. People say that Daladier acted under the influence of Patenôtre. A crisis would be rather awkward in view of the news coming from Germany and Spain. Herriot is apparently requested by everybody to form a National Government but this would spoil his further ambitions.' Churchill replied on the following day: 'I am sorry to hear what you say about Daladier. Any weakening of the French Government at this moment would add to our dangers.'

[3] The home of the Rt. Hon Major George Tryon, formerly Minister of Pensions (1922–24, 1924–29 and 1931–35) and Postmaster-General from 1935 to 1940. He was created Baron in April 1940.

have now recovered and if only Central Europe will keep quiet I hope to make up for lost time.

Yours sincerely,
Neville Chamberlain

Winston S. Churchill to the Duchess of Atholl

(*Churchill papers: 2/331*)

26 August 1938

My dear Duchess,

I regret I do not desire to join in a signed letter. I have always thought this was a very ineffective way of dealing with difficulties.

Winston S. Churchill to Robert Boothby

(*Churchill papers: 2/331*)

27 August 1938   Chartwell

Very many thanks for your most interesting letter and enclosures, which I return.

I hope, indeed, that the Government will do their utmost to avert war, which I personally think is very near to us at the present time.

Let me know your movements. It would be very nice if you could come down here for a night. I remain at Chartwell until September 15.[1]

---

[1] On 27 August 1938 Churchill had spoken at Theydon Bois, in his constituency. Speaking of the Czechoslovak crisis he said, as reported in *The Times* two days later: 'They all hoped and prayed that Lord Runciman's mission of conciliation to Prague would be successful, and certainly the Government of Czechoslovakia seemed to be doing their utmost to put their house in order, and to meet every demand which was not designed to compass their ruin as a State. . . . he could not believe there was the slightest reason why the people in that country should not come together in a good and lasting arrangement between themselves if only they were let alone to do it. But possibly outside forces, larger and fiercer ambitions, might prevent that settlement, and then Europe and the civilized world would have to face the demands of Nazi Germany, or perhaps be confronted with some violent action on the part of the German Nazi party, carrying with it the invasion of a small country with a view to its subjugation. Such an episode would not be simply an attack upon Czechoslovakia; it would be an outrage against the civilization and freedom of the whole world. Every country would ask itself, "whose turn will it be next?" '

The Duke of Windsor to Winston S. Churchill

(Churchill papers: 1/324)

28 August 1938   La Cröe
                                                     Cap D'Antibes

Dear Winston,

A parcel containing a copy of your new book 'Arms and the Covenant' arrived here from Mr Allen[1] whilst we were on our holiday in Italy. It was unpacked and placed in a bookshelf, and it was only on taking it out to-day that I discovered you had, as usual, signed this copy for me.

I therefore apologise sincerely for the delay in writing to thank you for the book, and assure you I shall lose no time in reading it.

Miss Maxine Elliott, who was dining with us the other evening, tells me she is expecting you to stop with her at 'L'Horizon' next month. I therefore look forward to an early meeting, and telling you how much of your book I agree with!

The Duchess and I hope you are well and that we shall have the pleasure of seeing you again soon.

                                                     Yours sincerely,
                                                     Edward

Sir Robert Waley Cohen to Winston S. Churchill

(Churchill papers: 2/330)

30 August 1938

My dear Churchill,

Very many thanks for the interesting Note of your interview with Herr Foerster. It is very amusing to see how the cloven hoof appeared in the last sentence & the interpreter knew better than to translate it! The Jewish 'problem' which they are creating is of course a purely artificial one in Dantzig, but there as elsewhere it forms an essential part of their attack on civilisation.

I believe you are the only man who could tell Hitler the truth & give him a true picture of the inclined plane on which he is dragging down his country through elementary barbarism to final collapse. He can never drag England into 'sympathy' still less 'cooperation' in that course.

                                                     Yours sincerely,
                                                     Robert Waley Cohen

---

[1] Albert George Allen, 1888–1956. Solicitor. On active service in France, 1914–18 (DSO, Military Cross, despatches twice). Private solicitor to Edward VIII, 1936. Knighted, 1952.

Winston S. Churchill to Louis Levy

(Churchill papers: 1/407)

31 August 1938
Private and Personal

I heard from your office that you are already on the ocean returning. I am sorry I did not see you before you left. I enclose you the last letter I have received from Peat. Naturally he is disappointed at losing the chance of making twenty-five thousand dollars out of my lecture tour, I am sorry to lose it too. I cannot readily believe that if so long a notice as nearly three months is given any great inconvenience will be caused to the various societies with whom he has contracts. What he says in paragraph two of his letter about my having given him personal assurances apart from the contract is quite untrue: on the contrary I always regarded myself as free to abandon the tour if circumstances should render it impossible. Is it true that he will be sued by these societies and that his business will be wrecked? I think it is all nonsense.

I should think that any one could see that with the European situation as it is, it may be my bounden duty to be in Parliament when the Session opens on November 2. On the other hand if matters clear up I might be able to go later and to the Californian part of the tour before Christmas, ending December 14. But it is no use encouraging him with vain hopes. I have told him to come to see you.

At any moment you advise I will remit you the four thousand dollars for the forfeit.

With kind regards
Believe me,
Yours sincerely,

Harold Nicolson: diary

(Nicolson papers)

31 August 1938

He[1] had seen the Cabinet people yesterday after their meeting and found them very pleased with themselves. On the other hand Vansittart and Winston Churchill both think that their instructions to Nevile Henderson are not firm or precise enough. Hitler still thinks we are wobbling and unless he is told definitely that we shall come to the help of the Czechs and the French he will think he can defy or ignore us.

[1] Robert Boothby.

Robert Boothby to Winston S. Churchill

(*Churchill papers: 2/331*)

31 August 1938
Private

Dear Winston,

I do hope you have written to Halifax on the lines you suggested.

An announcement that we have 'entered into consultation with France and Russia' would be a compromise between the Cabinet view that no further action is necessary at present, and Van's view that nothing but the threat of force can now deter Hitler.

And I believe it wd achieve its objective.

But it must come before Nuremberg.[1] Sorry to bother you, but in these days one doesn't want to leave a stone unturned.

Yours ever,
Bob

Winston S. Churchill to Lord Halifax

(*Foreign Office papers: 800/314*)

31 August 1938   Chartwell

My dear Edward,

If Benes makes good, and R[2] thinks it a fair offer, yet nevertheless it is turned down, it seems to me there are two things which might be done *this week* to increase the deterrents against violent action by H, neither of which would commit you to the dread guarantee.

First, would it not be possible to frame a joint note between Britain, France

---

[1] Hitler was due to speak at Nuremberg, at the annual Party Day ceremonies, on 12 September 1938. During the course of his speech Hitler declared, of the Sudetenland: 'I am in no way willing that here in the heart of Germany through the dexterity of other statesmen a second Palestine should be permitted to arise. The poor Arabs are defenceless and perhaps deserted. The Germans in Czechoslovakia are neither defenceless nor are they deserted, and folk should take notice of that fact. I feel that I must express this thought at the Parteitag at which for the first time the representatives of our German-Austrian shires (*Gaue*) take part. They know best how bitter a thing it is to be separated from the Motherland. They will be the first to recognize the significance of what I have been saying to-day. They will be the most ready to agree with me when I state before the entire people that we should not deserve to be Germans if we were not prepared to adopt this attitude and in one way or another to bear the consequences which follow from it' (quoted in Norman H. Baynes, editor, *The Speeches of Adolf Hitler, April 1922–August 1939*, London 1942, volume 2, pages 1497–8).

[2] Lord Runciman, who was still in Czechoslovakia, seeking to promote a solution of the Czech–Sudeten dispute.

and Russia stating (a) their desire for peace and friendly relations; (b) their deep anxiety at the military preparations of Germany; (c) their joint interest in a peaceful solution of the Czechoslovak controversy, and (d) that an invasion by Germany of Czechoslovakia would raise capital issues for all three powers. This note, when drafted, should be formally shewn to Roosevelt by the Ambassadors of the three powers, and we should use every effort to induce him to do his utmost upon it. It seems to me not impossible that he would then himself address H emphasising the gravity of the situation, and saying that it seemed to him that a world war would inevitably follow from an invasion of Czechoslovakia, and that he earnestly counselled a friendly settlement.

It seems to me that this process would give the best chance to the peaceful elements in German official circles to make a stand and that H might find a way out for himself by parleying with Roosevelt. However, none of these developments can be predicted, one only sees them as hopes. The important thing is the Joint Note.

The second step which might save the situation would be fleet movements, and the placing of the reserve flotillas and cruiser squadrons into full commission. I do not suggest calling out the Royal Fleet Reserve or mobilisation, but there are, I believe, five or six flotillas which could be raised to First Fleet scale, and also there are about two hundred trawlers which would be used for anti-submarine work. The taking of these up and other measures would make a great stir in the naval ports, the effect of which could only be beneficial as a deterrent and a timely precaution if the worst happened.

I venture to hope that you will not resent these suggestions from one who has lived through such days before.[1] It is clear that speed is vital.

Yours ever,
Winston S. Churchill

PS. Perhaps you may care to show this to the PM, if you think it worth while.

---

[1] For Churchill's decisions in July and August 1914, when he was First Lord of the Admiralty, see his own accounts on pages 1186 and 1400. Fifteen years earlier Churchill had recalled in *The World Crisis*, volume 2, pages 374–5, how, in May 1915, at the height of the Dardanelles crisis, after his own departure from the Admiralty had been announced, Lord Kitchener had called on him at the Admiralty: 'He spoke very kindly about our work together. He evidently had no idea how narrowly he had escaped my fate. As he got up to go he turned and said, in the impressive and almost majestic manner which was natural to him, "Well, there is one thing at any rate they cannot take from you. The Fleet was ready". After that he was gone. During the months that we were still to serve together in the new Cabinet I was condemned often to differ from him, to oppose him and to criticize him. But I cannot forget the rugged kindness and warm-hearted courtesy which led him to pay me this visit'.

September 1938

Harrods Ltd to Winston S. Churchill

(*Churchill papers: 1/332*)

1 September 1938

Dear Sir

We have pleasure in advising you that we are having a consignment of very rare Golden Orfe—a cold water fish for outdoor ponds and aquaria; the colour is red, white and blue. These Orfe of such unusual colouring are the first to enter this country, and the prices are as follows:—

2 inches long	10/- each.
3 ,, ...	15/- ,,
4 ,, ...	20/- ,,

The above are offered subject to being unsold upon receipt of your definite order, and we would mention that they should make good breeding stock for next year.

Arthur Mann[1] to Winston S. Churchill

(*Churchill papers: 2/331*)

1 September 1938   The Yorkshire Post
Personal   Leeds

Dear Mr Churchill

I see that you spent some time with Lord Halifax yesterday. The previous day Lord Halifax was good enough to give me an interview. I did not come

---

[1] Arthur Henry Mann, 1876–1972. Journalist; Editor of the *Evening Standard*, 1918, and founder of the 'Londoner's Diary'. Editor of the *Yorkshire Post*, 1919–39. Companion of Honour, 1941. Member of the Board of Governors of the BBC, 1941–6. A Trustee of the *Observer*, he resigned in November 1956 in protest against the paper's criticisms of the Suez policy. According to his obituary in *The Times* (28 July 1972): 'Although the *Yorkshire Post*

away with an impression that the dangers of the European situation were fully appreciated. I wonder what conclusions you drew.

Before I saw Lord Halifax I had sent him a Memo of which I enclose a copy. It was written a fortnight ago before the present crisis developed but presents the background to it, as it appears to me. I have just read Mr Attlee's article in today's 'Herald'[1] & feel that unless the Prime Minister comes, broadly speaking, into line with it the Conservative Party is in for trouble. Though for patriotic reasons we may not say so now, great numbers I fancy, are of opinion that our present menace has been invited by Mr Chamberlain's pursuit of 'appeasement' without any true regard for the realities of the European situation.

Yours sincerely,
Arthur Mann

Winston S. Churchill: paragraphs for the 'Londoner's Diary'
('Evening Standard')

1 September 1938

SPORT AT BALMORAL

The Prime Minister has wisely taken his fishing rods to Balmoral. For the King's Highland home is one of the finest sporting properties in Scotland.

King George V used sometimes to send the Minister in Attendance out deer stalking. Mr Winston Churchill, when First Lord of the Admiralty, on

---

was Conservative in politics, he never hesitated to express in it bold criticisms of policy or to deviate from the party line when convinced that it was right to do so. He gave many warnings against the dangers facing Britain, and vigorously opposed the appeasement policy of Neville Chamberlain before and during the Munich crisis of 1938. Criticisms of Chamberlain which he published displeased many leading Yorkshire Conservatives and some shareholders and directors of the newspaper company. But he was strongly supported by the Chairman, Rupert Beckett, who told the shareholders roundly that he would himself resign rather than let criticisms of Arthur Mann be pressed. It was a tense and successful battle for the independence of an editor.'

[1] On 1 September 1938 the main leader page feature in the *Daily Herald* was an article by Clement Attlee, Leader of the Opposition, praising Neville Chamberlain's statement of 24 March 1938 as 'a warning that there is a limit to the tolerance which has been given hitherto to Fascist aggression'. The 'crux of the situation' in Europe, Attlee added, was not the 'degree or amount of liberty to be conceded to the German minority' in Czechoslovakia, but the action of Hitler 'in using the minority question in Czechoslovakia to pursue his ambitious dreams of power'. If the Nazis had their way with Czechoslovakia, he warned, 'a step will have been taken towards the destruction of the independence of all States'. The nations of south-eastern Europe, 'some for the first time, some after the lapse of twenty years, will fall into complete dependence on the German Reich'.

one occasion shot three stags in one day. It was not perhaps without some trepidation that he returned home. But King George was delighted.

'What do you think I keep them for?' he remarked.

ENOUGH

This was a very different outlook from that of the old Duke of Westminster,[1] grandfather of the present Duke, who was a gracious but formidable host.

'How many did you shoot?' he asked a youthful guest. 'Four,' was the answer.

'Indeed,' said the Duke, 'then you have shot enough and I will have your carriage ordered for to-morrow morning.'

WAR AT CHURT

Mr Lloyd George has declared a private war. The enemy are rabbits.

Recently he took over 160 additional acres at Churt, and before he starts to cultivate he wants to wipe out the rabbit population. So he is inviting many of his friends to bring their guns.

His own family will provide two crack shots—Gwilym and Richard.[2]

Mr Lloyd George himself will be an onlooker. He does not shoot.

Winston S. Churchill: paragraphs for the 'Londoner's Diary'

('*Evening Standard*')

2 September 1938

CIVIL SERVICE LEADERS

It is often said that the leading figures in political life are by no means the equal of the pre-war statesmen. It cannot, however, be said that this decline, if decline there be, has extended to the Civil Service.

---

[1] Lord Hugh Lupus Grosvenor, 1825–99. Succeeded his father as 3rd Marquess of Westminster, 1869; raised to the Dukedom, 1874. Grandfather of Churchill's friend Bendor, 2nd Duke of Westminster.

[2] Gwilym, 1894–1967, later 1st Viscount Tenby, who served in Churchill's wartime coalition as Minister of Food (1941–2) and as Minister of Fuel and Power (1942–5); and Richard 1889–1968, later 2nd Earl Lloyd George, a civil engineer.

In Sir Robert Vansittart and Sir Horace Wilson, who have taken a notable part in the Czech discussions in London, and in Sir Frederick Leith-Ross[1] the Ministers have at their disposal official advisers whose qualities have never been surpassed.

Although the financial prizes of a great career in the Civil Service are comparatively small, it still attracts a perennial stream of the finest brains in the nation.

The fact that business and industry draw off distinguished civil servants to more lucrative spheres should not be regarded upon a long view as an evil. Indeed, the possibility provides an additional and alternative attraction to ability and ambition to enter the service.

THEN TOO

It was an earlier Central European crisis that led to the late Sir Francis Mowat's story of his conversation with Mr C. T. Ritchie, Chancellor of the Exchequer in 1902–3. Sir Francis was Permanent Secretary to the Treasury.[2]

The news had just arrived of the assassination of the King and Queen of Serbia, who were cut to pieces in their palace in June 1903 by mutinous Serbian officers.

Sir Francis, painfully affected by the news, went into the Chancellor's room to tell him about it. Mr Ritchie, who was writing, listened at first abstractedly.

'The King has been murdered.' 'Ah,' said the Chancellor. 'The Queen has been eviscerated.' 'Dear, dear,' said the Chancellor, turning again to his letter. 'Two of the Ministers have been killed.'

'The Ministers!' exclaimed Mr Ritchie, rising from the table. 'How shocking!'

---

[1] Frederick William Leith-Ross, 1887–1968. Educated at Merchant Taylors' School and Balliol College, Oxford. Private Secretary to H. H. Asquith, 1911–13. British Representative on the Finance Board of the Reparations Commission, 1920–5. Deputy Controller of Finance, Treasury, 1925–32. Chief Economic Adviser to the Government, 1932–46. Knighted, 1933. Member of the British War Debts Mission to Washington, 1933. Negotiated financial arrangements with Germany, October 1934 and with Italy, April 1935. Financial Mission to China, 1935–6. Chairman of the Economic Committee of the League of Nations, 1936 and 1937. Director-General, Ministry of Economic Warfare, 1939–42. Chairman, Inter-Allied Post-War Requirements Committee, 1941–3. Deputy Director-General of UNRRA, 1944–5. Governor of the National Bank of Egypt, 1946–51. Deputy Chairman, National Provincial Bank, 1951–66.
[2] Sir Francis Mowat (a friend of Lord Randolph Churchill, and Churchill's own mentor during the early phase of the Tariff controversy), was Permanent Under-Secretary at the Treasury from 1894 to 1903. Charles Ritchie was Chancellor of the Exchequer from August 1902 to October 1903.

REBEL

Mr Frank Pakenham,[1] 32-year-old brother of Lord Longford and a don at Christ Church, worked under Mr Neville Chamberlain at Conservative headquarters six years ago.

But his political views have changed since then. He has become a Socialist. He has also, and more recently, inherited £70,000.

Now he is carrying his rebellion into the Chamberlain camp. Part of the legacy has been invested in the purchase of a Birmingham Socialist weekly newspaper.

CANDIDATES

Mr Pakenham has at least two reasons for choosing Birmingham as his battle-ground.

He is prospective Socialist candidate for West Birmingham, which was Sir Austen Chamberlain's seat; and his scholarly and attractive wife[2] is Socialist candidate for King's Norton, Birmingham. Mrs Pakenham is a cousin of Mr Chamberlain.

---

[1] Francis Aungier Pakenham, 1905–   . 2nd son of the 5th Earl of Longford, who was killed in action at Gallipoli in 1915. Educated at Eton and New College, Oxford. Worked in the Conservative Party Economic Research Department, 1930–2. Lecturer in Politics, Oxford, 1932. Prospective Labour Party candidate for Oxford City, 1938. Personal Assistant to Sir William Beveridge, 1941–4. Parliamentary Under-Secretary of State, War Office, 1946–7. Chancellor of the Duchy of Lancaster, 1947–8. Minister of Civil Aviation, 1948–51. First Lord of the Admiralty, 1951. Succeeded his brother as Earl of Longford, 1961. Lord Privy Seal, 1964–5. Secretary of State for the Colonies, 1965–6. Lord Privy Seal, 1966–8. Knight of the Garter, 1971.

[2] Elizabeth Harman, 1906–   . Elder daughter of Nathaniel Bishop Harman, FRCS, and Katherine Chamberlain. Educated at Headington School, Oxford, and Lady Margaret Hall. M.A. (Oxon). Workers' Educational Association (WEA) and University Extension Lecturer, 1929–35. She married Frank Pakenham in 1931. Unsuccessful Labour candidate for Cheltenham, 1935. Labour candidate for King's Norton, 1935–43. Member of the Rent Tribunal, Paddington and St Pancras, 1947–54. Unsuccessful Labour candidate for Oxford, 1950. She published her first book, *Points for Parents*, in 1956. Among her other books are *Victoria R I* (1964), *Wellington: Years of the Sword* (1969), *Wellington: Pillar of State* (1972) an illustrated photographic biography of Churchill (1974) and biographies of Byron (1976) and Wilfrid Scawen Blunt (1969). A Trustee of the National Portrait Gallery, 1968–78. CBE, 1974.

Winston S. Churchill to Lord Halifax

(*Foreign Office papers: 800/322*)

2 September 1938   Chartwell
Private & Personal

My dear Edward,

I have received privately from an absolutely sure source[1] the following information, which I feel it my duty to report to you, although I was not asked to do so.

Yesterday, September 2, the French Chargé d'Affaires in Moscow[2] (the Ambassador being on leave) called upon M Litvinoff[3] and, in the name of the French Government, asked him what aid Russia would give to Czechoslovakia against a German attack, having regard particularly to the difficulties which might be created by the neutrality of Poland or Roumania.

Litvinoff asked in reply what the French would do themselves, pointing out that the French had a direct obligation, whereas the Russian obligation was dependent on the action of France.

The French Chargé d'Affaires did not reply to this question. Nevertheless, Litvinoff stated to him, first, that the Russian Soviet Union had resolved to fulfil their obligations. He recognised the difficulties created by the attitude of Poland and Roumania, but he thought that, in the case of Roumania, these could be overcome.

In the last few months the policy of the Roumanian Government had been markedly friendly to Russia and their relations had greatly improved. M Litvinoff thought that the best way to overcome the reluctance of Roumania would be through the agency of the League of Nations. If, for instance, the League decided that Czechoslovakia was the victim of aggression and that Germany was the aggressor, that would probably determine the action of Roumania in regard to allowing Russian troops and air-forces to pass through her territory.

[1] Lord Halifax had noted in the margin at this point: 'Maisky'.

[2] Jean Payart, 1892–1969. French diplomat. Attaché in Berlin, 1920–4. Consul-General in Cologne, 1930–1. Counsellor of Embassy, Moscow, 1931–9 (Minister Plenipotentiary, July 1939). Suspended from the Foreign Service by the Vichy authorities, 1943. Returned to duty, Conference Secretariat, 1945. Ambassador to Belgrade, 1949–50. High Commissioner (later Ambassador) to Austria, 1950–4. Ambassador to Saigon, 1956–8.

[3] Maksim Maksimovich Litvinoff, 1876–1951. Jewish; born Meyer Wallach. Educated in Bialystok. Became a Bolshevik on the formation of the Party in 1903. Lived for many years in London, where he married an English Jewess, Ivy Low, in 1916. In London at the time of the revolution. Appointed Soviet Representative in London, 4 January 1918. In Stockholm, 1918–19. Deputy Foreign Minister, 1921–30. Chief Soviet Delegate at the Geneva Disarmament Conference, 1927. Foreign Minister, 1930–9. Full member of the Central Committee of the Communist Party, 1934–41. Ambassador to Washington, 1941–3. Deputy Foreign Minister, 1943–6.

The French Chargé d'Affaires raised the point that the Council might not be unanimous, and was answered that M. Litvinoff thought a majority decision would be sufficient, and that Roumania would probably associate herself with the majority in the vote of the Council.

M Litvinoff, therefore, advised that the Council of the League should be invoked under Article 11, on the ground that there was danger of war, and that the League powers should consult together. He thought the sooner this was done, the better, as time might be very short.

He next proceeded to tell the French Chargé d'Affaires that staff conversations ought immediately to take place between Russia, France and Czechoslovakia as to the means and measures of giving assistance. The Soviet Union was ready to join in such staff conversations at once.

Fourthly, he recurred to his interview of March 17, of which you no doubt have a copy in the Foreign Office, advocating consultation among the peaceful Powers about the best method of preserving peace, with a view, perhaps, to a joint declaration, including the three great Powers concerned, France, Russia and Great Britain. He believed that the United States would give moral support to such a declaration.

All these statements were made on behalf of the Russian Government as what they think may be the best way of stopping a war. I pointed out that the news to-day seemed to indicate a more peaceful attitude on the part of Herr Hitler, and that I thought it was unlikely that the British Government would consider any further steps until or unless there was a fresh break-down in the Henlein-Benes negotiations in which the fault could not on any account be attributed to the Government of Czechoslovakia. We should not want to irritate Herr Hitler, if his mind was really turning towards a peaceful solution.

All this may, of course, have reached you through other channels, but I considered the declarations of M Litvinoff so important that I ought not to leave this to chance.[1]

Yours vy sincerely,
W

[1] For Article XI of the League Covenant, see page 441, note 1. Litvinoff's willingness to invoke Article XI was not in evidence nine days later, when he met Georges Bonnet in Geneva at a meeting of the League Council. According to Bonnet's account, Litvinoff again declared that the Soviet Government were ready to help Czechoslovakia; but he made it clear 'that no military action would be taken by Russia until France had first given assistance to Prague and until the League had persuaded Rumania to allow Soviet troops and aircraft to pass'. He took the line that the question of aircraft could not be separated from that of land forces, and was therefore not interested in the Rumanian Government's offer to 'shut their eyes' to aircraft. He repeated with emphasis that Soviet troops would not cross the Rumanian frontier without the consent of the Rumanian Government. Bonnet, for his part, told Litvinoff definitely 'that Rumania would refuse passage to Soviet land forces' (Georges Bonnet, *De Washington au Quai d'Orsay*, volume 1, Geneva, 1946, page 200).

Norman Hamilton[1] to Winston S. Churchill

(*Churchill papers: 8/610*)

2 September 1938   Evening Standard

Dear Mr Churchill,
    Very many thanks for your Diary paragraphs.[2]
    I used two yesterday and two today, and I hope to use the others as they come into the news.
    I should be grateful if you could let me have material in small doses of, say, three paragraphs, so that they will be topical and less likely to be crowded out of the Diary.

Winston S. Churchill to Richard Freund [3]

(*Churchill papers: 2/341*)

2 September 1938
Private & Confidential

My dear Sir,
    I am very much obliged to you for your most interesting and valuable letter which I have read and considered carefully. I have very strongly the feeling that the veto of France, Britain and Russia would certainly prevent the disaster of war. I hear from many quarters of grave technical hitches in

---

[1] Norman Hamilton, 1909–   . Entered journalism in Glasgow in the late 1920s. Worked later in Leeds. Joined the *Evening Standard* in 1933; Editor of the 'Londoner's Diary', 1936–9. Editor of the *Glasgow Evening News*, 1939–40. Joined the Royal Air Force, 1939; later Information Secretary to Brendan Bracken at the Ministry of Information. After the war he was first editor of the *Sunday Empire News*, then editor of the *Daily Graphic* and *Sunday Graphic*, 1947–8 (subsequently Editor-in-Chief).

[2] Norman Hamilton, the editor of the 'Londoner's Diary' in 1938, writes: 'I cannot take any credit for persuading Winston to contribute. I believe Randolph had to go for several months on military exercises, and that Beaverbrook arranged with Winston to "stand in" during his absence. I do not know if Winston was paid: I believe the arrangement was that Randolph's salary was continued in return for Winston's contributions' (*letter to the author, 21 April 1975*).

[3] Richard Henry Freund, 1900–   . Born in Berlin, of Czech origin and later nationality. Educated at Berlin and Heidelberg Universities. Came to England as a German newspaper correspondent, 1926; dismissed from his job, 1933; naturalized 1935. Published *Zero Hour: Policy of the Powers*, 1936 and *Watch Czechoslovakia*, 1937. Worked as a freelance for the *Yorkshire Post*; joined the *Manchester Guardian*, 1938; Financial Editor, 1939–65. Changed his name to Fry during the Second World War. An authority on Indian Affairs. CBE, 1965.

the German mobilisation; your figures seem to be upon the sanguine side, but in principle I view the position somewhat as you do.[1]

Winston S. Churchill to Lord Halifax

(Foreign Office papers: 371/21668)

3 September 1938
Very Private

My dear Edward,

The enclosed is from Colonel Tweed,[2] a highly competent officer & observer, who, as you know is on LG's staff. I thought it might be of interest, & report what he said to you. I can express no opinions about it. It certainly cuts both ways.[3]

Yours ever,
W

[1] In his letter, sent from the *Manchester Guardian* office in London on 30 August 1938, Richard Freund had pointed out that with the German partial mobilization of May 1938, 10 Divisions had been added to the 60 German and Austrian Divisions under arms, 'and it seems that these troops were not discharged afterwards'. Even putting aside 25 divisions for 'rear cover' on the French and Polish borders, this would leave Germany with 45 Divisions, or 700,000 men, as against a Czechoslovak force 'now permanently under arms' of some 25 Divisions, 'with a total of more than 400,000 men'. This did not give the Germans the 3 : 1 superiority which was the accepted ratio 'for the attack to crash through the defence to quick victory'. But, Freund noted: 'That problem they have solved by the present manoeuvres. If they have now 1,500,000 men under arms, they have the 3 to 1 superiority which is the minimum required for success against the Czechs even if no other power intervenes. But they have not quite got that, even now, as some 350,000 men must again be deducted for manning the French and Polish frontiers. The difference represents a risk which may be just small enough for the Germans to think it worth while to try their luck.' The current German manoeuvres, Freund added, 'have given Germany the first chance of attacking Czechoslovakia with any hope of quick success'.

[2] Thomas F. Tweed, 1890–1940. Educated at Liverpool Institute and Liverpool University. Liberal Agent for the Eccles Division of Lancashire. On active service, 1914–18 (MC). An underwriting member of Lloyd's. Secretary of the Manchester Liberal Federation, 1918–26. Chief Organizer of the Liberal Party, 1926–30, resigning in order 'to associate himself complete with Mr Lloyd George's opposition to the National Government'. Styled 'Chief of Staff and Political Adviser' to Lloyd George from 1926 until his death. Author of several novels, the most successful of which was *Rinehard*, which became extremely popular in the United States under the title *Gabriel Over the White House*, which was also the title of the film of the book.

[3] Tweed's report noted the 'complete breakdown of German mechanical units' during the German mobilization and commented that many of the battalions were 'largely composed of eighteen year old conscripts of unimpressive physique who found their equipment and packs irksome'. According to the report, between 40% and 50% were without rifles, while there was 'nothing in the attitude of the officers that suggested any tenseness or war excitement. It looked more like manoeuvres on a grand scale.' Michael Creswell noted, after reading the Foreign Office copy of the report, that confirmation 'that the mobilization was rendered necessary by shortcomings coming to light at the time of the seizure of Austria is interesting' *(Foreign Office papers: 371/21668)*.

Harold Nicolson: diary

(*Nicolson papers*)

4 September 1938

. . . Bob[1] also told me that he had persuaded Winston to see Halifax and to urge that some show of friendship or solidarity should be made with Russia. Halifax made no great objection.

Lord Halifax to Winston S. Churchill

(*Churchill papers: 2/331*)

5 September 1938   Foreign Office

My dear Winston,

A line to thank you for your letter of the 3rd September which I found on my return to the Office yesterday. I do not at present feel that action of the kind proposed under Article 11 would be helpful, but I shall keep it in my mind. For the present I think, as you indicated, we must review the situation in the light of the report with which Henlein has returned from Berchtesgaden. This I have not yet seen, but Gwatkin[2] telegraphed last night to say that on the whole it was satisfactory. I do not think we can build too much on this at present and the situation remains very anxious.

Yours ever,
Edward

Malcolm MacDonald to Winston S. Churchill

(*Churchill papers: 8/596*)

5 September 1938   Colonial Office

Dear Winston Churchill,

It was very kind of you to send me a copy of the last volume of 'Marlborough',[3] and I am delighted and proud to have it inscribed in your own

---

[1] Robert Boothby.

[2] Frank Trelawny Arthur Ashton-Gwatkin, 1889–1976. Educated at Eton and Balliol College, Oxford. Entered the Consular Service, Far East, 1913. Member of the British Delegation at the Washington Disarmament Conference, 1921–2; the Imperial Economic Conference at Ottawa, 1932; the World Monetary and Economic Conference, London, 1933; the Munich Conference, 1938. Counsellor of Embassy, Moscow, 1929. Member of Runciman's mission to Czechoslovakia, 1938. Policy Adviser, Ministry of Economic Warfare, 1939–40. Assistant Under-Secretary, Foreign Office, 1940–7. Novelist, under the *nom de plume* John Paris.

[3] Churchill's fourth Marlborough volume had been published by George G. Harrap & Co Ltd on 2 September 1938. The main edition was of 10,000 copies, with 155 copies of the limited, specially bound edition.

hand. I was enthralled by the first three volumes, and shall eagerly seize opportunities to read to the finish of the story. You must feel happy at seeing the set of volumes now standing completed, on your bookshelf. As for the rest of us, you have left us all gasping again at your amazing industry and productivity, and I should like to join in the chorus of congratulations.

With very many thanks,
Yours sincerely,
Malcolm MacDonald

Sir Terence O'Connor to Winston S. Churchill

(*Churchill papers: 8/596*)

5 September 1938

My dear Winston,

The last volume of Marlborough arrived here this morning and I feel intensely grateful for your kind thought. I had looked forward greatly to reading it ever since I finished the last volume. I am sure that the whole book will always survive as one of the most astonishing monuments of industry and care at a time when the author's other activities were themselves more than a normal human frame ought to be asked to undertake!

I feel much happier lately about the Foreign field. Edward H & Neville between them seem to be acting well & firmly and Neville's réclame in France is remarkable. It looks as though Hitler's bluff has at last been called & that one can look forward to the day when we shall be able to tell him, in the only kind of language a Hun can understand, exactly where he gets off. Until that moment there never can be any enduring peace in the world.

I hope that you are well & enjoying comparative rest. The AG[1] is away & I am holding the fort for a week or so with intermittent visits to London—a kind life with just the right quota of work, reading and golf. Last night I had to read some despatches of yours on NW Rhodesia, written years ago.

With again ever so many thanks & all kind thoughts.

Yours ever,
Terence

---

[1] The Attorney-General, Sir Donald Somervell (see page 485, note 2).

James Watt to Winston S. Churchill

(*Churchill papers: 2/311*)

5 September 1938   Manchester
Personal

My dear Mr Churchill,

Thank you a thousand times for so kindly inscribing your fourth volume of Marlborough and his times for me.

It is a delightful possession to have all four volumes signed by their author.

This French and English alliance needs strengthening on the lines you have suggested all along. 'If we are to have an offensive and defensive alliance, why not say so?'

How can there be a solution short of one side giving in?

Can you imagine the Irish Treaty ever having been signed if Ireland had been joined by land to a hostile continent?

In the end they will come to your point of view as they did in regard to defence and of course that will be your unforgivable sin—to have been right and not told lies like Baldwin.

I am trying to join the Territorials at the mature age of 35 and with a weight of far too many stone. It is very difficult for the middle aged to get in!

I read Liberalism and the Social Problem[1] again in the train. What fools our Party have always been. They will not take the trouble to understand what the ordinary people in the street want.

I saw in the paper that you saw Lord Halifax at the Foreign Office and hope you convinced him about the need for our making a clear stand for the balance of power. After all Germany only has to 'join the Club' if she wants to have a real reign of peace.

I wonder how long it will be before the approaching conflict becomes war?

With renewed thanks,

Yours sincerely,

James Watt

[1] Published in 1909, *Liberalism and the Social Problem* contained extracts from twenty-one speeches made by Churchill between 5 April 1906 and 9 October 1909. These speeches set out his principal social reform ideas on such matters as unemployment and national insurance, land tax and income tax, and the 'constitutional menace' of the veto powers of the House of Lords.

Sir Edward Marsh to Winston S. Churchill

(*Churchill papers: 4/2*)

5 September 1938

My dear Winston,

Ever so many thanks for the book—it's beautifully produced as usual, what delightful illustrations! You must be pining for a bad notice, for a change.[1]

I wish I knew what is going to happen.

From,
Eddie

Norman Hamilton to Winston S. Churchill

(*Churchill papers: 8/610*)

5 September 1938   Evening Standard

Dear Mr Churchill,

Many thanks for the Diary material which I received today.

I used the paragraphs on Lord Lloyd and the Epping newspaper and I have filed the remainder for the future.

The paragraph on Lord Rayleigh[2] is unfortunately too far out of date. I have to try to keep the Diary ahead of the news as far as possible, or at least abreast of it.[3]

Yours sincerely,
N. F. Hamilton

---

[1] The fourth volume of Churchill's *Marlborough: His Life and Times* was published on 2 September 1938. Reviewing it in the *Evening Standard* on the previous day, Horace Thorogood wrote: 'It is hard to imagine Mr Winston Churchill's history of "Marlborough and His Times" being superseded by any future work on the same associated subjects. In its historical exposition, its battle pictures, its animated human interest and its literary distinction it is a book that belongs with the foremost of its class,' The review in *The Times* on 2 September 1938 commented: 'Buffeted by tremendous storms up to the very entrance to its haven, Mr Churchill's great vessel finally drops anchor in calm and quietude.'

[2] Robert John Strutt, 1875–1947. Educated at Eton and Trinity College, Cambridge. Professor of Physics, Imperial College of Science, 1908–20. Succeeded his father as 4th Baron Rayleigh, 1919. Foreign Secretary of the Royal Society, 1929–34. Chairman of the Governing Body of Imperial College of Science and Technology, 1936–47. President of the British Association, 1938.

[3] Norman Hamilton, editor of the 'Londoner's Diary', writes: 'As I remember, Winston was conscientious in doing this strange job and every time I failed to use a paragraph I feared retribution from Beaverbrook or Winston. But whatever he thought in private Winston was always considerate to an awed young man' (*letter to the author, 21 April 1975*).

Winston S. Churchill: draft paragraphs for the 'Londoner's Diary'

(*Churchill papers: 8/610*)

5 September 1938

Lord Rayleigh was quite right when, in his speech to the British Association, he described how Sir William Roberts-Austen,[1] Assayer to the Royal
Mint, discovered in 1900 a gas of a deadly character. Lord Rayleigh was,
however, in error in stating that Sir William had no idea of the malignant
military use to which this gas could be put. On the contrary, he was extremely
miserable at making the discovery. He fully realised the shocking consequences if it should be used in war. For a long time he hesitated whether he
should not obliterate what he had discovered. Upon the whole, he considered
that his duty to science should prevail. After all, we could not anticipate in
1900 either the ugly direction in which thought would progress, or its speed.
He, therefore, decided to yield the fruits of his labours to science. We may
recall that Lord Dundonald, the great Cochrane, buried his secrets in the
bosom of the Cabinet, and how his grandson,[2] in the war of 1914, revealed it
to the Admiralty. It was poison-gas originated by sulphur, and would undoubtedly have been decisive in Crimean days.

*   *   *

There was a much greater stiffness and formality among politicians in
Victorian times than at the present day. Nowadays everyone buzzes along
quite happily and points of attitude and bearing are very rarely defined. A
thick veneer of civility and geniality covers most social and political relationships. But the previous generation were much more abrupt and decisive.
They seldom hesitated to say the direct unpleasant thing. Lord Kimberley,[3]

[1] William Chandler Roberts-Austen, 1843–1902. Educated at the Royal School of Mines.
Chemist and Assayer to the Royal Mint from 1870 until his death. Fellow of the Royal
Society, 1875. Professor of Metallurgy at the Royal School of Mines from 1880 until his
death. Knighted, 1899.

[2] Douglas Mackinnon Baillie Hamilton, 1852–1935. Succeeded his father as 12th Earl of
Dundonald, 1885. On active service at Khartoum (1898) and South Africa (1899–1900).
Promoted Major-General for Distinguished Service in the Field, 1900. In 1914 he brought
Churchill (then First Lord of the Admiralty), a secret formula devised by his great-grand-
father, Archibald Cochrane, 9th Earl of Dundonald 1748–1831, Rear-Admiral of the United
Kingdom, of whom *Burke's Peerage and Baronetage* commented (London, 1978): 'The Earl's
long life was principally devoted to scientific objects chiefly with the view of benefiting the
commercial and manufacturing interests. Great industries have since been founded on his
discoveries.'

[3] John Wodehouse, 1st Earl of Kimberley, served as Secretary of State for the Colonies
from 1870 to 1874 and again from 1880 to 1882. He was also three times Secretary of State
for India (1882–5, 1886 and 1892–4) and Secretary of State for Foreign Affairs (1894–5).
His grandson, Jack Wodehouse, who was Churchill's private secretary in 1924, was killed in
an air raid on 16 April 1941. The Kimberley county seat was Arwenack Manor House,
Falmouth, Cornwall.

Mr Gladstone's Colonial Secretary, from whom Kimberley takes its name, was a man very aloof. We may judge his methods and manners by the following incident. Lord Spencer,[1] a Cabinet colleague of old association and a nobleman of equal rank, wrote to him one day that he was speaking in the neighbourhood of (Lord Kimberley's country house—please furnish), and suggested that as there were some pressing public matters to discuss, he would like to dine and sleep. 'Please do no such thing,' replied Lord Kimberley.

* * *

Henry Chaplin,[2] a kind of political forerunner of Sir Henry Page-Croft, was a man who preserved this old-fashioned mode of precision and formality. In conversation one day in the Autumn of 1914, he was walking with Sir Edward Grey through the passage from the House of Lords to the Central Lobby of the House of Commons, after listening to a debate on Blockade in the Upper Chamber. Grey, in the easy manner of those days, said: 'Looking back upon things, I am very glad the Convention of London did not go through.' Chaplin immediately bridled. He said: 'You say this to me. I presume I am entitled to make your statement public.' Grey replied: 'No. We are talking privately,' but rejoined Chaplin 'You have VOLUNTEERED this statement to me.' I had this story from the man who heard the words uttered, and he told me that he never had before realised the full implications of the words 'VOLUNTEERED a statement', which evidently was a term of art among the by-gone generation. The question certainly deserves consideration; whether we ought to be more robust or more, shall we say Baldwinian. There is a certain sloppiness invading public life which may very easily manifest itself in a marked decline of the will to live, and still more of the will to rule.

* * *

Everyone knows that in the Boer War the City Imperial Volunteers were described as Chamberlain's innocent victims,[3] but as we have frequently

---

[1] Churchill's kinsman, John, 5th Earl Spencer, who was Lord Lieutenant of Ireland 1868 to 1874 and 1882 to 1885, and First Lord of the Admiralty from 1892 to 1895, as well as a member of the Prince of Wales's Council. In 1981 his great-niece, Lady Diana Spencer, married Charles, Prince of Wales.

[2] Henry Chaplin, 1840–1923. Educated at Harrow and Christ Church. Conservative MP, 1868–1906 and 1907–16. Chancellor of the Duchy of Lancaster, 1885–6. President of the Board of Agriculture, 1886–92; of the Local Government Board, 1895–1900. Created Viscount, 1916. A keen sportsman, famed for his prowess in the hunting field; nicknamed the Squire.

[3] Not only Joseph Chamberlain, but also Churchill himself, had been the butt of such a comment, for in 1914 the Royal Naval Division soldiers who were sent, most of them without any prior training, to the siege of Antwerp, were known as 'Churchill's innocent victims' (but also, more kindly, as 'Churchill's lambs').

pointed out in these pages, the mild Mr Baldwin went off into an ever-honoured retirement with a bunch of scalps dangling from his girdle. It is, therefore, interesting to know how some of these mutilated victims are bearing themselves at the present time. Lord Lloyd has just taken his 'Wings'. This is a test of some quality.

(Here, if you like, insert some details of the Test, which can be readily obtained from the Aero Club or other authorities). This is unusual for a man of fifty-eight. At the same time, as Chairman of the British Council and head of the Navy League, he discharges an extremely valuable and important function.

* * *

An old member of the House was telling me the other day about Lord Lloyd in the House of Commons before the War. He was one of the brightest of the younger Tory Members who sat below the Gangway and took a highly-combative part in the Opposition to Mr Asquith's Liberal and Radical Government. He, of course, being of military age, went out to the War at the beginning; served in the East, and was with Lawrence during much of his campaigns. He, therefore, naturally fell out of the political sphere and others, whose duties were of a less arduous character, gained precedence in Party estimation. [He did not figure in that noble chronicle 'Deeds That Won the MVO'.][1] It is pleasant, however, to note that after his distinguished governorships abroad, he still preserves an effective and untiring vitality.

* * *

Now that things appear to be taking a more favourable turn in the European arena, one wonders whether Sir John Simon's Lanark speech was really quite as successful as it had to be made out to be. A friend whom I met in Pall Mall made the comment: 'Enough to encourage the Czechs to obstinacy and not enough to discourage the Germans from violence.' Of course, it is very difficult for Ministers to make pronouncements of exactly the right poise. It is always a problem to use enough dynamite to blow in a door without blowing down the building. On the whole, however, it may be said that if Sir John did little good, at any rate, he did no harm. That already is a lot.

* * *

From all over the country reports reach me that the farmers continue to be horribly upset by Mr Chamberlain's Birmingham speech. In the Epping Division they have even started a new paper, the central feature of which is

---

[1] Churchill deleted this sentence in the draft diary entry. Churchill would often jest that one day he would write a book entitled 'Deeds that Won the MVO'.

the championship of food production. In this case, they are not likely to come in conflict with the local Member, who has frequently declared that the mobility of the British Navy depends upon its being largely relieved of the preoccupation of convoying foodships in time of War, and that we ought to have certainly six months, and preferably one year's, food supply in the Island—either growing in the fields or stored in the barns or warehouses.

*   *   *

Although the report of the Sandys' case is long-delayed and the issues are over-clouded by larger matters, it is well to repeat and inculcate the definite principle upon which Parliament, the Press and the Public will unite, namely, that the Official Secrets Act was intended for spies, crooks, traitors and traffickers in official information, and should never be invoked unless there is a prima facie case on these lines against anyone, be he journalist, Member of Parliament, or merely man-in-the-street.

Brigadier-General Sir James Edmonds to Winston S. Churchill
(*Churchill papers: 8/596*)

6 September 1938

My dear, even very dear, Mr Churchill,

It was kind of you to remember me and send me Volume IV of your Duke John inscribed, to complete the set. I value it greatly not only as a splendid piece of English literature, but also as a token that I count among your friends.

Yours sincerely,
'Archimedes' Edmonds

I hope to send you 1916 Volume ii, which completes the Somme battles, in a couple of months or so. I am reading the first galley proofs.[1]

---

[1] Sir James Edmonds' own life's work, which took him more than twenty-five years to complete, was the multi-volume official war history, *Military Operations: France and Belgium*, of which he personally wrote the following eleven volumes: 1914 volume 1 (published in 1922), 1914 volume 2 (1925), 1915 volume 1 (1927), 1915 volume 2 (1928), 1916 volume 1 (1931), 1917 volume 2 (1949) and 1918 volumes 1 to 5 (1935–45). In 1951 he published *A Short History of World War 1*.

Sir Maurice Hankey to Winston S. Churchill
(*Churchill papers: 8/596*)

6 September 1938

My dear Winston,

I returned early this morning from a business meeting at Paris to find a delightful surprise awaiting me—Vol IV of Marlborough. I shall read it with the same avidity as earlier volumes. I congratulate you on your wonderful persistence in completing this great and invaluable contribution to history.

I found Paris, outwardly, incredibly normal and calm, but it is the calmness of resignation. The provinces, I gathered, are even more anxious than Paris. A young artillery reserve officer, who was my companion in the train last night, and who was expecting to be called up any moment, told me that at a race meeting he was at on Saturday, an event for officers on the active list only had to be cancelled because, just before the meeting, they had all been called back to their regiments. '*C'est effrayant*' he kept saying. Some well-informed people I met, however, thought we should tide over this crisis, but only by creating conditions in Czecho-Slovakia which would make an even graver crisis inevitable next year.

Yours ever,
M. P. A. Hankey

Winston S. Churchill to Sir Kingsley Wood
(*Churchill papers: 25/16*)

6 September 1938

1. Aeroplanes move so fast that it will always be difficult, especially at night, for defending planes to make contact with them and for ordinary anti-aircraft fire to bring them down, unless the attacker is tied to some pre-determined course by the necessity of bombing some small known target. The menace of the bomber will be defeated by developing methods of rendering regions of the air unhealthy, if not fatal to hostile aircraft passing through them. If this can be done over a sufficient space, even a rough knowledge of the enemy's future course will suffice.

2. The simplest mode of doing this is the 'aerial mine'. This can be anchored, as in kite-balloons, or floating. Since kite-balloons have apparently not been developed in such a way as to enable them to rise above the ceiling of modern bombers, the floating mine, which can be placed in position at any

desired height by means of aeroplanes, shells or possibly rockets should be developed.

A few ounces of high explosive will damage an aeroplane to such an extent as to render its return to its base unlikely. Supported by a parachute or possibly a small balloon and hanging at the end of a wire of appropriate length, comparatively few mines of this nature will be enough to form a curtain impassable to aeroplanes without grave risk. (About one hundred such mines, weighing, say, 50 pounds altogether, spread in a curtain of a mile width and a thousand feet deep, would bring down one aeroplane in five flying through that zone.)

If the mines are to be laid by aeroplane, all the pilot need do is to get into position within a mile in width and a thousand feet in height some five minutes before the enemy's arrival, an infinitely easier task than actually making contact with him. The same applies if the mines are laid by gun or rocket.

3. There are, of course, other methods which may possibly be simpler in certain cases though their feasibility cannot be guaranteed with the same certainty as that of the aerial mine described.

It is not impossible that one could produce over a period of some scores of seconds, regions in which up-currents of such violence occurred that a high speed aeroplane meeting them at a small angle of incidence would be damaged, if not destroyed. If an aeroplane moving at a low angle of incidence at 200 mph, ie 300 feet a second, struck an up-current of say, 30 feet a second, the effective angle of incidence would be increased by nearly 6 degrees, which, with some wing sections at any rate, would put a huge if not fatal strain upon the machine. A comparatively few pounds of weight of suitable substance combining with oxygen either carried with the fuel or perhaps better taken from the air, can produce sufficient heat to cause a region of hot air many scores of feet in diameter. This hot air will naturally rise and at the end of some seconds, obtain a considerable velocity. A few comparatively simple experiments would show whether an up-current of sufficient size and velocity would persist for a long enough period to render this method effective. All one can say at this stage is that ample energy could be made available and that a prima facie case for the experiments seems to exist.

Winston S. Churchill to Nellie Romilly[1]

(Churchill papers: 2/331)

6 September 1938

I was shocked to see the enclosed in the Daily Express, and on making enquiries I have no doubt how this breach of confidence passed.[2] You ought not to have repeated Clemmie's conversation, which was purely private, in any circumstances without permission. In this case Dr B came under the strict guarantees of secrecy which I gave him personally, and the statement and the visit attributed to him may bring upon him serious consequences.

The matter causes me very great anxiety.

Nellie Romilly to Winston S. Churchill

(Churchill papers: 2/331)

7 September 1938

Dearest Winston,

I am so deeply grieved at what I did. Please forgive me is all I can say. It was an absolutely thoughtless act. It has made me very unhappy, that I could act in any way badly towards you.

Yours,
Nellie R

Winston S. Churchill to William Chenery

(Churchill papers: 8/604)

8 September 1938

Dear Mr Chenery,

I send you herewith my third attempt at the Irish article. I have practically re-written it, and in a rather more hopeful vein,—not as a result of the Irish position being better, but rather that other matters have become worse.

---

[1] Nellie Hozier, 1888–1957. Clementine Churchill's sister. Served as a nurse in Belgium, 1914. Captured by the Germans, but released almost immediately. In 1915 she married Colonel Bertram Romilly.

[2] On September 6 an item in the *Daily Express* gossip column noted: 'Latest of Winston Churchill's interesting guests has been German ex-Chancellor Bruening. He lunched with Churchill at Chartwell; seemed depressed by letter he had just received (by "underground") from Germany; begged Churchill to influence British Government to "speak plainly to Hitler".'

Will you kindly let me know what you would like for the sixth article? I would suggest something like: 'Is the Air a decisive weapon?', or 'How will the next War differ from the last?' I could write for you very easily on these subjects, which seem not irrelevant to present conditions.

Winston S. Churchill to a correspondent: unsent letter

(*Churchill papers: 2/331*)

8 September 1938

Dear Sir,

I am not at all surprised at your uneasiness lest British influence should be used to press the Czechs into making a virtual surrender of the essentials of their independence and sovereignty, and of the democratic freedom which their people enjoy. I cannot myself feel, however, that either Lord Runciman or the British Government would go beyond what they believe not only to be fair and just, but moreover workable and lasting.

It appears that the Czechoslovak Government are willing to make important and real concessions to their German-speaking fellow-countrymen, and if these commend themselves to world approval, I am of the opinion that a very definite situation would be placed before all the nations who desire the preservation of peace, and that they would find a meeting-ground upon which they might with good heart take a stand for freedom, should there be an outbreak of violence.

I was reassured by the official statement issued yesterday that the suggestion in The Times leading article, that the Czechoslovak Government should make 'Czechoslovakia a more homogeneous State by the secession of that fringe of alien population who are contiguous to the nation with which they are united by race', in no way represents the views of His Majesty's Government. Such a proposal, if entertained, would have the effect of handing over to the German Nazis the whole of the mountain defence line which marks the ancient boundaries of Bohemia, and was specially preserved to the Czechoslovak State as a vital safeguard of its national existence.

In taking the unusual course of dissociating themselves so promptly from this suggestion, made by an eminent and friendly newspaper, His Majesty's Government seem to make it clear that they would not countenance proposals which go so far beyond what reason and justice demand.

Professor G. M. Trevelyan to Winston S. Churchill
(*Churchill papers: 8/596*)

8 September 1938

Dear Winston,

Thank you very much indeed for so kindly sending me the last volume. I already know its excellence. I most heartily congratulate you on the completion of this great work, a monument *aere perennius*[1] both to yourself and to your glorious ancestor. If you ever undertake another *big* work of an historical character let it be *Napoleon* in two volumes (no more).

Your very truly,
G. M. Trevelyan

Neville Chamberlain to Winston S. Churchill
(*Churchill papers: 8/596*)

8 September 1938   10 Downing Street

My dear Winston,

On my return this morning I was very pleased to find that you had sent me the final volume of your great work on Marlborough.

Your inscription is appropriate though perhaps if I were translated to the eighteenth century I might think it was not a much 'better 'ole' than the one in which I find myself. But to read about it in your vivid pages will be a pleasure which I promise myself whenever I can see a prospect of undisturbed tranquillity, for the necessary time.

Meanwhile I send my grateful thanks and am always
Yours sincerely,
Neville Chamberlain

Anthony Eden to Winston S. Churchill
(*Churchill papers: 8/596*)

9 September 1938
Private

My dear Winston,

Thank you so much for your letter and for sending me the enclosed, which I return as I am not sure whether you have another copy.

---

[1] From Horace, *Odes* (III, 30, 1), where the poet expresses his confidence in the eternity of his written work. 'I have created a monument,' he says, 'whose days will last longer than bronze.'

I arrived back here yesterday, and only wish that I could pretend to find the news more cheerful. But I have found the Fourth Volume of Marlborough. Thank you very much for it. I propose to dive into it this very evening and seek to forget in its pages the haunting apprehensions of the present days.

Yours ever,
Anthony Eden

Eleanor Rathbone to Winston S. Churchill
(*Churchill papers: 2/331*)

10 September 1938

Dear Mr Churchill,

May I say how relieved I was to see that you are still in this country & had been to the Foreign Office. Everyone I meet—mostly not of your party—wonders what you are thinking about the Government's attitude and whether you do not favour a more plain-spoken warning to Hitler. Hearing nothing, we are left wondering whether you too believe that our military position is too weak for us to venture on that. Hitherto, only the Trade Union Congress of the Labour Party have spoken out in a way calculated to make Hitler believe that England may possibly mean business.

If you did feel able to say anything of the same sort, and especially if Mr Eden did too, I believe it would rally opinion in the country as nothing else would.

There is a great longing for leadership and even those who are far apart from you in general politics realize that you are the one man who has combined full realization of the dangers of our military position with belief in collective international action against aggression. And if we fail again now, will there ever be another chance.

Excuse my butting in. But as an admirer and an outsider to political parties who hears a good deal of talk from the undistributed middle of public opinion, I cannot help fearing that your silence and Mr Eden's may be misunderstood.

Yours sincerely,
Eleanor Rathbone

Sir Samuel Hoare: recollections

(*'Nine Troubled Years'*)

11 September 1938

When the talk ended and we left the Cabinet Room, we found Churchill waiting in the hall. He had come to demand an immediate ultimatum to Hitler. He was convinced it was our last chance of stopping a landslide, and according to his information, which was directly contrary to our own, both the French and the Russians were ready for an offensive against Germany.

Winston S. Churchill to Lord Moyne[1]

(*Churchill papers: 2/331*)

11 September 1938

I am most grateful to you for your invitation, and if it is humanly possible, I will try to join you at Antigua before Christmas.

Will you tell Evelyn[2] how kind I think it of her to leave behind the painting apparatus. I will send to the 'Rosaura' before she sails a small package of canvases and painting equipment.

I look forward so much to this interlude of sunshine and peace. Alas, a cloud of uncertainty overhangs all plans at the present time, as I cannot pretend to be at all hopeful of the outcome. Owing to the neglect of our defences and the mishandling of the German problem in the last five years, we seem to be very near the bleak choice between War and Shame. My feeling is that we shall choose Shame, and then have War thrown in a little later on even more adverse terms than at present.

Clemmie is looking forward so much to her trip. I think it will do her a great deal of good. She needs a thorough change and you know what a good traveller by sea she is.

---

[1] Walter Edward Guinness, 1880–1944. 3rd son of the 1st Earl of Iveagh. Educated at Eton. Wounded while on active service in South Africa, 1900–1. Conservative MP for Bury St Edmunds, 1907–31. On active service, 1914–18 (despatches thrice). Under-Secretary of State for War, 1922–3. Financial Secretary, Treasury, 1923–4 and 1924–5. Minister of Agriculture and Fisheries, 1925–9. Created Baron Moyne, 1932. A director of Arthur Guinness, Son, and Company, brewers. Elected to the Other Club, 1934. Secretary of State for the Colonies, 1941–2. Minister Resident, Cairo, 1944 (where he was murdered by Jewish terrorists).

[2] Lady Evelyn Hilda Stuart Erskine, youngest daughter of the 14th Earl of Buchan. She married Lord Moyne in 1903, and died in July 1939.

Cabinet minutes
(*Cabinet papers: 23/95*)

12 September 1938

The Secretary of State for Foreign Affairs reported that, with the Prime Minister, he had seen Mr Winston Churchill on the previous day. Mr Churchill's proposition was that we should tell Germany that if she set foot in Czechoslovakia we should at once be at war with her. Mr Churchill agreed that this line of action was in advance of the line of action which he had proposed some two or three weeks earlier, but he thought that by taking it we should incur no added risk.

Sir Henry Strakosch to Winston S. Churchill
(*Churchill papers: 8/596*)

12 September 1938

My dear Winston,

It was a delightful surprise to receive your letter & the complete set of your 'Marlborough', which you were good enough to present to me. I cannot tell you how much I appreciate your kind thought. I shall treasure your 'Marlborough' as I treasure all your other writings.

These are indeed fateful times. They call for vision & courage—gifts which you possess in such abundant measure. I am confident that the people of this country—indeed of the whole democratic world—would face with vastly greater confidence the grave issues with which they are confronted if they knew that you were taking the active & prominent part in the government of this country which is its due & to which you are so richly entitled.

Winston S. Churchill to Arthur Mann
(*Churchill papers: 2/331*)

12 September 1938

My dear Mr Mann,

Thank you very much for your letter of September 1, which I am ashamed to say I have only now found time to answer.

We are, I think, almost in complete agreement upon the past. I take the very gravest view of the immediate future. It seems to me we are having the worst of both worlds, namely, being deeply involved in war, should it come, and yet not making our weight felt while time remains to avert it.

No one can tell what the coming week will bring forth, but I can hardly see any solution that will not be grievous.

Pray keep in touch with me.

Winston S. Churchill to Dr Colijn
(Churchill papers: 8/596)

12 September 1938

I send you now the fourth and last volume of 'Marlborough'; and I hope you will feel that I have done justice to the grand effort of the Republic in the final stages of the War of the Spanish Succession.

You accepted my criticisms of Slangenberg and the Dutch Deputies in respect of the year 1705; but some of your countrymen were vexed at them. I have always resolved to be unsparing in my censures of my own countrymen in those times, and I think you will feel on reading this book that I have made this good.

It will, I daresay, be a relief to you to travel back from the twentieth century into the eighteenth. The horrible position into which the world has got is all due to lack of foresight and courage on the part of public men; and now perhaps the unfortunate peoples of the world may be hurled against each other in a meaningless and murderous confusion, whereas a firm, merciful and coherent action by the overwhelming forces on our side would have produced, and might still produce peace, progress, and a prosperity unobtainable in former ages.

Winston S. Churchill to the Duke of Windsor
(Churchill papers: 1/324)

12 September 1938

Sir,

I now send Your Royal Highness the final volume of 'Marlborough'.

Your ancestor, King George III, said to Mr Gibbon, who presented him with the fifth or sixth volume of his history of 'The Decline and Fall': 'What, Mr Gibbon, another great big volume. Always scribble, scribble, scribble!' Alas, I fear, Sir, that you might well say this to me.

I look forward to the day when I shall see these four volumes reunited on the shelves of Fort Belvedere.

I hope that we shall meet again soon.

I am very sorry not to be able to come to Maxine's this year, but anyone can see the reason.

Sir, things are going very badly, and I fear they are going to become much worse.

Your devoted, humble servant

General Sir Bindon Blood to Winston S. Churchill

(*Churchill papers: 8/596*)

13 September 1938   59 Cadogan Square,
London SW1

Dear Winston,

We have just returned from my son-in-law's place in Warwickshire, where we spent five pleasant weeks, & I was delighted to find here your handsome present of the 4th Volume of your biography of Marlborough, with the delightful inscription inside the cover. I have already had a part of the first chapter read to me, besides the Preface.

I really have great difficulty in thanking you sufficiently for this delightful present, the invaluable result of your ten years' hard work, which clears up many mysteries which have hitherto puzzled us, & will provide me with pleasant employment for a long time.

With my best salaams to Mrs Churchill & yourself, I am,

ever your affectionate General,
B. Blood

Josiah Wedgwood to Winston S. Churchill

(*Churchill papers: 2/331*)

14 September 1938

My dear Winston,

Do our folk really mean business? They seem to have seen everyone but you, & it is inconceivable to me that they should actually be facing up to war if they have not called you in,—inconceivable that we should not be disgraced without you.

You must have lots of good ideas. I am thinking of Northern Spain, Indian factories, the Baltic, Roumania, enlisting Jewish refugees, Minorca, Turkish co-operation,—& 100 things. Not one of these people had anything to do with the direction of the last war. They are babies, if not cowards. You or God will have to help if this country is now to be saved.

I shall be in town this week end. Can't you see me? Phone Whitehall 9060, Extension 60.

Yours ever & more than ever,
Josiah C. Wedgwood

Randolph Churchill to Winston S. Churchill
(Churchill papers: 1/325)

15 September 1938   Cavalry Club

Dear Papa—

I'm just off to Aldershot—to learn the goosestep. I'm afraid the fun & zest has gone out of my military career.

Please in future emulate my deep-seated distrust of Chamberlain & all his works & colleagues. There is no infamy of which they are not capable. When they are with you they are careful to talk in honourable terms; if I have read them more truly it is because their underlings are less discreet with me.

Three days ago we were insulted; now we have the submission you have so often predicted.[1] Bless you & please in future steer your own course un-contaminated by contact with these disreputable men.

Your loving son,
Randolph

Commander Owen to Winston S. Churchill
(Churchill papers: 8/596)

15 September 1938

Dear Mr Churchill,

I have waited until I had time to read some of Marl IV before writing to thank you for sending me a copy. I am enjoying it immensely. You make the difficult political part so plain, that I believe I like it the best of all, though it is hard to say which of the four volumes is the most engrossing.

---

[1] On the afternoon of 15 September 1939 Neville Chamberlain had flown to see Hitler. On the following morning Churchill telegraphed to Dr Revesz, in Paris, for distribution to the European papers. 'The personal intervention of Mr Chamberlain,' he said, 'and his flight to see Herr Hitler, does not at all alter the gravity of the issues at stake. We must hope that it does not foreshadow another complete failure of the Western Democracies to withstand the threats and violence of Nazi Germany.'

Politics and your other cares and interests notwithstanding, I suspect you have some feeling of loss now that the work is done—There is no excuse for a misunderstanding of Marlborough any longer. I am very glad you have brought out the personal and domestic side so fully—eg the letter from the Godolphin grandson.[1]

What a fine fellow Matthew Bishop [2] was to have in one's ship or regiment—I hope there are plenty like him about to-day.

Yours sincerely,
J. H. Owen

Lord Hailsham to Winston S. Churchill
(*Churchill papers: 8/596*)

15 September 1938   Privy Council Office
Whitehall

My dear Winston,

Once more I have to thank you for a very welcome and generous present. I found on my return to London the fourth volume of your 'Life of Marlborough' awaiting me.

I think you know how much I appreciate the gift. I regard you as probably the most brilliant writer of English prose in the present day and I always enjoy your books; but apart from that you have again shown your friendship to me by giving me a copy and writing my name in it.

Yours ever,
Douglas

---

[1] On 9 August 1711, Marlborough's grandson had written to him: 'I hope you will go on in winning of Battles, taking of towns & beating & routing the French in all manner of ways, and then come home with a good peace & look back upon those glorious toils . . .'

[2] Private (afterwards Corporal) Matthew Bishop, of whom Churchill wrote: 'A young man with some property and an insatiable desire for warlike adventure, he had served afloat till the end of 1704. When his ship was paid off he addressed his captain, with whom he had much credit, as follows: "Sir, I have a favour to beg . . . You know, sir, my behaviour hitherto . . . I am of a roving nature; and ever since I heard of the Action that was performed on the Danube by the Duke of Marlborough, I promised myself, in God's name, that if nothing prevented I would go and assist the Duke, for so noble a General cannot have too many good men; and as my inclinations are already with him, I hope your Honour will not deny me; There have been many instances that our enemies' defeat has been owing to the success of one blow, and it may be my fortune to strike that lucky blow; and if you please to release me I am determined to stand to all events, for I find there will be nothing more done at sea, and I will go where I can be employed, for I have . . . no ambition but to carry arms, so that I may call myself a Man of War and an Arms Bearer." The captain consenting, Matthew obtained his discharge from the Navy, took to himself a wife, upon whom he settled all his property, and set forth in Flanders as a private in Webb's regiment. Thenceforward he served in all the bloodiest fighting, and his account of his ordeal at Malplaquet is of high value.'

A. E. Woodward Nutt [1] to Sir Kingsley Wood

(*Air Ministry papers: 19/25*)

15 September 1938

I have the following comments to make on Mr Churchill's Memorandum.

(1) AERIAL MINES

Aerial mines have been the subject of theoretical and experimental work by the Air Ministry Scientific Research Staff, in consultation with the Committee for the Scientific Survey of Air Defence, since June, 1935. A statement of the work done up to June 1938 is attached for your information. Experimental work is still proceeding.

Briefly, our work has established that aerial mines of the original form suggested by Mr Churchill, Professor Lindemann and others in 1935–36 are not likely to be a useful form of defence; but with increasing accuracy of interception it is conceivable that another form of aerial mine may be useful under exceptional conditions, and experimental work with this form of mine is, therefore, in active progress.

Mr Churchill's remarks in the second and third paragraphs of section 2 of his memorandum give an entirely false picture of the position. We have established that an aerial mine of the parachute–cable–bomb type, if it is to have a reasonable likelihood of inflicting lethal damage upon an aircraft which strikes it, will weigh many times as much as Mr Churchill assumes. Further, the effectiveness of aerial mines is linked up with the accuracy with which enemy aircraft can be located and their course and height foretold, and many times the number of mines suggested by Mr Churchill would, in fact, be required to ensure bringing down one aeroplane out of five.

Aerial mines of the balloon–cable–bomb type are not suitable for release from aircraft, and if released from the ground the quantities required are out of all proportion to their possible destructive effect. The laying of aerial minefields by rocket or gun is not practicable, since no means have yet been discovered of packing an aerial mine of effective dimensions into, and discharging it from, a suitable projectile.

---

[1] Arthur Edgar Woodward Nutt, 1902–   . Seely Prizeman, Cambridge, 1923. Worked with the De Havilland Aircraft Company, 1924–5; at the Royal Aircraft Establishment, Farnborough, 1925–7 and 1934–8; at various aircraft experimental stations, 1927–34. In charge of the Air Defence Research Section, Air Ministry, 1938–41; Joint Secretary to the Committee of Imperial Defence Sub-Committee on Air Defence Research (the ADR Sub-Committee), and Special Assistant to the Director of Scientific Research, Air Ministry. Various directing appointments, Ministry of Aircraft Production, 1941–5; Ministry of Supply, 1945–58. Director-General of Aircraft General Services, Ministry of Aviation, 1958–65. Technical Adviser (civil), Ministry of Aviation, 1965–6.

(2) PRODUCTION OF ARTIFICIAL UP-CURRENTS

This problem has received considerable attention during the last few years, and it has been shewn that modern aircraft can fly at high speeds into even sharp-edged vertical gusts of up to 30 ft a second without being damaged. When an aeroplane meets such a gust, owing to its natural stability, the flexibility of its wings and other factors, the change of incidence is relatively gradual, with correspondingly low stresses. No up-current which can be produced artificially by any known means is, in fact, sharp-edged, and up-currents produced in the manner in which Mr Churchill suggests would seem to be quite innocuous.

If, however, his advisers can suggest, in a more precise and scientific form, means by which violent up-currents could be produced with a reasonable expenditure of energy, we could no doubt arrange to look into the matter again.

Oliver Harvey: diary

('*The Diplomatic Diaries of Lord Harvey of Tasburgh*')

15 September 1938

British press receives news of PM's visit[1] with marked approval. City is much relieved. Reaction in Germany also one of relief. In America it looks as if it were regarded as surrender. Winston says it is the stupidest thing that has ever been done.

Lady Desborough to Winston S. Churchill

(*Churchill papers: 8/594*)

16 September 1938

My darling Winston,

What a magnificent article, it must be one of the greatest utterances of modern times.[2] The facts so terrific, the statement so dignified & calm. One's

---

[1] To Berchtesgaden to discuss the Czech crisis with Hitler. This was the first of three visits to Hitler. The second was to Bad Godesberg, the third to Munich.

[2] Churchill's article 'Can Europe Stave Off War', was published in the *Daily Telegraph* on 15 September 1938. 'The ordinary smooth and balanced phrases of diplomacy,' Churchill wrote, 'with all their refinements and reserves, are of little use in dealing with the fierce chiefs of German Nazidom', and he added: Everyone will sympathize with the high-minded statesmen who have laboured so patiently for peace. But one must ask whether they would add appreciably to our danger by declaring themselves unmistakably, while time remains. If, for instance, Great Britain, France and Russia were even now to present a joint or simultaneous

spirit flies to meet it—after encountering all the shrieking & all the phoney.

I have been so utterly miserable, the past seems all too near, to those who remember. *May* some hope come of the enterprise today? I do feel it a great & imaginative effort.

Your devoted,
Ettie

Sir Eric Phipps to Lord Halifax

(*Foreign Office papers: 800/311*)

16 September 1938 British Embassy,
Paris

My dear Secretary of State,

Bonnet is perturbed because he has heard from the Czechoslovak Legation here that Masaryk had declared that I reported to you on September 13th having been told by Bonnet that France would not assist Czechoslovakia even if that State were attacked by Germany. Of course, as you know, I have never reported this, but I fear Masaryk may have picked up in the Foreign Office or elsewhere something of the substance of my telegram No. 244 Secret of September 13th. If some indiscretion has been committed in this respect it will place me in a very awkward position with Bonnet. On this occasion I was able to reply in all truth that I had not reported any such thing; but that I had in effect found him (Bonnet) 'très ému' on September 13th.

As a matter of fact he was even more moved than I reported, and he went so far as to exclaim 'Tout de même il ne faudrait pas que les Anglais nous poussent à la guerre!' I naturally denied this soft impeachment with some heat. From what Bonnet told me yesterday (and reported by me) about certain British MPs enquiring of him and other members of the French Government by telephone whether there had not been a change in the French attitude during the last few days, this must be what Bonnet wished to complain of, besides what he described as the bellicose attitude of part of the British Press. He actually mentioned Winston Churchill and Spears as being amongst those who had rung him up. Presumably the former breathed fire and thunder in order to binge Bonnet up. Our MPs should realise that what-

---

note to Herr Hitler personally, setting forth that an attack on Czechoslovakia would immediately be followed by common action; and if at the same time President Roosevelt would proclaim that this note carried with it the moral sympathy of the United States, with all that would follow therefrom—there would be good hopes, if not indeed almost a certainty, of warding off the catastrophe which may so easily engulf our civilisation.'

ever they say by telephone of any interest probably goes to the Germans and certainly to those French who had best not hear it.

Having reported to you, without comment, Daladier's brave words to me on September 8th, I felt bound to report the more cautious statement of Daladier and the panicky utterances of Bonnet on September 13th.

Bonnet repeated to me this morning that he and the French Government would accept any plan advocated by the Prime Minister or Runciman and impose it upon the Czechs. . . .

Vyvyan Adams to Winston S. Churchill

(*Churchill papers: 2/331*)

17 September 1938

Dear Mr Churchill,

I am loth to trouble you with a letter, but just now I had a telephone conversation with the Duchess of Atholl who is in Canada. She asked me, if I had the opportunity, to tell you of her conviction that we in Western Europe cannot afford to allow Czechoslovakia to lose her natural mountain frontier. Of course I entirely agree.

And let me say how fully I agreed—and agree with your article in Wednesday's Telegraph. The dismemberment of Czechoslovakia would mean another trench lost to decency. I beg you to use your immense prestige to impress this palpable fact on the Government and the public.[1]

Yours very truly,
Vyvyan Adams

Winston S. Churchill to A. H. Richards

(*Churchill papers: 2/343*)

17 September 1938
Private

Dear Mr Richards,

Many thanks for your letter.

I am delighted to hear of the advance in your organization, and of the expansion in the powers of 'Headway'.

---

[1] In his *Daily Telegraph* article of 15 September 1938 Churchill had written: 'To the wage-earning masses of every land, the word "Czechoslovakia", lately so unfamiliar to their ears, spells nothing less than "self-preservation". Thus I believe that should these dark designs, now so remorsely unfolding hour by hour, reach their appointed climax, Nazi Germany will find herself engaged in a world war, inexpiable in its character.'

If, as I fear, the Government is going to let Czechoslovakia be cut to pieces, it seems to me that a period of very hard work lies before us all.[1]

Shiela Grant Duff to Hubert Ripka

(Grant Duff papers)

18 September 1938

I have the impression that things are going very badly. The Labour people who saw Chamberlain yesterday (this is very confidential but quite exact) got a very bad impression. They are not allowed to talk but I have the distinct impression that Chamberlain has a plan, acceptable to Hitler, which he will impose on you, on the French and on public opinion here.

I informed Churchill at once and asked for reassurance. He said he had not been informed, has no idea what is going on but that he too has the impression that there is some 'miserable plan' which Chamberlain and the Government will try and get accepted. He is confident that if Chamberlain tries now to get you to capitulate to the Nazis, that it will let loose a tremendous campaign here and that the country will split. Churchill himself is going to make a very strong declaration on Wednesday. . . .

Churchill says everything depends on the willingness of the Czechs to fight at all costs. In that case, Germany will attack you and the situation here will change immediately.

He thinks Germany may attack any time, and the more you establish order in the Sudeten German districts, the more necessary this aggression becomes. In the case of a German attack, it is absolutely certain that we will march.

---

[1] On 17 September 1938 Anthony Eden's Principal Private Secretary, Oliver Harvey, dined with Harry Crookshank, a Conservative MP and since 1935 Secretary in the Mines Department of the Board of Trade. Harvey noted in his diary: 'He is very unhappy about his position. He was amazed to hear that HMG had not told Germany that Great Britain would march on the same day as France. I explained that we had only said that we might march if France became involved and were in difficulties. He said he is convinced British public has been misled by press on this and will be furious on learning the truth. He has seen AE I'm glad to say. He is all in favour of the Winston policy of organising all states who will be against aggression and of so confronting the gangsters with a ring of force. I am sure he is right. We shall only defeat the dictators if we show courage and resolution. He is disgusted at our pusillanimity and at our wish for 150% superiority before we attempt anything. He refuses to accept German estimates of their own strength at their face value.'

Sir Alexander Cadogan: diary

(*'The Diaries of Sir Alexander Cadogan'*)

19 September 1938

Came in on interview between H[1] and Winston. Latter seemed to be tamed somewhat, and I gather H told him good deal of the truth about the French.

Winston S. Churchill to Mortimer Wheeler

(*Churchill papers: 8/597*)

19 September 1938

Dear Mr Wheeler,

I should now very much like to pursue with you the matter dealt with in my letter of July 4 and your reply of the 11th.

Meanwhile I have been making some progress, and I send you herewith 50,000 words, which I have written and which are already in print, and will send about 12,000 more at the end of the week. I had expected to get to the Norman Conquest with about 40,000 words, but it seems that 65,000 or 70,000 will be required. I do not grudge this on account of the deep interest of these times, the fact that they cover a thousand years of history, and are so much a common foundation between all branches of the English speaking races.

I should be most deeply obliged to you if you would read this text for me. It is, of course, only the roughest provisional draft subject to every form of amendment, excision and expansion. I should be obliged if you would correct and annotate it for me, and then afterwards, let us have a night or two together down here where we can discuss outstanding points.

Pray let me know if you can do this for me, and we can easily fix up our time and medium later on. Meanwhile I am rolling forward towards Henry II.

It has been a comfort to me in these anxious days to put a thousand years between my thoughts and the twentieth century.

[1] Lord Halifax.

Dr Colijn to Winston S. Churchill

(*Churchill papers: 8/596*)

19 September 1938

My dear Mr Churchill,

Your letter of September 12th, accompanying the 4th and last volume of 'Marlborough', reached me the following day. Being eager to know what the last act of the drama would bring, I devoted half of the Saturday and the whole Sunday in reading the book. Although I am not a professional historian, I have read in the course of the years a considerable number of history books, biographies and memoirs. Consequently I am in the position to make comparisons and I do not hesitate to say that I consider your historical works as supreme. I think the opinion of Professor Trevelyan, as given on the back flap of the jacket, expresses in an admirable way what every intelligent reader feels.

Although I fully agree with you that the horrible position into which the world has got is all due to the lack of foresight and courage on the part of public men, I do not know whether we start at the same year with our complaint. For me the year 1919 is the origin of all evils that have befallen us. The biggest mistake has been the dissolution of the Habsburg monarchy. During the centuries the Habsburgs have always stood up against Prussianism, not always successfully, but still they were willing to fight Prussia and anyhow they were a considerable barrier against Prussian activity in Central Europe. Instead of strengthening this barrier, the people of Paris removed it and put up another barrier: Czecho-Slovakia. This barrier was too weak to fight its battles alone and Czech-Slovakia became consequently a danger for the peace of Europe. Only if France and Great Britain were willing to fight for its existence could it be kept alive, but that would mean a general European war.

I really see no other way out. I think above all it is time to face the facts as they are. The attempt to keep Czecho-Slovakia as it is will mean a prolongation of the present tension for years and years to come. There are about 6 million Czechs against 9 million non-Czechs in the Czecho-Slovakian state and even if you count all the Slovakians as friendly citizens of the state, there are still not more than 9 million Czechs against 6 of other stock. I admire the courage of Mr Chamberlain. Whether he brings it off or not, his moral courage will be unimpaired.

Believe me, dear Mr Churchill,
With respect and regard,
Yours sincerely,
H. Colijn

Winston S. Churchill: draft paragraphs for the 'Londoner's Diary'

(Churchill papers: 8/610)

[20 September 1938]

1. In the early days, flying was not thought the same easy routine as it has now become. One sat in a wicker chair with a footrail and a clear view of the earth beneath. In front was a vertical rudder, on the movements of which flight depended. Behind was the engine, of about 50 or 60 horse-power. Accidents were frequent, and often fatal. The modern generation of aviators take it for granted that the engine will go on running. In those days, it was only two or three to one against it cutting out in an hour's flight. A cross-country flight was an adventure. The rule was to fly as high as possible, and always have a gliding line to some practicable landing-place. One hated flying over extensive woods. As for the sea, it was a gamble with life, the odds being somewhat in one's favour.

2. Several politicians in those days were enticed into the air. There was an Air Display at Hendon in 1910, (?1909) which all the political and military world attended. Mr McKenna,[1] First Lord of the Admiralty, went up with Mr Grahame-White,[2] who brought him down in this flimsy apparatus in a very steep nose-dive, to the alarm of the whole concourse. However, he landed all right. Then two flights were made, both of which ended in accidents, though not serious. The next thing we saw was Mr Balfour, who, in his usual bland, detached air, immediately took his seat in the next 'plane, and was successfully piloted round the aerodrome.

3. Mr Churchill did not fly until a year after he had become First Lord of the Admiralty. He was taken up for the first time by Lieut Spenser-Grey,[3] whose tragical death a few months ago will be remembered.

[1] Reginald McKenna, 1863–1943. Liberal MP, 1895–1918. President of the Board of Education, 1907–8. First Lord of the Admiralty, 1908–11. Home Secretary, 1911–15. Chancellor of the Exchequer, May 1915–December 1916. Chairman, Midland Bank, 1919–43.

[2] Claude Grahame-White, 1879–1959. Educated at Bedford Grammar School. Established one of the first motor engineering businesses in Britain, 1900. Became interested in aeronautics, 1909, and started a school of aviation at Pau, in the Pyrenees. The first Englishman to be granted a certificate of proficiency as an aviator. Started the first British flying school. Founded the Grahame-White Aviation Company, 1911, proprietors of the London Aerodrome, Hendon. Flight Commander, 1914; resigned to superintend the carrying out of Government contracts for building aeroplanes. Resident in California from 1925.

[3] Spenser Douglas Adair Grey, 1889–1937. A descendant of Earl Grey (of the 1832 Reform Bill). Entered the Royal Navy, 1907. Sub-Lieutenant, 1909, by which time he was one of the very few officers of any rank to possess his own aeroplane. An aviator in one of the first sea plane experiments, 1911. In 1912 he took Churchill on his first flight, and later gave Churchill flying lessons. Seriously injured after his plane crashed, following a spin, 1913. Wing-Commander, Royal Naval Air Service, 1914. Awarded the DSO in October 1914, when he

Lieut Spenser-Grey was the first, or almost the first naval officer to own an aeroplane of his own. He spent all the money he had in the world on buying it. In 1911 he kept it at Portland, and used to take captains and admirals, who wished to test the new sensation, for joyrides round the Fleet. He had many passengers. One day, when flying alone, he had a rather serious accident. Mr Churchill had just become First Lord. The report was laid on his table at the Admiralty that this young officer had been injured while flying. He sent him a telegram of sympathy, saying: 'I hope you will soon be flying again.' As soon as Spenser-Grey got well, he went armed with this telegram and demanded to join the Royal Naval Air Service, which had just been founded. When they objected he was too junior, he produced the telegram from the First Lord, and said: 'He hopes I shall soon be flying again.' With this the portals of the infant Naval Wing were open to him, and he became one of its distinguished ornaments.

4. Mr Bonar Law flew only from motives of public duty. After the War, it was so much quicker to get to Paris by air than any other way, and from time to time when he had to join Mr Lloyd George there, he used the aeroplane in exactly the same way that a man would eat whatever dish was put before him at a friend's house. He could not help liking it however. 'I must say' he said, 'coming back from France the other evening, with all the clouds lighted by the sunset, it was lovely.' (He actually said: 'it was very pretty').

5. The great difference between flying now and those days is that now one expects to get there. Then, one thought this hope sanguine.

Consuelo Balsan to Winston S. Churchill

(Churchill papers: 8/596)

20 September 1938   Saint Georges Motel
                                                    Eure

My dear Winston,

I have just received your last volume of Marlborough's life. It has touched me very much that at such a critical time with all your thoughts elsewhere you should have remembered me. Thank you very much. I wish you would

---

commanded a flight of aeroplanes which flew over Cologne (8 October 1914), circling the city while under anti-aircraft fire, and discharging his bombs on a military railway station. Sent on an Admiralty mission to purchase six flying boats in the United States, December 1914. Commander, flying boat experimental tests, Hendon, March 1916. Liaison Officer with the United States Air Force, Paris, 1917. Invalided out of the Royal Air Force, with the rank of Lieutenant-Colonel, 1919. He died, at the age of 48, after falling nine stories while fixing a wireless aeriel on the roof of his flat.

write your own life now. With your gifts, your imagination and your powers of presenting a situation, you could create a book of extraordinary interest for coming generations.[1] What a time to have lived in—almost too hectic when one learns of bombs on one's homes in France and reads of a hurricane heading for Casa Alva in Florida. Mr Chamberlain has we hope saved the present situation, but how about the future of the Balkans! The Jewish press in the USA is very disappointed that there is to be no war—sentiment is hardening against them everywhere.

Thank you again dear Winston, and love from Jacques and myself to you and Clemmie

Aff,
Consuelo

Anthony Crossley: diary

(*Crossley papers*)

20 September 1938

Went to see Eden. I wanted to find out whether he was going to align himself with Churchill etc and I wanted to prevent him taking precipitate action. I therefore told him that we had been invited to a conference by Winston in Lord Lloyd's house; that we had decided not to go; that we didn't wish to align ourselves with the Cabal who were notorious for plots against the Government.

Oliver Harvey: diary

('*The Diplomatic Diaries of Lord Harvey of Tasburgh*')

20 September 1938

I hear Winston has left for France, presumably to ascertain the real state of opinion there. He too is in absolute despair at HMG's policy.

[1] Churchill's autobiography, *My Early Life*, had ended with his entry into Parliament in 1900. He was never to write his long-awaited 'volume two', spanning the years 1900 to 1914, nor any specifically autobiographical or personal study of the years after 1900. He did however cover some autobiographical and personal aspects of his life from 1910 to 1922 in *The World Crisis*, and further personal material for the years 1930 to 1945 in successive volumes of *The Second World War*. Further autobiographical fragments appear throughout his other writings, including those scattered throughout *Thoughts and Adventures*, *Great Contemporaries*, in *Painting as a Pastime*, and in several of the fifty books by other authors for which he wrote introductions (see also pages 1283 and 1332).

Wing-Commander Anderson to Winston S. Churchill
(*Churchill papers: 2/338*)

21 September 1938   Royal Air Force Station,
                                     Catfoss,
                                     Nr. Hull

Dear Mr Churchill,

You wished to see a diagram of the organisation of the Royal Air Force dated 31st August, 1938.

It will be observed that our strength is as follows:—

Bomber Squadrons.

There are 57 Regular Squadrons, and 15 Auxiliary Squadrons, making a total of 72 Bomber Squadrons.

Fighter Squadrons.

There are 26 Regular Squadrons and 7 Auxiliary Squadrons, making a total of 33 Fighter Squadrons.

New Equipment.

(i) Bomber Squadrons. Of the 72 Bomber Squadrons, only 32 have been equipped with new type aircraft.

(ii) Fighter Squadrons. Of the 33 Fighter Squadrons, only 12 have been equipped with new type aircraft.

2. I have starred the Squadrons which have received new equipment, and I also attach a list giving types of new equipment.

Yours very sincerely,
C. T. Anderson

Winston S. Churchill: press statement
(*Churchill papers: 9/132*)

21 September 1938   Chartwell

It is necessary that the nation should realize the magnitude of the disaster into which we are being led. The partition of Czechoslovakia under Anglo-French pressure amounts to a complete surrender by the Western democracies to the Nazi threat of force. Such a collapse will not bring peace or safety to Great Britain and France. On the contrary, it will bring both countries into a position of ever-increasing weakness and danger.

The neutralisation of Czechoslovakia alone means the liberation of twenty-five German divisions to threaten the Western front. The path to the Black

Sea will be laid wide open to triumphant Nazi-ism. Acceptance of Herr Hitler's terms involves the prostration of Europe before the Nazi power, of which the fullest advantage will certainly be taken.

The menace, therefore, is not to Czechoslovakia, but to the cause of freedom and democracy in every country. The idea that safety can be purchased by throwing a small State to the wolves is a fatal delusion. The German war power will grow faster than the French and British can complete their preparations for defence. If peace is to be preserved on a lasting basis, it can only be by a combination of all the Powers whose convictions and whose vital interests are opposed to Nazi domination. A month ago this would have been possible. But all was cast away.

Parliament should be called together without further delay, and duly informed upon these grievous matters which affect the whole life and future of our country.

Robert Boothby to E. L. Spears

(*Spears papers*)

22 September 1938   Carlton Parc Hôtel
                                                            Geneva

Dear Louis,

I am sorry that you gave Winston the impression that I was no longer interested in Czecho-slovakia. Because it is far from being the case. During the 20 minutes I was in your house I made 3 observations, and only 3.

I said I thought there was nothing which we as a group could do *that night*. (Surely it was obvious.)

I said I thought that Anthony would not come round (this proved to be right).

Finally I said that I myself could not possibly support the proposals which were at that time appearing (without official authority) in the Press. I said nothing else at all.

I know you feel passionately on the subject. But my own record is not so bad (vide the 'Daily Telegraph' during the past 3 weeks). It would be fatal to jump to premature conclusions about the extent of the betrayal, or the attitude of any particular individual; and, by taking precipitate & unco-ordinated action to risk a division of our forces. I have not changed my views by one iota, and am perfectly prepared to cross the floor of the House should the necessity arise.

Moreover, according to my present (still inadequate) information, I think the necessity will arise.

I wd be grateful if you wd make my position clear to anyone who may be under a misapprehension.

It is vital, in this emergency, that those of us who broadly share the same views, should stick together, and work together. I am returning to London by air tomorrow.

Yours ever,
Bob Boothby

Harold Nicolson: diary

(*Nicolson papers*)

22 September 1938

At about 11.30 Winston Churchill telephones. Would I come up to London for a meeting at 4.30 in his flat? I say that I shall be there . . .

As I approach the door I see the vulture form of Bob Cecil slipping into the flat. While I wait for the lift to descend Winston appears from a taxi. We go up together.

'This' I say 'is Hell.'

'It is the end of the British Empire.'

We gather in the drawing room. There are present Lords Cecil, Lloyd, Horne, Lytton and Wolmer. The only House of Commons people there are Archie Sinclair, Brendan Bracken and myself. Winston has just been to Downing Street. He says that the Cabinet are at last taking a firm stand. Chamberlain is to demand from Hitler (a) early demobilization (b) agreement that the transfer of the Sudeten territories should be undertaken gradually by an international commission (c) that there must be no nonsense about Polish or Hungarian claims (d) that what remains of Czechoslovakia should be guaranteed.

We say at once, 'But Hitler will never accept such terms.'

'In the case,' says Winston, 'Chamberlain will return tonight[1] and we shall have WAR.' We suggest that in that event it will be inconvenient having our Prime Minister in German territory. 'Even the Germans' flashes Winston, 'would not be so stupid as to deprive us of our beloved Prime Minister.'

. . . a telephone message from Jan Masaryk . . . the Czechs are withdrawing gradually from the Sudeten areas. Also Hodza[2] has resigned. . . .

---

[1] From his second visit to Hitler, at Bad Godesberg, on the Rhine.

[2] Milan Hodza, 1878–1944. The son of a Slovak Protestant pastor, and noted Liberal. Entered the Hungarian Parliament in Budapest, 1905, as the only representative of the Slovaks. Founder of the Club of Minority Nations' Deputies, which served as a nucleus for non-Magyar co-operation inside Hungary. Sentenced to nine months in prison for persistent

We continue the conversation. It boils down to this. Either Chamberlain comes back with peace with honour or he breaks off. In either case we shall support him. But if he comes back with peace with dishonour we shall go out against him. 'Let us form the Focus' says Winston. We say that indeed we will. . . . He stands there behind the fire screen, waving a whiskey and soda at us, rather blurry, rather bemused in a way. But dominant and in fact reasonable. I say that there is a worse thing. 'What worse than worse?' asks Winston. I say this point in the communiqué about a 'general agreement'. What can that mean? . . . It may mean surrender on fronts more extended than the Czech front and in return such quite valueless concessions as 'a fifty year peace', 'no bombing of open towns'. We all feel that it is terrifying that a man like Chamberlain should be exposed to such terror and temptations. We conclude (a) that we shall support the PM if it means war or a firm line. (b) that if he runs away again we shall join with the Opposition. (c) that we shall be summoned by Winston again if things go wrong.

All those of us who said 'we must make it stand' will be branded as murderers. I know that. But I also know that the real courage is to sacrifice everything for this fight against violence.

Imre Revesz to Winston S. Churchill: telegram

(*Churchill papers: 8/607*)

22 September 1938   Paris

Your declaration has made a deep impression here.[1] All the newspapers have published it.

---

criticism of the Government, 1914. Interned by the Austro-Hungarian authorities, 1914–18. First Diplomatic representative at Budapest of the Czechoslovak State, 1919. Member of the Czechoslovak Parliament, 1918. Successively Minister of Unification, of Agriculture (twice) and of Education. Prime Minister of Czechoslovakia,. 1935–8. Established Home Rule for Ruthenia, 1937. Resigned on the night of 21 September 1938, eight days before the Munich agreements. In exile on the Riviera, 1938–40, in London 1940–1 and in the United States, 1942–4. Vice-President of the Czechoslovak State Council (in exile), 1940–4. In 1942 he published *Federation in Central Europe*, in which he wrote that he had spent his life fighting 'the illusion that small states placed between colossal neighbours could preserve their sovereignties without the building up of a co-operative solidarity between themselves'.

[1] Churchill's public statement of 21 September 1938 (see pages 1171–2).

Patrick Donner to Winston S. Churchill

(*Churchill papers: 2/331*)

22 September 1938

Dear Mr Churchill,

Thank you for your letter of Sept 9.[1] I should have replied before but only returned yesterday from abroad and found your letter awaiting me.

I am glad to be able to give you the assurance for which you ask. I do so absolutely and without qualification. While therefore I can gladly give you my word of honour that I am in no way connected with the statements to which you refer, I can only regret that after the many kindnesses and hospitality which you have extended to me over several years you should have thought me capable of such conduct. Should I at any time think it my duty to disagree with you I will give expression to my belief in public or over my signature but in no other manner—and certainly not covertly. I am grateful to you however for giving me the opportunity—which I now take—of a complete denial.

Yours sincerely,
Patrick

Winston S. Churchill to Patrick Donner

(*Churchill papers: 2/331*)

23 September 1938
Personal

I am very glad to receive your letter, and to have your disclaimer.

The reason why I wrote was because a suggestion had been made to me that you had been the author of this paragraph, and I was so anxious there should be no cloud in our relations.

General Sir Hugh Tudor to Winston S. Churchill

(*Churchill papers: 2/331*)

23 September 1938   Newfoundland

My dear Winston,

You have been right all along about Hitler and his Germany. Also that the Tory Party and its associates have let the country down.

[1] Not found.

Simon and Runciman wanted to act 'La perfide Albion' in 1914. Halifax is a pious rabbit.

Chamberlain is said to belong to the Astor pro-Hitler group. It is astounding how he can negotiate with Hitler when the latter is already making war on the Czechs, by arming Henlein's party and letting him attack Czech outposts—surely an act of war. The only possible excuse he may have, is that our rearmament is still in so deplorable a state; that we cannot go to war, except with the odds on our defeat.

Even now he should ask you to replace Inskip. But, unless he has some quite unexpected success in his present parleys, his time as Prime Minister will be short. With you as Prime Minister and Eden as Foreign Secretary of a National Government of 'he-men', instead of rabbits, Hitler would at least realize that bluff is useless.

Eden was involved in what Theodore Roosevelt called the unforgivable crime of 'hitting softly' in the Abyssinian crisis; thus antagonizing Italy without stopping her. But he has no doubt learnt his lesson.

Would the Russian Army be as hopeless as ever against German troops?

If Chamberlain has ruined our, and France's, prestige, will Roumania and Yugoslavia dare to stand up with us, even with Russian help, against Italy and Germany?

The Labour party surely must realize now; that, if we are to pull our weight, we must have Universal training, at least in the Territorial Army.

We cannot help France or even hold Egypt and India without an efficient Army.

I left the Reserve of Officers about three months ago, but if war comes I might still be of some use somewhere. I suppose everyone with any experience will be wanted.

Yours ever,
H. Tudor

Lord Zetland to Lord Linlithgow

(*India Office papers*)

25 September 1938

Now that the prospect of immediate hostilities has been dissipated people are beginning to ask themselves at what price? Winston Churchill has dashed over to Paris, presumably to test for himself opinion in France and, so far as might be, to rally the forces opposed to what was now being spoken of as a shameful surrender to the Dictators.

Oliver Harvey: diary

('*The Diplomatic Diaries of Lord Harvey of Tasburgh*')

25 September 1938

PM very pleased with himself and thinks Hitler's offer not too bad and should be recommended to the Czechs. Winston, AE and Amery are horrified at the possibility of our urging Czechoslovakia to accept.

Winston S. Churchill: press statement

(*Churchill papers: 9/132*)

26 September 1938

There is still one good chance of preserving peace. A solemn warning should be presented to the German Government in joint or simultaneous notes by Great Britain, France and Russia, that the invasion of Czechoslovakia at the present juncture would be taken as an act of war against these Powers. The terms of this note should be communicated to all Neutral countries, some of whom may be balancing their action, and most particularly to the Government of the United States. If such steps had been taken a month ago, it is improbable matters would have reached their present pass. Even at the last moment, clear and resolute action may avert the catastrophe into which we are drifting.

Not only the German Government but the German people have a right to know where we all stand.

If the Government and people of the United States have a word to speak for the salvation of the world, now is the time, and now is the last time when words will be of any use. Afterwards, through years of struggle and torment, deeds alone will serve, and deeds will be forth-coming.

It will indeed be a tragedy if this last effort is not made, in the only way in which it may be effective, to save mankind from martyrdom.

Lord Rothermere to Winston S. Churchill: telegram

(*Churchill papers: 2/331*)

26 September 1938

Have just read your suggestion of a solemn warning to Germany. Think it is admirable. Have been staggered by Germany's further demands after what looked like a settlement. If it hadn't been for you and me the country would not be nearly as well prepared for the encounter as it is today

Harold

Anthony Crossley: letter to his mother

(*Crossley papers*)

26 September 1938

. . . we received a message from Winston (with whom as you will remember we had declined to co-operate) that his position was a very simple one. He believed that only a joint declaration by England, France and Russia could possibly save peace with honour. Throughout the last two days, we have disapproved the apparent ignoring of Russia by both our own and the French Governments. Even at the dictation of Hitler, the Prime Minister cannot annul geography.

Mary Borden: diary

(*Lady Spears papers*)

26 September 1938

Telegram from Winston asking B[1] to come to Morpeth Mansions at 4 p m

Harold Nicolson: diary

(*Nicolson papers*)

26 September 1938

We read on the tape that the Prime Minister has sent Horace Wilson to Berlin by aeroplane carrying a personal letter to Hitler in his hand. I was terrified that this means a further surrender. . . .

I then go on to Winston Churchill's flat. He is not there when I arrive as he has been summoned by the Prime Minister. The others there are Cecil, Grigg, Archie Sinclair, Lytton, Amery, Lloyd, Harold Macmillan,[2] Bob Boothby and Spears. We begin by discussing whether national service should

---

[1] B = Beaucaire, Mary Borden's private name for her husband (Brigadier–General Edward Louis Spears).

[2] Maurice Harold Macmillan, 1894–   . Educated at Eton and Balliol College, Oxford. On active service, Grenadier Guards, 1914–18 (wounded three times). Conservative MP for Stockton-on-Tees, 1924–9, and 1931–45. Author of *Reconstruction: A Plea for a National Policy*, 1933; *Planning for Employment*, 1935; *The Next Five Years*, 1935; *The Middle Way*, 1938; and *Economic Aspects of Defence*, 1939. Parliamentary Secretary, Ministry of Supply, 1940–2. Privy Councillor, 1942. Minister Resident, Allied HQ, North-West Africa, 1942–5. Secretary for Air, 1945. Minister of Housing and Local Government, 1951–4. Minister of Defence, 1954–5. Secretary of State for Foreign Affairs, 1955. Chancellor of the Exchequer, 1955–7. Prime Minister, 1957–63. Chancellor of the University of Oxford from 1960.

be proclaimed at once. Grigg is very insistent. Lytton wants a coalition government immediately and I agree with him. . . .

At that stage Winston bursts in. He says (as Rob Bernays had also told me) that the Cabinet were in a blue funk last night and that Simon was urging further retreat. But the younger people revolted and the Simon faction began to lose ground. Then came the French all brave and solid this time, plus Gamelin who restored confidence. In the end the Cabinet were all united in feeling how brave, how strong, how resolute they had always been. . . .

He (Winston) had urged the PM to mobilize the fleet at once and call up all reserves. . . . We discuss plans. If Chamberlain rats again we shall form a united block against him. . . .

Winston says (and we all agree) that the fundamental mistake the PM has made is his refusal to take Russia into his confidence. Ribbentrop always said to Hitler 'You need never fear England until you find her mentioning Russia as an ally. Then it means she is really going to war.' We therefore decide that Winston shall go at once to Halifax and tell him to put out some such notice before Hitler's speech. 'We have only got till nine' says Winston grimly. . . .

Leo Amery: diary

(Amery papers)

26 September 1938

Went to Spears' office in St Stephen House, where his usual half dozen conspirators were assembled. They were all desperately keen about pressing the Government to make clear that we are in direct touch with Russia in order to impress the Germans, who have taken our non-contact with Russia as a clear proof that we do not mean to go in—nothing will ever induce them to understand us. They also wished for some public declaration by us, as Conservatives, that we stood for cooperation with Russia, to which I strongly objected. At this moment it would only put off many of our people, while once war is declared they will only too readily welcome help from the Devil himself, and as for the effect on Germany I didn't think much of it, though I had no objection to the request going forward to Halifax without my name added.

We then adjourned to Winston's flat where I found a queer collection: Bob Cecil, Victor Lytton, Lindemann, George Lloyd and one or two others; later Archie Sinclair. Presently Winston came in having just had half an hour with Neville. His idea was that the letter taken by Horace Wilson was a suggestion for a conference to work out the details of transfer, accompanied by a private message to be given only if Hitler was negative to say that we regretted that he insisted on taking by force what was already conceded, but that if he did we and Russia would support France.

Some discursive talk about Spears and Boothby's Russian idea and Winston afterwards went to tell Halifax the gist of our views about Russia, myself again stipulating that this should be for his use and not for publication. He told the story about the German General von Beck[1] opposing war on the grounds that Germany's superiority in the air would be progressively less important as fighting went on and that numbers and trained officers would win in the end.

After the others went off I stayed with Archie Sinclair and we had some further chat. So now Winston and I are once more working together in the third war,—for I can hardly conceive Hitler changing his mind on the receipt of Wilson's message before his speech tonight,—in our lifetime. Hitler was to see Wilson at five and his speech is at eight o'clock. If only there were a chance of German soldiers stopping this madman. It will be too late once war has broken out, for even if they do they are likely to continue fighting.

Winston reported Neville as a very exhausted and broken man. The poor fellow, he has done his best valiantly, but he should never have attempted such a task with such slender qualifications for it, and though Germany's folly may cover the traces history will no doubt say that he made a ghastly muddle of things after his first visit to Hitler, who seems, to some extent, to have deluded him. He said to Winston that he thought Hitler sincere, to which Winston replied reminding him that there were some sixteen occasions on which Hitler had solemnly made promises which he had broken either to friends or internationally.

[1] Ludwig von Beck, 1880–1944. Entered the Field Artillery, 1898. Attached to the General Staff of the German Imperial Army, 1912–18. Major-General Commanding the Saxon Artillery, 1931. Lieutenant-General, 1932. Head of the Military Planning Section of the Reichswehr Ministry, 1933–5. Chief of the German General Staff, 1935–8. Resigned, 27 August 1938. A British Embassy assessment (Berlin, 4 January 1938) had described him as 'not in sympathy with the present regime', and he was one of those who had been shown Churchill's letter to von Kleist (see page 1121). At the time of the July plot of 1944 against Hitler, he was the conspirator's nominee as Chief of State (Regent) in the post-Hitler Government. Committed suicide, 20 July 1944.

Richard Law: [1] *recollection* [2]

(Churchill papers: 4/143)

I have been racking my brains over the meeting at Morpeth Mansions, but I am afraid I can remember very little about it. I think that there were eight or ten people there and that they were mostly from the Lords—or at any rate they were not from the Commons.

My impression—which is very sketchy—is that the talk was about the possibility, even at that late hour, of coming to terms with the Russians in order to hold Hitler in check. I think this was the occasion on which I invited you to join the Communist Party.

The only thing I am positive about, was that Bob Cecil was there, and the fact that I recollect him so clearly makes me think that the discussion probably centred on the possibility of re-creating a Collective System against Germany.

Winston S. Churchill: recollections [3]

(Churchill papers: 1/143)

My records show that I visited Mr Chamberlain at 3.30 pm on September 26 at No 10, Downing Street. According to my recollection I was present in the Cabinet Room during the drafting of this communiqué [4] and the discussion upon it, and I pressed most strongly for the insertion of the reference to Russia. I am sure also that Lord Halifax was present. This communiqué was in entire accord with my views and I certainly had a feeling that we had all come together upon the crisis. Somebody was there also from the Foreign Office. Who would it be?

There was a meeting that same afternoon at my flat at Morpeth Mansions

---

[1] Richard Kidston Law, 1901–1980. Youngest son of Andrew Bonar Law (two of his brothers were killed in action on the western front). Editorial Staff, *Morning Post*, 1927; *New York Herald-Tribune*, 1928. Conservative MP for Hull South-West, 1931–45; for South Kensington, 1945–50; for Haltemprice, 1950–4. Elected to the Other Club, 1936. Member of the Medical Research Council, 1936–40. Financial Secretary, War Office, 1940–1; Parliamentary Under-Secretary of State, Foreign Office, 1941–3. Privy Councillor, 1943. Minister of State, 1943–5. Minister of Education, 1945. Created Baron Coleraine, 1954. Chairman National Youth Employment Council, 1955–62.

[2] In a private letter to Churchill of 28 July 1947.

[3] In a private letter to Sir Orme Sargent of 23 July 1947.

[4] A communiqué issued by the Foreign Office on the evening of 26 September 1938, and published in the newspapers on the following morning, that in the event of a German attack on Czechoslovakia, 'France will be bound to come to her assistance and Great Britain and Russia will certainly stand by France'.

with a number of leading Conservatives, including Lord Cecil, all of whom were convinced that we must work with Russia and, according to my memory, which I am refreshing by various enquiries, I returned to them and reported the character, if not the terms, of the communiqué.

Lord Halifax: recollections[1]

(Churchill papers: 4/143)

[26 September 1938]

As regards the September 26 communiqué, I *think* your recollection is at fault. I have a recollection of our meeting in the Cabinet Room, when we no doubt spoke together and agreed together in the sense of the communiqué. But that evening at the Foreign Office, Rex Leeper[2] who was then Head of the Press Department, brought me in the 'Communiqué' for approval. I approved it, without reference to Neville, because I thought it was completely in accord with his thought and with what I imagine we had all been saying to each other at our meeting. But, greatly to my surprise, Neville was much put out when the Communiqué appeared, and reproached me with not having submitted it to him before publication. I never understood then, and I don't understand now, why he should have been vexed—unless it was that he thought it 'provocative'! and not fully consistent with his desire to make further conciliatory appeal to Hitler.

Bernard Baruch to Winston S. Churchill: telegram

26 September 1938   New York

In case war send children and expectant mother[3] to me.

Bernie

---

[1] In a private letter to Churchill of 24 July 1947.

[2] Reginald Wildig Allen Leeper, 1888–1968. Born in Australia. Educated in Australia, and at New College, Oxford. Intelligence Bureau, Department of Information, 1917. Entered the Foreign Office, 1918; Political Intelligence Department, 1918–24. First Secretary, Warsaw, 1924; Riga, 1924; Constantinople, 1925; Warsaw, 1927–9. Transferred to the Foreign Office, 1929; Counsellor, 1933. Assistant Under-Secretary of State for Foreign Affairs, 1940–2. Ambassador to Greece, 1943–6. Knighted 1945. Ambassador to the Argentine, 1946–8.

[3] Diana Sandys was expecting her second child in December (see page 1327).

Winston S. Churchill to Bernard Baruch: telegram

(Churchill papers: 1/324)

27 September 1938

Many thanks, but Diana is air-raid warden in London. Now is the time for your man to speak. Will cable again soon.

Winston

Jan Masaryk to Winston S. Churchill

(Churchill papers: 2/331)

27 September 1938   The Czechoslovak Minister,
                                                    London

My dear Mr Churchill,

Here are the facts of the preparation and execution of the 'Hitler-Chamberlain auction sale'. I am sending only the important ones. You have my full permission to use them—just please not verbatim so some of my 'friends' here will not have a pretext to send me away from London. The map will be ready tonight and I will either send it then or leave it here till your return to London.

I am very grateful.

My love to you and yours,

Sincerely,
Jan Masaryk

Shiela Grant Duff: recollections

(Grant Duff papers)

[27 September 1938]

Ripka telephoned me from Prague on the evening of 27th to say that we were again putting great pressure on the Czechoslovak Government. Not only were further propositions about the transfer of territory being put to them, but these were being accompanied by still worse threats. The British notes in Prague were not only warning them that 'Bohemia would be militarily crushed' and that 'that remained a fact whatever might be the result of a possible war' but also that 'whatever might be the result of a world war, the present Czechoslovak frontier would never be restored.'

I at once telephoned Churchill. He was very angry with me. He had, only the previous day, himself seen the Prime Minister and Foreign Secretary and they had assured him that all this was at an end. Did I he asked angrily really need to draw the attention of the Czechoslovak Government to the statement in the press that morning issued by the Foreign Office that should a German attack be made now on Czechoslovakia 'France will be bound to come to her assistance and Great Britain and Russia will certainly stand by France?' What more, he shouted, did the Czechs want. They were having me on and I better take care and he all but slammed down the receiver.

None of us in England then knew that Chamberlain had gone behind the back of all this brave front and despatched Sir Horace Wilson with yet another appeasing missive.

Harold Nicolson: diary

(*Nicolson papers*)

28 September 1938

From the Peers' gallery around the clock the calm face of Lord Baldwin peered down upon the arena in which he himself had so often battled . . . the French Ambassador, who arrived a few minutes late, found some difficulty in squeezing himself into a place. . . .

Mr Winston Churchill, who sits at the end of my own row, received so many telegrams that they were clipped together by an elastic band.[1]

Winston S. Churchill: Press statement

(*Churchill papers: 9/130*)

28 September 1938

I have wished the Prime Minister 'God-speed' in his mission, from the bottom of my heart. The indomitable exertions which he has made to preserve peace make it certain that should he be forced to declare that it is our duty to take up arms in defence of right and justice, his signal will be obeyed by a united nation and accepted by a united Empire.

The decision of His Majesty's Government announced by the Home Secretary, not to relax in any way the precautions now being taken upon a great scale, and to carry through the mobilisation of the Fleet, for which

---

[1] As MPs listened to Chamberlain giving an account of the Czech crisis, a message was brought in to him from Hitler inviting him to a Four Power Conference at Munich. Chamberlain cut short his speech to announce the invitation, and his acceptance of it. In the ensuing enthusiasm, Harold Nicolson remained seated (see page 1188) as the House rose to cheer. Churchill also rose, approaching Chamberlain and wishing him 'God-speed'.

credit is due to the First Lord of the Admiralty,[1] is another steadying factor of first importance.

The calm, resolute spirit of all classes, particularly the great mass of the people, in the face of danger, shows the strength of the British character in the hour of trial.

There must be no relaxation of moral vigilance. We have not lightly entered into this grave matter, nor must we quit the field upon which we have taken our stand without good reason and honour. The natural, intense desire for peace must not be misinterpreted in any quarter. We must not forget that Herr Hitler has gained all that he demanded at Berchtesgarten, and that the discussion is now proceeding only upon the methods and conditions of the transference of territories and populations from the Czechoslovak Republic to Nazi rule. We have a direct obligation to secure for the truncated Czechoslovakia a fair chance of safety and of economic life. We cannot abandon our duty, and we shall need all our firmness and persistence to discharge it. No one should therefore suppose that the danger is past. This new triumph of the Nazi regime and the great accessions of military strength which it brings them, weights the balance heavily against democracy and freedom in Europe.

Anthony Crossley to Winston S. Churchill

(Churchill papers: 2/331)

28 September 1938

My dear Churchill,

After yesterday's speech, I went with several Members to a club and drank to our relief. In the course of conversation, one or two of them expressed indignation at what they called, the disreputable intrigues which had been going on, and to be perfectly frank, your name was mentioned.

I am glad that I went to your house yesterday morning and the day before, and I only write this to say that if it was ever necessary or if you should ever desire it, I am perfectly ready and willing to stand up in the House and say that it is not true that you were party to intrigues, and that provided the Government took a firm line you were wholly willing to fall in with them as a loyal supporter whether you were asked to take an active part or not. In this matter I shall regard myself as wholly at your disposal and you may certainly use this letter in any way you wish.

Yours sincerely,
Anthony Crossley

[1] Alfred Duff Cooper, who resigned from the Cabinet three days later, in protest against the Munich Agreement (see page 1189, note 1).

Winston S. Churchill: draft paragraph for the 'Londoner's Diary'

(*Churchill papers: 8/610*)

28 September 1938

Mr Duff Cooper is to be congratulated upon having at last obtained authority to issue the necessary mobilisation orders to the Fleet.

In general, the main power of the Fleet does not require mobilisation, and all modern ships maintained in commission can go into action almost immediately. Nevertheless there are a great many important auxiliary services connected with the Fleet and its flotillas, for which the Reservists are required.

The measure taken is therefore most necessary, and it is a pity it was not done some weeks ago.

It should be realised that the main fighting strength of the Fleet has been disposed of in the best possible manner. Persons wishing to know where exactly our Fleets are, can immediately be informed: 'They are at sea.'

Mr Duff Cooper's action follows upon the Admiralty tradition of being well in advance of the final moves of diplomacy. In 1914, Mr Churchill, the First Lord of the Admiralty, arranged with the Prime Minister personally to send the Grand Fleet to the North on the Tuesday before the declaration of war. It was therefore able to pass through the Straits of Dover unmolested before the opening of hostilities, and was in its dominant position in the critical days which followed. The actual call for Reservists was not made until the night of 1st August. The Cabinet had not been willing in the morning to consent to this step, but on the German declaration of war against Russia, the First Lord sent out the summonses to the Reservists without waiting for the necessary Royal Proclamation. There was therefore no legal liability upon the men to attend. Out of 50,000 men, however, there were no willing absentees. The matter was regularized forty-eight hours later by the King in Council.

In this case, the Proclamation obtained this morning observed the correct Constitutional procedure.

P. J. Grigg to Winston S. Churchill

(*Churchill papers: 8/596*)

29 September 1938   India

My dear Winston,

The primary object of this letter is to thank you for Vol IV of 'Marlborough'. I am already half way through it & am enjoying it tremendously.

If a cat may look at a king I may say that a certain sombreness which I find in your later style makes it even better than it was before. The end of the chapter in which you describe how the good peace was lost is absolutely magnificent.

But of course I can't help being full of events in the West. Three times I have had to start my letter to you over again. At the moment it looks as if there won't be war this time but I feel very ashamed at our having forced the Czechs so far and I can't believe that we have done anything but buy a few months of uneasy & expensive peace. However I suppose that Neville had great difficulty with his Simons & his Kingsley Woods and I gather also that Eric Phipps kept on dinning into them that the French weren't going to fight whatever happened. I do wish you were in the Government but I daresay that unless & until war actually comes the minnows won't tolerate the presence of a triton.

I have only 7 months more to go out here & I shall be very glad when it is over. I am rather uneasy at what looks like developing into a policy of doing anything to keep that irreconcilable old Anglo-phobe Gandhi quiet.

Love from us both to you both and renewed thanks for your great generosity in sending me all your books.

Yours ever,
PJG

Harold Nicolson: diary

(*Nicolson papers*)

29 September 1938

To luncheon at the Savoy in a private room with Winston, Cecil, Lytton, Arthur Salter, Wickham Steed, Walter Layton, Archibald Sinclair, Arthur Henderson,[1] Liddell Hart, Norman Angell, Megan Lloyd George, Violet Bonham Carter etc.

Lord Lloyd makes the first speech. He says that Chamberlain is going to run away again and that we must stop him. Then Archie speaks in the same

---

[1] Arthur Henderson, 1893–1968. The son of Arthur Henderson, Member of the War Cabinet, 1916–17 and Secretary of State for Foreign Affairs, 1929–31. On active service, 1914–18. Labour MP, 1923–4, 1929–31, 1935–50 and 1950–66. Parliamentary Private Secretary to the Attorney-General (Sir William Jowitt), 1929–31. Joint Parliamentary Under-Secretary, War Department, 1942–3; Financial Secretary, War Office, 1943–5. Parliamentary Under-Secretary of State for India and Burma, 1945–7. Secretary of State for Air, 1947–51. Vice-President of the Council of Europe Assembly, 1960–1. Created Baron Rowley, 1966. His younger brother David was killed in action on the western front in September 1916, two months before his eighteenth birthday.

sense. Then I speak, saying that if he does run away I shall vote against him. Then Arthur Salter says that he is all for fighting the Germans, but he would first like to know whether we are likely to win.

Winston says that he has got a telegram which he proposes to send to the PM saying that if he imposes further onerous terms on the Czechs, we shall fight him in the House. He wants to get Eden to sign it.

They all agree that the Government is less resolute than the country and that if Chamberlain runs away now he will be running badly. It seems that my refusal to stand up yesterday when all the rest of the House was hysterical has made an impression. Everybody has heard of it. I was ashamed of the House yesterday. It was a Welsh Revivalist meeting.

I had meant to go down to Sissinghurst, but Winston asked me to stay on in London. At 7 pm we meet again in the Savoy Hotel. The idea had been to get Winston, Cecil, Attlee, Eden, Archie Sinclair and Lloyd to join in a telegram to the PM begging him not to betray the Czechs. We had been busy at it all afternoon. But Anthony Eden refused to sign on the grounds that it would be interpreted as a vendetta against Chamberlain. Attlee had refused to sign without the approval of his Party. There was thus no time. We sat there gloomily realising that nothing could be done. Even Winston seemed to have lost his fighting spirit.

Lady Violet Bonham Carter: recollections[1]

(Churchill papers: 4/49)

[29 September 1938]
early evening

In particular I remember our last Meeting, on the evening of Munich, at the Savoy, just before your Dinner with the Other Club. At that Meeting you suggested sending a message to Chamberlain at Munich, signed by leaders of the three Parties, urging that no more concessions should be made at the expense of the Czechs. Archie and George Lloyd were of course willing to sign, (Anthony refused on the telephone) and Noel Baker, who telephoned the Labour leaders for their consent, reported that it could not possibly be given until the Party had endorsed such action at their Conference at Whitsuntide!

---

[1] In a private letter to Churchill of 18 October 1948.

Alfred Duff Cooper: diary[1]

(*Norwich papers*)

29 September 1938   [Savoy Hotel]
late evening

I insulted Prof Lindemann—Bob Boothby and I insulted Garvin so that he left in a rage. Then everybody insulted everybody else and Winston ended by saying that at the next general election he would speak on every Socialist platform in the country against the Government.

Winston S. Churchill to Alfred Duff Cooper: note passed in the House of Commons

(*Norwich papers*)

30 September 1938

Your speech was one of the finest Parliamentary performances I have ever heard. It was admirable in form, massive in argument and shone with courage and public spirit.[2]

[1] Duff Cooper was at a meeting of the Other Club. Others present included Lloyd George, Brendan Bracken, Richard Law, Sir Archibald Sinclair and one other Cabinet Minister, Walter Elliot, the new Minister of Health. One of the youngest present, Colin Coote, later recorded how, during the dinner, Churchill was in 'a towering rage and a deepening gloom'. The failure to persuade Eden or Attlee to sign the telegram to Chamberlain had much upset him. Coote also recalled how Churchill 'turned savagely' upon the two ministers present, Duff Cooper and Walter Elliot. An 'echoing timbre' to his usual voice betrayed his deep emotion: 'it was not an echo, but a supersonic boom'. How, Churchill asked the two Ministers, 'could honourable men with wide experience and fine records in the Great War condone a policy so cowardly? It was sordid, squalid, sub-human, and suicidal' (*'Editorial', pages 173–4*). In the early hours of the morning, on learning that Chamberlain, Daladier, Hitler and Mussolini were about to reach agreement at Munich on the terms of the transfer of the Sudetenland to Germany, Duff Cooper left the room in a rage. As Churchill himself left shortly afterwards, he passed an open door leading into one of the hotel's restaurants. From inside the crowded room the sound of merriment assailed him. Churchill stopped in the doorway, silent and impassive. Then, as he turned away, he muttered, as if to himself: 'Those poor people! They little know what they will have to face' (*Lord Coleraine, in conversation with the author*).

[2] During the course of his resignation speech, Duff Cooper said: 'The Prime Minister has believed in addressing Herr Hitler through the language of sweet reasonableness. I have believed that he was more open to the language of the mailed fist. . . .' Duff Cooper ended his speech with the words: 'I remember when we were discussing the Godesburg ultimatum that I said that if I were a party to persuading, or even to suggesting to the Czechoslovak Government that they should accept that ultimatum, I should never be able to hold up my head again. I have forfeited a great deal. I have given up an office that I loved, work in which I was deeply interested, and a staff of which any man might be proud. I have given up associations in that work with my colleagues with whom I have maintained for many years the most harmonious relations, not only as colleagues but as friends. I have given up the privilege of serving as lieutenant to a leader whom I still regard with the deepest admiration and affection. I have ruined, perhaps, my political career. But that is of little matter; I have retained something which is to me of great value. I can still walk about the world with my head erect.'

Winston S. Churchill to Anthony Crossley

(*Churchill papers: 2/331*)

30 September 1938

Many thanks for your letter. I am entirely indifferent to such opinions as you mention. The last word has not been spoken yet.

Lord Rothermere to Winston S. Churchill

(*Churchill papers: 9/130*)

30 September 1938
Private and Confidential

My dear Winston,

Before the end of March, Germany will demand the return of her colonies with equivalents for those the British Government is unable to return, such as German South West Africa. The great thing now is to avoid a head-on collision on this question. Germany intends to get these colonies back, and my information is that an ultimatum of two or three weeks will be delivered in due course giving a date on which they must be returned.[1]

We must avoid signing on the dotted line, so the only thing now is to open negotiations with Germany in regard to this particular matter.

The only other matter on Germany's agenda for next year is a final clean up of Czecho-Slovakia. The agreement signed in the early hours of this morning will lead to much friction, and will end after a period of nine or ten months by the entry of German troops into parts of Czecho-Slovakia outside the territory she has just gained.[2]

A moribund people such as ours is not equipped to deal effectively with a totalitarian State.

You might like to hear this interpretation of the situation.

Yours,
Harold R

---

[1] No such ultimatum was ever delivered.

[2] Five and a half months after the signature of the Munich Agreement German forces entered Prague, and Bohemia and Moravia were declared a German 'Protectorate' (see page 1391, note 3 and pages 1396–7).

Robert Birley: [1] *recollections* [2]

(*Randolph Churchill papers*)

[30 September 1938]

On the day of the Munich agreement I did something I have never done before or since. I ran away from school. I simply could not face the school. So I asked the second master to carry on and my wife and I went up to London. We were walking miserably round St James's when we met Ronnie Cartland.[3]

We talked and very soon found that we felt exactly the same. We both agreed that your father would somehow in the end save us from the disasters which we felt were inevitable, and that, if it had not been for him, we should have felt absolutely hopeless. After our talk on the pavement of about half an hour I was restored and I was able to go back to school.

---

[1] Robert Birley, 1903–   . Educated at Rugby and Balliol College, Oxford. Assistant Master, Eton College, 1926–35 (where he was one of Randolph Churchill's teachers). Headmaster, Charterhouse, 1935–47. Head Master, Eton College, 1949–63. Knighted, 1967. Chichele Lecturer, All Souls College, Oxford, 1967. Professor of Social Science and Humanities, City University, London, 1967–71. Chairman of the Central Council of the Selly Oak Colleges since 1969.

[2] In a letter to Randolph Churchill of 26 January 1965.

[3] John Ronald Hamilton Cartland, 1907–1940. Brother of Barbara Cartland. Their father was killed in action on the western front on 27 May 1918. Educated at Charterhouse. Worked at the Conservative Central Office 1927–35. Conservative MP for King's Norton, 1935–40. Captain, 53rd Anti-Tank Regiment, Royal Artillery, British Expeditionary Force, 1940. Killed in action in France, 30 May 1940. Churchill wrote of him, on 7 November 1941 (in the preface to Barbara Cartland's book *Ronald Cartland*): 'At a time when our political life had become feckless and dull, he spoke fearlessly for Britain. His words and acts were instinct with the sense of our country's traditions and duty. His courage and bearing inspired those who met him or heard him.'

October 1938

Sir Alexander Cadogan: diary

('*The Diaries of Sir Alexander Cadogan*')

1 October 1938

Winston, G. Lloyd and others are intriguing with Masaryk and Maisky. But I don't feel suitably frightened. Duff Cooper resigned. Good riddance of bad rubbish.

Kathleen Hill to Winston S. Churchill

(*Churchill papers: 2/350*)

1 October 1938

Owing to the situation the BBC are submitting all talks to be broadcast to the Home Office.[1] They are therefore very anxious to have your talk on the Mediterranean. If you cannot let them have it at once, would you kindly see Mr Burgess[2] who is ready to come to Chartwell this afternoon or tomorrow.

---

[1] On 10 August 1938 the Director of Talks at the BBC, Sir Richard Maconachie, had written to Churchill asking him to give a talk in a planned series on the Mediterranean. The general adviser to the series was E. H. Carr, Professor of International Relations at Aberystwyth University. Other intended speakers included Professor R. W. Seton-Watson, F. A. Voigt, Sir Ronald Storrs, Arnold Toynbee and Gerald Crowther. Maconachie hoped that Churchill would agree to give the opening talk, on 6 October 1938. The fee offered was fifty guineas (*BBC Written Archives*).

[2] Guy Burgess, 1912–1963. The son of a naval officer (who died when Burgess was 12). Educated at Eton and Dartmouth. Left Dartmouth on account of his poor eyesight, and returned to Eton. History scholar at Trinity College, Cambridge, 1930–4; while at Cambridge he joined the Communist Party and the Anti-War Movement. Visited the Soviet Union in 1934, Germany in 1935. Joined the staff of the BBC, 1935; subsequently BBC representative at the House of Commons, responsible for the *Week in Westminster* programme. Joined the British Secret Service, December 1938. Involved in the preparation of Allied propaganda, 1939–40; returned to the BBC, 1941–3. Joined the Foreign Office News Department, 1943; Private Secretary to the Minister of State, 1946; British Embassy, Washington, 1950. Defected to the Soviet Union, 1951; subsequently resident in Moscow, where he died.

Guy Burgess to Winston S. Churchill
(Churchill papers: 2/350)

2 October 1938

Dear Mr Churchill,

I've put the broadcast position officially on another sheet. I cannot help writing more personally to thank you for the way you received me to-day and for your book & the inscription. The one unfortunately is already historic for the world, the other will be for me.

I feel I must in the situation we now find ourselves and since I myself try to feel as a historian (I was a scholar at Cambridge, where I taught for a while) put what I feel on paper to you who listened so sympathetically this morning & on whom, as I see it, so much now depends. You will excuse the exaggerations (tho I feel we are in a situation whose dangers cannot be exaggerated).

Traditional English policy since the reign of Elizabeth, the policy of Marlborough, of Pitt, of Eyre Crowe,[1] of Vansittart, has been blindly set aside to suit the vanity, the obstinacy, & the *ignorance* of *one* man, no longer young. We shall be told he has saved the peace, that anything is worth that. This is not true. He has made war inevitable, & lost it.

Of all the four men present at the 4 power conference, Mr Chamberlain was alone firmly seated in power, the Minister of a united contented and—still in time enough—powerful nation. He possessed also the unponderables of world moral support. Yet what was the outcome? He has quite possibly sacrificed for ever the safety of the Empire and its necessary continental ally, France. In addition he has strengthened our opponents to an incredible degree. You spoke of 30 divisions given to Hitler. It is not 30 divisions that have been given to Hitler, but Germany itself—and a Germany that he will in future and for the first time, be able to lead into war with the possibility of success. The accusation that Chamberlain gave Mussolini Italy is untrue, he merely gave it back to him. Ten million men —and he dared not mobilise one. The history of de Bono[2] & de Badoglio,[3] of Vittorio Mussolini & the

---

[1] Eyre Alexander Barby Wichart Crowe, 1864–1925. Born in Leipzig; educated at Dusseldorf and Berlin (his mother was German, his father British). Entered Foreign Office as a Junior Clerk, 1906. Knighted, 1911. Assistant Under-Secretary of State, Foreign Office, 1912–19. Attacked by a section of the Press in 1915 for his German origins, his integrity was upheld publicly by Sir Edward Grey. One of the British plenipotentiaries at the Paris Peace Conference, 1919. Permanent Under-Secretary of State, Foreign Office, 1920–5.

[2] Emilio de Bono, 1866–1944. A professional soldier in the Italian army. On active service at the battle of Adowa, 1896, and in the First World War. Joined the Fascist movement and participated in the march on Rome, 1922. Governor of Tripolitania, 1925. Commanded the forces in Ethiopia, 1935 (but replaced by Badoglio). Minister of State, 1942. Took part in the Grand Fascist Council which led to the overthrow of Mussolini. Arrested on Mussolini's orders, tried and shot (in Verona) 1944.

[3] Pietro Badoglio, 1864–1956. Chief of the Italian General Staff, 1919–21. Governor of

Prince of Piedmont proves how easily the King & the army could have rid Italy, Europe & us of that insane opportunist.

By fortune rather than foresight we had all the cards in our hands. The gamble of Hitler's deposition might not have been worth taking—one will be told it was 'only a gamble', the War Office, the Reichswehr could not be certain. Perhaps. But we needn't have accepted the risk. For *one* principle of politics one can discern in Hitler. A regard for the historical incidents of his struggle to power in Germany. That is where he learnt his political lessons. Now these past weeks have been the *International* crisis of national socialism. Turn to the *National* crisis of Hitler's struggle for power. When Hindenburg refused him the Chancellorship. Then as now Hitler was threatening force. The party was organised & commanded to seize Berlin if his demands were refused. They *were* refused. What did Hitler do? He did *not* march, he withdrew—and was nearly deposed by the infuriated Strassers[1] for so doing. And why did he withdraw? Again an incident in the party struggle. He has tried Force *once*—and it failed. The Hitler–Ludendorff putsch. He has never forgotten the broken shoulder & the fear of that fiasco.[2] Hitler uses force only against fear, he has been right in that till now, for the odds were against him. Soon they may be against us. That *is* the simple truth of this crisis—he took what he thought he could get. He even told Chamberlain so: 'I wld never have given those demands if I thought you'd accept'. C. took that as a threat of war. It was probably only the successful crook regretting not asking enough.

What is to be done? I hear as I write the news of Duff Cooper's resignation & Harold's speech.[3] So there is internal hope—pace the labour party. But

---

Libya, 1928–33. Commanded the Italian troops in Ethiopia, 1936 (including the occupation of Addis Ababa). Commander-in-Chief of the Italian Army, 1940. Opposed to war with Greece, 1941, and replaced. Following the fall of Mussolini in September 1943, head of the Italian Government (negotiating the armistice with the Allies and declaring war on Germany). Retired from politics, June 1944.

[1] Gregor and Otto Strasser (see page 543, note 1).

[2] On 8 November 1925 Hitler's armed followers had briefly captured the Government of Bavaria, and persuaded General Ludendorff to join their 'revolution'. On the following day armed police regained control. Fourteen of Hitler's followers were killed, and Hitler himself captured and imprisoned. Ludendorff was acquitted.

[3] Speaking at Manchester on 1 October 1938, Harold Nicolson had called the Munich agreement a 'surrender' that had achieved peace not for a generation, but only for six months. Of Neville Chamberlain, Nicolson had declared: 'He was offered one of the greatest opportunities that ever fell to the lot of any British statesman. He missed that opportunity. Had he taken a firm line at Munich he would have established perhaps forever the superiority of democratic faith over fascist conceptions.' Nicolson had also criticized the House of Commons' manifestation of relief over the agreement, calling it 'one of the most lamentable exhibitions of mass hysteria that that great institution has ever witnessed'. In the House of Commons, on 5 October 1938, Nicolson retracted this latter remark, telling the House that his statement had been 'not only ill-considered but ill-mannered'. 'I crave pardon,' he added. 'I apologize humbly.'

you alone have the force & the authority to galvanize the potential allies into action. Anyhow I know nothing of English politics—in Parliament.

But internationally? There seems now so little to work with. One thing it seems must be done at once to retrieve what may now have shrunk to only the chance of a victorious war as the alternative to disaster + war.

The guarantee of the new Czech Frontier must be made absolute, & gun tight. I suspect Chamberlain possibly to have wrung this concession from Simon & Hoare only by reminding them of W. Wilson—by saying the country will never ratify it.[1] But it would. Hitler *must* be prevented from obtaining the material resources which, (& not the Sudetens) he is really after. This must be made clear—and soon. Otherwise—and this is the danger—the new Czech state will follow its material interests & under the Agrarian Fascists join Hitler. A loan must be given as well as guarantees, for the Czechs are ruined as well as powerless. How otherwise can we expect the Czechs to fight for Great Britain—for that is what the Franco-Czech alliance amounted to. The story I told you of the experiences of my friend, the head of the British Institute in Prague is relevant here. He is English. His servant depuis 3 ans would no longer clean his boots. He could only pass through the crowds round the British Legation by speaking *German* (he *might* then have been a social democrat). It is to the advantage *now* of the new Czech state to come to terms with the German Reich—and this before we know it may be followed by Hitler's next move—the attempt to create some form of Balkan–Danubian confederation under German control. Here full advantage must be taken, if it is not too late, of the fright Mussolini has had; together we must build a new front in the Balkans.

Thirdly the French must reaffirm the Franco-Soviet pact & Russia must be induced to do this by the promise of consultations with us.

Above all the Tory party must be made to realise that politics really depend on realism, but that the realities are questions of power, economic, strategic & military, and *not* on sentiment, whether pacifist, class or Christian.

Privately I know something of the manoeuvres of the Cagoulards[2] both here & in France. They wish an agreement with Germany. So do we all and it is possible the present arrangement is not an agreement with Germany, it is a

---

[1] In 1919 Woodrow Wilson had been the principal United States' negotiator of the Treaty of Versailles. In 1920 the United States' Senate had refused to ratify the Treaty, to which the United States was therefore no longer a signatory, so that several central aspects of the Treaty, such as the proposed guarantee of a permanently demilitarized Rhineland, never became a part of United States policy.

[2] A name given by the French Press to the *Comité secret d'action révolutionnaire* (CSAR), an extremist right wing group established in 1932, and responsible for the assassination both of the Italian anti-fascist Roselli brothers in 1935, and of the French Minister of the Interior, Marx Dormoy, in 1940. With the coming of war, many Cagoulards were active collaborators with the Nazis, 1940–5, but some joined anti-Nazi resistance groups.

capitulation to the enemies of the Empire, the present regime in power. Mr Chamberlain has snatched defeat out of the very jaws of victory.

I'm sure you will not have read as far as this—if you have and would be prepared to meet again I wish you'd get your secretary to drop me a line. I'm in the London telephone book—or at the BBC.

With all wishes for your success.

Yours very gratefully,
Guy Burgess

A public subscription from the people for the Czechs—not Chamberlain.

Sir Maurice Hankey: diary

(*Hankey papers*)

2 October 1938

Winston Churchill's sudden visit to France[1] by aeroplane, accompanied by General Spears, and his visit *only* to the members of the French Government like Mandel, who is opposed to the policy of peace, was most improper— Bonnet, the French Foreign Minister, has complained about it, asking what we would say if prominent French statesmen did the same: he has also protested against being rung up by Churchill and Spears from London for information. . . .[2]

Harold Nicolson: diary

(*Nicolson papers*)

3 October 1938

We have a meeting called by Winston in Bracken's house. Present Winston, Amery, Wolmer, Harold Macmillan, Cartland, Derrick Gunston,[3]

---

[1] On 20 September 1938 (see page 1170).

[2] Hankey added that Phipps had also complained to him that Sir Robert Vansittart was 'almost certainly in touch with Churchill, Eden, the Labour Leaders and with Léger and the Quai d'Orsay'.

[3] Derrick Wellesley Gunston, 1891–   . Educated at Harrow and Trinity College, Cambridge. On active service, 1914–18; second-in-command, 1st Batallion Irish Guards, 1918 (Military Cross). Conservative MP for Thornbury, 1924–45. Parliamentary Private Secretary to Kingsley Wood (Minister of Health), 1926–9; to Neville Chamberlain (Chancellor of the Exchequer), 1931–6; to David Margesson (War Office), 1940–2. Created Baronet, 1938. One of his two sons was killed in the Second World War (see page 1507, note 1).

Sidney Herbert,[1] Spears, Emrys-Evans[2] and others. We discuss what to do. The idea is that if the Government put down a resolution we shall try and get the opposition to put down an amendment for which we can vote. They can scarcely withdraw the whip from thirty members especially if Duff and Anthony join us.

Roy Harrod [3] *to Winston S. Churchill*

(*Churchill papers: 2/332*)

4 October 1938   Oxford

Dear Mr Churchill,

May I for one hereby testify that I am absolutely convinced, in view of such contacts and experience as I have, that the majority of the country is on your side in the foreign policy issue. I am in favour of a fairly quick election because I believe that there is a tendency to relapse into lethargic optimism until the next crisis when an appeal will be too late.

Of course an electoral pact is essential, and, I believe, quite possible. In one way strong labour representation must help us—in regaining Russia.

May I appeal to you for two things. One, a Midlothian campaign carried out throughout the country. Two, initiative with regard to the electoral pact. There is far too much squeamishness at present. If you would go to your Berchtesgaden and talk and talk at Attlee, I believe you could do the trick. If you would have the sense of taking charge of the situation, being the

---

[1] Sidney Herbert, 1890–1939. Educated at Eton and Balliol College, Oxford. On active service in the Royal Horse Guards, 1915–18 (wounded, despatches). Captain, 1918. Private Secretary to Churchill (then Secretary of State for War), 1919–20. Conservative MP for Scarborough and Whitby, 1922–31; for Westminster, Abbey, 1932–9. Parliamentary Private Secretary to the Prime Minister (Baldwin), 1923–4 and 1924–7. Created Baronet, 1936. Elected to the Other Club, 1938. Died at his villa in Cannes, March 1939. A bachelor, his baronetcy became extinct.

[2] Paul Vychan Emrys-Evans, 1894–1964. Educated at Harrow and King's College, Cambridge. Lieutenant, Suffolk Regiment, 1914–17 (wounded in France, 1916). Foreign Office, 1917–23. Unsuccessful Conservative candidate, 1929. Conservative MP for South Derbyshire, 1931–45. Parliamentary Private Secretary, War Office, 1940; Dominion Affairs, 1940–1. Parliamentary Under-Secretary of State for Dominion Affairs, 1941–5. A strong supporter and close friend of Anthony Eden.

[3] Roy Forbes Harrod, 1900–1978. Economist. Lecturer at Christ Church, Oxford, 1922–4; Student of Christ Church, 1924–67 (tutor to Randolph Churchill), University Lecturer in Economics, 1929–37 and 1946–52. Nuffield Reader in Economics, 1952–67. Served under Professor Lindemann on Churchill's Private Statistical Staff, Admiralty, 1940, and in the Prime Minister's Office, 1940–2. Statistical Adviser to the Admiralty, 1943–5 Joint Editor, *Economic Journal*, 1945–61. Economic Adviser to the International Monetary Fund, 1952–3. Member of the Migration Board, Commonwealth Relations Office, 1953–66. Knighted, 1959.

biggest man of the lot, you would find yourself in virtual charge. After all the basis is right, because you agree on the vital and essential and indeed only problem of the moment. I could contribute my tiny mite to this situation, if it were of any value, Attlee's secretary being an old personal friend of mine, who has some respect for me. (John Dugdale.[1])

I tried talking to the Prof, with whom I usually pick these things over, this evening, but found him encased in such a massive iceberg of pessimism that conversation was impossible. He suggested that we did not wish much to win an election, since the legacy from Chamberlain made all lines equally hopeless. I am sure you will rise above this and be prepared to take the kicks which materialise.[2] I write very briefly having a sense of the pressure you are under.

Ys vy sincerely,
Roy Harrod

Guy Burgess: BBC internal circulating Memorandum
(BBC Written Archives)

4 October 1938

Subject: Part of Conversation with Mr Churchill on Saturday, October 1st.

Mr Churchill complained that he had been very badly treated in the matter of political broadcasts and that he was always muzzled by the BBC. I said I was not myself in possession of the facts and, in any case, had nothing to do with such matters, since I believed that the allotment of space was settled by arrangement and discussion between the BBC and the political parties. I imagine that he was referring to a past controversy that I believe (though I didn't say so) there was over India and election time.

He went on to say that he imagined that he would be even more muzzled in the future, since the work at the BBC seemed to have passed under the

---

[1] John Dugdale, 1905–1963. Educated at Wellington College and Christ Church, Oxford. Attaché, British Legation, Peking, 1926–7. Private Secretary to Clement Attlee, 1931–9. On active service (army), 1940–5. Labour MP for West Bromwich from 1941 until his death. Parliamentary Private Secretary to Attlee (Deputy Prime Minister), 1945. Parliamentary and Financial Secretary, Admiralty, 1945–50. Privy Councillor, 1949. Minister of State for Colonial Affairs, 1950–1. Chairman of the Commonwealth Society for the Deaf.

[2] Churchill did not share 'Prof' Lindemann's pessimism, writing in the *Daily Telegraph* on 4 October 1938: 'It is a crime to despair. We must learn to draw from misfortune the means of future strength. There must not be lacking in our leadership something of the spirit of that Austrian corporal who, when all had fallen into ruins about him, and when Germany seemed to have sunk for ever into chaos, did not hesitate to march forth against the vast array of victorious nations, and has already turned the tables so decisively upon them. It is the hour, not for despair, but for courage and rebuilding; and that is the spirit which should rule us in this hour.'

control of the Government. I said that this was not, in fact, the case, though just at the moment we were, as a matter of courtesy, allowing the Foreign Office to see scripts on political subjects. The point is WSC seems very anxious to talk.

G. Burgess

Ivan Maisky to Winston S. Churchill

(*Churchill papers: 9/130*)

4 October 1938

My dear Churchill,

In view of the statement made last night by Sir Samuel Hoare on the question of 'contacts' between the British and the Soviet Governments during the crisis, I take the liberty of sending to you for your information the enclosed statement of the facts about this.

Yours sincerely,
I. Maisky

Ivan Maisky: note

(*Churchill papers: 9/130*)

4 October 1938

1. The Soviet Ambassador, during the crisis, visited the Foreign Office three times; on the 8th and the 28th September—on both occasions to see Lord Halifax—and on the 30th to see Sir Alexander Cadogan.[1] Between the 8th and the 28th September, the Soviet Ambassador was at Geneva and consequently there was no contact between him and the Foreign Office, neither was there any contact in London between the Foreign Office and the Soviet Charge d'Affaires.

2. During his visit to Lord Halifax on the 8th various subjects were

---

[1] Alexander George Montagu Cadogan, 1884–1968. Seventh son of the 5th Earl Cadogan. Educated at Eton and Balliol College, Oxford. Attaché Diplomatic Service, 1908. British Minister to China, 1933–5; Ambassador, 1935–6. Knighted, 1934. Deputy Under-Secretary of State for Foreign Affairs, 1936–7; Permanent Under-Secretary, January 1938–February 1946. Permanent British Representative at the United Nations, 1946–50. Government Director, Suez Canal Company, 1951–7. Chairman of the BBC, 1952–7. One brother, William George Sydney Cadogan, born in 1879, was killed in action in France on 14 November 1914. Another brother, Edward Cecil George Cadogan was a Conservative MP from 1922 to 1945 and largely responsible for the abolition of judicial corporal punishment.

touched upon including the position in Central Europe but the talk on this particular problem was simply an exchange of views on the situation.

3. The talk with Lord Halifax on the 28th took place when the Prime Minister was already in Munich. In this talk Lord Halifax explained to the Soviet Ambassador the circumstances under which the Munich Conference was arranged, and, among other things, said that the British Government did not raise the question of the Soviet Union participating in the Munich Conference as it was known beforehand that Hitler and Mussolini would reject any such suggestion at the same time hinting that the British Government was not averse to continuing its present relationship with the Soviet Government.

4. On the 30th September Sir Alexander Cadogan informed the Soviet Ambassador of the Munich results and had an exchange of view on the Munich 'settlement'.

5. During the same period of crisis the British Ambassador in Moscow had not a single conversation with the Soviet Foreign Office on Czechoslovakia.

6. In Geneva, Mr Litvinov and the Soviet Ambassador were meeting practically daily in the meetings of the Commissions or at lunches and dinners, Mr Butler,[1] the British Under Secretary for Foreign Affairs, and on several occasions (in the course of his comings and goings between London and Geneva) Earl de la Warr. But these meetings consisted in the exchange of the latest bits of news which either side had of the developments in Czechoslovakia and in the various capitals of Europe.

7. The only one occasion which approached something like consultation between the Soviet and the British Governments on the crisis occurred in the afternoon of the 23rd September—the day when Herr Hitler produced his ultimatum in Godesberg—when Earl de la Warr and Mr Butler on instructions from London, invited Mr Litvinov and the Soviet Ambassador to join them in a conversation of a quite 'informal' character. (The word 'informal' was particularly stressed.) During this meeting the British representatives asked Mr Litvinov what would be the Soviet attitude in case the Chamberlain–Hitler negotiations broke down and Czechoslovakia was invaded by Germany. Mr Litvinov once more reiterated the firm resolve of the Soviet Government to fulfill all her obligations under the Soviet–Czech

---

[1] Richard Austen Butler, 1902–1982. Educated at Marlborough and Pembroke College, Cambridge. President of the Cambridge Union, 1924. Conservative MP for Saffron Walden, 1929–65. Under-Secretary of State, India Office, 1932–7. Parliamentary Secretary, Ministry of Labour, 1937–8. Under-Secretary of State for Foreign Affairs, 1938–41. Privy Councillor, 1939. Minister of Education, 1941–5. Minister of Labour, 1945. Chancellor of the Exchequer, 1951–5. Lord Privy Seal, 1955–61. Home Secretary, 1957–62. Deputy Prime Minister, 1962–3. Secretary of State for Foreign Affairs, 1963–4. Created Baron Butler of Saffron Walden, 1965. Master of Trinity College, Cambridge, 1965–78.

Pact (provided France fulfilled hers—as is stipulated in the Soviet–Czech Pact), and in turn he suggested certain measures which in his opinion it would be necessary to take forthwith. The British representatives undertook to report these suggestions to London, but nothing has transpired since that time.

8. All through this crisis the 'contacts' which the British Government had with the Soviet Government were: a) rare; b) in the nature of an exchange of views on the situation or information given to the Soviet Government on the already accomplished facts; c) except the meeting of the 23rd September at Geneva, which had no direct results, there was not a single case of consultation with the Soviet Government on the steps or measures contemplated by the British or by the British and French Governments in connection with the crisis. Therefore, all attempts which are being made at the present time to create an impression that the Soviet Government had something to do with the Anglo-French Plan of the 13th September or with the Munich 'settlement' are absolutely false.

Lady Violet Bonham Carter to Winston S. Churchill

(*Churchill papers: 2/332*)

5 October 1938   House of Commons

Dearest Winston,

1,000 congratulations & thanks—for a *marvellous* speech—(will it pierce the shell of those drowsy tortoises—? dragging us to our doom).[1]

All thanks & love,
Violet

---

[1] Speaking on 5 October 1938 Churchill told the House of Commons: '. . there never can be friendship between the British democracy and the Nazi Power, that Power which spurns Christian ethics, which cheers its onward course by a barbarous paganism, which vaunts the spirit of aggression and conquest, which derives strength and perverted pleasure from persecution, and uses, as we have seen, with pitiless brutality the threat of murderous force. That Power cannot ever be the trusted friend of the British democracy.' He continued: 'What I find unendurable is the sense of our country falling into the power, into the orbit and influence of Nazi Germany and of our existence becoming dependent upon their good will or pleasure. It is to prevent that that I have tried my best to urge the maintenance of every bulwark of defence—first the timely creation of an Air Force superior to anything within striking distance of our shores; secondly the gathering together of the collective strength of many nations; and thirdly, the making of alliances and military conventions, all within the Covenant, in order to gather together forces at any rate to restrain the onward movement of this Power. It has all been in vain. Every position has been successively undermined and abandoned on specious and plausible excuses.'

Harold Nicolson: diary

(Nicolson papers)

5 October 1938

A meeting at Brendan Bracken's house to decide what we are going to do. Are we to vote against the Government or are we to abstain? We agree that the effect of our action would depend upon its joint character. It would be a pity if some of us voted against, and some abstained. It would be far more effective (since there is little hope of many voting against), if we all abstained. Winston says he refuses to abstain, since that would mean that he half agreed with Government policy. We decide that we must all do what we think best.[1]

Sir Samuel Hoare to Neville Chamberlain

(Templewood papers)

5 October 1938

. . . the reconstruction of the Government is urgent. I do not believe that there is any basis of a working agreement between Winston and ourselves. But as to Anthony, I would get him back if and when you can.[2]

Sir Sidney Herbert to Winston S. Churchill

(Churchill papers: 2/332)

6 October 1938

My dear Winston,

Your speech yesterday was magnificent—but so is every speech you make, & I wish to God that the Govt had listened to you years ago.

[1] Following the 'Munich' debate, thirty Conservative MPs abstained, and twelve of these thirty, including Churchill, remained seated during the Division, as a further protest. This action, Harold Nicolson noted in his diary, 'must enrage the Government, since it is not our numbers but our reputation'. Those who remained sitting were Churchill, Derrick Gunston, Ronald Cartland, Duncan Sandys, Harold Nicolson, Richard Law, Brendan Bracken, Commander Bower, Sir Roger Keyes, Lord Wolmer, Vyvyan Adams and Captain Alan Graham. The abstainers included Eden, Duff Cooper, Amery, Sir Sidney Herbert, General Spears, Harold Macmillan and Anthony Crossley. Nicolson noted: 'That looks none too well in any list. The House knows that most of the above people know far more about the real issue than they do' (*Nicolson papers*). Those who supported the Government in the division included several who had earlier supported Churchill on India, including Sir Henry Page Croft, Patrick Donner, Alan Lennox-Boyd, Victor Raikes and Sir Murray Sueter.

[2] Chamberlain did not ask Eden to rejoin the Government. Nor did he ask Churchill to join it. The following changes were made: Lord Runciman became Lord President of the Council, Sir John Anderson was appointed Lord Privy Seal, Earl Stanhope replaced Alfred Duff Cooper as First Lord of the Admiralty, Malcolm MacDonald went to the Dominions Office and Earl De La Warr to the Board of Education.

I write now to thank you, from my heart, for all your help on Tuesday. First for your encouragement—secondly for giving me your seat to speak from—(the best that exists in the H of C if one cannot have the Treasury box) & thirdly for all the kind things you were good enough to say to me afterwards.

I remember that you said that I must have been very well fit to make such a speech. Actually I lay in bed from 2 to 4 pm in a mixture of Coma and Terror. I could write no proper notes, nor arrange my speech—& had it not been for you, I think I should have 'run out' on it. So I thank you the more for having both helped & 'gingered' me into a speech which has, I think, proved useful (to judge by the Press & my Fan Mail) to all the things that you & I have at heart.[1]

Let us go on without cease at the Govt. Tell me how to help—until we are fully re-armed & able to talk *almost* equally to a Dictator.

Bless & thank you

Yrs,
Sidney Herbert

Winston S. Churchill to General Sir Hugh Tudor

(*Churchill papers: 2/332*)

6 October 1938

Thank you so much for your letter. You will have seen all the stresses we have gone through. The Government have thrown everything away, and I am trying now to see what plans can be made to stop the Huns.

Forgive me for not writing more, as I am so pressed.

[1] On 4 October 1938, during the second day of the 'Munich' debate, Sir Sidney Herbert told the House of Commons: 'At the expense of much dishonour, we have gained a temporary respite of peace. In the name of all that is decent let us use that for rearmament,' and he went on to urge Chamberlain not to hold a General Election, as it had been rumoured he wished to do, simply in order to seek yet another large majority. It would be better, he argued, to broaden the basis of the Government, and to invite both Labour and the Trade Unions to join it. Above all, Herbert said, the pace of rearmament had been allowed to slacken, and must now be accelerated. Referring to the Sandys case, Herbert told the House of Commons: 'Even a child in my village knows that we have not got Bren guns in the numbers these ought to be for every battalion . . . what is the good of having the men if we are to send them like sheep to the slaughter without armaments. We have talked long enough about "the years which the locusts have eaten". I was led to suppose that the locusts had stopped nibbling about two years ago, but I can still hear the little jowls creaking yet under the Front Bench.'

Winston S. Churchill to Sir Arthur Longmore

(*Churchill papers: 2/336*)

6 October 1938

I am so distressed by the change in the situation that I haven't the heart to address myself to the task to which you invited me at present.

Thank you very much all the same for giving me a further opportunity.

Mary Borden: diary

(*Lady Spears papers*)

6 October 1938

Harold Macmillan, Archie, Winston all speak against adjournment of the House. Declare the House has been given no outline of Government policy.

Tittering laughter greets Winston from Conservative benches when he declares the country wants the House to be in session during period of national emergency. The PM our Dictator is adamant.

Neville Chamberlain to Winston S. Churchill

(*Churchill papers: 2/332*)

6 October 1938   10 Downing Street

Dear Winston,

I am sorry if you think that my remarks were offensive,[1] but I must say that I think you are singularly sensitive for a man who so constantly attacks others.

---

[1] Following the division on October 6, Chamberlain moved a motion to adjourn the House until November 1. This was at once opposed by Attlee and Sinclair, as well as by several Conservatives. Harold Macmillan declared: 'We are being treated more and more as a kind of Reichstag to meet only to hear the orations and register the decrees of the government of the day.' It was essential for Parliament to meet before November 1, in what was, Macmillan said, a situation 'more dangerous and more formidable, more terrible than at any time since the beginning of Christian civilization'. Churchill likewise urged an early recall of Parliament to meet before November 1, suggesting that they met for two days on October 18. 'It is derogatory to Parliament . . .' he said, 'that it should be thought unfit as it were to be attending to these grave matters, that it should be sent away upon a holiday in one of the most formidable periods through which we have lived.' When Chamberlain said that it was up to the Speaker when Parliament was recalled, Churchill interjected: 'But only on the advice of His Majesty's Government.' Such a remark, Chamberlain retorted, was 'unworthy'. To say that the Government were not aware of the gravity of the crisis was a 'repetition of tittle tattle'.

I considered your remarks highly offensive to me and to those with whom I have been working.

I had not regarded these remarks, wounding as they were, as requiring a breach of personal relations, but you cannot expect me to allow you to do all the hitting and never hit back.

Yours sincerely,
Neville Chamberlain

Winston S. Churchill to Sir Alexander Cadogan
(*Foreign Office papers: 371/21808*)

7 October 1938

I should be very much obliged if you would let one of your secretaries explain the points in this letter, because I have not got them clearly in my mind.[1]

I have merely written in a conciliatory but mournful style to the Ambassador.[2]

Winston S. Churchill to Count Edward Raczyński
(*Churchill papers: 2/332*)

7 October 1938

Very many thanks for your kind and courteous letter.

We are all in the trough here, but your country has also passed through tragic vicissitudes. I have always thought of Poland as a nation which possessed a strong historical sense. This makes me all the more grieved to contemplate the squalid events which are occurring in Central Europe.

Believe me, all comes out even at the end of the day, and all will come out yet more even when all the days are ended.

Thank you once more for your great courtesy in writing to me.

[1] The Polish Minister, Count Edward Raczyński, had tried to explain to Churchill the reason for Poland's occupation of the Czech town and region of Teschen, in the immediate aftermath of the Munich Conference.

[2] Edward Raczyński, 1891–   . Educated at Krakow and Leipzig Universities, and at the London School of Economics. Entered the Polish Ministry of Foreign Affairs, 1919. Polish Minister to the League of Nations and Polish Delegate to the Disarmament Conference, 1932–4; Ambassador to London, 1934–45. Acting Polish Minister for Foreign Affairs (in London), 1941–2; Minister of State for Foreign Affairs in General Sikorski's Cabinet, London, 1942–3. Chairman of the Polish Research Centre, London, 1940–67. President of the Polish Government in Exile since 1979.

Robert Boothby to Winston S. Churchill

(*Churchill papers: 2/332*)

7 October 1938

Dear Winston,

I have just seen Brendan. He did not know yesterday that I had abstained from voting on the Government motion, having previously ascertained from the Labour party that they intended to challenge it. So that's that.

I see they've taken another slice off Czechoslovakia this morning.

Yrs ever,
Bob

Winston S. Churchill to Robert Boothby

(*Churchill papers: 2/332*)

7 October 1938

Of course, you were perfectly free to vote as you chose, and I am very glad to note that you abstained from voting on the Government Motion.

I do not understand the agitation which seizes you in these moments of what is, after all only petty Parliamentary action. You get so distressed about these matters both at the beginning and at the end, and nearly all our friends thought you had crumpled under the strain. You will certainly live to see many worse things than you have seen at present.

I have sent a copy of your letter to Duncan.

R. E. Fearnley-Whittingstall[1] to Winston S. Churchill

(*Churchill papers: 2/336*)

8 October 1938   Lincolns Inn Fields

Dear Sir,

I am a subaltern in an Anti-Aircraft Unit of the Territorial Army, and as such have been made aware of certain aspects of the recent mobilisation

---

[1] Robert Ellison Fearnley-Whittingstall, 1906–   . Educated at Oundle and Corpus Christi, Cambridge. Admitted solicitor, 1931. Joined the Territorial Army on the day after Hitler's invasion of Austria, March 1938. 2nd Lieutenant in a Territorial Searchlight Battalion, Royal Engineers, 1938–9. Served in Anti-Aircraft Command, and later in the Judge Advocate-General's Office, 1939–45.

which I feel ought to be fully investigated. I shall be glad to know whether you will be kind enough to see me so that I may discuss them with you.

Yours truly,
R. E. Fearnley-Whittingstall

Neville Chamberlain to his sister

(*Templewood papers*)

9 October 1938   10 Downing Street

I must say that I found the 4 days debate in the House a pretty trying ordeal, especially as I had to fight all the time against the defection of weaker brethren & Winston was carrying on a regular campaign against me with the aid of Masaryk the Czech minister. They, of course, are totally unaware of my knowledge of their proceedings: I had continual information of their doings & sayings which for the nth time demonstrated how completely Winston can deceive himself when he wants to, & how utterly credulous a foreigner can be when he is told the thing he wants to hear. In this case the thing was that 'Chamberlain's fall was imminent', . . .

I tried occasionally to take an antidote to the poison gas by reading a few of the countless letters & telegrams which continued to pour in expressing in most moving accents the writer's heartfelt relief & gratitude. All the world seemed to be full of my praises except the House of Commons but of course that was where I happened to be myself so naturally its voice spoke loudest in my ear. However on Wednesday things began to mend.

Winston S. Churchill to Sir Sidney Herbert

(*Churchill papers: 2/332*)

9 October 1938   Chartwell

Thank you so much for your letter. You stopped the General Election by your speech; and as you spoke I seemed to hear the voice of that old Conservative Party I once honoured and not of this over-whipped crowd of poor 'whites'.

I hear of the greatest panic in inner circles about the state of their defences now and in the future.

I must send you a copy of my book, which will show how precise, prolonged and detailed have been the warnings I have given.

I am so glad that we are working together again. I should like to talk to you very much, and I wonder whether you could come and spend a night here during the next fortnight or so? You have never seen this small place, which I have constructed largely with my own hands.

Winston S. Churchill to Richard Acland
(Churchill papers: 2/332)

9 October 1938

The answer is that there has been for several years no chance of catching up except by a combination or grand alliance of Powers, great and small, coupled with intense national effort. The disaster of Czechoslovakia has annihilated all possibility of a combination which can restore the situation in Europe. Nevertheless, night and day work by the whole of France and England might put us in a position where the Dictators might find easier prizes elsewhere.

Anyhow, whatever happens, as you say in your last paragraph, we must do our best. I greatly fear, however, a demand to cease arming, backed with specious blandishments.

Winston S. Churchill to Paul Reynaud
(Churchill papers: 2/332)

10 October 1938

I feel deeply concerned about the position of France, and about our own course. I cannot see what foreign policy is now open to the French Republic. No minor State will risk its future upon the guarantee of France. I am indulging in no pretensions upon our own account. You have been infected by our weakness, without being fortified by our strength. The politicians have broken the spirit of both countries successively. In the end England was ready to be better than her word. But it was too late.

The magnitude of the disaster leaves me groping in the dark. Not since the loss of the American Colonies has England suffered so deep an injury. France is back to the morrow of 1870.

What are we to do?

I cannot tell what are the forces now governing French action. The accursed

Flandin[1] is surely only typical of very large interests and moods which are at work beneath the surface of French politics.

The question now presenting itself is: Can we make head against the Nazi domination, or ought we *severally* to make the best terms possible with it—while trying to rearm? Or is a common effort still possible?

For thirty years I have consistently worked with France. I make no defence of my own country; but I do not know on what to rest to-day.

Please show this letter to Monsieur Mandel: but keep it otherwise to yourself.[2]

Robert Boothby to Winston S. Churchill

(*Churchill papers: 2/332*)

10 October 1938   House of Commons

Dear Winston,

Very many thanks for your letter, which I greatly appreciate.

I confess that I was, and am, greatly distressed. On purely personal grounds—which are of negligible importance—because I have so far failed to carry my Association with me, and had been warned by my Chairman that failure to support the Government would mean that I could not expect to be nominated again in the Unionist interest. (I enclose a telegram which I received this morning from my Executive, in which they have actually gone to the length of trying to stop me holding meetings!)

On broad national grounds—which are of vital importance—I feel that the consequences of our defeat, for that is what it amounts to, are incalculable; and that we may well have witnessed the first definite step in the downfall of the British Empire. I certainly doubt that we can live to see any worse thing happen than military defeat at the hands of Germany. And I am con-

---

[1] Flandin, who had resigned as Foreign Minister in June 1936, had sent Hitler a telegram of congratulations on the outcome of the Munich Conference.

[2] Reynaud replied to Churchill, in French, on 20 October 1938. Among the points which Reynaud made were: 'France is, alas, in a worse situation than in 1871. She has, in effect, as her neighbour, a Germany whose youth has today been made fanatical, and whose population, then equal, is today almost double that of France.' But Reynaud also saw hope in the fact that, 'after having taken note of our weaknesses', he believed that in Japan an economic crisis threatened to curb their military advantages, that in Italy Mussolini's intervention in Spain was unpopular, and that in Germany the internal situation was unstable. 'We have therefore,' he ended, 'no reason to lose hope, while we have the good luck to possess, among our friends, men of your calibre. One of your colleagues, a Labour MP, told me of the very great success of your speech, and the increasing importance of your position in the country. I rejoice in it.'

vinced that the only chance of salvation lies in a national unity, which is not at present in sight, and the achievement of which was made much more difficult by the events which took place in the House.

I hear that Max is all out for a smash, wants a purge in the Conservative Party, and is furious with Neville for not having an Election. Given his way he will split this country from top to bottom—and what is the good of that?

I do not think I have 'crumpled'; but I confess I cannot regard the events of the past few days, which I sincerely believe portend the doom of at any rate my generation, without agitation.

Yours ever,
Bob

Winston S. Churchill to Robert Boothby

(Boothby papers)

11 October 1938   Chartwell
Private

My dear Bob,

I do not think you will have any serious difficulty with your constituents if you let them know that whatever they say or do you will fight the seat.

I return you the telegram which they have sent you. I think you should certainly meet them at the earliest moment.

Yours vy sincerely,
W

Winston S. Churchill to R. E. Fearnley-Whittingstall

(Churchill papers: 2/336)

11 October 1938
Private

Dear Sir,

I shall not be in London before Parliament meets, except by chance. I should be very glad if you would write me a short note on the points you have in mind. You may be sure that I shall use the information with the utmost discretion.

Winston S. Churchill to John Dafoe[1]

(Churchill papers: 2/332)

11 October 1938

Thank you so much for your letter. I am deeply gratified to see the manner in which you had presented my speech in the House to your readers.[2]

I am now greatly distressed, and for the time being staggered by the situation. Hitherto the peace-loving Powers have been definitely stronger than the Dictators, but next year we must expect a different balance.

With all good wishes,

Lord Zetland to Lord Linlithgow

(India Office papers)

11 October 1938

Why, when there is a crisis, does Mr Winston Churchill go to 10 Downing Street? Is he invited? I have got the greatest possible admiration for Mr Churchill's Parliamentary powers, and his artistic powers, but I have always felt that in a crisis he is one of the first people who ought to be interned.

John Churchill[3] *to Winston S. Churchill*

(Churchill papers: 2/332)

13 October 1938

Dear Winston,

I met yesterday the Czech delegation sent over to arrange about the £10 million. They fell on me with excitement when they heard my name and sent respects etc to you. The principal man had been in Berlin during the

---

[1] John W. Dafoe, 1866–1944. Born in Canada. Editor of the *Montreal Herald*, 1892–95; the *Winnipeg Free Press*, 1901–44. Represented the Canadian Department of Public Information at the Paris Peace Conference, 1919. Churchill had met him in Winnipeg in August 1929. In 1917 Dafoe had declined Cabinet Office in Ottawa on the grounds that journalism and politics could not be mixed. In 1934 he became Chancellor of the University of Manitoba.

[2] On 6 October 1938 the *Winnipeg Free Press* gave considerable prominence to Churchill's Munich speech. A front page headline across four columns read 'Democracies threatened', with the second headline: 'Churchill says Britain will Rue Day Munich Agreement was Signed'. The article, which was illustrated by a photograph of Churchill, began: 'Drawing on all the bitterness and force of his oratorical ability, Winston Churchill swept Wednesday into the leadership of Parliamentary forces arrayed against Prime Minister Chamberlain's bargain with Chancellor Hitler as incorporated in the Munich agreement.'

[3] Churchill's brother (see page 61, note 4).

International Commissions meeting. When he learned the final result he sent to the French Ambassador[1] for an explanation, pointing out that the Munich agreement had been scrapped and that even the Godesberg Ultimatum had been excluded. The Ambassador shrugged his shoulders and said 'Le Fuehrer est en rage, alors qu'est-ce que nous pouvons faire'! He wanted me to tell you that.

yr,
JSC

Ramsay Muir[2] *to Winston S. Churchill*

(*Churchill papers: 2/332*)

13 October 1938

Dear Sir,

I have never met you, and you have probably never heard of me. But as a Liberal not without influence in our decimated party, I implore you to do what you alone *can* do: take the lead in a movement of national regeneration, and start what I may call a 'National Opposition'. The hidebound Labour Party will probably not follow you; but some of its best men, like Noel Baker, probably will. I should hope you would have a substantial following among the younger Conservatives. And I think I can promise you the whole-hearted support of the Liberal Party, which is by no means so negligible as it looks, and whose ideas more nearly correspond to the prevailing opinion of the nation than those of either of the other parties.

You probably know, better than I do, how profound is the reaction against Chamberlain's terrible surrender. Conservatives are vowing that they will never vote Conservative again. Some of my Liberal friends hope to draw party advantage out of this. I don't want to let mere party considerations weigh in such a crisis. But if you feel that the enterprise suggested to you is all but hopeless without the backing of a party machine, may I suggest to you that our machine still exists, though it is rather decrepit in many parts

---

[1] Robert Coulondre, 1885–1959. Born in Nîmes. A Consul in the London Embassy, 1909. On the staff of the Foreign Minister, 1910. On active service, 1914–18. Department of Political and Commercial Affairs, French Foreign Ministry, 1920; Deputy-Director, 1934–5. French Ambassador to Moscow, 1936–8; to Berlin, 1938–9; to Berne, 1940. President of the Reparations Commission, 1945. In 1951 he published his diplomatic memoirs, *De Staline à Hitler, souvenirs de deux ambassades.*

[2] Ramsay Muir, 1872–1941. Historian; he published his first book, on Liverpool Municipal history, in 1906; his *Atlas of Modern History* in 1911. Co-author of a series of historical atlases, and a pioneer in the field of historical atlases. Liberal MP for Rochdale, 1923–4. Chairman of the National Liberal Federation, 1931–3; President, 1933–6. Vice-President, Liberal Party Organization, 1936. His autobiography was published posthumously in 1943.

of the country, and that it would quickly be revived in co-operation with the LNU, LG's Council of Action,[1] and other organisations.

Now is the supreme moment; and if you would form a group of leaders and make a bold stand when Parlt resumes, the most satisfactory results might quickly follow.

For God's sake do this. It would revive the *moral* of the nation. I don't care whether you call yourself a Liberal or not, though that is the most descriptive of all political designations. But let us see a *man* at work again in our politics; a Chatham routing our supine Newcastles.

Sincerely yours,
Ramsay Muir

Winston S. Churchill to Sir James Hawkey
(*Churchill papers: 7/46*)

13 October 1938

My dear Sir James Hawkey,

I wish to consult the Association upon the grave events which have occurred. Upon India and National Defence, we have always acted in common. War has only been averted by submission to wrong-doing. I am convinced that a supreme national effort must be made to place our country in a position of security, where we shall be beyond the reach of being blackmailed from the Air. Very great sacrifices and exertions will be required from all, if the name of England is not to fail.

Will you therefore kindly ask our friends to assemble, and take the necessary steps in accordance with the rules of the Association.

Yours very truly,

Winston S. Churchill: draft letter[2]
(*Churchill papers: 7/46*)

[13 October 1938]

Sir,

Are we treating our member fairly? A letter has appeared in some of the papers circulating in the Division which accuses him of instability of principle

---

[1] The League of Nations Union, and Lloyd George's Council of Action; two organizations which had attracted the support of many Liberals, and former Liberals, in the 1930s.

[2] Churchill, who drafted this letter, noted on it, for Sir James Hawkey: 'Suggested letter to be signed by some friends and sent to as many local papers as possible for the next issue.'

and makes many complaints against him, including his attitude about the long settled India controversy. Surely it should be remembered that Mr Churchill has taken no Parliamentary action, either by speech or vote, without having consulted the Unionist Association beforehand either at the time of election or by public speeches delivered from time to time.

As to India, it is well known that the Association supported him and authorised him to fight that long battle and supported him throughout by repeated decisions as to rearmament; that too was put before us in the most prominent manner at the last General Election. He fought his election upon rearmament and obtained an increased majority at a time when most Conservative polls were falling.

When we look back upon the five years during which he has been pleading, with a great deal of knowledge, for effectual measures to put our country in a safe state, one can only feel deep sorrow and even indignation that his competent and timely advice was not taken. If his warnings had not passed unheeded, we should not now be in our present plight. Everyone ought to remember how four years ago he warned the Government that the Germans were building an Air Force which would soon surpass our own, how Mr Baldwin contradicted him flatly in the House and brushed aside the figures which he gave, and how these figures were proved to be right and the figures of the Government wrong; and how Mr Baldwin had to openly admit that he was in error upon this matter, so vital to the whole security of our country and the peace of Europe.

Again, in the recent crisis, our Member has said nothing in Parliament that does not follow naturally from the policy he explained, with general assent, to the Constituency at the great meeting at the Royal Forest Hotel in May. Had the policy then outlined been followed, we might never have got into this very deep water, nor should we have had to pay the price, the hard and ruinous price, of peace upon the Dictators' terms. Of course, Herr Hitler is very anxious to pillory our member as a man who is trying to make a war. Naturally the Nazi Party would like to silence him and prevent him from urging the nation to take the measures which even now might put us out of danger. But everyone knows how monstrous it is to suggest that any English statesman would seek to make a war with Germany. As far as I understand it, all that Mr Churchill has been doing is to try to get us into a position where we shall not be defenceless if we are exposed to some fresh act of aggression. In this he has rendered the greatest service to peace, because it is quite certain that a careless undefended England would be the greatest temptation to the Dictators to put forward demands which might easily lead to war. There are not many independent Members in the House of Commons; there is none whose words carry so far, and we ought, instead of cavilling to strengthen Mr Churchill's hands in his ceaseless efforts to maintain the strength and safety of our country. Certainly we ought not to join with Hitler and the German propagandists in trying to hound him down at a time when a real national union is admitted on all hands to be essential.

It would surely be a great misfortune if a quarrel arose in the Epping Division, which could not fail to attract the attention of the whole world. If Mr Churchill had to appeal to the electors and won, that would be an embarrassment to the Government; if he were beaten, it would be an encouragement to all the enemies of our country in every quarter of the world. For my part I say let us go on together, strengthening each other and trying to do our best to come through all the perils by which we are encompassed.

Richard Law to Winston S. Churchill

(*Churchill papers: 2/332*)

14 October 1938

My dear Winston,

In the intervals of licking my wounds, I'd like to congratulate you upon your terrific speech in the House last week (as well as to thank you for your kind & generous reference to myself)[1] and upon your attitude throughout the whole of this affair—I mean from the beginning of 'Arms & the Covenant' & hope that one day you will come into your own, although from your own point of view it's not really of very much importance; & can't see that office, even the highest, can add much to your fame.

We're just off to America for ten days and hope we'll hear your speech[2] in mid-ocean.

With best wishes & great admiration

Yrs,
Richard Law

---

[1] During the course of his speech on 5 October 1938, in the 'Munich' debate, Churchill singled out for praise Richard Law's 'compulsive' speech of protest, which had revived, he said, 'the memory of his famous father, so cherished in this House, and made me feel that his gifts did not die with him'. Churchill also told the House that Richard Law had been 'quite right in reminding us that the Prime Minister has himself throughout the conduct of these matters shown a robust indifference to cheers and boos and to the alternations of criticism or applause'.

[2] Churchill's broadcast of 16 October 1938 (see pages 1216–1227).

Lord Rothermere to Winston S. Churchill

(Churchill papers: 2/332)

15 October 1938

My dear Winston,

I urge you to go slow in regard to your Constituency. Neville Chamberlain's reputation will be undimmed so long as he is Prime Minister and any member of his Party who challenges that fact may suffer a complete eclipse.

The public is so terrified of being bombed that they will support anyone who keeps them out of war. I always knew they had no desire to stand up to the Dictators and I always knew that when there was a sharp issue of peace or war ninety-five per cent of the electors would rally to the peace policy however humiliating such a policy might be.

I do hope you will soft pedal on the whole position. If you were not in the House it would be a national loss.

I don't trust the Epping electorate because Epping is on one of the routes by which enemy aeroplanes will approach London.

Ward Price[1] was very downright last evening in asserting this point of view. I entirely agree with him.

Yours always,
Rothermere

Winston S. Churchill: broadcast to the United States[2]

(Churchill papers: 9/132)

16 October 1938

I avail myself with relief of the opportunity
   of speaking to the people of the United States.

I do not know how long such liberties will be allowed.

---

[1] George Ward Price, 1886–1961. Educated at St Catherine's College, Cambridge. *Daily Mail* War Correspondent, in the first Balkan war. Official War Correspondent at the Dardanelles and with the Salonica army. A Director of Associated Newspapers Ltd and special foreign correspondent for the *Daily Mail* between the wars. War Correspondent in France, 1939; in Tunisia, 1943; in France, 1944.

[2] Printed here are the speech notes set out in the form in which Churchill delivered them. The words in italics were underlined by Churchill in the notes.

The stations of uncensored expression are closing down; the lights are going
    out;
      but there is still time for those
        to whom freedom and parliamentary government
          mean something,
            to consult together.

Let me then speak in truth and earnestness while time remains.

The American people, have, it seems to me,
    formed a true judgment upon the disaster
      which has befallen Europe.

They realise, perhaps more clearly
    than the French and British publics have yet done,
      the far-reaching consequences of the abandonment
      and ruin of the Czechoslovak Republic.

I hold to the conviction I expressed some months ago,
    that if in April, May or June,
      Great Britain, France and Russia had jointly declared
        that they would act together upon Nazi Germany
          if Herr Hitler committed an act of unprovoked
            aggression against this small State,
    and if they had told Poland, Jugoslavia and Rumania
      what they meant to do in good time,
        and invited them to join the combination
        of peace-defending Powers,

I hold that the German Dictator would have been confronted
    with such a formidable array,
      that he would have been deterred from his purpose.

This would also have been an opportunity
    for all the peace-loving and moderate forces in Germany,
      together with the chiefs of the German army,
    to make a great effort to re-establish
      something like sane and civilised conditions in their own country.

If the risks of war which were run by France and Britain
    at the last moment had been boldly faced in good time,
        and plain declarations made, and *meant,*
    how different would our prospects be to-day!
But all these backward speculations belong to history.

It is no good using hard words among friends about the past,
    and reproaching one another for what cannot be recalled.

It is the future, not the past,
    that demands our earnest and anxious thought.

We must recognise that the Parliamentary democracies
    and liberal, peaceful forces
        have everywhere sustained a defeat,
    which leaves them weaker, morally and physically,
        to cope with dangers which have vastly grown.

But the cause of freedom has in it
    a recuperative power and virtue,
        which can draw from misfortune
            new hope and new strength.

If ever there was a time
    when men and women who cherish the ideals
        of the founders of the British and American Constitutions
            should take earnest counsel with one another,
                that time is now.

All the world wishes for peace and security.

Have we gained it by the sacrifice of the Czechoslovak Republic?

Here was the model democratic State of Central Europe,
    a country where minorities were treated better than
        anywhere else.

It has been deserted, destroyed and devoured.

It is now being digested.
The question which is of interest
   to a lot of ordinary people, common people,
      is whether this destruction of the Czechoslovak
         Republic will bring upon the world a blessing or a curse.

We must all hope it will bring a blessing;
   that after we have averted our gaze for a while
      from the process of subjugation and liquidation,
   everyone will breathe more freely;
   that a load will be taken off our chests;
   we shall be able to say to ourselves:
      'Well, that's out of the way anyhow.
         Now let's get on with our regular daily life.'

But are these hopes well-founded,
   or are we merely making the best of what
      we had not the force and virtue to stop?

That is the question that the English-speaking peoples
   in all their lands,
      must ask themselves to-day.

Is this the end, or is there more to come?
There is another question which arises out of this.

Can peace, goodwill and confidence
   be built upon submission to wrong-doing
      backed by force?

One may put this question in the largest form.

Has any benefit or progress ever been achieved
   by the human race
      by submission to organized and calculated violence?

As we look back over the long story of the nations,
   we must see that, on the contrary,
      their glory has been founded
         upon the spirit of resistance to tyranny and injustice,
   especially when these evils seemed to be backed
      by heavier force.

Since the dawn of the Christian Era
  a certain way of life has slowly been shaping itself
    among the Western peoples,
  and certain standards of conduct and government
    have come to be esteemed.

After many miseries and prolonged confusion
  there arose into the broad light of day
    the conception of the right of the individual;
  his right to be consulted in the government
    of his country;
  his right to invoke the law
    even against the State itself.
Independent Courts of Justice were created
  to affirm and enforce this hard-won custom.

Thus was assured throughout the English-speaking world,
  and in France by the stern lessons of the Revolution,
  what Kipling called 'Leave to live by no man's leave
    underneath the law.'

Now in this, resides all that makes existence precious
  to man, and all that confers honour and health
    upon the State.

We are confronted with another theme.

It is not a new theme;
  it leaps out upon us from the Dark Ages—
    racial persecution, religious intolerance,
      deprivation of free speech,
        the conception of the citizen
          as a mere soulless fraction of the State.

To this has been added the cult of war.

Children are to be taught in their earliest schooling
  the delights and profit of conquest and aggression.

A whole mighty community has been drawn painfully,
  by severe privations,
    into a warlike frame.

They are held in this condition, which they relish no more than we
    by a party organization, several millions strong,
        who derive all kinds of profits, good and bad,
            from the upkeep of the régime.
Like the Communists, the Nazis tolerate no opinion
    but their own.
Like the Communists, they feed on hatred.
Like the Communists, they must seek, from time to time,
    and always at shorter intervals,
        a new target, a new prize, a new victim.

The Dictator, in all his pride,
    is held in the grip of his Party machine.

He can go forward; he cannot go back.

He must blood his hounds and show them sport,
    or else, like Actæon of old,
        be devoured by them.

All-strong without, he is all-weak within.

As Byron wrote a hundred years ago:
    'These pagod things of Sabre sway,
        with fronts of brass and feet of clay.'
No one must, however, underrate the power and efficiency
    of a totalitarian State.

Where the whole population of a great country,
    amiable, good-hearted, peace-loving people,
        are gripped by the neck and by the hair
            by a Communist or a Nazi tyranny,
    for they are the same things spelt in different ways,
    the rulers for the time being can exercise a power
        for the purposes of war and external domination,
    before which the ordinary free parliamentary societies
        are at a grievous practical disadvantage.

We have to recognise this.

And then on top of all comes this wonderful mastery of the Air,
   which our century has discovered,
      but of which, alas, mankind has so far
         shown itself unworthy.

Here is this Air power, with its claim to torture and
   terrorize the women and children,
      the civil population, of neighbouring countries.

This combination of mediaeval passion,
   a party caucus,
      the weapons of modern science
         and the blackmailing power of air-bombing,
  is the most monstrous menace to peace, order and
      fertile progress that has appeared in the world
         since the Mongol invasions
            of the 13th century.
The culminating question to which I have been leading
   is whether the world as we have known it,
      the great and hopeful world of before the War,
      the world of increasing scope and enjoyment for the common man,
      the world of honoured tradition and expanding science,
   should meet this menace by submission
      or by resistance.

Let us see then whether the means of resistance
   remain to us to-day.

We have sustained an immense disaster;
   the renown of France is dimmed.

In spite of her brave, efficient army,
   her influence is profoundly diminished.

No one has a right to say that Britain,
   for all her blundering, has broken her word;
   indeed, when it was too late,
      she was better than her word.

Nevertheless, Europe lies at this moment
   abashed and distracted before the triumphant assertions
      of dictatorial power.

In the Spanish Peninsula, a purely Spanish quarrel
   has been carried by the intervention,
      or shall I say the 'non-intervention'
        (to quote the current jargon),
  of Dictators into the region of a world cause.
But it is not only in Europe that these oppressions prevail.

China is being torn to pieces
   by a military clique in Japan;
      the poor, tormented Chinese people there
        are making a brave and subborn defence.

The ancient empire of Ethiopia has been overrun.

The Ethiopians were taught to look
   to the sanctity of public law,
      to the tribunal of many nations gathered
        in majestic union.
But all failed: they were deceived,
   and now they are winning back their right to live
      by beginning again from the bottom
        a struggle on primordial lines.

Even in South America, the Nazi régime
   begins to undermine the fabric of Brazilian society.
Far away, happily protected by the Atlantic and Pacific Oceans,
   you, the people of the United States,
      to whom I now have the chance to speak,
  are the spectators,
      and may I add the increasingly involved spectators
        of these tragedies and crimes.

We are left in no doubt where American conviction
   and sympathies lie:
      but will you wait until British freedom and
      independence have succumbed,
        and then take up the cause,
          when it is three-quarters ruined,
          yourselves alone?

I hear that they are saying in the United States
   that because England and France have failed
      to do their duty,
         therefore the American people
            can wash their hands of the whole business.

This may be the passing mood of many people,
   but there is no sense in it.

If things have got much worse,
   all the more must we try to cope with them.
For after all, *survey* the remaining forces of civilization;
   they are overwhelming.

If only they were united in a common conception of right and duty,
   there would be no war.

On the contrary, the German people, industrious, faithful,
   valiant, but, alas, lacking in the proper spirit of civic independence,
      if liberated from their present nightmare,
         would take their honoured place
            in the vanguard of human society.

Alexander the Great remarked that the peoples of Asia
   were slaves because they had not learned
      to pronounce the word 'No.'

Let that not be the epitaph of the English-speaking peoples
   or of Parliamentary democracy,
      or of France,
         or of the many surviving liberal States of Europe.

There in one single word is the resolve which the forces
   of freedom and progress, of tolerance and goodwill, should take.

It is not in the power of one nation, however formidably armed,
   still less is it in the power of a small group of men,
      violent ruthless men,
         who have always to cast their eyes back
            over their shoulders,
   to cramp and fetter the forward march of human destiny.

The preponderant world forces are upon our side;
   they have but to be combined to be obeyed.
   We must arm. Britain must arm. America must arm.

If, through an earnest desire for peace,
   we have placed ourselves at a disadvantage,
     we must make up for it by redoubled exertions,
   and, if necessary, by fortitude in suffering.

We shall no doubt arm.

Britain, casting away the habits of centuries,
   will decree *national service* upon her citizens.

The British people will stand erect,
   and will face whatever may be coming.

But arms—*instrumentalities*, as President Wilson called them—
   are not sufficient by themselves.

We must add to them the power of ideas.

People say we ought not to allow ourselves
   to be drawn into a theoretical antagonism
     between Nazidom and democracy;
       but the antagonism is here now.

It is this very conflict of spiritual and moral ideas
   which gives the free countries
     a great part of their strength.

You see these dictators on their pedestals,
   surrounded by the bayonets of their soldiers
     and the truncheons of their police.

On all sides they are guarded by masses of armed men,
   cannons, airplanes, fortifications, and the like,
     —they boast and vaunt themselves before the world,
   yet in their hearts there is unspoken fear.

They are afraid of words and thoughts:
  words spoken abroad, thoughts stirring at home
    —all the more powerful because forbidden—
      terrify them.

A little mouse of thought appears in the room,
  and even the mightiest potentates are thrown into panic.

They make frantic efforts to bar out thoughts and words;
  they are afraid of the workings of the human mind.

Cannons, airplanes, they can manufacture in large quantities;
  but how are they to quell the natural promptings of human nature,
    which after all these centuries of trial and progress
      has inherited a whole armoury of potent and
        indestructible knowledge?
Dictatorship—the fetish worship of one man—is a passing phase.

A state of society where men may not speak their minds,
  where children denounce their parents to the police,
    where a business man or small shopkeeper
      ruins his competitor by telling tales
        about his private opinions;
such a state of society cannot long endure
  if brought in contact with the healthy outside world.

The light of civilised progress with its tolerances and co-operation,
  with its dignities and joys,
    has often in the past been blotted out.

But I hold the belief that we have now at last got far
  enough ahead of barbarism,
    to control it, and to avert it,
      if only we realise what is afoot
        and make up our minds in time.

We shall do it in the end. We shall sure do it.

But how much harder our toil, for every day's delay.
Is this a call to war? Does anyone pretend that preparation for resistance
  to aggression is unleashing war?

I declare it to be the sole guarantee of peace.

The swift and organized gathering of forces
  to confront not only military but moral aggression;
  the resolute and sober acceptance of their duty
    by the English-speaking peoples
      and by all the nations, great and small,
        who wish to walk with them;
  their faithful and zealous comradeship would almost
    between night and morning
      clear the path of progress
        and banish from all our lives
          the fear which already darkens
            the sunlight
to hundreds of millions of men.

Sir Terence O'Connor to Winston S. Churchill

(*Churchill papers: 2/334*)

16 October 1938

Winston dear,

That astonishingly good speech of your's tonight did make me rejoice.[1]
You seem to have made unerring contacts with currents of feeling that are
vital to our country at this moment. And you have done so much to align &
validate the temper of England.

There has been nothing since C. J. Fox to compare with the frequency &
mastery of your parliamentary performance these days.

Bless you,
Terence

Lord Lloyd to Winston S. Churchill

(*Churchill papers: 2/334*)

[16 October 1938]

My dear Winston,

A line to express my admiration of your broadcast—especially useful just
now. I am alarmed at what Neville may have in his mind re negotiations
with Germany.

---

[1] Churchill's broadcast to the United States, printed in full above.

Sir Sidney Herbert to Winston S. Churchill

(*Churchill papers: 2/332*)

17 October 1938
Private

My dear Winston,

Thank you so much for your letter of October 9th. It is much too complimentary; however, I feel proud as Punch of it, and it has given me great help and encouragement at a time when I am feeling very tired and ill.

Thank you also a thousand times for sending me your book. It is one of my most treasured possessions. When I read it I am almost terrified to see how precise have been the warnings which you have given and how stupidly they have been disregarded. I have spent more time than most people know trying to convince Ministers of the truth of your warnings and of the dangers with which we were faced. I had fondly thought that from me, since I am no orator, this was the most useful method to adopt: but it appears that this is not so, so now, if my health will stand it, I must attempt more flamboyant methods.

Thank you so much for asking me to come down to stay at Chartwell. I should like to later on very much, but at present I am full of tiresome constituency meetings and dinners, and have got people staying with me for the weekends.

I am sure that the great part of the country will rally to our views, and indeed my mail, which for the first time in my life has been gigantic, confirms this.

I tried hard at Boyton[1] last night to listen in to your broadcast to America, but could not get through; but I read it this morning in the newspapers and should like to send you my warmest congratulations. It was a magnificent effort. One of the things which the Prime Minister appears consistently to ignore is American public opinion, and your broadcast did much to remedy this.

My best love to Clemmie.

Yours always,
Sidney

[1] Sir Sidney Herbert's country house, Boyton Manor, Codford, Wiltshire. His London home was at 32 Hill Street, Mayfair.

James Fell [1] *to Winston S. Churchill*

(*Churchill papers: 2/332*)

18 October 1938

Dear Winston,

Just a line to congratulate you on your last US broadcast. It was just what was wanted. But don't waste time on an unnecessary bye-election. The voters, for or against you, are only half informed and their opinion will be of no value. Stiffen the government, we may even have to get Lloyd George back!

We want conscription of *everything*—money, brains, and labour—voluntary effort is fine but it leads to amateurism, doing things by halves & doing things too late.

I met you last in Vancouver, where I live mostly—I know the States well, & your broadcast was just what they need.

Yours sincerely,
James P. Fell

Winston S. Churchill to Ramsay Muir

(*Churchill papers: 2/332*)

18 October 1938   Chartwell
Confidential

I am very glad to get your letter, and I find myself in full sympathy with much that you write. You will see from my broadcast last night the line I am taking.

I am having trouble in my Constituency, and have let it be known that unless I am accorded a renewed expression of their confidence, I shall appeal to the electors.[2] In that case a by-election would occur which, from the charac-

---

[1] James Pemberton Fell, 1872–1947. Born in England and educated at Harrow. After leaving Harrow he joined the Yorkshire Artillery Militia, reaching the rank of Captain. In 1910 he moved to Vancouver, British Columbia, where he organized and commanded the 6th Field Company, Canadian Engineers until 1914. On active service with the First Division of the Canadian Expeditionary Force, 1914–18, reaching the rank of Lieutenant-Colonel. After the war he returned to Vancouver, where he invested in property and carried out engineering projects for the city of Vancouver, including an improvement of the harbour, and the planning and development of the city and districts of North Vancouver. He had met Churchill in Vancouver in August 1929.

[2] On 5 November 1938 *The Times* reported that: 'After a private meeting of the central council of the West Essex Unionist Association at Winchester House, EC, at which Mr Winston Churchill was present, the secretary of the association stated that the following resolution had been passed: "We express our gratitude to the Prime Minister for his continuing and courageous efforts in the cause of peace, but we regret that the warnings given during the last five years by the member for the Division, the Rt. Hon. Winston Churchill, endorsed as

ter of the Constituency and other circumstances, would greatly assist the developments you have in mind. No doubt also when Parliament meets very sharp divisions will make themselves manifest upon the absolutely shameful mis-management, and indeed betrayal of our interests involved in the rearmament failure.

I am in close touch with Archie, and I should like very much to have a talk with you before Parliament meets. I wonder if I could persuade you to come down and lunch with me here one day next week. I am free Monday, the 24th.

Winston S. Churchill to Richard Law

(*Churchill papers: 2/332*)

18 October 1938

Thank you so much for your letter. I send you this in reply, which will no doubt await your return.

I hope you will not think of resigning your seat until we can have a talk and survey the whole ground. I was with Max when you rang up the other night. He is determined to help you in every way, irrespective of his own general opinion and, as you know, his capacity for friendship is very high.

I am having trouble in Epping and if it becomes serious, I shall certainly appeal to the constituency. However, this issue will not develop until the first week in November, and it may be that by then it will have faded away.

The last sentence of your letter to Chamberlain is dominant now. The exposure of the failure of our defences strips Ministers of all credentials to be judges of the national interests.

Let me know when you come home, and let us take counsel together as to how we can stem the ebb-tide of British fortunes.

Winston S. Churchill to Anthony Eden

(*Churchill papers: 2/332*)

18 October 1938

I have now found time to read the most interesting memorandum you have sent me about Abyssinia. I agree with the measures proposed by your

---

they have been by this association as well as by the National Union of Conservative Associations, about the proper and timely rearmament of our country, have not been hearkened to; because we feel that if these counsels had been heeded the Prime Minister would have found himself in a far better position to negotiate with the heads of the dictator States. We therefore urge Mr Churchill to continue his work for national unity and national defence, believing that this will be the surest foundation for that lasting peace which is our deep desire." '

correspondent at the end of his letter, especially the Anglo-French staff arrangements for the defence of Djibouti. My opinion is that the mere stoppage of supplies by the French over the Djibouti railway would produce an immediate food crisis in Addis Ababa, quite apart from any closing of the Suez Canal.

I do not believe that Khartoum, if defended by 3,000 or 4,000 British soldiers with Sudanese battalions, could be taken by a coup-de-main. As a base, if fortified with pill-boxes, etc., and well provisioned, its reduction would be a very serious operation and would certainly require at least 40,000 men, together with adequate artillery and ample munitions.

The control of the waterways by gunboats is also an important factor. But even if Khartoum were taken, it would not be possible to advance down the Nile into Egypt. The Dongola loop of the Nile is obstructed by cataracts and, provided the British flotilla is not allowed to fall in the enemy's hands, no large body of men could be moved northwards. The railway from Alm Hamed to Wady Halfa could, of course, almost immediately be destroyed, and the rolling stock moved northwards. Even after Wady Halfa there is a four hundred miles stretch to Luxor, all through rocky gorges and desert country of the worst description. It seems to me, therefore, that a period of at least six months could be counted on safely before any Italian advance northwards upon Egypt could be made—if, indeed, it could be made at all.

In this period the question of the command of the Mediterranean would have settled itself. If we lose the command of the Mediterranean, the direct Italian invasion of Egypt is a simple operation, carrying with it the canal, etc. But I consider the Mediterranean is our decisive battle-ground at sea, and there ought to be no doubt whatever that after the first six weeks of fighting the Anglo-French Naval Forces should be able to drive all Italian vessels off the sea and cow their submarines into port. I am glad to know that the later views of the Admiralty about the vital importance of dominating the Mediterranean at length correspond to my own. The command of the Mediterranean by Great Britain, once established, seals the fate of all Italian Forces in Africa wherever they may be.

This letter is for your own personal information, and please keep it under lock and key. I think, however, it might be a good thing, if you sent Steer's[1]

---

[1] George Lowther Steer, 1909–1945. Born in South Africa. Educated at Winchester and Oxford; a first class degree in Classics, 1932. Crime and baseball reporter for the Capetown *Argus*, 1932–3. Drama critic, *Yorkshire Post*, 1933–5. Special War correspondent for *The Times* in Addis Ababa, 1935–6; in Spain, 1936–7. Special correspondent for the *Daily Telegraph* in Africa, 1938–9. Married in 1939, the daughter of the British Minister at Addis Ababa. 2nd Lieutenant, Intelligence Corps, 1940; Staff Captain, Abyssinia, 1940; Madagascar landing, 1942; Lieutenant-Colonel, Indian Field Broadcasting Units, Burma, 1943. Despatches thrice. Killed in a motor accident in Bengal, 1945. Author of several books, including *Judgment on*

memorandum to the War Office and asked for assurances that the points in question have been carefully studied.

Consuelo Balsan to Winston S. Churchill
(Churchill papers: 2/332)

18 October 1938   Lou Sueil
                                                       Eze

My dear Winston,

It is reported in the French Press that in your broadcast to the United States you say that France's good name is tarnished. If this is the award meted to an ally for loyally subscribing to Mr Chamberlain's policy it is not one likely to create good feeling and I regret it.

Aff,
Consuelo

Winston S. Churchill to Consuelo Balsan
(Churchill papers: 2/332)

20 October 1938

The actual words used by me were: 'We have sustained an immense disaster. The renown of France is dimmed. In spite of her brave, efficient army, her influence is profoundly diminished.'

It is impossible to imagine any more moderate statement of the painful events that have occurred.

Sir Harry Goschen[1] to Sir James Hawkey
(Hawkey papers)

20 October 1938

My dear Hawkey,

I have received your letter of the 14th October, and am sorry that you had a motor mishap which I hope you are quite well from now.

German Africa, 1938; *The Tree of Guernika, A Field Study of Modern War*, 1938; *Germany's African Claims* (Reprinted from *Daily Telegraph*, 1939); and *Sealed and Delivered, A Book on the Abyssinian Campaign*, 1942.

[1] Harry William Henry Neville Goschen, 1865–1945. Educated at Eton. A Director of the Agriculture Mortgage Co-operative Ltd and of the Atlas Assurance Company. OBE, 1918. Prime Warden of the Goldsmiths Company, 1919–20. Chairman of the National Provincial Bank. Knighted, 1920. Created Baronet, 1927.

I know that the records that Churchill has made all through the division through his warnings have been fully fulfilled, or almost, but I cannot help thinking it was rather a pity that he broke up the harmony of the House by the speech he made. Of course he was not like a small ranting member, and his words were telegraphed all over the Continent and to America, and I think it would have been a great deal better if he had kept quiet and not made a speech at all.

I am sure you will have a good meeting, and I should like very much to hear what takes place at it, as a good many of the electors from some of the outlying divisions such as Harlow are up in arms about him. He seems to have been more violent in the House of Commons than when he was speaking at Theydon Bois and in the constituency.

A good many people have written to Douglas Pennant[1] and others about him. There is to be a meeting against him in Epping I hear, and altogether it seems to be a jolly mess up.

What do you think of the whole thing?

Yours,
Sir Harry Goschen

Winston S. Churchill: dictated message to 'The Patriot'

(*Churchill papers: 2/332*)

21 October 1938

Mr Winston Churchill presents his compliments to the Editor and to Captain J. F. Ruthven,[2] and begs to thank them for sending him a copy of 'The Patriot'.[3]

---

[1] Claud Douglas Pennant, 1867–1955. Educated at New College, Oxford (BA, 1891). Called to the Bar, Inner Temple, 1894. Unsuccessful Conservative candidate for Northamptonshire South, 1906. Active in the Epping constituency; Chairman of the local Agricultural Committee during the Second World War. His wife was the only daughter of Sir Harry and Lady Goschen. A director for many years of the Herts and Essex Water Company. A Justice of the Peace for Harlow. Resident at Sheering, Bishop's Stortford. A descendant of the 1st Baron Penrhyn.

[2] Jocelyn Fitzgerald Ruthven, of 28 Goldington Avenue, Bedford. He died on 13 June 1943.

[3] In the *Patriot* of 13 October 1938, Churchill was among those Conservative MPs who were criticized for their opposition to the Munich Agreement. The magazine wrote: '. . . Czechoslovakia has been saved from extinction, and the British Empire and the world at large from Armageddon, and yet here we cannot get members of Parliament to show unanimous approval. It is disconcerting, to say the least, to find that Conservatives like Duff Cooper, Churchill, Eden and Vyvyan Adams, to mention only a few, have joined with the Socialists in disparagement, and are so blind to the realities of the situation that they refused to come

Mr Churchill is surprised to find on page 290 that you quote with approval Mr McGovern's[1] attack upon Mr Churchill for opposing the late India Constitution Bill, but thinks you must have come down pretty low in politics to have to make a point like that, considering that you were in agreement with him for all the five long years of that fight.[2]

Generally speaking, Mr Churchill thinks that a combination of the Nazis and the Tory Right Wing offers the best chance of reducing Britain to a vassal State within the shortest possible time. He is astounded that you do not react when the whole life of your country is at stake.

As you have intruded upon him by sending him your publication, he feels bound to answer you as you deserve.

---

out on the side of the Government. A more honourable course was taken by Mr McGovern, who would generally be considered a Red and might be expected to be in violent opposition if anyone was so entitled. But he refused to subscribe to the view that because he is in opposition therefore everything done by the Conservative leader must be wrong. And he did service in recalling how Socialists in the Great War welcomed Russia's desertion of the Allies, and he refused to believe that there was any guarantee now that Moscow would have carried out any obligations in a war to-day for Czechoslovakia.'

[1] John McGovern, 1887–1968. Served first as an apprentice plumber, then as a master plumber, 1909–29. Member of the Glasgow Parish Council, 1929–31. Independent Labour Party MP for Glasgow Shettleston, 1930–47; Labour MP, 1947–59. In 1931 he had been carried out of the House of Commons by eight attendants, during his 'Free Speech Campaign'. In 1933 he was arrested in connection with the unemployed riots. In 1934 he led a hunger march from Glasgow to London. In 1962 he left Britain to settle in Australia.

[2] In its issue of 13 October 1938 the *Patriot* quoted with approval McGovern's remarks during the Munich debate in the House of Commons: 'The right hon. gentleman the Member for Epping (Mr Churchill) has spoken of the struggle for democracy. I remember the present Home Secretary (Sir Samuel Hoare) standing at that box for weeks engaged in the task of giving a limited constitution to India, but Mr Churchill's talk then was that no democratic Government should be given to the people of India in any shape or form. He talked last night about pagan Germany, and said that we must not bargain with them. He talked about the Germans having driven out the Jews and attacked the Catholics and the Social Democrats. But he made the same kind of speeches about "atheistic Russia" when he spent £100,000,000 of the British taxpayers' money in trying to destroy the Soviet Republic. His love of democracy is, to my mind, a very unreal one. Some people get slogans to suit the times, and I think in the right hon. gentleman's slogan last night he was simply speaking with his tongue in his cheek.'

Mrs P. J. Grigg[1] to Thomas Jones

(*Grigg papers*)

23 October 1938   New Delhi

What a beautiful speech that was of Winston's! We have just finished read-ing it in the Times of Oct 6, and I found both Lady Astor's interpellations singularly inept! It was *not* nonsense to say that insofar as Germany has gained in substance all she set out to gain, we have sustained a defeat.[2]

I thought it was such a *good* speech! not bellicose but yet so full of warning. It must surely be true that those Countries will, one after another, be drawn into this vast system of power politics—military & economic—radiating from Berlin? In a letter which I had from Mr Governor[3] this week he says the same thing:—'But economically it can't well escape penetration, or domination even by Germany.' It seems to me so wise to say that now while there may yet be time.

So many (& among them of course PJ and Maurice Gwyer[4] & heaps I could name) dread the power of Nazi Germany & of our becoming depen-dent upon their good will & pleasure. I can 'arise again & take our stand for freedom as in the olden time'. Grand words! & not only *words*—coming as they do from Winston—I never shall understand why we can't have him in the Government.

[1] Gertrude Charlotte Hough, younger daughter of Rev G. F. Hough. She had married P. J. Grigg in 1919. They had no children.

[2] During his speech during the 'Munich' debate on 5 October 1938 Churchill had just said: 'We have sustained a total and unmitigated defeat, and that France has suffered even more than we have.' At this point Lady Astor called out: 'Nonsense,' whereupon Churchill continued: 'When the Noble Lady cries "Nonsense," she could not have heard the Chancellor of the Exchequer admit in his illuminating and comprehensive speech just now that Herr Hitler had gained in this particular leap forward in substance all he set out to gain. The ut-most my right hon Friend the Prime Minister has been able to secure by all his immense exertions, by all the great efforts and mobilisation which took place in this country, and by all the anguish and strain through which we have passed in this country, the utmost he has been able to gain—[Hon Members: "Is peace."] I thought I might be allowed to make that point in its due place, and I propose to deal with it. The utmost he has been able to gain for Czechoslovakia and in the matters which were in dispute has been that the German dictator, instead of snatching his victuals from the table, has been content to have them served to him course by course.'

[3] Montagu Collet Norman, 1871–1950. Educated at Eton and King's College, Cambridge. On active service in South Africa, 1900–1 (despatches). A Director of the Bank of England, 1907–19. Governor of the Bank of England, 1920–44. Privy Councillor, 1923. Created Baron, 1944. His brother Ronald was Chairman of the BBC from 1935 to 1939.

[4] Maurice Linford Gwyer, 1878–1952. Educated at Westminster and Christ Church, Oxford; Fellow of All Souls, 1902–16. Lecturer in Private International Law, Oxford, 1912–15. Legal Adviser to the Ministry of Shipping, 1917–19; to the Ministry of Health, 1919–26. Solicitor to the Treasury, 1926–33. Knighted, 1928. Member of the Indian States Inquiry Committee, 1932. First Parliamentary Counsel to the Treasury, 1934–7. Chief Justice of India, 1937–43. Vice-Chancellor of Delhi University, 1938–50.

Sir Archibald Sinclair to a correspondent

(*Thurso papers*)

24 October 1938

Mr Harcourt Johnstone has told me that you were disturbed by a report of a speech of mine in which I recommended the appointment of Mr Churchill as Minister for the Co-ordination of Defence in place of Sir Thomas Inskip. It is certainly my view that the present Government have shown slackness and inefficiency in matters of national defence. Strongly believing, as I do, in the principles of the Covenant of the League of Nations, I thought it was a disaster when Mr Chamberlain compelled Mr Eden to resign and himself took over the control of foreign policy. He abandoned the principles of the League and proceeded to try and drive a series of weak—and to my mind immoral—bargains with Signor Mussolini and Herr Hitler. That is why I said in that speech that he would have done better to leave Mr Eden in control of foreign affairs and himself to have concentrated upon discharging the responsibilities which fall to every Prime Minister as Chairman of the Committee of Imperial Defence.

I am not a Pacifist, but I respect the Pacifist point of view. The point of view for which I have no respect is that of people who admit the necessity for armaments but who do not seem to realise that if we have them they must be efficient and adequate to support our policy. Therefore let us have the most competent administrator available in charge of this branch of policy.

At the same time and in the same speech I repeated what I had said before in the House of Commons and on other platforms—that I loathe war and power politics and that, if Germany and Italy will agree to a measure of general disarmament—for disarmament must be the acid test of the sincerity of any peace settlement—and to submit all disputes to impartial arbitration, there is no price that I should be unwilling to pay for their friendship, and for the friendship of every other nation, that is consistent with our obligations to the League of Nations, that justice and equity demand, and that third party judgment may assess. . . .

Lord Cavan to Winston S. Churchill

(Churchill papers: 8/595)

25 October 1938

My dear Winston,

When in Italy last week, my old friend Marshal Caviglia[1] asked me to lend him your Marlborough—when I offered him a present.

I have had the pleasure of sending him the Four Volumes. I think your account of the backstairs workings of Dk John & Harley almost the most enthralling part of the book, which I have now finished with intense delight. I can assure you that Italy *longs* to be friends with us—from the King[2] and Mussolini & the Under Secy of State for War[3] down to the humble folk of the Asiago—with *all* of whom I had some conversation. They do *not* like the Axis & it sd not be difficult to make it revolve slowly in our favour.

Yours sincerely,
Cavan

Winston S. Churchill to Sir Abe Bailey: telegram

(Churchill papers: 1/324)

25 October 1938

Cranes arriving. Thousand thanks. We are building them a dugout. Love,
Winston

[1] Enrico Caviglia, 1862–1945. Fought with the Italian Army in East Africa in the 1890s. Italian Military Attaché, Tokyo, 1904–5. On active service in the Italo-Turkish war, 1911–12, and in the First World War, when he distinguished himself in the battle of the Asiago Plateau, at Caporetto, during the retreat of the Piave, and at the offensive of Vittorio Veneto. Minister of War, January–June 1919. Commanded the Italian Forces which forced Gabrielle D'Annunzio to abandon Fiume, 1920. Subsequently Senator, and Marshal of Italy. He took no part in Fascist politics, and in 1940 caused a sensation in Fascist circles by writing, in a preface to a book, that no nation that was not economically and financially independent could be the arbiter of its destinies in a long war.

[2] Victor Emmanuel, 1869–1947. The first in his line to be born in direct succession to the Italian crown, he became King of Italy in 1900, following the assassination of his father, King Umberto, by anarchists. In 1915 he supported Italy's entry into the war on the side of Britain and France. Accepted the Imperial Crown of Ethiopia, 1936, and the Crown of Albania, April 1939. Following Mussolini's declaration of war on Britain in June 1940 he withdrew from political life. Survived an assassination attempt, 1941. Formally authorized the arrest of Mussolini, 1943, and escaped from German-controlled Rome. Withdrew from public life, 1944. Abdicated, 1946, and lived the last four months of his life in exile in Alexandria.

[3] Alberto Pariani, Italian Under-Secretary for War and Army Chief of Staff from 1936 to 1940 (when he was succeeded by Graziani). Mussolini himself was Secretary of State for War, as well as Prime Minister, Chief of the Government, Minister of the Interior, Minister of the Navy, Minister of the Air and Minister of Italian Africa. In March 1945 General Pariani was sentenced to 15 years' imprisonment by the Rome High Court.

Randolph Churchill to Winston S. Churchill

(*Churchill papers: 1/325*)

[26] October 1938   Aliwal Barracks
                                                    Tidworth

My dear Papa—

We are messing with the above until our own mess is ready next week.

I don't know if this point has occurred to you:— The Government are blaming their failure to rearm in public on the Labour Party & in private on Lord Baldwin. Quintin[1] has been doing the first at Oxford, while Baldwin is the scapegoat of all ministerialists in conversation. Neither B nor the Labour Party are blameless, B more probably more culpable than any other individual *BUT* the big 4 have all held high office in British Cabinet for at least a year longer than Hitler has been Chancellor. Three of them date back to '31 & Halifax to '32.[2]

From every point of view I'm sure it is advisable to shift criticism from the events of September to those of the last 7 years. I know your mind is at work on that argument & I thought this point might fit in.

Your loving son
Randolph

PS. Please give my regards to Ian Colvin. I'm sorry I won't be able to see him.

---

[1] Quintin McGarel Hogg, 1907–   . An undergraduate at Christ Church, Oxford, 1926–30: President of the Oxford Union Society, 1929. Fellow of All Souls College, Oxford, 1931–8. Barrister, Lincoln's Inn, 1932. Conservative MP for Oxford City, 1938–50; for St Marylebone, 1963–70. Parliamentary Under-Secretary of State for Air in Churchill's 'Caretaker Government', May–July 1945. Succeeded his father as 2nd Viscount Hailsham, 1950, but in 1963 disclaimed his peerage for life. First Lord of the Admiralty, 1956–7. Minister of Education, 1957. Lord President of the Council, 1957–9 and 1960–4. Lord Privy Seal, 1959–60. Minister of Science and Technology, 1959–64. Secretary of State for Science, 1964. Lord Chancellor, 1970–4. Created Baron (Life Peer), as Lord Hailsham of Saint Marylebone, 1970. Companion on Honour, 1974. The Oxford by-election, at which he was first elected to Parliament, was held on 27 October 1938.

[2] Neville Chamberlain had served continuously in the Cabinet (first as Minister of Health, then as Chancellor of the Exchequer and finally as Prime Minister) since 25 August 1931; Sir Samuel Hoare (as Secretary of State for India, Foreign Secretary, First Lord of the Admiralty and Home Secretary) since 25 August 1931, with a break from December 1935 to June 1936; Sir John Simon (as Foreign Secretary, Home Secretary and then Chancellor of the Exchequer) continuously since 5 November 1931, and Lord Halifax (as President of the Board of Education, Secretary of State for War, Lord Privy Seal, Lord President of the Council and Foreign Secretary) since 15 June 1932. Hitler had come to power on 30 January 1933.

Winston S. Churchill to Lord Cecil of Chelwood: telegram

(*Cecil of Chelwood papers*)

26 October 1938

As long as I accept the Conservative Whip it is not possible for me to take sides in a by-election against them except where two Conservative candidates are standing.[1]

Winston

Buckhurst Hill Branch, West Essex Unionist Association: resolution

(*Churchill papers: 7/46*)

26 October 1938

Whilst we very readily accord our continued support to Mr Winston Churchill in his advocacy of a more vigorous re-armament programme, and while we would approve the role of constructive critic, we feel increasingly uneasy at Mr Churchill's growing hostility to the Government, and to the Prime Minister in particular, at a time when unity is of vital importance.[2]

---

[1] On 27 October 1938, following the death of the Conservative MP for Oxford, Captain Robert Croft Bourne, a by-election was held in which the official Conservative candidate, Quintin Hogg (the thirty-two year old son of the 1st Viscount Hailsham, then Lord President of the Council) received 15,797 votes, as against 12,363 votes cast for the Independent Progressive candidate, A. D. L. Lindsay (Master of Balliol College, Oxford, 1924–49, created Baron Lindsay of Birker, 1945), who stood on an 'anti-Munich' platform. Lindsay had been supported by both the Oxford City Labour Party and the local Liberal Association, both of whom had withdrawn their own candidates when Lindsay agreed to seek election in a 'Popular Front' programme.

[2] Speaking at Buckhurst Hill in his constituency on 1 February 1939, Churchill said that his critics in the Constituency still complained of the speech he had made in the House of Commons upon the Munich Agreement. 'I do not withdraw a single word. I read it again only this afternoon, and was astonished to find how terribly true it had all come. I recognize, however, that the fact that the Prime Minister was known to be a sincere worker for peace has had a good effect upon the populations of the Dictator countries and that it has become more difficult for their machine-made propaganda to alarm those populations by the fear that Britain and France are animated by any hostile designs upon their peace and prosperity.' In conclusion Churchill said: 'I have been out of office now for ten years, but I am more contented with the work I have done in these last five years as an Independent Conservative than of any other part of my public life. I know it has gained for me a greater measure of goodwill from my fellow-countrymen than I have ever previously enjoyed. When the General Election comes in the autumn, as we are told it will, I look forward confidently to an even larger majority than the record figure gained last time. I ask you not only for the support of Conservatives who put country before Party but also from those patriotic Liberals and Labour men who are ready to support a vigorous re-armament of our country and look forward beyond these troubles to the re-building on a stronger and surer foundation of fair play and goodwill to all countries of a League of Nations which by its power and unity shall lay to rest not only the fears and suspicions of these unhappy times but the underlying causes from which they spring.'

Herbert Worsley[1] *to Ramsay Muir*

(*Churchill papers: 7/46*)

26 October 1938   Epping
Confidential

Dear Ramsay Muir,

Your letter of 24th Oct came only today. This is my information: two local Unionist Association Committees have carried votes against WC recently, one by a large and the other by a small majority. (There have probably been similar performances elsewhere; I know of these two because they are in this neighbourhood.) There is undoubtedly a serious split in their ranks. Many Conservatives have told me of their opposition, chiefly on the ground of his 'continued disloyalty' to the Government. Meanwhile, Conservative HQ have sent down a command or advice (as the case may be) that the opposition to him is not to go too far, as they don't want a by-election. How effective this will be I can't say. I believe (don't know) that some of his leading opponents have the name of an official Conservative candidate already in their pockets or in their minds. That is as to the Conservative Party here. As to my Party, I am not going now to sound my officers and friends generally. It would be too dangerous. It might split the Party hopelessly in advance of the need. But I do know the attitude of some of my colleagues, and, broadly speaking, it is in favour of not putting up a Liberal candidate at a by-election challenge by WC, simply because they agree with his criticism of the Government and believe that he would work for collective security through a re-formed League. That also is my attitude and I have said so privately to enquiring friends. *But*—I am sure the attitude of Liberals generally would be determined largely by what he called himself. If a Conservative or even an Independent Conservative, a few might vote for him but the great bulk of them would not. I don't blame them: they feel a genuine loyalty to their own cause and name. If a decent Labour man put up, some of these would vote for him. But the bulk would abstain. We couldn't expect him (WC) to stand as an Independent Liberal, though my own opinion is that that designation most nearly describes his real attitude (I have—more or less—*always* thought so).

If he were to stand as an 'Independent', I believe he would get the bulk of the Liberal vote, provided he also announced publicly his adherence to our recent statement on foreign policy and a (very short) list of Liberal aims: removal of artificial barriers to world trade, the personal liberty of the citizen whether challenged by Fascism or Socialism; thorough treatment by the

---

[1] Herbert Worsley. Chairman of the Liberal Party in the Epping Division since 1908.

State of derelict areas and unemployment generally, instead of belated and piecemeal attempts; and Proportional Representation or other practicable means of making our electoral system more worthy of an intelligent democracy. I think he would probably support all these Liberal aims, and if he did and were faced by an official Tory, a Labour man and no Liberal candidate, I shall support him openly—unless of course something unforeseen and quite conclusive happened, which doesn't seem likely. There is no need for me to tell *you* that having led the Liberal Party in the Epping Division for thirty years, consoled them in their recurrent defeats and fought every Election (including 1918) with them, I am under a heavy obligation of loyalty to them. Therefore, whatever is done must be done openly. If they disapprove, I must at once recognise their right to do so. But I will never give them the smallest justification for saying or thinking that I have not played the game with them.

I shall be at the Reform tomorrow (Thursday). Come and lunch with me, if agreeable. Say 12.50. If you think it would help matters to shew this letter to WC, I have no objection. In that case, I must apologise to him for my use of his initials throughout this letter—done to save writing.

Rams ay Muir to Winston S. Churchill

(*Churchill papers: 7/46*)

27 October 1938   London

Dear Mr Churchill,

After our talk I wrote to Worsley, our chief man in Epping, saying that I had seen you, and that we ought to consider the possibility of a by-election as a result of the line you had taken; & asking him what he thought would be the attitude of the Liberals in the division.

I enclose his reply, which is much less downright than I expected. Worsley is always honest, & never allows himself to be carried away by enthusiasm.

I was at Oxford last night. An excellent & enthusiastic meeting, but one expects that. I formed the conclusion that Lindsay will be beaten, by the women's vote, but not heavily. The canvass shows an unprecedented number of 'doubtfuls', which means that people are wavering. The Liberals, I am sorry to say, have *not* pulled their weight, but are expected to vote right. They had rebuilt their organisation, & were sick at having to stand down.

Sincerely yours,
Ramsay Muir

Colin Coote[1] to Winston S. Churchill

(*Churchill papers: 2/332*)

27 October 1938   The Times

Dear Mr Churchill,

I assume that all decent people must be considering how to excise from the body politic this contaminating canker which calls itself a Government.

Upon this assumption, from the post in the enemy's headquarters which you once enjoined me to keep, I send you my conclusions formed after hearing their plans.

These plans are the mixture of cowardice and cunning with which we have become familiar; but they can be defeated. You will have already observed that Mr Chamberlain has been transformed from the Archangel Gabriel, bringing back peace with honour, to the defendant on a charge of dereliction of duty. The great achievement of a resolute negotiator has become the inevitable surrender of a defenceless scuttler. Let us be satisfied with this change. A further inquest on the Munich Agreement is a sheer waste of time. If persisted in, Chamberlain will force a general election on the issue of the angels of peace versus the warmongers, and thanks to the female electorate he will win.

Let us therefore merely accept, and drive home the fact that the Govt. did what it did at Munich because our defences are inadequate. Defence is the Achilles heel of this Govt. If the arrow strikes it, not even the mercenaries in the House of Commons will be able to heal the wound. Let them therefore be attacked upon the gross scandals in our defence system revealed by the crisis. You have probably seen Liddell-Hart's memo on AA guns. Eady's[2] comments on ARP are public knowledge. If you want information about deficiencies

---

[1] Colin Reith Coote, 1893–1978. Educated at Rugby and Balliol College, Oxford. On active service in France and Italy, 1914–18 (wounded and gassed). Coalition Liberal MP for the Isle of Ely, 1917–22. On the staff of *The Times*, 1923–42. Elected to the Other Club, 1933 (and author of its history, 1971). Joined the staff of the *Daily Telegraph*, 1942; Deputy Editor, 1945–50; Managing Editor, 1950–64. Knighted, 1962. Biographer of Walter Elliot (1965). Edited Churchill's *Maxims and Reflections* (1947) and *Sir Winston Churchill: a Self Portrait* (1954). Published *The Other Club* (1971). Published his own memoirs *Editorial* (1965). Coote later recalled, to the author, how he was 'reproached' by several friends for not resigning from *The Times* during the 'Munich' period and he added: 'I went to Winston and asked him, "should I resign". He urged me not to, telling me: "I should very much like to have a friend in the enemy's camp." '

[2] Crawford Wilfred Griffin Eady, 1890–1962. Educated at Clifton and Jesus College, Cambridge. Junior Clerk, India Office, 1913; Home Office, 1914. Private Secretary to the Minister of Labour, 1919. Principal Assistant Secretary, Ministry of Labour, 1929–34. Secretary, Unemployment Assistance Board, 1934–8. Deputy Under-Secretary of State, Home Office, 1938–40. Knighted, 1939. Deputy Chairman, Board of Customs and Excise, 1940–1; Chairman, 1941–2. Joint 2nd Secretary, Treasury, 1942–52.

in the Air Force, Hore-Belisha will give them to you in the effort to divert attention from himself. The attack on the score of defence might fail if the Govt intended from now on to take defence seriously. But they do not. There will be no Ministry of Supply. All that will happen is a Cabinet Committee under Runciman, with instructions to allow manufacturers to profiteer. That is what they call cutting out red tape. There will be no Ministry of National Service. All that will happen is that some Minister will be instructed to play at drawing up a National Register on lines which will not do more than offer jobs to dug-outs. There are three main reasons why Chamberlain does not mean business.

1. He honestly thinks he can do a deal with Hitler and Mussolini.
2. He is afraid of the effect of large-scale rearmament on the pound sterling.
3. He fundamentally wants Nazi ideas to dominate Europe, because of his fantastic dislike of Soviet Russia.

I therefore beg you not to be sidetracked by any of his stupidities into attacking him upon anything except defence. The temptation will be great. He intends to propose ratification of the Anglo-Italian agreement because the Italians have withdrawn one-sixth of their forces from Spain (and, incidentally, have sent more than the number withdrawn to Libya). This leaves Mussolini in complete control of Majorca. Now that is a very tempting target, but it will do little good to hit it. I repeat that the really vulnerable spot is defence; and that the Govt is planning to jockey you and others into the role of warmongers if you criticise them on anything else.

I fear the Labour Party will allow themselves to be jockeyed into this position. But you need not. Make your position clear by moving an amendment to the King's speech on the Govt's defence policy. That policy is indefensible; and I have reason to know that such an amendment would rally critics far more than any inquest upon Munich.

As an old Liberal who has always known that a large section of the Tories are white-livered, I say to you that the time has come to try what has never been done before, namely, the division of the Conservative party into the sheep and the goats. I refuse to believe that all patriotic sentiments are dead in that party; and I therefore believe the attempt may succeed. I am encouraged in that belief by the manifest unhappiness of many who have contributed to the present *debâcle*. And I am sure, after 20 years' independent survey of the political field, that the only issue on which to win in this country is a domestic issue. Defence is such an issue. Nothing else that matters is.

It is, of course, possible that the British people themselves are rotted by bad leadership, and that they deserve the Chamberlain policy. But at least they should be given a chance to show whether they are decadent or not; and the defence issue will give them the chance.

Your sincerely,
Colin R. Coote

Harold Nicolson: diary

(*Nicolson papers*)

27 October 1938

Duncan Sandys comes to see me. He says that the abstentionists must form a nucleus. I say 'Nucleus of what?' He says that we must band together to oppose all weakness. I say that any such group will find themselves led by Winston and that this will kill them. He says, not at all, that Winston will not come out and that there is no hope of getting him and Eden and Duff Cooper to agree. The thing must arise from the back benchers. We must form our own group and we must not pea-shoot the PM but drive towards a truly national government. We must have no fribbles or backsliders. . . .

I assure him that on such terms I am with him to the end.

Winston S. Churchill to Lord Cavan

(*Churchill papers: 8/595*)

28 October 1938

I am most grateful to you for your letter, and its kindness.

I am so glad you enjoyed the last volume of 'Marlborough', and it is a great compliment to me that you should have presented it to your Italian colleague.

I agree with you that Italian interests and inclinations lie with us, but I think they have little choice which side to take in view of our collapse and the German position on the Brenner.

Winston S. Churchill to Sir James Hawkey

(*Churchill papers: 7/46*)

29 October 1938   Chartwell

My dear Hawkey,

I send you herewith (1) a letter from Worsley to Ramsay Muir (vy secret). I do not think it necessary to consider any of these situations at present. (2) A letter from the 'Joint Democrats Committee' which seems to deserve consideration, evidently nothing can be done at present, and may never have to be done; but perhaps you will let me have your comments so that I can answer my correspondent, who is probably a Jew[1] (Urgent). (3) The Buckhurst Hill resolution is not unreasonable if they feel that way, but by 'National unity', do they mean blind loyalty to this Government?

As to Mr Illingworth's[2] letter, I should have thought that the Harlow Branch were going beyond their powers in attempting to prescribe the procedure of the Central Council, which is the parent body and must be free to debate and vote upon any resolutions which are submitted. I return you both documents for your convenience.

I think the 'conversations' are not suitable to be brought into our Constituency affairs. The parties concerned might mention that I had been making use of these letters, and that would do harm.

There are a number of declarations made by Inskip and others which can be found in my volume of speeches, where indeed, the whole tale is set out. I have a few cuttings of Hore-Belisha's false statements, and I will try to look them out for you. I was going to use them myself in the course of my speech. I cannot get at them at the moment.

Yours vy sincerely,
Winston S. Churchill

PS. What a lovely hall that was last night![3]

---

[1] Henry A. Kahan, of Chingford, Acting Secretary of the Joint Democrats Committee (to co-ordinate the activity of individual democrats and democratic organisations in defence of liberty and freedom). His letter began: 'I am instructed to inform you that the above named committee representing 350 members of the Epping division electorate, consisting of all shades of political opinion, have at a recent meeting passed a vote supporting the courageous fight for security and the preservation of Democratic liberties, that is being made by their member the Rt Hon Mr Winston Churchill. A census of popular opinion taken by us in this area, has shown that while your recent attitude has lost you a certain percentage of conservative support, it has gained for you a considerably greater support from the mass of electors' (*Churchill papers: 7/46*).

[2] T. Midgley Illingworth, Chairman of the Harlow Branch of the West Essex Unionist Association, who, had written to Sir James Hawkey: 'At a meeting of the Committee of this Branch held on Friday evening last, strong resentment was voiced by a majority of those present, at the attitude adopted by our Member during, and since the debate in the House on the Munich Agreement. As, however, Mr Churchill had already expressed a wish to consult his supporters, for which purpose you have called a meeting of the Central Council for November 4th, members of my Committee refrained from submitting resolutions expressing disapproval with which they had come prepared, as it was felt that it would be fairer to hear first what the Member had to say' (*Churchill papers: 7/46*).

[3] On the evening of 28 October 1938 Churchill was the principal speaker at the Connaught Hospital dinner, presided over by the Duke of Kent.

Winston S. Churchill to Sir Kingsley Wood

(Admiralty papers: 199/1929)

29 October 1938   Chartwell
Secret

A NOTE ON A SPECIAL OPERATION

1. In a war with Germany the severance of the Kiel Canal wd be an achievement of the first importance. I do not elaborate this as I assume it to be admitted.

2. Plans shd be made to do this &, if need be, all the details shd be worked out in their variants by a special technical committee.

3. Owing to there being few locks, & no marked difference of sea-level at the two ends of the Canal, its interruption by HE bombs even of the heaviest type could swiftly be repaired.

4. If however many bombs of medium size fitted with time-fuzes, some set for a day, others for a week, and others for a month, etc., could be dropped in the Canal their explosions at uncertain intervals & in uncertain places wd close the Canal to the movement of warships or valuable vessels until the whole bottom had been deeply dredged.

Alternatively, special fuzes with magnetic actuation should be considered.

5. The operation cd be repeated.

WSC

Winston S. Churchill to Sir Henry Page Croft

(Churchill papers: 2/332)

29 October 1938
Private & Confidential

Thank you for your letter, and its direct and straightforward answers. I know from old experience that one can build on what you say.

Will you let me, in my turn, deal with the points of difference which at present exist between us?

I agree that nothing can justify leading the country into defeat in war. War may be better than shame, but shame is better than defeat, which has a shame of its own. I submit to your sense of fair play that I have had nothing whatever to do with the policy or the course of events which led us to within an ace of war. None of the advice I gave, either on the need for preparedness or upon the conduct of foreign affairs, was taken. An opposite policy was followed, and that policy brought us, largely unprepared, to the verge of war, from which peril we escaped only at a heavy price. The point I ask you to consider before declaring your difference from me is that I am in no way responsible for what has happened. The Government alone bear the responsibility. They have conducted the whole movement of affairs. They have made the bed on which we now have to lie. There cannot be any differences between us about that.

But you may say: 'you had an alternative policy, and this policy would have led to war, all unprepared though we be.' It is true I believe that if we and France had in the spring and summer gone round to all the different countries involved, to wit, Russia, Poland, Jugoslavia, Roumania and even countries like Turkey, Bulgaria and Greece, and had said: 'we are prepared to guarantee the integrity of Czechoslovakia, subject to the necessary reforms, provided that you all come in, or enough of you come in,' we should have created a block or combination of Powers so overwhelming that Herr Hitler would have been forced by his generals and by his moderates to lie quiet. Nor would I have given the guarantee of England, except conditionally upon enough others coming in.

You may justly contend that this policy carried with it the idea, if all other conditions were fulfilled, that we should go to war for Czechoslovakia. But I affirm that this risk, which I have never concealed, was much less than the risks which were in fact actually run, after things had been let drift into their extreme plight.

This, then, is my contention against the Government, that they risked war, albeit unprepared, at such a time and in such a way as to incur the immense danger, whereas by foresight and decision at an earlier period, and with no greater risk,—with even less risk—they might have secured success instead of discomfiture.

It is not true that I have advocated a preventive war. Resistance to aggression, wise or unwise, timely or not, is not a preventive war, which is in itself essentially an aggressive act designed to forestall the growing strength of an opponent. Such a war as Germany might force on us should she fear our armaments begin to overtake her, would be a preventive war. Nothing like this has been in my mind since Germany has become so strong that military operations were required. But it is true I have used, and still use the argument that what has happened to Czecho-Slovakia has placed England and France at a disadvantage more substantial than anything they may recover in the next two years by development of their own forces. I need not elaborate this, because you have it all in your mind.

A further point remains. How can the Government justify their failure to have us adequately protected? Are they even now ready to take the necessary measures? Surely upon this we can be agreed, and also I trust upon the new great effort which is required to place our country in a position of independence.

In view of the answers you have made to the questions I put to you, there seems to be a wide field in which we can each work together for our own object, which is the greatness and survival of the British Empire.

I see rifts coming in the near future. It seems to me that Hitler will require of Chamberlain to have an Election before he makes his bargain, and to give proofs that he is in a position, at any rate for several years, to 'deliver the goods.' I have no doubt where I stand in the event. It may be possible to fight within the ranks of the Conservative Party, but will there be any rally of the strong forces of the Conservative Party to defend our rights and possessions, and to make the necessary sacrifices and exertions required for our safety, or is it all to go down the drain as it did in the India business, through the influence of the Central Office and the Government Whips? If so, I know my duty.

Your attitude I regard as of great importance. You know how earnestly I have wished to see you occupying a position worthy of your services and political weight. If you tell me that our Party is definitely committed to the easy-going life, to the surrender of our possessions and interests for the sake of quietness, to putting off the evil day at all costs, and that they will go along with Chamberlain into what must inevitably be a state of subservience, if not indeed actual vassalage to Germany, and that you can do nothing to arrest this fatal tide, then I think the knowledge would simplify my course. It is for this reason that I have ventured to intrude upon you.

Yours vy sincerely,
Winston S. Churchill

Winston S. Churchill to Sir Kingsley Wood
(*Churchill papers: 25/14*)

30 October 1938

I learn that the meeting of the ADR Committee has again been postponed till November 14th. This leads me to draw your attention to what I wrote to you on June 9th, when you first took office as Air Minister. The importance of this subject to our safety has now become paramount. But the Committee, in my opinion, is failing in its task, and is in danger of becoming an actual barrier upon swift progress.

I therefore venture to ask you to consider reinforcing it by adding Professor

Lindemann to its numbers. This would enable me, with his assistance, to put before you a continuous stream of valuable ideas and also to criticize with technical knowledge, which I do not possess myself, the progress or non-progress on existing lines of enquiry. I make this suggestion to you with full knowledge of what has happened in the past and after maturely considering it in all its bearings. I am sure that this step would be in the public interest and is essential to a genuine effort being made to overtake the time that has been lost.

I can well imagine how busy you have been since taking this office, but I cannot feel that you have been able to address your mind to the issues involved, either personal or technical, which I mentioned to you in my letter.

Unless I can feel that the work of this Committee is going to receive a new impulse from your own personal direction, I should consider it my duty to free myself from the silence I have observed for three years upon this branch of our defence and, with due regard to the necessity for secrecy, to endeavour to get something done by Parliamentary action. If you will very kindly re-read my speech of June 7th, 1935, which is included in the book I sent you, you will see that I was in possession at that time, before the Committee was created, of practically all the root ideas which have since been discussed upon the Committee, and I should propose to take up my task from the point reached on pages 241 and 242.[1]

I hope, therefore, you will give your personal attention to this matter and believe that it is still my desire to assist you by any means in my power.

Meanwhile I send you the third paper which I promised you in my private letter of July 26th (Sub-section c).

---

[1] Speaking in the Debate on the Adjournment on 7 June 1935, Churchill told the House of Commons: 'I wish to draw the attention of the House and of the public to a question connected with air defence. This point is limited, and largely technical and scientific in its character. Nevertheless it is important. It is concerned with the methods which can be invented, adopted or discovered to enable the earth to control the air, to enable defence from the ground to exercise control—domination—upon aeroplanes high above its surface.' A few moments later he declared: 'My experience—and it is somewhat considerable—is that in these matters when the need is clearly explained by military and political authorities science is always able to provide something. "Seek and ye shall find" has been borne out. We were told that it was impossible to grapple with submarines, but methods were found which enabled us to strangle the submarine below the water, a problem not necessarily harder than that of clawing down marauding aeroplanes. Many things which were attempted in the War we were told were technically impossible, but patience, perseverance, and, above all, the spur of necessity under war conditions made men's brains act with greater vigour, and science responded to the demand. That being so, I venture to set the research side of air defence in a position of primary importance. I agree that there is nothing which can offer any substitute for an equal or superior force, a readiness to retaliate, but if you could discover some new method the whole of our affairs would be greatly simplified.'

Thomas Jones to an American friend

(Jones papers)

30 October 1938

Churchill's speech to America,[1] brilliant as it was in phrasing, is criticised here as not likely to be helpful on your side. . . .

Lord Londonderry to Winston S. Churchill

(Churchill papers: 2/332)

31 October 1938

My dear Winston,

I am sending you the enclosed which I think will interest you. It certainly interests me as it shows your intrepid character (as flying was no child's-play then) and also your progressive ideas.[2] Another reason is that it gives me an excuse to write to you which I have wanted to do for some time. You will remember the little episode at Grillion's Club. Never have I felt so wounded or so unhappy that my oldest friend and benefactor—because I attribute all I may have accomplished (not very much but still something) first of all to your friendliness and counsel when I first entered Parliament and next to the start you gave me in 1918 at the Air Ministry—should not turn on me so unjustly. One gets proud and aloof and altho' we patched it up I know that a gulf has existed between us. Except for personal reasons which mean much to me, it does not matter because I have left the arena and as I let Baldwin destroy me, I have fallen back on the endless resources with which Provi-

---

[1] Churchill's broadcast of 16 October 1938, over NBC (see pages 1216–1217).

[2] Churchill began flying in 1913, at the age of thirty-nine, at a time when thirty-two was considered the top age at which a man could take up flying, and he flew regularly, for more than a year, until his wife prevailed upon him to give it up, on account of the dangers, following the death of one of his flying instructors. On 6 June 1914 Churchill wrote to his wife: 'This is a wrench, because I was on the verge of taking my pilot's certificate. It only needed a couple of calm mornings; & I am confident of my ability to achieve it vy respectably. I shd greatly have liked to reach this point wh wd have made a suitable moment for breaking off. But I must admit that the numerous fatalities of this year wd justify you in complaining if I continued to share the risks—as I am proud to do—of these good fellows. So I give it up decidedly for many months & perhaps for ever. This is a gift—so stupidly am I made—wh costs me more than anything wh cd be bought with money. . . . Anyhow I can feel I know a good deal about the fascinating new art. I can manage a machine with ease in the air, even with high winds, & only a little more practice in landings wd have enabled me to go up with reasonable safety alone. I have been up nearly 140 times, with many pilots, & all kinds of machines, so I know the difficulties, the dangers & the joys of the air—well enough to appreciate them, & to understand all the questions of policy wh will arise in the near future.' Some of Churchill's Admiralty minutes on flying are printed in Main Volume Two of this biography, pages 689 to 694.

dence through a good constitution, the accident of birth and many friends has provided me.

There is no need for the gulf because you and I are on the same lines. We have only differed as to the method.

I wanted to get hold of the Germans when they were weak and defenceless and on the lines of the policy of Castlereagh and Wellington in regard to a beaten France in 1815. I never liked the Germans as Germans, I hate Nazism as much as I do Bolshevism and Fascism, but I would first of all [like] to give the Germans the chance of playing a great part with us and France in international affairs, and if we found that this was only a dream, to be in a position to hold them in subjection as long as it was right to do so. I did not send you my book and I do not expect you have read it. Altho' I had a great success with it, (a successful 5/- book only touches about 8,000 people) owing to Baldwin having destroyed me and the influential Press selling a bear of my political stock, I have not been able to get my policy 'across'. I wrote my book with a very definite purpose and a selfish one too. I was determined to set down in black and white the value of contacts (which I almost alone had much) and my belief in the four Great Western Powers of Europe settling on a definite policy of peace: because I foresaw the disasters which have now overtaken us. What do I find? My policy carried out, at the last minute of the 11th hour in the face of arrogant threats. I do feel that at the time Neville Chamberlain had no alternative, but if only I could have persuaded our benighted administration to listen to me four years ago. . . .

Sir Henry Page Croft to Winston S. Churchill

(*Churchill papers: 2/332*)

31 October 1938

My dear Winston,

Many thanks for your letter of 29th inst.

Had you and those who abstained with you made clear that your attitude was purely on the grounds of inadequate defence, I should not have found myself 'so far apart' from yourself. Where I was in fundamental disagreement with you was on the point that you apparently considered we should have sought, or at least risked, the arbitrament of war rather than make the Munich Settlement, when you had convinced me that we were in a hopeless disparity in the Air arm. Since, until we had built up an army of several millions, the war would have been purely an air war, I was at a loss to understand how anyone could urge a course different to that which Chamberlain took. Only if we had been definitely committed to fight for the Czechs could we have undertaken such a one-sided contest; then, of course, we must have fought however bloody the consequences.

In answer to your three points:—

(1) I stand precisely where I have always stood on the subject of ex-German Colonies.
(2) I am not in favour of any air pact with Germany or anyone else which accepts definite inferiority in the air.
(3) I am prepared to support any measure for the speeding up of armaments, although if we were in fact in a condition to fight Germany in the air at the time of the Munich Agreement (which I still cannot believe), the need for a Ministry of Supply with its inevitable dislocation of general trade would not appear to be so imperative as it was a year ago.

I shall be glad to have a yarn with you on these subjects when the House meets.

Yours always,
Henry P. Croft

Dr Terence Brand: recollections

(*Letter to the author, 19 November 1981*)

[31 October 1938]   [Chartwell]

We must have spent half an hour discussing all aspects of the case[1] and his very real concern was obvious. He then came downstairs to see me off and as we stood on the steps outside, he suddenly asked 'what did I, and the local people I met, think about the Munich appeasement approach to Hitler?' I think my reply was that opinions were very much divided, many hoped that it would help to avert the threatened war, but others were unhappy about it. He said words to the effect that it was a disastrous episode, and waved me goodbye.

[1] Violet Pearman's continuing illness (see also pages 1096–7).

November 1938

1 November 1938   Chartwell

My dear Mrs P,

I talked to Dr Brand yesterday, & have come to the conclusion that you need a good long rest, if you are to recover yr health. I have therefore decided to offer you a year's leave at a salary of £3 a week. If you feel able to look after the literary accounts & to do a little work with the Press cuttings, all the better. But it is just as you feel, & there is no need for you to do anything, unless it is a help to you in passing the time.

Of course if, as I hope, you make rapid progress, you can resume yr duties here.

Meanwhile please come & see us, & use this garden whenever you feel inclined, & the sun shines.

Yours vy sincerely,
Winston S. Churchill

2 November 1938

My dear Winston,

You were as usual, generous and kind enough yesterday, to ask me to tell you quite frankly whether I was with you or against you.

In my small way, believe me, you have no greater admirer of yourself than I am. The difference between the view expressed by you and that held by myself, is that I believe Germany would have gone to war and I knew as a layman, that this country was completely unprepared, and no one has done more than you to bring before the nation for the past six years, the state of affairs in which we find ourselves, due to the state of unpreparedness.

In consequence of this state of unpreparedness, I cannot see what other steps the Prime Minister could have taken, and I for one remained an optimist all through that crisis.

I am now venturing to enclose a memorandum showing the inefficiency of the Ministry of Transport. Don't bother to read this unless you think it can be of some use.

You asked yesterday, what could be done. I suggest that every Member of Parliament who holds a shred of Tory faith, press for your suggestion of a Committee of enquiry or investigation. That no effort should be relaxed in or out of the House of Commons to press for the removal of Inskip, Belisha, Burgin[1] and Hoare, all four of whom were collectively and individually responsible for the chaos, which was so evident in the crisis, and if I may say so, it was evident to people like myself before the crisis arose.

I could suggest many practical and useful solutions, but I will not weary you any further than to wish you every good luck, and you may rest assured that while I may disagree with the principle as to whether Germany would go to war or not, that appears to be over now and we have got to fight for all we are worth to see that no such situation arises again.

Violet Pearman to Winston S. Churchill

(*Churchill papers: 8/594*)

3 November 1938

Dear Mr Churchill,

Thank you very much for your letter of the 1st and for your kind offer. I hope I shall not be away as long as a year, and as soon as I am quite well, I shall return. I will certainly do the press cuttings and the literary account while I am home.

By doing my housework myself and living alone with Rosemary,[2] I can manage, and it will be quiet. This house is too small to need any help, and

---

[1] Edward Leslie Burgin, 1887–1945. Educated in Lausanne and Paris. Solicitor. Intelligence Officer, 1916–18 (on active service in Italy, despatches). Liberal MP for Luton, 1929–45 (Liberal National since 1931). Charity Commissioner, 1931–2. Parliamentary Secretary, Board of Trade, 1932–7. Privy Councillor, 1937. Minister of Transport, 1937–9. Minister of Supply, 1939–40.

[2] Rosemary Pearman, 1929–   . Educated at Wadhurst College, Sussex (Churchill contributed to the cost of her education). Joined the Land Army, 1946; worked on a farm for two years; then at the Ministry of Pensions; then at the United States Embassy in London. She married, first, in 1948, Joseph Tufts; then, in 1952, Airman First Class Joseph Everett, United States Air Force (Churchill, then Prime Minister, helped to accelerate the paperwork necessary for the marriage). They had four children. Later she recalled, of Churchill: 'He was like an impish, big child. He was very sweet to know. He was always interested in what other people were doing. I remember when he came to see me once, when I was four or five, he got down on his hands and knees, crawling around, pretending to be a bear—and growling like one' (*conversation with the author, 30 January 1982*).

doctor says that this will be ideal, as it will give me the peace and quiet I need, and also the exercise.

I will try to come and see you and Chartwell when I can, but as it is all uphill and these buses only come halfway in the daytime, I cannot manage the rest of the uphill. If however Cale can manage to fit fetching me in with his work, then I can come and get the necessary items for the literary account, also the press cuttings. So the journey will not be wasted. I can get home myself. . . .

With very kind regards to yourself and very many thanks for your kindness and understanding.

Yours sincerely,
Violet Pearman

Winston S. Churchill to Ramsay Muir

(*Churchill papers: 2/333*)

5 November 1938
Private and Confidential

Dear Mr Ramsay Muir,

Thanks for your letter and its enclosure.

About our talk the other day, you will have seen that I carried my Association on the critical division. We were 100 to 44 (These figures are secret). I think it quite possible that the minority may bring forward a candidate of their own, and this would be neither disagreeable nor disadvantageous to me.

I have been invited by the seventeen Branches of the League of Nations Union in the Division to address a meeting in the near future, and am disposed to comply with their request. In this I should have the support of my Chairman, Sir James Hawkey, although he disapproves of the League of Nations. This might be an occasion where prominent Liberals might come to this—the only common platform, that exists at the present time. I think it indispensable to place the larger causes before the people, because otherwise the exertions which are necessary will certainly not be forthcoming. We might indeed make the meeting a considerable rally for the principles of the League of Nations, more than ever indispensable now. I will let you know further how this progresses.

Meanwhile, I have sent Mr Worsley's letter to Sir James Hawkey, in strict confidence, and I daresay these two may come together privately.

I only write to let you know that I am moving steadily along those lines

we discussed for National strength and unity. The fact that I and my friends
are in full control of the Unionist Association does not make me less desirous
of gathering together the largest measure of support for the main issue. I will
keep you informed of developments, and I should be very glad if you would
continue to study the position.

We must 'put country before party', as the saying goes.

Winston S. Churchill to Lord Londonderry

(Churchill papers: 2/333)

5 November 1938

It was very kind of you to write to me so fully, and in spite of our intense
political differences, I always hope we shall be able to preserve the relations
of friendship and of kinship.

Your policy is certainly being tried, and I see nothing for it at the moment
but to await the results of Chamberlain's hopes and experiment.

I view the immediate future with the deepest anxiety, but I am comforted
to feel I have no responsibility either for the neglect of our defences or for
other aspects of the Government's policy. It is incredible that we should have
been brought so low in five short years. There is plenty more to come.

Winston S. Churchill to Sir James Hawkey

(Churchill papers: 7/46)

6 November 1938
Private & Confidential

My dear Hawkey,

Although I know your views on the merits of the League of Nations
Union, I am of the opinion that it would be very advisable to take up this
suggestion in the near future. You have met Mr Richards who is the secretary
of this group of all parties which has gathered around me. They are working
for rearmament and National Service, and as many of them have been life-
long pacifists, their convictions are impressive. We must have a truly national
basis if we are to save ourselves at this critical juncture. I propose, unless you
advise to the contrary, to write to Mr Richards and say that I should be
disposed to address such a meeting before Christmas. I have no doubt that
many of the leading Liberals will be on the platform, and I shall be able to

make a strong speech for rearmament and for resistance to the Nazi tyranny.

A meeting like this might well prevent a Liberal candidate from coming into the field, in which case our position approaching a General Election would be a very strong one.

As you know, Mr Chamberlain is Vice-President of the League of Nations Union, and the official position of the party is that Conservatives are to be encouraged to take part in the work of that body, and are perfectly free to speak upon its platforms.

We must, of course, have our own meeting in the Royal Forest Hotel a week or two beforehand.

Will you tell Dinah[1] that Friday the 18th November or Friday the 25th would suit me, if she can get the hall.[2]

Pray send me Mr Richards' correspondence back as soon as possible, as I wish to write to him. He organized my Manchester, Sheffield, Birmingham and Bristol meetings,[3] which were certainly very brilliant affairs, the leading people of all parties and all creeds being represented on the platforms.[4]

[1] Dinah Hawkey, Sir James Hawkey's daughter, and (as Mrs Edward C. Pratt), Honorary Secretary of the Epping Division of the West Essex Unionist Association.

[2] Churchill defended his political record at Harlow on 25 November 1938. His speech began: 'I am very glad we are not to have a By-Election. I have had no wish to force one upon the Constituency. I have an abiding sense of comradeship and goodwill towards the Association. They have stood by me and followed the guidance it was my duty to give during the last fourteen years. During the last four or five years I have been trying constantly, by every method of appeal and attack, to stimulate the Government to rearm the country on a scale and at a rate equal to our dangers. In all this I have received constantly the support and encouragement of the Association. It would have been very painful to me to take any course which would have divided us. We have one of the finest organizations in the country, which we have built up together, and I hope that we shall continue to work unitedly to maintain the strength of the British nation and Empire & the great causes for which they stand. That is the sole object for which I remain in public life, and I know that is the supreme desire and resolve of this intensely patriotic constituency. I must recognize, moreover, that since the Munich Agreement, Mr Chamberlain and his Government have announced or taken several important steps which are in accordance with and constitute an advance towards the views which I hold upon foreign policy. In the forefront I place the Trade Agreement with the United States, upon which the President of the Board of Trade has been earnestly labouring for nearly a year. That has now come to fruition amid general assent on both sides of the Atlantic. There is nothing more vital to the safety and peace of the world than the increasing unity of sentiment and principle between the peoples of the English-speaking world. It is inspiring to feel that the great American democracy has the same hatred of tyranny and persecution, and the same love of the free institutions and Parliamentary system which the genius of our race had produced, and which we cherish here in this Island. I rejoice that the United States is arming. I cannot feel the slightest anxiety at the growth of their naval power.

[3] Churchill's speeches at Manchester on 9 May 1938, at Bristol on 16 May 1938, at Sheffield on 31 May 1938 and at Birmingham on 2 June 1938.

[4] On 9 December 1938 Churchill set out his support for the League of Nations, and defended his opinions on Foreign policy, at a meeting at the Royal Forest Hotel, Chingford, in his constituency (see page 1311). At the end of the meeting he was asked by Colin Thornton-Kemsley, Chairman of the Chigwell Unionist Association, 'if it would not be more honour-

Winston S. Churchill to Lord Cecil of Chelwood

(*Cecil of Chelwood papers*)

6 November 1938   Chartwell

My dear Bob,

I shall be very glad to sign a letter with you in the sense you desire.[1] Pray add my name, if you will, to what you and Angell have put forward.

Yours ever,
W. S. Churchill

Adolf Hitler: speech

(*Foreign Office papers: 371/21708*)

6 November 1938   Weimar

Mr Churchill has declared openly that in his opinion the present régime in Germany should be abolished in cooperation with internal German forces who would put themselves gratefully at his disposal for the purpose. If Mr Churchill had less to do with emigrés, that is to say, exiled foreign paid traitors and more to do with Germans, then he would see the whole idiocy and stupidity of what he says. I can only assure this gentleman that there is in Germany no such power as could set itself against the present régime.[2]

---

able and courageous of him, in view of his attacks on their leader, Mr Chamberlain, to describe himself as an independent'. Churchill replied 'that he intended to fight that constituency at the next election whatever happened, and on exactly the same platform as he fought the last election' (*The Times, 10 December 1938*).

[1] A nomination for the Nobel Peace Prize, on behalf of President Beneš (see also page 1264).

[2] On October 28 the German Government had begun a mass expulsion of all 20,000 Polish Jews resident in Germany. The explusions, which took place amid terrible scenes of brutality and hardship, provoked the seventeen-year-old son of one of the families expelled to shoot a member of the German Embassy in Paris. The assassination took place on November 7. Two days later the German Press accused Churchill of being linked in the murder plot. The *Angriff* newspaper headlined the murder: 'The work of the instigator-international: A straight line from Churchill to Grynspan.' The article declared that it was 'no coincidence' that Grynspan took 'the same line as is pursued by Messrs Churchill, Eden, Duff Cooper and their associates', and it stated: 'While in London the Churchill clique, unmasked by the Führer, was busy with sanctimonious deception, in Paris the murder weapon spat in the hands of a Jewish lout and destroyed the last measurable remnants of credibility in the assertion that agitation for war and murder against the Third Reich has never been carried on or contemplated.' Hitler's attack on Churchill prompted *The Times* to comment on November 11: 'It is much worse than merely ludicrous. It is wholly intolerable. It demands official notice, and should receive it without delay.'

Olive Harrington[1] to Winston S. Churchill

(Churchill papers: 9/133)

6 November 1938
4.30 pm

The Press Association rang to advise you that Herr Hitler had referred to you in a speech, saying:

'He thinks he can set on one side the Germany of to-day; it would be better if Mr Churchill would associate less with people who are paid by Foreign States and more with German people.'

Then later on in the speech he talked of disarmament, and said:

'As long as others only speak of disarmament, we do not believe them, and think their only desire is to repeat 1918. I can assure Mr Churchill and his friends that that only happened once and will never happen again.' Do you wish to make any comment, please?

Winston S. Churchill: press statement

(Churchill papers: 9/133)

6 November 1938

I am surprised that the head of a great State should set himself to attack British members of Parliament, who hold no official position, and who are not even the leaders of parties. Such action on his part can only enhance any influence they may have, because their fellow-countrymen have long been able to form their own opinions about them, and really do not need foreign guidance.

Herr Hitler is quite mistaken in supposing that Mr Eden, Mr Duff-Cooper, myself and the leaders of the Liberal and Labour Parties are war-mongers. Not one of us has ever dreamed of an act of aggression against Germany. We are, however, concerned to make sure that our own country is properly defended, so that we can be safe and free, and also help others to

[1] Olive Harrington, a married woman who was brought in to help Kathleen Hill following Violet Pearman's illness, and working at Chartwell throughout the Munich crisis. An accurate shorthand typist, she was subject to moments of nervous overstrain, and forced to remain in bed. After a few months she left Chartwell. Her successor, Miss Millicent Broomhead, assisted Kathleen Hill, but was subject to heart trouble, and unable to make the necessary and frequent journeys to London. Miss Broomhead was succeeded by Miss Mary Shearburn, who remained at Chartwell as No 2 secretary until the outbreak of war, and then worked for Churchill at Admiralty House. A relative by marriage of the novelist Ethel Mannin, she subsequently married Churchill's detective, W. H. Thompson.

whom we are bound. Herr Hitler ought to understand this mood and respect it. I have always said that if Great Britain were defeated in war, I hope we should find a Hitler to lead us back to our rightful position among the nations. I am sorry, however, that he has not been mellowed by the great success which has attended him. The whole world would rejoice to see the Hitler of peace and tolerance, and nothing would adorn his name in world history so much as acts of magnanimity and of mercy and pity to the forlorn & friendless, to the weak and poor.

Since he has been good enough to give me his advice, I venture to return the compliment.

Herr Hitler also shows himself unduly sensitive about suggestions that there may be other opinions in Germany besides his own. It would be indeed astonishing if among eighty millions of people so varying in origin, creed, interest and condition, there should be only one pattern of thought. It would not be natural. It is incredible. That he has the power, and alas the will, to suppress all inconvenient opinions is no doubt true. It would be much wiser to relax a little, and not try to frighten people out of their wits for expressing honest doubts and divergences.

He is mistaken in thinking that I do not see Germans of the Nazi regime when they come to this country. On the contrary, only this year I have seen, at their request, Herr Bohle, Herr Henlein, and the Gauleiter of Dantzig, and they all know that in common with most English men and women I should like nothing better than to see a great, happy, peaceful Germany in the vanguard of Europe. Let this great man search his own heart and conscience before he accuses anyone of being a war-monger. The whole peoples of the British Empire and the French Republic earnestly desire to dwell in peace, side by side with the German nation. But they are also resolved to put themselves in a position to defend their rights and long-established civilisation. They do not mean to be in anybody's power.

If Herr Hitler's eye shd fall upon these words, I trust he will accept them in the spirit of candour in which they are uttered.[1]

---

[1] The first version of this statement ended: 'I hope Herr Hitler will be allowed by his own censors to read these words, and that he will accept them in the same spirit of candour in which they are uttered.'

Desmond Morton to Winston S. Churchill
(*Churchill papers: 2/337*)

7 November 1938

. . . Of draft laws, draft regulations and draft orders-in-council for pro-
mulgation on the outbreak of war we have a number ready, but my point,
and what I believe to be the vital issue at the present time is that although
much planning has been carried out, it is quite insufficient to meet the
requirements of modern war.

There are gaps and worse than gaps in the most important breastwork of
modern defence; in the Fourth Arm of Defence, the Economic Arm, which
covers the economic life of the Nation and the Higher Command of the
Nation in war; from which the Armed Forces themselves derive their men and
their material; on whose efficiency the Armed Forces must depend for their
very existence.

In order that planning may be undertaken to fill these gaps in war, I ask
for decisions upon wartime economic policy; alternative decisions if you
like, so that alternative plans can be made. Without decisions, it is impossible
to plan.

Lastly I ask that, when the necessary decisions have been taken, authority
may be granted for plans to be drawn up accordingly, so that the Higher
Command of *this* Nation in war, which does not yet exist, may be created.

I am not pressing wild, new theories upon you. The theory of totalitarian
war is at least twenty years old and has been accepted everywhere. I am
asking that steps should be taken to put the obvious counter measures into
practice.

The cost of doing so will be relatively negligible. The cost of failure to do
so may be incalculable.

Josiah Wedgwood to Winston S. Churchill
(*Churchill papers: 2/333*)

8 November 1938

Dear Winston,

. . . I am bringing out an Anthology on Liberty, half American and half
English, prose and verse, which I think will be useful as propaganda against
Hitlerism and for joint action across the Atlantic. I want to have samples
right through our History and I propose to wind up with your broadcast to
America.[1] I should like, also, to have your selection of your best speech on the

---

[1] Churchill's broadcast of 16 October 1938 (see pages 1216–27).

subject. If you make no selection, I shall take your introduction to the South
Africa Bill 1906.[1] Any way, give me your blessing and approval, also any
hints that strike you as being appropriate. . . .

Yours,
Josiah Wedgwood

Adolf Hitler: speech

(*Foreign Office papers: 371/21708*)

8 November 1938

The gentlemen of the British Parliament are no doubt at home in the
British Empire but not in Central Europe. There they have no knowledge
whatever of the conditions of events and circumstances. They will not and
must not take this statement as an insult for we are not after all so well
informed about India or Egypt or Palestine. I should however consider it
proper if these gentlemen with their enormous knowledge and the unfailing
wisdom which is their own would concentrate for the moment on Palestine,
shall we say. They could shower blessings there. For what is going on there
smells damned strongly of force and very little democracy. But I only give
that as an example, not as criticism, for I am only the representative of my
German people and not the advocate of others.

That is where I differ from Messrs Churchill and Eden who are the advocates of the whole world. I am only the representative of my people and I do
here what I think necessary. When Mr Churchill says to me, 'How can the

---

[1] In introducing the Transvaal Constitution Bill to Parliament on 31 July 1906, Churchill
then Under-Secretary of State for the Colonies in Campbell-Bannerman's Liberal government, had won widespread praise for his plea, at the end of his speech, for an all-Party
approach to the grant of responsible government. As he told the House of Commons: 'We are
prepared to make this settlement in the name of the Liberal Party. That is sufficient authority
for us; but there is a higher authority which we should earnestly desire to obtain. I make no
appeal, but I address myself particularly to the right honourable Gentlemen who sit opposite
who are long versed in public affairs, and not able to escape all their lives from the heavy
South African responsibility. They are the accepted guides of a Party which, though in a
minority in this House nevertheless embodies nearly half the nation. I will ask them seriously
whether they will not pause before they commit themselves to violent or rash denunciations
of this great arrangement. I will ask them, further, whether they will not consider if they
cannot join with us to invest the grant of a free Constitution to the Transvaal with something
of a national sanction. With all our majority we can only make it the gift of a Party; they
can make it the gift of England. And if that were so, I am quite sure that all those inestimable
blessings which we confidently hope will flow from this decision will be gained more surely
and much more speedily; and the first real step taken to withdraw South African affairs from
the arena of British Party Politics, in which they have inflicted injury on both political
Parties and in which they have suffered grievous injury themselves.'

Head of a State cross swords with a British Member of Parliament?' I answer him 'Mr Churchill, don't you feel honoured? You can see from the fact that in Germany even the Head of the State is not afraid to cross swords with a British Member of Parliament the high esteem in which British Members of Parliament are held. Moreover, I am not the Head of a State like a dictator or a monarch, but I am the German people's Leader. I could, you may be convinced, have had quite different titles. I have kept the old one and shall keep it as long as I live because I want to be nothing else and never think of it. I am satisfied.'

Mr Churchill and these gentlemen are deputies of the English people and I am a deputy of the German people. The difference is only that Mr Churchill received but a fraction of British votes and I represent the whole German people. Therefore, my old comrades in arms, when I call you and the whole German people to watchfulness I have a holy right to do it. I have secured great successes for the nation in these few years. It must understand that I am always caring for its security. I never want to live to make at the end of my days dark prophecies as I close my eyes such as Bismarck made. I want to keep that which we have toilsomely achieved and to keep it for ever by the tremendous power of the whole German nation. Thereby is a task fulfilled which our dead gave up. For this Germany they once marched with us with the same faith in their hearts as we.

Alastair Forbes[1] to Winston S. Churchill

(*Churchill papers: 2/333*)

8 November 1938

. . . I do not think the young men of this country are willing to be conscripted by a Government pressing the present foreign policy, but were it really national—on the lines you yourself hoped to see it reconstructed, with Labour and Tory represented, we would trust you.

I am not interested in politics for their own sake. I am a young man about to start life, I have no oratory and no command of words, but all my heart is in this appeal to you *now* at this election to make you stand.

Before it is too late and you lose the influence you have on the country. If Eden does not do the same he stands the risk of losing his ideals as well as his popularity. You cannot allow this to happen. You cannot allow yourself

---

[1] Alastair Grant Forbes, 1918–   . Third son of James Grant Forbes of Boston, USA. Educated at Winchester and King's College, Cambridge. Served as a volunteer in Finland, 1940; subsequently in the Royal Marines, and as a war correspondent. After the war he worked as a journalist and freelance writer. A friend of both Mary and Randolph Churchill.

to be blackmailed by Party considerations at this time. It would be unforgivable. . . .[1]

Harold Nicolson to his wife
(*Nicolson papers*)

9 November 1938

I went to a hush-hush meeting with Anthony Eden. Present: Eden, Amery,
Cranborne, Sidney Herbert, Cartland, Harold Macmillan, Spears, Derrick
Gunston, Emrys-Evans, Anthony Crossley, Hubert Duggan.[2] All good
Tories and sensible men. This group is distinct from the Churchill group.
It also includes Duff Cooper. We decided that we should not advertise our-
selves as a group or even call ourselves a group. We should merely meet together from time to time, exchange views, and organise ourselves for a revolt
if needed. I feel happier about this. Eden and Amery are wise people, and
Sidney Herbert is very experienced. Obviously they do not mean to do anything rash or violent. At the same time they are deeply disturbed by the fact
that Chamberlain does not seem to understand the gravity of the situation.
Unless we pull ourselves together and have compulsory registration in the
next few months, it will be too late. It was a relief to me to be with people
who share my views so completely, and yet who do not give the impression
(as Winston does) of being more bitter than determined, and more out for a
fight than for reform. I shall be happy and at ease with this group.

Winston S. Churchill to the Nobel Prize Committee
(*Churchill papers: 2/333*)

10 November 1938   Chartwell

Dear Sir,
    I understand that the name of Dr Eduard Beneš has been put forward as
a recipient of the Nobel Peace Prize.

---

[1] Forbes had expressed his 'considerable dismay' that Churchill had refused to support the
Independent Progressive Candidate, Vernon Bartlett, at Bridgewater (see page 1323, note 1).
[2] Hubert John Duggan, 1904–1943. Educated at Eton. 2nd Lieutenant, Life Guards, 1924–
8. Conservative MP for Acton from 1931 until his death. Parliamentary Private Secretary to
the Civil Lord of the Admiralty (Euan Wallace), 1931–5. Lieutenant, Life Guards, 1939;
Captain, 1940. Failing health prevented him from taking an active part in the war, and he
died on 25 October 1943, at the age of 39. 'He was one of the very small band of Conservatives
who supported the present Foreign Secretary (Anthony Eden) at the time of his resignation,
and one of the hardly larger number who protested against the settlement of Munich' (A
correspondent, *The Times*, 30 October 1943).

As a British Member of Parliament and a Privy Councillor I should like whole-heartedly to support his candidature.

I need not emphasise to you the unfailing devotion of Dr Beneš to the principles of the League of Nations nor his real contribution to international justice and the cause of Peace.

I am sure that such an award would not only be warmly welcomed as a recognition of his efforts, but also as a timely gesture of support for the Peace ideals of the world.[1]

R. J. Minney[2] *to Winston S. Churchill*

(*Churchill papers: 2/333*)

11 November 1938   Sunday Referee
                                                          London

Dear Mr Churchill,

I hope you will not think it impertinent of me, but I feel that I ought to write and suggest this to you.

The recent crisis has revealed how weak we are, and now that the danger has passed the country is being lulled again into a state of apathy. It needs rousing, and I can think of no one who could rouse it so well as you.

If you, like Gladstone, went round the country making speeches four and five times a week, you would not only attract large numbers of people, but your views would also obtain prominence in the local press; and your campaign would obtain for you, I am confident, a tremendous following.

There would, of course, be no need either to criticise Mr Chamberlain or to attack Hitler; but I am sure you will agree that the country needs rousing.

I am writing because I feel that the message is better conveyed personally in this manner to you.

With all good wishes,
Yours sincerely,
R. J. Minney

[1] No Nobel Peace Prize was awarded between 1939 and 1943. In 1944 it went to the International Committee of the Red Cross, Geneva, and in 1945 to Cordell Hull. Beneš was never a recipient.

[2] Rubeigh James Minney, 1895–1979. Educated at King's College, London. On the Editorial Staff of the *Pioneer*, Allahabad and of the *Englishman*, Calcutta. Represented *The Times* in Calcutta. Worked on the *Daily Express* and *Sunday News*, London. A novelist, he published his first novel in 1921. Editor of *Everybody's Weekly*, 1925–35. Editor of the *Sunday Referee*, 1935–9. Editor, the *Strand Magazine*, 1941–2. In films since 1942. Playwright and biographer. Among his biographies are those of Chaplin (1954), Lord Addison (1958), and Hore-Belisha (1960).

Basil Liddell Hart to Winston S. Churchill

(Churchill papers: 2/348)

11 November 1938

Dear Mr Churchill,

A few days ago I met Captain Orde Wingate,[1] who is of our GHQ Intelligence in Palestine, and who has been playing a Lawrence-like role (in the opposite way) in combating the Arab terrorist gangs in Palestine. You may possibly have noticed the hint of his activities which was contained in the announcement in September when he was awarded the DSO for his exploits. He is now back on leave and I think it might interest you to meet him if you have time to do so. In case you care to, the Army & Navy Club will find him—or where he is actually staying, a service flat, at 17 Nottingham Place, WELbeck 3591.

He told me how much he would like to have a chance of seeing you, which was my reason for effecting this introduction.

The methods he has been employing with marked success are outlined in the enclosed memorandum, which I am sending you confidentially. It was as a result of it that he gained permission to try them out and to form and train special night squads for the purpose. Unfortunately the possibility of expanding the success already achieved is hampered by the hesitation of politicals out there to give permission for the expansion of this special force to an adequate scale. Apart from its significance as a contribution to the solution of the present difficulties in Palestine, I think the memorandum is likely to interest your military mind.[2]

With all good wishes,
Yours very sincerely,
Basil Liddell Hart

---

[1] Orde Charles Wingate, 1903–1944. Born in India. Educated at Charterhouse. 2nd Lieutenant, Royal Artillery, 1923; Captain, 1936. Attached to the Sudan Defence Force (serving mostly on the Abyssinian frontier), 1928–33. On special appointment (Intelligence) in Palestine and Transjordan, 1936–9 (wounded, despatches, DSO); organized special Jewish 'night squads' to combat Arab sabotage. On active service, 1939–44 (despatches, two bars to his DSO), first in Abyssinia, and then, as Commander of the Special Force, India Command in Burma. Killed in an aeroplane crash during a tropical storm, while on a visit to one of his units, 24 March 1944.

[2] Churchill met Wingate for the first time on 30 November 1938, at Churchill's 64th birthday dinner, given by Venetia Montagu. In his memorandum, Wingate explained the principle of 'night squads': groups of armed men who would protect Jewish settlements and British military installations—both then under Arab attack in Palestine—not by waiting in a defensive perimeter, but by setting out stealthily at night on patrols whose aim was to ambush the armed groups before they came anywhere near their would-be target.

Evelyn Fleming[1] to Winston S. Churchill

(*Churchill papers: 1/324*)

11 November 1938

My dear Mr Churchill,

It was very nice of you to come to luncheon the other day. I felt I ought to do something about having you limned & I managed to get John[2] on the telephone this morning. He says (as I suspected) that he would love to paint you—& in fact has always wanted to. Can't something be done about it? I suggest a sketch of two sittings, & I imagine that that is all you need do about it, unless you *want* to buy it afterwards. He paints ever so much better when it is not a commission, which he loathes.

This is only a suggestion & if you don't want to do it I will just tell him you haven't time to sit.

I do hope you think that I have done well by Val's[3] boys. I enclose a little list of what they have done so far which I hope is only the beginning. They tell me that Peter speaks brilliantly & without notes.

Yours very sincerely,
Evelyn Fleming

Evelyn Fleming: notes

(*Churchill papers: 1/324*)

11 November 1938

Peter (Reserve of the Guards).
Eton, an OS and in Pop, the Headmaster's French prize, the King's French prize, the Duke of Northumberland's Spanish prize, Captain of the Oppidans, Editor of the Chronicle. Oxford, (Christchurch), Editor of the 'Isis', Presi-

---

[1] Evelyn Beatrice St Croix Rose, 1875–1964. Daughter of George St Croix Rose, and widow of Churchill's friend Valentine Fleming.

[2] Augustus E. John, 1878–1961. Portrait painter. Associate of the Royal Academy, 1921; Royal Academician, 1928. A Trustee of the Tate Gallery, 1933–41. Order of Merit, 1942. President of the Royal Society of Portrait Painters, 1945–53. President of the Royal Academy, 1948–53.

[3] Valentine Fleming, 1882–1917. Educated at Eton and Magdalen College, Oxford (BA Honours in History, 1905). Rowed in the Eton College Eight (1900) and the Magdalen College Eight three years (1903–5). Won the Ladies' Plate at Henley, 1904. Called to the Bar, Inner Temple, 1907. Conservative MP for South Oxfordshire (Henley Division), from 1910 until his death. Hunted a pack of Basset hounds. A partner in Robert Fleming and Company merchant bankers. Major, Oxfordshire Yeomanry. On active service in France and Flanders from August 1914; Lieutenant-Colonel, DSO; killed in action, 20 May 1917.

dent of the OUDS, took a 1st class in Literature, has written 'Brazilian Adventure', 'One's Company', 'News from Tartary', is on the staff of 'The Times'.[1]

Ian

Eton, and in Pop, won Victor Ludorum 3 years running, disqualified first year, as under 15 years, when he won 7 challenge cups out of 9. Won Public Schools hurdles for England. Passed as prize cadet into Sandhurst. Passed for the Diplomatic (only 2 candidates taken out of 63) and then entered Reuters. Was sent as English reporter to Moscow for the Vickers Case and was offered Shanghai by them. Was given the chance at the same time of a partnership in the city and took it. (This is not his métier really).[2]

Richard

Eton, in Pop and an OS. Captain of the Beagles, winner of the 'steeplechase' 1930, was one off being Captain of the Oppidans. Oxford (Magdalen), a second class in Modern Greats, Master of the Beagles, is now a Director of Robert Fleming. Director of London Insurance Co. Is a Lovat Scout.[3]

Michael

Eton, and refused to be 'educated' but was as good as gold. Would not go to Oxford and asked to go straight into business. Is a Director of Robert Fleming. Director of 8 companies (aged 24). A Territorial.[4]

[1] Robert Peter Fleming, 1907–1971. Educated at Eton and Christ Church, Oxford. In 1935 he had married Celia Johnson, the actress. In 1940 he published *Flying Visit 1940*. On active service, 1940–5 (including Norway, 1940, and Greece, 1941, where he was wounded). Among his post-war publications were *The Siege at Peking*, *Bayonets to Lhasa*, and *The Fate of Admiral Kolchak*. A landowner, he lived at Merrimoles House, Nettlebed, Oxfordshire. His daughter Kate published *The Churchills* in 1975.

[2] Ian Lancaster Fleming, 1908–1964. Educated at Eton and Sandhurst. Studied also at Munich and Geneva Universities. With Reuters, 1929–33. With Cull and Company, Merchant Bankers, 1933–5. With Rowe and Pitman, Stockbrokers, 1935–9. Served in Naval Intelligence during the Second World War (including as Personal Assistant to the Director of Naval Intelligence); Commander, Royal Naval Volunteer Reserve. Foreign Manager of Kemsley (later Thomson) newspapers, 1945–59. In 1952 he married Anne Charteris, the former wife of Esmond, 2nd Viscount Rothermere, and widow of the 3rd Baron O'Neill. Beginning in 1953, he published a series of 'James Bond' novels, which were subsequently made into feature films.

[3] Richard Evelyn Fleming, 1911–1977. Educated at Eton and Magdalen College, Oxford. In 1938 he had married Dorothy Charmian Herman Hodge, daughter of the 2nd Baron Wyfold. On active service, 1939–45, with the Lovat Scouts and 5th Battalion Seaforth Highlanders (Military Cross). A Trustee of the Pilgrim Trust, 1948–75 (Chairman, 1968–74). Member of the Advisory Committee of the Saudi Monetary Authority. Chairman of the Sun Alliance and London Assurance, 1968–71. A Curator of the Oxford University Chest. Chairman, Robert Fleming Holdings, 1966–74. A Director of Barclays Bank.

[4] Michael Valentine Paul Fleming, 1913–1940. Educated at Eton. 2nd Lieutenant, Oxfordshire and Buckinghamshire Light Infantry, 1936; Captain, 1939. On active service in

A. H. Richards to Winston S. Churchill

(*Churchill papers: 2/343*)

11 November 1938

Dear Mr Churchill,

Several Focus associates expressed to me today the great encouragement they have derived from Mr Eden's courageous speech in The House yesterday.[1]

Obviously our re-armament programme has not begun to even visualize parity with the Dictator powers. After our recent experiences, it's criminal we should be allowed to remain so utterly helpless and defenceless.

Parliament, or rather The Government is completely out of touch with the opinion of the people. I speak that I know, for I have been about the country quite a lot recently.

Until we get a Ministry of Supply we shall get no effective co-ordination of defence. It brooks of no delay, we must set about the task of its establishment in grim earnest. Our people want, even yearn, to feel safe and secure, they are ready aye willing for service and for whatever sacrifices that may be demanded.

I appeal to you to give us a lead. Now is the time. Our defence Ministers stand self-confessed and self-condemned of their ineptitude and failure to

---

France, 1940. Wounded, and taken prisoner-of-war near Cassel, during the retreat to Dunkirk, 29 May 1940, when his battalion was one of the British formations entrusted with the defence of the Dunkirk beachhead, as part of the 48th (South Midland) Division. Died of his wounds (while in captivity at Lille), 1 October 1940. Posthumously mentioned in despatches, 4 April 1941.

[1] Speaking in the House of Commons on 10 November 1938, Anthony Eden emphasized the efforts which would be needed to 'maintain our own liberties', telling the House: 'This will call for a measure of self-surrender by every citizen. It will call, certainly the wealthier classes, for some measure of sacrifice of present standards of life. It has done that in several ways already. It will call for a reorganisation and, above all, a speeding-up in the working of the democratic machine. The time factor is all-important in the modern world, and the democracies by comparison are painfully slow. It will mean, in short, something in the nature of a revolution in our national life. It can be done. No effort of which any other country is capable is beyond the power of our own people. But let us make no mistake. Unless such an effort is made there is no future for the British people and the things they stand for in this world except a progressive weakening of their authority and a slow sliding down the slope. Britain is a first-class Power or nothing. With her area, with her population, she literally cannot live as a second or a third-class Power.' Eden also told the House: 'Only if your armaments are commensurate with your needs has your diplomacy a fair chance. The knowledge that we are comparatively weak almost inevitably affects policy. It affects our attitude to other countries, and it affects, in the world as you have to-day, their attitude towards us. Hatred of war is good. It is sane and it is healthy. But fear of war is not so good, for fear of war paralyzes the will, and no policy that is based upon fear, no policy which makes an appeal to fear, can be a policy that this country should follow.'

protect our shores. Colossal extravagance, waste and dissipation of man power which achieves little.

If you approve, we might have a Focus luncheon at which both you and Mr Eden would speak, starting there, we could get a real drive on. Our Focus has done a great good. Our associates have been most faithful, in their rigid adherence to our policy, both in The House, and in The Country. Lord Cranborne has asked to be invited to the next luncheon.

Pardon my importunity, I do beg of you to give a date to meet the youthful and dynamic forces that I have got together, some of whom are parliamentary candidates, but all of whom stand ready to support your policy of Arms and The Covenant and even National Service. They are waiting to go forth in The Country. Might be a good plan to invite Mr Eden to this luncheon thus conveying to him in a practical way an idea of the powerful forces gathering around us.

Everyone is pleased with the decision of your Executive, particularly the labour elements.

Headway's sales this month will approximate to 90,000 (ninety thousand). Quite an achievement this, in the short space of two months.

We have received *many* letters expressing approval of and support for the policy outlined in your article and quite a goodly number of new *yearly* subscribers. This doesn't confirm that the country is solidly united behind Mr Chamberlain. What rot, it's a wish rather than a statement of fact.

Early in New Year I shall turn my attention to making Headway a weekly, a valuable spearhead this.

Don't you think Sir James Hawkey should be invited to our next Focus luncheon, he cannot fail to be impressed by the influential and resolute gatherings we now have.

Yours sincerely,
A. H. Richards

Winston S. Churchill to A. H. Richards

(*Churchill papers: 2/343*)

12 November 1938

I doubt if Mr Eden would come. He is very shy at present.

I could, of course, ask Lord Halifax, and indeed I had already made him some suggestions. I do not think he is so far gone as the Prime Minister, but perhaps you think it would be more useful that we should meet by ourselves. If you will send me a list of those who would be likely to attend, I will communicate with Lord Halifax, provided you are in the same mood.

By all means invite Sir James Hawkey. I could keep Wednesday, the 30th, for you if you wish.

I am very glad 'Headway' is doing so well.

Chingford. Sir James Hawkey is quite willing that I should attend such a meeting, and I think the idea of taking a Cinema under the LNU is a very good one. Pray let me know what your plans would be in detail. We could, of course, sell a certain number of seats, and I should hope that the leading Liberals in the Constituency would come. I should not bring in too many outsiders.

I quite agree with you about a Ministry of Supply.

Winston S. Churchill to Evelyn Fleming

(*Churchill papers: 1/324*)

12 November 1938

My dear Mrs Val,

I should indeed like to be sketched by Augustus John. I am afraid I could not afford to commission him to paint a picture, but I am sure it would have a marketable value coming from his pencil. I would try to fit in a few sittings, but I am not often in London except to beat up this caitiff Government.

What a wonderful record your four boys have. You have indeed set them on the highway.

Winston S. Churchill to Alastair Forbes

(*Churchill papers: 2/333*)

12 November 1938
Private

Dear Alastair,

It may not have escaped your notice that at the present time I enjoy the support of the West Essex Unionist Association and that they have recently renewed their confidence in me and urged me to continue my campaign for improving our defences.

I also receive the Conservative Whip. I should not think it compatible with either of these conditions to oppose a Conservative candidate unless he were opposed by another Conservative with whose views I felt myself more in agreement.

I gather from your letter, which is rather scolding and very lengthy, that you would advise me to break these associations. But this is a matter I feel sure you will, on reflection, realise I have to settle for myself. It certainly should not be settled in relation to a single by-election.

I am very glad you are interesting yourself so keenly in politics.

With best wishes,

Believe me,

Winston S. Churchill to Lord Londonderry

(Churchill papers: 2/333)

12 November 1938

My dear Charlie,

Many thanks for your letter. It is good of you to give me your mind.[1]

I am quite sure that there never was and there never will be any chance of a satisfactory arrangement between the German Nazi party and the British nation, and I am very sorry that we did not begin to arm on a great scale, especially in the air, when the menace of this violent party first appeared.

I do not know what Chamberlain's future policy will entail. I am afraid he is not in earnest about rearmament. I believe he means to surrender the Colonies, and above all things I fear that he may make some Disarmament Convention with Hitler which will stereotype our lamentable inferiority in the Air.

Upon all these matters I shall fight with what strength I have, and I fear that upon all of them you will take a different view.

I doubt very much whether Chamberlain will carry the country with him. He is certainly dividing it on vital matters as it has never been split before. I am ashamed to see the great Conservative Party looking forward to an Election where they will exploit the psychosis of fear, and hope that the old women of both sexes will give a renewal of the present incompetent régime.

We had a pleasant dinner at Grillion's the other night. I rather hoped you might be there.

[1] In his letter to Churchill of 10 November 1938, Lord Londonderry had written: 'The only difference that I can see between us is that I wanted to get hold of the Germans when they were weak and practically defenceless and try and make them good members of the comity of nations as Castlereagh did with France, and you on the other hand never believed that policy could succeed. I do not know who was right but my policy was never tried until it was, I regret to say it, too late. Now I expect our thoughts follow the same line.'

Winston S. Churchill to R. J. Minney

(*Churchill papers: 2/333*)

12 November 1938

Thank you very much for your letter. I am afraid that making speeches in the country no longer has the old effect. In the first place they are not reported or replied to as they used to be before the War.

I did five or six meetings in March and April, in order to warn the country of what was coming this autumn, and everywhere had very large meetings in the best halls and platforms representative of all three parties, but while the labour entailed was enormous, it did not seem to produce the slightest result.

However, I have three or four speeches to make in my Constituency, which is the best I can do with all my other work. Thank you very much for your suggestion all the same.

Stefan Lorant[1] to Winston S. Churchill

(*Churchill papers: 2/333*)

12 November 1938   Picture Post
                                                    London

Dear Mr Churchill,

I am writing to ask you something which, in ordinary circumstances, you would hardly grant and I should hardly ask you. But I think the condition of the world is such that you may be willing to overlook convention, and to sacrifice to some extent your own wish for privacy.

---

[1] Stefan Lorant, 1901–   . Educated at the Evangelical Gymnasium, and Academy of Economics, Budapest. Left Hungary in 1919, following the collapse of the Bela Kun Government. Helped by Franz Kafka to find a job, he played the violin in a cinema in Teschen. Photographer and film maker, first in Vienna and then in Berlin, 1920–5; his first film, on the life of Mozart, was made when he was 19. Wrote, directed and filmed *Foolscap of Love* (Vienna) and *His Majesty, the Child* (Berlin). Made the first screen test of Marlene Dietrich. Editor, *Das Magazin*, Leipzig, 1925; *Bilder Courier*, Berlin 1926. Berlin Editor of the *Münchner Illustrierte Presse*, 1927–33 (Chief Editor from 1928). A pioneer of the modern illustrated newspaper. Placed in 'protective custody' in Munich, March 1933; freed six months later following the intercession of the Hungarian Government. Editor of the Sunday Magazine of *Pesti Naplo*, Budapest, 1933–5. Published *I Was Hitler's Prisoner*, 1935 (of which Wickham Steed wrote, 'it will live longer than Hitler's Germany'). Founded a publishing house, Pocket Publications, in London, 1937. Founder and editor of *Lilliput*, 1937–40. Designed and edited *Picture Post*, 1938–40. Resident in the United States since 1940. Author; pictorial biographer of Abraham Lincoln and Theodore and Franklin Roosevelt; pictorial historian of *Pittsburgh*; author of a history of the American Presidency, *The Glorious Burden*, and of modern Germany, *Sieg Heil*.

I want to run your life story in PICTURE POST. This paper has only been going for two months but it has a sale of nearly a million copies every week: it is probably read regularly by five million people, and I think I can say that it is a paper with dignity.

I want to run your life story, not as a stunt, but because in the past years you have been consistently right in matters of foreign policy. Above all, in recognising the danger to this country which Nazi Germany constitutes. A long experience with papers has shown me that the most powerful way to state a case is not in long political articles, but in pictures with captions underneath.

The series of pictures I have in mind will constitute a complete defence and statement of your political views, only it will be in a form which ordinary people can at once take in.

If this life story in pictures is to have the importance it deserves, I must have first-rate personal records. You have all the pictures we should want. What I suggest is that you allow me to come down and go through these with your Secretary, choose out the ones I want and let you see what I have chosen, and tell you briefly how I mean to use them.

It is really important that this article should be done at once, and if it is in any way possible for you I should like to come down early next week, if possible on Monday, but, if not, on Wednesday or Thursday, to Westerham.

It is perhaps just worth mentioning as a proof of my personal sympathy that I was for nine years editor of the Munich Illustrated Press, I was imprisoned when Hitler came to power, and I am the author of the book 'I was Hitler's Prisoner'.[1]

Yours truly,
Stefan Lorant

---

[1] Churchill arranged to see Lorant at Chartwell on 21 November 1938, but telegraphed just after midnight on November 20: 'Please cancel your visit' (*Lorant papers*). The visit took place two months later, see also page 1351 and 1383 n.1. On 25 February 1939 *Picture Post* published a long article by Wickham Steed, illustrated by photographs of Churchill at Chartwell, and stating that 'the greatest moment of his life is still to come'. A second article on March 4 traced his family history in pictures, and a third, a week later, took the form of thirteen questions and answers: 'I think it will be necessary to form a government on a broader base', Churchill said in one of his answers, 'and ensure the cooperation of the working people if we are to carry through a strong foreign policy'. The questions and answers were prepared by Lorant, who went to Chartwell to put them to Churchill.

Oliver Harvey: diary

(*'The Diplomatic Diaries of Lord Harvey of Tasburgh'*)

13 November 1938

There is a deliberate German campaign to represent AE, Winston, etc as warmongers so as to debar their return to power, as it is felt in Germany that they are the only people who understand the danger and would be able to rouse this country to take appropriate action.

Lord Londonderry to Winston S. Churchill

(*Churchill papers: 2/333*)

14 November 1938

Thank you very much for your letter, and please do not bother to reply to this one, because I shall take an early opportunity of seeing you. I am sorry you think that Chamberlain is not in earnest about rearmament, but I have no political connection whatsoever with him, and I have never discussed any of these matters with him since I left the Government. I sincerely hope that you are not correct in your belief that he will surrender the colonies, because I can assure you there is no difference of opinion on this subject between us.

There really has been only one point of disagreement between you and me. Using the old fable, I wanted to bring the influences of Phoebus to bear upon the weak and defenceless Germans and at the same time to employ the influences of Boreas. I am quite sure that four years ago that was the line to take. When Phoebus was eventually brought in the psychological moment was then a thing of the past.

I have always regretted that you were not given the office which I should have called the Ministry of Defence, when Inskip was called upon to co-ordinate our defences, but it is no use looking back. We must go forward determined not to surrender one square inch of colonial territory until there is a very definite understanding between the great Powers on the vital questions of peace, and reduction of armaments. There are other matters relating to currency and exchange, which I need not dwell on here. I entirely agree with you about the psychosis of fear, and I regret what I call the Left Wing tendency, which is paralysing the Conservative Party and destroying those great ideals which they have supported in the past.

Yours affectionately,
Charlie

Randolph Churchill to Winston S. Churchill

(*Churchill papers: 1/325*)

14 November 1938   4th Queen's Own Hussars
                                                     Candahar Barracks
                                                     Tidworth
                                                     Hants

My dear Papa—

Jowitt[1] expressed himself as 'entirely happy' about your libel action. He thought damages would be £1,000 or £2,000. The worst that could happen would be £150.

At the same time we both inclined to the view that in these particular times there were disadvantages in your being involved in so trumpery an affair—more especially since the book has been withdrawn & cannot really be said to have damaged you seriously.

Jowitt said that if you wished he could easily sound out the other side with a view to a settlement without prejudice to the action. If they would pay £500 & indemnity costs we both thought there was a lot to be said for settling.[2]

I think you ought to have a talk to him yourself.

Did you read Group Captain Payne's[3] article in this morning's Telegraph? The relative figures he gives of the British & German Air Forces seem most important.[4]

[1] William Allen Jowitt, 1885–1957. Called to the Bar, Middle Temple, 1909. Liberal MP for the Hartlepools, 1922–4. Elected to the Other Club, 1925 (shortly before joining the Labour Party). Labour MP for Preston, 1929–31. Attorney-General, 1929–32. Knighted, 1929. Privy Councillor, 1931. Labour MP for Ashton-under-Lyne, 1939–45. In Churchill's wartime Coalition he served as Solicitor-General, 1940–2; Paymaster-General, 1942; Minister without Portfolio, 1942–4; and First Minister of Social (later National) Insurance, 1944–5. Created Baron, 1945. Lord Chancellor, 1945–51, in Clement Attlee's Labour Government. Created Viscount, 1947; Earl, 1951. General Editor of the *Dictionary of English Law*.

[2] Churchill agreed to a settlement on the basis proposed by Jowitt, and this was accepted by William Heinemann Ltd, the publishers of Geoffrey Dennis' book *Coronation Commentary* (see pages 1407 and 1419).

[3] Lionel Guy Stanhope Payne, 1894–1965. Educated at St Paul's School. Entered the Regular Army (2nd Lieutenant, Suffolk Regiment), 1912. Seconded to the Royal Flying Corps, 1916. Military Cross, 1918. Air Force Cross, 1919. Captain, 1919. Permanent Commission, Royal Air Force, 1919–45. Spanish Order of Military Merit, 1920. Wing-Commander, 1935, with the Directorate of Operations and Intelligence. Air Representative to the League of Nations, 1936. Group Captain, commanding the Air Armament School at Eastchurch, 1937–8. Retired, 1938. Air Correspondent of the *Daily Telegraph*, 1938–9 and 1945–61. On active service, 1939–45. CBE, January 1945. Retired, with the rank of Air Commodore, December 1945.

[4] The main leader page article in the *Daily Telegraph* on 14 November 1938 was by Group Captain Payne, described as a graduate of the Imperial Defence College, formerly attached to the British Delegation at the Disarmament Conference, with 'long experience' in the

I asked our Colonel some time ago whether there would be any harm in you making a reference to the 700 sabres and 700 riding breeches. Although this gaffe was perpetuated in the case of all the mechanised cavalry regiments he thought people would be sure to think it came from here & that it would therefore be better to say nothing on this point.

We all hope however that you will raise the unpreparedness of the Mobile Division (of which we are a part). During the crisis we showed our mobility by digging funkholes.

Your loving son,
Randolph

Committee of Imperial Defence: Sub-Committee on Air Defence Research: minutes
(Churchill papers: 25/15)

14 November 1938
11.30 am
Secret

To be Kept Under Lock and Key

It is requested that special care may be taken to ensure the secrecy of this document.

THE SUB-COMMITTEE agreed—

> To invite the Air Ministry in consultation with Sir Henry Tizard's Committee to submit a Memorandum setting out the 'pros' and 'cons' of a high altitude (35,000 feet) balloon barrage on the 'necklace' principle, as suggested by Mr Churchill, with armed cables, which might be strung out as a curtain round the coast from the Isle of Wight to the Tyne at intervals of approximately 170 yards.

---

department of the Chief of the Air Staff. Entitled 'Britain's Essential Need for Effective Air Arm', it stated that: 'The present proposal' (outlined by Kingsley Wood in the House of Commons on 10 November 1938) 'should therefore have the effect of increasing the first-line aircraft in this country to about 3,100', but was not to be completed until 1941. 'But there is reason to think that Germany's first-line strength already exceeds that figure by at least 1,000 machines'. The article concluded: 'Our war potential depends upon the productive capacity of industry. It now seems obvious that our capacity to produce aircraft cannot be increased in peace, let alone in war, without some substantial reorganization of our industrial resources.'

Sir Henry Tizard to Sir Thomas Inskip

(*Cherwell papers*)

16 November 1938

I must say that I feel in a personal difficulty about the suggestion.[1] I fully realise that Mr Winston Churchill's main object in anything he does is to strengthen the defences of the country, and therefore it seems wrong to oppose anything he suggests unless one has very strong reasons for doing so. But I also feel that the real reason behind Mr Winston Churchill's suggestion is that he does not altogether trust the advice I give, and that he prefers Professor Lindemann's advice. I could quite easily foresee occasions when Professor Lindemann and I should not agree on the advice we gave you. We do not want that kind of disagreement on the Committee.

Wing-Commander Anderson to Winston S. Churchill

(*Churchill papers: 2/333*)

16 November 1938   Catfoss

Dear Mr Churchill,

The following information may be of some use to you. The November Air Force Lists show that we have Nos 3, 4, and 5 Heavy Bomber Groups. In No 3 Bomber Group there are 10 heavy Bomber Squadrons, in No 4 Bomber Group there are also 10 heavy Bomber Squadrons, and in No 5 Bomber Group there are 9 heavy Bomber Squadrons; all these Squadrons are equipped with either obsolete Heyfords or Whitleys and Harrows; the latter have all been designed and produced since the expansion; these aircraft are fully referred to in the report.

It is intended eventually to equip the heavy Bomber Squadrons with the Wellington type of aircraft. This is a twin-engined aeroplane, and it is designed to fly with a full load from this country to Berlin and back. However, it will be many months before this type of aircraft will be in all the Squadrons. The present policy is to equip No 99 Bomber Squadron with Wellingtons in approximately three months time; it should however, be realised that there will be many difficulties with the new type of aircraft, as regards inability to bomb, bomb-racks, wireless, etc; again, it is regarded by

---

[1] Churchill's proposal, in a letter to Sir Kingsley Wood on 14 November 1938, that Professor Lindemann should be appointed to the Air Research Defence Committee. On 15 November 1938 Inskip wrote to Tizard: 'Mr Churchill has given Kingsley Wood an assurance on behalf of Professor Lindemann of what I may call good behaviour.'

the Air Staff only as a stop-gap. The ideal bomber is yet to be designed, at present it is on the drawing-board, and it has been and is the subject of many conferences; and there it remains.

I am particularly concerned regarding the number of fatal accidents which have occurred during the past eleven months. The number of pilots killed is now 209, but many more die later through injuries, and a large number are invalided out of the Service due to injuries received, and the number of officers and airmen pilots, air observers, etc, would amount to well over 600.

The Air Force List only shows officer pilots, and the November list gives a total of 22 killed and 4 invalided out of the Service.

We have, as you are well aware, an Accidents Branch who are responsible for investigating these accidents, and the Director of this Branch is able to communicate direct with the Secretary of State for Air, and can even short-circuit the Air Council itself if he so wishes. I have nothing to say regarding the Accidents Committee or their organisation, but I can say a great deal regarding the personnel who are on the Committee. The Chief Inspector of the Accidents was appointed 13 months ago, a Wing Commander of the RAF who had been passed over for promotion and who had received that information in an Air Council letter. He is Wing-Commander Vernon-Brown.[1] Immediately prior to this officer's appointment to the Committee, Major Cooper,[2] the late head of the Accidents Department, decided to retire and the vacancy of the appointment was advertised in the 'Times' and other public press.

I think I have said enough to show that for a retired Wing Commander who was permanently passed over for promotion to be appointed as Chief Inspector of Accidents is wholly wrong.

What we really need is a first class engineer, who has not necessarily served in the Air Force, but one who can probe into the mysteries of these accidents, get in touch with the aircraft manufacturers, and fearlessly report the results and findings direct to the Departments concerned.

In nearly all the accidents personnel were killed outright, and no evidence

---

[1] Vernon Sidney Brown, 1889–   . Educated at Eastbourne College and Jesus College, Cambridge. A civil engineer, 1910–15. 2nd Lieutenant, Royal Flying Corps, 1915. On active service, 1916–17. French Croix de Guerre, 1916. Served in Iraq and Egypt, 1919–25. Retired, at his own request, with the rank of Air Commodore, 1937. Chief Inspector of Accidents, Air Ministry, 1937–44; Chief Inspector of Accidents, Ministry of Civil Aviation, 1944–52. Knighted, 1952.

[2] James Percy Carre Cooper, 1883–   . Works Manager, 1913–15. 2nd Lieutenant, Royal Flying Corps, 1915; Major, 1919. On active service with the British Expeditionary Force, S Squadron, 1915–17; 9 Squadron, 1917; 14th Wing, 1917. Military Cross, 1916. Mentioned in Despatches, 1919. OBE, 1919. Deputy Controller of Civil Aviation, 1920; subsequently Head of the Accidents Department, Air Ministry. Retired, 1937.

could be obtained as to why the accidents occurred, but with the right type of people serving on the Committee, probing into the parts, undoubtedly a great deal could be found out, thus reducing accidents and so saving the loss of so many precious lives.

Neville Chamberlain: speech

('*Hansard*', *17 November 1938*)

17 November 1938   House of Commons

I have the greatest admiration for my right hon. Friend's many brilliant qualities. He shines in every direction. I remember once asking a Dominion statesman, who held high office for a great number of years, what in his opinion was the most valuable quality a statesman could possess. His answer was, judgment. If I were asked whether judgment is the first of my right hon. Friend's many admirable qualities I should have to ask the House of Commons not to press me too far.[1]

Wing-Commander Anderson to Winston S. Churchill

(*Churchill papers: 2/338*)

18 November 1938   Catfoss

Dear Mr Churchill,

I read in today's papers that the Minister of Defence stated that the Royal Air Force had only 23 types of aircraft in use.

There is no secrecy in the types of aircraft which are in daily use in the Royal Air Force, eg, Player's Tobacco Company are issuing with their present issue of cigarette cards a series which includes 50 types of aircraft of the Royal Air Force.

I attach a list of these types, showing those that are in constant use.[2]

---

[1] For Churchill's public answer to this remark, see pages 1301–2.

[2] The types listed by Anderson were: 'Armstrong Whitworth Whitley 2-engined Bomber; Handley Page 2-engined Harrow Bomber; Vickers Wellesley 1-engined long-distance Bomber; Bristol Blenheim 2-engined Bomber; Fairey Battle single-engined Bomber; Fairey Hendon 2-engined Bomber; Handley Page Hampden Bomber; Handley Page Heyford 2-engined Bomber; Vickers Virginia 2-engined trainer aircraft; Hawker Hind 1-engined Bomber (Hector, Osprey, and Demon are addition to the Hind type); Vickers Vildebeest torpedo Bomber; Fairey Swordfish Torpedo Spotter; Avro Anson General Reconnaissance Aircraft; Vickers Vincent General Purpose aircraft; Vickers Valentia Troop Carrier;

Alfred Duff Cooper to Winston S. Churchill

(*Churchill papers: 2/333*)

19 November 1938

My dear Winston,

I am very disturbed to hear that you resented the reference that I made to you in my speech in the House last Thursday. I cannot see why you should. I merely said that I thought that all the PM meant by his reference to 1914 was that any enquiry after mobilisation would always show up gaps and deficiencies and that therefore he had hardly merited the rebuke you delivered to him. I might of course have omitted all reference to you but I think it is always a good thing in debate to hang one's arguments on to previous speeches.[1] Nor was my position on Thursday quite simple. Your great philippic which I enjoyed immensely and admired still more was an onslaught on the Government's record over a period of three years, during the whole of which, except the last six weeks, I was a member of the Government. You could hardly expect me therefore to say that I entirely agreed with you and

---

Supermarine Walrus, amphibian; Supermarine Scapa, Flying Boat; Supermarine Stranraer, Reconnaissance Flying Board; Short Sunderland 4-engined Flying Boat; Short Singapore 4-engined Flying Boat; Saro London 2-engined Flying Boat; Gloucester Gauntlet Fighter; Gloucester Gladiator Fighter; Hawker Fury Fighter; Vickers Spitfire Fighter; Hawker Hurricane Fighter; Fairey Gordon Bomber and Towed Target Aircraft; Bristol Bombay transport aircraft; Miles Magister Training aircraft; Miles Master high speed trainer aircraft; Airspeed Oxford 2-engined Advanced Trainer aircraft; Avro Tutor training aircraft; Avro Cadet training aircraft; Avro Prefect Navigational training aircraft; De Haviland Tiger Moth trainer aircraft (of which there are 600 in constant use); Westland Lysander Army Co-operation aircraft; Hawker Henley high speed towing aircraft; Vickers Wellington (now in production–to be issued shortly); Westland Wallace target towing and communication aircraft'. Anderson added: 'Above I have named 40 aircraft in daily use in the Air Force. The Hawker 'Hind', 'Hector', 'Osprey', and 'Demon' I have counted as one. The construction of each of these aircraft is completely different from that of any other, both as regards maintenance and supply of spare parts etc.'

[1] Speaking in the House of Commons on 17 November 1938, Churchill had appealed for fifty Conservatives to support him in the call for the setting up of a Ministry of Supply. Only two Conservatives, Brendan Bracken and Harold Macmillan, had in fact voted with him. During the debate, Alfred Duff Cooper, who had resigned from the Government six weeks earlier, spoke in defence of Neville Chamberlain, telling the House of Commons: 'I think the attack made upon him this afternoon by the right hon. Member for Epping was not merited. I did not take the Prime Minister's remarks upon that occasion as criticizing in any way the preparations made in 1914. All he said was that if instead of the tragedy of war there had been a sudden demobilization in 1914 it would, of course, have been followed by an enquiry, and all the organizations that were bad, everything that was missing or lacking, would have had the full limelight played upon it. It would have been found that so far from our preparations being worse in 1938 than in 1914 we were very much better prepared. I believe that to be profoundly true.' Duff Cooper added: 'great credit is due to the Minister for the Co-ordination of Defence, rather than the jeers to which he is usually subjected, for the part he has played in perfecting these preparations'.

to vote accordingly. However I am not the less sorry to have hurt you, whether your reasons for feeling hurt are good or bad, and I hope you will forgive me because your friendship, your companionship and your advice are very, very precious to me.

Yours ever,
Duff

Winston S. Churchill to Lord Kemsley[1]

(Churchill papers: 8/595)

19 November 1938

I was deeply gratified by the award which the Book Fair has conferred upon me of a gold medal for my biography of John, Duke of Marlborough. I shall always preserve this testimonial as a most valued possession. I regret that my duties in the House of Commons prevented me from receiving it myself.

You give a great encouragement to modern literature by the Annual Book Fair, which has now become an established institution. There is no country in the world which could show the like. Any writer is fortunate to use the English language, which has a reading public beyond compare. But the focussing and display of our annual productions adds advantages and amenities to our work.

I am delighted to learn that the Book Fair this year has surpassed all its previous records, and I plume myself upon having been selected to bear a part in its success.

Winston S. Churchill to Thornton Butterworth

(Churchill papers: 8/605)

21 November 1938

. . . the principal matter of this letter concerns 'My Early Life', and in a lesser degree, 'Thoughts and Adventures'. Out of these two publications, I received in the accounting period £7. 0s. 0d., and the total sales are only 171

---

[1] James Gomer Berry, 1883–1968. Newspaper proprietor, and brother of Lord Camrose. Created Baronet, 1928. Created Baron Kemsley, 1936. Chairman, Kemsley Newspapers Ltd 1937–59; Editor-in-Chief, *Sunday Times*, 1937–59. A Trustee of Reuters, 1941 (Chairman, 1951–9). Created Viscount, 1945. One of his six sons was killed in action in Italy in 1944.

and 110 copies all told. This is really deplorable. Both these books ought to be sold to Book Clubs, where they would have great sales, and they certainly could not make less for me than they are doing at the present time. They are practically dead now in your Keystone Library. I attach great importance to these two books being published in a popular form. I have written to you before on this subject without receiving any response.

There will certainly be, if I live, further volumes of the autobiography. There is also, as you know, another volume of the essays, which has already been printed at my expense.[1] We have no agreement on the matter, but I have always hoped we should be able to make a satisfactory arrangement. But when I see two highly successful books—'My Early Life' and 'Thoughts and Adventures'—stagnating like this, I feel somewhat discouraged.[2]

Winston S. Churchill to Alfred Duff Cooper
(*Churchill papers: 2/333*)

22 November 1938
Private

Thank you very much for your letter, which I was very glad to get. In the position in which our small band of friends now is, it is a great mistake ever to take points off one another. The only rule is: Help each other when you can, but never harm. Never help the Bear. With your facility of speech it ought to be quite easy to make your position clear without showing differences from me. I will always observe this rule. Although there was nothing in what you said to which I could possibly object, yet the fact that you went out of your way to answer me, led several of my friends to wonder whether there was not some purpose behind it: for instance, the desire to isolate me as much as possible from the other Conservatives who disagree with the Government. I

[1] Churchill's American articles from the years 1929 to 1931. The volume, although set up in galley proof, was never published.

[2] On 12 October 1938 Churchill had signed an agreement with Messers George Newnes, publishers (who in 1933 and 1934 had published *The World Crisis* as a 26 part weekly series) for a further book in part form, *Europe Since The Russian Revolution*. Churchill was paid an advance of £500 on signature (the equivalent of £8,000 in 1981). Six years later, on 30 October 1944, Churchill refunded this advance, and cancelled the agreement. The book was never written. On 1 November 1944 Herbert Tingay, Managing Director of Messrs George Newnes, wrote to Churchill: 'Needless to say, speaking as publishers, we greatly regret that intervening events have deprived us of the privilege of publishing another book of yours, but this can be as nothing when considered in the light of the almost superhuman burdens you have been called on to carry in your inspiring and courageous leadership, of which all of us must feel justly proud and deeply grateful' (*Charles Sawyer Ltd, booksellers, supplement to catalogue 303*).

did not credit this myself, and I am entirely reassured by your charming letter. We are so few, enemies so many, the cause so great, that we cannot afford to weaken each other in any way.

I thought the parts of your speech which I heard very fine indeed, especially the catalogue of disasters which we have sustained in the last three years. I don't know how you remembered them all without a note.

I am, of course, sorry about the Debate. Chamberlain has now got away with everything. Munich is dead, the unpreparedness is forgotten, and there is to be no real, earnest, new effort to arm the nation. Even the breathing space, purchased at a hideous cost, is to be wasted. It was my distress at these public matters that made me grumpy when you suggested supper, for I did not then know what you had said in the early part of your speech.

But anyway count always upon,

your sincere friend,

W

Walter Layton to Winston S. Churchill

(*Churchill papers: 2/333*)

22 November 1938

My dear Winston,

I appreciated immensely every word of your vigorous speech to the Press Club this afternoon.[1] But I am moved to tell you in particular how intensely I agree with your remark that in recent times an undue responsibility has been thrown upon the press.

I was deeply conscious during August and September that the course of history might have been different if Parliament had been in session, and that while the press might throw out opinion day by day, it could not bring to bear upon the Government the reaction of public opinion in the same way that Parliament can do.

---

[1] Speaking at a Press Club Luncheon on 22 November 1938, Churchill told his audience: 'I was earning my living at journalism when most of you were in the cradle.' His theme was praise for the principle of freedom of the press: 'After all, we are, for good or ill, committed to the democratic system of life and government; we shall sink or swim by it. We cannot change now. There is no time; in the great trials we shall have to fight with all the strength and weakness of democracy—I am not speaking of war. We shall have to hold our own with all the strength and weakness of democracy. We cannot change now. And if that be so, it is absolutely necessary that the Press should have the power—as it has the duty—of explaining to the people about other systems, about totalitarian systems, whether of the Right or the Left, in order to let the working people—the wage earning masses and the man in the street—know what kind of things they would be up against in the kind of system in which they would find themselves shorn and curtailed of their liberties.'

I had, in fact, a sense of impotence in face of a task which was beyond our power to carry out. Holding this view, the fiasco when Parliament ultimately came together, was the more disappointing.

Yours ever,
W. T. Layton

Ian Colvin: memorandum[1]

(Churchill papers: 2/340)

23 November 1938

An expose made by Herr Hitler in October of his future policy after considering the Munich Agreement. Attended by three or four of the highest fuctionaries of the Foreign Ministry, among them Herr von Ribbentrop and Baron von Weizsäcker.[2]

It is difficult to approximate the date on which this speech was made. The source, which I am compelled to omit, was a person present. I have every confidence that his version is accurate and balanced. It agrees with every observation of the conduct and speeches of Herr Hitler since the beginning of October; some of the programme laid down in this speech has been fulfilled, the rest is in process of being fulfilled.

Herr Hitler began by producing a confidential report which had been brought to him. It was written by a Herr von Kries, correspondent of a German newspaper in London. He read the report to his listeners. The German journalist declared that on Monday 26th September, the representatives of Soviet Russia in London and Paris informed the British and French governments that Soviet Russia was not able to take military action in a European war.

Thereupon Herr Hitler turned and rated the assembled few, saying that he was surrounded by cowards and ignorant men. If he had been supplied with this report at the right moment, he would never have invited Mr Chamberlain to Munich, and would never have signed the Agreement. He then began to delineate his new policy.

[1] Churchill, who had sent a copy of this memorandum to Lord Halifax, did not reveal its source, but noted on it: 'This comes to me from a singularly well-informed source.' Colvin also sent copies to Lord Lloyd and James Duncan MP ('who will shake up Simon with it', Colvin to Lloyd, 23 November 1938, *Lloyd papers*).

[2] Baron Ernst von Weizsäcker, 1882–1951. Served first in the German Imperial Navy, then in the diplomatic service. Political Director at the Foreign Office, Berlin, 1936–8; Head of the Political Department, 1938–43. Ambassador to the Vatican, 1943–4. Sentenced to imprisonment by the Nuremberg military tribunal, 1946; released, 1950.

It was necessary, he said, to devote attention to internal policy first. He wanted to eliminate from German life the Jews, the Churches, and suppress private industry. After that, he would turn to foreign policy again.

In the meantime, Great Britain must be attacked with speeches and in the press. First the Opposition, and then Chamberlain himself. He had learned from the negotiations preceding Munich how to deal with the English—one had to encounter them aggressively (vor dem Bauch treten).

He would deal with England as he had done with France, where he had produced a confusion in political life. Flandin was for Germany, and there were also such men in England. He named Sir John Anderson[1] as possible leader of a Fascist Great Britain. His (Hitler's) aim was to overthrow Chamberlain. The Opposition would not then be capable of forming a new government, and the same would occur as in France. The political strength of Great Britain would be paralysed. In England too, Fascism would gain the upper hand.

He did not want in the near future to brand as a lie his promise not to make more territorial acquisitions in Europe. Therefore he was first turning to internal policy. But when Mr Chamberlain was no longer prime minister, he would no longer consider himself bound by the Munich Agreement. Memel would at any time fall into the lap of the Reich like a ripe fruit. Memel and Danzig were not urgent problems. Now it was for the Ukraine to be made into an independent State. He referred to the collaboration of Sir Henry Deterding[2] in the German plan. A vassal state was to be formed. Poland was to be squeezed (umklammert) as the Ukraine would be liberated against the will of Poland.

*   *   *

It may be commented upon this account, that evidently Herr Hitler was making a considered statement of policy, for he has held closely to it ever since. The socialisation of private industry is being prepared. I think it will

---

[1] John Anderson, 1882–1958. Educated at Edinburgh and Leipzig Universities. Entered the Colonial Office, 1905; Secretary, Northern Nigeria Lands Committee, 1909. Secretary to the Insurance Commissioners, London, 1913. Secretary, Ministry of Shipping, 1917–19. Knighted, 1919. Chairman of the Board of Inland Revenue, 1919–20. Joint Under-Secretary of State in the Government of Ireland, 1920. Permanent Under-Secretary of State, Home Office, 1922–32. Governor of Bengal, 1932–7. MP for the Scottish Universities, 1928–50. Lord Privy Seal, 1938–9. Home Secretary and Minister of Home Security, 1939–40. Lord President of the Council, 1940–3. Chancellor of the Exchequer, 1943–5. Chairman of the Port of London Authority, 1946–58. Created Viscount Waverley, 1952. Order of Merit, 1957. Member of the BBC General Advisory Council. In 1941 he married Ralph Wigram's widow, Ava.

[2] Henri Wilhelm August Deterding, 1866–1939. Director-General of the Royal Dutch Petroleum Company; a Director of the Shell Transport and Trading Company Limited. A Dutch citizen, he received an honorary knighthood in 1921. Committed suicide on the outbreak of the Second World War.

not be long before Mr Chamberlain is attacked. There are signs that the Ukraine is definitely the next objective, and that expansion eastwards will be carried out against the will of Poland, Hungary and Rumania.

A private understanding has been reached between the Governments of the Reich and Czechoslovakia that the new Czechoslovak fortifications shall not be built round Bohemia, as Germany will guarantee those frontiers, but along the narrow waist of Slovakia, so that the country can be held open for a German advance against the closing-up motion which Polish and Hungarian diplomacy still contemplates. The new forts are to be built out of the British loan.

It is worth remembering that in internal politics, the plan against the Jews was sketched out by Herr Hitler himself, and left to Marshal Goering and Dr Goebbels to work out, as is customary with the dirty work of the Reich, also that Hitler ordered personally the measures against the Confessional Church now taking shape. Apart from the newly emerged Ukraine plan, my outline of future aims remains unchanged in order—Memel, Danzig, Schleswig, Eupen Malmedy, Switzerland, Alsace Lorraine.

Ian Colvin to Winston S. Churchill

(*Churchill papers: 2/340*)

23 November 1938   Berlin W 35
                                                   Kluckstr 12

Dear Mr Winston Churchill,

Here is a report that will interest you. It shows the workings of Hitler's mind. The man is furious, vindictive, and more than ever ungovernable. The last excesses in Germany we owe solely to his temper, as you will see. The tyrant loaded all the dirty and unpopular work onto Goering, whose popularity he now fears, and onto Goebbels, whom he may wish to drop one day anyway.

The word 'squeeze' on page three means a disposition of troops in Silesia and East Prussia and Pomerania that will constitute a grave threat to Poland, and force her to agree to relinquish her share of the Ukraine—six million souls, already in disaffection and sporadic revolt.

Hitler's two principal chessmen in the game for the Ukraine, Hetman Skoropadsky[1] and Sir Henry Deterding, are both in Germany.

---

[1] Pavlo Skoropadsky, 1873–1945. A general in the Tsarist Army; from April to December 1918, ruler (Hetman) of the German-dominated 'independent' Ukraine. In exile in Berlin from 1919, he died near Berlin on 26 April 1945.

It was great fun laying bricks with you, and spending such a nice day in Westerham. Please remember me to Mrs Churchill, and to Mary.

As to the enclosed memorandum, I think it would be useful to show this to Sir Archibald Sinclair. I understand that Hitler is simply furious with Chamberlain, regards him as having spoiled his destiny, and thinks that he would be trampling through the Balkans by now but for the British Prime Minister.

If it interests you, I can send you a list of Jews murdered in the November riots. I believe they add up to eighty, and then deeds of bestiality inside camps, which I cannot either verify or count up.

Yours very sincerely,
Ian G. Colvin

Sir Robert Ho Tung[1] *to Clementine Churchill*

(*Churchill papers: 1/343*)

23 November 1938   Hong Kong

Dear Mrs Churchill,

With the coming of Christmas, I venture once again to send to you through Messrs Thomas Cook & Son for your kind acceptance two boxes of China tea with the best wishes of my wife and myself for every blessing at Christmas and throughout the coming year. Among its many other virtues, Christmas enables one to think a little more closely of one's friends. The value of this season increases as one gets older and it is of inestimable worth to one who, like me, has passed the allotted human span of three score years and ten. I do hope Dame Fortune will add abundantly to the many blessings which have been showered on you and your family in past years. These two boxes of China tea are a small tribute from a friend of yours over in China. Tea is one of the best links, I think, between the East and the West, in as much as this beverage is a daily companion to every household in England.

China is passing through a terrible ordeal. Living though we are in the security of a British Colony, we are still daily in contact with all the evidence of the cruelties of modern warfare. Refugees, wounded soldiers, wounded civilians and pauperised merchants have been pouring in to this little island refuge from all parts of China. Trade is practically at a standstill and it seems that after this upheaval many of the old business houses will have disappeared

---

[1] Robert Ho Tung, 1862–1956. Financier and real estate owner, Hong Kong. Knighted, 1915. Honorary Commissioner for Hong Kong at the British Empire Exhibition, Wembley, 1924 and 1925. Awarded the Gold Meritorious Medal of the National Chinese Government, 1938. His telegraphic address was 'Longevity': he died at the age of $94\frac{1}{2}$.

and their places taken over by others. And the most poignant point about the present hostilities out here is the futility of it all—at least it seems futile to me. For that reason and above all, because this is the season of goodwill, the hope of an early return of peace becomes more rosy than a few months ago. I do hope that when Christmas comes next month, a spirit of goodwill will prevail, both in the West and in the East.

My wife joins me in sending to your family kindest regards.

Yours sincerely,
R. Ho Tung

PS We read with great interest and admiration of the active part which Mr Churchill has been playing in the discussion of the House of Commons on the political situation of Europe.

Winston S. Churchill: speech

('Hansard')

24 November 1938   House of Commons

The situation in Palestine is lamentable. There is tragedy in Palestine. Blood is shed, murders are committed, executions are carried out, terror and counter-terror have supervened in the relationship between the Jews and the Arabs,[1] both of whom have a right to dwell in the land which the Lord hath given them. The whole economic revival of Palestine, which was in

---

[1] Since the outbreak of violence in Palestine in the spring of 1936, the victims had consisted principally of British troops and Jewish civilians killed in attacks by armed Arab bands (within the first month, 21 Jews had been killed by Arabs and 6 Arabs killed by the Palestine police). As the violence intensified, the Jewish Agency had instituted a policy of restraint. By October 1936 more than 80 Jewish civilians, 33 British soldiers, and 100 Arabs (many of them in armed bands) had been killed: the Arabs as a result of British military action. With the renewal of the conflict in 1938, however, Jewish restraint, while still the official policy of the Jewish Agency, was challenged by a small group of Jewish extremists. On 29 June 1938 an Arab terrorist threw a bomb at a Jewish wedding party at Tiberias: seven Jews were wounded, including three children. Nine Jews had been killed during June in Arab attacks on individual Jews throughout Palestine. Jewish terrorists struck back in violent acts of reprisal. On July 6, a single Jewish terrorist bomb killed twenty-five Arabs in Haifa. On July 11 Arabs killed two Jews in Haifa, and on July 12 an elderly Jew was stoned to death in the city. The killings and counter-killings continued: on July 21 four Jewish workers were killed at the Dead Sea, and four days later, in Haifa, a Jewish terrorists bomb killed 39 Arabs in the melon market. By the end of July 1938, 102 Arabs had been killed as a result of Jewish action, and 59 Jews had been killed by Arabs. These killings and counter-killings continued for several more months, and included the murder of many hundred Arab moderates by Arab extremists: between November 1938 and May 1939 more than 400 Arab moderates were murdered by followers of the Mufti.

active progress three years ago, has been cast down. From whatever angle you observe this scene, I say that it is painful. It is even horrible, and mark you, whether we feel it or not, it is humiliating to us in this country.

But where does the blame lie? I cannot doubt that a great portion of the blame—ill will there is in abundance, wrong deeds there are done—lies here in London and on the Treasury Bench. When I use the word 'blame' I do not mean to press it too sharply upon my right hon Friend. I do not wish to press it too much upon Ministers, and yet one must press it a certain amount. They will no doubt protest that their hearts are clean, they never willed the great calamity that has overtaken Palestine, they never meant it, no unworthy motive has inspired them for a moment.

All that is true. The path of the British Government is paved with good intentions. At every stage they have sought to practice good will and to do right. I admit it, and yet in practice they bear a responsibility which, if it be not blameworthy in a grievous sense, has nevertheless produced the same consequences as blameworthiness would have produced for bringing about a senseless, needless, and at the present moment, profoundly injurious exhibition of British incapacity.

What is the fault to which the Ministers of the Crown in my view lay themselves open? Kindly, humane, well-meaning men, what is the fault of which they have brought themselves to be accused, not only by their critics in the House of Commons, but in the eyes of the world—in the eyes of the whole world, friendly and hostile? What is this fault? It is the fault, very grievous in persons of high station—it is a fault which amounts to a crime—of not being able to make up their minds. It is a very grievous fault. Confronted with this problem of Palestine, a problem ever intensifying over the last three years, they have been utterly unable to come to a decision.

The court is august, the judges are incorruptible, their private virtues are beyond dispute, but the case is urgent, and all they have been able to do in three whole years of classic incapacity is to palter and maunder and jibber on the Bench.

I have spoken before of the inherent vice to which this National Government, with its overpowering majority, is addicted. It is the vice of infirmity of purpose, and following from that, an impotence of positive decision. They are suffering from 'a decreptitude of the will power' which can easily be traced in other greater and graver fields at this moment which are not relevant to the subject which we are debating this evening.

I accuse His Majesty's Government of having been, for more than three years, incapable of forming a coherent opinion upon the affairs of Palestine. All this time matters in Palestine have been going from bad to worse, and throughout all this period, when the situation was passing continuously out of control, the Government seemed to be constantly seeking the line of least resistance.

What is astonishing is that, considering how long they have been looking for the line of least resistance, their patient quest has not been attended with a greater measure of success. They have occasioned the maximum of delay of effort, and the maximum of distress with the minimum of advantage to the people who are the victims of their indecision.

A year passes, six months pass—we have a Debate on Palestine. Do not let it be forgotten that people are dying there, that they are being executed and meeting grisly deaths from day to day and week to week, while here all that can be done is to have from time to time Debates and pay each other compliments, and, above all, run no risks of taking any decision.[1]

Winston S. Churchill to Sir James Hawkey

(*Churchill papers: 7/46*)

26 November 1938

My dear Hawkey,

I think we ought to carry our fighting to closer quarters. If the Duchess of Atholl stands as a Unionist, I feel I ought to support her, should she desire it. The precedents are numerous for Conservative members taking sides when there are two candidates of the same Party in the field. There are also other precedents,—my own at Westminster, when although I stood as a Liberal candidate, twenty-seven Conservative members supported me.

If I should go North, it will of course hot up again the opposition in the Division, and will throw an extra burden upon you and Dinah. I hope you will feel able to bear this if, after full consideration, I judge it right to go. Naturally one would have to look at the ground very carefully beforehand,

---

[1] Of the Palestine problem itself, Churchill said: 'I entirely agree with the right hon. Member for Caithness (Sir A. Sinclair) that this great increase in the Arab population disposes at once of the suggestion that they are being driven out by Jewish immigrants. They are, on the contrary, being brought into Palestine, into the sunlight of life by the very process we are pursuing and which we are determined to pursue. It would seem that in the last 15 years an increase of 300,000 according to the census figures has taken place in the Arab population and 315,000 in the Jewish population. Therefore, it would seem to me, having regard to our wartime pledges, that it would obviously be right for us to decide now that Jewish immigration into Palestine shall not be less in any given period than the growth of the Arab population arising largely from the animating and fertilising influence of the Jews.' Churchill also proposed (to maintain the existing Arab–Jewish balance in its existing ratio of 60 Arab to 40 Jew): '. . . a plan based on the principle of perseverance, and it is a 10 year plan. Roughly, it is to fix the immigration of the Jews into Palestine for 10 years at a certain figure which at the end of the 10 year period will not have decisively altered the balance of the population as between Arab and Jew.' This scheme had originated with Lord Samuel (see page 780).

but I think this might be a practical step to take to rouse the country from its sloth and trance; and if it should bring back further repercussions in the Constituency, I am pretty sure that you will be strong enough to overcome them.

I have not come to any decision yet, and write only to let you know how my mind is moving, and to invite your counsel.

Winston S. Churchill to Sir James Hawkey

(*Hawkey papers*)

28 November 1938   Chartwell

My dear Hawkey,

I have written to Foster[1] to say I cannot commit myself to a luncheon in September, when I earnestly hope to be on my holiday.

Will you kindly look at the enclosed letter[2] and let me know what it is all

---

[1] Frank Savin Foster, 1879–1964. Company Director. Member of the Loughton Urban District Council, 1915–33. A Justice of the Peace for Essex, 1929; County Councillor, 1937. Chairman of the Chigwell Urban District Council, 1933–49. Chairman of the Epping Magistrates Court, 1943–55. Knighted, 1955. President of the Loughton (South) Conservative Association.

[2] Not traced. Among the many hundreds of letters which Churchill received from his constituents in 1938 was a request from Jennie Hall of Woodford Green to define tenancy rights in controlled houses; a request from Arthur Hands of Wanstead to become President of the Wanstead Branch of the League of Nations Union; a petition from Woodford Green, Loughton and Buckhurst Hill to support a proportional representation Bill; a request from Mrs J. F. Hart to join her house warming at the Warren Wood House Hotel at Buckhurst Hill; a request from Fred Horder of Loughton to help change the Hire Purchase regulations; a request from Mrs H. L. Head of South Woodford to support the Anti-Docking Bill to 'put an end to a very cruel practise'; a request from Hilary A. Howe of Snaresbrook to help end the use of the 'cat' in prisons ('the use of instruments of torture can never be regarded by any decent person as synonymous with justice'); and a letter from Elizabeth Fox Howard of Buckhurst Hill which asked Churchill 'to urge the Government to increase the existing facilities for the entrance of refugees from Germany and Austria into England and the Colonies. I know that a good deal is being done, but the Home Office in unable, with its present machinery, to cope effectively with the situation, not from any lack of good will. Since 1933 I have given up a great part of my time to helping the victims of the Nazi terror, both here and in Germany itself, where I have acquired a good deal of inside knowledge. I am a member of the German Emergency Committee of the Society of Friends, one of the two or three bodies with which the Home Office is working in close touch, but we feel most urgently that the problem has reached proportions far beyond the scope of private Committees, however influentially supported, and I therefore beg you to press for a really efficient international organization, to deal with the question of Jewish and other refugees. I had the opportunity, not long ago, of discussing the matter with Lord Halifax, and I had the impression that he was prepared to consider the suggestion favourably, if a well thought-out scheme could be laid before the Government. Hoping that you will use your influence to get the Home Office Procedure simplified and speeded up, and also to promote the speedy and effective tackling of the problem by an International body. . . .' (*Churchill papers: 7/46*).

about. We have no trace here of any communication of the kind being re-ceived, nor am I aware of any functions I discharge of this kind. I have made it a strict rule to answer every letter from the Constituency, and I cannot think such an oversight would have taken place.

Mrs Pearman is, I am glad to say, much better, but I cannot ask her about any business for some time.

That was a wonderful Meeting we had the other night. I hope you read the speech I made in the House on Wednesday.[1] The position of Ministers is shameful!

Yours vy sincerely,
Winston S. Churchill

Harold Nicolson: diary

(*Nicolson papers*)

30 November 1938

A Focus luncheon at the Savoy—Winston, Archie Sinclair, Arthur Henderson, Liddell Hart, Wickham Steed, Violet Bonham Carter, Megan Lloyd George and so on. Violet tells me that Anthony Eden's speech at the Queen's Hall last night was a flop. There were thousands wanting to see him and hear him and expectation was immense. But his speech might have been one delivered by Lord Halifax himself and there was great disappointment. The general feeling is that he is not a leader . . .

We have speeches. I do not make a good one as I was wholly unprepared. Winston does. He says that:

'the icy blast of Government disapproval will serve not to quench the fire which is in us but to spread it into crackling flames.'

---

[1] The House of Commons had just debated the Government's Palestine policy, and the decision not to proceed with the Partition Plan advocated by the Peel Commission in 1937 (for a Jewish State, an Arab State, and a separate Jerusalem-Bethlehem region under continu-ing British jurisdiction). Churchill had spoken on the Wednesday, 24 November 1938. In his speech he was critical of the speech of the new Secretary of State for the Colonies, Malcolm MacDonald because, as he told the House, 'there lay over the speech an air of detachment from the responsibilities of the past which, perhaps, my right hon. Friend was entitled to assume in his individual capacity, but which cannot be shared by those who have long fol-lowed the course of affairs in Palestine since the Great War'. During the course of his speech Churchill made a sustained attack on the method of Government of the National Govern-ment, published above (pages 1289–91).

R. E. Fearnley-Whittingstall to Winston S. Churchill
(Churchill papers: 2/336)

30 November 1938   Lincoln's Inn Fields

Dear Sir,

I have heard from your Secretary that it has been impossible to arrange an interview for me to discuss with you the matters referred to in previous correspondence and suggesting that I should write to you thereon.

I feel a little diffident in committing myself to paper upon a subject which may come within the scope of the Official Secrets Act, but I have been very gravely alarmed at the appalling shortage of equipment and the breakdown of organization under which the Defence Forces suffered during the September emergency. The individual details of this shortage which have come within my notice are not such as, in my opinion, can be explained otherwise than by gross incompetence, or justified on any ground, and from the point of view of ensuring that the position will not be repeated at a future date I feel that the matter has been treated far too lightly by those in authority.

It is now accepted that the Defence Forces were, for one cause or another, deficient in major items of equipment, and particularly in guns, but it has not, so far as I am aware, been accepted that certain units in the Defence Forces were totally deficient in any form of first-aid equipment, including so much as a bottle of iodine, in steel helmets and even in ammunition. These are matters of detail, but such details are primary and essential, and deficiencies of this sort should, in my opinion, be the subject of courts martial; not merely to punish those responsible for their ineptitude and gross breach of duty, but also to ensure that those people to whom these deficiencies are common knowledge shall not be discouraged, by fear of their repetition on a future occasion, from volunteering for the Defence Forces.

The second, and equally important, matter on which I wished to see you is one of general policy. I have always worked and voted for the Conservative Party ever since I was eligible to do so and I have always taken a considerable interest in political affairs, but the developments of the past few months have made it quite impossible for me to support either the Conservative Party or the National Government until a radical change of policy and leadership has been effected. I should like, if I may, to pay a sincere and grateful tribute to yourself for the warnings which you have given for some years past and for the unerring accuracy of your predictions, and I am appalled to think that those warnings have not been acted upon or taken proper advantage of. Since the crisis I have made it my business to canvass the views of people in all walks of life and I have been very much struck by the unanimity amongst supporters of the National Government in condemning its present stubborn and disastrous policy. I am convinced that the country is in real danger and that the inarticulate mass of the electorate is crying out for new leaders and a new party.

It is, I know, a tremendous undertaking, but something should and something surely can be done to save the country from the position into which it is being led by an old man who mistakes stubborness for strength, capitulation for appeasement and publicity for public approbation. The real trouble is that the Conservative Party has long ceased to represent the ideals for which it formerly stood or to put forward any policy which does not give immediate promise of support at the next election, and the reason why this is so is that in all but a handful of constituencies it is impossible for any candidate, however sincere and able, to obtain the party nomination unless he is in a financial position to outbid all other applicants.

I hope it will not weary you to discuss these matters with me and I should very much appreciate the opportunity of elaborating a point of view which is, I am sure, widely held, and which I feel is entitled to be heard.

Yours truly,
R. E. Fearnley-Whittingstall

December 1938

Winston S. Churchill to R. E. Fearnley-Whittingstall

(*Churchill papers: 2/336*)

1 December 1938

I am very much obliged to you for your letter. I have no doubt about the truth of what you say. I have myself a mass of information as to the gross neglect which has characterized our preparations.

I have also read with interest what you write in the latter part of your letter. The same views have been put to me literally by hundreds of people in the last two months, but I am sure if there were any reasonable alternative to the present Government, they would be chased out of power by the country. But the difficulties of organizing and forming a new Party have often proved insuperable.

Thank you very much also for your kind references to me.

Clementine Churchill to Winston S. Churchill: telegram

(*Churchill papers: 1/322*)

2 December 1938   via Portishead Radio[1]

All count of days and anniversaries lost in lonely vast Atlantic. No port of call till Jamaica, but like Sir Richard Grenville we passed the Azores near Flores. Belated but loving birthday hopes and wishes.

Clemmie

---

[1] Clementine Churchill was on her way to the West Indies, for a cruise with Lord Moyne on his yacht *Rosaura*. In August 1938 Lord Moyne had been appointed Chairman of the Royal Commission in the West Indies. The Commission issued its report in December 1939.

Kingsley Martin[1] to Winston S. Churchill

(*Churchill papers: 8/594*)

2 December 1938

Dear Mr Churchill,

So many are saying just now that it is impossible for democratic countries to hold their end up in face of totalitarian threats without themselves abandoning their democratic constitutions and liberties, that I have set myself the task of asking people of experience and authority how far, if at all, they think it is necessary to modify our institutions in order to become efficient. I naturally thought of you, partly because of the great stand you have been taking both for democracy and efficiency, and also because you are one of the few people now prominent in public life who have had experience of executive office in time of national emergency. The method I propose is a conversation in which I would ask a few questions about your experience of working democratic institutions in war time and your views about their adequacy to the present situation.

I have already had such a conversation with Mr Lloyd George and I hope to be able to obtain the considered views of several others whose opinions will carry weight. I very much hope you will agree to do this. I hope the idea will appeal to you for its own sake; I believe it is a very considerable political importance at the moment to set people's minds thinking about the degree of compulsion which may be necessary, and about the best ways in which we can preserve our liberties.

I do not know exactly what you would expect by way of fee for a conversation of an hour or so on this topic. Weekly papers cannot compete with dailies in this matter, but we should be able I think in this case to offer a really substantial sum.

If you are willing to consider the idea, as I very much hope you are, perhaps it would be best for us to talk it over for a few minutes beforehand. I could arrange to see you at the House of Commons or elsewhere at your convenience.

---

[1] Basil Kingsley Martin, 1897–1969. Educated at Mill Hill School and Magdalene College, Cambridge. A conscientious objector, 1914–18, he served as a hospital orderly in France. Assistant Lecturer in political science, London School of Economics, 1923–7. On the editorial staff of the *Manchester Guardian*, 1927–31. Editor of the *New Statesman and Nation*, 1931–60; Editorial Director, 1961–2. Author of several books, including *The British Public and the General Strike*.

Clementine Churchill to Winston S. Churchill

(Churchill papers: 1/322)

4 December 1938   SS Carare
                                                        Fyffes Lines

My Darling,

    . . . You wanted me to look out for a Harbour in the W Indies for the
American fleet; in anticipation. I have been studying the map. If you look
you will see that Porto Rico is one of the Greater Antilles (ie Cuba, Haiti,
Jamaica & Porto Rico) belongs to the United States. It is bigger than
Jamaica. Moreover several of the Virgin Islands (Lesser Antilles) also belong
to America; so they probably will be able to fend for themselves; which is a
pity as I should like them to be beholden to us.

Harold Nicolson: diary

(Nicolson papers)

5 December 1938

    Winston starts brilliantly and we are all expecting a great speech. He accuses
Hore-Belisha of being too complacent. The latter gets up and says 'When and
where?' Winston says, 'I have not come unprepared,' and begins to fumble
among his notes, where there are press cuttings. He takes time. He finds
them. But they are not the best cuttings, and in fact they have not been prepared properly. The ones he reads out excuse rather than implicate Hore-
Belisha. Winston becomes confused. He tries to rally his speech but the wind
has gone out of his sails and he flops wretchedly.[1] 'He is becoming an old

---

[1] In the House of Commons on 5 December 1938, Churchill, having accused Leslie Hore-
Belisha of 'saying all sorts of things' about anti-aircraft defences which the officers involved
'merely by looking round . . . find very difficult to accept at their face value', was challenged
to give 'the exact references'. He answered: 'I did not come altogether unprovided,' and
proceeded to read a series of newspaper extracts of Hore-Belisha's recent speeches. The
extracts did not bear out Churchill's charge, and Hore-Belisha interrupted Churchill's
speech to say: 'In view of the extracts which the right hon. Gentleman has read, perhaps he
will do me the courtesy of withdrawing the aspersions which he made preliminary to reading
those extracts. I have listened to this kind of statement many times, and it has never been
substantiated. In almost every speech that I have made I have made the statements which
are there quoted, that we must not be complacent in the matter, that we have much leeway
to make up, and that very great progress has been made in recruiting and the other matters. I
have no desire to discourage the Territorials, who have been joining in such large numbers,
by painting exaggerated and gloomy pictures, as the right hon. Gentleman has done. I have
no desire to exaggerate the position one way, and I hope he will not exaggerate it in the other
way, but as he has accused me of making misleading statements which I did not make and
which he has not substantiated, I hope he may disclose the information on which he bases
his accusations.' A few moments later Churchill told the House: 'Nothing is more dangerous
than for a Minister, a Service Minister above all, to let himself be surrounded by people who
say comforting things to him. Every Service Minister ought to have at least one brute close at
hand to thrust forward, in all secrecy, the ugliest and most unwelcome facts.'

man' says Bill Mabane[1] beside me. He certainly is a tiger, who, if he misses his spring is lost.

Alastair Forbes to Winston S. Churchill

(*Churchill papers: 2/334*)

5 December 1938
Private

Dear Mr Churchill,

I am very sorry that I missed you yesterday at Chartwell. If you had not 'knocked my block off' in the first place, which I should have richly deserved, I wanted to apologise for the impertinence of my two letters to you.

During the last week or so, I have had time to reflect and I confess that I realise that both letters merely had the effect of making me out to be a complete fool. I am only sorry that the process of discovering this has entailed the expenditure of much of your valuable time, both in reading and answering the letters involved.

I am not a supporter of this Government and therefore I do not agree that 'to admit the fault is half the battle'. But this is not a matter of defence, so I hope you will accept my apology in the spirit in which it is offered. I have learnt my lesson.

Both letters were written in something approaching a paroxysm of rage and despair that things were drifting so fast that it was perhaps too late to stop them. In the circumstances I feel I said many things which were both thoughtless and unreasonable, and yet I hope not rude. This is harder to excuse.

But if I am now deeply ashamed of uncontrolled and stupid outbursts which did not express my reasoned opinions at all, I am not ashamed of my zeal in wanting to know who was to come to the rescue of this country and when. Although I am still just as anxious, I appreciate much more your enormous difficulties in organising any sort of 'rescue party' at this point.

Lastly, I hope most fervently that my objectionable behaviour on this occasion will not entirely prejudice you against me in the future. And if on

[1] William Mabane, 1895–1969. On active service in France and the Near East, 1914–19. Warden of the University Settlement, Liverpool, 1920–3. Vice-President of the Building Societies Association, and a Director of Kemsley Newspapers Ltd. National Liberal MP for Huddersfield, 1931–45. A staunch supporter of Chamberlain's foreign policy, on 4 October 1938, in the Commons, he praised Chamberlain's 'brilliant initiative' in the Munich crisis. Assistant Postmaster-General, 1939. Parliamentary Secretary, Ministry of Home Security, 1939–42; Ministry of Food, 1942–5. Privy Councillor, 1944. Minister of State, 1945. Knighted, 1954. Chairman of the British Travel Association, 1960–3. Created Baron, 1962.

this occasion I showed lamentable disrespect, as I now realize I did, it is on record among my often exasperated friends that even in disagreement I have always had the greatest possible respect and admiration for you and your opinions.

I deserve a kick, in fact, from the feet at which I have sat for so long!

My inability to repress myself is carried to the point of genius. But I hope that this letter will be correctly interpreted for what it is. An honest apology.

Yours very sincerely,
Alastair Grant Forbes

My motive for sending my first letter via Mary was partly because I wished to ensure your getting it personally and partly because I knew you would then give it your personal attention at once. I realise now that I might seem to have hidden behind skirts in the matter. This is not the case. At the time of sending the letter I was unable to see that it was really beneath contempt. And therefore I was not ashamed of it. If I had been, I would neither have sent it direct or by anyone else. Another time however I shall not send letters and then be retrospectively ashamed of them. I shall think a bit instead.

Leslie Hore-Belisha to Winston S. Churchill

(*Churchill papers: 2/336*)

6 December 1938   War Office

Dear Winston,

I was glad to have your note on the Bench last night.

The Bren gun and anti-tank rifle position of the Guards Battalions is as follows:—

The war establishments of these two weapons are—

Bren guns   50 per Battalion.
Anti-tank rifles   22 per Battalion.

Of the 10 Guards Battalions, 8 Battalions have their full complement of both weapons, and the remaining 2 Battalions will complete their full complement by 17th December.

It was good of you to say that you would take occasion to express satisfaction with these results.

Yours sincerely,
Leslie Hore-Belisha

Winston S. Churchill to Alastair Forbes

(*Churchill papers: 2/334*)

7 December 1938

Thank you very much for your letter of the 5th. There is really no need for such excessive self-reproach.

I am very glad you are taking a keen interest in politics, and I feel as you do upon the great issues involved.

Do come and see us when you can.

Wing-Commander Anderson to Winston S. Churchill

(*Churchill papers: 2/338*)

8 December 1938   Royal Air Force Station,
                                                     Catfoss,
                                                     Nr. Hull
                                                     Yorks

Dear Mr Churchill,

I enclose a further printed copy of British Aircraft of 1938.

I have summarized the types of machine which are used daily by squadrons of the Royal Air Force.

Yours very sincerely,
C. T. Anderson

Churchill: speech at Chingford, in his constituency

(*Churchill papers: 9/133*)

9 December 1938

The most remarkable ministerial statement has been made by Lord De La Warr, Minister of Education who says 'there is a deep and growing feeling that there is nothing we can do that can satisfy Germany, that friendly words and friendly actions are mistaken for cowardice, and that only armaments can speak effectually'. When Mr Chamberlain was questioned about this in the House of Commons, he did not repudiate his colleague; he said it was not a statement of policy, but a statement of fact. That is indeed an impressive declaration. Why these are the very facts I have been trying to drive into the heads of the Nation, and especially into the heads of the heads of the Nation, for the last three of four years. But what has happened to our leading men that they have only found this out now? Should there be no foresight in statesmen? Is there to be no comprehension of the verities and the realities afoot in the world before they actually fall like thunderbolts upon us? What do we keep these high ministers & great departments of state for, if it is not that with their knowledge and information they should look ahead and form true judgments, and then tell us what to do in good time. What Lord De La Warr said, and what the Prime Minister does not deny, was just as true three years ago as it is now. But three years ago there was a great difference in our position. It would have been quite easy to agree with our adversary while in the way with him three years ago. Then we might have had a lasting settlement. Then, if real energy had been shown, we should feel and we should be, far stronger and far safer to-day. It is discreditable to Ministers of the Crown that they should only wake up to National dangers after the time has long gone passed when those dangers could easily and smoothly have been averted.

The Prime Minister said in the House of Commons the other day[1] that where I failed, for all my brilliant gifts etc, was in the faculty of judgment. I would gladly submit my judgments about foreign affairs and National defence during the last five years to comparison with his own. In February he said that the tension in Europe had greatly relaxed; a few weeks later Nazi Germany seized Austria. I predicted that he would repeat this statement as soon as the shock of the rape of Austria passed away. He did so in the very same words at the end of July; by the middle of August Germany was mobilising for those bogus manoevures which after bringing us all to the verge of a world war, ended in the complete destruction and absorption of the republic of Czechoslovakia. At the Lord Mayor's Banquet in November at the Guild Hall, he told us that Europe was settling down into a more peaceful state. The words were hardly out of his mouth before the Nazi atrocities upon the Jewish population resounded throughout the civilised world.

When earlier in the year the Prime Minister made a heart to heart settlement with Mr De Valera, and gave up to him those fortified ports on the South coast of Ireland which are vital to our food supply in time of war, he led us to believe that henceforward Mr DV and the country now called Eire were reconciled to us in friendship, but I warned him with my defective judgement that if we got into any great danger Mr DV would demand the surrender of Ulster as the price for any friendship or aid. This fell out exactly. For Mr DV has recently declared that he cannot give us any help or friendship while any British troops remain to guard the Protestants of Northern Ireland.

[1] In the House of Commons on 17 November 1938 (quoted on page 1280 of this volume).

Kingsley Martin to Winston S. Churchill

(*Churchill papers: 8/594*)

10 December 1938   The New Statesman and Nation,
                                                    London

Dear Mr Churchill,

. . . I believe that such an interview would be of very real importance. This paper is now very much the largest of the weekly reviews, has a large overseas as well as home circulation, and in particular goes to people with 'left centre' opinion, who are following your speeches and articles with great attention. You have constantly emphasised the need for defending our internal freedom as well as our national independence, and I know that to many people the stumbling-block is just the one about which I wish to obtain your opinion in the projected interview. People ask how far it is possible to embark upon the full military preparation and recruitment of man power that now seems necessary, without losing the substance of democratic liberty. I am myself inclined to believe that this dilemma is a false one, but I know that nothing would do so much to help my readers on this point as a discussion of it by you.

I am enclosing a pamphlet which we have just published, which you will see begins with a quotation from your speech after Munich and which deals with one aspect of this problem.

I very much hope that £50 will seem to you adequate remuneration. The interview should not take more than about an hour of your time and I can bring a shorthand-typist with me, if that would suit you best. Please let me know if you would like to see me for five minutes to talk it over beforehand. In any case I will fit in the time and place to suit your convenience.

Winston S. Churchill to Esmond Harmsworth

(*Churchill papers: 2/334*)

10 December 1938

The enclosed account, from the Daily Mail of to-day, of my meeting at Chingford last night seems to me as about unfair and misleading a piece of news as could be imagined.

Here was a meeting of 1,200 people, cordial and enthusiastic, who listened for an hour to a speech to which The Times and the Daily Express thought it worth while to give a column.

Two or three intruders, wearing the badges of the British Union of Fascists, made silly interruptions from time to time, and the audience demanded that they should be turned out. They did not in any way heckle me in the sense of asking questions, but simply made irrelevant comments now and again.

Anyone reading the Daily Mail account would suppose that the meeting had been disorderly and unfriendly. No other paper in the country gave such a wrong and biased account. Because I cannot believe you would wish this to be done, I venture to send you the enclosed cutting.[1]

Randolph Churchill to Winston S. Churchill

(Churchill papers: 1/325)

10 December 1938   70 Westminster Gardens

My dear Papa—

I have done as you suggested and am sorry that I should have allowed you to see that I resented your 'speaking to me violently'.

But since I made the mistake of showing my resentment I may as well explain on what it was founded.

I have repeatedly told you that it is a rule of mine that no information exchanged in private conversation may be published without specific permission asked and given. You are the only one of my friends whom I have apparently been unable to convince of the rigidity with which I maintain this principle.

You always treat me with great suspicion and often when others are present allow it to be seen how little confidence you have in my discretion. Such treatment is naturally distressing to me as your son; it is also prejudicial to me as a journalist. People are unlikely to be encouraged to have a good opinion of my trustworthiness if they see that it is lacking in you.

I have long been baffled as to why you should put such indignities upon me—particularly in front of others. For the last seven years I have worked in Fleet Street without printing anything that came from you without your permission. I am not aware that I have even repeated anything by word of mouth that has been prejudicial to your interests.

---

[1] Under the headline 'Churchill heckled for an Hour', the *Daily Mail* of 10 December 1938 wrote: 'When Mr Churchill spoke in his constituency, Epping, last night, his speech was interrupted for nearly an hour by one man who, whenever Mr Chamberlain's name was mentioned, commented, "You can trust him." Attacking the Government's refusal to adopt compulsory national service, Mr Churchill said: "In the first three weeks of war, when the crash of air attacks resounds in our cities, and multitudes are dispersing into the countryside; when frantic efforts are being made to make headway against the ruthless, ceaseless attack of a formidable enemy, then 50,000 enumerators will go about the country and make a complete survey of all the available resources. And then in that hour of agony we shall actually go so far as to make it compulsory for men and women in the prime of life to fill in their forms." '

Since I proceed upon the basis of no publication without permission it is necessary from time to time that I ask you if I may make use of some particular piece of information. If, when I do so, you insist on speaking violently to me (as though some great effort were needed on your part to deter me), it naturally upsets me.

There is no one to whom you speak so harshly as to myself and there is no one who speaks to me in such tones as you often employ. I do not know why you should reserve your greatest hostility and suspicion for your son and why I should have to accept violent explosions from none but my father.

Please forgive me for writing all this, but I have often wanted to tell you how I feel. In future I will endeavour to hide my feelings and to bear your violent rebukes in silence.

Your loving son,
Randolph

Randolph Churchill to Winston S. Churchill
(Churchill papers: 1/325)

11 December 1938   70 Westminister Gardens

My dear Papa—

Thank you for your nice letter.[1] I know you did not mean to be unkind to me, and it was silly of me to have got upset.

Since we have embarked on explanations I must refer to one thing in your letter. You say that you always tell strangers 'You can talk to R with perfect confidence, so long as you mark clearly what is or is not for publication.'

That is the reverse of the basis on which I wish to meet people socially. Nothing is for publication. If I happen to hear something which I think of interest and whose publication would not embarass my informant it is for me to ask permission, as I did of you the other night. Usually it is possible to raise such a question without thereby provoking a scene.

The one thing I most wish to avoid is being treated differently from my friends on account of my profession.

It is for me acutely disagreeable if, throughout a conversation among a number of people, I have to be periodically singled out for special admonitions of discretion.

By showing a fitting resentment when any acquaintance has so used me I find that I am rarely subjected to such slights.

But naturally if you set such an example it is likely to be emulated, parti-

[1] Not traced.

cularly by anyone who might wish to snub me. If they have heard you talk
to me in this vein I am on weak ground when I wish to correct them.

Far the most valuable stock in trade of a journalist is that he should be
absolutely trusted. I have ever been scrupulously careful to merit such trust
and have won it in large measure from numerous persons of influence and
consequence.

But I have always found you more grudging and suspicious in talking to
me than I have found anyone else—certainly among my friends.

I don't want you to tell me anything you would prefer to keep to yourself,
and would far rather not hear something than have it prefaced with a credit-
destroying injunction.

Your loving son,
Randolph

PS It is obviously legitimate & indeed necessary in conversation to indicate
that some information is private and ought not to be repeated. What I dislike is discrimination towards the Press! R S C

PPS On the particular 'casus belli' I would like to submit that my suggestion
was not as outrageous as is implied by your bare statement that you were
explaining the details of a private business transaction and that I wished to
'open it up' in the Londoner's Diary.

According to the story as you outlined it 4,000 people instead of 600 had
been persuaded to buy a book by threatening the exclusion of their names.
If the story is true quite a lot of people must know about this 'private business
transaction'.

Moreover my suggestion was to seek the permission of your informant. It
occurred to me that if, as you indicated, he has quarrelled with his associates
over this very point he might not be averse to a little ventilation!

Viscount Castlereagh[1] to Winston S. Churchill
(Churchill papers: 2/334)

11 December 1938

My dear Winston,

I have just returned from Belfast where I read a full Report of your admirable speech. I need hardly say that it was very warmly received in N Ireland.

[1] Edward Charles Stewart Robert Vane-Tempest-Stewart, Viscount Castlereagh, 1902–
1955. Only son of the 7th Marquis of Londonderry. Educated at Eton and Christ Church,
Oxford. Unionist MP for County Down, 1931–5. Assistant Managing Director of Londonderry Collieries Ltd. Served in she Royal Artillery, 1939–45. (Middle East, 1941–2). Succeeded his father as 8th Marquis of Londonderry, 1949. Member of the House of Laity,
Church Assembly, 1950–5.

I have listened to practically all your speeches since I have been in the House & your utterances have been strangely prophetic. In this time of emergency & crisis I should have thought that a 'Rather Spineless Cabinet' would have invited the co-operation of a man of energy & proved experience. No doubt when war breaks out you will be asked to compile a National Register, order some guns & quell a Rebellion in Eire. But not before.

I still have vivid recollections of my talk with Rudolf Hess[1] just over two years ago, about which I told you. He said: 'Why do you not have Winston Churchill in your British Cabinet, then we should know you meant business.' It is so true & MacDonald's pitiful cringe to de Valera merely encourages a creature like Göring to ask for more.

As an Ulster MP I appreciate your speech very much.

Ever yrs,
Robin

Clementine Churchill to Winston S. Churchill: telegram
(Churchill papers: 1/325)

11 December 1938

Staying Montego Bay with Governor[2] and Lady Richards. Walter fetches me Kingston tomorrow. Your speech and article[3] on Chamberlain's foreign policy reported Jamaican papers.

Clemmie

[1] Rudolf Hess, 1896–   . Born in Alexandria, Egypt, of a merchant family. Went to Germany for his education, 1908. On active service in the infantry, and later in the Flying Corps, 1914–18. Served in the Freikorps, fighting against the communists in Munich 1919. Joined Hitler, 1920; active in the unsuccessful Munich Putsch of 1923. Imprisoned with Hitler, in Landsberg, 1923–5. Hitler's private secretary, 1925–33. Hitler's deputy as leader of the Nazi Party, 1933–41, with a seat in the Reich Cabinet. Flew on a 'peace mission' to Britain, 11 May 1941, his fourth attempt since December 1940. Confined in Britain, 1941–5. Sentenced to life imprisonment at the Nuremberg Trials, 1946; in prison in Berlin (Spandau) since 1946, and, since 1966, the sole remaining prisoner there (following the release of Baldur von Shirach, the Nazi Youth Leader, and Albert Speer, Hitler's Minister for Armaments and War Production).

[2] Arthur Frederick Richards, 1885–1978. Educated at Clifton College and Christ Church, Oxford. Entered the Malayan Civil Service as a Cadet, 1908; Secretary to the High Commissioner for the Malay States, 1923; Under-Secretary to the Government, Federated Malay States, 1926–9. Governor of North Borneo, 1930–3. Governor and Commander-in-Chief, Gambia Colony, 1933–6; Fiji, 1936–8 (and High Commissioner for the Western Pacific). Knighted, 1935. Captain-General and Governor-in-Chief of Jamaica, 1938–43. Governor and Commander-in-Chief of Nigeria, 1943–7. Created Baron Milverton, 1947. President of the Association of British Malaya, 1948–50. British Empire Leprosy Relief Association, 1948–50. In 1927 he had married Noelle Brenda Whitehead, daughter of Charles Basil Whitehead of Torquay.

[3] On 1 December 1938 Churchill had written in the *Daily Telegraph*, in an article entitled 'France and England'; 'The bloodless conquest and virtual absorption of Czechoslovakia by

Winston S. Churchill to the Duchess of Atholl

(Churchill papers: 2/333)[1]

12 December 1938

My dear Duchess of Atholl,

I have considered the circumstances of your by-election, and have come to the conclusion that a number of important principles and causes are involved in your success or failure.[2]

The first of these is the independent status of Members of Parliament. The idea that they should be delegates of a Party organization has always been abhorrent to those who understand the spirit of the British Constitution: and the Conservative Party have for several generations rejected it. Party Associations are of course free to use their influence about candidatures, and have a continuous right of consultation with their representatives. On the other hand, Members of Parliament, once they are elected, become responsible for the welfare and security, not only of any one constituency, but of the nation as a whole.

In the face of the challenge which has been offered you by your Association, I do not see what other course you could adopt but to appeal broadly to your constituents. This is the course which I have always proposed to follow myself should circumstances require it. I therefore feel the fullest sympathy with you at the present juncture.

But the issues raised by your candidature go far beyond ordinary questions of Parliamentary or Party affairs. You stand for the effective rearmament of our country and for an end to the procrastination, half-measures and mis-

---

Nazi Germany has transformed the military position of France. All her system of Alliances in Eastern Europe has collapsed and can never be reconstituted, except, perhaps, after a lapse of years and in an entirely different form. Hitherto France and Britain have had the feeling that they were stronger than Germany. Henceforward a different order prevails.' Churchill's article ended: 'The two great peoples whose fortunes are interwoven should search their hearts. It is certain that they have only to rouse themselves in their true strength, and in the spirit of old days, to put themselves in a position of security amid present dangers. They still have the power to command and safeguard their future, with which are intertwined the liberties gained for all the world by the long forging of the British Parliamentary system, and the swift, hard lessons of the French Revolution. Above all, it is indispensable that renewed exertions and sacrifices should be made by the British and French peoples, and that they should repel as a mortal thrust any manoeuvre to separate them from each other.'

   [1] This letter was published in full in *The Times* on 13 December 1938 (page 18, column 4).

   [2] The Duchess of Atholl had resigned the National Government whip eight months earlier, in April 1938, in protest against the Government's non-intervention policy in Spain (hence her nick-name 'The Red Duchess'). In November 1938, following her criticism of the Munich Agreement, the Kinross and Western Conservative Association had voted by 273 votes to 167 to seek a new candidate at the next election. Five days after this vote, the Duchess announced that she would resign her seat at once, and fight the resulting by-election as an Independent, opposed to the Government's foreign policy.

management, which have led us from a safe position into a state of woeful unpreparedness and danger. The creation of a Ministry of Supply, which you have advocated, is an essential step in our rearmament; but besides that it would be a welcome symbol of earnestness and energy which could not fail to make an impression upon foreign countries, many of whom are beginning to think, some with pleasure, others with dismay, that British democracy is losing its will to live.

You are no doubt opposed by many Conservatives as loyal and patriotic as yourself; but the fact remains that outside our island your defeat at this moment would be relished by the enemies of Britain and of Freedom in every part of the world. It would be widely accepted as another sign that Great Britain is sinking under the weight of her cares, and no longer has the spirit and will-power to confront the tyrannies and cruel persecutions which have darkened this age.

On the other hand your victory as an Independent Member adhering to the finest principles of the Conservative and Unionist Party can only have an invigorating effect upon the whole impulse of British policy and British defence and will be a signal from Scotland of the strong and growing resolve of the British nation to remain a power for good among men.[1]

Yours very sincerely,
Winston S. Churchill

Edward Heath[2] *to Winston S. Churchill*

(*Churchill papers: 2/334*)

12 December 1938   From The President,
The Oxford Union Society

Dear Mr Churchill,

I am afraid I had only a brief moment in which to mention Oxford to you at the Youth Movement lunch last Thursday, so may I now more formally invite you to speak at a debate next term? The present generation of Oxford men has never had the opportunity of hearing you at Oxford, and if you

---

[1] The Duchess was defeated (see page 1329, note 4).

[2] Edward Richard George Heath, 1916–   . Educated at Chatham House School Ramsgate, and Balliol College, Oxford. President of the Oxford University Conservative Association, 1937. Chairman, Federation of University Conservative Associations, 1938. President of the Oxford Union, 1938–9. On active service, 1939–45 (despatches); Major, 1945; MBE, 1946. Conservative MP for Bexley, 1950–74; for Bexley Sidcup after 1974. Assistant Government Whip, 1951; Deputy Chief Whip, 1953–5; Chief Whip, 1955–9. Privy Councillor, 1955. Minister of Labour, 1959–60. Lord Privy Seal, 1960–3. Secretary of State for Industry, Trade and Regional Development and President of the Board of Trade, 1963–4. Leader of the Opposition, 1965–70. Prime Minister, 1970–4. Leader of the Opposition, 1974–6.

would return to repeat your triumphs of the past—which to us are as mighty legends told us by life-members—I can assure you that the Union Hall could not contain all those who would come to hear you. I cannot promise to find you opponents comparable with those you had in the past but I will willingly invite anyone you may like to suggest to debate opposite you, and the motion for debate would also of course rest with you. The subjects I had in mind were National Service, a National Opposition, or some aspects of Foreign Policy. The possible dates are Jan 19th and 26th, Feb 2nd and 16th, or March 9th. It would be splendid if you could come for the first debate of term.

Professor Lindemann will vouch for me as an excellent rebel Tory, which explains why I am so very anxious that you should come, although I realise that it has been many Presidents' ambition that you should. Perhaps however you will think these extraordinary times in which we now live sufficient justification for coming down again to the Union.

Yours very sincerely,
E. R. G. Heath

Clementine Churchill to Winston S. Churchill

(*Churchill papers: 1/322*)

13 December 1938   MY Rosaura
                                    at Sea between Jamaica
                                        & Porto Rico

. . . I must tell you (to return to Jamaica) that in a tiny highland village where the Foundation Stone of a School was being laid the Chairman welcomed me as the wife of the future Prime Minister of England upon which the whole pitch black Audience burst into 'loud & prolonged cheers'. The Chairman told me that they all know about you & follow your doings in the Jamaican Press. I was thrilled & moved but rather embarrassed, as this rather took off from the welcome to the new Governor who had never been to the spot before.

A. H. Richards to Winston S. Churchill

(*Churchill papers: 2/343*)

13 December 1938
Strictly Private and Confidential

Dear Mr Churchill,

My warmest thanks for your great service at Chingford on Sunday last.

I thought you delivered a tremendously powerful, effective and particularly forceful speech.[1]

You will be delighted to know that many new members were enrolled.

I feel that for you, it has been a year of great exertion, but not a labour in vain. There are indications that around you are gathering resolute and dynamic forces in your valiant and unsparing efforts for the preservation of our precious heritage, freedom.

I entirely agree with Cummings' comments in Tuesday's News Chronicle that on Sunday you struck the right note:—

'If resistance to dictatorships was to achieve real National unity, there must be an ideal larger than that of national or imperial greatness, larger even than that of national safety. There must be the consciousness that some august tribunal shall be established which will uphold and enforce and itself obey the rule of law.'

I think you will agree that the peoples of the world face one of the most critical problems of all times. Is the democratic way of life to survive? The answer of Great Britain will be decisive. In 1939 we must marshall all our forces to put forth the utmost exertion for the defence of freedom and the creation of active peace. By courage and sacrifice alone, shall we overcome the Nazis hordes; otherwise the present drift will rush us headlong into overwhelming disaster.

I pray 'England arise. God save the people.'

Yours sincerely,
A. H. Richards

---

[1] On 12 December 1938 *The Times* gave greater prominence to Churchill's Chingford Speech than to speeches that same day by Oliver Stanley, Clement Attlee, Lord De La Warr and Arthur Greenwood. For an extract from the speech, see page 1320, note 1.

Sir Alexander Walker[1] to Winston S. Churchill

(*Churchill papers: 1/324*)

13 December 1938

Dear Sir,

I am desired by Sir Alexander Walker to advise you that he has sent you two cases of Black Label Whisky, which he would be pleased if you would accept with his compliments and the very best wishes for Christmas and the New Year.[2]

Winston S. Churchill to Kingsley Martin

(*Churchill papers: 8/594*)

14 December 1938

Dear Mr Kingsley Martin,

I should be very glad to give you the interview on the terms proposed, if you would let me know a little more precisely the scope you have in mind for it.

Could you not come to luncheon here on Saturday the 17th. I could meet you at Oxted, which is forty minutes from Victoria. We could then have a talk. I have shorthand secretaries available. This I think would save you some trouble.[3]

[1] Alexander Walker, 1869–1950. Director of John Walker & Sons, Ltd, whisky distillers, of Kilmarnock. Knighted, 1920. After Churchill had sent him Christmas greetings in 1945, he replied (on 31 December 1945): 'I trust that you will not consider it an impertinence on my part if, as an aged veteran of 77 or thereby, I would have wished you had taken the opportunity to retire from the leadership of the Conservative Party and devote most of your leisure to the great book on the war which I assume you may be intending to produce. . . .' (*Churchill papers: 2/142*).

[2] Churchill commented, on receipt of this letter: 'Send Sir A. W. vol 4 of Marlboro, editon de luxe.'

[3] Churchill's interview with Kingsley Martin was published in the *New Statesman and Nation* on 7 January 1939. Kingsley Martin began his account: 'A famous journalist once told me of an alarming interview that he had with Mr Churchill some years before the last war. Mr Churchill happened to be in full Privy Councillor's uniform and emphasised his points with finely executed passes and slashes of his sword. Mr Churchill himself declares that this is a fairy tale; and certainly, when I went to see him the other day, he was wielding nothing more ferocious than the builder's trowel with which he was completing an arch in the house that he has built with his own hands this summer. He was not, however, too much absorbed to discuss very fully the problem of Democracy and Efficiency.' The central theme of Churchill's remarks was that the preservation of democracy entailed sacrifices of time and energy, but not of democratic procedures. During the interview, Churchill gave his definition of democracy 'as the freedom of the individual, within the framework of laws passed by Parliament, to order his life as he pleases, and the uniform enforcement of tribunals independent of the executive. These laws are based on Magna Carta, Habeas Corpus, the Petition of Right and

Sarah Gertrude Millin[1] to Winston S. Churchill

(*Churchill papers: 8/599*)

15 December 1938

Dear Mr Churchill,

Since you gave me 'Arms & the Covenant' (and I value it above all my books), may I tell you that, by the time I came to the words 'If mortal catastrophe should overtake the British nation & the British Empire, historians a thousand years hence will be baffled by the mystery of our affairs' I found myself weeping.

For not a thousand years hence, but now, this question brings one to despair.

The book reads like a toll & knell of doom. All that heartened me is that you yourself, as I saw, have still more heart than any other person I have met in England.

I profoundly, & with homage, wish you good fortune.

Yours sincerely,
Sarah Gertrude Millin

Winston S. Churchill to Brigadier-General Sir James Edmonds

(*Churchill papers: 8/597*)

16 December 1938

In my book I am now writing, 'The History of the English-speaking Peoples', I am assigning about ten thousand words to the American Civil

---

others. Above all, they secure the freedom of the individual from arbitrary arrest for crimes unknown to the law, and provide for trial by jury of his equals. Without this foundation there can be no freedom or civilisation, anyone being at the mercy of officials and liable to be spied upon and betrayed even in his own home. As long as these rights are defended, the foundations of freedom are secure. I see no reason why democracies should not be able to defend themselves without sacrificing these fundamental values.' Even in wartime, Churchill added, democracy was essential, and such basic features of the democratic system as debate and questions 'far from hindering the conduct of the war, frequently assist it by exposing weak points'. Churchill ended: 'War is horrible but slavery is worse, and you may be sure that the British people would rather go down fighting than live in servitude.'

[1] Sarah Gertrude Liebson, 1889–1968. Born in Lithuania, of Jewish parents. Authoress, novelist and playwright. Wife of Philip Millin, a Judge of the Supreme Court of South Africa. She published her most famous novel, *God's Step-Children*, in 1924; a biography of Cecil Rhodes, in 1933, and a two-volume biography of General Smuts in 1938. She also wrote two volumes of autobiography, *The Night is Long* (1941), and the *Measure of My Days* (1955). In 1966 she edited a volume of essays, *White Africans Are Also People*, in defence of the white people of Rhodesia and South Africa.

War. I have read a great deal about this myself, but I wondered whether I could persuade you to focus for me the military narrative of the four campaigns in their proper proportion with the crises and turning-points marked, and with the strategical issues explained. No one could do this better than you,[1] if you could spare the time. I should then take this as a digest on which to work.

It would be very kind of you if you could help me in this way, and of course I could offer you an honorarium which would I trust repay your trouble.

With all good wishes for Christmas,
Believe me,

Winston S. Churchill to Edward Heath
(*Churchill papers: 2/334*)

17 December 1938

I have had a talk to Professor Lindemann, and have told him how much I should like to come and support you in your period of office.

However, I find it very difficult indeed to make any engagements at the present time, as my work is so heavy, but perhaps you will let me keep it open and send you word if I find myself free.

Winston S. Churchill to Lord Castlereagh
(*Churchill papers: 2/334*)

17 December 1938

My dear Robin,

I was delighted to receive such a kind letter from you, and I am so glad that our friends in Ulster were pleased with what I said about De Valera's graceless response to Chamberlain's generosity at our expense.

---

[1] Edmonds was the co-author of W. Birbeck Wood and Sir J. E. Edmonds, *The Civil War in the United States*, published in London a year earlier, in December 1937.

Winston S. Churchill to Sir Kingsley Wood

(*Churchill papers: 2/339*)

17 December 1938
Private and Personal

I think you should see the enclosed letter,[1] and I hope that you may be able to look into this case yourself. This officer is a friend of mine, and he strikes me as being one of the ablest men I have met in the Air Force. I should have thought that you could ill afford, at the present juncture, to lose the services of a highly competent technical & military officer in the very prime of his faculties. I am sure he would greatly impress you if you met him. He is, of course, a critic of many things as exist at present, and no doubt from that point of view may have given umbrage.

I think your Under-Secretary Balfour[2] knows him personally. I have strongly dissuaded him from resigning. On the other hand, I heard from an indirect channel that it was he who had been asked to go. This I find it difficult to believe. Anyhow, trouble and publicity might easily arise out of such a case, and I should like to feel sure that you could spare time to give it your personal attention.

---

[1] The 'enclosed letter' was from Group Captain Lachlan MacLean to the Air Officer Commanding No. 3 (Bomber) Group, Mildenhall. Dated 17 November 1938, the letter was an application 'to be placed on the retired list'. In it, MacLean wrote: 'I have reluctantly reached the conclusion, as the result of experiences in recent years, that the standard and code of the Royal Air Force differs from that to which I have accustomed myself, with the result that I find myself, not only out of sympathy with the atmosphere of the Service, but in opposition to the methods of suppression and coercion which are employed to extinguish criticism, however important and constructive, and to quench initiative or originality, should it in any degree run counter to orthodox.' MacLean added: 'The experience of these latter years has caused a steady process of disenchantment and foreboding, which reached its culmination in a profound horror at the situation disclosed by the recent International crisis, with regard to the readiness of the Air Force and its ability to take any part in the active defence of this country. . . . Since it became abundantly clear to me that, in the event of war, subordinate commanders would almost inevitably have found themselves in the terrible position of being compelled to despatch aircraft crews on missions which they would have known to be foredoomed, I determined, knowing the situation as I do, and knowing also that no great change or improvement can possibly take place in the near future, that I should never allow myself to be placed in such a position' (*Churchill papers: 2/339*).

[2] Harold Balfour, Parliamentary Under-Secretary of State for Air from 1938 to 1944 (see page 174, note 1).

Winston S. Churchill and Mary Churchill to Clementine Churchill: telegram

(Churchill papers: 1/314)

17 December 1938

Do please send us messages. Distressed not hearing.

Winston and Mary

Clementine Churchill to Winston S. Churchill: telegram

(Churchill papers: 1/325)

19 December 1938   MY Rosaura

Telegraphed fourteenth. Since then, called Porto Rico, St Croix, St Thomas, and today Tortola. Most interesting. Have written two long letters. Thinking of you constantly. Tender love.

Clemmie

Winston S. Churchill to Clementine Churchill

(Spencer-Churchill papers)

19 December 1938   Chartwell

My darling,

It seems an age since you left. Yet vy little has happened that matters. I have been toiling double-shifts at the English SPs, & our score tonight is 180,000, or 30,000 above the tally of 100 a day from Aug 1. It is vy laborious & I resent it, & the pressure. But if nothing intervenes it will be done by about June. And then only improvements have to be considered. My life has simply been *cottage* & book, (but sleep too before dinner) I have slept here every night—& have only been to London for occasional Parl^t Debates.

I send you telegrams frequently: but in yr answers you do not tell me what I want to know—How are you? Are you better & more braced up! How is the voice? Have the sea & repose given you the means of recharging yr batteries. That is what I want to know: and even more—Do you love me? I feel so deeply interwoven with you that I follow yr movements in my mind at every hour & in all circumstances. I wonder what you are doing now. Yr dear letter from the ship arrived after my chiding telegram had been sent off. Do cable every few days, just to let me know all is well & that you are happy when you think of me.

There is a sharp cold spell: the temperature is bloody: Snow covers the scene: the mortar freezes: I envelope myself in sweaters & thick clothes & gloves: They say it will be worse. A white Christmas! Pray God it be not a Red New Year!

Mary & I go to Blenheim on Saturday (Christmas Eve) & we go to the Circus on Thursday. Then I return here & think to stay till the middle of the month. But you know I love to keep an option on movement.

Epping is vy healthy. One night R Forest Hotel crowded with thoroughly friendly ticket-admitted Tories from the branches. They let me say all I wished; & wd as lief have voted *confidence*, as thanks. The next—LNU meeting all the Liberals & Labour—equally friendly. I do not doubt the people are ours. 'Let 'em all come' is my electioneering motto. The Hawkeys are quite happy: & vy robust.

Tonight great sensation—Revolt of the Under Secretaries. Randolph has brought it all out in the E Stand! *with their acquiescence*.[1] This may lead far.

I do not think war is imminent for *us*. Only further humiliations in wh I rejoice to have no share.

Darling do always cable every two or three days. Otherwise I get depressed—& anxious about you & yr health.

Probably when this reaches you it will be in warm sunshine. How scrumptious!

My sweet Clemmie, good night & my blessings on you.

Always yr devoted &
loving husband
W

PS. Polly is vy cruel to me but the cat is affectionate.

---

[1] On 19 December 1938 the front page headlines in the *Evening Standard* read: 'Revolt in Government. Dismissal of 3 Government Ministers is demanded'. The article, by the 'Evening Standard Correspondent', in fact Randolph Churchill, read: 'Serious revolt has broken out in the Government. Three Junior ministers threaten to resign as a protest against the continuance of gaps in the nation's defences. They insist particularly that these members of the Cabinet must be replaced. The rebels are Mr Robert Hudson (Secretary, Department of Overseas Trade), The Marquess of Dufferin and Ava (Parliamentary Under-Secretary, Colonial Office), Lord Strathcona & Mount Royal (Parliamentary Under-Secretary, War Office). The three ministers whose dismissal is demanded are Hore-Belisha, Inskip, Winterton. The rebels insist that the ministers in question have failed to take advantage of the breathing space afforded by the Munich Agreement to push ahead vigorously with plans for national rearmament.' In sympathy with the rebels were Captain Crookshank (Mines) and the Earl of Feversham (Private Secretary to the Minister of Agriculture). The rebels, according to the article 'were content that the Prime Minister should pursue his endeavour to reach agreement with Italy and Germany on outstanding problems. They were insistent, however, that deficiencies in defence must be made good, and that a more effective national service scheme should be adopted.' Randolph Churchill also reported a movement among Conservative back-benchers which 'may develop into a revolt' under L. S. Amery.

Winston S. Churchill to Clementine Churchill
(Spencer-Churchill papers)

20 December 1938   Chartwell

My dearest Clemmie, you will be saddened to know that Sidney Peel[1] has died. I do not know the cause. Many are dying now that I knew when we were young. It is quite astonishing to reach the end of life & feel just as you did fifty years before. One must always hope for a sudden end, before faculties decay. But that is a lugubrious ending to my letter. I love to think of you in yr sunshine. But I hope & pray that some solid gains are being made in yr poise & strength. Give my love to Walter No 1 & my regards to W No 2.[2]

Tender love my dearest love

from your ever devoted husband W

[1] Sidney Cornwallis Peel, 1870–1938. Third son of the 1st Viscount Peel. Educated at Eton and New College, Oxford. Fellow of Trinity College, Oxford, 1893. Secretary to the Licensing Commission. Called to the Bar, Lincoln's Inn, 1898. On active service with the Oxfordshire Imperial Yeomanry, South Africa, 1900. In Egypt as a newspaper correspondent, 1901, when he became a protegé of Sir Ernest Cassell, and subsequently Chairman of the London Committee of the National Bank of Egypt, and Vice-President of the Morocco State Bank. Fell in love with Clementine Churchill in 1903 (when she was eighteen); they were twice secretly engaged. On 18 February 1914 he married Lady Adelia ('Delia') Margaret Spencer, daughter of the 6th Earl Spencer. Colonel Commanding the Bedfordshire Yeomanry, 1915–17 (DSO, mentioned in despatches). Financial Adviser to the Foreign Office, 1917–19, and a member of the British Delegation to the Paris Peace Conference. Conservative MP for Uxbridge, 1918–22. Chairman of the Export Credits Guarantee Department Advisory Committee from 1919 until his death. Deputy Steward of Oxford University, 1924. Member of the Oxford University Statutory Commission, 1924. British Plenipotentiary to the Tariff Conference in China, 1925–6. Member of the Municipal Banks Committee, 1926–7. Member of the special Committee of Enquiry into the relations of the Indian States with the British Government, 1927–9. Created Baronet, 1936. Author of *The Binding of the Nile and the New Soudan* and two books on regimental history. His younger brother, the Rev Maurice Peel, MC (1915) and bar (1917), was killed in action in May 1917, leaving a son, David Peel, MC, who was killed in action in September 1944. Sir Sidney Peel had no children. His wife was subsequently a Woman of the Bedchamber to the Queen. 1939–50, and an Extra Woman of the Bedchamber to Elizabeth the Queen Mother from 1950. Sir Sidney Peel had died on 19 December 1938.

[2] Lord Moyne (see page 1155, note 1), and his son, Bryan Walter Guinness, born in 1905, who succeeded his father as the 2nd Baron Moyne in 1944.

Committee of Imperial Defence: Sub-Committee on Air Defence Research: minutes[1]

(Churchill papers: 25/15)

20 December 1938
3.30 pm
Secret
To Be Kept Under Lock and Key

It is requested that special care be taken to ensure the secrecy of this document.

THE SUB-COMMITTEE agreed:—

(a) To take note that Sir Frank Smith had taken the necessary steps with the Radio Research Board of the Department of Scientific and Industrial Research for the construction early in the New Year of experimental valves for use with very short waves.

(b) To avail itself of Professor Lindemann's offer to conduct research at the Clarendon Laboratory, Oxford, into valves for use with very short waves.

Clementine Churchill to Winston S. Churchill: telegram

(Churchill papers: 1/322)

21 December 1938   Rosaura

My darling my thoughts are with you nearly all the time and though basking in lovely sunshine and blue seas I miss you and home terribly. Tender love.

Clemmie

---

[1] The members of the Sub-Committee present were Sir Kingsley Wood (in the Chair), Sir Thomas Inskip, Churchill, Sir Warren Fisher (Secretary to the Treasury), Vice-Admiral Sir Reginald Henderson (Third Sea Lord), General Sir Hugh Elles, Lieutenant-General Sir Maurice Taylor (Deputy Master-General of the Ordnance, War Office), Sir Frank Smith (Secretary, Department of Scientific and Industrial Research), Sir Henry Tizard (Rector of the Imperial College of Science and Technology), Air Vice-Marshal R. E. C. Peirse (Deputy Chief of the Air Staff), Wing Commander E. J. Hodsoll (Inspector-General, Air Raid Precautions Department, Home Office), Professor A. V. Hill (Secretary of the Royal Society) and Professor F. A. Lindemann. Also present were Edward Bridges (Secretary to the Cabinet), Major-General H. L. Ismay (Secretary, Committee of Imperial Defence), H. G. Vincent (Principal Assistant Secretary, Office of the Minister for Co-ordination of Defence) and Vice-Admiral Sir Harold Brown (Director-General of Munitions Production, War Office).

Winston S. Churchill to Clementine Churchill: telegram

(*Churchill papers: 1/325*)

21 December 1938   Chartwell

Horribly cold here. Thinking of you Darling in sunshine. Are you better. Your first letter received. Wrote you air mail 20th. Love and wishes for Christmas are sent by Moppet, Nellie, Bertram, Mary and not least

Winston

Sir Reginald Barnes to Winston S. Churchill

(*Churchill papers: 1/324*)

21 December 1938

My dear old Winston,

I can't let Xmas come without sending a line to wish you all that is best—now & for ever!

It was such a joy to me seeing something of you in October, & I felt almost intelligent after our talks. One thing is certain—that the belated moves we are now making in arming, are very largely due to the way you stuck to your guns! about it. It makes me sad that so many are so stupid as not to recognise it.

Well dear old pal, this is to send my love, & to assure you that I myself—& many others—perhaps not so stupid!—believe in you.

Reggie

A. H. Richards to Winston S. Churchill

(*Churchill papers: 2/343*)

21 December 1938
Strictly Private and Confidential

Dear Mr Churchill,

I have pleasure in sending you the enclosed cutting from a local Newspaper giving an account of the Great Meeting at Chingford on Sunday, 11th December.[1]

---

[1] Churchill spoke twice at Chingford in December 1938, on December 9 (see page 1257, note 4), and on December 11 at a meeting organized by the League of Nations Union. During this second speech he warned of further aggression by Hitler. 'We do not know which direction it will take,' he said. 'Since Munich and the destruction of Czecho-Slovakia he has had so

The local Police Authorities estimate that nearly 1,300 people were actually present at the meeting and nearly 800 people were turned away.

On the whole, I thought the National Press gave very good notice to your speech.

I am simply inundated with applications for meetings from all parts of Great Britain, and I am wondering whether you would, from January to March 1939, address say three really Great Demonstrations, which I would delight in organizing for you.

I think thereby you would greatly enhance your steadily rising prestige in this country—let there be no doubt of that!

In moving among people of all classes I find more than ever, that the general feeling is that had we heeded in time, your very wise counsel in the matter of Rearmament and the Covenant—so oft and so resolutely repeated during the past five years, we should not have drifted into such dire peril. . . .

Winston S. Churchill to R. S. Hudson[1]

(Churchill papers: 2/334)

21 December 1938
Private & Personal

Wolmer said to me in the Lobby last night that he had heard that Randolph had given you all away. I spoke to Randolph, who says there is no truth in this whatever.

---

many choices open that his trouble is which to take first, whether it should be Memel or Danzig, whether he will stir up Polish Ukrainians against Poland or the Transylvanian population against Rumania. No one can tell, but everything points to an early resumption of Nazi aggression and no concerted resistance being made against it.' Of the League of Nations, Churchill said: 'Across the turmoil and resurgence of these years, and all the efforts and sacrifice they will entail, there must be the assurance that some august international tribunal shall be established which will uphold and enforce and itself obey the rule of law. So far from abandoning what is left of the League of Nations, or whittling down its powers till it becomes a little more than a debate assembly, we must proclaim our resolve to clothe it with even greater powers, and by our exertions to furnish it with the armed force which will make its judgments respected.' Churchill's speech ended: 'What is our foreign policy? We shall be told it is a policy of peace, but peace is not a policy: it is the supreme aim upon which all parties in Great Britain and France have set their eyes. It is our heart's desire, but it is not a policy. Then we are told our policy is appeasement. If that be true, it is obviously failing' (*Yorkshire Post*, 12 December 1938).

[1] Robert Spear Hudson, 1886–1957. Educated at Eton and Magdalen College, Oxford. Attaché, Diplomatic Service, 1911; First Secretary, 1920–3. Conservative MP for Whitehaven, 1924–9; for Southport, 1931–52. Parliamentary Secretary, Ministry of Labour, 1931–5. Minister of Pensions, 1935–6. Secretary, Department of Overseas Trade, 1937–40. Privy Councillor, 1938. Minister of Shipping, April–May 1940. Minister of Agriculture and Fisheries, 1940–5. Created Viscount, 1952.

I enclose a copy of The Whitehall Letter which reached me last Friday, and in which you will see that the matter was virtually made public, I suppose to many hundreds of people, by this disclosure. I was much surprised to read this at the time, as I knew from various sources, but in confidence, what was going forward.

Let me however say that I think no harm has been done, but perhaps rather good, by what has been made public. I congratulate you upon your public-spirited and courageous action. I trust that good may come of it, but I fear it is very late in the day.

Winston S. Churchill to Leslie Hore-Belisha
(Churchill papers: 2/336)

21 December 1938
Private & Personal

Many thanks for your letter of December 6. I hope you will not resent it if I say that I still fear you are being misinformed. I wonder you do not ask the colonels of these battalions to tell you whether they have in fact 50 Bren guns and 22 Anti-tank rifles in their hands at the present time.

I see a paragraph in 'The Yorkshire Post' states that I am the inspirer of the present attack which is being made on you.[1] There is no truth whatever in this. At no time indeed, except when defending Sandys from the attack you made upon him, which naturally I felt very deeply, have I taken any action personally hostile to yourself.

---

[1] On 20 December 1938, in its 'London Notes and Comments' column, the *Yorkshire Post* reported that the 'rebel' Ministers, led by Robert Hudson, were demanding the replacement of Lord Winterton, Sir Thomas Inskip and Leslie Hore-Belisha 'by Ministers likely to pursue rearmament with greater vigour'. The article added: 'The drive against Mr Hore-Belisha owes much, it is believed, to the inspiration of Mr Churchill, and many who agree with Mr Churchill on other matters do not altogether do so in this. Mr Hore-Belisha is a man of energy and imagination in a Cabinet where these qualities do not abound. At the same time, there is grave concern in all parts of the House at the apparently slow progress of our anti-aircraft measures and of other defences for which Mr Hore-Belisha is responsible.'

Winston S. Churchill to Clementine Churchill

(*Churchill papers: 1/325*)

22 December 1938

My darling one,

We had remarkable spring weather during December. The trees were trying to bud, and the birds began to sing. A lemon-scented magnolia made a
bold bid for life. But four days ago the temperature dropped, at one time as
low as ten degrees above zero, and icy winds whirled around. To-day the sun
is shining brightly at Chartwell, and we have five or six inches of snow. This
has delayed the cottage. I have almost finished all the brickwork both outside
and in, but Jackson is unconscionably slow with the carpentering, and we
have no roof beyond what you saw when you went away. I hope, however,
that they will be ready to begin the tiling by the end of next week.

Maxine telegraphed me for the 8th January onwards, and I have decided
to go, at any rate for a fortnight. I do not need rest, but a change is good and
I love sunshine.

Politics tend towards a crisis. Hudson and some of the Under-Secretaries
have threatened to resign unless Inskip, Hore-Belisha, Winterton and Runciman are dismissed. This is a new development and very damaging to the
Government.[1] The talk now is of a big reconstruction at the end of January,
and of Eden being invited back. I do not know what would happen then. It
seems to me impossible that it should affect me, either in being asked, or in
accepting if I were. Everything goes to show that our interests are declining
throughout Europe, and that Hitler will be on the move again in February
or March, probably against Poland. Although Poland has lost French and
English sympathies by Colonel Beck's cynical, cold-hearted behaviour,[2] the
great accession to Nazi power which will follow from an eastward advance
affects us grievously. It is part of the price we pay for Munich.

The Constituency is getting into fine order. The two meetings in the Royal
Forest Hotel within 48 hours of one another, were both the best I have seen.

---

[1] Five days earlier, on 17 December 1938, a by-election had been held at Bridgewater, in
Somerset, following the appointment of the Conservative MP, R. P. Croom-Johnson, as a
High Court Judge. The by-election was won by the Independent Progressive candidate,
Vernon Bartlett, with 19,540 votes, against the 17,208 votes cast for the Conservative candi-
date, P. G. Heathcoat-Amory. Bartlett was supported by the local Labour Party, and stood on
a 'Popular Front' programme. He also received support from the local Liberal Association.

[2] On 4 October 1938, following the dismemberment of the Sudetenland, the Polish Government occupied the town and mining region of Teschen (in Czech, Těšin; in Polish, Cieszyn).
The region had been earlier part of Bohemia (1625–1723), of Austria (1723–1918) and
divided between Poland and Czechoslovakia (1919–38). In 1945 it was recovered by Czechoslovakia. In 1947 the Polish-speaking inhabitants were granted certain local autonomous
privileges by Czechoslovakia.

The Conservative meeting was by ticket from the branches, and consequently composed of our own people entirely. Their friendliness was evident.
They listened to all my criticisms of Chamberlain, and Kemsley[1] who asked
a rude question seemed to have only two or three people with him in the
room. The Liberals rallied in great force at the LNU meeting, and I feel in
a very strong position. This, at any rate, is satisfactory. It may be that after
some kind of reconstruction, Chamberlain will have an Election, but on the
whole I think the prospect has receded.

I have hardly been to London at all, and have only come up to-day to take
Mary to the Circus.[2]

Sir Kingsley Wood to Winston S. Churchill

(*Churchill papers: 2/339*)

22 December 1938   Air Ministry
Private and Personal

My dear Winston,

Thank you very much for your letter about Group Captain McLean. I
have, as a matter of fact, had his case before me already and I should like to
have a word with you about him sometime. Meanwhile I can say that there
is certainly no truth in the story that has reached you that he has been asked
to retire, and I personally am sorry that he should have thought it necessary
to sever his connection with the Air Force.

Yours ever,
Kingsley Wood

[1] Colin Norman Thornton-Kemsley, 1903–1977. Educated at Chigwell School and Wadham College, Oxford. A chartered surveyor. Active in local politics at Epping, 1925–39;
Honorary Treasurer, Essex and Middlesex Provincial Area, National Union of Conservative
and Unionist Associations, 1938–43. Conservative MP for Kincardine and West Aberdeenshire, 1939–50; for North Angus and Mearns, 1950–64. Served in the Royal Artillery, 1939–
45. Vice-Chairman, Conservative Parliamentary Committee for Agriculture and Food, 1950–
3. Member of the Public Accounts Committee, 1955–64. Chairman, Scottish Unionist Members Committee, 1957–8. Knighted, 1958. He published his memoirs, *Through Winds and
Tides*, in 1974.

[2] Two days later, on 24 December 1938, Churchill went for Christmas to Blenheim with
Randolph and Mary, leaving on December 27. Also at Blenheim that Christmas were his
brother Jack and sister-in-law Lady Gwendeline and their daughter Clarissa; Brendan
Bracken, Tommy Bouch, Paul Maze and his son Etienne, and Victoria Gilmour and her
children Diana and Ian (see page 868, note 1).

Winston S. Churchill to Brigadier-General Sir James Edmonds

(Churchill papers: 8/597)

23 December 1938

There is no hurry. If I had your epitome of the American Civil War by the end of March, it would be all right. It is not so much detail that is needed, and certainly not a level account of all that happened, but the selection of the crucial points and the great strategic proportion which your judgment will enable you to assign.

I should like you to stand back from your canvas of knowledge, and without looking up anything, give me your impression of that wonderful episode.

Winston S. Churchill to Lord Craigavon

(Churchill papers: 1/324)

24 December 1938   Chartwell

My dear James,

I cannot tell you how moved I have been by your charming and beautiful gift, and all the memories and inspirations it envokes. Coming as it does at this time of trouble and misunderstanding in which I feel much alone, tho' constant, it is grateful to me beyond words. I shall stand by the declarations you have inscribed upon the cup, and Randolph will also march forward along that path.

But what pleases me most is the care and thought—and taste—by which your friendship for me has been symbolised. That indeed is precious to me: for you are one of the few who have it in their power to bestow judgments which I respect.

Yours ever,
Winston Churchill

Winston S. Churchill to Clementine Churchill: telegram

(Churchill papers: 1/325)

28 December 1938   Chartwell

Yours of thirteenth received. How exciting. Are you getting stronger. All well here Thawing. Working at book and cottage. Cable frequently. Much love.

Winston

Winston S. Churchill to Arthur Mann

(*Churchill papers: 2/334*)

28 December 1938

This really is not so. I have taken no part against Hore-Belisha and had no prior knowledge of the movement against him. I think he is far less culpable and lethargic than the bulk of them.

I am not suggesting that you should do anything about this, but I feel you would not mind my letting you know the facts.

R. S. Hudson to Winston S. Churchill

(*Churchill papers: 2/334*)

29 December 1938   Department of Overseas Trade
Personal

My dear Churchill,

I am grateful for your kind letter. I wish there had been no publicity. It would have made it much easier for the PM to do what we wanted. As a matter of fact the Daily Mail got hold of the story on the Thursday evening. To their honour be it said that when I told them that and when I urged it wld do no good to us or to the cause we had at heart to publish, they suppressed it. I wish I had had as successful an influence over Mike Wardell[1] when Randolph brought him the detailed story a few days later. However it's no use crying over the past. The main point is to try and secure someone with more go and more willingness to work than Horeb and Tom.[2] I have hopes but it will need a lot of pushing yet. Meanwhile I much fear it may be too late.

Yours ever,
Rob Hudson

[1] Michael Wardell, 1898–   . Entered Lord Beaverbrook's circle, and his employment, in 1926. Manager of the *Evening Standard*. Editor of the *Farmers Weekly*. A friend of the Prince of Wales (later Edward VIII). On active service, 1940–5 (Brigadier). After the war he went to Canada, where he became the owner of the Fredericton *Gleaner*, and looked after Beaverbrook's business interests in New Brunswick. Known to Beaverbrook as 'The Captain'. On the evening of 23 August 1949 Wardell was at Beaverbrook's villa, La Capponcina, in the South of France, playing gin rummy with Churchill. At his bedroom door, Churchill had a sensation of paralysis, and told Wardell: 'The dagger is pointing at me. I pray it may not strike. I want so much to be spared at least to fight the election. I must lead the Conservatives back to victory. I know I am worth a million votes to them. Perhaps two million!' That night Churchill had a stroke, but soon recovered, telling Wardell: 'The dagger struck, but this time it was not plunged into the hilt. At least, I think not' (*quoted in A. J. P. Taylor, Beaverbrook, page 593*).

[2] Leslie Hore-Belisha (Secretary of State for War) and Sir Thomas Inskip (Minister for the Co-ordination of Defence).

Diana Sandys to Winston S. Churchill

(*Churchill papers: 1/325*)

29 December 1938

Darling Papa,

I am writing to thank you for the magnificent Christmas present which you have given us. Before long the young lady and I will step out and select some 'fine feathers' for ourselves.

We cannot make up our minds yet what to call her—whether it shall be Sally or Carol?[1] Anyway, we are experimenting with each of these names for a few days. I hope we shall reach a decision soon or I shall have a nervous breakdown!

Happy New Year dear Papa, & again many thanks for your wonderful present.

Your loving,
Diana

Winston S. Churchill to Clementine Churchill

(*Spencer-Churchill papers*)

29 December 1938

My darling Clemmie,

You will see by the enclosed cutting that Mary was not at all bored at the circus. I could only stay for half the time, but there were a lot of nice people there, and the young Birkenheads[2] looked after her. The best were the sea lions, who showed remarkable intelligence and aptitudes.

I cabled to you about Diana's baby daughter. It came most unexpectedly, was less than eight months old and weighed just over four and a half pounds. She was perfectly well in the afternoon, sitting up and could see me. The baby is tiny but perfect, and by my latest news, thriving.

---

[1] Edwina Sandys, 1938–   . Daughter of Duncan and Diana Sandys; Churchill's first granddaughter. In 1960 she married Piers Dixon, son of the diplomat Sir Pierson Dixon. They had two sons, Mark (born 1962) and Hugo (born 1963). Their marriage was dissolved in 1973.

[2] The 2nd Earl of Birkenhead (son of Churchill's friend 'FE') and his wife Sheila (second daughter of Lord Camrose), whom Birkenhead had married in 1935.

Duncan and Randolph are forming a new party to bust up all the old ones. The plan is to have a hundred thousand members, who pay a pound a head a year, but after the first hundred thousand are enlisted they are ready to go on even to a million, or more if necessary. No one may belong who is not doing war preparation work of some kind or who has not fought in the last war. Anyone who disagrees with Randolph or Duncan is to be immediately dismissed, and at any meeting only those are to be allowed to stay who are wholeheartedly in favour of the programme. The programme has not yet been settled. I have promised to accept the Presidency when the first hundred thousand is reached. Meanwhile Mary has joined, and has volunteered for any work.

Otherwise there is no political news worth speaking of. I enclose you the Whitehall Letter of this week, which is extremely well-informed. I do not know where they get all their information. They had the news of the Under-Secretaries' revolt a week before it got out in public. I knew only in the deepest secrecy. They had the story, which again I had only first hand in the deepest secrecy, of Bonnet trying to bribe the Ambassadors Theatre (where I spoke) not to allow Duff Cooper to speak. I do not know whether they are right about Chamberlain's change of mind. It may well be that he will have to yield to the force of events, and will adopt my view and policy, while disliking me all the more. I had a talk with Anthony after his return from America.[1] He says nothing will induce him to join the Government unless it is reconstructed in the most drastic manner, and the policy is changed. Even this is not impossible.

I have just heard from Mr Wood of Harraps that they have, printed and with the printer, one hundred and ninety two thousand words, so I hope to complete the two hundred thousand by the New Year. If we did two hundred thousand in five months, there should be plenty of time in the year to finish and polish. I am now doing the Wars of the Roses. They are deeply interesting, and have been much too lightly treated by modern opinion. The causes were deep, the arguments equally balanced, and immense efforts were made to avert the disaster which occurred. I have just finished writing about Joan of Arc.[2] I think she is the winner in the whole of French history.

---

[1] Encouraged to do so by Joseph Kennedy, and with Lord Halifax's approval, Eden had accepted one invitation to speak in New York, and told his audience that they were destined to live 'in a period of emergency of which none could see the end': subsequently, on 13 December 1938, he met President Roosevelt in Washington. Eden's critics called it 'the visit of a film star' (The Earl of Avon, *The Eden Memoirs*, volume 2, London 1965, pages 39–42).

[2] In the first volume of *A History of the English-Speaking Peoples* Churchill wrote, of Joan of Arc: 'There now appeared upon the ravaged scene an Angel of Deliverance, the noblest patriot of France, the most splendid of her heroes, the most beloved of her saints, the most inspiring of all her memories, the peasant Maid, the ever-shining, ever-glorious Joan of Arc.

The leading women of these days were more remarkable and forceful than the men.

We came back from Blenheim on the Tuesday, not over staying our welcome. It was very comfortable and pleasant. I won £20—at bezique from Mary and Tommy Bouch,[1] whom you know. Randolph made himself very agreeable all round, and we bestowed and received many gifts. Molly[2] sent me a very nice, old French silver snuff box. I think this may be because her friend James Stuart[3] had the cheek to tell me in his exultation about the Duchess's defeat[4] that I ought not to accept the whip any longer. I naturally told him to go to Hell or Epping, and I expect he carried this tale to Molly and was rebuked. Anyhow it was kindly meant.

All Mary's goats give promise of increase, and February is expected to be the date. We shall have troops of goats browsing on our pastures, and instead of Mary hammering in three iron pegs each day, she will have to hammer in about a dozen. The parrot is not behaving well, he makes a nasty clucking noise to show his dislike of the cold weather, and I have to turn him out of the room as it irritates me. He has not bitten me again because I have not

---

In the poor, remote hamlet of Domrémy, on the fringe of the Vosges Forest, she served at the inn. She rode the horses of travellers, bareback, to water. She wandered on Sundays into the woods, where there were shrines, and a legend that some day from these oaks would arise one to save France. In the fields where she tended her sheep the saints of God, who grieved for France, rose before her in visions. St Michael himself appointed her, by right divine, to command the armies of liberation. Joan shrank at first from the awful duty, but when he returned attended by St Margaret and St Catherine, patronesses of the village church, she obeyed their command. There welled in the heart of the Maid a pity for the realm of France, sublime, perhaps miraculous, certainly invincible.'

[1] Thomas Bouch, 1882–1963. Educated at Cheltenham and Magdalen College, Oxford. Served in the 10th Hussars, 1904–7. Master of Fox Hounds, Galway, 1908; Tipperary, 1910–11. Major, Cavalry Corps Headquarters. British Expeditionary Force, 1914–18. Author; among his books were *Storms in Teacups* and *Sentimentalities* (1926). Joint Master of Belvoir Hounds, 1912–25; Lord Bathurst's, 1933–5. In 1953 he published his memoirs, *Coat of Many Colours*.

[2] Vreda Esther Mary Lascelles, 1900–   . Known as 'Molly'. Elder daughter of Major William Frank Lascelles, Scots Guards (a grandson of the 2nd Earl of Harewood), and of Lady Sybil de Vere Beauclerk (daughter of the 10th Duke of St Albans). In 1921 she married the Earl of Dalkeith (later 8th Duke of Buccleuch and Queensberry). In 1937 she held the Queen's canopy at the Coronation.

[3] James Gray Stuart, 1897–1971. Third son of the 17th Earl of Moray. Educated at Eton. On active service, 1914–18 (Military Cross and bar). Conservative MP for Moray and Nairn, 1923–59. Entered the Whips' Office, 1935; Deputy Chief Whip, 1938–41; Government Chief Whip, 1941–5; Chief Opposition Whip 1945–8. Privy Councillor, 1939. Secretary of State for Scotland, 1951–7. Created Viscount Stuart of Findhorn, 1959.

[4] The Duchess of Atholl, standing as an Independent, was defeated in the by-election on 21 December 1938, polling 10, 495 votes as against 11,808 for the official Conservative candidate, W. M. Snadden. There were no other candidates.

given the chance. A heron was found dead by the middle pool. He stood so long waiting for the fish who all stayed at the bottom, that he died of cold, want of food and exposure. I would gladly have sent him food if I had known of his plight. The snow is thawing fast, and we hope soon to see the last of it. I have practically finished the brick-work of the cottage, but Jackson is so much behind with the carpentry that I have arranged with Southon to give him a man to help him next week. Hill's mother has died and he is off to the funeral tomorrow. Everything else here appears to be quite normal. I continue to lead my routine mechanically, reading the papers and letters, eating, building, correspondence, sleeping, dining and finally dictating until three o'clock in the morning.

Rothermere sent his cheque to-day, but I gather from his letter he does not propose to renew his wager in the coming year. I have, therefore, decided to abandon port and resume my old association with brandy.

I dined with Elizabeth K de G,[1] very pleasant, the other night. Duff and Diana were there and several friends. Fred Cripps[2] and Violet[3] were there. She is quite plain now, and he is opinionated, fat and stupid.

Your letter of December 13th is just to hand. I expect you will be able to put it right between the two Walters.[4] I must say I should love to see these islands in the way you are doing it. It is getting there that is the difficulty. I plan to go abroad on the 6th or the 7th, and I shall return just when I feel inclined.

The book has reached the stage where I can do a lot of work on the proofs in bed in the sunshine of that room you know at Maxine's.

---

[1] Elizabeth Koch de Gooreynd. A friend of Euan Wallace (the Financial Secretary to the Treasury from May 1938 to April 1939).

[2] Frederick Heyworth Cripps, 1885–1977. Second son of the 1st Baron Parmoor, and brother of Sir Stafford Cripps. Director of the Russian and English Bank, Petrograd, before 1914. On active service at Gallipoli (wounded), 1915, in Palestine (DSO and bar), 1918, and in France. In 1927 he married Violet, Duchess of Westminster (marriage dissolved, 1951). Lieutenant-Commander, RNVR, 1939. He published his memoirs, *Life's a Gamble*, in 1958. Succeeded his brother as 3rd Baron Parmoor, 1971.

[3] Violet Mary Geraldine Nelson, daughter of Sir William Nelson, Baronet. She married (1st) George Richard Francis Rowley, Coldstream Guards; (2nd) in 1920, and 2nd Duke of Westminster ('Bendor'); (3rd) in 1927, the Hon F. H. Cripps, DSO, 2nd son of Lord Parmoor (and himself 3rd Baron Parmoor). Her son Milo succeeded his father as 4th Baron Parmoor in 1977.

[4] Lord Moyne (see page 1155, note 1) and his son, with whom Clementine Churchill was cruising in the West Indies. The younger 'Walter', Bryan Walter Guinness, born in 1905, had been educated at Eton and Christ Church, Oxford. In 1930 he was admitted a Barrister-at-Law, Inner Temple. A poet and novelist, he succeeded his father as second Baron in 1944. Major, Royal Sussex Regiment. A Governor of the National Gallery of Ireland from 1955. His first wife, Diana Mitford, whom he married in 1929, subsequently married Sir Oswald Mosley.

I wonder what Chamberlain is going to do at Rome,[1] but it seems pretty clear that Mussolini is not going to get any more for nothing.

Winston S. Churchill to Lord Halifax

(*Churchill papers: 2/334*)

31 December 1938
Private

At the Guildhall you seemed inclined to accept the invitation of our 'Focus' to come to luncheon and you mentioned January, but now it seems to me, unless some troubles arise, the second week in February would be the best. Will you, therefore, give me some day in that second week; a Tuesday or a Thursday are the best, because you will have your Wednesday Cabinet.

I send you a list of the people who usually come, and who probably would be asked.

We have had a large number of these luncheons and not a word has ever transpired. I think it would be a good thing for you to meet some of the Liberal and Left Wing elements, many of whom are lifelong Pacifists, but who now think we must be prepared to make a stand, if there is no other way. Anyhow, you would receive a very warm welcome.

I venture to enclose an article I wrote this week about Spain for the DT, in the hopes you may find time to read it.[2] If Franco is held up, as I expect

---

[1] Chamberlain left England for Rome on 10 January 1939. To one of his sisters he wrote, five days later: 'I am satisfied that the journey has definitely strengthened the chances of peace. To give first my impressions of Mussolini, I found him straightforward and considerate in his behaviour to us, and moreover he has a sense of humour which is quite attractive.' Mussolini was 'emphatic', Chamberlain added, 'in his assurances that he intended to stand by his agreement with us, and that he wanted peace, and was ready to use his influence to get it' (quoted in Keith Feiling, *The Life of Neville Chamberlain*, London 1946, page 393). Lord Halifax, who was also present, recorded Mussolini's assurances that 'As to any idea of a German attack in the West, such a thing was absolutely out of the question. Hitler would never send the youth of Germany to fall on the frontier which he regards as already decided' (quoted in The Earl of Birkenhead, *Halifax*, London 1965, page 429).

[2] On 30 December 1938, in an article entitled 'The Spanish Ulcer', published in the *Daily Telegraph*, Churchill wrote: 'Nothing has strengthened the Prime Minister's hold upon well-to-do society more remarkably than the belief that he is friendly to General Franco and the Nationalist cause in Spain. But these sentiments on either side may be pushed beyond the bounds of British interest. It would seem that to-day the British Empire would run far less risk from the victory of the Spanish Government than from that of General Franco. I have always been deterred from espousing the cause of either side in Spain by the dread of what would happen to whichever side was vanquished. The spectacle of either a Franco Spain or a Negrin Spain, with the beaten half of the Spanish nation trampled underfoot, has always seemed to me so dark and cruel that, not being a Spaniard, I will not become a partisan. But it must be admitted that if at this moment the Spanish Government were victorious they would be so anxious to live on friendly terms with Great Britain, they would find so much

he will be, in this offensive, there may perhaps be a moment. I am thinking a great deal about this. Our interests are plainly served by a Franco defeat, but far more by a united Spain.[1]

I am going abroad on Saturday next for a fortnight or three weeks.

With good wishes for the New Year,

Believe me,

---

sympathy among the British people for them, that we should probably be able to dissuade them from the vengeance which would have attended their triumph earlier in the struggle. On the other hand, if Franco won, his Nazi backers would drive him to the same kind of brutal suppressions as are practised in the Totalitarian States.' Churchill went on to urge 'a lasting reunion' of all factions in Spain: 'The stubborn, unflinching Republican infantry who held the trenches around Madrid and across the Ebro, the dauntless Catalans with their long history, the unlucky, ill-guided and bewildered Basques, the heroic cadets, unconquerable in the Alcazar, the patriot Generals of the old army, their officers and faithful men—all have a common principle which should overpower the scent of newly-shed blood. Why should the ideals of religion and monarchy be incompatible with those of freedom and democracy? All flow together generously in our island. Why should they not mingle harmoniously in the Spanish Peninsula?'

[1] On 7 December 1938 Churchill wrote to a correspondent, about the Spanish Civil War: 'There is so much good on both sides, but I fear they are going to torture each other to death, and ruin their country whose independence and prosperity is so important to us' (*Churchill papers: 2/334*).

January 1939

Thornton Butterworth to Winston S. Churchill
(*Churchill papers: 8/636*)

3 January 1939

Dear Mr Churchill,

. . . I am deeply concerned to learn of your dissatisfaction at the position of 'My Early Life' and of 'Thoughts and Adventures', and that you consider that these books are stifled.

I have again and again impressed upon our travellers the importance of pushing these books. They have done their best, but in their last report this Christmas they say that booksellers state that there is now little demand for either, and of course the Library demand is finished. However, as I have said before, I feel sure that there will be a *materially* increased demand for 'My Early Life' when the second volume of your Autobiography is published. . . .

To turn to a more pleasant subject: 'Great Contemporaries' in its cheaper and extended edition has, I am happy to inform you, done well. The subscription sales were 1,209 Home and 693 Overseas, making a total of 1,902 copies. Up to the 31st December these sales were increased to: Home 2,892 and Overseas 737, making a total of 3,639. And orders are coming in and I expect will continue to do so daily for some time to come. . . .

In conclusion I would say that nothing would induce me to part with the Copyright in any work of yours which you have been good enough to entrust to me. I value them beyond such material consideration as £.s.d. I also would like to express the hope that notwithstanding your disappointment over the continued sales of the two books in question, you will in surveying our long connection feel that I am not really such a doubtful proposition after all.

With kindest regards and all good wishes for the coming year,

I am,
Yours sincerely,
Thornton Butterworth

Winston S. Churchill to Clementine Churchill: telegram

(*Churchill papers: 1/344*)

4 January 1939   Chartwell[1]

Your letter December 19th greatly enjoyed by Mary and me. All well here.
Am off to Maxine's on 7th.

Clementine Churchill to Winston S. Churchill

(*Churchill papers: 1/322*)

4 January 1939   Monserrat

We have now moved to Monserrat, a small but lovely & mountainous
island very green & luxuriant. It has been ravaged by 2 hurricanes within
four years and an earthquake.

My darling, do you know that I am starved for a letter from you. Mary,
Horatia,[2] Moppett & Sarah have written but Alas not you & I am rather
miserable. You telegraphed that you had posted a letter by Air Mail leaving
Dec. 20th. This should have reached me at Antigua before we left there.
And even if I had received it, my Darling, I had left home 4 weeks before.
Do you think you could dictate a few words every day to a Secretary & she
could send it off twice a week. Never mind about writing yourself. I used to
mind about that, but I'm accustomed to typewritten letters now & I would
rather have them than nothing. I feel quite quite cut off.

Your loving but sad,
Clemmie

I hate telegrams just saying 'all well, rainy weather. Love Winston'.

---

[1] Churchill's guests at Chartwell during 1939 included Alan Bullock (January 5–6), Bill
Deakin (January 5–6, January 28–30, February 11–13, March 12), Professor Lindemann
(January 5–7, February 4–6, February 10–13, February 24–25, March 19–20, March 25–27,
April 28–29, June 30–July 1, and August 28–29), Duncan Sandys (March 19, April 1–2 and
June 10–11), G. M. Young (April 22 and August 3–8), Venetia and Judith Montagu (May
2–3), Sir Archibald Sinclair (August 27–29), Ian Colvin (June 17–19), Julian Amery (July
18–19), Terence O'Connor (August 3–8), and General Sir Edmund Ironside (August 26–28).

[2] Horatia Seymour, 1881–1966. Clementine Churchill's friend. Daughter of Horace Seymour, Gladstone's Private Secretary, 1880–5, and Deputy Master and Comptroller of the
Royal Mint from 1894 until his death in 1902. Following her father's death, her mother was
raised to the rank of a Knight's widow. In 1908 she was a bridesmaid at Churchill's wedding.

Winston S. Churchill to Thornton Butterworth

(Churchill papers: 8/636)

5 January 1939

Many thanks for your letter and for all the information you give me. As you know, I have the greatest admiration for the enterprise and acumen with which your business is conducted, but I am quite sure that 'My Early Life' would have had a very good sale if it could be published at 6d or 9d. Although there is not much profit in such publication, I should like very much to see this book reach classes to whom it has hitherto been denied.

With kind regards,

William Elliot to Violet Pearman

(Churchill papers: 25/17)

5 January 1939   Committee of Imperial Defence
Secret

Dear Mrs Pearman,

I am so sorry for having been so long in thanking you for your letter of 22nd December—the reason being that I was away from Christmas until after the New Year.

Will you please thank Mr Churchill for the article from the American paper 'Liberty' on the subject of a liquid air bomb which the writer of the article states that the Germans are manufacturing in great quantities.

Mr Churchill might be interested to know that we had already made enquiries about the alleged use of this type of bomb in the attacks on Barcelona as described in the Press. At first we were inclined to discredit the idea of liquid air as an explosive. Although we still have no definite evidence to go on, I understand that the experts are now prepared to believe that liquid oxygen can be used as a principal component in an explosive bomb. There appear to be great technical difficulties about making the bombs safe for carriage in aircraft, but if this can be overcome (as seems possible) it is reasonable to suppose that the Germans might already be using such bombs experimentally in Spain.

It so happened that the first stories of liquid air bombs coincided with the heavy raids made on Barcelona in March last. During these raids bombs weighing over 1,000 lbs were extensively used for the first time. We were inclined therefore, to attribute the stories of the effects of these 'liquid air bombs' to the greatly increased effects of really large ordinary explosive bombs. Moreover, the fact that all the bombing on that occasion was done by the Italians, and not by the Germans, tends to confirm this belief. I would add that one of the best blast effects in Barcelona was caused by a bomb hitting a convoy of lorries carrying TNT.

However that may be these deductions in no way prove that liquid air bombs were *not* used at Barcelona, and we have therefore been trying to get more at the truth of the matter.

Yours sincerely,
William Elliot

Leslie Hore-Belisha to Winston S. Churchill

(*Churchill papers: 2/371*)

6 January 1939   War Office

Dear Winston,

On receiving your letter of 21st December in which you queried the information that I had previously given you that of the 10 Guards Battalions 8 had their full complement of both Bren guns and anti-tank rifles, I caused a special report to be issued by Commands showing the dates on which the Guards Battalions in their Commands were complete to establishment in the equipment mentioned. I send you a copy of the information as I have received it. You will see that all the Guards Battalions now have all their equipment of both Bren guns and anti-tank rifles.

I do not in the least resent it when you say that you fear I am being misinformed. I hope you will not resent it if I tell you that you may be. If, however, you are not satisfied with this statement of the facts and you can suggest any other means of checking it, needless to say I will endeavour to give you every satisfaction.

With regard to the second paragraph of your letter when you call my attention to a paragraph in the 'Yorkshire Post' suggesting that you were the inspirer of the recent attacks upon me, I had not previously seen the paragraph. I do not think you are correct in saying that I made any attack upon Sandys. I can assure you that I never did any more than cause him to be asked to assist in investigating what appeared to be at the time a dangerous leakage of military information which might, for all we then knew, have been a stream going into channels beyond our control.

Yours sincerely,
Leslie Hore-Belisha

Mary Penman: [1] *transcription from shorthand notebook*
(*Penman papers*)

6 January 1939

Mr Churchill's plans for Saturday 7th:
Catches plane at 9 am from Croydon
Arrive Le Bourget 10.15 am
Lunches Mons Paul Reynaud at Palace
Tea Sir Eric Phipps at British Embassy at 4 pm
Interviews Mons Blum at 4.45 pm
Catches 8 o'clock train to Cannes from Gare du Lyon
Dines on train
Arrives Cannes 10 am (8th January) [2]

Mary Penman: journal
(*Penman papers*)

7 January 1939   Hotel Ritz, Paris

I had not been there more than five minutes when I noticed a stir—
Monsieur Churchill Arrive! I rushed towards his beaming figure—he hailed
me from far off—I was never so glad to see anyone in all my life before. I felt
reassured and not lost anymore. He was accompanied by the stately figure
of Prof (Professor Lindemann).

[1] Mary Cordelia Penman, 1915–   . School certificate, 1932. Secretarial training,
Portch's School of Commerce, Croydon. Secretary to Sir Edgar Jones (Chairman of the
National Food Canning Council, formerly Controller of the Priority Department of the
Ministry of Munitions, 1915–18, including the years when Churchill was Minister of Muni-
tions). Moved with her parents to Four Elms, near Chartwell, 1932. Began work at Chartwell,
3 August 1938. Left Churchill's service at the end of June 1939, in order to marry Leslie John
Fox, an architectural student. Since her visit to the South of France with Churchill in January
1939, she never left Britain. Joined the Civil Defence Corps. 1958. Welfare Section Officer
(later Senior Welfare Defence Officer), 1960. Local organizer, Women's Royal Voluntary
Service, 1974, when she organized a Visiting Service for the lonely and the housebound.
After the Second World War her sister Bee Penman also became one of Churchill's secretaries.
Mrs Fox writes, of her eight months with Churchill: 'I took my full share of the work and as
I was young enough not to mind late nights, I did a large share of the night work when the
History of the English Speaking Peoples was being dictated. I made many journeys with
Mr Churchill in the brown Daimler, taking dictation as we travelled' (*Letter to the author, 8
December 1978*).
[2] The expenses of Churchill's visit to Paris and the South of France were charged to his
Literary Account for January 1939, under the heading: 'Visit to Literary Agent in Paris',
and with the items: 'Mr C, Air ticket Croydon-Paris' (£4.10.0), Expenses in Paris, hotel,
taxis etc' (£12), 'Secretary's fares, London–Cannes & return, registration of luggage, etc'
(£10), 'Expenses of Secretary for 3 weeks @ £1 per day' (£21) and 'Return fare Paris–
London plus expenses on journey' (£3.10.0): a total of £51 (*Churchill papers: 8/639*).

A suite was ordered and Mr Churchill bade me follow him to it as he had some work for me. The three of us passed through high double doors into the sitting room of the suite. It was most lofty, a long window, the full height of the room was opposite the door, it was netted in Parisian style (which only just misses being Victorian). There were stiff chairs and a sofa covered in blue tapestry, the woodwork and legs of the furniture were lacquered in that subdued putty shade which I now know to be synonymous with France.

Some men with whom Mr Churchill had an appointment now arrived to interview him. When they had gone Mr Churchill said he would like a cup of soup and Prof also, so it was ordered. In a few minutes a beautifully set table was born in by two footmen. Prof and Mr Churchill proceeded to sup their soup while I feeling rather hungry, sat and watched. Mr C suddenly remembered me and asked me if I would like some, I said yes I would, he rose and went to his bedroom, returned with a glass into which he ladelled some of the soup from his tureen. The soup was the colour of beetroot juice, quite clear, and it tasted better than anything I have had before or am likely to have again, though I drank it from a toothbrush glass.

I had not quite finished when he called me to start work, I went and sat at the writing table before the great high window. There was not much work really only a few instructions and telegrams. This done Mr C departed to lunch with M Paul Reynaud at the Palace Trianon at Versailles. I wrote out the telegrams, gave them to the concierge to despatch and started out to get some lunch. . . .

This time slipped by in silence, it was six, it was half past six and then seven. Mr Churchill had not returned. At a quarter past seven the Prof and I became restive. It was necessary that we should leave for the Gare de Lyon at half past seven at the very latest and before that the luggage must be got down. I went and packed up everything and locked the cases. Mr Churchill had intended to change, he would not be able to do that now. Prof called the men to take the bags and gave instructions for two taxis to be ordered. Prof was also going from the Gare de Lyon, only not on the same train, his went ten minutes later.

Just before half past seven Mr Churchill burst in, all excited and flushed like a school boy. He had had a long talk with Blum and Delbos. I tore down to see Prof's and our luggage on to the respective taxis, in a second Prof and Mr Churchill had leapt into one taxi and I into another with the bulk of the luggage. 'Gare de Lyon, Train Bleu' I told the taximan and off we dashed. We arrived and the taximan asked for what I thought was too much according to the indicator. I had a very heated argument with him, eventually I gave him 16 francs; on looking up my notes of expenditure I saw that for the same journey in the morning the Cook's man had paid 20 francs, so I must have cheated the poor man after all. The porters here were nasty and would not understand what I wanted, still Mr Churchill rushed along and I rushed after him, we reached the train with a few minutes to spare.

Before we got in the photographers took Mr Churchill's photograph, I hoped I'd be in it too, but I have not seen it anywhere. Then he went in and the reporters crowded round me, wanted my name and so on, quite a thrill. Then Mr Churchill came to the door and said 'Why don't you get in' most severely, so I hopped in quickly. I think it was nasty of him to hawk me in in this way. He had been glad enough to be photographed!

The attendant to our coach was a very nice old fellow, spoke good English. I was shown into a compartment next to Mr Churchill's. Along one side was a wide seat with a comfortable back, with head rests covered in white linen. The walls were panelled in light coloured wood, with mahogany strips between the panels. In the centre of the panels there was a pattern of flowers in inlay, rather sweet in pinkish shades and black. There were, I counted, nine different kinds of wood in each panel. Unlike the English trains, all was spotlessly clean. In the corner of the compartment two doors curved outwards. I opened these. Inside each door was a full length mirror and in the enclosure a decent wash basin, brackets holding glasses and water bottle etc, and at the back a further mirror. There was a special electric light for this little cubby hole. Over the basin were, of course, hot and cold taps, but the kind little old man attendant explained to me apologetically that owing to the snow and ice the pipes had frozen and the taps did not work, so would it be all right if he brought me some water in the morning. Naturally, I said it would be quite alright.

About ten minutes after we had left the station we went to dinner. Mr Churchill and I had a little table for two to ourselves, and as might be expected, all eyes were turned upon us. Mr Churchill is well known and loved by the French, and the English passengers were interested and a little curious also. On our table was a lamp and a vase with some mimosa and two bright salmon carnations. Mr Churchill asked me what I would drink and I said I would like something light, so he ordered Graves. He had champagne in a bucket of ice. I refused the aperitif because I was not quite sure what it was and Mr Churchill, the lazy thing, had not done the Daily Telegraph article and proposed doing it after dinner so I had to be awake and sober too.

Winston S. Churchill to Clementine Churchill

(*Spencer-Churchill papers*)

8 January 1939   Château de L'Horizon

My darling one,

Here I am in radiant sunshine though there is a nip in the air. We crossed —Prof & I—in a new Frobisher aeroplane in $1\frac{1}{4}$ hours, without seeing the sea or the ground—all mist. But they seem to make no difficulty about weather: & landed perfectly. I will tell you by dictation about my day in Paris when Miss Penman has finished her luncheon. The journey was vy comfortable & I slept blissfully.

Maxine was overjoyed to see me—there is no one here yet except the Drag. The Windsors dine tomorrow night. There is much to do about curtseying to the lady. Feelings run high on the point. But all accounts show them entirely happy and as much in love with each other as ever. I will write you more hereafter.

I propose to stay here for a fortnight and work hard on the book. I have been leading a life of unbroken routine at Chartwell—& have now got in print no less than 221,000 words i.e. 63 days ahead of the vy hard task I prescribed of 1,000 a day from August 1. At this rate I shd cover the whole ground by May, wh wd leave 7 months for polishing. It is a formidable grind; but if accomplished will put things on a vy satisfactory basis.

Mary has been twice out hunting & lives for it. She has been vy sweet and is growing into her beauty. I left all well behind me. During the fortnight or three weeks I hope to stay here, I have virtually stopped work upon the Cottage; because I like to be about it myself. Jackson will do some needed odd jobs and the two men have joined Hill's party in cutting wood—now become urgent. As usual I did not leave Chartwell without a pang. But now that I am here I am sure I shall enjoy it.

Tomorrow the Daily Herald begin distributing the new cheap edition of the World Crisis wh Odham's have printed. It can be sold at 3/9 for each of two volumes—a miracle of mass production. They expect to sell over 150,000! I like to feel that for the first time the working people will hear my side of the tale.

I had a long talk with Anthony before leaving London; he is resolved not to join the Government—& they have so far made him no advances. But there may easily be a big reconstruction after Chamberlain's visit to Rome, & before the end of the month. I cannot feel that after all I have said, they can be able to swallow me—it wd have to be 'horns & all'. But I can truthfully say I do not mind. It will be much better to await the situation wh will arise after the G Election—now probably in October. Meanwhile the book is the thing.

I am going to consult a good doctor here—either old Bres[1] or a vy famous German Jew exile whom Maxine recommends—about my trouble, wh certainly is no better—though not a serious inconvenience. And I am going to be rubbed every morning, & generally go in for beauty culture!

Your dressing gown is greatly admired, I do think it lovely. I wear it always & think of you.

I have had a wonderful little silver cup from Craigavon—the particulars of wh I will describe to you later. It is a proof of his approval of the course I have taken wh I greatly value.

I have received two lovely letters from you & have also been shown those you have written to Maria. You seem to be having a delightful & interesting cruise & seeing all sorts of places off the beaten track. Also the Commission must be an intelligent accompaniment, & I have no doubt you are taking interest in their work. But what you do not say in any of yr letters or telegrams is how you are in yourself. Is the voice better, and are you stronger, & able to get through whole days? Really my pussy cat you have had a vy rough year—toe—throat—tail, and general debility—It is too much. I feel great hopes that the voyage will do you lasting good. But do let me know.[2]

I am deeply grieved that no letters have yet reached you. This is my third, & I am ashamed that I did not inquire earlier. I shall now write you every mail.

Good bye my darling Clemmie.

Always your loving & devoted,

W

[Sketch of sun shining and pig]

I append some bulletin material wh will supplement my writing.

[1] Doctor Brès, Maxine Elliot's devoted companion of her latter years. The doctor was with Maxine Elliot when she died, on 5 March 1940, and wrote to Churchill that same day: 'I have in the ears her last words said this morning about you. "Winston knows how to take his responsibilities—nothing can frighten him—he should be Prime Minister".' In his reply Churchill wrote of how 'I shall always feel grateful to you for the tender care and skill with which you watched over her.' (*Churchill papers: 2/394*)

[2] Clementine Churchill's daughter Mary writes of 'tensions on board the yacht arising from political differences. There was a real blow-up one evening while they were in Barbados: the company was listening to a broadcast from England, in which Winston (and the anti-Government point of view in general) was attacked. Vera Broughton exclaimed in a loud voice, "Hear, Hear!", which angered Clementine, as it was evidently intended for her benefit; but what really wounded and enraged her was that Walter Moyne remained ostentatiously silent—thereby inferring his tacit agreement with Lady Broughton. Clementine was already yearning for home, and her mind was particularly full of Winston and of his embattled position, and this was the last straw' (Mary Soames, *Clementine Churchill*, London 1979, page 280).

Winston S. Churchill to Clementine Churchill

(*Churchill papers: 1/344*)

8 January 1939   Château de L'Horizon
Secret

Darling Clemmie,

I had a full and interesting day in Paris. I had lunch with Reynaud at Versailles where he was recuperating after his exertions and triumphs in French finance. The whole of France is united against Mussolini. Reynaud said that if he touched Djibouti 'France would spring into a fresh and joyous war'. There is an intense desire to take it out of Mussolini for the humiliation inflicted upon them by Hitler. There is some talk that perhaps Mussolini will propose to Chamberlain a truce in Spain, which he, Mussolini, could certainly bring about.[1] This would be a great event and everyone would rejoice at it. However, no doubt Mussolini would ask as his price the Balearic Islands and other favours at the expense of France. Therefore, there may be much loss as well as gain. I object very much to people being paid simply for leaving off doing wrong.

In the afternoon I had a long talk with the Ambassador[2] and Charles Mendl, and then I went to see Blum, who was the most informing of all. They all confirm the fact that the Germans had hardly any soldiers at all on the French frontier during the Crisis. And Blum told me, (secret) that he had it from Daladier himself that both Generals Gamelin and Georges[3] were confident that they could have broken through the weak unfinished German line, almost unguarded as it was, by the fifteenth day at the latest, and that if the Czechs could have held out only for that short fortnight, the German armies would have had to come back to face invasion. On the other side there is their great preponderance in the air, and it depends what value you put on that how you judge the matter.

I have no doubt that a firm attitude by England and France would have prevented war, and I believe that history will incline to the view that if the worst had come to the worst, we should have been far better off than we may be at some future date.

---

[1] See page 1356, note 1.
[2] Sir Eric Phipps.
[3] Joseph Georges, 1875–1951. Entered the French Infantry, 1897. Chief of Staff to Marshal Foch, 1918. Head of the French Economic Service in the Ruhr, 1923. Chief of Staff to Marshal Pétain, 1925–6. Chef de Cabinet in the Maginot Government, 1929. Commanded the 19th Corps in Algeria, 1931. Wounded in Marseilles at the time of the assassination of King Alexander of Yugoslavia, 1934. Created Generalissimo, 1934. Commander of the Forces and Operations in the North East, 1939–40. A member of the French Committee of National Liberation, 1943.

Blum lives in a flat above which resides Delbos, who was brought down en deshabille to join our talk. Both are very anxious. They fear that Mussolini is determined to have his share of the loot, Hitler having had everything so far and he nothing, and they believe that Hitler is bound to him and will support him. I put it to them that perhaps if Mussolini attacked France we might keep Germany out by saying that we would not come in if she did not. All the Frenchmen seemed quite content with this, as they are sure they could smash Italy in an affair a deux. But they doubt very much whether Hitler would stay out, even if he brought the British in against him.

It now looks as if he had some sort of deal with Colonel Beck, and that he is more likely in an eastern movement to press towards Hungary and Roumania. Blum seems to think that these two ruffians will be moving again quite soon.

In London there is a good deal of fear that Hitler may turn towards us and make demands upon us instead of going to the East. The Ambassador told me he heard tales of pessimism prevailing in so many quarters in London. My feeling is that it is not we who will be singled out at such a time. But what a state to let the world get into!

Meanwhile Chamberlain, in endorsing all that Roosevelt said, has made a great advance to my point of view.[1] Perhaps you will have noticed that he used the very phrase I have been repeating for the last two years, namely 'freedom and peace', and that he put, as I have always done, 'freedom' first.

All reports from behind the scenes indicate his great disillusionment with Hitler and despair about appeasement. Meanwhile, however, the disagreeable muddle in ARP continues. The trenches in the parks are full of water. They cannot either fill them in or drain them and make them useful. Indeed, they have had to hire special guardians to keep children from drowning themselves in these muddy troughs. The ARP volunteers are disgruntled and melting away because of the defective organisation. Sir John Anderson, although so recently made a minister, is skating at St Moritz, and this is a subject of continued comment in the press.[2] There is a total lack of drive and

---

[1] On 4 January 1939 President Roosevelt's message to Congress had called for defence against aggression, although stressing the need for 'methods short of war'. On the following day Neville Chamberlain issued the following statement: 'Nobody who is charged with the heavy responsibilities of Government could fail to be impressed by the solemn words with which the President of the United States yesterday greeted the elected representatives of the American people. In these islands, where there is so clear a realization that only through freedom and peace can we hope to maintain and develop for ourselves and those that come after us the benefits for which we have laboured for generations, the sentiments expressed by the President will be welcomed as yet another indication of the vital role of the American democracy in world affairs and its devotion to the ideal of ordered human progress.'

[2] On 31 October 1938 Sir John Anderson had succeeded Earl De La Warr as Lord Privy Seal, with special responsibilities towards Air Raid Precautions.

Chamberlain does not know a tithe of the neglects for which he is responsible. Indeed, I do not think it would be much fun to go and take these burdens and neglects upon my shoulders, certainly not without powers such as they have not dreamed of according.

Duncan launched his Party with Randolph's assistance, and almost everyone ratted at the last moment, Violet [1] in the van, followed by Liddell Hart. Duncan was miserable, and Diana rang me up saying he had lain awake all night. But I told them now that they had taken this plunge, if they could not advance to *mark time*, and let it die peacefully, and on no account to make a public retreat; and this they have done. I expect Norwood will be on his trail pretty soon!

The baby,[2] I hear, continues to thrive. Instead of being four pounds six ounces, which it was when born, it is now four pounds, eleven ounces. It is, therefore, gaining strength more rapidly than the political movement launched at the same time.

I was delighted to receive James Craig's cup, I think it very beautiful in design. It is quite small and a goblet shape, according to an old Gaelic model, and has been made especially with three supporters, a sword, a brush and a pen. All round are quotations from my father, from me and one from Randolph, about Ulster. I wish some of these dirty Tory hacks, who would like to drive me out of the Party, could see this trophy.

To be continued in my next.

Tender love,
Darling,
Your devoted,
W

Neville Chamberlain to his sister

(*Templewood papers*)

8 January 1939

I have just had a letter from G. Gwynne [3] in which he warns me that I am embarking on the most perilous adventure of my life & while quite approving

---

[1] Lady Violet Bonham Carter (see page 160, note 3).
[2] Edwina Sandys, Churchill's second grandchild.
[3] Neville Gwyn Gwynne, 1868–1951. Mechanical engineer. Educated at Lancing and Pembroke College, Cambridge. Director of Gwynne's Pumps Ltd and of William Foster and Co, Lincoln. A member of the War Pensions Committee, 1917–18. CBE, 1920. President of the London and District Engineering Employers. Chairman of the British Engineers' Association. Chairman of the Engine Section of the Society of British Aircraft Constructors.

of what I have done & being grateful for it, feels it would be much better now to cancel the Rome visit & make a grand alliance against Germany. In other words better abandon my policy & adopt Winston's! Fortunately my nature is as Ll G says extremely 'obstinate', & I refuse to change, but if anything happened to me I can see plainly that my successor would soon be off the rails & we should once more be charged with that vacillation which in the past has made other diplomats despair.

F. H. Sandford[1] to Violet Pearman

(Air Ministry papers: 19/26)

11 January 1939
Secret

Dear Private Secretary,
    You will remember sending me on the 12th December the enclosed letter which Mr Churchill had received from Mr H. S. Robertson[2] of Prague.
    On receiving your letter I immediately made enquiries of our Intelligence Directorate, and I find that the statements in Mr Robertson's letter about aircraft production in Czecho-Slovakia do not agree with our information. According to our intelligence, there has never been anything approaching mass production in Czecho-Slovakia. The average output in the first six months of 1938 was between 50 and 60 Service aircraft a month, while the output from the Avia factory alone did not exceed about 20 aircraft of various types; and according to information recently given to our Attaché in Prague[3] by the Czech Chief of the Air Staff the output has decreased since the cession of Sudetenland. The performance of aircraft built in Czecho-Slovakia is well below the standard in this country, and most of the types in construction at present are obsolescent. There is no information available in the Air Ministry about costs of production in Czecho-Slovakia.

[1] Folliott Herbert Sandford, 1906– . Educated at Winchester and New College, Oxford. Entered the Air Ministry, 1930; Private Secretary to successive Secretaries of State (Swinton, Kingsley Wood, Samuel Hoare and Archibald Sinclair), 1937–40. Attached to RAF Ferry Command, Montreal, 1941–2. Secretary, Office of Minister Resident in West Africa, 1942–4. Assistant Under-Secretary of State, Air Ministry, 1944–7; Deputy Under-Secretary of State, 1947–58. Knighted, 1959. Registrar of Oxford University, 1958–72.
[2] I have been unable to trace either Mr Robertson or his letter.
[3] Archibald Hugh Herbert Macdonald, 1899–1947. Educated at Gresham School and Sandhurst. 2nd Lieutenant, Norfolk Regiment, 1917; Lieutenant, 1919. Flying Officer, Royal Air Force, 1921; Squadron-Leader, 1936. Mentioned in despatches, North-west Frontier, India, 1921. Air Attaché in Prague, Vienna and Belgrade, 1938–9. On active service, 1939–45. Retired, 1946.

I am sorry that I have not sent an earlier reply to your letter, but certain facts required to be checked up with the Air Attaché in Prague. The necessary information was not in consequence available before the Secretary of State left England for a short holiday at Christmas, and I kept the papers to show him on his return yesterday before writing to you.

You will no doubt treat the information contained in this letter as confidential.

F. W. Deakin to Kathleen Hill
(*Churchill papers: 8/625*)

16 January 1939

The letter in German is from a shopkeeper in Bad Gastein where Mrs Churchill bought some hats and clothes. He & his wife are Jews and beg her to get them a permit for temporary residence in England. They have affidavits for future emigration to America. I suggest that you send the letter to the German Jewish Aid Committee, Woburn House W1 with a note saying that Mrs Churchill would like the case attended to. It seems to be a genuine letter.

Winston S. Churchill to Clementine Churchill
(*Churchill papers: 1/344*)

18 January 1939   Château de L'Horizon
                                                              Golfe Juan,
                                                            Alpes Maritimes

I told you about the aeroplane journey when we went in complete mist all the time. The very next day under practically the same weather conditions a Swiss plane got pulled down by icing and half were killed.[1] It is all right as long as it works well. If it is in other ways convenient, I shall go back by the ferry, as I think one should only fly when it is incomparably the easiest way.

It was bright sunshine for two days, but ever since we have had nothing but grey skies and cold winds. This has not, however, worried me because I

---

[1] A Swiss airliner travelling from Zurich to Paris crashed into a hillside near Senlis on 8 January 1939. The crash was blamed on icing on the wings. Five passengers were killed and twelve injured. Among the injured were five British subjects, all of whom recovered from their injuries.

have stayed in bed every morning and made great progress with the book. We have averaged fifteen hundred words a day, although nominally on holiday. I shall have a lot for you to read when you come home.

The Windsors dine here and we dine back with them. They have a lovely little place next door to La D.[1] Everything extremely well done and dignified. Red liveries, and the little man himself dressed up to the nines in the Balmoral tartan with dagger and jabot etc. When you think that you could hardly get him to put on a black coat and short tie when he was Prince of Wales, one sees the change in the point of view. I am to dine with him tomorrow night with only Rothermere. No doubt to talk over his plans for returning home. They do not want him to come, but they have no power to stop him.

Just as at Chartwell I divided my days between building and dictating, so now it is between dictating and gambling. I have been playing very long, but not foolishly, and up to date I have a substantial advantage. It amuses me very much to play, so long as it is with their money.

On Saturday I shall motor to Monte Carlo, lunching on the way with Mr R. Purbrick, who has Muriel's[2] 'Marylands'. At Monte Carlo I stay the night with Rothermere, and go on the next day to Cap Martin for a few days with Daisy.[3] After which I shall return home and resume building.

Chamberlain's visit to Rome did no harm. That is the most we can say of it. The question is what are these people going to do now against us. The bomb explosions in London and Manchester are no doubt the Irish trying to get hold of Ulster.[4] How vain it was for Chamberlain to suppose he could make peace by giving everything away! Everything looks as if he and his Government are stiffening up on foreign matters. They adopted my very phrase 'Freedom and peace' in support of Roosevelt's statements, and they certainly gave nothing to the organ grinder or his monkey; not even to pay

---

[1] La Dragonnière, Lord Rothermere's Villa.

[2] Muriel Wilson (see page 336, note 1).

[3] Daisy Fellowes (see page 885, note 2).

[4] The *Annual Register* for 1939 recorded: 'In the early morning of January 16 members of the Irish Republican Army in England brought about a number of bomb explosions at places in the central districts of London and Manchester, causing considerable damage and the loss of one life. This marked the beginning of a campaign designed to intimidate the British Government into consenting to the incorporation of Northern Ireland into Eire. For several months scarcely a week passed without one or more bomb outrages being attempted by Irish extremists in London and other large towns, most of them on a small scale, but some aiming at the destruction of larger objectives, such as the destruction of an electricity supply or the blowing up of a bridge.' On 20 January 1939 *The Times* reported that there had been bomb explosions on January 17 in Birmingham, Manchester, Southwark and Harlesden, on January 18 in Liverpool, and on January 19 in London (where public buildings were being guarded by the police). One person was killed and 15 injured when an IRA bomb exploded at Kings Cross station on 26 July 1939.

him to go into the next street. It looks almost certain there will be no election before November, which is a great relief, for it would be very awkward at present.

The Duncan–Randolph movement, the Hundred Thousand, has already over-passed its first hundred. Violet made herself very awkward. Just as she upset Eden's Queens Hall meeting by her violence against the Government, so now she broke up Duncan's little effort by bolting in alarm. I need scarcely say, I did all in my power to dissuade them from it. And no doubt it does me a certain amount of harm. I do not care at all.

We are very quiet and happy here and the days succeed one another peacefully. There is a very pretty dance which I have seen here. An old English dance called 'Under the Spreading Chestnut-Tree', like the Lambeth Walk, only not vulgarised and cockneyfied. There is a very accomplished dancer and her husband, who perform at the Casino, and we are all to have lessons tomorrow after lunch. We take three steps and give a hop. I always hop at the wrong time, which I am afraid, provokes small minded people to laugh.

My reports from Chartwell show that the building is getting on well. Of course, now the two men are simply cutting wood, but when I get back all will be ready for tiling the roofs, and after that the floors will go down. I had an estimate for the joinery of the doors, cupboards etc, which seems to me moderate at £55.[1] It will be a lovely place when it is finished, and I look forward so much to leading you round it when you return. The greatest pains are being taken to make it water proof and weather proof, in every way.

In the summer when I am sure the book will be finished, I think I will build a house on the ten acres. It would cost about three thousand pounds to give a lovely dwelling for a man and his wife, two children, one double and one single visiting bedroom, and I expect we could sell it for five or six thousand pounds with the bit of land. It would amuse me all the summer and give me good health. I should get Lutyens[2] down to give his views as to where it should be put and what it should look like etc. He will do this for nothing, I am sure, as he has always begged to give advice. He has been appointed President of the Royal Academy, so another member of the Other Club is in a distinguished position. My idea about a house of this kind is

[1] At the money values of September 1981, just over £850.
[2] Edwin Landseer Lutyens, 1869–1944. Architect; his works included the British Pavilion, Paris, 1900; Queen Mary's Doll's House; some of the last substantial country houses built in Britain (Heathcote, Ednaston Manor, Berrydown, Little Thakeham); Le Bois des Moutiers (near Dieppe); the Whitehall Cenotaph; and much of New Delhi, including Government House and the Viceroy's House. Knighted, 1918. Order of Merit, 1942. A member of the Other Club from 1911.

that every bedroom must have a bathroom and must be good enough to be a bed-sitting room. Downstairs you have one lovely big room. However, you may be sure nothing will be done until you have passed the plans. I have at least two months work ahead on the present cottage.

Vincent Sheean:[1] *recollections*
(*'Between the Thunder and the Sun'*)

[19 January 1939]

On the night when Tarragona fell (January 19, 1939) our party dined at the Windsors' house at Antibes. The fall of Tarragona was an event which made inevitable the final collapse of the Spanish Republic. Up until then it was possible to hope that some last-minute development might strengthen the remnants of the Republic for further resistance. From then on the further steps—the capture of Barcelona and the conquest of all Catalonia—were predetermined. It was clear that France would do nothing. . . .

The Windsors' dinner was very grand, and the guests consisted of assorted notables from up and down the coast, mostly English people of high rank who were holidaying in the South. My Lords Rothermere and Beaverbrook had been prevented from attending by colds. (Lord Beaverbrook recovered sufficiently to appear at the Casino, where we saw him afterward.) When some of the more overpowering guests had departed, after the long and stately meal in the white-and-gold dining-room, the Duke of Windsor and Mr Churchill settled down to a prolonged argument with the rest of the party listening in silence. The Duke had read Mr Churchill's recent articles on Spain and his newest one (out that day, I believe) in which he appealed for an alliance with Soviet Russia.

We sat by the fireplace, Mr Churchill frowning with intentness at the floor in front of him, mincing no words, reminding HRH of the British constitution on occasion—'When our kings are in conflict with our constitution, we change our kings,' he said—and declaring flatly that the nation stood in the gravest danger of its long history. The kilted Duke in his Stuart tartan sat on the edge of the sofa, eagerly interrupting whenever he could, contesting every point, but receiving—in terms of the utmost politeness so

---

[1] James Vincent Sheean, 1899–1975. Born in Illinois. Educated at the University of Chicago. Foreign correspondent in Europe and Asia, 1922–7. Author, essayist and reviewer. He described his prewar meetings with Churchill in his book *Between The Thunder and The Sun*, published in 1943. Biographer of Nehru, 1959. He married Maxine Elliot's niece, Diana Forbes-Robertson, in 1935: 'what I remember in particular', she later recalled, 'was that Churchill was so kind to the young and such *fun*' (*conversation with the author, 8 October 1981*).

far as the words went—an object lesson in political wisdom and public spirit. The rest of us sat fixed in silence; there was something dramatically final, irrevocable about this dispute.

Clementine Churchill to Winston S. Churchill

(*Churchill papers: 1/332*)

19 January 1939   MY Rosaura[1]
                                                               Barbados

My Darling

Four days ago I was sitting in the Public Library at Dominica, (this was before getting your last letter) reading up the back copies of the 'Times' and suddenly there was Sidney Peel[2] looking at me from the middle of the Obituary page—A young photograph, as I used to know him—I closed my eyes; Time stood still, fell away, and I lived again those four years during which I saw him nearly every day. He was good to me and made my difficult rather arid life interesting. But I couldn't care for him & I was not kind or even very grateful. And then my Darling you came and in that moment I knew the difference.

I am glad you wrote to me about it because at that moment I longed for you. I wanted to put my arms round you and cry and cry.

We have now reached Barbados & soon I think will come home. These islands are beautiful in themselves but have been desecrated & fouled by man. These green hills covered with tropical bush & trees rise straight out of the sea & fringing the coasts are hideous dilapidated crazy houses, unpainted for years with rusty corrugated iron roofs. Trade stagnating, enough starchy food to keep the population alive but under nourished. Eighty per cent of the population is ill. . . .

Lieutenant-Colonel A. H. Burne to Winston S. Churchill

(*Churchill papers: 8/626*)

21 January 1939

Dear Mr Churchill,

I have heard that, in the course of your studies for your History of England, you have been favourably impressed by the Ancient Britons. Also I read

---

[1] Lord Moyne's yacht.

[2] To whom Clementine Churchill had twice been engaged between 1903 and 1907 (see page 1318, note 1).

that you have taken 'ten tin boxes' of books with you to the Riviera for further study on the subject.

Hence I venture to think that the enclosed paper may be of some interest to you. It probably contains no facts with which you are not already aware, but the point of view is perhaps sufficiently unorthodox to interest you. If so, you are welcome to anything it may convey. . . .[1]

Stefan Lorant to Winston S. Churchill

(*Churchill papers: 8/635*)

23 January 1939   Picture Post,
                                                       London

Dear Mr Churchill,

I was in touch with you a few weeks ago on the question of my coming down to see you and to select a number of pictures which would compose a series to be used in PICTURE POST. I believe that you know that such a series of pictures, coupled with an article setting out your views over the past few years and the way in which they have been entirely justified by events, would be of real value at the present time. You'll remember, perhaps, that arrangements had been completed when it was necessary for you to go away.

I should like to ask you—if you can—to find a day in the near future when I can come down to see you and talk the matter over. It is perhaps worth adding that PICTURE POST's circulation has increased in the meantime to well over a million and a quarter. A preliminary enquiry shows, that each copy is read by 5 people, so that you will be reaching a worth while public.

Yours faithfully,
Stefan Lorant

Sir Roger Keyes to Winston S. Churchill

(*Churchill papers: 8/624*)

23 January 1939

. . . If NC does not *beg* you to take on our defences in Inskip's place, he will *not* be doing his best for the British Empire in these dangerous times.

---

[1] Colonel Burne enclosed a vindication of the often criticized submission to Caesar by the British leader Cassivellaunus. For Churchill's response, see pages 1381–2 and 1381, note 1.

Mary Penman: journal

(*Penman papers*)

23 January 1939

I left by train for Monte Carlo arriving at the Villa Zoraïde[1] in the afternoon. The Daily Telegraph article was due to be dictated. On the 23rd, at 3.15 pm I was still waiting for the DT article to be dictated and outside a mistral was blowing. It was due to appear in print on Thursday 26th. Mr Churchill did not do any work whilst at the Villa Zoraïde, most unlike him. On Tuesday I was asked to call at Cook's in Monte Carlo and book our seats home on the Blue Train leaving Monte Carlo that evening. The luggage was packed and I supervised the labelling and it was loaded on to the car in which Mr Churchill was driven to the station. As we passed the Casino he ordered the car to stop although we had little time to spare before catching the train. He jumped out and ran to the Casino entrance, his clothes flapping about him in the strong wind, looking a little shabby and untidy. He disappeared inside briefly and then came out still running, he waved his right hand triumphantly to me and grinned as he leapt into the car beside me. 'I have just won enough to pay for our fares home—What do you think of that?'

The DT article was still undictated and it was Tuesday evening. After dinner on the Blue Train Mr Churchill who was very tired went to bed in his berth and having called me into the compartment which was anything but spacious announced his intention to dictate the DT article. The only thing I could find to sit on was his hat box in which he packed his dirty linen, it was barely 12 inches high and the light was very poor indeed.

Somewhere near to midnight the article was finished and I stood up, my legs were very cramped, I stumbled through the door and turned left down the corridor of the train to my compartment which adjoined his, my numb legs crumpled up under me completely and I collapsed upon the floor. The attendant standing at the end of the corridor a few yards away offered no assistance at all but gave me a very sour look.

[1] Daisy Fellowes' villa near Monte Carlo.

Mary Penman: journal

(*Penman papers*)

24 January 1939   Hotel Ritz, Paris

I typed the DT article and despatched it.[1] Mr Churchill was out for part of the day and I went out and had my lunch at the same restaurant where I lunched on the 7th. We had to take a taxi at 9.20 pm to the Gare du Nord to board the Golden Arrow at 9.50 pm (the night ferry) Mr Churchill was preparing to leave his suite at the Ritz, as usual we had not too much time to spare and I could not think why he was delaying our departure and fussing around. Then he darted into the salon where I waited and said he had lost his dental plate and would I help him find it. I looked around the bathroom hastily and then went into his bedroom and lifted his pillow and there lay his small gold dental plate, where he had put it when he slept.

We made a rapid taxi journey to the Gare du Nord, grabbed a porter and made undignified haste towards the departure platform. I was carrying among other articles the old black leather hat box, the lid became unfastened and the mouth of the box tilted downwards revealing some underwear, only prompt action on my part avoided spillage, 'We must not wash our dirty linen in public' Mr Churchill said as we ran the last stretch to the barrier.

Mary Penman: journal

(*Penman papers*)

25 January 1939

We reached Victoria in sunshine at about ten on Thursday morning. Mr Churchill had given me some precise directions about the luggage and said avoid opening a particular case at the customs. Somehow or other I bungled things, widely opening for the customs officer to inspect a case full of bottles

---

[1] Writing in she *Daily Telegraph* on 30 Janaury 1939, Churchill declared: '. . . on the great field of Europe Germany has become the dominant, aggressive power. Austria has fallen; Czechoslovakia has been subjugated; German authority and German trade stride forward together down the Danube Valley. The steel-helmets of the German army glint upon the Brenner Pass. In the unequal partnership of the two Dictators, Hitler has gained everything, and Mussolini nothing. At the same time, the keeping of a large, wholly unproductive army in Abyssinia, without the slightest control of the country or chance of developing it, has imposed a grievous strain upon Italian finance and economy. The very large Italian forces maintained in Libya to-day are an aggravation.' Entitled 'Mussolini's Cares', the article ended: 'We must all devoutly hope that the Italian Dictator will count the cost before opening the flood-gates of carnage upon the world—and upon no part of the world more than the highly vulnerable country of which he has so long been the spirited and successful chief.'

of dutiable liquor. Poor Mr Churchill who had just said 'nothing to declare'
had to apologise and pay up.

We were met by Cale and drove straight to Chartwell. The sun was shining. Mrs Churchill had not yet returned from the West Indies.

Lady Gwendeline Churchill to Winston S. Churchill
(*Churchill papers: 1/343*)

29 January 1939

Dearest Winston,

Clarissa is in a family in Paris, following Cours at the Sorbonne—they go
on till end March.—Do you think I ought to get her back before anything
happens—or do you think I will be able to get her back when it does happen
—or do you think I better write to Lady Phipps & ask her to protect C—
(Can one do that?)

What a dilemma! but C is so happy in Paris, working very hard &
beautifully unconcerned—She found England gloomy, dull & indeed it is—
so I let her go to Paris three weeks ago.

O dear Winston, forgive this idiotic scrawl—but poor Jack is so *depressed*
& *rather cross*, & so I thought I would turn to you to help me, because *I* am
responsible.

Yrs affectionately,
Goonie

Winston S. Churchill to Lady Gwendeline Churchill
(*Churchill papers: 1/343*)

30 January 1939

I don't think danger is imminent, not, at any rate for a fortnight or so,
and as the Dictators hope to terrify us into submission, probably there will
be plenty of grimacing and warnings beforehand. I think you might write
to Lady Phipps, and ask her if she would kindly let Clarissa know when to
quit, should such need arise. I cannot think there would be any difficulty in
getting out of Paris, and it is easy to come back by Dieppe or by Havre in
case the Calais and Boulogne ports were crowded. Nothing could be more
safe than to be in the country, either in France or in England. All I should
do would be to write to Lady Phipps, asking her to give Clarissa the tip if
need be.

How indescribably bloody everything is!

Clemmie will be back on February 6.

Desmond Morton to William Strang

(Foreign Office papers: 371/22963)

30 January 1939   Department of Overseas Trade
Secret

I dined with Winston Churchill last night. He tells me that he is seeing the Secretary of State to-day or to-morrow and will tell him the following, amongst other things, but I thought you might also like to have the information.

Winston saw M Léger in Paris last week and the latter told him that they had absolutely sure information of thirty 'convoys of munitions' passing north to south across Czechoslovakia from manufacturing centres in northern Germany to create a large dump in the Ostmark.[1] From this M Léger was inclined to believe that before long there will be a German military demonstration against Hungary and/or Roumania.

My own reaction to this is that it is unfortunate that we do not know more precisely what is meant by a 'convoy of munitions'. If a large dump of shot and shell is being created in the Ostmark from German manufacture, one may assume that it is shot and shell of German types for German guns. Did the dump consist, however, not of munitions but of other sorts of armament stores which might equally be used by the Italians, there is an obvious suggestion alternative to that of M Léger's regarding its purpose.

Next, I suggest that if the dump is not of material which could readily be used by Italian troops—who, as you will remember, have their own types of rifles, guns and so on, which German types of shell will not fit—it is not impossible that it should serve as a base of supply for German troops operating in Italy, but not, of course, against the Italians.

Finally, it is always very possible that this movement of war stores is merely in connection with rearming the ex-Austrian Divisions to the German scale and with German weapons.

These doubtful points might be cleared up were it only possible to have some more precise information about the 'convoys of munitions', but Winston tells me that Léger imparted the information to him in strict confidence, saying that he had not told our Embassy, whence you may feel it to be rather difficult to ask them to clear up the matter.

Yours ever,
D. Morton

---

[1] The German name for Austria, following its annexation to Germany in March 1939.

Charles B. Cochran to Winston S. Churchill

(*Churchill papers: 8/624*)

30 January 1939

Dear Mr Churchill,

As one of many hundreds of thousands of very ordinary citizens may I express my thanks for the very clear exposition of the Italian position in to-day's DT.[1]

I think I speak for my fellows when I say we're apt to get muddled & lose sight of the facts by the nonsense which is so widely distributed by newspapers and radio.

Only sheer gratitude emboldens me to express my insignificant views to you.

Yours sincerely,
Charles B. Cochran

Professor Lindemann to Winston S. Churchill

(*Churchill papers: 25/17*)

Christ Church,
Oxford

30 January 1939

My dear Winston,

I enclose a few notes on the paper anent the necklace scheme. If the Air Ministry had started working on it earlier, so that it could be put into operation at once, it would appear, on their own showing, that we should be safe until the Germans had either developed a machine to shoot it down in daytime or introduced some method of countering it, a matter of one or

---

[1] In an article in the *Daily Telegraph* on 30 January 1939 Churchill wrote: '. . . it is in Spain that Italian blood, money and munitions have been most seriously engaged. The Germans have contented themselves with sending specialists, technicians and aviators, together with masses of war material from their overflowing factories. Mussolini has actually done a large part of General Franco's fighting for him. Italian stocks of munitions of all kinds have been drawn upon heavily, and the burden upon the Italian people has become ever harder for them to bear. During the last year, for the first time, criticism has been rife in the ruling circles of Italian life and politics; and although the repeated submissions of the Western democracies to Dictatorial demands have veiled the movement of forces, there is no doubt that both Italy and her leader are to-day in a condition at once strained and fragile.'

more probably two years, especially the latter plan which would mean re-designing the whole German bombing fleet. Of course, if one takes the line that it is not worth doing anything because the enemy can invent a counter, there is not much to be said. On that principle we might as well not put armour on ships as the enemy can use a bigger gun etc.

I enclose a copy of the letter I sent to Crow[1] to which he has not yet replied. As you will see, a great deal can probably be done with his existing weapon, especially for barrage fire. I think there is something to be said for attacking the propellers if it is really true that they occupy such a large fraction of the span, as we were told when it was desired to prove that attack on the wing was no use as the propeller would cut the wire. It was claimed, you may remember, that 60% of the span was covered by propeller blades. In the calculations in my letter to Crow, I have assumed 40%, so that I have allowed a good margin. Even so the answer seems quite promising.

I need scarcely reiterate that the mines could be discharged very easily from aircraft or even shells. Still, if only one can get experiments of any sort done, it will be a step in the right direction. If they are successful it will be difficult to refuse to consider using some other method of laying the mine-field.

I am looking forward very much to seeing you on Friday. I have to go down to Buckhurst on Saturday afternoon,[2] but if you thought it convenient, I could come back on Sunday for dinner and we could go up to the Committee together on Monday.

I think Chatfield is an improvement on Inskip, but it seems a dreadful confession of failure that no Member of the House of Commons is considered fit to assume the office.[3] Morrison seems to have been thrown to the wolves.[4]

---

[1] Alwyn Douglas Crow, 1894–1965. On active service, 1914–17, (wounded, despatches, OBE). Joined the Proof and Experimental Establishment, Royal Arsenal, 1917; Director of Ballistics Research, 1919–39; Chief Superintendent, Projectile Development, 1939–40; Director and Controller of Projectile Development, 1940–5. Knighted. 1944. Director of Guided Projectiles, Ministry of Supply, 1945–6. Head of Technical Services, Joint Services Mission, Washington, 1946–53.

[2] Speaking at Buckhurst Hill on 1 February 1939, Churchill said: 'There is a spirit of intolerance in some Party circles at the present time, which if not firmly resisted would destroy the quality of the House of Commons. Is it not very odd to see the Executive of the Labour Party trying to discipline their followers into mere delegates, and imitating those very methods of totalitarianism of which they disapprove so much when practised abroad? It will be an ill day for British Parliamentary institutions when Members of Parliament fail to set country before Party' (*Churchill papers: 9/136*).

[3] On 29 January 1939 Lord Chatfield had been appointed Minister for Co-ordination of Defence, in place of Sir Thomas Inskip (who had been holding that office since March 1936). Inskip himself became Secretary of State for the Dominions.

[4] On 29 January 1939 W. S. Morrison had been appointed Chancellor of the Duchy of Lancaster (having previously been since October 1936, Minister of Agriculture and Fisheries).

So far as I can gather, Hitler's speech was not too bad.[1] Let us hope Rome will conform.

Please excuse this hasty screed and believe me, as ever,

Yours,

FAL

[1] Speaking in the Reichstag on 30 January 1939, Hitler defended the annexation of the Sudetenland with the words: 'Germany restored the rights of self-determination to 10 million of her fellow-countrymen in a territory where neither the British nor any other Western nation have any business. By so doing she threatened no one, she merely offered resistance to attempted interference by a third party. And I need not assure you, Gentlemen, that in the future as well we shall not tolerate the Western States' attempting to interfere in certain matters which concern nobody but ourselves in order to hinder natural and reasonable solutions by their intervention.' Later in his speech Hitler declared: 'Our relations with the Western and Northern States, Switzerland, Belgium, Holland, Denmark, Norway, Sweden, Finland, and the Baltic States become all the more satisfactory with the increasing tendency in these countries to turn away from certain articles of the Covenant of the League of Nations which involve danger of war. No country appreciates better than Germany the value of genuinely friendly and neutral States on its frontiers. May Czechoslovakia, too, succeed in re-establishing internal order in a manner which will exclude any possibility of a relapse into the tendencies of the former President, Dr Beneš.' According to the leading article in *The Times* on 31 Janaury 1939, Hitler's speech 'has belied the more nervous prophets. By common consent peace must be the work of deeds, not words; but the words heard last night contain no such invocation to war as some of them had predicted'.

February 1939

Winston S. Churchill to Mortimer Wheeler

(Churchill papers: 8/626)

1 February 1939

I am greatly indebted to you for the care and kindness with which you have examined and commented upon my proofs. I feel so diffident about writing on these unfamiliar topics, that it is a relief to me that you do not find the proofs ridiculous or unworthy.

There was a thing you said to me in the train that I have incorporated on page 4:—'Britain was therefore still joined to Europe when the Pyramids were a-building, and when learned Egyptians were laboriously exploring the ancient ruins of Sakkara.' I am delighted to find that you leave this uncorrected; but it is a staggering statement, most wonderful, and hitherto undreamed of. Is there a controversy about it, or is it admitted now?

There are one or two general issues which I should like very much to discuss with you. I wonder whether you could come down to dine and sleep the night of Friday the 3rd? It is only about forty minutes from Victoria to Oxted. I could meet you at Oxted, and there are excellent trains in the morning to take you to your work. Professor Lindemann will be my only other guest, and I am sure you would find his conversation very stimulating. Pray let your secretary telephone on receipt of this, to let me know.

I enclose a cheque for the honorarium I ventured to suggest to you in my earlier letter.

Peter K. Peirson[1] to Winston S. Churchill

(Churchill papers: 2/357)

[1][2] February 1939   Brno,
                                                            Czechoslovakia

As you see from my address, I am no longer in Prague, having been sent on from there to the English Institute here. Brno is not at all like Prague. Here I am in Moravia, and the people are not such true Czechs as those in the capital city, which is extremely nationalist. Here, too, we are nearer the German frontier, and German influence is far more dominating. The population is at present reckoned to be between 40% and 60% German, owing partly to the huge influx of Jews.[3] . . .

. . . The English Institute has now 2,011 pupils and a staff of little over a dozen English, Czech and German teachers. The numbers are so high because there are so many people wishing to leave the country and go to England, America and the Colonies. When I get to know some of them better, I may be able to tell you some more exact information from divers sources. Already I have met and made friends with all types and nationalities among the inhabitants. . . .

Among the Czechs the prevailing feeling, as far as I have been able to discern (and they speak very freely to me), is not what people in England might expect. Of course, they hated and still hate Munich. They bear no grudge against England, but they do blame France. Here is the gist of various conversations that I have had with them: 'Hitler! Well, what can you expect,—an upstart from the gutter! It is not surprising. But Mr Chamberlain and Lord Halifax are gentlemen.' They say this with only a touch of sarcasm and a shrug of the shoulder. They consider that England has lost its battle for freedom and democracy before ever it has begun, out here in Czechoslovakia. The British Government, they consider, are blind fools, their policy sheer

---

[1] Peter Kenneth Peirson, 1916–   . The son of a Chartered Accountant. Educated at Berkhamsted School and Worcester College, Oxford. Graduated in English, 1937. Published a book of poems, *First Fruits*, in 1937. Worked in accountancy in the City of London, 1937–8. A teacher at the English Institute, Brno, January–July 1939. Reserve of Officers, 1938 (but not called up, despite volunteering twice after the outbreak of war). Joined the Local Defence Volunteers (Home Guard), 1939. Conscripted into the Pioneer Corps, August 1940; commissioned 1942; served in Egypt and Palestine. Diploma of Education, 1948. A teacher at Bridgnorth Grammar School, 1948–53. Studied at Lichfield Theological College, 1954, and ordained. Subsequently Curate at Coseley, Cannock, Friern Barnet and Kenton. Vicar, St John the Divine, Stamford Hill, 1961; St Martin, Edmonton, 1964. Rector, Preston with Ridlington and Wing with Pilton (Rutland), 1977.

[2] This letter is undated. Kathleen Hill replied to Peter Peirson on 9 February 1939: 'My friend read it with attention and found it very interesting' (*Churchill papers: 2/357*).

[3] For a 'correction' to this figure, see Peter Peirson's next letter of 11 February 1939 (quoted on page 1367).

madness. Nevertheless, they accept their fate philosophically and even make light of it with a laugh! If a war comes now, they say, it will not touch Czechoslovakia; and for that they are thankful. They imply politely that they don't care a hang what happens to England and France. I feel that it would take a lot to make them fight for democracy again, having already lost so much by it. However, you, Sir, are highly respected here, and some people think that there is still hope for democracy, a distant gleam, if you were to come into power. 'If Mr Churchill and Mr Eden had been in power last year, this would never have happened,' some of them say; but they don't like to dwell on the past. Yet some stirring event, such as the sudden fall of Hitler, might rouse again their national spirit.

But each day that passes makes the situation worse. Each day the Germans (the Nazis) are taking a bit more power. There have always been Germans here, but not always Nazis. Last week they were officially allowed to show the swastika flag on public buildings; they wear badges, green-corded black hats and white stockings, none of which were seen before October of last year, when they announced that Hitler was going to occupy Brunn. Everywhere the Nazi salute and 'Heil Hitler' are to be found, with pictures of the Fuehrer in the German restaurants, which have often become the headquarters of subversive political clubs. Bookshops, too, have been opened, in which there is nothing but Nazi literature. And the Germans are becoming somewhat arrogant at times, with their Deutsches Haus dominating the city. But they may not 'return' to the Reich, from which they never came; they are forbidden to go to Germany; Hitler must have his strong minority still in the country.

The amputation of Czechoslovakia has made everybody poor. They have lost nearly all the mineral wealth of the country, and industry is almost at a standstill. They are dependent on Germany for practically everything for their existence. And still they smile. But more than once, when speaking German in a Czech shop, I have been very coldly served; but if I have mentioned that I am English, then they cannot do enough for me. The large Jewish population is in a very uncertain position, and I am frequently asked what are the prospects in England for a job. But I can't tell them. The refugee problem everywhere will continue to be acute for a very long time, I think. And every person, of whatever nationality, is continually asking me what is the public opinion in England. Is the country behind Mr Chamberlain? Did the people approve of Munich? I can only answer (to the non-Nazis) that I don't think so and am sure that there is a vast majority who would support a new party under you leadership.

I have explained time and again that we were absolutely helpless to lift a hand to aid this country, for Parliament was not even called at the right time, and when it was called it was only to announce the end of the crisis and of Czechoslovakia as a free, democratic republic. Of course, I have told them that this is only my personal opinion, but that I base my opinion upon fact and observation. And they are very relieved that it was not the whole people of England who deserted and betrayed them in their hour of need. In England the results of Munich seemed heartrending enough, but here, if one can get beneath the skin of the people's stoicism, they are stark and mortal. The country is bankrupt and denuded; the people have lost their national pride and their freedom. You can see it in their faces and in their actions,— but I'm afraid I can't give you any tangible evidence. Later I may be able to do so, when I get into the confidence of more people. . . .

There is one matter of interest that I might mention. I stopped for five hours in Dresden on the way here; there I got into conversation with some Germans; they were extremely pro-British and were very critical of Hitler's policy; I gathered from them that he has not the widespread support in Germany which is generally credited to him. But doubtless you already know this.

I am certain that you have a huge following in England, and I wish you every success in all your enterprises for the betterment of democracy. I am only sorry that this letter has not been as informative as I had hoped.

Your obedient servant,
P. K. Peirson

Lord Perth[1] to Lord Halifax: telegram
(*Foreign Office papers: 371/23784*)

2 February 1939   Rome

Dr Gayda,[2] in this evening's press, sharply takes Mr Churchill to task for his article in the 'Daily Telegraph' of January 30th, which he holds up as proof that the Prime Minister's policy of 'good will and loyalty' is not the general expression of British views today. He describes the article as 'a typical document of that agitation with which the party of the incendiary firemen is trying hard to push the civilised world towards war. . . .'

[1] James Eric Drummond, 1876–1951. Entered the Foreign Office, 1900; Private Secretary to Sir Edward Grey, 1915–16, and to A. J. Balfour, 1916–18. Knighted, 1916. Attached to the British Delegation at the Paris Peace Conference, 1919. Secretary-General of the League of Nations, 1919–33. British Ambassador in Rome, 1933–9. Succeeded his half-brother as 16th Earl of Perth, 1937. Deputy Leader of the Liberal Party in the House of Lords, 1947.
[2] Virginio Gayda, 1885–1944. An Italian diplomat, who subsequently joined the Fascist Party. Editor of the *Giornale d'Italia* from 1926 until his death. Notorious for his attacks on the democracies, and in particular on Britain. Known outside Italy as 'Mussolini's mouthpiece'. Killed in an American air-raid on Rome, 14 March 1944.

Gayda refutes the point made by Churchill and says that Italo-German solidarity is not the result of a bargain; it means recognition of the Italian rights denied by the democracies, assistance if these rights are not satisfied, and ready cooperation in every eventuality.[1]

Winston S. Churchill to Sir Archibald Sinclair

(Churchill papers: 2/357)

3 February 1939

Many thanks for sending me your correspondence with Domvile,[2] and I am much obliged to you for standing up for me. I have certainly, to the best of my recollection, never referred to Hitler as a gangster, though I might easily have done so with great truth. If you think it worth while to use more powder and shot upon him, you should ask him for his references.

LG, dining with me the other night, said he thought your last speech was the most powerful he had ever heard you deliver. He spoke with deep appreciation of your work. He thought the peroration was a little bit dragged in, instead of arising naturally out of it, but he was remarkably impressed by the cogency and solidity of your argument, and also by its delivery. I thought you would like to know this.

Winston S. Churchill to Lord Halifax

(Churchill papers: 2/357)

3 February 1939

I send you the list of acceptances to date. You will see that though the gathering is not numerous, it is representative.

You may be sure of the most cordial welcome on personal grounds, and I even think that on the great issues we may be coming closer together.

[1] A Foreign Office minute, by Andrew Napier Noble, commented on Gayda's complaint: 'An attempt to suggest that the wolf is threatened by the big bad lamb.'

[2] Barry Edward Domvile, 1878–1971. Entered the Royal Navy as a Cadet, 1892. Lieutenant, 1898. Assistant-Secretary, Committee of Imperial Defence, 1912–14. On active service, 1914–19 (Captain, 1916; CMG). Director of Plans Division, Admiralty, 1920–2. Chief of Staff, Mediterranean, 1922–5. Commanded HMS *Royal Sovereign*, 1925–6. Director of Naval Intelligence Division, 1927–30. Vice-Admiral Commanding the Third Cruiser Squadron, Mediterranean, 1931–2. President, Royal Naval College, Greenwich, and Vice-Admiral Commanding War College, 1932–4. Knighted, 1934. Admiral, retired list, 1936. In his book *By and Large*, published in 1935, he wrote, of Nazi persecution of the Jews: 'Because we ourselves are tolerant of the aliens and Jews in our midst to the point of stupidity, there is no reason for our being so intolerant of the policy of others'. An active member of the Anglo-German Fellowship, 1936–9, he argued that there was a community of interest between Britain and Nazi Germany. One of his two sons was killed in action in 1941.

Winston S. Churchill to Lord Beaverbrook

(*Beaverbrook papers*)

5 February 1939   Chartwell
Private

My dear Max,

I was surprised to read the paragraphs about Epping in the Sunday Express. They are misleading as to the true state of affairs; & certainly most unhelpful to me.[1] I thought that although we differed on public policy, you were not desirous of assailing me personally or locally. I am therefore all the more sorry that you shd do so.

Yours vy sincerely,
Winston S C

Winston S. Churchill to Sir Alexander Cadogan

(*Churchill papers: 8/645*)

5 February 1939

Perhaps you would be so kind as to allow your South-Eastern Department to look at what I have said in this article about Yugoslavia. I don't expect there will be much to alter, but I am always anxious to know the Foreign Office view before sending out these widely-printed articles. Any general comments also would be welcome. Naturally I alone am responsible for what is ultimately said.[2]

---

[1] An item in Cross-Bencher's 'Politicians and Politics' column in the *Sunday Express* of 5 February 1939 read: 'Now that his own problems are over Sandys can perhaps spare a tear for the troubles of his father-in-law, Winston Churchill, in Epping. Trouble is being made for Churchill there. The campaign is strong, the campaigners determined. Strongest, most determined of them all is Mr C. N. Thornton-Kemsley, a chartered surveyor, a public figure of note, a member of Mr Churchill's executive. I rang him up and asked about his campaign. This is what he said: "Many of the branch associations in the division are in practically open revolt against the member. They demand a candidate who will support the Prime Minister and the National Government in place of a member who while he does not hesitate to shelter under the goodwill attaching to the name of a great party, constantly and almost, it seems, inevitably criticizes the policy and actions of the party's leader. My own view is that the House of Commons should not be deprived of Mr Churchill's services. So long as he has the Government whips and the support of the majority of his Central Council I would hesitate to split the vote by recommending an unofficial Conservative candidate against him." '

[2] In an article published in the *Daily Telegraph* on 9 February 1939, Churchill commented on the resignation that week of the Yugoslav Prime Minister, Stoyadinovitch, writing, of Yugoslavia: 'This large, powerful, virile country, with its warlike population and inferior equipment, watches with acute anxiety the movements of the two Dictator Powers upon its borders. The sudden fall of the Stoyadinovitch regime is due to forces hard to measure. At the root of it, however, lies the question of national defence. So bitter is the discontent of the

I shall be in London to-morrow evening, so if this copy is returned to: 11 Morpeth Mansions, Victoria, before dinner, there will be time to telegraph any necessary corrections before the foreign circulation is made.

Committee of Imperial Defence Sub-Committee on Air Defence Research: minutes[1]

(*Churchill papers: 25/18*)

6 February 1939
11.30 am
To Be Kept Under Lock and Key

It is requested that special care may be taken to ensure the secrecy of this Document

THE SUB-COMMITTEE agreed—

(a) to note that the Air Ministry (after consultation with Sir Henry Tizard's Committee) are of the opinion that, in view of the difficult technical problems involved, a 35,000 ft armed balloon barrage

---

Croats with the present structure and system of the Yugoslav Government that it would not be possible to mobilise the soldiers of Croatia. These indeed, would fight with a good heart for the defence of their country, but once arms were placed in the hands of this sturdy and trained peasantry, it is more than probable they would be used for the purposes of establishing a federal Constitution for the Kingdom of the Serbs, Croats and Slovenes. Evidently the need of basing the government of Prince Paul broadly upon the whole State has produced an internal spasm of resolve. Only by the ruling Serbs making common cause with the rest of the kingdom can its full strength, security and integrity be realised. Dr Stoyadinovitch was markedly pro-German, and to some extent pro-Nazi, in his policy. He was one of those European statesmen who found in the Munich Agreement and the fate of Czechoslovakia a vindication of the course he had pursued. His government had always believed that France would abandon the Czechoslovak Republic, and on the morrow of that event his opponents who had wished to associate themselves with the interests of the Western democracies appeared utterly confounded. We may judge, therefore, from his resignation that the stresses internal and external of Yugoslavia have reached a point where national self-preservation seems to be involved. It is idle to forecast the future course of events in these grim regions. One can only say that the stronger and more united are the three races who of their own free will became one State, the better for the peace of the Balkans and of the Danube Valley; and for larger causes as well.'

[1] The members of the Sub-Committee present at this meeting were Sir Kingsley Wood (in the Chair), Sir Thomas Inskip, W. S. Morrison (Chancellor of the Duchy of Lancaster), Leslie Hore-Belisha, Churchill, Sir Warren Fisher (Secretary to the Treasury), General Sir Hugh Elles, Lieutenant-General Sir Maurice Taylor (Deputy Master-General of the Ordnance, War Office), Sir Frank Smith, Sir Henry Tizard, Wing-Commander E. J. Hodsoll (Inspector-General, Air Raid Precautions Department, Home Office), Professor A. V. Hill (Secretary of the Royal Society), Professor Lindemann, Rear-Admiral F. T. B. Tower (Director of Naval Equipment) and Group Captain D. F. Stevenson (Deputy Director of Operations, Air Ministry).

could not be developed for some years, by which time they consider that the strategic value of such a barrage would not justify its very high cost, particularly in the light of the probable development of devices for detecting and cutting the balloon cables.

(b) that despite the opinion of the Air Ministry expressed in (a) above, further consideration should be given to the possibility of extending the experiments with balloons and kites, mentioned in paragraph 7 of Paper No ADR 130, with a view to assessing the practicability of raising an armed balloon cable to 35,000 feet in one hour.

(c) that, in view of the doubts expressed by Mr Churchill and Professor Lindemann on certain points in Paper No ADR 130, they should be given the opportunity of discussing these points, and also the question raised in (b) above, with Sir Henry Tizard and Mr Pye.[1]

Lord Halifax to Winston S. Churchill

(*Churchill papers: 2/357*)

6 February 1939   Foreign Office

My Dear Winston,

Thank you very much for your letter of the 3rd February enclosing a list of the acceptances to the luncheon on the 9th February. Despite your assurances I feel more than a little scared. However, if the critics really start to get at me I shall look to you for support.

Yours ever,

E

Winston S. Churchill to Sir Kingsley Wood

(*Churchill papers: 2/371*)

7 February 1939

I shall be in London Thursday afternoon (9th), and should like very much to come to Berkeley Square to see your graphs.

Would five o'clock be convenient?

---

[1] David Randall Pye, 1886–1960. Lecturer in Engineering Science, Oxford University, 1909–14. Experimental Officer, Royal Flying Corps, 1915; Royal Air Force, 1918. Lecturer in Engineering, Cambridge University, 1919–25. Deputy Director of Scientific Research, Air Ministry, 1925–37; Director, 1937–43. Member of the Aeronautical Research Council, 1943–6. Knighted, 1952.

Sir Kingsley Wood to Winston S. Churchill

(*Churchill papers: 2/371*)

8 February 1939   Air Ministry
Secret

My dear Winston,

I am delighted to hear that you can come and see the graphs at Berkeley Square House tomorrow.

I am arranging for Sir Wilfrid Freeman, the Air Member for Development and Production to be available, and Edward Campbell[1] will meet you at the door.

Sincerely,
Kingsley Wood

Peter K. Peirson to Kathleen Hill

(*Churchill papers: 2/357*)

11 February 1939   Brno,
                                                         Czechoslovakia

I have since found out that my figures were quite incorrect. I checked them up and found that 40% to 60% should be at the most 15%. I discovered also that my source of information was not friendly and was deliberately intended to mislead me, though not in the way that was imagined. There seems to be quite a lot of pro-German propaganda here coming from quite unexpected sources. There is an Englishman here who is undoubtedly pro-Nazi, though he would vigorously deny it if he were taxed with it. He doesn't conceal his intentions well enough, but his influence is decidedly bad. 'All Jews should be thrown into the sea and drowned.' 'Roosevelt is a pathological case; he is demented because of his deformity.' 'Streicher is the sanest and fittest man in Germany!' Such Nazi slogans are repeated in the typical Nazi manner of propaganda whenever he imagines that he has an obedient audience. It is dangerous if Czechs think that Englishmen are pro-Hitler, for there are not

---

[1] Edward Taswell Campbell, 1879–1945. Served as a private in the army, 1895–9. A tobacco planter in Sumatra, 1900–21. British Vice-Consul, Sumatra, 1914–20 (and acting French Consul). Conservative MP for North West Camberwell, 1924–9; for Bromley from 1930 until his death. Private Secretary to Sir Kingsley Wood (when Postmaster General, Minister of Health, Secretary of State for Air, Lord Privy Seal and Chancellor of the Exchequer), 1931–43. Knighted, 1933. Created Baronet, 1939. Chairman of the Royal National College for the Blind, and of the Anglo-Netherlands Society. The third of his three sons, a Flight Lieutenant, was killed on active service in December 1942.

many of us here, and we are constantly being asked our and England's opinion on foreign politics.

I have been doing my best to combat such erroneous impressions. I have let it be known among the Czechs I have met that I do not support Mr Chamberlain. I have now gained the real confidence of one or two who are intelligent thinkers, the sort of men who would take an active part in helping their country to regain her lost freedom if the opportunity arose.

They said to me in English: 'Tell your friends in England that we grind our teeth and have clenched hands in our pockets.' They are bitterly resentful and are waiting eagerly, patriotically for the chance that they are sure will come to them. They distrust every German and insist that they are spies; which may be true in a sense, for the Germans always have their ears open for any scrap of political conversation among the Czechs. There are bitter words about the unfair delineation of the new frontier. Whole Czech towns (90% and over) have been taken by Germany merely for economical reasons. Even Brno was nearly taken and it was impossible to travel from here to Prague direct at one time. There are only 250,000 Germans left in Czechoslovakia, which is a good thing; but there are now 1,000,000 Czechs in Germany—and I know that they are being oppressed.

The Czech government have to do what they are told, but they don't like it. The people realize this, but they do not blame the government at all. They know that the government will do the right thing at the right time and have implicit trust in them. The situation in Jugoslavia is creating great interest here. There are three things that the people here are anxiously hoping for: a democratic victory in Jugoslavia; a change of government in Great Britain; and a revolution in Germany. Are any of these things possible or likely? We simply cannot tell here, on account of the meagre news that we receive. I haven't seen the English papers to-day yet; there was two days ago an open letter in the once liberal Czech paper to Mr Attlee: large portions of the letter were left blank because of the censorship.

Meanwhile life is not unpleasant, as there is still a certain amount of free speech and unhampered private life among the inhabitants. Unfortunately I cannot tell you about the situation in Prague, where everything is quite different and feelings run much higher. But I may hear of something later on. I would like to settle down here for a time, provided that Czechoslovakia does not become completely a vassal state of Germany, for Brno is a pleasant town and work here is on the whole very congenial. If only the situation were clearer! I wonder if you could tell me what are the possibilities of Great Britain being dragged into a war,—or any other European country for that matter, as it does make such a difference to one's peace of mind. I should like to know if I can settle down here for a time with the assurance that my life will not be disturbed by a political upheaval which would force me to leave the country.

For the moment, then, I will say good-bye. Please give my very kindest regards and warmest good wishes to your friend and thank him for his interest.

Your obedient servant,
P. K. Peirson

Sir James Hawkey to Winston S. Churchill

(*Churchill papers: 7/56*)

13 February 1939

Dear Mr Churchill:

Thank you for sending on Lord Beaverbrook's letter. I cannot agree with him that the undue prominence given to Thornton-Kemsley, who was described as a well-known figure of public note, etc, in the paragraphs, was not positively unfriendly to you. It certainly has not deterred him in his attacks upon you in the Division which have since the article appeared been more intense than before. I am afraid I have not the copy of the 'Sunday Express' but I do not recall any pledge of Kemsley's that he would not attack you as long as you have the Government Whip. I am glad that Lord Beaverbrook gives an assurance that he will help you in Epping.

With Dinah, I went out to see Sir Harry Goschen yesterday afternoon, as Lady Goschen[1] had written me a very strong letter again asking that Sir Harry should not be persuaded to be re-elected as Chairman of the Association. I had a long chat with Goschen and Douglas-Pennant, who was most useful, and Sir Harry gave me a positive assurance that he would stand with me for re-election. Mrs Douglas-Pennant,[2] who—as you may remember—was most vehement in her attacks on Chamberlain at the time of the Harlow meeting, has unfortunately gone over completely to the enemy.

Dinah is seeing Mrs Churchill tomorrow and will give her a full account of the present situation in the Division.

Believe me to be,
Faithfully yours,
A. James Hawkey

[1] Christian Grant, daughter of Colonel James Augustus Grant, CB, CSI, of Househill, Nairn. She married Sir Harry Goschen in 1893.

[2] Christian Eleanor Margaret Goschen, only daughter of Sir Harry and Lady Goschen. She married Claud Douglas-Pennant in 1922. For many years she was Commandant of the local detachment of the Red Cross.

Winston S. Churchill to Harcourt Johnstone
(*Churchill papers: 1/343*)

14 February 1939

It is kind of you to give me these opportunities of meeting Professor Robin,[1] and you know with what pleasure I would dine with you. But it is absolutely necessary for me to be in the country every possible night this year, in order to complete the history I am writing. Unless I can get three or four nights by myself down here, there is no chance of doing what I have set myself.

I am accordingly refusing practically everything, and I hope, therefore, you will excuse me.

Winston S. Churchill to Daisy Fellowes
(*Churchill papers: 1/343*)

15 February 1939

I think we are approaching the show-down, but there is certainly more confidence and resolution here than before. Bonnet continues to puzzle us. We have lovely sunshine here, and as mild as May.

Winston S. Churchill to Brigadier-General Spears
(*Churchill papers: 8/624*)

15 February 1939

Thank you so much for your letter and for your invitation to speak at Carlisle. It would give me great pleasure to accept, but it is absolutely necessary for me to be in the country every possible night this year, in order to complete the history I am writing.

I am accordingly refusing practically everything, and I hope therefore you will excuse me.

[1] Professor Robin died in June 1951. His obituary was published in *The Times* on 27 June 1951, but only in the 5 star edition. I have been unable to locate a copy of this edition, or to find out any other information about Professor Robin.

Winston S. Churchill to Lord Halifax

(Churchill papers: 2/357)

15 February 1939

I asked, as you suggested, the Prof to write me a note on broadcasting for propaganda purposes into Germany. I enclose what he has written. I asked him to avoid undue technicalities.

It was nice of you to come to luncheon the other day, and I am sure your speech, and the frank talk which followed did good.

Professor Lindemann: note for Winston S. Churchill

(Churchill papers: 2/357)

15 February 1939

Every wireless sending station operates on a definite wave-length. Only stations 'tuned' to that particular wave-length can receive the message. If two stations are operating simultaneously on wave-lengths which are nearly equal, they are both apt to be picked up and to disturb one another. During a pause in a programme such interference (heterodyning) occurs if the wave-lengths are close together, but *not* if they are exactly equal.

To avoid difficulties of this nature, all stations have agreed, under an international convention, to confine their emissions to specified wave-lengths. The observance of this convention, admirable, of course, in normal times, seems to have become a fetish with the BBC. It will certainly not be permitted to interfere with our enemies' activities in time of crisis or war. We ought not to allow it to hamper us.

As an example of undue scruples of this nature one may instance the reluctance of our authorities to jam the Bari broadcasts. This could have been done at trivial expense and trouble by a station in Palestine. Even an X-ray outfit in a hospital, suitably adapted, would have sufficed, if one preferred to avoid official intervention. Yet the BBC apparently disapproved.

In case of war or crisis it will be essential to prevent so far as possible interference with our own broadcasts and to have means of communicating with the German people.

To avoid this latter the German government have put on the market sets only capable of receiving on the German wave-lengths. It is believed that the vast majority of German sets are of this type. To reach their owners it will therefore be necessary to send on German wave-lengths, if necessary confining one's comments to pauses in their programmes.

It appears that preparations for war conditions are not adequate at Broadcasting House. It is suggested:

(1) That the BBC should maintain at least two or three spare senders in London in case the existing one is damaged whether by accident or design. It may be important to change one's wave-length, a matter of some hours, even if only to avoid enemy jamming. In an emergency a temporary interruption of the radio might be very serious.

(2) The BBC should be prepared to send messages on the most important German wave-lengths. To avoid heterodyning the carrier wave must be made to conform accurately to the German wave. There are various ways of doing this, without great technical difficulty, if preparations are made in advance.

(3) The BBC should have plans to emit on different wave-lengths should jamming become insupportable or in case new foreign stations came into use.

James Woodward and Sons[1] *to Kathleen Hill*

(*Churchill papers: 1/351*)

16 February 1939

Madam,

We are in receipt of your letter dated January 31st and Mr Winston Churchill's guns arrived here on the 14th inst.

We have examined the guns, and we find to put them into good order the following work is necessary to be done to them.

Fit new trigger blade to single trigger mechanism of No 2 gun.

Fit new cross pins & re-joint 2 pairs of barrels (At present the barrels are very loose in the actions due to fair wear & tear).

Strip, clean & re-oil the entire mechanism of both guns.

The cost of this work will be £6-15/- net, and we shall await your instructions before putting the same in hand.[2]

---

[1] James Woodward & Sons, Gun and Rifle Manufactory, of 29 Bury Street, St James's, London. On receipt of this letter Churchill instructed Kathleen Hill: 'Yes; do so.'

[2] On 6 March 1939 Kathleen Hill wrote to the Commissioner of Police of the Metropolis (Special Branch): 'I am directed by Mr Winston Churchill to send you two further threatening letters which he has received this morning' (*Churchill papers: 1/351*).

Winston S. Churchill to G. M. Young[1]
(Churchill papers: 8/626)

17 February 1939

I asked Eddie Marsh to give me an introduction to you and I daresay you have heard from him by now. Some months ago I read with the greatest pleasure your all too flattering appreciation of some of my speeches and writings in the London Mercury.[2]

But I now have been delighted by your brilliant essay on Charles and Cromwell. I have certainly not read anything on the period which gave me such a clear view of the two years in question. I venture to quote several of your remarks, of course with fitting acknowledgements, in the History of the English-Speaking Peoples which I am writing now. I can only spare about thirty-five thousand words for the Great Rebellion, and I wondered whether you would be willing to read the proof for me in an incomplete and un-revised condition. It will soon all be in printed proof.

I should very much like to have a talk with you about this period, with which I am beginning to become acquainted, and perhaps you would be so kind as to lunch and dine with me one day in the next few weeks.

I particularly like your criticism of Gardiner's smug and biased history. How much finer is Ranke!

Sir Nevile Henderson to Lord Halifax
(Foreign Office papers: 371/22965)

18 February 1939   Berlin

I said[3] that I thought that he could have his rest without uneasiness as I did not believe in any immediate serious international trouble unless Italy made it.

General Goering at once replied that he wished that he was as confident as I was. What guarantee had Germany that Mr Chamberlain would remain

---

[1] George Malcolm Young, 1882–1959. Educated at St Paul's School and Balliol College, Oxford. British Mission to Petrograd, 1916–17. CB, 1917. Fellow of All Souls College, Oxford. Historian, he published his first book, on Gibbon, in 1932; his biography of Stanley Baldwin in 1952. A Trustee of the National Portrait Gallery, 1937–59 and Member of the Standing Commission on Museums and Galleries, 1938–59.

[2] In an eight-page review of *Arms and the Covenant*, published in the August 1938 issue of *The London Mercury*, and entitled 'The Oratory of Winston Churchill', G. M. Young wrote: 'The remarkable position to which Mr Churchill has in these last years attained in the House of Commons is a good example of the power of what I have called coherence: on the subjects with which he is particularly conversant, on Foreign Policy and Defence, all his ideas stand in a systematic relationship with each other.' Young also noted Churchill's 'picturesque banter with a tang in it', a device, he commented, 'which hardly ever fails to make an English audience happy, and therefore willing to listen'.

[3] In conversation with General Goering.

in office and that he would not be succeeded by 'a Mr Churchill or a Mr Eden' Government? That was Germany's main preoccupation. . . .

But what was the meaning of the vast sums of money for British rearmament? There were two explanations: either, he said, England sought to render her position unassailable by her preparations for defence, or she intended to use her armaments when completed, for a preventative war on Germany . . . many people believe that the second alternative would be the one followed if anything happen to Mr Chamberlain. . . .

I urged him moreover to realise that the policy of a preventative war, attributed to some British politicians, carried no weight at all with the great mass of British public opinion or had any influence except with a section of the intelligentsia and of London opinion as distinct from the Country.

Neville Chamberlain to his sister
(Templewood papers)

19 February 1939　　　　　　　　　　　　　　　　　　Chequers

. . . Although I see that Roosevelt is cutting short his holidays on account of disturbing rumours about the intentions of the autocracies, & though I am rather glad he is doing so, I myself am going about with a lighter heart than I have had for many a long day. All the information I get seems to point in the direction of peace & I repeat once more that I believe we have at last got on top of the dictators. Of course that doesn't mean that I want to bully them as they have tried to bully us; on the contrary I think they have had good cause to ask for consideration of their grievances, & if they had asked nicely after I appeared on the scene they might already have got some satisfaction.

Now it will take some time before the atmosphere is right but things are moving in the direction I want.

You may remember that in my B'ham speech I said it was time someone else made a contribution. Thereafter Hitler altered his speech at the last moment & made it more pacific. . . .

I think we ought to be able to establish excellent relations with Franco who seems well disposed to us, & then, if the Italians are not in too bad a temper we might get Franco-Italian conversations going & if they were reasonably amicable we might advance towards disarmament. At any rate that's how I see things working round, & if I were given three or four more years I believe I really might retire with a quiet mind. . . .

In his Reichstag speech of Jan 30th the Führer gave an indication of the lines which Anglo-German relations might follow. He said 'It would be fortunate for the whole world if our two peoples could cooperate in full confidence with one another.' These words of the Führer were all the more impressive because they were spoken at the end of a year which was full of international tension & crises, yet that year found solutions for problems which seemed almost insuperable. Special mention should be made of the fact that the course of the great historical events brought about for the first time personal contact between the head of British policy & the leader of the German Reich. All of us who have at heart the existence of close friendly relations between Germany & England, hope therefrom for a further clari-fication of international relations, & are convinced that a new & fruitful element for cooperation between the nations has been established. The speech then goes on to welcome the Anglo-German coal agreement recently con-cluded & the prospects of further industrial negotiations between the 2 countries which it says 'we shall follow with deepest interest'.[1]

Harold Nicolson: diary

(*Nicolson papers*)

20 February 1939

I have a talk with Winston and Amery. The latter suggests the danger of an Italian raid on Khartoum. Winston says that this may happen but the essential thing is to drive the Italian ships out of the Mediterranean. That would only take six weeks. He is quite happy about our own forces there.

---

[1] In their accounts of Hitler's Reichstag speech of 30 January 1939, neither Neville Chamberlain nor Professor Lindemann (see page 1358), made any reference to Hitler's declaration that: 'In the course of my life I have very often been a prophet, and have usually been ridiculed for it. During the time of my struggle for power it was in the first instance the Jewish race which only received my prophecies with laughter when I said that I would one day take over the leadership of the State, and with it that of the whole nation, and that I would then among many other things settle the Jewish problem. Their laughter was uproarious, but I think that for some time now they have been laughing on the other side of their face. To-day I will once more be a prophet: If the international Jewish financiers in and outside Europe succeed in plunging the nations once more into a world war, then the result will not be the bolshevization of the earth, and thus the victory of Jewry, but the annihilation of the Jewish race in Europe!' (Authorised English translation, published in pamphlet form, Berlin, February 1939). Only the *Manchester Guardian* gave this quotation in its report of the speech, but translated the word *vernichtung* (annihilation) as 'destruction'. The *News Chronicle* and the *Yorkshire Post* both claimed to have published the speech in full, but both omitted this quo-tation. The *Daily Telegraph* also made no reference to it, but did quote the passage: 'The Jewish race will have to adapt itself to sound, constructive activity, as others do, or soon it will succumb to a crisis of an unbelievable magnitude'.

Winston S. Churchill to F. W. Ogilvie[1]

(*Churchill papers: 2/382*)

21 February 1939

I read with interest in the newspapers your new plan for monthly discussions between official representatives of the three Parties; but ought you
not to make some provision for public men who have held high office, and
who are not likely to be chosen as the spokesmen of those Parties? Ought
there not in such a forum to be room for independent opinions expressed by
those who may be called 'elder statesmen'?

For instance, it is quite possible under the present plan that Mr Eden,
Mr Duff Cooper, Lord Cecil, Lord Horne, Mr Amery and myself, Mr Lloyd
George, Sir Stafford Cripps and Mr Lansbury would none of them have any
access to the microphone, yet it may be thought that they have a contribution
to make which would be of value, and that large numbers of your listeners
would like to hear what they have to say. The idea that no public men not
nominated by Party Whips should be allowed to speak on the radio is not
defensible in public policy.

I would suggest that your Council might be asked to consider whether a
Panel might not be formed from which one independent speaker, not chosen
by the Whips, should be selected in each month.

As you touched upon this view with sympathy when we met a few weeks
ago at dinner, I venture to write to you personally before making public
comment.

Harold Nicolson: diary

(*Nicolson papers*)

21 February 1939

The Prime Minister speaks on the Defence Bill. He has the whole House
with him and could have made the sort of speech which would have
impressed and satisfied everybody. Such, however, is his desire to score off,

---

[1] Frederick Wolff Ogilvie, 1893–1949. Born in Chile, the son of a British engineer. Educated
at Clifton and Balliol College, Oxford. On active service, 1914–18; severely wounded at Hill
60, as a result of which he lost his left arm. Demobilized with the rank of Captain, 1919.
Lecturer in Economics, Trinity College, Oxford, 1920–6. Professor of Political Economy,
Edinburgh, 1926–34. Principal and Vice-Chancellor, Queen's University, Belfast, 1934–8.
Director-General of the BBC (in succession to Lord Reith), 1938–42. Knighted, 1942. Served
with the British Council, 1942–4. Principal of Jesus College, Oxford, from 1944 until his
death.

that he embarked upon a mean and jeering attack upon the League of Nations. Winston Churchill was able to take him up on this and made a very excellent speech.[1]

Sir Henry Strakosch to Winston S. Churchill

(*Churchill papers: 2/374*)

22 February 1939
Personal

My dear Winston,

Here is the paper on Germany's Expenditure on Armaments of which I spoke to you this morning, and a copy of which I sent last night to John Simon.

The conclusion reached is that, in the fiscal year 1938/39, Germany has spent, directly and indirectly, on Armaments a sum of money equal, in our currency, to £1,176 millions. You will, of course, understand that this figure must be regarded merely as indicating the order of magnitude of Germany's expenditure, and does not pretend to be an exact estimate. Nevertheless, I believe the figure to be pretty near the mark, for it has been built up from various German statistical and other publications and inferences drawn from them.

I made a similar estimate in the Autumn of 1937, covering the period 1936/37. The figures which have become available since then go to confirm that that earlier estimate was near the mark.

It is interesting to calculate the relative burdens of Armaments in relation to the National Income of this country and Germany. I enclose a note on this matter, from which you will see that our Armaments expenditure in 1938 absorbed, roughly speaking, 9% of our National Income, and that in the fiscal year 1939 that percentage is raised to 12%. Germany, on the other hand, in the year 1938, devoted 26% of her National Income to Armaments, and will probably do the same in 1939. That gives a broad picture of the magnitude of the burden on the community, and therefore on its standard

---

[1] On 21 February 1939, during the Debate on the Defence Loan, Churchill criticized Chamberlain for Chamberlain's remarks about the failure of collective security and the League of Nations. 'I hope he will make it clear,' Churchill said, 'that it was in no spirit of airy satisfaction that he referred to the undoubted downfall of so many hopes and ideals which the Government had encouraged.' But the rest of Churchill's speech was favourable to the Government, promising his support in 'the very great exertions' which the Government were making for defence.

of life, in the two countries. It also indicates our superiority in staying power in this wicked Armaments race.

I look forward very much to your lunching here one day next week. . . .

Winston S. Churchill to Desmond Flower [1]
(*Churchill papers: 8/626*)

22 February 1939

The afternoon of either Monday 6th, or Wednesday 8th of March, would be convenient for me, but in view of Parliamentary exigencies I should prefer to fix the actual hour when I know what the business is.

The book is progressing rapidly. Three hundred and thirty thousand words are now in print, and the narrative with some gaps, has reached the Great Reform Bill of 1832. Unless some misfortune occurs I should hope to have covered the ground by May. Meanwhile the various sections already done are being carefully checked and revised by authorities on each period. Professor Wheeler of the London University, the eminent archaeologist, has written of the early and most difficult portion in the most complimentary terms, saying that he was completely carried away by the interest of the story in its new guise. There appear, therefore, to be good prospects of my delivering you the finished work in good time.

I may mention that for your convenience I am having a list prepared of suitable illustrations. Perhaps you will let me know how many you want. I suppose at least a thousand.

Winston S. Churchill to John Wheldon
(*Churchill papers: 2/357*)

22 February 1939

. . . You may be sure that England is not going to make war. I wish I could feel the same confidence about other countries.

---

[1] Desmond John Newman Flower, 1907–   . Only son of Sir Newman Flower. Educated at Lancing and King's College, Cambridge. Entered Cassell & Co, 1930; Director 1931; Literary Director, 1938; Acting Director, 1939–40. On active service, 1940–5 (despatches, Military Cross, 1944). As Deputy Chairman of Cassell & Co, 1952–8 and Chairman 1958–71, he supervised the printing, publishing and sale of Churchill's *The Second World War* and *A History of the English-Speaking Peoples*.

Lord Swinton to Winston S. Churchill

(*Churchill papers: 2/371*)

22 February 1939

My dear Winston,

I want to write a line to thank you for a generous allusion to myself in a very interesting speech.[1] The results are there (the harvest): & that is all that matters.

I think you are right about a Ministry of Supply today. I think it wd probably have been a mistake, for the Air Ministry at any rate, at a stage when an industry had to be created—new design, new technique—& the Air Staff, the Technical Staff, & the industry had to prove their way in day to day contact. That is a matter of opinion. But the position today is wholly different. Firms have a clear run on a single type for a year or 18 months; & they know what follows after. I believe therefore that the dislocation argument is grossly over-rated. But if it were sound, it is better to have dislocation now than in war. No one asked for compulsory powers. Those are for war. If necessary earlier, better vest in one ministry than 3. The sole or decisive question to my mind is: 'If this organisation is necessary in war, ought you not to create it & have it working in peace?'—((a) to be effective (b) as a deterrent).

Nor does it mean a vast new machine. My plan, which Trenchard & Milne[2] endorsed, wd brigade the 3 Service Supply Depts under a single Minister,—& each member for Supply wd remain a member of his Service Council, thus linking the Service General Staff with the Ministry of Supply.

Yrs ever,
Swinton

---

[1] During his speech in the House of Commons on 21 February 1939 (see page 1377, note 1), Churchill said, in a reference to Britain's air power: 'It is evident that the coming financial year will see a very great accretion to our defensive strength. For the first time, the great aircraft production factories will be earning sums upon a scale which has hitherto been attained only in Germany—and it should not be forgotten that most of them were created under the administration of a Minister who is no longer in office, Lord Swinton.'

[2] George Francis Milne, 1866–1948. Entered the Royal Artillery, 1885. Commanded a battery at Omdurman, 1898. Served on Kitchener's Intelligence Staff in South Africa, 1900–2. Brigadier-General, commanding the 4th Division artillery, 1913–14. He took part in the battles of Le Cateau, Marne and Aisne, 1914. Lieutenant-General commanding the British forces at Salonica, 1916–18. Knighted, 1918. Commanded the British Forces at Constantinople (Army of the Black Sea), 1919–20. General, 1920. Chief of the Imperial General Staff, 1926–33. Field-Marshal, 1928. Created Baron, 1933.

Winston S. Churchill to Lord Swinton
(*Churchill papers: 2/371*)

24 February 1939
Private

I am very glad you noticed my remark about yourself. The Press are such lackeys, and do not seem at all to understand that up to the present whatever aeroplanes there are, are due to you. I was shown the other day all the progress charts, which certainly are much better than I had expected. If only you had been in the House of Commons, you should I am sure have fought your way through. Everyone respects the dignity with which you have borne what must have been a most painful, though only I trust a temporary interruption of your political career. I know what I felt about leaving the Admiralty in the War, when I was convinced I was right and master of the event.

With every good wish,

Believe me,

F. W. Ogilvie to Winston S. Churchill
(*Churchill papers: 2/382*)

24 February 1939   Broadcasting House
Private

Dear Mr Churchill,

Thank you very much for your letter.

Oh no, I had by no means lost sight of the project which you and I discussed when I had the pleasure of meeting you at dinner the other day. The Corporation has long been anxious to increase the facilities for political broadcasting, and we have been working hard towards this end. It seemed best to proceed, *more Britannico*,[1] by asking the political parties, in the first instance, to agree to choose subjects and speakers for the time put periodically at their disposal. This agreement has been reached, and the first debate in the new series is to take place, as no doubt you know, on Monday, the 27th.

We are closely considering further stages in the development of political broadcasting, and are investigating various projects in detail, including the one which you were good enough to outline.

Yours very truly,
F. W. Ogilvie

[1] After the manner of the British; in British style.

Winston S. Churchill to Maxine Elliot

(*Churchill papers: 1/343*)

24 February 1939

The plans have arrived, and we are studying them very carefully.[1] I do not think the original plan was too big, as I have a lovely site perched up in a wood overlooking the Weald of Kent. Of course I shall not begin it for some time, and only if I am sure there is no immediate danger of a calamity.

My daughter Sarah, (Mrs Oliver), is staying on the Riviera for a few weeks at: La Voile d'Or, Saint Jean, Cap Ferrat. She is recuperating after a nose and throat operation, but by the time you get this, she will be able to go about. It would be very kind of you to let her come and lunch or dine with you one day. All her thoughts are on the stage, which she seeks to make her profession, and she would love to have a talk with you.

When are you coming back to England for your cure? If it is at Walton Heath, you are very close to us. Mind you let me know.

Winston S. Churchill to several correspondents: telegram

(*Churchill papers: 2/357*)

24 February 1939

Much regret am in bed laid up with influenza. Hope find another opportunity.

Winston Churchill

Winston S. Churchill to Lieutenant-Colonel Burne

(*Churchill papers: 8/626*)

27 February 1939

My dear Colonel Burne,

I must apologise for the long delay in answering your letter of January 21. It seems to have been mislaid among my literary papers.

I am much interested by your vindication of Cassivellaunus, and it seems to me that the case you make out is unanswerable. At any rate I shall

---

[1] The plans were for a new building at Chartwell, described by Maxine Elliot in a letter to Churchill of 1 February 1939 as looking like 'a *mansion* instead of a cottage, which indeed it *is*'.

incorporate your conclusions in one form or other in my account of the episode.[1] I hope you will let me keep your typescript for the present.

Thank you for the most appreciative review of Marlborough IV which I read with so much pleasure in the English Historical Review.[2]

Peter Peirson to Kathleen Hill
(*Churchill papers: 2/357*)

27 February 1939   Brno,
                                                                   Czechoslovakia

I trust that you and your friend are in the best of health and that everything is going well with you. Malicious rumours from Prague have reached my ears to the effect that he has had a stroke! There is no need for me to ask for a denial, but I thought I might mention this small item.

Things are not so bright here, and many people are very worried and unhappy because of the new alien laws which have been passed. All 'foreigners' have been told to leave the country by March 31st. . . .

Another matter of interest is that half-a-dozen German lorries, filled with Reich workmen, arrived outside the Deutsches Haus yesterday to start work on the new motor-road through this country from Germany. There was a skirmish not long ago, when some Nazis insulted some young Czechs. The police managed to disperse the combatants. At the Capitol Cinema here the German film 'Olympia' is showing. All the Nazis are itching to go, but there is a Nazi picket outside to prevent the students from going, because the cinema is owned by a Jew! It's a very ludicrous situation. Many Jews are now

---

[1] Churchill wrote (in *A History of the English-Speaking Peoples*, volume 1, pages 13–14): 'At this juncture Cassivellaunus, by a prudence of policy equal to that of his tactics, negotiated a further surrender of hostages and a promise of tribute and submission, in return for which Caesar was again content to quit the Island. In a dead calm "he set sail late in the evening and brought all the fleet safely to land at dawn". This time he proclaimed a conquest. Caesar had his triumph, and British captives trod their dreary path at his tail through the streets of Rome; but for nearly a hundred years no invading army landed upon the Island coasts. Little is known of Cassivellaunus, and we can only hope that later defenders of the Island will be equally successful and that their measures will be as well suited to the needs of the time. The impression remains of a prudent and skilful chief, whose qualities and achievements, but for the fact that they were displayed in an outlandish theatre, might well have ranked with those of Fabius Maximus Cunctator.'

[2] A. H. Burne's review was published in the *English Historical Review* in January 1939. Of the battle of Malplaquet, Burne wrote: 'while Mr Churchill has not managed to find much unpublished material, he has dealt astonishingly well with the material at his disposal'. Of earlier criticisms of Marlborough's generalship, Burne noted: 'Mr Churchill slurs over nothing.' Burne added: 'On the political side Mr Churchill's touch is as sure as ever.' The review ended: 'After nearly ten years' toil Mr Churchill may lay down his pen secure in the knowledge that his history of his mighty ancestor will rank among the greatest biographies in the English tongue.'

without jobs; all teachers have been asked to provide information about their religion and ancestry, including the English teachers at the English Institute. Isn't this an infringement of the authorities' rights? On May Day, when there is a public holiday and demonstrations by all sections of the community, another German wish is to be gratified: the rule of the road will be changed from the left to the right. This in itself is perhaps a good thing, since Czecho-Slovakia is, I believe, the last continental country still keeping its traffic to the left. I have noticed a large increase in the number of German cars in this town just lately, most of them gathered round the Deutsches Haus.

A short time ago I visited Hanák's Bierkellar 'Salvator'. Every arriving and departing customer was greeted with 'Heil Hitler!' by everyone in the restaurant. When my party left, a man started to Heil each one of us until forcibly stopped by the head-waiter! Every table had little swastika banners, Goebelsian and Streicherian politics were fervently talked everywhere, and frequently knots of people would retire to the little committee-rooms, with which the place is well provided. Each face was fanatically pro-Hitler, and every arm willing to rise at the slightest provocation. I cannot properly describe here the scene itself and the whole atmosphere. It left a nasty impression on my mind. . . .

Kathleen Hill: Chartwell Literary Account

(*Churchill papers: 8/639*)

February 1939

3rd   Editor of 'Picture Post' to luncheon to discuss proposed article (his own car).

5th   Tip to chauffeur to take DT article to London, special journey. 10 shillings.

6th   Dictation in car to London. Gave luncheon to Dr Wheeler (working on proofs of ESP).

9th   Dictation in car to London. Saw Sir Robert Vansittart in connection with DT political articles.

10th 2 taxis for Mr Pearson[1] of 'Picture Post', to collect photographs for article.

11th Mr Deakin for weekend.

15th Dictation in car.

---

[1] The editor of *Picture Post* in 1939, Stefan Lorant, writes of Pearson, that he was 'a fairly young man, probably under 30, who looked after our "library" (perhaps two dozen books) and the picture file' (*letter to the author, 12 November 1981*).

March 1939

Wing-Commander Anderson to Winston S. Churchill

(*Churchill papers: 2/372*)

1 March 1939   Royal Air Force
                                                          Catfoss

Dear Mr Churchill,

I mentioned the small number of Permanent Commissions which are being granted to Short Service Commission officers.

You will note on page 6 of enclosed Air Ministry Order N 170, that 159 officers reached the qualifying standard for a Permanent Commission but only 38 of the 159 have been selected and granted their Permanent Commissions.

For the past two years we have given approximately 2,800 Short Service Commissions and it is I submit a poor compensation when only 38 a year are given Permanent Commissions.

Yours very sincerely,
C. T. Anderson

Group-Captain Lachlan MacLean to Winston S. Churchill

(*Churchill papers: 2/358*)

3 March 1939   United Service Club

Dear Mr Churchill,

Thank you very much for your kind invitation for lunch on Sunday last, which I received through Wing-Commander Anderson. I was very disappointed at not being able to accept & I should have written to thank you before, but I saw that you had been stricken with the 'flu scourge.

I hope you have fully recovered and are feeling none of the usual ill effects.

Should you at any time wish for any information of a technical character which it may be in my power to give, I should be very happy if you would regard me as always at your disposal.

Yours sincerely,
Lachlan MacLean

Kathleen Hill to a correspondent
(*Churchill papers: 2/376*)

6 March 1939

. . . Mr Churchill is recuperating after an attack of influenza, and is not making any plans in the immediate future.

Kathleen Hill to Peter K. Peirson
(*Churchill papers: 2/358*)

8 March 1939

Dear Mr Peirson,

Thank you very much for writing to me so fully.[1] I should have acknowledged your letter earlier but my friend has been laid up with an attack of influenza, and I have had a great deal to see to. He hopes to be completely recovered this week.

I greatly appreciate your kindness in writing to me, but of course I do not wish to be a burden to you, and I shall not expect a letter unless you have any special news of yourself to give.

---

[1] Peter Peirson had first written to Churchill on 22 January 1939, on the eve of his departure to Czechoslovakia, offering to send him information about the situation there. It was agreed that he should send his letters through Kathleen Hill. Peirson's first letter reached Chartwell from Brno on 9 February 1939 (see page 1360, note 2).

Peter K. Peirson to Kathleen Hill

(*Churchill papers: 2/358*)

12 March 1939   Brno,
                                                      Moravia,
                                              Czecho-Slovakia

Dear Mrs Hill,

Thank you very much for your letter, which I read with great interest. I was just going to write to you when it arrived; in fact, I had started to reply very cautiously, when I realized the folly of pretending to hide something completely innocent. The fact is that your letter, which was couched in rather guarded language, prompted me to examine it closer. As far as I can gather, there is not now any censorship of letters, nor is there any reason why one Englishman should not be able to tell another his own impressions of a foreign country even when dealing with politics. I don't know whether you intended to warn me about anything in your letter, but, on close examination, it looks to me as if your letter had been opened. The state of the gum is suspicious. It may not be anything, but I am enclosing the envelope for your perusal. However, although you have said nothing definite, I am not going to restrain my impressions yet, unless I hear anything to the contrary.

I am very sorry to hear of your friend's illness and I hope that he will soon be completely recovered. Please give him my kindest regards and sympathy.

Several things have been happening together here. The Slovak situation has been causing great uneasiness here, and many people have been saying that this is the end of Czecho-Slovakia; and Hitler is coming to Vienna this week. News of the British Expeditionary Force is a little strange to us. Can you possibly tell me if there is anything in the wind? Shall I be able to settle down here at all? And what is my position if war breaks out between Great Britain and another country? You will, I am sure, understand my great interest, as peace of mind is so important these days, especially abroad in the centre of the boiling-pot, though we don't expect a war actually in this poor country, whose very electric light is now in German hands.

To-day has been a German festival. A great many buildings have been lavishly decorated with Swastika banners, though, of course, the Czech flag is flown alongside. This afternoon the whole population turned out to gaze curiously at the pro-Nazi centres and to wait and see if anything happened. The police had everything well under control. But this evening the fun started. All the Nazis gathered in or around the Deutsches Haus to sing and demonstrate. There have been many attempts to attract Czechs to the party's cause, and this was revealed by the decoration of the headquarters, for, though there were many swastikas flying on the Deutsches Haus, the biggest by far and the central one was the Czech flag, whereas, elsewhere, both Czech and German flags are always the same size. There were several attempts at counter-demonstrations outside, but the police succeeded in keeping the crowd moving nearly all the time. Then came a long and foolish procession of 'Whitestockings' right through the town, though a lot of it was efficiently closed by the police. The procession lasted for four hours, with, I suppose, a meeting. (I am writing before I have obtained any news from the newspapers, but these are merely my own personal impressions of what I have seen myself.) The spectators for the most part stood by and laughed openly at the marchers, who were shouting 'Sieg Heil!' and other slogans as they marched and singing the Horst Wessel song. They did look a foolish, motley crowd. Many Nazis are convinced that Hitler will come on March 15th and the greeting 'Heil März!' instead of 'Heil Hitler!' has been quite common for some weeks. The Jews too, are afraid that that may happen; but politics are in such a mess all round that one doesn't know which way to look.

I have read with great interest the articles in 'Picture Post' on your friend and am looking forward to receiving the next copy with his commentary on world affairs. That is the kind of guidance that we require nowadays.

You must have been very busy, and I am sorry to trouble you with stories of things that are probably of no interest. But it is such a crying shame to enslave such a kind and sympathetic race as the Czechs. I don't expect you to write to me, and I think it is very kind of you to do so at all. I myself have been keeping in fairly good health, except for a cold last week, due to some disgusting wet weather after two perfect spring days. To-day I went for a 30 kilometre walk round Obřany and Babića in alternating snow and sunshine. It was lovely. I am hoping to ask my sister here for a holiday in the summer for a tour round Slovakia, Hungary, Moravia, and Bohemia, if only the political situation will calm down.

Hoping that you are in the best of health and thanking you once more for writing,

Yours sincerely,
Peter K. Peirson

PS. There have been large numbers of police on foot & mounted, who have behaved superbly: also fire-engines have been patrolling the streets & visiting the Deutsches Haus.

Neville Chamberlain to his sister

(*Templewood papers*)

12 March 1939   Chequers

Meanwhile all the prodigal sons are fairly besieging the parental door. You may have seen Winston's eulogies as reported in the Saturday press.[1] Anthony loses no opportunity of telling me how cordially he approves the Govt policy. Duff Cooper is loud in his praises, young Jim Thomas[2] wants to be a Whip (!) Wolmer speaks in the country in the warmest & most admiring terms of the PM. Duncan Sandys is a reformed character & makes moving speeches in support of the Govt. Vernon Bartlett[3] says the PM is going to win & Harold Nicolson declares he is 'dead right'. . . .

[1] Speaking at Chigwell, in his constituency, on Friday, 10 March 1939, Churchill had praised Chamberlain's recent declaration affirming the solidarity of Britain and France. He had also supported the Government policy of distributing Anderson shelters for air raid protection. Churchill ended his speech with a comment on his own Munich speech of 5 October 1938: 'I do not withdraw a single word. I read it again only this afternoon, and was astonished to find how terribly true it had all come. I recognize, however, that the fact that the Prime Minister is known to be a sincere worker for peace has had a good effect upon the populations of the dictator countries, and that it has become more difficult for their machine-made propaganda to alarm those populations by the fear that Britain and France are animated by any hostile designs upon their peace and prosperity.'

[2] James Purdon Lewes Thomas, 1903–1960. Educated at Rugby and Oriel College, Oxford. Unsuccessful Conservative candidate, 1929; Conservative MP for Hereford, 1931–55. Assistant Private Secretary to Stanley Baldwin, 1931. Parliamentary Private Secretary to Anthony Eden, 1932–8 and 1940 (when Eden was Secretary of State for War). Lord Commissioner of the Treasury, 1940–3. Financial Secretary to the Admiralty, 1943–5. Vice-Chairman of the Conservative Party, 1945–51. Privy Councillor, 1951. First Lord of the Admiralty, 1951–6. Created Viscount Cilcennin, 1955.

[3] Vernon Bartlett, 1894–   . On active service, 1914–16. On the staff of the *Daily Mail*, 1916; of Reuter's Agency, 1917. Reuter's, and then the *Daily Herald* representative at the Paris Peace Conference. Joined *The Times*, 1919; correspondent in Poland, 1919–20 and in Italy, 1921–2. The first BBC broadcaster on Foreign Affairs, 1928–34. On the staff of the *News Chronicle*, 1934–54. Independent Progressive MP for Bridgewater, Somerset, 1938–50. South East Asia Correspondent of the *Manchester Guardian*, 1954–61. Since 1961, resident in Italy, growing grapes and making wine.

Chatin Sarachi[1] to Winston S. Churchill

(Foreign Office papers: 371/24081)

13 March 1939

When I had the honour to meet you in January at Madame Maxine Eliot's House, in Cannes, we discussed the possibility of Jewish Emigration to Albania. I have just arrived from Tirana where I had the opportunity to discuss the matter. I have been authorised to negotiate in case the question still exists.[2]

Winston S. Churchill: speech[3]

(Churchill papers: 9/136)

14 March 1939   Waltham Abbey

. . . Complaint has been made in some of the outlying parts of the Constituency of my speech on the Munich Agreement. In this I pointed out that a disaster of the first magnitude had befallen France and England. Is that not so? Why do you suppose we are making all these preparations? Why do you suppose that the French military service has been lengthened, and we are to promise to send nineteen divisions to the Continent? It is because in the destruction of Czechoslovakia the entire balance of Europe was deranged, and the great and growing German Army is free to turn in any direction.

[1] Chatin Pascal Sarachi (Catin Saraci). Born at the beginning of the century in Scutari, Albania; member of a leading Roman Catholic landowning family. Educated in Vienna. Active in the revolution which brought King Zog to power, 1923–4. Albanian Consul General in Vienna, 1926; first Secretary, Albanian Legation, London, 1933–8. Resident in London from 1939, and becoming a British subject, he devoted the rest of his life to painting. In 1960 he married Elizabeth Judd of Dublin. He died in London in 1974.

[2] Several hundred Jews did find refuge in Albania, and continued to be sheltered there during the period of the Italian occupation of Albania (April 1939 to October 1943), including many refugees from Yugoslavia, following the German invasion in April 1941. But following the fall of Mussolini, and the assumption of German control over much former Italian territory, some 400 Jews, mostly refugees, were deported from Albania to Belsen in the spring of 1944. Less than 100 survived the war.

[3] For four and a half months, Churchill had been disturbed by repeated criticism inside his constituency of his speech attacking the Munich agreement (see page 1257, note 4). In this speech at Waltham Abbey, made as the Germany Army was about to march into Bohemia and Moravia, and as Slovakia was about to declare its independence, he sought to answer those criticisms. German troops crossed the Czech frontier on the following day, 15 March 1939, when Hitler established the 'Protectorate of Bohemia and Moravia'. Slovakia declared itself an independent State on 16 March 1939, and supported the Nazi German interest throughout the war.

I pointed out that Munich sealed the ruin of Czechoslovakia. You remember the tales we were told, how they would have a better life after they were 'free' from their unwilling German subjects. Besides they were to have a German guarantee of their reduced frontiers, and there was to be a British and French guarantee. I held the view that these guarantees were not worth the paper they were written on, or the breath that uttered them. What is the position now? The Czechoslovak Republic is being broken up before our eyes. Their gold is to be stolen by the Nazis. The Nazi system is to blot out every form of internal freedom. Their army is to be reduced to negligible proportions, or incorporated in the Nazi power. They are about to lose all symbols of an independent democratic State. Does anybody deny it? I said that once the Czechs had given up their fortified line, a pretext could be found to take everything from them. We have seen exactly the same methods used as were used in September. Disturbances have been fomented in Slovakia, I have no doubt at Herr Hitler's instigation. And then the German Press has set to work to abuse the Czechs, and accuse them of violent aggression against the Germans. The next thing is to order them to reduce their army, and take whatever Ministers into their Government Germany chooses to order. They are being completely absorbed, and not until the Nazi power has passed away from Europe will they emerge again in freedom. Why should I have said all these things? It was the truth. It was my duty to say them. Can anybody dispute them?

Now I have defended this speech which has been attacked, and I say never did I make a truer statement to the House. Practically everything that I said has already proved true. And who are these people who go about saying that even if it were true why state the facts? Why mislead the nation? What is the use of Parliament if it is not the place where true statements can be brought before the people? What is the use of sending Members to the House of Commons who say just the popular things of the moment, and merely endeavour to give satisfaction to the Govt Whips by cheering loudly every platitude, and walking through the Lobbies oblivious of the criticisms they hear. People talk about our Parliamentary institutions and Parliamentary democracy, but if these are to survive, it will not be because the Constituencies return tame, docile, subservient Members, and try to stamp out every form on independent judgment.

Major Fraser[1] to Winston S. Churchill
(*Churchill papers: 2/358*)

15 March 1939

Dear Mr Churchill,

In 1916 when you were commanding a battalion of the Royal Scots Fusiliers, I was GSO 3 of the 9th Division; in 1917, when I was wounded, you were kind enough to come & see me in hospital at Eccleston Square. But all this is so long ago now, that I have great hesitation in writing to you.

I am now Chief Intelligence Officer of the ARP Dept and have been with that Dept since 1936.

I should be most grateful if you could spare me a few minutes, as I should like to discuss a certain matter with you and ask your advice.

Yours sincerely,
F. L. Fraser

Sir Neill Malcolm[2] to Winston S. Churchill
(*Churchill papers: 2/358*)

15 March 1939

Dear Mr Churchill,

I cannot tell you how much pleasure I derived from your speech of last night, as reported in this morning's Times.[3]

---

[1] Forbes Leith Fraser, 1885–1963. 2nd Lieutenant, Seaforth Highlanders, 1904; Captain 1914. General Staff Officer, Grade 3, 9th Division, 1917 (wounded). Joined the Air Raid Precautions Department, Home Office, 1936; Chief Intelligence Officer, 1938.

[2] Neill Malcolm, 1869–1953. Educated at Eton and Sandhurst. 2nd Lieutenant, 1899. On active service on the north-west frontier of India, 1897–8; in the Sudan, 1898–99 (despatches, DSO); in South Africa, 1899–1900 (severely wounded); in Somaliland, 1903–4; and on the western front, 1914–18 (despatches; Major-General; severely wounded 29 March 1918). British Military Mission, Berlin, 1919–21. General Officer Commanding, Malaya, 1921–4. Knighted, 1924. High Commissioner for German Refugees, 1936–8. Editor, *The Science of War*.

[3] During his speech of 14 March 1939, an extract from which is quoted earlier, Churchill declared: 'The Czechoslovakian Republic is being broken up before our eyes. They are being completely absorbed; and not until the Nazi shadow has been finally lifted from Europe— as lifted I am sure it will eventually be—not until then will Czechoslovakia and ancient Bohemia march again into freedom.' A few moments later he declared: 'It is no use going to their aid when they are defenceless, if we would not go to their aid when they were strong. Therefore I agree entirely with those who think we should not intervene at the present time. We cannot. That is the end of it,' but, he added: 'to suppose that we are not involved in what is happening is a profound illusion. Although we can do nothing to stop it, we shall be sufferers on a very great scale. We shall have to make all kinds of sacrifices for our own defence that would have been unnecessary if a firm resolve had been taken at an earlier stage. We shall have to make sacrifices not only of money, but of personal service in order to make up for what we have lost.'

I do not understand why our government is allowed to pursue its policy of funk even under its title of 'appeasement'.

I wish you would make a great speech taking as your text 'Roll up the map of Europe'.

Yours very truly,
Neil Malcolm

Winston S. Churchill to Admiral of the Fleet Lord Chatfield
(Churchill papers: 2/328)

16 March 1939

I find it necessary to speak about the Mediterranean in the Debate this afternoon and, according to my promise, let you see in private confidence what I propose to say.[1]

I hope your speech this afternoon will be, as I am sure it will, a great success.

Admiral of the Fleet Lord Chatfield to Winston S. Churchill
(Churchill papers: 2/328)

16 March 1939   House of Lords

My dear Churchill,

Thank you so much for sending me your views of this intriguing Mediterranean problem. I am sure it is best I should not handicap you, in any

---

[1] Speaking in the Navy Estimates debate on 16 March 1939 (from 6.04 pm to 6.43 pm), Churchill said that 'for Britain in time of war, the command of the Mediterranean must be the prime objective'. Even without the new ships under construction, 'there should be no difficulty in securing this', even if Britain was fighting without an Ally, 'and had at the same time to watch the debouches from the Baltic and the Elbe'. This superiority, he said, 'would become even more ample if the British and French Fleets were acting in combination'. He hoped that the school of thought which argued that the Mediterranean should be sealed off and left as a 'closed sea' would be rejected by the Admiralty. 'To gain and hold command of the Mediterranean in case of war,' he asserted, 'is a high duty of the Fleet. Once that is achieved, all European land forces on the shores of North Africa will be decisively affected. Those that have command of the Mediterranean behind them can be reinforced to any extent and supplied to any extent. Those that have no such command will be like cut flowers in a vase.'

way, by commenting on them—which could only be done at length. I much doubt however if Shakespeare[1] wd be able to say much in reply!

Yours very sincerely,
Chatfield

Thank you also for your good wishes.

Sir Horace Rumbold to Winston S. Churchill
(*Churchill papers: 2/358*)

16 March 1939

My dear Churchill,

You asked me last night what I thought of the present situation and I replied that I was profoundly disheartened. This was an under-statement. I have had several difficult and depressing situations to deal with in the course of my career and I have, on the whole, been inclined to optimism. But I have never felt so depressed or so nauseated as I feel now and this because it seems to me that our Government have for a year or more, failed to look ahead, or to understand the character of the man with whom they are dealing.

In April 1933 I warned the government of the nature of the beast and of the system which had arisen in Germany. My despatch was largely an analysis of the more salient passages in 'Mein Kampf' and was, I am told, called 'Mein Kampf dispatch'. That is my only consolation but a poor one for, as I see it, we have reached the position of speculating gloomily which country is going to be involved in the next act of brigandage knowing perfectly well, except, perhaps, in the case of Switzerland or Holland—that we shall do nothing about it. At the utmost our PM will utter a bleat in the House. Having now read his statement or speech of yesterday I consider that it was anything but à la hauteur, whilst his conception of a breach of faith is not that of the average Englishman.

I am inclined to think that the northern gangster may go for Memel next and that his fellow brigand in the south will try for Albania.[2] I only hope

---

[1] Geoffrey Hithersay Shakespeare, 1893–1980. Served in the Great War, at Gallipoli and in Egypt. President of the Cambridge Union, 1920. Private Secretary to Lloyd George, 1921–3. Called to the Bar, 1922. National Liberal MP for Wellingborough, 1922–3; Liberal MP for Norwich, 1929–31; Liberal National MP for Norwich, 1931–45. Liberal National Chief Whip, 1931–2. Parliamentary Secretary at the Ministry of Health, 1932–6; and at the Board of Education, 1936–7. Parliamentary and Financial Secretary, Admiralty, 1937–40. Parliamentary Under-Secretary of State, Dominions Office, 1940–2. Created Baronet, 1942.

[2] Hitler annexed Memel to the German Reich, by ultimatum to Lithuania, on 22 March 1939. Mussolini invaded Albania on 7 April 1939.

that it will not enter into the PM's head to pay Hitler another visit. The season ticket he took to Canosa last autumn is more than sufficient and there is no doubt that what the Arabs would call the 'father of appeasement' was outwitted and rouléd by the 'father of lies or treachery' ie Hitler at Munich.

The seizure of the Czech aeroplanes and gold etc is such an accession of strength to Hitler that I don't put it past him to challenge us now in a most direct manner. The cancellation of Stanley's and Hudson's visit to Berlin was the least the government could do.[1] First I would do more for I do not think it consistent with our dignity—if we have any left—to keep on our Ambassador at Berlin who ought to be recalled on indefinite leave. As you know, the Americans have done this in the case of their Ambassador.[2] They are, it is true, 4,000 miles away. But my gorge rises at the thought that the King should be personally represented at the Capital of a bandit government.

This requires no answer. It was some relief to my feelings to pour out some of my bitterness to you for I know you feel much the same as I do.

Yours sincerely,
Horace Rumbold

Winston S. Churchill to Sir Douglas Hacking[3]
(Churchill papers: 7/56)

18 March 1939
Private and Confidential[4]

When we chatted last night you said you were only doing your duty in

[1] Following the German occupation of Prague, the British Government postponed the imminent visit to Berlin of the President of the Board of Trade (Oliver Stanley) and the Secretary of the Department of Overseas Trade (Robert Hudson), on the grounds that the present moment would be 'inopportune' for such a visit.

[2] Hugh R. Wilson, appointed United States Ambassador in Berlin in February 1938, who was formally recalled from Germany on 20 March 1939, when the German Ambassador in Washington was informed that the United States declined to recognize the German occupation of Czechoslovakia.

[3] Douglas Hewitt Hacking, 1884–1950. On active service in France, 1914–16 (despatches, OBE). Conservative MP for the Chorley Division of Lancashire, 1918–45. Parliamentary Private Secretary, Ministry of Pensions, 1920; Admiralty, 1920–1; War Office, 1921–2. Conservative Whip, 1922–5. Parliamentary Under-Secretary of State, Home Office, 1925–7. Secretary, Department of Overseas Trade, Parliamentary Secretary, Board of Trade, and Parliamentary Under-Secretary of State for Foreign Affairs, 1927–9. Government Delegate, League of Nations, Geneva, 1933. Parliamentary Under-Secretary, Home Office, 1933–4; Dominion Affairs, 1935–6. Chairman of the Conservative Party Organization, 1936–42. Created Baronet, 1938; Baron, 1945.

[4] This letter was never sent. Kathleen Hill noted on the carbon copy: 'Can this be destroyed? I think the original was torn up, but am not sure.' Churchill noted: 'Put away. Not sent,' and thus the carbon copy remained among his private papers.

interfering in my Constituency and that the local Association must decide.

What has happened is that Mr Thornton Kemsley and one or two others who admit they are in close touch with the Central Office have been trying to gain control of several of the Branch Associations, with a view to obtaining a majority upon the parent body. In two or three cases this has been successful, and we shall see when the Central Association meets on April 17 what the results of their activities are.

I must mention, however, that there are twenty-six branches and one hundred and three thousand electors. Nearly seventy thousand of these lie in the densely populated destricts of Woodford, Wanstead and Chingford.

The opposition, such as it is, which you have been fomenting, operates chiefly in the rural areas. These have been very largely over-represented in order to encourage their activities.

For instance, at Matching, a village of three hundred and eighty-four voters, officers were elected by a handful of people giving five votes on the central body.

At Chigwell and Theydon Bois also there have been rather curious tactics which, we are assured, are instigated and approved by your office. A number of new members suddenly appeared who had never done any work for the Party in the district but who had paid their shilling, or had it paid for them, the night before the Meeting. Consequently some very experienced, trustworthy workers for the Party were turned off the Committee and replaced by persons representing the Central Office section of the Conservative Party. This has caused a great deal of feeling in these districts, which were taken by surprise by what happened, and of course measures are being enforced to reverse these decisions and to censure the proceedings which led up to them.

I am sure that these small tactical results do not at all represent the electors even in those districts, for I have never had Meetings like I am having now.

Of course, when a Committee is subverted by these methods I am forced to form a separate Branch Committee, for which alone I act.

At Chigwell, for instance, where we had a Meeting of over six hundred people, I could not allow any of the new Committee to appear on my platform, though the Meeting was one of the finest ever held in the district and characterised by the utmost goodwill.

The reason why I put all this before you is to show you what the consequences of your interference must be, namely, that two alternative Associations will gradually come into existence in all the districts where your tactics are successful.

I believe that I shall command a substantial majority upon the Association at the Meeting on April 17, but if this should not be so, I shall be left with a minority of delegates representing at least 75% of the Conservative electors.

We shall then form a separate Association on this basis, and you will have created a split, the consequences of which will not pass away when the existing political differences subside. A feud will have been started which may last a long time.

All this makes me wonder whether you are acting rightly in meddling in these matters. I should have thought that you should preserve relationships with the official Association, headed by Sir Harry Goschen and Sir James Hawkey, in which I hold up to the present at least a three to one majority. When you go behind the backs of this Association into all this petty work you are surely acting improperly towards the constituted officers for the time being, and I submit this is an absolutely wrong course for a Party Manager to pursue. I do not say this because I am in the slightest degree apprehensive of what the result may be, because we have always had agreeable relations and I feel it my duty to explain the position fully to you, and because perhaps you yourself have not been personally closely concerned in what has happened.

I must add, of course, that so far all reference to the Central Office has been avoided by me and by my friends, but Sir James Hawkey and other officers of the Association feel very strongly that you ought to have addressed yourself to them before attempting all this small work in the Branches.

I trust you will consider what I say very carefully, because it would not be very pleasant if these matters came into public controversy. Do not, however, suppose for the moment I am asking any favour at your hands, because I am quite sure that the overwhelming mass of the Electorate will support me at the next Election, and I hope even to improve upon the great majority of twenty thousand which I had last time.

Peter K. Peirson to Kathleen Hill

(Churchill papers: 2/358)

18 March 1939
Brünn,
Mähren,
Germany[1]

Dear Mrs Hill,

There is nothing that I can say,—you probably know more than I do myself about what has happened. We feel very cut off now, as news is scarce, though I am sometimes able to hear the wireless from England in the

---

[1] Six days earlier this address was: Brno, Moravia, Czechoslovakia (see page 1386).

evening, and the British Vice-Consul here has committed suicide.[1] The situation, as far as I am able to gauge it at present, is very serious, and the NC speech was rather alarming.[2]

We don't know what will happen to us and we have heard nothing important from Prague, where the headquarters of the Institute are. But I suppose we shall stay here until we are told to go. Lessons have been badly upset, though we hope to have more or less regular work going again next week. If we are allowed to stay, I have no intention of remaining after June. It's a great pity, as I shall not have had sufficient time to obtain good references, and when I return to England I shall be out of a job, unless it's to join up.

I saw the first German troops entering the town. It was rather unique, as there are only 8 Englishmen here. The local Germans were very enthusiastic, but the rest of the population have been extremely and amazingly quiet. Everything is now draped in swastikas. Yesterday morning Hitler paid a surprise visit: the reception was very cool, and he drove straight back and did not make his intended speech here in the evening. Few people saw him or recognized him.

Communications are severely interrupted. There may be a train to England. Letters come in, but I doubt if letters out get through properly, if at all; so I shall not be surprised if this letter never reaches you. Cables are very uncertain. Please give my kind regards to your friend: I hope he will be able to get about now and do something.[3]

Yours sincerely,
Peter K. Peirson

[1] Walter Villiers Neumarck, Vice-Consul at the British Legation at Brno, Czechoslovakia since 1929. He committed suicide on 16 March 1939 as German troops were invading his native land. On March 20 R. A. Butler, Under-Secretary of State for Foreign Affairs, reported Neumarck's suicide to the House of Commons, provoking cries of 'shame!' when he said that Neumarck 'had been in poor health for some time and was suffering from depression, and it would seem probable that the strain of recent events aggravated his condition'. On March 28 a correspondent to The Times remembered Neumarck as 'a true and sincere friend to this country over a great many years'.

[2] Speaking at Birmingham on 17 March 1939, Chamberlain asked: 'Is this the end of an old adventure, or the beginning of a new? Is this, in fact, a step in the direction of an attempt to dominate the world by force?' His speech ended: 'I feel bound to repeat that, while I am not prepared to engage this country by new unspecified commitments, operating under conditions which cannot now be foreseen, yet no greater mistake could be made than to suppose that, because it believes war to be a senseless and cruel thing, this nation has so lost its fibre that it will not take part to the utmost of its power in resisting such a challenge if it ever were made.'

[3] On receiving Peirson's letters, Kathleen Hill would reply, from Chartwell: 'Thank you so much for your letter. My friend read it with attention, and found it very interesting' (Churchill papers: 2/357).

Winston S. Churchill to Sir Horace Rumbold
(Churchill papers: 2/358)

19 March 1939

Very many thanks for your letter. It is an encouragement to me to feel that we are in so good agreement. Since you wrote it, events have told their unanswerable tale, and Chamberlain in his speech has admitted the altogether wrong opinion which he formed of men and things for which he is responsible.

I had not the slightest doubt ten days ago that another stroke was imminent, and it seems to me that Hitler will not stop short of the Black Sea unless arrested by the threat of a general war or by actual hostilities.

Margot, Countess of Oxford and Asquith to Winston S. Churchill
(Churchill papers: 2/358)

19 March 1939

Dearest Winston,

We are *old* friends (I *very* old!).

I think you shd go to 10 Downing St & offer yr services, in whatever the PM wishes to place you.

We *must* show Germany that we are united to a *man* against her wish to dominate Europe.

Affectionately,
yr Margot

Kathleen Hill to B. Lubetkin[1]
(Churchill papers: 2/371)

20 March 1939

Dear Sirs,

I am desired by Mr Winston Churchill to thank you for the book 'Planned ARP', which you have sent him.[2]

---

[1] Berthould Lubetkin, a Russian-born architect whose penguin pool at the London Zoo was among the world's 'finest designs' of the 1930s (Charles McKean, *The Times*, 30 June 1982). Designer of the elephant and giraffe houses at Whipsnade, and, with his practice Tecton, of Peterlee New Town. A farmer since the 1940s, in 1982 he was awarded the Royal Gold Medal for Architecture.

[2] The preface of *Planned ARP* states: 'Immediately after the crisis of September 1938, Messrs. Tecton, Architects, were approached by the Council of the Metropolitan Borough of Finsbury to advise on the suitability of the available basements for use as public shelters.' The result was a detailed study of the problem of air raid protection in general, and precise recommendations to the borough recommending systematically planned air raid protection

Mr Churchill has to-day studied this book with some attention, and has not been favourably impressed thereby. It appears to be inspired by a wish to exaggerate the dangers of air attack and to emphasize the futility of basement protection in the interests of some particular scheme with which you are associated. The wide circulation of such a book would not be helpful at the present juncture.

Mr Churchill understands from the Lord Privy Seal[1] that properly reinforced basements will give a very large measure of protection.

Winston S. Churchill: message[2]

(*'The Times'*, *21 March 1939*)

21 March 1939

The Royal Cancer hospital is doing work of which the Nation should be proud. It is fighting this fell disease—trying to establish its cause and discover a cure—providing beds for patients and keeping those who are inoperable free from pain. If those who have contemplated, even for an instant, the possibility of being one day themselves in the clutch of cancer, subscribe to the fund, the present difficulty of raising sufficient money to continue the work should be easily overcome.

---

for the people of Finsbury. The results were published as *Planned ARP*: 'based on the investigations of structural protection against air attack in the Metropolitan Borough of Finsbury', and published by the Architectural Press Ltd., in March 1939. Paul Reilly wrote, reviewing *Planned ARP*: 'For the first time A.R.P. has been lifted out of the realm of opinion and guesswork and pinned down to mathematical measurements by the calculation for each type of shelter of a definite danger coefficient' (*News Chronicle*, *22 March 1939*).

[1] Sir John Anderson (see page 1286, note 1).

[2] Published in *The Times* and other national newspapers as an advertisement by the Royal Cancer Hospital, Fulham Road, London, with a photograph of Churchill under the heading: 'Famous Men Plead Humanity's Cause'. The advertisement went on to say that 74,000 died every year of cancer in Britain alone. It did not mention the fact that Churchill's two closest cousins, 'Sunny' the 9th Duke of Marlborough, and 'Freddie' Guest, had both died of cancer, in 1934 and 1937 respectively.

Winston S. Churchill to Neville Chamberlain
(Churchill papers: 2/358)

21 March 1939

I venture to reiterate the suggestion which I made to you in the lobby yesterday afternoon, that the anti-aircraft defences should forthwith be placed in full preparedness. Such a step could not be deemed aggressive, yet it would emphasise the seriousness of the action HMG are taking on the Continent. The bringing together of these officers and men would improve their efficiency with every day of their embodiment. The effect at home would be one of confidence rather than alarm. But it is of Hitler I am thinking mostly. He must be under intense strain at this moment. He knows we are endeavouring to form a coalition to restrain his further aggression. With such a man anything is possible. The temptation to make a surprise attack on London or on the aircraft factories about which I am even more anxious would be removed if it was known that all was ready. There could, in fact, be no surprise, and, therefore, the incentive to the extremes of violence would be removed and more prudent counsels might prevail.

In August 1914 I persuaded Mr Asquith to let me send the Fleet to the North so that it could pass the Straits of Dover and the narrow seas *before* the diplomatic situation had become hopeless. It seems to me that manning the anti-aircraft defences now stands in a very similar position, and I hope you will not mind my putting this before you.

Neville Chamberlain to Winston S. Churchill
(Churchill papers: 2/358)

21 March 1939   10 Downing Street

My dear Winston,

Thanks for your note. I have been spending a lot of time on the subject you mention but it is not so simple as it seems.

I will have a word with you when I see you next.

Yours sincerely,
Neville Chamberlain

Sir Herbert Creedy:[1] *recollections*

(*Randolph Churchill papers*)

[22 March 1939]

At a big official reception in 1939 when President Lebrun[2] was in London, Churchill recognised me, came up to me, and asked me what I was doing. I told him I had retired. 'What,' he said, 'retired at your age—three years younger than me? I am on the threshold of my career.'

Wing Commander Anderson to Winston S. Churchill

(*Churchill papers: 2/372*)

23 March 1939

Royal Air Force,
Catfoss

Dear Mr Churchill,

It was extremely kind of you to invite MacLean and myself to lunch at Chartwell on Sunday.[3]

I have been in touch with MacLean and he informs me that unfortunately he will be away from London this week-end. As regards myself, I have two Squadrons, Nos 49 and 150 arriving at Catfoss on Saturday 25th and it is a time when the Commanding Officer should be on the spot, so I hope you will forgive me for being unable to attend.

---

[1] The former Permanent Under-Secretary of State for War (see page 69, note 2).

[2] Albert Lebrun, 1871–1950. French Minister of Colonies, 1911–13; of War, 1913; of Colonies, 1913–14; of Blockade, 1917–18; of the Liberated Regions, 1918–19. Vice-President of the Senate, 1925–9; President of the Senate, 1931–2. President of the French Republic from May 1932 to July 1940 (when he was succeeded by Marshal Pétain). He was in London on an official visit from 21–24 March 1939.

[3] On 21 March 1939 Lachlan MacLean had sent Churchill, from the United Services Club, a letter and note on aircraft speeds, petrol consumption and interception. Among the points which MacLean made in his note was: 'For purposes of defence it is not enough to oppose Germany's raiding squadrons by subjecting them to attack in the vicinity of their objectives and only during the last ten to fifteen minutes of their approach flights, or at the commencement of their return flight, as the cases may be. Opposition, to have any chance of success, must be commenced long before our shores are reached, and attack tactics must be applied relentlessly, commencing if necessary three hundred miles away in order to force the enemy to full speed flight and the maximum consumption of fuel for as long as possible, and in order to provide a reasonable period to allow of an adequate and *repeated series of* attacks being developed.' The passage in italics had been underlined by MacLean. (*Churchill papers: 2/371*).

In the course of the next few days I will forward you details of the five points I mentioned, namely,

(a) Unserviceability of aerodromes owing to heavy rains and necessity of laying concrete runways.
(b) The Policy of turning a number of our Fighter Squadrons into Bombers.
(c) The building of the Hispano cannon factory at Grantham.
(d) The need for bettering conditions of service for the Short Service Commission officers.
(e) The number of airmen, approximately 30 a day who are applying for discharge, mainly due to bad conditions of our Training Camps.

Could the S of S visit for example, Yatesbury Camp in Wiltshire where 3,000 airmen are under training.

Yours very sincerely,
C. T. Anderson

Winston S. Churchill to Margot, Countess of Oxford and Asquith
(Churchill papers: 2/358)

23 March 1939

Thank you very much for your letter which I greatly appreciate. The Government have now adopted the foreign policy which I and most Liberals have long been pressing, and consequently I am in very good relations with them, but I am sure it would be a great mistake to make any offer of the kind you suggest.

Winston S. Churchill to Sir Keith Price[1]
(Churchill papers: 2/374)

23 March 1939

I wonder if you have any notes of the scale on which you were making explosives at the end of the War?

There is so much loose talk going on about the Germans being able to throw a thousand tons of bombs each night into England, etc, that it has occurred to me to examine the relative supplies of explosives, by which of course I include propellent.

[1] Keith William Price, 1879–1956. Chairman of Price & Pierce Ltd. Joined the Explosives Department, War Office, 1914; Director of the Raw Materials Section, 1915. Deputy Director-General, Ministry of Munitions, 1916–17. Knighted, 1917. Member of Council (Explosives), Ministry of Munitions, 1917–19. Deputy Director-General, Ministry of Supply, 1939–45.

L. S. Amery to Winston S. Churchill

Churchill papers: 2/358)

24 March 1939

My dear Winston,

I enclose a revise of the suggested memorial on universal service. What we want to ask for is a Bill which provides for a normal system of youth training such as exists in other democratic countries, but, at the same time, would enable the Government at any moment now, if it thought the situation serious enough, to call upon any other age classes that it required. Obviously if it looked like war tomorrow it is not the boys of 18 but the young men from 20 to 25 that we should want to call up.

The one great merit of getting the legislation passed is not that we should call up anybody for the moment, but that all the other arrangements for training cadres, equipment, etc, would be put in hand at once and on the right scale. . . .

Winston S. Churchill to L. S. Amery

(Churchill papers: 2/358)

24 March 1939

As you probably know, there is a lively discussion going on inside the Cabinet about compulsion, and it may be that those who are pressing for measures stiffer than your resolution will prevail. I am not very much inclined to sign this 'round robin' in such circumstances.

I hope to see you next week.

Lord Lloyd to Winston S. Churchill

(Churchill papers: 2/358)

24 March 1939

My dear Winston,

It was indeed good of you and Clemmie to send me those lovely flowers and I appreciate your kind thought more than I can say.

I rejoiced to read of the wonderful welcome that was given to you in the

Guildhall the other day.[1] It makes me enraged that at a moment like this you—the one person who could lead this country to security—should not be used. I am sure that more and more people feel the same.

It was bad news about Rumania last night.[2] I have been warning Halifax for the last month that he would be too late over that business. Unless he can move faster over the tobacco question in Turkey, Bulgaria and Greece, he will fail to get Bulgaria over to our side—which we can easily do, even to-day, if we act promptly.[3]

I have had a horrible attack of flu and am feeling like a wreck, but hope to emerge on Monday.

Winston S. Churchill to Maurice Ashley
(*Churchill papers: 8/626*)

24 March 1939

I have been remiss in writing to thank you for the notes you wrote for me on Cromwell. You were kind enough to say you would like to read through this period of my book, of which you have made a study. I, therefore, send you a proof from James I to the beginning of James II. You will see that I have provisionally printed your Cromwell as it stands. I have now claimed from the publishers their agreement to extend the work by another thirty thousand words, and therefore I may be able to give a somewhat larger scope to Cromwell and Monk than is allowed here.

As you know from experience, my draft proof bears very little relation to the finished product. I have been deeply interested in this period, and have been far from satisfied with the rendering I have given it so far. You will see contradictions and errors, but I should greatly welcome any comments you care to make.

It is very hard to transport oneself into the past when the future opens its jaws upon us.

[1] At the *Drapers* Hall, on 16 March 1939, Churchill presided over the 97th Annual Meeting of the Early Closing Association. His speech was reported in *The Times* on the following day. 'Lying across the world,' he said, 'was the shadow of an arbitrary and aggressive power, manifested in a form which filled us with deepest sorrow and anxiety. If that shadow could be lifted an expansion of life could be offered immediately to millions of people in every land who could go to more abundantly filled tables, live lives of greater variety, and enjoy greater amenities and leisure. They could have a higher culture and higher hopes and move forward to a brighter age.'

[2] News of the Rumanian-German Trade Treaty, signed in Bucharest on 23 March 1939, creating a number of 'mixed German–Rumanian' companies, including a German–Rumanian oil company.

[2] As Chairman of the British Council, Lord Lloyd had made a number of visits to the Balkans. His son writes: 'In his opinion and in that of those who thought like him, it was very important to do everything to encourage a pro-British attitude in these countries and one of the best ways of helping them was to buy their tobacco,' (*letter to the author, 14 November 1981*).

Winston S. Churchill to John Wheldon

(*Churchill papers: 8/626*)

24 March 1939

I am getting rather hungry for your notes on Henry VIII, which you so kindly promised to give me. Do not let the better be the enemy of the good. Remember 'Sentimental Tommy' who lost his examination because he could not think of the right word in the opening sentence.[1] I know you have a great flair for this reign, and I look forward very much to seeing what you have to say about it.

Winston S. Churchill to Brigadier-General Sir James Edmonds

(*Churchill papers: 8/626*)

24 March 1939

I have read with deep interest the military 'backbone', which you have sent me on the Civil War. It will be a great help to me in my task. I have great confidence in your judgement in these matters, and I look forward to receiving a further instalment. To enable one to see more clearly the proportions of the story I am having your notes put into proof.

When one comes to look at it en bloc, the Confederates never had any chance at all. It was only a question of the North getting under way and the amount of time required to destroy, if necessary, every living soul in the Confederate states. The dramatic point is the wonderful resistance which they made.

Have you read 'Gone with the Wind'?[2] It is a terrific book, but I expect you are too pressed with your work to read. I hope during the summer you will be able to spare me a night, when we can go through the campaign on the map.

I hope you are as sanguine as you used to be about no war and our not getting scragged.

With kind regards,
Believe me,

---

[1] *Sentimental Tommy*, by J. M. Barrie, published in 1896, and its sequel, *Tommy and Grizel*, published in 1900, tell the story of a young man over-endowed with imagination who can never resist playing the hero. He met an accidental death by hanging.

[2] Margaret Mitchell, *Gone With the Wind*, first published in London in 1936, and subsequently turned into a film. It was set in the American Civil War, on which Edmonds was a leading authority.

Winston S. Churchill to G. M. Young
(*Churchill papers: 8/626*)

24 March 1939

You very kindly said I might send you what I have written on the Stuart period. I, therefore, enclose a very rough preliminary draft from James I to the beginning of James II. The part about Cromwell as Lord Protector may be regarded as a grouping of the facts rather than as the finished narrative. I should be so much obliged if you could find time to look through this and thereafter let me have the advantage of a talk with you about it.

I hope you will not be vexed if I venture to suggest an honorarium of fifty guineas for your advice and assistance in checking this period. I should not feel justified otherwise in trespassing upon your time and thought. If I have offended, pray forgive me.

Yours very truly,

Winston S. Churchill to Lord Lytton
(*Churchill papers: 2/378*)

25 March 1939

I have been invited to address probably a hundred League of Nations Union meetings during the past few months. In April last I undertook a very laborious campaign in favour of the policy which the Government have now tardily adopted, namely—a Grand Alliance on the basis of the Covenant of the League. We had magnificent meetings in the biggest halls, with all Parties present, and I am not aware that the slightest influence was exerted upon events.

I must keep what strength I have for the House of Commons, though there is not much hope of that either. Nothing but the terrible teaching of experience will affect this all-powerful supine Government. The worst of it is that by the time they are convinced, or replaced, our own position will be frightfully weakened.

Geoffrey Dennis to Winston S. Churchill

(*Churchill papers: 2/358*)

25 March 1939

Dear Mr Churchill,

I signed an official apology to you with regard to 'Coronation Commentary'. I desire to add a sincere private apology, & here express my real
contrition for the gratuitously offensive remark I allowed myself to make.
I hope you will feel able to accept this.[1]

There is no *practical* means open to me of showing my regret. But I can at
least send you my moral support in your present political activity. The
country is looking to you. To take a liberty (which I feel that the present
horrible danger may excuse), & to refer to one important aspect as to which
I am much better informed than most Englishmen:—I will say that I hope
you leave *Italy* out of your present timely warnings & denunciations. I live
in that country, & I know the present situation there fairly well. The chance
of a change—a vital change—is a *real* one. The hostile public opinion (to
Germany) is strong enough perhaps, in certain circumstances, to *affect* the
Duce's plans. We shd do nothing to direct or arrest the growing change in
that opinion—nothing in *words*;—almost everything short (of course) of
betraying France. Italy weaned away, the outlook wd be fairer for the world.

Yours sincerely,
Geoffrey Dennis

Winston S. Churchill: memorandum

(*Churchill papers: 25/17*)

26 March 1939

ROSES

('Roses, roses all the way!')

1. The main defence of England against air raids is the toll which can be
exacted from the raiders. One-fifth knocked out each go will soon bring the
raids to an end.

2. We must not get in the way of fighter aircraft, searchlights, or gunfire,
over the land. But it would be good if a new deterrent could be created on
the sea approaches or homeward returns. If Mine-Curtains or Mine-Spirals
can be dropped athwart the track of raiders crossing the seas, either going

---

[1] For the 'offensive remark' in *Coronation Commentary*, see pages 653–4 and 660, note 2.

or coming, a toll will be levied upon them additional to anything now arranged.

3. No aircraft allotted to existing war-plans need be detached. A mine-laying group could be formed of older, or perhaps even civilian machines. These based upon the coasts of Suffolk and Kent could rise seaward at any time after the first alarm and cruise till the raiders come and return. They must be in contact with the RDF Stations, and be told by wireless at what heights, places, and times to lay their Curtains or Spirals.

4. We must imagine the opening attack as a large affair crossing the sea in relays for many hours. Probably even when coming they will fly pretty straight; but certainly they will go home the shortest way. It should not, therefore, be impossible to drop a Curtain, or lethal drizzle, very unpleasant for aeroplanes to fly through either way across this main route. Later on you might have to extend or vary north or south.

5. But it is the first results of the air attack which will govern the future of the air-war. It is not child's play to come and attack England. A heavy proportion of casualties will lead the enemy to make severe calculations of profit and loss. As daylight raiding will soon become too expensive, we have chiefly to deal with random night bombing of the built-up areas. The results of this may prove out of all proportion to the expense of carrying the stuff and to the wearing down of the hostile Air Force.

6. Even if only a quarter could be copped coming or going back across the sea, this would be a decisive addition to all the other deterrents now in existence.

7. I ask, therefore,[1] (A) That the technical experiments to determine the weight of charge required and the length of wire convenient etcetera, to damage propellers or wings should be given the highest priority.

(B) That at least one hundred aeroplanes not needed for bombing or fighting should be stationed in the coastal areas and organised and trained as above-sea mine-layers.

(C) That at least ten million of the approved pattern parachute bombs should be ordered as soon as the experiments in (A) have defined the specifications, and that a capacity production of a million a week should be provided.

8. Only in this way in the next few months can the shortage of guns, the absence of UP,[2] and other deficiencies be supplemented.

---

[1] In the original of this memorandum, as received by Kingsley Wood, Churchill added at this point: 'for the urgent consideration of the following measures' (*Air Ministry papers: 19/26*).

[2] UP = Unrotated Projectile = rocket.

Oliver Lyttelton[1] to Winston S. Churchill

(*Churchill papers: 2/375*)

27 March 1939

Dear Winston,

I do not know if you have noticed a letter in 'The Times' from a friend of mine called Strathallan,[2] the son of Lord Perth.

His point seems to me to be a good one. Many of the Territorial Anti-Aircraft formations will be quite useless *if war comes before their annual camp*.[3] I think it would not be a matter of great difficulty to give them their annual camp at once.

If you can give his idea a shove, I think it would be worth while.

Please forgive me for bothering you.

Yours ever,
Oliver

[1] Oliver Lyttelton, 1893–1972. The son of Alfred Lyttelton, Balfour's Colonial Secretary. Educated at Eton and Trinity College, Cambridge. 2nd Lieutenant, Grenadier Guards, December 1914; on active service on the western front, 1915–18 (Military Cross, DSO, despatches three times, wounded April 1918). Entered merchant banking, 1919. Joined the British Metal Corporation, 1920; later managing director. Elected to the Other Club at the beginning of 1939. Appointed Controller of Non-Ferrous Metals, September 1939. President of the Board of Trade, and Privy Councillor, July 1940. Conservative MP for Aldershot, 1940–54. Minister of State, Middle East (based in Cairo), and Member of the War Cabinet, June 1941. Minister of Production, March 1942–May 1945. Chairman of Associated Electrical Industries, 1945–51 and 1954–63. Secretary of State for Colonial Affairs, 1951–4. Created Viscount Chandos, 1954. Chairman of the National Theatre Board, 1962; Life President, 1971. Knight of the Garter, 1970. One of his three sons was killed on active service in Italy in 1944.

[2] John David Drummond, Viscount Strathallan, 1907–   . Only son of the 16th Earl of Perth. Educated at Downside and Cambridge. Lieutenant, Intelligence Corps, 1939; seconded for work in the War Cabinet Office, 1942–3, the Ministry of Production, 1943–6. Succeeded his father, as 17th Earl of Perth, 1951. Minister of State for Colonial Affairs, 1957–62. First Crown Estate Commissioner, 1962–77. Chairman of the Ditchley Foundation since 1963, and a Trustee of the National Library of Scotland since 1968.

[3] On 27 March 1939 *The Times* published a letter from Lord Strathallan (from 37 Threadneedle Street, EC2, dated 25 March 1939) stating that the 'many hours' said by an earlier correspondent to be devoted to the mastery of weapons in the Territorial Army 'do not generally amount to four, and may often be but one or two'. Yet even during these hours 'little practice of the weapons—as, for example, in the case of the anti-aircraft regiments firing their guns or using their sound-locators under active service conditions—is to be had'. It was only at camp, Strathallan argued, that the necessary 'intensive firing' with the latest equipment could be had. 'Is the certainty of peace sufficient,' he asked, 'to warrant delay in camps being held?'

Winston S. Churchill to Kingsley Wood

(Churchill papers: 25/17)

27 March 1939   Chartwell
For Yourself alone

My dear Kingsley,

I hope you will be inclined to have a Meeting of the ADR Committee quite soon.

The device we talked about has made a certain amount of fitful progress during the last three to four years. It now represents the sole addition to your deterrents against air raids which can be made effective in the next three months. The guns are moving at the rates you know; the UP cannot play any part this year. The projectiles of the lingering character cannot be designed, still less manufactured before the crisis of this year is past. The tall balloon-barrage is unhappily a long-term plan but there still remains the Mine-Curtain. You will see that in my note of July 1935 I pressed upon the Committee this Lindemann proposal. All is there in theory in ADR 21, July 1935, Paragraph 19.[1] Read it please.[2] All might be here in fact now if the idea had [not been scientifically sabotaged in quarters not worth specifying at the moment.][3] received loyal encouragement.

However, we cannot now afford to recriminate. The sole point is to gain a reinforcement of our defences. You will no doubt be told that everything is going on all right, and that there is no need to disturb the ordinary train of research; and I dare say unless you intervene another year [might] may well be [gained by those who have obstructed this plan] lost. Nevertheless when I put to you the question: 'Where else can you look for help?', you may perhaps lend your authority to the comparatively small simple measures which are required.

I therefore enclose a memorandum which I ask should be printed and circulated before our next Meeting. What we need is an exceptional priority. We go buzzing along with a host of ideas and experiments which [will] may produce results in '41, '42, and '43. Where will you find anything that can operate in June, July and August of 1939? This is the only possible reinforcement. Never will it be more needed than in these months when so much else is lacking. In my personal view this idea may turn out to be as good as

---

[1] Churchill's memorandum 'Air Defence' of 23 July 1935, circulated to the Committee of Imperial Defence's Sub-Committee on Air Defence Research, as document ADR 21, and published in full in the previous document volume of this biography (volume V, Companion Part 2, 'The Wilderness Years', pages 1215–1224).

[2] In the final version of this letter, as received by Kingsley Wood, Churchill underlined the word '*please*' (*Air Ministry papers: 19/29*).

[3] The phrases in square brackets were deleted by Churchill in the final draft.

the Tank or the Anti-Submarine methods. [It has certainly had the same obstruction from the Authorities.]

On March 4 Lindemann sent six of these [tiny] cigar cylinders to Woolwich to be filled with explosive. Farnborough has been waiting ready to try them on propellers. It would have taken at most an hour to fill these tiny containers; but so far nothing has happened. [Another month has been gained to the obstructive forces.] These delays were mortal to progress. [This] There is a form of departmentalism very vicious to England. I therefore beg you to call a Meeting and, if the case is made, to order the highest priority for these experiments. They are so simple that if they were in friendly and resolute hands, a few weeks would suffice. After nearly four years we have not been [able to get them made.] given any definite results. The story is [shameful] lamentable and only the public interest prevents its being told to Parliament.

Now I do beg you to use your authority. It costs so little; it is such a [tiny] minute fraction of your sphere of responsibility. But unless you insist that the small primary steps shall be taken at once, day after day, nothing will happen except this vast prolonged grimacing.

T. L. Horabin[1] *to Winston S. Churchill*

(*Churchill papers: 2/358*)

27 March 1939

Dear Sir,

I should perhaps begin by explaining that I am prospective Liberal candidate for North Cornwall in succession to Sir Francis Acland.[2]

Last week I spoke at twelve meetings in the division on the foreign situation, at each of which I tried, with the help of a map of Europe, to give a plain, unvarnished statement of the facts.

My main proposal was that as leadership was all important you were the only possible man for Prime Minister in this hour of danger.

---

[1] Thomas Lewis Horabin, 1896–1956. Educated at Cardiff High School. Business consultant. Independent Liberal MP for North Cornwall, 1939–47; Chief Party Whip of the Independent Liberals, 1945. Joined the Labour Party, 1947; Labour MP, 1947–50.

[2] Francis Dyke Acland, 1874–1939. Educated at Rugby and Balliol College, Oxford. Liberal MP for Richmond, 1906–10; for North West Cornwall, 1910–22; for Tiverton, 1923–4; for North Cornwall for 1932 until his retirement due to ill-health. Under-Secretary of State for Foreign Affairs, 1911–15. Financial Secretary to the Treasury, 1915; Secretary to the Board of Agriculture, 1915–16. Succeeded his father at 14th Baronet, 1926. He died on 9 June 1939.

It may interest you to know how this proposal was received.

It came as a shock to people for a free Liberal to suggest you as Prime Minister. It took about two minutes for the idea to sink in, and then there was an outburst of applause.

The only question asked at any meeting was over your change of party. Here I pointed out that you had changed your parties but not your principles, which went over well.

I can say as a result of the obvious attitude of the people at the meetings and of the personal discussions afterwards, that everyone felt my proposal was the only solution—but how are we to get Chamberlain out in time?

At a divisional meeting of all district officials on Saturday, Sir Francis Acland also supported the proposal (which came as a shock to him, I think) and those present felt that the only way of getting a move on quickly was to prepare a petition which might spread to other divisions.

The only opposition came from one Tory lady, who thought I had dealt with 'dear Mr Chamberlain too brutally'.

I enclose a copy of my speech in case you are interested in the arguments which brought these North Cornish people to acceptance of you as the only possible Prime Minister at this critical moment.

Yours faithfully,
T. L. Horabin

Brigadier-General Sir James Edmonds to Winston S. Churchill
(Churchill papers: 8/626)

27 March 1939   Committee of Imperial Defence

My dear Mr Churchill,

The final instalments are very nearly ready. It has required two boilings down to expose the 'backbone'. Without foreign intervention the South had no chance.

I have read 'Gone with the Wind', also 'Action at Aquia' (dealing with the devastation of the Shenandoah valley) and most novels on the war including your namesake's 'The Crisis'.[1] I devour novels American, French and German, there is rarely a good English one.

I shall be delighted to run over the campaigns on the map later on.

Yes, I am still sanguine. Hitler won't fight without an Ally and Mussolini is 'not for it'. Still if the War House must lie, why not say 90 instead of 19 divisions, to encourage the small nations. The absurd little figure has made

---

[1] Hervey Allen's *Action at Aquia* had been published in London in 1938. The novel *The Crisis*, by the American writer Winston Churchill, had been published in London in 1901.

foreign military journals laugh. At any rate, we ought to have the *cadres* of
90 divisions. In March 1918, after losing a couple of million men, Germany
had in the field 248 divisions plus 16 brigades. However, Germany's scheme
is: first to secure her own supplies; then to blockade us.

Yours sincerely,
J. E. Edmonds

Winston S. Churchill to Neville Chamberlain

(*Premier papers: 1/345*)

27 March 1939
Private & Personal

My dear Neville,

I do not think you will mind my writing to you upon the subject of the
enclosed Memorandum. Knowing how busy you are, I have reduced it to
the shortest compass, stating conclusions rather than the arguments for them.

Yours vy sincerely,
Winston S. Churchill

Winston S. Churchill to Lord Halifax

(*Churchill papers: 2/371*)

27 March 1939
Private & Personal

I do not think you will mind my writing to you upon the subject of the
enclosed Memorandum. Knowing how busy you are, I have reduced it to
the shortest compass, stating conclusions rather than the arguments for them.

Winston S. Churchill to Leslie Hore-Belisha

(*Churchill papers: 2/371*)

27 March 1939
Private and Confidential

I send you a copy of the Memorandum I have given to the PM to-day. I
also sent a copy to Halifax. I think it would be better for you to keep this
entirely to yourself, as Chatfield might be offended if he thought I was
circulating it. I hope you will find yourself in agreement with the arguments,
and that you will be able to use them. The PM seemed to like them, and I
think things may settle themselves in this sense.

Winston S. Churchill: Memorandum on Sea-Power, 1939

(*Churchill papers: 4/96*)

27 March 1939
Secret

1. To Germany the command of the Baltic is vital. Scandinavian supplies, Swedish ore, and, above all, protection against Russian descents on the long, undefended northern coast-line of Germany (in one place little more than a hundred miles from Berlin) make it imperative for Germany to dominate the Baltic. We may therefore be sure that in the opening phase she will not compromise her command of this sea. Thus, while submarines and raiding cruisers, or perhaps one pocket-battleship, may be sent out to disturb our traffic, no ships will be risked which are necessary to the Baltic command. The German fleet, as at present developed, aims at this as its prime and almost its sole objective.

If this be true, no very large British naval forces will be needed to watch the debouches from the Baltic or from the Heligoland Bight. British security would be markedly increased if an air attack upon the Kiel Canal rendered that side door useless, even if only at intervals.

2. Assuming Italy is hostile, which we may perhaps hope will not be the case, England's first battlefield is the Mediterranean. All plans for sealing up the ends must be discarded in favour of decisive victory there. Our forces alone should be sufficient to drive the Italian ships from the sea, and secure complete command of the Mediterranean, certainly within two months, possibly sooner.

The submarine has been mastered, thanks very largely to Lord Chatfield's long efforts at the Admiralty. It should be quite controllable in the outer seas, and certainly in the Mediterranean. There will be losses, but nothing to affect the scale of events.

In my opinion, given with great humility (because these things are very difficult to judge), an air attack upon British warships, armed and protected as they now are, will not prevent full exercise of their superior sea power. The British domination of the Mediterranean will inflict inevitable injuries upon Italy which may be fatal to her power of continuing the war. All her troops in Libya and in Abyssinia will be, as I said: 'cut flowers in a vase'. The French and our own people in Egypt could be reinforced to any extent desired, while theirs would be overweighted if not starved. If the French fleet and French naval bases are added to our own, this task is what the Admiralty should readily accept. Not to hold the Mediterranean would be to expose Egypt and the Canal, as well as the French possessions, to invasion by Italian troops with German leadership. We cannot tolerate this on any account. Moreover, a series of swift and striking victories in this theatre, which might be obtainable in the early weeks of a war, would have a most healthy and helpful bearing upon the main struggle with Germany. Nothing should stand between us and these results, both naval and military.

3. On no account must anything which threatens in the Far East divert us from this prime objective. In war one only has to compare one evil with another, and the lesser evil ranks as a blessing.

If Japan joins the hostile combination, which is by no means certain, for she has her hands full, all our interests and possessions in the Yellow Sea will be temporarily effaced. We must not be drawn from our main theme by any effort to protect them. Only if the United States comes in against Japan could we supply even a squadron of cruisers to operate with them. On this tableau we must bear the losses and punishment, awaiting the final result of the struggle.

4. The farthest point we can hold in the conditions imagined is Singapore. This should be easy. A fortress of this character with cannon which can hold any fleet at arm's length only requires an adequate garrison and supplies of food and ammunition, preferably for a year; but even six months would probably do. Singapore must hold out till the Mediterranean is safe, and the Italian fleet liquidated.

Consider how vain is the menace that Japan will send a fleet and army to conquer Singapore. It is as far from Japan as Southampton from New York. Over these two thousand miles of salt water, Japan would have to send the bulk of her fleet, escort at least sixty thousand men in transports in order to effect a landing, and begin a siege which would end only in disaster if the Japanese sea-communications were cut at any stage.

One can take it as quite certain that Japan would not run such a risk. They are an extremely sensible people. They would have the opportunity of obtaining for the time being complete satisfaction for all their ambitions in the Yellow Sea. Their fleet protects their homeland and overseas empire from the worst perils. To send a large part of their strictly limited naval forces on a wild adventure such as the siege and reduction of Singapore, will never commend itself to them until England has been decisively beaten, which will not be the case in the first year of the war. If, *per impossible*, they were to attempt it, a British victory in the Mediterranean might be followed a few months later by a decisive naval relief of Singapore. Do not therefore let us worry about this bugbear. Minor naval dispositions may be made to increase the deterrents against an attack on Singapore, but you may be sure that, provided it is fully armed, garrisoned and supplied, there will be no attack in any period which our foresight can measure.

5. As long as the British Navy is undefeated, and as long as we hold

Singapore, no invasion of Australia or New Zealand by Japan is possible. We could give Australasia a good guarantee to protect them from this danger, but we must do it in our own way, and in the proper sequence of operations. Can one suppose that Japan, enjoying herself in the mastery of the Yellow Sea, would send afloat a conquering and colonising expedition to Australia? It is ludicrous. More than one hundred thousand men would be needed to make any impression upon Australian manhood. The sending of such an expedition would require the improvident diversion of the Japanese fleet, and their engagement in a long, desultory struggle in Australia. At any moment a decision in the Mediterranean would liberate overwhelming naval forces to cut any such expedition from its base.

One does not know what the attitude of the United States would be to an attempt by Japan to conquer and colonise Australia. It would be easy for the United States to tell Japan that they would regard the sending of Japanese fleets and transports South of the Equator as an act of war. They might well be disposed to make such a declaration, and there would be no harm in sounding them upon this very remote contingency.

I am aware of the promise that we made to send a powerful fleet to the Pacific, but this would be folly in the opening stages of the war, and I am sure if the strategic argument is laid before the Australian Commonwealth, they will play the game by us as they have always done. Tell them the whole story, and they will come along. In the first year of a world war they would be in no danger whatever in their homeland, and by the end of the first year we may hope to have cleared up the seas and oceans.

My main conclusion in this section is that there is no danger of Japan sending large expeditions against Singapore or Australia until matters have been decided in Europe; and that if they did so, so long as we hold Singapore, they would be placing themselves at a great disadvantage. No, they will take Hong Kong and Shanghai, and clean us out of all our interests there. But then, if we are still alive, we will put that right later on.

6. Assuming that the foregoing argument is accepted, and that events generally conform to it, that our command of the Mediterranean is unquestioned and that no expedition has been launched against Singapore or Australia, the question would arise where the next operation of the British Fleet should be. This is a matter we cannot attempt to decide at this stage. But clearly the one great naval offensive against Germany is the Baltic. If, for instance, we had to-day a superior fleet in the Baltic, one might almost say for certain that Germany would not declare war. We have not got the naval power to attempt this before the Mediterranean has been conquered, but there is no hypothetical operation which should be studied more carefully, and for which plans should be made for use should conditions allow,

than the domination of the Baltic. Here is the sole great offensive against Germany of British sea-power. Ardent officers should be set to work for a year upon the problems of entering the Baltic and living there in indefinite ascendancy. Kronstadt presents itself as the chief base.[1] However, much blood will have flowed under the bridges before any question of application can arise. But if we are happy in the Mediterranean, and no Japanese expedition had been launched (which it will not be) in the Pacific, this would be the sovran plan.

However by that time the entry wd probably be fortified, & Denmark in German hands. Therefore the whole idea is purely hypothetical as well as remote.[2]

Desmond Morton to Winston S. Churchill

(*Churchill papers: 2/371*)

27 March 1939   Earlylands

My Dear Winston,

1. I think that on page 4 you overstate the unlikelihood of Japan sending a force to try and reduce Singapore. I am with you in claiming that it is unlikely that Japan will succeed in *capturing* Singapore, so long as we take the precautions you have outlined.

2. You do not mention India and Indian sea-borne trade. I understand that the Government of India has strongly urged the sending of the main fleet to Far Eastern waters on the ground that the mere absence of the fleet would give heart to rebellious elements in India.

3. I would have thought that British *and French* public opinion would, in the event, never allow the despatch of the British fleet, which we have so consistently claimed to be our great war contribution, to the other side of the world.

4. Apart from Singapore, what after all, are our interests and possessions in the Yellow Sea?

Yours ever,
Desmond Morton

[1] But only in the event of an arrangement or alliance with the Soviet Union. On 17 June 1919, as part of the British Government's anti-Bolshevik activities, a British coastal motor-boat had penetrated the Soviet naval defences at Kronstadt, and torpedoed a 6,600 ton cruiser. Two weeks *later*, on 4 July 1919, the War Cabinet, presided over by Lloyd George, decided that 'our Naval forces in Russian waters should be authorized to engage enemy forces by land and sea, when necessary'. The First Lord of the Admiralty at that time was Walter Long; Churchill was then Secretary of State for War and Air.

[2] This last paragraph was added in Churchill's handwriting on the copy as received by Neville Chamberlain, 10 Downing Street. Chamberlain noted on the memorandum: 'Lord

Harold Nicolson: diary

(*Nicolson papers*)

27 March 1939

A meeting in 17 Great College Street to discuss the situation. Duff Cooper, Amery, Anthony Eden, Wolmer, Harold Macmillan. There are two schools of thought. Those who want to get a coalition Government and those who want conscription. We are not quite sure which is the cart and which the horse. . . .

We decide to put down a motion urging a national government. . . .

Duff promises to get Winston to join us.

Harold Nicolson: diary

(*Nicolson papers*)

28 March 1939

I go about trying to collect signatures to our motion. Churchill, Eden, Duff Cooper, and Amery have signed. I find other people sticky. They agree with the principle but do not wish to be associated with anti-Chamberlain groups. . . .

Rab[1] says our motion (with which he himself agrees) will be twisted by David Margesson into appearing as a personal attack on the PM.

Lord Halifax to Winston S. Churchill

(*Churchill papers: 2/371*)

28 March 1939   Foreign Office

My dear Winston,

Many thanks for sending me your memorandum. With no claim to any special knowledge, I find my thought going very much with yours.

I hope you have sent a copy to Chatfield.

Yrs ever,

E

Chatfield might care to see,' and minuted for his Private Secretary: 'I don't think it necessary to reply to Mr Churchill's letter & memo as I had a talk with him just after I received it' (*Premier papers: 1/345*).

[1] R. A. Butler, Under-Secretary of State for Foreign Affairs (see page 1200, note 1).

Winston S. Churchill to Geoffrey Dennis

(*Churchill papers: 2/358*)

28 March 1939

I am very much obliged to you for your letter which entirely removes the painful impression I sustained on reading what you wrote. I thank you for having written to me as you have done.

I thought there was a great deal of brilliant writing in 'Coronation Commentary', and am very sorry that trouble arose out of certain passages.

Many thanks for what you say about the general situation.

Winston S. Churchill to George Harrap

(*Churchill papers: 8/626*)

28 March 1939

Dear Mr Harrap,

In my 'History of the English-speaking Peoples' I have now reached the period covered by 'Marlborough', and I hope you will not mind if I summarise some of the passages which form the general background to the biography. I find it difficult to write of the same events differently. I do of course paraphrase and alter as I go along, but still the identity of the two versions would be noticeable. The passages in question come mainly in the reigns of James II and William III, because Queen Anne is told on a much wider scale. I should like, however, to be assured that you have no objection to this process. The total passages extracted or summarised would amount to about 15,000 words out of the nearly 800,000 which the four volumes of 'Marlborough' contain, and would be included in the 'English-speaking Peoples' of 400,000 words. Thus the proportions appear small. Of course I should insert a footnote that in this period I have followed largely the line taken in 'Marlborough', and also made quotations from it.

Cassell's will only be publishing in several parts during 1940, and the whole work will not appear in book form till 1941.[1] I hope, therefore, you will allow me to plagiarize myself to some extent.

I should be glad of an early answer, as I am actually in this period at this moment. I am most anxious to get this work finished by the end of this year,

---

[1] The first volume of *A History of the English-Speaking Peoples* was not in fact published until 23 April 1956, the fourth and final volume until 14 March 1958. Not only did war intervene, and Churchill's premiership, but also the writing and publication of his six-volume war memoirs, *The Second World War*.

so as to begin our book[1] early in 1940. It is very hard to write about the past when the present is so disturbing.

Upon what I mentioned to you this morning, I will certainly in the first instance submit the project to you. There are at least 75 fortnightly articles each averaging 1,200 words, making about 90,000 words. As the articles are coming out regularly every fortnight, one could count on at least 100,000 words for the volume. The articles are all written in my best style, and they form a continuous survey of the darkening scene. They would be interspersed with short notes between the chapters to make the whole story run easily.

All the articles have been reproduced in thirty to forty foreign and Imperial newspapers all over the world. They all bear upon the foreign situation, which will increasingly dominate attention; and under some such title as 'Step by Step' I should think they would have a very good sale. I should contemplate an early publication, I hope during the summer.

Pray let me know as soon as convenient whether you are interested, because I have no doubt Butterworth will be anxious to make an offer.[2]

Sir Kingsley Wood to Winston S. Churchill
(*Churchill papers: 25/17*)

28 March 1939

My dear Winston,

I have your letter to which we are giving immediate attention. I will speak to you about it as soon as possible. I will arrange for your Memorandum to be circulated & arrange for a meeting to be called at an early date.

Sincerely,
Kingsley Wood

[1] *Europe Since The Russian Revolution* (see page 1283, note 2).

[2] *Step By Step* was eventually published by Thornton Butterworth on 27 June 1939 (and by Putnams in New York on 25 August 1939). It contained all Churchill's articles printed in the *Evening Standard* between 13 March 1936 to 5 April 1938 and in the *Daily Telegraph* between 14 April 1936 to 18 May 1939. A total of 7,500 copies were printed. The book was subsequently translated into French, German, Italian, Swedish, Danish and Spanish. There were two English reprints: in November 1939 (1,500 copies), February 1940 (1,800 copies). In 1942 Macmillan republished the volume, and in 1947 Odhams reissued it. For Churchill's preface, written on 21 May 1939, see page 1504 of this volume.

Sir Kingsley Wood to Winston S. Churchill

(*Churchill papers: 25/17*)

29 March 1939   Air Ministry

My dear Winston,

I am writing to let you know that I arranged for Pye to get in touch with Lindemann this morning to suggest that they should visit Farnborough together so that Lindemann should have an opportunity of seeing the experimental work which was being carried on there on lines very similar to his own proposals; and I gather that Lindemann is arranging to meet Pye at Farnborough tomorrow. There are also certain experiments which are to be carried out at Mildenhall on Monday if the weather permits and Pye is suggesting that Lindemann should attend these experiments with him.

I am, in consequence, holding my hand about arranging a meeting until I have had a report on the outcome of these experiments.

Sincerely,
Kingsley Wood

Lord Chatfield: notes on Winston S. Churchill's memorandum on Sea Power

(*Premier papers: 1/345*)

29 March 1939

. . . Generally I consider they are sound and, of course, as is well known to members of the CID strategical Sub-Committee, the general policy proposed of immediate and decisive action in the Mediterranean has been approved.

FAR EAST

As regards the Far East, I concur generally that we must take some risk in the Far East while we are settling the Mediterranean, but I very much doubt whether the Mediterranean problem will be settled in two or three months. . . . If, however, we have the United States fleet at Honolulu, our Far Eastern position will at once become easier, and we do not know that Japan will immediately come into the war. It would seem much more likely that she will wait to see what losses we have in our fleet and how we get on generally in Europe before she decides to come in, if at all. . . .

BALTIC

It is quite possible after we have settled the Mediterranean problem and when the situation in the Far East is clear to consider some such action.

Air Chief Marshal Sir Hugh Dowding to Kathleen Hill
(Churchill papers: 1/343)

29 March 1939   Montrose,
                                                       Stanmore

Air Chief Marshal Sir Hugh Dowding is very grateful for the return of his pipe which he left behind him at Chartwell Manor last Sunday.

Lord Greenwood[1] to Winston S. Churchill
(Churchill papers: 2/358)

30 March 1939

My dear Winston,

I am so glad that you are coming to the Canada Club Dinner at the Savoy on April 19th and that you will propose Bennett's[2] health. He is overjoyed at the compliment you pay him. I think you ought to speak at least twenty minutes, or indeed as long as you like. We are living in critical times and your fine record over the past years gives you an unchallenged position and the right to help to unite and to lead the English speaking world.[3]

Ever yours,

---

[1] Hamar Greenwood, 1870–1948. Born in Canada, Served in the Department of Agriculture, Ontario. Liberal MP (at Westminster), 1906–22. Parliamentary Secretary to Churchill at the Colonial Office and Board of Trade, 1906–10. Baronet, 1915. On active service with the British Expeditionary Force in France, as a Lieutenant-Colonel, 1915–16. Deputy Assistant Adjutant-General, War Office, 1916. Under-Secretary of State, Home Office, 1919. Secretary, Department of Overseas Trade, 1919–20. Chief Secretary, Ireland, 1920–2, and one of the organizers of the 'Black and Tans'. Joined the Conservative Party, 1922. Conservative MP, 1924–9. Created Baron, 1929. Treasurer of the Conservative Party, 1933–8. Created Viscount, 1937.

[2] Richard Bedford Bennett, 1870–1947. Born in New Brunswick. Member of the Legislative Assembly of Alberta, 1909–11, and of the Canadian House of Commons, 1911–21. Defeated, 1921. Minister of Justice, 1921. Elected Leader of Conservative Party, 1927. Returned to House of Commons, July 1930, and immediately became Prime Minister, Minister of External Affairs, and Minister of Finance. Represented Canada at the Imperial Conference, London, 1927, when he was sworn in as an Imperial Privy Councillor. Created Viscount, 1941.

[3] Speaking on 19 April 1939 at a dinner given by the Canada Club in honour of R. B. Bennett, the former Canadian Prime Minister, Churchill told the assembled guests (including two former Governors-General of Canada, Lord Willingdon and Lord Bessborough) that it

Harold Nicolson: diary

(*Nicolson papers*)

30 March 1939

A meeting of the New Commonwealth which is to be addressed by Winston. It is with difficulty that we whip up a proper audience. They simply do not wish to hear what they fear will be painful things. Winston merely says that when the war is over, we must build up a League of Nations based upon organised force and not upon disorganised nonsense.

Winston S. Churchill to John Wheldon

(*Churchill papers: 8/626*)

30 March 1939

My dear Wheldon,

I am delighted with the notes you have sent me, which will be of the greatest value. I am having them provisionally printed, and will send you the proofs. I now enclose a cheque for £52.10.0. with my very best thanks.

It would be a great help to me if you would, for a similar fee, read the chapters which I have in print leading up to Henry VIII. These would comprise the Wars of the Roses, Richard III and Henry VII. I should not want you to do any additional research, but merely to write freely from your modern knowledge on the proofs, both in correction and improvement. I have so far not bent in any references to the Reformation, keeping that larger topic for a later phase. Perhaps you will let me know whether this will be agreeable to you, and I will send you the proofs. The more you can put on to them, the better for my final reading.

Mrs Churchill thanks you very much for your kind messages.

---

was 'refreshing to find' that in the United States as well as Canada, 'these same resolves to resist at all costs the new machine-made forms of tyranny and oppression were also instinctive and strong'. A few moments later he declared: 'If the British Empire was fated to pass from life into history, we must hope it would not be by the slow process of dispersion and decay, but in some supreme exertion for freedom, for right and for truth. In the British Empire we not only looked out across the seas towards each other but backwards to our own history, to Magna Carta, to Habeas Corpus, to the Petition of Right, to Trial by Jury, to the English Common Law, and to Parliamentary Democracy. These were the milestones and monuments that marked the path along which the British race had marched to leadership and freedom. And over all this, uniting each Dominion with the other and uniting us all with our majestic past, was the golden circle of the Crown. What was within that circle? Not only the glory of an ancient unconquered people, but the hope, the sure hope, of a broadening life for hundreds of millions of men' (as reported in *The Times*, 20 April 1939).

Winston S. Churchill to Lord Chatfield

(*Churchill papers: 2/371*)

31 March 1939

I sent a copy of the enclosed[1] to the PM. It is by way of being an amplification of the speech I made in the House. I thought perhaps you would like to have a copy.

Desmond Morton to Winston S. Churchill

(*Churchill papers: 2/374*)

31 March 1939   Earlylands

My dear Winston,

The only criticism I have on the clip of papers headed: 'Speech on 2nd reading of ARP Bill', is to recommend strongly the omission of the argument on page 3 regarding the German supply of Nitrogen. It is not well founded. The Germans do not require any Chili Nitrate. They only use a very small quantity in peace as fertiliser, and then, only because the Chileans refuse to trade with them unless they take an agreed weight of Chili Nitrate every year. Then there are now several other processes for the fixation of Nitrogen from the air, besides the Haber process. Germany has no war reserve of natural nitrates and does not need any. Her fixation capacity is enormous, amounting, in the old Reich alone, apart from smaller plants in the Ostmark and Bohemia, to about 100,000 tons per month *in terms of Nitrogen*. I attach some figures.

The chief arguments in the papers labelled II, seem to me to be very sound. I only suggest consideration of three small points:

(a) If you are going to advocate bombing only military targets, it is very desirable to define what is meant by this term. There is already great controversy over it in technical circles; and if you don't watch it, you will be involved in arguments as tortuous as the old one over 'Strength of an Air Force', and 'What is meant by First Line'.

(b) I do not follow the argument that the 7,000 guns used by the Germans for AA purposes would, in the last war, have been in the front line. The Germans (and everyone else) have an even greater proportion of guns in the front line nowadays than they had in 1918, apart from AA artillery.

---

[1] Churchill's 'Memorandum on Sea-Power, 1939' printed on pages 1414–17, and on which, at Chamberlain's request Chatfield had already commented on two days earlier (see page 1421).

(c) I am told that the Thames, or for that matter any river, stands up at night like a signpost, even if the moon is obscured, and on any night when there is not a new moon, ie any reasonable sort of moon at all.

As regards the paper marked III, I am certain that if the Germans want to start mere destruction, they will use incendiary bombs to a very great extent. I attach a table of bomb weights, fuel consumption &c, for the German types of bombers now in their Air Force.

As regards the paper marked IV: there are some rather dangerous arguments here.

(a) I strongly suggest no mention of Spain or China. HMG has some very complete information on air-bombing in both these spheres, which, if you could see it, would, I am sure, convince you that events in neither of these parts of the globe can in any way be taken as a precedent for what might happen in Europe between two countries, who did not expect to own the property they were destroying, so soon as the war was ended. Not one single air attack in Spain by either side can be shewn to have been an attempt to destroy morale. In fact both sides went out of their way to try and avoid killing civilians. Nearly everything printed about this in the Press, whether pro-Republican or Pro-Franco, has been nonsense. In China there has been a certain amount of indiscriminate bombing by the Japanese; but not nearly so much as the Press has made out. Conditions and circumstances are, however, quite at variance with a European war or European peoples.

(b) I would certainly not say that the German Air Force has no intention of bombing civilians. Our information is quite the contrary. Little secret is made by them of their lectures to their Air Force on the use of bombers in war. True, they do not officially advocate the 'Terror-tactics' save as a last resort; but they strongly advocate the bombing of targets behind the fighting line, which will inevitably entail the death of civilians. Their intention towards us is to destroy first of all the docks and harbours on our East Coast, and secondly our aircraft factories.

Neither of these points vitiates your main argument demanding the marking out of 'target areas', which I consider to be eminently sound.[1]

---

[1] During the debate on the European situation on 3 April 1939, Churchill urges the acceleration of measures of air defence, telling the House: 'Personally, I believe that the weapon of air terror cuts both ways, and I believe also, that it cannot in any case be decisive against the life of a brave and free people. Nevertheless, the ordeal to which we should be subjected is one which we should not underrate. Do not let us neglect anything. Let us take

I also return the letter speaking of a possible shortage in this country of light coal tar oils. I do not know the situation created by the new expansion of the Territorial Field Army; but prior to that there was no danger of shortage, I understand. This was mainly due to various very secret discoveries of alternative methods of making what I may call synthetic toluene. Plant exists for the hydrogenation of creosote into toluene in large quantities. They do not want this talked about. I can get you the exact and detailed figures for the last war, when I go back to London. They are all to be found in the Confidential History of the Ministry of Munitions. Have you got a copy?

Finally I attach some figures about Germany, which may be of use or interest to you.[1]

Yours very sincerely,
Desmond Morton

Sir Kingsley Wood to Air Chief Marshal Sir Hugh Dowding
(*Air Ministry papers: 19/26*)

31 March 1939

. . . I have arranged for Lindemann, who as you know is in close touch with Mr Churchill, to be put au fait with what is going on at Farnborough and with the experiments that are to be carried out at Lakenheath, and I should have no objection to your informing Mr Churchill of those experiments if you happen to see him.

---

every step to diminish this dangerous period and to abridge its duration. But precautions taken are not only safeguards; they may be preventatives.'

[1] Desmond Morton's figures were of German aircraft production and bomb loads, weight of fuel carried with full bomb load according to aircraft types, a breakdown of German liquid fuel stocks held as of 1 January 1939 (total Petrol Production: 2,500,000 tons), a breakdown of current production in 1939 (a total of 2,600,000 tons); a note on German fuel reserves (900,000 tons of crude); and a detailed calculation to show that in the first year of war Germany 'must import from somewhere over 3 million tons of petroleum products'. Morton's note continued: 'Be it noted that of the 1,500,000 tons of synthetic motor spirit produced in the year in Germany, about 850,000 tons is produced by processes which give a spirit capable of being used as aviation spirit after ethylisation. There is plenty of Tetra ethyl lead made and in stock in Germany for this purpose.' Churchill sent this note to Sir Henry Strakosch on 18 April 1939 (see page 1463).

Kathleen Hill: Chartwell Literary Account

(*Churchill papers: 8/639*)

March 1939

5th   Tip to chauffeur to take DT article to London (special journey), plus tips at Victoria £1

12th   Mr Deakin for one night.

18th   Meeting bookbinder at Oxted and return.

19th   Meeting Dr Revesz (literary agent) also Dr Ripka & Miss Grant-Duff at Oxted, 3 luncheons, and car back to Oxted Stn.

25th   Professor Lindemann for w/end.

27th   Book dictation in car to London.

April 1939

Victor Cazalet: diary

(*Robert Rhodes James: 'Victor Cazalet, A Portrait'*)

April 1939

He is in grand form. We talk from 8.30 to 1 am. He goes over faults of Government. As put by him, we do seem to have been very behindhand with everything. Naval unpreparedness in Mediterranean very difficult to explain. . . .

I feel now Winston should be in Cabinet. Personally I think Simon, Hoare, Stanhope, should go, and Winston, Eden be put in. There is a good deal of feeling that Halifax should replace Chamberlain, but I think it is out of the question. I suppose if Winston got into the Cabinet in any capacity he would be PM very soon after the war broke out.

Victor Cazalet: diary

(*Robert Rhodes James: 'Victor Cazalet, A Portrait'*)

April 1939

As to Winston and Anthony Eden there is a growing demand that Winston should be included in the Government. I spent five hours with him two days ago and there is no doubt that he could and would, serve with Chamberlain and obviously has a 'war' mind. He has been right about every thing for the last five years and his inclusion in the Government would do more to show Germany that we mean business than anything else. On the other hand, of course, Winston's disadvantages are obvious and his liabilities as a colleague are fully known to a good many members of the Cabinet. The real objection, of course, is that Simon and Sam foresee that all possible hopes of the Premiership for them are gone if Winston is in the Government. It is generally believed that Sam Hoare realises his chances of becoming Prime Minister are not very bright and that he would like to go to India in a few years' time.

Lord Chatfield to Winston S. Churchill

(*Churchill papers: 2/371*)

April 1939

My dear Churchill

Thank you very much for sending me the copy of the strategic paper which you have sent to the Prime Minister. I am very glad to have it.

I very much agree with nearly all you say and only put in the word 'nearly' so as to give myself a loophole of escape in case my mind may work on other lines gradually! The Baltic question will have to be left for a decision until that happy moment that you prophesy arrives when we have settled the Mediterranean question, and the Far East one has not developed dangerously. On your main plan we are all, I think, in agreement, ie as regards the Mediterranean.

Yours very sincerely,
Chatfield

Harold Nicolson: diary

(*Nicolson papers*)

3 April 1939
10.50 pm

I am seized upon by Winston and taken down to the lower smoking room with Maisky and Lloyd George. Winston adopts the direct method of attack. 'Now look here Mr Ambassador, if we are to make a success of this new policy we require the help of Russia. Now I don't care for your system and I never have, but the Poles and the Roumanians like it even less. Although they might be prepared at a pinch to let you in, they would certainly want some assurances that you would eventually get out. Can you give us such assurances?' Lloyd George, I fear, is not really in favour of the new policy and he draws Maisky on to describe the deficiencies of the Polish army. Apparently many of their guns are pre-revolution guns of the Russian army. Maisky contends that the Polish soldiers are excellent fighters and that the officers are well-trained. Winston rather objects to this and attacks Lloyd George. 'You must not do this sort of thing, my dear. You are putting spokes in the wheel of history.' The relations between these two are very curious. They have had bitter battles in the past and they have emerged from these combats with great respect for each other's talents and an affectionate sharing of tremendous common memories. It is curious that little way that Winston has when he speaks to Lloyd George of calling him 'my dear'.

We then get on to the question of Italy. Maisky takes the line that Russia will not come in to any coalition which includes Italy and that they will have no confidence in France or ourselves if we start flirting with Italy and opening negotiations with Mussolini. Winston takes the line that the main enemy is Germany and that it is always a mistake to allow one's enemies to acquire even unreliable allies. 'For instance' he says 'at the beginning of the war I felt that Turkey would be more of a liability to Germany than an asset. I rapidly changed that opinion.' Lloyd George contends that Italian action in the Mediterranean would be extremely damaging to us and weaken us considerably. Winston admits that we should have to divert our commercial tonnage round by the Atlantic but that the Navy could still operate decisively in Mediterranean waters. Winston wants me to come on to Pratts Club but I am sleepy and drive away with Randolph.

Sir Henry Strakosch to Winston S. Churchill

(*Churchill papers: 2/374*)

5 April 1939
Confidential

My dear Winston,

I enclose a note of Germany's Supply and Consumption of Mineral Oils at the present time, and a guess at her consumption in times of War. On the assumption that she secures free and exclusive access to Roumanian oil in times of war, she might be able to balance supply and consumption at least for a year. She would have to overcome certain transport difficulties, which, however, do not seem to be insuperable.

The conclusion I reach is that it is imperative for us to make all preparations to blow up the Roumanian oil wells as soon as hostilities begin—as was done in the Great War. In that connection, it is interesting to note that 55% of the oil produced in Roumania comes from British, French and Belgian-owned companies, 12% from American-owned companies, and 14% from companies jointly owned by Roumanian, British and French interests.

Yours ever,
H. Strakosch

Bernard Baruch to Winston S. Churchill: telegram
(*Churchill papers: 1/343*)

6 April 1939

My home open to all Grandchildren if trouble comes.

Bernie

Winston S. Churchill to Bernard Baruch: telegram
(*Churchill papers: 1/343*)

6 April 1939

Grateful your offer. Consider countryside fairly safe for children. Hope you are bringing your end along.

Winston

Winston S. Churchill to John Wheldon
(*Churchill papers: 8/626*)

6 April 1939

My dear Wheldon,

I send you herewith Richard III, Henry VII, Edward VI, Mary and Elizabeth.

You will see that Henry VII, Edward VI and Mary are in a very rudimentary form. Any improvements and expansions you can make to them, I shall be most grateful for. Elizabeth is more complete, but needs much improving.

I add Richard III, which is in a semi-final condition, as it leads up to the Tudor period.

Winston S. Churchill to Thornton Butterworth
(*Tresham Lever papers*)

6 April 1939
Private

Dear Mr Butterworth,

I wonder if you would be interested in a project of mine, to publish the series of fortnightly articles on world affairs, which I have written for THE EVENING STANDARD and THE DAILY TELEGRAPH, in one volume under some such title as 'Step by Step'?

There are at least seventy-five articles, each averaging 1,200 words, making about 90,000 words. As the articles are coming out every fortnight, one could count on at least 100,000 words for the volume. The articles are all written in my best style, and they form a continuous survey of the darkening scene. They would be interspersed with short notes between the chapters, to make the whole story run easily. All the articles have been reproduced in thirty to forty foreign and Imperial newspapers all over the world. They all bear upon the foreign situation, which will increasingly dominate attention, and I should think the book would have a very good sale. I should contemplate an early publication, I hope during the summer.

Pray let me hear from you whether you are interested.

Yours sincerely,
Winston S. Churchill

Sir Kingsley Wood to Winston S. Churchill
(*Churchill papers: 25/17*)

6 April 1939   Air Ministry
Secret

My dear Winston,

I have now had a brief report on developments since last Thursday.

I gather that the visit which Lindemann paid to Farnborough with Pye was most useful, and I understand that he was shown all the experiments in hand with the long wire mine. I also understand that the relative advantages of the long and the short wire mines were discussed and Pye gathered the impression that Lindemann was satisfied as to the probable greater efficiency of the 2,000 ft wire.

Unfortunately the weather proved unsuitable for the experiments at Mildenhall on Monday, but it was possible to carry them out on Tuesday, and I understand that they were most successful. Lindemann was present at these exercises; and as soon as I have a full report from Pye I will send you a copy.

As regards the filling of the explosives at Woolwich. We are arranging for Lockspeiser[1] of Farnborough to go over to Woolwich immediately after

---

[1] Ben Lockspeiser, 1891–   . Engaged in aeronautical research at the Royal Aircraft Establishment, Farnborough, 1920–37; Head of the Air Defence Department, Farnborough, 1937–9. Assistant Director of Scientific Research, Air Ministry, 1939–41. Deputy Director of Scientific Research, Armaments, Ministry of Aircraft Production, 1941–3; Director, 1943–5; Director-General, 1945. Knighted, 1946. Chief Scientist to the Ministry of Supply, 1946–9. Secretary to the Committee of the Privy Council for Scientific and Industrial Research, 1949–56.

Easter and explain to them the importance that we attach to early experiments and to give them any advice and assistance that he can. I have no doubt that Woolwich will be willing to proceed immediately with the work that is required, but if necessary I will have a word with Hore-Belisha.

I will write to you again as soon as I have a report on the Mildenhall experiments and hear the outcome of Lindemann's talks with Woolwich.

Yours ever,
Kingsley Wood

Arthur Christiansen: [1] *recollections*

('*Headlines All My Life*')

[6 April 1939]   [Stornoway House]

In the corner Lord Beaverbrook and Brendan Bracken, a young carroty haired MP, are playing backgammon.

Standing with his back to the log fire is Winston Churchill, who is clearly bored at being neglected by the backgammon players. It is our first meeting and I notice that he is smaller than I expected, but just as pink and baby-looking. He shakes me limply by the hand, but in spite of this he is enthusiastic to have me for his audience, an audience of one only but that is better than none.

'Where is the—ah—the British Fleet to-night?' he asked me, rolling the words around his palate and licking them before they are uttered. 'It ish lolling in the Bay of Naples. No doubt, the—ah—the Commander of the British ships at Naples is—ah—being entertained ashore, entertained no doubt on the orders of—ah—Mussholini himself at the Naples Yacht Club.'

Churchill glowered at me and chewed his cigar before continuing: 'And where should the British Fleet be to-night? On the other side of that long heel of a country called Italy. In the Adriatic Sea, to make the rape of Albania impossible.' [2]

'That is why, my boy, Mussholini is entertaining the British Fleet ashore at Naples to-night.'

---

[1] Arthur Christiansen, 1904–1963. Educated at Wallasey Grammar School. Joined the *Wallasey Chronicle*, 1920. News Editor of the *Sunday Express*, 1926–9; Assistant Editor, 1928–33. Editor of the *Daily Express*, 1933–57; Editorial Director, 1957–9. Director, Independent Television News, 1960–2. In 1961 he published his memoirs, *Headlines All My Life*.

[2] Italian forces invaded Albania on the following day, Friday, 7 April 1939.

Harold Macmillan: recollections

('*Winds of Change*')

Good Friday, 7 April 1939

I was lunching with Churchill at Chartwell when the news came of the Italian landings. It was a scene that gave me my first picture of Churchill at work. Maps were brought out; secretaries were marshalled; telephones began to ring. 'Where was the British fleet?' That was the most urgent question. That considerable staff which, even as a private individual, Churchill always maintained to support his tremendous outflow of literary and political effort was at once brought into play. It turned out that the British fleet was scattered throughout the Mediterranean. Of the five great ships, one was at Gibraltar, one in the Eastern Mediterranean, and the remaining three, in Churchill's words 'lolling about inside or outside widely-separated Italian ports. . . .'

I shall always have a picture of that spring day and the sense of power and energy, the great flow of action, which came from Churchill, although he then held no public office. He alone seemed to be in command, when everyone else was dazed and hesitating.

Lord Halifax's first reaction to Mussolini's blow was as characteristic as Churchill's. He is said to have exclaimed, when he heard of the sudden and treacherous attack: 'And on Good Friday too!'[1]

Winston S. Churchill: draft Press Statement[2]

(*Churchill papers: 9/136*)

8 April 1939

Last Tuesday night, April 4, the First Lord of the Admiralty made a speech, at a function on board the Ark Royal, the form of which caused alarm. It was officially explained that in times of tension the anti-aircraft

---

[1] On 8 April 1939 Sir John Simon told the Cabinet: 'We should so conduct ourselves so that we should not appear to condone aggression while, at the same time, we should not indulge in such strong rebukes as to make ourselves appear in a weak position.' At this same Cabinet, discussing the growing opposition demand for the recall of Parliament, an unnamed Minister pointed out that 'if the Prime Minister were to remain in Scotland for any long time his absence would be liable to be misrepresented' (*Cabinet papers: 23/98*).

[2] This statement was prepared for the Press, but not issued. That same day, Kathleen Hill had noted for Churchill: '12.30 Mr Randolph telephoned to say that in regard to the paragraph in the *News Chronicle*, he had spoken to Sir Roger Keyes and afterwards had got in touch with the Admiralty, and they confirmed the disposition of the Mediterranean Fleet, with the exception of the "Malaya" which was not at Algiers but at Mentone. This, he thinks, makes the story better.'

batteries of British warships are kept in a state of constant and instant readiness, and that all that Lord Stanhope had done was not to relax this precautionary vigilance which was deemed necessary. We may judge to what a point this has been carried by the fact that the guns' crews of the Ark Royal, lying in Portsmouth Harbour, were not even allowed to come down from their guns to the entertainment, although if they had, they could have regained their posts in two or three minutes.

Vigilance and precautions in the Royal Navy are always to be applauded, though even these virtues may sometimes be carried to lengths imposing needless strain upon the personnel. But how is this extreme state of tension and preparedness in the British Home Fleet to be reconciled with the simultaneous scattering of the Mediterranean Fleet over the whole of that sea? There is no secret about it. The position of all our ships has been published in the newspapers. The four battleships of the Mediterranean Command were widely dispersed. The Warspite was at San Remo; the Barham was at Naples; the Malaya at Mentone; and the Ramillies in the Eastern Mediterranean. The destroyers were divided between Corsican ports, Tunisian ports and Gibraltar. The bulk of the cruisers were at Malta. It is not possible to conceive a more unmilitary disposition or one which could more expose vital units of our sea power isolated to surprise attacks. Yet this routine was followed in the Mediterranean at the same time that the First Lord did not think it safe to allow the anti-aircraft gunners of the Ark Royal even to go below on their own ship to attend a performance. How is this extraordinary contradiction of policy to be explained?

At this juncture the Mediterranean was a theatre of special tension. It had been known for some days that the Italian Fleet was concentrating at the mouth of the Adriatic, and that large masses of troops with transports were being assembled in Eastern Italian ports. It was generally believed that a descent upon Albania was imminent. Apart from this, the British defensive alliance with Poland had just been concluded. Why then was the British Fleet in the Mediterranean allowed to be dispersed in this manner? It is quite possible that a British naval concentration off the coast of Greece would have prevented the invasion of Albania. Not only was a grave risk run but an opportunity of making sea power count was squandered.

We shall no doubt be told that the Mediterranean Fleet was merely carrying out the Admiralty programme published in February for the Easter holiday season; but if this is so, it surely makes matters worse. One can hardly doubt that the improvident dispersal of the British Fleet's announced dispositions was one of the conditions taken into consideration by Signor Mussolini in the timing of his stroke against Albania and might easily have played its part in the timing of other strokes.

No doubt these faulty dispositions have now been rectified, and one must ask how long is this sort of thing to go on? Will our rulers not remember the warning lines:

'A thousand years scarce serve to form a State,
An hour may lay it in the dust.'[1]

C. G. L. Syers[2] to Neville Chamberlain

(*Premier papers: 1/323*)

9 April 1939

Mr Winston Churchill rang up shortly after the delivery of the letter below to give the following message. He emphasised at the time, and went to the trouble later of ringing up once again to emphasise, that he was merely passing on information which he felt he ought to report; he could not in any way vouch for the information which he had given. His message was that he had heard from a sure source in touch with pro-British circles in Greece (in point of fact, Mme Venizelos)[3] that General Metaxas[4] is on the verge of joining the Rome–Berlin Axis; The King of Greece[5] is against any such step

---

[1] Lord Byron, *Childe Harold's Pilgrimage*, Canto ii, Stanza 84. This was a constant theme of Churchill's thought. In a speech to his constituents in the General Election of 1959 (the last Election speech of his career), he said: 'To build may have to be the laborious task of years. To destroy can be the thoughtless act of a single day.'

[2] Cecil George Lewis Syers, 1903–   . Educated at St Paul's and Balliol College, Oxford. Entered the Dominions Office, 1925; Assistant Private Secretary to the Secretary of State, 1930–4. Assistant Private Secretary to the Prime Minister (Chamberlain), 1937–40. Deputy High Commissioner, South Africa, 1942–6. Assistant Under-Secretary of State, Commonwealth Relations Office, 1946–8; Deputy Under-Secretary of State, 1948–51. Knighted, 1949. High Commissioner, Ceylon, 1951–7.

[3] Helena Stephanovic-Skylitsi (Schilizzi), 1875–1959. Born in London; member of a Greek family from the island of Chios. She married the Greek statesman, Eleftherios Venizelos, in London, in September 1921, as his second wife. (He died in 1936.) She devoted her life to charitable works. Resident in Paris, 1936–9; subsequently in London, where she died.

[4] Yanni Metaxas, 1870-1941. Fought in the Greek army against the Turks, 1897. Chief of the General Staff, 1913. A rival and opponent of Venizelos, he was against the entry of Greece into the war, on the side of Britain and France, in 1915. Formed the Party of Free Opinion, 1923. Deputy Prime Minister, 1935. Prime Minister, 1936, at the head of a Cabinet of ex-army officers and non-politicians. Ruled Greece as an autocrat from 1936 until his death.

[5] George II, King of the Hellenes, 1890–1947. Succeeded as King following the abdication of his father, January 1923. Deposed, December 1923, and lived in exile in England, a republic being proclaimed in Greece in 1924. Restored to the throne by plebiscite, November 1935. Following the German conquest of Greece in 1941, he temporarily resumed the duties of Prime Minister, setting up his headquarters on Crete. With the German conquest of Crete, he escaped to Egypt. Restored to the throne by plebiscite, September 1946 (69·7% of the votes being in favour of a restoration of the monarchy). On his death he was succeeded as King by his brother Paul.

as are all the people; but the pro-British element in Greece believe General Metaxas to be wavering and they are extremely perturbed. They believe that only swift action can save the situation and what they would like to see done is that the Mediterranean Fleet should be sent to Corfu and Crete which, in their view, would decide the action to be taken by Greece.

Mr Winston Churchill added that his friends in the French Government, with whom he had been in touch, assured him that France would support any vigorous action in this connection taken by us; but they felt that it rested with us to move first since the interest was primarily a British one and the question was a Naval one.[1]

Sir Robert Vansittart to Lord Halifax

(*Foreign Office papers: 800/318*)

9 April 1939

Mr Churchill rang up to say in supplement to his letter that he learns from Madame Venizelos, who lives in Paris & is in touch with all pro-British & pro-French Greek elements, that the latter are in great fear lest General Metaxas should commit Greece to the axis, & that the one step which could prevent this, is the one he recommended in his letter.

I thanked Mr Churchill but said that according to our information and the Greek Minister[2] here, Greece was very nervous but determined to resist any aggression.

---

[1] Chamberlain minuted on this note: 'I shd like this note & Mr Ch's letter when I preside at the Cabinet tomorrow morning.' When the Cabinet met on the morning of 10 April 1939 Lord Halifax reported that he had seen the Greek Minister on the previous (Sunday) morning, and that the Minister had said that Italy was reported to be about to occupy Corfu 'between the 10th and 12th April'. The Minister added 'that Greece would resist any Italian attack by force'. Halifax had also seen the Italian Charge D'Affaires, Signor Crolla, on the Sunday morning. Crolla had reported Mussolini's view that the Italian Government 'could not, however, allow Corfu, which was a vital strategic point, to be occupied by a foreign Power other than Greece'. No reference was made in the Cabinet to Churchill's suggestion, but Sir John Simon told his colleagues, in supporting some British involvement: 'A sharp distinction could be drawn between Albania, on the one hand, where Italian interests had long been recognised, and Greece and Turkey on the other hand' (*Cabinet papers: 23/98*).

[2] Haralambos Simopoulos, 1874–1942. Doctor in Law, University of Athens. Studied law in Germany and France. Entered the Greek Foreign service, 1901. Chargé d'Affaires in London, 1917. Minister in Prague and Budapest, 1920. High Commissioner in Constantinople, 1922. Minister in Washington, 1924–35; in London, 1935–40. Permanent Vice-Minister of Foreign Affairs, Athens, September 1940.

Winston S. Churchill to Neville Chamberlain

(*Premier papers: 1/323*)

9 April 1939   Chartwell
Private and Personal

My dear Prime Minister,

I am hoping that Parliament will be recalled at the latest on Tuesday, and I write to say how much I hope the statements which you will be able to make will enable the same united front to be presented as in the case of the Polish Agreement.[1]

It seems to me, however, that hours now count. It is imperative for us to recover the initiative in diplomacy. This can no longer be done by declarations or by the denouncing of the Anglo-Italian Agreement or by the withdrawal of our Ambassador.

It is freely stated in the Sunday papers that we are offering a guarantee to Greece and Turkey. At the same time I notice that several newspapers speak of a British Naval Occupation of Corfu. Had this step been already taken, it would afford the best chance of maintaining peace. If it is not taken by us, of course with Greek consent, it seems to me that after the publicity given to the idea in the Press and the obvious needs of the situation, Corfu will be speedily taken by Italy. Its recapture would then be impossible. On the other hand, if we are there first, an attack even upon a few British ships would confront Mussolini with beginning a war of aggression upon England. This direct issue gives the best chance to all the forces in Italy which are opposed to a major war with England. So far from intensifying the grave risks now open, it diminishes them. But action ought to be taken to-night.

What is now at stake is nothing less than the whole of the Balkan Peninsula. If these States remain exposed to German and Italian pressure while we appear, as they may deem it, incapable of action, they will be forced to make the best terms possible with Berlin and Rome. How forlorn then will our

---

[1] On 31 March 1939, two weeks after the German occupation of Prague, and the disintegration of Czechoslovakia into two regions (one the German Protectorate of Bohemia and Moravia, the other a new state, Slovakia), the British Government announced, a Polish Guarantee. Under it, Britain would intervene militarily if Poland's independence were to be endangered. But on 1 April 1939 *The Times* stated that this 'new obligation which this country yesterday assumed does not bind Great Britain to defend every inch of the present frontiers of Poland. The key word in the statement is not integrity but "independence".' Two days later, Chamberlain himself wrote, in a private letter to his sister, about the drafting of the Guarantee: 'It was of course mostly my own & when it was finished I was well satisfied with it. It was unprovocative in tone, but firm, clear but stressing the important point (perceived alone by The Times) that what we are concerned with is not the boundaries of States, but attacks on their independence. And it is we who will judge whether this independence is threatened or not' (*Neville Chamberlain papers*).

position become! We shall be committed to Poland and thus involved in the East of Europe while at the same time cutting off from ourselves all hope of that large alliance which once effected might spell salvation.

I write the above without knowledge of the existing position of our Mediterranean Fleet which should of course be concentrated and *at sea*, in a suitable, not too close supporting position.

> Yours very sincerely,
> Winston S. Churchill

Neville Chamberlain to his sister

(*Templewood papers*)

9 April 1939   10 Downing Street

It doesn't make things easier to be badgered for a meeting of pmt by the two Oppositions & Winston who is the worst of the lot, telephoning almost every hour of the day. I suppose he has prepared a terrific oration which he wants to let off. I know there are a lot of reckless people who would plunge us into a war at once but we must resist them until it becomes really inevitable.

I got several abusive telegrams from Communists yesterday & I see Mr Barnes[1] of the Co-ops is calling for my resignation. On the other hand wherever I go the people collect in crowds to give me their good wishes & I don't believe that Hitler & Mussolini have shaken my position.

Lord Davies to Winston S. Churchill

(*Churchill papers: 2/358*)

10 April 1939

My dear Churchill,

The pigeons are coming home to roost with a vengeance. What you prophesied in Sept is unfortunately coming true with each day that passes. During the last war it was part of my job to write appreciations for LlG.

---

[1] Alfred Barnes, 1887–1974. Educated at the LCC School of Arts and Crafts. Chairman of the Co-operative Party 1922–45, and Co-operative MP for South East Ham 1922–31 and 1935–55. A Lord Commissioner of the Treasury in the second Labour Government, 1929–30. Privy Councillor, 1945. Minister of War Transport 1945–6; of Transport 1946–51.

That is my excuse for inflicting upon you the enclosed Memo which I have sent to Halifax. Time is passing—can't you get them to act?

More power to your elbow!

Yrs v sincerely,

DD

Winston S. Churchill to Sir Kingsley Wood

(*Churchill papers: 25/17*)

10 April 1939

Many thanks for your letter of the 6th. Lindemann's view is that as the long wire mine has been fully worked out it should instantly be put into production. But the smaller mines with shorter wires should also be developed. One does not exclude the other; on the contrary, a mixed grill might give the best results. Do not however, after these three and a half years delay, let anything obstruct the mass production of the device on which we are agreed.

About Woolwich: all that is needed is that six small containers, made accordingly to already approved specifications, should be filled with HE. One man could do this in one hour. They were arranged to take the standard detonators, which must be available by the thousand. These six small containers were sent to Woolwich on March 4, but the one man and the one hour have been lacking for nearly six weeks.

No experiment can be made until the containers are filled. The experiment consists in flicking these small mines into a running propeller. All the facilities for this are ready at Farnborough, but by other regulations the lorry containing the propeller must be sent to Shoeburyness before the experiment is allowed. We are told that Farnborough and Shoeburyness will not delay in making the experiment. But how can they do it when the one man and the one hour at Woolwich cannot be spared?

Excuse me bringing these facts before you.[1]

[1] Sir Kingsley Wood replied, on the following day: 'My dear Winston, Thank you for your letter, which I have just seen on my return to Town. I have noted what you say about developing smaller mines as well as the long wire variety. As regards the question of filling the containers, I am sure that Woolwich will deal with this at the first possible moment, but you can of course rely on my following the position up and doing anything further that may seem advisable. I will write you again at an early date.'

Joseph E. Davies[1] *to Winston S. Churchill*

(*Churchill papers: 2/358*)

10 April 1939   Brussels

My dear Mr Churchill:

The hectic events of the last week have precluded my sending you a personal line to tell you how very much I appreciated and enjoyed the courtesy and hospitality that you extended so generously to me on the weekend of April 1st. Even now, we still are under pressure and I am begging you to excuse this stenographic form of letter for that reason.

It was with renewed admiration that I read your very powerful and masterful presentation of the case in the House of Commons on Monday, April 3rd.[2]

I have been reading Hansard's debates on foreign affairs for the past two years and nothing has impressed me more than the power of the great speeches which the distinguished husband of Mrs Churchill has made during this epoch-making time.

Your lovely home in the beautiful English countryside together with the charm and cordial welcome of the 'Lady of the Manor' and your fine self will remain with me for a long time. . . .

---

[1] Joseph Edward Davies, 1876–1958. Born and educated in Wisconsin. State Prosecuting Attorney, Wisconsin, 1902–6. Chairman, Democratic Party, Wisconsin, 1911–16. Western Manager, Campaign for the Election of Woodrow Wilson, 1912. US Commissioner of Corporations, 1913–15. Member of the War Industries Board, 1915–18. Chairman of the US Federal Trade Commission, 1915–16. Economic Adviser to President Wilson at the Paris Peace Conference, 1919. United States Ambassador to the Soviet Union, 1936–8; to Belgium, 1938–9. Special Assistant to the Secretary of State in Charge of War Emergency Problems and Policies, 1939–41. Chairman of the War Relief Control Board, 1942–6. President Roosevelt's Special Envoy to Stalin, 1943. President Truman's Special Envoy to Churchill, 1945. Special Adviser to President Truman at the Potsdam Conference, 1945.

[2] Speaking in the House of Commons on 3 April 1939, Churchill gave his support to the Polish Guarantee of 31 March 1939. There was, he said, 'almost complete agreement' on foreign policy between the Government and its former critics. 'We can no longer endure,' he said, 'to be pushed from pillar to post.' He was anxious that the new found firmness of the Foreign Office should be properly followed up, and fully understood, telling the Commons: 'There was a sinister passage in the Times leading article on Saturday similar to that which foreshadowed the ruin of Czechoslovakia, which sought to explain that there was no guarantee for the integrity of Poland, but only for its independence. . . . But the position of the British and French Governments seems to be perfectly clear. We are not concerned at this particular moment with particular rights or places, but to resist by force of arms further acts of violence, of pressure or of intrigue. Moreover, this is not the time for negotiation. After the crime and treachery committed against Czechoslovakia, our first duty is to re-establish the authority of law and public faith in Europe.' The 'slightest sign of weakness' Churchill warned would only serve to aggravate the dangers, not only for Britain but for the whole world. Above all, the Soviet Union must be encouraged to come forward as a partner in the gathering together of all threatened States.

PUNCH   2nd November 1938

A FAMILY VISIT

"IT WAS A GREAT WORK, AND I WISH YOU COULD NOW ADD ANOTHER
CHAPTER TO YOUR OWN CAREER."

THE OLD SEA-DOG

" ANY TELEGRAM FOR ME ? "   PUNCH   12th July 1939

R. D. Jones[1] *to Winston S. Churchill*

(*Churchill papers: 2/374*)

11 April 1939

Dear Mr Churchill,

Please forgive me for writing to you. I would like to put your mind at ease as regards the great number of submarines now being built in Germany. They are destined for Spain, Italy, Albania—packed in cases, marked Munich Beer. Some of them will be used as floating mines, some will be anchored and others will be adrift in the track of ships. Any shipmaster taking one for a real submarine & 'rams' it, will be very sorry for himself.

Wishing you well,

Yours respectfully,
R. D. Jones

[1] R. D. Jones of Llys-Wen, Bodorgan, Anglesey. For Desmond Morton's comment on this letter, see page 1457.

Kathleen Hill to Major Desmond Morton

(*Churchill papers: 2/374*)

11 April 1939
Personal

Dear Major Morton,

I have been requested by Mr Churchill to send you these figures, compiled by Sir Keith Price, on munitions production during the War.[1]

Mr Churchill would be obliged if you could give him the approximate German figures for the present year.[2]

Leslie Hore-Belisha: diary

('*The Private Papers of Hore-Belisha*')

11 April 1939   War Office

A message was brought to me during the Army Council meeting that Winston was on the line and had asked if I would go to Chartwell as he had a bad foot and could not come to London. He said he particularly wanted to have a talk to me. I guessed what he was feeling, being out of it all. I sent a message that I would go down as soon as the meeting was over.

Reached Chartwell about 10 pm. He opened the door himself. He had a felt slipper on his bad foot. We had dinner alone together. He recalled the difficulties he had had during the war, how he had advocated measures in the Cabinet, which had been turned down by his colleagues, and then had suffered violent opposition because these measures had not been carried out. I arrived back home about 2 am.[3]

---

[1] By 1918 the annual British production of explosives deliveries had reached 79,098 tons of High Explosives, 205,156 tons of Ammonium-Nitrate, and 130,196 tons of Propellant (letter from Sir Keith Price to Churchill, 9 April 1939).

[2] The German production of explosives in 1938, according to Desmond Morton (in reply to Kathleen Hill's letter), was 168,000 tons of High Explosives, including 30,000 tons from the three annexed factories in Czechoslovakia; 3 *million* tons of Ammonium-Nitrate; and 'upwards of 100,000 tons per annum' of Propellant (*Churchill papers: 2/374*).

[3] In the early hours of 12 April 1939. Later that same day, Churchill was at 10 Downing Street for a meeting with Neville Chamberlain. A *Daily Herald* front page headline on 13 April 1939 read: 'Churchill as Supply Chief?', and the article went on to report that Churchill had spent 55 minutes (45 minutes, according to the *Daily Telegraph*) with Neville Chamberlain at 10 Downing Street on the previous day. It was also expected that a Ministry of Supply was about to be established. 'It is understood that Mr Churchill may be invited to take charge of the Ministry.' A second article in the *Daily Herald* on April 15 began: 'Mr Churchill's early inclusion in the Government may be confidently expected.'

Winston S. Churchill to Maurice Ashley

(*Churchill papers: 8/662*)

12 April 1939

My dear Ashley,

I am most grateful to you for the deeply interesting and helpful letter you have written to me on the Stuart section, and also for your comments on the text.

At this stage, working against time, and with so many distractions, my aim has been to get the narrative through from the beginning to the end, leaving behind many omissions and many general questions. I hope this will be completed by the end of May, when I shall have surveyed the whole story and will know broadly what there is in it. I have then six months in which to step back and put the emphases and finishing touches. Until this stage is reached, I shall not finally decide on the judgment I tried to give about Cromwell and other figures. As you know, an enormous amount of changes are made by me after the first proof is printed.

In the main, the theme is emerging of the growth of freedom and law, of the rights of the individual, of the subordination of the State to the fundamental and moral conceptions of an ever-comprehending community. Of these ideas the English-speaking peoples were the authors, then the trustees, and must now become the armed champions. Thus I condemn tyranny in whatever guise and from whatever quarter it presents itself. All this of course has a current application.

I enclose you the five Slips about the death of Charles I, which were omitted from the proofs. You are quite right in supposing that two or three Slips have to be written about the Declaration of Breda and the early years of Charles II.

Let me once again thank you for your kindness, and the thought you have bestowed upon this jejune and largely unshaped draft.

Imre Revesz to Winston S. Churchill

(*Churchill papers: 8/634*)

12 April 1939   Paris

Dear Mr Churchill,

I have received your telegram asking whether we could transmit by wireless an article for Colliers. I have asked you on the telephone but was unable to reach you. So I am writing you as it would be too complicated to explain the situation in a telegram.

In principle, I could easily transmit the article by the Amsterdam station but everything depends whether Colliers could arrange the reception. I could not possibly ask the New York Herald Tribune to undertake such a work for another newspaper as they are very busy in receiving day and night their news from all the parts of the world and the reception of 4,000 words takes a considerable time.

The best solution would be the following: Colliers should make an understanding with the Radio Corporation of America who are in contact with the Holland Radio and charge them to receive this transmission. The Radio Corporation could easily arrange with the Holland Radio all details (wave-length, speed, time of transmission etc). They should cable Holland Radio that this article will be remitted by Cooperation in Paris and the transmission paid by us.

If you cable this to Colliers and if the Radio Corporation in America will get in touch with Holland Radio in Amsterdam, they could fix all technical details within a few hours.

The costs of the transmission depend entirely on the speed. The 4,000 words would cost at a speed of 30 words per minute about £15–20, at a speed of 70 words per minute about £8–10. The speed would depend upon the ability of the receivers and on atmospheric conditions. These figures only include the transmission of the wireless message, the costs of the reception ought to be paid by Colliers. But these are usually not very high.

In general, such wireless transmissions are only advantageous in case of a regular service. For an isolated transmission the ordinary presscable or Press Wireless might be preferable though considerably more expensive. Nevertheless, if you wish we can make a trial.

Please let me know about your decision.

Yours very sincerely,
I. Revesz

Winston S. Churchill: speech

(*'Hansard'*)

13 April 1939

Here let me say a word about the British Intelligence Service. After 25 years' experience in peace and war I believed it to be the finest service of its kind in the world. I believe the right hon Member for Caernarvon Boroughs (Mr Lloyd George), who had supreme responsibility in those years, will corroborate me. I have always believed, and foreign countries have always believed, that it was the finest in the world. Yet we have seen both in the case of the subjugation of Bohemia and in the case of the invasion of Albania that apparently Ministers of the Crown had no inkling or at any rate no conviction of what was coming.

I cannot believe that this is the fault of the British Secret Service. Several days before the stroke at Bohemia was made, Nazi intentions were known in many countries throughout Europe. The whole time-table was laid down, the whole programme was known beforehand. Similarly in the case of Albania, the Italian concentration and preparations were reported repeatedly in the Press.

We sneer at the Press, but they give an extremely true picture of a great deal that is going on, a very much fuller and detailed picture than we are able to receive from Ministers of the Crown. At any rate, it was quite well known that gathering of troops and ships was taking place in the Eastern ports of Italy. There was much talk that Albania was the quarry, although I quite agree that you could not tell in what form the assertion of Italian authority over Albania would be exerted, or to what extent the late King of Albania[1] and the Albanian people would make themselves accommodating parties to what took place.

How was it that on the eve of the Bohemian outrage Ministers were indulging in what was called 'sunshine talk', the golden age prospects?[2] How was it that last week holiday routine was observed at a time when, quite clearly, something of a very exceptional character, the consequences of which could not be measured, was imminent? I do not know.

I know perfectly well the patriotism and sincere desire to act in a manner of

[1] Ahmed Zog, 1895–1961. A Muslim. The son of the head of a leading Albanian clan. Educated in Constantinople. Fought against the Turks in 1913. On active service in the Austro-Hungarian Army, 1914–18. Albanian Minister of the Interior, 1920. Commander-in-Chief of the Albanian forces, 1921. Minister of the Interior (for the second time), 1921. Prime Minister, 1921–4. After an attempt was made on his life, he retired with his colleagues to the mountains on the Serbian–Albanian border. Proclaimed Albania a Republic, and elected President, 1925. Repressed the revolt of the northern Catholic tribes, 1926, and executed the Catholic priest who had inspired the revolt. Proclaimed King of Albania (as King Zog), 1928. Fled to Greece after the Italian invasion; and then to England (where he lived near High Wycombe). When Albania became Communist in December 1945, he went from England to Egypt, then to Long Island in the United States, and finally to Cannes. He died in hospital in Paris.

[2] On 10 March 1939 (five days before Hitler's occupation of Prague), Neville Chamberlain had told the Press Correspondents in the House of Commons that Europe was 'settling down to a period of tranquillity', while on that same day Sir Samuel Hoare had spoken publicly of the possibility that, if Hitler, Mussolini, Franco, Chamberlain and Daladier were to work together, they might in an 'incredibly short space of time transform the whole history of the world' by freeing Europe from the nightmare of war and the burden of arms expenditure. Such a friendly collaboration between the dictators and the democrats would be the means, Hoare added, of creating a new 'golden Age'.

perfect rectitude and render valuable services to the country which animates Ministers of the Crown, but I wonder whether there is not some hand which intervenes and filters down or withholds intelligence from Ministers. Certainly it was so in the case of the German aeroplane preparations four years ago. The facts were not allowed to reach high Ministers of the Crown until they had been so modified that they did not present an alarming impression.

It seems to me that Ministers run the most tremendous risk if they allow the information collected by the Intelligence Department, and sent to them I am sure in good time, to be sifted and coloured and reduced in consequence and importance, and if they ever get themselves into a mood of attaching importance only to those pieces of information which accord with their earnest and honourable desire that the peace of the world shall remain unbroken.

Colonel Moore-Brabazon to Winston S. Churchill

(*Churchill papers: 2/358*)

13 April 1939

Dear Winston,

Very Good indeed. You voiced the opinion of the House and it has had a great effect.[1]

Yours,
'Brab'

[1] During his speech in the House of Commons on 13 April 1939, a portion of which is printed above (pages 1446–8), Churchill also spoke in support of Chamberlain's offer of a guarantee to Greece, and a 'more effective' arrangement with Turkey. But he could not feel, he said, that the dispositions of the British Mediterranean fleet during the Albanian crisis 'conformed to the ordinary dictates of prudence'. At the very moment when the Mediterranean Fleet had been dispersed, he said, 'it was known that the Italian Fleet was concentrated in the Straits of Otranto and that troops were being assembled and embarked on transports, which presumably were intended for some serious enterprise'. Churchill added: 'It is incredible to me that, when all this intelligence had come to hand and when the First Lord of the Admiralty considered that a state of tension existed requiring the utmost precautions at home, the Mediterranean Fleet was not concentrated, and at sea. These matters touch the very life of the State and I trust that improvidences of this character will not be repeated in the anxious months which lie before us.' Churchill also spoke of Russia, telling the House of Commons: 'The other day I tried to show the House the deep interest that Russia had against the further Eastward extension of the Nazi power. It is upon that deep, natural, legitimate interest that we must rely, and I am sure we shall hear from the Government that the steps they are taking are those which will enable us to receive the fullest possible co-operation from Russia, and that no prejudices on the part of England or France will be allowed to interfere with the closest co-operation between the two countries, thus securing to our harassed and anxious combinations the unmeasured, if somewhat uncertain, but certainly enormous counterpoise of the Russian Power.'

Margot, Countess of Oxford and Asquith to Winston S. Churchill
(*Churchill papers: 2/358*)

13 April 1939

Dearest Winston,

You say in yr speech—reported to-day—that we are making ourselves 'ridiculous in the eyes of foreign countries' by refusing to fill in a form etc. Not *one* person in this house, nor *one* of my friends or servants have received a form to fill in. Where are they to be found?

Yours affectionately,
Margot

Winston S. Churchill to Margot, Countess of Oxford and Asquith
(*Churchill papers: 2/368*)

14 April 1939

I was speaking not of individuals, but was deploring the fact that the country has not been asked to have a National Register which everyone would be obliged to sign.

Thank you so much for writing.

Harold Nicolson: diary
(*Nicolson papers*)

14 April 1939

We are in a situation of the very gravest danger. I feel, as Winston said, twenty years younger.

Winston S. Churchill to Evelyn Walkden[1]
(*Churchill papers: 2/358*)

14 April 1939

Sir,

I notice in various newspapers a report of your speech to the National Union of Distributive and Allied Workers, at Southport, on April 10, in which you are quoted as saying:

'Sir Stafford had gone out of his way to arrange a compromise of all sorts of schemes with Winston Churchill, Sinclair and a whole host of others whose friendship he would not like to be certain of for five minutes at a time.'

I have never had any political relations direct or indirect with Sir Stafford Cripps and have never discussed any compromise with him. I know him only as a distinguished Member of the House of Commons. In these circumstances I hope you will withdraw the statement which you made.

Eric Long to Winston S. Churchill
(*Churchill papers: 2/371*)

14 April 1939

My dear Winston,

I hate troubling you at this moment, but I am gravely alarmed at certain aspects with regard to the raising of the Territorial Army.

Yesterday I was in Kent, and was shown a letter, under the signature of Lord Somers,[2] who is Deputy Commissioner for the whole of the Boy Scouts

---

[1] Evelyn Walkden, 1893–1970. Son of a Lancashire Miners' leader. Educated at Lancashire Evening Institutes. A student of the Workers' Educational Association. Joined the Lancashire Hussars, 1914. On active service as Salonica, 1916–19. An organizer of the National Union of Distributive and Allied Workers (a Union for Glass, Pottery, Chemicals, Food, Drink, Tobacco, Brushmaking and Distribution), 1928–41. A Borough Councillor, Sutton and Cheam. Founder of the Sutton Municipal Open Air Theatre. Unsuccessful Labour candidate (by 881 votes) at Rossendale, in the General Election of 1935. Elected in an unopposed by-election at Doncaster, 1941. Parliamentary Private Secretary to the Minister of National Insurance (Sir William Jowett), 1944–5. Re-elected (with a 23,051 majority over his Conservative opponent), 1945. Parliamentary Private Secretary to the Minister of Food (Sir Ben Smith), 1945–6. All-Party Parliamentary Mission to Greece, 1946. Defeated at the General Election of 1950.

[2] Arthur Herbert Tennyson Somers Cocks, 1887–1944. Succeeded his great uncle as 6th Baron Somers at the age of twelve. On active service, 1914–18 (DSO, MC). Governor of Victoria, Australia, 1926–31; acting Governor-General of Australia, 1930–1. President of the MCC, 1936–7. Deputy Commissioner, Boy Scouts Association for Great Britain and the British Commonwealth from 1941 until his death.

in this country, requesting County Commissioners to make arrangements for members of the Rovers Section of the Boy Scouts Association to attend a jamboree in the North of England or in Scotland this summer. The boys in this section of the Scouts are between the ages of 17 to 23. Surely, if any camps are to be attended by these fellows it should be within the Territorial Army. I know at least one Divisional Commissioner who feels very strongly on this matter, but if this sort of thing is allowed to continue no wonder people are getting a little nervous as to the real position in this country.

I know that I have probably reached the age when my services are no longer required. If so, I should like to be told that I am free to join the ARP, or any other such body without fear of being suddenly whisked off into something else without preparation.

In consequence of this, I wrote to the War Office a fortnight or so ago, explaining to them that I had been twenty three years in the Territorial Army, and that I knew something about raising men. I said I was prepared to do anything at this moment to help to raise and to train the men. Further, that I was prepared to work for four or five nights each week in London or round London, wherever I might be sent. The only reply I have received I now enclose.

In my office there is a young fellow, aged 25, who has been to no less than four different recruiting offices in London, and the only prospect he sees at the moment is that his name will be put down on a waiting list of over 400 in a London Territorial battalion, and who might be accepted amongst that number, but, in the meantime, they can hold out no hope for him that he can attend drills, (though he is offering his services as a private), or prepare him in any way for an emergency.

I hesitate to bring these affairs to your attention, but I really am one of many who, whilst supporting the Prime Minister a hundred per cent, am beginning to despair of such people as Hore-Belisha, who are in charge of the country's defence.

With all good wishes,

Yours ever,
Eric Long

Lord Londonderry to Winston S. Churchill

(*Churchill papers: 2/368*)

14 April 1939

My dear Winston,

I have read the excellent speech which you made yesterday in the House of Commons and what you said about the Secret Service.[1] I also have wondered why the British Government appear to have so little information about what is going on. In this connection, I want to refer to what you said in your speech.

> 'I certainly did say so in the case of the German aeroplane preparations four years ago. The facts were not allowed to reach high Ministers of the Crown until they had been so modified that they did not present an alarming impression.'

This really is a complete misapprehension on your part. I have had to suffer from it before and irresponsible people in the Press are inclined to quote you. As a matter of fact, I had full information on the German Air Force at that time, and if you doubt what I say, I should be glad if you would see Marshal of the Royal Air Force Sir Edward Ellington, and ask him to arrange for an interview with Medhurst;[2] I think he is Wing Commander. I know that you do not care very much about hearing arguments which destroy your case, but facts are facts, and everything that I said about the numbers of the German Air Force was substantially correct. . . .

I always felt that you did a very great service in persuading Neville Chamberlain to change his policy towards rearmament. For lots of reasons which I need not go into now, I was quite unable to do this, but if the Government here had realised that the Germans were quite incapable of taking any offensive, I am quite sure that we could have followed one of two courses. The first one was to make contacts with the Germans, and if after these contacts we realised, as I think we would have realised, that the Germans were not to be trusted, we were in a position then to have prevented their rearmament. The line to have taken was quite simple. We should have

---

[1] This section of Churchill's speech is quoted in full in this volume (pages 1446–8).

[2] Charles Edward Hastings Medhurst, 1896–1954. On active service, France and Palestine, 1914–18: Inniskilling Fusiliers, 1915; Royal Flying Corps, 1915–18 (Military Cross); Major, 1917. Royal Air Force, 1919. Served in Iraq, 1926–8. Instructor, RAF Staff College, 1931–3. Deputy Director of Intelligence, Air Ministry, 1934–7. Air Attaché, Rome, Berne and Berlin, 1937–40. Assistant Chief of the Air Staff (Intelligence), 1941; (Policy), 1942. Commandant, RAF Staff College, 1943–4. Commander-in-Chief, RAF Mediterranean Middle East, 1945–8. Knighted, 1945. Head of the Air Force Staff, Joint Services Mission at Washington, 1948–50. His only son was killed in action in 1944.

drawn attention before the League of Nations, which had some power then, to every breach of the Treaty of Versailles. Instead of that, France and England kept on making feeble protests but did nothing, with the result that the Germans rapidly increased their strength until they arrived at their present position. . . .

I should like to congratulate you on the speeches which you are making, but I am afraid you will find it a very difficult task to stimulate the Government into taking the proper line now, which is to go all out with enthusiasm and determination for the policy which you have outlined.

Yours ever,
Charley L

Winston S. Churchill to Lord Londonderry

(Churchill papers: 2/358)

15 April 1939

Many thanks for your letter. I am afraid I must hold very strongly to my view, but it would only be wearisome to insist upon it. I am sure you did what you thought best. You will remember how strongly I pressed you at the time to force your demands upon the Cabinet and warned you they would turn on you and make you responsible for our shortcomings, but in your book, which I have read, you say you reassured them.

Anyhow, I am very glad we are in agreement now and I still hope the worst may not happen.

Winston S. Churchill to Eric Long

(Churchill papers: 2/371)

15 April 1939

I think that Hore-Belisha is one of the most active of Ministers; but I fully agree with you that great confusion prevails.

Winston S. Churchill to A. H. Richards

(*Churchill papers: 2/376*)

15 April 1939

I am very glad to know that these Labour men[1] are coming to our luncheon on the 25th instant. Mrs Churchill will certainly come. It ought to be an important occasion.

Robert Boothby to Winston S. Churchill

(*Churchill papers: 2/358*)

15 April 1939   Edinburgh

Dear Winston,

I can't resist writing a line to thank you for, and to congratulate you on, the best speech I have ever heard in the House of Commons.[2] There was nothing more to be said.

No answer, of course—

Yours ever,
Bob

[1] The two Labour men who had agreed to come to the 'Focus' luncheon on 25 April 1939 were Arthur Greenwood (a former Minister of Health, and since 1935 Deputy Leader of the Labour Party) and John Marchbank, Secretary of the National Union of Railwaymen.

[2] Churchill's speech of 13 April 1939 (see page 1448, note 1). Churchill ended his speech: 'The danger is now very near. A great part of Europe is to a very large extent mobilised. Millions of men are being prepared for war. Everywhere the frontier defences are manned. Everywhere it is felt that some new stroke is impending. If it should fall, can there be any doubt that we shall be involved? We are no longer where we were two or three months ago. We have committed ourselves in every direction, rightly in my opinion, having regard to all that has happened. It is not necessary to enumerate the countries to which, directly or in-directly, we have given or are giving guarantees. What we should not have dreamt of doing a year ago, when all was so much more hopeful, what we should not have dreamt of doing even a month ago, we are doing now. Surely, then, when we aspire to lead all Europe back from the verge of the abyss on to the uplands of law and peace, we must ourselves set the highest ex-ample. We must keep nothing back. How can we bear to continue to lead our comfortable, easy life here at home, unwilling even to pronounce the word "compulsion," unwilling even to take the necessary measure by which the armies that we have promised can alone be re-cruited and equipped? How can we continue—let me say it with particular frankness and sincerity—with less than the full force of the nation incorporated in the governing instrument? These very methods, which the Government owe it to the nation and to themselves to take, are not only indispensable to the duties that we have accepted but, by their very adoption, they may rescue our people and the people of many lands from the dark, bitter waters which are rising fast on every side.'

Neville Chamberlain to his sister

(Neville Chamberlain papers)

15 April 1939   Chequers

... I asked D. Margesson to ascertain during Thursday evening whether my position had been shaken at all and he reported that he could not find any trace of it but I confess to feeling very dispirited & very lonely. Attlee behaved like the cowardly cur he is. I had seen him several times during the week when I told him everything and he appeared (and indeed I believe he was) completely satisfied.

On Thursday morning he asked to see me *before* the Cabinet, & brought Dalton along with him. I expected him to say he could not support me unless I denounced the agreement but he made no mention of it & only came to press for something to be said about Roumania as well as Greece. I told him that we should be discussing that in Cabinet & that I would report the views of himself & his friends. Just as I was going into the House I saw him in the Lobby & said 'I am going to include Roumania in the same assurance as we are giving to Greece' to which he said 'Good.'

I was therefore confident that he would give us full support & was dumb-founded when he led off by declaring his disappointment, went on to mis-represent my attitude, & finished with an ordinary party attack about our abandonment of the League & collective security. I heard afterwards that this had been decided on at the party meeting in the morning under the influence of Dalton, & Attlee made no effort to stem it, much to the indignation of A. Greenwood[1] who had been fogbound in the Channel the night before & had missed the meeting.

I have done with confidences to the Labour party. They have shown them-selves implacably partisan & this game in which they have all the advantages of a truce & none of the disadvantages is too one-sided for me to go on with it. I had already given up Archie Sinclair & was not surprised by his speech which was a really lamentable exhibition on such an occasion, but I had hoped for a better speech from Winston. I had sent for him in the hope of keeping the House as united as possible & I had given him much information after first telling him very flatly that I knew Randolph told journalists & others what his father had reported to him of his talks with me.

---

[1] Arthur Greenwood, 1880–1954. Lecturer in economics, Leeds University, and Chairman of the Yorkshire District Workers' Educational Association. Assistant Secretary, Ministry of Reconstruction, 1917–19. Labour MP for Nelson and Colne, 1922–31; for Wakefield, 1932–54. Parliamentary Secretary, Ministry of Health, 1924. Minister of Health, 1929–31. Privy Councillor, 1929; Deputy Leader of the Labour Party, 1935. Member of the War Cabinet, 1940–2. Lord Privy Seal, 1945–7. Chairman of the Labour Party, 1952.

W took this warning in very good part, expressed his entire approval of what we were doing & declared his intention of making a 'not unhelpful' speech. But there was an acid undertone which brought many cheers from Labour benches & again I felt depressed when he sat down. The first speech in fact which gave me any comfort was A. Eden's with which I thoroughly agreed & I sent him a friendly note & he replied in equally cordial terms.

I heard afterwards that when Winston got my message he thought I was going to offer him the Ministry of Supply & he was therefore smarting under a sense of disappointment, only kept in check by his unwillingness to do anything which might prevent his yet receiving an offer to join the Govt.

[Churchill saw David Margesson and expressed his 'strong desire' to enter the Cabinet.][1]

I told DM that I would let this suggestion simmer a bit. It caught me at a moment when I was certainly feeling the need of help, but I wanted to do nothing too quickly. The question is whether Winston, who would certainly help on the Treasury bench in the Commons, would help or hinder in Cabinet or in Council. Last Saturday for instance he was at the telephone all day urging that Pmt should be summoned for Sunday & that the Fleet should go & seize Corfu that night! Would he wear me out resisting rash suggestions of this kind?

Winston S. Churchill to Alan Bullock [2]

(Churchill papers: 8/626)

15 April 1939

I have now read with great interest your excellent annotation. On Galley 384 you make a suggestion which I send you back, because I agree with its importance. Will you not write two or three thousand words on the social history and institutional development of this period, showing the life of the people, their houses, their foods, their troubles, their habits, with quotations from contemporary authorities. I could then interweave this with the text as it stands.

It is quite true that in the first instance going over this long story I do dwell on battles and kings, but I am most anxious that the other side should

---

[1] For this section of Chamberlain's letter, see page 1461, footnote 2.

[2] Alan Louis Charles Bullock, 1914–   . Educated at Bradford Grammar School and Wadham College, Oxford. MA, 1936. 1st Class Modern History, 1938. A member of the BBC European Services, 1940–5. Tutor in Modern History, New College, 1945–52; he published *Hitler: A Study in Tyranny* in 1952. Biographer of Bevin (volume 1, 1960, volume 2, 1967, volume 3, 1982). Master of St Catherine's College, Oxford since 1960. Vice-Chancellor, Oxford University, 1969–73. Knighted, 1972. Created Baron, 1976.

be represented so far as it lends itself to narration. Of course people were living and dying all the time.

Will you talk to Deakin about this?

Winston S. Churchill to G. M. Young
(*Churchill papers: 8/626*)

16 April 1939

I have studied with great attention and pleasure your invaluable notes on the Stuart period, and I have the hope that you might be able to assist me in other parts of my work.

Could you spare me the week-end, Saturday 22, and Sunday, 23 April? Mr Deakin, who is helping me regularly, will be able to come at that time. We could go through the Stuart period, and also cast our eyes upon the text which covers some other epochs.

I find I omitted in the copy I sent you about five thousand words on the opening period of Charles II's reign, in which you will see some references to the Clarendon Code. Perhaps you will kindly look at this meanwhile.

Desmond Morton to Winston S. Churchill
(*Churchill papers: 2/374*)

16 April 1939   Earlylands

Were this correspondent's statement correct, I do not think it would 'put my mind at ease', as he hopes.

Germany is indeed building a certain number of submarines on order from other countries. The Turks have two on order, one is being delivered by sea, and is even now on her way; the other has been rejected by the Turkish Purchasing Commission owing to the bad metal she contains; has been returned to the stocks for an attempt to be made to recondition her.

It is not thought that there are many secret and undeclared submarines built; though there is some evidence that Germany possesses more than she should, having several submarines with duplicated numbers. There are also believed to exist a stock of large components of submarines, which, in the event of war would enable her to launch submarines with greater celerity than would seem possible on a superficial examination of her building capacity. The capacity of the latter is estimated at about 100 a year, assuming not more than 10% to be above 500 tons, and not more than 40% above 250 tons. The above information is, of course, confidential.

D M

Desmond Morton: note
(*Churchill papers: 2/371*)

17 April 1939   Earlylands

I would be delighted to discuss Eng Cmdr Mandeville's[1] proposals at Mr Churchill's convenience; but I doubt if the former has given us enough information about them to do so.[2] It is not fair to criticise them without hearing his reaction to certain apparent, immediate objections.

With this reservation, it seems to me that he is in error on two main points. (a) He is certainly wrong in saying that we have no-one considering such efforts in war. The Joint Planning Officers and the senior Joint Planning Sub-Committee of the CID do so regularly, especially the Joint Planning Officers, to whom is added, as Cmdr Mandeville himself suggests a mere 'lousy' civilian for co-ordination (and other) purposes, though I doubt if my Mr Owen[3] would be pleased at the reference to him as a mere 'lousy' civilian.

[1] Geoffrey F. Mandeville, 1901–1942. Midshipman, HMS *Indomitable* (Battle Cruiser), 1917; HMS *Wrestler* (Torpedo-Boat Destroyer), 1919. Sub-Lieutenant, 1921; Royal Naval Engineering College, 1922. Lieutenant (Engineer), 1922. Advanced Engineering Course, 1924. Served on HMS *Marlborough* (Battleship), 1925–7; at Portsmouth Dockyard, 1927–30; on board HMS *Berwick* (Cruiser), 1930–2. Lieutenant-Commander, 1930; Commander, 1934. Served on HMS *Despatch* (Cruiser), 1935–7; HMS *President* 1937–40; Engineer-in-Chief's Department, 1940–1; HMS *Eagle*, 1941. Died on 11 August 1942, when HMS *Eagle* was sunk by a German U-Boat (U.43) in the Mediterranean, while on convoy duty with the 'Pedestal' convoy bound for Malta.
[2] In a letter to Churchill, Engineer Commander Mandeville proposed, with supporting details, that Churchill should put forward in the House of Commons 'these aspects of England's strength': the ability to attack Spain through the Balearic Islands and Gibraltar (British forces), Morocco (French forces) and France (French forces); to attack Italy through Abyssinia (East African, Sudanese and Indian forces), Leros and Rhodes (Turkish and Greek forces), Libya (French–Tunisian and British–Egyptian forces), Albania (Greek, British, Australian and New Zealand forces) and France (French forces); and to attack Germany through Schleswig (British and Canadian forces), Fehren (British and Canadian forces), Rügen (Polish forces), the North-East coast (Polish forces), East Prussia (Polish forces) and France (French forces). Mandeville added: '. . . may I persuade you to gather together all those who believe in amphibian warfare? This was so neglected in 1914–18 that sea-land, or the *new* air–land amphibian wars will be the *surprise* of the next conflict. Do not leave it to the Italians to teach us, by example, the energy of this form of warfare.' Against Mandeville's reference to 'the new air–land amphibian wars' Desmond Morton noted: 'This may well be so.'
[3] Rowland Hubert Owen, 1903–   . Educated at Trinity College, Dublin. Department of Overseas Trade, 1926. Commercial Secretary, Residency, Cairo, 1935. Principal, Department of Overseas Trade, 1936–9; a member of Desmond Morton's Industrial Intelligence Centre after its enlargement in 1936; attached to the Joint Planning Sub-Committee of the Committee of Imperial Defence, 1936–9. Ministry of Economic Warfare, 1939 (Representative of the Ministry in the Middle East, 1942). Director of the Combined (Anglo-American) Economic Warfare Agencies, 1943. Senior UK Trade Commissioner, India, Burma and Ceylon, 1944. Comptroller-General, Export Credits Guarantee Department, 1953–8. Deputy Controller, HM Stationery Office, 1959–64. He later described Desmond Morton as 'a man of inexhaustible dynamism, a shrewd and penetrating observer with a great gift for interpretation and expression' (*letter to the author 28 October 1981*).

(b) Before considering any theoretic strategic plan it is essential to be sure on two points, (i) exactly who is fighting whom, and (ii) the real strength of the Forces of which we and our allies would dispose, and the enemy would dispose, on the date, and in the circumstances envisaged. There are, moreover, 4 'Forces' to consider. Naval, military, Air and Supply.

Whereas Cmdr Mandeville should know a deal about our naval strength, and may know about our air strength, he is apparently frightfully optimistic about our land and industrial and supply strength *at the present time*, and I fear lest our weakness in the latter directions may vitiate all his plans.

Rejecting better counsel, I am tempted and fall; so add that Cmdr Mandeville has raised what is, to my mind, a very important general point, and one which caused great trouble in the war of 1914. What is the value of the 'side-show'? Venturing to disagree with my late chief, Lord Haig, I would answer that, dependent upon circumstances, it may be very great indeed.

Secondly, I agree with Cmdr Mandeville, that in a future war, the side-show of combined operations between naval, military and air forces may be of supreme importance. But I have regretfully to admit that our forces as a whole do not seem to be adequate at present to indulge in these ventures. Declaring to Parliament that the Territorial Force is to be doubled does not double the Territorial Force. Even if the man-power is forthcoming, trained at that, where are the armaments? Answer: 'In a not very different position to that before the declaration.'

DM

Leslie Hore-Belisha: diary
(*'The Private Papers of Hore-Belisha'*)

17 April 1939

He[1] asked me what I thought of the idea of inviting Attlee, TUC leaders, Churchill, and others to attend the CID. I said it was a good idea, but I refused to believe that we would not stand up to opposition to compulsory military service from whatever quarter it came. . . .

In the evening Churchill rang up. He was apprehensive about Gibraltar. I told him that we were sending the Welsh Guards and that two battalions were on their way from Palestine and that they could be disembarked at Gibraltar. A reinforcement of guns and material had been despatched there. He urged me not to resign.

[1] Lord Halifax.

Winston S. Churchill to Lord Halifax
(*Foreign Office papers: 800/323*)

17 April 1939   Chartwell
Private and Confidential

My dear Edward,

I think I spoke a little too confidently to you last night about the re-assurance to be attached to the portion of the German fleet proceeding to Spain. I see they are not sending the two 26,000-ton battle-ships; so that they would have a force of some strength in the Baltic. It may be of course that they are prepared to sacrifice the two or three 'Deutschlands' to a Mediterranean adventure, in order to clinch the resolution of Spain and Italy to come in on their side. If so, these ships would be expected to play the part that the 'Goeben' did in Turkey in the late War.[1] It is possible therefore I was over-hopeful.

I find that Roger Keyes takes a more serious view. 'It may be,' he writes, 'that the German manoeuvres are a guarantee that the Germans do not contemplate doing anything while they are away. On the other hand, there are such very dangerous possibilities in Spain, that it may be that they con-template basing this small force on a well-defended Spanish port as a threat in the flank of our communications. If so, it would need a considerable force to contain it, including battlecruisers to overhaul the two pocket battleships.'

The dispositions of our Fleet are inexplicable. First, on Tuesday night, April 4, the First Lord showed that the Home Fleet was in such a condition of preparedness that the men could not even leave the anti-aircraft guns to come below. This was the result of a scare telegram, and was, in my opinion, going beyond what vigilance requires. On the other hand, at the same time, the Mediterranean Fleet was, as I described to the House, scattered in the most vulnerable disorder throughout the Mediterranean; and as photographs published in the newspapers show, the 'Barham' was actually moored alongside the Naples jetty.

---

[1] In October 1914, when Turkey was still neutral, the Turkish Minister of War, Enver Pasha, agreed to a German request that the *Goeben* and the *Breslau* steam into the Black Sea. On the morning of Thursday October 29 the *Goeben* and *Breslau*, commanded by a German Admiral but flying the Turkish flag, bombarded the Russian Black Sea ports of Odessa, Nikolaev and Sevastopol. Later that day Sir Edward Grey telegraphed to the British Am-bassador to Turkey that unless the Turks made 'immediate reparation to Russia', he did not see how war could be avoided; but he assured the Ambassador that Britain would not 'take the first step'. On October 30, however, he sent the Ambassador an ultimatum for transmis-sion to the Turks, demanding the dismissal of the German military and naval missions and the removal from the *Goeben* and *Breslau* of all German personnel within twelve hours. If this was refused, the Ambassador was instructed to 'ask for your passports and leave Constantinople with the staff of the Embassy'. On 1 November 1914, off Smyrna, two British destroyers began Britain's hostilities against Turkey.

Now the Mediterranean Fleet has been concentrated and is at sea, where it should be. Therefore no doubt all is well in the Mediterranean. But now the unpreparedness is transferred to home waters. The Atlantic Fleet, except for a few anti-aircraft guns, has been practically out of action for some days owing to very large numbers of men having been sent on leave. One would have thought at least the leave could be 'staggered' in times like these. All the mine-sweepers are out of action refitting. How is it possible to reconcile this with the statement of tension declared to be existing on Tuesday week? It seems to be a grave departure from the procedure of continuous and reasonable vigilance. After all, the conditions prevailing now are not in principle different from those of last week. The First Sea Lord[1] is seriously ill, so I expect a great deal falls upon Stanhope.

I write this to you for your own personal information, and in order that you can check the facts for yourself. Pray, therefore, treat my letter as strictly private, as I do not want to bother the Prime Minister with the matter, but think you ought to know.[2]

Lord Halifax to Lord Chatfield

(*Foreign Office papers: 800/323*)

18 April 1939

I enclose a letter from Winston Churchill about naval matters. I am sorry to bother you in these very busy days but I would be most grateful if you would supply me with an answer. You will see that the letter is 'strictly private' and will, I know, ensure that it is treated as such.

---

[1] Admiral of the Fleet Sir Reginald Backhouse, who died on 15 July 1939. He was succeeded as First Sea Lord by Sir Dudley Pound.

[2] In his letter to his sister on 15 April 1939, Chamberlain had written: 'I heard from D. Margesson after the debate that Winston had asked him to dinner and saying that this was no time for mincing words informed him bluntly of his strong desire to join the Govt. In reply to enquiries he assured David of his confidence that he could work amicably under the PM who had many admirable qualities some of which he did not possess himself. On the other hand he too had great qualities and could do much to help the PM to bear his intolerable burden, likely as it was to get worse as time went on. He would like the Admiralty but would be quite satisfied to succeed Runciman as Lord President. He thought Eden should be taken in too but observed that he could give much more help than Eden.'

Eleanor Rathbone to Winston S. Churchill

(*Churchill papers: 2/374*)

18 April 1939
Private

Dear Mr Churchill,

I was greatly interested in your remarks in Thursday's debate about the apparent inadequacy of the Government's Secret Service information from abroad. May I add some illustrative examples, just in case any of them have escaped you?

1. The attached Press letter [1] gives my summary of the apparent ignoring of evidence available in Prague of Hitler's intention to march in on March 15th.

2. A German refugee who escaped just after the march-in told another refugee (a man I know and trust) that he obtained his permit through a high-placed German officer (one of those in command of the troops who marched in) (he gave the name and rank, but I promised not to mention it) whom he had previously been friendly with. The Officer said: 'You ought to have got out long ago; I could have told you the date a month ago.'

3. When I was in Prague on refugee business (January 13th to 20th) I heard from everyone—refugee workers, journalists, etc—that the British Legation was completely aloof, uninterested and unhelpful over refugee questions. Yet apart from humane motives, they ought to have been closely in touch. The German refugees in Czechoslovakia included some of the men engaged in secret propaganda against Hitlerism and accustomed to going backwards and forwards over the German border. Should not a good Secret Service have its own ways of picking the brains of such men? In my refugee work, I frequently come across evidence of how much better informed they were of Germany's intentions than the Foreign Office was or appeared to be —evidence given before and not after the fact.

4. In February 1937 I was in Prague, Bucharest and Belgrade with the Duchess of Atholl. In Prague, the then British Chargé d'Affaires [2] was completely pro-Henlein and anti-Czech. In Bucharest, the British Minister [3] (as admitted to me by a member of his family) was strongly anti-Semite, though

---

[1] Not printed.

[2] Robert Henry Hadow, 1895–1963. Educated at Harrow and King's College, Cambridge. Entered the Diplomatic Service, 1919. Chargé d'Affaires in Prague, 1935, 1936 and 1937. Counsellor, Buenos Aires, 1942; Washington, 1944. Consul-General, Los Angeles, 1948. Knighted, 1953. Consul-General, San Francisco, 1954–7.

[3] Reginald Hervey Hoare, 1882–1954. A member of the banking family. Educated at Eton. Entered the Diplomatic Service, 1905. Counsellor, 1923. Minister at Teheran, 1931–4. Knighted, 1933. Minister in Bucharest, 1935–41. Remained in Government service until 1944, when he joined his family bank in Fleet Street.

the persecution of the Roumanian Jews had already begun. In all three capitals, one was struck with the aloofness of the British Legations from democratic sections of opinion. I am sure that at the end of a week's visit, we knew more about what the Trade Union, University, Peace Movement, Women's Movement leaders were thinking and feeling than the people at the Legation did. They may have been more 'discreet' than really ignorant, but I think one can tell the difference.

5. The British Consular Service seems generally suspect in democratic circles. This has been especially so in Spain and in Prague. They seem so often to have foreign wives or commercial connections of a definitely pro-Nazi kind. I won't trouble you with instances, though I could cite a good many, eg the present Passport Officer or British Consul (I am not sure which) in Prague is said to have a German wife who is strongly suspect. . . .

Winston S. Churchill to Sir Henry Strakosch

(Churchill papers: 2/374)

18 April 1939

I enclose a note on your paper about German oil resources. It is from a friend of mine and most secret. Please do not let the letter pass out of your personal possession. What he says may enable you to re-cast your figures, and I think it would be of great advantage if you would do so.

Will you send me the letter back when you have done with it.

Brendan Bracken to Bernard Baruch

(Baruch papers)

18 April 1939

Winston has won his long fight. Our Government are now adopting the policy that he advised three years ago. No public man in our time has shown more foresight. And I believe that his long, lonely struggle to expose the dangers of the dictatorships will prove to be the best chapter in his crowded life.

Leslie Hore-Belisha: diary
('*The Private Papers of Hore-Belisha*')

18 April 1939

I got home late and there was a message that Churchill had telephoned. I rang him and he said from information he had received about Gibraltar, he felt something was going to happen there. I told him that everything possible that the War Office could do, had been done, that extra gunners had been sent and that any personnel and material that could be spared had been despatched. I mentioned to him the difficulties I was having and he again advised me not to resign, that events would justify my objectives and that he would support me.

Lord Chatfield to Lord Halifax
(*Foreign Office papers: 800/323*)

19 April 1939
Secret

My dear Halifax,

Thank you for your letter from Winston.

There is, of course a good deal in all that he says, though one wishes he would not be quite so restless, because it implies a want of confidence in the Admiralty and ignores certain important considerations altogether.

The question of the change in the strategical position caused by the proceeding of the German Squadron to Spain is a matter on which the Admiralty alone can advise and they are fully qualified to do so. The First Lord informed me yesterday that they considered that this move was not a menace, particularly since the two German training ships, about which the Germans had also warned us, were proceeding to(?) the West Indies and passed down the Channel yesterday. Obviously this may be a Machiavellian move to deceive us though it is difficult to believe that this is the case. Whether the separation of this part of the German Fleet from the main body is a strategic move, and if so whether it is a good one, is again a matter on which the Admiralty alone can advise. If it was their intention to go to war during the next month and they intended to place these ships on our trade routes before the war started, they would be in a very good position to do so. At the same time it would be almost equally easy to move them *in advance* into the Atlantic if they were at Wilhelmshaven. Roger Keyes' more serious view is based, of course, on the intervention of Spain on the side of the Axis and if that occurs the strategical position would be so altered to our disadvantage that it would not be affected to a large extent by the presence of the German ships there now. Generally I may say I view this visit of the German ships to Spain as a serious step rather because of its influence on the Spanish mentality and the contacts that will be formed between the Spanish and German Navies, the plans for co-operation that can be made and the insistence, possibly of the Germans, that the naval bases shall be properly protected for the use of their ships. I do not see that we can in any case do anything about that at the moment unless we were to make a counter demonstration with the British Navy at Gibraltar. This is as I say again a matter for the Admiralty to advise.

As regards the criticisms as to the disposition of the Home Fleet, I asked before the Fleet went on leave whether the Foreign Office and the Admiralty had considered the desirability of this taking place and was informed that a decision had been arrived at by the Prime Minister in conjunction with you and the First Lord approving it, a decision which I have no doubt at the time was a right one, if I may say so. What Mr Churchill forgets invariably is that the British Fleet is *an old Fleet*, largely due to his own action when he was Chancellor of the Exchequer in opposing its reconstruction, though he is not entirely to blame as you will know. The result is that we are building up our Fleet too late as the DR Committee[1] emphasised five years ago. In consequence it is inevitable that our old ships should have frequent need of repairs and the only time they can do this is during these leave periods. It was only two days ago that I was informed that the 'Hood' our most valuable ship had turbine trouble, and was laid up two or three months—a disastrous situation. That is why I view, as I told you last night, the despatch of the 'Repulse', our only battle cruiser, to the other side of the Atlantic with such serious concern.[2] Whether the Home Fleet should be now sent to sea and the

---

[1] The Defence Requirements Committee of the Cabinet, set up in 1935. Its principal meetings are described in Main Volume V of this biography, on pages 640–2 (meeting of 30 April 1935) and pages 647–8 (meeting of 10 May 1935). It was at this latter meeting that the Chief of the Imperial General Staff, Sir Archibald Montgomery-Massingberd, warned that 'by aiming at parity with the German Air Force we were issuing a new challenge to Germany in a form of warfare in which we were most vulnerable. Germany was better placed than we were, not only geographically. Everything was in Germany's favour and they had a greater capacity to expand their Air Force than we possessed. We were challenging Germany to a race in air armament and in such a race, Germany was bound to win. Germany had three great advantages. She had conscription, we had not, and this counted for much, especially as her population was 66 million to our 44 million. Germany's preparations for industrial mobilisation were infinitely better than ours. Lastly, Germany could devote all her efforts to her home Army and Air Force; we had world-wide commitments, naval, military and air' (*Foreign Office papers: 371/18840*).

[2] The *Repulse* was intended to take King George VI and Queen Elizabeth on their Royal visit to Canada and the United States. In view of the crisis, the Admiralty chartered as a

men recalled from leave is a matter which no doubt we shall discuss this morning at the Cabinet. They are due to return on the 27th and I should have thought that such a step was unnecessary, especially if it would have the effect of sending some ships to sea before their repairs are completed, though no doubt some of them could be left behind if necessary to finish their repairs.

Then as regards the Mediterranean Fleet, I think he exaggerates when he talks of them being scattered in 'vulnerable disorder'. It is, of course, a matter of opinion whether paying a friendly visit to our potential enemy and fraternising with them is placing your ship in a state of jeopardy or the contrary, but you will remember that the Admiralty pointed out that the majority of the Fleet was at Malta all the time. We cannot maintain a continuous reasonable vigilance on our present system and if we have got to do so we must change our principles in my opinion, but you will remember that during the whole of the last twelve months there has been a state of strain and would Mr Churchill say that during the whole of those twelve months the British Navy should have been kept at their war stations?!

Yours sincerely,
Chatfield

Mortimer Wheeler to Winston S. Churchill
(*Churchill papers: 8/625*)

19 April 1939   The London Museum

Dear Mr Churchill,

On our return from Palmyra (whither we were driven by your Lebanese chauffeur of 5 years ago) we find *Marlborough* awaiting us in his glory. How very charming and gracious of you and your wife to send him to us! The book forms the nucleus, the focus, the rallying-point in one of our new bookshelves in our new establishment, and shines upon us in the London sunlight which welcomes us after the storms of the Syrian desert.

Thank you very much indeed—we shall both of us treasure your gift.

Yours sincerely,
R. E. Mortimer Wheeler

_____

substitute the Canadian Pacific liner, *Empress of Australia*, which sailed from Southampton on 5 May 1939.

Lord Tyrrell[1] to Winston S. Churchill
(*Churchill papers: 2/358*)

19 April 1939

My dear Winston,

I wish I could address you again as 'First Lord of the Seas' to congratulate you on your statesmanlike speeches of last & this week.[2] They have done more to pull the country together than any other. I do not often, if ever, agree with Wedgwood Benn,[3] but I did on Thursday in his comment on your speech.[4]

If I had my way I shd like to see you as Lord President in control of the Defence Cttee in its widest sense.

I am off to Switzerland tomorrow for a fortnight's rest: it is also a good intelligence centre which we of course neglect.

When I return, I wish you would let me come & see you. See to it that we keep the leadership which is virtually over now that we have conscription.

Yrs ever,
The Beaver

---

[1] William George Tyrrell, 1866–1947. Educated at Balliol College, Oxford. Entered the Foreign Service, 1889. Private Secretary to Sir Edward Grey, 1907–15. Knighted, 1913. Assistant Under-Secretary of State at the Foreign Office, 1919–25; Permanent Under-Secretary, 1925–8. Privy Councillor, 1928. Ambassador in Paris, 1928–34. Created Baron, 1929. President of the British Board of Film Censors, 1935–47. A member of the Other Club from 1924. His younger son, Hugo, died of wounds received in action, February 1915; his elder son, Francis, was killed in action in February 1918.

[2] Churchill's speeches of 3 April 1939, after the British Guarantee to Poland (see page 1441, note 2) and of 13 April 1939, after the Italian invasion of Albania (see page 1448). In approving, during this second speech, Chamberlain's announcement earlier in the debate that Britain had just offered a guarantee to Roumania, Churchill declared: 'One sees a great design which, even now at the eleventh hour, if it could be perfected, would spare the world the worst of agonies.'

[3] William Wedgwood Benn, 1877–1960. Liberal MP, 1906–27. A Junior Lord of the Treasury in Asquith's Government, 1910–15. On active service, 1915–19 (Royal Fying Corps, despatches twice). Joined the Labour Party, 1927. Labour MP, 1928–31 and 1937–42. Secretary of State for India in Ramsay MacDonald's second Premiership, 1929–31. Created Viscount Stansgate, 1941. Secretary of State for Air in Clement Attlee's Government, 1945–6. One of his three sons was killed in action in 1944; another, Anthony (Tony) Wedgwood Benn, disclaimed his father's title and was a member of the Labour Governments of 1964 and 1974, but unsuccessful contender for the Deputy Leadership of the Labour Party (1981).

[4] I have not been able to trace this comment, but Wedgwood Benn's son, Tony Benn, notes: 'Father was on the Committee looking into the Sandys case. He was very involved in that. He didn't see eye to eye with Churchill on most matters, including India, but he was in agreement over rearmament. He wouldn't have gone out of his way to say something friendly, but Churchill would have noticed if he had' (*conversation with the author, 1 February 1982*).

Group-Captain Lachlan MacLean to Winston S. Churchill

(*Churchill papers: 2/358*)

19 April 1939   United Service Club

Dear Mr Churchill,

I have heard that I am to be asked to speak before the Air Committee of the House of Commons in the near future. I have begun to prepare what I want to say, but of course I am quite inexperienced in foreseeing the pitfalls I may possibly encounter & in how best to present my subject to such a body.

I should be very grateful if you could spare me a few minutes for a word of advice. I could come to your flat at any time convenient to you next week.

Yours sincerely,
Lachlan MacLean

Winston S. Churchill to Harold Balfour

(*Churchill papers: 2/375*)

19 April 1939
Private

The passage marked in red (A) of this letter, seems to be a variant of the idea you mentioned to me the other day.[1]

I think also that the innocent process of establishing a factory in a foreign country, which factory would contain all the spares, etc, is one you should consider as an element in your plan.

I have merely sent an acknowledgment to my correspondent, but you are welcome to take him on if you think it is worth while.

---

[1] The passage marked in red read as follows: 'The matter I now will put before you, is a very important one, especially as I am convinced war will break out within a short time and is inevitable. In this case you have to give the Germans the first blow, of which they will never recover and this has to be made by aeroplanes, in a great number and incessantly, bombarding all the vital spots in Rhineland and Westphalia, as well as bridges and mainroads. Now if these machines have a starting point in Holland, it would facilitate matters very much, as now they are forced to start many hundred miles earlier, so that they cannot carry the same number of bombs, as they could from a much closer starting point. However as Holland is strictly neutral, so long as they are not attacked by the Germans (although I think they will try to get hold of our ports), the thing to do is to erect a factory of flying machines in this country, Haarlem would be an ideal place, near the North Sea, with Dutch directors (one of whom I should like to be) with Capital of British manufacturers (Lord Nuffield a.s.o.) so that in case of war, the flying machines would not only find a complete range of accessories, but also a point from which they could start, taking as a fact that Holland would be also attacked and be no longer neutral.' The writer of this letter was H. van Lier, of Haarlem, Holland.

Sir Henry Strakosch to Winston S. Churchill
(*Churchill papers: 2/374*)

20 April 1939
Personal

My dear Winston,

Thank you so much for your letter of the 18th, and for letting me see the comments of your friend on my paper about German Oil Supply and Consumption. I shall re-examine the question in the light of his comments, but I may say at once that my talk with Lindemann, when I had tea with you the other day, satisfied me that my figures for petrol and oil consumption of the German Air Force in times of war are too high. I shall let you know the result of my further investigation.

I shall, of course, treat the document you sent me as strictly confidential, and send it back to you when I have finished with it.

Yours very sincerely,
H. Strakosch

Frank Pakenham to Winston S. Churchill
(*Churchill papers: 2/358*)

21 April 1939   Christ Church,
                                                Oxford

Dear Mr Churchill,

Will you please forgive my troubling you with the enclosed cutting from to-day's Daily Telegraph. You have brought it on yourself, if I may say so, by your emergence as the one man of knowledge and purpose whom the public recognize as equal to the military necessities of the moment. *Please don't bother to reply to this letter*, but the point made in my letter to the Telegraph is one of a number that seem more likely to be cleared up if placed in your charge than in any other way.[1]

With further apologies

Yrs sincerely,
Frank Pakenham

[1] On 21 April 1939 the *Daily Telegraph* published a letter from Frank Pakenham critical of the 'Reserved List' system in preventing Dons over the age of 25 from serving in the Territorials. Part of his letter read: 'As a Socialist, I think that all who have not had the foresight to train themselves in advance should take their chance equally in a crisis like the present, and that it would do University men like myself a great deal of good, and could scarcely do the Army much harm, if we were all started off at the bottom. But the essential point is that a decision should be come to. At present there is a sharp conflict between the policy officially laid down and the advice tendered by military authorities to local applicants, with the result that the so-called "educated" man in his 30's, who is not already in the Territorials, is prevented from taking any steps to equip himself to render full-time service in event of war.'

Sir Keith Price to Winston S. Churchill
(*Churchill papers: 2/371*)

22 April 1939

Dear Mr Churchill,

I am enclosing a short statement on the Potato position which speaks for itself. I have no hesitation in saying that it is a crime, under present circumstances, to deliberately restrict the production of essential foodstuffs in such a way. . . .

Winston S. Churchill to Frank Pakenham
(*Churchill papers: 2/358*)

24 April 1939

Very many thanks for your letter, and for the admirable contribution you have made to the 'Daily Telegraph'. I am in hearty accord with it, and will make this point when the Supplementary Estimate is debated for the increased Territorial Forces.

Winston S. Churchill to Sir James Hawkey
(*Churchill papers: 7/56*)

24 April 1939   Chartwell
Private

My dear Hawkey,

I am sure you would be wise to reserve your fire until we see whether they attack, and how strong they are.

If they attack you and Dinah, I will make a case of your services and success, and of the ingratitude shown, especially taking advantage of a moment when your health is weak. This will give us a great advantage.

If, on the other hand, you opened by attacking them as they so richly deserve, it would give them the opportunity of saying that we had begun it.

I expect that the predominate feeling of the meeting will be to stand together in the hour of danger, and that we shall have very strong support on maintaining the Association unbroken under its present leadership. Once this is clear, it might well be right to make a complaint about the monstrous treatment that we have received.

Forgive my not signing this, as I am in the car.

Yours sincerely,
pp Winston S. Churchill
Private Secretary

Sir Kingsley Wood to Winston S. Churchill

(*Churchill papers: 25/17*)

24 April 1939 Air Ministry
Secret

My dear Winston,

I am sorry not to have written sooner in regard to Lindemann and the experiments.

First, as regards the 'smaller mines with shorter wires', I am not quite sure whether you have in mind the 100 ft mines or the light mines for attack against airscrews. The 100 ft mines were, as you will remember, abandoned at the end of 1936, and I am doubtful whether we should be justified in reconsidering them now. The light mines for attack against airscrews, on the other hand, have distinct possibilities. Their value depends upon what is the minimum weight of explosive which will do lethal damage to an airscrew blade when detonating in contact with it, and experiments to determine this are to be carried out using Lindemann's bombs.

As regards going into production on the long wire mine, there are, I am afraid, certain technical and tactical points which have still to be cleared up including the testing of the sample bombs which have not yet been completed and which will require testing for the functioning of the fuse. The examination of these points is, of course, being proceeded with with all possible speed.

Then as regards the filling of Lindemann's containers at Woolwich, I understand that there are two types, one with a specially sensitive filling requiring neither fuse nor detonator and intended to go off on impact with an airscrew blade and the other with detonators but also without fuses. Pye has been in touch with both the Ordnance Board and with the Director of Artillery at the War Office and he understands that the latter type have now been filled and that approval has been given for their testing. Arrangements for the trials will be pressed forward with all possible speed. On the other hand, he understands that the other type, those without detonators, are regarded by the War Office as so dangerous that they have not been willing to undertake the filling.

I have not, of course, been able to go into matters very fully in this letter, and I am inclined to think that it would be a good thing if you could find time to see Air Vice-Marshal Tedder and Dr Pye and discuss things with them more in detail. If this commends itself to you, perhaps you would let me know and I will arrange to put them in touch with you.

Yours ever,
Kingsley Wood

Harold Nicolson: diary

(*Nicolson papers*)

25 April 1939

A large Focus luncheon in the Pinafore Room at the Savoy. The luncheon is given in honour of the American Ambassador,[1] who arrives accompanied by his son.[2] The members of the committee are Winston, Anthony Eden, Lord Cecil, Reggie McKenna, Cranborne, Arthur Greenwood, Archie Sinclair, Violet Bonham Carter, Alderman Toole of Manchester and the Chairman of the NUR[3] etc etc. Kennedy makes a very excellent speech.

[1] Joseph Patrick Kennedy, 1888–1969. Born in Boston. Graduated from Harvard, 1912 Assistant General Manager, Fore River Plant, Bethlehem Shipbuilding Corporation, 1917–19. Investment banker. Chairman of the Securities Exchange Commission, 1934–5 and of the US Maritime Commission, 1937. Ambassador to London, 1937–41. Of his four sons, Joseph was killed in action in 1944; John (President of the United States) was assassinated in 1963; and Robert (a Senator) was assassinated in 1968.

[2] John F. Kennedy, later President of the United States, who was in Britain working on his Harvard senior year dissertation, which was subsequently published as the book *Why England Slept*, in July 1940. In the Introduction, Kennedy wrote: 'About two years ago Winston Churchill published a book entitled *While England Slept*. This book is an attempt to explain why England slept. I have started with the assumption that there is no short-cut to the answer to this problem. To me, it appears extremely short-sighted to dismiss superficially England's present position as the result of one man or one group of men's blindness. To say that all the blame must rest on the shoulders of Neville Chamberlain or of Stanley Baldwin is to overlook the obvious. As the leaders, they are, of course, gravely and seriously responsible. But, given the conditions of democratic government, a free press, public elections, and a cabinet responsible to Parliament and thus to the people, given rule by the majority, it is unreasonable to blame the entire situation on one man or group.' Kennedy added: 'I do not believe necessarily that if Hitler wins the present war he will continue on his course towards world domination. He may well be too exhausted, or he may be satisfied with what he has obtained. But, in the light of what has happened in the last five years, we cannot depend on it. A defeat of the Allies may simply be one more step towards the ultimate achievement—Germany over the world. Therefore, if Hitler succeeds in winning the present war, the position of America will be remarkably similar to that of England during the last decade.'

[3] John Marchbank, 1883–1946. Worked as a shepherd until the age of fourteen, then as a cattleman and dairyman. Began work on the railways, as a porter, at the age of eighteen. President of the National Union of Railwaymen, 1922–4; Assistant General Secretary, 1925; General Secretary, 1934–42. Elected to the Trades Union Congress General Council, 1933. Vice-President of the International Transport Workers Federation, 1935. Director of British Overseas Airways Corporation, 1943. In July 1944 he broadcast an appeal to the railway workers of Hungary not to allow Hungarian Jews to be deported to the death camps.

Hugh Cudlipp[1] to Winston S. Churchill: telegram

(*Churchill papers: 8/624*)

25 April 1939

Huge mail has reached me this morning following my Churchill article on Sunday.[2] Letters are overwhelmingly in your favour. Will let you know details by letter. I think they would interest you.

Hugh Cudlipp

Professor Lindemann to Winston S. Churchill

(*Churchill papers: 25/17*)

26 April 1939   Christ Church
                                                          Oxford

My dear Winston,

Many thanks for letting me know the Secretary of State's views.

Though I have always pressed that mines on wires should be developed, I have always maintained that the best length was a matter for investigation. I have no objection to the 2,000 ft mine, but I think it is a great pity to neglect the shorter mine, which we may for the sake of simplicity refer to as the 100 ft mine. The difference, in effect, is that the longer mine pulls up over the wing whilst the shorter one swings round on to it. The longer is therefore probably more likely to be cut by special cutters or perhaps even by the propellers. The shorter is much simpler to make and as we have shown you,

---

[1] Hugh Cudlipp, 1913–   . Entered provincial journalism, 1927; Features Editor of the London *Sunday Chronicle*, 1932–5; of the *Daily Mirror*, 1935–7. Editor of the *Sunday Pictorial* 1937–40 and 1946–9. On active service, 1940–6. OBE, 1945. Managing Editor, *Sunday Express*, 1950–2. Joint Managing Director, *Daily Mirror* and *Sunday Pictorial*, 1959–63. Chairman, Daily Mirror Newspapers, 1963–8; International Publishing Corporation, 1968–73. Director of Associated Television Ltd, 1956–73. Knighted, 1973; Baron, 1974.

[2] The whole front page, and all of page two, of the *Sunday Pictorial* of 23 April 1939 was devoted to what the headline called 'The Great Churchill Scandal', and to the question 'Why isn't Winston Churchill in the Cabinet?'. The answer, according to the article, was 'that the personal suspicions and fear and jealousies of others are crushing him out, and the desire of the nation is disregarded with contempt. Instead of utilizing Churchill's gifts, they are content, these enemies, to disseminate false legends of his "inconsistencies", his "temperament", his "erratic judgement", his "scare-mongering". This 'fantastic duel' should now cease, the paper demanded. 'Much has this man suffered from the incalculable caprices of political fortune: is the nation, too, to suffer for the incalculable vanity of his detractors? For the injustice of his expulsion is outweighed only by the criminal disservice to Britain which allows this state of affairs to go on.' The article ended by suggesting that Churchill should be appointed Lord President of the Council, in place of Lord Runciman, 'who has the impertinence to embark upon a four month's holiday without resigning . . .'

it is quite easy to devise a suitable, safe detonating mechanism. I think it could be made ready for production in a very few weeks given help and facilities.

As to utility, assuming an equal proportion of each type striking the wing will be effective, there is not much to choose. The 2,000 ft mine has a 20 times greater chance of collision than a 100 ft mine, but weighs some 20 times more. Provided the weight is equal, it must be a matter of indifference to the mine-layer whether he discharges 200 long mines or 4,000 short ones. What I would urge is that some type of mine be put into production with the greatest possible speed.

Our complaints about delay, however, were concerned mainly with the 'minelets' or 'bomblets' for attacking propellers. As the Secretary of State says, the first point is, what is the minimum weight of explosive necessary. To test this I sent half a dozen bomblets to Woolwich to be filled on the 4th March. These were arranged to take ordinary detonators since we were not concerned at this stage to investigate whether one could dispense with this complication. I am glad to learn from Pye to-day that there is every hope that the tests will be made on Monday, the 1st May.

An immense simplification in manufacture will, of course, be achieved if it is ultimately possible to dispense with detonators. In view of the extremely violent blow the bomblet will suffer from a propeller blade, I think it quite possible that the ordinary tetryl with which the present ones are being filled will explode without a special detonator. If so, there is no difficulty or danger whatsoever. If not, one may have to go to slightly more unstable explosives, but I feel confident such can be found. After all one is only looking for a substance safe to handle but which will detonate on being struck a blow far more violent than anyone can give with a hammer.

Do you think it would be a good idea for me to try and interest the ICI in such an investigation? It is quite easy to make. All one needs is a rotating steel bar to simulate a propeller into which miniature bomblets filled with the various explosives in question are swung.

If you decide to see Air Marshal Tedder and Dr Pye, I need scarcely say I shall be happy to come to the discussion should you think this desirable.

In haste,
Yours ever,
FAL

Hugh Cudlipp to Winston S. Churchill

(*Churchill papers: 8/633*)

26 April 1939   The Daily Mirror

Dear Mr Churchill,

So far, following my article last Sunday advocating your entry into the Cabinet, I have received 2,400 letters from readers.

They are overwhelmingly in your favour, and I have never known such an unqualified response. An analysis of the letters shows that they come from all classes. A huge section comes from ex-soldiers and men in the Service today. An interesting point, too, is your appeal to the young.

'No more boot-licking to Hitler' is the general line of comment. 'We want a strong man who is not afraid.' Etc.

So far only 73 out of the growing total of 2,400 letters are against you joining the Cabinet. A number of those are of the cranky type which describe me as a 'dirty Jew in Mr Churchill's pay'—the usual sort of abusive letter of no importance. The more serious objectors blame you for Gallipoli, and use other familiar lines of attack.

Your name on our street placards aroused tremendous interest, and there is not the slightest doubt of the overwhelming view of the country on this issue.

Yours very sincerely,
H. Cudlipp

Winston S. Churchill to W. S. Morrison[1]

(*Churchill papers: 2/371*)

26 April 1939

I send you a copy of a memorandum on potatoes prepared by Sir Keith Price, who was my member for explosives (X) in the Ministry of Munitions. It speaks for itself. If the planting season has now been lost it is little less than a scandal.

It is now nearly a fortnight since I mentioned the matter to you. Before, however, raising the matter in public, which I reserve full right to do, I should be glad to know whether anything has been done, or what can be done.

---

[1] Chancellor of the Duchy of Lancaster since January 1939 (see page 1093, note 6), with responsibility for Britain's Food Defence arrangements.

Winston S. Churchill to Admiral Sir Herbert Richmond[1]

(*Churchill papers: 2/371*)

26 April 1939

I have now read the paper you so kindly sent me, and I think we are in entire agreement. Of course, the proper steps to take against the 'Deutschlands', is to hunt them down with cruiser squadrons, each of which contains a battle cruiser, even suspending merchant traffic in the meanwhile. It should be easier to hunt them down in the coming war than in the last on account of the developments of wireless, seaplanes etc. It is therefore particularly unfortunate that at a time when the three 'Deutschlands' are being placed in their strategic positions we should have the 'Renown' undergoing a long re-fit, the 'Hood' with turbine trouble, and the 'Repulse' going to America. I hope this last act of unwisdom may be prevented.

I am very glad you are watching the situation so attentively.

Lieutenant-Colonel Eliot Crawshay Williams[2] *to Winston S. Churchill*

(*Churchill papers: 2/358*)

26 April 1939

My dear Winston,

Just a line to wish you every kind of success in your efforts to make us able to bear our part in whatever may be to come. I wish you were in the Cabinet.

In case you've time to glance at it here's a plea for Conscription written, I think, from a rather new angle, which I hope you may consider a useful contribution to your campaign.[3]

Yours ever,
Eliot Crawshay Williams

[1] Herbert William Richmond, 1871–1946. Entered Navy, 1885. Captain, 1908. Commanded HMS *Dreadnought*, 1909–11, Assistant Director of Operations, Admiralty, 1913–15. British Liaison officer, Italian Fleet, 1915. Commanded HMS *Commonwealth*, 1915–16; HMS *Conqueror*, 1917; HMS *Erin*, 1918, Commander-in-Chief, East Indies, 1923–5. Knighted, 1926. Commandant, Imperial Defence College, 1926–8. Admiral, 1929. Professor of Naval and Imperial History, Cambridge, 1934–6. Master of Downing College, Cambridge, 1936–1946. Naval historian.

[2] Eliot Crawshay Williams, 1879–1962. Educated at Eton and Trinity College, Oxford. Entered the Army in 1900. Unsuccessful Liberal Candidate, 1906. Assistant Private Secretary to Churchill (at the Colonial Office), 1906–8. Liberal MP for Leicester, 1910–13. Parliamentary Private Secretary to Lloyd George (at the Exchequer), 1910. Lieutenant-Colonel, Commanding the 1st Leicestershire Royal Horse Artillery, Egypt and Sinai, 1915–17. Author of more than sixty books and plays, the first being *Across Persia* (1907).

[3] Churchill replied on 29 April 1939: 'I am greatly indebted to you for the kindness of your letter, which is most encouraging to me in these difficult times.'

Winston S. Churchill to Sir Kingsley Wood

(*Air Ministry papers: 19/26*)

27 April 1939   Chartwell
Private

My dear Kingsley

I send you herewith a letter I have received from Lindemann on the points mentioned in your letter.

Everything moves forward so slowly that I fear nothing will be ready should trouble come. If we had several millions of these mines, both long wire and small propeller breakers, and a hundred aeroplanes not needed for fighting purposes, from which they could be laid, we should have a strong new additional protection for this country. Why will you not get us this? You have the power.

I also send you three other papers which have been written for me by Professor Lindemann. These ideas seem worthy of examination.

Yours vy sincerely,
Winston S. Churchill

Harold Nicolson: diary

(*Nicolson papers*)

27 April 1939

Winston . . . makes a fine defence of France.[1] It is the most moderate and effective speech that I have heard him make.

[1] Speaking during the conscription debate in the House of Commons on 27 April 1939, Churchill said that 'the most dangerous attack was on the loyalties of the two western democracies. Great Britain was as dependent on France as France was dependent on us'. Churchill then spoke of the 'insidious propaganda that was going on', intended apparently 'to drive a wedge between us and France'. Were such propaganda to succeed, he warned, 'the ruin of both countries would be speedy and final'.

Winston S. Churchill: broadcast to the United States
(Churchill papers: 9/136)

28 April 1939

The character and quality of Herr Hitler's speech[1] shows a certain improvement on any he has made before. This improvement is no doubt largely due to the action of the President of the United States in sending his memorable message of peace and warning to the world a fortnight ago.[2]

President Roosevelt is the object of a good many jibes and taunts from the German Führer. The President's high purpose and great station will enable him to rise superior to these. The American democracy is likewise subjected to ridicule. They will get over that.

Part of the service rendered to the cause of peace by the intervention of the President is apparent. It may well be also that designs we do not know of were prevented, or at least suspended, by a message which has earned the gratitude of almost the whole world.

The more prudent attitude adopted by Japan in refusing to join in an anti-democracy movement, which fact cannot have been absent from Herr Hitler's mind, is of course directly attributable to the movement of the United States fleet to the Pacific Ocean.

Any improvement in Herr Hitler's declaration is also due to the revival in Europe of a system of mutual aid against aggression, and to the active formation of a peace bloc of nations, great and small, which are all arming and ready to defend each other.

[1] On 28 April 1939 Hitler had summoned the Reichstag in order to tell it of his answer to Roosevelt's 'Peace Appeal'. He spoke for two hours. Long before America had been discovered he said, 'this Reich existed, not merely in its present extent, but with the addition of many regions and provinces which have since been lost'. He then attacked the 'Peace-Dictate' of Versailles, praised the desire for neutrality of Holland, Belgium, Switzerland and Denmark, announced that all territorial disputes between France and Germany were 'done away with', spoke of Germany's 'fortune' to be on good terms with Hungary and Yugoslavia, defended the annexation of Austria, Bohemia and Moravia, stressed his life-long public desire 'of a close friendship and collaboration between England and Germany', spoke of his 'sincere admiration' for the colonizing work of the Anglo-Saxon people, insisted that he was filled with 'profound regret' at the British view that war with Germany was inevitable ('the only claim I have ever made, and shall continue to make on England is that of a return of our Colonies'), proposed the return of Danzig 'into the framework of the German Reich' and a German-controlled railway line across the Polish corridor, and then set out a twenty-one point answer to Roosevelt's appeal. That same day, the German Government announced the abrogation of two agreements, the Anglo-German Naval Agreement of 18 June 1935 and the German–Polish Declaration of 26 January 1934. For Hitler's 'pro-British' remarks, see page 1483, note 1.

[2] On 14 April 1939 Roosevelt had sent both Hitler and Mussolini a 'Peace Appeal', in which he asked for assurances that the German armed forces would not invade Finalnd, Latvia, Estonia, Lithuania, Norway, Sweden, Denmark, the Netherlands, Belgium, Great Britain, Ireland, France, Portugal, Hungary, Rumania, Yugoslavia, Russia, Bulgaria, Turkey, Iraq, Syria, Palestine, Arabia and Iran. In his speech of April 28, Hitler read out this list in mocking tones, to the accompaniment of much laughter, especially when he reached 'Palestine'.

Finally, it is due to the consolidation of France, and to the rearmament of Britain.

Naturally we all welcome an improvement, even if only in the words spoken by the Head of so great a State. But after all we have gone through in the last year it must be plainly said that words and declarations cannot by themselves restore trust and confidence, unless and until they are made good by deeds and by conduct extending over a considerable time.

While eight million Czechs are held in bondage; while the violation of the Munich Agreement remains unrepaired, not to mention other painful difficulties, a formidable barrier exists between Nazi Germany and the peaceful law-respecting, liberty loving civilisation of the world.

The denunciation of the Anglo-German Naval Agreement need excite no regrets or alarm. The British Navy cannot be overtaken by any efforts which Nazi Germany may make. It would no doubt be better that those efforts should be diverted to building a German fleet than that they should be concentrated upon the growth of air power, which is a menace to all, or upon land armaments by which smaller neighbours can be over-run.

Stripped of its verbiage and trimmings, Herr Hitler's speech reveals a wish to isolate Poland and to present an issue to Poland in the most plausible form, backed by a sombre gesture.

The denunciation of the Non-Aggression Pact with Poland, which was not to end until 1944, must be regarded as the most serious feature of the speech and as a new cause for anxiety. The Hitler method has always been to take one step at a time and, while reassuring others, to get one country shut up with him alone.

For all these reasons it is of the highest consequence that there should be no slackening of the vigilance and preparation of the peace-seeking Powers of Europe and no diminution of the influence which the United States is exercising for the common good.

It is upon the continuance of these vast processes that any real escape from our dangers must depend. There are many passages in Herr Hitler's speech which would seem designed to induce Great Britain to abandon her precautions and to withdraw from the part she has pledged herself to play in Eastern Europe. Such blandishments have on several occasions been the prelude to acts of Nazi violence. They will not have any effect upon the now thoroughly awakened British public opinion. Above all, they will not in the slightest degree retard the growth of our defence forces.

It is quite natural that Herr Hitler should not like the way in which the Great War ended. He would rather it had ended in a German victory, and in the kind of peace treaties which Germany would have made, like the Treaty of Brest Litovsk, or the treaty with Rumania or like the terms which were to be enforced upon Belgium even up to the middle of 1918. Whatever may be said against the Treaty of Versailles it was a instrument mild in comparison with these German conceptions. In the German view, which H.H.[1] shares, a peaceful Germany and Austria were fallen upon in 1914 by a gang of wicked designing nations, headed by Belgium and Serbia, and would have defended herself successfully if only she had not been stabbed in the back by the Jews. Against such opinions it is vain to argue. It is a case of 'believe it or not'. But when H.H. complains of the reparations exacted from Germany, we are surely entitled to point out that far more than was ever extracted in reparations, was lent to Germany, partly by Britain, but mostly by the United States of America, the bulk of which is not likely to be repaid. The reparation clauses of the Treaty of Versailles were never enforced, and so far from bleeding Germany white, the victorious Allies and associated powers poured enormous wealth into Germany after the war, and thus enabled her to modernise her industries and revive her economic wellbeing. Unhappily Germany has sought to use these benefits to forge a hideous apparatus of slaughter to hold the world to ransom or subject it to servitude.

The system of compulsory service now introduced into Britain in peace time, or what is called peace time, implies the sacrifice of the most deeply-rooted habits of an island people. It is an act of faith and a symbol of Britain's resolve not to fail in her part of the conflict for individual liberty and public law which is now open. The great causes which are afoot must march forward until they are vindicated and securely enthroned. But all the more is it necessary to proclaim that we in Britain or in France—and I am sure, in the United States—ask no security for ourselves that we are not willing to share with a free, peaceful and happy Germany.

If there be encirclement of Germany, it is not military or economic encirclement. It is an psychological encirclement. The masses of the peoples in all the countries around Germany, are forcing their governments to be on their guard against tyranny and invasion, and to join for that purpose with other like-minded states. Nothing can now stop this process except a change of heart in the German leaders, or a change of those leaders. But there is no country in the Grand Alliance that is being formed in Europe with the full sympathy and approval of the United States, that would tolerate for one moment the idea of attacking Germany, or of trying to impede her peaceful development and legitimate growth. On the contrary the return of Germany to the circle and family of Europe, and to the wide, lofty uplands of a progressive, tolerant, prosperous civilisation, remains the sovereign hope of the British, French and American democracies. And this is what is going to happen in the end.

[1] Herr Hitler.

Lord Melchett to Winston S. Churchill

(*Churchill papers: 2/358*)

29 April 1939   Imperial Chemical House,
                                                             London

My dear Winston,

I have just read the report of your speech today, on the 'tape'.[1] It was truly splendid and gave one such inspiration and real joy, after all the 'mud' that has been fed to us.

It was splendid and vigorous, breathing the old glory of England and based on a real sense of the higher moral values.

From a colleague who returned today I hear that your name is on every tongue in America and Canada.

God bless you and prosper your efforts.

Yours,
Henry

Winston S. Churchill to Lieutenant-Colonel A. J. Muirhead[2]

(*Churchill papers: 2/358*)

29 April 1939

My dear Muirhead,

Enclosed is a record of F. W. Deakin who would like to join the Oxfordshire Hussars in their present artillery form. I can say from my own intimate knowledge of him for several years that he is in every way fitted to make an excellent officer.[3]

---

[1] Churchill's broadcast to the United States, quoted above.

[2] Anthony John Muirhead, 1890–1939. Educated at Eton and Magdalen College, Oxford. On active service in France and Italy with the Oxfordshire Yeomanry, and on the Staff, 1914–19 (MC and bar; despatches three times). Served in the Lithuanian Army, 1919–20. A member of the Oxfordshire County Council, 1925–37. Conservative MP for Wells, 1929–39. Parliamentary Secretary to the Minister of Agriculture (Sir John Gilmour), 1931–2 and to Walter Elliot, 1932–5. Parliamentary Secretary, Minister of Labour, 1935–7. Under-Secretary of State, Air Ministry, 1937–8. Parliamentary Under-Secretary of State for India and Burma, 1938–9. Commanded the 63rd (Oxfordshire Yeomanry) Anti-Tank Regiment, Royal Artillery, Territorial Army, 1939. He lived at Haseley Court, Oxford, and died on 20 October 1939.

[3] Bill Deakin's principal service in the Second World War was with Special Operations Executive (SOE), first in London and then in Cairo. In May 1943 he was parachuted into Yugoslavia at the head of a small British mission (2 officers and 4 other ranks) to make contact with Tito and his partisans, who were at that very moment engaged in a decisive battle with vastly superior German forces. The other officer who was parachuted with him was killed in an air attack in June 1943. Deakin remained with the Partisans until September 1943, when he

I understand that both my nephews, my brother's sons, John and Peregrine [1] Spencer Churchill, have been for some time applying to join the regiment, in which so many of their family have served, but that nothing seems to move, and they do not know what to do. The younger of them is now in touch with the Engineers—being a fully-qualified civil engineer [2]—but why does everything take such an enormous time? There seems a sort of catalepsy of action which communicates itself even to the smallest branches of the Administration. I should have thought that you, in your ministerial position, could easily clear minor obstructions out of the way. If, on the other hand, you do not need to recruit officers please do not hesitate to say so because other arrangements can no doubt be made. [3]

---

returned to Cairo to become Head of the SOE Yugoslav Section. In 1944 he was seconded to the staff of Harold Macmillan, Cabinet representative for the Mediterranean theatre, and was attached as adviser to the Balkan Air Force Command, which was responsible for all operations by land, sea and air into Central and South-Eastern Europe. In 1971 he published an account of his Yugoslav experiences, *The Embattled Mountain*.

[1] Henry Winston Spencer Churchill, 1913–   . Known as 'Peregrine'. Jack Churchill's younger son. Educated at Harrow and Cambridge. Inventor and Company Director.

[2] Peregrine Churchill had trained as a dock engineer, and was working with Guest, Keen and Baldwins, the steel manufacturers, on military hutting. He had joined the Oxfordshire Yeomanry in 1938 ('we had one gun and the wheel fell off. We were given pitchforks and sent to Belfast'). Returned to engineering, designing bomb shelters, including one for King George VI at Windsor. Commissioned in the Royal Navy, 1939. Returned almost immediately to Guest, Keen and Baldwins, to work on the setting out of coastal radar stations. While in a night Club in London (the Florida, in Berkeley Square) during the Blitz, he was buried in rubble during an air-raid, and unable to work for more than four months. Subsequently he worked for the Ministry of Aircraft Production, on bomb storage, and for Combined Operations, on invasion camouflage for the Dieppe and St Nazaire raids, and building the camouflage span across Newhaven harbour for D-Day, 'the largest camouflage span of the war'. (*Conversation with the author, 25 January 1982*).

[3] John Spencer Churchill ('Johnny') had joined the Queen's Own Oxfordshire Yeomanry Anti-Tank Gun Regiment in 1938. He received no military employment between April 1939 and the outbreak of war. In October 1939 he joined the Royal Engineers and Signals Board as a Civil Servant, and in November 1939 was posted to the Royal Engineers as a 2nd Lieutenant. Captain, 1st Corps, British Expeditionary Force, January 1940. Officer Commanding 102 Provost Company, advance to Brussels and retreat to Dunkirk, May 1940. Major, Anti-Aircraft Command (Concealment of Guns and Fortifications), June 1940. Army Photographic Interpretation Unit (with responsibility of reporting German Flak positions for Bomber and Fighter Command, and American Bomber Command), 1943–4. Inter-Service Liaison Officer, 21 Army Group Headquarters (Intelligence), 1944–5. Demobilized, 1945.

Sir Henry Strakosch to Winston S. Churchill

(*Churchill papers: 2/358*)

30 April 1939

My dear Winston,

The fish duly arrived last Thursday in excellent condition and are now—apparently—quite happy in my pond. Also, they seem to get on quite well with my gold fish.

It was awfully good of you to have thought of me & to have enriched my pond with such fine specimens. Ever so many thanks.

I am looking forward to seeing you on Thursday at the Other Club & to have your opinion on the situation in the light of Hitler's speech.[1] Though one ought to beware of attaching any real importance to anything he says one rather gets the impression that he is really afraid of war.

Ever yours,
H. Strakosch

---

[1] Following a 'peace appeal' to Hitler and Mussolini from President Roosevelt, Hitler told the Reichstag at a special session on 28 April 1939: 'During the whole of my political activity I have always expounded the idea of a close friendship and collaboration between Germany and England. In my Movement I found innumerable others of like mind. Perhaps they joined me because of my attitude in this matter. This desire for Anglo-German friendship and co-operation conforms not merely with sentiments which result from the racial origins of our two peoples, but also to my realization of the importance for the whole mankind of the existence of the British Empire. I have never left room for any doubt of my belief that the existence of this Empire is an inestimable factor of value for the whole of human cultural and economic life. By whatever means Great Britain has acquired her colonial territories—and I know that they were those of force and often brutality—nevertheless I know full well that no other Empire has ever come into being in any other way, and that in the final resort it is not so much the methods that are taken into account in history as success, and not the success of the methods as such, but rather the general good which the methods yield. Now there is no doubt that the Anglo-Saxon people have accomplished immeasurable colonizing work in the world. For this work I have a sincere admiration. The thought of destroying this labour appeared and still appears to me, seen from a higher human point of view, as nothing but the effluence of human wanton destructiveness. However, this sincere respect of mine for this achievement does not mean foregoing the securing of the life of my own people. I regard it as impossible to achieve a lasting friendship between the German and Anglo-Saxon peoples if the other side does not recognize that there are German as well as British interests, that not only is the preservation of the British Empire the meaning and purpose of the lives of Britishers but also that for Germans the freedom and preservation of the German Reich is their life purpose. A genuine, lasting friendship between these two nations is only conceivable on the basis of mutual regard.' Hitler added: '. . . the only claim I have ever made, and shall continue to make, on England is that for a return of our colonies. But I always made it very clear that this would never become the cause of a military conflict.'

Chartwell Literary Account Items: notes

(*Churchill papers: 8/639*)

30 April 1939

APRIL.
1. Professor Lindemann for week-end.
8.   ”   ”   ”
   and also luncheon party for 3 guests (literary).
9. Mr Mann ('Yorkshire Post') to lunch.
13. Dictation in car to London.
15. Mr Deakin for week-end.
19. Dictation in car to flat.
22. Mr Young and Mr Deakin for week-end.
    (History of E-SP)
24. Car journey to London.
28. Prof Lindemann for week-end. (History.)

May 1939

J. W. Farrell[1] to Winston S. Churchill

(*Churchill papers: 2/374*)

1 May 1939   Admiralty
Secret and Personal

Dear Sir,

With reference to the request you made to me this morning on the telephone I have ascertained that according to the Admiralty calculations the first of the German 35,000 ton battleships should be ready about the Autumn of 1940, and the second in the very early part of 1941. These dates of course would be liable to be changed should the German Government decide to hasten completion at all costs.

We do not, of course, make such information as this public, and I have, therefore, marked the letter Secret and Personal.

Yours faithfully,
J. W. Farrell

Lord Rothermere to Winston S. Churchill

(*Churchill papers: 2/359*)

1 May 1939   Portugal

My dear Winston,

Germany's denunciation of the Anglo-German Naval Pact is, I am sure, simply to free her hands so that she can build very great numbers of submarines.

---

[1] James William Farrell, 1913–   . Entered the Admiralty as an Assistant Principal, 1935; served in the Civil Establishments Branch, 1935–6; in Naval Law Division, 1936–8; the Military Branch, 1938. Private Secretary to the Civil Lord of Admiralty, 1938–9; to the Parliamentary and Financial Secretary, Admiralty, 1939–40. An Acting Principal, Military Branch, 1940–1; Commission and Warrant Branch, 1941–6. Transferred to the Ministry of Fuel and Power, 1946.

I am told she has all the parts of submarines in great quantities and that these can be assembled in a few weeks. I foresee it is possible Germany may have 200 submarines at the end of the next six months.

The only reply to submarines is apparently TBDs.[1] I wish you would press in the Commons for an addition of at least 100 TBDs to our present strength. The number may have to be 200 TBDs but now we are in this struggle what does the cost matter.

I was very gratified that you remembered my birthday. I owe you—and so do your fellow-countrymen—many many thanks. There may be an opportunity soon for all of us to show in what gratitude and esteem you are held by true blue Britishers.

I came here with a view of travelling through Spain but from what I hear Franco is not at all too friendly towards England so I am not going to risk a possible chance of being marooned in an enemy country should war break out.

Yours,
Harold R

Sir Edward Marsh to Winston S. Churchill
(*Churchill papers: 8/628*)

1 May 1939

My dear Winston,

The weather hasn't been such as to tempt me out of doors, & I was chucked for dinner, so I've done practically nothing all day except read these proofs—& I've just finished them at 1.15 am. They are the most splendid stuff—absorbing reading, & they preserve in an astonishing manner & with most salutary effect the balance between hope & fear, and they are all prodigious vindication of your foresight.[2]

I think there are surprisingly few repetitions—I've marked such as I've noticed, but most of them seem inevitable.

I observe that the first article mentioned in the index, *How we can restore the lost Glory* . . . , is not here.

I hope you will find any small comments of use.

Looking forward to the rest,

Yours ever,
Eddie

---

[1] Torpedo boat destroyers.

[2] Marsh was reading the proofs of Churchill's new book, *Step By Step* (see pages 1420 note 1, 1504–5, and 1542–4).

I suppose you deliberately adapted your style to the newspaper trick of printing almost every sentence on a separate paragraph—It has rather an odd effect in a book, but obviously it can't be helped.

PS. Tues morning—the second batch has just arrived, & I'm getting down to it.

Winston S. Churchill to G. M. Young
(*Churchill papers: 8/626*)

2 May 1939

I send you herewith a cheque for £50.0.0. covering the month of May, and I have given instructions to the Bank to make a similar payment on the first of each month for the five following months.

In spite of public distractions, I have made a deep dent on the reign of Anne this week.

It was very pleasant talking with you, and I greatly look forward to your aid.

T. L. Horabin to Winston S. Churchill
(*Churchill papers: 2/359*)

2 May 1939

Dear Mr Churchill,

Last week in North Cornwall I came out for full blooded compulsory National Service for finance, industry, man and woman power, before conscription was announced.

When the Conscription Bill was announced I went bald-headed for Mr Chamberlain for 'playing at shops'.[1]

---

[1] The Conscription Bill did not bring in conscription as such, but set up a 'register' to which all those of conscription age were to put their names, so that when needed, they could at once be located, and called up. But speaking at Cambridge on 19 May 1939, Churchill said of the new legislation: 'This Bill and its general acceptance is a great act of faith on the part of British democracy. At the beginning of the war of 1914 we soon had a million volunteers on our hands, for the bulk of whom no weapons were available. Ultimately over two million men demanded to be led to the Front. But after that the limits of voluntary recruitment were exhausted. The war continued and the armies could not be maintained. Then we had the hateful spectacle of volunteers who had been wounded twice or even thrice, being sent back to the trenches, and of regular soldiers who had served two whole years in the Front Line being deprived of the right to claim expiry of their contract. This proved intolerable to the national sense of justice. Moreover the two million households and families whose menfolk had borne the whole burden, were infuriated by the fact that there were very large

Feeling is very strong that the present conscription proposals are unfair and ineffective, and most people, liberal, labour and conservative alike, would prefer full blooded National Service. In fact they feel that if the situation is serious enough to introduce conscription at all, a thorough job should be made of it.

Feeling is the same amongst the people in London.

At the Cornwall meetings your name met with substantial applause the moment it was mentioned. Tories came up to me after some of the meetings and said they could only agree that you should be PM—in fact their expressions about their leader, Mr Chamberlain, are becoming lurid.

Amongst ordinary people of all parties the feeling that compulsion of wealth must be linked with compulsion of man power is strong, and unless proposals for this purpose are quickly published there will be a much deeper split in the country than appears at first sight.

On last week's showing I believe I could fight a bye-election successfully on compulsory National Service for everyone, but this would not, I imagine, help things forward now.

Yours very truly,
T. L. Horabin

Winston S. Churchill to Lord Beaverbrook

(*Beaverbrook papers*)

2 May 1939   Chartwell
Private

My dear Max,

Thank you for sending me the cuttings about Mr Baruch, which I am keeping a little longer, as I am going to ask him about the subject.

---

numbers of perfectly fit men remaining at home, filling at higher wages the jobs of those who had volunteered. It was this sense of wrong and injustice, which spread through the country in the Spring and Summer of 1916, that alone carried the Conscription Bill. How different now! Now to-day, before a shot has been fired, in cool blood we are taking this momentous step, and taking it with a very large measure of national acceptance. Nothing could more vividly mark the manner in which the wage-earning classes—without whom no armies can be formed—have realised the deadly nature of the assault which is being directed at their fundamental rights and liberties. What nearly two years of bloody war only attained with difficulty in 1916, is now practically conceded by the will of the Nation in a time of nominal peace. This is the point which should impress foreign countries, because it is the most explicit guarantee of the resolve of the British people to bear its part in what is now plainly a world cause' (*Churchill papers: 9/137*).

He is the author of the 'cash and carry' idea. This amendment of the
Neutrality Act would certainly be highly beneficial to us. I have very little
doubt in my mind that Baruch is taking this line in order to facilitate the
passing of the legislation, and I cannot conceive that his attitude is other than
intensely hostile to Hitlerism. However, of course I may be wrong.

Yours ever,
W

PS. Cutting returned, as I have now read it.

Wing-Commander Anderson to Winston S. Churchill: telephone message

(Churchill papers: 2/372)

2 May 1939

No 215 Bomber Squadron at the end of April dropped 28 (250 lb) General
Purpose High Explosive bombs, new issue. Eleven out of these 28 bombs
failed to explode. The bombs were dropped at Catfoss sea ranges.

Wing-Commander Anderson to Winston S. Churchill: telephone message

(Churchill papers: 2/373)

2 May 1939

No 49 Bomber Squadron, peace location Scampton, equipped with
Hampden bombers, establishment of aircraft 21, strength 16, average
serviceability eight aircraft.

Delays are experienced in obtaining spare parts, and are also caused by
the length of time required for carrying out inspections. For example, when
the aircraft has flown 120 hours, a 120-hour inspection is carried out, and
the aircraft is unserviceable for one month. The time taken to complete 120
hours flying is approximately eight weeks.

Wing-Commander Anderson to Winston S. Churchill: telephone message

(*Churchill papers: 2/372*)

2 May 1939

No 29 Fighter Squadron, Debden, is equipped with Blenheim fighters, ie an adaptation of the Blenheim bomber with extra turrets. Its role is that of a long-distance fighter, to operate from France. The establishment is 21 aircraft, strength is 16, and the number serviceable is 3.

This squadron has not a single Browning gun, although it is a fighter Squadron. Mountings and parts are being made by the Southern Railway but the plans and drawings have only just been issued. After completing 120 hours flying, the Blenheim aircraft are unserviceable for six weeks to carry out the inspection, the average time taken to complete 120 hours flying is eight weeks.

Lord Rothermere to Winston S. Churchill

(*Churchill papers: 2/359*)

4 May 1939   Portugal

My dear Winston,

I wrote to you a few days ago suggesting you might press the Government for more TBDs and auxiliary vessels to deal with the increasing menace from German submarines.

Garvin, in his article last Sunday, says definitely Germany is building submarines in sections so as to have them ready for assemblage at any moment. There is the wife of an oil man here who travels much in Germany. She says exactly the same view is held in Germany.

I had some confirmatory evidence nearly eighteen months ago on this point.

Germany was defeated in the Great War only because she had an insufficiency of submarines. If she had had 300 or 400 instead of the 40 which she kept at sea Britain would have been a German vassal state by 1918.

Yours always,

Harold R

Winston S. Churchill to Lord Camrose
(*Churchill papers: 8/630*)

6 May 1939   Chartwell

The three months for which you kindly renewed our arrangement finishes at the end of May, and therefore the last article I shall be writing for you will be the one to be published on May 18. I shall begin with The Daily Mirror on June 1. I hope this will be convenient to you.

Let me say I have much enjoyed working for The Daily Telegraph during these fourteen months, and I hope you have been satisfied with the character of the articles. Alas, they have mostly only proved too true.

Imre Revesz to Winston S. Churchill
(*Churchill papers: 8/638*)

6 May 1939   Paris

Dear Mr Churchill,

Last week I have received the visit of an English gentleman who came to see me on behalf of the Foreign Office. He wanted some information regarding the matter about which I have written to you already and which you have communicated with the Foreign Office.

During the past weeks the situation became worse in many countries and I should like to give you some new information regarding Poland, Rumania and Greece, our new allies:

1°) Poland. Your last article 'Poland's Peril' was not published in Warsaw and in spite of the change in policy no British article was published in the Polish press during the past weeks.

2°) Rumania. The German control over the press has become complete during the past weeks. Even the most francophile newspaper UNIVERSUL is now pro-nazi. The method of pressure is the following: there is an Under-secretary for Press and Propaganda, the Head of which is Mr Titeanu. Mr Titeanu is a great friend of a German lady, Frau Erika von Kohler, who is in Bukarest since several months and who happens to be the sister of Himmler, the Head of the Gestapo. This governmental organisation has monopolized the publicity in Rumania and newspapers can only get publicity through this department. The consequence is that the publicity revenue of a francophile paper has sunk from 400,000 Lei per month to practically zero. On the other side, the publicity revenue of the newspaper CURENTUL, controlled entirely by the Germans, has risen from 100,000 Lei to over 300,000 Lei per month. I think it is not necessary to comment this situation. I only should like to add that there are 22 German language newspapers in Rumania controlled directly by the Propaganda Ministry in Berlin.

3°) Greece. During the past months I have made very interesting arrangement with leading Greek newspapers ELEFTHERON VIMA, PROIA and ETHNOS, and though half of our articles have been censored by the Government I was always able to publish 6–8 articles in a month which was something. I have now received the April-report from my agent in Athens which is disastrous. Since Italy occupied Albania and Great Britain guaranteed the independence of Greece, no article criticizing fascism or nazism has been allowed to be published by the Greek press. The only three articles the publication of which the Government permitted were the following: an article by Virginio Gayda, an article by Senor de Madariaga[1] (rather favourable to Franco) and an English article which has shown some understanding of Germany. Since the 1st of April all the articles written by Winston Churchill, Anthony Eden, Duff Cooper, Wickham Steed, Major Attlee, Admiral Usborne[2] and all the French statesmen have been prohibited by the Greek censorship.

I have definite proofs that all these articles have been accepted by the newspapers for publication and that their publication has been prohibited afterwards by the Greek Government.

I am giving you this information because I feel sure you will agree with me that this situation is intolerable. I have also given some of this information to M Daladier. I hope to see him next week.

Something from Scandinavia: last week I have received in Paris the visit of Mr Trygger,[3] the Editor of the great conservative newspaper SVENSKA

[1] Don Salvador de Madariaga, 1886–1978. Born in Spain. Technical adviser, Spanish Northern Railway, 1911–16. Journalist, publicist and literary critic, London, 1916–21. Member of the Press Section, League of Nations Secretariat, Geneva, 1921–2; Director of the Disarmament Section, 1922–7. Professor of Spanish Studies at Oxford, 1928–31. Spanish Ambassador in Washington, 1931; in Paris, 1932–4. Spanish Permanent Delegate to the League of Nations, 1931–6. Author of more than thirty books on Spanish and international themes, including *Anarchy or Hierarchy* (1937) and *Theory and Practice in International Relations* (1938). Founder-President of the College of Europe (at Bruges). Resident in Oxford, 1939–76. In 1976 he returned to Spain, to take his place in the Spanish Royal Academy.

[2] Cecil Vivian Usborne, 1880–1951. Gunnery-Lieutenant, 1903. Commanded the mine-layer *Latona* off the Dardanelles, 1916. Captain, 1917. Senior Naval Officer, Salonica, 1917; Corfu, 1918. Commanded the Naval Brigade on the Danube, 1918–19. Deputy Director of Naval Ordnance, 1919. Deputy Director of the Gunnery Division, Naval Staff, 1922. Vice-President of the Chemical Warfare Committee, 1923. Director of the Tactical School, 1925. Captain, HMS *Malaya*, 1927; HMS *Resolution*, 1928. Rear-Admiral, 1928. Director of Naval Intelligence, 1930–2. Retired, 1933. Director of the Censorship Division, Press and Censorship Bureau, 1939–40. Special Service, Admiralty, 1941–5.

[3] Carl Trygger, 1894–   . Born in Uppsala, the son of Swedish Foreign Minister Ernst Trygger. Began work in a banking office in Stockholm, 1923; Assistant Director of the office 1929. Chief Editor of the *Svenska Dagbladet* (in which his father had a financial interest), 1934–40. Returned to banking, as a bank Director, 1940. Noted for his skill as a pilot.

DAGBLADET in Stockholm. You certainly remember him, we have lunched together in Chartwell last year. He was tremendously anxious to get your articles. Now he says that he cannot publish them anymore unless on non-political subjects. He also denounced my contract for Mr Eden's articles which he was anxious to sign last summer. He says that he cannot ruin his newspaper and if he would go on to publish articles by statesmen who 'do not understand Germany', he would get no more publicity at all and would be unable to pay any dividend to his stockholders. This is the situation.

Yours very sincerely,
I. Revesz

PS. I have read that you have delivered a broadcast to America last week. May I ask you for which network and whether you have received a fee for this broadcast or not? I want to take up my negotiations for the regular broadcasting service for America and it would be helpful for me if I would know under what conditions you have delivered that speech. I am sending you enclosed two letters which have been addressed to you by readers of PARIS-SOIR.

Winston S. Churchill to Imre Revesz
(Churchill papers: 8/638)

8 May 1939

Dear Doctor Revesz,

I am indeed sorry to hear that the net is closing round our activities, through fear of Germany. Luckily, you have already called in the New World to redress the balance of the Old.

I gave a broadcast to the United States, gratis and on public grounds, and it was a condition that the two great Agencies linked up together, which they did.

I have not yet received the accounts of the last four articles, and if their circulation has prospered. Will you please let me have them at your convenience.

When answering my previous letter about the Preface to the new book, perhaps you will give me a list of all the papers in all the countries which have at any time taken the articles in the series.

Winston S. Churchill to Sir Edward Marsh

(*Churchill papers: 8/628*)

8 May 1939

I send you an additional article which is new-laid,[1] and you will also have one more for the finale.[2]

I have incorporated practically all your corrections, and I think they are admirable. I had missed nearly all of them when I read them over. I hope to get the book out in June.

I enclose you a cheque with my very best thanks,

---

[1] Churchill's article 'The Russian Counterpoise', published in the *Daily Telegraph* on 4 May 1939, in the course of which he wrote that 'it must be vividly impressed upon the Government of Poland that the accession of Soviet Russia in good earnest to the peace bloc of nations may be decisive in preventing war, and will in any case be necessary for ultimate success. One understands readily the Polish policy of balancing between the German and the Russian neighbour, but from the moment when the Nazi malignity is plain, a definite association between Poland and Russia becomes indispensable. These are days when acts of faith must be performed by Governments and peoples who are striving to resist the spread of Nazidom.'

[2] 'The Anglo-Turkish Alliance', published in the *Daily Telegraph* on 18 May 1939, and praising the Anglo-Turkish alliance. 'The fact,' Churchill wrote, 'that Mr Chamberlain should have made this Alliance with Turkey shows how unfavourably the British Cabinet have been impressed by the conduct of the Italian Dictator during the later years of his memorable career. With a foresight which deserved commendation, Mr Chamberlain last year prepared the way by the grant of a ten million pounds loan to Turkey. This was warmly welcomed by the Turkish nation. The Alliance now contracted grew naturally out of mutual assistance and goodwill, and is a practical expression of the common interest of Great Britain and Turkey in the peace and freedom of the Eastern Mediterranean'. Churchill went on to praise the new Alliance and urged that it should be used to encourage the drawing in of Russia to the growing circle of allies. 'Both Turkey and Russia,' he wrote, 'have a common interest in the independence and integrity of Rumania. A Nazi advance down the Danube valley through conquered Austria and intimidated Hungary would carry with it mortal danger to Turkey and Russia. Already the Nazis have a powerful growing flotilla on the Danube. A Nazi capture of the mouths of the Danube would be speedily followed in the incursion into the Black Sea of numerous U-boats, transported in sections. If Russia and Turkey lost control of the Black Sea, any port on its shores might become the landing base for the long-talked of German "Drive to the East". In fact there never was a more obvious unity of interests than that prevailing among the Black Sea Powers. Unless they stand together, measureless miseries must be again their lot.'

Winston S. Churchill to T. L. Horabin

(*Churchill papers: 2/359*)

8 May 1939
Private

Dear Mr Horabin,

Many thanks for your letter.

I am puzzled to know what you mean by the phrase 'compulsion of wealth'. At the present time more than three-quarters of large incomes is taken, and more than a half of large estates at death.

Power will be taken, I presume, in the New Ministry of Supplies Bill to compel employers and firms to turn over to the necessary forms of war production irrespective of the prospects of their present trades.

I strongly favour the principle: 'Take the profits out of war,' which I take it means no-one must come out of a war richer than he went into it. I suggested this in Parliament a year ago, and the Government have now adopted it.

Finally, we are assured that the most stringent measures are to be taken against what is called 'profiteering'. Perhaps you will let me know whether you have in mind any additional measures. Do you mean a capital levy, or a forced loan at a low rate of interest? If so, I think it would be arguable that more damage would be done to our credit and to the general level of values in this country by such a step, than the results would justify. We cannot possibly fight a war except by the fullest use of our credit. If this is violently deranged, we should be crippled.

The Socialists of course would like to take over all the means of production, distribution and Exchange. The result would be chaos, a vast impoverishment, and an internal struggle of the most serious kind. I am sure you could not be in favour of this merely because 200,000 young men are called up for six months' military training.

Harold Nicolson: diary

(*Nicolson papers*)

9 May 1939

It is almost heartbreaking that at such a time we should not have Churchill in the Government.

Paul Maze: diary
(*Maze papers*)

10 May 1939

Met Blum at Margot Asquith's. Randolph joined us & he drove us to Chartwell. Winston welcomed us at the front door. Lunched in that charming dining room. Bonar Law's son [1] was there with his very dull wife. Conversation rendered difficult by Clemmie's constant interference in the conversation & her desire to translate to show up her French (which is very good). Very excellent lunch, then a walk about the garden when a group of photographers took snapshots. We had to leave early as Blum was expected at 3.45 by Halifax.

Henry Channon: [2] *diary*
(*Robert Rhodes James, 'Chips'*)

11 May 1939

Blum is in London. He is the real architect of many of our woes and it is revolting to see the Churchill gang kowtowing to this Jewish agitator who has done such infinite harm.

Winston S. Churchill to W. S. Morrison
(*Churchill papers: 2/371*)

11 May 1939

Thank you very much for your letter of May 9 returning the letter from the Clyde Cold Storage Company.

I think it is alarming that you 'have no power to interfere with the normal course of trade in time of peace'. Certainly this would be a very poor consolation should war come, and many deficiencies appear. Is it not possible for you to obtain the necessary powers to achieve the end which you recognise as desirable? Please excuse my pressing this point upon you.

[1] Richard Law (see page 1181, note 1). In 1929 he married Mary Virginia Nellis, of Rochester, New York.

[2] Henry Channon, 1897–1958. An American by birth. Educated privately, and at Christ Church, Oxford. In 1933 he married Lady Honor Guinness, elder daughter of the 2nd Earl of Iveagh. Conservative MP for Southend on Sea, 1935–50; for Southend on Sea (West), 1950–8. Parliamentary Private Secretary to the Under Secretary of State for Foreign Affairs (R. A. Butler), 1938–41. Knighted, 1957.

Air Chief Marshal Sir Hugh Dowding to Winston S. Churchill
(*Churchill papers: 1/343*)

12 May 1939

Dear Mr Churchill,

I am writing to ask if you would care to come out & see the Fighter Command Operations Room some morning soon, and if you and Mrs Churchill would lunch afterwards with my sister & myself. I know how busy you must be, & I shall not be surprised if you can't fit it in: but you will be very welcome if you can manage it. If it is a convenience I could send a car for you to London, & Mrs Churchill could spend an hour before lunch with my sister in the garden while we are busy. If the idea appeals to you, would you give me one or two alternative dates, or I could fix a date with your Secretary.

Yours sincerely,
H. C. J. Dowding

L. S. Amery to Winston S. Churchill
(*Churchill papers: 2/379*)

12 May 1939

My dear Winston,

I enclose a letter from Weizmann which he wished me to show you. I had meant to have given it to you in the House but you have not been there these last two days.

There is no doubt that the Government, through sheer drift and cowardice, have landed themselves in an impossible position over Palestine. Even if the Mandates Commission does not turn them down for direct breach of faith, they will now be faced with a situation in which neither Jews nor Arabs will cooperate in carrying out their so-called solution. The Arabs obviously will wish to exploit their victory by further violence and steadily increased demands, while the Jews will continue asserting their claim and will find their own way of making things difficult for the Government. Partition, if it would not have satisfied either side, had at any rate in it a certain element of finality. The Government proposals are likely to satisfy no one and to settle nothing.[1]

---

[1] On 17 May 1939 the Cabinet approved, and the Government published, a Palestine White Paper, restricting Jewish immigration to Palestine to 75,000 over the following five years (25,000 of whom were to be emergency or special cases). After five years, with the numerical balance thus still in favour of the Arabs, a constitution was to be devised giving a virtual veto on all future Jewish immigration to the Arab majority. The Jews were upset by the restrictions, and by their long term implications. Many Arabs, however, rejected the limitations as insufficient. For Churchill's comments, see page 1505, note 1.

The best hope will be to get a really strong body of Government supporters to vote against the Government, possibly on some motion refusing to accept the Government's view unless and until it has been approved by Geneva as a fulfilment of the pledges under the Mandate.

Yours ever,
Leo Amery

Sir Robert Vansittart to Winston S. Churchill
(Churchill papers: 2/359)

12 May 1939   Foreign Office

My dear Winston,

M Elie Bois[1] the Director of the 'Petit Parisien' is coming to London on May 18th for a few days and would much like to have an opportunity of a talk with you during his stay.

M Bois is a great friend of mine, and I very much hope that you will be able to give him an interview. He is a great deal more than the director of a powerful newspaper; he has very great personal influence in the French political world, and he is a friend of this country.

Yours ever,
Van

Winston S. Churchill to Lord Cecil of Chelwood
(Cecil of Chelwood papers)

13 May 1939   Chartwell

My dear Bob,

Thank you very much for sending me your correspondence with Anthony, but I do not see what I can do at the present time.

I suppose the Government will be very anxious not to provoke Japan unduly at a moment when everything hangs in the balance over here. It is astonishing how much they have adopted our policy.

Yours ever,
W

[1] Elie J. Bois. Born in Vichy in 1878. Entered journalism in Paris at the age of twenty, writing for the *Figaro*. Parliamentary Correspondent of the *Salut Public* (Lyon). Worked for the *Matin*, 1906–8; the *Temps*, 1908–14. Director of the *Petit Parisien*, 1914–40. Following the formation of Marshal Pétain's Government in June 1940, he came to Britain, where he published a book, *Truth on the Tragedy of France* (Hodder and Stoughton, 1941). Died, 1941.

John Hodsoll[1] *to Winston S. Churchill*

(*Churchill papers: 8/629*)

15 May 1939   Home Office, ARP Dept

Dear Mr Churchill,

Thank you for your letter of the 11th May.

I have read carefully through your article and as far as I can see there is nothing in it which is likely to require alteration in public interest.[2] There are just two points, however, which I would like to mention; on page 3 where I have put a pencil line, you speak of 50,000 gas masks being distributed in the last crisis, actually the figure was 38,000. Also, a little further down on that page you talk about the steel shelter being covered with sandbags. I expect you appreciate that if all the steel shelters are to be covered with sandbags we shall have an appalling job to get adequate supplies and there is always the trouble of filling them. Do you think you could possibly say 'covered with earth or sandbags or concrete'. If you could do this I think it would be a help because an article coming from yourself will, naturally, be widely read and we don't want to get into people's heads that they can only use sandbags to cover up the shelters. Earth or concrete is, of course, equally good and generally easier to do.

Yours sincerely,
E. J. Hodsoll

[1] John Hodsoll, 1894–1971. An engineer; worked in the Great Western Railway Works, Swindon, 1911–14. Joined the Royal Naval Air Service, 1914. Commanded the sea-plane base at Alexandria, 1918 (despatches twice). Air Ministry, 1919–22. HQ, RAF India, 1925–9. Assistant Secretary, Committee of Imperial Defence, 1929–35. Retired from the RAF, 1935. Assistant Under-Secretary of State, Home Office, in charge of the Air Raid Precautions (ARP) Department, 1935–7; Inspector-General, 1938–48. Knighted, 1944. Director-General, Civil Defence Training, 1948–54. Chief Civil Defence Adviser, in charge of the Civil Emergency Planning Section, North Atlantic Treaty Organization (NATO), 1954–61.

[2] Churchill's confidence in the effectiveness of Air Raid Precautions was evident in the article which he wrote in 1939: 'Bombs Don't Scare Us Now', for *Collier's*; as 'Air Bombing is no Road to World Domination', published in the *News of the World* on 18 June 1939, in the course of which he wrote, of possible German air 'terror tactics': 'The killing of noncombatants including women and children, on a large scale would infuriate the nation and the war would become what is called an inexpiable war. The attitude of the United States is also a tremendous factor for Nazidom to consider. Obviously, such an atrocity, unworthy even of the Dark Ages, would make every nation feel that mankind had reached a point beyond all ordinary questions of politics and war.' Churchill's article continued: 'There is nothing in this problem of air attack which the British nation cannot confront with its long proved doggedness and hardihood,' and he went on to recommand one of the existing 'small blast-proof shelters', or the basements of high buildings, adding: 'It is discreditable that these basements were not prepared after the rape of Austria or especially after Munich.'

Sir Henry Strakosch to Winston S. Churchill

(*Churchill papers: 2/371*)

15 May 1939

My dear Winston,

I enclose a note of an investigation which I had made regarding the possible use of liquid hydrogen in aviation. There is not a great deal of definite information available, and the calculations and conclusions of the note have therefore to be considered with a good deal of caution. I am sending a copy of the note to Professor Lindemann, who probably knows a good deal more about the subject than we have been able to ascertain in the course of our investigation.

Ever yours,
H. Strakosch

L. S. Amery to Winston S. Churchill

(*Churchill papers: 2/379*)

16 May 1939

My dear Winston,

I have just had the following cable from Smuts:[1]

'Please cooperate with other friends in last minute effort to prevent abandonment of Jews and Balfour policy. If real trouble comes Jews in Palestine and elsewhere will prove reliable friends. I favour temporising with Palestine settlement while European situation remains uncertain.'

It is of course too late now to prevent the Government making public their weakness and folly over the Palestine business. The fact is that they have had the 'jitters' about the whole Near Eastern situation, and have got it into their heads that Arab support against the Dictators depends entirely upon their giving way over Palestine. The real effect will be that the Arabs will be neither more nor less helpful than before, and that we shall alienate the Jews, who, not only outside but inside Palestine, are a far more effective

---

[1] Jan Christian Smuts, 1870–1950. Born in Cape Colony. General, commanding Boer Commando Forces, Cape Colony, 1901. Colonial Secretary, Transvaal, 1907. Minister of Defence, Union of South Africa, 1910–20. Second-in-Command of the South African forces that defeated the Germans in South-West Africa, July 1915. Honorary Lieutenant-General commanding the imperial forces in East Africa, 1916–17. South African Representative at the Imperial War Cabinet, 1917 and 1918. Prime Minister of South Africa, 1919–24. Minister of Justice, 1933–9. Prime Minister, 1939–48. Field-Marshal, 1941. OM, 1947. In 1917 he was made an honorary member of the Other Club.

force. I have no doubt if we laid ourselves out we could in three months raise a Jewish force in Palestine worth a great deal more from the fighting point of view than the whole Egyptian Army.

It is less than two years since the House refused to endorse the Government's partition policy because it was not convinced that this was an honest fulfilment of the Mandate. Now I suppose a docile and frightened majority will applaud what is, in effect, the complete abandonment of the Mandate. But there might be a revulsion of feeling, and I think those of us who can speak with effect ought to do so. I should like to get in on Monday if I can. I hope you will speak on one day or the other.[1]

Yours ever,
L. S. Amery

Winston S. Churchill to G. M. Young
(Churchill papers: 8/626)

17 May 1939

Dear Mr Young,

I send you herewith the revises of James I and Charles I and the Restoration, omitting the Cromwell period which I am going to reconsider later. These three reigns must now be regarded as in a very advanced state of completion. Would it not be well for you (if you can bear it) to read them through again while the text is fresh in your mind, and make sure we are not leaving anything behind us?

I send you also the copy from which these revises have been set up. You will see in red ink the corrections which you made, and which I have adopted. Will you kindly let me have this back, together with the revised proofs, at your convenience, with any suggestions you may care to make.

I think it is in fairly good order now.

W. S. Morrison to Winston S. Churchill
(Churchill papers: 2/371)

19 May 1939

My dear Winston,

I was not at all surprised to receive your letter of 11th May in which you urge the importance of the Government obtaining powers to interfere with the normal course of trade in foodstuffs. As you know, I have only been

---

[1] Churchill spoke on 22 May 1939, the second day of the Palestine White paper debate (see page 1505, note 1).

responsible for Food Defence arrangements since Easter but I am giving this particular problem urgent and serious consideration.

Yours sincerely,
W. S. Morrison

Cabinet Committee on Foreign Policy: minutes
(Cabinet papers: 27/624)

19 May 1939

SIR SAMUEL HOARE: . . . he had heard some gossip to the effect that at a dinner party at the Polish Embassy Mr Winston Churchill had said that he was in possession of an important letter from Poland, which he proposed to read in the course of the Parliamentary Debate. It was alleged that on the same occasion the Polish Ambassador had stated that so far from Poland being now opposed to a Triple Pact she was really in favour of it, but that it was necessary at the moment to maintain a façade of disapproval.

Jan Masaryk to Winston S. Churchill
(Churchill papers: 2/359)

20 May 1939

Dear Mr Churchill,

In answer to your telegram may I say:

My information was originally received from a high official in Prague who is minutely conversant with the relations between our former National Bank, the BIS[1] and the Bank of England. I naturally cannot quote him as it would mean a very quick removal to a concentration camp, but I can absolutely vouch for his authority and veracity.

The fact whether Mr Wohlthat[2] had negotiated with the Treasury in the last few days does not seem to me of primary importance. On the other hand, it was not denied that these conversations have taken place. I am told that a Director of the Bank of England knows well about the conversations. Perhaps

[1] The Bank of International Settlements.
[2] Helmuth Christian Heinrich Wohlthat, 1893– . Born in Wismar, Mecklenburg. Educated in Düsseldorf and Berlin. Entered the German Army (Field Artillery), 1912; Lieutenant, 1914. On active service, 1914–16. Studied commerce at Cologne University, 1919; at Columbia University, New York City, 1920–2. In commerce in the United States, 1922–32. Returned to Germany, 1932. Executive Director of the State Milk, Oil and Fat Production Directorate; 1933–5. Head of the Foreign Currency Directorate of the Ministry of Finance, 1935–7. Ministerial Director of the Four Year Plan, 1938–41. Conducted economic negotiations in Rumania, Spain and Britain, 1939. Ministerial Director of the German Delegation for German Japanese Trade, Moscow, 1941 and Tokyo, 1941–5. An adviser on foreign trade in Japan, 1945–8; in the United States since 1948, and in Germany (resident in Düsseldorf).

Bob Boothby could supply the details as I again do not want to mention any names.

According to information, which I took greatest possible care to get accurately, there are two salient facts:

1. Out of the Czecho-Slovak gold held by the Bank of International Settlement 23,087 kg gold has been assigned to the Reichsbank. This gold is also deposited in London and the transfer was made under strongest pressure by the German Government. This transaction has nothing to do with further negotiations to which I will refer in the following:

2. From the source which I mentioned at the beginning of this letter I have been notified and warned that negotiations between the Treasury and the representatives of Germany were to begin on the 15th of May and that no Czecho-Slovak representatives will take part, the object of these negotiations being the release of Czecho-Slovak balances blocked under the Banking Accounts Restriction Act.

That Germany's sole object is getting hold of gold and foreign assets belonging to the Czecho-Slovak National Bank and our nationals, there is no question of a doubt. This gold and these assets have been saved and earned by my unhappy people by 20 years of very hard work. Hence you will understand how I feel about it.

If, at this moment, nothing has been given to Germany I am very glad, but I will say that so far I have failed to see any authoritative denials of the two facts mentioned.

I confess that I was frightened by your telegram mentioning the PM as I would not be surprised if both your telegram and mine did constitute a rather interesting reading matter for some Munichites. I would be extremely obliged if you would quote me as little as possible. You know me well enough to realise that I am not saying this out of personal lack of courage, but a lot of innocent people could suffer if it were known that they were in touch with me.

With kindest greetings to you and yours

Sincerely,
Jan Masaryk

Winston S. Churchill to Brendan Bracken
(Churchill papers: 2/359)

21 May 1939

This is from Masaryk and may be of some help to you in clarifying the position. Please note his last paragraph. He is very shy.

Kindly let me have the letter back.

Winston S. Churchill to Jan Masaryk

(Churchill papers: 2/359)

21 May 1939

Many thanks for your letter. I think we shall stave it off all right.[1]

Have no fear about our telegrams being under surveillance by the Government. We have not got to that yet here. Anyhow you are entirely within your rights and duties.

Winston S. Churchill: Preface to 'Step By Step'

('Step By Step', page 9)

21 May 1939

During the last three years I have written a fortnightly letter mainly about Foreign Policy and Defence. When I came to read these letters through I was surprised to find that they seemed to tell the tale of these three eventful and disastrous years in a continuous flow. They are at once a running commentary upon events as they happened or were about to happen, and a narrative of what we have lived through. I therefore thought it would be right to present them to the readers of Great Britain, the United States, France and Scandinavia in this volume and its translations which I trust may be accepted as a faithful record.

I have not omitted a single letter nor have I altered what was written at the time in any essential. Where I have modified my opinion as the tale unfolded I have not concealed the change, the reasons for which emerge in the account. The reader may judge for himself how far these comments and forecasts, written in most cases before the events occurred, have been vindicated. It is a gratification to me that His Majesty's Government have at length by leisurely progress along their own paths of thought adopted even in detail the policy and theme set forth. I cannot conceal my sorrow that they did not reach these conclusions earlier. These contrary emotions lead me with all diffidence to present the story in a connected and permanent form.

---

[1] In the debate on 6 May 1939, arguing against the sending of £6 million of Czechoslovak Government gold to the new German rulers in Prague, Churchill told the House of Commons: 'Here we are going about urging people to enlist, urging them to accept new forms of military compulsion; here we are paying taxes on a gigantic scale in order to protect ourselves. If at the same time our mechanism of Government is so butterfingered that this £6 million of gold can be transferred to the Nazi Government of Germany, which only wishes to use it, and is only using it, as it does all its foreign exchange, for the purpose of increasing its armaments . . . it stultifies altogether the efforts our people are making in every class and in every party to secure National Defence and rally the whole forces of the country.'

Winston S. Churchill: Epilogue to 'Step By Step'

('Step By Step', p. 366)

21 May 1939

Here then, in an hour when all is uncertain, but not uncheered by hope and resolve, this tale stops.

Great Britain stands in the midst, and even at the head of a great and growing company of states and nations, ready to confront and to endure what may befall. The shock may be sudden, or the strain may be long-drawn: but who can doubt that all will come right if we persevere to the end.

Dr Chaim Weizmann to Winston S. Churchill: telegram

(Weizmann papers)

23 May 1939

Your magnificent speech may yet destroy this policy.[1] Words fail me express my thanks.[2]

Weizmann

[1] On 23 May 1939 Churchill spoke against the Government's Palestine White Paper policy, urging that the proposed restrictions on Jewish immigration to Palestine were both a betrayal of the Balfour Declaration of 1917, and a shameful act of appeasement to Arab threats. During the course of his speech he said: 'What will our potential enemies think? What will those who have been stirring up these Arab agitators think? Will they not be encouraged by our confession of recoil? Will they not be tempted to say: "They're on the run again. This is another Munich," and be the more stimulated in their aggression by these very unpleasant reflections which they make? After all, we were asked by the Secretary of State (Mr Malcolm MacDonald) to approach this question in a spirit of realism and to face the real facts, and I ask seriously of the Government: Shall we not undo by this very act of abjection some of the good which we have gained by our guarantees to Poland and to Rumania, by our admirable Turkish Alliance and by what we hope and expect will be our Russian Alliance. You must consider these matters. May not this be a contributory factor—and every factor is a contributory factor now—by which our potential enemies may be emboldened to take some irrevocable action and then find out, only after it is all too late, that it is not this Government, with their tired Ministers and flagging purpose, that they have to face, but the might of Britain and all that Britain means?'

[2] The Palestine White Paper of 1939 was neither destroyed nor modified as a result of Churchill's speech. Among those Conservatives who voted against the White Paper were Winston Churchill himself, Vyvyan Adams, Leo Amery, Brendan Bracken, Ronald Cartland, Victor Cazalet, Richard Law, Oliver Locker-Lampson, Harold Macmillan and Adrian Moreing. Others voting against included David Lloyd George, Sir Archibald Sinclair and Harold Nicolson. The final vote was 268 to 179 in favour of the Government's policy.

Nathan Laski to Winston S. Churchill

(*Churchill papers: 2/379*)

24 May 1939

Dear Mr Churchill,

May I congratulate you upon the great and statesmanlike speech you made on the Palestine question last night. I think it is not exaggerating to say that you will get the blessings of millions of Jews all over the world.

It requires a great statesman to take the stand you have done in the troubled times we are living. How a man like Inskip, a very religious man, can stand up and speak in a manner so dishonest as he did last night, is more than I can understand.[1] As an old man, I ask myself what is the matter with the English people that they sit down to allow a man like Chamberlain keep out of the Cabinet a great statesman, without any flattery, that you are; a man, whom, if his advice had been taken years ago, England would not be in the terrible position she is in today.

I can only hope that the time is not far distant when England will recognise that we have in you a man who can take charge of the affairs of this country and successfully overcome the blunders that others have made.

I intended coming to hear your son as I really have a great affection for him, but unfortunately I had to take the Chair at a meeting of the National Service Committee, of which I am a member.

With kindest regards and good wishes,

Believe me,

Yours very sincerely,

Nathan Laski

---

[1] Speaking immediately after Churchill in the Palestine debate on 23 May 1939, Sir Thomas Inskip (the Secretary of State for Dominion Affairs) said, of Churchill's speech: 'He described it as a melancholy occasion. I do not know whether the melancholy nature of the occasion was due to the fact that he was out of agreement with the views of the Government. If that was the case, he must by this time be fairly well inured to the buffets of fate. This is not the first occasion on which he has found himself in this situation.' Later in his speech Inskip said: '. . . the British race are peculiarly well-fitted as to reconcile a conflict of right with right. [Laughter] Hon. Members opposite may smile at that, but they know very well that in many a great reform in the history of the British race rights have been reconciled with rights. Our own common law teaches us that the individual rights that we ourselves enjoy are limited by the rights that other people enjoy, and the rights of the Jews in Palestine, as I am sure they would admit, must be limited by the rights of other people in Palestine. The only question is as to what effect that limitation may have on the exercise of a particular right. Here you have the Jews with ages, not centuries, of possession in Palestine, under the goad of savage persecution, sick with hope deferred, supremely efficient, but, on the other hand, you have the Arabs in possession, dominant, or their kith and kin dominant, in the greater part of the Arab Peninsula, members of a widespread political system, nurtured and supported by a fervour of religious enthusiasm which our colder Northern character cannot fully understand. How are we to satisfy the hopes, and how are we to allay the fears, of each? I can only

Winston S. Churchill to G. M. Young

(*Churchill papers: 8/626*)

24 May 1939

I was so glad to learn on enquiring to-day that you have so far recovered from your indisposition as to be allowed to leave hospital. I hope you will on no account strain yourself by too much work in the period of convalescence.

I am incorporating your corrections of the Stuart period in my copy. I think apart from Cromwell this is now in fairly good condition.

I am looking forward to seeing your corrections of the early period when you feel quite fit again.

I have the American Civil War on my hands now, which should take me about a fortnight.

With good wishes,
Believe me,

John Gunston[1] to Winston S. Churchill

(*Churchill papers: 2/359*)

25 May 1939   University Pitt Club
                                                      Cambridge

Dear Mr Churchill,

I am writing to thank you very much indeed for sending me your book 'My Early Life'. I read it when quite a small boy, and it was then that the admiration that I still have for you was born in my somewhat romantic mind! I am sure that on reading it again I shall enjoy it even more.

I am so glad that you liked the meeting and should like to thank you again for coming down during what must have been a very busy time for you.[2] You

---

say that if Palestine is the citadel of Jewish hopes, it is the native land of a large Arab population, and the task, intricate as it is, is to reconcile the hopes and the fears of those two populations.'

[1] John St George Gunston, 1919–1944. Son of Sir Derrick Gunston, MC, MP, 1st Baronet, (and in 1939 Conservative MP for Thornbury, see page 1196, note 3). Educated at Harrow School, 1932–6, and at Trinity College, Cambridge, 1937–40. 2nd Lieutenant, 1st Battalion, Irish Guards, 1940; temporary Captain, 1943. On active service in North Africa, 1943. Attached to the 2nd Special Air Service Regiment, 1943. On active service in Italy, 1943–4. Taken prisoner, 1944. Killed as a prisoner-of-war, March 1944.

[2] Speaking at Cambridge University on 19 May 1939, Churchill praised the desire of the student body to testify, through the new Conscription Act, 'its resolve and conviction in a time of serious public need'. It was the duty of all citizens he said, 'to make sure the cause is good', and it was to that point that he then addressed his argument, telling the assembled students: 'These totalitarian systems of government came into being from different causes. In Italy there was fear of Communism. In Germany there was the bitterness of defeat. Two

are the only man who could have made a success of such a meeting on a matter about which many of us feel very strongly, and I only wish that some of the members of our present Government could be able to write of themselves with truth but one chapter of the book which you have been so kind to send me.

Yours sincerely,
John Gunston

Winston S. Churchill to the Anglo-Foreign Information Bureau Ltd
(*Churchill papers: 2/359*)

27 May 1939

Dear Sirs,

The first real false move I have seen in your otherwise admirable accounts is on page 8 of letter No 64, about Czech funds, and I am much disturbed to know what are the motives behind this exceedingly venomous paragraph.

You will have no doubt read the debate in Parliament. There is no excuse whatever for delivering Czech money to Germany, and the mere pretence of using the Bank of International Settlement cannot be admitted by any who take your general view of the foreign situation.[1]

Robert Boothby to Winston S. Churchill
(*Churchill papers: 2/373*)

27 May 1939

Dear Winston,

I have now put all my papers relating to the crisis of last September into chronological order, for filing purposes. And it occurs to me that you might be interested to glance through them.

---

remarkable men rose on these strong tides to dictatorial authority. Both, in the early stages, rendered great service to their countries. But both were carried away by the habit of despotism and lust of conquest, and both at the present time seem ready to array themselves against the progress and freedom of the modern age. They cannot pursue their course of aggression further without bringing about a general war of measureless devastation. To submit to their encroachments would be to condemn a large portion of mankind to their rule; to resist them, either in peace or—which God forbid—in war, will be dangerous, painful and hard. There is no use at this stage in concealing these blunt facts from anyone. No one should go forward in this business without realising plainly both what the cost may be, and what are the issues at stake' (*Churchill papers: 9/137*).

[1] For Churchill's opposition to the transfer of Czech funds to Germany, see page 1504, note 1. As a result of the outcry, the gold remained in England.

They represent the spasmodic—and quite unavailing—efforts of one of
your back-bench supporters: and prove at least that the information I got
from continental sources was good. One of the few things in my life of which
I am proud is that in all matters of major policy during the past 5 years I have
hitched my waggon to your star.

Long after the names of the miserable creatures who are now supposed to
govern us have been lost in a merciful oblivion, the incredible services you
have rendered to this country since 1933 will be remembered.

Yours ever,
Bob

PS. My sole concrete political achievement to date is the blocking of the
Czech balances—which I did, with Waley's[1] help, in 24 hours, at the instance
of two Czech friends.

I certainly don't want to see the fruits of my labours thrown away. But
Waley tells me that, before he can gather them, he *must* get some information
from the Germans. If our claims are met, there will be no surplus.

RB

Arthur Serocold[2] to Winston S. Churchill

(*Churchill papers: 8/624*)

27 May 1939

Dear Mr Churchill,

Thank you very much for the copy of 'My Early Life', which I received
yesterday. I can hardly restrain myself from devouring it until after my
Tripos examinations next week. It is such an insidiously delightful book
that it is only by the strictest self-discipline that I manage to get any work
done at all.

I feel that if literature is to be the reward of meritorious behaviour last
Friday, then the University Library should be handed over to you, as a small
token payment of what we at Cambridge feel we owe to you.

Even now I overhear reminiscences of the meeting, and I am sure that it
will remain as a model in the minds of all who intend to hold a public meet-

---

[1] S. D. Waley, Principal Assistant Secretary at the Treasury since 1931 (see page 224, note
1).

[2] Arthur John Pearce Serocold, 1918–1942. Educated at Eton, 1931–6, and Cambridge,
1937–40. On active service, 1940–2; Captain, Welsh Guards, attached to the Hampshire
Regiment. Killed in action in December 1942.

ing at Cambridge. They will never, however, be able to secure the services of such a speaker.

Yours sincerely,
Arthur Serocold

Helen Kirkpatrick[1] *to Winston S. Churchill*
(*Churchill papers: 2/359*)

30 May 1939   Anglo-Foreign Information Bureau Ltd
London
Dear Sir,

Thank you for your letter of May 27th. We regret that you should feel we have made 'a false move', in the paragraph of Czech funds. We made a careful investigation into the matter, and took advice from a number of financial experts.

We were informed that legally neither the British Government, under existing Acts, nor the Bank of England were in a position to refuse the demand.

The point which you would, no doubt, have wished us to make refers to the action of the Bank of International Settlement in presenting a demand on the Bank of England which the latter was unable to refuse. Inasmuch as Sir Otto Niemeyer and Mr Norman are the British representatives on the BIS responsibility undoubtedly rests on them. Failure to question the *bona fides* of the 'Czech' demand must be laid at the door of the BIS and its directors, but not on the British Government, we are advised.

There were no sinister motives behind the account we gave, and we take steps this week to correct the impression that we approved this transfer, as the paragraph apparently implied.

Yours faithfully,
H. P. Kirkpatrick

[1] Helen P. Kirkpatrick, 1909–   . Born in Rochester, New York (Lady Randolph Churchill's birthplace). Educated at Smith College, Massachusetts, and at the University of Geneva. Joined the Foreign Policy Association, Geneva, 1935. Editor of *Geneva*, a monthly magazine on international affairs, 1935-7. A free-lance journalist writing from Geneva for the *Manchester Guardian, Daily Telegraph, News Chronicle* and *New York Herald Tribune*, 1936-7. Co-founder in 1937 of *The Whitehall News Letter*, (with V. Gordon Lennox), a weekly bulletin on international affairs, to which Churchill was a subscriber. Resident in London, 1937-9; London Correspondent of the Paris daily *L'Oeuvre*, 1937-9. Author of *This Terrible Peace* (about the Munich agreements), 1938, and *Under the British Umbrella*. 1939. Foreign and War Correspondent of the *Chicago Daily News*, 1939-45, in London, North Africa, Italy and France; Paris Bureau Chief, 1944-6. European Diplomatic Correspondent of the *New York Post*, 1946-9. Worked for the US Department of State, and Economic Cooperations Administration, Washington and Paris, 1949-53. Assistant to the President, Smith College, 1953-5. In 1954 she married Robbins Milbank.

June 1939

Winston S. Churchill to Alan Bullock
(*Churchill papers: 8/626*)

1 June 1939
Private

Dear Mr Bullock,

Many thanks for your notes on Australia, which will be very helpful. They give however inevitably a somewhat drab picture. There are so many convicts and penal settlements, that I wonder whether you could not lighten the tale by giving me some notes on:

(1) The geological severance of the Australian Continent from other parts of the world, and consequently the unique character of her animals, the kangaroo, the platypus, etc. From this come interesting points about animals introduced into Australia, like the rabbit (or the silkworm) which flourished abnormally in surroundings of almost another world, and thereafter played the devil with the balance of the local fauna.

(2) Australian love of sport; horse-racing; the Melbourne Cup; Adam Lindsay Gordon's[1] poems about all these.

(3) Something about the very fine type of manhood developing there. An exceptionally handsome race, with virile and martial qualities proved in the Great War. An equal land; a happy land; climate lovely apart from droughts,

---

[1] Adam Lindsay Gordon, 1833–1870. Born in the Azores, of Scottish parents. Spent his childhood in Spain and then England. Educated at the Royal Military College, Woolwich, and Merton College, Oxford. Expelled from Woolwich in 1851 for stealing a horse from the stables, in order to ride in a race. In 1853 his father sent him to South Australia. Rather than use the letters of introduction which his father had given him, he joined the mounted police as a trooper. His horsemanship was exceptional, and he became one of the best steeplechase riders in Australia. In 1864 he published his first book of verse, *The Feud*. He entered the Australian Parliament in 1866, but resigned in 1867 to live in the country, continuing his riding and developing his writing. He published two books in 1867: *Sea Spray and Smoke Drift* and *Ashtaroth*. Despite the popularity of his books, his financial position declined from gambling and drinking, and in 1870 he lost an expensive lawsuit aimed at recovering some family lands. In June 1870 he saw his last book *Bush Ballads and Galloping Rhymes* through the press, and on the following day he went out into the bush and shot himself.

which water-storage should eventually cure. Kipling wrote some fine verses about Australia.[1]

(4) We should have a page or so on New Zealand.

Perhaps you will see whether you can give me some notes on these points before I take up my task.

Yours sincerely,
Winston S. Churchill

Professor Lindemann to Winston S. Churchill
(*Churchill papers: 2/371*)

5 June 1939

Christ Church,
Oxford

My dear Winston,

Many thanks for your note with enclosure from Rothermere. He had already sent me the cutting and I enclose a copy of my reply.

As you know, I have always maintained that anti-aircraft guns are value-less for defending large areas. I think he must have generalised this statement to include the defence of battleships or small targets. I had always hoped anti-aircraft artillery was useful for this purpose, but the cutting from the Spectator makes me excessively uneasy.

I hope to see you on Thursday and remain,

as ever,
yours,
FAL

PS. I have just heard from the ICI that, as I had expected, they have suc-ceeded in making little bombs which will go off without requiring detonators.

Winston S. Churchill to Imre Revesz
(*Churchill papers: 8/638*)

5 June 1939

Dear Dr Revesz,

I am much interested in your proposal to negotiate with the American broadcasting companies for my special broadcasts to the United States.

---

[1] In his poem 'The Young Queen', written to celebrate the inauguration of the Common-wealth of Australia on New Year's Day 1901, Rudyard Kipling wrote of how the 'Old Queen of the Northland' gave her blessing to the 'Young Queen of the Southland' with the words: 'Ay, we be women together—I give thee my people's love.'

These would not exceed ten minutes, and would be either monthly or fortnightly. I shall be very glad to consider any concrete proposals you may lay
before me after your discussions on the spot, and for this purpose I accord
you exclusive rights of handling the matter. This, of course does not apply to
any public broadcasts I may give in the meanwhile.[1]

Winston S. Churchill to Sir Edward Marsh
(*Churchill papers: 8/626*)

6 June 1939

I have now got over 450,000 words of the English Speaking Peoples in
print, and some portions of it have reached a degree of completion which
would not be unworthy of your scholarly eye. I should like, therefore, to
begin sending you from time to time some of these ripe sections, in order that
you can make the necessary corrections. Would £20 per hundred thousand
words be agreeable to you?

I shall be deeply interested to know your opinion of the text.

Alan Bullock to Winston S. Churchill
(*Churchill papers: 8/626*)

6 June 1939

Dear Mr Churchill,

I am sorry you were disappointed with the section on Australia. That the
story should be a drab one is perhaps inevitable, if one only goes as far as
1860, the date at which I stopped, I should have thought that life in a 19th
century Australian town was crude, & monotonous and only relieved by the
rather tawdry orgies of the gold diggers. There is of course the other side to
Australian life which you mention, but that is a later development at the end
of the century. What I will try to do, therefore, is to send you some notes
as a sort of epilogue to the section I have already sent you. At the same time I
will send you a fuller account of the exploration of central Australia, an

[1] On 11 July 1939 Revesz and Churchill signed an agreement giving Revesz 'the exclusive
rights for handling his broadcasts outside Great Britain'. Churchill agreed to deliver 'monthly
broadcasts' to the National Broadcasting Company in New York. For each broadcast,
Revesz agreed to pay Churchill £100. But on 5 September 1939, with the coming of war,
Churchill cancelled the arrangement.

epic story in its way & one which might do something to relieve the dullness.

I believe Deakin has already given you the section on New Zealand: I hope you will find that satisfactory.

Yours sincerely,
Alan Bullock

I am so sorry: I forgot to acknowledge your cheque. Very many thanks.

Winston S. Churchill to Alan Bullock
(*Churchill papers: 8/626*)

7 June 1939

Many thanks for your letter.

I was not at all disappointed with what you wrote about Australia, but I felt that they would not be pleased if we stressed the convict side too much. Do do what you propose, and send me some notes for a sort of epilogue.

I like your section on New Zealand very much, though here again a little about the beauty of the country, the climate, the flora and fauna, the Yellowstone Terraces, etc, would be welcome.[1]

Winston S. Churchill to G. M. Young
(*Churchill papers: 8/626*)

7 June 1939

Very many thanks for the section 'Britannia', Galley 1–18, which I have dealt with. I have also received this morning the Vikings, Galley 58–82. Have you, however, sent me the intervening section, namely galley 18–58, or are you working on that now? I am not in any immediate hurry for it, and I only write in case it has gone wrong in the post.

---

[1] In the published version of *The History of the English-Speaking Peoples*, twelve pages were devoted to Australia and New Zealand (volume 4, pages 90–101).

Winston S. Churchill to the Austin Motor Co Ltd

(*Churchill papers: 1/351*)

7 June 1939

Dear Sirs,

Austin—Reg No FKT 180
Chassis No 54724.

The above particulars refer to a car recently purchased by me from the Austin Motor Co, Birmingham. Since its delivery to me it has failed to perform as a new car should. There has been a good deal of trouble with it, and the car has not been available for use on several days owing to time taken for repairs and adjustments.

The agents for the sale of the car, The Westerham Servicing Station (Wolfe Garage) first had to put right the speedometer which was not working when delivery was made at the end of last March. The second trouble was caused by the windscreen wipers, which were faulty, and the roof, which leaked. Thirdly there was the overdrive of the back axle. The repair of this was executed at Holland Park, and a new axle was substituted.

At great inconvenience I have had to send the car back to Holland Park a second time, to-day, as there is a noise which is audible at any speed, and according to my chauffeur, appears to be something to do with faulty shackles or springs.

I am extremely dissatisfied with the present working of the car, and very much surprised having regard to the very high reputation of your firm. I trust my complaint may receive the attention of the higher authorities in the Company, and I shall be glad to hear from you.[1]

---

[1] Two days later the Service Manager of the Holland Park Austin Service Department wrote to Churchill: 'We are in receipt of your letter of the 7th instant, and regret to learn of the trouble you have experienced with the car since purchase, and your feeling of dissatisfaction. When the car was here on the 5th instant to have the rear axle changed, the time at our disposal did not permit of a lengthy road test, but during the time the car was being tested there was no evidence of noise from the rear springs. When it came to us on Wednesday, the 7th instant, the sound was quickly located, and although unpleasant, was not in any way detrimental to the running of the car. The work necessary to eliminate it was carried out as speedily as possible. We trust that from now on the car will give every satisfaction and that there will be no further cause for complaint.'

Winston S. Churchill to Sir Edward Marsh

(Churchill papers: 8/626)

11 June 1939

Here is the Stuart section which is the most advanced at present, and I shall be very interested to know what you think of it; not only its general interest but particularly if you find parts which are below the level of the rest, or boring or redundant.

Winston S. Churchill to Brigadier-General Sir James Edmonds

(Churchill papers: 8/626)

11 June 1939

I send you herewith my proof of the Civil War down to the end of Chancellorsville. You will see that what you did was a great help; but, of course, I have spread myself a good deal more.

I hope to complete the tale to the death of Lincoln in 40,000 words.

I would be very much obliged if you would read this proof for me, and make any corrections and supply any omissions which occur to you.

I have Gettysburg and Vicksburg with the printers, and will send them in a day or two.

Winston S. Churchill to Lord Halifax

(Churchill papers: 2/359)

11 June 1939
Private

Naturally I was a little disturbed by your speech in the Lords;[1] but I understand that it does not imply any change of the policy upon which the country is in principle so united. I am sure you realise that to talk about giving back colonies, or *lebensraum*, or any concession, while nine million Czechs are still in bondage, would cause great division among us.

Very bad reports are coming from Bohemia and Moravia about the oppression and terrorism of the Nazi Regime upon these conquered people, and similar conditions are developing in Slovakia. At any moment bloody

---

[1] Speaking in the House of Lords on 8 June 1939, Halifax referred to 'the really dangerous element in the present situation, which is that the German people as a whole should drift to the conclusion that Great Britain had abandoned all desire to reach an understanding with Germany, and that any further attempt at such a thing must be once for all written off as hopeless'. He also spoke of 'rival claims adjusted on a basis that might secure a lasting peace'.

episodes may occur, and it is even said that many executions by the Gestapo have already taken place. Therefore, it seems to me quite impossible even to enter into discussions with Hitler at the present time.[1]

I read your speech, therefore, as a general restatement of our desire for an eventual reconciliation of British and German interests and aspirations at a time when the character of the present Nazi Regime shall have undergone a fundamental change.

I have undertaken with very great pleasure to propose your health at the 1900 Club Dinner on the 21st, and I learn that there will be many MPs and notables there to welcome you.[2] I should like to have a talk with you before-hand, and I wonder whether you could lunch with me Wednesday, the 14th or Thursday the 15th at 11, Morpeth Mansions. I stay as much as I can in the country during this beautiful weather, but I shall be in London on both these days, and if luncheon is impossible to you I could come and see you.

Winston S. Churchill to G. M. Young
(*Churchill papers: 8/626*)

13 June 1939

I spent a whole day and night upon your comments on Book I, and have adopted all but two or three which I have marked for discussion. I parted rather ruefully with some of my titbits, but I bow to knowledge. I have purposedly abstained from reading the whole text through, as I always try to keep my eye fresh for the final revise. We shall have reprints back by the end of the week, and I look forward to sending you a clean copy then.

I have nearly finished the American Civil War, and will also send you a copy of the new material on that. It runs to 40,000 words and has been pretty stiff work as there are so many facts.

The fifteen or sixteen Galleys which you have with you, carrying us down to the Conquest, are in a very weak condition, and stand much in need of improvement and fortification.

---

[1] Churchill had written in the *News of the World* a week earlier, on 4 June 1939, of Nazism: 'An almost religious flavour has been given to this vast conspiracy against German freedom; and the Catholic and racial ascendancy, bedecked with trappings of Thor and Odin, and with Herr Hitler as a Messiah at the summit. The most visible form of fervour which this hideous degeneration of the human mind manifests is the persecution, on grounds of race and faith, of the Jews, subjecting them to every form of insult and cruelty, and stealing their money, possessions, and the businesses and employments of their livelihood. The inculcation of race hatred against a helpless minority is the driving force. It is a cult of malignancy the like of which has never been witnessed on such a scale or with such power.'

[2] Churchill's speech at the 1900 Club dinner is printed in full on pages 1527–31 of this volume.

As soon as I have finished the American Civil War, I am going back to the Napoleonic period, the French Revolution, Waterloo 'and all that'.

Deakin is correcting and annotating Book II from the Norman Conquest to Wyclif, so perhaps you will let me know which Book attracts your prior interest.

Winston S. Churchill to John Wheldon
(Churchill papers: 8/626)

13 June 1939

My dear Wheldon,

I send you herewith a revised copy of the Henry VII chapter. I was particularly pleased with the help you gave me in this. The chapter could stand a slight addition. Perhaps you will try to add some notes on the text about Lambert Simnel, for I see you had a note that he was a more interesting figure than Perkin Warbeck.

I am looking forward greatly to receiving your further notes on the Edward VI–Mary period.

Harold Nicolson: diary
(Nicolson papers)

14 June 1939

Dine with Kenneth Clark in Portman Square. The Walter Lippmanns[1] are there, also Sibyl[2] and the Julian Huxley's[3] and Winston Churchill as the guest of honour.

[1] Walter Lippmann, 1889–1974. Educated at Harvard. Associate Editor, *New Republic*, 1914–17. Assistant to the Secretary of War, 1917; Captain, Military Intelligence, USA, 1918. Editor, *New York World*, 1919–31. Special writer to the *New York Herald Tribune* syndicate, 1931–62. Pullitzer Prize for International Reporting, 1962. In 1938 he married, as his second wife, Helen Byrne Armstrong.

[2] Sibyl Colefax (see page 113, note 2).

[3] Julian Sorell Huxley, 1887–1975. Educated at Eton and Balliol College, Oxford. Lecturer in Zoology at Balliol, 1910–12. Published his first (of nearly fifty) books, the *Individual in the Animal Kingdom*, in 1911. Professor of Zoology, the Rice Institute, Houston, Texas, 1912–16. Staff Lieutenant, GHQ, Italy, 1918. Senior Demonstrator in Zoology, Oxford University, 1919–25. Professor of Zoology, King's College, London, 1925–7. Professor of Physiology in the Royal Institution, 1926–9. Secretary of the Zoological Society of London, 1935–42. Fellow of the Royal Society, 1938. Director-General of the United Nations Educational, Scientific and Cultural Organization (UNESCO), 1946–8. Knighted, 1958. His books included *Essays in Popular Science* (1926), *Ants* (1929), *If I Were Dictator* (1934), *At the Zoo* (1936), *The Uniqueness of Man* (1941), *Democracy Marches* (1941), *On Living in a Revolution* (1944), *Biological Aspects of Cancer* (1957), *The Humanist Frame* (1961), and two volumes of *Memories* (1970 and 1972).

Winston is horrified by Lippmann's saying that the Ambassador Joe Kennedy had informed him that war was inevitable and we should be licked. Winston is stirred by this defeatism into a magnificent oration. He sits hunched there, waving his whiskey and soda to mark his periods, stubbing his cigar with the other hand:

'It may be true, it may well be true, that this country will at the outset of this coming and to my mind almost inevitable war be exposed to dire peril and fierce ordeals. It may be true that steel and fire will rain down upon us day and night scattering death and destruction far and wide. It may be true that our sea communications will be imperilled and our food supplies placed in jeopardy. Yet these trials and disasters, I ask you to believe me Mr Lippmann, will but serve to steel the resolution of the British people and to enhance our will for victory. No, the Ambassador should not have spoken so, Mr Lippmann, he should not have said that dreadful word. Yet supposing (as I do not for one moment suppose) that Mr Kennedy were correct in his tragic utterance, then I for one would willingly lay down my life in combat rather than, in fear of defeat, surrender to the menaces of these most sinister men. It will then be for you, for the Americans, to preserve and to maintain the great heritage of the English speaking peoples. It will be for you to think Imperially, which means to think always of something higher and more vast than one's own national interests. Nor should I die happy in the great struggle which I see before me, were I not convinced that if we in this dear dear island succumb to the ferocity and might of our enemies, over there in your distant and immense continent the torch of liberty will burn untarnished and (I should trust and hope) undismayed.'

Walter Lippmann: notes

(*Lippmann papers*)

14 June 1939

CHURCHILL: Change of opinion and attitude in England genuine. Government sincere; military preparations good. Replying to Kennedy and Vansittart view: air defense good enough to inflict 20% casualties which is a deterrent. Systematic day raiding no longer possible; night raiding can't reach military objectives; killing of civilians will make the 'inexpiable war' and may not be attempted. Air raids against shipping no threat for convoyed ships. Submarine has been mastered and can be hunted successfully. Great

Britain has nearly one million soldiers already. German army can't pierce French carapace; Spain negligible; British territorials can hold Spanish army and blockade of Spain would ruin her. Would rather Turks than Italians as allies. Italy a prey, Turkey a falcon. Would cut losses in Far East; no dispersion of the fleet; settle with Japan after the war. Central Europe mobilized as a unit in 1914. Then Germany had ten divisions from Czecho-Slovakia; now they need six divisions to hold it. Hungary, Jugoslavia, Rumania, dangerous and unreliable: Poland, a new force, and behind it, the Russian pad.

No use to say to Germany they are not being encircled. Better to over-whelm them with righteous indignation. Only argument that counts is force. No use shaping policy in accordance with Goebbels' propaganda. Take your own line and make them follow. In event of German mobilization, mobilize fleet; at first provocative action, cut German railway communications with Europe and defy them to do anything about it. As for negotiated peace, there never can be peace in Europe while eight million Czechs are in bondage.

Winston S. Churchill to Brigadier-General Sir James Edmonds
(Churchill papers: 8/626)

15 June 1939

Many thanks for your letter and the proofs.

I am very glad you think well of the story. I must tell you that I have been reading in detail your History, and I think it one of the best accounts I have ever read of this War, with which I was already much acquainted. I have visited nearly all the battlefields including Charleston, Gettysburg, the Peninsula, the Wilderness, Spotsylvania, Cold Harbor and Fredericksburg. I think it the most interesting of all the wars of which I have read. Your book gives such a just, level and comprehensive account, and it was a great pleasure to me to read it for the first time.

I now send you the missing pages about Chancellorsville, with a further batch, namely: Gettysburg, Vicksburg, Chickamauga, and 1864.

As you see, I am very nearly at the end. When I go through it for the second time, I shall add in a good deal more politics. Perhaps I may send it to you again when it is in its final form, so that you can judge the general proportions.

Would you be interested in seeing the section on 1812, of which two pages were sent you in error?

I think the Pakenham[1] repulse at New Orleans in 1815, where he lost two thousand men in an hour for only thirteen American casualties, influenced the whole thought of the American Army officers, hence McClellan's refusal to gratify Lincoln by frontal attacks, etc.

Sir Kingsley Wood to Winston S. Churchill

(*Churchill papers: 25/17*)

15 June 1939   Air Ministry
Secret and Personal

My dear Winston,

I have now seen a report by the Home Defence Committee on the note which you sent me recently suggesting that steps should be taken to guard against the landing of enemy troops by aircraft in the neighbourhood of munition works, bridges and other vulnerable points; and I think that you will be interested to know the opinion that they have formed.

They first took note of the fact that the increase in size of modern bombers and troop carriers requires prepared surfaces for landing and taking off, and in consequence they felt that the number of vulnerable points adjacent to fields where troop carriers could land would be very limited. For this reason they reached the conclusion that in most cases vulnerable points could more easily be destroyed by air bombardment or by sabotage than by an air-borne demolition party. In the case of a small vulnerable point which offered a difficult target to bombs, a raid might be attempted, but they thought it more probable that the demolition party would, in such circumstances, be landed by parachute rather than by troop-carrying aircraft.

The possibility of the landing of demolition parties from the air has been

---

[1] Sir Edward Pakenham, who had commanded a Division at Salamanca, in the Peninsular War, and who landed at New Orleans with 8,000 British troops. In his account (*A History of the English-Speaking Peoples*, volume 4, page 294), Churchill wrote: 'The swamps and inlets in the mouth of the Mississippi made an amphibious operation extremely dangerous. All men and stores had to be transported seventy miles in row-boats from the Fleet. Jackson hastened back from Florida and entrenched himself on the left bank of the river. His forces were much inferior in numbers, but composed of highly skilled marksmen. On the morning of January 8, 1815, Pakenham led a frontal assault against the American earthworks—one of the most unintelligent manoeuvres in the history of British warfare. Here he was slain and two thousand of his troops were killed or wounded. The only surviving general officer withdrew the army to its transports. The Americans lost seventy men, thirteen of them killed. The battle had lasted precisely half an hour. Peace between England and America had meanwhile been signed on Christmas Eve, 1814. But the Battle of New Orleans is an important event in American history. It made the career of a future President, Jackson, it led to the belief that the Americans had decisively won the war, and it created an evil legend that the struggle had been a second War of Independence against British tyranny.'

taken into account in fixing the strength and disposition of our home defence garrisons; and in addition all the really important vulnerable points, other than those which for practical purposes are not susceptible to sabotage, will be guarded by armed personnel or the National Defence Companies. Moreover, a considerable number of vulnerable points will be provided with light anti-aircraft guns or protected by balloon barrages against attack by low flying aircraft. These defences will provide a formidable deterrent to attempted landings by aircraft or by parachute.

In these circumstances, it is felt that it is unnecessary to take the special measures suggested in the last paragraph. I am, nevertheless, extremely grateful to you for having drawn my attention to this question and for giving me an opportunity of having the point considered by the Committee of Imperial Defence.

Yours ever,
Kingsley Wood

General Sir Edmund Ironside to Winston S. Churchill
(Churchill papers: 2/371)

17 June 1939   Government House,
                                                        Gibraltar

Dear Mr Churchill,

I am taking the liberty of writing to you upon giving up the Command here, which I do on the 26th. I am motoring up through Spain and hope to be able to see Franco en route.

Anyway, I leave this place better than I found it and my time has not been wasted. You cannot conceive what things were like when I took over and I hope I never find a show like that again.

I take over my new job on July 1st[1] and I have only a hazy idea of what I shall find. My job, to my mind, is a terrific one and I have very little time in which to get it going. The two principal things appear to me to be:—

1. The inculcation of a tactical doctrine. At the moment there is none in the Army & there has been no head to direct it.

2. The training of all the Corps Comdrs & their Staffs & the new Dist Comders & their Staffs. Many of them have never commanded anything in war and I am doubtful of the capacity of many, chosen as they have been at haphazard.

The other things are the Conversations with Foreigners & the Inspection of Overseas Garrisons, which will really not be possible.

---

[1] Ironside had been appointed Inspector-General of Overseas Forces (based in the United Kingdom), with his offices in Horse Guards Parade.

This Tientsin business must make people think and we cannot afford to start military operations in the Far East.[1] I do not believe that we shall. We may even have to strip India of all the British troops if the crisis develops, as I am convinced it will, and nothing should weigh against saving the Empire. I hope we have big enough men to release all our unnecessary commitments & concentrate upon the big thing.

I cannot believe that the Germans will attack the Maginot Line or we the Siegfried Line. Egypt & Palestine are the centre of the world & the Empire & here we can concentrate our Forces. Italy is the Achilles heel of the Berlin–Rome axis.

I do now wish that we had you in charge once more in the anxious times coming. I feel, as an old soldier, little confidence in some of our political leaders. They don't seem to have either the vision of big men or the guts either.

You cannot make an Army in a few months after years of neglect and I feel frightened of our lack of direction.

Yours very sincerely,
Edmund Ironside

Count Schlabrendorff: [2] *recollections*
(*'Offiziere gegen Hitler'*)

[17 June 1939]

Shortly before the outbreak of war I travelled myself to England. There I

[1] Japanese forces, while attacking deeper and deeper into China, had blockaded the British trading concession at Tientsin. The British Government had protested, but taken no military action; nor did Churchill see how they could do so. As he told the City Carlton Club, London on 28 June 1939 (during an appeal for a 'full and solid alliance' with Russia to be made 'without delay'): 'We ought not to send our Fleet to the Far East until we are sure of our position in the Mediterranean, and probably then it will not be necessary. I do not believe that Japan, deeply entangled in China—nay, bleeding at every pore in China—her strength ebbing away in a wrongful and impossible task, and with the whole weight of Russia upon her in the north of China, will wish to make war upon the British Empire until she sees how matters go in Europe. Therefore, we should approve both patience and firmness in the attitude of our Government towards the problem of the Far East.'

[2] Fabian von Schlabrendorff, 1907–   . A descendant of Queen Victoria's tutor, Baron Stockmar. A lawyer; from 1936, one of the small group of Government employees who sought to challenge Hitler and Nazism. On the Staff of Army Group Centre (Eastern Front), when he attempted, but failed, to find an opportunity to seize Hitler during a visit to the Centre Army Group headquarters, July 1941; closely involved in a similar unsuccessful attempt in March 1943, and again in the 'Bomb Plot' of 20 July 1944, when it was intended by the conspirators that he would be sent to Stockholm to open negotiations on behalf of the new Government with the western Allies (and preferably with a member of Churchill's staff). Tortured and interrogated, April–May 1945; liberated from Nazi custody in the South Tyrol by advancing United States troops, 4 May 1945. Returned to his law practice in Germany. Author of *Offiziere gegen Hitler*.

looked up Lord Lloyd, whom I was able to approach thanks to a contact made by our group—I was able to inform him that the outbreak of war was inevitable and would be prefaced by an attack on Poland, whatever proposals of mediation might be made. Further I told him that English attempts to reach an understanding with Russia would be double-crossed, as the conclusion of a pact between Hitler and Stalin was imminent. Hitler wanted to protect his rear through this agreement.

Lord Lloyd asked me to strengthen his hand by repeating both my messages to Lord Halifax, the British Foreign Minister. . . .

At that same time I had a discussion of the same nature with Winston Churchill. It took place at his country residence. As I introduced my remarks with the sentence 'I am no Nazi but a good patriot,' a smile played on Churchill's broad face, and he answered,

'So am I.'

P. J. Grigg to his father

(*P. J. Grigg papers*)

18 June 1939

On Thursday[1] I dined with Winston. He was looking younger if anything than two years ago & was most charming and friendly. He too regards a more or less early war as certain![2]

---

[1] Thursday, 15 June 1939.

[2] Writing in the *News of the World* on 4 June 1939, Churchill commented: 'If the world polled tomorrow and every grown man and woman recorded their opinion, ninety-nine out of a hundred would declare their desire for peace. There never was a time when there was so immense a volume of resolve for peace among hundreds of millions of thinking folk in every land. Yet they are all moving forward, step by step and day by day, towards the abyss. The helplessness of mankind to avert or control its destiny is more plainly apparent than ever before. All these vast populations long to be left alone to live their ordinary lives, better their conditions, bring up their families, cultivate their gardens. And yet everything is in train to make them fall upon and rend each other with teeth and claws incomparably more deadly than any ever used in any previous quarrel. The sovereign people, the enfranchised masses, the will of the majority, Parliamentary institutions, the mass-thought of mankind—all these seem to be utterly impotent to stop the approach of another World War. Why does the moth go to the candle? Its wings have been singed already: it has felt the bite of the flame, it would no doubt like to live its brief life. And yet it flies to the burning candle with universal and almost automatic resignation. All nations are now moving forward obdurately, blindly as if in a trance, towards the infliction of indescribable horrors upon one another. Such a contrast between the will of man and his actions seems to spring only from madness or from a seizure of herd passion.'

Winston S. Churchill to Sir Edward Marsh

(*Churchill papers: 8/626*)

18 June 1939

I now transport you across about one thousand years to another fairly completed island of the America Civil War, with the development of Canada as a preliminary.

I shall be most interested to know how this strikes you.

Sir Henry Tizard to Winston S. Churchill

(*Churchill papers: 25/17*)

19 June 1939

Dear Mr Churchill,

I shall be at Biggin Hill shortly before 10 am tomorrow (Tuesday) morning, & am looking forward to meeting you there. Watson-Watt, Director of Communications Research at the Air Ministry, will also be there. As you want to be back by 5 pm if possible, we shall only be able to show you three or four of the more important things.

I have had to have a slight operation to my jaw lately, & still have a good deal of pain. I mention this as it is just possible, though not likely, that I shall not turn up tomorrow. If I *should* fail you—which I don't intend to do if I can possibly avoid it—Watson-Watt will look after you & get you back in time.

Yours sincerely,
H. T. Tizard

Sir Stafford Cripps: diary

(*Copy, Churchill papers: 4/19*)[1]

19 June 1939

I had a long discussion with Baldwin on the subject of 'the immediate setting up of a Government of National concentration to warn our enemies and encourage our friends particularly Russia'.[2]

---

[1] When Churchill was writing his war memoirs in 1946, Cripps sent him copies of several diary entries (see also page 1531).

[2] Eleven days earlier, on 8 June 1939, Churchill had published an article in the *Daily Telegraph* arguing strongly in favour of an Alliance between Britain, France and Soviet Russia. In the course of his article he wrote: 'We often hear the clever-foolish question "How can Britain and France succour the Baltic States; or indeed Poland and Rumania, to whom

Winston S. Churchill to Colonel Bill[1]

(Churchill papers: 1/351)

20 June 1939

Dear Colonel Bill,

Pray see the enclosed. As I warned you some time ago there is now statutory authority for the compulsion of flat-owners to make the necessary provision, and I shall be very glad if you can inform me without delay what steps you propose to take to provide shelter in the basements of Morpeth Mansions.[2]

Alice, Lady Wimborne[3] *to Winston S. Churchill*

(Churchill papers: 1/343)

21 June 1939

My dear Winston,

Little Ivor and I want to tell you how touched by and grateful we are, for your visit to Ivor[4] & his last talk with you, at your coming round to see us

---

guarantees already have been given?' The answer is that if enough Nazi forces are held upon the Western Front, the States who are attacked in the East may be able to maintain themselves triumphantly. The whole possibility of establishing an effective Eastern Front depends upon the cordial aid of a friendly Russia in the East. We must not assume that the German army is all-powerful or that the life-thrust of the hard-pressed German people is capable of making head in every direction at the same time. No-one must under-rate the military prowess of the German army. That has been proved too often and too recently. But it is greatly to be doubted whether their military system, so newly reconstructed, is strong enough to bear the cumulative weight at the same moment of so many nations, great and small, provided that the military arrangements of all these states are loyally and thoroughly concerted.'

[1] James Gordon Bill, 1884–1960. 2nd Lieutenant, Royal Artillery, 1903. Captain, 1914. Major, 1918. Adjutant, Territorial Force, 1921. Retired from the Army, 1922. Subsequently Estate Manager, City and West End Properties Limited, London, including Morpeth Mansions. Lieutenant-Colonel, Regular Army Reserve of Officers, 1928.

[2] On 22 June 1939 Churchill wrote again to Colonel Bill: 'I think you should proceed rapidly, so that everything is ready before the end of July. By the way, you were wrong in supposing that a bomb falls obliquely. When cast from a certain height it falls vertically. Come and see me if you like about this one day.'

[3] Alice Katherine Sibell Grosvenor, 1880–1948. Younger daughter of the 2nd Baron Ebury. She married Ivor Guest (later 1st Viscount Wimborne) in 1902. On the death of the 1st Viscount, on 14 June 1939, their only son Ivor succeeded as 2nd Viscount Wimborne. Born in 1903, he had been Conservative MP for Brecon and Radnor, 1935–9; he was to be Parliamentary Under-Secretary of State for Air, 1943–5, and Liberal Whip in the House of Lords, 1944–8.

[4] Ivor Churchill Guest, 1873–1939. Son of Ivor Bertie Guest and Lady Cornelia Spencer Churchill (Churchill's aunt). On active service in South Africa, 1900. Conservative MP for Plymouth, 1900–6. Liberal MP for Cardiff, 1906–10. Created Baron Ashby St Ledgers, 1910. Paymaster-General, 1910–12. Succeeded his father as 2nd Baron Wimborne, 1914. Lord Lieutenant of Ireland, 1915–18. Created Viscount, 1918. Brother of 'Freddie' Guest (see page 50, note 2).

after he died, and by your coming down to Ashby to be there when he was buried in the home he created and loved so much. In his heart, there was Winston & Sunny;[1] and no one else he knew or liked in any way competed with these two, who were far more to him than any of his brothers or indeed than anyone else on earth except little Ivor & myself. He was never the same after Sunny went. It did not matter whether he saw you both or not. He did not need propinquity with people even those he loved best, though always happier for seeing them. But he loved as few people can. His point of view to everything was utterly original & that it was so never dawned upon his mind. He had a wonderful life and no husband or father was ever more deeply loved and venerated. Dear Winston I am desolate indeed in the loss of his never failing love & that complete & utter understanding we had together. No one & nothing could ever separate us. There were no secrets no deceptions no pettiness. We were the supreme factor in each other's lives. I can not contemplate life without him. He suffered so unspeakably for three years with that cruel illness I must not wish him back. I am ashamed that that thought does not bring me more consolation.

With all our thanks dear Winston for all that you always did for him, much happiness that at different times you brought him, much strength that you gave him and again for your presence near him in the last hours.

Your loving,
Alice

Winston S. Churchill: speech notes[2]
(*Churchill papers: 9/137*)

21 June 1939

Even if I were in strong political disagreement with our guest of the evening, it would be a pleasure to me to propose his health. We all know and

---

[1] Charles Richard John Spencer Churchill, 1871–1934. Churchill's cousin. Known as 'Sunny'. Succeeded his father as 9th Duke of Marlborough, 1892. Paymaster-General of the Forces, 1899–1902. Staff Captain and ADC to General Hamilton during the South African War, 1900. Under-Secretary of State for the Colonies, 1903–5. Lieutenant-Colonel, Queen's Own Oxfordshire Hussars, 1910. An original member of the Other Club, 1911. Employed at the War Office as a Special Messenger, 1914–15. Joint Parliamentary Secretary, Board of Agriculture and Fisheries, 1917–18.

[2] Churchill was speaking at a 1900 Club dinner, where Lord Halifax was the principal guest, and Lord Londonderry in the Chair. Among those present were Lord Halifax (the principal guest), Lord Londonderry (the President of the Club), Lady Londonderry, Clementine Churchill, the French, Polish and Turkish Ambassadors, Lord Zetland, Lord Lloyd, Sir John Reith, Major-General Sir Alfred Knox, Sir John Wardlaw Milne, Sir Murray Sueter, Brigadier-General Spears and Duncan and Diana Sandys. The Club members had been among the leading opponents of the Government's India Bill of 1935, and Churchill's strongest supporters during his five year campaign against the Bill, from 1930 to 1935.

admire his sterling qualities as an Englishman, a fox-hunter and a friend. I always look back with agreeable memories to the days when, on the morrow of the victory in the Great War, Edward Wood and I worked together at the Colonial Office.[1] Afterwards there came some difficulties. You are no doubt aware, Lord Halifax, that quite a number of members of the 1900 Club did not see what is called 'eye to eye' with you over the India Constitution Act. For five years we fought that policy. But this I can say without a doubt, that there never was a moment in that long controversy when we did not recognise the patriotism and sincere conviction of our Viceroy. And I think that he, for his part, will acknowledge that from the moment when the new Indian Constitution received the Royal assent, not one of us by word or deed, did anything to obstruct or prejudice the working out of that remarkable experiment in Oriental self-government. We were content to leave the question of who was right and who was wrong to history; and there—for the present at any rate—we leave it now.

We think it very good of you, to come here tonight because we know the grinding weight of the burden which rests upon your shoulders and upon the Prime Minister. There is no Office more exacting and more precarious than that of the Foreign Secretary. He has to be continually talking privately and publicly to Ambassadors, to Parliament, to the nation and to people of all kinds. A word put wrong may breed a mischief. A sentence wrested from its context may be twisted into, may even become a blunder or a crime. We realise that he must speak with particular circumspection. We are therefore doubly grateful to him for coming here tonight to talk to us, as I am sure he will, in candour and simplicity. We sympathise with him in the anxieties and vexations of the Foreign situation; not only in Europe but in the Far East. We know that now when the powers of evil are so strong we must walk warily, and that what can't be cured must be endured. We are sure that he is resolved to uphold the honour of the country, strictly to observe our public engagements, [and not to buy a precarious spell of peace for ourselves at the expense or ruin of friendly nations. We hope that is realised in all quarters. One of the uses of this gathering tonight is to make it realised in all quarters].[2]

History shows that Englishmen (and Scotsmen and Welshmen too) have often differed with one another about the Foreign policy of our island State. Some have favoured one Continental combination and others the opposite. Some have been for Intervention and others for standing aloof. But Lord Halifax, let me tell you that when we drink your health tonight it will be a sign that in principle there are no differences between us. We have all, from

---

[1] Churchill as Secretary of State for the Colonies; Edward Wood (as he then was) as Under-Secretary of State (from April 1921 until the fall of the Coalition in October 1922).

[2] Churchill deleted the sentences in square brackets before delivering his speech.

various standpoints, accepted the policy which you and the Prime Minister have now proclaimed. If differences remain, they will only be upon emphasis and method upon timing and degree.

Naturally I am a supporter of the foreign policy of His Majesty's Government. I thought a year ago that a Grand Alliance of peace-seeking States, in harmony with the principle of the Covenant, to resist aggression, and willing to remove where possible legitimate grievances, would in fact give almost the certainty of Peace. I cannot now feel the same assurance. Undoubtedly we ourselves are much better prepared than we were in September. Our Air Force has been equipped with the best machines. Our Air Defences are not only far better armed but constantly manned. Science has been brought powerfully to our aid against Air attack. Our organisation for internal defence has made great advances. The Army is stronger. The Navy is ready and relatively far stronger than in 1914. The methods for dealing with submarines are on an altogether higher level than any previously attained in war. There was no reason why this position should not have been reached a year ago—or even two years ago. There is every need that it should continue to be improved in the future. But the increase in our strength and preparedness is a real aid to the Foreign Secretary, and a potent factor for world Peace. Meanwhile, on the other hand, the Foreign situation has deteriorated and the balance in Europe has been seriously altered to our disadvantage. Others also have been preparing too. Therefore I cannot feel confident that the policy which I advocated last year will still be effective in preventing war. I feel bound to say that. But I sincerely believe that it gives us the best chance of preventing war: and that if war comes it offers the best chance of victory. Therefore I give it my support, and am glad on public as well as private grounds to commend this toast to you tonight.

As Lord Halifax no doubt knows, many in this Club would have viewed a year ago with very grave misgivings the guarantees we have given to Poland and Rumania. What has happened to bring us all together? It has been the flagrant and brutal manner in which the Munich agreement has been torn to pieces by the Nazi Government of Germany. We have in the Chair tonight my noble friend and kinsman Lord Londonderry. Certainly I have not always seen 'eye to eye' with him about the Nazi movement. It is a proof of the folly or the villainy of the Nazi outrage upon Bohemia and Moravia, that we should find ourselves in cordial and resolute agreement tonight.

But I must make one other reservation. This is no time for half measures, or half-hearted measures. Some have argued for a policy of Britain abandoning all interest in Eastern and Central Europe and letting events take their course there. More may be said for the policy which His Majesty's Government have now adopted of a Grand Alliance or Peace block. There is nothing to be said for not carrying out that policy in all its vigour and integrity. To go thus far, and not to take all the consequential and logical steps which are required, would be to combine the dangers of both courses without the security of either. For this reason I believe that most who are here tonight approve and endorse the willingness of His Majesty's Government to make an alliance with Soviet Russia, without which no effective stability can be created or long maintained in the East.

We all cordially join in complimenting His Majesty's Government upon the wisdom and foresight which led to the Anglo-Turkish Agreement, and we welcome the presence of the Turkish Ambassador[1] in our midst.

Above all we rejoice in the wonderful success which has crowned the Royal visit to Canada and the United States, and our hearts go out in gratitude to our beloved King and Queen for the inestimable service they have rendered to their faithful subjects.[2]

I think I speak for everyone when I say that we regard a prosperous, honoured and contented Germany, playing a leading part in guiding the European family, as one of the first, permanent interests of the British Empire. But that is not the prospect which we have to face tonight. We have to face a far less hopeful prospect. All Europe is at least half-mobilised. No-one knows when another blow will be struck against law and peace and freedom. No-one knows on whom that stroke will fall. But there are some things which we do know. The time has come when further acts of unprovoked aggression will be resisted by the united strength of Britain and of the Empire, of which we are the head. We believe that in such resistance we shall be moving in alliance or in companionship with at least three-quarters of the population of the globe.

We feel that our place in the world, our traditions, our interests, our duty,

---

[1] Tewfik Rushdi Aras, 1883–1972. Born at Çanakkale (Chanak), Dardanelles. Studied at Medical Universities in Beirut and Paris. Inspector-General of Public Health, Salonica, 1905. Active in the Young Turk revolution; subsequently Inspector-General of Public Health of the Ottoman Empire, and Medical Officer to the 1st and 5th Armies, 1914–18. Member of the First National Assembly of Turkey, and President of the Tribunal of Independence. Twice Minister of Health. Minister for Foreign Affairs, 1925–38. Turkish Ambassador in London, 1939–42.

[2] King George VI and Queen Elizabeth had just visited Canada and the United States, reaching Quebec on 17 May 1939. In Ottawa the King presided over the Canadian Parliament, and assented to legislation, as well as signing in person a Trade Treaty between Canada and the United States. On 9 June 1939 the Royal Train crossed into the United States. During the visit the King had several long conversations with President Roosevelt, and heard of Roosevelt's plan to establish a series of naval bases on British islands in the Caribbean, for the better protection of the American continent. The King also recorded Roosevelt's words to him: 'If London was bombed, USA would come in', and Roosevelt added: 'Offensive air warfare was better than defensive and he hoped we should do the same on Berlin.' (Quoted in John W. Wheeler-Bennett, *King George VI, His Life and Reign*, page 391).

compel us to stand in the forefront of the long array of States and Nations which is drawing up to encounter if need be a renewed act of physical and moral violence. We all hope it will not come. If there are any good offices which we can render to prevent it, we are sure they will not be lacking.

We have a Government which has proved, and over-proved,[1] its sincere desire for peace. We know that no taunts or minor affronts will stir them from that solid basis of sober, decent lawful life which is our hearts' desire. But we are here tonight to give to the Secretary of State for Foreign Affairs and the Prime Minister the assurance, that if after every resource and expedient has been exhausted, they feel it necessary to give the dread signal, a united Party, a united Nation, a united Empire will do their duty, and will do their best.

Sir Stafford Cripps: diary

(Churchill papers: 4/19)

22 June 1939

I saw Winston Churchill at his flat for more than an hour.

He inveighed strongly against the PM, said he Eden and others had been ready to join the Cabinet since Hitler went into Prague but would not be admitted as it would stop all possibility of appeasement. My article in the Tribune of June 30th is a reflection of our discussion on the PM.[2] He was opposed to the idea of Broadcasts (to Germany) as he was afraid the German Government would look upon it as appeasement and that it would not have any value otherwise. He agreed on the need of an all-in Government but despaired of any way of getting rid of or convincing Chamberlain.

I got the impression that he could do nothing at all in the matter though he agreed. It was a most interesting talk in which amongst other things he pointed out that but for Chamberlain's switch on Foreign Policy after the occupation of Prague, the Popular Front movement would have swept the country and I gathered he could have supported it!

I saw Kingsley Wood in the House a day or two later and pressed upon him the need for the all-in Government. He was interested and sympathetic but I felt he would not take any initiative in the matter.

---

[1] Churchill deleted the words 'and over-proved' before delivering his speech.

[2] This article, entitled 'Our Fuehrer!' was illustrated by a montage photograph of Chamberlain dressed as Hitler, in Nazi uniform, in front of the Houses of Parliament. Cripps wrote: 'A Cabinet of nonentities or "yes-men" has been collected together so that the Prime Minister may act the part of a giant amongst dwarfs thus preserving his dictatorial power'.

Winston S. Churchill to G. M. Young
(*Churchill papers: 8/626*)

22 June 1939

Very many thanks for sending me your second revise of the Early Period. I have incorporated the corrections, and I think it is in very good fettle now.

I am much concerned to learn that you are still in poor health. Pray let me know how you are getting on. I do hope the help you are giving me is not a burden to you.

I have sent a copy of your Norman Conquest to Deakin, and we will go into it together this week-end.

I think, from memory, that my point about the Druids' human sacrifices and its Carthaginian connection is from the opening chapter of Ranke, but I will look it up.

Winston S. Churchill to G. M. Young
(*Churchill papers: 8/626*)

24 June 1939

I shall consider the whole of this William the Conqueror piece with Deakin on Sunday. . . .

I am afraid I continue to take a sombre view of our affairs.

Winston S. Churchill to Sir Edward Marsh
(*Churchill papers: 8/626*)

24 June 1939

I have been through all your corrections of the Stuart period, and have adopted almost all.—*Note:* I spell 'judgement' 'judgment'. In this section the only part of which I was not sure is the latter part of Cromwell. I have reserved this for the final reading, because I have not yet decided upon my line about that large bloke.

The section about the Colonies should not have been printed in its present form, and I am sorry it reached you. It is probable a cut of 10,000 words will be administered to this section. I think it enormously improved by your comments.

With regard to Britannia, every word of this apart from quotations was mine, and some good judges, Wheeler for instance, a great archaeological expert, declared himself 'thrilled' by the presentation of the story. But I am very grateful to you for giving me your impression. Certainly I think the old hens of quotation must be boiled down into soup. There are many too many. In my final reading I shall probably cut 10,000 words out of this section, and will certainly try to lift the beginning to a higher plane than that of which I have as yet been capable. At the time I dictated the problem was words, now it is compression, which at any rate is healthy. I hope soon to have some more stuff for you. It has been a most educative ride for me. Though I have frequently had to dismount and talk politics to the wayfarers.

Winston S. Churchill to General Sir Edmund Ironside
(Churchill papers: 2/371)

27 June 1939
Private

I was delighted to hear from you, and am looking forward very much to seeing you as soon as you come home.

The situation is most serious, and I do not think you will have much inspecting to do. You will find here any quantity of first-rate soldiers, but except for a few Divisions they will have no weapons or equipment for a very long time to come.

Winston S. Churchill to Sir Kingsley Wood
(Air Ministry papers: 19/29)

27 June 1939

My dear Kingsley,

I found my visit to Martlesham and Bawdsey under Tizard's guidance profoundly interesting, and also encouraging. It may be useful if I put down a few points which rest in my mind:—

(1) These vital RDF stations require immediate protection. We thought at first of erecting dummy duplicates and triplicates of them at little expense; but on reflection it seems to me that here is a case of using the smoke-cloud.

Many of them are on or near the coast; therefore from a barge or buoy in the sea, or from a container a mile to the right or to the left along the coast, and another inland, it might be possible according to the wind by pressing an electric button on the alarm, which they will be the first to receive, to make a white sea mist which will envelope the towers and the buildings during the quarter of an hour of danger. This would be inexpensive, and above all, soon provided. Even when the B guns come, they could with their special appliances fire through the mist, which would prevent the actual towers or buildings being precisely located in daylight or moonlight.

(2) A weak point in this wonderful development is of course that when the raid crosses the coast it leaves the RDF, and we become dependent upon the Observer Corps.

This would seem transition from the middle of the 20th Century to the Early Stone Age. Although I hear that good results are obtained from the Observer Corps, we must regard following the raider inland by some application of RDF as most urgently needed. It will be some time before the RDF stations can look back inland, and then only upon a crowded and confused air theatre. Here is where the 'lambs' come in.

(3) The marvellous progress of the process of investing the 'lambs' with smelling-powder (as I saw at Martlesham) should give us exactly what we need. The 'lambs' directed by RDF would meet the raiders out at sea, and keep continually with hostile squadron formations, explaining their whereabouts as they go.

Tizard is keen on combining this service with dropping 'depth charges' (as I call them). This is an embellishment desirable in itself, but far less important than following Mary about precisely from place to place. It seems to me that prompt action in this field might bear speedy fruit.

(4) Everything I saw convinces me of the need of developing the mine-curtain. It is now more than six months since you seemed to be convinced of its possibilities, but alas, we are still far from mass-production! It seems essential to have a separate mine-curtain sub-command on the coast in close contact with the RDF stations. The large numbers of obsolescent aeroplanes which will be available should enable one or two groups of fifty each to be stationed on the East Coast at the most likely interception points. They will operate only over the sea, and perhaps only on the return journey of the raiders. The raiders will go straight home from a line drawn from the point where they have been throwing their bombs to their departure bases, and give fairly accurate interception. There would be no extra burden thrown on the fighting stations, or upon RDF, unless they want to take it on!

I see this process as a most important additional means of taking toll. Moreover there will be no harm in this becoming known and exploited as an additional deterrent. *Note:* Tizard suggested that it would be specially valuable for instance to defend an isolated key point, eg Malta, or indeed a fleet at sea, or in a Mediterranean harbour or floating base. This appears to me to be well worthy of the immediate thought of the Admiralty.

(5) The progress in RDF especially applied to range-finding must surely be of high consequence to the Navy. It would give power to engage an enemy irrespective of visibility. How different would have been the fate of the German battle-cruisers when they attacked Scarborough and Hartlepool in 1914, if we could have pierced the mist![1] I cannot conceive why the Admiralty are not now hot upon this trail. Tizard also pointed out the enormous value to destroyers and submarines in directing torpedoes accurately irrespective of visibility by night or day. I should have thought this was one of the biggest things that had happened for a long time, and all for our benefit.

(6) The method of discrimination between friend and foe is also of the highest consequence to the navy, and should entirely supersede recognition signals with all their peril. I presume the Admiralty know all about it.

I am glad you have another Meeting of our Committee. I should be very glad if you would circulate the operative parts of this letter, so that we could have a discussion thereupon.

Finally, let me congratulate you upon the progress that has been made. We are on the threshold of immense securities for our island. Unfortunately we want to go further than the threshold and time is short.

Yours vy sincerely,
Winston S. Churchill

Lord Lothian to Winston S. Churchill

(*Churchill papers: 2/359*)

28 June 1939

My dear Winston,

If you are in London on Tuesday or Wednesday, could I come and have a

---

[1] On 16 December 1914 a German naval force of 3 Battleships, 3 Cruisers and 5 Destroyers attacked three east coast ports, Hartlepool, Scarborough and Whitby. At Hartlepool, during the German bombardment, 113 civilians were killed and 300 wounded. At Scarborough 17 civilians were killed and 60 wounded. At Whitby 3 civilians were killed and 4 wounded. At Hartlepool, for a few days, the local authorities had tried to minimize the number of dead. Among the buildings damaged were private houses, a barracks, a lighthouse, a school and a hotel. Churchill told the War Council on the afternoon of the raid: 'It was believed that the enemy's object in making this raid was mainly as an act of retaliation for his recent defeat in the Falkland Islands; also to re-establish the prestige of the German navy in Germany and in neutral countries; and possibly to endeavour to influence the dispositions of our fleet and draw them into an area where they would be more accessible to the German submarines' (*Cabinet papers: 22/1*).

short talk to you about the United States and the present situation?[1]
Unfortunately I am fixed for lunch both days but I could come and see you
more or less at any time if your Secretary will ring up mine and make a
mutually convenient date.

Yours sincerely,
Lothian

PS. I'm going to Paris on Thursday, 6th.

Winston S. Churchill to G. M. Young
(*Churchill papers: 8/626*)

28 June 1939

Many thanks for the proofs returned this morning. The envelope in which
they came broke in the post, and was wrapped up again by the Post Office.
This makes me anxious about your 'typescript or ms notes of Magna Carta'
which you mention on Galley 286. They have not arrived, yet I am most
anxious to see them, because we are just coming on to the reconstruction of
the King John chapter.

If you have them by you, will you please send them as soon as possible. If
not, I wonder whether you can try to do them again for me?

In my last letter I asked about the Galleys of Book I which I have not yet
received, beginning at Galley 83–89, and Galleys 106–108, 422–424, and
617–619. This period of Edward the Confessor and Canute is in a very ragged
state, and I am shortly going to concentrate upon it. Will you let me know
whether you still have the Galleys by you, or if you have sent them and they
have gone astray. If so, I will send you duplicates.[2]

---

[1] Lord Lothian (see page 416, note 1) had just been appointed British Ambassador to the
United States.

[2] In order to try to complete work on the English-speaking peoples before the end of the
year, Churchill decided to employ an extra secretary, in addition to Mrs Hill. The lady
chosen was Miss E. R. Widgery. Aged 23 (in June 1939), she applied on 23 June 1939 for the
position of 'Secretary Shorthand Typist', advertised that day in the *Daily Telegraph*. She was
interviewed, and employed at a starting salary of £2.10.0 a week. For the pattern of secretarial work at Chartwell 'after hours', and for Mrs Pearman's successor, see page 1558, note 2.

Winston S. Churchill to G. M. Young

(*Churchill papers: 8/626*)

28 June 1939

To-night's post brought your new batch of proof, including the missing Edward the Confessor period. I am delighted with your survey of the growth of Parliament. The only thing about which I have any doubts now is whether you have written a note on Magna Carta which has gone astray.

This letter supersedes my previous one of to-day's date.

Sir Kingsley Wood to Winston S. Churchill

(*Churchill papers: 2/359*)

29 June 1939   Air Ministry

My dear Winston,

I am greatly indebted to you for the letter you have sent me following your visit to Bawdsey, and I am making arrangements to circulate your views at once to all concerned.

Many thanks too for the copy of your article in the 'News of the World'.[1]

Sincerely,
Kingsley Wood

---

[1] Churchill's article of 4 June 1939, already quoted in part on page 1524 note 1. Of the Air factor, and the likelihood of war in 1939, Churchill wrote: 'The main reason why Herr Hitler has been able to overawe France and England while he has been breaking his treaties and overrunning his weaker neighbours is the fears, or perhaps it would be truer to say the uncertainties, about the power of the Air Arm. The French know where they are about the Army. The British are very clear upon the Navy. But the Air belongs to what Bismarck called "the imponderabilia". Both the British and French Governments, through their incomprehensible slowness in developing Air power and Air defensive measures, were particularly sensitive lest they should be exposed on this score. But a more robust feeling is now growing on both sides of the Channel. The French military authorities are inclined to view Air attack as only a somewhat less efficient and more widely ranging form of artillery bombardment. The British are conscious of very rapid increases in strength and efficiency. Already the British Air Force is far stronger than in September, and all the arrangements for enduring Air attack have advanced. It is, perhaps, not too much to say that by 1940 the British Air Force and the British nation will feel a great measure of confidence so far as the defence of the British island is concerned. One may say, therefore, that a year's improvement in the Germany Army will be more than overmatched by a year's improvement in the British Air Force. All these aspects are, of course, profoundly weighed and studied in Berlin, and I mention no consideration which is not obviously present to trained, instructed minds of the leading General Staffs of Europe and the United States. It seems difficult to believe that Herr Hitler and Field-Marshal Goering would be content to see the blackmailing squeeze of Air-Terror gradually melt in their hands. This reflection also seems to count on the side of early action.'

Sir John Anderson to Winston S. Churchill

(*Churchill papers: 8/624*)

29 June 1939   Home Office

My dear Churchill,

It was very kind of you to take the trouble of sending me a copy of your article in the 'News of the World'.

As a matter of fact, I had taken steps to obtain a copy, immediately after you mentioned it to me, and had already read it. I was most interested to see it and, if I may say so, thought it very good indeed. I am sure it will have done a great deal of good, and I am very glad to think that you have used your great influence to get before the public some of the considerations which should be more clearly appreciated. I entirely agree with your view as to the danger of allowing the public to slip into a defeatist attitude in this matter.[1]

Two small comments on detail occur to me.

(1) We considered at the outset whether the steel shelters could be recommended for use *inside* buildings but could not get over the fire risk.

(2) Our standard concrete & brick shelters are I believe very good & more suitable than steel for certain locations.

Yours v sincerely,
John Anderson

Robert Hudson to Winston S. Churchill

(*Churchill papers: 2/365*)

30 June 1939
Private

Dear Winston,

I hesitate to worry you when you are so busy, and all the more as probably you already know most of what I am going to say. The seriousness of the situation, however, must be my excuse.

---

[1] Churchill's *News of the World* article of 4 June 1939, ended: 'If Nazidom should resolve to play the final stake and force another world struggle, we must all do our duty and do our best in whatever situation we happen to be. As was said aforetime: "God willing, we can do no other." Nor need there be fear about the final result. Although the sufferings of the assaulted nations will be great in proportion as they have neglected their preparations, there is no reason to suppose that they will not emerge living and controlling from the conflict. With blood and tears they will bear forward faithfully and gloriously the ark which enshrines the title deeds of the good commonwealth of mankind. Meanwhile the last chance of averting these ordeals lies in the unity of the peace-seeking nations, in the firmness of their attitude, and in their armed strength.'

Halifax's speech was I think absolutely first-class, but from such information as I can gather I am still in doubt whether it will serve its purpose of persuading Germany and especially Hitler, that we are really in earnest. Prytz,[1] the Swedish Minister for example, was lunching with one of my civil servants, and I met him at dinner last night, and I do not think that either of us succeeded in convincing him that we would carry our professed intentions to the bitter end.

Although since December I have scrupulously abstained from encouraging civil servants' confidences, in the last ten days I have had increasing evidence of a sort of administrative malaise arising from the lack of decision on the part of their elders and betters.

In my own experience I am appalled at the lackadaisical method in which we are dealing with the question of supplying the Poles, the Turks, and the Rumanians with munitions and raw materials of which they sorely stand in need, and the lack of any agreed plan between the French and ourselves how best to utilise what supplies we can afford.

It seems to me that if Halifax's speech fails as I am afraid it may, there is no alternative under present leadership but a steady drift into war.[2]

---

[1] Björn Prytz, 1887–1976. Born in Sweden. Educated at Dulwich College, London. Managing Director (in Philadelphia, USA) of a ball-bearing company, 1914–19; Managing Director of the parent company (in Sweden), 1919–38. Swedish Minister in London, 1938–47. After his return from London he became Chairman of the Swedish Export Council, of the Swedish Match Company, and Volvo Ltd. In a telegram to the Swedish Government in June 1940, after the fall of France (known as 'the Prytz telegram'), Prytz reported that in a conversation with R. A. Butler (then Under-Secretary of State for Foreign Affairs), he had been told that no occasion would be missed to reach a compromise peace with Hitler. According to Prytz, Butler had said that Churchill's attitude was not decisive and that the war would not necessarily have to be fought until a military decision was reached. Prytz said that during his talk Butler was called by Lord Halifax, then Foreign Secretary, and asked to convey to the Swedish Minister that 'common sense and not bravado' would govern British policy. The same day Prytz sent his telegram to the Swedish Foreign Ministry. It was placed before the Swedish Cabinet the next day, and the Swedish Government's much criticized decision to allow German troops to pass through Sweden on their way to and from Norway followed soon afterwards. In his memoirs, The Art of the Possible, published in 1971, Lord Butler denied giving Prytz 'grounds for supposing that any of us had become less bellicose'.

[2] Following the criticisms of his House of Lord's speech of 8 June 1939, Halifax spoke again at Chatham House on 29 June 1939, reiterating his earlier view that negotiations were still possible. 'If we could once be satisfied,' he said, 'that the intentions of others were the same as our own, and that we all really wanted peaceful solutions—then, I say here definitely, we could discuss the problems that are today causing the world anxiety.' But, he went on, 'this is not the position which we face to-day. The threat of military force is holding the world to ransom, and our immediate task is—and here I end as I began—to resist aggression. I would emphasize that to-night with all the strength at my command, so that nobody may misunderstand it. And if we are ever to succeed in removing misunderstanding and reaching a settlement which the world can trust, it must be upon some basis more substantial than verbal undertakings. It has been said that deeds, not words, are necessary. That also is our view' (quoted in Alan Campbell Johnson, Viscount Halifax, A Biography, London 1941, page 528).

I understand from a fairly good source that the Prime Minister in conversation a day or two ago, indicated that he felt his policy had failed, and that he was contemplating handing it over to someone else, according to my informant that someone else being Kingsley Wood.

Surely the time has come when we ought to form in this country a War Government. It seems to me that this is the only step left which might still at the eleventh hour convince Hitler and his entourage that we mean business.

Can't you and Halifax cut the Gordian knot?

Yours ever,
Rob

Lord Camrose to Winston S. Churchill
(*Churchill papers: 8/628*)

30 June 1939

My hearty congratulations on your speech on Tuesday![1] I should imagine that Halifax last night was not unfortified by your remarks.

Harold Nicolson: diary
(*Nicolson papers*)

30 June 1939

The vital thing is to bring into the Cabinet people who are known abroad to be pledged to a policy of resistance and whose willingness to enter the Cabinet would show to the whole world that there can be no further Munichs. . . . We then discuss how far the Prime Minister would be opposed to bringing in Winston Churchill and Anthony Eden. . . .

[1] Speaking at a City Carlton Club luncheon on 28 June 1939 (a Wednesday, not a Tuesday), Churchill spoke with confidence to the assembled businessmen of Britain's strength at sea and in the air. 'As to the Army,' he said, 'this nation, so long considered to be unmilitary, had no lack of men ready to serve. With the approach of danger, men came forward. How splendid it had been to see the Conscription Act carried by almost universal assent and to see all these young men coming forward, feeling it an honour to be called upon, grieved and crestfallen if from any physical disability they were prevented from taking their places in the ranks.' Churchill also argued that 'a full and solid alliance should be made with Russia without delay'. 'Finally,' he said, 'and most weighty among the factors which might preserve the peace of the world, there was the intimate comprehension of the cause of freedom now at stake in Europe which was shown by the United States. We asked favours from nobody. Every country must judge its own interests and its own duty for itself, but the understanding, good will, and sympathy of the great Republic and its eminent President were a very great encouragement to us in months and weeks of increasing anxiety' (*The Times*, 29 June 1939).

Camrose says that Winston is the vital figure.[1] . . . The difficulty is that the Prime Minister himself, as well as Hoare and Simon, are terrified of Winston and will put up the strongest resistance. It would be much easier for them to accept Anthony, Amery or Duff Cooper. 'Yet you must have Winston.'

Chartwell Literary Account: notes

(Churchill papers: 8/639)

30 June 1939

JUNE

5th	Double journey to London by car. Literary dictation both ways.		
,,	Cost of sending article to Paris by 'plane. . .	2.	6.
,,	Cost of car expenses to Croydon, and having to hire car while chauffeur away (article to Paris by 'plane) £1.	10.	0.
8th	Dictation in car.		
14th	,,		
19th	,, (double journey).		
,,	Cost of sending article to Paris by 'plane . .	2.	6.
,,	Cost of car journey to Croydon		
,,	Dictation in car to London (both ways).		
20th	,, ,, ,, one way.		
21st	,, ,, ,, ,,		
23rd	,, ,, ,, ,,		
25th	Mr Deakin stayed for 2 days.		
28th	Dictation in car (double journey).		
30th	Professor Lindemann stayed one night.		

[1] Four days after his talk with Harold Nicolson, Lord Camrose gave public expression to this feeling in a leading article in the *Daily Telegraph* (quoted on page 1544, note 1).

July 1939

Clement Attlee to Winston S. Churchill
(Churchill papers: 8/628)

1 July 1939

My dear Winston,

Thank you so much for sending me your book.[1] It must be a melancholy satisfaction to you to see how right you were. I am glad Halifax has at last made the speech which ought to have been delivered long ago.

The wheel has certainly come full circle since Hoare's speech at Geneva to which you refer in your third article.[2]

But what a loss in the meantime. Lets hope it's not too late.

With all good wishes,

Yours sincerely,
Clement Attlee

Desmond Morton to Winston S. Churchill
(Churchill papers: 8/628)

2 July 1939   Earlylands

Dear Winston,

Thank you so very much for sending me a copy of 'Step by Step'. I did not know it was in preparation. Many of the articles I read at their first appear-

---

[1] *Step by Step*, which had been published in London by Thornton Butterworth on 27 June 1939 (see page 1420, note 1).

[2] On 11 September 1934 Sir Samuel Hoare, then Foreign Secretary, told the League Council, meeting at Geneva to discuss the Italian invasion of Abyssinia: 'If risks for peace are to be run, they must be run by all. The security of the many cannot be assured solely by the efforts of a few, however powerful they may be. . . . In conformity with its precise and explicit obligations the League stands, and my country stands with it, for the collective maintenance of the Covenant in its entirety, and particularly for steady and collective resistance to all acts of unprovoked aggression. The attitude of the British nation in the last few weeks has clearly demonstrated the fact this is no variable and unreliable sentiment, but a principle of international conduct to which they and their Government hold with firm, enduring and universal persistence.'

ance, but not all. None of them lose by a second, or third or an oft-repeated study. Many years on, historians will read this and your speeches in Arms and the Covenant. They will wonder but I doubt if they will decide what devil of pride, unbelief, selfishness or sheer madness possessed the English people that they did not rise as one man, depose the blind guides, who have certainly 'swallowed camels' even if they have not 'strained at gnats', and call on you to lead them to security, justice and peace.

There is a Polish proverb about the Poles themselves: 'Mądry Polak po szkodzie', or 'wise is the Pole after the event'. The English electorate is growing more Polish daily.

Yours ever,
Desmond Morton

Sir Henry Strakosch to Winston S. Churchill

(*Churchill papers: 8/628*)

2 July 1939

My dear Winston,

Thank you so much for sending me your latest book 'Step by Step'.

I am delighted that you have published your fortnightly articles in this form. The average person who reads your articles in the daily press usually has only a hazy recollection of what you had written in your previous articles & does not therefore adequately appreciate how consistently right you have been in your appraisal of the trend of things & in your advocacy of the essential measures to meet it.

'Step by Step' brings this out in striking fashion, & ought to make the average person realise how badly those in charge of our National affairs have been floundering through these last fateful years. How different the map of Europe would have looked & how immeasurably higher would have stood our prestige & with it the prospect of peace & prosperity if they had had the courage & good grace to accept your advice. What a happier world we should be living in to-day if you had stood at the helm during the last few years.

Ever yours,
Henry Strakosch

Frederick Leathers to Winston S. Churchill

(*Churchill papers: 8/628*)

3 July 1939

Dear Mr Churchill,

I was proud to receive the signed copy of your new book 'Step by Step' and knowing something of your views over the period 1936/1939 I shall be much interested in reading the record of them and in the light of all that has happened subsequently.

I hope we may soon see you again at Cory Buildings and you know you are welcome at any time—meeting or no meeting.

My warmest thanks for your kind thought.

Sincerely yours,
F. Leathers

Lord Camrose: notes of a conversation with Neville Chamberlain

(*Camrose papers*)

3 July 1939

The Prime Minister said that he had not yet given up hopes of peace. He had now reason to believe that Hitler was aware, to some extent, at any rate, of the resolution of this country, and steps were being taken all the time to further inform him of it. If Hitler were asking for Danzig in a normal way it might be possible to arrange things, as Beck had intimated when he was over that if full protection could be devised and faith could be placed in German undertakings, Danzig should not be an insuperable problem.

He had, of course, read the leader in the Daily Telegraph,[1] and thought

---

[1] In its leading article of 3 July 1939 the *Daily Telegraph* described Churchill as 'a statesman not only schooled in responsibility by long and intimate contact with affairs of State, but possessing an unrivalled practical knowledge of the crucial problems which war presents, especially in the higher strategy. With vision and energy he unites a conspicuous gift of exposition and popular appeal, and in this strait pass the nation cannot prudently dispense with the great services which he is so capable of rendering.' The article added: 'Every public man has his defects; and every public man has made mistakes in his time. If they were to be counted as a bar to confidence, who would remain, except nonentities, to carry on the King's Government? The plain fact is that when people speak to-day of a reconstruction of the Cabinet, they are thinking first and foremost of the inclusion of Mr Churchill, and it is quite certain that no step would more profoundly impress the Axis Powers with the conviction that this country means business. It is impossible to ignore the welling up of the feeling not only inside the rank and file of the party, but also among some of its most distinguished members, that Mr Churchill's inclusion in the Government is an urgent need. The act of inviting Mr Churchill to join the Cabinet would be the most popular step which Mr Chamberlain could take, and, far from diminishing his stature and influence, it would enhance them. He must be

he would like to see me on it to explain his point of view. This was to the effect that, while he appreciated Churchill's ability, his own experience in Cabinet work with him had not been such as to make him feel that his (Churchill's) inclusion in the Cabinet would make his own task any easier. He admitted that Baldwin had not attempted to control his Cabinet, and that therefore Winston had had a much freer rein than he should have done. In any case, however, the result was that Winston's ideas and memoranda tended to monopolise the time of the whole Ministry. If you did not agree with him he was liable to lose his temper in argument and a number of his colleagues had found that the easier way was not to oppose him. Personally he had had two discussions with him which had ended in rather violent disagreement; but in each case he found that in a week's time Churchill had forgotten the matter and had some fresh idea which he regarded as being more important. His own personal relations with him were quite cordial and they had never had any lasting differences.

His own responsibility at the present time was so onerous that he did not feel that he would gain sufficiently from Winston's ideas and advice to counterbalance the irritation and disturbance which would necessarily be caused.

In our article we had suggested that other names came readily to the mind. One was, of course, Anthony (Eden). Well, Winston was Public Enemy No 1 in Berlin, and Eden was the same in Italy. Their inclusion in the Cabinet might strike both ways. So far as the latter was concerned, he still clung to the idea that Italy being the weaker and now the unwilling partner of the Axis, we ought not to eliminate all idea of being able to seduce her away from her present entanglement. Eden's appointment might have a detrimental effect on such a chance.

To my suggestion that all the present members of the Cabinet were not popular and that some, including Simon, were definitely distrusted, he replied that he knew very well that Simon was not liked or admired.

We agreed that the question of Eden ('while he has a following in the country') was not of the same consequence as that of Winston. He did not strongly demur to my emphasis of the psychological effect Winston's inclusion would have on the country, but he was the only person who could properly judge the question from every angle. Simon's judgment, and Hoare's, might have been wrong at times, but Winston's was notorious. As a recent instance, on the Saturday after the Italians marched into Albania the latter

---

acutely conscious today of the tremendous responsibilities which destiny has laid upon his shoulders, and he might well feel it to be a saving relief of his own strength to have the aid and counsel of those pre-eminently qualified to give help in such testing times.'

warned them persistently ('he was on the doorstep all day') to at once seize Corfu as the essential and immediate counterstroke. He emphasised the privacy of this statement.

Salisbury[1] was asked whether he could not find some means of getting Randolph back. S replied, 'If you have once got rid of a carbuncle do you make an effort to get it back?' He told me this as an amusing remark, not seriously applying it to the present situation.

He (C) was a man who was slow to make up his mind, and equally slow to change it once he had made his decision. He would not say that he would never ask W to join the Cabinet, but at the moment he did not intend to. Circumstances might arise which would make him feel that W could be of positive help to him—he did not rule that out. In the event of war W would, of course, be in the Cabinet and in the War Cabinet itself.

At the outset of his remarks on Winston he said, rather enigmatically, that although we appeared to have had some differences last year ('I have read of them') these matters were now over, and he had hoped that we should understand each other again and 'be like we used to be'. I formed the conclusion that he was a little nervous in making this statement and phrased it badly in consequence.

Harold Nicolson: diary

(*Nicolson papers*)

4 July 1939

Paul Evans[2] is at the Club. He says the real opponent to the inclusion of Winston is Kingsley Wood.

Henry Channon: diary

(*Robert Rhodes James, 'Chips'*)

4 July 1939

Jim Thomas is now annoyed by the Churchill plot, to which he originally subscribed, and by the fact that Winston is stealing all Anthony's thunder.

---

[1] The 3rd Marquess of Salisbury, Prime Minister in 1886, at the time of Lord Randolph Churchill's resignation (as Chancellor of the Exchequer).

[2] Paul Emrys-Evans, the Conservative MP (see page 1197, note 2).

Sarah Oliver to Winston S. Churchill

(*Churchill papers: 8/628*)

4 July 1939

Darling Papa,

Thank you so very much for the very valuable addition to our library.
It was sweet of you to think of sending me a copy. I am in the middle of
reading it now—why didn't—and oh why don't they listen to you!

Your loving,
Sarah

Lord Craigavon to Winston S. Churchill

(*Churchill papers: 8/628*)

4 July 1939

My Dear Winston,

Again I have to say 'Thank you' for an addition to my Churchill Library,
though where Cassandra comes into the picture I fail to see!

You have been simply wonderful throughout, and I earnestly hope that
we will not have long to wait till the Country has your services again at its
full disposal.

Yours ever,
James

Sir Reginald Barnes to Winston S. Churchill

(*Churchill papers: 8/628*)

4 July 1939

My dear old Winston,

How nice of you to send me your latest book. I have read some of the
letters, but not all, but to do so, is only to underline the fact, that I instinctively knew all the time, that you have been *right* about the Nazis.

It is a great triumph for you, dear old pal.

Now, our rather slow movers in command, having gone rather more than
the whole hog, & burnt their last remaining boat, seem to be realising *at last*,
that you might be of some help to them, in the fight that still seems to be
ahead. If we stick to this line, & continue to make our position all round
stronger, I can't believe that a nation of good soldiers like the Germans, will

embark on a war which they can't see a victorious end to. I pray I shall see you in the Cabinet soon.

Best love,
Reggie

I hope you will be able to manage to come down to Tidworth on the 22nd, & see the tanks!

Anthony Eden to Winston S. Churchill

(*Churchill papers: 8/628*)

5 July 1939

My dear Winston,

I am delighted with the present of 'Step by Step'. Thank you very much for sending it to me. The reading of it is somewhat painful, but no doubt salutary.

I see that Low[1] portrays us together 'on the Step' tonight.[2] Again, thank you so much.

Yours ever,
Anthony

Lord Wolmer to his father[3]

(*Selborne papers*)

5 July 1939

My friends in the H of C all think it would help very much if *you* would write a letter to The Times & urging Neville to bring into his Govt men like Anthony Eden & Winston just to prove to Hitler that England is united. . . .

---

[1] David Alexander Cecil Low, 1891–1963. Cartoonist and caricaturist. Born and educated in New Zealand. Joined the *Star*, London 1919; the *Evening Standard*, 1927; the *Daily Herald*, 1950 and the *Manchester Guardian*, 1953. Knighted, 1962.

[2] On 5 July 1939 the main Low cartoon in the *Evening Standard*, entitled 'Still on the Doorstep', showed Churchill and Eden standing outside 10 Downing Street. On the step itself, knocking at the door, was a man identified as 'Public Opinion', holding a newspaper on which was written: 'The Need for a Stronger Government'. Neville Chamberlain was also shown, peeping out of the window.

[3] William Waldegrave Palmer, 2nd Earl of Selborne (see page 400, note 2).

They do not think Neville will pay any attention to private representations but will take notice of a public demand. Vide yesterday's & today's DT.[1]

Sir Stafford Cripps to Winston S. Churchill

(*Churchill papers: 2/364*)

5 July 1939

My dear Winston Churchill,

As you will have gathered from our talk the other day I am most anxious to see a reconstruction of the Government even on limited lines, if nothing more can be attained.

May I make this suggestion to you as a possible way of breaking down the insane resistance of Chamberlain to your entry into the Cabinet.

Could you not make a public statement—to your Constituents or otherwise—stating your preparedness to give your services to the country and emphasizing the need for some spectacular act to confirm the avowed change in Foreign Policy. I feel that it would make a tremendous impact just now on the country and would intensify enormously the demand that is growing everywhere for your inclusion in the Government.

Somehow or another Chamberlain must be forced to yield to this demand, and such a clear statement by you would I believe make it much more difficult for him to hold out.

Please think this over and decide to act upon it!

Yours sincerely,
R. Stafford Cripps

---

[1] Following the *Daily Telegraph's* leading article of 3 July 1939, urging Churchill's inclusion in the Cabinet, the newspaper had published letters received supporting their stand. In one of these letters, published on July 5, the author and journalist Reginald Pound wrote: 'There is no doubt that Mr Churchill, for all those faults which are often hinted at but strangely seldom defined, has a greater capacity than any other political personality of our time for making the mass of people feel safer in the physical sense. It has not been forgotten up and down the country that it was he who had the Fleet ready in 1914: this was often quoted at me. "A loud sigh of relief would go up were Mr Churchill given scope for his energy and powers. He has been consistently defeated by mediocrity—frequently the fate of the creative brain that forswears the final touch of ruthlessness in its dealings with others." '

Sir Stafford Cripps: diary

(*Churchill papers: 4/19*)

5 July 1939

Today I sent letters to Kingsley Wood and Stanley begging them to act in this matter (reconstruction of the Govt). I also wrote to Winston Churchill and suggested he should make a public statement offering his services in order to put further pressure on Chamberlain who is 'digging his toes in' and refusing to change the Cabinet.

Yesterday I had a letter from Halifax in reply to mine urging Cabinet reconstruction, suggesting my proper course was to go and put the matter before the PM myself! I don't feel that our relationship would make this a helpful line of approach at the present!

Wing-Commander Anderson to Winston S. Churchill

(*Churchill papers: 2/372*)

5 July 1939

Nos 102 Bomber Squadrons from Driffield, and 78 Squadron from Ditchforth, completed three weeks air firing and bombing practice at Catfoss on 1st July 1939. No 102 Squadron had nine Whitley 3 Aircraft. The peace establishment of both these Squadrons is sixteen Aircraft each.

Squadrons only attend practice camp for air-firing and bombing for one period in every twelve months, and they should be equipped fully with aircraft and crews as instruments of war. The shortage of aircraft in these Squadrons is due to unserviceability, difficulty in obtaining spare parts, and the necessity of sending aircraft to manufacturers for installation of later type engines.

The grant of Permanent Commissions is far too small, and some seventy officers in the last Air Ministry Weekly Order who qualified for permanent commissions by passing the examination, but could not be accepted owing to lack of vacancies, have now attained the rank of Flight-Lieutenant, and are due out any time. In many cases, not wishing to extend their services by a further year. It will be realised that in many cases these Flight-Lieutenants who are the backbone of the Service have not unnaturally become discontented, and their interests lie in their future civilian careers, and their minds are not on the Service.

HENLEY AIRCRAFT. The latest type issued for target towing were issued to Armament Training Stations in May. It is quite impossible to get any spare parts for these aircraft, and the rate of serviceability is decreasing daily, which in turn reduces the air-firing facilities for visiting Squadrons.[1]

Winston S. Churchill to Sir Kingsley Wood

(*Churchill papers: 25/17*)

6 July 1939
Secret

I think it would be a good thing if Lindemann went down to Bawdsey before our next Meeting and saw what was being done. He knows the Head there, who suggested his going some time ago. If you would give permission, he would arrange it privately. There would be no necessity to have any special demonstrations with aeroplanes flying or ships moving, as Lindemann would take it all in quite readily.

Perhaps your Secretary would telephone me if you feel able to give the permission desired.

Robert Boothby to Winston S. Churchill

(*Churchill papers: 2/363*)

6 July 1939   House of Commons

Dear Winston,

Colin Coote writes (privately and confidentially) as follows:—'The paper[2] refuses to print your speech. It is in one of its worst moods about everything that it is not sure will please Mr C. You will have observed the agitation in favour of Mr Winston Churchill. I will offer you a small bet that the other Mr C won't listen to it for one moment; for his motto is still peace at any price except the loss of office, and he is rightly sure that the inclusion of Winston

---

[1] Churchill gave this letter to Sir Kingsley Wood on 11 July 1939, without revealing its source. But on 27 July 1939 Folliott Sandford noted, for the Permanent Under-Secretary of State for Air: 'You may like to know that the document was handed to him by Mr Churchill and I think that there can be little doubt that the author was the Camp Commandant at Catfoss who has been a frequent purveyor of information in the past to Mr Churchill' (*Air Ministry papers: 19/26*).

[2] *The Times*, on whose staff Colin Coote served from 1923 to 1942.

means his own proximate exclusion. So you will come to a Carlton Club meeting in the end, if the British Empire is to survive.'

I know nothing of what is happening here. But I know that Scotland is solid.

Yours ever,
Bob

L. S. Amery to Sir Robert Menzies[1]

(*Amery papers*)

6 July 1939

There is a considerable Press clamour for bringing back Churchill and a few other outsiders.[2] Nothing much may come of this in peace, for the Prime Minister is an autocrat and has no mind to be dictated to. But if it came to war, I imagine a Coalition would be inevitable.

---

[1] Robert Gordon Menzies, 1894–1978. Born and educated in Australia. Attorney-General, Minister for Railways and Deputy Premier of Victoria, 1932–4. Attorney-General, Commonwealth of Australia, 1934–39. Prime Minister of Australia, 1939–41 (he became Prime Minister in April 1939). Leader of the Opposition, 1943–9. Prime Minister for the second time, 1949–66 (and Minister of External Affairs, 1960–1). Companion of Honour, 1951. Head of the Mission to President Nasser to discuss the future of the Suez Canal, 1956. An Honorary Member of the Other Club, 1959. Knight of the Thistle, 1963. Chancellor of Melbourne University, 1967–72.

[2] On 3 July 1939 almost every newspaper had a leading article urging Chamberlain to bring Churchill into the Cabinet. According to the Communist *Daily Worker* of 4 July 1939, the driving force behind this campaign was not Churchill himself, but 'a curious group headed by Lord Lothian, the Ambassador-Designate to Washington, Lord Astor and Lord Trenchard, former police chief of London'. On 5 July 1939 the London evening *Star* had written: 'It is expected that Mr Churchill will shortly return to the Admiralty. No move would be more likely to convince the Nazis that the British Government is in earnest in its resolve to resist aggression. Reports reaching Whitehall show that even the recent speeches of Lord Halifax and the Opposition spokesmen have failed to dispel the illusion of the Nazis that Britain would remain passive before an attempt to change the status of Danzig by force. Those who know the Nazi psychology best say that the return of Mr Churchill and Mr Eden to the Cabinet would do more than a hundred speeches to convert the Nazis to a belief in the sincerity of our intentions. As an imaginative stroke of policy the reappearance of Mr Churchill at the Admiralty could hardly be bettered. Apart from its effect abroad it would inspire public opinion at home.' Similar accounts were put forward in the *Spectator* on 7 July 1939 and *Time and Tide* on 8 July 1939. But the *New Statesman and Nation's* London diarist noted, also on 8 July 1939: 'In the Cabinet I understand that Mr Chamberlain has strong personal objections to Mr Churchill's inclusion—perhaps the strongest is the fear that it would very quickly be Mr Churchill's Cabinet and that whatever last-minute hopes there are of appeasement over Danzig would be frustrated by his inclusion.'

Henry Channon: diary

(*Robert Rhodes James, 'Chips'*)

6 July 1939

. . . On this Churchill issue the Berrys[1] are themselves divided. Camrose being pro-Churchill, but Kemsley anti. The Astors surprisingly enough, take a strong pro-Churchill line. Lady Astor,[2] frightened by anonymous letters and gossip about the so-called 'Cliveden Set' has thrown over her principles and is urging Chamberlain against his better judgment, to take the plunge. He won't, David Margesson assures me.

Major-General James Marshall-Cornwall[3] to Lord Halifax

(*Foreign Office papers: 371/22974*)

6 July 1939

CONVERSATION WITH COUNT SCHWERIN[4]

Churchill is the only Englishman Hitler is afraid of. He does not take the PM or Lord Halifax seriously, but he places Churchill in the same category as Roosevelt. The mere fact of giving him a leading Ministerial post would convince Hitler that we really mean to stand up to him.

[1] The two brothers, Lord Camrose and Lord Kemsley (William Berry and Gomer Berry), owners respectively of the *Daily Telegraph* and the *Sunday Times*.

[2] Nancy Witcher Langhorne, 1879–1964. Born in Virginia. Married first, in 1897, Robert Gould Shaw (divorced, 1903); second, in 1906, the 2nd Viscount Astor. As the Conservative MP for Plymouth Sutton, 1919–45, she was the first woman to take her seat in the Westminster Parliament. Companion of Honour, 1937. Churchill wrote of her, in 1937: 'She reigns on both sides of the Atlantic in the Old World and the New, at once as a leader of fashionable society, and of advanced feminist democracy. She combines a kindly heart with a sharp and wagging tongue. She embodies the historical portent of the first woman Member of the House of Commons. She denounces the vice of gambling in unmeasured terms, and is closely associated with an almost unrivalled racing stable. She accepts Communist hospitality and flattery, and remains the Conservative member for Plymouth. She does all these opposite things so well and so naturally that the public, tired of criticising, can only gape.' (*Great Contemporaries*, in the essay entitled 'George Bernard Shaw'.)

[3] James Handyside Marshall-Cornwall, 1887–   . Entered Royal Artillery, 1907. Served as an Intelligence Officer in France and Flanders, 1914–18; Military Cross, despatches five times. Attended the Paris Peace Conference, 1919. Intelligence Officer Constantinople, 1920–2. Served with the Shanghai Defence Force, 1927. Military Attaché, Berlin, April 1928–April 1932. Took the surname Marshall-Cornwall, 1929. Director-General, Air and Coast Defence, 1938–9. Knighted, 1940. General Officer Commanding the British Troops, Egypt, 1941; Western Command, 1941–2. Editor-in-Chief, captured German archives, 1948–51. President, Royal Geographical Society, 1954–8. Military historian.

[4] Johann Ludwig (Lutz), Count Schwerin von Krosigk, 1887–1977. Born in Anhalt. Studied law at Oxford University. Served in the financial service of the Prussian Administra-

Send air striking force to France.

Gort[1] head army.

We[2] pointed out to Schwerin the obvious objections to his proposals. Naval demonstrations for instance are a particularly futile way of showing one's teeth, and Winston's entry into the Cabinet might make for discord rather than unity. . . .

Schwerin repeated that we must show our strength if we mean to stand up to Hitler, and that only deeds would impress him. Schwerin reiterated the point that Churchill's admission to the Cabinet would be the most effective measure. Otherwise trouble would start again very soon. . . .

Hitler was convinced that British foreign policy was thoroughly flabby. The fact that we had been floundering for three months in inconclusive negotiations with Russia only confirmed this opinion of his, and the fact that we allowed the Poles to lead in the Danzig negotiations instead of dictating policy to them.

Lord Wolmer to Winston S. Churchill

(*Churchill papers: 8/628*)

7 July 1939

My dear Winston,

How extremely kind of you to send me 'Step by Step' with such a charming inscription. I do appreciate it.

The book is a record of perspicacity and courage on your part. England owes you many apologies.

Yours ever,
Wolmer

---

tion for some years before 1924. Entered the Reich Ministry of Finance, 1924. One of the German delegates at the London Economic Conference, August 1931, and at the Experts Committee on Reparations at Lausanne, December 1931. Financial Secretary of the Reich (Reichsfinanzminister) under Papen, Schleicher and Hitler, June 1932–May 1945. Foreign Secretary during the Dönitz Government, May 1945. Imprisoned by an American military court, 1947; released 1951.

[1] Lord Gort, the Chief of the Imperial General Staff, was not appointed Commander-in-Chief of the British Expeditionary Force until the evening of 3 September 1939, following Britain's declaration of war on Germany. Until then, the position had been left vacant.

[2] Marshall-Cornwall was accompanied by Colonel Beaumont-Nesbitt.

Winston S. Churchill to G. M. Young

(*Churchill papers: 8/626*)

7 July 1939

Here is the note on Magna Carta, which I should be glad if you would alter and improve before I send it to the printer.[1]

I also send you a note on the Tudor Dictatorship, which has drafted amendments upon it. It seems to me that something will be required of this kind, and I am anxious to have your views upon it before I proceed to put it into its final form. Pray let me have it back, as it is my only annotated copy.

Winston S. Churchill to John Wheldon

(*Churchill papers: 8/626*)

7 July 1939
Private

My dear Wheldon,

I am much obliged to you for what you are sending me, to which I am now devoting my attention.

With regard to your wish for a Commission, you have only to let me know to whom you would like me to write on your behalf, and what is the precise point, and I will gladly do so. It is very likely that I may be able to smooth away some difficulties, but let me have exactly what you want me to say.[2]

---

[1] Of Magna Carta, Churchill wrote (*A History of the English-Speaking Peoples*, volume 1, pages 198–9): 'After forty years' experience of the administrative system established by Henry II the men who now confronted John had advanced beyond the magnates of King Stephen's time. They had learned to think intelligently and constructively. In place of the King's arbitrary despotism they proposed, not the withering anarchy of feudal separatism, but a system of checks and balances which would accord the monarchy its necessary strength, but would prevent its perversion by a tyrant or a fool. The leaders of the barons in 1215 groped in the dim light towards a fundamental principle. Government must henceforward mean something more than the arbitrary rule of any man, and custom and the law must stand even above the King. It was this idea, perhaps only half understood, that gave unity and force to the barons' opposition and made the Charter which they now demanded imperishable.'

[2] For Wheldon's military career, see page 104, note 1. He received his Commission on 26 July 1939.

Lieutenant-Colonel Gray[1] to Lord Halifax

(*Foreign Office papers: 371/22974*)

8 July 1939

CONVERSATION WITH COUNT SCHWERIN

I asked him what he thought the effect would be if Winston were included in the Cabinet. He said—there would be a tremendous outcry in Germany: but that Hitler thinks that Churchill is the only dangerous Englishman, and it might perhaps do good, because it might perhaps *make* him realize that Great Britain really intends to fight if there is any further aggression.

Winston S. Churchill to Sir Stafford Cripps

(*Churchill papers: 2/364*)

8 July 1939   Blenheim[2]
Private

Many thanks for your most kind letter which I have carefully weighed.

I am quite sure that any such demarche on my part would be unwise, and would weaken me in any discussion I might have to have with the gentleman in question.

Many thanks for writing.

Neville Chamberlain to his sister

(*Templewood papers*)

8 July 1939

This has been a comparatively quiet week only enlivened by the drive to put Winston into the government. It has been a regular conspiracy in which Mr Maisky has been involved as he keeps in very close touch with Randolph and no doubt Randolph was responsible for the positive statements in the

---

[1] Clive Osric Vere Gray, 1882–1965. 2nd Lieutenant, 1901; on active service on the north-west frontier of India, 1908 (dangerously wounded); in the European War (despatches eight times, DSO). Lieutenant-Colonel, 1918. One of His Majesty's Body Guard, Corps of Gentlemen at Arms from 1932 until his death.

[2] Churchill was at Blenheim from 7 to 10 July 1939, his last visit there before the outbreak of war. The other guests included Consuelo Balsan, Lady Maria Stewart (Lord Londonderry's youngest daughter), and Viscount Ednam (elder son of the 3rd Earl of Dudley).

Mail that it was all settled[1] as well as the less definite paragraphs in the Express. I don't mind them, but I am vexed that Camrose who used to be such a firm supporter should now have committed himself. As soon as I saw the leader in the Telegraph I sent for him and explained just why I was not prepared to invite Winston. I did not convince him, but perhaps the interview was useful as at any rate I was assured that there was no bitterness in his mind. But since his illness Camrose is a changed man.

Winston S. Churchill to Sir Emsley Carr
(Churchill papers: 8/629)

9 July 1939

My dear Emsley Carr,

It gives me great pleasure to receive your letter and to learn that you are satisfied with the articles. I thought the one about the Air was of very great importance, and after I had written it I showed it to Wing Commander Hodsall, who is in charge of ARP at the Home Office, and found that he was in complete agreement. I have also had a letter from Sir John Anderson, to whom I sent a copy, thanking me for the article. I feel therefore that your readers have had good advice on this matter.

In view of the uncertainties which may affect me personally I should like to get the series for 1940 in an advanced condition, or at any rate on the stocks, before the end of September, August and September being the months which I should normally reserve for this work.

[1] On 5 July 1939 the *Daily Mail* Political Correspondent, Wilson Broadbent, published an article which began: 'Mr Winston Churchill's early return to the Cabinet, most probably as First Lord of the Admiralty—a post he held in 1914—is certain. His inclusion in the Cabinet in this post, or some equally important position, has been discussed among leading Ministers for some time. Most of them are agreed that he will be a valuable asset to the National Government. Mr Chamberlain, like Lord Baldwin before him, has always recognised Mr Churchill's merit. In the past, however, there have been differences. These are now at an end. Mr Churchill will be ready to join the Government to fulfil what he regards as a national duty. He is whole-heartedly in support of the Government's foreign policy as stated by Viscount Halifax last week. The Prime Minister will shortly decide when it is convenient to make the necessary changes in the Cabinet to provide a place for Mr Churchill. It is assumed that if Mr Churchill is to become First Lord, Earl Stanhope, present holder of the office, will be transferred to Lord Runciman's post as Lord President of the Council. Lord Runciman, who has not been in the best of health, will probably retire . . .'

Winston S. Churchill to Newman Flower

(Churchill papers: 8/626)

9 July 1939
Private & Confidential

Dear Mr Newman Flower,

You will be glad to know that the 'Story of the English Speaking Peoples' is now practically complete. Four hundred and sixty thousand words are actually in print and more than half has undergone a second revise. I hope, therefore, to let you have the work ready for publication in plenty of time before the end of the year. I have borne in mind throughout the fact that you wish to publish it with illustrations, and consequently have leant upon narrative and episodes rather than dissertation. The American side has been very fully treated. There are, I think, over 70,000 words about the United States and Canada, and the story of the American Civil War is a small book in itself.[1] I thought this was most important to my scheme of making a book which would be acceptable both to English and American readers.

I have come across a great number of illustrations which I think would be suitable and would be very ready to help you in this matter when the time comes.

It has been a comfort at times in this anxious year to retire into the past centuries; but I have had to work very hard, and many a night have sat up until two or three in the morning.[2]

---

[1] The 111-page American Civil War section of *A History of the English Speaking Peoples* was published by Cassells in book form in 1961, three years after the main volume 4 had appeared. Entitled *The American Civil War*, 10,000 copies were published in March 1961, and a further 5,000 copies the following May. No change was made in the text, but Civil War photographs were added.

[2] This was no exaggeration. Kathleen Hill's notes of the end of the working day at Chartwell include the hours for herself, and for Mary Shearburn, the Secretary who had replaced Violet Pearman: on 26 April, 12.30 am for Mary Shearburn (Mrs Hill stayed until 1 am); 29 April, 2.45 am for Mary Shearburn; 30 April, 12.45 am for Mary Shearburn; 1 May, 2.15 am for Mary Shearburn; 2 May, 2.15 am for Mary Shearburn (Mrs Hill until 2 am); 7 May, 2 am (for both); 10 May, 1.30 am for Mary Shearburn; 21 May, 1 am for Mary Shearburn (2 am for Mrs Hill); 22 May, 2.30 am for Mrs Hill; 29 May, 2 am (for both); 30 May, 2.15 for Mary Shearburn; 31 May, 1 am for Mrs Hill; 24 June, 2 am for Mary Shearburn; 29 June, 2 am for Mrs Hill; 14 July, 2.45 am, for Mary Shearburn; 15 July, 1 am for Mary Shearburn and 16 July, 1.15 am for Mrs Hill. The latest hours recorded were during the 4 weeks in which Hitler occupied Prague, 3.15 am for Mrs Hill, and 2.45 am for her deputy, at that time Olive Harrington. Between 25 and 30 August 1939, as the Polish crisis developed, and the work on The History likewise intensified, 12.30 am was the earliest for another typist (Miss E. R. Widgery) and 2 am the latest (for Mary Shearburn), in which secretarial work ceased at Chartwell during six consecutive nights. For each 'Late Duty' Churchill paid an extra 2/6d.

Winston S. Churchill to F. W. Deakin
(*Churchill papers: 8/626*)

10 July 1939

Many thanks for your notes on Richard II and Wyclif. I send you back Richard II hoping you will be able to write in on the text the amendments you think desirable. I have no doubt you are right in wishing them to be made, but I cannot at this stage look it all up myself. You have the points in your mind and please make them as you see fit.

I am going over to Paris late on Thursday night[1] to see the Review, but I shall fly back by the four o'clock on Friday in plenty of time to receive you at Chartwell when I am expecting you.

Could you then bring with you Richard II in a form in which I could send it for a further reprint. I should hope also to have Bullock's amendments to Henry III and Edward I.

If we could run through these together on Friday night and Saturday morning, Book II would be in a very advanced form.

By that time also I shall have Edward III, and we can incorporate your amended Wyclif which I am keeping with me.

Sir Archibald Sinclair to Winston S. Churchill
(*Churchill papers: 2/360*)

10 July 1939
Personal and Confidential

My dear Winston,

You and I are agreed that Parliament ought not in the present critical situation to rise at the end of this, or at the beginning of next, month for a prolonged recess unless some means can be devised for maintaining touch between Ministers and members of all parties in the House of Commons. Moreover, if the situation gets worse during the recess, if there is a public demand for the meeting of Parliament, and if members of Parliament who are closely in touch with the situation sympathise with that demand, there ought to be some simple kind of machinery to enable consultations between Ministers and such members to take place.

You asked me to suggest a plan. My proposal is as follows:—

(a) All Privy Councillors who have been Cabinet Ministers to be invited by the Prime Minister to hold themselves in readiness for consultation during the Recess.

[1] Thursday, 13 July 1939 (see pages 1563–4).

NB. 1. No formal appointment of a Committee by the House of Commons.

2. Of the ex-Cabinet Ministers five are Conservatives, of whom only one (Sir John Gilmour[1]) was pro-Munich; nine are Socialists (including Attlee who as a matter of fact has never been in a Cabinet[2]); and two (Ll G and me) are Liberals.

3. The total number of ex-Cabinet Ministers is sixteen, so that in the event of a meeting with the Prime Minister and five or six other Ministers responsible for Foreign Affairs and Defence, the number present would be about the same as the membership of the Cabinet.

(b) It would be understood that meetings would be arranged by the Prime Minister either on his own initiative or on that of the Leader of the Opposition or of any three or four of the members of the panel.

(c) If the object of a meeting was to persuade the Prime Minister to ask the Speaker to re-call the House of Commons, three things might happen:—

Either (i)   The Prime Minister might consent to make the request to the Speaker;

or (ii)   The Prime Minister might convince those who were present that it would be inadvisable or untimely to recall Parliament;

or (iii) The Prime Minister might refuse to make the request to the Speaker, but others might remain convinced that Parliament ought to meet. In such circumstances agreement would probably be reached to meet again within a few days, and meanwhile everybody present, while bound by the obligation of secrecy in regard to everything that had passed at the meeting, would remain free to say what he thought about recalling Parliament.

NB.   In no case would any vote be taken, and the Prime Minister would of course be free to bring to the meeting as many Ministers and others as he wished.

I attach a list of Privy Councillors in the House of Commons who are not at present members of the Government, distinguishing between those who have, and those who have not, been members of a Cabinet.

---

[1] John Gilmour, 1876–1940. Educated at Edinburgh University and Trinity Hall Cambridge. Conservative MP for East Renfrewshire, 1910–18; for Glasgow Pollock, 1918–40. On active service in South Africa, 1900–1 (despatches twice), and in France, 1914–18 (despatches, DSO). Scottish Unionist Whip, 1919–22 and 1924. Succeeded his father as 2nd Baronet, 1920. Privy Councillor, 1922. Secretary of State for Scotland, 1926–9. Minister of Agriculture and Fisheries, 1931–2. Home Secretary, 1932–5. Minister of Shipping, 1939–40.

[2] From 2 March 1931 to 24 August 1931 Clement Attlee had been Postmaster-General in Ramsay MacDonald's Labour Government. The post had not, however, been in the Cabinet. In 1924, in the first Labour Government, Attlee had served as Under-Secretary of State at the War Office.

Do let me know what you think of this proposal. I have framed it on the assumption that if it was pressed upon the Prime Minister by you, Greenwood, Eden, Lloyd George and me, he would accept it. No other assumption seems worth considering because the House would not at present adopt this or any similar proposal if he asked them to reject it. On the other hand, he would probably hesitate to strain the loyalty of his followers by rejecting a practicable plan for removing a probable source of public anxiety in August and September.

Yours ever,
Archie

Harold Nicolson: diary
(*Nicolson papers*)

11 July 1939

. . . Chamberlain's obstinate exclusion of Churchill from the Cabinet is taken as a sign that he has not abandoned appeasement and that all gestures of resistance are mere bluff.

Sir Samuel Hoare to William Astor[1]
(*Templewood papers*)

11 July 1939

Internal politics here are on the whole quieter. Greenwood[2] has behaved very reasonably and responsibly over China, Danzig and the Anglo-Russian Pact.

The only excitement has been the drive to get Winston into the Government. Your father and mother have been, for some reason, very excited over this attempt—both of them being very anxious to get Winston in on the ground that his presence in the Government would act as a deterrent to Germany. I have adopted with them and other people a completely detached

---

[1] William Waldorf Astor, 1907–1966. Known as Bill'. Son of the 2nd Viscount Astor and Nancy Astor. Educated at Eton and New College, Oxford. Secretary to the 2nd Earl of Lytton on the League of Nations Committee of Enquiry in Manchuria, 1932. Conservative MP for East Fulham, 1935–45, and for Wycombe, 1951–2. Parliamentary Private Secretary to Sir Samuel Hoare, 1936–9. Lieutenant-Commander, RNVR, 1939. Succeeded his father as 3rd Viscount, 1952.

[2] Arthur Greenwood, Deputy Leader of the Labour Party (see page 1455, note 1), and Labour spokesman on Foreign Policy.

attitude, holding as I do the view that these personal matters are solely in the discretion of the Prime Minister.

As a matter of fact, I was convinced that the attempt would fail. Anything that Winston attempts is always overdone, and in this case it was so overdone that it has stirred up a great reaction against him. I believe that if there was a ballot of Conservative Back Bench Members on the subject, four out of five would be against him. This is to some extent the result of the papers of the Left and the important papers of the Right shouting with one voice for his inclusion.

All this has made Neville's position stronger rather than weaker.

Winston S. Churchill to Sir Kingsley Wood [1]

(*Air Ministry papers: 19/26*)

11 July 1939

S OF S

The only big thing you can get *quickly* is the mock-up smaller apparatus for the lambs. Would Dowding like to have (say) 20 by August 15th? Is this possible?

WSC

Neville Chamberlain to his sister

(*Templewood papers*)

12 July 1939

I hear that Winston himself is very depressed and he certainly looked it at the dinner at Buckingham Palace on Monday. In particular he is distressed by a couple of witty articles making fun of the suggestion that he would help matters in the Cabinet which appeared in Truth. [2]

---

[1] This note was passed to Sir Kingsley Wood by Churchill at the end of the meeting of the Air Defence Research sub-committee of the Committee of Imperial Defence. On the following day Kingsley Wood sent a copy to Air Vice-Marshal Peirse, the Deputy Chief of the Air Staff, for his comments.

[2] On 7 July 1939 the whole front page of *Truth* was devoted to belittling the idea of Churchill in the Cabinet. The article began: 'There is on foot an intrigue, backed by a blatant Press campaign, the purpose of which is to enable Mr Winston Churchill, with his satellites holding on to his apron-strings, to muscle into the Cabinet. MPs who are familiar both with these pro-Churchill manoeuvres and with the personalities behind them, pay little or no

Air Vice Marshal Peirse to Sir Kingsley Wood

(*Air Ministry papers: 19/26*)

14 July 1939
Secret

S OF S

I have got Sir Hugh Dowding's views on the point which Mr Winston Churchill raised at the conclusion of the ADR Meeting on 11th July.

2. The result of the recent trials of the RDF air to air set installed in the Battle at Martlesham was, as you are aware, most promising. I have accordingly put in train arrangements for 21 copies of this 'lash-up' set to be made. Four of these sets will be installed in specially screened Blenheims to enable Sir Hugh Dowding to undertake the development of RDF air to air tactics on the highest priority. We hope that the equipment and aircraft for this will be available during the last half of August.

3. A further 17 Blenheims will be screened, and these, with the remainder of the sets (likely to be available in September) will enable a full Squadron to be initially equipped in the event of a sudden emergency after that date.

R. E. C. Peirse

Consuelo Balsan: recollections

('*The Glitter and the Gold*')

14 July 1939

. . . We returned to Paris in time to witness the great military review held there on July 14, the national holiday.

---

attention to either. But as the public may be misled, it is necessary to declare that in the House of Commons itself there is no demand for Mr Churchill's inclusion in the Cabinet outside his particular coterie—numbering less than a dozen—who have been christened "the Glamour Boys". When we find a paragraph in the *Evening Standard* urging as an argument for Mr Churchill's inclusion in the Cabinet that it is supported by the *News Chronicle*, the *Manchester Guardian*, the *Yorkshire Post*, and the *Daily Mirror*, we realise what the game is. Those organs of public opinion—to give them a courtesy title—would seize any weapon with which to attack the Prime Minister, and their devices can be dismissed as of no account. The *Daily Telegraph* is in a different category, and though it has adopted the same line as those of its contemporaries I have named, assumes that it is not consciously a participator in the plot. But however unexceptionable its motives may be, its pro-Churchill reasoning is not. On July 3 the *Daily Telegraph* had a long leader which read like a love-lyric, with Mr Churchill in the role of the beloved.' For an extract from this 'love-lyric', see page 1544, note 1.

Winston Churchill, a guest of honour[1] in the reviewing stand, said to me afterwards, when I commented on the large tanks that had shaken the Champs Elysées in their progress: 'The Government had to show the French that their economies had been transferred from the idleness of the stocking to the safety of the tank.'

William Chenery to Winston S. Churchill
(*Churchill papers: 8/634*)

14 July 1939   Collier's,
                                                        New York

Dear Mr Churchill,

Mr Beck[2] brought me today the book you so generously sent me. I am grateful to you and I am old enough to be thrilled at the thought that three days ago 'Step by Step' was in your hands in London. America is closer to Britain in time than most of us imagined practicable so soon and I believe closer in sympathy than at any moment prior to April 1917.

I shall treasure your book, not least of all because more clearly than other statesmen you discerned the actual meaning of events. I still hope profoundly that war can be and will be honourably avoided. If it is, your frank speech will surely have aided mightily in the achievement of peace.

I am hoping soon to receive the articles on which you are at work. With appreciation and regards, I am

Sincerely yours,
William L. Chenery

Neville Chamberlain to his sister
(*Templewood papers*)

15 July 1939   Chequers

There are more ways of killing a cat than strangling it, and if I refuse to take Winston into the Cabinet to please those who say it would frighten

---

[1] Churchill's flight to Paris had led to a certain unease, as shown by a proposed Parliamentary question to which the Air Ministry were asked to draft an answer, on 18 July 1939, as to the delaying of the 'last service to Paris on Thursday last for the benefit of Mr and Mrs Winston Churchill' (*Air Ministry papers, 18/26*).

[2] James Montgomery Beck, Jr, 1892–1973. Born in Philadelphia. Son of a Solicitor General to the United States. Educated at Princeton. Associated with the American Motion Picture Producers Association, 1928–35. President of the English Speaking Union of Newport, Rhode Island, 1958–66. In 1928 he married a niece of Margot Asquith (see page 906, note 1).

Hitler, it doesn't follow that the idea of frightening Hitler or rather of convincing him that it would not pay him to use force need be abandoned.

In fact I have little doubt that Hitler knows quite well that we mean business. The only question to which he is not sure of the answer is whether we mean to attack him as soon as we are strong enough. . . .

Winston S. Churchill: unsent letter to a constituent

(*Churchill papers: 2/360*)

17 July 1939   Chartwell

I have taken no part in the movement in favour of broadening His Majesty's Government, in which my name has been mentioned. But in view of the assertions now so loudly made that I am concerned in an agitation to drive Mr Chamberlain from office, I think it right to state that this has not been, and is not, my wish, nor I am sure, the wish of any of those Conservatives with whom I am in political contact.

From the moment when the Prime Minister entered upon a policy of forming a strong block of peace-minded States in harmony with the Covenant of the League of Nations, in order to resist further acts of aggression, no major difference in principle has existed between me and the Government.

These are not times when considerations of tactics and personal interest should be a bar to plain speaking; and I therefore feel it is my duty to place on record that I am willing to serve under Mr Chamberlain on the basis of the policy declared by him and by Lord Halifax, and give him any loyal help in my power. The only condition which I should feel bound to make would be that the process of broadening the Government should include those Conservative ex-Ministers who have consistently advocated courses similar to that on which the Government is now embarked, and who have testified to their convictions on important occasions. Such a step would, to the best of my belief, have a unifying effect throughout this country, and be welcomed in all countries friendly to Great Britain. It might have a restraining effect on dangerous intentions elsewhere. It would prevent the growth of a schism at home, which might otherwise be serious. It would prepare the way and render more smooth that further broadening of the Government, which is upon all sides admitted to be necessary, should unhappily the Prime Minister's efforts to prevent war not be attended by success.

I feel sure that my fellow-countrymen will not think the less of me for speaking with the simplicity and frankness which the gravity of the hour requires from all.

Lord Rothermere to Winston S. Churchill
(*Churchill papers: 2/360*)

17 July 1939   Monte Carlo

My dear Winston,

I can very well see a great responsibility may be placed upon you at an early date. Everyone, including especially myself, will wish you to be in the finest fettle when the day arrives.

Shall you and I renew the old bet, say for six or twelve months from the day of the receipt of this letter. If so I bet you £600 that you will not be able to run from the given date to the same date next year without shewing your predilection for cognac. Is it a deal?

Carefully handled I don't think there will be war over Danzig. Hitler left upon me the indelible impression that overtly he will never take the initiative in resorting to bloodshed. I suppose when I had my long talk with him he mentioned this latter at least a dozen times.

All the same we must go on arming night and day using up if necessary whatever available resources we can lay our hands on.

I think Hitler has been badly handled. Instead of the language of reproach and rebuke constantly applied to him, I should have tried out the language of butter because these Dictators live in such an atmosphere of adulation and awestruck reverence that the language of guns may not go nearly so far as the language of butter.

I have never yet seen an authoritative statement made in England complimenting Hitler on his tremendous record of achievement in Germany.

Yours always,
Harold

PS. On the few occasions on which I have written to Hitler I have always interlarded my letter with plenty of compliments. Strange as it may seem he is a shy and solitary man. How few people know this.

Sir Kingsley Wood to Winston S. Churchill
(*Air Ministry papers: 19/26*)

17 July 1939
Personal & Secret

My dear Winston,

I have been in touch with Dowding and Peirse since the ADR Meeting on Tuesday, and I think that you will be interested to see a copy of the instructions which have now been issued.

Yours ever,

Victor Cazalet: diary

(*Robert Rhodes James: 'Victor Cazalet, A Portrait'*)

18 July 1939

. . . To lunch with Winston. He is very gloomy. 60 to 40 on War. As usual perfect host.

Winston S. Churchill to Alan Bullock

(*Churchill papers: 8/626*)

18 July 1939

Dear Mr Bullock,

Sir Edward Marsh, who has been reading the proofs for grammar etc, makes various comments on Henry VI which you kindly checked for facts. I have marked the particular points, and shall be much obliged if you will attend to them.

You will see that I have recast Henry VI largely in accordance with your corrections. Perhaps on reading it through again you may see further points besides those mentioned by Sir Edward Marsh.

Please mark your further corrections in black ink.

Many thanks for your full notes on Henry III. I have recast the chapter and sent it for a reprint.

I am looking forward very much to receiving Edward I. It is the only important link now missing up to the Napoleonic Wars.

Winston S. Churchill to G. M. Young

(*Churchill papers: 8/626*)

18 July 1939

My dear Mr Young,

I have now sent Book I, 47,000 words, for a further revise. It has still to undergo my final reading. As you know, I keep my eye fresh for this, otherwise one cannot spot errors. Meanwhile anything that may be suggested to you by the various documents I have sent can stand by for inclusion at the last minute.

Deakin has gone to camp, but is free from the end of July till Thursday, August 10, when he goes on his holiday. He will be coming down here a good deal in that period, and I am hoping to clean up the proofs as far as the nineteenth century by then. I wonder if you could give me a few days in this interval? I should greatly like it. Pray let me know.

I am not satisfied with Cromwell, and should like to re-do it then after discussion with you. Broadly speaking, I remain hostile to him, and consider that he should be condemned as a representative of the dictatorships against which all the whole movement of English history has been continuous.[1]

Sir Kingsley Wood to Winston S. Churchill

(*Air Ministry papers: 19/26*)

18 July 1939

My dear Winston,

As you may be aware, in recognition of the increasing importance of the Auxiliary Air Force and the Royal Air Force Volunteer Reserve in the scheme of national defence, we have recently decided upon the introduction of distinctive badges which could be used, with civilian dress, by members of these two organisations.

I am enclosing one of these badges which I hope you will accept as Honorary Air Commodore of No 615 (County of Surrey) Auxiliary Air Force Squadron.

Yours ever,
Kingsley Wood

[1] Churchill wrote (in *A History of the English-Speaking Peoples*, volume 2, pages 250–2): '. . . the dictatorship of Cromwell differed in many ways from modern patterns. Although the Press was gagged and the Royalists ill-used, although judges were intimidated and local privileges curtailed, there was always an effective vocal opposition, led by convinced Republicans. There was no attempt to make a party around the personality of the Dictator, still less to make a party state. Respect was shown for private property, and the process of fining the Cavaliers and allowing them to compound by surrendering part of their estates was conducted with technical formality. Few people were put to death for political crimes, and no one was cast into indefinite bondage without trial.' But, Churchill added: 'If in a tremendous crisis Cromwell's sword had saved the cause of Parliament, he must stand before history as a representative of dictatorship and military rule who, with all his qualities as a soldier and a statesman, is in lasting discord with the genius of the English race.'

Julian Amery: [1] *recollections*

(*Letter to the author, 30 October 1981*)

[18 July 1939]   Chartwell

I stayed at Chartwell for the 18th/19th July. Clarissa [2] took me there to escort her to John Astor's ball at Hever—I think the last great social occasion before the war.

Winston talked about nothing but the prospect of war over dinner and went on about it over the brandy until Clemmie ordered us out. He came to the ball and I sat close to him while he watched the firework display over the lake.

I slept the night in what I think was Randolph's room. I must have gone to bed after the dawn and was still in the room when he came in to see me. I told him how much I admired Randolph with whom I had debated at the Oxford Union a few weeks earlier, to which he said 'he has great guns but no ammunition'!

I seem to remember that before dinner the night of the ball he played one of the fashionable games of the day with Clemmie, either Chinese Chequers or Peggety.

Winston S. Churchill to Lord Rothermere

(*Churchill papers: 2/367*)

19 July 1939

It is nice of you to have such friendly thoughts about me. I accept the proposal which you make, in view of the many uncertainties of the future. The operative date will be to-morrow, July 20.

You may well be right about Danzig; but does it really matter very much what the thing is called? Evidently a great 'crunch' is coming, and all preparations in Germany are moving forward ceaselessly to some date in August.

[1] Julian Amery, 1919–   . Son of L. S. Amery. Educated at Eton and Balliol College, Oxford. A war correspondent in the Spanish Civil War, 1938–9. Attaché, British Legation, Belgrade (on special missions in Bulgaria, Turkey, Rumania and the Middle East), 1939–40. Sergeant, Royal Air Force, 1940–1; commissioned, and transferred to the Army, 1941; on active service in Egypt, Palestine and the Adriatic, 1941–2. Liaison officer (behind German lines) to the Albanian resistance movement, 1944. Churchill's personal representative with General Chiang Kai-Shek, 1945. Unsuccessful Conservative candidate for Preston, July 1945; Conservative MP for Preston North, 1950–66; for Brighton Pavilion since 1969, Parliamentary Under-Secretary of State, War Office, 1957–8; Colonial Office, 1958–60. Privy Councillor, 1960. Secretary of State for Air, 1960–2. Minster of Aviation, 1962–4; of Public Building and Works, 1970; for Housing and Construction, 1970–2. Minister of State, Foreign and Commonwealth Office, 1972–4. In 1948 he published his Albanian recollections, *Sons of the Eagle*. Biographer of Joseph Chamberlain's career from 1901–14 (in succession to J. L. Garvin). In 1950 he married Catherine, daughter of Harold Macmillan.

[2] Churchill's niece, see page 4, note 2.

Whether H will call it off or not is a psychological problem which you can probably judge as well as any living man. I fear he despises Chamberlain, and is convinced that the reason he does not broaden his Government is because he means to give in once Parliament has risen. But I do not know whether, in the present state of public opinion, this will in fact come to pass.

I am remaining entirely quiescent at the present time. Like you, I have given my warnings, and I am consoled for being condemned to inaction by being free from responsibility.

I am very glad to have my 'History of the English-speaking Peoples' to work at. It is now nearly finished, 480,000 words being in print. I shall look forward to sending you a copy.

Should I find my way to the Riviera in the latter part of August, I will propose myself to spend a night with you, if you can find room.

Kathleen Hill to Winston S. Churchill
(*Churchill papers: 2/376*)

19 July 1939

Mr Richards has telephoned to say he has seen Dr Beneš, who would be very much pleased to attend a private luncheon at which he would speak quite frankly. He could attend such a luncheon any day next week, with M Masaryk.

Shall I suggest Thursday next week, as you will be going to London for the Other Club?[1]

Winston S. Churchill to Sir Kingsley Wood
(*Air Ministry papers: 19/26*)

20 July 1939   Chartwell
Secret

My dear Kingsley Wood,

Many thanks for your letter of July 17, which I have burned, together with the enclosure. I am very glad we have got our teeth into something as a result of the ADR Committee.

I thank you also for the badge which you have sent me. If you and Neville will wear it, I will wear it too—at least until the Churchill badge becomes obligatory!

Let me congratulate you upon the very fine manner in which you are standing up to your great task.

---

[1] Beneš and Masaryk lunched with Churchill at the Savoy Hotel on Thursday 27 July 1939. The lunch was held under the auspices of the Focus (see page 1579).

The protection of the factories, both by active and passive defence, seems to be No 1. If we can only hatch them out, we can probably get through.

Yours vy sincerely,
Winston S. Churchill

Winston S. Churchill to E. L. Spears
(*Churchill papers: 2/367*)

20 July 1939

I have just finished the book.[1] I think it a great work, and one of the finest I have read in the literature of the War. I marked the copy as I went along, and would gladly have a talk with you about it.

I am so rarely in London now, and so busy on my 'History' that I find it difficult to make appointments, but why do you not come down and lunch with me one day? You have only to arrange it with my secretary.

Your book ought certainly to be read by all British and French field officers and upwards—especially upwards!

Winston S. Churchill to Alan Bullock
(*Churchill papers: 8/626*)

20 July 1939

Dear Mr Bullock,

I send you the print of Henry III, after I have carefully considered your emendations. I will now add to it the final piece.

The story goes well in the present form, but will you kindly read it again for accuracy, challenging any points on which you do not agree.

At this stage I am not cutting out any passages which have already been printed but which may be thought somewhat irrelevant, eg the Albigenses.

Winston S. Churchill to Sir Edward Marsh
(*Churchill papers: 8/626*)

20 July 1939

Your corrections keep on coming to hand, and I copy them all religiously on to my text. They are a lesson in good sense and good English.

Will you think over some rules to be given to the printer about Capitals? I am for the fewest possible. 'State' should only have a capital when it has a definite title, ie State of Virginia; 'Royal' surely only at the most ceremonial

---

[1] *Prelude to Victory* by Brigadier-General E. L. Spears, with an Introduction by the Rt Hon Winston S. Churchill, PC, MP. (See also page 1005, note 2.)

moments. 'North, south, east and west', no capitals except when they have a significance apart from geography. 'Realm', no capitals except in the title of an Act, like DORA.[1] We have such a lot of these words that the pages will be disfigured unless a strict rule is instituted.

I am staggering along to the end of this job, and am glad to have found the strength to have accomplished it.

Winston S. Churchill to General Gamelin
(*Churchill papers: 2/365*)

21 July 1939

You received very kindly the suggestion I made of visiting another sector of the Maginot Line. Upon reflection, I think I should like to see the Rhine front, as I know nothing of that country, whereas I have seen a lot of Flanders. If it would be in no way inconvenient, I should like very much to come about August 14, assuming all is quiet, and I should like to bring with me General Spears, MP, who is so well known to you.

I trust that all plans are being made to have the closest arrangements between the French and British munitionaire about the supply of steel forgings, etc. Should war come, I expect those other people will be able to fire at the same rate for a good many months without slackening, as they did last time.

It was a great pleasure for me to see the splendid parade of the French Army and the French Empire on July 14, and if I may say so, to feel your hand upon this situation, which clearly approaches another climax.

Compton Mackenzie:[2] *memoirs*
('*Octave Eight*')

23 July 1939

There must have been three dozen guests lunching at Taplow Court

[1] The Defence of the Realm Act (August 1914).

[2] Edward Montague Compton Mackenzie, 1883–1972. Known as 'Monty'. An infant prodigy, he taught himself to read at 22 months. Educated at St Paul's and Magdalen College, Oxford. Novelist; author of a hundred books. Editor of *The Gramophone*. Converted to Roman Catholicism in the Spring of 1914. On active service, 1914–18, on Sir Ian Hamilton's staff at the Dardanelles, and as an intelligence officer in the Aegean. He described his experiences in *Greek Memories*, for which he was prosecuted under the Official Secrets Act. His answer to prosecution was *Water on the Brain*, a satire about the Secret Service. After the abdication of Edward VIII he published *The Windsor Tapestry*. Deeply committed to Scottish Nationalism, he found a home in the Hebridean Island of Barra in the Second World War, commanding the island's Home Guard. Author of biographical sketches of Roosevelt, Beneš, Pericles and Bonnie Prince Charlie. The first volume of his memoirs, *My Life and Times*, was published in 1963, followed by annual volumes until 1971: the volumes being a tribute to his phenomenal memory.

on that louring Sunday, July 23rd. Besides the large dining-table there were several small tables for the lunchers. I had the luck to find myself at the table with Winston Churchill and Lady Balniel.[1]

I was sharply aware of the overriding question at the back of Churchill's mind. Was war coming? I recall saying I hoped if war did come that the British Government would behave more sensibly over Ireland than in the last war. He flushed and said almost truculently,

'We cannot let down those who have remained faithful to the Union Jack,' and then perhaps feeling he was talking too much like a Conservative candidate in the Khaki election of 1900 the blue eyes twinkled and he said,

'I've invented a wonderful new tank.'

We asked what kind of a tank it was.

'It can dig itself in and turn itself into a machine-gun post if required.'

Neville Chamberlain to his sister

(Templewood papers)

23 July 1939   Chequers

. . . One thing is I think clear namely that Hitler has concluded that we mean business and that the time is not ripe for the major war. Therein he is fulfilling my expectations. Unlike some of my critics I go further and say the longer the war is put off the less likely it is to come at all as we go on perfecting our defences and building up the defences of our allies.

That is what Winston and Co never seem to realise. You don't need offensive forces sufficient to win a smashing victory. What you want are defensive forces sufficiently strong to make it impossible for the other side to win except at such a cost as to make it not worth while. That is what we are doing and though at present the German feeling is it is not worth while *yet* they will presently come to realise that it never *will* be worth while, then we can talk. But the time for talk hasn't come yet because the Germans haven't yet realised that they can't get what they want by force and that is why I regret these premature disclosures.

[1] Mary Katherine Cavendish, 1903–   . 3rd daughter of Lord Richard Cavendish, and niece of the 9th Duke of Devonshire. Her sister Elizabeth married the 5th Marquess of Salisbury. Her sister Diana married Robert Boothby. She married Lord Balniel (later 28th Earl of Crawford) in 1925. Her son Lord Balniel (born 1927) served as Minister of State for Foreign and Commonwealth Affairs from 1972 to 1974. Her uncle Lord John Cavendish was killed in action in France on 20 October 1914.

Meanwhile there is I think a definite détente. Craigie[1] has with great skill got an agreement with the Japs about the preliminary formula and if only a little restraint can be exercised on our side the inflammation should gradually subside.

As for the Churchill episode it has in Joe Kennedy's picturesque phrase 'Fallen out of bed' and although I see Garvin in an insufferably dull and boring article tries to keep it alive it has lost all life and even Camrose has now dropped it in the Telegraph.[2]

Winston S. Churchill to Sir Edward Marsh
(Churchill papers: 8/626)

24 July 1939

My dear Eddie,

I send you three quarters of the chapter on Henry VIII and shall be very much obliged if you can read it for me as soon as convenient. Will you write your corrections either in pencil or in green ink so as to distinguish them from my many emendations. I am sending you the only corrected copy which I possess as it will save an extra reprint if I can send it to the printers plus your remarks.

[1] Robert Leslie Craigie, 1883–1959. Entered the Foreign Office, 1907. British Representative, Inter-Allied Blockade Committee, 1916–18. First Secretary, Washington, 1920–3; transferred to the Foreign Office, 1923; Counsellor, 1928; Assistant Under-Secretary of State, 1934–7. Knighted. 1936. Privy Councillor, 1937. Ambassador to Japan, 1937–41. UK Representative to the United Nations War Crimes Commission, 1945–8.

[2] But the Press demands for Churchill's inclusion in the Government had not ceased entirely. On 24 July 1939 the main leader in the *Edinburgh Evening News* began: 'It is one of the most extraordinary developments of our somewhat feverish public life to-day that Liberals continue to urge the inclusion of Mr Churchill in the Cabinet. It is pointed out by one of the leading Liberal newspapers that there is a volume of opinion that by taking Mr Churchill into his Cabinet Mr Chamberlain could win for his Government the wider confidence that it lacks and needs, and that such a step on the Prime Minister's part would be regarded not as a sign of weakness but as a proof that he is determined to carry his policy to success.' The leader writer added: 'There can be no doubt whatever that in the particular matter of Germany Mr Churchill has been unerringly well informed, but when he started out on his outspoken criticism there was still a strong belief in some influential quarters that a reasonable settlement might be reached with Germany. That belief was destroyed when Germany by an overwhelming display of force seized Austria, Bohemia, and Moravia.' Letters, urging Churchill's inclusion in the Cabinet appeared in the *Leeds Mercury* and the *Daily Sketch* (24 July), the *Yorkshire Observer* (25 July) and both the *Yorkshire Post* and *Nottingham Journal* (26 July). An appeal for both Churchill and Eden to be brought back into the Cabinet was published in the *Daily Telegraph* on July 28, from Mark Patrick, the Conservative MP for Tavistock since 1931, and former Parliamentary Private Secretary to Sir Samuel Hoare at both the India Office (1933–4) and the Foreign Office (1935). Patrick wrote: 'Many people who till lately had not lost a rather vague sense of optimism have come at last clearly to realise the immediate dangers of the times, and, having realised them, they wish simply and naturally that all the best brains and the stoutest hearts we can command should be in the actual service of the State.'

Kathleen Hill to Winston S. Churchill

(*Churchill papers: 7/56*)

24 July 1939

Sir James Hawkey says he has recently been inspecting some of the permanent trenches at Woodford and Wanstead and district, and the disgraceful part of the work is the narrow entrance, which consists merely of a hole, about 3 ft square, with just an ordinary ladder. It would be next to impossible for elderly people or children to scramble down this ladder quickly, especially in the event of a sudden attack, and there is no doubt it would cause a great deal of panic.

The authorities say that in the event of a war, a proper ramp would no doubt be provided, but of course this is absurd, as in the event of war probably the necessary labour would not be available, nor would Hitler give us the warning to get these things done!

K H

General Sir Edmund Ironside: diary

(*Ironside papers*)

25 July 1939

I made a night of it with Winston Churchill at Chartwell. I dined alone with him and then we sat talking till 5 am this morning.

What a man. Whisky and cigars all the time. A fascinating house overlooking the Weald of Kent. He inherited the house from someone[1] and has made it worth living in. His own room is very big, some 60 ft long and is like a barn with its old rafters and beams. Crammed with books and papers and notes. He remarked that he would have to pull in his horns considerably if he ever took office, because he would have to cease making money by writing. Last September, had there been a war, he would have been given the Admiralty. Now he might even be Prime Minister and perhaps the War Office. He had made friends with Belisha, because he says that it was Belisha who got conscription through, 'taking his life in his hands'. He nearly

---

[1] Chartwell had not been inherited, but bought in 1922 (for £5,000). Churchill found this sum from part of the publisher's advance for the first volume of his war memoirs, *The World Crisis*. This advance consisted of £9,000 from the English publisher (Thornton Butterworth), £5,000 from the American publisher (Scribner), £5,000 for *The Times* serial, £3,000 for the American serial and £3,000 for the Foreign rights. These sums also covered the further £15,000 which Churchill paid for rebuilding and decorating Chartwell according to a plan drawn up by the architect Philip Tilden. Churchill raised a further £10,750 in 1923 by the sale of his London house at 2 Sussex Square. At the time of the purchase of Chartwell, he also held stocks and shares to the value of £60,760. In September 1981 the money equivalent of £5,000 was in excess of £80,000.

got the sack and acted with great courage. He has had repeated conversations
with Belisha, who he says, repeats conversations pell-mell.

Neville Chamberlain is not a war Prime Minister. He is a pacifist at heart.
He has a firm belief that God has chosen him as an instrument to prevent this
threatened war. He can never get this out of his mind. He is not against
Winston, but he believes that chances may still arrive for averting war, and he
thinks that Winston might be so strong in a Cabinet that he would be prevented from acting. The PM has inspiration that he will be the instrument
for preventing war. He was smothered in an avalanche of letters after
Munich, thanking him for having averted war. Winston thinks that Munich
was a terrible disgrace.

Winston considered that it was now too late for any appeasement. The
deed was signed and Hitler is going to make war. He walked about in front
of the map and demonstrated his ideas, repeating 'You are destined to play a
great part, you will be C in C. You must be clear on what is going to happen':—

   (i)   The crippling or annihilation of Poland
  (ii)   The employment of Italy to create diversions. Mussolini has sold his
        country for his job
 (iii)   The capture of Egypt, chiefly by Italian forces
 (iv)   A pressing on to the Black Sea via Roumania
  (v)   An alliance with Russia, when the latter sees how the land lies.

I told Winston that I was sure that we were in for a bad time and that we
should have to have guts to withstand the first German and Italian rush.
We had no considered plans. No plans to deal with the war in general. Even
the hazy idea of attacking the Italians had not been put into even a framework. He showed me a paper that he had written on the Mediterranean,
praying for active action there and not a solemn bottling up of each end. I
told him about my difficulties with Pound,[1] now the First Sea Lord. He said
that he was horrified at the appearance of Pound, limping around as lame
as anything.

Winston then produced the idea of putting a Squadron of battleships into
the Baltic. It would paralyse the Germans and immobilize many German

---

[1] Alfred Dudley Pickman Rogers Pound, 1877–1943. Entered Navy, 1891. Torpedo
Lieutenant, 1902. Captain, 1914. Second Naval Assistant to Lord Fisher, December 1914–
May 1915. Flag Captain, HMS *Colossus*, 1915–17. Took part in the Battle of Jutland. Served
on the Admiralty Staff, 1917–19. Director of Plans Division, Admiralty, 1922. Commanded
the Battle Cruiser Squadron, 1929–32. Knighted, 1933. Second Sea Lord, 1932–5. Commander-in-Chief, Mediterranean, 1936–9. Admiral of the Fleet, 1939. First Sea Lord and
Chief of the Naval Staff, 1939–43. He declined a peerage in 1943, on account of his lack of
means. Order of Merit, 1943.

divisons. The submarine had been dealt with & would no longer be a menace. This idea of British ships in the Baltic was revolutionary and I was very surprised at how Winston was so navally-minded. All his schemes came back to the use of the Navy. It ran through my head that here was a grand strategist imagining things and the Navy itself making no plans whatever. Quite definitely, the man who is now First Sea Lord had no plan for his Mediterranean fleet when he was in command of it. He could give me no idea of any offensive plan for dealing with Italy. I am sure there is none now.

E. M. B. Ingram[1] *to Winston S. Churchill*

(*Churchill papers: 8/633*)

25 July 1939   Foreign Office

Dear Mr Churchill,

Many thanks for the typescript of your article entitled 'What of the Tyrol?' which your secretary sent me yesterday. . . .

3. . . . If I might be permitted a general criticism of the article, it is that you seem to lay greater emphasis on the mess Mussolini has got his nationals into through his Axis policy than on the cynicism of Hitler in his apparent abandonment of his co-racials. Personally I think more is to be gained by showing up Hitler for a villain than Mussolini for a mug.

4. This letter is of course a private one and does not commit either myself or the Foreign Office to any responsibility for your article, nor does it necessarily imply our approval of its tone and substance.[2]

Yours sincerely,
E. M. B. Ingram

[1] Ernest Maurice Berkeley Ingram, 1890–1941. Educated at Eton and King's College, Cambridge. General Staff, War Office, 1914–18. Entered the Foreign Office, 1919. Chargé d'Affaires, Berlin, 1926 and 1927; in Peking, 1931, 1933 and 1934. Counsellor, 1932. Chargé d' Affaires in Rome, 1934, 1936 and 1937. Foreign Office, 1938–9. Diplomatic Adviser, Ministry of Economic Warfare, 1939–41.

[2] Churchill's article was published in the *Daily Mirror* on 27 July 1939, with the changed title: 'Hitler Sells the Pass!' Its theme was that, in agreeing to remove the German-speaking peoples of the Tyrol to Germany, and to allow the Tyrol both to remain inside Italy, and to be populated with Italians, Hitler was so intent on war as to be willing to pay the price of his convictions and utterances in order 'to bind Mussolini to his chariot-wheels'. Even in Switzerland, Churchill pointed out, rifles and ammunition had been distributed to half a million soldiers 'to keep at their own homes'. His article ended: 'In this part of Europe, as in all countries which border upon Nazidom, the fear of being the victim of a sudden lightening attack by Germany dominates the minds not only of Governments but of peoples. Who shall say these fears are groundless while one man, with his Party confederates, his political police and his astrologers, holds the fate of all Europe in his hands? And who will say that this is the moment for the British House of Commons to separate for a three-months holiday?' (*Churchill papers: 8/650*).

Winston S. Churchill to E. M. B. Ingram

(*Foreign Office papers: 371/23809*)

26 July 1939

I am very much obliged for your specific comments, which I have adopted. Generally speaking, I still have hopes of detaching Italy.

General Sir Edmund Ironside: diary

(*Ironside papers*)

27 July 1939

I keep thinking of Winston Churchill down at Westerham, full of patriotism and ideas for saving the Empire. A man who knows that you must act to win. You cannot remain supine and allow yourself to be hit indefinitely. Winston must be chafing at the inaction. I keep thinking of him walking up and down the room.

Lord Kemsley: notes of an interview with Hitler [1]

(*Premier papers: 1/332*)

27 July 1939   Bayreuth

Lord Kemsley said that he was the owner of a large number of newspapers in England, and had used all his influence in consistent support of the Prime Minister. . . . He had met Mr Chamberlain a short time after his return from Munich, and he was absolutely convinced that Mr Chamberlain attached tremendous importance to the document which had been signed by Herr Hitler and himself. He looked upon the Munich Agreement not merely as a settlement of the Sudeten matter, but as the forerunner of a different relationship with Germany in the future.

Herr Hitler talked about the strength of the Opposition to the Prime Minister, and referred particularly to Mr Winston Churchill and his powers of expression. Lord Kemsley replied that in his opinion far more notice was taken abroad of the Opposition than in England, and whilst giving away every credit to Mr Winston Churchill for his ability as a writer and as a speaker, he reminded Herr Hitler that Mr Churchill had been unfortunate in his campaigns on at least four occasions in the past, starting with the Abdication of King Edward VIII.

[1] On 23 July 1939 Sir Nevile Henderson wrote to Sir Horace Wilson: 'I gave Kemsley my advice, for what it is worth, as to the line he should take' (*Premier papers: 1/3232:*).

As regards the Opposition. Believe me, you worry much more about it than we do. In England we have freedom of speech and a free press. You never seem to appreciate that virulent attacks are made even on the Prime Minister—sometimes much more serious than the references to Germany. But the Prime Minister still survives. You will never understand England unless you think of Neville Chamberlain as our Führer, as we have to think of the Führer as your Neville Chamberlain.

Harold Nicolson: diary

(*Nicolson papers*)

27 July 1939

A luncheon of the Focus is held at the Savoy Hotel in honour of Beneš who has returned from the United States. Winston Churchill takes the chair. . . .[1]

Winston makes a magnificent speech proposing Beneš's health and Beneš replies in rather ungainly English thanking him and us.

Winston S. Churchill to General Georges

(*Churchill papers: 2/365*)

29 July 1939

I am greatly obliged by your letter. General Spears and I will arrive in Paris on the 14th by the mid-day 'plane. We should like to call upon you in the early afternoon and make our way to Strasbourg thereafter. We presume that at Strasbourg we could pay our respects to the General at any hour convenient on the 15th.

I am particularly anxious not to be in the way of anything that may be happening at this time, so that I should quite understand a sudden cancellation of any arrangements that may be made. General Spears tells me that you have already written to him and whatever you say we will do.

I look forward very much, if it is not at all inconvenient, to a conversation with you in Paris on the afternoon of the 14th at whatever hour may be fixed. Will you very kindly convey my respects to General Gamelin.

---

[1] The other guests included Sir Archibald Sinclair, Anthony Eden, Arthur Henderson, Basil Liddell Hart, Lady Rhondda (editor of *Time and Tide*), Harold Nicolson, Henry Wickham Steed, J. L. Clynes, Lord Cecil of Chelwood, Lord Lytton, Megan Lloyd George, Paul Emrys Evans and Duncan Sandys.

Winston S. Churchill to Lord Wolmer
(Selborne papers)

29 July 1939

Try to come on Wednesday; because the scattering of Parliament is a serious snub.

Yours ever,
W

Neville Chamberlain to his sister
(Templewood papers)

30 July 1939   Chequers

. . . All my information indicates that Hitler now realises that he can't grab anything else without a major war and has decided therefore to put Danzig into cold storage. On the other hand he would feel that with all these demonstrations here, mobilization of the fleet, territorials and militia men training, bombers flying up and down France, he must do something to show he is not frightened. I should not be at all surprised therefore, to hear of movements of large bodies of troops near the Polish frontier, great flights of bombers and a crop of stories of ominous preparations, commandeering of buildings and cars, warning of doctors, calling up of civilians and so forth. That is part of the war of nerves and no doubt will send Winston into hysterics. But to summon Parliament to ask questions and to demand counter measures is to play straight into Hitler's hands and give the world the impression that we are in a panic.

Lord Wolmer to Winston S. Churchill
(Selborne papers)

31 July 1939

I am afraid I do not quite agree with you and Anthony about this. The assumption is I take it that Neville, having got rid of the House, proposes to do another Munich. Even if this were true I cannot believe that he would be deterred from making an agreement which he considered right, by anything that was said or done in the House of Commons. The House is so obedient to him that he can rely on securing a big majority for any policy he may like to propose.

The real tribunal before which he has to justify himself is the bar of public opinion, and that is in session whether the House of Commons is or not. Therefore, the demand that the House shall continue to sit seems to me unreal and pin-pricking.

Chartwell Literary Account: notes
(*Churchill papers: 8/639*)

31 July 1939

1st	Cost of taking Secretary to Wimborne[1] Dorset, for week-end, fares, accommodation etc.	£3. 10. 0.
3rd	Dictation in car London–Chartwell.	
4th	Mr Deakin stayed for one night.	
6th	Dictation in car to London.	
7th	Cost of taking Secretary to Woodstock, hotel bill, fares, etc.	£4. 0. 0.
	Telegrams sent from Blenheim.	19. 6.
,,	Cost of fetching proofs by car from Westerham.	3. 6.
10th	Lunch to Dr Revesz (Literary Agent) and Mrs Ogden Mills[2] (New York Herald Tribune).[3]	

[1] Churchill and his wife were again the guests, as they had been in May 1938 (see pages 1036 note 1 and 1045 note 2) of Lord and Lady Cranborne, at Manor House, Cranborne, Dorset, halfway between Salisbury and Wimborne Minister, and two miles from Wimborne St. Giles.

[2] Margaret Ogden Mills, widow of Ogden Livingston Mills, Republican Congressman and lawyer (who died in 1937).

[3] In a calculation which he made on 21 July 1939 of his likely income for the six months July to December 1939 Churchill's largest single forecast was the £7,500 final advance payment due on delivery of *The History of the English Speaking Peoples*. But he also planned continual articles, for July, *Picture Post* and the *Daily Mirror*; for August the *Daily Mirror* and *Collier's*; for September, the *Daily Mirror*, *Collier's* and *Tit Bits*; and for October to December the *News of the World* (£4,200), the *Daily Mirror* (£600), *Collier's* (£700) which, together with the income from Imre Revesz's European syndication, would total £15,780 (tax, £3,850), a total six monthly income *after* tax of £11,930 (or the September 1981 equivalent of more than £180,000).

August 1939

---

1 August 1939
Private and Personal

. . . Forgive me if I do not write fully to-day, but as you may imagine I am in a whirl of Cabinet Committees and Departmental meetings that always rain upon us in the last few days of the Session. Neville has had two consider-able successes in the House, one on the pensions resolution and the other in the foreign debate yesterday. The Winston opposition is going very thin.

Harold Nicolson: diary

(*Nicolson papers*)

1 August 1939

Spears who had been staying with Winston says that the old boy is deter-mined to speak with great violence and to vote against. This embarrasses Anthony who there and then rings Winston upon the telephone and begs him not to be too violent. Winston says he will press for assurances but that he will have to have the most explicit assurances if he is to be prevented from voting against the Government. It is no good Chamberlain saying he will summon Parliament 'if there is a change of situation'. He must promise to summon if any cloud arises at all. It is agreed that Harold Macmillan should ring up Winston later and try and persuade him.

Ronald Cartland to his sister

(*'Ronald Cartland'*)

2 August 1939

After Neville's speech [1] our little group drifted disconsolately into the lobby. Winston came out. 'Well,' I said to him, 'We can do no more.'

'Do no more, my boy?' he echoed, 'There is a lot more we can do. This is the time to fight—to speak—to attack!'

Neville Chamberlain to his sister

(*Templewood papers*)

5 August 1939   Chequers

The Wednesday debate in spite of the bitterness among our people and the Liberals, really went very well. When I got up to reply I had an extraordinary ovation; the cheering lasted for quite two minutes till it became almost embarrassing. I had seen Winston in the lobby before-hand and exhanged a few friendly words with him. But he is so sensitive to criticism that he couldn't stand even my joking remark about a tù quo que when he said he couldn't trust my judgement. That annoyed him so much that he actually went out of his way to associate himself with Sinclair's fatuous and imbecilic proposition that if Parliament had met earlier last September we could have mobilised a fleet, made an agreement with Russia, and saved the independence of Czechoslovakia. I did turn upon him savagely then and barked out that I totally and utterly disagreed with him. He was in a state of red fury after that and burst out at David Margesson whom he met subsequently in the lobby. But

---

[1] In the House of Commons on 2 August 1939, Sir Archibald Sinclair supported a Labour amendment for the recall of Parliament on 21 August 1939 (instead of October 3, the date proposed by the Government): 'a mere assurance', he said, 'that there will be no departure in policy, is not enough. We want to know for certain that before grave decisions are taken the House of Commons will have a chance to discuss the issues in public here. . . .' Churchill, who spoke immediately after Sinclair, also argued in favour of the earlier date. 'It might be,' he said, that Chamberlain's 'good faith' was in no way in question, 'but there might be a difference of judgement. I use the word "judgement" with some temerity, because my right hon. Friend twitted me some time ago about that notorious defect which I have in my composition.' Chamberlain's judgement, he added, might well be exercised on 'a legitimate and national topic upon which differences of opinion would arise between us'. Replying, Chamberlain referred to the 'stories of the militarization of Danzig, the Far East and so forth'. But he went on to dispute that Churchill's 'gloomy picture' was in fact cause to recall the House of Commons at the end of August, and he added: 'My right hon. Friend the Member for Epping (Mr Churchill) was good enough to say that he did not distrust my good faith; it was my judgement that he distrusted. I am rather inclined to say, *tu quoque*.'

yesterday he appeared to have recovered his temper and repeatedly cheered my remarks about Japan.[1]

That is Winston all over. His are summer storms, violent but of short duration and often followed by sunshine. But they make him uncommonly difficult to deal with.

Winston S. Churchill to Sir Kingsley Wood

(*Churchill papers: 2/371*)

5 August 1939

Yesterday's explosion[2] impresses very vividly upon one the danger which bombs falling in the streets over gas mains may well cause. I have no doubt this matter has been considered, and that arrangements have been made to cut off the gas when bomb raids are expected. Some of the mains, however, are so large that this may not suffice. I wonder whether the possibility of filling them in whole or in part with a neutral gas during air-raids has been considered? I do not know what is the size of the mains or how great the danger they would cause; if it is serious this possibility might be worth exploring.

Has anything been done about theatres, cinemas, etc? I am told that the Managements have not been told what to do about an ARP warning. Yet surely this should all be thought out beforehand, because the effect of a bomb falling in a crowded theatre would be very bad.

---

[1] Speaking in the House of Commons on 4 August 1939 (the last day of the 1938–9 Session of Parliament) Chamberlain said: 'Surely we must all the time, in the presence even of these insults and injuries which have been inflicted upon British subjects in China, remember what are the limits of what we can do at this particular time to help our people there. . . . We would much rather settle our differences with Japan by discussion and negotiation, provided we can do so without sacrificing what we conceive to be fundamental considerations of principles, than do it by resort to force. . . . Above all, let us not forget that there may be even nearer and graver problems to be considered in the course of the next few months. We must conserve our forces to meet any emergency that might arise.'

[2] On 4 August 1939 a gas main had exploded in the City of London, near St Paul's. The explosion took place at half past four on a Friday afternoon, after a subsidence in the street ruptured gas and water mains, and broke an electric cable. More than 100 people were injured, a block of old buildings marked for demolition collapsed, and windows in buildings within a radius of several hundred yeards, including St Paul's itself were shattered. Fortunately, the explosion occurred an hour after the subsidence, so that the immediate area had already been evacuated. In St Paul's, only windows of plain glass were shattered, the stained glass remaining intact.

General Sir Edmund Ironside to Winston S. Churchill
(*Churchill papers: 2/365*)

7 August 1939   Norfolk

Dear Mr Churchill,

I am up here for the holiday. I feel that things are hanging in the balance, and I can find no fire in getting our things in order. There is a calm of inaction all over the Govt Offices. We have improved in our preparations & people are beginning to get self-satisfied, but I can see so many holes that I can see no reason for this feeling. There is still no plan for action, certainly not in the Navy & the PM's statement that he might send a Fleet to the Far East shows no mastery of Imperial Strategy. Perhaps that is only talk.

I shall be going over to France shortly to see Gamelin & Georges and to see if I can get out of them something in the way of a plan. It is uphill work ferreting out how we now stand. I am sure that we are acquiescing too much & are having no effect upon the main strategy.

I'll come down & have another talk if I may when I come back.

Yours sincerely,
E. Ironside

Departmental Note to Sir Kingsley Wood
(*Air Ministry papers: 19/26*)

9 August 1939

In connection with your meeting with Mr Churchill tomorrow afternoon, you will probably like to see again his recent letter to you regarding the acquisition of a Town Centre in Croydon for No 615 (County of Surrey) Auxiliary Air Force (Fighter) Squadron, and the attached papers which also deal with the subject.

The position is that the property called 'Engadine' to which Mr Churchill refers, is apparently the only one which is suitable for the purpose, but its acquisition is being opposed not only by the Croydon Town Council, but also by the owners, the Ecclesiastical Commissioners.

Mr Churchill suggests compulsory purchase, but there are, as explained to him in Air Commodore Peake's[1] letter of the 26th July, legal and other

---

[1] Harald Peake, 1899–1978. Educated at Eton and Trinity College, Cambridge. On active service in the Coldstream Guards, 1918. As a Squadron-Leader, he raised and commanded Squadron No 609 West Riding, Auxiliary Air Force, 1936–48. Director of the Auxiliary Air Force, Air Ministry, 1938. Wing Commander (acting Air Commodore) attached to the Royal Air Force, 1939. Air Commodore, 1940. Director of Public Relations, Air Ministry, 1940–2. Special Duty List, Air Ministry, 1943–5. Resigned his commission, 1945. Chairman, Steel Company of Wales, 1955–62; of Lloyds Bank Ltd, 1961–9. Knighted, 1973. Chairman of the RAF Benevolent Fund, 1973.

difficulties about this. You can, however, tell him that we are consulting the Treasury solicitor for advice on the question of compulsory purchase (see minute 60 on the attached file).

A. H. Richards to Winston S. Churchill
(*Churchill papers: 2/276*)

11 August 1939

I should like to think that you too 'Sir' will be taking a much needed rest and change. Dread days loom before us and darken the skies and if we are to face with courage and confidence, the spectre of war stalking across Europe menacing our beloved land, I am persuaded that in the hour of dire need our people, with one voice will turn to you to deliver us and to lead us into the 'Paths of peace'.

Winston S. Churchill to Sir Kingsley Wood
(*Churchill papers: 25/17*)

13 August 1939

I send you two slips for your consideration. The first (A) is the draft of a letter which Lindemann thought of writing to the DT. There are a lot of rumours going about this atomic explosive, and Ribbentrop has made remarks to people on the subject. I expect Lindemann's view is right, ie that there is no immediate danger, although undoubtedly the human race is crawling nearer to the point when it will be able to destroy itself completely. Let me know whether you would advise publication or not. It is entirely as you say.

I also send you (B) a couple of points which have occurred to me.

I hope to be back before the end of the month, and it would give my Wife and me great pleasure if you could fit in luncheon here with one of your inspections. Like many others in this country, I feel grateful to you for what you are doing.

Professor Lindemann: draft letter

(*Air Ministry papers: 19/26*)

13 August 1939

Some weeks ago one of the Sunday papers splashed the story of the immense amount of energy which might be released from uranium by the recently discovered chain processes which take place when this particular type of atom is split by neutrons. At first sight this might seem to portend the appearance of new explosives of devastating power. In view of this it is essential to realise that there is no danger that this discovery, however great its scientific interest and perhaps ultimately its practical importance, will lead to results capable of being put into operation on a large scale for several years.

There are indications that tales will be deliberately circulated when international tension becomes acute, about the adaptation of this process to produce some terrible, new, secret explosive capable of wiping out London. Attempts will no doubt be made by the Fifth Column to induce us by means of this threat to accept another surrender. For this reason it is imperative to state the true position.

First, the best authorities hold that only a minor constituent of uranium is effective in these processes and that it will be necessary to extract this before large scale results are possible. This will be a matter of many years. Secondly, the chain process can only take place if the uranium is concentrated in a large mass. As soon as the energy develops it will explode with a mild detonation before any really violent effects can be produced. It might be as good as our present day explosives, but it is unlikely to produce anything very much more dangerous. Thirdly, these experiments cannot be carried out on a small scale; if they had been successfully done on a big scale, (ie, with the results with which we shall be threatened unless we submit to blackmail) it would be impossible to keep them secret. Fourthly, only a comparatively small amount of uranium in the territories of what used to be Czechoslovakia is under the control of Berlin.

For all these reasons, the fear that this discovery has provided the Nazis with some sinister, new, secret explosive with which to destroy their enemies is clearly without foundation. Dark hints will no doubt be dropped and terrifying whispers will be assiduously circulated, but it is to be hoped that nobody will be taken in by them.

Winston S. Churchill: notes

(Air Ministry papers: 19/26)

13 August 1939

There are many munition works, bridges, etc, whose destruction would seriously injure our war effort, in the neighbourhood of large fields in which aeroplanes could be landed. The exercises in landing troops by aeroplane which have been undertaken in Germany seem to indicate that this method is intended for use against valuable targets which might not be easy to destroy by aerial bombing. Only in the minority of cases could forces able to cope with fifty or one hundred armed men be rushed to the spot within an hour or so. If the landing is made close to the vulnerable spot, a few score of determined men could create immense havoc and very likely return to their aeroplanes and take off again without serious loss. At the worst they could surrender and would have to be treated as prisoners of war.

If this danger is real it can be guarded against by digging a few ditches in suitable spots across fields which are large enough for modern aeroplanes to land and near enough to valuable targets to render this action desirable.

Winston S. Churchill to General Sir Edmund Ironside

(Churchill papers: 2/365)

13 August 1939

I am off to-morrow for a three days' tour of the Maginot Line (Rhine Sector). Generals Georges and Gamelin are very kindly going to come with me a part of the time; and I expect we shall be able to have some talks on the matters we discussed.

When I come back about August 24 or 25, I shall probably have a lot which I should wish to talk over with you.

Of course I think this fortnight may enable us to see more clearly through the mist. Personally I take the graver view; but as we have lost the initiative, one is baffled by the many uncertainties.

I will ring you up when I come back.

Winston S. Churchill to G. M. Young

(*Churchill papers: 8/626*)

13 August 1939

My dear Young,

I send you herewith the Victorian Age.

I greatly need your aid in this last section. I am taking your own book away with me, and perhaps we may have a talk about this period towards the end of September (if we ever get there). Of course you have already read the American side of the nineteenth century, to which the Victorian Age is the counterpart.

I also send you a clean copy of the proofs of Books I and II so far as they have yet been sent by the printer. But we do not need to worry about these now. All the latest revises will reach you in due course as they come back.

You will be glad to hear my wife has recovered from her lumbago without having to adopt your remedy.

With good wishes,

Winston S. Churchill to Clementine Churchill

(*Spencer-Churchill papers*)

14 August 1939   Hotel Ritz, Paris

My darling,

This trip promises to be both agreeable & instructive. General Georges, who will command the Army in a war, has put all aside to conduct me. He met the aeroplane & drove me to the restaurant in the Bois where in divine sunshine we lunched; & talked 'shop' for a long time. I am in full accord with the views held here. It is thought that nothing will happen till the snow falls in the Alps, & gives to Mussolini a protection for the winter. This looks like early or mid-September; wh wd still leave Hitler 2 months to deal with Poland, before the mud season in that country. All this is of course speculation, but also reasonable. It seems to fit the German programme so far as it has been published.

The General is coming here in a few minutes to take me to the Gare de l'Est. We are to travel in a special Michelin train of extreme speed to Strasburg, dining en route. We are to have 2 vy long days on the line. The trip fits in with an Inspection, & it seems to suit their ideas to have me in these regions at this time. Anyhow everything is being done in the most considerate manner.

We came across vy nicely; & there was a smoking compartment on the plane.

I think you had better send any urgent message to me at the Ritz. I will ring up each morning in case. But I do not know exactly where I shall be. We sleep tonight Strasburg: tomorrow Colmar & Wednesday Belfort. I shall be back here 3 pm on Thursday. I think it is all going to be vy interesting.

Louis Spears is a gt friend to Georges. They were together in the war for a long time.

Keep all this to yourself.

Always yr ever loving husband
darling yr devoted
W

Captain A. H. Henderson-Livesey[1] to Winston S. Churchill

(*Churchill papers: 2/361*)

19 August 1939

Sir,

At this grave hour I write on behalf of some of my friends here informally assembled to say that we pray that God will give you health and strength to discharge the great task which awaits you.[2]

We feel that the continued exclusion of yourself from the ranks of the Government is a monstrous scandal which cannot long continue.

We note that you have been spending your vacation inspecting the defences of France while the First Minister of the Crown has been absorbed in the mysteries of rod and line in remote Highland streams.

At this juncture your name alone can do for the people of this country what that of Kitchener did in 1914.

I remain, Sir,
Your Obedient Servant,
A. H. Henderson-Livesey

---

[1] Alfred Herbert Henderson-Livesey, 1882– . Joined the Essex Yeomanry as a private, 1914. 2nd Lieutenant, 1915; Lieutenant, 1917. Captain, Army Educational Corps, 1920. Pharmacologist; in the Second World War his firm specialized in the treatment of pilots' burns.

[2] Henderson-Livesey wrote from the headquarters of the North Southwark Liberal National Party (66–68 Union Street, Borough, London S.E.1.).

Winston S. Churchill: recollections

(*Churchill papers: 4/114*)

20 August 1939

On my return from the Rhine front I passed some sunshine days at my cousin Madame Balsan's place, with a pleasant but deeply anxious company, in the old Château where King Henry of Navarre had slept the night before the battle of Ivry. Mrs Euan Wallace[1] and her sons were with us. Her husband was a Cabinet Minister. She was expecting him to join her. Presently he telegraphed he could not come, and would explain later why.

Other signs of danger drifted in upon us. One could feel the deep apprehension brooding over all, and even the light of this lovely valley at the confluence of the Eure and the Vesgre seemed robbed of its genial ray. I found painting hard work in this uncertainty.

Paul Maze: diary

(*Maze papers*)

20 August 1939

Winston came to paint the Moulin. I worked alongside him. He suddenly turned to me and said: 'This is the last picture we shall paint in peace for a very long time.' What amazed me was his concentration over his painting. No one but he could have understood more what the possibility of war meant, and how ill prepared we were. As he worked, he would now and then make statements as to the relative strengths of the German Army or the French Army. 'They are strong, I tell you, they are strong,' he would say. Then his jaw would clench his large cigar, and I felt the determination of his will. 'Ah' he would say, 'with it all, we shall have him.'

[1] Barbara Lutyens, 1898–1981. Eldest daughter of Sir Edwin Lutyens, the architect. In 1920 she married Euan Wallace (as his second wife). He already had two sons by his first wife, and they had three further sons. Of the two sons whom she 'inherited', David was killed in action in Greece and Gerard was killed in a flying accident in Canada during the Second World War. Of her own three sons, Peter, a Battle of Britain pilot, was killed in action, and Johnny died in his early twenties as a result of a general anaesthetic during a nose operation. 'My poor boys,' she used to say, 'only knew school and war.' Her third son, Billy, (a friend of Princess Margaret) died of cancer in 1977, at the age of 49. Barbara Wallace later married (as his second wife) the American writer and historian, Herbert Agar, who died in 1980.

Paul Maze: diary

(*Maze papers*)

21 August 1939

Winston came to paint again. We talked about his visit to the Maginot Line with Georges—very impressed with what he saw. Dined at the Chateau. Winston was fuming but with reason as the assemblée didn't see any danger ahead.

As Charteris[1] was walking up the stairs to go to his bed room he shouted to me, 'don't listen to him. He is a warmonger.' He was depressed as he left. I had written a letter to him 'only to read when he was over the Channel'. 'Don't worry Winston you *know* that you will be Prime Minister and lead us to victory.' Jessie[2] read the letter & said 'this will cheer him up'.

W. H. Thompson: recollections

('*Sixty minutes with Winston Churchill*')

[22 August 1939]   [between Dreux and Paris]

. . . my wife[3] travelled part of the way in Mr Churchill's car, taking notes for him. When he had finished his work he lapsed into silence, and she sat looking out of the window at the beautiful and peaceful country through which they were passing. The corn was ripe and, in its heaviness, it looked like the golden waves of a gently undulating sea.

Mr Churchill grew graver and graver as he sat wrapped in thought, and then said slowly and sorrowfully:

'Before the harvest is gathered in—we shall be at war.'

Winston S. Churchill: recollections

(*Churchill papers: 4/114*)

22 August 1939

On August 22 I decided to go home, where at least I could find out what was going on. I told my wife I would send her word in good time.

On my way through Paris I gave General Georges luncheon. He produced all the figures of the French and German Armies, and classified the divisions

---

[1] The Hon Sir Evan Charteris, KC (see page 736, note 3).

[2] Jessie Lawrie. In 1950 she married Paul Maze (as his second wife): their friendship had dated from the 1920s.

[3] Mary Shearburn (see pages 509, note 2 and 1259 note 1).

in quality. The result impressed me so much that for the first time I said: 'But you are the masters.' He replied: 'The Germans have a very strong army, and we shall never be allowed to strike first. If they attack, both our countries will rally to their duty.'

That night I slept at Chartwell.

Harold Nicolson: diary
(Nicolson papers)

23 August 1939

Archie . . . rings up Winston Churchill. The latter has just returned from Paris and is in high fettle. The French are not at all perturbed by the Russo-German pact[1] and are prepared to support Poland none the less. They are half mobilising. Winston had just rung up Paul Reynaud who asserts that all is going well. By which he means War I suppose.

Sir Kingsley Wood to Winston S. Churchill
(Air Ministry papers: 19/26)

23 August 1939

I should like very much to come and lunch with you one day at Chartwell if an opportunity offers. . . .

I hope that you found your visit to France interesting and encouraging.

Winston Churchill: notes
(Churchill papers: 2/371)

23 August 1939

I thought that I would set down some of the points in my mind as a result of my long talks over here. They are, of course, my own personal opinions.

1. Ought there not to be a liaison between the British and French supply organisations as intimate as that now established between the fighting forces. I have long felt that the superiority of the German organisation of industry

---

[1] Announced on 21 August 1939, and signed in Moscow two days later, by Ribbentrop and Molotov, who gave the Pact one of its names (also known as the Nazi-Soviet Pact).

for war is the greatest advantage they possess. In 1914 there was a lull after the first two months, everyone being short; but this will not repeat itself on the German side for a good many months. It seems essential to organise the supply not only of the British but the French army in respect of the movement of war materials particularly steel and explosives, both to Britain and America. The French factories will require to be fed with raw materials though they have vast capacities for the later processes. I have no doubt a great deal has been done in this direction, but they did not seem to know much about it over here.

2. The French front cannot be surprised. It cannot be broken at any point except by an effort which would be enormously costly in life and would take so much time that the general situation would be transformed while it was in progress. The same is true, though to a lesser extent, of the German side.

The flanks of this Front, however, rest upon two small neutral states. The attitude of Belgium is thought to be profoundly unsatisfactory. It is not true as Van Zeeland [1] told me a little while ago that the French High Command are content with the neutrality of Belgium. If an attack were made upon Belgium and the Belgians called for help, the French could reach the line of —— [2] before the Germans, but the advance positions behind the Albert Canal would be lost. Moreover, there are other possibilities in this quarter which would be greatly obstructed. The view which I expressed to Van Zeeland when I saw him was that the Belgians, though they remain technically neutral, should interpret their neutrality in such a way as to retain on their Front at least ten German divisions but that an attitude of pure indifference or impartiality did not accord either with what happened to Belgium in the past or Belgian interests in the future. Ought we not to press Belgium to show a definite bias in our favour. After all their existence depends upon an English–French victory. At present there are no military relations of any kind between the French and the Belgians.

At the other end of the line, about which I was able to learn a good deal, the French have done everything in their power to prepare against an invasion through Switzerland. This operation will take the form of a German advance down the Aar Valley, protected on its right by a movement into or towards the Belfort Gap. The Swiss arrangements are rudimentary. They have no Commander-in-Chief or Headquarters Staff. There are three Swiss

---

[1] Paul van Zeeland, 1893–1973. A Director of the Belgian National Bank, 1926; Deputy Governor, 1934. Prime Minister of Belguim, 1935–7 (when he devalued the franc by 28 per cent). President of the Co-ordinating Foundation for Refugees, 1939. In exile in England, 1940. Minister of Foreign Affairs, 1949–54.

[2] The blank words in paragraphs two and four were left blank in Churchill's copy of this note.

Corps Commanders, one of French connections and sympathies nearest France; one of German contacts nearest Germany; and one of Italian contacts nearest Italy. If an attempt were made to violate Swiss security, one of these would be nominated Commander in Chief. In the only case likely to occur it would no doubt be the Frenchified Swiss who would be chosen, but he has no Staff and would have to create one. In these circumstances the invader might penetrate very deeply, repairing the blown-up roads as they went. I do not see what more can be done about it because the French arrangements are very good.

However, I personally think it extremely unlikely that any heavy German attempt will be made either against the French Front or against the two small countries on its flanks in the opening phase.

3. It is not necessary for Germany to mobilise before attacking Poland. They have enough divisions already on a war footing to act upon their Eastern Front, and would have time to reinforce the Siegfried line by mobilising simultaneously with the beginning of a heavy attack on Poland. Thus a German mobilisation is a warning signal which may not be forthcoming in advance of war. The French, on the other hand, may have to take extra measures in the period of extreme tension.

4. The French say they have the power to mobilise six million men including the Colonials; but of course all these would not be needed immediately. They have at present a million under arms as against Germany's two millions. This disparity need cause no alarm so far as the safety of France is concerned in view of the arrangements made. They have prepared the —— for —— divisions. This is comparable to the German 130.

I asked particularly what would be the best moment for Germany to strike. I found general agreement with the view which I personally hold that time is now on our side, and that Hitler will be worse off next year than this. As to date, it is thought he would be wise to wait until the snow falls in the Alps and gives the protection of winter to Mussolini. During the first fortnight of September or even earlier these conditions would be established. There would still be time for him to strike heavily at Poland before the mud period of late October and early November would hamper a German offensive. Thus this first fortnight in September seems to be particularly critical, and the present German arrangements for the Nurembourg demonstration seem to harmonize with such a conclusion.

5. The object of the French would evidently be to hold as many German Divisions on their Front as possible, so as to take the weight off Poland. For this purpose they would have to engage actively all along the line and, without having any more Sommes or Passchendaeles, force the Germans to man their lines heavily. As the Front extends so many hundreds of miles it ought to

be possible to hold a very large number of German divisions in the West—how many no-one seemed inclined to estimate.

It is impossible not to be affected by the mood of calm confidence which prevails in the High Command and no-one can doubt the immense scale and high quality of the effort made to provide for national safety.

Harold Nicolson: diary

(*Nicolson papers*)

24 August 1939

I hear a rumour that the PM this morning offered to resign if war came andthat the King refused to accept his resignation. In the smoking room Winston and Lloyd George are talking together. I join them. Ll G is clamouring for a secret session of Parliament. He says we must be able to tell the PM that he must go.

Henry Channon: diary

(*Robert Rhodes James, 'Chips'*)

24 August 1939

At 2.45 the House met and soon the Prime Minister rose. He spoke in well modulated phrases and was clear and admirable, but with little passion or emotion, and I thought of the Munich crisis last September and all the excitement then. There was little resemblance to that hectic day this afternoon. The House was calm, bored, even irritated, at having its holiday cut short by Hitler.

I looked about me. Lloyd George opposite me, and Winston Churchill a little to the right below me, those twin apostles of Russian friendship looked old, and dejected. Winston held his face in his hands and occasionally nodded his head in agreement with the PM. I was directly behind Neville, and admired him immensely as he coolly unfolded the story of Russian perfidy and German aspirations. Everyone secretly or openly, whatever they may say, hopes that the Poles will climb down. But the whole House expect war.

Victor Cazalet: diary

(*Robert Rhodes James: 'Victor Cazalet, A Portrait'*)

25 August 1939

We had a very full meeting of Parliament on Thursday. Chamberlain made a good but not very impressive speech. I sat in Smoking Room with LG and Winston. Both v anti-Chamberlain. Think he has let us into this mess. We never ought to have given guarantees to Poland unless they had consented to allow Russian army across their frontiers.

General Sir Edmund Ironside: diary

(*Ironside papers*)

27 August 1939

Down to Chartwell for lunch yesterday. . . .

Winston was full of Georges, whom he had seen over in France. I found that he had become very French in his outlook and had a wonderful opinion of the whole thing he saw. He had General Spears with him. The burden of his song was that we must have a great Army in France, that we couldn't depend upon the French to do our effort for us. That we must get twenty Divisions by Christmas. I told him that we had no such plans in being. He showed me how the French were going to attack Italy and how they held the high ground round the Mont Cenis and looked down upon the Italians below them. I told him that the French had told him far more than they had told our General Staff, that I had been unable, as C-in-C designate, to get any clear plan out of things. Winston said that we were trying to get as much control in the conduct of affairs as if we had an Army of one and a half millions.

Geoffrey Parsons[1] to Winston S. Churchill: telegram
(Churchill papers: 2/361)

27 August 1939   c/o New York Herald Tribune
                                                          Paris

Returned Paris after day Berlin. Send you this report by telegraph, since hours are numbered. Impossible to exaggerate confidence of Hitler and German people that British will capitulate. Germans seems cheerful, loyal, as result nobody has expected anything but swift easy victory over Poles, having been fed idea British would never fight over Dantzig or Poland. Seems just beginning appreciate risk of general war. Signing British–Polish treaty[2] first real shock to German Government. My analysis for what it is worth would thus centre efforts around Hitler of British stand. General cynicism towards British attitude amazing to me after visit to London. But it exists in opinion of American observers in Berlin. Of course Hitler may have gone too far to withdraw or he may decide to fight anyway. But I doubt the latter. As a complete outsider, may I suggest that some bold action like immediate formation of War Cabinet would probably have more effect than anything else.

Sir Edward Marsh: diary
(Marsh papers)

29 August 1939

Winston rang me up asking me to represent him at Oc's[3] memorial service.
He said Hitler was evidently rattled, but he didn't see how he could climb down, which would cost him his life.

[1] Geoffrey Parsons, 1879–1956. Educated at Columbia University, New York. Police Reporter for the Brooklyn *Evening Sun*, 1900. Editorial writer for the New York *Sun*, 1901–13. Editorial writer for the *New York Tribune*, 1913. Chief Editorial writer of the New York *Herald Tribune*, 1924; Chief Editorial Adviser from 1952 until his death. In 1942 he was awarded the Pulitzer Prize; its citation praised his 'clearness of style, moral purpose and power to influence public opinion', and called his editorials an 'outstanding instance where political affiliation was completely subordinated to the national welfare'.

[2] On 25 August 1939, recognizing the immediate dangers of a German attack on Poland now that Russia had decided to stand aside, the British Government signed a formal Treaty of Alliance with Poland. Under this Treaty, Britain was obliged to go to war with Germany, should Germany attack Poland.

[3] Arthur Melland Asquith, 1883–1939. Known as 'Oc'. Sudan Civil Service, 1906–11. In business, 1911–14. Enlisted in the Royal Naval Volunteer Reserve, 1914. Served in the Royal Naval Division at Antwerp, Dardanelles and western front, 1914–16. Four times wounded. Controller, Trench Warfare Department, Ministry of Munitions (when Churchill was Minister of Munitions), 1918. Member of Council, Ministry of Labour, 1919. Company director. The son of H. H. Asquith, he died on 25 August 1939.

Duff Cooper: diary
(*Norwich papers*)

29 August 1939

Brendan had been assured by Van that our note to Hitler was everything that could be desired.[1] Winston rang up the Polish Ambassador while we were there, who said that he was now completely satisfied with the support he was receiving from our Government.

Winston S. Churchill to F. W. Deakin
(*Churchill papers: 8/626*)

29 August 1939

My dear Bill,

I have tried to fit these Galleys together. The present result is quite impossible. I send you my own copies, where the Galleys are arranged more or less in chronological order. It is no use mixing up sections about Pitt and George III with separate studies of the American colonies. What we want is a coherent account of the Seven Years War, featuring the rise of Chatham. This will include the 'Continental Struggle' and 'Frederick the Great', the Canadian section more or less complete, and the India one of which you are making me the draft. The Book called 'The First British Empire' will end with this chapter, which will be called either 'The Great Pitt' or 'The Seven Years War', the position of the First British Empire as it stands at the Peace of Paris 1763.

The next Book is called 'The Quarrels of the English Speaking Peoples', and opens after the Peace of Paris. This shows the home politics of the reign of George III plus the effects of the Seven Years War on the Colonies. See what you can do to link Chapter VII together before I start upon it. I send you the Galleys which have been excluded and left over for the 'Quarrels' book.

Will you let me have some books on the period covered by Chapter VII 'The Great Pitt'. While you are sending them to me, I am going on with 'Queen Elizabeth'.

[1] On 28 August 1939, in reply to Hitler's offer of an agreement with Britain once the 'anomaly' of Poland's frontiers was dealt with by negotiation, the British Government replied, declining any such negotiation, and noting that 'they could not, for any advantage offered to Great Britain, acquiesce in a settlement which put in jeopardy the independence of a State to whom they have given their guarantee'. To the alarm of some, however, the British reply supported direct negotiations between Germany and Poland, as a first step to a settlement guaranteed by all the powers.

Winston S. Churchill to Neville Chamberlain: not sent

(Churchill papers: 2/364)

30 August 1939   Chartwell
Private

My dear Prime Minister,

I think you are quite right to let things drag on, if they will; more especi-ally because one feels a certain hesitation on the other side as the *act* ap-proaches. But would it not be helpful to call up the reserves and mobilize the TA? If events turn out badly, it would prove a timely precaution. If they continue undefined, it would be an invaluable testing of machinery which is probably very rusty. Anyhow the effect would surely add to the force of your exertions to preserve peace; and the people involved would gladly respond.

I do not see myself how Hitler can escape from the pen in which he has put himself. But a victory without bloodshed would be the best; and this would help, not hinder it.

Yours sincerely,

Winston S. Churchill to Sir Kingsley Wood

(Churchill papers: 25/17)

30 August 1939   Kenley
Secret

1. USE OF HURRICANE OR SPITFIRE AIRCRAFT
   for air experience by new pilots just posted to the flights.
      Also for flight formation and air firing experience if possible.
   (This last point is particularly important).

RE: CROYDON AIRPORT

2. Scheme of Camouflage for Airport Buildings and concrete aprons not yet given to airport authorities: nor have they any instructions to proceed with Camouflage work although it is a very lengthy and extensive job.
3. Obstruction from the airport authorities to the digging of trenches outside the aerodrome boundary for the protection of pilots and crews standing by their aircraft dispersed around the aerodrome.
4. The scheme of underground shelters (being carried out by contractors) is proceeding far too slowly—no special extra shifts of workmen are employed—and they are very inadequate at present.

Winston S. Churchill to Josiah Wedgwood
(*Wedgwood papers*)

31 August 1939   Chartwell

It would never do for me to stand out of the many misfortunes which will follow a declaration of war, in order to safeguard my personal prospects. However, all you say is true.

Winston S. Churchill to Sir Newman Flower
(*Churchill papers: 8/624*)

31 August 1939

Thank you very much for procuring me this extra time for the Preface to the Life of Sir Austen Chamberlain.

I am, as you know, concentrating every minute of my spare life and strength upon completing our contract. These distractions are trying. However 530,000 words are now in print and there is only cutting and proof reading, together with a few special points, now to be done.

You will understand, more than anyone else, how difficult it is for me to spend a night upon another form of work. However, I still hope I may be able to serve you.

Winston S. Churchill to G. M. Young
(*Churchill papers: 8/626*)

31 August 1939

I wonder how you are getting on with the proofs I sent you.

I have completed the Commonwealth story (Lambeth and Monk), but have still not cleared away the Queen Elizabeth block. I am now working on the Chatham period, which is very inspiring.[1] I shall be very glad to hear from you. It is a relief in times like these to be able to escape into other centuries. Happily there are good hopes that Chamberlain will stand firm.

---

[1] Churchill wrote (*A History of the English-Speaking Peoples*, volume 3, page 132): 'William Pitt ranks with Marlborough as the greatest Englishman in the century between 1689 and 1789. "It is a considerable fact in the history of the world," wrote Carlyle, "that he was for four years King of England." He was not the first English stateman to think in terms of a world policy and to broaden on to a world scale the political conceptions of William III. But he is the first great figure of British Imperialism. Pitt too had brought the force of public opinion to bear upon politics, weakening the narrow monopoly of the great Whig houses. His heroic period was now over. "Be one people," he commanded the factions. Five years later he was to hold high office once more amid tragic circumstances of failing health. In the meantime his magnificent oratory blasted the policies of his successors.'

September 1939

General Sir Edmund Ironside: diary

(*Ironside papers*)

1 September 1939

I got to the Horse Guards as 10 am was striking and was immediately rung up by Winston from Westerham who said 'They've started. Warsaw and Cracow are being bombed now.' I rang up Gort at the War Office who said that he was off to a meeting. He didn't believe it. I urged him to tell Belisha. He did and Belisha was seen rushing off to Downing Street. I rang Winston again and he said he had the news definitely from the Polish Ambassador, who had told him $1\frac{1}{2}$ hours ago. . . . How could the War Office possibly be ignorant of this?

Lord Camrose: diary

(*Camrose papers*)

2 September 1939

Winston called me up at 11.30 and told me that he had accepted a place in the War Cabinet and was to be a Minister without portfolio.

Brigadier-General Angus McNeill[1] to Winston S. Churchill

(*Churchill papers: 2/366*)

2 September 1939   Haifa Yacht Club

My dear Winston,

—My best congratulations on being once more in the Cabinet, and lucky we are to have you!

Reminds me of the silly old jest many years ago. 'What's the good of a "Cabinet" without a WC?'—

Today is the 41st anniversary of Omdurman, & you & I little thought as we wiped the blood off our swords on that occasion, that we should live to see *two* wars with the Huns!

Good luck to you old friend—

Yrs ever,
Angus

Alfred Duff Cooper: diary

(*Norwich papers*)

2 September 1939

At about 10.30 I went round to Winston's flat, which he had asked me to do. . . . He considered that he had been very ill-treated, as he had agreed the night before to join the War Cabinet but throughout the day he had not heard a word from the Prime Minister. He had wished to speak that night in the House but feeling himself already almost a member of the Government had refrained from doing so.

There were present at his flat Anthony, Bob Boothby, Brendan Bracken and Duncan Sandys. We were all in a state of bewildered rage. Bob was convinced that Chamberlain had lost the Conservative Party forever and that it was in Winston's power to go to the House of Commons tomorrow and break him and take his place. He felt very strongly that in no circum-

---

[1] Angus John McNeill, 1874–1950. A contemporary of Churchill at Harrow. 2nd Lieutenant, Seaforth Highlanders, 1895. On active service in Crete, 1897, at Omdurman, 1898, in South Africa, 1899–1900 (despatches), and in Somaliland, 1901. Captain, 1901. On the staff of the Mounted Infantry School, 1904–8. Retired from the Army, 1910. Joined the Lovat Scouts Yeomanry, 1914; temporary Brigadier-General, 1917 (despatches five times, 1914–18; DSO, 1918). Commanded the Norfolk and Suffolk Infantry Brigade, Territorial Army, 1920–2. Commanded the Palestine Gendarmerie, 1922–6. Chief Stockbreeding Officer to the Government of Palestine, 1926–31. In 1899 McNeill had drawn the sketches for Churchill's book, *The River War*.

stances now should Winston consent to serve under him. On the other hand, if Winston now backed Chamberlain he could save him. Was it better to split the country at such a moment or bolster up Chamberlain? That seemed at one time the decision that Winston had to take.

He was himself very undecided, said that he had no wish to be Prime Minister, doubted his fitness for the position. He rang up the French Embassy. Was told that all was well—that we should see the situation from quite a different angle tomorrow which sounded very ominous to us. Anthony was also in a state of great perplexity. He was not to be a member of the War Cabinet but only Dominions Secretary. He did not relish the prospect.

We all argued that Winston should refuse to serve unless Anthony was included in the War Cabinet as otherwise he would be in a minority of one. Brendan pressed that he should also insist on my inclusion and that of Bobbety[1]—'the other Ministers' as he put it 'who had resigned for conscience sake'. Winston left us for a bit and went to draft a letter to the PM saying that the events of the day had created a new situation, and that he hoped he would make no announcement of his inclusion in the War Cabinet at present. It was to have been announced on that Saturday morning.

Later Winston succeeded in getting through to someone whom he described as 'a friend' who would be able to tell him what had taken place at the Cabinet. Unfortunately his secretary gave the show away by coming in and saying, 'Mr Hore-Belisha is on the telephone.' He was much annoyed. He came back with the information that after a very stormy Cabinet—stormy in every sense for it was attended by a terrific thunderstorm—it had been decided to deliver the ultimatum next morning.

This altered the whole situation. Our heated discussion cooled down. Winston said that he would send his letter to the Prime Minister none the less—and so in the small hours we wandered through the dark streets.[2]

---

[1] Lord Cranborne, who had resigned as Under-Secretary of State for Foreign Affairs in February 1938 (at the time of Eden's resignation as Foreign Secretary). He received no office in Neville Chamberlain's wartime Government, but was appointed Paymaster-General by Churchill on 15 May 1940, and held different Cabinet posts throughout Churchill's wartime and peacetime premierships.

[2] In anticipation of war, and of the inevitable black-out, Churchill had given instructions on 2 September 1938 for the immediate purchase of '1 Torch for Mrs Churchill; Dark material for door; Adhesive tape, gum and black paper' (*Churchill papers: 8/639*).

Winston S. Churchill to Neville Chamberlain

(*Churchill papers: 4/96*)

2 September 1939   11 Morpeth Mansions

My dear Prime Minister

Aren't we a very old team? I make out that the six you mentioned to me
yesterday aggregate 386 years or an average of over 64! Only one year short
of the Old Age Pension! If however you added Sinclair (49) and Eden (42)
the average comes down to $57\frac{1}{2}$.

If the Daily Herald is right that Labour will not come in,[1] we shall certainly
have to face a constant stream of criticism, as well as the many disappointments and surprises of which war largely consists. Therefore it seems to me all
the more important to have the Liberal Opposition firmly incorporated in
our ranks. Eden's influence with the section of Conservatives who are associated with him, as well as with Moderate Liberal elements also seems to me
to be a very necessary reinforcement.

The Poles have now been under heavy attack for thirty hours, and I am
much concerned to hear that there is talk in Paris of a further note. I trust
you will be able to announce our Joint Declaration of War at *latest* when
Parliament meets this afternoon.

The *Bremen* will soon be out of the interception zone unless the Admiralty take special measures and the signal is given today. This is only a
minor point, but it may well be vexatious.[2]

I have not heard anything from you since our talks on Friday, when I
understood that I was to serve as your colleague, and when you told me that
this would be announced speedily. I really do not know what has happened
during the course of this agitated day; though it seems to me that entirely

---

[1] Neville Chamberlain did not offer any Cabinet posts to the Labour leaders. When, in
May 1940, he sought to form an all-Party coalition, it was the refusal of the Labour leadership to accept his Premiership (the Labour party was then in Conference at Bournemouth)
that led to Churchill's emergence as Prime Minister.

[2] Seeking to return to Germany from the United States, the passenger liner *Bremen* took
refuge in the Soviet port of Murmansk. She was subsequently intercepted by the submarine
Salmon, but allowed to proceed according to the conventions of International Law, which
were, as Churchill wrote in his War Memoirs, 'observed rightly and punctiliously' (volume 1,
page 333). The ship reached Bremerhaven on 13 December 1939, but took no part in the
naval war, having been notified as a hospital ship in 1940; and on 18 March 1941 the official
German news agency (DNB) reported a serious fire on board, blaming it on German communist sabotage. The fire was confirmed by a British aerial photograph, published four days
later in the western Press, showing the ship burning. The cause of the fire turned out to be
the act of a young seaman who bore a grudge against the ship's Captain. The fire was so
severe that the ship never sailed again, but was sold for scrap in 1946. Built in 1929, of 51,656
tons, the ship was owned by the Norddeutscher Lloyd. It was the ship on which Sarah
Churchill had 'eloped' to the United States in 1936, to join Vic Oliver.

different ideas have ruled from those which you expressed to me when you said 'the die was cast'. I quite realise that in contact with this tremendous European situation changes of method may become necessary, but I feel entitled to ask you to let me know how we stand, both publicly and privately, before the Debate opens at noon.[1]

It seems to me that if the Labour Party, and as I gather the Liberal Party, are estranged, it will be difficult to form an effective War Government on the limited basis you mentioned. I consider that a further effort should be made to bring in the Liberals, and in addition that the composition and scope of the War Cabinet you discussed with me requires review. There was a feeling to-night in the House that injury had been done to the spirit of national unity by the apparent weakening of our resolve. I do not underrate the difficulties you have with the French; but I trust that we shall now take our decision independently, and thus give our French friends any lead that may be necessary. In order to do this we shall need the strongest and most integral combination that can be formed. I therefore ask that there should be no announcement of the composition of the War Cabinet until we have had a further talk.

As I wrote to you yesterday morning, I hold myself entirely at your disposal, with every desire to aid you in your task.

[1] In the House of Commons at 7.30 on the evening of 2 September 1939 Neville Chamberlain spoke, not of a midnight ultimatum with only 4½ hours to run—as agreed upon by the Cabinet three hours before—but of the possibility of further negotiations with Germany. Although the Germans had not yet replied to the earlier Anglo-French warning, Chamberlain said, this might be because they were considering a new Italian proposal for a conference to discuss a possible German–Polish settlement. 'If the German Government should agree to withdraw their forces,' Chamberlain announced, 'then His Majesty's Government would be willing to regard the position as being the same as it was before the German forces crossed the Polish frontier.' Were German troops to withdraw, Chamberlain added, 'the way would be open to discussions' between Germany and Poland, discussions with which the British Government would be 'willing to be associated'. Leopold Amery recalled in his memoirs: 'The House was aghast. For two whole days the wretched Poles had been bombed and massacred, and we were still considering within what time-limit Hitler should be invited to tell us whether he felt like relinquishing his prey! And then these sheer irrelevancies about the terms of a hypothetical agreement between Germany and Poland. . . . Was all this havering the prelude to another Munich? A year before the House had risen to its feet to give Chamberlain an ovation when he announced a last-moment hope of peace. This time any similar announcement would have been met by a universal howl of execration.' 'There was no doubt,' Churchill later recorded, 'that the temper of the House was for war. I deemed it even more resolute and united than in the similar scene on August 3, 1914, in which I had also taken part.'

Sir Reginald Dorman-Smith:[1] *recollections*

(*'Sunday Times'*: *6 September 1964*)

[2 September 1939]

After the stormy debate following the PM's statement to the House at 7.30 pm on September 2, I went out of the Chamber with my PPS, Sir Cedric Drewe,[2] to find myself cut by some of my greatest MP friends. A little later, someone told me: 'Do you know some of your colleagues are holding a meeting in the Chancellor's room?' I hurried there to find Sir John Anderson in the chair beside a phone linked directly to Number 10.

My colleagues already there had decided they would not leave that room until such time as war had been declared. As we sat there and waited by the phone and nothing happened, I felt like a disembodied spirit. It didn't seem real. We were on strike—like those poor little miners down there until yesterday,[3] you know.

. . . there was a feeling of great emotion. All of us were getting back to our natural selves. I became more Irish, and Hore-Belisha more Jewish—talking of rights and indignities and so on.

We had early on decided to send Sir John Anderson to No 10 to take over the line there. 'Shakes' Morrison had taken over our phone. As we waited, we got scruffier and sweatier. I don't remember we had any food brought in. To me, it was Malcolm MacDonald who stood out from us all. He was cool, calm and collected and even told a few jokes.

Eventually, the call came for us to go to No 10. I didn't know how to get there because it was pouring with rain and I had no car. Then Malcolm

---

[1] Reginald Dorman-Smith, 1899–1977. Educated at Harrow and Sandhurst. 2nd Lieutenant, Indian Army, 1918; served in the 15th Sikhs. Major, Queen's Royal Regiment (Territorial Force), 1930; honorary Colonel, 1937. A County Alderman, Surrey, 1931–5; Justice of the Peace, 1932. Conservative MP for Petersfield, 1935–41. President of the National Farmers Union, 1936–7. Knighted, 1937. Minister of Agriculture and Fisheries, January 1939 to May 1940. Privy Councillor, 1939. Governor of Burma, 1941–6. High Sheriff of Hampshire, 1952. A Justice of the Peace for Hampshire, 1960.

[2] Cedric Drewe, 1896–1971. Educated at Eton and the Royal Military Academy, Woolwich. Served with the Royal Field Artillery, 1914–19. A Devon landowner, farmer, and member of the National Farmers Union (of which Reginald Dorman-Smith was President). Conservative MP for South Molton, 1924–9; for Honiton, 1931–55. Parliamentary Private Secretary to the Minister of Agriculture (Reginald Dorman-Smith to May 1940; R. S. Hudson to 1943), and Chairman of the Small Pig Keepers Council (to promote pig clubs on bomb sites). Assistant Government Whip, 1943. Lord Commissioner of the Treasury, 1944–5. Conservative Deputy Chief Whip, 1949. Knighted 1951. Treasurer to King George VI, 1951–2; to Queen Elizabeth II, 1952–5.

[3] Two miners (Gershom Jones, aged 43 and Jim Pearce aged 34) who had stayed underground at Coventry Colliery, Keresley, Warwickshire, for eleven days, came up on 4 September 1964. They were seeking a bonus payment and an inquiry into the running of the pit, and had been dismissed after returning to surface on August 24. On surfacing 'both were heavily bearded and pale' (*The Times*, 5 September 1964.)

MacDonald offered me a lift. I got in his car and said: 'Malcolm, this means war. Your father would have been very distressed, wouldn't he?' He replied: 'My father—he wouldn't have been distressed—he would have recognised that he could have solved the whole thing in five minutes!'

We got to No 10, by now all of us really scruffy and smelly, and it rather shook us to find Halifax, who had been dining with the PM, and Cadogan in evening clothes.

The PM had evidently not changed for dinner. In we went to the Cabinet Room. Again, reports are quite wrong about stormy scenes. This was a plain diktat from the Cabinet.

At that moment, the Cabinet Office was on to Paris (Cadogan was talking to Bonnet). Jaspar Rootham,[1] a secretary in the Cabinet Office, was listening in and taking notes because he was the only other one who could speak French well.

Cadogan was saying that naturally, we should go in with France at the same moment, but Paris was saying that if you start war now, we cannot get our young people out of Paris like you (our children had already been evacuated from London). They were convinced Paris would be bombed so soon as war was declared. They were horrified and terrified at our determination for an immediate ultimatum and said: 'Are you going to have all our women and children killed?'

I remember that the PM was calm, even icy-cold, all the time we were there. I strongly believe that Chamberlain has been quite wrongly decried as the arch-appeaser (still a dirty word—though isn't appeasement what everyone's doing now?).

From my own dealings with him—for months I had been getting agriculture on to a war footing—I am convinced that ever since Munich, he had been seeking peace, in a spectacular manner, but had very quietly been preparing for war. I am quite certain that he was holding back now only because of the French. He was terribly worried that Paris might indeed be attacked from the air.

But now—facing a Cabinet on a 'sit-down strike'—he had no alternative. The climax came most dramatically. The PM said quietly: 'Right, gentlemen, this means war.'

---

[1] Jasper St John Rootham, 1910–   . Educated at Tonbridge School and St John's College, Cambridge. Entered the Civil Service, 1933; Private Secretary to the Prime Minister, 1938–9. On active service, 1940–5 (served in the Middle East, the Balkans and Germany; despatches). Acting Assistant Adviser, Bank of England, 1946; Adviser to the Governor, 1957; Chief of the Overseas Department, 1952; Assistant to the Governor, 1954; retired, 1967. Managing Director, Lazard Brothers and Company Limited, merchant bankers, 1967–75. Director of the Agricultural Mortgage Corporation, 1967–77. A poet, he published a volume of his collected poems in 1972, and a further volume of poems in 1975.

Hardly had he said it, when there was the most enormous clap of thunder and the whole Cabinet Room was lit up by a blinding flash of lightning. It was the most deafening thunder-clap I've ever heard in my life. It really shook the building.

I felt in a different world—it was like something out of Oppenheim.[1]

And, of course, we were in a different world. In the sunshine next day, we were listening to the PM on the radio announcing that a state of war existed between Britain and Germany and the first air-raid siren had sounded.

W. H. Thompson: recollections

('*Sixty minutes with Winston Churchill*')

[3 September 1939]   [Morpeth Mansions]

Within a few minutes of Chamberlain's broadcast telling the nation that we were at war with Germany, the air raid sirens sounded over London.

Churchill went outside and stood staring into the sky. What thoughts must have been crowding into his mind at that moment! It was with difficulty that we prevailed upon him to enter an air-raid shelter. He only agreed to go when it was pointed out that it was up to him to set an example.

Down we went into a basement, the Old Man with a bottle of brandy under his arm. There he paced up and down, just as he had done on that day over seventeen years before, when I had my first interview with him.

[1] Edward Phillips Oppenheim, 1866–1946. Born in London. Educated at Wygesston Grammar School, Leicester. Published his first novel at the age of twenty. Author of more than ninety books of mystery, adventure and espionage, as well as novels and volumes of short stories. One of his most popular novels, *Mr. Grex of Monte Carlo*, was published in 1915. In 1939 he published *Sir Adam Disappeared*. Resident on the Riviera between the wars, he moved to Guernsey in 1940. When the Germans occupied the Channel Islands, they used his house as Luftwaffe headquarters. In England during the war, he published his autobiography, *The Pool of Memory*, in 1941. In 1945 he returned to Guernsey, where he died.

Fritz Günther von Tschirschky: [1] *recollections* [2]

(*Martin Russell papers*)

[3 September 1939]

. . . in 1939 he was living in Morpeth Mansions (having left Germany in 1935). Churchill and his wife were also living there. On the occasion of the first air-raid warning, all the occupants of the building went down to the basement, except von Tschirschky who felt that a German would not be welcome. He remained in the flat where he was living (he was looking after it for a lady who had gone to the country). However, he knew the Churchills slightly, and when Mrs Churchill noticed his absence she sent her house-keeper to ask him to come down. He demurred, but when the house-keeper said it was an order he went down to the shelter.

There he found Churchill in a great state of indignation, stamping his foot, complaining there was no telephone and no portable wireless, and saying the Germans would have much better organized air-raid shelters. Von Tschir-schky said there was a portable wireless in the flat he was occupying. 'You Germans are so damned efficient—please be kind enough to fetch it,' said Churchill. The all-clear was sounded a few minutes later.

W. H. Thompson: recollections

('*Sixty minutes with Winston Churchill*')

As soon as the 'All Clear' sounded Churchill rushed up to the roof of Morpeth Mansions where he had his flat, and stood there trying to discern aircraft in the cloudless sky.

[1] Fritz Günther von Tschirschky, 1900–1980. Born in Silesia. Army Cadet School, 1914–18. Served in the 8th Dragoons, 1919–20. Became von Papen's personal assistant at the Vice-Chancellery, March 1933 (when Hitler was Chancellor). Arrested at the Vice-Chancellery and taken to Gestapo prison at Prinz-Albrecht-Strasse, 30 June 1934. After release on 6 July returned to Silesia. Went to Vienna as personal assistant to von Papen who was Ambassador, August 1934. Recalled to Berlin but went to Switzerland, February 1935. In April 1936 he and his wife went to Lausanne, then to Paris, later to London. His wife returned to Silesia in 1936. Interned in Isle of Man 1940. Released 18 November 1944. His family came to England, September 1946. Rejoined the German diplomatic service, 1952. Subsequently Counsellor in London, and Consul-General Lille, 1959. Retired 1963. Died in Munich, 9 October 1980.

[2] I am grateful to Martin Russell for this record of a conversation which he had with von Tschirschky on 1 May 1980, five months before von Tschirschky's death. Martin Russell adds: 'In 1954 when von Tschirschky was in the German diplomatic service he met Churchill again at a dinner attended by Adenauer. He asked Churchill if he remembered meeting him in 1939. Churchill replied "Yes, you were the German with the portable wireless" ' (*letter to the author, 31 December 1981*).

Next on that memorable Sunday, we went to the House of Commons when Churchill with characteristic generosity went out of his way to pay tribute to the good intentions of Mr Neville Chamberlain in the following words:

'In this solemn hour, it is a consolation to recall and to dwell upon our repeated efforts for peace. All have been ill-starred, but all have been faithful and sincere.'[1]

When the Commons adjourned he came to me and said briefly:

'10 Downing Street, Thompson.'

When he returned to the car after his interview with the Prime Minister he was smiling, and as the door was opened for him he called to Mrs Churchill, sitting waiting for him:

'It's the Admiralty. That's a lot better than I thought.'

Sir Maurice Hankey to his wife
(Hankey papers)

3 September 1939   United Services Club

. . . As far as I can make out, my main job is to keep an eye on Winston! I spent $1\frac{1}{2}$ hours with him yesterday morning. He was brimful of ideas, some good, others not so good, but rather heartening and big. I only wish he didn't give one the impression that he does himself too well!

I went into the House of Commons smoking room yesterday. The amount of alcohol being consumed was incredible! Winston was in a corner holding forth to a ring of admiring satellite MPs!

He has let it get into the Press that he will be in the War Cabinet—to the great annoyance of many.

[1] Churchill's speech in the House of Commons on the morning of 3 September 1939, which began: 'In this solemn hour it is a consolation to recall and to dwell upon our repeated efforts for peace. All have been ill-starred, but all have been faithful and sincere. This is of the highest moral value—and not only moral value, but practical value—at the present time, because the whole hearted concurrence of scores of millions of men and women, whose co-operation is indispensable and whose comradeship and brotherhood are indispensable, in the only foundation upon which the trial and tribulation of modern war can be endured and surmounted. This moral conviction alone affords that ever-fresh resilience which renews the strength and energy of people on long, doubtful and dark days. Outside, the storms of war may blow and the lands may be lashed with the fury of its gales, but in our own hearts this Sunday morning there is peace. Our hands may be active, but our consciences are at rest.' A few moments later Churchill declared: 'This is not a question of fighting for Danzig or fighting for Poland. We are fighting to save the whole world from the pestilence of Nazi tyranny and in defence of all that is most sacred to man. This is no war of domination or imperial aggrandizement or material gain; no war to shut any country out of its sunlight and means of progress. It is a war, viewed in its inherent quality, to establish, on impregnable rocks, the rights of the individual, and it is a war to establish and revive the stature of man.'

Robert Boothby to Winston S. Churchill

(Churchill papers: 2/363)

3 September 1939

Dear Winston,

You shd know that Greenwood told me just now that he demanded an interview with the Prime Minister immediately after the debate last night. He said: 'You couldn't see your supporters. I could. And I know the feeling of mine. I wish to tell you that unless you present an ultimatum to Germany before eleven o'clock tomorrow, neither you nor I nor anyone else on earth will be able to hold the House of Commons.' He added that the French Government had been informed this morning that the House of Commons would stand no further delay.

Your immediate task seems to have been made much easier by the PM today. His was not the speech of a man who intended to lead us *through* the struggle.

Yrs ever,
Bob

Your speech was splendid, so was Ll G's.

Paul Maze to Winston S. Churchill

(Churchill papers: 2/366)

3 September 1939   Moulin de Montreuil
                                          Saint-Georges-Motel
                                                Eure

My dear Winston,

I feel happy to know that the responsibility of the Navy is in your hands at this juncture.

I am writing this only a few yards from the spot where your easel stood ten days ago—now we are at war and we can meet the future with true confidence.

Sir Reginald Barnes to Winston S. Churchill

(*Churchill papers: 2/363*)

3 September 1939

My dear old Winston,

I am *so* glad that at last you are in your right place, & will knock that L--r Hitler out.

Personally I am miserable, as they say I am too old.[1] If there is any sort of job that I could do, that you may hear of, *please* remember me.

All success to you old pal,

Reggie

Sir Emsley Carr to Winston S. Churchill

(*Churchill papers: 8/629*)

3 September 1939

My dear Winston,

I cannot say with what pride and satisfaction I heard of the decision of the Prime Minister to place you in full charge of the Admiralty, and my pride is shared by the entire British people.

We know that you are the right man in the right place and that our beliefs will be fully justified by the success which will accompany your efforts.

I want also to assure you that you can rely upon the entire support of the great paper which I have the honour to control.[2]

As you are aware that—apart from our world wide circulation—we have more readers in the services than any other paper, and it will be my first and constant duty to encourage and support them on every occasion.

Again I heartily congratulate you and wish you the best of fortune in your great and momentous work.

---

[1] Barnes was three years older than Churchill (who was 65 years old on 30 November 1939).

[2] On 10 September 1939 an article by the political correspondent of Sir Emsley Carr's *News of the World* described how 'everyone in all Parties was delighted with the appointment of the ever-youthful Mr. Winston Churchill as a Member of the Cabinet in his old post as First Lord of the Admiralty, which he held in 1914, when with dramatic prescience he mobilized the Fleet. It was interesting that after ten years of vigorous work in helpful opposition he should come back to Office. But the satisfaction of the House was much more broadly-based. Everyone felt that Mr. Churchill would bring freshness and vigour to the task of winning the war, and that his mastery in tactics would be a national asset'.

Lord Southborough[1] *to Winston S. Churchill*
(*Churchill papers: 2/367*)

3 September 1939

My dear Churchill,

I cannot refrain from writing you a note to say how glad I am to have lived on to see you again in a position and an Office which brings back to me many recollections, and to feel that the road should be wide if not smooth to that premier place which should have been open to you long ago.

Yours,
Southborough

Winston S. Churchill to Lord Stanhope
(*Churchill papers: 2/367*)

4 September 1939   11 Morpeth Mansions

My dear Stanhope,

Fortune of war which chased me a quarter of a century ago from the Admiralty, has now reversed its action. I am sure you know that I have done nothing to disturb you. Indeed I had already accepted a deal in the War Cabinet 'without portfolio', when a change of plan brought me into this office. The few hours I spent there last night show me the excellent condition in which you have left it; and I have no doubt that this impression will be deepened as my knowledge grows. I should like very much however to learn from you the points you had especially in mind, in order that nothing may be overlooked in changing guard. Perhaps you will let me know when I may call upon you.

I hope we are to be colleagues, as well as neighbours,[2] and that I may count on your assistance.

Believe me,

Yours very sincerely,
Winston S. Churchill

[1] Francis John Stephen Hopwood, 1860–1947. Assistant Solicitor, Board of Trade, 1885. Knighted, 1901. Permanent Secretary, Board of Trade, 1901–7. Member of the Transvaal and Orange River Constitutional Enquiry, 1906. Permanent Under-Secretary of State for the Colonies, 1907–11 (Churchill being Under-Secretary of State from 1906–1908). Privy Councillor, 1912. Additional Civil Lord of Admiralty, 1912–17 (Churchill being First Lord from 1911 to 1915). Created Baron Southborough, 1917. Secretary to the Irish Convention, 1917–18. President of the Commission to India on Reform, 1918–19. President of the China Association. In 1911 he was one of the nine 'distinguished' outsiders elected to the Other Club (founded in that year by Churchill and F. E. Smith).

[2] Lord Stanhope's country house was Chevening, near Sevenoaks, only four miles from Chartwell. In London he lived at 111 Eaton Square.

Josiah Wedgwood to Winston S. Churchill

(*Churchill papers: 2/368*)

4 September 1939

My dear Winston,

Thank whatever God there be. Now we shall win. Think of me if you want a job of any sort well done.

1. Petrol seems to me to be the key, especially as the real war won't start till they have eaten Poland. That gives us 6 months to drain them of petrol, and you can bomb their petrol factories.

2. Their air raid warnings. Can't you send over one machine every 12 hours to make them give air raid warnings and stop all work?

Yours ever,
Josiah Wedgwood

Edouard Beneš to Winston S. Churchill

(*Churchill papers: 2/381*)

4 September 1939   Putney

My dear Winston Churchill,

It is for me a very agreeable occasion to express to you my sincerest congratulation on your appointment to the cabinet and I sincerely wish you every success in your very responsible work.

May I thank you once more for all the great services you have rendered to my unfortunate country during the last year and assure you of my warmest sympathies in this historical hour in which your great country is obliged to wage a war for its freedom, for the reestablishment of the sound principles in international politics and for justice towards small attacked peoples? I hope that even in this great struggle my people and myself personally we shall have the occasion to collaborate with you effectively for the victory of these principles, as was the case in the last war twenty five years ago.[1]

Yours very friendly,
Edouard Beneš

[1] In February 1919, as Czech troops fought in Russia against the Bolsheviks, Churchill had written to Balfour to support 'Beneš and the Czecho-Slovak project'. In July 1919 Beneš himself had written to Churchill, 'that in the Europe of the future the Czecho-Slovakia Republic will be the pivot of a new political system in Central Europe'. Beneš added, of the 'Czecho-Slovak nation': 'Its territory is four times as great as Belgium, and it will have a considerable population of about 14 millions. Prague will be the centre of western influence in Central Europe and a centre of observation, either towards Germany or towards Central Europe and the Balkans or towards Poland and Russia' (*Churchill papers: 16/20, 16/39*).

V. V. Tilea[1] to Winston S. Churchill

(*Churchill papers: 2/381*)

4 September 1939   The Roumanian Minister,
                                                          London

Your Excellency,

May I be allowed to add my congratulations to those of your host of
well-wishers, who appreciate the great services that you have rendered in
the past, and who are happy to know that once more your high intelligence,
vast experience and immense driving power are to be utilised in the service
of the British Nation at this time.

In congratulating you personally, I also congratulate the British people
on your appointment as First Lord of the Admiralty,—an appointment
which, by a happy coincidence places you once again, as in 1914, in control
of the British Navy in time of War.

I am confident that your great qualities of mind and heart will enable you
to accomplish successfully the high mission with which you have been entrusted by the Government and people of this Country.

Believe me, Your Excellency,
Yours very sincerely,
V. V. Tilea

F. J. Leathers to Winston S. Churchill

(*Churchill papers: 2/366*)

4 September 1939

My dear Mr Churchill,

The bright spot of yesterday, otherwise so black, was the official announcement of your appointment as First Lord and your inclusion in the War
Cabinet.

---

[1] Viorel Virgil Tilea, 1896–1972. Born and educated in the Transylvanian region of
Austria-Hungary, the son of a prosperous timber merchant. On active service in the Austro-
Hungarian cavalry, 1916–18 (including the occupation of Rumania). As a Rumanian citizen
from 1919, he built up a prosperous timber industry, introducing a private health service
for his 300 employees. Active from 1926 in seeking to form a Danube Confederation, and a
supporter of the Pan-Europe Movement. Founder of the Anglo-Rumanian Cultural Association, 1923. Negotiator of the first Anglo-Rumanian Trade Agreement 1930. Rumanian
Minister in London, 1938–40. Worked for the Rumanian Freedom Station during the
Second World War. In 1941 he refused to return to Nazi orientated Rumania, whereupon
his Rumanian nationality was cancelled, and all his properties seized. Resident in the USA,
1946–8, and in Britain from 1948 until his death. In his draft memoirs he wrote: 'For my
time, the lights have gone out in Eastern and Central Europe. But my time is a little moment
in history. We shall climb back to civilization in God's good time.' (*Tilea papers*)

It gladdened the hearts of your friends and gave immense assurance and satisfaction right through the country and beyond. Although you know the ropes at the Admiralty so well it would have been better for the country and fairer to you had you the opportunity of directing preparations months before but we are confident of your success and proud of your achievements.

Believe me

Yours sincerely,
F. J. Leathers

Lord Davies to Winston S. Churchill
(*Churchill papers: 2/364*)

4 September 1939

My dear Churchill,

First, let me offer you my sincere congratulations and best wishes on your inclusion in the Cabinet. At the Admiralty you will have the unique distinction of being responsible for the direction of the Navy in the two greatest wars in which this country has ever been engaged. But when called upon to assume this responsibility you might have responded in the words of Foch, when, during an even more acute crisis, he said, 'It is a hard task you offer me now; a compromised situation, a crumbling front, an adverse battle in full progress. Nevertheless, I accept.' Perhaps it is not quite as bad as this, but I hope that the Admiralty is only a stepping-stone, and that in the course of the next six months you may be called upon to assume the supreme direction of affairs. . . .

Margaret, Countess of Birkenhead [1] *to Winston S. Churchill*
(*Churchill papers: 2/363*)

4 September 1939   Charlton,
                                                            Banbury

My dear Winston,

A cry of 'Thank God' went up from the whole family when we read the good news, & I am sure the same cry has gone up from the whole nation.

---

[1] Margaret Eleanor Furneaux, 1878–1968. Daughter of the classical scholar Henry Furneaux. In 1901 she married F. E. Smith (later 1st Earl of Birkenhead), one of Churchill's closest friends, who had died in 1930.

I cannot tell you how thankful I am to feel that your great gifts & wonderful brain are being used in the War Cabinet, as there is no one else in the country to compare with you at a time like this. If only Fred was here to be working with you!

We all[1] send you our love & delighted congratulations.

Yours affectionately,
Margaret

Sir Ian Hamilton to Winston S. Churchill

(*Churchill papers: 2/365*)

4 September 1939

Lennoxlove,
Scotland

My dear Winston,

Heartfelt congrats on your attainment of the most vital of all the billets under the King, & congrats to all Britons also.

As some ambitious enemy bomber may let fly a shot at Chartwell tell Clemmie that if she likes to rest a spell in a Mediaeval Castle with 12 foot walls she is more than welcome.

Yours ever,
Ian Hamilton

L. S. Amery to Winston S. Churchill

(*Churchill papers: 2/363*)

4 September 1939

My dear Winston,

Thank heaven you are safely back at the heart of things. I dare say it may be a good thing that you should be giving the necessary impulse at the Admiralty during the opening phase. But I confess I should like to see you free, as soon as possible, in a real War Cabinet, coordinating the whole sphere of defence, if not the whole conduct of the war. However, that is as may be. For the present you will have all that you can cope with in the way of immediate tasks.

---

[1] Margaret Birkenhead had two children: the 2nd Earl of Birkenhead (Churchill's godson) who had married, in 1935, Sheila Berry, later Lady-in-Waiting to Princess Marina, Duchess of Kent; and Pamela, who had married, in 1936, Sheila Berry's brother Michael, later 1st Baron Lord Hartwell, Chairman and Editor-in-Chief of the *Daily Telegraph*.

For the moment apparently I am not being wanted to do anything, and for the first time for many years I feel that it matters whether I should be taking part in things or not. But all the qualities which have kept me out during these years are qualities which are of use in war and should be used. Meanwhile, if I can be of any service to you, in the way of working up memoranda on general policy outside the purely naval sphere, or in any other way, please command me. I shall be only too happy to work for you.[1]

Yours ever,
Leo Amery

A. H. Richards to Winston S. Churchill
(*Churchill papers: 2/387*)

4 September 1939

My dear Mr Churchill,

Warmest congratulations upon your accession to the War Cabinet elsewhere so aptly described as 'Mounting the Bridge'.

In this hour of trial it is indeed a source of great inspiration and strength, that your great gifts will be so ungrudgingly dedicated to the service of 'The Cause' that you have so nobly and courageously espoused.

How different the course of history would have been had your repeated warnings and foreshadowing of the doom stealing over Europe been acted upon and your constructive statesmanlike proposals accepted.

Today, plain ordinary people everywhere in simple faith and trust will look to you to lead us into the paths of peace—to banish from the Earth forever this evil Nazism—which shall be Peace indeed.

My own humble association with you, has been a great privilege, a rich and memorable experience, mellowed into profound affection.

In the coming stress may the God of all strength be your strength. . . .

I pray that God will bless and keep you, and make your service great, even unto the establishment of Peace on Earth, Goodwill Among Men, which shall merit His 'Well Done'.

Yours sincerely,
A. H. Richards

---

[1] L. S. Amery received no Government post in Neville Chamberlain's wartime administration; but in May 1940 was appointed by Churchill to be Secretary of State for India and Burma, a position which he held until July 1945.

Felix Frankfurter[1] to Winston S. Churchill

(*Churchill papers: 2/365*)

4 September 1939   Supreme Court of the United States

Dear Mr Churchill,

Since you are sponsoring the cause of free men everywhere, perhaps you will not decree it the act of an impertinent outsider for me to express satisfaction that you now are where you ought to be. In thought, this country is certainly not neutral. There is a unanimity of opinion for the democracies unlike the confusion of feeling in 1914. And since there is this clear conviction that Hitler has challenged our way of life and that you and the French are defending it, I have high hopes that we shall not be wanting in giving effective expression to our convictions.

With every good wish,

Yours very sincerely,
Felix Frankfurter

Lady Leslie[2] to Winston S. Churchill: telegram

(*Churchill papers: 1/343*)

5 September 1939   Glaslough,
                                   Co Monaghan

Feel safer now you are at Admiralty. Bless you.

Léonie

---

[1] Felix Frankfurter, 1882–1965. Born in Vienna, of Jewish parents. Taken to the United States at the age of twelve. Graduated from Harvard Law School, 1906. Joined Henry Stimson's law office in New York. Professor, Harvard Law School, 1914–39. A member of the Zionist delegation to the Paris Peace Conference, 1919. In 1931 he published an important article, 'The Palestine Situation Restated' in *Foreign Affairs*, critical of Britain's Palestine policy. A friend of President Roosevelt, he became a Supreme Court Justice on 17 January 1939, serving until 1962.

[2] Leonie Blanche Jerome, 1859–1943. Sister of Lady Randolph Churchill. She married Colonel John Leslie in 1884. Their younger son Norman was killed in action on 18 October 1914.

Sir George Arthur[1] *to Winston S. Churchill*

(*Churchill papers: 2/363*)

5 September 1939   Carlton Club

My dear Winston Churchill,

Please believe that among all the good wishes which attend you just now none are more sincere or more earnest than mine, and I dare to think that no one would rejoice more eagerly in your appointment than my dear Lord Kitchener. Superficial differences may have arisen between you in those days of heat, but I *know*, and can testify, that he had for you not only keen admiration but a sense of very *warm affection*.

I am

Yrs most truly,
Sir George Arthur

Lord Londonderry to Winston S. Churchill

(*Churchill papers: 2/366*)

7 September 1939

My dear Winston,

This is just a line to say how delighted I am to see that at last you have joined the (War) Cabinet. As you know, I wish you had been there for some time previously. At this time, it would be wrong for any of us to make any public criticisms, but I am not impressed by the majority of your colleagues in the War Cabinet, as I am quite sure there is not one of them who knows anything about waging war. . . .

You may be quite sure that all my good wishes are with you in your very important position.

Yours ever,
Charlie

[1] George Compton Archibald Arthur, 1860–1946. 3rd Baronet, 1878. Entered Army, 1880. Private Secretary to Lord Kitchener, 1914–16. Assistant to the Director of Military Operations, War Office, 1916–18. On several missions to France; he acted as interpreter between Sir Douglas Haig and General Nivelle before the battle of Arras, March 1917. His publications include *Life of Lord Kitchener* (3 vols, 1920) and *Concerning Winston Spencer Churchill* (1940). He gave his autobiography (published 1938), the title *Not Worth Reading*.

Colin Thornton-Kemsley to Winston S. Churchill
(*Churchill papers: 2/368*)

12 September 1939

You won't welcome a letter from me & it will not be a long one, but war puts things into proportion, and I should not be happy to go off to my job until I had said something which had been on my mind of late.

For fourteen years I worked as hard as most in your support, and from September until the time of my By-Election in March[1] (since when I have scrupulously refrained from taking any part at all in the affairs of your Division) I have opposed you as hard as I knew how for reasons, and in ways, which you know all about.

I want to say only this. You warned us repeatedly about the German danger & you were right: a grasshopper under a fern is not proud now that he made the field ring with his importunate chink.

Please don't think of replying—you are in all conscience busy enough in an office which we are all glad that you hold in this time of Britain's danger.

Winston S. Churchill to Colin Thornton-Kemsley
(*Churchill papers: 2/368*)

13 September 1939   Admiralty

I certainly think that Englishmen ought to start fair with one another from the outset in so grievous a struggle and so far as I am concerned the past is dead.

Alice, Lady Wimborne to Winston S. Churchill
(*Churchill papers: 2/368*)

16 September 1939

My dear Winston,

It was with real joy that I learnt you were back in the seat of power which you should never have been allowed to vacate. And moreover 'ruler' once more of the key of our defences. How that news brought back 1914 & onwards & nostalgia for the days when in spite of war the world seemed fine. I sleep happier at nights for that you are there.

I fear we are faced with a grim tragedy. . . .

---

[1] On 30 March 1939 Thornton-Kemsley had been elected Conservative MP for Aberdeenshire and Kincardineshire. He remained in Parliament for 25 years.

*   *   *

Winston S. Churchill: draft[1]

(Churchill papers: 4/114)

We shall hear in succeeding generations a lot of talk about the pacific virtues we displayed; how we exhausted every expedient; how we flaunted a magnificent patience; how we never lost our heads or were carried away by fear or excitement; how we turned the second cheek to the smiter seven times or more.

Some historians will urge that admiration should be given to a Government of honourable high-minded men who bore provocation with exemplary forbearance and piled up to their credit all the Christian virtues, especially those which command electioneering popularity; but who when their patience was at length worn out by repeated injury and peril turned upon their aggressor with their backs to the wall.

I hope it will also be written how hard all this was upon the ordinary common folk who fill the casualty lists of world wars. Under representative Government and Parliamentary institutions, they confide their safety to the Ministers and the Prime Minister of the day. They have just cause of complaint if their guides or rulers so mismanage their affairs that in the end they are thrust into the worst of wars with the worst of chances.

---

[1] Churchill wrote this passage in 1946 or 1947, for the first volume of his war memoirs, but deleted it before publication.

Biographical
Index

Compiled by the Author

For subject headings, see under the index
entry for Churchill (Sir) Winston Leonard Spencer.

a 'helpful' speech, 66; thanks Churchill for 'your very kind references to myself', 76–7; 'over-cautious', 114; and German arms expenditure, 122, 257; and 'peace conditions' in industry, 125; and critics of the Government's defence policy, 166, 1452; Churchill consults, 188 n. 1; and German intentions, 190 n. 1; and Baldwin's choice, as against 'the devil', 202; his political future, 206; his half-brother Austen's unease, 233; and the Defence Deputation, 258–9, 330; and Churchill's gift, 377, 1153; 'the villain of the piece', 407; critical of the League of Nations, 416 n. 2; and the second Defence Deputation, 425 n. 1; and the Abdication, 493–4; his Budget (of 1937), 521, 662–3, 668–9, 686, 689–92, 694; offers his sympathy to Churchill, 549; states British weakness to Cabinet, 559 n. 2; Baldwin's successor as Prime Minister, 575, 673, 685–8; and Churchill's political future, 582, 1084; Churchill sends Rowley-Atcherley Report to, 594, 698–9; his half-brother's death, 626–7; and the financial position of the Duke of Windsor, 634, 635–6, 638, 643, 644; Churchill's article on, 685–8, 709, 861; and the Nyon Conference, 766; 'has begun very well', 767–8; one of Churchill's 'numerous admirers', 775–6; and Lord Londonderry, 782; and the United States, 787; and a 'lie' about British air strength, 877–8; his conflict with Vansittart, 883 n. 1; 'threatened men live long', 891 n. 3; and Eden's resignation, 914 n. 1, 1236; and American lack of knowledge of, 927; and Churchill's hopes of a defence enquiry, 930–1, 932; and Churchill's Air notes, 936, 996, 1007; his attitude said to be 'contrary to our best instincts', 936–7; gives 'little indication of real policy', 937; his 'ghastly' inheritance, 940; 'that miserable wobbler', 941; and Czechoslovakia, 948 n. 3, 952–3, 1018 n. 1, 1022

n. 1, 1024, 1114; and Churchill's visit to Paris (March 1938), 966, 969; and Mussolini's intentions in Spain 993; and negotiations with Eire, 1009 n. 2, 1302, 1314; and the Anglo-Italian agreement, 1011 notes 1 and 2; 'satisfactory' remarks of, 1047; hopes of conscription from, 1051; preparations for a speech of, 1059 n. 1; and material for 'counter-attacking' Churchill, 1075; and Hore-Belisha, 1088 n. 1; and food supplies in war, 1093, 1147–8; and a German emissary (August 1938), 1120, 1121–2, 1126–7; and the Czechoslovak crisis (September 1938), 1131, 1133, 1142, 1156, 1162, 1164, 1165, 1167, 1173–4, 1177, 1178–80, 1181, 1184, 1187, 1189 n. 1, 1193–6, 1251, 1285; and the aftermath of 'Munich', 1194 n. 3, 1202, 1204–5, 1207, 1210, 1212, 1216; and the evolution of a post-'Munich' policy, 1227, 1242, 1243, 1244, 1248, 1256, 1257, 1264; his 'courage', 1167; 'our Dictator', 1204; his reputation 'undimmed', 1216; Churchill's growing bitterness towards, 1229 n. 2; his responsibilities (since 1931), 1238 n. 2, 1344; 'no need to criticize', 1265; his support a matter of dispute, 1270; Lord Halifax 'not so far gone as', 1270; 'not in earnest' about rearmament' (November 1938), 1272, 1275; attacks Churchill's 'judgment', 1280; reflects on the mobilization of 1914, 1281; 'has now got away with everything', 1285; Hitler 'furious' with, 1288; and German intentions (December 1938), 1301–2; 'you can trust him', 1304 n. 1; and the unlikelihood of a Government reconstruction, 1324; his alleged 'change of mind', 1328; in Rome, 1331, 1340, 1342, 1344, 1347; and Spain, 1331 n. 2; and a 'great advance', 1343; and Churchill's continued exclusion from the Government (January–August 1939), 1351; the Czech attitude to (in February 1939), 1360, 1368; Goering's fears of a

1660 BIOGRAPHICAL INDEX

Hitler, Adolf—*contd.*
1578–9; and the coming of war (August–September 1939), 1589, 1598, 1599, 1600, 1613

Hoare, Sir Reginald: 'strongly anti-Semite', 1462–3

Hoare, Sir Samuel (later Viscount Templewood): Churchill's letters to, 2–3; his supporters, 14; his future, 16; and 'the verities of life', 20; and defence, 55, 61–2; and Rhineland crisis, 68; and Abyssinia, 92, 99–101, 111, 787; returns to the Cabinet, 166 n. 1, 240 n. 3; opposes emergency powers for industry, 190 n. 1; and the Defence Deputation (of July 1936), 263 n. 2; at the Admiralty, 296–7, 302–3; and Churchill's correspondence, 314; the effect of his speeches, 365; and the Duke of Windsor, 493–4; and the Fleet Air Arm, 514; and battleship rivalries, 665–8, 697–8; becomes Home Secretary, 688 n. 2; and aliens in Britain, 707–8; and the Foreign Secretaryship, 920 n. 1; and the 'Munich' crisis, 1155, 1195, 1199; and the aftermath of 'Munich', 1202; and India, 1234 n. 2; his responsibilities (since 1931), 1238 n. 2; 'should go', 1428; foresees a 'Golden Age' (March 1939), 1447 n. 2; and Poland, 1502; 'terrified of Winston', 1541; his Geneva speech (of 1934) recalled, 1542; and the 'drive' to get Churchill in the Government (July 1939), 1561–2; and Chamberlain's 'considerable successes' (August 1939), 1582

Hobart, Brigadier (later Major-General Sir) P. C. S.: and defence, 371–2

Hobhouse, Charles: 680 n. 2

Hodsoll, Wing-Commander (Sir) John: 1082 n. 2, 1319 n. 1, 1365 n. 1; and bomb shelters, 1499, 1557

Hodza, Milan: and the Czech crisis (of 1938), 1021 n. 1, 1173

Hogan, Captain H.: and the 'Sandys case', 1093

Hogg, Quintin (later Lord Hailsham of Saint Marylebone): his by-election campaign (of October 1938), 1238, 1239

Hopkins, Sir Richard: Churchill seeks help through, 424

Hopkinson, Austin: 170

Horabin, T. L.: his by-election campaign (March–April 1939), 1411–12, 1487–8; and 'compulsion of wealth', 1495

Horace: quoted, 1153

Horder, Fred: 1292 n. 2

Horder, Sir Thomas: 454, 1075 n. 1

Hore-Belisha, Leslie (later Baron): 47 n. 2, 260, 299; and the gift of a key chain, 526; becomes Secretary of State for War (May 1937), 688 n. 2, 701 n. 1; and Gibraltar, 738–9; at Chartwell, 752; and a 'separate army' for India, 767; and Army command changes, 853–4, 857; abused, 908; and Spain, 940, 988–9; 'pained', 1052–4; 'you would not be dissatisfied', 1073; and the 'Sandys case', 1083 n. 1; Mae West on, 1086; 'deserves to be exposed', 1088; and air force deficiencies, 1242–3; his 'false statements', 1245; Churchill's ill-judged attack on (December 1938), 1298–9, 1300; his dismissal demanded, 1317 n. 1, 1322 n. 1, 1323, 1326; 'misinformed', 1322; defends himself, 1336; and Churchill's memorandum on sea power (March 1939), 1413; and explosives research, 1433; called to Chartwell (April 1939), 1444; 'one of the most active Ministers', 1453; and Gibraltar, 1459, 1464; urged not to resign, 1459; Churchill's praise for, 1575–6; and the outbreak of war, 1602, 1604, 1607

Horne, Sir Robert (later Viscount): 22, 50–1, 56 n. 1, 62, 68, 166, 173; and the Defence Deputation (of July 1936), 265 n. 2, 278, 285–6, 313; and the second Defence Deputation (November 1936), 425 n. 1, 436 n. 1; and *Arms and the Covenant*, 1099–1100; and the 'Munich' crisis, 1173; and broadcasting, 1376

Horstenau, General Glaise von: 245 n. 2, 934 n. 1